LESLIE HALLIWELL WITH PHILIP PURSER

HALLIWELL'S TELEVISION COMPANION

THIRD EDITION

GRAFTON BOOKS

A Division of the Collins Publishing Group

LONDON GLASGOW
TORONTO SYDNEY AUCKLAND

Grafton Books
A Division of the Collins Publishing Group
8 Grafton Street, London W1X 3LA

Published as *Halliwell's Teleguide* by Granada Publishing 1979
Second edition (retitled *Halliwell's Television Companion*) 1982
Third edition published by Grafton Books 1986

British Library Cataloguing in Publication Data
Halliwell, Leslie
    Halliwell's television companion.—3rd ed.
    1. Television programs—Great Britain—
    Dictionaries   2. Television programs—
    United States—Dictionaries
    I. Title   II. Purser, Philip
    791.45′0941   PN1992.3.G7

ISBN 0-246-12838-0

Typeset by CG Graphic Services, Aylesbury, Bucks
Printed in Great Britain by R. J. Acford,
Chichester, Sussex

Contents

LH's contributions to this edition of the *Television Companion* are dedicated to those old-time Hollywood movie stars who had the pioneering spirit to establish themselves in television series before 1960 (in some cases only just):

MILTON BERLE in *The Milton Berle Show*
JACKIE COOPER in *The People's Choice*
WILLIAM BENDIX in *The Life of Riley*
BORIS KARLOFF in *Starring Boris Karloff* (and later *Thriller*)
DAVID NIVEN, CHARLES BOYER, JACK LEMMON, BARBARA
    STANWYCK in *Four Star Theatre*
RED SKELTON in *The Red Skelton Show*
LUCILLE BALL in *I Love Lucy*
JOAN DAVIS in *I Married Joan*
J. CARROL NAISH in *Life with Luigi*
EVE ARDEN in *Our Miss Brooks*
GENE AUTRY in *The Gene Autry Show*
JACK BENNY in *The Jack Benny Show*
LORETTA YOUNG in *The Loretta Young Theatre*
RONALD COLMAN in *Halls of Ivy*
MICKEY ROONEY in *The Mickey Rooney Show*
ROBERT MONTGOMERY in *Robert Montgomery Presents*
SPRING BYINGTON in *December Bride*
RICHARD BOONE in *Medic*
RAY MILLAND in *The Ray Milland Show*
ROBERT YOUNG in *Father Knows Best*
ALFRED HITCHCOCK in *Alfred Hitchcock Presents*
RICHARD GREENE in *The Adventures of Robin Hood*
JANE WYMAN in *Jane Wyman Presents*
ROBERT CUMMINGS in *The Bob Cummings Show*
JIMMY DURANTE in *The Jimmy Durante Show*
. . . and PERRY COMO, and DINAH SHORE, and FRANK SINATRA
and of course BOB HOPE

PP dedicates his entries to the updated list of his heroes and heroines:

IAN and SUSAN WOOLDRIDGE
GERALDINE and CLIVE JAMES
TIM and ANNEKA RICE
KEN and GWEN and A. J. P. TAYLOR
And, once again,
BILLIE and WILLIE WHITELAW

Introduction to the Third Edition (1986)

by Leslie Halliwell

Readers who were inclined to consult the last edition of this compendium will recall that Philip Purser looks after the British scene, while I deal with the American programmes and the general shape of the book. This division of duty accords fairly precisely with our everyday labours. As buyer for ITV I am concerned mainly with American material, since the British companies make or generate their own; while Philip, in covering the British scene for the *Sunday Telegraph*, has little time to spare for the American shows, which he sees quite reasonably as mere commercial props to a schedule which otherwise might occasionally falter in the ratings. He, in other words, is mainly caring for the minority; I am mainly providing for the majority, for the up to twenty million British viewers who watch *Raiders of the Lost Ark* or *The A Team* or *Murder She Wrote*. Which of us is Dr Jekyll, and which Mr Hyde, must be left for the reader to decide; but it makes for an entertaining mix, and as before both Philip and I feel free, in so far as we are able, to disagree in print with each other's opinions.

The fact is that television is far too broad a field for one man – or even two – to cover adequately. As it is we have omitted news, current affairs, sport, and foreign-language programmes, apart from the briefest of generalizations; but we do now feel, I think, that the volume you hold in your hand is an adequate guide to what we might call transatlantic television. So far as both countries are concerned it goes back thirty years and more, the extent of our own memories; and we have both been diligent in adding such historical detail as can be researched. Our targets here are single plays, serials and films: every American TV movie, for instance, is detailed, a major enterprise in itself. We also look for personalities whose contribution to the art has been worth recording, and we add 'theme' notes where we can.

It may be observed that Philip takes a higher critical line than I do. This arises from the nature of the beast. British television on the whole is of a standard capable of interpretation by the *Sunday Telegraph*; American network television is more aptly summed up by a few wisecracks from *TV Guide*. It is undeniably a mass medium over there, aimed, as someone once alleged, at a fat little guy in Milwaukee, slouched in an armchair with a can of beer in his hand. This is the way things have happened in America: television is in the hands of the advertisers, and many viewers regret that. They have recourse to the privately subsidized network, ironically called public television, which finds its biggest hits in British exports (for which it pays very little); otherwise, Americans with high critical standards watch very little television apart from the occasional blockbusters such as *Roots* or *The Winds of War*, and telemovies on urgent subjects such as AIDS or the prospect of a third world war.

This is not to say that the regular commercial output is to be derided: after all, this country has cherished Hollywood for eighty years on the grounds that its studios offer in abundance glamour and adventure, necessary recreational facilities to us all, at standards we cannot ourselves attain because other countries see no reason to buy the results. No doubt the American networks would like to make more programmes on the level of *Hill Street Blues* and *Lou Grant*, but they have difficulty in keeping such shows on the market because the public shows a decided preference for domestic sitcoms and mindless mayhem. This is not to say that American television has not changed. In the four years since the last edition of this book the public has clearly set its face against movie rip-offs (*Shadow Chasers* from *Ghostbusters*, *Bring 'em Back Alive* from *Raiders of the Lost Ark*, *Stir Crazy* from *Stir Crazy*, all failures) and it has also shown a decided desire to laugh. *Hill Street Blues*, with its non-star group cast, not only led the way to other dramas such as *St Elsewhere*, it also encouraged half-hour comedies (following the freak success of *Taxi*) set in a bar (*Cheers*), the DA's office (*Foley Square*) and in a run-down newspaper city room (*Mary*). There was the surprising popularity of a comedy about old age, hitherto thought a taboo subject; but the ladies in *Golden Girls* are all stars of the past, handy with wisecracks, and added to them is a newcomer who pretends to be eighty but is in reality only sixty years old, so that the blow is cushioned, despite the sharpness of the dialogue. (Priest: 'I can't wait much longer. This is Miami, I have funerals backed up!') Imitations of other series are also being seen through rather rapidly: *Hollywood Beat* could not ride on the success of *Miami Vice*, nor *The Colbys* on *Dynasty*, nor *Lime Street* on *Hart to Hart*. Positive recent successes, however, are soap operas, which were once confined to daytime but now proliferate in prime; and there is a disturbing tendency, both in miniseries and in running shows such as *Hunter* and *Cagney and Lacey* and *The Equalizer* and *Lady Blue*, to dwell on the realistic details of violence instead of purveying the 'Mickey Mouse' variety of years ago. The heroine of *Lady Blue* ('One move and your future is cancelled') was obviously designed to cash in on the tremendous movie success of Clint Eastwood as *Dirty Harry* and Sylvester Stallone as *Rambo*, but the authorities may well see to it that this particular brand of popcorn for the masses, however instantly palatable, does not remain available for long. The final observation to be made is that blacks are now acceptable in America to audiences of every background: currently the most successful network comedy is *The Cosby Show*, which concerns the family problems of a well-to-do lawyer. Their colour is hardly ever mentioned.

The successes of American television are largely due not to stars but to scripts. Alas, there are insufficient trained or witty writers for more than a handful of successes a year, and it is to this sad fact rather than to their averagely proficient stars and acceptable premises that we must ascribe the disastrous reception by critics and public alike of such shows as *Glitter*, *Finder of Lost Loves*, and *Hell Town*; as *The Last Days of Pompeii*; and, as the sad attempt to turn a miniseries called 'V' into a weekly action thriller. A different reason can be adduced for the relentless boredom generated by so many TV movies; they are all required to run exactly the same length, 96 minutes for a two-hour slot, and many of them would be better cut down to an hour rather than having to halt the plot for time padding via five minutes of sexual banter or routine chasing. This problem stems basically from financial considerations: a two-hour movie holds the audience longer than a 90-minute one, and once into it viewers are not likely to switch off until it ends, even if parts of it are boring. Also, since union demands have sent up the cost of production to such astronomical figures, there is a reluctance to throw anything away. (Chaplin shot 20 hours of film for *City Lights*, which in the end lasted 85 minutes.)

Television makes its own stars these days. There are no cinema ones important to the viewers, who don't go to the pictures any more: and even the stars who have known success on TV can't count on audience loyalty unless their new vehicle is good: hence the recent disasters of Robert Blake and Robert Wagner. The immense success of Joan Collins in *Dynasty* was due not to her track record – her career might charitably have been assumed to be drawing to a close – but to the fact that her middle-aged character did incredibly naughty things. From that it was but one step to the depiction of rich American families as collections of scoundrels and perverts who never have much to do beyond dressing in tennis or evening wear and hanging around expensive but underpopulated sets from which flatly to deliver lines of naïve bitchery.

Change is inevitable, but will it be for the better? Some viewers may sigh for the days when television aimed for a quiet general competence interrupted by the occasional idea which engaged the brain rather than the eye: *The Streets of San Francisco* was as like the cinema as the medium was ever required to get. Desperate executives last year rummaged in their nostalgia trunks and came up with new versions of *The Twilight Zone* and *Alfred Hitchcock Presents*, while *The Equalizer* is a modern version of *Have Gun Will Travel*. They were modest successes at best, but at least they cost less to make than Steven Spielberg's *Amazing Stories*, equally backward-looking in everything but budget; so expensive indeed that its owners so far say they can't afford to release it to television stations abroad.

Thirty years ago television was a delightful extension of people's lives, a moving gallery of fresh faces and concepts which on the whole broadened one's horizons. Now it costs a hundred times as much, and the reaction of the average viewer is a shrug. Can the end of the eighties recreate it as the stimulating 'live' medium it once was? Of course not: money talks loudest, and the advertisers demand a crass commercialism. But it might help in America if the programme makers had a little more real contact with the people they are supposed to make the programmes for.

LH, April 1986

Explanatory Notes

Television is a vast and frightening wasteland in which treasures are occasionally to be found by the keen explorer. This book is an alphabetical catalogue, wherein some of those treasures are to be found.

What is *not* covered? Foreign-speaking programmes unless they have been well exposed in the western world. News and magazine items. Sports coverage. Music and art critiques. Studio discussions. Live or tape shows which were not preserved; pointless, usually, to record something which the student of the future can no longer consult, when so much else is pressing for inclusion. On the other hand I have tried to include all TV movies, bland as most of them are, partly because they are on film and partly because they form a record of the development of various careers.

It's a start: nearly twelve thousand items about an art (or craft) which has had little written about it beyond fan effusions, technical tomes and worthy but very boring pontifications about its proper use in an ideal society. Because it directly affects all our lives in so many ways, it must be important enough for a general handbook appreciating its achievements, and if the attitudes expressed on it in this still exploratory volume are not by common consent the right ones, I hope many people will write in and say so. Bouquets and brickbats, please, c/o Granada Television, 36 Golden Square, London W1, UK.

If a programme is sufficiently well documented, its details are set out in a format similar to that used in *Halliwell's Film Guide*:

First line: title and, if appropriate, one to four asterisks denoting the extent of its social/historical/artistic interest. If there is an alternative title (aka = also known as) it is given a line to itself under the title.

Second line:
(a) country and year of origin. (For American series the end date is that of the last September season start.)
(b) running time. Note that programmes designed to fit a commercial one-hour slot are normally rationalized as 50 minutes, though they may run as little as 47 minutes or as much as 53 minutes. 'Half-hours' are usually given as 25 minutes, 'two-hours' as 96 minutes, '90-minuters' as 74 minutes. Bear in mind also that American films run faster in the UK, by one minute in 25, so that a 74-minute film is only 71 minutes to an Englishman. It takes a mind more scientific than mine to explain the reason for this.

(c) if a TV movie (TVM); if recorded on tape (VTR). This last note is made only if the fact is surprising; most comedy series, studio-based programmes and British drama are on tape.

Third line: production credits, usually a series of companies and people joined by obliques. I have omitted trade distributors, as these tend to vary from country to country, but I have aimed to give first the station or network which originally transmitted (and usually commissioned) the programme. Then the production company(ies) which made it. A producer in brackets is an employee rather than a partner. Executive producers like David Gerber are often shown rather than line producers, as it is the former who have the real influence; but situations vary immensely.

Fourth line: synopsis.

Next: appraisal.

Then: artistic credits. Writer (*w*), director (*d*), photographer (*ph*), music score (*m*), production designer (*pd*), art director (*ad*), where available. In the case of series the original creator (*cr*) is normally given, and occasionally I have listed and credited each episode where the results seem interesting. In British credits, the creative overseer is still normally listed as producer rather than director, and in these and other cases further interpretation and research will be required.

Then: principal cast in order of importance.

Finally: additional notes and critical quotes, if any.

This amount of information simply cannot be found for many items which seem to be worth an entry; the format is also very space-consuming, therefore many entries have been compressed into paragraph form, with only selected information.

In the programme entries, contributions which seem to be especially meritorious are printed in SMALL CAPITALS. In people entries, a rosette (✻) admits the bearer to Halliwell's Hall of Fame, an accolade reserved to those whose contribution is so outstanding as to form a milestone in television's lengthy progress. Also in people entries, the most significant programmes are in SMALL CAPITALS.

The aim has been to ensure that all series or single items have been included which genuinely widen the boundaries of English-speaking television. Each reader however is bound to discover what to him are mistakes of emphasis, if only because of the temptation to give better coverage to the more easily accessible items. A better balance is constantly sought.

There is very little cross-referencing, except of alternative titles for series and pilot films. If you are looking up a programme, most of the chief contributors will have their own entries. If you are looking up a person, his or her most important productions will also be separately treated. If a practitioner has also had an extensive film career, reference to my *Filmgoer's Companion* is indicated.

The cut-off date for inclusion is roughly the end of 1985, but some programmes from the beginning of 1986 have been included.

To sum up what you may expect to find:

Series

TV movies

Individual plays, documentaries and other entertainments of significance

People who have made significant creative contributions (plus a few who simply appear a lot)

Companies and networks

Technical and trade terms

General subjects (such as lookalikes, stage management of life, etc.)

Books on television

Philip Purser's contributions are distinguished by the initials 'PP' at the end; all other items are by the undersigned. When we have disagreed with each other, we have made this clear by adding comments introduced by an 'LH' or 'PP'.

For many years now, archives in America and Britain have been collecting and preserving television programmes for posterity. I hope that this book will have some value for the student of the year 2000 and later, if only as a handy guide to the field. But primarily it is intended for the thoughtful viewer of the eighties, in search of useful information or instant nostalgia.

Acknowledgement

Grateful thanks are due to the correspondents who sent in corrections and suggestions, and in particular to David M. Drake and S. F. G. Rowntree.

L.H., January 1986

THE TELEVISION COMPANION
A-Z

'It picks up where *Jesus of Nazareth* left off!'
A.D. (Anno Domini)
US 1985 12 × 50m (various
  formats) colour miniseries
NBC/Proctor and Gamble/Vincenzo
  Labella

The early years of Christianity and the decline of the Caesars.
Flatly developed history with pauses for orgies and religiosity. Not a persuasive piece despite expensive production.

w Vincenzo Labella, Anthony Burgess *d* Stuart Cooper *ph* Ennio Guarnieri *m* Lalo Schifrin *pd* Enzo Bulgarelli

Anthony Andrews (Nero), James Mason (Tiberius), John McEnery (Caligula), Denis Quilley (Peter), Phillip Sayer (Paul), Diana Venora (Corinna), Cecil Humphreys (Caleb), Richard Kiley (Claudius), Ava Gardner (Agrippina), Ben Vereen (Ethiopian); and Colleen Dewhurst, Jack Warden, Neil Dickson, David Hedison, John Houseman, Ian MacShane, Jennifer O'Neill, Damien Thomas

'Tries mightily to ignite: it goes phffft.' – *Daily Variety*

† Some said the initials stood for 'awfully dull'.

A for Andromeda*
GB 1961 7 × 45m bw

BBC science fiction serial by Fred Hoyle and John Elliot, directed by Michael Hayes; now chiefly remembered for propelling an unknown drama student called Julie Christie into instant stardom. She played a lab assistant working on a sinister computer which earthlings had trustingly built to specifications received from outer space. Once complete, it set about mastering the world. The lab assistant, up till then a brunette, was killed and re-synthesized as a blonde (and extremely beautiful) android whose subsequent behaviour neatly summed up the philosophic proposition of the \story. Would she serve her inhuman master or warm to the pleadings of a flesh-and-blood lover? In other words, would science triumph over man, or man contain science? The answer came excitingly after a rather lumpish start, and the ideas were of the quality to be expected from the Cambridge Professor of Astronomy (Hoyle), but a sequel lacking Julie Christie, *The Andromeda Breakthrough*, also lacked comparable impact.   PP

A. J. Wentworth, BA
GB 1982 6 × 30m colour
Thames (Michael Mills)

Arthur Lowe's last role as the tetchy absent-minded schoolmaster created by the *Punch* writer H. F. Ellis. Gentle and amusing, but after years of Captain Mainwaring he didn't quite manage the cringeing to the headmaster also required of the character.

w Basil Boothroyd *d* Michael Mills

Arthur Lowe, Harry Andrews   PP

A Plus. Admirable British afternoon programme from Thames, for many years known as *Afternoon Plus* and going out daily on ITV. Now twice-weekly on Channel 4, usually comprising the interview of a celebrity guest by Mavis Nicholson.   PP

'When it can't be done, they do it!'
The A-Team *
US 1983–   × 50m colour
MCA/Stephen J. Cannell

Ill-assorted soldiers of fortune, themselves on the run from army law, assist victims of injustice.
A master of disguise, a black giant with 'bad attitudes', and a psychopath are three of these Four Just Men in the two-hour pilot film recycled the plot of *The Magnificent Seven*. The series alternated between boring badinage and senseless violence of the Mickey Mouse kind, but it certainly attracted the world's kids.

cr STEPHEN J. CANNELL, FRANK LUPO

GEORGE PEPPARD (Col. Hannibal Smith), MR T ('B.A.'), Dirk Benedict ('The Face'), Dwight Schultz ('Howling Mad Murdock'), Melinda Culea (first season), William Lucking, William Windom (pilot only)

'Juve behaviour, palsy pranks, impersonations and tricky escapes add up to accumulative numbness.' – *Variety*

'Tired guys who have spent the day drilling teeth or putting fenders on Fords may find an hour of uncomplicated diversion here.' – *TV Guide*

'No one admits liking it, but everyone watches it.' – *Hollywood Reporter*

A–Z. BBC entertainment of 1956–7, with a second series a year later, in which Alan Melville strung together sketches, songs, parodies and guest appearances to a different letter of the alphabet each week. Derived originally from a published format by Wolf Mankowitz, it was somewhat ahead of the sophistication of the day. An impersonation of Percy Thrower, gardening expert, giving advice on how to dispose of unwanted garden gnomes brought anguished letters objecting to such wilful destruction and offering kind homes for spurned statuary. Produced by Brian Sears.   PP

Aaker, Lee (1943–   ). American child actor of the fifties who had a long run in *The Adventures of Rin Tin Tin*.

Abba. A Swedish rock group, popular from the late seventies in many television specials. Members: Bjorn Ulvaeus, Agnetha Faltskog, Anni-Frid Lyngstad, Benny Anderson.

Abbot, Russ (*c* 1941–). Zany British comedian of the seventies/eighties who with his broadly farcical gang presents *Russ Abbot's Madhouse*.

The Abbott and Costello Show: see Abbott, Bud

Abbott, Bud (1895–1974) (William Abbott). Veteran vaudevillian crosstalker famed for his partnership with Lou Costello. In 1953, after the decline of their Hollywood careers, they reunited for a half-hour TV series (52 episodes) which revamped all their old routines and was still being played 25 years later. In 1966 Hanna–Barbera made 156 × 5-minute cartoons which weren't bad. (At least they used Abbott's voice.)

Abbott, Philip (1923–   ). Stolid but useful American actor, one of the team in *The FBI* and in occasional TV movies: *Tail Gunner Joe*, *Escape from Bogen County*, etc.

ABC (US). America's 'third network' which in the seventies, by a remarkable spurt, became number one in the ratings. (Its competitors are CBS and NBC.) ABC was formed in the forties by a merger between United Paramount Theatres and the proprietor of Life Savers. Its guiding spirit has been Leonard Goldenson, now chairman, and its most successful programme developments have included *The Wonderful World of Disney*, *Cheyenne* and *Maverick*, Movie of the Week, Monday night football and *Roots*.

ABC (GB). Independent TV contractor, an offshoot of the ABC theatre chain in which the major shareholders were ABPC (a production company) and Warners (who were bought out in the fifties). From 1955 ABC's territory was the Midlands and North of England at weekends, but as a result of the ITA's 1968 reshuffle it became leading partner, with Associated Rediffusion, in Thames TV, the London weekly company.

The Abdication**
GB 1976 56m colour (VTR)

An excellent 40th anniversary wrap-up of events leading to the abdication of Edward VIII; much use of contemporary newsfilm. Written and narrated by James Cameron; directed by Philip Geddes; produced by Gordon Watkins; for BBC.

† *The Abdication* is also the title of a Thames 1978 documentary about the history of Palestine after the British handed over; produced by Richard Broad.

The Abduction of St Anne *
aka: *They've Kidnapped Anne Benedict*
US 1975 74m colour TVM
Quinn Martin

A private eye is asked by a bishop to investigate the reported sainthood of a gangster's daughter.

This is called having it all ways. Oddly, the mixture works well enough in the revered Hollywood manner.

w Edward Hume, *novel The Issue of the Bishop's Blood* by Thomas Patrick McMahon d Harry Falk

Robert Wagner, E. G. Marshall, Lloyd Nolan, William Windom, Kathleen Quinlan, James Gregory

Abide with Me **
GB 1977 70m colour
BBC (Mark Shivas)

In a Cotswold village in the twenties, a 14-year-old girl goes to be maid and housekeeper to a 90-year-old lady.

Fascinating drama from life, of the kind that only the BBC seems to do.

w Julian Mitchell, *book A Child in the Forest* by Winifred Foley d Moira Armstrong

CATHLEEN NESBITT, ANN FRANCIS, Zena Walker, John Nettleton, Geoffrey Bayldon 'Full of loving touches and rich in human understanding.' – *Daily Telegraph*

Abigail's Party *
GB 1977 100m colour (VTR)

Drama about the events of a night, very frank in the modern manner and with occasional barbs of wit. Notable as the first full-length TV drama to be partly improvised. With Alison Steadman; devised and directed by MIKE LEIGH; produced by Margaret Matheson; for BBC.

About Britain. An umbrella title for a daytime half-hour slot on the ITV network since 1975. Regional companies are invited to fill it with films showing their own areas; the results have been variable to say the least.

PP: 'But there have been such oddities as a 1985 TVS contribution about a Southampton wife and mother who was convinced that her child was fathered "from beyond the grave" by a long-deceased pop singer.'

About Religion. The first regular weekly religious programme in Britain, running from 1956 to the late sixties. Produced for ATV by ex-actor Michael Redington, it immediately won the approval of the churches. Items varied from interviews with the archbishops of the day to a passion play called 'Christ in Jeans'.   PP

About Time (GB 1985 6 × 50m). Interesting idea to explore the way lives are organized by the clock and what it represents, with much perception from the series's guru, John Berger, but a little too much of Marxist theories of time as a capitalist invention. Produced by Christopher Lawrence for Third Eye and Channel 4.   PP

Abrams, Gerald W. (1939–). American executive producer. *Red Alert, Ski Lift to Death, The Defection of Simas Kurdika, Letters from Frank, Act of Love, Marion Rose White, Scorned and Swindled, Florence Nightingale*, etc.

Academy Awards Telecast. TV's bow towards the movies, this top-rating annual show, usually seen at the beginning of April, is networked live from Los Angeles and has been known to run more than three hours. The fact that it is staged for TV has made it rather a bore for those who actually attend, but it has its historical appeal as America's

major annual gathering of film stars, with nostalgia its trump card. The statuette awarded is known as Oscar, and awards began in 1927.

Academy of Television Arts and Sciences. America's group of TV professionals who annually present their version of Oscar, called Emmy by derivation from the image orthicon tube. Awards began in 1949 and are usually televised. The categories vary alarmingly from year to year and seem to be increasing in number.

Acapulco
US 1961 8 × 25m bw
NBC/UA/Libra

Veterans of the Korean war live it up in a ritzy resort, and give protection to a criminal lawyer.

Flop series attempting a sub-Hemingway approach to post-war wanderers.

James Coburn, Ralph Taeger, Allison Hayes, Telly Savalas

Accidental Family
US 1967 16 × 25m colour
NBC/Sheldon Leonard

A widowed Californian comedian turns farmer in order to bring up his son.
Forgettable schmaltz.

Jerry Van Dyke, Teddy Quinn, Lois Nettleton

According to the Rules * (GB 1972; 75m; bw). Superb, restrained documentary made by Robert Reid for the BBC about the lawsuit brought by Dr Wladislaw Dering, a London doctor, after being named for war crimes in a Leon Uris novel. The establishing compilation film and the reconstructed lawsuit were kept firmly separate. In the latter the limitations of the brief television extracts were always declared. The aim was to give an accurate impression rather than make a case, and the result was strangely moving: on the one hand, the victims reliving terrible days in the ordered calm of an English courtroom; on the other, an initially brave and good man who had become corrupted simply by survival in such a place as Auschwitz; vindictiveness alternating with forgivingness, candour with a refusal to admit the inadmissible; and from it all a stolid English jury extracting the one extraordinary verdict that was apt. The same case inspired the reprehensible *QB VII*. See also: *Auschwitz*.
PP

**Accounts ** (GB 1983). Farmer's widow and two sons try to make a go of a (Scottish)

Border hill farm, only to be let down by lousy book-keeping. Hence the title. 'Gently absorbing, pawky and truthful,' I wrote at the time. 'If you want to see how film-making can be understated, oblique and yet wonderfully lucid just watch the relationship evolve between the younger of the two boys and the friend of the family, as played by Jonathan Newth in one of the most subtle and consummate performances I've seen.' Written by Michael Wilcox, directed and produced by Michael Darlow for Partners in Production and Channel 4's *Film on Four*.   PP

Accused (US 1958). A half-hour courtroom drama which lasted one season on ABC. Drawn from a daytime programme called *Day in Court*, it presented re-enactments of famous criminal cases, usually presided over by law professor Edgar Allan Jones Jnr. Produced by Selig J. Seligman.

Ace Awards. American awards presented annually for original achievement by the national Association for Cable TV.

Ace Crawford Private Eye
US 1983 13 × 25m colour
(Viacom) Conway Enterprises
Adventures of an inept detective.
Get Smart it isn't . . . and the viewers agreed.
cr Ron Clark, Tim Conway
Tim Conway, Joe Regalbuto, Shera Danese, Billy Barty, Dick Christie

✳ **Ace, Goodman** (1899–1980). Outstanding American comedy writer for radio and TV, who in the fifties provided smart scripts for Milton Berle, Perry Como and Sid Caesar.

Acker, Sharon (1935–). American leading lady. TV movies include *A Clear and Present Danger*, *Hec Ramsey* (pilot), *The Stranger*, *The Hanged Man*, *The Hostage Heart*, *The Murder That Wouldn't Die*.

Ackerman, Bettye (19 –). American occasional actress, wife of Sam Jaffe and at his side in the *Ben Casey* series. TV movies include *Companions in Nightmare*, *Heat of Anger*, *Murder or Mercy*, *Doctors' Private Lives*.

Ackerman, Harry S. (1912–). American executive who after work in an advertising agency and with CBS programme development was supervisor and often

creator of Screen Gems' output in the sixties. The results included *Dennis the Menace*, *The Flying Nun*, *Hazel*, *The Farmer's Daughter*, *Bewitched* and *The Ugliest Girl in Town*.

Ackland, Joss (1928–). British character actor frequently on TV in single plays. Series: *The Crezz*, *Shadowlands*, 1985.

Ackroyd, David (1940–). American leading man. *Another World*, *Harvest Home*, *The Word*, *And I Alone Survived*, *The Sound of Murder*, *When Your Lover Leaves*, *The Sky's the Limit*, etc.

'Handicapped kids melt a tough guy's heart!'
The Acorn People
US 1980 96m colour
NBC/Rollings–Jaffe–Lorra–Brezner (Peter Katz)
Problems of physically handicapped children at a Texas summer camp.
By American standards an admirably discreet heartwarmer.
w/d Joan Tewkesbury *ph* Robert Jessup
Ted Bessell, LeVar Burton, Cloris Leachman, Dolph Sweet
'One of the better telefilms of recent memory. Having something to say, it says it and, having said it, closes down.' – *Daily Variety*

Act of Betrayal ✳✳
GB 1971 85m 16mm colour
BBC
A dramatization of the discovery of the Portland spy ring as seen by the neighbours and friends of those living at 45 Cranley Drive, Ruislip.
An early example of the modern art of faction which became prevalent at the end of the seventies; real events are woven into a web of supposition.
w Hugh Whitemore *d* William Slater
Zena Marshall, Marjorie Wimbush, Michael Gwynn
† See *45 Cranley Drive* for an earlier treatment of the same episode.

Act of Love
US 1981 96m colour
NBC/Paramount/Cypress Point (Gerald Abrams)
A young Polish-American promises his paralysed brother that he will kill him and end his misery.
Well-intentioned but unnecessary problem picture about euthanasia; nicely made, but

nothing at all new except the Seattle locations.

w Michael de Guzman, *novel* Paige Mitchell *d* Jud Taylor *ph* Michael D. Margulies *m* Billy Goldenberg

RON HOWARD, Robert Foxworth, Mickey Rourke, David Spielberg, Jacqueline Brookes

Act of Passion **
aka: *The Lost Honor of Kathryn Beck*
US 1984 96m colour TVM
CBS/Comworld/Open Road (John Nicolella)

An innocent girl is harassed by the police after spending the night with a suspected terrorist.
Americanization, shot in Chicago, of a German original; compelling drama, very well made.

w LORING MANDEL from the *novel* and film by Heinrich Böll *d* SIMON LANGTON *ph* Gordon Willis *m* Laurence Rosenthal *pd* Peter Larkin

MARLO THOMAS, KRIS KRISTOFFERSON, George Dzundza, Jon DeVries, David Rasche, Linda Thorson, Edward Winter

Act of Violence
US 1980 96m colour
CBS/Paramount

A liberal-minded divorcee is assigned to a teleseries on urban violence but is herself the victim of mugging.
Predictably earnest and psychologically harrowing melodrama of the moment. Well made but superfluous.

Elizabeth Montgomery, James Sloyan, Sean Frye

An Actor's Life for Me (GB 1985). Six half-hours of actors and actresses telling horror stories of their profession to the camera. Some *longueurs* and some hilarious, doubtless oft-rehearsed set pieces, with the honours going to Anton Rodgers, Maureen Lipman and Jack Shepherd. Produced by Tony Staveacre, for BBC.   PP

It's just another headline – until it happens to your child!'
Adam *
US 1983 96m colour TVM
NBC/Alan Landsburg (Linda Otto)

When his small son is kidnapped and found murdered, a man stands up against the FBI for children's rights.
Moderately gripping fictionalization of a true story which engrossed America in 1982.

w Allan Leicht *d* Michael Tuchner *ph* Mike Fash *m* Mike Post

DANIEL J. TRAVANTI, JoBeth Williams, Martha Scott, Richard Masur, Paul Regina

Adam Adamant. BBC 50-minute tape show of the mid sixties in which Gerald Harper played a period hero thawed out in the 20th century to pit his wits against modern evils. As a Saturday night time-filler, it had class.

PP: 'The collision of Edwardian clubland chivalry with the swinging London of the sixties had obvious potential but the execution was a bit hurried and skimpy. Created by Verity Lambert and Tony Williamson.'

✴ **Adam, Kenneth** (1908–78). Affable British executive, formerly in publicity, who as BBC-TV's first Programme Controller (and later Director) played a key part in fostering the great sunburst of creativity at the Television Centre during the sixties. On retirement became a part-time academic in the United States.   PP

Adam Smith *
GB 1972 39 × 25m colour (VTR)
Granada (June Howson)

After the death of his lady, a Presbyterian minister seeks the meaning of life while continuing to help his parishioners.
Gritty, determined and well-meaning combination of drama and religion, rather doleful to watch.

w Ben Rae (Trevor Griffiths) *d* Richard Martin
Andrew Keir, Tom Conti, Kara Wilson, Brigid Forsyth

Adam 12 *
US 1968–75 164 × 25m colour
NBC/Universal/Jack Webb (James Doherty)

Incidents in the lives of urban police officers in a cruiser car.
Popular, easy-going attempt to humanize the cops. Worth comparing with the much tougher British *Z Cars*, which used exactly the same premise except for taking 50 minutes to tell one story rather than 25 to tell four.

cr Jack Webb, Robert Cinader
Martin Milner, Kent McCord

Adams, Berle (1917–). American executive, long with MCA, and producer (*Brass Target*, TV specials). Latterly in distribution.

Adams, Brooke (1949–). American leading lady of the late seventies, mainly in theatrical films. TV movies include *The Daughters of Joshua Cabe*, *Who Is the Black Dahlia*, *Murder on Flight 502*, *Nero Wolfe*.

The Adams Chronicles **
US 1975 13 × 50m colour (VTR)
WNET (Jac Venza)
How succeeding generations of the John Quincy Adams family influenced American history.
Stalwart saga produced by public TV with the aid of grants: above the heads of the mass audience but with many pleasures, good historical sense, and the correct measured pace.
story editor Anne Howard Bailey
William Daniels, George Grizzard, John Houseman, Nancy Coleman, David Birney, JOHN BEAL, Wesley Addy, Leora Dana, Kathryn Walker (Emmy 1975)

✳ **Adams, Don** (1927–) (Donald James Yarmy). American entertainer, former impressionist who hit it big on *Tonight*, *The Bill Dana Show*, and later (1965–70) as the bumbling spy in GET SMART (Emmy 1966/67/68). In the mid-70s he failed to impress in a comedy called *The Partners* or as host of *Screen Test*, and a 1980 *Get Smart* film (*The Nude Bomb*) was disastrous.

Adams, Edie (1929–). American comedienne best remembered on shows of her husband Ernie Kovacs (1951–6). TV movies: *Evil Roy Slade*, *Superdome*, *Fast Friends*, etc.

Adams, Julie (1928–) (Betty May Adams). American leading lady of fifties films; makes occasional TV comebacks, notably in *The Jimmy Stewart Show*. TV movies include *The Trackers*, *Go Ask Alice*, *Greatest Heroes of the Bible*.

Adams, Mason (1920–). American character actor, familiar as LOU GRANT'S editor. TV movies include *The Deadliest Season*, *And Baby Makes Six*, *A Shining Season*, *Murder Can Hurt You*, *The Revenge of the Stepford Wives*.

Adams, Nick (1931–68) (Nicholas Adamschock). American actor, young in the fifties, who starred in series *Saints and Sinners* and *The Rebel*.

Adams of Eagle Lake. An American series for ABC which never got off the ground,
despite several efforts in 1975, when a TV movie, *Winter Kills*, and two one-hours were made, all based on the country sheriff played by James Garner in the cinema film *They Only Kill Their Masters*. In 1978 Andy Griffith, around whom the TV series was to be built, was still trying, with a slightly different character, in such TV movies as *The Girl in the Empty Grave* and *Deadly Game*. All were MGM productions. The format creator was John Michael Hayes.

Adam's Rib
US 1973 13 × 25m colour
ABC/MGM (Peter Stone, Peter H. Hunt)
Married lawyers are at odds both at home and in court.
Unsuccessful copy of a successful film, with willing leads no substitute for Tracy and Hepburn.
cr Peter H. Hunt *m* Perry Botkin Jnr, Gil Garfield
Blythe Danner, Ken Howard, Edward Winter, Dena Dietrich

Adamson, Peter (1930–). British character actor who played (exclusively) the rough diamond Len Fairclough in *Coronation Street* from the birth of the serial in 1960 until being famously written out in 1983.

The Addams Family **
US 1964–5 64 × 25m bw
ABC/Filmways (David Levy)
Daily doings of a macabre family based on the Charles Addams cartoons in the *New Yorker*.
A sophisticated black comedy idea became an unexpected popular success, largely owing to a catchy theme tune, a succession of good gags and snappy production values. *The Munsters*, a similar idea aired during the same season, was also popular but played more for sympathy.
JOHN ASTIN (Gomez), CAROLYN JONES (Morticia), JACKIE COOGAN (Uncle Fester), TED CASSIDY (Lurch), Blossom Rock (Grandmama), The Thing
† The hand of The Thing was played by Ted Cassidy.
†† A half-hour cartoon series of the same name passed without notice as did a 1979 special, *Halloween with the Addams Family*.

Addison, John (1920–). British composer whose TV scores include *Centennial* and *Pearl*.

Adelson, Gary (1954–). American producer, son of Merv. *The Winter of Our Discontent, Lace, House Detective*, etc.

Adelson, Merv (1929–). American producer associated with some of Lorimar's most successful productions: *The Waltons, Eight Is Enough, Dallas, Kaz, Knots Landing, Sybil, A Man Called Intrepid*, etc.

admags. A now forgotten alternative to the commercial spot in the early days of Britain's commercial television was the advertising magazine, in which performers were allowed to extol the virtues of various products during the course of a generally vapid quarter-hour of chat. *Jim's Inn*, presided over by Jimmy Hanley, was the best-known example. The facility was withdrawn by the ITA in 1963. PP

Adrian, Rhys (1928–). British writer of sharply individual, often wistful plays: *The Protest* (1960), *Thrills Galore* (1967), *The Foxtrot* (1971), *Evelyn* (1971), *The Buffet* (1976), *Mr and Mrs Bureaucrat* (1980), *Passing Through* (1982). PP

Adventure at Scott Island: see Harbormaster

The Adventurer
GB 1972 24 × 25m colour
ITC (Monty Berman)
A cloak and dagger series made on 16mm for an American prime-time access slot, with Gene Barry as a debonair villain-catcher against jetset backgrounds. It didn't catch anyone's imagination, despite the stalwart support of Stuart Damon, Barry Morse and Catherine Schell.
m Jerry Goldsmith (theme John Barry)

Adventures in Paradise
US 1959–61 91 × 50m bw
ABC/TCF (Martin Manulis)
Adam Troy runs a small schooner in the South Pacific.
Mindless adventures inspired by James Michener stories. The star, a sailing enthusiast, subsequently made a movie called *I Sailed to Tahiti with an All-Girl Crew*, which suggests the level of the series.
cr James A. Michener
Gardner McKay

Adventures in Rainbow Country
Canada 1972 26 × 25m colour
CBC/Manitou
A 14-year-old boy has fun growing up near Lake Huron.

Unexceptionable, and rather boring, open-air series for youngsters and indulgent adults.
Billy Williams, Lois Maxwell

Adventures of a Jungle Boy
GB 1957 13 × 25m colour
ABC/Gross–Krasne
A young Tarzan lives with a friendly cheetah in East Africa.
Harmless, unimaginative, plagiaristic nonsense.
Michael Carr Hartley

The Adventures of Aggie. An independent British half-hour comedy series of the fifties with Joan Shawlee as a fashion designer on international assignments.

The Adventures of Black Beauty *
GB 1972 26 × 25m colour
London Weekend/Fremantle
Two well-brought-up children, a horse, and a country estate in Victorian days.
Pleasantly made adventures with no relation to Anna Sewell's book.
William Lucas

The Adventures of Dick Turpin: see Dick Turpin

The Adventures of Don Quixote *
GB 1972 98m colour TVM
BBC/Universal
Easily assimilated but quite unremarkable compression of Cervantes's great novel.
w Hugh Whitemore *d* Alvin Rakoff
Rex Harrison, Frank Finlay, Rosemary Leach

The Adventures of Ellery Queen: see Ellery Queen

The Adventures of Gulliver (US 1980; 17 × 25m). Anaemic animated version of a classic which it in no way resembles. A Hanna–Barbera Saturday morning disaster.

The Adventures of Hiram Holliday *
US 1956 26 × 25m bw
A meek little reporter on a world tour has various adventures.
Modest comedy series from a Paul Gallico character, which confirmed the stardom of Wally Cox after *Mr Peepers*.
Wally Cox, Joel Smith

The Adventures of Huckleberry Finn
US 1981 96m colour TVM
NBC/Schick Sunn Classic (William
  Cornford)
Poor version of the Mark Twain classic.
w Tom Chapman d Jack Hively ph Paul
Hipp m Bob Summers
Kurt Ida, Dan Monahan, Brock Peters,
Forrest Tucker, Larry Storch, Lurene Tuttle,
Jack Kruschen, Mike Mazurki
'Marshmallow soft . . . thin-blooded indeed
. . . it's "Happy Days on the Mississippi"
time.' – *Daily Variety*
† See also *The New Adventures of Huckleberry
Finn*.

The Adventures of Jim Bowie
US 1956–7 78 × 25m bw
ABC/Louis Edelman
A frontiersman journeys to Texas after the
Louisiana Purchase.
Elementary western adventures for the
family, from the book *Tempered Blade* by
Monte Barrett.
Scott Forbes, Robert Cornthwaite, Peter
Hanson

The Adventures of Judge Roy Bean
US 1955 39 × 25m bw
Barrett/Quintet
Exploits of a rascally judge in the old west.
Acceptably amusing studio-bound western
series.
Edgar Buchanan, Jack Beutel

The Adventures of Kit Carson
US 1952–4 104 × 25m bw
Universal
Travels of a western scout.
Ho-hum family western series.
Bill Williams, Don Diamond

The Adventures of Long John Silver *
Australia 1955 26 × 25m colour
Isola del'Oro
Cramped, studio-bound adventures of a
rascally pirate, notable chiefly for preserving
a famous star performance.
ROBERT NEWTON, Connie Gilchrist, Kit Taylor

The Adventures of Muhammad Ali
US 1977 26 × 22m colour
TCF/Farmhouse Films (Fred Calvert)
Adventures of 'the greatest', in company with
his young niece and nephew, his public
relations man, and his dog.
Adequate cartoon time-passer, voiced by the
man himself.

The Adventures of Nellie Bly
US 1980 96m colour TVM
NBC/Schick Sunn Classic (James L.
  Conway)
The semi-factual story of one of New York's
first newspaperwomen.
Could have been fun; but the level of writing,
directing and acting was too low.
w S. S. Schweizer d Henning Schellerup
ph Stephen W. Gray m Bob Summers
Linda Purl, Gene Barry, John Randolph,
Paul Sylvan, Cliff Osmond, Elayne Heilveil,
J. D. Cannon

The Adventures of Nick Carter
aka: *Nick Carter*
US 1972 73m colour TVM
Universal (Stanley Kallis)
A private detective gets into colourful
company when investigating the death of a
friend.
Another attempt to revivify one of the
longest-lasting detectives of all; plot and cast
are uneasy, the nineties setting really does
not help.
w Ken Pettus d Paul Krasny
Robert Conrad, Shelley Winters, Brooke
Bundy, Dean Stockwell, Pat O'Brien,
Broderick Crawford, Neville Brand, Pernell
Roberts

The Adventures of Ozzie and Harriet *
US 1952–65 435 × 25m bw (last 26 in
  colour)
ABC/Stage Five (Ozzie Nelson)
Archetypal domestic family comedy: so bland
was the concept that the hero's occupation
was never mentioned in fourteen years, but
America lapped it up.
cr Ozzie Nelson
OZZIE NELSON, HARRIET (HILLIARD) NELSON,
their sons David and Rick and their
daughters-in-law June and Kris
† A feature film, *Here Come the Nelsons*, was
made in 1951. David and Rick's real-life
wives later became co-stars of the series, and
Rick became a top pop guitarist and vocalist.

The Adventures of Rin Tin Tin *
US 1954–6 52 × 25m bw
ABC/Columbia (Herb Leonard, Frederick
  Briskin)
A dog is a great asset at Fort Apache in the
1880s.
Often enjoyable family western.
Lee Aaker, Jim Brown, Joe Sawyer

The Adventures of Robin Hood **
GB 1955–9 143 × 25m bw
ITC/Sapphire (Hannah Weinstein)
Robin outwits the wicked sheriff and thwarts King John.
Generally spirited extensions of a favourite legend; they certainly hit the target at the time.
RICHARD GREENE, John Arnatt, Archie Duncan, Alexander Gauge, ALAN WHEATLEY

The Adventures of Sherlock Holmes
US 1955 39 × 25m bw
Sheldon Reynolds
Sloppy retreads of great stories, ill-cast and poorly filmed.
Ronald Howard, Howard Marion-Crawford

† See also *Sherlock Holmes and Dr Watson.*

The Adventures of Sherlock Holmes
GB 1984–5 13 × 52m colour
Granada (Michael Cox)
Granada built a length of Victorian Baker Street behind their permanent Coronation Street set for what they hoped would be the definitive Holmes series. It went down better abroad than at home but Jeremy Brett was certainly the most satisfactory Holmes TV has given us. Following Conan Doyle's example, episode 13 killed off the great detective at the Reichenbach Falls. Granada immediately brought him back to life in *The Return of Sherlock Holmes*, 1986.
w various *d* Paul Annett, John Bruce, David Carson, Ken Grieve and Alan Grint *design* Michael Grimes and others
Jeremy Brett, David Burke (as Watson) PP

The Adventures of Sir Francis Drake: see Sir Francis Drake

The Adventures of Sir Lancelot
GB 1956 30 × 25m bw
ITC/Sapphire
Legends of the court of King Arthur. Adequate, unexciting production.
William Russell, Jane Hylton, Ronald Leigh-Hunt (as King Arthur), Cyril Smith (as Merlin)

The Adventures of Superman *
US 1953–5 104 × 25m bw (52), colour (52)
Lippert/National Periodical Publications
A superbeing from the planet Krypton poses on earth as Clark Kent, a mild-mannered reporter, but zooms into action whenever the innocent need help.

Crude but likeable serial from a thirties comic strip. Superman had previously featured in a couple of low-budget theatrical features and a serial, *Atom Man vs Superman*; in the sixties he became a cartoon character in *The Batman–Superman Hour* and *Super Friends*. 1978 revived him as the hero of a super-budget feature.
GEORGE REEVES, Phyllis Coates, John Hamilton

The Adventures of the Falcon
US 1954 39 × 25m bw
Bernard Schubert
Mike Waring takes on hazardous assignments.
Roughneck version of the more famous film series.
Charles McGraw

Adventures of the Queen
US 1975 99m colour TVM
TCF (Irwin Allen)
A mad bomber is loose on an ocean liner. Overstretched failed pilot on the *Queen Mary* at Long Beach. Plot and performances make it very ho-hum.
w John Gay *d* David Lowell Rich
Robert Stack, Ralph Bellamy, David Hedison, Bradford Dillman, Sorrell Booke, Burr de Benning, John Randolph

Adventures of the Sea Hawk
US 1958 26 × 25m bw
Wesmore, Inc
Scientists travel in a floating electronics lab. Palatable early evening adventures, filmed in Bermuda.
John Howard, John Lee

Adventures of the Seaspray
Australia 1965 32 × 25m colour
Columbia/Roger Mirams
An 83-foot schooner sails the South Pacific. Moderate family fare.

The Adventures of Tugboat Annie
Canada 1956 39 × 25m bw
Normandie
Tugboat captains enjoy a friendly feud. Watchable extension of the feature film characters created by Norman Reilly Raine.
Minerva Urecal, Walter Sande

The Adventures of William Tell *
GB 1957 39 × 25m bw
ITC
The legendary Swiss folk hero defeats the evil Gessler.

Or, Robin Hood in the Alps. A location-filmed series with more than a spark of vitality.

Conrad Philips, Jennifer Jayne, Willoughby Goddard

Advice to the Lovelorn
US 1980 96m colour
NBC/Universal (Jon Epstein)
A newspaper columnist fails with her own love life.
Ho-hum failed pilot; watchable for those who like to be 10 minutes ahead of the movie.

w Howard Burk d Harry Falk

Cloris Leachman, Desi Arnaz Jnr, Donna Pescow, Tina Louise, Melissa Sue Anderson, Lance Kerwin, Paul Burke, Walter Brooke, Kelly Bishop

'The film flaps disconcertingly back and forth among the three tales: it's like automatic channel switching.' – *Daily Variety*

The Aerodrome * (GB 1983).
Glittering film dramatization of Rex Warner's ill-timed 1941 allegory of the attractions of Fascism, left as a period piece in details of dress and country life but with the military hardware updated to the fifties. 'The make-believe was perfectly set in sometime and nowhere, but I wonder how many viewers shared my original instinct to look around to see who it was aimed at.' With Jill Bennett, Peter Firth, Richard Johnson, Richard Briers. Written by Robin Chapman, directed by Giles Foster. Produced by Kenith Trodd, for BBC.   PP

AES Hudson Street (US 1978).
A shortlived half-hour tape comedy series about a black doctor (Gregory Sierra) in an incompetently run emergency hospital. (AES = Adult Emergency Services.) Created by Danny Arnold, Tony Sheenan, Chris Haywood.

The Affair ***
GB 1963 100m bw (VTR)
BBC (John Jacobs)
An unpopular college don is accused of cheating and defended by an older man who dislikes him.
Brilliant TV adaptation of a celebrated play and novel, with an all-star cast of its time.

w RONALD MILLAR, from his play and C. P. SNOW's novel d JOHN JACOBS

JOHN CLEMENTS, Alan Dobie, Michael Goodliffe, Felix Aylmer, Nigel Stock, Sheila Allen, Cyril Luckham

† Same story dramatized 1984 as part of C. P. Snow cycle *Strangers and Brothers*.

The Affair *
US 1973 74m colour TVM
ITC/Spelling–Goldberg
Extrovert lawyer falls in love with reclusive polio victim, but it doesn't work.
Watchable modern soap opera.

w Barbara Turner d Gilbert Cates ph Jerry Hirschfeld

Natalie Wood, Robert Wagner, Bruce Davison, Kent Smith, Pat Harrington

† A theatrical version was released at 92m.

affiliate station. A local American station which contracts with a network to take a proportion of its programmes.

The AFI Salute. The American Film Institute has taken to hosting an annual dinner at which a famous star or director of yesteryear is toasted. The resulting festivals of nostalgia, filled with star tributes and film clips, have invariably been televised. Recipients have included John Ford, James Cagney (Emmy 1974), Orson Welles, William Wyler, Bette Davis, Henry Fonda, Alfred Hitchcock, James Stewart, Fred Astaire, Lillian Gish, Frank Capra, Gene Kelly.

Africa **
US 1967 200m colour
ABC News (James Fleming, Blaine Littell)
Milestone four-hour documentary examining the new independent states of Africa; still one of the longest single programmes ever made for TV. Despite much ballyhoo, the public switched to other channels and the experiment was not repeated.

narrator Gregory Peck m Alex North

African Patrol
GB 1957 39 × 25m bw
Gross–Krasne
A mobile policeman in East Africa.
One of the shoddier adventure series of its time.

John Bentley

The African Queen (US 1977).
A 50-minute pilot made by Mark Carliner for CBS. It didn't take, despite good attempts at the famous film roles by Warren Oates and Mariette Hartley.

After a Lifetime *
GB 1971 80m colour (VTR)
LWT
A Liverpool family assembles for a funeral. Predictable realist drama with interesting credits.

w Neville Smith d Ken Loach
Bill Dean, Neville Smith, Peter Karajan

After Hours *. Michael Bentine's first Goon-type television series for ABC (GB) in 1959–60, trying out all the innovations, including cartoon figures by Bob Godfrey, which were to come to fruition in *It's a Square World*.   PP

After the Bomb: see Nagasaki – the Return Journey

After the Funeral *
GB 1960 52m bw (VTR)
ABC (Sydney Newman)
In the Armchair Theatre series; Alun Owen's second play for ABC. Two grandsons (and their wives) compete to look after an old sea captain after his wife's death. One is an ambitious Welsh academic who needs the old boy to bolster up his cultural standing in Swansea, the other an easy-going Liverpool merchant seaman who just thinks Grandad would be happier with them. Within the simple, localized human story was a clash of cultures as old as the Old Testament: the theoretical embalmed kind against the practical and living.
d Ted Kotcheff
Charles Carson, Hugh David, William Lucas, Sylvia Kaye   PP

Aftermash *
US 1983 22 x 25m colour
TCF/Larry Gelbart, Burt Metcalfe
After the Korean War, Colonel Potter, Father Mulcahy and Corporal Klinger find themselves on the staff of the same mid-western rehabilitation centre.
Spin-off attempt, unsuccessful because it doesn't have a star and its mood veers too frequently between farce and sentiment.

Afternoon at the Festival *
GB 1973 50m colour (VTR)
YTV
An agent and his ex-wife are involved in a new picture deal at the Cannes Film Festival. Amusing edgy comedy with undertones.
w David Mercer d Donald McWhinnie
Leo McKern, Adrienne Corri

Afton, Richard (1913–85). BBC light entertainment producer of the fifties (*Café Continental*, *Quite Contrary*, etc) who believed that no publicity was bad publicity, and was expert at attracting it. Discovered many performers from the Television Toppers to Mary O'Hara. In the seventies reappeared as television critic of the London *Evening News* until that paper's absorption into the *London Standard* in 1980. Retired to Florida and was seen posthumously in Whicker's *Living with Uncle Sam*.   PP

Against the Wind (Australia 1975; 13 × 50m miniseries). Popular soap opera about an Irish girl deported to Botany Bay. 'Strong story line and high production values. A real winner.' – *Variety*

The Agatha Christie Hour (GB 1982). Thirteen very mild one-hour dramas from Christie stories which did not concern straight detection. The viewers were muddled. From Thames.

An Age of Kings *** (GB 1960). Outstanding BBC re-orchestration of Shakespeare's history plays from Richard II to Richard III, via Henrys IV, V and VI, to make one 15-episode serial spanning 86 years. Individual episodes received new titles, e.g. *The Band of Brothers*, *The Boar Hunt*, and for the first time the full strength and stretch of the narrative became apparent. The medieval crown prefaced every instalment as the symbol of what it was all about: the lure, the power and the burden of kingship. With David William, Robert Hardy, Eileen Atkins, Paul Daneman. Directed by PETER DEWS. (See also: *Shakespeare*.)   PP

The Age of Uncertainty **
GB 1976 12 × 60m, 1 × 150m colour 16mm
BBC (Adrian Malone)
A series of lectures, with film and visual aids, depicting 'the rise and crisis in industrial society seen in the light of economic factors'. Perhaps just short of a brilliant achievement, but certainly a considerable one, culminating in a discussion with Henry Kissinger, Edward Heath, Shirley Williams, Jack Jones and Rolf Dahrendorf.
producers Dick Gilling, Mick Jackson, David Kennard
JOHN KENNETH GALBRAITH
'One of the great milestones in the world history of television.' – *Financial Times*
'Illuminating entertainment handled with elegant style.' – *Daily Express*
PP: 'Fiddling economic history; the producer's compulsion to illustrate every point didn't help. Milton Friedman, presenting the alternative monetarist interpretation two years later, was – for better or for worse – incomparably more effective.'

AN AGE OF KINGS. David William as Richard II in the BBC's stunning sequence of Shakespeare's historical plays.

The Ages of Man. John Gielgud's famous performance of extracts from Shakespeare as arranged by George Rylands was presented for CBS in 1965 by David Susskind and Daniel Melnick, and won an Emmy as best dramatic programme.

**Agony ** (GB 1979–81). Engaging comedy series about magazine agony column writer (the delicious Maureen Lipman) unable to order her own involvements as sensibly as she advises others. Originally hatched by Anna Raeburn, real-life exponent of the trade, in collaboration with Len Richmond. Later, Richmond took over. Produced by John Reardon, for LWT.   PP

Agran, Linda (1947–). Energetic British story editor and producer, into show business originally as an agent's secretary. From 1976 with Euston Films as script executive on all productions as well as producing *Widows* and sequel; 1981–6 director of scripts and development; executive producer, *Prospects*, 1986. Now freelance.   PP

Agutter, Jenny (1952–). British actress, young in the seventies, in all media. TV movies include THE SNOW GOOSE (Emmy 1972), *War of Children, Mayflower, Beulah Land, The Man in the Iron Mask.*

Aidman, Charles (1925–). American general-purpose actor. *The Red Badge of Courage, Amelia Earhart, Alcatraz, Prime Suspect, Marion Rose White,* etc. Many series guest spots.

Ain't No Time for Glory
US 1957 74m bw TVM
Columbia/Playhouse 90

During the Battle of the Bulge, an American officer talks a German commander into surrender.
Dull and respectable.
d Oscar Rudolph

Barry Sullivan, Gene Barry, John Drew Barrymore, Bruce Bennett

Airline (GB 1982). One-hour series from YTV, created by Wilfred Greatorex, about a civil airline started from scratch by two men demobilized in 1946. Interest limited by unsympathetic leads, Roy Marsden and Anthony Valentine; executive producer David Cunliffe.

PP: 'I thought it excellent.'

Airport *
GB 1978 3 × 50m colour
BBC (Shirley Fisher)

A documentary triptych showing in detailed and assured style how a major international airport (Heathrow) really works.
reporter Harold Williamson

Airwolf
US 1984– 1 x 96m, 57 x 50m colour
CBS/Universal/Bellisarius

A reclusive adventurer comes down from his mountain retreat to fly a specially equipped helicopter against the foes of America.
Serious-minded comic strip with a hero who plays the cello in his off moments. It looks better than it sounds, but its place in the schedule was always precarious.
cr Donald P. Bellisario

Jan Michael Vincent, Ernest Borgnine, Alex Cord

Aitken, Maria (1945–). Liquid-eyed British actress who branched out as chat show hostess after conducting editions of *Friday Night . . . Saturday Morning. Private Lives,* 1983–4. *Poor Little Rich Girls* (as actress), 1984. *Lizzie, an Amazon Adventure.*   PP

Akins, Claude (1918–). American character actor, a heavily-built, slow-moving fellow who throughout his Hollywood career was usually cast as a villain. TV, however, redeemed him, and after many guest star roles he starred in 1974 as the kindly truck-driving hero of the two-season series MOVIN' ON, in 1979 as the evil sheriff of *BJ and the Bear*, and in 1980 in his own series, *Lobo*, based on that character. TV movies include *Lock, Stock and Barrel*, *The Night Stalker*, *Death Squad*, *Eric*, *Kiss Me Kill Me*, *Killer on Board*, *Little Mo*, *Murder in Music City*, *The Concrete Cowboys*, *The Baron and the Kid*

Alan, Ray (1930–). British ventriloquist who learned to play the ukulele from George Formby. Famous for his aristocratic dummy Lord Charles.

Alas Smith and Jones (GB 1984–5). Successive comedy series punning on the title of the 1971–2 western and reuniting two of the *Not the Nine O'Clock News* team, Mel Smith and Griff Rhys Jones. Produced and directed by Martin Shardlow, for BBC.   PP

The Alaskans
US 1959 36 × 50m bw
ABC/Warner
During the 1898 gold rush two likeable adventurers work for Skagway's nefarious saloon keeper.
As tatty-looking and badly acted a series as ever came out of a major studio.
Roger Moore, Jeff York, Ray Danton, Dorothy Provine

Alberg, Mildred Freed (19 –). American drama producer associated with *Playhouse 90*, and in the seventies two religious specials, *The Story of David* and *The Story of Jacob and Joseph*.

❅ **Albert, Eddie** (1908–) (Eddie Albert Heimberger). Genial American actor, usually in light roles. A frequent guest star who also had two long-running series, GREEN ACRES and *Switch*. TV movies include *See the Man Run*, *Fireball Forward*, *Promise Him Anything*, *Evening in Byzantium*, *The Word*, *Beulah Land*, *Oklahoma City Dolls*, *Rooster*, *The Demon Murder Case*, *Burning Rage*

Albert, Edward (1951–). American actor, son of Eddie Albert. TV movies include *Killer Bees*, *Death Cruise*, *Black Beauty*, *Silent Victory*.

❅ **Albertson, Jack** (1907–81). American vaudevillian familiar for many years as straight man to Phil Silvers and Milton Berle; he subsequently enjoyed moderate success on Broadway and in Hollywood. In his later years he became a popular TV star in such series as *Ensign O'Toole*, *Dr Simon Locke*, CHICO AND THE MAN (Emmy 1975) and *Grandpa Goes to Washington*. TV movies include *The Monk*, *Once Upon a Dead Man*, *Congratulations It's A Boy*, *The Comedy Company*.

Albertson, Mabel (1901–82). American character comedienne, memorable as Grandma in *The Tom Ewell Show*.

Albright, Lola (1925–). American leading lady who after a rather disappointing movie career in wisecracking roles became a TV star in PETER GUNN. TV movies: *Delta County USA*, *Terraces*.

Alcatraz Express **
aka: *The Big Train*
US 1960 96m bw TVM
Paramount/Desilu/Quinn Martin
An attempt is made to rescue Al Capone on his way by train to Alcatraz.
Excellent suspense thriller made from two episodes of *The Untouchables*.
w William Spier *d* John Peyser
ROBERT STACK, NEVILLE BRAND, Bruce Gordon, Paul Picerni, Nicholas Georgiade, Abel Fernandez

Alcatraz: The Whole Shocking Story *
US 1980 2 × 96m colour
NBC/Pierre Cossette Productions (James H. Brown, Ernest Tidyman)
A young robber spends 27 years in jail, mainly in Alcatraz, but resists corruption.
Rather unwieldy and overlong but intermittently powerful dramatization of a true case, the subject of which advised on the script.
w Ernest Tidyman *d* Paul Krasny
ph Robert B. Hauser *m* Jerrold Immel
Michael Beck (as Clarence Carnes), Telly Savalas, Art Carney, Alex Karras, Will Sampson, Ronny Cox, Richard Lynch, James MacArthur, Ed Lauter
'A solid TV film whose roots reach back to some of the better prison films of yesteryear.' – *Daily Variety*

Alcoa. The Aluminum Corporation of America, a noted sponsor of dramatic anthologies in the late fifties including *One Step Beyond*, *Alcoa Première*, *Alcoa Theatre*

(*Turn of Fate*), and *The Alcoa Hour. Eddie*, an episode of *Alcoa Goodyear Theatre*, won an Emmy in 1958.

✻ **Alda, Alan** (1935–). American leading actor, son of Robert Alda. His great success has been on TV as Hawkeye in *M*A*S*H*, throughout the long run of which he proved himself a star of the first magnitude. Also on TV in *That Was the Week That Was* (US version), *The Glass House, Kill Me If You Can* (as Caryl Chessman), *Playmates, Isn't it Shocking?* Emmys 1976 and 1978 for *M*A*S*H* (episodes *Dear Sigmund, Inga*). In 1984 produced (to little effect) a series based on his film *The Four Seasons*.

Alda, Robert (1914–) (Alphonso D'Abruzzo). Italian–American leading man of 1940s movies, father of Alan Alda. Occasional TV movies include *Last Hours Before Morning, Supertrain, Perfect Gentlemen*.

Alderton, John (1940–). British juvenile lead who matured into a quirky character comedian. He didn't make it in films, but TV kept him busy in *Emergency Ward Ten*, PLEASE SIR, *Upstairs Downstairs, No Honestly, The Upchat Line, Thomas and Sarah* and *Father's Day*.

The Aldrich Family. A domestic comedy from the early days of US TV, this live half-hour series ran on and off from 1949 to 1953 and was based on the well-known Henry Aldrich teenage character created by Ezra Stone, a mid-America stereotype not far removed from Andy Hardy. In this version were Bob Casey, House Jameson and Barbara Robins. The series was created by Clifford Goldsmith, author of the original play *What a Life!*, which was filmed under this title in 1941 and had already led to a Paramount film series starring James Lydon.

Aldrich, Robert (1918–83). Overpraised American director of sixties films. Early TV work includes episodes of *China Smith, Adventures in Paradise, The Sundance Kid.*

Aldridge, Michael (1920–). Engaging, versatile British actor very funny in such early comedies as Giles Cooper's *Love and Penguins* or (later) in Tom Stoppard's and Clive Exton's *Eleventh Hour* runner, 1975. Series include *The Men in Room 17, Love for Lydia, Charters and Caldicott, Mussolini the Untold Story.*   PP

TERENCE ALEXANDER (1923–). One of the legions of familiar British supporting players, this lightest of light leading men found his most secure niche as friend to Channel Isles cop Bergerac.

Alexa (GB 1982). Steamy novelist Andrea Newman, of *Bouquet of Barbed Wire* fame, furnished this rather thin four-parter about high-powered news-hen (Isla Blair) descending on rural couple played by Christopher Blake and Joanne David, with predictable results. For BBC *Love Story*. PP

Alexander, Ben (1911–69) (Nicholas Benton Alexander). American actor, a former child star of the cinema who in later life played a second lead cop in *Dragnet* and *The Felony Squad.*

Alexander, Jane (1939–) (Jane Quigley). American character actress who has earned some distinctions. TV movies include *Welcome Home Johnny Bristol, Miracle on 34th Street, A Circle of Children*, ELEANOR AND FRANKLIN (as Eleanor), *Death Be Not Proud, A Question of Love*, PLAYING FOR TIME.

Alexander the Great. In 1964 ABC made an expensive 60-minute pilot with William Shatner; no series resulted. See also: *The Search for Alexander the Great.*

Alexander: The Other Side of Dawn
US 1977 96m colour TVM
Douglas Cramer

A teenage male prostitute tries to reform.
Vaguely repellent quasi-documentary.

w Walter Dallenbach d John Erman

Leigh J. McCloskey, Eve Plumb, Alan
Feinstein, Earl Holliman, Juliet Mills, Jean
Hagen, Frances Faye

Alexandra Palace. The world's first regular
television service was begun by the BBC on 2
November 1936 from a Victorian complex on
Muswell Hill. *Picture Page*, transmitted that
evening, became the first studio talk show.
PP

Alfred Hitchcock Presents ***
US 1955–61 260 approx × 25m bw
CBS (later NBC)/Universal/Shamley
(Norman Lloyd)

An anthology of twist-in-the-tail suspensers,
usually with a dash of comedy. Because the
villains often got away with their nefarious
schemes, the moral code obliged Hitchcock
to sign off in person with a throw-away moral
ending, and these tit-bits, plus corresponding
openings and a catchy theme tune, made the
show phenomenally popular, though Hitch
himself directed fewer than 20 episodes. The
stories, often drawn from semi-classic
sources, were always impeccably presented.
In 1962–4 the series moved from CBS to NBC
and became an hour for 93 episodes, but
many of these were unsatisfactory and almost
all seemed padded.

† The catchy theme tune was Gounod's
Funeral March of a Marionette.
The half-hour episodes were as follows:

Gentleman from America (w Francis Cockrell,
story Michael Arlen; d Robert Stevens; with
Biff McGuire, Ralph Clanton)

There Was an Old Woman (w Francis and
Marion Cockrell; d Robert Stevenson; with
Estelle Winwood, Charles Bronson)

Triggers in Leash (d Don Medford; with Gene
Barry, Darren McGavin)

The Vanishing Lady (d Don Medford; with
Pat Hitchcock, Mary Frobes)

Breakdown (d Alfred Hitchcock; with Joseph
Cotten, Raymond Bailey)

Revenge (w A. I. Bezzerides, Francis
Cockrell; d Alfred Hitchcock; with Ralph
Meeker, Vera Miles)

Don't Come Back Alive (w Robert C. Dennis;
d Robert Stevenson; with Sidney Blackmer,
Virginia Gregg)

Salvage (w Fred Freiberger, Dick Carr; d
Justis Addis; with Gene Barry, Nancy Gates,
Elisha Cook Jnr)

The Big Switch (w Richard Carr, story Cornell
Woolrich; d Don Weis; with George
Mathews, George E. Stone)

Place of Shadows (w Robert C. Dennis; d
Robert Stevens; with Mark Damon, Everett
Sloane)

The Legacy (w Gina Kaus; d James Neilson;
with Leora Dana, Jacques Bergerac)

Guilty Witness (w Robert C. Dennis; d Robert
Stevens; with Joe Mantell, Judith Evelyn)

Our Cook's a Treasure (w Robert C. Dennis,
story Dorothy L. Sayers; d Robert Stevens;
with Everett Sloane, Beulah Bondi)

And So Died Riabouchinska (w Mel Dinelli,
story Ray Bradbury; d Robert Stevenson; with
Claude Rains, Charles Bronson)

Premonition (d Robert Stevens; with John
Forsythe, Cloris Leachman, George
Macready)

The Older Sister (w Robert C. Dennis; d
Robert Stevens; with Joan Lorring, Pat
Hitchcock, Carmen Mathews)

Shopping for Death (w Ray Bradbury; d
Robert Stevens; with Jo Van Fleet, Robert
Harris, John Qualen)

Never Again (w Gwen Bagni, Irwin Gielgud,
Sterling Silliphant, story Adela Rogers St
John; d Robert Stevens; with Phyllis Thaxter,
Warren Stevens, Louise Allbritton)

The Case of Mr Pelham (w Francis Cockrell,
story Anthony Armstrong; d Alfred
Hitchcock; with Tom Ewell, Raymond
Bailey)

The Long Shot (w Harold Swanton; d Robert
Stevenson; with Peter Lawford, John
Williams, Robert Warwick)

Safe Conduct (w Andrew Solt; d Justis Addis;
with Claire Trevor, Jacques Bergerac, Werner
Klemperer)

The Hands of Mr Ottermole (w Francis
Cockrell, story Thomas Burke; d Robert
Stevens; with Theodore Bikel, Rhys Williams)

The Cheney Vase (with Patricia Collinge,
Darren McGavin, George Macready)

Momentum (w Francis Cockrell; d Robert
Stevens; with Joanne Woodward, Skip
Homeier)

You Got to Have Luck (w Eustace and Francis
Cockrell; d Robert Stevens; with John
Cassavetes, Marisa Pavan, Ray Teal)

A Bullet for Baldwin (no details to hand)

The Derelicts (w Robert C. Dennis; d Robert
Stevenson; with Robert Newton, Philip Reed)

Santa Claus and the Tenth Avenue Kid (w
Marian Cockrell; d Don Weis; with Barry
Fitzgerald, Arthur Space)

Back for Christmas (*w* Francis Cockrell, *story* John Collier; *d* Alfred Hitchcock; with John Williams, Isobel Elsom, Gavin Muir)

Whodunit (*w* Francis and Marian Cockrell; *d* Francis Cockrell; with John Williams, Alan Napier)

The Perfect Murder (*w* Victor Wolfson, *story* Stacy Aumonier; *d* Robert Stevens; with Mildred Natwick, Hurd Hatfield)

Help Wanted (*w* Robert C. Dennis; *d* James Neilson; with John Qualen, Lorne Greene, Madge Kennedy)

Wet Saturday (*d* Alfred Hitchcock)

The Orderly World of Mr Appleby (*w* Victor Wolfson; *d* James Neilson; with Robert H. Harris, Louise Larrabee)

Portrait of Jocelyn (*w* Harold Swanton; *d* Robert Stevens; with Philip Abbott, Nancy Gates)

The Belfry (*w* Robert C. Dennis; *d* Herschel Daugherty; with Jack Mullaney, Pat Hitchcock)

The Baby Sitter (*w* Sarett Rudley; *d* Robert Stevens; with Thelma Ritter, Mary Wickes)

Decoy (*w* Bernard C. Schoenfeld; *d* Arnold Laven; with Robert Horton, Cara Williams)

The Hidden Thing (*w* James P. Cavanagh; *d* Robert Stevens; with Biff McGuire, Judith Ames, Robert H. Harris)

Mink (*w* Irwin Gielgud, Gwen Bagni; *d* Robert Stevenson; with Ruth Hussey, Anthony Eustrel)

The Creeper (*w* James P. Cavanagh, *d* Herschel Daugherty; with Constance Ford, Steve Brodie)

Crackpot (*w* Martin Berkeley, Harold Gast; *d* John Lucas; with Biff McGuire, Mary Scott)

Malice Domestic (*w* Victor Wolfson, *story* Philip MacDonald; *d* John Meredyth Lucas; with Phyllis Thaxter, Ralph Meeker)

Mr Blanchard's Secret (*w* Sarett Rudley; *d* Alfred Hitchcock; with Mary Scott, Robert Horton)

Kill with Kindness (*w* A. J. Russell; *d* Herschel Daugherty; with Hume Cronyn, James Gleason, Carmen Mathews)

The Better Bargain (*w* Bernard Schoenfeld; *d* Herschel Daugherty; with Robert Middleton, Henry Silva)

Jonathan (*w* Bernard Schoenfeld, Sterling Silliphant; *d* John Meredyth Lucas; with Corey Allen, Douglas Kennedy, Walter Kingsford)

Conversation over a Corpse (*w* Norman Daniels; *d* Jules Bricken; with Dorothy Stickney, Carmen Mathews)

The End of Indian Summer (*w* James P. Cavanagh)

A Man Greatly Beloved (*w* Sarett Rudley, *story* A. A. Milne)

One More Mile to Go (*w* James P. Cavanagh; *d* Alfred Hitchcock; with David Wayne, Louise Larrabee)

John Brown's Body (*w* Robert C. Dennis, *story* Thomas Burke; *d* Robert Stevens; with Russell Collins, Leora Dana)

Manacled (*w* Sterling Silliphant; *d* Robert Stevens; with William Redfield, Gary Merrill)

The Cream of the Jest (*w* Sarett Rudley, *story* Fredric Brown; *d* Herschel Daugherty; with Claude Rains, James Gregory)

Number Twenty Two (*w* Joel Murcott, *story* Evan Hunter; *d* Robert Stevens; with Rip Torn, Russell Collins)

Vicious Circle (*w* Bernard Schoenfeld, *story* Evan Hunter; *d* Paul Henreid; with Dick York, George Macready)

Father and Son (*w* James P. Cavanagh, *story* Thomas Burke; *d* Herschel Daugherty; with Edmund Gwenn, Frederic Worlock)

The Indestructible Mr Weems (with Russell Collins, Robert Middleton)

A Bottle of Wine (*w* Sterling Silliphant, *story* Borden Deal; *d* Herschel Daugherty; with Herbert Marshall, Robert Horton, Jarma Lewis)

One for the Road (*w* Robert C. Dennis; *d* Robert Stevens; with Louise Platt, John Baragrey)

The Three Dreams of Mr Findlater (*w* Sarett Rudley, *story* A. A. Milne; *d* Jules Bricken; with John Williams, Isobel Elsom)

The Dangerous People (*w* Francis Cockrell; *d* Robert Stevens; with Albert Salmi, Robert H. Harris)

The Night the World Ended (*w* Bernard Schoenfeld; *d* Justis Addis; with Russell Collins, Edith Barrett, Harold Stone)

Martha Mason, Movie Star (*w* Robert C. Dennis; *d* Justis Addis; with Judith Evelyn, Robert Emhardt)

The West Warlock Time Capsule (*w* Marion Cockrell; *d* Justis Addis; with Henry Jones, Mildred Dunnock)

A Little Sleep (*w* Robert C. Dennis; *d* Paul Henreid; with Barbara Cook, Vic Morrow)

Listen, Listen! (*w* Bernard Schoenfeld, *d* Don Taylor; with Edgar Stehli, Dayton Lummis)

Bull in a China Shop (*w* Sarett Rudley; *d* James Neilson; with Estelle Winwood, Dennis Morgan, Elizabeth Patterson, Ellen Corby, Ida Moore)

The Equalizer (*w* Robert C. Dennis; *d* James Neilson; with Leif Erickson, Martin Balsam)

On the Nose (*w* Irving Elman; *d* James Neilson; with Jan Sterling, Carl Betz)

The Canary Sedan (*w* Sterling Silliphant, *story* Ann Bridge; with Jessica Tandy, Murray Matheson, Gavin Muir)

Lamb to the Slaughter (*w* Roald Dahl; *d* Alfred Hitchcock; with Barbara Bel Geddes, Harold J. Stone)

Guest for Breakfast (*w* James P. Cavanagh, C. B. Guilford; *d* Paul Henreid; with Joan Tetzel, Scott Mackay)

The Right Kind of a House (*w* Robert C. Dennis, *story* Henry Slesar; *d* Don Taylor; with Robert Emhardt, Jeanette Nolan)

Flight to the East (*w* Joel Murcott; *d* Arthur Hiller; with Gary Merrill, Patricia Cutts)

Disappearing Trick (*w* Kathleen Hite, *story* Victor Canning; *d* Arthur Hiller; with Robert Horton, Betsy Von Furstenburg)

Fatal Figures (*w* Robert C. Dennis; with John McGiver, Vivian Nathan)

The Festive Season (*w* James P. Cavanagh; *d* Arthur Hiller; with Carmen Mathews, Edmon Ryan)

Death Sentence (*w* Joel Murcott; *d* Paul Henreid; with James Best, Steve Brodie)

Post Mortem (*w* Robert C. Dennis, *story* Cornell Woolrich; *d* Arthur Hiller; with Steve Forrest, Joanna Moore, James Gregory)

Impromptu Murder (*w* Francis Cockrell, *story* Roy Vickers; *d* Paul Henreid; with Hume Cronyn, Valerie Cossart, Doris Lloyd)

The Crocodile Case (*w* Robert C. Dennis, *story* Roy Vickers; *d* Don Taylor; with Denholm Elliott, Hazel Court)

Little White Frock (*w* Sterling Silliphant, *story* Stacy Aumonier; *d* Herschel Daugherty; with Herbert Marshall, Julia Adams)

The Safe Place (*w* Michael Hogan; *d* James Neilson; with Robert H. Harris, Jerry Paris)

The Young One (*w* Sarett Rudley; *d* Robert Altman; with Carol Lynley, Vince Edwards)

The Glass Eye (*w* Sterling Silliphant, *story* John Keir Cross; *d* Robert Stevens; with Jessica Tandy, Tom Conway, William Shatner)

Last Request (*w* Joel Murcott; *d* Paul Henreid; with Harry Guardino, Hugh Marlowe)

The Diplomatic Corpse (*w* Robert C. Dennis, Alec Coppel; *d* Paul Henreid; with George Peppard, Peter Lorre)

The Percentage (*w* Bernard Schoenfeld; *d* James Neilson; with Alex Nicol, Nita Talbot)

The Mail Order Prophet (*w* Robert C. Dennis; *d* James Neilson; with E. G. Marshall, Jack Klugman)

The Perfect Crime (*w* Sterling Silliphant, *story* Ben Ray Redman; *d* Alfred Hitchcock; with Vincent Price, James Gregory)

Heart of Gold (*w* James P. Cavanagh, *story* Henry Slesar; *d* Robert Stevens; with Mildred Dunnock, Darryl Hickman, Nehemiah Persoff)

Reward to Finder (*w* Frank Gabrielson; *d* James Neilson; with Jo Van Fleet, Oscar Homolka, Claude Akins)

Miss Bracegirdle Does Her Duty (*w* Marian Cockrell, *story* Stacy Aumonier; *d* Robert Stevens; with Mildred Natwick, Gavin Muir)

Miss Paisley's Cat (*w* Marian Cockrell, *story* Roy Vickers; with Dorothy Stickney, Harry Tyler)

Enough Rope for Two (*w* Joel Murcott; *d* Paul Henreid; with Jean Hagen, Steven Hill) ·

Silent Witness (*w* Robert C. Dennis; *d* Paul Henreid; with Don Taylor, Pat Hitchcock)

Night of the Execution (*w* Bernard Schoenfeld; *d* Henry Slesar; with Georgiann Johnson, Pat Hingle)

Sylvia (*w* James P. Cavanagh, *story* Ira Levin; *d* Herschel Daugherty; with Ann Todd, John McIntire)

The Deadly (*w* Robert C. Dennis; *d* Don Taylor; with Phyllis Thaxter, Craig Stevens)

Return of the Hero (*w* Andrew Solt, Sterling Silliphant; with Jacques Bergerac and Susan Kohner)

A Dip in the Pool (*w* Francis Cockrell, *story* Roald Dahl; *d* Alfred Hitchcock; with Keenan Wynn, Louise Platt, Fay Wray)

Foghorn (*w* Frank Gabrielson, *story* Gertrude Atherton; *d* Robert Stevens; with Barbara Bel Geddes, Michael Rennie)

The Motive (with Skip Homeier and Carmen Mathews)

Together (*w* Robert C. Dennis, *story* Alec Coppel; *d* Robert Altman; with Joseph Cotten, Christine White)

Poison (*w* Casey Robinson, *story* Roald Dahl; *d* Alfred Hitchcock; with Wendell Corey, James Donald, Arnold Moss)

Six People, No Music (*w* Richard Berg, *story* Garson Kanin; *d* Norman Lloyd; with John McGiver, Peggy Cass)

The Waxwork (*w* Casey Robinson, *story* A. M. Burrage; *d* Robert Stevens; with Barry Nelson, Everett Sloane)

The Jokester (*w* Bernard Schoenfeld, *story* Robert Arthur; *d* Arthur Hiller; with Albert Salmi, Rosco Ates, James Coburn)

Don't Interrupt (*w* Sidney Carroll; *d* Robert Stevens; with Chill Wills, Biff McGuire, Cloris Leachman)

Invitation to an Accident (*w* Robert C. Dennis; *d* Don Taylor; with Gary Merrill, Joanna Moore)

The Crooked Road (*w* William Fay; *d* Paul Henreid; with Richard Kiley, Walter Matthau)

And the Desert Shall Blossom (*w* Bernard Schoenfeld; *d* Arthur Hiller; with William Demarest, Rosco Ates)

A Personal Matter (*w* Joel Murcott, *story* Brett Halliday; *d* Paul Henreid; with Wayne Morris, Joe Maross, Frank Silvera)

Mrs Herman and Mrs Fenimore (*w* Robert C. Dennis; *d* Arthur Hiller; with Mary Astor, Doro Merande, Russell Collins)

The Morning After (*w* Rose Simon Kohn, Robert C. Dennis; *d* Herschel Daugherty; with Robert Alda, Jeanette Nolan, Dorothy Provine, Fay Wray)

Two Million Dollar Defence (*w* William Fay; *d* Norman Lloyd; with Barry Sullivan, Leslie Neilsen)

Banquo's Chair (*w* Francis Cockrell, *story* Rupert Croft-Cooke; *d* Alfred Hitchcock; with John Williams, Kenneth Haigh, Reginald Gardiner, Max Adrian)

Design for Loving (*w* Ray Bradbury; *d* Robert Stevens; with Norman Lloyd, Marian Seldes)

Safety for the Witness (*w* William Fay; *d* Norman Lloyd; with Art Carney, Robert Bray, James Westerfield)

The Morning of the Bride (*w* Kathleen Hite; *d* Arthur Hiller; with Barbara Bel Geddes, Don Dubbins)

The Necklace (*w* Sarett Rudley; *d* Herschel Daugherty; with Claude Rains, Betsy Von Furstenburg)

Relative Value (*w* Francis Cockrell, *story* Milward Kennedy; *d* Paul Almond; with Denholm Elliott, Torin Thatcher, Frederic Worlock, Tom Conway)

A Man with a Problem (*w* Joel Murcott; *d* Robert Stevens; with Gary Merrill, Mark Richman, Elizabeth Montgomery)

Curtains for Me (*w* Robert C. Dennis, *story* Anthony Gilbert; *d* Leonard Horn; with Jane Greer, Kent Smith, Madge Kennedy)

Total Loss (*w* J. E. Selby; *d* Don Taylor; with Nancy Olson, Ralph Meeker)

The Last Dark Step (*w* William Fay; *d* Herschel Daugherty; with Robert Horton, Fay Spain)

Tea Time (*w* Kathleen Hite; *d* Robert Stevens; with Margaret Leighton, Marsha Hunt, Murray Matheson)

The Crystal Trench (*w* Sterling Silliphant, *story* A. E. W. Mason; *d* Alfred Hitchcock; with James Donald, Patricia Owens, Patrick Macnee)

The Impossible Dream (*w* Meade Roberts; *d* Robert Stevens; with Franchot Tone, Carmen Mathews, Mary Astor)

Out There, Darkness (*w* Bernard Schoenfeld; *d* Paul Henreid; with Bette Davis, James Congdon, Frank Albertson)

The Avon Emeralds (*w* William Fay; *d* Bretaigne Windust; with Roger Moore, Hazel Court, Alan Napier)

I'll Take Care of You (*w* William Fay; *d* Robert Stevens; with Russell Collins, Ralph Meeker, Ida Moore)

A Night with the Boys (*w* Bernard Schoenfeld; *d* John Brahm; with John Smith, Joyce Meadows)

The Dusty Drawer (*w* Halsted Welles; *d* Herschel Daugherty; with Dick York, Philip Coolidge)

Cheap Is Cheap (*w* Albert S. Lewin, Burt Styler; *d* Bretaigne Windust; with Dennis Day, Alice Backes)

Arthur (*w* James P. Cavanagh; *d* Alfred Hitchcock; with Laurence Harvey, Hazel Court, Robert Douglas)

The Kind Waitress (*w* William O'Farrell; *d* Paul Henreid; with Rick Jason, Olive Deering)

The Right Price (*w* Bernard Schoenfeld; *d* Arthur Hiller; with Allyn Joslyn, Eddie Foy Jnr)

Touché (*w* William Fay; *d* John Brahm; with Paul Douglas, King Calder)

Appointment at Eleven (*w* Evan Hunter; *d* Robert Stevens; with Clint Kimbrough, Clu Gulager)

The Human Interest Story (*w* Fredric Brown; *d* Norman Lloyd; with Steve McQueen, Arthur Hill)

Your Witness (*w* William Fay; *d* Norman Lloyd; with Brian Keith, Leora Dana)

Murder Me Twice (*w* Irving Elman; *d* David Swift; with Alan Marshal, Tom Helmore, Phyllis Thaxter)

The Baby Blue Expression (*w* Helen Nielsen; *d* Arthur Hiller; with Sarah Marshall, Peter Walker)

The Schartz-Metterklume Method (*w* Marian Cockrell, *story* Saki; *d* Richard Dunlap; with Hermione Gingold, Elspeth March, Doris Lloyd, Norma Varden, Pat Hitchcock, Tom Conway)

The Hero (*w* Bill S. Ballinger, *story* H. DeVere Stacpoole; *d* John Brahm)

I Can Take Care of Myself (*w* Thomas Grant; *d* Alan Crosland Jnr; with Myron McCormick, Linda Lawson)

Not the Running Type (*w* Jerry Sohl; *d* Arthur Hiller; with Paul Hartman, Robert Bray)

Graduating Class (*w* Sterling Silliphant; *d* Herschel Daugherty; with Wendy Hiller, Gigi Perreau)

Anniversary Gift (*w* Harold Swanton, *story* John Collier; *d* Norman Lloyd; with Barbara Baxley, Harry Morgan, Jackie Coogan)

Hitch Hike (*w* Bernard Schoenfeld; *d* Paul Henreid; with Suzanne Pleshette, John McIntire, Robert Morse)

Road Hog (*w* Bill S. Ballinger; *d* Stuart Rosenberg; with Raymond Massey, Robert Emhardt)

An Occurrence at Owl Creek Bridge (*w* Harold Swanton, *story* Ambrose Bierce; *d* Robert Stevenson; with Ronald Howard, Juano Hernandez, James Coburn)

No Pain (*w* William Fay; *d* Norman Lloyd; with Brian Keith, Joanna Moore)

The Blessington Method (*w* Halsted Welles; *d* Herschel Daugherty; with Henry Jones, Dick York, Elizabeth Patterson)

Coyote Moon (*w* Harold Swanton; *d* Herschel Daugherty; with Macdonald Carey, Collin Wilcox, Edgar Buchanan)

Dry Run (*w* Bill S. Ballinger; *d* John Brahm; with Robert Vaughn, Walter Matthau)

Speciality of the House (*w* Victor Wolfson; *d* Robert Stevens; with Robert Morley, Kenneth Haigh)

Man from the South (*w* William Fay, *story* Roald Dahl; *d* Norman Lloyd; with Peter Lorre, Steve McQueen)

The Cure (*w* Michael Pertwee, *story* Robert Bloch; *d* Herschel Daugherty; with Nehemiah Persoff, Cara Williams)

Special Delivery (*w* Ray Bradbury; *d* Norman Lloyd; with Steve Dunne, Beatrice Straight)

Craig's Will (*w* Albert E. Levin, Burt Styler; *d* Gene Reynolds; with Dick Van Dyke, Stella Stevens, Paul Stewart)

Dead Weight (*w* Jerry Sohl; *d* Stuart Rosenberg; with Joseph Cotten, Julie Adams)

Backward, Turn Backward (*w* Charles Beaumont; *d* Stuart Rosenberg; with Alan Baxter, Tom Tully)

The Day of the Bullet (*w* Bill S. Ballinger; *d* Norman Lloyd; with Barry Gordon, Glenn Walken)

Across the Threshold (*w* Charlotte Armstrong; *d* Arthur Hiller; with George Grizzard, Pat Collinge)

The Cuckoo Clock (*w* Robert Bloch; *d* John Brahm; with Fay Spain, Beatrice Straight, Don Beddoe)

The Ikon of Elijah (*w* Norah Perez, Victor Wolfson; *d* Paul Almond; with Oscar Homolka, Sam Jaffe)

Mother, May I Go Out to Swim? (*w* James P. Cavanagh, *story* Q. Patrick; *d* Herschel Daugherty; with William Shatner, Gia Scala, Jessie Royce Landis)

Madame Mystery (*w* William Fay, *story* Robert Bloch; *d* John Brahm; with Harp McGuire, Audrey Totter)

Escape to Sonoita (*w* James A. Howard, Bill S. Ballinger; *d* Stuart Rosenberg; with Burt Reynolds, James Bell)

Cell 227 (*w* Bill S. Ballinger; *d* Paul Henreid; with Brian Keith, James Best)

Forty Detectives Later (*w* Henry Slesar; *d* Arthur Hiller; with Jack Weston, James Franciscus)

The Little Man Who Was There (*w* Gordon Russel, Larry Ward; *d* George Stevens Jnr; with Norman Lloyd, Arch Johnson, Read Morgan, Robert Armstrong)

Insomnia (*w* Henry Slesar; *d* John Brahm; with Dennis Weaver, James Milhollin)

Party Line (*w* Eli Jerome; *d* Hilton Green; with Judy Canova, Royal Dano)

One Grave Too Many (*w* Eli Jerome; *d* Arthur Hiller; with Jeremy Slate, Neile Adams)

The Man Who Found the Money (*w* Allan Gordon; *d* Alan Crosland Jnr; with Rod Cameron, Arthur Hill)

Hooked (*w* Thomas Grant; *d* Norman Lloyd; with Robert Horton, Vivienne Segal)

Letter of Credit (*w* Helen Neilsen; *d* Paul Henreid; with Robert Bray, Bob Sweeney)

Make My Death Bed (*w* Henry A. Cogge; *d* Arthur Hiller; with Biff Elliott, Jocelyn Brando)

Pen Pal (*w* Hilary Murray; *d* John Brahm; with Katherine Squire, Clu Gulager)

Coming Home (*w* Henry Slesar; *d* Alf Kjellin; with Crahan Denton, Jeanette Nolan)

Cop for a Day (*w* Henry Slesar; *d* Paul Henreid; with Walter Matthau, Glenn Cannon)

The Hat Box (*w* Henry Slesar; *d* Alan Crosland Jnr; with Paul Ford, Billy Gray)

Gratitude (*w* William Fay, *story* Donn Byrne; *d* Alan Crosland Jnr; with Peter Falk, Paul Hartman)

Keep Me Company (*w* Henry Slesar; *d* Alan Crosland Jnr; with Anne Francis, Edmund Hashim)

The Greatest Monster of Them All (*w* Robert Bloch; *d* Robert Stevens; with Sam Jaffe, Robert H. Harris, William Redfield)

I, Spy (*w* John Collier, *play* John Mortimer; *d* Norman Lloyd; with Kay Walsh, Eric Barker, Cecil Parker, William Kendall)

The Five Forty Eight (*w* Charlotte Armstrong, *story* John Cheever; *d* John Brahm; with Zachary Scott, Phyllis Thaxter)

Oh, Youth and Beauty (*w* Halsted Welles, *story* John Cheever; *d* Norman Lloyd; with Gary Merrill, Patricia Breslin)

The Kiss-Off (*w* Talmadge Powell; *d* Alan Crosland Jnr; with Rip Torn, Mary Munday)

A Very Moral Theft (*w* Allan Gordon; *d* Norman Lloyd; with Betty Field, Karl Swenson, Walter Matthau)

Sybilla (*w* Charlotte Armstrong; *d* Ida Lupino; with Barbara Bel Geddes, Alexander Scourby)

Museum Piece (*w* Harold Swanton; *d* Paul Henreid; with Myron McCormick, Larry Gates)

The Contest of Aaron Gold (*w* William Fay, *story* Philip Roth; *d* Norman Lloyd; with Sydney Pollack, Frank Maxwell)

The Doubtful Doctor (*w* Jerry Sohl; *d* Arthur Hiller; with Dick York, Gena Rowlands)

A Secret Life (*w* Jerry Sohl, *story* Nicholas Monsarrat; *d* Don Weis; with Ronald Howard, Patricia Donahue, Arte Johnson)

A Change of Heart (*w* Robert Bloch; *d* Robert Florey; with Nicholas Pryor, Abraham Sofaer)

The Landlady (*w* Robert Bloch, *story* Roald Dahl; *d* Paul Henreid; with Patricia Collinge, Dean Stockwell)

Mrs Bixby and the Colonel's Coat (*w* Halsted Welles, *story* Roald Dahl; *d* Alfred Hitchcock; with Audrey Meadows, Les Tremayne, Stephen Chase)

The Honey (*w* Henry Slesar; *d* Alan Crosland Jnr; with Robert Loggia, Doris Dowling)

The Man with Two Faces (*w* Henry Slesar; *d* Stuart Rosenberg; with Spring Byington, Bethel Leslie)

The Last Escape (*w* Henry Slesar; *d* Paul Henreid; with Keenan Wynn, Jan Sterling)

Outlaw in Town (*w* Michael Fessier; *d* Herschel Daugherty; with Ricardo Montalban, Constance Ford)

Deathmate (*w* Bill S. Ballinger; *d* Alan Crosland Jnr; with Gia Scala, Les Tremayne)

Coming, Mama (*w* James P. Cavanagh; *d* George Stevens Jnr; with Eileen Heckart, Don Defore)

The Horseplayer (*w* Henry Slesar; *d* Alfred Hitchcock; with Claude Rains, Ed Gardner)

A Crime for Mothers (*w* Henry Slesar; *d* Ida Lupino; with Claire Trevor, Biff Elliott)

Incident in a Small Jail (*w* Henry Slesar; *d* Norman Lloyd; with John Fiedler, Richard Jaeckel)

A Woman's Help (*w* Henry Slesar; *d* Arthur Hiller; with Geraldine Fitzgerald, Scott McKay)

The Throwback (*w* Henry Slesar; *d* John Brahm; with Scott Marlowe, Joyce Meadows)

Summer Shade (*w* Harold Swanton; *d* Herschel Daugherty; with Julie Adams, James Franciscus)

Ambition (*w* Joel Murcott; *d* Paul Henreid; with Leslie Neilsen, Ann Robinson, Harold J. Stone)

A Pearl Weeps (*w* Peggy and Lou Shaw; *d* Don Weis; with Hazel Court, Ernest Truex, Jack Cassidy)

The Sorcerer's Apprentice (*w* Robert Bloch; *d* Joseph Leytes; with Brandon de Wilde, Diana Dors, Larry Kert, David J. Stewart)

The Pearl Necklace (no details to hand)

Servant Problem (*w* Henry Slesar; *d* Alan Crosland Jnr; with John Emery, Jo Van Fleet)

You Can't Trust a Man (*w* Helen Nielsen; *d* Paul Henreid; with Polly Bergen, Joe Maross)

The Gloating Place (*w* Robert Bloch; *d* Alan Crosland Jnr; with Susan Harrison, Henry Brandt)

Final Arrangements (*w* Robert Arthur; *d* Gordon Hessler; with Martin Balsam, Slim Pickens)

Self Defence (*w* John T. Kelley; *d* Paul Henreid; with George Nader, Audrey Totter)

Apex (*w* John T. Kelley; *d* Alan Crosland Jnr; with Vivienne Segal, Mark Miller)

Bad Actor (*w* Robert Bloch; *d* John Newland; with Robert Duvall, David Lewis)

Bang, You're Dead (*w* Harold Swanton, *story* Margery Vosper; *d* Alfred Hitchcock; with Biff Elliott, Lucy Prentiss)

Act of Faith (*w* Nicholas Monsarrat, *story* Eric Ambler; *d* Bernard Girard; with Dennis King, George Grizzard)

The Matched Pearl (*w* Henry Slesar; *d* Bernard Girard; with John Ireland, Ernest Truex)

Ten O'Clock Tiger (*w* William Fay; *d* Bernard Girard; with Robert Keith, Frankie Darro)

The Silk Petticoat (*w* Halsted Welles, Norman Ginsberg, *story* Joseph Shearing; *d* John Newland; with Michael Rennie, Antoinette Bower)

First Class Honeymoon (*w* Henry Slesar; *d* Don Weis; with Robert Webber, Jeremy Slate, John Abbott)

The Faith of Aaron Menefee (*w* Ray Bradbury, *story* Stanley Ellin; *d* Norman Lloyd; with Andrew Prine, Sidney Blackmer)

The Door without a Key (*w* Irving Elman; *d* Herschel Daugherty; with Claude Rains, John Larch)

You Can't Be a Little Girl All Your Life (*w* Helen Nielsen, *story* Stanley Ellin; *d* Norman Lloyd; with Caroline Kearney, Dick York)

The Old Pro (*w* Calvin Clements; *d* Paul Henreid; with Richard Conte, Sarah Shane)

The Big Score (*w* Bryce Walton; *d* Boris Sagal; with Rafael Campos, Evan Evans)

Beta Delta Gamma (*w* Calvin Clements; *d* Alan Crosland Jnr; with Burt Brinckerhoff, Severn Darden)

The Woman Who Wanted to Live (*w* Bryce Walton; *d* Alan Crosland Jnr; with Charles Bronson, Lola Albright)

Maria (*w* John Collier, *story* John Wyndham; *d* Boris Sagall; with Norman Lloyd, Nita Talbot)

Strange Miracle (*w* Halsted Welles; *d* Norman Lloyd; with David Opatoshu, Eduardo Ciannelli)

The Right Kind of Medicine (*w* Henry Slesar; *d* Alan Crosland Jnr; with Robert Redford, Russell Collins)

Most Likely to Succeed (*w* Henry Slesar; *d* Richard Whorf; with Howard Morris, Jack Carter)

The Last Remains (*w* Henry Slesar; *d* Leonard Horn; with John Fiedler, Ed Gardner)

A Jury of Her Peers (*w* James P. Cavanagh; *d* Robert Florey; with Ann Harding, Robert Bray)

The Test (*w* Henry Slesar; *d* Boris Sagal; with Brian Keith, Eduardo Ciannelli)

Services Rendered (*w* William Link, Richard Levinson; *d* Paul Henreid; with Steve Dunne, Hugh Marlowe)

Burglar Proof (*w* Henry Slesar; *d* John Newland; with Robert Webber, Paul Hartman)

The Twelve Hour Caper (*w* Harold Swanton; *d* John Newland; with Dick York, Sarah Marshall)

The Case of M. J. H. (*w* Henry Slesar; *d* Alan Crosland Jnr; with Barbara Baxley, Robert Loggia)

Profit-Sharing Plan (*w* William Link, Richard Levinson; *d* Bernard Girard; with Henry Jones, Ruth Storey)

Where Beauty Lies (*w* James P. Cavanagh, *story* Henry Farrell; *d* Robert Florey; with Cloris Leachman, George Nader)

Victim Four (*w* Talmadge Powell; *d* Paul Henreid; with Peggy Ann Garner, Paul Comi)

Golden Opportunity (*w* Bryce Walton, Henry Slesar; *d* Robert Florey; with Richard Long, Colleen Gray)

The Kerry Blue (*w* Henry Slesar; *d* Paul Henreid; with Gene Evans, Carmen Mathews)

The Children of Alda Nuova (*w* Robert Wallsten; *d* Robert Florey; with Jack Carson, Christopher Dark)

What Frightened You, Fred? (*w* Joel Murcott; *d* Paul Henreid; with R. G. Armstrong, Ed Asher)

The Big Kick (*w* Robert Bloch; *d* Alan Crosland Jnr; with Anne Helm, Brian Hutton, Wayne Rogers)

Alfred Hitchcock Presents *
US 1985–   x 25m colour
NBC/Universal (Andrew Mirisch)

A macabre joke which Hitchcock would have appreciated. New versions of the old stories, with some fresh ones thrown in, are prefaced by computer-colorized versions of the old Hitchcock intros. Quality variable, but the quartet which introduced the series, in the form of a two-hour TV movie compendium, was entertaining and efficient enough. The elements were:

Man from the South, now with John Huston, Melanie Griffith, Steve Bauer, Kim Novak, Tippi Hedren; directed and rewritten by Steve de Jarnatt

Incident in a Small Jail, now with Ned Beatty, Lee Ving, Tony Frank; directed and rewritten by Joel Oliansky

Bang! You're Dead, now with Gail Youngs, Lyman Ward, Billy Mumy; directed by Randa Haines, written by Harold Swanton and Christopher Crowe

An Unlocked Window, now with Annette O'Toole and Bruce Davison; directed and rewritten by Fred Walton

Alfred Marks Time *. Popular British entertainment series of the fifties and early sixties (Rediffusion) featuring the comedian, his wife Paddy O'Neil and guest stars, all introduced by the formidable ex-RSM Brittain.   PP

Alfresco (GB 1984 7 × 30m). Granada's version of the late-night, new wave comedy shows to be found on all channels in the mid-eighties, and – as usual – sharing with them some of the performers and most of the writers. Emma Thompson shone in both categories. Further series followed. Produced by John G. Temple.   PP

The Algerian War (GB 1984 5 × 52m). Sober, exhaustively researched history of the bitter struggle between Algerian nationalists and French settlers, and how de Gaulle solved it with the most magisterial U-turn in history. From Peter Batty Productions, for Channel 4.   PP

Ali, Muhammad (1942–   ) (Cassius Clay). Loud-mouthed and irresistibly entertaining professional prizefighter, three times world champion. TV movie: *Freedom Road*.

Alias Smith and Jones *
US 1970 74m colour TVM
Universal (Frank Price, Glen Larson)

Two bandits come to an arrangement with the government.
Comedy western, clearly modelled on *Butch Cassidy and the Sundance Kid*; it spawned a successful series.

w Glen Larson   d Gene Levitt   m Billy Goldenberg

PETE DUEL, BEN MURPHY, Susan St James, James Drury, Forrest Tucker, Earl Holliman

Alias Smith and Jones *
US 1971–2 48 × 50m colour
ABC/Universal

The series ran pretty true to the pilot, but the high spirits eventually proved no substitute for dramatic action, and westerns were in any case declining in audience appeal.
Pete Duel (who died after 37 episodes and was replaced by Roger Davis), Ben Murphy, Sally Field

Alice *
GB 1965 75m bw (VTR)
BBC

The story behind the writing of *Alice in Wonderland*.
An absorbing reconstruction of the puzzle of Lewis Carroll's personality.

w DENNIS POTTER   d Gareth Davies

GEORGE BAKER, Rosalie Crutchley, David Langton, Debbie Watling   PP

Alice
US 1978–84 209 × 25m colour
Warner/David Susskind

A widow works in a hash-house and brings up her teenage son.
Moderate transcription of the restaurant sequences from the film *Alice Doesn't Live Here Any More*. A raucous long-runner in the US, it didn't travel.

cr Robert Getchell

Linda Lavin, Philip McKeon, Vic Tayback

† Polly Holliday, who played the raucous Flo, left after awhile to star in her own series, *Flo*, which didn't work. She was replaced by Diane Ladd.

Alice in Wonderland
GB 1966 80m bw (VTR)
BBC

An unattractive version of the *Alice* books, with far too much of the adaptor, Jonathan Miller, breaking through the fine Victorian fabric.

m Revi Shankar

Anne-Marie Malik, Ralph Richardson, John Gielgud, Peter Cook, Wilfrid Brambell, Leo McKern, Michael Redgrave, Malcolm Muggeridge

PP: 'Or, alternatively and quite attractively, a glimpse of stuffy, boring, condescending, unpredictable, illogical adulthood as Jonathan Miller thinks Lewis Carroll thought Victorian children saw it.'

† Straightforward serial version, except for colour separation effects, came from Barry Letts for BBC, 1986. Kate Dorning was Alice.

Alice in Wonderland
US 1985 2 × 95m colour miniseries
CBS/Irwin Allen/Proctor and
   Gamble/Columbia

Mind-boggling TV version of an English classic, with tacky costuming and weird casting.

w Paul Zindel   d Harry Harris   ph Fred Koenekamp   m Mort Stevens   songs Steve Allen

Natalie Gregory (a cute nine-year-old Americanized Alice), Lloyd Bridges (White Knight), Red Buttons (White Rabbit), Sid Caesar (Gryphon), Carol Channing (White Queen), Imogene Coca (Cook), Sammy Davis Jnr (Caterpillar), Ann Jillian (Red Queen), Arte Johnson (Dormouse), Harvey Korman (White King), Karl Malden (Walrus), Jayne Meadows (Queen of Hearts), Robert Morley (King of Hearts), Roddy McDowall (March Hare), Anthony Newley (Mad Hatter), Louis Nye (Carpenter), Martha Raye (Duchess), Telly Savalas (Cheshire Cat), Jonathan Winters (Humpty Dumpty) and other stars in bit parts

The Aliens Are Coming *
US 1980 100m colour TVM
NBC/Quinn Martin (Philip Saltzman)

Skywatchers are menaced by aliens in search of energy sources and capable of absorbing human beings.
Handy amalgam of several well-worn themes, including Martin's own *The Invaders* as well as *Invasion of the Body Snatchers*. Special effects are the real stars.

w Robert W. Lenski   d Harvey Hart   ph Jacques Marquette   m William Goldstein

Tom Mason, Eric Braeden, Melinda Fee, Fawne Harriman

ALICE IN WONDERLAND. Of all the many, and sometimes perverse, interpretations of the Lewis Carroll classic, the most bizarre must be Irwin Allen's 1985 travesty for American TV, with its legion of unsuitable stars who all too clearly hadn't read the book. Here are Red Buttons as the White Rabbit, Sid Caesar as the Gryphon, Carol Channing as the White Queen, Imogene Coca as the Cook, Sammy Davis Jnr as the Caterpillar, and Patrick Duffy as the goat. (The goat?)

Alistair Cooke's America **
GB 1972 13 × 50m colour
BBC (Michael Gill)

Brilliantly filmed historical documentaries in which the knowledgeable and urbane Mr Cooke wanders across his adopted land and, aided by a first-class camera crew, picks up all the strands which have made up the present-day nation. Not only the series, but the book based on it, was a bestseller. The series won an Emmy and Mr Cooke got a British Academy Award.

All Creatures Great and Small *
GB 1974 96m colour TVM
EMI/Venedon (for Hallmark Hall of Fame)

Adventures of a country vet in Yorkshire of the thirties.
Unadventurous crowd-pleaser based on the autobiographical books of James Herriot. A theatrical sequel followed under the title *It Shouldn't Happen to a Vet* (US: *All Things Bright and Beautiful*); and see below for TV series.

w Hugh Whitemore *d* Claude Whatham *ph* Peter Suschitzky *m* Wilfred Josephs

Simon Ward, Anthony Hopkins, Lisa Harrow, Freddie Jones, Brenda Bruce

All Creatures Great and Small
GB 1977–80 41 × 50m colour (VTR)
BBC

A popular extension of the above, not markedly dissimilar in style and appeal from *Dr Finlay's Casebook*.

CHRISTOPHER TIMOTHY, Robert Hardy, Carol Drinkwater, Peter Davison

All for Love
GB 1982 6 × 52m colour
Granada (Roy Roberts)
Stories from Elizabeth Taylor (the novelist,
not the star), Francis King and, inevitably,
William Trevor, among others. Dramatized
and directed by various hands. The common
element was love of one sort or another.
Further six followed in 1983.   PP

All Gas and Gaiters * (GB 1966–70).
Enjoyable BBC character comedy which
broke new ground in allowing one to laugh
gently at the clergy. It starred WILLIAM
MERVYN (the bishop), Robertson Hare (the
archdeacon), DEREK NIMMO (the curate).
Nimmo went on to become a comic monk in
the equally long-running *Oh Brother!*
Creators: Edwin Apps, Pauline Devaney.

All in a Day ** (GB 1971–4). Intermittent
series of absorbing, often exciting
documentaries obtained by bringing a large
number of film cameras to bear on all aspects
of a predictable event, e.g. the launch of a
super-tanker ('If the chains don't hold her
we'll have a new bridge across the Tyne') or a
National Front march. A special edition
upped the number of cameras to assemble a
composite impression of one day in the
births, deaths, comings and goings of the City
of Sheffield. Produced by Mike Wooller; for
BBC.   PP

All in the Family ****
US 1971–7 160 approx × 25m colour
   (VTR)
CBS/NORMAN LEAR
A working-class bigot continually gets his
comeuppance but never learns his lesson.
A revolutionary comedy, adapted from
BBC's *Till Death Us Do Part*; watching it
quickly became a national pastime, and it
played no small part in encouraging viewers
to think about contemporary issues. It also
killed the old gentle style of American
domestic comedy which had been handed
down from the clean-living families of the
Hardys, the Aldriches and the Nelsons,
introducing a raucous acid note, bad language
and the discussion of ethnic, moral and
religious topics. By 1977, however, it had
served its purpose in its original form, and
became known as *Archie Bunker's Place*, the
central character having opened a bar. The
show won Emmys in 1970, 1971, 1972 and
1977, and the performers were also
honoured.
cr Norman Lear, Bud Yorkin
CARROLL O'CONNOR, JEAN STAPLETON, Sally
Struthers, Rob Reiner, Betty Garrett,
Beatrice Arthur

† Spin-offs included *Maude* and *The
Jeffersons*
PP: 'The show was seen in Britain (BBC) from
1972, when I observed: The great change is in
the Alf Garnett figure. The flow of prejudice
against the young, the Left and the blacks is
maintained, with some to spare for the
Mexicans and the Jews. But Alf was solid and
wooden and witless in his ignorance and, no
matter how Johnny Speight may have
protested otherwise, rather endearing. Deeply
ingrained in the American comedy tradition is
the need for everyone to be smart. So Archie
Bunker is also a wisecracker, sometimes
effectively so in Norman Lear's growly script.
Whether this will impair the durability of the
original idea remains to be seen.'

All Is Forgiven
US 1985   x 25m colour
Paramount/Charles Burrows (Ian Praiser,
   Howard Gerwitz)
Problems in the life of the lady producer of a
daytime soap opera.
Unlovable comedy format claustrophobically
set in soundproofed studios.
Bess Armstrong, Terence Knox, Shawnee
Smith, Carol Kane, David Alan Grier,
Valerie Landsburg, Judith-Marie Bergan

All My Children. American daytime soap
opera which began on ABC in 1970 and
shows no sign of being replaced. It concerns
the tribulations of two middle-class families in
Pine Valley, USA, and stars Ruth Warrick
and Mary Fickett. Creator: Agnes Nixon.

All My Darling Daughters *
US 1973 74m colour TVM
Universal (David Victor, David J.
   O'Connell)
A widower discovers that his four daughters
want to get married at the same time.
Amiable sentimental nonsense which needed
firmer control.
w John Gay *story* Robert Presnell Jnr and
Stan Dreben *d* David Lowell Rich
Robert Young, Raymond Massey, Eve
Arden, Darleen Carr, Judy Strangis, Sharon
Gless
† See also the following.

All My Darling Daughters' Anniversary
aka: *My Darling Daughters' Anniversary*
US 1974 74m colour TVM
Universal (David Victor, David J.
   O'Connell)
Inevitable sequel to the above: all the girls
have babies at the same time.
Dim.

w John Gay *d* Joseph Pevney

Robert Young, Raymond Massey, Ruth Hussey, Darleen Carr, Judy Strangis, Sharon Gless

All Our Working Lives **
GB 1984 11 × 50m colour/bw
BBC (Angela Holdsworth)

Excellent oral history series on traditional British industries and how they have either run down or adapted to changing times and new technology. Archive film of boom days (e.g. the aircraft factory in wartime) was intercut with the testimony of the veterans today.   PP

LH: 'The kind of social history which television was created to produce, it should be made available at regular intervals until the negative wears out.'

All Our Yesterdays. A British documentary series from Granada which ran from 1960 to 1973, usually in 20m form. By use of theatrical newsreels, each weekly issue covered the events of 25 years ago. Regular presenter: Brian Inglis. Chief producers: Tim Hewat, Douglas Terry. 638 programmes were made in all.

† West German television has the same idea, only 40 years on and using entire newsreels from various countries, under the title *Vor Vierzig Jahren*.   PP

All Star Secrets (GB from 1984). Pitiful game show in which celebrities attempt to attribute piffling bits of experience claimed by other celebrities. The public, as usual, is relegated to a supporting role: the latter-day Michael Parkinson is ideally cast as referee. Produced by Gill Stribling-Wright for LWT, with Little Joey Inc. and Action Time.   PP

All the Kind Strangers
US 1974 74m colour TVM
Cinemation/Jerry Gross

Seven orphans decoy strangers to their lonely farmhouse: some of the adults disappear.
Nuthatch melodrama with a certain amount of pizazz.

w Clyde Ware *d* Burt Kennedy

Stacy Keach, Samantha Eggar, John Savage, Robby Benson

'An untamed land. A turbulent river. Where a man and a woman could find all the adventure they ever dreamed of . . . and more danger than anyone should be asked to face!'

All the Rivers Run *
Australia 1983 4 × 96m colour
Crawford (Alan Hardy)

An orphaned British girl falls for the owner of a paddle steamer on the Murray River.
Visually satisfying romance set at the turn of the century. The plot is overstretched, but it delighted the ladies.

w Peter Yeldham, Vince Moran, Colin Free, Gwenda Marsh, *novel* Nancy Cato *d* GEORGE MILLER, PINO AMENTA *m* BRUCE ROWLAND

SIGRID THORNTON, JOHN WATERS, Charles Tingwell, Dinah Shearing, Gus Mercurio

'A handsomely mounted, well-acted, adroitly conceived production bristling with hooks to catch and keep the viewers' attention.' – *Variety*

All the Way Home
US 1981 98m colour
NBC/Paramount (Charles Raymond)

A Tennessee family survives the death of the father.
Rare (in its time) live performance of a standard play, recorded at the Bing Theatre of the University of California.

play by Tad Mosel from the *novel A Death in the Family* by James Agee *d* Delbert Mann

Sally Field, William Hurt, Ned Beatty, Ellen Corby, Ann Doran, Betty Garrett, Murray Hamilton, Polly Holliday, John McIntire, Jeanette Nolan

'I was reminded . . . what a treat it is to see and hear *real* people on television.' – Kay Gardella, LA *Daily News*

All the World's a Stage (GB 1984 13 × 40m). The history of the theatre as stodgily written and presented by Ronald Harwood with assorted actors in extracts from the plays, and Frankie Howerd for the instalment on classical comedy. 'What a waste of time and great expense,' said Sean Day-Lewis on behalf of a panel of critics voting it one of the six bummers of the year. Directed by Keith Cheetham; produced by Harry Hastings, for BBC.   PP

LH: 'The book of the series was remaindered with remarkable alacrity.'

All Together Now
US 1975 74m colour TVM
RSO (Ron Bernstein)

A teenage boy proves to the court that he and his young brother and sisters can make it on their own.
Adequate sentimental stuff.

w Jeff Andrus, Rubin Carson *d* Randall Kleiser

John Rubenstein, Glynnis O'Connor, Brad Savage, Bill Macy, Jane Withers, Helen Hunt

All You Need is Love **
GB 1977 13 × 50m colour
LWT/Theatre Projects
A history of the popular music of the 20th
century.
Often disappointing, sometimes brilliantly
assembled and presented, this solidly
researched series covered its ground
thoroughly and included much rare footage as
well as rounding up for interview all the big
surviving names. Historically, a most valuable
project.

p/d TONY PALMER

Allan, Andy (1943–). British producer
and executive, director of programmes at
Central since 1984. Previously with
Tyne-Tees and Rediffusion.   PP

Allan, Elkan (*c* 1930–). British journalist
and producer. In latter capacity responsible
for historic Vietnam documentary before
anyone had heard of Vietnam, *The Quiet
War*, 1961; also *Freedom Road*, 1964, and
Rebellion at Easter on the 50th anniversary
of the Irish Easter rising. As head of light
entertainment at A–R launched *Ready
Steady Go!* Left TV to compile and write the
first substantial Fleet Street programme
preview guide in the *Sunday Times*, 1969–78.
Nowadays in video and video journalism,
columnist *Video Week*.   PP

Allen, Corey (1934–). American director
(former actor and writer). TV movies include
*See the Man Run, Cry Rape, Yesterday's
Child, Stone, The Return of Frank Cannon*.

✳ **Allen, Dave** (1934–). Irish cabaret
comedian whose speciality is religious jokes
told from a high stool while he plays with a
cigarette. Favourite sign-off: 'Goodnight,
good luck, and may your God go with you.'
Popular in Britain and Australia from the
mid-sixties, in the mid-seventies he branched
out less successfully as a TV traveller and
interviewer of eccentrics. First TV drama
appearance: *One Fine Day* (1979).

Allen, Elizabeth (1934–) (Elizabeth
Gillease). American leading lady of sixties
theatrical films. TV series: *Bracken's World,
The Paul Lynde Show*. TV movie: *No Other
Love*.

Allen, Fred (1894–1956) (John F. Sullivan).
Mournful-looking American radio comedian
famous for his feud with Jack Benny. He
never quite made it in the movies, and
although he appeared frequently on TV from
1950 until his death it is for radio that he will
be remembered.

Allen, Irwin (1916–). American film
producer who made some rather
clodhopping fantasy spectaculars and then,
with remarkable success for a time, adapted
the same genre for TV. (*Fire, Flood,
Hanging by a Thread, Cave In*, etc.) Series
include VOYAGE TO THE BOTTOM OF THE
SEA, *Lost in Space, Time Tunnel*, LAND OF
THE GIANTS, *The Swiss Family Robinson,
The Return of Captain Nemo, Code Red,
Alice in Wonderland*.

Allen, Jim (1926–). Heavyweight British
writer of fiercely Left (but not Communist)
views, formerly building worker and miner.
Came to TV writing via a stint on *Coronation
Street* and made his first impact with *The
Lump* (BBC 1967), directed by Jack Gold.
Days of Hope (1976) brought him to the
precipice over which art topples into
propaganda, and his serious work remained
unseen for some years save for the admirable
and timely *The Spongers* (BBC 1978),
answering common beliefs about those who
subsist on social security, and the
misbegotten *United Kingdom* (BBC 1981).
Recent credits include *Willie's Last Stand*
(1982) and a north-country saga set mainly in
post-World War II years, *The Gathering
Seed* (1983).   PP

Allen, Patrick (1927–). British leading
actor, a lantern-jawed tough guy who became
famous as CRANE; subsequently the voice of
innumerable commercials and the star of
Hard Times.

Allen, Steve (1921–). American general
purpose comedian, commentator and
panellist of the fifties, still seen occasionally
as talk show host. TV movies: *Now You See It
Now You Don't, Rich Man Poor Man*.

'Allo 'Allo (GB 1984–5). Sitcom set in
occupied France with comic resistance
workers, black marketeers and cuddly
bungling German officers. You were either
scandalized or delighted. Written by Jeremy
Lloyd and David Croft, directed and
produced by Croft, for BBC.   PP
'It is time the BBC said Goodbye Goodbye
to the above. It is an insult to the many
people who were tortured or killed by the
Gestapo.' – reader's letter to the *Sunday
Telegraph*

All's Fair
US 1976 23 × 25m colour (VTR)
CBS/Norman Lear
An emancipated woman and her reactionary
husband find marriage an enjoyable strain.

Talky comedy which didn't quite hit the jackpot.

cr Rod Parker, Bob Schiller, Bob Weiskopf *d* Bob Claver

Richard Crenna, Bernadette Peters

Allyson, June (1917–) (Ella Geisman). American leading lady of the forties and fifties who also tried TV with a drama anthology, *The June Allyson Show*. Cuteness and charm were her forte. She still plays guest star roles and appears in occasional TV movies: *See the Man Run*, *Letters from Three Lovers*, *Curse of the Black Widow*, *Three on a Date*.

Aloha Means Goodbye
US 1974 100m colour TVM
Universal (Sam Strangis)
A girl in hospital discovers that if she dies she may become a heart donor for the surgeon's son.
Icky medical melodrama.
w Dean Riesner, Joseph Stefano, *novel'* Naomi A. Hentze *d* David Lowell Rich
Sally Struthers, James Franciscus, Joanna Miles, Henry Darrow, Larry Gates

Aloha Paradise
US 1981 13 × 50m colour
ABC/MCA/Aaron Spelling
Guests work out their love lives at a Hawaiian vacation resort.
Tepid multi-storey vehicle for a star who no longer seemed to shine.
Debbie Reynolds, Patricia Klous, Mokiha-Na
'This kind of show makes me feel like a sourpuss . . . I've heard speculation that someone writes the scripts, but that could be malicious gossip. I prefer to believe they're not written at all. The producers tear up old *Love Boat* and *Fantasy Island* scripts, toss them in the air and paste them together as they fall . . . There are glimpses of Hawaiian scenery, on blurry screens behind the actors, who are plainly thousands of miles away in a studio building, where they are in no danger of being struck by falling pineapples.' – Robert MacKenzie, *TV Guide*

Along Came a Spider **
US 1969 74m colour TVM
TCF (Alan A. Armer)
The widow of a scientist killed in an accident plots revenge on his careless colleague.
Efficient suspenser shot on a university campus.
w Barry Oringer *d* Lee H. Katzin

Suzanne Pleshette, Ed Nelson, Andrew Prine, Richard Anderson, Brooke Bundy

Almost Heaven
US 1979 74m colour
ABC/Paramount/Gloria Hickey
  Productions
Problems of a heavenly crisis and conscience centre.
Soap opera with a celestial slant. An idiotic idea which almost got picked up as a series.
w Dale McRaven *d* Bill Persky *ph* Lester Shorr *m* Paul Chihara
Eva Gabor, Robert Hays, Jay Leno

Alonzo, John A. (1934–). American cinematographer of theatrical films; turned director. Also directed a few rather flashy TV movies: *Champions*, *Belle Starr*, *Blinded by the Light*.

Alpha Beta *
GB 1974 65m colour
Memorial Enterprises (Timothy Burrill)
Enterprising but deadening telefilm version of a stage two-hander about two angry people locked in a dying marriage.
w E. A. Whitehead *d* Anthony Page
ALBERT FINNEY, RACHEL ROBERTS

The Alpha Caper *
GB theatrical title: *Inside Job*
US 1973 74m colour TVM
Universal/Silverton (Aubrey Schenck)
A parole officer, unjustly retired, plots a 30-million-dollar robbery with one of his protégés.
Reasonably entertaining comedy drama.
w Elroy Schwartz *d* Robert Michael Lewis *ph* Enzo Martinelli *m* Oliver Nelson
Henry Fonda, Leonard Nimoy, James McEachin, Larry Hagman, Elena Verdugo, John Marley, Noah Beery
'There's a good thesis to be written on the hermetic aesthetics of the TV movie: every element seems to follow a pre-ordained pattern whose points of reference are always other movies rather than real experience.' – *Monthly Film Bulletin*

The Alternative
Australia 1978 74m colour TVM
Paramount
An unmarried mother chooses between her ex-lover and a new protector.
Ho-hum Peg's Paper character drama.
w Tony Morphett *d* Paul Eddey
Wendy Hughes, Peter Adams, Tony Bonner, Carla Hoogeveen

Alternative 3 * (GB 1977; 52m; colour). Amusing spoof documentary about the disappearance of various high-IQ citizens, allegedly to form nucleus of a standby civilization on Mars against the coming End of the World. Sly parodies of fashionable breathless TV journalism sweetened the joke, ex-newscaster Tim Brinton held it all together with po-faced gravity and needless to say some supernature fanatics refuse to this day to accept that it was anything but gospel truth, although it was originally scheduled for April 1st. Written by David Ambrose; directed by Chris Miles; for Anglia.   PP

Altman, Robert (1925–). American cult movie director who got started in television and made scores of humdrum filmlets in the fifties for such series as *Bronco*, *Sugarfoot* and *Alfred Hitchcock Presents*. Only longform TV movie: *Nightmare in Chicago*.

Alvin and the Chipmunks *
aka: *The Alvin Show*
US 1961 26 × 25m bw
CBS/Ross Bagdasarian

Cartoon series featuring the producer's then-popular characters who (via electronic trickery) sang en masse in a high-pitched version of the producer's own voice. Also included was an adventure of inventor Clyde Crashcup.

Amahl and the Night Visitors ***. Gian-Carlo Menotti's opera about the shepherds welcoming the birth of Christ was written especially for TV and first produced by NBC in 1951. For many years, in various productions, it was an annual Christmas offering.

Amanda's
US 1983   × 25m colour VTR
Viacom/E & L (Eliot Shoenman, Len
  Rosenberg)

Days in the life of the outspoken owner of a seaside hotel.
Glum American transcription of the BBC's classic *Fawlty Towers*: the producers didn't dare to make Amanda churlish enough.

cr Eliot Shoenman

Beatrice Arthur, Fred McCarren, Simone Griffeth, Rick Hurst, Tony Rosato

Amateau, Rod (1927–). American director of a few light films and innumerable TV series episodes: *Lassie*, *Private Secretary*, *Dobie Gillis*, etc. 1980: supervising/directing *The Dukes of Hazzard/Enos*.

The Amateur Naturalist (GB/Canada 1983). Gerald and Lee Durrell agreeably demonstrating how to study wildlife wherever you happen to be, whether in your own garden, in a city or on holiday. A contest inspired by the series, *Amateur Naturalist of the Year*, followed in 1984. From Dorling Kindersley/Primedia/Primetime for Channel 4.   PP

Amateur Night at the Dixie Bar and Grill
US 1979 100m colour TVM
NBC/Universal/Motown (Rob Cohen,
  Lauren Shuler)

The proprietress of a dingy roadhouse tries to beef up business by staging a talent contest.
A rather dismal complex of character sketches which occasionally stirs the attention.

w/d Joel Schumacher *ph* Ric Waite *m* Bradford Craig

Victor French, Candy Clark, Rick Hurst, Louise Latham, Jamie Farr

The Amazing Chan and the Chan Clan (US 1976; 16 × 25m). Abysmal cartoon series with kids doing the detecting. The very bottom of the Hanna–Barbera barrel, its only interest being the voicing of Chan by Keye Luke, who once played Chan's number one son.

The Amazing Howard Hughes *
US 1977 2 × 96m colour TVM
EMI/Roger Gimbel (Herbert Hirschman)
The life of the millionaire aviator, inventor, film producer and recluse.
Informative and watchable biopic, rather slackly handled and with a disconcerting habit of stopping for a commercial break in the middle of a scene, then going on with something quite different.

w John Gay *d* William A. Graham *m* Laurence Rosenthal *ph* Michael Margulies

TOMMY LEE JONES, Ed Flanders, Carol Bagdasarian, James Hampton, Tovah Feldshuh

The Amazing Mr Malone (US 1951). Live half-hour mystery series on ABC, with Lee Tracy as a criminal lawyer. Based on a radio series, and novels by Craig Rice.

The Amazing Spiderman: see Spiderman (1978)

Amazing Stories *
US 1985 44 × 25m colour
NBC/MCA/Universal/Amblin (Steven
  Spielberg, David E. Vogel)
On the strength of his theatrical box-office

reputation, Spielberg got a huge budget and an unprecedented order for 44 of these slight and overproduced stories in the wake of *Twilight Zone*. Audience reaction was not too enthusiastic, but they stand as an interesting monument and an indication of how a clever filmmaker can play with mood on the small screen.

'Nothing new . . . too much of it felt like scenes spliced together from *ET*, *Close Encounters of the Third Kind*, *Poltergeist* and other Spielberg films.' – *Daily Variety*

The Amazing World of Kreskin
US/Canada 1972–3 ? × 25m colour (VTR)

Audience participation show featuring a genuinely bewildering bespectacled magician and mind reader.

'A beautiful young surgeon uncovers a deadly game plan in an undercover war against Men!'
Amazons
US 1984 96m colour TVM
ABC (Stuart Cohen)

Descendants of the original Amazons infiltrate American society and kill off the men in power above them.
Extreme example of Women's Lib, quite stylishly packaged as a thriller.

w David Solomon, Guerdon Trueblood *d* Paul Michael Glaser

Madeline Stowe, Jack Scalia, Jennifer Warren, Tamara Dobson, Stella Stevens, Peter Solari, Leslie Bevis

Amber Waves *
US 1980 100m colour TVM
ABC/Time–Life (Philip Mandelker, Stuart Kallis)

A selfish young New York model, stranded in Kansas, is taught a purpose in life by a travelling harvester who is desperately ill.
Sporadically absorbing and well-made message picture.

w Ken Trevey *d* Joseph Sargent *ph* DONALD M. MORGAN *m* John Rubinstein

DENNIS WEAVER, Kurt Russell, Mare Winningham, Fran Brill

'A hymn to integrity.' – *Daily Variety*

The Ambush Murders
US 1982 96m colour TVM
CBS/Charles Fries/David Goldsmith

When two policemen are gunned down, a black man is interrogated and spends four years proving his innocence.
Reasonably gripping account of a true 1971 case.

w Tony Kayden, from the *book* by Ben Bradle Jnr *d* Steven Hillard Stern *ph* Frank Phillips *m* Paul Chihara

JAMES BROLIN, DORIAN HAREWOOD, Alfre Woodard, Robert Denison, Amy Madigan

Ameche, Don (1908–   ). American film star of the thirties who later hosted a TV circus series and made occasional guest appearances: *Gidget Gets Married*, *Shadow Over Elveron*, etc.

Amelia Earhart *
US 1976 150m colour TVM
Universal/NBC (George Eckstein)

A biography of the American woman flyer of the thirties who disappeared over the Pacific.
Standard biopic, quite well done in television terms, with good performances, aerial sequences and music; but too long.

w Carol Sobieski *d* George Schaefer *costumes* Edith Head *m* David Shire *aerial sequences* Frank Tallman

SUSAN CLARK, John Forsythe, Stephen Macht, Susan Oliver, Catherine Burns, Jane Wyatt, Charles Aidman

America: see Alistair Cooke's America

America Salutes Richard Rodgers: The Sound of His Music (US 1976). Clumsily titled two-hour special for CBS, hosted by Henry Winkler and Gene Kelly. Good individual items are swamped by fulsome bookends. Nevertheless, it won an Emmy for director Dwight Hemion, and another for writers Alan Buz Kohan and Ted Strauss.

American Caesar *
Canada 1984 10 × 28m colour/bw
Cineworld (Ian McLeod)

Interesting undramatized series from William Manchester's biography of General Douglas MacArthur, American chief-of-staff long before World War II, Pacific supremo and last Shogun of Japan before colliding with the US President over the conduct of the Korean War. Unusually for the eighties, cast in half-hour format, with John Colicos as narrator and John Huston speaking MacArthur's words. Despite the brevity of the episodes, the research was excellent and the atmosphere of the times caught with the aid of such imaginative touches as having the only American survivor of the infamous Bataan death-march play the little harmonica tune he'd improvised to keep up spirits among the prisoners.   PP

An American Christmas Carol
US 1981 96m colour TVM
Smith–Hemion/Edgar J. Scherick/Stanley
  Chase/Joe Slan/ABC

Dickens's story is adapted to 1933 New
Hampshire. The modern Scrooge is Benedict
Slade, president of a finance company, who
during the Depression grinds his creditors
into the ground.
Difficult to object to the attempt, but the
star is finally unequal to the role and the
overall attempt is fairly tedious.

w Jerome Coopersmith   *d* Eric Till   *ph*
Richard Clupka *m* Hagood Hardy

Henry Winkler, David Wayne, Chris
Wiggins, Dorian Harewood, Susan Hogan

American Dream
US 1981 74m colour TVM
ABC/Mace Neufeld (Barney Rosenzweig)

Needing a bigger house, a Chicago
suburbanite has to move his family into the
inner city.
Neat treatment of an unrewarding subject.
Six one-hours followed, but it was never
really a goer as a series.

w Ronald M. Cohen, Barbara Corday, Ken
Hecht *d* Mel Damski *ph* Paul Vom Brack *m*
Artie Butler

Stephen Macht, Karen Carlson, Hans
Conried, Michael Hershewe, Tim Waldrip,
Andrea Smith, Scott Brady

'Shows how wise, funny and loving a TV
program can be' – *Daily Variety*

The American Dream (GB 1984).
Jonathan Dimbleby in search of same in four
hour-long reports on such dreamscapes as
Silicon Valley and Madison Avenue, winding
up – since this was Election Year – with the
simple frontier faith much invoked in
Reagan's re-election campaign. Neatly done
in Francis Gerard's production, for YTV. PP

An American Family **
US 1973 12 × 50m colour (VTR)
PBS (Craig Gilbert)

For one year, TV cameras invaded the home
of a well-to-do Californian family and
patched together from the resulting miles of
film 12 hours of what purported to be an
intimate glimpse into their real,
unadulterated private life, warts and all. The
series caused furious discussion, but by any
measurement was a television first. A year
later the BBC made its own variation, this
time using a working-class family from
Reading: they quickly became national
figures.

American Film Institute: see AFI Salute

The American Girls
GB title: *Have Girls, Will Travel*
US 1978 11 × 50m colour
CBS/Columbia (Harve Bennett, Harris
  Katleman)

Two girl reporters travel the US in a camper.
By *Charlie's Angels* out of *Route 66*, this
derivative but trend-conscious series set out
to peddle glamour and sex with a soupçon of
social awareness.

Priscilla Barnes, Debra Clinger, David
Spielberg, Dana Andrews

An American in Pasadena *
GB title: *Gene Kelly's Dancing Years*
US 1977 50m colour (VTR)
Viacom

From-the-stalls record of a charity show in
which Gene Kelly and guests talk, sing and
dance through his career. Irresistible
material, disappointingly staged and shot.

pd Marty Pasetta *w* Buz Kohan

guests Frank Sinatra, Liza Minnelli, Lucille
Ball, others

The American Short Story * (US 1977;
colour). Superior anthology of stories by
Stephen Crane, Scott Fitzgerald,
Hemingway, Henry James, John Updike and
others, made for educational release on
16mm or videocassette but earning
transmission on many TV stations. Executive
producer: Robert Geller; for Learning in
Focus Inc.   PP

The first 17 were as follows:

The Golden Honeymoon by Ring Lardner (*w*
Frederic Hunter; *d* Noel Black; with Teresa
Wright, James Whitmore; 50m)

Paul's Case by Willa Cather (*w* Ron Cowen;
d Lamont Johnson; with Eric Roberts,
Michael Higgins; 52m)

The Greatest Man in the World by James
Thurber (*w* Jeff Wanshel; *d* Ralph
Rosenblum; with Brad Davis, John
McMartin, Reed Birney, Howard da Silva;
49m)

Rappaccini's Daughter by Nathaniel
Hawthorne (*w* Hebert Hartig; *d* Dezso
Magyar; with Kristoffer Tabori, Kathleen
Beller; 56m)

The Jilting of Granny Weatherall by
Katherine Anne Porter (*w* Corinne Jacker; *d*
Randa Haines; with Geraldine Fitzgerald,
Lois Smith; 55m)

The Sky Is Gray by Ernest J. Gaines (*w*
Charles Fuller; *d* Stan Latham; with Olivia
Cole, Cleavon Little; 44m)

The Man That Corrupted Hadleyburg by Mark Twain (*w* Mark Harris; *d* Ralph Rosenblum; with Robert Preston, Fred Gwynne, Tom Aldredge; 38m)

Barn Burning by William Faulkner (*w* Horton Foote; *d* Peter Werner; with Tommy Lee Jones, Diane Kakan; 38m)

Parker Adderson, Philosopher by Ambrose Bierce (*w/d* Arthur Barron; with Harris Yulin, Douglass Watson; 37m)

The Blue Hotel by Stephen Crane (*w* Harry M. Petrakis; *d* Jan Kadar; with David Warner, James Keach, John Bottoms; 52m)

Soldier's Home by Ernest Hemingway (*w* Robert Geller; *d* Robert Young; with Richard Backus, Nancy Marchand; 39m)

Bernice Bobs Her Hair by F. Scott Fitzgerald (*w/d* Joan Micklin Silver; with Shelley Duvall, Veronica Cartwright, Bud Cort; 45m)

Almos' a Man by Richard Wright (*w* Leslie Lee; *d* Stan Latham; with LeVar Burton, Madge Sinclair; 37m)

The Displaced Person by Flannery O'Connor (*w* Horton Foote; *d* Glenn Jordan; with Irene Worth, John Houseman; 56m)

The Jolly Corner by Henry James (*w/d* Arthur Barron; with Fritz Weaver, Salome Jens; 41m)

I'm a Fool by Sherwood Anderson (*w* Ron Cowen; *d* Noel Black; with Ron Howard, Santiago Gonzalez; 36m)

The Music School by John Updike (*w/d* John Korty; with Ron Weyand, Dana Larson, Tom Dahlgren; 27m)

'Good news for anyone who had begun to think that American culture is summed up in disco.' – Robert MacKenzie, *TV Guide*

The Americans
GB title: *The Blue and the Grey*
US 1961 26 × 50m bw
NBC

In 1861 Virginia secedes from the Union, and two brothers take opposite sides.
Predictable but well-made historical actioner.

Darryl Hickman, Dick Davalos

Americans *
GB 1978 13 × 50m colour
BBC (John Bird)

Profiles of American figures of the types who have become over-familiar through the media: company president, schoolteacher, private detective, First Lady, Indian chief, immigrant, rancher, district attorney, etc.

w/d, narrator DESMOND WILCOX

'American history has been strengthened, American culture enriched and enlivened, by the presence of characters who have become familiar to us on our Saturday morning cinema screens, or in our television dramas. Fictionalizing these characters has often blurred the truth. But, in truth, they do exist. They may not always do so.' – Desmond Wilcox

'Stylish and engaging.' – *Daily Mail*

PP: 'The only flaw was to include celebrities such as juvenile film star Jodie Foster or Mrs Rosalynn Carter, the then President's lady, in a selection otherwise of unsung heroes.'

Ames, Leon (1903–) (Leon Wycoff). American character actor, in movies from the early thirties, usually in smooth, silent and not very interesting roles. He became a popular TV star in LIFE WITH FATHER, FATHER OF THE BRIDE and MISTER ED. TV movies include *Sherlock Holmes in New York*, *The Best Place To Be*.

Amos *
US 1985 96m colour TVM
CBS/Bryna/Vincent

A new resident at an old people's home suspects the matron of practising euthanasia, and resents it.
Curious but not unsuccessful attempt at a black comedy-drama, cast on a high level but tending to slackness in its second half.

w Richard Kramer, from the *novel* by Stanley West *d* Michael Tuchner *ph* Fred J. Koenekamp *m* Georges Delerue

Kirk Douglas, Elizabeth Montgomery, Dorothy McGuire, Pat Morita, James Sloyan, Ray Walston, Don Keefer

Amos Burke Secret Agent: see Burke's Law

Amos 'n' Andy. A famous radio comedy series in which caricatured black men were impersonated by whites, its translation to TV in 1951 was a brave attempt, but within two years it had been withdrawn because of protests from various organizations. The bewildered actors, who had been on radio since 1925, were Charles Correll and Freeman F. Gosden; they produced the CBS TV version, but had taken care to cast black actors for TV, namely Alvin Childers and Spencer Williams.

Ampex. The first successful brand of videotape was invented for the Ampex Corporation by Charles Ginsberg and Ray Dolby. Its acceptance by the TV industry in 1956 marked the end of live TV.

Amsterdam, Morey (1912–). American nightclub comedian chiefly familiar on TV as the hero's friend in *The Dick Van Dyke Show*.

Amy. Amy Johnson, pioneer aviatrix, has been the subject of three broadcast plays all called simply by her name. A Channel 4 film in the *Eleventh Hour* slot, 1982, predictably and boringly set her as a feminist in a 'non-goal-orientated' context. Roger Milner's 1984 BBC drama with Harriet Walter (*d* Nat Crosby) was a great improvement; but in many ways the most satisfactory exercise is still a 1973 BBC radio play by Mary-Jean Hasler with Rosalind Shanks, produced by Alan Burgess.   PP

Amy Prentiss: see Mystery Movie

Amyes, Julian (1917–). Veteran British drama director and producer, with Granada from their early days until official retirement, since then busier than ever. Favourite directing credits over the years include *Dial M for Murder*, 1952, *No Man's Land*, 1978, *Great Expectations*, 1980, *Jane Eyre*, 1982, and an Amyes family production, *A Wife Like the Moon*, 1983, written by Anne Allan (Mrs Amyes) with daughter Isabella in the cast.   PP

Anatomy of a Seduction *
US 1979 100m colour TVM
CBS/Filmways/Moonlight Productions
  (Frank Von Zerneck)

A middle-aged divorcee is unable to prevent herself having an affair with the son of her best friend.
Top quality soap opera with good performances.

w Alison Cross *d* Steven Hillard Stern *ph* Howard Schwarz *m* Hagood Hardy

Susan Flannery, Jameson Parker, Rita Moreno, Ed Nelson

Anatomy of an Illness *
US 1984 96m colour TVM
CBS/TCF/Hammer/Jerry Gershwin (Peter
  J. Thomson)

A senior journalist finds himself suffering from a degenerative disease, but cures himself through vitamin C and old comedy movies.
Curious but apparently true, this well-presented case history at least provides an upbeat exception to the doleful trend of TV's disease-of-the-week movies.

w Lawrence Roman, from the autobiographical book by Norman Cousins *d* Richard T. Heffron

ED ASNER, Eli Wallach, Millie Perkins, David Ogden Stiers, Lelia Goldoni

anchorman. The chairman or question master of a panel game, or the studio announcer in a current affairs show, linking together various reports and interpreting them for the viewers.

And Baby Makes Six
US 1978 100m colour TVM
NBC/Alan Landsburg Productions
  (Herbert Hirschman)

A 46-year-old mother with a grown family becomes pregnant.
Pleasant sentimental drama with nowhere to go.

w Shelley List *d* Waris Hussein *ph* Ric Waite *m* Bud Karlin

Colleen Dewhurst, Warren Oates, Timothy Hutton, Maggie Cooper, Mildred Dunnock, Mason Adams

And Did Those Feet *
GB 1965 75m bw (VTR)
BBC (James McTaggart)

A wealthy man hates his illegitimate sons.
Quirky play with interesting credits.

w David Mercer *d* Don Taylor

David Markham, Patrick Troughton, Willoughby Goddard

PP: 'An allegory about middle-aged innocents trying to escape from the big real world for which they are unfitted and finally succeeding – but, alas, only after some heavily jocular goings-on – in a deserted swimming pool, a truly magical scene. Candles burned on the surround and decked the diving boards. A menagerie of inflated rubber animals nodded gravely on the water. The light from the surface shimmered and danced. And high on their swings Mercer's twin heroes rocked gently to and fro in perfect contentment.'

And I Alone Survived
US 1979 100m colour TVM
NBC/Jerry Leider Productions (Burt
  Nodella)

A girl survives a mountain plane crash by walking over remote mountains in the Sierra Nevada.
Adequate elaboration of a true incident.

w Lane Slate, *book* Lauren Elder with Shirley Streshinsky *d* William Graham *ph* Jordan Cronenweth *m* Lawrence Rosenthal

Blair Brown, David Ackroyd, Maggie Cooper, Vera Miles, James G. Richardson

And Mother Makes Three. British (Thames) sitcom of the early seventies, written by Richard Waring, produced and directed by Peter Frazer-Jones, and starring WENDY CRAIG as a frantically coping mum. The show stemmed from another called *Not in Front of the Children*, and was eventually transformed into *And Mother Makes Five*.

And No One Could Save Her
GB 1972 73m colour TVM
Associated London (Robert Stigwood)
An American girl seeks her husband in Dublin; but there is no trace of him, so could he be a figment of her imagination?
Bunny Lake Is Missing all over again; not badly done.
w Anthony Skene d Kevin Billington ph Austin Dempster m Ron Grainer
Lee Remick, Milo O'Shea, Frank Grimes, Jennie Linden

And So We Say Farewell *
GB 1975 50m colour
BBC
A smart compilation of early film catalogues from the collection of Henry Fisher, introduced by Denis Norden.

And Your Name Is Jonah
US 1979 100m colour TVM
CBS/Charles Fries/Capital Cities (Norman Felton, Stanley Rubin)
A young mother discovers that her son, thought retarded, is merely deaf.
Likeable but overlong telefilm in the wake of *Mandy*.
w Michael Bartman d Richard Michaels ph David Myers m Fred Karlin
Sally Struthers, James Woods, Randee Heller, Jeff Bravin

Anderson, Barbara (1945–). American leading lady, former beauty queen; became familiar as assistant to Raymond Burr in *Ironside*, for which she won an Emmy in 1967. TV movies include *Visions*, *Don't Be Afraid of the Dark*, *Strange Homecoming*, *You Lie So Deep My Love*, *Doctors' Private Lives*.

Anderson, Daryl (1951–). American general purpose actor, remembered as Animal in *Lou Grant*. Also: *The Phoenix*, *Sweet Revenge*.

Anderson, Eddie (1905–77). Black American character actor familiar in Hollywood as the archetypal frightened manservant and on radio and TV as Jack

Benny's disgruntled manservant Rochester. Black self-consciousness in the sixties made the stereotype unacceptable, and when Rochester reappeared on a Benny special in 1970 and was asked to fetch the car, he made the famous retort: 'Massah Benny, we don' do dat no mo'!'

✲ **Anderson, Gerry** (1929–). American producer in Britain, specializing in stylish action hokum, usually enacted by puppets. Series include *Four Feather Falls*, *Supercar*, *Stingray*, *Captain Scarlet*, *Joe 90*, THUNDERBIRDS, *UFO* (live action), SPACE 1999 (live action), *Terrahawks*.

Anderson, Jean (1908–). Angular British character actress best remembered as the formidable mama in THE BROTHERS. Also prominent in *Tenko*.

Anderson, John (1922–). American general purpose actor. TV movies include *Scalplock*, *Call to Danger*, *Heatwave*, *Manhunter*, *Death Among Friends*, *Bridger*, *Once an Eagle*, *The Last Hurrah*, *Backstairs at the White House*.

Anderson, Dame Judith (1898–). Australian actress in America, ever famous for her Mrs Danvers in *Rebecca*. In TV, won an Emmy for her Lady Macbeth in 1954 and again in 1960. In her eighties, assumed a leading role in the soap opera *Santa Barbara*.

Anderson, Loni (1945–). Busty blonde American leading lady and comedienne. *WKRP in Cincinnati*, *Three on a Date*, *My Mother's Secret Life*, *Partners in Crime*.

Anderson, Melissa Sue (1962–). American leading lady who came to prominence as a child star in LITTLE HOUSE ON THE PRAIRIE. *The Brady Bunch*, *The Loneliest Runner*, *The Survival of Dana*, *Which Mother is Mine*, *Advice to the Lovelorn*, *First Affair*.

Anderson, Moira (1940–). Toothsome Scottish singer, a familiar face on British TV since 1960 when she turned up in *The White Heather Club*. For a while she introduced *Stars on Sunday*, and had several series of her own.

The Anderson Platoon *** (France 1967). Brilliant hand-held camera account of a US infantry platoon in Vietnam, both in action and at leisure. Directed by Pierre Schoendorffer. Never had the climate of war

been caught so faithfully and so vividly: the tension building up and winding down again, the sudden mirror-bright unreality of action.
PP

Anderson, Richard (1926–). American second lead/character actor, familiar on TV as Oscar Goldman in *Six Million Dollar Man* and *Bionic Woman*. TV movies include *Along Came a Spider*, *The Astronaut*, *The Longest Night*, *The Night Strangler*, *The Immigrants*, *Pearl*, *Murder by Natural Causes*.

Anderson, Warner (1911–76). American character actor, familiar on TV in *The Doctors*, *The Line Up*, *Peyton Place*.

The Andersonville Trial *
US 1970 120m colour (VTR)
KCET Los Angeles/Stanley Kramer

The trial in the 1860s of Henry Wirtz, camp commandant accused of the deaths of many Unionist prisoners.
Solid docu-drama.

w Saul Levitt *d* George C. Scott

Richard Basehart, Buddy Ebsen, Cameron Mitchell, William Shatner

† Emmys went to Stanley Kramer and Saul Levitt.

Andrews, Anthony (1946–). Boyish British actor who leaped to national fame as the subaltern hero of *Danger UXB* and to international renown as the doomed playboy of BRIDESHEAD REVISITED. Subsequently and not very rewardingly in *Z for Zachariah*, 1982, *Mistress of Paradise*, *Ivanhoe*, *The Scarlet Pimpernel* and *Sparkling Cyanide*. PP

Andrews, Dana (1909–). American leading man of the forties, brother of Steve Forrest. TV movies include *The Failing of Raymond*, *Shadow in the Streets*, *The First 36 Hours of Dr Durrant*, *The Last Hurrah*, *Ike*.

✷ **Andrews, Eamonn** (1922–). Irish sports commentator who came to Britain and became popular, despite his lack of conversational ability, as host and linkman (*What's My Line?*, *The Eamonn Andrews Show*, *Tonight*, *This Is Your Life*, *Time for Business*). He is now looking back on more than 30 years of such success.

Andrews, Edward (1915–85). American character actor with a shifty/genial persona, very busy in the early sixties in such series as *Thriller*. Series include *Broadside*, *Supertrain*. TV movies include *The Over the Hill Gang*, *The Intruders*, *How to Break Up a*

Happy Divorce, *Lacy and the Mississippi Queen*, *Undercover with the KKK*.

Andrews, Harry (1911–). Stalwart English character actor, in all media. TV movies include *Clayhanger* (series), *The Four Feathers*, *SOS Titanic*, *The Curse of King Tutankhamun's Tomb*, *The Seven Dials Mystery*.

Andrews, Julie (1934–) (Julia Wells). A British child singer who after success on Broadway and in Hollywood became a top international star and married Blake Edwards. An occasional TV guest star; see also *The Julie Andrews Hour*.

Andrews, Tige (*c* 1923–). American character actor, real name Andropoulos; chiefly familiar on TV as cop in *The Detectives* and *The Mod Squad*. TV movies include *Skyway to Death*, *Raid on Entebbe*, *The Return of the Mod Squad*.

The Andros Targets *
US 1977 13 × 50m colour
CBS (Bob Sweeney, Larry Rosen)

Adventures of an investigative journalist.
A smooth, snappy dramatic show inspired by *All The President's Men*. It failed because the masses found it too serious, while the intelligentsia were annoyed by its silly plots.
ᵗ*cr* Frank Cucci

James Sutorius, Pamela Reed, Alan Mixon

The Andy Griffith Show *
aka: *Andy of Mayberry*
US 1960–8 249 × 25m bw (last 100 in colour)
CBS/Mayberry

Adventures of a small-town sheriff.
Mid-American comedy, full of crackerbarrel philosophy and rural types. (It continued as *Mayberry RFD* when its star moved on to become *The Headmaster*.)

Andy Griffith, Don Knotts (in first 160), Ronny Howard

† *The New Andy Griffith Show* was unsuccessful.

Andy Pandy. A puppet series for children which played between 1953 and 1957 and later tended to give the BBC an old-fashioned image. Maria Bird was the human being in vision.

The Andy Williams Show. An American variety hour on NBC, very popular in the early sixties: it won Emmys in 1962, 1965 and 1966. The singing star began by playing it straight but was later subjected to a *Hellzapoppin* atmosphere which involved a talking bear. Bob Finkel was among the more influential producers.

Angel *
US 1960 39 × 25m bw
CBS

Tribulations of a young architect with a charming but scatterbrained French wife.
Pleasing comedy of its time with just a touch of sophistication.

Annie Fargé, Marshall Thompson, Doris Singleton, Don Keefer

Angel City
US 1980 96m colour TVM
CBS/Factor–Newland (John Newland, Alan Jay Factor)

A West Virginian, short of funds, takes his family to pick crops in Florida and falls foul of the boss of a civilian labour camp.
A latter-day *Grapes of Wrath*; well enough done, but why do it?

w James Lee Barrett, *novel* Patrick Smith d Philip Leacock ph James Pergola m Mark Snow

Ralph Waite, Mitchell Ryan, Paul Winfield, Jennifer Warren, Jennifer Jason Leigh, Red West, Bob Minor

'Taut little horror vidpic . . . should hold viewers by its grimness and its humanity.' – *Daily Variety*

Angel Death *
US 1979 50m colour
David Bell Associates/David Begelman

Harrowing documentary on the effects of phencyclidine hydrochloride, a new drug used by teenagers and likely to cause violence and brain damage.

w/p/d John Cosgrove, Charles Klasky *narrators* Paul Newman, Joanne Woodward

Angel Dusted
US 1981 96m colour TVM
NBC/NRW Features (Marian Rees)

An earnest student takes to drugs and goes on a psychotic binge.
Heavy-going case history, nicely made but very predictable.

w Darlene Craviotto, *book* Ursula Etons d Dick Lowry ph Frank Beascoechea m James Horner

Jean Stapleton, Arthur Hill, John Putch, Darlene Craviotto, Percy Rodrigues

'Tract-like development and a pat answer.' – *Daily Variety*

Angel on my Shoulder
US 1981 96m colour TVM
ABC/Viacom/Mace Neufeld/Barney Rosenzweig/Beowulf Productions

The devil sends a dead gangster's soul back into the body of an honest DA.
This heavy-handed variation on *Here Comes Mr Jordan* didn't really work as a 1946 film starring Paul Muni and Claude Rains, and this production is totally lacking in zest.

w George Kirgo, from the screenplay by Roland Kibbee and Harry Segall d John Berry ph Gayne Rescher m Artie Butler

Peter Strauss, Richard Kiley, Barbara Hershey, Janis Paige, Seymour Cassel, Murray Matheson, Anne Seymour

'Fantasy must have one foot in reality, one in the land of dreams; this just trudges blindly onwards.' – *Daily Variety*

Angel Pavement ** (GB 1958).
Outstanding four-part BBC serial by Constance Cox, from J. B. Priestley's novel of hard times in a small London business in the Depression: the first modern novel to be given the classic serial treatment, and an important trail blazer. With Maurice Denham, Alec McCowen.   PP

Angels.
Sporadic British (BBC) tape hour of the seventies, about a group of young nurses in a big London hospital. For home consumption; producers and directors various. Original (1976) cast included Erin Geraghty, Fiona Fullerton, Clare Clifford, Julie Dawn Cole, Karan David, Lesley Dunlop, Faith Brook, Janina Faye; devised by Paula Milne; produced by Ron Craddock. Returned 1979 as a 25-minute soap opera.

Angels are So Few
GB 1971 65m colour (VTR)
BBC

A young man thinks he's an angel.
Half-successful whimsy, a light-hearted trifle surprising from this author.

w Dennis Potter d Gareth Davies

Tom Bell, Christine Hargreaves

Angie
US 1979–80   × 25m colour
ABC/Miller–Milkis–Henderson/Paramount (Bob Ellison, Dale McRaven)

A New York waitress marries a millionaire.
Or, *The Beverly Hillbillies* revisited, but with a charmless yakkity-yak heroine and a strident laugh track.

cr Garry K. Marshal, Dale McRaven

Donna Pescow, Robert Hays, Doris Roberts, Sharon Spelman

Anglia. British commercial station originally responsible for the mainly agricultural counties of the east, and set up with the appropriate bias. But since the switch to UHF transmitters it has acquired considerable tracts of industrial midlands, including the new city of Milton Keynes, and has tried hard to change its image. Internationally it is chiefly known for the wildlife series *Survival* and the glossy *Tales of the Unexpected*.   PP

Animal Doctor
aka: *Woobinda, Animal Doctor*
Australia 1968 39 × 25m colour
Freemantle
Adventures of a vet in the outback.
Passable filler for young people.
Don Pascoe, Bindi Williams

Animal Olympians **
GB 1982 60m colour VTR
BBC Bristol Wild Life Unit
A remarkable documentary displaying the superlative physical feats of the animal world, written and produced by Jeffrey Boswall.

Animal Story. A British half-hour series, followed by *Animal Alphabet* and *A to Zoo*, produced in the early sixties by Granada TV in association with the Regent's Park Zoo Film Unit. Executive producer: Derek Twist. Examples in NFA.

Animal, Vegetable and Mineral. British (BBC) panel game of the fifties, in which eminent university dons and scientists, including Mortimer Wheeler and Glyn Daniel, were asked to identify odd museum pieces and archaeological artefacts.

Anka, Paul (1941–). Canadian boy singer of the fifties, subject of a famous documentary, *Lonely Boy*. Subsequently a pretty big marquee name for concerts and specials.

The Ann Sothern Show *
US 1958–61 93 × 25m bw
CBS/Anso Productions
Problems of running a New York hotel, with the star as assistant manager.
Lightly likeable sitcom, with the star fighting her waistline.
Ann Sothern, Don Porter, Ernest Truex
† The star had previously appeared with Don Porter in *Private Secretary*.

Anna and the King *
US 1972 13 × 25m colour
CBS/TCF (Gene Reynolds)
In Victorian times, the King of Siam hires an English governess to tame his many offspring.
Reasonably careful and engaging extension of the films *Anna and the King of Siam* and *The King and I*. It failed because the network placed it badly and wouldn't give it a second chance.
YUL BRYNNER, Samantha Eggar, Keye Luke, Eric Shea

Anna Karenina *. The BBC's 1978 production, in partnership with Time–Life and Polytel, is worth recording as a massive production achievement which carefully reconstructed 19th-century Russia much as the same producer's *The Forsyte Saga* reconstructed Edwardian England. The 10 × 50m episodes however proved over-generous in sheer footage for this basically simple human story of adultery and tragedy. With Nicola Pagett, Eric Porter, Stuart Wilson, Mary Morris; written (after Tolstoy) and produced by Donald Wilson for executive producer Ken Riddington; directed by Basil Coleman.   PP

Anna Karenina
US 1985 135m colour TVM
CBS/Colgems/Rastar (Hugh Benson)
A rather flat and flavourless television version.
w James Goldman Simon Langton *ph* Kelvin Pike *m* Barry Peters
Jacqueline Bisset, Christopher Reeve, Paul Scofield, Ian Ogilvy, Anna Massey, Joanna David, Judy Campbell

Annakin, Ken (1914–). British film director of the fifties who made few forays into TV. TV movies include *Hunter's Moon*, *Murder at the Mardi Gras*, *Institute for Revenge*, *The Pirate*.

The Annan Committee. Appointed by the British government to pronounce on the future of TV, this group under Lord Annan disgorged itself in 1977 of a long and unwieldy report which more or less recommended the offering of the fourth channel to the IBA as a holding point for independent producers.

Anne Hughes, Her Boke (GB 1978). Michael Croucher's BBC film reconstructing in loving detail the daily round of an 18th-century Herefordshire farmer's wife as she sets it down in her diary. Subsequently doubts were cast on the authenticity of the original material.   PP
'The perfect programme, without a flaw to pick at or a fault to find fun with.' – *Guardian*

ANNA KARENINA. Another well-revived classic received its flattest treatment in Columbia's 1985 version, and that despite the efforts of Jacqueline Bisset, Paul Scofield and Anna Massey.

Annie Oakley
US 1953–7 80 × 25m bw
ABC/Flying A Productions
Adventures of a female sharpshooter in the old west.
Annie Get Your Gun without the music; not very lively.
Gail Davis, Brad Johnson, Jimmy Hawkins

Annie, The Women in the Life of a Man *
(US 1969). One-hour special for CBS, exposing the many faces and talents of Anne Bancroft. It won Emmys as outstanding variety programme (executive producer Joseph Cates, producer Martin Charnin); and for its writing (Peter Bellwood, Gary Belkin, Herb Sargent, Thomas Meehan, Judith Viorst).

Annika *
GB/Sweden 1984 3 × 52m
Central/Sveriges TV2 and Baltic
   Producktions (Colin Nutley, Sven-Gosta Holst)
Yobbish English boy holiday-jobbing in the Isle of Wight falls for Swedish language student and follows her back to Stockholm. An attractive contemporary love story that for once gave both co-production partners a worthwhile result, very perceptive about the fine incompatibilities between nationality and nationality, class and class, generation and generation.
w Colin Nutley, Sven-Gosta Holst *d* Colin Nutley
Christina Rigner, Jesse Birdsall   PP

Annis, Francesca (1944–). British leading actress who became a star as LILLIE and consolidated her position in *Why Didn't They Ask Evans?*

Ann-Margret (1941–) (Ann-Margaret Olsson). Swedish–American musical entertainer and light actress who seems to be game for anything but will probably be best remembered for her specials.

announcers. The heyday of the announcer in Britain was the immediate postwar period on BBC television, when all programmes – including interludes – were linked by a

ANNIKA. This Anglo-Swedish love story introduced Christina Rigner to British screens.

smiling head in vision. The three best-known announcers then were Mary Malcolm, Sylvia Peters and McDonald Hobley. They became the first television personalities, in the case of the women as much fêted as the first women newsreaders were to be 20 years later. In 1951 Sylvia Peters appeared with the Crazy Gang in the Royal Variety Performance. If Mary Malcolm lost an earring it was front-page news. In-vision announcers were phased out in 1958, briefly brought back again (Judith Chalmers, Valerie Pitts) and finally retired from BBC-TV in the early sixties, though most ITV stations retain them in order to strengthen local identity. Channel 4 came on the air in 1982 with featured announcers but soon phased them out.   PP

Another Day
US 1978 4 × 25m colour
Domestic sitcom: the problems of a married couple who both have full time jobs. Not a success. Created by James Komack for Paul Mason/CBS; with David Groh, Joan Hackett.

Another Opening, Another Show * (GB 1976). A rather wistful BBC hour in which John Mills introduced some leading lights who were stars in his youth and showed that

they could still perform: Jessie Matthews, Anna Neagle, Jack Hulbert, Cicely Courtneidge, Barbara Mullen, Richard Murdoch. Produced by Yvonne Littlewood.

Another Sunday and Sweet FA *
GB 1972 52m colour (16mm)
Granada (Peter Eckersley)
Rivalries between two small football teams come to violence on the field.
Amusing north country comedy.
w JACK ROSENTHAL d Michael Apted
DAVID SWIFT, Duggie Brown, Joe Gladwin, Clare Kelly, Lynne Carol
† Critics' Circle Award.

'Her husband's past just walked into her life – will his illegitimate daughter end their marriage?'
Another Woman's Child
US 1983 96m colour TVM
CBS (Asa Maynor, Linda Lavin)
A childless couple take in the husband's illegitimate daughter by a woman who has just died.
Predictable domestic drama which gets bogged down in psychiatric discussion.
w Conrad Bromberg d John Erman ph Don Morgan m Billy Goldenberg
Linda Lavin, Tony LoBianco, Joyce Van Patten, Doris Roberts, Ron Rifkin

Another World. This title was used both by Granada TV for a travel and nature series produced by Douglas Fisher, and by the NBC network for a one-hour soap opera set in Bay City, USA, which began in 1963 and is still going strong.

Ansara, Michael (1922–). Heavy-featured American character actor often seen as Latin or Indian villain. In TV, played leads in *Law of the Plainsman* and *Broken Arrow*. TV movies include *Powderkeg, Call to Danger, Ordeal, Barbary Coast*.

Anspach, Susan (1939–). American general purpose actress. TV movies: *I Want to Keep My Baby, The Secret Life of John Chapman, Rosetti and Ryan, Mad Bull, The Last Giraffe, Portrait of an Escort, The First Time, The Yellow Rose, Deadly Encounter, Space*

answer print. The first available print on which sound and vision have been combined (though the quality may be capable of improvement).

Answers
US 1982 119m colour VTR
Orion (Frank Von Zerneck)
Three one-act plays by Ernest Thompson, all dealing with a response to an unexpected meeting.
Tolerable but unexciting trio of playlets depending largely on the actors.
w Frank Von Zerneck, Robert Greenwald, Michael Brandman d George Schaefer
A Good Time: Sam Bottoms, Patricia McCormack
The Constituent: Ned Beatty, Burgess Meredith
Twinkle, Twinkle: Eileen Brennan, Robert Webber

anthology. A dramatic series without a continuing character (though there may be a host).

Antiope. The name of the French teletext system.

Antiques Roadshow. BBC touring format originally produced by Robin Drake, whereby a team of decorative arts specialists from the major auction houses visits English country towns to identify and value treasures brought in by the public. Some rare pieces have come to light along with much agreeable entertainment. Conducted 1982–3 by Arthur Negus, since then by Hugh Scully.
                                                    PP

Antonio, Lou (1934–). American actor, writer and director, mostly in TV. *Partners in Crime* (a), *Sole Survivor* (a), DOG AND CAT (a), *Someone I Touched* (d), *The Girl in the Empty Grave* (d), *Something for Joey* (d), THE CRITICAL LIST (d), *Silent Victory* (d), *Breaking Up Is Hard to Do* (d), *The Star Maker* (d), *Something So Right* (d), *Rearview Mirror* (d), etc.

Antony and Cleopatra. ATV's 1974 version of Shakespeare's tragedy, starring Richard Johnson and Janet Suzman, and directed by Jon Scoffield, was chosen by BAFTA as best play of the year.

Any Second Now
US 1969 98m colour TVM
Universal (Gene Levitt)
A would-be wife murderer is on the run in Mexico.
Thinly stretched suspenser with attractive backgrounds.
w/d Gene Levitt ph Jack Marta m Leonard Rosenman

Stewart Granger, Lois Nettleton, Joseph Campanella, Dana Wynter, Katy Jurado, Tom Tully

Anyone for Tennis?
GB 1968 75m bw
J. B. Priestley ingeniously pursuing his preoccupation with time for a *Wednesday Play* in which that favourite entrance in the teacup theatre of the thirties – through the French windows brandishing a tennis racquet – became the threshold between one world and the next. Unhappily the plot turned on attitudes a little dated in the wrong way. Directed by Claude Whatham; produced by Graeme McDonald; for BBC.   PP

Applause! Applause! * (GB   1968). Interesting short series of memoirs of music hall greats with, for example, a highly candid account of the tortured marriage of Lucan and McShane. Produced by Marjorie Baker; for Thames.   PP

Apple Pie (US 1978). A shortlived half-hour comedy for CBS, set in 1933 Kansas. Rue McClanahan played a lonely hairdresser who built up family members by advertising for them.

Apple's Way
US 1974 24 × 50m colour
CBS/Lorimar (Lee Rich)
Tired of the rat race, a Los Angeles architect moves his family to a small town in Iowa.
Fashionable anti-urban family series in which the people were just too nice to be human.
cr Earl Hamner
Ronny Cox, Lee McCain, Malcolm Atterbury

Appointment with . . . (GB 1960–2; 39 × 26m; bw). Interview series from Granada TV in which Malcolm Muggeridge was found in conversation with the likes of Jacques Soustelle, Arthur Miller, W. H. Auden, Christopher Isherwood, Stephen Spender, Jo Grimond, Cyril Connolly and Oswald Mosley. Produced by Pat Lagone; preserved in NFA.

Appointment with Destiny *
US 1971–3 7 × 50m colour
David Wolper
A series of historical reconstructions which were staged and acted, then made to look like actuality film. The format was much criticized, though the films were exciting. Subjects: *The Crucifixion of Jesus*, *Showdown at OK Corral*, *Surrender at*

Appomattox, The Plot to Murder Hitler, The Last Days of John Dillinger, Peary's Race to the North Pole and *They've Killed President Lincoln.*

Apted, Michael (1941–). British wizard originally a researcher at Granada where his researches famously included finding the seven-year-olds for the historic *Seven Up.* Went on to direct, and under Granada's lateral mobility into drama, since when he has never looked back except to make all the *Seven Up* follow-ups. TV plays and films include *Country Matters*, KISSES AT FIFTY and many more. Now in the movies. PP

Aquaman. A cartoon character created in 1970 by Filmation. Son of a lighthouse keeper and a lady from Atlantis, he found himself in command of all sea creatures. His seven-minute adventures featured in *The Superman–Aquaman Hour.*

The Aquanauts
aka: *Malibu Run*
US 1960 13 × 50m bw
CBS/UA/Ivan Tors
Adventures of professional divers in Honolulu.
Thin hokum with glamour backgrounds, very similar to the same producer's *Sea Hunt.*
Keith Larsen, Jeremy Slate, Ron Ely

The Aquarians
US 1970 96m colour TVM
Universal (Ivan Tors)
Underwater scientists fight sharks, earthquakes and each other.
Routine ocean depths hokum, professionally but boringly handled.
w Leslie Stevens, Winston Miller, *story* Ivan Tors, Alan Caillou *d* Don McDougall *m* Lalo Schifrin
Ricardo Montalban, Jose Ferrer, Leslie Nielsen, Kate Woodville

Aquarius. British arts programme, LWT's very variable bid for culture on a Saturday night, marred by a succession of supercilious presenters. It ran from 1970 till 1977 and included films about Casals, Stanley Spencer, Arthur Rubinstein, Salvador Dali and Harold Acton. In 1978 it was succeeded by the *South Bank Show*, with a somewhat more down-to-earth approach.

Archard, Bernard (1922–). Aquiline British character actor whose moment of fame came in the fifties when for several seasons he played Colonel Oreste Pinto in *Spycatcher.*

Archer
US 1975 7 × 50m colour
NBC/Paramount
Adventures of Ross MacDonald's detective hero Lew Archer among California's idle rich.
A damp squib of a series, following the pilot *The Underground Man.* It seems the star just wasn't at ease.
Brian Keith, John P. Ryan

Archer, Anne (1947–). American leading lady. *The Pirate, The Sky's the Limit, Falcon Crest,* etc.

Archie Bunker's Place: see All in the Family

Arden, Eve (1912–) (Eunice Quedens). American character comedienne who graduated from the chorus, spent her Hollywood career as the heroine's tall, cool, wisecracking friend, then became a TV star in three successful series: OUR MISS BROOKS (Emmy 1953), *The Eve Arden Show* and *The Mothers in Law.* TV movies include *In Name Only, A Very Missing Person, All My Darling Daughters, A Guide for the Married Woman.*

Are You Being Served? *
GB 1974–   60 approx. × 30m colour (VTR)
BBC (David Croft)
Misadventures in the clothing section of a department store.
A single-set farce series relying heavily on outrageous characters and double entendres. A great success, it temporarily made a household word of John Inman as the gay Mr Humphreys.
w Jeremy Lloyd, David Croft
MOLLIE SUGDEN, JOHN INMAN, FRANK THORNTON, ARTHUR BROUGH, Trevor Bannister, Wendy Richard, HAROLD BENNETT, Arthur English
† A feature film version was made in 1977. An American version was tried out under the title *Beane's of Boston.*

'The most terrifying words a girl can hear!'
Are You in the House Alone?
US 1979 100m colour TVM
CBS/Stonehenge (Jay Benson)
A 17-year-old girl is menaced by an intruder who turns out to be a would-be rapist.
Rather muddled and overlong suspenser which turns out to have a serious point.
w Judith Parker, *novel* Richard Peck *d* Walter Grauman *ph* Jack Swain *m* Charles Bernstein

Kathleen Beller, Blythe Danner, Tony Bill, Robin Matson

'A half-baked survey of high school sexual mores, family relations and the effects of rape.' – Judith Crist

Arena. Umbrella title for BBC2's arty films about the arts since the late seventies. Some pretentious ones, some original triumphs such as the 1979 analysis of the innumerable hit versions of one song, 'My Way'. BAFTA award, 1982, to then Editor Alan Yentob. Now edited by Nigel Finch and Anthony Wall.   PP

The Aristocrats (GB 1983 6 × 50m). Robert Lacey, author of a best-seller about the Queen, touching his forelock to half a dozen characters lower down on the order of precedence, e.g. the Duke of Westminster and Prince Franz Josef II.   PP

Arkin, Alan (1934–). Intense American character actor who despite his qualities never seems to be box office. TV movies: THE OTHER SIDE OF HELL, *The Defection of Simas Kurdika.*

Arledge, Roone (1931–). American executive, former longterm sportscaster for ABC.

Arlott, John (1914–). Bass-voiced English cricket commentator and Hampshire topographer.

Armatrading, Joan (1950–). American singer, frequently in specials.

Armchair Theatre. The first drama series in Britain to achieve a personality all its own, launched by ABC Television (GB) in 1956 in an attempt to secure a toehold on a national network then dominated at the weekend by ATV's light entertainment and filmlet series. Under producer SYDNEY NEWMAN, lured over from Canada in 1958, a deliberate policy of contemporary plays on contemporary themes was forced through, relying at first on American and Canadian authors but gradually building up a stable of young native writers, among them Ray Rigby, Alun Owen and Robert Muller. Directors including Ted Kotcheff, Philip Saville and the veteran George More O'Ferrall maintained a remarkably solid, cinematic authority over what were still live video productions.

Despite complaints of unduly seamy realism ('Armpit Theatre', it was called jokingly), *Armchair Theatre* was required Sunday night viewing during the heyday seasons of 1959–61. With Newman's departure to the BBC in 1963, together with his story editors Peter Luke and Irene Shubik, the title inevitably lost some lustre but remained a respected one until the changeover of ITV contracts in 1968. ABC's successor, Thames, revived it briefly but without success in the early seventies. It belonged as firmly to the sixties as the Beatles. Preserved in NFA are: *Now Let Him Go* (1957), *Scent of Fear* (1959), *Hot Summer Night* (1959), *Lena O My Lena* (1960), *A Night Out* (1960), *The Rose Affair* (1961), *The Trial of Dr Fancy* (1964), *Prisoner and Escort* (1964).   PP

Armstrong, Moira (1930–). British drama director who shot to eminence with *Testament of Youth* and followed it up with *Something in Disguise, How Many Miles to Babylon,* etc. Recently: *CQ* and *Freud* (1984), *Bluebell* (1986).   PP

The Army Game *
GB 1957–62 153 × 25m bw VTR
Granada (Peter Eton)
Archetypal army farce series created by Sid Colin which was enormously popular in the UK and made stars of BERNARD BRESSLAW, ALFIE BASS and BILL FRASER (the latter pair went on to become *Bootsie and Snudge*) Charles Hawtrey and Michael Medwin were also involved, and in the first two years William Hartnell was the sergeant major. A film version was made in 1958 under the title *I Only Arsked.*
PP (1960): 'Snudge is a towering comic creation, perhaps the best that British TV has yet constructed from scratch. Snudge is a bully and a coward and a social climber, a warrior whose fiercest campaigns have been in the class war.'

❋   **Arnaz, Desi** (1915–) (Desiderio Alberto Arnaz y de Acha). Diminutive but explosive Cuban singer who became a bandleader, made a few films, married Lucille Ball, founded Desilu Studios, and starred with Lucy in the phenomenally successful comedy series *I Love Lucy.* Later divorced Lucy. Autobiography 1976: *A Book.*

Arnaz, Desi Jnr (1953–). American leading man, son of Desi Arnaz and Lucille Ball. TV movies include *Mr and Mrs Bo Jo Jones, She Lives, Having Babies, Flight to Holocaust, Black Market Baby, The Courage and the Passion, How to Pick Up Girls, Advice to the Lovelorn, The Night the Bridge Fell.*

Arnaz, Lucie (1951–). American leading lady, daughter of Desi Arnaz and Lucille Ball. On TV as child in her mother's series. TV movies as grown-up: *Who Is the Black Dahlia*, *Death Scream*, *The Mating Season*, *Washington Mistress*, *The Lucie Arnaz Show*.

❋ **Arness, James** (1923–) (James Aurness). Long, lean American actor, brother of Peter Graves; after small film roles became enormously successful as star and owner of *Gunsmoke*; reappeared, rather more grizzled, in 1976 as star of *How the West Was Won*. 1981: *McClain's Law* (series).

Arnhem: The Story of an Escape
GB 1976 85m colour
British army medical colonel eludes capture after the failure of the Arnhem air-drop in 1944. Based on a true-life account the production was able to utilize sets and props assembled for the movie *A Bridge Too Far*. Written by Hugh Whitemore from the Memoir by Graeme Warrack; directed by Clive Rees; produced by Innes Lloyd; for BBC.   PP

Arnie *
US 1970–1 58 × 25m colour
CBS/TCF (Rick Mittleman)
Slightly ethnic sitcom about a Greek–American blue collar worker suddenly promoted to managerial status. Moderate wit and pace made it appealing.
cr David Swift *ph* Leon Shamroy
HERSCHEL BERNARDI, Sue Ane Langdon, Tom Pedi, Roger Bowen, Herb Voland

Arnold, Jack (1916–). American director who made slick science fiction for Universal in the fifties and later reappeared sporadically as director of such TV series as *Perry Mason* and *McCloud*.

Around the World in Eighty Days. A rather feeble Australian half-hour cartoon series was made in 1972 but was not well received.

Arquette, Cliff (1906–74). American character comedian who appeared on TV for many years as rustic philosopher Charlie Weaver.

Arquette, Rosanna (1959–). American leading lady, grand-daughter of Cliff Arquette. *The Dark Secret of Harvest Home*, *James at 15*, *Zuma Beach*, *The Wall*, *The Executioner's Song*, *Johnny Belinda*, etc.

Arrest and Trial *
US 1963 30 × 74m bw
ABC/Universal
Crime series with a dour tone and an exploratory format: each story was in two halves, the first showing cops tracking down a suspect, the second the DA's success or failure in prosecuting him. The public seems to have found it complicated, but it was a clear step towards longform TV movies, needed to replenish the dwindling Hollywood variety.
Ben Gazzara, Chuck Connors

The Art of Crime
aka: *Roman Grey*
US 1975 74m colour TVM
Universal (Jules Irving)
A gypsy antique dealer doubles as a private eye.
Tolerable busted pilot.
w Martin Smith, Bill Davidson, *novel Gypsy in Amber* by Martin Smith *d* Richard Irving *ph* Jack Priestley *m* Gil Melle
Ron Leibman, David Hedison, Jill Clayburgh, Eugene Roche, Jose Ferrer

The Art of Persuasion * (GB 1985–6 × 25m). Good little series on advertising today, as revealed – for example – in a blow-by-blow account of the luckless shooting of a new Cinzano commercial or the views of an industry wizard such as David Ogilvie. Written and presented by Christopher Frayling; produced by Jeff Millard, for HTV and Channel 4.   PP

Artemis 81
GB 1981 185m colour
BBC (David Rose)
Infuriating, baffling, occasionally overwhelming apocalyptic blockbuster by David Rudkin in which the forces of darkness led by a brutish, Jutish old god were headed off in the nick of time from wreaking doom and destruction on the planet. I thought the powerful visions, such as of a 'city made sick' – all fumes and fog and insistent public-address voices in an alien tongue – were let down by high-faluting' language, too much left unexplained and an inadequately awesome climax. But a 17-year-old *Sunday Telegraph* reader, Sarah Jane Lawrence of Aylesbury, argued spiritedly for loose ends in imaginative drama. 'What a pity it would be if we understood absolutely everything or if ambitious projects were abandoned and all we ever saw were straightforward disaster films or detective series.'

d Alastair Reid *m* David Greenslade
Hywel Bennett, Dinah Stabb, Dan
O'Herlihy, Sting   PP
LH: 'Good to look at, but neither easy to
follow nor very entertaining.'

Arthur, Beatrice (1924–). Self-confident,
abrasive American character comedienne. A
hit as cousin Maude in *All in the Family*, she
quickly gained her own long-running series
MAUDE in which much fun was poked at the
American middle class. (Serious problems
such as abortion were also tackled.)

Arthur, Jean (1905–) (Gladys Greene).
Squeaky-voiced American leading lady of
many important American films in the thirties
and forties. Her sole excursion into series
television, *The Jean Arthur Show*, was not a
success.

Arthur Negus Enjoys (GB 1983 7 ×
25m). The much-loved antiques expert
swapping enthusiasm and expertise with
different companions as they tour favourite
stately homes. Produced by Robin Drake for
BBC.   PP

Arthur of the Britons
GB 1972 26 × 25m colour
Harlech TV (Patrick Dromgoole)
Realistic treatment of the legend of King
Arthur.
Oliver Tobias

'She thought Arthur was the stuff of
legend – until Camelot appeared before
her very eyes!'
Arthur the King
US 1983 142m approx. colour TVM
Comworld (Martin Poll)
A New York tourist falls down a hole at
Stonehenge and finds herself reliving the
story of Arthur.
A striking cast is wasted on a flabby
rendering which should have been retitled
'Alice in Merlinland'.
w J. David Wyles, David Karp *d* Clive
Donner *ph* Denis Lewiston *pd* Franco
Chianese
Malcolm McDowell (Arthur), Edward
Woodward (Merlin), Candice Bergen
(Morgan), Dyan Cannon (tourist), Rosalyn
Landor (Guinevere), Rupert Everett
(Lancelot), Lucy Gutteridge (Niniane),
Patrick Ryecart (Gawain)
† The production was sponsored by CBS,
who took one look and put it away. It finally
appeared in 1985.

Arthur's Treasured Volumes. Hit-and-miss
1960 comedy series for Arthur Askey by ATV,
whose initials were preserved in the title. Each
show was supposed to emerge from a book in
Arthur's library, but if parodies of literary
forms were intended they failed to show up. PP

As It Happened, by William S. Paley. A
fascinating published memoir by the founder
of the CBS network (Doubleday 1979).

As the World Turns. Long-running
American soap opera, on CBS since 1956,
about the residents of a middle-class suburb
(in Oakdale USA) and their secrets. Created
by Irna Philips and Ted Corday.

The Ascent of Man ★★
GB 1974 13 × 50m colour
BBC/Time–Life
Inspirational account by DR JACOB BRONOWSKI
of the philosophies evolved by man
throughout history. Sharp control gave the
series strong visual appeal, and Bronowski
proved himself a TV star.

Ash, Lesley (19 –). British *ingénue*, as
bright as she is blonde. First noticed in
Cupid's Darts, 1981. Subsequent credits
include *La Ronde*, 1982, *The Balance of
Nature*, 1983, *The Happy Apple* (series),
1984, and – alas – CATS EYES, 1985.   PP

Ashcroft, Dame Peggy (1907–).
Distinguished British character actress who
made her television debut in *Shadow of
Heroes* (BBC, 1959) but only came to
popular and critical acclaim with CREAM IN
MY COFFEE and CAUGHT ON A TRAIN, both
1980, then JEWEL IN THE CROWN, 1984, for
which she won all awards going. Also: *The
Last Journey*, *The Wars of the Roses*, *Little
Eyolf*, *Edward and Mrs Simpson* (as Queen
Mary).   PP

Asher, William (19 –). American
director who got an Emmy in 1965 for his
handling of *Bewitched*.

Ashley, Elizabeth (1939–) (Elizabeth
Cole). Promising American leading lady of
the seventies; never quite arrived. TV movies
include *Harpy*, *The Face of Fear*, *When
Michael Calls*, *Second Chance*, *The Heist*,
Your Money or Your Wife, *The Magician*,
One of My Wives Is Missing, *The War
Between the Tates*, *A Fire in the Sky*.

Ashley, Ted (1922–). American executive,
former head of Ashley Famous Agency and
president of Warner Brothers.

Ask Me Another. American (NBC) quiz game of the early fifties in which panellists had to guess the identity of hidden sporting celebrities by asking them questions.

Ask Pickles. Sentimental viewers' requests BBC programme of the fifties, with Wilfred and Mabel Pickles. See *magic wands*.   PP

Ask the Family. BBC quiz game of the sixties and seventies in which two families pit their wits against each other to answer questions which demand a high degree of intelligence. Quizmaster: Robert Robinson, who was still conducting the show in 1981.

❋ **Askey, Arthur** (1900–82). Diminutive British music hall comedian who was a TV regular throughout the fifties and made frequent appearances into the eighties. Recounted his life in 1979 in *The Old Boy Network*.

❋ **Asner, Ed** (1929–). American character actor who rose inexorably to the status of television star. Emmys 1970, 1971 and 1974 for THE MARY TYLER MOORE SHOW; 1975 for RICH MAN, POOR MAN; 1976 for *Roots*; 1977 for LOU GRANT. TV movies include *The Life and Assassination of the Kingfish* (as Huey Long), *A Small Killing*, *A Case of Libel*, *Anatomy of an Illness*. Recent series: *Off the Rack*. Inimitable at delineating a rumpled, genial, middle-aged idealist, and at suggesting that this is himself.

Aspel, Michael (1933–). British teleperson who soldiered through 30 years of pretty terrible chores, from *Ask Aspel* (children's programme) to hosting the British Academy Awards, to emerge as one of the most affable of the trade. Wields a nice unforced wit, not as studied as that of Clive James, without Terry Wogan's tireless twinkle, but all very understated and English, so that when there is a sting to it you are surprised and pleased. Own chat show, *Aspel & Company*, from 1984, for LWT.   PP

'*Aspen* is love! *Aspen* is mystery! *Aspen* is glamour! *Aspen* is murder! A jet-set killing at a glamorous ski capital . . . and the shocking, headline-making trial that followed!'
Aspen
GB title: *The Aspen Murder*
US second run title: *The Innocent and the Damned*
US 1977 3 × 95m colour
Universal/Roy Huggins (Jo Swerling Jnr)

A young attorney investigates a murder at a ski resort.
Mindless cobbling together, for the Best Sellers series of novelizations, of two flashy novels showing the rich at play.
w/d Douglas Heyes, *novels Aspen* by Bert Hirschfield and *The Adversary* by Bart Spicer
ph Isidore Mankowsky *m* Tom Scott, Mike Melvoir
Sam Elliott, Perry King, Michelle Phillips, John McIntyre, Gene Barry, Bo Hopkins, Tony Franciosa, Joseph Cotten, John Houseman
'Enough purple passion and rampant victimizing to turn all that snow into slush.' – *Daily Variety*

The Asphalt Cowboy
aka: *Culpepper*
US 1981 74m colour TVM
MCA (Michael Fisher, Mike Vejar)
A rugged policeman quits to run a security guard service with a roster of wealthy clients. Unsuccessful thick-ear pilot.
w Michael Fisher *d* Cliff Bole
Max Baer Jnr, Robin Dearden, Lory Walsh, Noah Beery, Richard Denning, James Luisi

The Asphalt Jungle
US 1960 13 × 50m bw
ABC/MGM
The Deputy Police Commissioner of a big city fights crime rings.
A competent cop show bearing little relation to the famous and much remade film.
m Duke Ellington
Jack Warden, Arch Johnson, Bill Smith

Assante, Armand (1949–). American leading man. TV movies: *Human Feelings*, *Lady of the House*, *The Pirate*, *Sophia Loren*, *Rage of Angels*, *Evergreen*.

The Assassin ❋❋. Absorbing West German drama-doc reconstructing the lone (and never satisfactorily motivated) attempt of one Georg Elser in 1939 to plant a bomb in a Munich beer-cellar where it would kill Hitler. Shown in Britain (BBC) 1972. With Fritz Hollenback as Elser; written by Hans Gottschalk; directed by Rainer Erler.   PP

Assault on the Wayne
US 1970 74m colour TVM
Paramount
Enemy agents try to seize a top-secret device from an atomic submarine.
Standard excitements, quite professionally put together.

w Jackson Gillis *d* Marvin Chomsky

Joseph Cotten, Leonard Nimoy, Lloyd Haynes, Dewey Martin, Keenan Wynn, William Windom

Assignment Foreign Legion
US 1957 26 × 25m bw
CBS/Anthony Bartley

A female foreign correspondent seeks the stories behind the men of the foreign legion. Unintentionally hilarious hokum with the star out of her depth amid production values decidedly below her norm.

Merle Oberon

Assignment Munich
US 1972 96m colour TVM
ABC/MGM (Jerry Ludwig)

A shady American saloon owner in Germany helps the US Army find loot stolen during World War II.

Pilot for a shortlived series which turned up as *Assignment Vienna*. (Vienna gave more facilities.) The aim was for a cross between *Casablanca* and *The Third Man*, but what came on the screen was pure hokum.

w Eric Bercovici, Jerry Ludwig *d* David Lowell Rich *m* George Romanis

Roy Scheider, Richard Basehart, Lesley Warren, Werner Klemperer, Robert Reed, Pernell Roberts, Keenan Wynn

† The series, *Assignment Vienna*, ran eight episodes in rotation with *The Delphi Bureau* and *Jigsaw*, under the umbrella title *The Men*.

Associated Rediffusion. British ITV
company which owned the weekday London franchise from 1954 but merged – and was submerged – with ABC to become Thames in the 1968 reshuffle.

Associated Television: see ATV

The Associates
US 1981 13 x 25m colour

The amusing aspects of life with a New York law firm headed by Wilfrid Hyde-White. A fairly promising concept which somehow didn't take. Produced by Paramount.

Astaire, Fred (1899–) (Frederick Austerlitz). American star dancer, singer and light romantic lead who after a dazzling Hollywood career turned to TV with a memorable series of specials: *An Evening with Fred Astaire* in 1958 won Emmys for best single programme, best musical special and best single performance, and in 1960 *Astaire*

Time won best performance and best variety special. In the late sixties played an engaging old rogue in many episodes of *It Takes a Thief*. TV movies: *The Over-the-Hill Gang Rides Again*, *A Family Upside Down* (Emmy 1977), *The Man in the Santa Claus Suit*. Recipient 1981 of the AFI Salute.

Astin, John (1930–). Heavily-moustached American comedy character actor, less successful in films than in TV, where he has starred in such series as *I'm Dickens He's Fenster*, THE ADDAMS FAMILY and *Operation Petticoat* as well as in TV movies like *Evil Roy Slade*, *Skyway to Death*, *The Dream Makers*. New series 1985: *Mary*.

Astin, Patty Duke: see Duke, Patty

Astro Boy. Half-hour cartoon series produced in Japan in 1963, about a robot boy who fights evil in the 21st century.

The Astronaut
US 1971 74m colour TVM
Universal

A civilian is asked to double for a famous astronaut who has been injured.

Tense melodrama which eventually runs out of plot.

w Gerald di Pego, Charles R. Juenstle *d* Robert Michael Lewis

Jackie Cooper, Monte Markham, Susan Clark, Robert Lansing, Richard Anderson, John Lupton

Asylum for a Spy
US 1967 74m colour TVM
Universal

A spy suffers a mental breakdown and a counterspy goes undercover in the hospital to pick his brains.

Tedious, talky suspenser, originally a Chrysler Theatre two-parter.

w Robert L. Joseph *d* Stuart Rosenberg *ph* Bud Thackery

Robert Stack, Felicia Farr, George Macready

At Ease
US 1983 14 × 25m colour
Warner/Aaron Spelling (Hy Averback, Jim Mulligan)

Comedy in an army camp.

Tolerable follow-on from innumerable predecessors.

cr John Hughes

Roger Bowen, Jourdan Fremin, Richard Jaeckel, Joshua Mostel, David Naughton, Jimmie Walker, Fred McCarren

'Somewhere back around the French and Indian war, someone probably first came up with the idea of a military comedy where mischievous enlisted men scheme to outwit their bumbling superiors. Little in the way of original material has been added to the genre since then, and *At Ease* carries on the dust-coated tradition with military precision.' – *Daily Variety*

At Home. Quaint BBC outside broadcast exercise of the fifties in which Richard Dimbleby (later, Berkeley Smith) would call on an eminence in his own home and engage him, and his family, in polite conversation. On one occasion Dimbleby was received by the butler, who then ushered him – and the millions of unseen viewers – into his lordship's presence.   PP
† Title and idea revived by HTV in 1983–4 with Derek Robinson calling on such west country worthies as Auberon Waugh and Field Marshal Lord Harding. Produced and directed by Terry Harding.

At Last the 1948 Show ** (GB 1967). Aggressively funny comedy series from Rediffusion, masterminded by David Frost though he didn't appear on the screen. Directed by Ian Fordyce; with Marty Feldman, Aimi Macdonald, Graham Chapman, John Cleese, Tim Brooke-Taylor. Feldman went on to plough his own furrow, the others to dream up *Monthy Python*.   PP

Atherton, William (1947–) (William Knight). American leading man. *Centennial*, *Tomorrow's Child*, *Malibu*, etc.

Atkins, Christopher (1961–). American leading man who started as juvenile in the film remake of *The Blue Lagoon*. *Child Bride of Short Creek*, *Dallas*, etc.

Atkins, Eileen (1934–). British actress of strength and distinction in both classic and contemporary roles from Joan of Arc in *An Age of Kings*, 1960, through to Tamora in *Titus Andronicus*, and John Osborne's much-maligned mum in *A Better Class of Person*, both 1985.   PP
LH: 'Her other claim to fame is as co-creator of *Upstairs Downstairs*.'

Atkinson, Rowan (1955–). Bulbous-eyed, adenoidal comedian of the aggressive type: became known through *Not the Nine O'Clock News* and *The Black Adder*. An acquired taste, though smoother in *Black Adder II*.

The Atlanta Child Murders *
US 1985 1 × 142m, 1 ×
    96m colour miniseries
CBS/Orion/Abby Mann/Finnegan/Gerald Rafshoon
An account of the 1979–82 killings and the subsequent trial of Wayne Williams. Spasmodically interesting but overlong docu-drama.

Abby Mann *d* John Erman *ph* Victor J Kemper *m* Billy Goldenberg
Jason Robards, James Earl Jones, Rip Torn, Morgan Freeman, Lynne Moody, Ruby Dee, Martin Sheen

Atom Ant and Secret Squirrel
US 1965 26 × 25m colour
NBC/Hanna–Barbera
A cartoon series from this studio's better days. Atom Ant, like Mighty Mouse, was a take-off of Superman; Secret Squirrel, a spy, was seen in a separate section with his friend Squiddly Diddly.

Attack on Fear
US 1984 96m colour TVM
Viacom/Tomorrow (Herbert Hirschman)
Married journalists expose irregularities within the drug rehabilitation foundation of Synanon.
Tepid piece of crusading which hadn't been adequately translated into dramatic terms.

w T. S. Cook, book *The Light on Synanon* by David Mitchell *d* Mel Damski *ph* Donald M. Morgan *m* Tony Berg
Paul Michael Glaser, Linda Kelsey, Kevin Conway, John Harkins, Alan Fudge

Attack on Terror
aka: *The FBI versus the Ku Klux Klan*
US 1975 198m (two parts) colour TVM
Warner/Quinn Martin
The alternative title says it all.
Flat, overlong cops and robbers in a very familiar vein.

w Calvin Clements *d* Marvin Chomsky *ph* Jacques Marquette *m* Mundell Love
George Grizzard, Rip Torn, Dabney Colman, Andrew Duggan, L. Q. Jones, Marilyn Mason, Peter Strauss, Wayne Rogers, Ed Flanders

✳ **Attenborough, Sir David** (1926–). British producer and presenter of innumerable international wildlife series, including ZOO QUEST and WILDLIFE ON ONE. In the mid-sixties became Controller of BBC2, then the BBC's director of programmes, but in 1972 returned to his favourite preoccupation. The British Academy gave him the Desmond Davis Award in 1970 and a fellowship in 1979, at the time of his most ambitious series, LIFE ON EARTH. This was followed by *The Living Planet* in 1984. Knighted 1985.

Attica *
US 1979 100m colour TVM
ABC Circle (Louis Rudolph)
Docu-drama reconstructing an upstate New York prison riot of 1971.
The expected compressions and distortions do not quite manage to blunt the power of this rather self-conscious but generally worthy piece.
w James Henerson, *book A Time to Die* by Tom Wicker *d* Marvin Chomsky *ph* Don Birnkraut
George Grizzard, Charles Durning, Arlen Dean Snyder, Anthony Zerbe, Roger E. Mosley

ATV (Associated Television). British commercial company which until 1968 operated in the midlands on weekdays and in London at weekends; subsequently ran a seven-day midlands operation. ATV's guiding light was originally Norman Collins, then master showmen Val Parnell and Lew Grade took over. Lew Grade virtually deserted TV for movie-making, but during his 20 or so years as ATV's programme chief he staged a wide variety of light entertainment, including *Sunday Night at the London Palladium*, several Anglo-American series such as those starring Julie Andrews and the Muppets, upwards of a dozen Gerry Anderson puppet series, and mid-Atlantic crime series shot expensively on 35mm film. Among the latter are *The Saint*, *Danger Man*, *The Prisoner*, *Man in a Suitcase*, *The Persuaders* and *Space 1999*. In 1981 the IBA forced ATV to reconstitute itself as Central.

Auberjonois, René (1940–). American character actor. TV movies: *Once Upon a Dead Man*, *The Birdmen*, *Shirts/Skins*, *Panache*, *The Rhinemann Exchange*, *The Dark Secret of Harvest Home*, *The Wild Wild West Revisited*.

Aubrey, James (1918–). American executive, former salesman and station manager, who in 1959 became president of CBS and was known as the smiling cobra for his competitiveness and ruthlessness. Hints of scandal caused his downfall; he went briefly to MGM but was subsequently little heard from.

Audience Flow. A measure of the change of audience between and during programmes.

**An Audience with . . . ** (GB 1982–4). Twice it was with Dame Edna Everage, supported the second time by Barrie Humphries' other and funnier character, Sir Les Patterson. A studio crowd composed largely of celebrities provided enthusiastic laughter and occasionally acted as foils. In between came one with Kenneth Williams, and in 1985 Billy Connolly. Overall producer: Richard Drewett, for LWT.   PP
LH: 'I can't *stand* Sir Les Patterson.'

Audley, Maxine (1923–). British general-purpose actress, adept at slightly sinister or mad ladies.

Audubon Wildlife Theatre. A Canadian half-hour series (78 episodes) made in 1970, showing the survival of rare birds and mammals; based on the researches of the famous naturalist.

Auf Wiedersehen, Pet *
GB 1984 13 × 52m colour
Central/Witzend Productions (Martin McKeand)
Adventures of a job lot of British building workers leaving wives and families behind in unemployment-hit Tyneside in order to seek work in West Germany. Doubts about the impenetrability of their Geordie accents quickly dispersed when Jimmy Seed, deploying the thickest accent of all, became the audience's favourite. The original idea came from the TV director Franc Roddam, and was mercifully developed by Dick Clement and Ian La Frenais as a comedy of character rather than a situation giggle, with no studio audience.
w Dick Clement, Ian La Frenais *d* Roger Bamford, Baz Taylor
Tim Healy, Jimmy Nail, Kevin Whately, Pat Roach, Gary Holton, Timothy Spall, Christopher Fairbank   PP
'In the very best tradition of British comedy.' – Anthea Hall, *Sunday Telegraph*
† Further series of 13 followed in 1986, set in Britain and Spain.

Aunt Mary
US 1980 100m colour TVM
CBS/Hallmark Hall of Fame/Henry Jaffe Enterprises
The true story of a woman, crippled by frostbite in childhood, who lives on welfare

and develops neighbourhood kids into a baseball team.
Overlong star character study.
w Burt Prelutsky, *story* Ellis A. Cohen *d* Peter Werner *ph* High Gagnier *m* Arthur B. Rubenstein

Jean Stapleton, Martin Balsam, Harold Gould, Dolph Sweet, Robert Emhardt

Aurora
US 1984 96m colour TVM
Roger Gimbel/Peregrine/Sacis (Alex Ponti)
To raise cash for the curing of her blind son, a woman convinces each of three former suitors that he is the father.
Sentimental hokum which becomes too much of a family affair. (Count the Pontis.)
w John McGreevey, Franco Ferrini, Gianni Menon, Maurizio Ponti *ph* Roberto Gerardi *m* Georges Delerue
Sophia Loren, Daniel J. Travanti, Ricky Tognazzi, Edoardo Ponti, Angela Goodwin, Philippe Noiret

Aurthur, Robert Alan (1922–). American writer, a graduate of the 'golden age' of TV drama, best remembered for *A Man Is Ten Feet Tall*.

Auschwitz. Taking this one name to represent the whole appalling apparatus of the Nazi extermination policy, the phenomenon has received due attention from the television networks of the world, but often diminution as well. Of fictional or dramatized treatments made in the West the controversial *Playing for Time* rises most honourably to the subject, with the last play in Ken Taylor's 1964 trilogy *The Seekers* (BBC) next and *Holocaust* shambling along in the rear. The definitive documentary account is *The Final Solution* (Thames 1975), a three-hour expansion by Michael Darlow of the 'Genocide' episode of *The World at War*. But as so often is the case in television, the marginal or oblique approach has better conveyed the enormity: *Kitty – Return to Auschwitz* by scaling it down to one woman's experience, recalled without visual aids; *According to the Rules* by filtering it through the calm processes of an English court 20 years later. PP
† See next entry, *Mengele* and *A Painful Reminder*.

Auschwitz and the Allies (GB 1982). Investigated a particular aspect of the preceding grim topic: why did the British and Americans refuse to believe stories of mass extermination filtering through from the East? When they did start to credit them, why did they do nothing? But Rex Bloomstein's answers were partial and partisan. His programme was itself a model of the very mystery or scandal or conspiracy it sought to uncover. It was accompanied (night before) by *The Gathering*, a straightforward account of the 1981 reunion of death-camp survivors in Israel which included harrowing personal reminiscences. 'If these had been available in 1943 or 1944,' I wrote at the time, 'perhaps history really would be different, for a woman's story of how she watched her baby starve to death, or another's of finding her own father in the mortuary, might have sunk in where bald numbers failed to lodge.' Both produced by Rex Bloomstein for BBC. See also *The Joel Brand Story*. PP

Austin, Ray (1932–). Anglo-American screenwriter and director who was heavily involved in *The Avengers* and *The Champions*. Later in Hollywood: *Magnum*, *Simon and Simon*, *Tales of the Gold Monkey*.

Australia. Four major channels are available, three commercial and one (ABC) government-sponsored and much akin to Britain's BBC. Home-produced product is variable at best, and all channels lean heavily on imports.

The Autobiography of Miss Jane Pittman **
US 1973 109m colour TVM
Tomorrow (Robert W. Christiansen, Rich Rosenberg)
In 1962, a 110-year-old negress in a southern state reflects on her early life as a slave and takes a drink from the 'Whites Only' fountain.
Ambitious and careful TV movie which did much in America to raise the sights of the genre.
w Tracy Keenan Wynn, *novel* Ernest J. Gaines *d* John Korty *ph* James Crabe *m* Fred Karlin *pd* Michael Haller
CICELY TYSON, Michael Murphy, Richard A. Dysart, Katherine Helmond
† Emmys 1973: best special, Cicely Tyson, John Korty, Tracy Keenan Wynn.

Automan
US 1983 1 x 74m, 12 x 50m colour
TCF/Glen A. Larson (Donald Kushner, Peter Locke)

To help in desperate situations, a Los Angeles cop with a bent for science summons a superman out of his computer. Tawdry comic strip stuff with a few visual gimmicks repeated far too often.

cr Glen A. Larson *sp* Donald Kushner

Desi Arnaz Jnr, Chuck Wagner, Robert Lansing, Heather McNair, Gerald S. O'Loughlin

Automania (GB 1984). Zippy history in 13 parts, of motoring and motor-car enthusiasts. Written and presented by Julian Pettifer, produced by Nigel Turner; for Central.   PP

Autry, Gene (1907–). American singing cowboy who after a long film career produced and starred in a popular half-hour series featuring himself, Pat Buttram and Champion the wonder horse (85 episodes between 1950 and 1953). He later became a station owner.

Avalon, Frankie (1940–) (Francis Avallone). American trumpeter and singer, in many concert specials.

Averback, Hy (1925–). American director who may have helmed more TV episodes than anyone else, most of them in the fifties. TV movies: *Richie Brockleman: The Missing 24 Hours*, *The Magnificent Magical Magnet of Santa Mesa*, *The New Maverick*, *A Guide for the Married Woman*, *Pearl*, *The Night Rider*.

The Avengers ***. This influential comedy suspense series actually began as a serial melodrama called *Police Surgeon*, made by Britain's ABC in 1960 and produced by Leonard White. This starred Ian Hendry as a man avenging his wife's murder, but a supporting character which caught the eye was that of PATRICK MACNEE as a dandified secret service agent (bowler hat and cane borrowed from a performance by Ralph Richardson in the film *Q Planes*). When Hendry wouldn't continue, MacNee became the lead of a retitled one-hour series, with HONOR BLACKMAN as his aide. Her judo and leather outfits became talking points, but she left the show after two series when it was still on black-and-white VTR. Thereafter *The Avengers* not only went on to colour film but gained an American network sale and lasted three seasons, two with DIANA RIGG and one with Linda Thorson; MacNee was in every episode. It had developed into a secret agent spoof, with fantasy violence, zany villains and macabre plots solved by amusing and ambiguous leading characters whose hair

never even got ruffled. The writer most responsible for its image was PHILIP LEVENE.

In 1976 Albert Fennell and Brian Clemens, who had been much involved with the production and writing of the old series, put together *The New Avengers*, with MacNee assisted by Joanna Lumley and Gareth Hunt, but the spark was fitful and the production beset by financial problems. It ran 26 episodes.

The 1961 series (black-and-white tape, with MacNee and Blackman) was not preserved.

The 52 black-and-white episodes produced on tape in 1962/3 with MacNee and Blackman were transferred to 16mm and are as follows:
Mr Teddy Bear
Propellant 23
The Decapod
Bullseye
Mission to Montreal
The Removal Men
The Mauritius Penny
Death of a Great Dane
The Sellout
Death on the Rocks
Traitor in Zebra
The Big Thinker
Death Despatch
Dead on Course
Intercrime
Immortal Clay
Box of Tricks
Warlock
The Golden Eggs
School for Traitors
The White Dwarf
Man in the Mirror
Conspiracy of Silence
Chorus of Frogs
Six Hands Across the Table
Killer Whale
Brief for Murder
Concerto
Nutshell
Golden Fleece
Death à la Carte
Man with Two Shadows
Don't Look Behind You
The Grandeur that Was Rome
The Undertakers
Death of a Batman
Build a Better Mousetrap
November Five
Second Sight
The Gilded Cage
The Medicine Men
Dressed to Kill
The White Elephant
The Little Wonders

The Wringer
Mandrake
The Secrets Broker
Trojan Horse
The Outside/In Man
The Charmers
Esprit de Corps
Lobster Quadrille

The titles of the MacNee/Rigg episodes were as follows:
1965 season:
The Town of No Return
The Gravediggers
The Cybernauts
Death at Bargain Prices
Castle De'ath
The Master's Minds
The Murder Market
A Surfeit of H_2O
The Hour that Never Was
Dial a Deadly Number
The Maneater of Surrey Green
Two's a Crowd
Too Many Christmas Trees
Silent Dust
Room without a View
Small Game for Big Hunters
The Girl from Auntie
The Thirteenth Hole
The Quick Quick Slow Death
The Danger Makers
A Touch of Brimstone
What the Butler Saw
The House that Jack Built
A Sense of History
How to Succeed at Murder
Honey for the Prince
1967 season:
From Venus with Love
The Fear Merchants
Escape in Time
The See Through Man
The Bird Who Knew Too Much
The Winged Avenger
The Living Dead
The Hidden Tiger
The Correct Way to Kill
Never Never Say Die
Epic
The Superlative Seven
A Funny Thing Happened on the Way to the Station
Something Nasty in the Nursery
The Joker
Who's Who
Return of the Cybernauts
Death's Door
The Fifty Thousand Pound Breakfast
Dead Man's Treasure
You Have Just Been Murdered

The Positive Negative Man
Murdersville
Mission Highly Improbable
The Forget Me Knot

The MacNee/Thorson episodes produced in 1968 were:
Game
The Super Secret Cypher Snatch
You'll Catch Your Death
Split
Whoever Shot Poor George Oblique Stroke XR 40
False Witness
All Done with Mirrors
Legacy of Death
Noon Doomsday
Look
Have Guns, Will Haggle
They Keep Killing Steed
The Interrogators
The Rotters
Invasion of the Earthmen
Killer
The Morning After
The Curious Case of the Countless Clues
Wish You Were Here
Love All
Stay Tuned
Take Me to Your Leader
Fog
Who Was That Man I Saw You With?
Homicide and Old Lace
Thingumajig
My Wildest Dream
Requiem
Takeover
Pandora
Getaway
Bizarre

'The saga of an American woman!'
The Awakening Land *
US 1979 3 × 100m colour
NBC/Warner/Bernstein–Kuhn–Sagal
 (Robert E. Relyea)
Superior but rather plodding miniseries about western pioneers and in particular a woman who overcomes all hardships.

w James Lee Barrett, Liam O'Brian, novels Conrad Richter d Boris Sagal m Fred Karlin

Elizabeth Montgomery, Hal Holbrook, Jane Seymour, Steven Keats, Tony Mockus, Louise Latham

'An epic drama rich in mood, detail and characterization.' – Los Angeles Times

The Awakening of Candra

US 1981 (networked
 1983) 96m colour TVM
CBS/Michael Klein

A bride is abducted while on a camping trip in the High Sierras.
Moderate teledrama based on a real case with insufficient substance for the film's length.

w Tom Lazarus   d Paul Wendkos   ph Richard C. Glouner   m Billy Goldenberg

Blanch Baker, Cliff de Young, Richard Jaeckel, Jeffrey Tambor

The Aweful Mr Goodall (GB 1974).

Curiously titled but rather pleasing series of six hours about a retired civil servant who pokes his nose into little mysteries. With Robert Urquhart; for LWT.

PP: 'Intermittently a spy series featuring a retired intelligence officer but also a commentary on the generation gap between those who experienced World War II and those who didn't. I found Richard Bates's idea increasingly complex and interesting and the performances of Robert Urquhart and Isabel Dean more and more rewarding.'

Ayckbourn, Alan (1939–). Phenomenally successful British author of lightweight plays reflecting the inanities of modern middle-class life. Those televised include *The Norman Conquests*, *Bedroom Farce*, *Absurd Person Singular*, *Just Between Ourselves Stranger*, *The Questor Tapes*, *Heatwave*, *Suddenly Love*.

Ayres, Lew (1908–) (Lewis Ayer). American movie star of the thirties who became a valued TV character actor. TV movies include *Earth II*, *She Waits*, *The*

Ayres, Pam (1947–). British television personality whose doggerel poetry, first exposed on *Opportunity Knocks*, rapidly grew hard to take.

B. Traven: A Mystery Solved ** (GB 1978; 75m; colour). Satisfying piece of literary detection (for BBC) by producer Will Wyatt and reporter Robert Robinson which actually came up with the answer – or anyway 95 per cent of it. The reclusive author of *The Treasure of the Sierra Madre* and other minor classics was positively named as Otto Feige, born in Poland. As in the best detective movies, the vital evidence was only turned up in the last reel. PP

Baa Baa Black Sheep
US 1976–8 1 × 95m, 35 × 50m colour
Universal (Stephen J. Cannell)
Adventures of 'Pappy' Boyington and his unconventional air crews during World War II in the Pacific.
Boisterous sentiment and melodrama amplify routine service antics in a rather dislikeable series which struggled over two seasons, latterly as *Black Sheep Squadron*. It could be viewed as a milder airborne version of *The Dirty Dozen*.
w/cr Stephen J. Cannell d Russ Mayberry *flying sequences* Tallmantz Aviation
Robert Conrad, Simon Oakland, Dana Elcar, Dirk Blocker

Babe *
US 1975 100m colour TVM
MGM/Norman Felton, Stanley Rubin
The story of woman athlete Babe Didrikson and her battle with cancer.
Careful but essentially tedious American hero-worship in the wake of *Sunshine*, *It's Good to be Alive*, etc.
w Joanna Lee, from *This Life I've Led* by Babe Didrikson d Buzz Kulik ph Charles F. Wheeler m Jerry Goldsmith
SUSAN CLARK, Alex Karras, Slim Pickens, Jeanette Nolan, Ellen Geer

Baby Comes Home
US 1980 96m colour TVM
CBS/Alan Landsburg (Shelley List)
A woman who has just had a baby at 48 worries about the future.
Dreary sequel to *And Baby Makes Six*. Nothing cheerful happens, and the session is largely devoted to talk about life and the menopause.
w Shelley List m Fred Karlin
Colleen Dewhurst, Warren Oates, Devon Ericson, Fred Lehne, Mildred Dunnock

Baby, I'm Back
US 1978 13 × 25m colour (VTR)
CBS/Charles Fries
A long-lost husband returns to disturb his wife's second marriage.
Black version of an old routine.
Desmond Wilson, Denise Nicholas, Ed Hall, Helen Martin
'The writers never exercise judgment at the expense of a joke.' – Robert Mackenzie, *TV Guide*

Baby Sister
US 1983 96m colour TVM
ITC/Moonlight (Frank Von Zerneck)
A young doctor falls for his girl friend's younger sister.
Tediously protracted nymphet melodrama, very sudsy.
w Jo Lynne Michael, Paul Haggard Jnr, Susan Title d Steven Hillard Stern ph Isidore Mankovsky m Fred Karlin
Ted Wass, Phoebe Cates, Pamela Bellwood, Efrem Zimbalist Jnr

The Baby Sitter
US/Canada 1980 96m colour TVM
ABC/Filmways–Moonlight (Frank Von Zerneck)
A nubile teenager wheedles her way into the household of a dentist and causes havoc.
Tedious variation on an old theme, last seen as *Three into Two Won't Go*.
w Jennifer Miller d Peter Medak ph Rexford Metz
William Shatner, Patty Duke Astin, Stephanie Zimbalist, John Houseman, Quinn Cummings
'Only lesson to be learned from the slow-paced vidpic is to demand references before hiring live-in help.' – *Daily Variety*

Bacall, Lauren (1924–) (Betty Perske).
Rangy American actress, widow of
Humphrey Bogart and a match for anybody.
TV movies include *Applause* (a version of her
Broadway success), *Perfect Gentlemen*.

Bach, Barbara (1945–). American starlet
of Austrian–Irish parentage; flirted briefly
with James Bond in *The Spy Who Loved Me*,
and equally briefly was one of *Charlie's
Angels*.

Bachelor Father *
US 1957–61 157 × 25m bw
CBS/Universal (later on NBC and ABC)
A bachelor lawyer is guardian to his teenage
niece.
One of the more pleasing sitcoms of its era,
with a smooth star performance.
John Forsythe, Noreen Corcoran, Sammee
Tong

Backstairs at the White House *
US 1979 1 × 150m, 3 × 100m colour
NBC/Paramount/Ed Friendly Productions
The life of Lillian Rogers Parks, black maid
at the White House for 30 years.
Skilfully produced mini-series which spends
rather too much time in the kitchen and too
little with its parade of presidents. On the
whole, a high-class drag.
w Gwen Bagni, Paul Dubov, from *My Thirty
Years at the White House* by Lillian Rogers
Parks d Michael O'Herlihy ph Robert L.
Morrison m Morton Stevens ad Morton
Hamon
Leslie Uggams, Olivia Cole, Lou Gossett,
Robert Hooks, Leslie Nielsen, Hari Rhodes,
Paul Winfield, Cloris Leachman; Julie Harris,
Victor Buono (as the Tafts); Celeste Holm,
George Kennedy (as the Hardings); Robert
Vaughn, Kim Hunter, Claire Bloom (as the
Wilsons); Ed Flanders, Lee Grant (as the
Coolidges); Larry Gates, Jan Sterling (as the
Hoovers); John Anderson, Eileen Heckart
(as the Roosevelts); Harry Morgan, Estelle
Parsons, Heather Angel (as the Trumans);
Andrew Duggan, Barbara Barrie (as the
Eisenhowers); Dana Wynter, Barry Sullivan,
Louise Latham
'It's like spending a day with Rich Little.' –
Daily Variety

Backtrack
US 1968 97m colour TVM
NBC/Universal
Adventures of four Texas Rangers.
Poor pilot for *Laredo*.
d Earl Bellamy
Neville Brand, Doug McClure, Peter Brown,
James Drury

Backus, Jim (1914–). American character
comedian with a fruity voice well known in
cartoons and commercials; the voice of Mr
Magoo. TV series include *I Married Joan*,
The Jim Backus Show (*Hot Off the Wire*),
Gilligan's Island, *Blondie*. TV movies: *Wake
Me When the War Is Over*, *The Magic
Carpet*, *Miracle on 34th Street*, *The Rebels*,
etc.

Bad Blood (GB 1981 90m TVM).
Backwoods farmer runs amok in wartime
New Zealand, killing seven people and
bringing on the fiercest manhunt ever known
in that country. An early starring role for
Jack Thompson and one of only two TVMs
to be made by Southern Pictures, short-lived
film subsidiary of Southern Television, which
lost its franchise at the end of the same year.
Written and produced by Andrew Brown,
from the book by Howard Willis, directed by
Mike Newell.   PP

'The hottest action on wheels!'
BAD Cats *
US 1980 74m colour TVM
ABC/Spelling–Cramer (Everett Chambers)
Two easy-going young cops work for
'burglary auto detail, commercial auto thefts'
in the 'SCPD' (Spelling–Cramer Police
Department?).
Pale imitation of *Starsky and Hutch*, with the
advantage of first-class car chases.
w Al Martinez d Bernard L. Kowalski ph
Jim Albert m Barry de Vorzon
Asher Brauner, Steve Hanks, Vic Morrow
† Seven 'one-hour' episodes followed, but the
viewers spotted a rushed copy.

The Bad News Bears (US 1979). 25-minute
comedy series from the movie series, with
Jack Warden reluctantly coaching a Little
League baseball team. 26 episodes were
made, but the show was not a success.
Produced by Huk Inc and Frog Inc; for
Paramount/CBS.

Bad Ronald
US 1974 74m colour TVM
Lorimar
A teenage killer is hidden in the attic by his
mother. When she dies, new tenants find him
still there.
Silly, tasteless melodrama, put over with
some style.
w Andrew Peter Marin, *novel* John
Holbrook Vance d Buzz Kulik
Kim Hunter, Scott Jacoby, Pippa Scott,
Anita Sorsaut, John Larch

The Bad Seed

US 1985 96m colour TVM
ABC/Warner/Hajeno (George Eckstein)

A widow wonders whether her nine-year-old daughter might possibly be a psychotic murderer.

Modest television remake which doesn't quite have the flair of the 1956 film or the theatrical original.

w George Eckstein, *play* by Maxwell Anderson and *novel* by William March *d* Paul Wendkos *ph* Ted Voightlander *m* Paul Chihara

Blair Brown, Lynn Redgrave, David Carradine, David Ogden Stiers, Richard Kiley, Carrie Wells

'Satisfyingly chilling . . . sure to raise hackles.' – *Daily Variety*

Badel, Alan (1923–82). Incisive, aquiline British leading actor whose TV appearances have been surprisingly rare but include a series, *The Count of Monte Cristo*, Pinter's *The Lover* (BAFTA award 1964), *Trilby* and *The Winslow Boy*. TV movie: *Shogun*.

Badge of the Assassin *

US 1985 96m colour TVM
CBS/Columbia/Blatt–Singer (Robert K. Tanenbaum)

Black terrorists in Harlem get their kicks from killing cops.

Reasonably exciting docu-drama which fails to come up with a point of view.

w Lawrence Roman, *book* by Robert K. Tanenbaum and Philip Rosenberg *d* Mel Damski *ph* John Lindley *m* Tom Scott

YAPHET KOTTO, James Woods, Alex Rocco, David Harris, Steven Keats

'It goes from point to point with a dry unfolding that occasionally spurts into life.' – *Daily Variety*

The Badge or the Cross

aka: *Sarge: The Badge or the Cross*
US 1971 98m colour TVM
Universal (David Levy)

When his fiancée is killed by a bomb meant for him, a cop becomes a priest, in which guise he later solves the crime.

Heavy-going pilot for a shortlived series. Another pilot was *The Priest Killer*.

w Don M. Mankiewicz *d* Richard A. Colla *m* Dave Grusin

George Kennedy, Ricardo Montalban, Diane Baker, Larry Gates

Badge 714: see Dragnet

Badham, John (*c* 1944–). American television director, mainly with Universal from 1970 on such series as *Night Gallery* and *The Bold Ones*. TV movies include *The Gun*, *Isn't It Shocking*, *The Godchild*, *Reflections of Murder*. He hit the big time theatrically with *Saturday Night Fever*.

Badiyi, Reza S. (*c* 1945–). American director associated with slick editing and sure camera placement, as in THE EYES OF CHARLES SAND and the title sequence of *Hawaii Five-O*. Career otherwise rather disappointingly restricted to series episodes.

Baer, Max Jnr (1937–). Giant-size American actor, seen almost exclusively as Jethro in the long-running *Beverly Hillbillies*.

Baez, Joan (1941–). American folk singer and occasional political activist. Appearances sporadic.

Baffled!

GB 1971 96m colour TVM
ITC/Arena (Philip Leacock)

A racing driver has a prophetic dream which leads him into a very involved murder plot.

Weird and fathomless hotchpotch which wastes a lot of talent.

w Theodore Apstein *d* Philip Leacock *ph* Ken Hodges *m* Richard Hill

Leonard Nimoy, Susan Hampshire, Vera Miles, Jewel Blanch, Rachel Roberts, Valerie Taylor, Ray Brooks, Angharad Rees

BAFTA: see British Academy of Film and Television Arts

Baggetta, Vincent (1947–). American leading man, star of THE EDDIE CAPRA MYSTERIES. TV movies: *In the Matter of Karen Ann Quinlan*, *The Rhinemann Exchange*, *Murder on Flight 502*, *Eischied* (pilot), *The Ordeal of Bill Carney*, *The Chicago Story*, *MacGruder and Loud*

Bailey, Pearl (1918–). Black American singer who makes occasional appearances in all media, latterly on TV in *Silver Spoons*.

Bailey, Raymond (1904–80). American character actor who after playing innumerable small film roles became a nationally known character as the harassed banker Mr Drysdale in THE BEVERLY HILLBILLIES.

Bailey, Robin (1919–). Tall, elegant British character actor who curiously became a star as the mufflered north country Uncle

Mort in the eccentric BBC series I DIDN'T KNOW YOU CARED. First in television as host of *The Sixty Four Thousand Dollar Question* in 1957; starring 1981 in *Sorry I'm a Stranger Here Myself*. Recently: *Going Home, A Midsummer Night's Dream, The Brandons, The Fosdyke Saga, Charters and Caldicott* and as the Brigadier in the spoken stories *Tales from a Long Room*.

The Baileys of Balboa
US 1964 39 × 25m bw
CBS/Richelieu (Bob Sweeney)

Episodes in the life of a beachcombing family.

Disappointing comedy series: no laughs.

Paul Ford, Judy Carne, Sterling Holloway, John Dehner

Baily, Leslie (1906–). British producer, remembered for his nostalgic 'Scrapbook' series on radio and TV.

Bain, Barbara (1932–). Cool American leading lady who starred with some success in *Mission Impossible* (Emmys 1966, 1967, 1968) and with less in *Space 1999*. TV movies include *Murder Once Removed, Goodnight My Love, Savage, A Summer without Boys*.

Bain, Conrad (1923–). Avuncular Canadian actor in American television. He graduated from a support role in *Maude* to the nominal lead in *Diff'rent Strokes*, though he allows Gary Coleman to steal all the scenes.

Baio, Scott (1961–). American juvenile actor of the seventies, in *Happy Days* and such TV movies as *The Boy Who Drank Too Much*. Recently: *Joanie Loves Chachi, Charles in Charge, How To Be a Man*.

Baird, John Logie (1888–1946). British inventor of the first mechanical system of television, also later of a colour system and videodisc.

The Bait *
US 1972 74m colour TVM
Spelling–Goldberg

An undercover policewoman lures a girl-killer into a trap.

Smart suspenser which oddly failed as a pilot; two years later along came *Police Woman*.

w Don M. Mankiewicz, Gordon Botler d Leonard Horn ph Gert Anderson m Jack Elliott/Allyn Ferguson

Donna Mills, Michael Constantine, William Devane, June Lockhart

Baker, Bob (1939–) **and Martin, Dave** (1935–). Talented British writing partnership specializing in droll but when necessary shocking thrillers (see *Thick as Thieves*), Bristol-based and given first encouragement by HTV. *Item* (1974), *Machinegunner* (1976), *Murder at the Wedding* (serial, 1979). They now write individually as well and Baker is script editor at HTV.   PP

Baker, Diane (1938–). American leading lady of the sixties. TV movies: *Trial Run, The Old Man Who Cried Wolf, Do You Take This Stranger, Killer by Night, A Tree Grows in Brooklyn, The Last Survivors*, etc. Produced *A Woman of Substance*.

Baker, Hylda (1908–). Jerky little British character comedienne, at her most exuberantly typical in *Nearest and Dearest*.

Baker, Joe Don (1936–). Thick-set American character actor of tough roles. Series: *Eischied*. TV movies: *Mongo's Back In Town, That Certain Summer, To Kill A Cop, Power*. Striking British début (and BAFTA nomination) in *Edge of Darkness*, 1985.

Baker, Richard (1925–). British newsreader and presenter, a sympathetic and familiar presence from the sixties; has a special interest in music.

Baker, Robert S. (1916–). British executive producer who with his partner Monty Berman was responsible for most of ATV's filmed adventure series: *The Saint, Gideon's Way, The Baron, The Persuaders*, etc.

Baker, Tom (1936–). Cheerful, tousle-haired British character actor who was the fourth to occupy the title role in the BBC's ever-running serial *Dr Who*, endowing the doctor with a long stripey scarf. Also introduced *The Book Tower* on children's TV.   PP

Bakewell, Joan (c 1942–). British presenter and interviewer whose greatest hour was on BBC's *Late Night Line Up* during the late sixties. More recently linking *Reports Action* and *On The Town*. Arts correspondent for *Newsnight* on BBC2.

balance. Material added to a schedule to give seriousness.

Balance Your Budget
(US 1952). Embarrassing American quiz of the early fifties in which contestants had to explain why they were in the red before getting a chance to put themselves in the black.

Balin, Ina (1937–). American leading actress who had a spotty career in the sixties. TV movies include *The Lonely Profession*, *Desperate Mission*, *Call to Danger*, *Panic on the 5.22*, *Danger in Paradise*, *The Immigrants*, *The Children of An Lac*.

Ball, Bobby: see Cannon, Tommy

Ball Four
US 1976 5 × 25m colour (VTR)
CBS (Don Segall)
Life in the locker room of a baseball club.
Awesomely unfunny comedy series.
cr Jim Bouton, Marvin Kitman, Vic Ziegel
Jim Bouton, Jack Somack, David-James Carroll

✻ **Ball, Lucille** (1910–). America's favourite female clown, who became nationally loved for her willingness to have a go at everything, even to fit her baby into the dictates of a weekly series. With her then husband Desi Arnaz she founded Desilu Studios and became her own producer and distributor; her comedy shows under various titles turned simple situations and knockabout into high art. I LOVE LUCY, HERE'S LUCY, THE LUCY SHOW, plus innumerable specials and guest appearances. A two-hour special, *CBS Salutes Lucy*, was shown in 1977 and encapsulates her career. She won Emmys in 1952, 1955, 1966 and 1967. Made a comeback 1985 as a bag lady in *Stone Pillow*.

Ball, Nicholas (1946–). Sharp British leading man who was noticed in *The Crezz* and subsequently shot to fame as HAZELL, an East End version of the California-type private eye.

The Ballad of Andy Crocker
US 1967 74m colour TVM
ABC/Spelling–Thomas
A Vietnam veteran can't settle to life in his old home town.
Would-be poetic, *Best Years of Our Lives*-style folksiness, with a brooding hero. Rather tiresome.
w Stuart Margolin *d* George MacCowan
Lee Majors, Pat Hingle, Jimmy Dean, Agnes Moorehead, Joey Heatherton, Jill Haworth, Bobby Hatfield

Ballard, Kaye (1926–) (Catherine Gloria Balota). American character actress, formerly in vaudeville. TV movie: *The Dream Merchants*. Series: *The Mothers-in-Law*.

The Balloon Game. Shortlived, alas, panel show on BBC2 in which contestants played the old game of arguing which of several nominated historical characters (Cromwell, Crippen, Rasputin, etc) should be dumped from a sinking balloon in order to save worthier passengers. What was amazing was that instead of licensed celebrities the players were ordinary university students.   PP

The Ballroom of Romance ✻✻ (GB Ireland 1982 50m). Plaintive masterpiece from the sensitive but uneven writer William Trevor, filmed in and around the rural dance-hall in the west of Ireland which inspired his story. Ageing spinster settles once again for redneck lecher instead of dream lover. Cyril Cusack (as the Manager) survives another night of dismal peacekeeping. Produced by Kenith Trodd for BBC/RTE.   PP

The Ballyskillen Opera House
GB 1980 6 × 25m colour (VTR)
Granada (John Hamp, Stephen Leahy)
An old Irish theatre is kept going by the bumbling manager and his devoted staff.
Sadly humourless farrago, mumbled through by an incompetent cast and oddly decorated each week by a guest artist.
w Linda Thornber *d* David Liddiment
Frank Carson, Anna Manahan, Charlie Roberts, Bernadette Shortt

Balsam, Martin (1919–). Distinguished American character actor whose first series TV was as second lead in *Archie Bunker's Place*. TV movies include *Money To Burn*, SIEGE, *Miles To Go Before I Sleep*, *The House on Garibaldi Street*.

Bam! Pow! Zapp! (GB 1969). Playwright Nigel Kneale's passionate swipe at the convention of violence in films and TV series and thick-ear fiction whereby a blow on the head leaves at worst a slight headache. In reality damage to the brain can result in long illness, paralysis and the destruction of the personality.
Kneale demonstrated this in a tight, claustrophobic story about a young yob who beat up a bank cashier and out of subsequent curiosity and shame was drawn into the ruined man's life, until in final expiation he pledged himself to look after his victim for evermore. With Clive Revill. Directed by William Slater; produced by Graeme McDonald; for BBC (*Wednesday Play*).   PP

Bamford, Roger (19 –). British drama director who made his debut with *Pit Strike* 1977, and his reputation with AUF WIEDERSEHEN, PET 1984, all but losing it again with *Blott on the Landscape*.   PP

Banacek: see Mystery Movie and Detour to Nowhere

Banana Splits *
US 1968–70 125 × 25m colour
Hanna–Barbera
Freewheeling miscellany for children: cartoons and a live adventure serial, hosted by a puppet rock group. Some bright ideas.

Banglestein's Boys *. Raucous British play about the exploits of a rugby team. Produced in 1969 by LWT, it established the writing talents of Colin Welland, and was produced by Kenith Trodd and directed by John McKenzie. In NFA.   PP

Banjo Hackett
US 1976 99m colour TVM
Columbia/Bruce Lansbury
Adventures of a wandering cowboy and a small orphan boy.
A failed pilot, and no wonder: aimless, slow-moving sentimental goo.
w Ken Trevey *d* Andrew V. McLaglen *ph* Al Francis *m* Morton Stevens
Don Meredith, Ike Eisenmann, Chuck Connors, Jennifer Warren

Banks-Smith, Nancy (1929–). Idiosyncratic British TV critic, appreciated more by her readers than by the industry. Formerly with the *Sun*; since the late sixties with the *Guardian*.   PP

Bannen, Ian (1928–). Scottish character actor, in all media. On TV, mainly single plays; also *Tinker Tailor Soldier Spy*, *Jane Eyre*, *Jesus of Nazareth*, *Johnny Belinda*, *Dr Jekyll and Mr Hyde*.

Banner, Bob (1921–). American producer and director, mainly of musical specials: Carol Channing, Dinah Shore, Peggy Fleming, Liberace, etc. Emmy 1957 for direction of *The Dinah Shore Chevy Show*.

Banner, John (1910–73). Austrian–American character actor, a chubby comedian or sometimes a heavy villain. TV series: *Hogan's Heroes*, *Chicago Teddy Bears*.

Bannister, Trevor (1936–). Sharp-featured British comedy lead who after exposure in *Coronation Street* and *The Dustbinmen* settled down as the somewhat overshadowed star of *Are You Being Served?*

Bannon, Jack (1940–). American character actor, son of Jim Bannon. Mainly familiar as a LOU GRANT regular; also in *Tail Gunner Joe*, *Amelia Earhart*, etc.

Banyon *
aka: *Walk Up and Die*
US 1971 97m colour TVM
NBC/Warner (Richard Alan Simmons)
Adventures of a Los Angeles private eye of the thirties.
Smart-looking nostalgia and not a bad plot for a pilot; but the hero is humourless and the show was shortlived (running only 13 episodes), as four years later was its almost indistinguishable successor *City of Angels*, which even used the same building for the hero's office.
w Ed Adamson *d* Robert Day *m* Leonard Rosenman
Robert Forster, Jose Ferrer, Darren McGavin, Herb Edelman

The Barbara Stanwyck Show (US 1960). A half-hour dramatic anthology series for NBC which was also used to try out pilots for new series, none of which ever got off the ground. The star introduced each story and appeared in half a dozen.

Barbary Coast *
GB title: *In Old San Francisco*
US 1975 74m or 98m (two versions)
    colour TVM
ABC/Paramount (Douglas Heyes)
A police detective with a penchant for disguise blackmails a saloon proprietor into helping him.
Ambitious pilot for a rumbustious nineties series. Alas, the elements did not jell.
w Douglas Heyes *d* Bill Bixby *m* John Andrew Tartaglia
William Shatner, Dennis Cole, Lynda Day George, Charles Aidman, Michael Ansara
† Dennis Cole may have been all at sea, but his replacement, Doug McClure, was merely stolid, and the show, retitled *Cash and Cable*, folded after 13 × 50m episodes. Producer: Cy Chermak.

Barbeau, Adrienne (1947–). American leading lady with sharp edges. A hit in *Maude*; later in demand as guest star. TV movies: *The Great Houdinis*, *Having Babies*, *Red Alert*, *Crash*, *Someone's Watching Me*, *The Darker Side of Terror*, *The Top of the*

Hill, Valentine Magic on Love Island, Tourist.

Barber, Glynis (19 –). Blonde South African-born actress who delighted everyone as *Jane* in the two comic-strip serials for BBC and was an instant hit in *Dempsey and Makepeace.*

The Barchester Chronicles
GB 1982 7 × 55m
BBC (Jonathan Powell)

Trollope's *The Warden* and *Barchester Towers* run together to make a spiky classic serial of intrigue and double-dealing amid cathedral cloisters.

w Alan Plater *d* David Giles

Donald Pleasence, Nigel Hawthorne, Geraldine McEwan, Susan Hampshire

The Last Chronicle of Barset, later in the sequence of novels, had been dramatized by Peter Black, 1959, with Hugh Burden as Mr Crawley and Olga Lindo as the Bishop's masterful wife, Mrs Proudie.   PP

Bardot, Brigitte (1934–). French star and sex symbol who has ventured only rarely into television. *Bardot Special* (RTF 1967, shown by BBC 1968) displayed her in a variety of outfits, and finally swathed in a French *tricolore* that was to have been transparent until the French authorities thought this might show disrespect to the flag. She also sang – but Bardot's vocal cords, as I observed at the time, are among her less interesting organs. *Brigitte Bardot – My Own Story* (1983) was a three-part series from Sygma/Antenne 2 shown in Britain by Channel 4. Bardot talked to Allain Bougrain-Dubourg, billed as writer, producer and former lover, with photographs, snippets from the movies and the testimony of family and friends stitched into the conversation: a venerable formula but one not always used so naturally. Directed by Catherine Poubeau.   PP

Bare, Richard L. (1909–). American producer with much Hollywood experience. *Green Acres, Run for Your Life, Nanny and the Professor, Alias Smith and Jones*, many others.

'Love her. Use her. Or destroy her. Everyone wants a piece of Tyger Hayes!'
Bare Essence: *The Love of Power, the Power of Love*
US 1983 6 x 50m (plus pilot) colour
NBC/Warner (Walter Grauman)

Love, lust, power and intrigue in the perfume business.

Would-be long-running soap whose aroma didn't linger.

w Robert Hamilton *d* (pilot) Walter Grauman

Genie Francis, Ian MacShane, Jennifer O'Neill, Jessica Walter, Michael Woods, John Dehner

Barefoot in the Park
US 1970 12 × 25m colour
ABC/Paramount

Life for young marrieds in a New York cold water flat.

Neil Simon's amusing play was rather pointlessly given a black cast. Nobody cheered.

Scoey Mitchell, Tracey Reed, Thelma Carpenter

Baretta *
US 1975–7 82 × 50m colour
ABC/Universal/Public Arts–Roy Huggins (Jo Swerling Jnr)

A redrafting of *Toma* when the star refused to continue. The new man is still a plainclothes cop with a penchant for disguise; this time he has a pet parrot and the urban milieu is overpowering; also, from the first episode he's hot to get the gangsters who shot his girl in mistake for him. (See *The Badge or the Cross.*) The mixture turned out to have great appeal to the young.

cr Stephen J. Cannell *m* Dave Grusin/Tom Scott

ROBERT BLAKE, Tom Ewell, Dana Elcar, Michael D. Roberts

❋   **Barker, Ronnie** (1929–). Cheerful, avuncular British character comedian; with Ronnie Corbett one of THE TWO RONNIES, and remarkable for his precision, his enunciation, his characterizations and his ability to smile his way through dubious material and make maiden aunts love it. Also popular solo as the old lag in PORRIDGE and *Going Straight*, and as the Lancashire shopkeeper in *Open All Hours*. BAFTA awards as best light entertainment performer 1971, 1975, 1977.

The Barkleys
US 1972 26 × 25m colour
NBC/Hanna–Barbera

Adventures of a family headed by a loud-mouthed suburbanite; they just happen to be dogs. A take-off of *All in the Family* which didn't quite work.

Barkworth, Peter (1929–). Leading British character actor who from playing affable young men matured into one of the finest exponents of middle-life crises, often in partnership with producer Mark Shivas. BAFTA award 1974 for *Crown Matrimonial*, as Edward VIII, then went on to play Edward's adversary, Stanley Baldwin, in *Churchill: The Wilderness Years*. Series: TELFORD'S CHANGE, 1979; THE PRICE, 1984; *Late Starter*, 1985, Read St Matthew's Gospel, 1986.   PP

Barlow, Thelma (*c* 1941–). British character actress who has been the tremulous Mavis in *Coronation Street* since 1971.

Barmitzvah Boy ***
GB 1976 75m colour
BBC (Graeme McDonald)

A boy finds the pressures too much and ducks out of his own barmitzvah.
Hilarious and moving Jewish domestic comedy which surprisingly failed as a stage musical and was never quite snapped up as a movie.
w JACK ROSENTHAL d MICHAEL TUCHNER
JEREMY STEYN, MARIA CHARLES, BERNARD SPEAR, ADRIENNE POSTA, Cyril Shaps

'If you missed it, do yourself a favour and seek out the repeat.' – *Daily Mail*
† BAFTA awards: best play, best writer.
PP: 'A great delight, funnier than anything Jack Rosenthal has written since – well, the last thing he wrote, and just as touching as the somewhat overpraised *The Evacuees*. The plot described a perfect sentimental parabola; the build-up of anticipation and mild foreboding as the ceremony loomed; its central figure's sudden walkout, the flattened summit while Momma wept and sister argued, and then momentum gathering for the swoop down to the happy-ironic ending.'

Barnaby Jones *
US 1973–79 175 × 50m colour
CBS/Quinn Martin (Philip Salzman)

A retired private detective takes over the practice when his son is killed.
Griff had the same idea at precisely the same time, but Lorne Greene flopped in one season while his rival carried through seven seasons with ease. Neat, interesting mysteries with high-life settings, adequately produced and with a highly personable old star.
m Jerry Goldsmith
BUDDY EBSEN, Lee Meriwether, Mark Shera

Barnes, Carol (1944–). British newscaster for ITN, formerly in radio.

❋ **Barnett, Isobel** (Lady Barnett) (1918–81). British television personality, especially popular in the fifties as one of the panellists on WHAT'S MY LINE?
PP: ' "Men found her discreetly sexy," said a *Radio Times* chronicler in 1969; "women saw her as the person their daughter was going to grow up into after she had married a titled millionaire." Later she became a radio personage. Her end was sad in the extreme: after a shoplifting charge she took her own life.'

Barney Miller *
US 1975– ? × 25m colour (VTR)
ABC/Columbia/DANNY ARNOLD (Chris Hayward)

'Realistic' but funny episodes in a New York police precinct house.
Raucous and often penetrating humour with tragic undercurrents gives this series much in common with *M*A*S*H* and *All in the Family*, but it travels somewhat less well. Outstanding comedy series 1982.
cr Danny Arnold, Theodore J. Flicker
HAL LINDEN, Barbara Barrie, ABE VIGODA, JACK SOO, Max Gail, Ron Glass, James Gregory
† In 1977 Abe Vigoda left the show and appeared in a spin-off, *Fish*; creators Danny Arnold, Theodore J. Flicker

The Baron
GB 1965 30 × 50m colour
ITC (Robert Baker, Monty Berman)

An antique dealer is really an undercover agent.
Routinely glossy adventures, pleasingly implausible plots, mid-Atlantic atmosphere, vaguely based on the John Creasey character.
script supervisor Terry Nation
Steve Forrest, Sue Lloyd, Colin Gordon

Baron, Alexander (1917–). British novelist who came to television during the fashion for everyday social realism of 1959–60 with *A Bit of Happiness*, *The Blood Fight* and *The Harsh World*. Since then he has contributed to many anthology series, made several serial adaptations and continued to furnish infrequent but always distinguished single plays, e.g. *Gentle Folk* (1980). Recent credits include *Jane Eyre* (1982), *Goodbye Mr Chips* (1984), *The Adventures of Sherlock Holmes* (1984–5).   PP

'A gambler plays for the biggest stake of his life ... his son!'
The Baron and the Kid
US 1984 96m colour TVM
Telecom Entertainment (Michael Lepiner, Ken Kaufman)

A wandering poolroom hustler teams up with the son he never knew he had.
Thin but quite pleasant telefeature relying primarily on the personality of its star.

w Bill Stratton d Gene Nelson ph John Lindley m Brad Fiedel

Johnny Cash, Darren McGavin, Greg Webb, Tracy Pollan, June Carter Cash

Baron, Lynda (1942–). British singer and performer who after making herself known in *Not So Much a Programme* took twenty years to re-establish herself on TV as the district nurse and object of Ronnie Barker's lust in *Open All Hours.*

Barr, Patrick (1908–). British character actor, a popular TV leading man of the fifties.

Barr, Robert (1910–). British writer of documentary television, drama-documentary and eventually drama pure and simple, in BBC-TV from early postwar days. *Germany Under Control* (1946 – beat that!); *Pilgrim Street*, six stories about a London police station; MEDICO, 1958, Italia prizewinner. Yet he went on to write expertly for Z CARS, MAIGRET and SOFTLY, SOFTLY. His personal masterwork was probably the superb SPYCATCHER series, followed by *Moonstrike*. Most recent credit, *Airey Neave*, 1980. PP

Barraclough, Jenny (19 –). British documentary director who leaped to distinction with the 'brilliant, unnerving and salutary' THE BOMB DISPOSAL MEN of 1974. Since then, many and varied subjects including *Hang On, I'll Just Speak to the World* (60 years of BBC radio), 1982; *Elizabeth, the First Thirty Years*, 1983; *Life of an Orchestra* (series), 1984; *Number 10 Downing Street*, 1985. PP

Barratt, Michael (1928–). Heavyweight British linkman forever associated with the *Nationwide* early-evening news round-up, though he left it before its end to set up a freelance film outfit. PP

Barrett, Rona (1934–) (Rona Burnstein). American columnist who covers Hollywood in print and latterly on TV.

Barrie, Barbara (1931–). American character actress. TV movies include *79 Park Avenue, Tell Me My Name, Summer of My German Soldier, Backstairs at the White House, Roots: The Next Generations.* Series: *Breaking Away.*

Barriers (GB 1983 20 × 30m). Orphaned teenager seeks out his true roots in a good children's serial from Tyne-Tees. Written by William Corlett, directed by Bob Hird and Tony Kysh, devised and produced by Margaret Bottomley. PP

Barris, Chuck (19 –). American quizmaster and impresario.

Barron, John (1920–). Tall, distinguished-looking British character actor. TV series include *Emergency Ward 10, All Gas and Gaiters, Doomwatch*, POTTER.

Barron, Keith (1934–). Deceptively good British leading actor equally at home in strong TV drama (three Dennis Potter plays), mid-brow serials (TELFORD'S CHANGE) and situation comedy (*New Adventures of Lucky Jim*, DUTY FREE). PP

Barry, Gene (1921–) (Eugene Klass). American entertainer and light actor who made his greatest mark on TV in a series of impeccably dressed roles with just the right amount of cuff showing. *Bat Masterson*, BURKE'S LAW, *The Name of the Game, The Adventurer.* TV movies include *Prescription Murder, Istanbul Express, The Devil and Miss Sarah, Ransom for Alice, Aspen.*

Barry, Jack (1918–84). American television anchorman, long associated with such quizzes as *Twenty One, Tic Tac Dough* and *The Joker's Wild.*

Barry, John (1933–) (John Barry Prendergast). British composer of scores of famous film themes. TV work includes *Love Among the Ruins, Eleanor and Franklin.*

Barry, Michael (1910–). BBC head of drama from early postwar days until shortly before Sydney Newman's takeover in 1963. Thought at the time to be too theatre-orientated, but nevertheless nurtured drama-doc experiments by Robert Barr, Duncan Ross, Colin Morris and others, not to mention the *Quatermass* serials, *1984*, and Iain MacCormick. PP

Barrymore, Michael (19 –). British comic with own series on Thames, 1983, but best known as compère of birdbrained BBC game show *Get Set Go.* PP

PETER BARKWORTH, undeniably a TV star of the first magnitude, tended in the mid-eighties to play too many wronged husbands. Here in *Late Starter* he has to start from scratch when his wife gambles away all his savings.

Barstow, Stan (1928–). Doughty British north country writer who has adapted his own novels to television, adapted other people's and furnished several originals, e.g. *The Pity of It All* (1966), *A Raging Calm* (1974), *A Brother's Tale* (1983). Was also involved in the conception of *A Family at War*. The novel with which he originally made his name, *A Kind of Loving*, became with its two sequels a 10-part series in 1982.   PP

Barter. An American commercial system by which a distributor gives programmes to a station in return for time slots.

Baryshnikov, Mikhail (1947–). Russian ballet dancer in America, a great TV success in the special BARYSHNIKOV ON BROADWAY.

Basehart, Richard (1914–84). American character actor, popular in films from the forties. TV series: *Voyage to the Bottom of the Sea*. TV movies: *Sole Survivor*, *City Beneath the Sea*, *The Birdmen*, *The Death of

Me Yet, Assignment Munich, The Bounty Man, Maneater, Time Travellers, 21 Hours at Munich, Flood, Stonestreet, The Critical List, The Rebels, Marilyn: The Untold Story.

The Basement * (GB 1967). Two men jostle for the possession not only of one girl but also – like animals – of territory, namely the basement flat they temporarily share. All conducted in the tight, ornate pattern of rivalry to be expected from HAROLD PINTER, including a famously startling cricket match played with a bass recorder for bat, a candelabra as stumps and a solitaire marble as the ball. The first ball was a bye that shattered a stained-glass window. The second struck the batsman's knee with agonizing force. The third he clouted back up the wicket to explode a tank of tropical fish. With Derek Godfrey, Pinter himself and Kika Markham. Directed by Charles Jarrott, designed by Eileen Diss, for BBC.
                                                        PP

Basic cable. An American system by which the subscriber gets a channel of programmes for a single fee per month (as opposed to *pay-cable* which implies payment per programme).

Basinger, Kim (*c* 1952–). American leading lady, former model. Series: *Dog and Cat, From Here to Eternity.* TV movies: *The Ghost of Flight 401, Katie: Portrait of a Centerfold,* etc.

Bass, Alfie (1920–). Diminutive British cockney actor who during the sixties was a national figure on TV as 'Excused Boots' Bisley, though when that particular star waned he found no further leading roles and returned to the stage. Series: *The Army Game, Bootsie and Snudge,* later episodes of *Till Death Us Do Part.*

❋ **Bassey, Shirley** (1937–). Dynamic Welsh-born singer, fond of stressing her Tiger Bay background and mixed heritage. One of the few real television stars, with a series to herself every year or two.

The Bastard
US 1978 2 × 95m colour
Universal for Operation Prime Time (John Wilder)
A combination of unlikely circumstances sends a French peasant boy of the 1780s to fame and fortune in America.
Stiff historical charade, from the first in a whole dynasty of novels. The actors appear to have been only recently introduced to their clothes, and for the first hilarious half-hour all speak with ze French accent.
w Guerdon Trueblood *novel* John Jakes *d* Lee H. Katzin *ph* Michael Hugo *m* John Addison
Andrew Stevens, Patricia Neal, Lorne Greene, Tom Bosley, Buddy Ebsen, William Daniels, James Gregory, Olivia Hussey, Cameron Mitchell, Henry Morgan, Eleanor Parker, Donald Pleasence, Barry Sullivan, William Shatner, Keenan Wynn
'As a serious contender in the field of telefilms, it falls on its face . . . as bloodless and unconvincing as a school pageant.' – *Daily Variety*
'Not even a top-flight cast can save this mini-series from terminal superficiality . . . the humour is inadvertent and certainly not enough to sustain interest throughout.' – *Hollywood Reporter*
† The film was shot in six weeks at a cost of three million dollars.

Bat Masterson *
US 1958–60 108 × 25m bw
NBC/United Artists
Adventures of a dandified gunfighter.
Silly but mildly amusing exploits which made a star of Gene Barry.

Bate, Anthony (1928–). British character actor with a slightly supercilious air; his best chance came with the lead in *Intimate Strangers.*

Bates, Alan (1934–). Distinguished British actor, very occasionally on TV, the most notable occasion being in the BBC serialization of *The Mayor of Casterbridge* (1978) and *An Englishman Abroad* (1983).

Bates, H. E. (1905–74). British novelist and short-story writer whose works have been much raided by television, usually to mutual advantage. *Country Matters* (1972); *Love for Lydia* (1977), *A Moment in Time* (1979), *Fair Stood the Wind for France* (1981). Richard Bates, the television producer, is his son. PP

Bates, Michael (1920–78). British character actor, familiar in early years of two series: *Last of the Summer Wine* and *It Ain't Half Hot Mum.*

Bates, Richard (1937–). British producer. *Please Sir, Public Eye, A Man of Our Times, Helen – A Woman of Today, Intimate Strangers, Love for Lydia, The Prime of Miss Jean Brodie, The Tripods.*

Batey, Derek (1928–). British game show host chiefly associated with *Mr and Mrs*; also an executive with Border TV which produces it.

Batman *
US 1965–7 120 × 25m colour
ABC/TCF/Greenway (William Dozier)
The first 'camp' TV series, based on the old comic strip by Bob Kane about the 'caped crusader' who dashes around in his Batmobile saving society from such supercriminals as the Riddler, the Joker and the Penguin. Adults soon tired of the stereotyped spoof, clearly shot on a shoestring, but kids enjoyed it, especially when exclamations such as Splat! and Zowie! appeared onscreen during the fight scenes. It was designed to play on two evenings a week, a nod to the old serial format.
m Neal Hefti, Nelson Riddle
Adam West, Burt Ward, Yvonne Craig, Alan Napier; with frequent guests Frank Gorshin (the Riddler), Cesar Romero (the Joker), Burgess Meredith (the Penguin).

BATMAN. Burt Ward was Robin and Adam West the caped crusader in the popular if slightly tacky television version of the Saturday morning movie serial.

† The production was spurred by the theatrical re-release of the old *Batman* serials, which were a great hit with campus audiences. In 1966 a movie feature was made. †† Guest villains have also included Tallulah Bankhead (the Black Widow), Joan Crawford (the Devil), Ethel Merman (Lola Lasagne), Vincent Price (Egghead), Ida Lupino (Dr Cassandra), George Sanders (Mr Freeze), Rudy Vallee (Lord Marmaduke Ffogg), Shelley Winters (Ma Parker), Milton Berle (Louis the Lilac), Liberace (Chandell).

Battered
aka: *Intimate Strangers*
US 1977 96m colour TVM
Charles Fries

A frustrated husband whose job is threatened becomes a wife-beater.
Exploitative social drama.

w Richard and Esther Shapiro *d* John Llewellyn Moxey

Dennis Weaver, Sally Struthers, Tyne Daly, Larry Hagman, Melvyn Douglas

Battered
US 1978 96m colour TVM
NBC/Henry Jaffe (Michael Jaffe)

Three studies of wife-beating at various levels of society.
Heavy-going case histories, well enough handled.

w Karen Grassle, Cynthia Lovelace Sears *d* Peter Werner *ph* John Bailey *m* Don Peake

Joan Blondell, Howard Duff, Karen Grassle, LeVar Burton, Mike Farrell, Diana Scarwid

Battlestar Galactica *
US 1978 140m colour
ABC/Universal/Glen Larson (Leslie Stevens)

Survivors from a distant galactic war work their way towards earth, hampered by the Cylons whose aim is to destroy mankind.
Lumbering, humourless space fantasy in the wake of *Star Wars*: the hardware is the undoubted star, but even that becomes repetitive, and the actors and script are boring.

w/d Richard A. Colla, Glen Larson *sp* JOHN DYKSTRA, Joe Goss, Karl Miller *costumes* Jean-Pierre Dorleac

Lorne Greene, Dirk Benedict, Richard Hatch

'A flashy, spectacular special effects display, a hardware store in the sky with all the emotional impact of a soggy doughnut.' – Dave Kaufman

† The hardware was salvaged for use in a one-hour series which began strongly but fell away as the 1978–9 season progressed. Further episodes however aired a year later as *Galactica 1980*.

Batty, Peter (1931–). British historical documentarist who after long experience with BBC and ATV went independent and regularly turns out such features as *The Battle of the Bulge*, *The Birth of the Bomb* and *Operation Barbarossa*. Recently: *Il Poverello* (1982), *Swindle!* (3 parts), *The Algerian War* (series).

Bavarian Night
GB 1981 75m colour

Andrew Davies parable about a school parent–teacher association's social evening at which a German band and lots of thigh-slapping lead upright citizens into sexual and political indiscretions. Civilization as we know it took a nasty turn, though it recovered more or less in the end. Jack Gold directed as if grateful for a comedy again. BBC *Play for Today* with Bob Peck, Sarah Badell. PP

Baverstock, Donald (1924–). British current affairs editor and programme executive. As a whizz-kid of the fifties he started the original (early-evening) *Tonight* on BBC-TV. Later, nursed *TWTWTW* on to the air. Head of BBC1 when second channel set up in 1964. Founder member and first programme director of Yorkshire Television 1968–73. PP

Baxter, Anne (1923–). American leading lady of forties movies, latterly in small screen guest roles. TV movies include *Companions in Nightmare*, *The Challengers*, *Ritual of Evil*, *The Catcher*, *The Moneychangers*, *Little Mo*, *East of Eden*, *Hotel*, *The Hands of Death*.

Baxter, Meredith (1947–) (aka Meredith Baxter-Birney). American leading lady who met her husband David Birney when they were both starring in BRIDGET LOVES BERNIE. TV movies: *The Cat Creature*, *The Stranger Who Looks Like Me*, *Target Risk*, *The Imposter*, *The Night that Panicked America*, *Little Women*, *The Family Man*, *Beulah*

Land. From 1982 a household word in *Family Ties*.

Baxter, Raymond (1922–). British sports and news commentator, long with BBC; in the sixties became best known for introducing a weekly science programme, *Tomorrow's World*.

Baxter, Stanley (1928–). Simian Scottish comedian and mimic who broke into national television with *On the Bright Side* 1959–60, followed by other BBC series until 1971. From 1974 to 1982 concentrated on annual showbizzy spectaculars for LWT, written by Ken Hoare, in which he took all parts, imitated famous acts and re-staged movie set-pieces; at best brilliantly sustained (the Pope interviewed by Joan Bakewell, *Upstairs Downstairs* sent up), other times reaching for too easy a flip exit. In 1985 back to the BBC. PP

Bay City Blues
US 1983 4 × 50m colour
NBC/MTM (Rick Wallace)

Stories of a small town baseball team.

The *Hill Street Blues/St Elsewhere* formula failed badly when applied to sport: technique was abundantly evident, but the viewers simply didn't care.

cr Stephen Bochco, Jeffrey Lewis

Michael Nouri, Pat Corley, Perry Lang, Michele Green, Patrick Cassidy, Barry Tubb, Ken Olin

'Could be pigeonholed as soap if the dialog, style and acting weren't so adroitly handled.' – *Daily Variety*

Bayldon, Geoffrey (1924–). Ascetic looking British actor, best known on TV in the title role of *Catweazle*, and later featured in *Worzel Gummidge*.

BBC (British Broadcasting Corporation). The 'voice of London' is not state controlled, but was founded by royal charter in 1927 and exists by virtue of a licence fee collected from all who have receivers on their premises. It now operates two TV channels and four national radio channels as well as local radio. In the days of its first director general, John Reith, it was undoubtedly puritanical and maiden-auntish, but the advent of commercial TV made BBC1 at least very competitive for top ratings.

BBC2. The second, 'cultural' channel of the BBC, which seldom goes for ratings unless BBC1 is going for culture. The two channels are scheduled in collaboration, with programme junctions where possible. BBC2 opened in 1964, and its first night was devastated by an electricity failure. It never managed to catch the imagination of the public at large, even with well-remembered programmes like *Late Night Line Up*, and has generally been content to address itself to a selection of minorities.

BBC3: see That Was the Week that Was

Beach, Ann (1938–). Diminutive British comedy actress who in 1984 became instantly recognizable as the neighbour in *Fresh Fields*.

Beach Patrol
US 1979 74m colour TVM
ABC/Spelling–Goldberg (Phil Fehrle)
A girl joins the beach patrol.
Cut from the same cloth as *Starsky and Hutch*, this is a thin, shoddy bid for a series which luckily wasn't offered. Even the beach buggy chases are tired, and the dialogue suggests that three monkeys typed it.
w Ronald Austin, James D. Buchanan *d* Bob Kelljan *ph* Arch Dalzell *m* Barry De Vorzon
Christine Delisle, Richard Hill, Jonathan Frakes, Robin Strand, Michael Gregory, Paul Burke

Beacham, Stephanie (1947–). Sultry British actress who came to fame as the bad girl in *Tenko* and weathered *Connie*, 1985. In between, *Sorrell and Son*, 1984. Now in the *Dynasty* spin-off, *The Colbys*.   PP

The Beachcomber
US 1960 39 × 25m bw
Filmaster (Nat Perrin)
A businessman throws up his career and goes to the South Seas in search of truth.
Vaguely inspirational dramas which don't really have enough punch.
cr Walter Brown Newman
Cameron Mitchell

Beachcombers
Canada 1972–4 39 × 25m colour
CBC
Children help a middle-aged man who prefers to live a rugged existence on the beaches north of Vancouver.
Moderately pleasant open-air series for young people.

Beacon Hill
US 1975 13 × 50m colour (VTR)
CBS/Robert Stigwood (Jacqueline Babbin, Beryl Vertue)
Life in an upper-class Boston home during the first part of the century.
An attempt to re-create the British success *Upstairs, Downstairs* for American audiences. It failed.
w Sidney Carroll *m* Marvin Hamlisch
Steven Elliott, Nancy Marchand, George Rose, Beatrice Straight, Don Blakely, Roy Cooper, David Dukes, Edward Herrmann

Beak, Ollie. Owl puppet with thick Liverpool accent and pronounced opinions on the life and culture of the day who enlivened A-R children's programmes in the sixties. Worked with skiffle singer Wally Whyton, Muriel Young and another puppet known as Fred Dog. Staged comeback in the late seventies.
                                                          PP

Bean, Orson (1928–) (Dallas Burrows). American comedian and talk show host, popular on TV from the mid-fifties to the mid-sixties. Brought to Britain by Granada.

Beany and Cecil
US 1961–2 78 × 25m colour
Bob Clampett
Adventures of a boy who can fly and a serpent who gets seasick.
Smoothly animated cartoon adventures.

Bearcats *
US 1971 15 × 50m colour
CBS/Filmways (David Friedkin, Morton Fine)
In 1914, two freelance investigators roam the southwest in a Stutz Bearcat.
Ambitious semi-western which didn't quite work: too many Mexican accents, perhaps.
cr/executive producer Douglas Heyes
Rod Taylor, Dennis Cole
† See also *Powder Keg*, which was the pilot.

A Beast with Two Backs **
GB 1968 75m bw
Innocent dancing bear is slaughtered by backward country folk to expiate a crime one of them has in fact committed. A powerful piece of myth-making (though set only in the 1890s) by DENNIS POTTER, with Patrick Barr as the bear's owner. A BBC *Wednesday Play* produced by Graeme McDonald, directed by Lionel Harris. In NFA.   PP

Beasts * (GB 1976). Six 50m plays by NIGEL KNEALE exploiting familiar and not altogether irrational suspicions of the animal world. The first, *Barty's Party*, directed by Don Taylor, set the mood as rats besieged the lonely home of a housewife whose only link with the outside world was via a radio phone-in. Produced by Nicholas Palmer, for ATV.									PP

The Beasts Are on the Streets
US 1978 95m colour TVM
NBC/Hanna–Barbera (Harry R. Sherman)

Wild animals escape from a safari park. Predictable panic and suspense movie, rather tortuously plotted and at its best when the beasts are in close-up.

w Laurence Heath *d* Peter Hunt *ph* Charles G. Arnold *m* Gerald Fried

Carol Lynley, Dale Robinette, Anna Lee, Billy Green Bush, Philip Michael Thomas

Beat the Clock (US 1950–7). Half-hour game show for CBS with Bud Collyer; participants had to perform difficult or messy stunts within a given number of seconds. (*Jeux sans Frontières* is the same idea on a grander scale. In the UK the show became a popular segment of *Sunday Night at the London Palladium*.)

The Beatles
US 1965 39 × 22m colour
King Features

Fragmented adventures and singalongs with the mop-headed quartet, quite well animated by Halas and Batchelor.

The Beatles at Shea Stadium (US 1966). A record of their American tour, directed by Andrew Laszlo.

The Beatles in New York: see Yeah! Yeah! Yeah!

The Beatles' Magical Mystery Tour (GB 1967). A little too zany and mystical, this BBC special on the lines of their movies was not generally liked. It was written and directed by the group.

Beaton, Norman (1934–). West Indian black actor in Britain; star of the first black serial *Empire Road*, and of the comedy series *The Fosters*.

'Alcohol was her tragedy – and her triumph!'
Beatrice
aka: *Life of the Party: the Story of Beatrice*
US 1982 96m colour TVM
Columbia/Ken and Mitzie Welch

In 1944, the alcoholic wife of a wealthy Texan cures herself and sets up a halfway house for alcoholic girls released from jail. An aimless saunter down Misery Street, based of course on a true story.

w Mitzie Welch *d* Lamont Johnson

Carol Burnett, Lloyd Bridges, Marian Mercer, Geoffrey Lewis, Gail Strickland

Beatty, Ned (1937–). Stocky American actor in all media. TV movies: *Footsteps*, *The Marcus Nelson Murders*, *Dying Room Only*, *The Execution of Private Slovik*, *Attack on Terror*, *The Deadly Tower*, *Tail Gunner Joe*, *Lucan*, *A Question of Love*, FRIENDLY FIRE, *Guyana Tragedy*, *All God's Children*, *Splendor in the Grass*, *The Violation of Sarah McDavid*, *Pray TV*, *A Woman Called Golda*, *Kentucky Woman*, *Celebrity*, *The Last Days of Pompeii*, *Robert Kennedy and His Times*

Beaumont, Hugh (1910–82). American leading man, father in *Leave It to Beaver*.

Beauty and the Beast *
US 1976 76m colour (VTR)
Hallmark Hall of Fame/Palm Productions
(Thomas M. C. Johnston)

A more or less faithful version of the classic fairy tale, with scenes filmed in England. Somewhat uninspired.

w Sherman Yellen *d* Fielder Cook *m* Ron Goodwin

George C. Scott, Trish Van Devere, Virginia McKenna, Bernard Lee

Beauty, Bonny, Daisy, Violet, Grace and Geoffrey Morton. Prizewinning (BAFTA 1974) Thames TV documentary about the rearing of farm horses, directed by Frank Cvitanovitch.

Beavers, Louise (1902–62). Big, warm-hearted, black character actress who in 1960 starred in the series *Beulah*.

Beck, John (*c* 1938–). Stalwart American actor, in all media. Series: *Flamingo Road*. TV movies: *The Silent Gun*, *Lock, Stock and Barrel*, *Sidekicks*, *The Law*, *Attack on Terror*, *Call of the Wild*, *Wheels*, *The Time Machine*, *Greatest Heroes of the Bible*, *The Buffalo Soldiers*, *The Great American Traffic Jam*, *Peyton Place: the Next Generation*

Beckett, Samuel (1906–). Irish writer and Nobel prizewinner luckily not much done on television, though his 1956 radio play *All That Fall* was translated to television by RTF as *Tous Ceux qui Tombe* in the early sixties, and most of the short works have been seen. In 1982 *Arena* presented a Beckett Festival on BBC2 comprising a new ballet *Quad*, a Don Pennebaker documentary about Beckett's best-known interpreter, Billie Whitelaw, rehearsing *Rockaby* at the National, and re-runs of four earlier productions: *Happy Days* and *Not I* with Billie Whitelaw, *Eh Joe* with the late Jack McGowan, and *Krapp's Last Tape* with the late Patrick Magee. Clips from these also figured in an 80-minute RTE biographical special by Sean O'Mordha, *Silence to Silence*, 1984.   PP

❉ **Beckinsale, Richard** (1945–79). British light leading man of the new school, familiar on TV in the series *The Lovers*, RISING DAMP and PORRIDGE.

The Bee Gees. A popular rock group of British north country brothers. Barry Gibb (1946–), Maurice Gibb (1949–), Robin Gibb (1949–).

Beeny, Christopher (1941–). Self-effacing British light character man, former child actor. *Upstairs, Downstairs*, *The Rag Trade*, *In Loving Memory*.

Beery, Noah Jnr (1913–). Dependable American character actor who graduated from rustic types to genial uncles. TV series include *Circus Boy*, *Hondo*, *Doc Elliott*, *The Rockford Files*.

Before and After *
US 1980 96m colour TVM
ABC/Franklin Koenigsberg (Sam Manners)
A well-to-do 40-year-old housewife tries various ways of reducing.
Comedy with a serious purpose, this examination of one of the lesser traumas of our time is amusing, well made, and pleasantly photographed in Seattle.
w Hindi Brooks, Jim Henerson *d* Kim Friedman *ph* Brianne Murphy *m* Jimmie Haskell
Patty Duke Astin, Bradford Dillman, Barbara Feldon, Art Hindle, Conchata Ferrell, Kenneth Mars, Rosemary Murphy, Betty White

Beg Borrow or Steal
US 1973 74m colour TVM
Universal (Stanley Kallis)
Three disabled men plan a museum heist.
Modest caper yarn which becomes tasteless in its effort to be different.

w Paul Playdon *d* David Lowell Rich
Mike Connors, Kent McCord, Michael Cole, Russell Johnson, Joel Fabiani, Henry Beckman

Begelman, David (1922–). American executive who began as an agent and rose through MCA and CMA to be president of Columbia, a post he was forced to leave in 1978 when prosecuted for fiscal irregularities. After producing a TV documentary called *Angel Death* he moved over to MGM.

Begg, Michael (1946–). British outside-broadcast director (e.g. Cenotaph Armistice Day Service and Old Man of Hoy rock climb, both 1984) who developed estimable sideline as producer of unsporting sports specials: THE FISHING RACE, 1976, and sequel *The Golden Maggot*, 1977; *Birdman of Jacksonville*, 1985. *Calum Kennedy's Commando Course*, made in 1980 but held up until 1985, extended the idea to rural show business. Also more straightforward treatment of virile topics in series *Behind the Lines*, 1985.   PP

Beggarman, Thief
US 1979 2 × 96m colour TVM
NBC/Universal (Jack Laird)
In 1968, members of the Jordache family in Beverly Hills, Antibes and West Germany are brought together by circumstance at the Cannes Film Festival.
Unseaworthy supposed sequel to *Rich Man, Poor Man*, to which it bears almost no relation at all.
w Art Eisenson, Mary Agnes Donahue, *novel* Irwin Shaw *d* Larry Doheny *ph* Robert Caramico *m* Eddie Sauter
Jean Simmons, Glenn Ford, Lynn Redgrave, Tovah Feldshuh, Andrew Stevens, Bo Hopkins, Tom Nolan, Jean-Pierre Aumont, Dr Joyce Brothers, Anne Francis, Alex Cord, Michael Gazzo, Anne Jeffreys, Christian Marquand, Susan Strasberg, Robert Sterling
'A rambling, disjointed mini-series peopled in the main by unpleasant characters who wallow in interminable personal crises.' – *Daily Variety*

Behind Closed Doors (US 1959). Half-hour anthology series for NBC, allegedly revealing secrets of naval intelligence in World War II, from the files of Rear Admiral Ellis M. Zacharias. Narrator: Bruce Gordon.

Behind the Badge: see A Killing Affair

The Beiderbecke Affair (GB 1985 6 x 50m). Amiable thriller involving jazz-loving hero, mysterious lot of Bix Beiderbecke records and mildly surrealist plunges into cubland (i.e. meeting place of Cubs, or junior Boy Scouts) as well as clubland; all set in north-eastern England. With James Bolam, Barbara Flynn, Dudley Sutton, Terence Rigby, Colin Blakely, Dominic Jephcot. Written by Alan Plater, produced by Anne W. Gibbons, for YTV.   PP

Being Normal (GB 1983 85m). Case-history play which rose considerably above the limits of a case-history to present the unharrowing but very worrying problem of the child who doesn't grow. Sympathetically written by Brian Phelan, directed by Pete Smith; with Anna Carteret, David Suchet; produced by Alan Shallcross, for BBC.   PP

Bel Geddes, Barbara (1922–   ). American leading actress, daughter of stage designer Norman Bel Geddes. In a few films between the late forties and the mid fifties, she only guested on TV until 1978, when she landed the mother role in DALLAS and won an Emmy for it in 1980.

Belafonte, Harry (1927–   ). Eminent black American ballad singer who had a sporadic film career from the mid-fifties. TV achievements include an Emmy in 1960 for *Tonight with Belafonte*.

Believe It or Not
aka: *Ripley's Believe It or Not*
US 1982–5 approx. 85 x 50m colour
Columbia/Rastar/Ripley International
Jack Palance introduces a magazine show of the bizarre and the unexplained.
A television extension of the long-lived newspaper strip, cheaply thrown together and often risibly enacted.
producers Jack Haley Jnr, Jack Kauffman
'Through scientific investigation and our own curiosity, oddities that once mystified us have now become more understandable, more human. The odd, the alien, the unbelievable are finally being seen for what they are, keys to increased knowledge about ourselves and the world around us.' – narration
'All oddities in the program have been authenticated by "Ripley's Believe It or Not!" board of directors.' – standard credit

The Bell * (GB 1982 4 × 55m). One of Iris Murdoch's more readable novels dramatized by Reg Gadney to make a gripping religio-erotic intrigue set in a convent of today with a lay vegetarian community attached. 'The mingled scents of sex, repression, summertime, stagnant waters, orangeade and cant,' I wrote at the time, 'are wafted headily from the screen.' With Ian Holm, Tessa Peake-Jones. Directed by Barry Davis. Produced by Jonathan Powell, for BBC.   PP

Bell, David (1936–   ). British light entertainment producer who has successfully handled Danny La Rue, Stanley Baxter, Bruce Forsyth and Benny Hill.

The Bell Telephone Hour. A splendid example of enlightened sponsorship, this show was a leading provider of light culture – ballet, opera, music – to American radio and television for nearly 40 years. Its years as a weekly TV offering were 1959–68, and in 1963 it won an Emmy as best musical programme. In 1976, to celebrate the centenary of the telephone, a superb variety special, *Jubilee*, was mounted by Gary Smith and Dwight Hemion; Bing Crosby and Liza Minnelli introduced many famous stars.

Bell, Tom (1933–   ). Cherokee-profiled British leading actor with long and honourable record in TV from *A Night Out* (1960) and other Armchair Theatre hits to series *Out* and *Holocaust* (both 1978) and, most recently, *The Detective*, 1985.   PP

Bellamy, David (1933–   ). British botanist and expert on effluents whose genial personality and bizarre diction have made him a favourite television pundit. *Life in Our Sea, Bellamy's Britain*, BOTANIC MAN and (as an explorer apparently scaled down to insect size), *Bellamy's Backyard Safari* (1981) and *Bellamy's Seaside Safari* (1985). To America for *Bellamy's New World*, 1983.   PP

Bellamy, Earl (1917–   ). American director who began in Universal programmers in the fifties and despite much TV has never made an individual mark. His credits range from *Alfred Hitchcock Presents* to *Starsky and Hutch*.

Bellamy, Ralph (1904–   ). Veteran American character actor who played second leads in Hollywood from the early thirties, became a stage star, and remains in demand for TV guest spots. Series include *Man Against Crime, The Eleventh Hour, The Most Deadly Game, The Survivors, Hunter, Wheels*. TV movies: *Wings of Fire, The*

Immortal, Something Evil, Search for the Gods, Murder on Flight 502, Return to Earth, The Boy in the Plastic Bubble, Once an Eagle, The Moneychangers, Testimony of Two Men, Wheels, The Clone Master, Billion Dollar Threat, Condominium, The Winds of War (as FDR), *The Fourth Wise Man, Space*, etc.

Bellamy's Backyard Safari * (GB 1981).
Four half-hour films in which naturalist David Bellamy is 'shrunk' by special effects to a height of 5 millimetres so that he can reveal the secrets of plants and insects in the domestic garden. Ingenious and quite successful. Directed by Paul Kriwaczek; produced by Mike Weatherley; for BBC.

Bellaver, Harry (1905–). American character actor who had considerable success in the early sixties as 'third banana' in *Naked City*. Subsequent appearances sparse but include a TV movie, *Murder in Music City*.

The Belle of Amherst
US 1976 78m colour VTR
PBS/Dome/Creative Image (Mike Merrick, Don Gregory)
A one-woman performance by Julie Harris of the life of Emily Dickinson as seen through her poems and letters.
w William Luce *d* Charles S. Dubin *pd* H. R. Poindexter

'How she became the west's most wanted – and most desired – woman!'
Belle Starr
US 1980 96m colour TVM
CBS/Hanna Barbera/Entheos (Doug Chapin)
The last days in 1889 of the famous woman outlaw.
Feminist version of an old warhorse; good-looking but dramatically empty.
w James Lee Barrett *d* John A. Alonzo *ph* John A. Alonzo *m* Dana Kaproff
Elizabeth Montgomery, Cliff Potts, Michael Cavanaugh, Jesse Vint, Fred Ward, Alan Vint, Geoffrey Lewis

Belushi, John (1949–82). Rotund American low comedian who developed from a college satirist to a star of Hollywood lampoons. A mainstay of NBC's *Saturday Night Live* 1975–9.

Ben Casey *
US 1960–5 153 × 50m bw
ABC/Bing Crosby Productions (James E. Moser)
Working title: *The Medical Man*

Cases of a tough, intense young doctor on the staff of a big hospital.
A downbeat show which succeeded partly because of its air of startling realism, and partly from the appeal of its young and old leads.
cr James Moser
VINCE EDWARDS, SAM JAFFE, Bettye Ackerman
'It has become popular because so many like to hear others talk about their operations.' – Don Miller
'It accurately captures the feeling of sleepless intensity in a metropolitan hospital.' – *Time*

Ben Hall
GB–Australia 1975 13 × 50m colour (VTR)
BBC–ABC
Stories of an Australian outlaw.
Modest, forgettable action series.
p Neil McCallum
Jon Finch, John Castle

Ben Spray **. A TV play by Peter Nichols about a sacked schoolteacher who goes to a hilarious party with a girl he has just met. In the *Lucky Jim* tradition. Originally produced by Granada in 1961 (Ian Hendry); revived by LWT in 1972, with John Alderton. In between came a sequel, *Ben Again*, with Dinsdale Landen as Ben (1963).

Benaderet, Bea (1906–68). American TV comedienne, the perfect neighbour for Gracie Allen in many seasons of *The Burns and Allen Show*; also in *Peter Loves Mary, Beverly Hillbillies* and later the star of her own *Petticoat Junction*.

Bendix, William (1906–64). American 'tough guy' comedy character actor. The first radio star of THE LIFE OF RILEY, he also played the role on TV between 1953 and 1958. Also on TV in *Overland Trail*.

Benedict, Dirk (1944–) (D. Niewoehner). American leading man of series *Chopper One, Battlestar Galactica*. TV movies: *Journey from Darkness, Cruise into Terror*.

Benjamin Franklin (US 1974). Four 75-minute tape documentaries by Glenn Jordan won an Emmy. Franklin was played at various stages by five different actors: Beau Bridges, Richard Widmark, Eddie Albert, Lloyd Bridges and Melvyn Douglas.

Benjamin, Richard (1938–). American leading comedy actor. Main contribution to television: series *He and She, Quark*.

✻ **Bennett, Alan** (1934–). British wit and writer who emerged from the *Beyond the Fringe* revue quartet to become an occasional performer but a sensitive TV playwright, with a nose for everyday fortitude and an ear for the richness of everyday speech, especially among fellow-northerners.

1965	*My Father Knew Lloyd George* BBC	
1966–7	*On the Margin* (comedy series, also starred)	BBC
1972	*A Day Out*	BBC
1975	*Sunset Across the Bay*	BBC
	A Little Outing	BBC
1978	*A Visit from Miss Prothero*	BBC
	Me – I'm Afraid of Virginia Woolf	LWT
	Doris and Doreen	LWT
1979	*The Old Crowd*	LWT
	Afternoon Off	LWT
	One Fine Day	LWT
	All Day On the Sands	LWT
1982	OBJECTS OF AFFECTION, comprising six plays: *Our Winnie, A Woman of No Importance, Rolling Home, Marks, Say Something Happened, Intensive Care*	BBC
1983	*An Englishman Abroad*	BBC
1986	*The Insurance Man*	BBC

As a performer in *The Drinking Party* (1965), BBC satirical shows 1964–6, *Alice in Wonderland* (1966), *The Merry Wives of Windsor* in the BBC Shakespeare. Narrator of nostalgic railway item for Yorkshire Television, 1985, and *Man and Music*, 1986. On *South Bank Show* 1979 talking about recent plays; subject of full assessment, same show 1984. PP

Bennett, Cyril (1929–76). Influential British current affairs producer and executive. Made Rediffusion's *This Week* the best programme of its kind 1960–3. Associated with David Frost in mid-sixties, programme controller of LWT from 1970. PP

Bennett, Harve (1930–) (Harvey Fischman). American series producer who concocted *Six Million Dollar Man, Bionic Woman* and *The Powers of Matthew Starr.*

Bennett, Harold (1899–1981). British character actor who came to television as an elderly man and is best remembered as 'young Mr Grace', frail but game, in *Are You Being Served?*

Bennett, Hywel (1944–). British character juvenile of the sixties. He had great success in such films as *The Family Way* and *The Virgin Soldiers*, but his youthful appearance did not help him get more mature roles. He re-emerged in the late seventies as a TV star of consequence, both in the series SHELLEY and as the murderous doctor of MALICE AFORETHOUGHT.

Bennett, John (1928–). Dark-eyed, lithe British character actor whose only series as star was an East End piece called *Honey Lane* in the early sixties; he is however familiar as cop or crook in hundreds of series episodes.

Bennett, Lennie (1939–) (Michael Berry). British comedian, the suaver half of Lennie and Jerry (Stevens). Formerly a Blackpool journalist. From 1982 host of *Punchlines*.

Bennett, Tony (1926–) (Angelo Benedetto). American concert singer, discovered in 1949 by Bob Hope. Many TV guest appearances; famous for theme song, 'I Left My Heart in San Francisco'.

Benny and Barney: Las Vegas Undercover
US 1977 74m colour TVM
NBC/Universal (Glen A. Larson)

Adventures of two Las Vegas car cops. Slick pilot which surprisingly didn't sell.

w Glen A. Larson *d* Ron Satlof

Terry Kiser, Timothy Thomerson, Jack Colvin, Jane Seymour, Jack Cassidy, Hugh O'Brian, George Gobel, Dick Gautier

The Benny Hill Show. An occasional one-hour show from Thames TV in which the star writes and performs all his own material, usually consisting of very old jokes turned into doggerel song, impressions of celebrities, and moderately blue sketches. Over the years his chief aides have been Bob Todd and Patricia Hayes, with John Robins as most frequent director. BAFTA award 1971, best light entertainment.

Typical jokes:
– I can give tit for tat.
– In that case, tat.

– I've got the face of a sixteen-year-old
– Give it back, it's getting wrinkles.

✻ **Benny, Jack** (1894–1974) (Benjamin Kubelsky). American stand-up comedian who made international trademarks of his meanness and his 'slow burn'. Admired everywhere, he had a reasonably distinguished film career but was if anything even more distinguished in radio and TV, both in situation comedy and musical specials, and became a national monument, winning Emmys in 1957 and 1958.

JACK BENNY got to be eighty, but his on-screen character never passed 39. Though he seldom cracked a joke, his warm humour was deeply missed.

Benson
US 1979 approx. 154 x 25m colour
ABC/Columbia/Witt–Thomas–Harris

A sassy butler goes to work for an incompetent governor.
Mildly political comedy of insult, a showcase for one of the stars of *Soap*.

cr Susan Harris

Robert Guillaume, James Noble, Inga Swenson, Caroline McWilliams

Benson, George (1943–). American singer and guitarist, in occasional specials.

Benson, Graham (1946–). British producer, there via an unusual route as floor manager and then unit manager. BBC *Première* seasons 1976–8, *Fox* for Euston Films, 1979. Since 1982: *Outside Edge*, RED MONARCH, *Meantime*, *Charlie* and three films for BBC2 including *Slip-Up* (1986). PP

Benson, Hugh (1917–). American producer with experience dating back to World War II and *The Ed Sullivan Show*. Recently: *Contract on Cherry Street*, *A Fire in the Sky*, *Goldie and the Boxer*, *The Dream Merchants*, *Goliath Awaits*, *The Blue and the Gray*, *The Master of Ballantrae*, *Hart to Hart*, *Anna Karenina*.

Benson, Robby (1955–) (Robert Segal). Teenage American actor who matured impressively. TV movies include *Remember When*, *All the Kind Strangers*, *The Virginia Hill Story*, DEATH BE NOT PROUD, *The Death of Richie*, *Two of a Kind*, *California Girls*, *Tough Cookies*

Bentine, Michael (1922–). Anglo-Peruvian comedian who has purveyed zany nonsense for 30 years in recurring series such as *The Goon Show*, *It's a Square World* and *Potty Time*.

Bentley, John (1916–). Stalwart British leading man of the fifties, of the strong silent type. Little TV between *African Patrol* in the fifties and *Crossroads* in the seventies.

Berenger, Tom (1950–). Tough young American leading man in the John Garfield/Paul Newman mould. TV movies: *Johnny We Hardly Knew Ye*, *Flesh and Blood*.

Berg, Gertrude (1899–1966) (Gertrude Edelstein). Amply proportioned American character actress famous as Molly in THE GOLDBERGS, which began on radio in the forties and on TV in various forms up to 1956. There was also a movie version in 1951. See also *Mrs G. Goes to College*. Emmy 1950: best actress.

Bergen, Edgar (1903–79). American ventriloquist who introduced Charlie McCarthy and Mortimer Snerd to an unsuspecting world. Many TV appearances, latterly as mild-mannered character actor.

Bergen, Polly (1930–) (Nellie Bergen). American leading lady of a few fifties films; retired to head cosmetics firm. Occasionally on TV: Emmy 1957 for best performance as *Helen Morgan*. Other appearances include *Death Cruise*, *Million Dollar Face*, *Born Beautiful*, *The Winds of War*, *Velvet*. TV movie: *Kiss of Gold*.

Bergerac
GB 1981 13 × 50m colour
BBC (Robert Banks Stewart)

Cases of a detective in the Channel Isles. Tepid and uninvolving Sunday night mysteries, just about saved by the unfamiliar location but not helped by a bland leading man.

cr Robert Banks Stewart

John Nettles, Terence Alexander

Bergman, Ingmar (1918–). Swedish writer-director always attracted by television, though some of his television works, notably *Fanny and Alexander*, have first been released abroad in abbreviated feature-film versions. Directed five plays on Swedish Television (SRT) in its early days, beginning with an adaptation from his namesake Hjalmar Bergman, *Mr Sleeman is Coming*, 1957. Main credits since:

1969 *The Rite* (*Riten*, in US *The Ritual*)
1970 *The Farö Document* (*Farö-dokument*)
     The Lie (*Reservatet*), *The Largest Theatre in the World*
1973 *Six Scenes from a Marriage* (*Scener ur ätt aktenskap*)
1975 *The Magic Flute* (*Trollflöjten*)
1976 *Face to Face* (*Ansikte mot ansikte*)
1979 *Farö-dokument 1979*
1983 *Fanny and Alexander* (*Fanny och Alexander*)
     After the Rehearsal (*Efter repetitionen*)   PP

Bergman, Ingrid (1915–84). Swedish film star with a distinguished Hollywood career. Occasional TV includes THE TURN OF THE SCREW (Emmy 1960), *24 Hours in the Life of a Woman*, *A Woman Called Golda* (Emmy 1982). Tribute, *Ingrid*, narrated by Sir John Gielgud 1984. A TV movie of her life appeared in 1986.

Berle, Milton (1908–) (Mendel Berlinger). Brash, disarming American vaudevillian who never quite managed movie fame but in the fifties became Mr Television and indulged in every known form of slapstick and schmaltz. His later career was sketchy but he never gave up guest appearances. Emmy 1949: outstanding kinescope personality. TV movies: *Evil Roy Slade*, *Seven In Darkness*, *The Legend of Valentino*. 1981: compering *Magic of the Stars*.

Berlin Affair
US 1970 97m colour TVM
Universal (E. Jack Neuman, Paul Donnelly)
A professional killer loses his value when he falls in love.
Complex, rather unpleasant international suspenser.

w Peter Penduik, E. Jack Neumann *d* David Lowell Rich

Darren McGavin, Fritz Weaver, Brian Kelly, Claude Dauphin, Pascale Petit

Berlin Alexanderplatz (W. Germany/Italy 1984; 14 x 60m). Curious hypnotic saga of released convict among the fleshpots of Berlin on the eve of the Nazi era. With Günter Lamprecht, Hanna Schygulla, Barbara Sukowa; written and directed by Rainer Werner Fassbinder for Bavarian Atelier/RAI/WDR.   PP

Berlin, Tunnel 21
US 1981 142m colour TVM
CBS/Filmways (Gerald W. Abrams, Bruce J. Salan)
In 1961, a US army lieutenant and his East German girlfriend are separated by the wall.
Predictable, sluggish melodrama.

w John Gay, *novel* Donald Linquist *d* Richard Michaels *ph* Igor Luther

Richard Thomas, Horst Buchholz, Jose Ferrer, Kenneth Griffith

Berman, Monty (1913–). See Baker, Robert S.

Berman, Shelley (1924–). American nightclub comedian and monologuist who mirrors life's frustrations.

The Bermuda Depths
US 1978 96m colour TVM
ABC/Rankin–Bass
In the Bermuda Triangle, scientists are threatened by a prehistoric sea creature.
Tolerable taradiddle.

w William Overgard *d* Tom Kotani *ph* Jeri Sopanen *m* Maury Laws

Burl Ives, Connie Sellecca, Leigh McCloskey, Carl Weathers

Bernardi, Herschel (1923–). American character actor, usually in sympathetic but lugubrious ethnic roles; a Broadway hit as star of *Fiddler on the Roof*. TV series: *Peter Gunn*, *Arnie*. TV movies: *But I Don't Want to Get Married*, *No Place to Run*, *Sandcastles*, *Seventh Avenue*, etc.

Bernette, Sheila (1941–). Perky, diminutive British comedienne, usually in supporting roles. Once a regular on *The Black and White Minstrel Show* and *Frost Over England*.

Berns, Seymour (1914–82). American executive producer and ideas man, latterly with Four Star and Columbia; formerly in radio and director of a wide range of shows.

Bernstein, Elmer (1922–). American composer. TV scores include *Hollywood the Golden Years*, *The Making of the President* (Emmy 1963), *Four Days in November*,

Guyana Tragedy, Moviola. Series: *Julia, Owen Marshall, The Rookies*, etc.

❀   **Bernstein, Leonard** (1918–). American orchestral conductor whose television concerts in the fifties did much to introduce young people to classical music. 'He turned the whole country into his classroom.' – Cleveland Amory.

❀ **Bernstein, Sidney** (Lord Bernstein) (1899–). British showman, film producer and tycoon who with his brother Cecil founded Granada Television and gave it its unique stamp. It could be more public spirited than any public service broadcasting, and at the same time more commercially astute than any commercial station. It could be stingy in small matters, lavish in large, and though both Bernsteins and their senior lieutenants were Londoners, they identified the company wholly with their allotted North of England (later North West) franchise. Bernstein himself scarcely ever appeared on the screen until at the age of 85 he commented on the sources of Granada's concentration camp programme A PAINFUL REMINDER. Life peerage, 1969.   PP
† Though Cecil (1905–81) was often thought of only as 'the other Bernstein', an administrator, he was in fact closely involved in programming in the early days, especially light entertainment. It was at Cecil's instigation that *The Army Game* and its successor *Bootsie and Snudge* were evolved.

'Where dreams come true – for a price!'
Berrenger's
US 1985 13 × 50m colour
Lorimar (Diana Gould)
Life in the executive suite of a New York department store.
Desperate attempt at a soap opera, lacking a single likeable character.
cr Diana Gould
Sam Wanamaker, Jeff Conaway, Jonelle Allen, Art Hindle, Yvette Mimieux, Ben Murphy, Claudia Christian, Melody Ashton, Anita Morris

Berry, Ken (*c* 1929–). American comic actor of the meek and mild type. Series include *F Troop, Mayberry RFD*. TV movies: *Wake Me When the War Is Over, The Reluctant Heroes, Every Man Needs One, Letters from Three Lovers*, etc.

Bert D'Angelo, Superstar
US 1976 13 × 50m colour
ABC/Quinn Martin (Mort Fine)
Clumsily titled and generally unhappy spin-off from *Streets of San Francisco*, with Paul Sorvino as a belligerent New York cop on loan-out.
The spin-off episode generated good tension between him and the regulars, but in the series he badly needed someone to spark with.
m Paul Williams

Beryl's Lot (GB 1973–6). Fitfully scheduled working-class series from Yorkshire TV, varying from 25 to 50 minutes, about a milkman's wife trying to better herself; with Carmel McSharry.

Bessell, Ted (1935–). American general purpose actor of extrovert types. Series include *That Girl, The Ted Bessell Show, Good Time Harry*. TV movies: *Two on a Bench, Your Money or Your Wife, Breaking Up Is Hard to Do, Scream Pretty Peggy, What Are Best Friends For?*

The Best Christmas Pageant Ever
US 1984 50m colour
Comworld/Schaefer–Karpf (George
  Schaefer)
Six mischievous children from a welfare family make a hit of the church Nativity pageant.
Moderately appealing mini-special.
w Barbara Robinson from her book
d George Schaefer *ph* Edward R. Brown
m John Elizalde
Loretta Swit, Jackson Davies, Janet Wright, Megan Hunt

'Her secret could cost her everything she loves!'
Best Kept Secrets
US 1984 96m colour TVM
ABC Circle (David Manson)
A policeman's wife discovers that she and her friends are the subjects of secret security files which are being used for political blackmail.
Media-conscious 'high impact television', unlikely to cause much fuss outside America.
w April Smith *d* Jerrold Freedman
Patty Duke Astin, Frederic Forrest, Meg Foster, Peter Coyote, Albert Salmi

The Best Little Girl in the World *
US 1983 96m colour TVM
Metromedia/Aaron Spelling (Lynn Loring)

A teenage girl embarrassed and confused by her budding adulthood develops anorexia nervosa.
Predictable but quite moving case-history.
w David Moessinger, *novel* by Stephen Levenkron *d* Sam O'Steen
Charles Durning, Eva Marie Saint, Jennifer Jason Leigh, Lisa Pelikan, Jason Miller

The Best of Families *
US 1977 8 × 50m colour (VTR)
PBS/Children's Television Workshop (Gareth Davies)
In New York between 1880 and 1900, the fortunes of three families, of very different social backgrounds, intermingle.
Social history rather than drama, this stylish production was surprisingly badly received by the critics.
cr Naomi Foner *w* Corinne Jacker and others
William Prince, Milo O'Shea, Guy Boyd, Victor Garber, William Hart

Best of Friends
US 1984 6 x 50m colour
Lorimar (Philip Capice)
Tribulations of two neighbouring families who help each other out in time of trouble . . . of which in this series there is plenty.
cr Carol Sobieski
Karen Carlson, Tom Mason, Janet Eilber, Michael Murphy, John McLiam

The Best of Groucho: see You Bet Your Life

Best of the West (US 1981). New half-hour series for the American 1981 season, a would-be comedy about the adventures of a tenderfoot and his family in the old west. With Joel Higgins, Carlene Watkins, Tom Ewell; created by Earl Pomerantz; for Weinburger–Daniels/Paramount/ABC.

The Best Place To Be
US 1979 2 × 96m colour TVM
ABC/Ross Hunter
A well-heeled widow gets used to her new life and ceases to rely on her family.
Awful slushy drama, mainly of interest to readers of *House and Garden*.
w Stanford Whitford, *novel* Helen Van Slyke *d* David Miller *ph* Terry K. Meade *m* Henry Mancini
Donna Reed, Efrem Zimbalist Jnr, Betty White, John Phillip Law, Stephanie Zimbalist, Madlyn Rhue, Timothy Hutton, Mildred Dunnock, Lloyd Bochner, Leon Ames
'All that's missing is a lace border for the TV screen.' – *Daily Variety*

The Best Play of . . .
GB 1976–8 6 × (variable) m colour
Granada (Laurence Olivier, Derek Granger)
As befitting a project with Olivier at its head, the idea was unlimited – to pick a best play from any, perhaps every, year this century and give it sumptuous new production. In the event only half a dozen were realized, of which the most publicized and most grandiose was also the turkey: Tennessee Williams's *Cat on a Hot Tin Roof* with Natalie Wood and Robert Wagner.
The most interesting choice was that of a television play, Harold Pinter's *The Collection*, to represent 1960 (should have been 1961, but never mind). With Olivier and Malcolm MacDowell taking the parts originally played by Griffith Jones and John Ronane, the homosexual current in the plot was all but reversed – a revealing glimpse of the way casting and direction (here Michael Apted) can modulate a script. A local classic, *Hindle Wakes*, made a good choice for 1912 with Olivier himself sharing the direction with June Howson. Lady Olivier (Joan Plowright) starred in James Bridie's *Daphne Laureola* for 1949 and Eduardo de Filippo's *Saturday, Sunday, Monday* for 1973. *Come Back, Little Sheba* by William Inge completed the six.
PP

Best Sellers. Umbrella title devised by Universal in 1976 to cover the novelizations, in various shapes and sizes, which followed *Rich Man, Poor Man*. They were *Captains and the Kings*, *Once an Eagle*, *The Rhinemann Exchange*, *Seventh Avenue*, *79 Park Avenue*, *Aspen*, *Wheels*, *The Dark Secret of Harvest Home*, *Brave New World* and *Women in White* and all are noted separately in this volume.
A separate series, commissioned for syndicated stations, was called *Operation Prime Time*, and the first four novels under this heading were *Testimony of Two Men*, *The Bastard*, *Evening in Byzantium* and *The Immigrants*.
In Britain the title was used in 1967–8 for a Rediffusion series about best-selling novelists, e.g. Paul Johnson on Trollope.

The Best Times
US 1985 6 x 50m colour
ABC/Lorimar (Michele Gallery)
A sixteen-year-old high school student finds life difficult when her divorced mother becomes her teacher.
Yucky series about modern teenage pangs; luckily it didn't last long.
Beth Ehlers, Janet Eilber, Jim Metzler, Liane Curtis, Darren Dalton

Bethune, Zina (1950–). American leading lady who starred in *The Nurses*, then moved over to daily soap opera.

Betjeman, Sir John (1907–84). British Poet Laureate and inimitable television performer–narrator, sometimes furnishing a commentary in verse. Favourite subjects: topography of the British Isles, architecture, churches, railways. In 1983 TIME WITH BETJEMAN (7 × 50m) reviewed the now wheelchair-bound poet's television output together with chats with old friends and companionable interrogation by producer Jonathan Stedall. BBC.

1955–6	*Discovering Britain*: 26 × 5m Shell soft-sell commercials for ITV, from Random Films (Peter Mills). All the rest for BBC
1959–68	*Monitor* contributions including own poems, chat with Philip Larkin, Festival Sites, cinemas
1960–67	*ABC of Churches* in *Meeting Point* religious magazine programme
1962	*John Betjeman Goes by Train*
1963	*Let's Imagine*: Branch-line railways
1964	*One Man's Country*: Cornwall
1965	*Pity About the Abbey*: BBC Wednesday Play, written by Betjeman with Stewart Farrar
1966	*Pride of Place*: Hardwick Hall, with Arthur Negus *Journey to Bethlehem*
1968	*Marble Arch to Edgware Contrasts*: Tennyson – A Beginning and an End
1969	*Bird's Eye View: An Englishman's Home* and *Beside the Seaside*
1970	*Four with Betjeman*: four programmes on Victorian architects *Look, Stranger*: Ellan Vannin
1971	*That Well-known Store in Knightsbridge*: Harrods
1972	*Betjeman's Australia*: four-part travelogue *Thank God It's Sunday*: two programmes
1973	METROLAND, which see
1974	*A Passion for Churches*
1976	*Vicar of this Parish*: Kilvert *Summoned by Bells*
1977	*The Queen's Realm Betjeman's Belfast*
1979	*Betjeman's Dublin* PP

The Betrayal
aka: *The Companion*
US 1974 74m colour TVM
Metromedia

A girl takes a job as companion to a lonely widow and sets her up as a robbery victim. Fairly well characterized suspenser which runs out of steam.

w James Miller d Gordon Hessler

Amanda Blake, Tisha Sterling, Dick Haymes, Sam Groom

Betrayal
US 1978 96m colour TVM
NBC/EMI/Roger Gimbel

A lesbian is seduced by her therapist under the guise of sex therapy, and sues him. Silly sex drama allegedly based on a real case. It would be interesting to know how, if the real heroine was also a typist, she paid her medico-legal bills.

w Jerrold Friedman, Joanna Crawford, *novel* Lucy Freeman and Julie Roy d Paul Wendkos ph Gayne Rescher m Paul Chihara

Lesley Ann Warren, Rip Torn, Richard Masur, Ron Silver, John Hillerman, Peggy Ann Garner

'The moment of triumph seems small indeed for all the misery the girl (and the audience) has endured.' – *Daily Variety*

Bette Midler – Ole Red Hair Is Back *
US 1977 50m colour VTR
NBC/Divine Television/Smith–Hemion

A spirited display of the star's bizarre talents, and the show which gained her a wider audience.

w various d Dwight Hemion *guests* Dustin Hoffman, Emmett Kelly

Better Late Than Never *
US 1980 96m colour TVM
NBC/Ten–Four (Bob Birnbaum)

Residents of a retirement home band together to assert their dignity and make something of their lives. Fairly successful comedy of elderly rebels, full of excellent performances.

w John Carpenter, Greg Strangis d Richard Crenna ph Ronald Browne m Charles Fox

Harold Gould, Strother Martin, Tyne Daly, Marjorie Bennett, Victor Buono, George Gobel, Lou Jacobi, Jeanette Nolan, Larry Storch, Donald Pleasence, Harry Morgan

Better Luck Next Time **
GB 1964 50m bw

Absolutely delightful British–American–

Canadian attempt at rueful New York comedy, about a professional co-respondent (Zhora Lampert, sad, slavonic, outstandingly funny) and her client, played by Michael Bryant. Written by Stanley Mann and directed by Silvio Narrizano for ATV's *Studio 64* drama experiment, which teamed writer and director to hatch a play between them.   PP

The Betty Hutton Show: see Goldie

The Betty White Show *
US 1977 13 × 25m colour
CBS/MTM
A middle-aged TV actress makes a police woman series with her ex-husband as producer.
Wisecracking comedy, smartly performed; but the public maintained its tradition of not liking backstage shows.
Betty White, John Hillerman
† The star had had a comedy variety series of the same title in 1958.

Between Friends
US 1983 96m colour TVM
HBO/Robert Cooper (Jonathan Estrin, Shelley List)
Two divorcees develop a friendship in their search for a man.
Slow-starting drama which rambles all the way through. Shot on location in Toronto.
w Jonathan Estrin, Shelley List, *novel Nobody Makes me Cry* by Shelley List *d* Lou Antonio *ph* Francois Protat *m* James Horner
Elizabeth Taylor, Carol Burnett, Barbara Rush, Henry Ramer

'How would you feel if you woke up one day and found 20 years of your life had vanished?'
Between the Darkness and the Dawn
US 1985 96m colour TVM
A woman recovers after a long coma and sets about enjoying the teenage life she didn't have.
Novelty melodrama which soon ceases to amuse
Elizabeth Montgomery, Karen Grassle, Dorothy McGuire, James Naughton

Between the Wars
US 1978 16 × 25m colour (VTR)
Alan Landsburg/Mobil
A documentary survey of diplomacy and politics between 1918 and 1938.
Fairly absorbing collage of old newsreels, but told entirely from the American point of view.
w Anthony Potter *host* Eric Sevareid

'Is blood thicker than water?'
Between Two Brothers
US 1981 96m colour TVM
Turman/Foster (Bill Finnegan)
An ambitious young politico finds that his cheerfully wild brother is involved in a series of burglaries.
Intense but not very interesting melodrama.
w Mike Robe *d* Robert Lewis
Michael Brandon, Pat Harrington, Helen Shaver, Brad Savage

Betz, Carl (1920–78). Solid American leading man of the fifties and sixties, best known for *The Donna Reed Show* and *Judd for the Defense*.

Beulah *
US 1950–3 c 100 × 25m bw
ABC
Trials and tribulations of a family with a sassy black cook.
Cheerful stereotyped comedy about a character who originated on radio's *Fibber McGee*. Many black actors as guest stars.
cr Marlin Hurt
ETHEL WATERS (later LOUISE BEAVERS), Percy Harris (later Dooley Wilson), William Post Jnr (later David Bruce), Ginger Jones (later Jane Frazee), Butterfly McQueen

Beulah Land
US 1980 3 × 96m colour
NBC/Columbia/David Gerber
A girl from Savannah marries a dull Georgia landowner because she covets his plantation.
Ingenuous revamp of elements from *Gone with the Wind*. Well enough made, but not so that you'd care.
w Jacques Meunier, *novels* Lonnie Coleman *d* Virgil Vogel, Harry Falk *ph* Andrew Jackson *m* Allyn Ferguson *ad* Edward Carfagno
Lesley Ann Warren, Michael Sarrazin, Meredith Baxter Birney, Eddie Albert, Hope Lange, Paul Rudd, Dorian Harewood, Paul Shenar, Martha Scott, Jenny Agutter, Allyn Ann McLerie
'Mush, it used to be called, and Sarah wades into it with a sure foot.' – *Daily Variety*
† The mini-series was beset by protests before it aired because of its supposedly low depiction of blacks.

The Beverly Hillbillies **
US 1962–70 212 × 25m 106 bw, 106 colour
CBS/Filmways (AL SIMON)

The Clampetts strike oil and move into Beverly Hills.

A hokey idea which surprised everyone by working at full steam for several years before the strain began to show: the Clampetts became America's favourite family.

cr PAUL HENNING *m* LESTER FLATT and EARL SCRUGGS

BUDDY EBSEN, IRENE RYAN (as Daisy Moses/Granny), DONNA DOUGLAS, MAX BAER JNR, RAYMOND BAILEY, NANCY KULP

† In 1981 Al Simon and Paul Henning produced *The Return of the Beverly Hillbillies*, with Imogene Coca standing in for the late Irene Ryan.

Beverly Hills Cowgirl Blues
US 1985 96m colour TVM
CBS/Leonard Goldberg

A lady cop from Laramie seeks killers in Beverly Hills.

A tired contraption which wears out its welcome early on.

w Rick Husky   *d* Corey Allen   *ph* Harry May   *m* Mark Snow

James Brolin, Lisa Hartman, David Hemmings, Irena Ferris, Michael C. Gwynne

'Stunningly badly written, it stumbles from cliché to triteness with ingenious dependability.' – *Daily Variety*

Bevin Boys (GB 1983). Useful documentary on the wartime direction of young men to the coal mines instead of the armed forces, with testimony from ordinary conscripts as well as such famous former Bevin Boys as Jimmy Savile and Brian Rix. Produced by Michael Partington, for Tyne-Tees.   PP

Bewes, Rodney (1937–). British light comic actor, familiar as one of *The Likely Lads*. Also played solo in *Dear Mother, Love Albert*.

Bewitched *
US 1964–71 252 × 25m colour
ABC/Columbia (Harry Ackerman/Bill Asher)

An attractive witch gets married and has a family, but is unable to resist the temptation to turn the magic on by twitching her nose.

Tolerable and popular fantasy comedy enlivened by the number of older stars who popped in occasionally as magical uncles and aunts.

cr William Dozier, Harry Ackerman   *m* Harry Sukman

ELIZABETH MONTGOMERY, Dick York (five seasons), Dick Sargent (thereafter), Agnes Moorehead, Maurice Evans, Marion Lorne, George Tobias

† When the star occasionally played her look-alike cousin Serena, she billed herself as Pandora Sparks.

Beyond the Bermuda Triangle
US 1975 74m colour TVM
Playboy (Ron Roth)

Sequel to *Satan's Triangle*: a businessman searches for friends who have disappeared in the fatal area.

Open-air melodramatic nonsense: quite watchable.

w Charles A. McDaniel   *d* William A. Graham

Fred MacMurray, Sam Groom, Donna Mills, Suzanne Reed

Beyond Westworld
US 1978 13 x 50m colour

A failed attempt to cash in on the success of the film *Westworld*, about a robot resort where your dreams can come true if nothing goes wrong. Any adult elements in the concept were replaced by Saturday morning space fiction. MGM.

Biberman, Abner (1909–77). American small-part actor who played Caribbean villains in many movies; later became a TV director of such series as *Wagon Train*, *Twilight Zone* and *The Virginian*.

Bicycling. The passing of programmes from one station to another without their returning to the distributor for checking.

Biff Baker USA
US 1953 26 × 25m bw
CBS/Universal

An American couple travels behind the Iron Curtain.

Ingenuous cold war thick-ear.

Alan Hale Jnr, Randy Stewart

Big Blue Marble *. American children's series showing how experience can be enjoyably enlarged; basically a magazine format with *Sesame Street* trimmings. Created and produced by Henry Fownes; musical director Norman Paris; animation by Ron Campbell; produced weekly from 1974 for the ITT Corporation.

Big Bob Johnson and His Fantastic Speed Circus
US 1977 96m colour TVM
NBC/Paramount/Playboy (Joseph Gantman)

A daredevil truck driver takes part in a long-distance race.

Empty-headed action extravaganza presaging the popularity of *The Dukes of Hazzard.*

w Bob Comfort, Rick Kellard d Jack Starrett ph Robert Jessup m Mark Snow

Charles Napier, Maud Adams, Constance Forslund, Robert Stoneman, William Daniels, Rick Hurst

'Curiously joyless nonsense.' – *Daily Variety*

Big Breadwinner Hog
GB 1969 8 × 50m bw (VTR)
Granada

An evil young London gangster stops at nothing to get his way.

Tawdry mixture of *Scarface* and *Brighton Rock*, much criticized for its violence.

w/p Robin Chapman

Peter Egan

The Big Client *
GB 1959 50m bw
ABC (Sydney Newman)

One in the *Armchair Theatre* series, a cracking satire set in a small advertising agency; unscrupulous partner intrigues to attract the account of an American company opening up in Britain, to the disapproval – but eventual discomfiture – of straitlaced colleague.

w Malcolm Hulke, Eric Paice d Ted Kotcheff

Ian Bannen, Peter Dyneley, Jack Hedley PP

Big Deal * (GB 1984–5 21 × 50m). Ray Brooks as a compulsive gambler and ever-optimistic chancer in an agreeable low-life series set in *Minder* territory. Sharon Duce was his girl friend, Donald Sumpter a sinister heavy latterly. Created by Geoff McQueen, also written by Gavin Grainger, Max Marquis, Neil Rudyard, etc. Directed by Jeremy Summers, Carol Wiseman, etc. Produced by Terence Williams, for BBC. PP

The Big Eat (GB 1962). Clive Exton comedy about an eating contest, rejected by *Armchair Theatre*, rescued by the BBC. William Kotcheff, who would have directed for ABC, obliged again. You needed an Alka-Seltzer afterwards.   PP

Big Eddie
US 1975 9 × 25m colour
CBS/Deezdemandoze/Persky–Denoff (Hy Averback)

Family problems of the owner of a New York arena.

Forgettable comedy.

cr Bill Persky, Sam Denoff

Sheldon Leonard, Sheree North, Quinn Cummings, Alan Oppenheimer

The Big Flame (GB 1969). Liverpool dockers take over their own docks and run them more efficiently than any hated capitalist. A powerful 'Wouldn't it be marvellous if . . . ' tract by Jim Allen, directed by Ken Loach, produced by Tony Garnett as a BBC *Wednesday Play* and weakened only by crude special pleading in script, casting and performance, with a British judge portrayed like Hitler's vengeance judge Roland Freisler and British troops as Fascist thugs.   PP

Big G: see Empire

Big Hawaii
GB title: *Danger in Paradise*
US 1977 13 × 50m colour
NBC/Filmways (Perry Lafferty)

A wanderer returns to the family's Hawaii ranch to help his ailing father.

Bland, uninteresting series developed from a promising pilot, *Danger in Paradise*. The scenery is all that's worth watching.

cr William Wood

Cliff Potts, John Dehner, Bill Lucking

'A rebel son and his brawling buddy take on all comers in a turbulent drama set against the allure of the islands.' – publicity

Big John
US 1983 50m colour
MGM–UA/Intermedia (Alan Godfrey)

A Georgia sheriff chases the murderer of his son to New York.

Warmed-over pilot for a series which, not surprisingly, wasn't picked up.

cr James Lee Barrett

Dale Robertson, Joey Travolta, Kaaren Lee, Natalie Klinger

Big Mo
US 1978 96m colour TVM
CBS/Frank Ross, Douglas Morrow

Incidents in the careers of two basketball players, Maurice Stokes and Jack Twyman.

Enough said.

w Douglas Morrow *d* Daniel Mann
Bernie Casey, Bo Svenson, Janet McLachlan,
Stephanie Edwards

The Big Rip Off
US 1974 97m colour TVM
A gambling con-man confounds his enemies
and solves a murder.
Slick, fairly entertaining pilot for a *Mystery
Movie* segment (*McCoy*).
w Roland Kibbee, Dean Hargrove *d* Dean
Hargrove
Tony Curtis, Roscoe Lee Browne, Larry
Hagman, John Dehner, Brenda Vaccaro

Big Rose
US 1974 74m colour TVM
TCF
Adventures of a middle-aged lady private
eye.
Not unentertaining for a failed pilot.
w Andy Lewis *d* Paul Krasny
Shelley Winters, Barry Primus, Lonny
Chapman, Peggy Walton, Joan Van Ark

Big Shamus, Little Shamus *
US 1979 13 × 50m colour
CBS/Lorimar (Fred Freiburger)
A divorced hotel detective in Atlantic City is
helped by his smart young son.
Over-sentimental but sharply observed
comedy–drama series which didn't really
have a hope of catching on but was worth the
effort.
cr Tracy Hotchner, Christopher Knopf *m*
Mike Post, Peter Carpenter
Brian Dennehy, Doug McKeon, George
Wyner, Kathryn Lee Scott

The Big Time * (GB 1978–   ). BBC series in
which Esther Rantzen waves her magic wand
and gives village cooks, reverend diarists or
amateur jockeys their chance to try it for real.
So see: *magic wands.*   PP

Big Town
US 1952–7 169 × 25m bw
CBS (later NBC)
Adventures of a crusading magazine editor.
Routine time-filler, syndicated under various
titles including *Heart of the City*, *By-Line
Steve Wilson*, *Headline* and *City Assignment*.
Patrick McVey (later Mark Stevens)

The Big Valley *
US 1965–8 112 × 50m colour
ABC/Four Star
Tales of a California ranching family in the
1870s.

Cleanly made stories, mostly domestic, with
plenty of guest stars.
m George Duning
BARBARA STANWYCK, Richard Long, Peter
Breck, Linda Evans, LEE MAJORS

The Biggest Aspidistra in the World.
Incisive history of the BBC by Peter Black.
First published by BBC Publications, 1972.

Biggins, Christopher (1948–   ). Plump
British character comedy actor and game
show personality, e.g. *On Safari*, *Surprise,
Surprise*.

Bilko: see You'll Never Get Rich

'Society forgot him – for 46 years!'
Bill *
US 1981 96m colour TVM
CBS/Alan Landsburg (Mel Stuart)
A mentally retarded man has managed to
survive in New York, but gets into trouble
when he is mistaken for a wino.
A true story thoughtfully transferred to the
screen, with a striking performance from its
star.
w Corey Blechman *d* Anthony Page
MICKEY ROONEY, Dennis Quaid, Largo
Woodruff, Kathleen Maguire

Bill Brand *
GB 1976 11 × 50m colour (VTR)
Thames/Stella Richman
Problems of a radical left-wing MP.
Downbeat dramatic series, revered by the
critics but rejected by the public.
w Trevor Griffiths *d* Michael Lindsay-Hogg
Jack Shepherd

The Bill Cosby Show (US 1969). Syndicated
NBC half-hour which ran two seasons. The
star played the athletic coach at a Los
Angeles high school, and the emphasis was
on warmth rather than comedy. Also starred:
Joyce Bullifant, Lee Weaver.

The Bill Dana Show (US 1965). NBC
half-hour comedy with the star in his familiar
portrayal of Latin immigrant Jose Jimenez,
here a bellboy in a New York hotel. It ran
one-and-a-half seasons, and featured Don
Adams, Jonathan Harris and Gary Crosby.

Bill: On His Own *
US 1983 96m colour TVM
CBS/Alan Landsburg (Linda Otto)
Continuing the story of retarded Bill Sackter
(who died as the film was finished). In this

chapter he runs a coffee shop on the university campus.

w Barry Morrow d Anthony Page

MICKEY ROONEY, Helen Hunt, Edie McClurg, Tracey Walter, Teresa Wright, Paul Lieber, Dennis Quaid, Largo Woodruff

Billington, Kevin (1933–). British documentarist and feature director. BAFTA 1967 best documentary: *Madison Avenue USA*. TV movies: *And No One Could Save Her*, *The Good Soldier*. Directed *Outside Edge* and *Henry VIII* in the BBC Shakespeare.

Billion Dollar Bubble* (GB 1976). 50-minute documentary re-enacting the circumstances which allowed an American computer to produce two million dollars' worth of phoney insurance. Written by Tom Clarke; directed by Brian Gibson.

Billion Dollar Threat
US 1979 96m colour TVM
ABC/Columbia/David Gerber (Jay Daniels)

A *bon vivant* American spy pits his wits against a madman about to destroy the ozone.

Tolerable nonsense in the wake of James Bond.

w James Sangster d Barry Shear ph Jack Woolf m Richard Shores ad Dale Hennesey

Dale Robinette, Patrick MacNee, Ralph Bellamy, Keenan Wynn, Ronnie Carol, Beth and Karen Specht

Billy * (GB 1980). BBC *Play for Today* by G. F. Newman about a four-year-old boy battered by his father. Produced by Kenith Trodd, directed by Charles Stewart.

'Marvellously acted, finely detailed film' – *The Times*

† Not to be confused with the 'Billy' trilogy of Graham Reid. See *Too Late to Talk to Billy*.

Billy Bunter (GB 1952–62). Gerald Campion became famous (though not lastingly so) playing the fat boy of the old Greyfriars school stories in intermittent BBC series fudged up around this character. Originally they went out live, twice over, every Friday – at 5.25 for children, at 7.25 for adults.   PP

The Billy Cotton Band Show: see Cotton, Billy

Billy Liar (GB 1973–4). The young northern fantasist created for novel and film by Keith Waterhouse and Willis Hall was turned by them quite successfully into TV situation

BILLY BUNTER, the famous fat boy of the Greyfriars Remove, had his most popular incarnation when he was played by Gerald Campion.

comedy. A minor stir was created by Dad's bad language, but generally speaking the half-hour series was popular even though it clearly lacked originality. Produced and directed by Stuart Allen, with Jeff Rawle and George A. Cooper. An American version was mooted in 1977 but didn't happen.

† An American copy called *Billy*, starring Steve Guttenberg, was briefly tried out in 1979.

Billy: Portrait of a Street Kid
US 1980 96m colour TVM
CBS/Mark Carliner

A black ghetto youngster tries to improve his life.

Utterly predictable from start to finish; never very engrossing, and aimed firmly at a black audience.

w,d Stephen Gethers

LeVar Burton, Michael Constantine, Ossie Davis, Tina Andrews

The Bing Crosby Show
US 1964 28 × 25m bw
ABC/Bing Crosby Productions

Domestic comedy about a middle-aged couple with two teenage daughters and a long-staying friend.

Moderately pleasant but entirely unremarkable.

Bing Crosby, Beverly Garland, Frank McHugh

Biography (GB 1970; 6 × 75m; colour). Crucial periods in the lives of Danton, Charles I, Kepler, Beethoven, Alexander Fleming and Byron as dramatized by Arden Winch, Ian Curteis and others, for BBC. Occasionally very effective, e.g. Beethoven (MICHAEL JAYSTON) sawing the legs off his piano, the better to feel its vibrations after deafness had set in; but a certain portentousness clung to the series as a whole. See: *lookalikes*.   PP

Bionic Woman *
US 1976–7 35 × 50m colour
MCA (Harve Bennett)
After the six-million-dollar man, a badly injured girl is scientifically reconstructed and put to work for the CIA.

Initially much effort was made to inject warmth and humanity into this comic strip idea, but within a season our heroine had become just another dumb dame who could run fast and lift weights, with dialogue to match. She and her bionic boyfriend were cancelled by the network in April 1978.

cr Kenneth Johnson *m* Jerry Fielding
LINDSAY WAGNER, Richard Anderson

The episode titles were as follows:
Welcome Home Jaime (two-parter)
Angel of Mercy
Mirror Image
Thing of the Past
Bionic Beauty
The Ghosthunter
Claws
The Deadly Missiles
Jaime's Mother
The Jailing of Jaime
Winning Is Everything
Fly Jaime
Assault on the Princess
Canyon of Death
In This Corner, Jaime Sommers
The Return of Bigfoot
Sister Jaime
Black Magic
The Vega Influence
Kill Oscar (two-parter)
Road to Nashville
Jaime's Shield (two-parter)
Deadly Ringer (two-parter)
Doomsday Is Tomorrow (two-parter)

Once a Thief
The De Jon Caper
Jaime and the King
Beyond the Call
Biofeedback
The Night Demon
Iron Ships and Dead Men
The Bionic Dog (two-parter)
Fembots in Las Vegas (two-parter)
Rodeo
Brain Wash
Motorcycle Boogie
African Connection
Escape to Love
Max
All for One
Over the Hill Spy
The Pyramid
The Martians Are Coming
The Antidote
Sanctuary Earth
Deadly Music
Which One Is Jaime?
Rancho Outcasts
Out of Body
Long Live the King
On the Run

† Also in for guest shots during the series were *Bionic Boy* (played by Vincent Van Patten) and *Bionic Dog*.

Birch, Paul (*c* 1904–69). Canadian actor who in 1958 starred as the burly truck driver in *Cannonball*.

bird. Slang term for satellite.

Bird, Michael J. (19 –). British writer who established himself with thriller serials relying on package-tour locations in the Greek islands, popular with audiences, unregarded critically except for the semi-mystical *The Dark Side of the Sun*, 1983. *The Aphrodite Inheritance*, 1979; *Who Pays the Ferryman*, 1982; *The Outsider*, 1983; *Maelstrom*, 1985; *The Winning Streak*, 1985.   PP

Bird of Prey *
GB 1982 4 × 50m colour
BBC (Michael Wearing)
Much-acclaimed thriller serial in which a mild-mannered, portly but persistent civil servant sniffs out gigantic international computer conspiracy. The plot sometimes seemed intelligible only to another computer but it made Richard Griffiths a star, and a sequel, *Bird of Prey II*, followed in 1984.

w Ron Hutchinson *d* Michael Rolfe

Bird of Prey II p Bernard Krichevsky *d* Don Leaver   PP

Birdman
US 1967 26 × 22m colour
NBC/Hanna–Barbera

An explorer is helped and blessed by the Egyptian sun god, and finds he has special powers to combat evil.
Derivative cartoon series.

The Birdmen
aka: *Escape of the Birdmen*
US 1971 96m colour TVM
Universal (Harve Bennett)

Prisoners of war escape from the Nazis by building a glider and soaring down from the castle parapets into Switzerland.
By *Colditz* out of *The Flight of the Phoenix*: phoney-looking but otherwise passable fantasy.

w David Kidd d Philip Leacock

Doug McClure, Chuck Connors, Richard Basehart, René Auberjonois, Don Knight, Max Baer, Tom Skerritt

**Bird's Eye View ** ** (GB 1969–71). A BBC series of helicopter travelogues of the British Isles, breathtaking to look at and worthy of frequent repeats. Edward Mirzoeff masterminded the series; Brian Branston directed *Bird's Eye View of Great Britain*, which is preserved in the NFA.

Birds of Prey **
US 1972 81m colour TVM
Tomorrow (Alan A. Armer)

A helicopter pilot on traffic duty tracks down an armoured car hold-up.
Smoothly-made actioner with pretensions.

w Robert Boris d William Graham m Jack Elliott/Allyn Ferguson

David Janssen, Ralph Meeker, Elayne Heilveil

Birney, David (1944–). American leading man who became known via *Bridget Loves Bernie*, in which he met his wife Meredith Baxter Birney, then known as Meredith Baxter. Later TV series: *Serpico*. TV movies: *Murder or Mercy, Only with Married Men, Testimony of Two Men, Someone's Watching Me, The Five of Me, Valley of the Dolls, St Elsewhere, Master of the Game, Glitter*

Birt, John (1944–). British producer and executive. At Granada started *Nice Time*, which guarantees him his place in Heaven. At London Weekend formulated, with David Elstein, the 'bias against understanding' criticism of current affairs output which much influenced thinking in the mid-seventies. Later headed Features and Current Affairs at LWT until appointed Programme Controller in 1981.   PP

Birth of a Nation **
GB 1983 4 × av. 85m colour
Central (Margaret Matheson)

Strictly, David Leland's four plays on the imperfections of the British education system are separate titles, but they were transmitted as a quartet and we follow suit. *Birth of a Nation* itself showed a state comprehensive under siege from ex-pupils aggrieved because it had not fitted them for life on the dole, while inside the classrooms formal tuition was unfavourably compared to the studies Leland evidently regarded as worthwhile, namely a laboratory full of little animals and sex education the rest of the time.

Flying into the Wind dealt sympathetically, fairly, even amusingly with parents in an isolated fenland small-holding who insisted on educating their small daughter themselves.

Rhino tackled the problem of a black girl labelled unteachable.

Made in Britain controversially analysed the behaviour and beliefs of a swastika-tattooed skinhead, unnervingly played by Tim Roth.

One star for the scale of Leland's overall design, another for the raw energy of the last play, a third for the unexpected generosity of *Flying into the Wind*, one star withdrawn for the way circumstances were set up, here and in *Birth of a Nation*, to suit his case.

d Mike Newell, Edward Bennet, Jane Howell, Alan Clarke

Jim Broadbent, Robert Stephens; Graham Crowden, Derrick O'Connor, Rynagh O'Grady; Deltha McLeod, Andrew Partridge; Tim Roth   PP

**The Birth of ITV ** * (GB 1976). A 21st anniversary round-up of news and views, produced by David Elstein for Thames, with many figures prominent at the time: Norman Collins, Selwyn Lloyd, Malcolm Muggeridge, Freddie Grisewood, Grace Wyndham Goldie, Mark Chapman-Walker. In NFA.

The Birth of Television **
GB 1977 90m colour/bw (VTR)
BBC

A memoir of TV's early days, with extracts from programmes and interviews with survivors. A valuable research tool.

w/p Bruce Norman

Gracie Fields, Dinah Sheridan, Arthur Askey, Cyril Fletcher, Leslie Mitchell

The Birthday Run **
GB 1971 50m colour

Two worlds, two nations, two cultures collide as a party of old-fashioned Socialist wheelers descend on a cyclists' hostel only to find the old place is now the posh residence of an ex-working-class novelist. Arthur Hopcraft had written nothing truer or funnier. With Gerald Flood, George A. Cooper, Mary Peach, Patsy Heywood, Barry Lowe. Directed by Richard Everitt; produced by Peter Eckersley; for Granada.   PP

Bishop, Joey (1918–) (Joseph Abraham Gottlieb). American nightclub comedian who had sporadic success in TV. See *The Joey Bishop Show*.

A Bit of a Lift **
GB 1973 50m colour
Thames (Joan Kemp-Welch)

Inspirational comedy by and with Donald Churchill, as a would-be suicide who has booked into a hotel with a bottle of brandy and an overdose of sleeping pills. Tramping the corridors is a fruity philanderer trying to remember the number of the room in which he has a lady friend waiting. By a sequence of events not too difficult to imagine the one takes the other's place in a triumphant affirmation of love as a literally life-saving force. But for one or two clumsy details in the plotting and even clumsier film inserts in the production it would have an extra star.

d Dennis Vance

Donald Churchill, Ronald Fraser, Anne Beach   PP

A Bit of an Experience ** (GB 1967; bw). Documentary account of a major brain operation and in particular the reactions of the woman patient's husband and children as they await the outcome. Honest, moving and eventually encouraging, it paved the way for many subsequent programmes of the same nature. Directed by Michael Latham; produced by Michael Latham and Gordon Thomas; for BBC.   PP

Bitter Harvest
US 1980 96m colour TVM
NBC/Charles Fries (Tony Ganz)

A farmer fighting a mysterious cattle ailment gets no help from the bureaucrats.
Well made but overlong social conscience drama which might have been more memorable as a documentary in a shorter time slot.

w Richard Friedenberg *d* Roger Young *ph* Gayne Rescher *m* Fred Karlin

Ron Howard, Art Carney, Richard Dysart, Tarah Nutter, Jim Haynie, David Knell

Bixby, Bill (1934–). Unassuming American light leading man, one of the most familiar faces on TV. Series include *My Favorite Martian*, *The Courtship of Eddie's Father*, THE MAGICIAN, THE INCREDIBLE HULK. TV movies: *Congratulations It's A Boy*, *The Couple Takes a Wife*, *Barbary Coast*, *Rich Man, Poor Man*, etc.

BJ and the Bear
US 1979 47 × 50m colour
NBC/MCA/Glen A. Larson

Adventures of a young trucker with a pet chimpanzee.
Briefly fashionable adventure series drawn from various components, e.g. the hero admits to having been 'the fastest Medivac pilot in Nam', and *Smokey and the Bandit* must also have been firmly in the producer's mind.

cr Glen A. Larson

Greg Evigan, Claude Akins

'A small amount of haw-haw horseplay and macho posturing goes a long way with me.' – Robert MacKenzie, *TV Guide*

The Black Adder (GB 1983 6 × 35m). Learned romp through some alternative history in the aftermath of Bosworth Field, with Rowan Atkinson as the last of the Plantagenets – a role he wrote for himself, with Richard Curtis. 'His nostrils gape. Sometimes he looks like a mad man. Whirring noises signal the cogitative process whereby he will think up the suggestion first made by someone else – the weakest of the running jokes.' Others were better, but only with a second series in 1986 did it really take off. Also with Brian Blessed, Peter Cook. Produced by John Lloyd, for BBC. PP
† *Black Adder II*, 1986, moved on to Elizabethan Times, with Ben Elton as co-writer to Curtis and Miranda Richardson and Tim McInnerny as queens.

The Black and White Minstrel Show. Long-running fast-moving BBC variety show, created by George Inns. Comedy turns alternated with medleys from the George Mitchell singers. Racial groups objected to the men's blackface make-up, but this added immeasurably to the old-fashioned style of the enterprise, and the show was an immense hit throughout the sixties, stimulating several touring versions of the show and creating such stars as DAI FRANCIS, TONY MERCER and JOHN BOULTER. It lasted 21 seasons, from 1958 to 1978.

PP: 'Mindless entertainment whose breathless progression from song to schmaltzy song won the first Golden Rose of Montreux, thereby setting back the cause of European television by two years. The men were blacked up as nigger minstrels, the girls remained white, and repeated challenges from this quarter to try reversing the convention and see how the audience liked *that* were ignored. A further idiocy was that everyone nevertheless dressed up to suit the style of each batch of songs, so that black-faced Hussars serenaded powdered Viennese ladies for Strauss and Friml, or black-faced Mounties wooed pale-faced Red Indian maidens in selections from *Rose Marie*. The show transferred to the London stage for several seasons before finally dying of incongruity.'

Black Arrow
US 1985 74m colour TVM
Walt Disney/Harry Alan Towers

A young nobleman combats the schemes of his wicked uncle.
Lustreless remake of an old warhorse. The cast seems even more tired than the script.

w David Pursall, Harry Alan Towers, *novel* by Robert Louis Stevenson d John Hough ph John Cabrera

Stephan Chase, Oliver Reed, Fernando Rey, Donald Pleasence

Black Beauty: see The Adventures of Black Beauty

Black, Cilla (1943–) (Priscilla White). British pop vocalist who from 1968 had several winter series of Saturday specials, in which she carefully nurtured her Liverpool accent and working-class gaucherie. Reappeared 1985 as host of *Surprise, Surprise*.

black crushing. Technical term for unsatisfactory lighting, under-exposed so that everything dark merges into one colour.

Black, Isobel (1943–). Attractive Scottish actress of the sixties, later in Australia. *The Girl Who Loved Robots, Calf Love, Mogul, The Lower Largo Sequence*. Comeback in 1980 in *The White Bird Passes*. Lately, *Boswell for the Defence, The Brief*. PP

Black, Karen (1946–). Vivacious, odd-eyed American leading lady, in all media. TV movies: *Trilogy of Terror, The Strange Possession of Mrs Oliver, Mr Horn, Power, Where the Ladies Go, Confessions of a Lady Cop*.

Black Market Baby
Theatrical title: *Don't Steal My Baby*
US 1977 96m colour TVM
ABC/Brut

A pregnant but unmarried college student plays into the hands of a 'babies for sale' racket.
Yucky teenage melodrama.

w Andrew Peter Martin, *novel A Nice Italian Girl* by Elizabeth Christman d Robert Day ph Richard C. Glouner m Richard Bellis, George Wilkins.

Desi Arnaz Jnr, Linda Purl, Bill Bixby, Jessica Walter, Tom Bosley, David Doyle

'She loves him and wants their baby, but a ruthless adoption ring wants it more!' – publicity

Black Noon *
US 1971 73m colour TVM
Columbia (Andrew Fenady)

In the old west, a young minister and his wife arrive at a remote town run by diabolists.
Preposterous nonsense with a winning way.

w Andrew J. Fenady d Bernard Kowalski

Roy Thinnes, Ray Milland, Yvette Mimieux, Gloria Grahame, Lynn Loring, Henry Silva

Black, Peter (1913–). Britain's first, and some would say only, television critic. Writing in a popular paper, the *Daily Mail*, from 1952 to 1973, his overnight review was arguably the single most beneficial force to bear on a developing medium. His best-known dictum, expanded in his book *The Mirror in the Corner* (Hutchinson, 1972), is that television only reflects the society that produced it, and that those who seek to control or censor television really want to get their hands on us. PP

Black Saddle
US 1958–9 44 × 25m bw
ABC/Four Star

A gunfighter turned lawyer tours the southwest after the Civil War.
Adequate western time-passer.

Peter Breck, Russell Johnson

Black Sheep Squadron: see Baa Baa Black Sheep

Black Water Gold
US 1969 75m colour TVM
Metromedia

A scuba diver finds lost treasure from a Spanish galleon, but has trouble profiting from it.

Naïvely made and written adventure piece.

w/d Alan Landsburg

Bradford Dillman, Aron Kincaid, Keir Dullea, Ricardo Montalban, France Nuyen

Blacke's Magic *
US 1986   × 60m colour
NBC/MCA/Universal (Peter S. Fischer)
A retired magician and his con-man father help the police to solve baffling cases.
Light-hearted mysteries from a reliable source.

cr Peter S. Fischer consultants Richard Levinson, William Link

Hal Linden, Harry Morgan

Blackman, Honor (1926–   ). British leading
lady from the Rank charm school; after years as an English rose, she blossomed forth in 1961 as the leather-garbed, judo-kicking Cathy Gale in the early series of THE AVENGERS; subsequently her best chances were in the theatre.

Blackout
US 1985 96m colour TVM
HBO/Roger Gimbel/Peregrine/Lee Rock
An obsessed Ohio detective works doggedly to trap a man he thinks is a murderer.
Reasonably tense and adult thriller of the forties film noir school; but somewhat lacking in real excitement.

w David Ambrose, Richard Smith, Richard Parks d Douglas Hickox ph Tak Fujimoto m Laurence Rosenthal

Richard Widmark, Keith Carradine, Kathleen Quinlan, Michael Beck, Gerald Hiken, Paul Drake

'Schlock shock, wrapped in a handsome package.' – Daily Variety

Blacks in TV. Black actors have always had a
place in TV, albeit an inferior one in the fifties, when Amos 'n' Andy, played by two whites in blackface, caused protests and had to be taken off the air. Subsequently blacks could be starred, but usually playing servants as in Beulah, or assistants as in East Side West Side, and NYPD. The breakthrough came in 1967 with I Spy, in which Bill Cosby was seen as Robert Culp's absolute equal in girl chasing as well as spy catching. Thereafter blacks were seen doing just as well as whites in The Mod Squad, Mission Impossible, Hogan's Heroes, The Silent Force, The Young Lawyers, Julia, Tenafly and many others.

From 1970 on, the success of Sanford and Son made all-black shows popular, and there have subsequently been two or three always on the air: That's My Mama, Barefoot in the Park, Good Times, The Jeffersons. The ultimate tribute was paid when TV movie specials began to atone for hundreds of years of black subordination: The Autobiography of Miss Jane Pittman, Roots, King.

PP: 'In Britain they were mostly represented by The Black and White Minstrel Show until 1978. Since then, in such mainly feeble sitcoms as Mixed Blessings (1978) or The Brothers McGregor. Their best deal has come from unassuming fiction series which have incorporated black personnel without making a virtue of it, e.g. Spearhead or Widows. In comedy shows, Kenny Lynch and Lenny Henry have achieved more than all the high-minded attempts to represent black interests. Black on Black was Channel 4's regular series for black viewers 1982–5. Ebony remains the BBC equivalent.'

The Blackwell Story
US 1957 74m bw TVM
Columbia/Playhouse 90
In the 1830s America's first woman doctor gains respect.
Very modest TV movie from the struggling early days.

d James Neilson

Joanne Dru, Dan O'Herlihy, Marshall Thompson, Charles Korvin, Keith Larsen

Blade on the Feather *
GB 1980 95m colour TVM
LWT/Kenith Trodd
An unexpected and sinister visitor imposes himself upon the household of a retired spy.
Mystifying Pinterish drama kept going by minor sensationalism and good acting; the actual story is so obvious that it needs all the confusing wrapping to maintain interest.

w Dennis Potter d Richard Loncraine ph Peter Hannan ad Andrew Drummond

Tom Conti, Donald Pleasence, Kika Markham, Denholm Elliott, Phoebe Nicholls

PP: 'Dennis Potter reopens the obsessions of his earlier play Traitor to bring retribution to a retired don who may or may not have been the "fifth man" who recruited Philby and Co. to the Soviet cause. The usual swipe at the ruling classes, but within a richly equivocal, sunny, often funny piece of invention.'

Blaine, Vivian (1924–   ) (Vivian
Stapleton). American leading lady of the forties who reappeared in character parts in

the seventies. TV movies: *Katie: Portrait of a Centerfold*, *The Cracker Factory*, *Fast Friends*, *Sooner or Later*.

Blair, Janet (1921–) (Martha Lafferty). American leading lady of the forties whose chief TV outing was as Henry Fonda's wife in *The Smith Family*.

Blair, Les (1941–). British director associated chiefly with improvised drama (see Improvisation). Edited Mike Leigh's *Bleak Moments*, 1974. Directed BLOOMING YOUTH, 1974; *The Enemy Within*, 1975; *The Whip Hand*, 1976; and the scripted quartet *The Nation's Health*, 1983; *Honest, Decent and True*, 1986.   PP

Blair, Linda (1959–). American juvenile actress of the seventies. TV movies: *Born Innocent*, *Sara T*, *Sweet Hostage*, *Victory at Entebbe*, *Stranger in Our House*.

Blake, Amanda (1929–) (Beverly Louise Neill). American leading lady of the fifties who after a desultory career in films and TV landed the role of Miss Kitty in GUNSMOKE and played it for 19 years.

Blake, Robert (1934–) (Michael Gubitosi). American character actor who started with Our Gang and developed along the lines of a Dead End Kid, finally discovering his star niche in BARETTA (Emmy 1964). Tried to repeat himself in *Joe Dancer*.

Blakely, Colin (1930–). Stocky British actor especially good at conveying suppressed power. *Son of Man* (as Jesus), *The Hanged Man*, *The Breaking of Colonel Keyser*, *Red Monarch* (as Stalin), *The Father*, *Operation Julie*.   PP
'His face is now so battered that he appears to be wearing a permanent stocking mask.' – Byron Rogers, *Sunday Times*

Blakely, Susan (1949–). American leading lady, former model, who came to the fore in RICH MAN, POOR MAN. TV movies: *Secrets*, *Make Me an Offer*, *A Cry for Love*, *Oklahoma City Dolls*.

Blake's Seven (GB 1978–). BBC junior science fiction, rather heavy going for grown-ups.

Blankety Blank (GB 1977–). Abysmal BBC game show maintaining the proposition of the equally hideous *Celebrity Squares* that only showbiz show-offs can be entertaining, and therefore the role of contestants from the general public will be limited to nominating which show-off shall compete on their behalf – in this case to furnish the missing words in some banal statement. Terry Wogan presided for the first few years and was replaced in 1984 by Les Dawson, who was even more insulting, much to the audience's delight.   PP

Blansky's Beauties
US 1977 13 × 25m colour
ABC/Paramount/Garry Marshall
A moral guardian is appointed to look after Las Vegas showgirls.
Fairly dire comedy series which gave its star no room to breathe.
cr Garry Marshall, Bob Brunner, Arthur Silver
Nancy Walker
† The format was tried again in 1978 as *Legs* (changed in mid-season to *Who's Watching the Kids?*).

Bleak House ***
GB 1985 8 × 50m
BBC (John Harris, Betty Willingale)
Masterly, meticulous serialization of Dickens's tenebrous novel of a Victorian lawsuit dragging on and on to impoverish or destroy all those caught up in it. The realism extended to real horse dung littering the re-created streets of London.
w Arthur Hopcraft   *m* Geoffrey Burgon   *design* Tim Harvey   *d* Ross Devenish
Diana Rigg, Denholm Elliott, Fiona Walker, Graham Crowden, Bernard Hepton, Peter Vaughan, Robin Bailey, Frank Windsor, T. P. McKenna
'Don't let the details get in your way. Just relax and enjoy eight weeks of great characters greatly portrayed, of Dickensian England brilliantly captured in all its mire, mirth and melodrama'. – *People* Magazine
† Only previous version *c* 1954, 12 × 30m, *w* Constance Cox.   PP

Bleasdale, Alan (1946–). British writer, formerly Liverpool schoolteacher, who to interest his tougher pupils devised classroom playlets featuring characters like themselves, later done on radio and finally television (1984) as *Scully*. Bleasdale had meanwhile leapt to fame with *The Boys from the Blackstuff* (1982).   PP

bleeding whites. Technical term for photography so over-exposed that white sections become 'hot' and run off into other areas.

Bless 'Em All (GB 1955). A BBC variety show produced by Derek Burrell-Davis to celebrate the tenth anniversary of VE-Day and featuring a number of stars of the time: Richard Dimbleby, Jean Metcalfe, Ralph Reader, Vera Lynn, Richard Murdoch, Kenneth Horne, Eric Barker, Pearl Hackney, Charlie Chester, Robertson Hare, Jack Warner, Sam Costa.

Bless Me Father (GB 1979–). Half-hour character comedy series out of LWT, starring Arthur Lowe as a feisty parish priest of the early fifties, Peter de Anda as his junior, and Gabrielle Daye as his housekeeper. Fairly sharp observation and wry humour make it watchable.

Bless This House. An absolutely straightforward British domestic type sitcom of the seventies which provided Sid James with his last good role, coping with teenage children and his own incompetence. Produced and directed by William G. Stewart for Thames TV, with Diana Coupland, Sally Geeson, Robin Stewart.

Blessed, Brian (1937–). Massive British character actor who gained national fame in z CARS and was Caesar Augustus in *I, Claudius*. Also in many films.

Bligh, Jasmine (19 –). British announcer, who helped to open the BBC service from Alexandra Palace in 1935, and also welcomed viewers back after the war in 1946.

Blind Ambition
US 1979 4 × 96m colour
CBS/David Susskind (George Schaefer)
Rather strained mini-series based at far too great length on the Watergate revelations of John Dean.
w Stanley R. Greenberg *books* John and Maureen Dean *d* George Schaefer
Martin Sheen, Theresa Russell, Rip Torn (as Nixon), Michael Callan, William Daniels, Ed Flanders, William Windom, John Randolph, Lawrence Pressman

Blinded By the Light *
US 1980 96m colour TVM
CBS/Time–Life (Philip Mandelker)
A girl trying to rescue her brother from religious fanatics almost succumbs herself.
Topical real-life horror story with plenty of punch but no real surprises.
w Robin Vate, Stephen Black, Henry Stern *d/ph* John Alonzo *m* Jonathan Tunick

Kristy McNichol, Michael McGuire, Jenny O'Hara, Philip R. Allen, Sandy McPeak, Anna Jackson, James Vincent McNichol
'A sharp study of the invasion of the soul snatchers.' – *Daily Variety*

Bloch, Robert (1917–). American thriller writer, famous as the author of *Psycho*. Television scripts include *The Cat Creature*, *The Dead Don't Die*.

Blondell, Joan (1906–79). Wisecracking American comedienne of the thirties cinema; later on TV in character roles. TV movies: *Winchester 73*, *Banyon*, *The Dead Don't Die*, *Winner Take All*, *Death at Love House*, *Battered*, *The Rebels*.

Blondie
US 1968 26 × 25m colour
CBS/King/Kayro
The farcical adventures of the Bumstead family, so popular as a comic strip and in the movies, did not work on TV: either the timing was wrong or the new cast failed to appeal.
Will Hutchins, Pat Harty, Jim Backus
† A previous series had run on NBC in 1957 with Arthur Lake and Pamela Britton.

Blood and Honour
West Germany 1982 5 × 50m
  colour miniseries
Beta/Daniel Wilson/Taurus/SWF (Linda Marmelstein)
The effect of the Hitler Youth on a non-Nazi family.
Stiff and clumsy miniseries which barely even convinces that its heart's in the right place.
w Robert Muller, Helmut Kissel *d* Bernd Fischerauer *ph* Hannes Hollman *m* Ernst Brandner
Jeffrey Frank, Gedeon Burkhard, Steven Rubling, Steven Higgs, Jacob Fruchtmann, David Weidner, Rolf Becker
'Too long, too ponderous . . . bogged down in pedantry.' – *Daily Variety*

'The chilling story behind the blazing headlines!'
Blood Feud
US 1983 2 × 96m colour
TCF/Glickman–Selznick
Bobby Kennedy comes head to head with Jimmy Hoffa, boss of the Teamsters.
A rather wearisome dogfight which could have been covered in half the time, especially since it admits to 'fictionalization and compression for dramatic reasons'.

w Robert Boris *d* Mike Newell *ph* Robert Morrison *m* Fred Steiner

Cotter Smith, Robert Blake, Danny Aiello, Edward Albert, Brian Dennehy, Douglas Dirkson, Sam Groom (as JFK), Ernest Borgnine (as J. Edgar Hoover), Jose Ferrer, Vito Scotti

Blood Money (GB 1981). Crime serial in six half-hours, about the kidnapping of a small boy. Good routine cop stuff. With Bernard Hepton, Michael Denison. Written by Arden Winch; directed by Michael E. Briant; for BBC.

The Blood of Others
US/France 1985 3 × 96m colour
Orion/Lamar Card (Denis Heroux, John Kemeny)

A selfish French girl during World War II becomes drawn through love into the Resistance.
Extraordinarily verbose and uncompelling treatment of a well-worn theme, with a leading lady who has grown up gracelessly.

w Brian Moore, *novel* by Simone de Beauvoir *d* Claude Chabrol

Jodie Foster, Michael Ontkean, Sam Neill, Stéphane Audran

Blood Sport
US 1973 74m colour TVM
Danny Thomas

A college boy fights his father's wish to make him a football star.
Predictable character melodrama.

w/d Jerrold Friedman

Ben Johnson, Gary Busey, David Doyle, Larry Hagman

Bloody Kids
GB 1980 96m colour TVM
ATV/Black Lion (Barry Hanson)

Teenagers turn to violence in a faceless urban environment.
Bleak and despairing look at a social problem which is probably best not treated fictionally since the real subjects could never be so articulate and the real surroundings are far less melodramatic than they are made to look here.

w Stephen Poliakoff *d* Stephen Frears

Derrick O'Connor, Gary Holton, Peter Clark

Bloomers (GB 1979). Last sitcom for the talented actor Richard Beckinsale, who died the same year. He played an unsuccessful actor working in a flower shop. With Anna Calder-Marshall. Written by James Saunders; for BBC.   PP

Blooming Youth *
GB 1973 75m colour

'Vwrs all ages, sexes, wntd to share enjoyment of off-the-cuff flmd comedy abt 4 yng people (3m, 1f) sharing s/c furn. flt.' An exercise in improvisation which really worked. With Colin Higgins, Philip Jackson, Peter Kinley, Lydia Lisle. Directed by Leslie Blair; produced by Tony Garnett; for BBC.   PP

Blott on the Landscape (GB 1985 6 × 50m). Tom Sharpe's supposedly uproarious novel of dirty tricks between proponents and opponents of a new motorway made a distinctly downroarious television serial. Among the casualties were George Cole, Geraldine James, David Suchet (as the ex-POW Blott), Simon Cadell and Julia McKenzie. Dramatized by Malcolm Bradbury, directed by Roger Bamford, produced by Evgeny Gridneff; for BBC.   PP

The Bloxham Tapes *
GB 1976 50m colour (VTR)
BBC (Jeffrey Iverson)

An account of the British hypnotist who can project selected subjects back into previous lives; two of them bring back details from 11th-century York and medieval France.
If it's a con trick, it's a good one, and the programme is valuable as a record of what appears to have happened.

The Blue and the Gray
US 1983 8 TV hours (various
  formats) colour miniseries
CBS/Columbia/Larry White/Lou Reda
  (Hugh Benson, Harry Thomason)

An account of the American Civil War as seen by a Virginia farmboy artist.
Fairly clodhopping miniseries which predictably wowed 'em in the States but was coolly received elsewhere. Acting, writing and direction range down from competent to numbingly bad.

w Ian McLellan Hunter, *story* by John Leekley, Bruce Catton *d* Andrew V. McLaglen *ph* Al Francis *m* Bruce Broughton

John Hammond, Stacy Keach, Diane Baker, Kathleen Beller, Lloyd Bridges, Rory Calhoun, Colleen Dewhurst, David Doyle, Warren Oates, Gerald S. O'Loughlin, Geraldine Page, Rip Torn, Robert Vaughn, John Vernon, Sterling Hayden (as John Brown), Paul Winfield, Julius Harris, Gregg Henry, William Lucking, Duncan Regehr . . . and Gregory Peck as Abraham Lincoln

The Blue and the Grey: see The Americans

The Blue Angels
US 1960 39 × 25m bw
NTA/Sam Gallu
Exploits of a naval four-man precision flying team.
Standard action series of its time.
Mike Galloway, Don Gordon, Dennis Cross, Warner Jones

The Blue Knight *
US 1973 195m approx. colour TVM
NBC/Lorimar (Walter Coblenz)
The life of a Los Angeles cop on the beat. The first superlength TV movie: the length is wasted on this mundane material, which resists all efforts to give it status.
w E. Jack Neuman, *novel* Joseph Wambaugh *d* Robert Butler *ph* Michael Margulies
WILLIAM HOLDEN, Lee Remick, Sam Elliott, Eileen Brennan, Joe Santos
† Emmy: best dramatic programme.

The Blue Knight
US 1975 74m colour TVM
CBS/Lorimar
Second try for the above: this time the pilot, though shorter, was even slower and duller, and the consequent series had a brief life.
w Albert Rueben *d* J. Lee-Thompson
George Kennedy, Alex Rocco, Glynn Turman, Verna Bloom
† The one-hour series which ensued from the George Kennedy pilot was less than a spectacular success and ran 13 episodes. Produced by Joel Rogosin for Lorimar; music by Henry Mancini.

The Blue Light
US 1965 17 × 25m colour
ABC/TCF
An American spy insinuates himself into Nazi Germany during World War II.
Poorly conceived tall stories.
Robert Goulet, Christine Carère
† Four episodes were cobbled together for theatrical release under the title *I Deal in Danger*.

Blue Money * (GB 1982 82m). Tim Curry as a cabby who finds a suitcase stuffed with banknotes left in his taxi, and tries to grab it to finance his dreams of stardom as a rock singer. A bright, bizarre adventure with music. Also with Debby Bishop, Billy Connolly, Dermot Crowley. Written by Stewart Parker, directed by Colin Bucksey, produced by June Roberts and Jo Apted; for LWT.   PP

Blue Peter. BBC1's half-hour magazine programme for young people has been a fixture most of the year since the mid-fifties, sometimes appearing twice a week.

Blue Remembered Hills ***
GB 1979 90m colour
BBC (Kenith Trodd)
Of the single plays of Dennis Potter, one of the undisputed masterpieces:* a bunch of seven-year-olds zigzag through an eventful, sunny day in wartime rural England to display the innocences, cruelties and manoeuvres of childhood. The novelty, tried out by Potter in a couple of scenes in one of his plays many years earlier, is to have grown-up actors in the parts, throwing a vivid new light on the business of being young.
d Brian Gibson *ph* Nat Crosby
Michael Elphick, Colin Welland, Helen Mirren, Janet Duvitski, Colin Jeavons, Robin Ellis   PP
* LH: 'Disputed by me: I didn't think it worked at all.'
† BAFTA award 1979: best play.

Blue Thunder
US 1984 13 × 50m colour
ABC/Columbia/Rastar/Public Arts (Roy Huggins)
Adventures of a heavily-armoured police helicopter.
Comic strip exploits with dialogue well suited to balloons. ('OK, that's it, from now on we're going to do it my way.')
cr David Moessinger, Jeri Taylor
James Farentino, Dana Carvey, Sandy McPeak, Dick Butkus, Bubba Smith
'Old-fashioned formula actioner. Same name as the 1983 film; everything down pat *à la* 1955 TV. Not much ventured, not much gained.' – *Daily Variety*

Bluey (Australia 1976). One-hour police series from Crawford Productions, with Lucky Grills and John Diedrich. Surprisingly popular in UK, but only 26 were made.

The Boat ****
Original title: *Das Boot*
W. Germany 1982 1 × 90m, 5 × 60m
Bavarian TV/WDR (Gunther Rohrbach)
Though previously released in the cinema in a compact version, it took the television deployment of six episodes over six evenings (BBC2, 1984) to bring out the full sweep and mounting tension of Wolfgang Petersen's epic story of a U-boat mission at the height of the Battle of the Atlantic in 1941. The

division into episodes was crucial: only once on a real how-they-gonna-get-outa-that cliff-hanger, but always on a note of anticipation to keep the story working on in the viewer's mind. Well-differentiated characters, lavatorial German humour and a marvellously solid U-boat replica completed a television achievement, I wrote at the time, which only *The Jewel in the Crown* had lately been able to match in ambition, scale and getting it right. 'The best war film I have ever seen,' said Ludovic Kennedy.

w and *d* Wolfgang Petersen, *novel* Lothar Gunther Buchheim *m* Klaus Doldinger

Juergen Prochonow (as the Skipper)   PP

Bob and Carol and Ted and Alice
US 1973 12 × 25m colour
ABC/Columbia/Mike Frankovich (Jim Henerson)

Flabby attempt to translate the wife-swapping film to TV without any wife-swapping.

cr Larry Rosen, Larry Tucker

Bob Urich, Anne Archer, David Spielberg, Anita Gillette, Jodie Foster

The Bob Crane Show
US 1975 13 × 25m colour
MTM/NBC (Norman S. Powell, Martin Cohan)

A 42-year-old insurance salesman quits to pursue a medical career.
An interesting comedy with a point to make. It didn't make it.

Bob Crane, Trisha Hart, Ronny Graham, Todd Susman, James Sutorius

The Bob Cummings Show: see Love That Bob

The Bob Newhart Show
US 1972–7 104 approx. × 25m colour
CBS/Mary Tyler Moore (David Davies)

A psychiatrist has his own family problems. Agreeable but unexciting sitcom with a grain of something more serious in it.

Bob Newhart, Suzanne Pleshette, Peter Bonerz

† Newhart's previous (tape) series won an Emmy in 1961.

The Body Human (US 1977–81). A series of seven 50-minute specials financed by the American Bankers' Association and produced by Tomorrow/Medcom for CBS. Alexander Scourby narrates, and each hour tackles an aspect of the human body: vision, the brain, the nervous system, etc. Emmy 1977.

The Body in Question ** (GB 1978). What the human body is made of, how it works and – not least – the infinitely variable personalities it enshrines: a philosophical, often funny and oddly reassuring series by Jonathan Miller combining for once his talents as physician, performer and artist. Produced by Patrick Uden; for BBC.   PP

The Body Show. British exercise-while-you-watch series of 1982–3 without the usual moral nagging or odour of keep-fit classes, thanks to the sunny personality of presenter Yvonne Ocampo, a former nudie dancer. The style was emulated on BBC Breakfast television in the person of the 'Green Goddess'. From 51% Productions for Channel 4.   PP

'The day England declared war on Australia!'
Bodyline *
Australia 1984 5 × 90m colour
Kennedy Miller/Ten Network (Terry Hayes, George Miller)

The 1932–3 Test Match cricket series in Australia, with the dastardly English team adopting bumpers bowled at the batsman's head or ribs in an effort to beat the run-scoring machine Don Bradman. A heavily Australian version of sporting history (though scripted by an Englishman) went back to the days of Imperial Raj to trace the roots of the English captain D. R. Jardine's ruthless will to win, while demon bowler Harold Larwood was shown as a dogged ranker from the coalfields who would obey orders to the bitter end. 'But for all its simon-pure Aussie heroes, its Daisy Ashford view of English society, its same small crowd of spectators, its ridiculously overblown commentary and sub-*Chariots of Fire* music,' I wrote at the time of its BBC2 transmission, 'it really did make a few cricketers and their attendants act out national attitudes and national circumstances.'

w Denny Lawrence, Lex Marinos, Terry Hayes, George Miller, George Ogilvie, Carl Schultz, Robert Caswell *d* Carl Schultz, George Ogilvie, Denny Lawrence, Lex Marinos

Hugo Weaving (Jardine), Gary Sweet (Bradman), Jim Holt (Larwood), Heather Mitchell, Julie Nihill, Rhys McConnochie, Frank Thring, John Gregg, John Walton

† *Forty Minutes* (BBC) had treated the same subject more objectively in documentary style, 1983.   PP

The Boer War ** (GB 1960). A fairly definitive Granada action stills documentary, written by Rayne Kruger and directed by Claude Whatham.

Bogart, Paul (1919–). Medium-range American TV director who also aspired to a few theatrical features. Credits most regularly seen on *The Defenders*, *Hawk* (which he also produced), *Nichols* and *Alice*. Emmy 1967 for DEAR FRIENDS (CBS Playhouse); 1969 for SHADOW GAME (CBS Playhouse); 1977 for an episode of *All in the Family*.

Bogie
US 1980 96m colour TVM
CBS/Charles Fries (Philip Barry)
Episodes from the life of Humphrey Bogart after 1934.
Mildly interesting biopic which simply isn't full enough to be anything like definitive, and says more about the domestic tantrums than the movies.
w Daniel Taradash, *book* Joe Hyams *d* Vincent Sherman *ph* Harry May *m* Charles Bernstein
Kevin O'Connor, Kathryn Harrold (as Lauren Bacall), Anne Wedgeworth (as Mayo Methot), Herb Braha (as Peter Lorre), Alfred Ryder (as Romanoff), Stephen Keep (as Leslie Howard)

Bognor (GB 1981). Unsuccessful 18-part half-hour series from Thames, about a low-key investigator from the Department of Trade. Somehow it just didn't catch on despite a nice performance from David Horovitch. Written by T. R. Bowen, from the novels by Tim Heald; directed by Robert Tronson.

Bokova, Jana (19 –). Czech-born director, early graduate of Britain's National Film School, with distinctive observational style in which the camera isn't just a fly on the wall, it's a participant. *Rent Boys* for LWT and *Living Room* for BBC, 1978; *I Look Like This*, Granada, 1979; *Blue Moon*, about the lamented Concert Mayol in Paris, and a profile of Anthony Quinn, both BBC, 1980; *Dallas – the Big Store*, about the fabled Neiman–Markus department store, BBC, 1981; *Sunset People*, BBC, 1984.   PP

✳ **Bolam, James** (*c* 1939–). Leading British character actor, familiar as one of THE LIKELY LADS; in more serious vein as the lead in three seasons of WHEN THE BOAT COMES IN, a one-hour serial about the Depression years on Tyneside; and as the conniving invalid in *Only When I Laugh*.

Bold Journey (US 1956–8). Half-hour film series for ABC, produced and narrated by Jack Douglas, who presented true-life accounts brought back by explorers.

The Bold Ones *
US 1969–71 98 × 50m colour
NBC/Universal (Roy Huggins/Cy Chermak/Jack Laird)
Interesting but unsatisfactory attempt to present rotating dramas about some of the pillars of our society. Hal Holbrook was a senator (pilots, *The Whole World is Watching*, *A Clear and Present Danger*, *A Continual Roar of Musketry*). E. G. Marshall, David Hartman and John Saxon were doctors (pilot, *Five Days in the Death Of Sergeant Brown*). Burl Ives and James Farentino were lawyers (pilots, *The Sound of Anger*, *The Long Morning After*). Leslie Nielsen was a police chief and Hari Rhodes a DA (pilot, *Deadlock*). George Kennedy was a cop turned priest (pilots, *The Badge and the Cross*, *The Priest Killer*). The one-hour series turned out to be a prestige offering which didn't grip the public imagination, and only doctors, lawyers and a DA were involved.
'The common theme is the contemporary world. The lawyer, the doctor, the urban situation and law-and-order . . . we focus on the young people in life who are trying to take over.' – Herb Schlosser, vp NBC
'What will actually emerge from this smorgasbord is impossible to predict.' – Dave Kaufman
† An Emmy was awarded in 1970.

Bold Venture
US 1959 39 × 30m bw
United Artists
An adventurer and his pretty young ward live on a hotel boat in Trinidad.
Unremarkable hokum based on a radio series.
Dane Clark, Joan Marshall

Bolger, Ray (1904–). Amiable eccentric dancer who after careers on Broadway and in Hollywood came to TV in 1953 as star of *The Ray Bolger Show* in which he played a hoofer in a touring company. It ran 59 episodes. TV movies: *Captains and the Kings*, *The Entertainer*, *Three on a Date*, *Heaven Only Knows*.

Bolwieser (Germany 1976). A 110-minute TV film written and directed by Rainer Werner Fassbinder from the novel by Oskar Maria Graf, about a twenties stationmaster who ruins his own reputation by lying to protect his unfaithful wife. All very solemn and over-acted, like *The Blue Angel* come alive again, it nevertheless has a hypnotic grip. With Kurt Raab and Elisabeth Trissenaar: from ZDF. Shown on BBC in 1981.

The Bomb. Jonathan Dimbleby has been the only operator to call a programme on nuclear arms by that simple title, in the run-up to the US Presidential election of 1980, with a follow-up next time. *Four Years On: the Bomb* in 1984 (*p* and *d* Francis Gerard, for YTV). But see more famous exercises in what it could mean under the titles *Doomsday for Dyson*, *The War Game*, *The Day After*, *Threads* and *On the Eighth Day*. PP

The Bomb Disposal Men ** (GB 1974). Documentary account of the Ordnance Corps ammunition technical officers whose duties include dealing with home-made bombs and booby-traps in Northern Ireland. Reporter Jack Pizzey shadowed a trio as they prepared for a tour of duty, culminating in a young captain's baptismal encounter with a dollop of gelignite. Brilliant, unnerving and salutary. Directed by Jenny Barraclough; for BBC. PP

Bomba. In 1949 the old 'Bomba the Jungle Boy' films starring Johnny Sheffield were edited to make 13 TV hours under the title *Ziv Bomba*.

Bonanza **
Syndication title: *Ponderosa*
US 1959–71 310 × 50m colour
NBC (DAVID DORTORT)

Adventures of the Cartwright family on their Ponderosa ranch near Virginia City.
Supremely popular and often engaging western series in which the action elements were mainly subordinated to soap opera. Women especially liked it because there was a man for most types: grizzled, wise Ben (LORNE GREENE) and sons Adam (Pernell Roberts, who left after six seasons), the enormous, slow-thinking Hoss (DAN BLOCKER, who died in 1972), and fresh-faced Little Joe (MICHAEL LANDON). David Canary joined later, and Sen Yung was around as the Chinese cook. The studio look didn't seem to matter.

cr DAVID DORTORT *story editor* John Hawkins *m* DAVID ROSE *theme tune* JAY LIVINGSTON, RAY EVANS

Bond, James. Legendary spy character created by Ian Fleming; examined early in his career in *Anatomy of the Hero* (ABC Tempo), 1962. Directed by Joe McGrath, produced by Peter Luke.

Bond, Julian (1930–). Tireless British writer in TV from the pioneering days of *Probation Officer*, 1958–60. Major credits include *A Man of Our Time* (1968), *The Ferryman* (1974) from Kingsley Amis, *Love for Lydia* (1977) from H. E. Bates, *The Far Pavilions* (1984) from M. M. Kaye, *Strangers and Brothers* (1984) from C. P. Snow. PP

Bond, Ward (1903–60). Veteran American character actor who after a lifetime in Hollywood became a TV star as Major Adams in WAGON TRAIN, which began in 1957. When he died in mid-season, John McIntire took over.

Bondi, Beulah (1892–1980). American character actress who emerged occasionally from retirement for TV roles in *The Waltons* and won an Emmy in 1976 for doing so. Only other TV movie: *She Waits*.

Boney
Australia 19   26 × 50m colour (16mm)
Global/STV/John McCallum
Cases of an Aborigine detective.
Slow-paced stories with a flaw at the centre, i.e. the lead is played by a white man in blackface.
w from books by Arthur Upfield
James Laurenson

Bonino (US 1953). Half-hour live comedy series for NBC, with Ezio Pinza as a widower with eight children. Naturally, he was also an opera singer.

Bono, Sonny (1936–). American singer who, with or without his ex-wife Cher, has had several series on American TV. TV movies: *Murder on Flight 502*, *Murder in Music City*.

The Book Game (GB 1982). Re-tread of the old *Take It or Leave It* panel show in which literary snippets are identified (or often not) and their authors discussed; with Robert Robinson again in charge. PP

book programmes. Of many, mostly shortlived, attempts over the years to deal with current writing and publishing the most durable was *The Book Programme* (BBC 1973–81) and even that was seasonal. It owed much to the vigorous and far from neutral chairmanship of presenter Robert Robinson, who latterly also edited the show. Paperbacks were served by *Read All About*

It (also BBC) conducted by Melvyn Bragg 1976–8 and for a further year by Ronald Harwood. In 1983 lacklustre new seasonal series were introduced on BBC2 and Channel 4, respectively *Bookmark*, presented initially by Simon Winchester, then by Ian Hamilton, and *Book Four*, from LWT, presented by Hermione Lee. See below for *The Book Tower*.   PP

The Book Tower (GB 1977–). A series of 25-minute programmes explaining books to young children. Initially narrated by Tom Baker, who was replaced by Stephen Moore and then Alun Armstrong. From YTV.

Booker Prize. Britain's richest literary award. Its presentation has been a television event since the late seventies, at first on BBC2, since 1984 on Channel 4. That year it was followed by *A Profile of Arthur James Mason*, a play by Kazio Ishiguro about a shy novelist which deliberately afforded some wry comparison with the high-minded hustling from the Guildhall.   PP

Bookie * (GB 1983). Wry comedy about a Glasgow bookmaker tangling emotionally with an attractive female punter, but not at the expense of his business principles, which led to a three-play series in 1986 with Robert Urquhart. Written by Allan Prior, for STV.
                                                              PP

Boone
US 1983   × 50m colour
NBC/Lorimar/Aminda/Earl Hamner
(Claylene Jones, John F. Perry)
In the forties, in backwoods America, the young son of poor but honest folks carves himself a career as a country music singer. Half *The Waltons*, half Elvis Presley: a big zero in the ratings.
cr Patty S. Schweitzer
Thomas Byrd, Greg Webb, Elizabeth Huddle, Barry Corbin, Kitty Moffat, Amanda Peterson

Boone, Debbie (1956–). American singer, daughter of Pat Boone. In occasional specials.

Boone, Pat (1934–) (Charles Eugene Boone). Gentle-mannered American singer who had his own show on American TV as early as 1957, and made a seventies comeback with his family.

Boone, Richard (1917–81). Craggy-featured American character actor who had mixed success on TV. Series include *Medic*, HAVE

GUN WILL TRAVEL, *The Richard Boone Show*, *Hec Ramsey*. TV movies: *In Broad Daylight*, *Goodnight My Love*, *The Great Niagara*, *The Last Dinosaur*, etc.

Boop Boop a Doop ** (US 1985). Well-informed 72m documentary tracing the creation of Max Fleischer's cartoon character, Betty Boop. Produced by Joshua Sugar for Crystal Pictures.

Booth, Shirley (1907–) (Thelma Ford Booth). American character actress who had a brief career in Hollywood after much Broadway success. TV series include HAZEL (Emmy 1961 and 1962 as best series actress), *A Touch of Grace*.

❈ **Boothby, Lord** (Robert Boothby) (1900–). British parliamentarian and prominent TV panel figure of the fifties and sixties.

Boothe, Powers (19 –). Dominant American actor who won an Emmy in 1980 for playing Jim Jones in GUYANA TRAGEDY. Also: *A Cry for Love*, *The Plutonium Incident*. Also played Philip Marlowe in *Chandlertown*.

Boots and Saddles
US 1957 39 × 25m bw
NBC
Life in the fifth cavalry during the 1870s. Mildly likeable western filler.
Jack Pickard, Pat McVey

Bootsie and Snudge ***. Originally (1960) *Bootsie and Snudge in Civvy Life*. British comedy series redeploying BILL FRASER's preposterous sergeant-major and ALFIE BASS's skiving squaddie from *The Army Game* as doorman and odd-job man in an old-fashioned London club. The format, created by Barry Took and Marty Feldman, gave Fraser ample opportunity for his grandiose aspirations and dropped aspirates; one of the 100 × 25m episodes consisted entirely of the two wondering what to do with an afternoon off, and in the end doing nothing. Milo Lewis directed most of the episodes, Peter Eton produced; for Granada. In 1974, after a 10-year lay-off, the show was revived (*p* and *d* Bill Podmore) but lasted only six episodes.   PP

Border TV. British ITV company serving a small area centring on Carlisle. Its relatively small turnover makes it a sensitive indicator of rises and falls in ITV's fortunes, and it has survived several financial crises.

The Borderers * (GB 1969–70). Spirited northern western set in the 17th-century Scottish Borders, complete with cattle and sheep rustling, mounted chases and antagonisms settled by sword or gun. Thanks to a towering performance by Iain Cuthbertson as the crafty warden (i.e. sheriff), there were also more subtle satisfactions. The format was by Bill Craig; produced by Peter Graham Scott; for BBC.
PP

Borge, Victor (1909–). Danish pianist–comedian, for many years an international TV and stage favourite with his one-man show.

The Borgia Stick **
US 1967 98m colour TVM
Universal (Richard Lewis)
An innocent-seeming suburban couple are blackmailed employees of a powerful and mysterious crime syndicate.
Well-paced and intriguingly unfolded thriller, one of the best of the early TV movies.
w A. J. Russell d David Lowell Rich
Don Murray, Inger Stevens, Fritz Weaver, Barry Nelson, Sorrell Booke
† The film was also released theatrically.

The Borgias
GB 1981 10 × 50m colour
BBC/Mark Shivas
In 1492 Roderigo Borgia bribes his way into being Pope and sets the scene for decades of villainy in high places.
Confused and unimpressive family farrago – could the Borgias ever be made dramatic or sympathetic? – with an added liability in the shape of its star's hilariously imperfect command of English. An expensive fiasco.
w John Prebble d Brian Farnham m Georges Delerue
Adolfo Celi, Oliver Cotton, Anne Louise Lambert, Alfred Burke

Borgnine, Ernest (1915–) (Ermes Borgnino). Star American character actor who has been solidly busy throughout middle age, going to Hollywood in the forefront of the TV invasion of the fifties, to star in *Marty*. TV work has included many guest roles and two series: *McHale's Navy, Future Cop*. TV movies: *Sam Hill, The Trackers, Future Cop, Jesus of Nazareth, Fire, The Ghost of Flight 401, The Cops and Robin, All Quiet on the Western Front, Carpool, Airwolf, The Last Days of Pompeii*, etc.

Born and Bred *
GB 1978 12 × 50m colour (VTR)
Thames (Peter Duguid)
Blackish comedy of the misadventures of a perfectly awful South London family.
Not at all a bad attempt, with many hilarious moments of the kind later familiar in *Soap*.
w DOUGLAS LIVINGSTONE d Baz Taylor
Max Wall, Gordon Kaye, Kate Williams, Ray Mort, Tony McHale, Trevor Peacock, Pat Ashton

Born Beautiful
US 1984 96m colour TVM
NBC/Proctor and Gamble (Michael Lepiner)
A top fashion model gives way graciously to a younger rival and herself becomes a photographer.
Glossy time-waster which aims to be the *All About Eve* of its milieu.
w Rose Leiman Goldemberg d Harvey Hart ph Michael J. Davis m Brad Fiedel
Erin Gray, Lori Singer, Polly Bergen, Ed Marinaro

Born Free *
US 1974 13 × 50m colour
NBC/Columbia/David Gerber (Paul Radin)
Agreeable TV adaptation of Joy Adamson's books and films about game wardens and a lion in East Africa. Unfortunately the network couldn't play it before 8 p.m., which was too late for the family audience, and its ratings disappointed.
Gary Collins, Diana Muldaur, Hal Frederick

Born Innocent
US 1974 74m colour TVM
Tomorrow
Problems of a 14-year-old girl in a tough detention centre.
Television thought it had grown up because the heroine was raped with a broom handle. Ho hum.
w Gerald di Pego d Donald Wrye
Linda Blair, Joanna Miles, Kim Hunter, Richard Jaeckel, Mitch Vogel
† This film, unfortunately first transmitted in the US at 8 p.m., is credited with assisting the anti-violence pressure groups which in 1976 were able to bring about 'family time' up to 9 p.m. and a stiff reduction in cop and crime shows after that. From this blow American TV took more than two years to recover.

Born to Be Small *
GB 1971 50m colour
Interesting documentary on the world of

dwarfs. Written and directed by Anthony Armstrong Jones (Lord Snowdon); produced by Derek Hart; for ATV.

Born to Be Sold
US 1981 96m colour TVM
NBC/Ron Samuels
A social worker attacks baby factories. Old-fashioned racket-busting melodrama.
w Karen Harris d Burt Brinckerhoff ph William Cronjager m Johnny Harris
Lynda Carter, Harold Gould, Philip Sterling, Dean Stockwell, Sharon Farrell, Lloyd Haynes, Ed Nelson

The Borrowers
US 1973 74m colour (VTR) TVM
TCF/Walt de Faria (Warren J. Lockhart)
A small girl finds that little people live under her kitchen floorboards.
Slow-moving family larks based on Mary Norton's book; good trick effects.
Eddie Albert, Tammy Grimes, Judith Anderson, Beatrice Straight, Barnard Hughes

Bosanquet, Reginald (1932–84). Endearing British newscaster, with ITN from its beginnings in 1955 until his abrupt departure during the ITV stoppage of 1979. At first a scriptwriter and reporter regarded only as a workaday understudy to more glamorous figures such as Chris Chataway and Ludovic Kennedy, he gradually became a character in the public's eye, renowned for his precarious delivery when the consonants were clustering against him, and his enjoyment of the good things in life. After 1979 made occasional appearances, including three *Nationwide* spots on BBC1 in which he fulminated against alimony and other evils. Autobiography *Let's Get Through Wednesday*, 1980.   PP

Bosley, Tom (1927–). Roly-poly American character actor who apart from film work has been much in evidence in TV series *The Debbie Reynolds Show, Happy Days*. TV movies: *Night Gallery, Vanished, No Place To Run, Death Cruise, The Last Survivors, Testimony of Two Men, The Bastard, With This Ring, The Triangle Factory Fire Scandal, The Return of the Mod Squad*, etc. Also the voice of Pop in *Wait Till Your Father Gets Home*.

Bosom Buddies (US 1980–1). A one-season half-hour comedy about two ad men who have to dress as women because a girls' hostel is the only one they can afford. A long way behind *Some Like It Hot*, and the situation was strained

even in the first episode. With Peter Scolari, Tom Hanks; created by Chris Thompson; for Miller–Milkis/Paramount/ABC.

Boss Cat: see Top Cat

Boss Lady (US 1952). Half-hour comedy series for NBC, with Lynn Bari as chief executive of a construction firm.

Boston Blackie
US 1951–2 58 × 25m bw
United Artists
Underworld adventures of the crook with a heart of gold.
Flatly handled variation on the long-running film series.
Kent Taylor, Lois Collier, Frank Orth

Bostwick, Barry (1946–). American leading man in the James Stewart mould. TV movies: *The Chadwick Family, The Quinns, Murder by Natural Causes, Once Upon a Family, Scruples, Moviola*. Series: *Foul Play*.

Boswall's Wild Life Safari to Mexico (GB 1978). Six half-hour films photographed by Douglas Fisher and 'starring' Jeffrey Boswall the naturalist; for BBC. Titles: *Across the Cactus Desert, The Sea of Cortez, To the Islands of the Sea Wolf, Through the Mangrove Marismas, Save the Jungle!, On the Scorpion Reef*. The same team previously went to Ethiopia and Argentina and also made *The Private Life of the Jackass Penguin*.

Boswell, James (1740–95). Scottish advocate and literatteur who inspired two quite dissimilar TV exercises in 1983–4. *Boswell for the Defence*, adapted from his account of his successful defence of an alleged sheep-thief by Mark Harris, made a strong 90-minute play with David McKail, Alec Heggie, Isobel Black, Andrew Keir and Rikki Fulton, directed by Gareth Davies, produced by Roderick Graham, for BBC Scotland. Less successfully from that source came *Boswell's London Journal*, series about the young Boswell in search of social advancement and sexual conquests, done as a low-budget series with video inlays and sketchy backgrounds. Ian Sharp played Boswell.   PP

Botanic Man (GB 1978). A 10 × 25-minute series for Thames TV in which David Bellamy traces the evolution and adaptation of living things. Produced by Terry Dixon.

Bottoms, Joseph (1954–). American leading man. TV movies: *Trouble Comes to Town, Unwed Father, Stalk the Wild Child, Holocaust, The Intruder Within*.

Bottoms, Sam (1955–). American leading man. TV movies: *Savages, Cage without a Key, Greatest Heroes of the Bible, East of Eden.*

Bottoms, Timothy (1951–). American leading man. TV movies: *The Money-changers, The Gift of Love, A Shining Season, Escape, East of Eden.*

Bough, Frank (1933–). British sporting commentator who also appeared on *Nationwide* and was the first host of the BBC's *Breakfast Time.*

Bouncing Back * (GB 1983 52m). Ingenious, very Schumanesque Howard Schuman comedy about a therapist who rehabilitates his patients with the aid of closed-circuit television, subjecting them to the false bonhomie of quiz shows, the fixed smiles of the song-and-dance spectacular and – most soothingly of all – the unction of the chat show. With John Gordon-Sinclair, Christopher Guard, Phoebe Nicholls, Eleanor Bron, Roger Lloyd Packer. Music by Andy Roberts, directed by Colin Bucksey, produced by Lynn Horsford; for Central. PP

The Bounder (GB 1982–3 13 × 30m). One of several attempts to use up the autumnal glories of George Cole not being fully stretched by *Minder*, here by *Rising Damp* writer Eric Chappell. Cole played a stuffy householder up against an unscrupulous character of a brother-in-law played by Peter Bowles. It never quite fired. With Isla Blair. Produced and directed by Vernon Lawrence, for YTV. PP

The Bounty Man
US 1972 74m colour TVM
Spelling–Goldberg
A hunter falls for the girl friend of his quarry. Glum pocket western.
w Jim Byrnes *d* John Llewellyn Moxey
Clint Walker, Richard Basehart, John Ericson, Margot Kidder, Gene Evans, Arthur Hunnicutt

Bouquet of Barbed Wire *
GB 1976 6 × 50m colour (VTR)
LWT (Tony Wharmby)
A father's obsessive love for his married daughter leads to tragedy.
Kinky saga which was much discussed and provoked a less satisfactory sequel, *Another Bouquet* (*p/d* John Frankau). Well made and acted, but less than convincing.

w Andrea Newman *d* Tony Wharmby
Frank Finlay, Susan Penhaligon, James Aubrey, Sheila Allen

Bourbon Street Beat
US 1959 39 × 50m bw
ABC/Warner
Exploits of two private eyes in New Orleans. Old-fashioned mysteries, adequately produced.
Richard Long, Andrew Duggan, Van Williams

Bowen, Jim (1937–). British comedian and anchorman (*Bullseye*); an ex-schoolteacher.

Bowen, John (1924–). British writer of versatility and stamina whose works range from studies of adolescence such as *The Essay Prize* (ATV 1960), in which Eileen Atkins had a one-line part, to complex thriller serials of recent times: *Rachel in Danger* (Thames 1979), *Dying Day* (1980). Somewhere in between come Bowen's rustic chillers (see *Robin Redbreast*), ghost stories and imaginative reworkings of the classics (*Heil Caesar*, 1974): author of *The McGuffin*, source of 1986 TVM. A producer at BBC Pebble Mill in the eighties. PP

Bowers, Lally (1917–84). British character actress and light comedienne who made occasional television appearances: *Pygmalion, The Importance of Being Earnest, A Fine Romance.*

Bowles, Peter (1936–). Heavily built British light actor with a neat touch for classy farce. Best known for continuing roles in TO THE MANOR BORN and *Only When I Laugh.* In 1982 *The Bounder* came to nothing much but *Lytton's Diary* (1985) extended him into more serious comedy.

Bowman, Lee (1914–79). American light leading man who had a thin film career but was busy in fifties TV series such as *Ellery Queen* and *Miami Undercover*. TV movie: *Fame Is the Name of the Game.*

Boxleitner, Bruce (1950–). American light leading man, striking in the series *How the West Was Won*. Also *Bring 'Em Back Alive, Scarecrow and Mrs King*. TV movies: *The Chadwick Family, A Cry for Help, Kiss Me Kill Me, Happily Ever After, The Gambler, East of Eden, Fly Away Home.*

The Boy David: see The Visit.

THE BOY DAVID. This three-part documentary about a Peruvian boy whose face was all but destroyed by disease was much acclaimed and quickly repeated.

The Boy in the Bush (Australia/GB 1984 4 × 60m). D. H. Lawrence had a hand in M. L. Skinner's yarn about a young Englishman trying his hand in the Australian outback in the early years of the century, but it seemed composed of fairly predictable characters and clashes. With Kenneth Branagh, Sigrid Thornton. Adapted by Hugh Whitemore, directed by Rob Stewart, produced for ABC and Channel 4 by Portman Productions.   PP

The Boy in the Plastic Bubble *
US 1976 96m colour TVM
Spelling–Goldberg/ABC (Joel Thurm, Cindy Dunne)
A boy without immunities has to live in a sterile environment.
Unusual and moving but inevitably over-extended fable.
w Douglas Day Stewart d Randal Kleiser
John Travolta, Glynnis O'Connor, Robert Reed, Diana Hyland (Emmy, best actress)

The Boy Who Drank Too Much
US 1980 96m colour TVM
CBS/MTM (Donald A. Baer)
Of two boys on the school hockey team, one is the thoughtful child of loving parents, the other a teenage alcoholic living with his despairing widower father.
Glum shocker which though well made and acted seems to have no particular point except an obvious warning of the dangers of drink.
w Edward DeBlasio, novel Shep Greene d Jerrold Freedman ph Allen Daviau m Michael Small
Scott Baio, Don Murray, Lance Kerwin, Ed Lauter, Mariclare Costello

Boyce Goes West (GB 1984). Baffling series with Welsh heart-throb Max Boyce trekking round the American rodeo circuit as a singing cowboy.   PP

Boyd QC. An early staple (from 1956) of British independent TV, this half-hour series by Associated Rediffusion cast Michael Denison as a barrister and Charles Leno as his clerk. Like Perry Mason, Boyd always won, but the court procedure was often intriguing.

❋ **Boyd, William** (1895–1972). Mature American leading man, familiar through films of the thirties and forties as the black-garbed Hopalong Cassidy. Edited for TV, these were a sensational success, and Boyd became a folk hero. See Hopalong Cassidy.

Boyle, Katie (1928–) (Katerina Imperiali di Francabilla). English-accented Italian lady who since the fifties has chosen to adorn English television as panellist or anchorwoman, while not being above writing beauty hints for the popular press and a problem page for TV Times.

The Boys from the Blackstuff ***
GB 1982 5 × av. 60m colour VTR
BBC (Michael Wearing)
Intemperate, indignant, somewhat over-hailed saga of unemployment on Merseyside which gave the Thatcher government's critics fresh ammunition and everyone a new catchphrase – 'Gizza a job', the recurring cry of the vehement character Yosser, played by Bernard Hill. The series was developed by Alan Bleasdale from a 1978 single play The Black Stuff about a gang of tarmac-layers who lost their jobs and their money moonlighting. What should have been the first episode, concentrating on their former boss as he went broke, was transmitted as The Muscle Market in 1981. The remaining five, ranging from 55 to 70 minutes in duration, followed the six members of the gang as they ran up against unfeeling social security clerks and stony police, with Yosser emerging as the folk hero of the day.
'A phenomenal performance by Bernard Hill,' I wrote, 'caught in a spiral of frustration, rage, as dignity, wife, family and finally home were taken from him, he was reduced to a head-banging zombie.'
w Alan Bleasdale d Philip Saville
† Texts published as a Granada paperback, 1982.   PP

Bozo the Clown. A character created in 1959 by Larry Harmon. Actors were trained to play him in local shows for children, and cartoons featuring him had to be included. As merchandising schemes go, this certainly had the old one-two.

Bracken's World *
US 1969–70 41 × 50m colour
NBC/TCF (Stanley Rubin)
How a big movie studio operates. In the first few episodes Bracken, the tycoon, was seen only as a hand and a cigar, but those who imagined Darryl F. Zanuck would not be far wrong. The series had a few interesting insights, but not surprisingly got itself bogged down in soap opera.
cr Dorothy Kingsley
Eleanor Parker (in first 16), Elizabeth Allen, Leslie Nielsen, Peter Haskell, Linda Harrison
'We deal with people at the workaday level, where there is identification.' – Stanley Rubin

Bradbury, Malcolm (1932–). British academic (Professor of American studies at the University of East Anglia) and writer whose original plays for TV (*The After Dinner Game*, 1975; *Love on a Gunboat*, 1977; *Standing in for Henry*, 1980) were eclipsed by the dramatization of his novel THE HISTORY MAN by another hand, Christopher Hampton, 1982. The reverse process worked less well when Bradbury adapted Tom Sharpe's *Blott on the Landscape*, 1985. Bradbury also writes authoritatively about television.   PP

Braden, Bernard (1916–). Canadian host and light actor who with his wife Barbara Kelly had varied success in Britain, notably as panellist and latterly host of a consumer guidance show, *On the Braden Beat*. BAFTA award 1964.

The Brady Brides (US 1981). Shortlived sequel to *The Brady Bunch*, with two of the girls grown up and about to be married. Not a starter. With Eve Plumb, Maureen McCormick, Robert Reed, Florence Henderson, Ann B. Davis. Written by Sherwood and Lloyd Schwartz; directed by Peter Baldwin; for Redwood/Paramount/NBC. What was originally designed as a TV movie actually aired as four half-hours.

The Brady Bunch
US 1969–73 117 × 25m colour
ABC/Paramount (Sherwood Schwartz)

A widower with three sons marries a widow with three daughters.

Yes, that old chestnut. Cheerful and sudsy, it worked well enough: the family even turned into a variety act and – in 1972 – sparked off a cartoon series, *The Brady Kids*, which ran 52 episodes.

cr Sherwood Schwartz *m* Frank de Vol

Robert Reed, Florence Henderson, Ann B. Davis . . . plus six kids, one dog and one cat

Brady, Scott (1924–85) (Jerry Tierney). American tough guy actor of forties films. TV movies include *The Night Strangler*, *Roll Freddy Roll*, *Kansas City Massacre*, *Law and Order*, *Wheels*, *When Every Day Was the Fourth of July*, *To Kill a Cop*, *The Last Ride of the Dalton Gang*, *Power*.

Braeden, Eric (19 –) (Hans Gudegast). German actor in America. *The Power Within*, *The Aliens are Coming*, *The Young and the Restless*.

Bragg, Melvyn (1939–). British novelist, and presenter and editor of arts programmes since joining BBC straight from university. Started paperback review *Read All About It*, also literary quiz *Take It or Leave It*. Associated with LWT's *South Bank Show* since its inception.   PP

Brahm, John (1893–). American director who after a stylish but low-key Hollywood career played himself out in television with episodes of the kind of crime series he had always favoured: *Alfred Hitchcock Presents*, *Naked City*, *The Twilight Zone*.

The Brains Trust. A phenomenon of wartime radio whose enormous popularity was won by the combination of erudition with a great deal of knockabout badinage and needling of each other by Professor C. E. M. Joad, Commander Campbell and Dr (as he was then) Julian Huxley. The BBC television version (1954–5) was altogether more donnish, with the speakers disposed in armchairs rather than huddled round a table and Sir Julian Huxley the only survivor from the old days, on one memorable occasion joined by his brother Aldous. It was no longer popular erudition and certainly not popular entertainment. But it had one thing going for it: it never recruited its speakers from showbiz. Created by Howard Thomas; produced (for TV) by John Furness.   PP

Brake, Patricia (1942–). British comedy actress who does a smart line in cockneys and was a hit in *Porridge*, *Going Straight* and *The Glums*.

Braker
US 1985 74m colour TVM
ABC/MGM–UA/Blatt–Singer/Centerpoint
(Joseph Stern)

Adventures of a Los Angeles homicide cop. Routine pilot which didn't sell.

w Felix Culver, Jim Carabatsos *d* Victor Lobi

Carl Weathers, Joseph Bottoms, Alex Rocco, Peter Michael Goetz

Brambell, Wilfrid (1912–85). British character actor specializing in dirty old men, e.g. the elder Steptoe in STEPTOE AND SON.

Brand, Neville (1921–). Thick-set American character actor who played Al Capone in *The Untouchables*. TV movies: *Lock Stock and Barrel*, *Two For the Money*, *Killdozer*, *Death Stalk*, *Barbary Coast*, *The Quest*, *Fire*, *Captains Courageous*, *The Seekers*, etc.

A Brand New Life *
US 1972 74m colour TVM
Tomorrow

A middle-aged wife discovers she is pregnant. Well acted but fairly predictable domestic drama.

w Jerome Kass, Peggy Chantler Dick d Sam O'Steen m Billy Goldenberg

Cloris Leachman, Martin Balsam, Wilfrid Hyde White, Mildred Dunnock, Gene Nelson, Marge Redmond

Branded
US 1964–5 48 × 25m bw (35 in colour)
NBC/Goodson–Todman

In the old west, a West Point graduate is cashiered as a coward and seeks to prove himself.

Good standard western.

Chuck Connors

Brando, Marlon (1924–). Leading American actor who seldom appears on TV; but he won an Emmy in 1978 for his appearance as the Nazi Lincoln Rockwell in ROOTS: THE NEXT GENERATIONS.

Brandon, Michael (19 –). American leading man. *The Red Badge of Courage, Queen of the Stardust Ballroom, James Dean, Red Alert, Vacation in Hell, A Perfect Match, Between Two Brothers, Deadly Messages, Dempsey and Makepeace*, etc.

Brass ***
GB 1983–4 26 × 30m colour
Granada (Bill Podmore)

Rich comedy series from two ex-*Coronation Street* writers piling together every cliché of north-country, trouble-up-at-t'mill fiction and embellishing the result with puns, jokes and inversions taken from every nook of popular culture. 'You don't need to be able to catch these flying allusions,' I wrote, 'but if you can, each one increases the savour.' Timothy West played Bradley Hardacre, heartless mill-owner, mine-owner and munitions manufacturer.

w John Stevenson, Julian Roach d Gareth Jones

Timothy West, Caroline Blakiston, Barbara Ewing, Geoffrey Hinsliff, David Ashton PP

Brass
US 1985 96m colour TVM
CBS/Orion/Carnan/Jaygee (Jerry Golod)

A widowed New York detective preserves his integrity at all costs.

Routine cop stuff, rather hysterically detailed, and designed as the pilot for a star series which didn't take.

cr Roy Baldwin, Matt Harris d Corey Allen ph Ronald M. Lautore m Joe Sherman

Carroll O'Connor, Lois Nettleton, Larry Atlas, Samuel E. Wright, Paul Shenar, Marcia Gross, Begona Plaza, Vincent Gardenia

Brass Tacks. British current affairs show emanating from the BBC's northern production centre in Manchester and therefore setting out to (1) bring northern no-nonsense attitudes to issues of the day; (2) expose same to no-nonsense studio audience; and (3) invite phone-in reactions via no-nonsense local radio stations. Sometimes it succeeds.   PP

Brasselle, Keefe (1923–81). Gangling young film actor who became a TV producer for James Aubrey and CBS and formed Richelieu Productions. When hints of scandals cancelled the projects, he wrote a satirical novel called *The CanniBalS*.

Brave Eagle (US 1955). Half-hour western for CBS, taking the Indian viewpoint, with Keith Larsen as the heroic brave and Bert Wheeler as an old scout.

Brave New World
US 1979 150m colour TVM
NBC/Universal/Milton Sperling
   (Jacqueline Babbin)

Six hundred years from now, child-bearing has been replaced by hatcheries, but chaos breaks out when a young man raised among 'savages' disrupts the even tenor of carefully controlled existence.

Originally shot as a four-hour mini-series, kept on the shelf for two years and released in edited form, this is a risible American attempt at an English modern classic, with limited sets and actors who clearly wish they were elsewhere.

w Robert E. Thomson, *novel* Aldous Huxley d Burt Brickerhoff ph Harry L. Wolf m Paul Chihara ad Tom H. John

Julie Cobb, Bud Cort, Keir Dullea, Ron O'Neal, Marcia Strassman, Kristoffer Tabori, Dick Anthony Williams

'Gimmicks and indifferent production values give the future a bad look.' – *Daily Variety*

Brave Stallion: see Fury

BRASS. In Granada's larger-than-life comic serial the grasping Bradley Hardacre, always at the centre of whatever mischief was afoot, was played by Timothy West.

The Bravos
US 1971 100m colour TVM
Universal

Post-Civil War problems of an army officer. Adequate, overlong mini-western.

w Christopher Knopf *d* Ted Post

George Peppard, Pernell Roberts, Belinda Montgomery, L. Q. Jones, Bo Svenson

Bray, Robert (19 –82). Stalwart American outdoor star of *Stagecoach West*.

Bread or Blood ***
GB 1981 5 × 75m colour
BBC (Ruth Caleb)

Marvellous evocation of rural life in a not so Merrie England of 150 years ago, derived from an account by W. H. Hudson who had taken it all down from an aged survivor. Birth, death, grinding poverty, the cruel enclosure acts bulk large, but all shouldered with dignity and rectitude by the shepherd hero.

w Peter Ransley *ph* Ray Orton *d* Peter Smith

Malcolm Storry   PP

Breakfast Television. A part of American life for more than 30 years, it was tried out in the UK on three occasions without catching on – in the London ITV area in the late fifties, in Yorkshire in the early seventies, in Scotland in a quaint BBC 'radiovision' experiment whereby the cameras were wheeled in on the morning radio news miscellany. Pressure from advertisers, it was claimed, led the IBA to offer a separate breakfast franchise at the time of the 1980–81 re-allocation of contracts. It went to TV-am, who opened their *Good Morning Britain* in February 1983. The BBC cheekily had slipped in first with *Breakfast Time* and for a long period completely outclassed the competition, but in so doing further stretched its already extended finances. Neither side has proved much need for television at this time of day in a country whose work and commuting patterns are different from those of the United States. PP

Breakfast Time. The BBC's breakfast show, little changed since it began in January 1983, with Frank Bough as comfy anchorman and a variety of Selina Scott replacements as his co-presenter. 'As with Milton Keynes,' I wrote after the first week, 'no one wanted it, but now it's there it's quite handy.' Original editor: Ron Neil. PP

Breaking Away
US 1980 8 × 50m colour
ABC/TCF (Herbert B. Leonard)
A small-town teenager loves bicycles and anything Italian.
Shortlived series based on the successful film. Not bad at all; just not strong enough.
Shaun Cassidy, Vincent Gardenia, Barbara Barrie, Jackie Earle Haley, Tom Wiggin, Thom Bray
'Nothing less than charming.' – *Daily Variety*

The Breaking of Colonel Keyser *
GB 1972 50m colour
Robert Holles play with Colin Blakely as a wild infantry officer sacked from his command on the eve of D-Day because of his harsh training methods. Obviously modelled on a real colonel who was court-martialled for making his troops shout 'Ho-de-ho' when he yelled 'Hi-de-hi!' – the same man gave Jimmy Perry and David Croft the title of their evergreen *Hi-de-Hi!* Neatly enshrined in Holles's story (for Thames Television) was one of the dilemmas of a civilized nation forced to wage war: do you leave it to the nice but less efficient soldiers or call in the thugs who are good at it? PP

The Breaking Point *
US 1963–4 52 × 50m bw
ABC/Bing Crosby Productions
Psychiatric case histories.
At least a bid towards adult drama at a time when it was sorely needed. The atmosphere however was a little too rarefied.
Paul Richards, Eduard Franz

Breaking Up *
US 1978 96m colour TVM
Time–Life/David Susskind (Frederick Brogger)
When her marriage ends, a woman fights to retain her personal identity.
Tolerable telefilm, smartly photographed in Toronto and New York.
w Loring Mandel d Delbert Mann ph Gil Taylor ad Ben Edwards m Walter Levinsky
Lee Remick, Granville Van Dusen, Vicki Dawson, David Stambaugh, Frank Latimore

Breaking Up Is Hard To Do
US 1980 2 × 96m colour TVM
Columbia
Four men with marital problems live it up at a beach house.
A rather sour drama with irritating characters and not much development.
w Jim Henderson d Lou Antonio
Robert Conrad, Billy Crystal, Ted Bessell, Jeff Conaway, Tony Musante, David Ogden Stiers

Breakout
US 1967 97m colour TVM
Universal (Richard Irving)
Escaped convicts in a blizzard stop to help a small boy.
Ripe Hollywood corn and not much action.
w Sy Gomberg d Richard Irving
James Drury, Kathryn Hays, Woody Strode, Sean Garrison

Brecht, Bertolt (1898–1956). Communist German poet and playwright whose works steadily turn up on television. In 1983–4 alone in Great Britain were two productions of the *Seven Deadly Sins* and a recital of Brecht songs by Robyn Archer as *A Song for Bad Times* (Channel 4 from Telekation) with stock footage of latter-day riots and other troubles crassly intercut into proceedings. PP

Breck, Peter (1930–). American 'second lead' who had a fair crack at series: *Black Saddle*, *The Big Valley*.

Brenda Starr, Girl Reporter *
US 1975 74m colour TVM
David Wolper
An intrepid newspaperwoman defends a millionaire from voodoo villains.
Comic strip derivative which didn't quite take, but provides some fair fun along the way.
w George Kirgo, *comic strip* Dale Messick *d* Mel Stuart
Jill St John, Jed Allan, Victor Buono, Sorrell Booke, Joel Fabiani

Brennan, Eileen (1937–). Thickset American character actress, in all media. TV series: *A New Kind of Family*, PRIVATE BENJAMIN. TV movies: *Playmates*, *The Blue Knight*, *My Father's House*, *The Night That Panicked America*, *The Death of Richie*, *Black Beauty*, *My Old Man*.

❊ **Brennan, Walter** (1894–1974). American character actor with a long and honourable Hollywood history including three Academy Awards; for the roles he played, he often did not require his teeth. He remained busy on TV to an advanced age, in long-running series: THE REAL MCCOYS, *To Rome with Love*, *Tycoon*, *The Guns of Will Sonnett*. He also starred in TV movies, notably *The Over the Hill Gang*, *The Young Country* and *Home for the Holidays*.

Brenner (US 1959). New York based, half-hour police series for CBS, with Edward Binns and James Broderick as father and son cops.

Brensham People
GB 1976 3 × 45m colour
BBC (Innes Lloyd)
Trilogy wrought by Hugh Whitemore from John Moore's fond novels of life in a Gloucestershire country town – actually Tewkesbury, where it was filmed.
Going, Going, Gone d Brian Parker
Master of Many Arts d Lawrence Gordon Clarke
William Hart-Wainwright d Peter Smith   PP

Bret Maverick (US 1981). James Garner returns in a one-hour series attempting to catch the flavour of the 20-year-old western comedy hit.

Brett, Jeremy (1935–) (Peter Jeremy Huggins). Personable British actor whose disdainful good looks and rather mannered, matinée-idol delivery had only to weather for a couple of decades to make him an ideal Sherlock Holmes, which they did in Granada's *Adventures of Sherlock Holmes*, 1984–5. A specialist in old-fashioned upright types. *The Good Soldier*, *Florence Nightingale*, *Deceptions*, etc.   PP

The Brian Keith Show
aka: *The Little People*
US 1972–3 48 × 25m colour
NBC/Warner
Easy-going comedy about a paediatrician in Hawaii.
Brian Keith, Shelley Fabares, Victoria Young, Roger Bowen, Nancy Kulp

Brian's Song *
US 1971 73m colour TVM
Columbia (Paul Junger Witt)
The true story of Brian Piccolo, a football star who died of cancer.
In the tradition of *The Pride of the Yankees*, this earnest sentimental piece was a big hit in its home country, and won a few plaudits for telemovies, but other countries saw it as one long cliché.
w William Blinn *d* Buzz Kulik *m* MICHEL LEGRAND
James Caan, Jack Warden, Billy Dee Williams, Bud Furillo, Shelley Fabares, Judy Pace
† Emmy 1971, best programme.

Brideshead Revisited ****
GB 1981 13 × 50m colour 16mm
Granada (Derek Granger)
An Oxford undergraduate finds his life dominated by his friendship with a wealthy Catholic family.
A massive undertaking which turned out at five million pounds more expensive than anyone dreamed, and was thought of not only as the *Caesar and Cleopatra* of British television but as an albatross round the neck of Granada. In fact its critical success was almost unanimous, and it was not a disaster in the ratings. More homosexually oriented than the novel, it aroused curiosity on this account and despite unavoidable slowness its camera was always in the right place and it never looked less than gorgeous. In the end its faults were those of the book, to which it was almost obsessively faithful.
w JOHN MORTIMER, *novel* Evelyn Waugh *d* CHARLES STURRIDGE, MICHAEL LINDSAY-HOGG *pd* PETER PHILLIPS *m* Geoffrey Burgon
JEREMY IRONS, ANTHONY ANDREWS, Diana Quick, Claire Bloom
guests: Laurence Olivier, JOHN GIELGUD, Mona Washbourne, Stéphane Audran, John Le Mesurier, Jane Asher

Bridger
US 1976 100m colour TVM
Universal (David Lowell Rich)

Adventures of a mountain man around 1830. Fairly pleasing western pilot which didn't make it.

w Merwin Gerard d David Lowell Rich ph Bud Thackery m Elliot Kaplan

James Wainwright, Ben Murphy, Dirk Blocker, Sally Field, William Windom

Bridges, Alan (1927–). British director whose most lauded television plays include *The Lie* (BAFTA 1970) and *The Traitor*.

Bridges, Beau (1941–). American leading actor, in all media; son of Lloyd Bridges. TV series: *United States*. TV movies: *The Man without a Country, The Stranger Who Looks Like Me*, MEDICAL STORY, *The Four Feathers, The President's Mistress, The Child Stealer*.

Bridges, Jeff (1949–). American leading man, son of Lloyd Bridges. TV movies: *Silent Night Lonely Night, In Search of America*.

✸ **Bridges, Lloyd** (1913–). Reliable American star actor whose physique belies his years. Apart from a successful film career he may well hold the record for TV guest shots and series. Among the latter: SEA HUNT, *The Loner, Water World, The Lloyd Bridges Show, San Francisco International, Joe Forrester, How the West was Won*. TV movies: *Silent Night Lonely Night, The Silent Gun, The Love War, A Tattered Web, The Deadly Dream, Haunts of the Very Rich, Crime Club, Death Race, Stowaway to the Moon, Roots, Telethon, The Great Wallendas, The Critical List, East of Eden, Disaster on the Coastliner, Moviola, Beatrice, The Blue and the Gray, Grace Kelly, George Washington, Paper Dolls*, etc.

Bridges to Cross (US 1986   × 50m). A project at press time was this romantic drama series with Suzanne Pleshette as a Washington magazine reporter trying to outsmart her ex-husband who works for the same paper. Also cast, Roddy McDowall, Jose Ferrer, Eva Gabor. Produced by Bill Blinn for Lorimar.

Bridget Loves Bernie *
US 1973 24 × 25m colour
CBS/Columbia/Douglas S. Cramer (Arthur Alsberg, Bob Nelson)

New York comedy: wealthy Irish Catholic girl falls for a Jewish cab driver.

Surprisingly agreeable updating of *Abie's*

Irish Rose: it was popular enough, but network pressures caused its demise.

cr Bernard Slade

MEREDITH BAXTER, DAVID BIRNEY (the stars later married in real life), Harold J. Stone, Bibi Osterwald, AUDRA LINDLEY, DAVID DOYLE, NED GLASS, Robert Sampson

The Brief (GB 1984). Mysterious little series from TVS about a barrister (Ray Lonnen) specializing in courts martial and thus forever whizzing off to Germany and the waiting charms of Sabina Postel while at home the charms of Isobel Black linger unappreciated. Written by Ray Jenkins and directed by John Frankau, it never quite justified its rather arbitrary milieu.   PP

Brief Encounter
GB 1975 74m colour TVM
ITC/Carlo Ponti/Cecil Clarke (Duane C. Bogie)

A suburban wife falls for an unhappily married doctor she meets on her weekly shopping trip.

Almost a word-for-word remake of the successful film, but with the wrong talent off form. A disaster.

w John Bowen d Alan Bridges

Richard Burton, Sophia Loren, Jack Hedley, Rosemary Leach, Anne Firbank, John Le Mesurier

✸ **Briers, Richard** (1934–). Dithery British light comedy actor, an engaging silly ass who appeared in several series as a young and not so young husband: BROTHERS IN LAW, THE MARRIAGE LINES, THE GOOD LIFE, *The Norman Conquests, The Other One, Goodbye Mr Kent*.

Briggs, Professor Asa (1921–). British historian and official chronicler of the BBC in ponderous *History of Broadcasting in the United Kingdom* for Oxford University Press. On screen, wrote and presented *Karl Marx in London*, 1982, and *Karl Marx – the Legacy*, 1984.   PP

Brimley, Wilford (19 –). American character actor specializing in craggy character types.

Brimstone and Treacle. Dennis Potter's 1976 play recorded by the BBC but never transmitted, on the grounds (as given by Alasdair Milne, then director of programmes) that its admittedly shocking scenes of an inert, brain-damaged girl being raped would provoke such outrage that the author's 'point of serious importance' would never get across. In fact a flawed, slipshod but deeply religious piece occupying a crucial place in a long sequence of agonized interior dramas which Potter had been writing. Two stage versions, neither very satisfactory, were mounted, and in 1982 a movie was finally realized, with Sting as the demonic young hero and Denholm Elliott as the girl's father, repeating his performance in the original TV show, which was produced by Kenith Trodd and directed by Alan Bridges. PP

Brinckerhoff, Burt (1936–). American TV director. TV movies include *The Cracker Factory*, *Can You Hear the Laughter?*, *Brave New World*.

'No animal can escape him. No man can outsmart him. No woman can resist him!'
Bring 'Em Back Alive
US 1982 17 × 50m colour
CBS/Schenck–Cardea/Columbia/
Thomson–Bernstein–Boxleitner
In 1939 Malaya, Frank Buck captures animals on commission but also gets mixed up with an assortment of spies.
Spoofy but too confused, this hokum is so pleased with itself that it seems to keep stopping to pat itself on the back.
cr Frank Cardea, George Schenck, Tom Sawyer
Bruce Boxleitner, Cindy Morgan, Clyde Kusatsu, Ron O'Neal, Roger Newman, John Zee, Harvey Jason, Kai Wulff
'All the trappings, allure and foolishness of long-ago Saturday afternoon serials at the Rialto mixed in with take-offs of w.k. past films, a smattering of Tarzan with his togs on, plenty of cliffhanging, and echoes of *Raiders of the Lost Ark*.' – *Daily Variety*

Bringing Up Buddy
US 1960 34 × 25m bw
CBS/MCA/Kayro
A young bachelor is cared for by his maiden aunts.
Mildly appealing comedy.
cr Joe Connelly, Bob Mosher
Frank Aletter, Doro Merande, Enid Markey

Brinkley, David (1920–). American commentator and anchorman, half (with Chet Huntley) of a famous newscasting team on NBC from 1956.

Brink's: The Great Robbery
US 1978 96m colour TVM
CBS/Quinn Martin

Dramatization of a Boston robbery of the fifties, from FBI files.
Routine real-life cops and robbers; the same case later featured as an unsuccessful theatrical movie.
w Robert W. Lenski *d* Marvin Chomsky
Carl Betz, Stephen Collins, Burr de Benning, Michael Gazzo, Cliff Gorman, Darren McGavin, Art Metrano, Leslie Nielsen

Britain in the Thirties (GB 1983 11 × 40m colour/bw). Usually, a particular issue was examined each week in this useful BBC series, e.g. the 1933 Oxford union debate in which pacifism carried the day, possibly to the encouragement of the dictators. Narrated by Andrew Faulds, produced by Christopher Cook. PP

British Academy of Film and Television Arts (BAFTA). The organization which gives annual merit awards. Formerly known as the British Film Academy, then as the Society of Film and Television Arts. It is operated from club premises in Piccadilly, London.

The British at War. 14-week compilation by Channel Four of two-hour programmes of official British documentaries of World War II, most of which had not been screened for forty years. Introduced from Churchill's war rooms, the programmes ran through the autumn of 1984 and were followed in the spring by AMERICANS AT WAR, consisting principally of Frank Capra's *Why We Fight* series.
PP: 'Umbrella title for masterly Channel 4 season of British World War II films in 1984, both features and propaganda or informational shorts, chosen by Leslie Halliwell. Followed by similar American season, 1985.'

British Broadcasting Corporation: see BBC

The British Empire
GB 1972 13 × 52m colour
Predictably running into disfavour with the Right for being too critical of British Empire-building and with the Left for being too adulatory, it was in fact a flabbily liberal history with the voices of individual contributors (Rene Cutforth, James Cameron among others) homogenized into one narrative read by Robert Hardy. Despite co-production resources the historical re-enactments were skimpy, too. A low-budget epic, a breathless spectacle with a cast of several. Edited by Max Morgan-Witts; for BBC/Time–Life. PP

Brittany, Morgan (1951–) (Suzanne Cupito). American leading lady. TV movies include *The Amazing Howard Hughes*, *The Initiation of Sarah*, *Stunt Seven*, *Samurai*, *The Dream Merchants*, *Moviola*, *The Wild Women of Chastity Gulch*, *Dallas*, *Glitter*, *Half Nelson*

Britton, Tony (1924–). Leading British actor, too often allocated roles lighter than his potential. Series: *The Nearly Man*, *Robin's Nest*, *Don't Wait Up*.

Broad, Richard (1942–). British documentary film-maker who first came to notice with a *This Week* special (Thames, 1975) applying that programme's reporting techniques to a vivid picture of Britain in 1844, complete with painful rural eviction. Subsequent works include the series *Palestine* (1978) and *The Troubles* (with Ian Stuttard, 1980). PP

Broadside
US 1964 32 × 25m bw
ABC/Universal (Edward J. Montagne)
Adventures of four Waves in the Pacific war. Flimsy service comedy.
Kathy Nolan, Edward Andrews
'Of genuine laughter there is little, of novelty none.' – Don Miller
† The series was a spin-off from *McHale's Navy*.

Brock's Last Case *
US 1972 98m colour TVM
Universal (Roland Kibbee)
A New York detective retires to a Californian citrus ranch but finds himself still up to his neck in murder.
Competent movie serving as the pilot for a series which later switched back to New York and the title of its original inspiration, *Madigan*.
w Martin Donaldson, Alex Gordon d David Lowell Rich m Charles Gross
Richard Widmark, Will Geer, John Anderson, Michael Burns, Henry Darrow

Broderick, James (1927–82). American character actor with a worried look, the father in FAMILY. TV movie: *The Shadow Box*.

❀ **Brodkin, Herbert** (1912–). American executive producer who won much respect for such projects as *The Defenders*, *Holocaust*, *Studs Lonigan*, *Siege*, *Skokie*. Originally a scenery designer.

Brokaw, Tom (1940–). American anchorman, host of NBC's *Today* since 1976.

Broke, Richard (1943–). British producer who came up by the story-editor route. Recent credits include *The Serpent Son*, *School Play*, *The Wilderness Years*, *Dr Fischer of Geneva*, *The Monocled Mutineer*. PP

Broken Arrow
US 1956–7 72 × 25m bw
ABC/TCF
An Indian agent tries to bring peace with the Apaches.
Contrived and rather glum rip-off of the famous film.
John Lupton, Michael Ansara (as Cochise)

Broken Glass (GB 1982). Compassionate drama on the painful subject of incest, written by James Andrew Hall, sensitively acted by James Grout and Bernard Hepton, rather oddly incorporated by Central in a Saturday night thriller series for ITV. PP

Broken Promise
US 1980 96m colour TVM
CBS/EMI/Roger Gimbel
A family of five abandoned children is helped by a juvenile services worker.
Pallid mixture of tears and smiles, always with a calculating eye on the viewer's heartstrings.
w Stephen Kandel, book Kent Hayes and Alex Lazzarino d Don Taylor ph Robert Jessup m Fred Karlin
Chris Sarandon, Melissa Michaelsen, George Coe, David Haskell

Brolin, James (1941–). American general purpose leading man who appeared regularly in *The Monroes* and rose to fame as the junior doctor in *Marcus Welby MD* (Emmy 1969). TV movies include *Short Walk to Daylight*, *Class of 63*, *Trapped*, *Steel Cowboy*, *White Water Rebels*, *Cowboy*, *Mae West*. Settled in as the resident manager of *Hotel*.

Bron, Eleanor (1940–). British revue actress who emanated from Cambridge during the Peter Cook period and became associated on TV with him and David Frost in their various variety formats.

Bronco
US 1958–61 68 × 50m bw
ABC/Warner
An ex-Confederate officer brings law to the west.

Below par spin-off from *Cheyenne*, one of a nap hand of hour westerns held by Warner at this period (*Maverick*, *Sugarfoot*, etc).

Ty Hardin

Bronk
US 1975 74m colour TVM
CBS/MGM

Alex Bronkov, a homicide detective on suspension, tracks down a narcotics ring. Utterly predictable crime hokum resting on its star, who carried the subsequent 50m series for 24 episodes.

cr Carroll O'Connor *w* Ed Waters, Al Martinez, Carroll O'Connor, Bruce Geller *d* Richard Donner *m* Lalo Schifrin

Jack Palance, David Birney, Tony King, Joanna Moore, Henry Beckman

† The series was produced by Bruce Geller.

Bronowski, Jacob (1902–76). British philosopher and historian whose great TV achievement was his 13-hour film series *The Ascent of Man*, aired by the BBC in 1975.

Bronson, Charles (1922–) (Charles Buchinski). Steely-eyed American star actor who before his Hollywood eminence was in two TV series: *Man with a Camera*, *The Travels of Jamie McPheeters*.

The Brontës of Haworth *
GB 1973 5 × 50m colour (VTR)
Yorkshire TV (Marc Miller)

A fresh look at the lives of the Victorian novelist sisters and their dissolute brother. Excellent semi-documentary drama with a genuine feeling for the period.

w Christopher Fry *d* Marc Miller

Alfred Burke, Michael Kitchen, Vickery Turner, Rosemary McHale, Ann Penfold

Brooke-Taylor, Tim (1940–). British lightweight comedy and cabaret actor, since 1970 one of *The Goodies*.

Brooks, James L. (1940–). American writer–producer involved in several long-running series: *Room 222* (creator), *The Mary Tyler Moore Show*, *Rhoda*, *Lou Grant*, *Taxi*, *The Associates*.

Brooks, Mel (1927–) (Melvin Kaminsky). American jokester who made a big killing in Hollywood in the seventies when there was a lack of anyone with a sharper sense of humour. His previous TV career included co-scripting *Get Smart* and having the original idea for *When Things Were Rotten*.

Brookside. British bi-weekly soap opera launched with Channel 4 in November 1982. Though set in the distressed city of Liverpool and always intended to reflect the problems of unemployment and inner-city decay, the actual location is a private housing estate on which the production company own a number of properties to act as a permanent set. Brookside families tend to be middle class or at least upwardly mobile, with the husband a redundant executive, white collar trade unionist or thrusting young executive. The young people are especially well done and the serial quickly won enough adherents to become Channel 4's top-rating regular programme. From Brookside Productions (Phil Redmond), created and masterminded by Redmond, for Channel 4.   PP

Brosnan, Pierce (1953–). Personable Irish leading man in America. *The Manions of America*, *Nancy Astor*, REMINGTON STEELE.

Brother to the Ox * (GB 1982 60m). Excellent picturization of Fred Kitchen's book about his days as an apprentice farm labourer in the early years of the century, with Graham Hill, a 16-year-old miner's son, enduring the long hours of toil, the mucking-out, the spartan comforts – but also the occasional celebrations and kindnesses. Written by Stephen Wakelam, directed and produced by John Willis, for YTV.   PP

The Brotherhood of the Bell *
US 1971 100m colour TVM
Cinema Center (Hugh Benson)

A secret fraternity takes stern measures against the enemies of its members. Unusual mystery, quite watchable and well done.

w David Karp *d* Paul Wendkos *ph* Robert Hauser *m* Jerry Goldsmith

Glenn Ford, Dean Jagger, Maurice Evans, Rosemary Forsyth, Will Geer, Eduard Franz, William Conrad

'One is her lover, the other a killer. Telling them apart is a matter of life and death.'

Brotherly Love
US 1984 96m colour TVM
CBS (Andrew Gottlieb)

A successful family man finds that his ne'er-do well twin brother has committed a murder and incriminated him. Slow-starting melodrama with a plot which might have worked well.

w Ernest Tidyman *d* Jeff Bleckner

Judd Hirsch, Karen Carlson, George Dzundza, Ron Karabatsos, Barry Primus

Brothers
US 1985 × 25m colour tape
Slightly unusual and outspoken sitcom made for cable: the misadventures of three brothers, one of whom is discovered to be homosexual.
Robert Walden, Paul Regina, Brandon Maggart. Created by Gary Nardino for Paramount.
'A delicate subject is handled intelligently, making its points by ridiculing bigotry.' – Don Merrill, *TV Guide*

The Brothers *
US 1956–7 78 × 25m bw
CBS
Two brothers run a photography studio in San Francisco.
Amiable comedy with excellent talent.
Gale Gordon, Bob Sweeney, Ann Morriss, Frank Orth

The Brothers. Long-running BBC 50-minute VTR serial of the seventies, about a family of brothers in the trucking business and their domination by their widowed mother. For a while it was a Sunday night must, but its appeal suddenly waned. Jean Anderson, Jennifer Wilson, Richard Easton, Robin Chadwick, Patrick O'Connell and Kate O'Mara were involved.

Brothers and Sisters (US 1979). Unsuccessful 13 × 25-minute comedy series about fraternity problems at a small midwestern college. With Chris Lemmon, John Cutler, Randy Brooks; for Jozak/Paramount/NBC.

The Brothers Brannigan
US 1960 39 × 25m bw
CBS/Wilbur Stark
Two private eyes are based in Phoenix.
Adequate, forgettable crime filler of its time.
Steve Dunne, Mark Roberts

Brothers in Law
US 1985 96m colour TVM
ABC/Stephen J. Cannell (Jo Swerling Jnr)
A team of battling lawyers works through loopholes.
Rather unattractive pilot which despite its premise contrives to include the usual ration of Cannell violence.
w Stephen J. Cannell *d* E. W. Swackhamer *ph* Don Birnkrant *m* Mike Post, Pete Carpenter
Mac Davis, Joe Cortese, Robert Culp, Daphne Ashbrook, Gerald S. O'Loughlin

Brothers, Joyce (1928–) (Joyce Bauer). American psychiatrist who had her own series in the fifties and sixties after winning top prizes on two quiz shows and becoming a national celebrity.

A Brother's Tale (GB 1983 3 × 52m). Good old-fashioned story-telling from Stan Barstow, dramatizing his own novel of fallen-hero footballer battening on his unsung brother and family. With Trevor Eve, Kevin McNally; directed by Les Chatfield, produced by Pauline Shaw, for Granada. PP

Brown, Blair (19 –). American leading lady. *The Oregon Trail*, *Captains and the Kings*, *Wheels*, *And I Alone Survived*, *The Child Stealer*, *Kennedy*, *The Bad Seed*, *Space*.

Brown, Bryan (1950–). Australian leading man. Television includes *Against the Wind*, *The Thorn Birds*, *Eureka Stockade*, A TOWN LIKE ALICE, *Kim*.

Brown, Faith (1947–). British impersonator, mainly of musical stars; she has had several specials and a series of her own.

Brown, Georg Sanford (*c* 1943–). Black American actor, in most media. *The Rookies*, *The Young Lawyers*, *Dawn*, *Roots*, *The Night the City Screamed*, *Grambling's White Tiger* (d only), *The Kid with the Broken Halo*, *The Jesse Owens Story*, etc.

❋ **Brown, Janet** (1927–). British impersonator, often in support of Mike Yarwood; does a splendid Margaret Thatcher.

Brown, Pamela (1917–75). British actress in all media. Her finest TV hour may have been her supporting role in Hallmark's *Victoria Regina*, for which she won a 1961 Emmy.

Brown, Robert (*c* 1931–). Stalwart American leading man, seen in *Here Come the Brides* and *Primus*.

Bruce Forsyth's Big Night (GB 1979). A striking failure of LWT's autumn Saturdays, this uneasy collection of interview, quiz, jokes, audience participation and revue numbers also marked the end of the public's infatuation with its star, who having been unable to do wrong could henceforth do no right, either with the public or the press. Producer: Richard Drewett.

PP: 'But he worked his way back to popularity with *Play Your Cards Right*, started the following year and still going strong when it latched up its 100th edition in 1985.

Brush, Basil. A foxy glove puppet familiar on British screens from the early sixties. The combination of an aristocratic voice, good jokes and catchphrases like 'Boom Boom' has endeared the simple entertainment to adults and children alike.

Bryant, Michael (1928–). Sensitive, ideal television actor whose knobbly face has more often registered suffering than delight in, for example, *Talking to a Stranger*, *The Seekers*, *Roads to Freedom* and an episode of *Colditz* in which he memorably feigned madness. PP

Buccaneer (GB 1980). Otherwise known as the Onecrate Line. BBC series with Bryan Marshall as skipper of the sole aircraft belonging to an embattled cargo airline, Clifford Rose the tycoon who took over the outfit at the urgings of a predatory wife. Never became quite airborne. PP

The Buccaneers
GB 1956 39 × 25m bw
ATV/Sapphire
In the 1620s, ex-pirate Dan Tempest protects British interests on the high seas.
Cut-price swashbuckler.

Robert Shaw

Buchanan, Edgar (1902–79). American character actor who vied with Walter Brennan for country philosopher roles and later made an equal killing in TV with roles in long-running series: *Judge Roy Bean*, *Petticoat Junction*, *Cade's County*. TV movies include *Something for a Lonely Man*, *The Over the Hill Gang*, *Yuma*.

Buck Rogers in the 25th Century
US 1950 39 × 25m bw
ABC
In 1919 a mining engineer is rendered unconscious by a mountain gas and awakes in 2430, helping to save his new society from evil forces.
A long-lost series version of the comic strip.
Ken Dibbs, Lou Prenis, Harry Deering

Buck Rogers in the 25th Century
US 1978 89m colour TVM
Universal/Glen Larson (Richard Caffey)
A camped-up version of the above, complete with helpful robot *à la Star Wars*. This pilot was released theatrically with some success.

w Glen Larson, Leslie Stevens *d* Daniel Haller *ph* Frank Beascoechea *m* Stu Phillips *ad* Paul Peters

GIL GERARD, Pamela Hensley, Erin Gray, Tim O'Connor, Mel Blanc (as the voice of Twiki), Henry Silva, Joseph Wiseman

† The resulting one-hour series limped hesitantly through two seasons and won a limited but vocal international following. There were 37 episodes.

Buckman, Peter (1941–). British critic and writer (*Dancing Country*, etc.) who branched out as student of soap opera in book *All for Love*, 1984. Latest screen credits: *All Together Now* and *All Passion Spent*. PP

Buckskin *
US 1958 39 × 25m bw
NBC/Betford/Revue
Life in a Montana town in wild west days.
Rather pleasing minor western series, too gentle to last.

Tommy Nolan, Sally Brophy

Bud 'n' Ches *
GB 1981 80m colour (VTR)
ATV (Jon Scoffield)
Flanagan and Allen think back over their music hall career.
Remarkably lavish musical extravaganza with a good feel for television despite some obvious cutting. The trouble is that dramatically there is nothing to say: Bud 'n' Ches were only interesting when they sang.

w Sid Colin *d* JON SCOFFIELD *pd* RICHARD LAKE
BERNIE WINTERS, LESLIE CROWTHER

'The men who kept America laughing while their own hearts were breaking!'
Bud and Lou
US 1978 96m colour TVM
NBC/Bob Banner (Robert C. Thompson, Clyde B. Phillips)
The rise and fall of a top comedy team.
Initially interesting but finally dreary re-creation of the ups and downs of two comics of the forties whose personal life was not at all funny.

w George Lefferts, *book* Bob Thomas *d* Robert C. Thompson *ph* Richard C. Clouner

Harvey Korman, Buddy Hackett, Michele Lee, Arte Johnson, Robert Reed

Budgie
GB 1971–3 30 approx. × 50m colour (VTR)
Thames (Verity Lambert)

Adventures of a London spiv.
Occasionally likeable but not especially interesting comedy dramas.
w Keith Waterhouse, Willis Hall
Adam Faith, Iain Cuthbertson, Georgina Hale

Buffalo Bill Jnr
US 1955 40 × 25m bw
Flying A (Gene Autry)
Self-explanatory meek-and-mild western.
Dick Jones, Nancy Gilbert

The Bugaloos
US 1970–1 17 × 25m colour
NBC/Sid and Marty Krofft
Adventures of a group of singing insects and their evil nemesis Benita Bizarre.
Screechy kiddy show in which most of the characters are played by puppets.
m Charles Fox
Martha Raye, Caroline Ellis, Wayne Laryea, John Philpott, John McIndoe

Bugs Bunny. Warners' famous cartoon rabbit has been well exposed on TV via various groupings of the old films. In the seventies several newly animated specials were made, but they were never up to the old standard.

Bullwinkle. A dumb moose cartoon character created by Jay Ward for innumerable segments of a long-running series usually called *The Rocky Show*, though Bullwinkle was certainly the more striking character. The cartoons originally appeared in the fifties, linked to such other segments, all quite wittily scripted, as *Peabody's Improbable History* and *Fractured Fairy Tales* (narrated by Edward Everett Horton).
† When Jay Ward later made *Fractured Flickers*, it was officially introduced as 'the biggest waste of time since *The Bullwinkle Show*'.

Bully (US 1978). A recording of James Whitmore's stage performance as Theodore Roosevelt. Too long at two hours, it pulls together some interesting facts about a little-known character. Written by Jerome Alden, directed by Peter H. Hunt, for Maturo/Image Corp.

Bulman * (GB 1985 13 × 52m). The tough, crafty, string-gloved detective of Granada's *Strangers* finally accorded his own series. Retired from the police, he sets up shop as a clock mender but is speedily drawn into private investigation. With Don Henderson gaining in stature as Bulman, especially in a strong closing episode, and Siobhan Redmond as his wee Scots assistant. Written mainly by Murray Smith, also by Paul Wheeler and Henry Livings, produced by Steve Hawes, for Granada. A further series was made in 1986.   PP

The Bunker
US/France 1980 150m colour TVM
Time–Life/SFP (David Susskind, Diana Karew, George Schaefer)
A conjectural account of Hitler's last days and suicide in the Berlin bunker.
Overlong and unconvincing wallow into a subject which has now been tried several times too often; the whole life of Hitler should be told; these last hysterical days alone have the air of being stranger than fiction.
w John Gay, *book* James O'Donnell *d* George Schaefer *ph* Jean Louis Picavet *m* Brad Fiedel
Anthony Hopkins (a grotesquely overplayed Hitler, but Emmy 1981), Richard Jordan, James Naughton, Cliff Gorman, Michel Lonsdale, Martin Jarvis, Andrew Ray, Piper Laurie, Susan Blakely
'The ultimate horror story.' – *Daily Variety*

A Bunny's Tale
US 1985 96m colour TVM
ABC/Stan Margulies (Joan Marks)
Personal problems of hostesses in the Playboy Clubs.
Dreary rehash of material culled from Gloria Steinem's 1963 book. Not really a goer.
w Deena Goldstone   *d* Karen Arthur *ph* Gayne Rescher *m* Paul Chihara
Kirstie Alley, Cotter Smith, Deborah Van Valkenburgh, Lisa Pellikan, Diana Scarwid

Buono, Victor (1939–82). Heavyweight American character actor. TV movies: *Goodnight My Love, Crime Club, Brenda Starr, High Risk, Man from Atlantis, Backstairs at the White House, The Return of Mod Squad, Better Late Than Never, Murder Can Hurt You.*

Burghoff, Gary (1940–). Unassuming-looking American character actor who scored a hit (and won an Emmy in 1977) as Radar in M*A*S*H. TV movies: *Casino, The Man in the Santa Claus Suit.*

Burke, Alfred (1918–). British character actor with a wry look, most memorably cast in *Public Eye* as the private detective who was always behind the eight ball. One of the more reliable constituents of *The Borgias*.

JAMES BURKE had an amiably quirky way of presenting scientific facts, but *The Day the Universe Changed* was not among his most popular projects.

Burke, James (1936–). British writer, presenter and frenetic science popularizer. Came to the fore via *Tomorrow's World*, general current affairs work and commentaries on space-shot relays. His attempts to relate scientific and technological ideas to everyday life (and each other) in, for example, the series *Connections* (BBC 1978) are admirable in intention if too often confused by fidgety presentation. In *The Day the Universe Changed* (1985) he finally blew it.   PP

Burke, Mick. British film cameraman killed on Everest assignment in 1975, whose name is commemorated in an annual BBC award for adventure or travel films.   PP

Burke, Paul (1926–). Serious-looking leading man who scored handsomely as the young cop in *Naked City* but subsequently found work a little scarce. Other series: *Noah's Ark*, *12 O'Clock High*. TV movies include *Crowhaven Farm*, *The Rookies*, *Crime Club*, *Little Ladies of the Night*, *Wild and Woolly*, *Beach Patrol*.

Burke's Law *
US 1963–5 81 × 50m bw
ABC/Four Star/Barbety (Aaron Spelling)
Murder cases of an elegant and eligible police chief.
A genial send-up of who-done-its which never quite managed enough wit and tended to waste its vast supply of guest stars, but created an engaging central character and a mind-boggling Beverly Hills atmosphere with an endless helping of glamour girls. Every episode title began 'Who Killed —?' and there was always a wide choice of suspects.
cr Ivan Goff, Ben Roberts (after a Dick Powell Theatre film by Ernest Kinoy) *m* Herschel Burke Gilbert.

GENE BARRY, Gary Conway, Regis Toomey
The episodes were as follows:
Who Killed Holly Howard? (*w* Albert Beich, William H. Wright; *d* Hy Averback; with Elizabeth Allen, William Bendix, Bruce Cabot, Rod Cameron, Fred Clark, Jay C. Flippen, Cedric Hardwicke, Stephen McNally, Suzy Parker, Zasu Pitts, Will Rogers Jnr)
Who Killed Mr X? (*w* Lewis Reed; *d* Don Weis; with Jim Backus, Barrie Chase, Ann Harding, Dina Merrill, Elizabeth Montgomery, Charles Ruggles, Soupy Sales)
Who Killed Harris Crown? (*w* John Meredyth Lucas; *d* Don Weis; with Lola Albright, Joan Blondell, Barbara Eden, Eva Gabor, Gene Nelson, Juliet Prowse, Don Rickles, Ruth Roman)
Who Killed Cable Roberts? (*w* Gwen Bagni, Paul Dubov; *d* Jeffrey Hayden; with Mary Astor, Zsa Zsa Gabor, Paul Lynde, John Saxon, Lizabeth Scott, Chill Wills)
Who Killed Julian Buck? (*w* Albert Beich; *d* Don Weis; with Ed Begley, Karl Boehm, Corinne Calvet, Rita Moreno, Terry-Thomas, Keenan Wynn)
Who Killed Alex Debbs? (*w* Harlan Ellison; *d* Don Weis; with Arlene Dahl, Sammy Davis Jnr, Diana Dors, John Ireland, Burgess Meredith, Suzy Parker, Jan Sterling)
Who Killed Sweet Betsy? (*w* Edith Sommer; *d* Hy Averback; with Richard Carlson, Gladys Cooper, John Ericson, Carolyn Jones, Michael Wilding)
Who Killed Billy Jo? (*w* Tony Barrett; *d* Hy Averback; with Nick Adams, Laraine Day, Howard Duff, Phil Harris, Ida Lupino, Tina Louise, Cesar Romero, Elaine Stewart, Tom Tully)
Who Killed Wade Walker? (*w* Bob O'Brien; *d* Stanley Z. Cherry; with Rhonda Fleming, Jay C. Flippen, Anne Francis, Martha Hyer, Frankie Laine, Nancy Sinatra, Dana Wynter)

Who Killed the Kind Doctor? (*w* Edith Sommer; *d* Don Taylor; with Joan Caulfield, Annette Funicello, Celeste Holm, James MacArthur, Dewey Martin, Sheree North, Susan Oliver)

Who Killed Purity Mather? (*w* Harlan Ellison; *d* Walter Grauman; with Janet Blair, Wally Cox, Charles Ruggles, Telly Savalas, Gloria Swanson, Nancy Kovack, Mary Ann Mobley)

Who Killed Cynthia Royal? (*w* Jameson Brewer, Day Keene; *d* Charles Haas; with Frankie Avalon, Macdonald Carey, Stubby Kaye, Marilyn Maxwell, Una Merkel, Kathy Nolan)

Who Killed Eleanor Davis? (*w* Herman Hoffman; *d* Don Taylor; with Nick Adams, Jane Darwell, Edward Everett Horton, Arthur Hunnicutt, Dean Jones, Elsa Lanchester, Terry Moore, Debra Paget)

Who Killed Beau Sparrow? (*w* John Meredyth Lucas; *d* David McDearmon; with June Allyson, Yvonne de Carlo, Jack Haley, Agnes Moorehead, Ken Murray)

Who Killed Jason Shaw? (*w* Lewis Reed; *d* Stanley Z. Cherry; with Tammy Grimes, Richard Haydn, Oscar Homolka, Burgess Meredith, Keenan Wynn)

Who Killed Snooky Martinelli? (*w* Gwen Bagni, Paul Dubov; *d* Robert Ellis Miller; with Hoagy Carmichael, Broderick Crawford, Arlene Dahl, Carl Reiner, Cesar Romero, Janice Rule)

Who Killed What's His Name? (*w* Tony Barrett; *d* Don Taylor; with Elizabeth Allen, Edgar Bergen, Dick Clark, Andy Devine, Reginald Gardiner, Virginia Grey, Spike Jones, Gena Rowlands)

Who Killed Madison Cooper? (*w* Lewis Reed; *d* Jeffrey Hayden; with Jeanne Crain, Marty Engels, Carolyn Jones, Dorothy Lamour, Kevin McCarthy, Terry-Thomas)

Who Killed April? (*w* Albert Beich; *d* Lewis Allen; with Eddie Bracken, Jack Carter, Hans Conried, Gloria Grahame, Martha Hyer)

Who Killed Carrie Cornell? (*w* Jay Dratler; *d* Byron Pau; with Michael Ansara, Jim Backus, Fernando Lamas, Diana Lynn, William Shatner, Joanie Sommers)

Who Killed His Royal Highness? (*w* Gwen Bagni, Paul Dubov; *d* Don Weis; with Linda Darnell, Sheldon Leonard, Elizabeth Montgomery, Bert Parks, Mickey Rooney, Telly Savalas, Gale Storm)

Who Killed Marty Kelso? (*w* Tony Barrett; *d* Don Taylor; with Herschel Barnardi, John Ericson, Glynis Johns, Diane McBain, Luciana Paluzzi, Don Taylor, Marie Wilson)

Who Killed Avery Lord? (*w* Lewis Reed; *d* Richard Kinon; with Broderick Crawford, Felicia Farr, Chill Wills, Ed Wynn)

Who Killed Andy Zygmunt? (*w* Harlan Ellison; *d* Don Taylor; with Ann Blyth, Macdonald Carey, Tab Hunter, Aldo Ray, Deborah Walley, Jack Weston)

Who Killed the Paper Dragon? (*w* Jameson Brewer, Day Keene; *d* Marc Daniels; with Howard Duff, Dan Duryea, James Shigeta, Miyoshi Umeki)

Who Killed Molly? (*w* Albert Beich; *d* Don Weis; with Hoagy Carmichael, Nanette Fabray, Jay C. Flippen, Jayne Mansfield, Arthur O'Connell)

Who Killed Who IV? (*w* Gwen Bagni, Paul Dubov; *d* Don Weis; with Lola Albright, Steve Cochran, Reginald Gardiner, Patsy Kelly, Fess Parker)

Who Killed Annie Foran? (*w* Tony Barrett; *d* Lewis Allen; with Don Ameche, John Cassavetes, Wendell Corey, Gena Rowlands)

Who Killed My Girl? (*w* Tony Barrett; *d* Don Taylor; with Richard Carlson, Jane Greer, Stephen McNally, Gene Raymond, Don Taylor)

Who Killed the Eleventh Best Dressed Woman in the World? (*w* Edith Sommers; *d* Don Weis; with Hazel Court, Jeanne Crain, Joanne Dru, Martha Hyer, Susan Strasberg)

Who Killed Don Pablo? (*w* Gwen Bagni, Paul Dubov; *d* Richard Kinon; with John Cassavetes, Cecil Kellaway, Patricia Medina, Agnes Moorehead, Cesar Romero, Forrest Tucker)

Who Killed Half of Glory Lee? (*w* Harlan Ellison; *d* Don Weis; with Joan Blondell, Nina Foch, Betty Hutton, Buster Keaton, Gisele MacKenzie)

Who Killed Vaudeville? (*w* Gwen Bagni, Paul Dubov; *d* Gene Nelson; with Jim Backus, William Demarest, Eddie Foy Jnr, Phil Harris, Gypsy Rose Lee, Gene Nelson, Gloria Swanson)

Who Killed 711? (*w* Gwen Bagni, Paul Dubov; *d* Sidney Lanfield; with Hans Conried, Broderick Crawford, Dan Duryea, Rhonda Fleming, Burgess Meredith, Mamie Van Doren)

Who Killed the Horn of Plenty? (*w* Tony Barrett; *d* Richard Kinon; with Vera Miles, Terry Moore, John Saxon, David Wayne)

Who Killed Lenore Wingfield? (*w* Leigh Chapman; *d* Don Weis; with Anne Helm, Victor Jory, Ida Lupino, Charles Ruggles, Dean Stockwell)

Who Killed Mr Cartwheel? (*w* Gwen Bagni, Paul Dubov; *d* Don Weis; with Nick Adams, Ed Begley, Fred Clark, Patsy Kelly, Sheldon Leonard, Diane McBain)

Who Killed Cassandra Cass? (*w* Lorenzo Semple Jnr; *d* Jerry Hopper; with Lola Albright, William Bendix, Shelley Berman, Elsa Lanchester, Louis Nye, Nehemiah Persoff)

Who Killed Cornelius Gilbert? (*w* Lewis Reed; *d* Don Taylor; with Edgar Bergen, Dane Clark, Barbara Eden, Nanette Fabray, Martha Hyer)

Who Killed the Tall One in the Middle? (*w* Tony Barrett; *d* Don Weis; with Eduardo Ciannelli, Steve Cochran, Hal March, Diane McBain, Juliet Prowse)

Who Killed the Surfboard Broad? (*w* Tony Barrett; *d* Don Taylor; with Theodore Bikel, Macdonald Carey, Dorothy Lamour, Dewey Martin)

Who Killed Everybody? (*w* William Link, Richard Levinson; *d* Richard Kinon; with Corinne Calvet, Arlene Dahl, June Havoc, Margaret Leighton, Alan Mowbray)

Who Killed Supersleuth? (*w* Lorenzo Semple Jnr; *d* Lawrence Dobkin; with Ed Begley, Zsa Zsa Gabor, Thomas Gomez, J. Carrol Naish, Carl Reiner)

Who Killed the Richest Man in the World? (*w* Stephen Kandel; *d* Gene Nelson; with George Hamilton, Diana Lynn, Ricardo Montalban, the Smothers Brothers)

Who Killed Merlin the Great? (*w* William Link, Richard Levinson; *d* Richard Kinon; with Nick Adams, Janet Blair, Charles Ruggles, Paul Richards, Jill St John)

Who Killed Davidian Jonas? (*w* Gwen Bagni, Paul Dubov; *d* Sam C. Freedie; with Broderick Crawford, Dennis Day, Reginald Gardiner, Ruta Lee, Sheree North, Cesar Romero)

Who Killed the Swinger on a Hook? (*w* Tony Barrett; *d* Lewis Allen; with Dick Clark, Gloria de Haven, Leif Erickson, Janice Page, Don Rickles)

Who Killed the Strangler? (*w* Larry Gordon; *d* Sam C. Freedie; with Frankie Avalon, Jeanne Crain, Annette Funicello, Una Merkel, Robert Middleton)

Who Killed the Jackpot? (*w* Gwen Bagni, Paul Dubov; *d* Richard Kinon; with Anne Francis, John Ericson, Steve Forrest, Nancy Gates, Louis Hayward, George Nader, Jan Sterling)

Who Killed Mother Goose? (*w* William Link, Richard Levinson; *d* Sam C. Freedie; with Lola Albright, Ann Blyth, George Hamilton, Jan Murray, Walter Pidgeon)

Who Killed the Toy Soldier? (*w* Lorenzo Semple Jnr; *d* Jerry Hopper; with Joan Caulfield, Martha Hyer, Abbe Lane, Louis Nye, Chill Wills)

Who Killed Wimbledon Hastings? (*w* Leigh Chapman; *d* Jerry Hopper; with Nick Adams, Edgar Bergen, Vic Dana, Debra Paget, Gale Storm, Marie Wilson)

Who Killed Rosie Sunset? (*w* Tony Barrett; *d* Paul Wendkos; with Eddie Albert, Hans Conried, Dennis Day, Sheree North, Russ Tamblyn)

Who Killed the Fat Cat? (*w* Gwen Bagni, Paul Dubov; *d* Jerry Hopper; with Macdonald Carey, Billy de Wolfe, Diana Hyland, Martha Raye, Don Rickles)

Who Killed the Man on the White Horse? (*w* David Giler; *d* Allen Reisner; with Barbara Eden, Fernando Lamas, Virginia Mayo, Robert Middleton, Telly Savalas)

Who Killed the Thirteenth Clown? (*w* Charles Hoffman; *d* Jerry Hopper; with Corinne Calvet, Joan Caulfield, Betty Hutton, Terry-Thomas, Jack Weston)

Who Killed the Rest? (*w* Lorenzo Semple Jnr; *d* Sam C. Freedie; with Theodore Bikel, Steve Cochran, Eartha Kitt, Cesar Romero, Janice Rule)

Who Killed Mr Colby in Ladies' Lingerie? (*w* Tony Barrett; *d* Jerry Hopper; with Joan Bennett, Edd Byrnes, Arlene Dahl, Paul Lynde, Bert Parks)

Who Killed Cop Robin? (*w* David P. Harmon; *d* Murray Golden; with Hal March, Ricardo Montalban, Terry Moore, Susan Strasberg, James Whitmore)

Who Killed Nobody Somehow? (*w* Gwen Bagni, Paul Dubov; *d* Jerry Hopper; with Lola Albright, Rory Calhoun, Tom Ewell, Diane McBain, Kevin McCarthy)

Who Killed Hamlet? (*w* Albert Beich, Lewis Reed; *d* Don Weis; with John Cassavetes, Eddie Foy Jnr, Edward Everett Horton, Agnes Moorehead, Basil Rathbone)

Who Killed the Rabbit's Husband? (*w* Tony Barrett; *d* Jerry Hopper; with Gloria Grahame, John Ireland, Una Merkel, Sal Mineo, Paul Richard)

Who Killed the Grand Piano? (*w* Larry Gordon; *d* Fred de Cordova; with Ed Begley, John Cassavetes, Martha Hyer, Marilyn Maxwell, Nehemiah Persoff)

Who Killed the Card? (*w* Gwen Bagni, Paul Dubov; *d* Jerry Hopper; with Eddie Bracken, Hazel Court, Wally Cox, Les Crane, Jill Haworth)

† Ill-advisedly, the format was changed in 1965 to *Amos Burke Secret Agent*, the atmosphere becoming more that of James Bond, with Carl Benton Reid as spymaster. The new show lasted 13 episodes.

Burnet, Sir Alastair (1929–). British journalist and former newspaper editor, he now heads Independent Television News. BAFTA award 1970 and 1979 (Richard Dimbleby award).

✳ **Burnett, Carol** (1934–). American lady comic, the plain Jane's Lucille Ball. Much loved by the American public and practically unknown elsewhere, she had her own weekly variety show throughout the seventies, and won Emmys in 1962, 1973 and 1974. TV movies: *The Grass Is Always Greener over the Septic Tank, Friendly Fire.*

Burnett, Hugh (1924–). Idiosyncratic British producer, film-maker and own reporter active from the fifties onwards, and in every kind of non-fiction programme from *Panorama* to *Face to Face* and Saturday night satire (*The Late Show*). Made many documentaries and documentary series, on subjects as varied as road carnage and South Africa, but if he has a particular stalking ground it is the twilit zone between religion, superstition and the paranormal. See *The Folklore of Christendom.*   PP

'Out of fear came courage. Out of despair, hope!'
The Burning Bed ✳✳
US 1984 96m colour TVM
NBC/Tisch–Avnet (Carol Schreder)

A battered wife finally murders her brutish husband by setting fire to his bed.
A case history taken from life, this TV movie was also judged remarkable for its central performance.

w Rose Leiman Goldemberg *d* Robert Greenwald *ph* Isidore Mankofsky *m* Charles Gross

FARRAH FAWCETT, Paul Le Mat, Richard Masur, Grace Zabriskie, Penelope Milford, Christa Denton, James Callahan

'She's an unwelcome stranger in a town where corruption runs deep and tempers run hot!'
Burning Rage
US 1984 96m colour TVM
CBS/Gilbert Cates (Jeffrey Benjamin)

A mineowner tries to play down the menace of dangerous fumes from an underground fire.
Ibsen invented the theme in *An Enemy of the People*, and made it more dramatic.

w Karon Ann Hoeffner, Clifford Campion *d* Gilbert Cates *ph* Isidore Mankofsky *m* Robert Drasnin

Barbara Mandrell, Tom Wopat, Bert Remsen, John Pleshette, Eddie Albert

Burnley, Fred (1933–73). British director, formerly film editor, a promising career cut short. *The Dream Divided* (BFA 1969), *Down These Mean Streets* (BFA 1969), *The Search for the Nile*, etc.

Burns, David (1902–71). Unassuming American character actor who won an Emmy in 1970 for *The Price*.

The Burns and Allen Show ✳✳
aka: *The George Burns and Gracie Allen Show*
US 1950–7 139 × 25m bw
CBS/McCadden

The celebrated comics used a simple format, starting and ending with a chat to the audience: she was scatty, he was indulgent, and in the central sketch their long-suffering neighbours got involved. (The format was being imitated as late as the seventies by Britain's *No, Honestly*.) It worked beautifully to the satisfaction of an entire nation.

GEORGE BURNS, GRACIE ALLEN, FRED CLARK/LARRY KEATING, BEA BENADARET, HARRY VON ZELL

† After eight seasons, Gracie retired; in 1958 *The George Burns Show* was moderately successful, with son Ronnie Burns playing a major role.

✳ **Burns, George** (1896–) (Nathan Birnbaum). American comedian with long vaudeville experience and even longer teamed with his wife Gracie Allen. His trademarks were a long cigar and his confiding monologues to the audience. After Gracie's death he appeared in *The George Burns Show* and *Wendy and Me*, and later emerged from semi-retirement to become a film star at the age of 80 and America's oldest star of specials. He wrote several volumes of reminiscence.

✳ **Burr, Raymond** (1917–). Heavyweight American character actor who unexpectedly became a major TV star in a succession of popular crime series: PERRY MASON, IRONSIDE, *Kingston Confidential*. Emmy 1958, best series actor. TV movies include *Mallory, 79 Park Avenue, The Jordan Chance, Centennial, Love's Savage Fury, Eischied* (pilot), *Disaster on the Coastliner, Perry Mason Returns.*

Burrud, Bill (1925–). American anchorman, former child star, who from the fifties hosted many travel and adventure series, sometimes from his own experience but often bought in.

The Burston Rebellion * (GB 1985 90m).
True-story film drama of East Anglian
schoolchildren who came out on strike in
1914, after their husband and wife
schoolteachers (Eileen Atkins, Bernard Hill)
had been sacked, allegedly for inflicting
corporal punishment. According to socialist
history their only offence had been to hold
enlightened educational views. Elaine
Morgan's script was directed by Norman
Stone, produced by Ruth Caleb, for BBC
Screen Two.   PP
† The same episode inspired a 1974
Yesterday's Witness, narrated by James
Cameron.

Burton, Humphrey (1931–). British
producer, presenter and overlord of arts
programmes, e.g. *Omnibus*, *Aquarius*. Has
headed departments at the BBC, London
Weekend and the BBC again, but lately has
concentrated on organizing and directing
television versions of outstanding musical
events, at which he has few peers when it
comes to communicating the sense of
occasion. Berlioz' *Te Deum* from St Paul's,
1969; Beethoven's Ninth from Berlin
conducted by Von Karajan, 1976; Andrew
Lloyd Webber's *Requiem* from New York,
1985.   PP

Burton, LeVar (1957–). Black American
actor, a hit in ROOTS. Other TV movies
include *Billy: Portrait of a Street Kid*, *One in a
Million*, *Dummy*, *Guyana Tragedy*.

Burton, Richard (1925–84) (Richard
Jenkins). Irrepressible Welsh actor who
frittered away his film career on silly parts
until *Wagner* came along, too late. TV
movies: *Divorce His Divorce Hers*, *Brief
Encounter*, *Ellis Island*.

Bus Stop *
US 1961 25 × 50m bw
ABC/TCF/Roy Huggins (Robert Blees)
Strangers passing through a small town find
their personal dramas coming to a head in the
bus stop café.
An unlikely premise, vaguely derived from
the William Inge film, produced a very
variable but usually watchable semi-
anthology.
Marilyn Maxwell, Joan Freeman, Richard
Anderson, Rhodes Reason
'Inge is "story consultant" for the series but if
he has personally approved any of the
episodes presented thus far, he must have
done so while thinking about something else.'
– Don Miller

† The violence of one episode, starring
Fabian Forte as a teenage tough, is alleged to
have caused the downfall of a network
president.

The Business Programme. Channel 4's
seasonal series on business and finance, from
Limehouse Productions.

Busman's Holiday (GB since 1985). Quiz
show in which teams from different
occupations (firemen, tennis coaches, etc.)
answer questions on travel, geography, their
own and their opponents' jobs. Winners get
a foreign jaunt to meet their opposite
numbers and see how their task is handled in
Brussels or Bangkok. Produced by Stephen
Leahy, for Granada.   PP

The Busters
US 1978 50m colour
CBS/MTM (Jim Byrnes)
Adventures of two rodeo cowboys.
Cliché-ridden pilot which didn't sell.
w Jim Byrnes *d* Vincent McEveety
Bo Hopkins, Brian Kerwin, Slim Pickens

Busting Loose
US 1977 ?13 × 30m colour
CBS/Paramount/Mark Rothman, Lowell
Ganz (Lawrence Kasha)
A young Jew determines to set up house away
from his mama.
Raucous ethnic comedy which succeeds,
more or less, on a hit-or-miss principle.
cr Mark Rothman, Lowell Ganz
Adam Arkin, Jack Kruschen, Pat Carroll,
Barbara Rhoades

But I Don't Want to Get Married
US 1970 72m colour TVM
Aaron Spelling
A widower is inundated with candidates to be
the mother of his family.
Pleasant comedy which is neither quite funny
nor quite moving enough.
w Roland Wolpert *d* Jerry Paris
Herschel Bernardi, Kay Medford, Shirley
Jones, Sue Lyon, Nanette Fabray

Butch Cassidy and the Sundance Kids
US 1973 13 × 22m colour
Hanna–Barbera
Four members of a rock group are actually
spies.
Inept cartoon masquerading under a come-on
title.

Butler, David (1927–). Scottish actor who made the big time by becoming a television writer, at first of biographical epics for Lew Grade, later of all kinds of series and American blockbusters. Has an actor's instinct for what is popular, is often top of the class, occasionally bottom. Achievements include contributions to EDWARD THE SEVENTH, 1975; *Helen – A Woman of Today*, 1973; and *Lillie*, 1978. *Disraeli* (1979) was dull, *We'll Meet Again* (1982), which he created, pretty dire. *Marco Polo* (1982), *The Scarlet and the Black* (1983), *Mountbatten, the Last Viceroy* (1985).   PP

Butler, Robert (19 –). Hard-working but unexciting American director whose career includes *Alfred Hitchcock Presents*, *Hogan's Heroes* and *Kung Fu* as well as some Disney features. In 1973 he won an Emmy for THE BLUE KNIGHT.

Buttons, Red (1919–) (Aaron Schwatt). American nightclub comic who had moderate success in TV and movies. Series: *The Red Buttons Show*, *The Double Life of Henry Phyfe*. TV movies include *Breakout*, *Telethon*, *Vegas*, *The Users*, *Alice in Wonderland*.

Buzzi, Ruth (1936–). Plain-faced American comedienne who scored a hit in *Laugh-In*.

By the Sword Divided (GB 1983–5). Saga of the English Civil War as experienced by a family split between Royalist and Roundhead sides. Created by John Hawkesworth and written by several hands, it was worthy, well researched and popular with the costume-drama public. Sharon Mughan, Timothy Bentinck, Rob Edwards and Lucy Aston were among those who went through the whole run.   PP

❋   **Bygraves, Max** (1922–). British cockney singer and entertainer, famous for his easy manner, his family humour and his waving hands. TV shows: mostly variety specials.

Byington, Spring (1893–1971). Favourite American character actress who made a big hit on TV in *December Bride* and was later featured in *Laramie*.

Byline (US 1951). Shortlived half-hour live mystery series for ABC with Betty Furness as a reporter on the trail of international criminals.

Byrne, Peter (1928–). Pleasing British second lead whose main success was as Jack Warner's son-in-law in the long-running *Dixon of Dock Green*.

Byrnes, Edd (1933–) (Edward Breitenberger). Blond American junior lead who established a vast following as Kookie in *77 Sunset Strip* but was not much heard from thereafter.

Byron – A Personal Tour ❋ (GB 1981). Expensive experimental biopic in which Frederic Raphael revisits the scenes of Byron's life and tips in its incidents via brief acted scenes in and out of which, as linkman, he is liable to walk, ride or even swim. An outrageous concept which nevertheless tells a good deal about its subject – and its author. With Malcolm Sinclair. Directed by Frank Cox; produced by Edward Mirzoeff; for BBC.

Cabbages and Kings (GB 1979–80). Attempt which didn't quite come off to repeat on TV (Granada) the popular cerebration of Nigel Rees's radio panel show *Quote, Unquote*. For TV it was thought necessary to augment the traditional sources of literature, newspapers and graffiti with some more visual teasers, e.g. film clips requiring identification, which was perhaps the trouble. PP

† *Quote, Unquote* was subsequently (1985–6) done on BBC TV under its original title.

Cable penetration: the percentage of households in an area equipped to receive cable transmissions.

cablevision. Improved method of TV transmission in which ground cables give a better defined picture in difficult reception areas. Big business in America, where it is controlled independently of the networks.

Cabot, Sebastian (1918–77). Bulky British character actor, from the mid-fifties in great demand on American TV. Series: *Checkmate*, *Family Affair*, *Ghost Story*.

Cadell, Simon (1950–). British light leading man with an air of perplexity which suits farcical hero roles. First lead in *Hi-De-Hi!*, as the entertainments officer. Lately in *Blott on the Landscape*.

Cade's County *
US 1971 24 × 50m colour
CBS/TCF/David Gerber (Charles Larson)
Cases of a New Mexico sheriff.
Well-made modern western which surprisingly ran only one season, perhaps because in recommended TV fashion the hero was given neither home nor personal life, appearing to exist only in his office (a device which did work for Jack Lord in *Hawaii Five-O*).

Glenn Ford, Edgar Buchanan, Peter Ford

✻ **Caesar, Sid** (1922–). American revue comic who never really recovered from being the toast of the nation in the fifties in YOUR SHOW OF SHOWS. Between 1954 and 1958 he had his own domestic comedy series *Caesar's Hour*, his 'wives' including Nanette Fabray and Janet Blair. A fairly frequent guest artist.

The Caesars **
GB 1968 7 × 50m bw (VTR)
Granada (Philip Mackie)
A history of the machinations which led to the decline and fall of Rome.
Freehand version of well-known historical facts, wittily written and incisively acted in a stylish studio production. At least the equal of the later *I, Claudius*.
w PHILIP MACKIE *d* Derek Bennett

FREDDIE JONES (Claudius), ANDRÉ MORELL (Tiberius), RALPH BATES (Caligula), Sonia Dresdel (Livia), Barrie Ingham, Roland Culver
PP: 'Endorsed absolutely.'

Caesar's Hour (US). A one-hour comedy show of the mid-fifties which won Emmys for Sid Caesar, Carl Reiner and others.

Cage without a Key
US 1975 100m colour TVM
Columbia/Douglas S. Cramer
A girl teenager is wrongly convicted of murder and sent to a penal institution.
By *Born Innocent*, out of *Caged* and *Woman's Prison* . . . every scene has been seen before.
w Joanna Lee *d* Buzz Kulik

Susan Dey, Michael Brandon, Jonelle Allen, Sam Bottoms

Cagney and Lacey
US 1981 96m colour TVM
Filmways/Mace Neufeld
A vicious murderer is caught by two New York lady cops, one a freewheeler and the other much married.
A very flabby pilot saved from boredom by Loretta Swit, who however could not be cast in the series which resulted. The actual plot is belatedly and inadequately explained.
w Barbara Avedon *d* Ted Post *ph* Bert Dunk *m* Mark Snow

LORETTA SWIT, Tyne Daly, Al Waxman, Joan Copeland, Ronald Hunter

CAGNEY AND LACEY. A pair of lady cops who quickly became household words.

† After being cancelled in its first season, the show was rescheduled by public request and ran for four years, with Sharon Gless replacing Meg Foster who replaced Loretta Swit.

Cahn, Sammy (1913–). Prolific American lyricist who has become a staple of talk shows on both sides of the Atlantic.

Caine, Marti (1945–) (Lynda Crapper). Lanky north country British singer and – that rare thing – female comic, who made a big hit on *New Faces*. Own BBC series from early eighties.

The Caine Mutiny Court Martial (US 1956). An adaptation of part of Herman Wouk's novel which appeared on CBS Four Star Jubilee and won Emmys for LLOYD NOLAN (as Captain Queeg), and for adaptors Paul Gregory and Franklin Schaffner.

Cain's Hundred
US 1961 30 × 50m bw
NBC/MGM (Paul Monash)
A young lawyer heads a government law enforcement agency, after being a legal adviser for the mob.
Smartish crime series somewhat handicapped by a cold lead.
Mark Richman
'Having accumulated damning data on an even hundred of the nation's top gangsters, he brings one to justice each week, unless the show is pre-empted by a special.' – Don Miller

Calamity Jane
US 1984 96m colour TVM
CBS (Herbert Hirschman, Jane Alexander)
The semi-legendary western heroine is revealed through letters she supposedly wrote, but never sent, to her daughter by Wild Bill Hickok.
Not a happy exercise: poetic flights and dark photography prevent much audience interest, and action is minimal.
w Suzanne Clauser   *d* James Goldstone   *ph* Terry K. Meade   *m* Fred Karlin
Jane Alexander, Frederic Forrest, Ken Kercheval, Walter Olkewicz, Walter Scott, Talia Balsam, David Hemmings

Calder, Gilchrist (1918–). Pioneer British producer–director who with Colin Morris devised famous BBC drama-docs in the fifties. Went on to be the Corporation's last staff drama director, working on almost every routine series while also turning out remarkable individual productions, e.g. James Hanley's *The Inner World of Miss Vaughan* (1965), Nigel Kneale's *Wine of India* (1970). Now active as freelance.   PP

Calder-Marshall, Anna (19 –). British leading lady who retired early but in 1968 won an Emmy for *The Female of the Species*.

Caleb Williams (GB/W. Germany 1983 6 × 85m). Rousing teatime serial from novel about capricious master, hard-done-by servant boy, dark secrets and furtive romance by the 18th-century radical William Godwin. With Mick Ford, Stephen Rea, Gunther-Maria Halmer, Chrissie Cotterill. Written by Robin Chapman, directed by Herbert Wise, produced by Tyne-Tees (Ted Childs and Norton Romsey) for C4.   PP

'The fantasy girls of the month, knocked off one by one. January. February. March. Poor Miss April!'
The Calendar Girl Murders
US 1984 96m colour TVM
Beautiful models are murdered by a mystery maniac.
Sexploitation thriller which looks a good deal better than it sounds.
w Scott Swanton, Gregory S. Dinallo   *d* William A. Graham   *ph* Robert Steadman   *m* Brad Fiedel
Tom Skerritt, Robert Culp, Barbara Parkins, Sharon Stone, Barbara Bosson, Robert Beltran, Robert Morse
'There isn't much credibility in the tired tale.' – *Daily Variety*

Calf Love (GB 1966 75m bw telerecording). English boy stays with German family to learn the language, falls first for one daughter then the other. Vernon Bartlett's autobiographical novel, dramatized by me, directed by Gilchrist Calder and produced by Peter Luke for BBC *Wednesday Play*, was a production rarity in that it was optically telerecorded on 35mm celluloid and subsequently edited as a film – a technique which speedily ended with the advent of colour in 1967: the equipment was capable only of monochrome. The production starred Simon Ward, Isobel Black, Warren Mitchell.   PP
† In 1985 West German television filmed the same story, updated from 1911 to 1939, as *Backfischliebe*. Written by Philip Purser and Rolf Hadrich, directed by Rolf Hadrich, produced by Heidi Steinhaus for WDR/NDR.

Calhoun, Rory (1922–   ) (Francis Timothy Durgin). American hero of co-features in the fifties; never made it big in TV but did star in *The Texan*. TV movies include *Flight to Holocaust, Flatbed Annie and Sweetiepie*.

California Fever (US 1979). Half-season 50-minute series about high jinks among the West Coast young. A bore for anyone over the age of 15. With Marc McClure, Jimmy McNichol, Michele Tobin, Lorenzo Lamas. Created by Stephen Kandel for Lou–Step/Warner/CBS.

The California Kid *
US 1974 74m colour TVM
Universal (Paul Mason)
The brother of a victim corners a psychotic small-town sheriff who forces speeders off the road to their deaths.
Oddball mixture of *Duel* and *Bad Day at Black Rock*; not unentertaining.
w Richard Compton d Richard Heffron
MARTIN SHEEN, Vic Morrow, Michelle Phillips, Stuart Margolin, Nick Nolte

The Californians
US 1957–8 69 × 25m bw
NBC/Louis F. Edelman
A young marshal has trouble in San Francisco in the 1850s.
Acceptable gold rush semi-western with plenty of rough stuff.
Richard Coogan, Adam Kennedy, Sean McClory

Call Her Mom
US 1972 74m colour TVM
Columbia (Herb Wallerstein)
A glamorous waitress becomes house mother for a college fraternity and sharpens up the ideas of the members.
Easy-going collegiate nonsense.
w Kenny Solms, Gail Parent d Jerry Paris
Connie Stevens, Van Johnson, Charles Nelson Reilly, Jim Hutton, Cyd Charisse, Corbett Monica, Gloria de Haven

Call Mr Diamond: see Richard Diamond

Call My Bluff. A panel game: devised by Mark Goodson and Bill Todman for NBC in 1965, it became a much longer runner on the BBC, with sides captained by Patrick Campbell and Frank Muir, and Robert Robinson as compere. After Campbell's death, Arthur Marshall took over. Three panellists give a definition of an obscure word; the other side has to decide which is telling the truth.

Call of the West: see Death Valley Days

The Call of the Wild
US 1976 96m colour TVM
Charles Fries/NBC (Malcolm Stewart)
Adventures of a dog which belongs to a Klondike gold prospector.
It moves in fits and spurts, but the scenery is great and it's reasonably faithful to Jack London's book.
w James Dickey d Jerry Jameson
John Beck, Bernard Fresson, Donald Moffat

A Call on Kuprin * (GB 1961). Excellent two-part dramatization of Maurice Edelman's thriller about a madcap British plot to kidnap a prominent Soviet citizen and supposed dissident, anticipating by many years the unheroic, equivocal spy stories which came into vogue in the seventies. With Marius Goring, Eric Portman, John Gregson, Natasha Parry. Written by Anthony Steven; directed and produced by John Jacobs; for BBC.   PP

Call the Gun Expert * (GB 1964). BBC series about Churchill's, the London gunsmiths, and the expertise that Robert Churchill would make available to the CID when investigating small-arms crimes. Notable for the way its present-day reporter (Macdonald Hastings) would step in and out of re-enactments of famous cases Churchill helped solve – a technique periodically re-invented ever since. The director, showing early originality, was Jack Gold.   PP

Call to Danger
US 1972 74m colour TVM
Paramount (Laurence Heath)
Adventures of an élite squad for the Justice Department.
Warmed-over crime busting in a failed pilot designed as a follow-up to *Mission Impossible*.
w Laurence Heath d Tom Gries
Peter Graves, Clu Gulager, Diana Muldaur, John Anderson, Tina Louise

'The thrilling adventures of high-flying men with a mission – and the explosively emotional personal lives they live with those who love them!'
Call to Glory
US 1984   × 50m colour
ABC/Paramount
The careers of a few friends in the US air force through the last two decades.
A propaganda piece weighted down by heavy theatrics; it began well in America, then plummeted in the ratings.

Callahan *
US 1982 25m colour
CBS/Carsey–Werner/Finnegan Associates
(David Misch)

A museum curator becomes involved in a
series of dangerous, exciting and romantic
adventures around the world.

Amusing spoof on *Raiders of the Lost Ark*.
No series resulted, perhaps because the pace
could not have been kept up.

w David Misch, Ken Finkleman

Jamie Lee Curtis, Hart Bochner, John
Harkins

Callan **
GB 1967–73 52 × 50m colour (VTR and
film)
Thames TV (Reginald Collin)

A cold-blooded secret service agent has his
own standard of ethics.

If only as a corrective to the James Bond
brand of spy glamour, this deserved to be a
success, and was. It was also very influential,
so that rather too many bleak and violent spy
melos followed.

cr JAMES MITCHELL

EDWARD WOODWARD, Michael Goodliffe,
Russell Hunter

† A 'one-off' named *Wet Job*, starring
Woodward as an ageing Callan, was made in
1981.

PP: 'Around 1970 Callan was potentially
killed off, then recalled the following season,
when I wrote, "*Callan* is back, its glum hero
no more dead than James Bond was at the
end of *From Russia with Love*. In a way the
set-up is very like that of the Bond saga,
except that Callan has always remained what
Ian Fleming set out to make Bond – "a blunt
instrument" – but soon forgot, and that of
course Callan is the outsider in the
establishment while Bond was very much the
insider. I've never been a fan of either but
have to recognize a loving and meticulous bit
of pop myth-making when I see it. *Callan*
almost transcends the spy convention, but
not quite. Would his loneliness and
intransigence be in the least interesting if he
weren't a professional killer?'

Callan, Michael (1935–   ) (Martin Caliniff).
American light leading man of the sixties. TV
series include *Occasional Wife*. TV movies:
In Name Only, *Blind Ambition*, *Donner Pass*.

Called Up (GB 1983). BBC documentary
about National Service, i.e. peacetime
conscription from 1945–56, as recalled
mainly by the famous, and (except for a vivid

memoir by Nicholas Harman of being
wounded in Korea) inferior as social history
to *Bevin Boys* the same season.   PP

Callie and Son
US 1982 142m colour TVM
CBS/Hemdale/Rosilyn Heller/City
    Films/Motown Pictures (Rosilyn Heller)

A poor girl marries a millionaire and years
later finds her illegitimate son and buys him
back.

Heavy blend of politics and mother-love, the
sort of thing Barbara Stanwyck used to
wallow in.

w Thomas Thompson   d Waris Hussein
ph Dennis A. Dalzell   m Billy Goldenberg

Lindsay Wagner, Jameson Parker, Dabney
Coleman, Jay Garrett, Michelle Pfeiffer,
James Sloyan, Andrew Prine

Calling Doctor Gannon: see Medical Center

Callow, Simon (1949–   ). Sardonic British
actor who made a name with a book on the
actor's trade *Being An Actor* and a cult hit
on television as the fate-prone hero of the
comedy *Chance in a Million* (1984). Also
played the composer Handel in C4's second
Handel biograph, *Honour, Profit and
Pleasure*, 1985.   PP

Calucci's Department
US 1973 13 × 25m colour (VTR)
CBS/Sullivan (Howard Gottfried)

Frustrations of a state unemployment office.
Claustrophobic studio comedy which proved
unsympathetic.

m Marvin Hamlisch

James Coco, Candy Azzara, Jose Perez, Jack
Fletcher

Calum Kennedy's Commando Course **
(GB 1980). Unkind, hilarious account of a
Scottish Highlands and Islands tour by a
concert troupe led by balladsinger Calum
Kennedy. Some artistes failed to turn up at
all, others surreptitiously deserted, and the
film petered out in a welter of litigation
which wasn't settled until 1985, when it was
finally screened with a one-minute cut.
Written and narrated by Ian Wooldridge,
produced by Michael Begg, for BBC.   PP

'A mockery of one in particular and Scotland
in general' – Calum Kennedy, quoted in
Aberdeen *Evening Express*.

Calvert, Phyllis (1915–   ) (Phyllis Bickle).
British leading lady of the forties; later
became a TV star in *Kate*.

Calvin and the Colonel (US 1961). Half-hour cartoon series for ABC in which a bunch of Southern animals take up residence in a Northern city. Created and voiced by Gosden and Correll, who played *Amos 'n' Andy* on radio for years.

Camera *
GB 1980 20 × 25m colour
Granada (Maxine Baker)
A history of photography and cinema, fronted by Gus McDonald.
A valuable archive series which isn't always compulsive viewing.

Camera in Action **
GB 1965 4 × 25m bw
Granada
Four historical documentaries using the rostrum camera technique to animate old photographs. (See *City of Gold*.) The titles were *Uprooted*, *A Prospect of Whitby*, *War of the Brothers*, *Photographer*.

❀ **Cameron, James** (1911–85). Distinguished British journalist and traveller, on TV as writer and presenter of highly personal programmes over many years, beginning with *All Our Yesterdays* and two *Men of Our Time* for Granada, thereafter mainly for the BBC. He contributed several times to the series ONE PAIR OF EYES and had his own intermittent *Cameron Country*. His favourite theme was the folly of nations and their leaders, at best elegiac and passionate, sometimes reaching too readily for the sackcloth and ashes.

His *Western Eye-witness in North Vietnam* was independently made when Western networks were suspicious of the invitation extended to Cameron by the Ho Chi Minh government. There was one TV play, *Distant Guns*, and one radio play, *The Pump* (inspired by his own heart attack), which won an Italia Prize and was subsequently adapted to TV.

In 1984 he was the subject and star of a five-part series *Once upon a Time* recapping his life and times and television travels. Titles drawn on included: *Gentlemen of the Press*, *Point of Departure*, *The Guns of Aphrodite*, *The Life and Death of Picture Post*, *Venice – the Vanishing Lady*, *Berlin: the Haunted House*, *Death of the Orient Express* and *Temporary Person Passing Through*.   PP

Cameron, Rod (1910–83) (Nathan Cox). Tough-looking American co-feature star of the forties who was popular in early TV series: *City Detective*, *Coronado 9*, *State Trooper*.

The Camerons (GB 1979; 6 × 50m; colour). Dreary *Roots*-type saga from the American author Robert Crichton's delvings into his Scottish ancestry, with Morag Hood ageing from 16 to 60 as its matriarch. Written by Bill Craig; for BBC Scotland.   PP

Camille
GB/US 1984 96m colour TVM
CBS/Viacom/Norman Rosemont
In the mid-19th century, a Paris courtesan conceives a true love for an innocent young man.
Woebegone travesty of a classic theme, with a lumbering plot line which starts too early and a distinguished cast all at sea.
w Blanche Hanalis, *novel by* Alexandre Dumas *fils d* Desmond Davis *ph* Jean Tournier *m* Allyn Ferguson
Greta Scacchi, Colin Firth, John Gielgud, Billie Whitelaw, Patrick Ryecart, Denholm Elliott, Ben Kingsley, Lila Kaye, Ronald Pickup, Rachel Kempson
'The mystique of Marguerite's singular character and her personal tragedy have been replaced by bloodless emotions and doubtful actions . . . sad stuff indeed.' – *Daily Variety*

Camp Runamuck
US 1965 26 × 25m colour
NBC/Columbia (David Swift)
Boys' and girls' summer camps are just across the lake from each other.
Flat comedy vaguely inspired by *The Happiest Days of Your Life*.
cr David Swift
David Ketchum, Arch Johnson, Dave Madden, Frank De Vol

Campanella, Joseph (1927–). American character actor. TV series: *Guiding Light*, *The Nurses*, *Mannix*, *The Bold Ones*. TV movies include *Any Second Now*, *Murder Once Removed*, *Drive Hard Drive Fast*, *Skyway to Death*, *Unwed Father*, *Terror on the 40th Floor*, *Hit Lady*, *Journey from Darkness*, *Sky Heist*, *Ring of Passion*.

Campbell, Cheryl (*c* 1951–). Star British character actress especially notable in *Pennies from Heaven* and *Testament of Youth*, rather less so in *The Seven Dials Mystery*.

Campbell, Patrick (1913–80). Actually the third Baron Glenavy, this gentlemanly stammerer and humorous columnist became one of BBC's unlikeliest stars, especially in the latter seventies in *Call My Bluff*.

Campus (GB 1983). Aspect-by-aspect study of one of Britain's 47 universities (actually Edinburgh) at a time of spending cuts and diminishing prospects at the end of the course. Produced by Patrick Turley, for BBC.

Can Ellen Be Saved?
US 1974 74m colour TVM
ABC Circle

A private eye rescues a teenager from a strange religious sect.
Adequate melodrama, treated rather more weirdly than it warrants.
w Emmett Roberts d Harvey Hart ph Earl Rath m The Orphanage
Leslie Nielsen, Michael Parks, John Saxon, Kathy Cannon, Louise Fletcher

Can You Hear the Laughter?
US 1980 96m colour TVM
CBS/EMI/Roger Gimble (Peter S. Greenberg)

The tragic real-life story of Freddie Prinze, star of *Chico and the Man*, who shot himself after problems of drugs and personal relationships.
Glum retread of unhappy events, for those who like to see others suffer.
w Peter S. Greenberg, Dalene Young d Burt Brinckerhoff ph Robert Caramico m Peter Matz
Ira Augustain, Kevin Hooks, Randee Heller, Julie Carmen
'The core of Freddie Prinze is never discovered, only the trappings.' – *Daily Variety*

Canadian Broadcasting Corporation: see CBC

Canary, David (1938–). Stalwart American actor who was added to the star line-up of *Bonanza* during its last few seasons.

Candid Camera. An American studio half-hour which originated in the fifties (host: Allen Funt) and lasted on and off for 20 years. (The English version was at its best when hosted by Jonathan Routh.) The format was to stage impossible situations – e.g. a car turns up at a garage without an engine – and to film, by hidden cameras, people's bewildered reactions.

Cannell, Stephen J. (1941–). American television writer who started on *Adam 12*; later became producer of *The Rockford Files*; then began to create and produce his own series, e.g. *Baa Baa Black Sheep*, *Baretta*, *The Greatest American Hero*.

Cannon
US 1970 100m colour TVM
CBS/Quinn Martin (Anthony Spinner, Alan A. Armer)

A fat private eye investigates a murder and finds small-town corruption.
Adequate, padded mystery serving as pilot for a successful series.
w Edward Hume d George McCowan m John Parker
WILLIAM CONRAD, Barry Sullivan, Vera Miles, J. D. Cannon, Lynda Day, Earl Holliman
† The series lasted five seasons (120 × 50m episodes).

Cannon, J. D. (1922–). Mean-faced American actor. TV series: *McCloud*. TV movies include *UMC*, *Sam Hill*, *Cannon*, *Testimony of Two Men*, *Killing Stone*, *Ike*, *Walking Through the Fire*.

Cannon, Tommy (1938–) and **Ball, Bobby** (1944–). British north country comedians being groomed for stardom by LWT. So far they have proved to be a seldom acquired taste.

Cannonball
Canada 1958 39 × 25m bw
Robert Maxwell/Rudy Abel

Adventures of a team of truck drivers plying between Canada and the US.
Acceptable comedy dramas, pleasantly played.
Paul Birch, William Campbell

Canova, Diana (1953–). American comedienne, daughter of film comic Judy Canova; notable in SOAP and *But I'm a Big Girl Now*. TV movie: *With This Ring*.

The Canterville Ghost *
GB 1974 50m colour (VTR)
HTV–Polytel (Joseph Cates)

A 17th-century earl is walled up alive in his own castle and comes back 200 years later as a benign ghost.
Careful and well-cast version of the Oscar Wilde story.
w Robin Miller d Walter Miller
David Niven, Flora Robson, James Whitmore, Audra Lindley, Maurice Evans

Cantor, Eddie (1892–1964) (Edward Israel Itskowitz). Ebullient American star of Broadway and the movies who in later life turned successfully to radio and TV, in the latter medium usually as host of specials and discoverer of young talent.

Captain America
US 1978 96m colour TVM
CBS/Universal (Allan Balter)

Dingy comic strip pilot with little to take the eye or hide the low concept.

w Don Ingalls d Rod Holcomb

Reb Brown, Len Birman, Heather Menzies, Steve Forrest

† A second pilot was made under the title *Return of Captain America*, but the project never took off.

Captain America II: Death Too Soon
US 1979 96m colour TVM
CBS/MCA (Allan Balter)

An ex-marine dons disguise to become a mysterious crimefighter, and tackles a terrorist using a drug which accelerates ageing.
Worse than the first, if such a thing were possible.

w Wilton Schiller, Patricia Payne d Ivan Nagy

Reb Brown, Len Birman, Connie Sellecca, Christopher Lee, William Lucking

The Captain and Tennille. A singing act which came to the fore in 1976 and briefly starred in their own weekly one-hour variety show for ABC. They are Daryl Dragon and Toni Tennille.

Captain David Grief
US 1956 39 × 25m bw
Jack London Productions/Guild Films

Adventures of a South Seas trader.
It seemed tolerable at the time.

Maxwell Reed

Captain Gallant
US 1955–6 65 × 25m bw
Frantel

Foreign Legion adventures, filmed in North Africa.
If revived, they could become a cult, they're so bad.

Buster Crabbe, Fuzzy Knight

† Also known as *Foreign Legionnaire* and *Captain Gallant of the Foreign Legion*.

Captain Kangaroo. An early morning studio show for small children, hosted since 1953 by Bob Keeshan. Two generations of American kids have grown up with it.

Captain Midnight
Syndicated title: *Jet Jackson, Flying Commando*
US 1954 39 × 25m bw
CBS/Screen Gems

A former air ace commands the Secret Squadron, a government organization designed to combat evil.
Ingenuous hokum which filled a need.

Richard Webb, Sid Melton, Olan Soule

Captain Nice
US 1966 15 × 25m colour
NBC (Buck Henry)

A secret formula turns a mild-mannered chemist into a crime fighter.
Unfunny attempt in a familiar mould.

William Daniels, Alice Ghostley

'Seems to have been concocted on the principle that if you make something sufficiently absurd people will laugh it to scorn.' – Jack Edmund Nolan

Captain Noah and His Floating Zoo *
GB 1972 25m colour
Granada (Douglas Terry)

The ark story, very stylishly animated.

w Michael Flanders d/*animation* Brian Cosgrove, Mark Hall m Joseph Horowitz

Captain Scarlet and the Mysterons
GB 1967 32 × 25m colour
ATV/Gerry Anderson

Martians invade the earth. Spectrum combats them.
Tolerable puppet series with a hero looking like James Garner.

Captain Video (US 1949–54). Low budget half-hour space opera for children, about a wealthy private citizen who took it upon himself to ensure the safety of the universe against marauders. With Richard Coogan (later Al Hodge). Created and produced by James Caddigan; written by Maurice C. Brock.

Captains and the Kings
US 1977 12 × 50m colour
MCA/Universal/Public Arts (Roy Huggins, Jo Swerling Jnr)

A boy who arrives in the US as an orphan immigrant starts an important political dynasty.
Hastily pasted together mini-series from a novel based on the Kennedy family. Only occasionally compulsive; structure weak and make-up especially poor in the later sequences.

w/d Douglas Heyes, Allen Reisner, *novel* Taylor Caldwell m Elmer Bernstein

Richard Jordan, Barbara Parkins, Vic Morrow, Joanna Pettet, Ray Bolger, Celeste Holm, Ann Sothern, Pernell Roberts, Robert Vaughn, Burl Ives, Jane Seymour

Captains Courageous
US 1977 93m colour TVM
Norman Rosemont

A rich boy, nearly drowned, is rescued by
New England fishermen.

An old chestnut, rather stolidly recreated,
and certainly no match for the MGM 1937
version.

w John Gay, *story* Rudyard Kipling *d*
Harvey Hart *ph* Philip Lathrop *m* Allyn
Ferguson

Karl Malden, Jonathan Kahn, Johnny Doran,
Neville Brand, Fred Gwynne, Charles
Dierkop, Jeff Corey, Fritz Weaver, Ricardo
Montalban

'At the centre the heart's missing.' – *Daily
Variety*

The Capture of Grizzly Adams
US 1982 96m colour TVM
Worldvision/Schick (Charles E. Sellier
  Jnr)

Exiled after being framed on a murder
charge, Grizzly Adams returns to claim his
young daughter.

Belated TV movie based on a surprisingly
successful series.

w Arthur Heinemann *d* Don Keeslar

Dan Haggerty, Kim Darby, Noah Beery Jnr,
Keenan Wynn, Chuck Connors, June
Lockhart

Car 54, Where Are You? **
US 1961–2 60 × 25m bw
NBC/Euopolis (Nat Hiken)

Misadventures of a precinctful of New York
cops.

A crack comedy series with real control in the
writing and excellent characterizations.

cr NAT HIKEN

FRED GWYNNE, JOE E. ROSS

'The funniest film show currently on the air.'
– Don Miller, 1962

Car Wash (US 1979). Abortive half-hour
series for NBC which never really surfaced, a
car wash station being a somewhat limited
setting for a comedy. With Danny Aiello,
Stuart Pankin. Written by Arne Sultan, Bill
Dana; directed by Alan Myerson; for
Leonard Stern/Universal.

The Cara Williams Show
US 1964 39 × 25m bw
CBS

In a company which prohibits the
employment of married couples, a
scatterbrained young woman tries to hide her
marriage to the efficiency expert.

CAR 54 WHERE ARE YOU? Joe E. Ross
and Fred Gwynne in the cop comedy
which could be seen as a funny
forerunner of *Hill Street Blues*.

Mild comedy which soon ran out of steam
when the secret had to be revealed.

Cara Williams, Frank Aletter, Paul Reed

Carey, Macdonald (1913–). American
second lead who after a fair innings in movies
came to TV in the fifties in *Dr Christian* and
Lock Up; ten years later settled in a
long-running soap opera, *Days of Our Lives*.
TV movies: *Gidget Gets Married*, *Ordeal*,
Who Is the Black Dahlia?, *Roots*, *Stranger in
Our House*, *The Rebels*.

Carey, Phil (1925–). American second lead
who never quite made it in pictures but
appeared in several TV series: *77th Bengal
Lancers*, *Philip Marlowe*, *Laredo*.

Carey, Ron (1936–). American character
actor who looks like a slimmer version of
Lou Costello; plays Officer Levitt in *Barney
Miller*.

Cargill, Patrick (1918–). Accomplished
British farceur of the sixties and seventies.
Series: FATHER DEAR FATHER, *Ooh La La*, *The
Many Wives of Patrick*.

Caribe
US 1975 13 × 50m colour
ABC/Quinn Martin (Anthony Spinner)

Adventures of a law enforcer in the Caribbean.
Dismally routine crimebuster with star and stories alike uneasy.

Stacy Keach, Carl Franklin, Robert Mandan

'Murder in the steamy tropics!'
A Caribbean Mystery *
US 1983 96m colour TVM
CBS/Warner/Stan Marguiles

Miss Marple solves a murder in a West Indian hotel.
Very watchable puzzler with good local colour (although shot in California).

w Sue Grafton, Steve Humphrey, *novel* Agatha Christie *d* Robert Lewis *ph* Ted Voigtlander *m* Lee Holdridge

HELEN HAYES, Barnard Hughes, Jameson Parker, Season Hubley, Swoosie Kurtz, Cassie Yates, Steven Keats, Maurice Evans, Brock Peters

'Just the thing for an evening's pleasure, with one of the great fictional busybodies chasing clues . . . and killers.' – *Daily Variety*

Carliner, Mark (1938–). American TV producer with an eye for a commercial subject (movies include *Coffee, Tea or Me?* and *Horror at 37,000 Feet*) but no luck with series: *Flying High* was his best crack.

Carlson, Richard (1912–77). American second lead who from the fifties alternated movies with acting in, and sometimes directing, TV series: *I Led Three Lives*, *McKenzie's Raiders*.

Carmen. Bizet's opera has been much televised, from an ill-starred studio production by Rudolph Cartier in 1962 which had Rita Hunter in a small part, to a sunny parody by Benny Hill. Peter Brook's three versions with three different casts were shown by C4 in 1984–5. The writing of the opera and its disastrous first performance were the subject of an excellent Christopher Nupen documentary *Carmen: the Dream and the Destiny* (1973).   PP

Carmichael, Ian (1920–). British light comedy star whose TV series (from the mid-sixties) have included *The World of Wooster*, *Bachelor Father* and *Lord Peter Wimsey*.

Carne, Judy (1939–) (Joyce Botterill). Vivacious British leading lady in Hollywood. Series include *Fair Exchange*, *The Baileys of Balboa*, *Love on a Rooftop*, *Laugh-In* (in which she was the sock-it-to-me girl).

Carney, Art (1918–). American comedy actor who began on TV as Jackie Gleason's stooge in *The Honeymooners* and in the sixties emerged as a star in his own right, especially in movies. Series: *Lanigan's Rabbi*. TV movies: *Death Scream*, *Katherine*, *Bitter Harvest*, *Fighting Back*, *Alcatraz*. Emmy 1953, 1954, 1955 as best supporting actor; also for a special in 1960, *The Art Carney Show*; and in 1966 and 1967.

The Carol Burnett Show: see Burnett, Carol

Carothers, A. J. (1931–). American writer who made an impression with *Nanny and the Professor*, and followed it up with the family type of TV movie.

Carpenter, Harry (1925–). British sports commentator, former linkman for BBC's *Grandstand*. Lent his name, willy-nilly, to 1982 boxing play *Harry Carpenter Never Said It Was Like This*.

Carpenter, John (1948–). American director of horror films. TV movies include SOMEONE'S WATCHING ME, *Elvis*; also wrote *Better Late Than Never*.

Carpenter, Richard (*c* 1933–). British writer of series for imaginative older children: *Catweazle*, *The Ghosts of Motley Hall*, *Robin of Sherwood*. Began as an actor in Granada's *Knight Errant*.

Carpenters, The (Richard Lynn Carpenter, 1946– , Karen Anne Carpenter, 1950–83). American poprock singers, brother and sister, most popular in early seventies.

Carpool *
US 1983 96m colour TVM
CBS/Charles Fries

Four commuters sharing a car to save petrol find themselves holding the loot from an armoured truck robbery.
Tepid comedy which occasionally rises to a fair height of entertainment.

w Stanley Z. Cherry, Carole Cherry *d* E. W. Swackhamer *ph* Dennis Dalzell *m* Jimmie Haskell

Harvey Korman, Peter Scolari, T. K. Carter, Stephanie Faracy, Chuck McCann, Ernest Borgnine

'Enough witty observations on life and gentle characters to lay a solid claim on laughs.' – *Daily Variety*

Carr, Thomas (1907–). American director who seemed only to surface in television, notably in the fifties and sixties in many episodes of *Rawhide* and *Superman*.

Carradine, David (1940–). Lean, thoughtful American actor, son of John Carradine. Pursues an eccentric movie career and has starred in two TV series: *Shane*, KUNG FU. TV movies: *Maybe I'll Come Home in the Spring*, *Mr Horn*, *Gauguin the Savage*, *High Noon Part Two*, *Jealousy*, *The Bad Seed*, *North and South*

Carradine, Keith (1950–). American actor, brother of David and son of John. *A Rumour of War*, *Chiefs*, *Scorned and Swindled*.

Carradine, Robert (1954–). American actor, brother of David and Keith, son of John. TV: *The Sun Also Rises*.

Carrillo, Leo (1880–1961). Mexican character actor who after a long career in films was seen on TV in the fifties as Pancho in the long-running *Cisco Kid* series.

Carroll, Diahann (1935–) (Carol Diahann Johnson). Black American singer and actress; star of *Julia* (TV series). TV movie: *I Know Why the Caged Bird Sings*.

Carroll, Leo G. (1892–1972). British character actor who after many years in Hollywood brought his dry personality to TV in three series: *Topper*, *Going My Way* and *The Man from UNCLE*.

Carrott, Jasper (1942–) (Robert Davies). British stand-up comic with thick Birmingham accent and no diffidence. Those who find him funny find him very funny indeed. Best with a live audience, best of all in a live show, i.e. *Jasper Carrott Goes Live* (LWT 1979) and an Election Night Special, 1983. *Carrott's Lib* (BBC) from 1982.   PP

Carry on Laughing. High and, better still, low moments from the British *Carry on* movies strung together to make a 30-minute Thames TV series and eventually (1985) an hour-long compilation.   PP

Carson, Jeannie (1928–) (Jean Shufflebottom). Vivacious British star who scored a great hit in one American series of the fifties, *Hey Jeannie!*

Carson, John (1927–). Elegant British character actor whose voice is almost indistinguishable from James Mason's. Often in classic serials.

Carson, Johnny (1925–). American stand-up comedian turned anchorman; breezy host of the TONIGHT show since 1962. Previously anchorman of *Who Do You Trust?*, *Earn Your Vacation* and *The Johnny Carson Show*. His 1981 attempt to get his show popular in London was ill-fated, mainly because of poor selection.

Carson, Violet (*c* 1901–84). British pianist and character actress who came to stardom in 1960 as the formidable Ena Sharples in Granada's long-running soap opera CORONATION STREET.

Carter Country (US 1977–8). Half-hour comedy series for ABC, about small-town goings-on in Georgia, 'just down the road from Plains', and in particular about a redneck police chief and his sassy black deputy. With Victor French, Kene Holliday.

Carter, Lynda (1951–). Very mildly talented American singer and leading lady. Main asset: the strapping body that got her the lead in *Wonder Woman*. Miss USA 1972. TV movies include: *The Last Song*, *The Baby Brokers*.

Carter's Army
US 1969 72m colour TVM
Thomas–Spelling
During World War II a white southern officer is given a black platoon to help in a dangerous assignment.
Formula action hokum.
w Aaron Spelling, David Kidd   *d* George McCowan
Stephen Boyd, Robert Hooks, Susan Oliver, Roosevelt Grier, Moses Gunn, Richard Pryor, Billy Dee Williams

The Cartier Affair *
US 1984 96m colour TVM
NBC/Hill–Mandelker (Joel Dean, Chris Nelson)
An ex-con pretends to be gay so as to get a secretarial job with a soap-opera queen he plans to rob.
Overstretched star movie which contains some amiable fooling.
w Eugenie Ross-Lemming, Brad Buckner *d* Rod Holcomb   *ph* Hanania Baer *m* Arthur Rubinstein
Joan Collins, David Hasselhoff, Ed Lauter, Randi Brooks, Telly Savalas, Rita Taggart

❋   **Cartier, Rudolph** (1908–). Austrian-born director, a staff writer with the German UFA film studios until the Nazis took over. After making one or two films in Britain, joined the BBC drama department in 1952 and became its best-known director for programmes like THE QUATERMASS EXPERIMENT, *1984*, *The Queen and the Rebels*, *Mother Courage*, *A Midsummer Night's Dream*, *The Aspern Papers*, *The Frog*, *An Ideal Husband*, *Lady Windermere's Fan*.

PP: 'He specialized in ambitious, action-filled epics regardless of the limitations of live studio production – eight shows a year, year in, year out. Also pioneered grand opera in the studio, e.g. *A Tale of Two Cities*, *Carmen*. No one man did more to extend the ambitions of television drama.'

Casablanca
US 1983 50m colour
NBC/Warner/David L. Wolper (Charles B. FitzSimmons)

Again it didn't work, especially not against overlit studio backdrops.

w James M. Miller

David Soul, Hector Elizondo, Patrick Horgan, Arthur Malet, Kai Wolff, Scatman Crothers, Trisha Noble

† Five episodes were all.

'The hour is acceptable. But following in the footsteps of such a predecessor calls for more than acceptable. It requires first rate, and *Casablanca* is way down the line from that.' – *Daily Variety*

Casablanca. In 1955 eight 50m episodes were made for a rotating series called *Warner Brothers Present*. It had the ambience of the movie though the stories were weak; Charles McGraw played Rick, Marcel Dalio was Renaud, and Clarence Muse was Sam.

Casanova *
GB 1971 6 × 50m colour (VTR)
BBC (Mark Shivas)

The life of Casanova.

Eyebrows were raised at language, nudity and sexual writhings in this otherwise downbeat though well-acted historical reconstruction.

w Dennis Potter d John Glenister

Frank Finlay

PP: 'For a second showing (1974) the six episodes were re-edited into four of 75 minutes each, which gave Potter's narrative style, jumping to and fro in time, more elbow room and resulted in a stronger continuity.'

Casanova '73 (GB 1973; 6 × 30m). Nothing to do with the previous item, but a Galton and Simpson comedy show for BBC spun off from a hilarious Comedy Playhouse single called *The Suit*. In both, Leslie Phillips played a sagging, seedy philanderer whose philandering was usually foiled by circumstances, but unusually in English silly-ass comedy he did look as if he might know his way around a double bed; which is doubtless why the format failed to catch on.
PP

Case, Allen (c 1937–). American 'second lead' who appeared in two western series, *The Deputy* and *The Legend of Jesse James*. TV movies: *The Magician*, *Man from Atlantis*.

A Case of Rape *
US 1974 98m colour TVM
Universal

A rape victim finds the legal system works against her.

Spirited warming over of documentary facts.

w Robert E. Thompson d Boris Sagal

Elizabeth Montgomery, Ronny Cox, Cliff Potts, William Daniels, Rosemary Murphy

The Case of the Dangerous Robin
US 1960 38 × 27m bw
Ziv

Cases of an insurance investigator.

Oddly titled but otherwise quite forgettable crime series.

Rick Jason, Jean Blake

Case on Camera (GB 1984–5). The American *People's Court* anglicized for C4 by Yorkshire (Paul Dunstan). Real-life litigants were persuaded to have their cases heard in a TV mock-up of a County Court small-claims session, with the retired Judge Alan King-Hamilton acting as arbitrator. Since the TV company were paying all awards and costs, the result was rather bloodless but undeniably droll from time to time.
PP

Casey Jones *
US 1957 32 × 25m bw
Columbia/Briskin

Adventures of a train driver in the wild west.

Lively adventure series which lingers pleasantly in the memory.

Alan Hale Jnr, Bobby Clark, Mary Laurence, Dub Taylor

Cash and Cable: see Barbary Coast

Cash, Johnny (1932–   ). American country and western star, in many TV specials. TV movie: *The Pride of Jesse Hallam*, *Murder in Coweta County*, *The Baron and the Kid*.

Casino
US 1979 96m colour TVM
ABC/Aaron Spelling
aka: *S.S. Casino*
A cruise ship proprietor has money problems. Busted pilot with some turgid plotting and unattractive characters.
w Dick Carr d Don Chaffey
Mike Connors, Gary Burghoff, Lynda Day George, Bo Hopkins, Barry Sullivan, Sherry Jackson, Robert Loggia, Robert Reed, Joseph Cotten

Casper and the Angels (US 1980; 13 × 22m). A baby ghost joins a team of lady cops. Cartoon series of mind-boggling tastelessness and inanity from Hanna–Barbera.

Cassidy, David (1951–   ). American pop singer of the seventies, one of the children of Jack Cassidy and Shirley Jones, who rocketed to solo stardom after *The Partridge Family*. Star of a shortlived series: *David Cassidy, Man Undercover*.

Cassidy, Shaun (1956–   ). Another Cassidy brother who appeared as one of *The Hardy Boys*, and in the series *Breaking Away*.

Cassidy, Ted (1932–79). Hulking seven-foot American character actor who played Lurch the butler in *The Addams Family* and later provided menace in *The New Adventures of Huck Finn*.

Cassie and Co (US 1982). Half-baked 50-minute series started by Carson Productions and Columbia, with Angie Dickinson as a private detective aided by various streetwise ethnic youngsters. It distinctly lacks style and humour, and the star needs more careful photography than she gets. With John Ireland, Alex Cord, A. Martinez and Dori Brenner.

Cassino: A Bitter Victory (GB 1985 60m). The only World War II battle in the west, anyway, to revert to the static slogging matches of W W I. Ken Grieve's well-researched film for Granada (producer Nick Skidmore) laid the blame squarely on bad weather and worse generalship but otherwise didn't add much to previous exercises: *The Battle for Cassino* (Peter Batty Productions, 1969) and a 1957 *This Week* (A–R) which brought opposing commanders into the studio.   PP

The Castaways on Gilligan's Island
US 1982 74m colour TVM
NBC/Universal/Redwood (Lloyd J. Schwartz)
The desert island gang is rescued, but their millionaire leader decides to build a hotel on the old site.
Update on the old comedy show *Gilligan's Island*, with most of the same cast but fewer laughs per minute.
w Sherwood, Al and Elroy Schwartz d Earl Bellamy
Bob Denver, Alan Hale, Jim Backus, Natalie Schaefer, Russell Johnson, Tom Bosley

Castle, Roy (1933–   ). British comedian, light entertainer and dancer popular from the fifties; originally a stooge in Jimmy James's drunk act.

The Cat Creature
US 1973 74m colour TVM
Columbia/Douglas S. Cramer
Death from a supernatural feline follows a stolen Egyptian amulet.
Poorly made, sluggishly written horror hokum which wastes its cast.
w Robert Bloch d Curtis Harrington m Leonard Rosenman
Meredith Baxter, Stuart Whitman, Gale Sondergaard, Keye Luke, David Hedison, John Carradine

Catalina C-Lab
US 1982 50m colour
NBC/Paramount/Marty Katz
A private company runs an undersea laboratory off Catalina Island.
Busted pilot which looked good but did not have the possibility of variety.
w Gordon Dawson d Paul Krasny ph Lamar Boren m Fred Karlin
Gary Prendergast, Bruce Weitz, Jeff Daniels, Malachy McCourt

The Catcher
US 1971 98m colour TVM
Columbia/Herbert B. Leonard
An ex-police detective offers his services in tracking down fugitives.
Tedious pilot which not surprisingly didn't get anywhere.
w David Freeman d Allen H. Miner m Bill Walker
Michael Witney, Jan-Michael Vincent, Tony Franciosa, Catherine Burns, David Wayne, Alf Kjellin, Anne Baxter

Cater, John (1932–). British general-purpose actor, on TV from 1953. *The Naked Civil Servant, The Duchess of Duke Street, Death of an Expert Witness*, many others.

Cates, Gilbert (1934–). American director. *To All My Friends on Shore, After the Fall, The Affair, Johnny We Hardly Knew Ye, Hobson's Choice, Burning Rage, Consenting Adult*, etc.

Cates, Joseph (1924–). American producer, brother of Gilbert Cates. *Annie: the Women in the Life of a Man, George M, Spoon River, Dames at Sea, A Johnny Cash Christmas, The Magic of David Copperfield, The Cradle Will Fall, Special People*, etc.

Cates, Phoebe (1964–). American leading lady whose first roles were in sexpot style. *The Baby Sister, Lace, Lace II.*

Catherine Cookson's The Mallens: see The Mallens

Catholics ***
GB 1973 74m colour TVM
CBS/Harlech TV
A remote abbey insists on sticking to the Latin mass and a young priest is sent to talk to the abbot.
Absorbing drama of ideas with splendid Scottish island backgrounds.
w BRIAN MOORE *d* JACK GOLD *ph* Gerry Fisher *m* Carl Davis
TREVOR HOWARD, MARTIN SHEEN, Cyril Cusack, Andrew Keir, Michael Gambon

Cathy Come Home **
GB 1966 95m bw
BBC (TONY GARNETT)
Documentary play dramatizing the plight of homeless young mothers.
A low-life saga which became one of TV's most discussed dramas.
w JEREMY SANDFORD *d* KEN LOACH
CAROL WHITE, RAY BROOKS
PP: 'The Wednesday Play at its Wednesday Playmost, in that it aroused public opinion and did genuine good. It was nevertheless a highly faultable work, dividing humanity into victims and victimizers and not shrinking from painting the latter in the blackest hues. I'm sure the play did a great service to social education, but I am certain it did a terrible disservice to television drama.'

C.A.T.S. Eyes
GB 1985 1 × 78m, 11 × 52m TVS (Rex Firkin)
Silly all-girl action series featuring three sleuthettes whose activities are 'secretly directed by the Home Office. Set in TVS's own Kent area.
cr Terence Feely *w* and *d* various
Jill Gascoine, Leslie Ash, Rosalyn Landor, Don Warrington
† In a second series, 1986, Tracy Louise Ward replaced Rosalyn Landor.

Cattanooga Cats
US 1969 17 × 48m colour
Hanna–Barbera
Adventures of a feline rock group (and other segments: *Auto Cat and Motor Mouse, Phileas Fogg Jnr, It's the Wolf*).
Unremarkable Saturday morning cartoon fare.

Catweazle *
GB 1969 26 × 25m colour
LWT
An 11th-century wizard accidentally transports himself to the 20th century and is helped by a small boy.
Imaginative comedy series for children, but in the final analysis it lacks charisma despite an excellent star performance. In 1981 the theme was borrowed by *Mr Merlin*.
w Richard Carpenter
GEOFFREY BAYLDON

Caught in a Free State ** (Ireland 1983 6 × 52m). Never very successful, often bumbling, exploits of German agents in neutral Ireland during 'the Emergency' of 1939–45, with the prize going to the spectacularly miscast courier Ernst Weber Drohl (Benno Hoffman) whose qualifications were as a chiropodist and circus strong-man. Written by Brian Lynch and directed by Peter Ormrod, for RTE. Shown by C4. PP

Caught on a Train **
GB 1980 80m colour (VTR)
BBC (Kenith Trodd)
On a packed night train through Germany, a young Englishman finds himself embarrassed by the autocratic behaviour of an old German lady.
An extremely well acted anecdote with little apparent point to make.
w Stephen Poliakoff *d* PETER DUFFELL *ph* Tony Pierce-Roberts, John Else *m* Mike Westbrook
PEGGY ASHCROFT (BAFTA 1980), Michael Kitchen, Wendy Raebeck

PP: 'The minor hazards of travel induce as much nail-biting as the wildest dangers in a more conventional thriller.'

Cave In!
US 1979 96m colour TVM
Warner/Irwin Allen
Rainstorms trap a killer in the Yellowstone Park Caverns.
Absolutely predictable pap from this producer, with a lot of rushing about but very little actually happening.
w Norman Katkov d Georg Fenady
Dennis Cole, Susan Sullivan, Ray Milland, Leslie Nielsen, Julie Sommars, James Olson

Cavett, Dick (1933–). American talk show host of the sixties and seventies, probably the most intelligent of his breed. A former actor.

❋ **Cawston, Richard** (1923–). Pioneer British documentary-maker, a film editor at Ally Pally in the late forties, producer of *Television Newsreel* 1950–4, BBC head of documentaries 1965–70. Films include *This is the BBC*, 1959; *Television and the World*, 1961; and *The Royal Family*, 1969; since when he has produced all the Queen's Christmas broadcasts.   PP

Cazenove, Christopher (1945–). British leading man, popular in *The Regiment*, *Jennie*, *The Duchess of Duke Street*.

CBC. Canadian Broadcasting Corporation, the official TV channel in that country, founded on similar lines to the BBC.

CBS. The Columbia Broadcasting System has nothing to do with Columbia Pictures. Beginning in 1927 as a chain of independent radio stations, and controlled from 1929 by William S. Paley, it grew into the most trusted and conservative of the American TV networks, managing in the sixties and eighties to be leader in entertainment too.

The Cedar Tree (GB 1976–9). Bi-weekly soaper set in the thirties and presumably hoping for some of the same nostalgic continuity enjoyed by *The Waltons*, i.e. the domestic goings-on of its country-house family taking place against distant backdrop of Munich, ARP, etc. Despite some scripts from the veteran screen-writer T. E. B. Clarke (almost his only television work), it petered out after two seasons. With Philip Latham, Joyce Carey, Cyril Luckham, Peter Copley. Created by Alfred Shaughnessy, produced by Ian Fordyce, for ATV.   PP

Ceefax. The BBC's form of data transmission system, providing instant access to a wide range of printed information.

Celebrity *
US 1984 1 × 125m, 2 ×
    96m colour miniseries
NBC Productions (Rosilyn Heller)
Three high-school buddies reach various kinds of fame but can never forget a rape-murder which they once concealed.
Heavy-breathing novelization with some good brooding passages but rather too much hysteria.
w William Hanley, *novel* by Thomas Thompson d Paul Wendkos *ph* Philip Lathrop m Leonard Rosenman
Michael Beck, Joseph Bottoms, Ben Masters, Hal Holbrook, James Whitmore, Karen Austin, Ned Beatty, Tess Harper, Dinah Manoff, Claude Akins
'Run-of-the-mill TV straining to be high drama.' – *Daily Variety*

Celebrity Playhouse
GB 1981 2 × 50m, 1 × 78m
YTV (David Cunliffe)
Three old war-horses of the theatre led out again to carry some big names into action:
Graham Greene's *The Potting Shed* with Celia Johnson, Paul Scofield, Anna Massey; d David Cunliffe
J. B. Priestley's *Eden End* with Eileen Atkins, Georgina Hale, Frank Middlemass, Robert Stephens; d Donald McWhinnie
G. B. Shaw's *Pygmalion* with Twiggy and Robert Powell; d John Glenister   PP

Celebrity Squares (GB 1976–80). Desperate game show for ATV derived from *Hollywood Squares* (US) in which rundown comics, superannuated sportsmen and other nonentities competed on behalf of the mere people who actually stood to win or lose on the outcome of proceedings too piffling to describe. Bob Monkhouse was your fun-master.   PP

Cellan-Jones, James. See Jones, James Cellan.

censorship. Though television in Britain or America has never been subject to the formal censorship accepted by the cinema in both countries, and the English theatre until 1967, all broadcasting organizations are to some extent bound by the terms of their licences to operate: from the FCC in the United States, from Parliament in Britain. In the case of the

British ITV companies, the Independent Broadcasting Authority acts as a supervisory body between them and the government.

In practice nearly every decision not to transmit a programme, or to have it altered, is taken within the broadcasting outfit, either for its own editorial reasons or in anticipation of the disfavour of politicians, advertisers or the public, and it has to be said that in Britain, at all events, controversial or tendentious programmes which have got on the air far outnumber those that have been impeded. But censorship is no more welcome for being self-imposed, nor is the measure of its effect necessarily the number of actual interventions. The danger of a timid or censorious atmosphere is not so much to programmes already made as to those that now will never be made.

Apart from the special case of Northern Ireland, censorship has mostly been exercised on the constantly shifting frontier of sex and morality, and with a little more justification against gratuitous scenes of violence.

Celebrated cases in Britain include a *World in Action* on defence spending banned by the ITA in 1962; Peter Watkins's *The War Game*, refused transmission by the BBC director-general Sir Hugh Greene on the grounds that it would unduly alarm the lonely and aged; Kenneth Griffith's impassioned tribute to the Irish patriot Michael Collins, *Hang Out Your Brightest Colours*, rejected by ATV. Among plays *Three on a Gasring* (ABC *Armchair Theatre*) was shelved in 1959 after being shown to an outside panel including a bishop; Dennis Potter's *Brimstone and Treacle* banned by Alasdair Milne, BBC director of television, because of its central rape of an inertly handicapped girl; Ian McEwan's *Solid Geometry* and Howard Schuman's *Censored Scenes from King Kong* for specific sexual imagery; Roy Minton's *Scum* because of sexual and general violence.

In 1961 Granada prepared a documentary (*p* Philip Mackie) on the subject of censorship, including television censorship. The programme was itself banned.   PP

Centennial *
US 1978 2 × 140m, 10 × 93m colour
NBC/Universal/John Wilder (Howard Alston)

Episodes adapted from James Michener's immense novel, bringing the story of a western town from Indian times to the present day.
A mammoth undertaking just fails to be the white man's *Roots*, which was clearly the intention.

w John Wilder and others *d* Virgil Vogel and others *ph* Duke Callaghan *m* John Addison

Robert Conrad, Richard Chamberlain, David Janssen, Raymond Burr, Sally Kellerman, Michael Ansara

'A story of reckless daring and reckless loving, of struggle and pain, of laughter and triumph. It's the story of the land, and the people who turned it into a nation!' – publicity

† NBC called the series 'the longest motion picture ever made'.

The Century Turns
aka: *Hec Ramsey*
US 1971 97m colour TVM
Universal (Jack Webb, William Finnegan)

An ex US marshal solves the double murder of a homesteading couple.
Tolerable pilot for a series which became part of *Mystery Movie*, about a western detective using scientific methods.

w Harold Jack Bloom *d* Daniel Petrie

Richard Boone, Rick Lenz, Sharon Acker, Harry Morgan, Robert Pratt

The Chadwick Family
US 1974 74m colour TVM
Universal (David Victor)

A writer discovers family problems when he is offered an important new job which involves a move.
Ho-hum domestic drama.

w John Gay *d* David Lowell Rich

Fred MacMurray, Kathleen Maguire, Darleen Carr, Barry Bostwick, John Larch, Margaret Lindsay

Chalk and Cheese (GB 1979). Only six
episodes were made of this much heralded 25-minute comedy series with Michael Crawford and Michael Gambon as neighbours who don't get on.

The Challenge
US 1970 74m colour TVM
TCF

To avoid a nuclear war, two countries poised to strike each other agree to settle their differences by an unarmed contest between one man from each side.
Silly panic button melodrama.

w Marc Norman *d* Alan Smithee

Darren McGavin, Mako, Broderick Crawford, Paul Lukas, James Whitmore, Skip Homeier

Challenge of a Lifetime
US 1985 96m colour TVM
ABC/Moonlight (Robert M. Sertner)

An LA divorcee tries to pick up the threads of her life in Hawaii.
Old-fashioned woman's picture with quite a strong star performance.

w Peachy Markowitz d Russ Mayberry ph Hector Figueroa m Mark Snow pd Mark Mansbridge

Penny Marshall, Richard Gilliland, Jonathan Silverman, Mary Woronov, Mark Spitz

'Except for the culminating athletic endeavours, not an overwhelmingly eventful scenario.' – Hollywood Reporter

The Challengers
US 1968 96m colour TVM
Universal (Roy Huggins)

International racing drivers compete in the Grand Prix.
You can compute this one before you switch on.

w Dick Nelson d Leslie H. Martinson

Darren McGavin, Sean Garrison, Nico Minardos, Anne Baxter, Richard Conte, Farley Granger, Juliet Mills, Sal Mineo, Susan Clark

The Challengers
GB 1972 6 × 52m colour
YTV (Peter Willes)

The first of what were to be three ITV fiction series about Members of Parliament within five years (the others: The Nearly Man, Bill Brand) but dwelling on two politicians, one Labour, one Tory.

w Edmund Ward d Marc Miller

Colin Blakely, Michael Gambon   PP

'Lifts the lid off constituency politics . . . the sets, the party faithfuls, the bitchiness all delightfully accurate' – The Times

Chalmers, Judith (1936–). British announcer whose BBC stints date back to the forties when as a child she announced Children's Hour. In the eighties became popular hostess of the holiday programme Wish You Were Here.

Chamberlain, Richard (1935–). Handsome, thoughtful American leading man who sprang to fame as TV's DR KILDARE. TV movies: F. Scott Fitzgerald and the Last of the Belles, The Count of Monte Cristo, The Man in the Iron Mask, Centennial, Shogun, Cook and Peary, Wallenberg.

Champion the Wonder Horse
aka: The Adventures of Champion
US 1956 26 × 25m bw
CBS/Flying A (Gene Autry)

A once wild horse befriends a 12-year-old boy in the 1880s southlands.
Adequate children's adventure, much revived.

Barry Curtis, Jim Bannon

The Champions
GB 1967 30 × 50m colour
ATV

A secret agent team is composed of three people with supernormal skills and powers.
Cheerful nonsense: it seemed rather childish at the time, which was before the advent of Six Million Dollar Man and Marvel Superheroes.

script supervisor Dennis Spooner

Stuart Damon, Alexandra Bastedo, William Gaunt

Champions: A Love Story
US 1979 96m colour TVM
CBS/Warner (John Sacret Young)

Two teenage ice skaters team up and fall in love.
Ho-hum content, neat production.

w John Sacret Young d/ph John A. Alonzo m John Rubinstein

James Vincent McNichol, Joy LeDuc, Shirley Knight, Tony LoBianco, Jennifer Warren, Richard Jaeckel

**Chance in a Million ** (GB 1984 6 × 30m). Delightful sitcom for the discerning about a strait-laced young fogey, his dizzy girl-friend and the part played by blind fate – not to say coincidence – in their affairs. Part of the appeal lay in the hero's mode of speech, omitting all definite and indefinite articles and starting every sentence with a verb. With Simon Callow, Brenda Blethyn; written by Andrew Norris and Richard Fegen; produced by Thames (Michael Mills) for C4; had to laugh.   PP

A Chance of Thunder * (GB 1961). Avant-garde BBC thriller serial about a threatened assassination whose climax occurs in the BBC's own studios; of interest as one of John Hopkins's first original TV scripts, with Peter Hammond directing and Peter Vaughan as the embattled police inspector hero.   · PP

Change of Direction (GB 1980). BBC series with Ludovic Kennedy in conversation with

some celebrated converts from one way of life to another, e.g. astronaut Buzz Aldrin, redeemed alcoholic and born-again Christian.
PP

Channel Four. Britain's newest (1982) broadcast channel, owing much in concept to a proposal from the Annan Committee for an 'open' or independent publishing channel, but implemented rather more realistically by the Tory government which came to power in 1979. It operates under the supervision of the IBA, is partly financed by the ITV companies and relies on them for a proportion of its contributions and services. The bulk of its new programmes, however, come from independent producers and though some strident minorities (notably the feminists) were over-evident and off-putting in the first two or three years, there can be no denying that C4 has immeasurably extended the variety and sources of television programming. It has also established a tradition of scholarly movie seasons, re-run classic series from television's past and bought-in serials from Brazil, Europe and Australia. The chief executive from inception has been Jeremy Isaacs.
PP

Channel Four News. Furnished by ITN but under its own editor and chief presenter, Peter Sissons. Running 50 minutes less commercial breaks, it is able to offer fuller coverage of obvious stories and to digress on less obvious items. During the 1984–5 miners' strike it was popularly regarded by the miners as the news service fairest to their cause, but this was at least partially due to the extra time available for presenting all sides in the various arguments.
PP

Channel TV. In Britain, the smallest ITV station, covering the Channel Isles.

Channing
US 1963 26 × 50m bw
ABC/Universal

A young college professor finds he has much to learn from an older colleague.
Dr Kildare transferred to the campus, with less happy results.

Jason Evers, Henry Jones

Channing, Stockard (1944–) (Susan Stockard). American comedienne who was handed two shots at a comedy series under her own name; neither worked. TV movies: *The Girl Most Likely To*, *Lucan*, *Silent Victory*.

Chapman, Graham (1941–). British light comedian, one of the *Monty Python* gang, and a former doctor.

Chapman, Robin (19 –). British writer of strongly individual flavour who has mostly preferred to work within the series format, and the crime series at that, though always choosing ambiguous heroes and heroines: *Spindoe* (1968), *Big Breadwinner Hog* (1969), *Holly* (1972), *Haunted* (1974), *Come the Revolution* (a satire on left-wing theatre politics, 1977).
PP

Chappell, Eric (1933–). Gifted British writer who in 1974 spun a comedy series off from his stage play *The Banana Box*, called it *Rising Damp*, and never looked back. *Only When I Laugh*, 1979, was another hit. *The Bounder* (1982) never quite caught on but DUTY FREE (1984, with Jean Warr) confirmed his place as one of the two (or at most three) funniest sitcom writers of the day.
PP

Chappell, Herbert (1934–). British director specializing in classical music productions; recently, *Sounds Magnificent* (1984) and two documentaries on the Tanglewood summer music school in Massachusetts, 1985.
PP

Charge! (GB 1969). Robert Morley's West End comedy of the fifties, *Hippo Dancing*, seems to have been the inspiration for this BBC sitcom he wrote for himself with Jeremy Paul. Morley played an outrageous suburban snob and tyrant who when asked to read the lesson in church, for example, turned the occasion into an extended one-man show. Funny but never caught on.
PP

Charles Endell Esquire (GB 1979). A series of 7 × 50m episodes with Iain Cuthbertson as a heavyweight Scots confidence man in Soho.

Charles in Charge
US 1984   × 25m colour
CBS/Universal/Scholastic (Michael Jacobs)

A house-boy looks after his employers' three children.
Ho-hum comedy with no real reason for being.

cr Barbara Weisberg, Michael Jacobs
Scott Baio, Julie Cobb, James Widdoes, Willie Aames

Charleson, Ian (19 –). Dour Scottish actor, much in favour after the movie *Chariots of Fire*. Best TV role in *Oxbridge Blues*.

'For some, the Civil War didn't end in 1865!'

Charleston
US 1978 96m colour TVM
NBC/Robert Stigwood (Beryl Vertue)
Three southern belles struggle for survival in the aftermath of the Civil War.
Cut-price *Gone with the Wind*, of no possible interest to anybody.

w Nancy Lynn Schwarz *d* Karen Arthur

Delta Burke, Lynne Moody, Patricia Pearcy, Jordan Clarke, Richard Lawson, Martha Scott

Charley Hannah
US 1985 96m colour TVM
CBS/Telepictures/Blacksheep (Roger Bacon)
During a chase, a Florida police captain accidentally shoots an innocent boy.
Failed pilot for more cop stuff with tears between the action.

w David J. Kinghorn *d* Peter Hunt

Robert Conrad, Red West, Shane Conrad, Joan Leslie

Charley's Aunt. This 1896 farce by Brandon Thomas is much revived. The most memorable TV production is probably the BBC's of 1969, with Danny La Rue as the undergraduate who impersonates his own rich aunt from Brazil (where the nuts come from). Coral Browne, John Standing and Dinsdale Landen were also involved, and direction was by John Gorrie.

Charlie (GB 1984 4 × 52m). David Warner as a lugubrious private investigator in a serial turning on trade-union intrigues. Also with Michael Aldridge, Frank Windsor, Maggie Steed. Written by Nigel Williams, directed by Martin Campbell, produced by Graham Benson, for Central.   PP

Charlie and Company
US 1985   × 25m colour VTR
CBS/TCF/Allan Katz, Bob Henry
The domestic tribulations of a Chicago highway worker.
A blue-collar version of *The Cosby Show*, but not so funny.

cr Michael Kagan

Flip Wilson, Gladys Knight, Ray Hirardin, Richard Karron, Kip King

Charlie and the Great Balloon Chase *
US 1978 96m colour TVM
NBC/Daniel Wilson (Fran Sears)

A 72-year-old fulfils his life's ambition to travel by balloon across the United States.
Easy-going romp which is always good to look at and often quite witty.

w Art Wallace *d* Larry Elikann *ph* Dennis Dalzell *m* Glenn Paxton

JACK ALBERTSON, Adrienne Barbeau, John Reilly, Slim Pickens, William Bogert
'Full of beauty and insight as well as laughs.'
– *Daily Variety*

Charlie Brown. The hero of the Snoopy cartoons, created by Charles M. Schultz, has appeared in a number of 25-minute cartoon specials since 1973, all written by the original author and produced by Lee Mendelson and Bill Melendez, with music by Vince Guaraldi. They are *Charlie Brown's Thanksgiving* (Emmy 1973), *Charlie Brown's Christmas* (Emmy 1965), *It's a Mystery Charlie Brown*, *It's the Easter Beagle Charlie Brown*, *Be My Valentine Charlie Brown*, *It's the Great Pumpkin Charlie Brown*, *It's Arbor Day Charlie Brown*, *Happy Anniversary Charlie Brown*, *You're a Good Sport Charlie Brown* (Emmy 1975), *You're the Greatest Charlie Brown*, *A Charlie Brown Celebration*, *Snoopy's Getting Married*.

Charlie Chan: Happiness is a Warm Clue
US 1971 96m colour TVM
Universal (Jack Laird)
aka: *Happiness is a Warm Clue*
A famous detective emerges from retirement to solve murders aboard a yacht.
Dismal comeback for a famous screen character: desperately poor writing, total lack of pace and unsuitable casting made sure that no series ensued.

w Gene Kearney *d* Daryl Duke

Ross Martin, Leslie Nielsen, Virginia Lee, Rocky Gunn

† See also *The New Adventures of Charlie Chan*.

Charlie Cobb: Nice Night for a Hanging
aka: *Nice Night for a Hanging*
US 1977 96m colour TVM
Universal/Richard Levinson, William Link
A private eye of the 1870s is hired to find a rancher's missing daughter.
Fair pilot which wasn't picked up.

w Peter S. Fischer *d* Richard Michaels *ph* Andrew Jackson *m* Mike Post, Pete Carpenter

Clu Gulager, Blair Brown, Ralph Bellamy, Christopher Connelly, Pernell Roberts, Stella Stevens

The Charlie Farrell Show
US 1956 13 × 25m bw
CBS

An ex-actor runs the Palm Springs Racquet Club.

In fact this ex-actor was the Mayor of Palm Springs, so the show went down well there, but not anyplace else.

Charlie Farrell, Charles Winninger, Richard Deacon, Anna Lee, Marie Windsor, Jeff Silver, Kathryn Card

Charlie Wild, Private Detective (US
1950–1). Half-hour live crime series for CBS, with Kevin O'Morrison as a New York private eye who always got into trouble.

Charlie's Angels **
US 1976 74m colour TVM
ABC/Spelling–Goldberg (Ivan Goff, Ben Roberts)

Three gorgeous girls with special skills work undercover on expensive, impossible cases for an employer they never see.

If it's smooth Hitchcockian hokum you are after, a very good pilot for a series that did make it. The plot is borrowed from all kinds of other movies including *Dark Waters*, the pace is snappy and the spirit of *The Avengers* and *Mission Impossible* hovers at hand.

w IVAN GOFF, BEN ROBERTS d John Llewellyn Moxey m Jack Elliott, Allyn Ferguson

KATE JACKSON, FARRAH FAWCETT-MAJORS, JACLYN SMITH, Diana Muldaur, Bo Hopkins, DAVID DOYLE, David Ogden Stiers

† The 50-minute series which followed was the hit of the 1976 season, to the despair of all intelligent telewatchers. In its second season Farrah Fawcett-Majors was replaced by Cheryl Ladd, though later, as Farrah Fawcett, she returned for occasional appearances. Tanya Roberts and Shelley Hack were further recruits before the final (121st) episode was made in 1981.

†† The unseen Charlie was voiced by John Forsythe.

Charlton, Michael (1927–). Australian cricket commentator who came to Britain and became a political journalist, especially on BBC's *Panorama*.

The Charterhouse of Parma
(Germany/Italy 1983 6 × 65m). Stendhal's epic of Napoleonic times reached C4 in this handsome co-production by Tele-Munchen and ITF, written by Jean Grualt, Enrico Medioli and Tafina Demby; with Marthe Keller, Andrea Occhipinti, Georges Wilson and Gian Maria Volonte. Directed by Mauro Bolognini, produced by Claudio Grassetti.

Charters and Caldicott *
GB 6 × 50m
BBC (Ron Craddock)

The cricket-obsessed clubland heroes on the sidelines of the pre-war movies *The Lady Vanishes* and *Night Train to Munich* warmed up from the deep-freeze as present-day figures only lately retired from vaguely diplomatic service activities, and plunged straightaway into a murder mystery.   PP

w Keith Waterhouse d Julian Amyes

Robin Bailey, Michael Aldridge

'Incredibly, Bailey and Aldridge, synonyms for sublime English pottiness, have never worked together before. Waterhouse and Craddock must feel like the chap who introduced Gilbert to Sullivan.' – Richard Last, *Daily Telegraph*.

LH: 'As a founder member (1938) of Charters and Caldicott I must protest that in this slow-moving production both they and the plot were too laid back.'

Chase
US 1973 74m colour TVM
NBC/Universal/Jack Webb

Four Los Angeles police officers, with special skills and motor cycles, form an élite squad. The mixture as before; it doesn't rise.

w Stephen J. Cannell d Jack Webb

Mitch Ryan, Reid Smith, Michael Richardson, Brian Fong, Wayne Maunder, Gary Crosby

† The 50-minute series which followed ran 24 episodes and was not accounted a success.

'Her best friend was murdered, and she must defend the man accused!'

Chase
US 1973 24 × 50m colour
NBC/Universal/Jack Webb

Routine action stuff.

Adventures of an élite police unit.

Mitch Ryan, Wayne Maunder, Reid Smith

Chase, Chevy (1943–) (Cornelius Crane Chase). American light leading man and comedian who won an Emmy in 1975 for SATURDAY NIGHT LIVE.

Chataway, Christopher (1931–). British long-distance runner of the forties. He came into TV as one of ITN's original newscasters; later a BBC commentator before entering politics.

❋ Chayevsky, Paddy (1923–81). Star American TV dramatist of the fifties. His MARTY, THE CATERED AFFAIR, THE BACHELOR PARTY and MIDDLE OF THE NIGHT were all made

CHARLIE'S ANGELS. The second season for the famous females gave us four for the price of one: Kate Jackson, Farrah Fawcett, Cheryl Ladd and Jaclyn Smith. David Doyle is the lucky man.

into movies. He went to Hollywood and seemed to lose most of his flair.

Cheaper to Keep Her
US 1983 96m colour TVM
Paramount

An ex-detective signs on as investigator for a feminist attorney.
Fairly lively busted pilot which doesn't quite manage to fill the space available.

d Ken Annakin

Mac Davis, Tovah Feldshuh, Rose Marie, Jack Gilford, Art Metrano

The Cheaters
GB 1960 26 × 25m bw
The Danzigers

An insurance investigator exposes defrauders.
Average crime series.

John Ireland, Robert Ayres

Checkmate
US 1959–61 70 × 50m bw
CBS/Revue

Adventures of three assorted private detectives in San Francisco.
Elementary but reasonably competent mystery series with a hero for each age group.

cr Eric Ambler

Anthony George, Sebastian Cabot, Doug McClure

'The laughs are on the house!'
Cheers ***
US 1982　　× 25m colour
Paramount/Charles Burrows Charles

Characters congregate in a downtown bar.
Often brilliantly amusing character comedy which went through various phases but always fulfilled its initial promise.

w Les and Glen Charles　*d* James Burrows

TED DANSON, SHELLEY LONG, Rhea Perlman, Nicholas Colasanto, George Wendt

'May well turn out to be the best of the new season sitcoms.' – *Daily Variety*

† Emmy 1983: outstanding comedy series (also writing and direction of individual episodes)

'The jokes in the show don't reproduce on paper, mostly, because they arise out of character instead of out of a gag file. It's a healthy sign.' – *TV Guide*

Chelsea at Nine (GB 1957–64). A sophisticated variety show originated by Granada TV from the Chelsea Palace. American directors were employed to give the latest transatlantic look to the show, and many American acts were imported.

The Chelsea Murders (GB 1981). Of all Lionel Davidson's superior thrillers the least superior; alas it's also the only one to be adapted to TV (by Jonathan Hales) for a neat Thames production with Dave King as the detective-inspector solving a series of literary-inspired killings among the Chelsea slob-set. PP

† But Davidson's children's story *Soldier and Me*, written under the pseudonym of David Line, was turned into a BAFTA-award winning children's serial by Granada (*d* Carol Wilkes) in 1973.

Cher (1946–) (Cherilyn Sarkisian). Armenian–American singer who has starred in variety series of the seventies both with and without her ex-husband Sonny Bono.

Chertok, Jack (*c* 1910–). Independent producer (*My Favorite Martian*, *The Lone Ranger*, etc).

Chessgame * (GB 1983 × 52m). Labyrinthine but absorbing spy series, actually three two-part adventures from novels by Anthony Price; with Terence Stamp as his learned, world-weary agent. Also with Michael Culver, Carmen du Sautoy, Robin Sachs. Written by Murray Smith and John Brason, directed by William Braine, Ken Grieve, Roger Tucker; produced by Richard Everitt, for Granada. PP

Chester, Charlie (1914–). British cockney comic who made a radio hit with his wartime show *Stand Easy* and did some television in the fifties.

The Chester Mystery Plays **
GB 1976 150m colour (VTR)
BBC (Cedric Messina)

A compilation of scenes from the 14th-century religious plays originally performed by the craft guilds of Chester.
A marvellous rendering of these crude but vigorous playlets, with much use of chroma-key enabling actors to play against backdrops which look like a brightly illuminated medieval manuscript.
modern version Maurice Ussey *d* Piers Haggard *m* Guy Wolfenden *designer* Stuart Walker
Michael Hordern (as God), Tom Courtenay (as Christ), Brian Glover, Joe Gladwin, Christine Hargreaves, Christopher Guard
'A superb example of a fusion of all the crafts.' – *Guardian*

Cheyenne *
US 1955–62 107 × 50m bw
ABC/Warner

Adventures of a western wanderer in the years after the Civil War.
Marathon western series in which right always prevailed and many episodes were cutdown variants on popular Warner movies, using the original stock footage. In general, satisfying to all classes, with a new giant star.
CLINT WALKER (as Cheyenne Bodie)
'No different from the low-budget westerns that kids used to see in movie theatres on Saturday afternoons.' – Don Miller, 1957

† During the run of the series the star caused so much trouble that the studio threatened him with replacements, two of which developed into successful series of their own: *Sugarfoot* and *Bronco*. For the latter years of its run *Cheyenne* alternated with them; earlier it had rotated with *Casablanca* and *King's Row* under the title *Warner Brothers Presents*.

Chicago (GB/US 1961; 60m; bw). Impressionistic study of the city by the British film-maker Denis Mitchell, though calling on the local knowledge and prejudices of novelist Studs Terkel. Some rather obvious cross-cutting between the abattoirs and the fleshpots of the city, but a powerful piece otherwise. For BBC and local station WBKB. PP

The Chicago Story
US 1981 96m colour TVM
NBC/MGM/Eric Bercovici (John Cutts)

Police, legal and medical teams interact following the inadvertent shooting of a small girl at play.
Top-heavy pilot for a proposed three-tier series featuring two cops, two doctors and

two lawyers. One can't think that all the stories will stand this treatment, but at least the location production is satisfying to the eye.

w Eric Bercovici d Jerry London ph Andrew Jackson m Lalo Schifrin

Vincent Baggetta, Dennis Franz, Kene Holliday, Jack Kehoe, Craig T. Nelson, Kris Tabori

Chicago Teddy Bears *
US 1971 13 × 25m colour
CBS/Warner

The owner of a Chicago restaurant in the twenties has trouble with gangsters.

Quite a lively comedy spoof of the *Untouchables* era, this amiable series failed to make its mark with the public.

Dean Jones, Art Metrano, John Banner, Marvin Kaplan, Jamie Farr, Huntz Hall, Mike Mazurki, Mickey Shaughnessy

Chico and the Man *
US 1974–7 approx. 75 × 25m colour (VTR)
NBC/Wolper/Komack (James Komack)

A crotchety old garage owner is helped and hindered by a young Chicano.

Phenomenally successful comedy series relying on characterization. When 'Chico' died in 1977, other young Chicanos were used in approximations of the role.

m Jose Feliciano

JACK ALBERTSON, FREDDIE PRINZE

'What happened in this town will haunt you forever!'
Chiefs *
GB title: *Once upon a Murder*
US 1983 3 × 96m colour
CBS/Highgate (Martin Manulis)

In a southern town, a murder in 1924 is unsolved and leads to others over a 40-year period.

Very tolerable miniseries with a genuine sense of place and some suspense.

w Robert W. Lenski, *novel* by Stuart Woods d Jerry London ph Michael Hugo m Michael Small

Charlton Heston, Keith Carradine, Stephen Collins, Brad Davis, Tess Harper, Paula Kelly, Wayne Rogers, Paul Sorvino, Victoria Tennant, Billy Dee Williams

'What might have been sheer melodrama instead is a look at the agonies of a community trying to find its way into the new life it's destined for.' – *Daily Variety*

Child Bride of Short Creek
US 1981 96m colour TVM
NBC/Metromedia/Lawrence Schiller/Paul Monash

North of the Grand Canyon, a strict religious sect of polygamists faces resentment from outsiders. Meanwhile two youngsters in love plan to escape.

Predictable 'exposé' which no doubt pleased the audience which welcomed it.

w Joyce Eliason d Robert Lewis

Christopher Atkins, Diane Lane, Conrad Bain, Kiel Martin, Helen Hunt, John Shawlee, Dee Wallace

Child, Julia (1912–). American cookery expert who has starred in several series.

Child of Glass
US 1978 96m colour TVM
Walt Disney (Jan Williams, Tom Leetch)

A family moving into an old house finds in possession the ghosts of a Victorian child and her dog.

Moderate ghost story for children, rather similar to the cinema film *The Amazing Mr Blunden*. Produced for *The Wonderful World of Disney*.

w Jim Lawrence, *novel The Ghost Belonged to Me* by Richard Park d John Erman ph William Cronjager m George Duning

Barbara Barrie, Biff McGuire, Anthony Zerbe, Nina Foch, Katy Kurtzman, Steve Shaw

The Child Stealer
US 1979 96m colour TVM
NBC/Columbia (Mike Wise, Franklin R. Levy)

A mother seeks the daughters who have been abducted by a former husband.

Nicely made but rather stretched out story for our time.

w Sue Milburn d Mel Damski

Beau Bridges, Blair Brown, David Groh, Cristina Raines, Eugene Roche

A Childhood ***
GB 1984 4 × 60m
C4 from Melrose Productions (Angela Pope)

Four portraits of young children obtained not by the fly-on-the-wall, as they superficially seemed to be, but by months of getting to know the subjects and then, if necessary, re-enacting key incidents. 'Children of children of the television age,' I wrote at the time, 'they take to it as effortlessly as they take to computers.'

John and Rebecca; children of Irish parents, mother in Brixton, father still in Belfast.

John, Tina and Julia; idyllic hols in the Scottish Highlands.

Angie; 10-year-old black girl, sweet and knowing.

Gavin; upper-middle-class achiever working up to and sitting private school entrance exams.

p and *d* Angela Pope   PP

Children in Crossfire ** (GB 1974 50m).

Historic and influential film about children in war-torn Belfast and Derry, shot by Michael Blakstad for BBC. Repeated in 1982, followed by 1981-made sequel, *A Bright Brand New Day*.   PP

'An unpretentious and paralysing documentary about what is happening to young minds growing up in Northern Ireland.' – Clive James, *Observer*.

Children in the Crossfire *
US 1984 96m colour TVM
NBC/Schaefer–Karpf/Prendergast/
   Brittcadia/Garylord (George Schaefer)

Americans organize summer holidays in the US for Catholic and Protestant Irish children, as a respite from the violence which surrounds them.

Well-meaning fictionalization of a touchy subject.

w Lionel Chetwynd   *d* George Schaefer *ph* Edward R. Brown, Walter Lassally *m* Brad Fiedel

Julia Duffy, Charles Haid, David Huffman, Karen Valentine

'It may skirt issues, but it lights up some truths.' – *Daily Variety*

The Children Nobody Wanted
US 1981 96m colour TVM
Warner/Blatt–Singer

A 19-year-old boy and a nurse become foster parents to the mentally handicapped.

True, or semi-true, story based on a newspaper item.

w Lee Hutson   *d* Richard Michaels   *ph* Reynaldo Villabobos   *m* Barry De Vorzon

Fred Lehne, Michelle Pfeiffer, Matt Clark, Noble Winningham

† The basis of the story was the Butterfield Youth Ranches of Missouri.

The Children of An Lac
US 1980 96m colour TVM
CBS/Charles Fries (Jay Benson)

In 1975 Saigon, two American women save orphans from the approaching Viet Cong.

Dullish war actioner with appeal mostly to women.

w Blanche Hanalis, *story* Ina Balin *d* John Llewellyn Moxey *ph* Don McAlpine *m* Paul Chihara

Shirley Jones, Ina Balin, Beulah Qua, Alan Fudge, Ben Piazza

'Truth may be stranger than fiction, but it doesn't have to be duller.' – *Daily Variety*

Children of Divorce
US 1980 96m colour TVM
NBC/Marble Arch/Christiana (Joanna Lee)

Three families are seriously affected when the parents split up.

Portmanteau case history with no great surprises.

w/d Joanna Lee   *ph* Harry J. May   *m* Raoul Kraushaar, Minette Alltan

Barbara Feldon, Lance Kerwin, Stacey Nelkin, Carmine Caridi, Stella Stevens, Greg Mullavey, Olivia Cole, Billy Dee Williams, Zohra Lampert, Fritz Weaver

Children of Fire Mountain (New Zealand 1979).

13-part half-hour children's serial set in 1900, with assorted villainy and an exploding volcano. With Paul Airey, Rachel Weston. Written by Roger Simpson; directed by Peter Sharp; produced by Roger Le Mesurier.

Children of the Night
US 1965 96m colour TVM
CBS/Robert Guenette (Conrad Holzgang)

A graduate student devotes herself to helping teenage prostitutes.

Another helping of exploitation disguised as social conscience.

w Vickie Patik, Robert Guenette, *story* by William Wood *d* Robert Markowitz *ph* Gil Hubbs *m* Miles Goodman

Kathleen Quinlan, Nicholas Campbell, Mario Van Peebles, Lar Park-Lincoln, Wally Ward

Children Playing ** (GB 1967; 78m; bw).

Remarkable television drama about schoolchildren staying at a vacation hostel and filling in the long summer day with games, alarms, constantly changing patterns of activity while on the perimeter two sinister adolescents threaten to invade the group. Not the fashionable improvised exercise it may sound, but the script by David Rudkin was realized with the aid of a professional playgroup leader, Marjorie Sigley. An absorbing, worrying, entertaining triumph. Directed by Peter Wood; produced by Cecil Clarke; for ATV.   PP

Children's Television Workshop. A non-profit, independently funded organization headed by Joan Ganz Cooney and dedicated to better TV for children. From its New York studios it has produced since 1967 *Sesame Street*, *The Electric Company* and special events such as *The Best of Families*.

Child's Play * (GB since 1984). Engaging game show, based on an American original, turning on cute sayings by children and saved from cuteness itself by the skill of the presenter, Michael Aspel. Produced by Keith Stewart, subsequently Richard Hearsey, for LWT.   PP

Childs, Ted (19 –). British writer, director, producer and executive, responsible in one capacity or another for many of Thames' and Euston Films' earlier thriller series, including *The Sweeney*, *Quatermass* and *Charlie Muffin*. Since 1984 Controller of Drama at Central. Recent writing credit: *Andy Robson* (Tyne-Tees serial), 1983.   PP

Chiller
US 1985 96m colour TVM
CBS/Polar/J. D. Feigelson

A wealthy woman revives her cryogenically preserved son but lives to regret it.
Essentially a monster-from-beyond-the-grave pic, with a side dressing of *Dallas*. None of it works.
w J. D. Feigelson *d* Wes Craven *ph* Frank Thackery *m* Dana Kaproff
'One that shouldn't have been unthawed.' – *Daily Variety*

'He's searching for his missing son. She's looking for a new beginning. Together they uncover a shocking secret!'
China Rose *
CBS/Robert Halmi

An American businessman arrives in Canton to find his son who disappeared in China 16 years previously.
Glossy-looking travelogue which turns out to have borrowed the plot of *The Third Man*, and handles it not half badly.
w David Epstein *d* ROBERT DAY *ph* ERNEST DAY *m* Charles Gross
George C. Scott, Ali MacGraw, Michael Biehn, Dennis Lill, David Snell

China Smith. Half-hour American series of the fifties, starring Dan Duryea as a sailor of fortune.

The Chinatown Murders
US 1974 98m colour TVM
Universal

Kojak tangles with Chinese Tongs when a top gangster is kidnapped.
Tedious Kojak double entry.
w Jack Laird *d* Jeannot Szwarc
Telly Savalas, Dan Frazer, Kevin Dobson, George Savalas, Michael Constantine, Sheree North

The Chinese Detective (GB 1981; 6 × 50m; colour). First British police series to have an ethnic hero, played by David Yip. Scripts by Ian Kennedy Martin, quite exciting, due ration of racial antagonism. Directed by Tom Clegg; produced by Terence Williams; for BBC.   PP

CHiPs *
US 1977–   × 50m colour
NBC/MGM (Cy Chermak, Rick Rosner)

Adventures of two motorcycle cops in the California Highway Patrol.
What might have made an acceptable half-hour series is relentlessly padded with talk, and generally operates at a low level of intelligence, but the action scenes and the two young stars save it.
cr Rick Rosner
LARRY WILCOX, ERIK ESTRADA, Robert Pine

'They were sod-busters, hell raisers, dream-makers, trail-blazers. They fought their way across a continent on fire!'
The Chisholms *
US 1978–9 6 × 96m (or varied format) colour
CBS/Alan Landsburg (Paul Freeman)

In 1844, a Virginia family heads for California.
Archetypal wagon train saga with plenty of incident after a sluggish start. Splendid production detail, attractive locations; but the incidents are a shade too diverse.
cr David Dortort *w* Evan Hunter *d* Mel Stuart *ph* Jacques Marquette *m* Elmer Bernstein, from Aaron Copland
ROBERT PRESTON, Rosemary Harris, Ben Murphy, Brian Kerwin, Jimmy Van Patten, Stacey Nelkin, Susan Swift, Charles Frank, Anthony Zerbe, Brian Keith
'The fate of the Chisholm family becomes something of consequence.' – *Daily Variety*

† Three episodes were made in 1978 and three in 1979, with two cast changes. Then a one-hour series was begun with Mitch Ryan subbing for Preston, whose character had died; but it didn't take.

The Choice
US 1981 96m colour TVM
NBC/Pat and Bill Finnegan

A college girl finds herself pregnant and discovers that her mother is also considering an abortion.
Very predictable 'social problem of the week' movie, full of intense emotional confrontations.

w Dennis Nemec d David Greene

Susan Clark, Mitchell Ryan, Jennifer Warren, Largo Woodruff

'Her only weapon was love!'
Choices of the Heart *
US 1983 96m colour TVM
NBC/Metromedia/Katz–Gallin/Half Pint
  (David W. Rintels)

The story of Jean Donovan, who went to El Salvador as a lay missionary and was mysteriously killed.
Flashback drama from life: more illuminating than the news headlines, but still thin for a two-hour drama.

w John Pielmeier d Joseph Sargent

Melissa Gilbert, Peter Horton, Helen Hunt, Pamela Bellwood, Mary McCusker, Martin Sheen, Mike Farrell, Rene Enriquez

Chomsky, Marvin (1929–). American TV director who has acquired a reputation for efficient if not very stylish presentations of epic mini-series, notably *Roots* (Emmy 1977) and such TV movies as *Attack on Terror*, *Danger in Paradise*, *Victory at Entebbe*, *Fireball Forward*, *The Magician*, *Mrs Sundance*, *Kate McShane*, *Hollow Image*, *Attica* (Emmy 1980), *King Crab*, *Dr Franken*.

Chopper One
US 1974 13 × 25m colour
ABC/Spelling–Goldberg (Ronald Austin,
  James Buchanan)

Adventures of a helicopter patrol team in the Los Angeles Police.
Acceptable crime hokum with good photography and plenty of action.

m Dominic Frontiere

James McMullen, Dirk Benedict

Episodes were as follows:
Ambush
The Hostage
Deadly Carrier
Bust out
Killing Time
The Boy Who Cried Wolf/
  The Informer/Downtime
The Hijack
The Cooperhead
Strain of Innocence
The Drop
The Scramble

Chopper   Squad   (Australia   1975). Empty-headed stories of helicopter rescue along the beaches; 24 hours about which comment would be superfluous.

The Christians *
GB 1977 13 × 50m colour
Granada (Norman Swallow, Mike
  Murphy)

The history of Christianity.
Basically a coffee-table series, pretty to look at but with insufficient hard information. Bamber Gascoigne proved less than hypnotic both as writer and as linkman.

Christie,   Agatha   (1891–76).   Boring British whodunit writer whose works became inescapable with the vogue for glossy international TV movies of the early eighties. LWT's *Why Didn't They Ask Evans?* and *The Seven Dials Mystery* (1981) led to a 10-part series *Partners in Crime* (1983). Meanwhile Thames had *The Agatha Christie Hour* (9 episodes) in 1982 and the BBC *Spider's Web*, same year.   PP
LH: 'I never thought her plots boring, but some of the adaptations certainly are. The strain currently continues with five American TV movies for CBS: *Murder Is Easy*, *Murder with Mirrors*, *Sparkling Cyanide*, *13 at Dinner*, *Dead Man's Folly*.'

A Christmas Carol **
GB 1971 25m colour
ABC/Chuck Jones, Richard Williams

A cartoon version of Dickens's story of Scrooge.
A potted but effective cartoon achievement, with drawings in the style of Victorian illustrations.

d RICHARD WILLIAMS md Tristram Cary
voices Alastair Sim, Michael Redgrave, Michael Hordern

The Christmas Coal Mine Miracle *
aka: *Christmas Miracle in Caulfield USA*
US 1977 96m colour TVM
TCF (Lin Bolen)

An account of a 1951 disaster in Pennsylvania, when a mine was rocked by explosions but miraculously no one was killed.

Good solid drama of a kind rarely encountered these days.

w Dalene Young d Jud Taylor ph Terry Meade

Mitch Ryan, Kurt Russell, Barbara Babcock, Don Porter, Andrew Prine, John Carradine

A Christmas to Remember
US 1978 96m colour TVM
CBS/George Englund

A city teenager stays with his farmer grandparents during the Great Depression of the thirties.

Superior schmaltz.

w Stewart Stern, novel The Melodeon by Glendon Swarthout d George Englund ph Gayne Rescher m Jimmie Haskell

Jason Robards, Eva Marie Saint, George Parry, Joanne Woodward, Bryan Englund

A Christmas without Snow *
US 1979 96m colour TVM
CBS/John Korty/Frank Konigsberg

Problems of a church choir struggling to rehearse The Messiah.

Somewhat unusual and quite palatable seasonal fare.

w John Korty, Richard Beban, Judith Nielsen d JOHN KORTY ph Michael Fash m Ed Bogas

Michael Learned, JOHN HOUSEMAN, Ramon Bieri, James Cromwell, Valerie Curtin, Ruth Nelson, Beah Richards

'Sentiment successfully milked.' – Daily Variety

Christopher Columbus
US/Italy/Germany/France 1985 6 ×
    50m colour miniseries
Lorimar/RAI/Bavaria Atelier/Antenne
    Deux (Silvio and Anna Maria Castellani)

Columbus persuades Ferdinand and Isabella to let him discover America.

Handsome but dramatically stilted historical pageant with a wooden lead.

w Laurence Heath d Alberto Lattuada ph FRANCO DI GIACOMO m Riz Ortolani pd Mario Chiari

Gabriel Byrne, Oliver Reed, Faye Dunaway, Rossano Brazzi, Virna Lisi, Raf Vallone, Max Von Sydow, Eli Wallach, Nicol Williamson, Michel Auclair, Massimo Girotti, Murray Melvin, Jack Watson, Larry Lamb

chroma key. An electronic device which allows a background studio space, by blue saturation, to be filled by a moving picture from another source. Much used in news broadcasts.

Chronicle. A BBC occasional one-hour series, relating and updating archaeological discoveries.

Chuckleheads. 150 × 5m bw comedies edited down in the fifties from two-reelers featuring Ben Turpin, Snub Pollard, etc. Distributor: Adrian Weiss.

Churchill and the Generals *
GB 1979 165m colour
BBC/Jack Le Vien/Australian Broadcasting
    Commission (Alan Shallcross)

When made prime minister in 1940, Churchill spends as much time fighting his own generals as fighting Hitler.

Fascinating sidelights into history with generally excellent performances.

w IAN CURTEIS d Alan Gibson m Wilfred Josephs

TIMOTHY WEST (Churchill), Eric Porter (Brooke), Patrick Allen (Auchinleck), Lyndon Brook (George VI), Richard Dysart (Eisenhower), Alexander Knox (Stimson), Patrick Magee (Wavell), Ian Richardson (Montgomery), Arthur Hill (Roosevelt), Joseph Cotten (Marshall)

PP: 'Like all impersonation dramas, in the end a trot through the waxworks to see who can identify the most exhibits without looking at the name cards. That's de Gaulle – quick or you'll miss him. But what was the point of such a lightning flash of ze troublesome Frenchman considering he did not figure again in the story?'

Churchill, Donald (1930–). As an actor (British), specializes in seedy middle-aged lovers; as a playwright, writes droll comedies about seedy middle-aged lovers. Not unexpectedly, stars in many of his own scripts. Over the years the outcome has generally been a bonus for everyone: Sharp at Four (1964), Room in Town (1970), A BIT OF A LIFT (1974), Feeling His Way (1975), etc. With Julia Jones wrote the Moody and Pegg series (1974) and the serial dramatization of Dickens's Our Mutual Friend (1976). In 1980 Churchill took over and transformed the role of the less than upright inspector in ATV's low-life police sitcom, Spooner's Patch. Goodnight, God Bless followed, 1983. Latest writing credit: screenplay of Mr Pye, 1986.

PP

Churchill, Winston (1874–1965). He hated television and scarcely ever appeared on it. In return, television hasn't done much for Churchill, though he evidently approved of Jack Le Vien's supposedly documentary series *The Valiant Years* (1961) with Churchillian voice-over supplied by Richard Burton. Burton went on to play the part in vision in *Walk with Destiny* (US 1974). Other impersonations of the Old Warrior have come from Leon Sinden, Nigel Stock and Timothy West, none achieving great physical resemblance. Warren Clarke was the young Winston in *Jennie* (1974), Robert Hardy is the Churchill of *Winston Churchill – The Wilderness Years*. *Churchill's People*, a series of studio plays inspired by his *History of the English-Speaking Peoples* (BBC 1975) was a dull dog. Ironically the great man's funeral yielded outside broadcast masterpieces from both BBC and ITV. See also *lookalikes*.   PP

Churchill's People
GB 1975 26 × 50m colour (VTR)
BBC/MCA
Stories from British history.
A genuinely disastrous attempt to breathe flesh into Churchill's *History of the English-Speaking Peoples*. A pretentious embarrassment.

Cider with Rosie * (GB 1971). One of the BBC's first all-film dramas, from poet Laurie Lee's artfully artless account of growing up – and learning about the birds and the bees – in rural Glos. With Rosemary Leach, Peter Chandler. Director Claude Whatham leans on juvenile charm, but it is pleasant to watch, and he went on to do a much truer period piece in *Fothergill* a decade later. Writer: Hugh Whitemore; producer: Ann Kirch.   PP

Cimarron City
US 1958 26 × 50m bw
NBC/Universal/Mont
The mayor keeps the peace in a western town.
Watchable *Destry*-style western.
George Montgomery, Audrey Totter, John Smith

Cimarron Strip
US 1967 23 × 74m colour
CBS (Philip Leacock)
A marshal keeps the peace between Kansas and Indian territory.
Standard, overlong western episodes.
Stuart Whitman, Percy Herbert, Randy Boone, Jill Townsend

† The series was CBS's attempt to emulate the success of NBC's western longform *The Virginian*.

Cinader, Robert A. (1925–84). American producer of television series and miniseries. *Emergency*, *Adam 12*, *The Silent Service*, *Boots and Saddles*, *Chase*, *The Two-Five*, *Quincy*, *Condominium*, *The Immigrants*, *Knight Rider*, etc.

Cinema * Long-running (1964–71) British film magazine show, a weekly half-hour from Granada, in which new releases were related to clips linked by theme, star or director. Successive hosts were Bamber Gascoigne, Derek Granger, Mark Shivas, Michael Scott, Michael Parkinson, Brian Trueman, Clive James (who killed it). It was succeeded by *Clapperboard*, which went for the family audience.

A Circle of Children *
US 1977 96m colour TVM
TCF/Edgar J. Scherick
Problems of a teacher of autistic children.
An earnest and well-written piece, but the feature film *A Child Is Waiting* was better.
w Steven Gethers, *book* Mary McCracken *d* Don Taylor *ph* Gayne Rescher *m* Nelson Riddle
Rachel Roberts, Jane Alexander, David Ogden Stiers
† *Lovey: A Circle of Children, Part 2* was an unnecessary sequel.

Circle of Fear: see Ghost Story

Circuit Eleven Miami (GB/US 1979; approx. 12 × 50m; colour). Cycle of programmes culled by BBC producer Mark Anderson from tapes of civil and criminal cases heard in Florida during an experimental 12-month period in which cameras were allowed into the courts. An English lawyer, Walter Merricks, explained American law and there were also out-of-court interviews with accused and counsel, but a straight transcript might have made truer television.   PP

Circus Boy *
US 1956–7 49 × 25m bw
NBC/Columbia/Herbert B. Leonard
A boy is adopted by a circus troupe.
Well-made children's drama series with a lively background of the early 1900s.
Noah Beery Jnr, Robert Lowery, Guinn Williams, Mickey Dolenz

The Cisco Kid
US 1951–5 156 × 25m colour
Ziv
Adventures of the masked rider of the old west.
Standard children's western.
Duncan Renaldo, Leo Carrillo
† The first TV series to be filmed in colour.

The Citadel
(GB 1983 6 × 50m). This version of A. J. Cronin's story of an idealistic young doctor threatened by success launched a minor vogue for serials, preferably about idealistic young doctors, from popular novels of the chain library era, e.g. *Sorrell and Son*, 1984, *My Brother Jonathan*, 1985. Don Shaw adapted this one, Peter Jefferies directed Ben Cross and Clare Higgins. Produced by Ken Riddington, for BBC.   PP

Cities at War **
GB 1968 3 × 50m bw (16mm)
Granada (Mike Wooller)
Documentary reconstructions of life in Leningrad, Berlin and London during World War II.
Excellent straightforward history on film.
w (respectively) Bruce Norman, Annemarie Weber, Bruce Norman *d* Michael Darlow

PP: 'With its fine balance of archive film, personal reminiscence and restrained hindsight, an exemplary piece of compilation by Mike Wooller and his team. The common denominator to the three essays was the extraordinary courage and humour shown by all three civil populations; the great common virtue was the instinct to survive.'

Citizen '63 (GB 1963). As a young director in the BBC's Bristol studios John Boorman had been churning out a half-hour film every week for a year when this modest series of profiles of representative West Country souls – a schoolgirl, a police officer, a sharp young businessman – made the network and was hailed by the critics as the first sustained exercise in the newly fashionable style of *cinema-vérité*. Ten years later his collaborator on the show, Michael Croucher, chased up some of the original subjects to see what had befallen them; none had fared so dramatically as Boorman himself, wafted to Hollywood and the Big Time largely as a result of his *Citizen '63* acclaim. See also *The Newcomers*.
                                                         PP

Citizen Smith (GB 1979). Laboured BBC sitcom about middle-class drop-out imagining he is dedicated revolutionary; all very tame and predictable.   PP

Citizen 2000 (GB since 1982). Long-term project by Thames Television (Catherine Freeman) to monitor an assortment of 1982 babies through to the adulthood which they officially attain at the turn of the millennium. So far, there have been only modest annual reports in off-peak hours. Later, presumably, attention will increase.   PP

The City *
US 1971 95m colour TVM
Universal (Frank Price)
The Indian mayor of a southwestern city wages a political war while he pursues a mad bomber.
Well-made telemovie set in Albuquerque, the pilot for a shortlived series.
w Howard Rodman *d* Daniel Petrie *m* Alex North
ANTHONY QUINN, Skye Aubrey, Robert Reed, E. G. Marshall, Pat Hingle

The City
US 1977 74m colour TVM
NBC/Quinn Martin (John Wilder)
Two cops scour Los Angeles in search of a psychotic with a deadly grudge.
Slick pilot; no series resulted.
w John Wilder *d* Harvey Hart *ph* Jacques Marquette *m* John Elizalde
Robert Forster, Don Johnson, Ward Costello, Jimmy Dean, Mark Hamill

City Beneath the Sea
GB theatrical release title: *One Hour to Doomsday*
US 1970 98m colour TVM
Warner/Kent/Motion Pictures International (Irwin Allen)
An undersea city is threatened by an errant planetoid.
Futuristic adventure from a familiar stable; it will satisfy followers of *Voyage to the Bottom of the Sea*.
w John Meredyth Lucas *d* Irwin Allen *ph* Kenneth Peach *m* Richard La Salle *ad* Roger E. Maus, Stan Jolley
Stuart Whitman, Robert Wagner, Rosemary Forsyth, Robert Colbert, Burr de Benning, Richard Basehart, Joseph Cotten, James Darren, Sugar Ray Robinson, Paul Stewart

City Detective (US 1953–4; 65 × 25m; bw). Stereotyped private eye series from MCA/Universal. With Rod Cameron.

City Hospital (US 1952). Half-hour live series for CBS, dramatizing routine crises of a New York hospital. With Melville Ruick, Ann Burr.

City in Fear: see Panic on Page One

City Killer
US 1984 96m colour TVM
NBC/Stan Shpetner
Turned down by the girl he loves, a mad
ex-army bomb expert starts blowing up city
buildings.
Slow-starting but generally watchable
suspenser.
w William Wood d Robert Lewis ph Fred
J. Koenekamp m John Rubinstein
Heather Locklear, Gerald McRaney,
Terence Knox, Peter Mark Richman,
Audrey Totter

City of Angels
US 1976 13 × 50m colour
NBC/Universal/Public Arts (Jo Swerling
Jnr)
Cases of a Los Angeles private eye in the
thirties.
More effort went into the period detail than
into the plots, and the films looked
unattractive, which is unforgivable.
cr Jo Swerling Jnr
Wayne Rogers, Clifton James, Elaine Joyce
† The first three episodes were cobbled
together and released in theatres as *The
November Plan.*

City of Gold **
Canada 1957 22m bw
National Film Board
Pierre Berton, born in the Yukon, re-creates
life there around the turn of the century by
the use of still photographs.
Pioneer example of the use of the rostrum
camera, and a highly successful and delightful
one.
w PIERRE BERTON

Civilization ***
GB 1969 13 × 50m colour (VTR)
BBC
Imposing documentary series, by and with
Kenneth Clark, tracing the arts which have
shaped western man.
PP: 'And into the bargain a splendid
refutation of the fad of the day for non-linear
documentaries and arts programmes relying
on the juxtaposition of images, or the
counterplay of sound and pictures.
Civilization depended on a single spool of
prose unrolled by Clark at his own pace. The
programme was itself highly civilized.'

Claire * (GB 1982). Superior mid-brow
serial by Alick Rowe about conscientious
couple who foster problem teenager, played
by Caroline Embling with wary eyes and
bristling fair hair. 'Every little scene,' I
wrote at the time, 'seems to ring horribly or
touchingly true, or sometimes both.' With
Lynn Farleigh and William Gaunt, directed
by John Gorrie, produced by Ron Craddock,
for BBC.   PP

clapperboard. Hinged board clapped
together to mark synchronization at
beginning of filmed action. Also
Clapperboard was the title of Granada's
weekly half-hour on the cinema, compiled
1970–80 by Graham Murray and introduced
by Chris Kelly.

Clark, Brian (1932–). British writer,
originally schoolteacher and drama coach,
who made an emphatic debut with *Whose
Life Is It Anyway?* (1972), about a paralysed
hospital patient demanding the right to die,
subsequently a stage success and movie.
Drew on his teaching experience to coach
child actors for his *Easy Go* (1974). Also,
The Saturday Party (1975), TELFORD'S
CHANGE (series, 1979), *Late Starter* (1985).
                                                                            PP

Clark, Candy (1947–). Distinctive
American leading lady, mainly in films. TV
movies: *James Dean, Amateur Night at the
Dixie Bar and Grill, Where the Ladies Go,
Rodeo Girl.*

Clark, Dane (1913–) (Bernard Zanville).
American leading man, mildly popular at the
end of the forties. A frequent TV guest actor;
series include *Wire Service, Bold Venture,
The New Perry Mason.* TV movies: *The Face
of Fear, The Family Rico, The Return of Joe
Forrester, James Dean, Once an Eagle,* etc.

Clark, Dr David Stafford (1916–). But
when he was one of the best-known faces on
television in the fifties his name couldn't be
given. He was billed simply as 'a consultant
psychiatrist', most commonly on the bizarre
agony column show *Is This Your Problem?*
He also appeared in *Panorama* and had his
own series *Lifeline* (1960), always as a calm
reassuring figure.   PP

Clark, Dick (1929–). American game show
host and linkman, famous since his pop music
programmes of the fifties. TV movies:
Telethon, Deadman's Curve.

Clark, Ernest (1912–). Familiar British character actor, usually as unsmiling nemesis, e.g. in the long-running *Doctor* series, and earlier in *All Gas and Gaiters*.

✳ **Clark, Kenneth** (1903–84) (Lord Clark). British art critic and connoisseur who became acquainted with television as the first chairman of the ITA, 1954–7. Only later did he venture on screen as a superb popularizer of art and culture. Series for Lew Grade's ATV, notably *Romantic Versus Classic Art* led to CIVILIZATION (BBC 1969), and the nickname of his last years, Lord Clark of Civilization.   PP

Clark, Petula (1932–). British cabaret singer, formerly child actress who had her own BBC TV series as long ago as 1952 (*Pet's Parlour*). More recently in occasional specials.

Clark, Susan (1940–). Canadian actress in Hollywood. TV movies: *Something for a Lonely Man, The Challengers, The Astronaut, Trapped,* BABE (Emmy 1976), *McNaughton's Daughter,* AMELIA EARHART, *Jimmy B and Andre, Maid in America, Webster.*

Clarke, Alan (19 –). Long-established British drama director still doing adventurous video productions (*Stars of the Roller Skate Disco*, 1984; *Contact*, 1985), as well as films. Credits include *Penda's Fen* (1974).   PP

Clarke, Arthur C. (1917–). British science-fiction writer, commentator and prophet of the relay satellites which have made television a global medium. Apart from many chat-show appearances, a member of CBS commentary team on Apollo moon-shot missions. Subject of YTV documentary 1972 and episode of BBC *Time Out of Mind* (1979). *Arthur C. Clarke's Mysterious World* (YTV series of 13, 1980) was concerned with curiosities rather than mysteries, and almost nothing to do with sci-fi, *Arthur C. Clarke's World of Strange Powers* (1985) even less so.   PP

✳ **Clarke, Cecil** (1917–85). British executive, originally in charge of the unit furnished by the H. M. Tennent management to produce plays for ATV, in 1964 joining ATV itself as head of drama. Eventually headed special projects to continue largely unsung but formidable record extending over more than a quarter of a century. Last series: *I Remember Nelson* (1982). Last production: *The Biko Inquest* (1984).   PP

Clarke, Roy (1930–). Busy British writer best known for the gentle senior-citizen comedy of the ever-running *Last of the Summer Wine* and the broader, funnier style of *Open All Hours*, 1978–83. The *Magnificent Evans* for the same star, Ronnie Barker, failed to click in 1984, and *Open All Hours* was recalled. Also wrote two six-part serials about the early days of the English film industry, *Flickers* (1981) and *Pictures*, 1983.   PP

Clarke, Tom (1920–). British playwright, not very prolific but of high standard, including two celebrated Jack Gold subjects, *Mad Jack* (1970), and *Stocker's Copper* (1972). Others include *A Brilliant Future Behind Him* (1967), *Billion Dollar Bubble* (1976), *Victims of Apartheid* (1978), *Muck and Brass* (1982), and *Caring* (1986).   PP

Class of '63
US 1973 74m colour TVM
Metromedia/Stonehenge (Dick Berg)
Old passions flare up at a college reunion. Adequate mini-drama.
w Lee Kalcheim *d* John Korty
Joan Hackett, James Brolin, Cliff Gorman, Ed Lauter

Clayburgh, Jill (1944–). Leading American actress of the later seventies. TV movies: *Female Instinct* (*The Snoop Sisters*), *Hustling, The Art of Crime, Griffin and Phoenix.*

Clayhanger ✳
GB 1976 26 × 50m colour (VTR)
ATV/Stella Richman
Two generations of a Potteries family, a step or two down from the Forsytes. Impeccably made but rather boring family saga.
w Douglas Livingstone, *novels* Arnold Bennett *d* John Davies, David Reid
Harry Andrews, Janet Suzman, Peter McEnery, Joyce Redman

A Clear and Present Danger ✳
US 1969 100m colour TVM
Universal (William Sackheim)
A senator's son determines to do something about smog.
Mildly enjoyable socially-conscious drama.

w A. J. Russell, Henri Simoun *d* James Goldstone

Hal Holbrook, E. G. Marshall, Jack Albertson, Joseph Campanella, Pat Hingle, Sharon Acker, Mike Kellin

Cleaver and Haven: see Future Cop

❋ **Cleese, John** (1939–). Tall, angular, eccentric British comedy actor, an essential ingredient of MONTY PYTHON and his own manic man in FAWLTY TOWERS (BAFTA best light entertainment performance 1979). In 1986 commercials for the BBC (on BBC TV) and for the Social Democratic Party.

Clemens, Brian (1931–). British writer–producer, associated with *The Avengers*, *The Persuaders* and *Thriller* (GB).

Clement, Dick (1937–). British comedy scriptwriter, with Ian la Frenais. Series: THE LIKELY LADS, PORRIDGE, *Going Straight.*

The Cleopatras
GB 1983 8 × 50m
BBC (Guy Slater)
Gorblimey chronicles of the line of Egyptian queens all called Cleopatra, culminating in the one everyone knows about. As a long-delayed follow-up to Philip Mackie's *The Caesars* of 1968 it was disappointing, but bare-bosomed handmaidens kept some of the audience watching and Michelle Newell as the last of the Cleos was one of the few I'd seen to suggest that the lady captivated her Romans with the aid of her sexual talents rather than romantic attachment or political wiles, which was just as likely a proposition, and more fun.

w Philip Mackie *m* Nick Bicât *d* John Frankau
Richard Griffiths, Graham Crowden, Robert Hardy, Michelle Newell, Christopher Neame
PP

Clews, Colin (19 –). British director, mainly of light entertainment shows (Palladium, Morecambe and Wise, etc). BAFTA award 1964.   PP

Cliff! (GB 1984 4 × 50m). Eternal rock star and wholesome performer Cliff Richard has his career traced from beginnings to his latest gig, with testimony along the way from Adam Faith, Jack Good, Marty Wilde.   PP

cliffhanger. Unresolved situation (e.g. the hero hanging off a cliff) at the end of an episode of a serial, designed to persuade viewers to tune in next week.

Cliffhangers (US 1978). An unsuccessful attempt by Glen Larson and Universal to make up a weekly hour of three episodes of various types of Saturday morning serial, plus trailers. Camp could go no further, and it didn't.

'The excitement of the chase! The lure of the exotic! The shock of the unexpected!' – publicity

'It's *sincere* trash, the only good kind . . . but it doesn't quite take me back to those afternoons at the Fruitvale Theatre. It's just not the same without the stale popcorn and the sticky carpets.' – Robert MacKenzie, *TV Guide*

† The weekly elements were: *Stop Susan Williams*, with Susan Anton; *The Secret Empire*, with Geoffrey Scott; and *The Curse of Dracula*, with Michael Nouri.

Climb an Angry Mountain *
US 1972 97m colour TVM
Warner/Herb Solow
A local sheriff trails an Indian escaped convict to the top of Mount Shasta.
Overlong but generally enjoyable location melodrama which failed to spark a series.
w Joseph Calvelli, Sam Rolfe *d* Leonard Horn *ph* Michel Hugo *m* George Duning
Fess Parker, Arthur Hunnicutt, Marj Dusay, Barry Nelson, Stella Stevens

Clipper Ship
US 1957 74m bw TVM
Columbia/Playhouse 90
On a ship returning to South America a girl falls for a condemned prisoner.
Talky melodrama with back-projected sails.
d Oscar Rudolph
Charles Bickford, Jan Sterling, Steve Forrest, Helmut Dantine, Evelyn Ankers

Clive of India * (GB 1983 100m). Glittering one-man show by Kenneth Griffith presenting the life, achievements and legacies (good and bad) of the empire-builder. Directed by Michael Pearce, produced by Tempest (Timothy O'Grady), for C4.   PP

The Clock (US 1949–51). Seminal half-hour suspense series for NBC, mainly live, in each episode of which a clock was prominently featured. Originally a radio show.

ARTHUR C. CLARKE. The science fiction writer found time at his Sri Lanka hideaway to introduce a series of true-life mysteries, and is seen here with one of them, Uri Geller.

The Clone Master
US 1978 96m colour TVM
NBC/Paramount/Mel Ferber (John D. F. Black)

A scientist clones 13 replicas of himself and sends them forth to fight evil.
Gimmicky pilot, quite watchable in its crazy way. No series.

w John D. F. Black d Don Medford ph Joseph Biroc m Glen Paxton

Art Hindle, Robyn Douglass, John Van Dreelen, Ralph Bellamy, Ed Lauter

Close-Up: Jessica Novak (US 1981). Hour series from TCF about a lady newscaster. Aspirations obvious to be a TV version of *Lou Grant*; success limited to seven episodes.

closed captioning: an American TV way of of saying sub-titling.

Cloud Howe (GB 1982 4 × 50m). Sequel 11 years later, to the nice rural Scottish serial *Sunset Song* (1971), but this gap exactly matched the time-interval between the original novels by Lewis Grassic Gibbon. Vivien Heilbron's Chris, widowed in the 1914–18 War, was now married to a minister of the kirk in an industrial town. Bill Craig again furnished the script, directed by Tom Cotter, produced by Roderick Graham, for BBC Scotland.
A third serial, *Grey Granite*, completed the Gibbon trilogy in 1983.   PP

Clouds of Glory *
GB 1978 2 × 50m colour (16mm)
Granada (Norman Swallow)

The lives of the Wordsworths and Coleridge. Historical re-creations with the director on top technical form, but also with some exploitation and distortion of fact. The Coleridge episode, *The Rime of the Ancient Mariner*, is to say the least eccentrically told, but it looks good.

w Melvyn Bragg, Ken Russell d KEN RUSSELL pd Michael Grimes ph DICK BUSH

David Warner, Felicity Kendal, David Hemmings

Coach of the Year
US 1980 96m colour TVM
NBC/Paramount/A. Shane

A partially paralysed pro-football player becomes a coach.
Heart-warming stuff, but nothing that hasn't been seen a hundred times before.

d Don Medford

Robert Conrad, Erin Gray, Ricky Paul, David Hubbard, Lou Carello

'Credibility gets the long stretch in this one.' – *Daily Variety*

Cobb, Lee J. (1911–76) (Lee Jacoby). Burly, distinguished American actor of all media. TV series: *The Virginian*. TV movies: *Double Indemnity, Dr Max, Heat of Anger, Trapped Beneath the Sea, The Great Ice Ripoff.*

Coburn, James (1928–). American leading man with an insolent air. TV: *The Dain Curse, Darkroom.*

❋   **Coca, Imogene** (1908–). American eccentric revue comedienne associated in the early fifties with Sid Caesar and *Your Show of Shows*. In 1954 she had her own variety hour, *The Imogene Coca Show*. Never subsequently found a niche except in *Grindl*, which lasted only one season, and the abysmal *It's About Time*. Emmy 1951: best actress. TV movie: *The Return of the Beverly Hillbillies.*

Cocaine and Blue Eyes
US 1983 96m colour TVM
NBC/Columbia (Daniel S. Mark)

A private eye becomes involved with drug smugglers when his card is found on the body of a murder victim.
Routine mystery with most of the expected situations.

w Kendall J. Blair d E. W. Swackhamer

O. J. Simpson, Candy Clark, Eugene Roche, Cindy Pickett, Cliff Gorman, Maureen Anderman, Keye Luke, Tracy Reed

'Predictability, compromise and convenience supersede plotting and invention.' – *Daily Variety*

Cocaine: One Man's Seduction
US 1983 96m colour TVM
NBC/Charles Fries/David Goldsmith

A middle-aged real-estate salesman tries cocaine to give himself a lift. Results predictable.
Modern road to ruin, nicely done, but not exactly compulsive.

w Barry Schneider d Paul Wendkos ph Chuck Arnold m Brad Fiedel

Dennis Weaver, Karen Grassle, James Spader, Pamela Bellwood, David Ackroyd, Jeffrey Tambor

Cock, Hen and Courting Pit *
GB 1966 75m bw (VTR)

Eloquent David Halliwell play about the nature of intense physical passion and how this is, in part, a fearful illness. When the young lovers meet again, ten years afterwards, they discover with relief that nothing remains between them; they are cured. Apart from its merits, interesting as an important step along the way to making drama on location and on film – less than a quarter of the finished production was done in the studio. It also came just before television ventured into the permissive era, so that when the couple bathe in their deserted mill pool they are wearing decorous swimsuits. With Maurice Roëves, Nicola Pagett. Directed by Charles Jarrott; produced by Peter Luke; for BBC.   PP

Coco, James (1929–). Chubby American comic actor with stage, screen and TV credits. Series: *Calucci's Department*.

Code Name: Diamondhead
US 1977 74m colour TVM
Quinn Martin/NBC

Adventures of a US counter-intelligence agent in Hawaii.
A predictable pilot which didn't sell.

w Paul King *d* Jeannot Szwarc *ph* Jack Whitman *m* Morton Stevens

Roy Thinnes, France Nuyen, Zulu, Ian MacShane

Code Name: Heraclitus
GB 1967 88m colour TVM
Universal

A war veteran dies briefly on the operating table; revived, he is emotionless and so makes an ideal spy.
So who said the six million dollar man was a new idea?

w Alvin Sapinsley *d* James Goldstone

Stanley Baker, Ricardo Montalban, Jack Weston, Leslie Nielsen, Sheree North, Kurt Kasznar

Code Name Jericho: see Jericho

Code of Vengeance
US 1985 96m colour TVM
NBC/Universal (Robert Foster)

In trouble, an Arizona family is helped by a Vietnam vet who discovers trouble in the community.
With a plot borrowed from *Shane*, this looks suspiciously like a pilot for a series about a wandering do-gooder . . . which is exactly what it became, under the title *Dalton*.

w Robert Foster *d* Rick Rosenthal *ph* Duke Callaghan *m* Don Peake

Charles Taylor, Erin Gray, Charles Haid, Randall Cobb, Keenan Wynn

Code R
US 1977 13 × 50m colour
CBS/Warner (Ed Self)

Adventures of an emergency rescue service on a Californian island (Catalina).
Simple-minded action for children, tourists and dogs.

cr Ed Self *ph* Richard Kelly *m* Lee Holdridge

James Houghton, Martin Cove, Tom Simcox, Susanne Reed

Code Red
US 1981 74m colour TVM
Columbia/Irwin Allen

Adventures of a family of firefighters.
Risible retread of *Emergency*, 'warmly' dedicated to the firefighters of the world.

w Laurence Heath *d* J. Lee Thompson

Lorne Greene, Sam Jones, Andrew Stevens, Julie Adams

† A 50m series was picked up for the 81/82 season.

Code Three
US 1956 39 × 15m bw
Hal Roach

Cases of the Los Angeles County Sheriff's office.
Below par crime filler.

Richard Travis

Codename: Foxfire
US 1985 96m colour TVM
NBC/Universal (Alex Beaton, Douglas Benton)

Three women secret agents work for the government.
Slackly handled and unattractively cast, this pilot spawned a series that lasted only half a dozen hours.

w Richard Chapman, Bill Dial *d* Corey Allen *ph* F. Pershing Flynn *m* Joe Sample

Joanna Cassidy, John McCook, Sheryl Lee Ralph, Henry Jones, Robin Johnson, Liliana Komorowska

'Credibility is jettisoned early in the running and never recovered.' – *Daily Variety*

Coe, Fred (1914–79). American producer associated with TV's 'golden age' of the fifties: many plays; series include *Mr Peepers*. Emmy 1955 for *Producer's Showcase*.

Coffee, Tea or Me? *
US 1973 74m colour TVM
Mark Carliner
An airline stewardess has one lover in London and another in Los Angeles.
So what else is new? Agreeable daffy comedy.
d Norman Panama
Karen Valentine, John Davidson, Michael Anderson Jnr

Coke, Cyril (19 –). Veteran British drama director, with A–R in early days of ITV, still going strong in the eighties. *Malice Aforethought*, *Pride and Prejudice*, *Flickers*, *The Consultant*.   PP

Cold Comfort Farm *
GB 1968 3 × 50m bw (VTR)
BBC (David Conroy, Peter Hammond)
A young woman finds her country relations to be grotesque caricatures of the popular urban conception of country folk.
Stella Gibbons's wryly amusing novel of the twenties, a splendid corrective to *The Archers*, was subtly transferred to TV in this memorable adaptation.
dramatized by David Turner
Alastair Sim, Fay Compton, Sarah Badel

Cold Harbour *(GB 1979; 60m; colour). Refugee girl from Chile is fixed up with marriage of convenience by her communard London hosts, it never occurring to them in their political zeal that she might also need some ordinary friendship and care. A perceptive impression of foreign-ness, written by Peter Prince; directed by Stephen Frears; for BBC. With Leticia Garrido, Anthony Sher.   PP

A Cold Night's Death *
US 1972 73m colour TVM
Spelling–Goldberg (Paul Junger Witt)
In a snowbound laboratory scientists are experimenting on apes . . . and someone is experimenting on *them*.
Reasonably tart and chilling sci-fi.
w Jarrold Freeman d Christopher Knopf
Robert Culp, Eli Wallach, Michael C. Gwynne

The Cold Room
GB/US 1984 96m colour TVM
HBO/Jethro/Forstater (Bob Weis, Mark Forstater)
A girl in East Berlin with her father discovers herself possessed by the soul of a girl who died there in World War II.
Muddled supernatural melodrama with insufficient plot to flesh out its theme.
w James Dearden, *novel* by Jeffrey Caine
d James Dearden ph Tony Pierce-Roberts
m Michael Nyman pd Tim Hutchinson
George Segal, Amanda Pays, Renee Soutendijk, Warren Clarke, Anthony Higgins, Elizabeth Spriggs, Ursula Howells

Cold Warrior (GB 1984 6 × 50m). Cold-war thriller serial featuring Michael Denison as the plummy spymaster Captain Percival, originally created by playwright Arden Winch in BLOOD MONEY (1981) and then *Skorpion* (1983). Now scripted by Murray Smith, John Brason and others, directed by Andrew Morgan. With Lucy Fleming, David Swift, Neil Stacy, Dean Harris. Produced by Gerard Glaister, for BBC.   PP

Colditz *
GB 1972–3 28 × 50m colour
BBC/Universal (Gerald Glaister)
Incidents during World War II in the crack German prisoner-of-war camp.
A good intelligent series which proved highly popular in the UK but was never even screened in the US.
Robert Wagner, BERNARD HEPTON, David McCallum, Anthony Valentine, Jack Hedley

Cole, Dennis (*c* 1941–). Bland American juvenile lead, in series *The Felony Squad*, *Bracken's World*, *Bearcats*. TV movies: *The Connection*, *Barbary Coast, Cave In*.

✵ **Cole, George** (1925–). British character actor who started as a juvenile in 1940, formed a famous stage partnership with Alastair Sim and appeared in many films as well as starring in the series *A Life of Bliss*. Memorable TV appearances include A MAN OF OUR TIMES and MINDER. Less memorable include *The Bounder* (1982), *Comrade Dad* (1984) and *Blott on the Landscape* (1985).

Cole, Nat King (1919–65) (Nathaniel Coles). Black American pianist and singer. In 1957 he was to have his own series, but it was cancelled, because southern stations threatened a boycott.

Cole, Olivia (19 –). Black American actress who won an Emmy in 1976 for her performance in *Roots*.

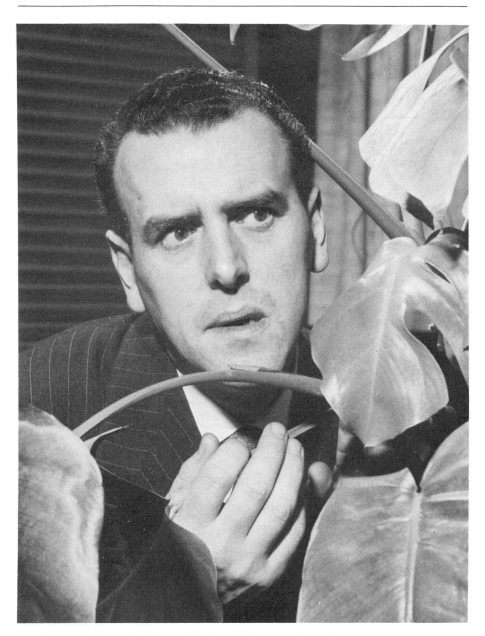

GEORGE COLE is so familiar to *Minder*-watchers as Arthur Daley that some may not recognize him in his 1961 persona as David Bliss in *A Life of Bliss*.

Coleman, Dabney (*c* 1937–). Useful American character actor, often in heavy comic roles. Starred on TV as *Buffalo Bill*; TV anchorman.

Coleman, David (1926–). British sports commentator, longtime host of *Sportsnight*, whose reckless prose style has given its name to a regular anthology of commentators' bloops in the magazine *Private Eye*.

❋ **Coleman, Gary** (1968–). Black child actor with star quality which showed in *Diff'rent Strokes*. His ebullient personality, which caused some people to allege he was a dwarf, was caused by a childhood illness. TV movies: *The Kid from Left Field, Scout's Honor, The Kid with the Broken Halo, The Kid with the 200 IQ, The Fantastic World of D. C. Collins*

Colicos, John (1928–). Bulky Canadian character actor in Hollywood. TV movies: *Goodbye Raggedy Ann, A Matter of Wife and Death, The Bastard, Battlestar Galactica.*

Colla, Richard J. (1918–). American director with a preliminary career in short films and a tendency towards experiment. TV movies include *The Tribe, The Questor Tapes, Live Again Die Again.*

The Collaborators
Canada 1975–6 14 × 50m colour
CBC
Stories of the pathologists who assist police work.
The stories in fact became very miscellaneous, and the series petered out, but essentially it was a competent imitation of American standards.

The Collection *
GB 1961 50m bw (VTR)
Ageing dress designer agonizes over whether or not his young protégé spent the night with pretty boutique owner. Typical early Harold Pinter TV play, produced by Peter Willes for A–R, directed by Joan Kemp-Welch, with Griffith Jones, John Ronane, Vivien Merchant. The same script was re-produced for Granada's *Best Play* series in 1976.   PP

College Bowl. American quiz show of the fifties, hosted by Allen Ludden, with college teams competing to answer difficult general knowledge questions (Emmy 1962, best game show). From it the British *University Challenge* was drawn.

Collingwood, Charles (1917–). American international correspondent, long with CBS.

Collins, Gary (*c* 1935–). Unassuming American leading man. Series include *The Wackiest Ship in the Army, Iron Horse, The Sixth Sense, Born Free.* TV movies: *Quarantined, Getting Away from It All, Houston We've Got a Problem, Roots, The Night They Took Miss Beautiful,* etc.

❋ **Collins, Joan** (1933–). British leading leading lady who after a desultory career in international films became a surprise hit in the soap opera *Dynasty*, in which she played the predatory Alexis. She became the envy of women all over the world who wouldn't mind looking as alluring as she does at her age. TV movies: *The Moneychangers, Paper Dolls, The Wild Women of Chastity Gulch, The Making of a Male Model, Her Life as a Man, The Cartier Affair.*

Collins, Lewis (1946–). British light leading man, one of *The Professionals*.

Collins, Norman (1907–). British executive instrumental in the creation of ITV and the founding of ATV. Also author of the novel, *London Belongs to Me* (serialized in 1977).

Collins, Pauline (1940–). Chubby British actress who scored a hit in the early episodes of UPSTAIRS DOWNSTAIRS and later appeared with her husband John Alderton in *Thomas and Sarah*, a kind of sequel.

Collision Course **
US 1976 100m colour TVM (tape)
David Wolper
The conflict between President Truman and General MacArthur which led to the latter's resignation.
Dogged dramatized documentary with some splendid moments between the padding.
w ERNEST KINOY *d* Anthony Page
E. G. MARSHALL, HENRY FONDA, John Randolph, Andrew Duggan, Barry Sullivan, Lloyd Bochner, Lucille Benson, Ann Shoemaker
† Another *Collision Course* was Granada's 75-minute 'faction' about the events leading up to the mid-air collision over Zagreb of two passenger planes; written by Martin Thompson.
†† While *Course for Collision* was Arthur Hailey's second aviation thriller (1958) after *Flight into Danger*. US president en route to Moscow by polar route finds his plane on course for collision with unidentified bomber heading for America . . .

Colonel Flack
US 1953   × 25m bw
CBS/Wilbur Stark
An elderly confidence trickster constantly eludes the law.
Mild but surprisingly popular comedy of its time, transmitted live.

JOAN COLLINS, just before she made it big in *Dynasty*, found time to play in one of Orson Welles' *Great Mysteries* for Anglia. The ever-reliable Anton Rodgers supported her.

cr Everett Rhodes Castle, from his published stories
Alan Mowbray, Frank Jenks

Colonel March of Scotland Yard
GB 1953 26 × 25m bw
Sapphire
Stories of the Department of Queer

Complaints, from the novels by Carter Dickson. Despite its star, a tacky series in which the sets always seemed about to fall apart.

Boris Karloff

† Episodes were as follows:

Hot Money
Death in the Dressing Room
The Invisible Man
Error at Daybreak
The Silver Curtain
The Invisible Knife
Death in Inner Space
The Missing Link
The Second Mona Lisa
The Talking Head
At Night All Cats Are Grey
The Abominable Snowman
Death and the Other Monkey
Passage at Arms
The Stolen Crime
Murder Is Permanent
The Case of the Lively Ghost
The Sorcerer
The Deadly Gift
The Strange Event at Roman Fall
The Devil Sells His Soul
The Silent Vow
The Case of the Misguided Missal
The Case of the Kidnapped Poodle
Present Tense
The Headless Hat

Colorado C1
US 1978 50m colour
CBS/Quinn Martin/Woodruff (Philip Salzman)

Two brothers lead an élite state police force. Competent standard cop show pilot which wasn't signed on.

w Robert W. Lenski *d* Virgil W. Vogel *ph* Jacques R. Marquette *m* Dave Grusin

John Elerick, Marshall Colt, L. Q. Jones, Laurette Spang, Christine Belford, David Hedison

Colossus: The Ship That Lost a Fortune *
GB 1978 2 × 50m colour (16mm)
BBC (Tony Salmon)

An account of the reconstruction of rare Greek vases which were smashed and lost in a 1798 shipwreck off the Scillies.
Precise and painstaking documentary paying as much attention to diving as to museum work. The kind of film report that only the BBC would mount.

narrator Dr Ann Burchall

colour. America began a colour system in 1953, Britain not until 1968, when technology was much more advanced and the system more satisfactory, with subtler tones and a much wider range. In each case colour sets were expensive and slow to sell, but by the mid-seventies were in the majority.

Colt 45
US 1958–9 67 × 25m bw
ABC/Warner

In the old west, a gun salesman is actually a government agent.
Passable western.

Wayde Preston, Donald May

Columbia Broadcasting System: see CBS

Columbo: see Mystery Movie

Combat! *
US 1962–6 152 × 50m bw (last 25 in colour)
ABC/Selmur

Adventures of an infantry platoon in the European theatre during World War II.
Smartly tooled films, much appreciated by war veterans, and of a high standard of scripting.

Rick Jason, Vic Morrow

Combat Sergeant (US 1956). Shortlived half-hour war adventure series for ABC, set during the North African campaign, with Michael Thomas and Cliff Clark.

Come Dancing. A perennial BBC series culminating in an annual ballroom dancing championship.

The Comeback Kid
US 1982 96m colour TVM
ABC (Louis Rudolph)

An ex-baseball player finds satisfaction in coaching street kids.
You don't have to see the film to imagine the warmth and humanity which ooze out of it.

w Joe Landon *d* Peter Levin

John Ritter, Doug McKeon, Susan Dey, Jeremy Light, James Gregory

The Comedian (US 1958). A *Playhouse 90* presentation for CBS, written by Rod Serling. Emmys for best writing, best single programme.

The Comedians. An influential format created by Granada TV in 1971. The acts of stand-up comics were sliced into individual jokes and re-edited into a shaped half-hour with musical bridges. It lasted well for two seasons and yielded several spin-offs. Creator: John Hamp. With Bernard Manning, Charlie Williams, Tom O'Connor, Mike Reid, Ken Goodwin, Frank Carson, Duggie Brown. The title and idea was briefly revived in 1985.

Comedians (GB 1979). A 95-minute adaptation of Trevor Griffiths's play about a retired comedian teaching young recruits at a night class. With Bill Fraser, Jonathan Pryce; directed by Richard Eyre; for BBC.

The Comedy Company
US 1978 93m colour TVM
CBS/MGM/Merit Malloy/Jerry Adler
Would-be comics at a try-out club save the owner from a takeover.
Rather woebegone modern treatment of an old-hat theme; not very entertaining.
w Lee Kalcheim d Lee Phillips ph Matthew F. Leonetti m Tom Scott
Jack Albertson, GEORGE BURNS, Lawrence-Hilton Jacobs, Susan Sullivan, Abe Vigoda, Michael Brandon, Herb Edelman

Comedy Playhouse. Umbrella title for intermittent British series of single half-hour comedies, originally all by Alan Simpson and Ray Galton, from which the more successful episodes might – and did – become series in their own right, e.g. *Casanova '73.*   PP

Comic Roots (GB 1982 4 × 40m). Four comedians revisit the landscape wherein they grew up and acquired their comic stock-in-trade: Les Dawson (Manchester); Roy Hudd (seaside summer shows); Paul Shane (Rotherham); Irene Handl (London bourgeoisie). From BBC.   PP

The Comic Strip (GB 1982–3 5 × 30m). Hit-or-miss parodies of various genres by young company taking their name from the fringe theatre where they'd started. Peter Richardson, Dawn French and Jennifer Saunders were the prime movers. The hits included *Five Go Mad In Dorset*, making happy mock of Enid Blyton, *Bad News Tour*, about a pop group on the road, and *Summer School*. The misses were the rest, and were total misses. From Michael White/Comic Strip Productions, for C4. Further episodes followed in 1984–6.   PP

Coming Next . . . (GB 1985). More anarchic comedy masterminded by Paul Jackson and this time entrusted to a quartet

of young performers led by Chris Barrie from *Carrott's Lib* and *Spitting Image*. Best feature was a louche inversion of the BBC's *East Enders* called *West Enders*. With Carla Mendonca, Gareth Hale, Norman Pace. Produced by Paul Jackson Productions, for C4.   PP

Coming Out *
GB 1979 75m colour
Covert homosexual writer finally declares himself, precipitating a domestic crisis.
Intelligent, witty *Play for Today* by James Andrew Hall with a solid, undemonstrative performance by Anton Rodgers, Nigel Havers as his gilded young friend, Richard Pearson as a bitchy rival and Hywel Bennett intruding sardonically as a 'straight'. Directed by Carol Wiseman; produced by Kenith Trodd; for BBC.   PP

Coming out of the Ice *
US 1982 96m colour TVM
CBS/Telepictures/Frank Konigsberg (Christopher Pearce)
A young American living in Russia refuses to change his citizenship, is arrested as a spy, and spends two decades in remote prisons and labour camps.
Adequate, unsurprising autobiographical piece, based on the experiences of Victor Herman.
w Alan Sharp d Waris Hussein
John Savage, Willie Nelson, Ben Cross, Francesca Annis

A Coming to Terms for Billy (GB 1984). Final play in Graham Reid's 'Billy' trilogy – see *Too Late to Talk to Billy*. Directed by Paul Seed, with Kenneth Branagh, Brid Brennan, James Ellis, Gwen Taylor. Produced by Chris Parr, for BBC Northern Ireland.   PP

Command 5
US 1984 96m colour TVM
ABC/Paramount (Anthony Spinner)
Adventures of an élite police force 'which is not restricted to conventional methods, nor state and territorial boundaries'.
In other words, to quote *Daily Variety*, 'a repugnant endeavour to glamorize another para-military band of thugs'. Lousy, anyway.
w Anthony Spinner d E. W. Swackhamer ph Dennis Dalzell m Lalo Schifrin
Stephen Parr, Wings Hauser, John Matuszak, Gregory Sierra, William Russ, Sonja Smits

Command in Battle
GB 1958 7 × 30m bw

Lord Montgomery re-fighting his great battles head-on to BBC cameras with the same unshakable self-confidence he had displayed in the field. Each instalment was introduced from the actual caravan he had used, or with the actual telephone to hand by which he had issued his orders, leading Alan Brien in the *Observer* to note that yes, this was indubitably the actual Montgomery we had used in the war.   PP

† Montgomery was also the subject of a 1963 BBC documentary, *Monty, Portrait of a Soldier* (w Fred Majdalany; p Maurice Harvey).

The Commanders * (GB 1972–3; 8 ×
50m). Originally four BBC studies of World War II commanders in the European theatre, beginning with Monty's adversary Rommel. On the repeat run four more were added from the Japanese campaigns, including an episode on Admiral Yamomoto written by Correlli Barnett which could serve as a model of the proper assessment of an enemy 30 years on. Frank Gillard narrated throughout.
                                                                PP

The Commanding Sea
GB 1981 6 × 50m colour 16mm
BBC/Malone–Gill

Clare Francis examines man's uses of the sea, from merchant shipping and herring trawling to her own single-handed sail across the Atlantic.
A rather disappointing series, muddily photographed and insecurely edited.

w/d Michael Gill, Anthony Mayer m Carl Davis narrator Laurence Olivier

Commercial Breaks (GB 1984–5 26 ×
50m). Gripping real-life stories of business coups and campaigns in Britain and America, filmed as they happen. Produced by David Dugan, for BBC.

The Common *
GB 1973 90m colour

Rich Tory family living one side of the suburban common tangles with poor and radical family on the other, the local school play bringing matters to a head. In retrospect the symmetry of it all was a little too satisfying, though no summary can take into account the wit and accuracy and plaintive undertones of anything Peter Nichols writes. *Play of the Month* with Peter Jeffrey, Vivien Merchant, Dennis Waterman, Gwen Taylor.   PP

❋ Como, Perry (1912–) (Pierino Roland
Como, once known as Nick Perido). Easy-going Italian–American ballad singer, a TV staple through the fifties and sixties, especially on *Kraft Music Hall*. Emmys 1954, 1955, 1956, 1958 as best male singer/personality. Still doing specials in the eighties.
'He gives his usual impression of a man who has been told to say cheese and simultaneously shot in the back with a poisoned arrow.' – Clive James

Compact (GB 1962–5). Bi-weekly BBC
soaper set in the offices of a women's magazine and the homes of its staff. An innovation was to be the introduction of 'real' celebrities into the story, e.g. the writer Ted Willis or the actor Ian Carmichael dropping in as themselves, but this was forgotten as the fiction proved it could hold a middle-class audience, anyway, in thrall without such help. Later, *Crossroads* borrowed the same idea. With Jean Harvey, Moray Watson, Marcia Ashton.   PP

† An international version of the same format under the title *Impact* was under development in 1985–6 by Limehouse (Susi Hush) with W. German and Luxembourg partners.

Companions in Nightmare *
US 1967 99m colour TVM
Universal (Norman Lloyd)

Murder at a group therapy session.
Slightly offbeat, rather pretentious whodunit.

w Robert L. Joseph d Norman Lloyd

Melvyn Douglas, Gig Young, Anne Baxter, Patrick O'Neal, Dana Wynter, Leslie Nielsen

Company (US 1971). A fascinating
50-minute documentary about an all-day rehearsal by the Broadway cast of a famous musical to make the record. With Elaine Stritch, etc; directed by Richard Leacock and D. A. Pennebaker; executive producer Danny Melrick.

Company of Killers
US 1969 87m colour TVM
Universal

A psychopathic killer is at large in the city.
Adequate chase thriller.

w E. Jack Neuman d Jerry Thorpe

Van Johnson, Ray Milland, Robert Middleton, John Saxon, Susan Oliver, Clu Gulager, Brian Kelly, Fritz Weaver, Diana Lynn

compilation. Programme made up chiefly from segments of other programmes, stock shots or library film.

Comrades * (GB 1985–6 12 × 45m). Twelve fly-on-the-wall pictures of Soviet life, attacked at first for accepting official facilities too readily and giving a honeyed view of military academy, magistrates' court or medical man. But later episodes centred on individuals (fashion designer, film director) sadly or bravely trying to beat the system, and the unfamiliar provincial or far-flung locations were a revelation in themselves. Produced by Richard Denton, for BBC.

Concealed Enemies **
US/GB 1984 4 × 50m
WGBH with Goldcrest/Comworld (Peter Cook)
The extraordinary story of Alger Hiss's doomed libel suit against Whittaker Chambers, obscure ex-communist journalist who had accused him of being a Soviet spy. The main British contribution to this co-production was the screenplay, but it was a useful one. 'And when it was all over,' I wrote at the time, 'you still weren't sure who done it, or indeed if anything had ever been did.' Shown in Britain, over two nights, on C4.
w Hugh Whitemore *d* Jeff Bleckner
Edward Herrman (as Hiss), John Harkins (as Chambers), Peter Riegert   PP

Concentration (US 1958). Half-hour quiz game for NBC, based on the old game of trying to pick two cards of the same denomination. Hosts, Jack Barry and (later) Hugh Downs. The format was successfully transferred to Britain.

The Concert. Tricksy little play, originally for radio, which was the first television drama to enjoy international renown. The author was a Canadian, Joseph Schull; his play, repeatedly done in the United States and Britain as well as his own country during the late forties and early fifties, depended on a dénouement: the unseen suitor of the pretty blind musician was, unknown to her, a black man. For TV it meant an early use of the subjective camera in order to preserve the secret, but the script was so rigged to score cheap points that it was hardly worth the trouble. For the record the last BBC production, *c* 1958, starred Diane Cilento and Earl Cameron.   PP

Concrete Beat
US 1983 74m colour TVM
ABC/Viacom/Picturemaker (Jay Daniel)
Adventures of a columnist on a Manhattan weekly.
Rather smug pilot for a series which wasn't ordered: the content was too slight to fit into the slick format.
w Glenn Gordon Caron *d* Robert Butler *ph* James Crabe *m* Artie Kane
John Getz, Darianne Fluegel, Ken McMillan, Rhoda Gemignani, Van Nessa L. Clarke, Dean Santoro

The Concrete Cowboys
US 1979 96m colour TVM
CBS/Ernie Frankel
Two Tennessee gents find adventure on the road to Hollywood.
Slackly handled comedy adventure which seldom rises to the occasion beyond a few chases and pile-ups.
w Jimmy Sangster *d* Burt Kennedy *ph* Alan Stensvold *m* Earle Hagen
Tom Selleck, Jerry Reed, Morgan Fairchild, Claude Akins, Roy Acuff, Barbara Mandrell
† A series emerged two seasons later, but ran only four episodes.

Condo
US 1984 13 × 25m colour
TCF/Witt–Thomas (Harry Waterson)
In a condominium complex, some inhabitants have moved down, and others have moved up.
Rather feeble comedy of neighbours who don't get on.
cr Sheldon Bull
McLean Stevenson, Yvonne Wilder, Luis Avalo, Brooke Anderson, Julie Carmen

Condominium
GB title: *Condominium: When the Hurricane Struck*
US 1980 2 × 96m colour
OPT/Universal (Gino Gimaldi, Hannah Shearer)
A jerry-built Florida apartment block collapses in a hurricane.
Standard *Bridge of San Luis Rey* treatment of hackneyed people with hackneyed problems.
w Stevan Hayes, *novel* John D. MacDonald *d* Sidney Hayers *ph* Frank Thackery *m* Gerald Fried
Barbara Eden, Steve Forrest, Dan Haggerty, Ralph Bellamy, Richard Anderson, Larry Bishop, Dane Clark, Macdonald Carey, Linda Cristal, Dorothy Malone, Don Galloway, Arte Johnson, Stuart Whitman,

Ana Alicia, Nehemiah Persoff, Pamela Hensley, Jack Jones.

'They shouldn't write 'em like this any more!' – *Daily Variety*

Condor
US 1984 74m colour TVM
ABC/Orion

In 2000, an agent for a Los Angeles anti-terrorist organization is assigned a beautiful robot partner.

Futuristic thick-ear with laughable dialogue: a pilot which didn't sell.

Ray Wise, Craig Stevens, Wendy Kilbourne, Carolyn Seymour

Confession
US 1957 74m bw TVM
Columbia/Playhouse 90

A reporter discovers that the public idol who is his subject had feet of clay.

Familiar exposé stuff, adequately put over.

d Anton M. Leader

Dennis O'Keefe, June Lockhart, Paul Stewart, Romney Brent

'Would his world fall apart before he pulled himself together?'

Confessions of a Married Man
US 1984 96m colour TVM
ABC/Comworld/Gloria Monty (Charles A. Pratt)

A middle-aged businessman defies his routine life by having an affair, but when his wife finds out the results are surprising.

Unsensational and mainly uninteresting domestic crisis worked out on all too familiar lines.

w,d Steven Gethers   *ph* Paul Lohmann
m Billy Goldenberg

Robert Conrad, Jennifer Warren, Ann Dusenberry, Mary Crosby, Lance Guest

The Confessions of Felix Krull (Germany
1982 5 × 60m). Thomas Mann's last, unfinished novel turned into a rather heavy romp through bedrooms and boudoirs, with the English actor John Moulder-Brown as its opportunist hero. Dramatized by Alf Brustellin, Bernhard Sinkel; directed by Bernhard Sinkel; produced by Peter Marthesheimer and Jotn Schroder; for Taurus Films/C4.   PP

The Confidence Course
GB 1965 75m bw (VTR)

Dennis Potter's first play. Three smooth operators trying to persuade a score of unfortunates to enrol in an expensive personality-building class are defeated by a kind of holy fool who converts everyone back to the comfort of being unconfident. A nice idea that never quite realized its potential. With Dennis Price, Stanley Baxter; directed by Gilchrist Calder; produced by James MacTaggart; for BBC.
                     PP

Conflict. Umbrella title used for a suspense anthology segment of *Warner Brothers Present*, a one-hour series which began in 1955. It included the pilots for *77 Sunset Strip* and *Sugarfoot.*

Congratulations, It's a Boy
US 1971 73m colour TVM
Aaron Spelling

A swinging bachelor's life changes when his grown son turns up.

Modest comedy with a few laughs.

w Stanley Cherry *d* William A. Graham

Bill Bixby, Diane Baker, Jack Albertson, Ann Sothern, Karen Jensen

Congressional Investigator
US 1959 26 × 25m bw
Sandy Howard

Government investigators uncover evidence for congressional hearings.

Syndicated series, a rare example of an attempt to make entertainment out of politics (not forgetting a little thick-ear).

Edward Stroll, William Masters, Stephen Roberts, Marion Collier

Conjugal Rights **
GB 1973 3 × 50m colour
YTV (Peter Willes)

Philip Mackie drama trilogy which came as near as anything to persuading the real Philip Mackie to stand up: an elegant permutation of three married couples in which, after his somewhat bleak view of marriage in *A Marriage* six months earlier, he offered a recipe for making it work. The philandering Michael (Ian Holm) acted as demonstrator, bedding both the other ladies without blunting the edge of his delight in his own wife or ever shaking her confidence in this respect. The secret was discretion allied to introspection: understanding the attraction other women held for him, and judiciously giving in to it, he was less likely ever to be bowled over. 'I plead for more self-knowledge . . . and a little considerate hypocrisy.'

d Marc Miller

Ian Holm, Barbara Ferris   PP

The Connection *
US 1973 74m colour TVM
Phil D'Antoni/Metromedia

A tough reporter mediates between jewel
thieves and insurance companies.

Complex, New York based thriller which
resolves itself into a pretty good chase
comparable with the same producer's *The
French Connection.*

w Albert Ruben *d* Tom Gries

Charles Durning, Ronny Cox, Zohra
Lampert, Dennis Cole, Dana Wynter,
Howard Cosell, Mike Kellin

Connell, Brian (1916–). Crusty British
interviewer and narrator, originally
anchorman on *This Week*. In recent years
associated chiefly with Anglia Television, for
whom he conducts *The Brian Connell
Interview*, necessarily restricted to Top
People since Connell's opening gambit is to
read out each subject's *Who's Who* entry.
Ironically, Connell himself is not listed in that
work.   PP

Connelly, Christopher (1941–). American
leading man, who became known in *Peyton
Place* and later played the lead in *Paper
Moon*. TV movies: *In Name Only, Incident in
San Francisco, The Last Day, Charlie Cobb,
Murder in Peyton Place, Crash, Stunt Seven,*
etc.

Connery, Sean (1930–). Before scooping
up riches and respect as James Bond in the
earlier and better Bond movies the rugged
Scottish actor carried off some superior roles
on BBC Television: *Requiem for a
Heavyweight* (1957); *Colombe* (1958);
Adventure Story (1961). His son Jason took
over the title-part in *Robin of Sherwood,*
1986.   PP

Connie
GB 1985 13 × 52m
Central (Nicholas Palmer)

Down to her last drachma, former fashion
tycoon returns from life in the Greek isles to
sleep and scheme her way back into the
family business.

A pretty barmy format to exploit (a) the
local industry of Central's new East
Midlands sub-franchise, (b) the Nottingham
studios it was required to build and (c) the
colourful charms of Stephanie Beacham.

w Ron Hutchinson *d* Alan Dossor, Michael
Rolfe, Paul Harrison

Stephanie Beacham, Brenda Bruce, Paul
Rogers

'Tries to do for Nottingham's rag trade what
Dallas does for Texas oil' – *Telegraph
Sunday Magazine*

Connolly, Billy (1942–). Hirsute Scottish
comedian whose vulgarity shows through his
impenetrable accent. Slowly gaining a kind of
respectability, he has been largely limited to
interview shows.

Connolly, Ray (1940–). British writer,
columnist and critic (London *Standard*)
originally associated with pop-music scene.
Television credits: *Honky-Tonk Heroes*
(series), *Forever Young* (TVM), *Lytton's
Diary*, 1985–6.   PP

Connor, Kevin (1939–). British director,
now mainly in TV. *Goliath Awaits, Master of
the Game, Mistral's Daughter*, etc.

Connors, Chuck (1924–) (Kevin
Connors). Lean, mean-looking action star,
former sportsman, who enjoyed a fairly
successful film career but did even better in
TV. Series: *Rifleman, Arrest and Trial,
Branded, Cowboy in Africa, The Thrill
Seekers*. TV movies include *The Birdmen,
Night of Terror, Set This Town on Fire,
Horror at 37,000 Feet, Banjo Hackett, Roots,
The Night They Took Miss Beautiful,
Standing Tall.*

Connors, Michael (1925–) (Kreker
Ohanian). Armenian–American leading man
who after a mild film career became a top TV
star in the action series *Tightrope*, MANNIX
and *Today's FBI*. TV movies: *Beg Borrow
or Steal, The Killer Who Wouldn't Die,
Revenge for a Rape, The Long Journey
Back, High Midnight, Casino, Nightkill,
Glitter*, etc.

Conrad, Michael (1925–83). American
character actor, the sergeant who took the
rollcall in *Hill Street Blues* (Emmy 1982).
Other TV: *Donovan's Kid, Edge of Night,
Delvecchio, Fire on the Mountain.*

Conrad, Robert (1935–) (Conrad Robert
Falk). American leading man. Series include
Hawaiian Eye, The DA, THE WILD WILD WEST,
Assignment Vienna and *Baa Baa Black
Sheep*. TV movies include *Weekend of
Terror, Five Desperate Women, The
Adventures of Nick Carter, The Last Day,
Smash-up on Interstate Five, Centennial, The
Wild Wild West Revisited, Breaking Up Is
Hard to Do, Will, A Man Called Sloane,
Coach of the Year, Confessions of a Married
Man, Hard Knox, Two Fathers' Justice,
Charley Hannah.*

Conrad, William (1920–). Portly
American character actor, the original Matt
Dillon on radio. Often a director for TV, but

CONNIE. Stephanie Beacham here seen in *Connie* before being allotted the Joan Collins lookalike role in *The Colbys*.

most famous as the long-running CANNON; less so as *Nero Wolfe*. TV movies include *The Brotherhood of the Bell*, *O'Hara US Treasury* (pilot), *Attack on Terror*, *Night Cries*, *Keefer*.

'Sometimes the truth can tear a family apart.'
Consenting Adult
US 1984 96m colour TVM
ABC/Martin Starger/David Lawrence/Ray Aghayan

A 20-year-old boy tells his mother he's homosexual, but dad can't be told because he's recovering from a stroke.
Predictable discussion drama, by no means as daring as it might once have been.

w John McGreevey, *novel* by Laura Z. Hobson *d* Gilbert Cates *ph* Frank Stanley *m* Laurence Rosenthal

Marlo Thomas, Martin Sheen, Barry Tubb, Talia Balsam, Ben Piazza

Consequence of Love
US 1984 96m colour TVM
CBS (Judith Parker)

A college girl falls for her professor's husband.
Peg's Paper romance, in no way remarkable.

w Judith Parker *d* Gus Trikonis

Melissa Sue Anderson, Loretta Swit

Conspiracy of Terror *
aka: *Enter Horowitz*
US 1975 74m colour TVM
Lorimar

A man-and-wife detective team encounter diabolism in the suburbs.
Curious mix of Jewish humour and macabre goings-on; a failed pilot.

w Howard Rodman *d* John Llewellyn Moxey *m* Neal Hefti

Michael Constantine, Barbara Rhoades, Mariclare Costello, Logan Ramsay

Conspiracy to Kill *
aka: *The DA: Conspiracy to Kill*
US 1970 97m colour TVM
Universal/Jack Webb
The DA of a small community tries a case
involving a local chemist who is also a fence.
One of two failed pilots for the same
non-series (see *The DA: Murder One*). Quite
watchable.

w Stanford Whitmore, Joel Oliansky *d* Paul
Krasny

Robert Conrad, William Conrad, Belinda
Montgomery, Don Stroud, Steve Ihnat

Constantine, Michael (1927–) (Con-
stantine Joanides). Familiar rumpled-
looking American character actor who
had a leading role in *Room 222*; also
appeared in *Hey Landlord*. Emmy 1969, best
supporting actor. TV movies include *The
Impatient Heart, Deadly Harvest, Suddenly
Single, The Bait, Big Rose, Death Cruise, The
Secret Night Caller, Conspiracy of Terror,
Twin Detectives, Wanted the Sundance
Woman, 79 Park Avenue, Summer of My
German Soldier, The Pirate, Crisis in
Mid-Air.*

The Consultant (GB 1983 4 × 50m).
Hywel Bennett as the specialist assassin in a
medium-rare thriller by John McNeil,
dramatized by Alan Plater. Also with
Donald Burton, Philip Jackson, Pamela
Salem. Directed by Cyril Coke, produced by
Ron Craddock, for BBC.   PP

Contact * (GB 1985 70m). British army
platoon on night patrol in Northern Ireland,
as depicted in a tense, almost wordless,
semi-improvised drama directed by Alan
Clarke. It opened the BBC's *Screen Two*
season of fiction films for TV but was
actually shot on hand-held video, often
through image intensifiers. Written by A. F.
N. Clarke, with Sean Chapman as the
platoon commander; produced by Terry
Coles.   PP
'So real it hurt . . . vividly captured the sense
of danger, the terror of feeling that any
second a bullet or a bomb can shatter life.' –
Daily Express

Conti, Tom (1941–). Leading British
character actor, usually in single plays apart
from *Adam Smith*, THE GLITTERING PRIZES and
THE NORMAN CONQUESTS. TV movies: *Blade
on the Feather, The Wall.*

Contract on Cherry Street
US 1977 148m colour TVM
NBC/Artanis/Columbia (Renee Valente)

A police lieutenant starts a private war on the
Mafia in revenge for the death of a pal.
Overlong, repetitive and ordinary cop saga,
Madigan-style, in which Sinatra saw fit to
make a comeback.

w Edward Anhalt *d* William A. Graham
ph Jack Priestley *m* Jerry Goldsmith

Frank Sinatra, Martin Balsam, Verna Bloom,
Harry Guardino, Henry Silva, Martin Gabel

'The cop show pattern emerges all too soon,
and even Sinatra can't stem the tedium.' –
Daily Variety

contrast. The relationship between the
lightest and darkest areas in a TV picture.

Contrast was the first and last serious
journal in Britain devoted wholly to
television; it lasted only five years, 1961–6.
Published by the British Film Institute,
edited first by Peter Black, then by David
Robinson.
† *Contrasts*, in the plural, is a local
documentary series in the Midlands of Great
Britain, often better viewing than that
offered by networked features. Producer:
Jim Berrow, for Central.   PP

convergence. Superimposition during
transmission of various colours of the picture
over each other. Bad convergence is almost
always a malfunction of the set.

Conversation Pieces * (GB 1983 5 × 5m).
Five-minute animations set to recordings of
real conversations, e.g. a young offender
negotiating with his probation officer, old
people re-living a foreign holiday, a
magazine being put together with amazing
unprofessionalism. An original idea which
made a funny little treat; from David
Sproxton and Peter Lord, for C4.   PP

Converse, Frank (1938–). Thoughtful
American leading man who has had a
sporadic TV career. Series: *Coronet Blue,
Movin' On*. TV movies: *A Tattered Web, Dr
Cook's Garden, Killer on Board, Cruise into
Terror, Sgt Matlovich vs the US Air Force,
Marilyn: The Untold Story, The Miracle of
Kathy Miller, Mystery at Fire Island*, etc.

Convoy
US 1965 13 × 50m bw
NBC/Universal
World War II adventures in the North
Atlantic.
Uninteresting war series with the chill wind of
failure about it.

John Gavin, John Larch, Linden Chiles

Convy, Bert (1934–). American leading man and singer, former baseball player. TV movies: *Death Takes a Holiday, The Girl on the Late Late Show, SST: Death Flight, Thou Shalt Not Commit Adultery, Dallas Cowboy Cheerleaders, The Man in the Santa Claus Suit, Ebony, Ivory and Jade, Hanging by a Thread, Help Wanted Male.*

Conway, Gary (1938–) (Gareth Carmody). Adequate American leading man who was briefly popular in the series *Burke's Law* and *Land of the Giants.*

Conway, Russ (1924–) (Trevor Stanford). British pianist popular during the fifties and sixties, especially in *The Billy Cotton Band Show.*

Conway, Shirl (1914–) (Shirley Crossman). American character actress, on the lighter side, who scored an unexpected hit in the series *The Nurses.*

Conway, Tim (1933–). American comic actor and writer. Rose to fame in *McHale's Navy*, briefly had a series of his own in 1970, joined Carol Burnett in 1975. Emmy 1976, best comedy support.

Coogan, Jackie (1914–84). American actor who made a great hit in 1921 as a child star and is still around in TV, where he scored his biggest hit as the grotesque Uncle Fester in *The Addams Family*. TV movies: *The Phantom of Hollywood, The Specialists, Sherlock Holmes in New York, Family Reunion*, etc. His reminiscences in Kevin Brownlow's *Hollywood* were pertinent and poignant.

Cook and Peary: The Race to the Pole *
US 1983 96m colour TVM
CBS/Wiener–Wilkie (Robert Halmi Jnr)
Dr Cook and Admiral Peary differ in their accounts of reaching the North Pole in the 1890s.
Stiff and not entirely reliable account of still mysterious doings in remote places.
w I. C. Rapoport *d* Robert Day *ph* Ernest Day *m* Charles Gross
Richard Chamberlain, Rod Steiger, Diana Venora, Michael Gross

Cook, Fielder (1923–). TV director of the fifties whose *Patterns* took him to Hollywood for the film version. Later career interesting but sporadic. TV movies: *Sam Hill, Goodbye Raggedy Ann, The Homecoming, Miracle on 34th Street, This Was the West That Was, Miles to Go Before I Sleep, Judge Horton and the Scottsboro Boys, Beauty and the Beast, Too Far to Go, I Know Why the Caged Bird Sings*, etc. Emmys 1966 (*Brigadoon*), 1970 (*The Price*).

Cook, Peter (1937–). British writer and performer of undergraduatish humour, moderately popular with Dudley Moore in a sporadic cabaret style sixties series called *Not Only But Also*. 1981 series: *The Two of Us.*

❋ **Cooke, Alistair** (1909–). Respected Anglo-American journalist and commentator who adds incisive wit to his urbane manner. Many TV appearances as host and commentator, mostly in America; his major project, however, was his 13-hour series *America*, which he wrote and narrated for BBC, winning an Emmy in 1972; also a special Emmy in 1974.

Cool Million
US 1971 97m colour TVM
Universal (David J. O'Connell)
A private eye whose fee per case is one million dollars locates a missing heiress.
Slick, glamorous and empty pilot for a shortlived (only four episodes) addition to *Mystery Movie.*
w Larry Cohen *d* Gene Levitt
James Farentino, Lila Kedrova, Patrick O'Neal, Christine Belford, Barbara Bouchet, John Vernon, Jackie Coogan

Coombs, Pat (1930–). British comedy actress who after years of playing timid souls in sketches found a secure place as foil to Peggy Mount in *You're Only Young Twice.*

Cooney, Joan Ganz (1930–). American executive and pioneer of Children's Television Workshop, which produces *Sesame Street.*

Cooper, Alice (1948–) (Vincent Damon Furnier). American rock singer with deliberately weird persona.

Cooper, Derek (1935–). British journalist and narrator. His voice helped set the tone of *World in Action* throughout its early years – businesslike, assertive, impersonal. As a food and eating-out reporter, the James Bond of the business, loping fearlessly through realms of pizza and black pudding. Series: *The Taste of Britain* (1975). Voice only, *The Living Body* (1984).   PP

Cooper, Giles (1918–66). British dramatist, arguably the most inventive to exploit the broadcast medium, first in radio, then TV. His plots were elegantly developed from one simple, striking idea, e.g. suburban neighbours who had secretly knocked down interior walls in their terrace of houses to make a communal residence (*The Long House*, 1965). He also worked as adaptor on the *Maigret* series and several serials, including the *Sword of Honour* trilogy from Evelyn Waugh. See *The Other Man*.   PP

Cooper, Jackie (1921–). American ex-child star who pursued a varied adult career as executive, producer and occasional actor. Features vividly in *Only You Dick Daring*. Series: *The People's Choice*, *Hennessy*. TV movies as actor include: *Shadow on the Land, Maybe I'll Come Home in the Spring, The Astronaut, The Day the Earth Moved, The Invisible Man, Mobile Two, Operation Petticoat*. Won an Emmy for his direction of an episode of *White Shadow*. Autobiography 1981: *Please Don't Hurt My Dog*.

Cooper, Joseph (1912–). Diffident British musical expert who chairs BBC2's occasional *Face the Music* series.

Cooper, Tommy (1921–84). Giant-size, fez-topped British comedian who made a speciality of getting magic tricks wrong. A star from the mid-fifties, almost always in a variety format.

Coote, Robert (1909–82). British character actor of the Dr Watson type, in international films. TV series: *The Rogues, Nero Wolfe*. TV movie: *Institute for Revenge*.

The Cop and the Kid
US 1975 6 × 25m colour
NBC/Paramount/Playboy (Jerry Davis)
A bachelor policeman fosters an unruly orphan and his dog.
Ho-hum sentimental comedy which didn't last.
cr Jerry Davis *m* Jerry Fielding
Charles Durning, Tierre Turner, Patsy Kelly

Copacabana
US 1985 96m colour TVM
CBS/Dick Clark/Stiletto (R. W. Goodwin)
A would-be singer gets a job tending bar at a swank night club.
Moderate spoof of forties musicals, helped by good numbers.

w James Lipton *d* Waris Hussein *ph* Bobby Byrne *m* Barry Manilow
Barry Manilow, Annette O'Toole, Estelle Getty, James T. Callahan, Ernie Sabella, Joseph Bologna
'A fond send-up, worth a smile or two of recognition.' – *Daily Variety*
'Sweet but not too sappy.' – *People* Magazine

Copperfield, David (1957–). Elegant young American magician who has had several specials featuring his elaborate tricks.

co-production. One financed and produced jointly by more than one company, usually in different countries. The danger of such enterprises is that the flavour of compromise may be the predominant one.

The Cops and Robin
US 1978 96m colour TVM
NBC/Paramount (Tony Wilson)
An ageing cop and his robot partner track down a mobster to Knotts Berry Farm.
Final attempt to create a new series about a robot cop, the idea having failed in *Holmes and Yoyo*. See also: *Future Cop*.
w John T. Dugan, Brad Radnitz, Dawning Forsyth *d* Allen Reisner *ph* Howard Schwartz
Ernest Borgnine, Michael Shannon, John Amos, Natasha Ryan, Carol Lynley
'Too much talk, too little action.' – *Daily Variety*

Corbett, Harry (1918–). Cheerful Yorkshire puppeteer, one of Britain's longest-running TV personalities. Created the famous glove puppet Sooty.

Corbett, Harry H. (1925–82). Burly British character actor whose finest hour was as the younger Steptoe in the innovative comedy series STEPTOE AND SON.

✵ **Corbett, Ronnie** (1930–). Diminutive Scottish comedian who has had several series of his own but is best known as one of THE TWO RONNIES, and with Ronnie Barker won a BAFTA award in 1971 as best light entertainment performer.

Corby, Ellen (1913–) (Ellen Hansen). American character actress who played Grandma in THE WALTONS, and won Emmys in 1974 and 1975 for so doing.

Cord, Alex (1935–) (Alexander Viespi). American leading man whose career has been spotty. TV movies: *The Scorpio Letters, Genesis II, Fire, Beggarman Thief, Hunter's Moon.*

Coren, Alan (1983–). British humorist (nevertheless Editor of *Punch*), frequent chat-show guest and contest-master of *Television Scrabble.* Also TV critic of *The Mail on Sunday* since 1984. TV series *The Losers*, 1978. Wrote a misguided *Omnibus* on the British Hero (in adventure fiction), 1973.   PP

Corey for the People
US 1977 74m colour TVM
Columbia/Jeni (Buzz Kulik, Jay Daniel)

A young assistant DA prosecutes a socialite for murder.
Competent standard courtroom stuff: no series resulted.

w Alvin Boretz   *d* Buzz Kulik

John Rubenstein, Eugene Roche, Carol Rossen, Ronny Cox, Joseph Campanella

Corey, Wendell (1914–68). Reliable American actor who usually played the other man or the deceived husband. TV series: *Harbor Command, Peck's Bad Girl, The Eleventh Hour.*

The Corn Is Green
US 1978 96m colour TVM
CBS/Warner (Neil Hartman)

In an 1890s Welsh village, a spinster schoolteacher prepares a young miner for an Oxford scholarship.
This TV version is at least superior to the 1946 film in substituting Welsh locations for very phoney sets, but the melodrama still gets in the way and only the star's performance maintains the interest.

w Ivan Davis, *play* Emlyn Williams *d* George Cukor *ph* Ted Scaife *m* John Barry

KATHARINE HEPBURN, Ian Saynor, Bill Fraser, Patricia Hayes, Anna Massey, Toyah Wilcox

The Corner Bar (US 1972). Half-hour tape comedy for ABC about the frequenters of a New York tavern. Hosts included Gabriel Dell and (later) Anne Meara and Eugene Roche. Produced by Alan King and Howard Morris.

Cornwell, Judy (1942–). Versatile British actress, in many plays. Series include *Moody and Pegg, The Good Companions.*

Coronado 9
US 1959 39 × 25m bw
Universal

A former Naval Intelligence officer operates as a private eye.
Routine mysteries agreeably set on the Coronado peninsula.

Rod Cameron

The Coronation (1953). Generally regarded as the broadcast which converted the British people to the idea of television. In the first half of 1952 326,000 bought or took out rentals on TV sets: in the same period of 1953, leading up to the Coronation the figure was 526,000. American viewers watched film or kinescopes flown across the Atlantic by RAF jet aircraft; reports of a chimpanzee called J. Fred Muggs who broke into proceedings there with commercial plugs caused some distress back home. Incidentally it was the second Coronation to be televised – the 1937 crowning of George VI was covered by the pre-war BBC service.
                                                                      PP

Coronation Street ***. Long-running British soap opera set in a terraced street in industrial Lancashire. Granada have made two half-hours a week since 1960, with the help of many producers and writers, though H. V. Kershaw has been the most consistent guiding light and the original format was devised by Tony Warren. Characters who became household names include Ena Sharples (Violet Carson), Elsie Tanner (Pat Phoenix), Minnie Caldwell (Margot Bryant), Albert Tatlock (Jack Howarth), Annie Walker (Doris Speed), Jack Walker (Arthur Leslie), Ken Barlow (William Roache) and Hilda and Stan Ogden (Jean Alexander and Bernard Youens). Arthur Lowe as Mr Swindley also gained his last step to stardom in the series.

'There is little reality in this new serial which apparently we will have to suffer twice a week. The programme is doomed from the outset, with its dreary signature-tune and grim scene of a row of terraced houses . . .' – Ken Irwin, *Daily Mirror*, 1960

Coronet Blue
US 1966 13 × 50m colour
CBS/Plautus/Herb Brodkin

An amnesiac seeks to uncover his past.
Promising series which was never allowed to get going, and ended before the mystery of its title could be revealed.

Frank Converse, Brian Bedford, Joe Silver

The Corsican Brothers
US 1985 96m colour TVM
CBS/Norman Rosemont (David A. Rosemont)

CORONATION STREET. Its twenty-five years plus are unlikely to be equalled by any other British soap opera: and William Roache (right) as Ken Barlow was there at the start and is still going strong. Julie Goodyear as Bet Lynch is another familiar figure; Richard Blain was a guest for plot requirements only.

Corsican twins try to end the family tradition of vendetta.

Drab TV presentation of an old standard: the confusions of the story are not counterpointed by any kind of narrative drive.

w Robin Miller, *novel* by Alexandre Dumas *père* *d* Ian Sharp *ph* Frank Watts *m* Allyn Ferguson

Trevor Eve, Geraldine Chaplin, Olivia Hussey, Nicholas Clay, Jean Marsh, Bendict Taylor, Simon Ward, Donald Pleasence, Margaret Tyzack, Jennie Linden

Cosa Nostra, Arch Enemy of the FBI

US 1966 97m colour TVM
Quinn Martin

A contract killer murders a grand jury witness.

Muddled cops and robbers, as cumbersome

as its title, put together from two episodes of *The FBI*.

w Norman Jolley *d* Don Medford

Efrem Zimbalist Jnr, Walter Pidgeon, Celeste Holm, Philip Abbott, Telly Savalas, Susan Strasberg

Cosby, Bill (1938–). Black American actor and comedian who made a major breakthrough in *I Spy* as the first black to get equal star billing in a series. (He won Emmys for it in 1965, 1966, 1967, and in 1968 another for a musical special.) Subsequently most effective as guest artist, though he has been involved in a couple of series, *Cos* and *Fat Albert and the Cosby Kids*, with special appeal to children. TV movies: *To All My Friends on Shore*, *Top Secret*.

The Cosby Show (US 1984). This half-hour sitcom, with the star as a lawyer adept at one-liners, confounded all predictions by becoming the great hit of its season, often getting more than a 50 per cent share of audience. Sample line: 'No boy should have a 95 dollar shirt unless he's on a stage with his four brothers.' Produced by Marcy Carsey, for NBC.

Cosell, Howard (1920–). American sports commentator and talk show host.

cost per thousand (homes or viewers): a means of comparing the relative sales efficiency of different programmes by determining how many people saw them, and dividing this into the cost.

Costello, Lou (1906–59) (Louis Cristillo). American comedian, the chubby half of Abbott and Costello (see *Abbott, Bud*).

Costigan, James (19 –). American writer of distinction. TV movies include *Little Moon of Alban* (Emmy 1959), *War of Children, Last of the Belles, In This House of Brede*, LOVE AMONG THE RUINS (Emmy 1975), *F. Scott Fitzgerald in Hollywood*, ELEANOR AND FRANKLIN (Emmy 1976).

A Cotswold Death * (GB 1983). Topical up-dating of the English country-house murder whodunit, with the victim a typical lord of the manor – these days an Arab sheik. Ian Richardson as a much-put-upon detective-inspector cracked it eventually to settle quite a droll, dry film written and directed by Tony Bicat. Also with Brian Cox, Robert Flemying, Edward Hardwicke, Daphne Heard and Timothy Spall. Produced by Michael Wearing, for BBC.   PP

Cotten, Joseph (1905–). American leading actor of stage and screen who in his older age guested in mainly unrewarding roles in TV movies: *Split Second to an Epitaph, The Lonely Profession, Cutter's Trail, Assault on the Wayne, Do You Take This Stranger, City Beneath the Sea, The Screaming Woman, The Devil's Daughter, The Lindbergh Kidnapping Case, Aspen, Return to Fantasy Island, Churchill and the Generals, Casino*. Also narrated series, *Hollywood and the Stars*.

Cotton, Bill (1928–). BBC light entertainment specialist (1962–77), son of Billy Cotton, below, who became controller of BBC1 1977–81 and, after a spell out of the swim in charge of future DBS plans, bounced back in 1983 to displace Aubrey Singer as managing director of BBC TV.   PP

✳ Cotton, Billy (1899–1969). Cheerful British bandleader who would have a go at anything and hosted a long-running BBC variety show with the emphasis on comedy. His son, Bill Cotton Jnr, subsequently became managing director of BBC1.

Cotton Candy
US 1978 96m colour TVM
NBC/Major H Productions (Ron Howard)

A high-school failure forms a rock band and makes good.
Time-passer for teenagers.

w Ron Howard, Clint Howard   *d* Ron Howard   *Ph* Robert Jessup   *m* Joe Renzetti

Charles Martin Smith, Clint Howard, Leslie King, Kevin Lee Miller

Count Dracula
GB 1977 145m colour (VTR)
WNET/BBC (Morris Barry)

An elongated and sex-ridden version of the classic vampire yarn, with too much unpleasant horror to sustain the romantic gothic mood which it obviously seeks, and too little room for its star to manoeuvre.

w Gerald Savory   *novel* Bram Stoker   *d* Philip Saville   *m* Kenyon Emrys-Roberts

Louis Jourdan, Frank Finlay, Susan Penhaligon, Mark Burns, Jack Shepherd, Judi Bowker

The Count of Monte Cristo
GB 1955 39 × 25m bw
ATV

Adventure series vaguely based on the Alexandre Dumas classic.

George Dolenz, Nick Cravat, Fortunio Bonanova

The Count of Monte Cristo
GB 1975 96m colour
ITC/Norman Rosemont

A man unjustly imprisoned escapes and revenges himself on his enemies.
Competent rather than inspired; one longs for the Robert Donat version.

w Sidney Carroll   *d* David Greene

Richard Chamberlain, Tony Curtis, Trevor Howard, Louis Jourdan, Donald Pleasence, Kate Nelligan, Dominic Guard

Countdown (GB since 1982). Afternoon word game which happened to be the first programme to go out on C4 and has continued seasonally ever since. Viewers are encouraged to join in at home, for fun rather than prizes. Produced by YTV (John Mead).   PP

THE COSBY SHOW. For no very good reason, this amiable show about a New York doctor and his family was the instant hit of the 1984–5 American season.

Countdown to Looking Glass *
US 1984 78m colour TVM
HBO/L & B/Primedia (W. Paterson Ferns)

A nuclear crisis is triggered when bank failures and the fall of a middle-eastern country coincide with confrontations on the Persian Gulf.

Disaster melodrama played as for real; one of the better ones, but as they proliferate so they lose most of their point.

w Albert Rubin d Fred Barzyk ph Miklos Lente

Scott Glenn, Michael Murphy, Heleb Shaver, Patrick Watson, with Eric Sevareid, Nancy Dickerson, Sen, Eugene McCarthy

'The question is, do we really need another speculative nuclear holocaust drama? Those involved no doubt have their intentions in the right place. But the trend of turning the unthinkable into the thinkable via ''speculative'' thinking is somewhat discomforting.' – *Hollywood Reporter*

counter programming: Playing on one channel a programme appealing to an audience differently constituted from the one watching the other.

The Counterfeit Killer
aka: *The Faceless Man*
US 1968 95m colour TVM
Universal

A cop with a criminal background goes undercover to solve the mystery of corpses being washed ashore.

Underdeveloped and rather boring mystery pilot.

w Harold Clements, Stephen Bocho d Josef Leytes

Jack Lord, Shirley Knight, Charles Drake, Jack Weston, Mercedes McCambridge, Joseph Wiseman

Counterspy
US 1958 39 × 25m bw
Screen Gems

Adventures of a governmental counter-intelligence agent.

Routine syndicated series which later spawned a couple of feature films, *David Harding Counterspy* and *Counterspy Meets Scotland Yard.*

Don Megowan

Country Cousins: see Green Acres

The Country Diary of an Edwardian Lady
GB 1984 12 × 28m
Central (Patrick Gambell)

Pretty-pretty adaptation from Edith Holden's posthumous best-seller and her subsequent life-story, ending with her death by drowning in the river at Kew. 'Did she fall,' I wondered, 'or could she no longer endure the classical muzak which poured from the sky whenever she contemplated nature?'

w Elaine Feinstein, Dirk Campbell *d* Dirk Campbell

Pippa Guard as Edith   PP

The Country Girls (GB 1983). Edna O'Brien's novel of two Irish girls discovering sex and love, in that order, with screenplay by the author, Sam Neill as a star name and Maeve Germaine and Jill Doyle as the girls. 'Here are the twin polarities of youth, innocence and wickedness perfectly incarnated in two remarkable young actresses,' said Peter Davalle in *The Times.* Directed by Desmond Davis, produced by London Film Productions (Aida Young), for C4.   PP

Country Gold
US 1984 96m colour TVM
CBS (Ann Weston, Marcy Gross)

A top girl country singer married to her manager finds herself at odds with a new young rival.

All about Eve set to country music, but without any of the wit.

w Priscilla English *d* Gilbert Cates *ph* Gerald Hirschfield *m* Billy Goldenberg

Loni Anderson, Earl Holliman, Linda Hamilton, Cooper Huckabee, Dennis Dugan

The Country Husband *
US 1957 74m bw TVM
Columbia/Playhouse 90

A middle-aged executive wonders whether to leave his wife and family for a young girl.
Routine domestic drama, quite well acted.

w Paul Monash, *story* John Cheever *d* James Neilson

Frank Lovejoy, Barbara Hale, Felicia Farr, Kerwin Mathews

**Country Matters ** **
GB 1972 13 × 50m colour (16mm)
Granada (Derek Granger)

An anthology of superior dramas linked only by their setting in the English countryside; drawn from the stories of H. E. Bates and A. E. Coppard. BAFTA 1972, best drama series.

'Consistently superb.' – *The Times*

A Country Practice (Australia since 1983). Soppy but irresistible soaper centred on small-town doctors' partnership, with Lorrae Desmond as the matronly receptionist and all human life coming in sooner or later for consultation. With Shane Porteous and Grant Dodwell on the stethoscopes, Brian Wenzel as the local cop, Penny Cook as his stepdaughter the vet, and Anne Tenney as a perpetually dizzy townie housewife.   PP

The Couple Takes a Wife
US 1972 73m colour TVM
Universal (George Eckstein)

An au pair girl becomes rather too well entrenched.
Simple domestic comedy.

w Susan Silver *d* Jerry Paris

Bill Bixby, Paula Prentiss, Myrna Loy, Nanette Fabray, Valerie Perrine, Robert Goulet, Larry Storch

The Courage and the Passion
US 1978 96m colour TVM
Columbia/David Gerber

The private lives of officers at an air force base.
Unsuccessful pilot for a soap opera series which didn't happen. Good flying sequences are submerged by half-a-dozen trivial sex plots.

w Richard Fielder *d* John Moxey *ph* John M. Nickolaus *m* Richard Shores

Vince Edwards, Desi Arnaz Jnr, Trisha Noble, Linda Foster, Robert Hooks, Paul Shenar, Monty Hall, Don Meredith, Robert Ginty

† Previously known as *Joshua Tree*; aka *The Power and the Passion.*

Courageous Cat. A five-minute cartoon series spoofing Batman, syndicated in the US in 1961, with music by Johnny Holiday.

Course for Collision: see Collision Course

Court Martial *
GB 1966 26 × 50m bw
ITC/Roncom (Robert Douglas, Bill Hill)
Cases of two officer–lawyers in the US Army during World War II.
Brisk, efficient and slightly unusual series made by Lew Grade for the ABC network.
Peter Graves, Bradford Dillman

The Court Martial of George Armstrong Custer
US 1977 93m colour TVM
Norman Rosemont
An imaginary reconstruction of the trial which would have happened had Custer survived the battle of Little Big Horn.
Rather flat considering the possibilities.
w John Gay, *book* Douglas C. Jones *d* Glen Jordan *m* Jack Elliott
James Olson, Brian Keith, Ken Howard, Blythe Danner, J. D. Cannon, William Daniels, Stephen Elliott, Biff McGuire

The Court of Last Resort
US 1957 26 × 25m bw
NBC/Paisano
A seven-man court of do-gooders aims to free prisoners wrongfully convicted.
Modest mystery series, based on a real organization founded by Erle Stanley Gardner.
Lyle Bettger, Paul Birch (as Gardner)

Courtenay, Tom (1937–).Undernourished-looking British actor who was in one TV movie, *I Heard the Owl Call My Name.*

The Courtship of Eddie's Father
US 1969–71 78 × 25m colour
ABC/MGM (James Komack)
A small precocious boy tries to get his widowed father remarried.
Popular but rather trying sentimental comedy.
m Harry Nilsson
Bill Bixby, Brandon Cruz, Miyoshi Umeki, James Komack

Cousteau, Jacques (1910–). French undersea explorer who from the mid-sixties appeared in a long-running documentary series for Metromedia. Emmys 1960, 1961; appeared 1978 in *The Cousteau Odyssey.*

Covenant
US 1985 74m colour TVM
TCF/Michael Filerman
A supernaturally evil family uses its powers in modern San Francisco.

Apparently aiming to go one better than *Dynasty*, this busted pilot astonishes by its ineptitude.
w J. D. Feigelson, Dan DiStefano *d* Walter Grauman *ph* James Crabe *m* Charles Bernstein
Jane Badler, Jose Ferrer, Kevin Conroy, Charles Frank, Whitney Kershaw, Barry Morse, Bradford Dillman
'It sails smartly along till it sinks of its own silliness.' – *Daily Variety*

Cover (GB 1981). Six-hour spy story for highbrows, with Alan Howard of the Royal Shakespeare Company making a debut as the cold spymaster. Of rather limited appeal. Written by Philip Mackie; directed by Alan Cooke; produced by Jacqueline Davis/John Frankau; for Thames. Sample episode title: *Pussy Passed By and She Peeped In.*

Cover Girls
US 1977 74m colour TVM
Columbia/David Gerber/NBC
Two glamorous fashion models are espionage agents.
Desperate flim-flam in the wake of *Charlie's Angels.*
w Mark Rodgers *d* Jerry London
Cornelia Sharpe, Jayne Kennedy, Vince Edwards, Don Galloway, George Lazenby

'Unofficial ... unstoppable ... undercover ... going wherever Americans are in trouble!'
Cover Up
US 1984 1 × 96m, 22 × 50m colour
CBS/TCF/Glen Larson (Harker Wade)
A fashion photographer and her male model are really spies when they go abroad on assignments.
Doleful rehash of old ingredients.
cr Glen Larson
Jennifer O'Neill, Jon-Erik Hexum (who after a few episodes died in a tragic accident and was replaced by Anthony Hamilton), Richard Anderson
† Sample line: 'Feel him out: I find him strangely suspicious.'
Or: 'Your eyes are undressing me.'
'Do you mind? There is an easier way.'
'The pair is constantly spouting preposterous dialogue, some of which is muffed, and is exposed to situations so dubious that the show becomes a parody of the actioner venue.' – *Daily Variety*

Covert Action
US 1979 91m colour TVM
CBS/G. B. Milesi

A former CIA agent in Athens is threatened when he begins to write his memoirs.
Like a serious *Hopscotch*, this pacy little thriller was filmed in Italy for theatrical release, but didn't achieve it.

w John Crowther, Vittorio Schiraldi *d* Romolo Guerrieri

David Janssen, Corinne Clery, Arthur Kennedy, Philippe Leroy

Coward of the County *
US 1982 96m colour TVM
CBS/Kraco (Ken Kragen, John Marias)

At the start of World War II, an easy-going Southern preacher defends a local conscientious objector.
Solid family entertainment with a good sense of time and place.

w Clyde Ware, Jim Byrnes, *song* by Roger Bowling and Billy Ed Wheeler *d* DICK LOWRY *ph* Steven Poster *m* Larry Cansler

KENNY ROGERS, FREDRIC LEHNE, Largo Woodruff, Mariclare Costello

'He's one man against an entire town!'
Cowboy *
US 1983 96m colour TVM
CBS/MGM–UA/Bercovici/St Johns
  (Richard R. St Johns)

An ex-schoolteacher escapes from the city and returns to the cattle-raising country where he was born.
Curiously old-fashioned but quite pleasing piece of nostalgia.

w Stanely and Carole Cherry, Dennis Capps *d* Jerry Jameson *ph* Robert Jessup *m* Bruce Broughton

James Brolin, Annie Potts, Randy Quaid, George DiCenzo, Michael Pataki, Ted Danson, Robert Keith

The Cowboy and the Ballerina
US 1984 96m colour TVM
CBS/Cowboy Productions (Jerry
  Weintraub, Lee Majors, Neil T. Maffeo)

An American rodeo star falls for a defecting Russian ballerina.
The title says it all: nobody bothered to invent a plot, and the pace is stultifyingly slow.

w Denne Bart Petitclerc *d* Jerry Jameson *ph* Ben Coleman *m* Bruce Broughton

Lee Majors, Leslie Wing, Christopher Lloyd, James Booth, John McIntire, Antoinette Bower, Angelica Huston

Cowboy in Africa
US 1967 26 .× 50m colour
ABC/Ivan Tors

A rodeo star is hired to capture and domesticate African wild animals.
Moderately pleasing variation on *Daktari*, from the pilot film *Africa Texas Style*.

Chuck Connors, Tom Nardini, Ronald Howard

The Cowboys
US 1974 13 × 25m colour
ABC/Warner

Seven boys help a widow run her ranch.
Disappointing extension of a popular western film.

Moses Gunn, Diana Douglas, Jim Davis

Cowboys * (GB 1980–1). Disgracefully funny situation comedy from Thames about rackety small building firm mismanaged by Roy Kinnear and employing Colin Welland and Dermot Kelly. Written by Peter Learmouth.   PP

Cowell, Adrian (1934–). British explorer and film-maker who burst on to the scene with a sequence of anthropological thrillers about remote peoples in remote places. The one best remembered is *The Tribe That Hides from Man* (ATV 1970) in which the quarry, the last aboriginal, uncontaminated Indian tribe in Brazil, duly eluded Cowell's camera; the evidences of their existence, in a hastily abandoned encampment, were strangely more effective than if they had actually been observed. But Cowell had been in South America before, for *The Destruction of the Indian* trilogy in the early sixties (BBC). His other happy hunting ground was the opium-growing bandit country of South-East Asia which gave him *The Opium Trail* (1966) and further programmes. Has continued ever since, but with decreasing frequency as inflation assails budgets that were impressive even without the employment of pricey cameramen such as Chris Menges and Louis Wolfers. *Decade of Destruction* (1984) was a five-part recapitulation of all he laments about the rape of the world's natural resources.   PP

Cowgill, Brian (1927–). British executive, rising in BBC hierarchy by way of outside broadcasts and sports programming to be Controller of BBC1 and briefly director of news and current affairs before going to Thames Television as managing director in 1977. Left in 1985 after bizarre dispute with fellow ITV hardheads over his hi-jacking of *Dallas* from the BBC. Joined publisher Robert Maxwell to head his cable and satellite interests.   PP

Cox, Barry (1942–). British current affairs producer and executive, lately controller of features and current affairs for LWT.   PP

Cox, Brian (1946–). British character actor, notable on TV as Henry II in *The Devil's Crown*.

Cox, Constance (19 –). British writer specializing in classical serial adaptations, responsible for many of the BBC's famous runners in the fifties, e.g. *Angel Pavement*, 1958; *Bleak House*, 1959.   PP

Cox, Sir Geoffrey (1910–). New Zealand-born journalist and (briefly) diplomat who took over the editorship of ITN in 1956 and turned it into the most successful television news operation in Europe, if not the world. Retired in 1969 but remained in TV as deputy chairman of YTV, then chairman of Tyne-Tees. Published valuable account of his days at ITN as *See It Happen*, The Bodley Head, 1983.   PP

Cox, Ronny (1938–). American general purpose actor who starred in the series *Apple's Way*. TV movies: *The Connection*, *A Case of Rape*, *Who Is the Black Dahlia?*, *Having Babies*, *Corey for the People*, *The Girl Called Hatter Fox*, *Lovey*, *Transplant*, *Alcatraz*, *The Last Song*.

Cox, Wally (1924–76). Bespectacled American comedy actor who made a hit as *Mr Peepers* and *Hiram Holliday* in the fifties. TV movies include *Quarantined*, *The Young Country*, *The Magic Carpet*, *The Night Strangler*.

CPO Sharkey
US 1977 ?34 × 25m colour
NBC/R and R (Aaron Ruben, Gene
   Marcione)
A petty officer commands a training unit at the San Diego Naval Station.
Another service comedy which didn't travel.
cr Aaron Ruben *d* Peter Baldwin
Don Rickles, Elizabeth Allen, Harrison Page

A Crack in the Ice * (GB 1964, 1985). Ronald Eyre's adaptation of a story by the Russian author Nikolai Leskov was the very first BBC *Wednesday Play* in 1964, with Bill Fraser in the cast, Eyre himself directing, produced by Peter Luke. Nobody remembered this when it was done again 21 years later, directed by Anthony Garner, produced by Rosemary Hill, for BBC *Summer Season*.   PP

The Cracker Factory
US 1980 96m colour TVM
ABC/EMI/Roger Gimbel (Richard Shapiro)
A frustrated housewife takes to drink and is rehabilitated in an asylum.
Fairly punishing snake pit saga sparked by an excellent star performance.
w Richard Shapiro *novel* Joyce Rebeta-Burditt *d* Burt Brinckerhoff *ph* Michael Hugo *m* Billy Goldenberg
NATALIE WOOD, Peter Haskell, Perry King, Juliet Mills, Vivian Blaine, Shelley Long

The Cradle Will Fall
US 1983 96m colour TVM
CBS/Cates Films Inc/Proctor and Gamble
   (Joseph Cates)
A lady DA happens to spot a mad gynaecologist disposing of one of his victims, and he goes after her.
Muddled suspenser made even odder by casting of daytime soap actors in subsidiary roles.
w Jerome Coopersmith, *novel* by Mary Higgins Clark *d* John Llewellyn Moxey *ph* Steve Poster *m* Elliott Lawrence
Lauren Hutton, Ben Murphy, James Farentino, Charita Bauer, Carolyn Ann Clark, Peter Simon

Craig, Bill (1930–). Scottish writer of long experience. Credits include the *Cloud Howe* trilogy and contributions to *Bergerac*, *The Irish RM* and *The Adventures of Sherlock Holmes*.

Craig Kennedy, Criminologist
US 1952 26 × 25m bw
Adrian Weiss
Adventures of a scientific detective.
Sherlock Holmes need have no fear.
Donald Woods

Craig, Michael (1929–). British leading man of fifties films who matured slowly into a strong character actor. British series include *The Second Time Around*, *Triangle*; in Australia he was in *The Timeless Land*.

Craig, Wendy (1934–). British comedy actress, popular in domestic comedy series including *Not in Front of the Children* (BAFTA 1968), *And Mother Makes Three*, *Butterflies*, *Nanny*, etc.

Crane. British one-hour series of the early sixties, with Patrick Allen as an adventurer abroad.

Crane, Bob (1929–78). Wry-faced American leading man, former drummer and radio comic. Most popular in *Hogan's Heroes*.

Crash *
US 1978 96m colour TVM
ABC/Charles Fries (Edward J. Montagne)

An investigation into the causes and results of the crash of flight 401 in Miami in 1972. Coldly clinical and quite awe-inspiring treatment of an incident treated a different way in *The Ghost of Flight 401*. Top-flight production makes it the more impressive.

w Donald S. Sanford, Steve Brown, *book* Rob and Sarah Elder *d* Barry Shear *ph* Jacques Marquette *m* Eddy Lawrence Manson *sp* Art Brewer

Eddie Albert, William Shatner, Adrienne Barbeau, Brooke Bundy, Christopher Connelly, Lorraine Gary, Sharon Gless, George Maharis, Ed Nelson, Artie Shaw

'It's a cinch not to make it as an inflight motion picture.' – *Daily Variety*

Craven, Gemma (1950–　). Popular British leading lady and light singer. Series include *Song by Song*, *Pennies from Heaven*.

Crawford, Broderick (1910–　). Burly American character actor, son of Helen Broderick. His lengthy film career included an Academy Award for *All the King's Men*. TV series include *Highway Patrol*, *King of Diamonds*, *The Interns*. TV movies include *The Challenge*, *A Tattered Web*, *The Adventures of Nick Carter*, *The Phantom of Hollywood*, *Mayday at 40,000 Feet*.

Crawford, Henry (1947–　). Australian producer. *A Town Like Alice*, *Five Mile Creek*, *Eureka Stockade*, etc.

❋ **Crawford, Michael** (1942–　) (Michael Dumble Smith). British light leading man and comedian, former child actor. After being accepted in a variety of roles he shot to fame as the accident-prone hero of SOME MOTHERS DO 'AVE 'EM, an extreme characterization which may have prevented his finding another vehicle apart from the unsuccessful *Chalk and Cheese*.

crawl. The roll-up credits which end most TV shows.

Crawlspace *
US 1971 74m colour TVM
Viacom/Titus

A lonely middle-aged couple take in a dangerous young man who comes to repair their furnace.
Unusual suspenser which keeps the interest.

w Ernest Kinoy, *novel* Jerbert Lieberman *d* John Newland

Teresa Wright, Arthur Kennedy, Tom Harper, Gene Roche

Crazy like a Fox *
US 1984　× 50m colour
CBS/Columbia/Schenck–Cardea/
　Brontosaurus/
　Wooly Mammoth (Roger Shulman,
　John Baskin)

A sloppy old private eye involves his smart lawyer son in various dangerous scrapes.
Smooth series of light detection yarns, with touches of wit and originality.

cr Roger Shulman, John Baskin, George Schenck, Frank Cardea

Jack Warden, John Rubinstein, Penney Peyser, Robby Kiger, Ed Lauter

Crazy Times
US 1981 96m colour TVM
Warner/Kayden/Gleason/George Reeves

Two groups of tough New York teenagers meet to make war.
Regrettable television extension of a debased movie fashion for plumbing the urban depths.

w George Reeves *d* Lee Phillips

Ray Liotta, David Caruso, Michael Pare, Talia Balsam

Cream in My Coffee *
GB 1980 95m colour
LWT/Pennies from Heaven (Kenith Trodd)

An elderly couple at a seaside hotel are overwhelmed by memories of the past.
A rather sourly nostalgic drama sparked by good performances. The Grand Hotel, Eastbourne, was taken over for the production, and the astronomical cost caused a hiccup in LWT's plans to commission prestige drama.

w Dennis Potter *d* Gavin Millar *ph* Ernest Vincze

PEGGY ASHCROFT, LIONEL JEFFRIES, Faith Brook, Martin Shaw, Shelagh McLeod, Peter Chelsom

PP: 'His most mature treatment to date of ordinary human experience, specifically the haphazard but extraordinarily durable relationship of marriage and the ire of growing old.'

Credo. London Weekend's long-running, sometimes controversial religious programme was for many years an institution, networked to nearly every ITV region at 6 p.m. on Sunday. In the late seventies and early eighties it alternated with ATV's *Jay Walking*, then was relegated to an afternoon slot and finally transferred to C4, leaving the spiritual welfare of ITV viewers in the care of Sir Harry Secombe and the folksy *Highway*.   PP

Creggan (GB 1981; 50m). Striking Thames documentary about the terrorist stronghold inside a Catholic estate in Londonderry. Director: Michael Whyte.

Crenna, Richard (1926–). Busy American leading man whose film career was desultory but who was popular enough on TV to star in several series: *Our Miss Brooks*, *The Real McCoys*, *Slattery's People*, *All's Fair*. TV movies include *Thief*, *Footsteps*, *Double Indemnity*, *Nightmare*, *Shootout in a One Dog Town*, *Honky Tonk*, *A Girl Named Sooner*, *The War Between the Tates*, *Centennial*, *Devil Dog*, *First You Cry*, *A Fire in the Sky*, *Fugitive Family*, *The Day the Bubble Burst*, *It Takes Two*, *Passions*, *London and Davis in New York*, *The Rape of Richard Beck*.

The Crezz *
GB 1977 12 × 50m colour (VTR)
Thames (Paul Knight)

An interesting but unsuccessful attempt at a light-hearted *Peyton Place* set in a genteel London suburb. Marks for trying rather than achievement.

w Clive Exton

Joss Ackland, Hugh Burden, Peter Bowles, Elspet Gray

Cribb (GB 1979–81). Exploits of a detective-sergeant in Victorian London derived by Peter Lovesey from his successful crime novels featuring the same character. The pilot, *Waxwork* (1979), invoking Madame Tussaud's and a little risqué photography, indicated straightaway Lovesey's zeal in researching the by-ways of 19th-century leisure (prize-fighting, walking marathons, etc) to yield his plots. See *Sergeant Cork*. Alan Dobie plays Cribb with surface modesty and much confidence below. Produced by June Wyndham-Davies; for Granada; 14 × 50m.

LH: 'Doses of whimsy and sometimes incoherent story-telling make interest variable; the treatment somehow is insufficiently full-blooded, and Alan Dobie seems a reticent star.'

Crime Club *
US 1972 74m colour TVM
CBS/Glicksman–Larson

A private detective investigates the fatal car crash of an old friend.
Entertaining mystery pilot which never got anywhere.

d David Lowell Rich

Lloyd Bridges, Barbara Rush, Victor Buono, Paul Burke

Crime Club
aka: *The Last Key*
US 1975 74m colour TVM
Universal (Matthew Rapf)

A Washington DC club comprises specialists who band together to combat crime.
Another failed attempt to promote this famous title into a series.

w Gene R. Kearney *d* Jeannot Szwarc

Robert Lansing, Scott Thomas, Eugene Roche, Barbara Rhoades, Biff McGuire

Crime Inc. * (GB 1984; 7 × 52m). Enterprising documentary investigation into the Mafia and its allies throughout the US, but made by the all-British Thames Television.

Crime of Innocence
US 1985 96m colour TVM
NBC/Ohlmeyer (Paul Radin)

An ill-disposed judge is responsible for teenagers being corrupted in prison.
Well-intentioned but rather muddy melodrama which sees its problem from too many angles.

w Michael Berk, Douglas Schwartz *d* Michael Miller *ph* Kees van Oostrum

Andy Griffith, Ralph Waite, Diane Ladd, Shawnee Smith, Tammy Lauren

'The potential remains locked away because of Hollywood heavy-handedness.' – *Daily Variety*

Crime Photographer (US 1951). Shortlived half-hour live crime series for CBS, with Richard Carlyle (later Darren McGavin) as a news photographer.

Crime Sheet. A half-hour British series of the early fifties introducing Raymond Francis as Lockhart of Scotland Yard. After a period under the title *Murder Bag*, the show became the long-running one-hour *No Hiding Place*.

Crimewatch (GB since 1984). Intermittent BBC vigilante series modelled on a West German idea, in which the circumstances of unsolved crimes are re-enacted in an attempt to jog memories and prompt information from the public. Initial misgivings about the opportunities likewise offered to start a witch-hunt or settle old scores seem not to have materialized, and there have been some successes. Introduced by Sue Cook and Nick Ross.   PP

Crisis. International title for the *Bob Hope Chrysler Theatre*, an anthology of 114 50m film dramas made between 1963 and 1966 by Universal. Also used in the fifties for syndicated versions of *Kraft Mystery Theatre*.

Crisis at Central High
US 1981 120m colour TVM
CBS/Time–Life/Levinson–Link

In 1957, the principal of a girls' school in Little Rock is determined to achieve peaceful integration.
Well-meaning, well-acted, historically interesting telemovie which like most of its kind is made yawnworthy by excessive length.
w Richard Levinson, William Link, *memoir* Elizabeth Huckaby *d* Lamont Johnson *ph* Donald M. Morgan *m* Billy Goldenberg
JOANNE WOODWARD, Charles Durning, Henderson Forsyth, William Russ, Calvin Levels

Crisis at Sun Valley
US 1978 96m colour TVM
Columbia/Barry Weitz

A skier becomes a sheriff in Sun Valley.
Casual coupling of two unsold pilots for a series variously touted as *Stedman* and *Deadly Triangle*. Barely watchable.
w Carl Gottlieb, Alvin Boretz *d* Paul Stanley *ph* Al Francis *m* Dick de Benedictis
Dale Robinette, Bo Hopkins, Tracy Brooks Swope, Paul Brinegar, Taylor Lacher, John McIntire, Ken Swofford

Crisis in Mid-Air
US 1980 96m colour TVM
CBS Entertainment (Roger Lewis)

An air traffic controller has a busy night.
Efficient routine melodrama on the lines of *Airport*.
w Sean Baine *d* Walter Grauman *ph* John Nickolaus *m* Bob Drasnin
George Peppard, Karen Grassle, Desi Arnaz Jnr, Michael Constantine, Greg Morris, Fabian Forte, Dana Elcar, Alan Fudge, Don Murray

Criss Cross Quiz. British title of *Tic Tac Dough*, a popular long-running quiz of the fifties in which correct and incorrect answers scored noughts or crosses on an electronic game board. Chief host: Jeremy Hawk.

The Critical List *
US 1978 2 × 96m colour TVM
NBC/MTM (Jerry McNeely)

Loosely connected mini-series about a doctor who fights a local battle for his staff and a national battle against government officials involved in a federal health fund fraud. Very slickly made.
w Jerry McNeely, *novel* Marshall Goldberg *d* LOU ANTONIO *ph* Charles Correll *m* James Di Pasquale
LLOYD BRIDGES, Robert Wagner, Buddy Ebsen, Lou Gossett Jnr, Barbara Parkins, Richard Basehart, Pat Harrington, Melinda Dillon, Ken Howard
'The four hours pass by without leaving much trace.' – *Daily Variety*

Croft, David (19 –). Consistent British comedy writer and producer, the writing usually in partnership. *Dad's Army*, *It Ain't Half Hot Mum* and *Hi-de-Hi!* with Jimmy Perry. *'Allo, 'Allo* (1984) with Jonathan Lynn.   PP

❋ **Cronkite, Walter** (1916–). American star newsman and commentator, with CBS from 1962. Many awards include a 1978 Emmy (Governors' Award).

The Crooked Hearts
US 1972 74m colour TVM
Lorimar

A policewoman goes undercover to catch a suave murderer who preys on wealthy members of a lonelyhearts club.
Rather unattractive comedy-drama, interesting for its stars.
w A. J. Russell *d* Jay Sandrich *m* Billy Goldenberg
Douglas Fairbanks Jnr, Rosalind Russell, Maureen O'Sullivan, Ross Martin

Crosbie, Annette (1934–). British character actress, popular in a few films but mainly notable on TV: *The Six Wives of Henry VIII* (as Catherine of Aragon: BAFTA award 1970), *Katherine Mansfield*, *Edward the Seventh* (as Queen Victoria: BAFTA award 1975), *The Disappearance of Harry* (1982).

❋ **Crosby, Bing** (1901–77). American crooner and light actor. One of the most memorable entertainers of his time, Bing made many guest appearances on TV and for many years up to his death provided a Christmas special. His only film series, a domestic comedy called *The Bing Crosby Show*, was not a great success when it aired in 1964. Later, he was the first choice for *Columbo*, but turned it down. TV movie: *Dr Cook's Garden*.

Crosby, Cathy Lee (1948–). American leading lady who hosted *That's Incredible*. TV movies: *Wonder Woman*, *Keefer*, *Roughnecks*.

Crosby, Nat (1930–). Outstanding British film cameraman who finally tried his hand as a director with *Amy* (1983). But the camera keeps him busy. Credits include *Blue Remembered Hills* (1979), *Going Gently* (1981), *Ballroom of Romance* (1982), *An Englishman Abroad* (1983), *Poppyland* (1984), *Silas Marner* (1985).   PP

Crosscurrent *
aka: *The Cable Car Murders*
US 1971 96m colour TVM
Warner (E. Jack Neuman)

The San Francisco police investigate when a man is found dead in a cable car.
Good competent police mystery.
w Herman Miller *d* Jerry Thorpe *m* Jerry Goldsmith

Robert Hooks, Jeremy Slate, Robert Wagner, Carol Lynley, Jose Ferrer, Simon Oakland, John Randolph

Crossfire
US 1975 75m colour TVM
Quinn Martin

A police volunteer for undercover work is 'caught' peddling drugs and ostracized by his colleagues.
Routine hokum, well enough made.
w Philip Saltzman *d* William Hale *m* Pat Williams

James Farentino, John Saxon, Roman Bieri, Patrick O'Neal, Pamela Franklin, Frank de Kova

Crossings (US 1986). Miniseries from the novel by Danielle Steele about pre-war encounters on a luxury liner. Cheryl Ladd, Lee Horsley, Jane Seymour, Christopher Plummer. Directed by Karen Arthur for Aaron Spelling/Warner.

Crossroads. British soap opera set in a generally underpopulated Midlands motel which began at the end of 1964 as a daily serial, later reducing to four and finally three episodes a week. This last cut was by command of the IBA and much to the displeasure of the show's loyal devotees, who also protested at the enforced departure of its mainstay, Noele Gordon, in 1981.

My comment when it started: 'Not, as you might think, the first daily serial that commercial has tried, but the fourth (previous attempts: *Sixpenny Corner*, *One Family*, *Home Tonight*). Whether it will last any longer than those is one of the minuscule imponderables of 1965. It seems to me to be the lowest, feeblest and laziest form of drama ever invented, as if they'd simply gone home and left the tap running.'

But Dorothy Hobson rode to the defence in a book: *Crossroads: the Drama of a Soap Opera* (Methuen 1982).   PP

† The title was also used in 1955 for an A–R series in which guests debated turning points in their lives with a panel.

Croucher, Michael (1941–). British producer and executive, long based in the BBC's Bristol studios, latterly as head of general programmes. *Citizen '63* (with John Boorman) and 10-years-after follow-up, *A Year in the Life Of*, *The Gamekeeper*, *The River Keeper*, etc.   PP

Crowhaven Farm *
US 1970 72m colour TVM
Aaron Spelling (Walter Grauman)

Local witches terrify a New York wife when she inherits a Connecticut farm.
Genuinely frightening supernatural high jinks in the *Rosemary's Baby* arena.
w John McGreevey *d* Walter Grauman

Hope Lange, Paul Burke, Lloyd Bochner, John Carradine, Virginia Gregg

Crown Court *. A long-running British daytime series from the seventies, produced by Granada TV. Based on *The Verdict Is Yours*, but with a rehearsed script, it gets through a court case in three half-hours, and is more entertaining than many peak-time offerings.

Crown Matrimonial (GB 1973). Reasonably distinguished televersion of the play by Royce Ryton about the abdication of Edward VIII as seen by the royal family. With PETER BARKWORTH (as Edward), Greer Garson (as Queen Mary), Robert Sansom, Maxine Audley, Anna Cropper, Andrew Ray. Directed by Alan Bridges; for LWT.

Crowther, Leslie (1933–). British comedy actor, the perpetual innocent. Series include *Crackerjack*, *My Good Woman*, *The Price is Right*.

❋ **Cruickshank, Andrew** (1907–). British character actor who made his greatest mark in TV as Dr Cameron in DR FINLAY'S CASEBOOK in the mid-sixties.

Cruise into Terror
US 1978 96m colour TVM
Aaron Spelling, Douglas Cramer (Jeff Hayes)

Passengers on a pleasure ship are menaced by evil spirits surrounding an Egyptian sarcophagus.
Lethargic nonsense with the usual quota of semi-stars and an unseaworthy script.

w Michael Braverman d Bruce Kessler

Hugh O'Brian, Ray Milland, John Forsythe, Dirk Benedict, Christopher George, Lynda Day George, Frank Converse, Lee Meriwether, Stella Stevens, Marshall Thompson

Crunch and Des
US 1955 39 × 25m bw
NTA

Adventures of two owners of a charter boat.
Predictable adventures in the studio tank.

Forrest Tucker, Sandy Kenyon, Joanne Bayes

Crusade in Europe (US 1949). Half-hour documentary series for ABC, assembled from combat footage of World War II and based by Fred Feldkamp on the book by Dwight D. Eisenhower. Produced by the *March of Time* unit under Richard de Rochemont.

Crusader
US 1955–6 52 × 25m bw
CBS/Universal

A current affairs reporter has a mission to right international wrongs.
Implausible thick-ear.

Brian Keith

Crutchley, Rosalie (19 –). British actress whose strong dark features led to her playing many a loveless spinster or bossy wife, from *The Garden in the Sea* (1955) onwards. Recent credits include *By the Sword Divided* (serial) and *The Testament of John* (1984).   PP

A Cry for Help ★★
aka: *End of the Line*
Universal/Fairmont-Foxcroft (Richard Levinson, William Link)

A cynical disc jockey desperately tries to help a suicidal girl who phones in.
Character drama with sufficient suspense.

w Peter S. Fischer d DARYL DUKE

ROBERT CULP, Elayne Heilveil, Ken Swofford, Chuck McCann

A Cry for Love
US 1980 96m colour TVM
NBC/Charles Fries/Alan Sacks

A drug-addicted divorcee falls for an incurable dipsomaniac.
Prime time entertainment it ain't, but if you have to have so negative a theme, it's done well.

w Renee Taylor, Joseph Bologna d Paul Wendkos ph Richard Glouner m Jimmie Haskell

Susan Blakely, Powers Boothe, Charles Sibert, Herb Edelman, Edie Adams, Gene Barry

Cry for the Strangers
US 1982 96m colour TVM
CBS/MGM–UA/David Gerber (Jay Daniel)

A Seattle psychiatrist and his wife move to a seaside community and find that a series of murders seems to be connected with the weather.
Mildly suspenseful, slow-moving melodrama of a mysterious community.

w J. D. Feigelson, *novel* John Saul d Peter Medak

Patrick Duffy, Cindy Pickett, Lawrence Pressman, Brian Keith, Claire Malis

A Cry in the Wilderness
US 1974 74m colour TVM
Universal/Lou Morheim

Bitten by a rabid skunk, a man chains himself in the barn while his wife fetches medical help. His home is then threatened by a flood . . .
Absurd piling-up of disaster situations: more laughs than suspense.

w Stephen and Elinor Karpf d Gordon Hessler

George Kennedy, Joanna Pettet, Lee H. Montgomery, Collin Wilcox-Horne

Cry of the Innocent
Eire 1979 96m colour TVM
Theodore P. Donahue/Morgan O'Sullivan/Tara

An insurance executive relentlessly tracks down the saboteur who accidentally killed his family.
Tolerable, predictable action melodrama.

w Sidney Michaels, *story* Frederick Forsyth *d* Michael O'Herlihy *ph* Robert L. Morrisson *m* Allyn Ferguson

Rod Taylor, Joanna Pettet, Nigel Davenport, Cyril Cusack, Walter Gotell, Alexander Knox, Jim Norton

Cry Panic *
US 1974 74m colour TVM
Spelling–Goldberg

In an unfamiliar town, a motorist accidentally kills a pedestrian. The body then disappears . . .
Efficient what-the-hell-happened melodrama with echoes of *Bad Day at Black Rock*.

w Jack Sowards *d* James Goldstone

John Forsythe, Earl Holliman, Anne Francis, Ralph Meeker, Claudia McNeil

Cry Rape *
US 1974 74m colour TVM
Warner

Various points of view on the trying of rape cases.
Dramatized documentary: nothing new, but persuasive.

w Will Lorin *d* Corey Allen

Peter Coffield, Andrea Marcovicci, Patricia Mattick

Cryer, Barry (1935–). British writer of zany comedy scripts after various American models. Occasionally, as in *Who Do You Do*, fancies himself a performer, and does a passable impersonation of Groucho Marx.

Crystal, Billy (1947–). Former American nightclub comedian who scored a hit as the gay son in SOAP. Also in *Human Feelings*, *Enola Gay*, *Breaking Up Is Hard To Do*.

CTV. Canadian channel of independent commercial stations, akin to Britain's ITV.

The Cuckoo Waltz *
GB 1976–81 26 × 25m colour (VTR)
Granada (John G. Temple)

Two impecunious young marrieds have his rich friend as boarder.
Modestly pleasing comedy series which never quite got to first base.

w Geoffrey Lancashire, John G. Temple

Diane Keen, David Roper, Lewis Collins

Cukor, George (1899–1983). Distinguished American film director who won a 1974 Emmy for *Love Among the Ruins* and followed it up with another telemovie, *The Corn Is Green*.

Culloden ****
GB 1964 70m bw (16mm)
BBC (Peter Watkins)

A brilliantly re-created, low-budget docu-drama account of the Battle of Culloden, presented as though modern TV cameras were on the spot. Vivid, exciting and highly influential.

w/d PETER WATKINS *ph* DICK BUSH *ed* MICHAEL BRADSELL

Culp, Robert (1931–). Tall, wolfish, American leading actor whose main TV success was the series *I Spy*. (He had previously starred in *Trackdown*, and later played a support role in *The Greatest American Hero*.) TV movies: *The Hanged Man*, *See the Man Run*, *A Cold Night's Death*, *Outrage*, *Houston We've Got a Problem*, *Strange Homecoming*, *A Cry for Help*, *Spectre*, *Flood*, *Last of the Good Guys*, *Roots: the Next Generations*, *Hot Rod*, *Woman in White*, *The Dream Merchants*, *The Night the City Screamed*, *Killjoy*, *Her Life as a Man*, *The Calendar Girl Murders*, *The Key to Rebecca*.

Cummings, Robert or **Bob** (1908–). American light leading man who after a moderate Hollywood career became a popular TV star in the fifties, usually as a harassed executive. *Love That Bob*, *The Bob Cummings Show*, *My Hero*, *My Living Doll*, etc. TV movies: *Partners in Crime*, *Gidget Grows Up*, *The Great American Beauty Contest*. Won Emmy 1954 for *Twelve Angry Men*.

Cunliffe, David (1935–). British director, producer and executive; since 1979 in charge of Yorkshire's drama. Personal credits include *The Potting Shed*, 1981.   PP

Cupid's Darts **
GB 1981 50m colour

Robin Bailey as a conventionally unworldly philosopher enjoying a liberating attachment to a latter-day groupie (darts players rather than pop musicians). In YTV's *Plays for Pleasure* season, to which David Nobbs's comedy belonged, there was always a little Christmas cracker motto to accompany the happy ending. Here, the philosopher thanked the girl (a sparkling performance by Leslie Ash) for teaching him to be able to walk away from their little affair without looking back. But funny, endearing and optimistic. Produced by Pat Sandys.   PP

Curry and Chips (GB 1969). Half-hour comedy series about a Pakistani at work in a British factory. An interesting early reflection of integration, but not particularly funny. With Spike Milligan, Eric Sykes. Written by Johnny Speight; produced and directed by Keith Beckett; for LWT.

PP: 'About as funny as a party political broadcast and twice as self-righteous.'

Curry, Tim (1946–). British leading actor who after pop music associations on the stage (*Hair*, *The Rocky Horror Picture Show*) played the lead in ATV's *Will Shakespeare*. Also in *Rock Follies*.

The Curse of King Tutankhamun's Tomb
GB/US 1980 96m or 80m colour TVM
Harlech TV/Columbia (Patrick Dromgoole, Peter Graham Scott)

An account of the 1922 discoveries in the Valley of the Kings, and of the strange events which followed.
Enjoyably absurd melodramatic version which makes no attempt to rationalize the facts by research and becomes reminiscent of an incomplete Saturday morning serial.

w Herb Meadow, *book* Barry Wynne *d* Philip Leacock

Robin Ellis, Harry Andrews, Angharad Rees, Wendy Hiller, Eva Marie Saint, Raymond Burr, Faith Brook, Tom Baker, Rupert Frazer; narrator Paul Scofield

Curse of the Black Widow
Re-run title: *Love Trap*
US 1978 96m colour TVM
ABC Circle (Steven North)

Murders are commited by a giant spider.
Nonsense mystery which passes the time.

w Robert Blees, Earl Wallace *d* Dan Curtis *ph* Paul Lohman *m* Robert Cobert

Tony Franciosa, Donna Mills, Patty Duke Astin, June Allyson, Sid Caesar

Curteis, Ian (1935–). British writer, formerly actor and director, who after a dreary trilogy *Long Voyage Out of War* (1971) wisely settled for biographical reconstructions, including plays about Beethoven, *Hess* (STV 1978), Sir Alexander Fleming, *Churchill and the Generals*, *Suez 56* and *Miss Morrison's Ghosts*. PP

Curtis, Dan (1926–). American independent producer who, after his success with the serial *Dark Shadows*, has concentrated on TV movies with a horror theme: *The Night Stalker*, *Dracula*, *Scream of the Wolf*; also *When Every Day Was the Fourth of July*, *Supertrain*, *The Last Ride of the Daltons*, etc.

Curtis, Jamie Lee (1958–). American leading lady, daughter of Janet Leigh and Tony Curtis. *Operation Petticoat*, *She's in the Army Now*, *Death of a Centrefold*, *Money on the Side*.

Curtis, Ken (1925–) (Curtis Gates). American character actor, a *Gunsmoke* regular.

Curtis, Tony (1925–) (Bernard Schwarz). Popular second level film star of the fifties who in middle age managed only occasional character roles. In TV, he played a number of guest roles, and co-starred in *The Persuaders*, *McCoy*, and *Vegas* (1st year). TV movies: *Third Girl from the Left*, *The Count of Monte Cristo*, *The Users*, *Kiss of Gold*, THE SCARLETT O'HARA WARS (as David O. Selznick), *Inmates*, *Million Dollar Face*, *Portrait of a Showgirl*, *Half Nelson*.

Cushing, Peter (1913–). British leading actor and horror star who in the mid-sixties, with fair success, played Sherlock Holmes in a long BBC tape series. TV movie: *The Great Houdinis*.

Custer
aka: *The Legend of Custer*
US 1967 17 × 50m colour
ABC/TCF (Frank Glicksman, Robert Jacks)

Legendary western exploits of the famous American general.
A fair western series which somehow failed to connect with the public, perhaps because Custer was presented as a whitewashed hero.

m Elmer Bernstein

Wayne Maunder, Peter Palmer, Slim Pickens, Michael Dante, Alex Davion, Robert F. Simon

The Cut Man Caper
US 1975 96m colour TVM
Columbia/Liam O'Brien, Carl Pingitore

Black policemen are assigned to investigate a series of ghetto finance companies.
Oddball ethnic cop melodrama, presumably a failed pilot.

w Larry Brody *d* Don Medford

Raymond St Jacques, Robert Hooks, Scoey Mitchell, Godfrey Cambridge, Lou Gossett

Cuthbertson, Iain (1930–). Bluff Scottish actor who played the second lead (Charlie Endell) in *Budgie*, leads in *Sutherland's Law* and *Charlie Endell Esquire.*

Cutter *
US 1973 74m colour TVM
Universal (Richard Irving)

Private eye seeks missing football player.
Snazzy black-oriented mystery pilot that didn't make it.

w/d Dean Hargrove *m* Oliver Nelson

Peter De Anda, Cameron Mitchell, Barbara Rush, Gabriel Dell, Robert Webber, Archie Moore

Cutter to Houston
US 1983 1 × 74m, 8 × 50m colour TVM
CBS/MGM–UA/Cypress Point (Gerald Abrams)

Adventures of an emergency unit in a modern community hospital three hours from Houston.
Youth-oriented medical show full of fast cars and helicopters. Not a hit.

w,d Sandor Stern *ph* Frank Stanley *m* Ry Cooder

Jim Metzler, Shelley Hack, Alec Baldwin, Noble Willingham, K. Callan, Susan Styles

Cutter's Trail *
US 1969 100m colour TVM
CBS/John Mantley

Adventures of the Marshal of Santa Fe in 1873.
Standard western pilot that wasn't picked up.

w Paul Savage *d* Vincent McEveety

John Gavin, Marisa Pavan, Joseph Cotten, Beverly Garland

Cvitanovich, Frank (19 –). Canadian documentary film-maker working in Britain who prefers to stand outside all fads and fashions of the moment. Favourite subjects are horses and football, though one of his first films, *Bunny* (1972), was about his own handicapped son. *The Road to Wigan Pier* (1973), *Saturday's Heroes* (trilogy, 1976), *A Day at the Races* (1978), *Murphy's Stroke* (1980), *Victoria Park* (1982). Has lately branched out with a musical *Down in the Valley* (1984) and John Osborne's dramatized autobiography, *A Better Class of Person* (1985).   PP

Cyprus: Britain's Grim Legacy (GB 1984 2 × 52m). The legacy, I rightly assumed at the time, would be the one Britain left behind, not one she inherited. Norma Percy's two programmes were pre-expanded from what was to be one episode of the 1985 Granada series on how we messed up *The End of Empire*, which see.
'An island shared by legendary enemies, the Greeks and the Turks – what stupid planning on the part of British colonists. And only 40 miles from the Turkish mainland! We should have moved it to another part of the Mediterranean altogether. No wonder it is now an island divided.'   PP

D-Day to Berlin. The WWII liberation of Europe was commemorated in one or two 25th anniversary specials in 1969 (see *Ten Men Went to War*) but much more exhaustively 40 years on in 1984–5. Essential runners were:

Destination D-Day. The elaborate preparations and deceptions recalled by Huw Wheldon in a BBC documentary written by Wheldon and Roy Davies, directed by Davies, produced by Harry Thompson.

D-Day 40 Years On (BBC) and *D-Day plus Forty* (ITN): live coverage of anniversary commemorations in France, Britain, the Channel Isles.

Nan Red: TVS documentary (Peter Williams, Graham Hurley) about one invasion beach, and the people who lived behind it.

Albert's War: edition of Thames afternoon show *A-Plus* (Alan Gluckman) tranporting an unenthusiastic 18-year-old British infantryman, as he was then, back to Normandy for an unheroic view.

Three Bob for D-Day: two Granada local programmes to much the same brief, taking their title from the private soldier's pay in 1944.

D-Day to Berlin (BBC): notable for colour footage shot by Hollywood director George Stevens and never before screened.

The Battle for Berlin: brilliant *Timewatch* special (BBC) by Charles Wheeler to reveal how the Russians won a political race as well as a military victory, if at horrendous cost.

Yanks Meet Reds: the historic join-up of American and Russian troops on the Elbe recalled and up-dated for YTV's *First Tuesday* (Kevin Sim).

The Day We Won the War: VE-Day memories assembled for BBC documentary (Peter Ceresole) narrated by Frank Gillard.

PP

The DA
US 1971 13 × 25m colour
NBC/Universal/Jack Webb

The problems of a conscientious district attorney.

A series which followed two successful pilots (see *Conspiracy to Kill* and *The DA: Murder One*) but failed to take off.

Robert Conrad, Henry Morgan

The DA: Murder One
US 1969 97m colour TVM
Universal (Harold Jack Bloom)

The District Attorney traps a homicidal nurse.

One of two competent pilots (see *Conspiracy to Kill*) made for a series that didn't go.

w Harold Jack Bloom d Boris Sagal

Robert Conrad, Howard Duff, Diane Baker, J. D. Cannon, David Opatoshu

Daddy I Don't Like It Like This
US 1978 96m colour TVM
CBS/Merrit Malloy

New York parents are accused of child abuse. Tasteless treatment of a subject better suited to a documentary.

w Burt Young d Adell Aldrich ph Donald M. Morgan m David Shire

Burt Young, Talia Shire, Doug McKeon, Erica Yohn

Dad's Army ***
GB 1968–77 50 approx. × 30m colour
BBC (Jimmy Perry, David Croft)

Adventures of a platoon of over-age local defence volunteers (Home Guard) in a small southern town in Britain during World War II.

At its best, an inimitable character comedy with a splendid company of old timers dispensing essentially British, throwaway humour. BAFTA 1971, best comedy series.

w/cr DAVID CROFT, JIMMY PERRY

ARTHUR LOWE, JOHN LE MESURIER, CLIVE DUNN, JOHN LAURIE, IAN LAVENDER, ARNOLD RIDLEY, JAMES BECK, FRANK WILLIAMS, BILL PERTWEE

† A feature film version was made in 1971.

Dagmar (*c* 1930–) (Virginia Ruth Enger). American vaudeville artist who traded on her superstructure in TV variety shows of the fifties.

Dahl, Roald (1916–   ). Norwegian–British writer of short macabre tales which were televised by Anglia as ROALD DAHL'S TALES OF THE UNEXPECTED.

Dahrendorf on Britain (GB 1984; 5 × 50m). Friendly dissertation on Britain's perennial industrial decline and how it might be reversed, by the German economist Ralf Dahrendorf shortly before he finished a spell as director of the London School of Economics. Produced by Adrian Milne, for BBC.   PP

Dailey, Dan (1914–78). American dancing hero of many a forties musical. Turned to TV in character roles, and series include *The Four Just Men, The Governor and J.J., Faraday and Company*. TV movies: *Mr and Mrs Bo Jo Jones, The Daughters of Joshua Cabe Return, Testimony of Two Men*.

The Dain Curse *
US 1978 3 × 96m colour
CBS/Martin Poll
A private eye in the twenties seeks missing diamonds and finds himself on a murder trail. Atmospheric film version of a classic mystery novel of considerable plot complication; but far too long for the material.

w Robert Lenski, *novel* Dashiell Hammett d E. W. Swackhamer ph Andrew Laszlo m Charles Gross

JAMES COBURN, Jean Simmons, JASON MILLER, Hector Elizondo, Paul Stewart, Beatrice Straight, David Canary, Paul Harding, Roland Winters

'Lush, thought-provoking . . . a fine puzzler.' – *Daily Variety*

† A 'feature version' running 110 minutes is called *Private Eye*.

The Dakotas *
US 1962 19 × 50m bw
ABC/Warner
Four men fight corruption after the Civil War.
An appropriately dour, tough western which didn't please generally but certainly created an atmosphere of its own.

Larry Ward, Jack Elam, Chad Everett, Mike Greene

Daktari *
US 1966–8 89 × 50m colour
CBS/MGM/Ivan Tors
Adventures centring on an African animal welfare compound.
Popular family series from the pilot *Clarence*

the Cross-Eyed Lion which was released theatrically.

m Shelly Manne

Marshall Thompson, Cheryl Miller, Hari Rhodes, Hedley Mattingley

† *Cowboy in Africa* and *Keeper of the Wild* (a 1978 failed pilot) adopted an almost identical format.

Dale, Margaret (19   –   ). British director, ex-dancer herself, who was undisputed queen of television ballet throughout the fifties and sixties, understanding that movement is all and therefore never going in so close as to mask it. Used a lot of overhead camera positions and made maximum use of shadows. *Nutcracker* and *The Sleeping Beauty*, both with Fonteyn, *Pineapple Poll* with Merle Park, many others.   PP

'A family ruthless in its quest for power and passion!'

Dallas *
US 1978–82   × 50m colour
CBS/Lorimar (Leonard Katzman)
A rich Texan family faces all kinds of trouble, mostly self-manufactured.
Good-looking but cliché-strewn family saga. Not bad for those who like this kind of thing.

cr/w DAVID JACOBS d Robert Day (pilot) ph Edward Plante m Jerrold Immel

Barbara Bel Geddes, LARRY HAGMAN, Linda Gray, Patrick Duffy, Victoria Principal, Ken Kercheval, Charlene Tilton, Steve Kanaly, Susan Howard, Jared Martin, Howard Keel, Leigh McCloskey

'A limited series with a limited future.' – *Variety*

'Basically it has the trashy elements people want from this kind of fare.' – *Daily Variety*

† In fact the show fascinated millions because of the ruthlessness of its hero–villain, J.R., who kept it at the top of the international ratings for several seasons. A spin-off series, *Knots Landing*, performed less spectacularly; but *Falcon's Crest*, a copycat affair set in the Napa valley, was a hit.

'What really goes on behind the scenes with the most gorgeous girls in America!'

The Dallas Cowboy Cheerleaders
US 1979 96m colour TVM
ABC/Aubrey–Hamner (Bruce Bilson)
A girl reporter is sent to Dallas to get the dirt on the cheerleaders by becoming one herself. Competent girlie show with melodramas on the sidelines. Compulsive rubbish.

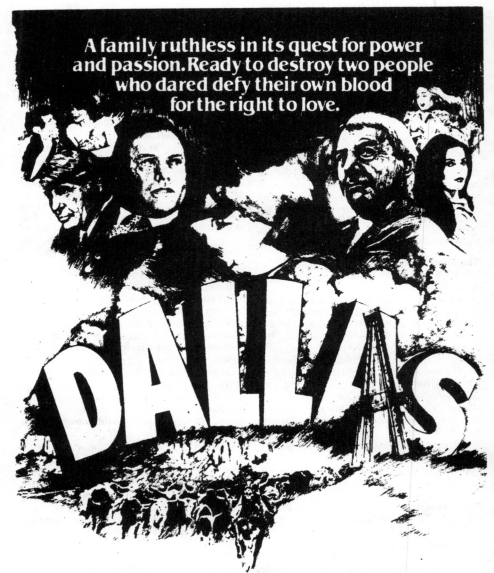

A family ruthless in its quest for power and passion. Ready to destroy two people who dared defy their own blood for the right to love.

DALLAS

Starring Larry Hagman, Patrick Duffy, Victoria Principal, Barbara Bel Geddes, Jim Davis, Charlene Tilton. Special Guest Star David Wayne.

10PM CBS◉2
NEW SERIES PREMIERE

DALLAS. An American ad published just before the show went on the air. *Variety's* review included the phrase 'a limited series with a limited future'.

w Robert Hamner *d* Bruce Bilson *ph* Don Birnkrant *m* Jimmie Haskell

Jane Seymour, Laraine Stephens, Bert Convy, Bucky Dent, Pamela Susan Shoup, Ellen Bry

Dallas Cowboy Cheerleaders II
US 1980 96m colour TVM
ABC/Aubrey–Hamner (Alan Godfrey)

Personal problems arise when the Cheerleaders set off for a tour of the Far East.

Competent repeat order.

w Stephen Kandel *d* Michael O'Herlihy *m* Carol Connors and the Waters Family

John Davidson, Laraine Stephens, Julie Hill, Roxanne Gregory, Candy Ann Brown, Natasha Ryan

Dalton (US 1985). New series starring Charles Taylor. See *Code of Vengeance* (pilot).

Daly, James (1918–78). Incisive American character actor, in a few films. TV series: *Foreign Intrigue, Medical Center.* Emmy 1965 as best supporting actor for *Eagle in a Cage.*

Daly, Tyne (*c* 1950–). Stocky American actress who shot to fame as the married half of *Cagney and Lacey* (Emmy 1983). *Greatest Heroes of the Bible, Better Late Than Never, The Women's Room.*

The Dame of Sark * (GB 1976). Two famous performances – those of CELIA JOHNSON and TONY BRITTON – are preserved in this rather thin play by William Douglas Home about events in the Channel Islands under Nazi occupation. Directed by Alvin Rakoff; for Anglia TV.

Damon, Cathryn (19 –). American actress who plays the less zany of the two sisters in SOAP (for which she won an Emmy in 1980). TV movie: *Friendships, Secrets and Lies.*

Damon Runyon Theater
US 1954 39 × 25m bw
CBS/Columbia

Anthology of low-life New York stories.

Host: Donald Woods

Dan August *
US 1970 26 × 50m colour
ABC/Quinn Martin (Adrian Samish)

Cases of a police detective in California. One of the better mystery series, from the pilot *The House on Greenapple Road* which however had Chris George in the lead. Despite its star, snappy pace and good production quality it failed to score high numbers.

m Dave Grusin

Burt Reynolds, Richard Anderson, Norman Fell

Episode titles:

In the Eyes of God
Murder by Proxy
The Murder of a Small Town
Quadrangle for Death
The Soldier
Love Is a Nickel Bag
The Law
The Color of Fury
The King Is Dead
Epitaph for a Swinger
When the Shouting Dies
Passing Fair
Invitation to Murder
The Union Forever
Death Chain
Trackdown
Days of Rage
The Titan
Dead Witness to a Killing
Bullet for a Hero
Circle of Lies
Prognosis Homicide
The Assassin
The Worst Crime
The Meal Ticket
The Manufactured Man

Dan Raven
US 1960 43 × 50m bw
NBC/Columbia

Cases of a police detective whose beat is Sunset Strip.

Fair cop show which failed to take off.

Skip Homeier

Dan Tempest: see The Buccaneer

Dana, Bill (1924–). American comedy actor who after displaying his fractured English in supporting roles was given *The Bill Dana Show*, but it didn't run. TV movies: *Rossetti and Ryan, A Guide for the Married Woman, Murder in Texas.*

Dance, Charles (1946–). British actor in suitably modest roles, e.g. in *The Last Day* (1983) until elevated to leading manhood by THE JEWEL IN THE CROWN. *Rainy Day Women* and *The Secret Servant* followed the same year, 1984. Episode of *Time for Murder*, 1985.   PP

CHARLES DANCE. One of the new stars born of Granada's famous production *The Jewel in the Crown*, here seen surveying the aftermath of the railway station massacre.

Dancing Girls (GB 1982; 4 × 60m). Real-life hard-luck stories of four dancers and a dance troupe transmitted over successive evenings on BBC2, leaving critics to wonder if in at least one instance the camera had not helped blight the chances of the poor nymphs. Made by Richard Denton, for BBC.   PP

Danger (US 1950–4). Half-hour live dramatic anthology for CBS, mostly mysteries. Directors included Sidney Lumet, John Frankenheimer and Yul Brynner.

Danger Has Two Faces
US 1967 89m colour TVM
TCF

A much disliked executive in Berlin is shot in mistake for an American agent, who promptly takes his place.
Re-edited episodes from *The Man Who Never Was*, a series which had nothing except the title to do with its movie namesake.
w Merwin Gerard, Robert C. Dennis, Judith and Robert Guy Barrows *d* John Newland *m* Nelson Riddle, William Lava, Gerald Fried

Robert Lansing, Dana Wynter, Murray Hamilton

Danger in Paradise
US 1977 98m colour TVM
CBS/Filmways/Perry Lafferty

An ailing Hawaiian rancher has to accept the help of his estranged ne'er-do-well son. Expensive but muddled pilot which looked fine but had too many sub-plots including the Mafia and a wicked stepmother. It led to a shortlived (13 × 50m) series, *Big Hawaii* (*Danger in Paradise* in GB).
w William Wood *d* Marvin Chomsky
Cliff Potts, John Dehner, Ina Balin

Danger Man ***
GB 1959 26 × 25m bw
GB 1961–2 45 × 50m bw (2 in colour)
Adventures of an independent spy working for the British Secret Service.
Crisp, sophisticated James Bondery with a star who had a clipped style of his own.
PATRICK MCGOOHAN

† The 50m films were known in the US as *Secret Agent*.

Danger UXB **
GB 1978–9 13 × 50m colour
Thames/Euston Films (Johnny Goodman, Christopher Neame)

Worthy, often exciting series about bomb disposal sappers in World War II, unaccountably undervalued at the time unless it was because the technical authenticity – derived from memoirs of Major A. P. Hartley – was ahead of the human authenticity. ANTHONY ANDREWS, later in *Brideshead*, played the subaltern hero, Maurice Roeves his stalwart sergeant.
cr John Hawkesworth, John Whitney *w* John Hawkesworth *d* Ferdinand Fairfax and others   PP

Dangerous Assignment (US 1952; 39 × 25m). Film series starring Brian Donlevy as a secret agent. Donlevy Productions for NBC.

Dangerous Company
US 1382 96m colour TVM
NBC/Lorimar (Bill Finnegan)
The story of a convict who engineered the first prison strike, and on his release became chief of security for a big corporation.
A basically true story which would have fared better as a documentary than as a TV movie.
from a book by Ray Johnson *d* Lamont Johnson
Beau Bridges, Carlos Brown, Jan Sterling

Dangerous Davies, the Last Detective
GB 1981 106m colour TVM
ATV (Greg Smith)
A bumbling London copper decides that a 15-year-old murder case should be reopened. Overlong but quite satisfying old-fashioned mystery with comedy overtones.
w Leslie Thomas *d* Val Guest
Bernard Cribbins, Bill Maynard, Joss Ackland, Bernard Lee, Frank Windsor, John Leyton, Maureen Lipman

The Dangerous Days of Kiowa Jones
US 1966 100m colour TVM
MGM/Max E. Youngstein, David Karr
Adventures of an ex-lawman in the old west. Dreary, talkative western which seems desperate to fill up its allotted time and go home.
w Frank Fenton, Robert E. Thompson, *novel* Clinton Adams *d* Alex March *ph* Ellsworth Fredericks *m* Samuel Matlovsky
Robert Horton, Diane Baker, Sal Mineo, Nehemiah Persoff, Gary Merrill, Robert H. Harris, Royal Dano

Daniel Boone
US 1964–9 165 × 50m colour (29 bw)
NBC/Arcola/Felspar/TCF (Aaron Rosenberg)

Adventures of the frontiersman of revolutionary days.

Rather sloppy adventure series with too much use of the studio backlot; but the kids lapped it up year after year, possibly for the title sequence which showed Dan'l splitting a tree with one throw of an axe.

story editor D. D. Beauchamp *m* Paul Sawtell

Fess Parker, Patricia Blair, Ed Ames

† In 1977 an attempt was made to revive the character as *Young Dan'l Boone*. It failed.

Daniel, Glyn (1912–). British archaeologist and Cambridge don who became one of Britain's first TV stars after his appearances on *Animal, Vegetable, Mineral*.

Daniels, Paul (1938–). North country British conjuror whose illusions tend to be familiar while his style is hardly on a par with those of the great magicians; but in lieu of other candidates he became TV's top illusionist of the early eighties.

Daniels, William (1927–). Neat-featured American character actor who apart from a few films has been seen in TV series as *Captain Nice* and as the detective in *Soap*. TV movies include *Murdock's Gang*, *A Case of Rape*, *Sara T*, *One of our Own*, *Killer on Board*, *The Bastard*, *Sgt Matlovich vs the US Air Force*, *The Rebels*, *Blind Ambition*.

Danner, Blythe (1945–). Leading American TV actress chiefly notable in series *Adam's Rib* and in a few TV movies: *Dr Cook's Garden*, *F. Scott Fitzgerald and 'The Last of the Belles'*, *Sidekicks*, *A Love Affair*, *Are You in the House Alone?*, *Too Far To Go*, *Inside the Third Reich*, *In Defence of Kids*, *Helen Keller: The Miracle Continues*, *Guilty Conscience*.

Danny Doyle: see I Spy

The Danny Kaye Show ** (US 1963). A season of elegant variety hours in a style now sorely missed, this easy-going but personality-packed series won an Emmy.

The Danny Thomas Show: see Make Room for Daddy

Dante
US 1960 26 × 25m bw
NBC/Four Star

A nightclub owner has his heart in the right place though he's always in trouble with the cops.

Or, Everybody Comes to Rick's. In this case the formula didn't work as well as in *Casablanca*.

Howard Duff, Alan Mowbray, Tom D'Andrea

† From a character played by Dick Powell in *Four Star Playhouse*

Dante's Inferno ** (GB 1967). A KEN RUSSELL film for BBC on the life of Dante Gabriel Rossetti. With Oliver Reed, Judith Paris, Andrew Faulds.

PP: 'For the first time in a Russell film I began to get restless. Time stopped skipping by and started to drag its feet. I stifled a yawn. What had gone wrong? Had Russell lost his touch? No, he hadn't. He had met his match. The truth is that the pre-Raphaelites were so bizarre, so extraordinary, that the grossest liberty that a film-maker could take with them would still be paler than the truth. Russell had Rossetti gulping Chloral from bottles inscribed in large letters, CHLORAL – in fact Rossetti not only did gulp Chloral but boosted its dubious effects with enormous chasers of Scotch whisky. The recovery of the poems from poor Elizabeth Siddal's grave was used to prompt ponderous Gothic fancies, involving spectral arms and faces, while omitting such truly grotesque details as the fact that each page was carefully washed in disinfectant and dried out before being restored to the poet.'

Daphne Laureola (GB 1978; 94m). James Bridie's play about the eccentric dowager with the ailing elderly husband was one of Granada's *The Best Play of . . .* series, and not the best received. Directed by Waris Hussein; with Joan Plowright, Laurence Olivier, Arthur Lowe, Clive Arundell.

PP: 'The only trouble was that Miss Plowright robbed it of half its import simply by being too young and plump, and even more by not bringing extravagant enough a personality to the proceedings. Though the age of the deep-drinking Lady Pitts is indicated somewhere in the text as 48, Bridie wrote the part for Edith Evans, then in her fifties and renowned for her playing of larger-than-life old ladies. It is also clear from the attitudes of other diners in the restaurant where she is discovered that her ladyship is to be thought distinctly *grande dame*.'

Dark Mirror
US 1984 96m colour TVM
ABC/Warner/Aaron Spelling (Sanford Schmidt)

An innocent girl almost gets the blame for her twin sister's murders.

Flatulent remake of the forties thriller, with psychiatry which now seems elementary.

w Corey Blechman, *screenplay* by Nunnally Johnson *d* Richard Lang *ph* Frank Stanley *m* Dominic Frontiere

Jane Seymour, Stephen Collins, Vincent Gardenia, Hank Brandt, Jack Kruschen, Cathleen Cordell

The Dark Secret of Harvest Home
US 1978 1 × 96m, 1 × 145m colour
MCA/Universal (Jack Laird)

A family of city dwellers move to the country but find themselves the object of dark satanic rites.

Protracted taradiddle with no narrative grip and not much in the way of characterization; but it occasionally looks good.

w Jack Guss, *novel Harvest Home* by Thomas Tryon *d* Leo Penn *m* Paul Chihara

Bette Davis, David Ackroyd, Joanna Miles, Rosanna Arquette, René Auberjonois

'Dreary, attenuated and tasteless.' – Judith Crist

Dark Shadows *. A mark for trying is deserved by this curious daily soap opera which between 1966 and 1970 notched up nearly a thousand VTR half-hours on ABC. Centring on a spooky New England house, it mixed vampires into its romantic brew and even tried to take them seriously. Those involved included Jonathan Frid, Joan Bennett and Mitch Ryan; creator was Dan Curtis.

Dark Victory
US 1975 150m colour TVM
Universal (Jules Irving)

A socialite finds she is dying of a brain tumour.

Absurdly extended remake of the 1939 film, which proved to be way out of fashion when remade in 1963 as *Stolen Hours*.

w M. Charles Cohen *d* Jules Irving

Elizabeth Montgomery, Anthony Hopkins, Michele Lee

'What happens when you created the world's first perfect human . . . and he turns out to be your wife's perfect lover?'

The Darker Side of Terror
US 1979 96m colour TVM
CBS/Shaner /Ramrus/Bob Banner

A university professor clones himself, but a flaw causes the double to take on overtones of Mr Hyde.

Agreeably silly science fiction with smooth production trappings.

w John Herman Shaner, Al Ramrus *d* Gus Trikonis *ph* Don Morgan *m* Paul Chihara

Robert Forster, Adrienne Barbeau, Ray Milland, John Lehne, David Sheiner, Eddie Quillan

Darkroom
US 1981   × 50m colour
ABC/Universal (Peter S. Fisher)

An anthology of strange stories, usually three to the hour, introduced by James Coburn. Most are overlong, and it would be hard to find one that really works.

'Most of the problems with the show's first outing seem to spring from the attempt to concentrate on cerebral suspense tales. Show will probably do better on week two, when it introduces elements like screaming girls and creatures lurking in the swamps – the sort of thing people are paying money to see these days.' – *Daily Variety*

Darlow, Michael (1934–   ). Forceful British director, equally at home in documentary or drama. In the former category, *Cities at War* (1968), the 'Occupation' and 'Genocide' episodes of *The World at War* (1974), *The Final Solution* (1975), biographical studies of Dickens, Hazlitt, Turner, *Great Expectations* (1978). In drama, *Crime and Punishment* (1978), *Suez* (1979), *Dancing Country* (1981), *The Barretts of Wimpole Street* (1982), *Mr Pye* (1986). Also an executive of production co-operative Partners in Production.   PP

Darts. After snooker, the unathletic, smoking-and-drinking game which lends itself best to TV, thanks to split-screen presentation offering a close-up of the board simultaneously with the player's moment of supreme concentration. The cosy commentary addressed to the contestants ('Eric, you need one hundred and two') also helps. Plays about darts have also been popular: *Cupid's Darts, One Hundred and Eighty!!!*.   PP

The DA's Man
US 1958 26 × 25m bw
NBC/Universal/Jack Webb

Adventures of an undercover agent working for the DA.

Forgettable crime series.

John Compton

Dastardley and Muttley in Their Flying Machines *
US 1969 17 × 22m colour
CBS/Hanna–Barbera

In World War I, an incompetent spy and his dog try to prevent American messages from getting through.
Rather a bright and original cartoon series.
voices Paul Winchell, Dick Messick *m* Hoyt Curtin

A Date with Judy
US 1952 39 × 25m bw
ABC
Adventures of a spoiled but lovable teenage girl in Santa Barbara.
A pre-Gidget Gidget, from the film and radio series.
Patricia Crowley, Judson Rees, Anna Lee

A Date with the Angels
US 1957 39 × 25m bw
ABC
The trials and tribulations of young marrieds. Unsurprising domestic comedy.
Betty White, Bill Williams, Russell Hicks, Isobel Elsom, Burt Mustin

The Dating Game. American daytime show, on ABC from 1965 and from 1973 in syndication. By asking questions of three men silhouetted behind a glass panel, a girl decides which she'd like to go out with. An early success for producer Chuck Barris.

Daughter of the Mind **
US 1969 74m colour TVM
TCF (Walter Grauman)
An international scientist believes that the ghost of his dead daughter is appearing to him, but the FBI exposes the trickery as the work of foreign agents.
Chilling little mystery which plays reasonably fair with the audience and works up quite a bit of excitement.
w Luther Davis, *novel The Hand of Mary Constable* by Paul Gallico *d* Walter Grauman *m* Robert F. Drasnin
Ray Milland, Gene Tierney, Don Murray, George Macready

**Daughters of Albion ** (GB 1979; 50m; colour). Three girls from a Liverpool biscuit factory find themselves at a student party, separated from the other guests by a yawning gulf of culture and expectations. What was so touching was how little the workers asked of life and how much one of them, at least, gave in return; namely a little painless graduation in the facts of life for one of the academics. Play by Willie Russell in YTV's first *Plays for Pleasure* season; produced by David Cunliffe.
PP

The Daughters of Joshua Cabe
US 1972 74m colour TVM
Spelling–Goldberg
A grizzled westerner finds that he will lose his property unless his three daughters to whom it is entailed come to live on it. He can't reach them, so he recruits three more . . .
Rather boring open-air comedy drama, like a heavy-handed *Petticoat Junction*.
w Paul Savage *d* Philip Leacock
Buddy Ebsen, Sandra Dee, Karen Valentine, Lesley Warren, Jack Elam, Leif Erickson
† Sequels: *The Daughters of Joshua Cabe Return, The New Daughters of Joshua Cabe.*

The Daughters of Joshua Cabe Return
US 1975 74m colour TVM
Spelling–Goldberg
One of the daughters is blackmailed by her own father.
Another attempt to turn a pilot into a series, with a new cast. No livelier than the first. (A third pilot appeared in 1976, and again failed: see *The New Daughters of Joshua Cabe.*)
w Kathleen Hite *d* David Lowell Rich
Dan Dailey, Christine Hart, Dub Taylor, Carl Betz, Ronne Troup, Brooke Adams, Kathleen Freeman

David Cassidy, Man Undercover (US 1978). A confused title for a dreadful cop show which sprang from a *Police Story* segment about a teenage cop involving himself with the high school drug scene. Produced by David Gerber, it ran to four episodes; for Columbia/NBC.

David Copperfield *
GB 1970 100m colour TVM
Omnibus/Sagittarius (Frederick H. Brogger)
A version for American TV, told in flashback as David muses on the Yarmouth sands.
Compressed but oddly tedious; performances are the saving grace.
w Jack Pulman *d* Delbert Mann *ph* Ken Hodges *m* Malcolm Arnold
Robin Phillips (David), Ralph Richardson (Micawber), Wendy Hiller (Mrs Micawber), Edith Evans (Betsey Trotwood), Ron Moody (Uriah Heep), Emlyn Williams (Mr Dick), Michael Redgrave (Mr Peggotty), Megs Jenkins (Nurse Peggotty), Susan Hampshire (Agnes), Corin Redgrave (Steerforth), Laurence Olivier (Creakle), Richard Attenborough (Tungay), James Donald (Murdstone), Cyril Cusack (Barkis), Pamela Franklin (Dora)

David Copperfield *
GB 1975 6 × 50m colour (VTR)
BBC/Time–Life (John McRae)
A solid, sensible serial version of Dickens's novel, with all the favourite characters well preserved.

w Hugh Whitemore d Joan Craft
Jonathan Kahn/David Yelland (David), Arthur Lowe (Micawber), Patricia Routledge (Mrs Micawber), Patience Collier (Betsey Trotwood), Martin Jarvis (Uriah Heep), Timothy Bateson (Mr Dick), Ian Hogg (Mr Peggotty), Pat Keen (Peggotty)

David Frost Presents the Guinness Book of Records (GB 1982). Some of the more fatuous stunts that earn a place in this fatuous work as observed by Frost or female colleague, Jamie Lee Curtis. One for the wallys from Paradine Productions/LWT. Further editions since.   PP

David Frost's Global Village *. An occasional series on Yorkshire TV from 1979, in which the man with the mike holds a discussion on some subject of interest with guests beamed in live by satellite as well as with the studio audience.

The David Niven Show (US 1959). A half-hour dramatic anthology for NBC, with the star more or less at ease. Later syndicated as part of *Four Star Theatre*.

Davidson, Jim (1954–). British quickfire comedian who sprang to minor fame on *New Faces* and after co-starring in *What's On Next* was handed *The Jim Davidson Show*. A Londoner, his cheeky humour is in the vein of Max Miller and Max Bygraves. *Jim Davidson's* FALKLANDS SPECIAL (1984).

Davidson, John (c 1945–). Young American leading man of the seventies. TV series: *The Girl with Something Extra*. TV movies: *Coffee Tea or Me?*, *Shell Game*, *Roger and Harry*.

Davies, Andrew (1936–). British TV playwright, formerly a teacher, with some bias to school subjects, e.g. *Bavarian Night*. But also *Fearless Frank*, about the Edwardian editor and lothario, later a stage success.   PP

Davies, Dickie (c 1942–). British sports commentator, long on ITV's *World of Sport*.

Davies, Freddie (1937–). British second-string comedian who makes spluttering noises and is known as Mr Parrotface. Most popular in the early seventies.

Davies, Geoffrey (1941–). British leading man mainly familiar as the most upright of the young doctors in *Doctor in the House*.

Davies, John Howard (1939–). British comedy director, former child star.

Davies, Rupert (1916–76). Solidly-built British character actor who after years of small parts, and indifferent series such as *Sailor of Fortune*, became a star as the pipe-puffing MAIGRET, a role which unfortunately typed him and harmed his later career.

Davies, Windsor (1930–). Welsh supporting actor who made a hit as the bellowing sergeant-major of *It Ain't Half Hot, Mum*.

Davis, Ann B. (1926–). Wry-faced American supporting comedienne. Series include *The Bob Cummings Show*, *The Brady Bunch*. Emmy 1958, best supporting actress.

Davis, Bette (1908–) (Ruth Elizabeth Davis). Celebrated American dramatic actress whose fairly regular TV work includes *Madame Sin*, *The Judge and Jake Wyler*, *Scream Pretty Peggy*, *The Disappearance of Aimee*, *The Dark Secret of Harvest Home*, STRANGERS (Emmy 1978), *White Mama*, *Skyward*, *Family Reunion*, *A Piano for Mrs Cimino*.

Davis, Carl (1936–). Amazingly fecund British composer whose music credits are as many as they are memorable, from *The World at War* and *The Naked Civil Servant* to *Late Starter*, taking in along the way the composition and conducting of new scores for Thames Television's reclamation of silent movie classics (*Napoleon*, *The Big Parade*, etc.) in the cinema. But only once has it worked round the other way, when his orchestral suite 'Variations on a Bus Route' inspired the hugely enjoyable BBC documentary *To the World's End*, 1985.   PP

Davis, Desmond. Confusingly, there have been two British drama directors of this name, unrelated. The first, who died in 1960, is commemorated by the British Academy's prestigious Desmond Davis award for 'outstanding creative contribution to television'. His textbook *The Grammar of Television Production* remains in use after a quarter of a century.

The latterday Desmond Davis has directed many video and film productions, including *Passing Through* and *Russian Night – 1941* (both 1982), *The Country Girls* (1983).   PP

Davis, Jim (1910/1915–80). Burly American actor who was mainly restricted to second feature westerns but made a belated hit as the head of the DALLAS clan. TV movies: *Satan's Triangle, Just a Little Inconvenience, Vanished, The Trackers, Deliver Us from Evil, Law of the Land, Killing Stone.*

Davis, Joan (1908–61). Rubber-faced American eccentric comedienne who after a solid film career became a TV star in *I Married Joan.*

Davis, Mac (1942–). American country and western singer.

Davis, Ossie (1917–). Black American actor. TV movies: *The Outsider, Night Gallery,* THE SHERIFF, *Billy: Portrait of a Street Kid, King, Teacher Teacher, Roots: The Next Generations, All God's Children.*

Davis, Steve (1957–). British snooker player, who despite many attempts to project his sparkling personality on chat and comedy shows remains a deeply boring young man. PP

Davison, Peter (19 –). Personable young British actor, fifth incumbent of *Dr Who.* Previously in *All Creatures Great and Small.* PP

Davy Crockett. Five one-hour segments of Disney's *Frontierland,* made in 1954 and 1955, were subsequently combined into two feature films, *Davy Crockett* and *Davy Crockett and the River Pirates,* which were theatrically released. The five titles were *Davy Crockett Indian Fighter, Davy Crockett Goes to Congress, Davy Crockett at the Alamo, Davy Crockett's Keelboat Race* and *Davy Crockett and the River Pirates.*

Dawber, Pam (1950–). American leading lady who allows herself to be perpetually upstaged by Robin Williams in *Mork and Mindy.*

Dawn: Portrait of a Teenage Runaway
US 1976 96m colour TVM
Douglas S. Cramer/NBC

A 15-year-old girl runs away and becomes a prostitute.
Exploitation masquerading as social conscience. Dreary, too.

w Dalene Young *d* Randal Kleiser *m* Fred Karlin

Eve Plumb, Bo Hopkins, Leigh McCloskey

Dawn University (GB 1963). Forgotten and shortlived attempt by ITV (Anglia) with Cambridge University to emulate the 'Sunrise Semesters' of American television. Generally much too imprecise, but probably contributed to the concept of the Open University as promulgated soon afterwards by Harold Wilson. PP

Dawson, Les (1933–). Glum Yorkshire comedian at his best in a variety format; pessimism is his forte, and he also does a passable impression of W. C. Fields.

Dawson, Richard (1935–). British light actor in Hollywood, mainly familiar as one of *Hogan's Heroes* and as host of the long-running game show *Family Feud.*

The Day After *
US 1983 135m colour TVM
ABC Circle (Robert A. Papazian)

A Russian nuclear bomb destroys a town in Kansas.
Documentary drama intent on showing the details of what might happen. Reasonably convincing on this level, but too slow and literal to be an artistic success.

w Edward Hume   *d* Nicholas Meyer
ph Gayne Rescher *m* David Raksin

Jason Robards Jnr, JoBeth Williams, Steve Guttenberg, John Lithgow, Bibi Besch, John Cullum

PP: 'The fourth nuclear cautionary tale on British television, and not the least pessimistic, except perhaps to take a kinder view than some of human nature in adversity. What was wrong with that? But the obligatory post-transmission debate *After the Day After* was the disaster which followed the disaster movie, coming in much too hard on the end of the film and cutting off a minute of the desolate ending as an unseen radio voice searches for a response from survivors, if any.'

The Day Before Yesterday *
GB 1970 6 × 50m colour/bw
Thames (Phillip Whitehead)

Political history of Britain from Attlee to Macmillan, assembled from archive film plus personal memoirs with commentary written and delivered by Robert Kee. PP

† In 1984 Whitehead went over an extension of the same ground in the C4 series *The Writing on the Wall.*

DAVY CROCKETT. The feature films which were so popular in Britain during the late fifties were actually composed of television half-hours roughly strung together. The real attraction, perhaps, was Fess Parker's coonskin cap.

'The greatest story as it's never been told before!'
The Day Christ Died
US 1980 142m colour TVM
CBS/TCF/Martin Manulis

Mildly interesting version of the events leading up to the crucifixion, somewhat controversial in view of its political implications but in any case entirely superfluous in view of other recent treatments such as *Jesus of Nazareth*.

w James Lee Barrett, Edward Anhalt d James Cellan Jones ph Franco di Giacomo m Lawrence Rosenthal

Chris Sarandon (Jesus), Colin Blakely (Caiaphas), Keith Michell (Pilate), Hope Lange (Claudia), Barrie Houghton (Judas), Jonathan Pryce (Herod)

'Someone decided rhetoric and naturalism were good replacements for reverence and true drama; they aren't.' – *Daily Variety*

'Talky, single-levelled and disappointing.' – *Variety*

Day, Dennis (1917–). (Owen Patrick Denis McNulty). High-voiced American comedian and singer, long associated with Jack Benny in radio and TV.

Day, Doris (1924–) (Doris Kappelhoff). Vivacious American singer and leading lady of the fifties and sixties; on TV *The Doris Day Show* went through four seasons and four formats.

day for night. Method of shooting night scenes in daytime and then darkening them in the lab. The system gives far more clarity than the more 'realistic' method of shooting at night, which all too often results in all the blacks 'crushing' into each other.

A Day in the Life of the World (GB 1977). How television news bulletins in 30 countries covered one day picked at random. A coup in Thailand following student riots, a military parade in Cairo and the sinking pound sterling were the most common items, but East of the Iron Curtain they all started with the First Secretary's latest speech or departure or arrival or handshake. Uganda led with Amin greeting a Yugoslav visitor. Red China's Angela Rippon (unseen) began, 'Comrades, we bring you the news of the evening.' Mexico had a jokey phone-in news show and an Australian newscast included a song by Ewan McColl and Peggy Seeger, confirming the long-held suspicion that at any given time this tedious pair are going on somewhere in the world. Presented by Olivier Todd; for BBC.
PP

The Day of the Triffids
GB 1981 6 × 30m colour (VTR)
BBC (David Maloney)

Carnivorous plants take over the earth. Disappointingly flat and uninvolving adaptation.

w Douglas Livingstone, *novel* John Wyndham *d* Ken Hannam *m* Christopher Gunning

John Duttine, Jonathan Newth, Maurice Colbourne, Emma Relph

A Day Out ** (GB 1972). A 50-minute nostalgic play by ALAN BENNETT, about friends cycling in the country in 1911 Halifax. With James Cossins, Fred Feast, Virginia Bell; directed by STEPHEN FREARS; for BBC2.

Day, Robert (1922–). Competent British film director of the fifties who went to Hollywood and became a reliable supplier of TV movies: *The House on Greenapple Road, In Broad Daylight, Death Stalk, Having Babies*, etc.

❋ **Day, Sir Robin** (1923–). Eminent British exponent of broadcast journalism, chiefly associated in the public's eye with the determined, even aggressive interviewing of politicians – 'an intimidating archangel' in the phrase of the late Maurice Edelman, MP. Began as one of the original ITN newscasters in 1955, quickly adding side role as parliamentary correspondent. With the BBC's *Panorama* from 1959 onwards, eventually as linkman 1967–72. His characteristically breathy delivery was also heard on radio from the mid-1970s, when he took over *The World at One*. A passionate believer in Parliament, he has long advocated the regular televising of its proceedings as a corrective to the violence and agitation which he believes to be unduly emphasized by ordinary television news coverage. BAFTA 1974: Richard Dimbleby Award; knighted 1981. Chairs BBC's weekly *Question Time*. PP

The Day the Bubble Burst
US 1981 142m colour TVM
CBS/TCF/Franklin R. Levy, Mike Wise (Marty Katz)

Several sets of people are caught up in the Wall Street crash of 1929.

A surprising attempt, and a lumbering failure, lacking clarity and the old Hollywood skills. For all the talk of expensive sets, it looks like a dress rehearsal on the backlot.

w Stanley R. Greenberg, *book* Max Morgan-Witts and Gordon Thomas *d* Joseph Hardy

Blanche Baker, Franklin Cover (as Hoover), Richard Crenna, Robert Vaughn, Robert Hays, Dana Elcar, Audra Lindley, Bill Macy, Donna Pescow, David Ogden Stiers

The Day the Earth Moved *
US 1974 74m colour TVM
ABC Circle

Aerial photographers track an incipient earthquake and try to persuade local townfolk to evacuate.

Fairly smart low-budget disaster movie.

w Jack Turley, Max Jack *d* Robert Michael Lewis *m* Bobby Sherman

Jackie Cooper, Stella Stevens, Cleavon Little, William Windom, Beverly Garland

The Day the Loving Stopped
US 1981 96m colour TVM
ABC/Paul Monash, Jerome Zeitman
 (Robert L. Jacks)

The teenage daughter of a psychiatrist is upset by her parents' impending divorce.

Tolerable if lethargic telefeature which treads a well-beaten path.

w Liz Coe, *book* Julie Autumn List *d* Daniel Mann *ph* Robert Hauser *m* Lee Holdridge

Dennis Weaver, Valerie Harper, Dominique Dunne, Sam Groom

'Wearying dramatization does little to create interest in the problem.' – *Daily Variety*

The Day the Universe Changed (GB 1985;
10 × 50m). Another expensive turkey from James Burke, this time intended to chart the radical changes to man's perception of the universe at various times in history. As usual it was whizz-whizz round the locations according to the Burke's Law that thou shalt stand on the spot to deliver a sentiment that shall most effectively distract attention from that sentiment. Since what he had to say was vulgarly and slangily expressed, it didn't much matter, though. Produced by Richard Reisz, John Lynch, for BBC.   PP

The Day the Women Got Even
US 1981 96m colour TVM
NBC/PKO/Otto Salomon

Four lady theatregoers stumble on a blackmail plot and help set matters right.

Curious comedy–melodrama, somewhat ineptly done but with a few slapstick laughs.

w Jud Scott, Gloria Gonzales *d* Burt Brinckerhoff *ph* Brian West *m* Brad Fiedel

Barbara Rhoades, Georgia Engel, Jo Ann Pflug, Tina Louise, Julie Hagerty, Gerald Gordon

'Lightweight piffle . . . an amiable but unremarkable effort.' – *Daily Variety*

The Day War Broke Out *
GB 1975 50m colour
Thames (John Robins)

Memories of World War II are revived by film clips and interviews with Ronnie Aldrich, Bing Crosby, George Elrick, Margaret Lockwood, Tommy Trinder, Jack Warner, etc.

A pleasant piece of social history.

Day-Lewis, Sean (1931–). Television editor of London *Daily Telegraph*, one of the best informed and most influential of journalists covering the scene.   PP

Days of Hope **
GB 1976 four films: 99m, 103m, 77m,
 132m colour
BBC/Polytel (Tony Garnett)

Four socialist-oriented plays tracing events in Britain between 1916 and 1926, through the lives of three poor people.

Hard tack, vigorously presented in grainy semi-documentary style. Not exactly entertaining, but compulsive once one gets into the mood.

1916: *Joining Up*
1921: *Lockout*
1924: *The First Labour Government*
1926: *The General Strike*

w JIM ALLEN *d* KEN LOACH

Paul Copley, Nikolas Simmonds, Pamela Brighton, Norman Tyrrel, Gary Roberts, Edward Underwood, John Phillips

'It made much else on television seem amateur and effete.' – *The Times*

'So manifestly superior to what we normally find on television that criticism was temporarily disarmed.' – *Sunday Times*

Days of Our Lives. American soap opera which has run five times a week on NBC from 1965. Those involved include Macdonald Carey, Susan Flannery and Susan Seaforth.

De Camp, Rosemary (1913–). American character actress adept at pleasant understanding wives. TV series include *Dr Christian*, *The Bob Cummings Show*, *That Girl*.

De Cordova, Frederick (1910–). American director of innumerable star comedy half-hours in the fifties and sixties.

De Felitta, Frank (1921–). American writer-director. *The Two Worlds of Jenny Logan*, *Dark Night of the Scarecrow*.

De La Tour, Frances (1944–). Homely British actress who rose to celebrity as Miss Jones in *Rising Damp*. Since then, *Duet for One*, *Flickers*.

De Patie, David (1930–). American producer, especially associated with Friz Freleng in the making of cartoon series.

De Paul, Judith (1944–). American entrepreneur in Britain. An ex-opera star,

Bo and Hope make Miami sizzle!

The heat is on as they close in on sunken treasure and Bo's hidden past!

Days of our Lives

TAKE THE PLUNGE! **1PM** **4** **WEEKDAYS**

DAYS OF OUR LIVES. American daytime soap operas rarely travel, since most foreign territories prefer their own. Britain has plenty, but the afternoons have been largely given over to Australian series such as *The Sullivans*, *A Country Practice*, and *Sons and Daughters*.

she sailed into production with a series of Gilbert and Sullivan operas and *Mountbatten the Last Viceroy.*

De Vol, Frank (1911–). American composer of hundreds of scores for series and TV movies.

Deacon, Richard (–1984). Bald-headed comic supporting actor most memorable in *The Dick Van Dyke Show.*

The Dead Don't Die *
US 1975 74m colour TVM
Douglas S. Cramer
A man wrongly executed becomes a zombie and helps find the real murderer.
Interesting low-budget attempt to reproduce a thirties horror thriller such as *The Walking Dead.* Script not quite good enough.
w Robert Bloch *d* Curtis Harrington
George Hamilton, Ray Milland, Ralph Meeker, Linda Cristal, Joan Blondell, James McEachin

Dead Ernest (GB 1982; 6 × 30m). Short-lived attempt by Central to take up the talents and fame of Andrew Sachs (Manuel in *Fawlty Towers*) in a sitcom set in a draughty Heaven, Ernest having perished with other Blackpool holidaymakers in a freak tidal wave. It didn't catch on, but the writers, John Stevenson and Julian Roach, went on to write *Brass*, so good came out of it all.   PP

Dead Man on the Run
aka: *New Orleans Force*
US 1975 74m colour TVM
Bob Sweeney
The head of an élite squad of federal investigators investigates his predecessor's murder.
Unnecessarily muddled and unrefreshing cop show.
w Ken Pettus *d* Bruce Bilson *m* Harry Geller
Peter Graves, Pernell Roberts, Diana Douglas, Katherine Justice

Dead Man's Curve
US 1978 96m colour TVM
EMI (Pat Rooney)
A fifties rock-and-roll singer becomes a vegetable after a car crash.
Dreary youth-oriented biopic of Jan Berry and Dean Torrence.

w Dalene Young *d* Richard Compton *ph* William Cronjager *m* Fred Karlin
Richard Hatch, Bruce Davison, Pam Bellwood, Floy Dean
'Facile approach to real-life drama.' – *Daily Variety*

Dead Men Tell No Tales *
US 1971 74m colour TVM
TCF (Walter Grauman)
A travelling photographer in Los Angeles is hunted by professional killers who have mistaken him for someone else.
Quite smartly-made chase mystery.
w Robert Dozier, *novel* Kelly Roos *d* Walter Grauman
Christopher George, Judy Carne, Patricia Barry, Richard Anderson

Dead of Night
US 1977 74m colour TVM
Dan Curtis/NBC
A trilogy of supernatural stories . . .
. . . none of them very good.
w Richard Matheson *d* Dan Curtis
Joan Hackett, Lee Montgomery, Horst Buchholz, Anjanette Comer, Patrick MacNee, Ed Begley Jnr, Ann Doran, Christina Hart

Dead on Target
US 1977 74m colour TVM (VTR)
TCF (Stanley Colbert)
An oil executive is kidnapped.
Feeble sequel to the theatrical features about *Our Man Flint.* No series.
w Norman Klenman *d* Joseph Scanlon
Ray Danton, Sharon Acker, Lawrence Dane

Deadline
US 1959 39 × 25m bw
Official
Anthology of dramatic stories about newspapermen.
Adequate late-night filler.
narrator Paul Stewart *m* Fred Howard

'3.5 million people held for ransom!'
Deadline
Australia 1980 96m colour TVM
9 Network/Hanna–Barbera/New South Wales Film Corporation (Hal McElroy)
Criminals explode a small nuclear device and hold the government to ransom.
Adequate action thriller with a few surprising twists.
w Walter Halsey Davis *d* Arch Nicholson
Barry Newman, Bill Kerr, Trisha Noble, Bruce Spence, Vincent Ball

Deadline Action: see Wire Service

Deadline Midnight. British fiction series set in Fleet Street newspaper office, produced by ATV in the early sixties with Arthur Christiansen, former editor of the *Daily Express*, as adviser. Fleet Street was not particularly appreciative. With Peter Vaughan, Glyn Houston. PP

Deadlock
US 1969 96m colour TVM
Universal (William Sackheim)

The police chief and district attorney of a large city disagree violently over the best means of solving local murders and preventing mob action.
Sobersided, socially conscious pilot for a series that didn't go.
w Chester Krumholtz, Robert E. Thompson, William Sackheim *d* Lamont Johnson

Leslie Nielsen, Hari Rhodes, Aldo Ray, Ruby Dee

The Deadly Dream *
US 1971 73m colour TVM
Universal (Stan Shpetner)

A weird dream about a death sentence begins to turn into reality.
A sufficiently engaging suspenser with an unconvincing outcome.
w Barry Oringer *d* Alf Kjellin *m* Dave Grusin

Lloyd Bridges, Janet Leigh, Leif Erickson, Carl Betz, Don Stroud, Richard Jaeckel

'They loved the same way they lived – dangerously!'
Deadly Encounter
US 1983 96m colour TVM
CBS/EMI/Roger Gimbel (Paul Cameron, Robert Boris)

An American helicopter pilot in Mexico goes on the run with his former girl-friend when gangsters are after her.
Frenzied chase adventure with good flying sequences.
w David J. Kinghorn, Robert Boris *d* William A. Graham *ph* Frank Holgate *m* Fred Karlin, Michael Hoenig

Larry Hagman, Susan Anspach, James Gammon, Michael C. Gwynne
'While the vidpic sparkles when it's up in the air, the story is fragile enough to fly off on its own.' – *Daily Variety*

The Deadly Game
US 1977 96m colour TVM
NBC/MGM

After a highway accident, a rural police chief finds himself on the track of terrorists.
Another attempt by the star to turn his country cop character into a series. (See *Winter Kill*, *The Girl in the Empty Grave*, *Adams of Eagle Lake*.) No takers, though the atmosphere is pleasant enough.
w/d Lane Slate
Andy Griffith, Sharon Spellman, Hunter Von Leer, Dan O'Herlihy, Claude Earl Jones

Deadly Harvest *
US 1972 73m colour TVM
CBS/Anthony Wilson

An East European defector in California finds himself the target for an assassin's bullet.
Efficient suspenser.
w Anthony Wilson, *novel Watcher in the Shadows* by Geoffrey Household *d* Michael O'Herlihy
Richard Boone, Patty Duke, Michael Constantine, Murray Hamilton

The Deadly Hunt *
US 1971 74m colour TVM
Four Star

A young couple on a forest holiday become unwitting targets for paid killers, and a forest fire helps them escape.
Silly but watchable action suspenser.
w Eric Bercovici *d* John Newland
Tony Franciosa, Peter Lawford, Anjanette Comer, Jim Hutton

Deadly Intentions
US 1985 2 × 96m colour miniseries
ABC/Green–Epstein (Neil T. Maffeo)

An innocent girl marries a doctor who turns out to be a psychopath. After their divorce, he continues to harass her to such an extent that he is eventually arrested for having 'deadly intentions' . . .
A true story which, spread over four hours, doesn't amount to much and even seems rather silly.
w Andrew Peter Marin, *book* by William Randolph Stevens *d* Noel Black *ph* Reynaldo Villalobos *m* Georges Delerue
Madolyn Smith, Michael Biehn, Cloris Leachman, Morgana King, Jack Kruschen, Cliff de Young
'The loopholes are almost as disturbing as the stupefying shocks.' – *Daily Variety*

Deadly Lessons
US 1983 96m colour TVM
ABC/MGM–UA/Leonard Goldberg (Ervin Zavada)

The headmistress of a girls' finishing school finds her pupils are being murdered . . .
Not a bad murder mystery, but it would have satisfied more if half an hour shorter.

w Jennifer A. Miller *d* William Wiard *ph* Andrew Jackson *m* Ian Freebairn-Smith

Donna Reed, Larry Wilcox, David Ackroyd, Diane Franklin

Deadly Messages
US 1985 96m colour TVM
ABC/Columbia/Paul Pompian

A girl who believes she has psychic powers is stalked by a mysterious killer.
Adequately suspenseful but essentially silly thriller in which the solution dispenses with the supernatural and relies too much on chance.

w Bill Bleich *d* Jack Bender

Kathleen Beller, Michael Brandon, Dennis Franz, Sherri Stoner

The Deadly Tide
US 1975 98m colour TVM
Spelling–Goldberg

Jewel thieves vanish into thin air from a waterfront warehouse . . . they become scuba divers.
Fragmented adventures of the *SWAT* team originally shown in two parts.

w Ben Masselink *d* Gene Levitt

Steve Forrest, Christopher George, Lesley Warren, Sal Mineo, Don Stroud, Susan Dey, Phil Silvers

The Deadly Tower *
US 1975 100m colour TVM
MGM

The capture of the University of Texas sniper who in 1966 caused many casualties before being caught by a single policeman.
Good documentary-style re-creation of an awesome event.

w William Douglas Lansford *d* Jerry Jameson

Kurt Russell, Richard Yniguez, Ned Beatty, John Forsythe, Pernell Roberts

Deadly Triangle
US 1977 74m colour TVM
Columbia

An Olympic skier becomes sheriff of Sun Valley.
Familiar crime stuff with unfamiliar but limiting background.

w Carl Gottlieb *d* Charles S. Dubin

Dale Robinette, Robert Lansing, Maggie Willman, Taylor Lacher

† See also *Crisis at Sun Valley*.

Deakin, Michael (1939–). British executive, formerly art dealer, who produced noteworthy documentaries for YTV (including *Johnny Go Home*) before joining the TV-am consortium as programme controller and in its bloodbath early days famously clashing with its starry presenters.
PP

Dean, Isabel (1923–) (Isabel Hodgkinson). Agelessly beautiful British actress whose credits are far too numerous to list *in extenso*, but they go back to the original *Quatermass Experiment* in 1953, must include *Man of Our Times* (1968), and keep on coming in the eighties.
PP

The Dean Martin Show *. A one-hour comedy variety spectacular which ran on NBC from 1965 to 1973. The star kidded himself and his friends, and was backed by a chorus line called The Gold Diggers.

Dear Detective
US 1979 96m colour TVM
CBS/Viacom/Dean Hargrove, Roland Kibbee

A lady detective-sergeant tracks down the murderer of leading politicians.
Scene-for-scene remake of a well-received French original. In American the mixture of whimsy and thrills didn't gell, and only four one-hour episodes of the much vaunted series were made.

w Dean Hargrove, Roland Kibbee, *original script* Philippe de Broca, Michel Audiard *d* Dean Hargrove *ph* Ric Waite *m* Dick and Dean de Benedictis

Brenda Vaccaro, Arlen Dean Snyder, Ron Silver, Michael MacRae

'Absurdity, not wit, seems to be the keynote.'
– *Daily Variety*

† The French film was known as *Tendre Poulet* (in England, *Dear Inspector*).

Dear Ladies (GB 1983; 6 × 30m). The genteel drag act of Hinge and Bracket whimsically acted out in picturesque village setting, to non-stop and baffling studio laughter. Produced by Mike Smith/Peter Ridsdale Scott, for BBC.
PP

Dear Phoebe
US 1954 39 × 25m bw
NBC/Chrislaw

A male reporter writes the Lonelyhearts column.
Passable comedy series.

Peter Lawford, Marcia Henderson, Charles Lane

Death Among Friends
aka: *Mrs R*
US 1975 74m colour TVM
Warner/Douglas S. Kramer

A lady cop solves a Beverly Hills murder.
Talkative whodunit.

w Stanley Ralph Ross *d* Paul Wendkos

Kate Reid, Martin Balsam, Jack Cassidy,
Paul Henreid, Lynda Day George

Death and the Maiden: see Hawkins on
Murder

Death at Love House *
US 1976 74m colour TVM
Spelling–Goldberg (Hal Sitowitz)

A long-dead silent film star appears to haunt
her Beverly Hills mansion.
Engaging supernatural nonsense with a most
agreeable cast entering into the spirit of the
thing.

w Jim Barnett *d* E. W. Swackhamer

Robert Wagner, Kate Jackson, Marianna
Hill, Sylvia Sidney, Joan Blondell, Dorothy
Lamour, John Carradine

'It has everything going for it except a
sensible script and intelligent dialogue.' –
Judith Crist

Death Be Not Proud **
US 1975 100m colour TVM
Westfall Productions/Good Housekeeping
(Donald Wrye)

An account of the death of journalist John
Gunther's son from a brain tumour.
Extremely well-made and acted wallow in a
real-life tragedy, for those who can take it.

w/d Donald Wrye, *book* John Gunther

Arthur Hill, Jane Alexander, ROBBY BENSON,
Linden Chiles

Death Car on the Freeway
US 1980 96m colour TVM
CBS/Stan Shpetner

A maniac cruises along the Los Angeles
freeways manoeuvring women into accidents.
Very competent action thriller of the simple
kind TV movies can manage.

w William Wood *d* Hal Needham

Shelley Hack, Peter Graves, George
Hamilton, Dinah Shore, Barbara Rush

Death Cruise
US 1974 74m colour TVM
Spelling–Goldberg

Holidaymakers on a luxurious cruise are
systematically murdered.
Mildly engrossing murder mystery on the
lines of *And Then There Were None.*

w Jack Sowards *d* Ralph Senensky *m* Pete
Rugolo

Edward Albert, Kate Jackson, Richard Long,
Polly Bergen, Celeste Holm, Tom Bosley,
Michael Constantine, Cesare Danova

'He killed her fiancé. Raped her. Tried to
frame her for the murder. And she
loved him.'

A Death in California
US 1985 2 × 96m colour miniseries
ABC/Lorimar/Mace Neufeld (Richard L.
O'Connor)

An escaped psychopath moves in with a
family, kills the husband and rapes the wife
. . . who later refuses to testify against him.
Based on a true case or not, this plays like
No Orchids for Miss Blandish all over again,
with a confused narrative, unpleasant
people, and more violence than one expects
from TV.

w E. Jack Neuman, *book* by Joan Barthel
d Delbert Mann *ph* Joseph Biroc *m* John
Cacavas

Sam Elliott, Cheryl Ladd, Alexis Smith,
Fritz Weaver, Granville Van Dusen, Barry
Corbin

'For those savoring their savagery undiluted,
their sadism rampant . . . it fills the bill.' –
Daily Variety

A Death in Canaan *
US 1978 120m approx. colour TVM
Warner/Robert W. Christiansen, Rick
Rosenberg

A teenage boy is accused of his mother's
murder.
Draggy fictionalization of a real-life case,
with vivid scenes and good acting but too
many unanswered questions.

w Thomas Thompson, Spencer Eastman,
novel Joan Barthel *d* Tony Richardson
ph James Crabe *m* John Addison

Stefanie Powers, Tom Atkins, Jacqueline
Brookes, Paul Clemens, Brian Dennehy,
Kenneth McMillan

'The areas between fact and fiction are
lamentably fuzzy.' – *Daily Variety*
'An absorbing and meaningful drama.' –
Judith Crist

Death Moon
US 1978 96m colour TVM
CBS/EMI/Roger Gimbel (Jay Benson)

An executive is overcome by a Hawaiian
curse.
Unintentionally funny poppycock of the old
school; much too long despite attractive
locations.

w George Schenk *d* Bruce Kessler *ph* Jack Whitman *m* Paul Chihara

Robert Foxworth, Joe Penny, Barbara Trentham, France Nuyen, Dolph Sweet

Death of a Centerfold

US 1983 96m colour TVM

NBC/MGM–UA/Larry Wilcox Productions

The story of the *Playboy* model who was murdered by her husband.

Straightforward account of a tragedy, later filmed as *Star 80*.

w Donald Stewart

Jamie Lee Curtis, Bruce Weitz, Robert Reed

Death of a Princess *

GB 1980 96m colour

ATV (Martin McKeand, Anthony Thomas)

One of the few television programmes to cause a full-scale diplomatic row, the Saudi Arabians objecting bitterly to its reconstruction of what they regarded as a perfectly proper act of Islamic justice but what the West inevitably saw as barbaric, messy murder – the execution of a royal princess and her lover for adultery. ANTHONY THOMAS's simulated documentary (with actors impersonating witnesses as well as participants to the drama) in fact ventured much beyond the rights and wrongs of the incident to ask how it had happened. Along the way it threw up some sharp insights into life in present-day Islam. Cooped up in the royal palaces, according to Judy Parfitt as a German nanny, the women would watch imported video movies hour after hour. 'Mein Gott,' she said, to bring the full horror home, 'we must have seen *The Sound of Music* twelve times.'

ph Ivan Strasburg, Nick Knowland

Suzanne Abou Taleb   PP

The Death of Adolf Hitler (GB 1973; 80m; colour). Ambitious reconstruction by Vincent Tilsley, for LWT, of the last hours in the Bunker, partly based on eye-witness accounts, partly on imagination and a rather unconvincing notion that the Monster's last obsession would have been to make sure he alone was to be given credit for the extermination of the Jews. With Frank Finlay as Hitler, Caroline Mortimer as Eva Braun and particularly good impersonations of Josef and Magda Goebbels by Oscar Quitak and Marion Mathie.   PP

Death of an Expert Witness *

GB 1983 7 × 52m

Anglia (John Rosenberg)

First of a clutch of adaptations from the superior whodunits of P. D. James, with Roy Marsden mini-toupéed as dour detective Adam Dalgleish.   PP

w Robin Chapman *d* Herbert Wise

Barry Foster, Geoffrey Palmer, Ray Brooks, Andrew Ray

The others were:

Shroud for a Nightingale (1983)

Cover Her Face (1985)

w Robin Chapman *d* John Davies

John Vine, Phyllis Calvert, Bill Fraser, Mel Martin

The Black Tower (1985)

w William Humble *d* Ronald Wilson

Pauline Collins, Martin Jarvis, Maurice Denham, Rachel Kempson

Death of a Salesman

US 1985 142m colour TVM (tape)

CBS/Roxbury and Punch (Robert F. Colesberry)

An unsuccessful middle-aged salesman is the victim of his own delusions and the American Dream.

Disappointingly tepid version of a play which now seems encased within its period.

w Arthur Miller *d* Volker Schlondorff *ph* Michael Ballhaus *m* Alex North

Dustin Hoffman, Kate Reid, Stephen Lang, Charles Durning, Louis Zorich, David S. Chandler, John Malkovitch

A Death of Innocence *

US 1971 74m colour TVM

Mark Carliner

A small-town woman goes to New York for her daughter's murder trial.

Emotional character drama, well presented.

w Zelda Popkin, from her novel *d* Paul Wendkos *m* Morton Stevens

Shelley Winters, Arthur Kennedy, Tisha Sterling, Ann Sothern

The Death of Me Yet *

US 1971 74m colour TVM

Aaron Spelling

A Russian spy who has apparently defected to California turns out to have been a US agent all the time.

Confused but watchable suspense drama.

w A. J. Russell, *novel* Whit Masterson *d* John Llewellyn Moxey

Richard Basehart, Doug McClure, Darren McGavin, Rosemary Forsyth, Meg Foster

The Death of Richie
US 1977 96m colour TVM
NBC/Henry Jaffe (Michael Jaffe)

The tragic family repercussions of a teenager's drug addiction.

Another case history from real life. It would be nice to watch one about a teenager who *didn't* go off the rails.

w John McGreevey, *book* Thomas Thompson d Paul Wendkos m Fred Karlin

Ben Gazzara, Robby Benson, Eileen Brennan, Lance Kerwin

Death or Glory Boy * (GB 1974; 3 × 50m; colour). Autobiographical dramatization by Charles Wood of a young soldier's disillusionment with the regular army – a sort of spoken opera with long arias from a succession of prima donna NCOs followed by staccato duets consisting mainly of repeated phrases, but deadly accurate in catching the fine tones of class snobbery in post-war Britain. Produced by Peter Willes for YTV; with Christopher Blake.   PP

Death Race *
US 1973 74m colour TVM
Universal (Harve Bennett)

In the Libyan desert during World War II, two grounded US pilots are relentlessly pursued by a German tank commander.

Fairly gripping war action suspenser.

w Charles Kuenstle d David Lowell Rich

Lloyd Bridges, Roy Thinnes, Eric Braeden, Doug McClure, Brendan Boone

Death Ray 2000: see A Man Called Sloane

Death Scream *
US 1975 100m colour TVM
RSO (Ron Bernstein)

The case history of a woman who was fatally stabbed in view of neighbours who ignored her cries for help.

Dramatized documentary about an American malaise – the 'don't get involved' syndrome.

d Richard T. Heffron

Raul Julia, Cloris Leachman, John Ryan, Nancy Walker, Philip Clark, Lucie Arnaz, Art Carney, Diahann Carroll, Kate Jackson, Tina Louise

Death Sentence *
US 1974 74m colour TVM
Spelling–Goldberg

A woman juror who discovers the truth about a murder case is threatened by the real killer – her husband.

Good watchable suspenser.

w John Neufeld, *novel After the Trial* by Eric Roman d E. W. Swackhamer

Cloris Leachman, Laurence Luckinbill, Nick Nolte, Alan Oppenheimer, William Schallert

Death Squad *
US 1973 74m colour TVM
Spelling–Goldberg

The police commissioner hires a tough ex-cop as undercoverman to expose a renegade policeman.

Good gritty cop show.

w James David Buchanan, Ronald Austin d Harry Falk

Robert Forster, Melvyn Douglas, Michelle Phillips, Claude Akins

Death Stalk *
US 1974 80m colour TVM
David Wolper/Herman Rush (Richard Caffey)

Escaped convicts abduct the wives of two campers, and an overland chase ensues.

Good outdoor suspenser.

w Stephen Kandel, John W. Bloch d Robert Day

Vince Edwards, Anjanette Comer, Robert Webber, Carol Lynley

Death Takes a Holiday
US 1971 73m colour TVM
Universal (George Eckstein)

Death comes to earth in handsome form, and falls in love.

Curious, would-be fashionable, tricksily photographed and mainly flat-footed updating of a dated concept.

w Rita Lakin, *play* Alberto Cosella d Robert Butler

Melvyn Douglas, Myrna Loy, Monte Markham, Yvette Mimieux, Maureen Reagan

Death Valley Days *. A half-hour western series sponsored and owned by the makers of Twenty Mule Team Borax. It went through over 600 episodes from 1952, and before that was on radio for 20 years. Hosts have included Robert Taylor, Dale Robertson, Ronald Reagan, and Stanley Andrews ('The Old Ranger'). Aka: *Call of the West.* Production standards are generally poor.

The Debbie Reynolds Show
US 1969 26 × 25m colour
NBC/Filmways/Harmon (Jess Oppenheimer)

Adventures of a scatty suburban housewife.
The star seems to have thought of herself as a

second Lucille Ball, but the viewers had other ideas.

cr Jess Oppenheimer

Debbie Reynolds, Don Chastain, Tom Bosley, Patricia Smith

The Debussy Film ** (GB 1965; 65m). One of the better composer-lives directed by KEN RUSSELL, full of visual invention. Written by Russell and Melvyn Bragg; with Oliver Reed, Vladek Sheybal, Annette Robertson; for BBC.
PP: 'As a piece of musicology it may well be suspect. As a contribution to *Monitor*'s bread-and-butter task of reporting on the world of the arts it is irrelevant. As a television film in its own right, as a play if you like, as an entertainment, it explodes like an extravagant and unpredictable firework; I wouldn't have missed it for anything.'

The Decade of Destruction (GB 1984; 5 × 52m). Adrian Cowell goes back to the Brazilian rainforests (*The Tribe That Hides from Man*, 1970) for a massive analysis of the threat to the world's climate and natural stability if the trees continue to be felled and the land cleared. Directed by Adrian Cowell, produced by Roger James, for Central.   PP

December Bride *
US 1954–8 146 × 25m bw
CBS/Desilu
An elderly widow thinks of herself as eligible. Amusing comedy with pleasing characters.
Spring Byington, Frances Rafferty, Dean Miller, Verna Felton, Harry Morgan (as Pete)
† Pete's wife Gladys was never seen, but in the spin-off series *Pete and Gladys* she was played by Cara Williams.

December Flower (GB 1984). Damp-hankie epic in which Jean Simmons, as newly widowed heroine, seeks to befriend surly old Aunt (Mona Washbourne). Written by Judy Allen, directed by Stephen Frears, produced by Roy Roberts, for Granada. With Bryan Forbes, June Ritchie, Pat Heywood.   PP

Deceptions
US 1985 2 × 96m colour miniseries
NBC/Columbia/Consolidated/Louis
   Rudolph (William Hill)
Twin sisters decide to exchange lives. Hilariously over-the-top melodrama with plenty of murder and adultery.

w Melville Shavelson, *novel* by Judith Michael *d* Melville Shavelson, Robert Chenault *ph* Ernest Day *m* Nigel Hess *pd* John Blezard
Stefanie Powers, Barry Bostwick, Gina Lollobrigida, Brenda Vaccaro, Jeremy Brett, James Faulkner, Sam Wanamaker
'Garish, profane and contemptuous, it even gives miniseries a bad name.' – *Daily Variety*

Decision * (GB 1976; 3 × 78m; colour). Three films for Granada by the American-in-London master of observational TV, Roger Graef. He set cinematographer Charles Stewart's cameras running during long hours of deliberation as (1) the British Steel Corporation decides whether or not to go ahead with a new plant in Scotland, (2) Hammersmith borough council wrestles with the rates and (3) an oil company counts the cost of North Sea exploration. Edited down, the results reveal much about the chancy business of making corporate decisions.   PP

Decoy *
aka: *Police Woman Decoy*
US 1957 39 × 25m bw
Pyramid
Adventures of an undercover police woman. A smart suspense series of its time with an attractive lead.

Beverly Garland

Dee, Simon (1935–) (Nicholas Henty-Dodd). British disc-jockey who had insubstantial television career in the late sixties, appearing on pop music shows and gladhanding the 1967 Miss World contest. His own chat show *Dee Time* began from Manchester studios, later moved to London and a prime Saturday spot, but suddenly ran out of favour. Further fling with LWT 1970–71.   PP

The Deerslayer
US 1978 74m colour TVM
NBC/Sunn Classics (Bill Conford)
Puerile version for the Classics Illustrated series of Fenimore Cooper's celebrated novel about Hawkeye and Chingachgook rescuing a chief's daughter from her enemies. Production elements all equally poor.

w S. S. Schweizer *w* Dick Friedenberg *ph* Paul Hipp *m* Bob Summers and Andrew Belling
Steve Forrest, Ned Romero, John Anderson, Charles Dierkop

The Defection of Simas Kudirka *
US 1977 96m colour TVM
Paramount/Jozak (Gerald I. Eisenburg,
  Gerald W. Abrams)

A Lithuanian radio operator on a Soviet
fishing vessel leaps hopefully to freedom in a
Massachusetts harbour.
Arresting, sober docu-drama from a true
incident.

w Bruce Feldman d David Lowell Rich
(Emmy award) ph Jacques Marquette m
David Shire

Alan Arkin, Richard Jordan, Shirley Knight,
Donald Pleasence, John McMartin, George
Dzundza

The Defenders ***
US 1961–4 132 × 50m bw
CBS/Plautus/Herb Brodkin (Robert
  Markell)

Cases of a father–son lawyer team.
Superior courtroom drama, usually with
serious issues at stake. A milestone in TV
series.

cr Reginald Rose

E. G. MARSHALL, ROBERT REED

† The pilot film, *The Defender*, was seen on
Studio One in 1957. It starred Ralph Bellamy
and William Shatner, with Steve McQueen as
their client.

definition. The sharpness of a picture on the
TV screen.

Dehner, John (1915–   ) (John Forkum).
American character actor with a tendency to
sharp comedy. TV series include *The Baileys
of Balboa*, *The Doris Day Show*, *Big Hawaii*,
Enos. TV movies include *Winchester 73*,
Something for a Lonely Man, *Quarantined*,
Honky Tonk, *The Big Ripoff*, *Missiles of
October*, *Young Maverick*.

Delancey Street: The Crisis Within
US 1975 74m colour TVM
Paramount (Emmet Lavery Jnr)

A dramatized account of a San Francisco
hostel for people in trouble.
Glum do-goodery which dramatically just
doesn't take off despite obvious earnestness
all round.

w Robert Foster d James Frawley

Walter McGinn, Carmine Caridi, Lou
Gossett, Michael Conrad, Mark Hamill

Delaney, Frank (1942–   ). Irish presenter,
into British television via BBC Radio book
programmes, and one of the more bearable
members of the Irish invasion. Own
chat-type series (6 × 45m) for BBC 1982. PP

Delderfield, R. F. (1912–72). British
playwright (*Worm's Eye View*, *Mayerling*) and
novelist whose big three-deckers enjoyed a
vogue as television serials in the late
seventies and early eighties. *The Avenue* and
A Horseman Riding By (1978); *To Serve
Them All My Days* (1980), *Diana* (1984). PP

Deliver Us from Evil *
US 1973 74m colour TVM
Warner/Playboy

Five men recover a fortune from a skyjacker
and fight their own greed and each other.
Smartly made open-air fable with predictable
outcome.

w Jack Sowards d Boris Sagal

George Kennedy, Jan-Michael Vincent,
Bradford Dillman, Jack Weston, Charles
Aidman

The Delivery Man * (GB 1967; 30m; bw).
Impressive directorial debut by film editor
Jim Clark with a heartening study for
Granada of a breezy obstetrician at a
Sheffield hospital, the sort who would safely
bring half a dozen babies into the world and
then shoot off for a game of rugger and a
piss-up afterwards. Though the doctor and his
patients were 'real', Clark interestingly made
use of actors to fill in some supporting roles.
Part of the *This England* series, produced by
Norman Swallow and Denis Mitchell.   PP

Della
US 1964 66m colour TVM
Four Star

An attorney visits a small town to negotiate
land purchase with a wealthy lady recluse.
Peyton Place-style pilot for a projected series
called *Royal Bay*, which didn't materialize.

d Robert Gist

Joan Crawford, Diane Baker, Paul Burke,
Charles Bickford, Richard Carlson

The Delphi Bureau
US 1972 99m colour TVM
ABC/Warner

An agency of gifted people with total recall is
responsible only to the President.
Ingenuous spy capers with the usual high
gloss and nonsense plot. This pilot led to a
series of eight one-hours, which was not a
success.

w Sam Rolfe d Paul Wendkos

Laurence Luckinbill, Joanna Pettet, Celeste
Holm, Bob Crane, Cameron Mitchell,
Bradford Dillman, Dean Jagger

† The series played as a rotating element of
The Men.

Delta County USA
US 1977 96m colour TVM
ABC/Paramount/Leonard Goldberg

Problems of young people in a southern city. *Peyton Place* all over again, not badly done.

w Thomas Rickman *d* Glen Jordan *m* Jack Elliott, Allyn Ferguson

Jim Antonio, Jeff Conaway, Joanna Miles, Peter Donat, Lola Albright, Robert Hayes, Ed Power

Delvecchio
US 1976 22 × 50m colour
NBC/Universal (William Sackheim, Lane Slate)

Stories of a tough cop with underworld connections.
Disappointing cop show headlining a new star who wasn't.

cr Sam Rolfe, Joseph Polizzi

Judd Hirsch, Charles Haid, Michael Conrad

Demarest, William (1892–1984). Veteran American comedy character actor with long vaudeville and film career. TV series: *Tales of Wells Fargo*, *Love and Marriage*, *My Three Sons*. TV movies: *Don't Be Afraid of the Dark*, *The Millionaire*.

demographics. The science of knowing what proportion of the total audience watches a given show and whether it appeals to certain age, sex and class groups.

The Demon Murder Case
US 1983 96m colour TVM
NBC/Dick Clark Productions

An ordinary young man about to be married is possessed by a pack of demons and turns to murder.
Confused rip-off of *The Exorcist*; plenty going on, but in the end not much to remember.

w William Kelley *d* Billy Hale *ph* John Lindley *m* George Allison Tipton

Kevin Bacon, Lione Landland, Charlie Fields, Joyce Van Patten, Andy Griffith, Cloris Leachman, Eddie Albert, Richard Masur

Dempsey
US 1983 142m colour TVM
CBS/Charles Fries (Jay Benson)

Episodes in the life of the famous American prizefighter.

Dempsey and Makepeace
GB 1985 1 × 75m, 20 × 50m
LWT (Tony Wharmby)

Shameful crime and/or security fantasy, teaming high-born English policewoman with – or against – thuggish New York cop on reluctant attachment to London. Hard to say which is the more offensive, the needling one to the other in the setting up of each episode or the clumsy violence which unites them by the end. The worst crime of all is the abuse of Glynis Barber, the delightful Jane in Mervyn Haisman's *Jane* cartoons, as Makepeace. Michael Brandon is Dempsey. Ray Smith ruthlessly masterminds their exploits.

cr Tony Wharmby *w* and *d* Various   PP

Dench, Judi (1934–). Jolly determined British actress who has done wonderful things on television, notably a *Z-Cars* appearance in a John Hopkins script which led to the *Talking to a Stranger* quartet (1966); the CBS *Midsummer Night's Dream* (1967); couple of other Shakespeares, Morecambe and Wise, *On Giant's Shoulders* (the dramatization of the story of Terry Wiles, thalidomide child, 1979), *Langrishe Go Down* (1980), *A Fine Romance* (1981), *Saigon – Year of the Cat* (1983).   PP

Denis, Armand (1897–1971) **and Michaela** (*c* 1920–). Television's first wild-life travellers (flourishing throughout the fifties) were a husband and wife who took it in turns to furnish the commentary in heavy French accents. She was blonde and mugged the camera, he twinkled. Together they made a double act much appreciated by mimics of the day.   PP

Denison, Michael (1915–). Plummy British actor who after a long career in the theatre and cinema became a TV star as *Boyd QC* in the fifties and again as Captain Percival in *Blood Money* and subsequent thrillers in the eighties.   PP

Denmark has had television from 1947, and the state now allows 50 hours per week on one channel (though Danes enjoy many other transmissions from neighbouring countries). About half these hours are filled by imported programmes.

Dennehy, Brian (1940–). Bulky American character actor. TV series: BIG SHAMUS LITTLE SHAMUS. TV movies: *Johnny We Hardly Knew Ye*, *It Happened at Lakewood Manor*, *Ruby and Oswald*, *A Death in Canaan*, *A Real American Hero*, *Pearl*, *A Rumor of War*, *Silent Victory*, *The Jericho Mile*, *Dummy*, *The Seduction of Miss Leona*, *Fly Away Home*.

DEMPSEY AND MAKEPEACE. Not Wilhelmina Tell, but Glynis Barber as one half of London Weekend's crime-solving duo, which bothered the critics because it was so obviously patterned after American models. Authority was concerned by the violence; the *Sun*-reading public wasn't bothered at all.

Denning, Richard (1914–) (Louis A. Denninger). Light American leading man of the forties; in TV played *Mr and Mrs North*, *The Flying Doctor* and *Michael Shayne* and later appeared occasionally in *90 Bristol Court* and as the governor in *Hawaii Five-O*.

Dennis, Les (*c.* 1952–). Light-charactered British comedy star who rapidly soared to fame as partner of the late Dustin Gee.

The Dennis O'Keefe Show
US 1959 39 × 25m bw
CBS

Tribulations of a widowed columnist and his young son.
Forgettable sentimental comedy series.
Dennis O'Keefe, Ricky Kelman, Hope Emerson

Dennis the Menace *
GB title: *Just Dennis*
US 1959–63 146 × 25m bw
CBS/Columbia/Darriel

Adventures of a mischievous small boy in a toney suburb.
The American answer to William, from Hank Ketcham's comic strip. A generally amusing series, notable for young Dennis's uneasy relationship with the next-door neighbour, Mr Wilson.
JAY NORTH, JOSEPH KEARNS, Gale Gordon, Herbert Anderson, Gloria Henry

Denton, Charles (1937–). British producer and executive, formerly head of features for ATV and programme controller for its successor, Central. Now in charge of Central's film-making outfit, Zenith.

Denver, Bob (1935–   ). Eccentric American comedy actor whose style is a cross between Stan Laurel and Jerry Lewis. TV series: *Dobie Gillis, Gilligan's Island, The Good Guys, Dusty's Trail.*

Denver, John (1943–   ) (Henry John Deutschendorf Jnr). American country and western singer; many TV specials and occasional films.

Department S
GB 1970 28 × 50m colour
ATV
Specialists investigate major international crimes for the government.
The British *Mission Impossible*, just about watchable.
Peter Wyngarde, Joel Fabiani, Rosemary Nichols

The Deputies
aka: *Law of the Land*
US 1976 98m colour TVM
Quinn Martin
Three young deputies and their elderly boss solve murders of local prostitutes.
Downbeat western detection, very dark, very slow and very boring. A failed pilot.
w John Wilder, Sam Rolfe *d* Virgil Vogel *ph* William Spencer *m* John Parker
Jim Brown, Barbara Parkins, Moses Gunn, Andrew Prine, Nicholas Hammond, Don Johnson, Glenn Corbett

The Deputy *
US 1959–60 76 × 25m bw
NBC/Top Gun
In the 1880s, a western marshal takes a reluctant deputy.
Modestly pleasing western series notable for Henry Fonda's comparatively few appearances as the marshal.
Henry Fonda, Allen Case

Deputy Dawg
US 1960 104 × 25m colour
CBS/Terrytoons
A simple-minded sheriff maintains law and order in the old west.
Amusing canine cartoons (four to the half-hour).
voice Dayton Allan

Derbyshire, Eileen (*c.* 1931–   ). British character actress, for twenty years one of the props of *Coronation Street* as a longtime old maid who eventually married but soon became a widow.

Design Matters (GB 1985; 10 × 30m). Nicely critical series on everyday design as it affects everyday surroundings, e.g. the concrete wastes of the South Bank. Produced and directed by Charles Mapleston, for Malachite/C4.   PP

Desilu. The studio formed in the early fifties by Desi Arnaz and Lucille Ball; later absorbed by Paramount.

Desilu Playhouse *
US 1958–9 54 × 50m bw
CBS/Desilu
Generally pleasing anthology drama series with top stars; hosted by Desi Arnaz.
Here are the episodes:
Bernadette. The story of Bernadette of Lourdes (*w* Ludi Claire; *d* Ralph Alswang, Claudio Guzman; with Pier Angeli)
The Case for Dr Mudd. The story of the man who helped Lincoln's assassin (*w* Don Brinkley; with Lew Ayres)
My Father the Fool. Cases of a Puerto Rican lawyer (*w* Adrian Spies; *d* Jerry Thorpe; with Eli Wallach, J. Carrol Naish)
Debut. A ballerina is torn between love and a career (*w* Paul Monash; *d* Arthur Hiller; with Susan Strasberg)
The Time Element. A man has a premonition of the Pearl Harbor attack (*w* Rod Serling; *d* Allen Reisner; with William Bendix)
The Night the Phone Rang. A man is forced to act as executioner for a crime syndicate (*w* Aaron Spelling; *d* Allen Miner; with Eddie Albert)
Silent Thunder. An American Indian seeks dignity in a white community (*w* James Edwards, John McGreevey; *d* Ted Post; with John Drew Barrymore, Earl Holliman)
KO Kitty. A dance teacher inherits a prizefighter (*w* Madelyn Martin, Bob Carroll Jnr; *d* Jerry Thorpe; with Lucille Ball, Aldo Ray, William Lundigan)
Crazy Hunter. A girl trains a blind horse (*w* Walter Newman; *d* Jerry Thorpe; with Franchot Tone, Jo Van Fleet)
Ballad for a Bad Man. Touring actors in the old west (*w* Bob Barash; *d* Jerry Hopper; with Jane Russell, Steve Forrest, Mischa Auer, Jack Haley)
Comeback. A has-been ballplayer revivifies a Little League team (*w* Stanley Niss; *d* Arthur Lubin; with Dan Duryea, William Frawley)
Happy Hill. Enemies of an escaped convict enlist the unwitting aid of his wife (*w* Barney Slater; *d* Robert Sinclair; with Claire Trevor, Royal Dano)

Chez Rouge. The proprietress of a Panama bistro is needled by her ex-husband (*w* Adrian Spies; *d* Allen Reisner; with Janis Paige, Harry Guardino, Ray Danton)

Trial at Devil's Canyon. A tough sheriff defies the army and the citizens (*w* Lowell Barrington; *d* Claudio Guzman; with Lee J. Cobb, Skip Homeier)

Symbol of Authority. A timid proof reader poses as a doctor (*w* Ernest Kinoy; *d* Robert Sinclair; with Ernie Kovacs, Jean Hagen)

Martin's Folly. A backyard shipwright has dreams of glory (*w* Calvin J. Clements; *d* Robert Ellis Miller; with Tony Randall, Maggie Mahoney, Carl Reiner)

Perilous. A lady spy falls for one of the enemy (*w* William Templeton; *d* Jerry Thorpe; with Joan Fontaine, Maximilian Schell)

Chain of Command. An army officer takes over his first unit (*w* Joseph Landon; *d* Jerry Thorpe; with Hugh O'Brian, Martin Milner)

A Diamond for Carla. Romance on a remote Caribbean island (*w* Sonya Roberts; *d* Claudio Guzman; with Anna Maria Alberghetti, Johnny Desmond)

Innocent Assassin. An IRA man in 1921 has to kill an informer (with James MacArthur, Piper Laurie)

The Hard Road. A bounty hunter finds himself on the run (*w* Douglas Heyes, Roy Erwin; *d* Douglas Heyes; with Barry Sullivan, Cliff Robertson)

Man in Orbit. The first astronaut is unofficially launched into space (*w* Joseph Landon; *d* Claudio Guzman, Dann Cahn; with Lee Marvin, E. G. Marshall, Martin Balsam)

Killer Instinct. A prizefighter's protégé becomes his enemy (*w* Joseph Landon; with Rory Calhoun)

So Tender, So Profane. A Cuban finds it hard to accept his sister's wayward past (*w* Adrian Spies; *d* Jerry Thorpe; with Desi Arnaz, Pedro Armendariz, Barbara Luna, Margo)

Two Counts of Murder. A political boss protects his grandson (*w* Henry Kenker; *d* Robert Ellis Miller; with Raymond Massey, David Janssen)

Come Back to Sorrento. An Italian immigrant girl finds love in Brooklyn (*d* James Sheldon; with Marisa Pavan, Robert Loggia)

The Day the Town Stood Up. An itinerant philosopher challenges an arrogant bandit (*w* Allen H. Miner, Lowell Barrington; *d* Allen H. Miner; with Joseph Cotten, Virginia Grey, James Gregory, Clu Gulager)

Border Justice. A Mexican law officer challenges a cattle baron (*w* Lowell Barrington, Albert Ruben; *d* Claudio Guzman; with Gilbert Roland, Bruce Gordon)

Six Guns for Donegan. An ageing sheriff risks death to protect the town weakling (*w* John Mantley; *d* Douglas Heyes; with Lloyd Nolan, Harry Townes, Jean Hagen, James Franciscus)

Meeting at Apalachin. A detective unmasks the head of a crime syndicate (*w* Adrian Spies; *d* Joseph M. Newman; with Jack Warden, Cara Williams, Luther Adler)

Lepke. The downfall of the chief of Murder Inc (*w* Adrian Spies; *d* Jerry Thorpe; with Walter Winchell, Lloyd Bridges, Joseph Wiseman, Sam Jaffe)

Murder in Gratitude. A doctor unmasks his brother's killer (*w* William P. Templeton; *d* Jerry Thorpe; with Trevor Howard, Robert Coote, Michael Pate)

The Hanging Judge. A judge launches a personal vendetta against evil (*d* Buzz Kulik; with James Whitmore, Jean Hagen, Buddy Ebsen)

Thunder in the Night. The operator of a North African casino becomes involved with fake passports (*w/d* Sheldon Reynolds – with a presumed nod to *Casablanca*; with Desi Arnaz, Akim Tamiroff, George Macready, Rod Taylor)

The Desilu Revue. Variety show with young talent (*w* Bob Schiller, Bob Weiskopf; *d* Claudio Guzman; with Lucille Ball, Desi Arnaz, Vivian Vance, William Frawley)

Night Panic. A girl is driven to hysteria by anonymous phone calls (*w* A. A. Roberts; *d* Richard Kinon; with John Ericson, Cloris Leachman)

Cry Ruin. The son of a politician turns to violence (*w* John Kneubuhl, John Mantley; *d* Paul Stanley; with Keir Dullea, Larry Gates, Richard Anderson)

The Problem in Cell 13. A scientist takes a bet that he can escape from a maximum security prison (*w* A. A. Roberts; *d* Richard Kinon; with Claude Dauphin, Everett Sloane)

Change of Heart. A blind criminologist solves a murder (*w* David J. Goodman; *d* Richard Kinon; with Robert Middleton, Dick Sargent)

The Sound of Murder. A student's future is threatened by blackmail (*w* William Templeton; *d* Robert Altman; with Alex Davion, Liam Redmond)

Circle of Evil. A private eye proves his client's guilt (*w* Robert Blees; *d* Jerry Thorpe; with Hugh O'Brian, Felicia Farr)

The Man in the Funny Suit. An old comedian tries to make a comeback (*w/d* Ralph Nelson; with Ed Wynn, Keenan Wynn, Red Skelton, Rod Serling)

City in Bondage. A district attorney exposes a much-loved policeman (*w* Adrian Spies; *d* Claudio Guzman; with Barry Sullivan, Ed Begley)

Murder Is a Private Affair. A wealthy retired gambler helps a frightened heiress (*d* Earl Bellamy; with Dina Merrill, David Brian, Adam West)

In Close Pursuit. A society woman turns to murder when her husband is unfaithful (with Jan Sterling, William Windom, Beverly Garland)

Death of a Dream. A woman finds that her husband is a thief (*w* Paul Savage; *d* Robert Altman; with Dianne Foster, Robert Vaughn)

Dead on Nine. A husband and wife, tired of each other, both decide on murder as a way out (*w* William Templeton, *play* Jack Popplewell; *d* William Claxton; with Louis Hayward, Signe Hasso, Maxwell Reed)

Desmond, Lorrae (1931–). All-Australian soap opera diva (Shirley in *A Country Practice*) whose brief career in British television in the fifties is perhaps just as well forgotten. She sang and smiled onto various light entertainments and co-starred with Jacqueline Mackenzie in a doomed but unusual sitcom *Trouble for Two*.   PP

'At Hamilton High, the kids get stoned, the pusher gets rich – and young lives get destroyed!'

Desperate Lives
US 1982 96m colour TVM
CBS/Lorimar (Lew Hunter)

A high-school counsellor combats the widespread use of drugs among teenagers. Ho-hum social-purpose drama with no surprises whatever.

w Lew Hunter *d* Robert Junter
Diana Scarwid, Helen Hunt, William Windom, Michelle Green, Doug McKeon

The Desperate Miles *
US 1975 74m colour TVM
Universal/Joel Rogosin

To prove his independence, a disabled war veteran undertakes a 130-mile road trip by wheelchair.

Impressive or foolish according to one's point of view: well enough put together and acted.

w Joel Rogosin, Arthur Ross *d* Daniel Haller
Tony Musante, Joanna Pettet, Jeanette Nolan, Lynn Loring, John Larch

Desperate Mission
US 1971 98m colour TVM
TCF/Ricardo Montalban

Episodes in the career of Joaquin Murieta. Moderate western fare fictionalized from the exploits of a real-life outlaw.

w Jack Guss *d* Earl Bellamy *ph* Jorge Stahl Jnr *m* Robert F. Drasnin
Ricardo Montalban, Slim Pickens, Earl Holliman, Ina Balin, Rosie Greer

Desperate Voyage
US 1981 96m colour TVM
CBS/Barry Weitz/Joe Wizan

A modern privateer terrorizes the Gulf of Mexico. Quite a solemn thriller with an absurd premise, pleasantly filmed around Catalina Island.

w Alvin Sapinsley, *novel Last Voyage of the Valhalla* by Ray Kyrtle *d* Michael O'Herlihy *ph* John C. Flinn III *m* Bruce Broughton
Christopher Plummer, Jonathan Banks, Cliff Potts, Christine Belford, Lara Parker, Nicholas Pryor

'Tense enough to make waves.' – *Daily Variety*

Desperate Women
US 1978 96m colour TVM
NBC/Lorimar (Robert Stambler)

In the old west, a wanderer releases three women convicts and finds himself in plenty of trouble. Desultory outdoor melodrama with moments of interest; would have made a good hour.

w Jack B. Sowards *d* Earl Bellamy *ph* Jorge Stahl *m* Dick de Benedictis
Susan Saint James, Dan Haggerty, Ronee Blakely, Ann Dusenberry, Randy Powell, Susan Myers, John Crawford

Destination America **
GB 1976 6 × 50m colour
Thames

A rather overpowering but monumental series of documentaries covering the various ethnic groups who fled from Europe to make modern America.

Destiny of a Spy
GB 1969 99m colour TVM
NBC/Universal

Spies on opposite sides fall in love.
Competent, forgettable, drawn-out espionage melodrama.

w Stanford Whitmore, *novel* John Blackburn *d* Boris Sagal

Lorne Greene, Harry Andrews, Anthony Quayle, Rachel Roberts, Patrick Magee, James Donald

Destry
US 1964 13 × 50m bw
ABC/Universal

The new young sheriff of Bottleneck doesn't wear guns.
Thin imitation of the famous films.

John Gavin, Mari Blanchard

The Detective *
GB 1985 3 × 50m
BBC (Sally Head)

As with Sainsbury's austerely named own packagings, the plain title concealed excellence – a dense, complex story of ramrod-straight Metropolitan police commander up against corruption in high places, with loyalties strained to breaking point and a fairly won surprise denouement.

w Ted Whitehead, *novel* by Paul Ferris *d* Don Leaver

Tom Bell, Mark Eden, Vivienne Ritchie, Terence Rigby   PP

Detective in the House
US 1985   × 50m colour
CBS/Lorimar (William L. Young)

A much-married engineer gives his life a change of direction by setting up as a detective.
Muddled mixture of domestic comedy and mystery: not on.

cr Judy Merl, Paul Eric Myers *d* Bill Bixby (pilot)

Judd Hirsch, Cassie Yates, Jack Elam, Connie Stevens

'A mix of *Father Knows Best* and the private eye genre, it offers the worst elements of each.' – *Daily Variety*

The Detectives *
US 1959–60 67 × 25m bw
US 1961 30 × 50m bw
ABC/Four Star

Captain Matt Holbrook gets his villains.
Clean, competent cop show.

Robert Taylor, Ursula Thiess (in half-hours), Tige Andrews, Adam West, Mark Goddard

Detour to Nowhere *
aka: *Banacek*
US 1971 98m colour TVM
Universal (George Eckstein)

A wealthy Polish Bostonian collects lost and valuable property for insurance companies . . . at a ten per cent finder's fee.
Overlong but fairly ingenious pilot about a gold heist in the desert with no getaway tracks. The subsequent series, *Banacek*, made a rather boring addition to *Mystery Movie*.

w Anthony Wilson *d* Jack Smight

George Peppard, Christine Belford, Ed Nelson

'They head for Vegas to gamble, but the game becomes survival!'
Detour to Terror
US 1980 96m colour TVM
NBC/Columbia/Playboy (Don Mark)

Kidnappers force a tour bus into the desert and put the lives of passengers in jeopardy.
Competent if predictable action thriller with some exciting chases by dune buggy.

w Sydney A. Glass, Mark Dodgers *d* Michael O'Herlihy *ph* John M. Nickolaus *m* Morton Stevens

O. J. Simpson, Anne Francis, Randall Carver, Richard Hill, Arte Johnson, Lorenzo Lamas, Kathryn Holcomb

Devane, William (1937–). American leading actor, on TV in *From Here to Eternity* (mini-series and series). TV movies: *Missiles of October*, *Fear on Trial*, *Crime Club*, *The Bait*, *Red Alert*, *Black Beauty*, *The Other Victim*.

Devenish
GB 1977–8 13 × 25m colour (VTR)
Granada (John G. Temple)

The other executives in a toy factory despise an irritating busybody.
Wholly unsympathetic comedy which doesn't begin to be funny despite a good cast.

w/cr Anthony Couch *d* Brian Mills

Dinsdale Landen, Terence Alexander, Geoffrey Bayldon, Geoffrey Chater, Veronica Roberts

The Devil and Miss Sarah *
US 1971 73m colour TVM
Universal (Stan Shpetner)

A man captures an outlaw and brings him to justice, but the outlaw – who may be the devil – turns the mind of the wife his way.
Oddball western semi-fantasy which drags more often than it sparkles.

w Calvin Clements *d* Michael Caffey

Gene Barry, James Drury, Janice Rule, Charles McGraw, Slim Pickens

Devil Dog, Hound of Hell
US 1979 96m colour TVM
CBS/Zeitman–Landers–Roberts (Lou Morheim)

The family pet of a well-bred suburbanite grows into a monster which spreads evil. Silly horror comic without the laughs that might have made it palatable.

w Stephan and Elinor Karpf *d* Curtis Harrington *ph* Jerry Finnerman *m* Charles Knight

Richard Crenna, Yvette Mimieux, Kim Richards, Ike Eisenmann, Victor Jory

'The suspense is contrived, stuck on a premise about as legitimate as a seven-dollar bill.' – *Daily Variety*

The Devil's Crown ***
GB 1978 13 × 50m colour (VTR)
BBC (Richard Beynon)

The history of the Plantagenets.
A strikingly written and played version in the modern vernacular, with deliberately artificial medieval-style sets.

w Ken Taylor *d* Alan Cooke *m* David Cain
BRIAN COX, Jane Lapotaire, Christopher Gable

The Devil's Daughter *
US 1972 74m colour TVM
Paramount (Edward J. Mikis)

When a girl turns 21, she finds that her dead mother had sold her soul to the devil. Moderately creepy black magic mumbo jumbo sparked by its star performance.

w Colin Higgins *d* Jeannot Szwarc *ph* J. J. Jones *m* Laurence Rosenthal

SHELLEY WINTERS, Robert Foxworth, Belinda Montgomery, Joseph Cotten, Jonathan Frid, Martha Scott, Diane Ladd

The Devil's Lieutenant (GB/West Germany 1984; 2 × 115m). Jack Rosenthal in unsmiling mood for once as he dramatizes Maria Fagyas's seamy murder mystery set among the officer corps in imperial Austro-Hungary. With Helmut Griem, Ian Charleson, Renée Goddard, directed by John Goldschmidt, produced by Bavaria Atelier, for C4.   PP

Devine, Andy (1905–77). Husky-voiced American comedy character actor, the fat sidekick in many a western. TV series: *Wild Bill Hickok* (as Jingles). TV movies: *The Over the Hill Gang*, *The Over the Hill Gang Rides Again*.

The Devlin Connection
US 1983   × 50m colour
NBC/Viacom/Mammoth Films/Jerry Thorpe (Cliff Gould)

The managing director of a cultural centre was once a CIA agent, and when a son he never knew about turns up out of the blue they join forces to solve mysteries.
Muddled series with a star ill-at-ease and a creator who hasn't decided what level to play for.

cr John Wilder

Rock Hudson, Jack Scalia, Jack Kruschen, Leigh Taylor Young

Devlins (US 1975; 16 × 22m). Bland cartoon series about three orphans who become a motor cycle stunt team. From Hanna–Barbera.

Dewhurst, Colleen (1926–). American character actress, in all media. TV movies include *The Story of Jacob and Joseph*, *Silent Victory*, *Studs Lonigan*, *And Baby Makes Six*, *Mary and Joseph*, *Death Penalty*, *Escape*, *Guyana Tragedy*, *The Women's Room*, *A Perfect Match*, *Baby Comes Home*.

Dhondy, Farrukh (1944–). Indian writer, in Britain since 1964, who graduated from ethnic-minority programmes to network series with *No Problem* (1982–3). Since then, seasons of short plays for BBC and a sitcom about rival Indian restaurants, *Tandoori Nights*. Now a commissioning editor at C4.
                                                            PP

Diagnosis Unknown
US 1960 39 × 25m bw
CBS

Cases of a New York pathologist.
Adequate medical mystery series.

Patrick O'Neal, Phyllis Newman, Cal Bellini, Chester Morris

Dial Hot Line
US 1970 98m colour TVM
Universal (William Sackheim)

A psychiatric social worker starts a clinic for those in desperate mental straits.
Ho-hum do-gooder which sparked a very short series, *Matt Lincoln*.

w Carol Sobieski *d* Jerry Thorpe

Vince Edwards, Chelsea Brown, Kim Hunter, June Harding

Dial M for Murder
US 1981 96m colour TVM
NBC/Time-Life/Freya Rothstein (Peter Katz)

Mike and Betty.
Just an average American couple.
They have a house, a car,
two kids, and one lovable dog—
possessed by the Devil.

DEVIL DOG:
HOUND OF HELL

(A Halloween Howler)
STARRING RICHARD CRENNA
AND YVETTE MIMIEUX

THE CBS TUESDAY NIGHT MOVIES
9PM CBS◉2

DEVIL DOG: HOUND OF HELL.   What can one say about something which is clearly supposed to be a Hollywood joke, but turns out not to be funny? Send the people who made it to see *Bride of Frankenstein*, that's what.

A financially embarrassed tennis player's attempt to murder his wife goes awry.
When Hitchcock filmed this, he did so with discretion but veered little from the original script, so there seems little point in a TV film which takes the same attitude.
w John Gay,   *play* by Frederick Knott
d Boris Sagal   *ph* Michael Hugo   *m* Billy Goldenberg
Angie Dickinson, Christopher Plummer, Ron Moody, Michael Parks, ANTHONY QUAYLE

Dial 999
GB 1958 39 × 25m bw
Stories of Scotland Yard.
Good elementary police thrillers.
Robert Beatty

Diamond, Neil (1941–). American rock singer, in TV concert appearances.

Diamond, Tessa (19 –). British writer who devised commercial television's first successful soap, *Emergency – Ward 10*, and wrote many episodes; after which a long silence until she re-surfaced in the eighties as a writer on *Smiffs* and creator of *Gems* (1985).   PP

Diamonds
GB 1981 13 × 50m colour (VTR)
ATV (David Reid)
Boardroom intrigues in the family diamond firm of Coleman and Son.
Disappointing soap opera on the *Dallas* model; it simply doesn't have star quality.
w John Brason *d* John Cooper
John Stride, Hildegarde Neil, Norman Wooland, Doris Hare, Simon Ward, Ian McCullouch, Mark Kingston

Diamonds in the Sky * (GB 1980). Seven one-hour BBC documentaries in which Julian Pettifer examines the impact of civil aviation on our lives and our world, a world in which 600 million people travel by air each year. Executive producer: Richard Cawston.

Diana
US 1973 13 × 25m colour
NBC/Talent Associates
A British divorcee finds her way in New York.
Disappointingly ordinary star comedy.
Diana Rigg, Richard B. Shull, David Sheiner, Barbara Barrie
'One marvels at American TV's capacity to reduce even the best to its level.' – Jack Edmund Nolan

Diana (GB 1983; 10 × 55m). Another mid-brow saga from R. F. Delderfield turned into a mid-brow family serial, this one a love story with World War II cloak-and-daggery intervening. With Kevin McNally, Jenny Seagrove; written by Andrew Davies, directed by David Tucker, produced by Ken Riddington, for BBC.   PP

Diary of a Maasai Village * (GB 1984 5 × 45m). For those patient enough to follow them, Melissa Llewellyn-Davies's films of daily life among Maasai tribesmen grew into a real soap opera, with the young warriors getting into trouble, much deliberation over the sale of cattle and the arrival of a new little Maasai. 'The ethnic film to out-eth all others,' I noted. For BBC.   PP

Diary of a Nobody. George and Weedon Grossmith's little classic of late Victorian humour came to the screen in a rather plodding BBC serialization, 1980, and a

potted but very funny Ken Russell version for the BBC2 *Six* anthology of 1964, accommodating in 43 minutes nearly all the famous accidents, aspirations and deflations. Brian Pringle was Mr Pooter.   PP

Diary of a Teenage Hitchhiker
US 1979 96m colour TVM
ABC/Stan Shpetner
A town where teenagers beg lifts from strangers is asking for trouble.
Feeble excuse for a movie; it turns into a standard girl-in-jeopardy routine.
w Robert Malcolm Young *d* Ted Post
ph Hector Figueroa
Charlene Tilton, Katherine Helmond, Dick Van Patten, James Carroll Jordan

Diary of a Village (GB 1976; 8 × 30m). Loving series of films of life in a Wiltshire village from the BBC's fly-on-the-wall department headed by Roger Mills, though hard on the heels of similar exercises by Granada (*Goostrey: A Village*) and Jonathan Stedall (*Away in a Village*, three parts) it couldn't help seeming a case of the mills of Rog grinding fine but grinding exceeding slow. Produced by Mark Anderson.   PP

Diary of a Young Man (GB 1964; 6 × 45m). Troy Kennedy Martin had earlier in the year published a long manifesto deploring the prevailing naturalism of television drama and urging a more direct style of storytelling. *Diary*, written with John McGrath for BBC and directed by John McGlashan, was intended to demonstrate the possibilities. Its account of two young Northerners seeking fame, fortune and girl-friends in the 'Swinging London' of the day made copious use of a voice-over commentary and riffles of still pictures but also revealed a wilful naïvety. The view of capital and labour was child-eyed, to say the least, while Victor Henry's narration wearily syllabized every word and stressed every 'the' and 'a'. Ironically, Martin and McGrath had done much more to realize their aims, perhaps without noticing it, when they set the style of *Z Cars* two years earlier, and taught the viewing public painlessly to follow a story without needing every dot to be joined up. PP

'Every time I hear a creak in the house or a step on the street outside, I'm sure they're coming for us!'

The Diary of Anne Frank
US 1980 96m colour TVM
NBC/TCF/Half Pint–Katz–Gallin (Raymond Katz)

When the Nazis invade Amsterdam, a Jewish family hides in an attic for two years. With the George Stevens movie still very much around, there seems very little point in making this inferior version from virtually the same script. The effect is claustrophobic without being inspiring.

w Frances Goodrich, Albert Hackett, from their play d Boris Sagal ph Ted Voigtlander m Billy Goldenberg

Melissa Gilbert, Maximilian Schell, Joan Plowright, James Coco, Scott Jacoby, Clive Revill, Melora Marshall, Doris Roberts, Erik Holland, Anne Wyndham

Dick and the Duchess (GB 1957). Half-hour comedy series starring Patrick O'Neal and Hazel Court, as an American insurance investigator in London and his noble wife.

The Dick Powell Show (US 1961-2). aka: *Dick Powell Theatre*
One-hour anthology for NBC, hosted and produced by Dick Powell for his company Four Star and NBC. Not only was a high standard of drama and production maintained, but several pilots were featured including those for *Burke's Law* and *Saints and Sinners*.
Episodes were as follows:

Who Killed Julie Greer? (w Frank Gilroy; d Robert Ellis Miller; with Nick Adams, Ralph Bellamy, Edgar Bergen, Lloyd Bridges, Jack Carson, Carolyn Jones, Ronald Reagan, Mickey Rooney, Kay Thompson, Dean Jones, Edward Platt. NB: This was the pilot for *Burke's Law*, and Dick Powell played Burke.)

Ricochet (w Adrian Spies; d Marc Daniels; with Van Heflin, John Doucette, Robert F. Simon)

Killer in the House (w Morton Fine, David Friedkin; d David Friedkin; with Edmond O'Brien, Earl Holliman, Wallace Ford)

John J. Diggs (w Albert Beich, William H. Wright; d Ralph Nelson; with Dick Powell, Rhonda Fleming, Jack Kruschen, Michael Parks)

Doyle Against the House (w Richard Alan Simmons; d Ralph Nelson; with Milton Berle, Jan Sterling, Ludwig Donath, Gavin McLeod)

Out of the Night (w Christopher Knopf; d David Friedkin; with Dick Powell, Charles McGraw, Ziva Rodann, Rosemarie Bowe)

Somebody's Waiting (w Adrian Spies; d Arthur Hiller; with Mickey Rooney, Susan Oliver, Tige Andrews, Leonard Stone, Warren Oates)

The Geetas Box (w Art and Jo Napoleon; d Thomas Carr; with Cliff Robertson, Charles Bickford, Dean Stockwell, Frank Albertson, Whit Bissell)

Goodbye Hannah (w Steve Fisher; d Marc Daniels; with Dick Powell, Carolyn Jones, Bill Berger, Addison Richards)

Up Jumped the Devil (w Frank D. Gilroy; d Otto Lang; with Hugh O'Brian, Otto Kruger, Josephine Hitchinson)

Three Soldiers (w Richard Alan Simmons; d Ralph Nelson; with James Donald, Robert Webber, Telly Savalas)

A Swiss Affair (w William Froug; d Robert Ellis Miller; with Dick Powell, Cecil Kellaway, Hazel Court)

The Fifth Caller (w Helen Nielsen; d Robert Butler; with Michael Rennie, Eva Gabor, Elsa Lanchester, George Macready, Mabel Albertson, Tom Conway)

Open Season (w Elizabeth Wilson, d Ray Milland; with Dorothy Malone, Thomas Gomez, Dennis O'Keefe)

Death in a Village (w Chris Knopf, Aaron Spelling; d Marc Daniels; with Gilbert Roland, Nehemiah Persoff, Thomas Gomez, Vladimir Sokoloff)

A Time to Die (w Aaron Spelling; d Marc Daniels; with Dick Powell, June Allyson, Edgar Bergen, John Saxon, Ernest Truex, Tuesday Weld, Andy Williams)

The Price of Tomatoes (w Richard Alan Simmons; d David Friedkin; with Peter Falk, Inger Stevens)

Obituary for Mr X (w Vic Tams; d Harry Keller; with Steve Cochran, Gary Merrill, Dina Merrill, Nancy Davis, John Ireland)

Squadron (w/d Walter Doniger; with Dick Powell, Pat Conway, Joanna Moore, Bruce Dern)

The Prison (w Richard Alan Simmons; d Don Medford; with Charles Boyer, Theodore Bikel, John Abbott)

Colossus (w Richard Alan Simmons; d Don Medford; with William Shatner, Geraldine Brooks, Robert Brown)

Epilogue (w Bruce Geller; d Bernard Kowalski; with Lee Marvin, Ricardo Montalban, Claude Akins)

Thunder in a Forgotten Town (w Richard Carr, Irving J. McCarthy; d Bernard Kowalski; with Jackie Cooper, Edie Adams, Milton Berle, Joey Bishop, Jackie Coogan, Gary Crosby, Robert Emhardt, David Janssen, Dewey Martin, Pat O'Brien, Susan Oliver)

Charlie's Duet (*w* Richard Carr; *d* Don Taylor; with Jim Backus, Anthony Franciosa, Zsa Zsa Gabor, James Gregory, Julie London, Cesar Romero)

Seeds of April (*w* Christopher Knopf; *d* Harry Keller; with Gene Barry, Nina Foch, Beverly Garland, Keenan Wynn)

The Legend (*w* Bob Barbash; *d* Marc Daniels; with Dick Powell, Sammy Davis Jnr, Robert F. Simon, Walter Sande, Gloria Jean, Everett Sloane)

The Hook (*w* Christopher Knopf; *d* Joseph H. Lewis; with Robert Loggia, Ray Danton, Ed Begley, Ted de Corsia)

View from the Eiffel Tower (*w* Alfred Brenner, Aaron Spelling; *d* Lewis Allen; with Dick Powell, Bella Darvi, Akim Tamiroff, Jane Powell)

The Clocks (*w* Charles Bennett; *d* Lewis Allen; with Joan Fontaine, David Farrar, Wayne Rogers)

Tomorrow the Man (*w* Bob Barbash; *d* Don Medford; with Eli Wallach, Kim Hunter, Larry Blyden, Susan Kohner)

Run Till It's Dark (*w* Turnley Walker; *d* Robert Ellis Miller; with Tuesday Weld, Fabian, Paul Newlan)

The Honorable Albert Higgins (*w* Ben Starr, Bob O'Brien; *d* Don Taylor; with Tom Ewell, Barbara Rush, Vaughn Taylor, Vito Scotti, John Litel)

In Search of a Son (*w* S. Lee Pogostin; *d* Buzz Kulik; with Dick Powell, Dean Stockwell, Gladys Cooper, Sebastian Cabot)

The Big Day (*w* Max Ehrlich; *d* Robert Florey; with Robert Morley, Joan Blondell, Jack Cassidy, Everett Sloane)

Special Assignment (*w* Bob O'Brien, Ben Starr; *d* Don Taylor; with Dick Powell, June Allyson, Edgar Bergen, Jackie Cooper, Lloyd Nolan, Mickey Rooney, Barbara Stanwyck)

The Sea Witch (*w* Allen H. Miner, Cecil Smith; *d* John Peyser; with Carolyn Jones, Harry Guardino, John Ericson, Gerald Mohr)

The Court Martial of Captain Wycliff (*w* Harry Julian Fink; *d* Buzz Kulik; with Dick Powell, Dina Merrill, Edward Andrews, Ed Begley, Robert Keith, James MacArthur, Alexander Scourby, Charles Ruggles, Robert Webber)

Everybody Loves Sweeney (*w* Bill Manhoff; *d* Don Medford; with Mickey Rooney, Joanne Linville, Ross Martin, Jack Albertson)

The Losers (*w* Bruce Geller; *d* Sam Peckinpah; with Lee Marvin, Keenan Wynn, Rosemary Clooney)

Pericles on 31st Street (*w* Harry Mark Petrakis, Sam Peckinpah; *d* Sam Peckinpah; with

Theodore Bikel, Carroll O'Connor, Arthur O'Connell)

Project X (*w* Collier Young; *d* Walter Doniger; with Michael Rennie, Gena Rowlands, Steve Forrest)

Crazy Sunday (*w* James Poe; *d* Jeffrey Hayden; with Dana Andrews, Vera Miles, Rip Torn, Barry Sullivan)

Borderline (*w* Albert Beich, William H. Wright; *d* Charles Haas; with John Payne, Hazel Court, Frank Silvera)

Days of Glory (*w* Richard Alan Simmons; *d* Marc Daniels; with Charles Boyer, Suzanne Pleshette, Lloyd Bochner)

The Doomsday Boys (*w* Richard Alan Simmons; *d* Elliot Silverstein; with Dick Powell, Alejandro Rey, Peter Falk, John Larch)

The Great Anatole (*w* Richard Alan Simmons; *d* Buzz Kulik; with Curt Jurgens, Dana Wynter, Lee Phillips, Leonid Kinskey)

Apples Don't Fall Far (*w* Les Pine; *d* Josef Leytes; with Johnny Crawford, Michael Kane, Joe de Santis, David Wayne)

The Judge (*w* Bruce Geller, Harry Mark Petrakis; *d* Bernard Kowalski; with Richard Basehart, Nico Minardos, Mary Murphy, Otto Kruger, Elisha Cook Jnr)

Luxury Liner (*w* Christopher Knopf; *d* Paul Wendkos; with Rory Calhoun, Carroll O'Connor, Jan Sterling, Ludwig Donath, Oscar Beregi)

The Rage of Silence (*w* Ed Spiegel, Jules Maitland; *d* Don Taylor; with Peter Falk, Carol Lynley, Frederick Beir)

Tissue of Hate (*w* Tony Barrett; *d* Marc Daniels; with Henry Fonda, Polly Bergen, Gloria Vanderbilt, Eduard Franz)

The Last of the Big Spenders (*w* Richard Alan Simmons; *d* Robert Gist; with Dana Andrews, Inger Stevens, Robert Redford, Herschel Bernardi, Norman Fell)

The Boston Terrier (*w* Lester Aaron Pine; *d* Blake Edwards; with John McGiver, Robert Pine, Robert J. Wilke, John Marley)

No Strings Attached (*w* Ben Starr, Bob O'Brien; *d* Hy Averback; with Dick Powell, Angie Dickinson, Mamie Van Doren, Barbara Nichols, John Litel, Leo Gorcey)

Savage Sunday (*w* Adrian Spies; *d* Buzz Kulik; with Nick Adams, Ann Blyth, Russell Thorson. NB: This was the pilot for the series *Saints and Sinners*.)

The Third Side of a Coin (*w* S. Lee Pogostin; *d* Marc Daniels; with June Allyson, John Forsythe, Hugh Marlowe)

Independence, SW (*w* Allan Sloane; *d* Samuel

Fuller; with William Bendix, Julie Adams, David McLean)

The Last of the Private Eyes (*w* Richard Carr, Robert L. Jacks; *d* Marc Daniels; with Robert Cummings, Eddie Rochester Anderson, William Bendix, Sebastian Cabot, Macdonald Carey, Linda Christian, Jeanne Crain, Jay C. Flippen, William Lundigan, Victor Buono, Janis Paige, Keenan Wynn)

The Old Man and the City (*w* John Pickard, Frank Provo; *d* William A. Graham; with Charles Ruggles, Bruce Dern, Charles Bickford, Edward Binns, John Larkin, Dennis Morgan, Alex Nicol, Gene Raymond, Joan Blackman. NB: This was the pilot for an unrealized series, *Adamsburg USA.*)

Dick Tracy *
US 1950 130 × 5m colour
ABC/UPA

Cases of the famous comic strip detective with the jut jaw (created by Chester Gould in 1931).
Slick but rather curious cartoons in which the celebrated detective stays home and sends his assistants out on the cases.

† A 1950 live-action half-hour series for ABC had starred Ralf Byrd.

Dick Turpin (GB 1980; 6 × 30m). Jaunty re-write of popular legend by the team that went on to do the same thing even more successfully with *Robin of Sherwood*. With Richard O'Sullivan, Michael Deakes; written by Richard Carpenter and others; produced by Paul Knight, for LWT. *Dick Turpin's Greatest Adventure* followed, 1982.   PP

The Dick Van Dyke Show ***
US 1961–5 158 × 25m bw
CBS/William Morris/Calvada (Carl Reiner)

The private life of a scriptwriter for the *Alan Brady Show*.
Phenomenally successful series which was half farce, half warm observation of a young married couple and their friends, with echoes of vaudeville from the supporting cast. Emmys 1964 and 1965. See *Van Dyke, Dick*.
cr CARL REINER (who originally hoped to play the lead himself but ended as the hero's boss)

DICK VAN DYKE, MARY TYLER MOORE, MOREY AMSTERDAM, ROSE MARIE, RICHARD DEACON, CARL REINER

† Among those closely involved in the production/direction were Jerry Paris and Sheldon Leonard.

†† The pilot film, aired in 1960, was *Head of the Family*.

Dickens, Charles (1812–70). Favourite Victorian novelist and performer, most of whose stories have been rendered on television many times. In 1985 alone, for example, no less than three Dickens serials ran on BBC TV: *The Pickwick Papers*, BLEAK HOUSE and *Oliver Twist*. Most substantial achievements in recent years are generally reckoned to be *Hard Times* (Granada 1977) and *Bleak House* (1985), both dramatized by Arthur Hopcroft, and the RSC production of *Nicholas Nickleby* translated to C4 in 1982. In addition to the bio-series below, Dickens was the subject of a Thames drama-doc *The Hero of My Life*, directed by Michael Darlow in 1970.   PP

Dickens of London
GB 1977 10 × 50m colour (VTR)
Yorkshire TV (David Cunliffe)

The ageing Dickens reviews scenes from his life.
Elaborate but singularly unpersuasive series with the star also playing Dickens's father.
w Wolf Mankowitz *d* Marc Miller *m* Monty Norman

Roy Dotrice, Diana Coupland, Karen Dotrice, Richard Leech, Adrienne Burgess

The Dickie Henderson Show. British half-hour star comedy vehicle, popular on Rediffusion in the fifties. The star played himself, more or less, with June Laverick as his wife.

Dickinson, Angie (1931–). Durable American leading lady who cheerfully moved over from films to TV. Series: POLICE WOMAN, *Cassie and Company*. TV movies: *The Love War*, *Thief*, *See the Man Run*, *The Norliss Tapes*, *Pray for the Wildcats*, *A Sensitive Passionate Man*, *Overboard*, *Pearl*, THE SUICIDE'S WIFE, *Dial M for Murder*, *Cassie and Co.*, *One Shoe Makes It Murder*, *Jealousy*, *A Touch of Scandal*, *Hollywood Wives*.

Dickinson, Sandra (19 –). British dizzy blonde of comedy and quiz programmes.

Did You See . . . ? ** (GB since 1980). The best television show about television ever, comprising a set piece on some aspect of the industry, a sharp résumé of the week's good and bad moments, and a discussion of three selected programmes by a panel of critics, all whipped along by Ludovic Kennedy. The critics are enthusiastic (or, more often, unenthusiastic) amateurs rather than professionals, but usually adroitly cast by producer John Archer.   PP

† BAFTA award, 1984

Diff'rent Strokes
US 1978–   × 25m colour tape
Long-running American comedy series about
a widowed millionaire who adopts two black
boys. The younger of them, GARY COLEMAN,
became a TV star of the first magnitude,
partly because it was known that his
ebullience concealed a serious kidney
problem. Conrad Bain, Charlotte Rae;
created by Jeff Harris and Bernie Kukoff for
Embassy/NBC.

Dig This! (GB 1959). The pop music show
which succeeded *Six-Five Special* on BBC
during the battle of pop music shows at this
time; produced by Francis Essex, with Bob
Miller and the Millermen and plucky singer
Barbara Young.   PP

Diller, Barry (*c* 1937–). American
executive who went from ABC (where he
instigated the TV movie, more or less) to
control of production at Paramount.

Diller, Phyllis (1917–). American stand-up
comedienne who had one not-too-successful
TV series, *The Pruitts of Southampton*;
otherwise in guest appearances.

Dillman, Bradford (1930–). Ever-reliable
but seldom-starred American leading man
who has given useful performances in all
media. TV movies include *Fear No Evil*,
Black Water Gold, *Longstreet*, *Revenge*, *The
Eyes of Charles Sand*, *Moon of the Wolf*,
Deliver Us from Evil, *Adventures of the
Queen*, *Widow*, *Street Killing*, *The Hostage
Heart*, *The Memory of Eva Ryker*, *Tourist*,
Before and After. Series: *Kings Crossing*.

Dimbleby, David (1938–). British
reporter, interviewer and anchorman, son of
Richard Dimbleby. His career with the BBC
has embraced stints on *Panorama*,
Nationwide; commentaries from live political
and ceremonial occasions; and his own
series, e.g. *David Dimbleby in Conversation*
(1982–3). In 1984 was infamously dropped
from covering TUC Conference because of
union pressure; the family newspaper group
which he also manages was using a 'blacked'
printing contractor.   PP

Dimbleby, Jonathan (1944–). British
tele-journalist, brother of David Dimbleby;
reporter for *This Week* and later investigator
on one-hour specials for YTV. Since 1982
has presented *First Tuesday* for same
company, and written and presented
documentary series *The Eagle and the Bear*
(1981), *The American Dream* (1984).

❄ **Dimbleby, Richard** (1913–65). The
voice of the BBC, it was said, from the war
years until Churchill's funeral. Began as
radio's first 'news observer', a job he
suggested himself; radio war correspondent
1939–45, including broadcasts from an RAF
bomber over Germany. For television he
became the commentator on all great state
occasions, earning a not altogether deserved
reputation for undue deference towards
royalty and the ruling classes; he was also
anchorman on *Panorama* 1957–63. In both
capacities his professionalism and ability to
cope with every kind of delay and disaster
were undisputed. In 1958 he made,
prophetically, a BBC holiday film starring
two of his three young sons. Both were to
carry on the family tradition – see entries for
David and Jonathan.   PP

Dimmock, Peter (1920–). British sports
commentator and executive who in the
mid-seventies took up an appointment with
the American ABC network.

Dinah. Half-hour morning talk show of the
seventies, syndicated in the US five days a
week, with Dinah Shore as hostess.

Dinenage, Fred (1942–). British
tele-nonentity on sports and game shows.

Dinner at the Sporting Club *** (GB 1978;
75m; colour). Superb play for BBC by Leon
Griffiths, with a tremendous performance by
John Thaw as the decent, gritty manager of a
young boxer just turned pro and booked to
fight in front of the dinner-jacketed toffs and
bounders of the Sporting Club. The best thing
on this subject since Ralph Peterson's *The
Square Ring* nearly 30 years before. Produced
by Kenith Trodd; directed by Brian Gibson.

Dinner Party (GB 1962–3). Forlorn attempt
by ATV to hold a live discussion show over
the debris of a meal that had actually been
consumed, with Lord Boothby as expansive
host to a variety of political or literary
luminaries. Never very successful, it
foundered altogether when camera and mike
had to try and avoid a guest whose glass had
been topped up too frequently.   PP
LH: I liked it.

The Dion Brothers
GB theatrical title: *The Gravy Train*
US 1974 96m colour TVM
Tomorrow (Roger Gimbel)
Two coal miners seek a quick fortune in the
city as armed robbers.
Adequate modern gangster stuff.

w Bill Kerby, David Whitney (Terrence Malick) d Jack Starrett m Fred Karlin

Stacy Keach, Frederic Forrest, Margot Kidder, Barry Primus

director. The creative talent who directs the actors and the camera.

'Thrilling! Audacious! Gut-wrenching!'
The Dirty Dozen: Next Mission
US 1984 96m colour TVM
NBC/MGM–UA (Harry Sherman)

A court-martialled officer is given an out if he recruits a team of ex-convicts to kill a German general.
More or less a remake of the 1967 movie, and to no good purpose: everything about it seems old and tired.

w Michael Kane d Andrew V. McLaglen ph John Stanier m Richard Harvey

Lee Marvin, Ernest Borgnine, Ken Wahl, Larry Wilcox, Sonny Landham, Richard Jaeckel, Gavin O'Herlihy

'Lackluster quality . . . little suspense is evoked.' – *Daily Variety*

Dirty Money
aka: *Sewers of Gold*
GB 1979 106m colour TVM
ATV

A would-be fascist dictator determines to get funds by robbing a bank in Nice.
Overlong thriller which gets stuck when the villains do, burrowing through the sewers.

w Francis Megahy, Bernie Cooper d Francis Megahy

Ian McShane, Warren Clarke, Stephen Greif, Nigel Humphreys, Christopher Malcolm

PP: 'Lew Grade made-for-TV heist movie (based on the real-life Albert Spaggiari's exploits) which had more going for it than was generally conceded, including an unwittingly brilliant solution to the old problem of conveying the idea that Anglo-Saxon actors are speaking a foreign language. Everyone sounded as if he had been dubbed.'

Dirty Sally
US 1974 13 × 25m colour
CBS/TCF (John Mantley)

In the old west, a young adventurer joins forces with a crusty old junk dealer.
Unsuccessful comedy western.

Jeanette Nolan, Dack Rambo

The Disappearance of Aimee *
US 1976 96m colour TVM
NBC/Tomorrow (Paul Leaf)

A reconstruction of the mysterious disappearance of evangelist Aimee Semple McPherson in 1926.
Lively historical drama which doesn't really explain anything.

w John McGreevey d Anthony Harvey m Steve Byrne

Faye Dunaway, Bette Davis, James Sloyan, James Woods, John Lehne, Lelia Goldoni, Severn Darden

The Disappearance of Flight 412
US 1974 74m colour TVM
Cinemobile

Two air force jets disappear while chasing a UFO.
Milk-and-water science fiction which adds up to very little.

w George Simpson, Neal Burger d Jud Taylor m Morton Stevens

Glenn Ford, Bradford Dillman, Guy Stockwell, David Soul, Robert F. Lyons, Kent Smith

The Disappearance of Harry (GB 1982). Vague thriller set in Nottingham and apparently pieced together from that city's best-known historical and geographical features. 'When they'd ticked them all off in the tourist literature,' I wrote, 'the story quietly fizzled out.' With Annette Crosbie, from Labrahurst Productions, for C4's *Film on Four.*   PP

Disappearing World **. A series of documentaries of varying lengths made by Granada TV in the seventies: Brian Moser visited native tribes in remote parts of the world. The results were highly acclaimed. BAFTA 1975: best documentary.

Disaster on the Coastliner *
US 1980 96m colour TVM
ABC/Filmways/Moonlight (Frank Von Zerneck)

A madman arranges for the computer-controlled Los Angeles–Frisco trains to collide.
Rather splendid all-star potboiler with action finales that wouldn't disgrace a big-screen spectacular.

w David Ambrose d RICHARD SARAFIAN ph Fred Koenekamp m Gerald Fried

Lloyd Bridges, Raymond Burr, Robert Fuller, Pat Hingle, E. G. Marshall, Yvette Mimieux, William Shatner, Paul L. Smith, Arthur Malet

Discovering English Churches (GB 1979). A series of 10 half-hours with Donald Sinden as he visits remarkable religious edifices. Unfortunately his plummy and unctuous tones give a comical air to the proceedings and quite spoil the intent. Produced by Dick Foster; for BBC.

The Discovery of Animal Behaviour (GB 1982; 6 × 60m). Historical-natural dramatizations of how observers or scientists made each breakthrough in understanding the way animals behave, and why. Written by John Sparks, produced by him and Michael Salisbury, for BBC Bristol.   PP

The Dismissal (Australia 1984; 6 × 52m). Dramatized version of the political schemozzle of the mid-seventies which led to Prime Minister Gough Whitlam being sacked by the Governor-General. What was no doubt riveting to Australians seemed long and complicated to others despite – or because of – some extra off-screen narration. All it did, I indicated at the time, was make a pretty wooden reconstruction even woodener. With Max Phipps as Whitlam, John Meillon as Sir John Kerr, John Stanton as Malcolm Fraser. Written by Terry Hayes and others, directed by various hands, produced by Terry Hayes for Kennedy–Miller, shown in UK by C4.   PP

❋   **Disney, Walt** (1901–66). American animator and master showman whose organization from the mid-fifties provided a weekly Sunday evening show for the ABC network.

Displaced Person (GB/US 1985; 50m). In postwar Germany a black child meets an army sergeant who he believes is his father. Schmaltzy but professional hour with undoubted appeal for certain audiences. Written by Fred Barron from the story by Kurt Vonnegut Jnr; with Julius Gordon, Rosemary Leach, Stan Shaw; for HTV/Hemisphere.

Disraeli – Portrait of a Romantic (GB 1979). Four-part drama series from ATV reconstructing the rise to power of the Victorian prime minister, with some emphasis on his love life. Without being riveting, it achieves a good solid standard of television drama. With Ian McShane, Mary Peach, Leigh Lawson, Margaret Whiting, Brett Usher, Mark Dignam. Written by David Butler; directed by Claude Whatham; produced by Lorna Mason/Cecil Clarke.

The District Nurse (GB 1984; 12 × 30m). Nerys Hughes as same in a gritty early-evening near-soaper, set geographically in Welsh mining landscape and historically back in time to catch the full flavour of district-nursing at its most pioneering. Written by Julia Smith, Tony Holland, *et al.*, produced by Julia Smith, for BBC.   PP

Diverse Reports * (GB since 1984). Simple but innovative idea to release current affairs TV from the constant need to observe impartiality (or anyway seem to be doing so) by balancing the people, not what they say. A squad of producer–presenters picked from the hard Left, libertarian Right and odd shades between take it in turn to be as partisan as they like on a chosen topic. Christopher Hird replaced Anna Coote in 1985 as principal Leftie, Peter Clarke remains chief scourge of the Left. Guest editors take over once a month, chosen to add a little celebrity, e.g. Paul Johnson, Max Hastings. Produced overall by David Graham and Diverse Productions, for C4.
                                                                                          PP

Divorce His, Divorce Hers
GB 1972 2 × 74m colour TVM
Harlech TV/John Heyman
Two films showing aspects of a divorce, one from the wife's viewpoint and one from the husband's.
Abysmally dull regurgitation of their own lives by the world's most boring showbiz couple.
w John Hopkins   *d* Waris Hussein   *m* Stanley Myers
Richard Burton, Elizabeth Taylor, Gabriele Ferzetti, Carrie Nye, Barry Foster, Rudolph Walker

Dixie: Changing Habits
US 1982 96m colour TVM
CBS/George Englund (Michael Greenburg)
A madame is released from jail into the custody of nuns, and teaches them something about commerce.
Predictable modern comedy which doesn't do much for religion.
w John Considine   *d* George Englund
ph Robert Jessup   *m* Jimmie Haskell
Suzanne Pleshette, Cloris Leachman, Kenneth McMillan, Geraldine Fitzgerald, John Considine, Susan Kellerman

Dixon, Ivan (1931–). Black American actor who was one of *Hogan's Heroes*.

Dixon of Dock Green **
GB 1955–76 250 approx. × 45m
  bw/colour (VTR)
BBC

Stories of an ageing cop in London's East
End.

George Dixon was the policeman killed in the
movie *The Blue Lamp*, but his co-creator
revived him and he lasted 21 years, until the
star playing him was 80. The early stories
tended towards the domestic, but later Dixon
became the station desk sergeant and action
was the main element, looked after by the
CID detectives.

cr TED WILLIS

JACK WARNER, Peter Byrne

Dizzy Feet ** (GB 1981). Trail-blazing,
deceptively simple, uncluttered compendium
of dance routines, from the immaculate tap
of veteran hoofer Honi Coles to a
thistledown fragment of ballet from David
Wall and Lesley Collier, all linked by droll
muppet-type talking feet. ATV's stylish
swansong – or swandance – before being
born again as Central; choreography by
Nigel Lythgoe, *m,d* Jack Parnell, produced
and directed by Jon Scoffield.   PP

Do Not Fold, Spindle or Mutilate **
US 1971 73m colour TVM
Aaron Spelling (Robert L. Jacks)

Four old biddies answer a computer dating
service as one fictitious glamorous girl, but
one of the applicants is a homicidal maniac.

Lively four-star comedy-thriller.

w John D. F. Black, *novel* Doris Miles Disney
d Ted Post *m* Jerry Goldsmith

Myrna Loy, Helen Hayes, Sylvia Sidney,
Mildred Natwick, Vince Edwards

Do They Mean Us? (GB since 1985).
Intermittent BBC series collecting together
reports on British life, social order, etc., as
seen on TV in other countries, with former
tabloid editor and professional cockney
Derek Jameson adding the Gorblimeys.
Inadequate on the rare occasions when the
programme tries to be serious, e.g. soccer
violence, but cheerful enough when
expressing comic disbelief at foreigners
having the temerity to investigate British
holiday camps or Kissogram services.   PP

Do You Remember Love? *
US 1985 96m colour TVM
CBS/Dave Bell (Wayne Threm, James E.
  Thompson)

A university professor learns she is a victim
of senile dementia: Alzheimer's Disease.

One of the better disease-of-the-week
movies, but sensitive acting and writing can't
entirely atone for a one-way plot.

w Vickie Patik *d* Jeff Bleckner *ph*
Bradford May *m* David Shire

JOANNE WOODWARD, Richard Kiley,
Geraldine Fitzgerald, Jim Metzler, Jordan
Charney, Jerry Hardin

'Nonclinical, startlingly human . . . packed
with memorable scenes.' – *Daily Variety*

Do You Take This Stranger?
US 1970 95m colour TVM
Universal/Roy Huggins

In order to inherit a million dollars, a
desperate man must engineer a switch of
identities.

Complex puzzle melodrama, good fun for
addicts.

w Matthew Howard *d* Richard Heffron

Gene Barry, Lloyd Bridges, Diane Baker,
Joseph Cotten, Sidney Blackmer, Susan
Oliver

Dobie, Alan (1932–). Rather stern-looking
British actor whose clear diction has brought
him a wide range of roles. First spotted on TV
in *The Plane Makers*; starring in *Cribb*.

Dobie Gillis
aka: *The Many Loves of Dobie Gillis*
US 1959–62 147 × 25m bw
CBS/TCF

Troubles of a frustrated teenager.
Hackneyed college comedy from the stories
by Max Shulman.

cr Max Shulman

Dwayne Hickman, Bob Denver, Frank
Faylen, Tuesday Weld, Warren Beatty,
Raymond Bailey

Dobson, Kevin (1944–). Leading
American actor who became familiar as an
aide to *Kojak*. Got his own series: *Shannon*.
TV movies: *Greatest Heroes of the Bible*, *The
Immigrants*, *Transplant*, *Hardhat and Legs*,
Mark I Love You, *Orphan Train*, *Reunion*.

Doc
US 1975 ? × 25m colour
CBS/Mary Tyler Moore

Anecdotes of a general practitioner in a poor
New York district.
Mild ethnic comedy.

cr Ed Weinberger, Stan Daniels

Barnard Hughes, Elizabeth Wilson, Audra
Lindley, David Ogden Stiers

Doc Corkle (US 1952). Shortlived half-hour comedy drama about a dentist and his family, with Eddie Mayehoff and Billie Burke. Only three episodes were telecast.

Doc Elliot
US 1973 15 × 50m colour
ABC/Lorimar (Sandor Stern)
The life of a country practitioner in the south-west, making house calls in a camper. Pleasant, modest, low-key country dramas.
m Marvin Hamlisch
James Franciscus, Neva Patterson, Noah Beery Jnr, Bo Hopkins

The Doctor (US 1952). Half-hour series for NBC in which Warner Anderson introduced dramatized case histories.

Dr Christian
US 1956 39 × 25m bw
UA
Stories of a small-town practitioner.
Rather limp elaboration on the forties films and later radio series.
Macdonald Carey

Dr Cook's Garden *
US 1970 74m colour TVM
Paramount (Bob Markell)
A small-town doctor nurtures the healthy and weeds out the sick.
Macabre comedy melodrama which tries hard but doesn't quite come off.
w Arthur Wallace, *play* Ira Levin *d* Ted Post
Bing Crosby, Frank Converse, Bethel Leslie, Blythe Danner

Doctor Dolittle
US 1970 17 × 22m colour
NBC/TCF/De Patie–Freleng
The doctor who talks to animals has various adventures aboard the good ship Flounder.
Tolerable cartoon adventures.

Dr Finlay's Casebook **
GB 1959–66 150 approx. × 50m bw (VTR)
BBC
Stories of an old and a young doctor, not forgetting their canny housekeeper, in a small Scottish town in the twenties.
Highly atmospheric and character-filled series which absorbed a nation for many a Sunday evening, as social history as well as drama.
cr A. J. Cronin
ANDREW CRUICKSHANK, BILL SIMPSON, BARBARA MULLEN

PP wrote, towards the end of the run: 'One of the few programmes which Mrs Whitehouse and her Daughters of the English Revolution have publicly condoned. I suppose it's not surprising that they should have picked on one of the few utterly detestable characters in television fiction. As so brilliantly played by Bill Simpson, Finlay is now slackening, thickening, greying, despite efforts – when he remembers – to simulate the youthful impetuosity he first brought to Tannochbrae. He is in fact smug, self-satisfied, self-righteous. He is also a bully. Last time he behaved unbearably to a very nice little body (Maureen Pryor) who'd hoped to raise a loan from Finlay's dad, enterprisingly played by Wilfred Pickles. I thought £50 a reasonable reward for the pleasure her companionship had given the old boy.'

Doctor Fischer of Geneva (GB 1984). Top-heavy TV film version of Graham Greene's mean, misanthropic little story about the Swiss millionaire who likes to see his guests grovel for lavish presents; with Alan Bates miscast as the sardonic observer but James Mason making the best of Dr Fischer. Also featuring Hugh Burden, Cyril Cusack, Barry Humphries. Directed by Michael Lindsay-Hogg, produced by Richard Broke, for BBC.   PP

Dr Franken
US 1980 96m colour TVM
NBC/Titus (Herb Brodkin)
The Frankenstein story is transplanted to modern New York.
And quite persuasive it is too, though once you appreciate the sheer cheek of the concept you know how it's going to progress and end, and the details are gory without being very arresting.
w Kee Thomas *d* Marvin Chomsky *ph* Alan Metzger *m* John Morris
Robert Vaughn, Robert Perrault, David Selby, Teri Garr

Dr Hudson's Secret Journal
US 1955–6 78 × 25m bw
Wesmor
Experiences of a brain surgeon.
Highly coloured medical hokum from a story by Lloyd C. Douglas.
John Howard

Doctor in the House *
GB 1970–3 90 × 25m colour (VTR)
London Weekend
Riotous adventures of medical students.
Zany comedy following after the film series;

this series was itself followed by *Doctor at Sea*, *Doctor at Large* and *Doctor on the Go*.

Barry Evans, Robin Nedwell, Ernest Clark, Geoffrey Davies

Dr Jekyll and Mr Hyde (GB 1981). Too long at 115 minutes, this slightly sexed-up version, with many invented scenes, has some good transformation sequences and an unexpectedly interesting central performance; otherwise it has the air of being curiously unnecessary. With DAVID HEMMINGS, Lisa Harrow, Ian Bannen, Clive Swift, Diana Dors, Toyah Wilcox. Written by Gerald Savory, from the novel by Robert Louis Stevenson (whose plot and development would have been better than the one offered); directed by Alastair Reid; produced by Jonathan Powell; for ABC.

Dr Kildare **
US 1961–4 142 × 50m bw
US 1965–6 58 × 25m colour
NBC/MGM/Arena

A young intern gets guidance and inspiration from a crusty old doctor.

Highly successful medical series based on the forties films and the stories by Max Brand. The half-hour episodes were semi-serialized.

m Jerry Goldsmith

RICHARD CHAMBERLAIN, RAYMOND MASSEY

† See also *Young Dr Kildare*.

Dr Max
US 1974 74m colour TVM
CBS/James Goldstone

A small-town doctor neglects his family to look after his patients.

Modest domestic drama.

Lee J. Cobb, Robert Lipton, David Sheiner, Janet Ward

Dr Scorpion
US 1978 96m colour TVM
Universal/Stephen J. Cannell

An ex-CIA agent defeats a criminal mastermind.

Humourless carbon copy of *Doctor No*, a yawn to sit through.

w Stephen J. Cannell *d* Richard Lang *ph* Charles Correll *m* Mike Post, Pete Carpenter

Nick Mancuso, Christine Lahti, Richard T. Herd, Sandra Kerns, Roscoe Lee Browne, Denny Miller

Dr Seuss. Pseudonym of Theodore Seuss Geisel (1904–   ), a highly successful American writer of illustrated stories for children which grown-ups also enjoy. Those transferred so far to TV, in half-hour special form, include *Horton Hears a Who*, *The Cat in the Hat*, *How the Grinch Spent Christmas*, *Dr Seuss on the Loose*, *The Hoober-Bloob Highway*. Animation has been by De Patie–Freleng.

Dr Simon Locke
Canada 1972 approx. 45 × 25m colour (16mm)
Chester Krumholz

Cases of an intense young doctor who joins an irascible old one in a small Canadian town.

Dr Kildare up north, all very cosy and predictable.

Sam Groom, Jack Albertson, Len Birman

† Dr Locke later moved to the city and became *Police Surgeon*.

Dr Strange
US 1978 96m colour TVM
CBS/Universal (Philip de Guere, Alex Beaton)

A New York occultist battles Morgan Le Fay and the forces of evil.

Lively, imaginative, but humourless and obscure fantasy, a cut above the usual Marvel Comics superheroes. No series resulted.

w Philip de Guere, from the characters created by Stan Lee *d* Philip de Guere *ad* William H. Tuntke

Peter Hooten, Jessica Walter, John Mills, Eddie Benton

Dr Who *. Highly coloured science fiction for older children, produced by the BBC in many hundreds of taped 25-minute segments since 1963. The leading character is a mystical gentleman (a 'Time Lord') who can travel through time and space in his 'Tardis' (which is disguised as a police box). His main opponents, a race of gravel-voiced robots called Daleks, became a household name. The series has been much criticized for its horrific monsters, but they always moved very slowly. The good doctor has been played by William Hartnell, Jon Pertwee, Patrick Troughton, Tom Baker, Peter Davison and Colin Baker. Terry Nation was chief deviser of this odd entertainment which has always been well mounted and accompanied by effective electronic music.   L.H.

† *The Five Doctors* (1983) re-mustered the first five in a special one-off, three of them in the flesh, two from old footage – plus, to add to the confusion, a sixth (Richard Hurndall) impersonating the first (William Hartnell). It also collected together in one neat demonstration package, I'm afraid, all that

had become gimcrack and silly about the serial over the years: hollow Daleks, Cybermen in baggy silver combinations and latter-day Time Lords in comic hats – they were all there.   PP

doctors. The classic formula in medical-men series comprised young doctor who had to learn that Experience and Wisdom still count, irascible old mentor who had occasionally to acknowledge that New Ideas can work, and a little medical propaganda ('If only she had come to see us six months earlier . . .'). *Dr Finlay's Casebook*, derived from A. J. Cronin's stories, may have set the formula, but *Dr Kildare* pursued it most determinedly, with every episode balancing one happy outcome against a less happy one and the theme music picked up on church bells if anyone actually died. Handsome and boyish in his white bum-freezer suit, Richard Chamberlain's Kildare won every mother's heart, and it was said that his chief rival, Dr Casey of *Ben Casey*, was deliberately created – all scowls and hairy forearms – to woo the American matron from dream son to dream lover. Vince Edwards played him, with Sam Jaffe as crusty senior. *Dr Simon Locke* applied the formula to a Canadian setting. Consult these practitioners individually.   PP

The Doctors. American soap opera which has played five times a week on NBC since 1964. James Pritchett, Lydia Bruce, Gerald Gordon portray life in Madison, USA.

The Doctors and the Nurses: see The Nurses

Doctors' Daughters (GB 1980). Abysmal half-hour comedy series about three old doctors giving up their country practice to three nubile young ministering angels. The mixture of high spirits, old jokes and slapstick simply doesn't work, and the cast is left to make bricks with no straw. With Lesley Duff, Victoria Burgoyne, Bill Fraser, Richard Murdoch, Jack Watling, Patrick Newell. Written by Richard Gordon and Ralph Thomas; directed and produced by Stuart Allen; for ATV.

Doctors' Hospital
US 1975 12 × 50m colour
NBC/Universal (Matthew Rapf, Jack Laird)
Problems of the staff and patients of a large metropolitan hospital.
Rather boring soap opera.

George Peppard, Zohra Lampert, Victor Campos

† See also pilot TV movie, *One of Our Own*.

Doctors' Private Lives
US 1978 96m colour TVM
ABC/Columbia/David Gerber (Robert Stambler)
Life and love in a general hospital.
A slab of soap opera which was meant to develop into a series, but lasted only four episodes.

w James Henerson d Steven Hillard Stern ph Howard R. Schwarz m Richard Markowitz

John Gavin, Donna Mills, Ed Nelson, Barbara Anderson, Bettye Ackerman, John Randolph

Document of a Death in the Family (Japan 1964). Cameraman Mashashi Ueno's hand-held-camera account of his father's decline and death from cancer, the very first snuff-show, as the Americans harshly term the genre. 'If there is a crumb of comfort,' I wrote after the 1964 Italia Prize screening, 'it is that even in a great hospital in a teeming city the death of an ordinary man is still a happening that for the moment resounds, that diminishes those that remain.'   PP

Dodd, Ken (1927–).   Rubber-faced, gap-toothed British comic from Knotty Ash (near Liverpool). Always in a variety format, he talks fast, sings quite well, employs a tickling-stick and created his own miniature chorus of Diddymen.

Does the Team Think? (GB 1982). Of itself, highly – but Jimmy Edwards's radio game show, transferred to TV by Thames with a predictable quartet of wags, only managed a non-simultaneous network screening, and that for not very long. With Jimmy Edwards, Beryl Reid, Frankie Howerd, Willie Rushton.   PP

Dog and Cat ✶✶
US 1977 74m colour TVM
(Paramount) Lawrence Gordon (Largo) (Robert Singer)
When his partner is shot, a police detective reluctantly accepts a slightly kooky lady replacement.
Amiable, slick, very entertaining pilot which pinches its plot from *The Maltese Falcon* but has a few extra tricks up its sleeve.

w Walter Hill d Robert Kelljan m Barry Devorzon

Lou Antonio, Kim Basinger, Richard Lynch, Charles Cioffi

† The resulting series disappointed and ran to only seven 50-minute episodes.

The Doll *
GB 1975 3 × 50m colour (VTR)
BBC (Bill Sellars)
A publisher meets and helps a mysterious woman who later disappears . . .
Complex, well-paced and thoroughly enjoyable suspense mystery in the author's usual sub-Hitchcockian and entirely British vein.
w Francis Durbridge d David Askey
John Fraser, Anouska Hempel, Geoffrey Whitehead, Derek Fowlds, Cyril Luckham, William Russell

The Dollmaker *
US 1984 142m colour TVM
ABC/Finnegan Associates/IPC/Dollmaker
  (Bill Finnegan)
During World War II, a hillbilly family has to move to the big city so that the father can get war work.
An eastward-trekking *Grapes of Wrath*, acted out in impenetrable accents and not very interesting even if it were understandable.
w Susan Cooper, Hume Cronyn, *novel* by Harriette Arnow d Daniel Petrie ph Paul Lohmann m John Rubinstein
Jane Fonda, Levon Helm, Geraldine Page, Amanda Plummer, Susan Kingsley
'Determinedly heartwarming, the tele-epic gets stuck in its own folksiness: it's just more than a body can bear.' – *Daily Variety*

Domestic Life
US 1984   × 25m colour
CBS/Universal/40 Share Productions
Domestic problems of a TV newsroom editor.
Unoriginal comedy which didn't take.
cr Steve Martin, Ian Praiser, Howard Gerwitz, Martin Mull
Martin Mull, Judith-Marie Bergan, Megan Follows, Christian Brackett-Zika, Robert Ridgely

Don Quixote: see The Adventures of Don Quixote

The Don Rickles Show
US 1968   × 25m colour (VTR)
ABC
A variety format starring the comedian, with Vic Mizzy's orchestra.

The Don Rickles Show
US 1971 13 × 25m colour
CBS/Sheldon Leonard
Stories of a suburbanite who is always behind the eight ball.
Fairly funny sitcom.
Don Rickles, Louise Sorel, Erin Moran, Joyce Van Patten, Robert Hogan, Edward Andrews

Donahue, Troy (1936–) (Merle Johnson). American juvenile lead of the fifties. TV series: *Surfside Six*, *Hawaiian Eye*.

Doniger, Walter (1917–). American writer–director. TV writing credits include *Bat Masterson*, *Maverick*, *The Survivors*, *Peyton Place*.

The Donna Reed Show
US 1958–65 275 × 25m bw
ABC/Screen Gems/Todon–Briskin (Tony Owen)
Standard star domestic comedy.
A long-runner, nimbly presented; it showed the ideal American house and family, in this case those of a pediatrician.
Donna Reed, Carl Betz, Shelley Fabares

Donnellan, Philip (1924–). Birmingham-based BBC film-maker, disciple of the radio producer Charles Parker who invented the 'ballad documentary'. Donnellan has inherited the same taste for mournful sung commentary (usually by Ewan MacColl) and leftish views, which led him into hot water when his *Gone for a Soldier* (1980) turned out to be one long diatribe against the British soldier. None of which should be allowed to diminish some real achievements, from *Joe the Chainmaker* (c 1958) onwards. In 1982 he started an intermittent series of people talking about work, *A Moment to Talk*.   PP

Donner Pass: The Road to Survival
US 1978 96m colour TVM
NBC/Sunn Classic (James Simmons)
Wagon train families trapped in a mountain pass are forced to become cannibals.
Faint-hearted treatment of an old American semi-legend. No excitement, no style.
w S. S. Schweizer d James L. Conway ph Henning Schellerup m Bob Summers
Robert Fuller, Andrew Prine, Michael Callan, Diane McBain, John Anderson

Donner, Richard (c 1936–). American director who hit the big time in movies after a long TV apprenticeship including *Have Gun Will Travel*, *Perry Mason*, *The Twilight Zone*, *The Fugitive*, *Cannon* and *Kojak*. TV movies include *Lucas Tanner*, *Sara T*, *Sons and Daughters*, *Bronk*.

Donny and Marie. A series of variety spectaculars with the toothiest hosts in the business, brother and sister Osmonds. Some of the guest numbers were inventively staged. The weekly one-hour series began in 1976 on ABC, produced by Sid and Marty Krofft, and lasted three seasons.

Donovan's Kid
US 1980 96m colour TVM
NBC/Walt Disney (Christopher Hibler)
One of two conmen touring the old west with a monkey learns he has a child in San Francisco.
Lethargic family entertainment from a tired stable.
w Harry Spalding, Peter S. Fischer *d* Bernard McEveety *ph* Al Francis *m* Jimmie Haskell
Darren McGavin, Mickey Rooney, Shelley Fabares, Murray Hamilton, Ross Martin, Michael Conrad

Don't Ask Me. YTV's lowbrow science and medicine show, 1975–9, in which a panel of experts showed off to a studio audience with the occasional aid of filmed bits. Dr David Bellamy was an early member. Dr Miriam Stoppard (playwright Tom's wife) and the tedious Dr Magnus Pyke were the regulars. *Don't Just Sit There* followed in 1980–1.   PP

Don't Be Afraid of the Dark *
US 1973 74m colour TVM
Lorimar/Allen Epstein
A young couple move into an old house and find supernatural creatures already in occupation.
Foolish but effective ghost story.
w Nigel McKeand *d* John Newland
Jim Hutton, Kim Darby, Barbara Anderson, William Demarest, Pedro Armendariz Jnr

Don't Be Silly * (GB 1979; 70m; colour). Marital drama by Rachel Billington ending in a knock-out, i.e. on the vexed subject of wife battery among the professional classes, and highly perceptive about the way a marriage could break in such an extreme way. Susan Fleetwood played the victim with just the right drowsy irritatingness, always puncturing the romantic moment, remembering to do the right thing at the wrong time, taking the blame as the easiest way out and in the end seeming to invite, even need, hubby's assault. 'If he didn't love me, he wouldn't bother to hit me.' With Christopher Godwin; directed by Kenneth Ives; produced by Innes Lloyd; for BBC.   PP

Don't Call Me Charlie
Working title: *Vive Judson McKay*
US 1962 26 × 25m bw
NBC
In post-war Paris, an American private forms a friendship with his eccentric colonel.
Curious but unsuccessful comedy series.
Josh Prine, John Hubbard, Cully Richard, Linda Lawson, Arte Johnson

Don't Do It Dempsey *
GB 1960 6 × 30m bw
Brian Reece as an amorous, thirsty, disorganized bachelor. Written for the BBC by Patrick Campbell and Vivienne Knight in a deliberate attempt to break away from the then-traditional British silly-ass hero, this engaging comedy series found no greater favour with the traditional English audience than the comparable *Casanova '73*.   PP

Don't Eat the Snow in Hawaii: see Magnum, PI

Don't Forget to Write ****
GB 1977–9 18 × 50m colour
BBC (Joe Waters)
Screenwriter Charles Wood's uproarious saga of a screenwriter very like Charles Wood up against writer's block, demon film directors and a chaotic home life. Developed from his contribution to YTV's *Ten Commandments* anthology in 1971. George Cole was again our hero, alternating between despair and a devious glee; Gwen Watford his wife, soaring into high alto tizzies of disbelief; Francis Matthews the fellow-writer friend supposedly based on Peter Nichols. Guest appearances were made by thinly disguised versions of such film industry luminaries as Dino de Laurentiis and director Pierre Schoendorffer. Dull BBC no-men argued that a professional writer's problems were too specialized for general amusement (though they had sustained *The Dick Van Dyke Show* long enough) and the series was axed after three short seasons.   PP
LH: I found it heavy going despite the star.

'Mary thinks there is something alive under her bed. Mary is right!'
Don't Go To Sleep
US 1983 96m colour TVM
ABC/Warner/Aaron Spelling (Richard Lang)
Murder in the family is the order of the day when a dead daughter reappears to her younger sister . . .
Teasing but not very satisfactory *Psycho*-style thriller.

w Ned Wynn *d* Richard Lang *ph* Chuck Arnold *m* Dominic Frontiere

Dennis Weaver, Valerie Harper, Ruth Gordon, Robin Ignico, Oliver Robins, Robert Webber

Don't Wait Up (GB 1983–6; 18 × 30m). Father and son keep house together after both their marriages have ended; not so much a sitcom as a sitcharm, played by Tony Britton and Nigel Havers with the gentlemanly virtues to endear them to a better class of audience. Written by George Layton; produced and directed by Harold Snoad, for BBC.   PP

Don't Look Back
US 1981 96m colour TVM
ABC/TBA Productions/Satie Productions (Danny Arnold)
The life of baseball star Leroy (Satchel) Paige.
A black makes good again. Lawks, Miss Scarlett, I think I'se seen this before.
w Ron Rubin, *book Maybe I'll Pitch Forever* by Satchel Paige *d* Richard A. Colla *ph* Hector Figueroa *m* Jack Elliott
Lou Gossett Jnr, Beverly Todd, Cleavon Little, Ernie Barnes, Clifton Davis, Hal Williams

Don't Push, I'll Charge When I'm Ready
US 1969 97m colour TVM
Universal
Adventures of an Italian POW in the US.
Drawn-out farce over-exploiting Italian volubility.
w Al Ramus, John Shaner *d* Nathaniel Lande
Enzo Cerusico, Cesar Romero, Soupy Sales, Sue Lyon

Don't Rock the Boat (GB 1982). Half-hour comedy series from Thames about a widower of 53 who against the advice of his children marries a girl half his age. Results unremarkable. With Nigel Davenport, Sheila White. Written by John Esmonde, Bob Larbey.

The Doomsday Flight *
US 1966 97m colour TVM
Universal
A mad bomber is discovered on a jet plane between Los Angeles and New York.
Obvious but effective suspenser.
w Rod Serling *d* William Graham
Jack Lord, Edmond O'Brien, Katherine Crawford, Van Johnson, John Saxon

Doomsday for Dyson * (GB 1958; 50m; bw). J. B. Priestley's dramatized tract on behalf of nuclear disarmament, historically of great interest but at the time rather an anti-climax, so great had been expectations or apprehensions. After a brilliantly chilly opening film sequence, proceedings reverted to a mannered trial and investigation reminiscent of progressive theatre of the thirties. With Ian Hunter. Directed by Silvio Narizzano; for Granada.
† The play was followed by the 'balanced' studio discussion then deemed essential (and sometimes still so) after a controversial programme. Taking part were Barbara Castle and Donald Soper for nuclear disarmament, Peter Thorneycroft and Emanuel Shinwell against.   PP

Doomwatch (GB 1970–71). Fashionable fiction series for BBC about élite corps of scientific watchdogs appointed to foil any threats to the environment, the human race, etc, posed by industry or technology. What its admirers never seemed to notice (apart from the tattiness of many of the stories) were the arbitrary, secret-police powers invested in our heroes, who included Robert Powell making his effective TV debut.   PP

Doonican, Val (1932–). Easy-going Irish singer, the popular host of many British variety series from the mid-sixties.

The Doris Day Show
US 1968–72 128 × 25m colour
CBS/Arwin (Terry Melcher)
A sitcom with four formats. To begin with the star played a country widow and mother, in the second year she was a secretary in San Francisco, in the third she brought her children to the city, and in the fourth she was a bachelor news reporter.
None worked particularly well, but the intentions were amiable.
Doris Day, Denver Pyle, Billy de Wolfe, Edward Andrews, Patrick O'Neal, Kay Ballard, John Dehner

Dors, Diana (1931–84). Jolly British sex symbol and actress (in later life stout actress) whose only TV series was *Queenie's Castle* (1970–2), but she popped up in many single plays, comedy bills and game shows.   PP

Dortort, David (1916–). American executive producer, notably of *Bonanza* and *High Chaparral*.

Dossers (GB 1984). Anthropologist Melissa Llewellyn-Davies (*Diary of a Maasai Village*, etc.) dropped her gaze to her own doorstep for this sharp study of London's down-and-outs who sleep rough. Directed by Michael Yorke.   PP

Dotrice, Roy (1923–). British character actor with a taste for senile impersonation which in 1969 won him a BAFTA award for his impression of John Aubrey in *Brief Lives*. Also notable in *Grand Babylon Hotel*, *Dickens of London*. TV movie: *Family Reunion*.

Dotto (US 1958). A half-hour quiz format for NBC, in which correct answers enabled contestants to link numbered dots on a board and gradually reveal the face of a celebrity. Also popular in Great Britain.

† *Dotto* has the distinction of being the first quiz show accused of rigging answers. An enquiry precipitated the quiz show scandals of 1959.

Double Dare
GB 1976 75m colour
Dennis Potter play about costive playwright holed up in hotel room with actress collaborator while elsewhere in the same hotel a call-girl played by the same Kika Markham visits boorish red-faced client. Cross-cutting between room dominated by typewriter and room dominated by bed makes a familiar Potter connection between sex and creativity, but a novel (for Potter) and much more interesting proposition, that everyone had somehow passed this way before – as in the Time plays of J. B. Priestley – is dumped in favour of what science-fiction enthusiasts call a solipsist explanation: actress and call-girl are one, the red-faced client is a projection of the hero and it's all in the mind. At the time I felt cheated: the time trip was a trip tease. But an absorbing intricately constructed, fiercely moral play. With Alan Dobie. Directed by Alan Bridges; produced by Kenith Trodd; for BBC.   PP

Double Dare (US 1984 × 50m). Shortlived action series with Billy Dee Williams as a burglar who helps the cops rather than go to jail. Where, oh where, have we seen it all before? With Ken Wahl, Joe Maher; produced by Terry Hughes for Warner/CBS.

The Double Deckers
GB 1970 17 × 25m colour
TCF (Roy Simpson)
Seven children use an old double-decker bus as their clubhouse and get into various scrapes.
Passable city version of the *William* books.
w Harry Booth, Glyn Jones *d* Harry Booth
Peter Firth, Bruce Clark, Brinsley Forde, Melvyn Hayes

Double Indemnity
US 1973 74m colour TVM
Universal (David Victor)
An insurance salesman helps a client to murder her husband.
A fair copy of the 1944 film without any of its character or effectiveness.
w from the original screenplay by Billy Wilder and Raymond Chandler and the novel by James M. Cain *d* Jack Smight *m* Billy Goldenberg
Richard Crenna, Samantha Eggar, Lee J. Cobb, Robert Webber

The Double Life of Henry Phyfe
US 1965 17 × 25m colour
ABC/Filmways
A meek clerk is plunged into espionage and intrigue.
Moderate, predictable comedy.
Red Buttons, Fred Clark

Double Your Money. British quiz based on *The 64,000 Dollar Question*: hosted by Hughie Green, it played for nearly 20 years from 1955.

'The only thing they had in common was the way they were murdered!'
Doubletake
US 1985 2 × 96m colour miniseries
CBS/Titus (Thomas de Wolfe)
A New York police lieutenant investigates the case of two decapitated corpses whose heads have been exchanged.
Ghoulish stuff with seamy trimmings, very watchable for those in the mood, hard to take for those who aren't.
w John Gay, *novel Switch* by William Bayer *d* Jud Taylor *ph* Barry Sonnenfeld *m* Arthur Rubinstein *pd* Charles C. Bennett
Richard Crenna, Beverly D'Angelo, Vincent Baggetta, Paul Gleason, Cliff Gorman, Drew Snyder, Julie Bovasso

Dougall, Robert (1913–). Dignified, popular British newsreader who on his retirement produced a book about TV, *In and Out of The Box*; also hosted *Stars on Sunday*, etc. Since 1982 has presented C4's magazine for the over-60s, *Years Ahead*.

DOOMSDAY FOR DYSON. A memento of the days when realism was not part of television drama. Ian Hunter was J. B. Priestley's doomed hero.

Douglas, Colin (1912–). Weighty British character actor who became a celebrity as Father in *A Family At War*.

Douglas, Donna (1933–) (Doris Smith). American leading lady who scored as the dumb Ellie May in *The Beverly Hillbillies* but was not much heard from subsequently. Appeared 1981 in TV movie, *The Return of the Beverly Hillbillies*.

Douglas Fairbanks Jnr Presents: see Fairbanks, Douglas Jnr

Douglas, Jack (1927–). Tall, gangling British comedian who made an act out of nervous tics. Stooge to many other comedians; joined the *Carry On* team in the late sixties; in series, *The Shillingbury Tales*.

Douglas, Kirk (1916–) (Issur Danielovich Demsky). American star actor seen on TV in *The Moneychangers*, *Victory at Entebbe*, *Mousey*, *Remembrance of Love*, *Draw!*, *Amos*.

Douglas, Melvyn (1901–81) (Melvyn Hesselberg). The immaculate American leading man of thirties and forties films and the impressive elder statesman of the American stage played many guest roles on TV from the mid-fifties, and appeared in a forgotten series called *Hollywood Offbeat*. Emmy 1967 for *Do Not Go Gentle Into This Good Night*. TV movies: *Companions in Nightmare, Hunters Are for Killing, Death Takes a Holiday, Death Squad, Murder or Mercy, Intimate Strangers*.

Douglas, Michael (1945–). American actor, son of Kirk Douglas; familiar as co-lead of *The Streets of San Francisco*. TV movie: *When Michael Calls*.

Douglas, Mike (1925–) (Michael Delaney Dowd Jnr). American linkman, host of a popular syndicated daytime talk show.

Dowager in Hot Pants (GB 1971). A rather deliberately unbalanced documentary on Hollywood, with interviews with Adolph Zukor, Betty Blythe and Stanley Kramer. Written and directed by Jack Gold; produced by Jeremy Isaacs; for Thames.

Down and Out * (GB 1981). BBC *Nationwide* reporter Tony Wilkinson's bold idea to live rough in London for a month, half a century after George Orwell had done the same thing for a book. A camera crew secretly filmed him while, pretending to be an unemployed northerner, he slept in doss-houses and washed up in hotel kitchens. The results, aired in four *Nationwide* segments, were scarifying, though to be fair at least one London borough, Camden, claimed that he had been unduly selective. PP

Down, Lesley-Anne (1954–). British leading lady who hasn't looked back since playing Lady Georgina in *Upstairs Downstairs*. Major subsequent TV achievement: Phyllis in THE ONE AND ONLY PHYLLIS DIXEY. Esmeralda in *The Hunchback of Notre Dame*; also *Murder is Easy*, *The Last Days of Pompeii*, *Arch of Triumph*, *North and South*.

Down to Earth (US 1985; × 25m). Low-budget domestic sitcom made for Ted Turner's cable network. An angel is sent to Earth to gain her wings, and becomes housekeeper for an ordinary family. All very claustrophobic and lacking in real zest. With Carol Mansell; produced by Rick Miner for the Arthur Company.

Downie, Nick (1946–). Lone-wolf British reporter, ex-SAS, who liked to cover war zones, notably Afghanistan, as his own cameraman and recordist, thus running into crossfire from the cinema and TV trade union ACTT as well as from Russian troops. Has now switched to non-warlike documentaries. *Survive* (series), 1984.   PP

Downs, Hugh (1921–). American talk show host, on the *Today* programme in the mid-sixties.

Doyle, David (1925–). American character actor, seen to advantage in *Bridget Loves Bernie* and *Charlie's Angels*.

Drabble, Phil (1914–). British country-life and field sports specialist who has presented *One Man and His Dog* since it began.

Dragnet ****
aka: *Badge 714*
US 1951–8 300 approx. × 25m bw
US 1967–9 98 × 25m colour
NBC/MCA/Jack Webb
Stories of Los Angeles police sergeant Joe Friday.

Simple but revolutionary cop show recording the minutiae of investigation, conversation and characterization in stretches of apparently flat but hypnotic dialogue. ('8.22 a.m. We were on our way downtown . . . All I want is the facts, ma'am.')

cr JACK WEBB, RICHARD BREEN *m* WALTER SCHUMANN

JACK WEBB, Ben Alexander (later Harry Morgan)

Dragnet *
GB title: *The Big Dragnet*
US 1969 97m colour TVM
Universal/Jack Webb
Sgt Joe Friday investigates the murder of several models.
Enjoyable rehash of the old *Dragnet* formula.
w Richard L. Breen d Jack Webb
Jack Webb, Harry Morgan, Vic Perrin, Virginia Gregg, Gene Evans

Dragon, Daryl (1942–). American musician, back-up for the Beach Boys before he teamed with his wife Toni Tennille as The Captain and Tennille.

The Dragon Has Two Tongues (GB 1985; 13 × 30m). Tennis-match history of Wales with Wynford Vaughan Thomas and Professor Gwyn Alf Williams batting the facts and the suppositions to and fro as one strove to support a romantic view and the other a Marxist interpretation. 'History with a giggle perhaps,' wrote Welsh critic Gethin Stoodley Thomas, 'but none the less impressive for that.' I thought it tiresome. Produced and directed by Colin Thomas, for HTV/S4C/C4.   PP

The Dragon's Opponent (GB 1973). Quaint bio-epic in two parts about Jack Howard, Earl of Suffolk, who crowned an adventurous life by making himself an expert on bomb fuses and was killed in World War II when trying to neutralize a new one; the quaintness came from the stilted dialogue handed over to lesser characters, especially the lower orders – unless it was meant to be a parody of dim British films of the period. With Ronald Pickup, Virginia McKenna; written by Colin Morris, for BBC.   PP

Drake, Charlie (1925–) (Charles Springall). Diminutive, roly-poly British comedian who scored a big hit in the fifties but subsequently grew tiresome.

drama-doc. The dramatized documentary dates from the early fifties, if not earlier, when BBC pioneers such as Colin Morris,

Tonight. A special <u>full</u> hour of...
DRACULA '79

- <u>Who</u> will save Mary from the horrifying kiss of the prince of darkness?
- <u>What</u> will happen to Kurt now that the count has sabotaged his car?
- <u>Why</u> have Dracula's fearsome Great Danes been unleashed on Mary?
- <u>When</u> will Dracula give up his endless pursuit of Kurt and Mary?
- Don't miss the most exciting Dracula chapters from the new suspense-filled "Cliffhangers" series!

THEY DON'T CALL 'EM
CLIFFHANGERS
FOR NOTHING.

8PM
TONIGHT!

4

DRACULA '79. The most filmed fiend in horror history even turned up as the hero of a chapter play when Universal thought it was a good idea to pack three serial episodes into an hour and called them CLIFFHANGERS. The public did not respond favourably, but Dracula quickly reappeared in several other guises.

Robert Barr and Duncan Ross were writing non-fiction scripts for actors acting out social and human problems: *The Pattern of Marriage*, *Woman Alone* (unmarried mum), *Rock Bottom* (alcoholic). Only when gamier or more controversial subjects were taken up (*Up the Junction*, *Cathy Come Home*) did purists start to demand a rigid separation. 'Is it a play or is it real? We have a right to be told.' In fact the hybrids were sometimes classed as plays, sometimes as documentaries. With the craze for biography and reconstructions of historical or recent events, e.g. *Culloden*, *45 Cranley Drive* (about the Lonsdale spy story) or *The Missiles of October* (Cuba missiles crisis), the element of actors playing named real-life characters was added, to the further distress of those who want fact and fiction compartmentalized. But the evidence is that most viewers take what is now a familiar convention in their stride. Why Granada should have pretended to be inventing it all over again in 1978 with a 'drama-doc' unit and a series of fairly unexceptional re-enactments of such exploits as the clandestine sale of the Mirage fighter to Israel is a mystery, though the hullabaloo was justified with the later special *Invasion.*   PP

Draper, Peter (1925–). British writer, one of the first to be put under regular contract (by ATV in 1958). Mostly gentle boy–girl comedies but occasional forays into more imaginative and striking plots, notably *A Touch of the Jumbos* for LWT (1970), in which power and promotion games within a multinational corporation are played out aboard a chartered Boeing 747.   PP

The Draughtsman's Contract * (GB 1982). Peter Greenaway's 'elegant piece of upthegardenpathmanship' (NFT programme note) about the 17th-century tease who hires an artist to sketch her husband's estate in return for a like number of sexual favours. Though thought of primarily as a cinema offering, it was in fact a C4 *Film on Four.* With Anthony Higgins, Janet Suzman, Anne Louise Lambert. Produced by the BFI, for C4.   PP

LH: 'The sort of piece that gives highbrows a bad name.'

Draw! *
US 1984 96m colour TVM
HBO/Astral/Bryna (Ronald I. Cohen)

A drunken sheriff is roused into action when his old adversary takes over the town.
Spoofy western which comes off pretty well until the halfway mark.

w Stanley Mann   *d* Steven H. Stern *ph* Laslo George   *m* Ken Wannberg

Kirk Douglas, James Coburn, Alexandra Bastedo, Graham Jarvis, Derek McGrath

A Dream for Christmas *
US 1973 100m colour TVM
Lorimar

A black parson moves from the Midwest to Los Angeles, and finds a whole new set of problems.
Pleasing family fare.

w John McGreevy   *d* Ralph Senensky

Hari Rhodes, Beah Richards, Lynn Hamilton, George Spell

Dream House
US 1981 96m colour TVM
CBS/Columbia/Philip Mandelker, Leonard Hill

A sophisticated lady architect from New York visits Georgia and is wooed by a local boy who pursues her back to the big city.
Mildly romantic comedy-drama which needed a stronger initial grip.

w Mike Lloyd Ross   *d* Joseph Hardy

John Schneider, Marilu Henner, Michael Gross, Miguel Fernandez

The Dream Machine (GB 1964). An interesting ATV documentary showing rehearsals for a light entertainment show, followed by the show itself. Written by S. C. Green and R. M. Hills; directed by Denis Mitchell; produced by Francis Essex.

The Dream Makers *
US 1975 74m colour TVM
MGM (Charles Robert McLain)

A college professor becomes a recording executive.
Unusual contemporary drama, not very exciting but convincingly done.

w Bill Svanoe   *d* Boris Sagal

James Franciscus, Diane Baker, John Astin, Kenny Rogers, Mickey Jones

Dream Stuffing (GB 1984; 10 × 30m). Up-to-the-minute sitcom about two young girls getting by on nothing very much, with blacks (one of them's father and the local DHSS officer) and homosexuals (their chum) fitted in without trying to make points. Written by Paul Hines and Su Wilkins, produced by Humphrey Barclay, for Limehouse/C4.   PP

Dreams
US 1984 13 × 25m colour
CBS/Lorimar/Centerpoint (Ronald E. Frazier)

Young Philadephia musicians form a rock group with the help of the local rich girl.
Pleasant but unoriginal early-evening programme filler.

cr Andy Borowitz

John Stamos, Jani Gertz, Cain Devore, Albert Macklin, Valerie Stevenson

Dreams of Leaving
GB 1980 75m colour

Joys and pains of an all-consuming but unconsummated love affair as suffered by a priggish young journalist arriving in Fleet Street en route – it was tempting to suspect – for his natural destination in Gray's Inn Road. David Hare's BBC play was oddly comparable (if also inferior) to David Halliwell's *Cock, Hen and Courting Pit* of 1966, down to an epilogue in which the participants reviewed the grand passion ten years later.   PP

Dreier, Alex (1916–). Portly American news commentator who gave it up for a chance to become this generation's Sydney Greenstreet, and somehow muffed it.

Dress Gray (US 1986; 2 × 96m). Miniseries produced by Warner for NBC, based on the novel by Lucian K. Truscott IV about a murder cover-up at West Point.

Drew, Robert (19 –) and **Leacock, Richard** (19 –). American pioneers of cinema (or television) *vérité*, the now commonplace technique of shadowing a chosen subject with hand-held camera and mike while trying to fade into the wallpaper yourself. Their films, initially for Time–Life *c* 1960, included studies of a racing driver on the eve of the Indianapolis 500, and a politician (John Kennedy) negotiating the Primary that was to set him on the road to the White House – the thinking then was that if the character were sufficiently engrossed by larger events he would more easily forget about the camera. This consideration was later found not to be vital; in any case Drew and Leacock were already beginning to move by 1963 towards the inclusion of some direct-to-camera observations, i.e. ceasing to pretend it isn't there. *The Chair*, that year, is an extraordinary account of the preparations for the execution of a convicted murderer in the US and last-minute attempts to win him a reprieve. Probably half the non-fiction films seen on TV today owe something to these two men and such fellow-innovators as the Maysles brothers.   PP

Drewett, Richard (19 –). British producer with LWT specializing in programmes on the frontier between light entertainment and something more ambitious, e.g. various Clive James shows, *An Audience With . . .* and, most notably, *The Trial of Richard III*. BAFTA award 1984.   PP

The Drinking Party ** (GB 1965; bw). Dreamy, pagan film directed by Jonathan Miller from Plato's *Symposium* of all things, shot in Stowe Park with Leo McKern as a rumbustious senior tutor of a Socrates enlightening a bevy of undergraduates as to the essence of love. A follow-up the next year, *The Death of Socrates*, failed to repeat an unusual success. Written by Leo Aylen; for BBC.   PP

Drive Hard, Drive Fast
US 1969 95m colour TVM
Universal (Jo Swerling Jnr)

A womanizing racing driver gets involved in a murder plot in Mexico City.

Unconvincing rigmarole padded out with local colour.

w Matthew Howard d Douglas Heyes
Brian Kelly, Joan Collins, Henry Silva, Joseph Campanella

Driving Ambition (GB 1984; 8 × 50m). Bleak feministic serial about housewife determined to muscle in on the male preserve of motor sport. With Donna Hewitt, Gavin Richards. Written by Paula Milne, directed by Michael Simpson, produced by Carol Robertson, for BBC. PP

Dromgoole, Patrick (1930–). British director, producer and executive, since 1968 with HTV, latterly as assistant managing director and executive producer of this company's ambitious co-production film ventures, including *Robin of Sherwood* (1984–5), *Return to Treasure Island* (1985), *D.P.* (1986). Directed *Man and Superman* (1982), *Chateau Arsenic* (1985).   PP

'He's quitting the rat race, burning his credit cards, and trying to convince his family it's for their own good!'
Drop-out Father
US 1983 96m colour TVM
CBS (Ann and Bob Shanks)

An executive disgusted with middle-class materialism decides to abandon success, but his family does not necessarily share his new values.

Half-assed social comedy which starts promisingly but gives up the ghost before halfway.

w Bob Shanks d Don Taylor ph Gerald Perry Finnerman m Peter Matz
Dick Van Dyke, Mariette Hartley, George Coe, William Daniels, Monte Markham

Drummonds (GB 1985; 10 × 52m). Cosy drama series set in a potty boys' prep school in the fifties, with Richard Pasco recycling his *Sorrel and Son* characterization to become the widowed headmaster. Problems on his problem-list included rebellious son, bank overdraft, squabbling staff and romance with a single parent. Created by Reg Gadney, also written by Maggie Wadey and T. R. Bowen. Produced by Colin Tucker, for LWT.   PP

Drury, James (1934–). Stalwart American leading man of the outdoor type. Series include *The Virginian*, *Firehouse*. TV movies: *Breakout*, *Alias Smith and Jones*, *The Devil and Miss Sarah*.

dry run. A dress rehearsal.

Dryer, Fred (*c.* 1951–). American leading man, a former sports star with a face like a composite of Richard Widmark and Clint Eastwood. Leaped into fame as *Hunter*.

The Duchess of Duke Street *
GB 1976–7 31 × 50m colour (VTR)
BBC/Time–Life (John Hawkesworth)
The *Upstairs, Downstairs* team virtually changed channels en bloc to make this rather similar series about a working-class cook who becomes the no-nonsense owner of a fashionable London hotel. It was based on the true story of Rosa Lewis and the Cavendish hotel.
Carefully reconstructed period drama, slightly marred by its strident central character and her eccentric cohorts, but usually very watchable.
cr John Hawkesworth
Gemma Jones, Richard Vernon, Christopher Cazenove, John Cater, Victoria Plucknett, John Welsh
'A winning mixture of nostalgia and down-to-earth realism.' – *Sun*

The Duck Factory
US 1984 6 × 25m colour
NBC/MTM (Allan Burns)
Problems for the staff of a Saturday morning cartoon factory.
The tone is too flip and the characters too zany for popularity, and the series folded quickly.
cr Allan Burns, Herbert Klynn
Jim Carrey, Julie Payne, Nancy Lane, Jay Tarses, Don Messick

Duel ***
US 1971 74 or 90m colour TVM
Universal (George Eckstein)
A car driver on the back roads of California is menaced by a petrol tanker.
Overlong (even longer for theatrical release) but brilliantly made TV movie which started its director off on a successful career. A simple suspenser, it pits one man against a huge anonymous threat as unexplained as the menace in *The Birds*.
w RICHARD MATHESON *d* STEVEN SPIELBERG *ph* JACK A. MARTA *m* Billy Goldenberg
DENNIS WEAVER (the others are bit parts)

Duel, Pete (1940–71) (Peter Deuel). Promising young leading man of the sixties, a suicide victim. TV series: *Love on a Rooftop*, ALIAS SMITH AND JONES.

Duff, Howard (1917–). American leading man/character actor of the forties and fifties. Played many guest roles on TV and starred in four series: *Mr Adams and Eve*, *Dante*, *The Felony Squad*, *Flamingo Road*. TV movies include *In Search of America*, *A Little Game*, *The Heist*, *Snatched*, *In the Glitter Palace*, *Ski Lift to Death*, *Battered*, *East of Eden*.

Duffell, Peter (19 –). British film and TV director around some years before jumping into prominence with CAUGHT ON A TRAIN (1980). Since then *The Far Pavilions*, *Experience Preferred But Not Essential*. PP

Duffy, Patrick (1949–). Gentle-mannered American leading man, a hit in THE MAN FROM ATLANTIS and a solid second lead in *Dallas*. TV movie: *Enola Gay*.

Duffy's Tavern
US 1954   × 25m bw
NBC
A televersion of the radio programme about a bar–restaurant on New York's Third Avenue and the types who congregate therein.
Ed Gardner, Alan Reed, Patte Chapman, Jimmy Conlin

Duggan, Andrew (1923–). American character actor who played numerous second leads in the movies and became a TV star in *Bourbon Street Beat*, *Room for One More* and *Lancer*. 1979: Eisenhower in *Backstairs at the White House*.

The Duke (US 1954). Half-hour comedy series for NBC, with Paul Gilbert as a boxer aspiring to become an artist.

The Duke
US 1979 96m colour TVM
NBC/Universal/Stephen J. Cannell
A 40-year-old Chicago prizefighter turns detective.
Ho-hum pilot for series that lasted four episodes. Not attractive in any way.
w Stephen J. Cannell *d* Lawrence Doheny *ph* Steve Poster *m* Mike Post, Pete Carpenter
Robert Conrad, Larry Manetti, Red West, Patricia Conwell

Duke, Daryl (1935–). Canadian director in Hollywood since 1964. Many series episodes; TV movies include *The President's Plane Is Missing*, *A Cry for Help*, *Jigsaw John*, *Griffin and Phoenix*.

Duke, Patty (1946–). American child star who grew up into a rather intense little actress of offbeat roles, married John Astin, and now calls herself Patty Duke Astin. Series: *The Patty Duke Show.* TV movies include *My Sweet Charlie, If Tomorrow Comes, She Waits, Deadly Harvest, Rich Man, Poor Man, Fire, Curse of the Black Widow, Killer on Board, The Storyteller, A Family Upside Down, Hanging by a Thread, Before and After, The Women's Room, The Baby Sitter, The Miracle Worker, Mom the Wolfman and Me, The Violation of Sarah McDavid.*

The Dukes of Hazzard
US 1979–84   × 50m colour
CBS/Warner/Paul Picard/Piggy
  Productions (Joseph Gantman)
Present-day examples of a moonshining family who are always in trouble with the law. A series which succeeded despite everybody's better judgement, car chases and smashes being the order of the day.
cr Gy Waldron

Tom Wopat, John Schneider, Catherine Bach, Denver Pyle, James Best, Sorrell Booke, Waylon Jennings

'Apparently the idea is to see that the south will never rise again – and that TV takes another step backwards.' – *Daily Variety*

Dullea, Keir (1936–). American actor. TV movies: *Black Water Gold, Law and Order, The Legend of the Golden Gun, Brave New World, The Hostage Tower, No Place to Hide.*

Dummy ** (GB 1977; 78m; colour). Moving case-history drama-doc about a deaf girl (played by Geraldine James) exploited by shoddy hearing people until she ends up in dock on a manslaughter charge. Hands fluttering, eyes bright at first with determination to make herself understood, then slowly dulling into acceptance, Geraldine James's performance was both a remarkable feat and a revelation. Written by Hugh Whitemore; directed and produced by Franc Roddam; photographed by Chris Menges; for ATV.   PP

Dummy
US 1979 96m colour TVM
Warner/Konigsberg (Sam Manners,
  Ernest Tidyman)
An illiterate deaf and dumb black youth is accused of murdering a prostitute; his court-appointed attorney is also deaf.
Fact-based courtroom drama which won an Emmy nomination.
w Ernest Tidyman *d* Frank Perry *ph* Gayne Rescher *m* Gil Askey

Paul Sorvino, LeVar Burton, Brian Dennehy, Rose Gregorio, Gregg Henry, Steven Williams

The Dumplings
US 1976 8 × 25m colour (VTR)
NBC/Norman Lear (Don Nicholl, Michael
  Ross, Bernie West)
Unsuccessful comedy series, based on a comic strip by Fred Lucky, about a happy, fat couple who decide to run a restaurant.

James Coco, Geraldine Brooks

Duncalf, Bill (19 –). Veteran British outside-broadcast producer who blossomed in mid-career as author-producer of strikingly original documentaries, from a 1959 reconstruction of the first surgical operation under chloroform in 1846 to *The Epic that Never Was.* Series: *They Made History*, 1960.
                                              PP

Duncan, Sandy (1946–). Gamine-like American star actress, usually in light comedy. Her series *The Sandy Duncan Show* (aka *Funny Face*) was not a success; more recently she played the title role in *Pinocchio.*

Dundee and the Culhane
US 1967 13 × 50m colour
CBS (Sam Rolfe)
In the old west, a wandering anti-violence lawyer has an assistant who protects him.
A western with a twist which didn't quite work.

John Mills, Sean Garrison

The Dunera Boys (Australia 1985; 2 × 115m). The transportation to Australia of a job lot of aliens, refugees and suspected Fifth Columnists in the first panic-stricken reaction to the German sweep through Europe in 1940 was hardly an edifying episode in British history, but this loony Aussie version got so much so comically wrong that only the embattled Australian camp commandant (Simon Chilvers) carried any credence. With Bob Hoskins, Warren Mitchell, Joseph Spano. Written and directed by Ben Lewin, produced by Bob Weis, for Jethro Films. Shown in GB by C4.
                                              PP

Duning, George (1908–). American composer of innumerable film and TV scores.

Dunkley, Chris (1944–). British critic (*Financial Times, Listener*) and frequent broadcaster on broadcasting matters. Series: *The Whistle-blowers.* Book: *Television Today and Tomorrow: Wall-to-Wall Dallas?*, 1985.

Dunlop, Michael (1945–85). British drama producer who started as a solicitor in Granada's contracts and copyright department. *A Family at War* (associate producer), first 99 episodes of *Crown Court*, etc. Produced and directed documentaries for ATV, 1979–82. Final credit: *Mapp and Lucia* for LWT, 1985.   PP

Dunn, Clive (*c* 1923–). British character comedian who has been playing old men for 30 years. Became familiar in *Bootsie and Snudge* and had his biggest hit in DAD'S ARMY.

Dunning, Ruth (1917–8). Popular British character actress, at her peak in the sixties playing an assortment of middle-aged types.

Dunninger, Joseph (1896–). American mentalist who had several TV series in the fifties and sixties.

Dunnock, Mildred (1904–). American character actress, usually of motherly types. TV movies: *A Brand New Life*, *A Summer without Boys*, *Murder or Mercy*, *The Best Place To Be*, *And Baby Makes Six*, *Baby Comes Home*.

✸ **Durante, Jimmy** (1893–1980). Classic American comedian who came late in life to TV but made a number of specials his own, and appeared regularly during the fifties in *All Star Revue*, *Colgate Comedy Hour*, *Texaco Star Theatre*, etc; his trademarks being his splendid nose or schnozzola and his sign-off line: 'Goodnight Mrs Calabash, wherever you are.' (Mrs Calabash was his pet name for his deceased wife.) Emmy 1952, best comedian.

Durbridge, Francis (1908–). British thriller writer who produced a number of splendid serials for the BBC: *Bat out of Hell*, *The World of Tim Frazer*, *The Doll*, etc.

Durning, Charles (19 –). Burly American actor who rose in the seventies almost to star status. TV movies; *The Connection*, *The Trial of Chaplain Jensen*, *Queen of the Stardust Ballroom*, *Switch*, *Captains and the Kings*, *Special Olympics*, *Studs Lonigan*, *Attica*, *A Perfect Match*, *Crisis at Central High*, *The Best Little Girl in the World*, *Dark Night of the Scarecrow*, *Eye to Eye*, *Death of a Salesman*

Duryea, Dan (1907–68). Laconic American character actor who in the earlier days of TV was *China Smith*, and died in harness on *Peyton Place*.

The Dustbinmen. British half-hour comedy series about a gang of roughneck garbage collectors. Credited with starting the seventies trend towards crudity in British comedy. Created by Jack Rosenthal; with Bryan Pringle, Trevor Bannister, Brian Wilde, Tim Wylton, Graham Haberfield.

Dusty's Trail
US 1973 26 × 25m colour
Metromedia/Sherwood Schwartz
Five wagons on the way west are separated from their friends.
Alarmingly incompetent rehash of *Gilligan's Island*, sadly lacking in jokes, pace and timing, and not helped by cheeseparing production.
w/cr Sherwood and Elroy Schwartz
Bob Denver, Forrest Tucker, Lori Saunders, Ivor Francis, Jeannine Riley, Bill Cort

Dutch Girls (GB 1985; 90m). Boys from minor Scottish public school on hockey-tour of Holland and failing to score on or off the pitch. Another tedious public schooldays confessional with elderly pupils (Timothy Spall, Colin Firth) redeemed only – and partially – by Bill Paterson as the accompanying sports master and Gusta Gerritsen as the nicest of the girls. Written by William Boyd, directed by Giles Foster, produced by Sue Birtwistle, for LWT.   PP

Duttine, John (1949–). Useful British actor in lean-heroic mould. *Spend, Spend, Spend* (1977), *People Like Us* and other R. F. Delderfield serials.   PP

Duty Free ****
GB 1984 12 × 30m
YTV (Vernon Lawrence)
Situation comedy to an entirely predictable formula (two couples holidaying in Spain) which somehow worked up and sustained a higher quotient of real laughter than almost any other. Though the original six-part batches were separated by six months and further delayed in the London area by a strike at Thames, it took only seconds to be wafted back to the series' unique fragrance of garlic, aftershave, duplicity and being horribly caught out.
'What makes this sitcom work while dozens fail,' I wrote, 'is the detail built into the four parts by the writers and performers. Joanna van Gyseghem's graciousness, Neil Stacy's complaisance, Keith Barron's desperate compulsions are the true springs of the comedy. There is no need for smart lines. They go only to the marvellous GWEN TAYLOR, and then are mostly battle cries as she fights to save her match.'
w Eric Chappell, Jean Warr *d* Vernon Lawrence
Carlos Douglas as Carlos the waiter
† A second series followed in 1986.   PP

GERALD DURRELL was one of the new breed of naturalists made famous by the television camera. Here seen in a 1983 programme with his wife Lee, he was known to more people than his celebrated writer brother Laurence.

Duvall, Robert (1931–). American star character actor whose best TV performance was as IKE. Also in *Fame Is the Name of the Game*.

Dying Room Only *
US 1973 73m colour TVM
Lorimar

A woman's husband mysteriously disappears from the washroom of a roadside café.
Adequate suspenser.

w Richard Matheson *d* Philip Leacock

Cloris Leachman, Ross Martin, Ned Beatty, Louise Latham

Dykstra, John (1947–). American special effects expert who won a 1979 Emmy for stylizing and producing BATTLESTAR GALACTICA.

Dylan, Bob (1941–) (Robert Zimmermann). American folk singer, in concert appearances.

Dynasty *
aka: *James Michener's Dynasty*
US 1976 100m colour TVM
David Frost

Problems of an Ohio pioneer family who become rich between the 1820s and the 1880s.
Satisfying through-the-years family drama with pioneer background: a projected series didn't go.

w Sidney Carroll, *novel* James A. Michener *d* Lee Phillips *m* Gil Melle

SARAH MILES, Stacy Keach, Harris Yulin, Harrison Ford, Tony Swartz

Dynasty
US 1981   × 50m colour
ABC/Aaron Spelling/Fox–Cat (E. Duke Vincent)

An oil-rich tycoon about to marry again has trouble with his family.
Witless, charmless imitation of *Dallas* which opened with a mind-boggling three-hour episode and struggled for half a season to

keep its head above water, but was later sent zooming to the box office heights by the entrance of Joan Collins as the evil Alexis, whose doings kept the world agog for several years.

cr Richard and Esther Shapiro

John Forsythe, Linda Evans, Pamela Sue Martin, Dale Robertson, Bo Hopkins, Al Corley, Pamela Bellwood

Dynasty II: The Colbys
US 1985–   × 50m colour
ABC/Warner/Aaron Spelling/Richard and Esther Shapiro

Dreary doings of a branch of the Carrington family, one with even more skeletons in the cupboard. Way over the top and not very amusing.

Charlton Heston, Barbara Stanwyck, Stephanie Beacham, Katharine Ross, John James, Emma Samms, Maxwell Caulfield, Tracy Scoggins, Ricardo Montalban, Joseph Campanella, Ken Howard, David Hedison, Ray Stricklyn

'Nice, dull, very rich folks.' – *Daily Variety*

'Too many thin plots, too many people, too little sense.' – *People* Magazine

The Eagle and the Bear
GB 1981 5 × 52m
YTV (Francis Gerard)

The Russian–American confrontation presciently examined by Jonathan Dimbleby early in the Reagan Presidency, late in the Brezhnev era, at the beginning of a 'Decade of Danger'. The opening and closing programme took a European view, the central three focused on three hotspots where Russian and American interests clashed – the Gulf, the Middle East and Dimbleby's pet obsession, the Horn of Africa.

w and *pres* Jonathan Dimbleby   *d* Francis Gerard   PP

Early Bird. The first communications satellite in synchronous orbit with the earth, i.e. appearing to remain in fixed station over the North Atlantic. Its debut as a global carrier of TV programmes in May 1965 could hardly have offered a more sensational promise of things to come. President Johnson harangued the governments of Europe, the American surgeon Michael de Bakey performed open-heart surgery for an audience of medics in Geneva, and a Canadian bank robber whose likeness was flashed on the screen was identified and arrested 2,000 miles away. Because of the high cost of renting TV time by satellite, however (each TV relay displaced much profitable telephone and telex traffic), Early Bird was soon restricted to hard news and major sporting events. As further satellites were launched usage increased again but still mainly for news, sport, special occasions and interviews. The relaying of entertainment programmes only became commonplace with the spread of commercial satellite distribution to cable operators in the eighties.   PP

An Early Frost *
US 1985 96m colour TVM
NBC (Perry Lafferty)

A young lawyer finds himself the victim of AIDS.
Serious, rather solemn telemovie decently exploring the new horror of the eighties: a disease which robs the body of its immunity and to which homosexuals are especially prone.

w Ron Cowen, Daniel Lipman   *d* John Erman

Ben Gazzara, Gena Rowlands, Aidan Quinn, Sylvia Sidney, D. W. Moffet

Earth II
US 1971 97m colour TVM
MGM/Wabe (William Reed Woodfield, Allan Balter)

A vast American space station is menaced by a Red Chinese nuclear weapon.
For its length probably the most expensive TV movie ever, scuttled by an entirely dull script and lack of humour.

w William Reed Woodfield, Allan Balter   *d* Tom Gries *ph* Michel Hugo *m* Lalo Schifrin
Gary Lockwood, Scott Hylands, Hari Rhodes, Anthony Franciosa, Mariette Hartley, Gary Merrill, Inga Swenson, Lew Ayres

Earthbound
US 1981 96m colour TVM
NBC/Taft (Michael Fisher)

A family from a distant galaxy finds itself grounded on Earth.
Simple-minded comedy which is a long way from either *The War of the Worlds* or *E.T.*

w Michael Fisher *d* James L. Conway *ph* Paul Hipp *m* Bob Summers

Burl Ives, Christopher Connelly, John Schuck, Meredith MacRae, Joseph Campanella

East End, West End (GB 1959). Jewish comedy series set among sharp operators and small businessmen in London, a first solo vehicle for Sid James, till then known only as Tony Hancock's foil. Written for him by Wolf Mankowitz but dimly executed by Rediffusion.   PP

East of Eden *
US 1981 4 × 96m colour
ABC/Mace Neufeld (Barney Rosenzweig)

A Connecticut farmer's two sons vie for father's affection; one of them later has trouble with his own two sons, whose mother was no good.

Lovingly photographed, slowly unfolding variation on the Cain and Abel theme, at times almost becoming the story of an evil woman; tension slackens at several points but as a job of film-making it's an impressive miniseries.

w Richard Shapiro, *novel* John Steinbeck *d* Harvey Hart *ph* FRANK STANLEY *m* Lee Holdridge

Timothy Bottoms, JANE SEYMOUR, Bruce Boxleitner, Karen Allen, Sam Bottoms, Hart Bochner, Lloyd Bridges, Warren Oates, Howard Duff, Anne Baxter, Richard Masur, Soon Teck-Oh

East 103rd Street (GB 1982). Extraordinary, unclassifiable, weirdly picturesque true-life film about a family of Puerto Rican drug addicts in New York's Spanish Harlem, made by the gifted cinematographer Chris Menges. Without going along with the fashionable liberal sentiments on the soundtrack about it all being a failure of the American Dream, it was undoubtedly the completest, most particular and most credible depiction ever of the circumstances of addiction.   PP

East Side West Side **
US 1963 26 × 50m bw
CBS/UA/Talent Associates

Problems of an urban social worker.
Solid drama series which tried to tackle issues of its day and was regarded as a milestone in series TV.

GEORGE C. SCOTT, Elizabeth Wilson, Cicely Tyson

EastEnders (GB since 1985). The BBC's bi-weekly soap opera set amid the everyday folk of the fictitious Albert Square in the imaginary London borough of Walford with the non-existent postcode of London E.20. Deliberately set up to challenge the 20-year domination of the north-country *Coronation Street*, it was heading the ratings within months, though only by adding in the audience for the Sunday compendium repeat – a feature never enjoyed by ITVs main-channel serials. Written and directed by various hands, produced by Julia Smith.
                                                            PP
LH: 'It also caused much controversy by bringing 'adult' language and behaviour into the family hour and Sunday afternoon.'

Eastwood, Clint (1930–). American leading man now known as the lean, cold-eyed hero of a score of action melodramas; older folk remember him as the

novice trail boss Rowdy Yates in the long-running series *Rawhide*.

Ebony. The BBC's long-running magazine programme for immigrant viewers. In 1985 producer John Wilcox introduced occasional specials devoted to one subject.

Ebony, Ivory and Jade
US 1980 74m colour TVM
CBS/Frankel Films (Jimmy Sangster)
The manager of a singing duo is an espionage agent.
Tolerable hokum with too much of the singing act.
w Jimmy Sangster *d* John Llewellyn Moxey *ph* Arch Dalzell *m* Earl Hagen
Bert Convy, Debbie Allen, Martha Smith, Claude Akins, Nina Foch, Frankie Valli

The Ebony Tower (GB 1984; 120m). Poor Laurence Olivier had somehow been inveigled into this dopey masturbation drama about an old artist, two nubile girls and a visiting wimp. These others were, respectively, Greta Scacchi, Toyah Wilcox and Roger Rees. Written by John Mortimer from the novel by John Fowles, directed by Robert Knights, for Granada.   PP

❋   **Ebsen, Buddy** (1908–) (Christian Rudolf Ebsen). American eccentric dancer who developed into a well-liked character actor and comedian, especially in two phenomenally popular series, *The Beverly Hillbillies* and *Barnaby Jones*. TV movies include *The Daughters of Joshua Cabe*, *Horror at 37,000 Feet*, *Tom Sawyer*, *The President's Plane Is Missing*, *Smash-up on Interstate Five*, *The Bastard*, *The Critical List*, *The Paradise Connection*, *The Return of the Beverly Hillbillies*.

EBU. The European Broadcasting Union; a union of broadcasters founded in 1950.

Eckersley, Peter (1936–81). Much-loved, influential British producer and executive, with Granada the whole of his 22 years in television. Adapted D. H. Lawrence, edited local nightly show *Scene at 6.30*, served as head of drama, produced *Hard Times* and *The Good Soldier*.   PP

The Ed Sullivan Show (originally *The Toast of the Town*): see Sullivan, Ed

The Ed Wynn Show
US 1958 15 × 25m bw
NBC/Screen Gems

Stories of a retired small-town judge and his orphan granddaughters.
Not quite this old vaudevillian's cup of tea.

Ed Wynn, Herb Vigran, Clarence Straight

† There had been a previous *Ed Wynn Show* in 1949 on CBS, a series of half-hour variety specials with famous comedy guests. This was the first series to originate live from Hollywood.

The Eddie Capra Mysteries
US 1978 13 × 50m colour
NBC/Universal (Peter S. Fischer)

A young lawyer prefers detection.
Old-fashioned whodunits, an improvement on the pilot, *Nightmare at Pendragon Castle*.

Vincent Bagetta, Wendy Phillips, Ken Swofford

'Perry Mason could not get a job in television today. No current TV lawyer would be caught dead in a tie.' – Robert MacKenzie, *TV Guide*

Eddington, Paul (1927–). British comedy actor of considerable style. Much on West End stage, but especially known on TV for THE GOOD LIFE and YES, MINISTER.

Edelman, Herb (1930–). American comedy character actor, in many guest roles, also series *The Good Guys*.

Edelman, Louis F. (19 –76). American independent producer whose hit series included *The Big Valley* and *Wyatt Earp*.

Eden, Barbara (1934–) (Barbara Huffman). Doll-like American comedy actress, known in TV for *I Dream of Jeannie* and *Harper Valley PTA*. TV movies include *The Feminist and the Fuzz*, *A Howling in the Woods*, *The Woman Hunter*, *Guess Who's Sleeping in my Bed*, *The Stranger Within*, *Let's Switch*, *How to Break up a Happy Divorce*, *Stonestreet*, *The Girls in the Office*.

Edge of Darkness ***
GB 1985 6 × 55m
BBC (Michael Wearing)

Dour north-country detective-inspector is drawn by the shocking death of his own daughter into investigating an international conspiracy to convert nuclear waste illegally into plutonium, essential ingredient of nuclear weapons.
Troy Kennedy Martin's Olympian screenplay mixed up-to-the-minute nightmares, intrigue, mysticism, necromancy and only a few loose ends to make the best cautionary thriller of the decade. 'There has been

nothing like it since the much undervalued *Quatermass* of 1979,' I wrote. And in the flamboyant CIA agent of Joe Don Baker, Orson Welles lived again!

w Troy Kennedy Martin *d* Martin Campbell
Bob Peck, Joe Don Baker, Joanne Whalley, Jack Watson, Charles Kay, John Woodvine, Kenneth Nelson, Ian McNeice

The original BBC2 transmission was immediately followed by a 3 × 105m BBC1 re-run.

† During the first run, C4 coincidentally aired a 90-minute documentary on the hazards and expediencies of nuclear waste disposal presented by Peter Sissons, *Waste Not? Want Not?*, produced by Peter Gillbe for John Gau Productions, just as valuable if not so exciting. PP

LH: 'OK, but I think two stars would be more than enough.'

Edge of Night. American soap opera which has played on CBS and NBC five times a week since 1956. Features Ann Flood, Laurence Hugo, Donald May.

The Edison Twins
Canada 1983   × 25m colour
CBC/Disney Channel/Nelvana Ltd (Ian McDougall)

Teenage siblings find that their adventures always require the solving of some scientific problem.
Half-hearted and rather poorly made semi-educational fillers.

cr Michael Hirsh, Patrick Loubert
Andrew Sabiston, Marnie McPhail

editor. 1. Creative technician who assembles pieces of film. 2. Creative producer of a current affairs series.

Edmonds, Noel (1949–). British disc-jockey and professional glad-boy who charmed his way to television celebrity – for what that's worth – via *Top of the Pops*, *Come Dancing*, *Multi-Coloured Swap Shop*, *The Late Late Breakfast Show*, *The Time of Your Life* and *Telly Addicts*. PP

Edna the Inebriate Woman **
GB 1971 90m colour (16mm)
BBC (Irene Shubik)

A vagrant woman gets all manner of help from the authorities but continues to go her own way.
Incisive drama-documentary.

w JEREMY SANDFORD *d* Ted Kotcheff
(BAFTA 1971, best director)

PATRICIA HAYES (BAFTA 1971, best actress), Barbara Jefford, Pat Nye

PP: 'Edna was allowed to be a victim of her own imperfections as well as society's. She got drunk and wet the bed and threw food about. She was even allowed to be comical at times. But I waited in vain for a real individual to emerge. She would say something salty and particular, then a few minutes later something equally salty and particular but particular to someone else altogether. Twice, much emphasis was placed on the tiny but important detail that she thought she was being accused of being *the* vagrant – not a vagrant – as if for her The Vagrant was a named villain like Jack the Ripper. In between came another scene when this quirk was quite forgotten. The impression was of snippets of dialogue transcribed from tape recordings and shared out, one for Edna, one for crony, another for Edna, one for another crony. I remember concluding of *Cathy Come Home* that if it was lousy art it was at least effective propaganda. *Edna* wasn't even that.'

Edvard Munch **
Norway/Sweden 1975 167m colour
Norsk Rikskringkasting/Sveriges Radio
The life and work of the Norwegian painter (1863–1944).
Punishingly long but often brilliant art film with most of the techniques expected of this film-maker.

w/d Peter Watkins ph Odd Geir Saether a/d Grethe Hajer

Geir Westby, Gro Fraas

Edward and Mrs Simpson ***
GB 1978 6 × 50m colour
Thames (Andrew Brown)
A sympathetic account of events leading up to the abdication of Edward VIII.
Stylish upper-class entertainment with great care given to period detail and royal facsimiles.

w SIMON RAVEN d Waris Hussein pd Allan Cameron

EDWARD FOX, CYNTHIA HARRIS, Peggy Ashcroft (Queen Mary), Marius Goring (George V), NIGEL HAWTHORNE (Walter Monckton), Andrew Ray (Duke of York), David Waller (Baldwin), Jessie Matthews (Aunt Bessie)

PP: 'What could so easily have been a pedestrian retelling of a familiar story gratifyingly turned out to be true art and history, thanks in particular to Edward Fox's performance as the King. His final abdication broadcast was modelled fluff for fluff on the original, yet still inspired – scarcely dropping

his eyes to the prepared text, as the real Edward must have done, and instead gazing desperately into the middle distance as if trying to see that huge, hurt audience.'

Edward the Seventh ****
US title: *The Royal Victorians* or *Edward the King*
GB 1975 13 × 50m colour (VTR)
ATV (CECIL CLARKE, JOHN GORRIE)
The complete life of Queen Victoria's heir, with insights into the other royal personages involved.
A superb piece of historical re-creation and one of the milestones of TV drama, with research, writing, production and acting alike impeccable.

w various, from the biography by Philip Magnus

TIMOTHY WEST, ANNETTE CROSBIE (Victoria), ROBERT HARDY (Albert), John Gielgud (Disraeli).

'It's all set out with loving craftsmanship, but with the kind of British deliberation that can give a Yank the fidgets.' – Robert MacKenzie, *TV Guide*

PP: Gave me the fidgets, too. I preferred intermittent impersonations of Teddy by Thorley Walters in *The Edwardians*.

† BAFTA 1975: best drama series; best design (Henry Graveney, Anthony Weller).

The Edwardians *
GB 1972 8 × 50m colour (VTR)
BBC (Mark Shivas)
Biographies of eight Edwardian figures: Conan Doyle, Lloyd George, Horatio Bottomley, E. Nesbit, Rolls and Royce, etc.

Edwards, Blake (1922–). American director known for big-screen comedy spectaculars. In TV he created PETER GUNN, *Richard Diamond, Mr Lucky* and *Dante*.

Edwards, Jimmy (1920–). Hectoring British comedian with wizard-prang moustaches (he had been a wartime Dakota pilot) who made his name in radio's *Take It From Here* and always rose most outrageously to material by its authors, Muir and Norden. On television his best outlet was *Whacko!* for the BBC in the mid to late fifties, playing the headmaster of a minor private school even more corrupt than in life. *The Seven Faces of Jim* (BBC 1961) cast him, obviously, in disparate episodes. After that there was a long interval before he returned, literally, to old form in revivals of the Glums segments from *Take It From Here* for London Weekend (1978–9), originally as part of *Bruce Forsyth's Big Night*, subsequently as *The Glums*.   PP

JIMMY EDWARDS, a comedy star from the radio days of *Take It from Here*, was an instant television hit when *Whacko!* came before BBC cameras in the late fifties.

Edwards, Ralph (1913–). American ex-announcer who came to fame in the fifties as host of *This Is Your Life*.

Edwards, Vince (1928–) (Vincento Eduardo Zoine). Intense American leading man who on TV had his greatest success as *Ben Casey* and never found another series to match it, certainly not *Matt Lincoln*; but played many guest roles.

Edwin (GB 1984; 90m). Retired judge and old neighbour bicker over the paternity of the former's son, finally deciding with relief that neither of them could have fathered such a go-getting, vegetarian, teetotal prig. John Mortimer's script sounded as if it might have passed around a few hands before Anglia finally picked it up (for C4), but Rodney Bennett's production was as handsomely done as it was cast: Alec Guinness, Paul Rogers, Renée Asherson. PP

Egan, Peter (1946–). Elegant leading actor remembered as the villain in *Big Breadwinner Hog*, Oscar Wilde in *Lillie*, and the next-door neighbour in *Ever Decreasing Circles*.

Egan, Richard (1921–). American leading man of the fifties who never quite fulfilled his promise. TV series: *Empire*, *Redigo*. TV movies: *The House That Would Not Die*, *Shootout in a One Dog Town*.

The Egg and I
US 1951   ? × 12m bw
CBS

TV series following the fortunes of the owners of a chicken farm; from the book by Betty McDonald and the popular film.

Patricia Kirkland, Frank Craven, Grady Sutton

Eggar, Samantha (1939–   ). British leading lady of the sixties. TV series: *Anna and the King*. Also played Billie Burke in *Ziegfeld: The Man and his Women*. Other TV movies: *Double Indemnity*, *All The Kind Strangers*, *The Killer Who Wouldn't Die*, *Hagen* (pilot), *For the Term of His Natural Life*.

Eh Brian It's a Whopper (GB 1984; 6 × 52m). Not the sitcom the title suggested, but a semi-serious social drama mainly about a Midlands fishing club, marginally about lean times in what had once been prosperous car-making country. 'Not terrifically gripping,' I said kindly. Written by Stephen Bill, with Roy Holder, Artro Morris, etc. Produced by David Dunn, for Central.   PP

Eight Is Enough
US 1977–80 105 × 50m colour
ABC/Lorimar (Robert L. Jacks)
A middle-class widower with eight children seeks a new wife.
Modestly pleasing family comedy–drama which recovered remarkably when its leading lady died after two episodes.
cr William Blinn, *book* Thomas Braden
Dick Van Patten, Diana Hyland (replaced by Betty Buckley), Grant Goodeve, Dianne Kay, Connie Needham

Eighteen Minutes to Balcombe Street (GB 1977). 50-minute documentary on the fugitive gunmen who held up a family in a London flat for several days while police surrounded the area. Written by John Shirley; directed by Stephen Frears; produced by Tony Wharmby and John Birt; for LWT.

84 Charing Cross Road *
GB 1975 75m colour (VTR)
BBC (Mark Shivas)
An American lady corresponds with a London bookshop over twenty years, and her pen friend dies before her first visit.
Charming, bookish playlet from published letters.
w Hugh Whitemore, *book* Helene Hanff *d* Mark Cullingham
Anne Jackson, Frank Finlay

87th Precinct *
US 1961 30 × 50m bw
NBC/Hubbell Robinson
Problems of hard-working police personnel in New York.
Likeable, crisply told cop stuff with domestic asides; the *Hill Street Blues* of its time.

cr Ed McBain
Robert Lansing, Norman Fell, Gregory Walcott, Ron Harper, Gena Rowlands

Einstein's Universe (GB 1979). A major 100-minute documentary celebrating Einstein's centenary, with Peter Ustinov honouring his memory and attempting to explain his theories in various spectacular if not entirely simple ways. Written by Nigel Calder; produced by Martin Freeth; for BBC.

Eischied: Only the Pretty Girls Die
US 1979 140m colour TVM
NBC/Columbia/David Gerber
An unorthodox New York cop with a bribery charge over his head traps a mad young man who is sniping at women.
Standard elements (apart from the initial unlikeability of the hero) meld in an overlong but well-made pilot for a series which didn't catch on, quite possibly because nobody could pronounce the hero's name.
w Mark Rodgers *d* Robert Kelljan *ph* Sy Hoffberg *m* John Cacavas
JOE DON BAKER, Alan Oppenheimer, Alan Fudge, Eddie Egan, James Stephens, Karen Valentine, Raymond Burr, Tom Ewell, Vincent Bagetta
† The leading character, and some of the abrasive style, were taken from the mini-series *To Kill a Cop*.
†† 13 one-hours were made in the 1979–80 season.

Elam, Jack (1916–   ). Genial, evil-faced American character actor, in innumerable films and TV guest roles. TV series: *The Dakotas*, *Temple Houston*, *The Texas Wheelers*, *Struck By Lightning*. TV movies include *The Over the Hill Gang*, *The Daughters of Joshua Cabe*, *The Red Pony*, *Sidekicks*, *Lacy and the Mississippi Queen*, *The Sacketts*.

Eleanor and Franklin **
US 1975 2 × 100m colour TVM
ABC/Talent Associates (David Susskind)
After Franklin Roosevelt's death his wife looks back on their years together.
Careful saga of a political marriage, well though not excitingly presented.
w James Costigan, *book* Joseph P. Nash *d* Daniel Petrie *m* John Barry
EDWARD HERRMANN, JANE ALEXANDER, Ed Flanders, Rosemary Murphy
† Emmy 1975: best programme.

Eleanor and Franklin: The White House Years *
US 1976 147m colour TVM
ABC/Talent Associates (David Susskind)

A well-received sequel, though sitting through it was a bit of a slog.

w James Costigan d Daniel Petrie ph James Crabe m John Barry

Jane Alexander, Edward Herrmann, Walter McGinn, Priscilla Pointer, Rosemary Murphy, Blair Brown, John Beal, Donald Moffat

† Emmys 1976: James Costigan, Daniel Petrie

Eleanor, First Lady of the World
US 1982 96m colour TVM
CBS/Embassy/Murbil (Fern Feld)

The life of Eleanor Roosevelt following FDR's death.
Predictably well-done historical document; but somehow not memorable.

w Caryl Ledner, Cynthia Mandelberg d John Erman ph Brian West, John McPherson m John Addison

JEAN STAPLETON, E. G. Marshall (Dulles), Coral Browne, Joyce Van Patten, Gail Strickland, Freddie Jones, Kabir Bedi

Eleanor Marx * (GB 1977; 3 × 75m; colour).
Trilogy of plays about the loves of Karl's daughter Tussie, as played by Jenny Stoller, with Alan Dobie as her husband Edward Aveling and Lee Montague as Marx, guttural in speech, wreathed in cigar smoke, afire with the irritation of boils, carbuncles and piles, and if now resting on his laurels – as much as the last complaint would allow – in his time no mean lover himself. Jenny Stoller was calm, comely, intelligent in a production which looked good and played better. Written by Andrew Davies; produced by Louis Marks for BBC.   PP

Electra
GB 1962 90m bw VTR

Rather surprising presentation (on the commercial network) of Greek tragedy in Greek, but as Lew Grade was rumoured to have observed, Aspassia Papathanassiou's bit of business with the vase of ashes would have been great in any language. Produced and directed for A–R by Joan Kemp-Welch; with Dimitri Malavetas, Dimitri Veakis.   PP

† A BBC *Play of the Month* version in English came in 1974, directed by Michael Lindsay-Hogg, with Eileen Atkins.

The Electric Company.
Children's Television Workshop's successor to *Sesame Street*, aimed at older children who have difficulty in reading.

Electric Folk in an Ancient Setting (GB 1974; 8 × 25m; colour).
Winsome title for what was in fact a nice little BBC series featuring the folk–rock group Steeleye Span performing in and around a sequence of stately homes.   PP

Elephant Boy
GB 1974 26 × 25m colour (16mm)
STV/Global

A native boy and his elephant on a Ceylon tea plantation have various adventures.
Mild and rather strained children's series with agreeable backgrounds.

The Elephant Man
US 1981 112m colour (VTR)
ABC/Marble Arch (Richmond Crinkley)

In Victorian England, a hideously deformed man is saved from a freak show by a surgeon and becomes a temporary pillar of society.
This true moral tale was told in several forms towards the end of the 1970s. This rather creaky transcription of the original Broadway play makes dull television because it is insufficiently adapted to a different medium; the hero's mere miming of his deformity seems silly to an audience accustomed to realism.

w Steve Lawson, *play* Bernard Pomerance d Jack Hofsiss

Philip Anglim, Kevin Conway, Penny Fuller, Richard Clarke

The Elevator *
US 1974 74m colour TVM
Universal (William Frye)

A variety of people including an escaping thief are trapped in a high rise elevator.
Tolerable panic situation melodrama which doesn't quite thrill as it should.

w Bruce Shelly, David Ketchum, Rhoda Blecker d Jerry Jameson m John Cacavas

James Farentino, Myrna Loy, Teresa Wright, Roddy McDowall, Carol Lynley, Don Stroud, Craig Stevens

The Eleventh Hour *
US 1962–3 62 × 50m bw
NBC/MGM/Arena

Stories of a psychiatrist's practice.
Downbeat, rather well-made dramas, often with endings a little too pat to be taken seriously.

Wendell Corey (later Ralph Bellamy), Jack Ging

The Eleventh Hour (GB 1975). Selfless BBC attempt to restore immediacy and danger to television drama. A pair of writers were closeted from Monday morning to write the script, rehearsals began mid-week, the play went out live on Saturday night. It really worked only once, when Tom Stoppard and Clive Exton knocked up a dizzy comedy about lexicographers and cricket for Michael Aldridge, Frank Thornton and Elvi Hale. PP
† The title was also used from 1982 for a Channel 4 outlet for experimental and often unwatchable films. In 1985 a season of same was devoted to nuclear topics.

The Eleventh Victim *
US 1980 96m colour TVM
CBS/Paramount/Marty Katz

A murderer of women is at large on Hollywood Boulevard.
Standard *Naked City*-type location thriller, and quite a slickly made one despite an ambiguous ending.
w Ken Friedman d Jonathan Kaplan ph Chuck Arnold m Michael Columbier
Bess Armstrong, Max Gail, Harold Gould

**Elgar ** (GB 1962). One of the earliest and best KEN RUSSELL composer–documentaries; with commentary by Huw Wheldon and production by Humphrey Burton (in black and white) for BBC.
† Elgar was also the subject of *Hope and Glory* (1984), excellent programme with Simon Rattle and the CBSO, produced by Jim Berrow, for Central.

Elizabeth R **
GB 1971 6 × 85m colour (VTR)
BBC (Roderick Graham)

A splendid pageant of the Renaissance queen and her age, with music by David Munrow.
'The Lion's Cub'
w John Hale d Claude Whatham
'The Marriage Game'
w Rosemary Anne Sisson d Herbert Wise
'Shadow in the Sun'
w Julian Mitchell d Richard Martin
'Horrible Conspiracies'
w Hugh Whitemore d Roderick Graham
'The Enterprise of England'
w Ian Rodger d Roderick Graham
'Sweet England's Pride'
w Ian Rodger d Roderick Graham
GLENDA JACKSON, Ronald Hines (as Cecil), Daphne Slater, Rachel Kempson, Bernard Hepton (as Cranmer), Rosalie Crutchley, John Ronane, Peter Jeffrey (as Philip)

'History without tears, and very addictive and successful into the bargain.' – *Daily Telegraph*
† The series won five Emmys.

Elizondo, Hector (1936–). American actor, in TV series *Freebie and the Bean*. TV movies: *The Impatient Heart, Wanted: The Sundance Woman, The Dain Curse.*

Elkie and Our Gang * (GB 1985; 60m). Socially aware song-and-dance show partly tacked together on the continuity idea of unemployed youngsters travelling to town to see an Elkie Brooks concert. With Elkie Brooks, Gemma Craven, Sam Harris. Produced and directed by Jon Scoffield, for Central.   PP

Ellery Queen
aka *Mystery Is My Business*
US 1954 32 × 25m bw
Norvin/Arrow

Adventures of the elegant sleuth.
Moderate series which never quite captured the atmosphere.
Hugh Marlowe

Ellery Queen
US 1974 22 × 50m colour
NBC/Universal/Fairmont-Foxcroft

Well-mounted revival, carefully set in the forties and featuring a final confrontation of suspects in a locked room. Despite the whodunit element, it lacked flair.
cr Richard Levinson, William Link m Elmer Bernstein
Jim Hutton, David Wayne, John Hillerman
'An old-fashioned Valentine to the classic movie mystery.' – NBC promotion

Episodes:
The Comic Book Crusader
The Twelfth Floor Express
Auld Lang Syne
The Lover's Leap
Miss Aggie's Farewell Performance
The Chinese Dog
The Mad Tea Party
The Pharaoh's Curse
The Blunt Instrument
Colonel Niven's Memoirs
The Black Falcon
The Sunday Punch
Veronica's Veils
The Judas Tree
The Eccentric Engineer
The Two Faced Woman
The Disappearing Dagger

Ellery Queen: Don't Look Behind You
US 1971 96m colour TVM
NBC/Universal (Leonard Stern)
Ellery catches a mad killer known as the Hydra.
Passable, over-padded mystery with sharp use of locations.
w. Ted Leighton, *novel Cat O'Nine Tails* by Ellery Queen d Barry Shear
Peter Lawford, Stefanie Powers, Harry Morgan, E. G. Marshall, Colleen Gray, Skye Aubrey

Ellice, Thomas (19 –). British writer with some classy adaptations to his name: *Silence of the Sea* from Vercors (1981), *The Wedding* from V. S. Pritchett and *Fräulein Else* from Arthur Schnitzler (both 1983). PP

Elliott, Denholm (1922–). Consummate British character actor who has heroically made the best of untold anti-heroic rôles on TV, including several by Dennis Potter – in *Follow the Yellow Brick Road, Brimstone and Treacle* and *Blade on the Feather* (BAFTA award for Elliott, 1980). Also *Let's Murder Vivaldi* by David Mercer and Don Taylor's *In Hiding*. Recently: *Bleak House* (1985).   PP

Elliott, John (1918–). British producer, writer and organizer. Made the BBC's first major documentary series, *War in the Air*, in the early fifties. Wrote *Andromeda* serials with Fred Hoyle. Many single plays and contributions to series but best-known writing credit is as creator of *The Troubleshooters*. For a while, head of programmes in BBC south and west region. Most recent credit: *Jet Trail* (BBC West, 1984) as writer and producer.   PP

Elliott, Michael (1931–84). British drama director, son of celebrated radio parson of the thirties, Canon W. H. Elliott. Into TV as BBC trainee 1956 and directed Tennessee Williams's *You Touched Me* same year. Notable classic productions ranged from *The Women of Troy* (1958) to the Olivier *King Lear* for Granada in 1983.   PP

Elliott, Nick (1944–). British producer and executive, chiefly responsible for building up success of *South Bank Show*. Now in charge of drama and arts at LWT including, alas, *Dempsey and Makepeace*. PP

Elliott, Sam (1944–). Easy-moving American leading actor who looks mean without his moustache. TV movies: *The Challenge, Assault on the Wayne, The Blue Knight, I Will Fight No More Forever, Once an Eagle, The Sacketts, Aspen, Wild Times, Murder in Texas, The Shadow Riders, Travis McGee, The Yellow Rose, A Death in California.*

Elliott, Stephen (19 –). American stage actor with a propensity for playing FDR. *Beacon Hill, A Miracle of Love, Jacqueline Bouvier Kennedy, My Body My Child, Hardcase, Winston Churchill The Wilderness Years, Prototype.*

Ellis Island
GB/US 1984 1 × 142m, 2 ×
    96m colour miniseries
CBS/Telepictures/Pantheon (Gabriel
    Katzka, Frank Konigsberg)
The adventures of various immigrants into America in 1907.
Stagily acted and set, this quickly becomes just another miniseries, its chief purpose to fill several hours of airtime. Performances and direction are sometimes wildly misjudged.
w Fred Mustard Stewart, Christopher Newman, from Stewart's *novel*
d Jerry London ph Jack Hildyard m John Addison
Peter Riegert, Greg Martyn, Claire Bloom, Judi Bowker, Kate Burton, Richard Burton, Faye Dunaway, Joan Greenwood, Ann Jillian, Lila Kaye, Stubby Kaye, Alice Krige, Cherie Lunghi, Milo O'Shea, Ben Vereen

Elphick, Michael (19 –). Barrel-chested British actor who can look as thick as two short planks but still give a sensitive performance. *This Year, Next Year* (1977), *Phyllis Dixey* (1978), *Blue Remembered Hills* (1979), *Private Schulz* (1981), *Pocketful of Dreams* (1982), *Masada* (1983), *Boon* (1986).   PP

Elvis
US 1980 140m colour TVM
ABC/Dick Clark (Anthony Lawrence)
Flashback biography of a rock singer. A fair lookalike performance grabs the interest, but there is too much padding and Colonel Parker's Svengali-like influence has been underplayed.
w Anthony Lawrence d John Carpenter ph Donald M. Morgan m Joe Renzetti
Kurt Russell, Shelley Winters, Pat Hingle, Season Hubley, Bing Russell, Melody Anderson, Ed Begley Jnr

Elvis and the Beauty Queen
US 1981 96m colour TVM
NBC/Columbia/David Gerber

A beauty queen becomes Elvis Presley's girl friend, lives with him for five years, and watches him deteriorate through drugs. Ghastly, empty exploitation item, more in the style of the yellow press than of TV.

w Julia Cameron *d* Gus Trikonis *ph* Thomas Del Ruth *m* Alan Ferguson

Stephanie Zimbalist, Don Johnson, Ann Dusenberry, Rick Lenz, Ann Wedgeworth

'All of this is less than gripping, and the tedious drama makes its way to an obvious conclusion.' – *Daily Variety*

Elwes, Polly (*c* 1925–). British TV hostess of comforting presence; married Peter Dimmock and virtually retired.

Ely, Ron (1938–) (Ronald Pierce). American athlete who became TV's *Tarzan*; also starred in *The Aquanauts*.

'Will Admiral Tom Mallory be forced to destroy the man his daughter secretly loves?'
Emerald Point N.A.S.
US 1983   × 50m colour
CBS/TCF/Richard and Esther Shapiro
(Freyda Rothstein)

The professional and family problems of a naval air station commander.
A runner-up in the *Dallas* stakes: it ran one season.

cr Richard and Esther Shapiro

Dennis Weaver, Maud Adams, Andrew Stevens, Charles Frank, Susan Dey, Patrick O'Neal, Richard Dean Anderson, Stephanie Dunnam, Jill St John, Doran Clark

Emergency
US 1971 100m colour TVM
Universal/Jack Webb

Adventures of a paramedic unit supervised by the city hospital and fire departments.
Rather dull multi-storied ambulance-chasing action drama which spawned a five-year series.

w Harold Jack Bloom *d* Christian Nyby *theme music* Nelson Riddle

Julie London, Randolph Mantooth, Robert Fuller, Bobby Troup

Emergency!
US 1972–7   × 50m colour
NBC/Universal/Jack Webb (Ed Self, Robert A. Cinader)

Paramedics work out of the Los Angeles Fire Department.
'Action without violence', with four or five stories per hour; in other words, *Adam 12*

writ large. Watchable in the sense that there is always something happening, but the acting and writing are flat and there is never anything to engage the mind. Which is presumably why it was a great success.

cr Harold Jack Bloom, R. A. Cinader *m* Nelson Riddle

Julie London, Randolph Mantooth, Kevin Tighe, Robert Fuller, Bobby Troup

† The run ended in 1977 with four 'two-hour' specials.

Emergency Plus Four
US 1973–4 24 × 22m colour
Universal/Mark VII/Fred Calvert

A cartoon spin-off from *Emergency* in which the para-medics are assisted by four kids. Doleful.

Emergency – Ward Ten. Britain's first twice-weekly serial, running from 1957 to 1967, the brainchild of a young scriptwriter Tessa Diamond who sold the idea to Lew (later Lord) Grade of ATV. Its most consistent star and heart-throb was the Australian actor Charles Tingwell, playing a house doctor. When the fashion changed to one-hour drama series in the sixties the weekly *Call Oxbridge 2000* took over the same fictitious setting and some of the same characters. Later, a new one-hour format *General Hospital* replaced *Ward 10* altogether, surviving until 1979 to maintain an ATV hospital-drama tradition that lasted over 21 years. Anthony Kearey was the key producer.   PP

† A movie version, *Life in Emergency Ward 10*, was released in 1960 to little effect.

Emerson, Faye (1917–). American leading lady who after a modest Hollywood career became a popular TV host and panellist in the fifties.

Emery, Dick (1918–84). Stocky British comedian with a bent for dressing up; highly popular in half-hour sketch shows in the early seventies, he lacked writers skilful enough to broaden his appeal. In 1982 he appeared in six very curious half-hours of a comedy-thriller called *Emery!* Last series, *Jack of Diamonds*, 1983.

The Emigrants (GB/Australia 1976; 4 × 75m; colour). Plodding cycle of plays about a British family emigrating to Australia, with Michael Craig as the least convincing artisan since the days of the Groves. Written by Brian Phelan; for BBC/ABC.   PP

Emmerdale Farm. British soap opera set in the Yorkshire dales and concentrating on a farming community: supplied twice weekly by YTV since 1972.

Emmy. See Academy of Television Arts and Sciences

Empire
GB title: *Big G*
US 1962 26 × 50m colour
NBC/Columbia (William Sackheim)
Action stories about the operation of the Garret family's huge ranch in New Mexico. Handsome, efficient family saga on the style of *The Big Valley*, *Bonanza* and *Dallas*.
cr Frank Nugent *m* Johnny Green

Richard Egan, Anne Seymour, Terry Moore, Ryan O'Neal
'TV's first major dramatic series set in the real west of today.' – publicity
† When the show failed, there followed a short half-hour series about the Egan character, called *Redigo*.

Empire, Inc (Canada 1982; 6 × 50m). Attempt at a period *Dallas* or *Dynasty*, set in Montreal between the wars, though sounding at times more like our *Brass* without the jokes. The despotic JR-type character was shot at the end of the first episode, which, as I pointed out at the time, had taken *Dallas* two years to reach. With Kenneth Welsh, Martha Henry, Jennifer Dale. Produced by CBC with the National Film Board of Canada.   PP

Empire Inc.
US 1984 6 × 25m colour
CBS/MGM/Humble Productions (Terry Hughes)
Strife in the boardroom of Empire Industries.
An attempt to re-do *Soap* with an executive setting. Miscasting and a lack of jokes threw it flat on its face.
cr Lawrence J. Cohen, Fred Freeman

Patrick MacNee, Dennis Dugan, Richard Masur, Michael McGuire, Edward Winter, Dick O'Neill, Howard Platt, Maureen Arthur

Encounter (GB). Well-researched religious half-hour series from Central on such topics as a reformed alcoholic becoming C. of E. priest or a bishop and a bad hat of the same name comparing notes.

End of Conflict * (GB 1963; 78m; bw). One of Anglia's first forays on to the ITV network with a play, and also one of the more interesting ones: a subaltern drama written by Barry England, with Barry Justice.   PP

End of Empire
GB 1985 14 × 52m
Granada (Brian Lapping)
Sour history of Britain's dissolution of the British Empire, concentrating on every handover that was accompanied by strife and/or partition, ignoring those that went smoothly and even blaming the British when independence was granted ahead of local demand as in Malaysia. Territories never part of the Empire, e.g. Palestine and Iran, were dragged in if they helped the overall picture of muddle and oppression. Cyprus not only had its episode here but also a separate two-part trailer in 1984, *Britain's Grim Legacy* (*p* Norma Percy).   PP
'Prejudiced and biased' – retired Indian administrator Donald MacPherson, CIE
'The loss of Empire is a painful, sometimes a tragic process. I believe our series pursued a great British tradition in reporting this process fairly.' – Brian Lapping
'No other nation is so dedicated to the destruction of its icons, or so careless of its history' – TV director David Wickes

End of the Line
GB 1984 5 × 60m
BBC Scotland (Tom Kinninmont)
Creditable attempt to assemble an anthology of films about employment and unemployment in one Scottish new town. On the whole, well written and well performed by up-and-coming Scottish authors and actors, plus some older hands (e.g. Andrew Keir) among the latter.
d Ian Knox and others   PP

Enemies of the State (GB 1983; 90m). Another of Granada's dramatized reconstructions of days of hope and years of despair behind the Iron Curtain, set in Czechoslovakia during the wan heyday of the Charter 77 movement, and conveying a rare whiff of the humdrum, everyday oppression of life in a one-party state. With Zoe Wanamaker, Paul Freeman. Written by Zdena Tomin, directed by Eva Kolouchava, produced by Mike Beckham.   PP

Enemy at the Door (GB 1978). One-hour drama series from LWT about life in the Channel Islands under Nazi occupation. With Alfred Burke, Bernard Horsfall, Ray Smith. Produced by Mark Chapman. It lasted two seasons.

L'Enfance du Christ ** (GB 1985; 100m). Berlioz' Christmassy oratorio on the Childhood of Christ semi-dramatized by Anthony Burgess to become almost an opera, and realized by director John Woods with the aid of electronic matte trickery which for once really worked. 'The ravishing music,' I wrote, 'swirled Joseph and Mary and Jesus across solid landscapes, amid real donkeys and lambs and oxen, but also – you suddenly realized – into the frames of half-remembered paintings by Holman Hunt or Simeon Solomon.' With Anthony Rolfe-Johnson, Richard van Allan, Fiona Kimm, William Schimell, Benjamin Luxon. Produced by John Woods and Michael Waterhouse, for Thames.   PP

England Their England (GB). Periodic documentary series from Central, usually for local transmission only, sometimes getting a daytime network showing. Executive producer Brian Lewis; producer in 1985 Jim Manson.   PP

English, Arthur (1913–). British 'wide boy' comedian of the forties who aged into a sympathetic TV actor in both plays (*Pygmalion*, as Dolittle) and series (*How's Your Father*, *Are You Being Served*).

English Family Robinson (GB 1957; 4 × 90m; bw live). Cycle of plays about British rule in India as witnessed by one empire-building family. At the root of almost every incident was the hostility between Hindu and Muslim; in the last play Dalpore, the imaginary setting throughout, was symbolically riven by the new frontier between India and Pakistan. Three generations of sweating family Robinson toiled (mainly at the top of their voices) to keep peace between the two factions while getting on with the job of developing the country; a now forgotten precursor to the great Raj vogue of 27 years later (*Jewel in the Crown*, *The Far Pavilions*), if at the end a much sourer one. 'Iain MacCormick,' I said at the time, 'wrote off India with the ill-grace of an admiral writing off a warship which had mutinied.' With Patrick Barr, Cyril Shaps, Ewen Solon, Peter Bryant, Eric Porter. Written by Iain MacCormick; for BBC.   PP

The English Garden *
GB 1980 7 × 25m colour
Thames (Diana Potter)

Sir John Gielgud takes us on a tour of some spectacular gardens and puts together a history of the garden through the ages.

Agreeable series clearly designed for the cassette market.

w Alan Gore, Laurence Fleming d Richard Mervyn

English Journey (GB 1984; 8 × 40m). Rum exercise which borrowed the title of J. B. Priestley's 1933 travelogue through slump-torn England for a trek over the same route, in roughly similar bad times, by Beryl Bainbridge. Excerpts from Priestley, read in his own fruity accents, only accentuated the shortcomings of the up-date. Produced by Bernard Hall, for BBC West.   PP

An Englishman Abroad ***
GB 1983 60m
BBC (Innes Lloyd)

Alan Bennett's screenplay from a story given him by actress Coral Browne, of how she met the traitor Guy Burgess in Moscow on a cultural-exchange theatre visit in 1958. It made a funny, brave little comedy, if a shade too ready to soften – or perhaps miniaturize – the enormity of what Burgess had done. 'Though I have no doubt the British Embassy in Moscow was staffed with dreadful young men,' I said at the time, 'every instinct tells me that they wouldn't have been dreadful in quite the teasing, twittering manner worn here.' But Alan Bates turned in a performance as Burgess reeking properly of garlic, mildew, stale vomit and dubious charm, plus a jauntiness that finally had to be applauded. Coral Browne carried off with aplomb a role that must have been puzzling to play – that of her own self 25 years younger but equipped with the mannerisms and knowingness of middle age.

w Alan Bennett d John Schlesinger
Charles Gray   PP
LH: 'Its sharp observation and wry dialogue make this for me one of the most enjoyable anecdotes ever televised.'

An Englishman's Castle *
GB 1978 3 × 50m colour (VTR)
BBC (Innes Lloyd)

The plight of a TV writer trying to tell the truth in a Britain 30 years after the Nazis won World War II.

A low-key dramatic trilogy which provides civilized dramatic entertainment without really surprising in any way.

w Philip Mackie d Paul Ciappesoni
Kenneth More, Isla Blair, Anthony Bate

An Englishman's Journey: See Priestley, J. B.

Enigma (GB 1982). Modest BBC Scotland series with Ludovic Kennedy re-telling some puzzling real-life mysteries of recent years. Usually he offered a reasonable explanation of what might have happened but was stumped by the case of Peter Gibbs, wartime fighter pilot, musician and leader of the BBC Scottish Symphony Orchestra until the light plane he was flying dived into the Atlantic off the Isle of Mull; his body was found months later high on the island, uninjured and bearing no traces of having been in salt water. 'A good series,' I wrote, 'because Kennedy never tries to drum up speculation, never ventures beyond the evidence he has shared with us.'   PP

Ennal's Point
GB 1982 6 × 50m
BBC Wales (John Hefin)
Stories of a lifeboat and its crew, too often left stranded on the shores of soapland.
w Alun Richards   d Gareth Davies (4), Myrfyn Owen (2)
Philip Madoc   PP

Enola Gay *
US 1980 140m colour TVM
NBC/The Production Company/Viacom
Events leading up to the dropping of the atomic bomb on Hiroshima in 1945, with special emphasis on the lives of the crew members of the plane involved.
Tiresomely protracted and mainly domestic inflation of a news event better suited to more documentary treatment.
w James Poe, Millard Kaufman, *book* Max Morgan-Witts and Gordon Thomas d David Lowell Rich ph Robert L. Morrison m Maurice Jarre
Billy Crystal, Patrick Duffy, Kim Darby, Gary Frank, Gregory Harrison, Richard T. Herd, Stephen Macht, Ed Nelson, James Shigeta, Robert Walden
'With all the material on hand, all the dramatic matter of one of the most extraordinary acts of mankind, TV puffs it up to something inconsequential – and dull.' – *Daily Variety*

'Three women, alone and struggling against all odds, find freedom and identity outside their traditional roles!'
Enormous Changes at the Last Minute
US 1983 110m colour TVM
ABC/Ordinary Lives Inc (Mirra Bank)
Three young women confront the problems of living alone in New York.

Minor drama produced by a network for specialized distribution: a prestige piece.
w John Sayles, *stories* by Grace Paley
d Mirra Bank, Ellen Hovde
Maria Tucci, Kevin Bacon, Ellen Barkin, Ron McLarty, Lynn Milgrim

Enos
US 1980   × 50m colour
CBS/Warner/Gy Waldron
The amiable but not too bright sheriff of Hazzard County joins the Los Angeles police force and goes out on patrol with a black partner.
Predictable easy laughs and chases are separated by the dullest wodges of inconsequential talk.
cr Gy Waldron
Sonny Shroyer, Samuel E. Wright, John Dehner
† A spin-off from *The Dukes of Hazzard*.

Ensign O'Toole
US 1962 26 × 25m bw
NBC/Four Star/Lederer
Predicaments of a young naval officer and his shipmates.
Mindless service comedy, all very predictable but occasionally funny.
Dean Jones, Jay C. Flippen, Harvey Lembeck, Jack Albertson, Beau Bridges

Enterprise (GB). Enterprising business series set up and still edited by John Swinfield, ex-*The Money Programme*, for Anglia TV, with special penchant for focusing on individual firms and individuals such as the Royal dress-designers the Emanuels, or Richard Branson, Virgin record and airline tycoon. Since 1982 plays (seasonally) on C4.   PP

The Entertainer *
US 1976 100m colour TVM
Robert Stigwood
A middle-aged vaudeville comedian considers his failure.
American TV adaptation of the famous play: it only springs into life when Ray Bolger's around.
w John Osborne m Marvin Hamlisch
Jack Lemmon, RAY BOLGER, Sada Thompson

The Entertainers *
GB 1965 50m bw (VTR)
Granada (Denis Mitchell)
A tour of pub entertainments which replaced music hall.

A vivid, smoky documentary which was temporarily banned by the IBA because a stripper twirled her tassels at the camera.

d John McGrath

Entertainment USA (GB since 1983). Fairly frenetic BBC2 half-hours shot in various US cities with the undoubtedly frenetic Jonathan King whizzing local musicians, local tourist features, current pop music hits into a breathless entertainment which has become a cult with young and old swingers.   PP

The Epic That Never Was ***
GB 1965 70m bw
BBC (Bill Duncalf)

Alexander Korda's 1937 film of *I, Claudius* was abandoned after two reels had been shot. This remarkable programme showed the remains and examined the reasons through interviews with the survivors, who included Merle Oberon, Josef Von Sternberg, Emlyn Williams and Flora Robson. Dirk Bogarde narrated.

w/d BILL DUNCALF

PP: 'It remains a classic of television and a memorial to a wondrous performance in the making, that of Charles Laughton as Claudius.'

The Equalizer *
US 1985   × 50m colour
CBS/Universal (Michael Sloan)

A cynical FBI agent retires and offers his services by newspaper ad to people in trouble.
Tough, stylish, not entirely settled in at mid-season, this curious series would remind most English viewers of the old spy hero Callan, magically transported to New York.

cr Michael Sloan

Edward Woodward, Robert Lansing

'Despite some flubs and hard-to-buy angles, it provides entertainment for the vigilantes in the crowd.' – *Daily Variety*
'Absurd and gratuitously violent.' – *LA Times*

Eric
US 1975 100m colour TVM
Lorimar

A teenage boy has an incurable disease.
One may suspect the motive and the point, but the thing is moderately well done.

w Nigel and Carol Ann McKeand, *memoir* Doris Lund *d* James Goldstone *m* Dave Grusin

John Savage, Patricia Neal, Claude Akins, Sian Barbara Allen, Nehemiah Persoff

Erman, John (19 –). American director. Many series episodes from the sixties. *Letters from Three Lovers, Green Eyes, Moviola, Roots, Eleanor, First Lady of the World, Who Will Love My Children, A Streetcar Named Desire, The Atlanta Child Murders, Right to Kill, An Early Frost.*

'The public hailed him as a comic genius, while his private agony was hidden from all!'
Ernie Kovacs: Between the Laughter
ABC Circle (David Levison)

A top comedian searches for his children, taken from him by his jealous ex-wife.
More jokes and less agony would have made for entertainment: this is soap opera.

w April Smith *d* Lamont Johnson

Jeff Goldblum, Madolyn Smith, Melody Anderson, Cloris Leachman, Edie Adams (as Mae West), John Glover, Joseph Mascolo

The Errol Flynn Theatre: see Flynn, Errol

Escapade
US 1978 50m colour
Quinn Martin/Woodruff (Brian Clemens)

Two carefree spies pursue another who vanishes.
Unsuccessful pilot for an American version of *The Avengers*.

w Brian Clemens *d* Jerry London *ph* Jack Swain *m* Patrick Williams

Granville Van Dusen, Morgan Fairchild, Len Birman, Janice Lynde

'All that is understandable about this pilot is the reason it didn't sell.' – *Daily Variety*

Escape
US 1971 74m colour TVM
Paramount

An escapologist becomes a spy.
Silly comic strip adventures with entertainingly hare-brained action climaxes.

w Paul Playdon *d* John Llewellyn Moxey

Christopher George, Avery Schreiber, Marlyn Mason, Gloria Grahame, William Windom, John Vernon, William Schallert

Escape
US 1973   × 25m colour
Jack Webb

Anthology dramas about people caught in hair-raising situations allegedly from real life.

narrator Jack Webb *m* Frank Comstock

Escape
US 1980 96m colour TVM
CBS/Henry Jaffe (Michael Jaffe)

A young American escapes from the Mexican prison where he has been imprisoned for smuggling drugs.
A pale shadow of *Midnight Express*, with characters inadequately explained and more time spent on talk than on action.

w Michael Zagor, *book* Dwight and Barbara Worker *d* Robert Lewis *ph* Isidore Mankofsky *m* James Di Pascuale

Timothy Bottoms, Kay Lenz, Colleen Dewhurst, Antonio Fargas

Escape from Bogen County
US 1977 96m colour TVM
Paramount–Moonlight–Aries (Frank von Zerneck, Robert Greenwald)

A corrupt state boss sends police after his runaway wife.
Rather   tiresome   melodrama   about unpleasant people.

w Judith Parker, Christopher Knopf *d* Steve Stern *ph* Fred Jackman *m* Charles Bernstein

Jaclyn Smith, Mitch Ryan, Michael Parks, Henry Gibson, Pat Hingle

Escape from Iran
US/Canada 1981 96m colour TVM
CBS/Canamedia (Stanley Rubin)

Canadian officials help some American diplomats to escape from captivity in January 1980.
Confusing   and   inadequately   explained treatment of a famous 'caper'.

w Lionel Chetwynd *d* Lamont Johnson *ph* Albert J. Dunk *m* Peter Jermyn

Gordon Pinsent, Chris Wiggins, Diana Barrington, Robert Jay, James B. Douglas, Tida Chang

Escape of the Birdmen: see The Birdmen

Escape of the One Ton Pet
US 1978 74m colour TVM
ABC/Tomorrow (Jean Moore)

A young girl raises a bull into a blue ribbon winner.
Agreeable movie for children, originally shown in three parts.

w Arthur Heinemann, George Lefferts *d* Richard Bennett *ph* Mario DiLeo

Stacy Swor, James Callahan, Michael Morgan

Escape to Mindanao
US 1968 95m colour TVM
Universal (Jack Leewood)

Two Americans escape from a Japanese POW camp.
Routine war action.

w Harold Livingston *d* Don McDougall

George Maharis, Willi Coopman, Nehemiah Persoff, James Shigeta

Espionage *
GB 1963 24 × 50m bw
ATV/NBC/Plautus

An anthology of spy stories, some of them partly true.
A somewhat gloomy but well-made series with excellent guest stars.

'The producer's overall thesis was that political intrigue degrades man, jeopardizes peace, and in the final analysis is ineffective. One quickly learned to expect a glum hour that would end in melancholia.' – Don Miller

Essex, Francis (1928–). British executive and writer who escaped from Chappells the music publishers to make his name in TV with pop music shows, notably *Dig This!* Subject of Denis Mitchell documentary *The Dream Machine*, 1966, when a light entertainment producer at ATV. After a period as programme controller at STV in the late sixties and seventies wrote *The Shillingbury Tales* (1981).   PP

Estrada, Erik (1949–) (Enrique Estrada). Puerto Rican leading man who made a hit as one of the heroes of *CHiPs*.

Ethel and Albert (US 1953–5). Half-hour comedy which had a season on each of the three networks. Based on a radio original, it featured an average family, the Arbuckles, and their average problems. With Alan Bunce, Peg Lynch.

Eureka Stockade
Australia 1983 2 × 96m colour
Eureka Stockade Film Partnership (Henry Crawford)

In the 1850s, Australian gold miners rebel against the British redcoats.
The incident made a boring feature film in 1948, and clearly can't spread to a four-hour miniseries in 1983. The yawns set in early, despite an ambitious production.

w Tom Hegarty *d* Rod Hardy *ph* Keith Wagstaff *m* Bruce Smeaton

Bryan Brown, Bill Hunter, Carol Burns, Amy Madigan, Brett Cullen, Penelope Stewart, Rob Mullinar

'Has everything to make a sweeping epic but thoroughly competent acting, urgency and an abiding interest.' – *Daily Variety*

European Broadcasting Union: see EBU

European Connections * (GB 1983; 6 × 30m). Profiles of Britons living and working in France, including a Roman Catholic parish priest in Normandy. Produced by Brian Lewis and Malcolm Feuerstein, for Central.   PP

Eurovision. Device by which members of the European Broadcasting Union can receive simultaneous telecasts of each other's programmes.

Eurovision Song Contest. Sadly, the one Eurovision link-up that regularly unites the whole of Western Europe, plus assorted Eastern and Mediterranean countries sneaking in. The songs are mostly dreadful, and in any case the occasion is more of a vote-counting contest than a musical one, but everyone watches, if only to see if Norway can score a zero again. In 1985 she fooled everyone by winning.   PP

EUROVISION SONG CONTEST

YEAR	COUNTRY	WINNER SONG	SINGER
1956	Switzerland	'Refrains'	Lys Assia
1957	Netherlands	'Net Als Town'	Corry Brokken
1958	France	'Dors, Mon Amour'	André Claveau
1959	Netherlands	'Een Beetje'	Teddy Scholten
1960	France	'Tom Pillibi'	Jacqueline Boyer
1961	Luxembourg	'Nous, les Amoureux'	Jean Claude Pascal
1962	France	'Un Premier Amour'	Isabelle Aubret
1963	Denmark	'Dansevise'	Grethe and Jørgen Ingmann
1964	Italy	'Non ho l'eta'	Gigliola Cinquetti
1965	Luxembourg	'Poupée de Cire, Poupée de Son'	France Gall
1966	Austria	'Merci Chérie'	Udo Jurgens
1967	United Kingdom	'Puppet on a String'	Sandie Shaw
1968	Spain	'La, la, la'	Massiel
1969	4 countries tied – each with 18 points:		
	Spain	'Viva Cantando'	Salome
	United Kingdom	'Boom-Bang-a-Bang'	Lulu
	Holland	'De Troubadour'	Lennie Kuhr
	France	'Un Jour, un Enfant'	Frida Baccara
1970	Ireland	'All Kinds of Everything'	Dana
1971	Monaco	'Un Band, un Arbre, une Rue'	Severine
1972	Luxembourg	'Après Toi'	Vicky Leandros
1973	Luxembourg	'Tu Te Reconnaitras'	Anne Marie David
1974	Sweden	'Waterloo'	Abba (Bjorn, Benny, Anna and Frida)
1975	Netherlands	'Ding Ding Dong'	Teach-In
1976	United Kingdom	'Save Your Kisses for Me'	Brotherhood of Man
1977	France	'L'Oiseau et L'enfant'	Marie Myriam
1978	Israel	'A-Ba-Ni-Bi'	Izhar Cohen and The Alphabeta
1979	Israel	'Hallelujah'	Milk and Honey
1980	Ireland	'What's Another Year'	Johnny Logan
1981	United Kingdom	'Making Your Mind Up'	Bucks Fizz
1982	West Germany	'A Little Peace'	Nicole
1983	Luxembourg	'Si La Vie Est Cadeau'	Corinne Hermes
1984	Sweden	'Diggo-Loo, Diggi-Ley'	Herrey Brothers
1985	Norway	'Let It Swing'	Bobbysocks

Euston Films. The first and by far the most successful film-making subsidiary set up by an ITV contractor, in this case Thames. Drama chief Lloyd Shirley cooked up the idea with George Taylor around 1970; their brainchild went on to make nearly all Thames's famous fiction series of the next two decades, including *Special Branch*, *The Sweeney*, *Danger UXB*, *Quatermass*, MINDER and *Widows*.

† Book: *Made for Television* by Manuel Alvarado and John Stewart, BFI/Thames Methuen, 1985.

The Evacuees ***
GB 1975 73m colour (16mm)
BBC (Mark Shivas)

Two Jewish boys are evacuated to St Anne's at the start of World War II, but try to escape back to Manchester.
Moving and amusing nostalgic comedy, impeccably realized.

w JACK ROSENTHAL *d* ALAN PARKER *ph* Brian Tufano

Gary Carp, Steven Serember, Maureen Lipman, Margery Mason, Ray Mort

'Stunning to look at and easy to feel.' – *Daily Mirror*

Evans, Barry (1945–). British leading man who during a rather desultory career starred in two TV series, *Doctor in the House* and *Mind Your Language*.

Evans, Gene (1924–). Reliable, tough-looking American character actor. Series include *My Friend Flicka*, *Spencer's Pilots*. TV movies include *The Intruders*, *The Bounty Man*, *Sidekicks*, *Matt Helm*, *Fire*, *The Sacketts*, *Wild Times*, *Casino*.

Evans, Linda (1942–). American leading lady with a long hiatus between her starring roles in *The Big Valley* and *Dynasty*.

Evans, Maurice (1904–). Welsh Shakespearian actor on Broadway; in the fifties he produced and starred in much Shakespeare for TV, and later acted in *Bewitched*.

The Eve Arden Show (US 1957). Half-hour comedy show for CBS, following on the success of *Our Miss Brooks*. This time the star was a widowed novelist, with Allyn Joslyn as the head of the lecture bureau which occupied her spare time.

Eve, Trevor (1951–). Unassuming young British actor who after scoring a local hit as the mild-mannered hero of *Shoestring*, went to Hollywood for *The Corsican Brothers* and *Shadow Chasers*.

Evening in Byzantium
US 1978 2 × 96m colour TVM
Universal/Glen Larson

A film producer at the Cannes Festival ponders his business and sexual problems. Mildly watchable novelization.

w Glen Larson, Michael Sloan, *novel* Irwin Shaw *d* Jerry London

Glenn Ford, Gloria de Haven, Shirley Jones, Eddie Albert, Vince Edwards, Patrick MacNee, Erin Gray, Gregory Sierra, Harry Guardino, Simon Oakland

An Evening with Fred Astaire (US 1958). A famous special produced and directed by BUD YORKIN; it won Emmys for best special, best writing, and best single programme.

Ever Decreasing Circles (GB 1984; 15 × 30m). Richard Briers over-enthusiastic in a rather prosaic sitcom from Bob Larbey and John Esmonde. With Penelope Wilton, Peter Egan. Produced and directed by Sydney Lotterby, for BBC. PP
LH: 'I warmed quite a lot to the characterizations: Briers as hopeless know-it-all, Wilton as long-suffering wife, Egan as too smooth neighbour.'

Everett, Chad (1937–) (Raymond Cramton). American leading man of the sixties whose main success was in the TV series *Medical Center*. Previously in *The Dakotas*; subsequently in *Hagen*. TV movies: *Centennial*, *The French Atlantic Affair*, *The Intruder Within*, *Mistress of Paradise*, *Malibu*.

Everett, Kenny (1944–). Elf-like, mischievous British disc jockey, parodist and comedian, into TV via *Nice Time*; starred in zany series such as *The Kenny Everett Explosion* and *The Kenny Everett Video Show*, usually based on an abundance of electronic techniques.

'A century of secrets, desires, fortunes and tragedies. The story of a lifetime!'
Evergreen
US 1985 6 × 50m colour miniseries
NBC/Edgar J. Scherick (Philip Barry)

TREVOR EVE, the easy-going and quiet-spoken hero of BBC's mystery series *Shoestring*, found himself at something of a loss when Hollywood beckoned and cast him in a shortlived imitation of *Ghostbusters* called *Shadow Chasers*.

An immigrant seamstress becomes the wife of a wealthy Westchester contractor.
Well-made but rather plodding fictional biography: a Jewish success story with asides for romance.

w Jerome Kass, *novel* by Belva Plain *d* Fielder Cook *ph* Woody Omens *m* Laurence Rosenthal *pd* Jan Scott

Lesley Ann Warren, Armand Assante, Ian McShane, Brian Dennehy, Patricia Barry, Ron Rifkin, Robert Vaughn

'Opulent, sentimental, and thorough, it wallows in suds.' – *Daily Variety*

Every Man Needs One
US 1972 74m colour TVM
Spelling–Goldberg

A swinging bachelor who steers clear of female attachments is forced to hire a woman assistant who takes him over.
Mild contemporary comedy.

w Carl Kleinschmitt *d* Jerry Paris

Ken Berry, Connie Stevens, Henry Gibson, Louise Sorel

Everybody Rides the Carousel *
US 1976 74m colour TVM
CBS/John and Faith Hubley

The works of psychiatrist Erik H. Ericson illustrate eight stages of man's life.
Ambitious cartoon with many inspired passages and just as many attacks of verbosity.

d John Hubley *m* William Russo

Everybody's Looking: see Tenafly

Everyman. The BBC's umbrella title for its Sunday religious slot, usually (from 1978) played after 10 p.m. and including a variety of excellent documentaries.

Everything Money Can't Buy
US 1976 13 × 25m colour
Columbia (Austin and Irma Kalish)

An angel in a bowler hat enables frustrated people to achieve their dreams.
A troubled comedy series, once called

Heaven Sent and finally shown as *Good Heavens*. A mixture of *Here Comes Mr Jordan* and *If I Had a Million*, it never worked with Jose Ferrer or Carl Reiner, largely because the stories were dim and the angel didn't have enough to do.

Evigan, Greg (c 1953–). American leading man of *BJ and the Bear*. TV movies: *Operation Runaway*, *Private Sessions*.

Evil Roy Slade *
US 1971 100m colour TVM
Universal (Jerry Belson, Gary Marshall)
The west's meanest outlaw reforms when he falls in love.
Overlong spoof, at its best better than *Blazing Saddles*.
w Jerry Belson, Gary Marshall d Jerry Paris
John Astin, Mickey Rooney, Pamela Austin, Dick Shawn, Henry Gibson, Dom De Luise, Edie Adams, Milton Berle

Ewell, Tom (1909–) (S. Yewell Tompkins). Crumple-faced American comedy character actor who in the fifties had a brief spell as a Hollywood star. TV series include *The Tom Ewell Show*, *Baretta*. TV movies: *Promise Him Anything*, *The Return of the Mod Squad*.

The Ewok Adventure
US 1984 96m colour TVM
ABC/Lucasfilm (Thomas G. Smith)
Separated from their parents when a spaceship crashes on Endor, two children are cared for by Ewoks who save all four from a giant.
Limited sets and limited interest (small children only) make this a rather boring telefeature, though on its home ground it racked up huge ratings.
w Bob Carrau d John Korty ph John Korty m Peter Bernstein
Eric Walker, Warwick Davis, Aubree Miller, Fionnula Flanagan

Ewoks: The Battle for Endor
US 1985 96m colour TVM
ABC/Lucasfilm
More of the same.
w,d Ken and Jim Wheat
Wilford Brimley, Warwick Davis, Aubree Miller, Siân Phillips

The Execution *
US 1984 96m colour TVM
NBC/Newland–Raynor (Oliver Crawford)

TOM EWELL had his own comedy show in the fifties, when he was cast as a family man with 'wall-to-wall women' – even the dog was female. Disappointingly, he deteriorated soon after in a crumpled old character actor.

Five lady concentration-camp survivors in Los Angeles recognize their old commandant and decide to execute him.
Uneasy revenge drama which succeeds chiefly on the hope that the audience will want to know what happens next.
w William Wood, Oliver Crawford, from Crawford's *novel* d Paul Wendkos ph Michael Margulies m Georges Delerue
Loretta Swit, Valerie Harper, Rip Torn, Jessica Walter, Sandy Dennis, Barbara Barrie, Robert Hooks, Alan Oppenheimer, Michael Lerner
'Cleverness isn't a substitute for depth.' – *Daily Variety*

The Execution of Private Slovik *
US 1973 120m colour TVM
Universal/Levinson–Link (Richard Dubelman)
During World War II an American soldier is executed for desertion.

Factual case history, earnestly but rather drearily retold.

w Richard Levinson, William Link, *book* William Bradford Huie *d* Lamont Johnson *ph* Bill Butler *md* Hal Mooney

Martin Sheen, Ned Beatty, Gary Busey, Warren Kemmerling, Mariclare Costello

The Executioner's Song *
US 1982 2 × 96m colour
NBC/Film Communications (Lawrence Schiller)

Fairly factual account of the last days of Gary Gilmore, psychopathic killer who elected to die in the electric chair rather than face life imprisonment.
For those who can take such a story, this is TV film making at its best; but it's downbeat all the way, and seems to serve no purpose.

w Norman Mailer, from his *book* *d* LAWRENCE SCHILLER *ph* Freddie Francis *m* John Cacavas

TOMMY LEE JONES, Rosanna Arquette, Eli Wallach, Christine Lahti, Jordan Clarke, Steven Keats, Mary Ethel Gregory

'It's like watching an untended wound fester.' – *Daily Variety*

executive producer. In TV, usually the head of a department (comedy, light entertainment, etc.), but also the moneybags in charge of a particular production and sometimes (as with Jack Webb) the creative force of the enterprise.

Executive Suite
US 1976 19 × 50m colour
CBS/MGM (Rita Lakin)

Boardroom and domestic problems of those who control a large corporation.
The pilot hour promised smart adult drama akin to the original movie, but compromise set in and the show was watered down to accommodate a youth element. As a serial it lacked cliffhangers, and was suddenly chopped without an end to the story. A cautionary tale for those interested in American TV practice.

cr Arthur Bernard Lewis, Norman Felton, Stanley Rubin

Mitch Ryan, Sharon Acker, Stephen Elliott, Madlyn Rhue, Leigh McCloskey, Brenda Sykes, Percy Rodrigues

Exoman
US 1977 96m colour TVM
Universal

Permanently paralysed after an attack by gangsters, a professor devises a super suit which makes him mobile enough to exact revenge.
Tasteless gimmick pilot.

w Martin Caidin, Howard Rodman *d* Richard Irving

David Ackroyd, Anna Schedeen, Harry Morgan, Jose Ferrer, Kevin McCarthy, A. Martinez

The Expert *
GB 1970–5 54 × 50m colour (VTR)
BBC (Andrew Osborn)

Cases of a pathologist.
Police mystery stories with a dry medical flavour and a self-effacing performance from the star.
MARIUS GORING

The Explorers **
GB 1975 13 × 50m colour
BBC (Michael Latham)

A series of documentary reconstructions of the lives of famous explorers, hosted by David Attenborough. The Amundsen episode, directed by David Cobham, won the BAFTA award for best documentary.

Exton, Clive (1930–). British playwright who in the fifties produced some memorable single plays (*No Fixed Abode*, *Soldier*, *The Trial of Dr Fancy*). Became a film scriptwriter, but gradually descended to routine efficiency.

Eye on Research *. Admirable BBC science programme of the early sixties in which the visits to laboratories and workshops took the form of live outside broadcasts, thus avoiding the possibility of an experiment being filmed six times before they got it to work properly, and, on occasion, achieving a spectacular candour when everything went wrong. Jet engines, computers and linear motors were among the projects reviewed, while the first moments of a baby's life in an edition on obstetric advances came by relay from Sweden. Raymond Baxter was the commentator, Aubrey Singer the producer.
PP

Eye to Eye
US 1984 6 × 50m colour
ABC/Warner/Skorpios (Steven A. Vail)

Adventures of a paunchy middle-aged private eye and a female eccentric.
Unsatisfactory format remembered from the movie *The Late Show*. Not a goer for series TV, especially not with this rather frenetic production and a grossly overweight star.

cr Rich Eustis, Michael Elias

Charles Durning, Stephanie Faracy, Maureen Stapleton

Eyes as Big as Canteloupes by Don Freeman. A sharply written book (US 1981) of commentaries on television of the seventies, especially the reasons why we get the programmes we do.

The Eyes of Charles Sand*
US 1972 75m colour TVM
Warner (Hugh Benson)

A young man with second sight solves a bizarre murder mystery.
Old-fashioned horror comic, well camped up.

w Henry Farrell, Stanford Whitmore *d* Reza S. Badiyi

Peter Haskell, Joan Bennett, Barbara Rush, Sharon Farrell, Bradford Dillman, Adam West

F.D.R.: The Last Year **
US 1980 150m colour VTR
NBC/Columbia/Titus (Herb Brodkin)

Episodes in the last year in the life of Franklin Delano Roosevelt.

An absorbing historical re-creation, concentrating on people rather than action.

w Stanley R. Greenberg, *book* by Jim Bishop

JASON ROBARDS, Eileen Heckart (Eleanor), Kim Hunter (Lucy Rutherford), Sylvia Sidney (cousin Polly), Edward Binns (Gen. Watson), Larry Gates (Admiral Leahy), Augusta Dabney, Michael Gross

F. Scott Fitzgerald and 'The Last of the Belles' *
US 1974 96m colour TVM
ABC/Titus (Herb Brodkin)

The first meeting of the novelist and his flamboyant wife Zelda, as shown in one of his short stories.

An interesting crack at comparing fact with fiction, well presented in all departments.

w James Costigan d George Schaefer ph Ed Brown m Don Sebesky ad Jack DeGovia

Richard Chamberlain, Blythe Danner, Susan Sarandon, David Huffman, Richard Hatch, James Naughton

F. Scott Fitzgerald in Hollywood *
US 1976 96m colour TVM
ABC/Titus (Herb Brodkin)

A comparison between Fitzgerald's two periods in Hollywood; 1927 as the triumphant author of *The Great Gatsby*, and 1937 as the alcoholic with the unbalanced wife.

A second extremely carefully mounted examination of the troubles besetting America's chronicler of the jazz age.

w James Costigan d Anthony Page ph James Crabe m Morton Gould ad Jack DeGovia

Jason Miller, Tuesday Weld, Julia Foster (as Sheilah Graham), Dolores Sutton (as Dorothy Parker), Michael Lerner, John Randolph

F Troop *
US 1965–6 65 × 25m 34 bw, 31 colour
ABC/Warner

Wacky goings-on at a fort in the old west. Pratfall army comedy, smartly enough presented to keep one laughing.

cr Richard M. Bluel

Forrest Tucker, Larry Storch, Ken Berry, Melody Patterson, Edward Everett Horton (as an Indian)

Fabares, Shelley (1942–). American leading lady, niece of Nanette Fabray. Series: *The Brian Keith Show*. TV movies include *Brian's Song*, *Two For the Money*, *Sky Heist*, *Pleasure Cove*.

Fabian of the Yard. British (BBC) half-hour series in the fifties of immense contemporary popularity, starring Patrick Barr in semi-fictional re-creations of famous police cases.

Fabray, Nanette (1920–) (Nanette Fabares). American comedienne, once a star of *Our Gang*. Many variety appearances. TV movies include *Fame Is the Name of the Game*, *But I Don't Want to Get Married*, *The Magic Carpet*, *The Couple Takes a Wife*.

The Fabulous Fifties (US 1960). An ABC flashback compilation which won an Emmy as best variety special.

The Face of Fear *
US 1971 72m colour TVM
Quinn Martin

A young woman who has (she believes) a terminal illness arranges for her own murder. And then . . .

An old chestnut adequately warmed over.

w Edward Hume, *novel Sally* E. V. Cunningham d George McCowan m Morton Stevens

Elizabeth Ashley, Ricardo Montalban, Jack Warden, Dane Clark

The Face of Rage
US 1983 96m colour TVM
ABC/Viacom/Hal Sitowitz (Neil T. Maffeo)

A divorcee is raped, and part of the therapy is to have her face and talk to a group of rapists in jail.

Only in America, one feels, could such an absurd 'cure' be offered by genuine doctors. True or not, it rings false from beginning to end.

w Hal Sitowitz, Donald Wrye d Donald Wrye ph Stevan Larner m Miles Goodman

Dianne West, George Dzundza, Graham Beckel, Jeffrey de Munn, Raymond J. Barry, Paul Bates, Stephanie Dunnam

'Words are being bounced around, and emotions are bared, but the confrontation fails to convince; someone's pulling a con job.' – *Daily Variety*

Face the Music. A long-running BBC2 musical quiz, presided over by pianist Joseph Cooper. Now superseded by *My Music*.

Face the Press (GB since 1968). Virtually the BBC's old *Press Conference* enterprisingly exhumed by Tyne-Tees as a networked ITV programme with some out-of-town viewpoint. Chaired latterly by Anthony Howard and (since 1985) Gillian Reynolds. From 1983 aired on C4.   PP

Face to Face ** (GB 1958–60). The first (and almost the last) sharp-edged interview series on British television; conducted by John Freeman, former *New Statesman* editor and Labour junior minister, future ambassador to Washington and chairman of LWT. Bertrand Russell, Edith Sitwell, Augustus John, Evelyn Waugh, Lord Reith, Victor Gollancz and Carl Jung were among immortals who consented to occupy the hard little chair a yard from Freeman's – 'Knee to Knee' would have been an apter title. Although Freeman was contemptuous of what he called the ceremonious, kid-glove questioning of public figures, he was never aggressive himself. He was inquisitive in a rather surgical way. The questions were designed to cut through superficial responses. He would never say 'How's your health?' or 'Do you enjoy good health?' but – if appropriate – 'Look, you have a record of poor health. Do you mind this?' There was a famous outcry when Gilbert Harding broke down and wept on the show but really this was an accident of Freeman blundering by chance into a private susceptibility of which he could have had no prior knowledge. Produced by Hugh Burnett; for BBC.   PP

faction. A neologism coined to describe the late seventies breed of TV movies purporting to give the factual lives of famous people, but invariably straying pretty far from the truth. Also called *docu-drama*.

The Facts of Life
US 1982–   × 25m colour VTR
Embassy
Problems of girls in a boarding school in upstate New York.
This being a tape show with limited sets, most of the action is confined to the dorm, with all the funny lines going to house mother. Precocious American teenagers are not for export.

Charlotte Rae, Lisa Whelchel, Nancy McKeon, Kim Fields, Mindy Kohn

'Exactly the sort of series that normally makes my teeth grind and my right eye twitch: wall-to-wall cute kids and one of those squeaky-clean, wholesome settings where the furniture looks edible . . . but the girls are likeable and you can always count on a funny line or two.' – Robert MacKenzie, *TV Guide*

Fade Out *
GB 1970 96m colour TVM
HTV (Patrick Dromgoole, Harry Field)
A television news team is involved in a top level government scandal.
Efficient power play.

w Leon Griffiths, *play* David Watson d John Nelson Burton

Stanley Baker, George Sanders, Geoffrey Bayldon, Ronald Hines, Ann Lynn, Francis Matthews, Faith Brook

Fadiman, Clifton (1904–). American literary man-of-all-trades who in the fifties became famous as the host of TV's *Information Please*.

The Failing of Raymond *
US 1971 73m colour TVM
Universal (George Eckstein)
An embittered student seeks revenge against the middle-aged lady teacher responsible for his not passing an exam.
Fairly good suspenser.

w Adrian Spies d George Eckstein m Pat Williams

Jane Wyman, Dean Stockwell, Dana Andrews, Murray Hamilton, Paul Henreid, Tim O'Connor

The Fainthearted Feminist (GB 1984; 6 × 30m). Another sitcom (like *Father's Day*) wrought from a newspaper column, Jill Tweedie's 'Martha' letters in *The Guardian*. There Ms Tweedie teased feminism on the surface, upheld it below. The BBC television version co-written by Christopher Bond tried to do both these things at the same time on the same level, and ended up with a stock of pert characters reduced to a few pert attitudes and idiosyncrasies; with Lynn Redgrave, Jonathan Newth, Sara Sugarman. PP

Fair Exchange
US 1962 14 × 50m bw
US 1963 13 × 25m bw
CBS/Desilu
An American and an Englishman exchange families for a year.
Halting comedy series which never made its mark.
Eddie Foy Jnr, Victor Maddern, Lynn Loring, Judy Carne

Fair Stood the Wind for France (GB 1981). Well-received televersion in four one-hour episodes of H. E. Bates's novel about an aircrew which baled out in occupied France during World War II. With David Beames, Cecile Paoli, Bernard Kay; adapted by Julian Bond; produced by Colin Tucker; for BBC.

Fairbanks, Douglas Jnr (1909–). American leading light actor, son of Douglas Fairbanks. Between 1954 and 1956 he produced and occasionally starred in at least 120 half-hour dramas of very variable quality. Made in England, they glutted the world's TV sets. TV movies as actor: *The Crooked Hearts*, *The Hostage Tower*.

Fairchild, Morgan (1950–). American leading lady. *Search for Tomorrow*, *Murder in Music City*, *Flamingo Road*, *The Dream Merchants*, *Time Bomb*, *The Zany Adventures of Robin Hood*, *Paper Dolls*.

Fairfax, Ferdinand (19 –). British director who came to notice with *Danger UXB* and *Speed King*. Lately *The Last Place on Earth*. PP

Fairley, Peter (1930–). British journalist who became science editor of ITN.

Fairly Secret Army (GB 1984; 6 × 28m). Lame sitcom featuring Geoffrey Palmer as retired military buffoon trying to raise private army to maintain civilization against the imminent breakdown of society, etc. With Diane Fletcher, Jeremy Child. Written by David Nobbs, directed by Robert Young, produced by Peter Robinson, for C4/Video Arts. PP

Faith, Adam (1940–) (Terence Nelhams). British pop star who turned to acting and had a hit with *Budgie* (1971–3). Lately, *Just Another Little Blues Song* (1984), *Minder on the Orient Express*. PP

Faith and Henry * (GB 1969; 52m; colour). Little film of young love, written by Julia Jones and shot by Jack Gold around some decaying industrial landscape in Lancashire. Through it ambled a boy and girl on the way home from school. The boy felt the spell of the scenery, the girl less so. They got to know each other, experienced the first nice pricklings of love, that's all. It was low on any sort of dramatic tension. Anyone in an unresponsive mood might have switched away in impatience. But anyone who did stay would have been charmed by the sweetness and optimism and the instinctive playing of the two youngsters. Produced by Kenith Trodd; for Kestrel/LWT. PP

The Falcon: see The Adventures of the Falcon

Falcon Crest
US 1981   × 50m colour
CBS/Lorimar/Amanda and MF (Malcolm R. Harding)
There's lots of infighting in the Channing family, owners of a valuable vine estate in the Napa Valley.
A lush-looking soap which struggled to success in the shadow of *Dallas* (i.e. it's made by the same producers and they scheduled the hit show right before it).
cr Earl Hamner *m* Bill Conti
Jane Wyman, Robert Foxworth, Susan Sullivan, Lorenzo Lamas, Mel Ferrer, Lana Turner
'On second look this is not a sister series to *Dallas*: more a second cousin, of cooler disposition and cleaner habits. Neither as warm as *The Waltons* nor as much fun as some of the broader soaps. On the other hand, a show that teaches us how to pronounce "cabernet sauvignon' can't be all bad.' – Robert MacKenzie, *TV Guide*

❋   **Falk, Peter** (1927–). Glass-eyed American character actor who scored his greatest hit as the shabby but perceptive detective COLUMBO, whose apparently diffident and casual harassment of murder suspects became one of the greatest bores of the seventies. Previously appeared in *The Trials of O'Brien*. Emmys 1961 for THE PRICE OF TOMATOES; 1971, 1974 and 1975 for *Columbo*. TV movies: *A Step Out of Line*, *Prescription Murder*, *Griffin and Phoenix*.

The Falklands War. As the first hot war to be fought by British forces since Korea, and one in which the broadcasting and Press presence was severely limited, its treatment inevitably came in for much criticism. Live coverage from 7,000 miles away was reduced to radio coverage, even on TV. One blind voice-over from Michael Nicholson ran on ITN for 11 minutes. The pictures took 18–23 days to arrive by sea and air. News of disasters and successes alike were dispensed first by a dour Ministry of Defence spokesman soon to be famous after a fashion, Ian MacDonald. Nevertheless several media reputations were forged during the brief campaign, notably those of BBC reporter Brian Hanrahan and Fleet Street's Max Hastings.

Key actuality broadcasts during and immediately after the campaign included the British Task Force setting sail, scenes in and around Downing Street when victory was gained, ecstatic Portsmouth welcomes for returning ships, and:

The Falklands: Where Will It End? Satellite-borne argie-bargie between studio assemblage of Argentinians actually in neighbouring Uruguay and equivalent British group in Leeds, refereed by David Frost, YTV, 5 May 1982.

Panorama (10 May 1982), notoriously airing dissenting voices from both Socialist and Tory politicians. That they should be heard was proper but not to such disproportionate length, said more reasoned critics, among them the programme's presenter Robert Kee who repudiated the show the next day.

Retrospective programmes, among them accusatory and/or dramatized items, included:

Panorama, again (21 June 1982), reporting from Argentina on life there in the latter days of the war, as led by a group of prosperous middle-class Señora Minivers.

Task Force South: BBC re-run of the campaign in 8 × 40m instalments, narrated by Brian Hanrahan, produced by Bernard Hesketh and John Jockel, July–August 1982.

First Tuesday (5 April 1983): uneasy letters from a young naval officer, David Tinker, who died in the campaign, set into context on YTV's monthly current affairs special.

Q.E.D. (same week). BBC Manchester's current affairs show on *Simon's War*, the long treatment and many operations needed by a Welsh Guardsman, Simon Weston, who suffered hideous burns in the *Sir Galahad* fire. A sequel followed two years later; the BBC Wales play *The Mimosa Boys* (1985) dealt with the circumstances leading up to the same disaster.

Heart of the Matter (17 April 1983): the BBC's religious series exploring the spiritual comfort experienced by families bereaved in the Falklands War.

The Falklands Factor: Don Shaw's dramatization of Dr Johnson's sentiments at the time of the 1770 Argentinian bid for the islands, as a corrective to ours two centuries later. With Donald Pleasence, *d* Colin Bucksey, BBC 1983.

The Waiting War: Maggie Wadey's play based on the experiences of three Navy families with menfolk aboard the doomed HMS *Sheffield*; *d* Tony Smith *p* Ruth Caleb, for BBC (1983).

Brass Tacks (14 November 1984): Enquiry into the sinking of the Argentinian cruiser *General Belgrano* conducted in quasi-official form by Lord Annan with Labour MP Ian Dalyell, needless to say, prosecuting and Tory Michael Mates defending; *p* Gerry Northam, for BBC Manchester.

The Fall and Rise of Reginald Perrin
GB 1976–80 20 approx. × 25m colour (VTR)
BBC (Gareth Gwenlan)

Frustrations of a middle-aged suburbanite with a dead-end executive job.

A frenetic comedy series rather lacking in funny jokes and tending to overuse the ones it has.

w David Nobbs

Leonard Rossiter, Pauline Yates, John Barron

The Fall and Rise of the House of Krupp *
GB 1965 60m bw
ATV (Peter Batty)

Impressive documentary history of the giant German iron, steel and arms firm, supposedly dismantled after World War II but already stronger than ever. Narrated by Bernard Archard; written and directed by Peter Batty.

The Fall Guy
US 1981 96m colour TVM
ABC/TCF/Glen Larson (Harker Wade)

A stunt man doubles as a bounty hunter.

Lumpy adventure pilot with comedy asides and a fairly stunning desert chase climax by car and helicopter.

w Glen Larson *d* Russ Mayberry *ph* Frank Beaschochea

Lee Majors, Jo Ann Pflug, Douglass Barr, Heather Thomas, Eddie Albert, Lou Rawls

† The one-hour series which resulted limped along for four seasons.

The Fall of Eagles
GB 1974 13 × 75m colour
BBC

Interminable (it seemed at the time) saga of the Hapsburg dynasty from the first Emperor Franz-Joseph to Kaiser Bill's departure into exile at the end of World War I, but along the way were solid performances.

w Robert Muller and others *d* Rudolph Cartier and others

Curt Jurgens (Bismarck), Gemma Jones (Princess Victoria), Patrick Stewart (Lenin), Barry Foster (Kaiser Wilhelm II), Marius Goring (Hindenburg)   PP

Fallen Angel *
US 1981 96m colour TVM
Columbia/Green–Epstein (Lew Hunter,
    Audrey Blaisdell-Goddard

The shy small daughter of a small-town widow is befriended by a recreation park coach who is also a scout for a child pornographer.
Subtly and strongly developed, this is a horror story in which nothing is actually shown. It is so persuasive that there were doubts whether it should be widely shown – too late, as it was the highest rated TV movie of its season.

w Lew Hunter *d* ROBERT LEWIS *ph* MICHAEL MARGUILIES *m* Richard Bella

DANA HILL, RICHARD MASUR, Melinda Dillon, Robby Cox

'It works well enough to scare parents and warn youngsters.' – *Daily Variety*

Fallen Hero
GB 1978–9 12 × 50m colour
Granada (June Howson)

Two six-parters about a professional rugby football player forced out of the game by injury and having to cope with a failing marriage as well as a vanishing career.
Gritty, honest.

w Brian Finch

Del Henney, Wanda Ventham   PP

Fame *
US 1982   × 50m colour
CBS/MGM/Jozak (Stanley C. Rogow)

Problems of the pupils at a New York dancing school.
A cleaned-up version of the film, with the usual assortment of ethnic types and generally plenty going on. Enthusiasm flagged after a couple of years; but when the network dropped the show, MGM produced a syndicated version for two more seasons.

cr Christopher Gore

Debbie Allen, Gene Anthony Ray, Lee Curreri, Tommy Aguilar, Lori Singer, P. R. Paul, Valerie Landsburg, Erica Gimpel, Carol Mayo Jenkins

PP: Fame is the holy grail to which all the kids aspire. Between bits of lacklustre hoofing they deliver smug little sermons to each other on the need to work for it, it doesn't just happen. The awful thing is that,

left to American audiences, the show would have died in 1983. Only the support of foreign buyers, including the BBC, kept it going.

The Fame Game (GB 1985). Talent-spotting contest from Granada (John Hamp) with a fancy computerized display to show the votes of a nationwide 'cross-section of the public' voting by interactive button, plus a less rarefied bit of technology in the form of a hook to haul off comics failing to please. With Tim Brooke-Taylor and Stan Boardman as tirelessly chirpy MCs.   PP

Fame Is the Name of the Game *
US 1966 100m colour TVM
Universal

A magazine reporter on assignment discovers a girl's body and traps her murderer.
Ho-hum glossy melodrama which sparked off a three-season series of telefeatures about the magazine, *The Name of the Game*.

w Ranald MacDougall *d* Stuart Rosenberg

Anthony Franciosa, Jill St John, Jack Klugman, George Macready, Lee Bowman, Nanette Fabray, Jay C. Flippen, Jack Warden

Fame Is the Spur (GB 1982). Adequate BBC serial in 8 × 50-minute parts, from Howard Spring's novel about the rise of the labour movement in Victorian Manchester. With Tim Pigott-Smith, David Hayman, Joanna David. Adapted by Elaine Morgan; directed by David Giles; produced by Richard Beynon.

Family *
US 1976–80 88 × 50m colour
ABC/Spelling–Goldberg (Mike Nichols)

Problems of a middle-class Los Angeles family. Impeccable production and nice manners make this look like the typical family of the commercials, but the show is well-meaning, the acting reliable and the stories usually plausible.

cr Jay Presson Allen *m* John Rubinstein

James Broderick, Sada Thompson, Gary Frank, Kristy McNichol, John Rubinstein, Elayne Heilveil

The Family **
GB 1974 12 × 30m colour (16mm)
BBC (Paul Watson)

A camera unit stays with the working-class Wilkins family of Reading for several months and gains a supposedly accurate portrayal of their behaviour.
A much criticized series, copying *An American Family*; it appeared to show up all the more

vulgar elements in the family's life, though it must be admitted that Mrs Wilkins emerged as a telly star.

† An up-date 10 years later, *The After Years*, was transmitted in December 1983.

Family Affair *
US 1966–70 138 × 25m colour
CBS/Universal/Don Fedderson (Edmund Hartmann)

A New York bachelor takes over the care of his nieces and nephew, much to the dismay of his English manservant.
Popular comedy with satisfactory style and performances.

cr Don Fedderson, Edmund Hartmann

Brian Keith, Sebastian Cabot, Anissa Jones, Johnnie Whittaker, Kathy Garver

A Family at War *
GB 1970–2 52 × 50m colour (VTR)
Granada (Richard Doubleday)

Tribulations of a Liverpool working-class family during World War II.
Earnest, moderately realistic chronicle, sometimes so glum as to give the impression of *Cold Comfort Farm*.

cr John Finch *d* June Howson and others

Margery Mason, Colin Douglas, Lesley Nunnerly, Shelagh Fraser, John McKelvey, Coral Atkins, Keith Drinkel, Colin Campbell, Barbara Flynn

Family Business
US 1983 74m colour TVM
South Carolina Educational TV Network (Hal and Marilyn Weiner)

Sons of a department store tycoon adopt various attitudes as the old man nears death. Solid televersion of a Broadway play, made for American Playhouse.

w Dick Goldeberg, from his *play* *d* John Stix *ph* Paul Raimondi

Milton Berle, Richard Greene, Jeffrey Marcus, David Garfield, David Rosenbaum

Family Feud.
An American panel game popular in the seventies on ABC from 1976; host Richard Dawson. The British version, via ATV, is *Family Fortunes* with Bob Monkhouse. A Goodson–Todman format in which families compete, it is very similar to *Ask the Family* on BBC.

Family Flight *
US 1972 73m colour TVM
Universal (Harve Bennett)

A light plane crashes in the desert and the family involved needs all its ingenuity to survive.

Taut, efficient action suspenser apparently inspired by *The Flight of the Phoenix*.

w Guerdon Trueblood *d* Marvin Chomsky

Rod Taylor, Dina Merrill, Kristoffer Tabori, Janet Margolin, Gene Nelson

Family Fortunes: see Family Feud

The Family Holvak
US 1976 13 × 50m colour
NBC/Universal (Dean Hargrove, Roland Kibbee)

Stories of a poor backwoods minister in the thirties, from the novel *Ramey* by Jack Farris. Rather dreary nostalgia, following on from the TV movie *The Greatest Gift*, and in the wake of *The Waltons*.

Glenn Ford, Julie Harris, Lance Kervin, Elizabeth Cheshire

The Family Kovack
US 1974 74m colour TVM
CBS/Warner/Playboy

A Chicago family bands together when the son is accused of bribing a city official.
Forgettable family drama distinguished by excellent location atmosphere, which was not enough to turn it into a series.

w Adrian Spies *d* Ralph Senensky

James Sloyan, Sarah Cunningham, Andy Robinson, Richard Gilliland

The Family Nobody Wanted
US 1975 74m colour TVM
ABC/Universal (David Victor)

A minister and his wife adopt a very miscellaneous family of twelve, but find they are resented in a new parish.
Old-fashioned sentimentality, laid on with a trowel.

w Suzanne Clauser, *book* Helen Doss *d* Ralph Senensky *ph* Jack Woolf *m* George Romanis

Shirley Jones, James Olson, Woodrow Parfrey, Ann Doran

Family Reunion
US 1981 2 × 93m colour
NBC/Columbia (Lucy Jarvis)

A small-town schoolteacher retires and is given a bus ticket for unlimited travel. She sets off to visit members of her family, then discovers that she has been got out of the way while a shopping mall on family property has been approved by the greedy town council.
Hesitantly developed, obscurely told and not very well acted (even by the star), this rather obvious moral story develops like a serious Ealing comedy but fails to be heartwarming.

w Allan Sloane *d* Fielder Cook *ph* Jack Priestley

Bette Davis, J. Ashley Hyman, Peter Weller, Roy Dotrice, Sally Prager, Chris Murray

The Family Rico
US 1972 73m colour TVM
CBS/George LeMaire

A crime syndicate leader is in trouble when his younger brother defects.
Shades of *On the Waterfront* and *The Brotherhood*, but actually from a Simenon novel previously filmed as *The Brothers Rico*. Enough is enough.

w David Karp *d* Paul Wendkos

Ben Gazzara, James Farentino, Sal Mineo, Jo Van Fleet, Dane Clark, Jack Carter, Leif Erickson, John Marley

Family Secrets
US 1984 96m colour TVM
NBC/Katz–Gallin/Half Pint/Karoger (Leora Thuna, Stefanie Powers)

A career woman finds on a family weekend that her mother and daughter have their problems too.
Glossy, slow-moving soap: watchable and instantly forgettable.

w Leora Thuna *d* Jack Hofsiss *ph* James Crabe *m* Charles Fox

Stefanie Powers, Maureen Stapleton, Melissa Gilbert, Gary Dontzig, Marion Ramsey

'Doesn't do much in the drama department.' – *Daily Variety*

Family Ties *
US 1982–   × 25m colour
NBC/Paramount/UBU Productions (Gary David Goldberg)

Two affluent parents of the let-it-all-hang-out generation find that their children tend towards conservatism.
Genuinely warm, affectionate comedy series which only occasionally presents a strained situation.

cr Lloyd Garber

Meredith Baxter Birney, Michael Gross, MICHAEL J. FOX, Justine Bateman, Tina Yothers

'Genuine people, genuine laughs, genuine heart. It's a fresh breeze.' – *Daily Variety*

'A family is more than the sum of its parts!'
The Family Tree
US 1983 6 × 50m colour
ABC/Comworld (Carroll Newman)

Two newlyweds have a ready-made family from their previous marriages.
Short-run series on a familiar theme. It was not extended.

cr Carl McKeand

Anne Archer, Frank Converse, James Spader, Martin Hewitt, Joanna Cassidy, Alan Feinstein, Ann Dusenberry

A Family Upside Down
US 1978 93m colour TVM
CBS/Ross Hunter–Jacque Mapes

An elderly man finds no reason to live on after the death of his wife.
Accurately observed but inevitably depressing soap opera.

w Gerald di Pego *d* David Lowell Rich *ph* Joseph Biroc *m* Henry Mancini

FRED ASTAIRE (Emmy), Helen Hayes, Efrem Zimbalist Jnr, Pat Crowley, Patty Duke Astin, Ford Rainey, Brad Rearden

The Famous Adventures of Mr Magoo *
US 1964 26 × 25m colour
NBC/UPA

Cartoon adaptations of literary classics.
A wheeze that works far better than might have been expected is to have Magoo 'play' characters in the stories, e.g. Frankenstein, Dr Watson, Dr Jekyll. The result, well animated, is an amusing series of pastiches.

Fancy Wanders (GB 1981). Unsuccessful half-hour comedy series with Dave King and Joe Marcell as a couple of fanciful tramps. Of less than absorbing interest. Written by Sid Green; for LWT.

'He's not your average teenage kid – unless you call a kid who turns into a wacky werewolf average!'
Fangface
US 1982 24 × 25m colour

The publicity tells the story of this Ruby–Spears cartoon series, which is neither better nor worse than one might expect from the saga of a boy who turns into a wolf.

Fanny and Alexander ***
Original title: *Fanny och Alexander*
Sweden 1982 300m
AB Cinematograph/SFI/SRTI/etc.

The original full-length, designed-for-television version of Ingmar Bergman's semi-autobiographical child's-eye treat, beginning in the bosom of a good-living theatrical family over a magical Christmastide, switching – after the death of the actor-paterfamilias and re-marriage of his widow – to a grim ecclesiastical household, and finally a return to somewhat happier times. The BBC2 three-part transmission (1984) ran the opening chunk before Christmas and then let four days (and the festivities) pass before showing the expulsion from Paradise.

w and *d* Ingmar Bergman

Gunn Wallgren, Borje Ahlstedt, Christina Schollin, Allan Edwall, Ewa Froling, Pernilla Allwin. Bertin Guve   PP

Fanny By Gaslight
GB 1981 4 × 50m colour
BBC (Joe Waters)

In 1868, the daughter of a brothelkeeper learns the true facts of her birth.

A wallow in the Victorian underworld which might have been more agreeable had the director not had the curious idea that the past was out of focus.

w Anthony Steven, *novel* Michael Sadleir *d* Peter Jefferies *m* Alexander Faris

Chloe Salaman, Anthony Bate, Michael Culver, Stephen Yardley

Fantasies *
US 1982 96m colour TVM
ABC/Monty (Leonard Goldberg)

The creator of a TV soap opera finds that her actors are being murdered one by one.

Old-fashioned jeopardy thriller with an off-putting title. Quite lively for a TV movie.

w David Levinson *d* William Wiard *ph* Richard L. Rawlings *m* James Di Pasquale

Suzanne Pleshette, Barry Newman, Robert Vaughn, Patrick O'Neal, Lenora May, Allyn Ann McLerie, Madlyn Rhue, Stuart Damon

The Fantastic Four
US 1967 19 × 25m colour
ABC/Hanna–Barbera

The passengers in a rocketship acquire fantastic powers when they pass through a radioactive belt.

Animated Marvel Comics adventures with a human torch, a stretcher, an invisible woman and a Thing.

Fantastic Journey
US 1977 74m colour TVM
NBC/Columbia/Bruce Lansbury (Leonard Katzman)

A small boatload of people, lost in a cloud in the Bermuda Triangle, find themselves on an island with different historical time zones, escaping from one weird adventure to the next.

Inept, cut-price science fiction nonsense which is boring when not laughable.

w/cr Merwin Gerard *d* Andrew V. McLaglen *m* Robert Prince

Jared Martin, Katie Saylor, Ike Eisenmann

† The resultant series, equally poor, ran to 13 50-minute episodes. Roddy McDowall joined the cast.

Fantastic Voyage
US 1967 17 × 22m colour
TCF/Filmation

Scientists are miniaturized and injected into an ailing human body so that they can repair it from inside.

Adequate cartoon transcription of the movie.

The Fantastic World of D. C. Collins
US 1984 96m colour TVM
NBC/Zephyr/Guillaume–Margo (Jim Begg)

The son of a diplomat spends his time daydreaming of adventure, then finds himself on the run from real spies.

It was all much funnier as *The Secret Life of Walter Mitty*.

w Phil Margo, Martin Cohan *d* Leslie Martinson

Gary Coleman, George Gobel, Pamela Segall, Jason Bateman, Shelley Smith, Bernie Casey

Fantasy Island *
US 1977–82 2 × 95m, approx. 120 × 50m colour
ABC/Spelling–Goldberg

For ten thousand dollars a weekend, the rich can go to a mysterious luxury island and have their wishes granted.

Despite two abysmally slow pilots, this mixture of *Outward Bound*, *Westworld*, *The Tempest* and *The Wizard of Oz* proved manna to the luxury-starved public.

Ricardo Montalban, Herve Villechaize

'For me, the character who epitomized *Fantasy Island* was the guy whose fantasy was to have lunch with Charlie's Angels. Not with Voltaire, mind you, or Orson Welles or even Sophia Loren, but with Charlie's Angels. The guy got his wish and probably deserved it.' – Robert MacKenzie, *TV Guide*

Far Out Space Nuts
US 1975 17 × 22m colour
TCF/Sid and Marty Krofft

Two ground-crew men are accidentally propelled into outer space.

Resistible cartoon adventures.

'A Love that defied an empire!'
The Far Pavilions
GB 1984 3 × 96m colour miniseries
HBO/C4/Goldcrest (Geoffrey Reeve)

An English cavalry officer in India loves a princess who has been promised to a despotic ruler.

Everything is thrown in but Rudolph Valentino as the Sheikh, but despite elaborate production the mixture never quite comes to the boil.

w Julian Bond, *novel* by M. M. Kaye d Peter Duffell ph Jack Cardiff m Carl Davis pd Robert Laing

Ben Cross, Amy Irving, Omar Sharif, John Gielgud, Christopher Lee, Rossano Brazzi, Benedict Taylor, Saeed Jaffrey, Robert Hardy

PP: 'My attention took a jolt early on when patrician Englishmen of the mid-19th century said: "You said it, not me," or: "She passed me over for some old fart in the Political Service – a geriatric." What avails it to stage mile-long wedding processions with camels and water-buffalo and, yea, elephants, if the producer, the director, the screenwriter and everyone else concerned with the production have recycled cardboard ears? I also decided that a long procession went a little way, and got very tired of protracted rear views of our hero (Ben Cross) strutting here and there in his tight britches and boots.'

Faraday and Company: see Mystery Movie and Say Hello to a Dead Man

Faraway Hill. Claimed as TV's first dramatic serial, this American half-hour effort of 1946 was actually a monologue for one woman (Flora Campbell) who, usually seen in close-up, spoke to a number of off-screen voices.

Farentino, James (1938–). Saturnine American leading man who appeared in many TV guest roles and the series *Cool Million* and *The Bold Ones*. TV movies include *Wings of Fire*, *Vanished*, *The Longest Night*, *The Family Rico*, *The Elevator*, *Crossfire*, *Jesus of Nazareth*, *The Possessed*, *Silent Victory*, *Son-Rise*.

Farewell to Manzanar
US 1976 105m colour TVM
Universal/NBC/John Korty

During World War II, many Japanese–Americans are interned.

Solid, solemn, not very compulsive communal guilt-shedding by film-makers who weren't involved.

w Jeanne Wakatsuki Houston, James D. Houston, John Korty d John Korty m Paul Chihara

Yuki Shimoda, Nobu McCarthy, Mako, Pat Morita

Farmers Arms (GB 1983; 60m). Sardonic view of modern farmers and farming life by Nick Darke. With Philip Jackson, Colin Welland, Brenda Bruce. Directed by Giles Foster, produced by Ann Scott, for BBC. PP

The Farmer's Daughter *
US 1963–5 101 × 25m bw (26 colour)
ABC/Columbia

A governess becomes influential in the home of a widowed congressman.

Reasonably intelligent sitcom after the movie.

Inger Stevens, William Windom, Cathleen Nesbitt

The Farming Year (GB 1959). Schools programme filmed for Rediffusion (on a Northamptonshire farm) and transmitted week by week throughout a full year, so successfully that it was repeated as an evening series.   PP

Farr, Jamie (1934–). Long-nosed American character comedian who was seen in *Chicago Teddy Bears* and (more memorably) as the transvestite Corporal Klinger in *M*A*S*H*.

'All she wants is to be a good DA! But her toughest case is being a woman!'
Farrell for the People
US 1982 96m colour TVM
NBC/MGM/InterMedia/TAL (Lin Bolen)

Adventures of the DA's new lady assistant.

Routine pilot which the start couldn't promote into a series.

w Larry Brody, Janis Hendler d Paul Wendkos ph Richard C. Glouner m Bill Conti

Valerie Harper, Gregory Sierra, Eugene Roche, Judith Chapman, Steve Inwood, Dennis Lipscomb

Farrell, Glenda (1904–71). Wisecracking American comedienne of the thirties who later made a comeback as a character actress and on TV won an Emmy in 1962 for her work in a *Ben Casey* episode.

Farrell, Mike (1942–). American actor who partnered Alan Alda in the latter years of *M*A*S*H*.

Farrow, Mia (1945–). American leading lady of the seventies, daughter of John Farrow

AFTER EIGHT YEARS WITH "M*A*S*H" MIKE FARRELL IS NOW ANOTHER KIND OF DOCTOR—

A detective with unusual methods for uncovering the truth. A best friend who listens to your dark sexual secrets.

Trust him.

PRIVATE SESSIONS

Make an appointment to see what goes on behind closed doors!

BLOCKBUSTER 2-HOUR MOVIE SPECIAL!

MIKE FARRELL is one of those familiar faces which most people can't place, and even devotees of *M*A*S*H* might find it hard to credit that he was second banana to Alan Alda for eight years. Alas, his TV movies were also fairly forgettable.

and Maureen O'Sullivan. She became famous as Alison in PEYTON PLACE but appeared in no other series; single TV appearances include *Johnny Belinda*, *Goodbye Raggedy Ann*, *Peter Pan*.

Farson, Dan (1930–). British–American interviewer in the early days of ITV, at first on *This Week* (where he famously brushed with Dylan Thomas's widow), then in usually brisk (15 minutes per episode) series of his own: *Member's Mail* (about MPs' constituency chores), *Out of Step* (minorities, yielding a celebrated edition with nudists), *Keeping in Step*, *Success Story*, *People in Trouble*, all for Rediffusion. Farson's flair was to be able to listen on camera as well as he talked. People volunteered amazing confidences. Drifted away from TV in the early sixties to live in Devon, but worked for HTV and on occasional metropolitan documentaries. Television critic, *The Mail on Sunday*, 1982–4, and deviser of *Gallery* for HTV/C4.
                                                                PP

Fast Boat to China (GB 1984; 4 × 55m). Alan Whicker tags along on a *QE2* cruise on which the mostly elderly passengers eat caviar because it's there. 'Mr Whicker's cheery commentary,' said Alexander Chancellor on behalf of a panel judging it one of the six turkeys of the year, 'served to deepen the sense of despair one felt watching those passive old people being delivered from one place to the next. A joyless spectacle.' Directed by Michael Tuchner, for BBC.   PP

Fast Friends
US 1978 96m colour TVM
Columbia/Green–Epstein/Sandra Harmon
A TV talk show host feuds with his head writer. Moderate, forgettable, semi-adult entertainment.

w Sandra Harmon *d* Steven H. Stern

Dick Shawn, Carrie Snodgress

Fat Albert and the Cosby Kids
US 1971–4 54 × 22m colour
CBS/Bill Cosby/Filmation

Adventures of a group of street kids. Tolerable children's cartoon series enlivened by Bill Cosby's voices.

Fatal Vision **
US 1984 2 × 96m colour miniseries
NBC (Richard L. O'Connor)

An army doctor claims that four hippies have murdered his family, but after years of investigation he is himself accused and finally convicted.

Soberly impressive re-enactment of a case which startled America and is currently still being argued. The narrative as filmed has some lapses, but seldom fails to grip.

w JOHN GAY, *book* by Joe McGinness *d* DAVID GREENE *ph* Stevan Larner *m* Gil Melle

Karl Malden, Eva Marie Saint, Gary Cole, Barry Newman, Andy Griffith, Mitchell Ryan

'A stunner of a docu-drama.' – *Daily Variety*

Father Brown *
GB 1974 26 × 50m colour (VTR)
ATV (Ian Fordyce)

Adventures of G. K. Chesterton's thoughtful clerical detective.

Not at all a bad interpretation of this rather difficult material, but it didn't appeal to an audience eager for easy sensation.

w Hugh Leonard *d* Robert Tronson

Kenneth More

Father Brown, Detective
aka: *Girl in the Park*
US 1980 96m colour TVM
NBC/Marble Arch (Martin Starger)

Father Brown, relocated in New York, solves the mystery of a body which keeps turning up to haunt the girl who witnessed its murder.

Very watchable, if overlong, transplantation of a famous character. The expected series, however, failed to materialize.

w Don M. Mankiewicz, Gordon Cotler *d* John Llewellyn Moxey *ph* Ronald Lautore *m* Allyn Ferguson, Jack Elliott

Barnard Hughes, Kay Lenz, George Hearn, Michael McGuire, Fred Gwynne, Donald Symington

'The suspense is dissipated by the length of the venture.' – *Daily Variety*

Father Charlie (GB 1982; 6 × 30m). Fairly desperate but not unfunny sitcom with Lionel Jefferies as an unruly ex-service Roman Catholic priest rashly posted to a nunnery as spiritual adviser. Written by Myles Rudge, directed and produced by Stewart Allen, for Central.   PP

Father Dear Father **
GB 1968–73 40 approx. × 25m colour (VTR)
Thames

A philanderer has trouble keeping his daughters under control.
Smart-paced farce, an excellent vehicle for a skilful star.

Patrick Cargill, Ursula Howells, Noel Dyson, Joyce Carey

† In 1977 Cargill appeared in seven more episodes made in Australia.

Father Figure
US 1980 96m colour TVM
CBS/Time–Life/Finnegan (William Finnegan)

After his wife's death, a man who has deserted his family attempts a reconciliation with his sons.
An involving study of tense family relationships.

w William Hanley, book Richard Peck d Jerry London ph Michael D. Marguilies m Billy Goldenberg

Hal Linden, Timothy Hutton, Jeremy Licht, Martha Scott

'A whiz of a vidpic.' – Daily Variety

Father Knows Best *
US 1954–9 191 × 25m bw
CBS/Columbia (Eugene B. Rodney)

The life of a typical American insurance man and his family.
As played, somewhere between the Hardys and the Joneses. And who can quarrel with success?

Robert Young, Jane Wyatt, Elinor Donahue, Billy Gray, Lauren Chapin

† In 1977 two taped 'reunion' programmes were made with all the members present.

†† The original sponsor dropped the show after the first 26 episodes, which shows what sponsors know.

The Father Knows Best Reunion
US 1977 74m colour (VTR)
Columbia (Renee Valente, Hugh Benson)

The Andersons celebrate their 35th wedding anniversary, and all the kids turn up.
Sentimental, obvious, and sure of a large audience.

w Paul West d Marc Daniels

Robert Young, Jane Wyatt, Elinor Donahue, Billy Gray, Lauren Chapin

† The title of the second special was Father Knows Best: Home for Christmas.

Father Murphy
US 1981 96m colour TVM
NBC/Michael Landon

A conman in the old west finds himself impersonating a priest in order to protect a band of orphans.
Carefully made opener for a series already committed; slow, but good to look at, with quiet humour. In its way a spin-off from Little House on the Prairie.

w/d/m Michael Landon
Merlin Olsen, Moses Gunn

Father of the Bride *
US 1961 34 × 25m bw
MGM (Robert Maxwell)

When the daughter of a prosperous family decides to marry, it's her father who suffers most.
Smooth comedy from Edward Streeter's book and the subsequent film.

LEON AMES, Ruth Warrick, Myrna Fahey, Burt Metcalfe

Fathers and Families (GB 1977; 6 × 50m; colour). Dinsdale Landen as a solicitor linking six plays by John Hopkins about families under strain, with the focus on the breadwinner. Produced by Mark Shivas; for BBC.   PP

Fathers by Sons: see Mothers by Daughters.

Father's Day
GB 1983 7 × 30m
C4/Picture Partnership Production (Brian Eastman)

One of two sitcoms around this time inspired by newspaper columns, in this case Hunter Davies's Punch saga of his teenage daughter, with John Alderton dressed and equipped to look like the source.

w Peter Spence, based on a moustache by Hunter Davies d Leszck Burzynski   PP

Faulk, John Henry (c 1918–   ). American commentator whose firing by CBS in the fifties, because of alleged Communist affiliations, and his subsequent lawsuit, formed a cause célèbre of the time and were recapitulated in the 1975 TV movie Fear on Trial.

Favourite Things (GB 1985; 6 × 30m colour). Roy Plomley, inventor and presenter of the radio programme that had run uninterruptedly since 1942, Desert Island Discs, devised a formula mixing bits of that entertainment with elements of television's old At Home and anyone's chat show. Beryl Reid, Phil Drabble, Antonia Fraser, Ian Botham, Les Dawson and the former Speaker of the House of Commons, Lord Tonypandy, described or demonstrated the particular pleasures of their lives – or at least all the ones suitable for revealing to a family audience.

† After Plomley's death later in the year the only edition that had been recorded for a second series was screened, with actress Judi Dench.   PP

Fawcett–Majors, Farrah (1947–) (formerly Farrah Fawcett). American pin-up actress of the seventies who became a national celebrity during the first year of *Charlie's Angels*. When she refused to sign up for a second year, she discovered her true worth. TV movies: *The Feminist and the Fuzz*, *The Great American Beauty Contest*, *The Girl Who Came Gift-Wrapped*, *Murder on Flight 502*, *Murder in Texas*, *The Red Light Sting*, THE BURNING BED. Divorce changed her name back to Farrah Fawcett.

Fawlty Towers **
GB 1975 6 × 30m colour (VTR)
GB 1979 7 × 30m colour (VTR)
BBC (John Howard Davies)
Misadventures of a manic hotel proprietor. Hilariously funny and original farce series with an inimitable if rather taxing performance from its star.

w John Cleese, Connie Booth
JOHN CLEESE, Connie Booth, Prunella Scales, ANDREW SACHS

'Low comedy with fast movement.' – John Cleese
'Outrageously funny . . . draws its humour from both the head and the bowels.' – *Sunday Telegraph*
PP: 'I think it deserves four stars.'
† BAFTA award best comedy series 1975, 1979.

Fay
US 1975 2 × 25m colour
NBC/Universal (Danny Thomas, Paul Junger Witt)
Adventures of a divorcee on the make. Sophisticated comedy series noted for the fastest cancellation in television history.

Lee Grant, Audra Lindley, Joe Silver

The FBI *
US 1965–73 208 × 50m colour
Warner/Quinn Martin
Case histories, largely fictional, and usually dividing the time available between the crooks' efforts to get away and the G-men's efforts to catch them.
Often a routine series, but the routine was tried and tested, and few people switched off.

m Bronislau Kaper
Efrem Zimbalist Jnr, Philip Abbott, William Reynolds

'Since the series artistically has been on the shoddy side, the FBI's close cooperation with the producer doesn't make the viewer think too highly of the FBI's acumen.' – Don Miller, 1965

The FBI versus Alvin Karpis, Public Enemy Number One
US 1974 100m colour TVM
Warner/Quinn Martin
J. Edgar Hoover personally joins in the case for a most wanted criminal of the thirties.
Long and flatly told crime-busting epic, one of a shortlived series of telefeatures which followed the one-hour series *The FBI* which ran nine years. See also: *Attack on Terror*.

w Calvin Clements *d* Marvin Chomsky
Robert Foxworth, Eileen Heckart, Kay Lenz, David Wayne, Harris Yulin, Gary Lockwood, Anne Francis

Fear No Evil
US 1969 98m colour TVM
Universal
A scientist dies after buying an antique mirror: a supernatural expert probes its secret.
Overlong scary suspenser which failed to start a series even after a second pilot, *Ritual of Evil*, was tried.

w Richard Alan Simmons *d* Paul Wendkos
Louis Jourdan, Bradford Dillman, Marsha Hunt, Wilfrid Hyde White, Lynda Day, Carroll O'Connor

Fear on Trial **
US 1975 100m colour TVM
Alan Landsburg (Stanley Chase)
The story of John Henry Faulk, a radio commentator who was caught up in fifties blacklisting but finally won his suit alleging wrongful dismissal.
Fascinating re-creation of recent history with a powerhouse performance from Scott as Louis Nizer.

w David Rintels *d* Lamont Johnson
GEORGE C. SCOTT, William Devane, Dorothy Tristan, William Redfield, David Susskind

Fearless Frank (GB 1978; 90m; colour). Bran-tub dip into the life and notorious loves of Frank Harris, played by Leonard Rossiter with much winking braggadocio. For anyone who had waded through the 900 pages of the memoirs he was here dictating to Susan Penhaligon as a continuity device, it seemed an arbitrary portrait, but it went on to be a stage hit in New York. Written by Andrew Davies; for BBC.   PP

Feast, Fred (1929–). Corpulent character actor, long seen as Fred Gee in *Coronation Street*.

Feather and Father
US 1976 74m colour TVM
ABC/Columbia (Larry White)

A smart lady lawyer solves cases with the help of her conman father and his underworld friends.

Dismal rehash of forties routines, a long way from Damon Runyon.

cr/w Bill Driskill d Buzz Kulik ph Gerald Perry Finnerman m George Romanis

Stefanie Powers, Harold Gould, John Forsythe, Frank Delfino, Bettye Ackerman, Jim Backus, Severn Darden

The Feather and Father Gang
US 1976 13 × 50m colour
ABC/Columbia/Larry White

An unenterprising series following from the above, with the same talents.

Feldman, Marty (1933–83). Bug-eyed British comedian who began as a writer and showed great promise, but whose talent seemed to decline in inverse ratio to his international acceptance. Various TV series include *Marty* (BAFTA award 1969) and *The Gold Diggers*.

Feldon, Barbara (1941–). American leading lady whose chief TV work was as the long-suffering female agent in *Get Smart*. TV movies include *Before and After*, *Children of Divorce*.

Feldshuh, Tovah (1953–). American leading lady who came to fame in *Holocaust*. TV movies: *The Amazing Howard Hughes*, *Terror in the Sky*, *The Triangle Factory Fire*, *Beggarman Thief*, *The Women's Room*, *Murder Ink*.

Felix the Cat. The original silent Felix cartoons by Pat Sullivan, made in the early twenties, have all been on TV, but the versions most seen were made in colour in the fifties by King Features, in semi-serialized form.

Fell, Norman (1924–). American character actor who was familiar in many films before he became a national figure in *Three's Company* and *The Ropers*. An earlier TV appearance was as part of the team in *87th Precinct*. 1982: *Teachers Only*.

Fell Tiger (GB 1985; 6 × 50m). Ace climber injured in fall tries new life running an adventure course for young executives. Predictable conflict-of-loyalties melodrama written by Christopher Green, with David Hayman, Jan Harvey, Alyson Spiro. Directed by Roger Cheveley, produced by Bob McIntosh, for BBC Scotland.   PP

The Felony Squad *
US 1966–8 73 × 25m colour
ABC/TCF (Walter Grauman)

On- and off-duty lives of three cops: old, young and medium.

Efficient cop show with strong stories and sleek production.

m Pete Rugulo

Howard Duff, Ben Alexander, Dennis Cole

Felton, Norman (1922–). Anglo-American producer of several successful Hollywood series including *The Man from UNCLE*, *Dr Kildare*, *Mr Novak*.

Female Artillery
US 1972 73m colour TVM
Universal (Winston Miller)

A western fugitive is protected from outlaws by a band of women who have been banished from a wagon train.

Failed mix of comedy and action.

w Bud Freeman d Marvin Chomsky m Frank de Vol

Ida Lupino, Dennis Weaver, Sally Ann Howes, Nina Foch, Linda Evans, Lee Harcourt Montgomery, Albert Salmi

The Female Instinct: see The Snoop Sisters

The Feminist and the Fuzz *
US 1970 74m colour TVM
Columbia

A cop and a women's-libber end up sharing an apartment.

Brisk romantic comedy with San Francisco backgrounds.

w Jim Henderson d Jerry Paris

David Hartman, Barbara Eden, Joanne Worley, Julie Newmar

Fenady, Andrew J. (1928–). American writer–producer whose series include *The Rebel*, *Branded*, *Hondo*.

The Fenn Street Gang: see Please Sir

Fennell, Albert (1920–). British independent producer, associated with *The Avengers* and *The Professionals*.

Fer de Lance *
GB theatrical title: *Death Dive*
US 1975 98m colour TVM
CBS/Leslie Stevens (Dominic Frontiere)

A submarine full of scientists is stuck on the ocean bed and terrorized by poisonous snakes.

Smooth but unlikely thriller.

w Leslie Stevens d Russ Mayberry m Dominic Frontiere

David Janssen, Hope Lange, Ivan Dixon, Jason Evers, Charles Robinson

Fernwood 2-Night *. American spoof talk show which lingered through the 1977 season after the demise of *Mary Hartman, Mary Hartman*, whose characters appeared in it. A rather uncomfortable entertainment.

Ferrer, Jose (1912–   ). Puerto Rican actor in Hollywood, in the forties a force to be reckoned with on Broadway. TV movies: *The Aquarians, Banyon, The Cable Car Murder, The Marcus Nelson Murders, The Missing Are Deadly, Medical Story, The Art of Crime, The Rhinemann Exchange, Exo-Man, The French Atlantic Affair, The Murder That Wouldn't Die, Gideon's Trumpet, The Dream Merchants, Pleasure Palace, Evita Peron, Peter and Paul, Berlin Tunnel 21, Blood Feud, Samson and Delilah, George Washington, Hitler's SS, Seduced, The Covenant*

Ferrer, Mel (1917–   ). American actor who had a fair Hollywood career and returned for occasional TV guest spots. TV movies: *Tenafly, Sharon: Portrait of a Mistress, Black Beauty, The Top of the Hill, The Memory of Eva Ryker, Fugitive Family, Falcon Crest, One Shoe Makes It Murder*

Ferrigno, Lou (1951–   ). American muscleman who found an unexpected niche in TV history as *The Incredible Hulk*. Subsequently in *Trauma Center*.

The Ferryman *** (GB 1974; 52m; colour). One of only two plays, as things turned out, to an umbrella title of *Haunted*, but a cracker. It was adapted by Julian Bond not from a ghost novel by Kingsley Amis but from a spoof radio talk the novelist gave pretending that the circumstances of his story had subsequently happened to him. With Jeremy Brett, Natasha Parry, Lesley Dunlop. Directed by John Irvin; produced by Derek Granger; for Granada. The other story came from Elizabeth Taylor, via Robin Chapman, directed by Michael Apted.   PP

Festival (GB 1963–4). Umbrella title for productions of established classics, as opposed to new TV plays, when Sydney Newman took over as BBC drama supervisor. The aim was to raid literature as well as the theatre but rushed on to the air at short notice the first season, anyway, had to fall back on the usual war-horses. An innovation was the use of location video-recording so that *Murder in the*

Cathedral and *Hamlet* could be produced in their actual locations, the latter to great effect. Produced by Peter Luke; for BBC.   PP

Fibber McGee and Molly
US 1959 26 × 25m bw
NBC

Adventures of a suburban husband who gets himself into trouble by exaggeration. Reliable sitcom based on the radio character.

Bob Sweeney, Cathy Lewis, Addison Richards, Hal Peary

Fiddick, Peter (1938–   ). British critic and commentator (*Guardian*); writer and presenter of two WTV series about TV, *The Television Programme*. With the rise of the 'art' of scheduling has also made himself a ratings-analyst for *The Listener*, etc.

Fidelio Finke, Where Are You Now? ** (GB 1973). Droll programme for BBC by and with André Previn chasing up some of the composers of yesteryear who *didn't* become immortals. The joke on funny names wore thin but samples of their owners' music were played respectfully and often gratifyingly by the LSO.
                                                            PP

Fiedler, Arthur (1894–1979). American impresario and conductor, famous on TV for his Boston Pop concerts.

Field, Sally (1946–   ). American juvenile actress of the sixties whose series include *Gidget, The Flying Nun, The Girl with Something Extra*. Won Emmy 1976 for SYBIL but by this time had become a film actress of some distinction.

Fields, Gracie (1898–1979) (Grace Stansfield). British music hall and concert singer, also film personality. Although she appeared on TV as early as 1936, most of her appearances were in her later years, when she spoke on talk shows and sang in religious programmes such as *Stars on Sunday*.

† She was the subject of two programmes in 1983–4: *Gracie*, a 'personal tribute' by Barbara Dickson (BBC Manchester); and impersonated by Polly Hemingway in a sprightly YTV special, *Pride of Our Alley*.

Fifty Fifty: see Partners in Crime

Fifty Years a Winner * (GB 1965; 50m; bw). Oddly engaging 75th birthday tribute to scientist Sir Lawrence Bragg, a Nobel prize winner before 1914 and still going strong at this time. Recorded at the Royal Institution where producer Philip Daly used a respectable version of the *This Is Your Life* format, with interviewer Barry Westwood cueing film snippets for the old boy's edification but with no studio audience. Written by Tony Jay.   PP

The Fight Against Slavery **
GB 1974 6 × 50m colour (16mm)
BBC/Time–Life (Christopher Ralling)

A dramatized history of the freeing of black slaves within the British Empire.

A first-class BBC job which puts *Roots* several degrees in the shade.

John Castle, Dinsdale Landen, Terence Scully, David Collings, Ronald Pickup, Willie Jonah

'Something like a masterpiece.' – *Sunday Telegraph*

Fight Night. Uncompromising title for fortnightly professional boxing relays from provincial halls for provincial audiences. Produced by Gary Newbon for, and with, Granada/Central/YTV.   PP

The Fighter
US 1983 96m colour TVM
CBS/Catalina/Martin Manulis (Ellen Levine)

An amateur boxer turns professional in order to care for his family.

Adequately made but rather uninteresting ringside drama with long domestic asides.

w Jerome Kass *d* David Lowell Rich *ph* Charles F. Wheeler *m* Patrick Williams

Gregory Harrison, Glynnis O'Connor, Pat Hingle, Steve Inwood, Susan Kellerman

Fighter Pilot
GB 1983 8 × 30m
BBC (Colin Strong)

The selection and training of RAF jet fighter pilots, at a cost now of more than two million pounds per head. From the group followed through the process, only one finally made it, though one or two more qualified to fly other types of aircraft. Others were dropped altogether along the way, setting a fashion for documentary series with a high failure quotient, e.g. *Behind the Lines* and *Queens': a Cambridge College* (both 1985).   PP

Fighting Back
US 1980 96m colour TVM
ABC/MTM (Jerry McNeely)

A Pittsburgh footballer gets back to the game after being wounded in Vietnam.

Smartly made telepic without a spark of originality. Of absorbing interest to Pittsburgh football fans.

w Jerry McNeely *d* Robert Lieberman *ph* Stevan Larner *m* Fred Karlin

Robert Urich, Bonnie Bedelia, Richard Herd, Howard Cosell, Art Carney

'Rocky Bleier as a dramatic figure never moves forward, let alone makes a touchdown.' – *Daily Variety*

The File on Jill Hatch
GB/US 1983 2 × 55m, 1 × 60m
BBC/NET (Alan Shallcross)

Repercussions 40 years on of a wartime marriage between black GI and white English girl. A worthy but strained attempt by the BBC and New York's public service station to make sense of the Brixton race riots of 1981.

w Kenneth Cavander *d* Alastair Reid

Tim Woodward, Penny Johnson, Frances Tomelty, Joe Morton

'The production has a raw power that is almost unfailingly gripping.' – *New York Times*   PP

Film '86, etc. Britain's most durable movie-review programme, updating its title every year to show how up-to-the-minute it is. What is supposed to be happening in the cinema in the long stretches when the show is not on the air has never been explained, but Barry Norman's cordial, choosy presentation of the clips – plus occasional interviews or location visits – maintains a high standard of mid-brow discernment.

When Norman vacated the seat in 1982 to present *Omnibus*, the programme's producer Ian Johnstone organized a macabre public audition during which three aspirants were tried out: Tina Brown, Miles Kington and Germaine Greer. Kington withdrew and in the end Johnstone took over himself for a couple of seasons, until Barry Norman and the arts in general decided they were not for each other and Barry resumed his seat at the pictures. Whereupon Johnstone went off to be film critic of the *Sunday Times*. Of such is the Kingdom of Heaven. Produced latterly by Jane Lush, for BBC.   PP

LH: 'The programme has given excellent service since the early seventies, but my grouch is that, owing to the shortage of interesting new films, too much time is given to Top Tens (including videos) and to clips of admittedly rubbishy films. Even the interviews and location reports usually turn out to concern films with no future. The time might more usefully be spent on backward looks to show how trends have developed.'

Film on Four. Channel 4's regular seasons of fiction films financed at least in part by C4 and all aiming at theatrical release as well as a television screening. The pet project of C4's senior commissioning editor David Rose, it has been hailed as a benison for British films by film enthusiasts and increasingly condemned by true television lovers as a senseless diversion of funds from television drama into a moribund film industry. The more successful productions have not been allowed on to the air until cinema takings have been mopped up, sometimes two years later. Mostly only those that have little hope of commercial success are dumped on TV first. First Love, a sub-division of Film on Four, is dealt with separately. PP

LH: 'I would take a somewhat more approving view, though I haven't personally liked many of the films (not enough cinematic pace) and the ones released to cinemas, even the successful ones, have had the unfortunate effect of robbing cinema of its old stature and reducing it to the more quiet and intimate level of television, which in the long run is not what people will pay money to see.'

Filthy Rich
US 1982   × 25m colour
NBC/Columbia/Larry White/Linda
  Bloodworth
A Tennessee land baron's will decrees that his heirs must live together harmoniously.
Noisy, frantic fun and games filled with dislikeable characters.

cr Linda Bloodworth

Delta Burke, Dixie Carter, Charles Frank, Jerry Hardin, Michael Lombard, Slim Pickens

Final Eye
US 1977 96m colour TVM
Paramount
A case for a private eye in the year 2001.
Lamebrained pilot for a series about the world's last practising private detective. A long way after Sherlock Holmes.
Susan George, Donald Pleasence, David Huddleston, Liam Sullivan

The Final Solution (GB/Thames 1975; 180m; bw). See: Auschwitz

The Final Test (GB 1951; 90m; bw live play). Veteran professional cricketer from the days when they were classed as 'players' as opposed to 'gentlemen' goes in to bat in his last Test Match. Terence Rattigan's play-for-TV gave the BBC a dash of prestige in Festival of Britain Year and Rattigan a second dividend from selling the screenplay to the movies, when Jack Warner played the hero. PP

Finch, John (19 –). British writer of prodigious stamina, originator and chief writer of A FAMILY AT WAR (1970–71), followed by lengthy sagas of northern life for which he has furnished every word: *Sam* (1973–5); *This Year, Next Year* (1977); *Flesh and Blood* (1980); *Spoils of War* (1981). PP

Finch, Jon (1942–). British general purpose actor whose movie stardom proved shortlived. TV: *Ben Hall, The Martian Chronicles, Peter and Paul.*

'You've lost someone you can't live without. And these two people could be your only hope!'
Finder of Lost Loves
US 1984   × 50m colour
ABC/Warner/Aaron Spelling
A rich widower devotes his life to finding other people's lost loves.
An emetic concept given appropriate treatment and comic-balloon dialogue. A supposed replacement for *Fantasy Island*, it died after one season.

cr Jill Baer, Christopher Vane, Bill and Jo LaMond

Anthony Franciosa, Deborah Adair, Richard Kantor, Anne Jeffreys
'They better stock up on the violin strings at Aaron Spelling Productions.' – *Daily Variety*
'There is so much love in this series, you almost wish for some violence.' – *TV Guide*
'A sort of *Love Boat* without the boat.' – *TV Guide*

Fine, Mort: see Friedkin, David

A Fine Romance * (GB 1981). Half-hour comedy series for LWT, a popular hit about the pursuit of a middle-aged single lady by a middle-aged available man, both a bit gauche about the business of romance. With JUDI DENCH and MICHAEL WILLIAMS (who are married to each other off the set). Written by Bob Larbey; produced and directed by James Cellan Jones.

Finland has had television since 1955, two channels since 1964. Domestic production fills 60 per cent of transmission hours.

Finlay, Frank (1926–). British general purpose actor who has been very well exposed on TV, in single plays such as *The Last Days of Hitler* and *Count Dracula* and in serials such as *Casanova* and BOUQUET OF BARBED WIRE. BAFTA award 1973 for *Don Quixote* (as Sancho Panza), *The Death of Adolf Hitler*, and *Candide*.

Finnegan, Begin Again
GB/US 1984 90m TVM
Consolidated/Jennie & Co./Zenith (Gower Frost)

Ageing journalist on the skids meets companionable widow, and love eventually triumphs again.

Despite its British involvement, with Central's film subsidiary Zenith putting up a major part of the budget, this benign yawnie was written and shot wholly in America.

w Walter Lockwood d Joan Micklin Silver

Robert Preston, Mary Tyler Moore, Sam Waterston, Sylvia Sidney, David Huddlestone   PP

Finnerman, Gerald Perry (1931–). American cinematographer who has done much television work.

Fire
US 1977 96m colour TVM
Warner/Irwin Allen/NBC

A forest fire threatens a mountain community. Cheapjack semi-spectacular.

w Norman Katkov, Arthur Weiss d Earl Bellamy m Richard La Salle

Ernest Borgnine, Vera Miles, Patty Duke Astin, Alex Cord, Donna Mills, Lloyd Nolan, Neville Brand, Ty Hardin

The Fire at Magilligan * (GB 1984; 50m). Respectable Ulster matron and prison visitor gives lift to hitchhiker who turns out to be an IRA youngster she had met when he was in Magilligan jail and she was on a disciplinary board. Harry Barton's was among the better plays to come out of a province where TV fiction has often afforded more insights than TV fact. With Dilys Hamlett. Directed by Jan Sargent, for BBC Northern Ireland. PP

A Fire in the Sky
US 1978 140m colour TVM
NBC/Columbia/Bill Driskill

A comet seems likely to devastate Phoenix, but nobody will listen to the astronomer's warning. Predictable disaster movie with far too much talk in the first hours, prefacing special effects which are only adequate.

w Dennis Nemec, Michael Blankfort, *story* Paul Gallico d Jerry Jameson ph Matthew F. Leonetti m Paul Chihara

Richard Crenna, Elizabeth Ashley, David Dukes, Joanna Miles, Lloyd Bochner, Andrew Duggan, Nicholas Coster

'If many of the characters are basically disagreeable, their destinies still bear watching.' – *Daily Variety*

Fire on the Mountain
US 1981 96m colour TVM
NBC/Bonnard (Robert Lovenheim)

A rancher doggedly resists the government takeover of his land.

Sluggish, padded, earnest treatment of a familiar theme.

w John Sacret Young, *book* by Edward Abbey d Donald Wrye

Ron Howard, Buddy Ebsen, Julie Carmen, Rossie Harris, Michael Conrad

The Fire Unleashed (US 1985). Three-hour news report on the future of nuclear power. Inevitably a downer but with much fascinating footage. Produced by Pamela Still and Richard Richter, for ABC. 'Should unnerve just about anybody. Don't sit too near the TV set.' – *Daily Variety*

Fireball Forward
US 1972 98m colour TVM
TCF

In World War II France, a general finds a spy in his division.

Adequate actioner with spy trimmings.

w Edmund North d Marvin Chomsky m Lionel Newman

Ben Gazzara, Eddie Albert, Ricardo Montalban, Dana Elcar, Anne Francis, Morgan Paull, L. Q. Jones

Fireball XL5
GB 1962 26 × 25m bw
ATV (Gerry Anderson)

Intergalactic adventures of Steve Zodiac and his crew.

Adequate puppet fantasies.

The Firechasers *
GB 1970 74m or 101m colour TVM
ITC (Julian Wintle)

An insurance investigator chases an arsonist. Lumpy, disjointed, watchable adventures.

w Philip Leven d Sidney Hayers m Laurie Johnson

Chad Everett, Keith Barron, Anjanette Comer, Joanne Dainton, Rupert Davies, Robert Flemyng, Roy Kinnear, John Loder, James Hayter

Firehouse
US 1973 74m colour TVM
ABC/Metromedia (Dick Berg)
Racist conflicts erupt in a city fire department
during an arson outbreak.
Totally unsurprising action yarn which
generated a shortlived series.

w Frank Cucci d Alex March

Richard Roundtree, Vince Edwards, Andrew
Duggan, Richard Jaeckel

Firehouse
US 1974 13 × 25m colour (16mm)
ABC/Metromedia/Stonehenge (Dick Berg,
  John Ireland, Richard Collins)
The shortlived series which spun off from the
TV movie had at least two adventures per
half-hour and a somewhat changed cast.
James Drury, Richard Jaeckel, Michael
Delano, Brad Davis, Bill Overton

First Affair
US 1983 96m colour TVM
CBS (Judith Parker, Andrew Gottlieb)
A lady professor finds that her student
babysitter is making a try for her husband.
Soupy, soapy romantic drama about kids
who should be getting on with their
homework.

w Judith Parker d Gus Trikonis ph Arthur
Ornitz m Lee Holdridge

Loretta Swit, Melissa Sue Anderson, Joel
Higgins, Kim Delaney

The First Churchills *
GB 1969 13 × 45m bw (VTR)
BBC (Donald Wilson)
A saga of the family of the Duke of
Marlborough.
Excellent high-style period soap-opera.

w/d Donald Wilson

John Neville, Susan Hampshire, James Villiers

First Lady (GB 1968–9). Thora Hird as a
crusading woman councillor in a
north-country series whose writers included
Alan Plater. Two series were made by the
BBC. 'Good bread and butter television
drama,' said *Television Today*.   PP

First Love. A warm corner of C4's Film on
Four institution during its first season,
sub-contracted to producer David Puttnam
and the Goldcrest film and TV independent.
Beginning with Jack Rosenthal's *P'Tang
Yang Kipperbang* on opening night, First
Loves were tailored to television's needs
rather than the cinema's, and mostly

appeared first on TV. 'Other noteworthy
titles included June Roberts' *Experience
Preferred but Not Essential* (d Peter Duffell),
Secrets, *Those Glory Glory Days*, and
Sharma and Beyond.
Oddly enough, Turgenev's *First Love* was
not a First Love: transposed from Russia to
Co. Wicklow in the 1840s as *Summer
Lightning* (an RTE production with Paul
Scofield, Tom Bell, Maureen Toal, David
Warner) it ran merely as a Film on Four.

The First Olympics
US 1984 1 × 96m, 1 × 142m colour
NBC/Columbia/Larry White–Gary Allison
  (William Hill)
An account of the Athens Games of 1896,
with special emphasis on the American team
which nearly didn't get there.
Heavy-going sporting history with rather too
much sport and insufficient leavening of
humour and insight.

w Gary Allison, William Bast d Alvin
Rakoff ph Paul Beeson m Bruce
Broughton pd Michael Stringer

David Ogden Stiers, Angela Lansbury,
Louis Jourdan, Gayle Hunnicutt, Honor
Blackman, Bill Travers, Virginia McKenna,
Alex Hyde White, Jason Connery, Hunt
Block, David Caruso

First Person Singular *
US 1953 ? × 25m bw
NBC
An anthology of stories using the subjective
camera technique in which the camera
becomes the eye of the protagonist. Developed
by Fred Coe; results interesting but not very
popular. See: subjective camera.

'Her courage and his determination
  turned a tragedy into a triumph!'
First Steps
US 1984 96m colour TVM
CBS (Ellis A. Cohen)
A girl high-school student is paralysed in a
car accident. An Ohio physiologist uses
computer electrodes to stimulate her wasted
muscles.
Grossly extended fictionalization of a real
case.

w Rod Browing d Sheldon Larry

Judd Hirsch, Amy Steel, Kim Darby,
Frances Lee McCain, James B. Sikking

The First 36 Hours of Dr Durant
US 1975 74m colour TVM
ABC/Columbia (James H. Brown)

A young surgeon reports to a city hospital and learns the realities of his career.
Dr Kildare rides again. Adequate for insomniacs who don't mind watching operations.

w Sterling Silliphant *d* Alexander Singer

Scott Hylands, Lawrence Pressman, Katherine Helmond, Karen Carlson

'The story of a young girl's sexual awakening!'
The First Time
US 1983 96m colour TVM
ABC/Orion (Frank Von Zerneck, Robert Greenwald)

An emotionally aware teenager follows her boyfriend when he goes to work on his father's fishing boat.
Reasonably intense family drama for those who like this sort of thing.

w Robie Robinson *d* Noel Nosseck *ph* Charles Correll *m* Fred Karlin

Susan Anspach, Jennifer Jason Keigh, Peter Barton, Harriet Nelson, Alex Rocco, Edward Winter

First Tuesday (GB since 1983). Monthly documentary outlet bagged on the ITV channel by Yorkshire (John Willis). Usually two items, which may be agitational, historical, sociological, agitational-historical, historical-sociological, etc. Introduced initially by Jonathan Dimbleby and Jane Walmsley, subsequently by Dimbleby only.
PP

'Talented, successful, glamorous. Then the tragedy every woman fears threatened to tear her world apart!'
**First You Cry ** **
US 1979 96m colour TVM
CBS/MTM (Philip Barry)

A TV journalist finds she has breast cancer.
If TV must make disease-of-the-week pictures, then this is the way to do them; but with no scourge left undocumented, enough is surely enough.

w Carmen Culver, *book* Betty Rollin *d* George Schaefer *ph* Edward R. Brown *m* Peter Matz
MARY TYLER MOORE, Anthony Perkins, Richard Crenna, Jennifer Warren, Richard Dysart, Florence Eldridge, Patricia Barry, Don Johnson

Fish
US 1977   × 25m colour (VTR)
ABC/Columbia/Mimus (Danny Arnold)

A spin-off from *Barney Miller*; Fish retires from the police to look after underprivileged children.
Not too successful.

Abe Vigoda, Florence Stanley, Barry Gordon

The Fishing Party * (GB 1972; 75m; colour).
Three Derbyshire miners escape from work and wives on a weekend's fishing; amiable comedy by Peter Terson, first of a trio of adventures featuring the same small gang, led by Brian Glover: *Shakespeare or Bust* and *Three for the Fancy* were the others. Directed by Michael Simpson; produced by David Rose; for BBC.
PP

The Fishing Race *** (GB 1976; 6 × 30m).
Delightfully   subversive   sporting   serial attacking the whole shaky ethos of angling as a contest of human versus fishy cunning, etc. The object was to land the maximum number of species in a set time, and garden ponds were raided for goldfish as ruthlessly as the nearest trout stream for trout. The funny commentator was Ian Wooldridge. Produced by Michael Begg; for BBC. A sequel the following year transferred the action to Scandinavia.
PP

The Fitzpatricks
US 1977 13 × 50m colour
CBS/Warner/Philip Mandelker (John Cutts)
Stories of a blue-collar family in Michigan.
Sentimental family series which proved a shade too icky to survive.

cr John Sacret Young

Bert Cramer, Mariclare Costello

Five Desperate Women
US 1971 73m colour TVM
ABC/Aaron Spelling
Five women on holiday find that one of two men on an island with them is a murderer.
Fair goosepimpler.

w Marc Norman, Walter Black *d* Ted Post *m* Paul Glass

Anjanette Comer, Joan Hackett, Denise Nichols, Stefanie Powers, Bradford Dillman, Robert Conrad, Julie Sommars

Five Fingers
US 1959 16 × 50m bw
NBC/TCF

Adventures of a US intelligence agent.
Strained unpersuasive stories which had nothing to do with the film nor, as alleged, with the book *Operation Cicero* by L. C. Moyzich.
David Hedison, Luciana Paluzzi

The 500 Pound Jerk
GB title: *The Strong Man*
US 1972 73m colour TVM
David Wolper (Stan Margulies)

A hillbilly giant is groomed as an Olympic weightlifter.
Mild satirical comedy.

w James B. Henderson *d* William Cronick

James Franciscus, Alex Karras, Hope Lange, Howard Cosell, Victor Spinetti

'Ann is married to five men. Her husband and his four hidden personalities!'

The Five of Me
US 1981 96m colour TVM
CBS/Jack Farren/Factor–Newland

A boy once threatened by his father grows up with five separate personalities, one of them psychotic.
Based allegedly on a genuine case, this comes over unpersuasively as a male version of *The Three Faces of Eve*. Dramatically it's rather boring.

w Lawrence B. Marcus, *book* Henry Hawksworth *d* Paul Wendkos *ph* Jack Woolf *m* Fred Karlin

David Birney, Mitchell Ryan, Dee Wallace, John McLiam, Ben Piazza

Flack, Roberta (1939–   ). American rock singer, at her peak in the early seventies.

The Flagstones: see The Flintstones

The Flame Is Love
US 1979 96m colour TVM
NBC/Friendly–O'Herlihy (Ed Friendly)

An innocent New York girl of 1890 goes to Europe to get married, and has alarming romantic experiences.
Ill-fated attempt to put high-flown romantic tushery on the screen. The production is hilariously undernourished to the point of showing TV aerials and yellow street lines; writing and acting are utterly dismaying.

w Hindy Brooks, *novel* Barbara Cartland *d* Michael O'Herlihy *ph* John C. Flinn III *m* Morton Stevens

Linda Purl, Timothy Dalton, Shane Briant, Joan Greenwood, Helena Carroll, Kathleen Barrington

'All the substance of a jelly bean.' – *Daily Variety*

A Flame to the Phoenix (GB 1983; 90m). Murray Smith, useful author of *Bulman* and other series, came a purler with this nonsensical melodrama set in Poland on the eve of the German invasion of 1939. On the way to its historically poignant conclusion, one of the Polish cavalry's forlorn charges against the Panzers, it embraced such barmy plottings as Gestapo men posing as hikers, a German spy plane piloted by a wizard RAF type and a pretty daughter of the household whose wont was to ride her horse naked through the woods by night. 'Tat-for-tit,' I noted glumly at the time, 'young officers stripped to the waist to practise their fencing with unbuttoned blades.' With Frederick Treves, David Haig. Directed by William Brayne, produced by Granada (Richard Everitt) for C4's *Film on Four* – where else?
PP

The Flame Trees of Thika
GB 1981 7 × 50m colour
Thames/Euston (Verity Lambert)

The life of an English family in Kenya in 1914.
Tolerable 'family' serial without much excitement between the shots of wild life.

w John Hawkesworth, *novel* Elspeth Huxley *d* Roy Ward Baker

Hayley Mills, David Robb, Nicholas Jones, Sharon Maughan, Ben Cross, Holly Aird

Flamingo Road
US 1980 96m colour TVM
NBC/Lorimar (Rita Lakin, Ed Feldman)

A lady drifter causes havoc when she settles in a small southern town which is simply seething with plots.
Shoddy redraft of the old Joan Crawford movie as the opener of a new series in the steps of *Dallas*. Characters and situations are simply not very interesting, the atmosphere is insufficiently steamy, and Howard Duff is no Sydney Greenstreet.

w Howard Lakin, *book* Robert Wilder *d* Edward H. Feldman *m* Gerald Fried

Cristina Raines, Howard Duff, Kevin McCarthy, John Beck, Peter Donat, Morgan Fairchild, Mark Harmon, Barbara Rush, Stella Stevens, Alejandro Rey

'All 99 and 44/100 pure soap, it should work up a nice lather.' – *Daily Variety*

† The series of one hours did moderately well in the 1980 season and was renewed.

Flanagan, Fionnula (1941–   ). Irish–American character actress. Series: *How the West Was Won*. TV movies: *The Godchild*, *The Legend of Lizzie Borden*, RICH MAN, POOR MAN (Emmy 1976), *Nightmare in Badham County*, *Mary White*, *Young Love First Love*.

Through Naked Eyes, Scorned and Swindled, The Ewok Adventure

Flanders, Ed (19 –). American character actor who won an Emmy in 1975 for A MOON FOR THE MISBEGOTTEN, and in 1976 for impersonating Harry S. Truman. Emmy 1983: outstanding lead actor (*St Elsewhere*).

Flatbed Annie and Sweetie Pie, Lady Truckers
US 1979 96m colour TVM
CBS/Filmways/Moonlight (Frank Von Zerneck)

Two lady truckdrivers try to escape a hijacker. The title says it all, except that the thing is one long chase. It has its funny moments but an hour would have been more than enough.

w Robie Robinson d Robert Greenwald ph William Jurgensen m Don Peak

Annie Potts, Kim Darby, Harry Dean Stanton, Arthur Godfrey, Fred Willard, Billy Carter

'Charm can only get you so far, and is no substitute for story.' – *Daily Variety*

Flemying, Gordon (19 –). Veteran British drama director originally with Granada (*The Younger Generation, Red Letter Day*, etc.). Recent credits: *The Wedding, Burgess, Philby and Maclean, One Summer*.

Flesh and Blood *
US 1980 2 × 93m colour TVM
CBS/Paramount/Gerald W. Abrams (Herbert Hirschman)

A tough young prizefighter is frustrated by his inability to cut the silver cord.
Slickly made, downbeat melodrama climaxing with what may be American television's first scene of incest. Impressive but not memorable.

w Eric Bercovici, *novel* Pete Hamill d Jud Taylor

Tom Berenger, SUZANNE PLESHETTE, John Cassavetes, Mitchell Ryan

'As compelling as it is disagreeable.' – *Daily Variety*

Flesh and Blood (GB 1980). Confusingly on the air in Britain at the same time as the above. A dynastic saga for the BBC by John Finch with Bill Fraser and Thora Hird. Well enough done but even its most loyal admirers would have been hard put to detect any significant differences from dozens of previous serials and series, and before them plays and films and novels, about self-made north country magnates with over-educated sons, ambitious daughters-in-law and trouble up at mill, or in this case up at cement works.   PP

Fletcher, Cyril (1913–). British comedian once known for his Odd Odes and odder voices; more recently a mainstay of the BBC consumer programme *That's Life*.

Flickers (GB 1981). A six-hour drama serial from ATV about the tribulations of a group of travelling film showmen at the turn of the century. No attitude is ever established, and the result is more off-putting than compelling. With Bob Hoskins, Frances de la Tour. Written by Roy Clarke; directed by Cyril Coke; produced by Joan Brown.

Flight *
US 1958 39 × 25m bw
NBC/McCadden

Stories of aviation from Kitty Hawk to Cape Canaveral.
Early docu-drama series, quite effectively presented.

Flight from Utopia * (GB 1984; 6 × 30m). Valuable architectural series partly facing up to the dreadful damage done by architects who imagined they were God, or at least engineers of society. Written and presented by Patrick Nuttgens, for BBC North.

Flight into Danger **
Canada 1956 50m bw
CBC (Stanley Newman)

An air disaster is narrowly averted when the entire crew goes down with food poisoning.
A key play in the history of television and of aviation movies. (It was filmed as *Zero Hour*, refilmed for TV as *Terror in the Sky*, and forms the inspiration for all the *Airport* movies as well as *Airplane*.) In TV it was one of the first dramatic entertainments to prove that what's on at home can keep the cinemas empty.

w ARTHUR HAILEY

Alex Webster, Cec Linder, James Doohan

Flight 90: Disaster on the Potomac
US 1984 96m colour TVM
NBC/Sheldon Pinchuk/Finnegan Associates (Bill and Pat Finnegan)

A docu-drama in the style of *The Bridge of San Luis Rey*, examining how passengers came to be on the ill-fated plane which crashed on take-off during a 1982 Washington blizzard.

w John McGreevey d Robert Lewis ph Fred Koenekamp m Gil Melle

Jeanetta Arnette, Barry Cobin, Stephen Macht, Dinah Manoff, Richard Masur, Donnelly Rhodes, K. Callan

'A vest-pocket *Airport* without the celebs.' – *Daily Variety*

The Flight of the Condor * (GB 1984; 3 × 55m). Much-praised wildlife survey of the Andes and the source of the Amazon, with no nature jockeys intervening. Written and produced by Michael Andrews, for BBC Bristol. PP

The Flight of the Dragons
US/Japan 1983 96m colour TVM
Telepictures/Rankin–Bass

A rather slackly developed cartoon feature set in 'the time between the waning Age of Magic and the dawning Age of Science': a quest for the Red Crown of Ommadon. Tolkien enthusiasts will not be impressed.

Flight to Holocaust
US 1977 96m colour TVM
A. C. Lyles/First Artists/NBC

Professional troubleshooters are called to the 20th floor of a skyscraper, into which a plane has crashed.
Modest action pilot with fairly good stunt effects.

w Robert Heverly *d* Bernie Kowalski *m* Paul Williams

Patrick Wayne, Christopher Mitchum, Desi Arnaz Jnr, Fawne Harriman, Sid Caesar, Paul Williams, Lloyd Nolan, Rory Calhoun, Greg Morris

The Flintstones **
Working title: *The Flagstones*
US 1960–5 166 × 25m colour
NBC/Hanna–Barbera

In the Stone Age, ebullient Fred Flintstone gets himself and his neighbour Barney Rubble into frequent bouts of trouble.
Amusing cartoon series for all ages, the Stone Age gimmick fitting in well with what sound like old Burns and Allen scripts, lightly worked over. Semi-animation was of a higher standard than we have seen since, and there always seemed to be something inventive going on. Emulating Lucy, the Flintstones had a baby during the series, and became a national institution; but later spin-offs such as *Pebbles and Bam Bam* (animated, 1971) were less successful. The 'live' characters also appeared in many specials and ice shows.

The Flip Wilson Show. A series of American one-hour specials which ran from 1970 to 1974 and won an Emmy in 1970.

Flipper *
US 1964–6 88 × 25m colour
NBC/MGM/Ivan Tors

In a Florida marine preserve, a boy makes friends with a dolphin.

Good looking animal series: the plots may have been strained but Flipper was always a delight.
Brian Kelly, Luke Halpin

The Flipside of Dominick Hide ** (GB 1980; 75m; colour). Witty, tongue-in-cheek science fiction by Jeremy Paul and Alan Gibson (who also directed) for BBC about a time-traveller from the future sniffing out his own genealogy, with a neat, sweet twist in the ending. With Peter Firth, Caroline Langrishe. Produced by Chris Cherry. PP
Sequel, *Another Flip for Dominic*, 1982

Flo (US 1980). Half-hour tape comedy series by Jim Mulligan/Warner for CBS, in which one of the denizens of *Alice* becomes the owner of a run-down bar in a small Texas town. Very raucous and wholly American; with Polly Holliday.

Flood
US 1976 96m colour TVM
NBC/Warner/Irwin Allen

A dam is breached and a small town is threatened.
Cut-rate spectacular in line with this producer's other TV efforts.

w Don Ingalls *d* Earl Bellamy *ph* Lamar Boren *m* Richard La Salle

Robert Culp, Martin Milner, Carol Lynley, Barbara Hershey, Richard Basehart, Teresa Wright, Cameron Mitchell, Roddy McDowall

'Before she was a legend, she was a woman!'
Florence Nightingale
US 1985 138m colour TVM
NBC/Columbia/Cypress Point (Tony Richmond)

The life of the 19th-century pioneer nurse who became famous in the Crimea.
Over-reverent, stilted but good-looking biopic which never really sparks into life.

w Ivan Moffat, Rose Leiman Goldenberg *d* Daryl Duke *ph* Jack Hildyard *m* Stanley Myers

Jaclyn Smith, Timothy Dalton, Jeremy Brett, Claire Bloom, Ann Thornton, Julian Fellows, Stephen Chase, Brian Cox, Timothy West

'It strains mightily to be dignified, refined and sobering: it turns out to be silly.' – *Daily Variety*

Florey, Robert (1900–79). French–American director who after a variable movie career turned to TV work and was a familiar name on the credits of *Four Star Playhouse*, *Wagon Train* and *Twilight Zone*.

The Flowering of Britain * (GB 1980; 50m; colour). How the wild flowers of Britain arrived and thrived and in some places still do: a fascinating dissertation for BBC by botanist Richard Mabey with no attempt to be emphatic in odd instances when he couldn't be sure, thus conveying total mastery of his subject.   PP

Fly Away Home
US 1981 96m colour TVM
CBS/Warner/An Lac (Sterling Silliphant)
The lives of several disparate groups of people are affected by their association with the war in Vietnam.
Curious portmanteau intended as the opener for a limited series. It wasn't given the chance.
w Sterling Silliphant   d Paul Krasny   m Lee Holdridge

Bruce Boxleitner, Tiana Alexandra, Michael Beck, Randy Brooks, Brian Dennehy, Olivia Cole
'Overladen scenes whose dialogue crashes of its own weight when it should sting.' – Daily Variety

Flying Boats ** (GB 1980; 3 × 30m). Spiffing archive compilation for BBC about the stately aircraft which plied pre-war Empire air routes, their World War II activities and final obsolescence.   PP

The Flying Doctor
Australia 1959 39 × 25m bw
Crawford
Cases of a doctor serving remote bush areas. Routine adventures, simply told.
Richard Denning, Peter Madden, Jill Adams, Alan White

Flying High
US 1978 96m colour TVM
CBS/Mark Carliner
Three girls from different backgrounds become airline stewardesses. ·
Pitifully thin time-passer which scored high enough ratings to warrant a series the following season.
w Marty Cohan, Dawn Aldredge   d Peter Hunt   ph William J. Jurgensen   m David Shire
Kathryn Witt, Pat Klous, Connie Sellecca, Howard Platt, Jim Hutton
'No sex, no action, no conflict, no problems, no interest. It makes Charlie's Angels look like Shakespeare by comparison.' – Daily Variety
'The hour is an adventure, or maybe it's a comedy. Apparently the producers weren't sure, either. They installed a laugh track, but just a teeny one. It titters along in a muffled

way, as though they have a studio audience in a gunnysack.' – Robert MacKenzie, TV Guide

Flying into the Wind: see Birth of a Nation

The Flying Nun
US 1967–9 82 × 25m colour
ABC/Columbia/Harry Ackerman (Jon Epstein, William Sackheim)
A novice nun discovers that she can fly.
How this very small and silly idea was stretched out to 82 episodes is a mystery, but it was, and people watched it.
cr Harry Ackerman, Max Wylie,   book The Fifteenth Pelican by Tere Ross
Sally Field, Alejandro Rey, Marge Redmond, Madeleine Sherwood
'Last year they took the wild route because ABC surveys indicated that's what the kids like. What the computers or somebody else forgot was that they would lose most of the other viewers. Those surveys, laid end to end, don't really mean a lot, but they do keep a lot of people off the unemployment rolls.' – Dave Kaufman, 1970

The Flying Tigers (US 1951). Shortlived half-hour action series about Pacific flyers in World War II. With Eric Fleming, Luis Van Rooten.

Flynn, Errol (1909–59). Tasmanian leading man who electrified Hollywood in the thirties. In the mid-fifties he lent his rather dissipated presence to a half-hour TV anthology called The Errol Flynn Theatre.

Foch, Nina (1924–   ). American general-purpose actress now making occasional forays into TV. Ebony Ivory and Jade, Shadow Chasers.

Foley Square *
US 1986   × 25m colour
CBS (Diane English)
A slice of life in the DA's office.
Hill Street Blues-style comedy with a few dramatic moments thrown in.
cr Diane English
Margaret Colin, Hector Elizondo, Michael Lembeck, Sanford Jensen, Cathy S. Silver, Richard C. Sarafian

The Folklore of Christendom * (GB 1965; 2 × 60m; bw). Extraordinary inventory of Christian teachings over the ages concerning the nature of Heaven and Hell, including specific dimensions, location and amount of remission to be earned in latter case by invoking the name of God. To astonish believers and non-believers alike. Produced by Hugh Burnett; for BBC.   PP

Follow the Sun
US 1961 30 × 50m bw
ABC/TCF
Three freelance writers have fun in Honolulu. Passable lightweight series of its time.

Barry Coe, Brett Halsey, Gary Lockwood, Gigi Perreau

Fonda, Henry (1905–82). American leading actor, a star in Hollywood for 40 years. Always busy, he also found time for TV series: *The Deputy*, *The Smith Family*. TV movies: *Stranger on the Run*, *The Red Pony*, *The Alpha Caper*, *Captains and the Kings*, *Home to Stay*, *Roots: the Next Generations*, *Summer Solstice*.

Fontaine, Frank (1920–). American zany comedian who became a minor star on Jackie Gleason's show from 1962.

Fontanne, Lynn (1887–1983). Distinguished Anglo-American stage actress who in 1964 won an Emmy for *The Magnificent Yankee*.

Fonteyn, Margot (1919–) (Margaret Hookham). British prima ballerina who made several TV appearances and in 1980 narrated the BBC's ambitious documentary series *The Magic of Dance*.

Food and Drink (GB since 1983). Seasonal series on just those things, unconvincingly introduced at first by the emaciated Henry Kelly, more appropriately by the better-nourished Chris Kelly. Produced latterly by Peter Bazalgette, for BBC.   PP

footprint: the geographic area within which a satellite transmission can be received.

Footsteps
US 1972 74m colour TVM
Metromedia (Dick Berg)
A tough coach is hired to whip a small college football team into shape.
Minor sporting drama.

w Alvin Sargent, Robert E. Thompson, *novel* Hamilton Maule *d* Paul Wendkos
Richard Crenna, Joanna Pettet, Forrest Tucker, Clu Gulager, Mary Murphy

For Heaven's Sake
US 1979 74m colour TVM
ABC/Blinn–Thorpe

An elderly angel helps improve the fortunes of a baseball team.
Similar to the failed *Heaven Help Us*, an attempt to turn sentimental other-worldly comedy into a series. It failed.

w William Blinn *d* Jerry Thorpe *ph* Chuck Arnold *m* John Rubinstein
Ray Bolger, Kent McCord, Joanna Pettet, Kenneth Mars

For King and Country
GB 1963 4 × 90m bw
Granada (Gerald Savory)
Characteristic Granada idea to exhume four World War I stage plays, all rather dreadful, and give them absolutely straightforward production. A glimpse of period drama in the version that was acceptable at the time, be it truth, half-truth or whopping lie.   PP

For Love and Honor
US 1983 96m colour TVM
NBC/MGM–UA/David Gerber (James H. Brown)
Life with the 88th Airborne Division of the American army.
Semi-soap set among the paratroopers: as a series (one-hour episodes followed), it failed to sell itself on either side of the Atlantic.

cr Leon Tokatyan and Diana Bell Tokatyan *d* Gary Nelson *ph* Gayne Rescher *m* Ian Freebairn-Smith
Cliff Potts, Yaphet Kotto, Shelley Smith, Rachel Ticotin, Amy Steel, Gary Grubbs

For Love or Money
US 1984 96m colour TVM
CBS/Robert Papazian/Henerson–Hirsch (Robert A. Papazian)
A lady researcher falls for a gambler.
Very slight romantic comedy with acres of time to fill and no way of filling it.

w James Henerson *d* Terry Hughes *ph* Harry J. May *m* Billy Goldenberg
Suzanne Pleshette, Gil Gerard, Jamie Farr, Ray Walston, Lawrence Pressman

For Lovers Only
US 1982 96m colour TVM
ABC/MGM–UA/Henerson–Hirsch/Caesar's Palace (Jay Daniel)
Honeymooners and wife swappers mingle at a Pennsylvania resort.
Arrant rubbish which begins foolishly and continues in the same vein.

w James G. Hirsch *d* Claudio Guzman *ph* Bill Jurgenson *m* Pete Rugolo

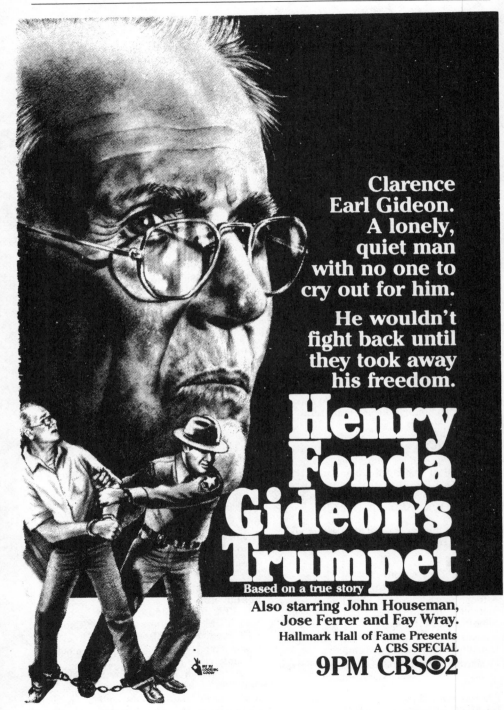

Clarence
Earl Gideon.
A lonely,
quiet man
with no one to
cry out for him.

He wouldn't
fight back until
they took away
his freedom.

HENRY FONDA Gideon's Trumpet

Based on a true story

Also starring John Houseman,
Jose Ferrer and Fay Wray.
Hallmark Hall of Fame Presents
A CBS SPECIAL
9PM CBS●2

HENRY FONDA made one of his finest appearances as Clarence Earl Gideon, but sadly it came close to the end of a marathon career.

Andy Griffith, Katherine Helmond, Gary Sandy, Sally Kellerman, Robert Hegyes, Gordon Jump

'Taste leaps out the window the moment the titles begin.' – *Daily Variety*

For Maddie With Love (GB 1980–81).
Lachrymose midday soap opera from ATV whose heroine learns she has only a few months to live. Despite this apparent terminus (admittedly handled rather movingly) the show resumed for a further run as her nearest and dearest learned to cope without her. With Nyree Dawn Porter, Ian Hendry.   PP

For Richer for Poorer (US 1977–).
Daytime soap opera for NBC about conflicts between the young and their elders. Created, if you'll pardon the expression, by Harding Lemay, with a varying cast.

For Tea on Sunday (GB 1963; 75m; bw).
Twice-done David Mercer play about young nutter who smashes up the furniture in his girl friend's flat, written and first produced when Mercer was over-taxed and much occupied with madness – he had lately finished his trilogy on wrestling with a socialist conscience in a capitalist world, its hero finally going bananas under the strain, and had also made a hit with *A Suitable Case for Treatment*, whose Morgan Delt flirted cheerfully with schizophrenia. Here the message that the mentally sick may have some private line to the Meaning of It All was easily rejectable, especially when Keith Baxter proved none too expert with the axe he was wielding. A second production in 1978 at least revealed some improved axemanship from Jonathan Pryce in the role. Directed both times by Don Taylor; for BBC.   PP

For the Love of Ada *
GB 1970–2 26 × 25m colour (VTR)
Thames

Two 70-year-olds fall in love and marry. Geriatric sitcom which really worked. The subsequent movie version didn't.

Irene Handl, Wilfred Pickles

For the Love of It
US 1980 96m colour TVM
ABC/Charles Fries/Neila (Stanley Ralph Ross)

Two young people find a clue to a murder and are pursued to San Diego by the FBI, the CIA, and enemy spies.
All-star attempt in the genre of *It's a Mad Mad Mad Mad World*, i.e. a chase punctuated by slapstick. Undernourished by wit, it seems merely silly.

w Stanley Ralph Ross *d* Hal Kanter *ph* William K. Jurgensen *m* Jimmy Haskell

Deborah Raffin, Jeff Conaway, Barbi Benton, Tom Bosley, Norman Fell, Henry Gibson, Adam West, Don Rickles. Jack Carter, Gil Lamb, Eddie Quillan, Pat Morita, Michael Kidd

For the People (US 1965).
Half-hour crime series for CBS, with William Shatner as an assistant DA, Howard da Silva as his boss, and Jessica Walter as his wife.

For the Term of His Natural Life
Australia 1983 6½ TV hours colour miniseries (Patty Payne, Wilton Schiller)

An innocent Englishman is driven from home and sent to Botany Bay.
A saga of injustice and adventure, from the novel by Marcus Clarke. Ill-cast and not especially exciting.

w Wilton Schiller, Patty Payne *d* Rob Stewart

Colin Friels, Anthony Perkins, Patrick MacNee, Samantha Eggar, Diane Cilento, Rod Mullinar, Susan Lyons

PP: 'Lurid melodrama of transportation to Australia in the 19th century, with innocent hero up against malefactors, sadists and a humane governor with pretty daughter. The governor was the only interesting character, played by a somewhat tubby Patrick MacNee, the jaw once braced debonairly above the cutaway collar and tightly-knotted tie of John Steed now wobbling up and down in a sea of jowl. Shown on BBC1 1985.'

For Us the Living
US 1983 74m colour TVM
Charles Fries (J. Kenneth Rotcop) for American Playhouse

Memoirs of the widow of Mississippi civil rights leader Medgar Evers.
A sincere tribute which somehow never becomes exciting.

w Ossie Davis, J. Kenneth Rotcop, *book* by Myrlie Evers *d* Michael Schultz *ph* Alan Kozlowski *m* Gerald Fried

Howard Rollins Jnr, Irene Cara, Margaret Avery, Roscoe Lee Browne

'In a world gone mad, they found each other!'

Forbidden
US 1985 96m colour TVM
HBO/Jazak Decade/Forstates
Clasart/Anthea (Mark Forstater)

During World War II in Berlin, an upper-class Nazi woman falls for a Jew.
Pattern play posing as character study as it weaves its way from one supposed suspense climax to another.

w Leonard Gross *d* Anthony Page *ph* Wolfgang Treu *m* Tangerine Dream

Jacqueline Bisset, Jurgen Prochnow, Irene Worth, Amanda Cannings, Avis Bunnage

'A young man. An older woman. A love story of the '80s!'

Forbidden Love
US 1983 96m colour TVM
CBS/Orion Jaffe–Blakely/Sama/Frank Von Zerneck (Marcy Gross, Ann Weston)

A young doctor falls for a fortyish businesswoman.
Glossy generation-gap idyll with a tearful finish. Like eating too much Turkish delight.

w Priscilla English, Laurian Leggett *d* Steven Hillard Stern *ph* Isidore Mankofsky *m* Hagood Hardy

Yvette Mimieux, Andrew Stevens, Jerry Hauser, Randy Brooks, John Considine, Jeffrey Lynn

Force Five
US 1975 74m colour TVM
CBS/Universal (Michael Gleason, David Levinson)

An undercover police unit is formed to control street crime.
Yet another élite force hopes and fails to make the grade as a series.

w Michael Gleason, David Levinson *d* Walter Grauman

Gerald Gordon, Nick Pryor, William Lucking, James Hampton, Roy Jenson, David Spielberg, Leif Erickson, Bradford Dillman

Ford, Anna (1943–). Pretty British teleperson, a newscaster for ITN 1978–81. Left to join TV-am with same delusions of grandeur as Angela Rippon's, and suffered same fate, early dismissal at the hands of Jonathan Aitken, over whom she famously threw a glass of wine. Now does odd voice-overs and presentation.   PP

Ford, Glenn (1916–) (Gwyllyn Ford). Stocky, virile Canadian–American film star of the forties and fifties. His forays into TV include innumerable guest roles and some series: *Cade's County, The Family Holvak, Havoc.* TV movies: *The Brotherhood of the Bell, Jarrett, The Disappearance of Flight 412, Punch and Jody, Once an Eagle, The 3000-Mile Chase, Evening in Byzantium, Beggarman Thief, The Sacketts.*

Ford, Paul (1901–76) (Paul Ford Weaver). American character actor, mainly in comic roles; most famous as Bilko's antagonist, the long-suffering Colonel Hall.

Ford, 'Tennessee' Ernie (1919–). American southern-style singer and presenter, popular throughout the fifties.

Foreign Exchange
GB 1969 72m colour TVM
ABC/Cohen–Sangster

A private eye is called back into the British Secret Service.
Espionage hokum which with *The Spy Killer* makes two failed pilots for the same non-series.

w Jimmy Sangster *d* Roy Baker

Robert Horton, Sebastian Cabot, Jill St John, Dudley Foster, Eric Pohlmann

Foreign Intrigue
US 1951–4 154 × 25m bw
NBC/Sheldon Reynolds

Adventures of foreign correspondents in Europe.
Punchy little 'behind the headlines' melodramas.

Jerome Thor, James Daly, Gerald Mohr (at different times)

† Syndicated as *Cross Current, Dateline Europe, Overseas Adventure.*

The Forest Rangers
Canada 1965 104 × 25m colour
ITC/ASP

Stories of a group of junior rangers in the Canadian Northwoods.
Flabbily shot outdoor adventure for kids.

Graydon Gould, Michael Zenon, Gordon Pinsent

Forever
US 1978 96m colour TVM
EMI (Marc Trabulus, Merrit Malloy)

Teenagers fall in and out of love in Northern California.
Yawnsville.

w A. J. Carothers, *novel* Judy Blume *d* John Korty *ph* Dave Meyers *m* Fred Karlin

Stephanie Zimbalist, Dean Butler, John Friedrich, Beth Raines, Diana Scarwid

'The scenes have all the compulsion of shampoo teleblurbs. . . the ironies of youthful romance are drawn out into tedium.' – *Daily Variety*

The Forgotten Man *
US 1971 73m colour TVM
ABC Circle (Walter Grauman)

GLENN FORD had a fair stab at television after his movie career faded, and was playing upstanding tough fellows into his sixties. *Cade's Country*, alas, was not quite the right vehicle for a long run, even though it used the same sets as *Peyton Place*.

Five years after being reported missing, a soldier returns from Vietnam, finds his wife remarried, and becomes desperate.
Well-filmed and rather poignant melodrama.
w Mark Rodgers *d* Walter Grauman
Dennis Weaver, Annie Francis, Lois Nettleton, Andrew Duggan, Percy Rodrigues

Forman, Sir Denis (1917–). British executive, with Granada TV from its formation in 1954, rising to become chairman on Lord Bernstein's retirement; highly respected and influential, has personally nursed many important series on to the air, notably *Jewel in the Crown*.

Forrest, Steve (1924–) (William Forrest Andrews). Reliable American actor, brother of Dana Andrews. Series: *The Baron, SWAT.* TV movies: *The Hanged Man, The Hatfields and the McCoys, Wanted: The Sundance Woman, Last of the Mohicans, Testimony of Two Men, Maneaters Are Loose, The Deerslayer, Captain America, Roughnecks, A Rumor of War.*

Forster, Robert (1942–). Sullen-looking American leading man of the seventies. TV series: *Banyon, Nakia.* TV movie: *The Darker Side of Terror.*

The Forsyte Saga ***
GB 1967 26 × 50m bw (VTR)
BBC/MGM (DONALD WILSON)
The story of a family of London merchants from the 1870s to the 1920s, and especially the story of unsympathetic Soames and his disastrous marriage.
A solid success, this expensive serial drama played around the world and its influence was much felt, all the way to the novelizations of the mid-seventies. The first half was undoubtedly the best, but so it is in John Galsworthy's books.
adaptor Lennox Philips, others *d* James Cellan Jones, David Giles *designer* Julia Trevelyan Oman
ERIC PORTER, NYREE DAWN PORTER, KENNETH MORE, SUSAN HAMPSHIRE, John Welsh, JOSEPH O'CONOR, Fay Compton, MARGARET TYZACK, Lana Morris
† BAFTA awards: best drama series; Eric Porter; Nyree Dawn Porter; Julia Trevelyan Oman.
PP: 'For the British audience a hidden significance was its function as a kind of communal family history, replete with lots of births, deaths and juicy scandals but also a nostalgia for what were imagined to be better days.'

Forsyth, Bruce (1928–). Jaunty British comedian who rose to fame in the fifties as compere of *Sunday Night at the London Palladium*, and consolidated his stardom in the seventies with *The Generation Game*. The critics were gunning for him, and *Bruce Forsyth's Big Night* was a disaster which cost him his public infallibility; but *Play Your Cards Right* was a modest success. *Hollywood or Bust*, 1984, busted.

❋ **Forsythe, John** (1918–) (John Freund). Pleasing, soft-spoken, American leading man who never quite made it in films but has enjoyed residuals from several successful TV series: *Bachelor Father, The John Forsythe Show, To Rome with Love, Dynasty.* The voice of Charlie in *Charlie's Angels.* TV movies include *See How They Run, Shadow on the Land, Murder Once Removed, The Letters, Cry Panic, The Healers, Terror on the 40th Floor, The Deadly Tower, Amelia Earhart, Tail Gunner Joe, Cruise into Terror, With This Ring, The Users.*

Fortress
Australia/US 1985 74m colour TVM
HBO/Crawford (Raymond Menmuir)

A schoolteacher and her charges are held to
ransom by hoodlums.
An old and never pleasant story is given
adequate gloss but no new twists.

w Everett de Roche, *novel* by Gabrielle
Lord d Arch Nicholson ph David Connell
m Danny Beckerman

Rachel Ward, Sean Garlick, Robin Mason,
Marc Gray

The Forty Eight Hour Mile
US 1970 97m colour TVM
NBC/Universal

A private eye pursues a tense triangle situation
which leads to murder.
OK who's-following-whom mystery.

d Gene Levitt

Darren McGavin, William Windom, Kathy
Brown, Carrie Snodgress

45 Cranley Drive ***
GB 1961 40m bw (16mm)
Granada (Tim Hewat)

Pioneering docu-drama recapitulating the
events leading to the arrest of the Portland
spies, rather more effectively than the
subsequent movie version (*Ring of Spies*).

d Mike Wooller

Forty Minutes (GB since 1982). Umbrella
title sheltering seasons of weekly 40-minute
documentaries masterminded by former
fly-on-the-wall specialist Roger Mills, for
BBC. Some are to this discipline but the
majority are traditional essays on subjects
chosen for their piquancy or for having been
long overlooked, e.g. an edition on unusual
facts about pigeons, and a trio of
programmes in 1985 devoted to the Eternal
Triangle of mistresses, wives, husbands.
Other topics have included: a neglected
World War II episode in which front-line 8th
Army troops were tried for desertion; female
circumcision; and Lady Lucia Lambton
exploring public lavatories (both sexes). In
1985 Edward Mirzoeff took over from Mills.
PP

Foster and Laurie *
US 1975 100m colour TVM
CBS/Arthur Stolnitz

The true story of two New York cops, shot in
the line of duty.
A well-intentioned tribute, but basically the
same old mean streets cops and robbers.

BARRY FOSTER, somehow, never quite
became a star, even after playing *Hamlet*
(for schools) in 1961 and going on to
become a very personable Van Der Valk.

w Albert Ruben, *book* Al Silverman d John
Llewellyn Moxey m Lalo Schifrin

Perry King, Dorian Harewood, Talia Shire,
Jonelle Allen

Foster, Barry (1930–   ). British actor of fair
hair, short stature but great presence. In TV
from *Incident at Echo Six* (1958) via many
plays and series to *Van der Valk*, *Orde
Wingate*, *The Three Hostages*, etc. Strength
is that he can be ordinary or just as easily be
flamboyant.   PP

Foster, Jodie (1962–   ). American teenage
actress of the seventies: made her first mark in
the shortlived 1974 series *Paper Moon*, in
which she took over the Tatum O'Neal role.

Foster, Julia (1942–   ). British leading
actress, mainly on TV, often in slightly fey
roles. Series include *Emergency – Ward Ten*,
Moll Flanders, *The Wilde Alliance*. Recent
credit: *Late Starter*.

The Fosters
GB 1976–7 22 approx. × 25m colour
LWT

Misadventures of a black family in London. A rather unattractive comedy series, vaguely borrowed from *The Jeffersons*.

Norman Benton, Isabelle Lucas

Fothergill ***
GB 1981 75m colour
BBC (Innes Lloyd)

Inventive yet faithful film drama wrought from John Fothergill's testy *An Innkeeper's Diary*, with Robert Hardy knocking off yet another consummate piece of impersonation to make this impossible snob of the twenties a human, even endearing, being.

w Robert Holles d Claude Whatham

ROBERT HARDY, Lynn Farleigh   PP

Foul Play (US 1980). An extremely shortlived one-hour series which mixed crime with zany comedy after the pattern of the film of the same name, but lacked a touch of genius to seal the mixture. With Deborah Raffin, Barry Bostwick. Created and written by Hal Sitowitz; for Miller/Milkis/Boyett/Paramount/ABC.

Found Money *
US 1984 96m colour TVM
NBC/Warner/Cypress Point (Jonathan Bernstein)

A bank computer expert and a security guard concoct an illicit scheme to distribute money to New Yorkers who do good deeds. Initially amusing comedy which runs out of steam.

w Michael Fairman, Richard Sanders d Bill Persky ph Larry Pizer m Jack Elliott

Dick Van Dyke, Sid Caesar, Shelley Hack, William Prince, Christopher Murney

'Comes off agreeable and often exceedingly wise.' – *Daily Variety*

The Four Feathers
GB 1976 96m colour TVM
NBC/Trident/Norman Rosemont

In the 1880s, a British officer redeems his cowardice by going under cover in the Sudan. Very thin TV version of a story magnificently filmed in 1938, with less memorable attempts in 1929 and 1956. This version is clearly superfluous.

w Gerald DiPego, *novel* A. E. W. Mason d Don Sharp

Beau Bridges, Robert Powell, Jane Seymour, Simon Ward, Harry Andrews, Richard Johnson, David Robb

444 Days . . . and Counting (GB/US 1982; 60m). The last-minute attempts by outgoing President Jimmy Carter to engineer the release of the American hostages in Iran, as preserved by privileged fly-on-the-wall cameraman Rolfe Teggem, lurking in the Oval Office the morning of Reagan's inauguration. Subsequent recollections and a rather superfluous commentary filled out this account. Though in the end the suspense gently subsided into neither climax nor anti-climax, an extraordinary fragment of history was preserved. Produced by Margaret Jay, for BBC.   PP

Four in One
US 1970 24 × 50m colour
MCA/Universal

A rotating series intended to break in four possible series, each running every fourth week. In fact only *McCloud* and *Night Gallery* went on to better things. The others were *San Francisco International*, with Lloyd Bridges, and *The Psychiatrist* with Roy Thinnes.

The Four Just Men *
GB 1959 39 × 25m bw
ATV

Four men agree to combat injustice throughout the world.

Not much to do with the Edgar Wallace book, but a convenient way of allowing four billed stars to work only every fourth week. Unfortunately the stories were disappointing and de Sica's English was a shade too fractured.

Jack Hawkins, Richard Conte, Dan Dailey, Vittorio de Sica

The Four Seasons *
GB 1981 4 × 40m colour
BBC (Marjorie Orr)

Four films about the experiences which most affect people's lives: birth, marriage, retirement, death.

Interesting documentary four-pack, reported by Bernard Falk.

Four Seasons of Rosie Carr
GB 1964 4 × 60m bw VTR

Ted Willis saga of warm-hearted Cockney woman making a new life in Australia in the early years of the century. Alas, Rosie Carr was of a goodness never seen on land or sea, ever ready with a brave smile, a kind word or her last sixpence for the poor of Spain, and eventually as unconvincing as the ritual bit of teeming London life with which producer–director Peter Graham Scott began each episode; for BBC.   PP

Four Star. An American television production company founded to utilize the talents of Dick Powell, Charles Boyer, Rosalind Russell and Joel McCrea. In fact the last two hardly contributed and David Niven was co-opted, with some assistance from Ida Lupino. The main drama output was channelled into *Dick Powell Theatre*, which was highly regarded.

Fourteen-day Rule. Accepted unofficially by the BBC in wartime, confirmed officially by Dr Charles Hill (later Lord Hill) as Postmaster-General in 1955, it forbade radio or TV discussion of any issue due to come up in Parliament within a fortnight. Scrapped 1957. PP

The Fourth Arm
GB 1983 12 × 50m
BBC (Gerard Glaister)
More undercover war heroics from the team that gave you *Secret Army*, *Kessler*, etc, with the scenario this time resembling intensive, competitive training programmes made familiar in contemporary real-life service epics such as *Police* and *Fighter Pilot*.
cr Gerard Glaister, John Brason w and
d various PP

The Fourth Wise Man
US 1985 74m colour TVM
Ellwood Kieser
A wealthy Persian physician devotes his life to finding the Messiah.
American Sunday evangelism runs riot in this somewhat amateur production which for all its good intentions doesn't hold water.
w Tom Fontana d Michael Ray Rhodes
Martin Sheen, Alan Arkin, Eileen Brennan, Ralph Bellamy, Richard Libertini, Lance Kerwin, Harold Gould

Fowlds, Derek (1937–). British actor with permanently surprised expression who matured from the *Basil Brush Show* to all series of *Yes Minister* and *Yes Prime Minister*.

Fowley, Douglas (1911–). American character actor who spent 30 years playing gangsters in movies, then moved to TV and played grizzled old fellows in such series as *Gunsmoke* and *Pistols 'n' Petticoats*.

Fox (GB 1980). A sort of Sarf London *Dallas*, with Peter Vaughan as the larger-than-life head of a sprawling family not without some shady connections, as well as assorted feuds and failing marriages. Forgettable. Written by Trevor Preston; for Thames/Euston Films. PP

Fox, Edward (1937–). Haughty-looking British leading actor who impressed as the Prince of Wales in EDWARD AND MRS SIMPSON.

Fox, Michael J. (1961–). American juvenile actor who plays younger than his years. *Palmerstown*, *Family Ties*, *Poison Ivy*.

Fox, Paul (1925–). British executive, into television as BBC news writer, 1950, thence via outside broadcasts to editorship of *Sportsview* (1953), then *Panorama* (1961). Controller of BBC1, 1967–8, director of programmes 1973, before joining YTV as Managing Director 1976. Reputedly a tough nut at inter-ITV meetings, he led the *Dallas*-inspired action against his former assistant Brian Cowgill in 1985. PP

Foxworth, Robert (1941–). American leading man. *Storefront Lawyers*, *Mrs Sundance*, *The Memory of Eva Ryker*, *Act of Love*, *Peter and Paul*, *Falcon Crest*.

❋ **Foxx, Redd** (1922–) (John Elroy Sanford). Black American character comedian who became a major star in SANFORD AND SON and subsequently starred in a weekly variety series.

Foxy Lady
GB 1984 7 × 30m
Granada (John G. Temple)
Diane Keen as predatory charmer who takes over north country provincial newspaper; fairly forgettable.
w Geoffrey Lancashire d Richard Holdhouse

Fractured Flickers
US 1961 26 × 25m bw
Jay Ward
Comedy series hosted by Hans Conried, featuring re-edited sequences from classic silent films with zany commentaries. Not likely to please film buffs.
'The biggest waste of time since *The Bullwinkle Show!*' – publicity

France. Had the world's second television service, beamed from the Eiffel Tower from 1938 on an extremely high-definition standard of 819 lines. After the war it also went it alone with the SECAM colour system, but French TV has never been able

MICHAEL J. FOX, because of *Back to the Future* and *Teen Wolf*, was the movie heart-throb of 1985, but television audiences in Britain at least failed to respond overwhelmingly to his long-running sitcom *Family Ties*. He is seen here on an Oxford location with his 'mother', Meredith Baxter Birney.

to escape government control or, in de Gaulle's case, government usage. Today all three channels are still administered by the State RTF organization. **PP**

France, Peter (1931–). Serious British teleperson, ex-colonial administrator and radio presenter into television via religious programmes. Since 1984 has conducted *Timewatch*; one-off specials include *Paisley . . . Child of Wrath, Man of God.* **PP**

Franciosa, Tony (1928–) (Anthony Papaleo). Beaming American leading man who is a bigger star on TV than in movies. Series include *Valentine's Day, The Name of the Game, Search, Rich Man, Poor Man, Wheels.* TV movies include *The Deadly Hunt, Earth II, The Catcher, This Was the West That Was, Matt Helm, Curse of the Black Widow, Aspen.*

Francis, Arlene (*c* 1908–) (Arlene Kazanjian). American character actress, a favourite TV panellist of the fifties.

Francis, Derek (1923–84). Owl-like, portly, British character actor, familiar from a multitude of roles, but never in a leading series part.

Francis Gary Powers: The True Story of the U-2 Spy Incident *
US 1976 96m colour TVM
Charles Fries/NBC (Edward J. Montagne, John B. Bennett)

In May 1960 an American spy plane is shot down over the Soviet Union.
Acceptable dramatization of a true incident.

w Robert E. Thompson, *book Operation Overflight* by Francis Gary Powers *d* Delbert Mann *m* Gerald Fried

Lee Majors, Nehemiah Persoff, Noah Beery Jnr, William Daniels, Lew Ayres, Biff McGuire, Thayer David

Francis, Raymond (1911–). British character actor who had a long run of success as Superintendent Lockhart in Rediffusion's Scotland Yard series of the fifties: *Crime Sheet, Murder Bag, No Hiding Place.*

Franciscus, James (1934–). American leading man of the sixties who didn't manage a big Hollywood career but proved adequate in several TV series: *Naked City, Mr Novak, Longstreet, Doc Elliott, Hunter.* TV movies include *Shadow over Elveron, Trial Run, Night Slaves, The 500 Pound Jerk, Aloha Means Goodbye, The Dream Makers, The Trial of Chaplain Jensen, One of My Wives Is Missing, Secrets of Three Hungry Wives, The Pirate.*

Frankenheimer, John (1930–). American director who scored his greatest successes in movies but had his roots in TV and went to Hollywood originally to film his successful TV production of *The Young Stranger.*

Frankenstein Jnr and the Impossibles
US/GB 1966–7 52 × 25m colour
Hanna–Barbera
Government agents and their 30-foot robot pose as a rock and roll group.
Witless cartoon series.

Frankenstein: The True Story
US/GB 1973 200m colour TVM
Universal (Hunt Stromberg Jnr)
It never was a true story anyway, this version doesn't stick to the book any more than the others, and at this length it is just an embarrassment, though good performances flicker through the tedium.
w Christopher Isherwood, Don Bachardy d Jack Smight
James Mason, Leonard Whiting, David McCallum, Michael Sarrazin, Jane Seymour, Nicola Pagett, John Gielgud, Margaret Leighton, Ralph Richardson, Michael Wilding, Tom Baker, Agnes Moorehead
† *The True Story of Frankenstein*, a 'dramatized collage' examining the myth was a BBC *Everyman* Special in 1986 (p Daniel Wolf).
†† A straightforward film-dramatization from YTV (1984) starred Robert Powell, David Warner, John Gielgud, Susan Wooldridge, Cary Fischer.

Franklin, Gretchen (–). Stalwart British actress with late-life celebrity as a pillar of *EastEnders*. PP

Franklyn, William (1926–). Smooth British general purpose performer who has been seen as actor, revue host, panellist, and especially as the voice-over in innumerable commercials.

Fraser, Bill (1907–). Heavyweight British character actor who became a TV star in the fifties for his appearances as the bullying sergeant in *The Army Game* and *Bootsie and Snudge*. Also appeared in many plays. Recent credits include *Puccini* (1984).

Fraser, John (1932–). British actor, a longtime juvenile who found it difficult to 'grow up'. In many single plays.

Fraser, Sir Robert (1904–85). Australian journalist and civil servant who became the ITA's first director general, 1954–70, for more kicks than ha'pence. PP

Fraser, Ronald (1930–). Parrot-like Scottish actor of fun and sensitivity, at his best in the sixties and early seventies, when he turned up sooner or later in every series and finally had his own, *The Misfit*. PP

Frawley, William (1887–1966). Crumple-faced American character comedian who after hundreds of Hollywood roles became a TV star as Lucille Ball's long-suffering neighbour in *I Love Lucy* and went on to play Grandpa in *My Three Sons*.

Frayn, Michael (19 –). British humorist and playwright who has written one or two fine comedies for television, beginning with *Jamie on a Flying Visit* (1968), also a series for Eleanor Bron. As a reflective, fastidious performer, a *One Pair of Eyes*; explorations of Berlin, Vienna, etc; the Australian journey in *Great Railway Journeys of the World*. PP

Frears, Stephen (19 –). British director, who came to notice as a film-maker (drama, documentary and all shades between) and only tried video when already established. His outstanding, assured productions include *Daft as a Brush* (1975), *Three Men in a Boat* (1976), *Last Summer* (1977), *Going Gently* (1981), *Walter* (1982), *December Flower* (1984), *A Song for Europe* (1985). PP

Fred *
GB 1982 7 × 30m
BBC Manchester (Don Haworth)
The daily round and meditations of Fred Dibnah, real-life steeplejack, traction-engine enthusiast and homely philosopher. An engaging series set on top of tall chimneys and church spires or, for relaxation, on the road under steam. PP

Free Country (US 1978). Briefly seen half-hour series for ABC, with Rob Reiner as

FRAGGLE ROCK, an amiably grotesque puppet show from the same stable as *The Muppets*, was not quite the same success.

a Lithuanian immigrant of 89 looking back on his young manhood.

free plug circuit. The traipse round chat shows and miscellany programmes made by authors, performers, etc, to promote a new book or film or album, usually arranged by their professional publicist. Regional miscellanies are the most accessible, then (in Britain) midday shows such as *Pebble Mill*. Hardest nut to crack used to be *Parkinson*, but its successor *Wogan* seems to be a soft touch for show-offs and phoneys of sufficient status.   PP

Freebie and the Bean
US 1980   × 50m colour
Warner (Philip Saltzman)

A cleaned-up series version of the film about two crazy cops with no sense of responsibility. Not only cleaned up but shorn of any possible interest.

cr Dick Nelson

Hector Elizondo, Tom Mason, William Daniels

'It had better pick up on the wit and charm departments if it's intent on hanging around.' – *Daily Variety*

† It lasted half a season.

Freedman, Jerrold (–   ). American director. *The Boy Who Drank Too Much*, *Victims*, *The Seduction of Gina*, *Best Kept Secrets*, *Seduced*.

Freedom
US 1981 96m colour TVM
ABC/Leonard Hill, Philip Mandelker

A difficult 15-year-old girl is allowed by her mother to go off and live on her own. She joins a carnival and learns the hard way. Absurd melodrama full of unreal people pretending they're normal.

w Barbara Turner *d* Joseph Sargent *ph* Donald M. Morgan *m* Janis Ian

Mare Winningham, Jennifer Warren, Tony Bill, Roy Thinnes, J. Pat O'Malley

Freedom Riders
US 1978 96m colour TVM
Columbia (Doug Benton)
aka: *My Undercover Years with the Ku Klux Klan*

An FBI undercover man infiltrates the Ku Klux Klan.

Reasonably interesting docu-drama.

w Lane Slate, Roger O. Hirson, *book My Undercover Years with the Ku Klux Klan* by Gary Thomas Rowe Jnr *d* Barry Shear

Don Meredith, James Wainwright, Albert Salmi, Clifton James, Edward Andrews, Slim Pickens, Maggie Blye, Michele Carey

Freedom Road *
GB 1964 50m bw
A–R (Elkan Allan)

Celebrated entertainment-with-a-message in which a programme of negro music gained poignancy both from Allan's deliberate interpolations and the chance circumstance of racial intolerance in America being reported in the news immediately before the show went on the air. I wrote at the time: 'Rarely can a handful of songs have taken on such fervour . . . the studio performance as restrained and orderly as a Wigmore Hall recital but the interleaved procession of old prints, photographs, snippets of film and snippets of prose all the time pushing up the emotional temperature. The singers seemed gripped by a great race-ache. . .' With Cleo Laine, Pearl Prescod, others. PP

Freedom Road
US 1979 2 × 95m colour
NBC/Zev Broun (Leland Nolan, Chet Walker)

After the Civil War, ex-slaves begin to seize their rights.

Interminable and stilted saga which shows little sign of the eight million dollars it allegedly cost.

w David Zelag Goodman, *novel* Howard Fast *d* Jan Kadar *ph* Charles Correll *m* Terry James, Coleridge-Taylor Parkinson

Muhammad Ali, Kris Kristofferson, Ron O'Neal, Edward Herrmann, Joel Fluellen, Bill Mackey

Freeman, John (*c* 1913–). British TV personality, the relentless interrogator of FACE TO FACE, who subsequently became British Ambassador to the US and chairman of London Weekend Television.

Freleng, Friz (1906–). American animator who after many years at Warner went into TV as half of De Patie–Freleng Entertainment.

Freud
GB/US 1984 6 × 60m
BBC/RCTV (John Purdie)

Ambitious bio-serial of der immortal shrink for which a decreasing few bothered to make an appointment. 'A mistaken compromise which went wrong in its writing. Complicated ideas were rendered down to suit the conventions of popular costume drama, yet all the attention was given to the ideas rather than the character exploration on which drama depends,' said Sean Day-Lewis on behalf of the *Telegraph* Sunday Magazine's panel picking the six best, or here the six worst, of the year.

w Carey Harrison *d* Moira Armstrong

David Suchet (as Freud), Suzanne Bertish, Anton Lesser, Michael Kitchen, David Swift, Michael Pennington, Dinsdale Landen

Freud, Clement (1924–). Lugubrious British TV personality who went on to become a Liberal MP.

The Friday Alternative (GB 1982–3). Innovative current affairs weekly operated in the first months of C4 by Diverse Productions (David Graham), using computer graphics and a panel of 250 'ordinary people' to bring vox pop values to the news of the day. Handicapped by a journalistic team at once inexperienced and transparently biased to the Left, it ran into disfavour and was axed at the end of the season, but paved the way for the much better *Diverse Reports* from the same producer. PP

Friday Night ... Saturday Morning. British (BBC) chat show (intermittently 1979–82) which tried to discover a new host every time – Sir Harold Wilson notoriously presided over two editions. Sooner or later they reached for Ned Sherrin again, though. PP

Friedkin, David (1939–). American director who together with **Mort Fine** (19 –) created and produced I SPY. Friedkin won an Emmy in 1962 for his direction of *The Price of Tomatoes* (*Dick Powell Theatre*), but his later work has been insignificant.

Friendly, Ed (19 –). American independent producer: *Little House on the*

Prairie, *The Young Pioneers*, *Backstairs at the White House*, etc.

'What happened to Peg Mullen happened to America!'

Friendly Fire *
US 1980 140m colour TVM
ABC/Marble Arch/Martin Starger (Philip Barry, Fay Kanin)

An Iowa mother goes to Vietnam to discover the real cause of her son's death.

Much praised on its first showing, this was an important telefilm for American audiences but did not touch the imaginations of others.

w Fay Kanin, *book* C. D. B. Bryan *d* DAVID GREENE *ph* Harry May *m* Leonard Rosenman

CAROL BURNETT, Ned Beatty, Sam Waterston, Denis Erdman, Timothy Hutton, Fanny Spiess

'One of the landmarks in the history of the medium.' – Boston *Globe*

† Emmys went to David Greene and to the film as 'best special'.

Friendly, Fred W. (1915–). Distinguished American journalist and commentator, long associated as producer with Edward R. Murrow and subsequently president of CBS News.

Friendly Persuasion
US 1975 100m colour TVM
ABC/International (Herbert B. Leonard)

At the outbreak of the Civil War a family of Quakers has to consider its position.

Modest remake of the 1956 movie in the hope of a series. The hope was forlorn.

w William P. Woods *d* Joseph Sargent

Richard Kiley, Shirley Knight, Michael O'Keefe, Tracie Savage

Friends (US 1978). A shortlived one-hour series for family audiences, about three 11-year-olds (one black) and their problems. Rather mechanical and obvious. With Charles Aiken, Jill Whelan, Jarrod Johnson. Created by A. J. Carothers; for Aaron Spelling/ABC.

Friends and Lovers
US 1974 13 × 25m colour
CBS/MTM (Steve Pritzker)

Misadventures of a violinist in the Boston Symphony Orchestra.

Vehicle for a new comedy star with a style which was too subdued to succeed in the ratings.

Paul Sand, Michael Pataki, Penny Marshall

Friendships, Secrets and Lies
US 1980 96m colour TVM
NBC/Warner/Wittman–Riche (Jacqueline Babbin)

Six sorority girls, all still living in their home town, are affected by a college tragedy.

Multi-angled melodrama by, with and for women. Not a great success.

w Joanna Jane Crawford, *novel The Walls Came Tumbling Down* by Babs H. Deal *d* Ann Zane Shanks, Marlena Laird *ph* Michael Marguilies *m* Angela Morley

Cathryn Damon, Shelley Fabares, Sandra Locke, Tina Louise, Paula Prentiss, Stella Stevens, Loretta Swit, Fran Bennett

'Tough going all the way for everyone, including the viewer.' – *Daily Variety*

Fries, Charles (1928–). American independent producer, formerly head of production for Metromedia: *The Word*, *The Martian Chronicles*, *A Rumor of War*, etc.

From a Bird's Eye View (GB 1970). Half-hour ITC (Lew Grade) comedy series with Millicent Martin as an air hostess.

From a Far Country
US/GB/Italy 1981 130m approx. colour TVM
NBC/Transworld/ITC/RAI/Film Polski (Giacomo Pezzali, Vincenzo Labella)

Episodes in the early life of Pope John Paul II.

Disjointed, almost incoherent glimpses of hardships in Poland under the Nazis, with occasional shots of a figure who turns out to be the future Pope. Reverence may have caused this standing back from the central figure; it certainly puts a test on the audience.

w A. Kijowski, J. J. Szczepanski, David Butler *d* Krzystof Zanussi *ph* Slawamir Idziak *m* Wojkiech Kilar

Cesary Morawski, Sam Neill, Christopher Cazenove, Lisa Harrow, Maurice Denham, Warren Clarke, Kathleen Byron, John Franklyn-Robbins

'Profound, reverential and confusing.' – *Daily Variety*

From Here to Eternity *
US 1979 6 × 50m colour
NBC/Columbia/Bennett–Katleman (Buzz Kulik)

Life on a Marine base in Hawaii at the time of Pearl Harbor.

TV retread of a somewhat overrated movie: plenty of power, and frankness remarkable for TV, but not much style.

The true story of the anguish and courage of one American mother.

What happened to Peg Mullen happened to America.

FRIENDLY FIRE

"One of the landmarks in the history of the medium."
—Boston Globe

Winner Of 4 Emmy Awards! Including Outstanding Drama.

Winner Of The Peabody Award!

Starring
CAROL BURNETT **NED BEATTY** and **SAM WATERSTON**

ABC MOVIE SPECIAL 8:00 PM 7 ⑧

FRIENDLY FIRE, a post-Vietnam melodrama, illustrates how local TV success can be. In America, a landmark in the history of the medium; in Britain, remembered by hardly anybody.

w Don McGuire, Harold Gast, *novel* James Jones *d* Buzz Kulik *ph* Jerry Finnermann *m* Walter Scharf
William Devane, Natalie Wood, Roy Thinnes, Peter Boyle, Steve Railsback, Joe Pantoliano, Kim Basinger
'If the steam at times seems more like forced air, the saga of wartime Hawaii has the kick, if not the wit, of *Dallas* gone khaki.' – *Daily Variety*
† A 'one-hour' series followed, but lasted only 13 episodes. It was 'developed' by Harold Gast, and written by Rudy Day and Tony Palmer. The 'survivors' of the original cast were joined by Barbara Hershey and David Spielberg.
PP: 'Natalie Wood was as unlike Deborah Kerr in the part as possible; underneath that whoopee exterior was a whoopee lady needing no awakening . . . Able to call on the momentum of expectation a good serial builds up, and having the elbow room to accommodate much more of the detail of James Jones's novel, this version was ultimately far better than the movie.'

From the Cradle to the Grave *
GB 1985 1 × 60m, 3 × 30m
YTV (John Willis)
Fairly scathing report on the welfare state after 40 years of catering – or failing to cater – for (1) the badly housed, (2) those looking after chronically handicapped loved-ones, (3) the long-term unemployed, and (4) the old-aged. Valuable but vitiated by a hectoring style if the chosen cases did not quite live up (or down) to scratch. Directed by Willis himself.   PP

Front Line (GB 1983; 60m). Loony assault on war correspondents from the Crimea to the Falklands by John holier-than-thou Pilger for Central, confused, inaccurate and prejudiced. The same week, the BBC (Adam Curtis) treated the same subject almost as fallibly in *Trumpets and Typewriters*.   PP

The Front Line (GB 1984). Sitcom wanly pitting two West Indian brothers against each other, the one born in Jamaica now a fully integrated citizen, indeed policeman; the one born in Britain perversely – but not very interestingly – a fuzzy Rastafarian. Written by Alex Shearer, produced and directed by Roger Race. With Paul Barber and Alan Igbon.   PP

The Front Page (US 1949). Early half-hour comedy series for CBS, based on the Hecht/McArthur play, with John Daly and Mark Roberts.

Front Page Detective (US 1951–2). Half-hour film series for the Dumont network, with Edmund Lowe as a newspaper columnist.

Frontier (US 1955). Half-hour anthology series for NBC, narrated by Walter Coy: 'This is the west. This is the land of beginning again . . .'

Frontier (GB 1968). British regiment on the North West frontier in the heyday of the Raj, with impetuous subalterns, Fulton Mackay as the curiously fragile adjutant, John Phillips the bluff colonel, James Maxwell the political officer frequently at odds with the army. But for some reason the authentic ingredients never quite combined as they should have done. Produced for Thames.   PP

Frontier (GB 1979). Three 52-minute documentaries from ATV about rich and poor in South America, the frontier in question being that of the minimum standards of civilization. For the first one, producer Brian Moser and his family lived for eight months in a shanty town. In 1983 he used the same title for a trilogy about the cocaine trade: among (1) the refiners in Colombia; (2) growers and coca-chewers in Bolivia; (3) smugglers and pushers in the USA.   PP

Frontier Circus
US 1961 26 × 50m bw
CBS/MCA/Calliope
A travelling circus has adventures out west. Unusual family western which didn't quite make it.
Chill Wills, John Derek, Richard Jaeckel

Frontiere, Dominic (1931–). American composer whose TV series scores include *The Outer Limits*, *Iron Horse* and *Twelve O'Clock High*.

❋ **Frost, David Paradine** (1939–). Ubiquitous tele-person of whom Malcolm Muggeridge's wife Kitty famously said, 'He rose without trace'. In fact, first came to notice as MC of a trio of little Rediffusion specials in 1961 devoted to the Twist (the craze of the day) as danced in London, Paris and on the Riviera. But it was *TWTWTW* a year later which established his mocking, headlinese delivery (with occasional lapses into cloying sincerity) first in Britain, then the USA. Between 1963 and 1965 he was commuting weekly to and fro across the Atlantic. In 1966 he divided himself another way: Frost the entertainer presided over *The Frost Report* (BBC 1966) and *Frost Over England* (1967), sharp revue-type series drawing on such performers as John Cleese, Ronnie Barker and Ronnie Corbett; he also supervised, without taking part in, *At Last the 1948 Show*. Meanwhile *The Frost Programme* (Rediffusion) marked the ascendancy of an alternative David: the aggressive interviewer and conductor of notorious, though defensible, 'trials by TV'. Moving to LWT, in which company he had an interest, Frost speedily lost favour through over-exposure. Since 1970 he has been mainly associated with heavyweight international packages, such as his interviews with ex-President Nixon in 1976, and occasional forum-type debates for YTV. One of the Famous Five who set up TV-am, and still turns up on it, once in a while. He remains an operator with a rare capacity to extract a passionate but purposeful debate from a host of speakers and a crowd on the floor.   PP

Favourite catchphrases: 'Hello, good evening and welcome'; 'We'll be back in a trice.'

Frost in May (GB 1982; 2 × 90m). Girlhood in a convent before World War I, and growing up in the world outside during it. Antonia White's novel popular in the thirties, a cult again in the eighties, newly dramatized with its sequel, *The Lost Traveller*, by Gerald Seymour; with Patsy Kensit, Elizabeth Spriggs, Janet Maw, John Carson, Sheila Burrell, Robert James, Elizabeth Shepherd, Daniel Day-Lewis, Charles Dance. Directed by Ronald Wilson, produced by Anne Head, for BBC.   PP

Frost Over England. Title of an occasional late sixties series in which David Frost, Ronnie Barker, Ronnie Corbett and John Cleese presented topical sketches. Winner at the 1967 Montreux Festival.

The Fugitive **
US 1963–6 120 × 50m bw (30 colour)
ABC/QUINN MARTIN

A doctor is on the run from an avenging policeman for the murder of his wife, and persistently tries to track down the real villain, a one-armed man.

Ingenious variation on *Les Misérables*; most of the episodes were more like *Shane*, with a mysterious stranger coming into a new

community each week, solving some of its problems and leaving. The format seized the imagination of a vast public, and the final episodes, which revealed all, emptied the streets all round the world. Generally speaking, the show was a professional job.

m Pete Rugolo

DAVID JANSSEN, BARRY MORSE, Bill Raisch (as the one-armed man)

† Emmy 1965: best drama series.

Fugitive Family
US 1980 96m colour TVM
CBS/Aubrey–Hamner (Ron Lyon)

A justice department lawyer is threatened by mobsters and has to take his family under an assumed name to start a new life.

Unusual, quite gripping suspense drama with an equivocal ending. Not at all bad as telefilms go.

w Tony Kayden, James G. Hirsch *d* Paul Krasny *ph* Robert Hauser *m* Morton Stevens

Richard Crenna, Diane Baker, Eli Wallach, Don Murray, Ronny Cox, Robin Dearden, Mel Ferrer

Fugitive Samurai. A Japanese property of the early seventies, offered around the world TV markets through America and in various forms: from 24 × 50m to a single 2-hour TV movie. The story concerned an unjustly betrayed samurai who escapes with his young son. Produced by the Nippon Television Network.

A Full Life (GB 1983; 6 × 30m). Reminiscences to Anthony Howard of assorted senior citizens: Lord Cudlipp, Lady Longford, Sir Roland Penrose, Admiral Sir Frank Twiss, Lord Beeching, John Arlott. Produced by Anthony Howard, for C4/TVS.

† Previously the title of the 1960 autobiography of World War II General and television performer Sir Brian Horrocks, published by Collins.

Fuller, Robert (1934–). Easy-going American second lead, in series from *Wagon Train* and *Laramie* to *Emergency*. TV movies include *Disaster on the Coastliner*, *Donner Pass*.

Fun and Games
US 1980 96m colour TVM
ABC/Warner/Kanin–Gallo (Fay Kanin, Lilian Gallo)

A woman factory worker refuses favours to the foreman in return for advancement.

Sexual harassment as TV's Social Subject of the Week. A rather obvious, loaded pattern play.

w David Smilow, Elizabeth Wilson d Alan Smithee ph Michel Hugo m Pater Matz

Valerie Harper, Cliff de Young, Max Gail, JoBeth Williams, Peter Donat, Art Hindle, Michael Nouri

'Seldom rises above the level of stereotypes.' – *Daily Variety*

The Funky Phantom *
US 1971 17 × 22m colour
ABC/Hanna–Barbera

Three teenagers release the timid ghost of an old colonial, who helps them to chase other ghosts.

Fairly lively cartoon updating of *The Canterville Ghost.*

Funny Business
US 1978 96m colour TVM
CBS/Universal/Heyday (Leonard B. Stern)

Walter Matthau introduces a collection of old comedy clips featuring Laurel and Hardy, the Marx Brothers, W. C. Fields, Abbott and Costello, Mae West, etc.

Fairly random ragbag which can hardly help being entertaining in spots, though poor print quality doesn't help.

w/d Richard Schickel m Henry Mancini

Funny Face
US 1971 13 × 25m colour
Paramount

A college student does TV commercials on the side.

Extremely mild comedy; no relation to the movie.

Sandy Duncan

Funny Man
GB 1980 13 × 50m colour
Thames

Despite the title, on the whole doleful annals of a music hall family act headed by Jimmy Jewel and based on his own father's company in the twenties and thirties. Times are hard, the wife dies, the kids are a problem. Barry Ingham cheers up things as a cad and Bob Todd as a drunk but the only moments deserving the word 'funny' are recurring glimpses of a knockabout furniture-moving sketch which Jewel mugs in forgotten period style. Created by Jimmy Jewel and Brian Thompson; produced by Peter Duguid.   PP

The Funny Side
US 1971 13 × 50m colour (VTR)
NBC/Bill Persky, Sam Denoff

Comedy variety series hosted by Gene Kelly, with sketches showing attitudes to modern life as revealed by five couples, including one black, one old and one working-class.

Warren Berlinger, Pat Finley, Jenna McMahon, Dick Clair, Michael Lembeck, Cindy Williams, John Amos, Teresa Graves, Burt Mustin, Queenie Smith

Funt, Allen (1914–). American funster, who after working on army concealment techniques in World War II evolved and presented the format of *Candid Camera.*

Further Adventures of Lucky Jim: see *New Adventures* of same

Fury
aka *Brave Stallion*
US 1955–9 114 × 25m bw
ITC

Adventures of a boy and his horse on a western ranch.

Innocuous action series for children.

Bobby Diamond, Peter Graves

Future Cop
aka: *Cleaver and Haven*
US 1976 96m colour TVM
ABC/Paramount/Culzean/Tovern (Gary Damsker, Anthony Wilson)

An old-fashioned cop is given a robot partner.

Uncertain mix of comedy, sentiment and action; it doesn't jell.

w Anthony Wilson, Allen Epstein d Jud Taylor

Ernest Borgnine, Michael Shannon, John Amos, John Larch

† Six one-hours followed, and in 1978 another movie (*The Cops and Robin*), but the producers were flogging a dead horse.

G.I. Brides (GB 1984). Mixed bag of case histories from World War II, built round a reunion at the time of the 1981 Royal Wedding. Commentary written by John Sandilands, produced and directed by Lavinia Warner for Warner Sisters/C4.
† Same subject treated same year in the BBC's *She Married a Yank*, narrated by Susannah York.   PP

Gabe and Guich (US 1981). New half-hour comedy about a New Yorker out west, starring Gabriel Kaplan; retitled *Lewis and Clark*.

Gable, Christopher (1940–). British light actor, former ballet dancer. TV work includes A SONG OF SUMMER, *The Dance of the Seven Veils*, and *The Jack Buchanan Story* (title role).

Gabor, Zsa Zsa (1919–). Decorative international beauty who settled in the USA and made the headlines by having several husbands. A frequent guest star on talk shows, she was Miss Hungary of 1936.

Gadney, Reg (1941–). British writer who after modest serializations of *Forgive Our Foolish Ways* and *The Bell, Last Love*, etc., hit the international big time with *Kennedy* (1983). In 1985 he created the school soap *Drummonds* for LWT.   PP

The Gaffer (GB 1981). A not very successful half-hour comedy series from Yorkshire TV, starring Bill Maynard as the proprietor of a small works, forever teetering on the brink of disaster. With Russell Hunter, Pat Ashton. Written by Graham White; produced and directed by Alan Tarrant.

Gala Performance (GB 1963–5). Periodically invoked title for a BBC programme of cultural bits and pieces introduced by someone like Richard Attenborough. On ITV it would be called *A Golden Hour* or *Golden Drama* and come with Lew Grade's compliments; either way it was pretty condescending and unsatisfying. Produced by Patricia Foy.   PP

Galactica: see Battlestar Galactica

Gale Is Dead **
GB 1969 50m colour (VTR)
BBC
A harrowing, pioneering documentary about the death of a young girl following drug addiction.

The Gale Storm Show
aka: *Oh Susannah!*
US 1956–9 125 × 25m bw
CBS (later ABC)/Roach/ITC
Problems of a social director on a luxury liner.
The original of *Love Boat*, this seemed quite amusing at the time.
Gale Storm, Zasu Pitts, Roy Roberts, James Fairfax

Gall, Sandy (1927–). British newscaster, long with ITN, and formerly a reporter for Reuter's. Has made himself a specialist on Afghanistan with several visits to rebel areas since the Soviet invasion. Special documentary, 1985.

The Gallant Men
US 1962 26 × 50m bw
ABC/Warner
Stories of war correspondents in World War II Italy.
Rather talky war adventures.
Robert McQueeney, William Reynolds

Gallery. BBC political programme which flourished during the sixties to the approval of politicians, who found it more respectful than the general current affairs shows. The audience, however, found it too clannish. PP

Gallery * (GB 1984). Agreeable little erudition show doing for painting what *Take It or Leave It* used to do for literature. Pictures have to be identified from a detail, but the talk that accompanies the process is more important than which side scores the points. Gallery professionals and art students made up the teams as well as art-loving celebs. Presented by George Melly, devised by Dan Farson, produced by Kenneth Price for HTV/C4. Further series 1986.   PP

The Galloping Gourmet. This soubriquet was mysteriously adopted by Graham Kerr, whose rather ragged cooking shows were a big daytime hit in the sixties with ladies across the world.

Galloway, Don (1937–   ). American second lead, best remembered as aide to Raymond Burr in *Ironside*. TV movies include *Lt Schuster's Wife*, *You Lie So Deep My Love*, *Cover Girls*, *Ski Lift to Death*.

✳ **Galton, Ray** (1930–   ). British scriptwriter who, with Alan Simpson, reached unique heights of comedy with HANCOCK and STEPTOE AND SON, after which the standard of invention and characterization seemed to fall somewhat alarmingly.
PP: 'But he combined with Johnny Speight to create the deplorably funny *Spooner's Patch*.'

Galway, James (1939–   ). Irish flautist of distinction, a familiar figure on British television.
PP: 'Too familiar.'

The Gambler
aka: *Kenny Rogers as the Gambler*
US 1980 96m colour TVM
CBS/Ken Kragen
A professional gambler rescues his ex-wife from her villainous husband.
Curious semi-western with a singer for star and not much pace. It looks good, though, especially the train shots.
w Jim Byrnes *d* Dick Lowry *ph* Joe Biroc *m* Larry Cansler
Kenny Rogers, Christine Belford, Bruce Boxleitner, Harold Gould, Clu Gulager, Lance LeGault

The Gambler – the Adventure Continues ✳
US 1983 2 × 93m colour TVM
CBS/Viacom/Lion Share (Neil T. Maffeo)
Brady Hawkes makes up a posse to rescue his kidnapped son.
Amiable western in which nobody comes to much harm. Despite one or two cast changes, and more white in the hero's beard, the action continues on the same train journey as was started three years previously.
w Jim Byrnes *d* Dick Lowry *ph* James Pergola *m* Larry Cansler
Kenny Rogers, Bruce Boxleitner, Linda Evans, Johnny Crawford, Cameron Mitchell, Mitchell Ryan, David Hedison, Gregory Sierra, Ken Swofford
'Tried and true Saturday matinée situations.'
– *Daily Variety*

Game for a Laugh (GB since 1981). Anglo-American game show seeming to owe much to the original studio-based *People Are Funny* of the forties and fifties, likewise *Truth or Consequences* which ran for 25 years on radio and TV. As developed by LWT, contestants undergo stunts of varying indignity before an audience of nerds. Conducted originally by Henry Kelly, Matthew Kelly, Sarah Kennedy and Jeremy Beadle. By 1985 only Beadle remained, now abetted by Lee Peck, Rustie Lee and Martin Daniels.   PP

The Gamekeeper. The gamekeeper's yearly round of rearing the young birds over whose slaughter he must eventually preside has inspired three British television films: (1) BBC (Bristol) documentary by Michael Croucher with this title (1975); (2) Thames documentary by Richard Broad, *The Shoot* (1978); (3) ATV fict-fact version, also called *The Gamekeeper*, from Barry Hines's novel and with the political nudges to be expected from producer Tony Garnett and director Kenneth Loach (1980).   PP

Games Mother Never Taught You
US 1984 96m colour TVM
CBS (Tristine Rainer)
A career woman invades the all-male executive suite, and makes a better breadwinner than her husband.
Adequately amusing comedy of the war between men and women.
w Liz Coe *d* Lee Phillips *ph* Ken Peach Jnr, Ronald M. Lautore *m* Mark Snow
Loretta Swit, Sam Waterston, David Spielberg, Ed Grover, Bill Marey, Eileen Heckart
'It settles on compromises for its final thesis.'
– *Daily Variety*

The Gangster Chronicles
US 1981 13 × 50m colour
Universal (Jack Laird)
The rise to fame and notoriety of Meyer Lansky, Lucky Luciano and Bugsy Siegel.
Long promised as a major television project which could run five years, this modern crime epic was so sloppily realized that 13 weeks did for it. Apart from the usual problem of presenting criminals in an attractive light, it also suffered from an excessively slow build-up and a total lack of style.
w Richard Alan Simmons *d* Richard Sarafian *ph* Gerry Finnermann
Michael Mouri, Brian Benben, Joe Penny, Richard Castellano, George DiCenzo, Alan Arbus, Madeline Stowe

Gangsters

GB 1976–7 1 × 110m, 13 × 50m colour
(VTR)

BBC (David Rose)

Birmingham is Britain's Chicago, riddled
with crime and vice, and in danger of being
taken over by the yellow peril.

Curious melodramatic serial which was not
much appreciated by viewers because it
began as realism and rose, or degenerated,
into spoof. Viewed as an update of *The Perils
of Pauline*, parts of it weren't bad, but the
attempt was somewhat foolhardy.

w Philip Martin *d* Alastair Reid

Maurice Colbourne, Elizabeth Cassidy,
Ahmed Khalil, Zia Mohyeddin, Saeed
Jaffrey, Chai Lee, Robert Lee

Garas, Kaz (1940–). Lithuanian-born
actor in Hollywood. *Strange Report, Riker,
Masserati and the Brain, Bay City Blues.*

Garden, Graeme (1943–). British comedy
performer, one of the Goodies.

Gardener's Calendar (GB since 1983).
Actress Hannah Gordon enlivens this
monthly hobbyist programme, produced by
Arthur Taylor for Granada/C4.

Gardenia, Vincent (1922–). Square-set
little Italian–American character actor. TV
includes THE DREAM MERCHANTS, *Breaking
Away.*

Gardner, Andrew (1932–). British
newscaster and presenter, with ITN and
Thames.

Gardner, Ed (1904–) (Edward
Poggenberg). American character actor,
host and linkman of the radio series *Duffy's
Tavern,* which came briefly to TV in the
fifties.

Gardner, Llew (1929–). Scots interviewer
and political commentator, rather impersonal
in style (except for dropping his final 'g's) but
renowned for driving a hard, thoroughly
prepared interview.   PP

Gargoyles *

US 1972 74m colour TVM

Tomorrow (Roger Gimbel)

An anthropologist and his daughter in
Mexico are menaced by ancient legendary
creatures.

Foolish but effective horror piece.

w Elinor and Stephen Karpf *d* B. W. L.
Norton

Cornel Wilde, Jennifer Salt, Grayson Hall

Garland, Beverly (1926–) (Beverly

THE GAMBLER. This good-looking but
slow-moving old-fashioned Western
began as a six-hour miniseries, all taking
place on a one-day train journey. Next
came a four-hour continuation following
the rest of the journey, though the star's
beard had grown whiter during
production. Further episodes are
currently promised, but will our heroes
ever reach San Francisco? Here are Linda
Evans, Bruce Boxleitner and Kenny
Rogers during a refreshment halt.

Fessenden). American leading lady of the
fifties who made a good impression in several
series: *Decoy, Coronado 9, The Bing Crosby
Show, My Three Sons.*

Garland, Judy (1922–69) (Frances Gumm).
Celebrated American singer, the story of
whose tragic decline after a Hollywood star
career is well known. Her chief contribution
to TV is the CBS 50m series of 1964 (24
specials with guest stars), and the story of that
was well told by Mel Tormé in his book *The
Other Side of the Rainbow.*

Garland, Patrick (1936–). British
producer–director, mainly on stage. His
contributions to TV include *Famous Gossips,
Brief Lives, The Snow Goose.*

❋ **Garner, James** (1928–) (James
Baumgarner). Easy-going American leading
man who after a pretty good Hollywood
career scored several hits in the TV series
field: *Maverick, Nichols, The Rockford Files*
(Emmy 1976), *Bret Maverick.* TV movies: *The*

Long Summer of George Adams, Heartsounds, The Glitter Dome, Space.

✱ **Garnett, Tony** (1936–). British drama producer, formerly actor, of declared Marxist views and considerable ability: *Cathy Come Home, Days of Hope, The Gamekeeper*, etc. Last appearance as actor in Mercer's *Birth of a Private Man*, 1963.

Garrett, Betty (1919–). American light actress, widow of Larry Parks. She pleased in a few films then retired more or less until her appearance as a regular in *All in the Family, Laverne and Shirley*

Garrison's Gorillas ✱
US 1967 26 × 50m colour
ABC/Selmur

During World War II, the US Army recruits convicts for use in dangerous missions behind enemy lines.
The producer had obviously seen *The Dirty Dozen*, but the point really is that this is an exciting, explosive series of war yarns, and why it wasn't renewed is one of the mysteries of TV.

Ron Harper, Cesare Danova, Brendon Boone, Christopher Cary, Rudy Solari

Garroway, Dave (1913–). American host and commentator, one of the famous telly men of the fifties and the originator of NBC's *Today* programme.

Gascoigne, Bamber (1935–). Intellectual British quizmaster, with *University Challenge* since 1962. In 1977 he wrote and presented a serious 13-hour study of *The Christians*.

The Gate of Eden (GB 1980; 3 × 50m). Sensitive if rather uneventful trilogy for YTV by William Corlett about a grumpy old recluse (Maurice Denham) briefly befriended by a schoolboy (Richard Gibson). A fine ear for the small embarrassments of family life.
PP

'A man for whom time is running out . . . and for whom life saves the very best for last!'
The Gathering
US 1977 96m colour
Hanna–Barbera (Harry R. Sherman)

A man who knows he has only a few months to live seeks reconciliation with his family. Talky, sentimental, wholly artificial Christmas piece, with the invalid appearing perfectly healthy as usual.

w James Poe *d* Randal Kleiser *ph* Dennis Dalzell *m* John Barry

Ed Asner, Maureen Stapelton, Rebecca Balding, Bruce Davison, Sarah Cunningham

† Emmy 1977, best special.

The Gathering, Part Two
US 1979 96m colour TVM
NBC/Hanna–Barbera

Two years after the death of her husband, Kate Thornton is running his business successfully and gets an offer of marriage. Padded sequel to a success; doesn't stand on its own.

w Harry and Renee Longstreet *d* Charles S. Dubin

Maureen Stapelton, Efrem Zimbalist Jnr, Lawrence Pressman

The Gathering Seed
GB 1983 6 × 45m
BBC (Colin Tucker)

Family saga beginning amid the hardships, togetherness, cobbles and clogs of pre-war northern terraces but after the first episode moving on to the hopes and let-downs of the brave new world of 1945 and onwards. The initial freshness and fierceness wore off.

w Jim Allen *d* Tom Clegg

James Ellis, Paul Copley, Christine Hargreaves, David Threlfall   PP

The Gathering Storm: see Walk With Destiny

Gau, John (1940–). British current affairs and documentary producer who left the BBC to set up as an independent, eventually with his own production outfit. *Lifeboat* (BBC) and *The Living Body* (for Goldcrest/Multimedia), 1984; *Soldiers* for BBC, 1985, *Assignment Adventure* and *Acceptable Risk* for C4. Also all Labour Party Political broadcasts 1983–6.   PP

Gautier, Dick (1939–). American leading man with a comic bent. Series: *Here We Go Again, When Things Were Rotten*. TV movie: *Marathon*.

Gavin, Barrie (1935–). British music and arts producer, editor of *Omnibus* 1975–8, at BBC Bristol 1978–81, an independent since. Recent credits include *The Tenor Man's Story* for Central (Jim Berrow) and *Rattle on Britten* for BBC.   PP

Gavin, John (1928–). Tall, serious American leading man of the sixties. He was the lead in two unsuccessful TV series, *Convoy* and *Destry*. TV movies: *Cutter's Trail, Doctors' Private Lives, The New Adventures of Heidi, Sophia Loren* (as Cary Grant).

The Gay Cavalier (GB 1953). Half-hour swashbuckling series set in 17th-century France, with Christian Marquand. Produced for Associated Rediffusion.

JILL GASCOINE, a hit as the policewoman of *The Gentle Touch*, seemed all at sea when asked to share *C.A.T.S. Eyes* with Leslie Ash (left) and Rosalyn Landor. But a second series was ordered, so the ratings must have been acceptable.

Gazzara, Ben (1930–). Glowering American leading man who had a modest Hollywood career punctuated by TV series: *Arrest and Trial*, *Run for your Life*. TV movies include *When Michael Calls*, *Fireball Forward*, *The Family Rico*, *Pursuit*, *Maneater*, *QB VII*, *The Death of Richie*, *The Trial of Lee Harvey Oswald*, *A Question of Honor*, *An Early Frost*

G.E. College Bowl: see College Bowl

Geer, Will (1902–78). American character actor who ran into trouble with the Un-American Activities Committee but resurfaced in old age as a key character actor and star of *The Waltons* (Emmy 1974). TV movies include *The Brotherhood of the Bell*, *Sam Hill*, *Brock's Last Case*, *Savage*, *The Hanged Man*, *Honky Tonk*, *Hurricane*, *Law and Order*, *A Woman Called Moses*.

Geeson, Judy (1948–). British leading lady who in her continuing role in *Danger UXB* showed that she has finally left behind the teenage sexpot roles that made her so boring in the sixties.

Geisel, Theodore: see Doctor Seuss

Geisha
US 1985 96m colour TVM
CBS/Stonehenge/Interscope (Richard L. O'Connor)

A lady anthropologist conducts research in a Tokyo geisha house.
Glutinously sincere whitewash of a much-mythologized institution. Unfortunately the picture has no sense of humour . . . and not enough plot.

w Judith Paige Mitchell, *book* by Liza Dalby *d* Lee Phillips

Pam Dawber, Richard Narita, Stephanie Faracy, Robert Ito, Dorothy McGuire

Geller, Bruce (1929–78). American producer. Series include *Mission Impossible* and *Mannix*, both of which he also created.

Gemini Man
US 1976 74m colour TVM
NBC/Universal (Leslie Stevens)

Recasting of the failed *Invisible Man* series; not much better.

w Leslie Stevens *d* Alan Levi *m* Lee Holdridge

Ben Murphy, William Sylvester, Katherine Crawford

† A series of 13 episodes followed.

Gems (GB 1985; 56 × 28m). Daytime soap set among the young fashion boutiques of Covent Garden, with fashions by Royal College of Art students plus designers Louise Walker and Jeff Banks. With Steve Mann, Cornelius Garrett, Cindy O'Callaghan, Margo Cunningham. Created by Tessa Diamond who had done the same for *Emergency – Ward 10* 28 years earlier. Produced by Brenda Ennis for Thames.   PP

The Gene Autry Show
US 1950–3 85 × 25m bw
CBS/Flying A

The boss of the Melody Ranch is a stickler for range justice.

Anaemic western series with songs.

Gene Autry, Pat Buttram, Gail Davis, Champion the Wonder Horse

† Syndicated as *Gene Autry's Melody Ranch*.

Gene Kelly's Dancing Years: see An American in Pasadena

General Electric Theater (US 1953–61). Long-running one-hour drama anthology for CBS, mainly hosted by Ronald Reagan. The general aim was to entertain, and top stars were showcased.

General Hospital. This is the title of a soap opera in the US and in Britain.

The General's Day **
GB 1973 60m colour (VTR)
BBC (Irene Shubik)

An elderly general woos a timid schoolmistress, but she finds that he has had sexual liaisons with his charlady.

A subtle, entertaining and moving play enshrining most of its author's preoccupations; most lovingly produced and acted.

w WILLIAM TREVOR *d* John Gorrie

ALASTAIR SIM, Annette Crosbie, Dandy Nichols

'Wholly convincing, with a hundred lovely touches on the way.' – *The Times*

General Strike Report * (GB 1976; 10 × 15m; colour). Bright idea to mark the 50th anniversary of the General Strike with a nightly 'news' bulletin given by Robert Kee following the course of events as if TV had existed in 1926. Produced by Michael Deakin for YTV, with *Nationwide*-type contributions from other companies. Midway through I wrote: 'What is so valuable is the unexpectedly vivid detail which a day-by-day compilation affords, such as the pit ponies seeing the light of day for the first time. And because the regional contributions really are researched and volunteered locally, the format resists any attempt to impose an overall and possibly fallacious interpretation of the Strike; a brave, forlorn and misguided undertaking shambles by.'   PP

Generation
US 1985 96m colour TVM
ABC/Embassy (Gerald DiPego)

An American family celebrates the end of 1999.

Strained pilot which didn't sell . . . after all, the turn of the century is just one more day.

w Gerald DiPego *d* Michael Tuchner *ph* Robert E. Collins *m* Charles Bernstein *pd* William Sandell

Richard Beymer, Hannah Cutrona, Priscilla Pointer, Cristina Raines, Beah Richards

The Generation Game. An elaborately produced game show produced by BBC for a winter season every year through the seventies, with BRUCE FORSYTH replaced in 1978 by LARRY GRAYSON. Each pair of contestants had to be related and of different generations, and their tasks included acting out a wildly farcical sketch.

generic title. One which groups together a number of disparate programmes, e.g. 'Million Dollar Movie', 'Mystery Movie'. Also called 'umbrella title'.

Genesis II
US 1972 74m colour TVM
Warner (Gene Roddenberry)

A space scientist is buried alive in a sealed

container and awakes in the 21st century, when mankind is formed into two tribes at war with each other.

Unpersuasive sci-fi with one splendid but overused effect of a shuttle train. Two more pilots were made (*Planet Earth*, *Strange New World*) but the show never got on the road.

w Gene Roddenberry *d* John Llewellyn Moxey *ph* Gerald Finnermann *m* Harry Sukman

Alex Cord, Mariette Hartley, Percy Rodrigues, Harvey Jason, Ted Cassidy, Titos Vandis

Gentle Ben
US 1967–8 56 × 25m colour
CBS/Ivan Tors (George Sherman)

A boy makes friends with a huge wild bear. Agreeable family fare.

Dennis Weaver, Clint Howard

Gentle Folk * (GB 1980; 90m; colour). Gently intriguing goings-on at an English country house party on the eve of World War I, with Denholm Elliott playing a character much like H. G. Wells, and Christopher Strauli suffering a vision of the carnage to come. Play by Alexander Baron; directed on location video by Rodney Bennet; for BBC.
PP

The Gentle Touch (GB 1979–). British one-hour series about the private and career life of a London policewoman. Tolerable rather than distinctive. With Jill Gascoine, Leslie Schofield. Created by Brian Finch; produced by Tony Wharmby; for LWT.

'Only his parishioners believe that this gentle priest is innocent – but is that enough?'
The Gentleman Bandit
US 1981 96m colour TVM
CBS/Linda Gottlieb (John E. Quill)

A priest finds himself under arrest for a series of hold-ups.

Amplification of a Delaware case which hit the headlines.

w Milan Stitt *d* Jonathan Kaplan

Ralph Waite, Julie Bovasso, Jerry Zaks, Joe Grifasi, Estelle Parsons

The Gentleman Bandit *
US 1981 96m colour TVM
CBS/Highgate (Linda Gottlieb)

In Delaware, a priest is picked out of an identification parade when a persistent bandit is being sought.

Fairly interesting presentation of a true

incident (the priest was later acquitted) with the emphasis on character. On a TV movie budget, you can't quite make it.

w Milan Stitt *d* Jonathan Kaplan *ph* John Lindley *m* Stanley Myers

Ralph Waite, Estelle Parsons, Jerry Zaks, Joe Grifasi, Julie Bovasso

Gentry, Bobbie (1944–). American folk singer whose chief hit was 'Ode to Billy Joe', which she also wrote.

George and Mildred *
GB 1976–80 approx. 30 × 25m colour
Thames

Misadventures of the social climbing Mrs Roper and her layabout husband.

Quite funny but vaguely unsympathetic vehicle for the landlords of *A Man about the House*.

w Johnnie Mortimer, Brian Cooke
YOOTHA JOYCE, BRIAN MURPHY

The George Burns and Gracie Allen Show: see The Burns and Allen Show

George Burns Comedy Week (US 1985; 6 × 25m). Anthology of hopefully comic playlets, introduced by the aged comedian. The concept didn't last long. Produced by Steve Martin and Carl Gottlieb for Universal/CBS. (One of the episodes, *The Couch*, spawned another shortlived series called *Liz and Leo*.)

The George Burns Show (US 1958). Half-hour comedy series for NBC. George, without Gracie, played a theatrical producer and did a lot of talking to the audience. His son Ronnie also made regular appearances.

George, Christopher (1929–83). Dependable, tough-looking American leading actor, seen almost entirely on TV. Series: *The Rat Patrol*, *The Immortal*. TV movies include *The House on Greenapple Road*, *Escape*, *Dead Men Tell No Tales*, *Man on a String*, *The Heist*, *The Last Survivors*, *Mayday at 40,000 Feet*, *Cruise into Terror*.

George of the Jungle
US 1967–8 51 × 25m colour
ABC/Jay Ward

Adventures of an accident-prone Tarzan.

Moderately amusing cartoon series, including segments devoted to *Super Chicken* and *Tom Slick*.

The George Sanders Mystery Theatre
US 1957 × 25m bw
NBC/Columbia

Stereotyped mystery playlets, hosted by the occasional star.

George Washington
US 1984 4 × 96m colour
CBS/MGM/David Gerber (Buzz Kulik)

The early life and times of America's first president and his fight against the British. Sober, earnest, good-looking and boring, this expensive miniseries with its thousands of extras was a hit in the homeland but not abroad.

w Richard Fielder, Jon Boothe *d* Buzz Kulik *ph* Harry Stradling Jnr *m* Laurence Rosenthal *pd* Alfred Sweeney

Barry Bostwick, Jaclyn Smith, Patty Duke Astin, David Dukes, Lloyd Bridges, Jose Ferrer, Hal Holbrook, Trevor Howard, Jeremy Kemp, Richard Kiley, Stephen Macht, James Mason, Rosemary Murphy, Clive Revill, Robert Stack, Anthony Zerbe

'Turns out the colonies weren't all quaintness and powder-horn.' – *Daily Variety*

Georgia Peaches
US 1980 96m colour TVM
CBS/New World (Roger Corman)

Tennessee moonshiners get into trouble with a crime ring as well as the Treasury Department.

Woebegone imitation of *The Dukes of Hazzard*.

w Mike Benderoth, Monte Stettin, William Hjortsburg *d* Daniel Haller *ph* David Sanderson *m* R. Donovan Fox

Tanya Tucker, Terri Nunn, Lane Smith, Sally Kirkland, Dennis Patrick, David Hayward

Gerard, Gil (1943–). Cheerful American leading man who did much to enliven the series BUCK ROGERS. TV movies: *Ransom for Alice*, *Killing Stone*, *Storming Home*, *International Airport*.

Gerber, David (1925–). American independent producer, responsible for such series as *Nanny and the Professor*, *Cade's County*, POLICE STORY (Emmy 1976), *Police Woman*, *Born Free*, *The Quest*, GIBBSVILLE, *Beulah Land*, *Once Upon a Spy*, *Power*, *Terror among Us*, *Elvis and the Beauty Queen*, *Today's FBI*, *Seven Brides for Seven Brothers*, *For Love and Honor*, *George Washington*, *Jessie*, *Lady Blue*.

Germany. The third most important television producer and consumer after the USA and Britain, West Germany maintains two public-broadcast systems: ARD, a federation of independent regional stations, and ZDF, a national service based in Mainz. Advertising is restricted to set periods. Sport, politics, the arts and programmes about health are the staples. Drama is good but has always been mostly shot on film, either on location or in movie studios. There was little tradition of studio video drama, as thrived in Britain until the eighties. PP

The Gertrude Berg Show: see Mrs G Goes to College

Get Christie Love
US 1974 74m colour TVM
ABC/David Wolper

Adventures of a black undercover policewoman.

The mixture as before; it led to a one-season series.

w George Kirgo *d* William Graham *m* Jack Elliott, Allyn Ferguson

Teresa Graves, Harry Guardino, Louise Sorel, Paul Stevens

† The series which followed consisted of 22 × 50-minute films, also produced by Wolper and starring Teresa Graves and Charles Cioffi.

Get Set Go. Baffling game show, ex-US, in which Michael Barrymore presides over rival teams trying to hustle their nominated guesser into guessing the right word. BBC.
PP

Get Smart **
US 1965–9 138 × 25m colour
Talent Associates/Heyday/NBC (Arne Sultan)

Adventures of a bumbling spy.

Highly amusing comedy spoof which managed to keep up its impetus until its final season.

cr MEL BROOKS, BUCK HENRY

DON ADAMS, BARBARA FELDON, Edward Platt

† Catchphrase for Adams: 'Sorry about that.'

Get Some In
GB 1974–7 approx. 30 × 25m colour (VTR)
Thames (Michael Mills)

The exploits of national service RAF recruits in the fifties.

Variable comedy series.

w John Esmonde, Bob Larbey *d* Michael Mills Tony Selby

Get the Drift ** (GB 1971–7). Likeable north country entertainment by and with playwright Henry Livings and folk-singer Alex Glasgow for BBC, developed from an earlier format, *The Northern Drift*. I wrote at the time: 'Livings is sly and bearded and looks as if he is a friendly satyr sent along by the Co-op's catering department. Alex Glasgow is more your Reader in Folk-song and Left-wing Satire at a North-Eastern university. They tell rambling stories and sing jolly ballads and wind up every show with a yet woozier version of that little classic of the day, the pub revolutionaries' marching song.' PP

Getting Away from It All
US 1971 74m colour TVM
Palomar

Two middle-class, middle-aged couples sell up and seek the simple life.
Fairly amusing contemporary comedy.
d Lee Phillips
Barbara Feldon, Jim Backus, Larry Hagman

Getting Married
US 1978 96m colour TVM
Paramount/Moonlight (Frank Von Zerneck, Robert Greenwald)

A TV newsroom apprentice falls for the lady newscaster and after a strenuous campaign finally – and unconvincingly – wins her.
Silly comedy drama with annoying stereotyped characters and not enough plot to stay the course.
w John Hudock *d* Steven Hillard Stern *ph* Howard Schwartz *m* Craig Safan
Richard Thomas, Bess Armstrong, Dana Dietrich, Fabian, Van Johnson, Audra Lindley, Mark Harmon, Katherine Helmond
'A cute idea that spends a long time getting nowhere.' – *Daily Variety*

Getting Physical
US 1984 96m colour TVM
CBS/Marcy Gross, Ann Weston (Ron Roth)

Assaulted one night, an overweight girl takes a cop's advice to get in shape, and becomes obsessed by body-building.
Something of a spectacle when the women are doing their workouts, otherwise distinctly lacking in plot.
w Laurian Leggett *d* Steven Hillard Stern *ph* Isidore Mankofsky *m* William Goldstein
Alexandra Paul, Sandahl Bergman, David Naughton, John Aprea, Janet Carroll

Getting Together
US 1971 15 × 25m colour
ABC/Columbia (Bob Claver)

Two young songwriters who live in an antique store try to carve themselves a Hollywood career.
Ho-hum vehicle for ho-hum stars.
Bobby Sherman, Wes Stern, Pat Carroll, Jack Burns, Susan Beher

Getty, Estelle (1923–). American stage actress who scored a great hit in 1985 as the forthright octogenarian in *The Golden Girls*.

ghost. A double image on a TV set, usually caused by waves bouncing off a nearby tall building.

The Ghost and Mrs Muir *
US 1968–9 50 × 25m colour
NBC (later ABC)/TCF (David Gerber)

A widow finds that her new house is haunted by the friendly ghost of a sea captain.
Pleasing fantasy comedy based on the 1947 film.
cr Jean Holloway *p/d* Gene Reynolds *m* Dave Grusin
HOPE LANGE, EDWARD MULHARE, Charles Nelson Reilly, Reta Shaw

Ghost Busters
US 1975 17 × 25m colour (VTR)
Filmation (Norman Abbott)

Kong and Spencer, with a gorilla named Tracy, set up as ghost hunters and confront legendary monsters.
Cheapjack knockabout which makes Columbia two-reelers of the early thirties look like *Gone with the Wind*.
cr Mark Richards *d* Norman Abbott
Forrest Tucker, Larry Storch, Bob Burns

'For Sarah Bowman, there could be no compromise!'
Ghost Dancing *
US 1983 96m colour TVM
ABC/Herbert Brodkin (Robert Berger)

The widow of a farmer takes violent action to prevent the Water and Power Department from encroaching on her land.
Reasonably engrossing story of a rather stupid woman; always good-looking and with the advantage, rare in TV movies, of an undoubted star performance.
w Phil Penningroth *d* David Greene *ph* Brian West *m* John Morris
DOROTHY MCGUIRE, Bruce Davison, Bill Erwin, Richard Farnsworth, Wings Hauser
'Shows that telefilms with something to say can be a dramatic success.' – *Daily Variety*

WINNER OF THE
1982 'ABC THEATRE AWARD'
FOR THE
BEST ORIGINAL SCRIPT
AT THE
EUGENE O'NEILL
NATIONAL PLAYWRIGHTS
CONFERENCE.

GHOST DANCING

For Sarah Bowman,
there could be no compromise.

Starring
DOROTHY McGUIRE
BO HOPKINS
BRUCE DAVISON
RICHARD FARNSWORTH

Written by PHIL PENNINGROTH
Directed by DAVID GREENE

ABC THEATRE PRESENTATION

9:00 PM 7 8

GHOST DANCING. One of America's occasional 'prestige' TV movies for which older actors who can normally get no work are lured back from retirement and then forgotten again.

The Ghost of Flight 401
US 1978 96m colour TVM
NBC/Paramount (Emmet Lavery)

When a passenger plane crashes, the ghost of the captain is subsequently seen on other planes in the area.
Flat transcription of an allegedly true story.

w Robert Malcolm Young, *book* John Fuller
d Steven Stern, Bob Rosenbaum

Ernest Borgnine, Gary Lockwood, Kim Basinger, Robert F. Lyons

Ghost Story
US 1972 24 × 50m colour
Columbia (William Castle)

An anthology of modern ghost stories, mostly too long or too silly. The title was changed at mid-season to *Circle of Fear*, the host disappeared, and the themes were not necessarily supernatural.

host Sebastian Cabot

A Ghost Story for Christmas. The BBC's generic title for a series of adaptations which appeared from 1971 within the octave of Christmas, all directed by Laurence Gordon Clark. 1971, *The Stalls of Barchester Cathedral* by M. R. James; 1972, *A Warning to the Curious* by M. R. James; 1973, *Lost Hearts* by M. R. James; 1974, *The Treasure of Abbot Thomas* by M. R. James; 1975, *The Ash Tree* by M. R. James; 1976, *The Signalman* by Charles Dickens; 1977, *Schalcken the Painter* (*w/d* Leslie Megahey from a story by Sheridan Le Fanu).

The Ghost Writer
US 1984 74m colour TVM
WGBH Boston/Malone Gill/BBC (Peter B. Cook) for American Playhouse

A novelist visits a famous writer who has become a recluse.
Modest, offhand anecdote with something for Jewish audiences but not much for others.

w Tristam Powell, Philip Roth, from Roth's story   d Tristam Powell   ph Kenneth MacMillan   m George Fenton

Rose Arrick, Claire Bloom, Macintyre Dixon, Mark Linn-Baker, Joseph Wiseman, Paulette Smit, Hope Lonoff

The Ghosts of Motley Hall *
GB 1976–7 20 × 25m colour (VTR)
Granada

The ghosts of a stately home resent intruders.
Lively comedy with effective trick work and a host of amusing characterizations.

Freddie Jones, Arthur English, Sheila Steafel

Gibbsville (TV movie): see The Turning Point of Jim Malloy

Gibbsville **
US 1976 13 × 50m colour
NBC/Columbia/David Gerber (John Furia Jnr)

Stories of a Pennsylvania mining town in the forties, based on John O'Hara's short stories and following on from the pilot film *The Turning Point of Jim Malloy*. The stories are seen through the eyes of two journalists.

cr Frank D. Gilroy   m Leonard Rosenman

John Savage, Gig Young, Biff McGuire, Peggy McKay

'A series that makes the commonplace a most exciting place.' – promotion

Gibson, Brian (19 –). British director, reaching drama and feature films by way of science documentaries for *Horizon*, including the memorable *Hospital 1922* (1972), *Joey* (1974), and *Billion Dollar Bubble* (1976), a very funny reconstruction (script Tom Clarke) of a gigantic computer swindle in the United States. Later Gibson productions include two Dennis Potter plays and *Gossip from the Forest* (1979).   PP

Gideon's Way *
GB 1964 26 × 50m bw
ATV (Robert S. Baker, Monty Berman)

Cases of a CID police inspector in London.
Standard cop show, efficient in all departments.

John Gregson, Alexander Davion, Daphne Anderson

Gidget
US 1965 32 × 25m colour
ABC/Columbia

Exploits of a California teenage girl with a passion for surfing.
Moderate domestic comedy for and with the empty-headed.

Sally Field, Don Porter

Gidget Gets Married
US 1971 73m colour TVM
Columbia (E. W. Swackhamer)

She was bad enough as a teenager, but the cast helps.

w John McGreevey   d E. W. Swackhamer

Macdonald Carey, Paul Lynde, Don Ameche, Joan Bennett, Michael Burns, Monie Ellis

Gidget Grows Up
US 1969 74m colour TVM
Columbia (Jerome Courtland)

See above.

w John McGreevey *d* James Sheldon

Karen Valentine, Robert Cummings, Edward Mulhare, Paul Lynde, Nina Foch, Warner Anderson

Gidget's Summer Reunion
US 1985 96m colour TVM
Columbia (syndication)/Ackerman Riskin

The teenage poppet is now a married woman running her own travel agency. With her marriage in trouble, she heads for Hawaii and finds love . . .

A beach party picture in which all the adolescents have grown up. Sticky.

w George Zatesio *d* Bruce Bilson

Caryn Richman, Dean Butler, Don Stroud, Anne Lockhart, Ben Murphy

Gielgud, Sir John (1904–). Distinguished British stage actor who took to films in his fifties and is not too choosy about his recent parts, though always a pleasure to watch. TV movies include *Probe, Frankenstein: The True Story, QB VII* and *Les Misérables*; he also played Sir Henry in *The Picture of Dorian Gray*, was in several Shakespeares, presented *The English Garden* and decorated LWT's two Agatha Christie thrillers. His stage performances in *Home* and *No Man's Land* were both recorded. 1981: *Brideshead Revisited*.

Gifford, Denis (1927–). British film buff and compiler of Thames's nostalgia series *Looks Familiar*.

The Gift of Laughter *
US 1981 130m approx. colour
MCA/Jack Haley Jnr

A film industry charity salute to the Los Angeles bicentennial. Carol Burnett, Dom DeLuise, Walter Matthau, Richard Pryor, Burt Reynolds and Jack Lemmon introduce clips from various eras of film comedy.

The Gift of Life
US 1984 96m colour TVM
CBS/Lawrence Turman, David Foster (Jerry London)

A family-oriented wife agrees to have a child for a couple unable to have children themselves.

Barely dramatized social issues tend to clog this movie after the first half-hour.

w Mike Robe *d* Jerry London

Susan Dey, Paul Le Mat, Cassie Yates, Edward Herrmann

'A poor little rich girl discovers the most wonderful gift of all!'

The Gift of Love
US 1978 96m colour TVM
NBC/Osmond (Mitchell Brower)

A penniless immigrant in old New York sells his watch to buy his wife combs for her hair, not knowing that she has sold her tresses to buy him a watch-chain.

Insanely extended version of O. Henry's short short story. Any interest has evaporated long before the punch line.

w Caryl Ledner *d* Don Chaffey *ph* Charles F. Wheeler *m* Fred Karlin

Marie Osmond, Timothy Bottoms, Bethel Leslie, June Lockhart, David Wayne

The Gift of Love: a Christmas Story
US 1983 96m colour TVM
CBS/Telecom/Amanda (Earl Hamner)

A middle-aged woman finds that her life is in pieces when her mother suddenly dies and her children seem about to go to the bad.

A bundle of rustic misery presented in a sentimental glow as a Christmas special. Those who like such things will probably love it.

w Earl Hamner, *story* by Bess Streeter Aldrich *d* Delbert Mann *ph* Larry Pizer *m* Fred Karlin

Lee Remick, Angela Lansbury, Polly Holliday, Joseph Warren, Mart Hulswit, Michael Pearlman

'Taking aim at the heart, it gets deflected on a soft shoulder.' – *Daily Variety*

Gilbert, James (*c* 1926–). British light entertainment producer whose outstanding shows have included *It's a Square World, Frost Over England, Not Only But Also, The Two Ronnies, Whatever Happened to the Likely Lads?, Last of the Summer Wine*.

Gillard, Frank (1908–). BBC radio executive who had second career on retirement as supplier of a voice-over much in demand – warm, educated but unstuffy. *Hospital 1922, The Commanders*, etc.   PP

Gillies, Jacques (19 –). British author of superior television thrillers in the sixties, mostly for ATV and directed by Quentin Lawrence. *The Gold Inside, The Takers, The Diamond Run*, etc.   PP

Gilligan's Island *
US 1964–6 98 × 25m bw (30 in colour)
CBS/Gladasaya/UA

Rich vacationers are marooned on an uninhabited island.

A surprisingly effective collection of old sight gags, mostly borrowed from Buster Keaton and Laurel and Hardy.

Jim Backus, Bob Denver, Natalie Schaefer, Alan Hale Jnr, Tina Louise

† A cartoon series, *The New Adventures of Gilligan*, was produced by Filmation in 1974, and a new live action pilot, *Return to Gilligan's Island*, appeared in 1978.

Gilmore, Peter (1931–). British leading man chiefly seen in *The Onedin Line*.

Gimme a Break (US 1981). Half-hour comedy series on tape, starring Dolph Sweet as a widowed policeman who has trouble with his sassy black housekeeper (Nell Carter). The style and the gags go all the way back to *Beulah*. Produced by Mort Lachman for Alan Landsburg/NBC.

'The world gave her hell! Now she's giving it back!'
The Girl Called Hatter Fox
US 1977 96m colour TVM
CBS/EMI (Roger Gimbel/George Schaefer)

A doctor in New Mexico rehabilitates a rebellious Indian teenager.
Powerful scenes in *Miracle Worker* vein don't quite atone for an aimless and overlong script.

w Darryl Ponicsan, *book* Marilyn Harris *d* George Schaefer *ph* Howard Schwarz *m* Fred Karlin

Ronny Cox, Joanelle Romero, Conchata Ferrell, Donald Hotten

The Girl from UNCLE
US 1966 29 × 50m colour
NBC/MGM/Arena (Norman Felton)

Insipid follow-on from *The Man from UNCLE*, which wasn't all that strong in the first place.

m Dave Grusin

Stefanie Powers, Noel Harrison, Leo G. Carroll

The Girl in the Empty Grave
US 1977 96m colour TVM
NBC/MGM/Richard O. Linke

Another case for the sheriff of Eagle Lake. And another failed attempt to get *Winter Kill/Adams of Eagle Lake* into a series.

w Lane Slate *d* Lou Antonio

Andy Griffith, Sharon Spellman, Hunter von Leer, Edward Winter

The Girl Most Likely To
US 1973 74m colour TVM
ABC Circle

An ugly college girl tries plastic surgery. Rather tasteless comedy with obvious situations.

w Joan Rivers, Agnes Gallin, *novel* Joan Rivers *d* Lee Phillips

Stockard Channing, Ed Asner, Warren Berlinger, Jim Backus, Joe Flynn

A Girl Named Sooner
US 1974 100m colour TVM
TCF

A hillbilly orphan girl inspires the devotion of an unhappy vet.
Slow-moving drama.

w Suzanne Clauser, from her novel *d* Delbert Mann

Cloris Leachman, Richard Crenna, Lee Remick, Don Murray, Susan Deer, Anne Francis

The Girl on the Late Late Show
US 1974 74m colour TVM
Columbia

A talk show executive tracks down a mysterious silent film star, and uncovers a guilty secret.
Patchy mystery drama with a muddled plot and too many stops for guest cameos.

w Mark Rodgers *d* Gary Nelson

Don Murray, Laraine Stephens, Gloria Grahame, Walter Pidgeon, Yvonne de Carlo, Van Johnson, Cameron Mitchell, John Ireland

Girl on the Run
US 1958 77m bw TVM
Warner (William T. Orr, Roy Huggins)

A hired killer menaces a beautiful nightclub singer.
The pilot for *77 Sunset Strip*, with Edd Byrnes, later a regular, playing a crazed killer.

w Marion Hargrove *d* Richard L. Bare

Efrem Zimbalist Jnr, Edd Byrnes, Erin O'Brien, Shepperd Strudwick, Barton MacLane, Vince Barnett

The Girl, the Gold Watch and Dynamite
US 1981 96m colour TVM
Operation Prime Time/Fellows–Keegan/ Paramount

The man with the magic watch prevents a flood and a land takeover.
Dim sequel to the following; grimly unfunny.

w George Zateslo *d* Hy Averback *ph* Bill Jurgenson *m* Bruce Broughton

Lee Purcell, Philip MacHale, Burton Gilliam, Zohra Lampert, Gene Barry, Jack Elam, Morgan Fairchild, Gary Lockwood, Tom Poston

The Girl, the Gold Watch and Everything
US 1980 96m colour TVM
Operation Prime Time/Fellows–Keegan/
Paramount

A young man invents a watch which can stop time and thwart evildoers.
Wet little fantasy designed for alternative viewing in half-hour segments. Either way, a bore.

w George Zateslo, *novel* John D. McDonald *d* William Wiard

Robert Hays, Pam Dawber, Jill Ireland, Ed Nelson, Macdonald Carey, Zohra Lampert, Maurice Evans

The Girl Who Came Gift-Wrapped
US 1974 74m colour TVM
Spelling–Goldberg

A publisher who has everything is given a beautiful girl for his birthday.
Empty-headed nonsense.

w Susan Silver *d* Bruce Bilson

Richard Long, Karen Valentine, Louise Sorel, Reta Shaw, Dave Madden, Tom Bosley

The Girl With Something Extra
US 1973 22 × 25m colour
NBC/Columbia/Bob Claver (Larry Rosen)

A young wife has psychic powers.
Feeble offering by producers looking for another *Bewitched.*

cr Bernard Slade

Sally Field, John Davidson, Zohra Lampert, Jack Sheldon

The Girls (US 1950). Half-hour comedy series for CBS, based on *Our Hearts Were Young and Gay,* the memoirs of Cornelia Otis Skinner and Emily Kimbrough. With Bethel Leslie/Gloria Stroock and Mary Malone. Originally called *Young and Gay.*

The Girls in the Office
US 1980 96m colour TVM
ABC Circle (Barry Oringer)

Four women are involved in different ways in the opening of a Houston department store.
Fair glossy fun aimed at a middle-class audience.

w Richard Danus *d* Ted Post *ph* Andrew Kostikyan *m* John Parker

Susan Saint James, Barbara Eden, Tony Roberts, David Wayne, Robyn Douglass, Penny Peyser, Joe Penny, Jonathan Goldsmith
'At best it's hammock TV.' – *Daily Variety*

The Girls of Huntington House *
US 1973 73m colour TVM
Lorimar (Robert L. Jacks)

Problems at a school for unwed mothers.
Well acted soaper.

w Blossom Elfman, from her novel *d* Alf Kjellin

Shirley Jones, Mercedes McCambridge, Sissy Spacek, William Windom

Girls of the White Orchid
US 1983 96m colour TVM
NBC/Hill–Mandelker (Claude Binyon Jnr)

A Tokyo nightclub enslaves American girls.
Dreary ragbag of old 'forbidden' clichés stolen from *The Shanghai Gesture.* Risible rather than provocative.

w Carole and Michael Raschella *d* Jonathan Kaplan *ph* John Lindley *m* Brad Fiedel

Jennifer Jason-Leigh, Thomas Byrd, Mako, Carolyn Seymour, Richard Narita, Soon-Tech Oh, Ann Jillian
'Gives the profession a bad name.' – *Daily Variety*

Girls on Top (GB 1985; 7 × 28m). Fairly desperate new-wave sitcom misusing Tracey Ullman, Dawn French, Jennifer Saunders and Ruby Wax as outlandish upstairs lodgers in a house owned by Joan Greenwood below. Written by Dawn French and Jennifer Saunders, produced and directed by Paul Jackson, for Central.   PP

Give 'Em Hell Harry
US 1975 102m colour

A recording of James Whitmore's much-acclaimed stage presentation of incidents in the life of Harry S. Truman.

Glaser, Paul Michael (1943–). American general purpose actor who shot to fame as the first half of STARSKY AND HUTCH, but was subsequently little heard from.

The Glass House *
US 1971 73m colour TVM
CBS/Tomorrow

Tensions mount between the inmates of a state prison.
Good acting, routine plot.

w Tracy Keenan Wynn, *story* Truman Capote *d* Tom Gries

Alan Alda, Vic Morrow, Clu Gulager, Billy Dee Williams, Dean Jagger, Kristoffer Tabori

The Glass Menagerie
US 1973 110m approx. colour TVM
David Susskind

A reclusive girl in old New Orleans admits her first gentleman caller.

Tiresome revamp of the famous play, with the star miscast as the awful mum.

w Tennessee Williams d Anthony Harvey m John Barry

Katharine Hepburn, Sam Waterston, Michael Moriarty (Emmy award), Joanna Miles

❊   **Gleason, Jackie** (1916–). Rotund American comic who after 1949 exposure in *Life with Riley* came to notice as star of *The Honeymooners*. Success subsequently went somewhat to his head, but after sundry Hollywood experiences he returned to TV as host of many variety specials.

Glencannon
GB 1958 39 × 25m bw
Gross-Krasne

Adventures of an old seafaring man.
Talkative, studio-bound comedies.

Thomas Mitchell

Gless, Sharon (1943–). American leading lady. TV movies include *All My Darling Daughters*, *Switch*, *The Islander*, *Centennial*, *Crash*, *The Immigrants*, *The Last Convertible*, *Hardhat and Legs*, *Moviola*, *Revenge of the Stepford Wives*, *The Miracle of Kathy Miller*, *Cagney and Lacey*, *Hobson's Choice*, *The Sky's the Limit*.

The Glitter Dome
US 1984 96m colour TVM
HBO/Telepictures/Trincomali (Frank Konigsberg)

Hollywood cops solve the murder of a movie mogul.
Moderately rough-textured cable movie, quite entertaining in an unremarkable way

w Stanley Kallis, *novel* by Joseph Wambaugh d Stuart Margolin ph Michael Watkins m Stuart Margolin

James Garner, John Lithgow, Margot Kidder, Colleen Dewhurst, John Marley, Stuart Margolin

† The title refers to a local bar used by the cops.

The Glittering Prizes ∗∗
GB 1976 6 × 75m colour (VTR)
BBC (Mark Shivas)

The lives of a group of people who met as undergraduates at Cambridge in the fifties.
A British equivalent of *The Group*, and almost as biting an indictment of its generation, with many scenes of great interest even though it comes to no especial conclusion.

w FREDERIC RAPHAEL d Waris Hussein, Robert Knights

TOM CONTI, Barbara Kellerman, Leonard Sachs, Angela Down, Malcolm Stoddart, Eric Porter, Dinsdale Landen

'The unmistakable feel of quality, as of rich cloth being taken between the fingers.' – *Daily Telegraph*

Globe Theatre (GB 1974). Umbrella title used by BBC for a series of foreign TV play productions, of which the most interesting were a very Germanic mock-documentary from West Germany, *Smog*, and a very Swedish social lament from Sweden, *Little Man Lasse*. A second season in 1978 included the West German *Interrogation of Machiavelli*. PP

† The title was revived in 1982 for a season including a clever Japanese whodunit, *Amaghi*, and again in 1986.

Gloria
US 1982 22 × 25m colour
CBS/Embassy

Archie Bunker's daughter becomes an assistant country vet.
No real relation to the *Bunker* series, just a mild comedy about animals and human eccentrics.

cr Dan Guntzleman, Steve Marshall

Sally Strothers, Burgess Meredith, Christian Jacobs, Jo DeWinter

The Glory Boys
GB/US 1984
YTV/Alan Landsburg Productions (Michael Glyn)

IRA thug and Arab terrorist join forces to assassinate Israeli scientist visiting London: from the line that produced *Harry's War*, it was strangely low in human interest or credibility, with the two assassins boringly contrasted in their fanaticism and their opponents lunatically miscast. The supposedly down-at-heel, insignificant British security agent was played by Anthony Perkins, his girl friend, an 'unattractive, dull little secretary', by Joanna Lumley who, as I said at the time, could be about as dull as a diamond. 'As for the target – well, he was intelligently played by Rod Steiger, but the only interesting thing about a target is whether it will be hit, and where.'

w Gerald Seymour, from his novel d Michael Ferguson

Alfred Burke, Gary Brown, Aaron Harris
PP

GIVE US A CLUE as a game was nothing more than charades, but the enthusiasm of team leaders Una Stubbs and Lionel Blair kept it in the Top Ten for several years. When Michael Aspel retired as chairman Michael Parkinson (centre) came in, but tended to look as though wishing himself elsewhere.

The Glums (GB 1979). Characters from a radio show of the fifties, *Take It From Here*, resurfaced in *Bruce Forsyth's Big Night* and were unwisely given their own series. They were funnier when unseen. Jimmy Edwards (in his old part), Patricia Brake (formerly Joy Nichols/June Whitfield), Ian Lavender (formerly Dick Bentley) played the blustering father, the prospective daughter-in-law, and the dimwitted son. Written by Frank Muir and Denis Norden; for LWT.

Glynis
US 1963 13 × 25m bw
CBS/Desilu (Jess Oppenheimer)

A lawyer's wife writes detective stories. Thin vehicle which didn't sustain.

Glynis Johns, Keith Andes

Go Ask Alice *
US 1973 74m colour TVM
Metromedia (Gerald I. Isenberg)

The diary of a teenage drug addict from a good family.

If we have to go through all this again, it's well done.

w Ellen Violett, from anonymous book *d* John Korty

William Shatner, Julie Adams, Andy Griffith, Jamie Smith Jackson, Ruth Roman, Wendell Burton

Go Go Gophers
US 1968 24 × 25m colour
CBS/Total TV/Leonardo

The adventures of two accident-prone Indians trying to keep the white man out of the west.

Uninspired cartoon series.

Go West Young Girl *
US 1978 74m colour TVM
Columbia/Harve Bennett, Harris Katleman
  (George Yanok)

In 1886 Arizona a newspaperwoman and an attractive widow are in search of Billy the Kid.
Amusing pilot for a comedy western.
w George Yanok *d* Alan J. Levi *ph* Gerald Perry Finnermann *m* Jerrold Immel
Karen Valentine, Sandra Will, Michael Bell, Cal Bellini, David Dukes, Charles Frank, Stuart Whitman, Richard Jaeckel

Gobel, George (1919–). Diffident American comic who caused a mild flutter in the fifties but was subsequently little heard from until *Harper Valley PTA* in 1980. Emmy 1953: most outstanding new personality. TV movie: *Better Late Than Never*.
† Catchphrase: 'Well, I'll be a dirty bird!'

God-in-a-Box (GB 1984). A religious TV programme about religious TV, presented by the Rev. Colin Morris, BBC head of religious broadcasting; but better known now as the title of the book on the same subject Morris published later the same year (Hodder), in which he urged a return to story-telling (as in the Bible) as the best means of spreading the word.   PP

God Rot Tunbridge Wells! ★★
GB 1985 120m
Ladbroke Productions/C4 (Tony Palmer)
George Frideric Handel grumbles and gossips his way through memories of his life and works as he prepares for bed after a dispiriting performance of *Messiah* in that Kentish borough a few days before his death. In style midway between the usual Tony Palmer extravaganza and the monologue of Roy Dotrice's *Brief Lives*, with 'Trevor Howard's bull-like stance, thin bristle of hair and features carved out by ancient glaciers,' I thought it one of the strongest and fullest likenesses of a great composer. Music-lovers disagreed.
w John Osborne *d* Tony Palmer   PP
LH: 'I disagreed too: it seemed totally over the top.'

God slot. In Britain, an offhand term for the 'Sunday break' or closed period, when religious or inspirational programmes must be shown.

The Godchild
US 1974 74m colour TVM
MGM/Mor/Alan Neuman
Three outlaws care for a baby whose mother has died.
Three Godfathers all over again; enough was enough.

w Ron Bishop *d* John Badham
Jack Palance, Jack Warden, Keith Carradine, Ed Lauter, Jose Perez

Goddard, Jim (19 –). Reliable British drama director (*Out*, 1978, etc.) who had the ill-luck to be taken up by the cinéaste clique of the British Film Institute but survived same to continue turning out reliable series such as *Kennedy* (1983).   PP

Goddard, Liza (1950–). British leading lady, often in slightly fey comedy. Series include *Yes Honestly*, *Pig in the Middle*.

Goddard, Willoughby (1932–). Corpulent British character actor. Series include *William Tell*, *The Mind of J. G. Reeder*.

The Godfather. When this film was transmitted on American TV in 1977 it was in a 10-hour version incorporating not only both released parts but an hour of footage previously edited out and now ploughed back by Francis Ford Coppola, who also spent months reshaping his massive TV movie to fit the requirements of commercial breaks.

Godfrey, Arthur (1903–83). One of America's first TV personalities, usually as host or talent scout.

Goff, Ivan (1910–). Australian writer in Hollywood, often in partnership with Ben Roberts. Series include *The Rogues*, *Burke's Law*, *Charlie's Angels*.

Going for a Song (GB 1968). Simple antiques quiz from BBC West modelled on old *Animal, Vegetable, Mineral?* which quickly became a national favourite and launched ARTHUR NEGUS as a personality.   PP

Going for the Gold
US 1985 96m colour TVM
CBS/ITC/Goodman Rosen (Dennis A. Brown)
The unusual story of top international skier Bill Johnson, who began as a car thief.
Unusual but not interesting, apart from the skiing sequences.
w Maxwell Pitt *d* Don Taylor *ph* Cristiano Pogany, Robert Jessup *m* J. A. C. Redford
Anthony Edwards, Sarah Jessica Parker, Deborah Van Valkenburgh, Wayne Northrop, Dennis Weaver, Ed Bishop

Going Gently ★★
GB 1981 75m colour
BBC (Innes Lloyd)

Two cancer patients bicker as both approach the end, which may not sound bewitching entertainment but becomes a sardonic and eventually very moving play as the disreputable one of the pair imparts to his stuffier room-mate the secret of acceptance.

w Thomas Ellice, *novel* Robert C. S. Downs *d* Stephen Frears

FULTON MACKAY, NORMAN WISDOM, Judi Dench   PP

Going My Way
US 1962 39 × 50m bw
ABC/Universal

Father O'Malley comes to a difficult New York parish.
Amiable retread of a favourite movie.

Gene Kelly, Leo G. Carroll, Dick York, Nydia Westman

Going Straight *
GB 1978 6 × 30m colour (VTR)
BBC (Sydney Lotterby)

Fletcher gets out of jail but finds that life on the outside is hard.
Disappointing sequel to *Porridge*, with funny lines but too many old situations.

w Dick Clement, Ian La Frenais

Ronnie Barker, Richard Beckinsale, Patricia Brake

The Going Up of David Lev
US 1971 74m colour TVM (16mm)
Hallmark

A boy learns how his father, a Jewish American, died in the Six Day War.
Modest Israeli adventure drama.

w Ernest Kinoy, Ephraim Kishon *d* James F. Collier

Topol, Claire Bloom, Melvyn Douglas, Brandon Cruz

Gold, Jack (1930–). British director who has excelled at every kind of television, starting with shorts for the old early-evening *Tonight*, but luckily for television has never scored so highly with features. *Death in the Morning* (with Alan Whicker), *Call the Gun Expert* (series), 1964; *The Lump*, 1967; *Faith and Henry*, 1969; *Stockers Copper*, 1972; *The Naked Civil Servant*, 1975; *The Sailor's Return*, *The Merchant of Venice*, 1980; *Praying Mantis*, 1982; *Red Monarch*, 1983; *Murrow*, 1985.

'A mysterious death sends two explorers on a deadly race for the legendary gold of El Dorado!'
Gold of the Amazon Women
US 1979 96m colour TVM
NBC/Mi-Ka (Stanley Ralph Ross)

Primitive statuesque women from the Amazon jungle follow their captors back to New York.
Arrant nonsense vaguely reminiscent of *King Kong*, though somewhat less entertaining.

w Sue Donen *d* Mark L. Lester *ph* David Quaid *m* Gil Melle

Anita Ekberg, Bo Svenson, Donald Pleasence, Richard Romanuz, Robert Minor

The Goldbergs. This comedy series about a Bronx Jewish family dates from the era of live TV, but in 1956 Gertrude Berg filmed 39 half-hours in which the family moved to the suburbs. Robert H. Harris played Jake.

Goldcrest. British independent production company with plentiful backing whose television wing under Mike Wooller provided much of C4's classy filmed drama in its first three years, including the First Love films and *Concealed Enemies*. Also *Robin of Sherwood* with HTV for the main ITV network, and the documentary series *The Living Body*. With financial troubles and takeovers in 1985 production was cut back and Wooller moved on.   PP

The Golden Age of Television (US 1981). An admirable series of representations, with interview and comment, of classic television dramas of the fifties, including Rod Serling's *Requiem for a Heavyweight* (1956, 88m) with Jack Palance, Kim Hunter, Ed Wynn; Paddy Chayevsky's *Marty* (1953, approx. 90m) with Rod Steiger, Nancy Marchand; Arnold Schulman's *Bang the Drum Slowly* (1956, 59m) with Paul Newman, George Peppard; J. P. Miller's *Days of Wine and Roses* (1957, 88m) with Cliff Robertson and Piper Laurie; Rod Serling's *The Comedian* (1957, 88m) with Mickey Rooney, Edmond O'Brien; Ibsen's *A Doll's House* (1959, 88m) with Julie Harris, Christopher Plummer, Jason Robards Jnr; Ira Levin's *No Time for Sergeants* (1955, 59m) with Andy Griffith. Distributed by Enter-Tel, Inc.

Golden Gate
US 1981 96m colour TVM
ABC/Warner/Lin Bolen Productions

A widow tries to keep a San Francisco newspaper going.
Not a bad attempt at a new *Dallas*-style series; alas, it never got further than the pilot.

w Stirling Silliphant *d* Paul Wendkos *ph* Isidore Mankofsky *m* Ralph Burns

Jean Simmons, Richard Kiley

'All-stops-out meller overplays its hand to the point of the absurd.' – *Daily Variety*

GOD'S WONDERFUL RAILWAY. A documentary about the GWR could scarcely have had a more appropriate host than Christopher Hughes, who was an underground train driver before he won Mastermind.

The Golden Gate Murders
US 1979 96m colour TVM
CBS/Universal (Carl Foreman)

A nun and a cop solve a series of strange murders in San Francisco.
Tolerably intriguing mystery with an implausible outcome.

w David J. Kinghorn *d* Walter Grauman *ph*
Jack Swain *m* Sol Kaplan

David Janssen, Susannah York, Lloyd
Bochner, Ken Tigor, Tim O'Connor, Alan
Fudge, Kim Hunter

'Religious aspects range from silly to
offensive in whodunit that delivers little if
any tension.' – *Daily Variety*

The Golden Girls **
US 1985   × 25m colour
NBC/Walt Disney/Witt–Thomas–Harris

Three women on the wrong side of fifty
share a Miami apartment with the sassy
mother of one of them.
A feast of one-liners as only these actresses
can deliver them, and rather surprisingly one
of the few genuine commercial hits of the
season.

cr SUSAN HARRIS

BEATRICE ARTHUR, RUE MCCLANAHAN,
BETTY WHITE, ESTELLE GETTY

'A shoo-in for viewers longing to laugh till it
hurts.' – *Daily Variety*
'Viewers from 16 to 60 should share a good
laugh.' – Hollywood *Reporter*

The Golden Land (GB 1983; 3 × 50m).
The Jews in the United States: success
stories (Tony Curtis, Sonia Mitchelson) and
other stories tracked down by Desmond
Wilcox. Produced by Colin Shindler, for
BBC.

Golden Moment
US 1980 2 × 96m colour
NBC/Don Ohlmeyer/Telepictures

At the Moscow Olympics, an American
footballer falls for a Russian girl athlete.
Or at least, he might have if the Americans
hadn't pulled out of Moscow because of
Afghanistan; the political move left this
miniseries with egg on its face. In its own
right it's a slow-moving sentimental wallow,
often indistinguishable from the intervening
soap commercials.

w David E. Peckinpah *d* Richard C.
Sarafian *ph* Stephen H. Burum *m* Perry
Botkin Jnr

Stephanie Zimbalist, David Keith, Richard
Lawson, Victor French, Merlin Olsen, Ed
McMahon, Salome Jens, O. J. Simpson,
Jack Palance, Nancy Marchand, James Earl
Jones

The Golden Shot. A popular British quiz
show which ran on ATV from 1967 to 1975:
contestants earned the right to answer

questions by shooting bolts at moving targets
from an elaborate rifle machine. Bob
Monkhouse was the most prevalent host.

The Golden Vision (GB 1968; 75m; bw).
One of the surprisingly few TV plays about
professional football and the spell it casts over
its fans – here in pre-rowdy days. Written by
Neville Smith and the newscaster Gordon
Honeycombe, with Ken Jones. Directed by
Ken Loach; produced by Tony Garnett; for
BBC.   PP

Goldenberg, Billy (1936–). American
composer whose TV themes include *Kojak*,
Rhoda, *Banacek*, *Columbo*, *Delvecchio*.

Goldengirl
US 1979 2 × 96m colour miniseries
NBC/Viacom/Goldengirl Inc (Danny
   O'Donovan)

A six-foot-two blonde bombshell is backed
by a consortium to make a splash in the
Olympics.
Overwrought sports melodrama which goes
on too long.

w John Kohn, *book* by Peter Lear *d* Joseph
Sargent

Susan Anton, James Coburn, Robert Culp,
Harry Guardino, Leslie Caron, Curt
Jurgens, Jessica Walter, James A. Watson
Jnr, Michael Lerner

'It took his wife and sons to show him
   that there was more than one way to
   become a man.'
Goldenrod *
US/Canada 1977 96m colour TVM
David Susskind/Film Funding (Lionel
   Chetwynd, Gerry Arbeid)

Problems of a rodeo hero in the 1950s.
Pleasingly made character drama on a rather
boring subject.

w Lionel Chetwynd, *novel* Herbert Harker *d*
Harvey Hart *md* Franklin Boyd

Tony Lo Bianco, Gloria Carlin, Donald
Pleasence

Goldenson, Leonard (1905–). American
executive, chairman of ABC.

Goldie
aka: *The Betty Hutton Show*
US 1959 26 × 25m bw
William Morris

A manicurist becomes the sole heiress of a
millionaire.
Modestly pleasing comedy series.

Betty Hutton, Tom Conway, Gigi Perreau, Richard Miles, Joan Shawlee, Jean Carson, Gavin Muir

'Like an old Jane Withers movie.' – Don Miller

Goldie and the Boxer
US 1980 96m colour TVM
NBC/Columbia/Orenthal (O. J. Simpson)

A black boxer on the skids finds himself guardian to a precocious child.
Sentimental hokum, expertly fashioned and spurred by the success of *The Champ*.

w David Debin, Douglas Schwartz d David Miller ph Isadore Mankofsky m Jimmie Haskell

O. J. Simpson, Melissa Michaelsen, Vincent Gardenia, Gordon Jump, Madlyn Rhue, Ned Glass, Phil Silvers

'The freight's too heavy for the frail vehicle!' – *Daily Variety*

Goldie and the Boxer Go To Hollywood
US 1981 96m colour TVM
NBC/Columbia/Orenthal (O. J. Simpson, Hugh Benson)

Joe and Goldie head for Hollywood, where he is offered a movie contract.
Lame sequel.

w Mel and Ethel Brez and Lew Hunter d David Miller

O. J. Simpson, Melissa Michaelsen, James Gregory, Jack Gilford, Reb Brown, Spanky Marcus

✱ **Goldie, Grace Wyndham** (1905–). British executive with a primary interest in current affairs. In her long career at the BBC she fostered the talents of many young producers while maintaining the Corporation's authoritarianism.

Goldschmidt, John (1943–). British film-maker and director who has maintained an extraordinarily consistent standard since playing himself in both as a straightforward documentarist (e.g. a profile of actress Helen Mirren) and a knowing stalker into the haunted fict–fact zone. *It's a Lovely Day Tomorrow* (ATV 1975) reconstructed a gruesome World War II air-raid shelter disaster. Since then, *Spend, Spend, Spend* (1977), *Life for Christine* (1980), *Egon Schiele* (1982), *The Devil's Lieutenant* (1984), *A Song for Europe* (1985).   PP

Goldstone, James (1931–). American director who graduated to features after a long TV apprenticeship. Series include *Court*

of Last Resort, *Rawhide*, *Voyage to the Bottom of the Sea*, *Star Trek*; TV movies include *Ironside* (pilot), *A Clear and Present Danger*, *Shadow over Elveron*, *Cry Panic*, *Dr Max*, *Things in Their Season*, *Journey into Darkness*, *Kent State*, *Charles and Diana*, *Rita Hayworth*, *Sentimental Journey*, *The Sun Also Rises*.

Goliath Awaits
US 1981 2 × 96m colour
NBC/Columbia/Larry White and Hugh Benson

Oceanographers discover a colony of survivors from a World War II luxury liner: they have learned to breathe under water.
Absurd without being endearing, this tedious fantasy of a Shangri-La of the deep said little for the public which gave it such high ratings.

w Richard Bluel and Pat Fielder d Kevin Connor ph Al Francis

Mark Harmon, Christopher Lee, Robert Forster, Frank Gorshin, Emma Samms, Jean Marsh, Alex Cord, John McIntire, Jeanette Nolan

Gomer Pyle USMC
US 1964–8 150 × 25m colour (1st 30 bw)
CBS/Ashland

Troubles of a naïve recruit to the Marines.
Pratfall service comedy with a particularly gormless hero.

Jim Nabors, Frank Sutton

Gone for a Soldier (GB 1980). Philip Donnellan's sour pull-together of songs, legends and horror-stories about the British army which very properly (for once) ran into trouble with loyal citizenry. Produced for BBC.   PP

† The title also used for an STV Remembrance Day tribute to Scottish troops, 1985.

The Gong Show. American syndication series in which an ebullient host encourages an assortment of abysmally poor amateur performers to do their stuff before a panel which has a choice of ways to banish them from the stage. Embarrassing to many, but the performers don't have to appear, and a large section of the public lapped it up, even in the UK where it was tried out in 1985 on Channel Four before a British version was commissioned.

Goober and the Ghost Chasers
US 1973 17 × 22m colour
Hanna–Barbera

A cowardly dog helps his owners to chase ghosts.
Inept cartoon series with below-par animation, a curiously quick copy of *Scooby Doo*.

Good and Bad at Games (GB 1983). Yet
another manifestation of the English public school writer's obsession with public schools (this time by William Boyd, using public school plot number 4e, revenge by victim on oppressors in later life). For C4's *Film on Four*.   PP

Good against Evil *
US 1977 74m colour
TCF (Ernie Frankel, Lin Bolen)
A baby girl is dedicated to Satan, and on her 21st birthday his emissary comes to fetch her. A surprisingly close rip-off of *The Exorcist* (not to mention *The Devil's Daughter*), this pilot is well made and acted but didn't make a series.

w Jimmy Sangster d Paul Wendkos

Dan O'Herlihy, Dack Rambo, Elyssa Davalos, Richard Lynch, Peggy McCay

Good Behaviour (GB 1983; 3 × 60m).
Molly Keane's novel of Irish life around the time of World War I, dramatized by Hugh Leonard and directed by Bill Hays, for BBC.

The Good Companions
GB 1980 9 × 50m colour
Yorkshire TV (David Cunliffe/Leonard Lewis)
The Dinky Doos travelling concert party is helped back onto its feet by three strangers: Miss Trant, Inigo Jollifant and Jess Oakroyd. Interminably elongated and generally misjudged musical treatment of J. B. Priestley's classic modern picaresque novel, which will doubtless survive for another day. Many good elements are dissipated by cute decoration and joyless casting.

w Alan Plater d Bill Hays

Judy Cornwell, Jeremy Nicholas, John Stratton, Jan Francis, Simon Green, Frank Mills, Vivienne Martin

The Good Dr Bodkin Adams (GB 1986;
74m). Story of the burly Eastbourne general practitioner accused in the fifties of murdering an old lady patient to speed up her legacy to him, acquitted by the jury but still struck off the medical register. Written by Richard Gordon (of the light-hearted *Doctor in the House* books); with Timothy

West as Adams, Nigel Davenport, James Villiers, Jean Anderson. Directed by Richard Stroud, produced by Innes Lloyd, for BBC.   PP

Good Girl *
GB 1974 6 × 52m colour
Julia Foster as the remorselessly innocent daughter of remorselessly sunny parents, wooed by grouchy, imperfect Peter Barkworth; an inverted *Taming of the Shrew* and a pleasing comedy. Written by Philip Mackie; produced by Peter Willes; for YTV.
PP

The Good Guys
US 1968 42 × 25m colour
CBS/Talent Associates (Leonard Stern/ Jerry Davis)
A cab driver and a restaurateur have delusions of grandeur.
Mild ethnic comedy.

w Jay Sandrich, Hal Cooper

Bob Denver, Herb Edelman, Joyce Van Patten

Good Heavens: see Everything Money Can't Buy

A Good Human Story *
GB 1977 62m colour (16mm) TVM
Granada (Julian Amyes)
Three journalists follow up clues to a murder in a seaside resort out of season.
Sharply observed, cynical talk-piece with a slightly disappointing ending.

w David Nathan d Gordon Flemyng

Warren Clark, Michael Elphick, Kenneth Haigh

'The first telly drama to catch the truth about Fleet Street.' – *People*

Good, Jack (1930–). British high priest of
pop and rock music programmes both sides of the Atlantic. As an ex-Oxford trainee producer at the BBC worked on the pioneer *Six-Five Special* from 1957. Moved to ITV (ABC) to create *Oh Boy!*, on to America in 1962 to produce *Hullaballoo*, etc. Much-advertised return to British television in the seventies never quite repeated the old magic. But while it had flowed he knew better than anyone how to dramatize the singers and their songs. Subject of *Master of Pop* from YTV, 1969.   PP

The Good Life
US 1971 15 × 25m colour
NBC/Columbia/Lee Rich (Claudio Guzman)

A suburban couple decide that the most comfortable life in these days of high taxes is as butler and housekeeper to a millionaire. A good idea lacking the writing to sustain it.

cr Fred Freeman, Lawrence J. Cohen

Larry Hagman, Donna Mills, David Wayne, Hermione Baddeley

The Good Life ***
GB 1974–8 30 approx. × 30m colour
BBC

A young draughtsman and his wife decide on self-sufficiency, and to the stunned disbelief of their neighbours bring pigs into their suburban garden.
Likeable and funny sitcom series with well-rounded characters.

w BOB LARBEY, JOHN ESMONDE

RICHARD BRIERS, FELICITY KENDAL, PAUL EDDINGTON, PENELOPE KEITH

'A happy and somewhat rare combination of intelligent writing and superb playing.' – *Daily Telegraph*

Good Morning Britain (GB since 1983). Title of ITV's breakfast television show put out by TV-am, about the only element of the original format to survive today.

Good Morning World
US 1967 26 × 25m bw
CBS/Discus/Bill Persky, Sam Denoff

The love lives of two disc jockeys in a Los Angeles radio station.
Abortive comedy series.

Joby Baker, Ronnie Schell, Julie Parrish, Billy de Wolfe, Goldie Hawn

The Good Old Days *. British old-time music hall show which since the mid-fifties has been irregularly transmitted from the City Varieties Theatre, Leeds, where the audience voluntarily dresses up in fashions of the 1890s and the chairman, excelling in fantastic feats of vernacular verbosity, has invariably been Leonard Sachs. Produced by Barney Colehan.

The Good Soldier * (GB 1981). Delicate two-hour film version of the Ford Madox Ford novel, superficially about two upper-class couples who meet regularly to take the waters at a German spa, more profoundly about passions that lurk under the stiff upper lip. With Robin Ellis, Susan Fleetwood, Jeremy Brett, Vickery Turner, Elizabeth Garvie. Directed by Kevin Billington; for Granada.   PP

A Good Sport *
US 1984 96m colour TVM
CBS/Warner/Ralph Waite Productions
(Christopher Morgan)

A sports columnist falls for a flighty fashion editor.
Sounds and plays like a remake of *Woman of the Year*, but that's uncredited. Pretty good fun anyway.

w Arnold Margolin   *d* Lou Antonio
ph Fred Schuler   *m* Mark Snow

Lee Remick, Ralph Waite, Sam Gray, Richard Hamilton, Delphi Harrington

'It not only moves quickly and happily, it has something to say about love and the approaches to it.' – *Daily Variety*

Good Time George ** (GB 1983–4; 13 × 30m). George Melly in his latter-day prime as a performer, recorded in a pretty little theatre in Bury St Edmunds; with John Chilton and the Feetwarmers plus guests. Great fun, good atmosphere.   PP

Good Times
US 1974–8   × 25m colour (VTR)
CBS/Tandem (Norman Lear)

Misadventures of a black family living in a poor section of Chicago.
Fairly routine ethnic comedy spun off from *All in the Family*.

cr Eric Monte, Mike Evans

Esther Rolle, John Amos, Jimmie Walker, Janet Du Bois, Bernadette Stanis

Goodbye Charlie (US 1985; 1 × 25m). Failed attempt at a revival of the play which was filmed with Tony Curtis: Susanne Somers now played the sex-changed ghost of the womanizer. Not a good idea. Written and produced by Patricia Nardo for TCF/ABC.

Goodbye Darling * (GB 1980). A series of eight 50-minute plays about the characters of an English village, all of them apparently intent on extramarital affairs. Usually smart and often funny, though with a tendency to go over the top. With Renée Asherson, Nigel Davenport, Moira Redmond, etc. Written by James Mitchell for BBC, who seem to have thought so little of it that they delayed transmission for eighteen months.

Goodbye Mr Chips (GB 1984; 6 × 30m). James Hilton's brief life of a much-loved old schoolmaster re-dramatized by Alexander Baron with Roy Marsden in the name-part. Directed by Gareth Davies, produced by Barry Letts, for BBC.   PP

Goodbye Mr Kent (GB 1982). Dispensable BBC comedy series with Richard Briers as Hannah Gordon's impossible lodger. Not much of an idea, and a very wobbly vehicle. Written by Peter Vincent and Peter Robinson; produced by Gareth Gwenlan.

Goodbye Raggedy Ann *
US 1971 74m colour TVM
CBS/Studio Center/Fielder Cook
A Hollywood starlet is driven to the point of suicide.
Well-made but rather obvious and unsympathetic mini-drama.

w Jack Sher *d* Fielder Cook

Mia Farrow, Hal Holbrook, John Colicos, Ed Flanders, Martin Sheen

Goodchild, Peter (1939–). British producer and executive into television drama by way of a chemistry degree and science programmes. Editor of Horizon 1969–78, when his productions included HOSPITAL 1922. Produced drama series *Marie Curie* (1977) and *Oppenheimer* (1981). Head of plays, BBC, since 1984.   PP

The Goodies *
GB 1973–8 40 approx. × 30m colour
BBC
Three goons get into trouble.
Anarchic farcical comedy, each episode starting at least as a spoof on some aspect of life but degenerating into a hopefully hilarious mess of sight gags, one-liners and elaborate visual trickery.

written by the performers GRAEME GARDEN, BILL ODDIE, TIM BROOKE-TAYLOR

'We think in terms of a human animated cartoon which inevitably means that half the humour is technical.' – Tim Brooke-Taylor

† The series won two Silver Roses at Montreux.

**Goodnight and God Bless ** (GB 1983; 6 × 30m). Good bad-taste sitcom with DONALD CHURCHILL as a realistically drawn television game show compère who cheats on tax, scrimps on the housekeeping, bullies his wife and preys on women. Owing at least a wink to the character he played in Peter Nichols's HEARTS AND FLOWERS, the scripts were by Donald Churchill himself with Joe McGrath, who was also executive producer. It didn't go down, of course, with the sucker public who love game show hosts; only one series was made. With Judy Loe, directed and produced by Alan Dossor, for Central.
                                                PP

Goodnight My Love **
US 1972 73m colour TVM
ABC Circle
Two private eyes – one a dwarf – are hired by a beautiful blonde to find her missing boy friend.
Successful spoof of a Chandler forties mystery, with good lines and excellent re-created Los Angeles settings.

w/d PETER HYAMS

RICHARD BOONE, MICHAEL DUNN, Barbara Bain, Victor Buono, Walter Burke

✳ **Goodson, Mark** (1915–). Former American scriptwriter who with Bill Todman became the world's most prolific inventor of panel games.

Goodson–Todman Productions. A company set up in 1946 to market game show formats, which it did most successfully, with *What's My Line?*, *Beat the Clock*, *To Tell the Truth*, *The Price is Right* and *Family Feud*. Their entry into series production in the sixties was less successful, *The Richard Boone Show* being their most prestigious effort. Mark Goodson and William Todman were both radio performers.

Goodyear TV Playhouse (US 1951–60). One-hour anthology series for NBC, produced by Fred Coe. Among its most notable originals were *Marty* and *The Catered Affair*, both by Paddy Chayefsky.

The Goon Show. Legendary British radio comedy which ran 1951–60, with Peter Sellers, Harry Secombe, Spike Milligan (who also wrote most of the material); Michael Bentine and Eric Sykes were associated with the team part of the time. All went into television, and one way or another their anarchic, surrealist humour was to influence TV comedy deeply. But only once did *The Goon Show* itself steal on to TV, as a one-off show for Thames in 1968, produced by its radio producer for five years, Peter Eton, with Sellers, Secombe, Milligan and – representing their natural heirs – John Cleese.   PP

Goostrey – A Village (GB 1976; 5 × 50m). One of a rash of chronicles of English village life about this time, but quite lightly done and the only northern choice. (Goostrey is in Cheshire.) Produced by Peter Carr; for Granada.   PP

✳ **Gordon, Gale** (1905–) (Gaylord Aldrich). American comedy actor who after his vaudeville days was prominent in such series as *Junior Miss*, *Dennis the Menace*, *Our Miss Brooks*, *Pete and Gladys* and *The Brothers* before becoming Lucille Ball's huffing, puffing boss or other nemesis on *Here's Lucy* and *The Lucy Show*.

Gordon, Hannah (1941–). Cool and pleasing British actress who has appeared in all forms of TV drama. Best known for her co-starring role in TELFORD'S CHANGE; also *My Wife Next Door*, *Miss Morrison's Ghosts*, *Goodbye Mr Kent*. Presents *Gardeners' Calendar* on C4.

Gordon, Noele (1922–). British character actress and linkwoman who had a long, long run in the soap opera *Crossroads*, before being fired in 1981.

The Gorge ** (GB 1968; 75m; bw). Bourgeois Bristol neighbours gather to admire a home movie of their greedy picnic (the title is doubled-edged) at Cheddar Gorge. Among the shots are some reminders of incidents unrumbled at the time, or anyway best forgotten, notably the pretty daughter who can't find her pants after sunbathing in the bracken. Delightful comedy by Peter Nichols; directed by Christopher Morahan; produced by Tony Garnett; for BBC. PP

Goring, Marius (1912–). British character actor who has been popular in all media but became most familiar on TV as the pathologist hero of *The Expert*.

Gorshin, Frank (1935–). Wiry American impressionist who on TV made a memorable impression in *Batman* as the Riddler. TV movies: *Sky Heist*, *Greatest Heroes of the Bible*, *Death Car on the Freeway*, *Goliath Awaits*.

Gortner, Marjoe (1944–). American actor, former travelling evangelist. TV movies: *The Marcus Nelson Murders*, *Pray for the Wildcats*, *The Gun and the Pulpit*, *Mayday at 40,000 Feet*.

Gosling, Ray (19 –). British place-taster increasingly turning to a line in popular anthropology. More interested in the people and social mix of a town than the architecture, and will wilfully enthuse about ribbon caravan development while sniffing at posh Chester or Cambridge; but a lot of good observation, zest and cheek. *One Man's View* (1969), *A Village for Christmas* (1974), *Gosling's Travels*, *Human Jigsaw* (1984–5). PP

Gossett, Lou Jnr (1934–). Striking black American actor. Series: *The Lazarus Syndrome*. TV movies: *Companions in Nightmare*, *It's Good to Be Alive*, *Sidekicks*, *Delancey Street*, ROOTS (Emmy 1977), *Little Ladies of the Night*, TO KILL A COP, *The Critical List*, *Backstairs at the White House*, *This Man Stands Alone*, *Don't Look Back*.

The Gossip Columnist
US 1979 96m colour TVM
Operation Prime Time/Universal (Jon Epstein)

A woman political columnist is sent to Hollywood and told to 'think trash'.

Incredibly tacky, predictable and old-fashioned 'woman's picture'; you can almost see the balloons coming out of the actors' mouths. Also available as five half-hours.

w Michael Gleason d James Sheldon ph Enzo Martinelli m Allyn Ferguson

Kim Cattrall, Bobby Vinton, Robert Vaughn, Dick Sargent, Conrad Janis, Joe Penny, Martha Raye, Sylvia Sidney, Bobby Sherman, Lyle Waggoner, Steve Allen, Jim Backus

Gossip from the Forest (GB 1979; 100m; colour). How the armistice terms were hammered out in 1918 in a railway carriage in the woods of Compiègne, with consequences generally reckoned to be disastrous for the world. Play adapted and directed by Brian Gibson from the novel by Thomas Keneally, strong on atmosphere and character but not remarkably so in revelations. With John Shrapnel as the German negotiator Matthias Erzberger and Hugh Burden as Foch; for Granada. PP

Gould, Harold (1923–). Sharp-featured American actor of incisive roles. Series: THE FEATHER AND FATHER GANG. TV movies: *Ransom for a Dead Man*, *How to Break Up a Happy Divorce*, *Medical Story*, WASHINGTON BEHIND CLOSED DOORS, *Eleventh Victim*, *Aunt Mary*, *The Man in the Santa Claus Suit*, *The Gambler*, *Moviola*, *King Crab*, *The Long Road Home*, *Better Late Than Never*.

The Government Inspector. Gogol's much-televised, much-filmed play about the humble traveller mistaken for a powerful functionary. TONY HANCOCK successfully took on the part for a BBC production in 1958 (p Alan Bromley). More recently (1983) a 3 × 30m BBC schools version by Ron Smedley starred Robin Nedwell, with Freddie Jones and Jack Wild. PP

The Governor and J.J.
US 1969 39 × 25m colour
CBS/Talent Associates (Leonard Stern,
  Arne Sultan, Reza Badiga)
A widowed governor is helped by his young
daughter.
Mildly political comedy which didn't really
appeal.
cr Leonard Stern
Dan Dailey, Julie Sommars, Neva Patterson

Grace, Nickolas (1949–). Magnetic
British actor who has made the most of being
the evil Sheriff of Nottingham in *Robin of
Sherwood* but graces other productions on
all brow levels.   PP

Graceless Go I
GB 1974 90m colour
HTV (Peter Miller)
One of the stumers of all time, a lurid
melodrama by David Storey featuring
psychiatrist, rugby player, randy hospital
administrator and their womenfolk, all of
whom have difficulty in keeping their clothes
on. The mystery is why HTV are so good
when they steal on to the network with
genuine local talents such as Bob Baker and
Dave Martin, so awful when one of their big
guns (here, Stanley Baker) and world
markets are involved.
d Patrick Dromgoole
Stanley Baker, Rachel Roberts, Angharad
Rees, Jack Watson   PP

❋ **Grade, Lord** (or Lord Lew Grade, as
Americans call him) (1906–) (Lew
Winogradsky). British impresario and
executive who after years as a vaudeville
dancer and an agent became Mr ATV in the
fifties and set out to sell British shows to
America, a policy which brought many
failures but can count among its successes *The
Saint*, *Danger Man*, *Thunderbirds*, *The
Persuaders*, *The Julie Andrews Hour*, *Space
1999* and *The Muppets*. In the seventies he
gradually abandoned TV for the production
of international multi-star movies which met
with varying success.

Grade, Michael (1943–). British
executive, nephew of Lord Grade. Began as
a sports journalist, then in family theatrical
agency until joining LWT, first as head of
light entertainment, subsequently (1977–81)
director of programmes. After three years in
the US as President of Embassy Television
and then a sub-contractor in his own name,
returned to Britain as Controller of BBC1.
A cheerful character never shy of speaking
up at industry conferences or on the air. PP

Grady *
GB 1970 3 × 52m colour
YTV (Marc Miller)
Anthony Bate rides into town like an
old-time gunfighter as a modern hero of
labour, a shop-floor loner interested only in a
bigger share of the loot for the workers,
contemptuous of all ideologues. One of
television's more successful attempts to wrest
drama from the industrial 1970s, and
certainly the first to imbue it with the values
of the Wild West of the 1870s.
w Edmund Ward *d* Marc Miller
Anthony Bate, Diana Coupland   PP

Grady (US 1975). Shortlived half-hour
comedy spun off from *Sanford and Son*;
Whitman Mayo moved from a black ghetto to
a racially mixed area.

Graef, Roger (1936–). American
film-maker long settled in Britain, the leading
exponent of patiently filming hour after hour,
day after day, at conferences, board
meetings, etc., and also behind the scenes of
same, to yield the raw material from which he
edits a full account of the way businesses,
delegations, councils and political parties
conduct their deliberations. *Inside the
Brussels HQ* (1975), *Decision* (from 1976),
British Communism (1978), POLICE (1982). PP

Graham, David (1943–). British current
affairs producer, ex-*Panorama*, who set up
the independent Diverse Productions,
responsible for *The Friday Alternative*, then
Diverse Reports on C4.   PP

Graham, Virginia (1912–). American
commentator, humorist and panellist (*Girl
Talk*, *The Jack Paar Show*).

Graham, William (1930–) (aka William
A. Graham). American director who went
through the television mill before graduating.
Series include *Kraft Theatre*, *Naked City*,
Route 66, *The FBI*, *Batman*. TV movies: *The
Doomsday Flight*, *Perilous Voyage*, *Trial
Run*, *The Thief*, *Jigsaw*, *Birds of Prey*, *Police
Story* (pilot), *Trapped Beneath the Sea*,
Minstrel Man, *21 Hours at Munich*, *The
Amazing Howard Hughes*, *Guyana Tragedy*,
etc.

Grambling's White Tiger
US 1981 96m colour TVM
NBC/Interplanetary Productions/
  Jenner–Wallach (Bert Gold, Micheline
  Keller)
A young footballer is the only white at a
black college.

Ho-hum sports melodrama with predictably boring asides.

w Zev Cohen, Lou Potter, Bill Attaway, *book My Little Brother Is Coming Tomorrow* by Bruce Behrenberg d Georg Stanford Brown *ph* Joe Wilcots *m* Michael Lloyd

Bruce Jenner, Harry Belafonte, LeVar Burton, Dennis Hayshort, Deborah Pratt

Grammar School
GB 1964 75m bw

Intriguing follow-up exercise by Don Haworth, for the BBC, to find out what had befallen the figures in a group photograph picked at random from the walls of Batley Grammar School in Yorkshire – the sixteen prefects of the year 1947, half a generation earlier. Disappointingly, perhaps, nearly every one had settled down sedately; two were in the church and others connected closely with it; no exotic success stories, no thoroughly bad lots. But if this sort of research is to transcend the mere satisfaction of curiosity it must be an honest account of the little bit of social history it picks on. PP

Granada TV. British independent TV company serving the Lancashire area, founded in 1955 by Sidney Bernstein. Somewhat more intellectual than the other ITV companies, it counts among its notable projects *World in Action*, *Disappearing World*, *Coronation Street*, *University Challenge*, *All Our Yesterdays*, *Country Matters*, *A Family at War*, *Cinema*, *Clapperboard*, *The Best Play of . . .*, and *Brideshead Revisited*.

Granada's Manchester Plays (GB 1958–60). Six stage plays originally produced at the Gaiety, Manchester, when it flourished under the rule of Annie Horniman. Granada's act of homage characteristically paid off as good television drama, too. Two each from Harold Brighouse, Stanley Houghton, Allan Monkhouse. Produced by Gerald Savory. PP

Grand Ole Opry. A variety show, popular in America in the fifties, exclusively devoted to country and western entertainers.

Grand Prix. Edited BBC2 recording on Sunday evenings in season of the afternoon's international motor-racing g.p., much savoured for the frantic commentary by Murray Walker plus expert interpolations by James Hunt. PP

Grand Strategy (GB 1972; 8 × 50m). Historian Michael Howard charts the great decisions of World War II, from Britain's to go it alone in 1940 to Goebbels's promulgation of Total War in 1944. Produced by Ronnie Noble; for BBC. PP

Grandpa Goes to Washington (US 1978). Shortlived 50-minute series about a retired professor who wins a senatorial election. Nothing to set the pulses racing. With Jack Albertson, Larry Linville, Sue Ane Langdon. Written by Noel Baldwin, Lane Slate; produced by Robert Stambler; for Paramount/NBC. 'Grandpa is one of those independent spirits salvaged from a Kaufman–Hart show by way of Will Rogers.' – *Daily Variety.*

Grandstand. The BBC's Saturday afternoon programme of sport.

Grange Hill. A BBC early evening serial which began in 1980 and aimed to present life in a modern provincial secondary school, warts and all. Devised by Phil Redmond and produced by Susi Hush, it provoked all the expected controversy; children themselves, whether or not they considered themselves libelled, appeared to enjoy it.

Granger, Derek (1921–). British producer, former theatre critic who went through the Granada mill (working in all departments) to wind up with the big one, *Brideshead Revisited*, but *Country Matters* (1972) is the one I cherish. PP

Grant, Lee (1929–) (Lyova Rosenthal). American character actress who had a moderate film career with several highlights. Her attempts at TV series have seldom got further than the pilot stage: *Fay* was cancelled after two episodes. TV movies include *Night Slaves*, *The Neon Ceiling*, *Ransom for a Dead Man*, *Lt Schuster's Wife*, *Partners in Crime*, *Perilous Voyage*, *The Spell*, *Backstairs at the White House*, *You Can't Go Home Again*.

The Granville Melodramas (GB 1955–6). Series of abbreviated Victorian melodramas staged in the old Granville Theatre, London, which Associated-Rediffusion acquired as a studio in the earliest days of commercial television. PP

The Grass Is Always Greener Over the Septic Tank
US 1980 96m colour TVM
CBS/Joe Hamilton

A lady novelist is sorry she persuaded her husband and family to move to the country.

As old as *The Egg and I*, but less funny and much more tiresome.

w Dick Clair, Jenna McMahon, *book* Erma Bombeck *d* Robert Day *ph* Steve Poster *m* Peter Matz

Carol Burnett, Charles Grodin, Alex Rocco, Linda Gray, Craig Richard Nelson, David Hollander

Grauman, Walter (1922–). Experienced American director responsible for some of the best episodes of *The Untouchables*, *The Fugitive* and *Streets of San Francisco*. TV movies include *Daughter of the Mind*, *Crowhaven Farm*, *The Old Man Who Cried Wolf*, *Paper Man*, *They Call It Murder*, *The Forgotten Man*, *Are You in the House Alone?*

Graves, Peter (1925–) (Peter Aurness). American leading man, much seen on TV, seldom in movies. Series include *Fury*, *Whiplash*, *Court Martial*, *Mission Impossible*. TV movies include *Call to Danger*, *The President's Plane Is Missing*, *Scream of the Wolf*, *The Underground Man*, *Where Have All the People Gone*, *Dead Man on the Run*, *SST: Death Flight*, *The Rebels*, *300 Miles for Stephanie*, *The Memory of Eva Ryker*, *The Winds of War*.

Graves, Teresa (*c* 1947–). Black American leading lady who starred in *Get Christie Love*. Also visible in *Laugh-In*.

Gray, Charles (1928–). Solidly-built British actor with incisive voice which he lent to Jack Hawkins when Hawkins lost his own. Many TV plays, plus series *The Upper Crusts*.

Gray, Donald (1914–78) (Eldred Tidbury). South African leading man who lost an arm in the war and despite this handicap – or perhaps because of it – made a popular hero of *Saber of London* in the early sixties.

The Gray Ghost
US 1957 39 × 25m bw
Lindsley Parsons

Civil War stories of a rebel daredevil.
Moderate action stuff with a special appeal in the South.

Tod Andrews, Phil Chambers

Gray, Simon (1937–). British playwright whose first work was for television though he now writes mainly for the stage. Close, intense plots about friendship, fidelity, involvement with others or the lack of same. *Plaintiffs and Defendants* and *Two Sundays*, following each other as BBC Plays for Today in 1975, starred the same leading actors, Alan Bates and Dinsdale Landen, but had them exchange characters between one play and the next. Also *Spoiled* (1968), *The Man in the Sidecar* (1971), others.   PP

Grayson, Larry (1923–). British comedian of the seventies, the first deliberately to suggest a gay persona; not otherwise remarkably talented, though his catchphrase 'Shut that door' and his stories of his friend Everard swept the land.

Great Acting (GB 1965–6). Extended interviews with Richardson, Redgrave and others intercut with clips of their work, sometimes vitiated by too reverential an approach by the interviewer and nearly always disdaining the great actor's television credits. But Olivier was forthcoming for Kenneth Tynan, and Noël Coward added a droll postscript to the series. Produced by Hal Burton; for BBC.   PP

The Great Adventure (US 1963–4). Ambitious one-hour anthology for CBS; each story dramatized a significant point in American history. Van Heflin narrated.

The Great American Beauty Contest
US 1972 73m colour TVM
Spelling–Goldberg (Everett Chambers)
A beauty contest is threatened by scandal. Acceptable comedy drama.

w Stanford Whitmore *d* Robert Day

Eleanor Parker, Bob Cummings, Louis Jourdan, Barbi Benton, Farrah Fawcett, Tracy Reed

The Great American Traffic Jam
US 1980 96m colour TVM
NBC/Ten–Four (Greg and Sam Strangis)

Various characters are caught up in a vast Los Angeles traffic jam which becomes a kind of mass celebration.
Thin rehash of *The Bridge of San Luis Rey*; good to look at and not much else.

w David Hackel, Stephen Hattman *d* James Frawley *ph* Crales Correll *m* Arthur B. Rubenstein

John Beck, Shelley Fabares, Desi Arnaz Jnr, Noah Beery, Phil Foster, James Gregory, Lisa Hartman, Ed MacMahon, Abe Vigoda, Lyle Waggoner

A Great American Tragedy *
GB title: *Man at the Crossroads*
US 1972 74m colour TVM
Metromedia (Gerald I. Isenberg)
A middle-aged executive loses his job and finds it hard to get another.
Convincing sketch of a familiar situation.

w Caryl Ledner *d* J. Lee-Thompson

GEORGE KENNEDY, Vera Miles, William Windom, Kevin McCarthy, Natalie Trundy

Great Britons
GB 1978 6 × 60m colour (VTR)
BBC (Malcolm Brown)

Distinguished biographies of famous men and women are turned into television documentaries.

A pleasing idea rather disappointingly carried out.

Horatio Nelson by David Haworth
Thomas Cook and Son by John Pudney
Florence Nightingale by Philippa Stewart
Robert Burns by David Daiches
David Lloyd George by John Gregg
Marlborough by Corelli Barnett

The Great Cash Giveaway Getaway *
US 1980 96m colour TVM
NBC/Penthouse/Cine Guarantors (Robert A. Papazian)

A young man accidentally steals a fortune from his crooked stepfather, and while on the run distributes most of it to charity.

Fairly pleasing open-air comedy adventure with excellent production values.

w Phil Reisman Jnr *d* Michael O'Herlihy

David Kyle, Elissa Leeds, Albert Almi, George Hamilton, James Keach

The Great Egg Race *.
Annual BBC2 contest originally in response to international challenge to see who could propel a standard egg the farthest distance in any contraption driven by a standard elastic band. The BBC added a supporting tournament in which teams of boffins from industry, the services, universities, etc compete to devise complex machines from everyday household components. In 1981 the egg race itself was discontinued. Demon professor Heinz Wolff remains in charge; producer Charles Huff.
PP

Great Expectations *
GB 1975 116m colour TVM
ITC (Robert Fryer)

Dickens's novel about the growing up of young Pip and his adventures with Miss Havisham, Estella and a convict named Magwitch.

So-so version planned as a musical but with the music removed.

w Sherman Yellen *d* Joseph Hardy *ph* Freddie Young *m* Maurice Jarre

Michael York, Sarah Miles, James Mason, Margaret Leighton, Robert Morley, Anthony Quayle, Rachel Roberts, Joss Ackland, Andrew Ray, Heather Sears

† Of several straight BBC serializations the best was *c* 1959, *p* Dorothea Brooking.

Great Expectations (GB 1978).
Non-fiction series from ATV, following a bunch of Tyneside school-leavers through their first years in adult life, together with improvised dramatizations of difficulties they encountered at home and work. Written by C. P. Taylor; directed by Michael Darlow.
PP

† The title was also used for a 10-part series on multi-cultural education, produced by John Twitchin for BBC, 1983.

The Great Gildersleeve
US 1955 39 × 25m bw
Finkel and Rapf

Anecdotes of a pompous small-town bureaucrat.

Modest comedy for the easily pleased, from the long-running radio show, a spin-off from *Fibber McGee and Molly*.

Willard Waterman, Stephanie Griffin

The Great Houdinis *
US 1976 96m colour TVM
ABC Circle

The career of the great escapologist told in retrospect.

Rather slow and gloomy to start, this curious biopic has enough guest cameos and restagings of famous tricks to hold the interest.

w/d Melville Shavelson *m* Peter Matz *technical advisor* Harry Blackstone Jnr

Paul Michael Glaser, Sally Struthers, Ruth Gordon, Vivian Vance, Adrienne Barbeau, Bill Bixby, Peter Cushing, Jack Carter, Nina Foch, Wilfrid Hyde White, Maureen O'Sullivan, Clive Revill

The Great Ice Rip-Off *
US 1974 74m colour TVM
ABC Circle/Dan Curtis

Four jewel thieves get away on an interstate bus.

Lively comedy-thriller.

w Andrew Peter Marin *d* Dan Curtis

Lee J. Cobb, Gig Young, Grayson Hall, Robert Walden

The Great Man's Whiskers
US 1971 96m colour TVM
Universal (Adrian Scott)

President-elect Abraham Lincoln agrees with a little girl's suggestion that he should grow a beard.

Whimsy based on fact, far too long for its substance.

w John Paxton, *play* Adrian Scott *d* Philip Leacock

Dennis Weaver, Dean Jones, Ann Sothern, John McGiver

The Great Movie Cowboys. An ingenious one-hour show evolved by NTA in the seventies. Old Republic second feature westerns were cut down to size and introduced by Roy Rogers.

The Great Niagara *
US 1974 74m colour TVM
ABC/Playboy

During the Depression, a river family helps guide those who challenge Niagara Falls.
Unusual, watchable open-air drama.

w Robert E. Thompson *d* William Hale *m* Peter Link

Richard Boone, Randy Quaid, Jennifer Salt, Michael Sacks, Burt Young

Great Railway Journeys of the World * (GB 1980; 6 × 75m). Pleasant idea to send six different travellers over exotic railway routes, though it became clear with the instalments set in India and South Africa that the real passion being catered for was train cranks' nostalgia for steam. Among those enjoying a freebie trip: Ludovic Kennedy, Michael Frayn, Michael Wood, and (on the Stamboul run) Anon. Produced by Roger Laughton; for BBC.   PP

.LH: 'Effectiveness varies, but the trip from Lima via Macchu Picchu to Paraguay is a corker, and the Australian and Indian journeys aren't far behind.'

† *Great Little Railways*, also seven in number, followed in 1983. Stanley Reynolds and Ray Gosling were among those who took narrow-gauge journeys in remote parts. *p* Colin Adams.

The Great Wallendas *
US 1978 96m colour TVM
NBC/Daniel Wilson

The story of a circus high-wire family.
Well-staged, unusual, but slightly disappointing account of a real family, the head of which was killed in a wire fall after the film was shown.

w Jan Hartman *d* Larry Elikann *ph* Robert Bailin *m* Joe Weber, Bill Soden

Lloyd Bridges, Britt Ekland, Taina Elg, John Van Dreelen, Ben Fuhrman, Bruce Ornstein

The Great War *
GB 1964 26 × 40m bw

Excellent history of World War I using still photographs and archive film which for the first time had been 'stretched' so that marching troops no longer seemed to be toddling along at a ludicrous pace. Written by John Terraine; produced by TONY ESSEX; for BBC. A follow-up, *The Lost Peace* (1966), was less impressive, possibly because the commentary, spoken by Sir Michael Redgrave, took on an unremittingly pessimistic tone from the outset.   PP

The Greatest American Hero
US 1981 96m colour TVM
ABC/Paramount/Stephen J. Cannell

A young teacher has a desert encounter with a flying saucer and is given a flying Superman suit but loses the instructions.
Oddball comedy which tries to be not only a comic strip but a spoof of same as well as showing that young people are really nice and having a message for our time. The disparate elements worked in the ratings despite clumsy flying sequences, and nobody will ever understand why. A series of one-hours followed, with the inept spaceman used by an FBI agent to do good.

w Stephen J. Cannell *d* Rod Holcomb *ph* Andrew Jackson *m* Mike Post, Pete Carpenter

William Katt, ROBERT CULP, Connie Sellecca, G. D. Spradlin, Michael Pare

'An extended joke . . . it may not be great comedy, but it plays for quick laughs and for flirtations with reality. That's not bad.' – *Daily Variety*

'The producers have the same relation to their creation as Katt has to his suit: they've got a great piece of gear but they aren't sure how to make it work.' – Robert MacKenzie, *TV Guide*

The Greatest Gift
US 1974 100m colour TVM
NBC/Universal

The life of a preacher in the midwest early in the century.
Slow, earnest, rather empty pilot for an unsuccessful series (*The Family Holvak*).

w Ben Goodman, *novel Ramey* by Jack Farris *d* Boris Sagal *m* Dick de Benedictus

Glenn Ford, Julie Harris, Lance Kerwin

'The legendary stories and the *real* people who lived them! The most *important* miniseries in television history! An all-new, *original* American production!'

Greatest Heroes of the Bible (US 1979). A series of flabby retellings of Bible yarns at various lengths, on the level to be expected of the producers, Sunn Classic, who are not above inventing episodes to fill the time slot. The effect is more risible than riveting. Actors involved include Hugh O'Brian, Lew Ayres, Robert Culp, John Marley, John Carradine, David Birney, Sam Bottoms, Anne Francis;

various writers laboured for inevitable producer Charles E. Sellier Jnr; for NBC, who should have known better. Total running time, about 10 hours.

The Greatest Show on Earth (US 1963). One-hour drama series for ABC, in colour, with Jack Palance as the boss of the Barnum and Bailey circus and Stuart Erwin as his sidekick. Richard Rodgers provided the theme tune.

'So much to live for, and so little time left! From cheers to tears, a very special love story!'
The Greatest Thing That Almost Happened
US 1977 96m colour TVM
CBS/Crestview (Charles Fries, Herbert Hirschman)
A high-school athlete is threatened by leukaemia.
Black variation on the medium's favourite theme.
w Peter Beagle, *novel* Don Robertson *d* Gilbert Moses *ph* Joe Wilcots *m* David Shire
Jimmie Walker, James Earl Jones, Deborah Allen

The Greatest Thinkers. A curious international co-production sponsored by the Swiss Broadcasting Corporation, Encyclopedia Britannica, Westdeutscher Rundfunk, Radio Telefis Eireann, IBM and Blackbox AG. In 13 half-hours Edward de Bono talks via television to famous thinkers and illustrates their teachings in various ways including sketches acted out by 'two young people' and 'a family'. An unsuccessful but fascinating piece of over-popularization. Subjects include Moses, Aristotle, Machiavelli, Jesus, Columbus, Descartes, Rousseau, Marx and Pavlov. Produced in 1980 by John Winistoerfer.

Greatorex, Wilfred (19 –). British story-editor and writer, creator of many successful formats: *The Plane Makers, The Power Game, Hine, The Man from Haven, 1990, Airline,* etc.   PP

Greek Drama. Television's highest-minded production ever was *Electra* in Greek, put out on the ITV network in 1962 by A–R. Eileen Atkins starred in a BBC *Play of the Month* version in English in 1974. *The Serpent Son* (1979) was a fairly gorblimey re-rendition of the *Oresteia* of Aeschylus by Frederic Raphael and Kenneth McLeish. *Antigone* has been given several times, both

in straightforward translation (though set once in a bull-ring) and in Anouilh's World War II version, notably with Dorothy Tutin in a BBC production of 1960. In 1986 Don Taylor was due to complete the recording of new translations by himself of Sophocles' Theban trilogy *Oedipus, Oedipus at Colonus* and *Electra,* for BBC.   PP

Green Acres
Working title: *Country Cousins*
US 1965–70 170 × 25m colour
CBS/Filmways (Paul Henning/Jay Sommers)
A city lawyer moves his luxury-loving wife out to a farm.
The Beverly Hillbillies in reverse: Ma and Pa Kettle style humour which amused America for five seasons.
cr Jay Sommers
Eddie Albert, Eva Gabor, Pat Buttram, Tom Lester, Alvy Moore

Green Eyes *
US 1976 96m colour TVM
Lorimar (David Seltzer, John Erman)
An American war veteran searches Vietnam for his illegitimate son.
Critically liked sentimental melodrama with production values above average.
w David Seltzer *d* John Erman *m* Fred Karlin
Paul Winfield, Rita Tushingham, Jonathan Lippe

The Green Hornet
US 1966 26 × 25m colour
ABC/TCF (William Dozier)
With the help of a karate expert, a masked crusader fights for justice.
Another form of *Batman,* from yet another comic strip and radio series. The punch didn't connect.
cr George W. Trendle *m* Billy May
Van Williams, Bruce Lee, Walter Brooke, Lloyd Gough

✸ **Green, Hughie** (1920–). Canadian/British juvenile actor, quizmaster (DOUBLE YOUR MONEY) and talent discoverer (OPPORTUNITY KNOCKS). His manner has been much mimicked.

Greene, David (1924–). British director who after sporadic film success became a pillar of American TV. Series include *The Defenders, Sir Francis Drake, Espionage.* Mini-series: RICH MAN, POOR MAN (part), *Roots* (part), *World War III.* TV movies: *Madame Sin, The Count of Monte Cristo, The Trial of Lee Harvey Oswald,* FRIENDLY FIRE, etc. He won Emmys for *The People Next Door* (1968, live), *Rich Man, Poor Man, Roots, Friendly Fire, World War III, Rehearsal for Murder, Take Your Best Shot, Ghost Dancing, Prototype, Sweet Revenge, Fatal Vision, Guilty Conscience*

Greene, Graham (1904–). Britain's most-filmed novelist is also much televised, though he would hardly have been flattered by the 1958 series spun off *The Third Man* with Michael Rennie as a resuscitated and rehabilitated Harry Lime. *Shades of Greene* (1976) was a huge improvement. Dramatizations of his novels range from a fine *The Power and the Glory* (BBC, 1959) with Sam Wanamaker, to a torrid *Stamboul Train* (BBC, 1963) and a miserable *Dr Fischer of Geneva* (1984). Also: *The Heart of the Matter*, 1983; *Monsignor Quixote*, 1985; *May We Borrow Your Husband?* with Dirk Bogarde, in production 1986.

Greene was interviewed off camera in a BBC *Omnibus* of the sixties but did not really appear on TV until he aired his complaint against the police in the South of France (where he lives) in *I Accuse*, 1983. Order of Merit, 1986.   PP

Greene, Hugh Carleton (1910–). British executive, brother of Graham Greene and ex-director-general of BBC. Biography, *A Variety of Lives* by Michael Tracey, 1983. PP: 'The greatest captain the BBC has ever had. He gave public broadcast television a role in the life of the country it had never had before, has already lost and will never enjoy again. It upset some, irritated others but excluded no one.'

❋   **Greene, Lorne** (1915–). Canadian character actor who, apart from a few films, devoted most of his career to TV and became one of its major stars. Series: *Sailor of Fortune*, BONANZA, *Griff, Battlestar Galactica, Code Red*. TV movies include *Destiny of a Spy, The Harness, Nevada Smith, The Moneychangers, SST: Death Flight, The Trial of Lee Harvey Oswald, Roots, The Bastard*.

Greene, Richard (1918–85). British leading man of Hollywood films in the late thirties; career later wandered, but he became TV's most famous face in 143 episodes of *The Adventures of Robin Hood*, after which he lived in comfortable semi-retirement.

Greene, Shecky (1925–) (Sheldon Greenfield). American stand-up comic known for blue humour and therefore restricted in his TV appearances.

Gregson, John (1919–75). Scottish leading actor with a busy film career. TV series: *Gideon's Way, Shirley's World, Dangerous Knowledge*.

Grenfell, Joyce (1910–79). British revue star and monologuist who made occasional appearances as such but became a much-loved personality in her last years through the panel show *Face the Music*.   PP

Grey Granite (GB 1983; 3 × 75m). Final serial in the Lewis Grassic Gibbon trilogy which began with *Sunset Song*. Written by Bill Craig again, starring Vivien Heilbron again, directed by Tom Cotter, produced by Roderick Graham.   PP

Grey, Joel (1932–) (Joseph Katz). Diminutive American musical comedy performer who became famous as the compère in *Cabaret*. TV movie: *Man on a String*.

Gries, Tom (1922–77). American general purpose director with good movie credits before he tackled TV. Series include *Richard Diamond, Checkmate, The Defenders, I Spy, Rat Patrol* (also created), *Batman*. TV movies: *Earth II, The Glass House, Call to Danger, The Connection, QB VII, The Healers, Helter Skelter*, etc.

Griff *
aka: *Man on the Outside*
US 1974 102m colour TVM
ABC/Universal (David Victor)

When his private eye son is murdered, an ex-cop takes over the business and hunts down the murderer.

Smooth pilot for an unsuccessful series.

w Larry Cohen d Boris Sagal m Elliot Kaplan

Lorne Greene, James Olson, Lorraine Gary, Lee H. Montgomery

† The resulting ABC series added Ben Murphy as Griff's aide but was a poor production and was easily beaten by the very similar *Barnaby Jones*. It ran to 12 × 50m episodes.

Griffin and Phoenix: A Love Story
GB theatrical title: *Today is Forever*
US 1976 96m colour TVM
ABC Circle (Tony Thomas)

Two people dying of incurable diseases fall in love.

TV moviedom's favourite theme in a double helping. Almost insufferable despite good production and performances.

KENNETH GRIFFITH was a memorable Napoleon in Granada's 1963 studio version of *War and Peace* (here with Nicol Williamson). The spirit moved him however in the direction of controversial documentaries which kept him as an actor away from the public eye.

w John Hill *d* Daryl Duke *m* George Aliceson Tipton

Peter Falk, Jill Clayburgh, Dorothy Tristan, John Lehne, George Chandler, Milton Parsons

Griffin, Merv (1925–). American talk show host who has been widely syndicated since the early sixties.

Griffith, Andy (1926–). Rangy, slow-talking American actor with a nice line in wily country boys. Series: THE ANDY GRIFFITH SHOW, *The Headmaster, Salvage.* TV movies: *The Strangers in 7A, Go Ask Alice, Pray for the Wildcats,* WINTER KILL, SAVAGES, *Street Killing, The Girl in the Empty Grave, Adams of Eagle Lake,* WASHINGTON BEHIND CLOSED DOORS, *Centennial, From Here to Eternity, Murder in Texas, For Lovers Only, Murder in Coweta County, The Demon Murder Case, Fatal Vision.*

Griffith, Kenneth (1921–). Sibilant Welsh actor and film-maker, in the latter capacity specializing in passionate denunciations of British imperialism in South Africa, Ireland and elsewhere. Has consequently had a number of efforts banned, though also one blacked by the trade union ACTT, so he can't be all bad. *The Man on the Rock* (1975) is a quaint but compulsive reconstruction of Napoleon's detention on St Helena with Griffith mooching in and out of all the parts. *Clive of India*, likewise, 1983.   PP

✻ **Griffiths, Leon** (1928–). British writer of occasional but expert single plays (*Dinner at The Sporting Club*, 1979) and contributor to anthology and crime series. Creator of *Minder*. Writers' Guild Award, 1964; BAFTA Writers Award, 1984.   PP

Griffiths, Richard (19 –). Corpulent British actor who rose to stardom as the dogged hero of the computer-fraud thriller *Bird of Prey* and sequel. Thereafter *The Cleopatras, A Captain's Tale*, and Henry in the BBC Shakespeare's *Henry VIII*.   PP

Griffiths, Terry (1947–). Welsh professional snooker player, more entertaining than most of the new generation of same.

Griffiths, Trevor (1935–). British TV dramatist of firm socialist views, came into television originally as an education officer. Debut with series *Adam Smith* which he wrote under the pseudonym of Ben Rae. Then:

1973	*The Silver Mask* (from Galsworthy)	LWT
1974	*All Good Men*	
	episode of *Fall of Eagles*	BBC
	Occupations	Granada
1975	*Through the Night*	BBC
1976	*Bill Brand* (series)	Thames
1979	*Comedians*	BBC
1981	*Sons and Lovers* (serial from D. H. Lawrence)	BBC
	The Cherry Orchard (Chekhov)	BBC
	Country	BBC
1982	*Oi for England*	BBC
1985	*The Last Place on Earth* (serial)	Central

Griffiths was subject of a *South Bank Show*, 1984.
Book: *Powerplays* by Mike Poole and John Wyver, 1984.   PP

Grigsby, Michael (19 –). British film-maker who came to notice with *Deckie Learner* (1965), charting an apprentice deck-hand's first trip with the trawler fleet. Subsequently, *Deep South* (1969), *Two Weeks Clear* (1974), others.   PP

Grindl *
US 1963 32 × 25m bw
NBC/Columbia (David Swift)
A middle-aged maid gets a new job, and a new adventure, every week.
The star tended towards the eccentric and the stories veered towards the macabre, which gave the show two pluses, and several episodes still stand up as very funny in their own right.
cr David Swift
Imogene Coca, James Milhollin

Grizzly Adams: see The Life and Times of Grizzly Adams

The Grove Family (GB 1953–6). The Groves survived a mere three years on BBC television, or 69 hours of screen time, a passing moment compared to *Coronation Street*'s 1,300-plus. But they were the pioneers, the first real soap opera team in Britain. Gran Grove, played by Nancy Roberts as a testy old matriarch, became a folk heroine much in demand for opening fêtes and new department stores. When a new actress took over the part of pretty daughter Pat it attracted as much attention as a Cabinet change. The family's social standing exactly matched the imagined standing of the television audience in the mid-fifties – lower-middle-class suburban, forever repairing the old car or painting the ceiling. *Grove Family* actors were the first victims of the dilemma which sooner or later faces every soap opera performer: the steady income was lovely but the longer they remained identified with one part the harder it became ever to get other parts. Those that did survive the struggle included Edward Evans, Ruth Dunning and Christopher Beeny, then a child, now the grown-up star of *Upstairs, Downstairs* and *In Loving Memory*. Written by Michael Pertwee, produced by John Warrington.   PP

Growing Pains
US 1985   × 25m colour
ABC/Warner (Arnold Margolin)
A Long Island psychiatrist moves his practice to his home so that his wife can resume her career as a reporter. *Mr Mom*, in fact.
Absolutely standard domestic sitcom with sassy kids behaving pretty badly.

cr Neal Marlens
Alan Thicke, Joanna Kerns, Kirk Cameron, Tracey Gold
'Trouble is, the territory's been trampled to death.' – Hollywood *Reporter*

The Grumbleweeds Radio Show. Precisely-named British (Granada) children's entertainment adapted from long-running BBC radio series.

Grundy (GB 1978). Unsuccessful half-hour comedy series for Thames, with Harry H. Corbett as a corner-shop owner with an eye for the ladies.

Grundy, Bill (1923–). British linkman, mainly for Granada and Thames. Easily bored, he hit the headlines in 1977 when he allowed a punk rock group to utter four-letter words on a live teatime show. Television reviewer, London *Standard*, 1978–82.

The Guardian *
US/Canada 1984 96m colour TVM
HBO/Robert
   Cooper/Levinson–Link/Stanley Chase
A New York apartment house under siege by junkies hires a protector who may or may not be psychopathic.
Intriguing crime melodrama with mystical asides.
w RICHARD LEVINSON, WILLIAM LINK
d David Greene   *ph* Richard Clupka
m Robert O. Ragland
Martin Sheen, Lou Gossett Jnr, Arthur Hill, Tandy Cronyn, Simon Reynolds, Anthony Sherwood
'Not only a tension builder, it says a mouthful.' – *Daily Variety*

The Guardians
GB 1971 13 × 50m colour
LWT (Rex Firkin)
Britain under a totalitarian regime of the near-future, the first of several such suppositions during the seventies (*The Donati Conspiracy*, *1990*, etc). The Guardians are a strong-arm political police force who drive up in yellow Unimogs; but the emphasis shifts from them by the end to dwell too narrowly on a small group of top people playing familiar power games.
cr Vincent Tilsley *w* Vincent Tilsley, John Bowen, Jonathan Hale
John Collin, Cyril Luckham, Derek Smith, Robin Ellis   PP

Guardino, Harry (1925–). American second lead, in many films and TV guest spots. Series: *The Reporter, Monty Nash, The New Perry Mason.* TV movies include *The Lonely Profession, The Last Child, Partners in Crime, Street Killing, Having Babies, Contract on Cherry Street, Pleasure Cove.*

Guess Who's Sleeping in My Bed?
US 1973 74m colour TVM
ABC Circle/Mark Carliner
A man and his overwhelming family, including a large dog, turn up to stay with his ex-wife. Thin, fairly likeable comedy.
w Pamela Herbert Chais *d* Theodore Flicker *m* Morton Stevens
Dean Jones, Barbara Eden, Kenneth Mars, Reta Shaw, Suzanne Benton

Guestward Ho!
US 1960 38 × 25m bw
ABC/Desilu
City slickers take over a dude ranch and are hindered by a wily Indian.
Very moderate comedy.
Joanne Dru, Mark Miller, J. Carrol Naish

'The movie for couples who want to fall in love – again!'
A Guide for the Married Woman
US 1979 96m colour TVM
NBC/TCF (Lee Miller)
A bored housewife decides to spice up her life. Unappetizing attempt to provide a distaff side of the same writer's *A Guide for the Married Man.* Not funny enough.
w Frank Tarloff *d* Hy Averback
Cybill Shepherd, Charles Frank, Barbara Feldon, Eve Arden

The Guiding Light. American soap opera, on CBS five days a week from 1952, mostly in a 15-minute slot. With Millette Alexander, Charita Bauer, Anthony Call.

Guillaume, Robert (1930–). Black American comedy star, former opera singer. SOAP, BENSON, *The Kid from Left Field, The Kid with the Broken Halo, The Kid with the 200 IQ.*

Guilty Conscience *
US 1985 96m colour TVM
CBS/Levinson–Link/Robert Papazian
A criminal lawyer thinks of various ways in which he might kill his wife; but reality takes him by surprise.
Rather like a more serious *Unfaithfully Yours,* this little suspenser has plenty of tricks up its sleeve.

w RICHARD LEVINSON, WILLIAM LINK *d* David Greene *ph* Stevan Larner *m* Billy Goldenberg
ANTHONY HOPKINS, BLYTHE DANNER, Swoosie Kurtz, Donegan Smith
'An entertainment requiring attention and a sense of humour – and an appreciation of class.' – *Daily Variety*

Guilty or Innocent: The Sam Sheppard Murder Case *
US 1975 156m colour TVM
Universal (Harve Bennett)
In 1954, a Cleveland doctor is convicted, then acquitted, of murdering his wife: he later gives up his practice and becomes a professional wrestler.
Pretty absorbing true-life stuff, but this is too long a time to spend on a tale with no end: the doctor died without revealing the truth.
w Harold Gast *d* Robert Michael Lewis *m* Lalo Schifrin
George Peppard, William Windom, Nina Van Pallandt, Walter McGinn, Barnard Hughes

Guinness, Sir Alec (1914–). Eminent British actor whose television debut in Britain was not until 1969, when he played opposite Sir John Gielgud in a shorty by Friedrich Durenmatt, *Conversation at Night,* in the BBC's *Thirty-Minute Theatre* slot. Subsequently *Caesar and Cleopatra* and the role of George Smiley in *Tinker, Tailor, Soldier, Spy* (BAFTA 1979) and *Smiley's People.* TV movies: *Little Lord Fauntleroy, Monsignor Quixote.*   PP

Gulager, Clu (c 1929–). American character actor, of Cherokee and Danish stock, mostly on TV and with a tendency to imitate James Stewart. Series: *The Tall Man* (as Billy the Kid), *The Virginian, Harry O.* TV movies include *San Francisco The International, Glass House, Footsteps, Call to Danger, Hit Lady, Once an Eagle, Charlie Cobb, Black Beauty, King, Ski Lift to Death, A Question of Love, Roots: The Next Generations, The Gambler, Skyward.*

Gummi Bears (US 1985; 13 × 22m). Disney animation featuring a Robin Hood-like band of medieval teddies who help good kings with their magic. Not a riotous success.

The Gun
US 1974 74m colour TVM
Universal (Richard Levinson, William Link)

A gun passes from hand to hand.
Shades of *Tales of Manhattan* . . . but the
mini-stories here are not very interesting.
w Richard Levinson, William Link *d* John
Badham

Steven Elliott, Pepe Serna, Edith Diaz,
Mariclare Costello, Jean Le Bouvier

The Gun and the Pulpit
US 1974 74m colour TVM
Danny Thomas
A gunslinger on the run masquerades as a
preacher.
Hesitant variation on *The Left Hand of God*.
w William Bowers *d* Daniel Petrie

Marjoe Gortner, Estelle Parsons, David
Huddleston, Slim Pickens

The Gun of Zangara *
US 1961 97m bw TVM
Desilu/Quinn Martin
An assassin's bullet marked for the President
hits the Mayor of Chicago.
Solidly entertaining *Untouchables* feature.
w William Spier

Robert Stack, Bruce Gordon, Joe Mantell,
Anthony George, Claude Akins

Gunn, Moses (1929–). Black American
actor, a formidable presence. TV movies:
Carter's Army, *The Sheriff*, HAUNTS OF THE
VERY RICH, *Roots*, *Law of the Land*. Series: *The
Cowboys*, *The Contender*.

The Guns of Will Sonnett *
US 1967–8 50 × 25m colour
ABC/Spelling–Thomas
An old man takes his grandson on a long
journey to find his gunfighter father.
Western saga ingeniously providing something
for everybody, including a main theme not
unlike *The Fugitive*.
Walter Brennan, Dack Rambo
† Since the series was abruptly cancelled, the
elusive gunfighter was never found.

Gunslinger (US 1961). One-hour western
series for CBS, with Tony Young as a Civil War
veteran working under cover for the army in the
person of Preston Foster.

Gunsmoke *
Syndication title: *Marshal Dillon*
US 1955–60 156 × 25m bw
US 1961–75 356 × 50m colour
CBS (Charles Marquis Warren, Norman
    McDonnell, John Mantley)
Marshal Dillon keeps law and order in a small
western town.

Phenomenally successful family western which
in its later years came perilously close to soap
opera.
JAMES ARNESS, AMANDA BLAKE, MILBURN STONE,
Ken Curtis, Glenn Strange and, in early years,
DENNIS WEAVER

Gunston, Norman (1948–). (Garry
McDonald). Comic Australian performer
who hit on the brilliantly simple idea of
making a chat show as openly inept and
cringing as most of them secretly were
beneath the suavity. Lank hair was
inexpertly draped across his bald patch,
scraps of tissue plugged the wounds of the
morning's shave. 'Mick Jagger,' he would
fawn, 'I have admired you since you were
with the Beatles.' After a single tape was
played unheralded and unexplained on
BBC2 *c* 1979 a series was bought by C4 in
1982–3 but failed to catch on. The outside
sketches which increasingly augmented the
chat segments, it has to be admitted, were
pretty dire.   PP

Gus Brown and Midnight Brewster
US 1985 74m colour TVM
NBC/Kaledonia/SCOMI (Scoey Mitchill)
After World War II, two veterans return
discontentedly to a rundown Oklahoma
farm.
A pilot, potentially, for another *Dukes of
Hazzard*: mercifully, it didn't sell.
w Scoey Mitchill *d* Jim Fargo *ph* Ronald
W. Browne *m* Harry Middlebrooks

John Schneider, Ron Glass, Teri Copley,
Gordon Jump

Guyana Tragedy *
US 1980 2 × 96m colour TVM
CBS/Koenigsberg (Ernest Tidyman, Sam
    Manners)
The career of self-styled priest Jim Jones and
the mass suicides at Georgetown which ended
his nefarious reign after the murder of a US
senator who had been sent to investigate his
cult.
Overlong but fairly powerful piece of television
journalism; nobody can know how close to the
truth it is, and it leaves several points
unexplained.
w Ernest Tidyman, from an account by staff
members of the *Washington Post d* William A.
Graham *ph* Gil Hubbs *m* Elmer Bernstein
POWERS BOOTHE, Ned Beatty, Irene Cara,
Rosalind Cash, Brad Dourif, Veronica
Cartwright
'It's like picking at a scab to watch a festering
sore.' – *Daily Variety*

Guyler, Deryck (1914–). North country British character actor and comedian noted for his resonant doom-filled voice. Long familiar as a support for Eric Sykes and as the caretaker in PLEASE SIR.

Gwillim, Mike (19 –). British actor, slight of build, who can nevertheless play the hero. After disappointing pop-fiction debut as the ex-jockey in *The Racing Game*, blossomed in classic roles, notably Pericles in the BBC Shakespeare. Also in *How Green Was My Valley*, *Coriolanus* (1984), *Antigone* (1986), *A.D. – Anno Domini*.   PP

Gwynne, Fred (c 1924–). Long-faced, lugubrious American comedy actor, seen to advantage in CAR 54 WHERE ARE YOU? and as Herman the Frankenstein-monster-like father in THE MUNSTERS.

Gypsy Warriors
US 1978 50m colour
Universal (Stephen J. Cannell)

In World War II, two Yanks in occupied France enlist the aid of a trio of gypsies.
Tepid pilot which didn't sell.

w Stephen J. Cannell, Phil deGuere *d* Lou Antonio *ph* Enzo Martinelli *m* Mike Post, Pete Carpenter

James Whitmore Jnr, Tom Selleck, Joseph Ruskin, Lina Raymond, Michael Lane

Hack, Shelley (19 –). American leading lady, one of Charlie's Angels. *Cutter to Houston, Trackdown, Found Money, Single Bars Single Women.*

Hackett, Joan (1934–83). American leading actress. TV movies: *The Young Country, How Awful About Allan, The Other Man, Five Desperate Women, Class of 63, Reflections of Murder, Stonestreet, The Possessed, Pleasure Cove, The Long Days of Summer, The Long Summer of George Adams.*

Hadleigh *. British one-hour drama series (Yorkshire TV) about the problems of a landowner in keeping up his stately home. The rather languid Gerald Harper scored in the lead, and the scripts were generally interesting, intelligent and unusual. Several seasons were presented during the seventies.

Hadley, Reed (1911–74) (Reed Herring). American radio actor who starred in one of the earliest TV film series, *Racket Squad.*

Hagen
US 1979 74 or 96m colour TVM
CBS/TCF/Chad Everett

A mountain man comes to San Francisco to solve the murder of an old friend, and stays to become a lawyer's eyes and ears.
Tolerable pilot for a series which quickly waned in interest. Nine 50-minute episodes were made.

cr Frank Glicksman, Charles Larson *d* Vincent Sherman
Chad Everett, Arthur Hill, Samantha Eggar

Haggard, Piers (1939–). British director who has made a few films but seems principally to be a wizard in the electronic medium, notably with the series *Pennies from Heaven.* INTENSIVE CARE, 1982; *Desert of Lies,* 1982.

Haggerty, Dan (1942–). Stalwart American leading actor who co-starred with a bear in THE LIFE AND TIMES OF GRIZZLY ADAMS. TV movies: *Desperate Women, Terror Out of the Sky, Condominium.*

Hagman, Larry (1930–). American comedy actor who pops up everywhere but took a long time to pick the right series. *I Dream of Jeannie, Here We Go Again, The Good Life,* DALLAS. TV movies: *Three's a Crowd, Vanished, A Howling in The Woods, Getting Away from It All, The Alpha Caper, Blood Sport, What Are Best Friends For, Sidekicks, Hurricane, Sara T, The Return of the World's Greatest Detective, Intimate Stranger, Last of the Good Guys, Deadly Encounter,* etc

Haigh, Kenneth (1929–). Introspective British leading actor often seen in bullying roles; well cast as *Man at the Top,* and in *The Search for the Nile. The Testament of John,* 1984.

Hale, Alan Jnr (1918–). American light character actor, as cheerfully burly as his father. TV series: *Casey Jones, Gilligan's Island.*

Hail to the Chief
US 1985 13 × 25m colour
Lorimar (Paul Junger Witt, Tony Thomas)

Problems for the first woman President of the United States.
Initially popular comedy show which curiously failed to sustain itself.

cr Susan Harris, Paul Junger Witt, Tony Thomas
Patty Duke Astin, Ted Bessell, Herschel Bernardi, Murray Hamilton

Hale, Barbara (1922–). Perky American leading lady of forties films; won an Emmy as best supporting actress in 1958 for her years of playing Della Street in PERRY MASON. 1985: back on screen in *Perry Mason Returns.*

Hale, William (1928–). American director who graduated to a few movies after much television work. Series include *Time Tunnel, Cannon, Kojak.* TV movies: *How I Spent my Summer Vacation, Nightmare, The Great Niagara, Crossfire, Red Alert, Stalk the Wild Child, Murder in Texas,* etc.

LARRY HAGMAN. Being Mary Martin's son did not notably assist his career for twenty years, but being cast as the bad guy in *Dallas* did.

Haley, Jack Jnr (1934–). Fashionable American impresario of the seventies. Won Emmy 1967 for direction of *Movin' with Nancy*, later noted for nostalgic compilations.

Half Hour Story * (GB 1967–8). Both Rediffusion in the person of Stella Richman and the BBC, in *Thirty-Minute Theatre* produced by Harry Moore, hit on the idea of seasons of short studio plays, partly as an economy move, partly from a kind of Pre-Raphaelite urge to get back to the roots of television drama in the live, contained performance. A few actually transmitted live. The experiment was generally beneficial: Tom Stoppard was one of several writers to cut his teeth on the 30-minute format and Alun Owen went on to write a whole clutch of two-handers. PP

Half Nelson
US 1985 1 × 96m, 6 × 50m colour
NBC/TCF/Glen Larson (Harker Wade)
A pint-sized New York cop goes to Hollywood to film his own life story. Rejected because he is too small, he becomes a private eye.

Unpromising series entry with rat pack guests and old-fashioned gangster comedy. It quickly folded.
cr Glen Larson, Lou Shaw
Joe Pesci, Victoria Jackson
'Looks like a moderate entry.' – *Daily Variety*

Hall, James Andrew (1939–). British writer who made his name with plays on such ticklish subjects as homosexuality in *Coming Out*, 1979, and incest in *Broken Glass*, 1982. *Lucifer*, 1984, also serializations of H. G. Wells's *The Invisible Man*, 1983, *My Brother Jonathan*, 1984, *Brat Farrar*, 1985, *Portrait of Clare*, 1986, etc. PP

Hall, Monty (1923–). American quizmaster and host, latterly with the daily *Let's Make a Deal*.

Hall, Willis (1929–). Prolific British writer, both of solo plays (e.g. *The Villa Maroc*, 1972) and in partnership with Keith Waterhouse for *TWTWTW* items and many comedy series: *The Upchat Line*, *Cowboys*. Dramadoc about George Orwell, *The Road to 1984*, 1984. PP

Hallelujah! (GB 1982; 7 × 30m). Thora Hird as a Salvation Army stalwart in a sitcom written by Dick Sharples. Patsy Rowlands lent less enthusiastic support. Produced by Ronnie Baxter for YTV. PP

Haller, Daniel (1929–). American director, previously known as art director for the Roger Corman/Edgar Allan Poe cycle. Series include *Owen Marshall*, *Ironside*, *Kojak*. TV movies: *The Desperate Miles*, *Black Beauty*, *Little Mo*.

Halliwell, David (19 –). British writer, best known for one of television's first (and best) tales of grand passion, *Cock, Hen and Courting Pit* (1976). Also: *Triple Exposure* (1972). PP

Hallmark Hall of Fame. Generic title for an irregular series of drama specials sponsored by Hallmark Cards since 1952. Either the plays or the performers usually have something classical about them.

Halls of Fame (GB 1984–5). More music hall nostalgia from Roy Hudd as he and guests recall legendary acts from the stages associated with them, e.g. Flanagan and Allen at the Victoria Palace. Produced by Barry Bevins and Rod Taylor, for BBC Manchester. PP

The Halls of Ivy *
US 1955 39 × 25m bw
CBS/TPA/ITC
Problems of a college president.
Charming, unusual comedy series carefully devised for its star.
Ronald Colman, Benita Hume

Hamann, Paul (1948–). British documentary film maker who hit the headlines when his 1985 *Real Lives* about rival Protestant and Catholic hard-liners in Londonderry was banned by the BBC governors. In fact he had made eight previous films in Northern Ireland and been associated with two more, including *Fighting for Life* and *Fighting Back*, both 1980, about surgery developed in Belfast for blast victims and the experiences of British troops undergoing it; *A Company*, 1984, about the first British army unit to have gone into action in the province. Non-Ulster subject: *Survivalists*, 1982.   PP

Hamill, Mark (1952–). American leading man who starred in *The Texas Wheelers* – and *Star Wars*!

Hamilton, David (1939–) (David Pilditch). Cheeky-faced British host and presenter, long with Thames.

Hamilton, Neil (1899–1984). American leading man of the silent screen; remembered in TV as the Commissioner in *Batman*.

Hamlet at Elsinore **
GB 1964 150m bw (VTR)
BBC (Festival/Peter Luke)
The extra two words are all-important. It's not just *Hamlet* recorded on location, it's *Hamlet* as a Renaissance play in a Renaissance setting, and possessed by it. Hamlet's 'Get thee to a nunnery' speech occurs to him in the ornate pulpit of the chapel; the players spill with their baggage cart into a great, sun-dappled courtyard; the duel rages through stately apartments hung with paintings, fires burning in the grates. Philip Saville couldn't have better demonstrated the infinite possibilities of location recording.
d Philip Saville
Christopher Plummer (Hamlet), Robert Shaw (Claudius), Michael Caine (Horatio), Jo Maxwell Muller (Ophelia), June Tobin (Gertrude), David McCallum (Fortinbras)
                                                            PP

Hammer and Sickle (GB 1977; 100m; colour/bw). Blockbuster history of the Soviet Union since the revolution with some rare archive footage but also actors to 'speak for' the four men who had ruled the state in that time, presumably to convey the flavour of their pronouncements without the distraction of overlaid translations. It worked rather well with Olaf Poolley's Lenin, and paradoxically best of all in his testament, which was presumably a written utterance. With the others, the need to find an approximate facial resemblance resulted in some personality matches so unlikely as to be equally distracting. David Burke's Stalin was positively gentle. Brian Glover had muted his usual cheery self so thoroughly that Khrushchev had also lost all ebullience. Paul Scofield's tiresomely portentous reading of the commentary completed the impression of a curiously doleful occasion. Written by Neal Ascherson; produced by Martin Smith; for Thames.   PP

Hammer House of Horror (GB 1979). One-hour thriller anthology on film, made for ATV by Roy Skeggs and Brian Laurence. The old Hammer themes of witchcraft, diabolism, reincarnation and possession were vigorously re-used, with too much emphasis on gore. In 1983 thirteen 90-minute formats were produced, but the scripts were padded; known in America as Fox Mystery Theatre.

Hammond, Peter (1923–). British juvenile actor of the forties who turned director and kept busy in British TV with series episodes and single plays.

Hamner, Earl (1923–). American writer who turned his memoirs of southern childhood into a movie (*Spencer's Mountain*) and then into a hit series (*The Waltons*). Subsequently writing and producing: *Apple's Way*, *Falcon Crest*, *Boone*.

Hampshire, Susan (1938–). Demure-seeming British leading lady best remembered on TV as Fleur in *The Forsyte Saga*, and later in *The Pallisers*.

Hancock, Sheila (1933–). Angular British comedy actress, married to John Thaw. TV series include THE RAG TRADE, *The Bed-Sit Girl*, *Mr Digby Darling*, *Now Take My Wife*.

✳ **Hancock, Tony** (1924–68). Ebullient British comedian who found his niche as the seedy, argumentative, bumptious, self-important buffoon of *Hancock's Half*

TONY HANCOCK being sketched by Feliks Topolski for his famous 1960 interview with John Freeman on *Face to Face*. In the expression can be seen an unhappy man whose inner inadequacies did much to wreck a career whose heights are still cherished.

Hour on radio and TV. Some of the early sixties scripts, such as *The Train*, *The Bowmans*, *The Reunion Party*, *The Blood Donor* and *The Missing Page* are classics by any definition; but the star's tragedy was that he refused to take advice.

PP: 'Hancock's drinking and allegedly agonized attitude to his work have inspired two TV impersonations, thinly-veiled in the case of *The Comic* (LWT 1969, with George Cole), declared as such in *The Lad Himself* (BBC 1980) in which Peter Corey claimed to reconstruct the comedian's lonely dressing-room ordeal before recording one of his classic half-hours, specifically *The Blood Donor* on 2 June 1961. This was immeasurably the better exercise. Corey had mastered the popping, expostulatory Hancock voice and even took on a little of the Hancock look, which was of a frog nearly but not quite transformed into a handsome prince by the kiss of a sub-standard princess. You still wondered if Hancock really did fill in time quoting Grock to himself on the need for comedy to be born of suffering, or whether he just had a nap.'

† *Omnibus* memoir, 1985; *p* Derek Bailey. BBC videos available.

The Hancocks
aka: *The Dark Side of Innocence*
US 1976 96m colour TVM
Warner (Jerry Thorpe, Philip Mandelker)

Problems of a well-to-do family, especially a young wife who feels she must leave her husband and children for a while.

High-class soap, slow-moving and pretentious; the technical sheen and the good life depicted make it look like a feature-length commercial.

w Barbara Turner *d* Jerry Thorpe

Joanna Pettet, Kim Hunter, Anne Archer, John Anderson, Lawrence Casey, Claudette Nevins, Robert Sampson, James Houghton

Handl, Irene (1900–). Cheerful, dumpy little British character actress, a popular favourite for many years. TV series: *For the Love of Ada*, *Maggie and Her*, *Metal Mickey*.

The Hands of Cormac Joyce
Australia 1972 74m colour TVM
Fielder Cook

A killer storm threatens a fishing community off the Irish coast.
Slow, folksy outdoor drama.

w Thomas Rickman, *novel* Leonard Wibberly *d* Fielder Cook *m* Bob Young

Stephen Boyd, Cyril Cusack, Colleen Dewhurst, Dominic Guard

The Hanged Man
US 1965 87m colour TVM
Universal (Ray Wagner)

A crook fakes his own death and goes under cover.
Complicated thieves-fall-out mystery set against a New Orleans mardi gras festival; a remake of the cinema film *Ride the Pink Horse*.

w Jack Laird, Stanford Whitmore *d* Don Siegel

Edmund O'Brien, Vera Miles, Gene Raymond, Robert Culp, J. Carrol Naish, Norman Fell, Archie Moore

The Hanged Man
US 1974 74m colour TVM
Bing Crosby Productions

A gunslinger is unjustly hanged, but recovers and becomes a mysterious avenger.
Doom-laden western comic strip which failed to take off as a series.

w Ken Trevey *d* Michael Coffey *m* Richard Markowitz

Steve Forrest, Cameron Mitchell, Sharon Acker, Dean Jagger, Will Geer

The Hanged Man (GB 1975; 6 × 50m).
Tough building-industry tycoon likewise pretends to be dead in order to track down the mysterious assailants who have tried three times to kill him. Interestingly written by Edmund Ward for YTV, with Colin Blakely in the part. (All three shows of this title take it from the name of one of the cards in a Tarot pack.)   PP

'Before the night is over, more than a cable will start to snap!'
Hanging By a Thread
US 1979 2 × 95m colour TVM
Warner/Irwin Allen (Arthur Weiss)

Eight people are trapped in an aerial tramway, and on the mountainside three men are out to kill one of them.
Dire and interminably mechanical suspense drama in which one cares nothing at all for the outcome and can't see much of the action since the show is filmed in the dark.

w Adrian Spies *d* George Fenady *ph* John Nickolaus *m* Richard La Salle

Donna Mills, Sam Groom, Michael Sharrett, Bert Convy, Burr de Benning, Patty Duke Astin, Cameron Mitchell

'A four-hour disaster telefilm that would just about fill out a 30-minute slot . . . most of the characters deserve to plunge down the 7,000 feet.' – *Daily Variety*

Hank
US 1965 26 × 25m colour
NBC/Warner

Adventures of an unregistered college student.
A series which didn't even please its intended young audience.

Dick Kallman, Linda Foster, Howard St John

Hanley, Jenny (1947–). British performer, daughter of Jimmy Hanley; she presided over *Magpie* for several years. *A Man about the House*, *Task Force*.

Hanlon
New Zealand 1984 8 × 50m colour
TNZ (Lex Van Os)

Stories of a lawyer of the Edwardian era.
Flabby courtroom dramas with some interesting moments, but not many.

w Felix Winner, Ken Catron

David Gwillim, Sylvia Rands, Robyn Nevin

Hanna–Barbera. A brand name that means cartoons, and especially those scores of indistinguishable yakkity-yak series which fill American TV screens on Saturday mornings. In fact William Hanna and Joe Barbera were the creators of Tom and Jerry, back at MGM in the thirties, and it was much later that they opened their TV factory with its economical system of semi-animation (which means that the characters had a very limited number of movements). The most striking products so far have been THE FLINTSTONES, THE JETSONS, SCOOBY DOO and WAIT TILL YOUR FATHER GETS HOME.

Hannah * (GB 1980; 4 × 35m). Agreeable mini-serial under the *Love Story* banner, wrought by Lee Langley from E. H. Young's novel *Miss Mouse* about a retiring single woman who finds romance in a seaside town. With Helen Ryan. Produced by Colin Tucker; for BBC.   PP

Hannibal's Footsteps (GB 1985; 4 × 30m). Columnist Bernard Levin retraces the conqueror's route across the Alps, with meditations along the way on food, drink, tourism and patriotism. Pleasant if rather neat. Produced by Bernard Clark, for John Gau Productions/C4.   PP

Happily Ever After
US 1978 96m colour TVM
CBS/Trimedia III Inc (Philip Barry)
A lumberjack takes a shine to the distaff partner of a singing duo.
Mildly likeable, pleasantly set sex comedy.
w Garry Michael White d Robert Scheerer ph Edward R. Brown m Peter Matz, Mitzie Welch

Suzanne Somers, Bruce Boxleitner, John Rubinstein, Eric Braeden, Bill Lucking

Happy
US 1960 26 × 25m bw
NBC/Roncom
Parents discover that their six-month-old baby not only talks but knows more than they do.
Unfunny variation on *Mister Ed.*

Ronnie Burns, Yvonne Lime

Happy
US 1984 96m colour TVM
CBS/Bacchus/Dom DeLuise (A. Marco Turk)
A nightclub clown witnesses a shooting and finds himself on the run.
The emphasis is on the tears behind the greasepaint, with nothing to laugh at at all. Grisly.
w Larry B. Williams, I. C. Rapoport d Lee Phillips ph Matthew F. Leonetti m Billy Goldenberg

Dom DeLuise, Dee Wallace, Henry Silva, Tony Burton, Gil Morey, Jack Gilford
'The moments meant to be touching border on maudlin.' – *Daily Variety*

The Happy Apple (GB 1983; 7 × 30m). Comedy set in a failing advertising agency, and not so lucky itself despite a script by Keith Waterhouse from a play by the late Jack Pulman and the involvement of Leslie Ash, Nicky Henson, John Nettleton, Jeremy Child and Derek Waring. Directed and produced by Michael Mills, for Thames.   PP

Happy Days **
US 1974–   × 25m colour
ABC/Paramount/Miller–Milkis (William S. Bickley)
Domestic crises of a small-town American family in the fifties.
A nostalgic series inspired by *American Graffiti*, this homely show was quickly taken over by the character of Fonzie, a braggart college drop-out friend of the young son, and this made it the top-rated comedy show of 1975 and 1976.
cr GARY MARSHALL

HENRY WINKLER, RON HOWARD, Tom Bosley, Marion Ross, Anson Williams, Donny Most

† The 'pilot' for the series was a sketch with Ron Howard included in *Love American Style.*

†† 209 episodes had been made by March 1982.

Happy Endings
US 1983 96m colour TVM
NBC/MGM–UA/Blinn–Thorpe
When a widow dies, her 18-year-old son struggles to keep the young family together. The echo you hear is from the previous films on the same subject.
w Chris Beaumont d Jerry Thorpe
Lee Montgomery, Jill Schoelen, Sarah Navin, Robert C. Kiger, Robin Gammell

Happy Endings
US 1985 96m colour TVM
NBC/Blinn–Thorpe (Christopher Beaumont)
An 18-year-old boy keeps the family together when his parents die.
Typical TV movie sob story, not really for export.
w Christopher Beaumont, *article* by Rubin Carson d Jerry Thorpe ph Chuck Arnold m J. A. C. Redford
Lee Montgomery, Jill Schoelen, Sarah Navin, Robert C. Kiger
'Moving at a glacial pace, it fails to make dramatic or social points.' – *Daily Variety*

Happy Ever After. Basic British sitcom from the seventies, with Terry Scott and June Whitfield as long-marrieds getting into farcical scrapes. A perennial BBC favourite, written by John Chapman and Eric Merriman.

Happy Ever After (GB 1970; 6 × 50m; colour). ATV anthology series with a happy ending required every time. Of contributing writers only Alfred Shaughnessy rose joyfully to the task with an ingenious three-hander starring Kika Markham, Michael Coles and John Alkin. Directed by John Nelson Burton.   PP

Happy Families * (GB 1985; 6 × 35m). Ingenious new-wave comedy with Jennifer Saunders as an ancient beldame trying to trace long-lost grand-daughters – whom she also played – and lure them to a last reunion. Her emissary was the sublimely thick Adrian Edmondson. The best episode mocked *Dallasty* junk-serials. 'Funny, fast and brutal,' I wrote of it, 'but I don't suppose it'll do any better than waggish critics in opening people's eyes to the lunacies of *D & D*.' With Dawn French. Written by Ben Elton, produced and directed by Paul Jackson.   PP

Happy Since I Met You * (GB 1981; 60m; colour). Boy meets girl, they love, fret, fight and try to patch it up. Inimitable Victoria Wood play with Julie Walters, Duncan Preston, filmed by Ray Goode; directed by Baz Taylor; for Granada. 'One of the funniest and saddest plays of the year.' – *Television Today*

Harben, Philip (*c* 1906–70). Diminutive British cookery expert, ever-present on TV in the fifties and sixties.

Harbor Command
US 1957 39 × 25m bw
UA

Stories of the harbour police.
Adequate action series.
Wendell Corey

Harbormaster
aka: *Adventure at Scott Island*
US 1957 26 × 25m bw
CBS/United Artists

Stories of a New England crime chaser in a sailboat.
Adequate action series of its time.
Barry Sullivan, Paul Burke, Nina Wilcox, Murray Matheson

Hard Knox
US 1984 96m colour TVM
NBC/Metromedia/A. Shane (Joan Conrad)

A Marine colonel grounded for health reasons takes over as commandant at his old military school.
It's *The Blackboard Jungle* come back to haunt us; and in the last reel all the nasty kids turn out to be regular fellows. (Just to show it, they douse the commandant with water.)

w David J. Kinghorn   *d* Peter Warner
ph George Kohut   *m* Mike Post, Pete Carpenter

Robert Conrad, Red West, Joan Sweeny, Bill Erwin, Dean Hill

Hard Times **
GB 1977 4 × 50m colour
Granada/WNET (Peter Eckersley)

A pompous northern industrialist takes an ex-circus girl as his ward.
Talkative televersion of a difficult Dickens novel, strengthened by good bravura acting and at the beginning some remarkable local colour in the Victorian factory town and circus setting.

w Arthur Hopcraft *d* John Irvin *design* ROY STONEHOUSE (BAFTA award)

PATRICK ALLEN, Timothy West, Edward Fox, Alan Dobie, Ursula Howells, Jacqueline Tong

'One of the most impressive achievements of the year.' – *Baltimore Sun*

PP: 'John Irvin and Arthur Hopcraft ended where they had opened, at the circus, with Harry Markham as Sleary, the riding master, giving the stern Gradgrind a little sermon in tolerance. I believe these lines and this performance to be the most truly Dickensian I have ever seen on TV and a beautiful rebuttal of the grim utilitarianism Dickens so hated.'

† The title was also used in 1970 for a documentary about the Welfare State poor by Ian Martin, for Thames, and again in 1982 for a BBC series on the 'new' poor of the recession.

The Hard Way (GB/Ireland 1980; 100m; colour). Anglo-Irish TVM to consolidate everyone's most cherished prejudices about the Irish. Patrick McGoohan played a professional assassin who had decided to retire to his white-washed cottage in the West but was coerced into carrying out (or purporting to carry out) one last job. At the critical moment he turned on his employer instead and the story ended, eventually, with the two men mutually gunning each other to death. Whereupon maudlin, caterwauling Celtic music filled the air. It is difficult to think of a more accurate representation of the sentimental necrophilia which for 60 years has glorified the Irish gunman in his own country. With Lee van Cleef, Edna O'Brien. Michael Dryhurst produced and directed, John Boorman must share the odium. For ATV PP

Hardcase
US 1971 73m colour TVM
Matt Rapf

A western adventurer returns home to find his ranch sold and his wife run away with a Mexican.
Tolerable quest western.
w Harold Jack Bloom, Sam Rolfe d John Llewellyn Moxey
Clint Walker, Stefanie Powers, Alex Karras, Pedro Armendariz Jnr

Hardcastle and McCormick
US 1983 96m colour TVM
ABC/Paramount/Stephen J. Cannell
  (Patrick Hasburgh)

An eccentric retiring judge blackmails an ex-con into helping him track down villains who have evaded the law.
Loud, action-packed and thoroughly dislikeable yahoo pilot for an early evening slot. The series is in its third season at press time: 67 hours so far.
w Patrick Hasburgh, Stephen Cannell d Roger Young ph Edward R. Brown m Mike Post, Pete Carpenter
Brian Keith, Daniel Hugh-Kelly, Faye Grant, John Saxon, Ed Lauter
'The plot tread's so worn it leaves no tracks.' – Daily Variety

Hardhat and Legs *
US 1980 96m colour TVM
CBS/Time–Life/Linda Yellen

A New York construction worker pursues a society divorcee.
Moderately abrasive sex comedy which gets by on its one-liners.
w Ruth Gordon, Garson Kanin d Lee Phillips
Sharon Gless, Kevin Dobson, Ray Serra, W. T. Martin, Elva Josephson

'Social comedies haven't been much in vogue since the Colbert–Lombard–Hepburn days, but Gordon and Kanin show how much there still is left to shine.' – Daily Variety

Hardin, Ty (1930–) (Orton Hungerford). American leading man who came from nowhere to be TV's *Bronco*, and subsequently had a very desultory film career. Australian series: *Riptide*.

✳ **Harding, Gilbert** (1907–60). British panellist and talk show guest who became popular in the fifties as the rudest man on TV, though he usually talked good sense. His crumpling under intense personal interrogation by John Freeman in *Face to Face* is a famous piece of television.

The Hardy Boys
US 1969 17 × 25m colour
TCF/Filmation
Adventures of two crime-solving teenagers who use a travelling rock group as a cover.
Animated Saturday morning filler.

The Hardy Boys/Nancy Drew Mysteries
US 1977–8 58 × 50m colour
Universal (Glen A. Larson)
Alternating stories from the books featuring famous teenage detective heroes.
For indulgent children. Miss Drew fares better than the awful Hardys; the films stray further and further from the books, and the contempt for the audience shows in appalling inattention to detail.
cr Glen A. Larson
Pamela Sue Martin, Shaun Cassidy, Parker Stevenson
† Only 10 Nancy Drew episodes were made.

Hardy, Robert (1925–). Intelligent and versatile British character actor who played Prince Hal/Henry V in *An Age of Kings*, the senior vet in ALL CREATURES GREAT AND SMALL and Churchill in THE WILDERNESS YEARS. *Fothergill* (1981) was another winner but recent credits have been on the whole unfortunate: *The Cleopatras*, 1983; *Jenny's War*, 1985, *Hot Metal*, 1986.
For another TV activity of his, see *The Picardy Affair*.

Hare, David (1947–). British playwright of left-wing views, best known in television context for *Licking Hitler* (1978), and *Saigon – Year of the Cat* (1983). Also grim Mao-ist text, *Fanshen*, c 1975; and a story of obsessive love, *Dreams of Leaving*, 1980. PP

Harewood, Dorian (c 1946–). Black American actor. TV movies: *Foster and Laurie, Panic in Echo Park*, SIEGE, *Roots: The Next Generations, An American Christmas Carol, Beulah Land, High Ice, The Ambush Murders, Trauma Center, The Jesse Owens Story*.

Hargreaves, Jack (1911–). British TV personality, an authority on country matters who began his career as a vet; latterly introduced various nature programmes for Southern TV, then Channel 4.

Hargrove, Dean (1938–). American screenwriter. *The Man from UNCLE*, *Columbo*, *McCloud*, etc. Also produced several series.

Harlech TV: see HTV

The Harlem Globetrotters on Gilligan's Island
US 1980 96m colour TVM
NBC/Sherwood Schwartz

A basketball team makes a forced landing on an island of castaways, and fails to foil a crazy scientist with ideas of his own for the sport.
Elongated two-reeler with enough gags for only one. A woebegone effort to make a new series out of a format which only just survived in the more tolerant sixties.

w Sherwood and Al Schwartz, David Harmon, Gordon Mitchell *d* Peter Baldwin *ph* K. C. Smith *m* Gerald Fried

Bob Denver, Alan Hale, Jim Backus, Natalie Schaefer, Connie Forslund, Russell Johnson, Martin Landau, Barbara Bain, Scatman Crothers, the Harlem Globetrotters

Harmon, Mark (1951–). Intense-looking American leading man. TV movies: *Eleanor and Franklin*, *Centennial*, *Little Mo*, *Getting Married*, *The Dream Merchants*, *Goliath Awaits*. Series: *Flamingo Road*.

The Harness *
US 1971 97m colour TVM
Universal (William Sackheim)

A California farmer finds his toughness gone when his wife becomes ill.
Adequate character drama which outstays its welcome.

w Leon Tokatyan, Edward Hume, *story* John Steinbeck *d* Boris Sagal *m* Billy Goldenberg

Lorne Greene, Louise Latham, Julie Sommars, Murray Hamilton, Lee H. Montgomery

Harper, Gerald (1929–). Languid, aristocratic British leading man who came to the fore in *Adam Adamant* and later personified the landowner HADLEIGH.

Harper, Ron (1935–). Tough-looking American leading man, once understudy to Paul Newman. Series include *87th Precinct*, *Wendy and Me*, *The Jean Arthur Show*, *Garrison's Gorillas*.

Harper, Valerie (1940–). American actress who after several seasons in *The Mary Tyler Moore Show* became star of her own half-hour, *Rhoda*. TV movies: *Thursday's Game*, *Night Terror*, *The Shadow Box*.

ROBERT HARDY as the Gestapo chief in *Jenny's War*. A sound actor for many years, his peak will undoubtedly be the lead in *Winston Churchill: the Wilderness Years*.

Harper Valley PTA
US 1980   × 25m colour
NBC/MCA/Redwood (Sherwood
  Schwartz)

Snobbish senior members of a small-town community look askance at the innocent goings-on of a young widow.
Antiquated farce series consisting, like most of this producer's work, of a series of very thin jokes followed by pratfalls. A somewhat dismaying ratings success.

w Sherwood and Lloyd J. Schwartz *d* Bruce Bilson and others

Barbara Eden, George Gobel, Fannie Flagg, Jenn Thompson, Anne Francine, Bridget Hanley

'None of their efforts came close to being even mildly funny.' – *Daily Variety*

† The series was based on a sexy low-budget movie, and also on its catchy theme song.

Harpers West One. British one-hour tape series of 1960, created by ATV and featuring the staff of a fictional department store.

Harpy

US 1969 100m colour TVM
CBS Cinema Center 100 (Gerald Seth
Sindell)

A divorced psychiatrist rehabilitates an
Indian boy who jealously trains his pet eagle
to kill anyone who comes between them.
A half-hour story stretched out to four times
its natural length.

w William Wood d Gerald Seth Sindell ph
Robert B. Hauser m David Shire

Hugh O'Brian, Elizabeth Ashley, Tom
Nardini, Marilyn Mason

Harriet * (GB 1974; 6 × 30m). Game
reporter Harriet Crawley tries George
Plimpton's trick of having a go at sky diving,
lion taming and taking part in Civil War war
games, all spiritedly directed by Tony
Palmer, for HTV. PP

Harrigan and Son

US 1960 34 × 25m bw
ABC/Desilu

A widowed lawyer conflicts with his son
about how to run the business.
Watchable at the time, but no *Defenders*.

cr Cy Howard

Pat O'Brien, Roger Perry

Harris Against the World (US 1964).
Half-hour comedy series for NBC, a section
of a weekly 90-minute portmanteau called
90 Bristol Court. Jack Klugman was a
much-married man, always behind the
eight-ball.

Harris, Anita (1942–). British singer who
found a successful niche in programmes for
children.

Harris, Julie (1925–). American character
actress who found movie and stage success in
gamin-like roles. Her television series (*The
Family Holvak, Thicker Than Water*) were
not long-runners, but she won Emmys in 1958
for *Little Moon of Alban* and in 1961 for
Victoria Regina.

Harris, Rolf (1930–). Bearded Australian
entertainer, who won fame as much by
sloshing around with pots of paint as by his
songs, which however include *Tie Me
Kangaroo Down, Sport* and *Nick A Teen and
Al K Hall*. Many variety series.

**Harry Carpenter Never Said It Was Like
This *** (GB 1982; 50m). Neat if
over-sermonizing little boxing drama by and
with ex-boxer Peter Cheevers, helped by

advice from Ian La Frenais. 'Could have
done with a little more small talk,' I wrote at
the time, 'some bits of life not being lived
solely to advance Cheevers's thesis of
gladiators trapped in a business that is
exploiting and destroying them . . . but he
has an interesting, humorous face and there
were some good jokes among the
carefully-tended lines.' Also with Barry
Lineham. Directed by Anthony Simmons,
for Central. PP

Harry O

US 1974 75m colour TVM
Warner (Jerry Thorpe)

An ex-cop private eye with a bullet in his
back lives in a beach shack and takes on
occasional cases.
Glum *policier* which took off as a series after
the second pilot, *Smile Jenny You're Dead*.

w Howard Rodman d Jerry Thorpe m Billy
Goldenberg

David Janssen, Martin Sheen, Margot
Kidder, Sal Mineo, Will Geer

† The resulting ABC series ran to approx. 50
50-minute episodes, all of adequate
production quality. Also starring Henry
Darrow/Anthony Zerbe; executive producer.
Jerry Thorpe; for Warner.

Episodes:
Harry O (pilot)
Smile Jenny You're Dead (second pilot)
Gertrude
The Admiral's Lady
Mortal Sin
Guardian at the Gate
Eye Witness
Coinage of the Realm
Material Witness
Shadows at Noon
Ballinger's Choice
Second Sight
Accounts Balanced
Forty Reasons to Kill
Elegy for a Cop
Silent Kill
For the Love of Money
The Counterfeit People
The Last Heir
Double Jeopardy
Sound of Trumpets
Street Games
Lester
Lester Two
Anatomy of a Frame
Portrait of a Murder
Book of Changes
Shades
One for the Road

Tender Killing Care
The Madonna Legacy
APB Harry Orwell
The Acolyte
Reflections
Mayday
Mister Five and Dime
Group Terror
Exercise in Fatality
Forbidden City
The Amazing Case of Lester and Dr Fong
Ruby
Death Certificate
Past Imperfect
Hostage
Victim

Harry's Game **
GB 1982 3 × 52m
YTV (Keith Richardson)

Undercover army captain in Northern
Ireland on trail of IRA assassin, the two men
coming together – fatally – only in the
closing minutes. If this sombre thriller by
Gerald Seymour (from his own 1975 novel)
did not accurately reflect the deep
sentiments of the British people when
assailed by the news from Northern Ireland,
I hazarded at the time, it would have been
rejected out of hand. My guess was that on
the contrary it would have scooped the
ratings. It did.

w Gerald Seymour   *d* Lawrence Gordon
Clarke

Ray Lonnen, Derek Thompson

† A single-shot re-run followed on ITV,
1983.   PP

Harry's Girls
US 1963 15 × 25m bw
NBC/MGM

A hoofer escorts girl dancers around Europe.
Disappointing comedy drawn from the films
Les Girls and *Idiot's Delight*.
Larry Blyden

Hart, Harvey (1928–.). Canadian director
who had little luck with theatrical movies but
became a reliable television choice. TV
movies include *The Young Lawyers*, *Murder
or Mercy*, *Panic on the 5.22*, *Can Ellen Be
Saved?*, *Street Killing*, *Goldenrod*, *The Prince
of Central Park*.

Hart of the Yard (*Nobody's Perfect*) (US
1980). Shortlived situation comedy series
with Ron Moody as an inept London
detective in San Francisco. The role was all
too clearly modelled on Inspector Clouseau,
but there just weren't enough jokes. Ron
Moody, Cassie Yates; produced by MCA for
NBC.

Hart to Hart
US 1978 96m colour TVM
ABC/Aaron Spelling

A jet-set millionaire and his sexy wife solve
murders at a health resort.
Tediously inflated pilot for a surprisingly
popular series which borrowed the couple
and even the dog from *The Thin Man* but
found borrowing scripts more difficult.

w/d Don M. Mankiewicz

Robert Wagner, Stefanie Powers, Roddy
McDowall, Lionel Stander

† The one-hour series ran from 1979 to 1984.

Hartley, L. P. (19 –). British novelist
whose sequence about a brother and sister,
The Shrimp and the Anemone, *The Sixth
Heaven* and *Eustace and Hilda*, made an
elegant dramatic trilogy in 1977–8, adapted
and directed by Alan Seymour; produced by
Desmond Davis; for BBC.   PP

Hartley, Mariette (1941–). Personable
American leading lady. TV movies: *Earth II*,
Sandcastles, *Genesis II*, *The Killer Who
Wouldn't Die*, *The Last Hurrah*, *The Love
Tapes*, *The Secret War of Jackie's Girls*, *No
Place to Hide*.

Hartman, David (1937–). Rather
awkward-looking American character actor,
the Donald Sutherland of TV. Series include
The Virginian, *The Bold Ones*, *Lucas Tanner*.
TV movies include *The Feminist and the
Fuzz*, *I Love a Mystery*, *Miracle on 34th Street*,
You'll Never See Me Again. Latterly host of
Good Morning America.

The Hartmans (US 1949). Shortlived
half-hour comedy series for NBC, with
dancers Paul and Grace Hartman as a
suburban couple.

Hartnell, William (1908–75). British
character actor who was the first to establish
two memorable figures: Dr Who and the
sergeant in *The Army Game*.

Harty, Russell (1934–). British talk-show
host since the seventies, notable for
interrupting his guests at the wrong moment.
In the eighties also blundered into summer
seaside specials, US visits, etc.

Harvest of Shame ***
US 1960 50m bw
CBS (Fred W. Friendly)

Classic documentary with a purpose, narrated
by Edward R. Murrow and exposing the

victimization of migrant agricultural workers in the Midwest; a latterday *Grapes of Wrath* which proved the influence of TV in government circles.

Hass, Hans (19 –). German diver and naturalist who with his decorative wife Lotte made a number of underwater series for the international market and in 1966 branched out with an anthropological saga *Man* (BBC/Australian Broadcasting Commission/Suddeutscher Rundfunk) in which the human race was studied as if by observers from outer space. PP

Hasselhoff, David (1952–). American leading man who came to notice in *Knight Rider*. Also: *Griffin and Phoenix, The Young and the Restless, The Cartier Affair*.

Hastings, Max (1945–). British reporter and presenter who made his name as a Falklands War correspondent and participant in post-mortem programmes on that campaign. Has since written and fronted *The War about Peace*, a shrewd rejoinder to anti-nuke documentaries, 1983, and *Alarms and Excursions*, 1985, rather limp Nile travelogue in the wake of General Gordon 100 years earlier. Now Editor of the *Daily Telegraph*. PP

The Hasty Heart
US 1985 135m approx. colour VTR
During World War II, a Scotsman finds he is terminally ill.
Unexceptional remake of the theatrical success of the forties.
w John Patrick *d* Martin Speer
Gregory Harrison, Cheryl Ladd, Perry King

Hatch, Richard (1947–). American leading man. Series: *Streets of San Francisco, Battlestar Galactica*. TV movies: *Crime Club, The Last of the Belles, The Hatfields and the McCoys, Deadman's Curve, The Hustler of Muscle Beach*.

The Hatfields and the McCoys
US 1975 74m colour TVM
Charles Fries
The story of the hillbilly feud which exploded because two young people wanted to marry.
Surprisingly botched retelling of a story which has so often been told before.
w/d Clyde Ware
Jack Palance, Steve Forrest, Richard Hatch, Karen Lamm

The Hathaways
US 1961 26 × 25m bw
ABC/Columbia (Ezra Stone)
A suburban family adopts three chimps. Elementary family farce which had trouble lasting a season.
Jack Weston, Peggy Cass

Haunted
US 1984 96m colour TVM
WGBH Boston/Post Mill (Stanley D. Plotnick) for American Playhouse
A woman leaves her husband, irritates her family, and latches on to a disturbed neighbour.
Irritating modern drama about characters who let it all hang out – over other people.
w,d Michael Roemer *ph* Franz Rath
Brooke Adams, Jon De Vries, Trish Van Devere, Ari Meyers
'These people need more patience than they deserve.' – *Daily Variety*

The Haunted Heroes * (GB 1984; 55m). Embittered Vietnam veterans who have gone to ground in the forests of North America, unable to come to terms with fellow citizens who only want to disown that whole episode. This haunting programme was a *World About Us* special, shot by a wild-life unit who came across the hermits when making a nature film in the woods. Italia Prize, 1985. Produced by Tony Salmon, for BBC. PP

'She fears him. She senses him. She loves him. She wants him. A man she's never seen!'
The Haunting Passion
US 1984 96m colour TVM
NBC/BSR/ITC (Paul B. Radin)
The owners of a splendid seaside house are haunted by lovers who died in it.
A long way behind *The Uninvited*, this ghost story starts slowly and never picks up pace. Mood and atmosphere are totally missing.
w Michael Berk and Douglas Schwatz *d* John Korty *ph* Hiro Narita *m* Paul Chihara
Jane Seymour, Gerald McRaney, Millie Perkins, Ruth Nelson

Haunts of the Very Rich **
US 1972 73m colour TVM
ABC/Lillian Gallo
Holidaymakers at a lush tropical resort find that they may be dead and this may be hell.
Smooth, palatable, exciting updating of *Outward Bound*, only marred by an unnecessarily tricksy and confusing finish.

w William Wood *d* PAUL WENDKOS
LLOYD BRIDGES, Cloris Leachman, MOSES GUNN, Anne Francis, Ed Asner, Tony Bill, Robert Reed, Donna Mills

Hauser's Memory *
US 1970 96m colour TVM
Universal (Jack Laird)

A scientist receives another man's memory by chemical transfer.
Variation on *Donovan's Brain*, quite pacy and likeable.

w Adrian Spies, *novel* Curt Siodmak *d* Boris Sagal
David McCallum, Lilli Palmer, Susan Strasberg, Robert Webber, Leslie Nielsen, Helmut Kautner

Have Girls Will Travel: see The American Girls

Have Gun Will Travel **
US 1957–62 225 × 25m bw
CBS (Julian Claman)

A retired gunfighter hires himself out to right wrongs . . . and becomes the Philip Marlowe of the old west.
A careful and effective mixture of western and detection, with the right star and clever little gimmicks. (The hero's name is Paladin and a chess knight is printed on his calling card.)
chief d Andrew McLaglen *m* Bernard Herrmann ballad theme sung by Johnny Western
RICHARD BOONE

'For all his educated ways, Paladin is nothing but a hired gun who has made violence a business.' – Don Miller

Have I Got You Where You Want Me? (GB 1981). Ho-hum seven-episode comedy series about a dentist and his teacher girlfriend who after seven years' engagement haven't quite decided to marry. Eminently forgettable. With Ian Lavender, Kim Braden. Written by Philip Harland and Paul Harris; directed by Malcolm Taylor; produced by Brian Armstrong; for Granada.

Havers, Nigel (1949–). Personable British actor, son of Attorney General in Thatcher government. His many credits include *Love for Lydia*, *A Horseman Riding By*, *Unity*, a superb performance as a homosexual in *Coming Out*, and the amiable sitcom *Don't Wait Up*.   PP

Haviland, Julian (1930–). British reporter/newscaster, with ITN since 1961.

Having Babies
US 1977 96m colour TVM
ABC/Paramount/Jozak (Lew Gallo)

Three couples experience the birth of a baby by 'natural' methods.
Heavy-going serious soap.

w Elizabeth Clark *d* Robert Day
Desi Arnaz Jnr, Adrienne Barbeau, Ronny Cox, Harry Guardino, Linda Purl, Jan Sterling, Jessica Walter, Karen Valentine, Abe Vigoda, Vicki Lawrence, Greg Mullavey

Having Babies II
US 1977 96m colour TVM
ABC/Paramount/Jozak (Gerald W. Abrams)

Cases of a woman obstetrician.
More of the above, but this time with the eye on a series.

w Elizabeth Clark *d* Richard Michaels *ph* Michael P. Joyce *m* Fred Karlin
SUSAN SULLIVAN, Tony Bill, Cliff Gorman, Carol Lynley, Paula Prentiss, Nicholas Pryor, Wayne Rogers, Cassie Yates, Lee Meriwether

† *Having Babies III* appeared in 1978, written by Pamela Chais and directed by Jackie Cooper, again with Susan Sullivan as Julie Farr. Guest stars included Mitchell Ryan, Patty Duke Astin and Richard Mulligan. In the same year *Having Babies* became a shortlived 50-minute series, sometimes known as *Julie Farr MD*. Mitchell Ryan stayed on as a regular.

Having It All
US 1982 96m colour TVM
ABC/Hill–Mandelker (John Thomas Lennox, Tristene Rainer)

A lady fashion designer finds herself unwittingly guilty of bigamy.
Frantic farce with insufficient steam for half its length.

w Elizabeth Gill, Ann Becket *d* Edward Zwick *ph* Michael D. Marguilies *m* Miles Goodman
Dyan Cannon, Barry Newman, Hart Bochner, Sylvia Sidney, Melanie Chartoff

'As a comedy, it has little if anything.' – *Daily Variety*

Havoc
aka: *When Havoc Struck*
GB 1977 13 × 22m colour
ITC

Glenn Ford narrates, with the help of the Sherman Grinberg film library, the stories of spectacular disasters. Modest international filler.

Hawaii Five-O **
US 1968 73m colour TVM
CBS/LEONARD FREEMAN

Adventures of a special investigation unit of the Hawaii state government.

Pilot for an immensely successful series.

d Leonard Freeman m MORTON STEVENS title sequence REZA S. BADIYI

JACK LORD, Nancy Kwan, Leslie Nielsen, Andrew Duggan, Lew Ayres, James Gregory

† The resulting series ran for more than 220 50-minute episodes. By denying its leading man any background characterization it was able to concentrate on the crime and its solution, and the exotic locations took away any bad smell of violence. The production team of Bill Finnegan and Bob Sweeney was replaced in the seventh season by Richard Newton and Philip Leacock. The last episode was screened in the 1979 season.

†† Jack Lord decided to live in Hawaii and fancied himself as an important local figure. The *LA Times* said of his characterization of McGarrett: 'He wears perhaps the only blue business suit in the islands.'

Hawaiian Eye
US 1959–62 134 × 50m bw
ABC/Warner

Cases of a team of private investigators in Hawaii.

Elementary crime stories aimed at the youth audience, with lots of surfing when crime got dull.

Robert Conrad, Grant Williams, Connie Stevens, Troy Donahue, Poncie Ponce

'Afflicted with a severe case of the cutes . . . as for the cases, Peter Gunn could have solved them before the opening commercial.' – Don Miller

Hawaiian Heat
US 1984 96m colour TVM
ABC/Universal/James D. Parriott (Douglas Green, Dean Zanetos)

Two disgruntled Chicago cops set up as private eyes in Hawaii.

Muddled pilot with good Chicago scenes followed by Polynesian tedium. A series resulted, but ran only 13 weeks.

w James D. Parriott d Mike Vejar ph Edward Rio Rotunno m Tom Scott

Robert Ginty, Jeff McCracken, Tracy Scoggins, Mako, Branscombe Richmond

'Little credibility in view and nothing to suggest trade winds. There's much of setting cars afire or dunking them, and the plotline's familiar enough for viewers to move their lips by.' – *Daily Variety*

Hawk *
US 1966 17 × 50m colour
ABC/Columbia/Hubbell Robinson (Robert Markell)

Stories of a Red Indian police detective in New York.

His racial origins didn't make much noticeable difference to the stories, but the shows were pretty crisp and cancellation was a surprise.

cr Alan Sloane

Burt Reynolds

Hawkesworth, John (1920–). British producer associated with nostalgic shows such as *Upstairs, Downstairs* and *The Duchess of Duke Street*. He also wrote many scripts for these and for *Blackmail*, *The Gold Robbers*, *Crimes of Passion*, *The Flame Trees of Thika*, *Q.E.D.*, *The Tale of Beatrix Potter*.

Hawkeye and the Last of the Mohicans
Canada 1956 39 × 25m bw
CBC/Normandie

Stories based on Fenimore Cooper's hero and his faithful Indian Chingachgook.

Modest schoolboy adventure.

John Hart, Lon Chaney Jnr

Hawkins on Murder *
aka: *Death and the Maiden*
US 1973 74m colour TVM
MGM (Norman Felton)

A famous homespun lawyer defends an heiress of a triple killing.

Careful, unexciting star pilot which ran to a short series of 74m follow-ups.

w David Karp d Jud Taylor m Jerry Goldsmith

James Stewart, Bonnie Bedelia, Strother Martin, Kate Reid, Robert Webber

Sequels:
Die, Darling Die (d Paul Wendkos)
Murder in Movieland (d Jud Taylor)
A Life for a Life (d Jud Taylor)
Blood Feud (d Paul Wendkos)
Murder in the Slave Trade (d Paul Wendkos)
Murder on the 13th Floor (d Jud Taylor)

Hawn, Goldie (1945–). American comedienne who became popular as the dumb blonde in LAUGH IN but went on to become a genuine movie star in a variety of roles; also made television specials.

Haworth, Don (19 –). BBC documentary film-maker working mainly in the north of England though never confined to northern themes. Indicative of his variety of subject are three titles plucked at random from the early sixties – *Time on Our Hands* (prophetic look at life 25 years on), *Operation Cave Rescue* (out with a potholers' rescue team), *Grammar School Boy* (survey of what had befallen the alumni of one grammar school sixth form graduating 20 years earlier). Also author of one TV play, *A Brush with Mr Potter on the Road to Eldorado* (1981).   PP

Hawthorne, Nigel (1929–). Urbane British actor who became a comedy star with *The Knowledge* and then *Yes, Minister*.   PP

Hayes, Helen (1900–). Diminutive, distinguished American actress who in her older age had fun in all kinds of roles in every media: even a teleseries, *The Snoop Sisters*. TV movies include *Do Not Fold, Spindle or Mutilate, The Moneychangers, Victory at Entebbe, A Family Upside Down*. Emmy 1952 as best actress.

Hayes, Patricia (*c* 1915–). British character actress who after years of stooging in comedy shows came into her own in the title role of EDNA THE INEBRIATE WOMAN.

Hayes, Peter Lind (*c* 1908–). Easy-going American comedy actor who with his wife Mary Healy was a staple of early TV variety shows.

Haynes, Arthur (1914–66). Moon-faced British comedian who sprang to deserved popularity in the early days of ITV and had several series of his own during the sixties, playing a likeable social pest whose self-assurance was proof against the combined forces of manners, learning and authority. His straight man was Nicholas Parsons, better known now as a game-show gladhander.   PP

Haynes, Lloyd (1932–). Black American actor who starred in *Room 222*.

Hays, Bill (19   –). British director with sheaf of fine credits, especially in video productions such as *Orde Wingate* (1976), episodes of *Rock Follies* and the TV operas *Trouble in Tahiti* and *The Mines of Sulphur, Good Behaviour*, 1983.   PP

Hays, Robert (1947–). American leading man. TV movies: *Young Pioneers, Delta County USA, The Initiation of Sarah, California Gold Rush, The Girl, the Gold Watch and Everything*. Series: *Angie*.

Hayward, Louis (1909–85). (Seafield Grant). South African juvenile lead in American films of the late thirties. Later in TV series: *The Lone Wolf, Climax, The Pursuers, The Survivors*.

'A whirlwind romance. A storybook marriage. A loving family. And enough tragedy to break two hearts!'

Haywire
US 1980 2 × 74m colour miniseries
CBS/Warner/Pando (William Hayward)
The fevered family life of actress Margaret Sullavan, who committed suicide in 1960.
Slick but sometimes confused miniseries from a best-seller. Acting and production are slicker than the script.
w Ivan Davis, Frank Pierson, *book* by Brooke Hayward   *d* Michael Tuchner *ph* Howard Schwartz   *m* Billy Goldenberg
LEE REMICK, Jason Robards, Deborah Raffin, Dianne Hull, Hart Bochner, Richard Johnson, Dean Jagger, Linda Gray
'Vidpic pokes into private places and invades areas that are no one's business; try and stop watching it.' – *Daily Variety*

Hazel
US 1961–5 154 × 25m bw
NBC/Columbia/Harry Ackerman (James Fonda)
Comedy series about a suburban household in which the maid is really boss.
Adequate domestic situations constructed for a likeable star.
cr William Cowley, Peggy Chantler, from a *Saturday Evening Post* cartoon character by Ted Key
SHIRLEY BOOTH, Don Defore, Whitney Blake

Hazell *
GB 1978 10 × 50m colour (VTR)
Thames (June Roberts)
Adventures of an ex-cop turned private eye in London's rougher districts.
Abrasive and generally likeable if slightly muddled attempt to translate Chandler's Marlowe to another setting. Not a complete success, and too violent, but good TV entertainment.
w various, *books* Gordon Williams and Terry Venables
Nicholas Ball, Roddy McMillan

Hazlitt in Love * (GB 1977; 50m; colour). Kenneth Haigh as the distinguished man of letters who became famously infatuated with a teenage girl: a vividly uncomfortable performance, shot in fish-eye close-up by Mike Fash, directed by Michael Darlow from a script by C. P. Taylor. Produced by Mike Wooller; for Thames.   PP

He and She *
US 1967 26 × 25m colour
CBS/Talent Associates (Arne Sultan)

Adventures of a serious young cartoonist and his slightly daffy wife.

Modern urban comedy with an agreeable dash of sophistication.

Richard Benjamin, Paula Prentiss, Jack Cassidy

Head, Ann (19 –). Esteemed British producer, ex-film industry and 12 years in Africa. For the BBC produced the L. P. Hartley trilogy *Eustace and Hilda*, *Donal and Sally*, *The Fatal Spring*.   PP

Head On (GB 1961). Shortlived Granada series in which the celebrity subject was confronted with filmed assessments of himself by friends, neighbours and rivals. It worked well when the person was someone like Randolph Churchill, less well with Dr Hewlett Johnson, the 'Red Dean' of Canterbury.

† The idea was subsequently re-invented as *Face Your Image* (BBC 1975) in which Lord Hailsham, Clive Jenkins, Germaine Greer and others were likewise exposed to flattering or unflattering views, with David Dimbleby in charge.   PP

Head, Sally (1948–). Rising British producer, ex-story editor, who chalked up a hit with *The Detective*, 1985. Previously, *Inside Out*, also 1985. Lately, *Lives and Loves of a She Devil*, *Breaking Up*.   PP

The Headmaster *
US 1970 14 × 25m colour
CBS/ADA/Aaron Ruben

Problems for the headmaster of a private school.

Pleasing but commercially unsuccessful star comedy.

Andy Griffith, Jerry Van Dyke, Parker Fennelly

Headmaster
GB 1977 6 × 50m colour

Frank Windsor as school head having to move down to deputy head when his school is merged with another: a dogged spin-off from a BBC *Play for Today* of the same title by John Challenor, who also furnished the scripts here.   PP

The Healers
US 1974 100m colour TVM
Warner

Life in a medical research hospital.
Boring, rather pretentious pap.

w John Furia Jnr, Howard Dimsdale d Tom Gries m David Shire

John Forsythe, Pat Harrington, John McIntire, Beverly Garland, Anthony Zerbe

Hear No Evil
US 1983 96m colour TVM

A San Francisco police detective is made deaf by a murder attempt but with the help of a hearing counsellor rounds up the evil Bay Riders.

Slow-starting, good-looking pilot for a series which never happened; possibly just as well, since stories for a deaf detective must be hard to find.

w Tom Lazarus d Harry Falk

Gil Gerard, Bernie Casey, Wings Hauser, Mimi Rogers, Christina Hart

'A tumultuous love story that is incredibly true!'
The Hearst and Davies Affair
US 1985 96m colour TVM
ABC Circle (Paul Pompian)

The story of the millionaire publisher who was the basis of *Citizen Kane* and his affair with a Ziegfeld girl whom he turned into a star.

Rather creaky probe into a famous scandal, with too many poor impersonations of famous people.

w Alison Cross, David Solomon d David Lowell Rich ph Charles Wheeler m Laurence Rosenthal

Robert Mitchum, Virginia Madsen, Fritz Weaver, Doris Belack

'Glitzy mounting may add up to entertainment for many viewers.' – Hollywood *Reporter*

'A father whose unfulfilled dream becomes a reality through the love and courage of his son!'
Heart of a Champion
US 1985 96m colour TVM
CBS/Sylvester Stallone, Robert Papazian

Boxer Ray Mancini, injured in World War II, is determined that his son Ray shall win the prizes which he didn't.

One more sporting biopic with smiles through the tears.

w Dennis Nemec d Richard Michaels

Robert Blake, Doug McKeon, Mariclare Costello, Curtis Conaway

'All the punch of a powder puff.' – *Daily Variety*

'In hard times a winner is a man who fights from the heart!'

Heart of Steel
US 1983 96m colour TVM
ABC/Beowulf (Peter Strauss, Gary Devore, Richard Briggs)

An Ohio steel mill closes, with dire results for the workers. After much depression, the men work the mill themselves for the sake of making a statement.

Self-pitying, rather arty proletarian drama which doesn't seem to have met with a favourable response.

w Gary De Vore d Donald Wrye ph Frank Stanley m Brad Fiedel

Peter Strauss, Pamela Reed, John Doucette, Barry Primus, John Goodman, Gary Cole

'More artful than convincing, more dramatic than persuasive.' – *Daily Variety*

Heart of the Dragon * (GB 1984). Outstanding series on life in contemporary China, including editions on food and eating out and another on the investigation and 'people's trial' of a petty wrong-doer which was to be oddly mirrored in the bigger and better-promoted series about Russia the following year, *Comrades*. This one was made by Ash Films, for C4.   PP

Heart of the High Country (GB/NZ 1985; 6 × 52m). Windy epic following the fortunes of a girl emigrant to New Zealand in the late 19th century, replete with rape, revenge and ups and downs in the world. Written by Elizabeth Gowans from an earlier NZ television script, *A Woman of Good Character*. With Valerie Gogan, Kenneth Cranham. Directed by Sam Pillsbury, produced by Lloyd Phillips and Rob Whitehouse for Central (Zenith Productions)/Phillips Whitehouse.   PP

The Heart of the Matter *
GB/West Germany 1983 4 × 65m
C4/Tele-Muenchen (Peter Weissenborn)

Graham Greene's oppressive yarn of adultery and guilt in wartime West Africa, rather unexpectedly – but effectively – filmed by Germans with an Italian director, English dialogue and Jack Hedley enterprisingly rediscovered to play the hero Scobie.

w Marco Leto, with Gerald Savory d Marco Leto

Jack Hedley, Erica Rogers, Manfred Seipold, Christiane Jean   PP

Heart to Heart *** (1962). Terence Rattigan's TV play about TV for The Largest

Theatre in the World. There were nine simultaneous productions by the BBC, RTF France, ORF Austria, SRT Sweden, NRK Norway, RTE Ireland, RAI Italy, NTS Holland and YLE Finland. The BBC production by Alvin Rakoff had Sir Ralph Richardson as a corrupt cabinet minister, Kenneth More as the TV interviewer David Mann in need of a sensational coup, Jean Marsh as Mann's wife and Wendy Craig as his little TV assistant.

With delegates to a European Broadcasting Union conference I saw excerpts from the other versions two months later. Sweden had the first David Mann to look tough and cerebral enough for the part; Ireland had Norman Rodway; Norway had very deft camera work, and a Peggy Mann who looked like a bleached Eartha Kitt; Italy's version remained distinctly Roman, though the setting was still supposed to be England. The French had the television girl leave by bus instead of small car, but everyone had managed to drum up a Bentley, Rolls or Mark X Jaguar for Mann.

† The title was also used by YTV, 1977, for an interview series in which Colin Morris talked to people facing, or who had faced, acute difficulties.   PP

Heartattack Hotel (GB 1983; 75m). Very black comedy by Andrew Davies taking place in luxury country hotel whose regime of rich meals, much drinking and violent exercise seems designed to achieve the threat of the title. With Robert Lang, Michael Gough, Madge Ryan. Directed by Mike Vardy, produced by Rosemary Hill, for BBC.   PP

Heartland (GB 1979; 6 × 50m; colour). Sequence of plays by John Bowen, Donald Churchill and others to the daisy-chain device of *La Ronde*, one partner in each affair striking up a fresh romance in the next episode. Produced for ATV and set geographically in their Midlands franchise to give the title an extra shade of meaning.   PP

Hearts and Flowers **
GB 1970 75m colour
BBC (Irene Shubik)

Middle-class family gathers for the father's funeral. A gentle, perceptive comedy by Peter Nichols with the humour flowing as unforcedly as the odd tear, which I interpreted at the time as evidence of a growing realization among drama departments that pessimism for pessimism's sake is as great a lie as sticking on a falsely happy ending, and usually a graver sin.

d Christopher Morahan

Anthony Hopkins, Donald Churchill, Priscilla Morgan   PP

Heartsounds
US 1984 120m approx. colour TVM
ABC/Embassy (Fern Field)

A prominent doctor suffers a series of heart attacks and is sustained in his last years by the love of his wife.
Good acting triumphs over a downbeat and long-drawn-out script.

w Fay Kanin, *book* by Martha Weinman Lear *d* Glenn Jordan

James Garner, Mary Tyler Moore

Heat of Anger *
aka: *Fitzgerald and Pride*
US 1971 74m colour TVM
Metromedia (Dick Berg)

A lady attorney and her young assistant defend a murderer.
Competent courtroom pilot which didn't make it.

w Fay Kanin *d* Don Taylor

SUSAN HAYWARD, James Stacy, Lee J. Cobb, Fritz Weaver, Bettye Ackerman

Heather Ann (GB 1983). Ambitious but stilted filmed drama from the company which had lately taken over the ITV south-west franchise. Set in that area it had Maurice Roeves as a fisherman who winches up an unexploded torpedo. With Susan Penhaligon, Jack Watson. Written by John Oakden. Directed by Christopher King, for TSW.   PP

Heatwave **
US 1974 74m Technicolor TVM
Universal (Harve Bennett)

An energy crisis topped by a heat wave incapacitates the city and sends people scurrying for the mountains.
Uncomfortably convincing and well-observed social melodrama.

w Peter Allan Fields, Mark Weingart *d* Jerry Jamison

Bonnie Bedelia, Ben Murphy, Lew Ayres, Lionel Johnston, Naomi Stevens, David Huddleston

Heaven and Earth **
GB 1956 90m bw TVM
ITC (Dennis Vance)

More people will read this entry than ever saw the extraordinary film it records, made by ATV's programme-making subsidiary in

the early days of commercial television and shown only once. Paul Scofield plays an agonized American evangelist aboard a transatlantic flight which runs into trouble. His fellow passengers decide he is the Jonah who is bringing them evil luck . . .
The accents and attitudes have dated. The special effects would win no prizes. 'But,' I wrote after a 1985 viewing, 'the story is gripping. The whole thing has a force, a spontaneity, a rawness long lost from television.'

w Denis Cannan, Peter Brook *d* Peter Brook *ph* Douglas Slocombe

Paul Scofield, Lois Maxwell, Leo McKern, Marjorie Stewart, Richard Johnson, Dorothy Bromiley, Thomas Heathcote, Peter Illing, Michael Goodliffe   PP

The Heaven Connection
US 1982 74m colour TVM
NBC/Universal (George Eckstein)

Three new arrivals are unable to enter Heaven until they perform a good deed back on Earth.
Celestial comedy of the kind which was done much better in the forties.

w George Eckstein *d* Philip Leacock

Jack Gilford, Doug Sheehan, Ilene Graff, Ray Contreras

Heaven for Betsy (US 1952). Half-hour comedy series for CBS, with Jack Lemmon and Cynthia Stone, real-life newlyweds, virtually playing themselves.

Hec Ramsey: see Mystery Movie

Heckart, Eileen (1919–). Rangy American character actress, in all media. TV movies: *The Victim, The FBI vs Alvin Karpis, Sunshine Christmas, Suddenly Love, Backstairs at the White House, White Mama, FDR: The Last Year* (as Eleanor Roosevelt).

Hedison, David (1926–) (Ara Heditsian). Handy American leading man of the second rank. TV series: *Five Fingers, Voyage to the Bottom of the Sea.* TV movies: *Crime Club, The Cat Creature, The Lives of Jenny Dolan, Murder in Peyton Place, The Power Within,* Kenny Rogers as *The Gambler II*; *A.D.* etc.

Hedley, Jack (1930–). Pleasant, diffident British leading man who scored a hit in *The World of Tim Frazer* but oddly never had another series to himself. A stalwart of *Colditz,* though, and the lead in the German-produced *The Heart of the Matter,* 1983.

Hee Haw
US 1969–74 95 × 50m colour (VTR)
Youngstreet/CBS
Lowbrow comedy variety show, a kind of hick version of *Laugh-In*.

Heffron, Richard T. (1930–). American director whose few TV movies are all quite interesting: *Do You Take This Stranger*, *Outrage*, *The Morning After*, *The California Kid*, *Locusts*, *Death Scream*, *A Rumor of War*, *A Killer in the Family*, *Anatomy of an Illness*, *The Mystic Warrior*, etc.

Heidi
US 1968 96m colour TVM
CBS/Omnibus (Frederick Brogger, James Franciscus)
An orphan girl is sent to live with her hermit grandfather in the mountains.
Respectable, good-looking but not very spirited version of a children's classic which is too frequently attempted.
w Earl Hamner Jnr, *novel* Johanna Spyri *d* Delbert Mann *ph* Klaus Von Tautenfeld *m* John Williams
Jennifer Edwards, Jean Simmons, Maximilian Schell, Michael Redgrave, Walter Slezak, Peter Van Eyck
† The network screening began on time, thus pre-empting the last few minutes of a delayed football game and causing furore throughout the USA. For this reason it deserves to be a footnote in television history.

Heil Caesar *
GB 1974 orig. 3 × 25m colour
John Bowen's brisk rewrite of Shakespeare's *Julius Caesar*, originally a three-parter for schools, subsequently re-edited as a single piece for an evening drama spot. Revolution and counter-revolution in modern terms, with Antony's rabble-rousing speech now a nationwide telecast, stem easily from Shakespeare's text though setting the action in a seedy banana republic rather diminishes his lofty ideals. With Anthony Bate, John Stride, Frank Middlemass. Produced by Ron Smedley; for BBC.   PP

Heiney, Paul (1949–). British have-a-go reporter and presenter from radio via the *That's Life* school. *The Big Time*, *In at the Deep End*.

The Heist *
GB title: *Suspected Person*
aka: *The Caper*
US 1973 73m colour TVM
Paramount (Edward J. Milkis)

An armoured car guard is framed for the robbery of his vehicle.
Competent routine crime melodrama.
w Lionel E. Siegel *d* Don McDougall *m* Robert F. Drasnin
Christopher George, Elizabeth Ashley, Howard Duff, Norman Fell, Cliff Osmond

Helen – a Woman of Today
GB 1973 13 × 50m colour (VTR)
Another round in the way-we-live-now chronicle begun by *A Man of Our Times*. A marriage breaks up, with particular attention this time to what befalls the wife. With Alison Fiske, Martin Shaw. Written by David Butler and others; produced by Richard Bates; for LWT.   PP

Helen Keller – the Miracle Continues
US 1984 96m colour TVM
OPT/TCF/Castle Combe Productions (David Lawrence)
The blind and deaf Helen Keller as a young woman is surprised to find herself the object of a young man's affections.
Rather clumsily told sequel to *The Miracle Worker*, and as it turns out an unnecessary one.
w John McGreevey, *book* Helen and Teacher by Joseph P. Lash *d* Alan Gibson *ph* Frank Watts *m* Jack Tiller
Blythe Danner, Mare Winningham, Perry King, Vera Miles, Jack Warden (as Mark Twain), Peter Cushing, Alexander Knox

'He's a priest with a heart of gold in a parish filled with crime. Anybody who preys on his people better pray for help!'
Hell Town
US 1985 1 × 96m, 8 × 50m colour
NBC/Breezy (Robert Blake)
A reformed convict is priest of a tough inner-city parish.
Revolting mixture of violence, sentimentality and unpleasant characters. Come back, Pat O'Brien, all is forgiven.
cr Robert Blake
Robert Blake, Whitman Mayo, Amy Green, Tim Scott, Fran Ryan
'It may be just a bit too down and dirty for most tube escapists.' – Hollywood *Reporter*
'Only an actioner with its collar turned round.' – *Daily Variety*

Hellinger's Law
US 1980 96m colour TVM
CBS/Universal (James MacAdams, Jack Laird)

A swank Philadelphia lawyer goes to Houston in response to pleas from the wife of an accountant accused of murder.
Predictable but glossy pilot for a series which surprisingly never happened.

w Lawrence Vail, Jack Laird *d* Leo Penn *ph* Charles Correll *m* John Cacavas

Telly Savalas, Rod Taylor, Morgan Stevens, Janet Dubois, Melinda Dillon, James Sutorius

'A time-worn puzzle; suspense is minimal.' – *Daily Variety*

Helmond, Katherine (1930–). American character comedienne who made a great hit as the zany Jessica in SOAP. TV movies: *Dr Max*, *Larry*, *Locusts*, *The Legend of Lizzie Borden*, *The Family Nobody Wanted*, *Cage without a Key*, *The First 36 Hours of Dr Durant*, *James Dean*, *Wanted: The Sundance Woman*, *Little Ladies of the Night*, *Getting Married*, *Pearl*, *Scout's Honor*, *World War Three*, *For Lovers Only*, *Rosie*, *Who's the Boss?*

Help! It's The Hair Bear Bunch
US 1972 16 × 22m colour
Hanna–Barbera

Animals try to improve living conditions at the zoo.
Unmemorable semi-animated cartoon series.

Help Wanted – Male
US 1982 96m colour TVM
CBS/QM Productions/Bill Brademan, Ed Self (Bruce Kane)

A wealthy lady publisher finds that her boy friend can't have children, so she hires a man to give her a baby and then divorce her.
A tedious, unfunny idea becomes a tedious, unfunny film.

w Max Shulman *d* William Wiard *ph* Thomas Del Ruth *m* Nelson Riddle

Suzanne Pleshette, Gil Gerard, Bert Convy, Dana Elcar, Harold Gould

'Desperately flippant lines, contrived motivations and tasteless observations.' – *Daily Variety*

Helter Skelter *
US 1976 2 × 100m colour TVM
Lorimar (Tom Gries)

A fictionalized account of the Manson murders.
Extremely powerful, *In Cold Blood* type treatment of a case which is certainly not entertaining and should possibly have been left in the newspaper files. The narrative is somewhat confusing, assuming too much prior knowledge.

w J. P. Miller *d* Tom Gries *ph* Jules Brinner

m Billy Goldenberg

George DiCenzo, Steve Railsback, Nancy Wolfe, Marilyn Burns, Christina Hart

Hemingway, Ernest (1898–1961). Television rights have been sparingly granted. Two serializations permitted to the BBC in 1965–6 were on strict video-only terms. Both were produced by Douglas Allen with Rex Tucker directing Giles Cooper scripts. *A Farewell to Arms* was the more successful, thanks to the presence of Vanessa Redgrave. Despite the good actor John Ronane as the hero Robert Jordan, *For Whom the Bell Tolls* was a turkey. See also *The Sun Also Rises*, 1985.

Hemingway (NBC 1966) was a useful biographical essay. Apart from a tendency to precede every commercial break (there were at least four) with a slogan summing-up, the assemblage was neat and dramatic and made the most of a limited supply of pictures; but Anthony Burgess analysed Hemingway's life and work to better effect in *Grace Under Pressure* (LWT *South Bank Show*, 1978). PP

Hemion, Dwight (1926–). American director of musical specials, usually working with Gary Smith. Emmys 1969, for *Singer Presents Burt Bacharach*; 1973, for BARBRA STREISAND AND OTHER MUSICAL INSTRUMENTS; 1976, for AMERICA SALUTES RICHARD RODGERS; 1977 for *Ben Vereen – His Roots*.

Henderson, Dickie (1922–85). British comedian, son of another, tremendously popular in the fifties as star of a domestic comedy series, *The Dickie Henderson Show*; in the sixties made progressively fewer regular variety appearances, concentrating on dancing; made a come-back in 1977.

Henderson, Don (1932–). Pugnacious British actor, ex-Royal Shakespeare Company, who identified himself passionately with the character of Detective-Inspector George Bulman in *The XYY Man*, *Strangers* and finally *Bulman*. This last brought him his reward in the form of critical acclaim and a second series. PP

Henderson, Florence (1934–). American operatic singer who found herself also in demand as a light actress and mother of *The Brady Bunch*.

Hendry, Ian (1932–84). British character lead, in innumerable plays and in guest parts in series. Star of the original *Police Surgeon* which spawned *The Avengers*. Also: *The Informer*, *The Lotus Eaters*.

Hennesey *
US 1959–61 96 × 25m bw
CBS/Hennesey Co/Jackie Cooper
Comedy adventures of a naval doctor at the San Diego base.
Lively service comedy which gave good value.
cr Don McGuire *m* Sonny Burke
Jackie Cooper, Roscoe Karns, Abby Dalton, James Komack

Henning, Doug (1947–). Canadian magician, noted for his slim, youthful appearance (absolutely nothing concealed about his person); also for his careful re-creations of elaborate classical illusions. Mainly seen in his own variety specials.

❊ **Henning, Paul** (1911–). American radio comedy writer who made a big hit in TV as creator of *The Bob Cummings Show*, *The Beverly Hillbillies*, *Petticoat Junction* and *Green Acres*.

Henry, Buck (1930–) (B. Zuckerman). American multi-talent whose chief service to TV has been as creator of *Get Smart* (with Mel Brooks), *Captain Nice* and *Quark*.

Henry, Lenny (1958–). British comic who made it via the talent-spotting show *New Faces*, thence *Tiswas* and, decisively, *Three of a Kind*. Has terrific energy and cheek, playing anything from classical characters to a comical Afro-demagogue. Survived *OTT* (1982) to have own BBC series from 1984.
PP

❊ **Henson, Jim** (1936–). American puppeteer, creator of *The Muppets* (which derived from his *Sesame Street* inventions).

Heidt, Horace (*c* 1905–). American bandleader, a familiar face on US television in the fifties. Became mayor of Van Nuys, California.

Hepburn, Katharine (1909–). Distinguished American film and stage actress whose very occasional forays into television include LOVE AMONG THE RUINS (Emmy 1974) and THE CORN IS GREEN.

Hepton, Bernard (1925–). British character actor of sensitivity and warmth. Series and serials include *Colditz*, *Sadie It's Cold Outside*, *Secret Army*, *Tinker Tailor Soldier Spy*, *Blood Money*, *Kessler*, *Mansfield Park*, *Bleak House*. Single plays from *The Mosedale Horseshoe* to *Broken Glass*.

Her Life as a Man
US 1983 96m colour TVM
NBC/Lawrence Schiller (Mimi Rothman)
A woman sportswriter disguises herself as a man in order to get a job.
Silly comedy-drama which can't sustain.
w Diane English, Joanna Crawford *d* Robert Ellis Miller
Joan Collins, Robert Culp, Robyn Douglass, Marc Singer

Her Revenge
US 1985 96m colour TVM
CBS/David Greene (Robert Papazian)
Lives and loves of officers on a military base. Pocket-size soap opera, of no memorable interest.
d David Greene
Kevin Dobson, Kelly McGillis, Helen Hunt, Alec Baldwin

The Herculoids
US 1967 26 × 25m colour
Hanna–Barbera
On a distant planet, mythical animals protect their king against monsters from other galaxies.
Cartoon series sadly lacking the imagination of its premise.

Here Come the Brides
US 1968–9 52 × 50m colour
ABC/Columbia (Paul Claver)
When Seattle was a village, its menfolk imported a boatload of brides from the east. Pastiche of *Seven Brides for Seven Brothers* which falls somewhere between comedy, adventure and *Peyton Place*.
Robert Brown, David Soul, Bobby Sherman, Joan Blondell, Mark Lenard

Here We Go Again *
US 1971 13 × 25m colour
ABC/Metromedia (Lew Gallow, Steve Pritzker)
Newlyweds are plagued by the constant intrusion of their former, over-friendly, spouses.
Fairly rare attempt for TV at sophisticated comedy of the Powell–Loy kind. It didn't last because of strong opposition, but it did try.
cr Bob Kaufman
Larry Hagman, Diane Baker, Dick Gautier, Nita Talbot

Here's Boomer (US 1980–81). Half-hearted attempt at a dog series for syndication, in the wake of *The Littlest Hobo* and *Benji*. Mildly

The hospital made one small mistake.

He's Not Your Son

Donna Mills   John James

WORLD PREMIERE!
CBS WEDNESDAY
NIGHT MOVIES

9PM CBS◉2

HE'S NOT YOUR SON. Producers of telemovies scour the earth for stories of personal heartbreak, and this was not the only one to discover melodrama in the possibility of babies being accidentally switched.

appealing moments were available, but allowing the dog to 'voice' the commentary was a mistake. Produced by A. C. Lyles for NBC.

Here's Lucy *
US 1968–73 144 × 25m colour
CBS/Lucille Ball Productions (Gary Morton)

Last of the Lucy half-hour series, this one finds her as a widow working in an employment agency; but the gags are much as before.

LUCILLE BALL, GALE GORDON, Lucie Arnaz

† See also *I Love Lucy* and *The Lucy Show*.

The Hero
US 1966 16 × 25m colour
NBC/Talent Associates

A western star is scared of horses.
A thin premise makes a thin comedy.

Richard Mulligan, Mariette Hartley

Heroes (GB 1984–5). Modest provincial BBC series in which a celeb selects the figures, living or dead, he most admires. Produced by Roger Burgess for BBC North-East, it earned a network repeat.
† Also the title of a 1981 John Pilger harangue on Vietnam veterans. PP

Herridge, Robert (1914–81). American TV producer who created and co-wrote such technically influential series as *Camera Three*, *Studio One*, *The Seven Lively Arts* and *The Robert Herridge Theatre*.

Herrmann, Edward (1943–). American character actor, a hit as FDR. Series: *Beacon Hill*. TV movies: ELEANOR AND FRANKLIN, *A Love Affair*, *Portrait of a Stripper*, *Freedom Road*, Alger Hiss in *Conceded Enemies*, Fred Friendly in *Murrow*.

He's Fired, She's Hired
US 1984 96m colour TVM
CBS (Stan Hough)

An advertising executive loses his job and can't find another, so he stays home while his wife becomes a copywriter . . . and rises fast.
Modest variation on a theme which rapidly became over-familiar.

w Bob Shanks, *novel Paper Castles* by Judy Rand d Mark Daniels

Wayne Rogers, Karen Valentine, Elizabeth Ashley, John Horton, Howard Rollins

'The hospital made one small mistake . . .'
He's Not Your Son
US 1984 96m colour TVM
CBS (Sam Strangis)

Carelessness in a hospital results in two new-born infants being switched.
Glutinous motherlove melodrama, with one of the babies developing a heart condition. For addicts of the genre.

w Alan Collis, Robert Friedl, Alida Van Gores, Arnold Margolin d Don Taylor ph Robert Jessup m Charles Fox

Donna Mills, Ken Howard, Ann Dusenberry, Michael C. Gwynne, Dorothy Malone

'Takes itself so soapsudily serious it leaves a ring in the bathtub.' – *Daily Variety*
'Brings new dimension to the word "contrived".' – Hollywood *Reporter*

Hess * (GB 1978; 50m; colour). Solid reconstruction by Ian Curteis of Rudolf Hess's baffling flight to Scotland in 1941, for STV.
Curteis's script neatly but unobtrusively slipped the maximum character and quirkiness into the few bare lines allowed each person – the Scottish village policeman mortified that he had no cell for this surprising prisoner, Ivone Kirkpatrick mourning his lost breakfast, the gallant Duke of Hamilton (whose luxuriant haircut was the production's one eyesore) starchily disconcerted at being the intended recipient of Rudi's calling card.
The hardware, also, was unusually solid: the Messerschmitt, the staff car, the uniforms, all looked right. Most valuably of all, in the German actor Wolf Kohler Scottish Television had a Hess whose muddled motives, fantasies, ignorance and superstition came vividly alive.
† Hess was also the subject of a BBC dramatized documentary *The Strange Case of Rudolf Hess*, 1970, when he was impersonated by Victor Beaumont, a German-born British actor who had once met him. PP

Hessler, Gordon (19 –). American director who spent years as story editor on *Alfred Hitchcock Presents* and later built a reputation in Britain as a horror man. TV movies: *Strangers at the Door, Scream Pretty Peggy, Skyway to Death, Hitchhike, Betrayal, The Strange Possession of Mrs Oliver, Kiss Meets the Phantom*, etc.

Heston, Charlton (1924–). Stalwart American leading man who after thirty years in movies began to dip his toe in TV: *Chiefs, Nairobi Affair, The Colbys*.

Hewat, Tim (c 1930–). Australian current affairs producer who, in Britain in the fifties and sixties, made his mark with *Searchlight* and *World in Action*, TV's equivalent of the best kind of penny press.

Hexum, Jon-Erik (1955–84). American 'hunk' who was cast in the lead of the series *Cover Up* but accidentally shot himself after a few episodes.

Hey I'm Alive *
US 1975 74m colour TVM
Charles Fries (Lawrence Schiller)

The true account of two people who survived a light plane crash in the frozen Yukon.
A good start, but it gets a bit gruelling and repetitive.

w Rita Lakin, *book* Helen Klauben d Larry Schiller m Frank de Vol
Ed Asner, Sally Struthers

Hey Jeannie *
US 1956 32 × 25m bw
CBS/Four Star/Tartan

A Scots girl in New York helps a taxi cab driver.
Simple-minded but pleasing comedy series, a good showcase for a star who subsequently retired from the scene.
JEANNIE CARSON, Allen Jenkins, Jane Dulo

Hey Landlord
US 1966 31 × 25m colour
NBC/Mirisch–Rich/UA

An aimless young man inherits a New York brownstone and has trouble keeping it in order.
Forgettable comedy series.
Will Hutchins, Sandy Baron, Michael Constantine, Pamela Rodgers

Hey Mulligan: see The Mickey Rooney Show

Heydays Hotel (GB 1976; 52m). Guests at a seaside hotel in 1938 aren't quite what they seem, nor is the hotel. Nor is it 1938. A *trompe-l'oeil* play by Philip Purser, with Tenniel Evans, Nigel Havers, Lesley Dunlop, Susan Wooldridge, Anne Reid; directed by Derek Lister, produced by Julian Amyes, for Granada.   PP
'Witty, subtle, admirably acted and produced.' – Peter Forster, *Evening Standard*
'No-go, napoo, Heigh-ho.' – Nancy Banks-Smith, *Guardian*

Heyes, Douglas (1923–). American writer–director. In TV, wrote and directed pilots for *The Outsider*, *The Bearcats*.

Hi-De-Hi! *** (GB 1980–). Half-hour comedy series set in a holiday camp in the fifties but concentrating on assorted vagaries of the camp staff: nervous, crooked, effete, man-mad, etc. Generally a worthy successor to *Dad's Army* and *It Ain't Half Hot, Mum* from the same team, though the public was slow to respond this time. With Simon Cadell, Paul Shane, Ruth Madoc, Jeffrey Holland, Leslie Dwyer, Felix Bowness. Written by Jimmy Perry and David Croft; produced by David Croft; for BBC.

Hickman, Dwayne (1934–). American juvenile lead of the forties. TV's *Dobie Gillis*.

The High Chaparral *
US 1967–71 98 × 50m colour
NBC/David Dortort/(James Schmerer)

The life of a rich Arizona rancher and his sons in the 1870s.
Bonanza under another name, but a good western series with excellent location work.
cr David Dortort m David Rose/Harry Sukman
Leif Erickson, Cameron Mitchell, Mark Slade, Linda Cristal, Henry Darrow, Frank Silvera

High Ice
US 1979 96m colour TVM
NBC/Eugene S. Jones

Three amateur climbers are rescued from a mountainside.
Good-looking but very thinly scripted open-air drama with barely enough incident to fill half an hour.
w Sy Gomberg d Eugene S. Jones ph Bob Collins m Robert O. Ragland
David Janssen, Tony Musante, Madge Sinclair, Dorian Harewood, Warren Stevens

High Midnight
US 1979 96m colour TVM
Universal/Mirisch (Andrew Mirisch)

A man accused of killing his own wife and daughter tracks down the policeman really responsible.
Clumsy, padded melodrama which substitutes brooding for suspense and offers very little entertainment value.
w Michael and Kathryn Montgomery d Daniel Haller ph Steven Larner m Jerry Fielding
David Birney, Mike Connors, Christine Belford, Granville Van Dusen, Edward Grover

High Office
GB 1981 4 × 50m colour
Granada (Brian Lapping, Norma Percy)
Another of Granada's exercises based on the US Ford Foundation technique of a sharp interlocutor (usually a law professor) taking a panel of former ministers, civil servants, diplomats etc., through a hypothetical but familiar scenario – such as a *coup d'état* in a friendly country – to establish how they would react and why. Often absorbing television.   PP

High Performance
US 1984 4 × 50m colour
ABC/Warner/Lou–Step (Albert J. Salzer)
An ex-racing driver runs a training school for top security men.
Boring series about yet another élite action unit. The network soon spotted its lack of worth.
cr David E. Peckinpah
Jack Scalia, Lisa Hartman, Rick Edwards, Mitch Ryan, Jason Bernard

High Risk *
US 1976 74m colour TVM
MGM/Danny Thomas (Robert E. Relyea)
A group of professionals with special skills take on impossible missions at a half million dollars a time.
Polished, predictable, highly derivative entertainment.
w Robert Carrington *d* Sam O'Steen
Victor Buono, Don Stroud, Joe Sirola, Joanna Cameron, Ronne Troup, Wolf Roth

High Tor. Claimed as the first telefilm, this 1955 American production took 12 days to shoot. In the Maxwell Anderson fantasy Bing Crosby starred as the dentist who refuses to sell his land on the Hudson and is visited by ghosts from America's past. Julie Andrews and Nancy Olson co-starred.

Highway Patrol **
US 1955–8 156 × 25m bw
Ziv
Stories of the California mobile cops.
An efficient series which had the whole world answering 'Ten four' for agreement.
BRODERICK CRAWFORD

'God knows it's time we had someone like him on our side!'
Highway to Heaven
US 1984 96m colour TVM
NBC/Michael Landon (Kent McCray)

An angel is sent for training on Earth and manages to make some disgruntled old people feel great.
A clodhopping fantasy which lacks wit, pace and even magic: the angel does nothing clever and is content to offer a few words of Christmas cracker wisdom. The show however was a considerable ratings hit, and in the one-hour series which followed he was soon helping the grieving mother of a mortally ill child with the opportunity to adopt an orphan after the death of her offspring.
w,d Michael Landon *ph* Brianne Murphy *m* David Rose
Michael Landon, Victor French, Helen Hayes, John Bleifer, Eddie Quillan

Hijack
US 1973 74m colour TVM
Spelling–Goldberg
A truck driver with a secret cargo has to frustrate several hijack attempts along his route.
Rather sluggish action melodrama.
w James D. Buchanan, Ronald Austin *d* Leonard Horn
David Janssen, Lee Purcell, Keenan Wynn, Jeanette Nolan, Tom Tully

❋ **Hiken, Nat** (c 1903–68). Outstanding American comedy writer who created SERGEANT BILKO (Emmy 1955, 1956, 1957) and CAR 54 WHERE ARE YOU? (Emmy 1961).

Hill, Arthur (1922–). Canadian actor in Hollywood. Teleseries include *Owen Marshall Counsellor at Law, Hagen.* TV movies: *The Other Man, Vanished, Ordeal, Death Be Not Proud, Judge Horton and the Scottsboro Boys, Tell Me My Name, Churchill and the Generals* (as Roosevelt), *Angel Dusted, Revenge of the Stepford Wives,* etc.

❋ **Hill, Benny** (1925–). Rotund British comedian who writes the scripts for his own variety specials, which consist of rude rhymes and burlesque-type sketches, which he gets away with because of his ability to charm his audience as a naughty boy. His impersonations are usually his best effects. In 1979 his old specials were cut up into a half-hour series which had astonishing success in American syndication.

Hill, Bernard (19 –). Aggressive British actor who shot to fame as the victim-hero of *The Boys from the Blackstuff.* Since then, *The Burston Rebellion,* as Lech Walesa in

BENNY HILL with a few of 'Hill's Angels'. At the age of sixty he is still getting laughs by behaving like a naughty schoolboy.

Squaring the Circle (1984) and as John Lennon in the disastrous *A Journey in the Life* (1985).   PP

Hill, James (19 –). British film and TV director associated with wild-life features,

e.g. *Born Free* and *The Wild and the Free* (US TVM, 1980) but also had a popular television success with *Worzel Gummidge* series. Wrote, directed and produced *The Young Visiters* (1984).   PP

Hill Street Blues **
US 1980   × 50m   colour
NBC/MTM
Tragic and farcical elements intermingle in
the daily routine of a rowdy urban police
station.
Ambitious though not entirely successful
attempt at a sanitized version of a Wambaugh
atmosphere such as is found in *The
Choirboys*. Obviously sharp and intelligent,
but hard to watch for a whole hour.

cr Steven Bochco, Mike Kozoll d (pilot)
Robert Butler m Mike Post

Michael Conrad, Daniel Travanti, Veronica
Hamel, Bruce Weitz

† After half a year of poor ratings, the
network surprisingly renewed the show in a
creditable attempt to encourage quality; and
in 1981 it won nine Emmys.
†† Emmy 1983: Outstanding drama series.

Hiller, Arthur (1923–).   Journeyman
American director who after a routine TV
career (*Climax*, *Hitchcock*, *Perry Mason*,
Wagon Train) had uneven Hollywood success
with *Love Story*, *The Hospital*, etc. No TV
movies.

Hillerman, John (c 1934–). American
comedy character actor, often of neat and
prissy types. On form in *The Betty White
Show*, *Magnum*. TV movies include *The
Great Man's Whiskers*, *The Law*, *The
Invasion of Johnson County*, *Kill Me if You
Can*, *Betrayal*, *Institute for Revenge*.

Hine ** (GB 1971; 13 × 50m; colour).
Barrie Ingham as a British arms salesman,
and a private entrepreneur at that. A role
guaranteed to offend every soft liberal
consciousness nevertheless turned up trumps,
thanks to the cunning of Wilfred Greatorex's
format, witty scripts by Greatorex himself,
Peter Draper and others, and Ingham's
debonair performance. In a world dominated
by giant corporations and agencies the lone
operator Hine emerged as the last honest
man. With Colin Gordon as a good bad-
tempered foil. For ATV.   PP

Hines, Barry (19 –). British writer of
leftish views combined with strong affection
for nature, author of the novel and movie
Kes. For television, *The Price of Coal* trilogy
(1977), *The Gamekeeper* (1977), *Looks and
Smiles* (1982), and the nuclear cautionary
tale *Threads*, 1984.   PP

Hines, Frazer (1944–).   British actor,
resident heart-throb on *Emmerdale Farm*
since it began. Turned up amusingly as such
in *Duty Free*.

Hines, Ronald (1929–).   British
general-purpose actor too often cast in
supine or suffering roles (the goodie-goodie
brother to Michael Elphick in *This Year,
Next Year*, Susannah York's husband in
We'll Meet Again clearly destined from
episode one to be crippled or cuckolded or
both). But perfectly capable of being strong
as well as good, as in the BBC Ford Madox
Ford trilogy of the sixties.   PP

Hinge and Bracket (Dr Evadne and Dame
Hilda). Genteel British drag act of extreme
unfunniness. Often on chat shows, and their
own BBC series *Dear Ladies*. Hinge is
George Logan, Bracket Patrick Fyffe.   PP

Hingle, Pat (1923–).   Tough-looking
American character actor, in all media. TV
movies include *The Ballad of Andy Crocker*,
The City, *If Tomorrow Comes*, *The Last
Angry Man*, *Escape from Bogen County*,
Sunshine Christmas, *Elvis*, *Disaster on the
Coastliner*, *Wild Times*.

Hiram Holliday: see The Adventures of
Hiram Holliday

Hird, Bob (1934–).   Scottish director,
ex-cameraman, who came to notice with *A
Family at War*, *Hadleigh*, *The Main Chance*,
etc. Made the serials *Huntingtower* and *Rob
Roy* for BBC Scotland.   PP

Hird, Thora (1913–). British north country
comic actress with very wide experience
including presenting *Songs of Praise* and
starring in TV series (*Meet the Wife*, *First
Lady*, *Flesh and Blood*, *Ours Is a Nice House*,
In Loving Memory, *Hallelujah!*).

Hirsch, Judd (1936–). American leading
actor of the rough diamond type. Series:
Delvecchio, *Taxi*. TV movies include *The
Law*, *Fear on Trial*, *The Legend of Valentino*,
The Keegans, *Sooner or Later*, *Detective in
the House*, *First Steps*, *Brotherly Love*
Emmy 1983: outstanding comedy actor
(*Taxi*)

Hirschman, Herbert (c 1919–85). American
producer, sometimes writer, with credits
stretching back from *Perry Mason* and *The
Defenders* through *The Men from Shiloh* to
Planet of the Apes.

His Mistress
US 1984 96m colour TVM
NBC/Warner/David L. Wolper (Hunt
Lowry)   •

A career woman falls for her married boss, and the liaison has a bad effect on her work. Self-pitying mix of strands from *Brief Encounter* and a dozen old Rosalind Russell movies.

w Beth Sullivan *d* David Lowell Rich *ph* Charles F. Wheeler *m* Billy Goldenberg

Robert Urich, Julianne Phillips, Cynthia Sikes, Tim Thomerson, Mark Shera, Linda Kelsey

'The sort of telefeature that critics tend to pan and viewers seem to adore.' – Hollywood *Reporter*

The History Man ***
GB 1981 4 × 75m
BBC (Michael Wearing)

Intrigues and treacheries of a fashionably left-wing lecturer in sociology (the title refers to another character who never appears) at a 'new' university in the early seventies.

Malcolm Bradbury's lethal satire zoomed Anthony Sher to fame as the monster in question and gave newspaper headline-writers a new catch-phrase for any story involving an academic. 'When he is scheming, which is most of the time,' I wrote, 'you can hear the microchips in his mind flicking through the possibilities. When he is caught out he takes refuge in bluster.' 'Anthony Sher,' Clive James said in the *Observer*, 'has found a way of making the word "sociology" a visual experience. His moustache and sideburns preach well-barbered rebellion. His woolly tank-top worn with nothing underneath proves that he is a man with his armpits bared to experience . . .'

w Christopher Hampton, *novel* Malcolm Bradbury *d* Robert Knights

Isla Blair, Nigel Stock   PP

Hit and Run * (GB 1965). Who was driving the Jaguar which killed a man and never stopped? BBC serial set in a milieu which any London exurbanite could recognize as a faithful copy of his local golfing, gin-and-tonic-swilling, mildly philandering, two-car-owning community. Certainly the dubious pleasures of recognition played a strong part in this serial's appeal, which remained astonishingly high almost to the very end. Evelyn Frazer's script, from a novel by Jeffrey Ashford, drove forcefully and naturally to a suspenseful climax each week; the acting of relative newcomers like John Tillinger (Steve) was well matched to that of veterans like Joseph O'Conor. Produced and directed by Paddy Russell.   PP

Hit Lady *
US 1974 74m colour TVM
ABC/Spelling–Goldberg

A glamorous lady artist is really a professional killer.

Ludicrously unlikely murder melodrama with predictable twists and glossy presentation.

w Yvette Mimieux *d* Tracy Keenan Wynn

Yvette Mimieux, Dack Rambo, Joseph Campanella, Clu Gulager, Keenan Wynn

Hitchcock, Alfred (1899–). See Alfred Hitchcock Presents

Hitched
GB title: *Westward the Wagon*
US 1973 74m colour TVM
NBC/Universal (Richard Alan Simmons)

Further adventures of the teenage newlyweds in the old west, first encountered in *Lock, Stock and Barrel*. No series resulted.

w Richard Alan Simmons *d* Boris Sagal *ph* Gerald Perry Finnermann *m* Pat Williams

Sally Field, Tim Matheson, Neville Brand, Slim Pickens, John Fiedler, Denver Pyle

Hitchhike!
US 1974 74m colour TVM
NBC/Universal (Jay Benson)

A woman driving off on vacation unwittingly gives a lift to a murderer.

Adequate tension piece without anything very memorable about it.

w Yale M. Udoff *d* Gordon Hessler *ph* Leonard J. South *m* Gil Melle

Cloris Leachman, Michael Brandon, Henry Darrow, Cameron Mitchell, Linden Chiles

Hitchhiker
US/Canada 1984 30 × 25m colour
Lorimar/Quintana

Stories with twists in the tail are linked by a wandering figure of doom.

Shades of *The Whistler*, but this series made for cable is usually a little over the top.

cr Riff Markowitz, Lewis Chesler, Richard Rothstein

The Hitch-Hiker's Guide to the Galaxy (GB 1981). Gallant attempt to translate in visual terms, as six half-hours, a successful Monty Pythonish radio serial which managed to send up space fiction while retaining serious overtones. The presentation was as way out as the subject matter, with the success/failure rate about fifty-fifty. With Peter Jones, Simon Jones, Joe Melia, Martin Benson, David Dixon. Written by DOUGLAS ADAMS; directed and produced by Alan J. W. Bell; designed by Andrew Howe-Davies; for BBC.

Hitler's SS: Portrait in Evil
US 1985 142m approx. colour TVM
NBC/Edgar J. Scherick (Aida Young)

Events in the life of a middle-class Stuttgart family under the Third Reich, as the elder brother becomes a devotee of Hitler.

Earnest, predictable, but rather clumsy telefilm which in the end gets nowhere.

w Lukas Heller d James Goddard
ph Ernest Vincze m Richard Hartley
pd Eileen Diss, Michael Porter

John Shea, Bill Nighy, Lucy Gutteridge, Robert Urquhart, Carroll Baker, Tony Randall, David Warner, Jose Ferrer, Michael Elphick, Stratford Johns

Hoare, Ken (1929–). British comedy writer, responsible for all Stanley Baxter shows of last 30 years.

The Hobbit
US 1977 74m colour TVM
NBC/Rankin–Bass/Xerox

A cartoon version of the book by J. R. R. Tolkien. The air of otherworldly fantasy is well sustained, though what passes for plot is insufficiently nourishing.

w Romeo Muller d Arthur Rankin Jnr, Jules Bass

(voices) John Huston, Orson Bean, Richard Boone, Otto Preminger, Cyril Ritchard, Hans Conried

Hobley, MacDonald (c 1915–). British announcer and light actor, one of TV's earliest personalities.

Hobson's Choice
US 1983 96m colour TVM
CBS (Blue Andre, Vanessa Greene)

A drunken shoemaker finds his eldest daughter is more than a match for his wiles. Yawnworthy transposition of the famous comedy from Lancashire to New Orleans. It suffers horribly in the crossing.

w Burt Prelutsky play by Harold Brighouse
d Gilbert Cates ph Isidore Mankofsky
m Robert Drasnin

Richard Thomas, Sharon Gless, Jack Warden, Lillian Gish, Bert Remsen, Wynn Irwin, Lenora May

'They have tossed out not only the delights but also jettisoned any sympathy for the characters or their plight.' – Daily Variety

Hodge, Al (–   ). American actor, a strong fearless type who five days a week in the 1950s starred as Captain Video. After six years he found himself hopelessly typecast and unable to get further acting jobs.

Hodge, Patricia (1946–). Statuesque British actress who has enlivened Edward and Mrs Simpson, Winston Churchill – the Wilderness Years, etc. Own series not so successful: Holding the Fort, Jemima Shore Investigates. PP

Hogan, Paul (1941–). Australian comedian specializing in 'ocker' (i.e. redneck or rough male) characterization. His Foster's Lager commercials went down better in Britain than his C4 series of 1982–3, re-edited from his Australian show with two programmes made in GB. PP

Hogan's Heroes **
US 1965–70 168 × 25m colour
CBS/Bing Crosby Productions (Edward H. Feldman)

American prisoners raise Cain in a German camp during World War II.

Based unofficially on Stalag 17, this is a rather tactless farce which comes off, chiefly because the Germans are likeable idiots. The level of plot invention is quite high, considering the constrained settings.

Bob Crane, WERNER KLEMPERER, JOHN BANNER, Robert Clary, Richard Dawson, Ivan Dixon

Holbrook, Hal (1925–). Diligent American actor who made a stage hit with his one-man show as Mark Twain. TV movies include A Clear and Present Danger, Suddenly Single, Goodbye Raggedy Ann, THAT CERTAIN SUMMER, THE PUEBLO AFFAIR (Emmy 1973), Sandburg's Lincoln (Emmy 1975), The Awakening Land, Murder by Natural Causes, The Killing of Randy Webster, George Washington, The Three Wishes of Billy Grier, 92 Grosvenor Street.

Hold the Back Page *
GB 1985 10 × 50m
BBC (Evgeny Gridneff)

Fleet Street sports writer moves from posh Sunday to tabloid daily, thereby encountering a different class of customer and a different set of values. Greeted by Fleet Street rather lukewarmly, the series went on to do quite nicely, thanks to ingenious plots and David Warner's lugubrious mug as the hero.

w Andrew Nickolds, Stan Hey
d Christopher Baker

David Warner, Richard Ireson, Tilly Vosburgh, David Horovitch PP

Holden, William (1918–81) (William Beedle). American film star whose television appearances included THE BLUE KNIGHT (Emmy 1973) and *21 Hours in Munich*.

Holding On (GB 1977). Serialization for LWT of Mervyn Jones's lifespan story of a London docker, via usual landmarks of two world wars, General Strike, Depression, Socialist struggles; worthy rather than exciting. With Michael Elphick; written by Brian Phelan.   PP

Holding the Fort (GB 1980). Strained half-hour comedy series about an executive who stays at home to run his own brewery and look after the children, while his wife goes back to army work. Strictly a filler. With Peter Davison, Patricia Hodge. Written by Laurence Marks, Maurice Gran; produced and directed by Derrick Goodwin; for LWT.

Holiday Lodge
US 1961 13 × 25m bw
CBS/J & M/Universal
Two incompetents are social directors at a summer resort.
A disappointing Hollywood excursion for Canada's favourite comics.
Johnny Wayne, Frank Shuster

Holles, Robert (1926–). British writer, ex-regular soldier (Korea) who put his experience in the ranks to effective, often subtle use in a score of service-life plays, e.g. *The Breaking of Colonel Keyser*, *The Discharge of Trooper Lusby*. But he also wrote the powerful *Michael Regan* and since *Vanishing Army* (1979) has abjured military subjects. *Fothergill* (1981) skilfully adapted John Fothergill's minor literary masterpiece, *An Innkeeper's Diary*.   PP

Holliman, Earl (1928–). American actor who graduated from weak roles to toughies. TV series include *Hotel de Paree*, *The Wide Country*, *Police Woman*. TV movies include *Tribes*, *Cannon*, *Desperate Mission*, *Trapped*, *Cry Panic*, *I Love You Goodbye*, *Alexander: The Other Side of Dawn*, *The Solitary Man*, *Where the Ladies Go*, *The Thorn Birds*

Hollow Image
US 1980 96m colour TVM
ABC/Titus (Herbert Brodkin)
A black fashion designer struggles to find her identity.
Yawnworthy urban *Roots*, very slick but very empty.
w Lee Hunkins *d* Marvin Chomsky *ph* Alan Metzger *m* Don Sebesky

Saundra Sharp, Robert Hooks, Dick Anthony Williams, Morgan Freeman
'Suds bubble up through the pretentious dialogue; stock characters abound.' – *Daily Variety*

Holloway, Stanley (1890–1982). British comedy character actor and music hall performer who tried almost everything during a long career. TV series: *Our Man Higgins*, *Thingummyjig*.

Holly
GB 1972 6 × 50m colour
Granada (Michael Cox)
Equivocal serial slightly reminiscent of *The Collector*, about pretty young woman held in semi-voluntary captivity by mentally oppressed hero. Better than a summary suggests but eventually unsatisfactory. Substitute white steed for battered van, hawk-visaged Arab sheik for disturbed visionary, and Holly could have been any heroine of romantic fiction 50 years ago.
w Robin Chapman *d* Gareth Davies, Brian Mills
Brigid Forsyth, David Burke   PP

Hollywood. The citadel of movie-making, which reacted so vigorously against television in the fifties, found the new medium necessary to its survival. With most 'movie movies' now shot on location, Hollywood studios were kept going only by television production, everything on film and almost everything on tape having been based in Los Angeles since the mid-sixties.

Hollywood *
GB 1979 13 × 50m colour
Thames (Mike Wooller)
Detailed, loving history of the great days of the movie capital, with a steady message that the silent films, so easily derided today, were in fact works of art when projected at proper speeds and accompanied by the cinema orchestras of their day. A saga of American history as well as cinema history.
w/d KEVIN BROWNLOW, David Gill *narrator* James Mason   PP
LH: 'I would give it at least three stars.'

Hollywood and the Stars *
US 1963 31 × 25m bw
NBC/Wolper/UA (Jack Haley Jnr)
Compilations of old movie scenes, introduced by Joseph Cotten. Those dealing with a theme (gangsters, monsters) are best.

Hollywood Beat
US 1985   × 50m colour
ABC/Warner/Aaron Spelling (Henry
  Rosenbaum)

Low-life adventures of undercover police
officers.

Nasty attempt to rip off *Miami Vice*. Nobody
was interested.

cr Henry Rosenbaum

Jack Scalia, Jay Acovone, Lane Smith, John
Matuszak, Edward Winter

'Repulsive.' – *LA Times*

The Hollywood Greats (GB 1978). A
continuing series of 50-minute investigations
into the appeal, the careers and the private
lives of dead stars, wittily put together and
presented (on a high budget) by BARRY
NORMAN, who in 1981 won BAFTA's Richard
Dimbleby Award for doing so and for
presenting a weekly analysis of films as they
come. Stars so far given the treatment include
Jean Harlow, Joan Crawford, Edward G.
Robinson, the Marx Brothers, Spencer
Tracy, Clark Gable and Ronald Colman; the
British series included Leslie Howard,
Robert Donat and Jack Hawkins. The format
also took in occasional looks at directors, as
in *Ready When You Are, Mr DeMille*.

Hollywood Off Beat
US 1953 13 × 25m bw
Marion Parsonnet

Dire private eye yarns wasting an excellent
star.

Melvyn Douglas

Hollywood or Bust * (GB 1984). Audience
participation show with Bruce Forsyth
shepherding the contestants through tiny
playlets allegedly based on *Gone with the
Wind* or other familiar epics. Inexplicably, it
failed to win favour and now seems to have
been written out of the annals. For the
record it was produced by Keith Beckett, for
Thames.   PP

Hollywood Palace. A regular feature of the
late fifties and early sixties, this American
hour-long series re-created an old-time
vaudeville bill, and most of the world's big
stars appeared in it.

Hollywood Squares. An elaborate quiz
show in which nine celebrities have to answer
the questions, and contestants guess whether
they are right, with scores like noughts and
crosses (tic tac toe). Popular throughout the
seventies, in Britain as *Celebrity Squares*.

Hollywood Wives
US 1985 3 × 96m colour miniseries
ABC/Warner/Aaron Spelling (Howard W.
  Koch)

Various revelations about their pasts rock
the Hollywood hierarchy – and there's a mad
killer on the loose.

Tacky visualization of an unreadable
best-seller, with more unintentional laughs
than anything else.

w Robert L. McCullough, *novel* by Jackie
Collins   *d* Robert Day   *ph* William M.
Spencer   *m* Lalo Schifrin

Candice Bergen, Angie Dickinson, Anthony
Hopkins, Rod Steiger, Joanna Cassidy,
Mary Crosby, Steve Forrest, Robert Stack,
Andrew Stevens, Stefanie Powers, Roddy
McDowall, Suzanne Somers, Daryl
Anderson, Julius Harris, Catherine Mary
Stewart

'Interiors look like set-ups from discount
department stores . . . lack of creativity
doesn't seem to bother anyone . . . as shiny
and thin as one of the many visible sequins.'
– *Daily Variety*

† On the first British transmission, the
penultimate reel was accidentally omitted.
Nobody rang up to complain.

Holm, Celeste (1919–). American
character actress. TV series: *Nancy*. TV
movies include *The Delphi Bureau*, *The
Underground Man*, *Death Cruise*, *Captains
and the Kings*, *Backstairs at the White House*,
Midnight Lace.

Holm, Ian (1932–). British character actor
of great range and presence. Series include
NAPOLEON AND LOVE, THE LOST BOYS.
Recently: *Singleton's Pluck*, *The Browning
Version* (1985). Also many voice-overs.

Holmes and Yo Yo
US 1975 13 × 25m colour
NBC/Universal (Leonard Stern, Jackie
  Cooper)

An experienced cop finds his new partner is a
robot.

Flat comedy in the wake of *Six Million Dollar
Man*. See also *Future Cop*, an attempt to take
the same subject seriously.

cr Jack Sher, Lee Hewitt

John Shuck, Richard B. Shull

Holocaust **
US 1978 9 × 50m colour
NBC/Herb Brodkin, Robert Berger

The story of a Jewish family under the Nazis.
Predictably harrowing, but gripping and
well-written though less than marvellously
made piece of fictionalized history. It caused
controversy wherever it was shown.

HOLLYWOOD WIVES. A selection of the unhappy rich folk of Tinseltown: Stefanie Powers, Rod Steiger, Steve Forrest, Andrew Stevens.

w Gerald Green *d* Marvin Chomsky

Joseph Bottoms, David Warner, MICHAEL MORIARTY, MERYL STREEP, Fritz Weaver, Rosemary Harris, Tovah Feldshuh, George Rose, Tom Bell, Marius Goring, Ian Holm, Robert Stephens, Blanche Baker

'The case against *Holocaust* is not that it is bad soap opera, but worse – much worse – that it is very good soap opera.' – Dennis Potter, *Sunday Times*

PP: 'The real regret must be that the enormity of the subject wasn't risen to, and now may never be.'

† Emmys: best limited series; Gerald Green; Marvin Chomsky; Michael Moriarty; Meryl Streep; Blanche Baker.

†† See also: *Auschwitz*.

Holton, Gary (1952–85). British actor and pop singer who won all hearts as Wayne in *Auf Wiedersehen, Pet*. He died of a drug overdose during the filming of the second series but was 'cheated' into uncompleted episodes by using a double and dubbed-on voice.   PP

Home ***
GB 1972 90m colour (VTR)
BBC

The reminiscences of two old men in a home for the elderly.

A feast of brilliant acting, primarily, and a record of a theatrical event; but the play itself may emerge as a classic.

w DAVID STOREY *d* LINDSAY ANDERSON

JOHN GIELGUD, RALPH RICHARDSON, Dandy Nichols, Mona Washbourne

Home and Away
GB 1972 7 × 50m colour

Julia Jones's feminist serial of a housewife (Gillian Raine) finding liberation as her children grow up and she makes a trip to Eastern Europe. Produced by Kenith Trodd; for Granada.   PP

Home Box Office. America's most successful cable TV company, a division of Time Inc. In 1983 it made a profit of 125 million dollars.

Home for the Holidays *
US 1972 74m colour TVM
Spelling–Goldberg (Paul Junger Witt)

Four daughters go home for Christmas and murders ensue.

Surprisingly grisly whodunit, quite exciting once it gets going.

w Joseph Stefano d John Llewellyn Moxey

Walter Brennan, Eleanor Parker, Jessica Walter, Julie Harris, Sally Field, Jill Haworth

The Home Front (GB 1983; 6 × 52m). Interesting, experimental but not very grabbing cycle of plays going on around – or inside the head of – a solitary sitcom writer, played by Warren Clarke. The stories plunged to and fro in time and some of them seemed to relate to novels by the author of the series, Peter Tinniswood. With Brenda Bruce, Malcolm Tierney, Cherith Mellor, Sue Robinson. Directed by Roy Battersby and Stuart Burge, produced by Nicholas Palmer, for Central.   PP

A Home of Our Own
US 1976 100m colour TVM
CBS/Quinn Martin

The true story of Father William Wasson, a Catholic priest who provided homes for Mexican orphans.

Well-meaning, uninteresting do-goodery.

w Blanche Hanalis d Robert Day

Jason Miller, Pancho Cordova, Pedro Armendariz Jnr

Home to Roost (GB 1985; 7 × 28m). Yet another permutation on sitcom family splinterings and re-formings, here the single dad (divorced) whose cosy home comforts are threatened by the grown-up son who descends on him, but robustly done by Eric Chappell (w), Vernon Lawrence (p), John Thaw and Reece Dinsdale; for YTV.   PP

Home to Stay *
US 1978 74m colour
David Susskind (Fred Brogger)

An Illinois farmer ponders whether to send his half-senile father into a rest home.

Poignant and well-acted domestic drama on a subject usually pushed under the carpet.

w Suzanne Clauser, novel Janet Majerus d Delbert Mann ph Reg Morris m Hagood Hardy

Henry Fonda, Michael McGuire, Kristen Vigard, Frances Hyland

'A whole can of family-relations worms is opened and left unexplored beyond obvious clichés and a pat solution suddenly provided.' – Judith Crist

Home Town (GB 1975). Passing attempt by the BBC to re-create on television the appeal of the long-running *Down Your Way* on radio, in which gentle interviewer descends on a locality, chats up selected inhabitants and plays their musical choices. Cliff Michelmore was the chatter-up here, but for some reason the series failed to win favour, though one of the communities visited, the carrier HMS *Ark Royal*, was to attain stardom the following year in *Sailor*.   PP

Home Video * and other video plays
GB 1984 3 × 60m VTR
Limehouse (Susi Hush) for C4

Making a virtue of economy, three video productions (which cost less than half as much as film) on the subject of video and related home technologies.

Home Video * was shot on a single hand-held camera to imitate the home video record of a grisly family celebration, full of unflattering angles, indiscretions and unplanned reflections. 'A funny, sad, intimate little hour of the kind of television that television seemed to have lost,' I wrote.

w Lesley Bruce d Alan Dossor

Colin Blakely, David Swift, Patricia Routledge

CQ spun a story about home computer buffs.

w Paula Milne d Moira Armstrong

Michael Elphick, Marjorie Yates, Michael Graham Cox

Tropical Moon Over Dorking ** (TX 1985) was the neatest of the lot, with Pauline Collins as a romantic novelist tapping up her chaste romances on a word-processor screen which by only a slight extension of the imagination turned into a visual display of her luckless hero and heroine rebelling at last against yet another unconsummated passion.

w Jeremy Burnham d Robert Chetwyn

Pauline Collins, Nicky Henson, Hetty Baynes   PP

The Homecoming *
US 1971 100m colour TVM
Lorimar (Robert L. Jacks)

Life for a poor country family in 1933.

Christmas sentimentality, slow-moving but well-detailed, this was the springboard for the highly successful series *The Waltons*, which surfaced the following year with a different cast.

w Earl Hamner Jnr, from his novel d Fielder Cook

HOLOCAUST. Two well-respected British actors play two of the most detested Nazis: David Warner as Heydrich, Ian Holm as Himmler.

Patricia Neal, Richard Thomas, Andrew Duggan, William Windom

† The original material had also been used as a cinema film, *Spencer's Mountain*.

Hometown

US 1985 10× 50m colour
CBS/Paramount/Stonehenge/Kirgette
  (Allan J. Marcil)

College friends from the sixties meet again in a New York suburb in the eighties.

Ensemble drama which simply didn't run because, despite the success of one-shots like *Diner* and *The Four Seasons*, there was absolutely no reason for it to work as a weekly series. It might have made a highbrow soap opera.

cr Julie and Dinah Kirgo

Jane Kaczmarek, Franc Luz, Andrew Rubin, Margaret Whitton, John Bedford-Lloyd, Christine Estabrook, Daniel Stern

Homeward Borne
US 1957 82m bw TVM
Columbia/Playhouse 90

A pilot back from the war feels unwanted because his wife has adopted an orphan.
Woman's magazine stuff, capably presented.
novel Ruth Chatterton *d* Arthur Hiller

Linda Darnell, Richard Kiley, Keith Andes, Richard Eyer

Homeward Bound
US 1980 96m colour TVM
CBS/Tisch–Avnet TV Inc

A 38-year-old man is pessimistic about life when he heads west to visit his father in the Napa vineyards; which is not surprising, as he's been divorced twice and his teenage son is dying of cancer.
A supposed actor's piece whose unnecessary glumness can't entirely be disguised by slick production.
w Burt Prelutsky *d* Richard Michaels *ph* Edward R. Brown *m* Fred Karlin

David Soul, Barnard Hughes, Moosie Drier, Jeff Corey, Carmen Zapata, Judith Penrod

Homicide. An Australian one-hour police series, by Crawford Productions. As live, tape or film it worked with its intended market for a period of nearly 10 years from 1967.

Hondo
US 1967 17 × 50m colour
ABC/Batjac/Fenady/MGM

Adventures of a cavalry scout during the Indian wars.
Rather ho-hum western, competent at best.
Ralph Taeger, Noah Beery Jnr, Kathie Browne, Michael Pate

Honestly, Celeste (US 1954). Shortlived half-hour comedy series for CBS, with Celeste Holm as a small-town journalist trying her luck in New York.

Honey West
US 1965 30 × 25m bw
ABC/Four Star

Cases of a lady detective who is also a judo expert.
Moderately amusing idea, pinched from *The Avengers*; less than moderate execution.
Anne Francis, John Ericson, Irene Hervey
† The character of Honey West was introduced in an episode of *Burke's Law*.

Honeyboy
US 1982 96m colour TVM
NBC/Estrada/Fan Fares (John Berry)

A fighter from the Bronx wins the middleweight crown but alienates all his supporters.
Reminiscent of a dozen old Hollywood movies, this tedious exercise lacks both a star and a good script.
w,d John Berry *ph* Gayne Rescher *m* J. A. C. Redford

Erik Estrada, Morgan Fairchild, James McEachin, Robert Castanza, Yvonne Wilder, Hector Elizondo, Sugar Ray Robinson
'Honeyboy may win bouts but he never wins sympathy.' – *Daily Variety*

Honeycombe, Gordon (1936–). British newscaster, long with ITN. A former actor, in 1976 he resigned from public life to write but resumed newsreading – with TV-am – from 1984.

Honeymoon Postponed * (GB 1961; 50m; bw; VTR). Bill Naughton's play which subsequently became a stage success under the title *All in Good Time* and the 1966 movie *The Family Way*, skimming lightly over a problem said to be commoner than you might think, the non-consummation (because of shyness, thin walls, having to live with the in-laws) of a marriage. Being a comedy it was oddly more sympathetic than any high-minded documentary would have been. The plot went soft at the end but Naughton's mastery of Lancashire idiom and Lancashire euphemism never flagged. 'The marriage,' as someone daintily put it, 'hasn't found itself yet.' With Paul Rogers, Patience Collier, Lois Daine, Trevor Bannister. Directed by John Knight, for ABC. PP

Honeymoon with a Stranger *
US 1969 74m colour TVM
TCF (Robert L. Jacks)

Some days after marrying an American woman, a wealthy European vanishes. Then an impostor arrives, claiming his rights . . .
This well-worn story started as an episode of *The Whistler*, was filmed as *Chase a Crooked Shadow*, became a play, *Trap for a Lonely Man*, and a TV movie, *One of My Wives is Missing*. It always works.
w David Harmon, Henry Slesar *d* John Peyser

Janet Leigh, Rossano Brazzi, Cesare Danova, Barbara Rush

The Honeymooners ***
US 1951–6 × 25m bw (VTR)
CBS

HOME TO ROOST. John Thaw, looking more mature than in his *Sweeney* days, welcomes as guest star his real-life wife, Sheila Hancock. The generation-gap comedy was remodelled in America for Jack Klugman.

Misadventures of a blundering bus driver, his wife and their married friends.

Simple-minded but classic TV comedy series: the male leads became national figures.

JACKIE GLEASON, ART CARNEY, AUDREY MEADOWS, Joyce Randolph

† The first three of the cast, with Jane Kean, got together for a 25th anniversary special in 1976.

†† The sketches were originally seen on *Cavalcade of Stars*, with Pert Kelton as Alice, to whom Gleason always said admiringly at the close: 'Baby, you're the greatest!' After Audrey Meadows, Sheila McRae took over the role.

† Catchphrase for Gleason: 'One of these days . . . one of these days . . . Pow! Right in the kisser!'

†† Book published 1985: *The Official Honeymooners Treasury* (Perigee Books).

Hong Kong
US 1960 26 × 50m bw
ABC/TCF

An American correspondent helps the British fight crime in the orient.

Fairly efficient but unremarkable studio-set adventures.

cr Robert Buckner

Rod Taylor, Lloyd Bochner

Hong Kong Beat (GB 1978; 7 × 40m; colour). Out with the Hong Kong Police on such routine tasks as rounding up drug pushers and intercepting clandestine migrants from mainland China; an occasionally controversial series which anticipated the stir that would be caused by *Police* four years later. Produced by John Purdie; for BBC.   PP

Hong Kong Phooey
US 1974 16 × 22m colour
Hanna–Barbera

A meek janitor has a double life as a disaster-prone super-detective.
Acceptable Batman-spoofing cartoon.

Honky Tonk *
US 1974 74m colour TVM
MGM

A con man meets his match in old Nevada.
Acceptable spin-off from the Clark Gable movie: it didn't make a series though.

w Douglas Heyes d Don Taylor ph Joseph Biroc m Jerry Fielding

Richard Crenna, Margot Kidder, Will Geer, Stella Stevens

Honky Tonk Heroes *
GB 1981 3 × 50m colour
ATV (Bill Hays)

Amiable satire on country and western enthusiasts in the home counties of England, with James Grout donning a precarious hillbilly accent as proprietor of a C & W club, and the music neatly integrated into the drama.

w Ray Connolly d Bill Hays

James Grout, Sheila Steafel, David Parfitt PP

Honor Thy Father *
US 1972 100m colour TVM
Metromedia (Charles Fries)

The everyday life of a New York Mafia family.
A mini-*Godfather*, watered down from a popular novel.

w Lewis John Carlino, *novel* Gay Falese d Paul Wendkos

Raf Vallone, Richard Castellano, Brenda Vaccaro, Joe Bologna

Honour, Profit and Pleasure * (GB 1985).
Another tricentenary dramatization of Handel's life, much less scratchy than Osborne's *God Rot Tunbridge Wells!* but just as pleasurable. With Simon Callow as the composer, written by Anna Ambrose and Peter Luke, produced and directed by Anna Ambrose for Spectre/C4.   PP

Hooks, Robert (1937–).
Black American actor. Series: *NYPD*. TV movies: *Crosscurrent*, *Trapped*, *Carter's Army*, *Backstairs at the White House*, *Hollow Image*, etc.

Hopalong Cassidy
US 1951 52 × 26m bw
William Boyd

Adventures of the black-garbed cowboy.
Tightly-paced little westerns, made to order when Hopalong's old movies caused a TV sensation.
William Boyd

Hopcraft, Arthur (1932–).
British writer, formerly a sports reporter, whose first plays turned on outdoor or athletic themes, e.g. THE MOSEDALE HORSESHOE (hill walking), *The Panel* (bowls) and *The Birthday Run* (cycling), all 1971. Since then, plays on varied themes, the series *The Nearly Man* (1974), *Nightingale's Boys* (part, 1975), *Hard Times* (from Dickens, 1976), *Tinker, Tailor, Soldier, Spy* (1979), *Bleak House*, 1985. BAFTA Writers Award, 1986.   PP

✳ Hope, Bob (1903–) (Leslie Townes
Hope). American wisecracking comedian, star of radio, movies and TV. His TV appearances have normally been in the form of one-hour specials, of countless number, but he has also guested in almost everyone else's shows, including *The Muppets*.

Hopkins, Anthony (1941–).
Stocky British actor in the Burton mould; he seemed for a while to be concentrating on TV and has appeared in such major projects as *War and Peace* (BAFTA award 1972), *QB VII*, *The Lindbergh Kidnapping Case* (Emmy 1975), *Victory at Entebbe*, *The Bunker* (as Hitler), *Mayflower*, *The Hunchback of Notre Dame* (as Quasimodo), *Peter and Paul*, *A Married Man*, *Arch of Triumph*, *Guilty Conscience*, *Hollywood Wives*.

Hopkins, Bo (1942–).
Burly American actor. TV movies: *The Runaway Barge*, *Kansas City Massacre*, *The Invasion of Johnson County*, *Dawn*, *Aspen*, *Thaddeus Rose and Eddie*, *Crisis in Sun Valley*, *The Last Ride of the Dalton Gang*, *Beggarman Thief*, *The Plutonium Incident*, *Casino*, *Rodeo Girl*, *Ghost Dancing*, *Dynasty*.

Hopkins, John (1931–).
British writer who came to the fore with a series of *Z-Cars* scripts and his own off-key thriller serial *A Chance of Thunder* (1961). In 1965 *Horror of Darkness*, the first of several plays obsessed by suicide, confirmed him as the serious dramatist whose quartet TALKING TO A STRANGER (1966) would be hailed as television's first authentic masterpiece. Hopkins was soon afterwards taken up by the cinema and has made only fitful contributions to TV since. Co-wrote *Smiley's People* with John Le Carré, 1982.   PP

A brilliant attorney
with a plan for murder.

His wife and his mistress
have a better idea.

Starring
ANTHONY HOPKINS

GUILTY CONSCIENCE

Also Starring
BLYTHE DANNER   SWOOSIE KURTZ

Written By **RICHARD LEVINSON** and **WILLIAM LINK** Directed By **DAVID GREENE**

WORLD PREMIERE CBS TUESDAY NIGHT MOVIES
9PM CBS ◉2

ANTHONY HOPKINS played most of the heavy roles in an actor's potential repertoire, so it was a relief to see him in modern dress in a modest suspenser.

Hopper, Jerry (1907–   ). American director who reliably produced co-features for many years and proved just as efficient at TV series like *Wagon Train*, *The Untouchables*, *Perry Mason* and *The Fugitive.*
102

Horace *
GB 1982 6 × 30m
YTV (Keith Richardson)
Mishaps and muddles of a simple-minded youth in a Yorkshire village. Developed by Roy Minton from a single BBC play, the series bravely borrowed the semblance of a half-hour sitcom to spin what were quite serious parables about the care of the handicapped. It was lovely for Horace to live amid an ordinary community instead of in some institution, able to stare into the pet shop window for hours on end or buy indiscriminate bargains at the church jumble sale; the price was the burden on his aged mother, stuck forever with the responsibility of a child. And what would happen to him when she could no longer cope?
w Roy Minton *d* James Cellan Jones
Barry Jackson as Horace   PP

Hordern, Sir Michael (1911–   ). Distinguished British stage actor whose occasional television appearances include *Edward the Seventh* and playing the Maugham character in CAKES AND ALE. Has played King Lear twice, Prospero in *The Tempest* many times. Also presented a C4 angling series, *Rod and Line.*

Horizon *. Umbrella title for a long-running BBC series of documentaries on scientific research and advance. (The brief is taken very loosely.) BAFTA award best factual programme 1972, 1974. Outstanding recent items have included *The Great Wine Revolution* and *The Case of the Ancient Astronauts*, the latter a debunking of the theories of Erich Von Daniken.
PP: 'Simply the best science series on British – and possibly the world's – television, despite many changes of emphasis over its decade and a half of existence as successive editors have inclined to medicine or politics rather than true science. The title has always covered self-contained filmed programmes rather than a magazine compilation, and several bright talents, notably Brian Gibson, have used the show as a display ground.'
† 21st anniversary compilation, 1985

Horizon 2002 *
GB 1977 55m colour (VTR)
BBC

An elaborate spoof showing what *Horizon* might be like 25 years on, when it surveys the (mythical) scientific advances which have happened in the meantime.

Horn, Leonard (1926–76). American director who made episodes of most major series from 1958. TV movies include *Climb an Angry Mountain*, *The Bait*, *Hijack*, *Nakia*, *The New Original Wonder Woman.*

Horne a'Plenty (GB 1968; 6 × 30m; bw). On radio the bluff humour and outrageous double-meanings of Kenneth Horne and his show *Round the Horne* became such a cult that transcripts were reprinted weekly in the BBC's august publication the *Listener.* Despite the participation of one of the same writers, Barry Took, this attempt to transfer Horne to vision (for Thames) failed to work, possibly because it lacked his radio foil Kenneth Williams, possibly because Horne never mastered the autocue and other aids to easy performance on TV, doubly essential when the show is live, as it bravely was here. With Sheila Steafel.   PP

Horrocks, Sir Brian (1895–1985). British World War II general who had unexpected but spectacular television career in the late fifties and early sixties, presenting series on various battles, commanders and men of action, including a controversial episode on the German SS hero Otto Skorzeny. As was suggested by Edward Fox's famous impersonation of Horrocks in the movie *A Bridge Too Far*, he was a natural performer.
PP

Horror at 37,000 Feet *
US 1972 73m colour TVM
Anthony Wilson
An evil power is set loose in a transatlantic jet from stones of an old English abbey which are being shipped to America.
Enjoyably arrant nonsense.
d David Lowell Rich
Buddy Ebsen, Chuck Connors, Tammy Grimes, France Nuyen, Lynn Loring, William Shatner, Roy Thinnes, Paul Winfield

Horror of Darkness *
GB 1965 75m bw
BBC (James MacTaggart)
Gloomy but impressive play by John Hopkins leading inexorably to the suicide (a Hopkins obsession at this time) of one of the participants in a triangle of sex and envy that for a while is played out only in looks and attitudes and music, with scarcely any dialogue.

d Anthony Page

Alfred Lynch, Nicol Williamson, Glenda Jackson   PP

A Horseman Riding By
GB 1977 13 × 50m colour
BBC (Ken Riddington)

Serial from novels by R. F. Delderfield that might have been designed to fit the BBC's then much-publicized impoverishment. An interminable, richly-textured pageant of English rural life, etc, thriftily scaled down to avoid too much actual (and expensive) pageantry; only one horseman, you noticed, and he was riding by. But a workmanlike production within the limits of the budget and the source, which is a three-decker novel written about half-a-century after the possibilities of the three-decker novel were exhausted.

w Alexander Baron, others

Nigel Havers, Prunella Ransome   PP

Horton, Robert (1924–) (Mead Howard Horton). American leading man of the fifties. Made a big hit in WAGON TRAIN but his only subsequent series was *A Man Called Shenandoah*, which was not a success.

Hoskins, Bob (1942–). British character actor, often of uncouth roles. *Thick as Thieves*, PENNIES FROM HEAVEN, *Flickers*, *Mussolini and I*.

Hospital **
GB 1977 9 × 45m colour (16mm)
BBC (Roger Mills)

Cinéma vérité documentaries showing, quite brilliantly, aspects of life in big general hospitals.
Riveting and disturbing.

w/d TIM KING

'Nerve-twistingly brilliant.' – *Daily Telegraph*
'It isn't possible to make a better documentary.' – *Guardian*

† BAFTA award 1977, best documentary (*Casualty* episode).

PP: 'Two hospitals in Bolton, Lancs, furnished the hopes, fears, sunshine and tears, plus a pettifogging industrial dispute. The title had earlier (1969) been used for a single ATV documentary by David Rea. ATV also screened (1980) the US *Lifeline*, shot in San Francisco General Hospital to the same department-by-department pattern as the BBC series but seeking to whip up dramatic tension more blatantly.'

Hospital 1922 ***
GB 1972 50m colour

Brilliant idea for the BBC *Horizon* slot, brilliantly realized, to re-create the everyday routines of a London hospital (Charing Cross) half a century earlier, including frock-coated physicians reaching diagnoses as elegant as their attire (and amazingly accurate) but treatment thereafter that still ran to leeches or mass teeth-extraction. The parts were taken not by actors but by real patients, nurses and doctors. Seeming to come alive from an old still photograph and at the end fading back into it, the reconstruction was almost faultless. Written and directed by Brian Gibson; produced by Peter Goodchild.
                                             PP

'Four ruthless terrorists are ready to kill. Sixty-five brave passengers aren't ready to die. It's time to fight back!'

Hostage Flight *
US 1985 96m colour TVM
NBC/Shooting Star (James Hay)

When terrorists take over a domestic flight to Detroit and kill some of the passengers, they are eventually overpowered. Before landing, the passengers discuss their revenge . . .
Competent and mildly intriguing telemovie with alternative endings: one ironic, the other with the terrorists hanged in the economy section.

w Stephen Zito, Felix Culver, *story* by Howard W. Koch and Harry Essex *d* Steven Hillard Stern *ph* King Baggot *m* Fred Karlin

Ned Beatty, Dee Wallace Stone, Rene Enriquez, Barbara Bosson, Ina Balin, Mitch Ryan, Jack Gilford, Kim Ulrich, John Sanderford, Kristina Wayborn, Frank Benard, John Karlen

The Hostage Heart
US 1977 96m colour
CBS/MGM/Andrew Fenady

Terrorists plan to infiltrate a hospital and hold up a delicate operation.
Good opportunities in a familiar suspense vein are thrown away by a boring script.

w Andrew J. Fenady, Charles Sailor, Eric Kalder, *novel* Gerald Green *d* Bernard McEveety *ph* Matthew F. Leonetti *m* Fred Karlin

Bradford Dillman, Loretta Swit, Vic Morrow, Sharon Acker, George DiCenzo, Cameron Mitchell, Paul Shenar, Belinda J. Montgomery

'All the elements – murder, doctors, terrorism, open-heart surgery, police, the FBI and a chase – have been dumped in the mixer to prove that mechanical suspense and plastic characters won't deliver a rewarding meller.' – *Daily Variety*

The Hostage Tower
US 1980 96m colour TVM
CBS/Jerry Leider (Burt Nodella, Peter Snell)

Mercenaries plot to kidnap the mother of the US President, holding her atop the Eiffel Tower after it has been packed with explosives.

Tedious would-be thriller which gives its interesting cast little to do.

w Robert Carrington, *story* by Alistair McLean *d* Claudio Guzman *m* John Scott

Douglas Fairbanks Jnr, Rachel Roberts, Peter Fonda, Billy Dee Williams, Celia Johnson, Keir Dullea, Maud Adams, Britt Ekland, Jack Lenoir

Hot Gossip. British dance group of the late seventies and early eighties whose mildly erotic costumes and routines helped give Kenny Everett's earlier series their stamp. Founded by Arlene Phillips, the troupe always had black boys and white girls. Its own show, *The Very Hot Gossip Show*, on C4 in 1982. PP

Hot off the Wire: see The Jim Backus Show

'Running from the cops. From a killer. And after the one person who can set them free!'
Hot Pursuit
US 1984 96m colour TVM
NBC/Kenneth Johnson Productions (Arthur Seidel)

A lady executive goes on the run when her boss's wife sets up her husband on a murder frame.

Glossy-looking but impenetrably narrated melodrama which set up a one-hour series about the couple on the run, avoiding the police and the bad guys while tracking down the real killer. It limped through 13 episodes.

w,d Kenneth Johnson *ph* John McPherson *m* Joe Harnell

Kerrie Keane, Eric Pierpoint, Mike Preston, Dina Merrill, Bradford Dillman

Hot Rod
US 1980 96m colour TVM
ABC Circle (Sam Manners)

A wandering car racer wins a small-town event while keeping one jump ahead of the law.

Mindless youth movie with good action sequences and agreeable small-town atmosphere.

w/d George Armitage *ph* Andrew Davis

Gregg Henry, Robert Culp, Pernell Roberts, Robert Mattson

The Hot Shoe Show (GB 1983; 6 × 35m). Dance entertainment with a dash of comedy of a kind, built round the talents of Wayne Sleep and Bonnie Langford. Other ballet stars taking part included Wayne Eagling and Lesley Collier. The music spanned classical, rock and jazz. Produced by Tom Gutteridge, for BBC PP

Hotel
US 1983 96m colour TVM
ABC/Warner/Aaron Spelling (Jerry London)

Personal stories of guests at a posh San Francisco hotel.

The aim seems to have been a seamy *Love Boat*, and the mixture was popular enough in the US, though viewers in other countries seemed to prefer more meat and less sauce. The one-hour series which resulted has run to more than 60 episodes at press time, but none has been memorable.

w John Furia Jnr, Barry Oringer *d* Jerry London *ph* Michel Hugo *m* Henry Mancini

Bette Davis, James Brolin, Connie Sellecca, Shea Farrell, Nathan Cook, Morgan Fairchild, Lloyd Bochner, Jack Gilford, Shirley Jones, Pernell Roberts, Mel Tormé, Lainie Kazan

† Bette Davis as the hotel's owner was intended to be the kingpin of the series, but illness intervened, and Anne Baxter (shades of *All About Eve*) took over as her sister.

Hot *I Baltimore
US 1975 13 × 25m colour (VTR)
ABC/TAT/Norman Lear (Ron Clark, Gene Marcione)

Peculiar characters converge in the lobby of a downbeat Manhattan hotel.

Unsuccessful attempt at a different kind of comedy: the critics latched on but the public didn't.

play Lanford Williams

Conchata Ferrell, James Cromwell, Al Freeman Jnr, Richard Masur

Four ruthless terrorists
are ready to kill.
Sixty-five brave passengers
aren't ready to die.
It's time to fight back.

HOSTAGE FLIGHT

GRIPPING WORLD PREMIERE MOVIE! 9PM 4

HOSTAGE FLIGHT. Most people in the world wanted to get back at terrorists, but when in this telemovie the passengers proved not too frightened to retaliate, a softer ironic ending was provided for countries which couldn't take the one in which they meted out capital punishment.

Hotel de Paree
US 1959 33 × 25m bw
CBS (Bill Self)

The Sundance Kid, a reformed character, hides out with his girlfriend at a frontier hotel.

Light western with some small claim to originality.

Earl Holliman, Jeanette Nolan, Judi Meredith, Strother Martin

hotelvision. A system pioneered in the early seventies by which hotel guests for a fee could see new movies on their TV set. It quickly descended to pornography and became an embarrassment.

'The surprise ending is only a scream away!'
Hotline
US 1983 96m colour TVM
CBS/Wrather/Ron Samuels

A woman is threatened by a whispering phone caller.

Interminable mystery with insufficient personal detail to maintain interest.

w David E. Peckinpah d Jerry Jameson
ph Matthew F. Leonetti m Johnny Harris

Lynda Carter, Steve Forrest, Granville Van Dusen, Monte Markham, James Booth

The Hound of the Baskervilles
US 1972 73m colour TVM
Universal (Stanley Kallis)

Sherlock Holmes investigates a spectral hound which roams Dartmoor.

Risible version with stolid acting and the most inappropriate sets.

w Robert E. Thompson, novel Sir Arthur Conan Doyle d Barry Crane

Stewart Granger, William Shatner, Bernard Fox, John Williams, Anthony Zerbe, Jane Merrow

The Houndcats *
US 1972 26 × 25m colour
NBC/De Patie–Freleng

Cat and dog agents combat evil.

Lively cartoon spoof of Mission Impossible.

m Doug Goodwin

'I suppose all that sex banter is supposed to make for adult comedy. But good adult comedies are like good adults: they have some grace and humanity.' – Robert MacKenzie, TV Guide.

House Calls (US 1979–81). 57 half hours were made of this variable comedy series; remotely based on the movie, it changed its

HOTEL. Bette Davis was to have been the star of this anthology series, but became ill after shooting one episode. Ironically she was replaced by Anne Baxter, who had famously replaced her many years previously in the plotline of All About Eve; and, even more ironically, Miss Baxter died suddenly two years later, just as Miss Davis was preparing a comeback. Also pictured: James Brolin.

format and regular cast more than once, but basically concerned the love life of the hospital staff. Wayne Rogers, Lynn Redgrave, David Wayne and Sharon Gless were all involved. Produced by MCA for CBS.

A House in Bayswater * (GB 1960; 30m; bw). An old London rooming house and its denizens, including garrulous landlady, faded dance teacher with tiny inept pupil, young photographer at work on pin-up portfolio with pretty model. At the end it was revealed to be all a memory: the house had been pulled down to make way for a nasty new office block. Ken Russell's first film except for a couple of Monitor items was re-screened in 1968, when it stood up remarkably well. Wasn't this a tiny but vital bridgehead in television history? – the very first darkling, demure, scrupulously shielded but unmistakably nude nude to insinuate herself into the nation's viewing rooms.　　　　　　　　　　　　　PP

House of Caradus (GB 1978). One-hour drama series about a family of provincial auctioneers. Despite interesting detail, the show simply didn't get up enough convincing dramatic steam. With Sarah Bullen, Robert Grange, Anthony Smee. Written by Bruce Stewart; directed by Marc Miller; produced by James Brabazon; for Granada.

The House on Garibaldi Street
US 1979 96m colour TVM
ABC/Charles Fries (Mort Abrahams)

The search for Adolf Eichmann in Argentina. Interestingly detailed historical account of the tracking down of a war criminal. It did not however stand up when released to cinemas.

w Steve Shagan d Peter Collinson ph Allejandro Alloa m Charles Bernstein

Topol, Nick Mancuso, Janet Suzman, Martin Balsam, Leo McKern, Charles Gray, Derren Nesbitt, Alfred Burke, John Bennett

'Crackles with authenticity and purposefulness.' – Daily Variety

The House on Greenapple Road *
US 1970 113m colour TVM
Quinn Martin

A suburban wife has apparently been savagely murdered . . . or has she?
Efficient and generally holding but awesomely long murder mystery, a premature pilot for the Dan August series which later emerged with a different lead.

w George Eckstein, novel Harold R. Daniels d Robert Day m Duane Tatro

Christopher George, Janet Leigh, Julie Harris, Tim O'Connor, Walter Pidgeon, Barry Sullivan

The House on the Beach (GB 1965; 50m; bw).
Denis Mitchell film about Synanon, the self-help hostel for drug addicts at Santa Monica, California, which enjoyed success and esteem at this time. Produced by Cyril Bennett; for Rediffusion/Intertel.   PP

The House on the Hill
GB 1981 6 × 50m colour

Glossy series to the reliable prescription of successive episodes in the history of one location, here a Glasgow town house from 1880 to 1980. Previous anthologies to the same idea include The Seasons (Granada, 1971) and Cottage to Let (ATV, 1977). Directed by Mike Vardy and Tina Wakerell; produced by Robert Love and Mike Vardy; for STV.   PP

† The title had previously been used for a single BBC play by Peter Ransley (1975), starring Elisabeth Bergner as a dotty old refugee.

The House that Wouldn't Die *
US 1970 72m colour TVM
Aaron Spelling

The owner of a Georgetown house feels threatened by an evil spirit and tries to exorcize it.
Single-minded and adequately chilling ghost story.

w Henry Farrell d John Llewellyn Moxey m Laurence Rosenthal

BARBARA STANWYCK, Richard Egan, Michael Anderson Jnr, Mabel Albertson

Housego, Fred (1944–). London taxi-driver who won Mastermind in 1980 and has been a radio and TV personality, mostly wasted, ever since.   PP

Houseman, John (1902–) (Jacques Haussmann). Distinguished American stage director and producer who in his seventies became an equally distinguished actor and starred in the series THE PAPER CHASE, based on his performance in the movie of the same name. TV movies include Meeting at Potsdam (unconvincing as Churchill), Fear on Trial, Captains and the Kings, Washington Behind Closed Doors, A Christmas without Snow, The Baby Sitter.

Houston, We've Got a Problem
US 1974 74m colour TVM
Universal (Harve Bennett)

A reconstruction of the Apollo 13 mission of 1970.
A rather unnecessary fictionalization of facts which speak for themselves.

w Richard Nelson d Lawrence Doheny m Richard Clements

Robert Culp, Clu Gulager, Gary Collins, Sandra Dee, Ed Nelson

How Awful about Allan *
US 1970 72m colour TVM
Aaron Spelling

A blind young man in his elder sister's care is tormented by strange voices . . .
Artful mystery chiller in the vein of the author's sagas about Baby Jane and Sweet Charlotte.

w Henry Farrell d Curtis Harrington m Laurence Rosenthal

Anthony Perkins, Julie Harris, Joan Hackett

How Green Was My Valley *
GB 1976 6 × 50m colour (VTR)
BBC/TCF (Martin Lisemore)

The life of the Morgan family in a Welsh mining valley between the wars.

Solidly professional transcription of a semi-classic novel.

w Elaine Morgan, *novel* Richard Llewellyn d Ronald Wilson

Stanley Baker, SIÂN PHILLIPS, Huw Justin, Rhys Powys

How I Spent My Summer Vacation
GB theatrical title: *Deadly Roulette*
US 1967 96m colour TVM
Universal (Jack Laird)

A young man accepts an invitation to a summer cruise aboard a millionaire's yacht, and finds himself among members of a crime syndicate.
Puffed-out and tediously flashy comedy adventure which soon wears out its welcome except as a tour round lush backgrounds.

w Gene Kearney d William Hale m Lalo Schifrin

Robert Wagner, Peter Lawford, Lola Albright, Walter Pidgeon, Jill St John, Michael Ansara

How It Is (GB 1968). Young persons' miscellany put on by the BBC, produced and frequently fronted by Tony Palmer. The emphasis was on music, both pop and classical, but there were lively, if usually inconclusive, interviews with selected adults. A late-night version, *How Late It Is*, followed in 1969.   PP

How Many Miles to Babylon? * (GB 1982; 115m). World War I story from Jennifer Johnston, author of *Shadows on Our Skin*, adapted again by Derek Mahon. With Siân Phillips, Barry Foster, Alan MacNaughton, Daniel Day-Lewis, Christopher Fairbank. Directed by Moira Armstrong, produced by Innes Lloyd, for BBC.   PP
'A play of ideas, exploring the connection between class and militarism with subtlety and intelligence.' – London *Standard*

How the West Was Won: The MacAhans
US 1976 120m colour
NBC/MGM (John Mantley)

A heavyweight but slow-starting pilot about a family moving west in the 1870s.

How the West Was Won *
US 1977 3 × 96m (1st season), 10 × 96m (2nd season) 11 × 96m (3rd season) colour
NBC/MGM/John Mantley

Episodes in the life of the wandering MacAhan family.

Expensive but stretched-out series following at some distance from the above pilot. Story line desultory but individual scenes well mounted.

d Bernard and Vincent McEveety, others m Jerrold Immel

James Arness, Bruce Boxleitner, Eva Marie Saint/Fionnula Flanagan. Guest stars include Christopher Lee, Lloyd Bridges, Ricardo Montalban, Horst Buchholz, Brian Keith, Cameron Mitchell, Mel Ferrer

How to Break up a Happy Divorce
US 1976 74m colour TVM
Charles Fries/NBC

A divorcee tries to get her husband back. Modestly sophisticated comedy.

w Gerald Gardner, Dee Caruso d Jerry Paris m Nelson Riddle

Barbara Eden, Hal Linden, Peter Bonerz, Marcia Rodd, Harold Gould

How to Impeach a President *
GB 1974 60m colour (VTR)
BBC (Tam Fry)

A modern treatment of the impeachment of Andrew Jackson, with interruptions from modern interviewers and TV techniques.
A documentary reconstruction produced at the time of the possible impeachment of Richard Nixon. Interesting in its own right, for its clever techniques, and as a precursor of the 1977–8 spate of docu-dramas presenting more questionable interpretations of climaxes in the lives of historical figures.

w John Lloyd d Alvin Rakoff

Walter Klavun, Robert MacNeil

'Packed with excitement, excellent oratory, and best of all it really happened.' – *Daily Mirror*

How to Pick up Girls
US 1978 96m colour TVM
ABC/King–Hitzig

A country cousin in New York learns about women from his self-assured buddy.
Curiously joyless farce which may appeal to teenage wallflowers.

w Jordan Crittenden, Peter Gethers, David Handler, Bill Persky, *book* Eric Weber d Bill Persky ph Alan Metzger m Don Sebesky

Desi Arnaz Jnr, Fred McCarren, Bess Armstrong, Polly Bergen, Richard Dawson, Alan King, Abe Vigoda, Deborah Raffin

'It ricochets from point to point and fails to make any of them.' – *Daily Variety*

How to Steal an Airplane
aka: *Only One Day Left before Tomorrow*
US 1970 100m colour TVM
Universal (Roy Huggins)

Two adventurers pose as tourists in a Latin American country to repossess a Lear jet stolen by the dictator's irresponsible son.
Modest, unremarkable adventure.

w Robert Foster, Philip de Guere Jnr d Leslie H. Martinson

Pete Duel, Clinton Greyn, Claudine Longet, Sal Mineo, Julie Sommars

How Wars End (GB 1985; 6 × 30m). A. J. P. Taylor lecture series on the to-ing and fro-ing and haphazard, even trivial circumstances – rather than noble aims being realized – which bring about armistices. The final one, on the end of World War II in Europe, was cunningly scheduled for the 40th anniversary of that event. Taylor's formula, I calculated at the time, was roughly 50 per cent scholarship, 25 per cent bluff and 25 per cent derring-do as he shuffled out on to the tightrope without notes or teleprompter. 'Nearly 80 years old now, he sometimes sways alarmingly, searches for a name. The suspense is unbearable. But he always recovers and gains the far bank, on cue, with a final tripping flourish.' Produced by Stacey Marking for History Today/C4.   PP

How We Used to Live (GB 1968–). Influential schools series from YTV originally re-creating a Victorian decade as experienced by 'ordinary' families. In 1981 the focus shifted to a more recent period, 1936–53. In 1984 20 new episodes covering the years 1922–6 were presented in dramatized form (by Freda Kelsall) with an out-of-school showing in addition, introduced by Thora Hird.

Howard, Alan (1937–). Virile British actor, son of Arthur, nephew of Leslie, seen mainly in Shakespearean roles, e.g. a spiffing Coriolanus in the BBC Shakespeare production, but also starred in the low-key spy serial *Cover* and as John Osborne's father in *A Better Class of Person*.   PP

Howard, John (1913–) (John Cox). American juvenile lead of the late thirties; retired from acting after early TV series *The Adventures of Sea Hawk, Dr Hudson's Secret Journal*.

Howard, Ken (1944–). Giant-size American leading man with Broadway and Hollywood credentials. Series: *Adam's Rib, Manhunter, The White Shadow*. TV movies include *Superdome, The Critical List, A Real American Hero, The Victims, Rage of Angels, The Thorn Birds, It's Not Easy, Glitter, He's Not Your Son*.

Howard, Ron (1953–). Fresh-faced American juvenile lead, former child actor. Series include *The Andy Griffith Show, The Smith Family, Happy Days*. TV movies include *The Migrants, Locusts, Huckleberry Finn, Act of Love, Bitter Harvest, Fire on the Mountain, When Your Lover Leaves*

Howard, Ronald (1918–). British light character actor, son of Leslie Howard. TV series: *Sherlock Holmes, Cowboy in Africa*.

Howard, Trevor (1916–). Distinguished British actor of increasingly raddled countenance. TV work includes *The Invincible Mr Disraeli* (Emmy 1962), CATHOLICS, *Night Flight, The Shillingbury Blowers*, STAYING ON, *God Rot Tunbridge Wells!, Inside the Third Reich, The Deadly Game, George Washington, Peter the Great*.

Howards' Way
GB 1985 13 × 50m
BBC (Gerard Glaister)

Redundant aerospace executive buys himself into south-coast family boat-building yard; meanwhile his wife is involved with a local wheeler-dealer; as for the teenagers . . .
Fairly brackish sea-water soap opera not helped by some stiff acting. Despite a possibly fatal conclusion, a further series seemed a certain threat.

devised Gerard Glaister, Allan Prior
w various d various

Maurice Colbourne, Jan Harvey, Dulcie Gray, Glyn Owen, Susan Gilmore, Stephen Yardley, Tony Anholt   PP

Howarth, Donald (1931–). British writer of the sixties with a private line to gentle, idiosyncratic goings-on among lonely northern characters, as in *All Good Children* and *A Lily in Little India*.   PP

Howarth, Jack (1897–1983). British character actor familiar as Albert Tatlock in *Coronation Street* for 23 years. Had previously spent 10 years in radio soap, *Mrs Dale's Diary*. MBE 1983.

Howdy Doody. American studio show for children hosted by a rather crude cowboy marionette. Immensely popular throughout its run (1947–60).

HOWARDS' WAY. A popular maritime soap opera for the BBC's Sunday evening audience, it infuriated viewers by following the American pattern of stopping its first season at an apparent catastrophe. Edward Highmore, Dulcie Gray, Tracey Childs, Maurice Colborne, Jan Harvey.

Howerd, Frankie (1922–) (Francis Howard). British eccentric comedian whose inimitable stumbling style is full of oohs and ahs and other curious exclamations. Many taped variety and sitcom series from the mid-fifties.

A Howling in the Woods *
US 1971 96m colour TVM
Universal

In a creepy house by Lake Tahoe, a girl is menaced by what appears to be a spectral dog, and a murder secret is unearthed.
Enjoyable spinechiller with not quite enough plot for its length.
w Richard de Roy d Daniel Petrie m Dave Grusin
Larry Hagman, Vera Miles, Barbara Eden, John Rubenstein

How's Your Father? (GB 1979; 6 × 30m; colour). Attempt by YTV to give Harry Worth a sitcom that got away from the single-handed muddles and misunderstandings he had been plying for 20 years. Alas, as a single-parent father with teenage son and daughter he was merely transferred to the familiar jumping-to-wrong-conclusions and mistaken-identity plots of every other family comedy.   PP

H. R. Pufnstuf *
US 1969 17 × 22m colour
NBC/SID and MARTY KROFFT

A boy finds a magic flute and sails away to a fantasy land threatened by a wicked witch.
Elaborate variation on *The Wizard of Oz*, peopled by talking things in elaborate costumes. Commendably high production standards.
Jack Wild
† A feature version was made, to rather less effect.

Hubley, John (1914–77). American animator, a founder member of UPA. Many specials for TV including *Everybody Rides the Carousel*.

Huckleberry Finn
US 1974 75m colour TVM
ABC Circle (Steven North)

Rough-edged TV version of Mark Twain's juvenile classic about adventures on the Mississippi.
w Jean Holloway d Robert Toten
Ronny Howard, Jack Elam, Merle Haggard, Donny Most, Sarah Selby, Jean Howard, Clint Howard, Royal Dano

Huckleberry Hound. A rather boring cartoon character with elements of Mickey Mouse. Introduced by Hanna–Barbera in 1958, he shared 195 half-hour shows with Pixie and Dixie and Hokey Wolf.

Hudd, Roy (1936–). Cheery, cheeky British comedian, originally a stand-up comic in the vein of Max Miller, whom he frequently impersonates. Came to notice in *Not So Much a Programme, More a Way of Life*, subsequently had his own series for BBC and YTV; now mainly in nostalgic exercises: *Halls of Fame, The Puppet Man*.

Hudson, Rock (1925–85) (Roy Scherer). American beefcake leading man of the fifties who proved willing to try anything. In TV this led him to *McMillan and Wife* in which, with or without moustache (or wife) he proved fairly adept at the old *Thin Man* type of mystery comedy. He subsequently starred in two mini-series, *Wheels* and *The Star Maker*; and in 1981 he came back to series with *The Devlin Connection*.

Hudson's Bay
Canada 1959 39 × 25m bw
North Star

Adventures of a trapper in the Canadian northlands.
Dull, flimsy adventure yarns partly redeemed by location shooting.
cr/d Sidney J. Furie
Barry Nelson, George Tobias

Huggins, Roy (1914–). American independent producer. TV series include *The Fugitive, Run for Your Life*.

Hugh and I. British (BBC) sitcom from 1962, teaming Hugh Lloyd and Terry Scott in the classical relationship of simple soul (Lloyd) getting the better of scheming friend.   PP

Hughes, Barnard (1915–). Grizzled American actor, in demand by all media; won an Emmy in 1977 for a *Lou Grant* episode, and has his own series, DOC and *Mr Merlin*. TV movies include *The Borgia Stick, Dr Cook's Garden, The Borrowers, The UFO Incident, Ransom for Alice, Kill Me If You Can, In the Matter of Karen Ann Quinlan, The Girl in the Park, Little Gloria, A Caribbean Mystery, The Sky's the Limit*.

Hughes, Nerys (1940–). British comedienne, one of *The Liver Birds*.

HUCKLEBERRY HOUND. That was the name of the series, but who remembers poor
Huckleberry? The real star was Yogi Bear, seen here with little Boo Boo.

Hull, Rod (1935–). Australian comedian
whose right arm manipulates the neck and
beak of a silent but highly aggressive emu.
Very popular in Britain in the seventies.

Hullabaloo (US 1965). One-hour
rock-and-roll variety series for NBC,
produced by Gary Smith.

The Human Factor. Regular and estimable
documentary series usually focusing on one
individual or group of individuals
overcoming adversity. Presented in turn by
Sue Jay, Kieran Prendiville, Peter Williams.

Human Feelings
US 1978 74m colour TVM
NBC/Crestview/Charles Fries (Herbert
  Hirschman)
God sends an angel to Vegas to find six
worthy souls; if he does, she'll spare the city.
He adopts human feelings to do the job, and
falls in love.

Jack Benny used to rib his own heavenly
comedy, *The Horn Blows at Midnight*, but
compared with this it was *Gone with the
Wind*.

w Harry Bloomstein *d* Ernest Pintoff *ph*
William J. Jurgensen *m* John Cacavas

Billy Crystal, Nancy Walker (as God), Squire
Fridell, Donna Pescow, Armand Assante,
Jack Carter, Pat Morita

'It'd take more than the dreadful
accompanying laugh track to get a yock.' –
Daily Variety

Human Jigsaw (GB 1984–5; 13 × 35m).
Extracts from *Disappearing World*
anthropological films re-cycled by Ray
Gosling, together with newly shot material
from nearer at hand, to draw comparisons
between the customs and taboos of tribal
peoples and those of our society. Um.
Presented by Ray Gosling, consultant
Professor Lorraine Baric, produced by Peter
Carr (1984). Sandy Ross (1985), for
Granada.   PP

ROY HUDD. An eager-to-please all-rounder, as stand-up comic, Max Miller impersonator, or (as here) provider of instant nostalgia for *Movie Memories.*

The Human Jungle *
GB 1963   × 50m bw
Parkyn–Wintle/ABC

Stories from a psychiatrist's case book. Lively melodramas with a whiff of *The Seventh Veil.*

Herbert Lom

Humble, William (1948–). British writer who came to notice – after a disputed credit – with *On Giant's Shoulders.* No dispute about the excellence of subsequent scripts, notably *Poppyland* and *The Black Tower,* both 1985.

Humperdinck, Engelbert (1936–) (Gerry Dorsey). British pop singer who hit the heights at home in the sixties and around the world in the seventies. TV appearances mainly in specials.

Humphries, Barry (1930–). Outrageous Australian comic who operates mostly as Dame Edna Everage, a permed, lacquered, irresistibly vain Sydney matron, though some find this creation soft-centred by comparison with Humphries's alternative role as Sir Les Patterson, lager-swilling cultural attaché of his country. Either way the result is rude and resourceful, especially with a responsive audience. *The Barry Humphries Show* (1977), *An Audience with Dame Edna Everage* (1981), etc.   PP

The Hunchback of Notre Dame (GB 1978). 96-minute tape version of an oft-filmed original, with Warren Clarke as Quasimodo, Kenneth Haigh as Frollo and Michelle Newell as Esmeralda. The attempt was unnecessary. Written by Robert Muller; directed by Alan Cooke; produced by Cedric Messina; for BBC.

The Hunchback of Notre Dame
US 1982 96m colour TVM
CBS/Columbia/Norman Rosemont

An expensive-looking TV version typical of this producer: much rhubarbing by the extras, desperate acting, and no film sense at all.

w John Gay *d* Michael Tuchner *ph* Alan Hume *m* Kenneth Thorne

Anthony Hopkins, Derek Jacobi, Lesley-Anne Down, John Gielgud, Robert Powell, David Suchet, Gerry Sundquist, Tim Pigott-Smith, Alan Webb, Nigel Hawthorne, Rosalie Crutchley, Roland Culver, Dave Hill

Hunniford, Gloria (1940–). Effusive Irish radio and TV presenter: local shows for LWT and panel quiz *We Love TV.*

Hunt, Gareth (1943–). Heavily handsome British leading man, familiar from *Upstairs Downstairs* and *The New Avengers.*

The Hunted Lady
US 1977 97m colour TVM
NBC/Quinn Martin (William Robert Yates)

A policewoman is framed for murder by the syndicate.

Confused but tolerable suspenser with a strong central performance.

w William Robert Yates *d* Richard Lang *ph* Paul Lohmann

Donna Mills, Robert Reed, Lawrence Casey, Will Sampson, Andrew Duggan

The Hunter (US 1952–3). Half-hour adventure series for CBS, with Barry Nelson as an American businessman involved in international intrigue.

Hunter
US 1977 7 × 50m colour
CBS/Lorimar (Christopher Morgan)

Adventures of a ruthless spy.
Smooth but intrinsically fifth-rate James Bondery.
cr William Blinn
James Franciscus, Ralph Bellamy

'She's no angel. He's no saint. Together, they couldn't be better!'

Hunter *
US 1984 96m colour TVM
NBC/Lorimar/Stephen J. Cannell (Chuck Bowman)

A plain-clothes police detective is persuaded to take a girl partner in his crusade to clean up Los Angeles street violence.
A half-assed *Dirty Harry* format with a star who looks half like Clint Eastwood and half like Richard Widmark. In the resulting one-hour series the team spent most of its time bucking the system while solving rather old-fashioned crimes: in the pilot it's the mad murderer who kills every Wednesday.
w Frank Lupo d Ron Satlof
Fred Dryer, Stepfanie Kramer

Hunter, Kim (1922–) (Janet Cole). American leading lady. TV moves: *Dial Hot Line, In Search of America, The Magician, Unwed Father, Born Innocent, Bad Ronald, Ellery Queen, The Dark Side of Innocence, Once an Eagle, Backstairs at the White House, The Golden Gate Murders, FDR: The Last Year, Skokie.*

Hunter, Ross (1916–) (Martin Fuss). American producer who tried TV when the market went cold for his style of glamour. TV movies: *Suddenly Love, The Best Place to Be, A Family Upside Down,* etc.

Hunter, Tab (1931–) (Andrew Arthur Gelien). American teenage rave of the early fifties; starred in *The Tab Hunter Show.*

Hunters Are for Killing *
US 1970 100m colour TVM
Cinema Center (Hugh Benson)

An ex-con finds himself in danger from his own family and his girl friend's father.
Complex suspenser which passes the time.
w Charles Kuenstle d Bernard Girard ph Gerald Perry Finnermann m Jerry Fielding
Burt Reynolds, Melvyn Douglas, Martin Balsam, Suzanne Pleshette, Larry Storch

Hunter's Moon (US 1978). A one-hour pilot for a series that never was, but aimed to become a new *Bonanza*. Cliff de Young, Leif Erickson, Morgan Stevens as the Randall family out west, with Alex Cord, Ty Hardin. Written and produced by David Dortort; directed by Ken Annakin; for TCF.

Hunters of the Reef
US 1978 96m colour TVM
NBC/Paramount/Writers Company (Stanley Kallis)

Marine salvagers in Florida are menaced by sharks.
Boring outdoor movie with predictable elements.
w Eric Bercovici d Alex Singer ph Andrew Laszlo m Richard Makowitz
Michael Parks, Mary Louise Weller, William Windom
'Excitement is kept to a minimum.' – *Daily Variety*

Hunter's Walk (GB 1973–4). Fairly routine police-routine series set in Northamptonshire; created for ATV by TED WILLIS. Ran two seasons.   PP

Huntley, Chet (1911–74). American news reporter and linkman, for many years an essential half of NBC's *Huntley–Brinkley Report.*

Hurricane
US 1974 74m colour TVM
Metromedia

Several people are caught up in a Gulf Coast hurricane.
Piffling multi-drama making far too obvious use of news footage at the expense of personal involvement.
w Jack Turley d Jerry Jameson m Vic Mizzy
Larry Hagman, Martin Milner, Jessica Walter, Barry Sullivan, Michael Learned, Will Geer

Hurll, Michael (1936–). Innovative British light entertainment producer with a bent for live shows and improvised settings.   PP

Hurt, John (1940–). British character actor who tends to play neurotics and eccentrics, and gave a notable performance as Quentin Crisp in THE NAKED CIVIL SERVANT (BAFTA award 1975).

Husbands, Wives and Lovers
US 1978 13 × 50m colour (VTR)
CBS/TCF (Hal Dresner)

Misdemeanours and attempted misdemeanours of a group of young married suburbanites.
Relentlessly 'funny' comedy series showing the lighter side of *No Down Payment* but not doing it very convincingly. The original pilot was called *Husbands and Wives*.

cr Joan Rivers, Hal Dresner w Harry Cauley and others d Marc Daniels and others m Ken and Mitzi Welch

Ron Rifkin, Jesse Willis, Eddie Barth, Lynne Marie Stewart, Mark Lonow, Randee Heller, Charles Siebert, Claudette Nevins, Tom Miller, Stephen Pearlman, Cynthia Harris

'Coarse and unfunny.' – *Daily Variety*

Hush, Susi (1945–). British drama producer, ex-*Coronation Street*, 26 episodes of *Crown Court*, *Grange Hill* fifth series, etc. Limehouse's video dramas, 1984. Now preparing *Impact*, international follow-up to old *Compact*.

Hussein, Waris (1938–). Indian drama director of sensitivity, with many credits from the mid-sixties on: early Simon Gray plays, *Shoulder to Shoulder*, EDWARD AND MRS SIMPSON.   PP

The Hustler of Muscle Beach
US 1978 96m colour TVM
ABC/John Furia, Barry Oringer

A penniless young New Yorker lives on Muscle Beach, California and grooms a retarded boy as a body-building champion. Ugh.

w David Smilow d Jonathan Kaplan m Earle Hagen

Richard Hatch, Kay Lenz, Tim Kimber, Jeanette Nolan

Hustling *
US 1975 96m colour TVM
ABC/Filmways/Lillian Gallo

A woman reporter tries to write the truth about New York prostitution.
Grainy, gritty, true-life semi-documentary. The fuzzy sound recording makes fiction or fact preferable to this well-meant compromise, but it tries hard.

w Fay Kanin, *book* Gail Sheehy d Joseph Sargent m Jerry Fielding

Lee Remick, JILL CLAYBURGH, Monte Markham, Alex Rocco

Huston, John (1906–). American writer–director who also acts, and has done so on TV in *The Word* and *Sherlock Holmes in New York* (as Moriarty). Voice of General MacArthur in *American Caesar*.

Hutchins, Will (1932–). Slow-speaking American actor who played the lead in *Sugarfoot* and was subsequently seen in *Blondie* and *Hey Landlord*.

Hutton, Betty (1921–) (Betty Jane Thornburg). Vivacious American leading lady of the forties whose star waned rather quickly. Her only TV series was *Goldie*.

Hutton, Jim (1938–79). American leading man. Series: *Ellery Queen* (lead). TV movies: *The Deadly Hunt*, *The Reluctant Heroes*, *They Call It Murder*, *Call Her Mom*, *Don't Be Afraid of the Dark*, *The Underground Man*, *Flying High*.

Hutton, Timothy (1960–). American juvenile lead of the seventies, son of Jim Hutton. TV movies; *Zuma Beach*, *The Best Place to Be*, *Friendly Fire*, *And Baby Makes Six*, *Young Love First Love*, *Father Figure*, *The Long Way Home*.

Hyams, Peter (1943–). American director, formerly newsman, who did a little TV work before graduating to the big screen. TV movies: *The Rolling Man*, *Goodnight My Love*.

Hylton, Jack (1892–1965). British showman and former band-leader sub-contracted by Associated-Rediffusion to furnish light entertainment in the very early days of ITV. He tried all sorts, including 24-minute versions of Strauss operettas and a desperate imitation of *The Army Game* set in the Marines, but only a few Alfred Marks shows had merit.   PP

hype: extra and often excessive promotion for a programme.

I Am the Law
US 1952 26 × 25m bw
Cosman
Cases of a city police inspector.
Routine cop show.
George Raft

IBA. The Independent Broadcasting Authority, a state-devised body which in GB controls commercial television and radio.

I Can Jump Puddles (Australia/GB 1983; 9 × 50m). Autobiographical serial about polio-crippled boy during the early years of the century, milking every tear-duct at every opportunity but also containing an admirable message for the Year of the Handicapped in which it was made. Thanks to the sturdy refusal of young Alan's schoolfellows to treat him any differently, he has fights, beatings and falls off horses or down a cliff at least twice every episode. And that was before he grew up. Written by Sonia Borg, Cliff Green and Roger Simpson, from book by Alan Marshall. Directed by Kevin Dobson, Keith Wilkes, Douglas Sharp. Produced by John Gauci for ABC/BBC.   PP

I Can't See My Little Willy (GB 1970; 75m). Comedy based on the saucy seaside postcards of Donald McGill, with Nigel Stock; written by Douglas Livingstone, directed by Alan Clarke, produced by Irene Shubik, for BBC *Play for Today* and not nearly as funny as the subject promised. Fifteen years later the same idea prompted *Kisses on the Bottom* (60m), with Peter Benson and Judy Cornwell, written by Stephen Lowe, directed by Jeremy Ancock, produced by Rosemary Hill, again for BBC and again not as cheeky as its title. 'Inside Judy Cornwell as the fat lady was a lot of padding trying to get out. Inside Stephen Lowe, judging by the accompanying article in *Radio Times*, was a serious social scientist rather than an inspired devotee.'   PP

I, Claudius ✱✱
GB 1976 13 × 50m colour (VTR)
BBC (Martin Lisemore)
The life and times of the eccentric Roman emperor.

A highly entertaining black comedy (when it isn't being too bloodthirsty), this celebrated series has some patches of splendid writing and acting, though the makeup at times verges on the ludicrous.

w Jack Pulman, *novels* Robert Graves

DEREK JACOBI (BAFTA award 1976), SIÂN PHILLIPS, Brian Blessed, George Baker, Stratford Johns, John Hurt

I Cover Times Square (US 1950). Shortlived half-hour crime series for ABC, starring Harold Huber, who also produced, as a crusading columnist.

I Deal in Danger
US 1966 89m colour TVM
TCF
In World War II, a member of the Nazi High Command is really an American spy.
Tall tale put together from bits of the series *The Blue Light*.

w Larry Cohen *d* Walter Grauman *m* Lalo Schifrin

Robert Goulet, Christine Carere, Donald Harron, Horst Frank, Werner Peters

I, Desire
US 1982 96m colour TVM
ABC/Columbia/Jim Greene, Allen Epstein (Audrey Blasdel-Goddard)
A coroner's aide tracks down a voluptuous female vampire.
Dreary variation on the old bloodsucking game, with a total lack of interesting detail.

w Bob Foster *d* John Llewellyn Moxey
ph Robert L. Marrison *m* Don Peake

David Naughton, Brad Dourif, Dorian Harewood, Barbara Stock, Marilyn Jones

I Didn't Know You Cared
GB 1975 approx. 25 × 30m colour (VTR)
BBC (Bernard Thompson)
Episodes in the lives of a phlegmatic Yorkshire family who usually look on the black side but have a laugh about it.
Uneasy example of the northern penchant for funereal comedy.

w Peter Tinniswood, from his books

ROBIN BAILEY, John Comer, Liz Smith, Anita Carey, Stephen Rea, Vanda Godsell, Gretchen Franklin, Deirdre Costello

'A rich ribald slice of Yorkshire pudding.' – *Daily Mail*

I Dream of Jeannie *
US 1965–70 139 × 25m colour (30 bw)
NBC/Columbia/Sidney Sheldon (Claudio Guzman)

An astronaut finds himself the master of a glamorous genie.

Amusing light comedy, pleasantly played; devised by the studio to extend the success of *Bewitched*.

cr Sidney Sheldon

Larry Hagman, Barbara Eden, Hayden Rorke

† An animated version, *Jeannie*, was made in 1973 by Hanna–Barbera.

I Dream of Jeannie . . . Fifteen Years Later
US 1985 96m colour TVM
NBC/Columbia (Hugh Benson)

Jeannie's husband is about to retire from NASA and wants to go on one last mission: their dispute nearly breaks up their marriage.

The participants are no better for being older, and half an hour of this kind of romantic fluff is surely as much as one should be expected to stand.

w Irma Kalish *d* William Asher

Barbara Eden, Wayne Rogers (replacing Larry Hagman), Hayden Rorke, Bill Daily, John Bennett Perry

I Had Three Wives
US 1985 6 × 50m colour
CBS/Warner/Brownstone (Donald A. Baer)

A private eye is helped by his three ex-wives.
A silly concept which had the briefest of network lives.

cr Donald A. Baer

Victor Garber, Maggie Cooper, Shanna Reed, Teri Copley, David Fastino

'Inept execution, a mediocre script, a lack of action and suspense.' – *Daily Variety*

'A child's love kept inside by fear. A mother's love kept alive by hope!'
I Heard the Owl Call My Name *
US/Canada 1973 74m colour TVM
Tomorrow (Daryl Duke)

A sickly young priest is sent to a remote Canadian Indian village and dies there.
Scenic, moving, slightly pointless personal saga.

w Gerald de Pego, *book* Margaret Craven *d* Daryl Duke *ph* Bill Butler *m* Peter Matz

Tom Courtenay, Dean Jagger

I Know Why the Caged Bird Sings
US 1978 96m colour TVM
CBS/Tomorrow (Jean Moore Edwards)

A black Mississippi girl in the 1930s learns to stand up for herself.
Well-meaning but dramatically under-developed fragment of autobiography.

w Leonora Thuna, *book* Maya Angelou *d* Fielder Cook *ph* Ralph Woolsey *m* Peter Matz

Diahann Carroll, Paul Benjamin, Ruby Dee, Roger E. Mosley, Esther Rolle

I Led Three Lives
US 1953–5 117 × 25m bw
UA

Or, I was a Communist for the FBI.
Dated cold war flagwaver.

Richard Carlson

I Love a Mystery
US 1967 98m colour TVM
Universal (Frank Price)

Three super-detectives seek a missing billionaire.
Woefully unfunny transfer to film of a spoof radio serial.

w Leslie Stevens, *serial* Carlton E. Morse *d* Leslie Stevens *m* Oliver Nelson

Ida Lupino, Les Crane, David Hartman, Jack Weston, Don Knotts

I Love Lucy ****
US 1951–5 179 × 25m bw
CBS/Desilu

The harebrained schemes of Lucy Ricardo (née McGillicuddy) tax the patience of her bandleader husband and their neighbours the Mertzes.

Classic TV comedy series which not only had the highest possible standard for script and performance quality but pioneered independent production as well as the three-camera quick-film system. Still irresistibly funny.

chief writers Madelyn Pugh and Bob Carroll

LUCILLE BALL, DESI ARNAZ, WILLIAM FRAWLEY, VIVIAN VANCE

† Frawley and Vance were hired when Gale Gordon and Bea Benaderet proved unavailable.

†† Emmys 1952 and 1953 as best situation comedy series.

I Love You . . . Goodbye
US 1974 74m colour TVM
Tomorrow

A suburban housewife leaves her family in an attempt to fulfil herself.
Mildly interesting character study.

w Diana Gould *d* Sam O'Steen

Hope Lange, Earl Holliman, Michael Murphy, Patricia Smith

I Married a Centerfold
US 1985 96m colour TVM
NBC/Frank Von Zerneck (Bob Sertner)

Poker players bet one of their number that he can't make a date with a centrefold girl. But he does, eventually, after much tedious and embarrassing comedy.

w Victoria Hochberg *d* Peter Werner

Teri Copley, Timothy Daly, Diane Ladd, Bert Remsen, Anson Williams

'When the nominations for sappiest telemovie of the month go out, it will be hard to overlook this one. The plot must have been snuck into the schedule on a microdot.' – *Daily Variety*

I Married Joan *
US 1952–6   × 25m bw
NBC/Volcano

Another dizzy wife comedy, her husband this time a long-suffering judge.
Funny but not marvellous.

Joan Davis, Jim Backus

I Married Wyatt Earp
US 1981 96m colour TVM
NBC/Osmond Television (Richard Lyons)

The story of Wyatt Earp's courtship.
Hilarious attempt to create a 'different' vehicle for the winsome Mormon star.

w I. C. Rapoport *d* Michael O'Herlihy
ph John Flynn

Marie Osmond, Bruce Boxleitner, John Bennett Perry, Ross Martin

'As a telefilm, this should be on the stage. The one leaving town.' – *Daily Variety*

I Never Said Goodbye
US 1974 74m colour TVM
NBC/Columbia (Wilford Lloyd Baumes, Jeff Myrow)

When a woman dies of cancer, the husband accuses the doctor of mercy killing.
Tearful melodrama ending in court.

w Jeff Myrow *d* Gloria Monty

June Lockhart, John Howard, David Naughton, Renne Jarrett, Jack Stauffer

I Remember Nelson **
GB 1982 4 × 52m
Central (Cecil Clarke)

The great sailor seen through the eyes, in turn, of wife, rival, loyal friend and hero-worshipping boy. Cecil Clarke's second and much bigger bite at the subject he'd first produced (to a Terence Rattigan script) in 1966 suffered rather than gained from being scheduled just as the Falklands War came to a head, especially as the spectacular finale of the Battle of Trafalgar was fatuously delayed for six months to spare a susceptible 1982 public the horrors of sawbones surgery on a red-painted deck in 1805. 'Kenneth Colley's affecting death scene,' I wrote at the time, 'was orchestrated as the climax to a whole symphony, not just the last movement.' It was still an intelligent and impressive play-cycle.

w Hugh Whitemore *d* Simon Langton
m Patrick Gowers *design* Anthony Waller, Henry Graveney

Kenneth Colley (as Nelson), Anna Massey (Lady N), Geraldine James (Emma Hamilton), John Clements (Sir William), Tim Pigott-Smith (Hardy)   PP

I Spy
US 1955 39 × 25m bw
Reah

Adequate anthology of spy stories, ancient and modern.

host Raymond Massey

I Spy **
working title: *Danny Doyle*
US 1965–7 82 × 50m colour
NBC/Sheldon Leonard

Two US spies travel around the world as tennis players.
Light-hearted suspense stories, very adequately played and produced. Notable as the first co-starring of black with white on TV.

m Earle Hagen

ROBERT CULP, BILL COSBY

I Take These Men
US 1983 96m colour TVM
CBS/MGM–UA (Lillian Gallo)

A wife of 15 years asks her husband for a divorce, and fantasizes marriage with three of the men at her anniversary party.
Frivolous comedy which needs more style than it gets.

w Richard Baer *d* Larry Peerce *ph* Michael D. Marguiles *m* Earle Hagen

Susan St James, James Murtaugh, Adam West, John Rubinstein, Brian Dennehy, Dee Wallace, Hermione Baddeley

I Want to Keep My Baby
US 1976 96m colour TVM
CBS (Joanna Lee)

A pregnant teenager makes a decision.
Competent exploitation piece.

w Joanna Lee d Jerry Thorpe m George Aliceson Tipton

Mariel Hemingway, Susan Anspach, Jack Rader, Vince Begatta

I Want to Live
US 1983 96m colour TVM
ABC/UA (Paul Pompian)

Barbara Graham, a girl with a criminal record, is arrested, tried and executed for a murder of which she claims to be innocent.
Lukewarm rehash of the celebrated 1956 film starring Susan Hayward. For those who want to watch this kind of thing, once is surely enough, especially since the film never makes up its mind about her guilt.

w Don M. Mankiewicz, Gordon Cotler d David Lowell Rich ph Charles F. Wheeler m Lee Holdridge

Lindsay Wagner, Martin Balsam, Ellen Geer, Pamela Reed, Harry Dean Stanton, Michael Alldredge, Dana Elcar

I Was a Mail Order Bride
US 1982 96m colour TVM
CBS/MGM–UA/Jaffe Brothers/Tuxedo (Michael Jaffe)

A lady journalist goes undercover to complete an assignment on men who get brides through mail order.
Tacky comedy which limps from start to finish.

w Stephen Zito d Marvin J. Chomsky ph Don H. Birnkrant m John Addison

Valerie Bertinelli, Ted Wass, Kenneth Kimmins, Karen Morrow, Holland Taylor, Sam Wanamaker, Jason Bernard

I Was Jesus (GB 1985). Nine actors who have played Jesus on stage or screen tell how the experience affected them. With Colin Blakely, Alan Dobie, David Essex, Frank Finlay, Tom Fleming, Robert Lindsay, Mark McManus, Kevin McNally, Paul Nicholas. Produced by Jim Murray, for BBC.   PP

I Will Fight No More Forever *
US 1975 101m colour TVM
ABC/Wolper (Stan Margulies)

The story of Indian chief Joseph who in 1877 led his people on a 1600-mile trek rather than live on a reservation.
Earnest historical account, a shade thin for its length.

w Jeb Rosebrook, Theodore Strauss d Richard Heffron m Gerald Fried

James Whitmore, Ned Romero, Sam Elliott

I Woke up One Morning (GB 1985; 6 × 30m). Situation comedy on the unpromising theme of alcoholics being dried out, the unpromise duly honoured. With Frederick Jaeger, Michael Angelis, Robert Gillespie, Peter Caffrey. Written by Carla Lane, produced and directed by Robin Nash, for BBC. Further series 1986.   PP

Ian Breakwell's Continuous Diary * (GB 1984; 21 × 5–11m). Dizzy late-night fillers based on quaint behaviour, quaint coincidences and quaint sights spotted by the artist Ian Breakwell over 20 years, e.g. three brown doors in Newport, Gwent, indoor market, one labelled 'GENTLEMEN', one 'LADIES' and one 'TROUT'. Produced by Anna Ridley, for C4.   PP

Ibsen, Henrik (1828–1906). Towering Norwegian dramatist who has been described as the ideal author for TV. Certainly his earlier, strongly realistic dramas lent themselves well to studio production in the fifties and sixties. *The Master Builder* was produced by both BBC and ABC (GB) within a few days of each other in 1958, the latter's version starring Sir Donald Wolfit. *John Gabriel Borkman* was chosen by Laurence Olivier for his return to TV in 1958 in an ATV production by Christopher Morahan. *Hedda Gabler* attracted a famous CBS/BBC co-production in 1963 by David Susskind, directed by Alex Segal, with Ingrid Bergman, Ralph Richardson, Michael Redgrave, Trevor Howard. A John Osborne version of the same play was done by YTV in 1980 with Diana Rigg as Hedda. Diana Rigg also starred in the rarely seen *Little Eyolf* in a BBC production by Michael Darlow, 1982.   PP

Iceland has a uniquely limited state television service which does not operate on Thursdays. It began operations in 1966 and imports 65 per cent of its programmes.

Ichabod and Me (US 1961). Half-hour comedy–drama series for CBS, with Robert Sterling as a small-town editor with a six-year-old son.

idiot board. Caption card held up out of camera range to assist star's failing memory.

Idiot Weekly, Price 2d. Probably not more than 100,000 people ever saw this late-night

show put out in the London area by A–R a total of six times in early 1956, but it was the beginning of a line of weird and wonderful comedy that was to lead eventually to *Monty Python* and *Not the Nine O'Clock News*. With Peter Sellers, Valentine Dyall, Kenneth Connor. Written by Spike Milligan; directed by Dick Lester. See: *A Show Called Fred*.   PP

If Britain Had Fallen
GB 1972 120m (3 parts) colour
BBC (Michael Latham)
Intriguing idea to speculate on how things might have turned out if Hitler had successfully invaded Britain in 1940, but wasted in execution by undue reliance on the experiences of the one small untypical outpost – the Channel Isles – which actually suffered this fate. One imaginative essay would have proved many times more illuminating and provoking.
w Basil Collier, Alun Chalfont, Richard Wade   PP

If the Crown Fits (GB 1961). Shortlived ATV comedy series with Robert Morley as the blustering monarch of a Ruritanian principality. Despite such modern touches as a princess in jeans and a court PRO, essentially the old Baron Hardup joke from pantomime. With Peter Bull, Tracey Lloyd.   PP

'For Janet, having an affair is the only way to hold a marriage together.'
If Things Were Different
US 1980 96m colour TVM
CBS/Bob Banner
Her husband's been hospitalized for a year, her teenage children have their own problems, so a Los Angeles woman starts a new career and a new love life.
Self-congratulating soap opera which will appeal to under-appreciated and overworked housewives.
w Bill Froelich, Mark Lisson *d* Robert Lewis *ph* Richard E. Rawlings *m* Lee Holdridge
Suzanne Pleshette, Don Murray, Tony Roberts, Arte Johnson
'Values are scuttled, and the problem telepic becomes the problem itself.' – *Daily Variety*

If Tomorrow Comes
US 1971 74m colour TVM
Aaron Spelling (Richard Newton)
Before Pearl Harbor, an American girl marries a Japanese. . .
Predictable tearjerker.
w Lew Hunter *d* George McCowan
Patty Duke, Frank Liu, James Whitmore, Anne Baxter, Pat Hingle

If You Had a Million: see The Millionaire (1954–9)

Ike **
US 1979 3 × 96m colour TVM
ABC Circle/MELVILLE SHAVELSON
How Dwight Eisenhower came to lead the Allied forces in World War II, and his alleged romance with Kay Summersby.
Generally vivid and extremely well-staged historical fantasia, with many sharp scenes and an interesting use of black and white newsreel footage tinted to blend with the new action.
w MELVILLE SHAVELSON, from the book by Kay Summersby and official records *d* Melville Shavelson, Boris Sagal *ph* Arch Dalzell, Freddie Young *m* Fred Karlin
ROBERT DUVALL, LEE REMICK, Dana Andrews, J. D. Cannon, Steven Roberts (as Roosevelt), WENSLEY PITHEY (as Churchill), Ian Richardson (as Montgomery), Laurence Luckinbill, Darren McGavin, Francis Matthews (as Noël Coward), Patricia Michael (as Gertrude Lawrence), Lowell Thomas (narrator)
'Shavelson offers pop history laced with men of stature who, inevitably, prove pushovers. Viewers will lap it up.' – *Daily Variety*
PP: 'An adoring blockbuster designed to represent the effete British in the most disparaging light possible, Churchill alone exempted. In the event, Mel Shavelson's script was so inept that the intended picture of the military genius and overlord of "Overlord" revealed instead a petty commander chiefly concerned at a crucial stage in the campaign to send his mistress on holiday to Washington. It was just as well that the assault on Europe was in fact planned by one Englishman (Morgan) and led by another (Montgomery), small points ignored or played down in this version of history.'

'She thought she knew the man she married . . . her search for the truth may lead to murder!'
Illusions
US 1984 96m colour TVM
CBS (Stanley Z. and Carole Cherry)
When her husband disappears on a business trip, a clothes designer has barely time to grieve before strange things begin to happen. Practised viewers will soon guess hubby's real business, and this oddly-titled entertainment soon reveals that it has nowhere new to go.
w Stanley Z. Cherry, Carole Cherry *d* Walter Grauman
Karen Valentine, Ben Masters, Brian Murray

I'm a Big Girl Now
US 1980 13 × 25m colour
ABC/Witt–Thomas–Harris (Don Richetta)
A divorced father moves in with his divorced daughter.
Smartish comedy with a too-restricted format.
cr Susan Harris
Diana Canova, Danny Thomas, Sheree North, Michael Short

I'm a Dreamer Montreal * (GB 1979; 50m; colour).
The title was explained in the closing moments: what a Belfast bus driver thought were the words of the old pop song 'I'm a dreamer, aren't we all?' It was the metaphor for a funny, inconsequential play by Stewart Parker which conveyed the essence of life in embattled Northern Ireland better than many a more portentous treatment. Produced by Robert Buckler; for Thames. PP

I'm Dickens He's Fenster *
US 1962 32 × 25m bw
ABC/Heyday (Leonard Stern)
Misadventures of two incompetent carpenters.
A deliberate attempt to revive slapstick, this was sometimes amusing but fell a long way short of Laurel and Hardy.
John Astin, Marty Ingels

Images of War * (GB 1981; 6 × 40m).
Enterprising short series from BBC about the work of British film cameramen and directors who were rather hesitantly assigned to the armed forces in World War II in an attempt to match Goebbels's highly organized propaganda output. PP

The Imitation Game
GB 1980 75m colour
BBC (Richard Eyre)
Idealistic girl joins the ATS (women's army) in World War II hoping to play a fitting role in the struggle, only to find herself restricted to menial tasks. Alas, the respected young novelist and short story writer Ian MacEwan had projected back to wartime days attitudes and obsessions which were never voiced and probably not even felt at the time. I commented in 1980: 'Women's rights and women's lib have become such an inescapable bore, propped up everywhere like hoardings covered with the same few posters, that it really is too much to send them back up the time tunnel and disfigure one of the few epochs when on the whole the British did get on rather well together.'
d Richard Eyre
Harriet Walter PP

Immel, Jerrold (19 –).
American composer. *Gunsmoke*, *The MacAhans*, *Harry O*, *Dallas*, *Oklahoma City Dolls*, *Knots Landing*, *Shadow Riders*, *The Yellow Rose*, *Berrenger's*, etc.

'The Lavettas ... the Levys ... Feng Wo and his beautiful daughter ... an unforgettable story of love and ambition, money and power!'
The Immigrants
US 1979 2 × 96m colour TVM
Operation Prime Time/Universal (Robert A. Cinader)
The rags-to-riches story of an Italian immigrant's son in San Francisco at the time of the earthquake.
Utterly predictable period pap for novel readers who can't be bothered. Production standards slightly below average.
w Richard Collins, *novel* Howard Fast d Alan J. Levi ph Frank Thackery m Gerald Fried
Stephen Macht, Sharon Gless, Aimee Eccles, Richard Anderson, Ina Balin, Lloyd Bochner, Kevin Dobson, Roddy McDowall, Susan Strasberg, Pernell Roberts, John Saxon, Barry Sullivan
'A picture in primary colours, a picture whose artist forgot to put in shadings and intelligent individuality.' – *Daily Variety*

The Immortal *
US 1969 74m colour TVM
ABC/Paramount (Lou Morheim)
Our hero has a rare blood type which gives immunity not only to disease but to ageing. . .
Superman rides again. Some fun, but the subsequent series was shortlived.
w Robert Specht d Joseph Sargent
Chris George, Barry Sullivan, Jessica Walter, Ralph Bellamy, Carol Lynley

The Impatient Heart
US 1971 95m colour TVM
Universal (William Sackheim)
A lady social worker tries to turn every relationship into a case.
Romantic comedy–drama: strictly for ladies.
w Alvin Sargent d John Badham m David Shire
Carrie Snodgress, Michael Brandon, Michael Constantine, Marian Hailey

The Imposter
US 1974 75m colour TVM
Warner
An actor hires himself out to the security

force as an impersonator of famous people. Tiresome idea, tiresome pilot; no series ensued.

w John Sevorg, Ken August *d* Edward Abrams

Paul Hecht, Nancy Kelly, Ed Asner, Meredith Baxter, John Vernon

The Imposter
US 1984 96m colour TVM   ,
ABC/Comworld/Gloria Monty (Nancy Malone)

A con artist just out of jail wins back his girl by taking over as a high-school principal. Muddled comedy–drama which irritates more than it interests.

w Eric Hendershot, Dori Pierson, Marc Rubel *d* Michael Pressman *ph* Andrew M. Costikyan *m* Craig Safan

Anthony Geary, Lorna Patterson, Jordan Charney, Penny Johnson, Billy Dee Williams

improvisation. Play made up by the actors as they work on it, though usually to a scenario which defines situation and character as precisely as any script, and always under the leadership of one of the directors who have specialized in this approach. There can be a gain in surface naturalism, even in humour, but what the improvisation is saying will too often turn out to be trite if not actually silly. Thus, of leading exponents, Leslie Blair scored hits with *Blooming Youth* (1974) and *Whip Hand* (about an apprentice jockey, 1976), but between these foundered with *The Enemy Within*, about a kind of Mrs Whitehouse figure; Mike Leigh pulled off a comic stroke with *Nuts in May* poking fun at earnest campers (1976), and then produced a chillingly disparaging view of life among the D-stream of humanity in *Grown-Ups* (1980).
PP

In at the Deep End **
GB 1982/4 12 × 50m
BBC (Edward Mirzoeff)

Amusing, lavish exercise in the reporter having a go at some activity rather than merely observing it, as demonstrated earlier by George Plimpton (US), or Harriet Crawley or John Noakes (GB). These two six-part series alternated Paul Heiney and Chris Serle and gained much from the latter's gangling (6ft 5in) build when tackling competitive ballroom dancing or professional snooker. Other challenges included writing a romantic story (it was terrible), dying both as a stand-up comic and as a fashion designer (Heiney); serving as a butler at a country-house weekend or as an auctioneer at Sotheby's (Serle).
PP

In Broad Daylight *
US 1971 74m colour TVM
ABC/Aaron Spelling

A blind actor plots revenge on his unfaithful wife and her lover.
Smart little suspenser from the days when TV movies seemed to have a bright future.

w Larry Cohen *d* Robert Day *ph* Arch Dalzell *m* Leonard Rosenman

RICHARD BOONE, Suzanne Pleshette, Stella Stevens, John Marley, Whit Bissell

'She risks everything to save them from a system they can't fight alone!'
In Defense of Kids
US 1983 96m colour TVM
CBS/MTM (Gene Reynolds)

A lady attorney sets up a firm to help young people.
A glum piece of do-goodery.

w Michele Gallery *d* Gene Reynolds *ph* William K. Jurgensen *m* Fred Karlin

Blythe Danner, Sam Waterston, Joyce Van Patten, Georg Stanford Brown

In Hiding * (GB 1980; 60m; colour).
Denholm Elliott as an adult who blunders into the private playground of a solitary child. A strange, dream-like play written and directed by Don Taylor, using a lightweight video camera as fluidly and elegantly as he would use film, replete with long interior vistas and even longer stillnesses. Elliott continues to turn out these extraordinary performances, each one making radically different use of his middle-aged pink good looks and darting eye. He made his entrance here as a pair of shabby shoes under shabby grey trousers purposefully descending a long staircase. But this Pinteresque air of mystery survived no longer than a perfunctory suspicion that he might be a Post Office robber, and the issue proved to be a man's freedom to spend his last months alive as he pleased.
PP

In Like Flynn *
US 1985 96m colour TVM
ABC/TCF/Astal/Glen Larson (Stewart Harding, Harker Wade)

A lady adventure writer finds her stories coming through in real life.
Fantasy adventure with touches of James Bond, *Romancing the Stone*, and *Remington Steele*. Not an entire success, but one is surprised that no series was called for.

w Glen Larson *d* Richard Lang *ph* Rene Verzier *m* Stu Philips

Jenny Seagrove, William Espy, William Conrad, Robert Webber, Eddie Albert, Stephanie Holden

IN AT THE DEEP END. An unusual but effective series in which Paul Heiney (left) and Chris Serle (right), both graduates from *That's Life*, were trained by professionals in various walks of life. Here model Michelle Paradise wears a suit which Paul has created.

'Well produced, cleverly plotted . . . better than average TV entertainment.' – *Daily Variety*

'Young women fell for his bedroom eyes. But she was a woman with a lot more to teach him!'

In Love with an Older Woman
US 1984 96m colour TVM
CBS/Charles Fries (Sharon Kovacs)

A lawyer who haunts singles bars makes a pass at an older woman who turns out to be in the same business.

Mildly amusing sex-comedy which wears out its welcome.

w Michael Norell, *novel* by David Laufelt *d* Jack Bender *ph* Tom Del Ruth *m* Lee Holdridge

John Ritter, Karen Carlson, Jamie Rose, Robert Mandan, Jeff Altman

In Loving Memory (GB 1979). 25-minute comedy series about a lady undertaker and her gormless nephew assistant, set in 1929. Curiously tasteless but not unfunny period comedy for a familiar star. With Thora Hird, Christopher Beeny. Written by Dick Sharples; directed and produced by Ronnie Baxter; for YTV.

PP: 'The pilot was produced as early as 1972 but shelved because of a shortlived BBC comedy series also about undertakers, *That's Your Funeral* by Peter Lewis, which was in fact rather funnier.'

In Name Only
US 1969 75m colour TVM
Columbia (E. W. Swackhamer)

Marriage brokers discover that ceremonies they performed in the past were not legal, and set out to make them so.

A well-worn theme, lamely tackled.

w Bernard Slade *d* E. W. Swackhamer

Michael Callan, Ann Prentiss, Paul Ford, Eve Arden, Elsa Lanchester, Ruth Buzzi, Chris Connelly

In Old San Francisco: see Barbary Coast

In Praise of Love (GB 1976; 50m; colour). Terence Rattigan's sentimental but touching play about gruff journalist trying to keep the truth of his wife's illness from her; later expanded into a full-length stage play. This original TV version for Anglia starred Kenneth More.

In Prison * (GB 1957; 40m; bw). Documentary shot inside Strangeways Gaol by Denis Mitchell and Roy Harris, the first-ever inside a British prison. When it was re-shown in 1981 to accompany the re-run of the series *Strangeways* it couldn't help seeming a little quaint both in content and form (Mitchell intervening as interviewer to ask polite questions of a prison officer, the governor making a set statement from his desk). For technical reasons a couple of brief scenes had actually to be contrived. It was still an extraordinary and sobering account for its time, with the prisoners exercising in the prison yard in insect-like patterns; their flat, defeated voices as they testified on Mitchell's wild-track sound; the insistent echoing of iron doors.   PP

In Search of . . . * (GB 1980). A series of 45-minute documentaries hosted by young historian Michael Wood, who roams locations seeking evidence of such luminaries as Boadicea, Eric Bloodaxe and Alfred the Great. Generally interesting if a little fatiguing. Produced by Derek Towers; for BBC.

In Search of America *
US 1970 72m colour TVM
Four Star

A family sets out to see the country by van, and to make its own mind up on contemporary values.

Naïve, patchy, sometimes agreeable semi-documentary.

d Paul Bogart

Carl Betz, Vera Miles, Jeff Bridges, Ruth McDevitt, Howard Duff, Kim Hunter, Sal Mineo

In Search of the Trojan War (GB 1985; 6 × 50m colour). Glamour-boy writer–presenter Michael Wood perambulates through time and geography to relive the 19th–20th-century archaeological quests for the site of Homer's Troy. His genuine enthusiasm for the subject lightened a repetitive and over-rhetorical narrative style. Produced by Bill Lyons, for BBC Manchester.   PP

In Sickness and In Health ***
GB 1985 7 × 30m
BBC (Roger Race)

Eleven years after the end of *Till Death Us Do Part*, Alf and Elsie Garnett are rediscovered in Welfare State retirement, his skinhead bonce little changed, but she grimmer, thinner and increasingly dependent on a wheelchair. Even if you never believed the sociological claims made for *Till Death* (e.g. that bigotry would be discredited by having Alf mouth it), it was good to see brusque hospital staff and thoughtless motorists shown up. 'The tirades are wonderful,' I wrote, 'and the human comedy better than ever.'

w Johnny Speight d Roger Race

Warren Mitchell, Dandy Nichols, guest appearance by Una Stubbs   PP

LH: 'Despite a couple of good laughs per episode, I found it a tasteless and generally pointless exercise in exhumation. Only one star for me, and that for its social history interest.'

In Tandem *
aka: *Movin' On*
US 1974 74m colour TVM
NBC/Metromedia/D'Antoni-Weiss

A pair of truckers help an orange farmer save his land.
Tense, well-characterized pilot with reminiscences of *Thieves' Highway* and *The Wages of Fear*; the resultant series ran two seasons, under the title *Movin' On.*

w Bob Collins, Herb Meadow d Bernard Kowalski m Don Ellis

CLAUDE AKINS, FRANK CONVERSE, Richard Angarola, Ann Coleman

In the Custody of Strangers
US 1982 96m colour TVM
ABC/Filmways (Frank Von Zerneck)

A teenage convict is brutalized by the adult prison system.
Predictable protest melodrama.

w Jennifer Miller d Robert Greenwald ph Isidore Mankofsky

Martin Sheen, Emilio Estevez (in real life Sheen's son), Jane Alexander, Kenneth McMillan, Ed Lauter, Virginia Kiser

In the Glitter Palace
US 1977 96m colour TVM
NBC/Columbia/Writers' Company (Stanley Kallis)

A lawyer detective defends his ex-girlfriend on a charge of killing her lesbian lover.
Apart from calling a spade a spade in sexual matters, this is a clean-cut old-fashioned murder mystery, and as such will do.

w Jerry Ludwig d Robert Butler ph Gerald Perry Finnermann m John Parker

Chad Everett, Barbara Hershey, Howard Duff, Anthony Zerbe, Diana Scarwid, David Wayne

In the Matter of Karen Ann Quinlan *
US 1977 96m colour TVM
NBC/Warren V. Bush (Hal Sitowitz)

Parents fight for the right to remove a life support machine from their comatose and incurable daughter.
Painful and not especially complete or enlightening rehash of a case which was already only too familiar from newspaper headlines. A solid stripe against docu-drama, despite earnest performances.

w Hal Sitowitz d Hal Jordan ph Arch Dalzell m Bill Conti

Brian Keith, Piper Laurie, David Huffman, David Spielberg, Biff McGuire, Stephanie Zimbalist, Louise Latham, Bert Freed

'At times, extremely moving . . . other times, it seems to be heading down avenues it never actually approaches.' – *Daily Variety*

In the Pink (GB 1982). Feminist revue of unrelenting, single-minded acrimony aired on opening night of C4. Two years later, same team mounted a second-birthday show, *The Raving Beauties Make It Work*, 'foully written and put over with the cordiality of a knee in the crotch,' as I winced at the time. With Anna Carteret, Sue Jones-Davies and Fanny Viner; produced by Tempest Films (Sheila Trezise).   PP

In This House of Brede *
GB 1975 105m colour TVM
CBS/General Electric Theater/Tomorrow (George Schaefer)

A widowed businesswoman becomes a nun.
Sincere, simplified Nun's Story: good watching.

w James Costigan, *novel* Rumer Godden d George Schaefer m Peter Matz

Diana Rigg, Judi Bowker, Pamela Brown, Gwen Watford, Dennis Quilley, Frances Rowe, Nicholas Clay

In Two Minds (GB 1967; 85m; bw). BBC play by David Mercer, directed by Kenneth Loach, produced by Tony Garnett, using documentary and interview conventions to chart the case-history of a schizophrenic.
What worried me was the remorseless – even conspiratorial – nature of this process. The girl stood no chance, or certainly none once her sympathetic doctor was booted out of the narrative half way through. Her parents were nagging, narrow-minded, venting their own guilts on to her. Her lover was indifferent (and unseen), her fellow-patient devious. The consultant was aloof and the nurse a cool, starched monster who planted darts of doubt and insecurity with the finesse of a bandillero.
Are people really as awful? Beneath the urgency and directness of their drama, which

rightly is the drama that now counts, the Garnett–Loach school suffer from a curiously old-fashioned and unwelcome reluctance to allow humanity in anyone of whom they disapprove.   PP

Inch High, Private Eye
US 1973 13 × 25m colour
Hanna–Barbera/NBC

Adventures of the world's smallest detective. Very moderate cartoon series.

Incident at Crestridge
US 1981 96m colour TVM
CBS/Jaffe–Taylor/MGM (Ervin Zavada)

A woman who takes up residence in a lawless Wyoming community with her executive husband is appalled at what she finds and wins an election as sheriff.
Sounds as though based on fact, but it isn't; once the lady's elected, the interest ends.
w Jim Byrnes d Jud Taylor ph William F. Geraghty m Arthur B. Rubinstein

Eileen Brennan, Pernell Roberts, Bruce Davison, Sandy McPeak, Cliff Osmond

'Okay dramatic fare, but it asks for a lot of gullibility.' – Daily Variety

Incident at Echo Six (GB 1958; 50m; bw).
One of some half-dozen TV plays about this time dealing with the troubles in Cyprus and the British army's anti-EOKA operations. Military messages mixed up with the dance music on the radio; mackintoshed policemen strolling into the front line of fighting; the colonel in a blazer – Gilchrist Calder's production seized avidly on such vivid touches to help paint its picture of a unique, joyless campaign. It also introduced two notable talents in author Troy Kennedy Martin, later to create Z Cars, and actor Barry Foster, playing a subaltern. Produced by Gil Calder; for BBC.   PP

Incident in San Francisco
US 1970 98m colour TVM
Quinn Martin

A man tries to help in a street brawl and finds himself accused of murder: he is saved by a crusading journalist.
Efficient but rather tedious melodrama.
w Robert Dozier, novel Incident at 125th Street by J. E. Brown d Don Medford m Pat Williams

Richard Kiley, Chris Connelly, Dean Jagger, Leslie Nielsen, Phyllis Thaxter, Ruth Roman, John Marley

Incident on a Dark Street
aka: The Guardians; Incident in a Dark Alley
US 1972 98m colour TVM
TCF

The US attorney's office makes a stab at organized crime.
Routine crime-fighting melodrama.
w David Gerber d Buzz Kulik

James Olson, Richard Castellano, William Shatner, David Canary, Gilbert Roland

'Gamma rays turn angry scientist into raging, seven-foot tall, green monster!'
The Incredible Hulk *
US 1978 2 × 93m   × 50m colour
CBS/Universal (Glen A. Larson)

A scientist studying human strength takes an overdose and when he gets angry turns into a jolly green giant.
Jekyll-and-Hyde comic strip hokum, played tongue-in-cheek by a producer who has clearly seen all the old Frankenstein movies.
Bill Bixby, Lou Ferrigno

† This began life as one of a series of Marvel Superheroes pilots but the first episode was so successful (in ratings terms) that it quickly became a series.

'Loved by the man she had to leave. Hated by the people she came to help!'
The Incredible Journey of Dr Meg Laurel
US 1979 142m colour TVM
CBS/Columbia/Ron Samuel

A lady doctor in 1932 returns to her childhood haunts in the Appalachian mountains.
Interminable as well as incredible, this load of rotting corn mercifully did not give birth to a series. Its most risible sight is that of Jane Wyman as the wise old woman of the mountains.
w Michael Berk, Douglas Schwartz, Joseph Fineman d Guy Green ph Al Francis m Gerald Fried

Lindsay Wagner, Jane Wyman, Dorothy McGuire, Andrew Duggan, Brock Peters, Gary Lockwood

The Incredible Machine *
US 1975 50m colour
National Geographic/Wolper (Irwin Rosten)

New techniques enable the camera to see the inner workings of the human body.
A remarkable documentary.
w/d Irwin Rosten narrator E. G. Marshall

The Incredible Mr Tanner (GB 1980). Shortlived 25-minute comedy series about the misadventures of a couple of street entertainers. With Brian Murphy, Roy Kinnear. Written by Johnnie Mortimer and Brian Cooke; directed and produced by Peter Frazer-Jones; for Thames.

Independent Broadcasting Authority: see IBA

independent station: in America, one not affiliated to a network.

Indict and Convict *
US 1974 100m colour TVM
Universal (David Victor)

The attorney-general's office investigates a murder which may have been committed by a public official.
Reasonably absorbing courtroom drama with attention to detail.
w Winston Miller *d* Boris Sagal

George Grizzard, Reni Santoni, William Shatner, Susan Howard, Eli Wallach, Myrna Loy, Harry Guardino

Information Please. American panel game of the early fifties in which viewers sent in questions in an attempt to stump the experts – usually Franklin P. Adams, Oscar Levant and John Kiernan, with Clifton Fadiman as moderator.

The Informer * (GB 1967). Ian Hendry as a disbarred barrister trying to repair career and marriage but meanwhile loyal to the relationships he had struck up in the half-world between crime and the law where he now operated; which sounds bleak but unexpectedly hauled itself into art, thanks to Hendry's performance and scripts by Jack Trevor Story, among others. Also with Heather Sears, Jean Marsh; for Rediffusion.
PP

Ingrams, Michael (1925–). Pioneering British reporter–director who made sympathetic social documentary series during the early days of ITV, e.g. *Our Street* (1961) about life in a terraced street in Camberwell. Fiction in the shape of *Coronation Street* starting later the same year displaced fact, and Ingrams unaccountably dropped out of television altogether.
PP

inherited audience. The one that remains with a programme from the previous show on the same channel, from being too idle to switch over.

The Inheritors
GB 1974 6 × 50m colour
HTV (Clifford Evans, Wilfred Greatorex)

Dynastic melodrama set in Welsh Wales as the young heir to the Gethin millions tries to save the ancestral acres from the joint assault of the tax man and mineral speculators.
Spirited but quickly forgotten.
cr Wilfred Greatorex *w* and *d* various

Peter Egan, Richard Hurndall   PP

'An innocent coed, a secret sorority, its bizarre rites of womanhood ... suddenly, a quiet college campus is plunged into an endless night of terror!'

The Initiation of Sarah
US 1978 96m colour TVM
ABC/Stonehenge/Charles Fries (Jay Benson)

A college girl finds her sorority riddled with strange goings-on, which unleash her own psychic powers.
Rather coy *Carrie* derivative with a few spooky moments.
w Don Ingalls, Carol Saraceno, Kenette Geller *d* Robert Day *ph* Ric Waite *m* Johnny Harris

Kay Lenz, Shelley Winters, Kathryn Crosby, Morgan Brittany, Morgan Fairchild, Tony Bill, Tisa Farrow

Inman, John (1936–). British comic actor, smart, smiling and effeminate, who soared to fame in ARE YOU BEING SERVED? but floundered a little when given his own series *Odd Man In*.

Inmates: A Love Story
US 1981 96m colour TVM
ABC/Finnegan Associates/Henerson–Hirsch

Life in a co-ed prison where the inmates are encouraged to be themselves; an embezzler falls for a lady thief.
Turgid claptrap, watching which is no light sentence.
w James G. Hirsch, Delia Jordan *d* Guy Green *ph* Al Francis *m* Dana Kaproff

Kate Jackson, Perry King, Shirley Jones, Tony Curtis

'Life in this zoo would seem fine to those without food or shelter ... punishment seems limited to staying behind barbed wire fences to enjoy sunsets, regular meals, cohabiting.' – *Daily Variety*

The Innes Book of Records (GB 1981–2; two series of 6 × 25m; colour). Somewhat recherché entertainment by and with Neil Innes, a singer-songwriter whose patent-leather hair and light baritone bespeak the thirties rather than the eighties; but lots of originality, style and slyness; should catch on eventually. Produced by Ian Keill; for BBC.   PP

† It didn't.

Innes, Hammond (1913–). British thriller-writer whose books are occasionally dramatized, e.g. *Golden Soak* (Australia 1980, shown by BBC) but has written for TV himself only sparingly. Notable: the Captain Cook episode in *Explorers*.   PP

The Innocent and the Damned: see Aspen

'It's his first crush, and it will change his mind forever!'
An Innocent Love
US 1983 96m colour TVM
CBS/TCF/Steve Binder (Buck Houghton)

Three university students help each other to understand love.

Not exactly the *ménage à trois* it sounds, this contains nothing that anyone over 18 would want to know.

w I. C. Rapoport

Melissa Sue Anderson, Doug McKeon, Rocky Bauer

Inside Britain's Bomb (GB 1985; 60m). Claimed to be the first detailed investigation into the manufacture, assembly and storage of Britain's nuclear weapons, but failing to uncover anything newly alarming. Produced by James Cutler as a *First Tuesday* special for YTV.   PP

Inside China (GB 1983; 3 × 52m). Two films on the newfound materialism and prosperity of many Chinese, *p* and *d* Leslie Woodhead; the third a more anthropological study of a minority tribal people, the Turkish Kazakhs, *p* and *d* Andre Singer. Executive producer Steve Morrison, for Granada.   PP

Inside Europe. A noble but short-lived scheme (1978) for six European networks and one US station to produce and share a series of current affairs reports on each of the countries involved. Granada represented GB. The other Europeans were Belgium, Denmark, Holland, Sweden and West Germany.

Inside George Webley (GB 1970; 6 × 25m; colour). Roy Kinnear and Patsy Rowlands in a YTV marital comedy by Keith Waterhouse and Willis Hall that deserved to fare better than it did. Kinnear fretted obsessively over a name he couldn't remember or whether he'd turned the gas off, Rowlands wanted only to sleep or eat.   PP

Inside Out (GB 1985; 6 × 50m). Contemporary comedy drama about an employment agency for ex-convicts; it escaped much attention but won an appreciative following. Written by Simon Moore, directed by Tony Smith and Pedr James, music by Phil Collins. Produced by Sally Head, for BBC.   PP

Inside Story * (GB 1979–80). Two series of BBC documentaries recording such processes as homosexuals reaching a decision to declare themselves as such, or aviation archaeologists in Kent digging up a Battle of Britain fighter (and the remains of its pilot) that had been buried in the mud for 40 years. It was also the series in which producer Roger Mills abandoned the purely observational, or fly-on-the-wall, approach to include interviews and direct-to-camera meditation.   PP

Inside the Third Reich *
US 1982 2 × 96m, 1 ×
   120m colour miniseries
ABC Circle/Paramount/E. Jack Neuman

The story of Albert Speer's recruitment into the Nazi party.

Reasonably interesting and plausible exposé of the Nazis in the thirties.

w E. Jack Neuman *d* Marvin Chomsky

Rutger Hauer, Derek Jacobi (as Hitler), Blythe Danner, John Gielgud, Trevor Howard, Robert Vaughn, Stephen Collins, Elke Sommer, Ian Holm, Viveca Lindfors, Randy Quaid, Maria Schell

The Insiders
US 1985 13 × 50m colour
ABC/Universal (Joel Blasberg, Stephen Cragg)

A young magazine reporter and his black ex-con buddy go undercover.

Fatiguingly noisy but otherwise very boring crime series which didn't find an audience.

cr Michael Ahnemann

Nicholas Campbell, Stoney Jackson, Gail Strickland

'The puerile nature of the plotting and the characters cries out for cartoon time.' – *Daily Variety*
'Stylistic slop.' – *LA Times*

Institute for Revenge
US 1980 96m colour TVM
NBC/Columbia/Bill Driskill/Otto Salomon

Cases of a computer-controlled detective agency.

Silly hokum which fails to entertain, mainly through lazy casting.

w Bill Driskill d Ken Annakin ph Roland Smith m Lalo Schifrin

Sam Groom, Robert Coote, Lauren Hutton, Lane Brinkley, Leslie Nielson, Kay Walston, George Hamilton, Robert Emhardt

'The mission unlikely splutters and stalls, never to ignite. In the words of IFR 7000, it doesn't compute.' – Daily Variety

Intensive Care ** See *Objects of Affection*

Interludes. The BBC's interlude fillers in the early days of television were in fact phased out well before 1960, but for some reason live on in popular myth as a feature of television that lasted until recent times. There were 14: The Windmill, The Weir, Messing about on the River, Palm Beach, Rough Sea on Rocks, The Kitten, Angel Fish, Spinning Wheel, Potter's Wheel, Gooney Birds Taking off, Piano Playtime, Road Works, Toy Fair, London to Brighton in Four Minutes.

Intermezzo (aka *Escape to Happiness*). The original screenplay by Gustav Molander and Gosta Stevens was not only filmed in Sweden in 1936 with Ingrid Bergman and Gosta Eckman, and again in Hollywood in 1939 with Bergman and Leslie Howard, but also – believe it or not – done as a live TV play in 1957 by ABC (GB). Ronald Howard honourably filled his father's old role of the great violinist but the Bergman part of the young girl who enjoys a brief idyll with the maestro went to someone called Adelaide Vandermoost, of whom not mooch more was heard. Dennis Vance directed.			PP

International Airport
US 1985 96m colour TVM
ABC/Warner/Aaron Spelling (Robert McCullough)

An airport manager staves off disaster for an airborne plane.

Tedious reworking of the old movie, not even well done on its own account.

w Robert McCullough, *novel* by Arthur Hailey d Don Chaffey, Charles S. Dubin ph Emil Oster m Mark Snow

Gil Gerard, Pat Crowley, Berlinda Tolbert, Kitty Moffat, Danny Ponce, Cliff Potts, Bill Bixby, Susan Blakely, George Grizzard, George Kennedy, Vera Miles, Susan Oliver, Robert Reed, Connie Sellecca, Robert Vaughn

'Barely satisfied the minimal standards for a potboiler.' – *Daily Variety*

International Detective
US/GB 1959 39 × 25m bw
Delry/A. Edward Sutherland/ABP

Stories of an international detective agency.

Quite a lively crime filler with a fake *March of Time* atmosphere.

Arthur Fleming

International Pro-Celebrity Golf. Like snooker or speedway, golf is one of the sports which television can take over, film and edit as artfully as it makes drama or comedy shows. It is canned sport, the actual play accomplished within a weekend but the results spun out to fill up to 13 half-hour shows. ABC in America were first in the field, now there are many entrepreneurs. *International Pro-Celebrity Golf*, a title used both sides of the Atlantic, is typical of the genre, with the added attraction of demonstrating how the ordinary golfer can partner a top professional, as long as he happens to be Frank Sinatra or Sean Connery.			PP

The Interns
US 1970 24 × 50m colour
CBS/Columbia (Bob Claver)

Stories of young doctors in a city hospital, following on from two feature films, *The Interns* and *The New Interns*.

A flop show in which nothing went right.

cr William Blinn

Broderick Crawford, Stephen Brooks, Chris Stone, Hal Frederick, Mike Farrell

Interpol Calling
GB 1959 39 × 25m bw
ATV/Rank/Wrather

Stories of the organization which chases criminals around the world.

Adequate potboilers.

Charles Korvin

The Interrogation of Machiavelli ** (Germany 1977). Excellent and widely shown version of the play by Lyda Winiewicz included in the BBC's 1978 Globe Theatre season. Machiavelli is faced with torture if he won't surrender the remaining manuscript of his dangerous work *The Prince*, but saved in the nick of time by the election of a new Pope, which means an amnesty for all political prisoners. With Hanns Messemer; directed by F-J Wild. An English-language version of the same play was done by the BBC (Innes Lloyd) in 1970 as *The Year of the Crow*.   PP

The Interrupted Journey *
aka: *The UFO Incident*
US 1975 100m colour TVM
Universal

A black man and his wife claim to have seen a flying saucer and to have been invited aboard. Overlong fictionalization of an incident reported in a book by John G. Fuller: quite amusing.

d Richard A. Colla

James Earl Jones, Estelle Parsons

interstitial programming: cable jargon for the short fillers which are used between programmes, especially if insufficient advertising has been sold.

Intertel. Consortium made up of Associated-Rediffusion (London), NET and Westinghouse (USA), ABC (Australia) and CBC (Canada) which pooled documentary programmes in the sixties. A–R's contributions included Robert Kee's *Children of the Revolution* about the postwar generation in Czechoslovakia and Paul Johnson's *A King's Revolution* (*d* Randall Beattie) about the Shah of Persia's drive to modernize his country. After 1968 Britain was briefly represented by the BBC instead.
                                                        PP

'Five minutes ago, her lover called. He said something he should have told her before. Something she will have to live with for the rest of her life.'
Intimate Agony
US 1983 96m colour TVM
ABC/Henerson–Hirsch/Robert Papazian

A resort community deals with a herpes outbreak.
Predictable melodrama with the villain a sexual disease instead of a shark.

w James G. Hirsch, James S. Henerson, Richard DeRoy *d* Paul Wendkos *ph* Thomas Del Ruth *m* Billy Goldenberg

Anthony Geary, Judith Light, Mark Harmon, Arthur Hill, Brian Kerwin, Penny Fuller, Robert Vaughn

Intimate Strangers *
GB 1974 13 × 50m colour
LWT (Richard Bates)

A television novel, as it billed itself, charting in exhaustive but eventually rather touching detail the effect on a middle-distance, jogging-along marriage when the husband has a heart attack and – apart from a radical change in their lifestyle – both partners are forced to re-examine the shifts and compromises they have accepted over the years.

cr Richard Bates

ANTHONY BATE, PATRICIA LAWRENCE   PP

'Only with so much love can there be so much hate!'
Intimate Strangers
US 1982 96m colour TVM
ABC/Charles Fries (Richard and Esther Shapiro)

The story of a compulsive wife-beater.
Okay melodrama for those who need to know.

w Richard and Esther Shapiro *d* John Llewellyn Moxey *ph* Robert Hauser *m* Fred Karlin

Dennis Weaver, Sally Struthers, Melvyn Douglas, Tyne Daly, Larry Hagman, Jack Stauffer

Into Thin Air
US 1985 96m colour TVM
CBS/Major H/Toby Ganz (Joseph Stern)

A woman's teenage son vanishes while on a trip.
Interesting true-life story with a tragic ending.

w George Rubino *d* Roger Young *ph* Charles Correll *m* Brad Fiedel

Ellen Burstyn, Robert Prosky, Sam Robards, Nicholas Pryor

The Intruder Within
US 1981 96m colour TVM
ABC/John Furia Jnr–Barry Oringer (Neil T. Maffeo)

Oilmen on an Antarctic rig uncover some incubating prehistoric monsters.
A misleading title conceals an old-fashioned monster rally with echoes of *The Thing* and *Alien*.

w Ed Waters *d* Peter Carter *ph* James Pergola *m* Gil Melle

Chad Everett, Joseph Bottoms, Jennifer Warren, Rickne Tarkington

'Not without holes, but . . . it's a good time.'
– *Daily Variety*

The Intruders
US 1967 95m colour TVM
Universal (Bert Granet)

Western townsfolk look to their reluctant marshal for defence against approaching gunmen.
High Noon style minor western: nothing surprising.

w Dean Riesner d William Graham

Edmond O'Brien, Don Murray, John Saxon, Anne Francis

The Invaders **
US 1966–7 43 × 50m colour
ABC/Quinn Martin

An architect is on the run from alien invaders, who want to shut his mouth . . . and no one else will believe him.
Ingenious variation on *The Fugitive* from the same producer, extremely well produced and quite imaginative, with villains who crumble into coloured dust when damaged.

cr Larry Cohen

Roy Thinnes, Kent Smith

Episode titles:

Beach Head
The Experiment
The Mutation
The Leeches
Genesis
Vikor
Nightmare
Doomsday Minus One
Quantity Unknown
The Innocents
The Ivy Curtain
The Betrayed
Storm
Panic
Moonshot
Wall of Crystal
The Condemned
Condition: Red
The Saucer
The Watchers
Valley of the Shadow
The Enemy
The Trial
The Spores
Dark Outpost
Summit Meeting 1 & 2
The Prophet
Labyrinth
The Believers
The Captive
Task Force
The Ransom

The Possessed
Counterattack
The Pit
The Organization
The Peacemakers
The Vise
The Miracle
The Lifeseekers
The Pursued
Inquisition

† There was some uproar when the show was unexpectedly cancelled without a final episode: it just stopped. (The same fate befell *Planet of the Apes*, *Executive Suite*, and a score of other series in which the hero was left in considerable trouble.)

Invasion *
GB 1980 100m colour
Granada (David Boulton/Eva Kolouchova/ Leslie Woodhead)

Drama-doc reconstruction of the 'Prague Spring' of 1968 and subsequent invasion by Soviet forces to wipe the smile off Dubcek's brand of communism with a smiling face, based on the detailed recollections of Zdenek Mlynar, former Czech Party secretary.

d Leslie Woodhead

Julian Glover, Paul Hardwick   PP

The Invasion of Johnson County
aka: *Brahmin*
US 1976 98m colour TVM
NBC/Universal (Roy Huggins)

A Bostonian con man in Wyoming prevents a private army from routing small-time ranchers.
What begins like a promising reprise of *Maverick* turns into a very limp outdoor drama, protracted way beyond its dramatic possibilities.

w Nicholas E. Baehr d Jerry Jameson

Bill Bixby, Bo Hopkins, John Hillerman, Billy Green Bush, Alan Fudge

Invasion of Privacy *
US 1983 96m colour TVM
CBS/Embassy/Dick Berg/Stonehenge (Allan Marcil)

An artist and her daughter go to live on a Maine island.
Solidly plotted telepic with stronger than usual characters and something of the feel of a real movie.

w Elaine Mueller, *novel Asking for It* by Joan Taylor d Mel Damski ph John Lindley m Tony Rains

Valerie Harper, Cliff De Young, Tammy Grimes, Carol Kane, Richard Masur, Jerry Orbach, Jacqueline Brooks

The Investigator (US 1958). One of the last 'live' crime series, a half-hour mystery with Lonny Chapman as a young private eye relying on the experience of his father (Howard St John).

The Investigators (US 1961). Briefly seen one-hour crime series about a team of New York insurance investigators. James Franciscus, James Philbrook, Mary Murphy and Al Austin starred.

The Invisible Man
GB 1958 39 × 25m bw
ATV (Ralph Smart)
A scientist uses his power of invisibility to solve crimes.
Smooth hokum. The name of the actor playing the invisible man was never revealed.
† The unseen star was later discovered to be Jim Turner.

The Invisible Man *
US 1975 74m colour TVM
NBC/Universal (Harve Bennett, Steven Bochco)
Quite a good updating of the theme; just occasionally it even catches the flavour of the original novel by H. G. Wells. The tricks are good, but the resultant series didn't work.
w Steven Bochco d Robert Michael Lewis m Richard Clements
David McCallum, Jackie Cooper, Henry Darrow, Melinda Fee
† This revised version led to a disappointingly brief series of 13 × 50m. The following season it was tried again as *The Gemini Man*. In Britain the BBC ran a straightforward serialization of H. G. Wells's novel in 1984.

The Invisible Woman
US 1983 96m colour TVM
NBC/Universal/Redwood (Sherwood Schwartz)
A girl reporter becomes suddenly invisible after visiting her uncle's lab.
Feeble rehash of old jokes from the *Gilligan's Island* stable; interest in the tricks does not sustain two hours.
w Sherwood Schwartz, Lloyd J. Schwartz d Alan J. Levi
Bob Denver, Alexa Hamilton, Harvey Korman, David Doyle, George Gobel

Invitation to Hell
US 1984 96m colour TVM
ABC/ITC/Moonlight (Frank Von Zerneck)
New arrivals in a high-tech community find that the Steaming Springs Country Club has a sinister basis . . .

Yawnworthy melodrama which begins by looking like a soap commercial and then takes us into Dante's Inferno. Not a success.
w Richard Rothstein d Wes Craven ph Dean Cundey m Sylvester Levay
Robert Urich, Joanna Cassidy, Susan Lucci, Joe Regalbuto, Kevin McCarthy

Ireland. A state service only, RTE, since 1961; now two channels, though many Irish are also able to receive British programmes via Welsh or Northern Irish transmitters.

Ireland: A Television History **
GB 1981 13 × 50m colour
BBC/RTE (JEREMY ISAACS)
Allegedly the first major attempt to tell the whole history of a country on television, this worthy endeavour seemed at times mercilessly padded, with not too much to take the eye and mind before the Troubles started. Full of marvellous stuff, it could have been edited down to seven hours and been more memorable.
w/presenter ROBERT KEE ph Philip Bonham-Carter, Ken Lowe
PP: 'Together with Thames's *The Troubles*, running simultaneously, the series answered a frequent complaint from the Left during the seventies that the roots of the Northern Ireland conflict were never examined, though inevitably Kee's painfully honest conclusion did not suit those whose opinions were already fixed one way or the other.'
† Previous attempts include *Ireland: Some Episodes from Her Past*; two programmes by Howard Smith, 1972.

Iris in the Traffic, Ruby in the Rain * (GB 1981; 70m; colour). Further attempt by playwright Stewart Parker to convey the looking-glass drama of life in Belfast today, with the signs of the internal siege encroaching everywhere into the background – armoured cars, slogans, shattered buildings – but his two heroines firmly preoccupied with the small problems of a broken shoe-strap or a streaming cold as they went their apparently unconnected ways. Then Ruby, the social worker (perfectly done by Frances Tomelty), was reluctantly drawn into a more complex muddle that might just possibly have had something to do with the Troubles at about fifth remove. John Bruce directed; for BBC.
PP

Irish Angle. Intermittent outlet for Irish (RTE and UTV) programmes re-broadcast on C4 in mainland Britain.

THE INVISIBLE MAN. 1975's television series was a long way from the 1933 movie original with Claude Rains and Gloria Stuart (seen below). Above, David McCallum shows Melinda Fee the source of his power.

Irish Love Stories (Ireland 1983; 6 × c 75m). Dramatizations from James Joyce, Sean O'Faolain, James Plunkett, Neil Jordan and William Trevor (two), one of whose was *Ballroom of Romance*, co-produced with Kenith Trodd and shown on BBC2. The others were screened in Britain by C4 in 1984/5. Produced by John Lynch, for RTE.
                                                                PP

The Irish R.M. (GB 1983–4; 13 × 52m). Adequate dramatizations by Hugh Leonard, Bill Craig and others of the much-loved stories of a resident magistrate during the innocent days of British rule in Ireland prior to the Free State, the realization owing much to Peter Bowles in the office. Also with Lisa-Ann McLaughlin, Bryan Murray, Sarah Badel. Directed by Roy Ward Baker, Robert Chetwynd. Produced by Barry Blackmore and Adrian Hughes for James Mitchell Productions/UTV. Shown in GB by C4.
                                                                PP

Iron Horse *
US 1966–7 47 × 50m colour
ABC/Columbia (Matthew Rapf, Fred Freiburger)
The building of railroads through the west in the 1870s, as seen by the fighting president of the BPS & D.
Adequate western series.
Dale Robertson, Gary Collins, Ellen McRae, Bob Random

Irons, Jeremy (1948–). Patrician British actor wafted to household fame when *Brideshead Revisited* (on TV) and *The French Lieutenant's Woman* (in the cinema) hit the world about the same time in 1981. But attentive viewers would have marked him in *Love for Lydia* and *Langrishe Go Down*. PP

Ironside *
GB title: *A Man Called Ironside*
US 1967 97m colour TVM
NBC/Universal (Collier Young)
San Francisco's chief of detectives is crippled for life after a shooting, but traps his attacker. Fair pilot for a series that ran eight years and was usually watchable though seldom stimulating.
w Don M. Mankiewicz, Collier Young *d* James Goldstone
RAYMOND BURR, Don Galloway, Barbara Anderson, Donald Mitchell, Geraldine Brooks, Wally Cox, Kim Darby
† The series which followed was phenomenally successful and ran to 177 × 50m and 8 × 96m episodes. It co-starred Barbara Anderson and Don Galloway. Creator: Collier Young; executive producer: Cy Chermak/Joel Rogosin, for Harbour Productions/Universal/NBC.

Irvin, John (19 –). British director. *Hard Times, Tinker Tailor Soldier Spy*, etc.

Irving, Richard (1917–). American producer–director who mainly functions in the former capacity, e.g. for *The Name of the Game, Six Million Dollar Man* and *Columbo*. TV movies as director include *Prescription Murder, Istanbul Express, Ransom for a Dead Man, The Art of Crime, Seventh Avenue, Exo Man, The Jesse Owens Story, Wallenberg*.

Is There Anybody There?
Australia 1976 74m colour TVM
Paramount/Gemini (David Hannay)
Two women are locked in a penthouse for the weekend with a murderer.
Mildly watchable, uninspired psycho-thriller.
w Bruce A. Wishart *d* Peter Maxwell *ph* Russell Boyd
George Lazenby, Wendy Hughes, Tina Grenville, Charles Tingwell

Is This Your Problem? (GB 1955–6). BBC panel show which was television's first agony column. Edana Romney, a South African actress who had enjoyed brief cinema stardom in the late forties, presided over a panel of advisers. The anonymous clients were glimpsed only in silhouette or oblique rear view as they took it in turn to confide to the experts (and everyone watching). Dr David Stafford Clark was a regular member, though by the medical conventions of the time, likewise unnamed. PP

❋ **Isaacs, Jeremy** (1931–). British producer with special interest in current affairs; especially noted for *The World at War*. Programme controller of Thames TV 1974–8. Chief Executive Channel Four 1981– . BAFTA: Desmond Davis Award, 1971; Fellowship, 1984.

'Torn between the man who loves her and the man who needs her. It's the toughest choice a woman can make – and she's enjoying every minute of it!'
Isabel's Choice *
US 1981 96m colour TVM
CBS/Stuart Miller/Pantheon (Gabriel Katzka)

A devoted secretary maintains her position after her boss leaves, and proves her importance to the firm.

Quiet little character study which would have been very effective at a more modest length.

w Oliver Hailey   *d* Guy Green   *ph* Frank Beascoechea   *m* Glenn Paxton

Jean Stapleton, Richard Kiley, Peter Coyote, Betsy Palmer, Mildred Dunnock

Isadora **
GB 1966 75m bw

Ken Russell's ebullient BBC film about Isadora Duncan, predating the movie by two years and fielding in Vivian Pickles a much more fitting (as well as jollier) actress than Vanessa Redgrave to play the 'Biggest Dancer in the World'. My paean then: 'Russell can break as many rules as he likes as long as he remains exuberant and inventive and unafraid of emotion. The marvellous things about *Isadora* were the things which would be the first to be eliminated by those grim Anglo-Saxon guardians, Good Taste and Moderation.' And the *Sun* declared: 'I was laughing at the beginning and crying at the end.'   PP

† Granada version, *Isadora*, 1982.

Ishi, the Last of His Tribe
US 1979 96m colour TVM
NBC/Edward and Mildred Lewis Productions

The story of the last of the Yahi Indians and how in 1911 he was taken under the wing of an anthropologist.

A painfully true yet basically undramatic incident is stylishly presented but prolonged beyond its means.

w Dalton and Christopher Trumbo   *d* Robert Ellis Miller   *ph* Woody Omens   *m* Maurice Jarre

Dennis Weaver, Eloy Phil Casadoz, Joseph Running Fox, Michael Medina

'Spellbinding . . . both for adults and for youngsters.' – *Daily Variety*

Island of Adventure: see The Swiss Family Robinson

The Islander
US 1978 96m colour TVM
CBS/Universal/Glen Larson

A mainland lawyer avoids urban pressures by taking over a rundown Hawaiian hotel.

Thinly stretched pilot which didn't enthuse anybody.

w Glen Larson   *d* Paul Krasny   *ph* Ron Browne   *m* Stu Phillips

Dennis Weaver, Sharon Gless, Peter Mark Richman, Bernadette Peters, Robert Vaughn

'The basic characters have escaped from so many series and telefilms that they've begun to wear out their welcome.' – *Daily Variety*

The Islanders
US 1960 24 × 50m bw
ABC/MGM

Two adventurers own a seaplane.
Happy-go-lucky Pacific idyll.

cr Richard L. Bare

William Reynolds, James Philbrook, Diane Brewster

Isn't It Shocking? *
US 1973 73m colour TVM
ABC Circle

In a sleepy New England town, someone is killing off the senior citizens.

Unusual black comedy. It doesn't quite work, but at least it's different.

w Lane Slate, Ron Bernstein, Howard Roseman   *d* John Badham

Alan Alda, Ruth Gordon, Louise Lasser, Edmond O'Brien, Lloyd Nolan, Will Geer

Istanbul Express
US 1968 94m colour TVM
Universal (Richard Irving)

Secret information is due to be exchanged on the train from Paris to Istanbul.

Underdeveloped and rather tedious spy caper.

w Richard Levinson, William Link   *d* Richard Irving

Gene Barry, John Saxon, Mary Ann Mobley, Jack Kruschen, John Marley, Moustache, Senta Berger

It Ain't Half Hot, Mum **
GB 1973–81 42 approx. × 30m colour (VTR)
BBC (David Croft)

In World War II India, a platoon of British soldiers is busy organizing a concert party.

Efficiently nostalgic army farce with a preponderance of gay jokes.

w DAVID CROFT, JIMMY PERRY

Michael Bates, Windsor Davies, Don Estelle, Melvyn Hayes, Donald Hewlett, Michael Knowles

It Came upon the Midnight Clear
US 1984 96m colour TVM
OPT/Colombia/Schenck–Cardea/LBS

An old man dies but is sent back to take his grandson on a mission of cheering up Manhattan.

There are surely enough versions around of *A Christmas Carol* without adding this embarrassingly limp variation overflowing with American schmaltz.

w George Schenck, Frank Cardea *d* Peter Hunt *ph* Dean Cundey *m* Arthur B. Rubinstein

Mickey Rooney, Scott Grimes, Barrie Youngfellow, George Gaynes, Gary Bayer, Lloyd Nolan

'The whimsy thickens as the plot thins.' – *Daily Variety*

It Couldn't Happen to a Nicer Guy
US 1974 74m colour TVM
Jozak (Arne Sultan)

A real estate agent is raped at gunpoint by a mysterious woman.

And it doesn't get any better after that. Silly, tasteless comedy.

w Arne Sultan, Earl Barrett *d* Cy Howard

Paul Sorvino, Michael Learned, Adam Arkin, Ed Barth

'Pleasure seekers trapped by a deadly menace from the depths of the earth.'
It Happened at Lake Wood Manor
aka: *Panic at Lake Wood Manor*; *Ants!*
US 1977 96m colour TVM
Alan Landsburg (Peter Nelson)

Resort guests are threatened by a plague of ants.

Mild horror filler.

w Guerdon Trueblood, Peter Nelson *d* Robert Scheerer

Suzanne Somers, Robert Foxworth, Lynda Day George, Gerald Gordon, Myrna Loy

'Telefilm moves smartly along and may leave some viewers scratching.' – *Daily Variety*

It Happened Like This (GB 1963). Series of videotaped adaptations of yarns by the between-the-wars thriller writer Sapper, attempting – but failing – to repeat the success of the same company's Somerset Maugham stories. Produced by Norman Marshall; for A–R.   PP

'With the help of a lovable angel, she discovers the meaning of life!'
It Happened One Christmas
US 1977 126m colour TVM
ABC/Universal (Marlo Thomas, Carole Hart)

When she contemplates suicide as a failure, a loan company operator is visited by her guardian angel who shows her how important her life has been.

Workaday rehash of *It's a Wonderful Life* which gives no clue as to why anyone thought it was a good idea.

w Lionel Chetwynd *d* Donald Wrye

Marlo Thomas, Wayne Rogers, Orson Welles, Cloris Leachman, Barney Martin, Ceil Cabot, Richard Dysart

It Takes a Thief *
US 1965–9 65 × 50m colour
ABC/Universal (Jack Arnold)

A master thief is paroled if he will do his thing for the government's behalf among the international jet set.

Some comedy, some suspense, but mostly fantasy, which was found in this case to be quite a saleable commodity.

cr Collier Young *m* Dave Grusin

Robert Wagner, Malachi Throne, Fred Astaire in some episodes

It Takes a Worried Man (GB 1983–4; 12 × 30m). Sitcom involving middle-aged man trying to survive broken marriage and job he doesn't like, written and impersonated by Peter Tilbury. Produced by Douglas Argent for Thames, the first six episodes went out on ITV, the second six – unusually – on C4.   PP

It Takes Two *
US 1982   × 25m colour
CBS/Columbia/Witt–Thomas–Harris (Greg Antonacci)

A marriage goes slightly awry when Daddy is a surgeon and Mummy becomes a prosecuting attorney.

Slightly sophisticated domestic comedy, too highbrow for the mass viewers.

cr Susan Harris

Richard Crenna, Patty Duke Astin

ITA. What the IBA was until the seventies: the Independent Television Authority.

Italia Prize. The most prestigious of all television awards, organized and presented by the Italian broadcasting authority RAI but determined by an international jury. There are three prizes, for drama, documentary and music programmes. Both BBC and ITV have been winners in all sections.   PP

IT TAKES TWO. Two competent actors, Richard Crenna and Patty Duke Astin, couldn't make a long-runner of this perhaps-too-intelligent sitcom about a married couple who are both professionals.

Italians (GB 1984). Lively series of documentaries on representational citizens, ranging from suave *glitterati* of the north to patriarchal Sicilian fisherman of the deep south. Produced by Jeremy Bennett, for BBC.

ITCA. A central company which services the ITV companies: the Independent Television Companies' Association. Its function is largely secretarial.

It'll Be Alright on the Night ** (GB 1977; 50m). Compilation of bloopers, gaffes and no-good film-takes from both television and the movies, a little too reliant on the latter, and especially on fits of the giggles by Peter Sellers, but strung together with much wit by Denis Norden, and in the best moments quite irresistibly funny. Further editions followed in 1981, 1984, etc., then 'Best of' skimmings and *It'll Be Alright Late at Night* (1985) with some x-ier moments. Written by Denis Norden, produced originally by Paul Smith; for LWT.   PP

ITN. Independent Television News, a production company which provides the daily news bulletins and is jointly financed by the ITV companies.

It's a Great Life
US 1954–5 78 × 25m bw
Raydic/NBC

Two young men try to make it in Hollywood. Palatable happy-go-lucky 'realistic' comedy.

James Dunn, Michael O'Shea, William Bishop, Frances Bavier

It's a Knockout: see Jeux Sans Frontières

It's a Living * (US 1980). 25-minute comedy series about waitresses in a nightclub. The rather confined format was opened out in the second season to take in their private lives outside the club, and the addition of a slightly zany character played by Louise Lasser gave the enterprise the feeling of a sequel to the departed *Soap*. With Susan Sullivan, Marian

Mercer, Gail Edwards. Written by Stu Silver; produced by Paul Junger Witt and Tony Thomas; for TCF.

† For the second and last season the title was changed to *Making a Living*.

It's A Long Way to Transylvania ** (GB 1967; 50m; bw VTR).

An instance of an anthology series, in this case ATV's *Love Story*, provoking an unexpected, unpredictable little treat. Robert Muller conjured up an old and long forgotten Mitteleuropean actor who had once specialized in horror films. When these suddenly become the object of a cult revival he is smitten by a young admirer and stages little occasions – a candle-lit dinner, a coach ride across the common – during which he attempts, with hairy masks and plastic fangs, to re-animate the vampire roles at which she half shivers, half giggles. It was MacLuhanism spelled out for all to see, the magic of the old medium being exploited literally to make the content of the new. More important, with the aid of a bizarre, ringletted performance by Peter Wyngarde and affectionate direction by Valerie Hanson it was touching and funny and, for anyone brought up in the cinema age, poetic; indeed, more truly poetic than that other celebrated re-working of the Beauty and Beast fable, Alun Owen's *The Rose Affair*. PP

It's a Man's World
US 1962 19 × 50m bw
Revue/NBC

Four young fellows live in a houseboat on the Ohio river.
An unsuccessful attempt to do something different. It was too understated for public acceptance.

cr Peter Tewksbury

Glenn Corbett, Ted Bessell, Randy Boone, Michael Burns

It's a Square World *.
British live/tape comedy series of the fifties and sixties, reprised to less effect in the seventies; built round its star Michael Bentine, who gives crazy illustrated lectures in which anything can happen, e.g. models and diagrams come to life. A pointer towards *Monty Python*.

It's About Time
US 1966 26 × 25m colour
CBS/Redwood/Gladasaya/UA

Two astronauts find themselves in a timewarp and land in the Stone Age.
Woeful attempt to make a live-action Flintstones: a promising cast has egg on its face.

cr Sherwood Schwartz

Imogene Coca, Joe E. Ross, Frank Aletter, Jack Mullaney, Mike Mazurki

It's Always Jan (US 1955).
Half-hour situation comedy series for CBS, with Janis Paige as a widowed nightclub singer with a 10-year-old daughter.

It's Good to be Alive *
US 1974 100m colour TVM
Metromedia

The story of baseball player Roy Campanella, paralysed after an auto accident.
Another 'inspiring' real life case of the miseries; sympathetically done, but not exactly riveting.

w Steven Gethers *d* Michael Landon

Paul Winfield, Ruby Dee, Lou Gossett, Julian Burton

It's Not Easy
US 1983   × 25m colour
ABC/TCF/Patricia Nardo/Frank Konigsberg

A divorced couple share joint custody of the children, and live across the street from each other.
A thin idea for a comedy: it didn't sustain.

cr Patricia Nardo

Ken Howard, Carlene Watkins, Bert Convy, Jayne Meadows

It's Your Move
US 1984 22 × 25m colour
NBC/Embassy (Katherine Green, Fred Fox Jnr)

A tricky teenager does his best to prevent Mum from marrying the struggling writer across the hall.
A kid who's so fast with one-liners is apt to pall, and the basic premise is thin, so this show had only one season in which to gather its fair quota of laughs.

cr Ron Leavitt, Michael G. Moye

Jason Bateman, David Garrison, Caren Kaye, Tricia Cast

ITV. An unofficial abbreviation for Independent (i.e. commercial) Television and all its companies; often confused with ATV, which was simply one of the companies. The network is made up of 15 stations, mainly created in the fifties. London is split between Thames and London Weekend; Granada has Lancashire, Yorkshire has Yorkshire, ATV the Midlands. At the 1968 contract changes TWW was replaced by HTV. In 1981 Southern was replaced by TV South and

Westward by TSW, while ATV reformed into CIT (Central Independent Television). The network is ruled, and the contracts awarded, by the Independent Broadcasting Authority, which has no show business orientations and is run by 1,330 bureaucrats and engineers.

ITV, This Is Your Life *
GB 1976 135m colour (VTR)
ITV
A handy retrospective of ITV's first 21 years, featuring most of the outstanding personalities connected with it.

Ivan the Terrible (US 1976). Briefly seen half-hour comedy series for CBS, with Lou Jacobi as a head waiter in Moscow.

Ivanhoe
US/GB 1982 142m colour TVM
Columbia/Norman Rosemont
Adventures of a mysterious avenger in the time of King John.
Slapdash period action, partially salvaged by an excellent cast.

w John Gay, *novel* Sir Walter Scott *d* Douglas Camfield

Anthony Andrews, James Mason, Olivia Hussey, Michael Hordern, Lysette Anthony, Ronald Pickup

I've Got a Secret. Highly successful American (Goodson–Todman) panel show of the fifties, a variation on *What's My Line?* in which the panel had to wrest from the contestant a 'secret' which had already been divulged to the viewers. Garry Moore was the regular host. The format continued on daytime into the seventies.

PP: 'Taken up in Britain first as *Top Secret*, 1982, Barry Took presiding; original title adopted 1984, with Tom O'Connor; on BBC.'

Ives, Burl (1909–) (Burl Icle Ivanhoe). Bald, bearded American folk singer and actor. Series: *OK Crackerby, The Bold Ones.* TV movies: *The Man Who Wanted to Live Forever, Captains and the Kings, Roots, The Bermuda Depths, The New Adventures of Heidi.*

'He's the ultimate fighting machine . . . the toughest terminator of all!'

J.O.E. and the Colonel
US 1985 96m colour TVM
ABC/Universal (Nicholas Corea)

Scientists develop a biologically perfect soldier . . . but he doesn't want to fight. Muddled sci-fi with a message, but with very little entertainment.

w Nicholas Corea *d* Ron Satlof *ph* William Cronjager *m* Joseph Conlan

Terence Knox, Gary Kasper, Aimee Eccles, William Lucking

'A rather strange package that doesn't quite fit together.' – *Daily Variety*

Jabberjaw
US 1977 17 × 21m colour
Hanna–Barbera (Iwao Takamoto)

A lovable shark helps four underwater teenagers.
Very mild Saturday morning cartoon fare.

cr Joe Ruby, Ken Spears

The Jack Benny Show: see Benny, Jack

Jack on the Box ★★
GB 1979 6 × 50m colour

Funny British novelist Jack Trevor Story (original author of Hitchcock's *The Trouble With Harry*) in a series of inimitable meditations on such subjects as death, work and patriotism, plus much fanciful autobiography. Disrupted by an ITV strike, the series finally emerged in two spasms a year apart, effectively killing a truly original contribution. Directed by Patricia Ingram; produced by John and Patricia Ingram; for ATV. PP

Jack Solomons's Scrapbook (GB 1955–6). Newsfilm snippets of old prizefights linked together by the boxing promotor Jack Solomons, whose woolly cardigan, turn of phrase and gruff East London accent made this ATV series a popular success among early ITV programmes. PP

Jacks and Knaves (GB 1961). Police series based on the interrogation methods of a legendary Liverpool detective-sergeant, entertaining in itself but of seminal importance as a forerunner of *Z Cars*. Written by Colin Morris; directed by Gil Calder; for BBC. PP

Jack's Game (GB 1984; 10 × 30m). Former footballer Jack Charlton celebrates his favourite sports, some of which turned out to be hunting and shooting and fishing, to the dismay of anti-bloodsports activists. Produced by Charles Flynn, for YTV/C4. PP

Jack's Horrible Luck ★ (GB 1961). Inconsequential, funny, wistful play (for BBC) about an encounter between young sailor and old busker, bringing together three talents due to flourish on TV in the next few years: writer Henry Livings, actors Barry Foster and Wilfrid Brambell. PP

The Jackson Five
US 1971–2 23 × 22m colour
ABC/Rankin–Bass

Misadventures of a rock group.
Hasty cartoon cash-in on a popular group of the time.

Jackson, Glenda (1937–). Leading British actress who became internationally popular through her TV performance as ELIZABETH R (Emmy 1971).

Jackson, Gordon (1923–). British character actor who after a lifetime in films playing everything from callow youths to spies became an international star as Hudson the butler in UPSTAIRS, DOWNSTAIRS, and followed this with *The Professionals*. TV movies: *Spectre, The Last Giraffe*.

Jackson, Jack (19 –). Pioneer British disc-jockey who also conducted a pioneer TV entertainment, *The Jack Jackson Show*, in the early days of commercial television (ATV). Made up of snatches of pop music and comedy, with mildly surrealist interruptions in funny voices, it was probably ahead of its time. PP

413

Jackson, Kate (1949–). American leading lady of the seventies, in two highly successful series: *The Rookies, Charlie's Angels.* TV movies: *Satan's School For Girls, Killer Bees, Death Cruise, Death Scream, Death at Love House, Topper, Thin Ice, Inmates,* etc.

Jackson, Michael (1957–). American pop singer whose video *Thriller* topped the charts in 1983. Formerly of the Jackson Five.

Jackson, Mick (19 –). British documentary director who moved emphatically into drama with *Threads*, 1984. BAFTA award that year. Had previously tested the subject with *A Guide to Armageddon*, 1982.   PP

Jackson, Paul (1948–). British director and producer who in 1985 was dubbed the Cecil Rhodes of the anarchic new comedy, buying up what he hadn't colonized himself. *The Young Ones* (1983), *Coming Next . . .* (1984), *Happy Families* and *Girls on Top* (1985).   PP

Jacobi, Derek (1939–). British character actor who distinguished himself in the title role of *I, Claudius* (BAFTA award 1976) and subsequently played MacLean in *Burgess, Philby and MacLean.* 1982: Frollo in *The Hunchback of Notre Dame.*

Jacobs, David (1926–). Genial British host, anchorman and disc jockey, in constant employment since the early fifties.

Jacobs, John (1924–). Accomplished British drama director and executive, brother of David. Responsible for many BBC successes before becoming head of drama at Anglia in 1962. Returned to freelance directing after a health breakdown in the late seventies. *Strange Interlude* (O'Neill trilogy), *A Call on Kuprin,* etc.   PP

Jacqueline Bouvier Kennedy
US 1981 142m colour TVM
ABC (Louis Rudolph)

A reasonably faithful account of an over-documented life, up to the assassination of JFK. Lush backgrounds made it a natural for the ratings game.

w,d Steven Gethers *ph* Isidore Mankofsky *m* Billy Goldenberg

Jaclyn Smith, James Franciscus, Rod Taylor, Stephen Elliott, Claudette Nevins, Donald Moffatt, Dolph Sweet

Jacques, Hattie (1924–80). Giant-size British comedy character actress, much on TV with Eric Sykes (as his sister).

Jaffe, Sam (1897–1984). Eccentric-looking American character actor whose big TV hit was as Dr Zorba in *Ben Casey.* TV movies: *The Old Man Who Cried Wolf, Quarantined, Sam Hill, QB VII,* etc.

Jailed by the British * (GB 1983; 2 × 60m). (1) How we rounded up and interned enemy aliens in the scary days of World War II, following the German conquest of Europe, all very shameful according to this version of the episode, but what other course was possible? (2) Our treatment of German PoWs, which turned out to be so imaginative and effective that only one escaped back to Germany and hundreds chose to stay on after 1945. Narrated by Eleanor Bron (1) and John Thaw (2). Produced and directed by Lavinia Warner for Dolphin Communications/C4.   PP

Jamaica Inn
GB 1983 3 × 60m
HTV (Peter Graham Scott)

Expensive (£2½m) and vain re-telling of the Daphne du Maurier yarn about 18th-century wreckers which hadn't done much for Hitchcock's reputation either, 45 years before. Everything went wrong except the wrecking scenes, and even they took place in a weird blue twilight which suggested some misjudged day-for-night cinematography.

w Derek Marlowe *d* Lawrence Gordon Clarke

Jane Seymour, Patrick McGoohan, Trevor Eve, John McEnery, Billie Whitelaw

LH: 'What *is* wrong with HTV's 16 mm cinematography? *All* their series look messily blue.'

James at 15
US 1977 13 × 50m colour
NBC/TCF (Martin Manulis)

The sexual awakening of an American teenager.
A well-made series which clearly would not be everybody's cup of tea.

Lance Kerwin, Lynn Carlin, Linden Chiles

James, Clive (1939–). Top gun among British television critics (though Australian by birth and upbringing) throughout the seventies, thanks to an idiosyncratic, joke-filled attack combined with shrewd judgements. At the same time a TV performer of wit and assurance in *Saturday Night People*, *A Question of Sex* and various specials, usually for LWT. From 1982 concentrated on this activity: *Clive James on Television*, *The Late Clive James*, etc.   PP

LH: 'These merits have so far remained hidden from me.'

James Dean *
US 1976 96m colour TVM
CBS/Jozak (William Bast, John Forbes)
The early career of the screen idol who was killed in 1955, as remembered by his former roommate William Bast.
Tolerably well presented, but probably more than we wish to know.

w William Bast *d* Robert Butler *ph* Frank Stanley *m* Billy Goldenberg

STEPHEN MCHATTIE (as Dean), MICHAEL BRANDON (as Bast), Candy Clark, Meg Foster, Jayne Meadows, Katherine Helmond, Dane Clark

James, Geraldine (1950–). British actress who came to notice as the deaf heroine of *Dummy* (1977) and went on to play the longest female role in *Jewel in the Crown* (1984). In between was Lady Hamilton in *I Remember Nelson* ('Geraldine James is lovely,' I wrote, 'wobbling around in diaphanous gowns, big inverted smile'). *Blott on the Landscape*, 1985.   PP

James, Sid (1913–76). Crumple-faced South African comic actor who became a great favourite in GB and a staple of the 'Carry On' comedies. Series include *Taxi*, *Hancock's Half Hour*, *Citizen James*, *Bless This House*.

Jameson, Jerry (19 –). American director who made a few suspense and adventure items before graduating to the big screen. *Heatwave*, *The Elevator*, *Hurricane*, *Terror on the Fortieth Floor*, *The Deadly Tower*, *The Secret Night Caller*, *The Lives of Jenny Dolan*, *Superdome*, *A Fire in the Sky*, *High Noon Part Two*, *Stand by Your Man*, *The Killing at Hell's Gate*, *Starflight*, *Cowboy*, *This Girl for Hire*, *The Cowboy and the Ballerina*, etc.

Jamie
US 1954   × 25m bw
ABC
After the death of his parents, a young boy goes to live with his grandfather.
Sentimental comedy which worked at the time.

Brandon de Wilde, Ernest Truex, Kathleen Nolan, Polly Rowles, Alice Pearce

Jamie, on a Flying Visit **
GB 1968 75m bw
BBC (Graeme McDonald)
Feckless rich butterfly impulsively looks up a college girlfriend of 10 years past, now sedately married and living in the suburbs. A train of exquisite social embarrassments, each one jolting off the next . . . a troop of Cossacks couldn't have made more impact on domestic routine than the vague, loud cheerfulness of someone insulated by money from everyday needs. The happiest *Wednesday Play* of its season.

w Michael Frayn *d* Claude Whatham

Anton Rodgers, Caroline Mortimer, Dinsdale Landen, Felicity Gibson.   PP

Jane **
GB 1982 5 × 15m
BBC (Ian Keill)
Delightful idea to bring to life the *Daily Mirror* cartoon character of the thirties and forties in a World War II adventure in which she suffered her usual morale-building difficulty in keeping her clothes on. The conventions and frames of a strip cartoon were cunningly preserved in the matte production.

w Mervyn Haisman *artwork* Graham McCallum *d* Andrew Gosling

Glynis Barber, Robin Bailey, Max Wall
'Gloriously escapist, creative, funny and nostalgic.' – *London Standard*

LH: 'I agree: why haven't we had more of the same, using other comic strips?'

† *Jane in the Desert*, also 5 × 15m, followed in 1984.   PP

'A woman without a memory, a detective without a clue, and a madman without a choice ... but to try and kill her again!'
Jane Doe
US 1983 96m colour TVM
CBS/ITC (Paul B. Radin)
GB title: *The Fifth Victim*
After being almost killed by the 'roadside strangler', a girl whose memory has gone tries to help the police.
Mystery suspenser of the old school; too long, but not bad.

w Cynthia Mandelberg, Walter Halsey Davis *d* Ivan Nagy *ph* Dennis Dalzell

Karen Valentine, William Devane, Eva Marie Saint, Stephen Miller, David Huffman
'A well-constructed exercise in terror.' – *Daily Variety*

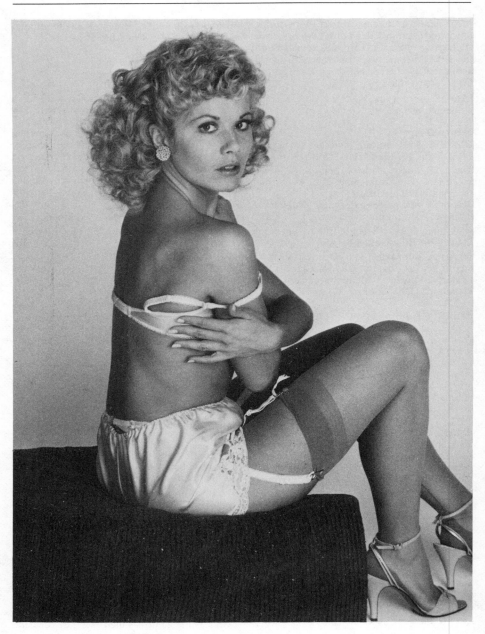

JANE. Glynis Barber was a decorative leading lady, but the real strength of the show was the skill with which she was popped in and out of cartoon backgrounds.

Jane Eyre *
GB 1971 108m colour TVM
Omnibus (Frederick H. Brogger)
A much-abused Victorian governess falls for
her moody master.
Over-bright teleplay with a strong Rochester
and not much else.

w Jack Pulman, *novel* Charlotte Brontë *d*
Delbert Mann *ph* Paul Beeson *m* John
Williams *ad* Alex Vetchinsky
GEORGE C. SCOTT, Susannah York, Jack
Hawkins, Nyree Dawn Porter, Ian Bannen,
Kenneth Griffith, Peter Copley, Rachel
Kempson, Jean Marsh, Constance Cummings

† BBC serials 1963, '73, '83.

The Jane Wyman Theatre
US 1956–60 163 × 25m bw
ABC/Lewman
Variable anthology series hosted by the star.

Janis, Conrad (1928–). American light
actor. Series: *Quark, Mork and Mindy.*

❋ **Janssen, David** (1930–80) (David
Meyer). Popular if rather glum American
leading man who had only moderate success
in feature films but was one of the staples of
TV, both in movies and series: *Richard
Diamond, The Fugitive, O'Hara US
Treasury, Harry O.* TV movies: *Night Chase,
The Longest Night, Moon of the Wolf, Birds
of Prey, Hijack, Pioneer Woman,
Fer-de-Lance, Stalk the Wild Child, Mayday
at 40,000 Feet, A Sensitive Passionate Man,
Superdome, Nowhere to Run, Centennial,
The Word, Panic on Page One, High Ice, SOS
Titanic.*

Japan has two public TV channels
supported by licence fees and operated by
NHK, the equivalent of the BBC, plus 13
major commercial stations.

Jarre, Maurice (1924–). French composer
who provided TV scores for *Shogun* and
Enola Gay.

Jarrett
US 1973 74m colour TVM
Columbia (David Gerber)
An adventurer combats a wily villain for the
possession of rare scrolls.
Foolish comic strip capers with a star far too
old for this kind of thing.

w Richard Maibaum *d* Barry Shear

Glenn Ford, Anthony Quayle, Forrest
Tucker, Laraine Stephens, Richard
Anderson

Jarvis, Martin (1944–). Neat, self-
contained British light leading man who
occasionally aspires to character roles as in
The Business of Murder. Series include
Nicholas Nickleby (title role), *The Pallisers,
Rings on their Fingers.*

Jason, David (1940–). British comedy
player with big doggy eyes and appealing
manner who rose to success as Ronnie
Barker's luckless errand boy in *Open All
Hours* and held it as Del in *Only Fools and
Horses.*

Jason King
GB 1971 26 × 50m colour
ATV
A famous thriller writer lends his sleuthing
services to the government.
Moderate spin-off from *Department S*, with
the leading man a shade too effete.

Peter Wyngarde

Jason, Rick (1929–). Smooth, slick
American leading man, star of TV series *The
Case of the Dangerous Robin* and *Combat.*

Jay, Peter (1937–). British journalist and
executive who won respect on television as
presenter of LWT's *Weekend World* from its
inception (winning BAFTA's Shell Award in
1974) until appointed British ambassador in
Washington by his father-in-law, James
Callaghan, in 1976. Headed TV-am until it
went on the air, when he was soon deposed.
Returned to front of camera with C4's *A
Week in Politics* from 1985.   PP

The Jayne Mansfield Story
US 1980 96m colour TVM
CBS/Alan Landsburg (Linda Otto, Joan
   Barnett)
A reconstruction of the career of the film star
tragically killed in the sixties, concentrating
on her extravagant lifestyle and her marriage
to Mickey Hargitay.
Tedious exploitation piece, ineptly assembled
and acted.

w Charles Dennis, Nancy Gayle *d* Dick
Lowry *ph* Paul Lohman *m* Jimmie Haskell

Loni Anderson, Arnold Schwarzenegger,
Raymond Buktenica, Kathleen Lloyd, G. D.
Spradlin

Jayston, Michael (1935–). Magnetic
British actor who made his name with *Mad
Jack* (1970). Series and serials include
Quiller and *Tinker, Tailor, Soldier, Spy.*

Jaywalking (GB). Periodic series of half-hour documentaries on social and religious issues, presented by Sue Jay for Central, initially as local shows, sometimes re-run on the network. PP

Jealousy
US 1984 96m colour TVM
ABC/Charles Fries (Alan Sacks)
Three playlets on the subject stated.
A trilogy with no apparent purpose other than to show off the talents of the star, who might have chosen more wisely.
w,d Jeffrey Bloom *ph* Gil Hubbs *m* Gil Melle, Jimmie Haskell
Angie Dickinson, Paul Michael Glaser, Richard Mulligan, David Carradine, France Nuyen, Bo Svenson, Susan Tyrrell, Julie Phillips

The Jean Arthur Show
US 1966 12 × 25m colour
CBS/Universal
Cases of mother-and-son lawyers.
Unsuccessful comedy–drama series with an uncomfortable star.
Jean Arthur, Ron Harper, Leonard Stone, Richard Conte

Jeavons, Colin (1929–). British general-purpose actor, in TV series *Billy Liar* and *The Hitchhiker's Guide to the Galaxy*.

Jefferson Drum
US 1958 26 × 25m bw
NBC/Columbia/Goodson–Todman
A newspaper editor fights corruption in an 1850s mining town.
Acceptable semi-western with no surprises.
Jeff Richards, Eugene Martin, Cyril Delevanti, Robert Stevenson

The Jeffersons
US 1975–83 183 × 25m colour (VTR)
CBS/Norman Lear (Don Nicholl, Michael Ross, Bernie West)
The black neighbours from *All in the Family* move to Manhattan's upper east side.
Ethnic spin-off which didn't appeal, perhaps because it was too reminiscent of *The Beverly Hillbillies*.
cr Don Nicholl, Michael Ross, Bernie West
Mike Evans, Isabel Sanford, Sherman Hemsley, Roxie Roker

Jemima Shore Investigates
GB 1983 12 × 52m
Thames (Tim Aspinall)
Glamorous investigative TV reportress duly investigates sundry crimes. The fatal flaw in the format, adapted from a literary series by Antonia Fraser, was that people who front TV shows never do anything for themselves, least of all investigate. That's done by researchers. 'In real life,' I said, 'Jemima would spend the day renegotiating her contract while others unravelled the mystery.' But there was at least one brilliant and original episode (from Peter Draper) and Patricia Hodge made a good Jemima.
w various *d* various PP

Jennie, Lady Randolph Churchill ****
GB 1975 7 × 50m colour (VTR)
Thames/Stella Richman (Andrew Brown)
The life of American Jennie Jerome, mother of Sir Winston Churchill.
Immaculately detailed period biography with precisely the right weight in every department.
w JULIAN MITCHELL *d* JAMES CELLAN JONES
LEE REMICK, RONALD PICKUP, Cyril Luckham, Rachel Kempson, Dan O'Herlihy, Barbara Parkins, Warren Clarke, Christopher Cazenove
'Constant enchantment.' – *Daily Express*

Jennifer: A Woman's Story
US 1979 96m colour TVM
NBC/Marble Arch (Martin Starger, Doris Quinlan)
A shipbuilder's widow tries to hold on to his business and becomes involved with boardroom intrigue.
Superior soap opera.
w Richard Gregson *d* Guy Green *ph* Michel Hugo *m* William Goldstein
Elizabeth Montgomery, Bradford Dillman, Scott Hylands, James Booth, Robin Gammell, John Beal

Jennifer Slept Here
US 1983 × 25m colour
ABC/Larry Larry/Columbia (Patricia Rickey)
The ghost of a glamorous movie star befriends the 14-year-old son of a family which moves into her old home.
Clumsy attempt to mix the old Topper strain with teenage sex-comedy.
cr Larry Tucker, Larry Rosen
Ann Jillian, John P. Navin Jnr, Georgia Engel, Brandon Maggart

JENNY'S WAR. Though apparently based on fact, this miniseries played as a highly unlikely story about one woman inside Nazi Germany wanting to get out. Even the determination displayed by Dyan Cannon failed to convince.

Jenny's War (GB/US; 4 × 52m). Loony melodrama about Anglo-American mum smuggled into wartime Germany to find PoW son, mixing bits of *Colditz*, bits of *Salon Kitty* and Robert Hardy once more as the suave Gestapo smoothie. With Dyan Cannon, Elke Sommer, Richard Todd, Denis Lill, Patrick Ryecart, Hartmutt Becker, Garfield Morgan. Written and directed by Steven Gethers from a novel by Jack Stoneley, produced by Peter Graham Scott, for HTV/Columbia/Rudolph Productions. PP

LH: 'Compulsively awful, including the old coffin trick from Ethel Vance's *Escape*, but one has to admit it got ratings.'

Jericho
aka: *Code Name Jericho*
US 1966 16 × 50m colour
CBS/MGM (Norman Felton)
In World War II, an allied spy team works behind enemy lines.
Rather flat adventure fare.
John Leyton, Marino Mase, Don Francks

The Jericho Mile *
US 1979 96m colour TVM
ABC Circle (Tim Zinnemann)
A convicted lifer keeps up his hobby of running, and eventually wins a chance to join the Olympic team.
Moderately effective yet somewhat confused tribute to the human spirit. It won Emmys for writers and star, but didn't survive when released on the big screen.
w Patrick J. Nolan, Michael Mann d Michael Mann ph Rexford Metz m Jimmie Haskell
Peter Strauss, Richard Lawson, Roger E. Mosley, Brian Dennehy, Billy Green Bush, Ed Lauter
'Energetic, often moving and purposeful.' – *Daily Variety*

The Jerk, Too
US 1984 96m colour TVM
NBC/Universal/40 Share (Ziggy Steinberg)
A naïve white man raised by blacks has adventures in Hollywood.
Frantic slapstick after the pattern of a movie which was inexplicably popular for a while; the TV version had no chance.
w Ziggy Steinberg, Rocco Urbisci d Michael Shultz ph Joe Biroc m John Sebastian, Phil Galston
Mark Blankfield, Ray Walston, Robert Sampson, Patricia Barry, Barrie Ingham, Stacy Nelkin, Thalmus Rasulala

'She deals with crime where it starts . . . in the heart and mind!'
Jessie
US 1984 96m colour TVM
ABC/MGM (Lindsay Wagner, Richard Michaels)
A lady psychiatrist is assigned to a traditional small-town police department.
In this pilot she tracks down a killer more by the use of force than science or even common sense; but the public was wise to the format's inadequacies, and the show closed after six one-hours.
w Felix Culver (Eric Bercovici) d Richard Michaels ph Matthew F. Leonetti m John Cacavas
Lindsay Wagner, Tony Lo Bianco, Celeste Holm, Tom Nolan, William Lucking

'Germany's supermen couldn't beat him . . . but America nearly did!'
The Jesse Owens Story
US 1984 96m colour miniseries
OPT/Paramount/Harve Bennett (Harold Gast)
The life and difficult times of the black runner who annoyed Hitler by winning his events in the 1936 Olympic Games.
The trouble is that there isn't enough story to fill four hours, since Owens never tried to be a hero or to lead the black cause. But as a mirror of past times the miniseries retains some interest.
w Harold Gast d Richard Irving ph Charles Correll m Michel Legrand
Dorian Harewood, Georg Stanford Brown, Debbi Morgan, Barry Corbin, Kal Wulff, Tom Bosley, LeVar Burton, Ronny Cox, Norman Fell, Greg Morris, Ben Vereen, George Kennedy

Jesus of Nazareth ****
GB 1977 2 × 150m colour
ITC/RAI (Vincenzo Labella)
The life of Jesus.
A star-packed spectacular, often sensational to look at; providing parts for many famous actors, it deliberately plays down the supernatural, but becomes a more gripping and emotional experience than any of the big-screen treatments of the subject.
w Anthony Burgess, Suso Cecchi d'Amico, Franco Zeffirelli d FRANCO ZEFFIRELLI m Maurice Jarre
ROBERT POWELL (Jesus), Anne Bancroft (Mary Magdalene), Laurence Olivier (Nicodemus), Ralph Richardson (Simeon), James Mason (Joseph of Arimathea), Anthony Quinn (Caiaphas), Peter Ustinov (Herod), Rod

Steiger (Pilate), Christopher Plummer (Herod Antipas); and Ernest Borgnine, Claudia Cardinale, Valentina Cortese, James Farentino, James Earl Jones, Michael York, Stacy Keach, Ian MacShane, Donald Pleasence, Fernando Rey, Olivia Hussey, Cyril Cusack

Jet Jackson, Flying Commando: see Captain Midnight

Jet Trail (GB 1984; 3 × 30m). History of jet aviation as seen from Bristol, where a lot of it – including Concorde – happened. Written and produced by John Elliott, for BBC West.

The Jetsons *
US 1962 24 × 25m colour
ABC/Hanna–Barbera

Problems of a 21st-century suburban family. A kind of reverse sequel to the successful *Flintstones*, this was an amusing cartoon series which somehow didn't hit the spot with the public.

voices Penny Singleton, Daws Butler, George O'Hanlon, Janet Waldo

Jeux Sans Frontières. Eurovision's other great popular success after the *Eurovision Song Contest*. Town teams competed in an annual Numbskulls' Olympics featuring greasy poles, giant carnival heads and lots of falling into water, all concocted with prodigious ingenuity. Preliminary British (BBC) rounds were held under the alternative title *It's a Knockout*, with Stuart Hall and Eddie Waring as MCs. Final programme 1982. An American version (Robert Stigwood) was tried out as *Almost Anything Goes.*   PP

The Jewel in the Crown **
GB 1984 14 × 52m
Granada (Christopher Morahan)

The rape of an English nurse sets in train a story of interlocking destinies in the last years of the British Raj in India. Though an odour of extreme self-satisfaction clung to this giant undertaking, there was good reason for it. Sir Denis Forman, Granada chairman, personally supervised the production, which grew from an earlier Granada dramatization of a Paul Scott novel, *Staying On* (1980), produced by IRENE SHUBIK. Shubik also schemed the general shape of *Jewel*, drawn from the four Scott novels known as the Raj Quartet; the screenplay thereafter was by Ken Taylor – 'a prodigious feat of story engineering,' I called

the result. Susan Wooldridge as Daphne Manners (the nurse), gawky yet sweet, her hair tightly bunned and kirbygripped, set the standard for at least half-a-dozen superb performances which followed. The whole show had a uniformly solid texture, whether filmed in India (as most of it was) or faked in England (e.g. the final railway-station scene after partition and a massacre, shot in Buckinghamshire).

w KEN TAYLOR *d* CHRISTOPHER MORAHAN, Jim O'Brien *m* George Fenton *design* Vic Symonds, Alan Pickford

PEGGY ASHCROFT, CHARLES DANCE, Saeed Jaffrey, GERALDINE JAMES, Rachel Kempson, ART MALIK, Zia Moyheddin, TIM PIGGOTT-SMITH, Eric Porter, SUSAN WOOLDRIDGE

See entry for Paul Scott.   PP

LH: 'Massive, much-lauded attempt to put on film a difficult series of novels. In the end the project may be seen to have succeeded for its acting and for a series of splendidly re-created sequences rather than as an epic whole.'

Jewel, Jimmy (1912–). Former British music hall comic (half of Jewel and Warriss) who emerged from retirement to become a more or less straight actor. Series include *Nearest and Dearest*, *Thicker Than Water*, *Spring and Autumn*; and FUNNY MAN, which was adapted at extreme length from his reminiscences.

Jigsaw *
US 1972 98m colour TVM
Universal (Stanley Kallis)

A disgraced policeman seeks the missing witness who can save him from a murder charge.

Sufficiently engrossing plot and some fine desert chases keep the pot boiling.

w Robert E. Thompson *d* William Graham

James Wainwright, Vera Miles, Andrew Duggan, Edmond O'Brien, Marsha Hunt, Irene Dailey, Richard Kiley

† A series of 50m episodes about the Missing Persons Bureau was begun, but only eight were made, all starring James Wainwright. They played under the title *The Men*, rotating with *The Delphi Bureau* and *Assignment Vienna.*

Jigsaw John
US 1976 13 × 50m colour
MGM/NBC (Ronald Austin, James Buchanan)

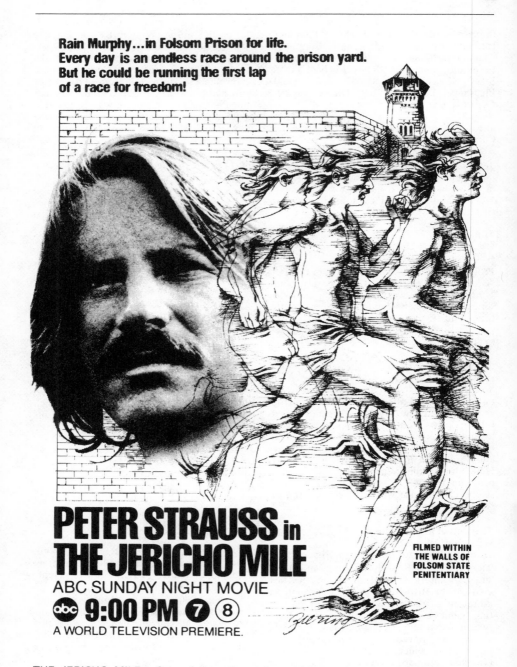

Rain Murphy...in Folsom Prison for life.
Every day is an endless race around the prison yard.
But he could be running the first lap
of a race for freedom!

**PETER STRAUSS in
THE JERICHO MILE**
ABC SUNDAY NIGHT MOVIE
🅰🅱🅲 **9:00 PM** ➐ ⑧
A WORLD TELEVISION PREMIERE.

FILMED WITHIN
THE WALLS OF
FOLSOM STATE
PENITENTIARY

THE JERICHO MILE. One of the telemovies which in some countries was thought good enough for theatrical release. But Peter Strauss never quite fulfilled the promise he showed in *Rich Man Poor Man*.

The adventures of a police detective whose real name was 'Jigsaw' John St John. Tolerable police series.

cr Al Martinez

Jack Warden, Alan Feinstein, Pippa Scott

† A 74m pilot film, *They Only Come Out at Night*, was aired the previous November.

Jillian, Ann (1951–) (Ann Jura Nauseda). American leading lady, former child actress. *Hazel, The Partridge Family, It's a Living, Mae West, Malibu, Jennifer Slept Here, Girls of the White Orchid, Ellis Island*.

The Jim Backus Show
aka: *Hot Off the Wire*
US 1960 39 × 25m bw
NBC/Ray Singer, Dick Chevillat

Adventures of a newspaper editor and owner perpetually striving to stave off bankruptcy. Adequate comedy series for syndication.

Jim Backus, Nita Talbot, Bob Watson

Jim Bowie: see The Adventures of Jim Bowie

Jim'll Fix It: see *magic wands*

Jimmy B and Andre
US 1979 96m colour TVM
CBS/Georgian Bay (Alex Karras)

A Detroit restaurateur forms a friendship with a deprived black child and tries to adopt him.
True-life heartwarmer, for susceptible viewers only.

w Douglas Graham, Charles Johnson d Guy Green ph Jules Brenner

Alex Karras, Susan Clark, Curtis Yates, Madge Sinclair, Eddie Barth

Jimmy Hughes, Rookie Cop (US 1953). Shortlived half-hour crime series for Dumont, with William Redfield avenging the death of his cop father.

The Jimmy Stewart Show *
US 1971 24 × 25m colour
NBC/Warner (Hal Kanter)

Domestic problems of a small-town anthropology professor.
Slightly disappointing but generally pleasing comedy vehicle, perhaps too perfectly tailored for its star.

cr Hal Kanter m Van Alexander

James Stewart, Julie Adams, John McGiver

Jim's Inn. The most popular and long-lived of the British advertising magazines, this ran from 1957 until the IBA banned the genre in the mid-sixties. Jimmy Hanley chatted to the regulars in his pub about new products on the market. Nobody loved it but the public.

Joanie Loves Chachi
US 1982   × 25m colour
ABC/Paramount/Miller–Milkis–Boyett/ Henderson (Terry Hart)

Teenage sweethearts sing disco duets in an Italian restaurant owned by his parents. Tepid spin-off from *Happy Days*.

cr Gary Marshall, Lowell Ganz

Erin Moran, Scott Baio, Al Molinaro, Ellen Travolta, Art Metrano

Joe and Mabel (US 1956). Briefly seen half-hour domestic comedy for CBS, with Larry Blyden as a city cab driver and Nita Talbot as his girl friend.

Joe and Sons (US 1975). Shortlived half-hour comedy series for CBS, with Richard Castellano as a widowed Italian–American factory worker.

Joe Dancer: The Big Black Pill
US 1980 96m colour TVM
NBC/Filmways (Robert Blake)

A Los Angeles private eye solves a murder. Routine murder mystery with interesting detail and a central character that harks back to Philip Marlowe.

w Michael Butler d Reza Badiyi ph Sherman Kunkel m George Romanis

Robert Blake, Jobeth Williams, Neva Patterson, Eileen Heckart, Veronica Cartwright, Ed Winter

† Two other *Joe Dancer* TV movies were made and shown, but no series resulted despite good ratings; this was allegedly because the star wanted everything too much his own way. Titles: *The Big Trade* (w Ed Waters, d Reza Badiyi), *Sweet Wine, An Old Line, One More Time* (w Robert Crais, d Burt Brinckerhoff).

Joe Forrester
US 1975 13 × 50m colour
NBC/Columbia (David Gerber)

Stories of the policeman on the beat in a rough area.
A spin-off from the TV movie *The Return of Joe Forrester*, this unexciting show debuted during the same season as *The Blue Knight*, which had the same subject and was only slightly better.

Lloyd Bridges, Pat Crowley, Eddie Egan

THE JEWEL IN THE CROWN. Though this much-praised miniseries focused on the younger generation, veteran actress Peggy Ashcroft (left, seen here with Fabia Drake) won much of the attention and quite a few of the prizes.

Joe 90 *
GB 1968 30 × 25m colour
ATV (Gerry Anderson)

A boy helps his father in advanced science. Smooth, entertaining puppet series.

The Joel Brand Story (GB 1965). West German dramadoc by Reinar Kipphardt, adapted and directed by Rudolph Cartier. Brand was the Hungarian factory owner who acted as go-between in a bizarre offer by the Nazi Adolf Eichmann to trade a million Jews for 10,000 army trucks, but failed to persuade the Allies to accept it. 'While professing to examine a set of fearful moral dilemmas the dramatization in fact ducked every one except the most emotional, the most dramatically convenient and – for the Germans – the most exculpatory.' With Cyril Shaps, Anton Diffring; produced by Peter Luke, for BBC. PP

**Joey ** ** (GB 1974; 50m). Unsentimental, uplifting dramatization of the autobiography of a 54-year-old spastic, Joey Deacon, who had spent all his life in institutions of varying grimness, imaginatively using the grammar of film (sub-titles, flickering scenelets) to convey the manner in which Joey had laboriously set down his story. Written by Elaine Morgan; directed by Brian Gibson; for BBC (*Horizon*). PP

† Repeated 1982 after Joey's death at age of 61.

The Joey Bishop Show
US 1961 26 × 25m bw
NBC/Danny Thomas/Bellmar

Domestic problems of a public relations man. Adequate star comedy vehicle.

m Earle Hagen

Joey Bishop, Marlo Thomas, Madge Blake, Warren Berlinger

† Another attempt was made in 1962–4 (97 episodes – 70 in colour); in this case the star was a nightclub comedian, and supporting players included Abby Dalton, Corbett Monica, Joe Besser and Mary Treen.

Joffé, Roland (1945–). British drama director of the left, associated with the Redgraves, Ken Loach and Jim Allen. *United Kingdom*, 1981, *'Tis Pity She's a Whore*. Into features, decisively, with *The Killing Fields*.

John and Yoko: a Love Story
US 1985 142m colour TVM
NBC/Carson (Aida Young)
The romance and marriage of John Lennon and Yoko Ono.
Not a lot can be said about this slow, unexciting and predictable wrap-up of near-facts.
w,d Sandor Stern *ph* Alan Hume *pd* Leo Austin
Mark McGann, Kim Miyori, Kenneth Price, Richard Morant, Rachel Laurence
'It generally entertains. As for depth, that's way out at sea.' – *Daily Variety*

John, Elton (1947–) (Reginald Dwight). Freakish-looking British pop singer.

The John Forsythe Show
US 1965 30 × 25m colour
NBC/Universal
Trials of the headmaster of a privately owned girls' school.
Unsurprising star comedy.
John Forsythe, Guy Marks, Elsa Lanchester, Ann B. Davis

John Gabriel Borkman **
GB 1958 78m bw
ATV (Caspar Wrede)
'To and fro paced the distinguished feet, overhead, unseen,' I dictated to the old *News Chronicle* as the transmission ended. 'Only after 20 minutes did the camera float up amid the falling snow to peer through misted windows into the upstairs room . . .'
There it found the greatest actor of his day, ending a 20-year sulk to make what was, effectively, his television debut. It *was* an occasion, and lived up to by Olivier in a fine intelligent performance, scaling down the trumpet voice, conveying Borkman's rising megalomania with little more than an impatience in conversation.
play by Ibsen *d* Christopher Morahan *design* Richard Negri
LAURENCE OLIVIER, Maxine Audley, George Relph, Pamela Brown, Irene Worth   PP

John Lennon: A Journey in the Life (GB 1985; 95m). Preposterous drama documentary using colour overlay ('a fancy way of making any programme look cheap and desperate'), with Bernard Hill as a morose lookunlike Lennon. Directed by Ken Howard, produced by Daniel Wolf as a BBC *Everyman* special.   PP

'An attack robbed her of her dignity . . . and now the man who loves her is fighting to get it back!'
Johnny Belinda
US 1982 96m colour TVM
CBS/MGM–UA/Lorimar/Dick Berg/Stonehenge (Stanley Bass)
A nutritionist on assignment to a poverty-stricken rural area discovers that the girl everyone thinks is retarded is only deaf and dumb.
Competent rehash of a once-popular film; the time now seems out of joint for it, and the elements don't really jell.
w Sue Milburn, *play* by Elmer Harris *d* Anthony Page *ph* Harry J. May *m* John Rubinstein
Richard Thomas, Rosanna Arquette, Dennis Quaid, Candy Clark, Roberts Blossom, Fran Ryan

Johnny Go Home ** (GB 1975; 2 × 50m). Famous (or infamous) report on the plight of homeless teenage boys in London which half-way through turns into a murder story. As a social document it caused enormous concern and led to the prosecution of at least one predator, but the propriety of observing and recording a scandal rather than bringing it immediately to the notice of the law could not easily be justified. Written and directed by John Willis; produced by Michael Deakin; for YTV. BAFTA award for best documentary.   PP

Johnny Midnight
US 1958 39 × 25m bw
MCA/Revue/Jack Chertok
A Manhattan actor turns detective and roams the Times Square area.
Predictable mysteries with a shade more flair than most.
Edmond O'Brien

Johnny Ringo
US 1958 38 × 25m bw
CBS/Four Star (Aaron Spelling)
A gunfighter turns sheriff of a lawless Arizona town.
Good routine western.
Don Durant

Johnny Staccato **

aka: *Staccato*

US 1959 27 × 25m bw

NBC/MCA/Universal

A jazz pianist in a Greenwich Village club turns detective.

Moodily-shot and performed mysteries with a good music score: a cut above the average crime series.

m Elmer Bernstein

John Cassavetes, Eduardo Ciannelli

Johnny, We Hardly Knew Ye

US 1977 96m colour TVM

NBC/Talent Associates/Jamel (David Susskind)

The early political background of John F. Kennedy.

Moderately compelling biopic; hard tack for the uninitiated.

w Lionel Chetwynd   *d* Gilbert Cates   *m* Garry Sherman

Paul Rudd, William Prince, Burgess Meredith, Shirley Rich, Kevin Conway, Tom Berenger

Johns, Stratford (1925–). Burly South African actor who scored in Britain as Inspector Barlow in the *Z Cars* series. As so often, his career floundered when he escaped from this typecasting, and *Barlow at Large* was much less popular.

Johnson, Celia (1908–82). Celebrated British stage and film actress. TV includes *Mrs Palfrey at the Claremont*, a play which won her a BAFTA award in 1973; also *The Dame of Sark*, *Staying On*.

Johnson, Don (*c* 1949–). American leading man. *Amateur Night, From Here to Eternity, The Rebels, Beulah Land, Revenge of the Stepford Wives, Elvis and the Beauty Queen, The Two Lives of Carol Letner,* MIAMI VICE, THE LONG HOT SUMMER.

Johnson, Kenneth A. (1942–). American writer–producer, creator of *The Bionic Woman* and *The Incredible Hulk*.

Johnson, Lamont (1920–). American director who graduated after critical plaudits to the big screen though his TV credits remain the more interesting. Series include *Peter Gunn, Have Gun Will Travel, Twilight Zone, The Defenders, The Trials of O'Brien.* TV movies: *Deadlock, My Sweet Charlie,* THAT CERTAIN SUMMER, *The Execution of Private Slovik,* FEAR ON TRIAL, *Crisis at Central High,* etc.

Johnstone, Paul (19 –). British producer associated through most of a long career with imaginative archaeological programmes, notably *Animal, Vegetable or Mineral?* and the *Chronicle* series.   PP

Jones, Carolyn (1929–84). Dark-haired American actress, once a TV hit as Morticia in THE ADDAMS FAMILY; emerged after retirement to play in *Roots* and *Little Ladies of the Night*.

Jones, David (19 –). British theatrical director who produced and presented BBC Arts magazines *Monitor* (1958–64) and *Review* (1971–2). Directed *Kean* and *Langrishe Go Down*, both 1978.

Jones, Dean (1933–). Busy American perennial leading man. TV series: *Ensign O'Toole, The Chicago Teddy Bears.* TV movies: *The Great Man's Whiskers, Guess Who's Sleeping in My Bed, When Every Day Was the Fourth of July.*

Jones, Elwyn (1923–82). British writer, script-editor and producer, instrumental in *Z-Cars, Softly, Softly* and all spin-offs thence.   PP

Jones, Freddie (1927–). British character actor, often enjoyably over the top, who came to the medium in middle age and made a big hit as Claudius in THE CAESARS. Most recent series: *The Ghosts of Motley Hall.*

Jones, Gemma (1942–). British character actress who became famous as *The Duchess of Duke Street.*

Jones, Griff Rhys (19 –). British comedy actor, the most normal one in *Not the Nine O'Clock News.* Later: *Alas Smith and Jones.*

Jones, Henry (1912–). American character actor. Series: *Channing, Phyllis.* TV movies include *The Movie Murderer, The Daughters of Joshua Cabe, The Letters, Roll Freddy Roll, Tail Gunner Joe.*

Jones, Jack (1942–). American popular singer, son of Allan Jones. Tried his hand at TV acting in *Condominium.*

Jones, James Cellan (19 –). British drama director and executive, head of BBC plays during the seventies. Credits date from *The Forsyte Saga* (1967), through to *Jennie, Lady Randolph Churchill* (1975), *A Fine Romance* (from 1981), *Horace* (1982) and *Oxbridge Blues* (1984).   PP

Jones, James Earl (1931–). Imposing black American actor who has portrayed Paul Robeson on the stage and had his own series, *Paris*. TV movies: *The UFO Incident, Jesus of Nazareth, The Greatest Thing That Almost Happened*, ROOTS: THE NEXT GENERATIONS, *Guyana Tragedy, Golden Moment, The Las Vegas Strip Wars, The Atlanta Child Murders, Me and Mom*

Jones, Julia (19 –). Prolific British writer, equally at home in single plays, serials and adaptations. *Home and Away* (1972) struck a mildly feminist note, otherwise free of fads of the day. *The Navigators* (1965); *Faith and Henry* (1969); *Moody and Pegg* series, with Donald Churchill (1974–5); *Our Mutual Friend*, from Dickens, also with Churchill (1976); *We, the Accused*, from Ernest Raymond (serial, 1980).   PP

Jones, Ken (1930–). Crumple-faced British north country comic actor, in such series as *The Wackers, Her Majesty's Pleasure, The Squirrels*.

Jones, Paul (1917–66). Much underrated British dramatist with a sharp eye for the comedy, and sometimes the bitterness, underlying the clipped niceties of middle-class behaviour. *The Winds of Love* (A–R, 1958) was perhaps the first-ever television play to deal unflinchingly with class. Also: *At Home, The Problem of Girl Friends, Fate and Mr Browne, A Couple of Dry Martinis*.   PP

Jones, Peter (1920–). British comedy character actor, a familiar face since 1950 but best known as the harassed boss in *The Rag Trade*.

Jones, Quincy (1933–). American composer who won an Emmy for his ROOTS score.

Jones, Shirley (1934–). American leading lady, singer and actress. She has appeared in many TV guest roles, but her sole series is *The Partridge Family*. TV movies: *Silent Night Lonely Night, The Girls of Huntington House, Winner Take All, Yesterday's Child, Who'll Save Our Children, A Last Cry for Help, The Children of An Lac, Shirley*, etc.

Jones, Steve (1945–). Bespectacled British TV and radio presenter and disc jockey.

Jones, Tom (1940–) (Thomas Woodward). Virile-looking Welsh pop singer who became an even bigger hit in America than at home. His 1970 series of specials for ATV was oddly unsuccessful in ratings terms. He tried again in 1981 and meanwhile was in a poor TV movie, *Pleasure Cove*.

Jones, Tommy Lee (1946–). Tall, rangy American actor who has sunk his teeth into a couple of good parts. *Charlie's Angels*, THE AMAZING HOWARD HUGHES, THE EXECUTIONER'S SONG.

Jonny Quest *
US 1964 26 × 25m colour
ABC/Hanna–Barbera

The young son of a famous scientist helps him in secret intelligence work.

Successful attempt at limited animation: the drawings have the look of a newspaper comic strip.

The Jordan Chance
US 1979 96m colour TVM
CBS/Universal/Roy Huggins (Jo Swerling Jnr)

An attorney who spent years in jail for a crime he didn't commit now seeks to defend other people wrongfully accused.

Ho-hum format for a tired star; it didn't take.

w Stephen J. Cannell *d* Jules Irving *ph* Enzo Martinelli *m* Pete Rugolo

Raymond Burr, Ted Shackelford, James Canning, John McIntire, Stella Stevens, Peter Haskell

'Jordan is thorough, calm and collected, but not necessarily interesting.' – *Daily Variety*

Jordan, Richard (1938–). American leading man who became noted on TV in *Captains and the Kings*; then *Les Misérables, The French Atlantic Affair, The Bunker, Washington Mistress*.

Jory, Victor (1902–82). Reliable American character actor who very often played saturnine villains. TV series: *Manhunt*. TV movies: *Perilous Voyage, Devil Dog*.

Josie and the Pussycats
US 1970–3 104 × 22m colour
CBS/Hanna–Barbera

Adventures of an all-girl rock group.
Middling cartoon series for Saturday morning.

† In 1972 the series was revived as *Josie and the Pussycats in Outer Space*, which was self-explanatory and stupid.

Jourdan, Louis (1921–). Elegant French actor who made a disappointing *Dracula* for BBC but was useful in some American TV movies: *Fear No Evil, Ritual of Evil, Run a Crooked Mile, The Great American Beauty Contest, The Count of Monte Cristo, The Man in the Iron Mask, The French Atlantic Affair, The First Modern Olympics.*

The Journal of Bridget Hitler
GB 1981 110m colour
BBC (Ann Head)
Messy treatment of the typescript supposedly by Hitler's Irish sister-in-law which tells of the future dictator's visit to Liverpool in 1912–13 and subsequent encounters with him in Germany. The reconstructed narrative with Maurice Roeves as a reasonably magnetic Adolf is forever being interrupted by a simulated interview with a latter-day Bridget or, worse, the backstage bickerings of the actors taking part in the dramatization.
w Beryl Bainbridge, Philip Saville *d* Philip Saville
Maurice Roeves, Siobhan McKenna, Julian Glover   PP

Journey from Darkness
US 1975 74m colour TVM
Columbia/Bob Banner
A blind student fights to enter medical school.
Another true weepie, more moving than dramatic.
w Peggy Chantler Dick *d* James Goldstone
Mark Singer, Kay Lenz, Wendell Burton, William Windom, Joseph Campanella, Jack Warden

Journey into the Shadows * (GB 1984; 90m). Anna Massey as Gwen John, sister of Augustus, model and mistress to Auguste Rodin, gifted artist in her own right. Gently beguiling play by Elaine Morgan, with Victoria Fairbrother, Mel Martin, Leigh Lawson; photographed by Colin Waldeck in pinks and oyster colours to look like Gwen's paintings; produced and directed by Anna Benson-Gyles, for BBC.   PP

Journey of a Lifetime (GB 1961). Quaint religious odyssey from ABC with John Bonney as a newly married water engineer sent to the Middle East and taking his bride (Anne Lawson) with him in lieu of a honeymoon. Their expeditions to biblical sites were accompanied by so much uxoriousness and carried out in such stylish outfits you suspected they carried matching bibles handtooled His and Hers.   PP

Journey to the Center of the Earth
US 1967 17 × 25m colour
ABC/TCF/Filmation (Lou Scheimer)
Adventures below ground of Professor Lindenbrook and his companions.
Pretty fair cartoon rendering of the Jules Verne adventure.

Journey to the Unknown *
GB 1968 17 × 50m colour
ABC/TCF/Hammer (Joan Harrison)
An anthology of weird stories. Quality very variable, but usually something of interest. No host, which killed it.
m Harry Robinson *story editor* John Gould

Joyce, James (1882–1941). Irish writer whose *Dubliners* and *Stephen D* were adapted to TV in the sixties. Centenary marked by *The World of James Joyce* (RTE, *p* Sean O'Mordha) shown on BBC2, and *Joyce in June*, comedy with music by Stewart Parker, *p* Terry Coles, *d* Donald McWhinnie, for BBC.   PP

Joyce, Yootha (1927–80). Angular British character actress who gained unexpected popularity as the landlady in *A Man About the House*, which led to co-star billing in *George and Mildred*.

Jubilee *
GB 1977 13 × 50m colour (VTR)
BBC (Pieter Rogers)
Separate plays trace the changing attitudes over the 25 years of the reign of Elizabeth II. An interesting concept with several good plays, but none proved very memorable or very popular.
d Peter Moffatt, Paul Ciapessoni, Valerie Hanson, Ruth Caleb

Judd for the Defense *
US 1967–8 50 × 25m colour
ABC/TCF (Paul Monash)
Cases of a big-time lawyer, Clinton Judd, who flies his own jet and only takes on cases he fancies.
Good solid courtroom series with an agreeable touch of the flamboyant; based on the career of F. Lee Bailey.
CARL BETZ, Stephen Young

The Judge and Jake Wyler
US 1972 100m colour TVM
Universal (Richard Levinson, William Link)
An eccentric lady judge, retired for health reasons, employs an ex-con as her 'legs' to solve murder cases.

Another comical pair of investigators, and this time their heart plainly isn't in it: they must have seen the script.

w David Shaw, Richard Levinson, William Link d Gil Melle

Bette Davis, Doug McClure, Eric Braeden

Judge Dee and the Monastery Murders
US 1974 96m colour TVM
ABC Circle (Gerald I. Isenberg)

A 7th-century Chinese judge solves a complex murder.

An interesting departure but an unlikely candidate for a series, with every role played by an Oriental.

w Nicholas Meyer, *novel* Robert Gulick d Jeremy Kagan ph Gene Polito m Leonard Rosenman

Khigh Dhiegh, Mako, Miiko Taka, Irene Tsu

† Granada TV of Britain staged a *Judge Dee* series in the sixties.

Judge Horton and the Scottsboro Boys *
US 1976 98m colour (VTR)
Tomorrow Entertainment (Paul Leaf)

A reconstruction of the 1931 court case in which nine black men in Alabama were accused of raping two white women.

A conscientious dramatic special which fails to shed fresh light on the subject.

w John McGreevey d Fielder Cook

Arthur Hill, Vera Miles, Lewis J. Stadlen

Judge Roy Bean: see The Adventures of Judge Roy Bean

Judgement: The Court Martial of Lt William Calley *
US 1975 100m colour (VTR)
Stanley Kramer/David Wolper

A reconstruction of the trial of the Vietnam war veteran accused of leaving civilians to die.

Well-intentioned and very adequately made docu-drama.

w Henry Denker d Stanley Kramer

Tony Musante, Richard Basehart, Bo Hopkins, Bill Lucking

Juke Box Jury. A popular panel show of the sixties in which guests were asked to judge new records, sometimes not knowing that the recording artist was behind a screen. It was to some extent superseded in the seventies by *New Faces*.

Julia *
US 1968–70 86 × 25m colour
NBC/Savannah/Hanncar/TCF (Hal Kanter)

A young Negro widow has a six-year-old son, an apartment in an integrated block and a job as a nurse.

Much-discussed, and quite successful comedy; the first to have an attractive black female lead on equal terms with whites, it veered between the slick and the sentimental.

cr Hal Kanter

Diahann Carroll, Lloyd Nolan, Marc Copage

The Julie Andrews Hour *
GB/US 1972 26 × 50m colour (VTR)
ABC/ITC (Nick Vanoff)

The star's best TV outlet, a series of stylish and varied musical hours with top guest stars: also Rich Little, Alice Ghostley, and Nelson Riddle and his Orchestra.

Juliet Bravo (GB since 1980). Popular 50-minute series about the northern police, somewhat reminiscent of *Z Cars*. Here the leading character is a lady inspector who is also a housewife. With STEPHANIE TURNER, David Hargreaves. Created by Ian Kennedy Martin; produced by Terence Williams; for BBC. Anna Carteret took over in 1983.

Jump, Gordon (1932–). American character comic, a regular on *WKRP in Cincinnati.*

The June Allyson Show
US 1959–60 57 × 25m bw
CBS/Four Star

Variable anthology series in which the hostess sometimes starred.

Jungle Jim
US 1955 26 × 25m bw
Columbia

Adventures of a white hunter and his son in the African jungle.

As if the old features weren't bad enough, here came a crappy series in the same mould . . .

Johnny Weissmuller, Martin Huston

Junior Miss. A 1953 American half-hour domestic comedy about a college girl (Barbara Whiting) and her temperamental father (Gale Gordon).

Junkin, John (1930–). British comedy actor with a clumsy act; writes material for himself and others.

Jury
GB 1983 13 × 55m
BBC (Colin Tucker)

PENNY JUNOR. A friendly face from Channel Four's consumer programme *For What It's Worth* (or, as they insisted on calling it, *4 What It's Worth*).

Members of a criminal court jury react in turn to the case they are hearing, and bring to their task the distractions of their own lives. A neat idea, weakened by individual episodes in which too much happened beyond the ken of the juror in question, e.g. a black woman's family problems expressed in scenes between her daughters which she was not present at and couldn't have known about.

w Peter Whalley, Andrew Lynch, Ken Blakeson, Dave Simpson *d* various   PP

Just a Little Inconvenience
US 1977 96m colour TVM
NBC/Universal/Fawcett-Majors (Allan Balter)

A Vietnam veteran tries to rehabilitate his best friend, who has become bitter after losing an arm and a leg in war action.
Tolerable and well-meaning drama which has rather too much footage for its own good.

w Theodore J. Flicker, Allan Balter *d* Theodore J. Flicker *ph* Duke Callaghan *m* Jimmie Haskell

Lee Majors, James Stacy, Barbara Hershey, Jim Davis, Lane Bradbury, Charles Cioffi
† Stacy, who played the invalid, was a genuine cripple after a motor cycle accident, and this film marked his return to acting.

Just Amazing! (GB 1984). Much-battered motorcycle ace Barry Sheene joined Kenny Lynch and Suzanne Danielle in presenting this wide-eyed wizzo children's programme, produced by John Fanshawe for YTV.   PP

Just an Old Sweet Song
US 1976 74m colour TVM
CBS/GE Theater/MTM (Philip Barry)

A black Detroit family goes on vacation to the south.
Rather an obvious parable; the expected series was never ordered.

w Melvin Van Peebles *d* Robert Ellis Miller *ph* Terry K. Meade *m* Peter Matz

Cicely Tyson, Robert Hooks, Beah Richards, Lincoln Kilpatrick, Minnie Gentry

Just Another Day (GB 1983–5; 8 × 30m; colour). Reporter John Pitman tagging along as everyday citizens earn their bread or enjoy themselves in ways that not everyone would envy, least of all in a hilariously anxious episode devoted to driving instructors. Other callings/institutions under examination included Selfridge's department store and cross-Channel ferries. Produced by Edward Mirzoeff, for BBC.   PP

Just Another Little Blues Song (GB 1984; 45m). And just another little play about a chancer having to raise the money in a hurry to stave off the attentions of a gangland creditor (see *Sammy*). This time it was Adam Faith on the spot, backed up by Gwen Taylor and Alun Lewis. Written by John Harvey, directed by John Bruce, for BBC.
    PP

Just Dennis: see Dennis the Menace

Just Like Coronation Street (GB 1984). Two programmes about street life supposedly – or ironically – in the style of the vintage soap. Produced by Diana Tammes and Seona Robertson for Reality Productions/C4.

Just Me and You
US 1978 96m colour TVM
EMI/Roger Gimbel (William S. Gilmore Jnr)

A girl answers an ad to drive across America with a man she doesn't know.

An interesting starting point, but the plot runs out of steam and the heroine is too neurotic to be sympathetic.

w Louise Lasser d John Erman ph Gayne Rescher m Fred Karlin

Louise Lasser, Charles Grodin, Julie Borvasso, Mark Syers

'Unfortunately the couple is not mismatched – both parties are abominable.' – Judith Crist

Just Our Luck
US 1983   × 25m colour
ABC/Lorimar/Lawrence Jordan (Ronald E. Frazier)

A meteorologist finds himself in command of a mischievous black genie.

Why a meteorologist? Why, indeed. Why in fact try this old chestnut when there is neither wit nor imagination to be had from the script?

cr Lawrence and Charles Gordon

T. K. Carter, Richard Gilliland, Ellen Maxted, Rod McCary

'Carter better bring in a wagonload of humour if the series is going to do anything but separate 8 pm from 8.30 pm.' – *Daily Variety*

Just Sex (GB 1984). Six-part series in which separate groups of men and women talked about just that thing. Produced by Veronyka Bodnarec for 51% Productions/C4.   PP

Just William *
GB 1976–7 26 × 15m colour (VTR)
London Weekend/Stella Richman

The adventures of Richmal Crompton's awful but imaginative child, very pleasingly done with authentic period settings.

Adrian Dannatt, Diana Dors (as Mrs Bott), Hugh Cross (as Mr Brown; in a previous film version he played William's brother Robert)

Justice (US 1954–5). Half-hour law series for NBC, with Gary Merrill as a lawyer dispensing legal aid to the poor.

Justice *
GB 1972–3 26 approx. × 50m colour (VTR)
Yorkshire (Jacky Stoller)

Cases of a lady barrister.

A solid vehicle for a star.

MARGARET LOCKWOOD, Anthony Valentine, John Stone

Kadar, Jan (1918–79). Hungarian director who did some Hollywood TV work: *Freedom Road, The Other Side of Hell.*

Kagan, Jeremy Paul (1945–). American director with limited TV output before big-screen work. TV movies include *Judge Dee and the Monastery Murders, Unwed Father, Katherine* (which he also wrote).

Kahn, Madeline (1942–). American comic actress whose principal TV exposure has been in one less-than-successful series, *Oh Madeline.*

The Kallikaks (US 1977). Briefly seen half-hour comedy series for NBC, with David Huddleston as a conniving coal miner who moves his large family to the good life of California.

Kane and Abel *
US 1985 1 × 142m, 1 × 96m colour
miniseries
CBS/Schreckinger/Embassy (Jud Kinberg, Michael Grade)
Worlds apart, a rich man and a poor man are born on the same day . . .
Well-plotted saga of ambition and rivalry during America's immigrant period.
w Robert W. Lenski, *novel* by Jeffrey Archer *d* Buzz Kulik *ph* Mike Fash *m* Billy Goldenberg
Peter Strauss, Sam Neill, Ron Silver, David Dukes, Fred Gwynne, Alberta Watson, Reed Birney, Jill Eikenberry, Veronica Hamel, Richard Anderson, Christopher Cazenove
'It covers six decades and seldom drops a stitch.' – *Daily Variety*

Kanin, Fay (19 –). American writer, wife of Michael Kanin. *Heat of Anger, Tell Me Where It Hurts, Hustling, Friendly Fire, Heartsounds.*

Kansas City Massacre *
US 1975 100m colour TVM
ABC/Dan Curtis

Melvin Purvis, the midwestern G-man who captured Dillinger, is ambushed when he transports a prisoner by train.
Pretty good gangster thriller, violent by TV standards.
w/d Dan Curtis
Dale Robertson, Bo Hopkins, Robert Walden, Scott Brady, Matt Clark

Kanter, Hal (1918–). American writer-producer. TV series created by him include *The George Gobel Show, Valentine's Day, Julia, The Jimmy Stewart Show, Chico and the Man.*

Kaplan, Gabriel (1946–). American comedy actor who starred in *Welcome Back Kotter.* Also: *Lewis and Clark.*

Karen
US 1975 13 × 25m colour
ABC/TCF (Gene Reynolds, Larry Gelbart)
Problems of a citizens' action group in Washington DC.
Curious comedy vehicle for a much trumpeted new star. Both failed.
Karen Valentine, Charles Lane
† A previous short-lived series named *Karen* was part of NBC's *90 Bristol Court* in 1964. Debbie Watson starred as a troublesome teenager.

Karl Marx – the Legacy * (GB 1984; 6 × 40m). Marx's influence in the world today as assessed for the BBC by the academic who is also – fittingly, some would say – the historian of the BBC. Written and presented by Asa Briggs. Produced by John Dekker.
PP

Karlin, Fred (1936–). American composer who wrote many TV scores including THE AUTOBIOGRAPHY OF MISS JANE PITTMAN (Emmy 1974).

Karlin, Miriam (1925–) (Miriam Samuels). British character actress, best remembered as the strike-prone Paddy in *The Rag Trade.*

Karloff, Boris (1887–1969) (William Pratt). British character actor, a tall, cadaverous but kindly gentleman forever associated with horror films. TV series include *Colonel March of Scotland Yard*, THRILLER.

Karras, Alex (1935–). Heavyweight American character actor, former pro football player. TV movies: *Hardcase, The 500 Pound Jerk, Babe, Mulligan's Stew, Mad Bull, Centennial, Jimmy B and Andre, Alcatraz, Maid in America, Webster*.

Kate
GB 1970–1 39 approx. × 50m colour (VTR)
Yorkshire TV
Private problems of the writer of a woman's page.
Moderately popular drama series.
Phyllis Calvert, Penelope Keith

Kate Bliss and the Tickertape Kid *
US 1978 96m colour TVM
ABC/Aaron Spelling (Richard E. Lyons)
A lady detective goes out west in disguise as a women's wear salesman.
Lively period comedy.
w William Bowers, John Zodorow *d* Burt Kennedy *ph* Lamar Boren *m* Jeff Alexander
Suzanne Pleshette, Don Meredith, Tony Randall, Harry Morgan, Burgess Meredith, David Huddleston, Gene Evans
'Full of high spirits.' – *Daily Variety*

Kate Loves a Mystery
aka: *Mrs Columbo*
US 1979 13 × 50m colour TVM
NBC/Universal (Richard Alan Simmons, Richard Irving)
Lt Columbo's wife solves her own murders. A flimsy format which didn't sell itself.
cr Richard Levinson, William Link
Kate Mulgrew, Henry Jones, Don Stroud

Kate MacShane
US 1975 100m colour TVM
CBS/Paramount (E. Jack Neuman)
A lady lawyer with an Irish family defends a socialite on a murder charge.
Tiresomely talkative and restless courtroom pilot with a highly unconvincing dénouement.
w E. Jack Neuman *d* Marvin Chomsky
Anne Meara, Sean McClory, Christine Belford, Charles Cioffi, Larry Gates
† A shortlived series (13 × 50m) followed, with E. Jack Neuman in charge.

Katherine *
US 1975 96m colour TVM
ABC/Jozak (Gerald I. Isenberg)
A young heiress becomes a political activist. Quite a well-composed moral tale of the sixties.
w/d JEREMY KAGAN *ph* Frank Stanley
Sissy Spacek, Art Carney, Henry Winkler, Julie Kavner, Jane Wyatt, Hector Elias
'An important lesson, well executed and well handled.' – *Daily Variety*

Katie, Portrait of a Centerfold
US 1978 96m colour TVM
Warner/Moonlight (Frank Von Zerneck)
An innocent girl, unused to the ways of the big city, arrives in Hollywood and is taken for a ride.
Elementary melodrama of the Awful Warning variety, very slickly packaged but of no real interest.
w Nancy Audley *d* Robert Greenwald *ph* Donald Morgan *m* Charles Bernstein
Kim Basinger, Melanie Mayron, Terri Nunn, Don Johnson, Dorothy Malone, Vivian Blaine, Don Stroud, Tab Hunter, Fabian

Katt, William (1951–). American leading man. *The Greatest American Hero, Pippin*.

Katzin, Lee H. (1935–). American director. Series work from 1965, followed by TV movies: *Along Came a Spider, Visions of Death, Voyage of the Yes, Ordeal, The Stranger, The Last Survivors, Sky Heist, The Quest, Man from Atlantis, The Bastard*, etc.

Kavik the Wolf Dog
US 1980 96m colour TVM
NBC/Pantheon/Stanley Chase (Jon Slan)
An Eskimo sled dog, mentally and physically injured in a plane crash, is nursed back to health by an arduous trek across the Alaskan wilderness.
Spectacular nonsense that takes its time but includes some good adventure bits.
w George Malko, *novel* Walt Morey *d* Peter Clark *ph* Bert Bunk *m* Murry Freedman
Ronny Cox, Linda Sorenson, Chris Wiggins, Andrew Ian McMillan, John Ireland

Kaye, Danny (1913–) (David Daniel Kaminsky). Master American comedian and entertainer whose one-hour series in 1966 had a little too much quality for popular success. His other stabs at TV have been modest, including *Peter Pan* (as Captain Hook), *Pinocchio* (as Gepetto, among others), and SKOKIE. Emmy 1963: best variety performer.

Kaz *
US 1978 × 50m colour
CBS/Lorimar
A crook gets a law degree while in prison,
and on his release teams up with a prestigious
defender.
Slick but unsuccessful character show in
which crime comes second.
RON LEIBMAN, PATRICK O'NEAL, Linda Carlson,
George Wyner
'Snappy writing and Leibman's nervy charm
have pumped one more head of steam into it.'
– Robert MacKenzie, *TV Guide*

Keach, Stacy (1941–). American
character actor, in all media. He starred in an
unsuccessful TV series, *Caribe*. TV movies:
*All the Kind Strangers, Dynasty, Jesus of
Nazareth, A Rumor of War, The Blue and
the Gray, Princess Daisy, Mike Hammer,
Mistral's Daughter*.

Kean. The outsize English actor Edmund
Kean (1787–1833) has been notably
impersonated twice on British television: by
Anthony Hopkins in Sartre's play *Kean*,
directed by James Cellan Jones, produced by
David Jones for BBC, 1978; and by Ben
Kingsley in a one-man play by Raymond
Fitzsimmons for C4 from YTV, 1983,
directed by Michael Ferguson.   PP

Kearns, Joseph (1907–62). Grouchy
American character actor best remembered
as the long-suffering neighbour in *Dennis the
Menace*.

Keating, Tom (1917–85). Grizzled British
painter who enjoyed a brief sunburst as a
television performer after he'd admitted
faking pictures by Samuel Palmer and other
English artists. *Tom Keating on Painters*,
1982; *Tom Keating on Impressionists*, 1984,
both 6 × 30m, produced by Richard
Beighton for The Moving Picture Co./C4.
'Keating doesn't know about television,
scarcely ever looks at the camera and just
gets on with his practical demonstration . . .
having long ago mastered the exact
workshop techniques employed by the
masters, he breaks the process down as
methodically as if he were taking his
audience step by step through changing the
engine and gearbox on a Volkswagen.'   PP

Kee and Levin (GB 1966). Whatever their
individual virtues, Bernard Levin and Robert
Kee made a forbidding duo when this
late-night inquisition was launched (for

Rediffusion), conducting a joint interrogation
of some luckless suspect like a pair of
dinner-jacketed Gestapo men. The show
relaxed and improved but didn't last.   PP

Kee, Robert (1919–). Respected British
reporter, interviewer and historian, originally
with ITN and back with them in the
mid-seventies as presenter of the midday
news show *First Report*, when he displayed an
endearing Rip van Winkle testiness, as if
having woken from a long intervening sleep
to find everyone talking round in the same old
circles. Between times a *Panorama* man
famously reporting from Algeria and a
member of the ill-fated freelance outfit
Television Reporters International, for whom
his *Rebellion* (about the Irish Rebellion of
1916) could later be seen as a try-out for the
magnum opus of his later career, the 13-part
Ireland: A Television History (BBC, 1980).
Briefly with TV-am as one of the 'Famous
Five' presenters. Latest series: *Something to
Declare*.   PP

Keefer
US 1978 74m colour TVM
Columbia/David Gerber (James H. Brown)
In 1942, a Lisbon café owner is also an allied
spy.
Shades of *Casablanca*, shot down by a
dullsville script.
w Bill Driscoll, Simon Muntner *d* Barry
Shear *ph* Gerald Perry Finnermann
m Duane Tatro
William Conrad, Jeremy Kemp, Michael
O'Hare, Cathy Lee Crosby, Marcel Hillaire,
Kate Woodville

The Keegans
US 1975 74m colour TVM
CBS/Universal (George Eckstein)
Problems of an Irish family living near
Boston.
Predictable to the last drop of blarney, this
cosy family drama suddenly turns into a
murder plot.
w Dean Riesner *d* John Badham
Adam Roarke, Judd Hirsch, Joan Leslie,
Spencer Milligan, Paul Shenar

Keel, Howard (1919–). Stalwart
American movie star and singer who late in
life settled down amid the cast of *Dallas*.

Keen, Geoffrey (1918–). Incisive British
character actor whose best series role was in
The Trouble Shooters.

BORIS KARLOFF spent a good deal of his later career before the television cameras, and starred in 26 episodes of *Colonel March of Scotland Yard*.

Keep It in the Family (GB 1980–). Absolutely standard domestic comedy about a family with problems. With Robert Gillespie, Pauline Yates, Stacy Dorning, Glyn Houston. Written by Brian Cook; produced and directed by Mark Stuart; for Thames.

Keeshan, Bob (1927–). American actor and host, the original and only *Captain Kangaroo* in the CBS programme for children.

Keir, Andrew (19 –). Rugged Scottish actor excelling in countless roles from *Soldier, Soldier* (1960) by way of *Sunset Song*, *King's Royal* and *The World Cup: A Captain's Tale* to *The Old Master*, 1984. PP

Keith, Brian (1921–) (Robert Keith Jnr). Burly, adaptable American character actor whose TV series have included *Crusader*, *The Westerner*, FAMILY AFFAIR, *Archer* and *The Little People* (re-titled *The Brian Keith Show*). TV movies include *Second Chance*, *The Quest*, *The Loneliest Runner*, *In the Matter of Karen Ann Quinlan*, *Centennial*, *The Chisholms*.

Keith, Penelope (*c* 1941–). British comedy character actress with a strong line in toffee-nosed virgins. She achieved sudden popularity in the mid-seventies as a result of work in such series as *Kate*, THE GOOD LIFE and *To the Manor Born*. BAFTA 1976 best actress (*The Norman Conquests*, *Saving It For Albie*); 1977 best light entertainment performer (*The Good Life*).

Kellerman, Sally (1936–). American general-purpose actress. *Centennial*, *For Lovers Only*, *Dempsey*, *September Gun*.

Kelly, Chris (*c* 1940–). Gentle-voiced British linkman, commentator and host, familiar from *Clapperboard* and *Wish You Were Here*. *Food and Drink* from 1984.

Kelly, Gene (1912–). Outstanding American singer and dancer. TV work includes the series *Going My Way* and numerous specials including *Jack and the Beanstalk* and a tribute to him called *An American in Pasadena*.

Kelly, Henry (1946–). Willowy Irish teleperson, ex-journalist, into television via BBC Radio 4. On television, jobs mostly beneath even his evidently limited aspirations, e.g. *Game for a Laugh*, *Good Morning Britain*, and *Food and Drink* until replaced by his robust namesake Chris Kelly.
PP

Kelsey, Linda (1946–). American leading actress who was popular in LOU GRANT. Also: *The Picture of Dorian Gray*, *Something for Joey*, *Eleanor and Franklin*, *A Perfect Match*, *Attack on Fear*, *His Mistress*.

Kemp-Welch, Joan (1906–). Outstanding British director, especially of the early TV plays of Harold Pinter. BAFTA 1964. Former actress.

Kendal, Felicity (1946–). British leading lady often in fey or mischievous roles; most famous for *The Good Life*.

Kendall, Kenneth (1924–). Distinguished-looking British BBC newsreader.

Kennedy **
GB/US 1983 1 × 165m, 2 × 110m
Central (Andrew Brown) in association
    with Alan Landsburg Productions (Joan
    Barnett)
JFK's story from the beginning of his Presidential campaign to the fateful day in Dallas. Hatched, written and mostly filmed in England, this lookalike epic nevertheless impressed American audiences as well as British, even if the show was stolen by Vincent Gardenia as J. Edgar Hoover, the sybilline FBI boss determined to catch the Kennedys out in their sexual excursions. As Christopher Dunkley pointed out in the *Financial Times*, this device usefully acknowledged the hero's imperfections without the need to show them.
w Reg Gadney *d* Jim Goddard *m* Richard Hartley
Martin Sheen (as JFK), John Shea (as Robert Kennedy), E. G. Marshall (as Joseph P. Kennedy), Blair Brown (as Jacqueline Bouvier Kennedy), Vincent Gardenia   PP

Kennedy, Arthur (1914–). Distinguished American character actor. His only TV series was the ill-fated *Nakia*. TV movies: *The Movie Murderer*, *A Death of Innocence*, *Crawlspace*, *The President's Plane Is Missing*.

Kennedy, Burt (1923–). American director who scored some big-screen hits after showing TV expertise as a writer–director of action items. TV movies include *Shootout in a One Dog Town*, *Sidekicks*, *All the Kind Strangers*, *Kate Bliss and the Tickertape Kid*, *The Wild Wild West Revisited*.

Kennedy, George (1925–). Imposing but rather bland American character actor who began by playing villains. TV series: *Sarge*, *The Blue Knight*. TV movies: *See How They Run*, *A Great American Tragedy*, *Deliver Us From Evil*, *A Cry in the Wilderness*, *Backstairs at the White House*, *The Jesse Owens Story*, *Half Nelson*, *International Airport*.

❋ **Kennedy, Ludovic** (1919–). Personable British television reporter, interviewer and link-man, also an author. Began as newscaster for ITN in 1955, thereafter mainly with BBC. For *Panorama* in 1961 obtained the first off-the-cuff interview in Britain of his namesake President John F. Kennedy. Intermittently on *Tonight* during the 1960s and sole presenter of its 1970s successor *Midweek*, when he was regarded by some as rather an establishment figure but in fact has always been a passionate defender of victims of injustice, with books and programmes on Timothy Evans, Stephen Ward and, most recently, the Lindbergh kidnapper Bruno Hauptmann. Many naval and travel documentaries. Since 1980 has chaired the television review of television, *Did You See . . . ?*   PP

The Kenny Everett Video Show * (GB 1978–80). Wildly inventive mix of comedy, music and mild erotics (furnished by a dance troupe called Hot Gossip) presided over by Everett in a variety of guises, including an animated cartoon version of himself for a sci-fi interlude featuring one Captain Kremmen. Required viewing for adolescents of all ages. Produced by David Mallet; for Thames. In 1981–2 Everett moved to BBC for much the same recipe, produced by James Moir, minus Hot Gossip.   PP

Kent State
US 1980 140m colour TVM
NBC/Interplanetary Productions
Events leading up to the killing by police of four students at an American university during 1970 riots.

A documentary-style re-enactment of unhappy events that might have been better treated at shorter length as pure documentary. Even Americans, to judge by the ratings, seemed unwilling to interest themselves in this approach.

w Gerald Green, Richard Kramer *d* James Goldstone *ph* Steve Larner *m* Ken Lauber

Talia Balsam, Jane Fleiss, Keith Gordon, Jeff McCracken

'A distasteful episode . . . until it's understood, it shouldn't be forgotten.' – *Daily Variety*

Kentucky Jones
US 1964 26 × 25m bw
NBC (Buzz Kulik)

Stories of a vet and horse trainer who adopts a small oriental boy.
Forgettable sentiment.

cr Albert Beich, William Wright

Dennis Weaver, Rickey Der, Harry Morgan

Kentucky Woman
US 1983 96m colour TVM
CBS/TCF/Walter Doniger

When her coalminer dad collapses with lung trouble, a waitress shows true grit and marches into the mine alongside the fellows. The idea was to show one of Charlie's Angels doing some acting, and once you get past the obvious guffaws she isn't bad; but the production is almost too slick and glossy to be in any way realistic.

w,d Walter Doniger *ph* Robert Jessup *m* George Romanis

Cheryl Ladd, Ned Beatty, Philip Levien, Sandy McPeak, Tess Harper

Kernan, David (1938–). British light actor and singer, most familiar for *That Was the Week That Was* and *Song by Song*.

Kerr, Graham (1934–). Genial British entertainer and occasional cook who in the late sixties made himself a darling of the ladies in *The Galloping Gourmet*; subsequently retired in search of truth.

Kerwin, Lance (1960–). American juvenile actor. *The Healers, The Family Holvak, Amelia Earhart, The Death of Richie, The Loneliest Runner, Salem's Lot, The Boy Who Drank Too Much, Side Show, A Killer in the Family, The Fourth Wise Man.*

Kessler (GB 1981; 6 × 50m; colour). The Gestapo heavy of the World War II series *Secret Army* uncompulsively rediscovered 35 years later as prosperous businessman and neo-Nazi, but with long-delayed retribution closing in from more than one quarter. With Clifford Rose, Alan Dobie, Nitza Saul. Devised by Gerard Glaister and John Brason; written by John Brason; directed by Tristan de Vere Cole; produced by Gerard Glaister; for BBC.   PP

Kestrel. Independent drama unit set up by Tony Garnett, Ken Loach, Kenith Trodd and others to furnish plays and films for London Weekend 1968–9. Ceased production when this contract was not renewed, save for one or two TV movies, e.g. *After a Lifetime* (1971).
                                                                        PP

The Key to Rebecca
US 1985 2 × 96m colour miniseries
OPT/Castle Combe/Taft (Robyn A. Watson, Adam Lawrence)

A Nazi spy in Cairo sends messages to Rommel about British troop movements. Uninvolving war story with more than the expected measure of sex and violence.

w Samuel Harris, *book* by Ken Follett *d* David Hemmings *ph* Mario Vulpiani *m* J. A. C. Redford

Cliff Robertson, David Soul, Season Hubley, Lina Raymond, Anthony Quayle, David Hemmings, Robert Culp

'Four hours of Silly Putty. With such bumbling on both sides, it's a wonder the war isn't still going on.' – *Daily Variety*

Key West
US 1972 91m colour TVM
Warner (Anthony S. Martin)

Documents incriminating a US senator are sought by crooks and agents on the Florida keys.
Ho-hum hokum.

w Anthony S. Martin *d* Philip Leacock

Stephen Boyd, Woody Strode, Sheree North, Earl Hindman, Tiffany Bolling, William Prince

The Keys of the Café (GB 1965). Edna O'Brien triangle drama featuring hairdresser, wife and driving instructor, the dialogue full of unexpected riches, strange shafts of reasoning delivered with beautiful gravity by Margaret Whiting, Peter Barkworth, Lois Daine and – making a slightly sinister debut as a straight actor – Ronnie Barker. Directed by Patrick Dromgoole; for ATV.   PP

Khan
US 1975 4 × 50m colour
CBS/Laurence Heath (James Heinz)
Cases of a Chinese private detective in San Francisco.
Disastrous attempt to revive the Charlie Chan syndrome. There's even a number one son.

Khigh Dhiegh, Irene Yah-Ling Sun, Evan Kim

A Kick up the Eighties (GB 1984). Alternative comedy from Scotland, though calling initially on established names from South of the Border, e.g. Tracey Ullman, Miriam Margolyes, 'Kevin Turvey'. The sketches were fairly indistinguishable from equivalent English entertainments, too, but it helped launch Robbie Coltrane. Directed by Brian Jobson. Produced by Colin Gilbert, for BBC Scotland.   PP

'Each brush with death brings them closer to the thrill of a lifetime!'
Kicks
US 1985 96m colour TVM
ABC Circle (David Levinson)
An odd couple of thrill seekers take to sex and crime.
A final chase around Alcatraz does not validate this somewhat perverse 'with it' telemovie.

w David Levinson d William Wiard
ph Bobby Byrne m Peter Bernstein

Anthony Geary, Shelley Hack, Tom Mason, Ian Abercrombie, Susan Ruttan
'A truly reprehensible project that barely deserved a full script reading.' – *Daily Variety*

The Kid from Left Field
US 1980 96m colour TVM
NBC/Gary Coleman Productions
An ex-baseball star reduced to selling peanuts gives tips to his small son, who is appointed team manager.
Sloppy and sentimental remake of a 1953 Dan Dailey vehicle.

w Kathryn Powers, Jack Sher d Adell Aldrich ph Frank Thackery m David Frank

Gary Coleman, Tricia O'Neil
'Fails to deliver the expected punch.' – *Daily Variety*

The Kid from Nowhere
US 1982 96m colour TVM
NBC/Cates–Bridges (Gilbert Cates)
A divorcee has a retarded boy who gets in the way of her social life until she falls for his new school coach, who enters Ricky for the Special Olympics.
Pleasant, padded-out introduction to mental handicap for those who haven't experienced it.

w Judy Farrell d Beau Bridges ph John A. Alonzo m Garry Sherman

Susan St James, Beau Bridges, Loretta Swit, Rick Wittman (a genuine Down's Syndrome boy), Fred Dryer, Nicholas Pryor

The Kid with the 200 I.Q.
US 1983 96m colour TVM
NBC/Guillaume–Margo/Zephyr (Jim Begg)
A young genius goes to college and causes resentment.
Very thin star vehicle which soon becomes wearisome.

w Oliver Hawthorne d Leslie Martinson ph Gary Grover m Dennis McCarthy

Gary Coleman, Robert Guillaume, Dean Butler, Karl Michaelsen, Mel Stuart, Harriet Nelson

'Someone you know is a victim of this crime!'
Kids Don't Tell
US 1985 96m colour TVM
CBS/Chris–Rose/Viacom (Barry Greenfield)
Documentary makers conduct research into child molestation.
Too pat an approach makes one wish that these film makers had stuck to the facts and let fiction alone.

w Peter Silverman, Maureen Hurley d Sam O'Steen ph Michael Margulies m Fred Karlin

Michael Ontkean, JoBeth Williams, John Sanderford, Leo Rossi, Ari Meyers, Jordan Charney

Kiley, Richard (1922–). American general purpose actor. TV movies: *Night Gallery, Incident in San Francisco, Murder Once Removed, Jigsaw, Friendly Persuasion, The MacAhans, Angel on my Shoulder, Golden Gate, Isabel's Choice, Pray TV, The Thorn Birds, George Washington, The Bad Seed, Do You Remember Love?*

Kilgallen, Dorothy (1913–65). American columnist who became a TV celebrity as a *What's My Line?* panellist in the fifties.

Kill Me If You Can
US 1977 98m colour TVM
NBC/Columbia (Peter Katz)
A reconstruction of Caryl Chessman's finally unsuccessful attempts to stave off execution as the 'red light' killer.
Tasteless and exploitative docu-drama with the star in a false nose and much lingering over the gas chamber scenes.
w John Gay d Buzz Kulik
Alan Alda, Talia Shire, Barnard Hughes, John Hillerman, Walter McGinn, Ben Piazza, John Randolph

Killdozer
US 1974 74m colour TVM
Universal (Herbert F. Solow)
A bulldozer affected by a strange meteorite murderously attacks a construction crew on a remote site.
And they can't run fast enough to get out of its way. Silly nonsense.
w Theodore Sturgeon, Ed MacKillop d Jerry London m Gil Melle
Clint Walker, James Wainwright, Carl Betz, Neville Brand

Killer **
GB 1983 3 × 52m
STV (Robert Love)
Superior police – or polis – serial set in Glasgow with Mark McManus as the dour Detective Chief Inspector Taggart later promoted to his own series, and already lumbered with wheelchair-bound bluestocking wife plus smart-arse university-trained assistant.
w Glen Chandler d Laurence Moody
Mark McManus, Neil Duncan   PP
† Not to be confused with trio of morbidly silly plays from YTV in 1984 called *Killer Exposed*, *Killer in Waiting*, etc.

The Killer Bees *
US 1974 74m colour TVM
ABC/RSO (Howard Rosenman, Bob Bernstein)
The elderly matriarch of a strange family is obsessed by bees and can use them to kill.
Flabby, over-talkative suspenser with a couple of good sequences; mainly notable for the reappearance of its star.
w Joyce and John William Corrington d Curtis Harrington m David Shire
GLORIA SWANSON, Edward Albert, Kate Jackson, Roger Davis, Craig Stevens

Killer by Night *
US 1971 100m colour TVM .
Cinema Center 100 (Fred Engel)
A doctor seeks a diphtheria carrier, a cop seeks a killer . . . and they're both looking for the same man.
Didn't this use to be *Panic in the Streets*? Well enough done again, anyway.
w David P. Harmon d Bernard McEveety
ph Robert B. Hauser m Quincy Jones
Robert Wagner, Diane Baker, Greg Morris, Theodore Bikel, Robert Lansing, Mercedes McCambridge, Pedro Armendariz Jnr

'Their only hope is desperate courage!
Their only comfort is desperate love!'
A Killer in the Family
US 1984 96m colour TVM
ABC/Stan Marguiles/Sunn Classic (Robert Aller)
Three sons help a convict to escape and find he isn't the innocent they imagined.
Pretty grim stuff for a TV movie, but not dramatically compulsive.
w Sue Grafton, Steven Humphrey, Robert Aller d Richard T. Heffron ph Hanania Baer m Gerald Fried
Robert Mitchum, James Spader, Lance Kerwin, Eric Stolz, Salome Jens, Lynn Carlin, Stuart Margolin

Killer in Waiting/Killer Exposed/Killer Contracted (GB 1984; 3 × 52m). Murky little murder stories hatched by Eric Wendell (2) and Robin Chapman, directed by Michael Ferguson and James Ormerod (2) for a YTV drama department which must have run out of ideas. With John Thaw, Diane Keen, Anthony Valentine, Dearbha Molloy; Edward Woodward, Kate Harper, Wanda Ventham.   PP

'500 desperate people trapped at sea and dying – one at a time!'
Killer on Board
US 1977 96m colour TVM
NBC/Lorimar (Sandor Stern)
A Pacific cruise is menaced by a mysterious disease.
Cliché-strewn suspenser without much suspense.
w Sandor Stern d Philip Leacock ph William H. Cronjager m Earl Hagen
Claude Akins, Patty Duke Astin, Frank Converse, William Daniels, George Hamilton, Murray Hamilton, Beatrice Straight

The Killer Who Wouldn't Die
aka: *Ohanian*
US 1976 96m colour TVM
ABC/Paramount (Ivan Goff, Ben Roberts)

An ex-detective takes to his boat when his wife is killed in mistake for himself, but finds himself harbouring a hired killer and avenging the death of a friend.

Lame crime pilot with the star using his own name and his own boat; it's all a mite too relaxed to make suspenseful melodrama.

w Cliff Gould *d* William Hale *m* George Garvarantz

Mike Connors, Samantha Eggar, Patrick O'Neal, Clu Gulager, Grégoire Aslan, Robert Hooks, Robert Colbert, James Shigeta, Mariette Hartley

The Killers *
US 1964 95m colour TVM
Universal (Don Siegel)

Zesty, brutal remake of the 1946 movie, intended for TV, but released theatrically because of its violence.

w Gene L. Coon *d* Don Siegel *ph* Richard L. Rawlings *m* Johnny Williams

John Cassavetes, Lee Marvin, Clu Gulager, Angie Dickinson, Ronald Reagan, Claude Akins

Killiam, Paul (1916–). American producer who specializes in restoring silent films and packaging them into such series as *Silents Please* and *Movie Museum*.

A Killing Affair
aka: *Behind the Badge*
US 1977 96m colour TVM
CBS/Columbia/David Gerber (James H. Brown)

A woman police detective falls in love with her black partner.

Heavy-going cop drama in which the action is relegated to the sidelines and the limelight reserved for some realistic – and boring – bed scenes.

w E. Arthur Kean *d* Richard Sarafian *ph* Al Francis *m* Richard Shores

Elizabeth Montgomery, O. J. Simpson, Dean Stockwell, Dolph Sweet, Todd Bridges, Todd Sussman

'An affair of overkill.' – *Daily Variety*

The Killing at Hell's Gate
US 1984 96m colour TVM
CBS (Ron Roth)

Whitewater canoeists are terrified when one of their number is shot down by snipers.

Adequate outdoors suspenser which would have made a good hour.

w Lee Hutson *d* Jerry Jameson

Robert Urich, Deborah Raffin, Lee Purcell, Paul Burke, Joel Higgins, George DiCenzo

The Killing of Randy Webster
US 1980 96m colour TVM
CBS/EMI/Roger Gimbel/Heller–Gutwillig

In 1977, an unhappy Houston teenager steals a van and is shot down by police.

Solemn re-enactment of a *cause célèbre*; despite meticulous detail, no new evidence is forthcoming.

w Scott Swanton *d* Sam Wanamaker *ph* Jules Brenner *m* Peter Matz

Hal Holbrook, Dixie Carter, James Whitmore Jnr, Jennifer Jason Leigh, Nancy Malone

'An aching realism and emotional slam which call for that worn out word, "gripping".' – *Daily Variety*

Killing Stone
US 1978 96m colour TVM
NBC/Universal (Michael Landon)

An innocent man is released after eleven years in prison, is funded by a publisher and becomes a private eye.

Proficient pilot which didn't take.

w/d Michael Landon *ph* Ted Voigtlander *m* David Rose

Gil Gerard, J. D. Cannon, Jim Davis, Nehemiah Persoff, Corinne Michaels, Matthew Laborteaux

† The title is a pun: the hero's name is Stone and people are out to get him.

Killjoy *
US 1981 96m colour TVM
CBS/Lorimar (Joe Wallenstein)

A determined cop tracks down the killer of an old girlfriend of his.

Reasonably slick and entertaining mystery.

w Sam Rolfe *d* John Llewellyn Moxey

Robert Culp, Nancy Marchand, John Rubinstein, Stephen Macht, Kim Basinger

Kilvert's Diary *
GB 1977 26 × 15m colour (VTR)
BBC

Incidents from the diary of a 19th-century country cleric.

Delightful series, just the right length, re-creating middle-class life of its time. The kind of production that only the BBC would do.

Kim
GB 1984 142m colour TVM
CBS/London Films (David Conroy)
During the Raj, a British youngster is raised
on the Indian streets and becomes a spy for
the army.
Somewhat elongated version of a story which
has proved intractable.

w James Brabazon, *novel* by Rudyard
Kipling d John Davies *ph* Michael Reed
m Marc Wilkinson

Peter O'Toole, Bryan Brown, John Rhys
Davies, Ravi Sheth, Julian Glover, Lee
Montague, Alfred Burke

A Kind of Alaska (GB 1984; 75m). Paul
Scofield and Dorothy Tutin in Harold
Pinter's stage two-hander about a woman
who wakes from a 30-year sleeping sickness
after treatment with the new drug L-Dopa.
Based on the book *Awakenings* by Dr Oliver
Sacks, directed by Kenneth Ives, produced
by Lynn Horsford for Central.

A Kind of Loving (GB 1982). The novel of
young lust in a grim northern town which
made STAN BARSTOW's name in 1960 (and
was filmed in 1962) finally reached television
(Granada) with its sequels *The Watchers on
the Shore* and *The Right True End* to make a
10 × 50m saga, dramatized by Barstow
himself, produced by Pauline Shaw.   PP

King
US 1978 3 × 96m colour
NBC/Filmways/Abby Mann (Paul
    Maslansky)
The life and times of Martin Luther King.
Protracted treatment of an over-familiar
subject, with reverence largely replacing
characterization.

w/d Abby Mann *ph* Michael Chapman *m*
Billy Goldenberg

Paul Winfield, Cicely Tyson, Ossie Davis, Al
Freeman Jnr, Steven Hill, Clu Gulager,
Roscoe Lee Browne, Cliff de Young

King and Castle (GB 1985; 52m). Derek
Martin and Nigel Planer teamed as
debt-collectors in a pilot for a low-life
replacement to *Minder*; created by Ian
Kennedy Martin, produced by Peter Duguid,
for Thames.

The King and Odie: see King Leonardo and
his Short Subjects

King, Dave (1929–). British cockney
comedian who was big in the fifties and even
succeeded in America, then had a long period
out of fashion before he returned in the
mid-seventies as a character actor. 1978:
Pennies from Heaven; 1980: *Fancy Wanders*
(series). 1981: *The Chelsea Murders*; 1984:
Last Love.

The King Family. An American singing
family who were popular in the sixties. As a
rule the show was limited to William King
and seven children, but on occasions it
swelled to as many as 36 family members.

King, Jonathan (1948–). Frenetic British
pop music fancier who mysteriously became
a cult figure with his *Entertainment USA*
reports on, and from, American cities. Also
does a feeble summer holiday show called
No Limits.   PP

King Kong
US 1966–8 78 × 25m colour
Videocraft
On a Javanese island, the son of a research
scientist befriends a 60-foot gorilla, and they
combat the evil Dr Who.
Bland cartoon rehash of a horror classic. Also
included in each half-hour is a segment of
Tom of T. H. U. M. B., about a dwarf spy.

King Lear **
GB 1983 180m approx.
Granada (Michael Elliott)
Laurence Olivier's last grand feat of acting,
in a role he'd first played at the age of 39.
This version in his infirmity, I wrote, was
'simple, transparent, heartfelt and in the end
enormously moving. The thin white hair
hung from a scalp as pink and defenceless as
a baby's. The eyes flickered longingly
towards the refuge of madness which the rest
of him so feared . . .'

d Michael Elliott *design* Roy Stonehouse
costumes Tanya Moiseiwitsch *m* Gordon
Crosse

Colin Blakely, Anna Calder-Marshall, John
Hurt, Jeremy Kemp, Robert Lang, Robert
Lindsay, Leo McKern, Diana Rigg, David
Threlfall, Dorothy Tutin   PP
LH: 'Sadly, by no means the equal of
Olivier's major Shakespeare films, but at
least an improvement on his *Othello*.'

King Leonardo and his Short Subjects
aka: *The King and Odie*
US 1960–2 39 × 25m colour
Leonardo TV

An African lion and his assistant Odie Calognie combat the evil influence of Itchy Brother and Biggy Rat.
Childish cartoon series.

King of Diamonds
US 1961 38 × 25m bw
Ziv/UA

Adventures of a security chief for the diamond industry.
Ham-fisted thick-ear.

Broderick Crawford, Ray Hamilton

King, Perry (c 1946–). American leading man. TV movies: *Foster and Laurie, Rich Man, Poor Man, Aspen, The Cracker Factory, Love's Savage Fury, Inmates, Golden Gate, The Hasty Heart, Helen Keller – the Miracle Continues.*

King's Row. One of the rotating segments of *Warner Brothers Present* in 1955 was a one-hour series derived from the famous film of a small town's dark secrets, the hero having now become a psychiatrist. Jack Kelly was Parris; Nan Leslie, Randy; Robert Horton, Drake; and Victor Jory played a revived Dr Tower.

King's Royal (GB 1982). BBC Scottish serial in 10 × 50-minute parts, from the novel by John Quigley about the fortunes of a Victorian whisky-distilling family. Missable except for people who will watch anything that moves. With Tom Bell, Eric Deacon, Louie Ramsay. Adapted by Ewart Alexander; directed by Andrew Morgan; produced by Geraint Morris.

Kingston
US 1976 96m colour TVM
NBC/Universal/David Victor

An elderly lady who owns a newspaper chain hires an investigator to find out why her editor has changed his policy.
Flabby pilot which was picked up solely on the strength of its star.

w Dick Nelson, David Victor d Robert Day
ph Sy Hoffberg m Leonard Rosenman

Raymond Burr, James Canning, Pamela Hensley, Bradford Dillman, Biff McGuire, Robert Mandan, Lenka Peterson

'Implausibility is evident throughout the very long two hours.' – *Daily Variety*
† 13 × 50m episodes followed, with Nancy Olson as co-star to Burr, but the show, rechristened *Kingston: Confidential*, never got off the ground.

Kingsway Corner. Why not just stick a camera out of the window? It must have occurred to many a desperate producer in the days of live television. A–R actually tried in 1956 – or anyway set up a camera and interviewer John Witty on the pavement outside Television House at the corner of Kingsway and Aldwych. It produced some interesting, low-pressure television until the site became too familiar and the innocence wore off.   PP

Kingswood – a Comprehensive School (GB 1982; 9 × 55m). Well-meaning answer to the fly-on-the-wall series *Public School* two years earlier, a comprehensive being the true public school (i.e. free) as other countries understand the term. Kingswood, in Northamptonshire, emerged well and its headmaster as a vigorous champion of state education, with only a little help from Richard Denton who produced and directed, for BBC.   PP
† A 45m discussion *Kingswood: an End of Term Report* followed.

Kinnear, Roy (1934–). Puffing British comic actor familiar in a multitude of minor roles and also as star of such series as *That Was the Week That Was, Inside George Webley* and *Cowboys*.

Kinvig (GB 1981). Curious half-hour series about a repairman who dreams of being seconded to another planet. Silly rather than funny, but played as though it's art. With Tony Haygarth, Patsy Rowlands, Colin Jeavons. Written by Nigel Kneale; produced and directed by Les Chatfield; for LWT.

Kiss Me, Kill Me
US 1976 74m colour TVM
NBC/Columbia (Stanley Kallis)

A lady investigator for the DA's office corners the murderer of a young teacher.
Adequate pilot which didn't sell.

w Robert E. Thompson d Michael O'Herlihy
ph Meredith Nicholson m Richard Markowitz

Stella Stevens, Michael Anderson Jnr, Dabney Coleman, Bruce Boxleitner, Claude Akins, Alan Fudge, Robert Vaughn

Kiss Meets the Phantom of the Park
US 1978 96m colour TVM
NBC/Hanna–Barbera (Terry Morse Jnr)

A bizarre rock group foils a mad scientist.
A musical curiosity vaguely derived from *The Phantom of the Opera*. Of no real interest at all.

w Jan-Michael Sherman, Don Buday *d*
Gordon Hessler *ph* Robert Caramico *m*
Hoyt Curtin

Kiss, Anthony Zerbe, Carmine Caridi

Kiss of Gold
aka: *Million Dollar Face*
US 1979 96m colour TVM
CBS/Robert D. Wood, Robert Hamner

A cosmetics tycoon becomes obsessed with
the girl who will model his new product.
Fairly lively boardroom melodrama.

w Jud Kinberg, Robert Hamner, *novel Kiss,
Inc.* by Lois Wyse *d* Michael O'Herlihy

Tony Curtis, Herschel Bernardi, David
Huffman, Polly Bergen, Lee Grant, Sylvia
Kristel, Gayle Hunnicutt

Kisses at Fifty ***
GB 1973 75m colour

Bill Maynard as a stolid working man knocked
off the rails in middle life by an affair with a
barmaid, and ready to forgo family, home and
home comforts (a chilly glimpse of a cold-
water shave in the pan of a public lavatory) to
pursue it. From my reaction at the time: 'Puts
Colin Welland back on the mountain top as a
playwright and seals Bill Maynard's transfer
from the comic's trade to the actor's . . .
Welland worked it all out with bleak honesty.
It was deep in his hero's character that he
would brave hostile stares and go back to give
his daughter away when she married; equally
in his character that he would leave again as
soon as the ceremony was over. He had made
his bed and would lie on it.' Directed by
Michael Apted; for BBC *Play for Today*.   PP

Kisses on the Bottom: see *I Can't See My
Little Willie* – which may not be the most
important cross-reference in this book but is
sure the neatest.

Kit Carson: see The Adventures of Kit
Carson

Kitty – Return to Auschwitz ***
GB 1979 100m colour
YTV (Peter Morley, Kevin Sim)

Kitty Hart, a Birmingham (England)
radiologist, shows her son around the
extermination camp to which she was sent as
a young girl but survived thanks to fortitude
and the impending collapse of the Nazi
regime. Peter Morley, also directing,
dispenses with the horrifying archive film
available. The only pictures are of Auschwitz
as it is preserved today, but Kitty's newly
awakened memories and occasional tears
convey the nature of the experience more
sharply than any of the dramatized attempts.
See: *Auschwitz*.   PP

† In 1985 *Kitty* was awarded the unique
Tokyo Prize at a World TV Festival in that
city and listed as one of the best 10 television
programmes (5 dramas, 5 documentaries) of
1975–85.

Kjellin, Alf (1920–). American director
(and occasional actor). Series include *Alfred
Hitchcock Hour*, *I Spy*, *Dr Kildare*, *The Man
from UNCLE*. TV movies: *The Girls of
Huntington House*, *The Deadly Dream*.

Klemperer, Werner (1919–). German–
American character actor, facially typecast to
play a monocled Nazi, which he did superbly,
with comic emphasis, in HOGAN'S HEROES
(Emmy 1967, 1968).

Klondike
US 1960 18 × 25m bw
NBC

Gold rush adventures.
Efficiently made adventure series which
didn't jell.

James Coburn, Ralph Taeger, Mari
Blanchard, Joi Lansing

❋ **Klugman, Jack** (1922–). Amiable,
worried-looking American character actor,
usually in slouchy comedy parts, who apart
from films has had his fair share of TV series:
Harris Against the World, THE ODD COUPLE,
QUINCY. Emmys: 1963 best actor (*The
Defenders*); 1970, 1972 (*The Odd Couple*). TV
movies: *Fame Is the Name of the Game*, *Poor
Devil*, *The Underground Man*, *One of My
Wives Is Missing*.

❋ **Kneale, Nigel** (1922–). Manx writer
with a leaning towards sci-fi and the
supernatural who, as a staff scriptwriter in
the early post-war days of BBC television,
hatched the QUATERMASS serials and
adapted *1984*. Otherwise (BBC except where
stated):
1955 *The Creature*
1956 *Mrs Wickens in the Fall*
1963 *The Road*
1964 *The Crunch*
1967 *The Year of the Sex Olympics*
1969 *Bam! Pow! Zap!*
1970 *Wine of India*
1972 *The Stone Tape*
1974 *Jack and the Beanstalk*
      Murrain (for ATV's *Against the
      Crowd*)
1976 *Beasts* (ATV)
1977 *Crow* (not made, ATV)
1979 *Quatermass* (Thames)
1981 *Kinvig* (LWT series).   PP

Knievel, Evel (1939–). Spectacular American stuntman who periodically appears on TV in pursuit of some death-defying feat.

Knight Errant
GB 1959–61 76 × 50m bw (VTR)
Granada (Warren Jenkins)
Stories of a debonair adventurer for hire. Lighter-than-air time filler which pleased in its day.
cr Philip Mackie
John Turner, Kay Callard, Richard Carpenter

Knight, Paul (1944–). British producer, ex-Granada (a junior on *A Family at War*) who scored with classic serials and then *Dick Turpin* and *Robin of Sherwood*.   PP

'Today's hero, driving the car of tomorrow!'
Knight Rider
US 1982–   × 50m colour
NBC/Universal/Glen Larson (Steven De Souza, Hannah Shearer)
A young man is bequeathed a prototype indestructible car which also talks back.
A perfectly silly idea which was pleasantly enough put over to justify a four-season run. The opener was a two-hour adventure with Richard Basehart as the dying inventor.
cr Glen Larson
David Haselhoff, Edward Mulhare
'The dialogue and acting are comic book and the plots are mostly hand-me-downs.' – Robert MacKenzie, *TV Guide*
'A kiddie show done on a childish level.' – *Daily Variety*

Knight, Shirley (1936–). American character actress. TV movies: *The Outsider*, *Shadow over Elveron*, *Friendly Persuasion*, *Medical Story*, *Return to Earth*, *21 Hours in Munich*, *The Defection of Simas Kurdika*, *Champions: A Love Story*, *Playing for Time*. For a while married to British TV writer John Hopkins, when she was billed as Shirley Knight Hopkins.

Knight, Ted (*c* 1925–) (Tadewurz Wladzui Konopka). American character actor who scored as the braggart announcer in *The Mary Tyler Moore Show* (Emmys 1972, 1975) and in 1978 began a rather unrewarding *Ted Knight Show*, a spin-off from *Busting Loose* in which he played the head of an escort agency. This was shortlived, and he joined *Too Close for Comfort*.

Knights, Robert (1942–). British drama director associated with all Malcolm Bradbury's plays, including *The History Man*. Also *Tender Is the Night*, 1985.

Knock on Any Door (GB 1965). ATV anthology series masterminded by Ted Willis to the social realism formula he had already defined in his own play *Look in Any Window*. At least the viewer was now symbolically invited to introduce himself, not merely peep.   PP

Knots Landing (US 1979). 50-minute series devised for CBS as a sequel/alternative to *Dallas*, with some character swapping. Basically a hothouse study of four married couples in a Californian cul-de-sac, it provides superior soap opera entertainment for those who don't find it all too funny for words. With James Houghton, Kim Lankford, Michele Lee, Constance McCashin, Don Murray, John Pleshette, Joan Van Ark, Ted Shackleford. Created and produced by David Jacobs; for Lorimar.
CBS calls it "a realistic exploration of modern marriage". Maybe it is, heaven help us.' – Robert MacKenzie, *TV Guide*

Knotts, Don (1924–). Sour-faced American character comedian who has appeared in several slapstick films and is a frequent TV performer. Series: *The Andy Griffith Show* (Emmys 1960, 1962, 1966).

The Knowledge ** ** (GB 1979; 78m; colour). Hilarious Jack Rosenthal comedy about the process by which aspirant London cabbies are forced to master a detailed topography of the capital and incidentally rid themselves of all fellow feelings. Consistently chuckleable-at, with a marvellous sado-comic performance by Nigel Hawthorne as the examiner. Produced by Euston Films (Christopher Neame) for Thames, directed by Bob Brooks. Also with Maureen Lipman, Mick Ford, Michael Elphick.   PP

Knox, Alexander (1907–). Canadian actor with careers in Hollywood and England. Series: *Tinker, Tailor, Soldier, Spy*. TV movies: *Run a Crooked Mile*, *Churchill and the Generals*, *Cry of the Innocent*.

Kodiak
US 1974 13 × 25m colour
ABC/Kodiak Productions (Stan Shpetner)
Adventures of the Alaska State Patrol. Acceptable action filler in an unfamiliar landscape.

KNIGHT RIDER, slotted against *Dallas* in the American schedule, seemed doomed to an early death. But its tricky car and its personable hero (David Haselhoff) enabled it to ride out four seasons.

cr Stan Shpetner, Anthony Laurence *m* Morton Stevens

Clint Walker, Abner Biberman, Maggie Blye

Kojak *

US 1973–7 110 × 50m colour
CBS/Universal (Matthew Rapf)

Cases of a bald-headed New York cop with a penchant for lollipops and fancy waistcoats.

Variable crime series which at its best gave an accurate picture of New York's seamier side and made a star and a so-called singer out of a character actor who had been busy playing villains.

cr Abby Mann *m* Billy Goldenberg (theme), John Cacavas (score)

TELLY SAVALAS, George Savalas, Dan Frazer, Kevin Dobson

Episodes:

Cop in a Cage with John P. Ryan

The Corrupter with Lola Albright, Robert Webber

Marker for a Dead Bookie with Roger Robinson

Dark Sunday with Richard Jordan

Siege of Terror with Harvey Keitel

One for the Morgue with Roger Robinson

Knockover with Alex Rocco

The Girl in the River with James Keach

Requiem for a Cop with Louise Latham

Web of Death with Hector Elizondo

Conspiracy of Fear with Larry Kert

Mojo with Ed Lauter

Die before They Wake with Harris Yulin

Death Is Not a Passing Grade with Mariclare Costello

Last Rites for a Dead Priest with Jackie Cooper

Deliver Us Some Evil with John Ritter

Eighteen Hours of Fear with Chuck McCann

Down a Long and Lonely River with Paul Michael Glaser

The Only Way Out with Lee H. Montgomery, John Hillerman

Dead on His Feet with Harry Guardino

Before the Devil Knows with Henry Darrow

Therapy in Dynamite with Steven Keats

Wall Street Gunslinger with Alan Feinstein

Best War in Town with Mark Shera, David Doyle

Elegy in an Asphalt Graveyard with Roger Robinson, Stephen Elliott

Slay Ride with Julie Gregg, Stephen McHattie

Loser Takes All with Leslie Nielsen

Hush Now Or You Die with Kathleen Quinlan

Unwanted Partners with Brad Dexter

You Can't Tell a Hurt Man How to Holler with Roger Robinson

Close Cover before Killing with Alex Rocco

A Very Deady Game with Art Lund

A Killing in the Second House with Martin Balsam

A Souvenir from Atlantic City with Jaime Sanchez

The Best Judge Money Can Buy with John Randolph

Nursemaid with Kay Medford

The Betrayal with Paul Anka

Cross Your Heart and Hope to Die with Andrea Marcovicci

Two Four Six for Two Hundred with Robert Loggia

Night of the Piraeus with Norman Lloyd

Acts of Desperate Men with Eugene Roche

The Trade-Off with Michael C. Gwynne

Queen of the Gypsies with Zohra Lampert

The Good Luck Bomber with Jack Ging

I Want to Report a Dream with Ruth Gordon

The Chinatown Murders parts one and two with Michael Constantine, Sheree North, Tige Andrews

Be Careful What You Pray For with George DiCenzo

Out of the Frying Pan with Eugene Roche

Secret Show – Deadly Snow with Robert Mandan

My Brother My Enemy with Sylvester Stallone

Deadly Innocence with Tige Andrews, Stephen Macht

Sweeter than Life with Neville Brand

On the Edge with Forrest Tucker

The Forgotten Room with George Pan

Life, Liberation and the Pursuit of Death with Joanna Miles

The Frame with Michael McGuire

Justice Deferred with Michael Ansara

No Immunity for Murder with Robert Alda

A Long Way from Times Square with Judith Lowry, Vincent Bagetta

A Grave Too Soon with Diana Hyland, Harold J. Stone, Daniel J. Travanti

Money Back Guarantee with David Ogden Stiers, Henry Brown

The Nicest Guys on the Block with Roger Robinson

Over the Water with Michael Christofer

A House of Prayer, a Den of Thieves with Eileen Brennan, Vincent Gardenia

Both Sides of the Law with David Opatoshu

Bad Dude with Roosevelt Grier

A Question of Answers parts one and two with Eli Wallach, Michael Gazzo

How Cruel the Frost, How Bright the Stars with Jesse Welles

A Wind from Corsica with Joseph Hindy

Law Dance with David Wilson

Sister Maria with Season Hubley

By Silence Betrayed with Cliff Osmond

The Pride and the Princess with Maria Schell

The Condemned with Paul Benjamin, Dorian Harewood

Dead Again with Simon Oakland

Birthday Party with Richard Gere

Where Do You Go When You Have No Place to Go? with Blair Brown

A Hair Trigger Away with Walter McGinn, Hurd Hatfield, Lynn Redgrave

Out of the Shadows with Ken Sylk

A Summer Madness with Fionnula Flanagan

When You Hear the Beep, Drop Dead with Eric Braeden, Susan Sullivan

An Unfair Trade with David Selby

The Godson with F. Murray Abraham

Black Thorn with Roosevelt Grier

A Need to Know with Hector Elizondo
Monkey on a String with Joseph Hindy
Lady in the Squad Room with Joan Van Ark, George Maharis
Kojak's Days parts one and two with Kitty Winn, Maud Adams
Kiss It All Goodbye with Carol Lynley, Christopher Walken
I Was Happy Where I Was with Tony Diaz
Another Gypsy Queen with Kathleen Widdoes
A Shield for Murder parts one and two with Geraldine Page
Case without a File with Angel Tompkins
I Could Kill My Wife's Lawyer with Joey Aresco
Tears for All Who Loved Her with Sam Jaffe
A Strange Kind of Love with James Sutorius
Letters of Death with Cristina Raines
Caper on a Quiet Street with Armand Assante
Cry for the Kids with Jack Ging
Laid Off with Michael Durrell
Once More from Birdland with Andrea Marcovicci
The Queen of Hearts Is Wild with Paula Kelly
The Summer of '69 parts one and two with Stephen McHattie, Diane Baker
No License to Kill with Kenneth McMillan
The Captain's Brother's Wife with Shelley Winters
Mouse with Ben Piazza
Sixty Miles to Hell with Priscilla Barnes
Justice for All with Charles Aidman
May the Horse Be with You with Mary Louise Weller
The Halls of Terror with Zohra Lampert
Chain of Custody with Jack Hogan
Photo Must Credit Joe Paxton with Tige Andrews, Arte Johnson
In Full Command with Danny Thomas

† See also *The Marcus Nelson Murders*, which served as pilot.

Kojak: The Belarus File
US 1984 96m colour TVM
CBS/Universal (Albert Ruben)
Kojak investigates the murders of Russian immigrants who survived the Nazi concentration camps.
Belated attempt to restart the series: despite moderately good reception, it failed.

w Albert Ruben *d* Robert Markowitz *ph* Alan Metzger *m* Joseph Conlan

Telly Savalas, Suzanne Pleshette, Max Von Sydow, Herbert Berghof, Dan Frazer, Alan Rosenberg, George Savalas

Kolchak: The Night Stalker
aka: *The Night Stalker*
US 1974 22 × 50m colour
MCA/Universal
A crime reporter has a penchant for getting mixed up with all kinds of monsters.
Self-consciously absurd comedy-horror spin-off from the high-rating TV movies *The Night Strangler* and *The Night Stalker*. The humour is thin, and the series ran out of monsters after half a dozen episodes.

cr Dan Curtis

Darren McGavin

Komack, James (1930–). American actor–writer–producer. Series include *Hennessey* (a/w), *The Courtship of Eddie's Father* (a/w/d), *Chico and the Man* (cr/d), *Welcome Back Kotter* (cr/d/p).

Kona Coast
US 1968 93m colour TVM
Warner/Richard Boone
The South Seas skipper of a fishing boat avenges his daughter's death from drugs.
Listless thick-ear which never made a series.

w Gil Ralston, *novel* John D. MacDonald *d* Lamont Johnson

Richard Boone, Vera Miles, Joan Blondell, Kent Smith

Konigsberg, Frank (19 –). American producer. *Pearl, It's Not Easy, Breaking Away, Guyana Tragedy, A Christmas without Snow, Divorce Wars, Coming out of the Ice, His and Hers, Rituals, Wet Gold, Ellis Island,* Surviving, *Right to Kill*.

'A brave venture into history.'
Korg: 70,000 BC
US 1974 16 × 22m colour
Hanna–Barbera
Oddball live action drama for children, purporting to illustrate the life of Neanderthal man.
Not a natural hit.

Korman, Harvey (1927–). Stalwart comedy actor who served for years with Carol Burnett. *Invisible Woman, Carpool, George Burns Comedy Week*.

Korty, John (1936–). American independent film-maker who makes occasional TV movies: *The People, The Autobiography of Miss Jane Pittman* (Emmy), *Go Ask Alice, Farewell to Manzanar*, etc.

Kossoff, David (1919–). Amiable, soft-spoken British character actor whose most successful appearances on TV were in the series *The Larkins* and *A Little Big Business* and as a Bible reader for all occasions.

Kotcheff, William T. (Ted) (19 –). Canadian director active in Britain in the late fifties and sixties, mostly for *Armchair Theatre. Hot Summer Night*, *The Big Client*, *The Last Tycoon*, many others.   PP

Kovacs, Ernie (1919–62). Big, burly, cigar-smoking American comedian whose shows of the fifties had an agreeable touch of satire. He is credited with the remark: 'Television is a medium, so called because it is neither rare nor well done.'

Kowalski, Bernard L. (1931–). American director who made some big-screen spectacles but seemed more his own man on TV. Series range from *The Westerner* to *Banacek* and *Baretta*. TV movies: *Terror in the Sky*, *Black Noon*, *Women in Chains*, *The Woman Hunter*, *In Tandem*, *Flight to Holocaust*, *The Nativity*.

Kraft Music Hall (US 1967–70). One-hour variety series for NBC, a revival of an old radio format starring Bing Crosby. Many top stars and experimental formats were featured in the TV version. Kraft also sponsored a Television Theatre (1947), a Suspense Theatre (1963–4), a Mystery Theatre (1961–2), etc.

Krantz, Steve (1923–). American producer. *Princess Daisy*, *Mistral's Daughter*.

Krasny, Paul (1935–). American director. TV movies include *The Adventures of Nick Carter*, *The Letters*, *Big Rose*, *The Islander*, *Centennial*, *When Hell Was in Session*, *Fugitive Family*, *Alcatraz*.

Kreskin, The Amazing (1935–) (John Kresge). American mentalist who had his own half-hour series in the seventies.

Kretzmer, Herbert (1925–). South African critic and songwriter long resident in Britain. His hit song *She*, sung by Charles Aznavour, was written as theme music for LWT's *Seven Faces of Woman* anthology and gave the sequel series its title. Since 1979 TV critic of the London *Daily Mail*.   PP

Krofft, Sid (19 –) and **Marty** (19 –). American puppeteers and comic costume designers, whose series for children have included H. R. PUFNSTUF and *Lidsville*.

The Krypton Factor (GB 1976–). A quiz programme devised by Granada TV to find overall superpersons who excel at physical stamina as well as intelligence and general knowledge. Sleek production helped it to become a hit, and in 1981 the format was sold to America. NB: Krypton is the planet on which Superman was born . . .

Kukla, Fran and Ollie. A puppet show for children which ran on NBC from 1947 until the mid-fifties. Fran was Fran Allison, the only live performer seen on the show. Puppeteer and creator was Burr Tillstrom; 'kukla' is Russian for 'doll'. Emmy 1953, best children's series.

Kulik, Buzz (1922–). American director whose television career dates back to *You Are There*, *Have Gun Will Travel* and *Perry Mason*. He made some undistinguished big-screen films, but returned to television as the whiz kid of major projects, not all of which performed as well as expected. *Vanished*, *Owen Marshall*, BRIAN'S SONG, *Pioneer Woman*, *Cage without a Key*, *Matt Helm*, *Babe*, *The Lindbergh Kidnapping Case*, *Corey for the People*, *Kill Me If You Can*, *Ziegfeld: The Man and His Women*, *From Here to Eternity*, etc.

Kulp, Nancy (*c* 1927–). Angular American comedy actress who became internationally popular as the banker's secretary in *The Beverly Hillbillies*.

Kung Fu ***
US 1971 75m colour TVM
ABC/Warner (Jerry Thorpe)

In the 1870s a half-American Buddhist monk flees to America with a price on his head.
Curious, likeable mixture of Oriental wisdom, western action and martial arts, impeccably photographed and fascinating to watch.

w Ed Spielman, Howard Friedlander *d* JERRY THORPE *m* Jim Helms

DAVID CARRADINE, Barry Sullivan, Keye Luke, Albert Salmi, Wayne Maunder

† The series which followed ran three years (72 × 50m) and because of its star and its style became an immense success in a world in which a more violent form of karate had been popularized by Bruce Lee. By the end of the second season, however, the plots had

worn very thin and the style, still remarkable for a TV series, was all that was left. Produced by Alex Beaton and Herman Miller for Jerry Thorpe and Warners; created by Ed Spielman.

Kuralt, Charles (1934–). American reporter, usually on special assignment for CBS.

Hurkos, Peter (1911–). Dutch psychic performer who made a stir in the early fifties.

Kurtz, Swoosie (1954–). American leading lady principally known for *Love, Jidney*.

La Frenais, Ian (c 1938–). British comedy writer, usually in tandem with Dick Clement.

La Rosa, Julius (1930–). American tenor who was a TV hit in the early fifties on *The Arthur Godfrey Show*.

La Rue, Danny (1927–). British (Irish?) comedian and female impersonator who toned down his nightclub act to make drag respectable. Actual talent minimal; willingness to please undeniable.

Lace
US 1984 1 × 120m, 1 × 96m colour
ABC/Lorimar (Preston Fischer)

A Hollywood sexpot tries to get back at her unknown mother for deserting her as a baby. Potted, bowdlerized televersion of a lurid best-seller. A great ratings success because of what it was thought to promise rather than what it actually offered.

w Elliott Baker, *novel* by Shirley Conran
d Billy Hale ph Phil Meheux m Nick Bicat
pd Allan Cameron

Phoebe Cates, Bess Armstrong, Brooke Adams, Arielle Dombasle, Anthony Higgins, Angela Lansbury, Herbert Lom, Anthony Quayle, Honor Blackman, Leigh Lawson, Nickolas Grace, Trevor Eve

PP: 'Just inching ahead of *Princess Daisy* in the department of unbelievable dramatics among the rich.'

Lace II
US 1985 2 × 96m colour miniseries
ABC/Lorimar (Preston Fischer)

The sexpot from *Lace* now goes on the trail of her unknown father.
Unintelligible international gibberish with pauses for sex and fashion shows.

w Elliott Baker d Billy Hale ph John Coquillon m Nick Bicat

Brooke Adams, Deborah Raffin, Phoebe Cates, Arielle Dombasle, Anthony Higgins, Christopher Cazenove, James Read, Patrick Ryecart, Michael Gough, Peter Jeffrey

'It can only be hoped that Lili doesn't have a missing brother or sister waiting in the wings.' – *Daily Variety*

Lacy and the Mississippi Queen
US 1978 74m colour TVM
Paramount/Lawrence Gordon (Lew Gallo)

Sisters who hardly knew each other wander through the old West avenging their father's murder.
Abysmal pilot for a show which could have been moderately entertaining. Slack handling prevents any reaction but boredom.

w Kathy Donnel, Madeleine DiMaggio-Wagner d Robert Butler ph Ted Voigtlander
m Barry Devorzon

Kathleen Lloyd, Debra Feuer, Jack Elam, Edward Andrews, James Keach

The Lad Himself: see Hancock, Tony

Ladd, Cheryl (1951–) (Cheryl Stoppelmoor). American leading lady whose tenure in *Charlie's Angels* encouraged her to make some rather dreary musical specials. *When She Was Bad*, *Kentucky Woman*, *Grace Kelly*, *The Hasty Heart*, *Romance on the Orient Express*, *A Death in California*.

The Lads *
GB 1963 50m bw
ATV/H. M. Tennent (Cecil Clarke)

Bit of bovver between local Cypriots and British soldiers on a night out in Famagusta, the latter dressed in sharp civvy suits and breaking repetitively into the neat little pastiche pop songs furnished for the occasion by Trevor Peacock, who also took part. (One of the songs, 'Mrs Brown You've Got a Lovely Daughter', later made the charts.) The ending included a bit of impersonation by Tom Courtenay not really consistent with the part he was playing, otherwise a lively and atmospheric play.

w Ronald Harwood d Caspar Wrede   PP

The Ladies
US 1984 96m colour TVM
NBC/Ed Friendly (Jackie Cooper, Robert Klane)

A woman deserted by her husband moves in on her recently divorced daughter.
Glossy soap opera tailor-made for female viewers.

LACE. The miniseries was less sensational than the book, but its various titillations attracted a large audience. Top, Brooke Adams; bottom, Phoebe Cates; right, Bess Armstrong; left, Arielle Dombasle.

w Robert Klane *d* Jackie Cooper

Patricia Elliott, Talia Balsam, Robert Webber, Steven Peterman, Michael Shannon

Ladies in Charge (GB 1985; 52m). Pilot for agreeable period series about emancipated flappers, ex 1914–18 war nurses, etc., who set up a problem-solving agency. Written by Alfred Shaughnessy, from an idea by Kate Herbert Hunting, for Thames. PP

Lady Blue
US 1985 1 × 96m , × 50m colour
ABC/MGM/David Gerber (Herb Wallerstein)

Cases of a female cop who shoots first.
Absurd but unpalatable hokum about an idiot lady at large in the streets of Chicago. Oddly enough this Dirty Harriet didn't make it in the ratings.

cr Robert Vincent O'Neil *d* (pilot) Gary Nelson

Jamie Rose, Danny Aiello

The Lady from Yesterday
US 1984 96m colour TVM
CBS/Comworld (Barry Weitz)

A Vietnam vet who has become a successful executive is visited by a dying Oriental woman who wants him to look after their son.
More glossy soap, well enough acted and presented.

w Tim Maschler, Ken Pettus *d* Robert Day
ph R. Michael Stringer

Wayne Rogers, Bonnie Bedelia, Pat Hingle, Tina Chen

Lady Killers
GB 1980 13 × 50m colour
Dramatized murder trials, all based on court transcripts, with some invented scenes in the cells. The first set dealt with crimes committed by women, the second – by a shift of emphasis in the title – with celebrated murderers of women, e.g. Crippen, George Smith, Neville Heath. Either way it was unedifying stuff, Granada seeking to make a virtue of parsimony by declaring proudly that the same courtroom set served as the High Court in Edinburgh one week, the Old Bailey the next. Introduced by Robert Morley; produced by Pieter Rogers. PP

LH: 'For me the invented scenes were not only boring but made the whole thing highly suspect.'

Lady of the House
US 1979 96m colour TVM
NBC/Metromedia/William Kayden

The life of Sally Stanford, the San Francisco brothel-keeper who stood for mayor.
No doubt a distorted version of the facts, but an acceptable mild shocker for female audiences.

w Ron Koslow *d* Vincent Sherman, Ralph Nelson *ph* Bob Morrison *m* Fred Karlin

Dyan Cannon, Armand Assante, Jesse Dixon, Zohra Lampert, Susan Tyrell, Maggie Cooper

† Sally Stanford died in 1981.

Lafferty, Perry (1922–). American executive producer, with CBS for many years. Series include *Hawaii Five O*, *Big Hawaii*.

Laine, Cleo (1927–) (Clementina Dinah Campbell). British high-note singer, wife of Johnny Dankworth and something of a cult figure.

Laine, Frankie (1913–) (Frank Paul Lo Vecchio). American pop singer of the fifties, much on TV as variety star and theme singer of *Rawhide*.

Lambert, Verity (1935–). British executive producer. Among programmes she has developed are *Dr Who*, *Adam Adamant*, *Somerset Maugham Stories* (BAFTA award 1969), *Shoulder to Shoulder*, *Budgie*, *Hazell*.

The Lambeth Boys (GB 1985; 3 × 60m). Karel Reisz's 1959 cinema documentary about south London Teddy Boys, *We Are the Lambeth Boys*, finally aired on TV, together with two 25-years-on follow-ups, directed and produced by Rob Rohrer, for BBC Manchester. PP

Lampert, Zohra (1937–). American leading lady. TV movies include *The Connection*, *One of Our Own*, *Black Beauty*, *Lady of the House*, *The Suicide's Wife*, *The Girl, the Gold Watch and Everything*, *Children of Divorce*. In GB, *Better Luck Next Time*.

Lancelot Link, Secret Chimp
US 1970–1 52 × 25m colour
ABC/Sandler–Burns

A chimpanzee spy working for APE (Agency to Prevent Evil) counters the machinations of CHUMP (Criminal Headquarters for Underground Master Plan).

Live action series for children with chimpanzees playing the roles with the aid of dubbed human voices. Different, anyway.

Lancer
US 1968–9 51 × 50m colour
CBS/TCF (Alan Armer)
A ranching family fights for survival in the San Joaquin Valley in the 1870s.
An attempt at another *Bonanza*, and rather a dull one.
cr Samuel A. Peeples, Dean Riesner *m* Jerome Moross
Andrew Duggan, James Stacy, Wayne Maunder, Elizabeth Baur

Land of the Giants *
US 1968–9 51 × 50m colour
ABC/TCF/Irwin Allen (Bruce Fowler)
A rocketship crashes on a planet ruled by giants.
Ingenious mixture of *Planet of the Apes* and *Dr Cyclops*. Very good trick photography and special sets are its chief recommendations.
cr Irwin Allen *m* John Williams *ad* Jack Martin Smith, Rodger E. Maus *special effects* L. B. Abbott, Art Cruickshank, Emil Kosa Jnr
Gary Conway, Steve Matheson, Kurt Kasznar, Don Marshall, Deanna Lund

Land of the Lost
US 1974 17 × 22m colour
NBC/Hanna–Barbera
A forest ranger and his children are caught in a time vortex and find themselves in a country populated by prehistoric monsters.
Curious attempt at a live action *Valley of the Dinosaurs*. Predictably, the monsters are not too convincing.
Wesley Eure, Kathy Coleman, Spencer Milligan

Landau, Ely (1920–). American executive, creator of NTA, film producer and guiding light of the American Film Theatre.

Landau, Martin (1933–). Sensitive-looking, rather glum American character actor who had leading roles in *Mission Impossible* and *Space 1999*. TV movies: *Welcome Home Johnny Bristol*, *Savage*.

Landen, Dinsdale (1932–). British light actor who has played everything from Dickens to drunks, with a tendency to overdo the farce. TV series: *Mickey Dunne*, *Devenish*, *Pig in the Middle*.

Landon, Michael (1936–) (Eugene Orowitz). American TV actor who became famous as Little Joe in BONANZA; later concentrated on writing and producing LITTLE HOUSE ON THE PRAIRIE. 1981: creator, producer and director of *Father Murphy*. TV movies (as writer–producer–director): *The Loneliest Runner*, *Killing Stone*. In 1984 produced and starred in another unlikely winner, *Highway to Heaven*, in which he played a rather useless angel.

Landsberg, Alan (1930–). American independent producer.

Lane, Carla (19 –). British comedy writer who swept to the top with *The Liver Birds* (co-writer Myra Taylor). Went solo with *Butterflies*, which ran five years. Lately increasingly serious, not to say solemn, sitcoms: *Leaving*, *I Woke Up One Morning*, *The Mistress*.   PP

Lange, Hope (1931–). Gentle-spoken American leading lady. TV series include *The Ghost and Mrs Muir*, *The New Dick Van Dyke Show*. TV movies: *Crowhaven Farm*, *That Certain Summer*, *The 500 Pound Jerk*, *I Love You Goodbye*, *Fer de Lance*, *The Secret Night Caller*, *Like Normal People*, *The Day Christ Died*.

Langford, Bonnie (1964–). British entertainer who developed from a precocious child performer to a precocious teenage one. Talented, though.

Langrishe, Go Down *
GB 1978 90m colour TVM
BBC (David Jones)
Three spinster sisters in a fading Irish mansion lose their equanimity – or in one character's case her virginity – when a German student stays in the lodge house. A Harold Pinter screenplay from the novel by Aidan Higgins was finally taken up by TV when it failed to go into production as a movie.
d David Jones *ph* Elmer Cossey
Judi Dench, Jeremy Irons, Harold Pinter, Margaret Whiting   PP

Lanigan's Rabbi
US 1976 98m colour TVM
NBC/Universal/Heyday (Leonard B. Stern)
A rabbi with a penchant for detection helps the local police chief solve a murder.
Initially pleasant but overlong and finally undistinguished pilot for a *Mystery Movie*

segment. See *Mystery Movie* for subsequent titles.

w Don M. Mankiewicz, Gordon Cotler, *novel Friday the Rabbi Slept Late* by Harry Kemelman *d* Lou Antonio *ph* Andrew Jackson *m* Leonard Rosenman

Stuart Margolin, Art Carney, Janet Margolin, Janis Paige

Lansing, Robert (1929–) (Robert H. Broom). American leading man, mostly on TV. Series: *87th Precinct*, *Twelve O'Clock High*, *The Man Who Never Was*. TV movies: *Killer by Night*, *The Astronaut*, *Crime Club*, *Widow*, *The Deadly Triangle*.

Lapotaire, Jane (1944–). British leading actress who played *Madame Curie*. Also repeated for TV her stage role as *Piaf*.

Laramie *
US 1959–62 124 × 50m 64 bw, 60 colour
NBC/Revue
Two friends own a trading station in Wyoming after the Civil War.
Passers-by each week meant a long guest list and a wide range of stories. A good family western series.
John Smith, Robert Fuller, Spring Byington

Laredo
US 1969–7 56 × 50m colour
NBC/Universal
Adventures of three Texas Rangers.
Unsubtle and rather charmless western series.
Neville Brand, William Smith, Peter Brown, Phil Carey

Large, Eddie: see Little, Syd and Large, Eddie

The Largest Theatre in the World. Idealistic project whereby European broadcasting organizations plus one or two elsewhere in the world would simultaneously put out their own versions of the same specially written TV play. Terence Rattigan set everyone off to a good start in 1962 with HEART TO HEART, ingeniously compounded from three ingredients which would transcend all frontiers – television itself, the behaviour of politicians and a little love. The home production (BBC) had Sir Ralph Richardson as a corrupt Cabinet Minister and Kenneth More as a failing TV interviewer out to rescue his career by exposing him. There were eight other productions, including one by French Television which was also taken by

neighbouring French-language services. All had managed to find a Rolls-Royce or a Jaguar for the hero, which led Sydney Newman (then head of BBC drama) to joke that whatever else the experiment had or had not achieved it had been a hell of an advertisement for British cars. Jean Cocteau, due to contribute the second script, died before he could do so. The third, *Someone in Your Midst* by Diego Fabbri, achieved only a limited take-up, the BBC being one of the defaulters. Harold Pinter's TEA PARTY in 1965 restored a sense of occasion. Fritz Hochwalder's *The Order* followed in 1967, then later the same year François Billetdoux's *Pitchi-Poi* varied the original formula: its saga of a wartime baby's search for her true parents was shot as a single co-operative venture, with each participating country supplying the location and facilities for a bit of the whole, even if it was no more than a wave as the characters whizzed through on a bus. Separate productions were resumed for THE LIE (1970), from Ingmar Bergman. Indeed the BBC version directed by Alan Bridges also transposed the action to Britain, though the tenor remained gloomily Swedish. The ball passed to Britain yet again in 1971 for *The Rainbirds*, by Clive Exton, a tirade against armies, the media, the medical profession, the church and possessive mothers which effectively brought the whole idea to a full stop.   PP

The Larkins *. British half-hour tape comedy of the fifties, about a cockney couple who keep a country pub. With David Kossoff, Peggy Mount. The inevitable feature film version was called *Inn for Trouble*.
PP: 'Peggy Mount as the battleaxe Ma Larkin was the whole show, with her hair scraped up from her neck in a tight roll of curls more intimidating than a fixed bayonet, and a voice to match. On one occasion, she snapped "Shut up" at a clock that dared to chime when she was in full tirade. It did, in mid-chime. Created by Fred Robinson; for ATV.'

Larry
US 1974 74m colour TVM
Tomorrow
A normally intelligent man of 26 has been considered mentally retarded and hospitalized since infancy.
Interesting case history based on fact.
w David Seltzer *d* William A. Graham
Frederic Forrest, Tyne Daly, Michael McGuire, Robert Walden

Larson, Glen (19 –). American producer–writer–director who seems to delight in borrowing themes from successful movies and turning them into long-running series. Thus *McCloud* (from *Coogan's Bluff*), *Alias Smith and Jones* (from *Butch Cassidy and the Sundance Kid*), *Six Million Dollar Man* (from James Bond), *Battlestar Galactica* (from *Star Wars*), *BJ and the Bear* (from *Smokey and the Bandit*), *Buck Rogers in the 25th Century*, *The Fall Guy*, *Rooster*, *Knight Rider*, *Trauma Center*, *Manimal*, *Automan*, *Masquerade*, *Cover Up*, *Half Nelson*, etc.

The Las Vegas Strip War
US 1986 96m colour TVM
NBC/George Englund (Mike Greenburg)
A hotel boss finds himself in the middle of a double cross between casino operators.
Uninteresting crime caper with a star at the end of his tether.

w,d George Englund *ph* Fred Koenekamp
Rock Hudson, James Earl Jones, Pat Morita, Robert Costanzo

Lasser, Louise (1939–). American comic character actress who scored a hit as the lead of *Mary Hartman, Mary Hartman* and moved on to *It's a Living*.

Lassie
US 1954–72 186 × 25m colour
CBS/Jack Wrather
A collie dog owned by a farmer protects him and his family.
Innocuous family fare. 15 × 20-minute episodes were also made, and several were combined to make movies.

Tommy Rettig, George Cleveland; then Jon Provost, Cloris Leachman; then Jon Provost, Hugh Reilly, June Lockhart; then Robert Bray

† Emmy 1954, best children's programme.

Lassie: The New Beginning
US 1978 96m colour TVM
Jack Wrather/Tom McDermott
When grandmother dies, Lassie accompanies the children on their way to a new home, but gets separated from them.
Rather muddled attempt to launch a new series; it gets by on the dog rather than any astuteness in plotting or characterization.

w Jack Miller *d* Don Chaffey *ph* Charles F. Wheeler *m* Jerrold Immel
Jeanette Nolan, John McIntire, John Reilly, Lee Bryant, Gene Evans, David Wayne
'If I were a collie, I'd sue.' – Judith Crist

Lassie's Rescue Rangers
US 1973–4 48 × 22m colour
Filmation
Lassie commands an all-animal rescue crew in the Rocky Mountains.
Clean but otherwise unremarkable cartoon series.

The Last Angry Man
US 1974 74m colour TVM
Columbia
The last cases of an old doctor in New York's poor quarters.
Unnecessary TV remake of the 1959 film. Quite flat.

w Gerald Green *d* Jerrold Freedman
Pat Hingle, Lynn Carlin, Tracy Bogart, Michael Margotta, Andrew Duggan, Sorrell Booke

**The Last Child *
US 1971 73m colour TVM
Aaron Spelling (William Allyn)
A future government denies married couples the right to more than one child; one family tries to escape.
Orwellian fantasy, rather better than *Zero Population Growth* which it resembles.

w Peter S. Fischer *d* John Llewellyn Moxey
Michael Cole, Janet Margolin, Van Heflin, Harry Guardino, Ed Asner

The Last Convertible
US 1979 3 × 96m colour TVM
NBC/Universal/Roy Huggins
The lives of five Harvard men from their graduation in 1940 to their reunion in 1969.
Watchable but shallow and over-extended novelization, with predictable reference to world events.

w Philip de Guere, Clyde Ware, Stephen F. McPherson, *novel* Anton Myer *d* Sidney Hayers, Gus Trikonis, Jo Swerling Jnr *ph* Thomas del Ruth, Edward Rio Rotunno *m* Pete Rugulo
Perry King, Deborah Raffin, Bruce Boxleitner, Edward Albert, Sharon Gless, John Shea, Michael Nouri, Kim Darby, Stuart Whitman, Vic Morrow, Martin Milner, John Houseman, Lisa Pelikan
'The characters are badly drawn Fitzgerald types who've stayed too long at the party.' – *Daily Variety*

A Last Cry for Help
US 1979 96m colour TVM
ABC/Viacom/Myrt–Hal Productions
The case history of a teenage girl with suicidal tendencies.

Another depressing symptom of American TV's disease-of-the-week syndrome.

w/d Hal Sitowitz ph Dennis Dalzell m Miles Goodman

Linda Purl, Shirley Jones, Tony Lo Bianco, Murray Hamilton, Grant Goodeve, Morgan Woodward

The Last Day *
US 1975 100m colour TVM
Paramount/A. C. Lyles

A retired gunman brings out his weapons to defend his town against the Dalton gang.
Trickily made western which would have played better straight but has some nice conceits and performances.

w Jim Byrnes, Steve Fisher d Vincent McEveety ph Robert Hauser m Jerrold Immel

Richard Widmark, Robert Conrad, Barbara Rush, Loretta Swit, Tim Matheson, Christopher Connelly, Richard Jaeckel

The Last Day (GB 1983; 75m). Dramatized reconstruction of the day the Americans quit Saigon in 1975, with Charles Dance playing the golden-haired reporter-hero. Written by the golden-haired reporter-nagger John Pilger it was less splenetically anti-American than might have been predicted, though the story was done better in *Saigon – Year of the Cat*. Also with Dan O'Herlihy, David Suchet; directed by Richard Stroud, produced by Peter Wolfes, for BBC.   PP

The Last Days of Pompeii
US 1984 1 × 120m, 2 ×
   96m colour miniseries
ABC/Columbia/David Gerber (Richard Irving, William Hill)

A $17 million Roman holiday based on the Bulwer Lytton novel about various types who were engulfed in the Vesuvius eruption of A.D. 79. Script and acting are hilariously variable, the special effects could have been better, and the whole plays like a pantomime from which the jokes have been omitted.

w Carmen Culver d Peter Hunt ph Jack Cardiff m Trevor Jones

Brian Blessed, Ned Beatty, Laurence Olivier, Siobhan McKenna, Ernest Borgnine, Nicholas Clay, Lesley-Anne Down, Olivia Hussey, Duncan Regehr, Franco Nero, Linda Purl, Anthony Quayle, Gerry Sundquist, Peter Cellier, Joyce Blair

'More like a Roman circus than a respectful adaptation, it gives kitsch a bad name . . . with miniatures looking like they were filmed in someone's garage.' – *Daily Variety*

† Reported pre-production announcement from the producer to a European salesman:
   'Well, don't say we never give you anything big. We're going to do *The Last Days of Pompeii*, and we're going to do it in Greece.'
   'Very nice, but why Greece?'
   'Why, isn't Pompeii in Greece?'
   'Not unless they moved it. It's near Naples.'
   'Oh. Well, Vesuvius is in Greece . . .'

The Last Dinosaur
US 1977 96m colour TVM
ABC/Rankin–Bass

A tycoon goes on a hunt in remote dinosaur country.
Crude but not unamusing entry in the King Kong stakes.

w William Overgard d Alex Grasshoff, Tom Kotani

Richard Boone, Joan Van Ark, Steven Keats, Luther Rackley

The Last Enemy *
GB 1956 90m bw

Brave attempt to dramatize Richard Hillary's autobiographical account of Battle of Britain pilot coming to terms with himself. Pete Murray was lightweight for such a complex and introspective character but the mix of film sequences and live studio production set new standards. Also with John Robinson, Patricia Driscoll, Tarn Bassett. Directed and produced by Peter Graham Scott; for A–R.

The Last Giraffe
aka: *Raising Daisy Rothschild*
US 1979 96m colour TVM
CBS/Westfall (Charles G. Mortimer Jnr)

A wildlife photographer in Kenya tries to protect the last examples of the Rothschild giraffe.
Good-looking but thinly scripted adventure in the *Born Free* mould.

w Sherman Yellen, book *Raising Daisy Rothschild* by Jock and Betty Leslie-Melville d Jack Couffer ph Ted Scaife m Fred Karlin

Susan Anspach, Simon Ward, Gordon Jackson, Don Warrington

Last Hours before Morning *
US 1975 74m colour TVM
MGM/Charles Fries

A hotel house detective is involved in a murder.
Chandleresque murder mystery, quite effectively done; it didn't go as a series.

w Robert Garland, George Yanok *d* Joseph Hardy

Ed Lauter, Rhonda Fleming, Robert Alda, Kaz Garas, Peter Donat, Don Porter

The Last Hurrah
US 1977 96m colour TVM
NBC/Columbia/O'Connor–Becker (Terry Becker)

An old politician has one last fling.
Competent but unnecessary retread of a semi-classic film.

w Carroll O'Connor, *novel* Edwin O'Connor *d* Vincent Sherman *ph* Gerald Perry Finnermann *m* Peter Matz

Carroll O'Connor, Mariette Hartley, Patrick Wayne, Jack Carter, Burgess Meredith, Robert Brown, Dana Andrews, Paul Picerni

Last Love * (GB 1983). Cheerful little senior citizenry romance between gracious widow sentenced by grasping family to old folks' home and retired Guards Sergeant-Major who rescues her. Written by Reg Gadney, directed by Nicholas Renton, for BBC.   PP

The Last Ninja
US 1983 96m colour TVM
ABC/Paramount/Anthony Spinner

A master Ninja, in the guise of a San Francisco antiques dealer, helps government departments in difficulty.
Sounds familiar, and it is, but the pilot was so stilted that it didn't sell.

w Ed Spielman *d* William A. Graham

Michael Beck, Nancy Kwan, John McMartin, Mako, Richard Lynch

The Last of the Belles: see F. Scott Fitzgerald and 'The Last of the Belles'

The Last of the Brave (GB 1960). One of the few television performances by the splendid old ham actor Sir Donald Wolfit. He played a retired French colonel of the old school who shoots his own son when the latter admits to cowardice in action. Also with Paul Massie, Rosemary Scott. Written by Stanley Mann; directed by Philip Saville; produced by Sydney Newman; for ABC (*Armchair Theatre*).   PP

Last of the Good Guys *
US 1978 96m colour TVM
CBS/Columbia (Jay Daniel)

A young cop starts an elaborate con game to ensure that the family of his dead buddy gets a pension.
Livelier than usual TV movie fodder.

w John D. Hess, Theodore J. Flicker, Clark Howard *d* Theodore J. Flicker *ph* Emmett Bergholz *m* Dana Kaproff

Robert Culp, Dennis Dugan, Richard Narita, Ji Tu Cumbuka, Larry Hagman, Marlyn Mason, Jonathan Harris

Last of the Great Survivors
US 1984 96m colour TVM
CBS (Doris M. Keating)

A social worker persuades a building inspector to reprieve a condemned house where her elderly charges live.
Strained, clumsily made comedy drama which fails to persuade on any level.

w Jim Kouf *d* Jerry Jameson *ph* James M. Glennon *m* Artie Butler

Pam Dawber, James Naughton, Thom Bray, Fritz Feld, Michael Callan, Maryedith Burrell

'If an orangutan can't pick up a guffaw or two, a telefilm's in trouble.' – *Daily Variety*

The Last of the Mohicans
US 1977 96m colour TVM
NBC/Schick Sunn Classic (Charles E. Sellier Jnr)

A white hunter is helped by Indians to escort two women through hostile country.
'Classics Illustrated' version of a novel which has been frequently adapted but never very well.

w Stephen Lord, *novel* James Fenimore Cooper *d* James L. Conway *ph* Henning Schellerup *m* Bob Summers

Steve Forrest, Ned Romero, Andrew Prine, Don Shanks

The Last of the Powerseekers *
US 1969 101m colour TVM
Universal

Complications and sudden deaths ensue when a banker accuses his son-in-law of embezzlement.
Ingenious stretch-out of several episodes from the unsuccessful Harold Robbins series *The Survivors*; most of the glamorous sequences are included, and the new plot hangs together remarkably well.

w/d Walter Doniger, Joseph Leytes, Paul Henreid

Lana Turner, George Hamilton, Ralph Bellamy, Kevin McCarthy, Louis Hayward, Diana Muldaur, Jan-Michael Vincent

Last of the Summer Wine **
GB 1974–   approx. 40 × 30m colour (VTR)
BBC

THE LAST PLACE ON EARTH.   The sad story of Scott's ill-fated trek to the South Pole.
Martin Shaw as Scott, Sylvester McCoy as Bowers.

Three old school friends in a Yorkshire village find themselves elderly and unemployed, so spend their days enjoying life..

Pleasing and unusual regional comedy which after years of familiarity became top of the ratings in 1982.

w ROY CLARKE

Michael Bates (later Brian Wilde), Bill Owen, Peter Sallis

'A new, mellow and gorgeous comedy series.' – *Guardian*

The Last Outlaw

Australia 1980 8 × 50m colour VTR
7 Network/Roger Le Mesurier/Ian Jones, Bronwyn Binns

The life and times of Ned Kelly.
Carefully detailed version of an oft-told tale.

w Ian Jones, Bronwyn Binns *d* Kevin Dobson, George Miller *m* Brian May

John Jarratt, Elaine Cusick, Debra Lawrance, Gerald Kennedy, Lewis Fitzgerald, Stephen Bisley

The Last Place on Earth **

GB 1985 1 × 75m, 5 × 50m
Central (Tim van Rellim) with Renegade Productions

The story of Captain Scott's doom-laden last expedition to the South Pole, re-told by Trevor Griffiths in line with the demythologizing biography by Roland Huntford plus an extra implication of his own that the fate of Scott's party was converted by the ruling classes into the stoical acceptance of suffering which would see us through two imperial wars and the Falklands adventure.

'What did emerge willy nilly from this

picture of Scott was – for all his vanity and rigidity and imprecision of orders – a special kind of nobility, a determination to keep working to the bitter end, writing innumerable letters and testaments. What was incontrovertible was that along the way Griffiths constructed a full-blown epic narrative, realized with striking godforsaken verisimilitude.'

w Trevor Griffiths *d* Ferdinand Fairfax

Martin Shaw (as Scott), Sverre Anker Ousdal (Amundsen), Susan Wooldridge (Kathleen Scott)   PP

† Previous versions of the story:
Scott's Last Journey, documentary by John Read, *w* Martin Chisholm, narrated by Richard Dimbleby, BBC 1962.
Shackleton, Episode 2, *w* Christopher Ralling, *d* Martyn Friend *p* John Harris, BBC 1983.
Terra Nova, studio (stage) play by Ted Tally, *d* John Bruce, with Michael N. Harbour, Knut Husebro, Kate Fahy, BBC 1984.

The Last Resort
US 1979 12 × 25m colour
CBS/MTM (Gary David Goldberg)
Madcap goings-on in the kitchen of a resort hotel.
Lame comedy which rattled around for a few weeks, and was then quietly disposed of.

cr Gary David Goldberg

Stephanie Faracy, Larry Breeding, Robert Costanzo, Zane Lasky

The Last Reunion ** (GB 1955).
Wartime RAF bomber crew assemble regularly for an 'aircrew breakfast' on the anniversary of their final operation, but this year – as every year – there are hints this will be the last time, especially if one of the party will insist on reviving old squabbles about something that happened that night over enemy territory. In a stunning *coup de télévision* the past takes over, and there's a further surprise in the ending. Kenneth Hyde's teaser, originally done by ATV, was the first play from ITV to enjoy a second production, by ABC *Armchair Theatre* in 1965 with Jeremy Kemp and Esmond Knight in the cast. At the time I said: 'Though the late Kenneth Hyde's dialogue is flat and uninspired the plot still engages like a meat-hook.'   PP

Last, Richard (1927–).
Redoubtable British critic, ex-opera chorus singer, with the *Daily Telegraph* since 1970, previously *The Sun*, not often taken in.   PP

The Last Ride of the Dalton Gang
US 1979 142m colour TVM
NBC/Dan Curtis (Joseph Stern)
In 1934, Emmet Dalton in Hollywood reminisces about his years out west with his outlaw brothers.
Nicely made but tediously long and rambling western which only occasionally sputters into gear.

w Earl W. Wallace *d* Dan Curtis *ph* Frank Stanley *m* Robert Cobert

Cliff Potts, Randy Quaid, Larry Wilcox, Sharon Farrell, Matt Clark, Royal Dano, Jack Palance, Dale Robertson, Bo Hopkins, R. G. Armstrong, Scott Brady

The Last Song
GB title: *Lady in Danger*
US 1980 96m colour TVM
CBS/Motown/Ron Samuels
An electronics expert is killed for a compromising tape, and his wife and daughter find themselves on the run.
Muddled melodrama which dissipates suspense by a concern for ecology.

w Michael Berk, Douglas Schwartz *d* Alan J. Levi *ph* Robert Hoffman *m* Johnny Harris

Lynda Carter, Ronny Cox, Nicholas Pryor, Paul Rudd, Jenny O'Hara, Dale Robinette, Don Porter

'Cliché situations and awkward motivations.'
– *Daily Variety*

Last Summer *
GB 1977 50m colour
Engagingly amoral tale of professional car thieves and car ringers, none of whom indulged the slightest scruple. Nemesis struck in the end when the new boy (Richard Mottau) panicked and reversed a disputed Jensen into his mentor's girl friend, which seemed to me to be fulfilling ethical rather than dramatic needs. Still, it was convincingly informative. How often do we complain that a man's work is the last thing ever to be examined in television drama? It was here. Richard Beckinsale gave a stunning performance, all world weariness, dark glasses and secret sentimentality. Written by Peter Prince; directed by Stephen Frears; for Thames.   PP

The Last Survivors
US 1975 74m colour TVM
Columbia/Bob Banner
After a sea disaster, an officer must decide which passengers shall remain in an overcrowded lifeboat.
Bathtub remake of the cinema film *Seven Waves Away*. Not as good (or even worse).

w Douglas Day Stewart d Lee H. Katzin
Martin Sheen, Diane Baker, Tom Bosley, Christopher George, Bruce Davison, Anne Francis, Percy Rodrigues, Anne Seymour, Bethel Leslie
† The theme was borrowed in both cases from the 1937 film *Souls at Sea.*

The Last Tenant
US 1980 96m colour TVM
ABC/Titus (Herbert Brodkin)
An ailing, ageing father prevents his son from marrying.
Earnest treatment of a familiar problem.
w George Rubino d Jud Taylor ph Sol Negrin m Dick Hyman

Last Train Through Harecastle Tunnel *
(GB 1969). Peter Terson comedy with Richard O'Callaghan as an ardent, spotty train-buff on one of those sentimental last trips as a railway line is closed down, and thereby coming into contact with a much more exotic cross-section of humanity than dreamed of by his patronizing office colleagues. Directed by Alan Clarke; produced by Irene Shubik; for BBC (*Wednesday Play*). PP

The Late Late Breakfast Show (GB since
1983). In fact an early evening Saturday show hosted by the ubiquitous Noel Edmonds with lots of stunts and silly contests, produced by Michael Hurll for BBC. PP
LH: 'In its fourth season, curiously, it began to get ratings. In television familiarity doesn't always breed contempt.'

The Late Late Show. An Irish institution,
the open-ended late-night chat, comedy, music, quiz and discussion show which has gone out live every Saturday night (initially, Friday) – except during summer – since 1962. In all that time it has been presented by Gay Byrne. In 1985 C4 screened edited extracts in the UK on Monday afternoons. Also produced by Gay Byrne, for RTE. Book: *To Whom It Concerns* (1972) by – guess who? – Gay Byrne. PP

Late Night Horror
GB 1968 approx. 7 × 30m colour
Series of half-hour horror playlets in fact recorded in 1967 partly as a training exercise in the use of colour equipment on the eve of BBC2's introduction of colour that year. The plays themselves weren't much, save for a Roald Dahl long anticipating Anglia's *Tales*

of the Unexpected and an unexpectedly erotic chiller called *The Bells of Hell*, but – perhaps because of the novelty of colour – the casting was weighty: Claire Bloom, Diane Cilento, Nora Nicholson, etc. Produced by Harry Moore; for BBC. PP

Late Night Line-Up: see Line-Up.

Late Starter **
GB 1985 8 × 50m
BBC (Ruth Boswell)
On the day he retires to what he hopes will be a life of comfy scholarship, the Professor of English at a Midlands university discovers that his wife, a secret gambler, has disappeared leaving him with ruinous debts. He starts life again in a North London bedsitter. Another gripping middle-class, mid-life-crisis series from the *Telford's Change* team, Mark Shivas hovering in the background as executive producer.
w Brian Clark d Barry Davis, Nicholas Mallett
Peter Barkworth, Rowena Cooper, Julia Foster, Beryl Reid, Jimmy Jewel PP
LH: 'Initially interesting, but dramatically with nowhere to go; and Barkworth really must stop playing the same self-apologizing character in different surroundings.'

Late Summer Affair **
GB 1962 90m bw
Tubby suburban paterfamilias suffering from the seven- (or rather, 17-) year itch packs wife and children off to seaside in expectation of saucy little holiday at home for himself. Sad–sweet comedy with Nigel Stock, blazered, baggy-flannelled, quietly distraught as the luckless lover; Reginald Marsh devastating as his odious friend and eventual usurper; Wendy Craig as the girl – she reproduced the type with marvellous accuracy, sudden changes of mood, highminded prattle, calculated unworldliness and all. Written by Leo Lehman; directed by Eric Tayler; for BBC. PP

The Lathe of Heaven
US 1981 96m colour TVM
WNET/The Television Laboratory/Taurus (David R. Laxton)
A psychiatrist finds that his patient's dreams really do come true, with devastating effects for urban civilization.
Public television's first telemovie is an oddly complex piece of science fiction, too messily told for wide public acceptance.

w Robert E. Swaybill, Diane English, *novel* Ursula K. LeGuin *d* David R. Laxton, Fred Barzyk *ph* Robbie Greenberg *m* Michael Small

Bruce Davison, Kevin Conway, Margaret Avery, Peyton Park

'The deadly serious telefilm loses its impetus as it attempts to impress visually.' – *Daily Variety*

Laudes Evangelii (GB 1962). Leonid Massine's dance-and-mime version of the Crucifixion, and events leading thereto, given a respectful, but less than overwhelming television production by Rediffusion. Directed by Joan Kemp-Welch.   PP

Laugh-In ***
US 1967–72 approx. 130 × 50m colour (VTR)
NBC/GEORGE SCHLATTER
Wildfire vaudeville series with injections of satire and many running gags: a mix of *Hellzapoppin*, *That Was the Week that Was* and *Monty Python's Flying Circus*. Catchphrases originating from this one show include:
(1) Beautiful downtown Burbank
(2) Very interesting, but stupid
(3) Sock it to me
(4) I forgot the question
(5) You bet your sweet bippy
(6) Here comes de judge
(7) Look it up in your Funk and Wagnalls
(8) I'll drink to that
(9) Is that a chicken joke?
Light entertainment all round the world was influenced by it, and famous people, including presidents, queued to be sent up on it, but a revival in 1977 produced hardly a ripple of interest.
DAN ROWAN, DICK MARTIN, GOLDIE HAWN, RUTH BUZZI, LILY TOMLIN, JOANNE WORLEY, TERESA GRAVES, ARTE JOHNSON, JUDY CARNE
† Emmys 1967, 1968: best variety show.

laugh track. Fake laughter added electronically to a comedy show which has been recorded without an audience. One of the banes of TV.

Laurel and Hardy. A five-minute cartoon series developed by Larry Harmon was syndicated in the US in 1966, with voices by John McGeorge and Larry Harmon. It did not match the originals, whose comedies have been playing on TV around the world since 1948.

Laurence Olivier Presents: see The Best Play of . . .

Laurenson, James (1935–). New Zealand actor who made his greatest mark on TV as the Aborigine detective in *Boney*, made in Australia.

Laurie, John (1897–1980). Fruity Scottish actor, a staple of British films for 30 years. On TV, best remembered as the doom-laden undertaker in DAD'S ARMY.

Laurie, Piper (1932–) (Rosetta Jacobs). Diminutive American leading lady who graduated into a character actress. TV series: *Skag*. TV movies: *In the Matter of Karen Ann Quinlan*, *Rainbow*, *The Bunker*, *Mae West*, *The Thorn Birds*, *Love*, *Mary*.

Lauter, Ed (1940–). Tough-looking American actor, usually in hard-boiled roles. *Last Hours before Morning*, *The Clone Master*, *The Jericho Mile*, *The Boy Who Drank Too Much*, *Undercover with the KKK*, *Guyana Tragedy*, *Rooster*, *The Three Wishes of Billy Grier*, *The Cartier Affair*.

Lavender, Ian (1946–). British juvenile actor who played the shy Private Pike in *Dad's Army* but subsequently found plum roles hard to locate: *The Glums*, *In Living Memory*.

Laverne and Shirley
US 1976–   × 25m colour
ABC/Paramount/Miller–Miklis/Henderson (Garry Marshall)
The adventures of two girls working in a Milwaukee brewery in the late fifties. Smileable spin-off from *Happy Days*.
cr Garry Marshall, Lowell Ganz, Mark Rothman *m* Charles Fox
Penny Marshall, Cindy Williams

The Law **
US 1974 120m colour TVM
NBC/Universal (William Sackheim)
The work of a public defender in a murder trial.
Harsh, sometimes quite brilliant drama documentary which goes on too long.
w Joel Oliansky *d* John Badham
Judd Hirsch, John Beck, Bonnie Franklin, Sam Wanamaker

The Law and Mr Jones
US 1960–1 45 × 25m bw
ABC/Four Star/Saxon
An honest lawyer helps the poor and needy. Obvious but quite appealing family drama.

cr Sy Gomberg
James Whitmore, Janet De Gore

Law and Order *
US 1976 144m approx. colour TVM
Paramount/PA (E. Jack Neuman)

An Irish Catholic New York cop has troubles stemming from the past as well as the present. Heavy-going if well-detailed crime chronicle with a confusing technique which means that the star always seems either too old or too young.

w E. Jack Neuman, *novel* Dorothy Uhnak *d* Marvin Chomsky *ph* Jack Marquette

Darren McGavin, Suzanne Pleshette, Will Geer, Art Hindle, Keir Dullea, Robert Reed, James Olson, Teri Garr, Biff McGuire, Jeanette Nolan

'An engrossing story of cop manners and morals.' – Judith Crist

Law and Order
GB 1978 4 × 75m colour

Four overlapping, uncompromising and disconcerting plays looking at crime and punishment through the eyes respectively of detective, criminal, lawyer and prison officer, with the implication that there was little to choose between them as flawed human beings. To make sure it registered, the final episode crammed every evil of the penal system into a few weeks of one man's sentence, thus arousing suspicions, at least in retrospect, that the exercise might not be wholly disinterested. Written by G. F. Newman; directed by Leslie Blair; produced by Tony Garnett; for BBC.   PP

Law of the Land
US 1976 96m colour TVM
NBC/Quinn Martin (John Wilder)

A frontier lawman searches for a psychopath with a vendetta against prostitutes.

Murky pilot for an unmade series to be called *The Deputies* which bid fair to expose the seamy side of the old west. A very similar script, substituting nuns for prostitutes, was used for the *Most Wanted* pilot.

w John Wilder, Sam Rolfe *d* Virgil W. Vogel *ph* William Spencer *m* John Parker

Jim Davis, Don Johnson, Cal Bellini, Nicholas Hammond, Darlene Carr, Barbara Parkins, Moses Gunn, Andrew Prine, Glenn Corbett

The Law of the Plainsman
US 1959 30 × 25m bw
NBC/Four Star/Cardiff

In 1885, an Apache is Marshal of part of New Mexico.

Adequate western.

Michael Ansara

Lawbreaker
aka: *Lee Marvin Presents Lawbreaker*
US 1963 32 × 25m bw
UA/Rapier/Maurice Unger

Dramatizations of actual criminal cases. Efficient latter-day *Crime Does Not Pay*.

host Lee Marvin

Lawford, Peter (1923–84). British leading man of the forties, in Hollywood since childhood. TV series: *Dear Phoebe, The Thin Man*. TV movies: *How I Spent My Summer Vacation, A Step Out of Line, Deadly Hunt, Ellery Queen: Don't Look Behind You, Phantom of Hollywood*.

The Lawgiver: see Moses

The Lawless Years *
US 1959–60 52 × 25m bw
Jack Chertok/NBC

A New York cop battles lawlessness in the twenties.

Another network's answer to *The Untouchables*. Not bad, but not very factual; allegedly based on the memoirs of a police lieutenant named Barney Ruditsky.

James Gregory

Lawley, Sue (1946–). British presenter, long with BBC and especially associated with *Nationwide*.

Lawman
US 1958–61 156 × 25m bw
Warner

Cases of the Marshal of Laramie.

Absolutely standard TV western, and very entertaining in its time.

John Russell, Peter Brown, Peggie Castle

Lawman without a Gun
aka: *This Man Stands Alone* (74m version)
US 1979 96m colour TVM
CBS/EMI (Roger Gimbel)

A black civil rights activist runs for sheriff in a southern town.

Self-conscious anti-racist melodrama.

w/d Jerrold Freedman *ph* Tak Fujimoto *m* Fred Karlin

Lou Gossett Jnr, Clu Gulager, Barry Brown, James McEachin, Mary Alice

Lawrence, D. H. (1885–1930). British novelist whose works have been variously dramatized for television. In 1966–7 Granada (GB) presented a series of 11 60-minute plays adapted from his stories; produced by Margaret Morris, the titles were as follows:

The White Stocking (*w* James Saunders, *d* Claude Whatham)

Daughters of the Vicar (*w* Peter Eckersley, *d* Gerald Dynevor)

New Eve and Old Adam (*w* James Saunders, *d* Gerald Dynevor)

Samson and Delilah (*w* John Hale, *d* Peter Plummer)

Tickets Please and *Monkey Nuts* (*w* James Saunders, *d* Claude Whatham)

The Blind Man (*w* Ken Taylor, *d* Claude Whatham)

Jimmy and *The Desperate Woman* (*w* Peter Eckersley, *d* Gerald Dynevor)

Two Blue Birds and *In Love* (*w* James Saunders, *d* Desmond Davis)

Strike Pay and *Her Turn* (*w* John Hale, *d* Richard Everitt)

The Blue Moccasins (*w* James Saunders, *d* Desmond Davis)

Mother and Daughter (*w* Patrick Garland, *d* Richard Everitt)

At the time I thought: 'For someone who preached love, Lawrence was extraordinarily intolerant of those lacking in love. The condemnation spat out in *Daughters of the Vicar* – "He's incomplete, like a six-months child" – would be an image of pity, not scorn, from any other writer.' Nearly 20 years later I felt the same when watching Alan Plater's play about Lawrence and Frieda Weekley, *Coming Through,* which see. What an unpleasant cove he must have been.

Earlier, *The White Stocking* was filmed (by Alan Tarrant) as *The Silk Stocking* in 1955 for ATV's Theatre Royal series. Lawrence's own play *The Widowing of Mrs Holroyd* was produced by Granada (*d* Claude Whatham) in 1961. *Sons and Lovers* was a successful BBC serial in 1981. *The Captain's Doll* was a BBC/Primetime co-production, *w* James Saunders, *d* Claude Whatham, *p* Louis Marks, with Jeremy Irons, Gila von Weitershausen, Jane Lapotaire. *The Boy in the Bush* (1984) came from an Australian novel in which Lawrence is supposed to have had a hand.   PP

Lawrence, Steve (1935–) (Sidney Leibowitz). American popular singer, usually with his wife Eydie Gorme.

Lawrence, Vernon (1940–). British comedy expert, producer–director of all YTV's Eric Chappell comedies, *Only When I Laugh, Rising Damp, The Bounder, Duty Free* and *Home to Roost.* Now Controller of Light Entertainment at YTV.   PP

Lawson, Sarah (1928–). Fresh-looking British leading lady of the fifties; by 1978 she had graduated to prison governess in *Within these Walls.*

Layton, George (1943–). Cheerful British light actor who took over the lead in *Doctor in the House* and was in *The Shillingbury Tales;* also wrote or co-wrote many series episodes.

The Laytons (US 1948). Early black domestic comedy series for the Dumont network; with Amanda Randolph.

The Lazarus Syndrome
US 1978 74m colour TVM
ABC/Viacom/Blinn–Thorpe (Robert Schlitt)

A black surgeon treats a journalist with a heart attack; he later recovers and becomes hospital administrator.

Slick pilot for a series which proved shortlived.

w William Blinn *d* Jerry Thorpe *ph* Jacques Marquette *m* Billy Goldenberg

Lou Gossett Jnr, Ronald Hunter, E. G. Marshall, Sheila Frazier

'Sudsy up to the eyeballs.' – *Daily Variety*

'Despite the high malarkey count and the trumped-up conflicts, this hospital tale hooked me and hauled me in.' – Robert MacKenzie, *TV Guide*

Le Carré, John (1931–) (David Cornwell).
Foremost spy-fiction writer whose original work for television has been eclipsed by later adaptations from his novels. *Dare I Weep, Dare I Mourn* was a 1966 attempt by Rediffusion to make the international TV film market with a 50-minute story of a ploy to smuggle a VIP refugee from East to West Berlin in the guise of a corpse. James Mason had little to do but breathe heavily and look alarmed. *End of the Line* (Thames *Armchair Theatre,* 1970) confined Ian Holm and Robert Harris in a locked railway compartment as agent facing double-agent in a cerebral game of strip poker, each player peeling off a layer of cover until one or another tells the truth. Skilful but just a little too arid. In 1979 Arthur Hopcraft's

dramatization of TINKER, TAILOR, SOLDIER, SPY made Le Carré a worldwide hit. *Smiley's People* (1982) followed.   PP

† Le Carré was subject of a *South Bank Show* profile 1983.

Le Mesurier, John (1912–83). Diffident-seeming British character actor, a familiar face from the mid-fifties. Acclaimed for his performance in TRAITOR; better known as Sergeant Wilson in DAD'S ARMY.

Le Vien, Jack (1918–). American documentary producer who persuaded Winston Churchill to give his consent to the series THE VALIANT YEARS, and a few specials, then made them very efficiently.

Leachman, Cloris (1928–). Angular but appealing American character actress willing to try her hand at anything. Series include *Lassie, The Mary Tyler Moore Show, Phyllis*. TV movies: *Silent Night Lonely Night, Suddenly Single, Haunts of the Very Rich, A Brand New Life, Crime Club, Dying Room Only, The Migrants, Hitchhike, Thursday's Game, Death Sentence, Someone I Touched, A Girl Named Sooner, Death Scream, The New Original Wonder Woman, It Happened One Christmas, The Long Journey Back, Backstairs at the White House, Willa, The Acorn People, Advice to the Lovelorn, Mrs R's Daughter, The Woman Who Willed a Miracle, The Demon Murder Case, Deadly Intentions*.

Leacock, Philip (1917–). British director who in the fifties seemed especially sensitive to subjects involving children; he went to the States and became a prolific director of TV episodes, including *Route 66, Gunsmoke, Hawaii Five-O*. TV movies: *The Birdmen, When Michael Calls, The Daughters of Joshua Cabe, Baffled, The Great Man's Whiskers, Dying Room Only, Key West, Killer on Board*, etc.

❋ **Lear, Norman** (1928–). American writer and producer who in the seventies scored enormous hits with a series of taped half-hour comedies, mostly on ethnic themes and always extending the borders of the permissible. ALL IN THE FAMILY, MAUDE, SANFORD AND SON, MARY HARTMAN, MARY HARTMAN, etc. Less successful were *Good Times, The Jeffersons, One Day at a Time, The Dumplings, Hot*l Baltimore, All's Fair* and *The Nancy Walker Show*.

Learned, Michael (*c* 1937–). American character actress who became a star as Mom in *The Waltons* and later *Nurse* (Emmy 1982). TV movies include *Hurricane, Widow, Little Mo, A Christmas Without Snow*.

'When his life was filled with pain, one small runaway boy gave him the courage to smile!'
Leave 'Em Laughing *
US 1981 96m colour TVM
CBS/Charles Fries (Julian Fowles)

A Chicago circus clown who enjoys entertaining children comes to terms with the fact that he is dying.
It sounds dreadful, but is saved from mawkishness by the star's vigorous performance.

w Cynthia Mandelberg and Peggy Chantler Dick, based on the life of Jack Thum *d* Jackie Cooper *ph* Howard Schwartz *m* Jimmie Haskell

MICKEY ROONEY, ELISHA COOK JNR, Anne Jackson, Allen Goorwitz, Red Buttons, William Windom

Leave it to Beaver
US 1957–62 234 × 25m bw
CBS/Revue

Domestic sitcom with emphasis on two mischievous small boys.
Small-town America as the clichés would have it – and extremely popular.

Jerry Mathers, Hugh Beaumont, Barbara Billingsley

Leave it to Charlie *
GB 1978   × 25m colour (VTR)
Granada (Eric Prytherch)

Adventures of an accident-prone young insurance agent in Bolton.
Cheerful character comedy with a genuine Lancashire feel, occasionally stymied by rather thin plots.

cr H. V. Kershaw *d* Eric Prytherch *m* Derek Hilton

David Roper, Peter Sallis, Jean Heywood, Gwen Cherrill

Leave it to Larry (US 1952). Half-hour domestic comedy series for CBS, with Eddie Albert as a shoe salesman and Ed Begley as his domineering father-in-law and employer.

Leave Yesterday Behind
US 1978 96m colour TVM
ABC Circle (Paul Harrison)

A young paraplegic retires bitterly from the world, but a young girl shows him he can still find love.
Yawnworthy if pretty-looking love story, its very obvious plot line dragged out interminably.

w Paul Harrison d Richard Michaels ph Ric Waite m Fred Karlin

John Ritter, Carrie Fisher, Buddy Ebsen, Ed Nelson, Carmen Zapata, Robert Urich

'A 78 disc love song played at 33 rpm.' – *Daily Variety*

Leaver, Don (1929–). British director with a flair for atmospheric thrillers, though has also followed James Cellan Jones on *A Fine Romance*, *Mitch* and *Bird of Prey II* (1984), *The Detective* (1985), *Unnatural Causes* (1986).   PP

Leaving (GB 1984–5; 13 × 30m). Newly divorced couple continue to be drawn to each other, despite the presence of new attractions. One of Carla Lane's increasingly solemn sitcoms, but though striving to be true and painful about the end of a marriage still willing to drop everything for a smart line. Keith Barron, Susan Hampshire, produced by John B. Hobbs for BBC.   PP

Lee Harvey Oswald – Assassin (GB 1966). Ponderous dramatization of the train of events that ended with President Kennedy's assassination and Oswald's own mysterious death a day or two later, derived – via a German documentary – from the Warren Report on the affair. My view then: 'That every line in the script can be substantiated in the Warren Report merely proves that the Warren Report wasn't written by Arthur Miller.' With Tony Bill as Oswald. Written by Rudolph Cartier and Reed de Rouen, from the original by Felix Lutzkendorf; directed and produced by Rudolph Cartier; for BBC.
PP

Lee, Joanna (19 –). American writer. *Cage without a Key*, *I Want to Keep My Baby*, *Mary Jane Harper Died Last Night*, *Tell Me My Name*, *Mulligan's Stew*, *Like Normal People*, *The Love Tapes*, *Children of Divorce*, *Hear Me Cry*.

Lee Marvin Presents Lawbreaker: see Lawbreaker

Leeds United! (GB 1974). A BBC *Play for Today*, Colin Welland's great oratorio to clothing workers who struck more or less

spontaneously in 1970 for an extra bob an hour – an increase which, even if they'd got it, would have been negated before the year was out by the escalation of prices and big boys' wages which was just getting under way. Proceedings went on at great length, repetitively, mostly at the tops of voices. The victims were the heroes. The unions were, if anything, worse than the unlikely employers. The Communists fared no better. Welland apparently cobbled it all together from local oral history, which is the way not to write a play by Colin Welland.   PP

Leeming, Jan (1942–). British newsreader and workaholic (seems on duty every weekend and Bank Holiday). Formerly in Australia and NZ.

The Legend of Custer: see Custer

The Legend of Jesse James *
US 1965 26 × 25m bw
ABC/TCF (David Weisbart)
The famous outlaw is presented as a kind of western Robin Hood.
Quite a slick and attractive series which didn't sustain.

cr Samuel A. Peeples

Chris Jones, Allen Case, Ann Doran

The Legend of Lizzie Borden *
US 1975 100m colour TVM
Paramount (George LeMaire)
An account of the Fall River murders of 1892, when the daughter of the house was suspected of having forty whacks at each of her parents . . .
A decently made film which takes a long time to produce no fresh evidence, and goes a bit overboard on the axe murders.

w William Bast d Paul Wendkos m Billy Goldenberg

Elizabeth Montgomery, Fritz Weaver, Katherine Helmond, Ed Flanders, Don Porter, Fionnuala Flanagan, John Beal

The Legend of Robin Hood (GB 1977). BBC serial in 12 25-minute segments, adopting a realistic approach to the familiar folk tale and alienating most of its audience in the process. With Martin Potter, Diane Keen, Paul Darrow. Written by Alistair Bell, Robert Banks Stewart, David Butler and Alexander Barron; directed by Eric Davidson; produced by Jay Rayvid.

The Legend of the Golden Gun
US 1979 96m colour TVM
NBC/Columbia/Bennett–Katleman (James D. Parriott)

In the old west, an innocent farmboy takes revenge on raider Quantrell, whose gang murdered his parents.
Uncertain spoof of the Lone Ranger, neither funny nor thrilling enough.

w James D. Parriott d Alan J. Levi ph Gerald Perry Finnermann m Jerold Immel

Jeff Osterhage, Carl Franklin, Hal Holbrook, Keir Dullea, Michelle Carey, R. G. Armstrong

'Whichever way it's supposed to be, there aren't many laughs or very much of interest.'
– Daily Variety

The Legend of Valentino
US 1975 100m colour TVM
Spelling–Goldberg

The alleged life and loves of the silent screen's sex idol.
A foolish fantasy which scarcely touches truth at all.

w/d Melville Shavelson ph Arch Dalzell

Franco Nero, Suzanne Pleshette, Yvette Mimieux, Judd Hirsch, Lesley Warren, Milton Berle, Harold J. Stone

The Legion Hall Bombing (GB 1978). A BBC Play for Today reconstructing the trial, under the Emergency Powers Act, of two Belfast youths accused of planting a bomb which went off at a British Legion whist drive in the city. Because of an editorial statement which the authors wished to superimpose the play was not transmitted during the season for which it had been produced, and only went out – minus this message – during a run otherwise made up of repeats. Caryl Churchill, who had edited the script from transcripts of the original case, and Roland Joffé, director, both took their names off the credits, evidently more concerned about the politics of the production than its content. PP

Legs. A 1978 one-hour pilot for a show about show-girls in Las Vegas. It was previously a failure as Mrs Blansky's Beauties; the title was eventually changed to Who's Minding the Kids? The producer so keen on his project is Garry Marshall.

Legs *
US 1983 96m colour TVM
ABC/Comworld (Franklin R. Levy, Ron Parker)

Stories behind the scenes with the Radio City Music Hall Rockettes.
Slick, predictable look at the careers of three chorus girls.

w, d Jerrold Freedman ph Allen Daviau

John Heard, Sheree North, Gwen Verdon, David Marshall Grant, Maureen Teefy

Lehman, Leo (1926–). Polish-born British dramatist who started with The Common Room, set among the teachers of a comprehensive school, and went on to produce some sensitive and often funny love stories, notably Late Summer Affair (1962). Since the early seventies he has written almost exclusively for West German Television, where his strongly anti-Left views are better appreciated. PP

Leibman, Ron (1938–). American leading actor, in series KAZ (Emmy 1979). TV movies: The Art of Crime, A Question of Guilt, Rivkin Bounty Hunter.

Leigh, Janet (1927–) (Jeanette Morrison). American leading lady of the fifties. TV movies: The Monk, Honeymoon with a Stranger, The House on Greenapple Road, The Deadly Dream, Murdock's Gang, Murder at the World Series, Telethon. Series: Hagen.

Leigh, Mike (19 –). British director specializing in improvisation, latterly devising comedies down among the dimmest and least appealing members of society which many critics find patronizing. Nuts in May (1976); The Kiss of Death (1977); Abigail's Party (1977); Grown-Ups (1980); Home Sweet Home (1982), Meantime (1983).

Leighton, Margaret (1922–76). British stage and film actress who in 1970 won an Emmy as Gertrude in HAMLET for Hallmark Hall of Fame. Also appeared in Frankenstein: The True Story.

Leisen, Mitchell (1898–1974). Stylish American film director who in his last years directed a few episodes of Twilight Zone, The Man from UNCLE, Wagon Train, etc.

Leland, David (19 –). British actor (Purvis in Jewel in the Crown), theatre director and author. For TV, Psy Warriors, Beloved Enemy and the screenplays of Central's four films about education beginning with Birth of a Nation, 1983.

Lena, O My Lena *
GB 1960 50m bw

Student working in factory during the vacation falls for one of the girls, whose kisses he can have but whose heart stays with her lorry-driver steady. Another clash of cultures from Alun Owen in which every endearment, every giggle, every uncomprehending stare was a reminder of the invisible ditch between the lovers. Peter McEnery's television debut; also with Billie Whitelaw, Colin Blakely. Directed by Ted Kotcheff; produced by Sydney Newman; for ABC (*Armchair Theatre*).   PP

Leonard, Hugh (1926–   ). Irish writer active in British television in the sixties, now working mainly for the Irish theatre, but a funny comedy of small-town bachelors, *The Virgins*, was a hit in 1974. *The Little World of Don Camillo* (1981). *Strumpet City* for RTE same year, episodes of *The Irish R.M.*   PP

Leonard, Sheldon (1907–   ) (Sheldon Bershad). American character actor who turned to producing TV shows and made quite a success of it: *I Spy*, *My Friend Tony*, *Big Eddie* (also acted). TV movies: *Top Secret*, *The Islander*.

Lester, Dick (1932–   ). American film director in Britain; started his rise to fame in TV, especially with the *Goon Shows* of the fifties.

Les Misérables: see under Misérables

Let Me Speak (GB 1964–5). Malcolm Muggeridge challenging youthful members of ardent minority groups on their beliefs and in one programme, when the tables were turned and he found himself defending Christianity to a bunch of young humanists, indicating for the first time the road to television sainthood he was about to tread. Young fascists were excluded from this BBC series, an instance of censorship often omitted from complaints about editorial control in television.   PP

Let There Be Love (GB 1982). Foolproof half-hour comedy series from Thames based on the old chestnut about the smoothie offering marriage to a young widow with three children and a large dog. One-liners and mistaken identities abound. With Paul Eddington, Nanette Newman. Written by Johnnie Mortimer and Brian Cooke.

Let's Go Naked * (GB 1979; 50m; colour). Delirious edition of the BBC human affairs miscellany *Man Alive* devoted to the – literally – spreading cult of naturism. From my review: 'On the evidence here the British bottom is already the equal of the German bottom and poised to challenge even the Dutch bottom. Adam Clapham's film was sober, responsible, repetitive and a great public service. It should have reassured all individualists that any holiday depending on everyone doing the same thing – whether surfing, exploring, being instructed in archaeology or taking their clothes off – is not for them.' Reporter, John Pitman.   PP

Let's Make a Deal. Long-running game show, on NBC several times a week from 1963, in which compere Monty Hall dares successful contestants to risk their winnings for even more loot. For some obscure reason he also encourages the contestants to dress in weird clothes. America loves it.

Let's Murder Vivaldi (GB 1968). David Mercer comedy of manners, written (in his own words) 'rather like a string quartet, very tight and formal'. Among other activities, Glenda Jackson is unloading her lover Denholm Elliott. Directed by Alan Bridges; produced by Graeme McDonald; for BBC (*Wednesday Play*).   PP

Let's Switch
US 1975 74m colour TVM
Universal (Bruce Johnson)
A woman's magazine editor and her old friend, a suburban housewife, decide to change places.
Smooth, predictable comedy.
w Peter Lefcourt, Chubby Williams, Sid Arthur, Ruth Brooks Flippen *d* Alan Rafkin *m* Harry Geller
Barbara Eden, Barbara Feldon, George Furth, Richard Schaal, Pat Harrington, Joyce Van Patten

The Letter *
US 1981 96m colour TVM
ABC/Warner/Hajeno (George Eckstein)
The wife of a Singapore plantation owner kills an 'intruder' who turns out to have been her lover.
This reliable vehicle for a star actress was immaculately filmed in 1940 by William Wyler and this is only a reach-me-down version, but the acting sees it through.
w Lawrence B. Marcus, *story* W. Somerset Maugham *d* John Erman
Lee Remick, Ronald Pickup, Jack Thompson, Jon Finch, Soon-Teck Oh, Kieu Chinh

'They didn't realize how much they loved their husbands – until they were faced with losing them!'

A Letter to Three Wives

US 1985 96m colour TVM

NBC/TCF/Michael Filerman (Karen Moore)

Three wives receive a letter from a friend to say that she has gone off with one of their husbands.

Uninspired updating of the 1949 semi-classic movie.

w Sally Robinson   d Larry Elikann   ph Laszlo George   m Johnny Mandel

Loni Anderson, Michele Lee, Stephanie Zimbalist, Ben Gazzara, Charles Frank, Michael Gross, Ann Sothern

'With edges softened, less pronounced performances, vid version suffices as a diverting morality tale.' – *Daily Variety*

The Letters *

US 1972 73m colour TVM

Spelling–Goldberg

Three important letters are delayed a year in delivery.

Multi-mini-drama, all quite watchable in its predictable way.

w Ellis Marcus, Hal Sitowitz, James G. Hirsch   d Gene Nelson, Paul Krasny

Barbara Stanwyck, John Forsythe, Dina Merrill, Ida Lupino, Leslie Nielsen, Ben Murphy, Jane Powell

Letters from Three Lovers

US 1973 74m colour TVM

Spelling–Goldberg

More delayed letters have dramatic consequences.

Success means a reprise.

w Ann Marcus, Jerome Kass   d John Erman

Barry Sullivan, June Allyson, Ken Berry, Juliet Mills, Martin Sheen, Belinda Montgomery, Robert Sterling

'Everyone knows what it's like to lose at love. But it's what you learn from it all that lets you love again!'

Letting Go

US 1985 96m colour TVM

ABC/ITC/Adam (Ervin Zavada)

A man in love with his wife is lost when she dies, but picks up with a girl who has been abandoned by her lover.

Would-be with-it, actually rather witless modern love story which seems at the end to have been mostly padding.

w Charlotte Brown   d Jack Bender   ph Rexford Metz   m Lee Holdridge

John Ritter, Sharon Gless, Joe Cortese, Kit McDonough

Levene, Philip (19   –   ). British writer, especially associated with *The Avengers*, to which he contributed most of the macabre stories.

Levenson, Sam (1911–80). American ex-schoolmaster who in the fifties was a popular talker, compere and light comedian.

Levin, Bernard (1928–   ). British journalist who made his name as a boy critic of ITV in its earlier days, for the *Manchester Guardian*. As a performer gained notoriety on *TWTWTW* with a series of outspoken confrontations with groups of farmers, nuclear disarmers, etc, during one of which he was famously sprayed with water from a plastic lemon. Another time a member of the studio audience took a swing at him, without connecting. Apart from panel spots on *Face the Music* has lately restricted his appearances to intermittent series of interviews under the title *The Levin Interview*, usually profound and increasingly concerned with spiritual rather than worldly matters. But *Hannibal's Footsteps* (1985) brought him down – or up – to earth again.

Levinson, Richard (1934–   ). American writer–producer, almost always with William Link. Together they created *Columbo* and *Mannix*, though many other attempts at series failed. TV movies include *My Sweet Charlie* (Emmy 1970), *Sam Hill*, *That Certain Summer*, *Savage*, *Partners in Crime*, *The Gun*, *Ellery Queen*, *The Storyteller*.

Levkas Man

GB/West Germany/Australia 1980

6 × 50m colour

Portman/Studio Hamburg/Australian Broadcasting Commission

A famous archaeologist is missing in Greece, and smuggling seems to be involved.

Muddled and styleless transcription of a pot-boiling novel; of no absorbing interest.

w Peter Yeldham, *novel* Hammond Innes   d Carl Schultz

Robert Coleby, Marius Goring, Kenneth Cope, Despo, Takis Emmanuel, Cyril Luckham

Lewis and Clark: see Gabe and Guich

Lewis, Emmanuel (1971–   ). Black, chubby American child star who achieved instant fame as *Webster*. At the age of 12 he was only 40 inches tall.

Lewis, Jerry: see Martin, Dean and Lewis, Jerry

Lewis, Robert Michael (19 –). American director, fairly adept at TV movies: *The Astronaut*, *The Alpha Caper*, *Message to My Daughter*, *Money to Burn*, *Pray for the Wildcats*, *The Day the Earth Moved*, *The Invisible Man*, *Guilty or Innocent*, *The Night They Took Miss Beautiful*, *Ring of Passion*.

Lewis, Robert Q. (1921–). American TV personality of the fifties, usually as host or panellist.

Lewis, Shari (1930–). Canadian ventriloquist and puppeteer whose most memorable creation is 'Lamb Chop'.

The Liars *
GB 1966 20 × 50m bw

Drama series ingeniously strung together from short stories of the twenties and thirties, and peopled by a constant group of characters. William Mervyn led the company of actors playing same. Written by Philip Mackie and Hugh Leonard; directed by Gordon Cunliffe and David Boisseau; produced by Philip Mackie; for Granada.   PP

Liberace (1919–) (Wladziu Valentino Liberace). American pianist and entertainer, all glitter and extravagance. Derided in the fifties, he showed his tenacity and in the eighties was still a big star of specials and cabaret.

PP (1959): 'Never mind about the four-minute mile. Hail the four-minute Tchaikovsky Concerto No. 1 by last night's pianist in the Palladium show. He wore a shimmery jacket with lace at the cuffs, and later tails and a diamanté bow tie. Apart from playing the piano, which for some reason had a transparent lid, he sang several songs and danced a few steps. At the end, he blew out the electric candles in his candelabra. He is certainly a performer. Whether what he performs is worth either the adulation or the scorn it seems to prompt is another matter.'

The Liberators * (GB 1954). A landmark in television drama, a 'big' original play by Iain MacCormick, one of a cycle of four (THE PROMISED YEARS), which made an impact on the early TV audience exceeded only by *1984* the same year. In the closing days of World War II in Italy an Allied patrol joins forces with local partisans to carry out an operation which will bring victory nearer – but at the expense of the partisans' own kinsfolk. Produced by Alvin Rakoff; for BBC.

The play was revived in 1960, when it lost some of its original impact, not so much because it was a repeat as because both attitudes to war and tastes in television storytelling had changed.   PP

The Liberty Man *
GB 1958 90m bw

Granada's first real excursion into native, purpose-written television drama, and a bit of a landmark. Adapted by Leo Lehman from a novel by Gillian Freeman, *The Liberty Man* was an adult love story of the times that sailed so close to the truth that when it did tell one or two fibs they hurt. Richard Pasco was a sailor on leave from the lower deck, Jane Barrett the pretty schoolteacher who taught his kid sister. He carried her case to the station and an attachment was born that precariously spanned the barriers of class and culture. Directed by Lionel Brett.   PP

library film. Another phrase for stock shot: one not made at the time of the production, but taken from a shelf.

License to Kill *
US 1984 96m colour TVM
CBS/Marian Rees/Dorothea Petrie

Parents of a girl killed by a drunk driver seek justice or revenge.
Solidly carpentered problem drama with more detail than is usual in a telepic.
w William A. Schwartz *d* Jud Taylor *ph* Robert Jessup *m* Laurence Rosenthal
James Farentino, Peggy Fuller, Don Murray, Millie Perkins, Ari Meyers, Donald Moffat, Jacqueline Brookes, Kristen Bigard

Licking Hitler (GB 1978). David Hare's World War II story about a sheltered girl working in the rackety world of propaganda, vivid and compelling but imposing on a wartime community attitudes of the author's own day, thereby distracting from what could have been an acute examination of the ethics of psychological warfare. With Kate Nelligan, Bill Patterson. Produced by Margaret Matheson; for BBC (*Play for Today*). See also *The Imitation Game*.   PP

Lidsville
US 1971 17 × 25m colour (VTR)
ABC/Sid and Marty Krofft

A boy is lost in a fantasy land where all the characters are hats.
Ingenious but limited modern fairy tale.

The Lie
GB 1970 90m colour
BBC Largest Theatre in the World (Graeme McDonald)

Ingmar Bergman's contribution to the simultaneous Eurodrama ideal, exporting to the other countries a very bleak, very Swedish view of sexual and human relations. The British version made this worse by attempting to transfer the scene to Britain as well. My review at the time:

'If they had kept a Scandinavian setting, it might just have got by as a parody of every neurotic Swedish movie ever made. But the names of characters, snatches of overheard radio, and other internal evidence confirmed that it was all supposed to be taking place in our own society, if a section of it that I have never encountered. Not even the children were allowed to smile . . .'

w INGMAR BERGMAN, Paule Britten Austin d Alan Bridges

Gemma Jones, John Carson, Joss Ackland
PP

The Lieutenant
US 1963 29 × 50m bw
NBC/Arena/MGM (Norman Felton)
Stories of a young officer in the peacetime Marines.
Very ho-hum.
Gary Lockwood, Robert Vaughn

Lt Schuster's Wife *
US 1972 73m colour TVM
Universal (Steven Bochco)
When a policeman is killed and slandered, his widow goes into action.
Adequate, well-paced pilot which didn't get anywhere.
w Bernie Kukoff, Steven Bochco d David Lowell Rich m Gil Melle
Lee Grant, Jack Warden, Don Galloway, Paul Burke, Eartha Kitt, Nehemiah Persoff, Murray Matheson

Life After Death (GB 1982; 75m). The BBC Play for Today shaping up to the last taboo – death and bereavement – for the first time since Peter Nichols's *Hearts and Flowers* of 1970, and doing so very intensely. With Dorothy Tutin and Ben Cross, written by Rachel Billington, directed by Anthony Simmons, produced by Innes Lloyd.   PP

The Life and Adventures of Nicholas Nickleby **
GB 1982 3 × 120m, 1 × 180m
Primetime/C4/RM Productions (Colin Callender)
The Royal Shakespeare's marathon Dickens adaptation re-shaped to TV. 'Theatrical setting and theatrical effects,' I wrote, 'combine perfectly well with the mobility of the single video camera, nosing in and out

the action, while the captive audience comes in with cheers, tears, standing ovations, to augment fireside emotions in the big climaxes.'
w David Edgar, from Dickens d Jim Goddard
Roger Rees (as Nicholas), David Threlfall (as Smike), Emily Richard, Jane Downs, John Woodvine   PP
LH: 'I would have thought it worth three stars: lighting, direction and camera placement brought the thing to life in a quite electric way.'

The Life and Assassination of the Kingfish *
US 1977 96m colour TVM
Tomorrow Entertainment (Paul Leaf)/NBC
The career and sudden death in 1937 of aggressive senator Huey Long.
Not an improvement on *All the King's Men*, but as a TV movie fairly commendable.
w/d Robert Collins
ED ASNER, Nicholas Pryor, Diane Kagan, Fred Cook

The Life and Death of Picture Post *
GB 1977 60m colour
BBC (John Ormond)
The rise and fall of an influential picture magazine which was begun in 1938 and at its height during World War II.
Fascinating journalism which collects together, before it's too late, all those involved, including Stefan Lorant, Tom Hopkinson, Fyfe Robertson and James Cameron.
w John Ormond narrator Rene Cutforth

The Life and Legend of Wyatt Earp *
US 1955–60 226 × 25m bw
ABC/Louis F. Edelmann/Wyatt Earp Enterprises
Stories of the Marshal of Tombstone.
A friendly western series with something to please almost everybody.
HUGH O'BRIAN

The Life and Times of David Lloyd George
GB 1981 9 × 60m colour (VTR)
BBC Wales (John Hefin)
Warts-and-all biography of a fiery statesman, with concentration on his love life and religious influences.
Heady stuff, marred by photography picturesquely out of focus.
w Elaine Morgan
Philip Madoc, Lisabeth Miles

The Life and Times of Eddie Roberts
(also known acronymically as 'L.A.T.E.R.')
US 1979 13 × 25m colour
Columbia/Marcstone
An assistant professor of anthropology has a
hectic off-campus life.
A failed attempt at an up-market *Mary
Hartman, Mary Hartman*, with Eddie as a
maladroit Everyman.
cr Ann and Ellis Marcus
Renny Temple, Udana Power, Stephen Parr,
Annie O'Donnell, Allen Case
'Within its framework scenes are enriched
with discussions of the issues of the day, or
about the stuff of life as everyone
experiences it. Family problems, marriage,
divorce, child-raising; health problems,
nutrition, running, cholesterol, meditation;
economics; the high cost of breakfast cereal
and vitamins; consumer problems; sex and
romance, crime and punishment, liberals and
conservatives; VD; life styles, metaphysics,
religions of the world, ESP, yoga, the occult;
the military–industrial complex; the Oedipus
complex; business versus labor; the space
age, the boundaries of the universe, the
meaning of life, life after death; the arts;
nuclear waste; lunch.' – publicity

The Life and Times of Grizzly Adams *
US 1976–7 34 × 50m colour (16mm)
NBC/Sunn Classic
A man escapes to the mountains after an unjust
accusation of murder, and lives there with an
old prospector and a pet bear.
Family fare made to order and
computer-controlled by a Mormon company.
High-class moving wallpaper with neither
animal nor human getting hurt.
m Bob Summers
Dan Haggerty, Denver Pyle
† The real Grizzly Adams was christened John,
and lived from 1812 to 1860. A wandering
trapper scarred by an arctic tiger, he left a wife
and four children in California to live alone in
the mountains. Badly mauled and injured by
years of hard life, he spent his declining days
being exhibited by P. T. Barnum.

The Life and Times of Lord Mount-
batten (GB 1969; 13 × 50m). Prolonged
autobiography-on-film as deliberately chosen
by the Admiral in preference to a conventional
written one, originally set up by Rediffusion
and inherited not altogether rapturously by
Thames when they took over the London
weekday contract. The archive footage, some
from Mountbatten's own hoard, was
remarkable but it was perhaps too early for his

lordship to give other than a fairly official
account of his exploits. Produced by Peter
Morley. Later, Mountbatten recorded some
franker memoirs for his own TV obituary, duly
screened after his assassination by the IRA in
1979.   PP

Life at Stake
GB 1978 8 × 50m colour (VTR)
BBC (Frank Cox)
Drama-documentaries reconstructing kid-
nappings, disasters and other terrorist
incidents of recent years.
Well made but somewhat unnecessary series.

Life Begins at Eighty (US 1950–6). Half-hour
panel game compered by Jack Barry, who
conversed with sprightly octogenarians. The
format was also popular in Britain under Brian
Michie's chairmanship.

Life Begins at Forty (GB 1978). Footling
series of 25-minute comedies from Yorkshire
TV, with Derek Nimmo as a middle-aged
incompetent.

Life for Christine
GB 1980 78m colour
Openly propagandist play based on the case of
a mentally disturbed girl seemingly doomed to
spend the rest of her life in prison, brought to
producer Gus Macdonald's notice by MIND,
an activist association concerned with mental
health. Powerful and effective if a little too
zealous in pointing a finger at those held to
blame. Written by Fay Weldon; directed by
John Goldschmidt; for Granada.   PP

Life Goes to the Movies *
US 1977 150m approx. colour
TCF/Time–Life (Jack Haley Jnr)
The story of America between 1936 and 1972 as
shown in the movies.
A spectacularly well-edited compilation which
gives the genuine flavour of Hollywood's
golden age.
w Richard Schickel *d* Mel Stuart

Life Goes to War *
aka: *The Movies Go to War*
US 1977 96m colour (VTR)
TCF/Time–Life
A companion piece to the above with more
emphasis on newsreels of World War II and the
activities of the movie stars of that period.

Life of an Orchestra ** (GB 1984; 4 ×
50m). Masterly series of peeps behind the
scenes as the London Symphony Orchestra

celebrates its 80th birthday, focusing on one or two key personalities each time. Directed and produced by Jenny Barraclough, for BBC.

A Life of Bliss (GB 1956). Another attempt to transfer a long-running radio comedy to television (BBC). PP: 'Basically there is only one joke – how George Cole puts his foot in it again and again and again. Sometimes it is because he is shy, sometimes because he is muddled, sometimes because he is both . . . in the end it mostly shows how a trivial misunderstanding can be magnified into a trivial misunderstanding.'

The Life of Riley. A half-hour American comedy series which had a season in 1949 with Jackie Gleason and Rosemary de Camp as the not-too-bright suburban riveter (1313 Blue View Terrace, Los Angeles) and his wife. It came back in 1953, and played five seasons, with WILLIAM BENDIX (who had created the character on radio in 1943) and Marjorie Reynolds. The show ran throughout on NBC, and won an Emmy in 1949.

† Catchphrase for Bendix: 'What a revolutin' development this is!'

Life of the Party: see Beatrice

Life on Earth **
GB 1979 13 × 50m colour
BBC (John Sparks)

Sir David Attenborough's rhapsodic but fascinating account of the arrival of living species on Earth, which as he frequently reminded his audience only took place in the comparatively recent moments of its existence as a planet.   PP

Life on the Mississippi *
US 1980 96m colour TVM
KCET/WNET/Nebraska ETV (William Perry)

Reminiscences of Mark Twain's youth as a river pilot.
Beautifully re-created nostalgic anecdotes from Public Broadcasting, first of a projected series of Mark Twain specials.

w Philip Reisman Snr d PETER H. HUNT ph WALTER LASSALLY m William Perry

Robert Lansing, David Knell, James Keane, Donald Madden

'Simply terrif . . . a wondrous world of grace and beauty.' – *Daily Variety*

Life With Father *
US 1954 26 × 25m bw
CBS/McCadden

Life in an upper-middle-class New York household at the turn of the century.
Amiable period comedy which manages a better atmosphere than the expensive film version.

Leon Ames, Lurene Tuttle

Life With Luigi
US 1952 39 × 25m bw
CBS

Problems of an Italian antique dealer in Chicago.
Adequate comedy series from a radio show.

J. Carrol Naish/Vito Scotti, Alan Reed/Thomas Gomez, Jody Gilbert/Muriel Landers, Sig Rumann

Lifeboat (GB 1984; 6 × 30m). Real-life exploits of the Humber lifeboat, filmed by a cameraman (Paul Berriff) who lived for four months in a caravan on its remote site. Produced by John Gau, for BBC.

Lifeline (US 1979). Hard-hitting series of one-hour documentaries from Tomorrow Entertainment, each 50-minute segment following the work of a particular surgeon. Not for the squeamish. Produced and directed by Alfred R. Kelman, it ran to 14 shows. 'As a series for the layman, it has all the charm of a scab lifting. Truth not only is stranger than fiction: it's far grimmer.' – *Daily Variety*

The Light of Experience. Intermittent BBC series of 15-minute direct-to-camera addresses by people who have suffered curious experiences, ordeals, conversions to faith, loss of faith, e.g. British nurse Rita Nightingale on being released from a Bangkok prison; Mrs Daphne Schild on her relationship with her daughter when both were held captive by Sardinian bandits. A religious format of uncommon interest and effectiveness, originally produced by Shirley du Boulay, later by John Wilcox.   PP

Lights Out (US 1949–51). Half-hour dramatic anthology for NBC, hosted by Jack La Rue/Frank Gallop and always presented live. The stories were almost all thunderstorm mysteries.

Like Mom, Like Me
US 1984 96m colour TVM
CBS

A recently separated woman and her teenage daughter cope with their new independence.
Somewhat boringly tearful drama with too little background detail.

w Nancy Lynn Schwartz *d* Michael Pressman

Linda Lavin, Kristy McNichol, Patrick O'Neal

TheLikelyLads ***
GB1965–9 × 30m bw/colour(VTR)
BBC

Escapades of two disaster-prone young men in Northumberland.

The funny side of *Saturday Night and Sunday Morning*, this comedy series made its mark through clever writing and acting.

cr/w IAN LA FRENAIS, DICK CLEMENT

RODNEY BEWES, JAMES BOLAM

† In 1973 came a final series of 26, *Whatever Happened to the Likely Lads?* This took up the story several years later, when Bolam returns from the army to find Bewes married to his girl.
†† An unrepresentative feature film version was released in 1976.

Lillie *
GB1978 13 × 50m colour
LWT(JackWilliams)

The life story of Lillie Langtry, friend of Whistler and Wilde who became a model, a society escort, the mistress of Edward VII and the toast of the American continent.

Irresistible period soap which adopts too plodding a pace in its middle section but as a whole is something of a triumph for all concerned.

w David Butler and John Gorrie *d* John Gorrie, Christopher Hodson, Tony Wharmby

FRANCESCA ANNIS, DENIS LILL (as Edward), PETER EGAN (as Wilde), DON FELLOWS (as Whistler), ANTON RODGERS

'Watching beautiful people behave scandalously is an infectious pastime . . . an invitation to wallow in vicarious luxury: marble palaces, silken gowns, chilled lobsters, warm bosoms.' – Robert MacKenzie, *TV Guide*

PP: 'Much better than you might have expected from David Butler's pedestrian account of Disraeli with which *Lillie* just overlapped. Here, with John Gorrie, he is furnishing a script nicely composed of small but telling domesticities – Langtry (Anton Rodgers) gargling before boarding the marital bed, Lillie gazing for hours through the window of their London rooms, content simply to be there.'

limbo. When applied to scenery, this means no scenery at all, just an illuminated cyclorama suggesting illimitable distance, or black velvet curtains.

Lime Street
US 1985 7 × 50m colour
ABC/Columbia/RJ/Bloodworth-Thomason
Mozark (Linda Bloodworth-Thomason)

An international insurance agency sends its sleuths on the trail of would-be defrauders.

Ho-hum crime series with Washington and Europe for backdrops: never a very happy concept, with too many domestic asides, it got off to a tragic start with the death of one of its young stars in a plane crash.

cr Linda Bloodworth-Thomason

Robert Wagner, JOHN STANDING, Patrick MacNee, Anne Haney, Lew Ayres, Samantha Smith, Maia Brewton

Limehouse. British independent studios (in London's former dockland) and production company headed until 1986 by Jeremy Wallington. Fiction includes video dramas for C4 and the late-night comedy *Coming Next . . .* In preparation: *Impact*, the re-born version of *Compact* with German and French partners. PP

Linda
US1973 74m colour TVM
ABC/Universal (William Frye)

A murderess frames her husband for the death of her lover's wife.

Neat little melodrama which filled most of TV's requirements.

w Merwin Gerard *d* Jack Smight *ph* Leonard J. South *m* John Cacavas

Stella Stevens, Ed Nelson, John McIntire, John Saxon, Ford Rainey, Mary-Robin Redd

The Lindbergh Kidnapping Case *
US1975 156m colour TVM
NBC/Columbia

The 1934 trial of Bruno Hauptmann for the kidnapping and murder of the Lindbergh baby. Lethargic semi-documentary of a famous trial. The film has nothing new to say, and expounds the facts without flair.

w J. P. Miller *d* Leonard Horn

ANTHONY HOPKINS, Cliff de Young, Sian Barbara Allen, Walter Pidgeon, Joseph Cotten, Martin Balsam, Keenan Wynn, Laurence Luckinbill

† Emmy 1975: Anthony Hopkins.
†† In GB the trial was devastatingly analysed by Ludovic Kennedy in *The Airman and the Carpenter*, 1984.

Linden, Hal (1931–) (Harold Lipshitz). Burly, cheerful American performer who made a hit in the title role of *Barney Miller* and also hit the nightclub circuit as a singer.

The Line-Up *
GB title: *San Francisco Beat*
US 1959 18 × 50m bw
CBS/Marjeff
One-hour version of *San Francisco Beat*, snappily made on the actual locations.
An excellent cop show.
Warner Anderson, Tom Tully

Line-Up. Introduced as a kind of genteel preface to the evening's programmes when BBC2 started in 1964, but soon converted to a late-night mulling-over of what had gone by, with the title changed for a while to *Late Night Line-Up*. It could be – and often was – smug and infuriating, but on occasion prompted some valuable set-pieces, as when Dennis Potter extemporized at length on the nature of treason following the transmission of his play *Traitor*. Its three main interviewers, Denis Tuohy, Michael Dean and Joan Bakewell, all went on to fruitful careers elsewhere in broadcasting.
PP

Link, William: see Levinson, Richard

Linkletter, Art (1912–). American talk show host of the fifties, concentrating in his *House Party* series on drawing out ordinary people from the audience to voice their opinions.

Linville, Larry (1939–). American character actor who made a hit in *M*A*S*H* as Hotlips' sneaky fiancé.

The Lion, the Witch and the Wardrobe
US/GB 1978 96m colour
Children's Television Workshop/Bill Melendez
Three children journey through a magic wardrobe to a land where good and evil are personified by a noble lion and a white witch. Unsatisfying and elongated cartoon version of a fantasy for intellectual kids.
w Bill Melendez, David Connell, *books* C. S. Lewis *animation direction* Bill Melendez
'The fantasy seems tired, the concept dry.' – *Daily Variety*
† The programme won an Emmy in the children's section.

Lions Led by Donkeys * (GB 1985; 60m). Last-chance documentary on the disastrous Battle of the Somme in 1916 to draw on testimony from survivors of same, by this time mostly in their nineties. Written by Peter Crookston, directed by Bill Duffy, produced by Brian Harding for Old Pals Productions/C4, the film did not muff the opportunity.
PP

❋ **Lipman, Maureen** (1946–). Entrancing British comedy actress, best known for the sitcom *Agony* but who ought really to be esteemed for the versatility which enabled her to be seen in four totally different performances between Christmas 1984 and New Year's Day 1985, including Shakespeare (*Love's Labour's Lost*) and the biting account of the music hall partnership of Lucan and MacShane, *On Your Way Riley!* In 1986, *All at Number 20*, *Shift Work*.
PP
LH: 'She's a highly competent performer, but I'd have held back the rosette for a year or two.'

Lisa Bright and Dark
US 1972 74m colour TVM
Hallmark
A mentally disturbed teenaged girl has days when she becomes dangerous.
Cheerless case history, rather well acted.
w John Neufeld, from his novel *d* Jeannot Szwarc *m* Rod McKuen
Kay Lenz, Anne Baxter, John Forsythe, Debralee Scott

Lisemore, Martin (1940–77). British TV director whose most notable achievements were *The Pallisers* and *I, Claudius*.

Listen to Your Heart
US 1984 96m colour TVM
CBS (Don Taylor)
Two executives face the pressures of working together while having an affair.
Thin comedy which turns into a shouting duet. Not the best.
w Christopher Beaumont *d* Don Taylor *ph* Jack L. Richards *m* James Di Pasquale
Kate Jackson, Tim Matheson, Cassie Yates, George Coe, Will Nye

Lithgow, John (1945–). American general-purpose actor. *The Oldest Living Graduate*, *The Day After*, *The Glitter Dome*.

A Little Big Business
GB 1964 14 × 25m bw (VTR)
Granada
A young man is taught the furniture business by his father.
Amusing, slightly offbeat, sitcom.
David Kossoff, Francis Matthews

Little, Cleavon (1939–). Black American comic actor often on TV including series *Temperatures Rising*.

A Little Game *
US 1971 73m colour TVM
Universal (George Eckstein)
A man suspects that his 11-year-old stepson
may be homicidal.
Quite a chilling little melodrama.
w Carol Sobieski, *novel* Fielden Farrington *d*
Paul Wendkos *m* Robert Prince
Ed Nelson, Diane Baker, Katy Jurado,
Howard Duff

Little Gloria . . . Happy at Last *
US 1983 2 × 96m colour miniseries
NBC/Metromedia/Edgar J. Scherick
(David A. Nicksay, Justine Heroux)
Events leading up to the 1934 custody trial
for young Gloria Vanderbilt.
Personal tensions among the idle rich,
impeccably presented but sometimes
obscurely narrated.
w William Hanley, *book* by Barbara
Goldsmith *d* WARIS HUSSEIN *ph* TONY IMI
m Berthold Carriere *pd* Stuart Wurtzel
Angela Lansbury, Bette Davis, Christopher
Plummer, Lucy Guttridge, Maureen
Stapleton, Martin Balsam, Glynis Johns,
John Hillerman, Barnard Hughes

Little House on the Prairie *
US 1974–   × 50m colour
NBC/ED FRIENDLY (MICHAEL LANDON)
The struggles of a family of homesteaders to
survive on the American plains a hundred years
ago, as seen through the eyes of the children.
Rather prettified but attractively made and
played version of the books by Laura Ingalls
Wilder.
cr MICHAEL LANDON *m* David Rose
Michael Landon, Melissa Gilbert

Little Ladies of the Night
US 1977 96m colour TVM
ABC/Spelling–Goldberg (Hal Sitowitz)
A pimp turns cop to help teenage prostitutes.
Glum exploitation piece with ideas above its
station.
w Hal Sitowitz *d* Marvin J. Chomsky *ph*
Dennis Dalzell *m* Jerry Fielding
David Soul, Lou Gossett Jnr, Linda Purl,
Clifton Davis, Carolyn Jones, Paul Burke,
Katherine Helmond, Dorothy Malone,
Kathleen Quinlan

Little Lord Fauntleroy *
GB 1981 96m colour TVM
CBS/Norman Rosemont (William Hill)

An American boy becomes an English lord and
melts the heart of his stern grandfather.
Pretty successful restoration of a period piece,
generally avoiding the pitfalls of sentimentality
and holding the interest.
w Blanche Hanalis, *novel* Frances Hodgson
Burnett *d* Jack Gold *ph* Arthur Ibbetson *m*
Allyn Ferguson
RICKY SCHRODER, ALEC GUINNESS, Eric Porter,
Colin Blakely, Connie Booth, Rachel
Kempson
'It will probably again win hearts and earn
tears.' – *Daily Variety*

Little Mo
US 1978 142m colour TVM
NBC/Mark VII (Jack Webb)
A biography of Maureen Connolly, tennis star
who died of cancer.
Tiresomely padded biopic.
w John McGreevey *d* Daniel Waller *ph* Harry
Wolf *m* Billy May, Carl Brandt
Glynnis O'Connor, Michael Learned, Anne
Baxter, Claude Akins, Martin Milner, Anne
Francis, Mark Harmon, Leslie Nielsen, Ann
Doran

A Little Night Music * (GB 1962; 50m).
Pleasing (and unusual for this outlet)
drawing-room comedy by Ronald Mavor as
members of the Edinburgh gentility needle
each other in exquisite Morningside accents
while rehearsing a string quartet. With Lally
Bowers, Paul Curran, Barbara Couper,
Geoffrey Whitehead. Produced by Sydney
Newman; for ABC (*Armchair Theatre*).   PP

The Little People: see The Brian Keith Show

Little Rascals. The TV name for the old *Our
Gang* comedies, made by Hal Roach between
the mid-twenties and the mid-forties, and still
going strong.

Little, Rich (1938–). American impressionist, famous for his Richard Nixon.

Little, Syd (1942–) **and Large, Eddie**
(1942–). British lowbrow comedians and
impressionists in the Abbott and Costello
mould, popular in the late seventies after an
introduction in *Who Do You Do?*

Little Women
US 1978 2 × 96m colour
NBC/Universal (David Victor)
Problems of the March sisters in Concord,
Massachusetts in 1861.

Pallid televersion of an oft-told sentimental tale which needs a lot of cunning to make it live. Here the actors look uncomfortable in their clothes.

w Suzanne Clauser, *novel* Louisa May Alcott d David Lowell Rich *ph* Joseph Biroc *m* Elmer Bernstein

Susan Dey, Meredith Baxter Birney, Ann Dusenberry, Eve Plumb, Dorothy McGuire, Greer Garson, Robert Young, Cliff Potts, William Shatner, William Schallert, Richard Gilliland, Virginia Gregg

'Pristine and gorgeous in aspect, and about as substantial as spun sugar.' – *Daily Variety*

† A short continuing series was attempted in 1979.

The Little World of Don Camillo
GB 1980 13 × 30m colour
BBC (Bill Sellars)

Spirited adaptation of a modern classic about the amiable feud in an Italian village between the wily priest and the communist mayor.

w Hugh Leonard, *books* Giovanni Guareschi d Peter Hammond

Mario Adorf, Brian Blessed

The Littlest Hobo
Canada 1963 57 × 25m bw
McGowan/Canamac

Adventures of a wandering Alsatian dog. Curiously titled, otherwise adequate children's series.

Live Again, Die Again *
US 1974 74m colour TVM
Universal (David Victor)

A woman kept frozen for forty years is revived and cured; returning home, she finds that someone is trying to kill her.
Nuthouse melodrama which early abandons its crionics theme and subjects the audience to every trick in the book: colour filters, distorted sound, surrealist montages, the lot. Unfortunately the plot is not strong enough to stand up to it.

w Joseph Stefano d Richard A. Colla

Donna Mills, Walter Pidgeon, Vera Miles, Geraldine Page, Cliff Potts, Mike Farrell

Live Aid ** (GB/USA 1985). The all-day pop concert relayed from Wembley and Philadelphia to an estimated 1½ billion worldwide audience, certainly reaching 30 million in Britain, or more than half the population, at peak moments. Organized by Bob Geldof, for the world.

Live from Pebble Mill (GB 1983; 5 × 30m live). Another attempt to recapture the thrill of live drama, mostly confusing that elusive quality with the brightly lit studio settings and pert, voluble dialogue of all the crummy, run-of-the-mill scripts of the live era that have long since been forgotten. Only the last playlet, *Japanese Style* by Michael Wall, achieved the right soap-bubble precariousness – and for organizational reasons it was also the only one that had been pre-recorded! Produced by Robin Midgley, for BBC Birmingham. PP

The Liver Birds *. British (BBC) half-hour tape comedy by Lew Schwartz, Myra Taylor and Carla Lane; it ran sporadically from 1969 until 1978. The distaff side of *The Likely Lads*, about the mainly amorous adventures of two lively Liverpool lasses, it originally starred POLLY JAMES and NERYS HUGHES, but there were several changes of cast and approach.

The Lives of Jenny Dolan *
US 1975 100m colour TVM
Paramount/Ross Hunter

A lady journalist investigates four puzzling deaths which prove to be connected.
Sleek, ambitious soaper which doesn't really work.

w Richard Alan Simmons, James Lee d Jerry Jameson *ph* Matthew F. Leonetti *m* Pat Williams

Shirley Jones, Stephen Boyd, John Gavin, Dana Wynter, Stephen McNally, James Darren, David Hedison, Farley Granger, Lynn Carlin, George Grizzard, Ian MacShane, Pernell Roberts, Percy Rodrigues

Lives of the Great Composers. Television loves nothing better. Whether the composers return the affection is another matter but, as Mahler said philosophically, no immortality is bad immortality.

Bach: Colin Nears; *The Cantor of St Thomas's*, 1985
Bartok: Ken Russell; *Bluebeard's Castle*, 1964.
Beethoven: episode of *Biography*, w Ian Curteis, 1970
Berlioz: weird Michael Ayrton film, 1969
Bizet: Christopher Nupen; *Carmen: the Dream and the Destiny*, 1973
Britten: Tony Palmer; *There was a Time*, 1980
Debussy: Ken Russell; *Debussy*, 1965
Delius: Ken Russell; *Song of Summer*, 1968
Elgar: Ken Russell; *Elgar*, 1962
  Jim Berrow; *Hope and Glory*, 1984

Handel: Tony Palmer/John Osborne: *God Rot Tunbridge Wells!*, 1985
Anna Ambrose/Peter Luke: *Honour, Profit and Pleasure*, 1985
Holst: Ken Russell; *The Planets*, 1983.
Messaien: Alan Benson; *The Music of Faith*, 1985.
Puccini: Tony Palmer/Charles Wood: *Puccini*, 1984
Scarlatti: Ann Turner: *Domenico Scarlatti*, 1985
Sibelius: Caspar Wrede, *c* 1968
Stravinsky: Tony Palmer, 1982
Strauss (Johann and family): *The Strauss Family* (series), ATV, 1973
Strauss, Richard: Ken Russell (infamously), 1970
Wagner: Tony Palmer/Charles Wood; *Wagner* (series), 1983
Walton: Tony Palmer; *At the Haunted End of the Day*, 1981
Vaughan Williams: Ken Russell: *South Bank Show*, 1984

Living Apart Together (GB 1983; 90m). Rock star returns to his native Glasgow for funeral of old friend and runs into a marital crisis. A musical Film on Four with real-life performer B. A. Robertson supplying his own songs and glamorously shot by Mark Littlewood to turn Glasgow into 'a Beverly Hills-on-the-Clyde where playboys toss their car keys to the bartender, taxis are whistled up in an instant and the passers-by don't bat an eyelid when everyone slips into a fully-orchestrated musical routine in the window of a music store'. With Barbara Kellerman; written and directed by Charles Gormley.   PP

The Living Body * (GB/France 1984; 26 × 26m). Limb-by-limb, organ-by-organ survey of same, enlivened by graphic presentation, extraordinary internal photography and a nice humour – an episode on the digestive process, for example, was hung on the framework of a robust midday meal being chomped by vineyard workers in the Médoc. British narrators: Derek Cooper and Miriam Margolyes; directed by Stuart Urban, Martin Weitz; written and produced by Karl Sabbagh for Goldcrest/Multimedia/C4 with Antenne II.   PP

Living in the Past (GB 1978). Quaint idea for a selected group of volunteers to live in a simulated Iron Age settlement for a year, quarantined from all contact with the modern world save a camera crew, sound engineer and BBC producer. It yielded eight 50m films.

Producer John Percival had earlier conducted an experiment in which people were dumped in the wilds of Exmoor to see how they could survive on natural resources only, and the prehistoric settlement idea had also been tried briefly in the Orkney Islands for an edition of the BBC *Chronicle* programme in 1957.   PP

Living It Up (GB 1958). Forlorn attempt by A–R to revive on TV the magic fun of Arthur Askey and Richard Murdoch's pre-war radio show *Band Waggon*, even to having them share a penthouse on top of Television House just as 20 years previously they had pretended to live in a flat over Broadcasting House. Unfortunately the script never settled enough to stick with the innocence of 1938 or go for contemporary in-jokes about TV commercials or Armand and Michaela Denis.   PP

The Living Planet * (GB 1984; 13 × 50m). Sir David Attenborough's sequel to his *Life on Earth*, concentrating this time on the interdependence of flora, fauna, geology and climate the world over. A much-loved and admired odyssey weakened by Attenborough's sloppy language ('less' cormorants and 'less' anchovies when he meant 'fewer') and his insistence that only man is fouling up the planet. This may be so, I noted at the time, but the pressure to do so comes not from man as a species but from *men* in their ever-increasing numbers. And short of a nuclear war there wasn't much that could be done about that.   PP
† The series was good-humouredly capped with an epilogue on its making – complete with funny out-takes – by Miles Kington.

Living Proof
US 1983 96m colour TVM
NBC/Proctor and
   Gamble/Melpemone/Telecom (Michael Lepiner)
The career of Hank Williams Jnr, who wrecked several lives as well as his own. Unengrossing saga of an unpleasant fellow.
w I. C. Rapoport, Stephen Kandel *d* Dick Lowry *ph* Robert M. Baldwin Jnr *m* ed. Michael Lloyd
Richard Thomas, Lenora May, Liane Langland, Ann Gillespie, Clu Gulager, Allyn Ann McLerie, Barton Heyman

Living with Uncle Sam * (GB 1985; 10 × 55m). How British expatriates have fared or are faring in the United States. Alan Whicker right back on form in this collection of 30 or 40 case-histories, many of them – as to be expected of Whicker – involving celebrities, successes or Joan Collins; but the best of the lot picking on such unsung, absorbing characters as the refined widow working as an assistant in a Palm Beach jewellery boutique and dreading old age and infirmity. Produced by Jonathan Stedall (who may have had something to do with the improvement), for BBC. PP

Livingstone, Douglas (1934–). British writer specializing in low-life drama such as *I Can't See My Little Willie* (1970), *Everybody Say Cheese* (1971), the South London dynastic saga *Born and Bred* (1979–80). A bit hit-and-missy but often funny. Also, straighter dramatizations, e.g. an excellent *Maria Marten* (1981). Not so good sitcom *Cockles*, 1984, but an excellent serious play about Northern Ireland, *We'll Support You Evermore*, 1985.
PP

Livingstone, Mary (*c* 1903–) (Sadye Marks). American comedienne, widow of Jack Benny; she appeared in most of his radio and TV shows.

Llewellyn-Davies, Melissa (1945–). British documentarist specializing in anthropological subjects, both conventional and unconventional: *Women of Marrakesh*, 1976; *Diary of a Maasai Village* and *Dossers* (*p*), both 1984.

The Lloyd Bridges Show *
US 1962 34 × 25m bw
CBS/Four Star/Loring–Caron

Adventures of a roving international journalist.
Virtually an anthology series, and a good one, in which the star not only hosts in one guise but plays a leading part in another.

Lloyd, Innes (19 –). British drama producer, BBC staff until 1980, with great flair for spotting unusual subjects and promising talent. Gave Stephen Frears, Brian Gibson and Ferdinand Fairfax their first directing assignments in drama. *The Snow Goose* (1971); Alan Bennett's *Day Out* (1972) and *Sunset Across the Bay* (1974); ORDE WINGATE (1976); *An Englishman's Castle* (1978); *Speed King* (1979); FOTHERGILL and *Going Gently* (1981). OBJECTS OF AFFECTION (Alan Bennett season, 1982). REITH (1983), AN ENGLISHMAN ABROAD (1983). PP
'The epitome of what a producer should be, tactful, good-humoured and, above all, an ally.' – Alan Bennett

Lloyd, John (19 –). British comedy expert, ex-radio writer and producer, into television 1979 with *Not the Nine O'Clock News*, *The Hitchhiker's Guide to the Galaxy* (assoc. producer), *The Black Adder*, since 1984 *Spitting Image*. PP

✳ **Loach, Ken** (1936–). Socially conscious British director, often working with producer Tony Garnett. UP THE JUNCTION, CATHY COME HOME, DAYS OF HOPE, *The Price of Coal*, etc. BAFTA award 1967. Lately: *Looks and Smiles*,1982; *Which Side Are You On?*, 1985.
PP

location video recording. Recurring dream in Britain in the sixties of using outside-broadcast facilities to liberate both factual and fictional television from the confines of the studio without the expense and other disadvantages of using film. Video cameras had ten times the latitude of film, needed no supplementary lighting and guaranteed a match with studio scenes. Anglia shot a David Bernstein comedy *They Don't Make Summers Like They Used To* in Suffolk, and immediately illustrated one of the temptations to be avoided. Dwelling too fondly on picture-book villages, director June Howson worked against a script which actually called for a rather spoiled countryside, idyllic only in sentimental fancy. *Armchair Theatre* tried out the idea to better effect with a David Mercer play, *A Way of Living*, set on the north-east coast. The slow opening survey of chimneys, roofs, slag-heaps and seashore told you as much about the people who lived there as twenty minutes of dialogue.
Meanwhile *Festival* (BBC) had made superb, if specialized, use of location VTR for *Murder in the Cathedral* in Canterbury Cathedral and, famously, HAMLET AT ELSINORE. On the documentary front Norman Swallow and Denis Mitchell achieved a notable triumph with A WEDDING ON SATURDAY and embarked upon an ambitious mobile VTR series around Manchester for Granada: *End of a Street*, self-explanatory; *Sharon*, about faith-healing; and *The Entertainers*, a somewhat contrived experiment in which Mitchell and Swallow set up a household of theatricals, two of whom happened to be strippers. Unhappily the last two programmes ran into silly censorship trouble, and though this had nothing to do with the method it did draw attention to the impossibility with VTR of snipping out a few token frames – editing was still a tricky business of transferring from one tape to another. The cumbersome presence of mobile control rooms and generator vans was

also proving a deterrent, and if their costs were counted in the budget, the great idea was no real saving on film. In the eighties the advent of lightweight cameras and recording gear reopened the possibilities. The very successful BBC serialization of *The Mayor of Casterbridge* (1978) was among the first use of this equipment.   PP

Lock, Stock and Barrel
US 1970 96m colour TVM
Universal

A runaway couple encounter savage animals, vengeful parents and natural hazards.
Slow starting adventure comedy featuring the couple later seen married in *Hitched.*

w Richard Alan Simmons *d* Jerry Thorpe *m* Pat Williams

Belinda Montgomery, Tim Matheson, Jack Albertson, Neville Brand, Burgess Meredith, Felicia Farr, John Beck, Robert Emhardt

Lock Up
US 1959–60 78 × 25m bw
United Artists

A lawyer helps the wrongly accused.
Adequate courtroom series.

Macdonald Carey

Lockhart, June (1925–). American actress, daughter of Gene Lockhart. TV series: *Lassie, Lost in Space, Petticoat Junction.* TV movies: *The Bait, Curse of the Black Widow, Loose Change, The Gift of Love, Walking Through the Fire,* etc.

Lockwood, Gary (1937–) (John Gary Yusolfsky). American leading man. TV series: *Follow the Sun, The Lieutenant.* TV movies: *Earth II, Manhunter, The FBI vs Alvin Karpis, The Ghost of Flight 401, The Incredible Journey of Dr Meg Laurel.*

Lockwood, Margaret (1916–) (Margaret Day). British film star who turned to the stage and TV when roles on the big screen became hard to find. Series: *The Flying Swan,* JUSTICE.

Locusts *
US 1974 74m colour TVM
Paramount

A discharged World War II pilot comes home in dejection but finds himself fighting a locust plague.
Very moderate personal drama gives way to very moderate special effects.

w Robert Malcolm Young *d* Richard T. Heffron *m* Mike Post/Peter Carpenter

Ben Johnson, Ron Howard, Lisa Gerritsen, Katherine Helmond

Loe, Judy (1947–). Good and good-looking British actress, widow of Richard Beckinsale. Credits include *Life after Death, Missing from Home, Goodnight and God Bless.*

The Log of the Black Pearl
US 1975 100m colour TVM
Universal/Jack Webb

A stockbroker inherits a ship and a clue to sunken treasure.
Rather like a modernized *Treasure Island,* but not so good by a long way.

w Harold Jack Bloom *d* Andrew McLaglen

Jack Kruschen, Glenn Corbett, Ralph Bellamy, John Alderson, Anne Archer, Kiel Martin

Logan's Run
US 1977 74m colour TVM
CBS/MGM

Two fugitives from a city of the future, in which one must die at the age of 30, meet various strange civilizations in the outside world.
Intriguing if rather plodding pilot which uses some of the more spectacular footage from its feature film original.

w William F. Nolan, Saul David *d* Robert Day

Gregory Harrison, Heather Menzies, Donald Moffat

† The resulting series ran only 13 × 50m episodes.

logo. An image or motif designed to implant a company, a film or a series in the public mind; e.g. MGM's lion, Fox's searchlights.

Lois Gibbs and the Love Canal
US 1982 96m colour TVM
CBS/Filmways (Robert Greenwald, Frank Von Zerneck)

A Niagara Falls housewife complains that her children are being poisoned by toxic wastes carried by underground streams.
Adequate filming of a true incident.

w Michael Zagor *d* Glenn Jordan *ph* Howard Schwartz

Marsha Mason, Robert Gunton, Penny Fuller, Roberta Maxwell, Louise Latham

London Belongs to Me
GB 1977 7 × 50m colour (VTR)
Thames (Paul Knight)

Various problems are faced by inhabitants of a dreary London lodging house before World War II.
Slightly disappointing, overstretched television of a solid novel which also made an excellent film.

w Hugh Leonard, *novel* Norman Collins *d* Raymond Menmuir

Derek Farr, Patricia Hayes, Peter Jeffrey, Fiona Gray, Madge Ryan

London Weekend Television. The ITV (commercial) company holding since 1968 the London franchise for Friday (from 7 pm: 5.15 pm from 1982) and the whole of Saturday and Sunday.

The Lone Ranger
US 1949–56 182 × 25m bw (39 colour)
ABC/Jack Wrather

A mysterious masked rider fights for justice. Pleasantly made comic strip western for children.

cr George W. Trendle, Fran Striker

Clayton Moore (occasionally John Hart), Jay Silverheels

† A series of Lone Ranger cartoons (26 × 25m) was made in 1966.

†† Tonto's famous greeting 'Kemo Sabe' is translated alternatively as 'faithful friend' or 'trusted scout'.

The Lone Wolf
aka: *Streets of Danger*
US 1953 39 × 25m bw
Gross-Krasne

Stories of a gentleman rogue who fights crime. An old reliable of the cinema failed to excite on TV.

Louis Hayward

The Loneliest Runner
US 1976 74m colour TVM
NBC (Michael Landon)

Problems of a teenage bed-wetter. An incredible subject, but by the end a rather touching little drama.

w/d Michael Landon

Lance Kerwin, Brian Keith

The Lonely Profession *
US 1969 96m colour TVM
Universal (Jo Swerling Jnr)

A private eye's client is murdered. Acceptable sub-Chandler goings on.

w/d Douglas Heyes

Harry Guardino, Dean Jagger, Troy Donahue, Joseph Cotten, Fernando Lamas, Dina Merrill

The Loner
US 1965 26 × 25m bw
CBS/Greenway/Interlaken/TCF

An ex-soldier tries to find himself after the Civil War.

Shane-styled western; atmosphere rather rarefied.

cr Rod Serling

Lloyd Bridges

The Lonesome Road * (GB 1962). Intrusive, button-holing stranger (Ronald Fraser) insinuates himself into suburban fireside. It turns out to be nothing sinister but a modern parable about the consolations of marriage. First transmitted in January, repeated in August, Giles Cooper's play was a popular and critical success. My comment at the time: 'Cooper here exploits the matter-of-fact idiom of TV drama which has sometimes ill served his richness of imagination. A plot which at first promises to be some kind of Jerome K. Jerome fantasy gradually circles down to earth like a light plane, and then neatly lands.' Directed by Donald McWhinnie; produced by Cecil Clarke; for ATV.   PP

The Long Day (GB 1963). Inside the notorious Dartmoor prison, now closed, with – for the first time – prisoners openly facing the camera to testify, plus prison officers, the deputy governor and the padre. The title came from an old lag who said, 'Looking back on the years I've done I consider it one long day . . . because nothing has happened day in and day out.' Produced by Mike Towers; for Television West and Wales (HTV's predecessor).   PP

The Long Days of Summer
US 1980 74m colour TVM
ABC/Dan Curtis (Joseph Stern, Lee Hutson)

In 1938 Bridgeport a Jewish family tries to protect a refugee against American Nazi bigotry. Slow but interesting memoir of past time.

w Lee Hutson, *story* by himself and Hindi Brooks *d* Dan Curtis *ph* Charles Correll *m* Walter Scharf

Dean Jones, Joan Hackett, Ronald Scribner, Donald Moffat, Andrew Duggan

Long Distance Information * (GB 1979). Neville Smith as a late-night disc-jockey and Elvis Presley fanatic on the night the news of Presley's death flashes round the world. Smith also wrote the play. My 1979 comment: 'Lots of dialogue that could be funny or sad at choice, and a powerful impression of the nostalgia that these days comes howling ever more closely after the sledge, so that even last week is bathed in a golden glow of lost happiness. Stephen Frears directed something slender but good'; for BBC (*Play for Today*).   PP

The Long Hot Summer *
US 1965 26 × 50m bw
ABC/TCF (Frank Glicksman)

Small-town troubles centre round a blustering local tycoon and his family.

Vaguely based on William Faulkner stories, but more clearly on the film of the same title, this domestic drama had a little more strength than *Peyton Place* but was handicapped by an intractable star and petered out when he was replaced.

cr Dean Riesner

Edmond O'Brien (later Dan O'Herlihy), Nancy Malone, Roy Thinnes, Ruth Roman

The Long Hot Summer *
US 1985 2 × 96m colour miniseries
NBC/TCF/Leonard Hill (Dori Weiss)

The macho son of a barnburner inveigles his way into the family of a wealthy southerner. Stretched-out version of the Paul Newman/Orson Welles film. It always looks good, but the content is pretty thin and rather muddled.

w Rita Mae Brown, Dennis Turner, *screenplay* by Irving Ravetch and Harriet Frank, *stories* by William Faulkner *d* STUART COOPER *ph* Reed Smooth, Steve Yaconelli *m* Charles Bernstein

DON JOHNSON, JASON ROBARDS JNR, CYBILL SHEPHERD, Ava Gardner, Judith Ivey, William Russ, Wings Hauser

'Teleadaptation of the 1958 film is road company version looking like outtakes from *Flamingo Road*.' – *Daily Variety*

'The sort of quality that doesn't show up frequently on TV unless it's a British import on PBS.' – *Weekly Variety*

Long John Silver: see The Adventures of Long John Silver

The Long Journey Back
US 1979 96m colour TVM
ABC/Lorimar (Robert Lovenheim)

An accident turns a girl into a brain-damaged amputee, but she fights her way back to a kind of contentment.

Painful and prolonged case history of a too familiar kind.

w Audrey Davis Levin *d* Mel Damski *ph* Stevan Larner *m* Fred Karlin

Mike Connors, Stephanie Zimbalist, Katy Kurtzman, Cloris Leachman

'Heavy going and too long, no matter how sterling the acting.' – *Daily Variety*

Long Past Glory (GB 1963). Doubly a rarity as novelist Len Deighton's only television play

and also one of the few from any quarter to try and sustain a *trompe l'oeil* until the final fade. A trio of filthy troglodytes living amid rats and mud, only venturing out to forage for supplies, were survivors neither of the nuclear holocaust as it was tempting to suppose, nor a second Flood. They were trench soldiers in World War I. Unfortunately the trick was not played straight enough to have the audience gratified rather than peeved at being taken in. With John Le Mesurier, Maurice Denham. Directed by Charles Jarrott; produced by Leonard White; for ABC (*Armchair Theatre*).   PP

Long, Richard (1927–74). Easy-going American leading man who proved an attractive series figure: *77 Sunset Strip*, *Bourbon Street Beat*, *The Big Valley*, *Nanny and the Professor*.

The Long Search **
GB 1977 13 × 50m colour (16mm)
BBC/RM (Munich)/Time–Life (Peter Montagnon)

Ronald Eyre travels around the world finding out what people's religions mean to them in modern life.

A solidly watchable, intelligent series in which only a few of the episodes would have been better at half the length.

'Has all the makings of a milestone.' – *Observer*

Long, Shelley (19 –). American leading lady, notable in CHEERS (Emmy 1983).

The Long Summer of George Adams
US 1983 96m colour TVM
NBC/Warner (Meta Rosenberg)

In 1952 in a small railroad town, a train engineer looks at his life and the folk around him.

Folksy and mildly sexy, this strange attempt at something different comes off in fits and spurts.

w John Gay, *book* by Weldon Hill *d* Stuart Margolin *ph* Andrew Jackson *m* Murray McLeod, Stuart Margolin, J. A. C. Redford

James Garner, Joan Hackett, Alex Harvey, David Graf, Anjanette Comer

A Long Way Home *
US 1981 96m colour TVM
ABC/Alan Landburg (Lida Otto)

A young man who was adopted tries to find his younger brother and sister.

Intriguing and rather moving drama with all the suspense associated with a quest.

w DENNIS NEMEC *d* ROBERT MARKOWITZ *ph* Don H. Birnkrant *m* William Goldstein

Timothy Hutton, Brenda Vaccaro, Rosanna Arquette, Paul Regina, George Dzundza, John Lehne, Bonnie Bartlett

The Longest Hundred Miles
US 1967 93m colour TVM
Universal

An American soldier in the Philippines leads a civilian flight away from the Japanese invasion. Routine war adventure.

w Winston Miller d Don Weis

Doug McClure, Katharine Ross, Ricardo Montalban

The Longest Night *
US 1972 74m colour TVM
Universal (William Frye)

A girl is kidnapped and buried alive in a coffin with a limited life support system.
Suspenseful crime melodrama based on an actual case.

w Merwin Gerard d Jack Smight

David Janssen, James Farentino, Phyllis Thaxter, Skye Aubrey, Charles McGraw, John Kerr

Longstreet
US 1970 74m colour TVM
ABC/Paramount (Joseph Sargent)

A New Orleans criminal insurance investigator is blinded in a chase but carries on.
Shades of Edward Arnold in *Eyes in the Night*. This very moderate mystery led to a one-season series.

w Sterling Silliphant d Joseph Sargent m Oliver Nelson

James Franciscus, Bradford Dillman, John McIntire, Jeanette Nolan

† The resulting series ran to 24 × 50m episodes, and featured Marlyn Mason and BRUCE LEE in support of Franciscus.

Look. Long-running BBC wildlife series conducted by Peter Scott throughout the fifties and sixties. PP

Look Back to Yesterday
US 1984 96m colour TVM
NBC/Ed Friendly (Kent McCray)

Charles Ingalls learns that his son has an incurable blood disease.
Oddball sequel to *Little House on the Prairie*, with the writer apparently determined to kill all the characters off.

w Vince R. Gutierrez d Victor French m David Rose

Melissa Gilbert, Dean Butler, Richard Bull, Victor French, Kevin Hagen, Dabbs Greer, Michael Landon, Matthew Laborteaux

Look in Any Window (GB 1958). Ted Willis play about an arid marriage whose title alone sums up the philosophy of television drama Ted Willis was trying to advance at the time – a drama of 'ordinary people' leading ordinary lives, as already pioneered in the United States by Chayevsky and others. With Joan Miller. Directed by Peter Cotes; for A–R. PP

Look What Happened to Rosemary's Baby
US 1968 96m colour TVM
Paramount/Culzean (Anthony Wilson)

A sequel to the 1968 film, with many of the same characters watching the devilish child grow up. Rather unattractive supernatural thriller.

w Anthony Wilson d Sam O'Steen m Charles Bernstein

Stephen McHattie, Ruth Gordon, Ray Milland, Patty Duke, Broderick Crawford, George Maharis, Tina Louise, Donna Mills, Lloyd Haynes

lookalikes. In the theatre the representation of the living or the lately dead was prohibited by the Lord Chamberlain until his powers of censorship were ended in 1967. In the cinema biopics were more common, but it was on television during the 1970s that the vogue for heroes and heroines drawn from recent history really took over, setting actors and casting directors a special problem. If the performance is to carry weight it must still derive mainly from the player's own interior and only secondarily from the make-up artist's skill, but the audience always expects a reasonable facsimile. In the case of immortals of great familiarity, e.g. Hitler, Churchill or Marilyn Monroe, the task is almost impossible. With lesser-known subjects there is more scope, and in *Churchill and the Generals* (1980), for example, Eric Porter's Sir Alan Brooke, the CIGS, came over as a richer impersonation than that of many a more extrovert original. In *The Missiles of October* (US 1975), recounting the Cuba missile crisis, Martin Sheen's Robert Kennedy was not only more persuasive than William Devane's John F, it was closer than his own J. F. Kennedy eight years later in *Kennedy* (GB/US). Noteworthy lookalikes have come from Barry Foster as Orde Wingate and Ian Richardson as Montgomery (both twice), Patrick Stewart as Lenin, Ian Holm as J. M. Barrie, Timothy West as Edward VII, Edward Fox as Edward VIII, Lee Remick as Jennie Churchill, Cheryl Campbell as Vera Brittain and Robert Hardy as Sir Malcolm Campbell, innkeeper John Fothergill and the Winston Churchill of the wilderness years. But in this last series

Peter Barkworth's Baldwin and Eric Porter's Chamberlain, again, were the uncanny ringers.   PP

Looking Back with Lord Reith: see Reith, John

Looking into Paintings (GB 1985; 6 × 30m). Average time spent in front of a picture at the National Gallery is only six seconds. This series linked to an Open University short course sought to show how to look longer, and what for. With Norbert Lynton, Alistair Smith, Robert Cumming. Produced by Nancy Thomas for Malachite Productions/C4.   PP

Looks and Smiles (GB 1982; 120m bw). Bleak drama of school-leavers in Sheffield unable to find work and drifting into petty crime or – by implication, even worse – into the army. The army bit gave away the political bias to be expected, alas, from this creative team, a young man already a soldier being shown with decreasing subtlety as a bully, a boor and an anti-Catholic bigot. Written by Barry Hines, directed by Ken Loach, produced by Irving Teitelbaum for Central, shot in black and white for effect.   PP

Looks Familiar. An easy-going nostalgia programme devised for Thames TV by Denis Gifford in the mid-seventies. Denis Norden chairs a panel of three 'experts' who identify clips of film of thirties and forties bandleaders, singers and film stars. The score is quite irrelevant: the gossip's the thing. (The series was originally a radio show called *Sounds Familiar*.) Producer, David Clark.

Loose Change
US 1978 3 × 96m colour
Universal (Jules Irving)

Three girls graduate from Berkeley in 1962 and we follow their subsequent lives.
Weary rehash of all the modern clichés – free love, student protest, politics, abortion – without much thought for professionalism or entertainment.
w Corinne Jacker, Charles E. Israel, Jennifer Miller, *book* Sara Davidson *d* Jules Irving *ph* John Elsenbach, Harry Wolfe *m* Don Costa
Cristina Raines, Laurie Heineman, Season Hubley, Theodore Bikel, David Wayne, Stephen Macht, Michael Tolan, Gregg Henry, Ben Masters, Kate Reid, June Lockhart

Lord, Jack (1922–) (John Joseph Ryan). Durable American leading man, in series *Stony Burke* and the long-running *Hawaii Five O*, which made him in his view one of the more important assets of the Hawaiian islands.

Lord Peter Wimsey. Ian Carmichael impersonated Dorothy L. Sayers's aristocratic detective of the twenties in three pleasing BBC serials in the early seventies.

Lord Reith Looks Back: see Reith, John

The Loretta Young Show *
US 1953–60 255 × 25m bw
NBC

Anthology dramas with introductions and occasional appearances by the star.
Superior series of its time, though Miss Young's dresses were often of more interest than the drama.

Lorimar. Independent production company headed by Lee Rich. Its first major success was *The Waltons*, and *Dallas* followed.

Lorne, Marion (1886–1968) (Marion Lorne MacDougal).   American   character comedienne who in 1967 won an Emmy as the dotty aunt in *Bewitched*.

The Lost Boys **
GB 1979 3 × 90m approx. colour
BBC (Louis Marks)

J. M. Barrie's involvement with the tragic Llewelyn Davies family changes his life and causes him to write *Peter Pan*.
Fascinating psychological study which is also a portrait of an era whose illusions were destroyed as totally as Barrie's.
w Andrew Birkin *d* Rodney Bennett *m* Dudley Simpson
IAN HOLM, Ann Bell, Tim Piggott-Smith, Anna Cropper, Maureen O'Brien
'I am sure such excellence would be beyond any other television service in the world.' – *Daily Telegraph*

Lost City (GB 1958). J. B. Priestley in search of the Bradford he knew half a century earlier, with BBC producer Richard Cawston making the most of smoky, Lowryesque skylines, jovial market hucksters, pies and peas, and using for the first time the now-familiar device of blending the signature tunes of favourite TV programmes into the evening sound of the city. At the time I wrote: 'Priestley himself, in broad-brimmed hat and flapping overcoat, strode through it all rather like a character from one of his plays.'   PP

Lost Flight
US 1969 105m colour TVM
Universal

After a plane crash in an island jungle, the
passengers learn to survive.

Memories of *Five Came Back*, and of another
ill-fated series called *The New People*. This one
didn't take – it wasn't very good – but the
seventies brought yet more pilots on the
theme.

w Dean Riesner *d* Leonard Horn *m* Dominic
Frontiere

Lloyd Bridges, Anne Francis, Bobby Van,
Ralph Meeker, Andrew Prine, Linden Chiles

Lost in London
US 1985 96m colour TVM
CBS/Emmanuel Lewis Entertainment
    Enterprises (Peter Manley)

A small black American boy gets lost in
London and falls in with street gangs.

Tedious update of *Oliver Twist* with Ben
Vereen and Freddie Jones sharing the Fagin
role. Presentation incredibly inept.

w Ron Rubin *d* Robert Lewis *ph* Terry
Gilbert *m* Ken Thorne

Emmanuel Lewis, Lynne Moody, Ben
Vereen, Freddie Jones, Basil Hoskins

Lost in Space
US 1965–7 83 × 50m colour
CBS/Irwin Allen/TCF

A family of the future, on its way to colonize
Alpha Centauri, is shipwrecked on an
unknown planet.

Cheerfully studio-bound adventure, mainly for
kids: too much talk for grown-ups.

Guy Williams, June Lockhart, Mark Goddard,
JONATHAN HARRIS, Marta Kristen, Billy Mumy,
Bob May (as robot)

The Lost Peace: see The Great War

The Lost Saucer
US 1975 16 × 22m colour (VTR)
TCF/Sid and Marty Krofft

Two androids in a flying saucer collect two
earth children and they all have adventures in
space.

Rather heavy-footed fantasy for children, with
good set design.

Ruth Buzzi, Jim Nabors

The Lost Tribe (GB 1980). Annals of a
warm-hearted Jewish family in Scotland,
beginning with the whimsical arrival of the
patriarch as a young refugee from Czarist
pogroms. Bound for America, he believes, he

is dumped by an unscrupulous shipper on the
dockside at Dundee. Written by Jack Ronder;
for BBC Scotland.   PP

A Lot of Happiness * (GB 1981; 78m;
colour). Profile-in-action of choreographer
Kenneth MacMillan creating a new ballet,
which is finally performed in the studio. A
deceptively straightforward, illuminating
record by film-maker Jack Gold, who also
asked the questions. Dancers: Birgit Keil and
Vladimir Klos. Produced by Norman
Swallow; for Granada.   PP

Lotsa Luck (US 1973). Half-hour comedy
series for NBC, based on Britain's hit show *On
The Buses*. It didn't travel, despite sterling
effort by Dom DeLuise and Kathleen
Freeman.

Lotterby, Sidney (19 –). British BBC
producer mainly associated with comedy, his
most generally acclaimed hit being *Porridge*.

Lottery!
US 1983 74m colour TVM
ABC/Orion/Rick Rosner (Robert
    Lovenheim)

Lottery prizes are distributed by a man from
the revenue and a jaunty Irishman.

Abysmal pilot with a witless frame and three
supremely boring stories. A long way below
the level of *Love Boat*, which is saying
something.

w David Engelbach *d* Lee Phillips
ph Matthew S. Leonetti *m* Mark Snow

Marshall Colt, Ben Murphy, Reni Santoni,
Christopher McDonald, Allen Goorwitz,
Renee Taylor

† The resulting one-hour series limped
through a season of 22 episodes.

Lou Grant **
US 1977–81   × 50m colour
CBS/Mary Tyler Moore (GENE REYNOLDS)

Dramas centring in the news room of a Los
Angeles daily newspaper.

A skilfully made and written if occasionally
rather earnest vehicle for a middle-aged star
from *The Mary Tyler Moore Show*.

ED ASNER, NANCY MARCHAND (as Mrs
Pynchon), MASON ADAMS, ROBERT WALDEN,
LINDA KELSEY, JACK BANNON

† Emmys (best drama series) 1978, 1979,
1980.

Louis Armstrong, Chicago Style *
US 1975 74m colour TVM
Charles Fries/Dick Berg

The famous musician struggles for his fame and fights the mob.

Presumably true anecdotes, quite well made and entertaining.

w James Lee d Lee Phillips

Ben Vereen, Red Buttons, Janet McLachlan, Margaret Avery

Louisiana
US/France 1984 2 × 96m colour
miniseries
Orion/International Cinema Corporation
(John Kemeny, Denis Heroux)

A pre-Civil War southern belle comes back from finishing school in Europe to find herself penniless; she marries her wealthy godfather and becomes a power in the land. Scarlett O'Hara's story was better than this dreary mid-Atlantic melodrama which seldom raises a flicker of interest.

w Etienne Perier, Dominique Fabre, Charles Israel, *novels* Louisiane and *Fausse-Rivière* by Maurice Denuzière d Philippe de Broca ph Michel Brault m Claude Bolling pd Jack McAdam

Margot Kidder, Ian Charleson, Andrea Ferreol, Lloyd Bochner, Victor Lanoux, Len Cariou, Raymond Pellegrin

'Surely there was some lightness in the Old South at one time or another; but then, misery loves company.' – *Daily Variety*

A Love Affair: The Eleanor and Lou Gehrig Story *
US 1977 96m colour TVM
NBC/Charles Fries

The private life of a baseball star who died of lateral sclerosis.

Superior in production and craftsmanship, this docu-drama contains nothing surprising.

w Blanche Hanalis, *book* My Luke and I by Eleanor Gehrig d Fielder Cook m Michel Hugo md Eddy Lawrence Manson

Blythe Danner, Edward Herrmann, Patricia Neal, Ramon Bieri, Lainie Kazan, Jane Wyatt, Gerald S. O'Loughlin, Georgia Engel

† The same story was told in the 1942 Gary Cooper film *The Pride of the Yankees*.

A Love Affair with Nature (GB 1985).
Look-at-art series with Edwin Mullins on the influence of the scenery and animals on English painters.

Love American Style *
US 1969 74m colour TVM
ABC/Paramount

Four comedy sketches on the theme of love: a successful series resulted.

w various d Charles Rondeau, Marc Daniels, Gary Marshall, Hy Averback

Don Porter, Marjorie Lord, Michael Callan, Penny Fuller, Greg Morris, Darryl Hickman, Robert Reed, Jeannine Riley

'We can do for situation comedies what *Laugh-in* did for variety shows.' – Arnold Margolin

† The series ran four seasons (112 × 50m). Creators: Douglas S. Cramer, Tom Miller; executive producers: Arnold Margolin, Jim Parker; for Paramount.

Love Among the Artists
GB 1979 5 × 50m colour
Granada TV (Howard Baker)

A disappointingly dull adaptation of Bernard Shaw's early novel about London society in the 1880s.

w Stuart Latham d Howard Baker, Marc Miller

John Stride, Geraldine James, Judy Campbell, Jane Carr, Martyn Jacobs

Love Among the Ruins **
US 1974 100m colour TVM
ABC Circle (Allan Davis)

An elderly actress turns to a former lover for legal counsel in a breach of promise case.

Splendid people are forced to overact because this high-class taradiddle goes on too long and makes their characters unconvincing. Still, it's a delight to have something so civilized.

w James Costigan, *novel* Angela Thirkell d George Cukor m John Barry

KATHARINE HEPBURN, LAURENCE OLIVIER, Richard Pearson, Colin Blakely, Joan Sims, Leigh Lawson, Gwen Nelson, Robert Harris

† Hepburn and Olivier won Emmys.

Love and Marriage *
US 1959 26 × 25m bw
NBC/Louis F. Edelman

Frustrations of a Tin Pan Alley music publisher.

Unusual comedy format with more than usual amusement.

William Demarest, Stubby Kaye, Kay Armen, Murray Hamilton

Love and Marriage (GB 1984; 6 × 52m).
Anthology of rather prosaic original video plays, other than James Andrew Hall's *Lucifer*. Produced by Pat Sandys, for YTV.

THE LOVE BOAT provided a safe haven for many ageing guest stars. Here are Douglas
Fairbanks Jnr and Ginger Rogers.

The Love Boat *
US 1977–   × 50m colour
ABC/Spelling–Goldberg

Comedies and dramas about passengers on a
pleasure boat cruise.

A hoary format scores more hits than misses.
(The 50m series was prefaced by three
experimental pilots, two at 96m and one at
74m.)

cr W. L. Baumes

Gavin MacLeod, Bernie Kopell, Fred
Grandy, Ted Lange, Lauren Tewes

'Everything I've tried to forget about the
movies is recaptured in this ABC hour.' –
Robert MacKenzie, *TV Guide*

Love Doubles (US 1980). Tennis players Bjorn Borg and his fiancée Mariana Simionescu pitted against Mr and Mrs Chris Evert Lloyd in a match in aid of charities.   PP

Love for Lydia **
GB 1977 13 × 50m colour
LWT (Richard Bates/Tony Wharmby)

Troubled but eventually triumphant serialization of H. E. Bates's novel about a *jeune fille fatale* of half a century earlier, and the young men she led such a dance. Apart from having to flesh out a slender work rather than the usual serialization chore of condensing a huge one, writer Julian Bond had to cope with a change of producer when at a late stage Richard Bates (H.E.'s son) was replaced by Tony Wharmby.

Mel Martin, Christopher Blake, Jeremy Irons, Beatrix Lehman, Rachel Kempson, Michael Aldridge   PP

Love for Rent
US 1981 96m colour TVM
ABC/Warren V. Bush

An Oklahoma girl runs away from home and becomes a Los Angeles prostitute.
The road to ruin, eighties style, with a backdrop of Hollywood tinsel.

w Andrew Britt *d* David Miller

Annette O'Toole, Lisa Eilbacher, Darren McGavin, Eugene Roche, Rhonda Fleming

Love, Hate, Love
US 1970 72m colour TVM
Aaron Spelling

Newlyweds are violently harassed by the girl's ex-suitor.
Rather unpleasant melodrama.

d George McCowan

Ryan O'Neal, Lesley Warren, Peter Haskell

Love in a Cold Climate
GB 1980 7 × 50m colour
Thames (Gerald Savory)

The lives of the Mitford girls and their eccentric family.
Caviare to the general, and poorly prepared at that, with a first hour full of badly rehearsed children. Some nice twenties atmosphere, and that's about it.

w Simon Raven, *books* Nancy Mitford *d* Donald McWhinnie

Judi Dench, Vivian Pickles, Michael Aldridge, John Moffatt, Michael Williams

'To hold the woman he loves in his arms, he must take his life in his hands!'
Love Is Forever
aka: *The Comeback*
US 1983 96m colour TVM
NBC/TCF/Michael Landon/Hall Bartlett

A CIA agent rescues his bride-to-be from Laos by swimming the Mekong river.
Extraordinarily overlong action melodrama with soppy romantic asides. Somewhere inside it a good one-hour action thriller is struggling to get out.

w,d Hall Bartlett *ph* Andrew Laszlo *m* Klaus Doldinger

Michael Landon, Moira Chen, Jurgen Prochnow, Edward Woodward, Priscilla Presley

'What reaches for romance really comes off as overcooked mush.' – *Daily Variety*

Love Is Never Silent
US/Canada 1985 96m colour TVM
NBC/Telepictures/Marian Rees Associates

A girl almost ruins her own life by caring for her deaf parents.
Moving but grossly overlong variation on the usual disease-of-the-week themes.

w Darlen Craviotto, *novel* by Joanne Greenberg *d* Joseph Sargent *ph* David Gribble *m* Billy Goldenberg

Mare Winningham, Phyllis Frelich, Ed Waterstreet, Cloris Leachman, Sid Caesar, Frederic Lehne

'A well-told story that relates to everyone.' – *Daily Variety*

Love Is Not Enough
US 1978 96m colour TVM
NBC/Universal (Stanley C. Robertson)

A black widower moves himself and his children from Detroit to a new way of life in Los Angeles.
Sentimental wallow for those who like that sort of thing.

w Arthur Ross *d* Ivan Dixon *ph* Lamar Boren *m* Coleridge-Taylor Parkinson

Bernie Casey, Renée Brown, Stuart K. Robinson

† A short run of one-hour episodes followed.

Love Leads the Way
US 1984 96m colour TVM
Disney/Hawkins/Perlmut (Jimmy Hawkins)

The story of the first Seeing Eye dog.
Tepid family movie with enough content for half its length.

w Henry Denker d Delbert Mann ph Gary Graver m Fred Karlin

Timothy Bottoms, Eva Marie Saint, Arthur Hill, Glynnis O'Connor, Susan Dey, Michael Anderson Jnr, Gerald Hiken

'The story of Susan Wallace and the terrifying choice she must make!'
Love Lives On
US 1985 96m colour TVM
ABC Circle (April Smith)

A 15-year-old drug addict learns she has cancer.
And she's pregnant too, and an alcoholic. Only confirmed disease-of-the-week addicts should switch on.

w April Smith d Larry Peerce ph Gerald C. Hirschfeld m James Di Pasquale

Christine Lahti, Sam Waterston, Ricky Goldin, Louise Latham, Joe Regalbuto

'Not only a downer, it's a cover-all-bases drencher.' – *Daily Variety*

Love, Mary
US 1985 96m colour TVM
CBS (Ellis A. Cohen)

A teenage girl, a dropout and drug addict, is sent to a reformatory, sees the light, and becomes a doctor.
True but incredible case history, tediously drawn out.

w Clifford Campion d Robert Day ph Frank Stanley m Robert Drasnin

Kristy McNichol, Matt Clark, David Paymer, Rachel Ticotin, Piper Laurie

'A heart-tugging drama that comes off like a series of cards flipping by.' – *Daily Variety*

Love of Life. Daytime soap opera, on CBS from 1951 to the eighties. The interminable story of two families in Rosehill, USA.

Love on a Rooftop
US 1966 26 × 25m colour
ABC/Columbia/Harry Ackerman (E.W. Swackhamer)

Newlyweds live in a top-floor flat in San Francisco.
Ordinary comedy.

cr Bernard Slade

Pete Duel, Judy Carne, Rich Little

Love on the Run
US 1985 96m colour TVM
NBC (Jay Benson)

A frustrated lady lawyer falls for her convicted client and goes on the run with him.

After a long unsteady start this peculiar telemovie makes next to nothing of the chase which one might expect to be its justification.

w Sue Grafton, Steve Humphreys d Gus Trikonis ph Philip Lathrop m Billy Goldenberg

Stephanie Zimbalist, Alec Baldwin, Constance McCashin, Ernie Hudson, Howard Duff, Madison Mason

'Vidpic says much about doom, about freedom and about realities; it says nothing about consequences – and it says nothing with high art.' – *Daily Variety*

The Love School
GB 1975 6 × 75m colour
BBC (Rosemary Hill)

Catchpenny title for what was in fact a dramatized history of the Pre-Raphaelite painters and all their posturings, coming vividly alive in a couple of episodes but making heavy weather of others. Excellent lighting by Dennis Channon.

w John Hale, Robin Chapman, etc

David Burke (Morris), David Collings (Ruskin), Ben Kingsley (Rossetti)   PP

Love Story
US 1973 13 × 50m colour
Paramount/NBC (George Schaefer)

An anthology of romances, usually two to an hour, this failed to repeat the success of the movie after which it was named.

PP: 'In Britain the title was used by ATV for several runs of an anthology series between 1965 and 1970. At its best, which was in the earlier days, it drew on contributions by Robert Holles, Edna O'Brien and Robert Muller, and touched off one outright masterpiece in *La Musica* from the formidable French novelist Marguérite Duras. The title is now used as an umbrella title for occasional mini-serials (usually 4 × 25m) produced by Colin Tucker and latterly Colin Shindler for the BBC, from 1979: *A Moment in Time* and *Fair Stood the Wind for France* from novels by H. E. Bates; *Sweet Nothings* by E. A. Whitehead; *Forgive Our Foolish Ways*, *Hannah*, *Alexa*, etc. Finally, it was also the title of a single play for Anglia (1974) by William Trevor, with Celia Johnson as a faded gentlewoman courted by rough Bill Maynard.'

The Love Tapes
US 1980 96m colour TVM
ABC/MGM/Christiana (Joanna Lee)

Stories of a videotape dating service.
Omnibus package which promises more than it produces.

w Elliot Shoenman, Joanna Emerson *d* Allen Reisner *ph* Robert Caramico *m* Billy Goldenberg

Loretta Swit, Martin Balsam, Michael Constantine, Mariette Hartley, Arte Johnson, Larry Wilcox, Wendy Philips

'Production has plastic values and situations worked out by numbers, and it'll go through the ratings roof.' – *Daily Variety*

Love That Bob: see Cummings, Robert

Love That Jill (US 1958). Shortlived half-hour comedy series for ABC, with Anne Jeffreys and Robert Sterling, married in real life, as heads of rival New York model agencies.

Love Thy Neighbour *. A tape comedy created in 1971 for Thames TV by Vince Powell and Harry Driver, about a working-class bigot with black neighbours. The cast (JACK SMETHURST, KATE WILLIAMS, RUDOLPH WALKER, NINA BADEN-SEMPER) made it work, though it never rose above the obvious. An American attempt in 1973 to repeat its success closed after 12 episodes.

† A feature film version was released in 1973.

†† Jack Smethurst starred in seven episodes of an Australian version which didn't take.

Love Thy Neighbour
US 1983 96m colour TVM
ABC/TCF/Patricia Nardo (Renee Valente)

Next-door neighbours change partners. Boring domestic comedy fluff.

w Chris Conrad *d* Tony Bill

John Ritter, Penny Marshall, Cassie Yates, Bert Convy, Constance McCashin

The Love War *
aka: *The Sixth Column*
US 1969 74m colour TVM
Spelling–Thomas

Killers attacking each other in a small California town are actually aliens from another planet fighting for control of Earth. Smooth, inventive, good-looking science fiction with plenty of suspense.

w David Kidd, Guerdon Trueblood *d* GEORGE MCCOWAN *m* Dominic Frontiere

Lloyd Bridges, Angie Dickinson, Harry Basch, Byron Foulger

Lovejoy, Frank (1912–62). Tough-looking American actor. TV series: *Meet McGraw.*

The Lover * (GB 1963; 52m). Harold Pinter's enamel-hard, much-honoured play about

out-of-town lovers whose subtly erotic preliminaries turn out to be a husband and wife's elaborate make-believe. With Alan Badel, Vivien Merchant. Directed by Joan Kemp-Welch; produced by Peter Willes; for Rediffusion. The same producer was responsible for a second version for YTV in 1977 with Patrick Allen replacing Alan Badel.   PP

The Lovers *. A tape comedy about a working-class courtship created in 1970 for Granada TV by JACK ROSENTHAL, distinguished by funny lines delivered in a highly stylized and artificial way. It made stars of PAULA WILCOX and RICHARD BECKINSALE.

† A feature film version was released in 1973.

Love's Dark Ride
US 1978 96m colour TVM
NBC/Mark VII (Joseph M. Taritaro)

When a designer is accidentally blinded he turns against his friends. Dislikeable and pathetic romantic melodrama with a predictable happy ending.

w Ann Beckett, Kane O'Connor, Dennis Nemec *d* Delbert Mann *ph* Robert Wyckoff *m* Tom Sullivan, John D'Andrea, Michael Lloyd

Cliff Potts, Carrie Snodgress, Jane Seymour, Granville Van Dusen, Shelly Novack, Tom Sullivan

'Viewers were probably hard put to stay awake.' – *Daily Variety*

Love's Savage Fury
US 1980 96m colour TVM
ABC/Aaron Spelling

Life on a Georgia plantation is disrupted by the outbreak of the Civil War. Risible attempt at a mini-budget soap opera that might be mistaken for *Gone with the Wind.*

w Calvin Clements Jnr *d* Joseph Hardy *ph* Richard L. Rawlings *m* John Addison

Jennifer O'Neill, Perry King, Robert Reed, Ed Lauter, Connie Stevens, Raymond Burr

'One to be taken with a box of chocolates and a grain of salt.' – *Daily Variety*

Lovey: A Circle of Children Part 2
US 1978 96m colour TVM
CBS/Time–Life (David Susskind)

More cases of a teacher of disturbed children. Unnecessary sequel to a rather good telemovie.

w Josh Greenfield *d* Jud Taylor *ph* Ron Lautore *m* Jerry Fielding

Jane Alexander, Ronny Cox, Chris McKeon, Jeff Lynas

✳ **Lowe, Arthur** (1915–82). Portly, self-important British character actor who after a career in bit parts became a TV star as Mr Swindley in *Coronation Street*. Subsequent series built around him included *Pardon the Expression* and *Turn Out the Lights*, but he really came into his own as the memorable Captain Mainwaring in DAD'S ARMY, and later as the star of BLESS ME, FATHER, POTTER and A. J. WENTWORTH BA.

Lowry, Judith (1890–1976). American small-part character actress who became famous in extreme old age as the game old lady in *Phyllis*.

Lowry, L. S. (1887–1976). British painter of industrial townscapes whose solitary life inspired at least three television works of art. *L. S. Lowry* (BBC, John Read, 1957) remains a classic impression of the man and his outlook. Material from it was used in *I'm Just a Simple Man*, 1977 obituary. *Mister Lowry* (Tyne-Tees, 1971) concentrated on a sojourn of the painter in the North-East but ended with him back in the Cheshire house, full of slowly ticking clocks, familiar from earlier TV portraits. *L. S. Lowry: a Private View* (Granada 1981) effectively dramatizes a memoir by Shelley Rohde, drawing on the recollections of a young woman friend of his last years. Script by David Wheatley; with Malcolm Tierney quite a respectable look-alike but an absolutely authentic sound-alike. Broadcasting Press Guild award, 1982.   Pʳ

Lubo's World (GB 1984; 5 × 15m). Shy joke deploying Jon Stephen Fink as a fictitious Russian 'life-style reporter' reporting back to Moscow on young people's fashions, the London pop-music scene etc. 'He has a nice comic-Russian idiom,' I thought, 'and looks the part, with round face and cap squarely on head, but what he finds isn't actually much fun.' Directed by Terry Winsor, produced by Sarah Radclyffe for Working Title Ltd/C4.   PP

Lucan
US 1977 74m colour
ABC/MGM/Barry Lowen

A boy brought up with wolves helps people in distress while trying to find his parents.
A surly hero with only moderately special powers seems unlikely for TV, but the idea, stemming from the real-life case recounted in Truffaut's *The Wild Child*, had been tried once before in *Stalk the Wild Child*. *Lucan* led to a series of 11 × 50m.
Kevin Brophy, John Randolph, Don Gordan

Lucas, William (1925–). Reliable British general purpose actor whose TV series include *Champion Road*, *Black Beauty* and *The Spoils of War*.

Lucas Tanner
US 1974 22 × 50m colour
NBC/Universal
A widowed baseball player/sportswriter becomes a suburban schoolmaster.
Modest character drama.
David Hartman, Rosemary Murphy

The Lucie Arnaz Show
US 1985 6 × 25m colour
Taft/Sam Denoff (Kathy Speer, Terry Grossman)
Adventures of a radio psychologist in Manhattan.
Poor adaptation of the British sitcom *Agony*. It didn't travel well.
w Susan Seeger
Lucie Arnaz, Tony Roberts, Karen Jablons-Alexander, Lee Bryant

Luckham, Cyril (1907–). Dignified British character actor long familiar in small roles: best role probably in *Angel Pavement*.

Luckinbill, Laurence (1934–). American leading man. Series include *The Delphi Bureau*, *The Secret Storm*.

The Lucy Show *
US 1962–8 156 × 25m colour (30bw)
CBS/Desilu (Gary Morton)
The middle section of Lucy's TV career, in which she played a gallant widow with Vivian Vance as her friend (for three seasons) and GALE GORDON as her boss. See also *I Love Lucy* and *Here's Lucy*.

Ludden, Allen (1918–81). American quizmaster, long in charge of *Password* and *College Bowl*.

Luke, Peter (1919–). Genial British writer and producer active in television before and after the 15-year bonanza of his stage hit *Hadrian VII*. Story editor for ABC *Armchair Theatre*, 1958–62, producer of *Tempo* arts programme 1962–3, of BBC *Festival* season 1963–5, and Wednesday Play 1965–6. Recent writing credits include *Honour, Profit and Pleasure* (1985), with Anna Ambrose.   PP

Luke's Kingdom
GB/Australia 1976 13 × 50m colour
YTV/Channel 9

Oliver Tobias as a young settler hacking out a chunk of the bush for himself in the Australia of the 1820s. 'It's a bastard of a place,' the local whore-mistress and Mother Courage-figure tells him. 'It takes a bastard to lick it.' Played with lowering self-confidence by Tobias, Luke duly does so. Breezy stuff, if a bit too dependent on skulduggery to ginger up the real drama of opening up a raw continent. PP

Lulu (1948–) (Marie Lawrie). British pop singer, in occasional acting roles.

Lumet, Sidney (1924–). American director who before his successful film career triumphed on TV with *You Are Here*, *Omnibus*, *Mama*, etc.

Lumley, Joanna (1946–). Pert British leading lady who shot to fame as Purdey in THE NEW AVENGERS.

The Lump ** (GB 1967). Jim Allen's first full-length play, famously directed by JACK GOLD and produced by Tony Garnett for BBC (*Wednesday Play*). My review at the time: 'I liked *The Lump* for the reasons I hated the previous play from the Red Wing of the Wednesday drama department. *Cathy* [*Come Home*] started with the propaganda and cast around for a victim to fit it. Jim Allen started with the human being and only got around then to shouting the odds about conditions in the building trade.' With Leslie Sands. PP

Lunghi, Cherie (19 –). Comely British actress whose good looks can as easily be sweet or sinister. *The Nearly Man*, *'Tis Pity She's a Whore*, *Praying Mantis*, *The Daughter in Law*, *Strangers and Brothers*.

Lunt, Alfred (1892–1977). Distinguished American stage actor who won an Emmy in 1964 for his performance in *The Magnificent Yankee*.

Lupino, Ida (1914–). British actress in Hollywood who towards the end of her film career turned director and handled many TV

episodes; also appeared in the series *Mr Adams and Eve*. TV movies (as actress): *Women in Chains*, *The Strangers in 7A*, *Female Artillery*, *I Love a Mystery*, *The Letters*.

Lynch, Joe (1925–). Irish comic actor in Britain. Best remembered in TV for *Never Mind the Quality Feel the Width*.

Lynch, Richard (1936–). Scarfaced American character actor, typecast as villain. TV movies: *Vampire*, *Alcatraz*, *Sizzle*, *The Phoenix*, *White Water Rebels*, *The Last Ninja*.

Lynde, Paul (1926–82). American character comedian with mournful face and funny voice. TV series: *The Paul Lynde Show*, *Temperatures Rising*. TV movies: *Gidget Grows Up*, *Gidget Gets Married*.

Lynn, Loretta (1935–) (Loretta Webb). American popular singer from the hillbilly belt, the original *Coal Miner's Daughter*.

Lynn, Dame Vera (1917–). British sentimental singer, World War II's 'sweetheart of the forces'. She still presents occasional musical hours.
PP (1960): 'She has some of the appeal of the Monarchy – a kind of permanence which transcends the fads of the day. Other singers may rise and fall; Vera goes on for ever.' In 1984/5 40th anniversaries of D-Day and VE-Day recalled her to the colours once again.

Lytton's Diary *
GB 1985–6 13 × 52m
Thames (Chris Burt)
Triumphs and temptations of a debonair Fleet Street gossip columnist troubled – but not every time – by too tender a conscience. Bright, intelligent series owing much to Peter Bowles as both star and begetter of the idea, with Philip Broadley.
w Ray Connolly d 1985, Herbert Wise, Peter Sasdy; 1986, Derek Bailey
Peter Bowles, Bernard Lloyd, Bernard Archard, Anna Nygh, Trevor Peacock (1985), Holly de Jong PP

M Squad *
US1957–9 117 × 25m bw
NBC/MCA/Latimer/Universal

Stories of a plainclothes detective in the Chicago police.

Good standard cop show, cleanly produced.

Lee Marvin

M Station: Hawaii
US 1979 96m colour TVM
CBS/Columbia (Fred Baum)

Oceanographers in Hawaii keep watch on the activities of enemy agents.

Tediously stretched-out pilot for a series that never was.

w Robert Janes d Jack Lord

Jared Martin, Jo Ann Harris, Andrew Duggan, Dana Wynter, Andrew Prine, Jack Lord, Tom McFadden

M.A.D.D.: Mothers Against Drunk Drivers *
US 1982 96m colour TVM
NBC/Universal (Michael Braverman)

When a girl is killed on the road, her mother forms a party to force new legislation through so that drunk drivers will be convicted.

Solid docu-drama based on real events.

w Michael Braverman d William A. Graham ph Dean Cundey m Bruce Broughton

MARIETTE HARTLEY, Paula Prentiss, Bert Remsen, Cliff Potts, John Rubinstein, David Huddleston, Grace Zabriskie, Alan Fudge

Mabey, Richard (1944–). Personable British botanist, not as extrovert as David Bellamy but equally knowledgeable and able to communicate enthusiasm. *In Deepest Britain* (1975), *The Flowering of Britain* (1980).   PP

The MacAhans
US1976 142m colour TVM
NBC/MGM/Albert S. Ruddy (John Mantley)

In 1860, a mountain man goes back to Virginia to help his family move west ahead of the impending war.

Rich but leisurely pilot for *How the West Was Won* (qv), whose soap opera elements were already more evident than the impending action.

w Jim Byrnes d Bernard McEveety ph Edward R. Plante m Jerrold Immel

James Arness, Eva Marie Saint, Richard Kiley, Bruce Boxleitner, Frank Ferguson, Ann Doran

MacArthur, James (1937–). American second lead who was content to appear as just that in *Hawaii Five-O* for 10 years. Career otherwise modest. Adopted son of Helen Hayes. TV movie: *The Night the Bridge Fell*.

McCalla, Irish (*c* 1931–). Well-endowed American leading lady who starred in the mid-fifties as *Sheena, Queen of the Jungle*. Retired 1962 to become an artist.

McCallum, David (1933–). Engaging British actor in Hollywood who scored a TV hit as Kuryakin in *The Man from UNCLE* and a lesser one in *Colditz* and as *The Invisible Man*. TV movies: *Hauser's Memory*, *She Waits*, *Frankenstein: The True Story*.

McClain's Law
US 1981 96m colour TVM
NBC/MGM/Eric Bercovici (Mark Rodgers, Robert H. Justman)

A San Pedro cop in his 50s has a 30-year-old partner.

Where have we heard that before? And the development is as old as the idea.

w Eric Bercovici d Vincent McEveety ph Sy Hoffberg m James Di Pasquale

James Arness, Marshall Colt, Conchata Ferrell, George DiCenzo, Gerald S. O'Loughlin, Scott Brady

'*Gunsmoke* had an unmistakable style. *McClain's Law* looks a lot like half a dozen other police shows.' – Robert MacKenzie, *TV Guide*

† The resulting series lasted 13 hours.

McClanahan, Rue (*c* 1925–). Sprightly little American comedy actress. MAUDE, *The Great American Traffic Jam*, *Word of Honor*, *The Day the Bubble Burst*, GOLDEN GIRLS.

McCloud: See Mystery Movie and Who Killed Miss USA?

McClure, Doug (1935–). Virile American action lead who grew up hopping from one series to another (*Checkmate, Overland Trail, The Virginian, Search*, etc.) before moving over to movies. TV movies: *The Longest Hundred Miles, Terror in the Sky, The Birdman, The Death of Me Yet, Playmates, The Judge and Jake Wyler, Shirts/Skins, Death Race, Satan's Triangle, Roots, SST: Death Flight, Wild and Woolly, The Rebels*.

MacColl, Ewan (1915–). Hard-Left Scottish folk-singer whose honking ballads accompanied many radio features in the forties and fifties, and some television documentaries thereafter. But he emerged rather likeably from a Granada 70th birthday special, *Daddy, What Did You Do in the Strike?*   PP

McCord, Kent (1942–) (Kent McWhirter). American leading man who made his big impact with *Adam 12* but hasn't been around much since.

MacCormick, Iain (1917–65). One of the first British TV playwrights and certainly the first to become a household name with his 1954 cycle of four full-length plays, *The Promised Years*, to his favourite theme of ordinary lives disrupted by war and war's aftermath. One of the four, *The Liberators*, was re-produced six years later. Another cycle, *English Family Robinson* (1957), covered British rule in India from the mutiny to partition as experienced by one family. A third saga, about English settlers in East Africa, was never produced. With the advent of small-scale domestic realism his larger style was out of fashion. *Nightfall at Kriekville* (1960), set in South Africa, was his last play to be realized.   PP

MacCorkindale, Simon (1953–). Elegant but scarcely compelling British leading man. *I Claudius, Jesus of Nazareth, The Manions of America, Manimal, Obsessive Love*.

McCowan, George (19 –). Efficient Canadian director in American TV. Sometimes condemned to such series as *Seaway, Cannon, Starsky and Hutch* and *Charlie's Angels*, he has also contributed some good telefeatures: *The Monk, The Ballad of Andy Crocker*, THE LOVE WAR, *Run Simon Run, The Face of Fear, Welcome Home Johnny Bristol, Murder on Flight 502*, etc.

McCowen, Alec (1925–). Sensitive British actor with long if widely-spaced list of credits from *Angel Pavement*, 1958, to *Mr Palfrey of Westminster* (1984–85). His one-man performance of *The Gospel According to St Mark* was transferred to TV by Thames for Easter 1979. Also one-man *Kipling*, 1984, and as Rudolf Hess in *The World Walk*, 1985.   PP

McCoy: see Mystery Movie and The Big Rip-Off

Macdonald, Gus (1940–). Scottish current affairs producer, presenter and executive: *World in Action* stints, *Union World* and many specials for Granada, including Election Night compilation of run-of-the-mill US television, 1983. From 1982, host of Channel Four's *Right to Reply*. Since 1986 director of programmes at STV.
                                                                          PP

McDonald, Trevor (1939–). First black British newscaster, long with ITN.

MacDougall, Peter (1947–). Scottish TV playwright who came to notice in 1975 with a timely piece about sectarian enmity, if in Glasgow rather than Belfast, *Just Another Saturday*. Also, *Elephants' Graveyard, Just a Boy's Game, A Sense of Freedom*. Latest work: *Shoot for the Sun*, 1986.   PP

McDowall, Roddy (1928–). British actor in America, former child star, who pops up in films and TV guest spots. He also played the leading ape in the series *Planet of the Apes*, and had a continuing role in *Fantastic Journey*. TV movies: *Night Gallery, Terror in the Sky, A Taste of Evil, What's a Nice Girl Like You, The Elevator, Flood, The Rhinemann Exchange, The Immigrants, The Thief of Baghdad*.

McEachin, James (1931–). Black American actor who played the title role in *Tenafly*. He also appeared in *The Alpha Caper* and many other telefilms.

McEveety, Bernard (19 –). American journeyman director. Series episodes range from *The Virginian* to *How the West Was Won*. TV movies include *A Step Out of Line, Killer by Night, The MacAhans, The Hostage Heart*.

McEveety, Vincent (19 –). American journeyman director, brother of Bernard. Series include *Bonanza, Gunsmoke, Petrocelli*. TV movies: *Cutter's Trail, Wonder Woman, The Last Day*, etc.

MacEwan, Ian (1950–). British writer of much-praised short stories and novels, represented on television first by the mispraised *The Imitation Game* (1980). His earlier *Solid Geometry* was untransmitted. A Film on Four, *The Last of Summer* 1983. PP

McGavin, Darren (1922–). Diligent, reliable American TV leading man and character actor. Series include *Mike Hammer*, *Riverboat*, *The Outsider*, *The Night Stalker*, *Kolchak*. TV movies include *The Challenge*, *The Challengers*, *Berlin Affair*, *Tribes*, *Banyon*, *The Night Stalker*, *Something Evil*, *Rookies*, *Say Goodbye Maggie Cole*, *The Night Strangler*, *Brink's: The Great Robbery*, *Law and Order*, *The Users*, *Ike*, *Love for Rent*, *The Martian Chronicles*, *The Return of Marcus Welby*, *The Baron and the Kid*, *My Wicked Wicked Ways*.

McGiver, John (1913–75). Owlish American character actor who was always welcomed by the public, whether in films or in TV series such as *Many Happy Returns*, *The Jimmy Stewart Show*.

❋ **McGoohan, Patrick** (1928–). Quirky Anglo-American leading actor who became a household word in DANGER MAN, went over the top in THE PRISONER, and made a brief comeback ten years later in *Rafferty*. The best thing about *Jamaica Inn*, 1983.

McGrath, John (19 –). Scottish director and film-maker of ardent left-wing views. Assistant director to Denis Mitchell and Norman Swallow on *The Entertainers* in 1963 and co-proponent with Troy Kennedy Martin the following year of the non-naturalistic drama represented by *Diary of a Young Man*. Also in 1964 masterminded *Six*, a BBC2 series of experimental short films commissioned from young directors, and contributed one himself. Adapted stories by George Mackay Brown as a Play for Today, *Orkney* (1971), and his own tendentious *The Cheviot, the Stag and the Black, Black Oil* (1974) alleging capitalist exploitations of Scotland over the centuries. In the eighties set up his own production company in Edinburgh, Gateway Films: *Sweetwater Memories* (documentary about National Service in 1956 Egypt); *Poets and People* (1984); *Blood Red Roses* (for US), 1986. ,PP

MacGraw, Ali (1939–). American leading actress. *The Winds of War*, *China Rose*, *Dallas*.

MacGyver
US 1985 22 × 50m colour
ABC/Paramount/Henry Winkler–John Rich (Mel Efros)
An adventurer with special skills is called in by the government for impossible missions.

cr Thackary Pallor

Richard Dean Anderson, Michael Lerner

'Big question is how he is going to rescue a weak plot and an unbelievable array of situations week after week.' – *Daily Variety*
'Poorly conceived, written and acted.' – *LA Times*

McHale's Navy
US 1962–5 138 × 25m bw
ABC/MCA/Sto–Rev/Universal
The wacky antics of a PT crew in the World War II Pacific, specifically on the island of Taratupa. Routine service goings-on à la Hollywood, and highly popular.

Ernest Borgnine, Joe Flynn, Tim Conway

† The series was first conceived as a drama under the title *Seven Against the Sea*. In 1964 it spun off a shortlived feminine counterpart, *Broadside*.

Machinegunner
GB 1976 74m colour TVM
Harlech TV (Patrick Dromgoole)
A Bristol debt collector uncovers a crime ring. Misleadingly titled but thoroughly predictable crime caper.

w Bob Baker, Dave Martin *d* Patrick Dromgoole

Leonard Rossiter, Nina Baden-Semper, Kate O'Mara, Colin Welland

PP: 'It was fun, though.'

Macht, Stephen (1942–). American leading man. TV movies: *Amelia Earhart*, *Raid on Entebbe*, *Loose Change*, *Ring of Passion*, *Hunters of the Deep*, *The Immigrants*, *Enola Gay*. Series: *American Dream*.

Mackay, Fulton (1924–). Scottish actor best known as the nemesis of Ronnie Barker in PORRIDGE, but notable in many plays including GOING GENTLY.

McKay, Gardner (1932–). American leading man, star of *Adventures in Paradise*; not much heard from since.

McKeever and the Colonel
US 1962 26 × 25m bw
ABC/Four Star

A military school cadet is in constant hot water. Forgettable comedy.

Scott Lane, Allyn Joslyn

Mackenzie
GB 1980 10 × 50m colour
BBC (George Gallachio)

The ups and downs of a man with determination to succeed, whoever or whatever stands in his way.
Steamy melodrama which spends a lot of time in the bedroom and was something of a censorship breakthrough for BBC. Not otherwise notable.

w Andrea Newman d Roger Cheveley

Jack Galloway, Kara Wilson, Lynda Bellingham, Toby Salaman, Richard Marner, Sheila Ruskin

PP (1980): 'No need to feel furtive if you are gripped by *Mackenzie*. It will not damage your health, or your social credibility if the neighbours get to know . . . The ambitious Scottish builder moving to London was convincingly drawn with his eventual undoing coming neither from success nor from his busy sex life but from a last spasm of his own Scottish Presbyterian rectitude.'

Mackenzie, Sir Compton (1883–1972).
Scottish man of letters and veteran TV performer (debut 1937) who had a popular cultural hit with *The Glory That Was Greece*, a BBC series of the late fifties produced by Stephen Hearst in which the scholarship was enlivened by passing observations on the undesirability of such varied features as the H-bomb, red tape and the top halves of bikinis.   PP

Mackenzie, Jacqueline (19 –).
Anglo-Scottish actress and mimic who had an ephemeral career as a funny reporter on *Highlight*, a BBC precursor of the early evening *Tonight* in the mid-fifties. She would imitate people, animals and even objects she encountered. Moving her on to more ambitious undertakings, notably a situation comedy with Lorrae Desmond prophetically called *Trouble for Two*, failed to sustain the spell, and by the sixties she had vanished from view.   PP

McKenzie, Julia (1942–).
Engaging British light comedienne and popular singer, notable in *Song by Song*, *Maggie and Her*, *That Beryl Marston*, etc. From 1984, a household word as the middle-aged heroine of *Fresh Fields*.

McKenzie, Robert (1917–81).
Canadian political scientist resident in Britain, best known for his participation in election specials, when he would habitually forecast the outcome early on. But also a formidable interviewer for *Panorama*, *24 Hours*, *Tonight* and his own series *The Pursuit of Power* (1981).   PP

The Mackenzies of Paradise Cove
aka: *Wonderland Cove*
US 1978 74m colour TVM
ABC/Viacom/Blinn–Thorpe

Five children, whose parents were lost at sea, live in Hawaii under the protection of a wandering sailor.
Innocuous family fare which led to an unsuccessful series of six one-hours.

w William Blinn d Jerry Thorpe

Clu Gulager, Sean Roche, Lory Walsh, Sean Marshall, Randi Kiger, Keith Mitchell

McKenzie's Raiders
US 1958 39 × 25m bw
United Artists

Stories of the independently commanded outfit which brought law and order to the southwest. Passable western.

Richard Carlson

McKern, Leo (1920–).
Australian character actor in Britain since 1946, in all international media. Televiewers know him best as RUMPOLE OF THE BAILEY, but many other resounding performances including the painter J. M. W. Turner in *The Sun Is God* and the writer–hero of David Mercer's *On the Eve of Publication*.

TV movies: *The House on Garibaldi Street*, *King Lear*, *Reilly Ace of Spies*, *Murder with Mirrors*, *Monsignor Quixote* (1985).

PP: 'The splendid Leo McKern with his moon-cratered face and squashed nose, glinting eyes and bassoon voice. . .'

✳ Mackie, Philip (1918–85).
Prolific British playwright and producer, into television 1954 by way of documentary films for government agencies. As a contract writer at the BBC, along with Nigel Kneale and Donald Wilson, adapted Mazo de la Roche's *Whiteoaks* saga, Morrison's *The Hole in the Wall*, etc. At Granada 1958–70 wrote and/or produced *Saki*, *Paris 1900*, *The Liars*, THE CAESARS, besides being head of drama. As a freelance writer thereafter his most celebrated achievements were THE NAKED CIVIL SERVANT, *The Organization* and *An Englishman's Castle*; also *Therese Raquin*. Winner of many prizes. From so

many styles and adaptations it is difficult to pin down a personal Mackie contribution, but it probably lies in his unsentimental, heartfelt view of the institution of marriage, bleakly at first in the single play *A Marriage* (1972), more optimistically in the trilogy *Conjugal Rights* six months later.   PP

Last work: *The Cleopatras* for BBC, *Praying Mantis* (two-part thriller) for Channel 4, *East Lynne* for BBC, unproduced mini-serials for USA.   PP

MacKintosh, Ian (1940–79). British writer and script editor, formerly a naval officer, who created the successful *Warship* series and subsequently *The Sandbaggers*, about an SAS-type military squad. While researching an episode for the latter, MacKintosh mysteriously disappeared on a light plane flight in Alaska.   PP

McLaglen, Andrew V. (1920–). American film director, son of Victor. After years of *Perry Mason*, *Have Gun Will Travel* and *Gunsmoke*, he graduated to big screen actioners, but this phase waned and he returned to telemovies: *Log of the Black Pearl*, *Banjo Hackett*, *Murder at the World Series*, etc.

Maclaine, Shirley (1934–) (Shirley MacLean Beaty). American performer from Broadway and Hollywood. Many TV musical specials, also an unsuccessful series, *Shirley's World*.

The McLean Stevenson Show
US 1976 13 × 25m colour (VTR)
NBC/M and M (Monty Hall)
Domestic problems of the owner of a hardware store.
Archetypal star domestic comedy.
McLean Stevenson, Barbara Stuart, Ayn Ruymen
11

MacLeod, Gavin (1931–). American general-purpose actor. *Hogan's Heroes*, MARY TYLER MOORE, THE LOVE BOAT, *Captains and the Kings*, *Murder Can Hurt You*.

McLuhan, Marshall (1911–81). Canadian sage whose philosophy of a new era in human communications, freed from the word-by-word dispensation of print, influenced television thinking in the 1960s. His most durable concept is probably that of the Global Village, i.e. the peoples of the world brought closer together by the shared, instantaneous news of radio and TV, but it has so far failed to demonstrate itself in practice.   PP

McMahon, Ed (1923–). American character actor, Johnny Carson's announcer and feed on the *Tonight* show. Former circus clown, host of *The Big Top*.

MacMahon, Horace (1907–71). American character actor with a prizefighter's face. He spent many years playing gangsters in movies, then on TV became a household word in *Naked City*, and retired after his next, *Mr Broadway*.

McMillan (and Wife): see Mystery Movie and Once Upon a Dead Man

MacMurray, Fred (1907–). American leading man of Hollywood's golden age. He came to TV in the long-running series *My Three Sons* and has done occasional guest spots. TV movies: *The Chadwick Family*, *Beyond the Bermuda Triangle*.

McNaughton's Daughter
US 1976 96m colour TVM
Universal/David Victor (David J. O'Connell)
The daughter of a successful defence lawyer wants to follow in father's footsteps.
Ho-hum courtroom melodrama which spun off three one-hour episodes and collapsed.
w Ken Trevey *d* Jerry London
Susan Clark, Ralph Bellamy, Vera Miles, Louise Latham, Mike Farrell

✻ **MacNee, Patrick** (1922–). Elegant British leading man who created the character of the suave John Steed in THE AVENGERS, borrowing most of it from Ralph Richardson in the cinema film *Q Planes*. TV movies: *Billion Dollar Threat*, *Mister Jerico*, *Matt Helm*, *Sherlock Holmes in New York*, *Evening in Byzantium*, *Stunt Seven*, *Rehearsal for Murder*, *The Return of the Man from UNCLE*, *For the Term of His Natural Life* (miniseries; Australia), *Empire Inc*, *Lime Street*

MacNeil/Cornelius/Emlyn (GB 1969). ATV trilogy of half-hour plays by Alun Owen, packaged together for the USA with links by Laurence Olivier, shown separately in Britain. Good little plays by the master of two-handed drama were swamped by the showbiz-cum-good-works razzmatazz with which they were served up – apart from the Olivier introductions much was made of the fact that the stars, Sean Connery, Michael Caine and Paul Scofield, were only taking part because their fees were going to charity. That is, either ATV wasn't prepared to pay the rate such names could commercially demand, or

PATRICK MacNEE's one great role was as Steed in *The Avengers*. It gave him a passport to Hollywood, where, curiously enough, he tended to play the kind of villain he had been more used to catching.

Connery, Caine and Scofield were saying that normally they wouldn't have deigned to stoop to TV; whichever the explanation, it was pretty patronizing. The consolation was Anna Calder-Marshall, who went through all three playlets.   PP
LH: 'The trilogy in America was known as *The Male of the Species*.'

MacNeil, Robert (1921–). Rangy Canadian reporter and presenter into radio as an all-night disc jockey, into TV via ITN, NBC and the BBC's *Panorama*. Has latterly co-hosted PBS's nightly news show *The MacNeil/Lehrer Report*. Book: *The Right Place at the Right Time*, 1982.   PP

McNichol, Kristy (1963–). American juvenile actress. *Family, Summer of My German Soldier, My Old Man, Blinded by the Light*.

McQueen, Steve (1930–80). Tough American leading man who before his film fame starred in a TV series, *Wanted Dead or Alive*.

McRaney, Gerald (1948–). Rangy, balding American leading man, a hit as one of the brothers in *Simon and Simon*. Also: *Where the Ladies Go, The Law, The Trial of Chaplain Jensen, The Jordan Chance, Roots II, Memories Never Die, City Killer*.

MacTaggart, James (1926–74). Scottish director, producer and occasional writer, in charge of BBC *Wednesday Play* during the controversial 1965 season which included Dennis Potter's debut, Mercer's *And Did Those Feet?* and *Up the Junction* but also the disgrace of *For the West*, a lurid tract about mercenaries in Africa by Michael Hastings. Returning to the floor he directed such key productions as *Moonlight on the Highway* (1968), ROBIN REDBREAST (1970), *Orkney* (1971) and Adrian Mitchell's *Man Friday* (1972). With *Candide* MacTaggart tried hard to promote a non-naturalistic style of drama making extensive use of chromakey and other electronic effects, which didn't catch on. His own play *Boys and Girls Come out to Play* (1975) was a nice spooky idea let down – ironically – by too naturalistic, not to say plodding, a dénouement. A man of great warmth and fun, MacTaggart is remembered by a lecture given in his name at the Edinburgh Festival each year.   PP

MacWhinnie, Donald (1920–). Able British drama director, ex-radio, at first associated with Samuel Beckett and other 'difficult' writers, but over the years proving his ability to adjust to all brow-levels. A major achievement is the Evelyn Waugh trilogy SWORD OF HONOUR (1968).   PP

Macy, Bill (1922–). American character actor, nationally famous as the husband of *Maude*.

Mad Bull
US 1977 96m colour TVM
Filmways (Richard M. Rosenbloom)

A tough wrestler falls in love and helps to catch a dangerous fanatic.
Muddled comedy-melodrama which takes an age to get into its stride.
w Vernon Zimmerman *d* Walter Doniger, Len Steckler *ph* Jacques Marquette
Alex Karras, Susan Anspach, Nicholas Colasanto, Danny Dayton, Elisha Cook Jnr

The Mad Death
GB 1983 3 × 55m
BBC Scotland (Bob McIntosh)

Rabies breaks out after pet cat is smuggled into Britain. Lurid but fairly gripping thriller as police and animal welfare track down suspected carriers.
w Sean Hignett, *novel* Nigel Slater *d* Robert Young
Richard Heffer, Barbara Kellerman, Richard Morant, Ed Bishop, Brenda Bruce, Jimmy Logan   PP

Mad Jack ***
GB 1970 75m colour

Superb film about World War I poet Siegfried Sassoon and his single-handed protest against the carnage on the Western Front. Michael Jayston was absolutely right as Sassoon, whose individuality was contained behind a

conventional huntin', shootin', fishin' exterior. JACK GOLD's direction was precise and unobtrusive and – when required to be – striking. Who would have thought it possible to discover a new image of horror from trench warfare, 1914–18? In his one spare, shocking excursion to the front-line Gold did so: a white drowned face floating just below the surface of a water-filled shell-hole. Written by Tom Clarke; produced by Graeme McDonald: for BBC (*Wednesday Play*).   PP

Madame Bovary * (GB 1964 and 1975).
Flaubert's bored provincial deceiver inspired the very first of the classic serials which have graced BBC2 ever since, with Nyree Dawn Porter in the role. Her story is also of interest as one of the few adaptations (here by GILES COOPER) to be twice produced. The second version, in colour, starred Francesca Annis, who made the lady femininely impossible and impossibly authentic; directed by Rodney Bennett; produced by Richard Beynon.   PP

Madame Butterfly *** (West Germany 1976). Creamy production of Puccini's opera with Placido Domingo and Mirella Freni. Conducted by Herbert von Karajan; directed by Jean-Pierre Ponnelle.   PP

Madame Sin *
GB 1971 73m colour TVM
ITC (Lou Morheim)

A former CIA agent is brainwashed by a ray gun and forced to work for a female mastermind operating out of a Scottish castle. High camp for star fans: not much fun for anyone else.
w Barry Oringer, David Greene *d* David Greene *ph* Tony Richmond *m* Michael Gibbs
Bette Davis, Robert Wagner, Denholm Elliott, Gordon Jackson, Dudley Sutton, Catherine Schell
† An 88m cinema version was also released.

Madame X
US 1981 96m colour TVM
NBC/Universal/Levenback–Riche Productions

A woman with a past shoots a blackmailer and is defended by her daughter who doesn't know her.
Ancient melodramatic warhorse, quite unnecessarily remade for TV after several movie versions.
w Edward Anhalt, *play* Alexandre Bisson *d* Robert Ellis Miller *ph* Woody Omens *m* Angela Morley

Tuesday Weld, Granville Van Dusen, Eleanor Parker, Jeremy Britt, Len Cariou, Robert Hooks

'If the updating of the dusty story creaks at times, it's also a boost for romanticism, something in short supply these days.' – *Daily Variety*

Madden, Cecil (1902–). British pioneer of television entertainment. As programme organizer and senior producer in the prewar BBC service he devised the quintessential show *Picture Page*, with which BBC TV officially began on 2 November 1936, and edited all 264 editions of it. On resumption of television in 1946 occupied same job for a year, then became first head of children's TV and assistant to the Controller, TV.   PP

Made in Britain: See Birth of a Nation

Madigan: see Mystery Movie and Brock's Last Case

Madison, Guy (1922–) (Robert Moseley). Lean American leading man who became TV's *Wild Bill Hickok*, then vanished in a flurry of Italian westerns.

Madoc, Philip (1934–). Welsh actor who made his name as Lloyd George in *The Life and Times of Lloyd George*. Since then, *Ennal's Point* and many single plays and films. To play Tito in forthcoming series.   PP

Madoc, Ruth (1943–). British actress and dancer, former wife of Philip (above), ex-Black and White Minstrel. Best known as Gladys in *Hi-De-Hi!*

Maelstrom
GB 1985 6 × 50m
BBC/Gryphen Productions (Vere
   Lorrimer)
Having evidently exhausted the possibilities for making thrillers out of Greek island scenery, Michael J. Bird switched to Norway. Fjords, fishing boats and wooden houses now occupied the screen while the characters painstakingly invited each other out to discuss the plot. But the mix of mystery, love story, old secrets and some sinister dolls found an appreciative audience.
w Michael J. Bird   *d* David Malone
Tusse Silberg, David Beames, Ann Todd, Susan Gilmore, Christopher Scoular   PP
LH: 'By the end, a repetitive and intolerable bore.'

Maestro (GB 1984). Profiles of legendary sporting figures of the recent past, e.g. cyclist Reg Harris, footballer George Best; conducted by Barry Davies, produced by Jeff Goddard, for BBC.   PP

Maggie (US 1981). New half-hour comedy for ABC, with Miriam Flynn as a contemporary midwestern housewife. Created and written by Erna Bombeck; produced by Charlie Hauck; with James Hampton.

Maggie Briggs
CBS 1984   × 25m colour
Lorimar/Charlie Hauck (Tom Cherones)
A smart cityside reporter is shifted to the feature section.
Despite its star, this comedy series entirely lacked focus and wit, and quickly went the way of a hundred others.
cr Charlie Hauck, Suzanne Pleshette
Suzanne Pleshette, Kenneth McMillan, Shera Danese, Stephen Lee, John Getz
'A sitcom that seems to have been pulled from a 1950s time capsule.' – *Daily Variety*

The Magic Carpet *
US 1971 97m colour TVM
Universal (Ranald MacDougall)
A pretty American student in Rome becomes a tourist guide.
A pleasant tour of Italy, with some nonsense going on in the foreground.
w Ranald MacDougall   *d* William A. Graham
m Lyn Murray
Susan St James, Robert Pratt, Nanette Fabray, Jim Backus, Wally Cox

The Magic of Dance *
GB 1980 6 × 50m colour
BBC (Patricia Foy)
Margot Fonteyn reflects on the world of ballet and the history of dancing.
Absorbing and fairly definitive treatment of its subject.

Magic Rays of Light * (GB 1981; 55m). Bright little memoir of the earliest days of British television to mark the BBC's final departure from its original television studios in Alexandra Palace. Directed by Michael Cocker; produced by David Nelson; for BBC.   PP

magic wands. Wilfred and Mabel Pickles's *Ask Pickles* in the last years of the BBC monopoly was the first show on British TV which set out to make innocent viewers' dreams come true. Many of the requests were no more momentous than to hear some favourite song by some conveniently available singer; others trafficked fairly shamelessly in sentiment to present a little lame girl with the pony of her dreams or allow a broken-down old violinist to realize his ambition of playing a Stradivarius, just once. 'If the Almighty writes the script,' said Wilf, 'it's got to be good.' Despite heading the BBC audience ratings for two years the programme did not long survive the advent of ITV. Pickles blamed the critics.

Since the mid-seventies the idea has been revived on a more jocular basis in *Jim'll Fix It*, with Jimmy Savile wielding the magic wand and the requests drawn from children only. Dreams fulfilled have ranged from a small girl transported to Austria to sing 'The Hills Are Alive with Music' on the actual *Sound of Music* location to a small boy allowed to act, for one day, as butler to a titled family. Esther Rantzen's *The Big Time* extends the big opportunity to adult aspirants in the form of separate 50-minute documentary accounts of vicar conducting newspaper gossip column, housewife preparing banquet or, most famously, small-time singer Sheena Easton making pop record and thereby being launched on professional career.   PP

Magical Mystery Tour (GB 1967). Witless, narcissistic, conceited film by, with and the property of the Beatles. My impression in 1967: 'What depressed me was not that the *Magical Mystery Tour* shambled arbitrarily from set-piece to set-piece but that the set-pieces were so boring and bad and sloppy when we got there. The motor-race, the spaghetti-shovelling, pretty well every fancy dragged on too long. A banal bit with the lads as magicians in their den had McCartney twice smirking at his own feeble line, like a tenth-rate amateur actor.' Produced by Denis O'Dell; for Nems.
                                                              PP

The Magician *
US 1973 73m colour TVM
NBC/Paramount

A professional magician uses his trickery to outsmart kidnappers.

Polished nonsense which led to a one-season series of the same ilk (24 × 50m).

w Laurence Heath *d* Marvin Chomsky *m* Pat Williams

BILL BIXBY, Kim Hunter, Barry Sullivan, Elizabeth Ashley, Signe Hasso, Joan Caulfield, Keene Curtis

Magilla Gorilla
US 1964–5 58 × 25m colour
Hanna-Barbera

A mischievous gorilla causes havoc in the pet shop.

Quite a lively cartoon series, from the firm's better days. Also included each week: a segment featuring *Ricochet Rabbit*, a western spoof.

The Magnificent Evans (GB 1984; 6 × 30m). Sitcom with Ronnie Barker as a small-town photographer in Wales; never quite developed. Written by Roy Clarke, produced by Sydney Lotterby, for BBC.   PP

The Magnificent Magical Magnet of Santa Mesa
aka: *The Adventures of Freddie*
US 1977 74m colour TVM
Columbia/David Gerber

A young scientist invents a magnet which can solve the world's energy crisis.

Footling slapstick farce with a few obvious laughs.

w Gerald Gardner *d* Hy Averback

Michael Burns, Susan Blanchard, Harry Morgan, Tom Poston, Keene Curtis

The Magnificent Thief *
aka: *A Thief Is a Thief Is a Thief; It Takes a Thief*
US 1967 100m colour TVM
Universal (Frank Price)

A master thief is promised parole if he becomes a US agent.

Smooth, silly pilot for a long-running series (*It Takes a Thief*).

w Roland Kibbee, Leslie Stevens *d* Leslie Stevens

Robert Wagner, Senta Berger, John Saxon, Susan St James, Malachi Throne

Magnum P.I.
US 1980– × 50m colour
CBS/Universal/Bellisarius/Glen Larson (Donald P. Bellisario)

Cases of an ex-Vietnam private eye who lives free in the Hawaiian guest house of a wealthy writer for whom he once did a favour.

Formula crime capers with strong comedy elements, a sleek new leading man and rather too many extraneous characters (saloon owner, chopper pilot, etc.). It could hardly fail to be a commercial success, but one might have hoped for a little more wit and clarity.

cr Donald P. Bellisario, Glen Larson

TOM SELLECK, JOHN HILLERMAN, Roger E. Mosley

† The pilot, *Don't Eat the Snow in Hawaii*, ran 96 minutes and was grossly padded out with Vietnam flashbacks and in-jokes.

Magnusson, Magnus (1929–) (Magnus Sigursteinnson). Icelandic–Scottish presenter and writer best known for the stern omniscience with which he puts the questions in MASTERMIND – Smugness Smugnesson, the critic Sylvia Clayton called him. Into TV via *Tonight* and popular archaeological programmes: *Chronicle, Living Legends, The Vikings, Archaeology of the Bible Lands*.   PP

Magpie. British twice-weekly magazine programme for children, produced by Thames Television.

Maharis, George (1928–). Smooth American leading man who has had a fairly successful career in both films and TV. Series: ROUTE 66, *The Most Deadly Game, Rich Man, Poor Man.*

Mahoney, Jock (1919–) (Jacques O'Mahoney). Stalwart American leading man, a former Tarzan. Series include *The Range Rider, Yancy Derringer.*

Maid in America
US 1984 96m colour TVM
CBS (Norman I. Cohen)

A burly construction worker forces an attorney to consider him for an advertised job as a live-in maid.
Obvious comedy with very little wit in the development.

w Peter Feibleman   *d* Paul Aaron
ph Norman Leigh   *m* David Frank

Susan Clark, Alex Karras, Fritz Weaver, Mildred Natwick, David Spielberg

'The style is out of fashion and the script fails to charm.' – *Daily Variety*

Maigret ***. A superb series of 50-minute tape dramas produced by the BBC in the late fifties, with RUPERT DAVIES as Simenon's pipe-smoking Parisian sleuth who gets results from studying character rather than clues. Producer: ANDREW OSBORN.
PP: 'Surely one of the BBC's more over-rated successes. The first glimpse of Simenon's legendary detective in a Sunday night play, with Basil Sydney in the title role, was fine. After the mechanical plot-unfolding of conventional whodunits and the retributive zeal of American crime series it was a revelation to have a murder story in which the murderer wasn't even shown; he wasn't important; the emphasis was on the cabaret girl victim and the needlessness of her lost life. This element of concern survived in the *Maigret* series proper that followed – for one thing many of the scripts would be written by the same

adapter, Giles Cooper. The trouble was the Maigret impersonation no longer fitted such a philosophical approach. If Sydney had been too heavy and withdrawn, Rupert Davies wasn't heavy enough. A reflective sniff and much business with his pipe couldn't alter the impression that he seemed less like a policeman who'd come to solve the crime than an insurance man who'd come to check on the details of the victim's policy.'
† Georges Simenon was profiled with particular reference to Maigret, in *Mirror of Maigret* (GB 1971), an ATV documentary by John Goldschmidt.

The Main Attraction * (GB 1983). Clean, bright, un-emceed variety series enshrining some classic turns – Tommy Cooper with his box-of-hats routine, Warren Mitchell as Alf Garnett. Directed by John Bishop, produced by John Fisher, for BBC.   PP

The Main Chance * (GB 1969–75; 45 × 50m). Long-running, perpetually breathless series about a go-getting solicitor, created by Edmund Ward and produced by David Cunliffe for YTV. My opinion at the time: 'Leaving aside John Stride's vigorous and intelligent performance, it's not difficult to see why Main has become popular. Like Wilder or Steed in their respective hey-days, he's a man of nerve and impatience and instant decision. No matter how equivocal the rights and wrongs of the case, he bulldozes in. He acts out everyone's secret dreams of busting through the trammels of over-organized, over-taxed, over-regulated society.
'More than that, he acts out a national interior tussle between conscious liberal sentiment and blind reactionary instinct. When the underdog is being denied his rights or the coloured couple being prevented from adopting a white child, Main is as impeccably progressive as a current affairs producer. When it's a matter of his own children being taken away from private education and sent to a state school in a rough neighbourhood, the eloquent left hand is put away and the clenched right fist hammers down.
'Close your eyes and listen and Edmund Ward's dialogue is too often composed of exchanges of information skilfully wrapped in twangy, epigrammatic language. But it isn't taking place on the Moon; throttled back and flattened out, it could be our story; calmed down, Main could be a member of the race.'
PP

MAIGRET was a series with a lived-in quality, and probably did more than any other entertainment to endear the French to British audiences. Here Rupert Davies seems a shade suspicious of the victim's widow, played by Jean Anderson.

Mainstream (GB 1979). Doomed attempt (by Humphrey Burton and others for BBC) to concoct a live and dashing arts survey, in jeopardy from the moment co-founder Tony Palmer pulled out on the eve of its debut. PP

Major Adams, Trailmaster: see Wagon Train

Majors, Lee (1940–). Beefcake American leading man. Series include THE BIG VALLEY, *The Men from Shiloh*, *Owen Marshall*, SIX MILLION DOLLAR MAN, *The Fall Guy*. TV movies: *The Ballad of Andy Crocker*, *Weekend of Terror*, *Frances Gary Powers*, *Just a Little Inconvenience*.

Make a Wish *
US 1971–5 96 × 22m colour (VTR)
ABC News and Public Affairs/Lester Cooper

Informational series for children, the instruction being applied with a gentler hand than in *Sesame Street*, but equally effectively.
w/d Lester Cooper *host and songwriter* Tom Chapin

Make Me an Offer
US 1980 96m colour TVM
ABC Circle (Carter de Haven)

When her husband leaves her, a woman finds a new interest selling real estate in Beverly Hills. Comedy–drama which seems to have very little point but generally amuses and interests.
w Pamela Chais *d* Jerry Paris
Susan Blakely, Bruce Bauer, Patrick O'Neal, John Rubinstein, Stella Stevens
'Erratic but entertaining.' – *Hollywood Reporter*

Make Room for Daddy *
US 1953–5 and 1957–63 199 × 26m bw
ABC/T & L

A Copa Club entertainer has family trouble. Efficient long-running star comedy, later known as *The Danny Thomas Show*. It was followed in 1970 by 26 hours of *Make Room for Granddaddy*, in colour, but this was not a success.

DANNY THOMAS, Marjorie Lord (Jean Hagen first three seasons)

† Emmys: 1953, best new series; 1954, best situation comedy.

Makin' It
US 1979 9 × 25m colour
ABC/Paramount/Miller–Milkis (David
  Duclan, Deborah Leschin, Jeff Ganz)

Adventures of an Italian-American high-school student constantly distracted from academic matters.

Feeble addition to the teen cycle.

cr Mark Rothman, Lowell Ganz

David Naughton, Greg Antonacci, Denise Miller, Ellen Travolta

Making a Living: See *It's a Living*

Making Cars (GB 1983; 4 × 30m). Car workers and former car workers talking to camera, mostly about the old days of Morris Motors and Pressed Steel, obtained by setting up studio in a Cowley shopping centre and letting them drop in. Backed up sparingly with archive film, they dispensed nostalgia, resentment, eloquence and pride in about the right proportions, plus much vivid detail. Produced by Greg Lanning for Television History Workshop/C4.   PP

Making Faces (GB 1975; 6 × 30m). Sequence of BBC playlets written by Michael Frayn covering 16 years in the life – and endless talk – of a Jewish girl, a kind of rarefied *Rhoda*. My reaction in 1975: 'It came to an end leaving me rather hungry for a hamburger, just too civilized and urbane and meticulous and localized and bloodless. There is something about Eleanor Bron's performance that makes you feel you ought to have an appointment to watch her.'   PP

The Making of a Male Model
US 1983 96m colour TVM
ABC/Warner/Aaron Spelling (Lynn Loring,
  Elaine Rich)

The lady boss of a New York model agency falls for a cowboy and makes him a star. Hokum which promises more than it delivers.

w A. J. Carothers *d* Irving J. Moore
ph Richard Rawlings *m* Artie Butler
Joan Collins, Jon-Erik Hexum, Jeff Conaway, Ted McGinley, Kevin McCarthy, Arte Johnson, Robert Walker

'It all comes off as a variation on a 1930s filmusical in which the ingenue, leaving contentment behind, goes after stardom only to discover the true cost.' – *Daily Variety*

The Making of America (GB 1966; 10 × 30m). Useful educational history of the USA, repeated as a late-night show in 1968. Produced by Peter Dunkley; for BBC.   PP

The Making of Mankind *
GB 1981 7 × 50m colour
BBC (Graham Massey)

A documentary survey of the origins of our species.

First-rate information series which may offer rather more than most people want.

w/presenter Richard Leakey

PP: 'Leakey's theories, derived from his discovery in Africa of fossil relics pre-dating the normally accepted estimate of man's span on earth, were first aired, when still controversial, in an Anglia documentary *Bones of Contention*, 1976.'

Making the Grade (US 1982). Half-hour comedy series for CBS, apparently an Americanization of the British series *Please, Sir*. The scene is an inner city high school in which the teachers are afraid of the pupils. With James Naughton, Jack Feldspar. Produced by Gary Goldberg; for Paramount.

Malatesta * (GB 1964; 90m). PATRICK WYMARK, riding high on his *Plane Makers/Power Game* characterization, made a bid for bigger things in this version of Henry de Montherlant's stage play about a Renaissance despot, and nearly – but not quite – succeeded. My reaction at the time: 'In an early fit of rage Malatesta beat his breast, barked, butted his way through a door in a strangely Victorian gesture and flung himself on his bed like a male Joan Crawford. Some of director Christopher Morahan's fashionable giant close-ups, all jowl and nostril, emphasized that the Wymark breathing wasn't quite up to grand drama, which is physically as demanding as grand opera.'

Also with Jessica Dunning, Cyril Shaps, John Glyn-Jones. Translated by Jonathan Griffin; produced by Peter Luke; for BBC (*Wednesday Play*).   PP

✳ **Malden, Karl** (1913–) (Mladen Sekulovich). Intense American character actor who after years of second leads in Hollywood was promoted by TV to the top rank in *Streets of San Francisco*, and followed it with the ambitious but unsuccessful *Skag*. TV movies: *Word of Honor*, *Miracle on Ice*, *Intent to Kill*, FATAL VISION

The Male of the Species: see MacNeil/Cornelius/Emlyn

Malibu
US 1983 2 × 96m colour miniseries
ABC/Columbia/Robert Hamner (Peter J. Thompson)

Dramas of the idle rich who live on the Malibu seafront.
A kind of West Coast *Coronation Street* without any of the interest. Acting, dialogue and situations are alike risible, emanating from the oldest clichés in the business, not to mention some of the oldest actors.

w Elliott Baker, *novel* by William Murray *d* E. W. Swackhamer

Kim Novak, James Coburn, George Hamilton, Eva Marie Saint, Steve Forrest, Ann Jillian, Valerie Perrine, Susan Dey, William Atherton, Richard Mulligan, Anthony Newley, Chad Everett

Malibu Run: see The Aquanauts

Malice Aforethought *
GB 1979 4 × 50m colour
BBC (Richard Beynon)

A country doctor plots to murder the wife who stands between him and an affair.
Delightfully observed caricature of English country life in the thirties, with most of the suspense of the original novel maintained.

w Philip Mackie, *novel* Francis Iles *d* Cyril Coke

HYWEL BENNETT, Judy Parfitt, Cheryl Campbell, Harold Innocent

'How low would they go to top each other?'

Malice in Wonderland
US 1985 96m colour TVM
CBS/ITC (Jay Benson)

The rival careers of Hollywood columnists Hedda Hopper and Louella Parsons.
Moderately amusing for insiders only, with plenty of lookalikes to be recognized.

w Jacqueline Feather, David Seidler, *book Hedda and Louella* by George Eels *d* Gus Trikonis *ph* Philip Lathrop *m* Charles Bernstein

Elizabeth Taylor (Louella), Jane Alexander (Hedda), Richard Dysart, Joyce Van Patten, Jon Cypher, Leslie Ackerman

'It's fanciful, sometimes amusing, but misses the actual strength of two powerful women.' – *Daily Variety*

The Mallens (GB 1978–80). Attempt by Granada to draw on the perennial popularity of romantic fiction. Catherine Cookson's story of a wild squire with a white streak in his hair who littered the surrounding moorlands with bastard children exhibiting the same trademark was, unfortunately, tosh. A second series dealing with some of the offspring was an improvement, thanks to the performances of Juliet Stevenson and Gerry Sundquist as star-crossed lovers. PP

Mallory
aka: *Circumstantial Evidence*
US 1976 96m colour TVM
Universal (William Sackheim)

A once successful lawyer now operates under a cloud of suspicion since he was jailed (unjustly, of course) for perjury.
Failed pilot featuring the star in a curly wig, which tends to distract from an efficient story.

w Joel Oliansky *d* Boris Sagal *m* James di Pasquale

Raymond Burr, Mark Hamill, Robert Loggia

Malone, Dorothy (1930–). American leading actress who did pretty well in Hollywood, and even better in TV (as the star of PEYTON PLACE) until her career suddenly seemed to peter out. TV movies: *The Pigeon*, *Rich Man, Poor Man*, *Little Ladies of the Night*, *Murder in Peyton Place*, *Katie: Portrait of a Centerfold*, *Condominium*.

Mama. Live half-hour comedy show on CBS for eight seasons (1949–56), with Peggy Wood as the head of a Swedish–American family; based on the film *I Remember Mama*, and the book *Mama's Bank Account* by Kathryn Forbes; with Judson Laire, Dick Van Patten, Rosemary Rice.

Mama Malone
US 1983 13 × 25m colour
CBS/Columbia/BEL (Paul Bogart, Terrence McNally)

An Italian matriarch in New York copes with her family while being the star of a TV cooking show.
Confusing format in which all the action seems to happen while the show is on air. It didn't take.

w Terrence McNally *d* Paul Bogart *m* John Kander, Fred Ebb

Lila Kaye, Randee Heller, Evan Richards, Richard Yniguez, Ralph Manza

The Man *
US 1971 100m colour TVM
Lorimar/ABC Circle

The US gets its first black president.
Solid mini-screen adaptation of a successful novel.

w Rod Serling, *novel* Irving Wallace *d* Joseph Sargent

James Earl Jones, Martin Balsam, Burgess Meredith, William Windom, Barbara Rush, Lew Ayres, Anne Seymour

A Man About the House *
GB 1973–6 39 × 25m colour (VTR)
Thames

Two girls share their flat with a man because he is an expert on cookery.
Very slightly daring farce which became much more so when translated to American TV as *Three's Company*. The dumb landlord and his wife were sufficiently popular to qualify for a series of their own, *George and Mildred*.

w JOHNNIE MORTIMER, BRIAN COOKE

RICHARD O'SULLIVAN, PAULA WILCOX, SALLY THOMSETT, YOOTHA JOYCE, BRIAN MURPHY

Man Against Crime (US 1949–55). Half-hour private eye series for CBS, with Ralph Bellamy prowling the streets of New York.

Man Alive *. BBC documentary series which ran from 1965 until the mid-seventies, edited by Bill Morton and Desmond Wilcox and specializing in stories of the human predicament. 'They wheel a plague cart through the world,' I said, 'crying "Bring out your dread".' But there were some memorable films.   PP
† In 1983 *Man Alive* reporter Harold Williamson revisited and up-dated some of his stories for a series called *Only Time Would Tell*.

The Man and the Challenge
US 1959 36 × 25m bw
NBC/United Artists (Ivan Tors)

A scientist tests problems of human survival. Unusual semi-documentary series with the accent on space training.
George Nader

The Man and the City
US 1971 13 × 50m colour
ABC/MCA/Universal

Problems of the widowed mayor of a southwestern city.
A carefully made series, following the pilot *The City*, which despite a powerful star never got off the ground.
Anthony Quinn, Mike Farrell, Mala Powers

Man at the Top *
GB 1971–3 approx. 39 × 50m colour (VTR)
Thames (Jacqueline Davis)

Further adventures of Joe Lampton, the aggressive hero of the cinema film *Room at the Top*.
Plain-spoken Monday night adult entertainment which led to yet another film, this time based on the series.

w Tom Brennand, Roy Bottomley, after John Braine

Kenneth Haigh, Zena Walker

The Man Behind the Badge
US 1954 38 × 25m bw
CBS/Buckeye

True-life police stories, hosted by Charles Bickford.
Predictable formula stuff.

A Man Called Intrepid
GB/Canada/US 1979 3 × 96m colour
NBC/Lorimar/Astral (Peter Katz)

On Churchill's orders, Canadian William Stephenson sets up an espionage sector under the name Intrepid.
Flabby mish-mash of fact and fiction, with good sequences let down by an overplus of talk, romance and self-pity.

w William Blinn, *book* William Stevenson *d* Peter Carter *ph* Brian West *m* Robert Farnon

David Niven, Michael York, Barbara Hershey, Gayle Hunnicutt, Paul Harding, Flora Robson, Peter Gilmore, Renée Asherson, Nigel Stock, Ferdy Mayne

'Not merely a travesty of fact, it is also a wanton insult to living memory and living people.' – Hugh Trevor-Roper

A Man Called Ironside: see Ironside

A Man Called Shenandoah *
US 1965 34 × 25m bw
ABC/MGM

After the Civil War, an amnesia victim seeks his true identity.
Fairly stylish, sombre western which didn't take.
Robert Horton

A Man Called Sloane (US 1979). 13 hours were transmitted of this half-hearted James Bond rip-off in which Robert Conrad played the indefatigable counter-intelligence agent with Dan O'Herlihy as his boss. Created by Cliff Gould for QM Productions/NBC.

The Man Called X
US 1955 39 × 25m bw
UA

Hokum crime series.

Barry Sullivan

Man Friday
GB 1972 75m colour (VTR)

Liberal inversion of the Robinson Crusoe story to show it from the black man's viewpoint. Instead of upright Englishman (or in historical fact, Scot) civilizing the savage, it is the savage who tries to civilize his mentor. Written by Adrian Mitchell; directed by James MacTaggart; produced by Graeme McDonald; for BBC (*Play for Today*). My comment in 1972: 'Unfortunately the revised version proved to be even more loaded than the original. The blacks to whom the story was being told were uniformly wise, beautiful and dignified, if ultimately a bit short on charity. . . Bounced against such natural virtue, Crusoe's poor old Western values couldn't help but look ridiculous. Mitchell had a lot of simple fun at the expense of our notions of property, wages, industry and education, but when it came to his repressed sexual urges I fast grew restive.

'Whose reactions were these supposed to be? Certainly not Defoe's, nor of anyone of his time. Of the Victorian, empire building Crusoe of later children's editions and picture books? – ah yes, perhaps. But we're in 1972 (I think), not 1872. If, as the Press handout says, the play was meant to be offering a contemporary understanding of the Man Friday role, it cheated by pitting him against an archaic interpretation of Crusoe.'
Colin Blakely   PP

Man From Atlantis
US 1977 3 × 96m, 1 × 74m, 13 × 50m
   colour
NBC/Taft H–B/Herb Solow

An amnesiac with webbed hands is found washed up on the beach and because of his undersea skills is co-opted by the US Navy. A hokum idea which was initially handled with some charm and imagination, but lost its minimal style in translation to a one-hour series.

Patrick Duffy, Belinda J. Montgomery, Alan Fudge, Victor Buono

The Man From Black Hawk
US 1959 37 × 25m bw
ABC/Columbia/Stuart–Oliver

Cases of an insurance investigator in the old west.
Standard crime series, watchable in its day.

Robert Rockwell

The Man From Haven (GB 1972; 6 × 50m). Ian Holm as an unsporting financial operator who ferrets out the identity of five shady holders of numbered Swiss bank accounts and blackmails one of them in each succeeding episode. Created by Wilfred Greatorex; for ATV. As I wrote at the time: 'The Left won't like Wilfred Greatorex's new anti-hero any more than they took to Hine, his arms salesman, last year. . . But those who pause a moment before shouting will perhaps see that it's also a sharp satire on Capitalism.'   PP

Man From Interpol
GB 1959 39 × 25m bw
Danzigers

Adventures of a Scotland Yard special agent. Like an old Monogram second feature, but shorter.

Richard Wyler

A Man from the Sun * (GB 1956). Historic drama-doc about West Indian immigrants to Britain, at least 10 years before anyone else suspected there might be problems. 'Studio-shot with location film inserts,' said the programme note when the NFT showed it in 1985, 'it embraces issues which remain depressingly familiar.' With Errol John and Cy Grant; written and produced by John Elliott, for BBC.   PP

The Man From UNCLE *
US 1964–7 99 × 50m colour
NBC/MGM/Arena (Norman Felton)

Adventures of Napoleon Solo, Ilya Kuryakin and Mr Waverly, leading lights of an international spy organization on the right side, its headquarters located in Manhattan behind Del Floria's tailor shop.
Sometimes amusing, sometimes silly imitation of James Bond with its tongue firmly planted in its cheek.

cr Norman Felton, Sam Rolfe (with 'guidance' from Ian Fleming) m Jerry Goldsmith

Robert Vaughn, DAVID MCCALLUM, Leo G. Carroll

Episodes:
The Vulcan Affair with Patricia Barry
The Iowa Scuba Affair with Slim Pickens

The Quadripartite Affair with Anne Francis
The Shark Affair with Robert Culp
The Deadly Games Affair with Alexander Scourby
The Green Opal Affair with Carroll O'Connor
The Giuoco Piano Affair with Anne Francis
The Doubles Affair with Senta Berger
The Project Strigas Affair with William Shatner, Peggy Ann Garner
The Finny Foot Affair with Kurt Russell
The Neptune Affair with Henry Jones
The Dove Affair with Ricardo Montalban
The King of Knaves Affair with Madlyn Rhue
The Deadly Decoy Affair with Ralph Taeger
The Fiddlesticks Affair with Dan O'Herlihy
The Yellow Scarf Affair with Linden Chiles
The Mad Mad Tea Party Affair with Richard Haydn
The Secret Sceptre Affair with Gene Raymond
The Bow Bow Affair with Susan Oliver
The Four Steps Affair with Luciana Paluzzi
The See Paris and Die Affair with Lloyd Bochner
The Brain Killer Affair with Elsa Lanchester
The Hong Kong Shilling Affair with Richard Kiel, Glenn Corbett
The Never Never Affair with Barbara Feldon, Cesar Romero
The Love Affair with Eddie Albert
The Gazebo in the Maze Affair with George Sanders, Jeanette Nolan
The Girls of Navarone Affair with Sharon Tate
The Odd Man Affair with Martin Balsam, Barbara Shelley (end of first season)
The Alexander the Greater Affair (2 parts) with Rip Torn, Dorothy Provine
The Ultimate Computer Affair with Charles Ruggles
The Foxes and Hounds Affair with Vincent Price, Patricia Medina
The Discotheque Affair with Ray Danton
The Re-collectors Affair with George Macready
The Arabian Affair with Michael Ansara
The Tigers Are Coming Affair with Jill Ireland
The Deadly Toys Affair with Angela Lansbury, Jay North
The Cherry Blossom Affair with France Nuyen
The Virtue Affair with Mala Powers
The Children's Day Affair with Eduardo Ciannelli
The Adriatic Express Affair with Jessie Royce Landis, Juliet Mills
The Yukon Affair with George Sanders

The Very Important Zombie Affair with Claude Akins
The Dippy Blonde Affair with Joyce Jameson
The Deadly Goddess Affair with Victor Buono, Daniel J. Travanti
The Birds and the Bees Affair with John McGiver
The Waverly Ring Affair with Larry Blyden
The Bridge of Lions Affair (2 parts) with Maurice Evans, Vera Miles
The Foreign Legion Affair with Howard Da Silva
The Moonglow Affair with Kevin McCarthy
The Nowhere Affair with Diana Hyland, Lou Jacobi
The King of Diamonds Affair with Ricardo Montalban
The Project Deephole Affair with Jack Weston, Barbara Bouchet
The Round Table Affair with Don Francks, Reginald Gardiner
The Bat Cave Affair with Martin Landau
The Minus X Affair with Eve Arden
The Indian Affairs Affair with Joe Mantell, Ted de Corsia (end of second season)
The Her Master's Voice Affair with Estelle Winwood
The Do It Yourself Dreadful Affair with Jeannine Riley
The Galatea Affair with Joan Collins
The Super Colossal Affair with Shelley Berman, J. Carrol Naish
The Monks of St Thomas Affair with Celeste Yarnell
The Pop Art Affair with Sherry Alberoni
The Thor Affair with Bernard Fox
The Candidate's Wife Affair with Diana Hyland, Richard Anderson
The Come with Me to the Casbah Affair with Pat Harrington
The Off Broadway Affair with Shari Lewis
The Concrete Overcoat Affair (2 parts) with Janet Leigh, Jack Palance, Eduardo Ciannelli, Joan Blondell, Allen Jenkins, Jack La Rue, Elisha Cook Jnr, Vince Barnett
The Abominable Snowman Affair with Anne Jeffreys
The My Friend the Gorilla Affair with Alan Mowbray
The Jingle Bells Affair with Akim Tamiroff
The Flying Saucer Affair with Nancy Sinatra
The Suburbia Affair with Victor Borge
The Deadly Smorgasborg Affair with Robert Emhardt
The Yo-ho-ho and a Bottle of Rum Affair with Dan O'Herlihy, Eddie Quillan
The Napoleon Bonaparte's Tomb Affair with Kurt Kasznar, Fritz Feld

The It's All Greek to Me Affair with Harold J. Stone

The Hula Doll Affair with Pat Harrington, Patsy Kelly

The Pieces of Fate Affair with Theo Marcuse, Grayson Hall

The Matterhorn Affair with Bill Dana

The Hot Number Affair with Sonny and Cher, George Tobias

The When in Rome Affair with Cesare Danova

The Apple a Day Affair with Robert Emhardt, Gil Lamb

The Five Women Affair (2 parts) with Joan Crawford, Herbert Lom, Curt Jurgens, Telly Savalas, Terry-Thomas

The Cap and Gown Affair with Henry Jones (end of third season)

The Summit Affair with Albert Dekker

The Test-tube Killer Affair with Paul Lukas, Christopher Jones

The J for Judas Affair with Broderick Crawford, Chad Everett

The Prince of Darkness Affair (2 parts) with Bradford Dillman, John Carradine, Carol Lynley, Lola Albright

The Master's Touch Affair with Jack Lord

The Thrush Roulette Affair with Michael Rennie

The Deadly Quest Affair with Darren McGavin

The Fiery Angel Affair with Perry Lopez

The Survival School Affair with Richard Beymer

The Gurnius Affair with George Macready

The Man from Thrush Affair with Barbara Luna

The Maze Affair with Anna Capri

The Deep Six Affair with Alfred Ryder

The Seven Wonders of the World Affair (2 parts) with Eleanor Parker, Barry Sullivan, Leslie Nielsen, Hugh Marlowe, Tony Bill, Dan O'Herlihy, Ruth Warrick

In Great Britain the following 'feature films' were released in cinemas:

To Trap a Spy from *The Vulcan Affair* and *The Four Steps Affair*

One Spy Too Many from *The Alexander the Greater Affair*

One of Our Spies Is Missing from *The Bridge of Lions Affair*

The Spy in the Green Hat from *The Concrete Overcoat Affair*

The Karate Killers from *The Five Daughters Affair*

How to Steal the World from *The Seven Wonders of the World Affair*

The Spy with My Face from *The Double Affair*

The Helicopter Spies from *The Prince of Darkness Affair*

'The weekly perils of Solo and Co have been damned by most critics with the faint praise that they're good clean fun. I don't think they're much fun, and I'm certain they aren't good. I also have doubts about their cleanliness.' – Don Miller, 1965

† See also *The Girl from UNCLE.* (The letters stand for 'United Network Command for Law and Enforcement'.)

The Man Hunter
US 1969 98m colour TVM
Universal (Don Roth)

A banker hires an African white hunter to track down and kill the murderer of his son. Watchable action/chase nonsense.

w Meyer Dolinsky, *novel* Wade Miller *d* Don Taylor

Roy Thinnes, Sandra Dee, Albert Salmi, Sorrell Booke, David Brian

Man in a Suitcase *
GB 1967 30 × 50m colour
ATV

Adventures of a bounty-hunting secret agent. Competent espionage thick-ear.

Richard Bradford

The Man in Room 17 (GB 1965–6; 30 × 50m). For most of the run there were actually two men, played by Richard Vernon and Michael Aldridge (later, Denholm Elliott), solving crimes by logic without ever leaving their eyrie. Separate writers and directors were responsible for the 'Room' sequences and the outside action, to keep the detection process as detached as possible. *The Fellows* (1967) translated the men to even more rarefied heights as academic criminologists whose own behaviour was supposed to throw light on the criminal urge. *Spindoe* (1968), as the title accidentally suggested, was a further spin-off, picking up the story of a gang-leader (Ray McAnally) trying to resume career and authority after a prison sentence imposed on him at the end of *The Fellows*. Along the way the sequence demonstrated an interesting progression from straightforward whodunitry to the ambiguous social commentary of Robin Chapman. Other writers: Dennis Woolf, Eddie Boyd, John Kruse. Directed by David Cunliffe and others; produced by Richard Everitt; for Granada.   PP

The Man in the Iron Mask *
US/GB 1977 96m colour TVM
Norman Rosemont/ITC

The half-brother of Louis XIV is imprisoned for years in the Bastille and rescued by D'Artagnan.

Modest swashbuckler which despite effort all round can hardly compete with the 1939 film.

w William Bast *d* Mike Newell *m* Allyn Ferguson

Richard Chamberlain, Patrick McGoohan, Louis Jourdan, Jenny Agutter, Ian Holm, Ralph Richardson, Vivien Merchant, Brenda Bruce, Esmond Knight

The Man in the Santa Claus Suit
US 1980 96m colour TVM
NBC/Dick Clark

Three New Yorkers in trouble at Christmas are helped by a mysterious character who appears in different guise to each of them.
Club-footed fantasy which aims to hover somewhere between *Harvey* and *Here Comes Mr Jordan*, and fails.

w George Kirgo, *story* Leonard Gershe *d* Corey Allen *ph* Woody Omens *m* Peter Matz

Fred Astaire, Gary Burghoff, John Byner, Bert Convy, Tara Buckman, Brooke Bundy, Nanette Fabray, Harold Gould

'Mildly diverting fantasy, a combination of *Dear Abby* and *Mr Fixit*.' – *Daily Variety*

Man of Many Faces: see Toma

A Man of Our Times ***
GB 1968 13 × 52m bw (VTR)

Accept subordinate job or strike out on his own? GEORGE COLE as the blue-chinned manager of a small furniture works taken over by a big firm acted out a common enough predicament of the day to inaugurate what became an intermittent sequence of serials over the years dealing – on the whole faithfully – with changes of life among the middle-aged middle classes: Julia Jones's *Home and Away* (children grown up, what to do next) from Granada (1972); Richard Bates's *Helen, a Woman of Today* (divorce) and *Intimate Strangers* (illness, early retirement, marriage under strain) from LWT (1973 and 1974); Adele Rose's *Second Chance* (divorce again) from YTV (1981). For hosts of viewers it was Their Story. But 'A Man' was the pioneer. Also with Isabel Dean. Written by Julian Bond; for Rediffusion.   PP

Man of the Month (GB 1969). Regular ATV documentaries over a period of about six months normally picking one eminence in the news, e.g. Levi Eshkol, then Prime Minister of Israel, but on one occasion – as *Woman of the Month* – a representative old age pensioner. PP

Man of the World
GB 1962 20 × 50m bw
ATV

Adventures of a roving photographer.
Very moderate, glossy actioner.

Craig Stevens

Man on a String
US 1971 73m colour TVM
Columbia

An ex-policeman goes undercover with the mob.
So routine you don't even need to watch it.

w Ben Maddow *d* Joseph Sargent

Christopher George, Joel Grey, William Schallert, Jack Warden

Man on the Outside: see Griff

The Man Who Could Talk to Kids
US 1973 73m colour TVM
Tomorrow

A frustrated child finds one adult with whom he can express himself.
Tedious taradiddle, well-meaning but dull.

w Douglas Day Stewart *d* Donald Wrye

Peter Boyle, Robert Reed, Scott Jacoby, Collin Wilcox-Horne

The Man Who Died Twice *
US 1970 100m colour TVM
Cinema Center 100 (Steve Shagan)

An American artist in Spain finds it convenient to sham dead, which leads to complications.
Slightly unusual, location-shot drama which keeps the interest.

w Jackson Gills *d* Joseph Sargent *ph* Gabriel Torres *m* John Parker

Stuart Whitman, Brigitte Fossey, Jeremy Slate, Bernard Lee, Severn Darden

The Man Who Married a French Wife
(US/GB 1982; 90m). Three classic Irwin Shaw stories packaged for an odd little co-production between WNET (educational network), USA, and the BBC, who contributed the title segment, directed by John Glenister, with Bob Sherman in the role. The other two stories were *The Girls in Their Summer Dresses*, bafflingly brought forward to modern times, and the best of the bunch, *The Monument*, with Charles Durning as a stalwart New York barman of the thirties. Both these were directed by Nick Havinga; all three dramatized by Kenneth Cavander.   PP

The Man Who Never Was
US 1966 18 × 25m colour
ABC/TCF (John Newland)

An unpleasant German is impersonated by his double, a US agent.

Cheeky melodrama inspired less by the film of the same name than by the old Chevalier vehicle *Folies Bergère*.

cr John Newland, Teddi Sherman, Judith and Julian Plowden

Robert Lansing, Dana Wynter

Man with a Camera
US 1958 29 × 28m bw
ABC/MCW (Lewis and Sharpe)

A freelance photographer gets involved in mysteries.

Punchy melodramas somewhat enlivened by an emerging star.

Charles Bronson

The Man with the Power
US 1977 96m colour TVM
Universal

A man whose father hailed from another planet has the power to perform amazing feats through eye concentration, and rescues a kidnapped princess.

Lead-footed fantasy pilot.

w Allan Balter *d* Nick Sgarro

Bob Neill, Persis Khambatta, Tim O'Connor, Vic Morrow

The Man without a Country *
US 1973 73m colour (16mm) TVM
Norman Rosemont

In the 18th century a young man damns his country and is sentenced never to set foot on it again.

Well-acted presentation of an American fable which in the end seems rather foolish.

w Sidney Carroll, *story* Edward Everett Hale *d* Delbert Mann

Cliff Robertson, Beau Bridges, Peter Strauss, Robert Ryan, Patricia Elliott, Walter Abel

Mandrake (the Magician)
US 1954 × 25m bw

Young Mandrake, who learned his secrets by ancient Tibetan tradition, crusades against evil with his servant Lothar.

Enthusiastic comic strip hokum.

Coe Norton, Woody Strode

Mandrake the Magician
US 1978 96m colour TVM
NBC/Universal (Rick Husky)

Mandrake operates as an undercover agent for the government.

Inept and styleless updating: miscasting plus a snail's pace produce boredom.

w Rick Husky *d* Harry Falk *ph* Vincent A. Martinelli *m* Morton Stevens

Anthony Herarra, Simone Griffith, Ji-Tu Cumbaka, Robert Reed, Gretchen Corbett, Peter Haskell, David Hooks

'Impossible, but Husky has pulled off the magic feat: he's made Mandrake and his pals dull to the point of stupefaction.' – *Daily Variety*

Mandrell, Barbara
(1948–). American country singer who got her own network series in 1980.

Maneater
US 1973 74m colour TVM
Universal (Robert F. O'Neill)

Holidaymakers are trapped in a wild animal quarry whose mad owner releases tigers to stalk and kill them.

The Hounds of Zaroff ride again, but not very excitingly.

w Vince Edwards, Marcus Demian, Jimmy Sangster *d* Vince Edwards *m* George Romanis

Richard Basehart, Ben Gazzara, Sheree North, Kip Niven

Maneaters Are Loose!
US 1978 96m colour TVM
CBS/Mona/Finnegan (Robert D. Wood, William Finnegan)

A small town is menaced by escaped tigers. Choppy, cliché-ridden suspenser which doesn't thrill but does irritate.

w Robert W. Lenski, *book Maneater* by Ted Willis *d* Timothy Galfas *ph* Hugh Gagnier *m* Gerald Fried

Tom Skerritt, Steve Forrest, G. D. Spradlin, Harry Morgan, Frank Marth, Diana Muldaur

'It includes, beyond abysmal dialogue and inane plotting, a guilt-ridden tiger hunter; a cop with a rotten superior and an ever-loving wife; a porno operation headed by a church deacon; a sexy cocktail waitress; an ex-drunk, once-famous reporter; corrupt county officials; a philandering county treasurer and his upright bossy wife; a woman who drinks too much; and even a forest fire. No actors' names, please, to protect the innocent.' – Judith Crist

Manhunt
Working title: *Underwater Car*
US 1959–60 78 × 25m bw
Columbia (Jerry Briskin)

Stories of the San Diego Police Department. Crime on location, quite efficient.

Victor Jory

Manhunt
GB 1970 26 × 50m colour

World War II series/serial about RAF pilot, girl and Resistance leader on the run in occupied France, with Robert Hardy gradually hogging the story as the high-living, lone-operator Abwehr sergeant Gratz – a character based on a real-life original. Also with Peter Barkworth, Cyd Hayman, Alfred Lynch. Written by Vincent Tilsley; created and produced by Rex Firkin; for LWT.

My assessment in 1970: 'The essential, unforgivable mistake has been to ascribe to a straightforward hot-war situation sophistications of conscience and intricacies of loyalty that belong to the Cold War. It's rather like old *Wagon Train*, in which urban problems of the 1950s were back-projected into the raw West of 100 years earlier.

'Alfred Lynch's Squadron-Leader Jimmy (Porter) is a total anachronism. The one strand in the saga that has struck me as authentic is the suspicion between patrician and Communist resistance movements. The one character who has been consistently believable – and most impressive – is Peter Barkworth's Vincent. The only times I have been reminded of the cruelty and terror of Nazism, or moved by the heroism of those who opposed it, have been when he has been in the foreground.'   PP

Manhunter *
US 1974 74m colour TVM
CBS/Quinn Martin

In 1933, when his fiancée is killed by public enemies, an ex-marine becomes a travelling G-man dedicated to their capture.

Dour pilot with a good period feel and a hulking Superman hero; the one-season series which followed was surprisingly dull.

w Sam Rolfe d Walter Grauman

Ken Howard, Gary Lockwood, Tim O'Connor, James Olson, Stefanie Powers

Manilow, Barry (1946–). American popular singer, in many concert specials.

Manimal
US 1983 96m colour TVM
CBS/TCF/Glen Larson (Harker Wade)

A university professor can transform himself into any animal at will.

And does so, of course, in the interests of justice; though what happens to his clothes is never made clear. Absurd taradiddle which even the American kiddult audience sniffed at; the one-hour series ran 13 episodes.

w Donald R. Boyle, Glen Larson d Russ Mayberry

Simon MacCorkindale, Glynn Turman, Melody Anderson, Terry Kiser, Lloyd Bochner

'The kind of series that gives television a bad name.' – *Daily Variety*

The Manions of America
US 1981 3 × 96m colour
ABC/EMI/Roger Gimbel (Stanley Kallis)

In the 19th century members of an Irish family, divided among themselves, make a new life in the New World.

Sluggish mini-series of primary interest to Irish-Americans.

w Rosemary Anne Sisson, *story* Agnes Nixon d Joseph Sargent; Charles Dubin ph Hector Figueroa, Lamar Boren, Frank Watts m Morton Stevens pd Paul Barnes

Kathleen Beller, Simon MacCorkindale, David Soul, Peter Gilmore, Nicholas Hammond, Kate Mulgrew, Barbara Parkins, Linda Purl, Anthony Quayle, Steve Forrest, Pierce Brosnan

'Evening soap opera flinging itself from distress to despair with little to relieve it.' – *Daily Variety*

❋ **Mann, Abby** (1927–). Prolific playwright of American TV's 'golden age', noted for JUDGMENT AT NUREMBERG, *The Marcus Nelson Murders, King, This Man Stands Alone, Skag, The Atlanta Child Murders* and many others.

❋ **Mann, Delbert** (1920–). American TV director who gained a huge reputation with such plays as MARTY, MIDDLE OF THE NIGHT and THE BACHELOR PARTY. His subsequent career in Hollywood was less inspired. TV movies: *The Man without a Country, Torn between Two Lovers, All Quiet on the Western Front, To Find My Son, All the Way Home, The Gift of Love, Love Leads the Way, A Death in California.*

Mannix *
US 1967–74 192 × 50m colour
CBS/Paramount/Bruce Geller (Ivan Goff, Ben Roberts)

Cases of a private investigator.

Well-made, action-filled crime show.

cr Richard Levinson, William Link m Lalo Schifrin

Michael Connors, Gail Fisher, Joseph Campanella, Robert Reed

Mantooth, Randolph (1945–). American leading man, half-Seminole, who leaped to stardom in *Emergency.*

Many Happy Returns
US 1964 26 × 25m bw
CBS/MGM/Lindabob
Business and domestic trials of the complaints
manager of a department store.
Engaging but unsuccessful star vehicle.
John McGiver, Elinor Donahue, Mark
Goddard

The Many Loves of Arthur
US 1978 50m colour
MTM (Philip Barry)
A gentle vet and an insecure stewardess fall in
love after being hurt by past romances.
Pleasant but not outstanding two-character
comedy which failed to sell a series.
w Gerald DiPego d Bill Bixby ph Chuck
Arnold m Paul Williams
Richard Masur, Silvana Gallardo, Constance
McCashin, Robert Ridgely

The Many Loves of Dobie Gillis: see Dobie
Gillis

Mapp and Lucia *
GB 1985 5 × 60m
LWT (Michael Dunlop)
E. F. Benson's exquisite comedy of
small-town life and rivalry in the twenties
nicely realized by Michael Dunlop (his last
show before he died), if appealing more to
fans of the six novels featuring Miss Mapp
and Mrs Lucas – separately or together –
than to the audience in general.
w Gerald Savory, novels E. F. Benson
d Donald McWhinnie
Geraldine McEwan, Prunella Scales, Nigel
Hawthorne   PP
LH: 'I felt it never got the spirit of the
books, and would alienate potential readers.'
† A further series of five followed in 1986.

Marathon
US 1979 96m colour TVM
CBS/Alan Landsburg
Middle-aged pals enter for the 26-mile New
York marathon.
Mild comedy with dramatic moments. The
locations are the best part.
w Ron Friedman d Jackie Cooper ph William
K. Jurgensen m Joe Renzetti
Bob Newhart, Herb Edelman, Dick Gautier,
Anita Gillette, Leigh Taylor-Young, John
Hillerman
'Affectionate jousting at the subject leaves
little dent.' – Daily Variety

Marchand, Nancy (1928–). Statuesque
American theatrical actress who scored a
television hit as Mrs Pynchon in LOU GRANT
(Emmy 1982).

'His greatest fight was to keep the
woman he loved!'
Marciano
US 1983 96m colour TVM
ABC (John G. Stephens)
The ups and downs of a prizefighter's career.
Nothing surprises even mildly in this
warmed-over version of a familiar story.
w Paul Savage d Bernard Kowalski
Tony Lo Bianco, Vincent Gardenia, Belinda
J. Montgomery, Michael O'Hare

The Marcus Nelson Murders *
US 1972 148m colour TVM
Universal (Abby Mann)
A New York detective tries to help a black
youth wrongly arrested for the murder of two
women.
Dour, unrecognizable pilot for Kojak: the
series was much more escapist in tone than this
grimly accurate exploration of New York
ghettoes.
w Abby Mann, from files on record d Joseph
Sargent (Emmy 1972) m Billy Goldenberg
TELLY SAVALAS, Marjoe Gortner, Gene
Woodbury, Jose Ferrer, Ned Beatty

Marcus Welby MD
aka: A Matter of Humanities
US 1968 98m colour TVM
ABC/Universal (David Victor)
An elderly Santa Monica doctor with heart
trouble takes on a young assistant and together
they help a small boy who can't speak or write.
A dullish pilot for a long-running series; it
nevertheless won Emmys for Brolin and
Young, who subsequently got a more stylish
haircut.
w Don M. Mankiewicz d David Lowell Rich
ROBERT YOUNG, JAMES BROLIN, Anne Baxter,
Pete Duel, Susan Strasberg, Lew Ayres
† The resulting series ran nine seasons;
172 × 50m episodes, created and produced by
David Victor. Syndication title: Robert Young
Family Doctor.

Margaret and the Saturday Night Ladies
US 1985 96m colour TVM
ABC/Poolhouse (Neil T. Maffeo)

A nun starts a rehabilitation house for convicted women.

Without even seeing the movie you can feel the thick mixture of smiles, tears and melodrama.

w Terry Louise Fisher and Steve Brown d Paul Wendkos

Bonnie Franklin, Jeanetta Arquette, Trazana Beverley, Rosemary Clooney

Margie

US 1961 26 × 25m bw
ABC/TCF

Scrapes of a twenties college girl.
Mild comedy, loosely based on the movie.

Cynthia Pepper, Penny Parker

Margin for Murder

US 1980 96m colour TVM
CBS/Metromedia/Robert Hamner (Alex Lucas)

Mike Hammer avenges the murder of his bouncer friend.

Reasonably lively private eye fable in the tough tradition expected of this author.

w Calvin Clements Jnr, from characters created by Mickey Spillane d Daniel Haller ph Michael C. Marguiles m Nelson Riddle

Kevin Dobson, Charles Hallahan, Cindy Pickett, Donna Dixon, Aarika Wells

Marie Curie **

GB 1977 5 × 50m colour (VTR)
BBC/Time–Life/Polytel (Peter Goodchild)

The life of Marie Curie, discoverer of radium.

A harsher attitude than usual, based on fresh research, but a complete picture, impeccably produced.

w ELAINE MORGAN, book Robert Reid d John Glenister

JANE LAPOTAIRE, Nigel Hawthorne, Penelope Lee, William Sleigh

'An exceptional piece of work.' – *Observer*

† BAFTA award 1977, best series.

Marilyn Monroe: Say Goodbye to the President (GB 1985). The doomed film star's relationship with John and Bobby Kennedy before she died from a drug overdose. Unpleasantly self-satisfied documentary written and directed by Christopher Olgiati, produced by George Carey, for BBC.   PP

Marilyn: The Untold Story *

US 1980 142m colour TVM
ABC/Lawrence Schiller

The life of Marilyn Monroe.

Yet another attempt – in the same year as it was done in *Moviola* – to make sense of *non sequiturs* and throw light on dark corners. Nothing new emerges, but the imitations of famous people are interesting.

w Dalene Young, book Norman Mailer d John Flynn, Jack Arnold, Lawrence Schiller ph Terry Meade m William Goldstein

Catherine Hicks, Richard Basehart (Hyde), Frank Converse (DiMaggio), John Ireland (Huston), Viveca Lindfors (Lytess), Jason Miller (Arthur Miller), Sheree North (Monroe's mother), Larry Pennell (Gable), Priscilla Morrill (Louella Parsons)

Marine Boy

US–Japan 1966 78 × 25m colour
Seven Arts

Adventures of a young agent for Ocean Patrol, an international undersea defence organization.

Stereotyped cartoon adventures.

Marion Rose White

US 1982 96m colour TVM
CBS/MGM/Gerald Abrams/Cypress Point (Steve Nicolaides)

A young girl is wrongly sent to a state hospital for the feeble-minded, and sterilized before the truth is discovered.

A fairly chilling true story of a woman who spent 30 unwarranted years behind bars.

w Garry Rusoff d Robert Day ph Richard Glouner m Billy Goldenberg

Nancy Cartwright, Charles Aidman, Ruth Silveira, Valerie Perrine, Katharine Ross, Frances Lee McCain

Mark, I Love You

US 1979 96m colour TVM
CBS/James T. Aubrey (William L. Hayward)

Grandparents try to claim a small boy away from the custody of his divorced father, whose life is thought to be bohemian.

Tedious fatherlove drama vaguely based on a real case but insufficiently dramatized.

w Sue Grafton d Gunnar Hellstrom ph Thomas Del Ruth m Jimmie Haskell

James Whitmore, Kevin Dobson, Cassie Yates, Dana Elcar

'Tedious and repetitive.' – *Daily Variety*

MANN'S BEST FRIEND. Fulton Mackay as the caretaker of a seedy apartment house, and Bernard Bresslaw as his aide, in a comedy series that never really caught on.

The Mark of Zorro
US 1974 74m colour TVM
TCF
Much-filmed adventure story about a Robin Hood of old California.
Modestly competent TV version.
w Brian Taggert d Don McDougall m Alfred Newman, adapted by Dominic Frontiere
Frank Langella, Ricardo Montalban, Gilbert Roland, Louise Sorel, Yvonne de Carlo, Robert Middleton

Mark Saber. Two separate crime series of the fifties featured this rather characterless character. In the American version he was a police inspector played by Tom Conway. In the British, played by Donald Gray, he was a one-armed private eye. In both cases he was inept, and so were his films.

Markham *
US 1959–60 60 × 25m bw
CBS/Markham/Universal
Adventures of a globe-trotting attorney who fancies himself as an investigator.
Fairly polished cops-and-robbers.
Ray Milland

Markham, Monte (1935–). American leading man who appears fairly exclusively on TV but never made a real hit. Series: *The Second Hundred Years*, *Mr Deeds Goes to Town*, *The New Perry Mason*. TV movie: *Death Takes a Holiday*.

Marks, Alfred (1921–). British comedian and actor whose series *Alfred Marks Time* was one of the few bearable entertainments in the early days of ITV. Now wholly an actor, and a good one. *Albert and Victoria*, a domestic comedy series, 1970–71.   PP

Marks, Louis (19 –). British producer. Entered industry 1959 as writer and later script editor on numerous series including *Dr Who*, *No Hiding Place*, *Main Chance*. Created ATV's *Honey Lane*. Joined BBC 1970. Productions include *Eleanor Marx*, *The Lost Boys* (RTS and Pye Awards), *Fearless Frank*, *St Joan*, *The Dybbuk*, *Grown-ups*, *Bavarian Night*, *Sheppey*, *Unity*, *The Crucible*.. Has lately concentrated on theatre classics including *Time and the Conways*, *Vicious Circle* and *A Month in the Country*, all 1985.

Marlowe, Hugh (1914–) (Hugh Hipple). American second lead of the fifties. TV series: *Ellery Queen*.

Marlowe – Private Eye *
GB 1984 6 × 60m
David Wickes Productions (David Wickes)/LWT
Cheeky but successful series of Raymond Chandler stories with Los Angeles exteriors but London standing in for 'Bay City' indoors; art-deco interiors along the Great West Road were just right. And of Powers Boothe as Marlowe I wrote, 'Has an easy smile, lots of integrity and a wide-jawed face that can endure a savage beating-up with only a swollen lip and a few grazes to show for it next day.'
w Jesse Lasky Jnr, Pat Silver, Jo Elsinger, David Wickes d Peter Hunt, Bryan Forbes, Sidney Hayers, David Wickes   PP
'What fun! What sleuthing! . . . What tailoring! . . . more! more! – *LA Times*
† A further series of six followed in 1986, with Canadian money (and Toronto locations) replacing LWT's involvement.

The Marriage (US 1954). Half-hour domestic comedy which ran five weeks on NBC in 1954, starred Hume Cronyn and Jessica Tandy, and was the first series to be transmitted in colour.
† Also the title of a perfectly dreadful documentary series (6 × 50m) following the preparations, wedding and first year of marriage of a foolhardy Welsh couple, produced and spelled out by Desmond Wilcox for BBC Scotland, 1986.   PP

Marriage Is Alive and Well
US 1980 96m colour TVM
NBC/Lorimar (Paul Waigner)
A wedding photographer gets four glimpses of the state of the institution of matrimony.
Whimsical multi-part comedy; presumably someone thought it might develop into a series on the lines of *Love American Style*. It didn't.
w Lee Kalcheim d Russ Mayberry ph Hector R. Figueroa m Fred Karlin
Joe Namath, Jack Albertson, Melinda Dillon, Judd Hirsch, Fred McCarren, Susan Sullivan, Nicholas Pryor, Deborah Baltzell

Marriage: Year One
US 1970 100m colour TVM
Universal/Norman Felton (Stephen Karpf)
Problems of lovers who marry while still at college.
The kind of problems most adult viewers at least can do without.
m David Shire
Sally Field, Robert Pratt, William Windom, Agnes Moorehead, Neville Brand

A Married Man
GB 1983 4 × 60m
LWT (John Davies) for C4
Solid, well-fleshed saga of marital doldrums, with Anthony Hopkins delivering (for him) an attractive and restrained performance.

w Derek Marlowe, *novel* Piers Paul Read
d Charles Jarrott

Anthony Hopkins, Ciaran Madden, Lise Hilboldt, Tracey Childs, Clive Francis, Kenneth Farrington, Geoffrey Chater, John Le Mesurier   PP

LH: 'Mainly dreary and always predictable.'

'She was almost a woman. He was almost a man. And all the world couldn't tear them from each other's arms.'

Married: The First Year
US 1979 4 × 50m colour
CBS/Lorimar
Contemporary problems face a newly married couple.
Hopeless sudser which barely got off the ground.

Leigh McCloskey, Cindy Grover, Claudette Nevins, Martha Scott

Marsden, Roy (1941–). Taciturn British actor who excels in taciturn roles: *The Sandbaggers*, *Airline*, *Goodbye Mr Chips* and Anglia's four P. D. James whodunit serials. For 1986 suggested the newspaper series *Inside Story* and stars in it.   PP

Marsh, Jean (1934–). British general purpose actress who scored a great personal hit, especially in the US, as Rose the maid in UPSTAIRS, DOWNSTAIRS.

Marshal Dillon: see Gunsmoke

The Marshal of Gunsight Pass (US 1950).
Half-hour western for ABC, starring Russell Hayden and Rosco Ates.

❋ **Marshall, E. G.** (1910–) (Everett G. Marshall). Distinguished American character actor. TV work includes THE DEFENDERS (series: Emmy 1961) and *The Bold Ones* (series) and an excellent impersonation of Truman in *Collision Course*. TV movies: *A Clear and Present Danger*, *Vanished*, *The City*, *Ellery Queen: Don't Look Behind You*, *Pursuit*, *Money to Burn*, *The Abduction of St Anne*, *Disaster on the Coastliner*.

Marshall, Garry (1934–). American series producer, associated with comedies such as *Happy Days*, *Laverne and Shirley*, *Mork and Mindy*.

Marshall, Penny (1943–). American comedy actress, a semi-regular in *The Odd Couple* and a co-star of *Laverne and Shirley*. TV movies: *Let's Switch*, *More Than Friends*.

Marshall, Peter (19 –) (Pierra la Cock). American anchor man, longtime host of *Hollywood Squares*.

Marshall, Roger (19 –). Veteran British writer of superior thrillers, by way of *The Sweeney* and all the other cop series to his own series and serials – in 1984 alone, *Missing from Home*, *Mitch* and *Travelling Man*.   PP

The Martian Chronicles
US/GB 1980 3 × 75m colour
Charles Fries Productions (Andrew Donnelly and Nelson Subotsky)
Ray Bradbury's sci-fi novel *The Silver Locusts* and sequels turned into an ambitious three-part saga but alas, plodding, humourless and too late. Nothing dates like a vision of the future – the screenplay may have been written only a year or two before and the hardware given a contemporary look, but the 30-year-old source of the story betrayed itself in a dozen ways.

w Richard Matheson d Michael Anderson

Rock Hudson, Darren McGavin, Gayle Hunnicutt, Fritz Weaver, Roddy McDowall, Maria Schell   PP

Martin, Dave: see Baker, Bob

Martin, Dean (1917–) (Dino Crocetti) and **Lewis, Jerry** (1926–) (Joseph Levitch). The American comedy team made their name on TV, in the Colgate Comedy Hour between 1950 and 1952. Later, as singles, Martin did better than Lewis with his long-running series of specials.

Martin, Ian Kennedy (1936–). British writer, best known for crime and spy series. Created *The Chinese Detective* (1981).

Martin Kane, Private Eye (US 1949–53). Long-running half-hour crime series for NBC, from a radio hit about a wisecracking private eye in New York. The lead was played in turn by William Gargan, Lloyd Nolan, Lee Tracy and Mark Stevens, and in 1957 there was a season with Gargan of *The New Adventures of Martin Kane*, in which the scene changed to London.

Martin, Mary (1913–). American star of stage and film musicals. Won an Emmy in 1955 as TV's PETER PAN; in 1979 appeared in a TV movie, *Valentine*.

Martin, Millicent (1934–). British songstress who came to the fore in *That Was the Week that Was* and later had her own series *From a Bird's Eye View*.

Martin, Pamela Sue (1959–). American juvenile actress of the seventies, TV's *Nancy Drew*. TV movies: *The Girls of Huntington House*, *The Gun and the Pulpit*, *Human Feelings*, *Dynasty*.

Martin, Ross (1920–81) (Martin Rosenblatt). American character actor, best known on TV for *The Wild Wild West*; also an unsuccessful Charlie Chan in *Happiness Is a Warm Clue*.

Martin, Troy Kennedy (1932–). British writer, brother of Ian, who made his debut with *Incident at Echo Six* in 1958, created the original z-CARS format and wrote the first episode, and in 1964 published a famous attack on naturalism in TV drama. *Diary of a Young Man*, with John McGrath, translated his alternative proposals into action, to no lasting avail. Since then, several plays and many series contributions, including the final *Z-Cars* episode (1978), *The Old Men at the Zoo*, *Reilly – Ace of Spies*, 1983, EDGE OF DARKNESS, 1985.   PP

Martine, Ray (1929–). Pert British comedian who had brief heyday in the mid sixties as compere of *Stars and Garters*.

Martinson, Leslie H. (19 –). American director whose contributions to screens small or big seem equally average. TV movies: *The Challengers*, *How to Steal an Airplane*. Series include *Cheyenne*, *Maverick*, *Bronco*, *77 Sunset Strip*, *Lawman*, *No Time for Sergeants*.

Marty ***
US 1953 53m bw
NBC (Fred Coe)
The play that ushered in the brief 'golden era' of original TV drama in America and with it, by showing that an ordinary, ugly butcher could have feelings, the whole vogue for everyday solid realism. 'The documentary of the human heart', Chayevsky himself called it. In America its very uneventfulness soon lost out to action series from the growing telefilm industry; in Britain it survived to the seventies.

w Paddy Chayevsky *d* Delbert Mann, Gordon Duff

Rod Steiger, Nancy Marchand   PP

Marty * (GB 1968). Marty Feldman's first autonomous series (for BBC), following his transition from comedy scriptwriter to comic performer in *At Last the 1948 Show*. At the time I wrote: 'The underground surfaces in a wild and wonderful outcrop which, for the present anyway, I would not lightly miss.' *Marty Amok* followed in 1970, co-starring Robert Dhéry from France.   PP

The Marva Collins Story
US 1981 96m colour TVM
CBS/Warner/NRW (Marian Rees)
A black schoolteacher, disenchanted with the system and its red tape, determines to start her own school.
True-life do-goodery.
w Clifford Campion *d* Peter Levin *ph* Don H. Birnkrant *m* Fred Karlin
Cicely Tyson, Morgan Freeman, Roderick Wimberly, Mashaune Hardy

Marvin, Lee (1924–). Leading American heavy who briefly became a somewhat improbable star. TV series: *M Squad*, *Lawbreaker*.

❋ **Marx, Groucho** (1890–1977) (Julius Marx). American comedian, the leading zany of the Marx Brothers, who in later life became a TV personality, allegedly conducting a quiz show, but in fact mostly insulting his guests with off-the-cuff quips. Emmy 1950, most outstanding personality. See YOU BET YOUR LIFE.

Mary (US 1978). Shortlived (three episodes) hour-long variety format in which Mary Tyler Moore tried in vain to demonstrate her versatility. Creator, Jim Hirschfield; for MTM and CBS.

'It makes life worth laughing!'
Mary *
US 1985 18 × 25m colour
CBS/MTM (David Isaacs, Ken Levine)
A divorcee tries to make a living on a down-at-heel Chicago newspaper.
Very tolerable wisecrack comedy with amusing characters.
cr David Isaacs, Ken Levine
Mary Tyler Moore, James Farentino, John Astin

Mary and Joseph: a Story of Faith
US 1979 147 minutes colour TVM
NBC/Lorimar (Gene Corman)
Interminable re-telling of events leading up to the birth of Jesus. Not for the impatient or the intolerant.

w Carmen Culver *d* Eric Till *ph* Adam Greenberg

Blanche Baker, Jeff East, Stephen McHattie, Colleen Dewhurst, Lloyd Bochner

† A foreword ran to this effect: 'Owing to the lack of reliable historical detail about the times in which Mary and Joseph lived, some of their story is presented as it *might* have happened.'

Mary Hartman, Mary Hartman *
US 1976 325 × 25m colour (VTR)
Tandem/Norman Lear (Viva Knight)

Semi-spoof soap opera, its appeal a little hard to determine for any but hardened daytime viewers, about a suburban community where the most awful things happen. Its producer sold it direct to syndicated stations, and for half a season it was a fashionable late-night attraction, but its appeal soon waned and production became uneconomic. It pointed the way for the more concentrated *Soap* which arrived the following year; its own unsuccessful sequels included *Forever Fernwood* and *Fernwood 2 Nite*.

cr Gail Parent, Ann Marcus, Jerry Adelman, Daniel Gregory Browne

LOUISE LASSER, Victor Kilian, Greg Mullavey, Graham Jarvis, Mary Kay Place

'We are simply taking a look at our life and times through another kind of prism. Of course, the prism may appear to have been fashioned by a drunken lens maker in a darkly wooded German forest.' – Norman Lear

'The most vicious crime in America is being committed by those who love their victims most.'

Mary Jane Harper Cried Last Night
US 1977 96m colour TVM
Paramount/Christiana (Joanna Lee)

A neurotic wife takes to beating her infant daughter.
Resistible case history.

w Joanna Lee *d* Allen Reisner *ph* Gayne Rescher *m* Billy Goldenburg

Susan Dey, Bernie Casey, Tricia O'Neill, John Vernon, Kevin McCarthy

The Mary Tyler Moore Show ***
US 1970–4 120 × 25m colour
CBS/Mary Tyler Moore (Ed Weinberger, Stan Daniels)

A bachelor girl works in the news room of a Minneapolis TV station.
Simple, efficient comedy show, filmed on two sets with three cameras, which worked by filling its heroine's two lives, at home and at work,

with funny people saying funny things. It won Emmys in 1970, 1974, 1975 and 1976, and led to three direct spin-offs, *Rhoda*, *Phyllis* and *Lou Grant*. See *Moore, Mary Tyler*.

cr/executive p JAMES L. BROOKS, ALLAN BURNS *m* Sonny Curtis

MARY TYLER MOORE, CLORIS LEACHMAN, VALERIE HARPER, ED ASNER, TED KNIGHT, GAVIN MCLEOD, GEORGIA ENGEL, BETTY WHITE

Mary White *
US 1977 96m colour TVM
Radnitz/Mettel (Robert B. Radnitz)

Friends remember the 16-year-old daughter of William Allen White, who died in 1921 after a riding accident.
A well-engineered compound of nostalgia and emotion, not too true to the facts.

w Caryl Ledner (Emmy) *d* Jud Taylor *ph* Bill Butler *m* Leonard Rosenman

Ed Flanders, Fionnula Flanagan, Tim Matheson, Donald Moffatt, Diana Douglas

'An almost perfect example of the TV movie as an art form.' – *LA Times*

Masada *
US 1981 8 × 50m (or variant formats) colour
ABC/Universal (George Eckstein)

In AD 73, Jews struggle against the forces of the Roman legions.
Mammoth, slow-moving mini-series which did surprisingly well in the American ratings but died overseas in shortened theatrical form as *The Antagonists*. Allegedly the most expensive film ever made for television.

w Joel Oliansky, *novel* Ernest K. Gann *d* Boris Sagal

ph Paul Lohmann *m* Jerry Goldsmith, Morton Stevens *pd* John H. Senter

Peter O'Toole, Peter Strauss, Barbara Carrera, Nigel Davenport, Alan Feinstein, Anthony Quayle, Denis Quilley, Anthony Valentine, Timothy West, David Warner, Richard Pearson, Jack Watson, Joseph Wiseman, Warren Clarke, Michael Elphick, Norman Rossington, Giulia Pagano, David Opatoshu

'A fine telefilm pointing up the triumph of dedication.' – *Daily Variety*

M*A*S*H ****
US 1972–84 255 × 25m colour
CBS/TCF (GENE REYNOLDS, LARRY GELBART)

Frustrations, mainly medical and sexual, of a mobile army surgical unit in Korea.
Bitter, hilarious and occasionally tragic comedy about carrying on with a wisecrack in

MAPP AND LUCIA may have been caviare to the general, but E. F. Benson's witty stories found a strong minority following. Geraldine McEwan, Prunella Scales.

the most impossible conditions. Its success as a concept is greater than that of the film from which it stemmed, and the effect of that success on TV comedy is incalculable.

m JOHNNY MANDEL ('Suicide Is Painless')

ALAN ALDA, MCLEAN STEVENSON, LORETTA SWIT, LARRY LINVILLE, JAMIE FARR, William Christopher, Wayne Rogers, GARY BURGHOFF, (later) HARRY MORGAN, Mike Farrell

The Mask
US 1954 14 × 50m bw (live)
ABC

Cases of brother defence attorneys.
Cited as TV's first live one-hour mystery series, and who's arguing?

Gary Merrill, William Prince

The Mask of Janus (GB 1965). Low-pressure BBC spy series with Dinsdale Landen as an ex-grammar school vice-consul getting involved in a little skulduggery and which led to the more ambitious *The Spies* the following year. My reaction in 1965: 'Stylish and not without wit and pleasing visual invention. It recognizes the game-like quality of espionage. At the same time it never forgets that the game is played with live human beings.'   PP

The Mask of Sheba
US 1970 100m colour TVM
MGM

Experts from the Foundation of Man fly to Ethiopia to seek a previous expedition and a priceless heirloom.
Inept adventure hokum which never seems to get going.

w Sam Rolfe *d* David Lowell Rich *m* Lalo Schifrin

Eric Braeden, Stephen Young, Inger Stevens, Joseph Wiseman, Walter Pidgeon, William Marshall

Mason, James (1909–84). Brooding British actor who had played small parts on pre-war BBC television but as a film star – one of the last of the ironclads, I called him – only came back to it in late life, and then not very profitably, e.g. *Dr Fischer of Geneva*. Subject of excellent Granada memoir *James Mason – the Star They Loved To Hate*, 1984, incorporating extended interview by Shelley Rohde.   PP

Masquerade
US 1983 74m colour TVM
ABC/TCF Renee Valente/Glen Larson (Harker Wade)

Unknown experts in their own fields are recruited by the CIA to take on evildoers in foreign fields.
Semi-comic version of *Mission Impossible*, with the heroes all looking like tourist types.

w Glen Larson *d* Peter H. Hunt *ph* Paul Lohman *m* Stu Phillips

Rod Taylor, Kristie Alley, Greg Evigan, Ernest Borgnine, Rue McClanahan, Howard Da Silva, Robert Morse, Oliver Reed, Austen Pendleton, Cybill Shepherd, Robert Sterling, Richard Roundtree, Daniel Pilon

'Lacks style, substance and imagination: otherwise it's just fine.' – *Daily Variety*

† A series of 13 hours followed.

Massacre at Sand Creek
US 1956 74m bw TVM
Columbia/Playhouse 90

An Indian-hating colonel leads his troops unnecessarily into battle.
Adequate mini-western.

d Arthur Hiller

Everett Sloane, John Derek, Gene Evans, H. M. Wynant

Masserati and the Brain
US 1982 96m colour TVM
ABC/Metromedia/Aaron Spelling (Charles B. Fitzsimons)

Adventures of a soldier of fortune and his brilliant 10-year-old nephew.
Failed pilot with not much sense but lots of action: car chases, helicopters, mysterious islands.

w George Kirgo *d* Harvey Hart *m* Billy Goldenberg

Daniel Pilon, Peter Billingsley, Ann Turkel, Camilla Sparv, Christopher Lee, Markie Poast, Christopher Hewett

Massey, Anna (1937–). Accomplished British actress, daughter of Raymond, sister of Daniel, who can make herself severe, sinister or sweet. Mrs Danvers in *Rebecca*, 1979; *You're Not Watching Me, Mummy* (Osborne play), 1980; Lady Nelson in *I Remember Nelson*, 1982; Gwen John in *Journey into the Shadows*, 1984; *Hotel du Lac*, 1986.   PP

Massey, Raymond (1896–1983). Popular Canadian actor whose long career included two TV series, *I Spy* and DR KILDARE. TV movies: *All My Darling Daughters*, *My Darling Daughters' Anniversary*, *The President's Plane Is Missing*.

'He's the supreme warrior. Even his eyes can kill you. His student is the supreme heartthrob. His eyes can melt you!'
The Master
US 1984 13 × 50m colour
CBS/Viacom

An American who has become a samurai returns home to right wrongs, but is followed by his enemies.
Comic-strip violence with some pretensions to style.

Lee Van Cleef

The Master Game (GB 1975–8). Intermittent series of 25-minute chess games for TV with the innovation of wiring the players so that their spoken thoughts can be heard in moments of decision. The device was extended to Bridge in *Grand Slam* (1981).   PP

Master of the Game
US/GB 1984 3 ×
146m colour miniseries
CBS/Viacom/Rosemont Productions (Norman Rosemont)

A matriarch reflects on her family history, which runs from South African gold mines at the turn of the century to Wall Street in the thirties and Europe through World War II.
Fragmented miniseries, not such a good look as the book was (presumably) a good read. Acting very variable.

w John Nation, Paul Yurick, Alvin Boretz, *novel* by Sidney Sheldon *d* Kevin Connor, Harvey Hart *ph* Arthur Ibbetson, Ronnie Taylor, John Coquillon *m* Allyn Ferguson

Dyan Cannon, Harry Hamlin, Ian Charleson, Cliff De Young, Fernando Allende, Liane Langland, Donald Pleasence, Johnny Sekka, Jean Marsh, Cherie Lunghi, Barry Morse, Angharad Rees, David Suchet, Leslie Caron, Shane Rimmer, David Birney

'What might have been a masterful TV occurrence dribbles into the inconsequential: relationships after part one have the strength of tissue paper.' – *Daily Variety*

Mastermind. A relentlessly highbrow BBC quiz which grew in popularity through the seventies, in which successful contestants must have more than one special subject as well as wide general knowledge. The questions are at university level and the atmosphere extremely tense. Bill Wright produced the first eight seasons, and Magnus Magnusson remains questionmaster.

PP: 'Not really highbrow at all. Like all quizzes, mainly a test of recall.'

Match of the Day. The BBC's weekend League football game, a national institution since 1964. Until 1979 it went out on Saturday night though European viewers could see it live during the afternoon. In 1980 ITV secured Saturday rights and the BBC had to make do with Sunday afternoon. Since then has alternated, except for most of the 1985–6 season when no League soccer was shown at all. Introduced latterly by Jimmy Hill; edited by Mike Murphy.   PP

Mather, Berkely (19 –). Regular army officer who retired in 1956 to pursue lucrative career as furnisher of mystery and thriller playlets. Later became screenwriter who worked on the early James Bond movies.   PP

THE MASTER. Martial arts were a fading fancy when this mildly intriguing series hit the world's screens. Despite the strong presence of Lee Van Cleef, it didn't have a chance of equalling the popularity of David Carradine in *Kung Fu*.

Matheson, Margaret (1946–). British drama producer and executive, formerly story editor (of *Elizabeth R*, *The Edwardians*, etc). In charge of BBC *Play for Today* 1976–8, including *Stronger than the Sun* and *Scum*. Then head of drama at Central and producer of *Muck and Brass* (series), 1982. Now with Central's film-making subsidiary, Zenith Films.   PP

Matheson, Tim (1949–). American leading man. TV movies include *Lock, Stock and Barrel*, *Hitched*, *Remember When*, *The Runaway Barge*, *The Last Day*, *The Quest*, *Mary White*.

Mathis, Johnny (1935–). American ballad singer who makes fairly frequent concert appearances.

Matinee from the Met. Regular satellite relays on Britain's C4 from the Metropolitan Opera, New York, usually shown the following (Sunday) afternoon and always with eye-popping principals.   PP

The Mating Season
US 1980 96m colour TVM
CBS/Highgate (Linda Gottlieb)
A lady lawyer on holiday falls for a birdwatcher.
Would-be zany comedy which lacks any funny ideas.
w Larry Grusin *d* John Llewellyn Moxey
ph Norman Leigh *m* John Morris
Lucie Arnaz, Laurence Luckinbill, Diane Stilwell, Joel Brooks, Swoosie Kurtz

Matt Helm
US 1975 74m colour TVM
ABC/Columbia
An ex-CIA agent becomes a Los Angeles private eye.
Unrecognizable from the movie series starring Dean Martin, and as routine as can be.
w Sam Rolfe *d* Buzz Kulik
Tony Franciosa, James Shigeta, Patrick MacNee, Laraine Stephens
† The series ran 13 × 50m episodes. Developed by Sam Rolfe; music by Morton Stevens; producers Charles FitzSimmons, Ken Pettus

Matt Houston
US 1981 96m colour TVM
ABC/Warner/Largo/Aaron Spelling
(Richard Lang)

A Texas millionaire turns private detective.
The luxurious trappings are as thick as the
Texas accents, but although the resulting
series ran for several seasons it did so only
on a low fuse. There were 66 one-hour
episodes.

w Ken Trevey, Richard Christian Danus
d Richard Lang ph Michel Hugo
m Dominic Frontiere

Lee Horsley, Pamela Hensley, John Aprea,
De De Howard, Cal Bellini, Barbara
Carrera, Jill St John, Art Metrano, Dale
Robertson

'A format so worn it has saddle sores.' –
Daily Variety

Matt Lincoln
US 1970 16 × 50m colour
NBC/MCA/Universal/Vince Edwards

A psychiatrist goes to the people who really
need him: the poor.
Rather dreary drama series with a social
conscience.

Vince Edwards

† See also *Dial Hot Line* (pilot).

A Matter of Choice for Billy (GB 1983).
Second play in the Graham Reid trilogy
which began with *Too Late to Talk to Billy*,
which see.   PP

A Matter of Degree * (GB 1960; 4 × 30m).
One of the first serials (BBC) on a tranquil,
non-thrillerish theme, written by ELAINE
MORGAN. Welsh miner's daughter wins place at
Oxford but eventually renounces it in favour of
home, hearth, looking after crippled Auntie
and marriage with dour redbrick boyfriend.
With Anita Morgan, Hugh David, Meredith
Edwards, Jessie Evans.   PP

A Matter of Humanities: see Marcus Welby
MD

A Matter of Life and Death
US 1980 96m colour TVM
CBS/Lorimar (Robert Jacks)

A lady doctor determines to deal exclusively
with dying patients, and becomes a national
celebrity.
Disease-of-the-week movie in spades.

w Lane Slate, based on the experiences of
Joy Ufema d Russ Mayberry

Linda Lavin, Charles Tyner, Peter Donat,
Gerald S. O'Loughlin, Salome Jens

A Matter of Sex
aka: *The Women of Willmar*
US 1984 96m colour TVM
NBC/Orion (Everett Chambers)

Female employees of a bank fight sex
discrimination.
Tedious docu-drama with a catchpenny title.

w Joyce Eliason d Lee Grant ph Fred
Murphy m Matthew McCauley

Jean Stapleton, Dinah Manoff, Judge
Reinhold, Pamela Putch, Gillian Farrell

'The drama is a plodding one, with endless
shots of women picketing and discussing
their hapless situation.' – *Daily Variety*

A Matter of Wife and Death
aka: *Shamus*
US 1975 74m colour TVM
Columbia

Adventures of another tough private eye.
Boring.

w Don Ingalls d Marvin Chomsky

Rod Taylor, Tom Drake, Anita Gillette, Joe
Santos

Matthews, Francis (1931–). Nimble
British leading man, familiar on TV for 20
years, notably as star of long-running *Paul
Temple* series.

Maude ***
US 1972–7 140 approx. × 25m colour
(VTR)
CBS/Tandem (Norman Lear, Bud Yorkin)

A middle-class woman in Tuckahoe NY can't
cope as well as she thinks.
Realistic social comedy which spun itself off
from *All in the Family* and proved at least an
equal success. In its later seasons it began to
tackle serious subjects such as abortion and
rape, always with an eye for character nuances
and an ear for a funny line. The leading
character became an American classic.

BEATRICE ARTHUR, BILL MACY, ADRIENNE
BARBEAU, Conrad Bain, Hermione Baddeley

Maunder, Wayne (1942–). American
leading man who surfaced in *Custer* and
Lancer, then disappeared.

Maupassant **
GB 1960 13 × 50m bw (VTR)
Granada (Philip Mackie)

Short stories by Guy de Maupassant, usually
two or three to the hour with a framing link.
At the time an original television style, with
high gloss and entertainment value.

cr PHILIP MACKIE *d* Silvio Narizzano, Claude Whatham, Henry Kaplan, Derek Bennett, Gordon Flemyng and others

Gwen Watford, Derek Francis, Thorley Walters

'A cracking pace and a great sense of period.' – *Guardian*

Maverick **
US 1957–61 138 × 50m bw
ABC/Warners

One of the family of cowboy heroes Warners created at this time, Maverick was a cowardly good-looking gambler who got out of trouble by the skin of his teeth, and the scripts had more humour than the usual western action. (One show turned Sheridan's *The Rivals* into a western.) When Bret Maverick wasn't available, his brother or his cousin took over. JAMES GARNER (Bret); Jack Kelly (Bart); Roger Moore (Beau)

† James Garner also appeared occasionally as Pappy Beauregard.

†† Emmy 1958, best western series.

††† Garner reprised the character in 1981 in *Bret Maverick*, the third attempt at resurrection and the only near-success.

Max   Headroom   (1985–).
Computer-generated British android who presents a pop video show of that name on C4, having been programmed to maintain a never-flagging stream of flip expertise. The first series ran 13 weeks. To introduce and explain their creation, the producers hastily devised a pilot narrative *Rebus: the Max Headroom Story* ** in which Max emerged triumphantly from much chicanery and counter-chicanery in a slightly future world of countless TV channels competing against one another 'necessity was revealed,' I wrote, 'as the Mother of some bright invention.' To come clean, Max is played by actor Matt Frewer. Also with (in the pilot) Nickolas Grace, Hilary Tindall, Amanda Pays, Paul Spurrier. Written (the pilot) by Steve Roberts, with music by Midge Ure and Chris Cross; directed by Rocky Morton and Annabel Jankel; produced by Peter Wagg for Chrysalis/C4.   PP
LH: 'I liked the introductory discussion, all very po-faced, except that it was shown on April Fool's Day.'

Maxwell, James (–).
Dependable British actor from the fifties onwards, e.g. the commanding officer in *Private Potter*, 1961. Recent credits: *Under the Hammer*, 1984.

Maya
US 1967 18 × 50m colour
NBC/MGM/King Brothers

An American boy in modern India searches for his white hunter father.

Uncompelling series from a feature film original. Nice scenery and elephants.

Jay North, Sajid Khan

Mayall, Rik (1958–).
British alternative comic with spiky hair and mad glare, on to television scene with Comic Strip appearances, *The Young Ones*, etc.

Maybe I'll Come Home in the Spring
US 1970 74m colour TVM
Metromedia (Charles Fries)

A teenage runaway comes back home and tries to see her parents' point of view.

Well detailed domestic drama, just a wee bit over-earnest.

w Bruce Feldman *d* Russ Metty

Eleanor Parker, Jackie Cooper, Lane Bradbury, Sally Field, David Carradine

Mayberry RFD
US 1968–70 78 × 25m colour
CBS/Paramount/RFD (Richard O. Linke, Andy Griffith)

Doings of a small town and its councillors. Small beer.

cr Bob Ross

Ken Berry, George Lindsay, Arlene Golonka, Paul Hartman, Jack Dodson

Mayberry, Russ (19 –).
Hard-working American series director (*Marcus Welby*, *Alias Smith and Jones*, *Six Million Dollar Man*, etc) whose occasional TV movies have been reasonably interesting: *Probe*, *A Very Missing Person*, *Fer de Lance*, *Stonestreet*, *The 3,000 Mile·Chase*, etc.

Maybury
GB 1981 13 × 50m colour

Enlightened if over-reassuring (some say) semi-serial set in a psychiatric hospital with six or seven overlapping story lines coming up during the 13 episodes and Patrick Stewart holding it all together as the resident psychiatrist Dr Roebuck. Written by Jim Hawkins, Anthony Minghella and David Blunt; directed by Richard Stroud, Don Taylor and others; produced by Ruth Boswell; for BBC.   PP
A further seven episodes followed in 1983.

Mayday at 40,000 Feet
US 1976 96m colour TVM
Warner/Andrew J. Fenady

A convict under escort goes berserk on a transcontinental plane.
Boring, overstretched suspenser.

w Austin Ferguson, Dick Nelson, Andrew J. Fenady d Robert Butler

David Janssen, Don Meredith, Christopher George, Ray Milland, Lynda Day George, Broderick Crawford, Maggie Blye, Tom Drake, Jane Powell

'You will never forget it – because every American still lives it!'
Mayflower
US 1980 96m colour TVM
CBS/Linda Yellen

An account of the first voyage of the Pilgrim Fathers and their arrival at Plymouth Rock. Fairly ambitious, slightly stilted but quite watchable historical drama.

w James Lee Barrett d George Schaefer

Anthony Hopkins, Richard Crenna, David Dukes, Trish Van Devere, Jenny Agutter, Michael Beck

'Exhilarating, inspiring, informative and beautifully produced.' – TV Guide

Mayhew, Christopher (19 –). British MP and television journalist of the fifties and sixties who wrote and delivered, in a dry incisive manner, series such as Crime and Does Class Matter?   PP

Maynard, Bill (1928–). Indifferent British comic who became an accomplished British actor. Looks about as lively as a sandbag, with big open mug and worried grin, but can astonish with such performances as in Paper Roses (1971), and KISSES AT FIFTY (1973). Series: Oh No It's Selwyn Froggitt, Trinity Tales, The Gaffer.   PP

The Mayor of Casterbridge *
GB 1978 7 × 50m colour
BBC (Jonathan Powell)

Hardy's novel dramatized by Dennis Potter and noteworthy, apart from intrinsic merits, as a successful revival of the old dream of location video recording, now using the lightweight gear which had become available.

d David Giles

Alan Bates, Anne Stallybrass, Anna Massey, Janet Maw, Jack Galloway   PP

Mayor of the Town
US 1954 39 × 25m bw
Rawlings–Grant, Gross–Krasne

Small-town dramas linked by the benevolent mayor.
Mildly satisfactory tales with a moral.

Thomas Mitchell

'Players in a dangerous game – risking their hearts, their minds, their lives!'
Mazes and Monsters *
US 1983 96m colour TVM
CBS/McDermott Productions (Tom McDermott)

Four undergraduates are psychologically affected by a game involving medieval fantasies.
Based on the Dungeons and Dragons syndrome, this good-looking teleplay might puzzle anyone over 30, but it will probably keep them watching.

w Tom Lazarus, novel by Rona Jaffe d Steven Hillard Stern ph Laszlo George m Hagood Hardy

Tom Hanks, Wendy Crewson, David Wallace, Chris Makepeace, Lloyd Bochner, Peter Donat, Anne Francis, Murray Hamilton, Vera Miles, Louise Sorel, Susan Strasberg

Mc: see under Mac

MCA. Music Corporation of America, a talent agency founded in the twenties by Jules Stein. It later acquired Universal Studios, Decca Records and Revue Productions, and when prodded by the government gave up the talent business entirely. It is now known chiefly as a TV distributor for Universal products.

Me and Maxx (US 1980). Shortlived half-hour sitcom about an 11-year-old girl who lives with her divorced father. All the jokes can be seen a mile off. Joe Santos, Melissa Michaelsen. Created by James Komack for NBC.

'Kate's looking for a killer. Her mom's looking for excitement. Together they find being private eyes can be murder!'
Me and Mom
US 1984 4 × 50m colour
ABC/Viacom (Hal Sitowitz)

A mother, a daughter and a retired cop form a detective agency.
Uninteresting comedy-drama series with a silly premise and unlikeable characters.

cr Marsha Miller

Lisa Eilbacher, Holland Taylor, James Earl Jones

Me and the Chimp
US 1971 13 × 25m colour
CBS/Paramount

A family adopts a chimp.
See *The Hathaways*. Simple-minded would be a charitable way of describing the level of humour.
Ted Bessell

Me! I'm Afraid of Virginia Woolf **.
First of six filmed plays by Alan Bennett which LWT put out over a three-month period in 1978–9. Here, a secret homosexual finally owns up, at least to himself, and Bennett suggests the love of one man for another can be as gentle, comforting and innocent as that of Daphnis and Chloe.
Also with Thora Hird.

† Other titles in the sextet include *The Old Crowd*, ONE FINE DAY, *All Day on the Sands*.
PP

Meadows, Audrey
(1929–) (Audrey Cotter). American comedy actress who made few appearances subsequent to her celebrated star role as Jackie Gleason's wife in THE HONEYMOONERS. Emmy 1954, best series actress.

Meadows, Jayne
(1925–) (Jane Cotter). American actress and TV personality, wife of Steve Allen, familiar in *I've Got a Secret* and *Masquerade Party*. TV movies: *Now You See It Now You Don't*, *James Dean*, *Sex and the Married Woman*.

Medic **
US 1954–5 59 × 25m bw
NBC

Filmed in hospitals, this docu-drama series told suspense stories about diseases to illustrate medicine's latest advances.
Clinical, well-told stories related in a manner which then touched a new note of authenticity.
Richard Boone (as the narrator, Dr Styner)

Medical Center
GB title: *Calling Doctor Gannon*
US 1969–75 170 approx. × 50m colour
CBS/MGM/Alfra (Frank Glicksman, Al C. Ward)

Stories of a young surgeon in a university hospital.
Long-running drama series which tinged on the sensational but usually gave good value for money.
cr Frank Glicksman, Al C. Ward *m* Lalo Schifrin
CHAD EVERETT, James Daly, Audrey Totter
† See *Operation Heartbeat* (pilot).

The Medical Man: see Ben Casey

Medical Story **
US 1975 100m colour TVM
NBC/Columbia (David Gerber)

An idealistic intern has some successes but loses his most valued patient.
Sharply made, hard-hitting and realistic hospital drama, pilot for a shortlived series.
w Abby Mann, *d* Gary Nelson *m* Arthur Morton, *theme* Jerry Goldsmith
Beau Bridges, Jose Ferrer, Harriet Karr, Shirley Knight, Carl Reiner, Claude Akins
† The subsequent series consisted of 13 × 50m episodes, all of high production quality but depressing content.

Medico (GB 1958). A documentary that could hardly go wrong. Ship steaming for land with injured man aboard, air crackling with urgent messages, doctor going to aid – this is the stuff of public service drama. Robert Barr's script tied it all together most professionally, and stopped just at the right moment. Things weren't resolved completely. Life went on, one felt, after the credits.
PP

Meet Corliss Archer
US 1954 39 × 25m bw
CBS/United Artists

Scrapes of a scatty teenage girl, from the play and film *Kiss and Tell*.
Witless pre-Gidget Gidgetry, transmitted live.
Lugene Sanders, Bobby Ellis

Meet McGraw
US 1957 39 × 25m bw
NBC/MM/Sharpe–Lewis

A private eye wages a one-man crusade against crime.
Adequate mystery series.
Frank Lovejoy

Meet Millie (US 1952–5). Half-hour comedy series for CBS, with Elena Verdugo as a New York waitress living with her mother (Florence Halop).

Meet Mr McNutley
US 1953 39 × 25m bw
CBS

Problems of a drama professor at a girls' college.
Acceptable star froth.
Ray Milland, Phyllis Avery, Minerva Urecal, Gordon Jones

Meeting at Potsdam *
aka: *Truman at Potsdam*
US 1976 74m colour (VTR)
David Susskind/PBS

A recreation of the 1945 international conference which brought World War II to an end.
Solid drama-documentary marred by an unsatisfactory imitation of Churchill.

w Sidney Carroll d George Schaefer

Ed Flanders (Truman), Jose Ferrer (Stalin), John Houseman (Churchill), Alexander Knox (Stimson), Barry Morse (Byrnes)

Melba
US 1985 6 × 25m colour
ABC/Columbia/Saul Ilson

A black career woman maintains her links with the family to whom her mother was servant.
Moderate but forgettable comedy format.

cr Marshall Karp

Melba Moore, Gracie Harrison, Barbara Meek, Jamila Perry, Michael Tucci

Melly, George (1926–). Rumbustious British jazz singer (*Good Time George*, etc.) who also has expert interest in surrealist painting and has taken part in *Arena* and other arts programmes. Was television critic of *The Observer* throughout most of the sixties. Wrote and presented jazz documentary *Whatever Happened to Bill Brunskill?* 1984, and chaired panel show *Gallery* same year, also 1986.   PP

Melvin Purvis G-Man *
GB theatrical title: *The Legend of Machine Gun Kelly*
US 1974 74m colour TVM
AIP/Dan Curtis

In 1933, a midwestern G-man captures Machine Gun Kelly.
Adequate gangster thriller which didn't make a series. See also *Kansas City Massacre*.

w John Milius, William F. Nolan d Dan Curtis ph Jacques Marquette m Richard Cobert

Dale Robertson, Margaret Blye, Harris Yulin, Dick Sargent, David Canary

The Member for Chelsea
GB 1981 3 × 50m colour (VTR)
Granada (June Wyndham-Davies)

In 1885 London society is scandalized by a sexual scandal involving a noted Liberal, Sir Charles Dilke.
Woebegone attempt to be permissive and intellectual at the same time, with much explicit sex overlaid by references to *Alice in Wonderland*.

w Ken Taylor d John Gorrie m Joseph Horovitz

Richard Johnson, Annette Crosbie, Eleanor David, Faith Brook

Memorial Day
US 1983 96m colour TVM
CBS/Charles Fries (Jay Benson)

A reunion with buddies from Vietnam makes a lawyer remember the time his platoon accidentally shot a group of children.
An almost operatic scenario of self-torment, not easy to watch.

w Michael Bortman d Joseph Sargent ph Hector Figueroa m Billy Goldenberg

Mike Farrell, Shelley Fabares, Robert Walden, Keith Mitchell, Bonnie Bedelia, Edward Herrmann

Memories Never Die
US 1982 96m colour TVM
CBS/Universal/Groverton/Scholastic (David Victor, Robert F. O'Neill)

A woman recovering from six years of suicidal depression goes home to look after her two children while her estranged husband recovers from a coronary.
A three-handkerchief affair by intention, this never begins to grip or convince.

w Ken Trevey, *novel Stranger in the House* by Zoa Sherburne d Sandor Stern ph Dennis Dalzell m Morton Stevens

Lindsay Wagner, Gerald McRaney, Melissa Michaelsen, Peter Billingsley, Jay Robinson, Barbara Babcock, Barbara Cason

'Too many emotions are on the sleeve.' – *Daily Variety*

The Memory of Eva Ryker
US 1980 142m colour TVM
CBS/Warner/Irwin Allen

A writer is hired by a millionaire to find out the truth about the sinking in 1939 of a liner in which his wife perished.
Rather clumsy compilation of film clichés which have all provided enjoyment in more skilled hands: switched identities, smuggling, the life of the idle rich, mysterious cloaked figures, murders and a frightened lady. Here they don't work.

w Laurence Heath, *novel* by Donald A. Stanwood d Walter E. Grauman ph John M. Nickolaus m Richard La Salle

Natalie Wood, Robert Foxworth, Ralph Bellamy, Roddy McDowall, Bradford Dillman, Jean-Pierre Aumont, Peter Graves, Mel Ferrer, Robert Hogan, Morgan Fairchild

The Men. Umbrella title for an American series of one-hour action thrillers: *Assignment Vienna*, *The Delphi Bureau* and *Jigsaw*. On NBC in 1972.

Menace. A title used at least twice in British television: the first time by playwright Arnold Wesker in 1967 with a muddled play about life under the imminent threat of nuclear war; again in 1973 for a not very menacing BBC anthology series of thrillers.   PP

Men at Law
aka: *Storefront Lawyers*
US 1971 10 × 50m colour
CBS/Leonard Freeman

Young lawyers join a big old-fashioned firm. Mixed-up series which made two format changes, then quietly died.
Gerald S. O'Loughlin, Robert Foxworth, David Arkin, Sheila Larkin

The Men from Shiloh
US 1970 24 × 74m colour
MCA/Universal

New name given to the last season of *The Virginian* after several cast changes.
m Ennio Morricone
Stewart Granger, James Drury, Doug McClure, Lee Majors

Men into Space
US 1959 28 × 25m bw
United Artists

The USAF prepares for space exploration. Docu-dramas, informative but repetitive.
William Lundigan

Men of Anapolis
US 1957 39 × 25m bw
United Artists

Stories of the US naval academy. Predictable uplifters and flagwavers.

Men of Ideas ** (GB 1978; 15 × 40m). Bryan Magee talks to fifteen leading philosophers of the day, including fashionable structuralists and the guru of the revolting students of 1968, Herbert Marcuse. Set down in print the conversations read as well as they sound on the air. Produced for BBC.   PP

Men of Iron (GB 1969; 120m). Episodic BBC history of the building of the first railway tunnel through the Pennines in 1840, from the partnership of Keith Dewhurst and Herbert Wise that had already produced *The Siege of Manchester*.   PP

Men of our Time (GB 1963). Eight assessments drawing on Granada's hoard of old Movietone newsreels but owing as much to the assessor as the assessed: Malcolm Muggeridge on Ramsay MacDonald and Stanley Baldwin; A. J. P. Taylor on Mussolini and George V; James Cameron on Gandhi and Lenin; Max Beloff on Roosevelt; Kingsley Martin on Hitler.   PP

Men of the Dragon **
US 1974 74m colour TVM
David Wolper (Stan Margulies)

A young American in Hong Kong combats a sinister organization to get back his kidnapped sister.
It's well-staged action all the way in this Kung Fu penny dreadful. Great fun.
w Denne Bart Petitclerc *d* Harry Falk *m* Elmer Bernstein
Jared Martin, Joseph Wiseman, Katie Saylor, Robert Ito

Men Who Love Women: see Rossetti and Ryan

Mengele (GB 1985; 90m). Definitive documentary on the crimes and subsequent secret life of Dr Josef Mengele, the Auschwitz 'Angel of Death', whose body – if it was his – was found in South America during the filming. A star participant was Mengele's son Rolf. Directed and produced by Brian Moser, for Central.   PP

Menges, Chris (19 –). British film cameraman associated with many outstanding documentaries for Adrian Cowell, John Goldschmidt and others; and a director in his own right with *Wild and Free Twice Daily*, 1969, and *East 103rd Street*, 1982.   PP

❋ **Mercer, David** (1928–80). British TV playwright whose work was shaped by three enduring influences: his own working-class upbringing; a struggle to reconcile his passionate socialism with the repressive regimes of Eastern Europe which he had at first admired (and for a while lived under); and an obsession with psychiatry and mental health following a nervous breakdown. A fascination with the aristocracy (*And Did Those Feet?*, *The*

Parachute, The Cellar and the Almond Tree) he acquired somewhere along the way. My assessment in 1968: 'If recordings of television plays could be bought for private playback David Mercer's would be the sleeves you'd leave lying on the coffee table, but Peter Nichols's or Dennis Potter's tapes you'd be more likely to wear out.

'With a dozen mostly eventful pieces in six or seven years Mercer is easily the most considerable author. I only wish I could enthuse about him as consistently as I admire him . . .

'He hates the violation of innocent, if wayward, minds by psychiatry. He dislikes orderliness, inaction, the civilized acceptance of wrongs. He is a socialist never quite sure whether he has failed socialism or socialism has failed him – at the end of his trilogy *The Generations* the activist-hero was symbolically shot down as he bestrode the Berlin Wall cursing both sides equally.'

Television plays transmitted:

1961   *Where the Difference Begins* BBC
1962   *A Climate of Fear* BBC
       A Suitable Case for Treatment BBC
1963   *The Buried Man* ATV
       The Birth of a Private Man BBC
       For Tea on Sunday BBC
       A Way of Living ABC
1965   AND DID THOSE FEET? BBC2 *Wednesday Play*
1967   *In Two Minds* BBC1 *Wednesday Play*
1968   THE PARACHUTE BBC1 *Play of the Month*
       Let's Murder Vivaldi BBC1
       On the Eve of Publication BBC1 *Wednesday Play*
1970   *The Cellar and the Almond Tree* BBC1
       Emma's Time BBC1
1972   *The Bankrupt* BBC1
1973   *You and Me and Him* BBC2
       An Afternoon at the Festival YTV
       Barbara of the House of Grebe (based on Thomas Hardy; Episode 6 in series *Wessex Tales*) BBC2
1974   *The Arcata Promise* YTV *Sunday Night Theatre*
       Find Me BBC *Omnibus*
1976   *Huggy Bear* YTV
1977   *A Superstition* YTV
       Shooting the Chandelier BBC2
1978   *The Ragazza* YTV
1980   *Rod of Iron* YTV   PP

Merchant, Vivien (1929–83) (Ada Thompson). British character actress especially associated with the plays of Harold Pinter, to whom she was married during the sixties and early seventies.

Meriwether, Lee (*c* 1939–). American leading lady, former Miss America, in series *Time Tunnel*, *Batman* (as Batwoman), *Barnaby Jones*. TV movies: *Having Babies II*, *Cruise into Terror*, *True Grit*.

Mervyn, William (1912–76). Portly British character actor who played many lords and bishops. Starred in several TV series including MR ROSE, *All Gas and Gaiters*, *Saki*, *The Liars*.

Message for Posterity
GB 1967 75m bw
BBC *Wednesday Play* (Lionel Harris)

Dennis Potter's fable prompted by stories of Churchill sitting reluctantly for his 80th birthday portrait by Graham Sutherland and rumours, perhaps, of what had befallen the painting, only now the artist was a fiery old Red deeply suspicious of his sitter. At first all went unexpectedly gently, ironically, between them. But Potter was still the angry young Potter then. As if dismayed by the sunny turn his play was taking he reached for a violent ending like a panicky missile controller destroying a wayward rocket.

d Gareth Davies

Joseph O'Conor, Patrick Magee   PP

Message to My Daughter
US 1973 74m colour TVM
Metromedia/Gerald Isenberg

A girl learns much about herself and her stepfather while listening to tapes recorded by her mother, now dead.
Icky and unconvincing weepie.

w Rita Lakin *d* Robert Michael Lewis

Bonnie Bedelia, Martin Sheen, Kitty Wynn, Neva Patterson

Messina, Cedric (19 –). South African producer, long resident in Britain, for many years in charge of the BBC's Play of the Month and, after a brilliant *Merchant of Venice* with Maggie Smith (1972) which he also directed, originator and first producer of the BBC Television Shakespeare project. Recent credits: *Tartuffe* and *Molière*, both with Antony Sher, 1985.   PP

Metal Mickey (GB 1979–81). Bright children's comedy series about a household and its helpful robot, who frequently out-acts the flesh-and-blood performers. Written by Colin Bostock-Smith, produced by Michael Dolenz; for LWT.   PP

meter: an automatic electronic measurement device used to determine viewing patterns in a cross-section of homes.

The Method
GB 1958 90m bw
First British studio programme to stay on the air after midnight – a late (11 p.m.) start was deliberately chosen so that actors working in the theatre could watch a blockbuster history of the Stanislavskyan acting method from its origin in the Moscow Arts Theatre to its latter-day fame after Marilyn Monroe had attended classes at the New York Actors' Studio. Arthur Miller, Tennessee Williams and Elia Kazan were among those taking part. Dan Farson was link-man. Directed by Silvio Narizzano; produced by Kenneth Tynan; for ATV. PP

Metro–Goldwyn–Mayer. The giant Hollywood film studio has made its share of TV series, but they have been somewhat half-hearted when compared with its great days of movie-making.

Metroland *** (GB 1973). SIR JOHN BETJEMAN's honeyed recollection (for BBC) of London's Metropolitan Railway as it pushed out into the country in the early years of the century to create the leafy suburbs once advertised as Metroland. Affectionate, funny, inimitable. PP

Metromedia. American broadcasting network which in the seventies went into TV production (briefly) and distribution.

Miami Undercover
US 1961 38 × 25m bw
Schenk–Koch
An investigator works with the police to keep Miami crime-free.
Old warmed-over hokum in a glamorous setting.
Lee Bowman, Rocky Graziano

'Two young cops in a city of temptation. Everything has its price – except them!'
Miami Vice
US 1984 96m colour TVM
NBC/Universal/Michael Mann
A laid-back Miami undercover cop, who lives on a boat with a pet alligator, is joined by a black New Yorker investigating the death of his brother.
Seamy side cop melodrama laced with rock music. Not to everybody's taste, but the resulting one-hour series became a long-term hit.
cr Anthony Yerkovitch d (pilot) Thomas Carter

Don Johnson, Philip Michael Thomas, Saundra Santiago, Michael Talbott, John Diehl, Gregory Sierra
'The same old formulas always will yield the same old products.' – Daily Variety

Michael Shayne
US 1960 32 × 50m bw
ABC/Four Star
Cases of Brett Halliday's happy-go-lucky detective.
Adequate mystery filler.
Richard Denning, Jerry Paris, Patricia Donahue, Herbert Rudley

Michell, Keith (1926–). Australian leading actor in Britain, whose fame got a lift when he played the king in The Six Wives of Henry VIII (Emmy 1971). TV movie: The Day Christ Died.

❋ **Michelmore, Cliff** (1919–). Cheerful, avuncular British anchorman, quizmaster and general TV personality who found his niche in the fifties with Tonight. Subsequently quizmaster and host in a variety of programmes.

Mickey
US 1964 17 × 25m bw
ABC/Selmur
A family man inherits a luxury California hotel. Not a bad comedy series, but it didn't collect ratings.
Mickey Rooney, Sammee Tong, Emmaline Henry

Mickey Mouse Club. A Walt Disney format of the fifties, revived in the seventies, consisting largely of clips from old Disney material plus a newly shot serial, linked by groups of kids marching around and singing the club's theme tune. Regular members were known as Mouseketeers. Jimmy Dodd and Roy Williams led the revels.

The Mickey Rooney Show (US 1954). Half-hour comedy series for NBC, with the star as a page at the NBC studio. Also known as Hey, Mulligan.

Mickey Spillane's Mike Hammer
US 1956–8 78 × 25m bw
MCA/Revue
Adventures of a tough private eye.
And they did seem tough in those days, even though humour had been injected to sweeten the pill. Generally an entertaining series.
Darren McGavin
† See under Mike Hammer for 1983 revival with Stacy Keach

Ricardo Tubbs' brother has been blown away. Sonny Crockett's marriage has fallen apart. Now, the only ones they can count on are each other!

MIAMI VICE

It has a grip all its own.

2-HOUR MOVIE PREMIERE!

SNEAK WEEK!

9PM 4

Let's All Be There!

MIAMI VICE. Whether it was the girls, the alligator or the pop music backing, this slick American import caught a late-night audience and held it tight.

Microbes and Men *
GB 1974 6 × 50m colour (VTR)
BBC (Peter Goodchild)

Stories of the elimination of various diseases by dedicated scientists.

Like visiting the Warner biopics of the thirties all over again. Riveting stuff.

w Martin Worth, John Wiles, Bruce Norman

Arthur Lowe, Robert Lang

Midas Valley
US 1984 96m colour TVM
ABC/Warner/Edward S. Feldman

A multi-story of rich and dissatisfied people in Silicon Valley.

Expensive pilot for a series that never made it.

cr Ann Beckett, Clyde Phillips   *d* Gus Trikonis

Robert Stack, Jean Simmons, Linda Purl, France Nuyen, George Grizzard, Philip R. Allen, Brett Cullen, Stephen Elliott, Joseph Hacker

Middlemass, Frank (1919–). British actor with reliable, usually kindly, always watchable face. Quintessential part was Messala, the professional soldier, in *Heil Caesar*. Also: *War and Peace*, *Kean*, *To Serve Them All My Days*, *Lace* and *The Invisible Man*. Latterly played Dan Archer in eternal radio soap *The Archers* until the character was killed off in 1986.

Midler, Bette (1945–). American burlesque singer noted for her strident voice and vulgarity; she has made several rather startling TV specials.

The Midnight Hour
US 1985 96m colour TVM
ABC Circle (Ervin Zavada)
At Hallowe'en, a group of high school pranksters unwittingly revive the cemetery dead.
Tasteless romp in the Spielberg mode.
w Bill Bleich *d* Jack Bender *ph* Rexford Metz *m* Brad Fiedel
Shari-Belafonte-Harper, LeVar Burton, Lee Montgomery, Dick Van Patten, Kevin McCarthy, Joanna Lee, Jonelle Allen
'A deadly dull Hallowe'en party . . . styleless imitation of genuine fright films.' – *Daily Variety*

Midnight Lace
US 1980 96m colour TVM
NBC/Universal/Four R (Leonard Rosenberg)
A rich woman hears threatening voices and thinks she is going insane.
Unforgivably thin remake of a 1960 movie which had nothing but top dressing going for it. This has nothing at all.
w Jerry Ludwig, *play Matilda Shouted Fire* by Janet Green *d* Ivan Nagy *ph* Isidore Mankofsky *m* Stu Phillips
Mary Crosby, Gary Frank, Celeste Holm, Robin Clark, Shecky Greene, Carolyn Jones, Susan Tyrrell
'Doesn't raise a ripple, let alone a goosebump.' – *Daily Variety*

Midnight Offerings
US 1981 96m colour TVM
ABC/Paramount/Stephen J. Cannell
A demented girl student turns to witchcraft and murder to get her own way.
Tedious and dimly photographed campus capers, of no interest to grown-ups.
w Juanita Bartlett *d* Rod Holcomb *ph* Hector Figueroa *m* Walter Scharf

Melissa Sue Anderson, Mary McDonough, Cathryn Damon, Gordon Jump, Patrick Cassidy
'Witchcraft brings on polite, glassy stares; so do vidpics with such limited dimensions.' – *Daily Variety*

A Midsummer Night's Dream **
GB 1964 78m bw (VTR)
Rediffusion (Joan Kemp-Welch)
One of the most successful Shakespeare productions of all time, with BENNY HILL given star billing as Bottom while the Athenian royals were only listed down the credits, which as I said at the time was putting the arse before the court. Flanders and Swann, the revue entertainers, wrote in to ask if my remark was not putting the coarse before the art. But the Victorian Romantic mood, with Mendelssohn's music and a corps de ballet, worked very nicely. With Peter Wyngarde (as Oberon), designed by Michael Yates, p r o d u c e d a n d d i r e c t e d b y J o a n Kemp-Welch.   PP

Midweek. Title used by the BBC1 late evening current affairs show in the mid-seventies, after *Twenty-four Hours* and before *Tonight*.   PP

The Mighty Continent *
GB 1975 13 × 50m colour (VTR)
BBC/SDR Stuttgart/Time–Life (Peter Morley)
A history of Europe in the 20th century.
Solid schoolbook extension at sixth-form level.
w John Terraine
PP: 'Ambitious history of Europe as a political and economic entity which somehow misfired, perhaps because Morley's idea of having a personal view split between two persons was a contradiction in terms, underlined by Peter Ustinov's lacklustre delivery as one of them.'

The Mighty Hercules. An American five-minute cartoon series syndicated in 1960, based pretty loosely on the Greek legends.

Mighty Moments from World History *
GB 1985 4 × approx. 50m
Artifax/C4 (Andrew Snell)
Comical but oddly touching versions of the legends of King Arthur, Lawrence of Arabia, the Dawn of Man and Boadicea, as staged on a shoestring by the double act of Desmond and Bernard, otherwise known as the National Theatre of Brent. They had previously (1984) done their very low-budget 'Messiah' on this channel.

w Patrick Barlow *d* Jude Kelly, John Stroud

Patrick Barlow (Desmond), Robert Austin (Bernard) PP

Mighty Mouse. A cartoon spoof of Superman which ran in the fifties, usually in six-minute segments but sometimes built up into half-hours.

The Migrants

US 1974 74m colour TVM

CBS/Tom Gries

Problems of migratory farm workers.

Almost an update of *Grapes of Wrath*, this striking drama won six Emmy nominations but no awards.

w Lanford Wilson, *story* Tennessee Williams *d* Tom Gries *ph* Dick Kratina *m* Billy Goldenberg

Cloris Leachman, Ron Howard, Sissy Spacek, Cindy Williams, Ed Lauter, Lisa Lucas

Mike Hammer *

aka: *Murder Me, Murder You*

US 1983 96m colour TVM

CBS/Columbia/Jay Bernstein (Lew Gallo)

Hammer, tough private eye and now a Vietnam vet, roars into action when his girl friend is killed and his new-found daughter is kidnapped.

A lively pilot while it keeps going, but a bore when it stops for sentiment, which luckily is not often. The twist ending however is somewhat foreseeable.

w Bill Stratton, based on characters created by Mickey Spillane *d* Gary Nelson *ph* Gayne Rescher *m* Earle Hagen

Stacy Keach, Tanya Roberts, Don Stroud, Delta Burke, Tom Atkins, Kent Williams

'Loaded with femme teasers, hard-boiled saloon-style fighting, good location filming.' – *Daily Variety*

† The resulting one-hour series ran 24 episodes before being interrupted by the star's jail sentence for possessing drugs. It returned in 1986.

Miles, Michael (1919–71). Quizmaster in Britain, popular from 1955 in the appalling *Take Your Pick*.

Miles to Go before I Sleep *

US 1974 75m colour TVM

Tomorrow

A lonely elderly man fulfils himself by helping teenage delinquents.

Yes, very worthy, and well acted, but not exactly compelling.

w Judith Parker, Bill Svanoe *d* Fielder Cook

Martin Balsam, Mackenzie Philips, Kitty Wynn, Elizabeth Wilson

Milland, Ray (1905–) (Reginald Truscott-Jones). Welsh-born leading man of the American cinema. He turned into a fairly considerable actor, and became a TV star in two series, *Markham* and *Meet Mr McNutley*. In his seventies he was to be found playing guest roles. TV movies: *Daughter of the Mind*, *River of Gold*, *Black Noon*, *The Dead Don't Die*, *Rich Man Poor Man*, *Look What Happened to Rosemary's Baby*, *Mayday at 40,000 Feet*, *Seventh Avenue*, *Testimony of Two Men*, *Cruise into Terror*, *The Darker Side of Terror*, *Cave In*.

Millar, Gavin (19 –). British film critic and director who presented Cinema programmes 1976–80 and shot *Omnibus* items on Gene Kelly (1974) and Busby Berkeley (1975). Wrote, presented and made *Travels with a Donkey* (1978) but his directing career took off with Dennis Potter's *Cream in my Coffee* (1980), followed by *Intensive Care* (1982), *Secrets* (1983), *The Weather in the Streets* (1984), *Unfair Exchanges* (1985) and *The Russian Soldier*, 1986. PP

Mille Miglia * (GB 1969; 75m). Michael Bryant impersonates racing driver Stirling Moss as he prepares to join the epic race (now discontinued) which used to be run over public roads in Italy. The script came, rather surprisingly, from Athol Fugard, otherwise known for plays to a very different meaning of the word 'race' set in his native South Africa. Directed by Robin Midgley; produced by Ronald Travers. First shown on BBC2, the show was rerun as a BBC1 *Play for Today* in 1970. PP

Miller, Arthur (1915–). Foremost US dramatist whose plays have all been done on TV, though more often in live or early VTR days, e.g. *Death of a Salesman* by Granada, 1957, with Albert Dekker; *The Crucible*, same company, 1959; *A View from the Bridge*, Rediffusion, 1966, with Raf Vallone; *The Price* (US) shown by LWT, 1971, with George C. Scott. Miller also wrote the screenplay of *Playing for Time*, 1980. PP

Miller, Joan (*c* 1910–). British TV presenter, an early (1936) host of *Picture Page*.

❋ **Miller, Jonathan** (1934–). British humorist, performer, medical man and director who arrived on the television scene by way of the revue *Beyond the Fringe* with Dudley Moore, Peter Cook and Alan Bennett. Unsuccessfully edited *Monitor* 1964–5; made films from Plato and M. R. James and the celebrated *Alice* with Gielgud and Malcolm Muggeridge. Produced the BBC Shakespeare directing a number of the plays himself. His varied skills came together most completely in *The Body in Question* (1978), which he wrote and presented. Went back to medicine in 1982 but couldn't stay altogether away from television or his other great love, producing opera. Presented *States of Mind* (13-part series on psychology, 1983); produced *The Beggars' Opera* with pop star Roger Daltry as McHeath, also 1983; prominent in *Staging an Opera* (6 × 30m series from TVS, 1983) about his production of *Fidelio* for Kent Opera; presented and took part in an extraordinary edition of *Horizon* for BBC, 1984, about a Parkinson's Disease victim, Ivan Vaughan. Presented *Origins*, 1986.   PP

Miller, Mitch (1911–). American oboeist and impresario who became a household word in the fifties with his pop music show *Sing Along with Mitch*.

Milligan, Spike (1918–). Zany British comedian, an acquired taste, who pops up in all media. Series include *Idiot's Weekly*, *A Show Called Fred*, *Milligan at Large*, *Q5*, *Curry and Chips*, *Oh In Colour*, *Q6*, *Q7*, etc. Subject of a C4 documentary, 1986.

Million Dollar Infield
US 1981 96m colour TVM
CBS/Rob Reiner, Peter Katz
The love life of four softball players. Dreary time-filler.

w Philip Mishkin, Rob Reiner, Dick Wimmer *d* Hal Cooper *ph* Tom Del Ruth *m* Artie Kane

Rob Reiner, Bonnie Bedelia, Bob Constanzo, Christopher Guest, Bruno Kirby

The Million Dollar Ripoff
US 1976 74m colour TVM
Charles Fries/NBC (Edward J. Montagne)
A gang plans to rob the payroll of a big city transport system.
Fair sub-Rififi caper melodrama.

w William Devane, John Pleshette *d* Alexander Singer

Freddie Prinze, Allen Garfield, Brooke Mills, Joanna de Varona

The Million Pound Grave (GB 1965). Originally a live show about the Sutton Hoo archaeological dig in 1939 which unearthed a 7th-century royal burial in Suffolk. Such is the continuing interest in the treasures discovered that in 1985 a telerecording of the programme was put out, followed by a new documentary, *Sutton Hoo*.   PP

The Millionaire
aka: *If You Had a Million*
US 1954–9 188 × 25m bw
CBS (Don Fedderson)
Michael Anthony, secretary to unseen multi-millionaire John Beresford Tipton, presents one million dollars, tax free, to a different needy person each week.
Wholly American fantasy comedy with the obvious moral that money isn't everything; based on the 1932 movie *If I Had a Million*.
Marvin Miller

The Millionaire
US 1978 96m colour TVM
CBS/Don Fedderson
Lethargic retread of the old warhorse (see above).

w John McGreevey *d* Don Weis *m* Frank De Vol

Robert Quarry, Martin Balsam, Edward Albert, John Ireland, Ralph Bellamy, William Demarest, Jane Wyatt

† A proposed one-hour series to follow quickly bit the dust.

Mills, Annette (1894–1955). Gentle-mannered British personality who in the fifties presented a puppet called Muffin the Mule.

Mills, Sir John (1908–). British actor, originally a song-and-dance man, on television (like many old cinema stars) comparatively late in his career, and then not very rewardingly (*The Zoo Gang*, *Young at Heart*). Best achievement in the 1979 *Quatermass* serial. PP

Mills, Roger (19 –). British docu-mentarist, responsible as producer or executive producer for most of the BBC's major observational series: *Inside Story*, *Sailor*, *Hospital*, *Hong Kong Beat*, *Circuit Eleven Miami*, *Public School*, *Strangeways*, *Forty Minutes*. BAFTA Desmond Davis Award, 1980.   PP

Milne, Alasdair (1931–). Scottish current affairs specialist and executive, since 1982 Director General of the BBC with his fair share of hot potatoes. A BBC trainee in

1954, into TV two years later to create the original early-evening *Tonight* with Donald Baverstock. Out of the BBC for a spell as a freelance, when he edited ITV's *This Week*.

Milner, Martin (1927–). American actor who aged rather quickly from callow youths to character roles. TV series: *The Trouble with Father, The Life of Riley, Route 66, Adam 12*. TV movies: *Emergency, Runaway, Hurricane, The Swiss Family Robinson, Flood, SST: Death Flight, Black Beauty, Little Mo, Crisis in Mid-Air*.

Milner, Roger (19 –). British actor-turned-writer specializing in biographical drama: *Speed King* (Sir Malcolm Campbell), *PQ17, Reith, Amy* (Johnson). As actor, played John Osborne's grandfather in *A Better Class of Person*. PP

Milton the Monster
US 1965–6 26 × 25m colour
ABC/Hal Seeger

Adventures of the world's most lovable monster, who lives on Horrible Hill in Transylvania.
Adequate Saturday morning cartoon filler, also featuring a segment on *Fearless Fly*.

Mimieux, Yvette (1942–). Sporadically ambitious American leading lady. Series: *The Most Deadly Game*. TV movies: *Hit Lady, Black Noon, Death Takes a Holiday, Disaster on the Coastliner*.

The Mind of J. G. Reeder
GB 1971 16 × 50m colour (VTR)
Thames

A clerk in the office of the Director of Public Prosecutions has a nose for unravelling mysteries.
Pleasant but unmemorable re-creations of Edgar Wallace's twenties crime stories.
Hugh Burden, Willoughby Goddard

Mind Over Murder
US 1979 96m colour TVM
CBS/Paramount (Jay Benson)

A girl foresees a plane crash and a killer on her tail.
Contrived shocker which delivers pretty fair entertainment of its kind.
w Robert Carrington *d* Ivan Nagy *ph* Dennis Dalzell *m* Paul Chihara
Deborah Raffin, David Ackroyd, Bruce Davison, Andrew Prine, Christopher Cary, Penelope Willis

'It may seem improbable but it sure has its breathcatchers.' – *Daily Variety*

Minder *
GB 1979–   × 50m colour
Thames/Euston Films

Adventures of a professional London bodyguard hired out by his shady employer to take care of other people's property.
Lively crime comedy–dramas, in which the second lead took most of the honours.
cr Leon Griffiths
Dennis Waterman, GEORGE COLE

PP: 'Funny about crime without making crime funny, equipped with two dreadfully endearing characters, the series is in a class all its own. I would add a fourth star.'

Minder on the Orient Express **
GB 1985 96m TVM
Euston Films/Thames (George Taylor)

First of the *Minder* movies made as soon as the series proper finished, and thriftily using up rolling-stock and other props furnished for *Romance on the Orient Express*. If the story tipped deeper into farce than regular episodes had, especially in the treatment of the luckless Det. Sgt Chisholm, it was still superior dodgy drama.
w Andrew Payne *d* Francis Megahy
George Cole, Dennis Waterman, Patrick Malahide, Glynn Edwards, Honor Blackman, Adam Faith, Ronald Lacey, Robert Beatty, Maurice Denham, Ralph Bates, Linda Hayden, Amanda Pays, Peter Childs   PP

Miner, Worthington (1900–). American TV producer of the fifties: *The Goldbergs, Medic, Studio One*.

The Miners' Strike (1984–5). Britain's longest major strike for half a century predictably generated much controversy, both in itself and over its coverage. Did television's appetite for action footage (a) exaggerate or (b) encourage picket-line violence? Was the striking miners' case fairly put? They claimed that only Channel Four News got it right, but this was chiefly because C4, with its 50-minute bulletin, was able to devote more time to all sides. It also had the bright idea, about half-way through, of giving the opposing chairmen (Arthur Scargill, NUM; Ian McGregor, NCB) a camera crew and 11 minutes of airtime apiece to present their own cases. As a performer Scargill won easily; as a strategist McGregor lasted out the better.
Another notable occasion was the whole evening, from 8 pm onwards, allotted to the

dispute by ITV on the eve of its first anniversary and – as things turned out – its collapse:

View from the Coalfields: presented by Jonathan Dimbleby, *p* John Edwards
The Strike and the Nation: Brian Walden, *p* David Aaronvitch, Peter Mandelson
Learning the Lesson: Brian Walden with Neil Kinnock, David Owen and Norman Tebbit, *p* John Wakefield

Feature programmes, mostly subsequent to the strike, include:
Which Side Are You on? Songs and poems by striking miners and their families pulled together by director Ken Loach, for LWT/C4, 1985.
Ms Rhymney Valley: Sanctimonious semi-dramatization of how fund-raising beauty contest in Welsh mining community is deflected by feminist heroine to reward imprisoned miners' wives instead. Written and directed by Karl Francis, for BBC, 1985.
Scab: the dispute through the eyes of a Yorkshire mining community. Powerful play by Geoffrey Case, directed by Gordon Flemyng, produced by Keith Richardson, for YTV, 1986. PP

Mini Pops (GB 1983). Fairly nauseating series, mercifully soon discontinued, in which winsome child performers were auditioned for adult song-and-dance routines. PP

mini-series. A term given in the mid-seventies to serializations of famous novels, which tended to appear in four to six episodes of various lengths, often scheduled on successive nights.

Minnelli, Liza (1946–). Vibrant American singer and actress, daughter of Judy Garland. TV appearances usually in musical specials.

Minstrel Man *
US 1976 98m colour TVM
Tomorrow/First Artists (Mitchell Brower, Bob Lovenheim)

A dramatized account of the 19th-century minstrel shows.
Unusual, well-produced musical period piece.
w Richard and Esther Shapiro *d* William A. Graham

Glynn Turman, Ted Ross, Stanley Clay, Saundra Sharp

Minton, Roy (19 –). British TV playwright specializing in harsh stories set in enclosed worlds, e.g. *Funny Farm* (mental hospital,

1975), and the banned *Scum* (Borstal institution), but occasionally allowing himself a nice line in comedy, as in *Sling Your Hook* (1969), *Horace* (series) 1982. PP

The Miracle of Kathy Miller
US 1981 96m colour TVM
CBS/Universal (Bernard Rothman, Jack Wohl)

An Arizona teenager overcomes massive brain damage after a car crash, and becomes an international athlete.
Rather flatly handled true story.
w Mel and Ethel Brez *d* Robert Lewis
Sharon Gless, Frank Converse, Helen Hunt, Bill Beyers

The Miracle of Life *** (Sweden 1982; 50m). Brilliantly microphotographed account of human reproduction. 'All you ever wanted to know about sex and were too big to find out,' I wrote at the time. Produced and directed by Lennart Neilssen, for SRT. Shown in GB in BBC *Horizon* slot. BAFTA Best Foreign Television Programme, 1983.

Miracle on Ice
US 1981 142m colour TVM
ABC/Filmways/Moonlight (Frank Von Zerneck, Robert Greenwald)

How the US Olympic hockey team took the 1980 gold medal at Lake Placid.
Well-mounted but interminable pap for sporting patriots.
w Lionel Chetwynd *d* Steven H. Stern *ph* Howard Schwartz *m* Fred Karlin
Karl Malden, Andrew Stevens, Steve Guttenberg, Jerry Houser, Eugene Roche, Jessica Walter
'Loaded with quality, energy and heart.' – *Daily Variety*

Miracle on 34th Street
US 1973 100m colour TVM
TCF

A department store Santa Claus claims to be the real thing.
Dull TV remake of the 1947 film with too much footage and inadequate talent.
w Jeb Rosebrook *d* Fielder Cook
Sebastian Cabot, Roddy McDowall, Jane Alexander, David Hartman, Jim Backus, Suzanne Davidson

The Miracle Worker
US 1980 96m colour TVM
NBC/Katz–Gallin/Halfpint (Fred Coe)

MINDER. The most popular success of the early eighties was without doubt this wry comedy drama. Dennis Waterman, as a bodyguard with a record, was the supposed star, but George Cole as his grafting boss was the one who really caught the public fancy. Between them, Royce Mills.

Helen Keller, blind and deaf, is taught by young Annie Sullivan to behave like a human being.

Over-stylized version of a play which while remaining faithful to the truth presented it in a stagey way which doesn't entirely suit television, giving a flat and unreal result.

w William Gibson, from his play *d* Paul Aaron *ph* Ted Voigtlander *m* Billy Goldenberg

Patty Duke Astin, Melissa Gilbert, Diana Muldaur, Charles Siebert, Anne Seymour

Mirren, Helen (19 –). Buxom and intelligent British actress whose many notable television performances include those in *The Duchess of Malfi*, *As You Like It* and *A Midsummer Night's Dream* in the BBC Shakespeare, *Blue Remembered Hills*. The subject of a John Goldschmidt documentary profile early in her career.   PP

Mirror, Mirror
US 1979 96m colour TVM
NBC/Christiana (Joanna Lee)

Three women facing emotional crises resort to plastic surgery.

Moderately intelligent upper-crust soap opera.

w Leah Appet, Charles Dennis *d* Joanna Lee *ph* Ben Colman *m* Jimmie Haskell

Loretta Swit, Janet Leigh, Lee Meriwether, Robert Vaughn, Peter Bonerz, Walter Brooke

Mirzoeff, Edward (1936–). Able British documentary film-maker and producer who first spread his (rotating) wings with helicopter-borne travelogues. Credits since then include Frederic Raphael's *Byron: a Personal Tour* (1981), *Year of the French* (1982), *The Other Half* (1984). Took over as producer both of *Real Lives* and of *Forty Minutes*, 1985.   PP

A Miserable and Lonely Death * (GB
1977; 30m). Effective reconstruction of the inquest into the death of Steve Biko, leader of a Black South African movement, while in police custody. Written by John Blair and Norman Fenton; directed by Michael Darlow; produced by David Elstein; for Thames (*This Week*).   PP

† The same case inspired *The Biko Inquest*, 1984, with Albert Finney; directed by Graham Evans, produced by Cecil Clarke, for United British Artists/C4.

Les Misérables
GB 1978 142m colour TVM
CBS/ITC/Norman Rosemont

The story of Jean Valjean, who after stealing a loaf of bread escapes from slavery and is hounded by the relentless Inspector Javert. A good example of this producer's superficial gloss, but there have been many better versions of the story than this.

w John Gay, *novel* by Victor Hugo *d* Glenn Jordan *ph* Jean Tournier *m* Allyn Ferguson *ad* Wilfred Shingleton

Richard Jordan, Anthony Perkins, Cyril Cusack, Claude Dauphin, John Gielgud, Ian Holm, Celia Johnson, Joyce Redman, Flora Robson, Christopher Guard, Caroline Langrishe, Angela Pleasence, Dave Hill

The Misfit (GB 1970). Ronald Fraser as the last of the Empire builders home after half a lifetime in the Far East to see with a fresh eye the less acceptable aspects of life in the 'permissive' Britain of the late sixties. The character was developed from one like him in a *Troubleshooters* episode also starring Fraser and written by the same author. Apart from a slight tendency to stop and moralize, funny and quite percipient. Written by Roy Clarke; directed by James Gatward; for ATV.   PP

Misfits of Science
US 1985 1 × 96m, 13 × 50m colour
NBC/Universal/James D. Parriott (Alan J. Levi)

Two scientists recruit oddballs with supernatural powers to help combat crime. Woefully inept comic strip adventures, a kind of human Fantastic Four with too much flat dialogue and too few special effects.

cr James D. Parriott

Dean Paul Martin, Kevin Peter Hall, Mark Thomas Miller, Courteney Cox, Jennifer Holmes, Mickey Jones

Miss All-American Beauty
US 1982 96m colour TVM
CBS/Marian Rees (Marcy Gross, Ann Weston)

Backstage at a beauty pageant. Routine multi-story exposé which just about occupies the space before one's eyes. But only just.

w Nancy Audley, Emily Tracy *d* Gus Trikonis *ph* Robert Jessup *m* Paul Chihara

Diane Lane, Cloris Leachman, David Dukes, Jayne Meadows, Alice Herson

Miss Jones and Son *
GB 1977–8 14 × 25m colour (VTR)
Thames

An unmarried mother looks after her child and greets life with a smiling face. Smart comedy which caused a few raised eyebrows but won a large following.

cr Peter Waring

Paula Wilcox

† An American version was attempted under the title *Miss Winslow and Son*.

Miss Lonelyhearts *
US 1983 52m b/w
American Film Institute/H. J. Holman; for American Playhouse

The work of a columnist giving advice to the lovelorn brings on tragedy. Incisive reshaping of a standard 20th-century classic; but afterwards it doesn't seem *that* much better than an episode of *Lou Grant*.

w Michael J. Dinner, Robert Bailey *d* Michael J. Dinner *ph* Juan Ruis-Anchia *m* Leonard Rosenman

Eric Roberts, Arthur Hill, Conchata Ferrell, John Ryan, Sally Kemp

Miss Marple
GB 1984–5 2 × 165m, 2 × 100m colour
BBC (Guy Slater, George Gallaccio)

Joan Hickson as Agatha Christie's spinster detective in dramatizations of her vintage (thirties and forties) cases, split into mini-serials when shown in the UK.

The Body in the Library (*w* T. R. Bowen, *d* Silvio Narizzano; with Gwen Watford, Andrew Cruikshank, Moray Watson, Valentine Dyall, Frederick Jaeger)
A Murder Is Announced (*w* Alan Plater, *d* David Giles; with Ursula Howells, Renee Asherson, Sylvia Sims, Joan Sims, Mary Kerridge, Ralph Michael, John Castle, Paola Dionosotti)
The Moving Finger (*w* Julia Jones, *d* Roy Boulting; with Michael Culver, Richard Pearson, Dilys Hamlett)

A Pocketful of Rye (w T. R. Bowen, d Guy Slater; with Peter Davison, Clive Merrison, Timothy West, Stacey Dorning)   PP

LH: 'A word for the generally fine recreation of pre-war British village life, also for the catchy music.'

† Two more titles followed in 1986: *The Murder at the Vicarage*, d Julian Amyes; *Sleeping Murder*, d John Davies. Another two were in production: *At Bertram's Hotel*, *Nemesis*.

Miss Morrison's Ghosts * (GB 1981). Intriguing dramatized account of a supposed time-slip in 1901 when two woman academics visiting the Palace of Versailles were convinced they had encountered Marie Antoinette and members of her court strolling along paths that had ceased to exist a century earlier. With Hannah Gordon, Wendy Hiller. Written by Ian Curteis; directed by John Bruce; produced by John Rosenberg; for Anglia.   PP

LH: 'Only the early reels were true to the original account: the main plot about college politics and female emancipation was entirely imaginary. And despite many enjoyments along the way, the ending was unsatisfyingly ambiguous.'

Miss World. Annual beauty contest held in London, a rival to the US-inspired Miss Universe. Was televised by the BBC until 1982, when ITV won the contract and I wrote: 'It is customary to have fun with the artless utterances of the girls and the witless utterances of the commentators, but this only conceals the real truth that the contest is the most boring, pointless, philistine event in the calendar. Miss Germany won only because she's got the biggest teeth.'   PP

The Missiles of October ***
US 1974 150m colour (VTR)
Viacom (IRV WILSON, BUZZ BERGER, HERB BRODKIN)

President Kennedy deals with the Cuban missile crisis of 1962.
Gripping political drama which began the mid-seventies fashion for 'factions' or reconstructions with actors of real-life events.

w STANLEY R. GREENBERG d ANTHONY PAGE

WILLIAM DEVANE, Martin Sheen, Howard da Silva, Ralph Bellamy, John Dehner, Andrew Duggan

The Missing Are Deadly
US 1974 74m colour TVM
Allen Epstein

A mischievous youth steals a rat from a laboratory and nearly starts a plague. Obvious, uninteresting suspenser.

w Kathryn and Michael Michaelian d Don MacDougall

Ed Nelson, Leonard Nimoy, Jose Ferrer, Marjorie Lord

Missing Children: a Mother's Story
US 1982 96m colour TVM
CBS/Warner/Kayden–Gleason (Jay Benson)

An abandoned wife puts her children in care till she finds employment; but then she finds that they have been adopted.
Painful but not entirely convincing mother-love yarn; a very extended piece of film-making.

w Jim Lawrence, Nancy Sackett d Dick Lowry

Mare Winningham, Polly Holliday, Jane Wyatt, Anne Haney, Lenora May, John Anderson, Scatman Crothers, Richard Dysart

Missing from Home ** (GB 1984; 6 × 52m). Apparently happily-married commuter fails to come home one evening. A superior mystery gradually deepening into an examination of mid-life and mid-marriage crises, with Judy Loe as the quintessential eighties heroine. Also with Jonathan Newth; written by Roger Marshall, for BBC.   PP

Missing Pieces *
aka: *A Private Investigation*
US 1983 96m colour TVM
CBS/Entheos (Doug Chapin)

With the help of a rumpled private eye a woman tracks down the killers of her political reporter husband.
Very tolerable telemovie with some smart dialogue and action.

w,d MIKE HODGES, *book A Private Investigation* by Karl Alexander ph Charles Correll pd Fred Harpman

Elizabeth Montgomery, Ron Karabatsos, John Reilly, Louanne Robin, Robin Gammell, Julius Harris

Mission Impossible *
US 1966–72 171 × 50m colour
CBS/Paramount/Bruce Geller (Stanley Kallis, Bruce Lansbury)

A special unit of spies and saboteurs is trained to attempt the impossible.
Clean-limbed adventure series with a good deal of silent action and teamwork, prefaced by

instructions irresistibly delivered on a self-destructing record. (The phone would have been simpler and safer.)

cr BRUCE GELLER *m* Lalo Schifrin

Steven Hill, Martin Landau, Barbara Bain; later Peter Graves, Greg Morris, Leonard Nimoy, Peter Lupus, Lesley Warren, Lynda Day George

† Emmys 1966, 1967: best drama series.

Mission Magic
US 1973 26 × 22m colour
Filmation

Miss Tickle and her students enter fantasy land through a magic blackboard.
Bland cartoon adventures.

The Mississippi *
US 1983 50m colour
CBS/Warner/Ralph Waite/Hajeno (Bob Crais)

A lawyer leaves the rat race for a Mississippi riverboat, but takes on cases as required at his various ports of call.
Courtroom stuff with a pleasant variety of locations; just the scripts take it a little above routine.

cr Darryl Ponicsan

Ralph Waite, Linda G. Miller, Stan Shaw

Mr Adams and Eve *
US 1956–7 66 × 25m bw
CBS/Bridget

The disagreements of a couple of married movie stars.
Borrowed from the cinema film *Simon and Laura*, but in itself no worse for that. A moderately astringent comedy for its time.

Ida Lupino, Howard Duff

Mr and Mrs Bo Jo Jones *
US 1971 74m colour TVM
TCF (Lester Linsk)

A young couple have to get married, and do well despite parental interference
Convincing, well-scripted domestic drama.

w William Wood, *novel* Ann Head *d* Robert Day

Desi Arnaz Jnr, Chris Norris, Susan Strasberg, Dan Dailey, Tom Bosley, Dina Merrill, Lynn Carlin

Mr and Mrs North
US 1953–4 57 × 25m bw
NBC/Bernard L. Schubert

A young wife constantly stumbles across murders.
Thin Man imitation, quite passable.

Barbara Britton, Richard Denning

Mr Belvedere
US 1985 × 25m colour
ABC/TCF/Lazy B/FOB (Patricia Rickey)

An arrogant male baby sitter takes command of a California household with sassy children.
Witless revamp of the 1948 movie *Sitting Pretty*: utterly predictable and seldom even superficially amusing.

cr Frank Dungan, Jeff Stein

Christopher Hewett, Ilene Graff, Bob Uecker, Rob Stone, Tracy Wells

Mr Broadway *
US 1964 13 × 50m bw
CBS/Talent Associates

Adventures of a New York public relations man.
Sophisticated drama series with a good local flavour; but somehow it seemed to be neither fish, flesh nor good red herring.

cr Garson Kanin

Craig Stevens, Horace McMahon

Mr Deeds Goes to Town
US 1969 17 × 25m colour
ABC/Columbia (Harry Ackerman, Bob Sweeney)

A country cousin finds himself heir to a 50-million-dollar city enterprise.
Carbon copy of the old movie without the old flair.

cr Harry Ackerman, Bernie Slade *m* Shorty Rogers

Monte Markham, Pat Harrington

Mr District Attorney
US 1954–5 78 × 25m bw
ABC/United Artists

Stories from a DA's case book.
Slick courtroom stuff.

David Brian

Mister Ed *
US 1960–5 143 × 25m bw
CBS/Filmways (Al Simon)

A suburbanite has a horse which talks only to him.
Televersion of the *Francis* movies, rather restricted in setting but often quite amusing.

ALAN YOUNG, Connie Hines, Leon Ames, Florence McMichael

† Larry Keating and Edna Skinner played the neighbours in the first 78 films.

Mr Garlund (US 1960). Half-hour mystery series for CBS, with Charles Quinlivan as a financial wizard who affected the life of a variety of people.

THE MISSISSIPPI. Ralph Waite (left) was fresh from his success in *The Waltons* when he devised for himself this series about a lawyer who gives up the big city for a life on the river, but though amiable it wasn't a big success. With him, Stella McMullen and Stan Shaw.

Mr Halpern and Mr Johnson (GB/US 1984; 65m). Theatrical two-hander with Laurence Olivier and Jackie Gleason mulling over a boring involvement of the past. Written by Lionel Goldstein, directed by Alvin Rakoff, for C4/HTV/Edie Ely Landau/Primetime. PP

Mr Horn
US 1979 2 × 96m colour TVM
CBS/Lorimar (Robert L. Jacks)

Episodes in the life of a western bounty hunter.
Good-looking western with an undernourished
plot line, the first two hours being an aimless
string of incident.

w William Goldman d Jack Starrett ph Jorge
Stahl Jnr m Jerry Fielding

David Carradine, Richard Widmark, Karen
Black, Richard Masur

'Plodding and repetitious.' – *Daily Variety*

Mr I. Magination (US 1949–51). Live CBS
half-hour series for children with Paul Tripp
staging impromptu playlets based on viewers'
letters.

Mr Inside, Mr Outside *
US 1973 74m colour TVM
Metromedia/Phil D'Antoni

One of a pair of cops goes undercover to trap
diamond smugglers.
Adequate location *policier*.

w Jerry Coppersmith d Alex March

Hal Linden, Tony Lo Bianco, Phil Bruns, Paul
Benjamin

Mr Jerico *
GB 1969 85m colour TVM
ITC (Julian Wintle)

Adventures of a con man.
Pleasant chase-and-caper yarn.

w Philip Levene d Sidney Hayers

Patrick MacNee, Connie Stevens, Herbert
Lom, Marty Allen

Mr Lucky
US 1959 34 × 25m bw
CBS/Spartan/Sharpe–Lewis (Jack Arnold)

Adventures of the owner of a gambling ship
(loosely based on a 1943 Cary Grant film).
Very moderate comedy-drama series.
supervisor Blake Edwards m Henry Mancini
John Vivyan, Ross Martin

Mr Magoo. A myopic cartoon character
created by UPA in the late forties and voiced by
Jim Backus. The adventurous old codger who
never knew whether he was talking to a cop or a
phone box later appeared in everything from
five-minute episodes to features and half-hour
series; most notable was *The Famous
Adventures of Mr Magoo.*

Mr Merlin *
US 1981 22 × 25m colour
CBS/Columbia/Larry Larry (Larry Rosen,
  Larry Tucker)

An amiable old sorcerer helps a boy out of
various jams.
Pleasant magical farce which couldn't quite
keep up the pace.

cr Larry Rosen, Larry Tucker
BARNARD HUGHES, Clark Brandon

Mr Novak
US 1963–4 60 × 50m bw
NBC/MGM

Experiences of a young schoolteacher.
Goodish American drama which didn't travel.

James Franciscus, Dean Jagger (later Burgess
Meredith)

Mr Palfrey of Westminster (GB 1984; 6 ×
52m). Pleasant low-key spy series featuring
Alec McCowen as a strictly non-violent, civil
service operative. A second series followed
in 1985. Produced by Michael Chapman, for
Thames.   PP

Mr Peepers *
US 1952–4 105 approx. × 25m bw
NBC

Adventures of a shy but dependable science
teacher.
Likeable comedies which are still fondly
remembered in the USA.

Wally Cox, Tony Randall, Marion Lorne,
Georgiana Johnson, Pat Benoit, Ernest Truex,
Norma Crane

Mr Roberts
US 1965 30 × 25m colour
NBC/Warner

Adventures of a young naval lieutenant on
board ship in wartime.
Watered-down version of the movie and stage
play.

Roger Smith, George Harmon, Steve Ives,
Richard X. Slattery

Mr Rogers' Neighbourhood. American
public TV chat show for and about children and
their attitudes to the serious matters of life and
death. Fred Rogers, the host, was a
Presbyterian minister. It ran from 1968 to 1974.

Mr Rose *
GB 1967–70 30 approx. × 50m bw (VTR)
Granada (Philip Mackie)

A retired Scotland Yard inspector continues to
solve murder cases.

Influential great detective format with two young legmen: a direct predecessor of *Ironside*, but with aspirations to sophistication.

cr Philip Mackie *d* Michael Cox, David Cunliffe

WILLIAM MERVYN, Donald Webster, Gillian Lewis

PP: 'In every Mackie entertainment there is a faint nostalgia for the light fiction of his own boyhood. The shades of Blackshirt or even Raffles lurk in the background, ever ready to slip into the 1967 scene some sentiment from 1937. But Mr Rose himself, played by William Mervyn as if slipping on a comfy smoking jacket, conceals beneath that infuriatingly bland exterior a genuine regard for truth and equity; and in my book there will always be plenty of room for the crime story resolved by a stroke of logic rather than a karate chop.'

Mr Smith
US 1983 13 × 25m colour
NBC/Paramount/Weinberger–Daniels
 (Ralph Helfer)

An escaped orang-utan takes an intellectualizing potion and becomes a Washington politician.
A somewhat wasted comedy premise with only the occasional touches of humour.

cr David Lloyd

Leonard Frey, Tim Dingan, Terri Garber, Laura Garber

'Is it possible the producers were referring to their own new series when they had Mr Smith denounce all television as mindless drivel?' – *Daily Variety*

Mr Smith Goes to Washington
US 1963 13 × 25m colour
ABC/Screen Gems

Adventures of an honest country politician in the Capitol.
Thin transcription of the famous movie.

Fess Parker, Sandra Warner, Red Foley

Mr Sunshine
US 1985   × 25m colour
ABC/Paramount/Henry Winkler–John
 Rich (Bob Ellison)

A drily witty English professor carries on despite an accident which has left him blind.
Ho-hum, would-be sassy comedy of weak one-liners.

cr David Lloyd

Jeffrey Tambor, Leonard Frey, Nan Martin, Cecilia Hart, David Knell, Barbara Babcock

Mr T (1952–) (Lawrence Tero). Massive black American performer who became a household word after appearing in *The A Team*. Also: *The Toughest Man in the World*.

Mr T and Tina
US 1976 13 × 25m colour
ABC/James Komack

A Japanese inventor in Chicago hires a Nebraska governess for his children.
Anna and the King played for farce: too eager to please.

cr James Komack, Stan Cutler, George Tibbles

Pat Morita, Susan Blanchard

Mr Terrific
US 1967 13 × 15m colour
CBS

A mild scientist turns into an all-powerful giant when he swallows a certain pill.
Comedy variation on the Jekyll/Hyde formula, rather ineptly done.

Stephen Strimpell, Dick Gautier, John McGiver

Mrs G. Goes to College
aka: *The Gertrude Berg Show*
US 1961 26 × 25m bw
CBS/Four Star/JAHFA

An elderly widow becomes a college freshman.
Curious to say the least, but the stars seemed to enjoy it.

Gertrude Berg, Cedric Hardwicke

Mrs Reinhardt * (GB 1981; 60m; colour).
Helen Mirren as a well-heeled, well-stacked woman seeking escape from a failing marriage in a dream-like but eventually ugly affair with a young American. Interesting sensual story by Edna O'Brien, filmed by Elmer Cossey in lush Brittany settings, directed by Piers Haggard, produced by Alan Shallcross; for BBC. With Brad Davis as the young man, Ralph Bates as the lady's husband.   PP

Mrs R's Daughter
US 1981 96m colour TVM
NBC/Dan Curtis

A woman becomes obsessed by her determination to bring to justice the man who raped her daughter.
Curiously unsympathetic character study.

w George Rubino *d* Dan Curtis *ph* Paul Lohmann

Cloris Leachman, Season Hubley, Donald Moffat, John McIntire

MISS MORRISON'S GHOSTS was an intriguing piece of what the trade calls 'faction', based on the famous memoir *An Adventure* about two English ladies who, visiting Versailles in 1901, saw some 18th-century ghosts. Hannah Gordon, Wendy Hiller.

Mrs Sundance
US 1973 74m colour TVM
TCF

The widow of the outlaw tries to go straight and becomes a schoolmistress, then finds she isn't a widow at all.

Disappointing western considering the possibilities: it takes too long to get going.

w Christopher Knopf d Marvin Chomsky m Pat Williams

Elizabeth Montgomery, Robert Foxworth, L. Q. Jones, Lurene Tuttle, Dean Smith, Arthur Hunnicutt

Mrs Thursday. A 1966 one-hour series contrived by Ted Willis as a vehicle for favourite character actress Kathleen Harrison, who retired shortly afterwards. She played an elderly cockney charwoman who inherits the controlling interest in an industrial empire.

PP: 'If I were a capitalist I'd be grateful for the warning of this series: to take my money out of any enterprise that ever fell into the hands of a humble, indomitable, lovable, uncomplaining, golden-hearted, ignorant old bird like Mrs Thursday.'

'His genius brought him tragedies and triumphs ... and three generations of women rewarded him with their love!'
Mistral's Daughter *
US 1984 2 × 142m, 1 ×
  96m colour miniseries
CBS/RTL/Steve Krantz (Herbert
  Hirschman, Suzanne Wisenfled)

The life of a selfish, womanizing Parisian painter from the mid-twenties to the mid-sixties.

Good-looking novelization which holds the interest pretty well and makes little secret of being based on Picasso.

w Rosemary Anne Sisson, Terence Feely, novel by Judith Krantz d Douglas Hickox, Kevin Connor ph Jean Tournier, Pierre Lhomme m Vladimir Kosma paintings John Bratby pd Alain Negre

Stacy Keach, Stephanie Powers, Lee Remick, Robert Urich, Timothy Dalton, Ian Richardson, Stephanie Dunnam, Alexandra Stewart, Joanna Lumley, Philippine Leroy Beaulieu, Caroline Langrishe

The Mistress (GB 1985; 6 × 30m). Doleful sitcom from Carla Lane to the fashionable notion that mistresses were to be pitied as outcasts without rights. With Felicity Kendal, Jack Galloway, Jane Asher. Produced by Gareth Gwenlan, for BBC. PP

'He brought her ecstasy. Then he taught her fear!'
Mistress of Paradise
US 1983 96m colour TVM
ABC/Lorimar (R. W. Goodwin)

In 1843 a Northern heiress marries a dashing Creole and goes with him to his wuthering Louisiana mansion.

A rip-off of *Rebecca* and *Jane Eyre*, complete with sinister housekeeper. At least it raises a laugh or two.

w Bennett Foster, William Bast d Peter Medak ph Ken Lamkin m John Addison

Genevieve Bujold, Chad Everett, Anthony Andrews, Carolyn Seymour, Olivia Cole

'Thankfully, they rarely make 'em like this any more.' – *Daily Variety*

Mitch *
GB 1984 10 × 52m
LWT (Peter Cregeen)

Fleet Street crime reporter turns up all human life. A good gritty series never glamorizing the seedy and often sad circumstances of crime, and keeping all the loose ends, which is perhaps one reason it sat on the shelf for two years before being scheduled.

cr Roger Marshall w various d Don Leaver, Peter Cregeen, Terry Green, Gerry Mill

John Thaw   PP

Mitchell, Cameron (1918–). (Cameron Mizell). Burly American character actor who has turned his hand to every kind of part. TV series: *The Beachcomber, High Chaparral.* TV movies: *Thief, The Delphi Bureau, Hitchhike, The Rookies, The Hanged Man, The Swiss Family Robinson, The Quest, Flood, The Hostage Heart, The Bastard, Hanging by a Thread,* etc.

❋ **Mitchell, Denis** (1912–). Truly innovatory British film-maker (with one or two essays in video) who began in BBC radio and pioneered the use of pre-recorded wildtrack voices when he turned to television in 1955. At first his films were mainly impressionistic studies of northern life. Later he tackled more specific subjects, including portraits of individual characters (e.g. a Soho busker) or cities (Chicago, Beirut), an African trilogy and European travelogues with Rene Cutforth. As a tutor he coached Dennis Potter in his first (and only) documentary, *Between Two Rivers,* and produced with Norman Swallow the *This England* series whose young directors included Michael Grigsby, Michael Apted, Francis

MR PALFREY OF WESTMINSTER. Alec McCowen as the diffident but ultra-shrewd spymaster.

Megahy, John Irvin, Richard Eyre, Frank Cvitanovich and Mike Newell. Since the end of the seventies Mitchell has returned to small, impressionistic films made under his own badge, DMF Productions.

'A vision of the world that is as personal and as intense as the creations of the most serious poet or painter, novelist or dramatist.' – Norman Swallow

Programmes transmitted:
1955   *On the Threshold*; BBC 'Special Inquiry' – Young Londoners.
1957   IN PRISON; BBC Manchester, with Roy Harris.
       Night and the City; BBC Manchester, with Roy Harris.
1958   ON TOUR; BBC Manchester, with Roy Harris.
1959   *Morning in the Streets*; BBC Manchester, with Roy Harris.
       A Soho Story; BBC – Study of a busker.

1960   THE WIND OF CHANGE; BBC – 1. Main Street Africa. 2. A View from the Farm. 3. Between Two Worlds.
1961   CHICAGO; BBC/ABC–WBKB.
       Grass Roots; BBC – Small-town America.
       Ed and Frank; BBC – Contrasted glimpses of conformist salesman and bohemian artist.
1962   *Summer in Lebanon*; BETA (W. Germany).
       The Intruders Ten Years After – follow-up to *On The Threshold*.
1963/4 *Sharon*; Granada (video) with Norman Swallow – See: *location recording*.
       The Entertainers; Granada (video) with Norman Swallow – See: *location recording*.
       The Dream Machine; ATV – Television.

MISTRAL'S DAUGHTER. Stacy Keach's carroty hair did not disguise his character's resemblance to Picasso in this eventful miniseries from the novel by Judith Krantz.

1965 *The House on the Beach*; Rediffusion/Intertel – Drug addicts' self-help in California.
1966 *Spring in Ethiopia*
1967 *Epitaph for a Young Man*; Granada – *This England*.
1969 *The Republic of Rhodesia*; Granada.
1970 *Seven Men*; Granada – Profiles of the mainly unsung: Quentin Crisp was an exception.
1970/71 *World in Action*; Granada – Six editions incl. *Pigs* about US police forces; American commercial radio; Quentin Crisp again.
1972 *European Journey*; Granada – West European countries.
1973 *European Journey*; Granada – East Europe: Rene Cutforth was the reporter both times.
1975 PRIVATE LIVES; Granada – 13 more profiles of the unsung.
1977 *Never and Always*; Granada – Study of Mitchell's own village in Norfolk.

1979 *Maryport*; Granada *This England* – With Ray Gosling as reporter.
1980 *The Pennines*; Granada *This England* – With Ray Gosling as reporter.
1981 *Impressions*; BBC/DMF Productions – 10-minute films.   PP

Mitchell, James (19 –). British writer, best known for the long-running series *Callan* and *When the Boat Comes In*.   PP

Mitchell, Julian (19 –). British writer mainly associated with adaptations from other sources but always inventive and imaginative. *A Family and a Fortune*, *Staying On*, *The Weather in the Streets*.

Mitchell, Leslie (1905–85). Veteran British commentator and compere, a pioneer BBC presenter who was still going strong in the late seventies as presenter of *Those Wonderful TV Times*, a Tyne Tees nostalgia offering. Subject of *This Is Your Life*, 1983.

Mitchell, Thomas (1892–1962). Outstanding Irish–American character actor who in his later days tackled TV series: *Mayor of the Town*, *O. Henry Playhouse*, *Glencannon*. Emmy 1952, best actor.

❋ **Mitchell, Warren** (1926–). British character actor who after years of being unnoticed shot to national fame as the bald-headed bigot Alf Garnett in TILL DEATH US DO PART, the forerunner of *All in the Family*. After the show ended in 1974 Mitchell was too identified with the character to find success in other fields, but eventually he became a respected star of the National Theatre. In 1981 he unwisely made a comeback as Alf Garnett in ATV's *Till Death*, but the 1985 BBC up-date *In Sickness and in Health* was a second triumph.

Mitzi and One Hundred Guys *
US 1975 50m colour (VTR)
CBS/Green Isle (Mort Green)

A streamlined variety special, extremely well-drilled, in which by clever cut-ins the star appeared ⁊ be dancing with a 'million-dollar chorus' inc ⁊ing Bob Hope, Bill Bixby, Andy Griffith, Ro₋s Hunter, Dean Jones, Leonard Nimoy and William Shatner.

w Jerry Mayer *d* Tony Charmoli

Mitzi Gaynor, Jack Albertson, Michael Landon

Mixed Blessings
GB 1978   × 25m colour (VTR)
LWT (Derrick Goodwin)

A university student wants to marry a black girl and both sets of parents disapprove.
Vulgar comedy turning up every cliché in the book.

w Sid Green *d* Derrick Goodwin

Christopher Blake, Muriel Odunton, Joan Sanderson, Sylvia Kay, George Waring, Carmen Munro

Mobile Two
US 1975 74m colour TVM
Universal/Jack Webb (Mike Mesehoff)

Adventures of a TV news reporter.
Tolerable pilot.

w David Moessinger, James M. Miller *d* David Moessinger

Jackie Cooper, Julie Gregg, Jack Hogan, Edd Byrnes

† A shortlived one-hour series followed under the title *Mobile One*, with the same two stars under producer William Bowers. It ran to 13 × 50m episodes.

ROBERT MITCHUM was well into his sixties when he played the fortyish lead in *The Winds of War*, a miniseries blockbuster, but he gave a great performance, even in the love scenes, and might well have starred in the sequel if the producers hadn't taken so long to make up their minds about it.

Moby Dick and the Mighty Mightor
US 1967 26 × 25m colour
Hanna–Barbera

Double-header cartoon series featuring a whale who protects shipwrecked children and a meek and mild boy who changes into a crusading giant.
Uninspired Saturday morning fillers.

The Mod Squad
US 1968–72 124 × 25m colour
ABC/Thomas/Spelling (Harve Bennett, Tony Barrett)

Reformed hippies help the Los Angeles Police Department.
Fairly slick adventures but boring people.

cr Aaron Spelling, Buddy Ruskin, Sammy Hess *m* Earle Hagen

Peggy Lipton, Michael Cole, Clarence Williams III, Tige Andrews

† In 1979 a TV movie called *The Return of the Mod Squad* failed to generate much interest.

Moffat, Geraldine (19 –). British actress peculiarly identified with Alun Owen's half-hour plays of the late sixties.

Mog (GB 1985; 13 × 30m). Witless, tasteless and unrealistic sitcom about petty thief (Enn Reitel) taking refuge in a mental home. Written by Dick Clement and Ian La Frenais from novel by Peter Tinniswood; directed by Nic Phillips; produced by Tony Charles for Witzend/Central. PP

Mogul * aka: *The Troubleshooters* (GB 1965–70; approx. 78 × 50m). BP was the model for writer John Elliott's admirable and long-running series about an oil company. Initially it ranged over all departments uncovering some subtle gradations in the social order of a big organization. Inevitably the emphasis switched first to the young go-getters (Ray Barrett, Robert Hardy) who acted as the company's troubleshooters and gave the show the title used in Britain from 1966 onwards (overseas it remained *Mogul*), then to the most durable characters: Stead, the managing director (Geoffrey Keen) and Willy Izzard the financial wizard (Philip Latham). It remained a solid and realistic entertainment. Script editor: Anthony Read; produced by Peter Graham Scott; for BBC. PP

Mom, the Wolfman and Me
US 1979 colour 96m TVM
CBS/Time–Life (David Susskind)

The 11-year-old illegitimate daughter of a Manhattan photographer with a crazy lifestyle steers her mum into marriage with an unemployed teacher.
Sharply made modern comedy about people who tend to be irritating.

w/d Edmond Levy, *novel* Norma Klein

Patty Duke Astin, David Birney, Danielle Brisebois, John Lithgow, Keenan Wynn, Viveca Lindfors

A Moment to Talk (GB 1982). Groups of workers talking among themselves in 15-minute segments over several evenings: a novel idea (then) and with lots of natural eloquence emerging; but were all the people chosen for their dissatisfaction with (a) their jobs, (b) the absence of same, or (c) both? Produced by Phillip Donnellan, for BBC Birmingham. PP

Mona McCluskey
US 1965 26 × 25m bw
United Artists/NBC (George Burns)

A glamorous film star tries to lead a double life as an ordinary housewife.
Dud vehicle for a bright star.

Juliet Prowse, Denny Miller, Herbert Rudley

Money on the Side
US 1982 96m colour TVM
ABC/Columbia/Green–Epstein/Hal Landers

Three outwardly respectable women turn to prostitution as a way to make money.
Yellow press-style time-filler of no particular social or entertainment value.

w Eugene Price, Robert Collins, Mort Fine d Robert Collins ph Fred Koenekamp m Richard Bellis

Karen Valentine, Jamie Lee Curtis, Linda Purl, Christopher Lloyd, Richard Masur

The Money Programme. What its name implies: a chatty programme about business and finance which has run on BBC2, under a succession of editors, since 1966. PP

Money to Burn
US 1973 74m colour TVM
Universal (Harve Bennett)

A crooked couple work out a counterfeiting caper even though the husband is in prison.
Initially ingenious crime comedy which suddenly peters out.

w Gerald di Pego d Robert Michael Lewis m Oliver Nelson

E. G. Marshall, Mildred Natwick, Cleavon Little, Alejandro Rey, David Doyle, Charles McGraw

The Moneychangers *
US 1976 3 × 96m (or varying format) colour
NBC/Paramount/Ross Hunter, Jacque Mapes

In the banking business, two ambitious vice-presidents become rivals.
Smooth and fairly palatable televersion of what is not one of the author's best novels.

w Dean Riesner, Stanford Whitmore, *novel* Arthur Hailey d Boris Sagal ph Joseph Biroc m Henry Mancini

Kirk Douglas, Christopher Plummer, Anne Baxter, Ralph Bellamy, Timothy Bottoms, Joan Collins, Susan Flannery, Robert Loggia, Jean Peters, Lorne Greene, Patrick O'Neal, Helen Hayes

† Emmys went to Christopher Plummer and to the show as Outstanding Series.

Mongo's Back in Town *
US 1971 73m colour TVM
Bob Banner

A professional killer is hired by his brother to kill a rival.
Tough, competent gangster thriller.

w Herman Miller, *novel* E. Richard Johnson
d Marvin Chomsky

Telly Savalas, Sally Field, Anne Francis, Martin Sheen, Joe Don Baker, Charles Cioffi, Ned Glass

Monitor ***. Famous BBC arts magazine which ran through the fifties and early sixties, introduced by Huw Wheldon.
PP: 'An institution: Sunday nights were never quite the same after it was axed in 1965. Like all institutions it could be infuriating. It was sometimes only too easy to remember that the dictionary definition of "monitor" is one who admonishes. As front man, Huw Wheldon seemed to expect the artists he interviewed to stick to their accustomed paths, and would register faint damning surprise if J. B. Priestley, say, was publishing a *thriller*. At the same time he was a brilliant editor, steering his way deftly between the latest nine-day wonders on one side and the entrenched despots of the arts on the other. He escaped from the studio confines by commissioning films of artists in their own environment, and in doing so fostered the talents of Ken Russell, John Schlesinger and a whole school of exuberant film-making for TV and, in due course, the cinema.'

The Monk
US 1969 74m colour TVM
Spelling–Thomas

A private eye guards an envelope, but it is stolen and his client killed.
Adequate mystery with San Francisco backgrounds.

w Tony Barrett d George McCowan

George Maharis, Janet Leigh, Jack Soo, Raymond St Jacques, Jack Albertson, Carl Betz, Rick Jason

'A combination of uninhibited young talents, visual innovation and infectious music.'
The Monkees **
US 1966–7 28 × 25m colour
NBC/Columbia

Four musical friends have mad adventures.
Ingenious and deliberate re-creation of the Beatles in American terms, complete with Dick Lester-style tricks, zany humour and speeded-up photography. The series culminated in a way-out motion picture called *Head*, and won a 1966 Emmy as best comedy series.

md Don Kirshner

David Jones, Peter Tork, Mickey Dolenz, Mike Nesmith

Monkey (Japan 1979). The BBC made a British serial version of this epic production by NTV and Kokusai Hoei. As translated by Arthur Waley, it's a fairy-tale version of the origins of Buddhism, but too strange for the European palate. English adaptation by David Weir.

Monkhouse, Bob (1928–). British comedian and host of game shows such as *The Golden Shot*, *Celebrity Squares* and *Family Fortunes*. In 1984 acquired his own show (BBC), a showcase for comedy acts – some rare – from both sides of the Atlantic. Also *Bob's Full House*, BBC quiz show, p Marcus Plantin.   PP

The Monroes *
US 1966 26 × 50m colour
ABC/TCF/Qualis (Frederick Brogger)

Orphaned children in the Old West struggle to hang on to their parents' homestead.
Spirited western drama with admirable scenery.

ph Monroe Askins, Jack Marta m David Rose

Michael Anderson Jnr, Barbara Hershey, Keith and Kevin Schultz, Tammy Locke, James Brolin, Ben Johnson

Montalban, Ricardo (1920–). Lithe, handsome Mexican actor in Hollywood. Never quite a star in films, but won an Emmy for *How the West Was Won* and became a household word as white-suited Mr Roarke in FANTASY ISLAND.

The Montefuscos
US 1975 13 × 25m colour (VTR)
NBC/Persky–Denoff

Three generations of an Italian–American family live in Connecticut.
Witless shouting match which soon outstayed its welcome.

cr Bill Persky, Sam Denoff
Joe Sirola, Naomi Stevens, Ron Carey

Monteith, Kelly (1942–). American comedian who became popular in Britain as star of late-night monologues, with intervening sketches about his sex life.

Montgomery, Belinda J. (c 1949–). American leading lady; in series *Man from Atlantis*. TV movies: *Ritual of Evil, The Bravos, Women in Chains, Crime Club, The Hostage Heart, Murder in Music City*.

Montgomery, Elizabeth (1933–). American leading lady (daughter of Robert Montgomery) who starred for many seasons in *Bewitched*. TV movies: *The Victim, Mrs Sundance, A Case of Rape, The Legend of Lizzie Borden, Dark Victory, A Killing Affair, The Awakening Land, Jennifer: A Woman's Story, Act of Violence, Belle Starr, When the Circus Came to Town, Rules of Marriage, Missing Pieces, Second Sight*

Montgomery, George (1916–) (George Montgomery Letz). American leading man who after a moderately successful career in films made a western TV series: *Cimarron City*.

Montgomery, Robert (1904–81) (Henry Montgomery Jnr). Smooth, elegant American leading man of the thirties who before retiring from show business to politics hosted in 1950–6 a one-hour anthology series, *Robert Montgomery Presents* (Emmy 1952, best drama series).

Month of the Doctors * (GB 1982; 2 × 50m). Gripping documentary reconstruction of how Yale University scientists struggled to identify and isolate a lethal virus infection introduced to the United States from Nigeria. Produced by Ruth Caleb, for BBC.
PP

A Month in the Country
GB 1955 90m bw TVM
A–R/John Clements

Turgenev's play, filmed at Shepperton to feature standards, was commercial television's first prestige drama, one of a small batch so made under the JOHN CLEMENTS PRESENTS umbrella. Much too costly by the accounting of the day even if the infant ITV hadn't been in dire financial straits, the series was quickly dropped, and moviemaking on this scale was not to return to British television for 20 years.

d Robert Hamer

Margaret Leighton, Laurence Harvey   PP

† A BBC production by Louis Marks, directed by Bill Hays with Eleanor Bron and Richard Briers was run of the mill in 1985.

Monty Nash
US 1971 14 × 25m colour
Four Star/Almada

Cases of a travelling State investigator. Predictable thick-ear.

Harry Guardino

Monty Python's Flying Circus ***
GB 1969–74 approx. 45 × 30m colour (VTR)
BBC (IAN MACNAUGHTON)

Zany variety show written and performed by an ex-Cambridge group which never shirks from incomprehensibility or bad taste, and often prefers to have the beginning of the show at the end, but frequently reaches heights of inspired lunacy. Its sketches always end abruptly or *segue* into others without reaching a curtain line.

JOHN CLEESE, GRAHAM CHAPMAN, ERIC IDLE, MICHAEL PALIN, TERRY GILLIAM, TERRY JONES

† BAFTA 1972: best light entertainment programme.

Moody and Pegg (GB 1974). Spinster Pegg (Judy Cornwell) and ex-married Moody (Derek Waring) converge on the same apartment to let, and agree to share it. Amiable comedy series with some very funny mishaps. Written by Donald Churchill and Julia Jones; for Thames.   PP

Moody, Ron (1924–). British comedian and actor with lop-sided face, india-rubber gait and a busy, inquisitive manner whose genius television has only rarely accommodated. *Moody in Storeland* (BBC, 1961) was all right until anyone opened his mouth and the script showed. *Hart of the Yard* (US, 1980) cast him amusingly as a Scotland Yard sleuth seconded to California, but probably his most successful deployment was in an arena show amid an active audience for YTV in 1968 called simply MOODY and produced by John Duncan. Latest credit: *Hideaway*, 1986.   PP

Moon landing. Arguably the most famous television relay ever, certainly attracting the largest simultaneous audience until then. As Neil Armstrong took the first human step on another world, 600 million are estimated to have been watching. Even in Britain, where it happened at 3.46 a.m. local time, eight million were still sitting up.   PP

Moon of the Wolf *
US 1972 74m colour TVM
Filmways (Everett Chambers)

A southern town is terrorized by a werewolf. Horror hokum which looks pretty silly in modern dress, but packs a scare or two.

w Alvin Sapinsley d Daniel Petrie

David Janssen, Barbara Rush, Bradford Dillman, John Beradino

Moonlight

US 1982 74m colour TVM
CBS/Universal (David Chase)

A delivery boy becomes a vital witness to a political murder case and although put under security by the CIA escapes to track down the murderer.

Failed pilot which entertains in fits and starts.

w David Chase d Alan Smithee ph Howard Schwartz m Patrick Williams

Robert Desiderio, Michelle Phillips, William Prince, Anthony Ponzini, Benson Fong

Moonlight on the Highway ** (GB 1969;
50m). Dennis Potter's first raid on the mythology of popular music, with Ian Holm as an anguished loner running a society dedicated to the memory of Al Bowlly, the crooner killed in the London Blitz. Aggressive, haunting. Directed by James MacTaggart; produced by Kenith Trodd; for LWT/Kestrel.   PP

Moonlight Sonata * (GB 1981; 50m;
colour/bw). Valuable documentary about the Coventry Blitz (under this code-name) 40 years earlier. Testimony from former RAF and Civil Defence staff finally dispelled the old rumour that Churchill deliberately sacrificed the city in order to preserve the secret that the British were already breaking German codes. That a massive raid was imminent was known, but not its target. Produced by Brian Lewis and John Pett; for ATV.   PP

Moonlighting *

US 1985 1 × 96m,   × 50m colour
CBS/ABC Circle/Picturemaker (Jay Daniel)

An international model, swindled by her advisers, finds she owns a small detective agency and, instead of selling it, teams up with the unwilling incumbent.

After a promising start, this would-be sophisticated comedy thriller series tended towards yards of unwitty banter between the conventional action stretches. But some Americans were reminded of Tracy and Hepburn.

cr Glenn Gordon Gould

Cybill Shepherd, Bruce Willis

† Also the title of a boring 1982 Film on Four with Jeremy Irons, directed by Jerzy Skolimowski.   PP

Moonstrike (GB 1963). BBC series about the
RAF squadron which landed agents in occupied Europe during World War II and brought others back to England; well written by ROBERT BARR but handicapped by low budget

and, despite resourceful special effects by Jack Kline, the fact that no Lysander aircraft (the type used) was then flying. Ironically, one was restored too late to take part.   PP

Moore, Brian (1932–). British soccer commentator, long with *World of Sport*.

Moore, Dudley (1935–). British pianist and light entertainer, one of the original 'Beyond the Fringe' team; usually seen on TV with Peter Cook in *Not Only But Also*.

Moore, Garry (1915–) (Thomas Morfit). American comedian and linkman popular in the fifties, especially as host of *I've Got a Secret*.

❋ **Moore, Mary Tyler** (1936–). Cute American leading lady who started her TV career in *Steve Canyon*, proceeded to be a sexy unseen voice in *Richard Diamond*, scored a big hit in THE DICK VAN DYKE SHOW and her own smash long-runner THE MARY TYLER MOORE SHOW. She subsequently preferred to withdraw her apple pie personality from the tube and become head, with her husband Grant Tinker, of MTM Productions. After their divorce she appeared more frequently as an actress. TV movies: *Run a Crooked Mile*, *First You Cry*, *Heartsounds*. For the British production company Zenith, a subsidiary of Central, she starred in *Finnegan Begin Again*, 1984. 1985: new series, *Mary*.

Moore, Patrick (1923–). Bulky British astronomer, host for many years of *The Sky at Night*.

Moore, Roger (1928–). British leading man who had a long TV career in *Ivanhoe*, *The Alaskans*, *Maverick*, *The Saint* and *The Persuaders* before becoming the cinema's James Bond. TV movie: *Sherlock Holmes in New York* (totally miscast in the title role).

Moorehead, Agnes (1906–74). Sharp-featured American character actress with long film career. TV series: *Bewitched*. TV movies: *The Ballad of Andy Crocker*, *Marriage: Year One*, *Suddenly Single*, *Rolling Man*, *Night of Terror*, *Frankenstein: The True Story*.

Morahan, Christopher (1929–). British drama director, producer and executive, head of plays at the BBC 1972–6, then at National Theatre. First major credit as a director: *John Gabriel Borkman*, with Olivier, 1958; most famous: *Jewel in the Crown* (producer and co-director).

More, Kenneth (1914–82). Jaunty British leading actor whose career was largely confined to stage and movies, though he made occasional TV appearances and starred with effect in *The Forsyte Saga*, *Father Brown* and *An Englishman's Castle*.

More O'Ferrall, George: see O'Ferrall, George More

More Than Friends
US 1978 96m colour TVM
ABC/Columbia/Rob Reiner, Phil Mishkin (Norman S. Powell)

A boy and girl who were school friends go through various relationships before deciding to stick together.
Sluggish Jewish comedy which scarcely holds the interest through its excessive length.
w Rob Reiner, Phil Mishkin *d* Jim Burrows
Penny Marshall, Rob Reiner, Dabney Coleman, Kay Medford

More Wild Wild West
US 1980 96m colour TVM
CBS/Jay Dernstein (Robert L. Jacks)

Two former government agents are brought out of retirement to chase a western villain who can make himself invisible.
Further farcical exploits tagged onto the end of a series which was already very tired.
w Bill Bowers, Tony Kayden *d* Burt Kennedy
Robert Conrad, Ross Martin, Jonathan Winters, Harry Morgan, Victor Buono

❋ **Morecambe, Eric** (1926–84) (Eric Bartholomew). British comedian, the bespectacled half of Morecambe and Wise, top comic team of British TV in the sixties and seventies. Owed much to Laurel and Hardy and Abbott and Costello, but had his own inimitable range of expressions. See also *Wise, Ernie*.
PP: 'What he brought most valuably of all to the Morecambe and Wise act were the English virtues of irreverence, levity and Philistinism. Insulting his enemies and patronizing his friends, getting names wrong and identities wilfully confused, or, if all else failed, displacing his spectacles sideways to turn himself into an instant low-brow Picasso figure, he dragged everything he touched down to his own sublime depths. There won't easily be another like him.'

Morell, André (1909–79) (André Mesritz). English character actor, a fine speaker; many appearances include Tiberius in *The Caesars*.

Morgan, Elaine (1920–). Welsh TV writer since the fifties, coming to the fore with the serial *A Matter of Degree*. Contributed to many series, especially *Dr Finlay's Casebook*. Best known in latter years for *A Pin to See the Peepshow*, *Joey* for Brian Gibson, the *Lloyd George* biographical saga and, drawing on a feminist interest, her flawless 1979 adaptation of Vera Brittain's TESTAMENT OF YOUTH. *The Burston Rebellion*, 1985.   PP

Morgan, Garfield (1931–). Balding British character actor whose best continuing role was in *The Sweeney*.

Morgan, Henry or **Harry** (1915–) (Harry Bratsburg). Reliable American character actor who apart from innumerable movies and TV guest shots has appeared in a number of series: *Kentucky Jones*, *Dragnet*, *December Bride*, *Pete and Gladys*, *Oh Those Bells*, *The Richard Boone Show*, *The DA*, *M*A*S*H*. TV movies include *The Feminist and the Fuzz*, *Sidekicks*, *Exoman*, *Maneaters Are Loose*, *The Bastard*, *Murder at the Mardi Gras*, *Backstairs at the White House*, *The Wild Wild West Revisited*.

Moriarty, Michael (1941–). American actor whose best TV role has been as the Nazi in *Holocaust*. Other TV movies: *A Summer without Boys*, *The Glass Menagerie*, *The Deadliest Season*, *The Winds of Kitty Hawk*, *Too Far to Go*.

Mork and Mindy *
US 1978–81 95 × 25m colour
ABC/Paramount/Henderson–Miller–Miklis

A space alien takes root in Boulder City, but only the girl who befriends him knows his true nature.
Interesting comedy series with echoes of Capra and a star of indefinable qualities. Unfortunately the scripts are often repetitive, and one feels it would have been livelier on genuine locations rather than confined basically to one or two sets.
cr Garry Marshall, Dale McRaven, Joe Glauberg
ROBIN WILLIAMS, Pam Dawber, Conrad Janis, Elizabeth Kerr

Morley, Peter (*c* 1926–). British documentary producer. BAFTA award 1964 (with Cyril Bennett) for *This Week*. Tokyo Prize, 1985, for *Kitty – Return to Auschwitz*. Now in video industry.

Morley, Robert (1908–). Expansive British actor, a favourite guest on chat shows both sides of the Atlantic. In situation comedies *If the Crown Fits* (1961), and *Charge!* (1969). Introduced *Lady Killers* (1980–81).   PP

The Morning After *
US 1974 74m colour TVM
David Wolper (Lawrence Turman, Stan Margulies)

A businessman becomes an alcoholic. An actor's piece which doesn't really convince.

w Richard Matheson d Richard Heffron m Pete Carpenter, John Lennon

DICK VAN DYKE, Lynn Carlin, Don Porter, Jewel Blanch

Morning in the Streets *
GB 1959 30m bw
BBC Manchester (Denis Mitchell, Roy Harris)

Mood piece conveying taste of life in unlovely, inimitable northern towns. Its only thesis was to draw a shadowy comparison between times as they are and times as they were – but everywhere and all the time Denis Mitchell caught the true sticky thumbprints of humanity. PP

Morris, Colin (1916–). British playwright (*Reluctant Heroes*) and voluntary social worker with BBC from 1954 as writer of pioneering social drama-docs in collaboration with Gil Calder: *Rock Bottom*; *Without Love*; *Who, Me?* Since then, occasional plays and serials including the Churchillian *Walk with Destiny*. Originated *The Newcomers* (1965). As an interviewer, presented *Heart to Heart* for YTV (1977), a series in which he talked to an agoraphobic, a compulsive gambler and others facing acute difficulties. Some of these cases he followed up in *Turning Point* four years later. Series *My Marriage* (7 × 30m), 1985. All of which makes it easy for him to be confused with the Rev. Colin Morris, BBC religious broadcaster and executive. He's not. PP

Morris, Greg (1934–). Black American actor, in series *Mission Impossible, Vegas.*

✳ **Morris, Johnny** (1916–). Cheerful, avuncular British TV personality who in his friendly, jokey style has conducted travel series and children's animal documentaries since the early fifties.

Morse, Barry (1919–). British light actor who made his main career in Canadian theatre. TV series: *The Fugitive* (as the relentless Lt Gerard), *Zoo Gang, The Adventurer, Space 1999, Whoops Apocalypse.*

Mortimer, John (1923–). British playwright and (as a barrister) champion of free speech. His earliest plays were first done on radio, including *The Dock Brief* (1958), a distant forerunner of his RUMPOLE OF THE BAILEY 20 years later. *A Voyage Round My Father, Will Shakespeare*, BRIDESHEAD REVISITED (from Evelyn Waugh). *Edwin*, 1984, *The Ebony Tower*, 1985. PP

Morton, Bill (1928–85). British producer teamed for many years with Desmond Wilcox on *Man Alive*. He went on to edit the arts magazines *Full House* and *Second House* on BBC2, and originated *100 Great Paintings*, which will probably continue to be seen, somewhere in the world, as long as there is television. PP

The Mosedale Horseshoe **
GB 1971 52m colour
Granada (Peter Eckersley)

Arthur Hopcraft's assured debut (though owing much to his director, Michael Apted). Four oddly assorted friends meet for their annual hill-walking weekend in the Lakes. There's a new landlord at the pub, not quite the same old atmosphere. The 12-mile expedition that is their aim this year defeats them. They quarrel and come together again with the healing aid of a few healing bottles of plonk.

Mosel, Tad (1922–). American playwright of the 'Golden Era' of the fifties, and the best according to Paddy Chayevsky. Specialized in 'the quiet joys and sadness of ordinary men'. *My Lost Saints, The Haven, Other People's Houses*, etc. PP

Moser, Brian (1935–). British film-maker specializing in anthropological series, e.g. *Frontier, Disappearing World*; but occasionally bumping up against newsier subjects, as when he happened to be in on the death of Che Guevara. In 1985 shot documentary on the Nazi war criminal Josef Mengele, thought to have holed up in South America since World War II. PP

Moses *
aka: *The Lawgiver*
GB/Italy 1976 6 × 50m colour
ATV/RAI (Vincenzo Labella)

The life of Moses.

Sober biblical account, filmed in Israel and rather slow; an unexpected popular success.

w Anthony Burgess, Vittorio Bonicelli d Gianfranco DeBosio

Burt Lancaster, Anthony Quayle, Ingrid Thulin, Irene Papas, Laurent Terzieff

Moshinsky, Elijah (19 –). Australian theatre director who scored with four BBC Shakespeare productions: *Midsummer Night's Dream, Cymbeline, Coriolanus, All's Well that Ends Well.* PP

Mossman, James (1926–71). Rangy British reporter and interviewer of the sixties, a James Bond of current affairs until his untimely death. *Panorama*, member of freelance outfit TRI, documentaries, editor/presenter of arts programme *Review*. PP

The Most Deadly Game
US 1970 12 × 50m colour
ABC/Aaron Spelling (Joan Harrison)

A sophisticated team solves unsolvable crimes. Polished detective story nonsense.

cr David Fine, Mort Friedkin

Ralph Bellamy, Yvette Mimieux, George Maharis

Most Wanted *
US 1976 74m colour TVM
ABC/Quinn Martin

An élite force is formed and tackles the capture of a maniac who rapes and murders nuns. What starts as a serious police drama becomes totally conventional and eventually hilariously inept.

w Larry Heath *d* Walter Grauman *m* Lalo Schifrin

Robert Stack, Sheree North

† The series which followed consisted of 22 × 50m episodes.

Mother and Daughter – the Loving War
US 1980 96m colour TVM
ABC/MTM/Edgar J. Scherick (S. Bryan Hickox)

A woman whose daughter was illegitimate finds that the same problem recurs in the next generation.
Woman's weepie which adequately fills its time slot.

w Rose Leiman Goldenberg *d* Burt Brinckerhoff *ph* Richard L. Rawlings *m* Lee Holdridge

Tuesday Weld, Kathleen Beller, Frances Sternhagen, Jeanne Lang, Ed Winter

Mothers by Daughters *** (GB 1983; 6 × 50m). Barbara Windsor, Bernadette Devlin, Sheila Hancock, Lynn Symour and Elizabeth Lutyens musing on the influence of their late mothers to Bel Mooney, plus Maureen Lipman on her very-much-alive Jewish momma. A bright idea, produced by Britt Allcroft for the Moving Picture Company/C4. PP

† *Fathers by Sons* followed in 1985; Terry Scott, Colin Welland, Denis Healey, Marcus Sieff, Tom Wakefield, Corin Redgrave.

The Mothers-in-Law *
US 1957–8 56 × 25m colour
NBC/Desi Arnaz

Two neighbouring suburban families are linked through their offsprings' marriage.
Mildly amusing domestic vehicle for two contrasting stars.

Eve Arden, Kaye Ballard, Herbert Rudley, Richard Deacon

Motives (GB 1983; 7 × 40m). Fashionable psychiatrist Anthony Clare extracting unedifying confessions of why they'd done what they'd done from such transgressors as footballer George Best and disappearing politician John Stonehouse. Produced by Chris Mohr, for BBC. PP

Moult, Ted (1926–). Cheerful, rural-sounding British farmer–broadcaster who for a while was a popular panellist on such game shows as *What's My Line?*, after which he more or less retired to farming – and commercials.

Mount, Peggy (1916–). British comedy character actress, a gargantuan presence with a stentorian voice. Series: *The Larkins, George and the Dragon, You're Only Young Twice.*

Mountbatten, the Last Viceroy *
GB 1985 6 × 50m colour miniseries
George Walker/Mobil/Judith de Paul

After World War II, Lord Mountbatten goes to India to help the country achieve independence.
Well-mounted but essentially rather nerveless historical drama which concentrates less on the Mountbattens than on Gandhi, Jinnah and Nehru.

w David Butler *d* Tom Clegg

Nicol Williamson, JANET SUZMAN (as Edwina), Ian Richardson (as Nehru), Sam Dastor (as Gandhi), Vladek Sheybal (as Jinnah), Nigel Davenport (as Ismay), Wendy Hiller (as Princess Victoria), Malcolm Terris (as Churchill)

The Mouse Factory *
US 1972 24 × 22m colour (16mm)
Walt Disney

Guest stars 'signing on' at the Disney studio theme-link such items as cars, houses and ghosts with footage from old Disney movies. An ingenious bringing together of some classic scenes; only the commentary is resistible.

Mousey *
GB theatrical title: *Cat and Mouse*
GB 1973 74m colour TVM
RSO (Beryl Vertue, Aida Young)
An unhinged schoolteacher taunts his ex-wife with murder threats.
Unusual psychological thriller.
w John Peacock *d* Daniel Petrie *ph* Jack Hildyard *m* Ron Grainer
Kirk Douglas, Jean Seberg, John Vernon, Sam Wanamaker, James Bradford, Bessie Love

The Movie Maker **
US 1967 91m colour TVM
Universal (Harry Tatelman)
The last of the old-time movie tycoons finds his life and his career falling apart.
Sympathetic portrait of a Louis B. Mayer or Darryl F. Zanuck type.
w Rod Serling, Steven Bochco *d* Josef Leytes
ROD STEIGER, Robert Culp, James Dunn, Sally Kellerman, Anna Lee

The Movie Murderer *
US 1970 99m colour TVM
Universal (Jack Laird)
An insurance investigator traps an arsonist who tries to destroy the negative of a movie in which he was filmed.
Lively   suspense   thriller   with   good performances.
w Stanford Whitmore *d* Boris Sagal
Arthur Kennedy, Tom Selleck, Warren Oates, Jeff Corey, Nita Talbot, Robert Webber, Severn Darden

Movie of the Week. Name given by the American ABC network in 1969–74 to its weekly slot for newly produced TV movies. *Movie of the Weekend* followed. Both slots took 74-minute films.

Movies from TV series have been surprisingly successful, at least in their country of origin. The first cinema movie from a TV source may have been *Life in Emergency Ward Ten*, back in 1959; other British examples include *Inn for Trouble* (The *Larkins*), *Bless This House*, *Steptoe and Son* (and *Steptoe and Son Ride Again*), *The Likely Lads*, *Porridge*, *Dad's Army*, *Father Dear Father*, *Till Death Us Do Part* (and *The Alf Garnett Saga*), *I Only Arsked*

(from *The Army Game*), *That's Your Funeral*, *Nearest and Dearest*, *On the Buses* (and two sequels), *The Lovers*, *A Man about the House*, *Rising Damp*, *Callan*, *The Sweeney* (and *Sweeney Two*), *Love Thy Neighbour*, *For the Love of Ada*. Americans have not tended to this fashion – the borrowing has been mostly the other way – and the only major attempt at revamping television material has been the *Star Trek* movies.

The Movies Go to War: see Life Goes to War

Movin' On *
US 1974–5 48 × 50m colour
NBC/D'Antoni–Weltz (Joe Gantman)
Adventures of two gypsy truckers, following on from the TV movie *In Tandem*.
A comfortable, friendly series sometimes let down by silly stories but benefiting from two likeable stars.
m Don Ellis (theme by Merle Haggard)
Claude Akins, Frank Converse

Moving * (GB 1985; 6 × 28m). The ordeals of moving house; a sitcom resourcefully fragmented by Stanley Price from his own stage play. Funny, mercifully devoid of a studio audience and with Penelope Keith in maximum form. Also involved: Ronald Pickup, Prunella Gee; produced and directed by Les Chatfield, for Thames.

Moviola **
US 1980 3 × 96m colour miniseries
NBC/Warner/David L. Wolper–Stan Marguilies
Three plays about Hollywood, from the book by Garson Kanin: all have entertaining passages for buffs, but the last is the best sustained.
This Year's Blonde: Marilyn Monroe is helped to stardom by the agent who loves her.
w James Lee *d* John Erman
Lloyd Bridges, Constance Forslund, Norman Fell, Michael Lerner, John Marley
The Silent Lovers: Garbo and Gilbert have an ill-fated affair.
w William Hanley *d* John Erman
Kristina Wayborn, Barry Bostwick, Harold Gould (as L. B. Mayer)
The Scarlett O'Hara War: David O. Selznick casts his biggest picture.
w William Hanley *d* John Erman

TONY CURTIS (D.O.S.), Bill Macy (Myron Selznick), George Furth (George Cukor), Harold Gould (Louis B. Mayer), Carrie Nye (Tallulah Bankhead), Clive Revill (Charles Chaplin), Sharon Gless (Carole Lombard), Barrie Youngfellow (Joan Crawford), Edward Winter (Clark Gable)

Mower, Patrick (1940–). British general purpose actor, almost entirely on TV: *Haunted, Callan, Special Branch, Target.*

Moxey, John Llewellyn (1930–). British film director who went to Hollywood and turned out innumerable TV movies of no especial merit: *The House that Would Not Die, The Last Child, Taste of Evil, The Death of Me Yet, The Night Stalker, Hardcase, The Bounty Man, Home for the Holidays, The Strange and Deadly Occurrence, Charlie's Angels* (pilot), *Conspiracy of Terror, Smash Up on Interstate Five, Panic in Echo Park, The President's Mistress, Sanctuary of Fear, The Power Within, The Children of An Lac,* etc.

MTM Much admired US production company founded in 1970 by Mary Tyler Moore (whence the initials) to make her own comedy show. Series since include *Rhoda, Lou Grant, Hill Street Blues* and *St Elsewhere.* Subject of NFT Season, London, 1984, and C4 documentary *Cat among the Lions* (p John Wyver) same year, the title deriving from MTM's mewing-kitten logo cheekily modelled on MGM's lion.   PP

Muck and Brass *
GB 1982 6 × 50m colour
Central (Margaret Matheson)
Mel Smith, previously thought of only as comic (*Not the Nine O'Clock News,* etc) scored as a ruthless young property developer in a fictitious Midland city where corruption and chicanery were part of everyday commerce.
w Tom Clarke d Marek Kanievska, Martin Campbell
Mel Smith, Darien Angadi, John Sharp   PP

'Mother, cop, woman – how can she be all three, when she has to put her life on the line?'
Muggable Mary: Street Cop
US 1983 96m colour TVM
CBS (Neal Maffeo)
A divorced woman joins the police force to get money for her ailing son, and jumps at the opportunity to do undercover work.
Tolerable time-passer veering between crime and domesticity.

w,d Sandor Stern
Karen Valentine, John Getz, Anne DeSalvo, Robert Christian, Michael Pearlman, Vincent Gardenia

❋ **Muggeridge, Malcolm** (1903–). British journalist, wit and pontificator: a reporter and interviewer for *Panorama* in the fifties, conversational interviewer for Granada in *Appointment with . . .* , debunker of great men and lost causes for anyone. His well-known progress from man of the world to ascetic Christian could be tracked by the attentive viewer: the clouds of cigarette smoke which had enveloped his early appearances suddenly disappearing; the scepticism with which he had reported from Lourdes for *Panorama* replaced by humility in a later documentary; and in the series *Let Me Speak* (BBC 1964–5), in which he challenged the beliefs of ardent minorities, Muggeridge finding himself defending his own faith against a determined group of Humanists. Perceiving this, producer Jonathan Stedall raided the archives for the eight-part *Muggeridge Ancient and Modern* (BBC 1981) in which St Mugg, as he is affectionately known, commented on clips from his past to yield a unique visual autobiography and self-assessment.
Documentaries:
1957 *The Thirties;* BBC (Andrew Miller Jones)
1962 THE TITANS: two programmes – USA and USSR; BBC (Therese Denny)
      The Long Struggle (British Welfare State); BBC
1964 *Men of Our Time:* Stanley Baldwin; Granada (Patricia Lagone)
      Twilight of Empire; BBC (Kevin Billington)
1965 LADIES AND GENTLEMEN, IT IS MY PLEASURE: mocking his own lecture tour of America; BBC (Jack Gold)
      Pilgrimage to Lourdes; BBC (Michael Tuchner)
      The American Way of Sex; BBC (Michael Tuchner)
1966 *The English Cardinal* (Heenan); BBC (Kevin Billington)
      A SOCIALIST CHILDHOOD (autobiog.); BBC (Kevin Billington)
1967 *A Hard Bed to Lie On;* BBC (Lawrence Gordon Clarke)
      An Unredeemed Intellectual (Leonard Woolf); BBC (Stephen Peet)
      Remembering Virginia (Woolf); BBC (Stephen Peet)
      LORD REITH LOOKS BACK (three progs); BBC (Stephen Peet)

1968 A LIFE OF CHRIST (series); BBC (Christopher Martin)

1969 *A Winter in Moscow*; BBC (Patsy Meehan)
Our Own Correspondent; BBC (Charles Denton)
A Quest for Gandhi; BBC (Peter Chafer)
SOMETHING BEAUTIFUL FOR GOD (Mother Theresa of Calcutta); BBC (Peter Chafer)

1971 *St Paul: Envoy Extraordinary* (series); BBC (Peter Chafer)

1972 *Tolstoy: Riches to Rags*; BBC (Jonathan Stedall)

1973 *Pilgrim of the Absolute* (Simone Weil); BBC (Vernon Sproxton)
A 20th Century Testimony; EDNL (Holland) (Jeremy Murray-Brown)

1974 *The Third Testament*; essays on Tolstoy, Bonhoeffer, St Augustine, Pascal, Kierkegaard, Blake; CBC (Jeremy Murray-Brown)

1978 *Dostoievsky*; Richard Price Assoc. (Pat Ferns)

Other appearances:

1952–7 at least 12 *Press Conference* appearances; BBC

1953–60 approx 66 *Panorama* interviews and reports; BBC

1955–7 about 8 *Brains Trust* participations; BBC

1959–60 two *Small World* participations; CBS

1960–61 39 *Appointment with* . . . interviews; Granada

1964–5 approx 10 *Let Me Speak*: confrontations with minority groups; BBC

1966 *Alice in Wonderland*, as the Gryphon; BBC

1968 *The Question Why*: studio discussions with MM as interlocutor; BBC

1981 MUGGERIDGE ANCIENT AND MODERN: 8 programmes, as above; BBC

1982 *A Week with Svetlana* (Stalin's daughter); BBC (Jonathan Stedall)

1983 *180 Not Out*, in conversation with centenarian Salvation Army warrior Catherine Bramall; BBC (Patti Steeples)
Also dialogues with Solzhenitsyn and ex-nun Karen Armstrong, C4 from Griffin.   PP

✱ **Muir, Frank** (1920–). British humorist and TV personality, originally a radio comedy writer with Denis Norden. Pops up in panel games like *Call My Bluff* and gives a touch of easy-going old-English wit; delights in puns.

Muldaur, Diana (1943–). Gracious American leading lady, a frequent guest star. Series: *Hec Ramsey, McCloud, Born Free*. TV movies: *Call to Danger, Ordeal, Planet Earth, Pine Canyon Is Burning, Black Beauty, To Kill a Cop, Maneaters Are Loose, The Word*, etc.

Mulgrew, Kate (1945–). American actress long familiar on the soap opera *Ryan's Hope*, then as the shortlived *Mrs Columbo*.

Mulhare, Edward (1923–). Irish leading man in America, most familiar as the naval spectre in *The Ghost and Mrs Muir* and the contact man for *Knight Rider*.

Mullard, Arthur (1912–). Burly British cockney actor, familiar in cameos for 20 years but never a star until *Romany Jones* and *Yus My Dear*.

Mullen, Barbara (1914–79). Irish character actress who after a solid film career made a big hit as Janet, the all-knowing housekeeper in DR FINLAY'S CASEBOOK.

Muller, Robert (1925–). German-born British writer formerly a magazine journalist and theatre critic. His first two TV plays, *Afternoon of a Nymph* and *Night Conspirators* (both *Armchair Theatre*, 1962), indicated two of his favourite themes – showbusiness and the Nazis, from whom he had escaped as a boy refugee in 1938. Later he developed a penchant for Gothic horror and historical subjects. Since the mid-seventies has worked mainly for West German television. *Die Welt in Jenem Sommer* (The World That Summer, 1980). UK credits lately: *Russian Night 1941* for BBC, 1982; pilot for Thames's *Storyboard*, 1983, called *Secrets*.   PP

Mulligan, Richard (1932–). Lanky, twitchy American comic actor who had a series as long ago as *The Hero* but didn't make it big until SOAP. Emmy 1980, best comedy actor.

Mulligan Stew
US 1977 74m colour TVM
Paramount/Christiana (Joanna Lee)

The parents of five children adopt four orphans.

Relentlessly cute family comedy after the style of *Yours Mine and Ours* and *Room for One More*.

w Joanna Lee d Noel Black

Elinor Donahue, Lawrence Pressman, Johnny Whitaker, Alex Karras

† A series of 13 × 50m episodes followed.

MunsterGoHome
US 1966 96m colour TVM
NBC/Universal (Joe Connelly, Bob Mosher)

Herman Munster inherits an English castle.
Not too bad a collection of ancient gags and
wheezes, with the Munster concept still fairly
fresh. (Not a pilot, as it came *after* the popular
comedy show.)

w George Tibbles, Joe Connelly, Bob Mosher
d Earl Bellamy ph Benjamin H. Kline m Jack
Marshall

Fred Gwynne, Yvonne de Carlo, Al Lewis,
Hermione Gingold, Terry-Thomas, John
Carradine, Butch Patrick, Debbie Watson

The Munsters **
US 1964–5 70 × 25m bw
CBS/MCA/Universal (Joe Connelly)

A suburban family consists of the Frankenstein
monster, a couple of vampires and a wolf-boy.
Dad works for the Gateman, Goodbury and
Graves Funeral Home, and they think other
people are odd.
Slightly cruder than *The Addams Family*,
which came out the same season, this amiable
horror spoof got by on winning
characterizations and a catchy music theme. In
a comical way it also had a message.

cr Joe Connelly, Bob Mosher

FRED GWYNNE, Yvonne de Carlo, Al Lewis

The Munsters' Revenge
US 1981 96m colour TVM
NBC/Universal (Edward J. Montagne)

A villain uses look-alike Munster robots to
carry out robberies.
Unnecessary and unsuccessful revamp of a
17-year-old formula which could never fill
more than 25 minutes.

w Don Nelson, Arthur Alsberg d Don Weis
ph Harry L. Wolf m Vic Mizzy

Fred Gwynne, Yvonne de Carlo, Al Lewis,
K. C. Martel, Jo McDonnell, Sid Caesar, Ezra
Stone, Howard Morris

'All the fun of a trip on the *Titanic*, or a return to
Vietnam.' – *Daily Variety*

The Muppet Show ****
GB 1976–80 130 approx. × 25m colour
(VTR)
ATV/Henson Associates (Jim Henson, Jon
Stone)

Puppets put on a weekly variety show.
The puppets vary from glove puppets to men
dressed up, and have an agreeable madness in
their design. The format comes from
Hellzapoppin, the jokes and the songs are old
and good, and characters such as Kermit the

Frog, Fozzie Bear and aged hecklers Statler
and Waldorf are already part of TV history.
The Muppets graduated from *Sesame Street*
through *The Julie Andrews Hour* to become
stars in their own right. A human guest star
appears each week to be sabotaged.

cr FRANK OZ, JIM HENSON

'The Muppets make you smile even when the
script-writers don't . . . Jim Henson and his
puppeteers invest their little characters with
love, which is the same as making them live.' –
Robert MacKenzie, *TV Guide*

† BAFTA 1976, 1977, best light entertainment
series; Emmy 1977, best variety series.

Murder at the Mardi Gras
US 1977 96m colour TVM
Paramount/Jozak/Richard Nader

A Philadelphia cashier wins a ticket to New
Orleans and finds her life in danger.
Glum, overstretched whodunit without even
the usual roster of guest stars.

w Stanley Ralph Ross d Ken Annakin ph
Roland Smith m Peter Matz

Barbi Benton, Didi Conn, Bill Daily, David
Groh, Gregg Henry, Harry Morgan, Joyce
Van Patten, David Wayne, Ron Silver,
LaVerne Hooker

'Anyone expecting a taut, slick mystery
telefilm better not look.' – *Daily Variety*

'Out for revenge he stalks his victims . . .
in a stadium packed with 45,000
screaming fans.'
Murder at the World Series
US 1977 96m colour TVM
ABC Circle (Cy Chermak)

Various people are drawn into a kidnapping
plot during a baseball game.
Dreary multi-star time-filler.

w Cy Chermak d Andrew V. McLaglen m
John Cacavas

Janet Leigh, Lynda Day George, Karen
Valentine, Murray Hamilton, Gerald S.
O'Loughlin, Michael Parks, Hugh O'Brian,
Nancy Kelly, Joseph Wiseman, Bruce
Boxleitner

Murder Bag (GB 1956–9). Half-hour crime
series from A–R introducing Superintendent
Lockhart (Raymond Francis) who was later
promoted to the 50-minute *No Hiding Place*.
PP

'Passion without love. Murder without
warning. Suspense without end.'
Murder by Natural Causes **
US 1979 96m colour TVM
CBS/Time–Life/Richard Levinson, William
Link

A mentalist takes elaborate steps to avoid being murdered by his wife and her lover. Smart twister with echoes of *Les Diaboliques* and *Dial M For Murder*. Good stuff, and for once not obviously padded.

w RICHARD LEVINSON, WILLIAM LINK *d* ROBERT DAY *ph* Jack Swain *m* Dick DeBenedictis

HAL HOLBROOK, Katharine Ross, Richard Anderson, Barry Bostwick

'Not only an intriguing who (or whether) dunnit but a literate, adult dramatic puzzle with an apparently endless series of twists.' – Alvin Marill

Murder: By Reason of Insanity

US 1985 96m colour TVM
CBS/LS Entertainment (Lawrence Schiller)

A man beats his wife, is locked up in a mental hospital, but still threatens to kill her.

Suspenseful but still unsurprising case history which makes its points for more care with dangerous patients.

w Scott Swanton *article* by Marilyn Goldstein *d* Anthony Page *ph* Alexander Gruszynski *m* John Cacavas

Candice Bergen, Jurgen Prochnow, Hector Elizondo, Eli Wallach, Lee Kessler, Kent Williams

Murder Can Hurt You!

US 1980 96m colour TVM
ABC/Metromedia/Aaron Spelling (Robert L. Jacks)

A Man in White sets out to murder all members of the Some of the Best Cops in the World Club.

In the wake of *Murder By Death*, an unfunny parody involving impersonations of several TV detectives. Feeble.

w Ron Friedman *d* Roger Duchawny *ph* Arch Dalzell *m* Artie Kane

Victor Buono (Ironbottom), Burt Young (Palumbo), Gavin McLeod (Nojack), Jamie Farr, John Byner (Studsky and Hatch), Tony Danza (Lambretta), Buck Owens (MacSky), Connie Stevens (Salty)

Murder in Coweta County

US 1983 96m colour TVM
CBS/Telecom/International Picture Show (Gene Nelson)

A true 1948 murder case in Georgia: a moonshiner is killed by a political boss who defies arrest.

Another 'only in America' eyebrow-raiser, this will carry conviction for those who can catch the accents.

w Dennis Nemec, *book* by Margaret Anne Barnes *d* Gary Nelson *ph* Larry Pizer *m* Brad Fiedel

Johnny Cash, Andy Griffith, Earl Hindman, Ed Van Nuys, Jo Henderson, June Carter Cash

Murder in Music City

US 1979 96m colour TVM
NBC/Frankel Films/Gank Inc (Jimmy Sangster)

A hard-pressed songwriter becomes a private eye to solve the mystery of the corpse in his own bathtub.

Muddled mystery with musical interludes. A time-passer at best.

w Jimmy Sangster, Ernie Frankel *d* Leo Penn *ph* Alan Stensvold

Sonny Bono, Lee Purcell, Claude Akins, Belinda Montgomery, Lucille Benson, Michael MacRae, Morgan Fairchild, Harry Bellaver

Murder in Peyton Place

US 1977 96m colour TVM
TCF/Peter Katz

A recap of events in America's most famous small town, and new trouble in which two of its most celebrated characters are done in.

Curious up-date of the successful soap opera of the sixties, not too badly done.

w Richard DeRoy *d* Robert Hartford-Davis, Bruce Kessler *ph* Gert Andersen *m* Laurence Rosenthal (theme by Franz Waxman)

Dorothy Malone, Ed Nelson, Tim O'Connor, Christopher Connolly, Joyce Jillson, David Hedison, Stella Stevens, James Booth, Kaz Garas

Murder in Texas *

US 1981 2 × 96m colour
NBC/Dick Clark/Billy Hale

An account of the murder of a Texas heiress, from a book by the second wife of the doctor–husband who was suspected.

Stranger than fiction, all right; all concerned appear to have acted with extreme stupidity. But as a picture of how the rich live in America's richest state the movie is something of an eye-opener.

w John McGreevey, *book Prescription Murder* by Ann Kurth *d* William Hale *ph* Donald M. Morgan *m* Leonard Rosenman

Sam Elliott, Katharine Ross, Farrah Fawcett, Andy Griffith, G. W. Bailey, Barry Corbin, Pamela Myers

'A strong, even riveting teleplay . . . incidents flow past with startlingly realistic actions . . . it's *Columbo* time without the detective.' – *Daily Variety*

Murder in the Cathedral (GB 1936 and 1964). T. S. Eliot's play about the murder of Thomas à Becket was the very first to be broadcast on a public television service, by the BBC on 19 October 1936, produced by George More O'Ferrall. In 1964 it was recorded in Canterbury Cathedral as an early demonstration of the possibilities of location VTR, with long cloistered vistas and the actors' breath misting on the air. Unfortunately the presence of real stones and mortar imposed a stones-and-mortar realism ¬which ill suited Eliot's rag-bag of styles. With Cyril Cusack, Denis Quilley, John Bennett, Esmond Knight, John Carson. Directed by George R. Foa; produced by Peter Luke; for BBC (*Festival*).   PP

Murder Is Easy *
US 1981 96m colour TVM
CBS/Warner/David L. Wolper–Stan
  Marguilies
A visiting American solves murders in an English village.
Complex but followable, and certainly very good looking, adaptation of a medium Agatha Christie who-done-it.
w Carmen Culver *d* Claude Whatham
ph Brian Tufano *m* Gerald Fried
Bill Bixby, Lesley-Anne Down, Olivia de Havilland, Helen Hayes, Patrick Allen, Shane Briant, Freddie Jones, Leigh Lawson, Jonathan Pryce, Timothy West, Anthony Valentine

Murder Not Proven (GB 1984; 3 × 55m). Classic murder cases which attracted the unique Scottish verdict 'Not Proven,' reviewed once again with Andrew Keir as narrator. Produced by Bob McIntosh, for BBC Scotland.   PP

Murder of a Moderate Man (GB/Italy 1985; 6 × 50m). Mafia-cum-spy thriller of a complexity not justified by the interestingness of the John Howlett novel on which it was based. 'And Dennis Quilley,' I wrote, 'is much too commanding a figure to play a hero who is apparently meant to be some kind of has-been fallen on lean days. The result is one of those co-productions which try to please both parties and succeed with neither.' Also with Susan Fleetwood; produced by John Bowen for BBC.   PP

Murder on Flight 502 *
US 1975 100m colour TVM
Spelling–Goldberg (David Chasman)
Murder on a jet airliner: will the killer strike again?
Watchable old-fashioned suspenser.
w David P. Harmon *d* George McCowan
Ralph Bellamy, Polly Bergen, Theodore Bikel, Sonny Bono, Dane Clark, Laraine Day, Fernando Lamas, George Maharis, Hugh O'Brian, Molly Picon, Walter Pidgeon, Robert Stack

Murder Once Removed *
US 1971 74m colour TVM
Metromedia (Bob Markell)
A doctor finds his wife is unfaithful and plans the 'perfect' murder.
Carefully plotted, very watchable will-he-get-away-with-it suspenser.
w Irving Gaynor Neiman *d* Charles Dubin
John Forsythe, Richard Kiley, Barbara Bain, Joseph Campanella, Wendell Corey

Murder One: see The DA: Murder One

Murder or Mercy?
US 1974 74m colour TVM
Quinn Martin
An attorney emerges from retirement to defend a man who killed his terminally ill wife.
Good acting in a human drama which isn't especially dramatic.
w Douglas Day Stewart *d* Harvey Hart
Melvyn Douglas, Bradford Dillman, Denver Pyle, Mildred Dunnock, David Birney, Don Porter, Robert Webber, Kent Smith

Murder She Wrote
aka: *The Murder of Sherlock Holmes*
US 1984 96m colour TVM
CBS/Universal/Levinson and Link (Robert F. O'Neill)
A Maine widow writes a best-selling mystery novel and helps to solve a murder case.
Overlong pilot for a highly successful one-hour series clearly modelled on Agatha Christie's Miss Marple. A change at least from screeching tyres, but the format quickly became tedious.
w Peter S. Fischer *d* Corey Allen *ph* Mario DiLeo *m* John Addison
Angela Lansbury, Eddie Barth, Jessica Browne, Brian Keith, Bert Convy, Herb Edelman, Ned Beatty, Arthur Hill, Raymond St Jacques

Murder with Mirrors

GB 1985 96m colour TVM
CBS/Warner/Hajeno (Neil Hartley)

Miss Marple suspects that an old friend is being poisoned.

Uneasy transcription of a standard detective story: a leaden script, poor pace, and some miscasting militate against it.

w George Eckstein, *novel* by Agatha Christie *d* Dick Lowry *ph* Brian West *m* Richard Rodney Bennett

Helen Hayes, Bette Davis, John Mills, Leo McKern, Liane Langland, Dorothy Tutin, Anton Rodgers, Frances de la Tour, John Woodvine

Murdock's Gang

US 1973 84m colour TVM
Don Fedderson

After serving a prison term, a flamboyant attorney becomes a private eye with a staff of ex-cons.

Unpersuasive time-passer.

w Edmund H. North *d* Charles Dubin

Alex Dreier, Janet Leigh, Murray Hamilton, William Daniels, Harold Gould, Don Knight

Murphy, Ben (1942–). Virile-looking American leading man. Series: *Alias Smith and Jones*, *Griff*, *Gemini Man*, *The Chisholms*. TV movies: *The Letters*, *Runaway*, *Heatwave*, *This Was the West that Was*, *Bridger*, *The Secret War of Jackie's Girls*, *Uncommon Valor*, *The Winds of War*, *The Cradle Will Fall*, *Lottery*, *Berrenger's*, *Gidget's Summer Reunion*.

Murphy, Brian (1933–). British character actor who played the landlord in *A Man About the House* and went on to star as the same obtuse character in *George and Mildred*. L *for Lester*, 1982; *On Your Way, Riley!*, 1985.

Murphy, Eddie (1961–). Sassy black American comic who started on *Saturday Night Live* before making a big name for himself in movies.

**Murphy's Stroke ** (GB 1980). Sunny film by Frank Cvitanovich reconstructing an ingenious betting ploy which in 1974 almost made a syndicate of Irishmen a nice killing. Always a lyrical director when horses are about, Cvitanovich made it very good to look at; a cast of mostly unfamiliar actors made it sound right. Written by Brian Phelan; for Thames.
                                                        PP

Murray, Arthur (1895–) (Arthur Murray Teichman). American dancing instructor ('Arthur Murray taught me dancing in a hurry') who in the fifties hosted, with his wife, TV's *Arthur Murray Dance Party*.

MURDER SHE WROTE had an unmistakeable, if unacknowledged, resemblance to Agatha Christie's Miss Marple stories, but despite Angela Lansbury's pleasant performance as the indomitable sleuth it lacked the background detail which makes a classic.

Murray, Don (1929–). Earnest American leading man who never quite hit stardom. TV movies: *The Borgia Stick*, *Daughter of the Mind*, *The Intruders*, *The Girl on the Late Late Show*, *The Sex Symbol*, *A Girl Named Sooner*, *Rainbow*, *Crisis in Midair*, *The Boy Who Drank Too Much*, *Confessions of a Lady Cop*, *Fugitive Family*. Series: *Knots Landing*.

Murray, Ken (1903–) (Don Court). American comedian, an inveterate Hollywood party-goer whose home movies have bolstered up many a TV show.

✳ **Murrow, Ed** (1908–65). American current affairs reporter, never separated from his cigarette, noted for hard-hitting current affairs shows like SEE IT NOW (which started the downfall of Senator McCarthy) and personality link-ups like SMALL WORLD and PERSON TO PERSON. Famous too were his broadcasts from London during the Blitz, and he by-lined many controversial documentaries including *Harvest of Shame*. Emmys 1953, 1955, 1956, 1957, 1958: most outstanding personality.

† Subject of TV biopic *Murrow*, 1986.

Musante, Tony (1936–   ). American leading actor often cast as a hoodlum but with an interesting range. Series: *Toma*. TV movies: *The Desperate Miles*, *Nowhere to Hide*, *My Husband is Missing*, *High Ice*, *Breaking up Is Hard to Do*, *Rearview Mirror*, *Magruder and Loud*.

The Muscle Market (GB 1981). Strikingly original, engrossing but ultimately rather unpleasant *Play for Today* (BBC) by Alan Bleasdale about a dodgy, self-made tarmacadam contractor in the process of going bust and thereby discovering that friendship is a rapidly disposable commodity. Would have been the first episode of *Boys from the Blackstuff* had it not been produced ahead of that series. The Boys were his work force.   PP

Music by Jerome Kern *
GB 1977 60m colour (VTR)
BBC/ABC Australia/CBC Canada (Kenneth Corden)

A slickly produced recap of the songs of Jerome Kern, styled on the lines of *Side by Side by Sondheim* but set in a TV studio with some dexterous camera movement.

w Arthur Schwartz, Benny Green *choreo* Gillian Gregory d Ron Isted *musical arrangements* Dennis Wilson

ARTHUR SCHWARTZ, David Kernan, Elizabeth Seal, Julia McKenzie, Teddy Green

The Music of Lennon and McCartney *
GB 1965 60m bw

30 numbers by Lennon and McCartney staged before a wildly enthusiastic audience and delivered by their chosen performers, including the other two Beatles, Cilla Black, Lulu, Marianne Faithfull and PETER SELLERS, who recited 'A Hard Day's Night' in his Olivier/Richard III imitation. Directed by Philip Casson; produced by John Hamp; for Granada.   PP

La Musica ** (GB 1965). Another masterpiece incorporated into a routine anthology series. Michael Craig and Vanessa Redgrave as man and wife chance to meet the night their divorce becomes absolute, each about to begin a new chapter but suddenly wanting – in dry, whispered exchanges – to prolong the old. It was box-office (biggest audience for any single play of 1965 according to TAM) as well as art, which should have pleased Lew Grade. Written by Marguérite Duras, translated by Barbara Bray; directed by John Nelson Burton; for ATV (*Love Story*).   PP

Mussolini: The Decline and Fall of Il Duce
US/Italy 1985 2 ×
96m colour miniseries
HBO/RAI/Antenne 2/Beta (Mario Gallo)

A picture of the last years of a failed dictator, with the emphasis on his daughter Edda, wife of Count Ciano.
Second of two quite unnecessary peeps into the home life of a monster; this performance was the more derided.

w Nicola Badalucco, Alberto Negrin d Alberto Negrin ph Armando Nanuzzi m Egisto Macchi

Susan Sarandon, Anthony Hopkins, Bob Hoskins (as Mussolini), Annie Girardot, Barbara de Rossi, Fabio Testi

'A madman who would stop at nothing to conquer everything!'
Mussolini – The Untold Story
US 1985 1 × 142m, 2 ×
96m colour miniseries
NBC/Train/Katz–Sofronski (Stirling Silliphant)

The story of Mussolini from his 1922 seizure of Rome to his ignominious end in 1945.
A lumpy and indigestible piece of contemporary history with a star quite unequal to the sympathizing of a monster.

w Stirling Silliphant w William A. Graham m Laurence Rosenthal pd Harry Lange

George C. Scott, Lee Grant, Mary Elizabeth Mastrantonio, Virginia Madsen, Raul Julia, Gabriel Byrne, Robert Downey

'Not much more than a bore.' – *Daily Variety*

My Father's House *
US 1975 96m colour TVM
Filmways

A high pressure executive has a heart attack and recalls family life with his father who suffered a similar fate.
Watchable but somewhat padded and elementary personal drama.

w David Sontag, David Seltzer, *novel* Philip Kunhardt Jnr d Alex Segal

Robert Preston, Cliff Robertson, Rosemary Forsyth, Eileen Brennan

My Father's House
GB 1981 7 × 50m colour
Granada (June Howson)

A schoolgirl grows up torn between her divorced parents and reluctantly discovering their secrets.
Rather routine soap opera, for addicts only.

w Paula Milne, *novel* Kathleen Conlon *d* Alan Grint

Judy Holt, Helen Ryan, Terrence Hardiman, Steven Mann, Anne Reid

My Favorite Husband
US 1953–4 approx. 78 × 25m bw
CBS

A young banker has a scatterbrained wife. Stereotyped domestic comedy.

Joan Caulfield/Vanessa Brown, Barry Nelson, Bob Sweeney, Alexandra Talton

† The series was based on a radio series which, starring Lucille Ball, set her on the path to her immense broad comedy success.

My Favorite Martian
US 1963–5 107 × 25m bw (32 colour)
CBS/Jack Chertok

A stranded Martian adopts a young newspaperman as his nephew and nobody else can see him.

Moderately amusing adaptation of the *Mister Ed* format.

Ray Walston, Bill Bixby, Pamela Britton

† A half-hour cartoon version was subsequently made by Filmation under the title *My Favorite Martians*.

My Friend Flicka
US 1956 39 × 25m colour
CBS/TCF

The small son of a midwestern family loves his horse.

Archetypal family show from the film and book by Mary O'Hara. Technical accomplishment modest, popularity wide.

Johnny Washbrook, Gene Evans, Anita Louise

My Friend Irma
US 1952–3 70 approx. × 25m bw
CBS

Two New York secretaries share an apartment, and one is beautiful but dumb.

Inept comedy, mainly remembered because the film version introduced Martin and Lewis to the big screen.

Marie Wilson, Cathy Lewis/Mary Shipp, Sid Tomack, Hal March, Sig Arno, Donald MacBride

My Friend Tony
US 1968 16 × 50m colour
NBC/Sheldon Leonard

A criminology professor is helped by a young Italian swinger.

Forgettable mystery series: the elements didn't jell.

James Whitmore, Enzo Cerusico

My Hero
aka: *The Robert Cummings Show*
US 1952 33 × 25m bw
NBC/Sharpe–Lewis

Domestic problems of a happy-go-lucky real estate agent.

Mild comedy which started the TV bigtime for its star.

Robert Cummings, John Litel, Julie Bishop

My Husband Is Missing
US 1980 96m colour TVM
NBC/Shaner–Ramrus/Bob Banner

A woman goes to Vietnam to find out what really happened to her husband.

Tedious romantic drama with enough plot for an hour.

w John Herman Shaner, Al Ramrus *d* Richard Michaels *ph* Michael Marguilies *m* Joseph Weiss

Sally Struthers, Tony Musante, James Hong, Jeff David

'He got bored.' – *Daily Variety*

My Kidnapper, My Love
US 1981 96m colour TVM
NBC/EMI/Roger Gimbel (James Stacy)

A rich girl falls for the crippled newsagent who helps kidnap her for ransom.

An extremely boring idea (remember Miss Blandish?), rather interestingly handled but far too long for its substance.

w Louie Elias, *novel* Oscar Saul *d* Sam Wanamaker *ph* Michael Marguilies *m* Fred Karlin

James Stacy, Glynnis O'Connor, Mickey Rooney, J. D. Cannon, Jan Sterling, Ellen Geer

'Fully textured . . . a daring, rich production.' – *Daily Variety*

My Little Margie
US 1952–4 126 × 25m bw
CBS/Hal Roach Jnr/Roland Reed

A slightly hare-brained 21-year-old hinders rather than helps her widowed father.

Family relationships through rose-tinted spectacles. Credited as the first series to be 'stripped', i.e. played five days a week at the same time.

Charles Farrell, Gale Storm

My Living Doll
US 1964 26 × 25m bw
CBS/Jack Chertok

A psychiatrist gets custody of a glamorous female robot.

Daffy comedy with some laughs, but too restricted to be a long-runner.

Robert Cummings, Julie Newmar, Doris Dowling, Jack Mullaney

My Mother the Car
US 1965 30 × 25m colour
NBC/United Artists/Cottage
  Industries/NBC

A suburbanite buys an old car which turns out to be the reincarnation of his dead mother, who continues to domineer over him.

Thought at the time to mark the outer limits of TV idiocy, this comedy has long been surpassed and now seems merely inept.

Jerry Van Dyke, the voice of Ann Sothern

'She learned how to love from the daughter she never wanted!'

My Mother's Secret Life
US 1984 96m colour TVM
ABC/Furia–Oringer

A 16-year-old girl discovers that her mother is an expensive hooker.

Tepid teleplay which exploits what it's supposed to expose.

w John Furia Jnr, Barry Oringer d Robert Markowitz ph Robbie Greenberg m Brad Fiedel

Loni Anderson, Paul Sorvino, Amanda Wyss, James Sutorius, Sandy McPeak

My Music * Long-running British radio panel show which since the early eighties has had a batch of editions each year simultaneously recorded for BBC TV. Frank Muir, Denis Norden, John Amis and Ian Wallace answer questions, identify tunes and sing songs set by host Steve Race, but no one bothers about the score; the fun's the thing.
PP

My Old Man
US 1979 96m colour TVM
CBS/Zeitman–McNichol–Halmi (Robert Halmi)

A 16-year-old girl whose mother has just died finds life rather odd with her oafish, boozy horsetraining dad.

Dreary distortion of a Hemingway story previously filmed (equally distortedly) as *Under My Skin*.

w Jerome Kass d John Erman ph Larry Pizer m Dominic Frontiere

Warren Oates, Kristy McNichol, Eileen Brennan, Joseph Maher

My Partner the Ghost: see Randall and Hopkirk (Deceased)

My Sister Eileen *
US 1960 26 × 25m bw
CBS/Columbia/Harry Ackerman (Dick Wesson)

Two midwestern sisters arrive in New York and set up housekeeping in a basement flat in Greenwich Village.

Friendly, zany comedy with agreeably mixed characters and a definite plus in its star.

ELAINE STRITCH, Shirley Bonne, Leon Belasco

My Son Jeep (US 1953). Shortlived, live, half-hour comedy series for NBC, with Jeffrey Lynn as a widowed doctor looking after two children.

My Son Reuben
GB 1974 13 × 25m colour (VTR)
Thames

The love/hate relationship of an overprotective Jewish mother and her errant son who runs a dry cleanery.

Modest, obvious comedy.

w Vince Powell

Bernard Spear, Lila Kaye

My Sweet Charlie *
US 1970 96m colour TVM
Universal (Bob Banner)

In a deserted beach house a young girl and a black man hide out from society for different reasons.

Well made but slow and pretentious character drama.

w Richard Levinson, William Link, *novel* David Westheimer d Lamont Johnson

Patty Duke (Emmy 1970), Al Freeman Jnr, Ford Rainey

My Three Sons *
US 1960–71 369 × 25m bw
ABC/Don Fedderson (Edmund Hartmann)

A widower watches his children grow up.

Simple, effective domestic comedy which dragged on rather longer than anyone intended.

cr Peter Tewksbury m Frank de Vol

FRED MACMURRAY, WILLIAM FRAWLEY (later WILLIAM DEMAREST), Beverly Garland, Stanley Livingston, Tim Considine

'When he was good, he became a star. When he was bad, he became a legend!'

My Wicked Wicked Ways
US 1984 142m colour TVM
CBS (Doris Keating)

The story of Errol Flynn up to his 1943 rape charge.
A very tentative affair which only occasionally comes to life.

w Doris Keating, Jill Trump, James Lee, Don Taylor, from Flynn's *memoirs* d Don Taylor

Duncan Regehr, Barbara Hershey (as Lili Damita), HAL LINDEN (as Jack L. Warner), Lee Purcell (as Olivia de Havilland)

My World and Welcome to It **
US 1969 26 × 25m colour
NBC/Sheldon Leonard (Danny Arnold)

A cartoonist sees his home life in terms of his drawings.
Ingenious and friendly domestic comedy drawn from James Thurber material, with interpolated cartoons an added plus. It was, of course, too good for the public.

cr MEL SHAVELSON

WILLIAM WINDOM, Joan Hotchkis, Liza Gerritsen, Harold J. Stone

'Deserves an A for effort.' – Jack Edmund Nolan

Mysteries of Chinatown (US 1949).
Half-hour live crime series for ABC, with Marvin Miller as Yat Fu, amateur sleuth and curio shop proprietor.

The Mysterious Island of Beautiful Women
GB title: *Island of Sister Theresa*
US 1979 96m colour TVM
CBS/Alan Landsburg (Paul Freeman)

Flyers who have run out of gas land on a Pacific island ruled by women who as children were refugees from French Indo-China.
Silly enough to be funny, but too long for a joke.

w Gary Sherman, Sandor Stern d Josep Pevney ph Al Francis m William Loose, Jac. Tillar

Stephen Keats, Jaime Lyn Bauer, Jayne Kennedy, Kathryn Davis, Peter Lawford, Clint Walker

'The ladies in particular deserve a nod: not one breaks up in laughter at the dialogue handed them.' – *Daily Variety*

The Mysterious Two
US 1979 96m colour TVM
CBS/Alan Landsburg (Gary Credle, Sonny Fox)

A man and a woman arrive in a pentagram to collect their chosen people of tomorrow and take them off to outer space.
Obviously designed as a mini-version of *Close*

Encounters, this is so inept from the word go that the network which ordered it didn't bother to play it.

w/d Gary Sherman ph Steve Poster m Joe Renzetti

John Forsythe, Priscilla Pointer, James Stephens, Robert Pine, Karen Werner, Noah Beery, Vic Tayback

The Mysterious World of Arthur C. Clarke
(GB 1980). British half-hour popular science series (13 episodes) introduced from a Sri Lanka beach by the well-known science fiction writer. We are then given remarkably little information about a number of strange phenomena from rainstorms of frogs to the moving rocks of Death Valley. A waste of a good opportunity, but a good promotion for the inevitable book. Produced by Simon Welfare, John Fairley; for Trident TV.

† His *World of Strange Powers* (1985) similarly muffed the opportunity to evaluate the paranormal.

Mystery and Imagination (GB 1965–70; approx. 26 × 50m, 6 × 78m). Occasional groupings of adaptations from mystery or horror literature begun by ABC and expanded to larger format by Thames. The autumn 1968 trio included *Frankenstein* (written by Robert Muller, directed by Voytek) and a DRACULA, directed by Patrick Dromgoole, in which Denholm Elliott – in the part – visibly disintegrates at the end; a remarkable stroke of special effects. In 1970 the selection was R. L. Stevenson's *The Suicide Club*, adapted by Robert Muller; *Sweeney Todd*, by Vincent Tilsley; *The Curse of the Mummy*, from Bram Stoker by John Russell Taylor.   PP

Mystery Is My Business: see Ellery Queen (1954)

Mystery Movie. In 1971 Universal began making films for this NBC slot which required either 74 or 97 minutes. Most of the films were too long at either length for their plots, and few were genuine mysteries, but some of the detective characters became household words. They included the shabby police detective *Columbo*, who usually got his man by annoying him; *McCloud*, a policeman who treated New York City like the open west where he came from; *McMillan and Wife*, a Thin Man-like pair who banteringly saved San Francisco from violent crime. These heroes were played respectively by Peter Falk, Dennis Weaver, Rock Hudson and Susan St James. Less successful, and shorter-lived, were the New

MY WORLD AND WELCOME TO IT, a Thurberish comedy mix of cartoon and live action, had a splendid central performance from William Windom, who subsequently toured the world with a one-man Thurber show.

York cop *Madigan* (Richard Widmark); the private eyes *Faraday and Company* (Dan Dailey, James Naughton); the elderly thriller writers *The Snoop Sisters* (Helen Hayes, Mildred Natwick); the western detective *Hec Ramsay* (Richard Boone); the black detective *Tenafly* (James McEachin); the con man *McCoy* (Tony Curtis); the man-for-millionaire-hire in *Cool Million* (James Farentino). A moderate success was the expensive loot-finder *Banacek* (George Peppard). See also: *Four in One*.
The series ended with the 1977 season.
The films were as follows (74m unless otherwise stated):

Columbo (see *Prescription Murder*).
Creators and executive producers:
Richard Levinson and William Link

Ransom for a Dead Man
Murder by the Book
Dead Weight
Short Fuse
Blueprint for Murder

Suitable for Framing
Lady in Waiting
Death Lends a Hand
Dagger of the Mind (96m)
Double Shock
Etude in Black (97m)
The Greenhouse Jungle
The Most Crucial Game
The Most Dangerous Match
Requiem for a Falling Star
A Stitch in Crime
Any Old Port in a Storm (96m)
Candidate for a Crime (96m)
Double Exposure
Lovely but Lethal
Mind Over Mayhem
Publish or Perish
Swan Song (97m)
A Friend in Need (97m)
An Exercise in Fatality (97m)
Negative Reaction (96m)
By Dawn's Early Light (96m)
Playback
A Deadly State of Mind
Troubled Waters (97m)
Forgotten Lady (97m)
A Matter of Honour
A Case of Immunity
Identity Crisis (98m)
Last Salute to the Commodore
Now You See Him (89m)

McMillan and Wife (see *Once Upon a Dead Man*)
Creator and executive producer: Leonard Stern

Easy Sunday Murder Case
Murder by the Barrel
Husbands, Wives and Killers
The Face of Murder
Death is a Seven-Point Favourite
Till Death Us Do Part
An Elementary Case of Murder
Blues for Sally M
Cop of the Year
The Fine Art of Staying Alive
Night of the Wizard
No Hearts, No Flowers
Terror Times Two
Two Dollars on Trouble to Win

Cross and Double Cross (96m)
Death of a Monster, Birth of a Legend
The Devil You Say
Free Fall to Terror
The Man Without a Face (96m)
Reunion in Terror
Downshift to Danger (97m)
Game of Survival (97m)
Buried Alive (97m)
Guilt by Association (98m)
Night Train to L.A. (97m)
Love, Honour and Swindle (96m)
Deadly Inheritance (97m)
Requiem for a Bride (97m)
Aftershock (97m)
Secrets for Sale (97m)
Greed (97m)
Point of Law (97m)
The Deadly Cure (98m)

McCloud (see *Who Killed Miss USA?*)
Creator and executive producer: Glen Larson
Encounter with Aries
Fifth Man in a String Quartet
Somebody's Out to Get Jennie
Top of the World, Ma
Disposal Man
A Little Plot at Tranquil Valley
The Barefoot Stewardess Caper (96m)
The Million Dollar Round-Up (96m)
The New Mexican Connection
The Park Avenue Rustlers
Showdown at the End of the World
Butch Cassidy Rides Again (96m)
The Colorado Cattle Caper
The Solid Gold Swingers (98m)
Cowboy in Paradise (97m)
This Must Be the Alamo (96m)
The 42nd Street Cavalry (96m)
The Gang That Stole Manhattan (96m)
The Concrete Jungle Caper (96m)
The Barefoot Girls of Bleecker Street (99m)
Shivaree on Delancy Street (98m)
The Lady on the Run (97m)
Return to the Alamo
Sharks (98m)
Park Avenue Pirates (97m)
Three Guns for New York (98m)
Showdown at Times Square (97m)
Fire! (99m)

Our Man in the Harem (98m)
The Day New York Turned Blue (98m)
Night of the Shark (98m)

Madigan (see *Brock's Last Case*)
Executive producer: Frank Rosenberg
The Manhattan Beat
The Midtown Beat
The Lisbon Beat
The London Beat
The Naples Beat
The Park Avenue Beat

Banacek (see *Detour to Nowhere*)
The Greatest Collection of Them All
Let's Hear it for a Living Legend
A Million the Hard Way
No Sign of the Cross
Project Phoenix
To Steal a King
The Two Million Clams of Cap'n Jack
Ten Thousand Dollars a Page
A Horse of a Slightly Different Color
If Max Is So Smart, Why Doesn't He Tell Us Where He Is?
Rocket to Oblivion
Fly Me – if You Can Find Me
No Stone Unturned
Now You See It, Now You Don't
The Three Million Dollar Piracy
The Vanishing Chalice

Hec Ramsey (see *The Century Turns*)
Executive producer: Jack Webb
The Mystery of Chalk Hill (96m)
The Mystery of the Yellow Rose (96m)
The Green Feather Mystery
Hangman's Wages
Dead Heat (95m)
The Detroit Connection
A Hard Road to Vengeance (98m)
Scar Tissue (97m)
Only Birds and Fools (96m)

Cool Million (see *Cool Million*)
Executive producer: D. J. O'Connell
The Abduction of Bayard Barnes
Assault on Gavaloni
Hunt for a Lonely Girl
Million Dollar Misunderstanding

Faraday and Company (see *Say Hello to a Dead Man*)
Executive producer: Leonard Stern
Fire and Ice
A Matter of Magic
A Wheelbarrow Full of Trouble

The Snoop Sisters (see *The Snoop Sisters* aka: *The Female Instinct*)
Executive producer: Douglas Benton
Corpse and Robbers
A Black Day for Bluebeard
Fear Is a Free Throw
The Devil Made Me Do It

McCoy (see *The Big Rip-Off*)
Bless the Big Fish
Double Take (96m)
In Again Out Again (98m)
New Dollar Day

Amy Prentiss
Executive producer: Cy Chermak
The Desperate World of Jane Doe (96m)
Profile in Evil
Baptism of Fire (99m)

Tenafly (see *Tenafly*)
Executive producers: Richard Levinson and William Link
The Cash and Carry Caper
Joyride to Nowhere
Man Running
The Window That Wasn't

See also: *Quincy*

The Mystery of Loch Ness ✶✶
GB 1976 50m colour (16mm)
BBC (Peter Dale, Hugh Burnett)
An open-minded account of the evidence for and against a monster in Loch Ness.
Excellent documentary with clear statements.
w/commentator HUGH BURNETT

'N' Division: see Police

Nabors, Jim (*c* 1932–). Moonfaced American comic actor, former opera singer; a hit as the foolish Gomer Pyle in *The Andy Griffith Show*, later on his own in *Gomer Pyle USMC*.

Nader, George (1921–). American leading man after a modest success in the fifties disappeared from view, but not before making TV series: *Ellery Queen*, *Shannon*, *The Man and the Challenge*. TV movie: *Nakia*.

Nagasaki – the Return Journey (GB 1985). Two Britons are taken back to the city that suffered the second atomic bomb – Geoffrey Sherring, who had been a PoW in Nagasaki at the time, and Leonard Cheshire, the bomber ace and latterday saint who had watched the attack as an official RAF observer. As Denys Blakeway's film (narrator Philip Tibenham) took pains to make clear, the latter was not welcome. 'In the programme's careful balance of the rights and wrongs of the Allied action there seemed to be a lingering assumption that Cheshire's defence of the bomb as the most humane end to the war was faintly embarrassing, if not distasteful.' Neither here nor in any of the other British or British-shown items marking the 40th anniversary of Hiroshima and Nagasaki was there any consideration of just how bloody an alternative ending (i.e. an invasion of the Japanese home islands) might have been. That was left to a special edition of the regular ABC *Nightline* in America, introduced by Barrie Dunsmore, which had obtained the detailed invasion plans and casualty estimates from Pentagon files.

† Other BBC anniversary programmes, grouped together under the umbrella title *After the Bomb*, comprised two discussions, a re-run of *Threads* and the first TV screening of *The War Game*, 20 years after it was made. Channel 4 showed *The Day After Trinity* (US), *The Nuclear Holocaust* (Japan) and *Acceptable Risk* (GB), a report on cancer incidence among workers at an old radium plant in Pennsylvania, *p* and *d* Peter Gillbe for John Gau Productions.

†† Two former Nagasaki PoWs had also been taken back there, some months earlier, for an edition of YTV's *First Tuesday*.   PP

Nairn, Ian (*c* 1925–79). British place-taster of sorrowful mien but ardent likes and dislikes, always travelling by Morris Minor tourer as tubby as himself. *Nairn's Europe* (1970), *Nairn's Journeys* (1978).   PP

Nairobi Affair
US 1984 96m colour TVM
CBS/Robert Halmi (David Kappes)
Father and son in Kenya – one a white hunter, the other a policeman chasing ivory poachers – quarrel over a girl.
Insipid outdoor melodrama relying too much on its wildlife.

w David Epstein   *d* Marvin J. Chomsky *ph* Ronnie Taylor   *m* Charles Gross

Charlton Heston, John Savage, Maud Adams, John Rhys-Davies, Connie Booth, Shane Rimmer, Thomas Baptiste

'Peters out before its potential can be realized.' – *Daily Variety*

Naked City ***
US 1958–62 39 × 25m, 99 × 50m bw
ABC/Columbia/HERBERT B. LEONARD
Cases of an old and a young cop on the New York force.
First-rate location-shot crime-in-the-streets series with strong stories, excellent guest stars, and a tendency to crazy titles. A milestone in TV production.

cr STERLING SILLIPHANT, after the film story by Mark Hellinger *theme music* Billy May

James Franciscus, John McIntire (half-hours); PAUL BURKE, HORACE MACMAHON, NANCY MALONE (hours)

† There follows a complete list of one-hour episodes, with writer, director and stars.

A Death of Princes (*w* Sterling Silliphant; *d* John Brahm; with Eli Wallach, George Maharis)

The Pedigree Sheet (*w* Sterling Silliphant; *d* John Brahm; with Eric Portman, Suzanne Pleshette)

A Succession of Heartbeats (w Sterling Silliphant; d Paul Wendkos; with Felicia Farr, Frank Overton)

Down the Long Night (w Charles Beaumont; d Paul Wendkos; with Nehemiah Persoff, Geraldine Brooks, Leslie Neilsen)

To Walk in Silence (w Barry Trivers; d Roger Kay; with Telly Savalas, Stephen Bolster)

Killer with a Kiss (w Leonard Praskins, Sloan Nibley; d Lamont Johnson; with Burt Brinckerhoff)

Debt of Honor (w W. R. Burnett; d Tay Garnett; with Lois Nettleton, Steve Cochran)

The Human Trap (w Ellis Kadison; d Lamont Johnson; with Ruth Roman, Jack Lord)

The Man Who Bit a Diamond in Half (w Howard Rodman; d Buzz Kulik; with Luther Adler, Walter Matthau, Elizabeth Allen)

Bullets Cost Too Much (w Sam Marx; d Buzz Kulik; with James Caan, Bruce Dern, Betty Field)

Murder Is a Face I Know (w Howard Rodman; d Arthur Hiller; with Keir Dullea, Theodore Bikel)

Landscape with Dead Figures (w Barry Trivers; d Elliot Silverstein; with Myron McCormick, Alfred Ryder)

A Hole in the City (w Howard Rodman; d David Lowell Rich; with Sylvia Sidney, Robert Duvall)

The Well Dressed Termite (w Jay Dratler; d Laslo Benedek; with Jack Klugman, Philip Abbott)

The Day It Rained Mink (w Howard Rodman; d David Lowell Rich; with Keenan Wynn, Abbe Lane)

Button in the Haystack (w Howard Rodman; d Tay Garnett; with Albert Salmi, Peggy Ann Garner)

Shoes for Vinnie Wineford (w Ellis Kadison; d Elliot Silverstein; with Dennis Hopper, Sylvia Miles)

Deadly Guinea Pig (w Jay Dratler; d William A. Graham; with Viveca Lindfors, Eugenie Leontovitch, George Voskovec, Barry Morse)

Vengeance Is a Wheel (w Gil Ralston; d Elliot Silverstein; with Gerry Jedd, Ben Piazza)

Fault in Our Stars (w Barry Trivers; d William A. Graham; with Roddy McDowall)

Tombstone for a Derelict (w Howard N. Ehrenman; d Elliot Silverstein; with Robert Redford, Polly Rowles)

A Memory of Crying (w David Chantler, Howard Rodman; d Alex March; with Luther Adler, Betty Field, Philip Abbott)

New York to LA (w Howard Rodman; d Elliot Silverstein; with Martin Balsam, Robert Blake)

A Very Cautious Boy (w Gil Ralston; d William A. Graham; with Peter Falk, Ruth White)

An Economy of Death (w Sy Salkowitz; d Boris Sagal; with Sam Jaffe, Sandor Szabo)

$C_3H_5(NO_3)_3$ (w Gilbert Ralston; d William A. Graham; with Hume Cronyn, J. D. Cannon)

Make Believe Man (w Sy Salkowitz; d Elliot Silverstein; with Chester Morris, Eduardo Ciannelli)

To Dream without Sleep (w Barry Trivers; d William A. Graham; with Gerry Jedd, Lois Nettleton)

A Kettle of Precious Fish (w Gilbert Ralston; d William Conrad; with Albert Dekker, Anthony Dawson)

Sweet Prince of Delancey Street (w Sy Salkowitz; d Alex March; with Dustin Hoffman, James Dunn, Robert Morse)

The Day the Island Almost Sank (w Jerry Thomas; d William Conrad; with Paul Hartman, Roger Carmel)

Take and Put (w Arnold Ellis; d Elliot Silverstein; with Mildred Natwick, Roland Winters, Nancy Carroll)

Take Off Your Hat When a Funeral Passes (w Howard Rodman and Anthony Spinner; d Jules Bricken; with Lee J. Cobb, Geraldine Fitzgerald, Alfred Ryder)

Dead on a Field of Honor (w Betty Andrews; d Jack Smight; with Cathleen Nesbitt, Jeremy Slate)

The Corpse Ran Down Mulberry Street (w Howard Rodman; d Boris Sagal; with Nehemiah Persoff, Joe de Santis, Sorrell Booke)

The Fingers of Henry Tourelle (w Jerome Ross and Howard Rodman; d Arthur Hiller; with Nina Foch, Luther Adler, Robert Loggia, Jerome Cowan)

A Wednesday Night Story (w Jerome Ross, Howard Rodman; d Arthur Hiller; with Ulla Jacobsson, David Janssen)

The Tragic Success of Alfred Tiloff (w Howard Rodman; d Alex March; with Jan Sterling, Jack Klugman)

Which Is Joseph Creeley? (w Gilbert Ralston; d Arthur Hiller; with Martin Balsam, Jack Kruschen, Murray Hamilton)

Show Me the Way to Go Home (w Shimon Wincelberg; d William A. Graham; with Burt Brinckerhoff, Lois Nettleton, Louise Allbritton)

The Hot Minerva (w Ernest Kinoy; d Paul Wendkos; with Glynis Johns, William Redfield, Kurt Kasznar)

Requiem for a Sunday Afternoon (*w* Howard Rodman; *d* Paul Nickell; with Jay Novello, Marisa Pavan)

Oftus Goofus (*w* Howard Rodman, Jo Pagano; *d* Arthur Hiller; with Mickey Rooney, Maureen Stapleton)

Bridge Party (*w* Gilbert Ralston; *d* William Conrad; with Fred Clark, Albert Dekker, James Barton)

The Face of the Enemy (*w* Peg and Lou Shaw; *d* William A. Graham; with Jack Warden, Kim Hunter)

Portrait of a Painter (*w* Howard Rodman, Mel Goldberg; *d* David Lowell Rich; with William Shatner, Theodore Bikel, Barry Morse, Lou Antonio)

The Night the Saints Lost Their Halo (*w* Abram S. Ginnes; *d* Elliot Silverstein; with Jo Van Fleet, Peter Fonda, George Voskovec)

The Contract (*w* Norman Lessing, Howard Rodman; *d* Paul Nickell; with James Shigeta, Abraham Sofaer)

One of the Most Important Men in the World (*w* Howard Rodman; *d* Paul Nickell; with Richard Conte)

A Case Study of Two Savages (*w* Frank Pierson; *d* William A. Graham; with Tuesday Weld, Rip Torn)

Let Me Die Before I Wake (*w* Abram S. Ginnes; *d* Paul Nickell; with Jack Klugman, James Farentino, Joanne Linville)

To Walk Like a Lion (*w* Ken Trevey, Howard Rodman; *d* Robert Gist; with Orson Bean, Barbara Barrie)

Today the Man Who Kills Ants Is Coming (*w* Howard Rodman, Kenneth Rosen; *d* Robert Gist; with John Larch, Geraldine Fitzgerald)

A Run for the Money (*w* Howard Rodman; *d* David Lowell Rich; with Keenan Wynn, Eli Wallach, Lois Nettleton)

The One Marked Hot Gives Cold (*w* Abram S. Ginnes; *d* David Lowell Rich; with Edward Andrews, Robert Duvall, Jean Muir)

Without Stick or Sword (*w* Les Pine; *d* Paul Stanley; with William Shatner, Martin Balsam)

Lament for a Dead Indian (*w* Joel Carpenter; *d* Robert Gist; with Peter Falk, Neville Brand)

The Sweet Smiling Face of Truth (*w* Gilbert Ralston; *d* James Sheldon; with Nina Foch, Shirl Conway)

And If Any Are Frozen, Warm Them (*w* Abram S. Ginnes; *d* Robert Gist; with Ludwig Donath, Akim Tamiroff, Nehemiah Persoff, Lilia Skala)

Strike a Statue (*w* Roland Wolpert, Howard Rodman; *d* John Newland; with George C. Scott, Paul Richards)

The Multiplicity of Herbert Konish (*w* Ernest Kinoy; *d* David Lowell Rich; with David Wayne, Jean Stapleton, Nancy Marchand)

The King of Venus Will Take Care of You (*w* Joel Carpenter; *d* David Lowell Rich; with Jack Warden, Barbara Baxley)

The Rydecker Case (*w* Gene Roddenberry; *d* John Brahm; with Martin Gabel, Michael Tolan)

Memory of a Red Trolley Car (*w* Abram S. Ginnes; *d* Lawrence F. Doheny; with Gladys Cooper, Barry Morse; Beatrice Straight)

Goodbye, Mama, Hello Auntie Maud (*w* Sy Salkowitz; *d* Robert Gist; with James Coburn, Salome Jens, Carroll O'Connor)

Hold for Gloria Christmas (*w* Joel Carpenter; *d* Walter Grauman; with Burgess Meredith, Herschel Bernardi, Eileen Heckart)

Idylls of a Running Back (*w* Ernest Kinoy; *d* John Peyser; with Aldo Ray, Sandy Dennis)

Daughter, Am I in My Father's House? (*w* Shimon Wincelberg; *d* David Lowell Rich; with Dan Duryea, Barbara Harris)

And By the Sweat of Thy Brow (*w* Abram S. Ginnes; *d* Irvin Kershner; with Barbara Barrie, Richard Jordan)

Kill Me While I'm Young So I Can Die Happy (*w* Abram S. Ginnes; *d* Denis Sanders; with Maureen Stapleton)

Five Cranks for Winter, Ten Cranks for Spring (*w* Sterling Silliphant; *d* Paul Stanley; with Shirley Knight, Robert Duvall, Ludwig Donath)

Go Fight City Hall (*w* Ben Maddow; *d* David Lowell Rich; with George Rose, Joseph Buloff)

Torment Him Much and Hold Him Long (*w* Sterling Silliphant; *d* Robert Gist; with Robert Duvall, Barbara Loden, Jesse White)

Make It Fifty Dollars and Add Love to Nona (*w* Shimon Wincelberg; *d* George Sherman; with Luther Adler, Ed Begley)

A Horse Has a Big Head, Let Him Worry (*w* Abram S. Ginnes; *d* Denis Sanders; with Diahann Carroll, Sorrell Booke)

Dust Devil on a Quiet Street (*w* Anthony Lawrence, Howard Rodman; *d* George Sherman; with Robert Walker, Richard Basehart, Barbara Barrie)

The Virtues of Madame Douvay (*w* Paula Fox; *d* Robert Gist; with Claude Dauphin, Denise Darcel)

King Stanislaus and the Knights of the Round Stable (*w* Abram S. Ginnes; *d* James Sheldon; with Jack Klugman, John Larch)

Spectre of the Rose Street Gang (w Alvin Sargent, Jerome Gruskin; d James Sheldon; with Jack Warden, Bethel Leslie, Carroll O'Connor)

Don't Knock It Till You've Tried It (w Joel Carpenter; d Alex March; with Walter Matthau, Sally Gracie)

Her Life in Moving Pictures (w Sidney Boehm, Howard Rodman; d George Sherman; with Eileen Heckart, Bradford Dillman)

Robin Hood and Clarence Darrow, They Went Out with Bow and Arrow (w Abram S. Ginnes; d Stuart Rosenberg; with Eddie Albert, Michael Strong)

The Apple Falls Not Far from the Tree (w Arnold Perl, Les Pine; d William A. Graham; with Keir Dullea, Alexander Scourby)

Beyond This Place There Be Dragons (w Shimon Wincelberg; d George Sherman; with Frank Gorshin, Sorrell Booke)

Man without a Skin (w Abram S. Ginnes; d James Sheldon; with George Segal; Gabriel Dell)

Prime of Life (w Sterling Silliphant; d Walter Grauman; with Gene Hackman, Richard Hamilton)

Bringing Far Places Together (w Howard Rodman; d Irvin Kershner; with Alejandro Rey)

The Highest of Prizes (w Arnold Perl; d James Sheldon; with Robert Culp, Akim Tamiroff)

Alive and Still a Second Lieutenant (w Shimon Wincelberg; d Ralph Senensky; with Jon Voight, Robert Sterling)

Stop the Parade, a Baby Is Crying (w Abram S. Ginnes; d William A. Graham; with Diana Hyland, Jack Klugman)

On the Battlefront Every Minute Is Important (w Howard Rodman; d Robert Ellis Miller; with Kurt Kasznar, David Hanssen)

Howard Running Bear Is a Turtle (w Alvin Sargent, B. Schweig; d Harry Harris; with Juano Hernandez, Paul Richards, Perry Lopez)

No Naked Ladies in Front of Giovanni's House (w Abram S. Ginnes; d Ralph Senensky; with Marisa Pavan, Al Lewis)

Color Schemes Like Never Before (w Alvin Sargent; d Ralph Senensky; with Johnny Seven, Lou Antonio)

Carrier (w Howard Rodman; d Robert Ellis Miller; with Bruce Gordon, Anthony Zerbe)

The SS American Dream (w Frank R. Pierson; d Allen H. Miner; with John Larch, Roger C. Carmel)

Golden Lads and Girls (w Ernest Kinoy; d William A. Graham; with Robert Webber, Elizabeth Allen, Murray Matheson)

Barefoot on a Bed of Coals (w Shimon Wincelberg; d James Sheldon; with Steven Hill, Zohra Lampert, Dustin Hoffman)

The Naked Civil Servant ***
GB 1975 80m colour (16mm)
 Thames

The life of acknowledged homosexual Quentin Crisp.

Brilliant documentary drama using captions and other Brechtian alienation effects. It created a new career for its elderly hero, who became a TV celebrity, and it won many awards.

w PHILIP MACKIE d JACK GOLD

JOHN HURT

PP: 'The unexpected masterpiece of the year. The Crisp character was perhaps nicer than he makes himself out to be, but the humour, courage and occasional tenderness of this homo's odyssey were marvellously caught.'

† *An Evening with Quentin Crisp* (US 1983; 100m) featured the real Q.C. batting questions from a New York audience. Produced by Ken Fix Productions, shown by C4.

Nakia
US 1974 15 × 50m colour
ABC/Columbia/David Gerber (Charles Larson)

An Indian becomes deputy sheriff of a New Mexico town.

Self-consciously socially conscious modern western which didn't take. Filmed near Albuquerque.

Robert Forster, Arthur Kennedy, Gloria de Haven, Taylor Lacher, George Nader

The Name of the Game. This series of
74-minute movies which sprang from *Fame Is the Name of the Game* (qv) ran three seasons (1968–70). The films were watchable but almost always over-padded, better on the crime themes than the social concern. Gene Barry played the managing editor of *Fame* magazine, with Robert Stack looking after crime and Tony Franciosa current affairs; they usually appeared on a rotating basis. Susan St James was Barry's secretary. Executive producer: Richard Irving; producers: George Eckstein (Stack), Dean Hargrove (Barry), Gene L. Coon (Franciosa). For NBC.

The titles were as follows:

Ordeal (RS, Farley Granger, Martha Hyer, Jessica Walter)

Witness (GB, RS, Victor Jory, Joan Hackett)

The Bobby Currier Story (RS, Brandon de Wilde, Julie Harris)

The Fear of High Places (GB, TF, Zsa Zsa Gabor, Jeanne Crain, John Payne)

The Taker (GB, TF, Bradford Dillman, Laraine Day, Estelle Winwood)

The Inquiry (RS, Barry Sullivan, Jack Kelly, Gia Scala)

Shine On, Shine On, Jesse Gil (TF, Darren McGavin, Juliet Prowse)

Nightmare (RS, Martin Balsam, Troy Donahue)

The White Birch (GB, Boris Karloff, Lilia Skala, Roddy McDowall)

An Agent for the Plaintiff (GB, Honor Blackman, Maurice Evans)

The Protector (GB, Robert Young, Anne Baxter, Ralph Meeker)

High on a Rainbow (RS, June Allyson, Broderick Crawford, Van Johnson)

Lola in Lipstick (GB, Ed Begley, Dana Wynter, William Windom)

Incident in Berlin (GB, Kevin McCarthy, Dane Clark, Geraldine Brooks)

The Suntan Mob (RS, Suzanne Pleshette, Wilfred Hyde White)

Collectors' Edition (TF, John Saxon, Senta Berger, Nina Foch, Paul Lukas)

The Revolutionary (GB, Harry Guardino, Simon Oakland)

The Third Choice (GB, Shirley Jones, Ossie Davis)

Swingers Only (RS, Robert Lansing, Ann Blyth, Jack Klugman)

Love-in at Ground Zero (GB, Keenan Wynn, Tisha Sterling)

Pineapple Rose (GB, Mel Tormé, Susan Strasberg)

The Black Answer (TF, Abby Lincoln, Ivan Dixon)

The Incomparable Connie Walker (TF, GB, Ivan Dixon, Dina Merrill)

A Wrath of Angels (RS, Ricardo Montalban, Edward Andrews)

Keep the Doctor Away (TF, Robert Goulet, Vera Miles)

Breakout to a Fast Buck (RS, Barry Nelson, Arthur O'Connell)

Give Till It Hurts (RS, Diane Baker, Dennis Weaver)

The Garden (RS, Richard Kiley, Anne Francis, Brenda Scott)

Chains of Command (RS, Sidney Blackmer, Dorothy Lamour, Pernell Roberts)

The Civilized Men (RS, Jack Kelly, Rod Cameron, Jill St John)

The Emissary (GB, Craig Stevens, Charles Boyer)

The Takeover (GB, Anne Baxter, David Sheiner, Michael Ansara)

Brass Ring (RS, Celeste Holm, Van Johnson)

Man of the People (GB, Fernando Lamas, Vera Miles, Robert Alda)

A Hard Case of the Blues (RS, Keenan Wynn, Sal Mineo, Russ Tamblyn)

The Power (RS, William Conrad, Broderick Crawford, Gene Raymond)

The Skin Game (RS, Rossano Brazzi, Suzanne Pleshette)

Goodbye Harry (GB, Darren McGavin, Dane Clark)

Lady on the Rocks (GB, Janice Rule, Nigel Davenport, James R. Justice)

The Tradition (GB, Ina Balin, Nico Minardos)

The Prisoner Within (TF, Steve Forrest, Ron Hayes)

High Card (GB, John Colicos, Gene Raymond, Barry Sullivan)

The Perfect Image (GB, Ida Lupino, Hal Holbrook, Clu Gulager)

Blind Man's Buff (TF, Broderick Crawford, Jack Klugman)

Island of Gold and Precious Stones (TF, Lee Meriwether, Henry Jones)

Laurie Marie (TF, Mark Richman, Antoinette Bower)

The Other Kind of a Spy (TF, Ed Begley, Leslie Nielsen, Joseph Campanella)

The King of Denmark (TF, Joseph Cotten, Margaret Leighton, Noel Harrison)

Echo of a Nightmare (RS, Ricardo Montalban, Arthur Hill)

One of the Girls in Research (GB, Brenda Vaccaro, Will Geer)

Tarot (GB, William Shatner, Luther Adler, Jose Ferrer)

Jenny Wilde Is Drowning (TF, Pamela Franklin, Frank Gorshin)

Aquarius Descending (GB, William Smithers, Arthur Hill, Hermione Gingold)

The Time Is Now (GB, Jack Klugman, Yaphet Kotto, Roscoe Lee Browne)

A Love to Remember (GB, Lee Grant, Ray Milland, J. D. Cannon)

The War Merchants (RS, Robert Wagner, Scott Brady)

The Broken Puzzle (GB, Chuck Connors, Pat Crowley, Alex Dreier)

Battle at Gannon's Bridge (RS, Darren McGavin, Jan Murray, Joan Blondell)

Why I Blew Up Dakota (RS, Jose Ferrer, Carolyn Jones, Clu Gulager)

The Glory Shouter (RS, William Shatner, Dina Merrill, Howard Duff)

So Long, Baby, and Amen (RS, Julie Harris, James Gregory)

All the Old Familiar Faces (GB, Burgess Meredith, Michael Constantin)

The Savage Eye (RS, Pete Duel, Jim Hutton, Marianne Hill)

Cynthia Is Alive and Living in Avalon (GB, Robert Culp, Mickey Rooney, Barbara Feldon)

Little Bear Died Running (Robert Culp, Steve Forrest)

The Enemy Before Us (TF, Orson Welles, Martin Balsam, Katina Paxinou)

A Sister From Napoli (Peter Falk, Geraldine Page, Tom Ewell, Kurt Kasznar)

Beware of the Watchdog (RS, Richard Kiley, Pernell Roberts, Diana Muldaur)

LA 2017 (GB, Barry Sullivan, Edmond O'Brien, Paul Stewart)

The Man Who Killed a Ghost (Robert Wagner, Janet Leigh, David Hartman)

Appointment in Palermo (GB, Brenda Vaccaro, Harry Guardino)

A Capitol Affair (GB, Suzanne Pleshette, Larry Hagman, Mercedes McCambridge)

The Showdown (GB, Warren Oates, Albert Salmi, Jack Albertson)

Seek and Destroy (RS, Leif Erickson, John Vernon, John McGiver)

I Love You, Billy Baker (two parts) (TF, Sammy Davis Jnr, Joey Bishop)

Name That Tune (US 1953–8). Simple half-hour musical quiz for NBC (later CBS). The format duly moved into daytime and turned up in Britain in the seventies as the centrepiece of Thames's *Wednesday Night Out*.

The Name's the Same (US 1951–4). Half-hour quiz show from Goodson–Todman for ABC. A panel had to guess the identity of a guest whose name was the same as that of a famous personage.

Nana (GB 1968; 4 × 50m). BBC costume serial adapted by Robert Muller from Zola's story of a heartless courtesan which aroused male interest, at least, thanks to the heroine's occasional uncostumed scenes. With

Katharine Schofield and Freddie Jones. In 1983 C4 part-financed and screened a French version (6 × 65m) with Véronique Genest as Nana, Guy Tréjan, Patrick Préjean, Albert Simone, and the same attractions, only more so. Written by Maurice Cazenove, produced by Cyril Grize and Armand Tabuteau, for Antenne 2. PP

Nancy
US 1970 17 × 25m colour
NBC/Columbia (Sidney Sheldon)
What it's like to be the 21-year-old daughter of the President.
Whimsical comedy which never gained much attention.
cr Sidney Sheldon
Rennie Jarrett, Celeste Holm, Robert F. Simon, John Fink

The Nancy Drew Mysteries: see The Hardy Boys/Nancy Drew Mysteries

The Nancy Walker Show
US 1976 13 × 25m colour
ABC/Norman Lear/TAT (Rod Parker)
A talent agent has trouble with her family.
Ho-hum star filler.
cr Norman Lear, Rod Parker
Nancy Walker, William Daniels, Ken Olfson, Beverly Archer, William Schallert

The Nanette Fabray Show: see Yes, Yes, Nanette

Nanny * (GB 1981–). Wendy Craig as she in an excellent BBC series set in the heyday of the British nanny, the thirties. Written by Charlotte Bingham and Terence Brady; produced by Guy Slater; for BBC. PP

Nanny and the Professor *
US 1969–71 54 × 25m colour
ABC/TCF (David Gerber)
A widower with three children is helped by a nanny with apparently magical powers.
Second-rate *Mary Poppins* with occasional ingratiating charm.
cr A. J. Carothers
Richard Long, Juliet Mills

Napoleon and Love
GB 1974 9 × 50m colour (VTR)
Thames
Stories of the women in Napoleon's life.
An ambitious series which strangely failed to appeal.
w Philip Mackie
Ian Holm

NARAL. A British ITV trade term meaning Nett Advertising Revenue After Levy, figures which affect the proportional payments of the various independent companies for any programme.

Narizzano, Silvio (c 1927–). Canadian director in Britain. TV highlights include *Death of a Salesman* and *Oscar Wilde on Trial.*

narrowcasting: scheduling programmes aimed at specific limited-interest groups.

The Nashville Grab
US 1981 96m colour TVM
NBC/Taft International (Charles E. Sellier Jnr)
A rock show at a women's prison serves as the cover for a kidnap scheme.
Wild and woolly action comedy full of cornpone clichés and wholesale destruction.
w David O'Malley, Thomas Chapman d James L. Conway ph Paul Hipp m Tom Summers
Jeff Conaway, Cristina Raines, Gary Sandy, Slim Pickens, Henry Gibson

Nashville 99
US 1977 4 × 50m colour
TCF/Ernie Frankel (Richard Newton)
A Nashville police lieutenant is also a farmer when he finds time for it.
Muddled action series with a sentimental side. Four episodes were made as a try-out and that was it.
d Andrew V. McLaglen
Claude Akins, Lucille Benson, Jeannine Riley, Jerry Reed

National Broadcasting Company: see NBC

The National Dream *
Canada 1975 6 × 50m colour (16mm)
CBC/BBC
The story of the building of the Canadian Pacific Railroad, as described in Pierre Berton's book.

National Educational Television: see NET

National Velvet
US 1960–1 58 × 25m bw
NBC/MGM
A girl brought up with horses dreams of winning the Grand National.
Well-made, thinly scripted stories for well-brought-up children; from the movie and Enid Bagnold's book.
Lori Martin, Ann Doran, James McCallion, Arthur Space

The Nation's Health
GB 1983 4 × 90m
Euston Films/Thames (Irving Teitelbaum) for C4
A young woman doctor is witness to (1) a hospital surgical team whose work is either careless or vainglorious, more interested in prestige than the welfare of the patient; (2) a family doctor of the old school struggling to give his patients proper care; (3) an aged couple separated by insensitive geriatric care and hospital closures; (4) a teenager confined in a psychiatric ward over-relying on drugs and expensive technology but again handicapped by NHS cutbacks.
G. F. Newman's fourfold swipe at consultants, hospital administrators and much medical practice on the one hand, and at National Health Service economies on the other, might have been more persuasive if anyone had realized these two attacks to some extent cancel each other out. If the health care favoured by the NHS is so wrong, cut-backs can only mean an improvement. It would also have helped if he hadn't made his heroes all saintly while equipping his villains – the surgeons for instance – with such comically unpleasant side-traits as gluttony or racism.
w G. F. Newman d Les Blair
Vivienne Ritchie   PP
† Each play was followed the next evening by a discussion *Follow the Nation's Health*, chaired by Joan Shenton, produced by Meditel Productions for C4.

Nationwide. BBC early evening magazine programme built on contributions from the regions as well as London, fairly silly in tone, which ran until 1984, when replaced by the *Six O'Clock News* and regional news magazines.

'The greatest family story of all time. A man, a woman, and the child who changed the world!'
The Nativity
US 1979 96m colour TVM
ABC/TCF/D'Angelo–Bullock–Allen (William P. D'Angelo)
Joseph courts Mary against a background of anti-Roman revolution in Israel.
Stolid biblical semi-spectacular.
w Millard Kaufman, Mort Fine d Bernard Kowalski ph Gabor Pogany m Lalo Schifrin
Madeleine Stowe, John Shea, Jane Wyatt, Paul Stewart, Audrey Totter, George Voskovec, Julie Garfield, Freddie Jones, John Rhys-Davies, Morgan Sheppard

The Natural World. Regular British wildlife programme from BBC Bristol which has also produced some remarkable specials – *On the Eighth Day* (1984) about the nuclear winter which would follow nuclear war, *On the Edge of the Sand* (1985) about Edward Lear, and the two-part *Kingdom of the Ice Bear* (also 1985). That was produced by Mike Salisbury and Hugh Miles. Series editor Peter Jones.   PP

Nature Watch (GB 1981–2; 26 × 30m). Natural history and wildlife series which surveyed these subjects by focusing each week on a different naturalist, with Julian Pettifer as intermediary. 'An original and intriguing angle to take,' said the *Daily Express*, 'since the personalities interviewed turn out every bit as colourful and exciting as the plants and animals.' Produced by Robin Brown, for Central.

† A further series followed in 1986.   PP

Natwick, Mildred (1908–). American character actress seen too seldom; at her best in eccentric roles. One of THE SNOOP SISTERS (Emmy 1973); also in *Do Not Fold, Spindle or Mutilate* and *Money to Burn*.

Naughton, James (1945–). American leading man. Series: *Faraday and Company*, *Planet of the Apes*. TV movie: *The Bunker*.

Navy Log
US 1955–7 102 × 25m bw
CBS/Sam Gallu
Anthology of stories about the navy, with guest stars.
Competent flagwaver.

NBC. National Broadcasting Company, one of America's three major networks; an offshoot of RCA, its progress has been dogged and competent rather than sparkling, and its innovations have often been further developed by competitors. It introduced early-morning and late-night talk shows, TV movies, press conferences, two-man newscasts, mini-series and longform series such as *Mystery Movie*.

Neal, Patricia (1926–). American character actress. TV movies: *The Homecoming*, *Things in Their Season*, *Eric*, *Tail Gunner Joe*, *A Love Affair*, *The Bastard*, *All Quiet on the Western Front*. The story of her recovery from a brain seizure was told in *The Patricia Neal Story* (*Pat and Roald*) in 1981.

Nearest and Dearest
GB 1968–72 47 × 25m colour (VTR)
Granada
When the aged owner of a Lancashire pickle factory dies, the ne'er-do-well son returns to help his frumpish maiden sister.
Archetypal north country farce borrowed from Stanley Price's *The Dear Departed* and later itself plagiarized for the John Inman series *Odd Man In*. Undoubted lavatory humour, its vulgarity had a certain vigour. An American version was attempted under the title *Thicker than Water*.
Hylda Baker, Jimmy Jewel, Joe Baldwin

The Nearly Man *
GB 1974 53m colour (16mm)
Granada (Peter Eckersley)
An erstwhile socialist intellectual MP finds himself on the rocks in middle age.
Vivid, fairly absorbing character drama.
w Arthur Hopcraft *d* John Irvin
TONY BRITTON, Ann Firbank, Michael Elphick, Wilfred Pickles
'It unmercifully strips the superficial glint from the life of a politician.' – *Daily Express*
† Broadcasting Guild award, best play.
†† A series of 7 × 50m plays followed.

Nedwell, Robin (1946–). British comedy actor seen in LWT's 'Doctor' series.

Needham, Hal (1931–). American director, former stunt man. TV movies: *Death Car on the Freeway*, *Stunts*.

Needles and Pins
US 1973 14 × 25m colour
NBC/Columbia/David Gerber (Herb Wallerstein)
An American *Rag Trade*, set in a dress manufacturer's workroom in New York's garment district.
A little more realistic than most American comedies, but not to the public taste.
cr Adele and Burt Styler *m* Marvin Hamlisch
Norman Fell, Deirdre Lenihan, Louis Nye, Bernie Kopell, Sandra Dee

❋ **Negus, Arthur** (1903–85). Genial British commentator on antiques in programmes of the sixties and seventies: GOING FOR A SONG, *Antiques Roadshow*, etc. Birthday tribute *Arthur Negus at Eighty* from the BBC, 1983, *Arthur Negus Enjoys*, BBC2 1983.

Nelson **
GB 1966 78m bw
ATV (Cecil Clarke)

Terence Rattigan's play about the great hero to the suggestion of Prince Philip and later expanded for the stage as *A Bequest to the Nation*. The period is the last brief sojourn in England before Trafalgar, when Nelson is enjoying connubial bliss with Lady Hamilton to the chagrin of poor Lady Nelson. How could a hero renowned for his grace behave so ungraciously towards his wife? 'Rattigan's explanation was that he was driven to it by Lady Nelson's relentless forgivingness – "Jesus taught us how to answer a blow on the cheek, but how do you answer a kiss?"

'With Rachel Roberts as an over-ripe, whoopee Emma Hamilton, Celia Johnson as poor Lady N and Michael Bryant in a stunning impersonation of the central character.' Directed by Stuart Burge.   PP

† In 1982 Cecil Clarke returned to the subject with the series *I Remember Nelson* written by Hugh Whitemore, who preferred to ascribe Nelson's ungallant behaviour to the scars of war.

Nelson, Ed (1928–   ).
American general purpose actor who came to the fore as Mr Rossi in *Peyton Place* and was subsequently starred in *The Silent Force*. TV movies include *A Little Game*, *The Screaming Woman*, *Tenafly*, *Runaway*, *Linda*, *The Missing Are Deadly*, *Murder in Peyton Place*, *Superdome*, *Leave Yesterday Behind*, *Crash*, *Anatomy of a Seduction*.

Nelson, Gene (1923–   ) (Leander Berg).
American dancer who turned director and did some good TV work, especially *Washington Behind Closed Doors*. TV movies: *Wake Me When the War Is Over*, *The Letters*.

Nelson, Ozzie (1906–75).
Unassuming American bandleader who with his wife Harriet Hilliard and their children starred for nearly 20 years in the archetypal domestic series *The Adventures of Ozzie and Harriet*. He made a small comeback in *Ozzie's Girls*.

The Neon Ceiling *
US 1970 97m colour TVM
Universal (William Sackheim)

A runaway wife and her daughter take temporary refuge in a desert shack with a colourful dropout.
Talkative but ingratiating and very well acted three character drama.

w Carol Sobieski, Henri Simoun   d Frank Pierson

GIG YOUNG, LEE GRANT (Emmy 1970), Denise Nickerson

Nero Wolfe
US 1977 96m colour TVM
ABC/Paramount/Emmet Lavery Jnr
(Everett Chambers)

The orchid-loving detective investigates the apparent persecution of a lady tycoon.
Meticulous televersion of a literary sleuth; not exciting, but restful to watch.

w/d Frank Gilroy, *novel The Doorbell Rang* by Rex Stout   ph Ric Waite   m Leonard Rosenman

Thayer David, Tom Mason, Anne Baxter, Brooke Adams, Biff McGuire, John Randolph, David Hurst, John Hoyt

'The production should have pleased the late author.' – *Daily Variety*

† For inscrutable reasons the movie was not played until 1979, and then after midnight. In 1980 a 50m series began on NBC with William Conrad and Lee Horsley. Unsuccessful in ratings terms, it was produced by Ivan Goff and Ben Roberts and ran to only 13 episodes.

NET. National Educational Television: the company which supplies programmes for America's public broadcasting channel.

network. In America, one of the major broadcasting organizations which commissions and broadcasts programmes in prime time through its chain of affiliated stations. In Britain, usually refers to the ITV (commercial) channel, where a programme is said to be networked if all the stations (i.e. the entire country) are taking it.

Nevada Smith
US 1975 74m colour TVM
MGM/Martin Rackin

Thin pilot with the hero a wandering, sometimes revengeful, do-gooder.

w John Michael Hayes, Martin Rackin   d Gordon Douglas

Cliff Potts, Lorne Greene

Never a Cross Word (GB 1968).
Marital comedy series from LWT involving Nyree Dawn Porter, Paul Daneman and all the usual muddles.   PP

Never Mind the Quality, Feel the Width
GB 1967–9 27 × 25m colour (VTR)
Thames

Manny Cohen and Patrick Kelly run a tailoring business in London's east end.
Friendly farce comedy with all the expected ethnic jokes.

w Vince Powell, Harry Driver
Joe Lynch, John Bluthal

Never the Twain (GB 1981). Half-hour comedy series about two antique dealers who can't end their feud even when their children fall in love. With Donald Sinden, Windsor Davies. Written by Johnnie Mortimer; directed and produced by Peter Frazer-Jones; for Thames.

The New Adventures of Batman
US 1977 15 × 22m colour
Filmation (Don Christensen)
A cartoon version using the voices of Adam West and Burt Ward.

The New Adventures of Charlie Chan
GB 1957 39 × 25m bw
Vision/ITC
Rather scruffy cases for the oriental detective, with a star plainly unhappy in the role.
J. Carrol Naish

The New Adventures of Gilligan
US 1974 17 × 22m colour
Filmation
A cartoon version using the voices of the *Gilligan's Island* stars.

The New Adventures of Heidi
US 1979 96m colour TVM
NBC/Pierre Cossette/Max Appelbaum (Charles B. FitzSimons)
A sweet child sent to live with her grandfather in the mountains puts various people's problems to rights.
Styleless rehash of an old, old vehicle, this time with songs added. Not a starter.
w John McGreevey *d* Ralph Senensky *ph* John Nickolaus *m/ly* Buz Kohan
Burl Ives, Katy Kurtzman, John Gavin, Marlyn Mason, Sean Marshall, Charles Aidman

The New Adventures of Huck Finn *
US 1968 20 × 25m colour
NBC/Hanna–Barbera
Not much to do with Mark Twain, more about three kids who go through caves to various fantasy lands, but an ingenious blending of live actors and cartoon backgrounds.
Michael Shea, Ted Cassidy

The New Adventures of Lucky Jim (GB 1967). Pallid BBC sitcom owing little to Kingsley Amis's immortal misfit and failing to benefit, either, from scripts by Dick Clement and Ian La Frenais. With Keith Barron. PP
† *The Further Adventures of Lucky Jim* followed in 1982, 7 × 30m, again written by Clement and La Frenais, with Enn Reitel, Glynis Barber; produced by Harold Snoad, for BBC.

The New Adventures of Martin Kane: see Martin Kane, Private Eye

The New Adventures of Perry Mason
US 1973 13 × 50m colour
CBS/Cornwall Jackson/TCF
The old sleuthing and courtroom format simply didn't work with even a touch of realism added, and different actors (perhaps because they were *better* actors) were resented. See *Perry Mason.*
Monte Markham, Harry Guardino, Sharon Acker, Dane Clark

The New Andy Griffith Show
US 1972 10 × 25m colour
CBS/Ada
Problems for the mayor of a small town in North Carolina.
A format which didn't work for a star who needed one that did.
Andy Griffith, Lee Meriwether, Marty McCall

The New Breed
US 1961 36 × 50m bw
Quinn Martin/Selmur/ABC
Activities of a select squad of the Los Angeles Police.
Competent, forgettable cop show.
Leslie Nielsen, John Beradino, Greg Roman, John Clark

The New Daughters of Joshua Cabe
US 1976 74m colour TVM
Spelling–Goldberg
Josh is unjustly imprisoned on a murder charge and his three 'daughters' evolve an escape plan. Tired time-filler.
w Paul Savage *d* Bruce Bilson
John McIntire, Jeanette Nolan, Jack Elam, Liberty Williams, Renne Jarrett, Lezlie Dalton
† See also *The Daughters of Joshua Cabe.*

The New Dick Van Dyke Show
US 1971–3 72 × 25m colour
CBS/Cave Creek (Dick Van Dyke)
Our hero is now an Arizona disc jockey who enjoys the simple life. (The third season moved him to Hollywood but did not repair falling ratings.)
A sequel that failed to equal its predecessor. Perhaps the supporting cast wasn't right; or perhaps the star was just a little too old. See *The Dick Van Dyke Show.*

Dick Van Dyke, Hope Lange, Barbara Rush, Dick Van Patten, Henry Darrow, Richard Dawson, Chita Rivera, Marty Brill, Fannie Flagg

New Faces
GB 1973–8 100 approx. × 55m colour (VTR)
ATV

Long-running talent scout show in which new professional acts are judged by a panel of showbiz personalities.

host Derek Hobson

The New Healers
aka: *The Paramedics*; *The Storm*
US 1972 74m colour TVM
Paramount

Three ex-armed-forces medical students help the doctor of a rural area and are accepted after a flood.
Predictable, watchable medico-action drama which didn't make a series.

w Sterling Silliphant *d* Bernard L. Kowalski
Leif Erickson, Kate Johnson, Robert Foxworth, Jonathan Lippe, Burgess Meredith, William Windom

The New Land *
US 1974 15 × 50m colour
ABC/Warner/William Blinn (Philip Leacock)

Scandinavian immigrants scrape a living in 1850s Minnesota.
Earnest outdoor dramas inspired by the Swedish film.

Scott Thomas, Bonnie Bedelia, Kurt Russell, Donald Moffat

The New Loretta Young Show (US 1962).
Half-hour comedy drama series for CBS. The star, previously so successful as hostess of an anthology (see *The Loretta Young Show*) lasted only one season in a firm format as a widow with seven children.

The New Maverick
US 1968 96m colour TVM
ABC/Warner/Meta Rosenberg

Conmen Bret and Bart Maverick emerge from retirement to help their second cousin.
As a comeback try, this seems like much ado about nothing, as it doesn't have either the style of the original series or anything to offer in its place.

w Juanita Bartlett *d* Hy Averback *ph* Andrew Jackson *m* John Rubinstein

James Garner, Jack Kelly, Charles Frank, Susan Blanchard, Eugene Roche, Woodrow Parfrey

'Better to take all the talents involved and move on to something else.' – *Daily Variety*
† See also *Maverick, Bret Maverick.*

The New Original Wonder Woman
US 1975 74m colour TVM
Warner/Douglas S. Cramer

See *Wonder Woman*. More nonsense adventures, slightly more firmly strung together with a World War II backdrop.

w Stanley Ralph Ross *d* Leonard Horn
Lynda Carter, Cloris Leachman, Lyle Waggoner, Red Buttons, Stella Stevens, Kenneth Mars, John Randolph

The New Pacific (GB 1985; 8 × 60m).
Up-to-date survey of an unregarded part of the world as it is transformed by Japanese hi-tech industries, cut-price tourism and US military needs. Produced by Mike McIntyre, for BBC.   PP

The New People
US 1969 17 × 50m colour
ABC/Spelling–Thomas/Rod Serling (Harold Gast)

Survivors of a plane crash make a new life on a deserted island where an abandoned town once housed atom test personnel.
Idealistic youth hokum, vaguely political and rather dull. The idea had been tried several times before.

cr Aaron Spelling, Larry Gordon
Richard Kiley, Tiffany Bolling, Lee Jay Lambert, Kevin Michaels, Brenda Sykes, David Moses

The New Phil Silvers Show
US 1963 30 × 25m bw
CBS/Gladasaya/United Artists (Rod Amateau)

Ruses of a conniving factory foreman.
Eagerly awaited sequel to *Bilko*, with none of the old spark.

Phil Silvers, Herbie Faye, Elena Verdugo

The New Temperatures Rising: see
Temperatures Rising

New York Confidential
US 1958 39 × 25m bw
ITC

Stories of an adventurous newspaper columnist.
Walter Winchell, more or less; but even the real Winchell couldn't make it on TV.

Lee Tracy

The Newcomers (GB 1964). John Boorman's follow-up to *Citizen '63*, and last series (for BBC) before going off to make feature films, broke new ground attempting to shape the goings-on of a young husband and wife and their friends into a superior, real-life soap opera. The shaping process was unhappily noticeable at times, as when the hero's going in to bat in a friendly cricket match was dressed up to evoke Alan Ladd taking on the gunfighter in *Shane*. The chosen community of Bristol literati was also a little precious. By the time the pregnant wife had finally been delivered of twins, however, a certain spell was being exerted. The couple were Anthony and Alison Smith, their twins will now be grown up, but whatever happened to their best friend? He was a local newspaper reporter called Tom Stoppard. Ten years later the idea of the programme was re-invented for the hideous *The Family*. In 1966 the title was also used for a conventional BBC soap opera set among new residents in an expanding community.   PP

Newell, Mike (19 –). British drama director associated with improvisation but with many scripted plays and films to his credit, including *Bad Blood* (1981).   PP

Newhart *
US 1982–   × 25m colour TVM
CBS/MTM (Sheldon Bull)

A New Yorker takes over an old dilapidated Connecticut inn.

The star is always worth watching, but as a vehicle, despite its quota of laughs and wisdom, this format proved slightly disappointing.

BOB NEWHART, Mary Frann, Steven Kampmann, Jenniefer Holmes, Tom Poston

'A comedian who was made for television, effortlessly practising a perfected style.' – Robert MacKenzie, *TV Guide*

Newhart, Bob (1929–). American comedian who usually plays the underdog. *The Bob Newhart Show* ran 144 episodes from 1972, with the star as a psychiatrist and Suzanne Pleshette as his wife; produced by MTM for CBS. In 1982 MTM produced another series simply called *Newhart*, with the star taking over a dilapidated Connecticut inn (see below); despite variable material, it ran for three seasons.

Newington, Peter (19 –). British director who whizzed to notice with *Monitor* arts films in the late fifties and sixties, made *The Picardy Affair* with Robert Hardy and

then dropped out of sight as a film teacher at the Royal College of Art. Has re-emerged lately to direct the jazz documentary *Whatever Happened to Bill Brunskill?*, 1984.
    PP

Newland, John (*c* 1916–). American actor and director best remembered as the cold-eyed host of ONE STEP BEYOND.

Newley, Anthony (1931–). Hard-to-take British vocalizer, formerly a likeable teenage star. Mainly concert appearances plus one early series, *The Strange World of Gurney Slade*.

The Newlywed Game (US 1967–70). Half-hour quiz show for ABC in which host Bob Eubanks asked young husbands questions about their wives (and vice versa) while the spouse was out of earshot. The format went on to daytime, and was adapted in Britain in the seventies by Border TV as *Mr and Mrs*.

Newman, Barry (1939–). American general purpose actor who starred in the movie *The Lawyer*, then in the same role did a TV pilot *Night Games* and finally ran two seasons with it as *Petrocelli*.

Newman, G. F. (19 –). Formidable British writer best known – if not loved – for his accusatory blockbusters *Law and Order* (1978) and *The Nation's Health* (1983). In between came the sensitive *Billy*, about child-battering, produced by Kenith Trodd, directed by Charles Stewart.   PP

❊   **Newman, Sydney** (*c* 1915–). Canadian drama producer, formerly commercial artist, who earned his medals producing live CBC dramas (e.g. *Flight into Danger*) to compete with the American networks available to 80 per cent of the Canadian audience. Lured to Britain first as producer of ABC Armchair Theatre (1958–63) and then BBC drama supervisor (1963–8), he revolutionized the TV play scene by encouraging topical social realism. Also receptive to science fiction and sketched out the initial idea and characters for *Doctor Who*.

Returned to Canada as a Film Commissioner and chairman of the National Film Board, but came back to Britain in 1985 to produce two series for C4.   PP

News at Ten. In Britain, ITN's main news bulletin since 1967, when it went up to a full half-hour for the first time and borrowed the American practice of sharing the load between two newscasters.   PP

The News on Good Friday (GB 1960; 20m; bw). Christ's crucifixion, and events leading thereto, as if reported on a TV newscast of the day, with eye-witness accounts, statements by Pilate and Barabbas, random street interviews and – back in Rome – the Emperor summing up the Middle Eastern situation now that this little local disturbance had been cleared up. 'Things,' he said, 'look pretty good.' Smart little Easter special, written by Christopher Hollis; for ATV.   PP

Newsnight. BBC2's Monday–Thursday late evening news summary plus special reports or interviews, launched 1980 though reviving a title used earlier in the seventies. On Fridays *Newsweek* takes a deeper look at one topic. PP

Newth, Jonathan (19 –). Sensitive British actor, lately at his best in *Accounts* and *Missing from Home*, less happily off in *The Fainthearted Feminist*.   PP

Newton-John, Olivia (1948–). British singer in international shows and films; several TV specials.

A Nice Pleasant Deadly Weekend
aka: *A Masterpiece of Murder*
US 1986 96m colour TVM
TCF/Andrew J. Fenady (Terry Morse)

A security detective and an ex-cat burglar join forces to solve a murder.

Drawn out vehicle for the stars whose average age is 80 plus.

w Andrew J. Fenady, Terry Nation
d Charles S. Dubin

Bob Hope, Don Ameche, Jayne Meadows, Yvonne de Carlo, Jamie Farr, Anne Francis, Kevin McCarthy, Stella Stevens

Nice Time **** (GB 1968). At first a silly-season fill-in in the Granada region only, eventually promoted to the network. The funniest, most inventive, least consequential entertainment of all time. In theory it was supposed to answer viewers' requests for favourite moments from comic movies, etc. In practice the team of Jonathan Routh, Kenny Everett and the then unknown Warwick University lecturer Germaine Greer engineered such bizarre turns as an Oxford and Cambridge boat race rowed on a seedy canal

between a Mr Oxford and a Mr Cambridge, massed ventriloquists' dummies singing 'Congratulations' and a chorus of male soprani, in kepis and baggy pants, rendering the Legionnaires' hymn from *The Desert Song.* Produced by Mike Murphy and JOHN BIRT.   PP

LH: 'It had its (occasional) moments, but I can't see how it could justify more than two stars.'

Nichols *
US 1971 26 × 50m colour
NBC/Warner/Cherokee (Meta Rosenberg)

Stories of the motorcycling sheriff of a small western town in 1915.

Easy-going semi-western littered up with too many cute characters and ideas (such as killing off the hero and bringing back his 'tougher' twin brother).

James Garner, Neva Patterson, Margot Kidder, Stuart Margolin, John Beck

Nichols, Dandy (1907–86). British character actress who became a national character as Alf Garnett's wife Else in TILL DEATH US DO PART. Reappeared 1985 in *In Sickness and in Health.*

Nichols, Mike (1931–) (Michael Igor Peschkowsky). American film director who began as a TV cabaret turn and later was executive producer of the series *Family.*

Nichols, Peter (1927–). British dramatist who emerged via a contest for new TV writers and quickly became one of the funniest and most inventive on the scene, until his success in the theatre and a growing disaffection with the naturalism required of television drama dried up his enthusiasm. An autobiographical series planned for 1980 under the title *Mixed Feelings* (BBC) never materialized. Plays produced:
1959 *A Walk on the Grass*; BBC
     PROMENADE; Granada
1961 BEN SPRAY; Granada
     The Reception; Granada
     The Big Boys; BBC
1963 *The Continuity Man*; BBC
     BEN AGAIN; Granada
     The Heart of the Country; ATV
     The Hooded Terror; ATV
1964 *The Brick Umbrella*; ATV
1965 *When the Wind Blows*; ATV
1968 *Daddy Kiss It Better*; YTV
     THE GORGE; BBC1 Wednesday Play
     Majesty (based on a story by F. Scott Fitzgerald in series *The Jazz Age*); BBC2

Winner Takes All (based on a story by Evelyn Waugh in series *The Jazz Age*); BBC2

HEARTS AND FLOWERS; BBC1 Play for Today

1972 *Ben Spray* (revival); LWT Sunday Night Theatre
1973 THE COMMON; BBC1 Play of the Month
1975 *Forget-Me-Not Lane* (TV version); BBC1 Playhouse   PP

Nicholson, Mavis (1930–). British presenter, mainly of daytime programmes such as *Afternoon Plus*.

Nielsen, Leslie (1925–). Tall Canadian actor often seen as villain or weakling. A frequent guest star; series include *The Bold Ones*, *The New Breed*, *Bracken's World*. TV movies include *See How They Run*, *Shadow over Elveron*, *Companions in Nightmare*, *Trial Run*, *Deadlock*, *Night Slaves*, *The Aquarians*, *Hauser's Memory*, *They Call It Murder*, *Snatched*, *The Letters*, *Can Ellen Be Saved*, *Brink's: The Great Robbery*, *Little Mo*, *Backstairs at the White House*, *Institute for Revenge*, *Cave In*, *The Night the Bridge Fell*.

Nielsens. American Nielsen ratings supplied by the A. C. Nielsen Company. In each area a statistical sample of homes is supplied with an audimeter which records what channel, if any, is being watched during each minute. This information is converted into graph form and a rating and share of audience produced for each programme.

Night Chase
US 1970 100m colour TVM
Cinema Center 100 (Collier Young)

A wealthy businessman on the run from police is nearly trapped in Los Angeles.
Overlong chase melodrama with attractive locations.

w Marvin A. Gluck *d* Jack Starrett *ph* Fred J. Koenekamp *m* Laurence Rosenthal

David Janssen, Yaphet Kotto, Victoria Vetri, Elisha Cook Jnr, Joe de Santis

Night Conspirators
GB 1962 50m bw

Ingenious chiller by Robert Muller about a senile Adolf Hitler smuggled back to Germany after holing up in Iceland since 1945, worked out with excitement and a kind of harsh logic which indicated that the nightmare ending was to be taken as a cautionary tale rather than an objective piece of make-believe. Directed by Philip Saville; produced by Sydney Newman; for ABC (*Armchair Theatre*).   PP

Night Court
US 1984   × 25m colour
NBC/Warner/Starry Night (Reinhold Weege)

An extremely unorthodox young man is appointed night court judge.
Zany, slightly black comedy which is more tiresome than funny.

cr Reinhold Weege

Harry Anderson, Karen Austin, John Larroquette, Selma Diamond, Gail Strickland, Richard Moll

Night Cries
US 1977 96m colour TVM
ABC/Charles Fries

A woman is tormented by cries which seem to be those of her own dead baby.
Watchable suspense melodrama.

w Brian Taggert *d* Richard Lang

Susan St James, William Conrad, Michael Parks, Dolores Dorn, Cathleen Nesbitt, Diana Douglas

Night Gallery *
US 1969 98m colour TVM
NBC/Universal (William Sackheim)

Three short stories of the supernatural, introduced by Rod Serling through paintings.
Not a bad package: the first is the best.

w Rod Serling *d* Boris Sagal, Steven Spielberg, Barry Shear

Ossie Davis, George Macready, Roddy McDowall, Joan Crawford, Barry Sullivan, Richard Kiley, Sam Jaffe

† The one-hour series which followed kept the same format and ran to 28 episodes, followed by about 50 half-hours. It repeated most of the plots from *Twilight Zone*.

Night Games
US 1974 74m colour TVM
Paramount (Thomas L. Miller, Edward J. Milkis)

A small-town lawyer defends a socialite on a murder charge.
The pilot for the series *Petrocelli*; routine competence in all departments.

w E. Jack Neuman *d* Don Taylor *m* Lalo Schifrin

Barry Newman, Susan Howard, Albert Salmi, Stefanie Powers, Anjanette Comer, Ralph Meeker, Henry Darrow

Night Heat
Canada 1985–   × 50m colour
Grosso Jacobson Productions

Police detectives operate the night shift in a big city.

Filmed in Toronto, this gritty melodrama has the advantage of two producers who were well-known city cops: Sonny Grosso and Eddie Egan. Otherwise it seems rather less remarkable than *Hill Street Blues*.

Scott Hylands, Allan Royal, Jeff Wincott, Susan Hogan

Night of Terror *
US 1972 73m colour TVM
Paramount (Edward J. Milkis)

A young woman is terrorized by an unknown assailant.

Nothing new, but plenty of suspense and inventive use of locations.

d Jeannot Szwarc

Donna Mills, Eddie Egan, Martin Balsam, Chuck Connors, Agnes Moorehead

A Night Out * (GB 1960). Tom Bell as a young clerk who goes berserk first from the nagging of his possessive mother, then from the chattering girl he picks up on his bid for freedom – the night out of the title. ABC claimed it as Harold Pinter's first TV play though the author lists a radio version first in *Who's Who*. What is incontrovertible and impressive is that a comedy by a notoriously 'difficult' writer was the first play ever to head the Top Ten ratings for the week. Pinter played a small part himself. Also with Madge Ryan, Vivien Merchant, Arthur Lowe. Directed by Philip Saville; produced by Sydney Newman; for ABC (*Armchair Theatre*).   PP

'By day, they're two average housewives. At night, they're out looking for trouble. The problem is they just might find it!'
Night Partners
US 1983 96m colour TVM
CBS/ITC/Moonlight (Robert M. Sertner)

Two Bakersfield housewives volunteer to help crime victims in times of stress.

Over-melodramatized fiction based on a scheme which is working well in parts of America.

w Judy Merl, Paul Eric Myers   *d* Noel Nossek   *ph* Isidore Mankofsky   *m* Fred Karlin

Yvette Mimieux, Diana Canova, Arlen Dean Snyder, Larry Linville, M. Emmet Walsh, Patricia McCormack, Dick Anthony Williams

'CBS in one fell swoop unravels any good Cagney and Lacey might have done for the femme cause in the police line-up; these poor dears couldn't make it at knitting.' –
Daily Variety

Night Rider
US 1978 74m colour TVM
ABC/Universal/Stephen J. Cannell
(J. Rickley Dumm)

Brought up by a rich woman, Chock Hollister poses as a fop to revenge himself on those who orphaned him.

Shades of the Scarlet Pimpernel, Zorro, the Count of Monte Cristo and the Lone Ranger! Mildly entertaining pastiche.

w Stephen J. Cannell   *d* Hy Averback   *ph* Steve Poster   *m* Mike Post, Pete Carpenter

David Selby, Percy Rodrigues, Pernell Roberts, George Grizzard, Anna Lee, Van Williams, Hildy Brooks

**Night School ** ** (GB 1960). Young man puts territory (his room) before romance (girl lodger) and realizes too late that he has won the wrong contest. At the time I found it 'funny, perceptive and finally rather wistful'. One of the two Harold Pinter TV plays embodying the word 'Night' in ·the title which went out within four months of each other and helped establish him as a leading dramatist in all outlets. Directed by Joan Kemp-Welch; produced by Peter Willes; for A–R.   PP
† Willes re-produced the play for YTV in 1978.

Night Slaves *
US 1970 74m colour TVM
Bing Crosby Productions (Everett Chambers)

In a small peaceful hotel, a man wakes up to find that his wife has been abducted by alien forces which have taken over the town.

Unexpected, intriguing sci-fi.

w Everett Chambers, Robert Specht   *d* Ted Post

James Franciscus, Lee Grant, Leslie Nielsen, Tisha Sterling, Andrew Prine

The Night Stalker *
US 1971 73m colour TVM
Aaron Spelling

A vampire stalks Las Vegas.

Horror comic with a sense of humour. (See also below.)

w Richard Matheson   *d* John Llewellyn Moxey
m Robert Cobert

Darren McGavin, Carol Lynley, Simon Oakland, Claude Akins, Charles McGraw, Barry Atwater, Elisha Cook Jnr, Kent Smith

The Night Strangler *
US 1972 74m colour TVM
Aaron Spelling/Dan Curtis

The reporter who tracked down the night stalker turns his attention to Seattle and a multi-murderer 120 years old.

More horror nonsense, rather less effective than before, but highly watchable. The two films led to a monster series called *Kolchak: The Night Stalker* (which made no sense); a more stylish pilot had been tried in *The Norliss Tapes*.

w Richard Matheson d Dan Curtis m Robert Cobert

Darren McGavin, Jo Ann Pflug, Simon Oakland, Scott Brady, Margaret Hamilton, Wally Cox, John Carradine

Night Terror
US 1977 74m colour TVM
Charles Fries/NBC

A woman has to flee for her life because she has witnessed a murder.

Old-hat screamer, very roughly assembled.

w Carl Gabler, Richard De Neut d E. W. Swackhamer m Robert F. Drasnin

Valerie Harper, Richard Romanus, Michael Tolan, Beatrice Manley

The Night That Panicked America *
US 1975 100m colour TVM
Paramount (Anthony Wilson, Joseph Sargent)

An account of Orson Welles's 1938 broadcast of *The War of the Worlds* and the effect it had on the nation.

The studio re-creation is excellent, but the film bogs down when it deals with the domestic dramas, which are totally predictable.

w Nicholas Meyer, Anthony Wilson d Joseph Sargent

Vic Morrow, Cliff de Young, Michael Constantine, Paul Shenar, Walter McGinn, Meredith Baxter, Tom Bosley, Will Geer

The Night the Bridge Fell Down
US 1980 2 × 96m colour
NBT/Warner/Irwin Allen

Eight people including a bank robber are trapped on a collapsing bridge.

When so-called suspense films are as long and tedious as this, San Luis Rey has something to answer for.

w Arthur Weiss, Ray Goldstone, Michael Robert David d George Fenady

James MacArthur, Desi Arnaz Jnr, Char Fontane, Richard M. Filliland, Barbara Rush, Leslie Nielsen, Gregory Sierra, Eve Plumb

The Night the City Screamed
US 1980 96m colour TVM
ABC/Columbia/David Gerber (Mel Swope)

Violence gets out of hand when an electrical storm knocks out a city's power.

Adequate multi-story melodrama: most viewers however will be ten minutes ahead of every incident.

w Larry Brody d Harry Falk

Clifton Davis, David Cassidy, Raymond Burr, Robert Culp, Don Meredith, Linda Purl

The Night They Saved Christmas
US 1984 96m colour TVM
ABC/Robert Halmi

An oil company dynamites territory near the North Pole and also near the central headquarters of Santa Claus.

Childish whimsy which doesn't come off – by a mile.

w James C. Moloney, David Niven Jnr d Jackie Cooper ph David Worth m Charles Gross

Jaclyn Smith, Art Carney, Paul LeMat, Mason Adams, June Lockhart, Paul Williams

'All the charm of a lump of coal.' – *Daily Variety*

The Night They Took Miss Beautiful
US 1977 96m colour TVM
Don Kirshner (George Lefferts)

A plane with five beauty contestants is hi-jacked.

Tediously incompetent caper story.

w George Lefferts d Robert Michael Lewis

Phil Silvers, Gary Collins, Chuck Connors, Henry Gibson, Peter Haskell, Sheree North, Stella Stevens, Gregory Sierra

Nightingale's Boys *
GB 1975 7 × 50m colour (VTR)
Granada (Brian Armstrong)

A schoolmaster on the brink of retirement meets again members of his most remarkable class.

Rather disappointing drama series, the plays being too different in tone for any kind of unity in the *Carnet de Bal* style.

cr Arthur Hopcraft *w* Arthur Hopcraft, Jack Rosenthal, C. P. Taylor, Colin Spencer, John Finch, Alexander Baron *d* Richard Everett, Les Chatfield, Peter Plummer, Roger Tucker, June Howson

Derek Farr

Nightkill
US 1980 96m colour TVM
NBC/Cine Artists (David Gil, Richard Hellman)

A wealthy woman's lover plots to kill her husband.
Uninventive thriller with some spooky house atmosphere.

w Joan Andre, John Case *d* Ted Post *ph* Tony Richmond *m* Gunther Fischer

Robert Mitchum, Jaclyn Smith, Mike Connors, James Franciscus, Fritz Weaver, Sybil Danning

Nightmare *
US 1973 75m colour TVM
Mark Carliner

A man in a Manhattan apartment witnesses a murder and becomes the quarry of the killers. The old old story, excitingly filmed but foolish in detail.

w David Wiltse *d* William Hale *m* Peter Link

Richard Crenna, Patty Duke, Vic Morrow

Nightmare in Badham County
US 1976 96m colour TVM
ABC Circle/Douglas S. Cramer

Two innocent college girls escape from a women's prison farm.
Predictable melodrama.

w Jo Heims *d* John Llewellyn Moxey *m* Charles Bernstein

Deborah Raffin, Lynne Moody, Chuck Connors, Fionnula Flanagan, Tina Louise, Robert Reed, Ralph Bellamy

Nightmare in Chicago
US 1964 80m colour TVM
Universal

A hunted killer finds himself trapped by police road blocks and commits more violence in an attempt to escape from the city.
Rough, occasionally vivid police story which eventually becomes tiresome to watch.

w David Moessinger *d* Robert Altman *m* John Williams

Robert Ridgeley, Charles McGraw, Philip Abbott

† Originally shown as a two-parter.

'There's only one rule: there are no rules!'

Nightside
US 1980 74m colour TVM
ABC/Universal/Stephen J. Cannell/Glen Larson (Alex Beaton)

A nightshift cop on the streets of LA gets a new young partner.
So what else is new? This is a failed pilot which shouldn't even have got to first base.

w Stephen J. Cannell, Glen Larson *d* Bernard Kowalski *ph* Arthur R. Botham *m* John Andrew Tartaglia

Doug McClure, Michael Cornellson, John DeLancie, Roy Jensen, Jason Kincaid

'Screeching brakes, auto crashes and a throbbing score emphasize the inanities.' – *Daily Variety*

Nil Carborundum * (GB 1962). Funny–anarchic picture of RAF life, centred on the cookhouse, by Henry Livings. Though already seen on the stage it was originally written for television and now done by the BBC. Amid all the chicanery and graft and playing at war the true hero was the phlegmatic man of peace (John Thaw) who got on with the job of maintaining human life on the planet, in this case by making tea and knocking up egg and chips. Graham Crowden was a great hit as the wing commander.   PP

Nimmo, Derek (1931–). British comic actor, adept at the bashful curate type which he played to perfection in ALL GAS AND GAITERS, *Oh Brother* and *Oh Father*. Also 'Bertie' in *The World of Wooster*.

Nimoy, Leonard (1931–). American general purpose actor, a rave in STAR TREK as the point-eared outer space denizen Mr Spock. Also appeared in *Mission Impossible*. TV movies: *Rex Harrison Presents Three Stories of Love, Assault on the Wayne, Baffled, The Alpha Caper, The Missing Are Deadly*.

Nine O'Clock News BBC1's main 25m newscast of the day, since 1971 at the hour and on the hour which the old Home Service radio bulletin turned into a national institution during World War II. Though dual presentation was adopted as early as 1973, the newsreaders were not featured as a double act until 1985, when a loony new titles sequence was also introduced, apparently showing intercontinental ballistic missiles homing in on London.   PP

Nine to Five *
US 1982   × 25m colour
ABC/TCF/IPC (Jane Fonda, Bruce Gilbert)

Three secretaries in a giant corporation are constantly at war with their overbearing boss and his office spy.

Despite some offbeat ideas, this slick comedy is more sharply amusing than the feature film from which it sprang.

RITA MORENO, Valerie Curtin, Rachel Dennison, Jeffrey Tambor, Jean Marsh

1911: a Year in Musical History ** (GB 1984; 4 × 90m).
Very bright art-house idea to pick on one year when 20th-century culture was flexing its muscles. After an introductory programme taking in all the arts, Sibelius and Mahler (two programmes) were featured in turn, with Simon Rattle conducting the CBSO. Directed by Barrie Gavin, produced by Kenneth Corden, for BBC.   PP

1915 *
Australia 1982 7 × 50m colour
Australian Broadcasting
  Commission/Lionheart (Ray Alchin)

Small-town rivals for the same girl, one sober, one a tearaway, agree to join up if war comes, and end up at Gallipoli. 'All the now-familiar ingredients of the Australian outback saga are there,' I wrote during the BBC's 3 × 120m presentation, 'and most of the time-honoured elements of the World War romance . . . but I don't remember them knitted together so persuasively and purposefully.'

w Peter Yeldham, novel by Roger McDonald d Chris Thomson ph Peter Hendry m Bruce Smeaton

Scott McGregor, Scott Burgess, Sigrid Thornton, Bill Hunter, Lorraine Bayly, Ilona Rogers

1984 *** (GB 1954).
Famous shocker from George Orwell's gloomy vision of a Stalinist England, with Peter Cushing, Yvonne Mitchell and André Morell, originally transmitted live on a Sunday evening with customary repeat performance mid-week. Faint-hearts and busybodies tried to have the latter cancelled but Michael Barry, then BBC head of drama, held firm and indeed introduced the repeat himself. Produced by Rudolph Cartier. Eleven years later Nigel Kneale's script was given a fresh production with David Buck, Jane Merrow and Joseph O'Conor, which failed to shock anyone. But in the year 1984, when attention was inevitably focused on the book again, a telerecording of Cartier's 1954 production – actually of the Thursday repeat performance – was shown at the National Film Theatre and stunned a predominantly young audience (few would have been born by 1954) into silence and then an ovation. It couldn't be shown again or re-broadcast because the makers of a new movie version had acquired all rights in the story. In Orwellian language, one of TV's great landmarks now unexisted.   PP

See Orwell

1990
GB 1977 16 × 50m colour (VTR)
BBC (Prudence Fitzgerald)

In the last decade of the 20th century in Britain the concept of common good is replacing the rights of the individual.

Not a bad effort, but 1984 said it all much more succinctly.

cr Wilfred Greatorex w Wilfred Greatorex, Edmund Ward, Arden Winch

Edward Woodward, Robert Lang, Yvonne Mitchell, Lisa Harrow, Clive Swift, Tony Doyle, Barbara Kellerman, Paul Hardwick

'The right mixture of honest suspense with growing paranoia.' – Variety

PP: 'An interesting, muted, so far non-violent speculation as to the form a consensus tyranny might take – the best of its genre there has been.'

90 Bristol Court
US 1964 13 × 74m bw
NBC

A trio of unrelated comedies all set in the same apartment block: Harris Against the World, Karen and Tom Dick and Mary. They quickly failed, though Karen was allowed to finish the season.

Niven, David (1909–83).
Debonair British star of international films who in the mid fifties became one of the four stars of Four Star Television and appeared in The David Niven Theatre, The Rogues, etc. Later TV work included The Canterville Ghost, A Man Called Intrepid.

Nixon, David (1919–78).
Bland bald British magician with a deceptively nervous manner; had his own occasional series from the early fifties, and was also a favourite panellist on shows such as What's My Line? and My Wildest Dream.

LEONARD NIMOY is one of those actors known for a single performance, in his case the long-eared Mr Spock in the much revived series *Star Trek*. In one episode he expressed a desire to return to his own planet and spawn, like a salmon. 'But Mr Spock,' expostulated Captain Kirk, 'you're not a fish!' Well, perhaps not quite.

The Nixon Interviews
GB/US 1977 4 × 50m colour

David Frost's celebrated set of sessions with the deposed president, made by his own outfit using local Californian facilities and with Australia, America and BBC backing. Produced by David Frost and John Birt; for Paradine.   PP

Nixon, Richard (1913–). The deposed American president's interviews with David Frost caused an international sensation in the spring of 1977 (see above).

Nizer, Louis (1902–). American show business lawyer, played by George C. Scott in *Fear on Trial*.

No Country for Old Men **
GB 1981 75m colour
BBC (Tristam Powell)

The last angry years of Jonathan Swift in St Patrick's Deanery, Dublin.
A brilliantly detailed and thoroughly depressing re-creation.
w DAVID NOKES d TRISTAM POWELL ph John Hooper m George Fenton
TREVOR HOWARD, Cyril Cusack, James Ellis

No Excuses
GB 1983 7 × 52m plus 52m reprise
Central (Simon Mallin)

Good times and bad times of a female rock star. An ambitious serial with music, which suffered from following too closely on Granada's comparable, though inferior, *Studio*, and even more from an extraordinarily ill-judged, noisome scene early in the run when an old butler was grossly humiliated. By the end I thought it was giving a passable idea of life on the road when, as the heroine said, 'Every night has to be party night, night after night after night,' but the show went into the annals as the graveyard of several reputations.
w Barrie Keeffe d Roy Battersby *songs* Andy J. Clark

Charlotte Cornwell, Donald Sumpter, Alfred Burke, Tony Melody

† Episode 8 was a reprise of the musical numbers only, under the title *Encore*. Another sequel was the High Court libel case in 1985 when Charlotte Cornwell was awarded £10,000 damages against TV critic Nina Miskow who said, among other things, that the star's bottom was too big.   PP

No Fixed Abode *
GB 1959 50m bw (VTR)

Clive Exton's classic first play, set in a common lodging house or 'Spike'. With Wilfrid Brambell, Michael Gwynn, Jack Hedley, Jack Rodney. Directed by James Ormerod; produced by Philip Mackie; for Granada.   PP

No Hiding Place *
GB 1959–66 170 approx. × 50m bw (VTR)
Associated Rediffusion (Ray Dicks)

Favourite, straightforward Scotland Yard mystery series, with Raymond Francis as Superintendent Lockhart and Eric Lander as his assistant. Clean if not very clever.

† Eric Lander was promoted after three seasons into his own series, *Echo Four Two*, but it was shortlived.

No, Honestly. A comedy format presented by LWT in 1974, from scripts by Charlotte Bingham. Much in the manner of Burns and

Allen, John Alderton and Pauline Collins, as patient husband and scatty wife, topped and tailed a comedy sketch by speaking directly to the audience. They were later replaced by Donal Donnelly and Liza Goddard, and the title was changed to *Yes, Honestly*. In all cases production was by Humphrey Barclay.

No Man's Land
US 1984 96m colour TVM
NBC/Warner/Jadda (Juanita Bartlett)

In the 1870s, a lady sheriff has three daughters, each by a different husband.
Curious western which doesn't seem to decide whether or not it's a spoof. As a pilot, it didn't catch fire.

w Juanita Bartlett *d* Rod Holcomb *ph* Ted Voigtlander *m* Mike Post, Peter Carpenter

Stella Stevens, Terri Garber, Melissa Michaelsen, Donna Dixon, John Rhys-Davies, Dack Rambo, Robert Webber, Janis Paige

'Spins too many wheels before it gets into action.' – *Daily Variety*

No Other Love
US 1980 96m colour TVM
CBS/Tisch–Avnet

The love affair of two mentally retarded people.
The effect of two hours of this situation with very little plot can be well imagined.

w Edwin Francis Kaplan *d* Richard Pearce *ph* David Myers *m* Charles Gross

Richard Thomas, Julie Kavner, Frances Lee McCain, Norman Alden, Elizabeth Allen

No Place to Hide
US 1981 96m colour TVM
CBS/Metromedia (Jay Daniel, S. Bryan Hickox)

A young heiress-to-be thinks that someone is trying either to kill her or to drive her mad.
We've heard it all before, and from the same author, but this is still a mildly effective shocker.

w Jimmy Sangster, *story* Harriet Steinberg *d* John Llewellyn Moxey *ph* Robert Hauser *m* John Cacavas

Mariette Hartley, Keir Dullea, Kathleen Beller, Arlen Dean Snyder, Gary Graham

'Vidpic offers some good jumps for viewers, and maybe that'll do for now.' – *Daily Variety*

No Place to Run
US 1972 73m colour TVM
Spelling–Goldberg

An old man flees to Canada with his orphan grandson of whom he can't get legal custody.
Patchy action drama with weepy interludes.

w James G. Hirsch *d* Delbert Mann

Herschel Bernardi, Larry Hagman, Stefanie Powers, Neville Brand, Scott Jacoby

No Time for Sergeants
US 1964 34 × 25m bw
ABC/Warner

A hillbilly is recruited to the Air Force.
Or, see *Gomer Pyle*. Obvious service humour.

Sammy Jackson, Harry Hickox, Kevin O'Neal, Andy Clyde

No Trams to Lime Street **
GB 1959 50m bw (VTR)
ABC (Sydney Newman)

Three sailors have a night out in Liverpool.
One of the most famous Armchair Theatre plays, in the Paddy Chayefsky *Bachelor Party* style.

w ALUN OWEN *d* Ted Kotcheff

Billie Whitelaw, Jack Hedley, Alfred Lynch, Tom Bell

† Revived by the BBC in 1965 and 1970.

Noah's Ark
US 1956 23 × 25m bw
NBC/Universal/Jack Webb

Experiences of a vet.
Very obvious animal series.

Paul Burke, May Wynn, Vic Rodman

Nobbs, David (19 –). British writer of satirical sketches and sitcoms who makes only rare but fruitful forays into drama. *Our Mr Wigram* (1976), CUPID'S DARTS (1981).　　PP

Noble, Peter (1925–). British show business personality, scriptwriter and occasional actor; author of, among other publications, *The Negro in Film* and *The Fabulous Orson Welles*. Editor of *Screen International* and *The British Film and Television Year Book*.

Nobody's Perfect (GB 1980). Limited 25-minute series from LWT about a strident wife and an understanding husband. Elaine Stritch and Richard Griffiths don't really make it work, and although the only writing credit is 'adapted by Elaine Stritch', what they're adapted from is *Maude*. Produced by Humphrey Barclay.

Nobody's Perfect (US): see Hart in San Francisco

Nolan, Kathy (1934–). American leading lady of *The Real McCoys* and *Broadside*; subsequently became president of Screen Actors' Guild.

Nolan, Lloyd (1902–). American actor in a long movie career as a tough guy. In TV, won an Emmy in 1955 as Queeg in THE CAINE MUTINY COURT MARTIAL and played the doctor friend in *Julia*.

Nolte, Nick (1940–). Rangy, powerful American leading man who shot to prominence in RICH MAN, POOR MAN, though his subsequent career never really took off. TV movies: *Winter Kill, The California Kid, Death Sentence, The Runaway Barge.*

Non è Mai Troppo Tardi (It's Never Too Late). Pioneering Italian programme of the fifties and early sixties aimed at teaching the country's many illiterates to read and write: so successful and popular that it was studied and emulated in numerous other parts of the world. In Britain, *On the Move* was launched in 1975.   PP

Norby (US 1955). Briefly seen half-hour comedy for NBC, with David Wayne as a small-town banker. Notable as the first series in colour.

Norden, Denis (1922–). British comedy scriptwriter (formerly with Frank Muir), panellist, wit and interlocutor of Thames's nostalgia programme *Looks Familiar* and LWT's *It'll Be Alright on the Night*. In all cases a little too fond of complex puns.

The Norliss Tapes **
US 1973 74m colour TVM
Metromedia/Dan Curtis
A supernatural investigator looks into the case of a woman whose diabolist husband has risen from the dead a ravening monster.
Smoothly made, fast-paced and genuinely frightening horror movie, an example of what can be done on a low budget.
w William F. Nolan *d* DAN CURTIS *m* Robert Cobert
Roy Thinnes, Angie Dickinson, Claude Akins, Hurd Hatfield

Norma (GB 1974; 60m). Four linked vignettes as a young married woman disposes of a lover, consults a friend, harangues her lawyer and encounters a childhood contemporary, all taking place in a park shelter. A late play – for British TV –

from Alun Owen, with Mary Healey; directed by June Howson, produced by Peter Eckersley, for Granada.   PP

Norman, Barry (1933–). Quizzical British writer–presenter mainly covering the movies, to which he brings a nice turn of phrase and a certain scepticism. (Son of Leslie Norman, film director.) *The Hollywood Greats* (1978–9), *The British Greats* (1980), *Barry Norman on Broadway* (1981), and regular seasons of the review programme *Film 80, Film 81*, etc. In 1982 became presenter of *Omnibus* but after one season returned to his true love.   PP

The Norman Conquests **
GB 1977 3 × 100m (approx.) colour (VTR)
Thames/WNET
Three plays showing the same awful family weekend from different angles.
Civilized, funny plays by Alan Ayckbourn, given precisely the right TV treatment, unspectacular and unhurried but just right. A rare treat.
d Herbert Wise
RICHARD BRIERS, PENELOPE KEITH, TOM CONTI, DAVID TROUGHTON, PENELOPE WILTON

North and South *
US 1985–6 24 × 50m colour miniseries
ABC/Warner/David Wolper (Robert Papazian, Paul Freeman)
Two families with different loyalties are caught up in the long conflict leading up to the American Civil War.
Teleblockbuster which starts as it means to go on: not as history but as *Dynasty* in fancy dress, with the heroine being endangered every other minute. The trappings are more than adequate for this purpose.
w various, *novels* by John Jakes *d* Kevin Connor, Richard Heffron
Lesley-Anne Down, David Carradine, Kirstie Alley, Philip Casnoff, Patrick Swayze, James Read, Georg Stanford Brown, Genie Francis; and guest stars Johnny Cash, Robert Guillaume, Hal Holbrook, Gene Kelly, Robert Mitchum, Elizabeth Taylor, Jean Simmons, Inga Swenson, Lloyd Bridges

North Beach and Rawhide
US 1985 96m colour TVM
CBS (Roni Weisberg)
Two young brothers are sent to a prison ranch for stealing and find themselves in charge of a tough ex-convict.

NO HIDING PLACE, a Monday night must for several years in the fifties, starred Raymond Francis (right) as Chief Superintendent Lockhart, with Eric Lander as Sergeant Baxter. Neither actor found a subsequent role of such substance.

Good open-air photography is the saving grace of this tired concept.

d Harry Falk

William Shatner, Tate Donovan, Christopher Penn, James Olson

North, Jay (1952–). American child actor who played *Dennis the Menace*; grew up a little and appeared in *Maya*; then left the industry.

North, Sheree (1933–). American character actress, formerly groomed as rival to Marilyn Monroe. TV movies: *Then Came Bronson*, *Vanished*, *Rolling Man*, *Trouble Comes to Town*, *Snatched*, *Maneater*, *Keye West*, *Winter Kill*, *Shadow on the Street*, *Most Wanted*, *The Night They Took Miss Beautiful*, *A Real American Hero*, *Amateur Night at the Dixie Bar and Grill*, *Women in White*, *Portrait of a Stripper*, *Marilyn: The Untold Story*.

Northstar
US 1985 74m colour TVM
ABC/Warner/Daniel Grodnik/Clyde Phillips (Howard Lakin)

Ultra-violet rays turn an astronaut into a walking time bomb but also give him special powers to combat evil.

And where have we heard *that* before? They find an antidote by the end of the movie, but it still didn't take as a series.

w Howard Lakin *d* Peter Levin

Greg Evigan, Deborah Wakeham, Mason Adams, David Hayward

Northwest Passage
US 1957 26 × 25m colour
NBC/MGM

Rogers' Rangers fight the French-Indian wars. North-western based on the movie rather than the book. The low budget shows.

Keith Larsen, Buddy Ebsen, Don Burnett

Norway has one television channel, NRK, under a state monopoly, and transmits about 50 hours a week, mostly of imported material.

Not for Hire
US 1959 39 × 25m bw
NBC

Cases of a Honolulu cop.
Average thick-ear.

Ralph Meeker

Not in Front of the Children. British half-hour domestic comedy series of the sixties, from BBC, starring Wendy Craig. From it were derived *And Mother Makes Three*, etc.

Not in Front of the Children
US 1982 96m colour TVM
CBS/TCF/Edward S. Feldman/Tamtco (A. Marco Turk)

When another man moves in with his ex-wife, an enraged divorcé sues for custody of the children.
'Emotionally charged' domestic drama with not a single surprising element.

w Cynthia Mandelberg *d* Joseph Hardy

Linda Gray, John Getz, John Lithgow, Stephen Elliott, George Grizzard

'A story about a nice girl – who's trying to stay that way!'
Not Just Another Affair *
US 1982 96m colour TVM
CBS/Ten Four/Sam Strangis

A Los Angeles attorney courts a charming marine biologist but finds she has old-fashioned ideas about sex and marriage. Reasonably sharp and sometimes witty battle of the sexes; above average for a TV movie.

w Philip Mishkin, Rick Podell, Mike Preminger *d* Steven Hillard Stern

Victoria Principal, Gil Gerard, Robert Webber, Richard Kline, Albert Hague

Not My Kid
US 1985 96m colour TVM
CBS/Finnegan/Beth Polson/Viacom (Pat Finnegan)

A father is shocked to find that his 15-year-old daughter is hooked on drugs.
So what else is new? Not enough to fill this telemovie's aching voids, despite careful work all round.

w Christopher Knopf *d* Michael Tuchner *ph* Fred J. Koenekamp *m* Mark Snow

George Segal, Stockard Channing, Andrew Robinson, Gary Bayer, Nancy Cartwright, Viveka Davis

'A good dramatic vehicle and an excellent lesson.' – *Daily Variety*

Not Only . . . But Also (GB 1965). Revue-type entertainment with Peter Cook and Dudley Moore originally contrived fortnightly on BBC2 but rerun as a weekly show on BBC1, when it became a cult hit and deservedly so, even if the Dud & Pete numbers, in which Cook and Moore philosophized on art and life in shabby raincoats, now seem rather patronizing. There were some funny visual jokes, e.g. a ballet of leaping nuns, from the director, Joe McGrath.
PP

Not So Much a Programme, More a Way of Life: see That Was the Week That Was

Not the Nine O'Clock News **
GB 1979–82 28 × 30m colour
BBC (John Lloyd, Sean Hardie)

Irreverent satirical revue which minced no words and spared nobody. At its best irresistibly funny, at its worst ramshackle and tasteless. Subsequent repeats and compilations of best gags, spin-off publications and discs.

d Bill Wilson

MEL SMITH, ROWAN ATKINSON, PAMELA STEPHENSON, GRIFF RHYS-JONES

PP: 'Erratic and fitful but emits at least two beautiful jokes every week.'

† Winner of the Montreux Bronze Rose. BAFTA Award and Emmy, 1980.

Now and Then (GB 1983; 6 × 30m). Minor but quite sweet sitcom of contemporary South London father trying to instruct his son while being flashbacked to his own World War II childhood. With Bernard Holley, John Alford, Liz Smith. Written by John Esmonde and Bob Larbey, directed by Derrick Goodwin, produced by Humphrey Barclay, for LWT.
PP
LH: 'In my view a delightful and much undervalued piece of social history.'

NORTH AND SOUTH. American television's 24-hour answer to *Gone with the Wind* emphasized two pairs of young lovers divided by war: James Read, Wendy Kilbourne, Patrick Swayse, Lesley-Anne Down.

Now Get out of That (GB 1983–4). Quaint contest-series in which rival teams of Americans and Brits, each two men and two women, had to act out an adventure-story scenario set in Wild Wales and involving tests of ingenuity, daring and physical endurance. Bernard Falk was the soft-skinned commentator drawing attention to sexism among the home team or sexual tensions among the visitors. Directed by Brian Strachan, produced by Philip Franklin, for BBC.   PP

Now Let Him Go * (GB 1957). J. B. Priestley's play possibly inspired by the bizarre circumstances of Tolstoy's death. Old artist lies dying in railway hotel bedroom, and with his last strength plots to prevent his waiting relatives from acquiring his pictures. With Hugh Griffith, June Thorburn. Directed and produced by Dennis Vance; for ABC (*Armchair Theatre*).   PP

Now You See It, Now You Don't
aka: *Midnight Oil*
US 1967 96m colour TVM
Universal (Roland Kibbee)

An art appraiser plans to sell a fake Rembrandt to a Middle Eastern prince. Woebegone, overlong comedy with much mugging from the star.

w Roland Kibbee *d* Don Weis

Jonathan Winters, Luciana Paluzzi, Steve Allen, Jayne Meadows, Jack Weston

Nowhere to Hide
US 1977 74m colour TVM
Mark Carliner/Viacom

A marshal is assigned to protect a former syndicate hit man.
Pretty fair action suspenser.

w Edward Anhalt *d* Jack Starrett

Lee Van Cleef, Russell Johnson, Tony Musante, Charlie Robinson, Edward Anhalt, Lelia Goldoni

Nowhere to Run *
US 1978 56m colour TVM
MTM/NBC (Jim Byrnes)

An accountant plans to make a killing at Las Vegas so that he can afford to ditch his nagging wife.

Elaborate but slow-starting suspenser with a good tense finale.

w Jim Byrnes, *novel* Charles Einstein d Richard Lang *ph* Chuck Arnold *m* Jerrold Immel

David Janssen, Stefanie Powers, Allen Garfield, Linda Evans, Neva Patterson, John Randolph

'A slick, wryly amusing coincidence stretcher.' – *Daily Variety*

Number 10 (GB 1983; 7 × 52m). Stories of British Prime Ministers written by Terence Feely and set mainly in a studio mock-up of the official residence-cum-office (see below). Denis Quilley as Gladstone, Ian Richardson as Ramsay MacDonald, Bernard Archard as the Duke of Wellington, John Stride as Lloyd George, David Langton as Asquith, Richard Pasco as Disraeli, Jeremy Brett as William Pitt the Younger. Produced by YTV.

Previously the title of a single play, from the novel by William Clark, produced by John Finch for Granada, 1968.

Number 10 Downing Street *
GB 1985 2 × 50m
BBC (Jenny Barraclough)

Part 1: Potted history of the prime ministerly residence and Cabinet offices, mainly from Asquith's tenure onwards, with reminiscences by surviving daughters or, in the case of those still living, the ex-premiers themselves.
Part 2: The sitting tenant at the time, Mrs Thatcher, and husband, discoursing on the old place.

w and narrator Christopher Jones   PP
See also The Woman at Number 10

Nurse
US 1980 96m colour TVM
CBS/Robert Halmi

When a doctor dies, his wife resumes her career as a nurse in a New York hospital.

Tangily photographed in New York, this is otherwise very predictable material from Dr Kildare's old files, and the actors are encouraged to stand around smiling at each other's niceness.

w Sue Grafton, *novel* Peggy Anderson d David Lowell Rich *ph* Peter Sova *m* Charles Gross

Michael Learned, Robert Reed, Cynthia Belgrave, Antonio Fargas, Jon Matthews

† A one-hour series followed in 1981 and was better received by the public than by the critics.

The Nurses *
aka: *The Doctors and the Nurses*
US 1962–4 103 × 50m bw
CBS/Plautus

What goes on in a large hospital.

Slickly made soap opera which doesn't always pull its punches.

Shirl Conway, Zina Bethune, Michael Tolan, Joseph Campanella

NYPD (New York Police Department) *
US 1967–8 49 × 25m colour (16mm)
ABC/Talent Associates (Danny Melnick)

Cases of New York's 27th precinct.

Vivid, rough-looking street cases dressed up as fiction, with plenty of screaming tyres.

cr Albert Ruben

Frank Converse, Robert Hooks, Jack Warden

Nye (GB 1982; 110m). Unexciting BBC drama-doc of the life of Welsh politician Aneurin Bevan with John Hartley in the role and Audrey Nicholson as Jennie Lee.

O Happy Band! (GB 1980). Short-flight comedy series about a village brass band. Not in the *Dad's Army* class. With Harry Worth, Jonathan Cecil, John Horsley. Written by Jeremy Lloyd and David Croft; produced by David Croft; for BBC.

The O. Henry Playhouse
US 1956 39 × 25m bw
Gross–Krasne

Anthology of short stories about old New York, introduced by Thomas Mitchell. Not at all bad.

O'Brian, Hugh (1925–) (Hugh Krampke). Adequate, unsmiling American leading man who after a good start in TV made little headway in movies; series include THE LIFE AND LEGEND OF WYATT EARP, *It's a Man's World*, *Search*. TV movies: *Wild Women*, *Harpy*, *Probe*, *Murder on Flight 502*, *Benny and Barney*, *Fantasy Island*, *Murder at the World Series*, *Cruise into Terror*.

O'Brien, Edmond (1915–85). Irish–American character actor who grew from a slim youth to a fat slob but was always eminently watchable. TV series: *Johnny Midnight*, SAM BENEDICT, *The Long Hot Summer*. TV movies: *The Hanged Man*, *The Doomsday Flight*, *The Outsider*, *The Intruders*, *River of Mystery*, *What's a Nice Girl Like You*, *Jigsaw*, *Isn't It Shocking?*

O'Brien, Edna (1936–). Irish novelist and playwright, rarely but interestingly represented on television: *The Keys of the Café*, 1965; *Mrs Reinhardt*, 1981; screenplay of her own *The Country Girls* for *Film on Four*, 1983. Not so happy: an acting role in *The Hard Man*. PP

O'Brien, Jim (19 –). British director, graduate of the National Film School who made his debut with *Shadows on Our Skin* and his name with *The Jewel in the Crown*. *The Monocled Mutineer*, 1986.

Objects of Affection ✱✱✱
GB 1982 7 × various, 45–60m
BBC (Innes Lloyd)

Six new and one old examples of comedy wobbling on the edge of tragedy and vice versa by Alan Bennett – three are set in hospital, four end in death or dying, and twice the nurse or the grieving relative misses the loved one's last breath because he's indulging in a little nookie.

'The smallest small-talk,' I wrote, 'has been lovingly sifted to yield the maximum savour and locate the speaker in his or her exact social substratum. People don't talk to each other, they conduct parallel monologues . . . sometimes it teeters over the edge into the picturesque and to be honest I find the whole convention a little dated, reminiscent of "the poetry of everyday speech" people were discovering in the heady days of television drama around 1960. But neither subject nor style can impair the decent, truthful, kindly perception of life and life's ironies.'

Intensive Care: d Gavin Millar; Alan Bennett, Thora Hird, Julie Walters

Our Winnie: d Malcolm Mowbray; Elizabeth Spriggs, Constance Chapman, Sheila Kelley

A Woman of No Importance: d Giles Foster; Patricia Routledge

A Day Out: Repeat of 1972 production, d Stephen Frears

Rolling Home: d Piers Haggard; John Barrett, Pat Heywood, Maureen Lipman, David Threlfall

Marks: d Piers Haggard; Marjorie Yates, Dandy Nichols, Ian Targett

Say Something Happened: d Giles Foster; Thora Hird, Julie Walters, Huw Lloyd   PP

† Book: *Objects of Affection*, 1982, also includes text of *An Englishman Abroad*.

'Making love on somebody else's time . . .'
Obsessed with a Married Woman
US 1985 96m colour TVM
ABC/Sidaris Cambe/Feldman–Meeker
   (Beverly J. Cambe, Arlene Sidaris)

A young writer falls in love with his married boss.

Slick, sophisticated melodrama which sounds a bit hollow by the end.

w C. O'Brien, Dori Pierson, Marc Rubel *d* Richard Lang *ph* Hannania Baer *m* Billy Goldenberg

Jane Seymour, Tim Matheson, Richard Masur, Dori Brenner, Claudia Cron

'Romantic slush . . . like something Kay Francis, Ann Harding or Joan Crawford used to suffer through . . . but with their clothes on.' – *Daily Variety*

'Her fantasy is to possess him!'
Obsessive Love
US 1984 96m colour TVM
CBS/ITC/Onza/Moonlight (Robert M. Sertner)

A mousey small-town girl wangles her way into the life of the soap opera hero she adores; but when he resists she becomes dangerous.

Stretched-out psychological study with a suspenseful conclusion.

w Petru Popescu, Iris Fruedman *d* Steven Hillard Stern *ph* Fred Koenekamp *m* Matthew McCauley

Yvette Mimieux, Simon MacCorkindale, Constance McCashin, Kim Shriner, Jill Jacobson, Louise Latham

'Anyone looking for another *Play Misty for Me* better look for the genuine article.' – *Daily Variety*

Occasional Wife
US 1966 30 × 25m colour
NBC/Columbia/Harry Ackerman (Robert Claver)

A bachelor executive hires a wife when he needs one for social occasions.

Mildly amusing comedy.

cr Fred Freeman, Lawrence J. Cohen

Michael Callan, Patricia Harty

❋ **O'Connor, Carroll** (1922–). American general purpose actor who after 10 years of secondary film roles became a national figure as Archie Bunker in ALL IN THE FAMILY, which in 1979 dwindled into *Archie Bunker's Place*. Emmys 1976, 1977, 1978. TV movies: *Fear No Evil*, *The Last Hurrah*.

O'Connor, Des (1932–). British comedian and singer who graduated from a holiday camp.

O'Connor, Donald (1925–). Sprightly American child actor and later song-and-dance man. When musicals died he became popular in TV as a talk show host, having won an Emmy in 1953 as best musical series star.

O'Connor, Tom (1940–). British comedian, ex-schoolteacher, into TV via *The Comedians*, *Opportunity Knocks*, *Wednesday at Eight*. Various own shows and conducts game shows and *I've Got a Secret*.

Octopus – Power of the Mafia ✱✱
Italy 1985 6 × 60m
RAI/Telecip/Taurus/C4/Escort Cine TV

Ambitious Roman detective accepts posting to Sicily to try and solve murder of local anti-Mafia police inspector. For Sean Day-Lewis in the *Daily Telegraph* the most intelligent and realistic crime series of the season, 'Telling both in its psychological explorations and in the onion-skin construction of its plot, each peeling producing a new outlook on the crime under investigation.'

w Ennio de Concini *d* Damiano Damiani

Michele Placido, Barbara Del Rosso, Florinda Bolkan, Flavio Bucci, François Perrier   PP

The Odd Couple ✱✱
US 1970–4 90 × 25m colour
ABC/Paramount (Garry Marshall, Sheldon Keller)

Two divorced men share an apartment and get on each other's nerves.

Successful extension of the Neil Simon play: skilful writing and playing keep the laughs flowing free.

Tony Randall, Jack Klugman, Al Molinaro, Penny Marshall, Janis Hansen, Elinor Donahue

† In the very last episode, Felix moved out to remarry his wife.

The Odd Man ✱
GB 1962 32 × 50m bw
Granada (Jack Williams)

Unusual offkey thriller series by the Scottish writer Edward Boyd, whose husband-and-wife private eyes had originally practised in BBC radio serials. For television (directed by Gordon Flemyng) they became more complex, with Edwin Richfield taking over the character previously played by the pop vocalist Teddy Johnson. Sarah Lawson was the wife. Couched in a clipped rhythmic dialogue rather like unsung lyrics, the show led on to *It's Dark Outside* (1964) and a recognizably Granadan style of *film noir*. A police-inspector in both series played by William Mervyn inspired and featured in a rather different, jollier spin-off called *Mr Rose* (1967).   PP

The Oddball Couple
US 1975   × 22m colour
De Patie–Freleng

A messy dog shares premises with a neat cat.
Anthropomorphic cartoon version of the stage
and film success.

voices Paul Winchell, Frank Nelson

Oddie, Bill (1941–   ). British comedy writer
and actor, since 1970 one of *The Goodies.*

Of Mice and Men
US 1981 124m colour TVM
NBC/Metromedia/Mickey (Alan Godfrey)

An itinerant worker tries to protect his
hulking, retarded brother Lenny from
getting into trouble.
The star designed this old warhorse to show
himself off, but despite good production the
premise became a comic cliché many years
ago.

w E. Nick Alexander, *novel* by John
Steinbeck *d* Reza Badiyi

Robert Blake, Randy Quaid, Lew Ayres,
Mitch Ryan, Pat Hingle, Cassie Yates

O'Ferrall, George More (1907–82). British
drama director and producer, the very first in
the world. When BBC TV started in 1936 he
was 'the drama producer'. First production
was T. S. Eliot's *Murder in the Cathedral* in
October of that year, followed by some 20
others. With the BBC again after the war he
produced a *Hamlet* with John Byron and
Muriel Pavlow, 1948. As a freelance after a
spell in the film industry he directed many
early *Armchair Theatre* shows, including one
of its rare ventures into the classics, *Ghosts.*
Anglia television's first head of drama, 1959–
64. RTS Gold Medal, 1973.   PP

Off Sides: see *The Pigs vs the Freaks*

Off the Minnesota Strip
US 1980 96m colour TVM
ABC/Universal (Meta Rosenberg)

A country girl in New York falls into the
clutches of a pimp.
The Road to Ruin in a new but not very
interesting version.

w David Chase *d* Lamont Johnson

Hal Holbrook, Michael Learned, Mare
Winningham, Ben Marley, Ronald Hunter

Off the Rack *
US 1984   × 25m colour
CBS/Warner/Brownstone/Mugwump
   (Frank Badami II)

A garment factory owner finds that he must
take into partnership his dead colleague's
widow.
A vivid sparring match between two
well-balanced protagonists. Good dialogue
makes laughs inevitable; but it didn't please
the audience.

cr DAN GUNTZELMAN, STEVE MARSHALL

ED ASNER, EILEEN BRENNAN, Pamela Brull,
William Brian Curran

Ogilvy, Ian (1943–   ). British light leading
man who starred in *The Return of the Saint.*

Oh Madeline
US 1983 19 × 25m colour
ABC/Viacom/Carsey-Werner

A busily married woman gets innocently
involved with her best friend's husband.
Based originally on the British comedy series
Pig in the Middle, this rapidly dwindled into
a standard domestic comedy about a nutty
wife, played as farce. Either way, the star
was hard to take.

cr Irma Kalish

Madeline Kahn, James Sloyan, Louis
Giambalvo, Jesse Welles

Oh No It's Selwyn Froggitt
GB 1976–   × 25m colour (VTR)
Yorkshire (Ronnie Baxter)

Adventures of an accident-prone handyman
with an irritatingly cheerful disposition.
Slightly unusual but generally resistible star
comedy.

w Alan Plater

Bill Maynard

Oh Susanna!: see The Gale Storm Show

Oh Those Bells! *
US 1962 13 × 25m bw
CBS

Adventures of the custodians of a Hollywood
prop shop.
Zany, amusing vehicle for under-used stars.

THE WIERE BROTHERS, Henry Morgan

O'Hara US Treasury
aka: *Operation Cobra*
US 1971 98m colour TVM
CBS/Universal/Jack Webb

Suddenly widowed by an accident, a deputy
sheriff from the midwest becomes a customs
agent and cracks a narcotics ring.
Semi-documentary thick ear which led to a
moderately successful series.

w James E. Moser *d* Jack Webb

David Janssen, Lana Wood, Jerome Thor, Gary Crosby, William Conrad

† The series which followed consisted of 52 × 50m episodes.

O'Herlihy, Michael (1929–). Irish director in Hollywood. Several films for Disney, but mostly TV. Series include *Maverick*, *Gunsmoke*, *Hawaii Five-O*. TV movies: *Deadly Harvest*, *The Young Pioneers*, *Kiss Me, Kill Me*, *Peter Lundy and the Medicine Hat Stallion*, *Backstairs at the White House*, *Cry of the Innocent*, *Desperate Voyage*, *A Time for Miracles*, *Million Dollar Face*, *I Married Wyatt Earp*.

Ohms
US 1979 96m colour TVM
CBS/Grant, Case, McGrath (Neil T. Maffeo)

A midwestern power company is defied by farmers who resent intrusion on their land. David beats Goliath again. A neatly made movie, though the outcome is never in doubt.

w Gene Case *d* Dick Lowry *ph* Jim Pergola *m* Elizabeth Swados

Ralph Waite, David Birney, Talia Balsam, Dixie Carter, Charley Long, Cameron Mitchell, Leslie Nielsen

Oi for England (GB 1982). Trevor Griffith's compressed vision of a city rent by unemployment and street violence as a skinhead band meets to rehearse in a beleaguered basement. Shot in video on a single set, it was directed by Tony Smith, produced by Sue Birtwistle, for Central. PP

Oil Strike North
GB 1976 13 × 50m colour (VTR)
BBC/TCF (Gerard Glaister)

Lives of men who work on an offshore oil rig. Tolerably well-made drama series which just didn't catch on.

Nigel Davenport, Barbara Shelley, Michael Witney, Angela Douglas, Callum Mill

OK Crackerby
US 1965 17 × 25m bw
ABC/United Artists/Beresford

A self-made millionaire wants his children to break into society.
Careful but unfunny star comedy.

cr Abe Burrows, Cleveland Amory

Burl Ives, Hal Buckley

The Oklahoma City Dolls
US 1981 96m colour TVM
ABC/Columbia/Ike Jones/Godmother (Matthew Rapf)

In the cause of equal rights, a woman forms a ladies' football team in competition with the men of the company for which she works.
A one-joke comedy which fills two hours.

w Ann Beckett *d* E. W. Swackhamer

Susan Blakely, Waylon Jennings, Eddie Albert, David Huddleston, Ronee Blakely

'It struggles through slogans and purpose to find warmth, but it's like snuggling up to a signboard.' – *Daily Variety*

The Old Boy Network * (GB 1979/81; 12 × 40m). Delightful idea to give music hall veterans (they had to be at least 70 and still working) a little theatre, an audience, an accompanist, and let them tell the story of their lives in any manner they chose. Arthur Askey batted first and there has been one Old Girl rather than Old Boy, Doris Hare. Others: Sandy Powell, Leslie Sarony, Chesney Allen, Richard Murdoch, John Laurie, Fred Emney, Jack Warner. Produced by Donald Sayer; for BBC. PP

† In 1983, four more entertainers, not necessarily over 70, were given the same opportunity under the title *Spotlight*: Alfred Marks, Dickie Henderson, Jimmy Edwards, Spike Milligan. Donald Sayer again produced.

Old Country (GB since 1982). Jack Hargreaves dispensing rustic lore in half-hour shows, directed by Stephen Wade for Limehouse/C4, just as he used to in *Out of Town* on ITV. PP

The Old Crowd (GB 1979). Alan Bennett's lurch into the pretentious in his season of six plays for LWT. I said at the time: 'The Old Crowd, you assumed, was just a protracted send-up of the works of Harold Pinter, down to the participation of an almost dumb waiter of sinister mien. It is troubling to learn that Alan Bennett apparently regarded it as a serious comedy of civilization (or anyway the middle classes) dancing on the brink of the abyss, his version of *Heartbreak House*.' PP

LH: 'I thought its models were Bunuel films: *The Exterminating Angel* or *The Discreet Charm of the Bourgeoisie*. But I enjoyed it just the same. Lindsay Anderson directed.'

The Old Grey Whistle Test. Mysterious title for BBC2's long-running token pop music show. The title was in fact explained as an old music hall myth: if the grey-haired doorman is heard whistling your tune, you're a hit.

The Old Man Who Cried Wolf *
US 1970 74m colour TVM
Aaron Spelling

An old man sees his friend beaten to death but the police don't believe him: only the killer does.

Modestly effective, predictable suspenser.

w Luther Davis d Walter Grauman

EDWARD G. ROBINSON, Martin Balsam, Diane Baker, Ruth Roman, Percy Rodrigues

The Old Men at the Zoo (GB 1982; 5 × 55m). Angus Wilson's cautionary novel of contemporary intrigues and future doom as dramatized by Troy Kennedy Martin; with Marius Goring, Roland Culver, Andrew Cruikshank. Directed by Stuart Burge, produced by Jonathan Powell, for BBC. PP

The Oldest Living Graduate
US 1981 96m colour
NBC/Gideon (Gareth Davies)

In 1962 in Bradleyville, Texas, there is tension in the household of an old, old soldier.

A 'from the stalls' treatment of a tolerable play, presented as the network's first live drama in 20 years. As entertainment, commendable but not marvellous.

w Preston Jones d Jack Hofsiss

Henry Fonda, Cloris Leachman, George Grizzard, Penelope Milford, Harry Dean Stanton, David Ogden Stiers

Oliver, Stephen (19 –) (Stephen John Walzig). American juvenile lead who appeared in series *Bracken's World*, *Peyton Place*.

† Another **Stephen Oliver** (19 –) is the British composer and opera buff who has presented an opera series for LWT and written music for many TV shows, including *Laurence Olivier – A Life*, below.

❉ **Olivier, Sir Laurence** (Lord Olivier) (1907–). On TV for the first time as Macbeth in a prewar Old Vic production which Lillian Bayliss let the BBC have for £75 complete with props, but offended by the high-handedness of the deal he refused any further truck with television for 20 years, other than selling the US première of his *Richard III* movie to CBS in 1956. Relented to appear in celebrated ATV production of Ibsen's *John Gabriel Borkman* (1958); thereafter a few select roles both sides of the Atlantic, plus voice-over commentary for *The World at War* (1974). Emmys: 1960, for THE MOON AND SIXPENCE; 1972, for LONG DAY'S JOURNEY INTO NIGHT; 1974, for LOVE AMONG THE RUINS. In 1976–7 he masterminded a grandiose

Granada project to present the Best Play of a number of given years. In the event only half a dozen were done, with Olivier himself starring in Pinter's *The Collection* and playing smaller parts in three others. He also made his television directorial debut, with June Howson, in *Hindle Wakes*. In 1981 played Lord Marchmain in *Brideshead Revisited* and John Mortimer's father in the remake of *Voyage Round My Father*, and two years later crowned his television career with *King Lear*. Since then, appearances of increasing unwisdom, e.g. *The Last Days of Pompeii* and *The Ebony Tower*, both 1984.

Extended interviews with Olivier by Kenneth Tynan in *Great Acting* (BBC 1966) and Dick Cavett in his US show screened by the BBC, 1974. *Olivier* was a three-part documentary without his participation produced by Bridget Winter for BBC, 1980. *Laurence Olivier – a Life*, a 2 × 90m special from LWT's *South Bank Show* team, 1982 (p Bob Bee), was built round a rather proprietorial interview by Melvyn Bragg but could not – nor would have wanted to – dim the magnitude and magnetism of a talent, I wrote, which had enriched the whole world of make-believe for the past 50 years. PP

O'Loughlin, Gerald S. (1921–). American character actor. Series: *The Rookies*. TV movies include *Murder at the World Series*, *Something for Joey*, *A Love Affair*, *Wheels*, *Crash*, *The Return of Mod Squad*, *Blind Ambition*, *Detour to Terror*, *Pleasure Palace*.

The Olympiad (US 1976). Generally overblown compilation series timed to cash in on the 1976 Olympics, but the final episode, devoted to Jesse Owens and his four gold medals at Hitler's 1936 Olympics, could hardly go wrong, and didn't. PP

The Omega Connection
US 1980 96m colour TVM
NBC/Disney (Dan Williams)

An American agent in London tracks down the baddies who have kidnapped a European professor.

Junior James Bondery, quite watchable; released to cinemas in the UK.

w Gail Morgan Hickman, David E. Boston, Davis Assael, Joshua Brand, Martha Coolidge d Robert Clouse ph Godfrey Godar m John Cameron

Jeffrey Byron, Larry Cedar, Roy Kinnear, Lee Montague, Mona Washbourne, David Kossoff, Frank Windsor, Walter Gotell, Nigel Davenport, Kathleen Harrison, Dudley Sutton, Julian Orchard, Percy Herbert

LAURENCE OLIVIER was seventy when he starred as the alcoholic Doc in *Come Back Little Sheba*, but the strength of his acting was undiminished.

Omnibus. A cultural hour transmitted on ABC from 1951 to 1956, produced by Robert Saudek and introduced by Alistair Cooke: the equivalent of BBC's *Monitor*. It included dramatizations of semi-classic material, and occasional musical specials. Emmys 1953, 1954, 1956, 1957.

PP: 'In Britain by a species of reverse lease-lend, the title was then adopted for *Monitor*'s midweek replacement from 1965 onwards. Under this heading the programme has accommodated individual essays as impressive as anything, including *Find Me* (1974), David Mercer and Don Taylor's thinly fictionalized homage to the *Ashes and Diamonds* actor Zbigniew Cybulski, but the magic that attached to the name of *Monitor* never quite reappeared, which is perhaps why Barry Norman was brought in to present the show in 1982. Editors have included Norman Swallow, Mike Wooller, Barrie Gavin and Christopher Martin.'

On Giant's Shoulders *
GB 1979 75m colour
BBC (Mark Shivas)

True-story play about Thalidomide child Terry Wiles whose adoptive parents gave themselves to his upbringing with rare dedication, the husband designing and constructing ingenious vehicles to give Terry a measure of independence. With Terry shedding various quantities of years to play his own cheeky, indomitable self, the play coursed on to a conclusion as uplifting and moving as any I've dispensed a tear over.

w William Humble, Anthony Simmons, *book* Marjorie Wallace, Michael Robson *d* Anthony Simmons

Bryan Pringle, Judi Dench, Terry Wiles as himself   PP

On Our Own (US 1977). One-season half-hour comedy for CBS, with Lynnie Greene and Bess Armstrong as two New Yorkers in the advertising business.

On the Bright Side * (GB 1959–60). Stanley Baxter's first TV series, transforming him from Scottish pantomime comic into nationwide favourite and setting the style of mimicry and much guying of Hollywood movies and other TV programmes which would keep him going for the next 25 years. With Betty Marsden. Produced by James Gilbert; for BBC.   PP

On the Buses *. British half-hour comedy series tending towards the cheerfully crude and vulgar, about a bus conductor, his mum, his homely sister and idle brother-in-law, his driver friend and their dim-witted inspector. Some fun on the comic postcard level. More than 60 episodes were produced by LWT between 1970 and 1975. With REG VARNEY, Cicely Courtneidge (later DORIS HARE), ANNA KAREN, MICHAEL ROBBINS, BOB GRANT, STEPHEN LEWIS.

On the Edge of the Sand ** (GB 1985). Dramatized account of the withdrawn life of Edward Lear, landscape and bird painter by profession, writer of nonsense rhymes in popular affection. Written by Alan Plater, directed by John Glenister, produced by Michael Andrews for BBC *Natural World* and sensitively acted by Robert Lang, it deserved better than my limerick summary.

On the Edge of the Sand, about Lear,
Never made it really quite clear
Whether Ed
Would have wed
Or was glad to remain vaguely queer.   PP

On the Eighth Day (GB 1984; 60m). Documentary prediction of the 'nuclear winter' which would follow the blotting out of the sun's rays by dust and moisture in a nuclear war. The programme, written and produced by Michael Andrews as a BBC *Natural World* special, accompanied the first transmission of the cautionary drama to the same proposition, *Threads*, which see.   PP

On the Eve of Publication (GB 1968; 55m). David Mercer play introducing the cantankerous old novelist Robert Kelvin who subsequently hovered unseen on the edge of *The Cellar and the Almond Tree* and figured posthumously in *Emma's Time*. Here was in the all too solid, if somewhat ravaged flesh of Leo McKern, busy composing an interior address to his young mistress and brooding over familiar Mercerian disillusions with socialism and his own part in the socialist struggle. Also featuring Michele Dotrice, Thorley Walters. Directed by Alan Bridges; produced by Graeme McDonald; for BBC (*Wednesday Play*).   PP

On the Line (GB 1982; 6 × 52m). Short-lived series which tried to do for car manufacture what *The Plane Makers* had done for the aircraft industry 20 years before, to little effect. Written by Jim Hawkins, directed by Paul Harrison, produced by Colin Rogers, for Central.   PP

On the March * (GB/US 1985; 10 × 30m). The story of the legendary *March of Time* news magazines which played in cinemas in America, Britain and Europe between 1935 and 1951, together with copious extracts from their various editions. Produced by Victoria Wegg-Prosser for C4/Flashback Television/SF Media Corporation.   PP

† In 1986, C4 continued with straightforward *March of Time* examples.

On the Move. A BBC ten-minute series of the mid-seventies, entertainingly instructing adults who can't read or write. BAFTA award 1976, best special programme of the year; producer David Hargreaves.

On the Rocks
US 1976 13 × 25m colour (VTR)
ABC/Metromedia/John Rich

The schemes of inmates of a minimum security prison.

Unsuccessful transposition to America of the British hit *Porridge*.

w Dick Clement, Ian La Frenais *d* John Rich

Jose Perez, Mel Stewart, Hal Williams, Rick Hurst, Bobby Sandler, Tom Poston

On Tour **
GB 1958 30m bw
BBC (Denis Mitchell, Roy Harris)

On the road with a shabby touring revue in the last days of the music hall circuit in Britain. Denis Mitchell's fifth film, a contribution to an otherwise forgotten series of half-hour films under the umbrella title of *Eye to Eye* and a vivid demonstration of his technique of counterpointing the pictures with wildtrack voice-over. Each overheard fragment of conversation became a kind of inner reflection on outward scenes. You saw the exotic dancer, you heard the ordinary girl underneath.   PP

On Trial *
GB 1962 10 × 50m bw (VTR)
Granada (Peter Wildeblood)

Courtroom re-creations of the trials of
Casement, Wilde, Dilke, Stead, Cowper,
Byng, Joseph Wall, Horatio Bottomley, the
Tichbourne claimant and the Edward VII
baccarat scandal.
Absorbing 'faction' TV.

† The American series under the same title
(ABC, 1950–1) was a current affairs debate
presided over by David Levitan.

**On Your Way, Riley! ** ** (GB 1985). The
bizarre marriage behind the music-hall
partnership of Arthur Lucan and Kitty
McShane – she a termagant, he
downtrodden, cuckolded and restricted to a
few pounds pocket money, yet with an odd
sort of love binding them. 'Our much-loved,
much-laughed Maureen,' I wrote of
Maureen Lipman as Kitty, 'turned into
something at once ludicrous, pitiable and
frightening. Brian Murphy cuddled into the
part of Lucan as if it were an old cardigan.'
Written by Alan Plater, from his own stage
version; directed by John Glenister,
produced by YTV (Margaret Bottomley) for
C4.   PP
LH: 'I didn't care for this at all. I find more
of the true relationship in the surviving Old
Mother Riley movies than in this strained
rehash.'

† See *Applause! Applause!*

Once an Eagle
US 1977 9 × 50m colour
NBC/Universal (William Sackheim, Peter
  Fischer)

The lives of two friends intertwine through
two world wars.
Lumbering mini-series from the doorstop
novel by Anton Myrer. Something of a slog,
with a few lively segments.

w Peter Fischer *d* E. W. Swackhamer,
Richard Michaels *ph* J. J. Jones *m* Elmer
Bernstein, Dana Kaproff

Sam Elliott, Cliff Potts, Darleen Carr, Glenn
Ford, Clu Gulager, Lynda Day George, Amy
Irving

Once in a Lifetime *
GB 1977–80 14 × 50m colour
YTV (Barry Cockcroft)

Barry Cockcroft was making documentaries
about hard lives lived close to the soil for
several years before they erected this umbrella
title above them. *Too Long a Winter* (1973) is
still the most famous example. Others include

an unfortunate follow-up to that one, *Hannah
Goes to Town* (1977); *The Underground Eiger*
(1979), about a fearful pot-holing operation;
Men of the Wet Sahara (1981), tideland
shrimpers of Morecambe Bay; *Another
Bloody Sunday* (1981), make or break time for
a spectacularly unsuccessful Rugby League
club. Further batches of three films followed
in 1982, 1985.   PP

**Once They Marched Through a Thousand
Towns**: see Skokie.

Once Upon a Brothers Grimm
US 1977 100m approx. colour (VTR)
Vidtronics/Bernard Rothman, Jack Wohl

The Brothers Grimm, stranded in a forest,
become involved with the problems of some of
their own creations.
Bland, studio-bound family special which
seldom rouses itself out of lethargy.

w Jean Holloway *d* Norman Campbell *m*
Mitch Leigh *ly* Sammy Cahn *choreo* Ron
Field

Dean Jones, Paul Sand, Ruth Buzzi, Chita
Rivera, Cleavon Little, Arte Johnson, Clive
Revill, Teri Garr

Once Upon a Dead Man **
US 1971 100m colour TVM
NBC/Universal (Leonard B. Stern)

San Francisco's police chief and his zany wife
uncover an art racket.
Easily digestible, hard-to-follow mystery
climaxing in a cycle chase. Pilot for the
McMillan and Wife series.

w Leonard B. Stern, Chester Krumholtz *d*
Leonard B. Stern

Rock Hudson, Susan St James, Jack
Albertson, René Auberjonois, Kurt Kasznar,
Jonathan Harris, Herb Edelman, John
Schuck, James Wainwright

† See *Mystery Movie.*

Once Upon a Family
US 1980 96m colour TVM
CBS/Universal (Jacqueline Babbin)

When his wife walks out, father and kids make
a new life.
Adequate 'woman's picture' with no surprises,
in the wake of *Kramer vs Kramer.*

w Alvin Sapinsley *d* Richard Michaels *ph*
Ronald W. Browne *m* Fred Karlin

Barry Bostwick, Maureen Anderson, Lee
Chamberlin, Jonathan Goldsmith, Jeremy
Licht, Nancy Marchand

Once Upon a Spy
US 1980 96m colour TVM
ABC/Columbia/David Gerber (Jay Daniel)

A computer expert is recruited into the secret service.
James Bond spoof with a reluctant hero. Good for a few laughs.

w Jimmy Sangster d Ivan Nagy ph Dennis Dalzell m John Cacavas

Ted Danson, Eleanor Parker, Christopher Lee, Mary Louise Weller, Leonard Stone

Once Upon a Time * (GB 1984; 5 × 50m). James Cameron became the fourth British television figure to have his life's work re-run before his eyes, but the first to comment on it without the help of an interviewer. Produced by Jenny Cropper, for BBC; see CAMERON.   PP

The One and Only Phyllis Dixey
GB 1978 115m colour
Thames (Mike Wooller)
Expensive, expansive biography of Britain's pioneer stripper and wartime morale-booster, with musical numbers re-created by Alf Ralston and intermittent testimony from Dixey's aged mother, agent and other survivors. Not a hit in Britain but popular elsewhere; in West Germany it went out twice as *Striptease für England*.

w Philip Purser d Michael Tuchner ph Mike Fash
Lesley-Anne Down, Chris Murney, Michael Elphick   PP

'Lesley-Anne Down, who has a tall kind of beauty, all nobility and dimples, was quite wrong for the Phyllis role – photos of Miss Dixie show her to be of the eager shopgirl type – but she kept going and made a good job of the naughty lady's decline into datedness, bankruptcy and terminal disease.' – Russell Davies, *Sunday Times*

'Lesley-Anne Down is simply splendid.' – Howard Rosenberg, *Los Angeles Times*

One Cooks, The Other Doesn't
US 1983 96m colour TVM
CBS/Lorimar/Kaleidoscope (Ron Roth)
It's embarrassment all round when for financial reasons a husband allows his first wife and her family to move in with his new menage.
Silly comedy which does provide enough jokes for about half its length.

w Larry Grusin d Richard Michaels ph Reynaldo Villalobos
Suzanne Pleshette, Joseph Bologna, Rosanna Arquette, Evan Richards, Robin Strand

'Good characters give the slight comedy zing; cut to 90 minutes it could have clicked 100%.' – *Daily Variety*

One Day at a Time
US 1975   × 25m colour (VTR)
CBS/Norman Lear/TAT (Dick Pensfield, Perry Grant)
A newly divorced woman has two teenage daughters.
Mostly pleasing comedy series.
cr Whitney Blake, Allan Mannings d Herbert Kenwith
Bonnie Franklin, Mackenzie Phillips

One Fine Day * (GB 1979). The unexpected success of the six filmed Alan Bennett plays for LWT: DAVE ALLEN, the Irish talking-head comedian, played a disenchanted estate agent camping out in a white-elephant office block – a very pretty visual metaphor.   PP

One Happy Family (US 1961). Half-hour comedy series for NBC, with Dick Sargent as a newlywed living with his in-laws.

100 Great Paintings *
GB 1980–82 100 × 10m colour
BBC (Bill Morton)
Rewarding idea to preface evening programmes on BBC2 with ten minutes of expert enthusiasm for a particular painting, always filmed in the gallery (or private collection) where it belongs. Transmission is not continuous, but broken into groups of five pictures to a weekly theme, e.g. 'bathing' or 'hunting'. Three or four groups are aired, then the series is rested for a while. Presenters include Sir Hugh Casson, Milton Brown, David Piper and the creator and editor of the show, Edwin Mullins.   PP

† Though the series ended on BBC2 in 1982, repeats and foreign screenings continue indefinitely.

199 Park Lane (GB 1965). '*Coronation Street* for toffs' – a BBC soap opera set in an expensive block of flats which, despite being devised and scripted by the veteran screen writer William Fairchild, was axed after a run of only four weeks. With Isabel Dean, Edwin Richfield.   PP

One in a Million: The Ron Le Flore Story
US 1980 96m colour TVM
CBS/EMI/Roger Gimbel (William S. Gilmore Jnr)
A black ghetto kid recovers from early imprisonment to become a baseball star.
The synopsis says it all; why bother to watch the movie?

w Stanford Whitmore, from Le Flore's memoirs *d* William A. Graham *ph* Jordan Cronenweth *m* Peter Matz

LeVar Burton, Madge Sinclair, Paul Benjamin, James Luisi, Billy Martin

One Life To Live (US 1968). American daytime soap opera, on ABC from 1968; it became an hour in 1978. Set in Llanview, USA.

One Man and His Dog * (GB since 1982). Television sheepdog trials launched on the premise that if snooker could be popularized by TV (*Pot Black*) why not this country test of skills? So it proved, even if sheep-lovers were pained to see dogs and handlers given star billing while the sheep were just sheep. Presented by Phil Drabble and Eric Halsall, directed (1983) by Michael Kerr, produced by Ian Smith, for BBC.   PP

One Man's Family (US 1949–51). Half-hour serial for NBC, from the radio original created by Carlton E. Morse; with Bert Lytell and Marjorie Gateson.

One Man's Week (GB 1971–2). Self-explanatory BBC series in which a worthy, e.g. Sir Hugh Greene, was sheepishly observed at work and play during one week, and heard reflecting on same. Ten years later the idea was revised as *A Year In the Life of*, the longer span adding to the variety of events but not much else.   PP

One Minute Please (US 1954). Panel game for Dumont in which the accolade went to the best one-minute speech on an absurd subject.

One of My Wives Is Missing **
US 1975 97m colour TVM
Spelling–Goldberg (Barney Rosenzweig)

A man arrives at a holiday resort and reports to the police that his wife has vanished. A woman he has never seen before then turns up claiming to be his wife. . . .
Satisfying what's-it-all-abouter which plays pretty fair and deals suspicion like a pack of cards. The plot is borrowed from *Chase a Crooked Shadow* and other sources.

w Peter Stone, *play Trap for a Lonely Man* by Robert Thomas *d* Glen Jordan *m* Billy Goldenberg

James Franciscus, Jack Klugman, Elizabeth Ashley, Joel Fabiani

One of Our Own
US 1975 98m colour TVM
NBC/Universal (Matthew Rapf, Jack Laird)

The chief of a large hospital faces numerous crises.
Predictable pilot for the unsuccessful series *Doctors' Hospital*.

w Jack Laird *d* Richard Sarafian

George Peppard, Oscar Homolka, William Daniels, Louise Sorel, Strother Martin, Zohra Lampert, Albert Paulsen

One of the Boys (US 1982). Half-hour taped comedy series starring Mickey Rooney as a feisty old codger who goes to live with his student grandson and gets in the way. Easy laughs are the order of the day, but the star could play himself in over a long run. Written and created by Saul Turtletaub and Bernie Orenstein for their own Toy II Productions and Columbia.

One Pair of Eyes **** (GB 1967–75; 76 × 50m). Intermittent BBC series of first-person films to the simple, brilliant notion of inviting an outside contributor to choose any theme he or she fancied, write a script and collaborate with a bright young director on the realization. Though trips down Memory Lane were the commonest (Kenneth Tynan back to Oxford, Georgia Brown to East End Jewish roots), there was always some moral reflection and some clients entertainingly tackled openly philosophical matters, e.g. Michael Frayn on the nature of travel in general and Tom Stoppard on the nature of travel on the M4 motorway in particular. The series eventually fell victim to inflation, as it became increasingly hard to find luminaries able to give up several months of their free time in exchange for a modest fee. Produced by Christopher Ralling and successors.   PP

'On the way to find a killer . . . they found each other!'
One Shoe Makes It Murder
US 1982 96m colour TVM
CBS/Lorimar/Fellows–Keegan (Mel Ferrer)

An ex-cop is hired by a Tahoe gambler to find his missing wife.
Glum Philip Marlowe imitation with over-age stars.

w Felix Culver, *novel So Little Cause for Caroline* by Eric Bercovici *d* William Hale *ph* Terry K. Meade *m* Bruce Broughton

Robert Mitchum, Angie Dickinson, Mel Ferrer, Jose Perez, John Harkins

'Texture appears more important than text.'
– *Daily Variety*

One Step Beyond **
US 1958–60 94 × 25m bw
ABC/Collier Young (Merwin Gerard)

Unexplained real-life experiences which tend towards the supernatural. 'Have you ever walked down a street and had the feeling that you knew what lay beyond the unturned corner?'

Simply staged occult series which did a good deal for TV production by its use of limbo sets and having its narrator walk in and out of the action.

cr MERWIN GERARD *host* JOHN NEWLAND *m* Harry Lubin

PP: 'Some episodes were made or remade in Britain by Associated-Rediffusion in 1960–1, using local actors but with John Newland still inviting the audience in his New England tones to explahr with him the amazing wahld of the unknown and take that Wan Stup Beyahnd.'

† In 1978 the format was revived for prime access time under the title *The Next Step Beyond*, but the old style was not evident.

One Summer *
GB 1983 5 × 52m
YTV (Keith Richardson)

Two unruly Liverpool teenagers run away to try to recapture the one happy interlude either of them can remember – a school camping trip in Wales. Funny and touching, it was first screened on C4, re-run on ITV in 1985.

w Willy Russell *d* Gorden Flemyng

David Morrissey, Spencer Leigh   PP

O'Neal, Patrick (1927–).
Smooth American actor whose infrequent appearances are generally welcome. Series: *Dick and the Duchess*, KAZ, TV movies: *Companions in Nightmare,*, *Crossfire*, *The Moneychangers*, *The Deadliest Season*, *The Last Hurrah*, *To Kill a Cop*, *Fantasies*, *Emerald Point*, *Spraggue*.

The Onedin Line *
GB 1974–8 50 × 50m colour (VTR)
BBC

The saga of a Liverpool shipping family. 19th-century open-air adventure mixes with boardroom and bedroom drama: an irresistible combination for Sunday nights.

cr Cyril Abraham

Peter Gilmore, Howard Lang, Jessica Benton, Brian Rawlinson, Mary Webster, Jill Gascoine, Anne Stallybrass

† Exterior locations: Exeter and Dartmouth.

Only Fools and Horses . . . * (GB since
1981). Unheralded half-hour situation comedy about low-life brothers left to cope alone, which grew in popularity, thanks to superior scripts and characterization, and finally received the left-handed compliment of being promoted to a 90-minute TVM version scheduled against the first *Minder* movie at Christmas 1985. Written by John Sullivan, produced and directed by Ray Butt for BBC. With David Jason, Nicholas Lyndhurst and Lennard Pearce as their grandad. On Pearce's death in 1984 Buster Merryfield came in as Uncle Albert.   PP

Only in America
GB 1980 3 × 50m colour
Thames (Michael Houldey)

Three films about the American dream beginning to go sour, though still good to look at thanks to Mike Fash's photography: Puerto Rican detectives; contemporary cowboy; black New Yorkers returning to Southern roots.   PP

The Only Way Out Is Dead
aka: *The Man Who Wanted to Live Forever*
Canada 1970 100m colour TVM
Palomar

A man determined to live forever selects other people's organs for his future use.
A talky rather than gruesome, but still rather tasteless suspenser.

w Henry Denker *d* John Trent

Burl Ives, Sandy Dennis, Stuart Whitman, Ron Hartman, Robert Goodier

Only When I Laugh (GB 1979–84). Cheerful
hospital comedy half-hours by Eric Chappell with James Bolam, Peter Bowles and Christopher Strauli as evidently incurable patients and ingenious little situations spun around new nurses, stuffy doctors, visiting hours and the hospital broadcasting system. Produced by Vernon Lawrence; for YTV. PP

Only with Married Men *
US 1974 74m colour TVM
Spelling–Goldberg

A sexy girl who only wants to date married men meets a sly bachelor who pretends to be married so as not to get involved.
Brash, bright sex comedy which sustains well for most of its length.

w Jerry Davis *d* Jerry Paris

David Birney, Michele Lee, John Astin, Judy Carne, Dom DeLuise

Ooh La La! *
GB 1973 6 × 50m colour (VTR)
BBC (Douglas Argent)
Six adaptations of Feydeau farces, impeccably presented with a star who was made for them.
adaptors Caryl Brahms, Ned Sherrin
PATRICK CARGILL

Open All Hours (GB 1978–). Half-hour comedy series written by Roy Clarke for Ronnie Barker, who plays a bluff north country shopkeeper with David Jason as his rather dense nephew and Lynda Baron as the nubile district nurse he covets. It provides easy laughs without stretching the star's talents. Produced by Sydney Lotterby; for BBC.

PP: 'I would give it two stars plus an extra one for Ronnie Barker's b-b-bad taste stammer. The show was laid off in 1984 to make way for *The Magnificent Evans* and happily brought back when that failed.'

Open All Night (US 1981). Half-hour comedy series about a small urban store frequented by strange characters. As American as *Open All Hours* is British. With George Dzundza, Sandra McCabe; produced by Bernie Brillstein; for ABC.

Open Door. BBC2's late night access programme, open to any minority groups who prove they can stage an interesting and fair programme. Later it changed its name to *Open Space* and moved to early evening.

Open Night (GB 1971–2). Television debates on aspects of television with Mike Scott in charge and with contributions from critics, programme-makers and the studio audience. Produced by Peter Heinze and Derek Granger; for Granada.   PP

Open Secret (GB 1980). Investigative series by and with Peter Williams, doughty ex-*This Week* reporter at this time with BBC, on such topics as dangers in the lead industry, shoddy architecture.   PP

The Open University. Britain's home-study university dreamed up by Prime Minister Harold Wilson as a 'university of the air' but in practice dependent mainly on postal tuition backed up by local tutorials and summer schools. Accompanying TV and radio courses carried by the BBC from Open U studios in Milton Keynes are an important but not dominant feature. Since it began in 1969 some 80,000 people have gained degrees.   PP

open-ended programme. One which does not have to finish at a specific time, or can be programmed to its full length instead of being cut to fit another network junction.

Operation Cobra: see O'Hara US Treasury

Operation Heartbeat *
aka: *UMC*
US 1969 100m colour TVM
MGM (A. C. Ward)
Life at a university medical centre.
Competent pilot for the long-running series *Medical Center*.
w A. C. Ward   *d* Boris Sagal
Richard Bradford, James Daly, Edward G. Robinson, Maurice Evans, Kevin McCarthy, William Windom, Kim Stanley, J. D. Cannon

Operation Julie *
GB 1985 3 × 52m
Tyne-Tees (Keith Richardson)
The reconstruction of a police operation to nab a multi-million-pound drug ring, comically handicapped by accidents and pinch-penny economies (police cars which wouldn't start, bugging cables eaten by goats) but eventually triumphant – whereupon the task force was disbanded and its leader posted to traffic duties. Thanks particularly to Colin Blakely as the dogged Inspector Lee, it gripped well, I thought. 'His dumpy frame, baggy tweeds and brave disbelief at the ingenuity with which things can go wrong finally took on heroic proportions.'
w Gerry O'Hara, Bob Mahoney, Keith Richardson, *book* by Dick Lee   *d* Bob Mahoney   PP

Operation Petticoat
US 1977 96m colour TVM
ABC/Universal (Leonard Stern)
Life on an antique submarine during the Pacific War.
Tedious rehash of an old movie which wasn't particularly inspired to begin with.
w Leonard Stern   *d* John Astin
John Astin, Richard Gilliland, Jackie Cooper, Craig Cassidy
† A half-hour series followed. In the second season the leads changed to Randolph Mantooth and Robert Hagan.

Operation Prime Time: see Best Sellers

Operation Runaway: No Prince for My Cinderella
US 1978 96m colour TVM
NBC/Quinn Martin (William Robert Yates)
A lawyer tracks down missing teenagers. Dreary pilot which unaccountably sold a series. It didn't last long.

w William Robert Yates d William Wiard ph William W. Spencer m Richard Markowitz

Robert Reed, James Olson, Terri Nunn, Karen Machon

'Robert Reed's job is to track down runaway teenagers. And he's pretty good at it. Unfortunately the show provides no compelling reason for wanting them back.' – *Daily Variety*

Opinions (GB since 1982). Regular series of half-hour meditations or fulminations on a subject of the presenter's choosing, e.g. Mike Brearley on a cricket captain's sufferings, Germaine Greer on Mrs Thatcher as a Great British Nanny. Produced by Nicholas Fraser (originally) for Griffin Productions/C4.   PP

Oppenheimer * (GB 1981). The story of the American professor who became 'father of the atomic bomb'. A curious choice of subject for British producers, but a solidly interesting series. With Sam Waterston. Written by Peter Prince; produced by Peter Goodchild; for BBC.
PP: 'Oppenheimer's security hearing had been previously reconstructed by Stuart Hood in *On Trial* (BBC, 1970).'

Oppenheimer, Jess (1918–). American comedy writer: *I Love Lucy*, *Angel*, *Glynis*, (creator) *The Debbie Reynolds Show*.

The Oppermanns ** (West Germany 1983; 2 × 110m). A wealthy Jewish family faces the threat of the Nazis. An independently made blockbuster, from the novel by Lion Feuchtwanger, which in a poignant revival of the *Largest Theatre in the World* togetherness of the sixties went out on the same two evenings throughout Europe, exactly 50 years after Hitler came to power. The carrier in Britain was BBC2. Written and produced by Egon Monk, for Gyula Tresitch Productions.   PP

Opportunity Knocks. A British talent scout show which ran on a weekly basis for most of each year from 1956 to 1977. Hughie Green presided and was much imitated for his smarmy introductions. About a score of the finalists achieved significant careers.

The Optimist (GB 1983; 7 × 30m). Drab sitcom, for some reason silent except for sound-effects, with Enn Reitel as hero aspiring to attract girls, wind-surf, attract girls, etc. Written by Robert Sparks, directed by Peter Ellis, produced by Robert Sidaway, for C4/New Century Films/ Charisma.   PP

Oracle. ITV's version of Teletext (qv).

Orchard, Julian (1930–79). British character comedian, frequently seen as beaming, effeminate foil to stars.

Orde Wingate **
GB 1976 3 × 75m colour (VTR)
BBC (Innes Lloyd)
Remarkable biographical study of the wartime Chindit leader, Arabic-speaking Zionist and gentile founder of the Israeli army. Each of the three episodes started and finished on a realistic filmed simulation of Wingate's jumping-off point on his last operation in 1944, but all flashbacks to his previous life were done as stylized tableaux in the studio. Written by Don Shaw; directed by Bill Hays; designed by David Myerscough-Jones.
My verdict at the time: 'In its use of lighting, its wonderfully economic mustering of information simply propelled on to the sound track, its unashamed commemoration of a weird and wonderful hero, *Orde Wingate* must be the drama adventure of the year.'

Barry Foster, Nigel Stock, Denholm Elliott
PP
† Barry Foster repeated the characterization less accurately in *A Woman Called Golda*, 1982.

Ordeal *
US 1973 74m colour TVM
TCF
An injured businessman is left for dead in the desert by his wife and her lover.
Remake of *Inferno*, considerably less effective.
w Francis Cockrell, Leon Tokatyan d Lee H. Katzin m Pat Williams

Arthur Hill, Diana Muldaur, James Stacy, Michael Ansara, Macdonald Carey

The Ordeal of Bill Carney
US 1981 96m colour TVM
CBS/Comworld/Belle (Jerry London)
The divorced father of two small boys loses custody of them because he is disabled. Lugubrious weepie based on a true case.
w Tom Lazarus d Jerry London ph Gerald Perry Finnerman m Billy Goldenberg

Richard Crenna, Ray Sharkey, Betty Buckley, Vincent Baggetta, Martin Milner

The Ordeal of Dr Mudd
US 1980 142m colour TVM
CBS/Marble Arch/BSR (Paul Radin)
The trial of the surgeon who treated Abraham Lincoln's assassin.
Unnecessary extension of a theme treated in 90 minutes by John Ford in 1936's *Prisoner of Shark Island* and in 50 minutes by *Desilu Playhouse* in the fifties.
w Michael Berk, Douglas Schwartz *d* Paul Wendkos *ph* Hector Figueroa *m* Gerald Fried
Dennis Weaver, Susan Sullivan, Richard Dysart, Michael McGuire, Nigel Davenport, Arthur Hill, Larry Larson
'A slow, handsome study of a basically dull man.' – *Daily Variety*

The Ordeal of Patty Hearst
US 1980 142m colour TVM
ABC/Paradine/William Finnegan
The kidnapping of the San Francisco heiress as seen by the FBI agent in charge of the case.
Harrowing and overextended restatement of a well-known story, with no further clarification.
w Adrian Spies *d* Paul Wendkos *ph* Hector Figueroa *m* John Rubinstein
Dennis Weaver, Lisa Eilbacher, David Haskell, Stephen Elliott, Tisa Farrow, Rosanna Arquette, Dolores Sutton

Orders from Above *** (GB 1975). Bitter but compelling investigation, partly based on Nicholas Bethell's *The Last Secret*, into the forcible repatriation by the Allies of Russian renegades, prisoners of war, slave workers and other strays after World War II. Normally resistant to the recriminations of the committed moralists whose watchword is 'My country right or wrong – but preferably wrong', I had nevertheless to proclaim *Orders from Above* a truly harrowing and shaming indictment. Produced by Robert Vas; for BBC.   PP

The Oregon Trail
US 1975 100m Technicolor TVM
NBC/Universal
A pioneer family heads west.
Talky mini-western pilot, making lavish use of clips from older and better movies, but with a certain integrity of purpose.
w Michael Gleason *d* Boris Sagal *m* David Shire
Rod Taylor, Blair Brown, Douglas Fowley, Andrew Stevens

† The series which followed more than a year later was poorly conceived and produced, and limped along for 13 × 50m episodes, not all of which were played. Rod Taylor again starred, but the presentation was perfunctory in the extreme.

The Organization *
GB 1972 6 × 50m colour
Elegant satire on jockeying for power and favour in the PR department of a large company – supposedly in the soft drinks business but thought by many in television to be modelled on an organization much nearer home. Written by Philip Mackie; for YTV.
My review at the time: '. . . never flagged as week by week it paired off its denizens of the public relations department for a little two-step in the centre of attention, rather like a Scottish country dance. The ending, with the last protuberances of particularity gently smoothed from young Pershore (Peter Egan) was satire of the urbanest quality. Donald Sinden's voice might have been bubbled through black velvet.'   PP

Orkin, Harvey (–1975). American scriptwriter, notably for Phil Silvers, and resident wag on the British satire show *Not So Much a Programme. . .*

Orkney *
GB 1971 90m colour
Three stories by the Orkney poet George Mackay Brown, adapted by John McGrath, directed by James MacTaggart and filmed in the beautiful (if unreliable) light of those islands. With Roddy McMillan, Hannah Gordon, Maurice Roëves, Claire Nielsen. Produced by Graeme McDonald; for BBC (*Play for Today*).   PP

Orlando, Tony (1944–) (Michael Cassivitis). American pop singer, usually with Dawn, his back-up group.

Ormond, John (19 –). Welsh poet and producer steadily turning out good, if unsung, BBC programmes from *Borrowed Pasture* 1960 to *Poetry In Its Place*, 1982.   PP

Orphan Train
US 1980 142m colour TVM
CBS/EMI/Roger Gimbel (Dorothea G. Petrie)
In 1854, a determined woman takes orphans from New York to find foster homes in the west.

Tolerable open-air fictionalization of a factual event; would have been better at half the length.

w Millard Lampell *d* William A. Graham *ph* Terry K. Meade *m* Laurence Rosenthal

Jill Eikenberry, Kevin Dobson, Linda Manz, Melissa Machaelsen, Morgan Farley

'It's a long, long trail unwinding.' – *Daily Variety*

Orson Welles Great Mysteries
GB 1973 26 × 25m colour (VTR)
Anglia (John Jacobs)

Anthology of strange stories, hosted by a cloaked Orson Welles (who does not appear in any of them).

Some quite good playlets, some very bad ones, and too much variation in the level to allow an effective series.

Orwell, George (1903–50) (Eric Blair). British literary lion whose famously gloomy vision of the future *1984* inevitably brought him much attention when that year dawned:

Orwell on Jura *** (GB/West Germany, 90m). How the dying author came to write *1984* on the remote Scottish island of Jura. With Ronald Pickup as Orwell, Fiona Walker as his sister; also with David Swift and Kit Thacker. Written by Alan Plater, filmed by Dick Johnstone, directed by John Glenister, produced by Norman McCandlish, for BBC Scotland/TPI.

George Orwell ** (GB; 5 × 40m). Exhaustive biography largely told by amazing roll-call of key witnesses – 'From childhood to deathbed almost every stage in Orwell's life seemed to have been imprinted on someone's mind.' Written and produced by Nigel Williams – who also unwisely delivered Orwell's words in quite the wrong accent – for BBC *Arena*.

The Road to 1984 * (GB 90m). Another dramatization, time-jumping and cross-referencing through the whole life, and handicapped – after the preceding film – by Granada's habitual economy in choosing locations. Their Isle of Jura compared unfavourably with the BBC's real thing. With James Fox as Orwell; written by Willis Hall, directed by David Wheatley, produced by Steve Morrison, for Granada.

Orwell – a Personal View (GB) by Anthony Burgess; C4 from Thames.

1984 (US 50m) Walter Cronkite on how closely reality had caught up on Orwell's fictional world; for CBS.

Beyond 1984 (GB; 3 × 30m). Wuffling over the same predictable question, as did an edition of *Forty Minutes*; both BBC.   PP

See also: *1984*.

Osborn, Andrew (1912–85). British producer (former actor): MAIGRET, DR FINLAY'S CASEBOOK, etc. BBC's head of series, 1964–74. Back to producing with *When the Boat Comes In*, *Walk with Destiny*.

Osborne, John (1930–). His historic theatre debut with *Look Back in Anger* in 1956 was followed by a 90-minute Granada TV version of the same play only six months later, directed again by Tony Richardson. *A Subject of Scandal and Concern*, reconstructing an 1840s trial for blasphemy, was his first play specifically for television, written for ITV but eventually (1960) produced by the BBC. Subsequent TV scripts ranged from the sublime THE RIGHT PROSPECTUS (1970), via *A Gift of Friendship* (1974), and *Almost a Vision* (1976) to the gorblimey *Very Like a Whale* (1980). As an actor played the aristocratic hero of Mercer's *The Parachute*. Interviewed unsatisfactorily (e.g. without reference to his TV work) in the *South Bank Show*, 1981.

In 1985, after some years' absence from the limelight, Osborne furnished two major works for TV: *God Rot Tunbridge Wells!* (which see) and a dramatization of his own chapter of autobiography *A Better Class of Person*, with Eileen Atkins as his implacably despised mother and Alan Howard as his father. Despite direction by Frank Cvitanovich and production by Lloyd Shirley, for Thames, this turned out somewhat ordinarily. 'It also has to be said that little Johnny grew into a singularly unattractive and graceless adolescent. Ah, but what did it matter so long as he loved his old mother?'   PP

Oscar: see Academy Awards Telecast

Oscar *
GB 1985 3 × 50m
BBC/Consolidated Productions (Carol Robertson)

Oscar Wilde at the peak of his success as a West End playwright; his fatal libel suit and consequent trial on charges of homosexuality; in prison and afterwards.

Wilde's sheer social dazzle at the outset wasn't very well communicated, but as the story grew tougher so did the production. 'And from Michael Gambon's dignified, increasingly apt impersonation you were left with a picture of Oscar Wilde that might have changed from the one you had before, and would certainly have offered one or two new insights.'

w John Hawkesworth *d* Henry Herbert

Michael Gambon, Robin Lermitte (as Lord Alfred Douglas), Norman Rodway (as Queensberry), Emily Richard (as Constance Wilde)   PP

Osmond, Donny (1957–). American juvenile singer, usually with his sister Marie and their brothers and sisters (the Osmond family, proudly Mormon). Weekly variety show, *Donny and Marie*, ran 1976–9; for it a new production complex was built in Salt Lake City and subsequently devoted itself to TV movie production.

Osmond, Marie (1959–). See above. Her TV movies include *The Gift of Love* and *I Married Wyatt Earp*, but she is too sweetly smiling to be a versatile actress.

The Osmonds
US 1972–3 26 × 22m colour
ABC/Rankin–Bass/Halas & Batchelor
The Osmonds rock group are appointed goodwill ambassadors by the United States Music Committee.
Passable cartoon series with music.

'Their good cheer is awful because you know that they are never not like that. The Osmonds are not even phoney: they are sincerely vacuous.' – Clive James

OSS
GB 1958 26 × 25m bw
ITC/Buckeye
Exploits of the Office of Strategic Services during World War II.
Adequate espionage series.
Ron Randell, Lionel Murton

O'Sullivan, Richard (1944–). British leading light actor, former child star. Series: A MAN ABOUT THE HOUSE, *Doctor in Charge*, *Robin's Nest*, *Dick Turpin*.

The Other 'Arf (GB 1980). ATV sitcom with model Lorraine Chase, elevated to stardom on the strength of a much-loved Campari commercial ('No, Luton Airport'), as the ever-so-common consort of posh Tory MP John Standing. As predictable as it sounds. PP

The Other Half
GB 1984 6 × 30m
BBC (Edward Mirzoeff)

Real-life marriages (four) or other enduring liaisons (two), as reviewed by those concerned in front of Mirzoeff's politely nosey camera. 'The British,' I wrote, 'have recognized television's role as national confessional, and when the call comes they accept as a citizen's duty the obligation to talk about themselves and their affairs within well-defined limits of candour.'

Agony Aunt Claire Rayner and husband; jockey John Francome and wife; dancer Gillian Lynne and husband; littérateur Sir Angus Wilson and companion Tony Garrett; MP Edwina Currie and husband; ex-*Playboy* chief Victor Lownes and friend Marilyn.   PP

The Other Lover
US 1985 96m colour TVM
CBS/Columbia/Larry Thompson (Hugh
  Benson)
An author calls on his publisher to complain about the cover of his new novel, and falls for the marketing director . . .
Straightforward rehash of the elements of *Brief Encounter* . . . tolerable while it's on, but not worth staying home for.

w Judith Parker, Susan Title *d* Robert Ellis Miller *ph* Fred J. Koenekamp *m* Lee Holdridge

Lindsay Wagner, Jack Scalia, Max Gail, Millie Perkins, John Bennett Perry

'Sentiment reigns supreme . . . surprising strengths and drawing power.' – *Daily Variety*

The Other Man *
GB 1964 140m bw
Granada (Gerald Savory)
Ambitious if rather pinch-penny exercise in the sub-genre of fiction known as the 'alternative present'. Writer Giles Cooper's initial make-believe was that Churchill had been killed in 1940 and his successor sued for peace. The story followed the career of a British subaltern as he rose to command a regiment serving the Nazis in a protracted racial war in Asia. The point was to show how any nation's military virtues could easily have been corrupted by an evil regime. Inside every decent man is this 'other man' waiting to take over.

d Gordon Flemyng
Michael Caine, Siân Phillips   PP

The Other Man
US 1970 96m colour TVM
NBC/Universal (William Frye)

A woman fears that her district attorney husband may have murdered her lover. Very adequate suspenser.

w Michael Blankfort, Eric Bercovici, *novel* Margaret Lynn *d* Richard A. Colla *ph* E. Charles Straumer *m* Michel Colombier

Roy Thinnes, Arthur Hill, Joan Hackett, Tammy Grimes, Rodolfo Hoyos

The Other Side of Hell *
US 1978 150m colour TVM
NBC/James T. Aubrey, Ronald Lyon

A man who has attempted suicide is committed to a hospital for the criminally insane.

Quite a powerful and compassionate study of the state of modern therapy, with several strong performances.

w Leon Tokatyan *d* JAN KADAR *ph* Adam Holender *m* Leonard Rosenman

ALAN ARKIN, Roger E. Mosley, Morgan Woodward, Seamon Glass, Leonard Stone

The Other Side of the Tracks (GB since 1983). Thinking man's (and woman's) pop music review on Channel 4, alternating weekly (1983) or seasonally (since 1983) with other formats. Introduced by Paul Gambaccini, produced by Rod Taylor for Partners in Production.   PP

The Other Woman
US 1974 74m colour TVM
Columbia (John Conboy)

A plain 35-year-old librarian finds herself pregnant as the result of one unexpected wild night, and learns that the wife of the father would like to keep the baby.

Woman's page melodrama of no absorbing interest.

w Peggy O'Shea *d* Peter Levin

Joel Fabiani, Katherine Helmond, Beverlee McKinsey, Pat O'Brien

The Other Woman
US 1984 96m colour TVM
CBS (Lila Garrett)

A middle-aged man can't keep up with his young wife, and meets a woman of his own age . . .

Fairly amusing romantic comedy with a few original twists.

w Anne Meara, Lila Garrett *d* Mel Shavelson

Anne Meara, Hal Linden, Madolyn Smith, Warren Berlinger, Joe Regalbuto, Janis Paige, P. J. Soles, Selma Diamond, Jane Dulo, Nita Talbot, Jerry Stiller

'The family's only hope for survival is each other!'

Otherworld
US 1984 8 × 50m colour
CBS/Universal (Philip de Guere)

A family on holiday is lost in a time warp. Would-be educational or inspirational claptrap, quite amusing as long as it sticks to action in the Forbidden Zone.

Sam Groom, Gretchen Corbett

OTT (GB 1982). Abysmal late-night live happening from Central in which incompetent new entertainers are separated by studio explosions and nubile girls over whom large quantities of custard are regularly poured. A very bad idea, but we were warned, as *OTT* stands for 'Over the Top'. Devised by Howard Imber, Chris Tarrant, Peter Harris. NB. The idea was apparently to make an adult version of the company's very noisy kiddie show, *TISWAS* ('Today Is Saturday, Wear a Smile').

'All we want to do is send people to bed early on a Sunday morning with a smile on their faces and perhaps a few mucky thoughts.' – Chris Tarrant

Our Family Business
US 1981 74m colour TVM
ABC/Lorimar (Lee Rich)

Problems for an Italian Mafia family in LA. Complex sub-Godfather goings-on. Even if the plots and counterplots were clear, there is no appetite among the TV audience for a Mafia soap opera, which is what this intended to be.

w Lane Slate *d* Robert Collins *ph* Reynaldo Villalobos *m* Tom Scott

Sam Wanamaker, Ted Danson, David Morse, Vera Miles, Ray Milland, Chip Mayer

Our Family Honor
US 1985 1 × 96m, 13 × 50m colour
ABC/Lorimar/Lawrence Gordon/Charles Gordon (Ronald E. Frazier)

Boy meets girl, but his is a Mafia family and hers consists of Irish cops . . .

A pretty intolerable basis for a soap opera in prime time, but they tried it . . . and failed.

cr John Tanner, Arthur Bernard Lewis, Richard Freiman

Eli Wallach, Kenneth McMillan, Daphne Ashbrook, Tom Mason, Michael Madsen

'Someone better come up with something interesting about at least one of the characters, or there goes *Our Family Honor*.' – *Daily Variety*

ORSON WELLES GREAT MYSTERIES (no apostrophe, by order) was a variable anthology with no relation to Welles except for his brief introductions in an outfit that looked as though he'd just come from advertising port wine. Here Eli Wallach stars in *Compliments of the Season*.

GEORGE ORWELL was the subject of several programmes when 1984 came round. Here Ronald Pickup plays him in a docu-drama.

Our House * (GB 1984; 6 × 30m). Families who have lived at least 50 years in the same house show the cameras round, whether it's a stately home or a suburban semi; the idea came from Robert Robinson, who was going to present the show but selflessly decided the householders could better speak for themselves, and it worked out very nicely. Produced by David Pearson, for BBC.   PP

Our Lives (GB 1983; 8 × 40m). Carefully researched dramadocs about young people up against the times. Produced by Riverfront Pictures for C4.

Our Man at St Mark's. Early sixties British half-hour comedy from Rediffusion, its hero being a likeable young British vicar, played by Donald Sinden/Leslie Phillips, with Joan Hickson as the housekeeper. The British answer to *Going My Way*.

Our Man Higgins *
US 1962 34 × 25m bw
ABC/Columbia

An American suburban family inherits a British butler.

Adequate, predictable star vehicle with its star in very good form.

cr Paul Harrison, from the radio series *It's Higgins, Sir*

STANLEY HOLLOWAY, Frank Maxwell, Audrey Totter

Our Miss Brooks *
US 1952–6 127 × 25m bw
CBS/Desilu

Misadventures of a high-school teacher. Lively star vehicle.

EVE ARDEN, GALE GORDON, Robert Rockwell, Richard Crenna

Our Private World (US 1965). Unsuccessful CBS peak-time soap opera, a spin-off from *As The World Turns*; with Eileen Fulton, Geraldine Fitzgerald.

Our Street *
GB 1960 7 × 30m bw
A–R (Michael Ingrams)

Pioneering documentary series shot in one small London street (Ulric St, Camberwell) on the eve of promised – or threatened – redevelopment. When the series was rerun two years later a few things had changed. 'But,' as I wrote at the time, 'most of the people in the street have still lived there all their lives; rehousing is still promised and just as far off; the pub is still the principal focus; everyone knows everyone else. It is curious how this documentary series anticipated so many of the features of the fictional *Coronation Street*: there's even a sort of Ena Sharples, only nicer-natured. How urbanely and uncondescendingly Ingrams captured it all.'   PP

Our Town *
US 1977 96m colour (VTR)
Hartwest (Saul Jaffe)

A new production, carefully styled for TV, of Thornton Wilder's no-scenery play about life in a New Hampshire town at the turn of the century.

d George Schafer *p/d* Roy Christopher

Hal Holbrook, Glynnis O'Connor, Robby Benson, Ronny Cox, Barbara Bel Geddes, Ned Beatty, Sada Thompson, Don Beddoe

Our Winnie: see Objects of Affection

Out * (GB 1978; 6 × 50m). Superior retribution thriller with Tom Bell as a hard man of crime out of prison after eight years, obsessed by only one aim: to find out who shopped him and settle the score. Written by Trevor Preston; directed by Jim Goddard; produced by Barry Hanson; for Thames. My view at the time: 'Like the contentious *Law and Order*, but without that series' political purpose, it rejects the customary division of its characters into cops mostly on our side and robbers mostly on the other side. Life is seen as a match between two dirty teams, neither of which have much to commend them and to whom allegiance is mainly a matter of accident.

'Meanwhile the scenery is littered with victims of both sides, from Ross's deranged wife and forlorn son to bystanders like the ex-whore Cimmie (an excellent performance by Katharine Schofield) who had tried to start a new life. At the centre is Tom Bell's Ross, head tilted warily, the pallor of prison on his bony face, so hard a hard man that he has practically ossified. . . .

'On its chosen terms it is a well-written, well-directed, well-acted and consistent piece of invention. It allows the virtues of loyalty (Ross's old mates played by John Junkin and Brian Croucher) and acknowledges the dogged rectitude of the steady copper (Robert Walker). Nor does it ever suggest that its hero's chosen livelihood has brought him anything but bleakness.'   PP

Out of Court (GB). Half-hour magazine programme on legal issues of the day, usually each week for four or five months. Produced by Hugh Purcell, for BBC.

'One of the most compelling current affairs series on television.' – Chris Dunkley, *Financial Times*

'He threw a city into terror – and dared the cops to stop him!'
Out of the Darkness *
US 1985 96m colour TVM
CBS/Centerpoint/Columbia/Grosso–Jacobson

In 1976–7 New York is terrorized by a gunman styling himself Son of Sam.
Good factual docu-drama which manages to avoid exploitation.

w Tom Cook *d* Jud Taylor

Martin Sheen, Jennifer Salt, Matt Clark, Eddie Egan

'A piece of suspenseful TV filmwork. It's all in order.' – *Daily Variety*

Out of the Undertow (GB 1984). Real-life experiences of trying to weather the economic depression (by setting up small businesses, etc.) rather oddly embellished with a playlet to the same topic by Fay Weldon and a homily from social savant Richard Hoggart. A six-part BBC series, with Miriam Margolyes in the playlets.   PP

Out of the Unknown *
GB 1965–6 26 × 50m bw
BBC (Irene Shubik)

Science fiction stories dramatized by mostly expert hands and including some of the best examples of the genre. Irene Shubik had previously story-edited a similar season for ABC (GB) under the title *Out of This World*.
                                                      PP

OSCAR WILDE's story was told in a three-part dramatization. Back row: Jonty Lovell, Pat Quayle, Jonathan Haley. Front row: Robin Lermitte, Michael Gambon, Emily Richard.

The Outcasts *
US 1968 26 × 50m colour
ABC/Columbia (Jon Epstein)
After the Civil War, a white and a black man pair up as bounty hunters. Good tough western.
Don Murray, Otis Young

The Outer Limits ***
Working title: *Please Stand By*
US 1963–4 49 × 50m bw
ABC/United Artists/Daystar (Leslie Stevens, Joseph Stefano)
Anthology of science fiction thrillers. A mainly stylish collection over which cultists still enthuse, discussing such episodes as *It Crawled Out of the Woodwork*, *Galaxy Being*, *Corpus Earthling*, *Behold Eck!*, *The Hundred Days of the Dragon*, *The Zanti Misfits*, *The Soldier* and *Demon with a Glass Hand*. In between these high spots lay quite a bit of junk, but the main title disarmed criticism.

cr LESLIE STEVENS

Episodes were as follows:
The Galaxy Being (w/d Leslie Stevens; with Cliff Robertson, Jacqueline Scott). A radio engineer tunes in a 3-D being from Andromeda.
The One Hundred Days of the Dragon (w Albert Balter; d Byron Haskin; with Sidney Blackmer, Phil Pine). The President is impersonated by an oriental agent who can change skin structure.
The Architects of Fear (w Meyer Dolinsky; d Byron Haskin; with Robert Culp, Geraldine Brooks, Leonard Stone). Scientists create a fake monster from space to frighten nations into peace.
The Man with the Power (w Jerome Ross; d Laslo Benedek; with Donald Pleasence, Edward C. Platt). A mild professor acquires uncontrollable powers.
The Sixth Finger (w Ellis St Joseph; d James Goldstone; with David McCallum, Edward Mulhare, Jill Haworth). Experiments thrust an uneducated miner into the biological future.
The Man Who Was Never Born (w Anthony Lawrence; d Leonard Horn; with Martin Landau, Shirley Knight). An astronaut passes through a time warp and returns to find Earth full of monsters.
OBIT (w Meyer Dolinsky; d Gerd Oswald; with Peter Breck, Jeff Corey). Government investigations reveal that we are being surveyed by another world.
The Human Factor (w David Duncan; d Abner Biberman; with Gary Merrill, Harry Guardino, Sally Kellerman). An experiment accidentally transposes the brains of two men.
Corpus Earthling (w Orin Borstein; d Gerd Oswald; with Robert Culp, Salome Jens). Rocks plan to take over the Earth.
Nightmare (w Joseph Stefano; d John Erman; with Ed Nelson, James Shigeta, Martin Sheen). Aliens attack the Earth and take prisoners.
It Crawled Out of the Woodwork (w Joseph Stefano; d Gerd Oswald; with Scott Marlowe, Barbara Luna). Black dust feeds on energy and becomes an uncontrollable monster.
The Borderland (w/d Leslie Stevens; with Mark Richman, Nina Foch). Scientists propel themselves into the fourth dimension.
Tourist Attraction (w Dean Riesner; d Laslo Benedek; with Ralph Meeker, Henry Silva, Janet Blair). A tycoon captures a monstrous lizard fish.
The Zanti Misfits (w Joseph Stefano; d Leonard Horn; with Michael Tolan, Bruce Dern). Exiles from another planet are sent to Earth in insect form.
The Mice (w Bill Ballinger, Joseph Stefano; d Gerd Oswald; with Henry Silva, Diana Sands). A convict volunteers to be exchanged with someone from another planet.
Controlled Experiment (w/d Leslie Stevens; with Barry Morse, Carroll O'Connor). Martians explore the quaint customs of Earth.
Don't Open Till Doomsday (w Joseph Stefano; d Gerd Oswald; with Miriam Hopkins, Melinda Plowman). Eloping teenagers find in their bridal suite a box containing a creature from another planet.
Z-z-z-z-z (w Meyer Dolinsky; d John Brahm; with Philip Abbott, Marsha Hunt). A queen bee assumes human form.
The Invisibles (w Joseph Stefano; d Gerd Oswald; with Don Gordon, George Macready). A secret society plans to conquer mankind by attaching parasites to people's spinal cords.
The Bellero Shield (w Joseph Stefano; d Gerd Oswald; with Martin Landau, Sally Kellerman, Chita Rivera). A captured space creature protects itself by an invisible shield.
Children of Spider County (w Anthony Lawrence; d Leonard Horn; with Lee Kinsolving, Kent Smith). Five young geniuses return to the other world from whence they came.
Specimen Unknown (w Stephan Lord; d Gerd Oswald; with Stephen McNally, Russell Johnson). Mushroom-like organisms attack a space station.

Second Chance (*w* Lou Morheim, Lin Dane; *d* Paul Stanley; with Simon Oakland, Don Gordon). A spaceship ride in an amusement park is commandeered by an alien.

Moonstone (*w* William Bast; *d* Robert Florey; with Ruth Roman, Alex Nicol, Tim O'Connor). Astronauts on the moon discover something alive.

The Mutant (*w* Allan Balter, Robert Mintz; *d* Alan Crosland Jnr; with Warren Oates, Julie Betsy Jones). A scientist on another planet mutates after being caught in the rain.

The Guests (*w* Donald S. Sanford; *d* Paul Stanley; with Gloria Grahame, Geoffrey Horne). A wanderer stumbles upon a strange house where time stands still.

Fun and Games (*w* Robert Specht, Joseph Stefano; *d* Gerd Oswald; with Nick Adams, Nancy Malone). On a strange planet, the national sport is pitting creatures from other planets against each other.

The Special One (*w* Oliver Crawford; *d* Gerd Oswald; with Richard Ney, Macdonald Carey). Earth children are trained by an alien to plot their planet's destruction.

A Feasibility Study (*w* Joseph Stefano; *d* Byron Haskin; with Sam Wanamaker, Phyllis Love). Six city blocks are transported to another galaxy.

Production and Decay of Strange Particles (*w/d* Leslie Stevens; with George Macready, Signe Hasso). A nuclear reactor goes out of control and produces strange creatures.

The Chameleon (*w* Robert Towne, Joseph Stefano, Lou Morheim; *d* Gerd Oswald; with Robert Duvall, Henry Brandon). An intelligence agent infiltrates a party of aliens.

The Forms of Things Unknown (*w* Joseph Stefano; *d* Gerd Oswald; with Vera Miles, Barbara Rush, Cedric Hardwicke, David McCallum). A madman's machine brings the dead back to life.

The Soldier (*w* Harlan Ellison; *d* Gerd Oswald; with Lloyd Nolan, Michael Ansara, Tim O'Connor). An Earth soldier of the future comes back through a time warp.

Cold Hands, Warm Heart (*w* Dan Ullman, Milton Krims; *d* Charles Haas; with William Shatner, Geraldine Brooks). An astronaut circles Venus and comes back feeling changed.

Behold Eck! (*w* John Mantley; *d* Byron Haskin; with Peter Lind Hayes, Joan Freeman). A pair of spectacles enables the wearer to see monsters.

Expanding Human (*w* Francis Cockrell; *d* Gerd Oswald; with Skip Homeier, Keith Andes). A drug expands human consciousness.

Demon with a Glass Hand (*w* Harlan Ellison; *d* Byron Haskin; with Robert Culp, Abraham Sofaer). The last survivor on Earth is hunted by soldiers from an alien planet.

Cry of Silence (*w* Louis Charbonneau; *d* Charles Haas; with Eddie Albert, June Havoc, Arthur Hunnicutt). Animated tumbleweeds stalk tourists.

The Invisible Enemy (*w* Jerry Sohl; *d* Byron Haskin; with Adam West, Rudy Solari). Astronauts on Mars are menaced by monsters.

Wolf 359 (*w* Seeleg Lester, Richard Landau; *d* Laslo Benedek; with Patrick O'Neal, Sara Shane). A professor makes a miniature version of a distant planet and finds it alive.

I, Robot (*w* Otto Binder; *d* Leon Benson; with Red Morgan, Howard da Silva). A robot is on trial for murdering its creator.

The Inheritors (two-parter) (*w* Sam Newman, Seeleg Lester, Ed Adamson; *d* James Goldstone; with Robert Duvall, Steve Ihnat, Ivan Dixon). A meteor is melted down into bullets which have an unusual effect on those they wound.

Keeper of the Purple Twilight (*w* Milton Krims; *d* Charles Haas; with Warren Stevens, Robert Webber). An alien exchanges his intellect for an Earthman's emotions.

The Duplicate Man (*w* Robert Dennis; *d* Gerd Oswald; with Ron Randell, Constance Towers). A space anthropologist creates a duplicate of himself.

Counterweight (*w* Milton Krims; *d* Paul Stanley; with Michael Constantine, Jacqueline Scott). A simulated flight to another planet turns out to be real.

The Brain of Colonel Barham (*w* Robert C. Dennis; *d* Charles Haas; with Grant Williams, Anthony Eisley). A computer is activated by a human brain.

The Premonition (*w* Sam Rocca, Ib Melchior; *d* Gerd Oswald; with Dewey Martin, Mary Murphy). A test pilot is saved from death by a sudden suspension of time.

The Probe (*w* Seeleg Lester; *d* Felix Feist; with Mark Richman, Peggy Ann Garner). Survivors of a plane crash find themselves motionless on a solid sea.

Outlaws *
US 1960–1 50 × 50m bw
NBC

In the old West, two lawmen go after the remaining badmen.
Pretty satisfying action series which at the time was criticized for its violence.

Bruce Yarnell, Don Collier, Barton MacLane

THE OUTER LIMITS usually concerned some scientist hero afflicted by monsters from outer space, or from the lab, or even from the id. Here Cliff Robertson is warning the world.

The Outlaws
US 1982 74m colour TVM
ABC/Universal/Limekiln/Templar (Les Sheldon)

A plumber and his inventing partner are unjustly sent to prison; escaping, they find themselves on the run from the Mafia.

Zany comedy which seems to have been intended as a series, a farcical *Fugitive*.

w Robert Wolterstorff, Paul M. Belous d James Frawley ph Dennis Dalzell m Jerrold Immel

Christopher Lemmon, Charles Rocket, Joan Sweeny, Charles Napier, Robert Mandan

Outrage **
US 1973 74m colour TVM
ABC Circle/Michael Green

A well-to-do businessman is harassed at home by marauding teenagers and finds himself powerless to do anything about it.

Based on a true case of a man who finally took the law into his own hands, this is a chilling and well-observed piece of unpleasantness.

w William Wood d Richard Heffron

Robert Culp, Marlyn Mason, Beah Richards, Thomas Leopold

Outrage
US 1985 96m colour TVM
CBS/Columbia/Irwin Allen

When his daughter is raped and murdered, and his wife dies of shock, a man takes the law into his own hands.

Sounds familiar, but this is a gripping and well-acted variation, its second half consisting of the courtroom proceedings.

w Henry Denker

Robert Preston, Beau Bridges, Linda Purl, Anthony Newley

**Outside Edge ** (GB 1982; 105m). Very funny cricket-club comedy by Richard Harris, with Paul Eddington, Prunella Scales, Maureen Lipman. Directed by Kevin Billington, for LWT. PP

The Outsider *
US 1968 26 × 50m colour
CBS/Universal/Public Arts (Roy Huggins)

Cases of a Los Angeles private eye.

Philip Marlowe in all but name, with the right cynical flavour; pilot film was *The Lonely Profession*.

cr Roy Huggins

Darren McGavin

The Outsider (GB 1983; 6 × 50m). Goodish thriller set in and about a provincial newspaper, with John Duttine, Joanna Dunham, Carol Royle. Written by Michael J. Bird; directed by Roger Cheeveley and Frank W. Smith; produced by Michael Glynn, for YTV. PP

The Over the Hill Gang *
US 1969 74m colour TVM
ABC/Spelling–Thomas

Retired – really retired – Texas Rangers bring law and order to a corrupt town.

Mildly amusing comedy western full of old faces.

w Jameson Brewer d Jean Yarborough

Pat O'Brien, Walter Brennan, Chill Wills, Edgar Buchanan, Jack Elam, Andy Devine, Gypsy Rose Lee, Rick Nelson, Edward Andrews

The Over the Hill Gang Rides Again
US 1970 74m colour TVM
ABC/Spelling–Thomas

Three retired Texas Rangers rescue a drunken friend and make him a marshal.

More of the above, not exactly inspired.

w Richard Carr d George McCowan

Walter Brennan, Fred Astaire, Edgar Buchanan, Chill Wills, Andy Devine

Overboard
US 1978 96m colour TVM
ABC/Factor–Newland

While a rich man tries to find his wife who has fallen overboard from their yacht, both of them think back to the problems of their marriage.

Unlikely but effective suspense drama with both stars in good form.

w Hank Searles d John Newland ph Robert C. Moreno m Mark Snow

Cliff Robertson, Angie Dickinson, Andrew Duggan, Lewis Van Bergen, Stephen Elliott, Skip Homeier

Overland Trail
US 1960 17 × 50m bw
NBC/Stagecoach/Revue

Adventures of a stagecoach driver and his young assistant.

Adequate western.

William Bendix, Doug McClure

overnights: rapidly assembled and not always reliable audience ratings available the day after the broadcast.

Owen, Alun (1926–). Welsh–Irish–Liverpool writer who did as much as anyone to make TV the most exciting theatre in Britain around 1960. *The Ruffians* was written first, for the BBC, but ABC got on to the air ahead of it with NO TRAMS TO LIME STREET (1959), such a hit that they immediately commissioned two more: *After the Funeral* and *Lena, O My Lena. The Rose Affair* (1961) was a conscious and misbegotten attempt to escape the bonds of naturalism. In the later sixties Owen concentrated increasingly on short (30-minute) two-handers, culminating in an over-sold trilogy for the transatlantic market *MacNeil, Cornelius* and *Emlyn* (1969) with introductions by Olivier and high-priced stars appearing for charity. Owen's last series was *Forget-Me-Not* (piffling adventures of a girl reporter, 1976) since which he has been little represented on British TV. In his first flush he was indubitably the poet of television drama, writing about particular people in particular places in a way that spelled the truth for anyone.   PP

† Recent credits: *Norma*, 1974; *Kisch, Kisch*, 1983, with Ian Richardson, Anthony Bate, *d* Keith Williams, John Hefin; *Lovers of the Lake*, 1984, in *Irish Love Stories* series, RTE/C4.

Owen, Bill (1914–) (Bill Rowbotham). Bantam north country British character actor, best known on TV for his dirty old man in *Last of the Summer Wine.*

Owen Marshall: Counselor at Law
US 1971 100m colour TVM
ABC/Universal/David Victor (Douglas Benton)

A California lawyer defends a young man accused of rape and murder.
Comfortable, over-prolonged courtroom stuff which turned into a series.
w Jerry McNeely *d* Buzz Kulik
Arthur Hill, Vera Miles, Joseph Campanella, William Shatner, Bruce Davison
† The series ran to 69 × 50m episodes.

Owen Wingrave (GB 1971). Benjamin Britten's only opera purposely written for TV, and a rather sombre tract in favour of pacifism based on a Henry James story. But an event, an event.   PP

Owner Occupied (GB 1977). Feeble comedy from Thames set in wartime Channel Isles. Richard Murdoch deserved better, Hannah Gordon went on to better things, Robert Hardy played a comic Kraut much removed from his refined Sgt Gratz in *Manhunt.*   PP

Oxbridge Blues **
GB 1984 7 × approx. 75m
BBC (James Cellan Jones)
Razor-sharp, marginally-linked plays about college days at Oxford or Cambridge and what befalls the glittering graduates in later life, adapted by Frederic Raphael from his collections *Oxbridge Blues* and *Sleeps Six.* The period had sometimes been wrenched on from the fifties and sixties and early seventies to which they really belonged, but Raphael was the only television writer of the year to keep his contribution more prominent than his director's or his players'.
w Frederic Raphael *d* James Cellan Jones, Richard Stroud, Frederic Raphael *m* Richard Holmes
Ian Charleson, Malcolm Stoddard, Amanda Redman, Rosalyn Landor, Diane Keen, Michael Elphick, Roger Hammond, Clifford Rose   PP
† The closing credits were sung in Latin each time, ending with 'Vivat Collegium Sancti Johannis Evangelistae apud Universitatem Cantabrigiensem quod erat Iacobi Fredericique alma mater tolerantissima' (May the College of Saint John the Evangelist in the University of Cambridge, which was for James and Frederic a most tolerant mother, live for ever).

Ozzie and Harriet: see The Adventures of Ozzie and Harriet

Ozzie's Girls
US 1973 24 × 25m colour (VTR)
Filmways
The Nelsons rent out their sons' bedrooms to two college girls.
Lukewarm comedy for ageing fans, following what seemed like a lifetime of *Ozzie and Harriet* and their family.
Ozzie Nelson, Harriet Nelson

PQ 17 (GB 1982; 75m; colour). Straight-forward dramatization by Roger Milner of the subsequent ordeals of Capt. Jack Broome, the officer who was disastrously ordered to abandon a wartime Russian convoy to its fate, with an excellent performance in the part by Richard Briers, better known for silly ass roles. With Rowena Cooper, Patrick Troughton. Directed by Frank Cox; produced by Innes Lloyd; for BBC.   PP

Paar, Jack (1918–). American talk show host who made *Tonight* popular on NBC between 1957 and 1962. After that, showbiz saw little of him.

Packin' It In *
US 1983 96m colour TVM
CBS/EMI/Roger Gimbel/Jones–Reiker
  (Christopher Seitz)
An executive and his somewhat inert family move from Los Angeles to Oregon and opt for the simple life.
Overtones of *Mr Blandings* and *The Good Life* do not mar the freshness of this mild but pleasing comedy.
w Patricia Jones, Donald Reiker *d* Jud Taylor *ph* Robert Collins *m* Mark Snow
Richard Benjamin, Paula Prentiss, Tony Roberts, Andrea Marcovicci, Kenneth McMillan
'Makes no overbid for the big yock; contents itself with characters and wry observation. That suffices.' – *Daily Variety*

Page, Anthony (19 –). British theatre director with a few TV credits, notably *Horror of Darkness*, 1965, and *The Parachute*, 1968.

Page, Geraldine (1924–). Leading American actress who won Emmys in 1966 for *A Christmas Memory* and in 1968 for *The Thanksgiving Visitor*. TV movies include *Trilogy*, *Something for Joey*.

Page, Patti (1927–) (Clara Ann Fowler). American band singer who had her own TV series in the middle and late fifties.

Pagett, Nicola (1945–). British leading lady. *Upstairs, Downstairs*, *Napoleon and Love*, *Anna Karenina*, etc.

Pagnamenta, Peter (1941–). British current affairs producer and department head. Started *Real Lives* in 1984.

A Painful Reminder * (GB 1985). The horrors of the German concentration camps again, but as a programme within a programme. The 86-year-old Sidney Bernstein (Lord Bernstein) made a rare personal appearance to comment on film of the camps he had ordered, as an Allied officer, so that no future Germans could deny their existence. Alfred Hitchcock advised on the production but the result had never been screened publicly until now; by the time it was completed, the priority was to enlist the help of the Germans in getting Europe on its feet again. Also taking part in the programme were cameraman, film editors and three survivors of Auschwitz. Directed by Brian Blake, researched by Liz McLeod, produced by Steve Morrison, for Granada.   PP

Palance, Jack (1920–) (Walter Jack Palanuik). Gaunt American leading man who proved pretty durable. Series: *Bronk*. TV movies: *Dracula*, *The Godchild*, *The Hatfields and the McCoys*, *The Last Ride of the Dalton Gang*, *The Golden Moment*. Won Emmy in 1956 for REQUIEM FOR A HEAVYWEIGHT. From 1982 to 1985, introducing *Ripley's Believe It Or Not*.

Palestine (GB 1978; 4 × 60m). Pains-takingly researched (by Taylor Downing, Isobel Hinshelswood and others) history of Palestine from the beginning of British administration in 1917 to the birth of the State of Israel in 1948. With Jewish and Arab historians to provide rival glosses on the archive material, the series set the pattern for the same team's *The Troubles* two years later. Directed and produced by Richard Broad; for Thames.   PP

Palin, Michael (1943–). British comic actor and writer, one of MONTY PYTHON'S FLYING CIRCUS, and the creator of RIPPING YARNS.

The Pallisers *
GB 1975 26 × 50m colour (VTR)
BBC (Martin Lisemore)
The saga of a Victorian semi-noble family with political leanings.
Elaborate, expensive serial which didn't quite catch the public fancy.
w Simon Raven, *novels* Anthony Trollope *d* Hugh David, Ronald Wilson
Susan Hampshire, Roland Culver, Philip Latham, Fabia Drake, Carolyn Mortimer, Sonia Dresdel, Sarah Badel, Gary Watson
PP: 'Susan Hampshire did her best to live up to the flighty reputation ascribed to Lady Glencora but the show was stolen, for as long as he was allowed to survive, by Barry Justice as the disreputable Burgo – the character perhaps closest to Simon Raven's own sympathies.'

Palmer, Geoffrey (1927–). British actor with long lugubrious face, mostly in sitcoms these days (*Fairly Secret Army, Butterflies, Hot Metal*) but a superb Quince in the BBC Shakespeare *Dream*; also in the very funny single comedy *Radio Pictures*. 1985.   PP

Palmer, Tony (1935–). British writer–director, former pop music critic, with a special interest in musical themes; originally prickly in temperament and uneven in performance, he has now matured into a very considerable film-maker whose studies of Britten (1980) and Walton (1981) achieved the unprecedented feat of winning the music section of the Italia Prize two years running.
1967   *Twice a Fortnight*; BBC – comedy series with Bill Oddie, etc
1968   *How It Is*; BBC – teenage pop and chat show
1969   *How Late It Is*; BBC – teenage pop and chat show
Films
1967   *Britten and his Festival*; BBC – Aldeburgh
1968   *All My Loving*; BBC – The Beatles
1969   *Will the Real Mr Sellers. . . ?*; BBC – Profile of Peter Sellers
1974   *The World of Hugh Hefner*; YTV – The *Playboy* Millionaire
1976   *Harriet*; HTV – Series with Harriet Crawley
1977   *All You Need Is Love*; LWT – 13-part history of pop music
1980   *There Was a Time*; LWT – Life and music of Benjamin Britten

1981   *At The Haunted End of the Day*; LWT – Likewise, William Walton
1982   *Stravinsky*; LWT
1983   *Wagner* (epic series); C4
1984   *Puccini*; C4   PP

Palmerstown USA *
US 1980 1 × 96m, 16 × 48m colour
CBS/Embassy
A black boy and a white boy grow up together in the 30s in a rural southern town.
Painstaking attempt by the author of *Roots* to provide an autobiographical follow-up.
cr Alex Haley, Norman Lear
Jonell Allen, Beeson Carroll, Michael J. Fox, Bill Duke, Janice St John

Panache *
US 1976 76m colour TVM
Warner
Adventures of a 'second team' of the king's musketeers in 17th-century France.
A mark for trying, but both acting and production are very laboured.
w Duke Vincent *d* Gary Nelson
René Auberjonois, David Healy, Charles Seibert

Pandora * (GB 1971; 65m). Hugh Leonard's play about a lethal love affair; directed by Brian Mills; produced by Peter Eckersley; for Granada. My view at the time: 'This was really very good, written straight from the heart or perhaps from pride, as if Leonard were working an old infatuation out of his own system.'

Panic!
US 1957 31 × 25m bw
McCadden/NBC (Al Simon)
Anthology about people in jeopardy situations. The most memorable had James Mason and his family marooned for the weekend on the top floor of an office skyscraper.
cr Al Simon *narrator* Westbrook Van Vorhees

Panic in Echo Park
US 1977 74m colour TVM
Edgar J. Scherick
Problems of a doctor in a minority community.
Heavy-going failed pilot.
w Dalene Young *d* John Llewellyn Moxey
Dorian Harewood, Catlin Adams, Robin Gammell

Panic on Page One
aka: *City in Fear*
US 1979 135m colour TVM
Transworld

A city newspaper's treatment of a mass murderer is thought to be inflaming the situation.

Moderately tense and intelligent urban thriller which is still likely to have been better done in black and white in the late forties.

w Albert Ruben *d* Alan Smithee *ph* John Bailey *m* Leonard Rosenman

David Janssen, Robert Vaughn, Perry King, Mickey Rourke, William Prince, Susan Sullivan, William Daniels

'Energetic and sporadically entertaining.' – *Daily Variety*

Panic on the 5.22 *
US 1974 74m colour TVM
Quinn Martin

Wealthy train passengers are terrorized by three incompetent hoodlums who are exasperated at finding credit cards instead of money.

Smooth, odd little suspenser which goes on too long and submerges in cliché philosophy. Some smart moments, though.

w Eugene Price *d* Harvey Hart

Lynda Day George, Laurence Luckinbill, Ina Balin, Andrew Duggan, Bernie Casey, Linden Chiles, Dana Elcar, Eduard Franz, Reni Santoni

Panorama. The BBC's flagship current affairs hour, which has run on Monday evenings since 1957, sometimes stuffily, but sooner or later reasserting itself as the Corporation's Old Thunderer with important or controversial editions (see *Falklands War*). Presenters over the years have included Malcolm Muggeridge, Richard Dimbleby, David Dimbleby, Robert Kee, though it's safe to say no one remembers the very first incumbent: Pat Murphy, a Fleet Street promotions man.   PP

Panton, Louise (19 –). British documentarist who made much impact with *Heart Transplant*, 1982, and a distressing *Forty Minutes*, 1984, on female circumcision. Also a *Real Lives*, 1985, on Mormon wives in Salt Lake City.   PP

Papa Doc: The Black Sheep (GB 1969; 50m). Notable scoop by Alan Whicker, whose documentary on the notorious 'Papa Doc' Duvalier, gangster president of Haiti, included an interview Whicker obtained by happening to notice the presidential Telex number in the local directory and tapping his request directly into Duvalier's study. Dupont International Journalism Award, UCLA 1971. Photographed by Frank Pocklington; for YTV. My comment in 1969: 'As an account of Haiti it was graphic but scrappy . . . what Whicker is so good at is a superior version of getting his foot in the door. The encounters with Papa Doc were creepy and really quite tense, like Philip Marlowe finally coming face to face with Mr Big. And Whicker's gleeful account of how he managed the second one, with the aid of a Telex, helped convey the weird ambience of a ramshackle but lethal dictatorship.'   PP

Papazian, Robert A. (19 –). American producer, formerly network executive. *Murder by Natural Causes*, *The Seeding of Sarah Burns*, *Crisis at Central High*, *Stand by Your Man*, *Intimate Agony*, *Prototype*, THE DAY AFTER, *For Love or Money*, *Guilty Conscience*, *The Rape of Richard Beck*.

The Paper Chase *
US 1978   × 50m colour
CBS/TCF (Robert C. Thompson)

Problems of a group of older students at law school.

Pleasing but uncommercial rewrite of the feature film, with John Houseman reprising his ferocious professor.

w JAMES BRIDGES *d* Joseph Hardy

JOHN HOUSEMAN, James Stephens, Tom Fitzsimmons, Katherine Dunfee Clarke, Robert Ginty, James Keane

'Hot passions, high fashions!'
Paper Dolls
US 1982 96m colour TVM
ABC/MGM–UA/Leonard Goldberg
(Michele Rappoport)

Two teenage girls become high-fashion photographic models, and get their lives ruined in the process.

Glossy, slightly bewildering and utterly resistible peep behind the scenes of an unattractive industry.

w Casey T. Mitchell and Leah Markus *d* Edward Zwick

Joan Collins, Joan Hackett, Jennifer Warren, Daryl Hannah, Marc Singer, Antonio Fargas, Craig T. Nelson, Alexandra Paul

Paper Dolls
US 1984 9 × 50m colour
ABC/MGM–UA/Mandy Films (Leonard
Goldberg)
An attempt to make a series from the TV
movie with a different cast. It didn't work at
all and was cancelled almost in
mid-sentence.
w Jennifer Miller
Lloyd Bridges, Dack Rambo, Morgan
Fairchild, Brenda Vaccaro, Jennifer Warren

Paper Man *
US 1971 74m colour TVM
TCF (Tony Wilson)
Students come to grief when they redesign a
computer to make money for them.
Complicated melodrama which finally loses
the interest after a very smart beginning.
w James D. Buchanan, Ronald Austin d
Walter Grauman
Dean Stockwell, Stefanie Powers, James
Stacy, James Olson, Elliott Street

Paper Moon *
US 1974 13 × 25m colour
ABC/Paramount/The Directors' Company
A bible-selling con man and a smart little girl
team up in the farm belt during the thirties.
A fair copy of the movie; some said it was
better. But it didn't please.
Christopher Connelly, Jodie Foster

Paper Roses ** (GB 1971; 55m). Dennis
Potter play directed by Barry Davis and
produced by Kenith Trodd for Granada; of
which I said at the time: 'Comedian Bill
Maynard sags bravely into the role of a
boring 64-year-old journalist for an unfair,
wickedly funny and secretly nostalgic
send-up of Fleet Street by Dennis Potter –
his best since *Moonlight on the Highway*
[1969]. Joke headlines punctuate the action
and a somnolent TV critic comments upon
it, finally delivering himself of a hostile
review of the play you have just seen.'   PP

Para Handy (GB 1960). BBC comedy series
from the stories, much loved by the Scots, of a
little Clyde steamer and its thirsty crew. With
two great Scottish comic actors, Duncan
Macrae and Roddy McMillan, as skipper and
engineer, it exerted much pawky charm. A
separate attempt on the same source and
under the same title in 1974, again with
Roddy McMillan, was scuppered by an
inexplicable decision to winch the action
forward to the present day.   PP

The Parachute **
GB 1968 75m bw
David Mercer's striking fable of the
aristocracy toying with Nazism, with John
Osborne as the fastidious Werner Von Ragen
who breaks his back testing a new parachute
for the regime he despises. Also with Jill
Bennett, Isabel Dean, Lindsay Anderson,
Alan Badel. Directed by Anthony Page; for
BBC (*Play of the Month*). My 1968 review:
'What Mercer was trying to enshrine here was
a chunk of 20th-century mythology, a part of
our own times but already so remote and
grotesque it's sometimes hard to believe it
isn't a nightmare dredged up from some
ancient tribal memory. I was never tempted
to think I was watching a literal re-creation
of the Germany of 25 years ago. I did feel I
might have been watching a rush advance
copy of the kind of intelligent, interpretative
version of it that will be made in, say,
another 25 – or 2,500 – years.'   PP

Parade. Umbrella title for 27 Granada arts
programmes, mostly of performers in
performance, 1972–3. Produced by Peter
Potter.   PP

The Parade
US 1984 96m colour TVM
CBS/Hill–Mandelker (Claude Binyon Jnr)
Three generations of women in a Kansas
town are set to considering their lives by the
return of one of their men from prison.
Front-porch drama of the type familiar in the
fifties from the pen of this author and
William Inge. It now seems like a mass of
clichés dating right back to *Our Town*.
w N. Richard Nash, Emily Tracy, from
Nash's *story* d Peter H. Hunt *ph* Paul
Lohmann *m* Arthur B. Rubinstein
Michael Learned, Frederic Forrest, Rosanna
Arquette, Maxwel Caulfield, James Olson,
Geraldine Page
'The central storyline turns feet up in the
dying Kansas burg.' – *Daily Variety*

Paradise Connection
US 1979 96m colour TVM
CBS/QM/Woodruff (Buddy Ebsen)
A Chicago trial lawyer goes to Maui in search
of his missing son.
Very routine mystery with a South Seas
background.
w Brigitt and Jon Christiansen d Michael
Preece *ph* William W. Spencer *m* Bruce
Broughton
Buddy Ebsen, Marj Dusay, Brian Kerwin,
Bonnie Ebsen, Paul Lambert, John Colicos

'Saturday morning thriller stuff.' – *Daily Variety*

Paradise Restored (GB 1968). Poet John Milton enduring blindness, bereavement and disillusion in the aftermath of the Commonwealth but finally overcoming these obstacles, with some help from Andrew Marvell, to start work again on *Paradise Regained*. A stern and eloquent film by Don Taylor for *Omnibus* (BBC), with John Neville as Milton.   PP

The Paradise Run
GB 1976 52m colour
Thames *Plays for Britain* (Barry Hanson)
Howard Brenton's simplistic allegory about British troops in Northern Ireland. My review at the time: 'The notion of the young soldier (Kevin McNally) and his officer (Ian Charleson) being equally ignorant of what they were doing in the troubled zone was interesting but unexplored, unverified, just used. The soldier was so vague about the world that he thought Churchill was still Prime Minister; when Brenton needed it, though, he had an inquiring enough mind to start yelling questions in mid-patrol.'   PP

The Paras (GB 1983; 7 × 30m). Selection, training and weeding out of volunteers for the British Parachute Regiment, all very tough and not much fun, despite Glyn Worsnip as reporter. Produced by David Harrison, for BBC.
† *Behind the Lines* (1985; 8 × 50m) did the same for the Royal Marines' exclusive Arctic and Mountain Warfare Cadre, their grim survival exercises lightened by the wit of the R.M. instructors. The old firm of Ian Wooldridge (writer–narrator) and Michael Begg (producer) helped too.   PP

Paris
US 1979   × 50m colour
CBS/MTM (Steve Bochco)
Adventures of a black city detective who's a criminologist on the side.
Uneasy crime series with very variable stories and a star who doesn't seem happy with his role.
cr Steve Bochco
James Earl Jones, Lee Chamberlain, Hank Garrett

Paris, Jerry (1925–). American actor turned director, most successfully with *The Dick Van Dyke Show* (Emmy 1963, best comedy director) and *Happy Days*.

Paris 1900 *
GB 1964 6 × 50m bw
Granada (Philip Mackie)
Six Feydeau farces trimmed and tweaked up for television, and played for all they were worth by a stock company led by Kenneth Griffith and Alfred Marks, including Judy Cornwell, Adrienne Corri and Paul Whitsun-Jones; directed by Silvio Narizzano. My 1964 review: 'Philip Mackie hit on a stylish way of playing costume fiction in *Saki*, almost lost it with *Maupassant*, extended it with *The Victorians* and now brings it to a final polish. The screen imperceptibly goes oval, black-and-white becomes sepia-and-cream, and the action jerks along as if it were What the Butler Saw.
'Feydeau, admittedly, is the most inspired and ingenious *farceur* ever. But with a dispersed audience comedy is difficult enough at the best of times – the communal belly-laugh is out of the question. . . The ruthless but scrupulous abridgement here, the zest, the beguiling decorations and titles, add up to a result whose outstanding quality I should have mentioned earlier: it's very funny.'   PP

Paris Precinct
US 1953–5 26 × 25m bw
Etoile
French Sûreté inspectors clean up crime in Paris.
Cop show modelled on New York patterns.
Louis Jourdan, Claude Dauphin

Paris 7000
US 1969 10 × 50m colour
ABC/Universal
An American attached to the embassy staff helps visiting countrymen in Paris.
Inept hokum hurriedly conceived to use up the star's contract when *The Survivors* was cancelled.
George Hamilton, Gene Raymond, Jacques Aubuchon

The Park Is Mine
US 1985 96m colour TVM
HBO/Astral (Denis Heroux)
A Vietnam vet, who finds that his dead buddy has mined Central Park, takes over and defies the city.
Somewhat hysterical suspenser with a familiar message: don't give them guns.
w Lyle Gorch *d* Steven Hillard Stern
ph Laszlo George *m* Tangerine Dream
Tommy Lee Jones, Helen Shaver, Yaphet Kotto, Eric Peterson

Parker, Alan (1944–). British director, now into films, but with TV experience. *No Hard Feelings*, THE EVACUEES (BAFTA award, 1975). *A Turnip-head's Guide to the British Cinema*, 1986.

Parker, Eleanor (1922–). American star actress who when movies failed her made occasional forays into TV, the most successful of which was the series *Bracken's World*. TV movies: *Maybe I'll Come Home in the Spring*, *Vanished*, *Home for the Holidays*, *The Great American Beauty Contest*, *Fantasy Island*, *The Bastard*, *She's Dressed To Kill*, *Once Upon a Spy*.

Parker, Fess (1925–). American leading man of the fifties. TV series: *Daniel Boone*, *Mr Smith Goes to Washington*. TV movie: *Climb an Angry Mountain*.

Parker, Stewart (1941–). Northern Irish playwright whose comedies of Northern Irish life skirt around the troubles: *Catchpenny Twist*, 1978; *I'm a Dreamer, Montreal*, 1979; *Iris in the Traffic, Ruby in the Rain*, 1981; funny non-Irish subject, 1985, *Radio Pictures*.

Parker, Willard (1912–) (Worster van Eps). American leading man of a few forties films. TV series: *Tales of the Texas Rangers*.

Parkin, Leonard (1929–). British newscaster, long with ITN; former journalist.

Parkinson, Michael (1936–). Yorkshire reporter turned talk show host. His north country good sense and ability to get the best out of his guests were offset by his constant references to 'my show'. In the eighties he grew big in Australia but decayed into compering witless game shows in Britain, before being rehabilitated by sound radio as the Roy Plomley replacement on *Desert Island Discs*.

Parks, Bert (1915–). American compere and quizmaster of the fifties; later became associated with the Miss America pageant.

Parks, Michael (1938–). American leading man who once appeared to be following in Brando's footsteps. Series: *Then Came Bronson*. TV movies: *Stranger on the Run*, *The Young Lawyers, Can Ellen Be Saved?*, *The Story of Pretty Boy Floyd*, *Perilous Voyage*, *The Savage Bees*, *Murder at the World Series*, *Escape from Bogen County*, *Night Cries*, *Hunters of the Reef*, *Rainbow*, *Fast Friends*, *Reward*.

Parsons, Nicholas (1928–). British light actor and quizmaster; once a stooge for the comedian Arthur Haynes, in the seventies he became inseparable from *Sale of the Century*.

Part Two Walking Tall: see Walking Tall

The Partners
US 1971 20 × 25m colour
NBC/Universal/Don Lee
A black and a white cop find themselves in as much trouble as the criminals.
Integrated comedy chase show which quickly ran out of steam.

cr Don Adams

Don Adams, Rupert Crosse

Partners in Crime
US 1973 74m colour TVM
Universal (Jon Epstein)
A retired lady judge and a reformed crook set up a detective agency.
A recast version of *The Judge and Jake Wyler* with a plot about an amnesiac robber who can't find his own loot. Still no takers.

w David Shaw *d* Jack Smight, Jon Epstein

Lee Grant, Lou Antonio, Harry Guardino, Richard Jaeckel, Bob Cummings, Lorraine Gary, Charles Drake

'This morning their husband was alive. Now he's gone and given them the business!'
Partners in Crime
US 1984   × 50m colour
NBC/Carson Productions/Columbia (Bill Driskill)
The two wives of a late detective carry on his agency.
Light-hearted crime fluff which failed to appeal.

cr Bill Driskill, Robert Van Scoyk

Loni Anderson, Lynda Carter, Leo Rossi, Walter Olkewicz

'Guilty as charged, no matter what charge.' – *Variety*

Parton, Dolly (1946–). Amply-bosomed American country and western singer, in occasional specials.

The Partridge Family *
US 1970–3 96 × 25m colour
ABC/Columbia (Bob Claver, Larry Rosen)
Five singing kids tour with their widowed mother.
Amiable comedy with music which became a teenage rave when David Cassidy soared to stardom.

cr Bernard Slade *m* Hugo Montenegro
Shirley Jones, DAVID CASSIDY, Susan Dey,
Danny Bonaduce, Dave Madden

Party Manners (GB 1950; 90m bw; live).
Mild political comedy by Val Gielgud,
brother of John and head of BBC radio
drama, which incredibly prompted the first
and only instance of programme banning by
the BBC Governors (or in this case their
chairman) until the *Real Lives* hoo-hah 35
years later. After the first performance on
the Sunday night, the play was much
attacked for its depiction of Labour
politicians leaking atomic secrets; Labour
peer Lord Simon of Wythenshawe, BBC
chairman, cancelled the second performance
scheduled for the Thursday evening;
Norman Collins, then in charge of BBC TV,
resigned in protest and went off to drum up
the case for an alternative commercial TV
system.   PP

Pasco, Richard (1926–). Companionable
British actor whose round face has been
bruised by life in many fine performances,
from the TV version of *Look Back in Anger*
and *The Liberty Man* and *The Tin Whistle
Man* of the fifties through to *Sorrell & Son*
and *Drummonds* in the eighties.   PP

Pasetta, Marty (1932–). American musical
producer.

Passage to Britain (GB 1984). Four-part
documentary series on immigration to
Britain, from the Huguenots of the 17th
century to the Bangladeshi of today, well
researched and imaginatively located but let
down by a questionable take-it-or-leave-it
commentary. Produced and directed by
David Cohen, for TVS/C4.   PP

A Passage to England * (GB 1975).
Engaging and ingenious comedy about
smuggling Asians into Britain by fishing boat,
the innocent passengers turning out to be not
quite so innocent as first supposed. With Colin
Welland, Niall Padden, Tariq Yunns. Written
by Leon Griffiths; directed by John
Mackenzie; for BBC (*Play for Today*).   PP

A Passage to India * (GB 1965). Twenty
years before the David Lean movie the BBC
had a video go at E. M. Forster's story via a
stage script by Santha Rama Rau. 'This was
so relatively excellent,' wrote *The Observer*'s
Maurice Richardson with careful abandon,
'that I feel half-inclined to rave about it.

There was plenty of movement but none of
those self-conscious camera capers you get
when TV tries to compete with cinema on its
own ground.' With Sybil Thorndike, Virginia
McKenna, Zia Moyheddin, Cyril Cusack.
Directed by Waris Hussein, produced by
Peter Luke, for BBC *Play of the Month*. PP

Passage West *
GB 1975 2 × 50m colour (16mm)
BBC/National Film Board of Canada (Philip
  Donnellan)
A study of the great British emigration across
the Atlantic, told through two cases, one
today and one a hundred years ago.
Solidly engrossing documentary stuff.
m John Faulkner

Passing Through * (GB 1982; 55m).
Railway worker's evening routine of a drink
in the pub, as regular and predictable as the
trains whizzing by, is broken by a
button-holing stranger. An old-fashioned TV
play by Rhys Adrian which had that quality,
I wrote at the time, that films never seem
able to capture, of going on long after the
credits have rolled and the studio crew
packed up and gone home. With Lee
Montague, Ian Richardson; directed by
Desmond Davis, for BBC.   PP

Passions
US 1984 96m colour TVM
CBS/Columbia/Carson/Wizan (Bobbi
  Frank)
Wife and mistress clash after a businessman
suffers a heart attack.
Superior soap opera which presumes to
'explore human strengths as well as frailties'.
w Janet Greek, Robin Maxwell, Sandor
Stern *d* Sandor Stern *ph* Frank Stanley
m Bruce Broughton
Joanne Woodward, Lindsay Wagner,
Richard Crenna, Viveca Lindfors, Heather
Langenkamp
'There are plenty of confrontations: no
wonder the businessman isn't up to
recovery.' – Hollywood *Reporter*

The Patricia Neal Story *
US 1981 96m colour TVM
CBS/Lawrence Schiller (Don Silverman)
An actress slowly recovers from a crippling
stroke.
Everybody seems a little too earnest not to
get any of the details wrong in this overcast
true-life story.

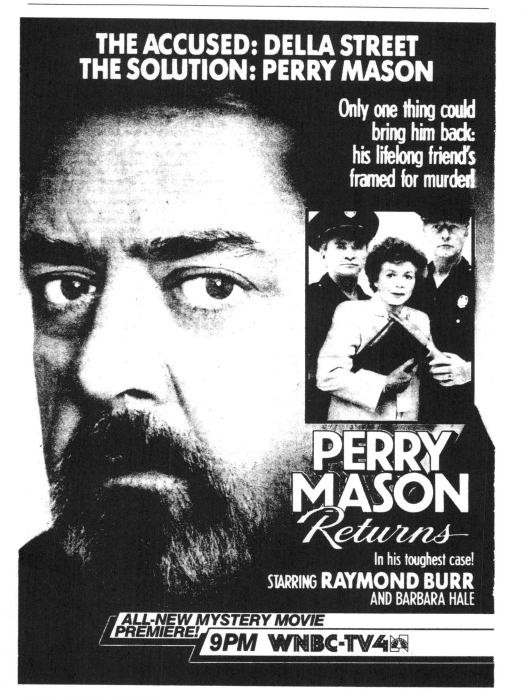

**THE ACCUSED: DELLA STREET
THE SOLUTION: PERRY MASON**

Only one thing could bring him back: his lifelong friend's framed for murder!

PERRY MASON *Returns*

In his toughest case!

STARRING **RAYMOND BURR**
AND BARBARA HALE

ALL-NEW MYSTERY MOVIE PREMIERE! 9PM WNBC-TV4

PERRY MASON RETURNS. Twenty years after their previous long-running series, Raymond Burr as Perry and Barbara Hale as Della had another stab at their famous roles.

w Robert Anderson, *book Pat and Roald* by Betty Farrell *d* Anthony Page *ph* Reynaldo Villalobos, Mike Fash *m* Lawrence Rosenthal

Glenda Jackson (Patricia Neal), Dirk Bogarde (Roald Dahl), Ken Kercheval, Jane Merrow, John Reilly, Mildred Dunnock

'The vulgarly curious will be disappointed: it's a story of fighting back, using humour and anger, and beating the odds.' – *Daily Variety*

Patrol Boat
Australia 1980 13 × 50m colour

Stories of 19 young men on an Australian naval patrol boat.
Routine action yarns, indifferently presented.

Andrew MacFarlane, Robert Coleby, Danny Adcock, Tim Burns

A Pattern of Morality: pilot title for Owen Marshall, Counselor at Law

Patterson, Neva (1925–). American character actress. TV series: *The Governor and J. J., Nichols.* TV movies: *The Stranger Who Looks Like Me, Message to My Daughter, The Runaways, Nowhere to Run.*

The Patty Duke Show
US 1963–5 104 × 25m bw
ABC/Chrislaw (William Asher)

A New York high school girl welcomes her identical European cousin for a visit.
Predictable family capers.
cr Sidney Sheldon *m* Sid Ramm, Harry Geller
Patty Duke, William Schallert, Jean Byron

Paul, Jeremy (1939–). Industrious British series writer with credits from *Country Matters* through to *Jemima Shore Investigates* and *By the Sword Divided*, also the two Dominick Hide plays and *Sorrell and Son*.
PP

Paul, John (1921–). British actor who became a national figure as *Probation Officer*, but when that show finished was little heard from. Also successful in *Doomwatch*.

The Paul Lynde Show
US 1972 26 × 25m colour
ABC/Columbia (Harry Ackerman, William Asher)

Domestic problems of an attorney.
Flustered generation gap comedy tailored for its star.
cr Sam Clark, Ron Bobrick, *stage play Howie*
Paul Lynde, Elizabeth Allen, John Calvin, Herb Voland

Paul Robeson *
GB 1978 65m colour
BBC (Geoffrey Baines)

A very adequate survey of the troubled career of a black American singer with 'red' leanings. With Peggy Ashcroft, Flora Robson, Elisabeth Welch. Research: Anita Sterner.

Paul Robeson: Tribute to an Artist * (US 1982; 30m colour). Outspoken documentary showing how a fine artist's career was ruined by political entanglements.

The Paul Sand Show *
aka: *Paul Sand in Friends and Lovers*
US 1974 13 × 25m colour
CBS/MTM

Adventures of a bachelor bass player with the Boston Symphony Orchestra.
Slightly unusual and quite likeable situation comedy.
Paul Sand, Michael Pataki, Penny Marshall

Pavarotti, Luciano (1935–). Italian operatic tenor, a popular TV guest.

Pay TV. A wired system tried out in Westminster, London, 1965–8, enabling subscribers to receive more expensive entertainment of their choice – movies, special events – by putting money in the slot. The Indianapolis 500 motor race live by satellite cost 10s (50p) an hour. It didn't catch on but most present-day cable systems have provision for pay-to-view billing for special events.
PP
LH: 'In America it was subdivided into **pay-cable**, normally indicating an overall monthly or weekly subscription charge, or **pay-per-view**, a coin-in-the-slot method of watching specific events.'

PBS. America's public broadcasting system, set up in 1969 and dependent on voluntary contributions, state and federal grants and corporate sponsorship. Mobil Oil funded the purchase of many British series aired under the umbrella title of *Masterpiece Theatre*.

Peabody Awards. Merit awards made annually to radio/television people and stations; awarded since 1940 in honour of George Foster Peabody, a New York banker.

The Peacock Committee. Set up in 1985 to enquire into the BBC's finances, under the chairmanship of Professor Alan Peacock. Due to have reported in July 1986, and expected to recommend against any wholesale change in the licence system.

Peacock, Michael (19 –). Accomplished British current affairs producer and executive who had the ill luck to be elevated to boy wonder in order to launch BBC2 in 1964, with only partial success; then briefly in charge of BBC1 before even briefer sojourn at newly formed LWT. Since the early seventies in transatlantic operations and VCR production.   PP

Peacock, Trevor (19 –). Seasoned British actor once on the pop-music scene (he wrote the song *Mrs Brown, You've Got a Lovely Daughter* for a TV play *The Lads* which re-surfaced years later as a hit); subsequently a Royal Shakespeare player. Recent TV includes *Lytton's Diary*, Titus in *Titus Andronicus*.   PP

peak time. Usually thought of in the UK as between 7.30 and 10.30 p.m. and in the US (which calls it prime time) as between 8 and 11 p.m. The half-hour between 7.30 and 8 p.m. is known in the US as prime access time. The need to define it at all is because in peak or prime time, when most people are supposed to be watching, maximum rates can be charged.

Pearce, Alice (1913–66). Adenoidal American actress who won an Emmy in 1965 for BEWITCHED.

'The explosive epic of love and war!'
Pearl
US 1978 3 × 96m colour
ABC/Warner/Silliphant–Konigsberg Co
(Sam Manners)

Life with the military in Honolulu just before Pearl Harbor.

Undistinguished rip-off of *From Here to Eternity*.

w Sterling Silliphant *d* Hy Averback *ph* Gayne Rescher *m* John Addison

Angie Dickinson, Robert Wagner, Lesley Ann Warren, Tiana Alexandra, Gregg Henry, Katherine Helmond, Alan Arkin, Brian Dennehy, Audra Lindley, Richard Anderson, Dennis Weaver, Max Gail

'Stereotyped soap characters make war look like a welcome purgative.' – *Daily Variety*

Peckinpah, Sam (1926–84). American director with a taste for violence. In his earlier days he created and sometimes directed such TV series as *The Rifleman*, *Klondike* and *The Westerner*.

Peck's Bad Girl
US 1959 39 × 25m bw
ABC

Misadventures of a 12-year-old girl.

Absolutely unsurprising suburban comedy.

Patty McCormack, Wendell Corey, Marsha Hunt

Peet, Stephen (*c* 1920–). British non-fiction film-maker who latterly specialized in head-to-camera reminiscences of historic events and epochs, e.g. *Yesterday's Witness*, *Tales of India*.

Penda's Fen (GB 1974). BBC *Play for Today* by David Rudkin: pubescent youth becomes caught up with spirit of the old pagan God of the locality (the Malvern Hills). I watched with admiration tempered by an occasional consciousness of being plunged from the sublime to the gorblimey. With Leo McKern. Directed by Alan Clarke, produced by David Rose.   PP

penetration, The extent to which TV is capable of being watched in specified areas; put a simpler way, the percentage of people having TV sets.

Penhaligon, Susan (1950–). British leading lady best remembered for *Bouquet of Barbed Wire*. Since then *Fearless Frank*, *A Fine Romance* (as Judi Dench's sister), *A Kind of Loving*, *Heather Ann*. In 1983 presented *A Kind of Living*, instructional series about self-sufficiency and growing your own high-fibre diet.   PP

Penmarric (GB 1979). BBC costume tushery set in Cornwall, with nothing said that wasn't either snarled or proclaimed.   PP

Penn, Leo (19 –). American director in TV from the early sixties: *Dr Kildare*, *Ben Casey*, *The Virginian*, *Marcus Welby*, etc. TV movies include *Quarantined*, *The Dark Secret of Harvest Home*, *Testimony of Two Men*, *Murder in Music City*.

'It helps us to look at our own world with an alert and sardonic eye. And there is no reason why we should not hum a tune and tap our feet as we do so.'
Pennies from Heaven **
GB 1978 6 × 75m colour (VTR)
BBC (Kenith Trodd)

In the mid-thirties, a frustrated song salesman tells himself that everything will be all right, but it isn't.

A unique concept, not entirely satisfactory but impeccably assembled, in which the more depressing the story gets (and it ends with the hero's execution and rebirth), the more

SUSAN PENHALIGON became a familiar face in *Bouquet of Barbed Wire*, and is here seen with Maurice Roëves in a fisherfolk drama called *Heather Ann*.

frequently the leading characters break into song and dance, or rather mouth to recordings of the time. Undeniably overlong and repetitive, it is superbly acted and directed, and the musical sequences, though their purpose remains slightly mysterious, often equal in delight those of many a major film musical.

w Dennis Potter *d* PIERS HAGGARD *choreo* TUDOR DAVIES

BOB HOSKINS, Gemma Craven, Cheryl Campbell, Kenneth Colley, Freddie Jones, Hywel Bennett, Ronald Fraser, Dave King

'Sparkling, brave, clever and caring.' – *Daily Mail*

People. Based on *People* magazine, this is a half-hour magazine format created for the 1978 season by Time–Life, with stylish segments corresponding to the feature pages of a modern illustrated magazine. It failed.

The People *
US 1971 74m colour TVM
Metromedia

A young teacher takes a job in a remote town and finds that her employers and pupils are aliens from another planet.

Quiet, understated science fiction with plenty of charm but not enough get-up-and-go.

w James M. Miller *d* John Korty

Kim Darby, Dan O'Herlihy, William Shatner, Diane Varsi

People and Politics (GB 1973–4). Useful late-night Thames series conducted mainly by Llew Gardner.   PP

People Are Funny (US 1954–60). Half-hour live comedy show for NBC, in which Art Linkletter chose people from the audience to indulge in stunts which often proved only embarrassing. It had been a radio favourite since 1942. In Britain (1955–6) it took the form of filmed stunts replayed before the studio audience, reappearing in the eighties as *Game For a Laugh*.

People from the Forest (GB 1981). The 60th birthday of perhaps the most imposing of Soviet dissidents, the nuclear physicist Andrei Sakharov, prompted this expressionistic BBC drama-doc (some of it deliberately in the style of the early Soviet cinema) telling his story and presenting both his case and that of the Russian State which now holds him in disgrace. With John Shrapnel as Sakharov. Written by Stephen Davis; directed by Mick Jackson.   PP

People to People (GB). Umbrella heading for various social documentaries and series on C4, e.g. *Just Like Coronation Street*, a two-parter on a terraced-house quarter in Oldham before and after drastic 'slum clearance', produced by Seona Robertson and Diane Tammes for Reality Productions; and *City General*, six-part hospital series shot in Stoke-on-Trent, produced by Sharon Goulds and Marilyn Wheatcroft for TV History Workshop.   PP

People versus Jean Harris *
US 1981 147m colour TVM (tape)
NBC/PKO/George Schaefer (Paul Klein)

A cardiologist and slimming-cure expert is shot by his mistress.
True-life courtroom drama based on the official transcripts. A little on the long side, and sometimes confusing, but gripping stuff nonetheless.

w George Lefferts *d* George Schaefer
ELLEN BURSTYN, MARTIN BALSAM, Richard Dysart, Peter Coyote

The People's Choice
US 1956–8 104 × 25m bw
NBC/Norden Productions

A politically ambitious young man loves the mayor's daughter.
Wholly American comedy which went down well with the voters.

Jackie Cooper, Patricia Breslin

Peppard, George (1929–). American leading man who came to TV with moderate success as *Banacek*. TV movies: *The Bravos*, *One of Our Own*, *Guilty or Innocent*, *Crisis Mid-Air*, *Torn Between Two Lovers*. From 1983, a mainstay of *The A-Team*.

Perenchio, Jerry (1930–). American executive, former agent. Joined Norman Lear in formation of Embassy Communications.

Perfect Gentlemen
US 1978 96m colour TVM
Paramount/Bud Austin (Jackie Cooper)

Four women whose husbands are in jail decide to steal back a large bribe to a go-between. Slow-starting comedy which disappoints despite its star cast.

w Nora Ephron *d* Jackie Cooper *ph* William K. Jurgensen *m* Dominic Frontiere
Lauren Bacall, Ruth Gordon, Sandy Dennis, Lisa Pelikan, Robert Alda, Stephen Pearlman
'Intrinsically a caper telefilm, show doesn't get hopping till the second hour, and then only fitfully.' – *Daily Variety*

A Perfect Match
US 1980 96m colour TVM
CBS/Lorimar (Andre Guttfreund)

A businesswoman finds she has a rare disease which requires the discovery of a donor with matching bone marrow; a search is therefore made for her own illegitimate daughter.
Indigestible mix of soap opera and case history, quite lushly mounted.

w John Sayles *d* Mel Damski
Linda Kelsey, Charles Durning, Michael Brandon, Lisa Lucas, Colleen Dewhurst

Perilous Voyage
US 1969 97m colour TVM
Universal (Jack Laird)

A revolutionary hijacks a ship and its cargo of machine guns.
Highly-coloured adventure story with plenty of action but not much sense.

w Oscar Millard, Sid Stebel, Robert Weverka *d* William Graham
William Shatner, Lee Grant, Michael Parks, Michael Tolan, Frank Silvera, Louise Sorel

The Perils of Pauline *
US 1967 98m colour TVM
Universal (Herbert B. Leonard)

An orphan girl has international adventures but finally marries the richest man in the world.
Sometimes engaging burlesque of the silent serial, afflicted by an attack of the cutesy-poos.

w Albert Beich *d* Herbert B. Leonard, Joseph Shelley *ph* Jack Marta *m* Vic Mizzy
Pat Boone, Pamela Austin, Terry-Thomas, Edward Everett Horton, Kurt Kasznar, Leon Askin

The Perils of Penelope Pitstop
US 1969–70 17 × 22m colour
Hanna–Barbera

A lady racing driver travels round the world combating her evil rival the Hooded Claw. Acceptable cartoon humour.

voices Janet Waldo, Paul Lynde, Mel Blanc

Perkins, Anthony (1932–). American actor, often of eccentric or sinister characters. TV movies: *How Awful About Allan*, *First You Cry*, *Les Misérables*, *For the Term of His Natural Life*, *The Glory Boys*.

Perrine, Valerie (1943–). American actress who has had some film success after graduation from TV where her movies include *The Couple Takes a Wife* and *Ziegfeld: The Man and his Women*.

Perry, David (19 –). British author of bizarre comedies, beginning with *Stuff and Nonsense* (1960), in which matter-of-fact characters gravely pursued their hobbies (in this case taxidermy) to logical but macabre extremes. *The Trouble With Our Ivy* (ABC *Armchair Theatre*, 1961) had a suburban householder cultivating a giant tropical creeper in his garden in order to spite the neighbours, and ended with both families reverting to apehood among the dense growth: a little masterpiece of humour unfortunately not matched by *Little Doris* (also ABC, 1963) featuring a pet sea monster. Perry, a theatre director, has written only once more for TV: *The Frobisher Game* (1969).

Perry Mason ***
US 1957–65 245 × 50m bw (last episode in colour)
CBS/Paisano (GAIL PATRICK JACKSON)

Cases of a defence lawyer who, aided by a smart secretary and a friendly detective, always proves his client innocent and someone else guilty. From stories by Erle Stanley Gardner.

Totally formalized and immensely popular, this cleanly made show was a worldwide success and its characters welcome in almost everybody's living-room, especially the DA who never won. Its mystery plots were complex but generally capable of being followed, and watching the show gave something of the satisfaction gained by crossword addicts.

RAYMOND BURR, BARBARA HALE, WILLIAM TALMAN, WILLIAM HOPPER, RAY COLLINS

† In the last episode, *The Case of the Final Fadeout*, guest stars included Erle Stanley Gardner as the judge.

†† In *The Case of the Constant Doyle*, when Burr was ill, Bette Davis played a lawyer friend who also won her case.

'Only one thing could bring him back: his lifelong friend's framed for murder!'
Perry Mason Returns *
US 1985 96m colour TVM
NBC/Viacom/Intermedia/Strathmore (Barry Steinberg)

Della Street is accused of murder.

Quite successful reprise of an old warhorse.

w Dean Hargrove *d* Ron Satlof *ph* Albert J. Dunk *m* Dick De Benedictis

Raymond Burr, Barbara Hale, William Katt, Holland Taylor, Richard Anderson, Cassie Yates, Kerrie Keane

Person to Person. Long-distance interview series created by and featuring Ed Murrow. It ran successfully from 1953 to 1960 on CBS.
PP: 'The title was also used in Britain by David Dimbleby for a series of filmed interviews (BBC, 1979) with Arthur Scargill, Mary Whitehouse, Lord Denning, Sir Peter Hall, Sir Freddie Laker, Sir James Goldsmith, mostly a little too bland and unchallenging to be really effective.'

Personal Report *
GB 1977–8 6 × 50m colour
ATV

A stab at the *One Pair of Eyes* format, if a little more argumentative and political in content, e.g. Auberon Waugh inveighing against strikes or Peter Odell, an economist, against British North Sea Oil taxation. John Pilger visited Czechoslovakia and in the best of the bunch Jack Trevor Story surveyed the new town of Milton Keynes and, in the episode's sub-title, advised *I'd Turn Back If I Were You, Doris*.   PP

The Persuaders *
GB 1971 24 × 50m colour
ITC

Two wealthy adventurers fight corruption all over the world.

Not much more serious than the 'Road' films, this series conveyed plenty of fun and its American failure was a mystery.

m John Barry

ROGER MOORE, TONY CURTIS, Laurence Naismith

Persuasion *
GB 1969 5 × 50m colour (VTR)
Granada (Howard Baker)

Anne Elliott rejects the man she loves but later wins him back.
Diligent adaptation of Jane Austen's last romantic novel, filmed in Dorset and Somerset.

w Julian Mitchell d Howard Baker

Ann Firbank, Bryan Marshall

Pertwee, Jon (1919–). Elongated British comic actor whose TV peaks are a period as *Dr Who* and another as *Worzel Gummidge.*

Pete and Gladys
US 1960–1 70 × 25m bw
CBS

Archetypal domestic comedy, a spin-off from *December Bride.*

Harry Morgan, Cara Williams, Verna Felton, Gale Gordon

Pete Kelly's Blues
US 1959 13 × 25m bw
NBC/Universal/Jack Webb

Adventures of a trumpet player in Kansas City in the twenties.
An unsuccessful, moody reprise of an unsuccessful, moody movie.

William Reynolds, Connee Boswell

Peter and Paul
US 1981 2 × 96m colour TVM
MCA (Stan Hough)

After the Crucifixion, two men keep the Christian faith alive.
Dreary Bible-in-pictures, with actors uncomfortable in their clothes and direction which apparently can afford no action beyond talking heads.

w Christopher Knopf d Robert Day

Anthony Hopkins, Robert Foxworth, Raymond Burr, Eddie Albert, Jean Peters, Herbert Lom, Jose Ferrer, David Gwillim, Jon Finch

Peter Gunn ***
US 1958–60 114 × 25m bw
NBC/Spartan (Blake Edwards)

Cases of a big city private eye.
Amusing tongue-in-cheek semi-spoof of the genre, with performances and production in key and from the star a fine impersonation of Cary Grant. A movie, *Gunn*, was subsequently made.

cr BLAKE EDWARDS m Henry Mancini

CRAIG STEVENS, LOLA ALBRIGHT, Herschel Bernardi

Peter Loves Mary
US 1960 32 × 25m bw
NBC/Four Star

The private lives of a show business couple.
Standard domestic farce.

Peter Lind Hayes, Mary Healy

† A previous format with musical interludes had played in 1950 as *The Peter Lind Hayes Show.*

Peter Lundy and the Medicine Hat Stallion
US 1977 96m colour TVM
NBC/Ed Friendly

A Pony Express rider recalls his youth in Nebraska.
Overlong pilot which caused no enthusiasm.

w Jack Turley, *novel* Marguerite Henry d Michael O'Herlihy ph Robert L. Morrison m Morton Stevens

Leif Garrett, Mitch Ryan, John Anderson

Peter Pan. The legendary TV production of the J. M. Barrie classic was the one originally presented live in 1955 by NBC, directed by Michael Kidd, with Mary Martin and Cyril Ritchard. Taped the following year, it was repeated many times.

Peter Pan
GB 1976 96m colour (VTR)
ITC (Gary Smith)

A stagey version, lacking in inspiration throughout.

adaptors Andrew Birkin, Jack Burns d Dwight Hemion *songs* Leslie Bricusse, Tony Newley

Mia Farrow, Danny Kaye

Peter Potamus
US 1964 42 × 25m colour
Hanna–Barbera

Adventures of a globe-trotting purple hippo and his monkey assistant So-So. Other segments introduce Breezely and Sneezely, a polar bear and a seal; and Yippy, Yappy and Yahooey, three dogs.

Peter the Great *
US 1986 8 × 50m colour miniseries
NBC/Viacom/Lawrence Schiller

The life and times of the czar of Russia who in the 17th century did much to civilize his country.
Ambitious and impressively filmed history, but few people wanted to know.

w Edward Anhalt, *book* by Robert K. Massie d Marvin J. Chomsky ph VITTORIO STORARO pd Alexander Popov

Graham McGrath/Jan Niklas/Maximilian Schell (as Peter), Lilli Palmer, Vanessa Redgrave, Laurence Olivier, Omar Sharif, Trevor Howard, Hanna Schygulla, Helmut Griem, Ursula Andress, Elke Sommer, Mel Ferrer, Jeremy Kemp

'It has all the elements of a Russian *Roots*.' – Brandon Tartikoff, President, NBC Entertainment

LH: 'I seldom buy shows in which the characters leave the room backwards.'

Petrie, Daniel (1920–). American director who moves from big screen to small and won an Emmy in 1976 for *Eleanor and Franklin: The White House Years*. Other TV movies: *Silent Night, Lonely Night, The City, A Howling in the Woods, Moon of the Wolf, Trouble Comes to Town, Mousey, Eleanor and Franklin, Sybil, The Quinns, The Dollmaker*, etc.

Petrocelli
US 1974 48 × 50m colour
NBC/Paramount (Thomas L. Miller, Edward J. Milkis)

A lawyer of Italian origin practises in a southwestern cattle town.
Courtroom series drawn from the TV movie *Night Games*, which was itself derived from the theatrical movie *The Lawyer*. Quite efficient, not very likeable. Filmed in Tucson.
cr Sidney J. Furie, Harold Buchman, E. Jack Neuman
Barry Newman, Susan Howard, Albert Salmi

Petticoat Junction *
US 1963–9 148 × 25m colour
CBS/Filmways (Al Simon/Charles Stewart)

Misadventures in a rural hotel and the train which serves it.
Studio-bound farce, quite nimbly presented by an engaging cast.
cr Paul Henning
BEA BENADERET, Edgar Buchanan, Linda Kaye, Douglass Dumbrille, Charles Lane, Rufe Davis, Smiley Burnette, Meredith McRae, Lori Saunders (June Lockhart replaced Bea Benaderet who died during fifth season)

Pettifer, Julian (1935–). British roving reporter: *Panorama, 24 Hours*, etc. BAFTA award 1969 for his coverage of the Vietnam war. Later: *Diamonds in the Sky, Nature Watch, The Shogun Inheritance, Automania. Fit for a King* (about Gordonstoun School) and the quiz show *Busman's Holiday*.

Peyton Place ***
US 1964–8 514 × 25m colour (1st two seasons bw)
ABC/TCF (Paul Monash)

Twice-weekly serial revealing the dark secrets of a small town.
Initially at least a superior piece of dramaturgy, cleverly directed, photographed and cast. The inevitable lapse came well before the end, with the departure of the first set of characters.
cr PAUL MONASH, *novel* Grace Metalious
DOROTHY MALONE, Ed Nelson, MIA FARROW, Christopher Connelly, George Macready, Dan Duryea, BARBARA PARKINS, RYAN O'NEAL, TIM O'CONNOR

† An unsuccessful – and dreadful – daytime soap opera, *Return to Peyton Place*, occupied the 1972 season. A telemovie, *Murder in Peyton Place*, appeared in 1977.

†† The original idea for a twice-weekly prime time soap opera was widely thought to derive from the British success with *Coronation Street*.

Peyton Place: The Next Generation
US 1985 96m colour TVM
NBC/TCF/Michael Filerman (Karen Moore)

The orphaned daughter of Alison MacKenzie turns up in town and sets off a series of violent events.
Hazy long-long-after sequel to a soap opera which would have been better left to gather semi-classic status.
w Rita Lakin *d* Larry Elikann *ph* Neil Roach *m* Jerrold Immel
Dorothy Malone, Barbara Parkins, Tim O'Connor, Ed Nelson, Pat Morrow, Evelyn Scott, Ruth Warrick, Chris Connelly, John Beck

'Their lives are about as interesting as the traffic on Sunset Boulevard.' – *Daily Variety*

The Phantom of Hollywood *
US 1974 74m colour TVM
MGM

When a film studio's back lot is bulldozed, mysterious deaths are caused by a masked figure.
Cheeky transplanting of *The Phantom of the Opera*; unfortunately the script isn't quite up to it.
w George Schenck *d* Gene Levitt
Jack Cassidy, Peter Lawford, Skye Aubrey, Jackie Coogan, Broderick Crawford, Peter Haskell, John Ireland

Phantom of the Opera
US 1983 96m colour TVM
CBS/Robert Halmi

A mad disfigured 'phantom' lurks below the opera house and advances the career of a singer who resembles his dead wife.

A crafty mix of the original story (whose author is not credited) and a 1944 film called *The Climax* which Universal made to use up the sets. As a pastiche, not too bad at all, but it's an old story however you vary the details.

w Herman Yellen d Robert Markowitz ph Larry Pizer m Ralph Burns

Maximilian Schell, Jane Seymour, Michael York, Jeremy Kemp, Diana Quick, Philip Stone, Paul Brooke, Andras Miko

The Phil Silvers Show: see You'll Never Get Rich

Philby: A Ruthless Journey (GB 1973). Documentary attempt to determine what motivated the third and most effective of the Foreign Office traitors, relying overmuch on film of Philby lately shot in Moscow by his son in which he revealed nothing. Comments from Hugh Trevor-Roper and ex-CIA man Miles Copeland. Written by Leslie Mallory; directed and produced by Peter Hunt; for BBC.   PP

Philby, Burgess and MacLean *
GB 1977 78m colour (16mm)
Granada (Jeremy Wallington)

A dramatized reconstruction of how the famous trio of Foreign Office officials became red spies and absconded to Moscow.

A fascinating piece of character drawing which touches a few nerves.

w Ian Curteis d Gordon Flemyng

DEREK JACOBI, Anthony Bate, Michael Culver, Elizabeth Seal, Arthur Lowe

'Ninety spellbinding minutes of insight and revelation.' – *Sunday Express*

Philip Marlowe (US 1959). Reasonably slick half-hour private eye series for NBC, with Philip Carey as the Raymond Chandler character.

'Any resemblance between this character and the Philip Marlowe created by the late Raymond Chandler is vestigial.' – *News Chronicle*

Phillips, Siân (1934–). Elegant Welsh actress, most memorable in *How Green Was My Valley* and *I, Claudius*; played Clemmie in *Churchill: The Wilderness Years*.

Philpott, Trevor (19 –). Unflamboyant British TV reporter, at his unbeatable best on some such low-pressure assignment as sailing down the Mississippi on a barge-train or following a pair of grotesquely overweight professional wrestlers on their profitable round of being hated and baited by the audiences. Less good when he has a social contention, e.g. the use and abuse of alcohol. His series usually embody his name in the title: *The Philpott File*, *Philpott in America*, etc. PP

The Phoenix
US 1982 74m colour TVM
ABC/Mark Carliner (Anthony and Nancy Lawrence)

An ancient god of light, buried in a Peruvian tomb, is brought to life but finds his new environment very strange.

Uneasily literary variation on *The Six Million Dollar Man*, with a superhero who looks pretty puzzled and does very few tricks.

w Anthony and Nancy Lawrence d Douglas Hickox m Arthur B. Rubinstein

Judson Scott, E. G. Marshall, Shelley Smith, Fernando Allende

† An extremely brief series followed but was promptly buried.

Phoenix, Patricia (1922–). British character actress, CORONATION STREET's Elsie Tanner.

Phyllis *
US 1975–6 39 × 25m colour
CBS/Mary Tyler Moore (Ed Weinberger, Stan Daniels)

Phyllis, a character from *The Mary Tyler Moore Show*, is always behind the eight ball. When her husband dies, she goes to live in San Francisco with her unsympathetic in-laws. Initially an amusing comedy full of cranky people, this had worn out its welcome by the end of its first season.

cr Ed Weinberger, Stan Daniels

CLORIS LEACHMAN, Henry Jones, Barbara Colby, JUDITH LOWRY

The Phyllis Diller Show: see The Pruitts of Southampton

A Piano for Mrs Cimino *
US 1982 96m colour TVM
CBS/EMI/Roger Gimbel (George Schaefer)

An elderly widow is in danger of being pronounced senile, but access to a piano saves her.

Satisfactory emotional binge with star acting.

w John Gay, *book* by Robert Oliphant *d* George Schaefer *ph* Edward R. Brown *m* James Horner

BETTE DAVIS, Keenan Wynn, Penny Fuller, Alexa Kenin, George Hearn, Graham Jarvis

The Picardy Affair **
GB 1963 60m bw

Playing Henry V in *An Age of Kings*, Robert Hardy became obsessed by the Battle of Agincourt and made himself an expert on the longbow, the weapon which won the day. Director Peter Newington took him to the site of Agincourt for an imaginative BBC evocation of Henry's campaign and the battle. Only one actor in costume helped out, perhaps not altogether necessarily: Esmond Knight, playing a representative English bowman. Later, Knight worked up his own one-man show on the theme, *The Archer's Tale*, also seen on TV. Hardy came back to the subject himself in *The Longbow* (1973). PP

Picking up the Pieces
US 1985 96m colour TVM
CBS (Dorothy G. Petrie)

A working mother carries on when her husband refuses to maintain her.
Dogged domestic drama climaxing in a courtroom. All too heavy for anyone to care.

w Gordon Cotler *d* Paul Wendkos *ph* Philip Lathrop *m* Paul Chihara

Margot Kidder, David Ackroyd, James Farentino, Ari Meyers, Joyce Van Patten, Barbara Rhoades, Herb Edelman, Stephen Young

Pickles, Vivian (1933–). British character actress who has made occasional hit appearances, notably as Isadora Duncan.

Pickles, Wilfred (1904–78). Yorkshire compere and comedian at his height in the forties; came back in the sixties as a character actor and was prominent in *For the Love of Ada* and *The Nearly Man*.

Pickup, Ronald (*c* 1940–). British stage actor who was notable on TV as Randolph Churchill in *Jennie* and George Orwell in *Orwell on Jura*.

The Picnic
GB 1975 30m colour (16mm)
BBC (Terry Hughes)

Silent comedy about the disasters which befall a crusty general and his family when they picnic by a river.

Disappointing, rather ill-timed pratfall farce, like Jacques Tati on an off day.

w David Huggett, Larry Keith

Ronnie Barker, Ronnie Corbett, Madge Hindle, Barbara New, Patricia Brake

† *By the Sea* followed in 1982.

The Picture of Dorian Gray
GB 1976 100m colour (VTR)
BBC

A lethargic adaptation of Oscar Wilde's famous story about an evil young Victorian who stays young while his portrait gets older and more raddled. Distinguished by Gielgud as Henry Wotton, but let down by Firth's impossibly pansy and broad-accented Dorian.

adaptor John Osborne *d* John Gorrie

JOHN GIELGUD, Peter Firth, Jeremy Brett

Picture Page. Archetypal BBC TV programme of the prewar (1936–9) service from Alexandra Palace. Joan Miller was the switchboard girl who would pretend to call up the celebrities, entertainers and quaint characters booked to appear and plug them into vision with the words 'You're through.' Started during the experimental period prior to the official opening of the service, the show ran to 264 editions, all edited by Cecil Madden, BBC senior producer and programme organizer. Leslie Mitchell was the interviewer (the interviews were always conducted standing up) and the performers lured to the studios for a £25 fee included Sophie Tucker, Maurice Chevalier and the young Danny Kaye. PP

Picture Parade. The BBC's first popular review of new cinema films on release, conducted by Robert Robinson in the early sixties. In the late seventies the format was revived as *Film 79*, etc., with Barry Norman in charge. PP

Picture Post (1938–57). Britain's most influential and, while it lasted, most successful picture news magazine, founded by Sir Edward Hulton. Victim of the television age, it ironically endowed television with some of its most enduring talents: reporters James Cameron, Trevor Philpott and Fyfe Robertson, all of whom were to have documentary series of their own; TV playwright Robert Muller; TV cameramen Slim Hewitt and Frank Pocklington. The publication was itself commemorated in a BBC documentary in 1978, *The Life and Death of Picture Post*.

'I have always regarded your magazine not as a picture paper but as an illustrated diary. I can't keep looking back at my TV.' – reader's letter, final issue   PP

Pictures
GB 1983 7 × 52m
Central (Joan Brown)

Roy Clarke digging away again at the early days of the English cinema (see *Flickers*), this time in the twenties, with Peter McEnery as an aspirant studio writer, Harry Towb as a stereotyped go-getting producer, Barry Dennen as a demon Slav director, and dialogue that matched the period only in the most superficial way. Also with Wendy Morgan as screen-struck ingenue, Anton Rodgers as fading star.

w Roy Clarke *d* Carol Wiseman   PP

Pig in the Middle (GB 1979–). Would-be sophisticated half-hour series about a fortyish man who decides to set up house with his wife's best friend. In the 1983 series of seven, the participants were Joanna Van Gyseghem, Liza Goddard and Terence Brady. Written by Charlotte Bingham and Terence Brady; produced by Les Chatfield; for LWT.

The Pigeon
US 1969 70m colour TVM
Spelling–Thomas

A black private eye tries to protect a family from the Mafia.
Unoriginal detection caper.

w Edward Lask *d* Earl Bellamy

Sammy Davis Jnr, Dorothy Malone, Ricardo Montalban, Pat Boone, Roy Glenn Snr, Victoria Vetri

Pigott-Smith, Tim (1946–). British actor excelling in authoritarian roles (*School Play*, *The Jewel in the Crown*) but also capable of gentility, Captain Hardy in *I Remember Nelson*; *The Lost Boys*; *Measure for Measure* in the BBC Shakespeare.   PP

The Pigs vs the Freaks
aka: *Off Sides*
US 1984 96m colour TVM
NBC/Sam and Greg Strangis

A small-town police chief runs into trouble when his son becomes a drop-out.
Faintly amusing domestic comedy set in a period, the late sixties, which Americans see with a rosy glow.

w Gordon Dawson *d* Dick Lowry *ph* Frank Beascoechea *m* Mark Snow

Tony Randall, Eugene Roche, William Windom, Grant Goodeve, Gloria de Haven, Adam Baldwin, Patrick Swayze, Elisha Cook Jnr, Penny Peyser

Pilger, John (*c* 1940–). Australian investigative journalist of untiringly Left-wing, anti-American disposition and accusing manner. Recent tracts: *Heroes* (1981) about spurned Vietnam veterans in America; *The Truth Game* (nuclear arms race propaganda) and *The Front Line* (war reporting), both 1983; *Burp! Pepsi versus Coke in the Ice Cold War*, 1984; *The Secret Country* (how we slaughtered the Australian Aborigines) 1985. Also a C4 series of interviews with fellow-whingers from Down Under, *The Outsiders*, and a TV play about the American scuttle from Saigon, *The Last Day*, both 1983.   PP

pilot. A film made in order to test a format and its public reaction. At one time the pilot simply became the first episode, but in the seventies for economic reasons it became normal to make a two-hour pilot even for a half-hour comedy. This resulted in some exceptionally boring pilots which squandered promising ideas.

The Pilots
GB 1963 60m bw
BBC (Richard Cawston)

Documentary about airline pilots, then in the first flush of flying jets and earning the heady sum of £2,000 p.a. It seemed informative but the critic Robert Vas, destined to be a notable documentarist himself, thought it 'a comfortable, detached and impersonal inquiry, executed with much hollow professionalism but never taking any risks' (*Contrast* magazine).   PP

Pine Canyon Is Burning
US 1977 74m colour TVM
Universal

A fireman leaves the city to begin a one-man country rescue operation.
Busted pilot, spun off from *Emergency*. Very routine.

w R. A. Cinader *d* Chris Nyby III
Kent McCord, Diana Muldaur, Dick Bakalyan, Andrew Duggan

The Pink Panther. A cartoon character from the title sequence of the film of the same name. *The Pink Panther Show* was a series of half-hours composed of the theatrical cartoons by De Patie–Freleng featuring the Panther and accident-prone Inspector Clouseau.

Pinky and Perky. Two puppet pigs, very popular on British TV in the fifties and early sixties.

Pinocchio *
US 1976 74m colour (VTR)
Vidtronics/Bernard Rothman, Jack Wohl

Musical version of the Collodi story of a puppet who becomes human.
Rather stiff at the joints, this old-fashioned TV studio production nevertheless finds the stars in good form.

w Herbert Baker d Ron Field, Sidney Smith
songs Billy Barnes

Danny Kaye (as Gepetto, Stroganoff and Collodi), Sandy Duncan, Flip Wilson, Clive Revill, Gary Morgan

Pinter, Harold (1930–). British playwright whose dialogue falls splendidly on the ear but whose meaning is often impenetrable. Work specifically written for TV includes A NIGHT OUT, TEA PARTY, THE LOVER. Has lately adapted stage two- and three-handers to television, including *A Kind of Alaska* (1984), *One for the Road* (1985).

Pioneer Woman *
US 1973 74m colour TVM
Filmways

Even after her husband is killed, a western-bound woman sets up house with her family.
Earnest sodbusting epic which unfortunately never made a series: it's convincingly done.

w Suzanne Clouser d Buzz Kulik m Al de Lory

Joanna Pettet, David Janssen, William Shatner, Lance Le Gault

The Pirate
US 1979 2 × 96m colour
CBS/Warner/Howard W. Koch

Romance and international intrigue surround an Arab oil tycoon.
A variety of lusty incidents fails to add up to drama, or even melodrama.

w Julius J. Epstein, novel Harold Robbins d Ken Annakin ph Ozzie Smith m Bill Conti

Franco Nero, Anne Archer, Olivia Hussey, Ian MacShane, Christopher Lee, Michael Constantine, James Franciscus, Armand Assante, Stuart Whitman, Eli Wallach, Jeff Corey, Ferdy Mayne

Pisier, Marie-France (1944–). French leading lady. TV movies: *The French Atlantic Affair, Scruples*.

Pistols 'n' Petticoats
US 1966 26 × 25m colour
CBS/Universal

Adventures of the long-suffering family of two rootin' tootin' hillbilly women.
Dismal farce which unhappily ended the career of its star.

Ann Sheridan, Ruth McDevitt, Douglas Fowley

Pit Strike (GB 1977). Alan Sillitoe's one television play, and only half an hour at that; for BBC (*Première*). My review at the time: 'Brewster Mason, too rarely seen on TV, was upright Joshua Reed, Bible-reading Nottinghamshire pitman sent down to London to picket power stations during the 1974 action, and billeted on a family of smart Socialist academics who assumed the workers were interested in power. Joshua was only interested in a decent wage, he said. Whatever the motive, it was in retrospect an ironic fable. That 1974 strike toppled the Heath government, ensured the election of Mrs Thatcher as Tory leader and sowed the seeds for the disastrous 1984–5 pit strike – from which Nottingham miners abstained. Also with Jenny Linden; directed by Roger Bamford. PP

Pitchi Poi *
European Broadcasting Union 1967 135m bw
RTF (Jacques Krier) with BBC, RTE, BRT, ARD, etc

The only Largest Theatre in the World contribution (from France) done as a co-operative Eurodrama, with eight countries each chipping in a segment of the saga as the hero Mathieu, a French peasant, plodded round Europe with the baby girl who had been thrust into his arms by a young Jewess fleeing from the Germans in World War II. His stubborn determination to restore her to her own family took 20 years, required several changes of actress in the part of the girl and accommodated a bit of scenery from every participant country, if only a passing wave (Luxembourg) or a glimpse from a bus window (Denmark). Written by François Billetdoux; overall producer: Jacques Krier; GB contributors: writer Peter Meyer, director Roderick Graham, producer Michael Bakewell. PP

† The BBC print was rerun in 1969 as a *Play for Today*.

Pitman, John (1940–). British try-it-yourself TV reporter schooled by Bernard Braden and still having a go. *Braden's Week*, *Man Alive*, *The Big Time*, *Let's Go Naked*, *The Other Half*, *Just Another Day*.   PP

The Pity of It All (GB 1966). The first, alas unlikely to be the last, account of mad, bad and dangerous driving on the roads. Produced by Hugh Burnett; for BBC. My view at the time: 'Burnett's account of road carnage on and around the M1 must be the documentary of the year, and not simply for its immediate kinetic effect on the beholder . . . Much television today is concerned with man and his environment. Well, this was the basic, literal collision of man and environment; this was the battlefield where the statistics are charted in blood and the sociology reduces to the smashed, spindly legs of a child.'   PP

The Plane Makers *
GB 1963   × 50m bw (VTR)
ATV
Drama series about management and union disputes in an aircraft factory.
A solid series which gradually spotlighted the performance of Patrick Wymark as John Wilder. After two seasons the centre of interest moved entirely to the board room and the title was changed to *The Power Game*.
cr WILFRED GREATOREX
PATRICK WYMARK, Barbara Murray, Jack Watling, Reginald Marsh

Planer, Nigel (1953–). British actor and comic, the quietest and sanest of *The Young Ones*. Recently: *Roll Over Beethoven*, *King and Castle*.   PP

Planet Earth
US 1974 74m colour TVM
ABC/Warner (Gene Roddenberry)
An American astronaut cast into the future finds himself enslaved by a society of women. One of three longform pilots for the same series, the others being *Genesis II* and *Strange New World*. None worked.
w Gene Roddenberry, Juanita Bartlett d Marc Daniels ph Arch R. Delzell m Harry Sukman
John Saxon, Janet Margolin, Ted Cassidy, Christopher Cary, Diana Muldaur

Planet of the Apes **
US 1974 14 × 50m colour
CBS/TCF (Herbert Hirschman)

Two astronauts lost in a time warp land on a planet where the apes are masters.
Clever retread of a powerful movie in a format somewhere between *The Fugitive* and *Gulliver's Travels*. Unfortunately it was badly scheduled, and the usual public indifference to quality merchandise caused a sudden cancellation, so that the astronauts are never rescued.
m Lalo Schifrin
Ron Harper, James Naughton, Roddy McDowall, Booth Colman, Mark Lenard
† A cartoon series, *Return to the Planet of the Apes*, was made in 1975 by De Patie–Freleng.

✿ **Plater, Alan** (1935–). Prolific British TV playwright, born in the North East and locating many of his stories there. Started on *Z-cars* (1963–5), since then many series, serials, single plays, even the odd musical. Note particularly:
1964   *Ted's Cathedral*; BBC
1968   *To See How Far It Is* (trilogy); BBC
1969   *Close the Coalhouse Door*; BBC, *Wednesday Play*
1974   *The Land of Green Ginger*; BBC, *Play for Today*
1975   *Trinity Tales*; BBC, six-part series
1977   *Middleman*; BBC, six-part series
1980   *The Good Companions*; YTV, eight-part serial from J. B. Priestley
1982   *The Barchester Chronicles*; BBC classic serial
1983   *Pride of Our Alley*; YTV
1984   *Orwell on Jura*; BBC
1985   *On Your Way, Riley!*; YTV
         The Beiderbecke Affair; YTV six-part serial
         On the Edge of the Sand; BBC
         Coming Through; Central   PP

Play for Today. The BBC's *Wednesday Play* retitled when transmission was switched first to Thursday evening, later Tuesday. Final season 1984.   PP

Play of the Month. Originally a regular monthly BBC1 occasion, latterly seasonal, always on a Sunday evening and nearly always an old warhorse of the theatre. But the title embraced some original works including Mercer's *The Parachute*, Nichols's *The Common* and some epic teutonic reconstructions by Rudolph Cartier. As an institution, finally abandoned in 1985.   PP

Play Things (GB 1976). Odd little filmed play about a misfit working as a professional playground warden; Stephen Frears's first collaboration with writer Peter Prince (from the latter's own novel) and second (after *Daft as a Brush*) with actor Jonathan Pryce. Also with Colin Campbell. Produced by Innes Lloyd; for BBC.   PP

Play Your Cards Right. British version of *Card Sharks* (US) re-worked to rescue Bruce Forsyth from the ruins of his *Big Night Out* show. Has run on ITV since 1980, produced and directed by Alasdair Macmillan, for LWT.   PP

Playhouse 90. Ambitious for its time (1958), this CBS season of '90-minute' film dramas supplied by Columbia marked the real beginning of the TV movie. Producer: Hubbell Robinson. Emmys: 1956, best new series; 1957, best dramatic anthology; 1960, best dramatic programme.

Playing for Time *
US 1980 140m colour TVM
CBS/Syzygy (Linda Yellen)

How women in a Nazi concentration camp survived by forming an orchestra; from the memoir of a Jewish cabaret singer.

Very heavy-going and overstretched, but in some ways a notable television occasion, with a grim reminder of the holocaust and some fine acting. A mild sensation was caused by the casting of Redgrave, an avowed anti-Zionist, as the Jewish Fania Fenelon.

w Arthur Miller, *book* Fania Fenelon *a* Daniel Mann *ph* Arthur Ornitz *m* Brad Fiedel

VANESSA REDGRAVE, Shirley Knight, Jane Alexander, Maud Adams, Marisa Berenson, Viveca Lindfors

Emmy 1981: Best Drama Special.

PP: 'Incomparably superior to *Holocaust*. A powerful screenplay by Arthur Miller begins aboard the train of cattle trucks carrying the prisoners across Europe . . . the arrival at the camp is brutal and squalid. Throughout, Vanessa Redgrave's bony skull and strong square face dominate the action, even when she is giving Fania maximum hesitancy and diffidence. She renders an honourable service to the play, to the person of Fania Fenelon and to the fortitude of those who in real life managed to survive Auschwitz. But she does this by taking over the part. A lesser actress might have entered it.'

Playing with Fire
US 1985 96m colour TVM
NBC/Zephyr (Jim Begg)

A troubled teenage arsonist is helped by society.

Boringly earnest melodrama which doesn't suit the chirpy star of *Diff'rent Strokes*.

w Lew Hunter *d* Ivan Nagy *ph* Gary Grauer *m* Dennis McCarthy

Gary Coleman, Cicely Tyson, Yaphet Kotto, Ron O'Neal, Salone Jens, Tammy Lauren

'A mediocre affair bogged down with repetitious situations and unlikeable people.' – *Daily Variety*

Playmates **
US 1972 74m colour TVM
Lillian Gallo

Two divorced men from different backgrounds become friends when taking their kids to the park. Later each begins to date the other's ex-wife.

Amusing modern comedy, smartly scripted and edited.

w Richard Baer *d* Theodore J. Flicker

Alan Alda, Doug McClure, Connie Stevens, Barbara Feldon

Plays for Britain (GB 1976; 5 × 52m, 1 × 70m). Attempt by Thames television in 1976 to endow a season of single plays with the committed, progressive, contentious (etc) qualities which got the rival *Play for Today* so talked about. All they succeeded in achieving was such strident and silly pieces as Howard Brenton's *The Paradise Run*, but Stephen Poliakoff's stage play *Hitting Town* (the lone 70-minute runner) went a long way to retrieving matters.   PP

Plays for Pleasure. Umbrella title for sextets of sunny plays from YTV in 1979 and 1981. Three contributions, at least, lived up to the claim: Willy Russell's *Daughters of Albion* (1979), *The Reason of Things* and *Cupid's Darts* (1981). Produced by David Cunliffe/Pat Sandys.   PP

Plays for Tomorrow (GB 1982; 6 × 55m). The then-familiar *Play for Today* umbrella title adapted to an anthology of scripts commissioned to show life about 25 years ahead. Nothing very imaginative emerged; the best (by Michael Wilcox) had a village cricket team picking its XI by computer. Series produced by Neil Zeigler, for BBC.   PP

Please Don't Eat the Daisies
US 1965–6 58 × 25m colour
NBC/MGM

Comedy of a suburban family, including a wife who writes and a shaggy dog. From the book (and film) by Jean Kerr.

Unexceptionable and unexceptional.

Pat Crowley, Mark Miller, King Donovan, Dub Taylor, Ellen Corby

Please Sir *
GB 1968 40 approx. × 25m colour (VTR)
London Weekend

A young schoolmaster has trouble with a rough mixed class.

Watchable sitcom depicting the lighter side of *The Blackboard Jungle* and *To Sir with Love*; borrowed in the US by the makers of *Welcome Back Kotter*. The staff room scenes were the most amusing. When the star departed the kids continued as *The Fenn Street Gang*.

JOHN ALDERTON, Erik Chitty, Joan Sanderson, DERYCK GUYLER

Please Stand By: see The Outer Limits

Pleasence, Donald (1919–). British character actor in all international media, usually as villain. TV movies: *The Bastard, All Quiet on the Western Front, Blade on the Feather, The French Atlantic Affair, Gold of the Amazon Women, Better Late Than Never.*

Pleasure at Her Majesty's *
GB 1976 100m colour (16mm)
Amnesty (Roger Graef)

A charity stage show, with peeps backstage.

A bit of a shambles, but useful as a record of some of the best sketches of the *Beyond the Fringe* and *Monty Python* teams, not to mention Barry Humphries and the Goodies.

Alan Bennett, John Bird, Eleanor Bron, Tim Brooke-Taylor, Graham Chapman, John Cleese, Peter Cook, Graeme Garden, Barry Humphries, Jonathan Miller, Bill Oddie, Michael Palin

Pleasure Cove
US 1978 96m colour TVM
NBC/Columbia/David Gerber (Lou Shaw)

Guests at a Florida hotel have a variety of problems.

Such as a terrible script.

w Lou Shaw d Bruce Bilson ph Jack A. Whitman Jnr m Perry Botkin Jnr

Tom Jones, Constance Forslund, Joan Hackett, Harry Guardino, Shelley Fabares, Ron Masak, Barbara Luna

'There's TV precedence for Lou Shaw's premise – *Fantasy Island* – but it's no excuse. This piece could give vacations a bad name.' – *Daily Variety*

Pleasure Palace
US 1980 96m colour TVM
CBS/Marble Arch/Norman Rosemont

An international gambler is called in to save the fortunes of an overextended Las Vegas hotel.

Thin but glossy comedy–drama with plenty to look at but not much to feed on.

w Blanche Hanalis d Walter Grauman ph Jack Swain m Allyn Ferguson

Omar Sharif, Jose Ferrer, Victoria Principal, Hope Lange, J. D. Cannon, Gerald O'Loughlin

Pleasure Palaces (GB 1982; 3 × 60m). The good old days of going to the pictures, from the silent era to the coming of the Talkies, as recalled by the fans. Produced by Seona Robertson and Dee Dee Glass, for C4/Reality Productions.   PP

Pleshette, Suzanne (1937–). American leading lady, familiar in many movies and on TV in the long-running *Bob Newhart Show.* TV movies: *Wings of Fire, Along Came a Spider, Hunters Are For Killing, River of Gold, In Broad Daylight, The Legend of Valentino, Law and Order, The Missing 24 Hours, Kate Bliss and the Tickertape Kid, Flesh and Blood, If Things Were Different, The Star Maker, Fantasies, Help Wanted: Male, Dixie: Changing Habits, One Cooks The Other Doesn't, Maggie Briggs, For Love or Money*

Plimpton, George (1927–). American investigative reporter who in the early seventies appeared in several specials showing him getting right inside the activity concerned: a professional footballer, a bit part player in a John Wayne western, an auto racer, etc. Generally more foolhardy than valiant.

Plowright, David (1931–). British executive, almost his whole career with Granada, which he joined in 1958. Programme Controller 1969, joint managing director 1975, sole m-d since 1981.   PP

Plummer, Christopher (1929–). Canadian actor in international films; despite many good roles he never quite managed star status. TV movies: THE MONEYCHANGERS (Emmy 1977), *Jesus of Nazareth,* THE SHADOW BOX, *Desperate Voyage, When the Circus Came to Town, Little Gloria Happy at Last, The Scarlet and the Black, The Thorn Birds, Prototype.*

The Plutonium Incident *
US 1980 96m colour TVM
CBS/Time–Life/David Susskind

A technician at a nuclear plant points out the possibility of plutonium contamination. Arrogant pinch of the plot of *The China Syndrome*, in itself sufficiently exciting and well acted.

w Dalene Young *d* Richard Michaels

Janet Margolin, Bo Hopkins, Powers Boothe, Joe Campanella

Pocketful of Dreams * (GB 1982; 60m). London villains pretend to be film-makers staging a bank robbery and at the last minute turn it into the real thing; an ingenious plot in *Minder* territory with some good jokes as the gang mastered the expertise of film-making and nearly became more interested in art than crime, but also a curiously hurried climax as if everyone was settling for an anecdote rather than a play. With Michael Elphick at his stubbornest and thickest, Philip Jackson; written by Jim Hill, directed by Stuart Urban, produced by Terry Coles, for BBC. PP

Poets and People * (GB 1985; 3 × 45m). Lively series in which contemporary poets read their works to appreciative audiences amid reasonably convivial surroundings, though working best of all in the case of the dry, abrupt Norman McCaig in the well-bred surroundings of an Edinburgh cultural society. Also, Tony Harrison, Douglas Dunn. Produced, directed and introduced by John McGrath for Freeway Productions/C4. PP

Points of View. Ultra-bright little abstracts of viewers' letters about BBC programmes, originally hatched to fill a five-minute gap before the news and briskly conducted throughout the early sixties by Robert Robinson. There was also a junior version for children. After a change of Robinson (from Robert to Kenneth) the programme was eventually taken off, until revived in the late seventies by Barry Took. PP

† The title had previously (1955) been used by A–R for 15-minute discussion fillers.

Poison Ivy
US 1985 96m colour TVM
NBC (Marvin Miller)

High jinks at a summer camp.
Thin teenage farce, like a polite Porky's. Very little discernible appeal to anybody.

w Bennett Tramer *d* Larry Elikann *ph* Bob Jessup *m* Miles Goodman

Michael J. Fox, Nancy McKeon, Robert Klein, Caren Kaye, Adam Baldwin

'Mild amusement is the best this production can muster.' – Hollywood *Reporter*

Polaris – the Secret World (GB 1971; 50m). First documentary to be shot aboard a Royal Navy Polaris submarine by a civilian crew (YTV) though other programmes followed suit, e.g. *Midweek* (BBC) three years later. PP

Poldark
GB 1976–7 29 × 50m colour (VTR)
London Films/BBC (Tony Coburn, Richard Beynon, Morris Barry)

A serial adaptation of Winston Graham's novels about the adventures of a squire in 18th-century Cornwall.
Moderately popular period tushery, as well done as need be.

w Jack Pulman, Paul Wheeler, Peter Draper, Jack Russell, Alexander Baron, John Wiles, Martin Worth *d* Christopher Barry, Paul Annett, Kenneth Ives, Philip Dudley, Roger Jenkins

Robin Ellis, Angharad Rees, Jill Townsend, Eileen Way, Judy Geeson, Ralph Bates

Poliakoff, Stephen (1952–). British playwright of rare and exact talent. *Hitting Town* (originally for the stage) and *City Sugar* (1976), *Stronger than the Sun* (1977), *Caught on a Train* (1980), *Soft Targets* (1982), *Strawberry Fields* (1986). PP

Police **
GB 1982 11 × 50m colour
BBC (Roger Graef, Charles Stewart)

Remarkable fly-on-the-wall series filmed during a nine-months sojourn with a division of the Thames Valley police based on Reading. Episodes featuring the humiliation of an aspirant detective constable and the insensitive investigation of a woman's complaint of rape aroused great controversy. In another bizarre episode the CID laid an elaborate trap for thieves known to be planning to burgle a local duchess, only to frighten off the attempt. Generally the detective branch showed up poorly; against this, the uniformed men and women going about the routine policing of the neighbourhood emerged as gratifyingly patient, good-humoured and understanding.

d Roger Graef *ph* Charles Stewart, Diana Tammes PP

LH: 'The effect is generally somewhat muddled though full of intriguing moments.'

† In the Midlands Central simultaneously screened *'N' Division* (6 × 30m; colour) monitoring Nottinghamshire police going about their duties but with the policemen voicing their own view of the job on the soundtrack. The detectives still came off worst.

†† *Operation Carter*, later the same year, chronicled a national round-up of professional villains shopped by an informer, as organized by the Thames Valley crime squad. Same credits as *Police*, 5 × 50m.

Police Five: see Taylor, Shaw

Police Squad (US 1982). A series of six half-hour comedies ordered by ABC from the makers of the spoof movie *Airplane!* Leslie Nielsen stars as the po-faced, accident-prone cop, sunk in a stew of verbal and visual gags which on the whole number more hits than misses. Produced by Bob Weiss; for Zucker/Zucker/Abrahams and Paramount.

Police Story **
US 1975–8 84 × 50m, 8 × 95m colour
NBC/Columbia/David Gerber (Stanley Kallis)

Anthology of serious dramas showing the human and social side of police work.
At its best, a compelling series, but the lack of a continuing thread made it easy to miss.

† A previous CBS half-hour series of this title, aired in 1952, had presented case histories from various law enforcement agencies.

Police Surgeon
Canada 1972–3 52 × 25m colour (16mm)
CIV–Colgate (Wilton Schiller)

Dr Simon Locke (qv) moves into the big city. Tolerable series with the doc encountering more criminals than Mike Hammer.

Sam Groom, Len Birman, Larry D. Mann

† *Police Surgeon* was also the title of an ABC (GB) bw tape series out of which grew *The Avengers*.

Police Woman *
US 1975–9 91 × 50m colour
NBC/Columbia/David Gerber (Douglas Benton)

A more hokey extension of *Police Story*, spun off from an episode entitled *Dangerous Games*. The star is decorative but doesn't do much except get herself into rather foolish and repetitive jeopardy situations. Production values high, though.

ANGIE DICKINSON, Earl Holliman, Charles Dierkop, Ed Bernard

Police Woman Decoy: see Decoy

'She put on a uniform and risked her life ... but when she took it off, she risked everything!'
Policewoman Centerfold
US 1983 96m colour TVM
NBC/ITC/Moonlight (Frank Von Zerneck)

A lady cop gets into trouble when she poses for a girlie magazine.
Silly though true, this slim story does not contain enough material to fill two hours, and the strain shows early on.

w Jan Worthington *d* Reza Badiyi *ph* Woody Omens *m* Fred Karlin

Melody Anderson, Ed Marinaro, Donna Pescow, Greg Monaghan, Bert Remsen, David Spielberg

Pollard, Su (1949–). British actress and comedienne, best known as Peggy in *Hi-De-Hi!*, but also in *Two Up, Two Down*.

Ponderosa: syndication title for Bonanza

Ponnelle, Jean-Pierre (19 –). French director who has revolutionized television opera with his versions of *Carmina Burana*, *Carmen* and above all his 1976 *Madame Butterfly* for German TV when I wrote: 'If he's a member of the Burgundy wine-shipping family of Pierre Ponnelle, he finally answers Omar Khayyam's old question as to what a vintner might buy one half as precious as that he sells: he can buy singers of the calibre of Placido Domingo and Mirella Freni, and Herbert von Karajan to conduct.' PP

Pony Express
US 1959 39 × 25m bw
NBC

Exploits of the pony express riders.
Quite acceptable youth western.
Grant Sullivan

Poor Devil
US 1972 73m colour TVM
Paramount

An aide of Satan fails to persuade a book-keeper to sign one of his contracts.
Grimly unfunny heavenly pantomime with all concerned ill at ease.

w Arne Sultan, Earl Barrett, Richard Baer *d* Robert Scheerer

Sammy Davis Jnr, Christopher Lee, Jack Klugman

Poor Little Rich Girls (GB 1984; 7 × 30m). Maria Aitken and Jill Bennett as dazzlers who can twist men round their little fingers etc. Temporarily out of husbands and money, they joined forces in what proved to be a forgettable combination. Granada. PP

Pope, Angela (1946–). British film-maker whose early baptism of notoriety came with *Yesterday's Men* (1971); a *Panorama* film about a comprehensive school likewise caused controversy. Lately she has concentrated on imaginative documentaries often about children: *A Childhood* (series), 1984; *The Treble* 1985; and a first fiction subject, *Shift Work*, 1986. PP

Pope John Paul II
US 1984 142m approx. colour TVM
Taft/Cooperman–De Paul (Burt Nodella)
A dutiful but scarcely enlightening biography, not very much better than *From a Far Country*.
w Christopher Knopf d Herbert Wise
ph Tony Imi m Wilfred Josephs
Albert Finney (with Michael Crompton as the younger John Paul), Alfred Burke, Brian Cox, Nigel Hawthorne, John McEnery, Lee Montague, Ronald Pickup, Andrew Ray

Popeye. The original 234 Max Fleischer cartoons of the spinach-eating sailorman were gobbled up by TV, and King Features Syndicate in 1961 made 220 new ones running five minutes each, but without the old spark. 17 half-hour shows followed in 1978.

Popi
US 1976 13 × 25m colour
CBS/ITP/Allied Artists (Herbert B. Leonard)
Adventures of a lower-class Puerto Rican New Yorker.
Dismal ethnic comedy drama.
cr Tina and Lester Pine, from the film of the same name m George Del Barrio
Hector Elizondo, Edith Diaz, Anthony Perez

The Poppy Is Also a Flower
GB title: *Danger Grows Wild*
US 1966 105m colour TVM
Comet/Euan Lloyd/TelsUN
United Nations agents destroy a narcotics ring.
All-star do-goodery sponsored by the United Nations; not much of a film.
w Jo Eisinger, *theme* Ian Fleming d Terence Young
Yul Brynner, Omar Sharif, Trevor Howard, Angie Dickinson, Rita Hayworth, E. G. Marshall, Gilbert Roland, Anthony Quayle, Eli Wallach, Stephen Boyd, Jack Hawkins, Marcello Mastroianni

Poppyland ** (GB 1985). Clement Scott, theatre critic and essayist of the *Daily Telegraph* in the 1890s, discovers a dream haven on the Norfolk coast but, under the eternal curse of the travel writer, destroys what he loves by writing about it. 'It was,' I noted, 'as if your favourite weekend hotel were suddenly to be filled by Terry Wogan, Joan Collins, Jeffrey Archer and Des O'Connor.' A curious, haunting, unclassifiable film with Alan Howard as Scott, Phoebe Nicholls as the personification of Poppyland. Written by William Humble from an idea by Richard Broke, who also produced, for BBC. PP

Porridge ***
GB 1974–7 30 approx. × 30m colour (VTR)
BBC (Sidney Lotterby)
An old lag in prison knows all the angles. Hilarious, sometimes thoughtful comedy of prison life, undoubtedly one of Britain's top sitcoms, largely because of its brilliant but unselfish star but partly because of the best comedy dialogue since *Steptoe and Son*. BAFTA 1974, 1976: best situation comedy.
cr/w IAN LA FRENAIS, DICK CLEMENT
RONNIE BARKER, RICHARD BECKINSALE, FULTON MCKAY, BRIAN WILDE
† In 1978 began *Going Straight*, a sequel showing Fletcher's attempt to adapt himself to his old home life.

Porter, Don (1912–). American second lead of the forties who grew into a useful character actor via TV roles in the series *Private Secretary*, *Our Miss Brooks*, *The Ann Sothern Show* and *Gidget*.

Porter, Eric (1928–). Gaunt British actor who achieved worldwide fame as Soames Forsyte in the 16-part *Forsyte Saga* and has deservedly retained a good measure of it with many excellent performances and at least two remarkable lookalike roles: as Sir Alan Brooke in *Churchill and the Generals* and as Neville Chamberlain in *Winston Churchill: The Wilderness Years*. In *The Jewel in the Crown* he played the enigmatic Count Bronowsky.

Porter, Nyree Dawn (1940–). Attractive New Zealand leading lady who landed a plum role as Irene in *The Forsyte Saga*. Also appeared in *The Protectors*.

Portrait *
GB 1978 6 × 25m colour (16mm)
BBC (Michael Begg)

Six people are painted by famous artists, and chat about their feelings as the portrait goes through its various stages.

A simple but effective idea, though the degree of interest must vary widely with the subject.

Robert Morley painted by David Poole, Chris Bonington by Alexander Goodie, Twiggy by Peter Blake, Eric D. Morley by Michael Noakes, the Earl of Lichfield by Lorne McKean, Ted Willis by Jim Mendoza

† In each case the model's fee was the portrait!

Portrait of a Rebel: Margaret Sanger
US 1979 96m colour TVM
CBS/Marvin Minoff, David Paradine
(Christopher Morgan)

The life and career of the advocate of birth control.

Rather demure and formal biopic which leaves a lot of questions unanswered.

w Blanche Hanalis d Virgil Vogel ph Don Birnkrant m Arthur B. Rubinstein

Bonnie Franklin, David Dukes, Richard Johnson, Milo O'Shea, Albert Salmi, William Windom

'Any insight is suspended in favour of historic images and tract-like statements.' – Daily Variety

Portrait of a Showgirl
US 1982 96m colour TVM
CBS/Metromedia/Robert Hamner

A girl dancer has problems in Las Vegas. Totally predictable wallow in show-business clichés.

w Bob Merrill d Steven Hillard Stern m Jimmie Haskell

Lesley Ann Warren, Tony Curtis, Rita Moreno, Dianne Kaye, Barry Primus, Howard Morris

Portrait of a Stripper
US 1979 96m colour TVM
CBS/Filmways/Moonlight (James Walsh)

A widow becomes a stripper to support her small son.

Lively exploitation piece which could have done without its sentimental tug-of-war over child custody.

w Ben Masselink d John A. Alonzo ph John A. Alonzo m Arthur E. Rubinstein

Lesley Ann Warren, Edward Herrmann, Vic Tayback, Sheree North, Allan Miller

Portrait of an Escort
US 1980 96m colour TVM
CBS/Filmways/Moonlight (Frank Von Zerneck)

A divorcee employed by an escort bureau gets into all kinds of trouble.

Romantic melodrama with touches of suspense thriller: an entertainment that goes off in too many directions at the same time.

w Ann Beckett d Steven Hillard Stern ph Howard Schwartz m Hagood Hardy

Susan Anspach, Tony Bill, Cyd Charisse, Kevin McCarthy, Edie Adams, Todd Susman

The Possessed
US 1977 74m colour TVM
Warner/NBC (Philip Mandelker)

A defrocked minister fights the devil in a girls' school.

Gloomy screamer, yet another attempt to bring The Exorcist to TV. (See Spectre, Good Against Evil.)

w John Sacret Young d Jerry Thorpe m Leonard Rosenman

James Farentino, Joan Hackett, Claudette Nevins, Eugene Roche, Harrison Ford

Post, Ted (1925–). American director with credits going back to the golden days of live television. Series episodes include Schlitz Playhouse, Zane Grey Theatre, Gunsmoke, Twilight Zone, Rawhide, Wagon Train. TV movies: Night Slaves, Dr Cook's Garden, Yuma, Five Desperate Women, Do Not Fold, Spindle or Mutilate, The Bravos.

Poston, Tom (1927–). American light comedian who in 1958 won an Emmy as best supporting actor on The Steve Allen Show. Subsequent film career nothing to shout about, but he played a supporting role in the Newhart series (1982–4).

Pot Black *
GB 1969–86 16 × 15m annually colour
BBC (Reg Perrin)

Annual made-for-TV snooker tournament which can be fairly said to have elevated a minority sport to a national entertainment. As a result major snooker tournaments now occupy many hours of TV several times a year, but Pot Black's highly-charged miniature format (only one frame per game) retained its popularity. I wrote in a review: 'The atmosphere of these games, staged in Birmingham, could be richer. The audience is ultra-respectful and there's not a pint of Black and Tan to be seen, not an eddy of cigar smoke. But the players in their dress trousers, bow ties and Cosa Nostra waistcoats . . . maintain the illusion of a secretive, serious, uncompromisingly masculine preserve. You won't see snooker players kissing.'

Original director: Jim Dumighan   PP

Potter * (GB 1979). Anecdotes about an intolerant retiree and his friendship with the rather eccentric local vicar. Star comedy series which sometimes hits, more often misses. With ARTHUR LOWE, JOHN BARRON, Noel Dyson. Written by ROY CLARKE; produced by Peter Whitmore in 14 half-hours; for BBC.

PP: 'Some funny moments and a nice line in pompous locution for Lowe, but it had that fatal whiff of a character run up to fit an actor rather than one striving for life on his own account.'

❋ **Potter, Dennis** (1935–   ). British TV playwright, arguably the most consummate and certainly the most versatile. He draws extensively on his Forest of Dean boyhood and later life, including a crippling illness, but only for the framework of his plays, not the wide-ranging imaginative content. Recurring elements in his plots include loyalty, patriotism, the artist's relationship with his work, the legacy of Christianity and the pop music of the thirties and forties. Also TV critic successively for the *Daily Herald*, the *New Statesman* and the *Sunday Times* between 1962 and 1978. As I said of him in an issue of the *Radio Times* (1979): 'Dennis Potter is to television as Robin Day is to news or Fiona Richmond to love, i.e. he simultaneously makes it, pronounces upon it and is passionately involved in it.'

Television plays:
1965	*The Confidence Course*;	BBC1
	Wednesday Play	
1965	*Alice*; BBC1 Wednesday Play	
1965	*Cinderella* (not produced)	
1965	*Stand Up, Nigel Barton*;	BBC1
	Wednesday Play	
1965	*Vote, Vote, Vote for Nigel Barton*;	
	BBC1 Wednesday Play	
1966	*Emergency Ward 9*; BBC2 Thirty	
	Minute Theatre	
1966	*Where the Buffalo Roam*; BBC1	
	Wednesday Play	
1967	*Message for Posterity*; BBC1	
	Wednesday Play	
1968	*The Bonegrinder*; Rediffusion	
1968	*Shaggy Dog*; LWT 'Company of Five'	
1968	*A Beast with Two Backs*; BBC1	
	Wednesday Play	
1969	*Moonlight on the Highway*; LWT/	
	Kestrel	
1969	*Son of Man*; BBC1 Wednesday Play	

1970	*Lay Down Your Arms*; LWT/Kestrel
1970	*Angels Are So Few*; BBC1 Play for Today
1971	*Paper Roses*; Granada
1971	*Traitor*; BBC1 Play for Today
1971	*Casanova* (6 parts); BBC2
1972	*Follow the Yellow Brick Road*; BBC2
1973	*Only Make Believe*; BBC1 Play for Today
1973	*A Tragedy of Two Ambitions* (in series *Wessex Tales*); BBC2
1974	*Joe's Ark*; BBC1 Play for Today
1974	*Schmoedipus*; BBC1 Play for Today
1975	*Late Call* (4 parts); BBC2
1976	*Double Dare*; BBC1 Play for Today
1976	*Brimstone and Treacle*; BBC1 Play for Today (not transmitted)
1976	*Where Adam Stood*; BBC2
1978	*The Mayor of Casterbridge* (4 parts); BBC2
1978	*Pennies from Heaven* (6 parts); BBC1
1979	*Blue Remembered Hills*; BBC1 Play for Today
1980	*Blade on the Feather*; LWT/PFH
1980	*Rain on the Roof*; LWT/PFH
1980	*Cream in My Coffee*; LWT/PFH
1985	*Tender is the Night*; BBC 6-part serial from Scott Fitzgerald's novel
1986	*The Singing Detective*; BBC 6-part serial

Other television:
1960	*Between Two Rivers*; BBC documentary film
1983	*Shakespeare in Perspective*: Cymbeline

In 1978 Potter was the subject of a *South Bank Show* (LWT) in which his work was assessed and he was interviewed by Melvyn Bragg.   PP

Pottery Ladies (GB 1985; 4 × 50m). Lives and works of three celebrated women artists who worked as designers in the Potteries in the art-deco heyday of the thirties and forties. A novel mix of art, industrial and social history with the ladies themselves – one of them 92 by this time – taking part. Produced by Jenny Wilkes for Metropolis Pictures/C4.   PP

Potts, Cliff (*c* 1942–   ). Tough-looking American leading man. Series: *Once an Eagle*, *Big Hawaii*. TV movies: *San Francisco International*, *The Magic Carpet*, *Live Again Die Again*, *A Case of Rape*, *Trapped Beneath the Sea*, *Nevada Smith*, *Love's Dark Ride*, *Little Women*, *Desperate Voyage*.

Powder Keg *
US 1970 93m colour TVM
Filmways

PLEASE SIR! The long-running TV sitcom received the supreme accolade of a feature film version, in which star John Alderton was joined (left to right) by Carol Hawkins, Liz Gebhardt and Jill Kerman.

In the 1914 southwest, two car-driving troubleshooters agree to get back a hijacked train from Mexico.

Ambitious pilot which flags between the action highlights. The resulting series, *Bearcats*, was shortlived.

w/d Douglas Heyes *m* John A. Tartaglia

Rod Taylor, Dennis Cole, Michael Ansara, Fernando Lamas, Tisha Sterling, John McIntire, Luciana Paluzzi, Reni Santoni

❋ **Powell, Dick** (1904–63). American leading man and singer of Hollywood in the thirties; in the forties he proved himself an actor and then, with David Niven and Charles Boyer, founded Four Star Television (there was no fourth) which in the fifties was quite a driving force of the industry. Before the camera, he hosted *Dick Powell Theatre*, which won many awards, and *Zane Grey Theatre*.

Powell, Robert (1946–). Blue-eyed British leading actor whose chief contributions to TV have been *The Four Feathers* and the title role in JESUS OF NAZARETH and *Frankenstein* (1984).

Powell, Vince (19 –). British scriptwriter, often with Harry Driver.

Power

US 1980 2 × 96m colour

NBC/Columbia/David Gerber (Jay Daniel)

The life of a labour trouble maker who is finally corrupted and imprisoned.

A television rip-off of *FIST*, this unspools like an old James Cagney movie with echoes of *On the Waterfront*; it never achieves the zest of any of its models.

w Ernest Tidyman *d* Barry Shear, Virgil Vogel *ph* Jacques Marquette *m* Jerrold Immel

Joe Don Baker, Karen Black, David Groh, Howard Da Silva, Tom Atkins, Ralph Bellamy, Scott Brady, Victor Jory, Red Buttons, Brian Keith, Suzanne Lederer, Bill Lucking, Paul Stewart, Jo Van Fleet

'Familiar to the point of banality.' – *Daily Variety*

The Power Game. An ATV monochrome VTR series of the mid-sixties which followed its predecessor *The Plane Makers* into the boardroom and made a star of PATRICK WYMARK as John Wilder, the power-hungry executive whom everybody loved to hate. Also much involved were Barbara Murray and Jack Watling. WILFRED GREATOREX created both series.

The Power Within
US 1980 74m colour TVM
ABC/Aaron Spelling (Alan S. Godfrey)

An unhappy young man is full of electrical energy because his mother was exposed to radiation.

You'd think there'd be a comic strip series in a hero who can shoot lightning from his fingertips, but this busted pilot bungles even that.

w Edward J. Lasko *d* John Llewellyn Moxey
ph Emil Oster *m* John Addison

Art Hindle, Edward Binns, Joe Rassulo, Eric Braeden, David Hedison, Susan Howard

'No one involved distinguishes himself.' – *Daily Variety*

The Powers of Matthew Star
US 1982 96m colour TVM
NBC/Paramount/Harve Bennett (Robert Earll)

A teenage hero and his black guardian are both from outer space, incognito on earth until invaders are ousted from their planet.

And ousting our baddies meanwhile, of course. A stylish pilot gave way to a very silly series with insufficient trickery to maintain the interest except perhaps for uncritical female teenagers.

cr Steven E. DeSouza

Peter Barton, Lou Gossett Jnr, Amy Steel, Judson Scott

† The one-hour series was interrupted by the young star's accident, and ran a total of 22 episodes.

Powers, Stefanie (1942–). American leading lady, in series *The Girl from UNCLE, The Interns, The Feather and Father Gang,* HART TO HART. TV movies: *Five Desperate Women, Sweet Sweet Rachel, Paper Man,* *Don't Look Behind You, Hardcase, No Place to Run, Shootout in a One Dog Town, Skyway to Death, Manhunter, Night Games, Sky Heist, Return to Earth, Washington Behind Closed Doors, Nowhere to Run, A Death in Canaan, Mistral's Daughter, Hollywood Wives.*

The Practice
US 1976–7 30 × 25m colour
NBC/MGM/Danny Thomas (Paul Junger Witt)

Conflict arises between an old New York doctor and his son who shares the same practice.

Reasonably lively Jewish comedy series.

cr Steve Gordon *story consultant* James Ritz
m David Shire

Danny Thomas, David Spielberg

The Practice (GB 1985; 13 × 50m). Determined attempt by Granada to emulate the Aussie *A Country Practice* in Coronation Street territory. The doctors were John Fraser, Brigit Forsyth and Tim Brierley. Enough viewers registered with them for a second series in 1986 with Rob Edwards replacing Brierley. Created by Mike Stott, produced by Sita Williams. PP

Praed, Michael (1960–). Saturnine young British actor, a romantic Robin in *Robin of Sherwood* before being tempted to Hollywood to become the soppy Prince Michael of Moldavia in *Dynasty.*

Pray for the Wildcats *
US 1974 100m colour TVM
ABC/Tony Wilson

Four business associates take a motor cycle trip into a remote region, but they end up fighting natural obstacles and each other.

A timid version of the cinema film *Deliverance*: not bad on its level.

w Jack Turley *d* Robert Michael Lewis

Andy Griffith, Marjoe Gortner, Robert Reed, William Shatner, Angie Dickinson, Janet Margolin, Lorraine Gary

Pray TV *
US 1982 96m colour TVM
ABC (Peter S. Greenberg)

A young minister discovers corruption in the evangelistic organization for which he works.

Interesting if exaggerated exposé of the religiosity which swamps American television every Sunday.

w Lane Slate *d* Robert Markowitz *ph* Don Birnkrant *m* Dannis McCarthy

John Ritter, Ned Beatty, Richard Kiley, Madolyn Smith, Louise Latham

'As for humanity, fervour, depth and truth, telefilm badly needs the Sinclair Lewis touch.' – *Daily Variety*

Praying Mantis *
GB 1982 2 × 78m
Portman Productions (Ian Warren) for C4

Classic French provincial murder plot as only French provincials nurture them, complete with goatish professor, beautiful wife, disloyal assistant and a Swiss insurance policy to give them all ideas. 'I didn't believe a word of it and wouldn't have missed a frame.'

w Philip Mackie, *novel* Boileau and Narcejac *d* Jack Gold

Carmen du Sautoy, Jonathan Pryce, Cherie Lunghi   PP

Prentiss, Paula (1939–) (Paula Ragusa). Elegant American leading lady who after the series *He and She* looked as though she was going places, especially as she was married to Richard Benjamin; but the promise was never fulfilled. TV movies: *The Couple Takes a Wife, Having Babies II, The Top of the Hill, Packin' It In, Mothers Against Drunk Drivers*.

Prescription Murder **
US 1967 99m colour TVM
Universal (Richard Irving)

A smoothie doctor murders his wife, but a dim-looking police lieutenant is on his trail. Actually the first *Columbo* (see *Mystery Movie*) made four years before the series proper began. One of the best, with the formula intact.

w Richard Levinson, William Link, from their play *d* Richard Irving

Peter Falk, Gene Barry, Katharine Justice, Nina Foch, William Windom

presentation. The department in a TV company responsible for getting the programme on to the air, supervising announcements, making timings, checking prints, meeting network junctions, etc.

The President's Mistress *
US 1978 96m colour TVM
Stephen Friedman/Kings Road/Richard Bright (Herbert Hirschman)

The American president's secret mistress is suspected by the CIA of being a Russian spy. Intriguing suspenser set in high places.

w Tom Lazarus, *novel* Patrick Anderson *d* John Llewellyn Moxey *ph* Robert Morrison *m* Lalo Schifrin

Beau Bridges, Joel Fabiani, Larry Hagman, Karen Grassle, Don Porter, Thalmus Rasulala, Gail Strickland

'A swift, attention-getting telefilm with good suspense and sharp twists.' – *Daily Variety*

The President's Plane Is Missing *
US 1971 94m colour TVM
ABC Circle

Air Force One disappears with the President aboard . . .
Rather mild political suspenser which disappoints despite a strong cast.

w Mark Carliner, Ernest Kinoy *d* Daryl Duke *m* Gil Melle

Buddy Ebsen, Peter Graves, Arthur Kennedy, Rip Torn, Raymond Massey, Tod Andrews, Mercedes McCambridge, Joseph Campanella

Press Conference. Popular BBC programme of the fifties which was exactly that – a politician or other newsworthy figure questioned by three or four journalists under a chairman, latterly Francis Williams.   PP

† See *Face the Press*.

Preston, Robert (1917–) (Robert Preston Meservey). Spirited Hollywood leading man of the forties who found greater fame on Broadway. *My Father's House, The Chisholms, Rehearsal for Murder, September Gun, Finnegan Begin Again*.

Pretty Boy Floyd
US 1974 74m colour TVM
Universal (Jo Swerling Jnr)

The hunt for a 1930s public enemy. Routine law-and-gangster stuff.

w/d Clyde Ware

Martin Sheen, Michael Parks, Kim Darby, Ellen Corby

Preview * (GB 1982; 80m; colour).
Ingenious, amusing and slightly creepy play by television critic Sylvia Clayton about a job lot of television critics assembling to see preview of a worthy documentary but instead being shown a home-made surrealist movie which has some nasty home truths for one and all. For the larger audience there was also the proposition, painlessly delivered, that TV

PRETENDERS. Costume adventures from semi-classical material are always popular in Britain, though the BBC usually does them best. Here are Frederick Jaeger and Frances Cuka in one of HTV's lesser serials.

may just about be acceptable as an alternative to life but never as substitute for it. With Anton Rodgers, Anna Cropper, Will Knightly and Cherie Lunghi. Directed by Jon Amiel; produced by Rosemary Hill; for BBC.   PP

LH: 'The play itself seemed to have only the most obvious points to make, but its form was imperfectly assimilated from a number of classic entertainments including *An Inspector Calls*, *Last Year in Marienbad*, *Outward Bound*, *La Ronde*, *Alice in Wonderland* and *Dear Brutus*.'

Previn, André (1929–). German–American composer–arranger, in Hollywood from childhood; latterly a presenter–performer of music programmes in Britain. PP: 'And a most entertaining one. *André Previn's Music Night*; *Sounds Magnificent* (1984); *Previn on Concertos* (1986).'

The Price *
GB/Ireland 1985 6 × 50m
Astramead/RTE (Mark Shivas) for C4

Wife and daughter of Irish-domiciled industrialist are kidnapped and held to ransom by the IRA, throwing a giant strain on to a marriage already flimsy. 'A subdued thriller from our own time and our own islands, alas,' I noted. 'The characters fit it. How they behave comes out of what they are. What they are thinking is apparent in what they don't say as much as what they do say.'

w Peter Ransley, idea by Peter Barkworth
d Peter Smith

Peter Barkworth, Harriet Walter   PP

LH: 'I found it all too much, amounting to self-parody. One star at most.'

The Price Is Right. American game show, showing since the late fifties, sometimes on several nights a week. Contestants are involved in guessing the value of various items of merchandise, sometimes via complex games, and the remarkable thing about the show is the amount of hysteria generated. Presented by Goodson–Todman for CBS.

PP: 'It didn't reach Britain until 1984 when I wrote, "The brilliant innovation is to make the prizes the game. Why waste time with general knowledge or simple tests of skill? What things are worth and how much you want them are all that matters." But Leslie Crowther is a genial master of cupidities whose "Come on down" has become a universal catch-phrase. Produced by William G. Stewart for Central.'

The Price of Coal
GB 1977 2 × 75m colour
BBC (Tony Garnett)

Linked plays by Barry Hines about the miner's lot. *Meet the People* had the colliery and the community fussing over the preparations for a Royal visit in Jubilee year; a genial, sharp-eyed if not exactly loyalist comedy making good use of the northern club comedians whom director Ken Loach pressed into service as actors. In *Back to Reality* disaster struck underground and predictably the production team showed its political teeth, contrasting the sentimental concern for miners in danger with the hostility when they demand more pay. Unfortunately the lesson was hammered home with scenes of reporters and TV crews ghoulishly importuning rescue workers and waiting wives. All they were trying to do, as I wrote at the time, was present the story as best they could. 'For all their fervour, for all their slogans, for all their high seriousness, Tony and Ken and Barry are doing exactly the same.'

Bobby Knutt, Jackie Shinn, Haydn Conway
                                                                            PP

Price, Richard (1933–). Leading British programme entrepreneur, originally handling LWT's overseas sales, now also in production with his company, Primetime.

The Pride of Jesse Hallam *
US 1981 96m colour TVM
CBS/Frank Konigsberg

An illiterate Kentucky coal miner is confused by the big city when he has to take his daughter to hospital.
Well-made dramatization of the universal problem of people who can't read or write.

w Suzanne Clauser *d* Gary Nelson *ph* Gayne Rescher *m* Johnny Cash

Johnny Cash, Brenda Vaccaro, Ben Marley, Eli Wallach, Guy Boyd, Chrystal Smith

'It tells a lot about Americanism without preaching.' – *Daily Variety*

Pride of Our Alley **
GB 1984 78m
YTV (Michael Ferguson)

The story of Gracie Fields, the Lancashire lass who became a movie star and the world's highest-paid singer, upped to art by the gutsy performance of Polly Hemingway, playing Gracie from seven to seventy. 'Here was that rare phenomenon, a bit of show business schmalz with an outstanding talent at its centre,' said Richard Last in the *Daily Telegraph*.

w Alan Plater *d* Michael Ferguson

Polly Hemingway, Barry Jackson, Michael Angeli, George Pravden   PP

LH: 'The girl was good, but the rest stiff and stagey. No stars for me.'

† *Gracie*, a one-woman tribute by singer Barbara Dickson, produced and directed by Mike Stephens, came from BBC Manchester, 1985.

Pride of the Family
US 1953 40 × 25m bw
ABC/Revue

Misadventures of a family in which the husband can't do anything right.
Primitive sitcom.

Paul Hartman, Fay Wray, Natalie Wood

The Priest Killer *
US 1971 100m colour TVM
Universal

San Francisco's law forces combine to catch a madman who murders Catholic priests.
Oddball cop show in which Ironside meets Sarge, and between them they get their man. Originally intended as two episodes of *Ironside*.

w Robert Van Scoyk, Joel Oliansky *d* Richard A. Colla *m* David Shire

Raymond Burr, George Kennedy, Don Galloway, Louise Jeffries, Don Mitchell, Anthony Zerbe

Priestland, Gerald (19 –). British presenter and God-botherer, for many years BBC religious correspondent on both radio and TV. Series: *Priestland Right and Wrong* (1983; 7 × 30m), produced by Angus Wright for TVS/C4.

Priestley, J. B. (1894–1984). Eminent British man of letters who had already written for the stage, the movies and radio and would clearly be intrigued by the new outlet of television. He was. His play *When We Are Married* was the first to be televised in full from a London theatre in 1938. After the war he was the first established dramatist to write for TV, with a satirical comedy *Whitehall Wonders* in 1949. Subsequent television works include:

1955 *You Know What People Are*; BBC – Series of non-naturalistic sketches of human behaviour, directed by Tony Richardson

1957 *Now Let Him Go*; ABC – Armchair Theatre play about a dying artist

1957 *The Stone Faces*; BBC – Rather lurid tale of a film star on the run from publicity, with Luise Rainer

1958 *Doomsday for Dyson*; Granada – Anti-nuclear fable of considerable impact

1958 *Lost City*; BBC – Documentary about his native Bradford by and with J. B. P., producer Richard Cawston

1968 *Anyone for Tennis?*; BBC – Wednesday Play to his favourite trick of playing with time

1977 *An Englishman's Journey*; BBC – LH: 'Disappointing trudge through the Midlands and North, revisiting old haunts for three half-hours produced by George Green.'

Of adaptations of his novels and stage plays, the most successful was a BBC serial from *Angel Pavement* (1958). The unexpected flop was YTV's musical version of *The Good Companions* (1980). As a personality he made occasional appearances. His 80th birthday in 1974 was marked by a YTV documentary and an absorbing BBC conversation with Robert Robinson. In 1984 his voice was heard reading extracts from his 1934 travelogue *English Journey* during a retracing of his itinerary by Beryl Bainbridge to the same title. On his death later that year, documentary tributes came from Robert Robinson in *J. B. Priestley Remembered* (BBC, *p* David Cheshire) and his son Tom Priestley as director of *Time and the Priestleys* (Central, *p* Jim Berrow).   PP

A Prime Minister on Prime Ministers
GB 1977 13 × 50m colour
YTV (Anthony Jay and Peter Morley)

Unencumbered by false modesty, Sir Harold Wilson discoursed on twelve assorted predecessors, with help from David Frost. Directed by Peter Morley. My view at the time: 'From the opening sequence of prime ministerly heads, beginning and ending with Harold's own, to the floorwalker attentiveness of David Frost as he feeds the questions, the implication is that to have been a prime minister is to have belonged to an exclusive profession which only a fellow-professional can really understand (rather as some dramatists believe that only fellow-dramatists can pronounce on their plays); and, furthermore, that this particular professional is certainly not less than *primus inter pares* in the roll.'   PP

The Prime of Miss Jean Brodie *
GB 1978 7 × 50m colour
Scottish TV

Adaptation of Muriel Spark's novel about a headstrong spinster schoolteacher in thirties Edinburgh.
Better frissons than the film, but too extended.

Geraldine McEwan

Prime Suspect
US 1982 96m colour TVM
CBS/Tisch–Avnet

An average man is suspected of being a multi-murderer, and has a hard time proving he isn't.
Compound from-the-headlines drama mainly concerned to criticize the media.
Not bad for a thriller with an axe to grind.

w Douglas Graham *d* Noel Black *ph* Reynaldo Villalobos *m* Charles Gross
Mike Farrell, Teri Garr, Veronica Cartwright, Lane Smith, Barry Corbin, James Sloyan

prime time: see peak time

Prime Time. A 1979 book by Marlo and Mina Lewis about the early years of American network TV, with anecdotes about Phil Silvers, Ed Murrow, Jackie Gleason, Frank Sinatra, Walter Winchell, etc.

primetime access rule: an American FCC insistence that not more than three hours between 7 and 11 pm shall be devoted to network programming. In practice networking starts at 8 pm.

Primus
US 1971 16 × 25m colour
Metromedia/Ivan Tors

An undersea expert fights crime as well as sharks.
An updated *Sea Hunt*, quite good to look at.

cr Michael and Andy White *m* Leonard Rosenman
Robert Brown, Will Kuluva

The Prince of Central Park *
US 1977 74m colour TVM
Lorimar (Harvey Hart)

Two children make a Shangri-La of the big city park.
Rather unusual, well-made little idyll.

w Jeb Rosebrook *novel* Evan H. Rhodes *d* Harvey Hart *m* Arthur B. Rubenstein

Ruth Gordon, T. J. Hargrave, Lisa Richard, Brooke Shields

Prince, Peter (19 –). British author of very occasional but interesting TV plays, usually directed by Stephen Frears. *Play Things* (1976), *Last Summer* (1977), *Cold Harbour* (1978).   PP

The Princess and the Cabbie
US 1981 96m colour TVM
CBS/Columbia/Freyda Rothstein

A cabbie helps a dyslectic rich girl.
The Cinderella story combined with disease of the week. Not a pretty sight.

w Edward Pomerantz *d* Glenn Jordan

Valerie Bertinelli, Robert Desiderio, Peter Donat, Cynthia Harris, Shelley Long

Princess Daisy
US 1983 2 × 96m colour miniseries
NBC/Steve Krantz (Lillian Gallo)

Adventures of the orphan daughter of a Russian prince and an American movie star. Expensive jet-set backgrounds include the Riviera and the fashion and cosmetics businesses.
Nobody loved this but the public.

w Diana Hammond, *novel* by Judith Krantz *d* Waris Hussein *ph* Charles Rosher, Tony Imi *m* Lalo Schifrin *pd* Dean Mitzner

Paul Michael Glaser, Lindsay Wagner, Robert Urich, Stacy Keach, Claudia Cardinale, Rupert Everett, Sada Thompson, Barbara Bach, Ringo Starr, Merete Van Kamp

Principal, Victoria (1950–). American leading lady who came to the fore in *Dallas*. TV movies: *The Night They Took Miss Beautiful*, *Last Hours Before Morning*, *Pleasure Palace*.

Prinze, Freddie (1953–76). Puerto Rican light actor, a suicide victim during the run of his big hit CHICO AND THE MAN.

Prior, Allan (1922–). British novelist and TV playwright, author of one-shot plays in the late fifties, then one of the founding stalwarts on *Z-Cars* and since then mainly associated with police and other series. Lately: *Bookie* (1983) and ensuing series (1986) for STV; co-devised *Howard's Way* for BBC, 1985. PP

The Prison *
GB 1975 78m colour TVM
Thames/Euston Films

A businessman is told that his wife has killed her sister out of jealousy.
Tortuous suspenser, quite neatly packaged.

w Geoffrey Gilbert *novel* Georges Simenon *d* David Wickes

James Laurenson, Ann Curthoys, James Maxwell, Kenneth Griffith, André Morell, Philip Madoc, George Murcell
'A first-class all-location job.' – *Daily Express*

The Prisoner **
GB 1967 17 × 50m colour
ATV (PATRICK MCGOOHAN)

An ex-secret agent is captured and brainwashed in a curious Shangri-La civilization from which he finds he can never escape.
Downright peculiar, sometimes fascinating, often irritating and trendy melodrama in which the episodes, though well made and acted, tended towards repetition. The much-awaited final episode explained nothing and fell apart almost completely, the intention apparently being to make a statement about Vietnam.

Patrick McGoohan

† Revived in 1976, the show turned into a minor cult, and Portmeirion, the private Welsh village in which it was filmed, again attracted unwelcome hordes of tourists. A re-run on Channel 4 in 1983/4 caused an outcry among fans because one episode was shown out of order. An accompanying documentary *Six into one: The Prisoner File* came from Illuminations/Yo-Yo Films.

The episodes were as follows:

Once upon a Time: *w*,*d* Patrick McGoohan; with Leo McKern
Do Not Forsake Me Oh My Darling: *w* Vincent Tilsley; *d* Pat Jackson; with Zena Walker, Clifford Evans, Nigel Stock
Living in Harmony: *w*,*d* David Tomblin; with Alexis Kanner
The Girl Who Was Death: *w* Terence Feely; *d* Don Chaffey; with Kenneth Griffith, Justine Lord

Dance of the Dead: w Anthony Skene; d Don Chaffey; with Mary Morris, Duncan MacRae
A Change of Mind: w Roger Parkes; d Pat Jackson; with Angela Browne, Don Sharpe
Hammer into Anvil: w Roger Woodis; d Pat Jackson; with Patrick Cargill, Victor Maddern
The General: w Joshua Adam; d Peter Graham Scott; with Colin Gordon, John Castle
It's Your Funeral: w Michael Cramoy; with Derren Nesbitt, Mark Eden
The Chimes of Big Ben: w Vincent Tilsley; d Don Chaffey; with Leo McKern, Nadia Gray, Finlay Currie, Richard Wattis
Checkmate: w Gerald Kelsey; d Don Chaffey; with Ronald Radd, Patricia Jessel, Peter Wyngarde, Rosalie Crutchley, George Coulouris
Free for All: w Paddy Fitz; d Patrick McGoohan; with Eric Portman
A, B and C: w Anthony Skene; d Pat Jackson; with Katherine Kath, Colin Gordon
Many Happy Returns: w Anthony Skene; d Joseph Serf; with Donald Sinden, Patrick Cargill, Georgina Cookson
Arrival: w George Markstein, David Tomblin; d Don Chaffey; with Virginia Maskell, Paul Eddington, George Baker, Guy Doleman
Fall Out: w,d Patrick McGoohan; with Alexis Kanner, Leo McKern, Kenneth Griffith

A Prisoner in the Caucasus *** (USSR, screened by BBC 1980).

Tolstoy's story could have been a North-West Frontier yarn by Kipling or G. A. Henty: dashing young officer captured by tribesmen finally escapes but within an ace of gaining safety seems certain to be shot by his pursuers – until the noble Pathan knocks aside his marksman's rifle as he fires.

It was in fact set among the Tartars when Tsarist troops were trying to put down a rising. Only Stalin finally tamed them by his customary drastic measures. Since they spoke a different language from Russian, dialogue in the screenplay was limited, even when our hero was joined by a spineless brother officer. It was therefore easy to overlay Alan Dobie's voice as a kind of interior monologue by the officer, but still smart of someone to spot this. The locations, the photography, the direction were all ravishing, and the relationship between the captive and the little Tartar girl wonderfully fresh and unhackneyed.   PP

Prisoner without a Name, Cell without a Number

US 1982 96m colour TVM
NBC/Chrysalis–Yellen (Linda Yellen)

The story of an Argentinian newspaper publisher whose accounts of political prisoners got him into hot water with the junta.

Rather lumbering dramatization of facts which should have carried themselves.

w Jonathan Platnick, Linda Yellen, Oliver P. Drexell Jnr, *autobiography* of Jacobo Timerman d Linda Yellen ph Arthur Ornitz m Brad Fiedel

Roy Scheider, Liv Ullman, Terrance O'Quinn, Sam Robards, Trini Alvarado

Prisoners of the Lost Universe

US 1983 96m colour TVM
Showtime/Marcel/Robertson (Harry Robertson)

A time travel machine catapults two people to the planet Vonya.

Unassuming adventure intended for children of all ages, but not really up to it.

w Harry Robertson, Terry Marcel d Terry Marcel ph Derek Browne m Harry Robertson

Richard Hatch, Kay Lenz, John Saxon, Peter O'Farrell, Ray Charleson

A Private Battle

US 1979 96m colour TVM
CBS/ Procter and Gamble/Robert Halmi

Author Cornelius Ryan learns that he has terminal cancer.

Sensitive and praiseworthy but dreadfully overlong dramatization of a courageous book.

w John Gay, *book* Cornelius Ryan and Kathleen Morgan Ryan d Robert Lewis ph Larry Pizer m Charles Gross

Jack Warden, Anne Jackson, David Stockton, Rachel Kelly, Frederick Rolf, Rebecca Schull

Private Benjamin

US 1981 39 × 25m colour
CBS/Warner (Madelyn Davis, Bob Carroll Jnr)

Slapstick adventures of a girl army recruit.

Just what it says: the Jewish princess of the movie has disappeared, and with her any trace of satire.

cr Don Reo

Lorna Patterson, Eileen Brennan, Hal Williams

'Some things intrinsically aren't worth doing, and one of them is turning a good movie into a bad television show.' – Robert MacKenzie, *TV Guide*

THE PRISONER. This 17-hour series, filmed in Portmeirion (standing in for a mysterious security village which might have been anywhere in the world), was largely masterminded by its star Patrick McGoohan. It was too sophisticated to be a great popular success, and its final episode had a tinge of lunacy, but more than 20 years later it still has a fan club and Portmeirion still sells penny-farthing lapel badges.

Private Lives (GB 1983; 6 × 35m). Chat show conducted by actress Maria Aitken in which the celebs were invited to volunteer reminiscences prompted by favourite meals, fragrances, pop songs – she took her title from the line about the potency of cheap music she had been uttering nightly on the stage in a revival of Coward's *Private Lives*. Beryl Reid, Kingsley Amis, Yehudi Menuhin and A. J. P. Taylor were among the clients who obliged. A further run followed in 1984. Produced by Lavinia Warner, for BBC.   PP

Private Potter *
GB 1961 52m bw
ATV/H. M. Tennent (Cecil Clarke)
Original, touching, funny–peculiar episode of army life by Ronald Harwood and Casper

Wrede. Young soldier goes rigid and screams while on anti-terrorist operation in Cyprus, causing the death of another trooper. He says later that it was a vision of God which threw him – a claim which his padre and commanding officer eventually uphold, but not, predictably, the topmost brass. Later filmed with Tom Courtenay.

d Casper Wrede

Tom Bell, James Maxwell, Leo McKern   PP

Private Schulz *
GB 1981 6 × 50m colour
BBC (Philip Hinchcliffe)
Comedy World War II serial inspired by an actual German plot to flood Britain with forged £5 notes and thereby destroy the economy, greeted with some misgivings on

grounds of taste. Could a just and honourable war be presented in terms of farce? To which the short answer was that frequently it *was* a farce . . . Michael Elphick reinforced the verdict with his funny performance as the stoical underling appointed to implement the scheme. Also with Ian Richardson, Billie Whitelaw. Written by Jack Pulman; directed by Robert Chetwynd. PP

Private Secretary *
aka: *Susie*
US 1952–3 104 × 25m bw
CBS/ITC/Ann Sothern

The secretary in a talent agency has more power than the boss.
Amusing sitcom with stars working well in tandem.

Ann Sothern, Don Porter

† See *The Ann Sothern Show.*

'A detective with unusual methods for uncovering the truth. A best friend who listens to your dark sexual secrets!'
Private Sessions
US 1985 96m colour TVM
NBC/Raven's Claw/Seltzer–Gimbel/
  Comworld (Thom Thomas)

Cases from a psychiatrist's salon.
Rather lame pilot for a series which didn't happen.
w Thom Thomas, David Seltzer *d* Michael Pressman *ph* Mike Fash *m* Lalo Schifrin

Mike Farrell, Maureen Stapleton, Denise Miller, Kelly McGillis, Tom Bosley

Prix Italia. An international merit prize established in 1948 by RAI. The competition is held each year in an Italian city and programmes can be submitted under drama, music and documentary headings.

Prix Jeunesse. An international merit prize established for excellence in the production of TV programmes for children awarded every other year in Munich by a foundation sponsored by the EBU and UNESCO.

Probation (GB 1985; 6 × 50m). A quarter of a century after the fiction (below), real-life case-histories from the probation service; marriage guidance one week, keeping an eye on a lifer on prison release another. 'Whether or not the producer, Steve Timms, ordained it so,' I wrote half-way through the run, 'these gentle prefects of the Welfare State have so far shown patience, tact and firmness in just the right proportions.' BBC South West. PP

Probation Officer. Seminal British one-hour series of the late fifties, which made stars of Honor Blackman, John Paul and David Davies, who failed to stay the course. Written by Julian Bond, produced by Tony Kearey, for ATV.

Probe *
aka: *Search*
US 1972 97m colour TVM
Warner (Leslie Stevens)

CIA agents are monitored by implanted radio devices.
Childlike James Bond stuff which works very well because it has a sense of humour and the bigger than usual budget is well spent. The resultant series, however, fell apart because of rotating leads. It was retitled *Search*.
w/d RUSSELL MAYBERRY *m* Dominic Frontiere

Hugh O'Brian, John Gielgud, Angel Tompkins, Elke Sommer, Burgess Meredith, Lilia Skala, Kent Smith

Prochnow, Jurgen (1941–). German leading man in international media. *Das Boot, Forbidden.*

producer or director? Much heartache is suffered, probably needlessly, by television producers and directors who fear that the distinction between their roles eludes the general public and that the other person is being given the credit (though never the blame, of course) that properly belongs to oneself. The confusion stems from television's divided roots in radio (where the producer is solely responsible for a programme) and the cinema (where the producer is more of an impresario while the director actually makes the picture). In light entertainment and outside broadcasts the producer may still be in creative control, especially in the BBC, but elsewhere the film industry convention is now generally observed. How a story or a report unfolds on the screen is wholly the director's business, from the camera angle in one fleeting scene to the casting and the locations. *What* unfolds on the screen is the producer's doing. He is perhaps the original begetter of the idea. He certainly acts (or should act) as counsellor, friend and critic to the director, also as a buffer between the director and the top brass. Most important of all, the good producer brings together talents that might not otherwise have met and make things happen that might otherwise not have happened. Producers of this sort include (in drama alone): Sydney Newman, Stella Richman, Innes Lloyd, Irene Shubik, Verity Lambert, Cecil Clarke, Mark Shivas, Kenith Trodd, Jonathan Powell and the late Peter Eckersley. PP

The Profane Comedy
aka: *Set This Town on Fire*
US 1969 96m colour TVM
Universal (Roy Huggins)

A convict is pardoned and announces that he will run for Lieutenant Governor.
Hard-to-like, awkwardly paced and obscurely narrated melodrama.

w John Thomas James *d* David Lowell Rich

Chuck Connors, Carl Betz, Lynda Day George, John Anderson, Jeff Corey

Professional Foul **
GB 1977 80m colour (VTR)
BBC (Mark Shivas)

An academic in Prague for a conference is asked by a former student to smuggle a manuscript out to the free world.
Undoubtedly superior but only patchily engrossing tragi-comedy from a fashionable playwright who suffers from verbal diarrhoea.

w Tom Stoppard *d* Michael Lindsay-Hogg
PETER BARKWORTH

'Funny, engrossing and suspenseful.' – *Daily Telegraph*

'A serious response by a writer of comedies to Amnesty's Prisoner of Conscience Year.' – Mark Shivas

PP: 'Stoppard's delight in philosophical wranglings was kept firmly relevant to the action, though the metaphor of the play, as well as its title, came from the football international that was also taking place in the city. The play pulled off the rare feat of being funny, engrossing and suspenseful whether watched as an adventure of ideas or as adventure with people.'

The Professionals
GB 1978 × 50m colour
LWT/Avengers (Albert Fennell, Brian Clemens)

An élite squad of MI5 deals with dangerous cases.
Derivative thick-ear which turned out not to be the *Sweeney* of the spy world.

Gordon Jackson, Martin Shaw, Lewis Collins

PP: 'Of all the rotten new breed of thuggish cops and secret agents, and here it is not even clear which they are supposed to be, this little gang is the least attractive. The curly-headed one reminds me fatally of Harpo Marx, the other of a tailor's dummy, while Gordon Jackson trying to be a ruthless taskmaster is doing nothing for the reputation of Gordon Jackson.'

Project UFO
US 1978 23 × 50m colour
NBC/Jack Webb (Col. William T. Coleman)

Investigations into flying saucer sightings.
The trouble is too much build-up for what must strictly speaking be a letdown, and the terse Webb style doesn't help in this case: three stories could have been got into each hour.

William Jordan, Caskey Swain, Edward Winter

'If it is a fact that space visitors have been flitting over the prairies for the past 30-odd years, astonishing farmers and frightening truck drivers, isn't it about time they came down to the city and said hello, or glorp, or something?' – Robert MacKenzie, *TV Guide*

Promenade *
GB 1959 50m bw (VTR)
Granada

Peter Nichols's study, directed by Julian Amyes, of the awfulness of adolescence in a seaside town, plotted and worked out with astonishing economy and skill considering it was only his second play. My 1959 review: 'The boredom and heartache are bad enough for anyone. For those who have the money and leisure to prolong them indefinitely they must be hell. So it was with most of last night's gang, roaming from pub to party and party to pub, combing their seaside town for something to do. They talked smart talk and cuddled on the beach, drifted in and out of love and hurt each other more than they guessed.

'Peter Nichols's . . . sharply distinguished little character studies, interpreted for the most part by young and unknown players, made it a rewarding journey. In particular Tom Bell gave a nicely restrained performance as a young labourer somehow mixed up with a middle-class gang, and Trader Faulkner dazzled in the only dazzling part.' PP

Promise Him Anything
US 1975 74m colour TVM
Seven Arts (Stanley Rubin)

Having suggested on her computer dating card that 'anything goes', a girl is taken to court when she doesn't produce.
The comedy doesn't produce either.

w David Freeman *d* Edward Parone

Eddie Albert, Meg Foster, Frederic Forrest, William Schallert, Tom Ewell

The Promise of Love
US 1980 96m colour TVM
CBS/Pierre Cossette (Jay Benson)

PROBATION OFFICER. This earnest series gave actor John Paul his one real claim to fame. Here he tries to straighten out one of his charges, played by William Ingram.

An 18-year-old war widow learns to cope. Thin little tragedy, hard to take for anybody over 21.

w Harry and Renee Longstreet, Carol Saraceno d Don Taylor ph Don Birnkrant m Paul Chihara

Valerie Bertinelli, Jameson Parker, Andy Romano, Joanna Miles, David James Carroll

'More than its title but less than its subject.' – *Daily Variety*

'Only one thing could keep a father from his son. The past!'
Promises to Keep
US 1985 96m colour TVM
CBS/Sandra Harmon/Green–Epstein

A wanderer, discovering that he may be dying, calls to see his son and grandson but finds nobody happy to see him.

Turgid family drama with gimmick casting its only hope of ratings appeal.

w Phil Penningroth d Noel Black ph Dennis A. Dalzell m Michel Legrand

Robert Mitchum, Christopher Mitchum, Bentley Mitchum, Claire Bloom, Tess Harper, Merritt Butrick, Jane Sibbett

'The Mitchum clan will hardly go down as an acting dynasty.' – *Daily Variety*

Prostitute I Am, Common I'm Not *
GB 1981 50m colour
Thames (Judy Lever)

Interviews with five acknowledged prostitutes, remarkable chiefly as a milestone in the march of permissiveness.

researcher Alexandra Sumner d Judy Lever

The Protectors
GB 1971 26 × 25m colour (16mm)
ITC
International assignments for top private detectives.
Routine hokum, competently presented.
Nyree Dawn Porter, Robert Vaughn, Tony Anholt

The Protectors
US 1982 74m colour TVM
ABC/Metromedia/Aaron Spelling (Jeffrey Hayes)
An unremarkable pilot episode for a cop show which became T. J. Hooker (qv).
cr Rick Husky
William Shatner, John Gladstein, Adrian Zmed, Richard Lawson

The Protest **
GB 1960 90m bw
Granada (Philip Mackie)
Rhys Adrian's debut as a TV writer with a quirky comedy of life among the organization men, a newly discovered social category at this time. With Tenniel Evans, Jack Hedley. Directed by Silvio Narizzano. My comment in 1960: 'Rhys Adrian dived headlong into the horrors of the annual dinner party and came out with an armful of hilarious, off-beat and wistful scenes. The company lecher patted his double bed and practised his razor smile; the company drunk rowed with his wife and practised a dreary anecdote; the chairman droned on and on and the company rebel staged his tiny demonstration by walking out. "If he is going to make the same speech year after year," he grumbled, "what proof have we got that a year has passed?" '   PP

Prototype
US 1982 96m colour TVM
CBS/Levinson–Link/Robert Papazian
A government-financed team of scientists develops a humanoid.
Frankenstein gets another dusting down, with entirely predictable results.
w Richard Levinson, William Link d David Greene ph Harry May m Billy Goldenberg
Christopher Plummer, David Morse, Arthur Hill, Frances Sternhagen, James Sutorius, Stephen Elliott
'It has so much going for it that it seems carping to say that the adventure lacks substance.' – Daily Variety

Provine, Dorothy (1937–). American leading lady who was scarcely noticed in The Alaskans but made a hit as the singer in The Roaring Twenties. It subsequently emerged that she couldn't really sing.

Prowse, Juliet (1936–). South African dancer and leading lady who once had her own series.

The Pruitts of Southampton
aka: The Phyllis Diller Show
US 1966 30 × 25m colour
ABC/Filmways
Stories from Patrick Dennis's novel House Party about the eccentric old pillar of Long Island society who protects her family's reputation.
Unfortunately the character and the actress meet in head-on collision, and the result is uneasy farce.
Phyllis Diller, Reginald Gardiner, Grady Sutton, John McGiver, Richard Deacon, Gypsy Rose Lee

Psy Warriors (GB 1981). Supposed terrorists in an army interrogation centre turn out to be soldiers undergoing a macabre psychological exercise. A BBC Play for Today by David Leland, directed by Alan Clarke; with John Duttine, Rosalind Ayres, Derrick O'Connor, whose brilliant trompe-l'oeil beginning was not sustained by the contrivedly anti-military, anti-West resolution.   PP

The Psychiatrist: God Bless the Children
US 1970 97m colour TVM
NBC/Universal (Edgar Small, Norman Felton)
A psychoanalyst helps a small town fight a school drug epidemic.
Ho-hum social conscience stuff.
w Jerrold Freedman d Daryl Duke
Roy Thinnes, Pete Duel, Luther Adler, Katherine Justice

P'tang Yang Kipperbang **
GB 1982 90m
Goldcrest/Enigma (David Puttnam) for C4
The first Film on Four and also the first First Love (umbrellas under umbrellas!), on Channel 4's opening night: Cricket-mad schoolboy hankers ineffectually after pretty classmate. 'Funny and sweet and made inspired use of an imagined John Arlott cricket commentary,' I reported, 'but did schoolchildren say "dishiest" already in 1948? Even more, did they say "sod off"? Bet they didn't.'
w Jack Rosenthal d Michael Apted   PP

The Pub Fighter ** (GB 1968; 28m). Jim Allen's concentrated little play based on childhood memories of illegal bare-knuckle matches in Midland pubs. Directed by Marc Miller; produced by Stella Richman; for Rediffusion (*Half Hour Story*). My 1968 review: 'Allen seems to be strongest on rough male society and stubborn male pride. The physical action here depended on a sexual situation which was perhaps a notch less persuasive but I accepted it. With a tremendous impersonation by John Collin – can't think of anyone else who could have done it – and a nasty little one by Peter Reynolds, *The Pub Fight* tasted to me like a distillation at just about as high a proof as you can get.'   PP

Public Defender
US 1953–4 59 × 25m bw
CBS/Hal Roach
Stories of the counsel appointed to give free legal aid to the poor.
Modest courtroom dramas.
Reed Hadley

Public Eye **
GB 1969–73 33 × 50m 21 colour, 12 bw
Thames
Cases of a down-at-heel private eye.
Moderately realistic detective dramas with a likeable hero who even goes to jail at the end of the series.
Alfred Burke

Public School
GB 1980 10 × 50m colour
BBC (Roger Mills)
Life under the camera's scrutiny in yet another closed institution, namely the British public school, which means private school. The example chosen was Radley, near Oxford, and as in the preceding *Sailor*, a different aspect of school routine was surveyed each week within a rough chronological scheme. But reactions were less concerned with the form of the series than its content, the nation dividing sharply into those who found everything about the school admirable and those who deplored its whole existence. The star of the show turned out to be the eccentric but endearing second master.   PP

public television: in the US, a service supported by state, local or private funding. In practice, the only way to see minority programming.

Puccini **
GB 1984 100m
Ladbrook/RM Productions (Tony Palmer)
for C4
The episode in the composer's life when his adored but insanely jealous wife accused a village servant girl of being his mistress. Mortified, the girl killed herself. Puccini, innocent for once, was deeply affected. Tony Palmer counterpointed the story with Puccini's opera *Turandot* which reproduces some of the circumstances and some of the composer's confused feelings. Unfortunately Palmer also intercut footage of himself directing the opera in Glasgow, falling out with the cast and slagging his critics, which costs him a third star but cannot diminish a visually and aurally stunning film.
w Charles Wood *d* Tony Palmer
Robert Stephens as Puccini, Virginia McKenna as Elvira Puccini, Bill Fraser, Peter Woodthorpe and William Squire as village elders and the models for Ping, Pang and Pong in *Turandot*   PP

Pueblo **
US 1973 100m colour TVM (VTR)
Titus (Herb Brodkin)
An American ship is seized by the North Koreans.
Dramatic documentary, very powerfully made.
Hal Holbrook, Andrew Duggan, Richard Mulligan, George Grizzard, Gary Merrill, Mary Fickett

Pulman, Jack (1925–80). British TV playwright of Polish–Irish parentage who made an impact in the late fifties with sensitive semi-autobiographical subjects: *A Book With Chapters in It*, *All You Young Lovers*, *Nearer to Heaven*. *You Can't Have Everything*, about a young couple forced to choose between getting a house and having a child, was the first British TV script to be bought by American TV, for the US Steel Hour. For the next 20 years, though, Pulman's name was seen mainly on serial adaptations, including the BBC's *War and Peace* and *I, Claudius*. A return to original writing with the World War II comedy serial *Private Schulz* was only realized, sadly, after his death. At the time he was working on *The Winds of War*, thereafter taken on by the author of the original novel, Herman Wouk.   PP

Punch and Jody
US 1974 74m colour TVM
Metromedia

An executive leaves his wife and joins the circus as a clown. 15 years later his daughter comes looking for him.

Drippy drama, awash in sentimentality and self-pity.

w John McGreevy *d* Barry Shear

Glenn Ford, Pam Griffin, Ruth Roman, Kathleen Widdoes

'Is there room in your cold, mean old heart for an adorable lost little girl and her dog?'

Punky Brewster
US 1984–   × 25m colour
NBC (David W. Duclon)

A small orphan and her dog are cared for by a crusty apartment manager.
But Shirley Temple she ain't.

Soleil Moon Frye, George Gaynes

The Puppet Man * (GB 1985; 6 × 40m). Nice little series re-creating the travels and encounters of Walter Wilkinson, who toured the West Country with a fit-up puppet show in the twenties, with Roy Hudd in the part and puppets newly copied from Wilkinson's drawings. Written, directed and produced by David Furnham for David Furnham Productions/C4.   PP
'Well in the tradition of gentle eccentric English comedy.' – *Time Out*

Purdie, John (19 –). British fly-on-the-wall film-maker (*Sailor*) who moved into dramatized subjects with less success, e.g. *Freud*, 1984.   PP

Purl, Linda (1955–). Diminutive American leading lady. TV movies: *Bad Ronald, The Oregon Trail, Eleanor and Franklin, Young Pioneers, Having Babies, Testimony of Two Men, Little Ladies of the Night, Black Market Baby, A Last Cry for Help, Women at West Point, Like Normal People, The Flame Is Love, The Night the City Screamed.*

The Pursuers
GB 1963 39 × 25m bw
Jack Gross

Scotland Yard stories, involving the use of police dogs.
Very moderate mysteries.

Louis Hayward

Pursuit **
US 1972 74m colour TVM
ABC/Circle (Lee Rich, Robert L. Jacks)

An extremist steals nerve gas and threatens to decimate a city where a political convention is being staged.
Admirably suspenseful thriller, just what a TV movie should be.

w Robert Dozier, *novel Binary* by Michael Crichton *d* MICHAEL CRICHTON *ph* Robert L. Morrison *m* Jerry Goldsmith

Ben Gazzara, E. G. Marshall, William Windom, Joseph Wiseman, Martin Sheen

The Pursuit of Power * (GB 1981). Relaxed and generally revealing interviews with ambitious politicians by Robert McKenzie, including Anthony Wedgwood Benn, Enoch Powell, Norman St John Stevas, David Steel and Roy Hattersley. With the possible exception of the Hattersley programme, when McKenzie gently hustled his man into Labour Party dissensions of the day, the series was a last demonstration of his gift for drawing out rather than steering his clients. He died later the same year.   PP

Puttnam, David (19 –). Highly successful British film producer, who moved into TV to mastermind the *First Love* series on C4 and has kept his interest in the medium.

Pygmalion
US/Canada 1984 96m colour TVM
(VTR)
TCF/Astral (Dan Redler)

A routine production of Bernard Shaw's comedy, with Peter O'Toole, Margot Kidder, Donald Ewer and John Standing

Pyke, Dr Magnus (1908–). British TV personality of the seventies, a scientist who on *Don't Ask Me* and other shows displayed a propensity for talking very fast and waving his arms around, thus making himself famous as an easy target for impressionists. He was soon doing commercials.

QB VII *
US 1974 315m colour
Columbia/Douglas Cramer

An American author in a novel accuses a Jewish doctor of war crimes; the doctor sues. Thinly disguised fact from the book by Leon Uris; as drama rather overstretched and patchily directed and acted, the fact being more remarkable than the fiction. Its interest is as the first of the very long TV novelizations of the seventies: it was played in two 'three-hour' segments and its qualified success led to *Rich Man, Poor Man* and *Best Sellers*.

w Edward Anhalt *d* Tom Gries *m* Jerry Goldsmith

Anthony Hopkins, Ben Gazzara, Juliet Mills, Leslie Caron, Edith Evans, Jack Hawkins, Lee Remick, John Gielgud, Dan O'Herlihy, Anthony Quayle

† Emmys: Jerry Goldsmith, Anthony Quayle

PP: 'For anyone in Britain who had seen R. W. Reid's documentary reconstruction of the same case, *According to the Rules* (1972), a travesty of the truth, with the Uris-hero given a glamorous RAF-pilot past and his adversary equipped with a son who would add to his humiliation by publicly denouncing him. I'd ram that star up the producer's nose.'

Q.E.D. (GB since 1981). Documentary
outlet, usually occupied by a film essay, which originates in BBC Manchester. Subjects range from the case-history of a soldier cruelly burned in the Falklands War to a 30-minute whizz round Britain's entire coastline obtained by speeding up a Betamax tape from a camera aboard a jet fighter. Editor (1986) David Filkin.   PP

Quaid, Randy (1950–). Lanky American
actor, usually of gauche characters. TV movies: *Getting Away from It All*, *The Great Niagara*, *The Last Ride of the Dalton Gang*, *Guyana Tragedy*.

Quarantined
US 1970 74m colour TVM
Paramount

A case of cholera hits a hospital just as a kidney donor is needed.
Medical suspenser, not very interesting.

w Norman Katkov *d* Leo Penn

John Dehner, Gary Collins, Sharon Farrell, Wally Cox, Sam Jaffe

Quark
US 1978 50m colour
NBC/Columbia/David Gerber (Bruce Johnson)

Adventures of a garbage collector in outer space.
Woefully unfunny opening episode for a shortlived half-hour series (eight of them made it).

cr Buck Henry *w* Steve Zacharias *d* Hy Averback *ph* Gerry P. Finnerman *m* Perry Botkin Jnr

Richard Benjamin, Conrad Janis, Hans Conried, Henry Silva, Tim Thomerson, Richard Kelton, Douglas Fowley

Quarterback Princess
US 1983 96m colour TVM
CBS (Gary M. Goodman, Barry Rosen)

A schoolgirl determines to become a pro football player.
Unsurprising account of events which for those who lived through them must have had a measure of surprise.

w Rod Browning, recollections of Tami Maida *d* Noel Black *ph* Isidore Mankofsky *m* James Di Pasquale

Helen Hunt, Don Murray, Dana Elcar, Barbara Babcock, John Stockwell

Quatermass *** (GB 1953–9 and 1979).
The Apollo moonshot was 16 years away when *The Quatermass Experiment* became the first TV serial to have the whole country (or such parts as could receive television) agog, yet it anticipated all later misgivings about manned space-flight as well as the excitement, the techniques and even some of the jargon (though in 1953 the word 'computer' evidently hadn't entered the language – the scientists referred to their 'predictor'). Returning to earth in a spacecraft which had wandered off course, a

luckless astronaut developed an infection which slowly turned him into a vegetable monster. In two sequels author Nigel Kneale developed his theme of science, especially military science, running ahead of human wisdom, with his hero Professor Quatermass (played in turn by Reginald Tate, John Robinson and André Morell) increasingly in the role of a kind of watchdog for mankind. Despite being limited to a small element of filming, Rudolph Cartier's productions spectacularly burst out of the studio confines. *Quatermass and the Pit*, a brilliantly inventive amalgam of cautionary tale and fictional mythology, ended with the annihilation of half London.

20 years later Kneale recalled his hero, by now an old man, for an ambitious morality set in a Britain of the near-future in which law and order had broken down while from space some predatory life-form harvested the human race like a trawler fishing the sea-bed. When the production was cancelled by the BBC on cost grounds, Thames picked it up, Sir John Mills becoming the fourth actor to play Quatermass (a name originally picked from the London telephone directory). Though generally rated something of an anti-climax after so long an interval, it was in fact just as well conceived and rather stronger on human qualities than the earlier cycle. What may have diminished its force, oddly, was a switch from six shorter episodes (the original BBC format) to four longer ones, which seemed to upset Kneale's narrative rhythm.

1953   *The Quatermass Experiment* 6 × 30m, BBC (Rudolph Cartier, also *d*); with Reginald Tate, Isabel Dean, Moray Watson, Ian Colin, Katie Johnson
1955   *Quatermass II* 6 × 30m, BBC (Rudolph Cartier); with John Robinson, Hugh Griffith, Monica Grey
1958–9 *Quatermass and the Pit* 6 × 30m, BBC (Rudolph Cartier); with André Morell, Cec Linder, Christine Finn, Anthony Bushell
1979   *Quatermass* 4 × 50m, Thames (Ted Childs), *d* Piers Haggard; with John Mills   PP

LH: 'I was transfixed by the first three serials (each of which was commendably filmed) but the fourth seemed to cover its lack of plot with tedious scenes of mass hysteria.'

Quayle, Anthony (1913–). Distinguished British stage actor, occasionally in other media. TV movies: *Destiny of a Spy*, *Jarrett*, *QB VII* (Emmy 1977), *Great Expectations*,

Moses, *21 Hours at Munich*, *Masada*, *The Testament of John*, *The Manions of America*, *Lace*, *The Last Days of Pompeii*, *The Key to Rebecca*. .

The Queen and I
US 1968 13 × 25m colour
CBS/Ed Feldman
Fun on a pleasure cruiser.
Tepid comedy.
Billy de Wolfe, Larry Storch, Carl Ballantine, Pat Morita

Queen for a Day. American daytime show, a big hit between 1955 and 1964 after 10 years of similar success on radio. Five contestants competed to tell sob stories about why they needed a particular expensive item, and audience applause decided which of them should win. The nadir of American TV.

Queen of the Stardust Ballroom **
US 1975 109m colour TVM
CBS/Robert Christianson, Rick Rosenberg
A middle-aged Bronx widow finds a new interest in life – the local dance hall.
Charming, well-written, homely drama reminiscent of *Marty*
w Jerome Cass *d* Sam O'Steen
MAUREEN STAPLETON, Charles Durning, Michael Brandon, Michael Strong

Queenie's Castle (GB 1970–2; 18 × 30m). Diana Dors equipped with a northern accent to rule the roost in a YTV sitcom. Scripts by Waterhouse and Hall gave it a rude cheerfulness if not much else.   PP

Queens': a Cambridge College (GB 1985; 10 × 50m). Theme-by-theme survey of life in an Oxbridge college, with some emphasis – then much in fashion – on applicants who failed to gain places at the college or undergraduates dropped after their first-year exams. The Master, the dons, sporting and recreational activities also came under inspection. Produced by Michael Waldman, for BBC.   PP

The Queen's Realm (GB 1977). Helicopter-shot travelogues of the British Isles as part of the BBC's celebration of the Queen's Silver Jubilee. Sir John Betjeman furnished a commentary in verse, plus contributions from Shakespeare, Milton, Blake, Auden, etc.   PP

QUATERMASS, a name originally picked at random from the telephone directory, came to promise science fiction of the most urgent and topical kind. Here is the creator of the original serials, Nigel Kneale.

Quentin Dergens MP *
Canada 1966 20 approx. ×
  50m colour (VTR)
Ronald Weyman/CBC

Problems of a Canadian MP.
Solidly interesting series which might have been expected to do more for its star's career.

cr George Robertson

Gordon Pinsent

The Quest *
US 1976 100m colour TVM
NBC/Columbia/David Gerber (Christopher Morgan)

Two brothers seek their sister who years ago was abducted by Indians.
Expensive but glum pilot.

w Tracy Keenan Wynn *d* Lee H. Katzin

Kurt Russell, Tim Matheson, Brian Keith, Neville Brand, Cameron Mitchell, Keenan Wynn, Will Hutchins

† The resulting series flopped through being too dour and violent: it lasted 13 × 50m episodes. Producers: Mark Rodgers, James H. Brown.

The Quest
US 1982 96m colour TVM
ABC/Paramount/Stephen J. Cannell (John Ashley)

Four Americans are found to be descended from the royal line of a tiny Mediterranean kingdom, and are given a series of trials to see which shall succeed.
Absurd extravaganza which might just have got by as a single feature. The intent however was a series, and the strain began to show very early, despite lavish trimmings.

cr Juanita Bartlett

Perry King, Noah Beery, Ray Vitte, Karen Austin, Ralph Michael

The Question of . . . Though never claimed as such, the umbrella title for occasional BBC specials on major issues of the day, usually taking the form of a public meeting with chief speakers on stage plus invited comments from the floor, and chaired by either Ludovic Kennedy or Robin Day. *The Question of Ulster* (1974); *of Television* (1977); *of Immigration* (1978); *of Life and Death* (1981).   PP

A Question of Guilt
US 1978 96m colour TVM
Lorimar (Peter Katz)

A loose woman is accused of murdering her two children, and public opinion and a prejudiced cop almost convict her.
Heavy-going socially conscious melodrama: they don't bother to tell us who did kill the kids.

w Jack and Mary Willis *d* Robert Butler
ph Rich Waite *m* Artie Kane

Tuesday Weld, Ron Leibman, Peter Masterson, Alex Rocco, Viveca Lindfors, Lana Wood

'It strains credulity too often to be believable.' – *Daily Variety*

A Question of Leadership (GB 1981). The 13-week steelworkers' strike of 1980 as mulled over by the strikers themselves plus other workers whose jobs depend on steel, and all highly critical of their union leadership. Independently made by a team whose political sympathies with the Left are undisguised, the film eventually went out only in ATV's own Midland area, followed by a studio discussion in which two union mandarins had the opportunity to challenge their critics. Compiled by Barry Hines; directed and produced by Kenneth Loach; for ATV.   PP

A Question of Love *
US 1980 96m colour TVM
ABC/Viacom/Blinn–Thorpe

A divorcee faces loss of custody of her child because she is a lesbian.
Having said that, the rest is predictable, but the acting is good.

w William Blinn d Jerry Thorpe ph Chuck Arnold m Billy Goldenberg

Gena Rowlands, Jane Alexander, Ned Beatty, Clu Gulager, Bonnie Bedelia, James Sutorius

'Interesting but not compelling.' – *Daily Variety*

A Question of Sex (GB 1979). LWT adult-education series with Anna Raeburn and Clive James which attracted attention because an earlier, more practical, series from Thames had been shelved unseen. Unless it was the implied threat that too much of it would leave you looking like Clive, this one seemed to be less about sex than about differences between the sexes. PP

Question Time. BBC public-forum programme since 1979 in which Sir Robin Day presides over a panel of four answering questions put by the audience – in other words a TV version of radio's eternal *Any Questions*.   PP

The Questor Tapes
US 1973 100m colour TVM
Universal

A superstrong robot is partly human but has no emotions.
A rather boring bit of science fiction which was elbowed out of the series stakes by *Six Million Dollar Man*.

w Gene Roddenberry, Gene L. Coon d Richard A. Colla

Robert Foxworth, Mike Farrell, John Vernon, Lew Ayres, Dana Wynter, James Shigeta

Quick Draw McGraw *
US 1959–62 135 × 25m colour
Hanna–Barbera

A dim-witted horse tries to maintain law and order in the old west.
The cartoon series which followed the phenomenally successful *Huckleberry*

Hound. Superior by TV standards. Also involved: *Snagglepuss*, a trouble-prone lion with a Bert Lahr voice; *Snooper and Blabber*, another cat and mouse team; *Augie Doggie and Doggie Daddy*, a generation gap comedy.

The Quiet War *
GB 1961 50m bw
Rediffusion (Elkan Allan)

Probably the very first documentary about the Vietnam war, before most people had ever heard the name. Retransmitted at the height of the war in 1968 with an introduction by Robert Kee, it may have seemed a little dated in style but poignant in content. I wrote on this second showing: 'There was the great issue, the disaster of our time, still an obscure and relatively innocuous little skirmish carried on amid cultivated rice fields with leaves on the trees, empty skies and only a handful of American "military advisers": a minor fire which could surely be extinguished if people put their minds to it. And instead . . . As Kee also said, it was like going back in a time machine, knowing what was going to happen and unable to do anything about it.'   PP

Quiller
GB 1975 13 × 50m colour (VTR)
BBC/TCF (Peter Graham Scott)

A top level government agent sometimes has doubts about his superiors.
Po-faced spy stuff, full of the clichés of the genre.

Michael Jayston, Moray Watson, Sinead Cusack

Quilley, Dennis (1927–). Leading British stage actor who dabbles in other media and can also sing. *Murder in the Cathedral*, *Contrabandits*, *Masada*, *A.D.*

Quincy *
US 1976– × 50m colour
Universal/Glen A. Larson

A medical examiner in the coroner's office can't resist poking his nose in and finding cases of murder.
Despite the number of corpses about, this is a light-hearted series and its star often triumphs over necessarily unconvincing scripts.

cr Glen A. Larson, Lou Shaw

JACK KLUGMAN, Robert Ito, Garry Walberg

† The series began as part of *Mystery Movie*, with four 96m episodes. See also: *A Star is Dead*.

Quinn, Anthony (1915–). Virile, dominating Mexican–American character actor with a long career in films. His one TV series, *The Man and the City*, was unsuccessful. Also on TV in *Jesus of Nazareth*.

The Quinns
US 1977 74m colour TVM
Daniel Wilson

Life with a family of New York Irish who have been firefighters for four generations. Tolerable failed pilot.

w Sidney Carroll d Daniel Petrie m John Scott

Barry Bostwick, Susan Browning, Liam Dunn, Pat Elliott, Geraldine Fitgerald

quiz game scandal. In 1959 quiz shows were competing with each other to give the highest prizes, and in the US contestants like Charles Van Doren were national celebrities from remaining unbeaten champions on shows like *Twenty One* and *The 64,000 Dollar Question*. It was then revealed that Van Doren and others had been briefed with answers to the tougher questions, and the entire nation felt cheated. The House of Representatives was brought in, heads rolled, the networks promised to take greater responsibility for their shows. Among the long-term results were a shift away from sponsorship of complete programmes towards time-buying, and the replacement of quiz and game shows by filmed series.

The Quiz Kid (GB 1979; 50m). A craze for general knowledge quizzes in northern pubs, with rival teams competing in a league, inspired J. C. Wilsher's first TV play, with Helen Mirren and Michael Elphick; directed by Bill Hays. It was pretty feeble in itself but paved the way for his interesting *Sin With Our Permission* which followed.   PP

quizzes. Roy Ward Dickson, a Canadian, claimed to have started the first broadcast quiz show in 1935, *Professor Dick and His Question Box* from station CKCL, Toronto. Radio and then television cash quizzes became massively popular in North American until scandal (see above) blighted them. In Britain they were only introduced with the advent of ITV in 1955, but by 1958 there were always a dozen versions on the air, many owned and at least partly managed by independent entrepreneurs such as John P. Wynn (*Ask Me Another, Hit the Limit*), Arlington Radio (*Double Your Money*), Michael Miles (*Take Your Pick*) and Ross Radio (*Can Do*). Granada had UK rights in *Criss Cross Quiz* (the American *Tic-Tac-Dough*), *Twenty One* and *Spot the Tune*, ATV in *Dotto, Keep It In the Family* and *The 64,000 Question* in which the figure initially represented not dollars, as in the USA, but sixpences, i.e. a top prize of £1,600 (later doubled). The biggest win in Britain was £5,580, by an actor, Bernard Davies, on *Twenty One*. Soon afterwards quiz shows fell under suspicion as a consequence of the American experience, and though local editions were cleared of dishonesty after internal investigation they did not long survive. 15 years later *Mastermind*, offering only a single modest trophy, was to eclipse them all in popularity.
         PP

Quo Vadis? * (Italy 1985; 6 × 105m). Respectable extended televersion of the much-filmed novel of Nero's reign of terror over ancient Rome, with early Christians coming in for much incidental oppression. Shown in Britain by C4, 1986, in three double helpings. With Klaus Maria Brandauer (as Nero), Frederic Forrest, Cristina Raines, Barbara de Rossi, Max Von Sydow. Made by Franco Rossi for RAI and co-production partners.   PP

quota. Most countries are obliged to fill a quota of home-produced material. In GB this is as high as 86 per cent for ITV, which means that only 14 per cent can be bought in from abroad. The BBC operates a similar, but vaguer, control.

Rachel and the Roarettes (GB 1985; 60m). Feminist fantasy in which multi-coloured lesbian motorcyclists liberate a bride-to-be from the enslavement of marriage while simultaneously flashing back to the 18th century to act out some Beggars' operatics. 'Silly writing, strident acting and the most drivelling lyrics ever heard on the air,' I said generously. With Josie Lawrence (as Rachel), Jean Hart, James Grout. Words and music by Jude Alderson, directed by Rob Walker, produced by Roger Gregory for BBC Pebble Mill. PP

The Racing Game (GB 1979). Tatty 50-minute series based on Dick Francis's name as a writer of horsey whodunits rather than his *oeuvre*, with Mike Gwilym as a crippled steeplechase jockey setting up as an on-course private eye. Written by Terence Feely and others; produced by Lawrence Gordon Clark; for YTV. My view at the time: 'Whizzes both television and the art of the thriller back to the era of Edgar Wallace.' PP

Racket Squad
US 1951–3 98 × 25m bw
Hal Roach
The police expose corruption.
Formulary cop show.
Reed Hadley

Radio Pictures * (GB 1985; 60m). Delirious chamber comedy by Stewart Parker making fun of the rum business of recording a radio play. With Dinsdale Landen, Frances Tomelty, Geoffrey Palmer; directed by Nicholas Renton, produced by Rosemary Hill, for BBC.

Rae, Charlotte (1926–) (C. Lubotsky). Motherly American character actress who became a star in *Diff'rent Strokes* and *The Facts of Life*.

Rafferty *
US 1977 13 × 50m colour
Warner
Cases of an eccentric but concerned doctor in a general hospital.

It turned out more like the Patrick McGoohan Show, with the star giving a richly hammy performance. But the writing and production were good, and the public's lack of interest was surprising.
Patrick McGoohan

Raffin, Deborah (1953–). American leading lady. TV movies: *Nightmare in Badham County, Ski Lift to Death, How to Pick Up Girls, Willa, The Last Convertible, Mind over Murder, Haywire, For the Love of It, Foul Play, The Killing at Hell's Gate, For Lovers Only, Threesome, Lace II.*

Raffles *
GB 1975 78m colour (VTR)
Yorkshire TV
An adaptation of the E. W. Hornung stories about a turn of the century gentleman cracksman.
Stylish but slightly disappointing new version of an old yarn, let down by the look of the thing, with too many hot colour tones.
w Philip Mackie *d* Christopher Hodson
Anthony Valentine
† A series of 13 × 50m episodes followed.

The Rag Trade. A British comedy half-hour which began on BBC in the 1950s and was revived, rather surprisingly, twenty years later with Peter Jones and Miriam Karlin from the original cast. Set in a dressmakers' workroom, showing how the girls take advantage of their long-suffering boss, it had grown cruder in the interim. Missing from the revised version were Sheila Hancock and Reg Varney; added were Anna Karen and Christopher Beeny. Creators: Ronald Wolfe, Ronald Chesney.

Rage
US 1980 96m colour TVM
NBC/Charles Fries/Diane Silver
A man convicted of rape admits his guilt under psychological pressures from the prison doctor.
Powerful stuff, in fact a bit much in every way; there simply isn't any respite from mounting hysteria.

w George Rubino *d* Bill Graham *ph* Alan Daviau *m* Laurence Rosenthal

David Soul, James Whitmore, Yaphet Kotto, Caroline McWilliams, Vic Tayback

'Men rage to have her, to own her, to destroy her!'
Rage of Angels
US 1983 2 × 96m colour
NBC/Furia–Oringer (Richard L. O'Connor)

Despite the enmity of the DA, a young lady lawyer whizzes to the top, with the help of a few dubious but romantic characters.

Action-packed miniseries which strains the credibility but fulfils most of the requirements of a commercial sensation. Oddly enough, it wasn't.

w Robert L. Joseph, *novel* by Sidney Sheldon *d* Buzz Kulik *ph* Ronald Lautore *m* Billy Goldenberg

Jaclyn Smith, Armand Assante, Ken Howard, Kevin Conway, Ron Hunter, Joseph Wiseman, George Coe, Wesley Addy, Deborah May

'Blessed with the texture of a chocolate eclair.' – *Daily Variety*

The Ragged Trousered Philanthropists *
(GB 1967). A triumph of abstraction by Stuart Douglass and director Christopher Morahan. From 500 pretty dense pages they fashioned a series of little vignettes, each one separately framed, which together embodied all the essentials of Robert Tressell's impatient, improving, often marvellously human and funny story of life in the building trade around 1905. With John Rees, Bryan Pringle.   PP

Raid on Entebbe *
US 1977 150m colour TVM
Edgar J. Sherick/TCF/NBC

How the Israeli commandos rescued a planeload of hostages from Uganda.

Probably the best treatment of this subject. (The others: *Victory at Entebbe* and the Israeli movie *Operation Thunderbolt*.)

w Barry Beckerman *d* Irvin Kershner *m* David Shire

Charles Bronson, Peter Finch, Yaphet Kotto, Jack Warden, Martin Balsam, Horst Buchholz, Eddie Constantine, Robert Loggia, John Saxon, Sylvia Sidney

The Raid on Top Malo (GB 1985; 50m). Reconstruction, partly round the sand-table, of a single isolated exploit in the Falklands War, and almost the only soldiering programme to emerge from that conflict.

Re-enacted and described by the squad from the Royal Marines' Mountain and Arctic Warfare Cadre which performed the original raid, it preceded the series *Behind the Lines* from the same producer, Michael Begg. Narrator Ian Wooldridge, for BBC.   PP

The Raiders
US 1964 75m colour TVM
Universal

Bushwhacked cattle drivers get some famous westerners to help them.

Mildly fanciful western.

w Gene L. Coon *d* Herschel Daugherty

Robert Culp, Brian Keith, Judi Meredith, Alfred Ryder, Simon Oakland

Rainbow
US 1978 96m colour TVM
NBC/Ten–Four (Peter Dunne)

The young life of Judy Garland. Interminably slow-starting biopic which develops some interest (too late) in its MGM sequences.

w John McGreevey *d* Jackie Cooper *ph* Howard Schwartz *m* Charles Fox

Andrea McArdle, Don Murray, Piper Laurie, Martin Balsam (as Louis B. Mayer), Moosie Drier (as Mickey Rooney), Michael Parks, Jack Carter (as George Jessel)

Rainy Day Women (GB 1983; 75m). Loony World War II melodrama in which *Dad's Army* volunteers turn into ravening rapists. With Charles Dance, Lindsay Duncan, Suzanne Bertish; written by David Pirie, directed by Ben Bolt, for BBC.   PP

Rakoff, Alvin (1927–   ). Canadian director active in Britain since the fifties, best on 'strong' meaty scripts, from *The Caine Mutiny Court Martial* (1958), to *Romeo and Juliet* in the BBC Shakespeare (1978) and the remake of *A Voyage Round My Father* (1982). Still resident in Britain though working chiefly in Canada and the USA.   PP

Ramar of the Jungle
US 1952–3 52 × 25m bw
Jon Hall

Adventures of a doctor in Africa.
Correction: on somebody's back lot. Jungle Jim Rides Again.

Jon Hall

Rambo, Dack (1941–   ). American leading man. TV series: *Dirty Sally*, *The Guns of Will Sonnett*, *Sword of Justice*. TV movies: *River of Gold*, *Hit Lady*, *Good Against Evil*, *Waikiki*, *All My Children*, *No Man's Land*, *Paper Dolls*.

Randall and Hopkirk (Deceased)
US title: *My Partner the Ghost*
GB 1972 26 × 50m colour
ATV

A private detective, killed on a case, comes back as a ghost but is invisible except to his partner.

Mister Ed meets *Here Comes Mr Jordan*: fair fun once you accept the premise, but it would have been better at half the length.

Kenneth Cope, Mike Pratt, Annette Andre

Randall, Joan and Leslie. Husband-and-wife team popular in the early days of British TV, as panellists, advertising announcers and actors in their own serial soap opera.

Randall, Tony (1920–). American character comedian, long a familiar figure in films. TV series: *Mr Peepers, The Odd Couple, The Tony Randall Show, Love Sidney*. TV movie: *Hitler's SS*.

The Range Rider
US 1951–2 76 × 25m bw
Flying A (Gene Autry)

A mysterious do-gooder rides the range. Standard kids' western, not unlike *The Lone Ranger*.

Jock Mahoney, Dick Jones

The Rangers
aka: *Sierra*
US 1974 74m colour TVM
Universal/Jack Webb (Edwin Self)

Problems of rangers in Yosemite National Park.
Typical Webb multi-drama in which the more exciting rescue bits look fake. The resulting series, *Sierra*, was a dead loss.

w Robert A. Cinader, Michael Donovan, Preston Wood *d* Chris Nyby Jnr *m* Lee Holdridge

James G. Richardson, Colby Chester, Jim B. Smith, Laurence Delaney

Rango
US 1966 17 × 25m colour
ABC/Spelling–Thomas

Misadventures of a bumbling Texas Ranger. Spoof which didn't quite work.

Tim Conway, Guy Marks, Norman Alden

Rankin–Bass Productions. Arthur Rankin Jnr and Jules Bass formed an animation company in the late fifties and have had considerable success, some of the work being done in Japan. Series include *The Jackson Five*

and *The Osmonds*; specials, *Frosty the Snowman* and the perennial *Rudolph the Red-Nosed Reindeer*. They vary between cartoon and puppetry, and despite their proficiency have never achieved a house style in the same way as UPA.

Ransley, Peter (1931–). British writer who after modest beginnings (*The House on the Hill*, 1975) won critical acclaim with *Bread or Blood*, 1981, and all-round success with *The Price* (serial, 1985) leading to *Inside Story*, 1986. In between came *Shall I Play Mother?*, BBC Play for Today, 1983.
PP

Ransom for Alice
US 1977 96m colour TVM
NBC/Universal (Franklin Barton)

Deputy marshals search for a young girl on the Seattle waterfront of the 1880s.
A failed pilot of no particular interest.

w Jim Byrnes *d* David Lowell Rich

Gil Gerard, Yvette Mimieux, Gene Barry, Barnard Hughes, Harris Yulin

Rantzen, Esther (1940–). Toothy and toothsome British anchorlady who started as assistant to Bernard Braden and succeeded him as host of a light-hearted consumer programme, *That's Life*. Produced *The Big Time* in which ordinary folk achieved their wildest dreams. *That's Family Life*, 1984.

Rape and Marriage – The Rideout Case *
US 1980 96m colour TVM
CBS/Lorimar/Stonehenge/Blue Greene
(Blue Andre, Venessa Greene)

The true case of an Oregon wife who claimed that her husband raped her.
Startling and persuasive semi-documentary which might have been even better as pure documentary.

w Hesper Anderson *d* Peter Levin *ph* Robert Caramico *m* Gil Melle

Mickey Rourke, Linda Hamilton, Rip Torn, Eugene Roche, Conchata Ferrell, Gail Strickland

'A fine, fine telefilm.' – *Daily Variety*

The Rape of Richard Beck
US 1985 96m colour TVM
ABC/Robert Papazian

A tough cop is raped by thugs.
And suffers like a woman, as did Lawrence of Arabia before him. Long and rather profitless.

w James G. Hirsch *d* Karen Arthur *ph* Thom Neuwirth *m* Peter Bernstein

Richard Crenna, Meredith Baxter Birney, Pat Hingle, Frances Lee McCain, Cotter Smith, Joanna Kerns

'The idea's a sincere concept; the execution comes off as unconvincing drama.' – *Daily Variety*

Rapf, Matthew (1920–). American writer of many series episodes; also producer of *Kojak*.

Raphael, Frederic (1931–). British writer and occasional performer (as in *Byron: a Personal Tour*, 1981, in which he mooched in and out of the dramatized scenes while providing the narration). Otherwise best known for his serial *The Glittering Prizes* and the deft screenplay of *Rogue Male*, both in 1976; the quaint rewrite of Greek tragedy (with Kenneth McLeish), *The Serpent Son*, plus *School Play*, both 1979; and *Oxbridge Blues*, 1984.   PP

Rascals and Robbers
US 1983 96m colour TVM
CBS (Hunt Lowry)

New adventures of Tom Sawyer and Huck Finn.

Adequate family entertainment which still manages to end up in the Indian caves.

w David Taylor, Carlos Davis *d* Dic Lowry

Patrick Creadon, Anthony Michael Hall, Anthony Zerbe, Allyn Ann McLerie

Rasputin Was a Nice Old Man (GB 1963). On the surface a blackish comedy duologue between a professed murderer and the reporter sent to buy his story, this early play by Leon Griffiths developed into an ingenious commentary on the stage-management of life by art. The market for confessions prompts the crime which is suitable for confession. With Alfred Lynch. Produced by Cecil Clarke; for ATV (*Drama 63*).   PP

The Rat Catchers *
GB 1961–3 39 × 50m bw (VTR)
Associated Rediffusion

Activities of a group of government spymasters.

Fairly absorbing melodramas which cast a commendably cold eye on the spy game after the excessive glamour of James Bond.

Gerald Flood, Glyn Owen, Philip Stone

The Rat Patrol
US 1966–7 58 × 25m colour
ABC/United Artists/Mirisch–Rich

Allied commandos harass the Nazis in North Africa during World War II.

A moderately competent production which caused all hell to break loose in GB because of the British Army's apparently minuscule contribution to the success of the operations; not since Flynn conquered Burma was there such an uproar.

Christopher George, Gary Raymond, Lawrence Casey, Justin Tarr

Rather, Dan (1931–). American newsman, long with CBS.

ratings. The star which TV programmers steer by. By a variety of methods, broadcasters discover to their own satisfaction how many people watched each particular show, and the rating is the proportion of TV sets tuned in out of those available in that area. As some of these may not be in use, a secondary figure, the share, is also given: this represents the proportion of those actually watching TV who tuned in to this particular show.

The Ratings Game **
US 1984 74m colour TVM
Imagination/New Street Productions (David Jablin)

A trucking magnate has a burning ambition to write TV scripts, and in Hollywood succeeds by accident.

Entertaining satire on the commercial aspects of American television; something you certainly wouldn't find on the networks.

w JIM MULHOLLAND, MICHAEL BARRIE *d* DANNY DE VITO *ph* Timothy Suhrstedt *m* David Spear

Danny de Vito, Rhea Perlman, Gerrit Graham, Bernadette Birkette, Barry Corbin, Huntz Hall, Kevin McCarthy

'Television gets skewered as the ratings system gets fixed. It's a joy!' – *Daily Variety*

Rattigan, Sir Terence (1911–77). Not the first world-class dramatist to write for television (that was Priestley) but surely the second with *The Final Test* (1951), about an ageing professional cricketer, later made into a movie. In 1962 he inaugurated the Largest Theatre in the World project with *Heart to Heart*, produced in eight countries, and in 1966 wrote *Nelson*, a 'study in miniature' for ATV which went on to become the stage success *A Bequest to the Nation*. His last TV script was *In Praise of Love* for Anglia in 1976, with Kenneth More facing the death of a loved one. On the last day of 1985 his much-revived short play *The Browning Version* was a critical hit in a new BBC production by Shaun Sutton, with Ian Holm and Judi Dench.

Rattigan was the subject of a 1977 TV tribute by Michael Darlow, for BBC.   PP

Raven, Simon (1927–). British novelist who produced a string of distinctive TV plays in the sixties, usually in closed community settings (army, college, school) only to cease – it seemed – as soon as he had enough scripts to make a published collection. *Royal Foundation*, *The Move Up Country*, *The Gaming Book*, *Soiree at Bossom's Hotel*. Since then his name has figured mainly on the lengthy serialization of *The Pallisers* (1975) and the masterly *Edward and Mrs Simpson* (1979).   PP

The Raving Beauties: see In the Pink

Rawhide *
US 1958–65 144 × 50m bw
CBS

Adventures on a cattle drive to Kansas.
Dour western series with a memorable theme tune and imitable characters and catchphrases ('Git 'em up . . . move 'em out!'). The trail stopped so frequently for miscellaneous dramas that it was a wonder the cattle ever arrived at their destination.

singer Frankie Laine *song* Ned Washington, Dmitri Tiomkin

ERIC FLEMING, CLINT EASTWOOD, PAUL BRINEGAR

The Ray Bolger Show
aka: *Where's Raymond?*
US 1955 39 × 25m bw
ABC

The romantic and comic adventures of a song and dance man.
Amiable star vehicle.

Ray Bolger, Margie Millar, Richard Erdman, Charles Smith

The Ray Milland Show
US 1954 39 × 25m bw
CBS/Revue

Problems of a drama professor at a co-ed college.
Time-filling star froth, the only difference from the previous season's *Meet Mr McNutley* being that that was set at a girls' college.

Ray Milland, Phyllis Avery, Lloyd Corrigan

Ray, Robin (*c* 1934–). British linkman and quizmaster, son of Ted Ray; has a special interest in music.

Raye, Martha (1916–) (Maggie O'Reed). Rubber-faced, wide-mouthed American slapstick comedienne who had a youthful career in the movies and later came to TV, primarily in 1955–6 in *The Martha Raye Show* but later in *The Bugaloos* and *McMillan*.

Read All About It (GB 1974–9). The Beatles' song *Paperback Writer* ushered in this lively BBC review of new paperback books and their authors, started by Melvyn Bragg and taken over by Ronald Harwood when Bragg went to the *South Bank Show*. As with all television book programmes, though, it was crazily restricted to short seasons once or twice a year regardless of the fact that publishing is a continuous activity. In 1981 it was replaced by an inferior programme called *Paperbacks*. PP

Read, John (19 –). Pioneering British arts-film producer whose subjects ranged from painter L. S. Lowry to Scott's Antarctic photographer Herbert Ponting, and the fatal expedition he accompanied. A retrospective season of Read's films in 1983 was introduced by Huw Wheldon.   PP

read more about it. The literature on television would now fill a sizeable barge, and incidentally sink it. Of the hundreds of titles in or out of print the following are both readable and worth reading.
T.C. Worsley: *Television: The Ephemeral Art* (Alan Ross, London 1970).
Peter Black: *The Mirror in the Corner* (Hutchinson, London 1972); the coming of ITV in Britain, wrapped up in a wise disquisition on the medium as a whole.
Erik Barnouw: *Tube of Plenty* (OUP, New York 1975); marvellous history of American television.
Clive James: *Visions Before Midnight*, *The Crystal Bucket* and *Glued to the Box* (Cape, London 1977, 1980 and 1983); his funny reviews, though not so persuasive as when they twinkled newly on the back page of the *Observer* review section.
Robert Sklar: *Prime-Time America* (OUP, New York 1980); informed essays on popular programmes by a lively academic.
Edwin Diamond: *Sign Off* (MIT Press, Cambridge, Mass. 1982). First of the gloomy predictions of the end of television as we know it.
Kenneth Passingham: *The Guinness Book of TV Facts and Feats* (Guinness Superlatives, London, 1984); beneath the catchpenny title a mass of information.   PP

Ready Steady Go! With Cathy McGowan and Keith Fordyce presenters, one of the more acceptable of the teenage pop shows which flourished in Britain in the sixties, put out by Rediffusion from 6 to 7 p.m. on Fridays with the slogan 'The weekend starts here'. When Rediffusion was amalgamated with ABC in the 1968 contracts reshuffle the tapes of the programme were acquired by the pop musician Dave Clark, later a programme entrepreneur. In 1985 C4 screened 7 × 30m compilations plus an Otis Redding special. Original producer: Francis Hitching.   PP

Ready When You Are, Mr McGill **
GB 1976 50m colour (VTR)
Granada (Michael Dunlop)

An actor who has always been an extra gets two lines to speak and can't manage them. Plain funny comedy, many of the jokes being at the expense of TV.

w JACK ROSENTHAL d MIKE NEWELL

Joe Black, Barbara Moore-Black, Diana Davies, JACK SHEPHERD

A Real American Hero
US 1978 96m colour TVM
CBS/Bing Crosby Productions (Samuel A. Peeples)

Tennessee sheriff Buford Pusser wages war on a local moonshiner.
Unnecessary small-screen version of a subject already explored in three *Walking Tall* movies, first with Joe Don Baker and then with Bo Hopkins.

w Samuel A. Peeples d Lou Antonio ph Charles Correll m Walter Scharf

Brian Dennehy, Forrest Tucker, Brian Kerwin, Sheree North, Lane Bradbury

† A brief TV series followed in 1981: see *Walking Tall.*

Real Lives ** (GB 1984–5; 12 × 50m).
Two series of documentary films, unrelated in subject matter save for aiming to show it through the eyes of those most intimately involved, e.g. the astronauts themselves on a shuttle mission or the couple picked by a romantic fiction magazine as living exponents of a True Romance. A 1985 episode, *At the Edge of the Union*, featuring opposing Nationalist and Unionist hard-liners in Northern Ireland, caused a political storm and one-day strike by BBC journalists when its transmission was blocked for three months by the Board of Governors. Produced by Peter Pagnamenta (1984) and Edward Mirzoeff (1985), for BBC.   PP

The Real McCoys *
US 1957–62 224 × 25m bw
ABC and CBS/Brennan–Westgate

Misadventures of a hillbilly family in rural California.
Some people said this show set back TV's development by ten years . . . until *The Beverly Hillbillies* came along. It was efficiently written and it made people laugh.

Walter Brennan, Richard Crenna, Kathy Nolan, Andy Clyde

The Real West **
US 1961 50m bw
NBC (Donald Hyatt)

An outstanding edition of the Project 20 series which tried to sum up the truth behind the fiction of the wild west, this memorable documentary also marked host Gary Cooper's last appearance before the cameras.

w Philip Reisman Jnr

Rear View Mirror
US 1984 96m colour TVM
NBC/Warner/Simon–Asher/Sunn Classic (Kip Gowans, Deborah Simon)

A woman out touring in a camper is taken hostage by escaped convicts who won't stop at rape or murder.
Unpleasantly chilling melodrama with all stops out.

w Lorenzo Semple Jnr, *novel* by Caroline B. Cooney d Lou Antonio ph Frank Watts m William Goldstein

Lee Remick, Tony Musante, Michael Beck, Jim Antonio, Don Galloway

'On-the-brink psychopaths could tilt with this one.' – *Daily Variety*

The Reason of Things (GB 1981; 52m). Alec McCowen as a celibate antique dealer revisiting the seaside town whither he was evacuated in World War II to thank the schoolmarm who had taught him that it didn't matter if he wasn't quite like the other little boys. A gentle, cheerful play by a first-time writer, with an irresistible performance by Margaret Tyzack as the teacher. Written by Freda Kelsall; directed by John Bruce; produced by Pat Sandys; for YTV (*Plays for Pleasure*).   PP

A Reason to Live
US 1985 96m colour TVM
NBC/Columbia/Robert Papazian

An out-of-work man is saved from suicide by his teenage son.
There seem to be Americans who warm to this kind of thing, but I never meet any.

w Robert Lewin *d* Peter Levin

Peter Fonda, Ricky Schroder, Carrie Snodgress, Deidre Hall

Rebecca ** (GB 1979). Creamy, seductive serialization of Daphne du Maurier's romantic classic, careful never to steer the same line as the Hitchcock movie. Written by Hugh Whitemore; directed by Simon Langton; produced by Richard Beynon; for BBC. My 1979 review: 'The spell-setting first line, "Last night I dreamed I went to Manderley again"', was spoken not by a disembodied voice but by one substantial if shadowed figure to another – presumably the de Winters in their eventide home, mulling over the old days. Max would be pushing 90 by now and no doubt just as moody.

'Jeremy Brett is terrific casting, with a hint of military brusqueness and even military bone-headedness beneath the saturnine glitter. Joanna David's anxious, watchful face and uniquely unimaginative hair style are also spot on, with such a nice smile beaming through whenever she can relax. And who would have thought of Anna Massey, an ingénue only yesterday, as the sinister Mrs Danvers? Richard Beynon or Simon Langton did, and she's great.' PP

LH: 'I never felt the menace of Miss Massey at all (Hitch's trick with Judith Anderson was never to show her moving). As for Julian Holloway as Favell, he might have sold Morris Minors but never Rolls-Royces. And the supposedly flame-filled sky at the end came up green. Back to Hitchcock for me.'

The Rebel
US 1959–60 76 × 25m bw
ABC/Goodson–Todman

Johnny Yuma, a Confederate soldier, settles in the west after the Civil War.
Reasonably thoughtful western.
Nick Adams

Rebellion (GB 1963; 60m). The Irish Revolution 1913–23, charted by Robert Kee in an early try-out for his massive *Ireland – a Television History*, 18 years later. Produced by Kee for TRI. PP

Reckless Disregard *
US/Canada 1985 96m colour TVM
Showtime/Telecom/Polar (Chris Dalton, Wayne Fenske)

An investigative TV journalist provokes a lawsuit for slander.
Smartly made and reasonably exciting docu-drama, though it does go in for special pleading.

w Charles Haas *d* Harvey Hart *ph* Rene Verzier *m* Gil Goldstein

Tess Harper, Leslie Nielsen, Ronny Cox, Frank Adamson, Lily Franks, Tony De Santis

'Should interest viewers who keep abreast of media trends.' – Hollywood *Reporter*

Recollections (GB 1985; 6 × 30m). Celebrities show Mary Parkinson (wife of Michael) their favourite keepsakes: another attempt (like *Private Lives* and *Favourite Things*) to come up with a visual equivalent of the *Desert Island Discs* format. Produced by Kenneth Price, for HTV. PP
† *The Glass Box* (Granada) is a variant on the same idea.

Red Alert *
US 1977 96m colour TVM
Paramount (Barry Goldberg)

Things go dangerously wrong on an atomic plant.
Excellent suspenser.

w Sandor Stern, *novel Paradigm Red* by Harold King *d* William Hale
William Devane, Michael Brandon, Adrienne Barbeau, Ralph Waite

The Red Badge of Courage *
US 1974 74m colour TVM
TCF/Norman Rosemont

During the American Civil War, a shy youth gets his first taste of battle.
Adequate, uninspired TV remake of the MGM feature film of 1950.

w John Gay, *novel* Stephen Crane *d* Charles B. Fitzsimons
Richard Thomas, Michael Brandon, Wendell Burton, Warren Berlinger, Charles Aidman

Red Flag: the Ultimate Game
US 1981 96m colour TVM
CBS/ITC/Marble Arch (Peter S. Greenberg)

American air force pilots carry out manoeuvres over the Nevada desert.
The usual rivalries can't obscure the fact that the show really consists of high-speed aerial shots, and those who like them will like it.

w T. S. Cook *d* Don Taylor *ph* Don H. Birnkrant, Rexford Metz, Art Scholl *m* Allyn Ferguson
Barry Bostwick, William Devane, Joan Van Ark, Fred McCarren, Linden Chiles, Arlen Dean Snyder

Red Letter Day *
GB 1976 7 × 50m colour
Granada (Michael Dunlop)

An anthology series to a prescription (a special day in someone's life) that prompted a good proportion of winners – Jack Rosenthal's *Ready When You Are, Mr McGill* and *Well Thankyou, Thursday*, with Judy Parfitt as a registrar of births, marriages and deaths; a typical Donald Churchill comedy, *The Five Pound Orange*; Howard Schuman's science-fiction tease, *Amazing Stories*. Also: *Matchfit* by Willis Hall, with Roddy McMillan as a football manager ill in a sanatorium; *For Services to Myself* by C. P. Taylor, with Alan Dobie as a socialist academic forced to review his lifelong principles as he goes to collect an OBE from the Queen; *Bag of Yeast* by Neville Smith, a young Catholic's ordination as priest. The last three and *Mr McGill* were filmed on location. **PP**

The Red Light Sting
US 1984 96m colour TVM
CBS/Universal/Jon Epstein

A government agent, with the help of a local madam, nails a big-time crook in San Francisco.

Not much of a follow-up to a very successful film.

w Howard Berk, *article The Whorehouse Sting* by Henry Post *d* Rod Holcomb *ph* Woody Omens *m* James Di Pasquale

Farrah Fawcett, Beau Bridges, Harold Gould, Paul Burke, Conrad Janis

'With a hero and heroine offering little charm, lots of innuendoes and no interest, telefilm never ignites.' – *Daily Variety*

Red Monarch **
GB 1983 115m
Enigma (Graham Benson) for
  Goldcrest/C4

Stalin's reign over Soviet Russia presented as a grim farce, on the sound principle that only knockabout comedy can do justice to the mixture of sycophancy, caprice and tyranny at the heart of all dictatorships, and this one in particular. 'Exuberant, funny and instructive,' I reported.

w Charles Wood, *sketches* by Yuri Krotkov *d* Jack Gold

Colin Blakely (as Stalin), David Suchet (as Beria), Carroll Baker, David Kelly **PP**

The Red Pony *
US 1973 100m colour TVM
Universal/Omnibus (Frederick Brogger)

When his pony dies after an illness a farmer's son loses faith in his father.

Well-meaning, overlong and dullish TV remake of the 1949 cinema film.

w Robert Totten, Ron Bishop *d* Robert Totten *m* Jerry Goldsmith (Emmy 1973)

Henry Fonda, Maureen O'Hara, Ben Johnson, Clint Howard

Redcap *
GB 1964–6 30 approx. × 50m bw (VTR)
ABC

Stories of the military police.

Brisk yarns of characters in action, as cold and crisp as one would expect.

cr Jack Bell

John Thaw

The Redd Foxx Show (US 1986; 13 × 25m). Half-hour comedy series with the grizzled star as proprietor of a newsstand/coffee shop in New York. With Rosana De Soto, Pamela Segall; produced by Rick Kellard and Stuart Sheslow for Lorimar/ABC.

Reddy, Helen (1941–). Australian ballad singer in America; occasional specials.

Redgrave, Lynn (1943–). Statuesque British actress who lost weight and became an American favourite. Series: HOUSE CALLS, *Teachers Only*.

Redgrave, Vanessa (1937–). British actress whose left-wing and anti-Zionist affiliations caused a minor uproar when she was cast in PLAYING FOR TIME but have never impaired a style of utter, eloquent naturalism which makes her arguably the ideal television actress: *Maggie* (1964), *La Musica* and *A Farewell to Arms* (1965). **PP**

Redigo
US 1963 15 × 25m colour
NBC/Columbia/Wilrich

Problems of a modern rancher.

Misguided half-hour series left over when *Empire* was cancelled.

Richard Egan

Redmond, Phil (1949–). British writer-producer who made his name with *Grange Hill* and went on to set up Mersey Productions and *Brookside* for C4. **PP**

Reed, Donna (1921–) (Donna Mullenger). American leading lady of forties films. Made a fortune with THE DONNA REED SHOW and returned to TV many years later in *The Best Place To Be*. Subsequently spent a year in *Dallas*.

Reed, Robert (1932–) (John Robert Rietz). American leading man, one of the busiest in TV. Apart from innumerable guest appearances, he has been in two of the most successful series, *The Defenders* and *The Brady Bunch*.

Reflections of Murder
US 1974 96m colour TVM
ABC Circle (Aaron Rosenberg)
At a remote boys' school, the headmaster's wife and mistress plot to murder him.
Dismal remake of *Les Diaboliques*, totally without pace or atmosphere.
w Carol Sobieski *d* John Badham *ph* Mario Tosi *m* J. S. Bach, adapted by Billy Goldenberg
Sam Waterston, Joan Hackett, Tuesday Weld, Lucille Benson

Regan *
GB 1974 78m colour (16mm) TVM
Thames/Euston Films (Ted Childs)
A Flying Squad detective breaks all the rules in his hunt for the killer of a young policeman.
Solidly watchable pilot for *The Sweeney*.
w Ian Kennedy Martin *d* Tom Clegg
John Thaw, Dennis Waterman, Lee Montague, Garfield Morgan, David Daker, Janet Key, Maureen Lipman
'Spanking direction and excellent deadpan acting.' – *Guardian*

The Regiment *
GB 1972–3 26 × 50m colour (VTR)
BBC (Anthony Coburn)
Stories from the officers' mess in the days of the Raj.
Elegant little melodramas which usually entertain, and always look good.
w Jack Ronder, Robert Holmes, others
Malcolm McDowell, Christopher Cazenove

Rehearsal for Murder *
US 1982 96m colour TVM
CBS/Levinson–Link/Robert Papazian
A Broadway playwright aims to find out who killed his fiancée by staging a reading of his new play.
Ingenious suspenser, a cut above the usual level.
w Richard Levinson, William Link *d* David Greene *ph* Stevan Larner *m* Billy Goldenberg

Robert Preston, Lynn Redgrave, Patrick MacNee, Lawrence Pressman, William Russ, Jeff Goldblum, William Daniels, Madolyn Smith

Reid, Alastair (1939–). British drama director whose credits include *Artemis '81* and the David Hemmings *Dr Jekyll and Mr Hyde*. Lately, *Slimming Down*, 1984, *The Houseman's Tale*, 1986.   PP

Reid, Beryl (1920–). British comic actress who is sometimes too much of a not particularly good thing. As a comedy act, she invented her invisible companion 'Marleen'; has more recently concentrated on comic cameos and occasional specials.

Reid, Graham (1945–). Northern Irish writer, formerly schoolteacher, who has stayed at home to write about that embattled region in the three *Billy* plays, *The Wrong Curriculum* and *Ties of Blood*.   PP

Reid, Robert (1933–). British documentarist, usually on scientific or medical themes and always of outstanding probity. Not content to close the file on a 1968 film about mentally disturbed children apparently being redeemed by a visiting American miracle worker, he returned to the subject for *The Broken Bridge* six years later and found them back to square one. In the fifties he produced *Eye on Research* and brought the BBC's first programme from Soviet Russia. For another notable Reid achievement see *According to the Rules*. Scripted *The Voyage of Charles Darwin*, 1978. Now in video production.   PP

Reilly – Ace of Spies *
GB 1983 1 × 78m, 11 × 52m
Euston Films (Chris Burt) for Thames
Exploits of a legendary Russian-born British agent and entrepreneur in the first 30 years of this century. Two main stories acted as mini-serials within the series, punctuated by one or two minor adventures and many affairs – a not entirely satisfactory format. There was also some inadequate period dialogue. But a finely written, directed and very moving conclusion atoned for much.
w Troy Kennedy Martin, *book* by Robin Bruce-Lockhart *d* Jim Goddard, Martin Campbell
Sam Neill (as Reilly), Leo McKern (as arms magnate Basil Zaharoff), Norman Rodway, Jeananne Crowley, Tom Bell, Kenneth Cranham (Lenin)   PP

Reilly, Charles Nelson (1931–   ). American comic actor, in series *The Ghost and Mrs Muir* and *Match Game*.

✳ **Reiner, Carl** (1922–   ). American actor, writer, jack of all trades, associated above all with Sid Caesar and Dick Van Dyke. Starred in series *Heaven Help Us*. Emmy 1956, best supporting actor, *Caesar's Hour*; 1961, 1962, 1963, best comedy writer, *The Dick Van Dyke Show*. TV movie as actor: *Medical Story*.

Reiner, Rob (1945–   ). American actor who played the idle son-in-law in *All in the Family* (Emmy 1973, 1977). Also produced and starred in *Free Country*. Son of Carl Reiner.

Reitel, Enn (19 –   ). Scottish-born comedy star of consistently witless series: *The Further Adventures of Lucky Jim*, *The Optimist*, *Mog*. Supplies voices for *Spitting Image*.   PP

✳ **Reith, John (Lord Reith)** (1889–1970). British administrator, the original general manager of the BBC, its first director-general and imposer of the 'Auntie' image. He failed to come to grips with TV, but his influence was felt until the sixties.

† The BBC preserved its founder's stamp in a trio of conversations with Malcolm Muggeridge under the title of *Lord Reith Looks Back* (1967, produced by Stephen Peet), starting off in Reith's native Glasgow before moving to London. The three 75-minute segments were: 1. 'I was meant to do something in the world'; 2. 'I found the BBC or the BBC found me'; 3. 'I was not fully stretched'. A compilation, *Looking Back with Lord Reith*, followed in 1971.

PP: 'Muggeridge seemed determined to exceed his client in the austerity of his views. I was reminded of Kenneth Tynan's *bon mot* about Donald Wolfit and Ernest Milton in a religious epic "stealthily upstaging each other to the greater glory of God".'

Reith
GB 1983 2 × 90m
BBC (Innes Lloyd)

The dramatized account of the life and work of the above, concentrating on politics and power with scarcely a reference to the BBC's business of making and putting out programmes; even on its chosen ground it is history edited to improve Reith's image. In the *Financial Times* Christopher Dunkley listed four inconvenient points omitted from the crucial episode of Reith's handling of the

General Strike in 1926. But there were few reservations about Scottish actor Tom Fleming's portrayal of the founding father.
w Roger Milner
Tom Fleming, Dinah Stabb   PP

Release. The title first used by BBC2 in a long and unavailing struggle to devise an arts magazine programme of quality. It was followed by *Review* with James Mossman proving that a tough reporter doesn't necessarily make a tough critic. Finally came *Mainstream*, of which the less said the kinder. Meanwhile *Arena*, devoted to single-subject film essays, has quietly excelled.   PP

Relentless
US 1978 74m colour TVM
CBS (Fredric Baum)

Bank robbers are hampered by a snowstorm which grounds their getaway airplane.
Efficient, routine chase and caper film.
w Sam H. Rolfe, *novel* Brian Garfield *d* Lee H. Katzin *ph* Jack Whitman *m* John Cacavas
Will Sampson, Monte Markham, John Hillerman, Marianna Hill
'The plot's whiskers have turned white despite the contemporary trappings' – *Daily Variety*

The Reluctant Heroes
aka: *The Egghead on Hill 656*
US 1972 73m colour TVM
Aaron Spelling

A knowledge of history helps a lieutenant on foot patrol during the Korean War.
Thin war comedy, a long way before *M*A*S*H*.
w Herman Hoffman, Ernie Frankel *d* Robert Day
Ken Berry, Cameron Mitchell, Warren Oates, Jim Hutton, Ralph Meeker

Remember When *
US 1973 96m colour TVM
Danny Thomas

Problems of a Connecticut family in wartime.
Rather untidily assembled nostalgia with a warmly sentimental core.
w Herman Raucher *d* Buzz Kulik
Jack Warden, Nan Martin, William Schallert

'It took her father 38 years to find the woman he couldn't forget!'
Remembrance of Love
US 1983 96m colour TVM
NBC/Comworld/Doris Quinlan

Onetime lovers, survivors of the holocaust, are reunited in Israel after forty years.

Rather too determined four-handkerchief weepie, marred by clumsy sub-plots.

w Harold Jack Bloom, *article* by Rena Dictor LeBlanc d Jack Smight ph Adam Greenberg m William Goldstein

Kirk Douglas, Pam Dawber, Chana Eden, Yoran Gal, Robert Clary

'It proves good intentions aren't enough.' – *Daily Variety*

Remick, Lee (1935–). American leading actress, in international films and TV. Best-known on the small screen for JENNIE (BAFTA award 1974), *Wheels*, and IKE. Other TV movies: *And No One Could Save Her*, *The Blue Knight*, *QB VII*, *Hustling*, *A Girl Called Sooner*, *Breaking Up*, *Torn Between Two Lovers*, *The Women's Room*, *The Letter*, *The Gift of Love*, *Mistral's Daughter*, *Rear View Mirror*.

Remington Steele
US 1982– × 50m colour TVM
NBC/MTM (Michael Gleason)

A lady private eye invents a dashing head of her agency, and he suddenly turns up.
A slightly bizarre premise with a hint of the supernatural inaugurates a series which looks slick but lacks true sophistication. To everyone's surprise it became a success in America, but died in Britain.

cr Michael Gleason

Stephanie Zimbalist, Pierce Brosnan

'Could move into higher gear if the actors can convince themselves that they can be, as well as look, worldly; otherwise, it's *Hart to Hart* in Pasadena.' – *Daily Variety*
'They're such a fun couple . . . wouldn't you just love to send them on a smart cruise? To Fiji, say, in a two-man canoe?' – Robert MacKenzie, *TV Guide*

Renaldo, Duncan (1904–) (Renault Renaldo Duncan). American leading man; TV's Cisco Kid.

Rendezvous Hotel
US 1979 96m colour TVM
CBS/Mark Carliner

Problems for the manager of a resort hotel . . .
. . . are equalled only by the problem the viewer may have in sitting through them.

w Austin and Irma Kalish, Clayton Baxter d Peter Hunt ph William J. Jurgensen m Jonathan Tunick

Bill Daily, Jeff J. Redford, Teddy Wilson, Bobbie Mitchell, Talya Ferro, Edward Winter

'Dialogue and situations are not apt to inspire anyone.' – *Daily Variety*

The Renegades
US 1983 96m colour TVM
ABC/Paramount/Lawrence Gordon

Seven hoodlums are recruited by the police as undercover agents.
Witless attempt to have your cake and eat it, by showing that the street gangs who filled American screens in the early eighties can have a social purpose.

w Bobby Zavatini d Nicholas Corea

Patrick Swayze, Randy Brooks, Paul Manes, Tracy Scroggins, Brian Tochi

Rep (GB 1982; 6 × 30m). Stingy Granada sitcom, nearly all conducted in the actors' digs, about a shabby seaside repertory company in the forties. Best thing about it was Iain Cuthbertson as its devious, bullying proprietor. Also with Stephen Lewis, Patsy Rowlands, Caroline Mortimer. Written by Digby Wolfe and Ray Taylor, directed and produced by Brian Izzard.   PP

The Reporter *
US 1964 13 × 50m bw
CBS/Richelieu (Keefe Braselle)

Investigations of a columnist for the New York Globe.
Smooth, very adequate comedy–drama entertainment.

cr Jerome Weidman

Harry Guardino, Gary Merrill, George O'Hanlon

Reputations (GB 1979–81). Occasional but excellent BBC series of assessments by Anthony Howard of political figures of recent years, e.g. Richard Crossman, Beaverbrook. Further 60m edition on Kenneth Tynan, 1982.   PP

Requiem for a Heavyweight ** (US 1956; GB 1957; 88m; live BW). Rod Serling's classic TV drama about a fighter on the way down demands a place in the annals, and not only for the players who dared the hazards of a live show to make it work: in America (CBS), Jack Palance as the dignified, dazed hero, Ed Wynn as his old trainer and Keenan Wynn as his manager; in Britain (BBC), Sean Connery, Warren Mitchell and George Margo, with Alvin Rakoff as producer. A kinescope of the US version figured in the 1981 Golden Age of Television season in America, and was one of the recordings to be screened in Britain by C4 in 1983.   PP

re-runs. It used to be an infallible rule that the American TV season lasted 39 weeks, from September to May, and was followed by 13 selected re-runs. As costs rose, the number of new programmes dwindled to the present 22/25, and re-runs consequently increased, though a show may be pre-empted at any time of the year for special programming. Once the network has finished with a show, it can of course start a new life in syndication – if there are enough episodes to make it usable as a strip. As for the British, they tend to re-run the wrong things and even then at inaccessible times.

Rescue 8
US 1958–9 73 × 25m bw
Columbia/Wilbert (Herbert B. Leonard)

Exploits of a two-man emergency rescue team.

Adequate location action filler.

Jim Davis, Lang Jeffries

residuals. Sums of money which must be paid to artists, musicians, etc, if and when a show is played in another territory.

The Restless Gun
US 1958–9 77 × 25m bw
NBC/Revue/Window

Adventures of a trouble shooter in the old west.

Standard half-hour western series.

John Payne

Retreat (GB 1967; 100m; bw). Sombre epic about British troops withdrawing to the sea in the Peninsular War which never quite plumbed its chosen depths of mysterious soldierly morale. With Leslie Sands, Ewen Hooper. Written by John Hale, directed by HERBERT WISE, produced by Cecil Clarke for ATV.   PP

Return Engagement
US 1978 74m colour VTR
NBC/Hallmark Hall of Fame (Mike Wise, Franklin R. Levy)

A former vaudeville star becomes a college professor; when she falls for a student, they make up a double act.

Mm. More curious than satisfying, but certainly different.

w James Prideaux d Joseph Hardy m Arthur B. Rubinstein

Elizabeth Taylor, Joseph Hardy, Peter Donat, Allyn Ann McLerie

**Return Flight ** (GB 1972). Peter Barkworth as an airline pilot plying between Hamburg and Luton who locks on to the lingering corporate fear of a bomber crew in trouble over Germany thirty years earlier: a really chilling contemporary ghost story by *Dr Who* writer Robert Holmes and just about the best thing in a spooky BBC series called *Dead of Night* which also included Don Taylor's *The Exorcism*.   PP

The Return of Captain Nemo
US 1978 3 × 50m colour
CBS/Warner/Irwin Allen (Arthur Weiss)

Captain Nemo is melted out from an ice cupboard and saves the modern world.

Flatulent seafaring hokum with too much dialogue and not enough humour.

w Norman Katkov, Preston Wood, Lamar Boren d Alex March ph Paul Rader m Richard La Salle a/d Eugene Lourie

Jose Ferrer, Burgess Meredith, Burr de Benning, Tom Hallick, Warren Stevens

'Both situation and dialogue are pitched strictly at the kidvid audience.' – *Daily Variety*

The Return of Frank Cannon *
US 1980 96m colour TVM
CBS/QM (Michael Rhodes)

Cannon avenges the death of a friend from the CIA.

Acceptable whodunit set rather unconvincingly among the horsey aristocracy.

w James David Buchanan, Ronald Austin d Corey Allen ph William Cronjager m Bruce Broughton

William Conrad, Allison Argo, Burr De Benning, Arthur Hill, Taylor Lacher, Diana Muldaur, Ed Nelson, Joanna Pettet

'If the story seems weary from overuse, the cast and crew give it all a good shake.' – *Daily Variety*

The Return of Joe Forrester *
US 1975 74m colour TVM
NBC/Columbia (Christopher Morgan)

Problems of a cop on the beat.

Adequate pilot for an adequate series, *Joe Forrester*, relying heavily on its star.

w Mark Rodgers d Virgil W. Vogel

Lloyd Bridges, Pat Crowley, Jim Backus, Dane Clark, Charles Drake, Dean Stockwell, Della Reese, Janis Paige, Edie Adams, Tom Drake, Eddie Egan, Hari Rhodes

The Return of Marcus Welby

US 1984 96m colour TVM
ABC/Universal/Marstar (Dennis E. Doty)

Old Dr Welby consoles a brilliant young doctor who seems to be losing everyone he loves to cancer.

Failed attempt to resurrect an old medical warhorse; the star refused to do more than the pilot.

w John McGreevey, Michael Braverman *d* Alexander Singer *ph* Edward R. Plante *m* Leonard Rosenman

Robert Young, Darren McGavin, Morgan Stevens, Elena Verdugo, Cristina Raines, Jessica Walter

The Return of the Beverly Hillbillies: see

The Beverly Hillbillies

The Return of the Gunfighter

aka: *As I Rode Down from Laredo*
US 1967 98m colour TVM
MGM

An ex-gunslinger avenges the deaths of a Mexican girl's parents.

Sluggish low-budget western.

w Robert Buckner *d* James Neilson *m* Hans Salter

Robert Taylor, Chad Everett, Ana Martin, Lyle Bettger, Michael Pate

The Return of the King

US 1985 96m colour TVM
ABC/Rankin–Bass

Second attempt to make a cartoon feature of characters from Tolkien's *The Hobbit*. This one looks good but is far too long and ends up confusing its potential audience. Narrated by John Huston; made in Japan.

'A challenge if not an appetizer.' – *Daily Variety*

The Return of the Man from UNCLE

US 1983 96m colour TVM
CBS/Viacom/Michael Sloan (Nigel Watts)

Solo and Kuryakin emerge from retirement when THRUSH steals an atom bomb.

Limp attempt to revive a sub-James Bond formula: moderate action sequences cannot atone for the tedium in between.

w Michael Sloan *d* Ray Austin *ph* Fred J. Koenekamp *m* Gerald Fried

Robert Vaughn, David McCallum, Patrick MacNee, Gayle Hunnicutt, Anthony Zerbe, Keenan Wynn, Simon Williams, George Lazenby

The Return of the Mod Squad

US 1979 96m colour TVM
ABC/Thomas–Spelling (Lynn Loring)

Three young cops return from 'retirement' to find out who is trying to murder their former chief.

Feeble reprise of a format which should have been forgotten.

w Robert Janes *d* George McCowan *ph* Arch Dalzell *m* Shorty Rogers, Mark Snow

Michael Cole, Clarence Williams III, Peggy Lipton, Tige Andrews, Victor Buono, Roy Thinnes, Tom Bosley, Ross Martin, Tom Ewell

Return of the Rebels

US 1981 96m colour TVM
CBS/Filmways/Moonlight (Frank Von Zerneck)

Members of a motorcycle gang reunite 20 years later.

Slambang, mindless nonsense for retarded five-year-olds.

w Robi Robinson ˙*d* Noel Nosseck *ph* Rexford Metz *m* Michael Melvain

Barbara Eden, Don Murray, Robert Mandan, Jamie Farr, Chris Connelly

'The kind of drivel that causes many people to consider the airwaves a vast wasteland.' – *Daily Variety*

The Return of the World's Greatest Detective

aka: *Alias Sherlock Holmes*
US 1976 74m colour TVM
NBC/Universal (Roland Kibbee, Dean Hargrove)

A motor cycle cop has an accident and recovers believing himself to be Sherlock Holmes.

Inept spoof apparently inspired by *They Might Be Giants*, and originally intended to become a series within *Mystery Movie*. No way.

w Roland Kibbee, Dean Hargrove *d* Dean Hargrove *ph* William Mendenhall *m* Dick de Benedictus

Larry Hagman, Jenny O'Hara, Nicholas Colasanto, Woodrow Parfrey, Ivor Francis

Return to Earth

US 1976 74m colour TVM
NBC/King–Hitzig (Jud Taylor)

The effects of Apollo 11 space flight on astronaut Buzz Aldrin, who had a nervous breakdown resulting in marital problems.

Interesting, understated case history.

w George Malko, *book* Buzz Aldrin *d* Jud Taylor *ph* Frank Stanley *m* Bill Goldenberg

Cliff Robertson, Shirley Knight, Charles Cioffi, Ralph Bellamy, Stefanie Powers

Return to Eden
Australia 1984 3 × 96m, 22 × 50m colour miniseries
Hanna Barbera/Hal McElroy

Amazing attempt to do an Australian *Dallas*, with a heroine menaced at every turn, notably by a crocodile which leaves her in need of plastic surgery. After falling in love with her surgeon she makes a new life as a fashion model, and takes her revenge on her murderous husband. That's the first six hours: the 22 take place seven years later, when more dark deeds in the family start to disturb the even tenor of her days. Audiences loved it; critics were helpless.

co-p,cr Michael Laurence

Rebecca Gilling, James Reyne, Wendy Hughes, James Smilie, Olivia Hamnett

'Torpid meller, in reaching for tension, barely rolls over.' – *Daily Variety*

Return to Fantasy Island: see *Fantasy Island*. This was a second 96-minute pilot, even drearier than the first. George McCowan directed from a script by Marc Brandel; actors included Adrienne Barbeau, Horst Buchholz, Joe Campanella, George Chakiris, Joseph Cotten, Laraine Day, George Maharis, Cameron Mitchell, France Nuyen and Karen Valentine, as well as Ricardo Montalban and Herve Villechaize.

Return to Peyton Place
US 1972 50 × 22m colour (VTR)
NBC/TCF (George Paris)

Incredibly inept daytime soap opera sequel to the famous twice-weekly peak-time serial.

d Allen Pultz, Frank Pacelli

Bettye Ackerman, Frank Ferguson, Katherine Glass, Julie Parrish, Warren Stevens, Guy Stockwell

Returning Home
US 1975 74m colour TVM
ABC/Lorimar/Samuel Goldwyn (Herbert Hirschman)

War veterans return to a small American town in 1945, and have various difficulties in settling down.

A potted version of *The Best Years of Our Lives*, intended as a pilot for a series that never was. Those who knew the movie found that this version trivialized it; those who hadn't weren't interested.

w John McGreevey, Bill Svanoe *d* Daniel Petrie *ph* Richard L. Rawlings *m* Ken Lauber

Dabney Coleman (Fredric March role), Tom Selleck (Dana Andrews), Joan Goodfellow (Teresa Wright), James R. Miller (Harold Russell), Whitney Blake (Myrna Loy), Sherry Jackson (Virginia Mayo)

Reunion *
US 1980 96m colour TVM
CBS/Barry Weitz

A middle-aged man is unsettled by attending his class reunion.

Warmly interesting drama with excellent performances.

w Sue Millburn *d* Russ Mayberry *ph* Hector Figueroa *m* George Romanis

Kevin Dobson, Joanna Cassidy, Linda Hamilton, Lew Ayres, George DiCenzo, Conchata Ferrell, Rick Lenz

Reunion at Fairborough *
GB 1985 96m colour TVM
HBO/Columbia/Alan Wagner/Alan King (William Hill)

A US Army Air Force squadron holds its 40th reunion in England, and one of its members discovers not only a lost love but a grand-daughter he never knew he had.

Pleasant, stretched-out star vehicle which serves its purpose.

w Arthur Ruben *d* Herbert Wise *ph* Tony Imi *m* Nigel Hess

Robert Mitchum, Deborah Kerr, Red Buttons, Judi Trott, Barry Morse, Shane Rimmer, Ed Devereaux

'Ably directed, well worth the time spent.' – *Daily Variety*

Revelations (1983; 6 × 30m). Celebs questioned by Eric Robson on some moment in life which afforded them a spiritual revelation. Iris Murdoch was supposed to be the catch, but the much-exposed Kenneth Williams unfolded the most vivid, touching and self-evidently truthful reminiscence. Produced by Nick Evans, for Border.   PP

Revenge!
US 1971 73m colour TVM
ABC/Aaron Spelling (Mark Carliner)

A man is lured and locked up in a cellar by a crazy woman who thinks he has wronged her. Heavy-going melodrama with the star well over the top.

w Joseph Stefano, *novel* Elizabeth Davis *d* Jud Taylor

Shelley Winters, Bradford Dillman, Carol Rossen, Stuart Whitman

Revenge for a Rape
US 1977 96m colour TVM
ABC/Albert S. Ruddy (Alan P. Horowitz)
When his wife is raped, a man takes the law into his own hands.
Death Wish all over again. One is enough.

w Yabo Yablonsky *d* Timothy Galfas *m* Jerrold Immel

Mike Connors, Robert Reed, Tracy Brooks Swope, Deanna Lund

The Revenge of the Stepford Wives
US 1980 96m colour TVM
NBC/Edgar J. Scherick (Scott Rudin)
A lady journalist finds herself in danger in a New England town where the men have had all their women turned into complaisant robots.
Listless and pointless sequel, treading much the same ground as the 1975 movie and to less purpose.

w David Wiltse *d* Robert Fuest *ph* Ric Waite *m* Laurence Rosenthal

Sharon Gless, Arthur Hill, Julie Kavner, Don Johnson, Audra Lindley, Mason Adams
'Uneven horror meller . . . a fitful adventure.'
– *Daily Variety*

Revolver. Fortunately doomed attempt by ATV and British record producer Mickie Most to concoct a teenage pop music show whose presenter, Peter Cook (posing as a dance hall manager), actively hated the music on offer – this during the brief Punk era of the late seventies.   PP

Reward
US 1982 74m colour TVM
ABC/Lorimar/Jerry Adler/Esprit
A disgruntled San Francisco cop smashes a drugs ring.
Failed pilot which promises more than it delivers.

w Jason Miller *d* E. W. Swackhamer *ph* Fred Jackman *m* Barry DeVorzon

Michael Parks, Richard Jaeckel, Louis Giambalvo, Malachy McCourt, Andrew Robinson, Annie McEnvie
'Fine film technique can't hold viewers without better material.' – *Daily Variety*

Rex Harrison Presents Three Stories of Love
aka: *Three Faces of Love*
US 1974 100m colour TVM
Universal
Three stories ranging from uninteresting to inept. *Epicac* by Kurt Vonnegut, *Kiss Me Again Stranger* by Daphne du Maurier, *The Fortunate Painter* by Somerset Maugham. Harrison doesn't help.

w Liam O'Brien, Arthur Dales, John T. Kelley *d* John Badham, Arnold Laven, Jeannot Szwarc

Julie Sommars, Bill Bixby, Roscoe Lee Browne, Lorne Greene, Leonard Nimoy, Juliet Mills, Agnes Moorehead

❋   **Reynolds, Burt** (1936–). American leading man with an insolent grin. After years of TV apprenticeship he rather surprisingly became a major movie star; his best remembered TV series are *Riverboat*, *Gunsmoke* (three seasons as an Indian), *Hawk* and DAN AUGUST. TV movies: *Hunters Are for Killing*, *Run Simon Run*.

Reynolds, Debbie (1932–) (Mary Frances Reynolds). Petite American light actress and entertainer, long with MGM. On television, attempts at series (*The Debbie Reynolds Show*, *Aloha Paradise*) have not been notably successful, but she has occasional musical specials.

Reynolds, Gillian (1935–). British radio critic and television performer, since 1985 chairing *Face the Press*. Previously the looking-good part of a keep-fit series with Richard Stilgoe, *Looking Good, Feeling Fit*. Wrote and presented *The Last Cathedral*, 1985.   PP

Reynolds, Sheldon (1923–). American international reporter who turned producer with *Foreign Intrigue* and *Sherlock Holmes*. In 1979/80, made *Sherlock Holmes and Dr Watson* in Poland.

Reynolds, William (*c* 1929–). American all-purpose actor. Series: *Pete Kelly's Blues*, *The Islanders*, *The Gallant Men*, *The FBI*.

The Rhinemann Exchange
US 1977 2 × 96m, 1 × 50m colour
NBC/Universal (George Eckstein, Richard Collins)
At the outbreak of World War II, an escape specialist is sent to Argentina on a dangerous espionage mission.
Adequate capsule version of a bestseller.

w Richard Collins, *novel* Robert Ludlum *d* Burt Kennedy *ph* Alex Phillips Jnr *m* Michel Colombier

Jeremy Kemp, Stephen Collins, Lauren Hutton, Pedro Armendariz Jnr, Claude Akins, René Auberjonois, Vince Edwards, Larry Hagman, John Huston, Roddy McDowall

Rhoda **
US 1974–8 110 approx. × 25m colour
CBS/Mary Tyler Moore

Adventures of a slightly kooky girl in New York.
Well written and characterized comedy, spun off from *The Mary Tyler Moore Show* and enriched by its new Jewish milieu. During the first two seasons Rhoda got married and divorced.
cr/executive p James L. Brooks, Allan Burns *m* Billy Goldenberg

VALERIE HARPER, Nancy Walker, Harold Gould

Rhodes, Hari (or Harry) (1932–). Handsome black American actor. Series: *The Bold Ones*.

rhubarb. What crowd actors are always supposed to mutter over and over again when they have no lines.

Rice, Anneka (1958–). Sunny British teleperson who started on Hong Kong radio but panted to fame as the 'sky-runner' in C4's *Treasure Hunt*. 'What you see most of her,' I observed, 'is what you see most of when anyone pretty and feminine is running away from camera and dressed in a one-piece overall, and very pleasant, too, though it is odd that with all that frenzied exercise it never grows less.' Also *Sporting Chance*, *Family Trees* and the travel show *Wish You Were Here*. PP

Rice, Tim (1944–). Successful British lyricist, until the eighties in partnership with Andrew Lloyd Webber, who had his own chat show in 1983 (7 × 40m, *p* David F. Turnbull, for BBC). In 1985, subject of *Lyrics by Tim Rice*, 90m showcase introduced by Paul Gambaccini, produced by Ian Bolt, for YTV. PP

Rich, David Lowell (1923–). American director, mostly for TV, where he has been competent if never outstanding since the days of *Studio One*, *Big Town* and *Route 66*. TV movies: *See How They Run*, *Wings of Fire*,

The Borgia Stick, *Berlin Affair*, *Lt Schuster's Wife*, *All My Darling Daughters*, *Set This Town on Fire*, *The Horror at 37,000 Feet*, *Brock's Last Case*, *Beg Borrow or Steal*, *Satan's School for Girls*, *Death Race*, *The Sex Symbol*, *Aloha Means Goodbye*, *You Lie So Deep My Love*, *Ransom for Alice*, *Telethon*, *The Defection of Simas Kurdika*, *A Family Upside Down*, *Little Women*, *Enola Gay*, etc.

Rich, John (1925–). American director who made a few movies in the sixties but is mainly associated with the days of live TV. Emmys as best comedy director: 1962 for THE DICK VAN DYKE SHOW, 1971 for ALL IN THE FAMILY.

Rich, Lee (19 –). Independent producer, head of Lorimar Productions (*The Waltons*, *Helter Skelter*, *Dallas*, *Knots Landing*, etc). He was formerly a partner in Mirisch–Rich Productions.

Rich Man, Poor Man ***
US 1975 12 × 50m (or 6 × 95m) colour
ABC/Universal (Frank Price)

The fortunes of two sons of an immigrant baker, from the end of World War II to the seventies.
The cinematic equivalent of a good read, this pioneering mini-series was well produced and acted, and kept its melodramatic excesses within check. It was an enormous and somewhat unexpected hit, and novelizations were in. See *Best Sellers*.
w Dean Riesner, *novel* Irwin Shaw *d* David Greene, Alex Segal *m* Alex North

PETER STRAUSS, NICK NOLTE, Susan Blakely, Dorothy McGuire, Ed Asner, Ray Milland, Craig Stevens, William Smith, Fionnula Flanagan

'Glossy melodrama, with the suds occasionally armpit deep.' – Alvin H. Marill

† Emmy awards: Ed Asner, Fionnula Flanagan, David Greene.

Rich Man, Poor Man: Book Two *
US 1976 22 × 50m colour
ABC/Universal (Frank Price)

The fortunes in industry of the surviving brother Rudy from *Rich Man, Poor Man*, and his relationships with his stepson and nephew. A totally artificial extension of a smash success, this lengthy serial gave the impression of being made up as it went along, and of not knowing when to stop. (In fact the hero was killed off at the actor's own request.) All that can be said in its favour is that it filled a slot just about adequately.

Peter Strauss, Gregg Henry, James Carroll Jordan, Susan Sullivan

The Richard Boone Show **
US 1963 25 × 50m bw
NBC/Classic/Goodson–Todman

An anthology of original and somewhat ambitious dramas, performed by a repertory and hosted by the star.

A smoothly carpentered concept which failed to catch the public fancy. Contributors included Rod Serling, Clifford Odets, Robert Dozier.

consultant Clifford Odets

RICHARD BOONE, Warren Stevens, Bethel Leslie, Lloyd Bochner, Robert Blake, Guy Stockwell, Harry Morgan, Jeanette Nolan, Ford Rainey

'A serious effort to raise the standards of television drama.' – Don Miller

Richard, Cliff (1940–   ) (Harold Webb).
Ever-youthful British pop singer who after immense success went religious but still makes occasional special appearances. In 1982 the BBC fêted his 20 years in show business with a four-part series, *Cliff!*

Richard Diamond *
Syndication title: *Call Mr Diamond*
US 1959–60 51 × 25m bw
CBS/Four Star

Cases of a smart young city detective.

Streamlined wisecracking crime series.

David Janssen, Mary Tyler Moore, Barbara Bain, Russ Conway, Regis Toomey

Richard the Lionheart
GB 1962 39 × 25m bw
Danziger

Uneasy period adventures which seemed to be aimed at neither children nor adults.

Dermot Walsh

Richard, Wendy (19 –   ). General
purpose British actress in both sitcoms (*Spooner's Patch*, *Are You Being Served?*) and soaps (*EastEnders*).

Richardson, Ian (1934–   ). Consummate
British actor whose many TV appearances range from *Tinker, Tailor, Soldier, Spy* (as the mole) and two impersonations of General Montgomery to playing Nehru in *Mountbatten – the Last Viceroy*.   PP

Richardson, Keith (1942–   ). British
producer and executive, head of drama at Tyne-Tees for two years before returning to YTV as deputy controller, drama. Produced *Second Chance*, *Horace*, *One Summer*, *The Glory Boys*, *The Wedding* (Tyne-Tees).

Richardson, Sir Ralph (1902–84). Eminent
British actor sparing of his television appearances but making them weighty when he did do one: *Heart to Heart*, 1962; *Hedda Gabler*, 1963; one or two US costume epics. In 1982 subject of *Sir Ralph at Eighty*, with Bernard Levin, produced by Bridget Winter, for BBC.

'Everybody underestimates Richie. He counts on it.'

Richie Brockelman, Private Eye
US 1977 1 × 74m (and 4 × 50m) colour
NBC/Universal (Steven J. Cannell)

Cases of an earnest 23-year-old private eye who is ridiculed by his family and friends.

Mildly amusing mini-series based on a character from *The Rockford Files*.

w Steven J. Cannell, Steven Bochco *d* Hy Averback

Dennis Dugan, Suzanne Pleshette, Lloyd Bochner, Norman Fell

'I would guess Richie's chances of turning 24 are faint.' – Robert MacKenzie, *TV Guide*

Richman, Stella (1925–   ) British executive
producer, formerly actress (a bit part in *The Quatermass Experiment*) and story editor. *Half Hour Story*, *Jennie*, *Clayhanger*, *Just William*, etc. Was briefly programme controller at LWT.   PP

Rickles, Don (1926–   ). American comedian
known for insulting his audience; not internationally renowned.

Ridley, Arnold (1895–1984). Venerable
British actor and playwright (*The Ghost Train*) who found late-life stardom as the pacifist Private Godfrey in *Dad's Army*.

Riesner, Dean (c 1930–   ). American
screenwriter, mostly for TV: *Rich Man, Poor Man* was the peak of his achievement.

The Rifleman *
US 1958–62 168 × 25m bw
ABC/Four Star/Sussex

Problems of a widowed rancher and his young son.

Good family western.

Chuck Connors, Johnny Crawford

Rigg, Diana (1938–   ). Intelligent British
leading lady of stage and screen. On TV, created Emma Peel in THE AVENGERS and after many years of trying had an American series to herself; but *Diana* was a failure, as was *The*

Diana Rigg Show on BBC. Other appearances include *In This House of Brede*, *Witness for the Prosecution*, *King Lear*, *Bleak House*.

'Their love was deeper than life itself!'
Right of Way
US 1983 96m colour TVM
HBO/Schaefer–Karpf (George Schaefer)

When a grandmother becomes ill, she and her husband plan a suicide pact.
Not exactly a bundle of laughs, this stretched-out teleplay defeats even the skills of its distinguished players.

w Richard Lees, from his *play* *d* George Schaefer *ph* Howard Schwartz

Bette Davis, James Stewart, Melinda Dillon

The Right Prospectus *** (GB 1970). Dream-like, singular, bemusing TV play from John Osborne in which a middle-aged couple shop around for a suitable public school, not for any son of theirs but for themselves. And no one at the school considers it in the least unusual when a blue-chinned, liverish George Cole and delectable gym-slipped Elvi Hale appeared in their midst. Also with Tom Criddle, Christopher Witty. Directed by Alan Cooke; produced by Irene Shubik; for BBC (*Play for Today*). My 1970 review: 'I think the point of the metaphor was to indicate, by reversing the normal order of things, just how arbitrary are the prospects of success and happiness. A man of substance in adult life, Newbold failed miserably as a schoolboy while his wife thrived. Why? Because although he had chosen his school with great care, Newbold reasoned, he had no choice as to which house he was assigned. And it was the house which ruled which values mattered, which alone could have provided the right stimulus for him. It's possible I've got it all wrong, but at least I enjoyed doing so.'   PP

Right to Reply. Channel 4's only regular self-produced programme, and a valuable one. The aggrieved can answer back to the producers of any C4 programme, either by invitation to the studio or simply by dropping into the channel's offices in London, Glasgow or Birmingham, and recording their complaint in an unmanned 'video box'. Conducted by Gus Macdonald, produced by Clare Paterson.   PP

Right to Kill?
US 1985 96m colour TVM
ABC/Wrye–Konigsberg/Taper–Media/
   Telepictures (Jack Clements)

A teenage boy kills his psychopathic father. Yet another melodramatic case history 'from the files'; a bit too much for the audience.

w Joyce Eliason *d* John Erman *ph* Gayne Rescher *m* Paul Chihara

Frederic Forrest, Christopher Collet, Karmin Murcelo, Justine Bateman, Ann Wedgeworth

Riker
US 1981 4 × 50m colour
CBS/Columbia/David Gerber

An ex-cop goes under cover for the attorney-general.
Surprisingly ho-hum cop stuff for this producer. Unsurprisingly, it failed to grab an audience.

cr Jerry Ludwig

Josh Taylor, Michael Shannon, Elyssa Davalos, Dane Clark

Rin Tin Tin: see The Adventures of Rin Tin Tin

Ring of Passion
aka: *Rehearsal for Armageddon*
US 1978 96m colour TVM
TCF

Political shadows of the Max Schmeling–Joe Louis fight in New York in the thirties.
Good: overall feeling strong, detail sometimes naïve.

w Larry Forrester *d* Robert Michael Lewis

Stephen Macht, Bernie Casey, Allen Garfield

Rings on Their Fingers (GB 1979–). Half-hour sitcom about a bright young couple who decide to get married after living together for years. At its best, quite lively, but not entirely dissimilar from the same author's *The Marriage Lines* of 20 years previously. With Diane Keen, Martin Jarvis. Written by Richard Waring; produced by Harold Snoad; for BBC.

Rintels, David W. (*c* 1935–). American writer responsible for *Clarence Darrow* (1974), FEAR ON TRIAL (Emmy 1975), WASHINGTON BEHIND CLOSED DOORS and *Gideon's Trumpet*.

Ripcord
US 1961–2 76 × 25m bw
Rapier/United Artists (Ivan Tors)

Two unusual detectives are trained skydivers. The ultimate in eccentric ideas becomes hokum.

Larry Pennell, Ken Curtis

Ripley's Believe It or Not
US 1982–5 88 × 60m colour

A rough-edged magazine format introduced by Jack Palance. Weird, supposedly true stories were acted out but all too often left unproven, and there was no sense of accurate scientific investigation, while the humour of the classic comic strip was missing. Produced by Ripley Productions for Columbia.

Ripping Yarns ** (GB 1979). A series of high-spirited half-hour comedies spoofing the horror film, the sealed room mystery, the *Boy's Own Paper* adventure, etc. By and starring Michael Palin; for BBC. BAFTA award for best light entertainment programme.

Rippon, Angela (1944–   ). Except for a brief stint by Nan Winton in the late fifties, Britain's first woman newsreader, initially (1975) on BBC2's *News Extra*, subsequently on the main *Nine O'Clock News* on BBC1. Branched out with motoring, country life and reporting programmes and quit news reading in 1980. Briefly with TV-am, 1983, followed by two years in Boston (USA) as a TV arts reporter. Now mostly on radio.

LH: 'Her appeal is devastating to some and a mystery to others.'

Riptide
US 1984 96m colour TVM
NBC/Paramount/Stephen J. Cannell (Jo Swerling Jnr)

Two easy-going private eyes on Manhattan Beach solve cases with the help of a gadgets genius and a helicopter.

All the worst elements of a Cannell pilot were combined in this slack, noisy adventure piece. The series which followed wasn't any better, but it ran three seasons.

cr Stephen J. Cannell, Frank Lupo

Perry King, Joe Penny, Thom Bray

'What an idea! You take *A-Team* action without Mr T, blend in a *Simon and Simon* detective team, without the rapport; add *Magnum* beefcake without Tom Selleck; mix in *Knight Rider* gadgetry, without the black Firebird; and you come up with *Riptide*, an action-adventure goulash without the tasty appeal of any of the shows on which it is based.' – *Daily Variety*

Rising Damp **
GB 1974–8 28 × 25m colour (VTR)
Yorkshire (Ronnie Baxter)

In a run-down apartment building, tenants tease the mean and sneaky landlord.

Virtually a single-set comedy series in which laughs constantly rise from the grime because of funny scripts and great ensemble acting.

w ERIC CHAPPELL

LEONARD ROSSITER, DON WARRINGTON, RICHARD BECKINSALE, FRANCES DE LA TOUR

'She was the most desired woman in the world . . . except by the men she loved!'
Rita Hayworth – the Love Goddess
US 1983 96m colour TVM
CBS/David Susskind (Andrew Susskind)

Skin-deep biopic which treats its subject more as a commodity than a woman, and arranges for some reason to avoid mentioning World War II.

w E. Arthur Kean *d* James Goldstone *ph* Terry K. Meade *m* Lalo Schifrin

Lynda Carter (Rita), Michael Lerner (Harry Cohn), John Considine (Ed Judson), Edward Edwards (Orson Welles), Alejandro Rey (Edward Cansino), Aharon Ipale (Aly Khan)

'Everyone's attempting to be legendary, but legends require distinctiveness and validity, not a good try.' – *Daily Variety*

Ritter, John (1948–   ) (Jonathan Ritter). American leading man, son of Tex Ritter the singing cowboy. Best known for the series *Three's Company*, TV movies: *Leave Yesterday Behind*, *The Comeback Kid*, *Pray TV*, *In Love with an Older Woman*, *Sunset Limousine*, *Three's a Crowd*, *Letting Go*.

Ritual of Evil
US 1969 98m colour TVM
Universal (David Levinson)

A psychiatrist who is also a supernatural investigator loses one of his patients to a witchcraft ritual.

An interesting theme is spun out and becomes nonsense.

w Robert Presnell Jnr *d* Robert Day *m* Billy Goldenberg

Louis Jourdan, Anne Baxter, Diana Hyland, John McMartin, Belinda Montgomery

The Ritz * (GB 1981; 55m). Documentary for BBC presenting a day in the life of one of London's most exclusive hotels. Full of fascinating insights. Presented by John Pitman, produced by Edward Mirzoeff.

The Rivals of Sherlock Holmes *
GB 1972–3 26 × 50m colour (VTR)
Thames

An anthology of stories about Victorian
detectives.
Variable but generally interesting selection
from anthologies published by Hugh Carleton
Greene.

River Journeys (GB 1984; 6 × 60m). After
two series of great and little railway
journeys, half-a-dozen intrepid – or just
lucky – travellers sail down great rivers,
notably explorer Christina Dodswell in New
Guinea.   PP

River of Gold
US 1970 74m colour TVM
Aaron Spelling

Two American divers in Mexico become
involved in the undersea search for a relic.
Below-average adventure hokum.

w Salvatore C. Puedes d David Friedkin m
Fred Steiner

Dack Rambo, Roger Davis, Ray Milland,
Suzanne Pleshette, Melissa Newman

River of Mystery
US 1969 96m colour TVM
Universal (Steve Shagan)

Two oil wildcatters in Brazil are lured into
helping rebels
Jungle thick-ear: quite unremarkable.

w Albert Ruben d Paul Stanley

Vic Morrow, Claude Akins, Niall MacGinnis,
Edmond O'Brien, Nico Minardos, Louise
Sorel

Rivera, Chita (1933–) (Conchita del
Rivero). Electrifying American dancer and
singer, an occasional TV guest. TV movie:
The Marcus Nelson Murders.

Riverboat *
US 1959–60 44 × 50m bw
NBC/Revue/Meladre

Adventures on a Mississippi steamboat in the
1840s.
The setting made for a refreshingly different
series, though most of the writing was pure
corn.

Darren McGavin, Burt Reynolds

Rivers, Joan (1937–). American comedienne who emerged from the Second City
improvisational troupe; on TV, makes guest
appearances.

Riviera Police
GB 1964 26 × 50m bw (VTR)
Associated Rediffusion

Rumour has it that the title, which says it all,
was offered in a spirit of humour and snapped
up seriously by a programme controller who
shall be nameless.

Geoffrey Frederick, Noel Trevarthen

Rivkin: Bounty Hunter *
US 1981 96m colour TVM
CBS/Ten–Four (Art McCaird, Frank Ballou)

A streetwise New Yorker rounds up crooks
who've jumped bail.
Slick busted pilot based on a real character:
good Manhattan–Jewish atmosphere and
even better action scenes.

w Peter Lefcourt d Harry Harris ph Richard
Kratina m Arthur B. Rubinstein

Ron Leibman, Harry Morgan, Harold Gary,
Verna Bloom, George DiCenzo, John Getz,
Harry Bellaver

'The pace is so sharp it could put out an eye.' –
Daily Variety

Rix, Brian (1924–). British actor–manager,
a latter-day doyen of stage farces who
appeared in more than 70 TV versions in the
fifties and sixties. Host of series for the
mentally handicapped, *Let's Go.*

Roache, William (1932–). British actor
who has played only one part on television
and that continuously since 1961: Ken
Barlow in *Coronation Street.* By 1985 he was
the last remaining founder-member of the
cast.   PP

The Road * (GB 1963; 55m bw). Chilling
science fiction play by Nigel Kneale in which
a new motorway is haunted by the ghosts of
a future catastrophe. 'As obsessive,
well-argued and worrying as all the best
science fiction aims to be,' said critic Philip
Oakes. With James Maxwell, John Phillips;
directed by Christopher Morahan, for BBC.
                                                    PP

The Road Runner. Character featuring in a
series of Warner cartoons, an imperturbable
bird who always escapes from the clutches of
Wile E. Coyote.

The Road West *
US 1966 16 × 50m colour
NBC/Universal

A widower with three children joins a wagon
train in the 1850s and settles on the prairies.
Adequate sodbusting saga. The first two

episodes were joined together and released theatrically as *This Rugged Land.*

Barry Sullivan, Andrew Prine, Brenda Scott, Kelly Corcoran

Roads to Freedom (GB 1970; 13 × 50m). Tedious BBC serialization of three Jean-Paul Sartre novels of life, politics and defeat in France 1938–40, chiefly interesting as the first drama marathon to include real-life characters – Daladier, Hitler, Chamberlain and Halifax. With Michael Bryant, Daniel Massey, Georgia Brown, Rosemary Leach, Norman Rossington.   PP

The Roaring Twenties *
US 1960–1 45 × 50m bw
ABC/Warner

Two reporters during prohibition find most of their best stories coming out of one night club. Ho-hum series given a special sparkle by its use of (a) a famous backlot and (b) the catchiest songs of the period.

Rex Reason, Donald May, DOROTHY PROVINE

Robards, Jason Jnr (1922–). Distinguished American character actor who has given a lift to some pretty routine dramas. TV movies: WASHINGTON BEHIND CLOSED DOORS, *A Christmas to Remember, Haywire.*

Robbery Under Arms
Australia 1985 3 × 96m colour
    miniseries
South Australian Film Corp. (Jock Blair)

Adventures of a mid-19th-century highwayman.
The trouble with any adaptation of this rambling novel is that Captain Starlight is hanged two-thirds of the way through, with interest passing to his young aides. This version has not licked the problem, and is massively overlong, even in the feature film version which appeared first and sank into oblivion.

w Graeme Koestveld, Tony Morphett, *novel* by Rolf Boldrewood *d* Ken Hannam, Donald Crombie *ph* Ernest Clark *m* Garry McDonald, Laurie Stone

Sam Neill, Steven Vidler, Christopher Cummins, Liz Newman, Deborah Coulis, Susie Lindeman, Ed Devereaux

Robbins, Jerome (1918–) (Jerome Rabinowitz). American choreographer who won Emmys in the fifties for his work on productions of *Peter Pan.*

The Robert Cummings Show: see My Hero

JASON ROBARDS JNR – not too many people remember Jason Robards Snr – has given distinguished performances in a large number of causes. Here he plays Franklin Roosevelt in *FDR: The Last Year.*

Robert Kennedy and His Times
US 1985 1 × 142m, 2 ×
    96m colour miniseries
CBS/Columbia/Chris–Rose (Bob
    Christiansen, Rick Rosenberg)

Yet another long and repetitive study of a family whose peccadilloes are becoming all too familiar. A good professional job is all one can say.

w Walon Green *d* Marvin J. Chomsky *ph* Michael D. Margulies *m* Fred Karlin *pd* William J. Kenney

Brad Davis, Veronica Cartwright (Ethel), Cliff De Young (J.F.K.), James Read (Teddy), Ned Beatty (J. Edgar Hoover), G. D. Spradlin (L.B.J.), Jack Warden (Joseph Kennedy), Beatrice Straight (Rose)

'It may not be history, but it's beguiling TV' – *Daily Variety*

Robert Montgomery Presents *
US 1950–6 150 approx. × 25m bw
Anthology dramas hosted by the star, who occasionally performs.
A series of generally high standards.

Robert Young Family Doctor: see Marcus Welby MD

Roberts, Ben (1916–84) (Benjamin Eisenberg). American screenwriter, usually with Ivan Goff. Series created include *The Rogues*, *Charlie's Angels*, *Mannix*.

Roberts, Pernell (1930–). American character actor who was a long time between his hit series *Bonanza* and *Trapper John*. TV movies: *The Silent Gun*, *San Francisco International*, *The Bravos*, *The Adventures of Nick Carter*, *Dead Man on the Run*, *The Deadly Tower*, *The Lives of Jenny Dolan*, *Charlie Cobb*, *Centennial*, *The Immigrants*, *The Night Rider*, *Hot Rod*, *High Noon Part Two*.

Roberts, Rachel (1927–80). Welsh character actress, latterly in Hollywood. TV movies: *Destiny of a Spy*, *Baffled*, *Great Expectations*, *A Circle of Children*, *The Hostage Tower*.

Robertson, Cliff (1925–). Sober-looking American leading actor who is occasionally seen on TV (WASHINGTON BEHIND CLOSED DOORS) and in 1953 played the title role in *Rod Brown of the Rocket Rangers*. TV movies: *The Sunshine Patriot*, *The Man Without a Country*, *A Tree Grows in Brooklyn*, *My Father's House*, *Return to Earth*, *Overboard*, *The Key to Rebecca*.

Robertson, Dale (1923–). American western star, former schoolmaster. TV series: *Tales of Wells Fargo*, *The Iron Horse*, *Dynasty*. TV movies: *Melvin Purvis G-Man*, *Kansas City Massacre*.

Robertson, Fyfe (1903–). British reporter, an emaciated bearded Scot who has been a familiar TV figure since the early fifties.

Robin Redbreast *** (GB 1970). One of the select band of single plays which have initiated a whole strand of drama, John Bowen's rustic chiller was twice repeated. In his story of a woman newly thrown on her own company who goes to live in an isolated cottage, he condensed all the matter-of-fact malevolence of the country which a town-dweller can sometimes experience. With Anna Cropper, Bernard Hepton, Freda Bamford. Directed by James MacTaggart; produced by Graeme McDonald; for BBC (*Play for Today*). Subsequent ventures in the same strain include the mini-serial *Harvest Home* (US), and Bowen's own two-part *Dark Secret* for LWT in 1981.   PP

Robin of Sherwood ***
GB 1984–6 2 × 100m, 24 × 50m
HTV/Goldcrest (Paul Knight)

The old legend newly invested with folklore, magic and necromancy; Robin is now the semi-mortal offspring of the pagan god Herne the Hunter – a circumstance which proved useful when after two seasons Michael Praed had to be replaced by Jason Connery. All the traditional heroes and villains are featured, plus an interesting addition in the form of a thick upper-class law-enforcer, Guy de Gisburne. Not only the best *Robin Hood* I'd ever seen, I said, but one to restore Robin to the First Division of legends.

cr Richard Carpenter *d* Ian Sharp and others *m* Clannad

Michael Praed (1986, Jason Connery), Judi Trott (Maid Marian), Nickolas Grace (Sheriff of Nottingham), Robert Addie (Guy de Gisburne), John Abineri (Herne the Hunter)   PP

LH: 'I disliked it fairly intensely, not least because it all looked so *green*. And who needs a supernatural Robin Hood? By the way, Basil Rathbone played Guy of Gisbourne in the 1938 Errol Flynn film, and the character also figured in the earlier Douglas Fairbanks version.'

Robin's Nest *
GB 1977–81   × 25m colour
Thames

A second spin-off from *A Man About the House* with Richard O'Sullivan now equipped with a steady companion (later, wife) in the person of Tessa Wyatt and a new situation in the form of running a little restaurant. A bonus for the series was that having grinned and borne it so long as odd man out in *A Man*, O'Sullivan was licensed to converse tirelessly in the jokes and wisecracks and contrived fantasies which when stuffed into the mouths of lesser characters in lesser series merely draw attention to the poverty of the whole. Tony Britton was the father-in-law. Written by Johnnie Mortimer and Brian Cooke.   PP

Robinson Crusoe
GB 1974 100m colour
BBC (Cedric Messina)

A straightforward retelling of Defoe's classic desert island yarn.

w/d James MacTaggart *ph* Brian Tufano *m* Wilfred Josephs

Stanley Baker, Ram John Holder

ROBIN OF SHERWOOD presented the legendary outlaw as modern young people seem to like him; older viewers would have preferred Errol Flynn. Here are Michael Praed and Judi Trott.

Robinson, Hubbell (1905–). American executive producer who oversaw CBS drama in the fifties.

Robinson, Robert (1926–). British journalist and host of programmes ranging from game shows (*Call My Bluff, Ask the Family*) to *The Book Programme* which latterly he also edited. Renowned for his carefully conserved hair style, but if there is any justice in the world esteemed for a precise, hard-thought-out turn of speech that makes most of his contemporaries sound as if they are area-bombing the target. In 1977 conducted the amazingly successful literary investigation, *B. Traven – Mystery Solved*, with Will Wyatt. Recent credits include *The Book Game*, 1982; *Robinson Country* (TVS

series) and *Our House* (co-deviser), both 1984; *In Trust – Houses and a Heritage* (National Trust film for C4), 1985.   PP

Robotech (US 1985; 85 × 22m). Japanese-made animation, produced and distributed by Harmony Gold, about a 21st-century battle of the planets.

Robson, Dame Flora (1902–84). Distinguished British actress who had difficulty finding leading roles but was always a welcome presence. *Heidi, A Man Called Intrepid, Les Misérables, Gauguin the Savage, A Tale of Two Cities.*

Rochdale. British parliamentary constituency where for the first time, at a by-election in 1958, TV cameras covered the rival party campaigns and interviewed the candidates. Until Granada single-handedly put it to the test here it had been assumed by everyone that the Representation of the People Act made such coverage illegal. As a result of this successful skirmish the General Election the following year was Britain's first 'TV Election'. Oddly, one of the candidates at Rochdale was the television professional Ludovic Kennedy. PP

Rock Follies *
GB 1976–7 12 × 50m colour (VTR)
Thames (Andrew Brown)

Three girls on a seedy tour aspire to be the world's greatest rock group.
Pithy modern drama with Busby Berkeley-style fantasy sequences, an interesting contrast with *Pennies from Heaven* though less meaningful.

w Howard Schuman d BRIAN FARNHAM, JON SCOFFIELD m Andrew Mackay

Charlotte Cornwell, Julie Covington, Rula Lenska

† BAFTA 1977: best drama series.

PP: 'The second series was called *Rock Follies of '77*, though a strike at Thames meant most of the run was held up until the following year. I wrote when it started: "*Rock Follies of '77* turns the usual law of smash-hit sequels upside down: it resumed better than the original *Rock Follies* began and, remembering how that first series rather tailed away, it also looks more durable. Is it because the author, Howard Schuman, now has the confidence, relaxation and/or desperation to go once more for the transatlantic wayfarers he used to mock so beautifully in plays like *Verité*? A honey made a late entrance here in the bulgy person of Kitty Shrieber (Beth Porter), high-powered American agent and packager." '

Rocket Robin Hood
Canada 1967 52 × 25m colour
Trillium Productions

In AD 2000 New Sherwood Forest is a floating asteroid.
Undistinguished cartoon capers.

The Rockford Files *
US 1974 74m colour TVM
Universal/Cherokee/Public Arts (Meta Rosenberg)

An ex-con private eye investigates 'closed' cases and helps a young woman to find out whether her father was murdered.

Lively pilot for a moderately successful series, shot in Los Angeles and the desert and maintaining a nice sense of humour.

w Stephen J. Cannell d Richard Heffron

JAMES GARNER, Lindsay Wagner, Noah Beery Jnr, William Smith

† The resulting series ran until 1980, and won an Emmy in 1979. Creators: Roy Huggins, Stephen J. Cannell; producer: Roy Huggins; for Universal/Cherokee/Public Arts.

Rocky and his Friends **
US 1959–60 158 × 25m colour
Jay Ward

A cartoon ragbag with some splendid items. Rocky the flying squirrel appears in a serial with his dim-witted moose friend Bullwinkle (the real star of the show), combating the machinations of Boris Badenov. Other segments include *Fractured Fairy Tales*, narrated by Edward Everett Horton; *Dudley Do-Right*, a simple-minded mountie; *Aesop's Fables*; and *Peabody's Improbable History*. Throughout is evident a distinct vein of wit.

Rocky Jones Space Ranger
US 1953 39 × 25m bw
Roland Reed

An interplanetary adventurer has an atomic space ship.
Kiddie fare, not a patch on Flash Gordon.

Richard Crane, Sally Mansfield

Rocky King (US 1950–3). Half-hour live crime series for Dumont, with Roscoe Karns as a New York police detective.

Roddenberry, Gene (19 –). American producer, creator of *Star Trek*, after which he didn't seem able to manage another hit.

Rodeo Girl
US 1980 96m colour TVM
CBS/Marble Arch/Len Steckler

The wife of a rodeo rider decides to try her luck at the game.
Rather ordinary domestic drama with rodeo backing; for minority audiences.

w Katharyn M. Powers d Jackie Cooper ph Howard Schwartz m Al DeLory

Katharine Ross, Bo Hopkins, Candy Clark, Jacqueline Brooks, Parley Baer

Rodgers, Anton (1933–). Engaging British actor of donnish appearance: *Fresh Fields* (sitcom), *Something in Disguise* and *An Actor's Life for Me* among recent credits.
PP

Rodgers, Richard (1902–79). Celebrated American song composer, partnered both with Hart and with Hammerstein. Television scores include VICTORY AT SEA (Emmy 1952), THE VALIANT YEARS (Emmy 1960).

Roger and Harry
US 1977 74m colour TVM
Columbia/Bruce Lansbury (Anthony Spinner)

Our two heroes offer a service: they recover missing objects, including people.
Highly derivative failed pilot.
w Alvin Sapinsley d Jack Starrett m Jack Elliott, Allyn Ferguson

John Davidson, Barry Primus, Susan Sullivan, Richard Lynch, Carole Mallory, Harris Yulin, Biff McGuire

Roger Doesn't Live Here Any More *
GB 1981 6 × 30m colour
BBC (Dennis Main Wilson)

The highbrow runner in a spate of situation comedies that year about lately separated or divorced men forming new attachments. This one at least had inventive, if wayward, scripts by John Fortune, some genuinely funny moments and no studio laughter.
d John Hobbs

Jonathan Pryce, Diane Fletcher, Kate Fahy
PP

Rogers, Ginger (1911–). Believe it or not she starred in a live BBC musical *Carissima* in 1959. Even harder to believe, the part afforded her not one step to dance, nor one note to sing. It was the idea of Eric Maschwitz, author of the show and at the time an otherwise successful head of the light entertainment department. '*Mediocrissima*' commented the *News Chronicle*.   PP

Rogers, Kenny (1938–). Rotund American western singer who eased comfortably into a number of TV movies. *The Gambler*, *Coward of the County*, *The Gambler – the Adventure Continues*, *Wild Horses*.

Rogers, Paul (1917–). Stolid British actor in all walks of television, from *Honeymoon Postponed* (1961) to *Butterflies*, *Barriers*, *Edwin* and, in 1985, *Connie*.   PP

Rogers, Ted (1934–). Fast-talking British stand-up comic, familiar from *Sunday Night at the London Palladium* to *Three-Two-One*.

ROBERT ROBINSON seems over-conscious of his thinning locks, and either scrapes his side hair over his pate or, when outdoors, wears old-fashioned headgear. After untold years of compèring quizzes, he is occasionally rewarded with a series of his own. Here in *Robinson Country* he starts a tour of Britain's south-west.

Rogers, Wayne (1933–). American leading man whose series include *M*A*S*H*, *City of Angels* and *House Calls*. TV movies: *Attack on Terror*, *Having Babies II*, *It Happened One Christmas*, *Thou Shalt Not Commit Adultery*.

Rogue Male *
GB 1976 96m colour (16mm) TVM
BBC/TCF (Mark Shivas)

Before World War II, a British aristocrat whose fiancée has been murdered by the Nazis sets out to shoot Hitler, narrowly misses, and is hounded back to England by the SS.
Deliberately cold-blooded film of a cold-blooded book (previously filmed by Fritz Lang as *Man Hunt*). Sequences impress, but the whole thing becomes rather silly and unpleasant.

w Frederic Raphael, *novel* Geoffrey Household *d* Clive Donner

Peter O'Toole, Alastair Sim, John Standing, Harold Pinter

PP: 'I dissent. Apart from Frederic Raphael's gratuitous conversion of the villain from German agent to British Fascist in his screenplay, a faithful and extremely exciting version of Household's classic. It was to have been the first of a full collection of between-the-wars Clubland Hero adventures produced by Shivas with Richard Broke as story editor. In the event only two more were shot, again directed by Clive Donner: *The Three Hostages* and *She Fell Among Thieves* (both 1978).'

The Rogues **
US 1964 29 × 50m bw
NBC/Four Star (Collier Young)

Adventures of a family of upper-class con men, who always do the right thing in the end. Motto: 'Honor before honesty'.

Jet-set Robin Hoods, they are seen in all the best places and headquartered in foggy London. An amusing and skilful series, too light in touch to catch the public fancy.

cr Collier Young

GIG YOUNG, CHARLES BOYER, DAVID NIVEN, GLADYS COOPER, ROBERT COOTE

Rogues' Gallery (GB 1968–9; 10 × 55m). Quaint but merited idea by Peter Wildeblood (who also wrote the scripts) for a sequence of plays set in Newgate Gaol and featuring all the legendary denizens of its heyday. For Granada.   PP

Rohde, Shelley (19 –). Capable and comely British interviewer who has conducted a succession of afternoon chat shows for Granada; also *The Glass Box* in which the guests have to choose items to be buried away for posterity. Special on James Mason, 1984.   PP

Roland Rat. British muppet-type figure with aggressive manner who rescued TV-am from disappearing audiences in 1983 and was signed up by the BBC two years later for series of his own plus guest appearances, e.g. top billing on the *Wogan* show.   PP

Roll, Freddy, Roll
US 1975 74m colour TVM
Persky–Denoff

In order to win a place in the Guinness Book of Records, a mild-mannered computer programmer lives for seven days on roller skates.

Slow-starting but finally quite hilarious comedy.

w Bill Persky, Sam Denoff *d* Bill Persky *m* Jack Elliott, Allyn Ferguson

Tim Conway, Jan Murray, Henry Jones, Scott Brady, Ruta Lee

Roll on Four O'Clock *
GB 1971 57m colour (16mm)
Granada (Kenith Trodd)

The plight of a sensitive boy in a tough school. A serious theme played effectively for comedy.

w Colin Welland *d* Roy Battersby

Colin Welland, Clive Swift, George A. Cooper

† *Sun* award, best play.

Roll Over Beethoven *
GB 1984–5 13 × 30m
Central/Witzend (Tony Charles)

Piano teacher takes on rock star as pupil, and love blooms. Pleasant sitcom set in country village the better to sharpen up its contrasts, and quite nicely done thanks to the likeability of the principals.

w Laurence Marks, Maurice Gran *d* Nic Phillips

Liza Goddard, Nigel Planer, Richard Vernon   PP

Rolling Man *
US 1972 73m colour TVM
Aaron Spelling

An ex-con tries to find his sons who have been farmed out to foster homes. Efficient, slightly unusual melodrama.

w Steve and Elinor Karpf *d* Peter Hyams

Dennis Weaver, Don Stroud, Agnes Moorehead, Donna Mills, Jimmy Dean, Sheree North

Rollout
US 1973 13 × 25m colour
CBS/TCF (Gene Reynolds, Larry Gelbart)

Exploits of the Red Ball Express, suppliers of resources to the fighting men at the front in World War II. Curiously unsuccessful black comedy which attempted to extend the success of *M*A*S*H*.

Stu Gilliam, Billy Hicks, Mel Stewart, Ed Begley Jnr

Roman Grey
aka: *The Art of Crime*
US 1975 74m colour TVM
Universal (Richard Irving)

ROLL OVER BEETHOVEN had class distinction as its basis, but the fans tuned in because they liked Nigel Planer as the pop star falling for the rich girl (Liza Goddard, seen behind him).

A New York gypsy antique dealer tries to save a friend on a murder charge.

Uninspired and rather desperate pilot which didn't go.

w Martin Smith, Bill Davidson d Richard Irving

Ron Leibman, Jose Ferrer, David Hedison, Jill Clayburgh, Eugene Roche

The Roman Holidays (US 1972). A 25-minute kiddie cartoon series (13 episodes) about an allegedly typical family of Roman times. From Hanna–Barbera; for NBC.

Romance **
GB 1977 6 × 50m colour (VTR)
Thames (PETER DUGUID)

Adaptations of six romantic novels, mostly bestsellers, from Victorian times to the present.

The treatments are variable, but the high style applied to such famous but unread books as *Moths* by Ouida (writer Hugh Whitemore, director Waris Hussein) and *Three Weeks* by Elinor Glyn (writer Gerald Savory, director Waris Hussein, star Elizabeth Shepherd) make them TV classics, and Ethel M. Dell's curious *The Black Knight* was made by adaptor John Kershaw and director Peter Hammond to seem much more interesting than it probably is.

'On a train bound for Paris, could one night of love change a woman's life forever?'
Romance on the Orient Express
GB 1985 96m colour TVM
Yorkshire TV/Frank Von Zerneck (James Hay)

An old romance is rekindled aboard the Orient Express.

Less plot than *Brief Encounter*, and considerably less interest. For people who like riding on expensive trains.

w Jan Worthington d Lawrence Gordon Clark ph Peter Jackson pd Richard Jarvis

Cheryl Ladd, Stuart Wilson, John Gielgud, Renee Asherson, Ralph Michael, Ruby Wax, Julian Sands

'While the story shuttles handsomely between the past and the present, the train barely leaves the station.' – *Daily Variety*

Romantic versus Classic Art (GB 1973; 1 × 60m, 14 × 30m). Scholarly and thorough history of the Romantic Revolution by Lord Clark of *Civilization*. Though less popular than that epic, and with a less catchy title, it was made by ATV.   PP

Romper Room. American format which was sold continuously around the world from 1953. The aim was to entertain and instruct the very young, and to this end props, toys, scripts and even a teacher were supplied so that the local station could make the programme.

Ronstadt, Linda (1946–). American singer, on TV in concert appearances.

The Rookies *
US 1971 73m colour TVM
ABC/Aaron Spelling

Recruits adjust to police life in a big city.

Semi-documentary cop show, tersely narrated.

w William Blinn d Jud Taylor

Darren McGavin, Cameron Mitchell, Paul Burke

† The resulting series ran to 68 × 50m films over four seasons. Gerald S. O'Loughlin was added to the regular cast of George Stanford Brown, Sam Melville, Bruce Fairbairn and Kate Jackson. Producers: Hal Sitowitz, Rick Husky.

Room for One More
US 1961 26 × 25m bw
ABC/Warner

The parents of four children adopt two more. Winsome televersion of a barely tolerable film.

Andrew Duggan, Peggy McCay

Room 222 *
US 1969–72 113 × 25m colour
ABC/TCF (Gene Reynolds)

The history teacher at Walt Whitman High is a Negro.

Character comedy borrowed from *To Sir with Love* and vaguely mirroring social progress. Everybody is very nice indeed to each other.

cr James Brooks, Gene Reynolds

LLOYD HAYNES, MICHAEL CONSTANTINE, KAREN VALENTINE, Denise Nicholas

Rooney, Mickey (1920–) (Joe Yule Jnr). Diminutive, enthusiastic American performer who was a great hit in his teenage years but was nearly 60 before he had the pleasure of a comeback. TV movies: *Evil Roy Slade*, *My Kidnapper My Love*, LEAVE 'EM LAUGHING, *Bill* (Emmy, 1982). Series: *Mickey*, *One of the Boys*.

ROMANCE ON THE ORIENT EXPRESS. A telemovie confection supposed to give the viewers just what they want. In fact it performed rather poorly, perhaps because Cheryl Ladd is not quite big enough, as stars go, to carry such a wispy plot.

Rooster

US 1982 96m colour TVM
ABC/TCF/Tugboat/Glen E. Larson (Harker Wade)

A 5'2" police psychologist tracks down criminals with the help of an insurance investigator and the latest in electronic equipment.

Unappealing comic-strip stuff which mercifully did not lead to a series.

cr Glen E. Larson, Paul Williams

Paul Williams, Pat McCormick

The Root of All Evil (GB 1968–9; 13 × 50m; colour). Anthology series split over two seasons chiefly memorable for airing one of Charles Wood's two preliminary runs with the characters he was to immortalize in *Don't Forget to Write*. They were already played by George Cole and Gwen Watford, with Edward Woodward intruding as a demon Italian film producer. Directed (this contribution) by Marc Miller; produced by Peter Willes; for YTV.   PP

Roots **

US 1977 12 × 50m colour
ABC/DAVID WOLPER (STAN MARGULIES)

The saga of a black family from the capturing of an African slave to the time of the Civil War.

Scene for scene this heavily socially conscious epic was not too compelling, but America needed it as a kind of expiation, and when it played on eight consecutive nights during a week of blizzards the ratings were unprecedented and it immediately became a TV landmark. As a British executive said rather cynically, its success may have been due to the fact that one third of America was snowed up, another third is black and the rest watch ABC anyway.

w William Blinn, Ernest Kinoy, James Lee, M. Charles Cohen, *book* Alex Haley *d* David Greene, John Erman, Marvin J. Chomsky, Gilbert Moses *ph* Stevan Larner, Joseph Wilcots *m* Quincy Jones, Gerald Fried

Ed Asner, Chuck Connors, Carolyn Jones, O. J. Simpson, Ralph Waite, Lou Gossett, Lorne Greene, Robert Reed, LeVar Burton, BEN VEREEN, Lynda Day George, Vic Morrow, Raymond St Jacques, Sandy Duncan, John Amos, Leslie Uggams, MacDonald Carey, George Hamilton, Ian MacShane, Richard Roundtree, Lloyd Bridges, Doug McClure, Burl Ives

† Haley's claim that the book told the story of his own ancestors was challenged after detailed research by international news reporters.

Roots: The New Generations *

US 1979 6 × 96m colour
ABC/David Wolper (Stan Margulies)

Alex Haley traces his forebears from 1882 to the 1970s.

Rather less compelling because less original than its predecessor, this sequel does have more identifiable situations and more outstanding performances as opposed to cameos.

w Ernest Kinoy, Sidney A. Glass, Thad Mumford, Daniel Wilcox, John McGreevey *d* John Erman, Charles S. Dubin, George Stanford Brown, Lloyd Richards *ph* Joseph M. Wilcots *m* Gerald Fried

JAMES EARL JONES (as Haley), George Stanford Brown, Olivia de Havilland, Henry Fonda, Greg Morris, Richard Thomas, Dorian Harewood, Ruby Dee, Ossie Davis, George Voskovec, John Rubinstein, Pam Grier, Percy Rodrigues, Beah Richards, Robert Culp, Paul Winfield, Dina Merrill, Brock Peters, Andy Griffith, Marlon Brando (Emmy as Rockwell, the Nazi), Michael Constantine, Damon Evans, Avon Long, Fay Hauser

'A compelling, humane production.' – *Daily Variety*

Roper, David (1944–). North country British leading man of comedy series *The Cuckoo Waltz* and *Leave It to Charlie*.

The Rose Affair

GB 1961 50m bw
ABC Armchair Theatre (Sydney Newman)

Alun Owen's misguided attempt to break away from everyday realism with an arch re-write of the Beauty and the Beast fable. I lamented at the time: 'Oh dear, how did someone of Owen's very special talent come to replace the true poetry of human speech, which he understands better than anyone, with gobbets of ornate doggerel?' Nevertheless the play was re-produced by the BBC, at Newman's urging, four years later.

d Charles Jarrott *design* Voytek

Natasha Parry, Anthony Quayle, Harold Lang, Dudley Foster, Naunton Wayne, Joseph O'Conor   PP

Rose, David (1924–). British drama producer and executive (original *Z Cars* producer, first Pebble Mill drama chief) who has been C4's senior commissioning officer since 1981. Last production credit: *Artemis '81*.   PP

✻ **Rose, Reginald** (1921–). American TV playwright, one of the props of the 'golden age' of the fifties. His contributions included TWELVE ANGRY MEN, THUNDER ON SYCAMORE STREET and A MAN IS TEN FEET TALL. He also created THE DEFENDERS.

Rosemont, Norman (1924–). American producer, usually of music specials or semi-classic one-offs: *The Man without a Country*, *The Man in the Iron Mask*, *Les Misérables*, *The Count of Monte Cristo*, *Captains Courageous*, *Little Lord Fauntleroy*, *Ivanhoe*, *The Hunchback of Notre Dame*, *Witness for the Prosecution*, *Master of the Game*, *Camille*, *The Corsican Brothers*, etc.

Rosenberg, Stuart (1928–). American director who after years in television (*Alfred Hitchcock Presents*, *The Untouchables*, *Twilight Zone*) made a name for himself on the big screen, but couldn't seem to keep it. TV movie: *Fame Is the Name of the Game*.

Rosenman, Leonard (1924–). American composer. Many TV scores include SYBIL (Emmy 1977), FRIENDLY FIRE (Emmy 1979).

✻ **Rosenthal, Jack** (1931–). Much-lauded British dramatist with a special flair for comedy. THE LOVERS (series), *The Dustbinmen* (series), *Another Sunday and Sweet F.A.*, *Mr Ellis Versus the People*, THE EVACUEES, *Sadie It's Cold Outside* (series), READY WHEN YOU ARE, MR MCGILL, BARMITZVAH BOY, *Spend Spend Spend*, *The Knowledge*, *P'tang Yang Kipperbang*, *The Devil's Lieutenant*.

Rosie (GB 1979–). Half-hour BBC series about the off-duty problems of a young policeman. Tolerable but forgettable filler. With Paul Greenwood, Tony Haygarth. Written by Roy Clarke; produced by Bernard Thompson.

Rosie: the Rosemary Clooney Story
US 1982 96m colour TVM
CBS/Charles Fries/Alan Sacks (Jackie Cooper)
Biopic charting the life of a band singer who made it big in Hollywood but suffered a breakdown due to drugs and hard times. Tolerable stuff of its kind, with a regulation happy ending.
w Katherine Coker, *book* *This for Remembrance* by Rosemary Clooney *d* Jackie Cooper *ph* Howard Schwartz *m* Frank Ortega *vocals* Rosemary Clooney

Sondra Locke, Tony Orlando, Penelope Milford, John Karlen, Cheryl Anderson, Katherine Helmond, Kevin McCarthy

Ross, Diana (1944–). Black American singer who went solo after being one of the Supremes.

Ross, Joe E. (1905–85). American nightclub comedian with a frenzied manner. Series include CAR 54 WHERE ARE YOU?, *It's About Time*.

Ross, Katharine (1943–). American leading actress. TV movies: *The Longest Hundred Miles*, *Wanted: The Sundance Woman*, *Murder by Natural Causes*, *Murder in Texas*, *Rodeo Girl*, *Marion Rose White*, *The Shadow Riders*, *Travis McGee*, *Secrets of a Mother and Daughter*.

'The playboy and the ex-cop . . . like no lawyers you've ever seen!'
Rossetti and Ryan
aka: *Men Who Love Women*
US 1977 96m colour TVM
Universal (Leonard B. Stern)
Two elegant lawyers, one an ex-cop, solve a murder case.
Fated attempt to put Starsky and Hutch in the courtroom: too much chat and not enough plot.
w Don Mankiewicz, Gordon Cotler *d* John Astin
Tony Roberts, Squire Fridell, Bill Dana, Patty Duke, Jane Elliot, Susan Anspach
† A subsequent 50m series ran to eight episodes.

Rossiter, Leonard (1927–84). British character actor whose wolfy features were equally adept at conveying menace, frustration or comic envy. So many classic sitcom roles, notably as Rigsby in *Rising Damp*, *The Fall and Rise of Reginald Perrin*, *The Losers* and his last series, *Tripper's Day*. On the serious side, *The Resistible Rise of Arturo Ui* (Brecht); in between, *Machinegunner*.   PP

rotating series. A scheduling pattern in which three series are rotated so that each appears every third week. This was tried out in the US with *The Men* (unsuccessfully) and *Mystery Movie* (successfully). In the UK, the BBC have occasionally tried it, but it seems to weaken the appeal of all the series involved.

Rough Justice. British (BBC) legal watchdog programme which ran into trouble in 1985 after a judge accused its reporter and producer of intimidating a witness; and is due to return in 1987 under new management.   PP

Rough Riders
US 1958 39 × 25m bw
United Artists

After the Civil War two Union officers journey west to find a new life.

Kent Taylor, Jan Merlin, Peter Whitney

Roughnecks
US 1980 96m colour TVM
Operation Prime Time/Golden
    Circle/Metromedia (Douglas Netter)

Oil drillers run into various kinds of trouble. Routine miniseries with a story line just as sloppy as the above suggests.

w Michael Michaelian *d* Bernard McEveety
ph John C. Flinn III *m* Jerrold Immel

Wilford Brimley, Cathy Lee Crosby, Sam Melville, Stephen McHattie, Steve Forrest, Vera Miles, Kevin Geer, Harry Morgan, Ana Alicia

'Slow-paced to the point of stupor.' – *Daily Variety*

Round the World with Orson Welles (GB 1955). Curtailed Rediffusion series of travelogues by and with the wayward Welles, of which two editions on bull-fighting in Spain attracted the most attention. Another one, supposed to be about English pubs, ended up as a conversation piece with Chelsea Pensioners. After less than half a projected 13-part series had been shot, the show ran out of money and was dropped.   PP

The Rounders
US 1966 17 × 25m colour
ABC/MGM (Ed Adamson)

Adventures of two idle, woman-chasing modern cowboys.
The soporific atmosphere got through to the audience.

Ron Hayes, Patrick Wayne, Chill Wills

The Rousters
aka: *Marshal of Sladetown*
US 1983 74m colour TVM
NBC/Columbia/Stephen J. Cannell (Jo
    Swerling Jnr)

Adventures of a bouncer and all-round troubleshooter at a smalltime travelling carnival.

The intention may have been a modern-day *Wagon Train*, but the characters were not sufficiently interesting to survive more than 13 × 50m episodes of the series which followed: indeed, the trade was surprised that they didn't call it quits at the pilot.

cr Stephen J. Cannell

Chad Everett, Hoyt Axton, Jim Varney, Maxine Stuart, Timothy Gibbs

† The running gag was that Everett played the great-grandson of Wyatt Earp, whose name he bore.

'Deprived of imagination, wit or coherence.' – *Daily Variety*

**Route 66 ** **
US 1960–3 116 × 50m bw
CBS/Columbia/HERBERT B. LEONARD

Two youthful wanderers travel across America in search of adventure.

A precursor of *Easy Rider*, this well-made show borrowed its plots from well-known movies. (The first, *Black November*, was *Bad Day at Black Rock*.) Towards the end it got a little sentimental and even eccentric, as in the unsatisfactory *Lizard's Leg and Owlet's Wing* which brought together, and wasted, Boris Karloff, Peter Lorre, Lon Chaney Jnr and Martita Hunt.

m Nelson Riddle

GEORGE MAHARIS (later Glen Corbett), MARTIN MILNER

† The idea was frequently borrowed by other series, e.g. 1978's *The American Girls*.

†† The title was also deliberately used for a 100m documentary account of the old road, made by John T. Davis for Central (GB) in 1985.

††† There follows a complete list of episodes, with writer, director and guest stars for each:

Black November (*w* Stirling Silliphant; *d* Philip Leacock; with Everett Sloane, Patty McCormack, Keir Dullea)

A Lance of Straw (*w* Stirling Silliphant; *d* Roger Kay; with Janice Rule, Thomas Gomez)

The Swan Bed (*w* Stirling Silliphant; *d* Elliot Silverstein; with Betty Field, Henry Hull, Murray Hamilton)

The Man on the Monkey Board (*w* Stirling Silliphant; *d* Roger Kay; with Lew Ayres, Alfred Ryder, Bruce Dern)

The Strengthening Angels (*w* Stirling Silliphant; *d* Arthur Hiller; with Suzanne Pleshette, Harry Townes)

Ten Drops of Water (*w* Howard Rodman; *d* Philip Leacock; with Burt Brinckerhoff, Deborah Walley, Sara Haden)

Three Sides (*w* Stirling Silliphant; *d* Philip Leacock; with E. G. Marshall, Johnny Seven, Joey Heatherton)

Legacy for Lucia (*w* Stirling Silliphant; *d* Philip Leacock; with Jay C. Flippen, John Larch)

Layout at Glen Canyon (*w* Stirling Silliphant; *d* Elliot Silverstein; with Charles McGraw, Bethel Leslie)

The Beryllium Eater (*w* Alvin Ganzer; *d* Richard Collins; with Inger Stevens, Edward Binns, Edgar Buchanan)

A Fury Slinging Flame (*w* Stirling Silliphant; *d* Elliot Silverstein; with Leslie Nielsen, Fay Spain)

Sheba (*w* Stirling Silliphant; *d* William Claxton; with Lee Marvin, Whitney Blake)

The Quick and the Dead (*w* Stirling Silliphant; *d* Alvin Ganzer; with Frank Overton, Regis Toomey)

Play It Glissando (*w* Stirling Silliphant; *d* Lewis Allen; with Anne Francis, Jack Lord)

The Clover Throne (*w* Herman Meadow; *d* Arthur Hiller; with Jack Warden)

Fly Away Home (two-parter) (*w* Stirling Silliphant; *d* Arthur Hiller; with Michael Rennie, Dorothy Malone)

Sleep on Four Pillows (*w* Stirling Silliphant; *d* Ted Post; with Patty MacCormack, Larry Gates)

An Absence of Tears (*w* Stirling Silliphant; *d* Alvin Ganzer; with Rin Tin Tin, Martha Hyer)

Like a Motherless Child (*w* Howard Rodman; *d* David Lowell Rich; with Sylvia Sidney, Jack Weston)

Effigy in Snow (*w* Stirling Silliphant; *d* Alvin Ganzer; with Scott Marlowe, George Macready)

Eleven the Hard Way (*w* George Clayton Johnson; *d* William A. Graham; with Walter Matthau, Edward Andrews)

Most Vanquished, Most Victorious (*w* Stirling Silliphant; *d* William D. Faralla; with Beatrice Straight, Royal Dano)

Don't Count Stars (*w* Stirling Silliphant; *d* Paul Wendkos; with Dan Duryea)

The Newborn (*w* Stirling Silliphant; *d* Arthur Hiller; with Albert Dekker, Robert Duvall)

A Skill for Hunting (*w* Jack Turley, M. Gelman; *d* David Lowell Rich; with Gene Evans, Joanna Moore)

Trap at Cordova (*w* Stirling Silliphant; *d* Arthur Hiller; with Thomas Gomez, Dianne Foster)

The Opponent (*w* Stirling Silliphant; *d* David Lowell Rich; with Darren McGavin, Lois Nettleton, Ed Asner)

Welcome to Amity (*w* Will Lorin; *d* Arthur Hiller; with Martha Scott, Susan Oliver)

Incident on a Bridge (*w* Stirling Silliphant; *d* David Lowell Rich; with Nehemiah Persoff)

A Month of Sundays (*w* Stirling Silliphant; *d* Arthur Hiller; with Anne Francis, Conrad Nagel)

Blue Murder (*w* Stirling Silliphant; *d* Arthur Hiller; with Suzanne Pleshette, Claude Akins, Gene Evans)

Goodnight Sweet Blues (*w* Will Lorin; *d* Jack Smight; with Ethel Waters, Juano Hernandez)

Birdcage on My Foot (*w* Stirling Silliphant; *d* Elliot Silverstein; with Robert Duvall, Mike Kellin)

First Class Mouliak (*w* John Vlahos; *d* William Conrad; with Nehemiah Persoff, Robert Redford, Martin Balsam)

Once to Every Man (*w* Frank L. Moss; *d* Arthur Hiller; with Janice Rule, Murray Matheson)

The Mud Nest (*w* Stirling Silliphant; *d* James Sheldon; with Betty Field, Lon Chaney, Ed Asner)

A Bridge Across Five Days (*w* Howard Rodman; *d* Richard Donner; with Nina Foch, James Dunn)

Mon Petit Chou (*w* Stirling Silliphant; *d* Sam Peckinpah; with Lee Marvin)

Some of the People Some of the Time (*w* Stirling Silliphant; *d* Robert Altman; with Keenan Wynn, Lois Nettleton)

The Thin White Line (*w* Leonard Freeman; *d* David Lowell Rich; with Murray Hamilton)

And the Cat Jumped Over the Moon (*w* Stirling Silliphant; *d* Elliot Silverstein; with Milt Kamen, James Caan, Martin Sheen)

Burning for Burning (*w* Stirling Silliphant; *d* Charles Haas; with Inger Stevens, Beulah Bondi)

To Walk with the Serpent (*w* Will Lorin; *d* James Sheldon; with Dan O'Herlihy, Simon Oakland)

A Long Piece of Mischief (*w* Stirling Silliphant; *d* David Lowell Rich; with Albert Salmi, Audrey Totter)

1800 Days to Justice (*w* Jo Pagano; *d* David Lowell Rich; with John Ericson, Noah Beery Jnr)

City of Wheels (w Frank Chase; d David Lowell Rich; with Bethel Leslie, Steven Hill)

How Much a Pound Is Albatross? (w Stirling Silliphant; d David Lowell Rich; with Julie Newmar, Frank McHugh)

Aren't You Surprised to See Me? (w Stirling Silliphant; d James Sheldon; with David Wayne, James Brown)

You Never Had It So Good (w Stirling Silliphant, Frank L. Moss; with Peter Graves, Patricia Barry)

Shoulder the Sky, My Lad (w Mort Thaw; d David Lowell Rich; with Ed Asner, Lili Darvas)

Blues for the Left Foot (w Leonard Freeman; d Arthur Hiller; with Elizabeth Seal, Akim Tamiroff)

Go Read the River (w Stirling Silliphant; d Arthur Hiller; with John Larch, Lois Smith)

Even Stones Have Eyes (w Barry Trivers; d Robert Gist; with Barbara Barrie, Paul Tripp)

Love Is a Skinny Kid (w Stirling Silliphant; d James Sheldon; with Tuesday Weld, Cloris Leachman)

Kiss the Maiden All Forlorn (w Stirling Silliphant; d David Lowell Rich; with Douglas Fairbanks Jnr, Arthur Hill, Zina Bethune)

Two on the House (w Gil Ralston; d David Lowell Rich; with Ralph Meeker, Henry Jones)

There I Am – There I Always Am (w Stirling Silliphant; d John Newland; with Joanna Moore, Emile Genest)

Between Hello and Goodbye (w Stirling Silliphant; d David Lowell Rich; with Susan Oliver, Herschel Bernardi)

A Feat of Strength (w Howard Rodman, Joseph Petracca; d David Lowell Rich; with Jack Warden, Signe Hasso)

Hell Is Empty, All the Devils Are Here (w Stirling Silliphant; d Paul Stanley; with Peter Graves, Michael Pate)

From an Enchantress Fleeing (w Stirling Silliphant; d William A. Graham; with Arthur O'Connell, Anne Helm)

One Tiger to a Hill (w Stirling Silliphant; d David Lowell Rich; with David Janssen, Signe Hasso)

Journey to Nineveh (w William R. Cox; d David Lowell Rich; with Joe E. Brown, Buster Keaton)

Man Out of Time (w Larry Marcus; d David Lowell Rich; with Luther Adler, Frank McHugh, Glenda Farrell)

Ever Ride the Waves of Oklahoma? (w Stirling Silliphant; d Robert Gist; with Jeremy Slate)

Voice at the End of the Line (w Larry Marcus; d David Lowell Rich; with Sorrell Booke, Frank Campanella)

Lizard's Leg and Owlet's Wing (w Stirling Silliphant; d Robert Gist; with Boris Karloff, Lon Chaney Jnr, Peter Lorre, Martita Hunt, Conrad Nagel)

Across Walnuts and Wine (w Stirling Silliphant; d Herbert B. Leonard; with Nina Foch, Betty Field, James Dunn)

Welcome to the Wedding (w Howard Rodman; d George Sherman; with Rod Steiger, Ed Asner)

Every Father's Daughter (w Anthony Lawrence; d Richard L. Bare; with Madlyn Rhue, Jack Kruschen)

Poor Little Kangaroo Rat (w Les Pine; d Walter E. Grauman; with Leslie Nielsen, Ronny Howard)

Hey, Moth, Come Eat the Flame (w Stirling Silliphant; d James Sheldon; with Harry Guardino, Mike Kellin)

Only By Cunning Glimpses (w Stirling Silliphant; d Tom Gries; with Theodore Bikel, Lois Smith)

Where Is Chick Lorimer, Where Has She Gone? (w Larry Marcus; d George Sherman; with Vera Miles, Martha Scott)

Give the Old Cat a Tender Mouse (w Stirling Silliphant; d Tom Gries; with Julie Newmar, Robert Webber)

A Bunch of Lonely Pagliaccis (w Stirling Silliphant; d Tom Gries; with Barry Sullivan, Warren Stevens, Vivian Blaine)

You Can't Pick Cotton in Tahiti (w Shimon Wincelberg; d Robert Ellis Miller; with Richard Basehart, Pat Engstrom)

A Gift for a Warrior (w Larry Marcus; d David Lowell Rich; with James Whitmore)

Suppose I Said I Was the Queen of Spain? (w Stirling Silliphant; d David Lowell Rich; with Lois Nettleton, Robert Duvall)

Somehow It Gets to Be Tomorrow (w Stirling Silliphant; d David Lowell Rich; with Roger Mobley, Lesley Hunter)

Shall Forfeit His Dog and Ten Shillings to the King (w Stirling Silliphant; d Tom Gries; with Steve Cochran, Kathleen Crowley)

In the Closing of a Trunk (w Stirling Silliphant; d Ralph Senensky; with Ed Begley, Ruth Roman)

The Cage Around Maria (w Jesse Sandler; d George Sherman; with Elizabeth Ashley, Beatrice Straight)

Fifty Miles from Home (w Stirling Silliphant; d James Sheldon; with Susan Oliver, Robert Emhardt)

Narcissus on an Old Red Fire Engine (*w* Joel Carpenter; *d* Ralph Senensky; with Anne Helm, Alan Hale Jnr (Glenn Corbett now replacing Maharis)

The Cruelest Sea of All (*w* Stirling Silliphant; *d* James Sheldon; with Diane Baker, Edward Binns)

Peace, Pity, Pardon (*w* Stirling Silliphant; *d* Robert Ellis Miller; with Alejandro Rey, Michael Tolan)

What a Shining Young Man Was Our Gallant Lieutenant (*w* Howard Rodman; *d* James Goldstone; with Dick York, James Brown, John Litel)

But What Do You Do in March? (*w* Stirling Silliphant; *d* Robert Ellis Miller; with Janice Rule, Susan Kohner)

Who Will Cheer My Bonny Bride? (*w* Shimon Wincelberg; *d* James Goldstone; with Gene Hackman)

Shadows of an Afternoon (*w* Leonard Freeman, Eric Scott; *d* James Sheldon; with Kathryn Hays, Richard Hamilton)

Soda Pop and Paper Flags (*w* John McGreevey; *d* Fred Jackman; with Joseph Campanella, Alan Alda)

Same Picture, Different Frame (*w* Stirling Silliphant; *d* Philip Leacock; with Joan Crawford, Patrick O'Neal)

Come Out Come Out Wherever You Are (*w* Richard Jessup, Anthony Basta, Stirling Silliphant; *d* Alvin Ganzer; with Diane Baker, Lon Chaney Jnr)

Where Are the Sounds of Celli Brahms? (*w* Stirling Silliphant; *d* Allen Miner; with Tammy Grimes, Horace MacMahon, Harry Bellaver)

Build Your Houses with Their Backs to the Sea (*w/d* Frank L. Pierson; with William Shatner, Pat Hingle)

And Make Thunder His Tribute (*w* Lewis John Carlino; *d* Leonard Horn; with J. Carrol Naish, Alfred Ryder, Lou Antonio, Michael J. Pollard)

The Stone Guest (*w* Stirling Silliphant; *d* Allen Miner; with Jo Van Fleet, Lee Philips)

I Wouldn't Start From Here (*w* Ernest Kinoy; *d* Allen Miner; with Parker Fennelly, Rosemary Forsyth)

A Cage in Search of a Bird (*w* Stirling Silliphant; *d* James Sheldon; with Dan Duryea, Stefanie Powers)

A Long Way from St Louis (*w* Stirling Silliphant; *d* Alvin Ganzer; with Jessica Walter, Virginia Wing)

Come Home Greta Inger Gruenschaffen (details not available)

Ninety Three Per Cent in Smiling (*w* Alvin Sargent; *d* Philip Leacock; with Albert Salmi)

Child of a Night (*w* Stirling Silliphant; *d* Allen Miner; with Sylvia Sidney, Chester Morris)

Is It True That There Are Foxes at the Bottom of Landfair Lake? (*w* Alvin Sargent; *d* John Peyser; with Geoffrey Horne)

Like This It Means Father; Like This Bitter; Like This Tiger (*w* Stirling Silliphant; *d* Jeffrey Hayden; with Larry Blyden, Eugene Roche)

Kiss the Monster, Make Him Sleep (*w* Stanley R. Greenberg; *d* Allen Reisner; with James Coburn)

Cries of Persons Close to One (*w* William Kelley, Howard Rodman; *d* Allen Miner; with Michael Parks)

Who in His Right Mind Needs A Nice Girl? (*w* Joel Carpenter; *d* Jeffrey Hayden; with Lee Philips, Lois Smith)

This Is Going to Hurt Me More Than It Hurts You (*w* Stirling Silliphant; *d* Alvin Ganzer; with Soupy Sales, Roland Winters)

Follow the White Dove with the Broken Wing (*w* Alvin Sargent; *d* Denis Sanders; with Lee Kinsolving, Bert Freed)

And Then There Were Two (two-parter) (*w* Stirling Silliphant; *d* Alvin Ganzer; with Roger C. Carmel, Nina Foch, Patrick O'Neal, Barbara Eden, Chill Wills)

I'm Here to Kill a King (*w* Stirling Silliphant; *d* Allen Reisner; with Robert Loggia, Tina Louise)

Roving Report. ITN's first and almost only non-news series, habitually regarded with suspicion by programme companies reluctant to share whatever credit was available for 'serious' programming but nevertheless surviving for over seven years, plus another three as *ITN Reports*, before being finally swallowed by *News at Ten* in 1967. The little films (originally 17 minutes, later 24) were sometimes brought back as by-products of news missions, more often shot on a shoestring by a reporter and crew dispatched on a quick foray to some quarter of the globe. Robin Day made the first 15, Reginald Bosanquet scores of later ones. The original producer was Michael Barsley. PP

† In 1986 Worldwide Television News (WTN) in which ITN is a partner acquired the title for a weekly cassette release.

Rowan, Dan (1922–). American comedian, the straight-man half of Rowan and Martin, who co-hosted *Laugh-In*.

The Roy Rogers Show
US 1951–6 100 × 25m bw
CBS/Roy Rogers

A rancher in Mineral City is also the owner of a diner.

Light modern western allowing the star to do his thing.

Roy Rogers, Dale Evans, Pat Brady, Harry Lauter

Royal Family ***
GB 1969 110m colour
BBC (RICHARD CAWSTON)

An informal look at the private life of Queen Elizabeth II.

A charming, easy and fresh documentary which managed not to put a foot wrong and was mainly responsible for bringing the monarchy down from its pedestal.

PP (1969): 'Richard Cawston's *Royal Family* proved to be a remarkable bit of work, but will he get the CVO or the Queen's Award for Industry for it? Is it a sales job or an apologia? Though very nicely and unstuffily scripted by Tony Jay, the film took up a noticeably defensive attitude to its subject, stressing the age of the royal Rolls-Royces (eight years) and how the *Britannia* exercises with the Fleet when not on royal business.'

† He got the CVO.

Royal Foundation * (GB 1961). Simon Raven's first TV play, with Richard Carpenter, Alex Scott, Joseph O'Conor. My 1961 review: 'The military court-martial, always rich in conflict, was here used to display an epic clash between high-camp Army and high-camp Academe. Was the impossible young national service subaltern in a posh regiment justified in pulling rank on his colonel within the precincts of his posh college? – the point being that he had just been made a Fellow of the latter. Raven never made the mistake of manipulating his characters; they responded impeccably to their own selves.'   PP

Royal Heritage **
GB 1977 9 × 50m colour (16mm)
BBC (Michael Gill, Ann Turner)

A tour of the royal collection of paintings, antiques and ancient buildings.

Slightly reverent but undeniably impressive walk through fabled halls overflowing with history and artistic richness.

w HUW WHELDON, J. H. PLUMB narrator HUW WHELDON d David Heycock ph Kenneth MacMillan

'Worthy to stand beside *Civilization* and *America*.' – *Financial Times*

'The BBC's jubilee export number, nimbly and enthusiastically presented.' – *The Times*

The Royal Romance of Charles and Diana
US 1983 96m colour TVM
CBS/Chrysalis–Yellen (Linda Yellen)

One of a pair of headline-hunting soap operas mirroring the royal event of 1982. It is difficult to say which was the worse.

w Robert L. Freedman, Selma Thompson, Jonathan Platnick, Linda Yellen d Peter Levin

Catherine Oxenberg, Christopher Baines, Ray Milland, Olivia de Havilland (as the Queen), Stewart Granger (Prince Philip), Dana Wynter, Barbara Caruso

'Excruciating.' – *Daily Variety*

The Royal Victorians: see Edward the Seventh

The Royalty (GB 1958; 6 × 30m; bw). Pioneering BBC serial – neither classic adaptation nor whodunit – set in a genteel London hotel facing a take-over. Written by Donald Wilson and Michael Voysey, it should have starred Margaret Lockwood and her daughter Julia, but the latter was eliminated by a hazard of live TV (she caught 'flu) and Carol Marsh substituted.   PP

Royce
US 1976 50m colour
MTM (William F. Phillips)

A new sheriff settles in Arizona in the 1870s. Sleek pilot, but westerns were not in favour.

w Jim Byrnes d Andrew V. McLaglen m Jerrold Immel

Robert Forster, Maybeth Hurt, Michael Parks

Ruby and Oswald
aka: *Four Days in Dallas* (120m version)
US 1978 140m colour TVM
CBS/Alan Landsburg (Paul Freeman)

A semi-documentary account of the assassination of President John Kennedy in Dallas in 1963.

Solid techniques don't necessarily make this the right way to handle history.

w John and Michael McGreevey d Mel Stuart ph Matthew F. Leonetti

Michael Lerner, Frederic Forrest, Doris Roberts, Lou Frizzell, Gordon Jump

'If the networks would only rebroadcast the newsfilm in their archives instead of re-enacting it, they would waste less of their money and less of the audience's time.' – *Time*

Rudkin, David (1936–). British writer of complex, sometimes mystic plays. *The Stone Dance*, *Children Playing*, *Penda's Fen*, *Artemis '81* and, most recently, *Across the Water*, 1983.   PP

Rudolph the Red-Nosed Reindeer *
US 1964 48m colour
Videocraft (Arthur Rankin Jnr, Jules Bass)
A reindeer with a red nose is derided by his friends but becomes the leader of Santa Claus's troupe.
Puppet fantasy which while not outstanding in itself did give us a universally known song and became an American annual event.

w Romeo Muller *d* Larry Roemer *narrator* Burl Ives

Ruff 'n' Reddy
US 1957–9 156 × 25m colour
Hanna–Barbera
Ruff the Cat and Reddy the Dog fight the forces of evil.
Routine cartoon capers.

The Ruggles
US 1950 13 × 25m bw
ABC
Archetypal domestic comedy.

Charles Ruggles, Erin O'Brien Moore, Margaret Kerry

Ruggles, Charles (1886–1970). Dapper American comic actor whose career in Hollywood dates from the late twenties. In his later years he had several TV series including *The Ruggles*, *The World of Mr Sweeney*.

Rule Britannia
GB 1981 6 × 50m colour
Reporter James Bellini taking a critical look at British institutions in the eighties and finding them still class-ridden and archaic. Produced by Alan Bell; for ATV.   PP

The Rules of Marriage
US 1982 2 × 96m colour
CBS/TCF/Brownstone/Enthios (Harry R. Sherman)
Problems arise in the 15-year marriage of a successful writer.
Fairly highbrow soap, suffering from rather boring characters and a lack of humour.

w Reginald Rose *d* Milton Katselas

Elizabeth Montgomery, Elliott Gould, Michael Murphy

The Rules That Jack Made (GB 1964). Imaginative if sometimes anachronistic reconstruction of the Spithead naval mutiny with Ewen Hooper in towering form as Valentine Joyce, its hero. Written by John Hale; produced by Cecil Clarke; for ATV.   PP

A Rumor of War
US 1980 2 × 96m colour
CBS/Stonehenge/Charles Fries (David Manson)
A restless young man joins the Marines and is the first in Vietnam.
Routine war saga which barely hangs together and certainly doesn't make the points it seems to intend.

w John Sacret Young, *autobiography* Philip Caputo *d* Richard T. Heffron *ph* Jorge Stahl Jnr, Stevan Larner *m* Charles Gross

Brad Davis, Keith Carradine, Michael O'Keefe, Richard Bradford, Brian Dennehy, Christopher Mitchum, Steve Forrest, Stacy Keach

'Not only does it show that war can dehumanize; it shows how human Americans are, too.' – *Daily Variety*

Rumour *
GB 1974 76m colour (16mm) TVM
Thames (Mike Hodges)
A Fleet Street columnist is given a tip about a cabinet minister being blackmailed, but finds he is being used to start a non-existent scandal.
Complex but exciting thriller, shot entirely on location.

w/d MIKE HODGES

Michael Coles, Ronald Clarke, Mark Baxter, Joyce Blair

Rumpole of the Bailey ****
GB 1978–83 18 × 50m
Thames Television (Irene Shubik)
Triumphs and failures of an ageing rank-and-file barrister operating at the Central Criminal Court, Old Bailey, London, who takes on defence briefs only, and, on top of legal adversaries, hard-hearted judges and dodgy clients, has to survive internal schemings in his chambers and the sublime distractions of his formidable wife, 'she who must be obeyed'.
A droll format which miraculously worked better and better as author John Mortimer reluctantly brought it back after several times terminating it, he thought. Rumpole evolved from a single BBC *Play for Today* in 1976, though some would trace his inspiration back to a radio and TV play of Mortimer's in the fifties, *The Dock Brief*.

See below for an extended special, *Rumpole's Return*, 1981. As a final compliment, the name of our hero's favourite wine bar, Pomeroy's (obviously modelled on El Vino's), was bestowed on a real establishment in 1985. Jackie Davies followed Irene Shubik as producer after the first Thames series of six. A fourth was in production in 1986.

w John Mortimer *d* various, including Donald McWhinnie, Robert Knights

LEO MCKERN (as Rumpole), Peggy Thorpe-Bates (as Mrs R.), Richard Murdoch, Peter Bowles, Bill Fraser, Patricia Hodge PP

Rumpole's Return *
GB 1981 120m colour TVM
Thames

Early special bringing the old war-horse back from supposed retirement in Florida, sniffing blood, to win a notable trial – at last – before his old antagonist Mr Justice Bullingham. That his triumph owed not a little to an arm of coincidence roughly as long as the distance between London and Miami we will pass over. The closing scene, as Rumpole cheerily annexed his old place in Chambers, represented John Mortimer's gift for creating thoroughly satisfactory occasions, and Leo McKern's for handling them at their fruitiest best. Bill Fraser as Bullingham. PP

Run a Crooked Mile
GB 1969 100m colour TVM
Universal (Ian Lewis)

An amnesiac is manipulated by a mysterious group of businessmen on whose secret he has accidentally stumbled.

Absurd sub-Hitchcock hokum with the hero disbelieved by everybody until . . .

w Trevor Wallace *d* Gene Levitt

Louis Jourdan, Mary Tyler Moore, Wilfrid Hyde White, Stanley Holloway, Alexander Knox, Laurence Naismith

Run Buddy Run
US 1966 16 × 25m colour
CBS/Talent Associates

The underworld is after a frightened book-keeper who has overheard secret information.

A comic *Fugitive*, and quite a good one, but spoofs are seldom popular.

Bernie Kopell, Jack Sheldon, Bruce Gordon, Malcolm Atterbury

Run for Your Life *
US 1965–7 85 × 50m colour
NBC/Universal/Roy Huggins

When told he has two years to live, a middle-aged man decides to seek rewarding adventures.

It's really *The Fugitive* all over again, and they let him off the hook at the end. Good popular drama.

cr Roy Huggins

Ben Gazzara

† Although the hero was given only two years to live, the show ran three seasons.

Run Joe Run
US 1974 26 × 25m colour
NBC/TCF/D'Angelo (William P. D'Angelo)

A German shepherd dog is on the run, accused unjustly of attacking his master.

A doggy *Fugitive*, or Rin Tin Tin rides again. Purely for kids.

Arch Whiting, Chad States

Run Simon Run
US 1970 74m colour TVM
ABC/Universal

An ex-con Indian seeks revenge against the real murderer of his mother.

Tedious but good-looking open-air melodrama which shifts from suspense to racial discussions.

w Lionel E. Siegel *d* George McGowan

Burt Reynolds, Inger Stevens, James Best, Royal Dano

Runaway *
US 1973 74m colour TVM
Universal (Harve Bennett)

A ski train carrying holidaymakers down a mountain has no brakes.

Modestly effective mini-disaster movie, quite watchable.

w Gerald di Pego *d* David Lowell Rich

Ben Murphy, Ben Johnson, Vera Miles, Martin Milner, Ed Nelson, Darleen Carr, Lee Harcourt Montgomery

The Runaway (GB 1973; 70m colour).
Perverse, maddening BBC *Omnibus* film by Don Taylor about a progressive woman novelist's crisis of political conscience but with such incidental pleasures as Angela Scoular, loosely involved as someone's friend, and a picnic in the grounds of a decaying mansion. With Sylvia Kay, Peter Bowles. PP

The Runaway Barge
aka: *The Rivermen*
US 1975 75m colour TVM
Lorimar

Three men earning a living on a Mississippi boat become involved in a kidnapping.
Slow starting, heavily accented adventure which didn't make a series.

w Stanford Whitmore *d* Boris Sagal *m* Nelson Riddle

Bo Hopkins, Tim Matheson, Jim Davis, Nick Nolte, James Best, Clifton James

The Runaways
US 1975 74m colour TVM
Lorimar

A teenage boy and a leopard meet in the wilderness: both have run away from insoluble problems . . .
Silly–serious extravaganza which looks good but dramatically makes little impact.

novel Victor Canning *d* Harry Harris

Dorothy McGuire, Van Williams, John Randolph, Neva Patterson, Josh Albee

87

Running Out
US 1984 96m colour TVM
CBS

A French girl returns to New York to rediscover the family she abandoned 12 years earlier.
Routine soap opera unenlivened by any sharpness in acting or direction.

w Elissa Haden Guest *d* Robert Day

Deborah Raffin, Tony Bill

Rushton, William (1937–). Portly British entertainer who began his career in *That Was the Week That Was* and writes for *Private Eye*. His TV series such as *Rushton's Illustrated* have not worked.

Russ Abbot's Madhouse (GB 1980–5). Frenetic comedy show aimed at a young audience, which helped London Weekend's Saturday schedules for five years. Also specials: *Russ Abbot's Christmas/Scottish Madhouses*, *Russ Abbot's Madhouse Annual*. Whatever else, they kept his name up front.   PP

✻ **Russell, Ken** (1927–). British director, the *enfant terrible* of the big screen who makes amazing extravaganzas out of serious subjects. His TV work, however, has mainly been sharper, wiser and occasionally tinged with genius, presumably because in this medium he is not tempted by big budgets. TV films include

ELGAR, BARTOK, DEBUSSY, ROUSSEAU, ISADORA, DANTE'S INFERNO, A SONG OF SUMMER (Delius), *Richard Wagner*, *Clouds of Glory*.

Russell, Kurt (1947–). American leading man, long familiar as a Disney juvenile. TV series: *The Travels of Jamie McPheeters*, *The New Land*, *The Quest*. TV movies: *Search for the Gods*, *The Deadly Tower*, *Christmas Miracle in Caulfield USA*, *Elvis*.

Russell, Willy (1947–). British (Liverpudlian) playwright; *Daughter of Albion* (1979), *One Summer* (serial, 1983).

Rutherford, Norman (19 –). British actor and theatre producer who was assistant head of drama at the BBC during the late fifties and briefly in charge in 1962–3. In the eighties he reappeared as an actor. *Jewel in the Crown* (Mr Maybrick), *Shadowlands*. PP

Ryan, Irene (1903–73) (Irene Riorden). Diminutive comedy character actress who after a lifetime in minor film roles became a national institution as Granny in THE BEVERLY HILLBILLIES.

Ryan, Mitch (1928–). Stalwart American character actor who has had series leads in *Dark Shadows*, *Chase*, *Executive Suite* and *The Chisholms*. TV movies: *Chase*, *The Entertainer*, *Escape from Bogen County*, *Peter Lundy and the Medicine Hat Stallion*, *Having Babies II*, *Sgt Matlovich vs the US Air Force*, *Angel City*, *The Five of Me*, *Uncommon Valor*, *Robert Kennedy and His Times*, *Fatal Vision*.

Ryan's Four
US 1983 74m colour TVM
ABC/Paramount/Fair Dinkum/Groverton
(Ervin Zavada, Roger Birnbaum)

The director of interns at an LA hospital takes on four new members.
You can write the script of this one while you're still tuning in. The resulting 50m series ran to just four episodes.

w Howard Rodman *d* Jeff Bleckner *m* Randy Edelman

Tom Skerritt, Lisa Eilbacher, Timothy Daly, Dirk Blocker, Albert Hall

'The group is demographically perfect enough to make A. C. Nielsen proud.' – *Daily Variety*

Ryan's Hope. ABC soap opera (born 1975) dealing with the young hopefuls of New York; with Bernard Barrow, Helen Gallagher, Michael Hawkins, Frank Latimore.

S4C (Sianel Pedwar Cymru), the Welsh fourth channel which went on the air at the same time as C4. In response to much pressure most of the programmes are in the Welsh language.

Sabbagh, Karl (19 –). British producer, ex-*Horizon*, specializing in medical series: *The Body in Question*; *The Living Body* (writer and producer).

Saber of London: see Mark Saber

Sabrina (c 1931–) (Norma Sykes). British glamour girl, amply endowed; introduced as figure of fun by Arthur Askey in the fifties.

Sachs, Andrew (1930–). German-born comic actor in British television, most famous as Manuel in *Fawlty Towers*. Only other sitcom *Dead Earnest* never took off, but he has done nice one-offs since.

Sachs, Leonard (1909–). British general purpose actor who found a comfortable niche as chairman of *The Good Old Days*. Never remembered is that he played a small but important part in the original *1984*.

The Sacketts
US 1979 2 × 96m colour TVM
NBC/Douglas Netter/NB Scott/Shalako
The three Sackett brothers of Tennessee head west and have various adventures.
Mainly enjoyable old-fashioned western with a somewhat ramshackle structure.

w Jim Byrnes, *books* Louis L'Amour *d* Robert Totten *ph* Jack Whitman Jnr *m* Jerrold Immel

Jeff Osterhage, Tom Selleck, Sam Elliott, Glenn Ford, Ben Johnson, Mercedes McCambridge, John Vernon, Marcy Hanson, Gilbert Roland, Gene Evans, Jack Elam, Slim Pickens, L. Q. Jones

'Four-hour telefilm gives back the western its good name.' – *Daily Variety*

Sackheim, William (1919–). American executive producer, in charge of development at Universal. Series include *The Flying Nun*, *Night Gallery*. Former writer with widespread credits.

Sacred Hearts (GB 1983; 90m). Girls at a convent boarding school in World War II East Anglia face adolescence and Adolf Hitler, in that order. An unconvincing overwrought Film on Four, with Anna Massey dusting off her Mrs Danvers act to play stern Sister Thomas. Also Oona Kirsch, Katrin Cartlidge; written and directed by Barbara Rennie, produced by Dee Dee Glass for Reality Productions/C4.   PP

Sadat *
US 1983 2 × 96m, colour miniseries
Operation Prime
  Time/Columbia/Blatt–Singer
The last 30 years in the life of the Egyptian premier who was assassinated.
Respectful (perhaps too respectful) and ambitious but often impenetrable biopic in which the western viewer is seldom sure where his sympathies should be. Confusion is worse confounded by having the Egyptian played by a black man. The show was tactfully withdrawn after dissension about it in the Middle East. It had been filmed in Mexico.

w Lionel Chetwynd *d* Richard Michaels *ph* Jan de Bont *m* Charles Bernstein
Lou Gossett Jnr, John Rhys-Davies (heavily made up as Nasser), Madolyn Smith, Jeremy Kemp, Eric Berry, Anne Heywood, Ferdy Mayne, Barry Morse, Nehemiah Persoff

Safe at Home
US 1985   × 25m colour
Turner (Arthur Annecharico)
A 15-year-old girl cellist moves in with her 33-year-old sportscaster brother.
Feeble *Odd Couple*-style comedy presented as a semi-soap opera for the big new uncritical daytime audience.

cr Arthur Annecharico
Martha Nix, Michael J. Cutt

Sagal, Boris (1923–81). American director who made some big-screen movies but generally settled for TV. Series include *77 Sunset Strip, The Alfred Hitchcock Hour, T.H.E. Cat* (also produced), *Mystery Movie.* TV movies: *Destiny of a Spy, The Movie Murderer, Hauser's Memory, The Harness, The Failing of Raymond, Deliver Us from Evil, Indict and Convict, A Case of Rape, The Dream Makers, Griff, Rich Man, Poor Man, Sherlock Holmes in New York, The Moneychangers, The Awakening Land, Ike, The Diary of Anne Frank,* etc.

Sahl, Mort (1927–   ). Iconoclastic Canadian comedian who was immensely popular and influential in the fifties but seemed unaccountably to lose his national TV standing. Now works locally in Los Angeles.

Saigon – Year of the Cat (GB 1983; 105m). The Americans' last days in Saigon, with an off-hand affair between Englishwoman and CIA man to counterpoint the off-hand disengagement of a powerful country from a doomed one, but a fairer picture than John Pilger's earlier *The Last Day*; with Judi Dench, Frederic Forrest; written by David Hare, directed by Stephen Frears, for Thames. PP

Sailor **
GB 1976 13 × 50m colour
BBC (John Purdie)
At sea with the aircraft carrier *Ark Royal* of the post-war years.
Appealing, well-shot series. The episode entitled *The Rescue* won a BAFTA award.
PP: 'A marvellous and surely elegiac series – unless reprieved to take part in some Socialist crusade against Iceland, Ibiza or the Isle of Man, the *Ark Royal*'s days must be numbered. Patrick Turley's dazzling camerawork in the title sequence – the ship seen first from high above, then from a low-approaching jet – has romanticized for all time, just in time, the image of the carrier as the supreme symbol of warlike power.'
So it proved, after a poignant BBC outside broadcast of her final home-coming.
In 1984 *Sailor* was re-run with a postscript produced by Patrick Turley, who shot the original series. The Captain was now in charge of Britain's lifeboats, the Padre in charge of other padres, the steward who married in Florida no longer married. All that was left of the *Ark Royal* herself was a section of rusting hull in the breaker's dock. Tom Wilkinson, the sterling Master at Arms on the television voyage, was moved to tears by the sight of it, and with him most of the audience.

Sailor of Fortune
GB 1956 26 × 50m bw
A seafaring wanderer helps people in trouble. The studio sets killed this one, but its star went on to better things.
Lorne Greene, Rupert Davies

The Sailor's Return
GB 1980 110m colour TVM
Thames/Euston Films (Otto Plaschkes)
Jack Gold's version of the David Garnett novella about a seafarer (Tom Bell) home from the sea with a black wife and the money to acquire a country pub. A mid-Victorian warning of race prejudice to come, let down by the suspicion that it was not so much the presence of the gracious Tulip (Shope Shoedeinde) behind the bar that drove away the customers as Tom Bell's piercing stare.   PP
w James Saunders
LH: 'Dramatically it far exceeded its natural length and provided almost nothing in the general way of entertainment.'

The Saint **
GB 1963–8 114 × 50m 71 bw, 43 colour
ATV/Baker-Berman
Stories of Simon Templar, the Robin Hood of crime, from the books by Leslie Charteris. On the whole the most satisfactory incarnation of this durable fantasy figure, with the right kind of lightweight star.
Roger Moore
† 1978 brought *The Return of the Saint* with Ian Ogilvy, from the same stable.

Saint, Eva Marie (1924–   ). Leading American actress. TV series: *How the West Was Won.* TV movies: *A Christmas to Remember, The Curse of King Tutankhamun's Tomb, When Hell Was in Session, Splendor in the Grass, Malibu, Jane Doe, Fatal Vision.*

St Clair, Isla (1952–   ). Scottish presenter popular on BBC's *The Generation Game.*

'It gets you where you feel!'
St Elsewhere **
US 1982–   × 50m colour
NBC/MTM (Bruce Paltrow)
Drama mixes with comedy among staff and patients at an old Boston teaching hospital called St Eligius.
A medical *Hill Street Blues* which was allowed to develop its popularity slowly, though its vein of black humour made it the hardest possible sell for a soap opera.

cr Bruce Paltrow, Joshua Brand, John Falsey *m* Dave Grusin (theme), J. A. C. Redford

Ed Flanders, David Birney, Norman Lloyd, William Daniels, Christina Pickles, Ed Begley Jnr, Cynthia Sikes, David Morse, Kavi Raz, Terence Knox

'If any program can get American viewers voluntarily to sit through an hour that includes stories about severe burn victims, the decision to shut off life support for a comatose nun, a boyfriend–girlfriend squabble over an abortion, an impending nurses' strike and a doctor's attempt to rebound from a rape arrest, this is it.' – *Daily Variety*

St James, Susan (1946–   ) (Susan Miller). American leading lady of the slightly kooky kind; made an impression as the second half of *McMillan and Wife*. Also in *The Name of the Game*. TV movies: *Alias Smith and Jones*, *The Magic Carpet*, *Scott Free*, *Night Cries*, *Desperate Women*, *The Girls in the Office*, *Sex and the Single Parent*, *SOS Titanic*, *How to Beat the High Cost of Living*, *The Kid from Nowhere*, *I Take These Men*, *Kate and Allie*.

Saints and Sinners *
US 1962 18 × 50m bw
NBC/Four Star/Hondo
Human stories uncovered by the reporters of a city newspaper.
Once again a better-than-average series bites the dust.
Nick Adams, John Larkin

'To the Soviet Union he is an enemy. To the world he is a hero!'
Sakharov *
US 1984 96m colour TVM
HBO/Titus (Robert Berger)
The story of Russian nuclear physicist Andrei Sakharov, whose outspoken views on human rights earn him internal exile in Gorky.
Unsurprising account of events very well known from the headlines. Acting impeccable, but a fresh angle was needed.
w David W. Rintels *d* Jack Gold *ph* Tony Imi *m* Carl Davis *pd* Herbert Westbrook
JASON ROBARDS, GLENDA JACKSON, Nicol Williamson, Frank Finlay, Michael Bryant, Paul Freeman, Anna Massey, Joe Melia, Lee Montague

Saki **
GB 1962 13 × 50m bw (VTR)
Granada (PHILIP MACKIE)

An elegant compendium of the witty stories of H. H. Munro.
w PHILIP MACKIE *d* Gordon Flemyng
MARTITA HUNT, FENELLA FIELDING, WILLIAM MERVYN, RICHARD VERNON
PP: 'The stylistic innovation was to string together a variable number of stories per episode and contrive that each should introduce the next. Mackie also rationalized Saki's characters so that his standard figures (clubman, *ingénue*, etc) could be played throughout by the same actor or actress. So successful was the format that it was subsequently applied to Feydeau farces (*Paris 1900*) and *The Liars* (1966), stitched together from short stories by many hands but all linked by William Mervyn and Nyree Dawn Porter as tall-story-telling hosts.'

Sale of the Century. A popular GB quiz show from Anglia TV, with three contestants answering increasingly difficult questions and using their scores to buy discounted goods. Nicholas Parsons as host.

Sales, Soupy (1926–   ) (Milton Hines). American comedian, usually seen performing corny jokes and slapstick in children's time.

Sallis, Peter (1921–   ). Unassuming British actor most familiar as one of the trio in *Last of the Summer Wine*.

Sally (US 1957). Half-hour situation comedy series for NBC, with Joan Caulfield as the companion of a wealthy widow. Gale Gordon and Arte Johnson were also involved.

Salomon, Henry Jnr (–1957). American documentary producer, noted for *Victory at Sea* and several NBC *White Papers* including *The Twisted Cross*.

Salty
US 1974 26 × 25m colour
Salty Co/TCF (Kobi Jaeger)
Adventures of an intelligent sea lion and his young owner.
Infallible kids' stuff.
Mark Slade, Julius Harris, Johnny Doran

Salvage *
US 1979 96m colour TVM
ABC/Columbia/Bennett–Katleman
A junk dealer plans to go to the moon and recover valuable litter left by astronauts.
Amusing fantasy with a fair measure of spectacle.
w Mike Lloyd Ross *d* Lee Phillips *ph* Fred Koenekamp *m* Walter Scharf

THE SAINT. Though there were later aspirants to the role, the television audience still identifies it with Roger Moore. Here he is seen with Paul Stassino, Quinn O'Hara, and Lois Maxwell (whom he would meet again as Miss Moneypenny in quite a different series).

Andy Griffith, Joel Higgins, Trish Stewart, J. Jay Saunders, Raleigh Bond, Jacqueline Scott

'A comedy of situations that's aimed at belly laughs and hits widely diversified targets.' – *Daily Variety*

† A series of 50m episodes followed, but the subjects had to be much more down-to-earth and the first engaging lunacy watered down. Audiences dwindled, and only 13 were made.

Sam **
GB 1973–5 39 × 50m colour (VTR)
Granada (Michael Cox)

How a boy grew up among the poor of a Pennine mining town.

Ambitious drama serial which tended to wear out its welcome; as Sam grew up, interest shifted from him to his redoubtable grandfather, and towards the end it all smacked of *Cold Comfort Farm*.

w/cr JOHN FINCH

Barbara Ewing, Ray Smith, MICHAEL GOODLIFFE, James Hazeldine, John Price, Althea Charlton

Sam
US 1978 7 × 25m colour
CBS/Jack Webb (Leonard B. Kaufman)

Cases of a police dog.

Four incidents to a segment: the principle didn't work so well as with *Adam 12*.

cr Jack Webb, Dan Noble

Mark Harmon, Len Wayland

Sam Benedict **
US 1962 28 × 50m bw
NBC/MGM

Cases of an adventurous lawyer and his assistant.

Smooth, superior courtroom drama with action interludes. Unbelievable, but palatable.

cr E. Jack Neuman, based on the career of Jake Ehrlich

Edmond O'Brien, Richard Rust

Sammy (GB 1958). Smart little telephone-solo thriller (a device also used in the movie *Sorry, Wrong Number* and Cocteau's play *La Voix Humaine*), starring the then unknown Anthony Newley as a shady operator who had to drum up a packet of money in three hours or face a nasty deputation from the local Mr Big. My review at the time: 'The action was confined to his telephonic manipulation of enough quick deals to give him the necessary profit. I begin to distrust the sentimental and – I suspect – superficial Jewishness we always get in fiction about the shadier side of commerce. Does every question have to begin with "So"? But otherwise *Sammy* was a little masterpiece of TV drama. The situation was plausible, the suspense authentic and the ending genuinely chilling.' Written, directed and produced by Ken Hughes; for BBC.   PP

'The seduction. The betrayal. The redemption. The story of a man and a woman.'
Samson and Delilah
US 1984 96m colour TVM
ABC/Comworld/Catalina (Franklin R. Levy)

High school version of a tale which wasn't done much better (but a little) by Cecil B. DeMille. As a gesture to film buffs, Victor Mature (who starred in that version) appears in a small part.

w John Gay d Lee Philips ph Gerry Fisher m Maurice Jarre

Antony Hamilton, Belinda Bauer, Max Von Sydow, Stephen Macht, Clive Revill, Daniel Stern, Victor Mature, Jose Ferrer, Maria Schell

Samson and Goliath
US 1967   × 25m colour
Hanna–Barbera

Whenever a boy utters magic words, he is turned into a superman and his dog into a lion. Derivative cartoon series.

Samurai
US 1978 74m colour TVM
ABC/Universal/Danny Thomas (Allan Balter)

Cases of a Frisco lawyer with a Japanese mother, a Japanese butler, and nothing much else to distinguish him from other television crime fighters.

Busted pilot with little to commend it.

w Jerry Ludwig d Lee Latzin ph Vincent Martinelli m Fred Karlin

Joe Penny, James Shigeta, Beulah Quo, Charles Cioffi, Dana Elcar, Morgan Brittany, James McEachin

'Not an attention-getter.' – *Daily Variety*

San Francisco Beat *
aka: *The Line-Up*, qv for 50m series
US 1954–8 183 × 25m bw
Desilu

An old and a young cop combat crime on the streets.

Who said *Streets of San Francisco* was a new idea? This pacy cop show preceded it by nearly 20 years.

Warner Anderson, Tom Tully

San Francisco International Airport **
US 1970 96m colour TVM
NBC/Universal (Frank Price)

A day's problems for the manager of a big airport.

No mad bomber, otherwise a mini-*Airport* and quite slick and entertaining.

w William Read Woodfield, Allan Balter d John Llewellyn Moxey

Pernell Roberts, Clu Gulager, Beth Brickell, Van Johnson, Nancy Malone, David Hartman, Cliff Potts, Tab Hunter

† A subsequent series of 6 × 50m episodes was aired as part of *Four In One*.

San Pedro Beach Bums
US 1977 1 × 74m, 11 × 50m colour
ABC/Spelling–Cramer (E. Duke Vincent)

Adventures of a noisy harbour gang whose hearts are in the right place.

Or, The Bowery Boys Go Boating. Noised as the start of a sensational new trend, it performed the remarkable feat of seeming too crass for the average American public, and submerged.

w E. Duke Vincent d (pilot) Barry Shear

Chris Murney, Jeffrey Druce, John Mark Robinson, Stuart Pankin, Barry McCullough

Sand, Paul (c 1943–). Amiable American character comedian who was tried out in his own TV series *Friends and Lovers*.

The Sandbaggers (GB 1978–80). Exploits of an intelligence strong-arm squad clearly modelled on the army's SAS units, with Roy Marsden as the laconic director of operations. It got better, but earlier episodes showed a certain paucity of resources either on the part of the production or the might of Britain it was dramatizing. The opening operation was carried out by two men flown into action aboard an elderly 748 turboprop. Directed by Michael Ferguson, created by Ian Mackintosh for YTV.

Sandcastles
US 1972 74m colour TVM
CBS/Metromedia (Charles Fries, Gerald I. Isenberg)
A girl has a romance with the ghost of the victim of an auto accident.
Dreary nonsense involving much moonlight walking on the beach. Technically interesting as the first TV movie shot on videotape and transferred to film; the difference showed in loss of quality and the technique was abandoned.

w Stephen and Elinor Karpf, James M. Miller
d Ted Post ph Alan Stensvold m Paul Glass

Herschel Barnardi, Bonnie Bedelia, Jan-Michael Vincent, Mariette Hartley, Gary Crosby

The Sandy Duncan Show
US 1972 13 × 25m colour
CBS/Paramount/Jefferson–Sultan
Misadventures of a student teacher at UCLA. A threadbare format which was tried out when *Funny Face* didn't work. This one didn't either.

Sandy Duncan, Tom Bosley, Marian Mercer

Sanford and Son **
US 1972–6 136 × 25m colour (VTR)
NBC/Bud Yorkin, Norman Lear/NBC (Saul Turteltaub, Bernie Orenstein)
Father and son run a junk yard in Los Angeles.
Black version of *Steptoe and Son*, a great American success which in this form didn't travel.

Redd Foxx, Desmond Wilson

† A 1977 spin-off called *Sanford Arms* failed to work.

Sangster, Jimmy (1927–). British writer who after scripting some of the better Hammer horrors found a niche in Hollywood's TV industry. *A Taste of Evil*, *Murder in Music City*, *Billion Dollar Threat*,

The Concrete Cowboys, *Once upon a Spy*, *No Place To Hide*, *The Toughest Man in the World*.

Santa Barbara (US 1984;   × 50m). NBC daytime serial about the lives and loves of four families in a beach community. Chief point of interest was the starring in it of 86-year-old Judith Anderson, who lives in Santa Barbara. Writer–creators, Jerome and Bridget Dobson.

Sapphire and Steel * (GB 1979–82; 39 × 50m). Interesting, undervalued, under-regarded sci-fi thriller serials in which angel-agents codenamed Sapphire (Joanna Lumley), Steel (David McCallum) and Silver (David Collings) roam through time and place to lay ghosts and rectify ancient wrongs. Written by P. J. Hammond, directed and produced by Shaun O'Riordan, for ATV.   PP
LH: 'In my book only weird.'

Sara
US 1975 13 × 50m colour
CBS/Universal (George Eckstein)
The life of a spinster schoolteacher in a burgeoning town in the old west. From a novel by Marian Cockrell.
Too quiet a show to suit the western background; these stories could have happened anywhere.

Brenda Vaccaro, Bert Kramer, Albert Stratton

Sara Dane
Australia 1981 8 × 50m colour
South Australia Film Corporation (Jock Blair)
In the early days of the Australian penal settlement, a girl unjustly deported as a thief marries a ship's officer and sets out on a new tempestuous life.
Adequate novelization with a nice feel for its period.

w Alan Seymour, *novel* Catherine Gaskin d Rod Hardy, Gary Conway

Juliet Jordan, Harold Hopkins, Brenton Whittle, Barry Quin, Sean Scully

Sarah T: Portrait of a Teenage Alcoholic *
US 1975 100m colour TVM
Universal (David Levinson)
A case history of a schoolgirl alcoholic.
Sensationalized documentary drama, the most popular TV movie of its year in America.

w Richard and Esther Shapiro d Richard Donner

ST ELSEWHERE.   Some of the constant cast factors in a hospital which seems to be always on its uppers. Bottom: Eric Laneuville, Norman Lloyd. Second row: Mark Harmon, Cynthia Sikes, Ed Flanders, Ellen Bry. Third row: Denzel Washington, Ed Begley Jnr, Christina Pickles, William Daniels. Top: David Morse, Howie Mandel, Stephen Furst.

Linda Blair, Verna Bloom, William Daniels, Larry Hagman

Sarafian, Richard (1932–). American director, in TV from the days of *Hawaiian Eye* and *The Roaring Twenties*. His more recent big-screen films have not impressed, but some of his TV movies have style: *Shadow on the Land, One of Our Own, A Killing Affair, Golden Moment, Disaster on the Coastliner, The Gangster Chronicles, Splendor in the Grass*, etc.

Sarandon, Chris (1942–). American leading man. TV movies: *You Can't Go Home Again, The Day Christ Died* (title role), *A Tale of Two Cities, Broken Promise*.

Sarge. See also *The Badge or the Cross, The Priest Killer*. The series, which had started in *Four In One*, ran to 13 × 50m episodes.

Sargent, Dick (*c* 1937–) American light leading man. TV series: *One Happy Family, Broadside, Bewitched.*

Sargent, Joseph (1925–) (Giuseppe Danielle Dargente). American director whose TV career began with *Lassie, Bonanza* and *The Man from UNCLE*. TV movies are a variable lot: *The Sunshine Patriot, The Immortal, Tribes, Longstreet, Man on a String, The Marcus Nelson Murders, The Man Who Died Twice, Sunshine, Hustling, The Night That Panicked America*, etc.

✱ **Sarnoff, David** (1891–1971). American executive, founder of the NBC network, president of the RCA corporations; also the radio operator who first heard the distress signals of the *Titanic* when it sank in 1912.

Satan's School for Girls
US 1973 74m colour TVM
Spelling–Goldberg
A schoolmistress fights the devil for control of a girls' school.
Lunatic farrago which might have been more suspensefully narrated and produced.
w Arthur A. Ross   *d* David Lowell Rich
Roy Thinnes, Kate Jackson, Pamela Franklin, Jo Van Fleet, Lloyd Bochner

Satan's Triangle *
US 1975 74m colour TVM
ABC/James Rokos–Danny Thomas
Dead bodies are found in a drifting boat in the Bermuda mystery area.
Good-looking hocus pocus which doesn't make much dramatic sense.

w William Read Woodfield   *d* Sutton Roley
Kim Novak, Doug McClure, Alejandro Rey, Jim Davis, Ed Lauter

satellite. An orbiting space station which, unmanned, picks up and relays television information from continent to continent. Satellites have been in use since 1960.

Saturday Live (GB 1985; 90m). Live bill of mostly 'alternative' comedy plus music and a spoof soap-serial called *Rich* which led to a regular season in 1986, hosted each week by a different star, e.g. Pamela Stephenson or Ben Elton or the Ven. Peter Cook, most of whom tend to be emphatic, aggressive and strong on rude words, because that's what makes them alternative. Produced by Paul Jackson and Geoff Posner, for LWT/C4.   PP

Saturday Night Affairs (GB 1984). Short-lived salon in which a selected nonentity (e.g. hairdresser Vidal Sassoon) played host to a job lot of other nonentities at a buffet party in the BBC's fabled Pebble Mill studios – to adapt Oscar Wilde, the unspeakable hovering over the uneatable. Produced by Tony Haygarth, it was axed after three programmes.   PP

Saturday Night People ✱✱✱
GB 1979–80 approx. 20 × 60m colour VTR
LWT (Barry Cox)
Dreamed up by Barry Cox, once a newspaper diarist, as the television equivalent of a gossip column, the format combined elements of a superior chat-show with one or two set-piece reports by the regular luminaries, Clive James and Janet Street-Porter, all more or less held together by Russell Harty. Give or take a couple of editions when some humourless left-winger soured the mix, it was the most civilized, erudite and funny television salon ever, and therefore, needless to say, spurned by many of the ITV regions and dropped by LWT itself after two seasons.   PP

LH: 'I would drop the three asterisks and insert a lemon. The one virtue of the show seemed to be that it wrapped up in one hour a week my three *bêtes noires*, who might otherwise have infected a programme each.'

Saturday Night Thriller (GB 1982; 6 × 52m). Misleadingly titled season from LWT which included only one out-and-out nail-biter (*Walk in the Dark* by Brian Finch, with Denis Quilley as a blind tycoon up against a silent killer) but did find room for a compassionate treatment of the painful

SALE OF THE CENTURY. Anglia's long-running quiz was hosted by Nicholas Parsons, with occasional assistance from the likes of Carole Ashby and Karen Loughlin.

subject of incest which was never meant to be thrilling at all, *Broken Glass* by James Andrew Hall, with Bernard Hepton and James Grout.
Other writers included Anthony Skene, Roger Marshall; directors, Christopher Hodson, Paul Annett and Peter Cregeen, two apiece.   PP

The Saturday Party (GB 1975; 90m; colour). It's thrown by a stockbroker to celebrate the fact that he has lost his job – now he can do something useful. Wife and family take a more practical view. Brian Clark's play (for BBC) was perhaps the first to be inspired by the recession which was just setting in. With Peter Barkworth in an early try-out of the role he was to enlarge in *Telford's Change*. More immediately a sequel to this play, *The Country Party*, followed in 1976. Produced by Mark Shivas; for BBC.   PP

Saturday Review (GB since 1984). BBC2's old arts review of the sixties and seventies under the title *Release* and then *Review*, born again in the eighties with Russell Davies, former TV critic of the *Sunday Times*, in charge on screen and John Archer, producer of *Did You See . . . ?*, the power behind the scenes. Sometimes it even considers something you might like to go and see or hear.   PP
LH: 'But not often.'

Saturday's Heroes
GB 1976 3 × 50m colour
Thames (Frank Cvitanovich)
Three films about professional football, which goes rarely documented considering it is supposed to be the national obsession. The first one dramatized a crisis in the career of a player of the twenties, Jimmy Seed. The other two dealt more conventionally with the contemporary scene.   PP

Savage *
US 1972 74m colour TVM
Universal (Paul Mason)
Adventures of the hard-hitting front man of a news commentary team.
Smooth topical melodrama which didn't run to a series.
w Mark Rodgers, William Link, Richard Levinson *d* Steven Spielberg
Martin Landau, Barbara Bain, Will Geer, Barry Sullivan, Louise Latham, Pat Hingle, Susan Howard

The Savage Bees
US 1976 96m colour TVM
Alan Landsburg/Don Kirshner/NBC

Killer bees invade New Orleans during the Mardi Gras.
Satisfactory stunt thriller, not outstanding but certainly better than the very similar, much heralded theatrical movie *The Swarm*.
w Guerdon Trueblood *d* Bruce Geller *m* Walter Murphy
Ben Johnson, Michael Parks, Paul Hecht, Horst Buchholz, Gretchen Corbett

Savages *
US 1974 74m colour TVM
Spelling–Goldberg
An unarmed youth in the desert flees from a deranged hunter.
Adventure suspense, not badly done.
w William Wood, *novel Death Watch* by Robb White *d* Lee H. Katzin
Andy Griffith, Sam Bottoms, Noah Beery Jnr, James Best, Randy Boone

Savalas, Telly (1924–) (Aristotle Savalas). Bald, beaming Greek-American character actor who achieved instant stardom as KOJAK. TV movies: *Mongo's Back in Town*, *Visions*, *The Marcus-Nelson Murders*, *She Cried Murder*, *Alcatraz*, *Hellinger's Law*, *My Palikari*, *The Cartier Affair*, *Kojak: The Belarus File*.

Savile, Jimmy (*c* 1925–). Silver-topped, platinum-blond British disc jockey and TV personality; an acquired taste.

Saville, Philip (*c* 1930–). British TV director with innumerable top shows to his credit. A few of the most memorable: *A Night Out,* · *Prisoner and Escort*, *The Rainbirds*, *Secrets*, *Gangsters* (pilot), *Count Dracula*. In 1982 he crowned his long career with *The Boys from the Blackstuff*, BAFTA Desmond Davis Award, *Those Glory Glory Days* and *Quest for Love*, 1983.

Savory, Gerald (1904–). British playwright with a famous thirties hit, *George and Margaret*, who in the fifties became an authoritative television drama ideas man and producer. For Granada he adapted their six classic 'Manchester' plays in 1960, plus others by Priestley and Arnold Bennett. At the BBC, as head of serials and then head of plays, 1966–72, he devised *The Six Wives of Henry VIII*, *Elizabeth R* and *Take Three Girls*. In 1985–6 adapted *Mapp and Lucia* for LWT.   PP

Say Goodbye, Maggie Cole *
US 1972 73m colour TVM
Spelling–Goldberg

A widow returns to medical practice in a tough slum area.
Efficient woman's tearjerker.

w Sandor Stern d Jud Taylor

Susan Hayward, Darren McGavin, Michael Constantine, Dane Clark, Beverly Garland

Say Goodnight to Your Grandma *
GB 1970 50m colour
Thames

Robust Colin Welland comedy set in the disputed territory that Welland had made peculiarly his own, where the rough male togetherness of pub and rugby club fights a losing battle against creeping domesticity. This time there was a whiff of the war of the generations, too, with scheming ma-in-law shamefully discomfited by resolute wife. Welland has the actor–writer's ear for dialogue which is funny but unforced, and Madge Ryan was super.   PP

Say Hello to a Dead Man *
US 1972 73m colour TVM
NBC/Universal

Escaping from 15 years in a South American jungle prison, a private eye returns to his old practice (which is being run by his son) and finds it difficult to adjust.
A silly premise at least provides some good jokes and chases. Pilot for *Faraday and Company* (see *Mystery Movie*).

d Gary Nelson

Dan Dailey, James Naughton, Sharon Gless, Craig Stevens, Geraldine Brooks, David Wayne, Howard Duff

Sayle, Alexei (1952–). Aggressive bristle-headed British alternative comedian, strictly for those who like aggressive, bristle-headed alternative comedians. *OTT*, *The Young Ones*, *Whoops Apocalypse*.

Scales, Prunella (1932–). British comedy actress who can disguise her pretty self with amazing selflessness, notably as Mapp in *Mapp and Lucia* and the managing Sybil in *Fawlty Towers*. Also *Outside Edge*, *Marriage Lines*, *Slimming Down*.   PP

Scalplock
US 1967 100m colour TVM
Columbia

A gambler wins a railroad.
Western pilot for *The Iron Horse* series. Prolonged but watchable.

w Stephen Kandel d James Goldstone

Dale Robertson, Robert Random, Diana Hyland

Scandal Sheet
US 1985 96m colour TVM
ABC/Metromedia

A woman newspaper reporter is hired by a high-circulation tabloid to deliver the inside story of a drunken ex-star who is married to a friend of hers.
Watchable, predictable melodrama.

w Howard Reidman d David Lowell Rich

Burt Lancaster, Robert Urich, Lauren Hutton, Pamela Reed

'They're partners – undercover and under fire!'
Scarecrow and Mrs King
US 1983–   × 50m colour
CBS/Warner/B and E/Shoot the Moon (Bill McCutchen)

An ordinary housewife unwittingly becomes involved in a spy game, and thereafter is called on from time to time by the FBI.
Mindless fluff which depends for its success on funny lines and inventive situations, which aren't that easy to come by in a weekly series; but the leads are decorative.

cr Brad Buckner, Eugenie Ross-Leming

Kate Jackson, Bruce Boxleitner, Beverly Garland, Mel Stewart

'It kicks off with a stab at distinction, and not many new shows can make that claim.' – *Daily Variety*
'Harmless fun is the category, I guess.' – Robert MacKenzie, *TV Guide*

Scarf Jack
GB 1981 6 × 25m colour
Southern TV (Chris McMaster)

A mysterious figure helps the oppressed Irish against the English occupying forces in 1798. The same story as the Rock Hudson movie *Captain Moonlight*, an odd choice for a British company in the middle of the Irish troubles, and one that caused some comment. Otherwise a somewhat tedious serial for older children.

w P. J. Kavanagh, from his *novel* d Chris McMaster

Roy Boyd, Keith Jayne, Jo Kendall

The Scarlet and the Black
US/Italy 1983 142m colour TVM
CBS/ITC/RAI/Bill McCutchen

The story of Monsignor Hugh O'Flaherty, a Vatican priest who during World War II helped several Allied soldiers and civilians to escape from the Nazis.

A film on this subject can hardly fail to be of some interest, but the narrative is muddled, the tone erratic and the acting not what it might be. Occasional scenes excite.

w David Butler, *book The Scarlet Pimpernel of the Vatican* by J. P. Gallagher *d* Jerry London *ph* Giuseppe Rotunno *m* Ennio Morricone

Gregory Peck, Christopher Plummer, John Gielgud, Raf Vallone, Ken Colley, Walter Gotell, Barbara Bouchet, Julian Holloway, T. P. McKenna

The Scarlet Pimpernel
US/GB 1983 142m colour TVM
CBS/London Films (David Conroy)
Sir Percy Blakeney, a London fop, is the brains behind the escape of several French aristocrats from the guillotine.
Twice as long as the 1935 film, and seeming it, this telepic is overburdened with sets and costumes at the expense of drama; nor are the performances all that might have been expected.

w William Bast, *novel* by Baroness Orczy *d* Clive Donner *ph* Dennis Lewiston *m* Nick Bicat

Anthony Andrews, Jane Seymour, Ian McKellen, James Villiers, Eleanor David, Dennis Lill, Ann Firbank, Malcolm Jamieson

Scars of Autumn (GB 1979). Three former correspondents reliving the German (and subsequently Russian) invasion of Poland which they had covered 40 years earlier: Sir Hugh Greene, Clare Hollingworth, the Earl of Lauderdale. Together, they re-traced their fitful progress eastwards in that curious, unbelievable twilight of a nation. Even as the heavens were falling, Sir Hugh recalled, Polish society continued to don white tie and tails to dine out. Produced by Peter Foges; for BBC.
PP

Scene of the Crime
US 1984 6 × 25m colour
NBC/Universal/Jon Epstein
Curious format in which a murder playlet stops just before the revelation, and guest celebrities are invited to say who done it.

Schaefer, George (1920–). American director with long TV experience, mainly in literal transcriptions of theatrical material. TV movies/specials: *Macbeth* (1960), *Victoria Regina*, *The Magnificent Yankee, A War of*

Children, F. Scott Fitzgerald and 'The Last of the Belles', In This House of Brede, Amelia Earhart, Truman at Potsdam, The Girl Called •*Hatter Fox, First You Cry, Who'll Save Our Children, Blind Ambition, Mayflower,* etc.

Schaffner, Franklin (1920–). American director, in television from 1953 and a pillar of its golden age, with such credits as TWELVE ANGRY MEN (1954), *The Caine Mutiny Court Martial* (1955) and PATTERNS (1955). Won an Emmy for *The Defenders* in 1961, then graduated to the big screen.

Scherick, Edgar J. (*c* 1922–). American producer. *A Circle of Children, Raid on Entebbe, The Seduction of Miss Leona, Revenge of the Stepford Wives, Little Gloria . . . Happy at Last, He Makes Me Feel like Dancing, Evergreen.*

Schifrin, Lalo (1932–). Argentinian composer in Hollywood. TV scores include *Mission Impossible, Mannix, Starsky and Hutch, Bronk, Most Wanted.*

Schindler (GB 1983; 78m). Documentary account of the high-placed Sudeten German playboy who cosseted 1,000 Jews to safety throughout the Nazi holocaust, as thinly fictionalized by Thomas Keneally in his Booker Prize novel *Schindler's Ark* some months before. Narrated by Dirk Bogarde, directed and produced by Jon Blair, for Thames.
PP

Schlatter, George (1932–). American writer–producer who won two Emmys for LAUGH IN.

Schlesinger, John (1926–). British film director who began with filmlets for the early-evening *Tonight* in the fifties, switched more enjoyably to *Monitor* items for Huw Wheldon and went on to make features. More recent TV credits include *An Englishman Abroad.*
PP

Schneider, John (1954–). American leading man. *The Dukes of Hazzard, Happy Endings, Gus Brown and Midnight Brewster.*

School Play *
GB 1979 75m colour
BBC
The obsession of the English upper classes with their schooldays under glittering reappraisal by Frederic Raphael. The device of having grown-up actors play their young

selves had less impact than in *Blue Remembered Hills*; the age gap was less bizarre and there was an anomaly in the participation of Jenny Agutter as the young cook, who logically should have been played by a middle-aged woman. But dazzling performances from Jeremy Kemp, Tim Pigott-Smith, Michael Kitchen and, best of all, Denholm Elliott.   PP

Schuck, John (1941–). Lumpy, bewildered-looking American character actor who scored in comic roles in *McMillan and Wife* and *Holmes and Yoyo*. TV movies: *Hunter*, *Roots*.

Schuman, Howard (1942–). American-reared, British-domiciled writer of usually funny, strongly idiosyncratic subjects derived from adult observation and adolescent memories of movies, pop songs and science fiction. VERITÉ and *Captain Video's Story* (1973), *Censored Scenes from King Kong* (censored, 1974), *A Helping Hand*, *Carbon Copy* and an episode of *Churchill's People* (1975), *Amazing Stories* in Granada's Red Letter Day anthology and ROCK FOLLIES (1976); *Rock Follies of '77* and *Anxious Annie* (1977); *Bouncing Back* and *Videostars* (both 1983).
                                                          PP

Schwartz, Sherwood (19 –). American producer and creator of comedy formats which are all basically the same: *Gilligan's Island*, *The Brady Bunch*, *Dusty's Trail*, *Harper Valley*.

Scoffield, Jon (1932–). British director, formerly designer, with amazing range of successes to his name, from Shakespeare through *Rock Follies* to Stanley Baxter shows. Recent hits include BUD 'N' CHES and DIZZY FEET. Now controller of music and entertainment for Central.   PP

Scofield, Paul (1922–). British actor of few but distinguished appearances on television, often for ATV. *Hamlet*, *Dance of Death*, *Emlyn*, *The Potting Shed*, *Summer Lightning*, *A Kind of Alaska*. See also Heaven and Earth   PP

Scooby Doo, Where are You? *
US 1969–71 72 × 22m colour
CBS/Hanna–Barbera

Four teenage ghost-hunters are hindered by their cowardly dog.
Another cartoon variation on a familiar theme (*The Funky Phantom*, *Goober and the Ghost Chasers*) but this one certainly provokes laughs and proved the most popular.

'What kind of man marries 82 women? What kind of woman does it take to stop him?

Scorned and Swindled *
US 1984 96m colour TVM
CBS/Columbia/Cypress Point (Nick Anderson)

A mature woman finds that her second husband is a con artist, and joins up with another man seeking him for revenge purposes.
Surprisingly tight and interesting telefeature with only a few of the vices of the genre.
w Karol Ann Hoeffner, Jerome Kass, *article* by Cable Neuhaus d Paul Wendkos ph Gil Hubbs, Peter Smokler m Billy Goldenberg
Tuesday Weld, Keith Carradine, Peter Coyote, Sheree North, Fionnula Flanagan

The Scorpio Letters
US 1967 98m colour TVM
MGM

British government agencies compete to smash a blackmailing ring.
Ho-hum spy hokum.
w Adrian Spies, Jo Eisinger d Richard Thorpe
Alex Cord, Shirley Eaton, Laurence Naismith

Scorpion Tales (GB 1978). Anthology series of 50-minute plays for ATV in which, as the title suggests, the plots have a sting in the tale. The best was by Bob Baker and Dave Martin, with Jack Shepherd as a merchant bank computer expert tempted to turn a private game of pretending to play the money market into an actual coup. I wrote at the time: 'It was good to see self-interest slowly steal across the brooding visage, cleft chin and down-turned mouth so often applied to the portrayal of upright figures such as Bill Brand, MP.'   PP

Scott Free
US 1977 74m colour TVM
NBC/Universal (Meta Rosenberg)

A Las Vegas gambler has contacts which enable him to solve difficult cases.
Busted pilot. Its fate is unsurprising in view of its unattractive presentation.
w Stephen J. Cannell d William Wiard
Michael Brandon, Susan Saint James, Robert Loggia, Michael Lerner
† The same punning title was used by British presenter and reporter Selina Scott for a 1986 away-from-the-studio series . . . and, many years earlier, for something similar with Michael Scott.

Scott, George C. (1926–). Leading American character actor. TV work includes a series, *East Side West Side*; guest appearances

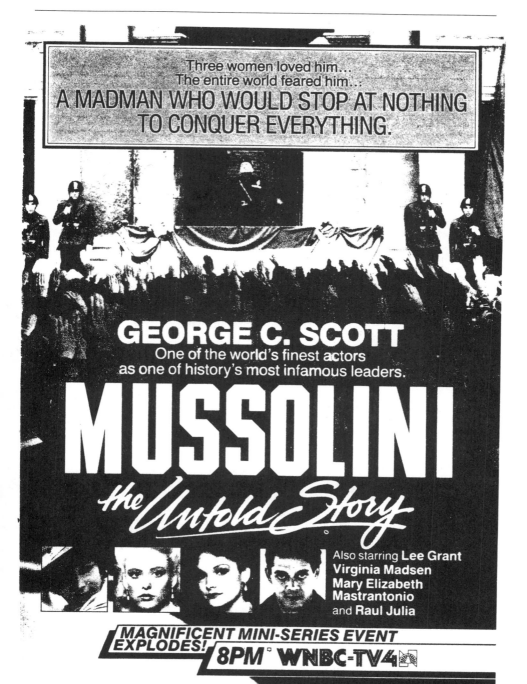

GEORGE C. SCOTT in *Mussolini – The Untold Story*. This was one of two Mussolini exposés which a surprised and not very interested world had to face in 1985.

in many others, including *The Road West* and *The Virginian*; and specials such as *The Andersonville Trial*. TV movies: *Jane Eyre*, *Fear on Trial*, *Beauty and the Beast*, *Oliver Twist*, *China Rose*, *A Christmas Carol*, *Mussolini the Untold Story*.

Scott, Jack (1923–). Senior British BBC weatherman from the seventies.

Scott Joplin: King of Ragtime
US 1978 96m colour TVM
NBC/Universal (Stan Hough)

The life of the composer of *The Sting*.
Downbeat ghetto biopic, relieved by the music (arranged and played by Richard Hyman).

w Christopher Knopf d Jeremy Paul Kagan

Billy Dee Williams, Art Carney, Clifton Davis, Godfrey Cambridge, Seymour Cassel

Scott, Martha (1916–). American leading lady of forties films; made a TV character comeback in the seventies. Series: *The Secrets of Midland Heights*. TV movies: *The Devil's Daughter*, *Thursday's Game*, *The Abduction of St Anne*, *Medical Story*, *The Word*, *Charleston*, *Married*, *Beulah Land*, *Father Figure*.

Scott, Michael (1931–). British linkman, long with Granada, especially on *Cinema*. Also producer of current affairs programmes: *Nuts and Bolts of the Economy*, etc. Appointed Granada's Programme Controller 1980.

Scott, Paul (1920–78). British author and publisher, famous as the source of *Staying On* and THE JEWEL IN THE CROWN, also the godfather of M. M. Kaye's novel which yielded *The Far Pavilions*. What is quite forgotten now is that he adapted two of his Indian novels himself for television in the early days: *Lines of Communication* (from *Johnny Sahib* 1952) and *Alien Sky* (1956). Both were directed by Ian Atkins, for BBC (Michael Barry).   PP

Scott, Peter Graham (1923–). British producer/director with flair for developing popular fiction series, e.g. *Mogul/The Troubleshooters* (1965–9), *The Borderers* (1969–70), *The Onedin Line* (1970–75), *Quiller* (1975), etc. Single productions include *The Last Enemy* and *The Quare Fellow* in the early days of ITV. Last 10 years chiefly with HTV: *Into the Labyrinth* (series), *Kidnapped*, *Jamaica Inn*, *Jenny's War*.
                                        PP

Scott, Selina (1951–). Dewy British TV journalist and presenter. ITN newscaster 1981–3, BBC *Breakfast Time* since – 'the girl you'd prefer to wake up to,' I suggested. Series *Scott Free*, 1986.   PP

Scott, Terry (c 1933–). Tubby British character comedian. Series include *Hugh and I*, *Scott On*, *Son of the Bride*, *Happy Ever After*.

Scout's Honor
US 1980 96m colour TVM
NBC/Gary Coleman (Jim Begg)

A middle-aged scoutmistress is harassed by a small boy telling tall tales.
Abysmally extended family comedy which would have been effective at half an hour, built around the small black boy whose timing and pacing have made him the biggest child star since Shirley Temple.

w Bennett Foster d Henry Levin

Gary Coleman, Katherine Helmond, Wilfrid Hyde White, Harry Morgan

Scream of the Wolf *
aka: *The Hunter*
US 1974 74m colour TVM
ABC/Metromedia/Dan Curtis

What appears to be a mad killer animal is actually a werewolf.
Adequately scary piece with not much sense in its script.

w Richard Matheson d Dan Curtis

Clint Walker, Peter Graves, Jo Ann Pflug, Phil Carey

Scream, Pretty Peggy *
US 1973 74m colour TVM
Universal (Lou Morheim)

A girl student takes a summer job in a sinister house, and chooses the wrong allies.
Fairly obvious but well presented Grand Guignol.

w Jimmy Sangster, Arthur Hoffe d Gordon Hessler

Bette Davis, Ted Bessell, Sian Barbara Allen, Charles Drake

The Screaming Woman *
US 1971 73m colour TVM
Universal (William Frye)

A woman recently ill thinks there is a woman buried somewhere in the grounds of her house. And there is.
Predictable suspenser with a nice cast.

w Merwin Gerard, *story* Ray Bradbury d Jack Smight

Olivia de Havilland, Joseph Cotten, Walter Pidgeon, Ed Nelson, Laraine Stephens

Screen Directors' Playhouse *
US 1955 39 × 25m bw
NBC/Eastman Kodak

Anthology dramas directed by Hollywood's top talents.

None of these playlets compares with the directors' top Hollywood product, but glimmerings of style can be seen. Among those represented are John Ford (with John Wayne starring), Leo McCarey, H. C. Potter, Norman Z. McLeod, Tay Garnett, Fred Zinnemann, George Waggner, William A. Seiter, George Marshall (with Buster Keaton starring) and John Brahm.

Screen Gems. Columbia's TV subsidiary; in the seventies it was renamed Columbia Pictures Television.

Screen Test. A 1975 format pioneered (unsuccessfully) by Universal for syndication. Don Addams showed film clips and then persuaded members of the audience to act them out.

† Presumably the inspiration for Bruce Forsyth's *Hollywood or Bust*, GB 1984.

Scruples
US 1980 3 × 96m colour TVM
CBS/Warner/Lou–Step (Leonard B. Kaufman)

A young but predatory widow opens a boutique in Beverly Hills.

Fashionable mishmash of sexual aberration with a few of the more glamorous kinds of crime. Just the thing for the *Dallas* audience.

w James Lee, *novel* Judith Krantz *d* Alan J. Levi *ph* Joe Biroc *m* Charles Bernstein

Lindsay Wagner, Barry Bostwick, Marie-France Pisier, Efrem Zimbalist Jnr, Connie Stevens, Nick Mancuso, Robert Reed, Gene Tierney, Louise Latham, Michael Callan, Sarah Marshall, Anna Lee

'Characters are sticks, or props, to fill out the plotline crammed with sex and money.' – *Daily Variety*

† In the following year a pilot was made for a one-hour series, but there were no takers.

Scully
GB 1984 6 × 30m, 1 × 60m
Granada (Steve Morrison)

A series of his own for the unruly football-mad Liverpool school-lad originally created by local playwright Alan Bleasdale when he was a teacher, to give his slow-learners something to read that might interest them more than *Janet and John* reading books. Scully stories were broadcast on BBC radio. Scully was given his own show on Radio City and featured on a Saturday morning children's entertainment. He turned up in a BBC Play for Today, *Scully's New Year's Eve*, and finally this series. At first it wasn't easy to see what the fuss was about; but by the end, with Scully blowing his chance of playing with Liverpool FC and plunging into an orgy of vandalism, a comic-strip for bad times was making uncomfortable viewing.

w Alan Bleasdale *d* Les Chatfield

Andrew Schofield, Ray Kingsley; with appearances as themselves by Kenny Dalglish, Elvis Costello   PP

Scum. A *cause célèbre* of 1978: Roy Minton's version of life in a Borstal, produced by Margaret Matheson as a *Play for Today*, was refused transmission by the BBC as being too violent, though its depiction of the institution as corrupt and vindictive probably didn't help either. Minton's story subsequently re-surfaced as a novel and a movie. The latter, ironically was shown on C4 in 1983. Alan Clarke directed both times.   PP

Sea Hawk: see The Adventures of the Sea Hawk

Sea Hunt *
US 1957–60 155 × 25m bw
Ziv

An ex-navy frogman hires himself out for underwater adventure.

Simple, well-made, popular show. The wonder is how they managed to find 155 underwater stories.

Lloyd Bridges

Sea Lab 2020 (US 1972). 13 22-minute episodes of inept animation from Hanna–Barbera, about an underwater colony of the future.

The Sea of Faith **
GB 1984 6 × 50m
BBC (Peter Armstrong)

Don Cupitt, Cambridge don and collar-and-tie churchman, charts the blows to blind faith in God which science and history have dealt since the Middle Ages, but ends up by finding that God is alive and well within each human conscience. Fashionably opulent in its locations but austere in its argument, the series was followed by a discussion, *Christianity in Charge*, in which Cupitt defended his thesis with the sureness of a snooker champ clearing the table. PP

Sea Song
GB 1974 78m colour TVM
Thames (Peter Hammond)

A young tycoon on a single-handed ocean race discovers a stowaway in the shape of an attractive journalist.

A quite agreeable comedy adventure which doesn't add up to much but looks good while it's on.

w Guy Slater *d* Peter Hammond

Tom Bell, Kika Markham

Sea Tales (GB 1979–80). Two short series of low-budget film dramatizations from BBC West, relying a lot on voice-over narration, but sometimes quite effective. Developed from similar *Country Tales* and followed by some spooky yarns culled from local viewers' letters. PP

Seapower
GB 1981 7 × 30m colour

History of same in a BBC series by Admiral of the Fleet Lord Hill-Norton, an unexpected personality with a line in smiles nearly as wide as his hat and a trick of diving down one hatch in full uniform and reappearing up the next in his woolly. I observed at the time: 'Meanwhile one learns much. The battleship used to be the back-bun of the Naveh, if no more. On the surface the captain of a submarine can't see very fah. On the other hand, the vessel is itself vulnerable to gun fah. Seapah takes many forms. The archive film is often remarkable and the enthusiasm catching.' PP

Search
US 1972 24 × 50m colour
NBC/Warner/Leslie Stevens

World Securities has agents primed for international protection of the wealthy.

A poor variation on a much zippier pilot called *Probe*. The fact that each star was seen every third week didn't help.

Hugh O'Brian, Doug McClure, Tony Franciosa, Angel Tompkins

The Search for Alexander the Great
US 1981 4 × 50m colour
KCET/Time Life/Video Arts (Michael Peacock, Haidee Granger)

Contemporaries of Alexander the Great explain his brief life.

Pleasantly filmed in Greece, but condescendingly structured, this is education for the subnormal.

w George Lefferts, Simon Raven *d* Peter Sykes *ph* Peter Jessop *m* Robert Sharples

Nicholas Clay, Jane Lapotaire, Robert Stephens, Julian Glover, Ian Charleson, Michael Williams, James Mason (narrator)

Search for the Gods *
US 1975 100m colour TVM
ABC/Warner/Douglas S. Cramer

A rare medallion sends three adventurers seeking evidence of ancient visitors to earth. Overstretched action hokum with pleasing moments.

w Herman Miller, Ken Pettus *d* Jud Taylor

Kurt Russell, Stephen McHattie, Ralph Bellamy, Victoria Racimo, Raymond St Jacques

The Search for the Nile **
GB 1971 6 × 60m colour (16mm)
BBC/Time–Life (CHARLES RALLING)

Dramatized historical documentaries of a very high standard, showing how explorers traced the source of the Nile.

w DEREK MARLOWE, MICHAEL HASTINGS

Kenneth Haigh, John Quentin, Norman Rossington, Michael Gough

Search for Tomorrow. American soap opera, on CBS since 1951. Small-town goings-on starring Mary Stuart, Larry Haines, Carl Low.

Searchlight. Hard-hitting British documentary series created for Granada by Tim Hewat in the fifties before *World in Action* took over.

Seasons of the Year
GB 1971 6 × 50m colour
Granada (Peter Potter)

Six plays set in the same country house over a period of a century and a half – an idea to be used again in *The House on the Hill* ten years later. These, written by Anthony Skene, seemed to be pastiches of Victorian and Edwardian styles.

d Richard Everitt (4), David Reid, Brian Parker. PP

Seaway *
Canada 1965 30 × 50m bw (2 colour)
ASP/CBS/ATV

Special police guard the St Lawrence seaway. An efficient, well-made series which somehow didn't excite.

Stephen Young, Austin Willis

Secombe, Sir Harry (1921–). Heavyweight Welsh singer who gave up an operatic career to be a comedian and court jester. After *The Goons*, his contributions to TV have mainly been specials.

Second Chance
US 1971 74m colour TVM
Metromedia
A stockbroker buys a Nevada ghost town and decks it out as a new community for people like himself.
Sluggish comedy drama.
w Michael Morris *d* Peter Tewkesbury
Brian Keith, Elizabeth Ashley, Juliet Prowse, Rosie Greer, Pat Carroll, William Windom

Second Chance
GB 1981 6 × 50m colour
YTV (Keith Richardson/David Cunliffe)
Susannah York and Ralph Bates facing up to divorce in the Our Story tradition of taking a familiar bad patch in middle-class lives and exploring it with an honesty and effectiveness above the normal level of soap opera. Written by Adele Rose. Directed by Gerry Mill and Richard Handford.   PP

LH: 'Nothing at all new, but a cinch for what *Variety* calls the femme audience.'

Second City Firsts. Not so much an umbrella as a swordstick title, guaranteed to drive innocents away from what were in fact two or three seasons of half-hour plays from new writers, commissioned and produced by David Rose, Tara Prem and Barry Hanson when Rose (ex *Z-Cars*) was posted to Birmingham (England's second city) to inaugurate a programme of drama from the new Pebble Mill studios. *Centre Play*, because Pebble Mill was officially a network production centre and Birmingham is in the centre of the country, was another bum designation.   PP

The Second Family Tree
US 1982 96m colour TVM
ABC/Comworld (Carroll Newman)
When divorced people marry, their families don't get on at once.
Would-be primetime soap opera which lasted only four 'one hours' after the pilot.
Anne Archer, Frank Converse

The Second Hundred Years
US 1967 26 × 25m colour
ABC/Columbia
A prospector is thawed out after 70 years in an Alaskan glacier, and finds himself a military secret.
Goofy comedy which proved too complicated despite enthusiasm all round.
Monte Markham, Arthur O'Connell, Frank Maxwell

Second Sight: a Love Story
US 1984 96m colour TVM
CBS/TTC/Entheos Unlimited (William Watkins)
A blind girl becomes bitter and disagreeable, what with falling in love, training a dog, and fearing an operation.
Muddled drama with no central thrust. The dog is the most likeable character.
w Dennis Turner, *book Emma and I* by Sheila Hicken *d* John Korty *ph* James M. Glennon *m* Dana Kaproff
Elizabeth Montgomery, Barry Newman, Nicholas Pryor, Michael Horton

Secret Agent: see Danger Man

Secret Army (GB 1979–81; 39 approx. × 50m; colour). The Belgian resistance organizes the escape of Allied agents, shot-down airmen and escaped PoWs during World War II. With Bernard Hepton masterminding operations from the cover of a black market restaurant catering for the occupiers and Clifford Rose as his Gestapo adversary, later featured in a follow-up series *Kessler*. Effective period series on well-worn theme created by Gerard Glaister and John Brason; for BBC.   PP

The Secret Country (GB 1985; 60m). John Pilger turns his baleful glare on his Australian homeland and its 'secret history' of oppressing if not quite exterminating the aboriginal population. Latter-day bomb tests and greedy mine-operators also come in for pilging, but there's better news on the civil rights front. An early if unfestive runner-up to the 1988 Australian Bicentenary, produced and directed by Alan Lowery, for Central.   PP

The Secret Diary of Adrian Mole, Aged 13¾ *
GB 1985 13 × 50m
Thames (Peter Sasdy)
The aspirations, ordeals and awful knowingness of adolescence as suffered by

Sue Townsend's gangling schoolboy, a paperback and radio institution long before coming to TV. Feckless Mum (Julie Walters) is separated from ineffectual Dad (Stephen Moore). Adored-one Pandora is infected with silly attitudes. In fact the whole rich cast of friends, relations and enemies could have been distilled from radio phone-ins and torn-up pages of *TV Times*. As Adrian, Gian Sammarco moves through it all with bespectacled solemnity.

w Sue Townsend d Peter Sasdy   PP

Secret Hospital ** (GB 1979). Celebrated one-hour documentary from Yorkshire TV, exposing horrifying conditions at Rampton Mental Hospital.

The Secret Life of John Chapman
US 1977 74m colour TVM
CBS/Paramount/Jozak (Gerald W. Abrams)

A respected college president decides to work as a common labourer.
Unconvincing story of a seeker after truth. Rather boring, too.

w John R. Coleman, from his novel *Blue Collar Journal* d David Lowell Rich

Ralph Waite, Susan Anspach, Elayne Heilveil, Brad Davis, Pat Hingle

The Secret Lives of Waldo Kitty *
US 1975 17 × 22m colour
Filmation

When his lady friend is threatened by a bulldog, a tomcat has dreams of being a hero. The derivation is obvious, the technique is slightly innovative, as the animals are real until the fantasy starts – in animation.

d Don Christensen *animation director* Rudy Larriva

The Secret Night Caller *
US 1975 74m colour TVM
Charles Fries/Penthouse

An otherwise respectable man has a compulsion to make obscene phone calls . . . Fairly interesting psycho-drama.

w Robert Presnell Jnr d Jerry Jameson

Robert Reed, Hope Lange, Michael Constantine, Sylvia Sidney, Elaine Giftos

Secret Orchards *
GB 1980 104m colour TVM
Granada (James Brabazon)

The true story of a millionaire banana importer, Roger Ackerley, who in the twenties had a bigamous second family. Obscurely narrated family saga which, told

with more style and polish, might have had a lot going for it.

w William Trevor, *books* J. R. Ackerley and Diana Petre d Richard Loncraine

FREDDIE JONES, Judy Parfitt, Joseph Blatchley

PP: 'I thought it a remarkable, precarious performance by Freddie Jones. But see below.'

† Roger Ackerley's son, J. R. Ackerley, played here by Joseph Blatchley, was also the subject of a BBC *Omnibus* film *We Think the World of You* three months later in which as an older man he came to terms with the homosexuality he had tried to confess to his father in the earlier film. This was written by Tristram Powell and Paul Bailey, directed by Powell and had Benjamin Whitrow as J.R. As I said at the time: 'In these two utterly disparate productions, one classed as a play, the other as an arts documentary, you could see all that is true and fine and gently stated in British television still thriving in 1980.'

The Secret Servant (GB 1984; 3 × 50m). SAS officer detailed to safeguard British spokesman at arms limitations conference runs up against Cold War mysteries. A Gavin Lyall thriller dramatized by Brian Clemens, with Charles Dance and Dan O'Herlihy, it was – unusually for BBC1 – stripped over three consecutive evenings. PP

The Secret War **
GB 1977 6 × 30m colour
BBC (Brian Johnson)

Fascinating history of secret weapons and weapon research on both sides during World War II, expanded from a single programme 15 years earlier. My 1977 review: 'On its chosen ground informative and extraordinarily thorough. They re-enacted the disarming of the magnetic mine the other week, using the actual mine. Here, every stage in the Messerschmitt Gigant's career from beginnings as a glider to Valhalla as six-engined power plane had been caught on newsfilm.'   PP

The Secret War of Jackie's Girls
US 1980 96m colour TVM
NBC/Universal/Penthouse/Public Arts (Dorothy J. Bailey)

Exploits of American lady fliers in Britain in 1940.
Curious blend of comedy and action melodrama, now lacking the propaganda motive which might once have sustained it.

w Theodore Jonas, D. Guthrie d Gordon Hessler *ph* William Cronjager *m* Fred Karlin

JENNY SEAGROVE sets out to conquer America in *A Woman of Substance* before turning into Deborah Kerr. The show won Channel 4 its highest drama rating to date when it was screened in Great Britain in 1985.

Mariette Hartley, Lee Purcell, Dee Wallace, Tracy Brooks Swope, Caroline Smith, Ann Dusenberry, Ben Murphy

'First requirement of suspension-of-disbelief forms of entertainment is to establish a basis in fact; no such observation is in evidence here.' – *Daily Variety*

Secret Weapons

US 1985 96m colour TVM
NBC/ITC/Goodman–Rosen (Judith A. Polone)

Young Russian girls are trained by the KGB to spy on American businessmen in Moscow. Over-the-top spy melodrama which rapidly loses interest.

w Thomas Baum, Sandor Stern *d* Don Taylor *ph* Richard Ciupka *m* Charles Bernstein

Sally Kellerman, Linda Hamilton, Hunt Block, Viveca Lindfors, Geena Davis, Barrie Ingham, James Franciscus

'Should be a miniseries – it's too hard to take in one sitting.' – *Daily Variety*

Secrets

US 1977 96m colour TVM
Paramount/Jozak (Gerald W. Abrams)

A woman who has always done exactly as she pleased finds herself unsatisfied. Woman's magazine stuff, adequately presented.

w Joanne Crawford *d* Paul Wendkos

Susan Blakely, Roy Thinnes, Joanne Linville, John Randolph

Secrets (GB 1983; 90m). Adolescent uncertainties at a girls' boarding school further confused by the pupil who brings back her late father's Masonic kit. Though qualifying as a *First Love* only on a sophistry (a suspected but in fact non-existent romance), Noella Smith's little non-plot has freshness and originality. With Anna Campbell Jones; directed by Gavin Millar, produced by David Puttnam, for C4.   PP

† Also the title of a 1983 *Storyboard* (Thames) pilot by Robert Muller about a security investigator, with John Castle and Barbara Kellerman.

Secrets of a Married Man

US 1984 96m colour TVM
NBC/ITC (R. W. Goodwin)

In wandering from the domestic path, an aircraft engineer finds himself in a bushel of trouble.

The Road to Ruin, Hollywood style. Of no absorbing interest.

w Dennis Nemec *d* William A. Graham *ph* Robert Steadman *m* Mark Snow

William Shatner, Cybill Shepherd, Michelle Phillips, Glynn Turman

'In showing the wages of sin, the writer stands by that old tradition: be sure to show the sin.' – *Daily Variety*

Secrets of a Mother and Daughter

US 1983 96m colour TVM
CBS/Stan Shpetner

A widow finds romance with a restaurant owner while her daughter separates from her husband and lands up with the same man. Tedious and shallow chunk of soap opera.

w Laurian Leggett *d* Gabrielle Beaumont *ph* Frank Stanley *m* John Rubinstein

Katharine Ross, Linda Hamilton, Michael Nouri, Bibi Besch

'It's tough to work up much compassion for creatures as wasteful as these two.' – *Daily Variety*

The Secrets of Midland Heights
US 1980 10 × 50m colour
CBS/Lorimar (Joseph Wallenstein)

The inhabitants of a college town spend more time on sex and intrigue than on learning.

Curious, fated attempt to do a teenage *Dallas* with a warmed-over script and a second team of actors.

w David Jacobs

Bibi Besch, Robert Hogan, Jordan Christopher, Mark Pinter, Lorenzo Lamas, Doran Clark, Martha Scott

'All it proves is that sludge can be ladled out as effortlessly as gravy.' – *Daily Variety*

'He gave every woman a reason to kill him. Finally, someone did!'
Secrets of Three Hungry Wives
US 1978 96m colour TVM
NBC/Penthouse/Cine Guarantors

Which of three traduced women murdered the sadistic millionaire bachelor?

Exploitation piece which dwindles into a murder mystery and will entertain most people whether or not they admit it.

w Jo Heims *d* Gordon Hessler *ph* William Cronjager *m* John Parker

Jessica Walter, Gretchen Corbett, Heather MacRae, James Franciscus, Eve Plumb, Craig Stevens, Raymond St Jacques

'Weaves a fine spell . . . slick and involving.' – *Daily Variety*

Sedaka, Neil (1939–   ). American pop rock star, on TV in occasional concert appearances.

Seduced
US 1985 96m colour TVM
CBS/Catalina/Comworld (Franklin R. Levy)

A state's attorney explores the mystery death of a millionaire who was married to his ex-girlfriend.

Fairly intriguing melodrama which dissipates itself in a romantic trip to the Virgin Islands, then recovers for an ironic finale.

w Charles Robert Carner *d* Jerrold Freedman *ph* Tak Fujimoto *m* Patrick Williams

Cybill Shepherd, Gregory Harrison, Jose Ferrer, Michael C. Gwynne, Ray Wise, Paul Stewart, Jordan Christopher, Mel Ferrer

'It struggles along to make its points, but they aren't worth the time.' – *Daily Variety*

The Seduction of Gina
US 1984 96m colour TVM
CBS/Bertinelli–Jaffe (Jack Grossbart)

The 20-year-old wife of a medical intern becomes addicted to gambling.

Nothing new in that. A film with little development and almost no interest.

w Judith Parker *d* Jerrold Freedman *ph* Tak Fujimoto *m* Thomas newman

Valerie Bertinelli, Michael Brandon, Frederic Lehne, Ed Lauter, John Harkins

The Seduction of Miss Leona
US 1980 96m colour TVM
CBS/Edgar J. Scherick

A frustrated lady professor lets her inhibitions go and chases two married men at the same time.

Not a farce but a heavy psychological study, though the publicity describes it as a romantic comedy. Marks for trying, but it's really as confused as all this suggests.

w Don Wakefield, *novel Bliss* by Elizabeth Gundy *d* Joseph Hardy *ph* Richard L. Rawlings *m* Robert Prince

Lynn Redgrave, Anthony Zerbe, Brian Dennehy, Conchata Ferrell, Elizabeth Cheshire

See How She Runs *
US 1978 96m colour TVM
CLN (George Englund)

A 40-year-old teacher, downtrodden by her family, decides to do something for herself – become a long-distance runner.

A telefilm of some quality which could nevertheless have been compressed into a single hour. It exhausts its welcome before half-time.

w Marvin A. Gluck *d* Richard Heffron *ph* Ron Lantore *m* Jimmy Haskell

Joanne Woodward, John Considine, Barnard Hughes, Lissy Newman

See How They Run *
US 1975 100m colour TVM
Universal (Jack Laird)

The children of a spy are menaced by neo-Nazis and helped by a G-man.

Lively chase adventure with good use of New York locations.

w Michael Blankfort *d* David Lowell Rich

John Forsythe, Senta Berger, Franchot Tone, Jane Wyatt, Leslie Nielsen

See It Now ****. CBS half-hour document-ary series which handled controversial news matters, including the witch hunts of the fifties; it is credited with starting the downfall of McCarthy. It ran from 1951 to 1958 and was created and produced by Fred W. Friendly and Edward R. Murrow; the latter also introduced it.

† The McCarthy exposé was transmitted 9 March 1954. Kinescopes were preserved. One was shown at a World TV Festival in London, 1963.

See the Man Run *
US 1971 73m colour TVM
Universal (Stan Shpetner)

An actor devises a means of easy money but finds himself in the middle of a kidnap plot. Ingenious suspenser which starts well and keeps its end up.

w Mann Rubin d Corey Allen

Robert Culp, Angie Dickinson, June Allyson, Eddie Albert, Charles Cioffi

'Sarah is single, pregnant, and about to give birth to another woman's child!'
The Seeding of Sarah Burns
US 1979 96m colour TVM
CBS/Michael Klein (Robert Papazian)

A girl offers to carry another woman's embryo, then finds that she doesn't want to give up the baby.
Well acted though rather obvious parable sustained by good presentation.

w/d Sandor Stern, story Marc Ray ph William Cronjager m John Mick

Kay Lenz, Martin Balsam, Cassie Yates, Charles Siebert, Cliff de Young

Seeds of Despair ** (GB 1984; 52m). Six months before the world woke up to the famine in Ethiopia, a year before the Live Aid concert, Charles Stewart's documentary gave warning of what was already beginning to happen, and what would certainly get worse if help were not sent. No one paid any attention.
Stewart broke off to shoot the above while in Africa making *Seeds of Hope* (GB 1985; 6 × 30m) focusing on the long-term programme to rectify the tree-felling and bad husbandry which had turned good land into desert.
Photographed and directed by Charles Stewart, sound by Malcolm Hirst. Produced by Richard Creasey, for Central with UN Environment program.   PP

THE SECRET DIARY OF ADRIAN MOLE. Having been successful as book, radio serial and stage play, the best seller about a pimply adolescent surprised nobody by topping the television ratings. Here is Gian Sammarco in the title role.

Seeger, Pete (1919–). American folk singer and composer, doyen of the current generation of balladeers.

The Seekers
US 1979 2 × 96m colour TVM
Operation Prime Time/Universal (Robert A. Cinader)

Jarod Kent becomes a Boston printer, with history happening all around him.
Second of the 'Kent chronicles' from the novels by John Jakes: *The Bastard* came first and *The Rebels* last, with *The Seekers* marginally the best, though the actors still seem only just introduced to their clothes. As Harry Cohn said, it's always unwise to make a movie in which the characters go out of the room backward.

w Steven Hayes d Sidney Hayers ph Vince Martinelli m Gerald Fried

Randolph Mantooth, Edie Adams, Neville Brand, Delta Burke, John Carradine, Rosey Grier, George Hamilton, Brian Keith, Ross Martin, Gary Merrill, Martin Milner, Vic Morrow, Hugh O'Brian, Robert Reed, Barbara Rush, Stuart Whitman

'Late 1700s in the US didn't miss a beat when it came to rape, whippings, white slavery, homosexuality, drunkenness, murder, syphilis, cruelty, enraged Indians and even cremation . . . folks sure had lots to do before TV. Well-known actors flip up in cameo roles like a deck of playing cards.' – *Daily Variety*

† Also the title of a 4-play cycle on the theme of man's need for God, 1964, by Ken Taylor (BBC).

Segal, George (1934–). American leading man, who after a career in movies began to look towards TV. *The Deadly Game*, *Trackdown*, *The Cold Room*, *The Zany Adventures of Robin Hood*, *Not My Kid*.

Seizure: The Story of Kathy Morris
US 1980 96m colour TVM
CBS/Jozak (Gerald I. Isenberg)

A pretty singer has a brain operation, and recovers.
Extremely graphic case history which shows more than most people will care to see. Uninspired treatment makes the whole enterprise seem ghoulish.

w Jack and Mary Willis with Robert Lewin, *book* Charles L. Mee Jnr *d* Gerald I. Isenberg *ph* Hector Figueroa *m* George Aliceson Tipton

Leonard Nimoy, Penelope Milford, Christopher Allport, Fredric Lehne, Linda G. Miller

'Anyone contemplating surgery will sure have a moment's hesitation.' – *Daily Variety*

Self, William (1921–). American producer and executive, head of Twentieth Century–Fox Television 1959–74.

Sellecca, Connie (1955–). American leading lady. *The Bermuda Depths*, *Flying High*, *She's Dressed To Kill*, *Captain America*, *Beyond Westworld*, *The Greatest American Hero*, *Hotel*, *International Airport*.

Selleck, Tom (1945–). Tall, commanding, humorous American leading man who after years of trying, notably in *The Sacketts* and *The Concrete Cowboys*, became an undoubted television star in MAGNUM PI.

semi-animation. General term for a number of processes which reduce cost by reducing the number of drawings necessary and producing a stylized but aesthetically unappealing effect: e.g. in conversation, the mouth will open and close repeatedly while the rest of the figure remains static.

Send in the Girls
GB 1978 7 × 50m colour (VTR)
Granada (June Wyndham-Davies)

Stories of girls on a sales promotion team.
Virtually an anthology of variable and highly resistible comedies and dramas.

Annie Ross, Anna Carteret, Diana Davies, Floella Benjamin

Senior Trip
US 1981 96m colour TVM
CBS/QM Productions/Kenneth Johnson (Daniel Kibbie)

Senior high school students from the midwest make their first trip to New York City.
Multi-story comedy-drama combining love and admission: one student even gets backstage at *Sugar Babies* and meets Mickey Rooney. The New York backgrounds are the best part.

w Ken Johnson, Dan Kibbie *d* Ken Johnson *ph* John McPherson *m* Joe Harnell

Scott Baio, Randy Brooks, Ralph Davies, Patti Kate Walsh, Jane Hoffman, Faye Grant, Liz Callaway

'All in all, it's a long visit.' – *Daily Variety*

Senior Year
US 1974 74m colour TVM
Universal

Family and college problems in 1955.
Inspired by *American Graffiti*, this became a tedious but brief series called *Sons and Daughters*.

w M. Charles Cohen *d* Richard Donner

Gary Frank, Glynnis O'Connor, Scott Columby, Barry Livingston

A Sense of Freedom *
GB 1981 104m colour TVM
STV/Jeremy Isaacs

The partial story of Jimmy Boyle, a convicted murderer who seemed to reform despite alleged brutalities in his prison treatment.
Unsympathetic treatment of a moderately true story which might have seemed more worth doing had one been sure where fact stops in this treatment and imagination

begins. As it is, nauseating detail and thick Glaswegian accents make it difficult to sit through.

w Peter MacDougall d John Mackenzie ph Chris Menges m Frankie Miller

David Hayman (as Boyle), Alex Norton, Fulton Mackay

PP: 'Unfortunately the film left as many questions about its own intentions hanging in the air, like its almost total preoccupation with brutality and violence while paying the most perfunctory – indeed, laughable – lip service to other essential processes going on inside Boyle.

A Sensitive, Passionate Man *
US 1977 96m colour TVM
NBC/Factor–Newland (Alan Jay Factor)

An aerospace scientist loses his job and takes to drink.
Polished restatement of a familiar theme.

w Rita Lakin, *novel* Barbara Mahoney d John Newland

David Janssen, Angie Dickinson, Todd Lookinland, Justin Randi, Rhodes Reason

Sentimental Agent
GB 1966 13 × 50m bw
ATV

An import–export agent finds himself rooting out criminals.
Flimsily-premised adventure series with a personable star.

Carlos Thompson, Clemence Bettany, John Turner

† The leading character first appeared in a segment of *Man of the World*.

'The child she always wanted does not want her!'
Sentimental Journey
US 1984 96m colour TVM
CBS/TCF/Lucille Ball/Smith–Richmond (Harry R. Sherman)

After a miscarriage, a lady producer on Broadway adopts a child, not entirely to the approval of her actor husband.
This has remarkably little to do with the old movie on which it is allegedly based, and on its own account seems to have no purpose.

w Darlene Craviotto, Frank Cavestani d James Goldstone ph Dick Kratina m Billy Goldenberg

Jaclyn Smith, David Dukes, Maureen Stapleton, Jessica Rene Carroll

'It gradually sinks into a tub of suds.' – *Daily Variety*

'Meet the oldest gun in the west . . . the nun and the madam who help him tame the town!'
September Gun
US 1983 96m colour TVM
CBS/QM Productions/BrademanSelf

An ageing gunfighter comes to the aid of a nun protecting Apache orphans.
Very slow and unsurprising western.

w William Norton d Don Taylor ph Gerald Perry Finnerman m Larry Gansler

Robert Preston, Patty Duke Astin, Geoffrey Lewis, Sally Kellerman, Christopher Lloyd

Sergeant Cork (GB 1963–4). Ted Willis thought up a series (for ATV) about a 19th-century Metropolitan police detective (played by John Barrie) some 15 years before Granada took up Peter Lovesey's *Cribb*. Unfortunately he and his writers never thought to research the gamey social and sporting undercurrents of Victorian life Lovesey draws on, and the result was usually a routine whodunit in fancy dress. PP

Sergeant Matlovich vs the US Air Force
US 1978 96m colour TVM
NBC/Tomorrow (Paul Leaf)

A sergeant in the Air Force is accused of homosexuality and expelled.
Overly restrained treatment of a court case that doesn't even end in victory for the oppressed. Daunting.

w John McGreevey d Paul Leaf ph Mario Tosi m Teo Macero

Brad Dourif, Marc Singer, Frank Converse, William Daniels, Stephen Elliott, Mitchell Ryan, David Spielberg

'A sluggish-moving, superficial drama which has little emotional impact.' – *Daily Variety*

Sergeant Preston of the Yukon
US 1955–7 78 × 25m bw
CBS/Wrather

A Mountie and his dog enforce law and order in the wilds.
Acceptable *Boy's Own Paper* stuff.
Richard Simmons

Sergeant Ryker
US 1963 85m colour TVM
Universal (Frank Telford)

In Korea, army lawyers prepare the trial of a sergeant accused of being a traitor.
Muddled courtroom drama which began life as two episodes of the anthology series *Crisis* and also served as pilot for a one-hour series *Counsellors at War*, also known as *Court Martial*.

w Seeleg Lester, William D. Gordon *d* Buzz Kulik

Lee Marvin, Bradford Dillman, Peter Graves, Vera Miles, Lloyd Nolan, Murray Hamilton, Norman Fell

Serle, Chris (1943–). Gangling British reporter whose height and dignity make him an ideal stool-pigeon reporter on *In at the Deep End*. Originally a radio producer, into TV via *That's Life!*. Serious TV includes *Greek Language and People*.   PP

❋ **Serling, Rod** (1924–75). American playwright who created TWILIGHT ZONE and its alter ego *Night Gallery*; also wrote in the mid-fifties such classic TV plays as PATTERNS, *The Rack*, REQUIEM FOR A HEAVYWEIGHT and *The Velvet Alley*.

The Serpent Son
GB 1979 3 × 75m colour
BBC (Richard Broke)

Much-mocked re-rendition of Greek tragedy (the Oresteia of Aeschylus) by Frederic Raphael and Kenneth McLeish, with outlandish costumes and too many friendly old character actors looking embarrassed at having to appear with bare flanks and painted faces to utter doom-laden sentiments. But Diana Rigg rose above it all with gusto as an enamelled, imperious Klytemnestra. Directed by Bill Hays.   PP

Serpico
aka: *The Deadly Game*
US 1976 98m colour TVM
NBC/Paramount/Emmet Lavery

A New York cop exposes corruption in the force: a true story which made a popular cinema film.

This is a TV remake/pilot, dour in mood and hard to follow: for New Yorkers who enjoy having their noses rubbed in the dirt.

w Robert Collins

David Birney, Tom Atkins

† The resulting series lasted half a season: 15 × 50m episodes.

Sesame Street ****. One-hour series aimed at underprivileged city children learning to read and write. Produced by JOAN GANZ COONEY through her Children's Television Workshop for PBS, it used every kind of cartoon and puppet trick, aped commercial techniques and brought in *Hellzapoppin*-type gags. By any standard superior TV and great entertainment for all ages, its Muppet

creatures, the brainchild of JIM HENSON, eventually had a successful series of their own. Hundreds of episodes were produced from 1969. Characters included Big Bird, Cookie Monster and Kermit T. Frog.

Sessions *
US 1983 96m colour TVM
NBC/Thorn EMI/Sarabanda (David Manson)

A call girl confesses all to her psychiatrist. Nicely made melodrama with an element of suspense.

w Barbara Turner *d* Richard Pearce *ph* Fred Murphy *m* Charles Gross

Veronica Hamel, Jeffrey DeMunn, Jill Eikenberry, David Marshall Grant

Sevareid, Eric (1912–). American news commentator, with CBS from 1939, and notable for his coverage of World War II in Europe.

Seven Brides for Seven Brothers
US 1982 74m colour TVM
CBS/MGM–UA/David Gerber (James M. Brown, Richard Fielder)

A rancher marries a waitress without telling her that back home he has six brothers for her to look after.

Listless, demusicalized version of a famous formula. The resultant 50m series became increasingly infantile, but ran to 22 episodes.

cr Marshall Herskovitz

Richard Dean Anderson, Terri Treas, Roger Wilson, Peter Horton

'The producers are dealing with folklore, but have opted to alter the fantasy-like charm of the movie by imposing realism that won't endure weekly exposure.' – *Hollywood Reporter*

Seven Days (GB since 1982). Channel 4's periodic religious series, produced for them by YTV, presented until 1984 by Michael Charlton and Helene Hayman, since then by Ann Loades and Robert Kee. Edited (since 1984) by Barbara Twigg, produced by Chris Jelley.   PP

† Also the title of a TVS regional current-affairs programme in the South of England.

Seven Days in the Life of Andrew Pelham
GB 1971 7 × 30m colour
BBC (Innes Lloyd)

Donald Sinden as an airline pilot who survived

SESAME STREET. Big Bird, one of the original characters, grew so popular that he was given his own 'specials'. Here he shares his bird seed with a real pigeon in New York's Central Park.

a crash in which many lives were lost and is now trying to survive the aftermath, both professionally and personally. Described as a cycle of playlets rather than a serial, it was an interesting format which deserved a less penny-pinching production. Created by Derek Hoddinot; written by Derek Hoddinot and Don Shaw; directed by Gilchrist Calder.

PP

Seven Deadly Sins *
GB 1966 7 × 52m bw
Rediffusion (Peter Willes)

Septet of single plays which teasingly refrained from identifying the sin under review until the final credits. *Seven Deadly Virtues* (1967) demonstrated still more teasingly how a particular boring virtue (thrift, modesty, etc) could lead to ends the opposite of those intended. Among writers rising to these pleasing briefs were Frank Marcus and Leo Lehman. PP

The Seven Deadly Sins (GB 1984). Brecht and Weill's ballet-with-songs (aka *Anna, Anna*) with Alessandra Ferri dancing one element of the heroine, Marie Angel singing the other, in a handsome Granada production designed by Roy Stonehouse, directed by Derek Bailey, produced by Steve Hawes. Straightforward BBC version with one Anna (Elise Ross), directed by Barrie Gavin, 1983. PP

The Seven Dials Mystery
GB 1981 140m approx. colour TVM
LWT (Jack Williams)

Following the murder of two foreign office officials, clues lead Lady Brent to a secret society in Soho.
One of Agatha Christie's most foolish novels is brought to the screen at too great a length and with insufficient attention to the kind of detail that makes people continue to watch. Small-part acting and the two country houses steal the show.

w Pat Sandys *d* Tony Wharmby *m* Joseph Horovitz

Cheryl Campbell, James Warwick, Harry Andrews, John Gielgud, Terence Alexander, Lucy Guttridge, Rula Lenska, Leslie Sands, Brian Wilde, Joyce Redman

Seven Faces of Jim * (GB 1962–3; 7 × 30m). As the title suggests, series of disparate larks for Jimmy Edwards written by Galton and Simpson for BBC and including a first visualization of the Glums, from radio's *Take It From Here*, as pursued 15 years later by LWT. Followed by *More Faces of Jim*. PP

Seven in Darkness
US 1969 74m colour TVM
Paramount

A chartered plane crashes in a mountainous region, and all the survivors are blind.
For connoisseurs of unlikely situations.

w John W. Bloch, *novel Against Heaven's Hand* by Leonard Bishop *d* Michael Caffey

Milton Berle, Dina Merrill, Sean Garrison, Arthur O'Connell, Alejandro Rey, Lesley Ann Warren

Seven Up. A Granada documentary of 1963 which selected seven children from various backgrounds and analysed their chances. At the appropriate times further programmes were made under the titles *Seven Plus Seven*, *Twenty One* and *Twenty Eight Up*, showing whether or not the children had achieved their ambitions. Michael Apted was researcher on the first programme and director of the others.

Seventh Avenue *
US 1977 3 × 96m colour
NBC/Universal (Franklin Barton, Richard Irving)

A young Jew makes it big, but loses his integrity, in New York's garment district in the thirties and forties.
One of the best of the early *Best Sellers* (it came fourth), but not the most popular.

w Lawrence Heath, *novel* Norman Bogner *d* Richard Irving

Steven Keats, Dori Brenner, Kristoffer Tabori, Jane Seymour, Alan King, Anne Archer, Eli Wallach, Jack Gilford

79 Park Avenue
US 1977 3 × 93m colour
MCA/Universal

The progress of a young New York whore and her involvement in a sensational murder case. Dismally made backlot epic; the tawdry look suits its subject.

w Richard de Roy, *novel* Harold Robbins *d* Paul Wendkos

Lesley Ann Warren, Raymond Burr, Polly Bergen, Michael Constantine, Peter Marshall, Albert Salmi, Marc Singer, Jack Weston

77 Sunset Strip *
US 1958–63 205 × 50m bw
ABC/Warner

A firm of private eyes operates from offices on Sunset Strip.
Long-running crime and glamour series which seems tatty now but hit the spot at the time.

m Mack David and Jerry Livingston
Efrem Zimbalist Jnr, Roger Smith, Edd Byrnes, Louis Quinn

'Like most Warner TV films, they abound with corner-cutting, uninspired direction and distressing scripts.' – Don Miller

77th Bengal Lancers

aka: *Tales of the 77th Bengal Lancers*
US 1956 26 × 50m bw
Columbia/Herbert B. Leonard

Stiff-upper-lip capers in turn-of-the-century India.
Not too bad apart from the Yank accents.

Phil Carey, Warren Stevens

Seville, David (1919–72) (Ross Bag-dasarian). American music executive who created the singing Chipmunks by speeding up three taped tracks of his own voice. A cartoon series, *Alvin and the Chipmunks*, followed.

Sex and the Married Woman

US 1978 96m colour TVM
Universal/NBC (George J. Santoro, Jack Arnold)

An authoress becomes famous when she publishes a dissertation on the sexual mores of 50 American women, but her own marriage founders.
Obvious marital comedy, sloppily constructed and very padded out, but with a few good lines.

w Michael Norell *d* Jack Arnold

Joanna Pettet, Barry Newman, Keenan Wynn, Dick Gautier, Fannie Flagg, Nita Talbot, Jayne Meadows

Sex and the Single Parent

US 1979 96m colour TVM
CBS/Time–Life (Stanley Kallis, Freyda Rothstein)

A man whose wife has left him meets a woman whose husband has left her – with three small daughters.
A would-be bright modern comedy which gets nowhere, especially when it gets serious.

w Sue Grafton, *book* Jane Adams *d* Jackie Cooper *ph* Bill Jurgensen *m* Fred Karlin

Susan Saint James, Mike Farrell, Dori Brenner, Warren Berlinger, Natasha Ryan, Katy Kurtzman

The Sex Symbol

US 1974 98m or 110m colour TVM
Columbia/Douglas S. Cramer

The private life of a Hollywood glamour queen.

Obsessively silly exposé obviously patterned after Marilyn Monroe.

w Alvah Bessie, from his novel *The Symbol d* David Lowell Rich *ph* J. J. Jones *m* Jeff Alexander

Connie Stevens, Shelley Winters, Don Murray, William Smith, James Olson, Nehemiah Persoff, Jack Carter

The Sextet *

GB 1972 8 × 50m colour (VTR)
BBC (Roderick Graham)

An attempt to create a TV repertory company. The actors were excellent but some of the dramas rather less.

Michele Dotrice, Ruth Dunning, Denholm Elliott, Richard Vernon, Dennis Waterman, Billie Whitelaw

Seymour, Gerald (1941–). British reporter and newsreader, with ITN from 1963 until he withdrew to concentrate on his thrillers, two of which have been turned into YTV blockbusters – *Harry's Game*, 1982, and the less successful *The Glory Boys*, 1984. PP

Seymour, Jane (1951–). British leading lady in Hollywood, who made a breakthrough as the evil heroine in *East of Eden*. Also in *Dallas Cowboy Cheerleaders, Captains and the Kings, The Four Feathers, The Scarlet Pimpernel, The Haunting Passion, Dark Mirror, The Sun Also Rises, Obsessed with a Married Woman, Jamaica Inn.*

Sez Les. Les Dawson's often very funny YTV show, originated by John Duncan in 1969 and running until 1976, a total of 51 editions plus four specials and six called *Les Sez* instead. PP

SFTA. The Society of Film and Television Arts, a British institution now combined with the British Film Academy in BAFTA, the British Academy of Film and Television Arts.

Shackleton ***

GB 1983 4 × 60m
BBC (John Harris) with Seven Channel, Australia

Efficient, handsome adventure–history of Scott's great rival for the South Pole – before Amundsen intruded, that is – realized to the same master plan as the same team's *Voyage of Charles Darwin* (1978). Hire a bunch of good young actors not yet expensive or impatient enough to mind spending weeks at sea, invest the rest of the budget in a working lookalike boat, and leave it to God to paint the scenery. 'An outdoor epic,' I wrote in *Stills* magazine, 'which at the same time draws continually on the intimacy television likes.'

w Christopher Ralling   *d* Martyn Friend
ph David Waitson   *m* Francis Shaw

David Schofield (as Shackleton), David Rodigan, Anthony Bate   PP

Shades of Darkness (GB 1983; 7 × 50m). Low-key hauntings from various published sources, few of them, alas, done well enough to impart a shiver. The most reliable frisson came from the opening titles against sinister rolling clouds. Produced by June Wyndham-Davis, for Granada.   PP

† Two more followed in 1986.

Shades of Greene *
GB 1975 13 × 50m colour (VTR)
Thames (Alan Cooke)

A very careful, but not entirely successful, attempt to dramatize Graham Greene's short stories, some of which defy TV interpretation. Top names, including Paul Scofield and John Gielgud, were employed, and sometimes there was more than one story to the hour. The entire enterprise was caviare to the general.

'The lighter side of dying!'
The Shadow Box **
US 1980 96m colour TVM
ABC/Shadow Box Film Co (Jill Marti,
   Susan Kendall Newman)

The last days of three people in a terminal hospice.
A clinical job of direction and acting – for those who can take it. The fact that there are comic elements tends to make it more harrowing.

w Michael Cristofer   *d* PAUL NEWMAN   *ph* Adam Holender   *m* Henry Mancini

CHRISTOPHER PLUMMER, Sylvia Sidney, James Broderick, Joanne Woodward, Melinda Dillon, Valerie Harper, Ben Masters, Curtiss Marlowe, John Considine

Shadow Chasers
US 1985 1 × 96m, 6 × 50m colour
ABC/Warner/Kenneth Johnson/Brian
   Grazer (Craig Schiller)

Two young psychic investigators combat malevolent spirits.
Shameless rip-off of *Ghost Busters*, which in itself was very nearly not a success. This lamebrain copy, with its hysterical characters and witless scripts, would not even make the pages of a penny comic.

cr Kenneth Johnson

Trevor Eve, Dennis Dugan, Nina Foch

Shadow in the Street *
US 1975 74m colour TVM
NBC/Playboy (Edward L. Rissien)

A tough ex-convict becomes a parole agent. Routine socially conscious melodrama, well put together.

w John D. F. Black   *d* Richard Donner

Tony Lo Bianco, Sheree North, Dana Andrews, Ed Lauter, Jesse Welles

The Shadow Line (GB/Poland 1976). Joseph Conrad's autobiographical story of a young seaman crossing the 'shadow line' from youth to manhood during a becalmed voyage in the East Indies, dramatized by Boleslaw Sulik and opulently filmed by ANDREZJ WAJDA but never quite impressing what they had co-produced. My reaction at the time: 'How did a play come to be sailing under documentary colours, especially when it was neither, but a feature film all the time? Despite a clever performance (and the best voice, with those pure round o-sounds) by Marek Kondrat, it remained a noble endeavour rather than a night to remember.'   PP

Shadow of the Cloak (US 1951). Half-hour espionage series for Dumont with Helmut Dantine as a master agent.

Shadow on the Land
US 1968 96m colour TVM
NBC/Columbia (Matthew Rapf)

A secret underground force battles a totalitarian American state.
Not a bad entry in the Awful Warning category, except that everybody shouts too much.

w Nedrick Young   *d* Richard Sarafian   *ph* Fred Koenekamp   *m* Sol Kaplan

Jackie Cooper, John Forsythe, Gene Hackman, Carol Lynley, Marc Strange, Janice Rule

Shadow over Elveron *
US 1968 100m colour TVM
Universal (Jack Laird)

An evil midwestern sheriff commits murder and is unmasked by the new young doctor. Heavy melodrama on familiar lines, with the cinema films *Hot Spot* and *The Tattered Dress* for models.

w Chester Krumholz, *novel* Michael Kingsley   *d* James Goldstone

Leslie Nielsen, James Franciscus, Shirley Knight, Franchot Tone, James Dunn, Don Ameche

'Brothers at home, enemies on the battlefield ... fighting together to save the women they love!'

The Shadow Riders
US 1982 96m colour TVM
CBS/Columbia/Pegasus (Hugh Benson)

After the Civil War, the Traven family tries to reassemble itself.

Extremely desultory western which offers sporadic excitement but never builds up any suspense.

w Jim Byrnes, *novel* by Louis l'Amour
d Andrew V. McLaglen *ph* Jack Whitman
m Jerrold Immel

Tom Selleck, Sam Elliott, Ben Johnson, Geoffrey Lewis, Jeffrey Osterhage, Gene Evans, Katharine Ross, R. G. Armstrong, Jane Greer, Harry Carey Jnr

'Spinning its wagon wheels, telefilm is long on promise, short on fulfilment.' – *Daily Variety*

Shadow Squad. An early (1957) half-hour British tape series from Associated Rediffusion about a couple of private eyes; with Peter Williams and Rex Garner.

Shadowlands ** (GB 1985; 90m). The tragic love affair and bereavement of the Oxford don and children's book author C. S. Lewis, elevated by a touching performance from Joss Ackland as Lewis. With Claire Bloom; written by William Nicholson, directed by Norman Stone, produced by David M. Thompson, for BBC Wales/*Everyman*. BAFTA Awards: best play and best actress (Bloom), 1986.   PP
† The original transmission of this film was also the occasion of a fierce critical attack on competitive scheduling. All four British channels were showing items likely to appeal to the same section of the audience: *Shadowlands* on BBC1, *The Death of the Heart* on ITV, *The Mysteries* (medieval church plays brought to life by the National Theatre) on C4 and the movie *The French Lieutenant's Woman* on BBC2.

Shadows on Our Skin *** (GB 1980). A BBC *Play for Today*, written by Derek Mahon, from the novel by Jennifer Johnston; directed by Jim O'Brien; produced by Kenith Trodd. A beautifully unstressed parable of life and conflicting loyalties in Northern Ireland as experienced by an 11-year-old in the Catholic Bogside of Londonderry. Played by local schoolboy, Macrae Clark, with tow hair, angel face, upper lip stubbornly enfolding lower and a little gruff, blurting-out voice, he scuffed his way past the barricades or idly noted the army patrol as if both were part of the firmament.
PP

Shaft *
US 1974 7 × 74m colour
CBS/MGM

A toned-down televersion of the film series about a black private eye. Skilfully made, but addicts seemed to miss the violence.

Richard Roundtree

Shaka Zulu
US 1986 10 × 50m colour miniseries
Harmony Gold/South African Television
(Ed Harper)

The story of a king of the Zulu nation who in the 19th century confronted the white invaders.

Extravagant, sincere but rather dogged historical melodrama in which the white folk get only an occasional look-in.

w Joshua Sinclair *d* William C. Faure
ph Alec Mills *m* David Polecutt

Henry Cele, Dudu Mkize, Edward Fox, Robert Powell, Fiona Fullerton, Trevor Howard, Christopher Lee, Gordon Jackson, Erica Rogers, Roy Dotrice, John Carson

Shakespeare. The Old Vic production of *Macbeth* with Laurence Olivier, hired lock, stock and barrel for £75, and a modern-dress version of *Julius Caesar* were among offerings from the BBC's infant television service 1936–9. Since then every play in the canon has been performed at least once and the old favourites several times, but not until 1978 did the BBC systematically tackle the complete works. The aim of providing a uniform visual edition of Shakespeare was unfortunately lost in a welter of different styles, so that even under Cedric Messina, originator of the series, one production would be starkly confined to the studio while the next was shot on location with picture postcard realism. Jonathan Miller, taking over after two years, added a further idiom by arbitrarily choosing an artist or artistic period to determine the look of the show – Dutch interiors for *The Merchant* and a splendid *Taming of the Shrew* with John Cleese, Veronese for *Antony and Cleopatra*. Individually, however, there were palpable hits. Shaun Sutton succeeded Miller for the last two years of the project.

Earlier BBC groupings include the 1960 serialization of the histories as *An Age of Kings*, a later and less imaginative version of the same cycle from the RSC's *Wars of the Roses*, and a sequence of the Roman plays under the title *The Spread of the Eagle*. *Will Shakespeare* (1978), John Mortimer's bio-series for ATV, with the playwright played by Tim Curry, was not wholly unsuccessful, but offering considerably more insight into

Shakespeare's genius were two acting seminars given by RSC actors in *The South Bank Show* (LWT) in 1979.

Play-by-play top thirty (director's name in brackets)

Love's Labour's Lost
BBC SHAKESPEARE (ELIJAH MOSHINSKY), 1985 with Maureen Lipman as a thweetly lithping Printheth of Franthe.

Midsummer Night's Dream
1. REDIFFUSION (JOAN KEMP-WELCH), 1964, with translucent cobwebby forest by Michael Yates, pointed ears for Oberon, Benny Hill as Bottom.
2. CBS (PETER HALL), 1969 filmed at Compton Wynyates with Judi Dench leading a corps of fairies pleasingly dressed in green paint.
3. BBC SHAKESPEARE (ELIJAH MOSHINSKY), 1981 with Helen Mirren, Peter McEnery, Brian Glover and a studio pond.

Romeo and Juliet
None so far worth singling out. But an interesting modernization from TV Globo, Brazil, *Romeo y Julieta* (Paulo Alfonso, Grisolli) turned up on C4, 1983, with R & J as students in the baroque city of Ouro Preto.

Titus Andronicus
BBC SHAKESPEARE (JANE HOWELL), 1985, with Trevor Peacock a bowed, beat-up Titus, Eileen Atkins as Tamora and a superb Aaron from Hugh Quarshie.

Richard II
BBC SHAKESPEARE (David Giles), 1978, with Derek Jacobi, lots of good support, nasty studio setting.

Henry IV
BBC AN AGE OF KINGS (Peter Dews), 1960, episodes 3–6.

Henry V
Likewise, episodes 7–8, Robert Hardy as Hal throughout. A good one in the BBC SHAKESPEARE (David Giles) with David Gwillim, 1979. Or the OLIVIER movie, available on Rank Video 78000100.

Richard III
Hungarian Television, 1978, all in monochrome close-ups with an interesting, petulant Richard. Or the Olivier movie.

The Merchant of Venice
BBC PLAY OF THE MONTH (Cedric Messina), 1972, with Maggie Smith as Portia, Frank Finlay as Shylock. Olivier played Shylock for ATV (Jonathan Miller), 1974, in Edwardian togs, but neither this nor the BBC Shakespeare version (Jack Gold), 1980, come up to Messina's.

The Taming of the Shrew
BBC SHAKESPEARE (Jonathan Miller), 1980, with John Cleese as a commendably male chauvinist Petruchio and Sarah Badel as Katharine.

As You Like It
BBC SHAKESPEARE (Basil Coleman), 1978, location VTR'd at Glamis Castle, of all places, with Helen Mirren as Rosalind.

Twelfth Night
ATV (JOHN DEXTER), 1970, in a lush Italianate setting with Alec Guinness making Malvolio a Tudor chartered accountant who'd strayed into show business.

Julius Caesar
BBC (Dallas Bower), 1938, in Fascist uniforms must have been sensational but survives in very few memories now. Same idea, updated, in *Heil Caesar* (BBC, Ron Smedley, 1974). Best straightforward productions have been Stuart Burge's for BBC, 1959, with Eric Porter as Brutus, and ALAN BRIDGES's also for BBC, 1967, with Robert Stephens as a sleek sealion of an Antony, 'honking that wicked wanton speech to the mob until they turned on their self-appointed liberators'.

All's Well That Ends Well
BBC/RST (JOHN BARTON), 1968, with Clive Swift and Lynn Farleigh.

Hamlet
Paul Scofield was famously sung to rest not by flights of angels but the commercials in a commercial break prematurely terminating ATV's 1956 live production by Peter Brook. Richard Chamberlain for the same company, 1971, was boring, as – surprisingly – was Derek Jacobi in the BBC Shakespeare version, 1979. So it has to be either HAMLET AT ELSINORE (BBC, Philip Saville), 1964, or once again wait for the Olivier movie to come round.

Measure for Measure
BBC SHAKESPEARE (DESMOND DAVIS), 1979, with Kenneth Colley as the Duke, Kate Nelligan as Isabella and Tim Pigott-Smith as Angelo.

Othello
Settle for Verdi.

Macbeth
1. BBC/Old Vic (George More O'Ferrall), 1938.
2. THAMES/RST (TREVOR NUNN), 1979, bare of scenery, 'black curtained in a locational vacuum' (Sean Day-Lewis). Ian McKellen, Judi Dench.

The BBC SHAKESPEARE version (Jack Gold) was let down by Nicol Williamson's sheep-like mien and bleating voice in the part -- a sort of Ramsay Macbeth.

King Lear
ORSON WELLES in a live CBS production from New York (Peter Brook), 1953, surely qualifies. Michael Hordern played Lear twice in productions by Jonathan Miller, 1975 and 1982, the latter for the BBC SHAKESPEARE. But the plum must be OLIVIER's 1983 performance for Granada (MICHAEL ELLIOTT).

Antony and Cleopatra
1. BBC *Spread of the Eagle* (Peter Dews), 1962, episodes 7–9 with Mary Morris as an ageing Cleo, Keith Michell as a boy Antony.
2. ATV/RST (JON SCOFFIELD), 1974, with Janet Suzman, Richard Johnson.
3. BBC SHAKESPEARE (Jonathan Miller), 1981, with Jane Lapotaire, Colin Blakely, ambience modelled on Veronese.

Coriolanus
BBC SPREAD OF THE EAGLE (Peter Dews), 1962, episodes 1–3 with Robert Hardy, Beatrix Lehmann, Jerome Willis; and the BBC SHAKESPEARE (Elijah Moshinsky), 1984, with Alan Howard, Irene Worth, Mike Gwilym.

The Tempest
It's always Michael Hordern.

Pericles, Prince of Tyre
BBC SHAKESPEARE (David Jones), 1984, with Mike Gwilym and Juliet Stevenson.

The Winter's Tale
BBC SHAKESPEARE (Jane Howell), 1981, a stunning production with Jeremy Kemp as Leontes and everyone in fur hats.   PP

Shakespeare in Perspective (GB 1978–85; 37 × 15m). Introductions to each BBC Shakespeare production, broadcast on the preceding evening or afternoon. The speaker could be a scholar or a show-off, oft-times traipsing through a location thought appropriate. Jilly Cooper did *The Merry Wives of Windsor*, Clive James *Hamlet*, General Sir John Hackett *Coriolanus*.   PP

Shakespeare Lives (GB 1983; 6 × 30m). Tiresome seminars on the performance of Shakespearean roles, before a keen audience, conducted by theatre director Michael Bogdanov. Produced by Victor Glyn and Mike Ockrent, for Quintet Films/C4.   PP

Shakespeare or Bust (GB 1974). A further adventure for Peter Terson's trio of jolly miners first encountered in *The Fishing Party*. This time they had hired a canal holiday boat with the aim of reaching Stratford-upon-Avon and seeing a Shakespeare production. There were no seats left at the theatre but the two more cultural pilgrims were rewarded with a private performance by Richard Johnson and Janet Suzman of their *Antony and Cleo* listed above, while the third member fulfilled a rather more enviable ambition to go skinny-dipping in the Avon with a girl from another boat whose man-friend had conveniently turned out to be more interested in boys: a fairy-story all round. Produced by David Rose; for BBC (*Play for Today*).   PP

Shalit, Gene (1931–). Bushy-haired and opinionated American co-host of NBC's *Today*.

Shallcross, Alan (1932–). British drama producer who first listed himself as a 'panellist' on *Nationwide*, *At the Eleventh Hour*, etc. Recent producer credits: *The Last Evensong* and the *Star Quality* season of Coward plays, 1985; *The Russian Solder*, 1986.   PP

Shane *
US 1966 17 × 50m colour·
ABC/Paramount/Titus (Herb Brodkin)

TV series in the shadow of a famous cinema western about a frontier family.

David Carradine, Jill Ireland, Tom Tully

Shane, Paul (1940–). Stout British comedian who came to popularity with *Hi-De-Hi!* and burnished it in *Muck and Brass*.

Shannon
US 1961 36 × 25m bw
Columbia/Robert Sparks (Jerry Briskin)

Cases of an insurance investigator who covers ten states in a car laden with gimmicks. It seemed quite stylish at the time.

cr John Hawkins

George Nader, Regis Toomey

'Action will predominate, with room for human interest, humor, pathos. The stories will be good for family audiences in that they will concentrate on people in trouble, not trouble in people.' – promotion

Shannon

US 1981 13 × 50m colour
CBS/Universal/the Aubrey Company
(Alvin Sapinsley)

A widowed New York detective moves with his son to San Francisco.

Sluggish cop show which spends too much time on personal relations and too little on crime-solving.

cr Albert Ruben

Kevin Dobson, Charlie Fields

share: the percentage of viewing households tuned to a specific programme at a specific time.

Sharing Time (GB 1984; 6 × 60m). BBC

anthology series with every episode taking place in the same country-house apartment, 'time-shared' by a number of part-owners; a further variation on the idea previously used in *The House on the Hill*, *Cottage to Let* and *The Seasons*, and here showing signs of terminal fatigue. PP

Shark Kill

US 1976 74m colour TVM
ABC/D'Antoni–Weitz (Barry Weitz)

Two men set off after the great white shark. Routine adventure not uninfluenced by the success of *Jaws*.

w Sandor Stern d William A. Graham ph Terry K. Meade m George Romanis

Richard Yniguez, Phillip Clark, Jennifer Warren, Elizabeth Gill, David Huddleston

Sharma and Beyond * (GB 1984; 90m).

Pleasing *First Love* film with science-fiction overtones as indecisive hero is torn between homage to the reclusive sci-fi author he worships and the attractions of the latter's daughter. With Michael Maloney, Suzanne Burden and Robert Urquhart; written and directed by film-school graduate Brian Gilbert, for Goldcrest/Enigma/C4. PP

Sharon and Elsie (GB 1984–5; 13 × 30m).

Harmless sitcom in a greetings-card company, with Brigit Forsyth, Janette Beverley, John Landry. Written by Arline Whittaker, produced by Roger Race (1984), Mike Stephens (1985), for Central. PP

'She could only love a man who loved his wife!'
Sharon: Portrait of a Mistress

US 1977 96m colour TVM
NBC/Paramount/Moonlight (Frank von Zerneck)

In San Francisco a rich man's mistress is driven into paranoia by her position.

Watchable character study.

w Nancy Greenwald d Robert Greenwald ph Fred Jackman m Roger Kellaway

Trish Van Devere, Patrick O'Neal, Janet Margolin, Sam Groom, Gloria de Haven, Mel Ferrer, Salome Jens

Shatner, William (1931–). Canadian leading actor who has displayed some integrity in hundreds of guest roles. Series: *For the People*, STAR TREK, *Barbary Coast*. TV movies: *The Sole Survivor*, *Vanished*, *Owen Marshall Counsellor at Law*, *The People*, *The Hound of the Baskervilles*, *Incident on a Dark Street*, *Go Ask Alice*, *Horror at 37,000 Feet*, *Pioneer Woman*, *Indict and Convict*, *Pray for the Wildcats*, *Barbary Coast*, *Perilous Voyage*, *Testimony of Two Men*, *The Bastard*, *Little Women*, *Crash*, *Disaster on the Coastliner*, *The Baby Sitter*, *T. J. Hooker*, *Secrets of a Married Man*, *North and South*.

Shattered Vows

US 1984 96m colour TVM
NBC/Bertinelli–Pequod (Robert Lovenheim)

A nun suffers several years of discipline but finally feels that her place is in the outside world.

Those who have seen *The Nun's Story* should try another channel, for this is equally heavy going without the inner conviction.

w Audrey Davis Levin, book *Nun: A Memoir* by Mary Gilligan Wong d Jack Bender ph Mikhail Suslov m Lee Holdridge

Valerie Bertinelli, David Morse, Caroline McWilliams, Millie Perkins, Patricia Neal

Shaughnessy, Alfred (1915–). High-placed British writer (his stepfather was equerry to Edward VIII) who in his own words achieved 'a mild form of fame and success at the age of 56' as story editor of UPSTAIRS, DOWNSTAIRS and author of many of its best episodes. His own earlier plays were uneven in quality, though at least a couple deserved more attention than they got. His daytime soap opera *The Cedar Tree* ran 1976–8. Latest credit: *Ladies in Charge*, 1985. PP

Shavelson, Melville (1917–). American writer–creator who after a long film career has been involved with such TV projects as *Make Room for Daddy*, MY WORLD AND WELCOME TO IT, IKE.

739   **She Waits**

Shaw, Don (1934–   ). British writer with military background and strong Derbyshire roots, best known for his ORDE WINGATE trilogy (1976) and *Lone Patriot* (1977), about the German resistance figure Dietrich Bonhoeffer, which later became a stage play. *The Falklands Factor*, 1983.   PP

Shaw, Irwin (1913–84). American writer with long experience of radio and TV, which he put to early good use in the novel *The Troubled Air*, 1950, about the anti-communist witch-hunt against broadcasters. His bestseller *Rich Man, Poor Man* became a pioneering miniseries. See also *The Man Who Married a French Wife*.
                                                              PP

Shaw, Martin (1945–   ). British actor who weathered thick-ear fame in *The Professionals* to notch up sensitive leads in *Cream in My Coffee* and *The Last Place on Earth*. Early good performance' as the no-good husband in *Helen – A Woman of Today*.   PP

Shawn, Dick (1929–   ) (Richard Schulefand). American comedian of whom enough is usually too much, as his normal level is over the top.

Shazam!
US 1974 24 × 22m colour (16mm)
Filmation/Warner
A radio announcer when he utters the magic word transforms himself into the all-powerful Captain Marvel.
Shoddy live-action retread of a hoary theme.

Michael Gray, John Davey, Les Tremayne

† Not to be confused with *Shazzan!* a 1967 Hanna–Barbera series of 26 × 22m cartoons: here a magic ring transports children to the Arabian Nights.

She
GB 1977 6 × 50m colour
LWT (Paul Knight)
Anthology series prompted by success of an earlier (1975) stab at the same idea, *The Seven Faces of Women*. This one had Elizabeth Jane Howard, Lynne Reid Banks and Howard Schuman among its authors but is probably best remembered for Herbert Kretzmer's title song, as sung by Charles Aznavour.   PP

'She's America's ultimate secret weapon!'
SHE
US 1980 96m colour TVM
CBS/Martin Bregman

Adventures of a lady spy with a penchant for disguise.
The attempt at a female James Bond simply doesn't come off, the plot being too limp and the actors too embarrassed.
w Richard Maibaum *d* Robert Lewis *ph* Jules Brenner *m* Michael Kamin
Cornelia Sharpe, Omar Sharif, Anita Ekberg, Robert Lansing, William Traylor, Isabella Rye
'Romantic adventure evaporates into a mindless fog.' – *Daily Variety*

She Cried Murder *
US 1973 74m colour TVM
Universal (William Frye)
A model witnesses a murder, and the policeman who comes to investigate is the murderer.
A ripe chestnut, nicely shot on New York locations.
w Merwin Gerard *d* Herschel Daugherty
Telly Savalas, Lynda Day George, Mike Farrell

She Fell Among Thieves *
GB 1978 80m colour TVM
BBC (Mark Shivas)
A British adventurer in Europe clashes swords with an evil but fascinating woman.
Interesting attempt to recapture the flavour of a dated popular author, the flavour being a mixture of John Buchan, Sherlock Holmes, Bulldog Drummond and Anthony Hope. Heady but enjoyable.
w Tom Sharpe, *novel* Dornford Yates *d* Clive Donner
Malcolm McDowell, Eileen Atkins, Michael Jayston, Sarah Badel, Karen Dotrice, Freda Jackson, Richard Pearson

She Lives
US 1973 74m colour TVM
ABC Circle
College newlyweds find that the wife is dying of a rare disease.
Dreary copy of *Love Story*.
w Paul Neimark *d* Stuart Hagmann
Season Hubley, Desi Arnaz Jnr

She Waits *
US 1971 74m colour TVM
Metromedia
A bride is possessed by the evil spirit of her husband's first wife.
Obvious ghost story with a few frissons and a good cast.
w Arthur Wallace *d* Delbert Mann

Dorothy McGuire, Patty Duke, David McCallum, Lew Ayres, Beulah Bondi

Shear, Barry (1923–79). American director who rose from TV via such series as *The Man from UNCLE* and *The Name of the Game* to make a few big-screen movies of the grittier kind. TV movies: *Night Gallery, Don't Look Behind You, Short Walk to Daylight, Jarrett, Punch and Jody, Starsky and Hutch, San Pedro Bums, Keefer, Crash.*

Sheen, Fulton (1895–). American Catholic bishop who became a leading TV personality with his fifties series *Life is Worth Living.*

Sheen, Martin (1940–) (Ramon Estevez). American leading man who had some good chances. TV movies: *Then Came Bronson, Goodbye Raggedy Ann, Mongo's Back in Town, Welcome Home Johnny Bristol, That Certain Summer, Pursuit, Letters from Three Lovers, Catholics, Message to My Daughter, The Execution of Private Slovik, The Story of Pretty Boy Floyd, The California Kid, The Last Survivors, Sweet Hostage, Blind Ambition, The Long Road Home.*

Sheena Queen of the Jungle
US 1955 26 × 25m bw
Nassour
Adventures from the comic strip about a female Tarzan.
Hilarious hokum with a splendidly Amazonian lead.
Irish McCalla, Christian Drake

Shell Game *
US 1975 74m colour TVM
CBS/TCF/Thoroughbred (Harold Jack Bloom)
A con man fleeces the crooked head of a charity fund.
Pleasant comedy suspenser on the lines of *It Takes a Thief.*
w Harold Jack Bloom *d* Glenn Jordan
John Davidson, Tommy Atkins, Marie O'Brien, Jack Kehoe, Joan Van Ark

Shelley (GB 1972). Modern-dress semi-dramatization of the poet's life and death written by John Elliott and directed by Alan Bridges for BBC. At the time I found it 'totally misconceived and, in at least one respect, miscast. The proposition that the poet's revolutionary fervour is so akin to present-day ideals that he could as easily have belonged to 1972 as to 1822 is perhaps tenable but to have modern settings, raucous pop music and sports cars, while retaining the diction of 150 years ago (not to mention the pistols and the scientific equipment), was a wilful piece of arrogance.' With Robert Powell, Jenny Agutter.   PP

Shelley (GB 1980–84). Periodic seasons of a sitcom starring Hywel Bennett as a smooth university drop-out living on his wits and social security, though after a while he did get (a) married and (b) a job. Written by Peter Tilbury; produced by Anthony Parker; for Thames.   PP

Shepherd, Cybill (1950–). American leading lady who battled back to the top after a rocky start in movies. *The Yellow Rose, Secrets of a Married Man, Seduced, Moonlighting, The Long Hot Summer.*

Shepherd, Jack (1940–). Gloomy-eyed but versatile British leading actor, notable in *The Girls of Slender Means, Ready When You Are Mr McGill, Bill Brand, Count Dracula.*

The Sheriff *
US 1970 74m colour TVM
Columbia (Jon Epstein)
A black sheriff gets into race trouble on a rape case.
Routine adequately-made melodrama.
w Arnold Perl *d* David Lowell Rich
Ossie Davis, Ruby Dee

Sherlock Holmes. For principal series featuring this much-performed hero (1955 and 1984–5) see The Adventures of Sherlock Holmes. Serials include *The Hound of the Baskervilles* (GB 1982) with Tom Baker, for BBC. Other titles, apart from those below, include *Young Sherlock* (GB 1982, 8 × 52m) *w* Gerald Frow, *d* Nicholas Ferguson; with Guy Henry, June Barry, Heather Chasen, John Fraser

Sherlock Holmes
GB 1967 26 × 50m bw (VTR)
BBC
A careful series with a miscast star. Faithful to the original stories, but some needed too much padding out to fill the hour.
Peter Cushing, Nigel Stock

Sherlock Holmes and Dr Watson (Poland 1980). A series of 25-minute episodes produced by Quentin Reynolds. Many episodes directed by Val Guest. Geoffrey Whitehead was an uneasy Holmes, Donald Pickering a punctilious Watson; most of the actors were English, but the Polish sets, and a remarkably unsuitable music score, made this one of the least satisfactory results of international co-production. Almost all the stories were originals by Sheldon Reynolds.

Sherlock Holmes in New York
US 1976 96m colour TVM
TCF/NBC (Nancy Malone, John Cutts)

Sherlock Holmes crosses the Atlantic to rescue Irene Adler from the clutches of Moriarty.

An appealing prospect, but the script and production prove boring and almost every actor is miscast.

w Alvin Sapinsley d Boris Sagal m Richard Rodney Bennett

Roger Moore, Patrick MacNee, John Huston, Charlotte Rampling, David Huddleston, Signe Hasso, Gig Young, Leon Ames, John Abbott, Jackie Coogan

Sherrin, Ned (1931–). British producer, associated chiefly with *That Was the Week that Was*; also debater and general teleman.

She's Dressed to Kill *
US 1979 96m colour TVM
NBC/Grant–Case–McHugh Enterprises/
  Barry Weitz

A fashion show takes place at an isolated Arizona mansion where a murderer lurks.
Old-fashioned screamer which takes a while to get going but then delivers, and maintains a fair level of surface interest throughout.

w George Lefferts d Gus Trikonis ph Thomas del Ruth m George Romanis

John Rubinstein, Eleanor Parker, Jessica Walter, Connie Sellecca, Jim McMullan, Gretchen Corbett, Corinne Calvet, Clive Revill, Marianne McAndrew

'If there's a superficial resemblance to *And Then There Were None*, it's also an amusing take-off on the world of high fashion.' – *Daily Variety*

She's in the Army Now
US 1981 96m colour TVM
ABC Circle (Harry R. Sherman)

Incidents in the army career of a girl uncertain of her future.
A curious pilot for a series which was intended to be half comedy and half melodrama, but in fact never happened at all.

w Earl W. Wallace d Hy Averback ph William Jurgensen m Artie Butler

Kathleen Quinlan, Jamie Leigh Curtis, Susan Blanchard, Melanie Griffith, Dale Robinette

Shillingbury Tales
GB 1981 6 × 60m colour
ATV (Greg Smith)

Winsome series set in a picture-book English village, developed from an earlier one-off, *The Shillingbury Blowers* with Trevor Howard.

cr/w Francis Essex d Val Guest
Robin Nedwell, Diane Keen, Jack Douglas, Bernard Cribbins.   PP

† Spin-off *Cuffy* with Cribbins and Douglas and Linda Hayden, 1983. p Paul Harrison (Central).

Shine on Harvey Moon (GB 1982; 6 × 30m; colour). Disarming light comedy series about the demob in 1946 of an RAF clerk, catching the austerity and optimism of post-war Britain better than many a more pretentious exercise. With Kenneth Cranham, Elizabeth Spriggs, Maggie Steed. Written by Laurence Marks and Maurice Gran; directed by Baz Taylor; produced by Tony Charles; for Central/Witzend Productions.   PP

† The series returned later the same year in 60m format and then annually until final batch in 1985.

A Shining Season
US 1979 96m colour TVM
CBS/Columbia/Green–Epstein/TM (Harry Thomason)

A long-distance runner and college coach, knowing he is dying of cancer, takes on the last challenge of training the handicapped.
Though based on a true case, this is almost a parody of the 'disease of the week' syndrome of American TV movies. How much inspiration can American viewers need or take?

w William Harrison, *book* William Buchanan d Stuart Margolin ph Andrew Jackson m Richard Bellis

Timothy Bottoms, Allyn Ann McLerie, Connie Forslund, Ed Begley Jnr, Mason Adams, Rip Torn

Shirley
US 1979   × 50m colour
NBC/Universal/Ten Four (Bob Birnbaum, Gwen Bagni)

A widow moves west with her several children, and makes a new life at Tahoe.
Unexceptional, unobjectionable, rather boring series which was soon found out.

cr Greg Strangis, Gwen Bagni, Paul Dubov

Shirley Jones, Peter Barton, Rosanna Arquette, Ann Doran

Shirley, Lloyd (1931–   ). Canadian drama producer in television since 1954, all but a few years with ABC (GB) or Thames after the 1968 ABC/Rediffusion merger. Set up Euston Films in 1970 with George Taylor. Now Thames's controller of drama.   PP

Shirley Temple Storybook: see Temple, Shirley

Shirley's World
GB 1971 17 × 25m colour
ATV (Sheldon Leonard)

Assignments of a photo journalist.
Unpleasing comedy drama series with a star ill-at-ease.

cr Sheldon Leonard
Shirley Maclaine, John Gregson

Shirts/Skins *
US 1973 74m colour TVM
MGM

Six young businessmen turn themselves into competing teams on a crazy bet.
Spasmodically funny, erratically scripted comedy.

d William Graham

René Auberjonois, Bill Bixby, Leonard Frey, Doug McClure, McLean Stevenson, Robert Walden, Loretta Swit

Shivas, Mark (*c* 1942–   ). Influential British producer, originally a film critic and editor of *Movie* magazine who briefly presented Granada's *Cinema*. Production career began as an assistant in same company's story department, then BBC before setting up the Astramead freelance group that made *Telford's Change*, *The Price* and *Late Starter*. For Southern TV produced *Winston Churchill – the Wilderness Years*. Also: *The Six Wives of Henry VIII* (1970), *The Glittering Prizes* and *Rogue Male* (1976), *On Giant's Shoulders* (1979), *The History Man* (1980), *The Borgias* (1981), *Moonlighting* (1982).   PP

The Shock of the New
GB 1980 7 × 60m colour
BBC

Robert Hughes's assertive treatise on the modern movement in art and architecture. My 1980 reaction: 'Every time we were whizzed to a new location, which was about every two minutes, there was Robert with a change of clothes to suit the mood – open-necked shirt and casual jacket for Paris when evoking the hullabaloo of 1968, dark suit and striped shirt for Turin or the Tate.
'For every allusion there had to be an illustration, e.g., a biplane in the air when Blériot's name was mentioned, though the biplane had nothing to do with Blériot and in fact dated from about 30 years later . . . There seemed to be a compulsion to drive home a definitive verdict on every mode and every artist who had come up, like mounting butterflies with a rivet gun.'   PP

Shoestring *
GB 1979–80 26 × 50m colour
BBC (Robert Banks Stewart)

Trevor Eve as a phone-in Galahad, investigative reporter on a West Country local radio show who takes on mysteries brought his way by listeners or (quite often) colleagues. Superior and civilized thriller series, created by Robert Banks Stewart.   PP

Shogun *
US 1980 6 × 96m or variant formats colour
NBC/Paramount (James Clavell, Eric Bercovici)

A 16th-century seaman is captured by the Japanese and learns to respect a local warlord. What our hero accomplishes in the first four hours could have been managed by Errol Flynn in ten minutes, and that about sums up the pace of this long, solemn foxtrot through oriental customs, much of it in Japanese with the occasional *hara kiri* or beheading to keep viewers awake. It can really be justified only by its prettiness.

w Eric Bercovici, *novel* James Clavell *d* Jerry London *ph* Andrew Laszlo *m* Maurice Jarre
Richard Chamberlain, Toshiro Mifune, Yoko Shimada, Damien Thomas, Alan Badel, Michael Hordern, Vladek Sheybal, John Rhys-Davies, Frankie Sakai, George Innes
Emmy 1981: outstanding limited series
'A lazily-paced, opulent romance . . . handsome, respectful, and for the first five hours dull.' – *Daily Variety*
† The project reputedly cost 22 million dollars. Overseas a more violent two-hour version was released theatrically, but made no great impact.

The Shogun Inheritance * (GB 1981; 7 × 40m; colour). Stylish, informative series on present-day Japan in the light of its middle history, written and narrated by Julian Pettifer; produced by Michael MacIntyre; for BBC.   PP

Shooting Stars
US 1983 96m colour TVM
ABC/Metromedia/Aaron Spelling (Richard Lang)

SHINE ON HARVEY MOON was a wryly comic chronicle of post-war life among the upper working class. Here Harvey (Kenneth Cranham) stands in the background while his mother (Elizabeth Spriggs) marries her Geoff (Tenniel Evans).

A pair of TV detectives whose show is cancelled strike out on their own.
These actors soon had a chance to do the same, for this was yet another pilot which didn't take.

w Michael Fisher d Richard Lang ph Dick Rawlings Jnr m Dominic Frontiere

Billy Dee Williams, Parker Stevenson, John P. Ryan, Edie Adams, Fred Travelena

Shooting the Chandelier * (GB 1977).
David Mercer's last excursion to his favourite ideological battleground of an East European country in the process of coming under Marxist rule. A Czech country house lately vacated by the Nazis is commandeered by two Red Army officers whose mutual antagonism sparks off a glittering political debate. With Edward Fox, Denholm Elliott. Directed by Jane Howell; for BBC (*Play of the Week*). PP

Shootout in a One Dog Town
US 1974 74m colour TVM
NBC/Hanna–Barbera (Richard E. Lyons)

A small-town western banker finds himself alone against a vicious gang of robbers.
Virtually a small-screen version of *High Noon*, and as such not bad at all.

w Larry Cohen, Dick Nelson d Burt Kennedy ph Robert B. Hauser m Hoyt Curtin

Richard Crenna, Stefanie Powers, Jack Elam, Arthur O'Connell, Michael Ansara, Gene Evans, Dub Taylor, Richard Egan, Michael Anderson Jnr

❋ **Shore, Dinah** (1917–) (Frances Rose Shore). American popular songstress who in mid-career turned talk show hostess and through most of the seventies had her daily half-hour aimed mainly at women.

Short Walk to Daylight *
US 1972 73m colour TVM
Universal (Edward J. Montagne)

Eight people are trapped in the New York subway by an earthquake.
Unfortunately most of the excitement is at the beginning, but at least it's a good idea.

w Philip H. Reisman Jnr, Steven Bochco, Gerald di Pego d Barry Shear

James Brolin, Don Mitchell, James McEachin, Abby Lincoln, Brooke Bundy

Shotgun Slade
US 1959–60 78 × 25m bw
MCA/Revue/Shotgun (Frank Gruber)

Cases of a private detective in the old west. Cheerful hokum, put together with some spirit.

m Gerald Fried

Scott Brady

Shoulder to Shoulder *
GB 1974 6 × 50m colour (VTR)
BBC/Warner (Verity Lambert)

The story of the suffragettes.

Rather perfunctory dramatizations of the lives of six women who led the movement; careful but not exactly compelling.

w Ken Taylor and others

Siân Phillips, Angela Down, Pamela Quinn

PP: 'This co-operative undertaking by Verity Lambert, Georgia Brown, Midge Mackenzie and Warner Brothers – Brothers? – was strangely soft-centred at times, not least in the sentimental elevation of Sylvia Pankhurst's honest working-class wing of the movement over the bourgeois followers of Emmeline and Christabel. To allow the latter to end up as instant Conservative blue-rinsers, charming the vote from Lloyd George after a display of wartime jingoism while Sylvia mourned lost ideals in the rain, is wriggling around in history.'

A Show Called Fred **
GB 1956 6 × 25m bw
Associated-Rediffusion (Dick Lester)

It grew out of an even earlier show called Idiot Weekly, Price 2d, and owed a lot to the GOONS, but can be justly identified as the first real manifestation of the surrealist television comedy that would bud with It's a Square World and come to fruition with Monty Python. The studio was open, the cameras in vision, just as TWTWTW would re-invent. In an archetypal gag a theatre audience waited expectantly as the curtains parted to reveal another audience, facing the first. Graham Stark, as a bird-man, laboriously failed to take off. Peter Sellers imitated Olivier's Richard III so intensely that it was obvious he would rather have created than mimicked the performance. A custard pie was ritually applied to the sunny face of Patti Lewis, Canadian vocalist. Valentine Dyall was also

involved. Written by Spike Milligan and others. Son of Fred followed, and The Best of Fred was a 1963 condensation of high moments from both.   PP

Shrapnel, John (19 –). Commanding British actor who has carried more than one TV production on his shoulders. The White Guard (1982 production), the BBC Shakespeare Lear, Sorrell and Son.   PP

Shubik, Irene (1935–). British producer, formerly academic historian, who came into television in the late fifties as a story editor for Sydney Newman. Graduated to production with the science fiction series Out of the Unknown, then Thirteen Against Fate (Simenon stories) and seasons of Play for Today. Notable productions include Sling Your Hook, Last Train through Harecastle Tunnel, The Right Prospectus, Hearts and Flowers, The General's Day, Wessex Tales and (for Granada) Staying On, which led to Jewel in the Crown which she set up but did not produce. Stinkers include The Rainbirds. Author of valuable book Play for Today (Davis–Poynter, 1975).   PP

Shull, Richard B. (1929–). American comedy character actor. Series: Diana, Holmes and Yo Yo.

Shulman, Milton (19 –). Canadian theatre critic resident in Britain since World War II who had a television career in the late fifties and sixties as producer of Zoo Time for Granada and then assistant controller of programmes at Rediffusion. In 1964 he pulled out of TV to lambast it instead in a weekly column in his paper, the London Evening Standard, and two books: The Least Worst Television in the World and The Ravenous Eye, both 1973. In the latter he came out ahead of most against violence on TV, gaining Brownie points for prescience but black marks for intemperance. Author of one TV play, Kill Three, 1967.   PP

Shut That Door! (GB 1972–7). Variety-cum-chat show concocted by ATV to display the talents of their limp-wristed, gentle discovery Larry Grayson; heavily dependent on guest performers but it kept Larry occupied until the call came to take over The Generation Game.
                                                                    PP

The Sid Caesar Show *
GB 1958 15 × 30m bw
BBC (Hal Janis)

Quixotic but determined attempt by the BBC to regain ground from ITV, which by this time commanded 72 per cent of the audience. Caesar and his company, unknown in Britain, were lured across the Atlantic for the summer to try to reproduce the success of *Your Show of Shows*. If their wild and inventive comedy (writers included Neil Simon, Larry Gelbart and the young Mel Brooks) never quite captivated the masses it certainly opened many eyes to new possibilities in humour. My review at the time: 'I had hoped to avoid saying the obvious thing about Sid Caesar's British debut – that he came, he saw, he conquered. There's no getting away from it though, Sid did. His first show for the BBC last night finally came up to every expectation.'

† The series went out live except for the last two shows, pre-recorded for transmission after Caesar's return to the USA for a new season of his American show, with Shirley Maclaine joining the team. The BBC also bought and screened this series.   PP

†† One or two editions were re-run on BBC2 in 1983 as part of a Sid Caesar reprise with Mel Brooks.

Side Show
US 1979 96m colour TVM
NBC/Sid and Marty Krofft (George Kirgo)
In a travelling circus, various odd or dramatic stories intermingle.
Since all the characters are from melodrama and there is an undue emphasis on freaks, this so-called slice of life inspires little empathy.
w George Kirgo d William Conrad ph Jack E. Swain m Ralph Burns
Lance Kerwin, Connie Stevens, William Windom, Red Buttons, Barbara Rhoades, Albert Paulsen, Tony Franciosa
'Circus folk have a mystique that still lures youngsters, but they've concealed it under a tent in this one.' – *Daily Variety*

Sidekicks
US 1974 75m colour TVM
Warner/Cherokee
A black and a white con man get in and out of scrapes in the old west.
Rather dreary action comedy based on the cinema film *The Skin Game*. No go as a series.
w William Bowers d Burt Kennedy
Lou Gossett, Larry Hagman, Blythe Danner, Jack Elam

Sidney Shorr: A Girl's Best Friend
US 1981 96m colour TVM
NBC/Warner/Hajeno (George Eckstein)

An ageing New York homosexual takes in a pregnant actress and becomes absorbingly fond of her baby daughter whom he later tries to adopt.
Homosexuality being referred to only fleetingly, this is less daring than it sounds, the relationship for a while resembling that of *The Odd Couple*. In fact it's a talkative, mostly well acted but drawn-out way of introducing a half-hour tape series in which the homosexual will adopt the little girl: see *Love Sidney*.
w Oliver Hailey d Russ Mayberry
Tony Randall, Lorna Patterson, David Huffman, Kaleena Kiff, Ann Weldon, John Lupton

Sidney, Sylvia (1910–) (Sophia Kosow).
American star actress of the thirties; busy on television as an elderly lady. TV movies: *Do Not Fold, Spindle or Mutilate, The Secret Night Caller, Winner Take All, Death at Love House, Raid on Entebbe, Snowbeast,* SIEGE, *The Gossip Columnist, FDR: The Last Year,* THE SHADOW BOX, *A Small Killing, Having It All, Finnegan Begin Again, An Early Frost.*

Siege *
US 1978 96m colour TVM
CBS/Titus (Herbert Brodkin)
Senior citizens in a New York apartment house are terrified by hoodlums.
Fairly holding if unnecessary melodrama which almost sustains its length.
w Conrad Bromberg d Richard Pearce ph Alan Metzger m Charles Gross
MARTIN BALSAM, SYLVIA SIDNEY, Dorian Harewood, James Sutorius

The Siege of Manchester *
GB 1965 120m bw (VTR)
Blockbuster to mark the coming of BBC2 to the North of England, but more than just a promotional gesture or snook at Granada on its own patch. Alan Dobie played Captain Rosworm, the German mercenary hired to defend Manchester (then a small township) during the Civil War, as a true professional. Herbert Wise elevated a studio production to epic stature. Written by Keith Dewhurst.   PP

Sierra
US 1974 13 × 50m colour
NBC/Universal/Jack Webb (Robert A. Cinader)
Cases for the rangers in Yosemite National Park (where Universal, by a strange coincidence, had just bought up the concessions).

Singularly inept attempt to do *Adam 12* in the open air, with badly matching stock footage; a short issue from the TV movie *The Rangers*.

James G. Richardson, Ernest Thompson, Mike Warren, Jack Hogan

Sigley, Marjorie (19 –). Children's drama teacher taken up by British television in the sixties, leading to her own children's shows and also a decisive hand in coaching the juvenile performers in a remarkable single play of 1967, *Children Playing* (ATV). In charge of children's programmes at Thames, 1983–6.   PP

Sigmund and the Sea Monsters
US 1973–4 24 × 22m colour
Sid and Marty Krofft

Two boys who live near the California beach befriend a sea monster but keep his presence a secret.
Modest live-action fantasy.

w Si Rose, John Fenton Murray, Jack Raymond, Fred Fox, Seaman Jacobs *d* Bob Lally
Bill Barty, Johnny Whittaker, Scott Kolden

Silas Marner * (GB 1985; 90m; TVM). Highly-praised tearjerker from George Eliot's novel about lonely man who adopts foundling child. With Ben Kingsley, Jenny Agutter, Patrick Ryecart; photographed by Nat Crosby, music by Carl Davis; written by Louis Marks and Giles Foster, directed by Foster, produced by Marks, for BBC.   PP

The Silence *
US 1975 74m colour TVM
Palomar

For violating West Point's honour code, a cadet is shunned by his associates.
Mildly interesting story based on fact.

d Joseph Hardy
Richard Thomas, Gunnel Lindblom, Jorgen Lindstrom

Silence of the Heart
US 1984 96m colour TVM
CBS/Tisch–Avnet/David A. Simons
(James O'Fallon)

The reasons for the suicide of a teenage boy. Another indictment of society, spreading guilt around rather aimlessly but with a certain old-fashioned professionalism.

w Phil Penningroth *d* Richard Michaels *ph* Isidore Mankofsky *m* Georges Delerue
Mariette Hartley, Dana Hill, Howard Hesseman, Chad Lowe, Silvana Gallardo

Silence of the Sea *. Vercors's famous story of the passive resistance of a father and daughter to the cultured young German officer billeted on them during the Occupation has been twice dramatized for BBC TV. First by Denis Johnston for the reopening of the service after World War II in June 1946; secondly by Thomas Ellice in 1981, directed by Philip Bonham-Carter in perhaps unconscious emulation of just such an early fixed-camera production.   PP

The Silent Force
US 1970 15 × 25m colour
ABC/Aaron Spelling

Undercover specialists work for the government.
Mission even more impossible. It failed.

cr Luther Davis
Ed Nelson, Percy Rodrigues, Lynda Day

The Silent Gun *
US 1969 74m colour TVM
Paramount (Bruce Lansbury)

A former gunfighter who has shunned weapons is appointed sheriff of his home town.
Adequate minor western

w Clyde Ware *d* Michael Caffey
Lloyd Bridges, John Beck, Ed Begley, Edd Byrnes, Pernell Roberts, Susan Howard

The Silent Lovers: see Moviola

Silent Minority *
GB 1981 50m colour
ATV (Nigel Evans)

A controversial report on life inside Britain's mental handicap hospitals. Lack of staff and funds were said to be the worst problem. Written and directed by Nigel Evans.

Silent Night, Lonely Night *
US 1969 98m colour TVM
Universal (Jack Farren)

Two lonely people with problems fall in love at Christmas in a small New England inn.
Acceptable rueful love story.

w John Vlahos, *play* Robert Anderson *d* Daniel Petrie
Lloyd Bridges, Shirley Jones, Carrie Snodgress, Lynn Carlin

The Silent Service
US 1957–8 78 × 25m bw
Twin Dolphins/NBC

Re-creations of true-life submarine adventures.

Adequate docu-drama making ample use of stock footage.

host Rear-Admiral Thomas M. Dykers

Silent Victory: The Kitty O'Neill Story
US 1980 96m colour TVM
CBS/Channing–Debin–Locke (R. J. Louis)

How a stunt woman overcame the handicap of deafness.

Remarkably tedious 'true-life' anecdote which the writer has immense difficulty in stretching out to fit the slot.

w Steven Gethers *d* Lou Antonio *ph* Michel Hugo *m* Jimmie Haskell

Stockard Channing, James Farentino, Colleen Dewhurst, Edward Albert, Brian Dennehy

Silent Witness
US 1985 96m colour TVM
NBC/Robert Greenwald (Conrad Bromberg)

A wife feels obliged to tell the truth when her brother-in-law is accused of rape and the family provides him with a fake alibi.

Good routine courtroom drama, but rape is surely an overused subject these days.

w Conrad Bromberg *d* Michael Miller *ph* Rexford Metz *m* Michael Hoenig

Valerie Bertinelli, John Savage, Chris Nash, Melissa Leo, Pat Corley, Steven Williams

'A sharp, convincing portrayal of the demands of honour.' – *Daily Variety*

Silents Please ***
US 1962–3 40 × 25m bw
ABC/Paul Killiam/Gregstan

Potted versions of silent film classics, with informative commentary.

A service to American cinema, and a very entertaining job of work. Apart from compilation episodes, films compressed into 25m include *Tempest, Don Juan* (two parts), *The Hunchback of Notre Dame, Son of the Sheik, Lilac Time, The Black Pirate, Blood and Sand, Dr Jekyll and Mr Hyde* (1921), *The Thief of Bagdad, The Eagle, Nosferatu, The General, The Sea Beast* and *Intolerance*.

Silliphant, Stirling (or Sterling)
(1918–). American TV writer responsible for some of the best episodes of NAKED CITY, ROUTE 66 and *Longstreet*. Now works primarily in movies, but in 1981 wrote a pilot for a Vietnam series that didn't happen, *Fly Away Home*, and subsequently did the scripts for *Mussolini the Untold Story* and *Space*.

Sills, Beverly (1929–) (Belle Silverman).
American opera singer, an occasional TV guest artist.

Silver Spoons
US 1982– × 25m colour
NBC/Embassy (David W. Ducion)

A spoiled, childish rich man is joined by his almost forgotten 12-year-old son from an old marriage.

Not much of a premise, but with the help of other juvenile characters and an occasional irascible grandfather (played by John Houseman) it became a long runner.

cr David W. Ducion, Ron Leavitt, Michael G. Moye, Howard Leeds, Ben Starr, Martin Cohan

Ricky Schroder, Joel Higgins, Jason Bateman

Silverman, Fred (1938–).
American executive who during the seventies was head of programming for CBS, ABC and NBC respectively. Moved over to MGM and found himself no longer a household name.

❋ Silvers, Phil (1912–85) (Philip Silver).
American burlesque and nightclub comedian who after a moderate success in films became one of the top TV stars of the fifties in YOU'LL NEVER GET RICH, in which he created the character of conniving Sergeant Bilko and which was promptly rechristened *The Phil Silvers Show*. After a respite, *The New Phil Silvers Show* cast him as a factory foreman, but failed to take. He subsequently made guest appearances. TV movies: *The Night They Took Miss Beautiful, Goldie and the Boxer*.

Simard, Rene (1960–).
French–Canadian pop singer who became something of a national star in a half-hour series of zany comedy items interlaced with music.

Simmons, Jean (1929–).
British star actress with a few TV credits: *The Dain Curse, Beggarman Thief, Golden Gate, A Small Killing*. In GB, *December Flower*.

Simon and Simon
US 1982–5 88 × 50m colour
CBS/Universal (Philip DeGuere)

Adventures of brother private eyes in San Diego.

A light-hearted detective series, thinly written and produced, which after a shaky start unaccountably built itself up into a long-running ratings hit.

PHIL SILVERS.   Not many people remember *The New Phil Silvers Show*, an intended follow-up to Bilko. It was set on the factory floor and ran only one season. Silvers, so recently a household word, never again found a successful format. Also seen: Herb Meadows.

cr Philip de Guere

Jameson Parker, Gerald McRaney

Simpson, Alan (1929–). British scriptwriter who with Ray Galton created *Hancock* and *Steptoe and Son*.

Simpson, Bill (1931–). Scottish actor known almost entirely as Dr Finlay in DR FINLAY'S CASEBOOK.

Simpson, O. J. (1945–). American black actor, former footballer; mostly in TV movies: *Roots*, *A Killing Affair*, *Goldie and the Boxer*, *Goldie and the Boxer Go to Hollywood*, *Detour to Terror*.

Sin on Saturday (GB 1982; 4 × 35m). Misbegotten provincial (BBC Scotland) attempt to build a chat show round the seven deadly sins. 'The bummer of the season,' I said, 'because it rests a catchpenny but perfectly workable format on lazy assumptions, lazy research and cheap notoriety.' In the event, the show was axed with three deadly sins still to come. With Bernard Falk.   PP

Sin with Our Permission **
GB 1981 50m bw/colour
ATV (Colin Rogers)

Ingenious, slightly futuristic play about a new city whose inhabitants are kept under surveillance and discreetly brainwashed via the community cable-TV service – its daily soap opera conditions them to behave according to the civic plan. What we were seeing, in fact, was an instructional dossier on how to manage dissidents, compiled from surveillance tapes (bw) and relevant extracts of the soaper (in colour). Not in the end a 1984-type story of oppression but a cautionary tale about trying to build heaven on earth . . . The aim was to give the citizens comfort and security and relieve them of the cruel illusion of freedom. With Paul Eddington; written by J. C. Wilsher; directed by Paul Harrison.   PP

Sinatra, Frank (1915–). American popular singer, in all media and a frequent TV guest as well as star of his own specials. TV movie: *Contract on Cherry Street*.

Sinden, Donald (1923–). Versatile British stage, screen and TV actor. Series include *Our Man at St Mark's*, *The Organization*, TWO'S COMPANY, *Discovering English Churches*, *Never the Twain*. Autobiography 1982: *A Touch of the Memoirs* (Hodder).

Sing Along with Mitch. Cheerful series of one-hour pop song shows produced by NBC in the early sixties. Mitch was Mitch Miller, who conducted a strong team of vocalists.

Singer, Aubrey (1926–). British executive who began as a trainee film editor with Gaumont-British; into television in the early fifties as outside broadcast producer; started BBC science features department; later chief of BBC2 before leaving television temporarily to direct BBC radio. Managing director BBC–TV, 1982–4. Now runs own TV film outfit, White City Films.

'Come right in. Find a lover. Or a friend. Or both. For an evening. Or forever . . . in a place where fantasies come alive!'
Single Bars, Single Women
US 1984 96m colour TVM
ABC/Universal/Tom Werner, Marcy Carsey/Sunn Classic (Stuart Cohen)

Comedy and drama in a singles bar.
Insubstantial offering 'based' on a hit song. Someone should have written a script.
w Michael Bortman   *d* Harry Winer
ph Juan Ruiz-Anchia   *m* Basil Poledouris
Tony Danza, Paul Michael Glaser, Keith Gordon, Shelley Hack, Christine Lahti

Singleton, Valerie (1937–). British presenter, for many years on *Blue Peter*, later *The Money Programme*, etc.

Sins
US 1986 3 × 96m colour miniseries
CBS/Worldvision/New World (Steve Krantz)

An ambitious woman builds the world's most successful magazine empire.
Easy watching for those who like to see rich folk disporting themselves in exotic locations. A sore trial for devotees of quality.
w Laurence Heath, *novel* by Judith Gould
d Douglas Hickox
Joan Collins, Joseph Bologna, Capucine, Giancarlo Giannini, Gene Kelly

The Sins of Dorian Gray
US 1983 96m colour TVM
ABC/Telepictures/Rankin–Bass

A gorgeous fashion model arranges for her perfect video test to grow old while she retains its bloom.
Jaded 'updating' of a minor classic. It would he hilarious if it weren't so depressing.
d Tony Maylam
Anthony Perkins, Barbara Bauer, Olga Karlatos, Joseph Bottoms

'A film about passion, courage, honour and betrayal. And the redemption that comes with love.'

Sins of the Past
US 1984 96m colour TVM
ABC/MGM–UA/Leonard Goldberg Sinpast (Stuart Cohen)

Ex-prostitutes who have remained friends are murdered one by one.
Seamy thriller which amused its intended audience.

w Steve Brown, David Solomon d Peter Hunt ph Paul Lohmann m Arthur Rubinstein

Barbara Carrera, Anthony Geary, Kim Cattrall, Kirstie Alley, Debbie Boone, Tracy Reed

Sir Francis Drake
GB 1962 26 × 25m bw
ATV

Adventures of Queen Elizabeth's master mariner.
Tolerable cloak and sword stuff.

Terence Morgan, Jean Kent

Sir Lancelot: see The Adventures of Sir Lancelot

Sir Thomas at Lincoln's Inn
GB 1958 30m bw

A curiosity: Sir Thomas Beecham rehearses a concert for the Bar Musical Society with the Royal Philharmonic Orchestra; is interviewed by Peter Brook of all people; a snatch of the actual concert. But of more enduring interest than *Tommy*, a centenary tribute to Beecham from the same company in 1979. Produced by Herbert Wise; for Granada.   PP

Sirota's Court
US 1976 8 × 25m colour (VTR)
Universal/NBC/Peter Engel

The comic cases which are seen in a night court.
Mildly exasperating comedy with everybody trying too hard.

Michael Constantine

Sissons, Peter (1942–). Admirable British news reporter and newscaster, with ITN from traineeship in 1964; industrial correspondent, 1974; presenter *News at One*, 1978; anchorman of C4's news since 1982. PP

sitcom. TV jargon for situation comedy.

Six
GB 1964 6 × approx. 45m bw
BBC (John McGrath)

Six short story-films commissioned from youngish directors at McGrath's suggestion – TV was using a lot of films, wasn't it time it put something into film-making? The fruits relied overmuch on fashionable images of the day – long Antonioni pans and statuesque groupings – but had a certain energy.

Diary of a Nobody, from the Grossmiths' book, d Ken Russell

Andy's Game, w Michael Hastings, d David Andrews

The Logic Game, w Jane Arden, Philip Saville, d Philip Saville

Don't I Look Like a Lord's Son?, w/d Joe Massot

The Chase, w Troy Kennedy Martin, d Michael Elstor

The Day of Ragnarok, w/d John McGrath

† *Five More* followed in 1966–8, without making the same impact. Writer–directors were McGrath and Saville again, John Irvin, Ronald Eyre and Mamoun Hassan.

Six Centuries of Verse (GB 1984). Excellent series of English and American verse readings by classy readers, e.g. Lee Remick articulating Emily Dickinson, Julian Glover grappling with *Beowulf*; edited by Anthony Thwaite, for Thames/C4.   PP

Six English Towns *
GB 1979–81 12 × 40m colour
BBC (Denis Moriarty)

Thanks to a second sextet *Six More English Towns*, a dozen small towns had the benefit of Alec Clifton-Taylor's expert eye (especially for the part played by local building materials) plus his enthusiasm and impatience with discordant new development.   PP

Six Faces
GB 1972 6 × 50m colour
BBC (Stella Richman)

Kenneth More as a world-weary man-of-our-times who was supposed to be seen each week through the acquaintance of a different participant – employer, wife, daughter, mistress. In the event it was the usual camera-eye view, as I wrote in my review at the time: 'Indeed, when it was the delicious Kika Markham's turn she spent a large part of the episode waiting for her lover-boy, who was observed independently chafing over business appointments, glancing at his watch and hailing taxis. And Kenneth More obstinately remained Kenneth More, regardless of whose consciousness he was meant to be filtered through: same chops stuffed with gob-stoppers, same maddening savoir-faire, crinkly smile, expensively-lubricated voice.'

Six Feet of the Country (Lesotho/GB 1982). Seven stories of varying length by the South African novelist Nadine Gordimer. Various directors for Profile Productions (Lesotho). Shown in Britain by C4.

Six Fifty-five Special (GB 1982). Short-lived chat show and Free Plug Circuit outlet from the BBC's Pebble Mill studios in Birmingham, trying to prove they were just as worldly as London W12. David Soul of *Starsky and Hutch* was teamed with local girl Sally James (a good deal more fun) as joint hosts.   PP

Six-Five Special (GB 1957–8). Television's first teenage pop music show, slipped into the BBC schedules as a lightweight Saturday complement to *Tonight* when the old 6–7 p.m. gap was closed. Originated by JACK GOOD, fronted by Pete Murray, Jo Douglas and former pugilist Freddie Mills, it quickly became a cult and threw off a movie, two stage shows, and a concert version. After a disagreement over the last-named Good lost his BBC contract; Denis Main Wilson took over as producer and Jim Dale as presenter – 'a pleasant young man who might have been run up in the BBC props department to do the job', as I said at the time. Well, that was 22 years before *Barnum*. The opposition countered first with Jack Jackson, then Jack Good's *Oh Boy!* The *Six-Five Special* was derailed and replaced by *Dig This!*   PP

The Six Million Dollar Man *
US 1972 74m colour TVM
ABC/Universal (Richard Irving)

An astronaut injured in a crash is remade with powerful artificial limbs and becomes a superhuman, bionic spy.
A slow starter for an immensely popular science fiction series which injected love interest by later spinning off *The Bionic Woman*. Two other 74m starters were made before the show settled down into a one-hour slot; *Wine, Women and War* and *The Solid Gold Kidnapping*.

w Henri Simoun, *novel Cyborg* by Martin Caiden *d* Richard Irving

Lee Majors, Darren McGavin, Martin Balsam, Barbara Anderson

† The resulting series reached its sixth season, with a virtually unchanged format, before cancellation in 1978.

The Six Proud Walkers (GB 1954; 6 × 30m; bw live). Said to be the BBC's first adult cliffhanger serial and certainly the first anywhere to incorporate a fictitious but authentically silly TV panel show into the plot. Donald Wilson's script was reproduced 10 years later by Douglas Allen, again for BBC, when the upright and gentlemanly detective-inspector couldn't avoid seeming a little old-fashioned but the plot still enmeshed everyone satisfactorily. With (this time) Julia Lockwood, Tony Britton, Lana Morris.   PP

Six Scenes from Marriage
original title: *Scener ur ett aktenskap*
Sweden 1972 6 × 50m colour
SRT (Ingmar Bergman)

Ingmar Bergman's dissection of a superficially happy marriage emptied the streets and closed the theatres the nights it was shown in Sweden. Dubbed for British consumption (BBC 1975) it didn't have quite the same impact, partly because the English voices seemed to fit the Swedish faces about as well as a moustache on the Mona Lisa, partly because of the extreme introspection of the characters. I wondered at the time: 'Do people really talk like that even when their lips haven't stopped moving?'

w Ingmar Bergman, *trans* Alan Blair *d* Ingmar Bergman

Liv Ullmann (dubbed by Annie Ross), Erland Josephson (John Carson), Bibi Andersson, Gunnel Lindblom   PP

The Six Wives of Henry VIII **
GB 1970 6 × 50m colour
BBC/Mark Shivas (Ronald Travers)

Historical pageant and character study, one play per wife. Its star made a brave try but was not quite' up to the older Henry. Scripts and production were however in the BBC's best style, and the project was popular in the US. It was also compressed into a disappointingly flat film, *Henry VIII and his Six Wives*.

w Jean Morris, Beverly Cross, Rosemary Anne Sisson

KEITH MICHELL, Annette Crosbie, Barbara Leigh-Hunt, Patrick Troughton, Elvi Hale, Angela Pleasence, Sheila Burrell

Sixpenny Corner (GB 1955). British television's first daily serial, put out by A–R Monday to Friday, in 15-minute episodes, when ITV opened. Written by former *Mrs Dale's Diary* hands Jonquil Antony and Hazel Adair, it was set in and around a corner garage in a new town, and didn't last. With Patricia Dainton, Howard Pays.   PP

The Sixth Sense
US 1971 25 × 50m colour
ABC/Universal

A professor investigates ESP and psychic phenomena.
Rather too dry and scientific semi-occult chiller series with a few authentic jolts.
Gary Collins

The Sixty Four Thousand Dollar Question
(US 1955–7). Half-hour quiz show for CBS from a radio original; answers doubled in value as the contestant proceeded. (The original British version was called *Double Your Money*.) A development, offering even more money, was *The Sixty Four Thousand Dollar Challenge* (1956–7).

Sixty Minutes (CBS 1968–). One-hour weekly news analysis covering the world scene in depth.

Sixty Years of Seduction
US 1981 96m colour
ABC/Columbia/Rastar–Brice–Green

James Garner, Angie Dickinson, Robert Urich and Victoria Principal present romantic clips from old movies.
Abysmally naïve and arch compilation job, totally lacking in genuine wit or observation. And all the clips are familiar.
w Buz Kohan *d* Jeff Marolis *m* Peter Matz
'It goes for the obvious like a leopard goes for the throat.' – *Daily Variety*

Sizzle
US 1981 96m colour TVM
ABC/Metromedia/Aaron Spelling (Lynn Loring, Cindy Dunne)

Newcomers in Chicago in the twenties are influenced by the shady owner of a speakeasy.
Spoofy melodrama which aims on too low a budget to re-create the roaring twenties.
w Clyde Ware, Richard Carr *d* Don Medford
Loni Anderson, John Forsythe, Michael Goodwin, Roy Thinnes, Leslie Uggams, Richard Lynch.

Skag *
US 1979 145m colour TVM
NBC/Lorimar (Abby Mann, Douglas Benton)

A steelworker is felled by a stroke and recovers to find that his family have a fresh realization of his value.
Heavy-going actor's piece, quite watchable on its own account though the thought of a weekly hour of misery was daunting.

w Abby Mann *d* Frank Perry *ph* Edmond Koons *m* Billy Goldenberg
KARL MALDEN, Piper Laurie, Craig Wasson, Peter Gallagher, Kathryn Holcomb, Leslie Ackerman
'A powerful and moving drama enriched with dimensional characters.' – *Daily Variety*
† The promised one-hour series was not a success and ended after eight episodes.

Skeezer
US 1982 96m colour TVM
NBC/Marble Arch/Blue Marble/Margie Lee/Bill McCutcheon (Lee Levinson)

An ex-nurse uses her dog to help emotionally upset youngsters.
Flabby tearjerker which just above lives up to its humble pretensions.
w Robert Hamilton, *book Skeezer, a Dog with a Mission* by Elizabeth Yates *d* Peter H. Hunt *ph* Harry J. May *m* Arthur B. Rubinstein
Karen Valentine, Leighton Greer, Mariclare Costello, Tom Atkins, Justin Lord

❋ **Skelton, Red** (1910–) (Richard Skelton). Durable American comic from the burlesque school; a big name in TV specials of the fifties and sixties, till excess drove him from the scene. Also a popular film star in the forties.

Skene, Anthony (1924–). British writer who came to notice with ingeniously plotted contributions to series such as *Trapped* or *The Root of All Evil*. I wrote of him then: 'Evidently he likes the challenge of writing to a prescription . . . his contributions have included at least two fizzing satires on the executive scramble and some solid military themes.' As an originator he has been less impressive. *The Seasons of the Year* (six plays, one setting), 1971. Recently: *The Adventures of Sherlock Holmes*.   PP

Ski Lift to Death
US 1978 96m colour TVM
Paramount/Jozak (Richard Briggs, Bruce J. Sallan)

Four groups of people at Lake Louise are trapped in a ski lift.
Routine, meandering suspenser of which only the last 20 minutes are worth watching.
w Laurence Heath *d* William Wiard *ph* Ozzie Smith *m* Barry DeVorzon
Deborah Raffin, Charles Frank, Howard Duff, Don Galloway, Gail Strickland, Clu Gulager, Don Johnson
'Anyone expecting a neat murder mystery better not bother.' – *Daily Variety*

Skippy the Bush Kangaroo
Australia 1966–8 91 × 25m colour
Norfolk International

A game ranger makes an unusual pet.
Enjoyable children's series with a prepossessing star.
Skippy, Gary Pankhurst, Ed Devereaux

Skokie *
US 1981 124m colour TVM
CBS/Titus (Robert Berger)
GB title: *Once They Marched through a Thousand Towns*

Dramatization of the late seventies Chicago riots when American Nazis planned to demonstrate in a Jewish area.
Overlong but generally gripping study, with some excellent performances.

w Ernest Kinoy *d* Herbert Wise *ph* Alex Thomson

DANNY KAYE, JOHN RUBINSTEIN, ELI WALLACH, Kim Hunter, Carl Reiner, Brian Dennehy, Ed Flanders, James Sutorius, Lee Strasberg, George Dzundza

Skorpion (GB 1982; 6 × 50m). Second serial featuring Michael Denison as the plummy-voiced security chief, Captain Percival. Also with Mary Wimbush, Terence Hardiman; written by John Brason, from an idea by Arden Winch; directed by Michael Hayes, produced by Gerard Glaister, for BBC.

The Sky at Night. Immensely long-running BBC item on stars (and latterly man-made satellites) visible each month, conducted by Patrick Moore; comforting reminder of the stability of British institutions. PP

Sky Heist *
US 1975 100m colour TVM
NBC/Warner/Jack Webb (Rick Rosner)

Holidaymakers rescued by the Aero Bureau of the Los Angeles County Sheriff's office turn out to be criminals with a major robbery in hand.
Exciting but overlong caper yarn intended as a pilot for a helicopter series.

w William F. Nolan, Rick Rosner *d* Lee H. Katzin

Don Meredith, Joseph Campanella, Larry Wilcox, Ken Swofford, Stefanie Powers, Frank Gorshin, Shelley Fabares

Sky King
US 1953–4 72 × 25m bw
ABC/Jack Chertok

A modern ranch owner keeps law and order from his private plane.
Acceptable hokum series of its time.
Kirby Grant, Gloria Winters

The Sky Trap
US 1978 96m colour TVM
NBC/Walt Disney (Jerome Courtland)

A young glider pilot nabs some smugglers coming in from Mexico.
Adequate action adventure for the family.

w Jim Lawrence, *book* D. S. Halacy Jnr *d* Jerome Courtland *ph* Rexford Metz *m* Will Schaefer

Jim Hutton, Marc McClure, Patricia Crowley, Kitty Ruth, Kip Niven

Skyhawks
US 1969 17 × 25m colour
Pantomime/Ken Snyder

Assignments of a daredevil air transport and rescue service.
Cleancut cartoon adventures.

The Sky's No Limit
US 1984 96m colour TVM
CBS/Lorimar/Palance–Levy (David Lowell Rich)

Female astronauts compete to be the first American woman in space.
Apart from the hardware, this script was all seen before in the early thirties.

w Renee and Harry Longstreet *d* David Lowell Rich *ph* Mike Fash *m* Maurice Jarre

Sharon Gless, Dee Wallace, Anne Archer, Barnard Hughes, David Ackroyd
'Applying a contemporary theme or two to formula stuff, it takes a bath in soapsuds.' – *Daily Variety*

Skyward *
US 1980 96m colour TVM
NBC/Major–H–Anson (Anson Williams, John Kuri)

A 14-year-old paraplegic girl is taught to fly by an ex-stuntwoman.
Another inspirational movie, but this time the elements pull together so that viewers will be rooting for success.

w Nancy Sackett *d* Ron Howard *ph* Robert Jessup *m* Lee Holdridge

Bette Davis, Clu Gulager, Howard Hesseman, Suzy Gilstrap, Ben Marley, Marion Ross
'A salute to the independence of the spirit.' – *Daily Variety*

Skyway to Death *
US 1974 74m colour TVM
Universal (Lou Morheim)

A mountain cable car gets stuck with passengers aboard.

Routine disaster/suspense adventure, dullish when everyone talks, okay when the action begins.

w David Spector d Gordon Hessler

Bobby Sherman, Stefanie Powers, John Astin, Joseph Campanella, Ross Martin

Slade, Bernard (19 –). American scriptwriter, creator of *The Flying Nun*, who went on to write the smash play *Same Time Next Year*.

Slater, John (1916–75). British character actor, often of cockney roles. Series: *Johnny You're Wanted*, *Z Cars*. .

Slattery's People *
US 1964 36 × 50m bw
CBS/Bing Crosby Productions (Matthew Rapf)

Cases of a state investigator.

Well-mounted political dramas which suffered the fate common on American TV with programmes of quality.

cr James Moser

Richard Crenna, Alejandro Rey, Francine York, Kathie Browne

Slay Ride *
US 1972 97m colour TVM
TCF

A New Mexico sheriff clears an Indian of a murder charge.

Competent outdoor murder mystery originally shown as two episodes of *Cade's County*.

w Anthony Silson, Rick Husky d Marvin Chomsky

Glenn Ford, Edgar Buchanan, Victor Campos, Peter Ford, Tony Bill

The Sleeping Ballerina *
GB 1964 30m bw

Touching, dignified film about Olga Spessivtzeva, a Russian ballerina to be ranked with Pavlova until she went mad in 1942. After twenty years in mental institutions in America, new drugs restored her to normal life. Ludovic Kennedy's film marked a deliberate attempt by the freelance outfit Television Reporters International to broaden from the current affairs output which they had set out to furnish and which was already running into trouble in the face of the ITV companies' reluctance to screen independents' work. Alas, it came too late. Shown in Britain by the BBC. PP

Sling Your Hook * (GB 1969). A BBC *Wednesday Play* from Roy Minton, directed by Michael Tuchner and produced by Irene Shubik. My 1969 review: 'Chronicle of a boozy weekend in Blackpool by a group of Nottingham miners which looked as if it were going to be just an extended dossier of quirky behaviour but in fact escalated nicely into a sort of *Ten Little Niggers*, with the members of the outing gradually peeling away until finally only the organizer was left morosely drinking light ale in the returning coach. The point was, of course, that it was a kind of allegory of the drift from the mines, a cheerful "up you" to a declining industry – if you don't need us we don't need you – though not without a residual bitterness.' PP

Small and Frye
US 1983 6 × 25m colour TVM
CBS/Walt Disney (Nick Arnold)

One of a pair of private eyes can shrink to any size at will.

A very strained gimmick for a very feeble comedy.

cr George Schenck, Ron Friedman

Darren McGavin, Jack Blessing

A Small Killing *
US 1981 96m colour TVM
CBS/Orgolini–Nelson/Motown (Neil T. Maffeo)

A lady professor goes undercover to help the police find the murderer of an old street-woman.

Interesting acting is defeated by a flabby script.

w Burt Prelutsky, *book The Rag Bag Clan* by Richard Barth d Steven Hillard Stern
ph Howard Schwartz m Fred Werner

Ed Asner, Jean Simmons, Sylvia Sidney, Kent Williams, Andrew Prine, J. Pat O'Malley

Small Miracle *
US 1973 74m colour TVM
Hallmark

Remake of the film *Never Take No for an Answer*, about a small boy who takes his sick donkey to the Pope.

Effective in its modestly sentimental way.

w John Patrick, Arthur Dales, *novel* Paul Gallico d Jeannot Szwarc m Ernest Gold

Marco della Cava, Vittoria de Sica, Raf Vallone

Small Wonder (US 1985; 22 × 25m; colour TVM). An inventor makes a small robot girl and tries her out as a member of the family. Flatly conceived novelty sitcom. Dick Christie, Marla Pennington, Tiffany Brisette. Created by Ed Jurist; for Metromedia. 'It has the aura of a sixties sitcom making an eighties debut.' – *Variety*

Small World. American talk show, on CBS in the fifties, the creation of Ed Murrow, who by means of international link-ups was able to discuss matters of the moment with three famous guests in their own homes in different parts of the world.

PP: 'Only a radio link in fact; three separate film crews recorded the participants; all was edited together afterwards. But a clever simulation of immediacy in pre-satellite days.'

† Title used in 1985 for four programmes on minority peoples in different parts of the world, e.g. the Cree Indians of Canada, native Corsicans in Corsica. *p* Gwynn Pritchard, HTV for C4.

Smash-up on Interstate Five
US 1976 96m colour TVM
Filmways (Roger Lewis)
After a freeway pile-up, we see how some of those involved came to be there.
Once you've seen the crash, there's no point in waiting: it's *The Bridge of San Luis Rey* all over again, and that was better written.
w Eugene Price, Robert Presnell Jnr, *novel Expressway* by Elleston Trevor *d* John Llewellyn Moxey *m* Bill Conti
Robert Conrad, Buddy Ebsen, Vera Miles, David Groh, Harriet Nelson, Sue Lyon, Scott Jacoby, Donna Mills, Herb Edelman, Terry Moore

Smedley, Ron (–). British schools TV producer whose shoestring versions of Shakespeare (*Heil Caesar*) and *The Government Inspector* were re-transmitted as peak-hour shows. Also responsible for 1982 history of schools TV, *Over My Dead Body*.

Smight, Jack (1926–). American director who cut his teeth in TV. Emmy in 1958 as best director of a single programme for *Eddie*. Series include *Twilight Zone*, *Arrest and Trial*, *Mystery Movie*. TV movies: *The Screaming Woman*, *The Longest Night*, *Partners in Crime*, *Double Indemnity*, *Linda*, *Frankenstein: The True Story*. Big-screen movies generally unremarkable.

Smile Jenny, You're Dead *
US 1974 90m colour TVM
Warner
A private eye protects a cover girl from murder.
Second pilot for *Harry O*; smoothly made.
w Howard Rodman *d* Jerry Thorpe
David Janssen, Andrea Marcovicci, Jodie Foster, Zalman King, Clu Gulager

Smiley's People *
GB 1982 6 × 60m
BBC (Jonathan Powell)
Wearier than ever at being involved in the affairs of a second-class Power doomed to play in the First Division of cloak-and-daggery, the veteran intelligence consultant of *Tinker, Tailor, Soldier, Spy* engineers the defection of his old adversary, the Soviet spymaster Karla. The ending, however powerful, left the Smiley saga curiously unfinished, I thought, like a bridge poking out across a chasm but not quite resting on the other side.
w John Le Carré, John Hopkins, from Le Carré's *novel d* Simon Langton *m* Patrick Gowers
Alec Guinness, Curt Jurgens, Eileen Atkins, Barry Foster, Michael Gough, Anthony Bate, Vladek Sheybal, Bernard Hepton, Rosalie Crutchley, Bill Paterson, Patrick Stewart (as Karla)   PP

The Smith Family *
US 1971–2 39 × 25m colour
ABC/Don Fedderson
The domestic and professional life of a city policeman.
As demonstrated by these stars, it's all too hygienic to be true, but the show, a curious attempt to present a family who looked as though they'd stepped right out of a commercial, was always mildly watchable.
cr Edmund Hartmann
Henry Fonda, Janet Blair, Darleen Carr, Ronny Howard, Michael-James Wixted, John Carter, Charles McGraw

Smith, Gary (1935–). American musical producer, usually with Dwight Hemion.

Smith, Howard K. (1914–). American news correspondent, with CBS and ABC.

Smith, Jaclyn (1947–). American leading lady of the late seventies, one of *Charlie's Angels*. TV movies: *Probe*, *Switch*, *Escape* *from Bogen County, The Users, Jacqueline Bouvier Kennedy, Rage of Angels, George Washington, Sentimental Journey, The Night They Saved Christmas, Florence Nightingale.*

Smith, John (1931–) (Robert Van Orden). Mild-mannered American second lead. TV series: *Cimarron City, Laramie*.

Smith, Kate (1909–). Amply proportioned American popular singer who had her own radio shows, followed by much TV in the fifties.

Smith, Maggie (1935–). Inimitable British actress and film star sparingly but usually memorably on TV from Peter Draper's *Sunday Out of Season*, 1960, through Cedric Messina's *Merchant of Venice* (as Portia), 1972, to *Mrs Silly*, a little piece in the *All for Love* anthology series, 1983, which she elevated to perfect art with the edge of her voice, the way she held herself, her resigned acceptance of the certainty that she would make a fool of herself again.   PP

Smith, Ray (1936–). Welsh actor excellent in masterful roles, which have lately included the harsh father in *We'll Meet Again* and, unfortunately, the taskmaster in *Dempsey and Makepeace*.

Smith, Roger (1932–). American leading man, formerly of *77 Sunset Strip*. Now manages career of wife Ann-Margret.

The Smothers Brothers: Tom (*c* 1932–) **and Dick** (*c* 1934–). This rather self-effacing comic duo with musical talent built themselves up to be a national American institution before suddenly fading from popularity and view. In 1965 they had a half-hour comedy series in which one played an apprentice angel coming back to earth to seek his brother's help; for the two following seasons they had a variety hour series. A 1975 attempted comeback was notably unsuccessful, as was 1981's *Fitz and Bones*.

SMS/Somerset Maugham Hour **
GB 1960–63 approx 40 × 50m bw
live/VTR
Associated–Rediffusion (Norman Marshall)

First British anthology series to be sold on its author's name (*SMS* standing for Somerset Maugham stories) and embarked upon only after some bizarre research by A–R. In a poll in which people were asked to identify names in a miscellaneous list of celebrities Maugham

was the writer to score most heavily, coming ninth after Bruce Forsyth. Tommy Steele came first. In another experiment 1,000 people were asked to name the writers who sprang to mind. Maugham came fourth, after Agatha Christie, Nevil Shute and Enid Blyton. Shute and Mrs Christie having written few short stories, and Noddy being considered too horrific for the family audience, Maugham was chosen. The result was a popular and critical success. Written by Stanley Miller and others; music by Sacha Distel.

† The title change to *Somerset Maugham Hour* came in 1962. In 1970 the BBC trudged over some of the same ground for a BBC2 series.   PP

Smuggler (GB 1981). Half-hour action series for the family, from HTV, set in 1802, with Oliver Tobias as an ex-naval officer turned smuggler. Written by Richard Carpenter; produced by Paul Knight and Sidney Cole.

The Smugglers
US 1968 100m colour TVM
Universal (Norman Lloyd)

American ladies on holiday in Europe are pawns for an international smuggling ring. Lively adventure comedy.

w Alfred Hayes, *novel* Elizabeth Hely *d* Norman Lloyd

Shirley Booth, Gayle Hunnicutt, Michael J. Pollard, Kurt Kasznar, Carol Lynley, David Opatoshu

Snatched *
US 1972 73m colour TVM
Spelling–Goldberg

The wives of three wealthy businessmen are kidnapped for ransom. Slick, tough action melodrama.

d Sutton Roley

Howard Duff, Leslie Nielsen, Sheree North, Barbara Parkins, Robert Reed, John Saxon

Snooker. Popularized by *Pot Black*, it was by the eighties the supreme television sports entertainment in Britain. The World Snooker Final in April 1985, admittedly a nail-biter between Steve Davis and Dennis Taylor only settled by the last ball on the table, pulled an audience of 14.40 million on BBC2 compared with soccer's FA Cup Final (BBC1, 10.35m) or the European Cup Winners' Cup Final (ITV, 12.55m) three weeks later. Re-run as *The Final Frame* in May, the snooker scored another 3.7m. Half-a-dozen major snooker tournaments, all sponsored by tobacco or other industries, now occupy TV screens for a week or more apiece, plus one billiards championship and one Pool contest. PP

The Snoop Sisters
aka: *The Female Instinct*
US 1972 96m colour TVM
NBC/Universal (Douglas Benton)

Two elderly lady mystery writers annoy their policeman nephew by investigating the death of a film star.

A promising format didn't really work despite the talent applied. See *Mystery Movie* for subsequent episodes.

w Leonard B. Stern, Hugh Wheeler d Leonard B. Stern

Helen Hayes, Mildred Natwick, Art Carney, Paulette Goddard (in a minuscule role), Craig Stevens, Bill Dana

Snoopy: see Charlie Brown

The Snow Goose *
GB 1971 50m colour
MCA/Universal/BBC

At the time of Dunkirk, a wounded goose in the Essex marshes brings together an orphan girl and a crippled artist.

Sufficiently moving and capable version of Paul Gallico's carefully sentimental story.

Richard Harris, Jenny Agutter

Snow, Peter (1938–). British newscaster and reporter, with ITN from 1962.

Snowbeast
US 1977 96m colour TVM
NBC/Douglas Cramer

A ski resort is terrorized by a half-human, half-animal creature.

The yeti comes to Colorado. Overstretched chiller.

w Joseph Stefano d Herb Wallerstein

Bo Svenson, Clint Walker, Yvette Mimieux, Sylvia Sidney, Robert Logan

Snowdon on Camera
GB 1981 2 × 60m colour
BBC (Ian Johnstone)

Two programmes with Lord Snowdon cheerfully demolishing the mystique of photography. Taking good ones, he says, needs only daylight and luck. In the second show he doubts the exaggerated values now placed on the photographer's art. Written by Lord Snowdon and Ian Johnstone; directed by Ian Johnstone.

† As a film-maker Lord Snowdon has made several valuable TV documentaries, from *Don't Count the Candles* (old people) with Derek Hart (1968) to *Peter, Tina and Steve* (on 'family placement' fostering for delinquent teenagers instead of Borstal, 1977). PP

The Snowman (GB 1982; 30m). Much-praised (by adults anyway) children's cartoon about a flying snowman. I thought him hopelessly unaerodynamic. Drawn and written by Raymond Briggs, produced by John Coats, for Snowman Enterprises/C4. PP
LH: 'Say what you like about the style, but overall it contrived to have at least two stars' worth of charm.'

Snyder, Tom (c 1939–). American anchorman, host of NBC's late night show *Tomorrow.*

So Soon to Die
US 1957 74m bw TVM
Columbia/Playhouse 90

An unemployed actor is employed to kill a girl, but falls for his prey.

Obvious, old-hat melodrama.

d John Brahm

Richard Basehart, Anne Bancroft, Sebastian Cabot, Torin Thatcher

So You Think You Can Drive * (GB 1965). The first and most valuable in an intermittent series of visual question-and-answer shows in which the audience at home was invited to compete against studio teams of experts, celebrities, etc. Traffic problems were filmed during a typical drive round a provincial town and the frame frozen at the point where the contestants had to choose between three or four alternative courses of action. With Cliff Michelmore, Magnus Magnusson; edited by Patricia Owtram, produced by Tim Slessor. Later subjects included everyday law, medicine and money matters, but only the driving edition has so far rated further, updated productions (1973 and 1981). PP

Soap ***
US 1977–80 80 approx. × 25m colour (VTR)
ABC/(Columbia) Witt–Thomas–Harris (Paul Junger Witt, Tony Thomas)

The families of two sisters, one rich and one poor: both have lots of secrets.

Controversial black comedy series, supposedly a spoof of soap operas but actually a light satire of all kinds of trends in today's entertainment, including homosexuality, religion, sex and the Mafia. Sample remark of mother to gay son whom she finds trying on her clothes: 'I've told you a hundred times, that dress fastens at the back . . .'

cr/w SUSAN HARRIS

RICHARD MULLIGAN, CATHRYN DAMON, ROBERT MANDAN, KATHERINE HELMOND, DIANA CANOVA, BILLY CRYSTAL, ROBERT GUILLAUME, Arthur Peterson, Robert Urich, Jennifer Salt, Ted Wass, Charles Lane

'Some of the jokes have nothing going for them but bad taste, which isn't always enough. Is it funny? Yes, it is, mostly, and I guess that constitutes redeeming social value.' – Robert MacKenzie, *TV Guide*

soap opera. Strictly speaking, unending daily serials going out all year, as first tried out on American daytime radio in the thirties and so called because they were sponsored (and indeed produced) by the big soap corporations realizing that here was a cheap way of keeping their names in front of the very audience they wanted to reach, the housewives. By 1939, Procter & Gamble alone ran 21 different soaps. They had titles such as *The Guiding Light*, *The Road of Life* or *One Life to Live* (known to the cast as *One Leg to Lift*) which summed up the pokerwork-motto philosophy on offer. When television came in after the war, many of them transferred to the new medium; one or two still survive, now 50 years old, but they have long been eclipsed by the peak-hour super-soaps *Dynasty* and *Falcon Crest* and *Dallas*, of course.

In Britain, the only perfect soaper these days is *The Archers* on radio. Though ITV tried daily serials, none caught on. The closest was *Crossroads*, before it was cut back to three days a week by diktat of the IBA. *Coronation Street* has never been more than twice weekly, but this exceptional, well-written, affectionately performed saga offers the best illustration of the authentic spell. It is an alternative slice of life, an extra set of neighbours.

For many people soap opera is as important an amenity as the electricity, gas or water coming into the house. But already the newer soaps, *Albion Market* and *EastEnders*, are pushing in much more plot, more extravagant happenings, bringing them slowly closer to the insane melodramatics of *Dallas* and *Dynasty*, the television equivalent of glue sniffing.

Recommended reading: *The Wonderful World of Soap Operas* by Robert LaGuardia, Ballantine 1974; *All for Love* by Peter Buckman, Secker 1984.   PP

Soft Targets (GB 1982; 75m). The Cold War as glimpsed through the eyes of an insignificant literary attaché in the Russian diplomatic compound in London who convinces himself that he is being set up by British security; an unusual comedy with unsettling overtones. With Ian Holm, Helen Mirren; written by Stephen Poliakoff, directed by Charles Sturridge, for BBC Play for Today.   PP

Softly Softly *
GB 1966–76   × 50m colour (VTR)
BBC
Perennially popular stories of a mythical Midlands police force.
Originally a spin-off from *Z Cars*, to follow the fortunes of Inspector Barlow, its cast suffered several changes and in its latter years the title became, rather clumsily, *Softly, Softly: Task Force*. Frank Windsor was on hand more or less throughout, as were Norman Bowler and Terence Rigby. Elwyn Jones was prominent among the writers, as were Robert Barr, Keith Dewhurst and Alan Plater.
'You can only sit rooted to your seat in joyful and generally fulfilled expectation.' – *Daily Express*

A Soiree at Bossom's Hotel
GB 1966 75m bw
BBC (Peter Luke)
Simon Raven's play about the last days of a little Mayfair hotel-cum-house of assignation obviously modelled on the old Cavendish. At the time I found it 'witty, un-memorable, easy to enjoy'.

d Gilchrist Calder

FABIA DRAKE, Wallas Eaton, Sarah Lawson, Roddy Maude-Roxby   PP

Soldier, Soldier * (GB 1960). With *Sergeant Musgrave's Dance* a hit in the theatre, playwright John Arden propelled another rough trooper into a bleak northern town for a first, bustling TV play. Of ANDREW KEIR in the part, I wrote in 1960: 'Swaggering, bragging, bullying, now foul-mouthed, now dropping into the rough poetry of a barrack-room Burns, he proclaimed a particular military tradition as old as war itself. The Lowland blend of boorishness and dubious charm was exact: did Keir contribute some of it himself? If so, it was the final touch to a part that fitted him as trimly as his tartan trews.' Also with Maurice Denham, Frank Finlay, Margaretta d'Arcy.   PP

Soldiers
GB 1985 13 × 50m
BBC (John Gau)

Ambitious series rashly mixing demonstration footage, personal testimony, re-enactment and old movie clips to analyse the allure/horror of warfare. Infantry, armour, artillery, etc. were considered arm by arm, together with episodes on legendary commanders and the general experience of battle. The result fell between two coffee tables – neither romantic enough to suit romantics nor practical enough to suit military buffs. Thriller writer Frederick Forsyth, said to be one of the latter, acted as presenter.

w John Keegan, Richard Holmes *episode producers* John Bird, Malcolm Brown, Ian Taylor, Robert Toner, Christopher Warren, Ivan Rendall   PP

Soldiers of Fortune
US 1955–6 52 × 25m bw
MCA/Revue

Two international adventurers offer themselves for hire.
Okay action series.

John Russell, Chick Chandler

The Sole Survivor *
US 1969 100m colour TVM
CBS/Cinema Center

A brigadier general helps to investigate the crash 17 years earlier of a plane which he, navigated, and the ghosts of the dead watch helplessly.
Interesting but overstretched supernatural melodrama.

w Guerdon Trueblood d Paul Stanley ph James Crabe m Paul Glass

Vince Edwards, William Shatner, Richard Basehart, Lou Antonio, Patrick Wayne

The Solid Gold Kidnapping: see The Six Million Dollar Man

The Solitary Man
US 1980 96m colour TVM
CBS/John Conboy

The life of a middle-class worker is shattered when his wife announces her intention of divorcing him.
Mildly interesting but repetitive psychological study of a man suddenly lost.

w James Byrnes d John Llewellyn Moxey ph Robert L. Morrison m Jack Elliott

Earl Holliman, Carrie Snodgress, Nicholas Coster, Lara Parker, Dorrie Kavanagh

Solo (GB 1970; 10 × 40m). Actors hamming their way through single-handed impersonations of the famous and infamous: Jeremy Brett as Byron, Eileen Atkins as Mary Kingsley, Michael Jayston as Wilfred Owen, etc. Produced by Cedric Messina; for BBC. PP

Solzhenitsyn, Alexander (1918–). Russian novelist who after his release to the West in 1976 gave a memorable interview on *Panorama*, scolding the West for its apathy to Soviet imperialism, and prompting the former Labour minister Lord George Brown to resign from the Labour Party next day. 'Not often,' I wrote, 'does the authentic wrath of God come funnelling into the living room.' Further appearances have been rare; the most recent was in conversation with Malcolm Muggeridge, on C4 in 1983. Solzhenitsyn's play *The Love Girl and the Innocent* was done by BBC TV in 1972, with Michael Bryant; his story *Russian Night 1941*, dramatized by Robert Muller, in 1982.
PP

Some Kind of Miracle
US 1980 96m colour TVM
CBS/Lorimar (George LeMaire)

A man becomes bitter when a swimming accident makes him impotent.
There can't be many diseases or disabilities left for TV movie producers to tackle. This is one that doesn't fill the slot without the help of assorted minor problems such as quadroplaegia.

w Mary and Jack Willis, from their book d Jerrold Friedman ph Tak Fujimoto m Jimmie Haskell

David Dukes, Andrea Marcovicci, Nancy Marchand, Michael C. Gwynne, Art Hindle, Stephen Elliott

Some May Live
GB/US 1966 100m colour TVM
(RKO) Foundation Pictures (Philip N. Krasne)

A woman army intelligence agent in Saigon passes classified information to her husband, a communist.
Boring political espionage adventure.

w David T. Chantler d Vernon Sewell ph Ray Parslow m Cyril Ornadel

Joseph Cotten, Martha Hyer, Peter Cushing, John Ronane

Some Mothers Do 'Ave 'Em *
GB 1974–9 30 approx. × 30m plus specials colour (VTR)
BBC (Michael Mills)

Adventures before and after marriage of the

world's worst accident-prone misfit.

The star's curiously effeminate character-ization proved much to the public taste, and some of the stunts were magnificently conceived. Otherwise the series was necessarily repetitive and quickly began to wear out its welcome.

w Raymond Allen

MICHAEL CRAWFORD, Michele Dotrice

Someone I Touched *
US 1975 74m colour TVM
ABC/Charles Fries (Wayne Weisbart)

A woman and her husband come to terms with each other when they find they have venereal disease.

Adequate 'outspoken' social melodrama.

w James Henderson *d* Lou Antonio

Cloris Leachman, James Olson, Glynnis O'Connor, Andy Robinson, Allyn Ann McLerie, Kenneth Mars

Someone's Watching Me *
US 1978 96m colour TVM
NBC/Warner (Robert Kobritz)

A lady TV director is terrorized by an apparent peeping tom whose motives may be even more sinister.

Smooth, competent screamer with a let-down solution and at least one suspense set-up too many.

w/d John Carpenter *ph* Robert Hauser *m* Harry Sukman

Lauren Hutton, David Birney, Adrienne Barbeau

Somers, Suzanne (1946–) (Suzanne Mahoney). American leading lady, a household word after *Three's Company*.

Somerset Maugham Hour: see SMS/Somerset Maugham Hour

Something about Amelia *
US 1984 96m colour TVM
ABC/MGM/Leonard Goldberg (Michele Rappoport)

A man commits incest with his teenage daughter after objecting to her first date.

Reasonably strong TV movie, though one suspects that the idea for a sensational subject came first and the story was built around it.

w William Hanley *d* Randa Haines *ph* Edward R. Brown *m* Marc Snow

Ted Danson, Glenn Close, Olivia Cole, Roxana Zal, Lane Smith, Kevin Conway

Something Beautiful for God * (GB 1969).
Malcolm Muggeridge's account, produced by Peter Chafer for BBC, of Mother Teresa of Calcutta, a decade before she was awarded her Nobel Peace Prize. My 1969 review: 'Whether according dignity and love to dying destitutes who in life had known neither, or caring for unwanted babies, or conducting a toddlers' play group or trying to organize the improvident fishermen of Malabar, her Order demonstrated the Christian ethic at its simplest and rarest.

'Mother Teresa herself, with her calm eyes and puckered mouth, managed to convey by appearance alone how she continually looked upon the worst of the world but saw only the best.'   PP

Something Evil *
US 1971 73m colour TVM
Bedford Productions

A young couple and family move into a haunted farmhouse.

Flashy supernatural thriller with not enough plot.

w Robert Clouse *d* Steven Spielberg

Sandy Dennis, Darren McGavin, Ralph Bellamy

Something for a Lonely Man
US 1968 98m colour TVM
Universal (Richard E. Lyons)

An old steam-engine brings prosperity to a western town.

Mildly enjoyable family western.

w John Fante, Frank Fenton *d* Don Taylor

Dan Blocker, Susan Clark, John Dehner, Warren Oates, Don Stroud

Something for Joey
US 1977 96m colour TVM
NBC/MTM (Jerry McNeely)

A college footballer looks after his younger brother who has leukaemia.

Depressingly slow disease-of-the-weeker, taken from real life but no better for it.

w Jerry McNeely *d* Lou Antonio *ph* Gayne Rescher *m* David Shire

Geraldine Page, Gerald S. O'Loughlin, Marc Singer, Jeff Lynas, Linda Kelsey, Kathleen Beller, Paul Picerni, Brian Farrell

Something in Disguise **
GB 1982 6 × 52m
Thames (Moira Armstrong)

Eccentric country-house family comedy turning into touching love story for Anton Rodgers and the adorable Elizabeth Garvie.

'The most consummate soap opera ever,' I wrote. 'It has life, death, birth, love, tragedy and something underhand going on as well.' If it also accommodated a few dreadful clichés of the soap opera, it did so in a good cause.

w Elizabeth Jane Howard, from her own novel *story consultant* Richard Bates d Moira Armstrong

Anton Rodgers, Elizabeth Garvie, Richard Vernon, Ursula Howells, Clare Clifford, Barry Stanton, David Gwillim   PP

Something So Right
US 1982 96m colour TVM
CBS/Tisch–Avnet/List–Estrin (Jonathan Estrin, Shelley List)

A boy warms to his divorced mother's new friend.

It's a switch that he likes him, but otherwise every reaction is pure routine, copied from a dozen films of the forties.

w Jonathan Estrin, Shelley List d Lou Antonio ph Gayne Rescher m Charles Gross

Ricky Schroder, Patty Duke Astin, James Farentino, Fred Dryer, Annie Potts

Son of Man (GB 1969). Dennis Potter's play about Jesus, seen as a barrel-chested journeyman carpenter with a simple, enormous message of love, but his divinity left somewhat in doubt. That this provoked resentment rather than indignation among those who disagreed, while inspiring respect rather than enthusiasm in those willing to accept the doubts, is probably an indication that this production, anyway, was inconclusive and the script ought to be re-realized some time, preferably minus some slangy locutions in the dialogue and in a less stagey studio setting. As it was it looked oddly old-fashioned, 'like animated illustrations from a Humanist Sunday School Bible', as I said at the time. Produced by Graeme McDonald; for BBC.   PP

'A very special love story for everyone who has hope!'
Son-Rise: a Miracle of Love
US 1979 96m colour TVM
NBC/Filmways/Rothman–Wohl (Richard M. Rosenbloom)

The case history of an autistic child.

A lovingly made film, but a documentary would have been more satisfying – and probably shorter.

w Stephen Kandel, Barry and Suzi Kaufman, *book* Barry Kaufman d Glenn Jordan ph Matthew F. Leonetti m Gerald Fried

James Farentino, Kathryn Harrold, Stephen Elliott, Carry Sherman, Michael and Casey Adams

Song by Song (GB 1978–80; 13 × 50m). A songwriter at a time, with the exception of one composite British edition, with Ned Sherrin sketching his life and times and a trio of singers to sing the numbers. A pleasant YTV entertainment developed from a live concert show *Side by Side by Sondheim* which Sherrin devised with Millicent Martin, David Kiernan and Julia McKenzie, and which served as a pilot for this series. Songwriters included Jerome Kern, Irving Berlin, Noël Coward, E. Y. Harburg, Sammy Cahn.   PP

A Song for Europe
West Germany/GB 1985 100m
Stern TV for C4 and ZDF (Johann Heinrich Gerhard)

High-minded Briton working for Swiss pharmaceutical giant leaks secrets of unfair trading practices to Common Market bureau, and for his pains loses wife, job, liberty and wealth. Unconcealedly based on the real life story of Stanley Adams (who shopped Hoffman La Roche) this Film on Four neatly conveyed – mostly between the lines – the motives and doubts of such a public-spirited Eurocitizen, but the pace was relentlessly uniform and Maria Schneider's performance as the wife absurdly spelled gloom and doom when he had scarcely embarked upon his course of action.

w Peter Prince d John Goldschmidt m Carl Davis

David Suchet, Maria Schneider, Reinhard Glemnitz, Ernst Schroeder, Dietmar Schoenherr, Robert Freitag, Georges Claisse
                                                                   PP

Song of Summer *** (GB 1968). KEN RUSSELL's account of how Eric Fenby, a young Scarborough cinema organist, volunteered to help the blind and paralysed composer Frederick Delius: funny, unsentimental, moving. With Max Adrian as Delius, Christopher Gable as Fenby, David Collings as Percy Grainger. For BBC.   PP

Songs of Praise. Half an hour of hymn-singing from a different church or chapel each Sunday, the former nicely rehearsed and the latter packed for the occasion. What used to be a filler before weightier religious items on Sunday evening is these days often the only religious item on BBC1. Thora Hird introduces seasonal compilations called variously *Your Songs of Praise Choice* or *Praise Be!*   PP

The Songwriters (GB 1978). A BBC series of 7 × 50m documentaries tracing the life and songs of outstanding British composers of this century, including Leslie Stuart, Lionel Monckton, Noël Coward, Lennon and McCartney. Pleasingly produced and written (on a modest budget) by Tony Staveacre.

Sons and Daughters
US 1974 13 × 50m colour
CBS/Universal/Barney Rosenzweig
Stories of small-town high-school students in the fifties.
Lame imitation of *American Graffiti*. See also *Senior Year* (pilot).
Gary Frank, Glynnis O'Connor

Soo, Jack (1917–79) (Goro Sozuki). Japanese–American character actor best remembered as one of the *Barney Miller* team.

'How far should a girl go – the first time?'
Sooner or Later
US 1980 96m colour TVM
NBC/Laughing Willow Company (Carole Hart)
A 13-year-old girl has a crush on a rock singer. Who needs to know? Or to waste a talented cast in telling about it?
w Bruce and Carole Hart *d* Bruce Hart *ph* Edward R. Brown *m* Stephen Lawrence
Denise Miller, Rex Smith, Barbara Feldon, Lynn Redgrave, Vivian Blaine, Judd Hirsch, Lilia Skala, Morey Amsterdam

Sooty. A glove puppet manipulated by Harry H. Corbett; popular in Britain throughout TV's postwar decades, and one of the medium's first stars.

Sophia Loren: Her Own Story
US 1980 140m colour TVM
NBC/EMI/Roger Gimbel (Alex Ponti, Peter Katz)
A potted version of the star's autobiography, including her romance with Cary Grant.
A bit of a plod.
w Joanna Crawford *d* Mel Stuart *ph* Alberto Spagnoli *m* Fred Karlin
Sophia Loren (also playing her own mother), John Gavin (as Cary Grant), Armando Assante, Rip Torn, Ritz Braun, Edmund Purdom (as Vittorio de Sica)
'Interesting but scarcely compelling'. – *Daily Variety*

The Sophisticated Gents *
US 1981 2 × 95m colour miniseries
NBC/Daniel Wilson (Fran Sears)

The 25th-year reunion of seven black athletes has unexpected repercussions.
Multi-story miniseries which was generally well received but achieved poor ratings.
w Melvin Van Peebles, *novel The Junior Bachelor Society* by John A. Williams *d* Harry Falk *ph* Terry Meade *m* Benny Golson
Sonny Jim Gaines, Paul Winfield, Bernie Casey, Rosie Grier, Thalmus Rasulala, Robert Hooks, Raymond St Jacques, Ron O'Neal, Dick Anthony Williams, Rosalind Cash, Bibi Besch
'A telefilm of depth and compassion, of richness and complexity.' – *Daily Variety*

Sophisticated Ladies *
US 1982 120m approx. colour
Black Tie Network (Brice Brandwen)
Pay-per-view telecast of a Broadway musical; not enough people forked out 15 dollars to make it a forerunner of such shows on a regular basis.
d Clark Jones
Hinton Battle, Paula Kelly, Phyllis Hyman, Robert Guillaume, Mercer Ellington and the Duke Ellington Orchestra
'An interesting footnote to telecommunications history – the first live theatrical production of a still-running Broadway musical to be sold on a national PPV basis via satellite, cable and subscription TV . . . The delivery system makes little difference to viewers: the medium is not the message, the show is.' – *Daily Variety*

Sorrell and Son * (GB 1984; 6 × 50m). Ex-officer and gentleman left as a penniless single parent in the aftermath of World War I buckles down as a hotel porter in order to send his son to school and teaching hospital. A dramatization from the 1925 best-seller by Warwick Deeping which inspired story editors to search out several other old chain-library favourites. With Richard Pasco, Peter Chelsom, Stephanie Beacham, John Shrapnel. Dramatized by Jeremy Paul, produced and directed by Derek Bennett, for YTV.   PP

The Sorrow and the Pity **
Original title: *Le Chagrin et la Pitié*
France 1971 270m bw
RTF (MARCEL OPHULS)
The first of the great blockbusters, in Britain making up a whole evening on BBC2: a candid view of life under the Nazi Occupation, centred on one locality, Clermont-Ferrand. Perhaps a

dozen witnesses gave evidence, including the former prime minister Pierre Mendés-France, a British SOE operative and a veteran of the Charlemagne Division which fought for the Germans; but each one had time to talk himself out. Contemporary newsreels (German, French and British) were likewise quoted in full. At the time I wrote: 'Deftly adapted to the English language by David Francis, Ophuls's film gave me not only the flavour of the Occupation but also the equivocation and inconsistency which I recognize as truth.'   PP

Sorry! (GB since 1982). Extremely British sitcom with Ronnie Corbett as an eternal Mummy's boy. Dispiriting. With Barbara Lott; written by Ian Davidson and Peter Vincent, produced by David Askey, for BBC.   PP

SOS Titanic
US 1979 140m colour TVM
ABC/EMI/Argonaut/Roger Gimbel

The one and only transatlantic voyage of the ill-fated *Titanic* in 1912.
Stilted and unsupple retread of all the gimmicks first seen in 1956's *A Night to Remember*. In this tedious version there isn't even an icy breath in the chill air.

w James Costigan d Billy Hale ph Christopher Challis m Howard Blake

David Janssen, Cloris Leachman, David Warner, Susan St James, Antoinette O'Reilly, Gerald McSorley, Harry Andrews, Ed Bishop, Warren Clarke, Ian Holm, Bessie Love, Helen Mirren, Ronnie Stevens, Philip Stone

'Vigorous if limited TV history.' – *Daily Variety*

† The budget was more than 5 million dollars.

Sothern, Ann (1909–) (Harriet Lake). Pert, wisecracking American leading lady of movies in the thirties and forties; in the fifties made a big name for herself as star of *Private Secretary* and *The Ann Sothern Show*. TV movies: *The Outsider, Congratulations It's a Boy, A Death of Innocence, The Weekend Nun, The Great Man's Whiskers, Captains and the Kings, A Letter to Three Wives*.

Soul, David (1943–) (David Solberg). American leading man who had a phenomenal success in *Starsky and Hutch*, and became a folk singer. TV movies: *The Disappearance of Flight 412, Little Ladies of the Night, Swan Song, Rage, Salem's Lot, World War III, The Manions of America, Casablanca, The Yellow Rose, Through Naked Eyes, The Key to Rebecca*.

The Sound of Anger
US 1968 100m colour TVM
Universal (Roy Huggins)

A team of lawyers defend teenage lovers accused of murdering the girl's father.
Moderate pilot for the series *The Bold Ones*. It achieves its purpose.

w Dick Nelson d Michael Ritchie

Burl Ives, James Farentino, Dorothy Provine

The Sound of Laughter *
GB 1975 100m colour (VTR)
BBC

Reminiscences of early radio comedians and writers.
Rather a disappointing programme, but immensely valuable historically as a record of what was said.

Arthur Askey, Richard Murdoch, Maurice Denham, Deryck Guyler, Frankie Howerd, Barry Cryer

The Sound of Murder
US 1982 96m colour TVM (tape)
OPT/Lorimar/Michael Brandman

An author plots with the help of a dictaphone to kill his wife and her lover.
Routine theatrical suspenser, somewhat dated by its hardware.

w William Fairchild d Michael Lindsay-Hogg

Michael Moriarty, Joanna Miles, Pippa Scott, Leonard Frey, David Ackroyd

Sounder
US 1976 74m colour TVM
ABC Circle

Problems of a poor black family in the thirties. Adventures of the Sounder family: a TV pilot that didn't take.

d William Graham

Ebony Wright, Harold Sylvester, Daryl Young

Sounder Part 2
US 1976 96m colour TVM
ABC (Terry Nelson)

A black father struggles to build a schoolhouse for his children.
Somewhat idealized idyll of the old south.

w Lonnie Elder III d William A. Graham m Taj Mahal

Harold Sylvester, Ebony Wright, Taj Mahal, Annazette Chase, Darryl Young

**Sounds Magnificent ** ** (GB 1984; 6 × 90m). André Previn discoursing on the evolution of the symphony and conducting examples by Haydn and Mozart, Beethoven, Berlioz, Brahms, Tchaikovsky and Shostakovich, with the Royal Philharmonic Orchestra. In sleeveless tunic and floppy shirt he looked like a cross between a snooker champion and one of the lovers in *As You Like It*, but it was a beguiling exercise in popular enlightenment. Produced by Herbert Chappel, for BBC.   PP

† *Previn on Concertos* followed in 1986.

South Africa. The last developed country to hold out against TV as a matter of policy, reluctantly introducing a service only in 1976. Its advent was chronicled at rather undue length in four episodes of *The Philpott File* that year for the BBC.   PP

The South Bank Show ***. British arts programme, arguably the best ever, certainly the best since *Monitor*'s heyday. Succeeding LWT's earlier *Aquarius* in 1978 it has made its reputation by choosing the right subjects (including adequate attention to television itself), and giving them ample treatment, whether in the form of film essays (e.g. Tony Palmer's on Britten and Walton) or studio performances such as the masterly Shakespeare seminars of 1979. Melvyn Bragg's interviews, especially with writers, constitute a third asset. Its formative producer was Nick Elliott.   PP

South of the Border (GB 1985; 7 × 28m). Stalwart northerner forced by closure of his local pit to venture south. Sitcom with some topicality and a little bite by Peter Tinniswood; with Brian Glover in t'part. Produced and directed by Derrick Goodwin, for BBC.   PP

South Riding *
GB 1974 13 × 50m colour (VTR)
Yorkshire (James Ormerod)

An adaptation of Winifred Holtby's book about a mythical Yorkshire community in the mid-thirties.
Produced with standard efficiency, it met with moderate success. BAFTA judged it best series of the year.

w Stan Barstow

Dorothy Tutin, Hermione Baddeley, Nigel Davenport

Soviet Union. TV in Russia is entirely state-controlled, and although there is a reasonable mix of entertainment programmes, everything is made to toe the party line. The bigger cities may have several channels, remote rural areas only one.

Space *
US 1985 3 × 142m, 3 ×
    96m colour miniseries
CBS/Paramount/Stonehenge/Dick Berg
(Martin Manulis)

Six characters are followed from World War II to their eventual destinies as part of the US space programme.
Complex, heavygoing, good-looking miniseries from the novel by James A. Michener, a production on the *Winds of War* level.

w Stirling Silliphant *d* Joseph Sargent, Lee Phillips *ph* Hector Figueroa, Gayne Rescher *m* Miles Goodman, Tony Berg

James Garner, Susan Anspach, Beau Bridges, Blair Brown, Bruce Dern, Melinda Dillon, David Dukes, Harry Hamlin, Michael York, Martin Balsam, James Sutorius, G. D. Spradlin, David Spielberg, Ralph Bellamy, Roscoe Lee Browne, Clu Gulager

'Pure television, a thing of wonderment.' – *New York Times*
'Order up a dozen Emmys.' – *TV Guide*
'Evokes the changing eras with panache.' – *Time*
'One of the three or four most distinguished projects in the history of television.' – Norman Cousins
'An exhilarating mission that floats effortlessly amid fact, fancy and fireworks.' – Associated Press

The Space Between Words
GB/US 1972 5 × 70m colour
BBC (ROGER GRAEF)

Five essays in leaving the camera running while people talk, argue or plan, supposedly to demonstrate how they fail to communicate. In at least one episode (family life) they seemed to be communicating only too inexorably, and boring each other to despair. But the fifth programme, dwelling on United Nations diplomats trying to set up a directorate to co-ordinate disaster relief, finally demonstrated that speech is indeed a product of the use to which it's put: three weeks were expended on mulling over the fine shades of meaning in the one word to 'direct'. The three other areas were work, school and politics.   PP

Space Ghost
US 1966–8 20 × 22m colour
NBC/Hanna–Barbera

Exploits of an interplanetary crime fighter who can render himself invisible.
Very ordinary cartoon frolics, including a 'prehistoric' segment featuring Dino Boy.

DAVID SOUL. After *Starsky and Hutch*, he seemed intent on showing his versatility: as champion skier, rapist, Nazi spy, tough westerner, even as Humphrey Bogart in an ill-fated attempt to re-do *Casablanca* for television. But he was never a real star except in the part which brought him fame. Here he plays opposite Cliff Robertson in *The Key to Rebecca*.

Space 1999 *
GB 1975–6 48 × 50m colour
ATV/Gerry Anderson

A space station breaks away, travels through the universe and encounters alien civilizations.

Star Trek in all but name; an ambitious and sometimes imaginative production, handicapped by a lack of pace and humour and two very doleful leads.

Martin Landau, Barbara Bain, Barry Morse, Catherine Schell

Spacek, Sissy (1950–). American leading lady. TV movies: *The Girls of Huntington House*, *The Migrants*, *Katherine*.

The Spanish Civil War *
GB 1982 6 × 60m
Granada (Steve Morrison)

Admirable, doggedly-digging history of a conflict so messy that it was often a war within a war, as when communists turned on communists in Barcelona. Written by Neal Ascherson and James Cameron, narrated by Frank Finlay, produced by David Kemp, John Blake and David Hart.   PP

The Spanish Farm Trilogy *
GB 1968 4 × 60m bw
BBC (David Conroy)

Effective condensation by Lennox Phillips of R. H. Mottram's 800-page chronicle of a war-torn farm in Flanders during and after World War I, with Caroline Mortimer sustaining the heroine's epic stubbornness. Also with Cavan Kendall, Jack Woolgar.   PP

Sparkling Cyanide
US 1983 96m colour TVM
CBS/Warner/Stan Marguilies

Complications arise at a dinner party when a rich man's wife is poisoned.

Shifted from England to Pasadena, this

puzzle is boring, flat and difficult to follow as is the *raison d'être* of the part played by the hero.

w Robert Malcolm Young, Sue Grafton, Steven Humphrey, *novel* by Agatha Christie *d* Robert Lewis *ph* Ted Voigtlander *m* James DiPasquale

Anthony Andrews, Deborah Raffin, Pamela Bellwood, Nancy Marchand, Josef Sommer, David Huffman, Christine Belford, June Chadwick, Barry Ingham, Harry Morgan

Spearhead ** (GB 1978–81). Annals of an infantry platoon in Northern Ireland, Hong Kong and at home in Britain, excellently done. Created by Simon Theobalds; written by Nick McCarty; directed by James Ormerod; for Southern. The central character was initially a colour-sergeant played by Michael Billington, with Jacqueline Tong as his wife; later, a fellow sergeant took over as hero, played by Roy Holder.   PP

special. A term which in TV was originally applied to variety entertainments but came to mean any kind of non-fictional one-shot.

Special Branch
GB 1969–73 approx 50 × 50m colour
Thames/Euston Films

Cases of Scotland Yard's security department. Practised, competent cop show which made no great waves.

George Sewell, Patrick Mower

Special Bulletin *
US 1983 96m colour TVM
NBC/Metromedia/Ohlmeyer (Marshall Herskovitz, Edward Zwick)

A national newscast covering a dock strike uncovers terrorists armed with a nuclear bomb.
Striking docu-drama which entertains while getting across all the political points it may or may not intend.

w,d Marshall Herskovitz

Christopher Allport, Kathryn Walker, Ed Flanders, Roxanne Hart, David Clennon, David Rasche, Rosalind Cash

'Meaningful, timely . . . and scary as hell.' – *Variety*

Emmy 1983: outstanding drama special

A Special Kind of Love
US 1978 96m colour TVM
CBS/EMI/Roger Gimbel (Merrit Malloy, Marc Trabulis)

A mentally retarded teenager wins the Special Olympics.

Or, see *The Kid from Nowhere.* Conventionally heartwarming emotional binge.

w John Sacret Young *d* Lee Phillips *ph* Matthew F. Leonetti *m* Peter Matz

Charles Durning, Irene Tedrow, Mare Winningham, Philip Brown, Herb Edelman, Kevin Condit

'A retarded boy's courage unites his family in a special moment of joy!'
Special Olympics
aka: *A Special Kind of Love*
US 1978 96m colour TVM
EMI (Merritt Malloy, Marc Trabulus)

A widowed truck driver has three teenage sons, one of whom is mentally retarded.
Slow, heavy-going family drama which ends in a fine burst of love and sentimentality but takes a hell of a while to get there.

w John Sacret Young *d* Lee Phillips *ph* Matthew F. Leonetti *m* Peter Matz

Charles Durning, Irene Tedrow, George Parry, Mare Winningham, Philip Brown
'Worthy causes don't necessarily make worthy drama.' – *Daily Variety*

'When all the world saw only their limitations . . . all she could see were possibilities!'
Special People
US 1984 96m colour TVM
CBS/Joe Cates (Bruce Raymond)

Mentally handicapped young adults are moulded into a successful theatre company.
Somehow very unlikeable and unconvincing piece of do-goodery in which the hapless handicapped end up with precious little sympathy, despite the fact that the story is true.

w Corey Blechman *d* Marc Daniels *ph* Mark Irwin *m* Eric N. Robertson

Brooke Adams, Liberace, David Gardner; and the Special People

The Specialists
US 1974 74m colour TVM
Universal (Robert A. Cinader)

US public health experts trace an epidemic. Lacklustre pilot.

w Preston Wood, R. A. Cinader *d* Richard Quine

Robert York, Jack Hogan, Maureen Reagan, Kyle Anderson, Tom Scott

'Supernatural forces invade a millionaire's mansion!'

Spectre
GB/US 1977 96m colour TVM
NBC/TCF/Gene Roddenberry (Gordon
L. T. Scott)

A criminologist specializes in the occult and exposes a coven of aristocratic devil worshippers in London.

Hilariously inept *Exorcist* rip-off with a starry cast all at sea. Special nude scenes were shot for a theatrical version which was never released.

w Gene Roddenberry, Sam Peeples *d* Clive Donner *m* John Cameron

Robert Culp, Gig Young, Gordon Jackson, James Villiers, Ann Lynn, John Hurt, Jenny Runacre

Speed Buggy
US 1973–4 48 × 22m colour
CBS/Hanna–Barbera

Adventures of three teenagers in a car with personality.
Made to order cartoon series.

Speed, Doris (1901–). British character actress who since 1960 has played the formidable Annie Walker in *Coronation Street*.

Speed King **
GB 1979 90m 16mm colour
BBC (Innes Lloyd)

Robert Hardy as the racing driver, Movietone commentator and domestic tyrant Sir Malcolm Campbell, and having to compete hard not to be upstaged by the 28-foot model of the Bluebird car with which Campbell broke the world land speed record in 1935. The record attempt was ingeniously simulated using the mock-up plus archive newsfilm whose absence of colour didn't show against the bleached backdrop of the Utah salt flats. The play ended with his 14-year-old son Donald christening the speed-boat to which Sir Malcolm next turned, and which was to kill Donald 30 years later.

w Roger Milner *d* Ferdinand Fairfax

Robert Hardy, Jennifer Hillary, Jack Galloway, Neil Nisbet   PP

Speight, Johnny (1921–). British writer, a former milkman with not much style but a sharp ear for the vernacular. Creator of Alf Garnett in *Till Death Us Do Part*.

The Spell
US 1977 74m colour TVM
Charles Fries (David Manson)

SPACE. James Garner seemed to leap from the laconic hero of *The Rockford Files* into middle age, as shown here in *Space*. His trouble was that his character had to start in his twenties, which may be what is giving Mr Garner food for thought.

An overweight adolescent is possessed by the devil.

The author of *The Exorcist* should sue. Otherwise a fair spinetingler.

w Brian Taggert *d* Lee Philips *m* Gerald Fried

Lee Grant, James Olson, Susan Myers, Barbara Bostock, Lelia Goldoni

✻ **Spelling, Aaron** (1928–). American producer who made a small corner in empty-headed glamorous entertainment series harking back to the old innocent Hollywood, from *Burke's Law* to *Charlie's Angels* and *The Love Boat*. The style began to run out with *Fantasy Island*, *Dynasty* and *Strike Force*, but still Spelling could do no wrong with the fat little beer-drinking guy in Milwaukee who according to the demographics is Mr Average American.

Spencer's Pilots
US 1976 13 × 50m colour
CBS/Sweeney/Finnegan (Larry Rosen)

Adventures of pilots for hire based at a small Midwestern airfield.

Despite an expensive first episode about barnstormers, this fated venture had the tired air of an old Monogram B feature.

cr Alvin Sapinsley m Morton Stevens

Christopher Stone, Todd Susman, Gene Evans

Spend, Spend, Spend **
GB 1977 90m colour (16mm)
BBC (Graeme MacDonald)

The story of a woman who won £152,000 on the football pools and spent it all, her husbands all dying of drugs and car accidents. An obvious moral tale about vulgar people. Brilliantly made, it also has the merit of being true.

w JACK ROSENTHAL book Vivian Nicholson d JOHN GOLDSCHMIDT ph Phil Meheux

Susan Littler, John Duttine, Helen Beck, Joe Belcher

'Working-class adrenalin in agonizing quantity . . . a heartbreaking piece.' – *Sunday Times*
'Beautifully organized . . . very funny.' – *Sunday Telegraph*

† BAFTA award 1977, best play.

Spenser: For Hire
US 1 × 96m, × 50m colour
ABC/Warner/John Wilder (Dick Gallegly)

A Boston private eye who is also a bit of a philosopher combines love and duty while generally on the run.

Pretentious thick ear without the saving grace of humour. At least the Boston locations are fresh.

cr John Wilder, novels by Robert B. Parker

Robert Urich, Barbara Stock

'Urich doesn't convince as a character who idiosyncratically bears no first name, drops partial quotes as if they were pearls, plays friend to all the little people who frequent his world.' – *Daily Variety*
'Insufferable hero. Banal writing. Is this a parody?' – *LA Times*

Spiderman
aka: *The Amazing Spiderman*
US 1978 74m colour TVM
CBS/Charles Fries (Edward J. Montagne)

A scientist infected by a spider finds he can scale walls and spin webs.

A comic strip notion humanized without much flair, humour or variation on the single idea. Strictly for kids.

w Alvin Boretz d E. W. Swackhamer Nicholas Hammond

† A series of 13 × 50m episodes ensued.

Spiderman *
Canada 1967–8 52 × 22m colour (16mm)
Grantray–Lawrence Animation

Cartoon version of the comic strip, quite stylishly done.

Spielberg, Steven (1947–). American director who hit the big time on the big screen with *Jaws*. TV work rather more interesting: *Night Gallery*, *Murder by the Book (Columbo)*, DUEL, *Something Evil*, *Savage*.

Spindoe (GB 1968; 6 × 52m; bw). Oblique crime series featuring the impassive gang leader convicted in the previous *The Fellows*. With Ray McAnally, Colette O'Neil, Anthony Bate; directed by Mike Newell, written and produced by Robin Chapman, for Granada.   PP

spin-off. An episode which introduces new characters and situations that are the projected starting-point for a different series. Also, the resulting series.

Spirit of Asia (GB 1981). A series in eight one-hours in which David Attenborough explores the art and religions of the less frequented East. Produced by Michael MacIntyre; for BBC.

Spitfire! (GB 1979). Copybook memoir of the fighter plane, originally produced for local consumption by BBC South and West where the immortal aircraft was designed and built. My 1979 review: 'With seeming effortlessness, John Frost interwove the technical, productional and romantic strands of the story. The Germans delivered a press vital to its quantity manufacture in the nick of time before the outbreak of war. Turning the exhaust ports backwards to give jet thrust added 15 mph. ACW Margaret Norton, inadvertently borne aloft on a Spitfire's tail, lived to tell her story, here. The plane now goes into mythology.'

† *Spitfire MH 434* was a less satisfactory history of one particular plane by Frank Cvitanovich for Thames (1979).   PP

Spitting Image (GB since 1984). Detestable satirical show animating life-size three-dimensional caricatures of the Queen,

769

SPIDERMAN was too silly a character to last long on television – all he really did was climb unnoticed up buildings in an absurd costume – but audiences being what they are, several episodes when padded out were successful as cinema films which people actually paid to see.

SPITTING IMAGE. No prizes for guessing the identity of these puppets from television's most vitriolic satirical review.

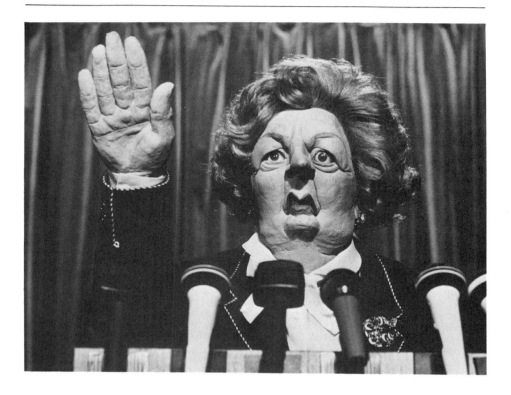

President Reagan, Mick Jagger and other heroes and monsters of the day; scripts sometimes sharp, but not often enough to excuse the ugly, inimical and repellent figures, which are by the partnership of Luck and Flaw (Peter Fluck, Roger Law). Produced by John Lloyd and others, for Central.

LH: 'Also against the tide, I have to admit finding it all a bit too much but not funny enough.'

† Compilations *The Beast of Spitting Image*, 1984, and *Second Beast*, 1985. Bronze Rose, Montreux, 1985; Best Comedy Banff; and our Julius Streicher Award for ethnic caricature.   PP

Splendor in the Grass
US 1981 96m colour TVM
NBC/Warner (Arthur Lewis)

In a Kansas town in the mid-twenties, a teenage pair are tempted but confused by parental ideas of sex.

Hotted-up version of the well-known sixties film. No obvious reason to make the effort.

w from the novel by William Inge *d* Richard Sarafian

Melissa Gilbert, Eva Marie Saint, Ned Beatty

The Spongers ** (GB 1978). Powerful and finally shocking Jim Allen play about a mother and her four children, deserted by the man of the family, up against an uncaring bureaucracy as they try to make ends meet. Ironically set against the background of the Jubilee celebrations the year before, it took its title – and its sting – from popular criticisms of idle families living gaily on state hand-outs. With Christine Hargreaves. Directed by Roland Joffe; produced by Tony Garnett; for BBC (*Play for Today*).   PP

Spooner, Dennis (1932–). British series writer with many contributions to *The Champions*, *Department S*, *Randall and Hopkirk (Deceased)*, *Jason King*, *The Avengers*.

Spooner's Patch ** (GB 1979–82). Louche comedy set in a small, corrupt police station which only earned its stars when Donald Churchill took over the name part of Inspector Spooner the second season. Written by Ray Galton (of Galton and Simpson) in partnership with Johnny Speight. Also with Patricia Hayes.　　　　PP

Sporting Chance (GB since 1984). Annual have-a-go series in which celebs take on a sport of their choice they've never tried before, with coaching from an expert. Anneka Rice tried orienteering one year, Martin Shaw gliding, Suzy Quatro clay-pigeon shooting. Produced by Peter Ramsden, for BBC.　　　　PP

Sportsview (GB 1954–70). Weekly sports review which in many ways anticipated the more aggressive and demotic style which the BBC was going to have to adopt in order to compete with ITV. Fronted by Peter Dimmock in the guise of a slightly raffish sporting gent, and calling on all the great sporting names of the day, it addressed viewers with a man-to-man directness only later emulated by *Tonight* or *Panorama*. In techniques it introduced to Britain the split-screen device for interviews between participants in studios miles apart. It mounted its cameras, with exciting results, aboard a Le Mans Jaguar, a TT motor cycle and a Cresta bobsleigh. The founding editor was Paul Fox, later chief of BBC1 and overlord of YTV. His successor, Brian Cowgill, followed him via a similar route to the managing directorship of Thames Television.　　　　PP

Spot the Tune. Long-running (209 editions) game show, self-explanatory, put out by Granada 1956–60 with Marion Ryan and Jackie Rae in charge.　　　　PP

Spraggue
US 1983 96m colour TVM
ABC/Lorimar (Michael Filerman)

A wealthy Bostonian and his Aunt Mary solve the murder of a beautiful woman on a train.
Facetious pilot for a series that didn't happen.
w Henry Olek, *novel* by Henry Barnes *d* Larry Elikann

Michael Nouri, Glynis Johns, James Cromwell, Mark Herrier

Spy! (GB 1980). Reconstructions of real-life espionage coups, e.g. the KGB's recruitment of the Admiralty spy John Vassall, or the 'turning' of a German agent dropped by parachute in Britain in 1940.　　　　PP

Spy Force
Australia 1970–1 42 × 50m colour (16mm)
Paramount/Roger Mirams

Army Intelligence tracks the Japs during World War II.
Spy stuff from an unfamiliar angle, but a show which bites off rather more than its budget can chew and is often uncomfortably violent.

The Spy Killer
GB 1969 74m colour TVM
Cohen–Sangster

An ex-secret agent is blackmailed into looking for a mysterious notebook.
Companion piece to *Foreign Exchange*; no better.
w Jimmy Sangster *d* Roy Baker

Robert Horton, Sebastian Cabot, Jill St John, Eleanor Summerfield, Barbara Shelley

Spy Trap (GB 1972; 20 × 25m). Three four-part serials, then twice-weekly mini serials, by ROBERT BARR applying to the contemporary counter-espionage world the expertise he had learned in his World War II *Spycatcher* series 13 years before.　　　　PP

Spycatcher **. British (BBC) half-hour show of the fifties, written by Robert Barr, featuring BERNARD ARCHARD as Lt-Col Oreste Pinto, one of Army Intelligence's chief interrogators of suspected spies. Most of the shows consisted of a single across-the-table duologue, and were both tense and convincing, though not always quite true to fact.

Spyship *
GB 1983 6 × 55m BBC Pebble Mill (Colin Rogers)

British trawler vanishes in northern waters. Was she carrying secret surveillance equipment? Labyrinthine but absorbing Cold War skulduggery with Tom Wilkinson excellent as dogged local journalist who won't be put off the scent, good Norwegian locations and Norwegian bit-part players.
w James Mitchell, *book* by Tom Keene, Brian Haynes *d* Michael Custance

Tom Wilkinson, Lesley Nightingale, Peter Eyre, Michael Aldridge　　　　PP

Squadron
GB 1982 10 × 50m
BBC (Joe Waters)

Exploits of a fictional 'rapid deployment' squadron of the RAF. Good clean-limbed adventure for old air-minded boys, with usual service-life rivalries.

SPYCATCHER. Another case of television creating a star, whose exploits are watched avidly every week, and then dumping him into the ranks of small-part actors. Bernard Archard (centre) is still around, but never again got a chance equal to that of playing Col. Oreste Pinto, seen here with Norman Mitchell and Terence Knapp.

w various   *d* Tristan de Vere Cole and others

Michael Culver, Malcolm Stoddard   PP

Square Pegs
US 1983 22 × 25m colour
CBS/Embassy (Anne Beatts)

High jinks in high school.
Unattractive comedy series about girls out to get boys to the detriment of their education.

cr Anne Beatts

Sarah Jessica Parker, Amy Linker, Merritt Butrick, John Femio, Tracy Nelson

'Quite promising, but not very funny.' – *Variety*

Squaring the Circle (GB 1984). Further reconstruction of much-reconstructed events in Poland as the Solidarity movement was born and put to trial, only jollied up now by playwright Tom Stoppard to yield a messy version half transcript, half caper. With Bernard Hill (as Lech Walesa), Alec McCowen, Roy Kinnear, John Woodvine. Directed by Mike Hodges, for TVS/Metromedia/Britannic Films/C4.   PP

Squires, Charles (1925–74). British film-maker of jolly cockney nature who made some outstanding documentaries, notably *The Grafters* (1964) in praise of street markets and their traders.   PP

The Squirrels
GB 1974–6 40 approx. × 25m colour (VTR)
ATV (Shaun O'Riordan)

Misadventures of the workers in a small office.
Middling comedy series.

w Eric Chappell   *d* Shaun O'Riordan

Bernard Hepton, Ken Jones, Patsy Rowlands

SST: Disaster in the Sky
aka: *SST: Death Flight*
US 1977 96m colour TVM
ABC Circle (Ron Roth)

Sabotage threatens a supersonic airliner with an explosion if it lands.
Fairly watchable all-star jeopardy melodrama.

w Robert L. Joseph, Meyer Dolinsky d David Lowell Rich m John Cacavas

Robert Reed, Peter Graves, Doug McClure, Lorne Greene, George Maharis, Martin Milner, Brock Peters, Tina Louise, Susan Strasberg, Burgess Meredith, Bert Convy, Misty Rowe

Staccato: see Johnny Staccato

✳ **Stack, Robert** (1919–) (Robert Modini). Cold-eyed American leading man who after an indifferent Hollywood career became a TV superstar when he played Eliot Ness in THE UNTOUCHABLES. His later series (*The Name of the Game, Most Wanted, Strike Force*) failed to achieve the same impact. TV movies: *The Strange and Deadly Occurrence, Adventures of the Queen, Murder on Flight 502*.

Stacy, James (c 1941–). American leading man who after appearing in *Lancer* was seriously injured in a car crash. TV movies: *Paper Men, Heat of Anger, Ordeal*, (after his accident) *Just a Little Inconvenience, My Kidnapper My Love*.

Stacy, Neil (19 –). Clean-cut, very British British actor, at home in thrillers like *Cold Warrior* but a surprise and delight as the stiff-upper-lipped Robert in DUTY FREE.
PP

stage management of life. *The Tunnel* was a desperately exciting *cinéma-vérité* record of the successful escape of 59 refugees from East Berlin to West by tunnelling under the infamous Wall (NBC 1963, *ph* Peter and Klaus Dehmel). Unfortunately it later transpired that the US networks had been competing to subsidize such exploits, casting grave doubts on the true spontaneity of the result. The manipulation of real-life characters to furnish suspenseful actuality has remained properly suspect ever since, but is very easily fallen into by sloppy practitioners. An example was the follow-up to *Too Long a Winter*, Barry Cockcroft's brilliant film about a lonely spinster hill-farmer, Hannah Hauxwell, for YTV. In the sequel the lady was brought to London and deliberately propelled round sleazy Soho (an area she would have been unlikely to encounter naturally) in order to furnish bemused reactions. More serious accusations of stage-management were levelled against news camera crews in Katanga, Angola and other war-torn countries when guerrillas or mercenaries were said to have set up skirmishes, even executions, for payment. In Northern Ireland foreign TV crews have been accused of paying young sectarians to attack the troops; British current affairs and news programmes have been condemned for seeming to connive with terrorist organizations by filming staged exercises, etc. While the degree of complicity varies widely the only really honourable stance for television is the same as that for the Press, which is as a disengaged observer.   PP

Stagecoach West (US 1960). One-hour western series for ABC, with Wayne Rogers and Robert Bray as drivers.

Stalin – the Red Tsar (GB 1978). Grim history of the Russian dictator and his crimes. Written by Boleslaw Sulik and Paul Neuburg; directed by Howard Ross; produced by Paul Neuburg; for LWT.   PP

Stalingrad *
GB 1963 120m bw
BBC (Rudolph Cartier)

Epic studio play reconstructing the last days of the beleaguered German garrison in World War II. My 1963 review: 'What came across so arrestingly, so vividly, was the *feel* of being in the closing trap – the strange mixture of apocalypse and cosy routine; the way in which even as the heavens were falling the lunatic administrative machine of the army clanked on, promoting colonels to the command of non-existent divisions, carrying out sentence on a shocked simpleton of a deserter.'

w Claus Hubalek/Rudolph Cartier d Rudolph Cartier

André Van Gyseghem, Peter Vaughan, Albert Lieven, Harry Fowler   PP

Stalk the Wild Child
US 1976 74m colour TVM
NBC/Charles Fries (Stanley Bass, Paul Wendkos)

A university doctor tries to tame a boy raised by wild dogs.
Unusual for a TV movie, this item was borrowed from Truffaut's *L'Enfant Sauvage* and led to the unsuccessful series *Lucan*.

w Peter Packer d William Hale ph Harry May m John Rubinstein

David Janssen, Trish Van Devere, Joseph Bottoms, Benjamin Bottoms, Jamie Smith Jackson

'One husband tried to steal her children, another was an alcoholic!'
Stand by Your Man
US 1981 96m colour TVM
CBS/Robert Papazian/Peter Guber–Jon Peters

The career and unhappy marriages of singer Tammy Wynette.

Tolerable rip-off of *Coal Miner's Daughter*; not without interest to fans.

w John Gay *d* Jerry Jameson *ph* Matthew F. Leonetti *md* Earle Hagen

Annette O'Toole, Tim McIntire, Cooper Huckabee, James Hampton, Helen Page Camp

Stand Up, Nigel Barton * (GB 1965). Scholarship boy's progress from village school to dreaming spires. First of a pair of obviously autobiographical plays by Dennis Potter in the then newly fashionable style of jumping to and fro in time and place, plus at least one little device – having the schoolkids played by adult actors – which was all Potter's own, and which he would famously revive for *Blue Remembered Hills*. Directed by Gareth Davies; produced by James MacTaggart; for BBC (*Wednesday Play*).
† *Vote, Vote, Vote for Nigel Barton*, inspired by Potter's unsuccessful parliamentary candidature in 1964, went out in the same slot a week later.   PP

Stand Your Ground (GB 1983; 12 × 30m). Self-defence for women demonstrated with good humour by Kaleghl Quinn. Produced and directed by Jenny Wilkes, for Moving Picture Co/C4.   PP

Stander, Lionel (1908–). Durable, rasping American character actor who belatedly found a TV niche as Max in *Hart to Hart*.

Standing, John (1939–). British actor, son of Hollywood Brit Sir Guy Standing. Best esteemed on TV for *Rogue Male* (1976) and *The Other 'Arf* with Lorraine Chase. PP

Standing Tall
US 1978 96m colour TVM
NBC/Quinn Martin (Marty Katz)

In 1934, a small-time cattle rancher is harassed when he refuses to sell his property. Moderately tense modern western.

w Franklin Thompson *d* Harvey Hart
Robert Forster, Chuck Connors, Linda Evans, Will Sampson, L. Q. Jones

Stanley
US 1956 26 × 25m bw
NBC

Stories of the bumbling proprietor of a hotel news stand.
Forgotten routine comedy.

Buddy Hackett, Carol Burnett

Stanton, Frank (19 –). American executive, president of CBS 1946–72; a politician rather than a programmer.

✿ **Stanwyck, Barbara** (1907–) (Ruby Stevens). Durable American star actress who made several excursions into television. In 1970 she won an Emmy for her series BARBARA STANWYCK THEATRE, and another in 1965 for *The Big Valley*. TV movies: *The House That Would Not Die*, *The Letters*, *A Taste of Evil*. In 1980 she was badly treated in a disastrous pilot for a *Charlie's Angels* spin-off called *Tony's Boys*.

Stapleton, Jean (1923–). American character actress who scored a hit as the long-suffering Edith in ALL IN THE FAMILY. TV movies: *Angel Dusted*, *Aunt Mary*, *Isabel's Choice*, *Eleanor: First Lady of the World*.

Stapleton, Maureen (1925–). American character actress. TV movies: *Tell Me Where It Hurts*, QUEEN OF THE STARDUST BALLROOM, *Cat on a Hot Tin Roof*, *The Gathering*, *Letters from Frank*, *Little Gloria . . . Happy at Last*, *Family Secrets*, *Sentimental Journey*, *Private Sessions*.

A Star Is Dead *
aka: *Quincy*
US 1976 74m colour TVM
Universal (Lou Shaw)

A pathologist investigates the death of a young actress.
Pilot for a *Mystery Movie* character: brisk, amusing and efficient but not exciting. The character however survived several seasons.
w Lou Shaw, Michael Kozoll *d* Noel Black
JACK KLUGMAN, Donna Mills, Robert Foxworth, June Lockhart, William Daniels

Star Maidens
GB 1975 13 × 25m colour
Global/Scottish

Astronauts are marooned on a planet ruled by women.

Humourless hokum whose only chance was to play for laughs.

Dawn Addams

'Making movies . . . making love . . . it's a Hollywood legend!'
The Star Maker
CBS/Columbia/Channing–Debin–Locke/ Carson Productions (John J. MacMahon)

The love life of a Hollywood director.

Unrevealing wallow in the film city's seamier side; it needed the wit of a Billy Wilder to make it effective.

w William Bast *d* Lou Antonio

Rock Hudson, Suzanne Pleshette, Brenda Vaccaro, Ed McMahon, Teri Copley, Cathie Shirriff, April Clough, Jack Scalia

Star of the Family
US 1982 13 × 25m colour
ABC/Paramount/RJMB and Little Andrew Enterprises (Stu Silver, Paul Waigner, Jack Seifert)

A local fireman can't stand the strain of his teenage daughter becoming a pop star.

Tedious comedy series which ran to only 13 episodes.

cr Stu Silver

Brian Dennehy, Kathy Maisnik, George Deloy, Todd Susman, Michael Dudikoff

Star Performance
GB/USA mid-1960s approx. 6 shows bw
Rediffusion/Talent Associates (David Susskind)

Imprecise collaboration yielding a new TVM version of *Laura*, an adaptation of Katherine Anne Porter's *Noon Wine*, and in the words of my review at the time 'a wordless and also mindless exercise called *Saturday Night Around the World* which to a smoochy score by Richard Rodgers showed young couples dancing, drinking, gazing into each other's eyes and occasionally patting each other's bottoms in seven assorted cities. Most of them looked like advertising models, and about as real. I was mainly saddened to see the name of Irvin Gitlin, a great documentary producer, attached to it.' PP

Star Quality
GB 1985 6 × 75m
BBC/Quintet (Alan Shalcross)

Stories by Noel Coward newly dramatized and lushly produced, but a cautious debut for the independent outfit Quintet which includes some of Britain's best writers and directors.

w Stanley Price (3), Jack Rosenthal, Ken Taylor, T. R. Bowen *d* (title story) Alan Dossor

Ian Richardson, Peter Chelsom, Pam Ferris; in other episodes, Carroll Baker, Paul Daneman, Judy Parfitt, Nigel Havers, Patricia Hayes, Max Wall, Paula Wilcox, Judi Dench, Ian Holm, Tom Courtenay, Nichola McAuliffe

Star-Spangled Soccer (GB 1978). Report by
IAN WOOLDRIDGE for YTV on English football as enthusiastically dressed up and razzmatazzed in the USA. I used the occasion for a homily on television's increasing stage-management of sport as well as of life, with the crowd's responses manipulated by outsize computer displays. PP

Star Trek ***
US 1966–8 79 × 50m colour
NBC/Paramount/Norway/NBC (Gene Roddenberry)

An American space ship of the future reconnoitres the universe.

And finds monsters and mysteries at each stop. A highly successful space fiction concept, with simple but streamlined sets, imaginative dialogue, and a few parlour tricks such as a dematerialization process and an interplanetary crew member with pointed ears. The show became a cult.

cr GENE RODDENBERRY

WILLIAM SHATNER, LEONARD NIMOY, De Forrest Kelley

† 17 episodes of a half-hour cartoon version were produced in 1973 by Filmation. The expensive feature film version (*Star Trek – The Motion Picture*) made in 1979 was not a success.

Starcrossed
US 1985 96m colour TVM
ABC/Charles Fries (Robert Lovenheim)

A girl from another planet is on the run from two outer-space hoods.

Shades of *The Invaders*, but this fantasy thriller stands up pretty well on its own feet.

w,d Jeffrey Bloom *ph* Gil Hubbs *m* Gil Melle

Belinda Bauer, James Spader, Pater Kowanko, Clark Johnson, Jacqueline Brookes

'It bursts forth with enough eeriness and suspense to gather viewers from all ages.' – *Daily Variety*

'A tough Kansas cop. A gorgeous Vegas dealer. Tracking down his missing sister. Turning up a deadly crime!'

Stark *
US 1985 96m colour TVM
CBS (David H. Balkan)

A private eye from Wichita arrives in Vegas to look for his younger sister.

Tough, competent, good-looking mystery pilot which surprised the trade by not selling.

w Ernest Tidyman, Bill Stratton d Rod Holcomb ph Frank Beascoechea m Peter Myers

Nick Surovy, Marilu Henner, Pat Corley, Seth Jaffe, Arthur Rosenberg

'Snappy crime drama with vitality and tension.' – Daily Variety

The Starlost
Canada 1973 16 × 50m colour (VTR)
Glen–Warren/TCF

The last survivors of earth travel through space looking for a new home.

Confused, inept sci-fi which never grips the imagination.

cr Douglas Trumbull

Keir Dullea

Starr and Company
GB 1958 77 × 25m bw
BBC (Barbara Burnham)

The Corporation's first attempt at a bi-weekly soaper in emulation of ITV's *Emergency – Ward 10*. Set in a small family firm making buoys it became a moderate success if not exactly a buoy wonder.

cr Donald Bull w Allan Prior, Ray Rigby, etc d Morris Barry, Chris McMaster

Philip Ray, Nancy Nevinson, Patricia Mort, Brian McDermott   PP

Starr, Freddie (1944–). Zany British comedian, former boxer, who came to the fore in *Who Do You Do?*

Starrett, Jack (1936–). American director. TV movies: *Night Chase, Roger and Harry, Nowhere to Hide, Thaddeus Rose and Eddie, Big Bob Johnson and his Fantastic Speed Circus, Mr Horn, The Survival of Dana.*

Stars and Garters ** (GB 1963–4). Entertainment spun off from a 1962 Dan Farson documentary about pub entertainers. A fictitious pub setting was constructed in the studio and the real pub stalwarts (Queenie Watts, Tommy Gowers) gave way to regular performers such as Clinton Ford and Kathy

Kirby but at first, anyway, with Ray Martine as compère the essential conviviality was preserved. Directed by John P. Hamilton, Daphne Shadwell; produced by John P. Hamilton; for Rediffusion. A second series produced by Elkan Allan, with Jill Browne in charge, effectively ended the format.   PP

The Stars Look Down *
GB 1975 13 × 50m colour (VTR)
Granada (Howard Baker)

Hard times for Northumbrian miners in the thirties.

Rather deliberately woebegone adaptation of a best-seller, with undeniably impressive sequences.

w Alan Plater, novel A. J. Cronin

Avril Elgar, Norman Jones, James Bate, Rod Cuthbertson

Stars of the Roller Skate Disco (GB 1984; 75m). Unemployed youngsters circle, sit out and argue the toss round a roller-skate rink under Big-Brotherly surveillance until such time as – if ever – the computer comes up with a job for them. A vivid metaphor of the near future by Michael Hastings, vitiated by the hero, boringly written and played to make all the approved political points. 'He was also such a whinger that his loyal girlfriend finally effed off without him, preferring to take even a lousy job than wait for ever for a dream one. I'm not sure this was the moral Hastings really intended.' With Perry Benson, Cathy Murphy; directed (on video) by Alan Clarke, for BBC.   PP

Stars on Sunday. An ingenious semi-religious concept devised by Yorkshire TV in 1969; it ran almost continuously until 1977 as part of the Sunday religious break. Well-known stars respond to listeners' requests for popular semi-religious songs; the sets are determinedly archaic, the atmosphere is reliably comforting, and the linkman is always a personality well-loved by the public. The production costs are kept down by recording several songs from each star on the same day and then intercutting.

Starsky and Hutch *
US 1975 75m colour TVM
ABC/Spelling–Goldberg

Two undercover cops are subject to murder attempts, and want to find out why.

Rough-and-tumble cop show with lots of car chases; it led to a successful series.

w WILLIAM BLINN d Barry Shear m Lalo Schifrin, Mark Snow

STARSKY AND HUTCH. It wasn't the plots that attracted audiences, it was the fast cars and the two young guys. David Soul we still see, but whatever happened to Paul Michael Glaser?

DAVID SOUL, PAUL MICHAEL GLASER, Buddy Lester, Richard Lynch

† The resultant series ran five seasons, its success stemming from the personalities of its stars rather than the writing or production. The anti-violence campaign resulted in a strong injection of romance and sentimentality from the third season on.

State of the Nation. Umbrella title periodically invoked since 1966 for Granada specials or series on the British economy, British politics, etc. These may be conventional documentaries, studio debates or Roger Graef's fly-on-the-wall accounts of institutions in the process of deliberation. PP

State of Things to Come (GB 1982; 120m). Television looks at its own future – cable, satellite, deregulation. Ambitious survey with Melvyn Bragg, Jonathan Dimbleby, Michael Grade, Brenda Maddox, Tony Wilson, Fred Friendly; organized and presented by Gus Macdonald, for Granada.
PP

State Trooper
US 1957–9 104 × 25m bw
MCA/Revue

Stories of the Nevada State Police.
Adequate cop filler.

Rod Cameron

Stay With Me Till Morning
GB 1981 3 × 50m colour
YTV (Michael Glynn)

Elementary and totally dispiriting account of extra-marital coupling among the northern middle classes.

w John Braine d David Reynolds

Nanette Newman, Paul Daneman, Keith Barron, Kate Coleridge

Staying On ★★
GB 1980 120m colour
Granada (Irene Shubik)

A near-flawless dramatization of Paul Scott's novel about the army couple who stayed on in

India after Independence because he was 'too young to retire, too old to try anything new'. Now old age and ill-health and the fear of losing their home are ganging up: funny, brave, touching and finally desolate as Lucy is left alone.

w JULIAN MITCHELL *d* Silvio Narizzano

CELIA JOHNSON, TREVOR HOWARD, Zia Mohyeddin   PP

† It led, of course, to *The Jewel in the Crown*. See also entry for Paul Scott.

Stedall, Jonathan (1938–). British documentary director who incidentally became a sympathetic interviewer when making *Time with Betjeman*. Previously, *Muggeridge Ancient and Modern*. Lately: *Living with Uncle Sam* (Alan Whicker). In preparation: *The Seven Ages of Man*.   PP

'Love and murder on the open road!'
The Steel Cowboy
US 1979 96m colour TVM
ABC/EMI Roger Gimbel (R. J. Louis)

A tough lorry driver is persuaded to transport stolen cattle.
Stark highway melodrama, watchable and forgettable.

w Douglas Wheeler, Bill Kerby *d* Harvey Laidman

James Brolin, Rip Torn, Jennifer Warren, Strother Martin, Melanie Griffith, Michael McGuire

Steele, Tommy (1936–) (Thomas Hicks). British cockney entertainer whose TV appearances have been limited to the occasional special.

A Step Out of Line *
US 1970 100m colour TVM
CBS/Cinema Center 100 (Steve Shagan)

Korean War buddies use their skills in a daring civilian robbery.
Okay crime comedy.

w Steve Shagan, S. S. Schweizer *d* Bernard McEveety *ph* James Crabe *m* Jerry Goldsmith

Vic Morrow, Peter Falk, Peter Lawford, Jo Ann Pflug, Lynn Carlin, Tom Bosley, John Randolph

Stephens, James (1951–). American leading actor, notable for *The Paper Chase*. TV movies: *True Grit*, *Eischied*.

Stephens, Robert (1931–). British actor of considerable presence and powerful, even

PAMELA STEPHENSON. The girl who would do anything for a laugh tended to wear out her welcome after *Not the Nine O'Clock News*, but continues to be seen in movie comedies of the 'in' kind.

honking voice. Credits range from *Suez* (as President Nasser) to *Puccini* (as Puccini), debits from *Holocaust* to *Studio*. Was also in *By the Sword Divided*.   PP

Stephenson, Pamela (19 –). Extrovert Australian comedienne who arrived in *Not the Nine O'Clock News* and has since adorned *Saturday Night Live* in America and *Saturday Live* in GB.   PP

Steptoe and Son ****
GB 1964–73 approx 40 × 30m bw, later colour (VTR)
BBC

The love–hate relationship between a frustrated rag-and-bone man and his exasperating old dad.
All kinds of barriers were broken by this earthy comedy series, each episode of which was at one time a national event and which was redrafted by the Americans as *Sanford and Son*. The standard fell off towards the end, but a dozen classical duologues remain.

w RAY GALTON, ALAN SIMPSON

HARRY H. CORBETT, WILFRID BRAMBELL

Stern, Leonard (c 1930–). American independent producer who has been mainly associated with light-hearted crime series: *The Governor and J.J.*, *Faraday and Company*, *McMillan and Wife*, *Rossetti and Ryan*.

Stern, Sandor (1936–). Canadian director. *Say Goodbye Maggie Cole*, *Where Have All the People Gone*, *Red Alert*, *Killer on Board*, *True Grit*, *The Seeding of Sarah Burns*, *To Find My Son*, *Muggable Mary*, *Memories Never Die*, *Passions*, *Secret Weapons*.

Stern, Steven Hillard (1937–). American director. *The Ghost of Flight 401*, *Anatomy of a Seduction*, *Fast Friends*, *Portrait of an Escort*, *Miracle on Ice*, *A Small Killing*, *Not Just Another Affair*, *Forbidden Love*, *The Baby Sister*, *Still the Beaver*, *An Uncommon Love*, *Getting Physical*, *Obsessive Love*.

Steve Canyon
US 1958–9 39 × 25m bw
Pegasus/NBC
Stories of an Air Force pilot on special assignment.
Juvenile hokum.
Dean Fredericks

Steve Randall (US 1952). Half-hour crime series for Dumont, with Melvyn Douglas as a lawyer sleuth.

Stevens, Andrew (1955–). American leading man. Series: *The Oregon Trail*, *Code Red*. TV movies: *The Last Survivors*, *Secrets*, *Once an Eagle*, *The Bastard*, *The Rebels*, *Women at West Point*, *Topper*, *Beggarman Thief*, *Miracle on Ice*, *Forbidden Love*, *Emerald Point*, *Hollywood Wives*.

Stevens, Connie (1938–) (Concetta Ingolia). American leading lady of the sixties. Starred in TV series *Hawaiian Eye*. TV movies: *Mister Jerico*, *Call Her Mom*, *Playmates*, *Every Man Needs One*, *The Sex Symbol*, *Love's Savage Fury*.

Stevens, Craig (1918–) (Gail Shekles). Mature American leading man of the fifties, later in character roles. His biggest success was on TV, where he seemed to impersonate Cary Grant. Series: *Peter Gunn*, *Man of the World*, *Mr Broadway*. TV movies: *The Elevator*, *Killer Bees*, *Rich Man, Poor Man*, *Secrets of Three Hungry Wives*.

Stevens, Leslie (1924–). American independent writer–producer. Series: *The Outer Limits*, *Stony Burke*, *Search*, *The Invisible Man*, *Battlestar Galactica*.

Stevens, Stella (1936–) (Estelle Eggleston). Hard-working American leading lady, often in hard-boiled roles. TV movies include *In Broad Daylight*, *Climb an Angry Mountain*, *Linda*, *Honky Tonk*, *The Day the Earth Moved*, *Kiss Me, Kill Me*, *Murder in Peyton Place*, *The Night They Took Miss Beautiful*, *Cruise into Terror*.

Stevenson, John (1937–). British comedy writer, ex-newspaper reporter, who worked on *Coronation Street* and *Nearest and Dearest*, and with collaborator Julian Roach hatched *Dead Ernest* and then the immortal BRASS.   PP

Stevenson, McLean (c 1932–). Tall, gangling American comedy actor who came into the limelight as Colonel Blake in *M*A*S*H* (a show which rather cheekily killed him off when he decided to leave). Also: *The Doris Day Show*, *The McLean Stevenson Show* (a simple-minded domestic comedy which ran 13 weeks in 1977), *Hello Larry*.

Stewart, Ed (1941–). British disc jockey, known as 'Stewpot'.

Stewart, James (1908–). American star actor, one of the great names in movies of the thirties, forties and fifties. Made two TV series, neither particularly successful: *The Jimmy Stewart Show* and *Hawkins on Murder*.

Stewart, William G. (–). British comedy and light entertainment producer for ATV and then Central. Current success: *The Price is Right*.

Sticking Together
US 1978 74m colour TVM
Viacom/William Blinn, Jerry Thorpe
A family of orphans in Hawaii persuade a conman to impersonate their Uncle Willy.
An attack of the cutes, well presented for those who can stomach that kind of thing.
w William Blinn d Jerry Thorpe ph Chuck Arnold m John Rubenstein
Clu Gulager, Sean Roche, Lori Walsh, Sean Marshall
† A short series followed under the title *The Mackenzies of Paradise Cove*.

Stilgoe, Richard (1943–). British light comedian, often seen as pianist–composer–singer, e.g. in *And Now The Good News*, *That's Life*. In 1982 chaired *Scoop*, a video version of *The News Quiz*.

Still the Beaver
US 1983 96m colour TVM
CBS/Universal (Nick Abdo)

The mischievous boy of *Leave It to Beaver* is now a widower with two troublesome sons, and still looks to his older brother for help. Fated attempt to revamp an old premise. The anticipated series did not materialize.

cr Brian Levant, Nick Abdo

Jerry Mathers, Tony Dow, Barbara Billingsley, Janice Kent, Joanna Gleason, John Snee

'The Cleavers have misplaced the winsome touch.' – *Daily Variety*

Stingray *
GB 1965 39 × 25m colour
ATV/Gerry Anderson

Adventures of a super submarine of the future.

Superior puppet adventure series.

'When you can't call the cops, call Stingray!'

Stingray
US 1985 96m colour TVM
Columbia/Stephen J. Cannell (J. Rickley Dumm)

A mysterious adventurer in a black 1965 car turns up just when people are in trouble.
Back to *The Scarlet Pimpernel* and *The Mark of Zorro*, but in modern dress. Silly action stuff to rival *Knight Rider*, but the network picked up only 6 hours after the pilot.

cr Stephen J. Cannell *d* Richard Colla

Nick Mancuso, Susan Blakely, Robyn Douglas, Gregory Sierra

'More package than content.' – *Daily Variety*

Stir Crazy
US 1985 13 × 50m colour
CBS/Columbia/Larry Larry (Larry Rosen, Larry Tucker)

Two innocents on a smalltown murder rap go on the run with a redneck lady sheriff in pursuit.
Farcical version of *The Fugitive*: the laughs can't be kept up, and the bits in between are awesomely boring.

cr Tucker, Rosen, Bruce Jay Friedman

Larry Riley, Joseph Guzaldo, Jeannie Wilson

'Silly, undistinguished and predictable.' – *Daily Variety*
'Much huffing and puffing over nothing.' – *LA Times*

JAMES STEWART. Big movie stars didn't always succeed in television, and James Stewart was no exception, even as a crafty trial lawyer in *Hawkins on Murder*.

The Stockard Channing Show (US 1980). Shortlived half-hour series with the star as assistant to a TV consumer's advocate. Written and produced by Aaron Ruben; with Ron Silver; for Columbia/CBS.

Stocker's Copper *
GB 1971 85m colour (16mm)
BBC (Graeme McDonald)

Cornwall 1913. A policeman becomes friendly with one of the strikers he is supervising.
A raw political play whose power in this production is undeniable.

w Tom Clarke *d* Jack Gold

Bryan Marshall, Jane Lapotaire, Gareth Thomas

Winner of the 1972 BAFTA and Writers' Guild awards.

'It's always exciting to watch a Jack Gold film because he always gets everything right.' – *Daily Mail*

Stone
US 1978 96m colour TVM
ABC/Universal/Stephen J. Cannell

A police detective gets into trouble with his principals for airing his views in novels and on television.

Slick pilot about a character clearly borrowed from Joseph Wambaugh.

w Stephen J. Cannell d Corey Allen

Dennis Weaver, Pat Hingle, Roy Thinnes, Joby Baker, Vic Morrow

† To everyone's surprise the resulting series was a failure and fewer than half a dozen episodes aired.

The Stone Faces (GB 1957). Rare appearance, on British TV anyway, of Luise Rainer, playing someone very like herself (or Garbo) on the run from publicity in a bad play by J. B. Priestley. My reaction at the time: 'Neither the scenes he sketched nor the dialogue he gave to his characters offered much evidence in support of Priestley's contention that happiness lay in wait if only nasty people (i.e. the Press) would leave nice people alone. Only Miss Rainer, in some Hollywood style closeups, suggested fleeting, snatched happiness with her unaided trembling lip and melting eyes. She deserved better from the script.'   PP

Stone, Milburn (1904–80). American character actor who after playing a hundred shady types in movies became a fixture as 'Doc' in *Gunsmoke*.

'For years she's made you laugh. Tonight, She'll touch your heart!'

Stone Pillow

US 1985 96m colour TVM

CBS/Schaefer–Karpf (Terry Donnelly)

A Manhattan bag-lady becomes friendly with a social worker.

Runyonesque comedy drama apparently designed as a stunt for its ageing star. Not bad, but it needed more salt and pepper.

w Rose Leiman Goldemberg d George Schaefer ph Walter Lassally m Georges Delerue

LUCILLE BALL, Daphne Zuniga, William Converse-Roberts, Stephen Lang, Susan Batson, Stefan Schnabel, Rebecca Schull

'It's Ball's show, no matter how it's sliced.' – *Daily Variety*

Stonestreet: Who Killed the Centrefold Model?

US 1977 74m colour TVM

NBC/Universal (David J. O'Connell, Leslie Stevens)

A female private eye goes undercover as a porno actress to solve a disappearance and a murder.

Watchable but unsuccessful pilot in a well-worn groove.

w Leslie Stevens d Russ Mayberry ph Terry K. Meade m Pat Williams

Barbara Eden, Richard Basehart, Joseph Mascolo, Joan Hackett, Louise Latham

Stoney Burke

US 1962 32 × 50m bw

ABC/United Artists/Daystar

Experiences of a rodeo rider.

Well-made series which fell somewhere between action and drama and hadn't really enough going for it.

cr Leslie Stevens

Jack Lord, Bruce Dern, Warren Oates

Stookie (GB 1985; 6 × 30m). Good and bad teenagers whose gangland is the Clyde riverbank just down from Glasgow, these days reclaimed by nature, green and grassy and teeming with wildlife. Nice teatime serial with David McKay; written by Allan Prior, for STV.   PP

Stoppard, Dr Miriam (1937–). Eager, bright-eyed British reporter and presenter, mostly on popular medicine topics in *Don't Ask Me* or *Where There's Life*, but has added occasional interview series, *Woman to Woman*.

Stoppard, Tom (1937–). Intellectual, tongue-twisting, paronomasiac British playwright whose great TV success was PROFESSIONAL FOUL. He also contributed a not very satisfactory version of *Three Men in Boat*, likewise of the Solidarity story in Poland, *Squaring the Circle*.

PP: 'But two brilliant half hours, *Teeth* (1968) and an *Eleventh Hour* contribution (1975) with Clive Exton.'

Storch, Larry (1923–). American entertainer who started with Jackie Gleason and went on to *F Troop* as well as cabaret acts. TV movies: *Hunters Are For Killing*, *The Couple Takes a Wife*, *The Woman Hunter*, *Better Late Than Never*, etc.

Storefront Lawyers: see Men at Law

Storm, Gale (1922–) (Josephine Cottle). American leading lady of a few forties films. In the fifties she rather surprisingly became a TV star in series *Oh Susanna!* (*The Gale Storm Show*) and *My Little Margie*.

Stormin' Home
US 1985 96m colour TVM
CBS (James A. Westman)

A ten-times loser who has alienated his wife and daughter finds his style in motorbike racing.
And whoever thinks you can fill two hours with that should be fired.

w Jerry Jameson, James Booth, George Yanok d Jerry Jameson ph Robert Jessup m Bruce Broughton

Gil Gerard, Lisa Blount, Pat Corley, Joanna Kerns, John Pleshette

'It never leaves the post.' – Daily Variety

A Story of David
GB 1960 99m colour TVM
William Goetz/Scoton/Mardeb (George Pitcher)

David's trouble with King Saul.
Competent biblical mini-epic.

w Gerry Day, Terrence Maple d Bob McNaught ph Arthur Ibbetson m Kenneth V. Jones

Jeff Chandler, Basil Sydney, David Knight, Barbara Shelley, Richard O'Sullivan, Donald Pleasence

The Story of David
US 1976 200m colour TVM
ABC/Columbia/Milburg Theatrical
(Mildred Freed Alburg)

David's life from his battle with Goliath to the end of his reign.
Ho-hum religious biopic, overlong and sententious.

w Ernest Kinoy d Alex Segal, David Lowell Rich m Laurence Rosenthal

Timothy Bottoms, Keith Michell, Anthony Quayle, Jane Seymour, Susan Hampshire, Norman Rodway, Brian Blessed, Barry Morse

The Story of Jacob and Joseph
US 1974 100m colour TVM
ABC/Columbia/Milburg Theatrical
(Mildred Freed Alburg)

Another biblical biopic, rather patchy and obliquely narrated.

w Ernest Kinoy d Michael Cacoyannis m Mikis Theodorakis

Keith Michell, Tony Lo Bianco, Colleen Dewhurst, Herschel Bernardi, Harry Andrews, Alan Bates (narrator)

'Probably the feature film most faithful to the Bible as a source.' – Jack Edmund Nolan

Storyboard. In advertising, the strip-cartoon presentation of a projected commercial, i.e. a demonstration. So intermittent series of try-outs for possible series by Thames TV go under the Storyboard umbrella. In earlier days (the late fifties) it had been used even more aptly for short experimental plays in non-naturalistic form on BBC.   PP

The Storyteller *
US 1977 96m colour TVM
NBC/Universal Fairmount–Foxcraft
(Richard Levinson, William Link)

A TV scriptwriter is troubled when a mother charges that his play caused her son's death.
Extended seminar on TV violence and its effects surprising from this source. A thoughtful piece, well made.

w William Link, Richard Levinson d Bob Markowitz ph Terry K. Meade m David Shire

Martin Balsam, Patty Duke Astin, Doris Roberts, James Daly, David Spielberg, Rose Gregorio

'Courageous, impressive . . . a valiant try.' – Daily Variety

Stowaway to the Moon
US 1974 100m colour TVM
CBS/TCF (John Cutts)

An 11-year-old boy stows away on a space flight.
Prolonged juvenile adventure.

w William R. Shelton, Jon Boothe d Andrew V. McLaglen

Lloyd Bridges, Michael Link, John Carradine, Pete Conrad, Jeremy Slate

Straight, Beatrice (1918–). American character actress. TV movies: The Borrowers, Killer on Board, The Dain Curse, Chiller, Robert Kennedy and His Times.

Straightaway (US 1961). Half-hour action series for ABC, with Brian Kelly and John Ashley as garage owners and racing car designers.

The Strange and Deadly Occurrence *
US 1975 74m colour TVM
NBC/Alpine/Charles Fries

A couple feel that their brand new house is haunted.
Stylish but rather strained suspenser with a lame ending.

w Sandor Stern d John Llewellyn Moxey

Robert Stack, Vera Miles, L. Q. Jones, Herb Edelman, Margaret Willock

Strange Homecoming
US 1974 74m colour TVM
NBC/Alpine/Charles Fries

A burglar and murderer goes home for the first time in years and his family think him charming.
Anyone seen *Shadow of a Doubt* lately? It was better.

w Eric Bercovici d Lee H. Katzin

Robert Culp, Glen Campbell, Barbara Anderson, Whitney Blake

Strange New World
US 1975 100m colour TVM
ABC/Warner (Walon Green, Robert F. Graham)

Three scientists return to earth after 200 years in a time capsule and find things very changed: women rule.
Third attempt at a new space fiction format. The other pilots were *Genesis II* and *Planet Earth*, and after this one they gave up.

w Al Ramrus, Ronald F. Graham, Walon Green d Robert Butler

John Saxon, Kathleen Miller, Keene Curtis, James Olson, Martine Beswick

The Strange Possession of Mrs Oliver
US 1977 74m colour TVM
NBC/Columbia (Stan Shpetner)

A woman is possessed by the personality of someone long dead.
Adequate creepy thriller.

w Richard Matheson d Gordon Hessler

Karen Black, George Hamilton, Robert F. Lyons, Lucille Benson

The Strange Report
GB 1968 13 × 50m colour
ATV

A criminologist and his young aides outsmart the police.
Good conventional mystery series.

Anthony Quayle, Kaz Garas, Annake Wills

The Strange World of Gurney Slade (GB
1960). Anthony Newley in a whimsical ATV series of the days before whimsy gave way to sex. Surrounded by lovely girls, he spoke to trees and animals, and they answered!   PP

The Stranger *
US 1972 98m colour TVM
Bing Crosby Productions (Alan A. Armer)

An astronaut crashes on another planet and becomes a fugitive from the authorities.
Lively chase pilot which just didn't catch on.

w Gerald Sanford d Lee H. Katzin

Glenn Corbett, Cameron Mitchell, Lew Ayres, Sharon Acker, Dean Jagger, Tim O'Connor, George Coulouris

The Stranger at Jefferson High
US 1978 96m colour TVM
NBC/Lyman Dayton

A healthy-minded 17-year-old from a Wyoming sheep ranch is misunderstood and harassed when he moves to a Los Angeles high school.
Amazingly old-fashioned moral fable about right triumphing in the end. For the pure of heart.

w Keith Merrill d Lyman Dayton ph Arthur Botham m Les DeAzevedo

Stewart Petersen, Dana Kimmell, Philip Brown, Shannon Farnon

'For anyone asking for any depth, dramatic involvement, or characters who'll surprise, it's a yawn.' – *Daily Variety*

Stranger in Our House
US 1978 96m colour TVM
NBC/Interplanetary/Finnegan Associates

When a distant cousin comes to stay with a California family, she seems to bring with her a little more than bad luck.
Vaguely occult suspenser which takes rather too long to get to its final revelation but is quite stylishly made.

w Glenn Benest, Max A. Keller, *novel* Lois Duncan d Wes Craven ph William K. Jurgensen m Michael Lloyd, John D'Andrea

Linda Blair, Lee Purcell, Jeremy Slate, Jeff McCracken, Jeff East, Carol Lawrence, Macdonald Carey

Stranger on the Run *
US 1967 97m colour TVM
Universal (Richard E. Lyons)

A tramp arrives in a western town and becomes a murder suspect.
Routine western with the usual messages about goodwill towards men.

w Dean Riesner, *story* Reginald Rose d Don Siegel

Henry Fonda, Michael Parks, Anne Baxter, Dan Duryea, Sal Mineo

The Stranger Who Looks Like Me
US 1974 74m colour TVM
Filmways

An adopted girl searches for her real mother.
Efficient tearjerker.

w Gerald di Pego d Larry Peerce

Meredith Baxter, Beau Bridges, Whitney Blake, Walter Brooke, Neva Patterson

The Stranger Within *
US 1974 74m colour TVM
Lorimar

A pregnant mother is bizarrely controlled by her own unborn child.

The start of the monstrous baby cycle (*The Devil within Her*, *It's Alive*, *I Don't Want to Be Born*, etc). More subtle than most.

w Richard Matheson d Lee Philips

Barbara Eden, George Grizzard, Joyce Van Patten, David Doyle, Nehemiah Persoff

Strangers (GB 1980-2). Rough crime-busting series from Granada originally with John Ronane, Mark McManus, Fiona Mollison, Dennis Blanch and Don Henderson as the stubborn, string-gloved Chief-Inspector Bulman, formerly of *The XYY Man*. Henderson alone went on to have his own series *Bulman* in 1985-6. Written mainly by Murray Smith, produced by Richard Everitt.   PP

Strangers and Brothers (GB 1984). Plodding BBC serial from C. P. Snow's fairly plodding sequence of novels of life in the ruling classes, with regular pauses for the characters to declare their beliefs or otherwise react to events. Julian Bond's script had people in the twenties and thirties talking of non-events and disadvantaged backgrounds, clichés not to be moulded for another half-century.   PP

The Strangers in 7A *
US 1972 75m colour TVM
CBS/Palomar/Mark Carliner

The superintendent of an apartment building becomes a hostage in a robbery plot.

Adequate suspenser.

w Eric Roth, *novel* Fielden Farrington d Paul Wendkos

Andy Griffith, Ida Lupino, Michael Brandon, Suzanne Hildur

Strangers: The Story of a Mother and a Daughter *
US 1978 96m colour TVM
CBS/Chris–Rose Productions

After 21 years of separation, a woman comes home to her widowed mother in New England.

An intense little two-header for skilled actors, this has a dramatic zing not often associated with TV movies.

w Michael de Guzman d Milton Katselas ph James Crabe m Fred Karlin pd Harry Horner

Bette Davis (who won an Emmy), Gena Rowlands, Ford Rainey, Donald Moffat, Whit Bissell, Royal Dano

Strangeways **
GB 1980 8 × 40m colour
BBC (Rex Bloomstein)

Masterly impression of life in a chronically overcrowded jail – coincidentally the same one penetrated by Denis Mitchell for *In Prison*, made in 1957. As with other series from the documentary division headed by Roger Mills, the purely observational fly-on-the-wall stance was now modified to include direct statements to camera by prisoners, prison staff and the impressive Governor of Strangeways, Norman Brown. The series ended at Christmas with Christmas inside.   PP

LH: 'The result is probably as honest as any attempt could hope to be, though there is the usual BBC tendency to side with the underdog even when he's a criminal.'

Strategy of Terror
US 1967 90m colour TVM
Universal

A New York police officer thwarts a plot to murder a UN leader.

Adequate chase thriller, originally a two-parter in the *Crisis* anthology.

w Robert L. Joseph d Jack Smight

Hugh O'Brian, Barbara Rush, Neil Hamilton, Harry Townes

The Strauss Family **
GB 1973 1 × 73m, 12 × 50m colour (VTR)
ATV (Cecil Clarke, David Reid)

The private lives of the father-and-son composers.

Superior, expensively-staged biography with music; in TV's best middlebrow tradition.

w Anthony Skene, David Reid, David Butler

Eric Woolfe, Stuart Wilson, Tony Anholt, Anne Stallybrass, Lynn Farleigh

Strauss, Peter (1942–). Gentle, conventional American leading man who after a few film roles became a national figure as Rudy Jordache in RICH MAN, POOR MAN (Books One and Two). TV movies: *The Man without a Country*, *Attack on Terror*, *Young Joe the Forgotten Kennedy*, *The Jericho Mile*, *A Whale for the Killing*, *Masada*, *Heart of Steel*, *Tender Is the Night*, *Kane and Abel*.

Stravinsky **
GB 1982 180m colour/bw
LWT (Tony Palmer)

Impressive, captivating account of the life and works of the Russian musical 'inventor,' as he called himself rather than 'composer,' on the centenary of his birth. His three surviving children testified on television for the first time, as did his widow (second wife) and latter-day musical assistant, Robert Craft. But most potently of all, Tony Palmer was able to draw on footage from an extended CBS interview made not long before his death and never screened.   PP

Street Killing *
US 1976 74m colour TVM
ABC Circle (Richard Rosenbloom)

A public prosecutor connects a street mugging to a Napoleon of crime.
Tense, slightly unusual crime melodrama.

w Bill Driskill *d* Harvey Hart *ph* David M. Walsh *m* J. J. Johnson

Andy Griffith, Bradford Dillman, Harry Guardino, Robert Loggia, Don Gordon

Street-Porter, Janet (1946–) (Janet Bull). British presenter with an affected cockney accent and a deliberately unattractive manner.
PP: 'She's lovely.'

A Streetcar Named Desire
US 1984 124m colour TVM
ABC/Telepictures/Keith Barish (Marc Trabulus)

Televersion of the celebrated play about a pretentious southern belle who goes from bad to worse when she takes refuge in her sister's New Orleans household. It can't really hold a candle to the film version, but it does try.

w Oscar Saul, *play* by Tennessee Williams *d* John Erman *ph* Bill Butler *m* Marvin Hamlish

Ann-Margret, Treat Williams, Beverly D'Angelo, Randy Quaid

Streethawk
US 1984 74m colour TVM
ABC/Universal (Bob Wolterstorff, Paul Belous)

A jet-black turbo-designed motorcycle helps a cop to get his revenge on the crooks who killed his partner.
Childish but efficient pilot for a series which faltered in the shadow of *Knight Rider*.

cr Bob Wolterstorff, Paul Belous

Rex Smith, Joe Regalbuto

Streets of Danger: see The Lone Wolf

'His wife and child were murdered. He's taken everything one man could take. Now he's fighting back!'
Streets of Justice
US 1985 96m colour TVM
NBC/Universal (Alan Barnette)

A Manhattan resident who shoots would-be muggers is hailed as a hero.
Adequate drama from the headlines.

w,d Christopher Crowe *ph* Mario De Leo *m* Junior Homrich

John Laughlin, Robert Loggia, Lance Henriksen, Jack Thibeau, Cristina Raines, Paul Shenar

The Streets of San Francisco **
US 1972 98m colour TVM
ABC/Warner/QUINN MARTIN

An old and a young police detective discover who murdered a young girl.
Highly efficient pilot for long-running location series.

w Edward Hume, *novel Poor Poor Ophelia* by Carolyn Weston *d* Walter Grauman

KARL MALDEN, MICHAEL DOUGLAS, Robert Wagner, Kim Darby

'Sometimes a fairish script, more often pointless chasing about San Francisco's hills.' – Jack Edmund Nolan

† The resulting series ran five seasons (120 × 50m episodes) and became an absolutely reliable action-packed crime entertainment. In the last season Michael Douglas was replaced by Richard Hatch.

Streisand, Barbra (1942–). Strong-voiced American singer with a tendency to arrogance; in occasional specials.

Stride, John (1936–). British general purpose actor who played leads in *The Main Chance* and *The Wilde Alliance*.

Strike Force *
US 1975 75m colour TVM
NBC/D'Antoni–Weitz

An élite police force is set up to counter organized crime.
Rough, tough, realistic cop show which didn't take.

w Roger Hirson *d* Barry Shear

Cliff Gorman, Donald Blakely, Richard Gere, Edward Grover

Strike Force
US 1982 74m colour TVM
ABC/Metromedia/Aaron Spelling (Joe Naar, Michael Fisher)

The police call in a special Strike Force to catch a bizarre murderer.
Absolutely routine special with an aged star. The series ran to 19 × 50m episodes.

cr Lane Slate

Robert Stack, Dorian Harewood, Richard Romanus, Michael Goodwin, Trisha Noble, Herb Edelman

'The years since *The Untouchables* have not dimmed the glitter in his stern blue eyes nor softened the clench in his jaw as he contemplates the disgusting fact that some criminals are still walking around in lead-free condition.' – Robert MacKenzie, *TV Guide*

Strike It Rich (US 1951–4). Half-hour quiz series for CBS; the contestants all needed money and had to say why. 'A despicable travesty on the nature of charity.' – *TV Guide*.

Strindberg, August (1849–1912). Stalwart anti-feminist Swedish author whose plays are regularly done on TV, especially *Miss Julie*, *The Strongest* and *The Father* (e.g. 1985 with Dorothy Tutin, Colin Blakely on BBC). Paul Scofield did *The Dance of Death* for ATV in 1965; a memorable production of *The Ghost Sonata* by Stuart Burge figured in a BBC season of World Theatre, 1958. In Sweden, Strindberg's novels have been handsomely serialized: *The People of Hemso*, *The Red Room* and *In the Outermost Archipelago*, all adapted by Herbert Grevenius and directed by Bengt Lagerkvist.   PP

stripping. Playing a series five days a week at the same time.

Stritch, Elaine (1922–). Lanky, rasp-voiced, American comedienne and singer, an under-used talent. Series: *My Sister Eileen*, *Two's Company*, *Nobody's Perfect*.

Stronger Than the Sun (GB 1977). Lab girl at a nuclear plant steals sample of plutonium in order to try and draw attention to the dangers of the programme. Gripping, and in the end desolate, but leaving too many inconsistencies and unexplained motives to be mulled over. With Francesca Annis, Tom Bell. Written by Stephen Poliakoff; directed by Michael Apted; for BBC (*Play for Today*).   PP

Struck by Lightning (US 1979). Shortlived 25-minute comedy series about a nervous descendant of Dr Frankenstein who inherits an old inn of which the eccentric handyman is the original monster. More or less limited to a single set, and flatly presented, this doesn't get the laughs one might expect, but JACK ELAM as the monster is a delight. With Jeffrey Kramer. Created by Terry Keegan; for Fellows–Keegan/Paramount/CBS.

The Struggle for Israel
GB 1970 2 × 50m bw
YTV (Tony Essex, Michael Deakin)
My 1970 review: 'A piece of film archaeology – as always from Essex – of great thoroughness (he'd unearthed some remarkable footage of pioneering Jewish settlers in the early years of the century); but put together in that authorial, rather than authoritative, way which becomes increasingly hard to take . . . It's not enough any longer simply to comb the archives for the most telling sequences and string them together with an omniscient voice-of-God commentary (a task once again delegated by God to Sir Michael Redgrave).' Written by Michael Deakin. See also *Palestine*.   PP

Strumpet City (Ireland 1980; 7 × 50m; colour). Solid, atmospheric version by Hugh Leonard of James Plunkett's novel of Dublin in the last days of British rule. With Cyril Cusack leading a fine cast.   PP

Struthers, Sally (1947–). Pint-sized, hoarse-voiced American actress who made a big hit as the daughter in *All in the Family*. TV movies: *Aloha Means Goodbye*, *Hey I'm Alive*, *The Great Houdinis*, *Intimate Strangers*, *My Husband Is Missing*, *And Your Name Is Jonah*.

The Stu Erwin Show: see The Trouble with Father

Stuart, Mel (1928–). American director, former documentary producer (in the sixties, three-time Emmy winner for *The Making of the President*). TV movies: *Brenda Starr*, *Ruby and Oswald*, *The Triangle Factory Fire Scandal*, *The Chisholms*, *Sophia Loren*.

Stubbs, Una (1937–). British light actress who became famous as Alf Garnett's daughter in *Till Death Us Do Part*.

Students in Revolt (GB 1968). BBC studio inquiry with Robert McKenzie trying to find out, in the wake of the Paris *événements*, just what students were protesting at, what it was about society they wanted to see changed, and what they proposed to put in its place, and getting the usual gobbledegook from Tariq Ali, Daniel Cohn-Bendit and others.   PP

JANET STREET-PORTER.   One of the most fearsome sets of gnashers in the business, with a voice so gruesomely adenoidal that one hopes for her friends' sake it is assumed.

Studio
GB 1983 7 × 52m
Granada (June Howson)

Comings and goings, temptations and tantrums in a country-house recording studio set up by pop-music tycoon Robert Stephens. A stinker which mainly served to drag down the slightly superior *No Excuses* which followed the same season.

w Anthony Minghella, Bob Mason *d* David Carson, Sebastian Graham-Jones *m* Bob Mason, Kevin Malpass

Robert Stephens, Michael Feast, Carol Leader   PP

Studio Four. Umbrella heading for a series of experimental plays (BBC) in the early sixties, taking over from a still earlier format called *Storyboard* in which the emphasis was on a brisk, non-naturalistic narrative style. Though never much appreciated by the audience at the time, the techniques were to influence the succeeding *Wednesday Play* and *Theatre 625* outlets, especially through directors such as Alan Bridges and James MacTaggart who had worked on *Studio Four*. The presiding spirit was story editor Roger Smith.   PP

Studio One (US 1949–57). Anthology drama series for CBS, produced mainly by Worthington Miner with emphasis on the visual.

Studio 64. Play series from ATV, obviously in 1964, in which a writer and director were teamed to hatch a play between them. It worked well at least a couple of times to yield *Better Luck Next Time* (Stanley Mann, Silvio Narizzano) and *The Crunch*, a thriller from Nigel Kneale and Michael Elliott about a Third World embassy in London which tries to hold Britain to ransom with a nuclear bomb in its own basement.   PP

Studs Lonigan *
US 1979 3 × 96m colour
NBC/Lorimar (Harry R. Sherman)

An Irish–American grows up in Chicago in the 1920s.
Solid transcription of a famous novel.

w Reginald Rose, *novel* James T. Farrell *d* James Goldstone

Harry Hamlin, Colleen Dewhurst, Charles Durning, Diana Scarwid, Michael Mullins, Brad Dourif

'A slow-to-get-started, cumbersome vehicle . . . startlingly realistic performances by Dewhurst and Durning . . . sets a tough measuring stick for other miniseries.' – *Daily Variety*

Stunt Challenge (GB since 1982). Annual contest between professional stuntmen to perform most spectacular feat, mostly involving motor cars. Produced by George Sawford, for Thames/Transworld International.   PP

stunting. Cancelling regular weekly programmes in favour of special events.

Stunts Unlimited
US 1980 74m colour TVM
ABC/Paramount/Lawrence Gordon

Three stunt men are recruited by army intelligence to invade the stronghold of a foreign gun runner and retrieve a military secret weapon.
Slick pilot of the *Mission Impossible* school.

w Laurence Heath *d* Hal Needham *ph* Mike Shea *m* Barry deVorzon

Chip Mayer, Susanna Dalton, Sam J. Jones, Glenn Corbett

subjective camera. When it shows you the action through the eyes of the main participant. It was tried hesitantly in the cinema, by Robert Montgomery in *The Lady in the Lake* from the Raymond Chandler story – curiously, Thames Television considered using the same device for their Chandleresque *Hazell* series but decided against. It was actually sustained on TV only in a series called *You Take Over* in the late fifties. But occasional flashes of subjective camerawork have become quite commonplace, e.g. in untold medical soap operas when the hospital corridors are seen from the point of view of a patient being wheeled to the operating theatre. *Sportsview* famously took the viewer round the Le Mans circuit behind the wheel of Mike Hawthorn's Jaguar. Jack Gold simulated the fox's eyeview of being hunted for *Death in the Morning.*   PP

† Also tried out in US series *First Person Singular*, developed by Fred Coe in early fifties.

Submarine * (GB 1984; 6 × 30m). Life underwater in the Royal Navy. Two programmes apiece for (1) testing would-be submarine captains at £1 million a head; (2) a hunter-killer sub on a NATO exercise; (3) a nuclear Polaris submarine preparing to leave base and families on patrol, and the 18-week cruise under the sea. Highly atmospheric fly-on-the-bulkhead series written and produced by Jonathan Crane, for BBC.   PP

Subterfuge
GB 1968 92m colour TVM
Intertel/Commonwealth United

An American agent runs into trouble in London.
Second-rate espionage thick-ear.

d Peter Graham Scott

Gene Barry, Joan Collins, Michael Rennie, Suzanna Leigh, Richard Todd

Success Story. Title used at least twice in GB, first by Rediffusion for a Dan Farson series of 15-minute interviews in 1959. Among the 11 successes chosen were Lady Lewisham (now Countess Spencer), Charles Forte and the racehorse Hyperion. In 1974 Alan Yentob and Julian Jebb used it for a short series of longer assessments: Christopher Isherwood's stories of the English girl in Berlin he called Sally Bowles which inspired a play, the musical *Cabaret* and two movies; Enid Blyton; John Osborne and *Look Back in Anger*; and the all-time best-seller among popular prints, Tretchikoff's *The Green Lady.*   PP

Suchet, David (19 –). Attentive British actor who suddenly became noticed with *The Last Day* and *Being Normal*. *Red Monarch*, *Freud*, *Blott on the Landscape* and *A Song for Europe* followed.   PP

Suchet, John (1944–). British reporter and newscaster with ITN since 1981.

Suddenly Love
US 1979 96m colour TVM
NBC/Ross Hunter

An underprivileged Brooklyn girl falls in love with a wealthy lawyer with heart trouble.
Thin tearjerker from several thirties models.

w Katherine Coker *d* Stuart Margolin *ph* Robert Hauser *m* Dave Rose

Cindy Williams, Paul Shenar, Eileen Heckart, Scott Brady, Kurt Kasznar, Joan Bennett, Lew Ayres

Suddenly Single *
US 1971 73m colour TVM
Chris–Rose

A newly divorced man joins a California singles community.
Reasonably amusing contemporary comedy.

w Elinor and Stephen Karpf d Jud Taylor

Hal Holbrook, Agnes Moorehead, Barbara Rush, Harvey Korman, Margot Kidder, Michael Constantine

Suez 1956 **
GB 1979 180m colour
BBC (Cedric Messina)

A play showing the government-eye-view of Middle East events which caused President Nasser to threaten the Suez Canal and Sir Anthony Eden to retaliate with military action.
Very well documented and sufficiently compelling.

w Ian Curteis d Michael Darlow

Michael Gough (Eden), Robert Stephens (Nasser), Peter Cellier (Selwyn Lloyd), Wensley Pithey (Churchill), Richard Vernon (MacMillan), Patrick Troughton (Monckton), Oscar Quitak (Gaitskill), Alexander Knox (Dulles)

PP: 'Whatever else you make of these enormous animated waxworks of Ian Curteis's, there is no doubt about the solid narrative drive, clanking away under the surface all the time like the cable on to which the San Francisco cable cars latch. However bald and flavourless a scene could be (and some consisted of nothing more than a few exchanges taken directly from published memoirs or records) it always answered at least one little what's-going-to-happen-next posed in the previous scene and set up at least one fresh one.'

Sugarfoot
US 1957–60 69 × 50m bw
Warner

A young western wanderer helps people in trouble.
Passable western which filled a need but is barely remembered.

cr Michael Fessier

Will Hutchins

Sugden, Mollie (1924–). North-country British character comedienne who usually plays a posh-talking but vulgar working-class lady. Series: *The Liver Birds*, ARE YOU BEING SERVED?.

'After her husband's death she felt angry, guilty, hurt . . . and more hungry for life than ever before!'
The Suicide's Wife
US 1979 96m colour TVM
CBS/Factor–Newland (Alan Jay Factor)

An analysis of the shock to a well-to-do woman when her husband inexplicably commits suicide.
Superior misery movie for those who can appreciate the controlled talents operating amid the grief.

w Dennis Nemec, *novel* David Madden d John Newland ph Michael D. Margulies

Angie Dickinson, Gordon Pinsent, Peter Donat, Zohra Lampert, Todd Lookinland, Lane Davies

A Suitable Case for Treatment
GB 1962 60m bw
BBC

David Mercer's first 'madness' play, directed by Don Taylor, subsequently (1965) filmed by Karel Reisz as *Morgan: A Suitable Case for Treatment*. My 1962 review: 'The play took the idea of the hero as a goon already propounded by Peter Nichols and others, only took it much further. Hovering on the brink of a breakdown, trying to resist the loss of his wife to a grotesquely smooth rival, reluctant to enmesh himself with a new girl, Morgan Delt zig-zagged from predicament to self-imposed predicament.
'Between times there were some striking hallucinations and dream sequences, and throbbing through Ian Hendry's high-comedy performance a true and distressing sense of the man's *plight*. When he finally reached for salvation in the shape of the new girl you wished him luck, but dubiously.'   PP

Sullivan, Barry (1912–) (Patrick Barry). Reliable American leading man of the forties, later character actor. A frequent TV guest star. Series: *The Man Called X, The Tall Man, Adventures at Scott Island, The Road West, The Immortal*. TV movies include *Night Gallery, The House on Greenapple Road, Yuma, Cannon, Kung Fu, The Magician, Savage, Hurricane, Once an Eagle, The Bastard, Backstairs at the White House*.

❋ **Sullivan, Ed** (1902–74). American linkman, former columnist. His *Ed Sullivan Show*, on CBS from 1948, was the medium's best showcase for vaudeville talent.

Sullivan, Susan (1944–). Elegant American leading lady of the seventies: star of *Julie Farr MD*. TV movies include *No Place to Run*, *Roger and Harry*, *Deadman's Curve*, *The Comedy Company*, *The New Maverick*. Series: *Falcon Crest*.

Sullivan's Empire
US 1967 90m colour TVM
Universal

Three sons seek their missing father in the South American jungle.
Watchable adventure hokum.

w Frank Chase *d* Harvey Hart, Thomas Carr

Martin Milner, Linden Chiles, Don Quine, Clu Gulager, Karen Jensen

Summer Fantasy
US 198 96m colour TVM
NBC/ITC/Moonlight (Frank Von Zerneck, Robert M. Sertner)

Two young Southern California girls become lifeguards on Venice beach and have various romantic intrigues.
Not much for the mature mind in this modern version of *The Millgirl's Romance*.

w Rena Down *d* Noel Nosseck *ph* Fred Koenekamp *m* Peter Bernstein

Julianne Phillips, Ted Shackleford, Michael Gross, Dorothy Lyman, Paul Keenan

Summer Girl
US 1983 96m colour TVM
CBS/Lorimar/Finnegan/Bruce Lansbury/Roberta Haynes

A teenage summer help turns out to be over-sexed, covetous and murderous.
Yawnworthy melodrama in which viewers are likely to be always ten minutes ahead of the action.

w A. J. Carothers, *novel* by Caroline Crane *d* Robert Lewis *ph* Fred Koenekamp *m* Angela Morley

Barry Bostwick, Kim Darby, Martha Scott, Murray Hamilton, Diane Franklin

'The pot may boil over a couple of times, but CBS has a good suspenser.' – *Daily Variety*

Summer of My German Soldier
US 1979 96m colour TVM
NBC/Highgate (Linda Gottlieb)

In Georgia during World War II, a Jewish teenage girl has a romance with a German prisoner-of-war.
Ironic idyll which might have been perfect at an hour.

w Jane-Howard Hammerstein, *book* Betty Greene *d* Michael Tuchner *ph* Peter Sova *m* Stanley Myers

Kristy McNichol, Bruce Davison, Esther Rolle (Emmy), Michael Constantine, Barbara Barrie

Summer Solstice *
US 1981 50m colour TVM
ABC/Boston Broadcasters Inc. (Stephen Schlow)

Two old people on the beach reminisce about their 50-year marriage.
A slight but pleasant duet for two top actors.

w Bill Phillips *d* Ralph Rosenblum *ph* Bob King *m* John Nagy

HENRY FONDA, MYRNA LOY, Stephen Collins, Lindsay Crouse

† The script was the winner of a 1979 New England playwriting contest

A Summer To Remember
US 1985 96m colour TVM
CBS/Interplanetary (Micheline H. Keller, Edward Gold)

An intelligent orang-utan gets lost and has various adventures.
Old-fashioned entertainment for that old-fashioned family audience.

w Scott Swanton *d* Robert Lewis *ph* Stephen M. Gray *m* Charles Fox

James Farentino, Tess Harper, Bridgette Anderson, Sean Justin Gerlis, Burt Young, Louise Fletcher, Taylor Lacher

'Should fill the bill for the juve set – and lots of their animal-loving elders.' – *Daily Variety*

A Summer Without Boys *
US 1973 74m colour TVM
Playboy

At a holiday resort during World War II, a woman becomes involved with a younger man and her daughter resents it.
Adequate woman's picture.

w Rita Lakin *d* Jeannot Szwarc

Barbara Bain, Michael Moriarty, Kay Lenz, Mildred Dunnock

The Sun Also Rises
US 1985 2 × 96m colour miniseries
NBC/TCF (John Furia)

Adventures of Americans in Paris who won't go home after World War I.
Dull, pretentious version of Hemingway's modern classic.

w Robert L. Joseph *d* James Goldstone

THE SUN ALSO RISES. Rise is what this miniseries version failed to do, despite its promising cast: Ian Charleson, Hart Bochner, Robert Carradine, Jane Seymour, Zeljko Ivanek, Leonard Nimoy. Perhaps Mr Spock put a spell on it.

Jane Seymour, Hart Bochner, Zeljko Ivanek, Robert Carradine, Ian Charleson, Leonard Nimoy

Sunday Afternoon (GB 1955–6). Miscellany programme produced by John Irwin for ATV in earliest days of commercial television. Noteworthy for a comic idea to poll viewers as to which of its nine regular contributors should be discarded when after 13 weeks the format was cut from 40 to 30 minutes. On receipt of lawyers' letters from some of the nine, this scheme was hastily abandoned. The nine were: artist Mervyn Levy, debutante Penny Knowles, actress Chin Yu, 'memory man' Leslie Welch, Tom Driberg, Edith Sitwell, Ludovic Kennedy, Jill Craigie and Anthony Wedgwood Benn.
PP

The Sunday Break (GB 1958–63). The first programme to invade the 6–7 p.m. slot on Sundays which until the late fifties was a closed period in order to encourage church-going. Masterminded by Penry Jones, later to be an

elder statesman of religious broadcasting at both the IBA and the BBC, it mixed religion, pop music and teenage affairs, with Julie Stevens as youthful anchorman.
PP

Sunday in September (GB 1961; 30m; bw). Historic, if loaded, actuality film, transmitted the day after a mass nuclear disarmament sit-down in London coincided with a patriotic Battle of Britain turn-out. God and the government were all too clearly on the side of the military spectacle, life on the side of the pacifists. Produced by Tim Hewat, for Granada.
PP

Sunday Night at the London Palladium. A live one-hour variety show from the stage of the world's most famous variety theatre, this ATV presentation was a weekly event from 1954 until 1965 and included the most famous names in show business as well as a 'Beat the Clock' game interlude. Compères included Tommy Trinder, Bruce Forsyth, Norman Vaughan and Jim Dale. The show was revived in the early seventies but for no good reason seemed less popular, though the format was identical; perhaps the talent was missing.

PP (1959): 'Sunday Night at the London Palladium is a 20th-century rite. Imperishable, immovable, above criticism, it occupies its pole position in the week as securely as football holds Saturday afternoon. Its ceremonial is as unchanging as an Order of Service. The congre— the audience, I should say, settles down with relief to one of life's reassuring certainties.

'Cheery compère will succeed high-stepping girls; "Beat the Clock" will follow a couple of lesser turns; finally, there will be the Big Star, and all the lush splendour of the revolving-stage finale. It is Val Parnell's benison on every loyal viewer.'

Sunday's Child (GB 1959). Runner in an ITV fashion about this time for comedy series featuring semi-orphans. Here it was former child star Mandy Miller looking after widowed Mummy, with scripts by Peter Lambda. On simultaneously was *Don't Tell Father* with Julia Lockwood doing same for bereft Daddy. They should have joined forces.   PP

Sunley's Daughter
GB 1974 3 × 50m colour
YTV (Barry Cockcroft)

True-life love story featuring austerely religious farmer, daughter and the hired hand, all taking place against the stern backdrop of the Cleveland Hills. My review at the time: 'There is in all these beautiful and engaging documentaries of rural life made by Barry Cockcroft and his team a certain Mary Webbish romanticism, an awe for the austerity and unremitting toil of the farm which in old Sunley's case could be eased overnight with the aid of the local electricity board. But apart from that one question, a decent reticence was maintained; self-acting demands were kept to a minimum, and in the extraordinarily attractive, acceptant Mary they have a super heroine.'   PP

Sunset Across the Bay *
GB 1975 70m colour (16mm)
BBC (Innes Lloyd)

A manual worker retires and he and his wife go to live at Morecambe.
Sensitive but rather painful tragi-comedy of old age and death.

w ALAN BENNETT d Stephen Frears ph Brian Tufano

HARRY MARKHAM, GABRIELLE DAYE, Bob Peck, Albert Modley, Betty Alberge, Madge Hindle

'A moving work, modest on the surface, richer and deeper in memory.' – *Daily Mail*

Sunset Limousine *
US 1983 96m colour TVM
CBS/ITC/Witzend (Allan McKeon, Robert Vehon)

A stand-up comedian makes a living as a limousine driver and gets mixed up with gangsters.
Easy-going, amusing romp with good lines.

w DICK CLEMENT, IAN LA FRENAIS d Terry Hughes ph Dennis Dalzell m Frank Denson

John Ritter, Susan Dey, Paul Reiser, Audrie J. Neenan, Martin Short, George Kirby, Louise Sorel, James Luisi

'The mixture works well . . . the cast carries the brightness unflaggingly.' – *Daily Variety*

Sunset People (GB 1984; 120m). Impressionistic documentary about the street that wriggles for 28 miles through Los Angeles' otherwise rectilinear street-map, and seeming at times almost as long; but full of droll real-life mini-dramas and loquacious out-of-work actors. Made by Jana Bokova, for BBC *Arena*.   PP

Sunset Song * (GB 1971). Lewis Grassic Gibbon's novels of life close to the earth in North-East Scotland, nicely shot and better acted to make a fine, unhackneyed serial. With Vivien Heilbron, Paul Young, Andrew Keir. Written by Bill Craig; for BBC Scotland.   PP

† Two sequels followed 11 and 12 years later: *Cloud Howe* and *Grey Granite*.

Sunshine
US 1973 121m colour TVM
NBC/Universal

A young wife finds she is dying of cancer.
Unbearably icky sudser which was popular among teenagers.

w Carol Sobieski d Joseph Sargent ph Bill Butler m John Denver

Cliff de Young, Brenda Vaccaro, Cristina Raines

† A short-lived series ensued (13 × 25m) starring Cliff de Young as the sadly coping widower (producer: George Eckstein; director: John Badham). There was also a second TV movie, *Sunshine Christmas*, and a theatrical feature of 1976, *My Sweet Lady*, which was made up from fragments of the series.

The Sunshine Boys
US 1978 50m colour
Ray Stark/MGM/NBC (Michael Levee)

Two long-retired vaudeville comics are still squabbling with each other.
Interesting attempt to make a television series of the hit play and film. The pilot didn't jell.

w Neil Simon d Robert Moore

Red Buttons, Lionel Stander

The Sunshine Patriot *
US 1968 98m colour TVM
Universal (Joel Rogosin)

A Russian secret agent takes the place of his double, an American businessman.
Adequate espionage suspenser.

w Gustave Field, Joel Rogosin, John Kneubuhl d Joseph Sargent

Cliff Robertson, Dina Merrill, Wilfrid Hyde White, Lilia Skala, Antoinette Bower, Donald Sutherland, Luther Adler

The Super
US 1972 13 × 25m colour (VTR)
ABC/Metromedia

Problems for the janitor of a semi-derelict New York apartment building.
Unattractive comedy series which didn't last.

Richard Castellano, Margaret Castellano

Super Friends
US 1973–4 26 × 45m colour
Warner/Filmation

Adventures of a group of friends with special powers: Superman, Batman and Robin, Aquaman, Wonder Woman.
Enough is too much, especially of a semi-animated cartoon.

The Super Globetrotters (US 1979). 13 22-minute episodes of Saturday morning animation from Hanna–Barbera about a crime-fighting basketball team.

Super Troupers (GB 1985; 7 × 30m; colour). Legendary music hall acts and musical comedy performances re-created by today's adepts, e.g. Barry Cryer as Billy Bennett, Anita Harris as Gertie Lawrence. Hosted by Tony Bilbow from the stage of the New Tyne Theatre, Newcastle, with interruptions from Eddy Angel and Tommy Trinder. Produced by Heather Ging, directed by Royston Mayoh. From Tyne Tees for C4.   PP

See Halls of Fame

LH: 'I was appalled by the fact that on its opening credits this so-called tribute misspelled the names of at least four top stars.'

Superdome *
US 1978 96m colour TVM
ABC Circle (William Frye)

A security guard is murdered during a big football game in New Orleans.
Pretty suspenseful, well-written telemovie which passes the time without exhausting the patience.

w Barry Oringer d Jerry Jameson ph Matthew F. Leonetti m John Cacavas

David Janssen, Jane Wyatt, Edie Adams, Clifton Davis, Peter Haskell, Ken Howard, Susan Howard, Van Johnson, Donna Mills, Ed Nelson, Vonetta McGee

Supergran (GB 1984; 13 × 30m). Cheerful children's series about a gentle old lady accidentally endowed with supernatural powers. With Gudrun Ure, Iain Cuthbertson. Written by Jenny McDade from the books by Forrest Wilson. Produced by Keith Richardson, for Tyne-Tees.

Superman
US 1952–6 104 × 25m 52 colour, 52 bw
National Periodical Publications

The all-powerful hero from the planet Krypton masquerades as mild-mannered reporter Clark Kent.
Fairly ragged, watchable kiddie show from the comic strip.

George Reeves, Noel Neill

superstation: one which feeds its programming by satellite, to other stations, for a fee

w Earl W. Wallace d Dan Curtis ph Dennis Dalzell m Bob Cobert

Steve Lawrence, Char Fontane, Don Stroud, Keenan Wynn, Deborah Benson, Ron Masak, Don Meredith, George Hamilton, Stella Stevens, Nita Talbot

† The pilot was subsequently released as *Express to Terror*

'I have an idea that may cut NBC's losses: let *Salvage-1* haul that train away and sell it for scrap.' – Robert MacKenzie, *TV Guide*

Supertrain
US 1979 96m colour TVM
NBC/Dan Curtis (Rod Amateau)

Adventures aboard America's most modern train, which includes a nightclub and swimming pool.
Dim pilot for a much-heralded but ignominiously shortlived series (eight episodes). Huge train and platform sets were built at gigantic cost (in television terms) but

the project never got off the ground as far as the audience was concerned, because nobody knew how to be either funny or thrilling. The real creator was Fred Silverman, wonder boy of two networks who failed at a third; continuing characters included Robert Alda and Edward Andrews.

Surfside Six
US 1960–1 74 × 50m bw
ABC/Warner

Three detectives live on a houseboat at Miami Beach.
Very moderate mystery series aimed at teenagers.
Troy Donahue, Lee Patterson, Van Williams, Diane McBain

Surrender Value *
GB 1961 50m bw (VTR)
ATV *Theatre 70*

William Lucas as caddish estate agent fiddling his expenses, rigging his commission, cuddling his secretary, seducing Maxine Audley, abusing his wife and generally observing two moral codes as sharply differentiated as his telephone voice for clients and his telephone voice for others. My review at the time: 'The disconcerting thing was that you couldn't help liking him and the refreshing thing was that he got away with the lot. No one seemed to have heard of Compensating Moral Value, the concept beloved of censors, that the scoundrel must always get his come-uppance. In a wry closing scene he even got an unearned bonus of affection and gratitude from his wife.' Written by Geoffrey Bellman and John Witney.   PP

† Co-author John Whitney is now, via commercial radio, director-general of the IBA.

Survival *. Half-hour wild-life film series which has been produced by Anglia TV at the rate of 13 or more episodes per year since the fifties. There have also been a number of one-hour specials including *The Flight of the Snow Goose*, *Tiger, Tiger* and *Gorilla*.

Survive * (GB 1984; 6 × 60m). Excellent series of first-hand reminiscences of survival in Arctic wastes, open boats or concentration camps, with the practicalities backed up by present-day survival training in various armed forces, but due attention also on the mental and temperamental qualities needed. Filmed and directed by Nick Downie, produced by Leon Clifton, for N Lee Lacy/C4.

'Blood-curdling, energetic . . . lively viewing.' – *Sunday Mirror*

Surviving
US 1985 142m colour TVM
ABC/Telepictures (Hunt Lowry)

The effect on the families of a teenage suicide pact.
Good intentions can't really atone for this extended wallow in gloom and despondency.
w Joyce Eliason   *d* Waris Hussein
ph Alexander Gruszynski   *m* James Horner
Ellen Burstyn, Len Cariou, Zach Galligan, Marsha Mason, Molly Ringwald, Paul Sorvino
'A painful, lovely telefilm full of riches and desperations.' – *Daily Variety*

The Survivors *
US 1969 15 × 50m colour
ABC/Universal (William Frye, Gordon Oliver, Walter Doniger)

Embezzlement and murder are just a couple of the things that happen in a millionaire's family.
An ill-starred attempt at a novel for TV by Harold Robbins. Chief fault was that the characters were rich but not interesting, and the Riviera story which was shot as a pilot was not shown until the series folded and portions of it were used, with much dramatic contrivance, as a wrap-up. A TV movie called *Last of the Powerseekers* was also extracted from the general muddle, which was compounded by dissensions among staff and cast.
cr Harold Robbins   *story editors* John Wilder, Michael Gleason
Lana Turner, George Hamilton, Kevin McCarthy, Ralph Bellamy, Rossano Brazzi, Louis Hayward, Jan Michael Vincent, Diana Muldaur

Survivors
GB 1975–7 39 × 50m colour
BBC

From the *Doomwatch* team, a doomsday saga of existence after a virus epidemic has wiped out most of the human race. Should have tapped, and sometimes did, everyone's dreams of self-sufficiency and starting all over again. At the time I said: 'The trouble was that as communications improved between isolated colonies of survivors, ideas became more important than immediate tasks of raising sheep or making cheese and ideas were what the series seemed least able to dramatize.'

w Terry Nation, Martin Worth

Carolyn Seymour, Lucy Fleming, Peter Copley, Dennis Lill   PP

Susie: see Private Secretary

Suspect *
GB 1969 76m colour (16mm)
Thames (Mike Hodges)

A crime is committed in a remote village, and the life of a family is affected.

Detailed, circumstantial police suspenser, well above average.

w/d Mike Hodges

Rachel Kempson, Michael Coles, George Sewell

PP: 'Of some historic note as Thames's first colour drama and first to be filmed wholly on location. It led to the formation of Euston Films.'

Suspense (US 1949–53). Half-hour live anthology drama for CBS. Ten years later it turned up briefly as a film series, now hosted by Sebastian Cabot.

Suspicion *
US 1957 21 × 50m bw
NBC/Revue/Alfred Hitchcock

An anthology of suspense stories. (Hitchcock was not involved except as executive producer.)

A mixed bag, but the level of technical accomplishment was quite high.

Bette Davis, Ida Lupino, Nancy Kelly, etc.

✱ **Susskind, David** (1920–). American independent producer and entrepreneur, usually involved with worthwhile material. Series include *East Side West Side*, GET SMART, and shows for *Kraft Theater* and *Play of the Week*. He also acted as moderator in a discussion programme, *The David Susskind Show*.

Sutherland, Muir (1933–). British executive who began with Border TV; successively in charge of sales, purchasing and presentation of Thames Television; ran the international operation before becoming director of programmes 1982–6. Now back with Border.

Sutherland's Law (GB 1976). Iain Cuthbertson in BBC stories of a procurator-fiscal, who in Scottish law is a kind of district attorney or investigative prosecutor, plus the bonus of an attractive west coast setting.   PP

Sutton, Shaun (1919–). Writer–director of pioneering children's serials, e.g. *The Silver Sword*, who became BBC Head of Drama. After occupying this post 1969–81, produced last batch of plays in the BBC Shakespeare.
BBC Book: *The Largest Theatre in the World*, 1982.

Suzman, Janet (1939–). South African actress in Britain, a notable Cleopatra in *Antony and Cleopatra*, 1974; played Lady Mountbatten in *Mountbatten – The Last Viceroy*, 1986.

Svengali
US 1983 96m colour TVM
CBS/Viacom/Robert Halmi

A voice-coach turns a teenage rock singer into a national sensation.

Absurd modernization with acting which can at best be described as disinterested.

w Frank Cucci, Sue Grafton *d* Anthony Harvey *ph* Larry Pizer *m* John Barry

Peter O'Toole, Jodie Foster, Elizabeth Ashley, Larry Joshua, Pamela Blair

'Telefilm flirts with generation differences, loyalties, incipient jealousy, but never comes away with anything deep, despite posh packaging.' – *Daily Variety*

Swackhamer, E. W. (19 –). American director, working from 1964. TV movies: *In Name Only*, *Gidget Gets Married*, *Death Sentence*, *Death at Love House*, *Once an Eagle*, *Night Terror*, *Spiderman*, *The Dain Curse*, *The Winds of Kitty Hawk*, *Vampire*, *The Death of Ocean View Park*, *Tenspeed and Brown Shoe*, *Reward*, *Oklahoma City Dolls*, *Foul Play*, *Bring 'Em Back Alive*, *Malibu*, *Carpool*.

Swallow, Norman (1921–). British executive producer, often in tandem with Denis Mitchell; with BBC and Granada. BAFTA 1977: Desmond Davis Award. Last undertaking: the ambitious but unappreciated *Television* series.

Swallows and Amazons Forever! (GB 1982; 4 × 25m). One of Arthur Ransome's messing-about-in-boats stories serialized by Michael Robson with a third-generation Dimbleby – Henry, son of David and Josceline – playing a decent sort of boy. Also with John Woodvine, Colin Baker and Andrew Burt. Directed by Andrew Morgan, produced by Joe Waters, for BBC.   PP

Swan Song
US 1980 96m colour TVM
ABC/TCF/Renee Valente/Topanga
A brilliant amateur skier turns pro and goes for the money.
Meandering outdoor drama which looks good but has precious little tension or point.
w Michael Mann, Ron Koslow, Jeffrey Bloom d Jerry London ph Michael Marguilies m Jonathan Tunick
David Soul, Bo Brundin, Jill Eikenberry, Murray Hamilton, Leonard Mann, Slim Pickens
'Loitering too long, it misses the mark.' – Daily Variety

S.W.A.T. *
US 1975–6 34 × 50m colour
ABC/Spelling–Goldberg (Robert Hammer)
For tough cases the police call in a special weapons and tactical team.
Cop show much criticized for its toughness; it was cancelled because of the anti-violence lobby. It did however manage some rousing action sequences, though its situations were repetitive.
cr Robert Hammer
Steve Forrest, Robert Urich, Rod Perry, James Coleman, Mark Shera
† The pilot was a 96m episode of *The Rookies* called *S.W.A.T.* Two other 96m episodes were made, *Deadly Tide* and *Running Man.*

Swayze, John Cameron (c 1913–).
American radio and TV newscaster of the forties and fifties: he always began with 'And a good evening to you' and closed with 'Glad we could get together.'

Sweden has a non-commercial parent company, Sveriges Radio, and its television organization began transmissions in 1957. There have since 1969 been two channels, each broadcasting about 40 hours per week, half of the programmes being imported.

The Sweeney **
GB 1974–8 52 × 50m colour
Thames/Euston Films
Cases of Scotland Yard's Flying Squad.
Rough, tough crime-in-the-streets cop melodrama, with much bad language, low life and violence, not to mention a villain-hating hero. Despite some unnecessarily impenetrable plots, a thoroughly professional job.
JOHN THAW, DENNIS WATERMAN, Garfield Morgan
† The pilot for the series was a TV movie called *Regan.*

Sweeney, Bob (19 –).
American comic actor who played Fibber McGee and was one of *The Brothers.* Later he turned producer: *Hawaii Five O, The Andros Targets.*

Sweeney Todd (US 1984; 139m).
A multi-camera version of the stage production of Stephen Sondheim's musical play: an interesting record which doesn't really come to life on television. With Angela Lansbury, George Hearn; directed by Terry Hughes; for RKO.

Sweepstakes (US 1978).
Shortlived one-hour comedy–drama series about runners-up in a million-dollar lottery. With Edd Byrnes; created by Thomas L. Miller and Robert Dozier; produced by Ben Kadish; for Miller–Milkis/Paramount/NBC.

Sweet, Dolph (1920–85).
Short and stocky American character actor who made it big in GIMME A BREAK. Also: *Another World, When the Whistle Blows, Jacqueline Bouvier Kennedy, The Two Worlds of Carol Letner.*

Sweet Hostage
US 1980 96m colour TVM
ABC/Brut (Richard E. Lyons, Sidney D. Balkin)
A man escapes from a mental asylum, kidnaps a farmer's daughter, and lives idyllically with her in a mountain hut.
Tedious romantic melodrama with a deranged hero who quotes poetry all the time.
w Ed Hume, novel *Welcome to Xanadu* by Nathaniel Benchley d Lee Phillips ph Richard C. Glouner m Luchi de Jesus
Linda Blair, Martin Sheen, Jeanne Cooper, Bert Remsen
'Fails to enchant . . . finds itself clogged by the tedious pace.' – Daily Variety

Sweet Revenge *
US 1983 96m colour TVM
CBS/David Greene/Robert Papazian
At an army post, a junior officer's wife finds she has good reason to hate her colonel, and does something about it.
Slightly unusual melodrama which grips once it gets into its stride.
w Andrew Peter Marin d David Greene ph Harry J. May m Gil Melle
Kevin Dobson, Kelly McGillis, Alec Baldwin, Savannah Smith, Wings Hauser
'Telefilm bristles with life, purpose and vengeance.' – Daily Variety

THE SWEENEY. John Thaw and Dennis Waterman in their glory days.

Sweet Sixteen (GB 1983; 6 × 30m). Yukky sitcom fielding Penelope Keith as imperious building tycoon amorously entangled with architect (Christopher Villiers) 16 years her junior, hence the title if nothing else. Written by Douglas Watkinson, for BBC. PP

Sweet Sweet Rachel *
US 1971 73m colour TVM
Stan Shpetner

An ESP expert tries to find out how a beautiful woman is being driven mad.
Reasonably chilling semi-supernatural thriller.
w Anthony Lawrence *d* Sutton Roley
Alex Dreier, Stefanie Powers, Pat Hingle, Louise Latham, Brenda Scott

Swenson, Inga (1934–). Tall American actress with a good line in sharp-tongued ladies, as demonstrated in BENSON. TV movies: *Earth II, Testimony of Two Men, Ziegfeld: The Man and His Women.*

Swift, David (1919–). American producer who at one point had a high reputation for the creation of comedy series: *Mr Peepers, Grindl, Camp Runamuck.*

Swindle! (GB 1983; 3 × 60m). Detailed documentary investigation of the IOS/Cornfeld/Vesco case, a notorious financial scandal of the era. Filmed by Slim Hewitt, directed and produced by Peter Batty, for Peter Batty Productions/C4.   PP

The Swiss Family Robinson
GB title: *Island of Adventure*
US 1975 74m colour TVM
ABC/TCF/Irwin Allen
A family has to fend for itself when shipwrecked on a desert island.
Abysmal remake heralding a likewise series.
w Ken Trevey *d* Harry Harris
Martin Milner, Cameron Mitchell, Pat Delaney, Michael Wixted, John Vernon
† The series ran to 24 × 50m episodes

Swit, Loretta (1938–). American character actress with comedic bent, a sensation as Hot Lips Houlihan in *M*A*S*H.* TV movies: *Shirts/Skins, The Last Day, The Hostage Heart, The Love Tapes, Cagney and Lacey, The Kid from Nowhere, Games Mother Never Taught You, First Affair, The Execution.*

Switch **
US 1975 74m colour TVM
CBS/Universal (Glen A. Larson)
A con man and an ex-cop are partners in an investigation agency and pull the wool over the eyes of a conniving police officer.
Fast moving, funny, not very comprehensible pilot based on the appeal of *The Sting.* Unfortunately the resultant series (66 × 50m) was tolerated rather than popular.
w Glen A. Larson *d* Robert Day
Robert Wagner, Eddie Albert, Charles Durning, Sharon Gless

Sword of Freedom
GB 1957 39 × 25m bw
ATV/Sapphire
Adventures of a 15th-century Italian Robin Hood.
Tolerable costume hokum.
Edmund Purdom

Sword of Honour *
GB 1967 3 × 90m bw
BBC
Solid, faithful version of Evelyn Waugh's World War II trilogy with Freddie Jones making his name as the mysterious Ludovic, Ronald Fraser as Apthorpe and Edward Woodward as the wan hero. Written by Giles Cooper; directed by Donald McWhinnie.   PP

In the tradition of such literary classics as *The Scarlet Pimpernel* and *The Count of Monte Cristo*, action and adventure combine with human emotion and sophisticated humour.'

Sword of Justice
US 1978 96m colour TVM
NBC/Universal (Glen Larson)
A playboy is framed on an embezzlement charge which has also caused the death of his parents. On his release from jail, having acquired special criminal skills, he sets about avenging himself on those responsible.
Doleful pilot which unaccountably resulted in a series order. Our hero will of course use his doubtful skills to help the oppressed.
Dack Rambo, Alexander Courtney, Bert Rosario
cr Glen Larson, Michael Gleason
† The series was cancelled after 13 × 50m episodes.

Sybil *
US 1976 2 × 96m colour
Lorimar/NBC (Jacqueline Babbin)
The investigation of a girl with sixteen different personalities.
Docu-drama which goes thirteen better than *The Three Faces of Eve.* Conscientious but a little long.
w Stewart Stern, *book* Flora Rheta Schreiber
d Daniel Petrie *m* Leonard Rosenman
Joanne Woodward, Sally Field, Brad Davis, Martine Bartlett, Charles Lane, William Prince

Sykes, Eric (1923–). British comedian and writer, who from the fifties to the seventies had regular series on BBC, with Hattie Jacques as his sister, Richard Wattis (early shows) as a neighbour, and (latterly) Deryck Guyler as a friendly policeman. They were always funny in an amateurish way.

Sylvester, Victor (1902–78). British orchestra leader who ran the BBC's Dancing Club for many post-war years. Famous for his measured tempo: 'slow, slow, quick quick slow'.

syndication. What happens to shows after the networks have finished with them: they are sold to local stations, either singly or in groups.

Szysznyk
US 1977 6 × 25m colour
CBS/Paramount/Four's Company (Jerry
  Weintraub)

An ex-Marine becomes a playground supervisor.

Dullsville sentimental comedy series. The title didn't help.

cr Jim Mulligan, Ron Landry

Ned Beatty, Olivia Cole, Susan Lanier

The Tab Hunter Show
US 1960 32 × 25m bw
NBC/Famous Artists (Norman Tokar)
Romantic misadventures of the playboy artist of a popular comic strip.
Tolerable comedy filler series.
Tab Hunter, Richard Erdman, Jerome Cowan

Tabitha
US 1977 13 × 25m colour
ABC/Columbia (Robert Stambler)
The daughter of the witch of *Bewitched* grows up and works in a television station.
Awful, youth-oriented sequel.
Lisa Hartman, Robert Urich, Mel Stewart

Taeger, Ralph (c 1929–). Standard American leading man. Series: *Acapulco*, *Klondike*, *Hondo*.

Taggart **
GB 1985–6 9 × 52m
STV (Robert Love)
Further cases, each 3 × 52m, of the detective chief-inspector (first seen in *Killer*) whose face is as genial as the front end of a Volvo. 'Peopled with good Glasgow characters played by good Glasgow actors,' I wrote. 'The dialogue is terse and the stories satisfyingly involved.'
w Glenn Chandler *d* Laurence Moody
Mark McManus, Neil Duncan

Tail Gunner Joe *
US 1977 150m colour TVM
Universal/NBC (George Eckstein)
The career of Senator Joe McCarthy.
Some absorbing material is a little too fancily presented in flashback, but the show gets marks for trying.
w Lane Slate *d* Jud Taylor *m/d* Billy May
Peter Boyle, Burgess Meredith, Patricia Neal, John Forsythe, Heather Menzies, Ned Beatty, Charles Cioffi, Andrew Duggan, Jean Stapleton, Henry Jones

Take a Letter, Mr Jones
GB 1981 7 × 25m colour
Southern (Bryan Izzard)

A female boss has a male secretary.
A bad idea for a sitcom, unredeemed by the handling.
w Ronald Wolfe, Ronald Chesney *d* Bryan Izzard
John Inman, Rula Lenska

Take It or Leave It **. BBC literary panel quiz of the sixties, conducted first by Robert Robinson, then by Alan Brien, in which getting the right answer was less important than the ruminations along the way. At the time I thought: 'If you shut your eyes at home when they identify each quotation on the screen you can join in the speculation; once the authorship is established the quotation remains to give the conversation a key, a piece of concrete evidence to go on. The talk is properly contained and yet it is also absolutely spontaneous.'   PP
† Briefly revived as *The Book Game*, 1982, with Robert Robinson again.

Take Six (GB 1979–80). Showcase, rather like the BBC's *Six* in 1964, for short films on any subject by directors new to television. Two series displayed interesting débuts by, among others, Peter Greenaway and Nick Gilbey with Derek Jones. Produced by Udi Eichler; for Thames.   PP

Take the High Road. Thrice-weekly Scottish soaper which since the early eighties has had a daytime network screening. Set in the Western Highlands and Islands, it is actually filmed in the village of Luss, on Loch Lomond. The regulars include Alec Monteath, Caroline Ashley, Kenneth Watson, Eileen McCallum, Gwyneth Guthrie and the singer Ian Wallace. Writers include Bill Craig. Produced (1985) by Brian Mahoney, for STV.   PP

Take Three Girls
GB 1969–71 26 × 50m colour
BBC (Gerald Savory)
Exploits of three girls sharing a London flat – at the time I thought it 'a feeble device to smuggle an anthology drama series into the schedules without actually calling it that. All it

achieves is to restrict most of the stories to the particular and on the whole extremely boring bits of society which modish London girls are supposed to frequent.' But individual episodes did rise to better things, notably an excursion to Austria by Robert Muller in which the journalist member of the trio went to interview a legendary prewar opera singer played by none other than Elisabeth Bergner.

w Guy Meredith; Julia Jones; Terence Brady and Charlotte Bingham; Lee Langley d Richard Martin; Roger Bamford; Les Chatfield; Julian Amyes p Gerald Savory

Susan Jameson, Lisa Goddard, Angela Down   PP

† *Take Three Women* (1982; 4 × 55m) revisited the same three heroines 13 years on; one episode apiece and one which brought them all together.

Take Your Best Shot *
US 1982 96m colour TVM
CBS/Levinson–Link/Robert Papazian

A once-successful television actor finds life frustrating when producers don't call.
Unusual and reasonably probing analysis of the life of a Hollywood also-ran.

W RICHARD LEVINSON, WILLIAM LINK d David Greene ph Stevan Larner m Peter Matz

Robert Urich, Meredith Baxter Birney, Jeffrey Tambor, Jack Bannon, Claudette Nevins, Susan Peretz, Michael Bell, Jennetta Arnette, Matthew Faison

Take Your Pick. An extremely tatty quiz show inflicted on the British for nearly 20 years from 1955 by Associated Rediffusion. Winners had the choice of opening a mystery box which would contain anything from a fortune to a dried prune. Michael Miles was the jokester in charge.

Taking Sides (GB 1984). A 'radiovision' collaboration between BBC1 and Radio 4 in which debates on various topics were broadcast live on both outlets, with Paul Sieghart as a patronizing and much too organizing moderator. 'A glittering performance,' I said, 'but one I'm happy to distrust.' So were the Broadcasting Complaints Commission, evidently, when in 1986 they upheld a complaint from the moralist and advocate of parental responsibility Mrs Victoria Gillick, who had appeared on the show in November 1984. PP

Talbot, Nita (1930–) (Anita Sokol). American wisecracking comedy actress, in

evidence through the fifties and sixties. *Hot off the Wire*, *The Movie Murderer*, *Here We Go Again*.

The Tale of Beatrix Potter (GB 1983; 90m). Soulful biopic of the creator of the Flopsy Bunnies, etc, with Penelope Wilton as the lady, Donald Gee, Jerome Willis. Narrated by Michael Hordern, written by John Hawkesworth from the biography by Margaret Lane; music by Carl Davis; directed by Bill Hays, produced by Carol Robertson, for BBC.

A Tale of Two Cities
US 1980 140m colour TVM
CBS/Marble Arch/Norman Rosemont

A drunken lawyer sacrifices himself for another during the French Revolution.
Bland classic from the producer who has adapted so many without deserving much praise for the way he does it.

w John Gay, *novel* Charles Dickens d Jim Goddard ph Tony Imi m Allyn Ferguson

Chris Sarandon (playing both Darnay and Carton), Peter Cushing (Manette), Billie Whitelaw (Mme Defarge), Kenneth More (Lorry), Alice Krige (Lucy), Barry Morse (the Marquis), Flora Robson (Miss Pross), George Innes (Cruncher)

'Romance, intrigue, honour, handsome production values, equally impressive costumes and plenty of candles.' – *Daily Variety*

Tales from the Darkside
US 1985–   × 25m colour
Embassy/JayGee/Laurel/Tribune (T. J. Castronova)

Series for syndication, very similar to *Twilight Zone*, *Night Gallery* and their ilk. Patchy, to say the least.

Tales of India *
GB 1978 6 × 40m colour (VTR)
BBC (Stephen Peet)

Interviews with survivors from the time of the Raj.
Invaluable social history, though it is surprising how little photographic and newsreel material is available.

d/narrator Christopher Cook

PP: 'The reminiscences to Peet's tried and trusted *Yesterday's Witness* formula included the ripping, not to say gripping, yarn of a young girl who was kidnapped by Pathan warriors, and her subsequent rescue by negotiation, of which I wrote: "Apart from affording eerie intimations of arbitrary terrorism and subtle peace-keeping which seem to belong so firmly to the present day, Peet was able to tell the story dramatically and cleanly using only a few talking heads, a few smudgy photographs and one (unattributed) clip from an old television programme." '

Tales of the Gold Monkey
US 1982 96m colour TVM
ABC/Universal/Donald P. Bellisario
(Donald A. Baier)

In a remote chain of South Pacific islands in 1938, an adventurer operates a seaplane service.
Flabby rip-off of *Raiders of the Lost Ark* (not to mention *Casablanca* and *The Maltese Falcon*), with every ingredient from volcanoes to extras in gorilla suits.

w Donald P. Bellisario d Ray Austin
ph Fred J. Koenekamp m Mike Post, Pete Carpenter

Stephen Collins, Caitlin O'Heaney, Jeff MacKay, Marta DuBois, Ron Moody, John Hillerman, Johnny Sekka

'Replete with stereotyped characters, feeble comedic attempts, and ho-hum situations that contain very little action or adventure.' – *Variety*

'As the old writer's adage goes: if you steal from one writer it's plagiarism; if you steal from several it's research.' – *TV Guide*

PP: 'I loved it for its rugged, 45-year-old, all-American star – the hero's 1937 Grumman Goose amphibian, which out-acted everyone.'

Tales of the Klondyke *
Canada/GB 1983 7 × 60m
Norfolk Communications/CBC/Primetime
(William Macadam)

Stories of the Gold Rush by Jack London vividly filmed on the right locations, and deriving from David Cobham's pioneering *To Build a Fire* for BBC2 in 1970. Cobham acted as series consultant, and directed three episodes. Orson Welles was narrator.

w various   story editor Peter Wildeblood
d various

Players included Robert Carradine, Cherie Lunghi, Neil Munroe   PP

Tales of the Long Room * (GB 1985; 13 × 15m). Tall stories of the cricket field as told by Robin Bailey pretending to be a bluff brigadier of the old school, inventive but a bit ornate. Written by Peter Tinniswood, produced by Vernon Lawrence, for YTV.
                                                    PP

LH: 'Funnier – and that means very funny indeed – on radio.'

Tales of the 77th Bengal Lancers: see 77th Bengal Lancers

Tales of the Texas Rangers
US 1955–6 52 × 25m bw
ABC/Columbia

Present-day yarns, from a radio series starring Joel McCrea. Not too bad, but no better than it needed to be.

Willard Parker, Harry Lester

Tales of Twelve Cities (GB 1981; 12 × 40m; colour). One each from all the BBC regions, including one from BBC East about Cambridge don Hugh Sykes Davies who had been a crony of the spies Guy Burgess and Anthony Blunt, and a final London contribution on the controversial GLC leader Ken Livingstone. A nice idea masterminded by James Dewar.   PP

Tales of the Unexpected
GB title: *Twist in the Tale*
US 1977 1 × 96m, 7 × 50m colour
NBC/Quinn Martin

An unsuccessful anthology of thrillers with twist endings.

Tales of the Unexpected *
GB 1979–84 × 25m colour (VTR)
Anglia (John Woolf)

Sardonic stories written (among others) and introduced by Roald Dahl.
Good sophisticated entertainment, though some of the stories linger defiantly on the printed page. Neat little performances from a rich assortment of actors make the series memorable.

The first 49 episodes were as follows:
The Man from the South (w Roald Dahl; d Michael Tuchner; with Jose Ferrer, Michael Ontkean, Pamela Stephenson)

Mrs Bixby and the Colonel's Coat (w Roald Dahl; d Simon Langton; with Julie Harris, Michael Hordern, Richard Greene)

William and Mary (w Roald Dahl; d Donald McWhinnie; with Elaine Stritch, Marius Goring)

Lamb to the Slaughter (w Roald Dahl; d John Davies; with Susan George, Brian Blessed)

The Landlady (w Roald Dahl; d Herbert Wise; with Siobhan McKenna, Leonard Preston)

TALES OF THE UNEXPECTED. When the show ran out of Roald Dahl stories, it found plenty of other twisty tales with surprise endings. In *Harmless Vanity* Sheila Gish (top) is the wife and Phoebe Nicholls the mistress, but who's going to do what to whom?

Neck (*w* Roald Dahl; *d* Christopher Miles; with John Gielgud, Joan Collins, Peter Bowles, Michael Aldridge)

Edward the Conqueror (*w* Roald Dahl; *d* Rodney Bennett; with Wendy Hiller, Joseph Cotten)

A Dip in the Pool (*w* Roald Dahl; *d* Michael Tuchner; with Jack Weston)

The Way Up to Heaven (*w* Roald Dahl; *d* Simon Langton; with Julie Harris, Roland Culver)

Royal Jelly (*w* Roald Dahl; *d* Herbert Wise; with Timothy West, Andrew Ray, Susan George)

Skin (*w* Roald Dahl; *d* Herbert Wise; with Derek Jacobi)

Galloping Foxley (*w* Roald Dahl; *d* Claude Whatham; with John Mills, Anthony Steel)

The Hitch Hiker (*w* Roald Dahl; *d* Alastair Reid; with Rod Taylor, Cyril Cusack)

Poison (*w* Roald Dahl; *d* Graham Evans; with Anthony Steel, Andrew Ray, Judy Geeson, Saeed Jaffrey)

Fat Chance (*w* Roald Dahl; *d* John Gorrie; with John Castle, Sheila Gish)

Taste (*w* Roald Dahl; *d* Alastair Reid; with Ron Moody)

My Lady Love, My Dove (*w* Roald Dahl; *d* Herbert Wise; with Elaine Stritch, Shane Rimmer)

Georgy Porgy (*w* Roald Dahl; *d* Graham Evans; with Joan Collins, John Alderton)

Depart in Peace (*w* Roald Dahl; *d* Alan Gibson; with Joseph Cotten, Gloria Grahame)

Genesis and Catastrophe (*w* Roald Dahl; *d* Herbert Wise; with Helmut Griem)

Mr Botibol's First Love (*w* Roald Dahl; *d* John Gorrie; with Jack Weston, Anna Massey)

Back for Christmas (*w* John Collier; *d* Giles Foster; with Richard Johnson, Siân Phillips)

The Orderly World of Mr Appleby (*w* Stanley Ellin; *d* John Gorrie, with Robert Lang, Elizabeth Sprigge)

The Man at the Top (*w* Edward D. Hoch; *d* Claude Whatham; with Peter Firth)

The Flypaper (*w* Elizabeth Taylor; *d* Graham Evans; with Alfred Burke)

A Picture of a Place (*w* Doug Morgan; *d* Giles Foster; with Jessie Matthews, Bill Maynard)

Proof of Guilt (*w* Bill Pronzini; *d* Chris Lovett; with Roy Marsden, Jeremy Clyde)

Vengeance Is Mine Inc. (*w* Roald Dahl; *d* Alan Gibson; with Betsy Blair)

A Girl Can't Always Have Everything (*w* Tonita S. Gardner; *d* Graham Evans; with Joan Collins, Pauline Collins)

Parson's Pleasure (*w* Roald Dahl; *d* John Bruce; with John Gielgud, Bernard Miles)

The Stinker (*w* Julian Symons; *d* Alan Gibson; with Denholm Elliott, Joss Ackland)

I'll Be Seeing You (*w* Robert Quigley; *d* Philip Dudley; with Anthony Valentine, Hilary Tindall)

The Party (*w* Doug Morgan; *d* Giles Foster; with Robert Morley, Joyce Redman)

Would You Believe It? (*w* Raymond Edmond Alter; *d* Barry Davis; with Richard Johnson, Nigel Havers)

Vicious Circle (*w* Donald Honig; *d* Philip Dudley; with Siobhan McKenna)

The Boy Who Talked with Animals (*w* Roald Dahl; *d* Alan Gibson; with Stuart Whitman)

The Best of Everything (*w* Stanley Ellin; *d* John Bruce; with Judi Bowker, Rachel Kempson)

A Woman's Help (*w* Henry Slasar; *d* Bert Salzman; with Tony Franciosa, Shirley Knight)

Shatterproof (*w* Jack Ritchie; *d* John Jacobs; with Eli Wallach)

The Sound Machine (*w* Roald Dahl; *d* John Gorrie; with Harry Andrews, James Warwick)

Never Speak Ill of the Dead (*w* John Collier; *d* John Corrie; with Colin Blakely)

The Best Policy (*w* Ferenc Molnar; *d* Ray Danton; with Gary Burghoff)

The Last Bottle in the World (*w* Stanley Ellin; *d* John Gorrie; with Anthony Quayle, Nigel Hawthorne)

Kindly Dig Your Grave (*w* Stanley Ellin; *d* Alan Gibson; with Micheline Presle)

Completely Foolproof (*w* Robert Arthur; *d* John Jacobs; with Rita Gam, Telly Savalas)

There's One Born Every Minute (*w* Bill Pronzini; *d* Alan Gibson; with Frank Finlay, Heather Sears, Jo Rowbottom)

Bosom Friends (*w* Dana Lyon; *d* Graham Evans; with Rachel Kempson, Joan Greenwood)

Glowing Future (*w* Ruth Rendell; *d* John Peyser)

The Way to Do It (*w* Jack Ritchie; *d* Alan Gibson; with Elaine Paige, Andrew Ray)

'They tick like 30-minute time bombs.' – *TV Guide*

Tales of the Vikings
US 1960 39 × 25m bw
United Artists/Brynaprod (Stanley
  Margulies)
Self-explanatory action item, rather risible.
Jerome Courtland, Buddy Baer

Tales of Wells Fargo *
US 1957–61 167 × 25m, 34 × 50m bw
NBC/Universal/Overland
Stories of the stagecoach line during
California's gold rush days.
Fairly rousing western adventures which
showed the west not as it was but as we like to
think it was.
Dale Robertson

Talkback (GB 1967–71). A BBC attempt to
allow the customer to comment on television
programmes and challenge their producers. In
practice it was soon given over to pressure
groups and 'planted' subjects. My view at the
time: 'Television doesn't have much luck in its
dialogue with itself. As a complaints column
of the air *Talkback* has so far attracted
contributions only from Disgusted and Pro
Bono Publico.'   PP

Talking to a Stranger **
GB 1966 4 × 90m bw (VTR)
BBC (Christopher Morahan)
In a famous judgement by George Melly in the
Observer, 'the first authentic masterpiece
written directly for television'. John Hopkins's
four plays go over and over one doom-laden
weekend in the dissolution of a suburban
family, as seen in turn from the viewpoints of
daughter, father and the quietly desperate
mother who takes her own life. What should
be the son's episode is rather mysteriously
presented as old-fashioned household drama
without flashbacks or interior visions, the
camera standing back to observe impassively.
If this betrays some vital reservation in the
conception of the quartet, it's still a monolith
along the way of television story-telling.
d Christopher Morahan
Judi Dench, Maurice Denham, Margery
Mason, Michael Bryant   PP

The Tall Man *
US 1960–1 75 × 25m bw
NBC/Universal
Sheriff Pat Garrett is helped by Billy the Kid.
An extraordinary perversion of history, but
quite a slick entertainment.
Barry Sullivan, Clu Gulager

Tallahassee 7000
US 1959 26 × 25m bw
Columbia
Cases of a Florida sheriff.
The star carries it, but some of the plots are
weak.
Walter Matthau

The Taming of the Shrew **
GB 1980 135m colour (VTR)
BBC (Jonathan Miller)
Directed by Jonathan Miller, in the BBC
Shakespeare series. My view at the time:
'Hardly a hint of Basilio Faulti clung to John
Cleese's excellent, grave, intelligent
Petruchio; those long legs braced once or
twice as if ready to hare off on some doomed
effort to retrieve the pie containing the dead
mouse before Egon Ronay could sink his teeth
into it, a certain briskness of manner with
menials; otherwise it was an object lesson in
serving Shakespeare while serving the
present-day audience.' Also with Sarah Badel,
Susan Penhaligon, John Bird.   PP

Tammes, Diane (19 –). British
camerawoman, director and producer, one
of the first graduates of the National Film
School. Worked on *Police* and other
observational series, shot *Sacred Hearts*
(Film on Four), co-produced *Just Like
Coronation Street*; much else.

Tammy (US 1965). One-season half-hour
comedy for ABC, based on the Ross Hunter
movies about an engaging backwoods girl.
With Debbie Watson and Denver Pyle. The
cast of the series also appeared in a 1967
movie, *Tammy and the Millionaire*.

Tandoori Nights (GB 1985; 6 × 28m).
Rivalry between two north London Indian
restaurants, one called The Jewel in the
Crown, the other The Far Pavilions – which
was about the best joke in a comedy series
which scored on affection rather than belly
laughs. With Saeed Jaffrey, Zohra Segal.
Written by Farrukh Dhondy, directed by Jon
Amiel, produced by Malcolm Craddock, for
Picture Palace/C4.   PP

'Terror and death stalk through a
  defenceless town!'
Tarantulas: The Deadly Cargo
US 1977 96m colour TVM
CBS/Alan Landsburg (Paul Freeman)
Deadly spiders in a banana consignment get
loose and multiply in a southern town.
Routine mini-monster thriller, twice as long as
it needs to be.

w Guerdon Trueblood, John Groves *d* Stuart Hagmann

Claude Akins, Charles Frank, Pat Hingle, Sandy McPeak, Deborah Winters

Tarbuck, Jimmy (1940–). British north country comedian, cheerful but not very clever. Popular in the sixties, subsequently often used as quizmaster.

Target
US 1951 38 × 25m bw
United Artists
Suspense anthology, vaguely centred on people of determination.

Adolphe Menjou (host and occasional star)

Target
GB 1977–8 22 × 50m colour (16mm)
BBC (Philip Hinchcliffe)
Cases of a regional crime squad.
Tough police thriller series, in direct opposition to *The Sweeney* but without the saving grace of humour.

Patrick Mower, Philip Madoc, Brendan Price, Vivien Heilbronn

† Much criticized for its violence, the first series was curtailed. The last 13 were more restrained.

Target Risk
US 1975 74m colour TVM
Universal
Bonded couriers combat thieves and blackmailers.
Abysmal crime pilot marking a desperate shortage of style and ideas.

w Don Carlos Dunaway *d* Robert Scheerer

Bo Svenson, Meredith Baxter, John P. Ryan, Robert Coote, Lee Paul

Target the Corruptors *
US 1961 35 × 50m bw
ABC/Four Star/Velie–Burrows–Ackerman
An investigative reporter reveals corruption in high places. Based on articles by Lester Velie.
Well-made gangster exposé with a remarkable amount of acting talent in the guest spots.

Stephen McNally, Robert Harland

Individual titles and stars were as follows:

The Million Dollar Dump: Walter Matthau, Peter Falk
Pier 60: Jack Klugman
The Platinum Highway: Dan O'Herlihy
The Invisible Government: Edmond O'Brien, Felicia Farr
The Poppy Vendor: Gena Rowlands, Robert Loggia

Bite of a Tiger: Ed Begley, Thomas Gomez
Touch of Evil: Lee Kinsolving, Ray Walston
Mr Megalomania: Wendell Corey
The Golden Carpet: Ed Asner, Larry Blyden
To Wear a Badge: Robert Culp, Robert Vaughn
Silent Partner: Luther Adler, Everett Sloane
Prison Empire: Preston Foster
The Fix: Frank Lovejoy
Quicksand: Richard Long, Steve Forrest
A Man Is Waiting to Be Murdered: Brian Donlevy
One for the Road: Walter Matthau, David Brian
Play It Blue: Dean Jones, Harold J. Stone
Chase the Dragon: Jack Klugman, Keye Luke
The Middleman: David Janssen, Vaughn Taylor
Viva Vegas: Jack Oakie, Suzanne Pleshette
Fortress of Despair: June Vincent, Joyce Van Patten
The Wrecker: Luther Adler, Linden Chiles
Babes in Wall Street: Harry Guardino, Barbara Eden
My Native Land: Cesar Romero, Jerome Cowan
The Malignant Hearts: Sidney Blackmer, James Gregory
A Man's Castle: Scott Marlowe, Robert Emhardt
Journey into Mourning: Keenan Wynn, Parley Baer
The Blind Goddess: Margaret Hayes, MacDonald Carey
A Book of Faces: Shirley Knight, Martin Balsam
Licence To Steal: Harold J. Stone, Gene Evans
Yankee Dollar: Alan Hale, Alfred Ryder
The Organizer Part One: Jack Warden, Brian Keith, Richard Anderson
The Organizer Part Two: Jack Warden, Brian Keith
Nobody Gets Hurt: Kevin McCarthy, Michael Parks
Goodbye Children: John Ericson, Don Haggerty

Tarrant, Alan J. (19 –). Pioneer British jack-of-all-trades; with ATV from early days as writer, director and producer: *Theatre Royal* 30-minute drama series, admags, light entertainment including *Sunday Night at the London Palladium*, sitcoms including *The Larkins* and *The Gaffer*. Latterly with YTV.
PP

Tarzan *
US 1966–7 57 × 50m colour
NBC/Banner (Sy Weintraub)

Tarzan returns to his jungle and helps the oppressed.

Neatly made jungle adventures, a little lacking in humour.

Ron Ely, Manuel Padilla Jnr

Taste of Evil *
US 1971 96m colour TVM
ABC/Aaron Spelling

A young woman comes home after having been raped and institutionalized, only to find that someone is trying to drive her insane.

Smooth, suspenseful variation on the author's own movie *Taste of Fear*.

w Jimmy Sangster d John Llewellyn Moxey
  ph Arch Dalzell m Robert Drasnin

Barbara Stanwyck, Barbara Parkins, Roddy McDowall, William Windom, Arthur O'Connell

Tate (US 1960). Shortlived half-hour series for NBC, with David McLean as a one-armed Civil War veteran turned wandering gunfighter.

A Tattered Web **
US 1971 74m colour TVM
Metromedia (Bob Markell)

A police detective protects himself by taking the law into his own hands.

Complex, satisfying crime melodrama with a twist or two.

w Art Wallace d Paul Wendkos

Lloyd Bridges, Broderick Crawford, Murray Hamilton, Ann Helm

Taxi *
US 1978–   × 25m colour
ABC/Paramount/John Carles Walters

Tape comedy mainly set in a New York cabmen's shelter: mainly tough humour with some sentiment, concerning a bunch of ethnic types. With Judd Hirsch, Jeff Conway, Danny de Vita. Created by James L. Brooks, Stan Daniels, David Davis, Ed Weinberger; produced by Glen and Les Charles. Emmy 1978, 1980, 1981: best comedy series.

'It will make you miss New York, unless you've been there.' – Robert McKenzie, *TV Guide*

† *Taxi* was also the name of a BBC one-hour series of the fifties, with Sid James and Ray Brooks as London cabbies.

Tayback, Vic (c 1931–   ). Burly American actor who can provide either menace or comedy. *Honor Thy Father*, *Getting*

Married, ALICE, *Moviola*, *The Great American Traffic Jam*, *The Night the City Screamed*, *The Jesse Owens Story*.

Taylor, A. J. P. (1906–   ). British historian, elfin in appearance, formidable of intellect, originally into television as a member of the knockabout *In the News* debating team of the fifties but best remembered for the ATV (later BBC) lectures he gave without notes or teleprompter and preferably live. He liked to stroll into the lights, plunge directly into his chosen subject and wind up with an elegant flourish within 20 seconds, either way, of his allotted time. He also scripted one or two documentaries (see *Men of Our Time*) and for Granada in 1980 made a personal series, *The Edge of Britain*, about his upbringing on the Lancashire coast. His 75th birthday in 1981 was marked by a BBC2 tribute. In 1985 he returned to lecturing with *How Wars End*.
                                                                        PP

Taylor, Baz (1945–   ). British director, initially with Granada, proficient in drama, documentary and commercials. Credits include *Adam Smith*, *Moody and Pegg*, *Born and Bred*, *Bernard Manning in Las Vegas* and *Irish Cheese*.

Taylor, Cecil P. (c 1931–82). British writer from the north-east whose credits included *Revolution*, 3 × 30m plays about Cromwell, Lenin and Fidel Castro, 1970; and the 1978 non-fiction series *Great Expectations*. Author of down-to-earth guidebook *Making a TV Play*, 1970.
                                                                        PP

Taylor, Dennis (1950–   ). Cheery Northern Irish snooker player who wrested the World Championship from Steve Davis in the 1985 thriller final. He lost it the next year in the first round.
                                                                        PP

Taylor, Don (1936–   ). Formidable British writer–director responsible for mounting the early plays of David Mercer, and sharing with him a recurring obsession with the failure of Socialism to create Utopia in Eastern Europe. Other passions are the role of the artist or thinker in an inimical society and the impulse that makes actors act. Credits as writer–director include *Prisoners* (1971), *Actor*, *I Said* and *The Exorcism* (1972), *The Roses of Eyam* and *The Runaway* (1973), *When the Actors Come* (1978), *In Hiding* (1980). Directed Nigel Kneale's *Beasts* (1971), Mercer's *Find Me* for Omnibus (1974), episodes of *Maybury* (1981), *The Critic* and *The White Guard*, 1982; *Two Gentlemen of*

A. J. P. TAYLOR. Almost from the beginning of television he was giving historical lectures straight to camera and at the age of eighty he was still going strong. Here in 1961 his subject was the Second World War.

Verona in the BBC Shakespeare and Testament of John, 1984; Sophocles' Theban Plays, 1986.   PP

Taylor, Don (1920–). American director, former actor (the young cop in Naked City, the bridegroom in Father of the Bride) who has done some television work. Series: M Squad, 87th Precinct, Burke's Law, etc. TV movies: Something for a Lonely Man, Wild Women, Heat of Anger, Night Games, Honky Tonk, A Circle of Children, Broken Promise, Drop Out Father, September Gun, He's Not Your Son, My Wicked Wicked Ways, Secret Weapons, Going for the Gold.

Taylor, Gwen (19 –). British actress and comedienne whose plump charms and lethal delivery are immortalized in DUTY FREE; other credits include Just Another Little Blues Song, the very serious 'Billy' plays about Northern Ireland, and Ties of Blood, likewise.   PP

Taylor, Jud (19 –). American director who has made more than his share of TV movies: Weekend of Terror, Suddenly Single, Revenge, The Rookies, Say Goodbye Maggie Cole, Hawkins on Murder, Winter Kill, The Disappearance of Flight 412, Search for the Gods, Future Cop, Return to Earth, Woman of the Year, Tail Gunner Joe, Mary White, The Christmas Coalmine Miracle, The Last Tenant, Lovey, Flesh and Blood, Incident at Crestridge, A Question of Honour, Packin' It in, License to Kill.

Taylor, Ken (1922–). British writer, author of many TV plays in the fifties and sixties, such as China Doll (1960), The Tin Whistle Man and Into the Dark (1962) and the ambitious trilogy The Seekers (1964). In recent years known chiefly for costume fiction; co-writer of The Borgias (1981), solo on Mansfield Park and, of course, THE JEWEL IN THE CROWN.

Taylor, Kent (1907–) (Louis Weiss). American leading man of the thirties; when roles grew few in Hollywood, he played in Rough Riders and Boston Blackie on TV.

Taylor, Rod (1929–). (Robert Taylor). Australian leading man in Hollywood; TV series between film roles include Hong Kong, Bearcats, The Oregon Trail. TV movies: Family Flight, A Matter of Wife or Death, Cry of the Innocent, Hellinger's Law, Jacqueline Bouvier Kennedy, Charles and Diana, Masquerade, Half Nelson.

Taylor, Shaw (1924–). British linkman and host who from the mid-sixties has been engaged in devising and presenting Police Five, a brief weekly programme in which the police ask for the public's help in solving crimes.

Teachers Only (US 1982). Half-hour comedy series by Carson Productions/ Columbia with Lynn Redgrave, Norman Fell and Adam Arkin as teachers in an especially odd American high school. The jokes are feeble and the subject matter often unfunny.

Tears in the Wind
GB 1956 50m bw (live)
ABC (Dennis Vance)
Rates a mention both for the whimsical accident of its title and as the first real Armchair Theatre play ever – there had been two isolated try-outs in the summer, but this adaptation of André Gide's Symphonie Pastorale inaugurated the first regular season

in September 1956. It was supposed to have been called *Tares in the Wheat*; a misreading of her shorthand outline by the producer's secretary went into the schedules before anyone could stop it. 'It was just as good a title,' said Vance philosophically.

w Millicent George *d* Dennis Vance

Joan Greenwood, André Morell, Barbara Mullen, Ian Bannen   PP

teaser. A trailer that whets the appetite without giving full details.

The Ted Knight Show (US 1978). Self-conscious half-hour comedy for CBS, with the bouncy star, late of *The Mary Tyler Moore Show*, running a scatty escort service.

telecine. The apparatus which projects a film programme and converts it into electronic signals for transmission.

telefilm. What would now be called a TV movie.

telementary. A rather unnecessary neologism describing a documentary made for TV.

teleplay. A word used in the fifties and sixties as script credit on TV fiction. It grew into disuse.

telerecording (in US, kinescope). An early method of recording television pictures optically on to 35mm or 16mm film to be played back on the telecine equipment (see above). Such early TV programmes as survive were recorded in this way, e.g. the BBC's 1953 Coronation footage and the 1954 production of *1984*. One or two plays were telerecorded in the studio and subsequently edited in the cutting-room, notably *Calf Love* and Mercer's *And Did Those Feet*, both 1966. With the switch to colour in 1967–9 the system was dropped, the monochrome equipment not being replaced.   PP

Teletext. The British system which turns specially adapted sets into a newspaper: hundreds of informational 'pages' can be obtained by pressing various number combinations on a remote control handset. The BBC system is called Ceefax, the ITV Oracle.

telethon. A live discussion programme during which members of the public may ring in with their opinions, and guest stars appear to aid a charity.

Telethon
US 1978 96m colour TVM
ABC Circle (Robert Lovenheim)

Serious problems face several of the people involved in a charity-fund-raising broadcast from Las Vegas.

Moderate multi-story entertainment relying chiefly on the tawdry glitter of its setting.

w Roger Wilton *d* David Lowell Rich *ph* Jacques Marquette *m* Peter Matz

Lloyd Bridges, Janet Leigh, Polly Bergen, Red Buttons, Edd Byrnes, Dick Clark, John Marley, Kent McCord, Jill St John

Television
GB 1985 13 × 52m
Granada (Norman Swallow)

Ambitious study of TV itself which inexplicably muffed the opportunity, possibly because a straightforward chronological approach was allowed only in one expert episode (the second) dealing with the early days of television. Thereafter it was theme by theme, jumping about in time and place, often missing the point of the marvellous programme extracts which jostled on to the screen, and relying much too much on an assertive, take-it-or-leave-it commentary.

d various *narrator* Ian Holm   PP

LH: 'Agreed, agreed. All the same, it's such a marvellous compilation job that I'd like to have my own set of videos.'

Television Dancing Club. The original BBC ballroom dancing programme, running from 1948 until its replacement by *Come Dancing*, and dedicated to the greater glory of its presiding genius Victor Sylvester. He taught a new step each week, his strict tempo orchestra supplied the music and his daughter-in-law Patti Morgan acted as the programme hostess.   PP

television on television. Broadcasters have examined their own activities generally half-heartedly. In Britain the most cerebral analysis comes in series classed as adult educational or otherwise put on in out-of-the-way hours. *Look Here* (Rod Allen) had regular seasons on LWT but was taken by only one or two other small stations. *The Television Programme* (Westward) ran to two six-part series on the lunch-time network, written and presented by the *Guardian*'s television correspondent Peter Fiddick. Chris Dunkley of the *Financial Times* has presented two BBC1 late-night series, the more recent being *The Whistle Blowers* about investigative journalism on TV.

Democratic discussion of television output, and in particular the recurring bogeys of sex, violence, bias and background music, has been attempted twice – by the BBC with *Talkback* in the mid-sixties and Granada with *Open Night* in 1971–2. More specialized reviewing of programmes has been tried by the BBC in *Line-Up* from 1964, *More than Meets the Eye* (1965), *In Vision* (1974) and, most successfully, *Did You See?*, since 1980. *Worldwide* was an admirable series by Maryse Addison on television in other countries, *Clive James on Television* is a whoopee version of the same.

Specials on television matters have included Dennis Mitchell's *The Dream Machine* (ATV, 1966) contrasting the work and ideals of a song-and-dance show producer, Francis Essex, with the cerebrations of a critic and an academic; *The Question of Television* (BBC, 1977) in the wake of the Annan report; a ten-hour compilation of American programmes by Gus Macdonald which Granada put out on its own region during the US Election night of 1980, and *The State of Things to Come* (cable, satellites, etc), also by Gus Macdonald, 1982. For Granada's ambitious *Television* series, see above.   PP

**The Television Programme ** ** (GB 1980–1). A series of 12 × 25-minute programmes from Westward TV, in which Peter Fiddick, with the aid of special effects, explains to the layman how various aspects of television programming work. See above.

Television Reporters International/TRI. British freelance outfit set up in 1963 by Robert Kee, Ludovic Kennedy, Malcolm Muggeridge, James Mossman and Lord Francis-Williams, with backing from Michael Astor and Jeremy Murray-Brown, ex-*Panorama* producer, as administrator. About 20 documentary films were made, mostly under contract to ATV, but the other companies were reluctant to share the credit for 'prestige' programming with outsiders, while Granada refused altogether to take them. The contract with ATV was not renewed and until Channel Four began to commission in 1981 the opportunities for truly independent production units remained almost non-existent within the British television system.   PP

Television Scrabble (GB 1984–5; each year 50 × 30m). Just what it says: the favourite old word game played Monday to Friday on TV over a 10-week tournament, plus the inevitable celebrity guests. The prize in 1985 was a gold and silver Scrabble set by Aspreys. Conducted by Alan Coren; produced by Paul Smith, Philip Livingstone, for Celador/Callendar/C4.   PP

Television South (TVS). British ITV contractor appointed by the IBA to replace Southern Television as from January 1982. The decision caused much bad feeling and gnashing of teeth, Southern having operated successfully since 1958.

PP: ' "Judging between someone's unkept promises," I said at the time, "and someone else's unkeepable promises." '

Aggrieved book: *The Franchise Affair* by Asa Briggs and Joanna Spicer, 1986.

Television South West (TSW). British ITV company appointed by the IBA to replace Westward Television as from January 1982. This move was fairly predictable following Westward's long series of boardroom squabbles.

Telford's Change *
GB 1979 10 × 50m colour
BBC (Mark Shivas)

Co-operative venture whereby leading actor Peter Barkworth, writer Brian Clark and producer Mark Shivas worked as a freelance group to make the series with BBC facilities but retain property rights in it. This novelty apart, it was a superior soap opera about high-placed banker (Barkworth) who tries to return to the grass roots of his profession as a provincial branch manager. My view at the time: 'The everyday stories of simple country clients are proving to be unexpectedly gripping. What I'm less persuaded by is the running saga of Telford and his missus (Hannah Gordon), who has insisted on staying behind in London to pursue a career in showbiz. The tussle of divergent aims is there; indeed it is what the series is all about; but so far it has been indicated only in bright smiles and brave phone calls. It's time they had a real row, and over something squalid and recognizable, like who is going to pay the bills for those sumptuous homes at each end of the line.' Also with Keith Barron; directed by Barry Davis.   PP

'A popular drama to keep the mind alive.' – *Guardian*

Tell Me My Name
US 1977 96m colour TVM
CBS/Talent Associates (Donald W. Reid)

An illegitimate adopted girl finds her own mother and the confrontation changes both their lives.

Tolerable middle-class drama; you don't really have to see it to know exactly what it's like.

w Joanna Lee, *book* Mary Carter *d* Delbert Mann *ph* Zale Magder *m* Hagood Hardy and Mickey Erbe

Arthur Hill, Barbara Barrie, Barnard Hughes, Valerie Mahaffey, Douglas McKeon

Tell Me Where It Hurts *

US 1974 74m colour TVM
CBS/Tomorrow (Herbert Hirschman)

A discontented housewife organizes a discussion group and changes the lives of her closest friends.

Witty comedy–drama which won an Emmy for best script.

w Fay Kanin *d* Paul Bogart *ph* David Walsh *m* David Shire

Maureen Stapleton, Paul Sorvino, Doris Dowling, Rose Gregorio, John Randolph, Louise Latham

Tell the Truth. Tepid game show which as *To Tell the Truth* ran for 23 years in America before dribbling on to Channel 4 in Britain from 1983. Graeme Garden presided over the panel of four nonentities endeavouring to identify which of three challengers – all purporting to be the same person – was telling the truth. Produced (in GB) by Brian Wesley for LWT/C4.   PP

Telstar. The first communications satellite to relay television pictures, launched in 1962. Whizzing round the earth in low orbit it was able to link Eastern and Western hemispheres for only 22 minutes at a time, but in the three years between its appearance and the first satellite in high synchronous orbit, Early Bird, it did much to foster interest in intercontinental television and incidentally helped dispel some of the more romantic notions of 'see it now' actuality which satellites were thought to offer. An inaugural relay from the United States to Europe included a herd of buffalo only too obviously cued to start stampeding the moment the producer called in the location. Among Europe's reciprocal goodies was a live excerpt from *Tosca* in Rome, which was more functional, but the one really significant item in the exchange was an eavesdrop on President Kennedy's regular news conference.   PP

Telly Addicts (GB from 1985). Yet another quiz show on the subject of television itself, zippier than *Those Wonderful TV Times* and marginally more searching than *I Love TV*

but still geared to soaps, sitcoms and other game shows. It benefited during its first season from an unbroken run of wins over three months by one family team, the Pains, ended only by a special Christmas edition in which they faced a panel of professionals. Conducted by Noel Edmonds, produced by John King, Juliet May, for BBC Pebble Mill.
                     PP

Temperatures Rising

US 1972 24 × 25m colour
ABC/Columbia/Harry Ackerman (William Asher)

The lighter side of hospital life . . .

. . . seemed to be inconceivable to both writers and cast.

James Whitmore, Cleavon Little, Joan Van Ark, Nancy Fox, David Bailey, Reva Rose

† The following season, 22 more episodes were made without Whitmore, under the title *The New Temperatures Rising*. Paul Lynde starred.

Temple Houston

US 1963 26 × 50m bw
NBC/Warner

A lawyer travels the old west.

Tolerable semi-western, rather too low key.

Jeffrey Hunter, Jack Elam

Temple, Shirley (1928–   ). American child film star, the multi-talented sensation of the thirties. Her main contribution to TV was a series of 14 × 50m fairy tales called *Shirley Temple Storybook*, produced in 1960 by William Asher. She starred in every third show.

Tempo (GB 1961–4). ABC's prestigious arts programme suggested and first edited by Kenneth Tynan. Later editors included Peter Luke and Clive Goodwin. Tynan could call on impressive names (Olivier, Gordon Craig, Zeffirelli, Truman Capote, Graham Sutherland, with Lord Harewood as regular link-man) and had good ideas, e.g. an examination of the face of Christ in art through the ages written by John Whiting and delivered by the poet Cecil Day Lewis; but some of them were carried out inconclusively and, poorly scheduled by ITV as a Sunday afternoon show, the programme rarely fulfilled Tynan's aim of letting art speak directly to the mass audience without the intervention (or the jargon) of critics and academics.   PP

The Ten Commandments
GB 1971 10 × 50m colour (VTR)
YTV (Peter Willes)

Having contrived a successful anthology series
for Rediffusion around the seven deadly sins
and the seven deadly virtues, Peter Willes set
this one up after he moved to Yorkshire in
1968. The most interesting play of the ten was
Charles Wood's *A Bit of a Family Feeling*, an
early try-out for his *Don't Forget to Write*.   PP

Ten Days in May (GB 1985; 50m). A
footnote to VE-Day 40th-anniversary
programmes: four months later, Granada
aired this rather reverential account of the
modest Russian city of Vitebsk as its
inhabitants commemorated their hardships
and eventual victory in the 'Great Patriotic
War'. Produced by John Blake.   PP

Ten Days That Shook the World
GB 1967 80m bw
Granada/Novosti (Norman Swallow,
  G. Alexandrov)

Creepy co-production with the Russians to
mark the 50th anniversary of the Revolution,
making no mention (for example) of the
British lecturer Gerald Brooke then held in a
Soviet jail for distributing a few pamphlets.
My reaction at the time: 'Participation with
the Russians was obviously a tempting
prospect. But did it not occur to anyone that
Granada's independent, gritty, sometimes
bloody-minded attitude to public affairs was
more valuable than all the facilities in the
world?' Directed by Michael Darlow.   PP

Ten Men Went to War (GB 1969). One of
the few 25th-anniversary commemorations of
D-Day, compared with the plethora of
programmes 40 years on. Produced by Terry
Johnston for Southern. Another runner was
D-Day 25 Years On, written and presented
by Brian Inglis, directed by Mike Wooller,
produced by Walter Butler for Granada.   PP

Tenafly *
aka: *Everybody's Looking*
US 1972 74m colour TVM
NBC/Universal/Levinson–Link (Jon
  Epstein)

A black private eye with domestic problems
solves the murder of the wife of a talk show
host.
Adequate pilot for what became a one-season
addition to *Mystery Movie*.

w Richard Levinson, William Link *d* Richard
A. Colla

James McEachin, Mel Ferrer, Ed Nelson,
John Ericson

Tender Is the Night *
GB 1985 6 × 55m
BBC (Betty Willingale)

F. Scott Fitzgerald's novel of love, madness
and redemption inspired – or inflicted on
him – by his marriage to Zelda. A
sumptuous production to a perceptive
rearrangement of the story by Dennis Potter,
with classy performances and shimmering
camerawork. But you wondered if there
wasn't something closer to home in more
urgent need of such treatment.

w Dennis Potter, *novel* F. Scott Fitzgerald
d Robert Knights *ph* Ken Westbury
m Richard Rodney Bennett

PETER STRAUSS, MARY STEENBURGEN, John
Heard, Sean Young, Edward Asner (guest
appearance)   PP

LH: 'Despite its sheen I found it impossible
to watch. But then I find Fitzgerald almost
impossible to read.'

Tenko
GB 1981 10 × 50m colour
BBC (Ken Riddington)

During World War II, European women
are interned by the Japanese.
Prisoner-of-war heroics and sufferings,
distaff version. Ably enough done, and a
popular success.

cr Lavinia Warner *w* various *d* Pennant
Roberts *m* James Harpham

Ann Bell, Stephanie Beacham, Renée
Asherson, Burt Kwouk, Claire Oberman,
Joanna Hole, Wendy Williams

† Ten further episodes followed in 1982,
then another 10 in 1984, covering the Allied
victory and liberation of the camps.
d Jeremy Summers, Michael Owen Morris.
  Finally came *Tenko Reunion* (1985, 110m
TVM) reassembling the women in Singapore
for a 1950 reunion and a nasty little murder
plot. *w* Jill Hyem *d* Michael Owen Morris
p Ken Riddington.

Tennille, Toni (1943–). American singer,
usually with Daryl Dragon ('the Captain').
Hosted own network variety series 1976–7.

Tenspeed and Brown Shoe *
US 1980 96m colour TVM
ABC/Paramount/Stephen J. Cannell

A black hustler and a young stockbroker team
up to solve crimes.
Polished, fast-moving crime caper, which a
network executive called the best pilot he'd
ever seen.

w/d Stephen J. Cannell

BEN VEREEN, Jeff Goldblum

TENDER IS THE NIGHT. The miniseries from F. Scott Fitzgerald's novel was boosted as a BBC production but actually it was co-produced with American partners who must have called some of the shots. In Britain at least it was caviare to the general, though it got good reviews. Mary Steenburgen, Peter Strauss.

† The one-hour series which followed, alas, was too cute for its own good, and died after 10 episodes.

The Tenth Level
US 1984 96m colour TVM
CBS (Tony Masucci)

A psychologist is disturbed by the results of an experiment he conducts on a group of willing volunteers.
Somewhat sluggish but well-intentioned and generally mature drama.

w George Bellak d Charles S. Dubin

William Shatner, Lynn Carlin, Ossie Davis, Estelle Parsons, Viveca Lindfors

The Tenth Month
US 1979 122m colour TVM
CBS/Joe Hamilton (Ray Aghayan)

Problems of a middle-aged unmarried mother. Interminable account of a mixed-up and not very interesting divorcee's determination not to marry the father of her child.

w/d Joan Tewkesbury, book Laura Z. Hobson ph Charles Rosher m Peter Matz

Carol Burnett, Keith Michell, Dina Merrill, Melissa Converse, Cristina Raines, Richard Venture

'Oddly cold and dispassionate.' – *Daily Variety*

Terraces
US 1977 74m colour TVM
Charles Fries

Crises in the lives of three women in a high-rise apartment block.
Tepid cross-cut domestic dramas.

w Lila Garrett, George Kirgo d Lila Garrett

Julie Newmar, Lloyd Bochner, Bill Gerber, Eliza Garrett, Kim McDonough, James Phipps

Terrahawks (GB 1983–4). 'The Earth year is 2020. Alien space ships have destroyed the ASA base on Mars. Commanded by the hideous Zelda, the aliens sweep all before them in their conquest of the universe. Only one man stands in their way: Dr Tiger Ninestein, leader of the unique fighting force known as the Terrahawks . . .' Another puppet epic from Gerry Anderson for Anderson Burr/LWT.   PP

Terrible Joe Moran
US 1983 96m colour TVM
CBS/Robert Halmi/Viacom

An aged veteran of the boxing ring is reunited with his granddaughter and gets her boy friend off the hook with the Syndicate.
Smooth sentimental piece, valuable chiefly as a showcase for its elderly star.

w Frank Cucci d Joseph Sargent ph Mike Fash m Charles Gross

JAMES CAGNEY, Art Carney, Ellen Barkin, Peter Gallagher, Joseph Sirola

Terror among Us
US 1981 96m colour TVM
Columbia/David Gerber (James H. Brown)

A paroled rapist is provoked and turns into a murderer.
Self-righteous social pleading ill befits the outrageous melodrama which this basically is; best to enjoy it for the suspense sequences.

w Dallas and Joanne Barnes d Paul Krasny

Don Meredith, Ted Shackleford, Sarah Purcell, Jennifer Salt

Terror and the State *
GB 1984 4 × 60m
Granada (Andrew McLaughlin)

Valuable 'hypotheticals' in which statesmen, civil servants, soldiers, judges, editors and television executives – some but not all by now retired from active office – were quizzed on their reactions to imaginary scenarios involving 1) kidnap of a prominent hostage; 2) dealings with a tyrant head of state; 3) terrorist bombings; 4) attempts to suppress the truth.   PP

d Eric Harrison

General Alexander Haig, James Schlesinger, Admiral Lord Lewin, George Ball, Alan Protheroe (BBC deputy DG), Harry Evans, etc

Terror in the Sky *
US 1971 74m colour TVM
Paramount (Matthew Rapf)

All the crew of a jet liner are stricken with food poisoning and the plane has to be brought down by a passenger.
Competent remake of the cinema film *Zero Hour*, from the radio play and novel *Flight into Danger* by Arthur Hailey.

d Bernard Kowalski

Leif Erickson, Doug McClure, Roddy McDowall, Keenan Wynn, Lois Nettleton, Kenneth Tobey

Terror on the Beach
US 1973 74m colour TVM
TCF

A family outing is ruined by violence from beach bums.

Unsurprising melodrama.

w Bill Svanoe d Paul Wendkos

Dennis Weaver, Estelle Parsons, Susan Dey, Kristoffer Tabori, Scott Hylands

Terror on the Fortieth Floor
US 1974 96m colour TVM
ABC/Metromedia (Ed Montagne)

Seven people are trapped in a skyscraper penthouse when fire breaks out.

Very faint carbon copy of *The Towering Inferno*; no contest.

w Jack Turley d Jerry Jameson ph Matthew F. Leonetti m Vic Mizzy

John Forsythe, Joseph Campanella, Lynn Carlin, Anjanette Comer, Laurie Heineman, Don Meredith, Kelly Jean Peters

Terror Out of the Sky
US 1979 96m colour TVM
CBS/Alan Landsburg (Peter Nelson)

A virulent strain of killer bee poses a hazard to a city.

Entirely unnecessary sequel to *The Savage Bees*; it makes little sense and certainly doesn't thrill.

w Guerdon Trueblood, Peter Nelson, Doris Silverton d Lee H. Katzin ph Michel Hugo m William Goldstein

Efrem Zimbalist Jnr, Tovah Feldshuh, Dan Haggerty, Bruce French, Ike Eisenman, Richard Herd

'As dopey as its special effects are amateurish.' – *TV Guide*

The Terry Fox Story *
US/Canada 1983 96m colour TVM
HBO/Robert Cooper Films II

A youth dying of cancer endures a marathon run for research.

Earnest and affecting true story, which however stands in the shadow of a one-hour documentary starring the real Terry Fox.

w Edward Hume d Ralph L. Thomas ph Richard Ciupko m Bill Conti

Eric Fryer, Robert Duvall, Michael Zelniker, Christopher Makepeace

'Beautiful, totally persuasive . . . a salute to the human spirit.' – *Daily Variety*

Terry-Thomas (1911–) (Thomas Terry Hoar-Stevens). Aristocratic British gap-toothed comic, much on TV in the fifties before graduating to films; mostly in variety format.

Terson, Peter (19 –). British playwright of exuberance and also tenacity – of his first 13 TV plays, written between 1958 and 1962, only two were accepted and none produced. But after the National Youth Theatre production of his stage play *Zigger-Zagger* was televised by the BBC in 1967 he was commissioned by Irene Shubik. *Mooney and His Caravans* (1968), *The Apprentices* and *Last Train Through Harecastle Tunnel* (1969). Three plays about a trio of Yorkshire miners (led by Brian Glover) in pursuit of meaningful leisure-time activity, *The Fishing Party*, *Shakespeare or Bust* and *Three for the Fancy*, followed in 1972–4.   PP

Tesler, Brian (1929–). British executive, now chairman and managing director of London Weekend. Into television 1952 as trainee producer, light entertainment, straight from Oxford. Controller ABC Television 1961–8, director of programmes at Thames, 1968–74. Managing director of LWT since 1976.   PP

The Testament of John (GB 1984). Socialist elder faces up to dark accusations about his behaviour in the Spanish Civil War, 44 years earlier. An eloquent, sedentary, unsurprising drama written (in verse) and directed by Don Taylor; with Anthony Quayle, Jane Lapotaire, Kenneth Haigh, Rosalie Crutchley. Produced by Louis Marks, for BBC.   PP

Testament of Youth **
GB 1979 5 × 50m colour
BBC (Jonathan Powell)

An adaptation of the autobiography of Vera Brittain, who suffered loss and hardship during World War I.

Spellbinding television serial with high emotional value and rich detail.

w ELAINE MORGAN d MOIRA ARMSTRONG

CHERYL CAMPBELL, Jane Wenham, Emrys James, Michael Troughton, Rupert Frazer

† Vera Brittain was the mother of politician Shirley Williams.

PP: 'The collision of idealism and carnage in 1914–15 is deftly invoked by the odd bits of archive film, snatches of Rupert Brooke and the echoes of bugles and distant gunfire in Geoffrey Burgon's score. If that sounds second-hand, it's not: it's making legitimate use of associations that have been set up over the years by Remembrance Services and Cenotaph ceremonies.'

Testimony of Two Men
US 1977 3 × 96m colour
OPT/Universal

The fortunes of two doctors in a small town
after the Civil War.

Uneasy costume drama, no *Gone with the
Wind* but rising at the end to a fine pitch of
frenzy. The actors work hard rather than
effectively, and the low budget shows in the
limited camera set-ups.

w William Hanley, James Miller, *novel* Taylor
Caldwell d Larry Yust, Leo Penn

Steve Forrest, Margaret O'Brien, Barbara
Parkins, David Birney, Ralph Bellamy,
Theodore Bikel, Tom Bosley, J. D. Cannon,
Ray Milland, Linda Purl, William Shatner,
Inga Swenson

† This 'novelization' was the first production
of *Operation Prime Time*, a project involving a
collection of local stations in a bid to provide
major entertainment material in competition
with the networks. It worked pretty well.

The Texan
US 1958–9 78 × 25m bw
CBS/Rorvic/Desilu

A cowboy wanders through the old west.
Easy-going adventure series, quite proficient
of its kind.

Rory Calhoun

The Texas Wheelers
US 1974 13 × 25m colour (VTR)
ABC/Mary Tyler Moore (Dale McRaven,
  Chris Hayward)

Misadventures of a family of idle Texans.
The idea was too negative; the series folded.

cr Dale McRaven

Gary Busey, Jack Elam, Mark Hamill, Tony
Becker

Thaddeus Rose and Eddie
US 1978 96m colour TVM
CBS (Don Paulson, Rod Sheldon)

Two Texas bachelors decide to try their luck in
the world outside.
Amiable, ambling comedy which despite good
elements doesn't hold the attention.

w William T. Wittliff d Jack Starrett ph
Robert Jessup m Charles Bernstein

Johnny Cash, Diane Ladd, Bo Hopkins, June
Carter Cash

Thames Television. The British ITV
company formed in 1968 from an
amalgamation of ABC and Associated
Rediffusion. It operates the weekday
franchise in London.

That Certain Summer **
US 1972 74m colour TVM
Universal (Harve Bennett)

A teenager discovers that his father is a
homosexual.
Much acclaimed drama: TV comes of age, etc.
Actually it takes a while to get started, but the
acting is fine.

w Richard Levinson, William Link d Lamont
Johnson

HAL HOLBROOK, Hope Lange, Scott Jacoby,
Martin Sheen, Joe Don Baker, Marlyn
Mason, James McEachin

That Girl *
US 1966–70 136 × 25m colour
ABC/Daisy (Bill Persky, Sam Denoff)

A midwestern girl arrives in New York
determined to be an actress.
Predictable but likeable and refreshing
comedy.

Marlo Thomas, Ted Bessell, Rosemary De
Camp, Lew Parker

That Was the Week that Was *.** A
late-Saturday-night satire show which burst
upon the nation in 1963 and changed the face
of British – and later American – viewing.
Suddenly we had so much satire that nothing
and no one was sacred; then equally suddenly
the boom ended and satire has scarcely been
heard of since. *TW3*, as it was familiarly
known, was produced by NED SHERRIN and
encouraged by Donald Baverstock. It made a
star of a very nervous young DAVID FROST and
established reputations for MILLICENT MARTIN,
DAVID KERNAN, BERNARD LEVIN, WILLIAM
RUSHTON and others. Presented before an
audience, it took the form of a very
rough-edged revue, with lots of barriers
broken, especially rude words and abuse for
the then Home Secretary, Henry Brooke, and
more amiable spoofing of the then Premier,
Harold Macmillan. It was aimed at readers of
the posh Sundays, and most viewers didn't
understand what the fuss was about.

† Subsequent versions (much the same,
really) were *Not So Much a Programme, More
a Way of Life* and *BBC3*.

That's Hollywood *
US 1977 26 × 22m colour (VTR)
TCF (Jack Haley Jnr)

Themed compilations of clips from the TCF
library.
A bit restricted in scope, and saddled with a
blah commentary, this series nevertheless
reminded us of many first-class scenes from

THAT'S FAMILY LIFE. Producer-performers Desmond Wilcox and Esther Rantzen, married to each other, were always on the look-out for a high-rating documentary subject, and when they did a series on families, what could be more natural than that they should start with their own?

the past. Unfortunately it was made on VTR, with loss of film transfer quality.

† Episodes include *The Great Detective*, *Here Come the Clowns*, *Masters of Disaster*, *The Song and Dance Men*.

That's Life. Light-hearted British consumer guidance show compered by Esther Rantzen, with Glyn Worsnip, Kieran Prendeville and Cyril Fletcher. Its investigations are made amusing rather than tragic. A BBC production, it has attracted large audiences since 1975. In the 1978–9 season Paul Heiney and Chris Serle replaced Worsnip and Prendeville.

PP: 'The consumer-watchdog element which is its justification was pinched from the least endearing feature of the old *Braden Show*, in which Esther Rantzen and John Pitman were quizzed by Braden on the funny things that PROs had told them on the phone. Only now (i.e. since 1973) it is la Rantzen in charge with

a succession of young wags reporting to her, and cheaper than ever. There are also market place pranks with the same few members of the public every week. And instead of Ronald Fletcher, Cyril.'

† In 1984 a number of editions of *That's Family Life* reflected Ms Rantzen's interests as her own much-publicized babies grew up.

That's My Boy (US 1954–8). Half-hour comedy series for CBS, with Eddie Mayehoff as an ex-athlete trying to turn his anaemic son in the same mould. With Rochelle Hudson, Gil Stratton Jnr, Mabel Albertson, John Smith. Mayehoff had appeared in the 1951 movie of the same title.

That's My Boy (GB since 1981). Intermittent adoption sitcom with Christopher Blake as a young doctor torn between Clare Richards as his adoptive mother and Mollie Sugden as his real mum.

Written by Pam Valentine and Michael Ashton, produced by Graeme Muir, for YTV.

That's My Mama
US 1974 24 × 25m colour (VTR)
Columbia/Allan Blye, Chris Bearde

Problems of a Negro barber in Washington, especially when his mother interferes in his life.
Unappealing black comedy with too much shouting.
cr Dan T. Bradley, Allan Rice
Clifton Davis, Theresa Merritt, Theodore Wilson, Lynne Moody

That's the Way of the World
US 1975 96m colour TVM
UA/Lorimar (Sig Shore)

A record producer is told by the Mafia to drop the new group he is developing and finds that corruption engulfs the whole industry.
Everyone always thought so, surely? A routine teleplay which will interest few besides pop-music fans.
w Robert Lipsyte *d* Sig Shore
Harvey Keitel, Ed Nelson, Cynthia Bostick, Bert Parks

That's Your Funeral *
GB 1971 6 × 25m bw

Droll series by Peter Lewis exploring the comic possibilities of the undertaking trade, with Bill Fraser in charge. A surrealist episode turned on the interment of a pet alligator in an alligator-shaped coffin.   PP

Thaw, John (1942–). Tough, unsmiling British leading actor, in series *Redcap*, *Thick as Thieves*, *The Sweeney*.

T.H.E. Cat
US 1966 26 × 25m bw
NBC (Boris Sagal)

A super-bodyguard prefers jobs in which he can fight crime.
A rather pretentious suspense series with nothing to be pretentious about. The initials are for Thomas Hewitt Edward, and the Cat suggests that the hero might have been a cat burglar and is adept at hair-raising climbs.
Robert Loggia, R. G. Armstrong

Them and Us (GB 1985; 6 × 25m). Cases before a juvenile court in a little drama series intelligently offering juvenile viewers plenty of audience-identification possibilities.

Written by Roger Parkes, directed by David Foster, produced by John Cooper, for Central.   PP

Then Came Bronson
US 1968 95m colour TVM
NBC/MGM

Adventures of a drop-out who is motorcycling around America.
Slow-moving, amiable pilot for a one-season series.
w Denne Bart Petitclerc *d* William A. Graham
Michael Parks, Bonnie Bedelia, Sheree North, Akim Tamiroff, Gary Merrill
'It's a romantic adventure, a romance not in the sense of boy–girl, but in terms of his love with life.' – Robert Justman
† The series lasted 26 × 50m episodes.

There Comes a Time (GB 1985; 6 × 25m). Having already been killed off in *Dead Ernest*, Andrew Sachs was now faced with terminal illness in a sitcom which always kept death neat and clean and not too certain. With Judy Cornwell. Written by Wally K. Daly, produced by Ronnie Baxter, for YTV.

There Was a Time **
GB 1980 105m colour
LWT (Tony Palmer)

Benjamin Britten's life, work and chief influences on same as reconstructed from his music, the tributes and reminiscences of others and lots of fascinating home-movie material. A *South Bank Show* special. Italia Prize 1980.   PP

There's Something Wrong in Paradise (GB 1984). Updated version of musical comedy chestnut as real band Kid Creole and The Coconuts are supposed to be shipwrecked on mythical Caribbean island where revolution is brewing . . . Also with Karen Black, the Three Degrees. Music and lyrics by August Darnell. Written by Mustapha Matura, directed by David Liddiment; produced by Steve Morrison, for Granada.
LH: 'Why it was conceived will remain a mystery. And if it had to be made, couldn't someone have thought of a better title?'

These Are the Days (US 1974). 16 22-minute cartoons about a rural family at the turn of the century. Insufficiently well done to be educational. From Hanna–Barbera; for ABC.

These Men Are Dangerous (GB 1966; 3 × 30m). Speculative glimpses of three nasty dictators as young men, over-saturated with significance. I thought at the time: 'The cadet Mussolini, Hitler and Stalin were required to voice comprehensive summaries of the urges that the world would rue, etc. The most successful, I thought, was that Hitler one, because Rudolph Cartier deliberately inflated it into a kind of apocalyptic vision.' Written by Jean Benedetti; for BBC. PP

They Call It Murder
US 1971 97m colour TVM
TCF/Parsons (Walter Grauman)

The District Attorney investigates a swimming pool murder.
Smooth pilot which got nowhere, featuring Erle Stanley Gardner's DA character.

w Sam Rolfe d Walter Grauman

Jim Hutton, Lloyd Bochner, Jessica Walter, Carmen Matthews, Leslie Nielsen, Nita Talbot, Robert J. Wilke, Ed Asner

They Made History (GB 1960). Pioneering biopics on television, e.g. of the forger Van Meegeren. Written and produced by Bill Duncalf, for BBC.

They Only Come Out at Night: see Jigsaw John

Thick as Thieves***
GB 1972 74m colour TVM
HTV (Patrick Dromgoole)

Account of seedy provincial safe-robbery as worked out, ingeniously enough, by upper class amateur and executed by such professional talent as he can recruit: exciting, droll, and deeply rooted in its Bristol setting: even the nasty ending (one of the gang getting his face blown off) is consonant with the logic of the play. At the time I felt that *Thick as Thieves* came second only to Kelly's Directory in getting the street numbers right. Leonard Rossiter's shifty, insecure, vicious grimace was, like the locale, absolutely specific and therefore universal.

w Bob Baker, Dave Martin d Patrick Dromgoole

Leonard Rossiter, Corin Redgrave, George Woodbridge, Horace James, Nina Baden-Semper PP

Thick as Thieves (GB 1974). LWT sitcom with Bob Hoskins as a comic crook back from prison to find his wife and best friend (John Thaw) living together in his absence. Though the scripts by Dick Clement and Ian La Frenais were as strong on jokes, character and predicament as to be expected, for John Thaw, anyway, the success of the TV movie *Regan* three days after the opening episode of *Thick as* must have pointed there and then to a more rewarding road ahead in *The Sweeney*. PP

Thicker than Water. Shortlived 1973 American version of *Nearest and Dearest* with Julie Harris and Richard Long. For ABC.

Thief *
US 1971 74m colour TVM
Metromedia (Dick Berg)

A smooth jewel thief outsmarts himself.
What seems to start as a light comedy later goes sour; a curious mixture.

w John D. F. Black d William Graham

Richard Crenna, Angie Dickinson, Cameron Mitchell

A Thief Is a Thief Is a Thief: see The Magnificent Thief

The Thief of Baghdad
GB/US 1979 96m colour TVM
NBC/Palm Films (Aida Young)

In old Baghdad, a thief helps a prince to outwit a wicked wazir.
Very thin version of an oft-told tale. Muddled in conception and execution, it won't erase memories of the Fairbanks or the Sabu films.

w A. J. Carothers d Clive Donner ph Denis Lewiston m John Cameron

Peter Ustinov, Roddy McDowall, Terence Stamp, Marina Vlady, Kabir Bedi, Frank Finlay, Ian Holm, Neil McCarthy

'It does move fast though its first hour, though the second could use some genuine levitation to get it off the ground.' – *Daily Variety*

Thin Ice
US 1979 96m colour TVM
CBS Entertainment (Mel Sokolow, Norman Cohen)

A history mistress has an affair with an 18-year-old student.
Who cares?

w David Epstein d Paul Aaron ph Andrew Laszlo m Earl Rose

Kate Jackson, Gerald Prendergast, Louise Latham, Lillian Gish, Mimi Kennedy, James Greene

'The idyllic love stuff seems oddly tarnished . . . self-denial somewhere along the line would have been more than tolerable.' – *Daily Variety*

The Thin Man *
US 1957–8 78 × 25m bw
NBC/MGM

Nick and Nora Charles, sophisticated New York sleuths, and their dog Asta solve a crime or two while having a good time.

A passable light entertainment which seemed rather better than the later *Thin Man* movies though certainly not up to the first.

Peter Lawford, Phyllis Kirk

'The films started the vogue for comedy–mysteries distinguished by wit, pace and incisive cutting. The TV series lacks all these.' – Don Miller

The Thing (US 1980). 13 half-hour cartoons from the comic strip about a timid teenager who has another life as an impregnable monster. From Hanna–Barbera; for syndication.

The Things I Never Said
US 1974 74m colour TVM
CBS/Columbia (Wilford Lloyd Baumes, Albert J. Simon)

A married couple don't get on, but have a mysterious idyll on the night when he is killed in a plane crash.

Supernatural romance which had a few takers at the time.

w Pat Fielder d Bill Glenn

Joseph Campanella, Diana Hyland, Brooke Bundy

Things in Their Season
US 1974 75m colour TVM
Tomorrow

A Wisconsin farm woman learns that she has leukaemia at a time when the family has other problems.

Another undramatic dying fall. *Dark Victory* has a lot to answer for.

w John Gay d James Goldstone

Patricia Neal, Ed Flanders, Marc Singer, Meg Foster

A Thinking Man as Hero *
GB 1973 2 × 75m colour
BBC

Curious but ultimately successful attempt by Hugh Whitemore to convey some of the philosopher Ludwig Wittgenstein's ideas by way of a conventional expenses-account-life drama, e.g. the word 'Cancer' and all its associations oppressing the characters far more than the illness it was – erroneously, as things turned out – identifying. At the time I wrote: 'The thinking man as viewer will have

been entertained, informed or educated, or in my case all three.'

d John Glenister

Keith Barron, Mary Miller   PP

Thinnes, Roy (1938–). Virile American action lead. Series: *The Long Hot Summer, The Invaders, The Psychiatrist, From Here to Eternity.* TV movies: *The Other Man, Black Noon, Horror at 37,000 Feet, The Norliss Tapes, Satan's School for Girls, Death Race, The Manhunter, Secrets, Code Name Diamondhead, The Return of Mod Squad.*

Third Girl from the Left *
US 1973 73m colour TVM
Playboy

An ageing nightclub chorus girl tries to improve her lot.

Smart but not very interesting comedy drama.

w Dory Previn d Peter Medak

Tony Curtis, Kim Novak, Michael Brandon

The Third Man * (US 1959–61). A slick series for its time (39 × 25m) but one which had nothing to do with Graham Greene's Harry Lime. Michael Rennie as Lime was a smooth international operator with a penchant for helping damsels in distress; Jonathan Harris was popular as his prissy manservant. Produced by Third Man Corporation in association with BBC.

Thirteen at Dinner
US 1985 96m colour TVM
CBS/Warner (Neil Hartley)

An American film star schemes to do away with her English husband.

Rather flat rendering of the Agatha Christie mystery *Lord Edgware Dies.*

w Rod Browning d Lou Antonio ph Curtis Clark m John Addison

Peter Ustinov, Faye Dunaway, David Suchet, Allan Cuthbertson, Diane Keen, John Stride, Lee Horsley, John Barron, Bill Nighy

'A characterless puzzle.' – *Daily Variety*

13 Queens Boulevard (US 1979). Shortlived 25-minute comedy series with Eileen Brennan as a tough-talking housewife. Produced by Bud Yorkin; for ABC.

Thirty Minute Theatre (GB 1967–72). Half-hour plays on BBC, originally live and many of them lost for ever, as revived on both

channels (see *Half Hour Story*) about this time. Harry Moore, a former New York actor and story editor, attracted early works by Dennis Potter (*Emergency Ward Nine*) and Tom Stoppard (*Teeth*) as well as luring Sir Alec Guinness on to British television for the first time in Durrenmatt's *Conversation at Night.* PP

This Child Is Mine
US 1974 74m colour TVM
CBS/Columbia/Douglas S. Cramer
  (Wilford Lloyd Baumes)

Foster parents fight an unmarried mother who wants her child back.
Routine 'woman's picture'.

w Richard DeRoy *d* Gloria Monty

Stephen Young, James Craig, Don Galloway, Rosemary Prinz, Robin Strasser, Marjorie Lloyd

This Child Is Mine
US 1985 96m colour TVM
NBC/Telepictures/Beth Polson/Finnegan

Adoptive parents and a real mother fight for the custody of an infant.
One for the ladies.

w Charles Rosin *d* David Greene *ph* Harry J. May

Lindsay Wagner, Chris Sarandon, Nancy McKeon, Michael Lerner, John Philbin, Kathleen York

'Thoughtful, touching, and even moving at times.' – *Daily Variety*

This England
GB 1965–8 30 × 30m bw
Granada (Denis Mitchell, Norman
  Swallow)

Series of personal, impressionistic films partly set up as a forcing ground for young directors – those who went on to make it include Michael Apted, Michael Beckham, Francis Megahy, Frank Cvitanovich, John Irvin and Mike Newell. Subjects ranged from a nuclear power station to Liverpool FC supporters flying to Eastern Europe for a match. In 1979 the title was revived for a few more films, in colour, including a couple shot by Denis Mitchell himself. Further series, 1986. PP

This Girl for Hire
US 1983 96m colour TVM
CBS/Orion/Barney Rosenzweig

A female private eye solves the murder of a well-known author.
Superficial and self-knowing take-off of the murder mysteries of the forties; far too arch for comfort.

w Terry Louise Fisher, Steve Brown *d* Jerry Jameson *ph* Robbie Greenberg *m* Bruce Broughton

Bess Armstrong, Celeste Holm, Cliff DeYoung, Hermione Baddeley, Jose Ferrer, Scott Brady, Howard Duff, Beverly Garland, Roddy McDowall, Percy Rodriguez, Elisha Cook Jnr

This House Possessed
US 1981 96m colour TVM
ABC/MGM/Leonard Goldberg (David
  Levinson)

A young woman becomes enmeshed in terror when she feels that her house is alive and determined to prevent her from escaping.
Slow-moving screamer, not badly done but severely lacking plot twists.

w David Levinson *d* William Wiard *ph* Thomas Del Ruth *m* Billy Goldenberg

Parker Stevenson, Lisa Eilbacher, Joan Bennett, Slim Pickens, Shelley Smith, Bill Morey

This Is Noël Coward *
GB 1972 96m colour (16mm)
Charles Castle

A valuable record of the life and career of Noël Coward, with film clips and interviews. The script also produced a book called *Noël*. Those appearing include Coward himself, John Gielgud, Maurice Chevalier, Richard Burton, David Niven, Lilli Palmer, Brian Aherne, Yul Brynner, Danny La Rue, Earl Mountbatten, John Mills, Gladys Cooper, Edith Evans, Hermione Gingold, Anna Neagle, Cecil Beaton, Sybil Thorndike, Joyce Grenfell, Celia Johnson. The wealth of original material makes the programme a valuable historical record despite the disappointing quality of the processing.

w/d Charles Castle *ph* Dick Bush *cartoons* Osbert Lancaster

This Is the Day (GB since 1984). Simple, touching Sunday morning format in which an informal religious service is broadcast live from a private household. Presented by Margaret Collingwood and others, produced (1986) by David Craig, for BBC. PP

This Is the West That Was
US 1974 74m colour TVM
Universal (Roy Huggins, Jo Swerling Jnr)

Wild Bill Hickok, Calamity Jane and Buffalo Bill fight each other and the baddies. Lame western spoof.

w Sam H. Rolfe, Jo Swerling Jnr d Fielder Cook

Ben Murphy, Kim Darby, Matt Clark, Jane Alexander, Tony Franciosa, Stuart Margolin

This Is Waugh *
GB 1976 3 × 25m colour
ATV (Derek Hart)

Splendidly reactionary, if rather guileless, surveys of the class system by Auberon Waugh, hedged with elaborate disclaimers by an IBA which turned not a hair at covert, or even overt, contributions from the Left.   PP

This Is Your Life. A half-hour 'live' show popular in America and Britain since the fifties, in which a celebrity is surprised by a party of his friends who recount his life story. Ralph Edwards has been the American host, Eamonn Andrews the British; and since it became the practice to record the show, embarrassment has been avoided. *This Is Your Life* has become the epitome of popular TV.

This Is Your Right (GB since 1970). Long-running social-aid programme put out three times weekly by Granada in its own region. Originally set up and presented by Michael Winstanley, doctor and (temporarily) Liberal MP.   PP

This Land of England (GB 1985; 4 × 60m). Revisionist history of English country life to upset as many cherished beliefs as possible. It wasn't stable, orderly or tranquil, argue historians David Starkey (who presented) and David Souden (behind the scenes). Produced and directed by Bruce MacDonald, for Mirageland/C4.   PP

This Man Dawson
US 1959 39 × 25m bw
United Artists

A law enforcement agency works on government missions.
Routine hokum.

Keith Andes

This Office Life (GB 1985). Unexpectedly flimsy one-off from Keith Waterhouse designed as some sort of homage to the Ealing comedies of the forties and fifties, complete with non-stop jaunty music and a

credit to that studio's favourite screenwriter, T. E. B. Clarke, as 'consultant', but working out more Shepherd's Bush than Ealing.   PP

This Week ** (GB 1956–78). The first 27-minute edition included eight items, ranging from a filmed story on Dr Otto John's defection in West Germany to a studio interview with that week's winner of a television quiz. By 1965 it was down to a single subject each week and regarded as the best current affairs show on British television, a position it held on and off until its pointless replacement by *TV Eye* in 1978. Its editors over the years included Peter Hunt, Cyril Bennett, Jeremy Isaacs, Phillip Whitehead and David Elstein; its reporters Robert Kee, Paul Johnson, Peter Williams, Peter Taylor, Jonathan Dimbleby. Put out by Thames TV, previously Rediffusion. Born again, 1986. PP

'Every man's fantasy . . . a woman who'll do everything you want . . . and you don't have to marry her!'
This Wife for Hire
US 1985 96m colour TVM
ABC/Comworld/Belle/Guillaume–Margo (Don Segall, Phil Margo)

A bored wife runs a business supplying housekeepers for busy bachelors.
Mildly suggestive comedy which runs out of steam before the end.

w Don Segall, Phil Margo d James R. Drake ph Rexford Metz

Pam Dawber, Robert Klein, Laraine Newman, Dick Gautier, Ann Jillian

'Too cute, pat and predictable.' – *Daily Variety*

This Year, Next Year
GB 1977 13 × 50m colour
Granada (Howard Baker)

Another lengthy John Finch serial, about jaded townie (Ronald Hines) yearning to return to the simple life already enjoyed by his brother (Michael Elphick). My review at the time: 'Touched a common day-dream of the era but wasn't the antithesis between idyllic Yorkshire dales and seedy London rather absurdly rigged? The sun shone on Jack's wedding, the girls floated round in lawn dresses, the good ale flowed. Back in the Smoke it was tepid keg in airless bars and Harry's missus (Virginia Stride) going to bed with his business partner in a borrowed bedsitter, fortified by a bottle of non-champagne like refugees from *Another Bouquet*, only without their style.'   PP

Thomas, Anthony (19 –). British documentary film-maker at best when his passionate curiosity is uppermost, less persuasive when his passionate convictions take over. *The South African Experience*, a 1977 ATV trilogy, strove too calculatedly to express Thomas's abhorrence of racialism in that country, where he had lived for some years. But the controversial *Death of a Princess* (1980) afforded keen insights into life in present-day Islam. Also: *Where Harry Stood* (beautifully simple life and times of a steel worker, 1974), *The Japanese Experience* (trilogy, 1974), *The Arab Experience* (trilogy, 1975), *The Good, the Bad and the Indifferent* (the Church of England, 1976), *The Most Dangerous Man in the World* (1982).   PP

✳ **Thomas, Danny** (1914–) (Amos Jacobs). American nightclub comedian whose most successful career was in TV, with the long-running *Danny Thomas Show* (*Make Room for Daddy*) and later *Make Room for Granddaddy*.

Thomas, Howard (1909–85). British executive, former radio producer (creator of *The Brains Trust*) and director of the fortunes of ABC Television; after its merger with Thames he became chairman of the joint company. Autobiography 1977: *With An Independent Air*.

Thomas, Lowell (1892–1981). American journalist (with Lawrence in Arabia) and radio commentator; came to TV primarily as host of a travel series, *High Adventure*.

Thomas, Marlo (*c* 1934–). American leading lady, daughter of Danny Thomas. *That Girl*, *Free to Be: You and Me*, *It Happened One Christmas*, THE LOST HONOR OF KATHRYN BECK (*Act of Passion*), *Consenting Adult*.

Thomas, Philip Michael (1959–). Black American leading man who became a star in *Miami Vice*. 'If Freud were around to analyse his ego, he'd need two couches.' – *People*

Thomas, Richard (1951–). American juvenile lead, the popular John Boy of *The Waltons*. TV movies: *The Homecoming* (from which sprang *The Waltons*), *The Red Badge of Courage*, *The Silence*, *Getting Married*, *Roots:*

The Next Generations, *No Other Love*, *To Find My Son*, *Berlin Tunnel 21*, *Johnny Belinda*, *Living Proof*, *Fifth of July*, *Hobson's Choice*, *The Master of Ballantrae*.

Thompson, Sada (1929–). American character actress who won a 1977 Emmy for *Family*.

'More than a love story – the magnificent adventure of a bold pioneer family. Fighting the furies of nature and the passions of men on the beautiful and brutal Australian frontier!'
The Thorn Birds *
US 1983 7 × 50m colour miniseries
ABC/Warner/David L. Wolper–Stan
  Marguilies/Edward Lewis

A priest discards his vows for a brief romantic fling, and has a son.
Rather tiresome, but highly commercial, miniseries from a notorious bestseller. Irritatingly reverent in its dealings with the church, slow all the way, and bathed in a golden glow of self-importance.
w Carmen Culver, *book* by Colleen McCullough *d* Daryl Duke *ph* Bill Butler *m* Henry Mancini *pd* Robert MacKichan
Richard Chamberlain, Barbara Stanwyck, Rachel Ward, Jean Simmons, Bryan Brown, Christopher Plummer, Ken Howard, Mare Winningham, Piper Laurie, Richard Kiley, Earl Holliman, Allyn Ann McLerie
'If it staggers lamentably in its final hours, story offers emotional impact, controversy and logical progression.' – *Daily Variety*
† Emmy 1983: outstanding lead actress, also supporting actor and actress: Barbara Stanwyck, Richard Kiley, Jean Simmons.
PP: 'Kiss, Kiss, ugh, ugh.'

Thornton, Frank (1921–). British comedy actor, usually of snooty types, e.g. Captain Peacock in *Are You Being Served?*

Thornwell
US 1981 96m colour TVM
CBS/MTM (Mark Tinker)
True account of a black American soldier who in 1961 was brainwashed by the Army in relation to stolen documents; he later sued the army, and won.
A tale which has been more compactly told in documentary form; the fictionalizing and extra length seem unnecessary.
w Michael de Guzman *d* Harry Moses *ph* Stevan Larner *m* Fred Karlin

Glynn Turman, Vincent Gardenia, Craig Wasson, Todd Susman, Maidie Norman, Edward Bell

'Fails to generate the expected dramatic build-up.' – *Daily Variety*

Thorpe, Jerry (*c* 1930–). American independent producer/director, son of Richard Thorpe. Series: *The Untouchables*, *Kung Fu*, *Chicago Teddy Bears*, *Harry O.*

Those Glory Glory Days * (GB 1983; 120m; TVM). Soccer-mad schoolgirls strive to beg, buy, wheedle or steal Cup Final tickets. Two hours meant some slow patches, especially in the build-up to Julie Welch's autobiographical comedy, but sprightlier invention developed and at the end there was a rueful postscript when the heroine, 20 years on and by now a Fleet Street football reporter, met the idol of her youthful escapade, footballer Danny Blanchflower (played by himself). Directed by Philip Saville, produced by David Puttnam for Goldcrest/Enigma/C4. It ran as a *First Love*.
                                                                                PP

Those Radio Times (GB 1982; 50m). Nicely assembled memoir of the BBC radio heyday 1922–53, with John Snagge, Sidonie Goossens, Arthur Askey, Elsie Waters, Henry Hall, George Chisholm, Vera Lynn, Wynford Vaughan-Thomas, David Davis, Molly Weir, Noel Johnson. Produced by Adam Low, for BBC.   PP

Those Wonderful TV Times (GB 1976–8). Panel quiz put out by Tyne-Tees in which contestants drawn from showbiz or journalism had to answer questions on, or identify clips from, past and present television output. All winnings went to charities of their choice. Madeline Smith was hostess.   PP

Thou Shalt Not Commit Adultery
US 1980 96m colour TVM
NBC/Warner/Edgar J. Scherick
The wife of a paraplegic contemplates an affair.
Tedious adult soap, part of an incomplete and risible project to make a movie on each of the Ten Commandments.

w Calder Willingham, Del Reisman *d* Delbert Mann *ph* Robert Hauser *m* Paul Chihara
Louise Fletcher, Robert Reed, Wayne Rogers, Bert Convy, Hal Williams, Lucy Lee Flippen

'What could have been an intelligent study turns instead to something ripped from a true confessions mag – and about as convincing.' – *Daily Variety*

Threads
GB 1984 115m
BBC (Mick Jackson)
Britain's fourth shock-horror simulation of the unthinkable – nuclear attack and its aftermath, the latter here prolonged and made even grislier, if that is possible, by the proposition of a nuclear ice-age brought on by clouds of debris in the atmosphere. Unbearably well done as regards atmosphere and gruesome special effects, but with minatory off-screen commentator plus captions too reminiscent of agitprop drama of the sixties. 'Propaganda first and cautionary drama second,' I summed up.

w Barry Hines *d* Mick Jackson
Karen Meagher, Rees Dinsdale

As usual, the transmission was followed by discussion programmes, and backed up scientifically on its nuclear winter proposition by a documentary *On the Eighth Day*.

† Mick Jackson had previously (1982) made *A Guide to Armageddon* for the BBC *Q.E.D.* series, an ironic demonstration by a London family of how to survive a nuclear attack according to official government guidance.

†† The other nuke-attack scenarios were *Doomsday for Dyson* (1958), *The War Game* (1965, not transmitted until 1985), a CBS documentary simulation in 1981, and *The Day After* (1983).   PP

Three After Six (GB 1964–6). Transparently low-cost Rediffusion local talk-show featuring three talkers who mulled over the day's news and gossip shortly after 6 p.m. – hence the title. Thanks to the amiability of Jack Hargreaves as one of the regulars and the loquacity and good stories of Alan Brien as the other, it caught on so well that other stations started to join in. In April 1965 the team was flown to New York to conduct ITV's first Early Bird relay. Third place was customarily occupied by a female, e.g. Gillian Reynolds or Dee Wells.   PP

Three Days in Szczecin
GB 1976 90m colour
Granada (Leslie Woodhead)
Dramatized documentary about the Polish shipyard workers' strike of 1971 which was a kind of try-out for the more successful

confrontation of 1980 which led to the formation of the independent trade union Solidarity. Leslie Sands played the Communist leader Gierek, Kenneth Colley the leader of the strikers, Edmund Baluka. Written by Boleslaw Sulik; directed by Leslie Woodhead.   PP

Three for the Road
US 1975 74m colour TVM
Mary Tyler Moore

A photographer widower travels across America on jobs, with his two sons, in a camper.
Acceptable family fare which led to a shortlived series.

w Jerry McNeely d Boris Sagal m David Shire

Alex Rocco, Vincent Van Patten, Leif Garrett, Julie Sommars

† The series ran to 13 × 50m episodes. Producer: Jerry McNeely; music: David Shire and James Di Pasquale; with Alex Rocco, Vincent Van Patten, Leif Garrett.

The Three Hostages *
GB 1977 85m colour (16mm)
BBC (Mark Shivas)

Richard Hannay reluctantly takes on the job of exposing a crime syndicate which has taken three significant hostages.
Well conceived and intriguing but in the event a disappointing entertainment which lacks pace and humour.

w John Prebble, novel John Buchan d Clive Donner

Barry Foster, John Castle, Diana Quick, Peter Blythe

300 Miles for Stephanie
US 1980 96m colour TVM
NBC/Edward S. Feldman (Antonio Calderon)

A man vows to run 300 miles to the Church of the Miracles if God will spare his terminally sick child.
A true anecdote with good moments but which in no way fills its slot.

w/d Clyde Ware

Tony Orlando, Julie Carmen, P. J. Oliveras

Three Men in a Boat *
GB 1975 65m colour
BBC (Rosemary Hill)

Jolly version of Jerome K. Jerome's manly idyll on the Thames, with a due reminder of sadder goings-on when the three encounter the drowned corpse. Written by Tom Stoppard; directed by Stephen Frears.   PP
LH: 'It didn't work for me; but then I'm an absolute devotee of the book.'

Three More Men in a Boat
(GB 1983; 75m). Misbegotten attempt to retrace the journey above by three ponderous latter-day wags, Benny Green, Christopher Matthew and Tim Rice. Produced by Richard Denton, for BBC.

Three of a Kind *
(GB 1981; 6 × 30m; colour). Promising little revue series by the talented trio of Lenny Henry, Tracy Ullman and David Copperfield, at least two of whom seemed destined for stardom. Produced by Paul Jackson, Associate Ian Davidson; for BBC.   PP
† Further series followed in 1982–3 and, yes, both Ullman and Henry became stars, Lenny Henry of his own show.

Three on a Date
US 1978 96m colour TVM
ABC Circle (David Shapiro)

Four couples on a game show win a Hawaiian holiday.
Yawnworthy multi-comedy, a landlocked Love Boat.

w Dale McRaven, book Stephanie Buffington d Bill Bixby ph Charles W. Short m George Aliceson Tipton

June Allyson, Ray Bolger, Loni Anderson, John Byner, Gary Crosby, Didi Conn, Patrick Wayne

Three on a Gas Ring
GB 1960 60m bw (VTR) (not transmitted)
ABC Armchair Theatre (Sydney Newman)

Rates a mention as one of the first television plays to be recorded but denied transmission after being shown privately to ITA officials and the Bishop of Coventry. The offence of David Osborn's play was that its heroine, an unmarried girl sharing a Chelsea houseboat with a man and another woman, was apparently unrepentant at finding herself pregnant. Within 15 years comparable situations were to be the stuff of witless situation comedies going out at peak time.

Joanna Dunham, Alan Bates, Sheila Allen PP

Three Piece Suite
GB 1977 4 × 25m colour
BBC (Michael Mills)

Show-off series for Diana Rigg, each programme consisting of three little sketches coaxed from the fashionable comedy writers of the day. It took off only with a sequel to *Brief Encounter* postulated by Keith Waterhouse and Willis Hall 30 years after the events of Noël Coward's play. At the time I found the other bits 'just as derivative (frumpish spinster, soft-porn film star) but being derived from general stereotypes rather than a particular source they ended up as unfunny caricatures.'   PP

Three Roads to Rome
US/GB 1960 78m
ABC/Rediffusion (Fred Coe, Arthur Penn)

Three love stories set in Rome, at the turn of the century, the thirties and the then present day, linked by Deborah Kerr as the heroine in every case. An early outbreak of co-production between Britain and the US.

w Tad Mosel, from stories by Martha Gellhorn, Edith Wharton, Aldous Huxley d Ronald Marriott

1. *Venus Ascendant*, with Anthony Newlans, Isabel Dean
2. *Roman Fever*, with Celia Johnson
3. *The Rest Cure*, with Jeremy Brett, Allan Cuthbertson   PP

Three Sovereigns for Sarah
US 1985 3 × 50m colour miniseries
PBS/Night Owl (Victor Pisano)

A survivor of the Salem witch hunts tries to clear the name of her dead sisters.
Solemn, interesting historical melodrama.

w Victor Pisano d Philip Leacock ph Larry Pizer m Charles Gross

Vanessa Redgrave, Patrick McGoohan, Phyllis Thaxter, Kim Hunter, Shay Duffin, Ronald Hunter

The Three Thousand Mile Chase
US 1977 96m colour TVM
NBC/Universal (Roy Huggins)

A professional courier and an importer are chased across country by gangsters.
Another attempt (see *Target Risk*) to get a series out of the courier business. This one was competent, but nothing happened.

w Philip DeGuere Jnr d Russ Mayberry

Cliff De Young, Blair Brown, Glenn Ford, David Spielberg, Priscilla Pointer

3–2–1 (GB since 1978). Undemanding and uninteresting game show with comedian Ted Rogers in charge. Produced by Don Clayton, previously Ian Bolt.

The Three Wishes of Billy Grier
US 1985 96m colour TVM
ABC/I & C (Jay Benson)

A teenager finds he has a rare and fatal ageing disease.
The 'disease-of-the-week' syndrome among TV movie producers must be reaching the bottom of the barrel after this one: even the make-up is unconvincing.

w,d Corey Blechman ph Frank Stanley m Brad Fiedel

Ralph Macchio, Betty Buckley, Hal Holbrook, Season Hubley, Jeffrey Tambor, Lawrence Pressman, Conchata Ferrell, Viveca Lindfors

† The three wishes are: playing the saxophone, making love, and finding his long-lost dad.

'Exploitative, insensitive meller.' – *Daily Variety*

Three's a Crowd
US 1969 74m colour TVM
Columbia

Erroneously thinking his first wife dead in a plane crash, a businessman remarries . . .
The cinema film *My Favourite Wife* revamped; each time to less effect.

w Buck Henry d James Frawley

Larry Hagman, E. J. Peaker, Jessica Walter, Norman Fell, Harvey Korman

Three's a Crowd
US 1984   × 25m colour
ABC/NRW/Bergmann–Taffner (Martin Rips, Joseph Staretski, George Sunga)

The man in between in *Three's Company* settles down with his choice, while his dad backs a restaurant for him.
Routine comedy stemming from the British *Robin's Nest*; all developments are predictable.

cr Michael Ross, Bernie West, George Burditt

John Ritter, Mary Cadorette, Robert Mandan

'This show is so despicable that my main reaction is amazement.' – Robert MacKenzie, *TV Guide*

Three's Company *
US 1977–   × 25m colour (VTR)
ABC/NRW/TTC

A young man moves in to share a flat with two girls.
Sexy American version of the British *A Man About the House*; it became a phenomenal success in the American ratings.

w various *d* Bill Hobin *m* Joe Raposo
John Ritter, Joyce de Witt, Suzanne Somers, Audra Lindley, Norman Fell

'There are some things even best friends won't share!'
Threesome
US 1985 96m colour TVM
CBS (Ron Roth)
A wealthy bon vivant passes on his girl friend to his roommate and then decides he wants her back.
Modern sex comedy, long on farce and melodrama, short on wit.

w Lawrence B. Marcus, *novel Salt* by Herbert Gold *d* Lou Antonio *ph* Adam Hollander *m* Angela Morley

Stephen Collins, Deborah Raffin, Joel Higgins, Susan Hess, Addison Powell

Thriller **
US 1960–1 67 × 50m bw
NBC/Revue/Hubbell Robinson (William Frye)
An anthology of horror stories, hosted by Boris Karloff, who also stars in several.
A patchy series, but the best items had a genuine chill, e.g. *The Incredible Dr Markesan*, *Pigeons from Hell*, *The Hungry Glass*.

The episodes were as follows:

The Twisted Image (*w* James P. Cavanaugh; *d* Arthur Hiller; with Leslie Neilsen, George Grizzard)

Worse Than Murder (*w* Mel Goldberg; *d* Mitchell Leisen; with Christine White, Constance Ford)

Man in the Middle (*w* Howard Rodman; *d* Fletcher Markle; with Mort Sahl, Werner Klemperer)

The Mark of the Hand (*w/d* Maxwell Shane; with Shepperd Strudwick, Mona Freeman)

Rose's Last Summer (*d* Maxwell Shane; with Mary Astor, Lin McCarthy)

The Watcher (*w* Donald S. Sanford; *d* John Brahm; with Martin Gabel, Oliver Sturgess)

Child's Play (*w* Robert Dozier; *d* Arthur Hiller; with Tommy Nolan, Bethel Leslie)

Girl with a Secret (*w* Charles Beaumont; *d* Mitchell Leisen; with Myrna Fahey, Rhodes Reason, Fay Bainter)

The Guilty Men (*w* Maxwell Shane; *d* Ray Nazarro; with Everett Sloane, Jay C. Flippen)

The Impulse (*w* Philip MacDonald, Maxwell Shane; *d* Gerald Mayer; with Conrad Nagel, Elisha Cook)

The Prediction (*w* Donald S. Sanford; *d* John Brahm; with Boris Karloff, Audrey Dalton)

The Purple Room (*w/d* Douglas Heyes; with Rip Torn, Richard Anderson)

The Big Blackout (*w* Oscar Millard; *d* Maurice Geraghty; with Jack Carson, Nan Leslie)

Knock Three One Two (*w* John Kneubuhl; *d* Herman Hoffman; with Warren Oates, Beverly Garland)

The Cheaters (*w* Robert Bloch; *d* John Brahm; with Henry Daniell, Jack Weston)

The Hungry Glass (*w* Douglas Heyes, *story* Robert Bloch; *d* Douglas Heyes; with Donna Douglas, William Shatner)

The Poisoner (*w* Robert H. Andrews; *d* Herschel Daugherty; with Murray Matheson, Sarah Marshall)

Man in the Cage (*w* Maxwell Shane; *d* Gerald Mayer; with Philip Carey, Guy Stockwell)

The Merriweather File (*w* John Kneubuhl; *d* John Brahm; with Bethel Leslie, James Gregory)

The Fingers of Fear (*w* Robert H. Andrews, *play* Katherine and Dale Eunson; *d* Jules Bricken; with Robert Middleton, Nehemiah Persoff)

Hayfork and Billhook (*w* Alan Caillou; *d* Herschel Daugherty; with Kenneth Haigh, Audrey Dalton)

Well of Doom (*w* Donald S. Sanford; *d* John Brahm; with Henry Daniell, Ronald Howard, Torin Thatcher)

Choose a Victim (*w* George Bellak; *d* Richard Carlson; with Larry Blyden, Susan Oliver)

The Ordeal of Dr Cordell (*w* Donald S. Sanford; *d* Lazlo Benedek; with Robert Vaughn, Kathleen Crowley)

Trio for Terror (*w* Barry Lyndon; *d* Ida Lupino; with Michael Pate, John Abbott, Reginald Owen)

Papa Benjamin (*w* John Kneubuhl, *story* Cornell Woolrich; with John Ireland, Robert H. Harris)

Late Date (*w* Donald S. Sanford, *story* Cornell Woolrich; *d* Herschel Daugherty; with Larry Pennell, Edward Platt)

Yours Truly Jack the Ripper (*w* Barry Lyndon, *story* Robert Bloch; *d* Ray Milland; with John Williams, Donald Woods)

The Devil's Ticket (*w* Robert Bloch; *d* Jules Bricken; with Macdonald Carey, Joan Tetzel, John Emery)

Pigeons from Hell (w John Kneubuhl; d John Newland; with Brandon de Wilde, David Whorf, Ottola Nesmith)

A Good Imagination (w Robert Bloch; d John Brahm; with Edward Andrews, Ed Nelson)

Parasite Mansion (w Donald S. Sanford; d Herschel Daugherty; with Pippa Scott, James Griffith, Jeanette Nolan)

Dark Legacy (w John Tomerlin; d John Brahm; with Harry Townes, Henry Silva)

Mr George (w Donald S. Sanford; d Ida Lupino; with Virginia Gregg, Howard Freeman)

The Grim Reaper (w Robert Bloch; d Herschel Daugherty; with William Shatner, Natalie Schaefer, Henry Daniell)

Terror in Teakwood (w Alan Caillou; d Paul Henreid; with Guy Rolfe, Hazel Court)

The Prisoner in the Mirror (w Robert Arthur; d Herschel Daugherty; with David Frankham, Frieda Inescort, Henry Daniell)

Letter to a Lover (w Donald S. Sanford; d Herschel Daugherty; with Ann Todd, Murray Matheson)

Guillotine (w Charles Beaumont, story Cornell Woolrich; d Ida Lupino; with Robert Middleton, Alejandro Rey)

The Innocent Bystanders (w Hardy Andrews; d John English; with George Kennedy, John Anderson)

What Beckoning Ghost (w Donald S. Sanford; d Ida Lupino; with Judith Evelyn, Tom Helmore)

The Weird Tailor (w Robert Bloch; d Herschel Daugherty; with Henry Jones, George Macready, Abraham Sofaer)

The Premature Burial (w William D. Gordon, story Edgar Allen Poe; d Douglas Heyes; with Boris Karloff, Sidney Blackmer, Patricia Medina)

Waxworks (w Robert Bloch; d John Brahm; with Oscar Homolka, Booth Colman, Martin Kosleck)

The Closed Cabinet (w Kay Lenard, Jess Carneol; d Ida Lupino; with David Frankham, Isobel Elsom, Olive Sturgess)

Masquerade (w Donald S. Sanford; d Herschel Daugherty; with Tom Poston, Elizabeth Montgomery, John Carradine)

Flowers of Evil (story Hugh Walpole; d John Brahm; with Luciana Paluzzi, Jack Weston, Vladimir Sokoloff)

God Grante That She Lye Stille (w Robert R. Andrews, story Lady Cynthia Asquith; d Herschel Daugherty; with Sarah Marshall, Ronald Howard, Henry Daniell, Victor Buono)

A Third for Pinochle (w Mark Ranna, Boris Sobelman; d Herschel Daugherty; with Edward Andrews, Doro Merande)

The Return of Andrew Bentley (w Richard Matheson, story August Derleth; d John Newland; with John Newland, Antoinette Bower)

The Bride Who Died Twice (w Robert H. Andrews; d Ida Lupino; with Joe de Santis, Eduardo Ciannelli, Robert Colbert)

Friend of the Dead (w Robert Arthur; d Herschel Daugherty; with Boris Karloff, Ed Nelson)

Welcome Home (w Robert Arthur; d Herschel Daugherty; with Boris Karloff, Ed Nelson, Estelle Winwood)

The Last of the Somervilles (w R. M. H. Lupino; d Ida Lupino; with Boris Karloff, Phyllis Thaxter, Martita Hunt)

The Storm (w William D. Gordon; d Herschel Daugherty; with Nancy Kelly, James Griffith)

An Attractive Family (w Robert Arthur; d John Brahm; with Joan Tetzel, Richard Long, Otto Kruger, Leo G. Carroll, Will Wright)

Portrait without a Face (w Jason Wingreen; d John Newland; with John Newland, Jane Greer)

The Remarkable Mrs Hawk (w Donald S. Sanford; d John Brahm; with Jo Van Fleet, John Carradine)

La Strega (w Alan Caillou; d Ida Lupino; with Ursula Andress, Alejandro Rey, Jeanette Nolan, Ramon Novarro)

A Wig for Miss Devore (w Donald S. Sanford, story August Derleth; d John Brahm; with Patricia Barry, John Fiedler)

The Incredible Dr Markesan (w Donald S. Sanford, story August Derleth; d Robert Florey; with Boris Karloff, Dick York, Carolyn Kearney)

Till Death Do Us Part (w Robert Bloch; d Herschel Daugherty; with Henry Jones, Reta Shaw)

The Hollow Watcher (w Jay Simms; d William Claxton; with Audrey Dalton, Sean McClory)

Cousin Tundifer (w Boris Sobelman; d John Brahm; with Edward Andrews, Vaughn Taylor)

The Specialists (*w* John Kneubuhl; *d* Ted Post; with Lin McCarthy, Ronald Howard, Robert Douglas)

Kill My Love (*w* Donald S. Sanford; *d* Herschel Daugherty; with Richard Carlson, K. T. Stevens)

Man of Mystery (*w* Robert Bloch; *d* John Newland; with John Van Dreelen, Mary Tyler Moore, William Windom)

The Lethal Ladies (two-parter) (*w* Boris Sobelman; *d* Ida Lupino; with Rosemary Murphy, Howard Morris)

Through Naked Eyes *
US 1984 96m colour TVM
ABC/Charles Fries (Paul Pompian)

Murders have happened in a Chicago apartment house, and a flautist and the girl across the way find themselves suspecting each other.

Thin suspenser with echoes of *Rear Window* and a dozen other low-budget thrillers of the fifties. Watchable for those with nothing more sustaining in sight.

w Jeffrey Bloom *d* John Llewellyn Moxey *ph* Jack L. Richards *m* Gil Melle

David Soul, Pam Dawber, Rod McCary, William Schallert, Fionnula Flanagan, Dick Anthony Williams

'It doesn't always ring true, but it's fun, and it even has a jump or two.' – *Daily Variety*

Through the Night *
GB 1975 75m colour

Trevor Griffith's play based on a diary kept by his wife when she went into hospital for a routine biopsy and came round from the anaesthetic to discover she had had a breast removed. Not an attack on surgical ruthlessness but on the accompanying doctorly attitudes, with a fairly optimistic ending and a dedicated performance by Alison Steadman. Directed by Michael Lindsay-Hogg; produced by Ann Scott; for BBC (*Play for Today*). PP

Thrower, Percy (1913–). British gardening expert, on BBC for many years.

Thunderbirds ***
GB 1966 32 × 50m colour
ATV/Gerry Anderson

Men and women with special skills help to combat world criminals.

Like the later Muppets, this is a children's series, i.e. a puppet spoof of the James Bond syndrome, which has genuine sophistication, gaiety and adult appeal.

Thursday's Child
US 1983 96m colour TVM
CBS/Viacom/Catalina (Peter Katz)

A young man and his family both suffer when he has to undergo a heart transplant. Somewhat padded but dramatically lively docu-drama for those who like hospital stuff.

w Gwen Bagni-Dubov, *book* by Victoria Poole *d* David Lowell Rich *ph* Charles F. Wheeler *m* Lee Holdridge

Gena Rowlands, Don Murray, Jessica Walter, Rob Lowe, Tracy Gold

Thursday's Game *
US 1974 96m colour TVM
ABC Circle (James L. Brooks, Lew Gallo)

When their Thursday night poker game breaks up, two men fail to inform their wives and continue to have more daring nights out. Pretty lively adult comedy originally intended for the big screen.

w James L. Brooks *d* Robert Moore *ph* Joseph Biroc *m* Billy Goldenberg

Gene Wilder, Bob Newhart, Ellen Burstyn, Cloris Leachman, Martha Scott, Nancy Walker, Valerie Harper, Rob Reiner, Norman Fell, Dick Gautier

Tic Tac Dough. American quiz game of the fifties (British title *Criss Cross Quiz*). Contestants used their correct or incorrect answers to play noughts and crosses on an electronic board.

Tidyman, Ernest (1928–). American screenwriter, former journalist. TV movies: *To Kill a Cop, Dummy, Power, Guyana Tragedy, Alcatraz.* Series: *Shaft.*

Ties of Blood *
GB 1985 6 × 60m
BBC (Tim Ironside Wood)

Six plays about the British army in Northern Ireland as seen by a 'neutral' Northern Irishman, with the emphasis on routine rather than action: a cook corporal drawn into a little romance, an infantry patrol thoughtlessly knocking down an old man's wall, three young soldiers on leave before their tour of duty, nursing sisters in the military wing of a Belfast hospital; all of them being brought face to face with some unwelcome reality sooner or later.

Low-key and rather flatly produced, but another attempt by playwright Graham Reid to plumb the individual complexities of the Troubles.

d James Ormerod
J. G. Devlin, Dearbha Molloy, Kenny Ireland, Tyler Butterworth, Denys Hawthorne, Gwen Taylor   PP

The Tigers Are Burning
GB 1965 50m bw
ATV (Anthony Firth)

Producer Firth was evidently convinced that the great tank battle at Kursk in July 1943 not only marked the turn of the tide in World War II but had been unaccountably overlooked in Western war histories, because he twice reconstructed the scene in Hitler's headquarters as the German General Staff watch him send his Panzer divisions to destruction. Here it was done by actors in everyday clothes, with Norman Rodway making Adolf a terrible class of a fella that had such a temper to him he would have over-run us all if Thanks Be the Russians hadn't stopped him. Seven years later Firth included a fresh version in a trio of documentaries called *Turning Point*, this time with the actors in uniform, and made up, but an even odder Hitler – Jewish in his speech rhythms! – from David Graham.   PP

Tigris
GB/Norway 1979 4 × 50m colour
BBC/Thor Heyerdahl

Last and not particularly engrossing expedition by the action-scholar who made a life's work out of retracing the migrations of early civilizations in reconstructions of the craft they would have had at their disposal; in this case, the Sumerians and the reed ships in which they sailed from Mesopotamia to the Indies. Written and produced by Bruce Norman.

Tightrope *
US 1957 37 × 25m bw
CBS/Columbia

An undercover police officer joins the mob. Sharply made but unavoidably repetitive gangster suspense series.

cr Russel Rouse, Clarence Greene
Michael Connors

Till Death Us Do Part ****
GB 1964–74 50 approx. × 30m bw, later colour (VTR)
BBC

A loud-mouthed working-class bigot gets himself and his family into hot water.
A comedy series which seldom strayed from a tiny set and was often poorly plotted yet changed the face of TV by means of what it said and how it said it. Alf Garnett was held up as a monster yet he voiced opinions which many people secretly held, so people had a sneaking sympathy for him when he got into trouble. He and his long-suffering wife Else were magnificent comic creations in the Dickensian mould, superbly acted; and the series, with its frequent tirades about race and religion and royalty, could hardly fail to make the headlines or to change the face of TV comedy. The Americans picked up the format rather carefully, but it became a roaring success for them as *All in the Family*.

cr/w JOHNNY SPEIGHT

WARREN MITCHELL, DANDY NICHOLS, Una Stubbs, Anthony Booth

† A sequel *In Sickness and In Health* appeared in 1985, cut short by the death of Dandy Nichols soon after the first run of seven.

The Tim Conway Show (US 1970).
Half-hour comedy series for CBS, about a clumsy pilot. With Joe Flynn, Anne Seymour.

'She will blow you away!'
Time Bomb
US 1984 96m colour TVM
NBC/Universal/Barry Weitz

Trucker buddies foil a ruthless terrorist gang attempting to hijack a nuclear armoured vehicle as it travels across Texas.
Failed pilot with good photography and adequate suspense.

w Westbrook Claridge   *d* Paul Krasny
ph Don Reddy *m* Sylvester Levay
Billy Dee Williams, Joseph Bottoms, Morgan Fairchild, Merlin Olsen, Anne Kerry

Time Express
US 1979 4 × 50m colour
CBS/Warner/Ivan Goff, Ben Roberts (Leonard Kaufman)

A mysterious train takes people back in time to a turning point in their lives where they get a second chance.
Inanely executed variation on *Fantasy Island*; the endpapers in the deserted station are the best part, but the star is over the top. It didn't catch on.

cr Ivan Goff, Ben Roberts *w* Gerald Sanford and others
Vincent Price, Coral Browne

A Time for Love
US 1973 100m colour TVM
Paramount (Sterling Silliphant)

Two love stories of different types.
A format which didn't jell, even after the
success of *Love Story*. No takers.

w Sterling Silliphant *d* George Schaefer,
Joseph Sargent

Jack Cassidy, Bonnie Bedelia, John
Davidson, Lauren Hutton, Christopher
Mitchum

A Time for Miracles
US 1980 96m colour TVM
ABC Circle (Jimmy Hawkins, Beverlee
Dean)

The story of Elizabeth Seton, born in 1774 and
the first American saint.
Religious charade in which all concerned seem
to be reading the script for the first time.

w Henry Denker *d* Michael O'Herlihy *ph*
Don Birnkrant *m* Fred Karlin

Kate Mulgrew, Jean-Pierre Aumont, Rossano
Brazzi, Lorne Greene, John Forsythe,
Leonard Mann, Robin Clark

Time for Murder
GB 1985 6 × 52m
Granada (Pieter Rogers)

Star-studded new plays on the theme of
sudden death, shot in the studio and
generally forgettable, even when written by
Charles Wood or especially when written by
Antonia Fraser.

Mister Clay, Mister Clay! *w* Antonia Fraser
  d Brian Mills; Ian Ogilvy, Eleanor Bron,
  Joan Hickson
The Murders at Lynch Cross *w* Frances
  Galleymore *d* Patrick Lau; Jill Bennett,
  Joanna David, Barbara Jefford, Sylvia
  Sims
This Lightning Always Strikes Twice
  w Michael Robson *d* David Carson;
  Claire Bloom, Charles Dance, Trevor
  Howard
Bright Smiler *w* Fay Weldon *d* David
  Carson; Janet Suzman, Jane Asher
Dust to Dust *w* Charles Wood *d* Brian
  Parker; Patricia Hodge, Michael Jayston,
  Judy Campbell
The Thirteenth Day of Christmas *w* Gordon
  Honeycombe *d* Patrick Lau; Patrick
  Allen, Elizabeth Spriggs PP

The Time Machine
US 1978 96m colour TVM
NBC/Schick Sunn Classic (Charles E.
  Sellier Jnr)

A computer genius builds a machine which
will take him into the past and the future.
And in this interfered-with version of the
H. G. Wells classic, he learns nothing at all
from either. Sheer rubbish in the accustomed
Classics Illustrated mould.

w Wallace Bennett *d* Henning Schellerup *ph*
Stephen W. Gray *m* John Cacavas

John Beck, Priscilla Barnes, Andrew Duggan,
Jack Kruschen, Rosemary de Camp, Whit
Bissell, John Doucette

The Time of Your Life *
GB 1958 90m bw
ABC (Sydney Newman/Jean Dalrymple)

An *Armchair Theatre* special: William
Saroyan's American tragedy in a star-studded
production sent over under State
Department sponsorship to play at the
Brussels Exposition and hijacked on its way
home by Newman.

d Philip Saville

Franchot Tone, Susan Strasberg, Ann
Sheridan, Dan Dailey PP

The Time of Your Life (GB 1985).
Celebrities look back on a crucial year in
their lifetime, e.g. Michael Parkinson on
1963, the year he entered television; with the
cheery support of Noel Edmonds. An
undemanding, entertaining format produced
by Henry Murray, for BBC. PP

Time on Our Hands
GB 1962 60m bw
BBC (Don Haworth)

Ingenious, if wayward documentary fore-
telling everyday life and excessive leisure
25 years ahead, i.e. 1987. Aldous Huxley
urged the discovery of a safer solace – in the
motor car age – than alcohol. Kingsley Amis
deplored the dilution of academic standards.
The evolution of fixed-term marriages was
plausibly explained. My 1962 review: 'The
trouble, as with all these confident exercises,
was the unBritish smoothness and
purposefulness with which everything had
happened. The new cities, new schools, new
universities had sprung up, all in 25 years;
there was even a local rocket station, with
departures for the planets. In reality the sites
for the new towns and new buildings would
still be the subject of Local Inquiries, while
Blue Moon, the first British space vehicle,
would just have been cancelled as obsolescent
prior to trials. The only safe prediction for
1987 is that I shall still be paying off my
mortgage.' How right I was. PP

Time Out. Before the title was appropriated
by the published leisure guide for Londoners it
was used briefly in Britain (1964–5) for an
occasional series of staged outside broadcasts,

THE TIME OF YOUR LIFE. An ingenious nostalgia format which had a celebrity recalling the year that meant most to him; other notables of the period then turned up for interview, and there was studio audience participation as well. Here Noel Edmonds introduces Steve Davis.

e.g. a spectacular rock climb in Yorkshire. Of that I said: 'The ultimate attraction was suspense – would anyone fall? With its floodlit beetling stage, its unseen audience and chorus of motor-horns, its skilfully matched leading players (one taciturn, one jokey) it was pure theatre, and theatre which could have turned at any time into the cruel kind.' Edited by Christopher Brasher.   PP

The Time Travelers
US 1976 74m colour TVM
ABC/TCF/Irwin Allen

Scientists go back in time and rescue a girl from the Chicago fire.

Scruffily-made fantasy with great chunks of tinted footage from *In Old Chicago*.

w Jackson Gillis, *story* Irwin Allen and Rod Serling *d* Alex Singer *a/d* Eugene Lourie

Sam Groom, Tom Hallick, Richard Basehart, Trish Stewart

† The expected series didn't happen.

Time Tunnel *
US 1966 30 × 50m colour
ABC/TCF/Irwin Allen

Scientists build a time tunnel and get caught in the fourth dimension.

A well-contrived piece of juvenile science fiction which deserves a nod for sheer audacity as our heroes each week get caught up in chunks of old Fox movies. The episode called *The Ghost of Nero* is a lulu, with footage from *A Farewell to Arms*.

cr Irwin Allen

James Darren, Robert Colbert, Lee Meriwether

Episodes were:

Rendezvous with Yesterday
One Way to the Moon
End of the World
The Day the Sky Fell Down
The Last Patrol
The Crack of Doom
Revenge of the Gods
Massacre
Devil's Island
Reign of Terror
Secret Weapon
The Death Trap
The Alamo
The Night of the Long Knives
Invasion
Robin Hood
Kill Two by Two
Visitors from Beyond the Stars
The Ghost of Nero
The Walls of Jericho
Idol of Death

Billy the Kid
Pirates of Dead Man's Island
Chase Through Time
The Death Merchant
Attack of the Barbarians
Merlin the Magician
The Kidnappers
Raiders from Outer Space
Town of Terror

† In 1976 Fox made an ill-advised effort to revive the project with a TV movie called *The Time Travelers* in which an attempt was made to prevent the Chicago fire (see above).

Time with Betjeman **
GB 1983 7 × 50m
BBC (Jonathan Stedall)

A year before he died, and much subdued by Parkinson's Disease, Sir John became the third Briton (after Malcolm Muggeridge and Alan Whicker) to have bits and pieces of his television past re-run before his eyes. The extracts were backed up by some affectionate probing from Jonathan Stedall; there were also encounters with friends and fans, sometimes falling flat (Barry Humphries), sometimes heavy-going (John Osborne), but sooner or later arousing the Betjeman glee and prompting that delighted Betjeman laugh.   PP

'Jonathan Stedall should be congratulated for attempting to preserve Sir John for the nation with this worthy series on the Poet Laureate's work and ways.' – Stanley Reynolds, *Guardian*

Timewatch * (GB since 1982). Monthly magazine re-examining and sometimes revising odd bits of history, usually two or three in each but occasionally devoting the whole hour to one topic, e.g. specials on the Norman Conquest and the 1945 Battle for Berlin. Presented originally by John Tusa, latterly by Peter France. Edited by Bruce Norman, produced by Timothy Gardam, for BBC.   PP

Timothy, Christopher (1940–). British leading man who scored a hit in ALL CREATURES GREAT AND SMALL.

Timothy's Second Diary **
GB 1960 60m bw
Granada (Tim Hewat)

Wonderful idea (by Leslie Halliwell) to show Humphrey Jennings's idealistic little World War II film *A Diary for Timothy* (in which a newborn baby is told about the world into which he will grow) and afterwards chase up its participants to see what had befallen them in

16 years, and how their ideals stood now. My 1960 review: 'The miner had become a pit-head baths superintendent with dusty lungs, the pompous young fighter pilot a relaxed psychiatrist in Canada, the engine driver a retired engine driver (on a railway pension of seven bob a week). And Timothy himself? The drowsy baby born on the eve of Arnhem was now a schoolboy shaping up to his GCE, shy, rather nervous, a hesitant but fairly contented member of the space age.' If the questions posed by Jennings were still hanging – and would be even more so now – it was a reminder of some changes for the better.

d W. Fielding   PP

Tingwell, Charles (1917–). Bland Australian actor; in England during the fifties, he became a familiar face in *Emergency Ward Ten*. Also appeared in *Homicide*.

Tinker, Grant (1926–). American executive, ex-husband of Mary Tyler Moore and in charge of the production company which bore her name but became MTM. 1981: appointed programme controller of NBC.

Tinker, Tailor, Soldier, Spy *
GB 1979 7 × 50m colour
BBC/Paramount (Jonathan Powell)

George Smiley comes back from retirement to track down a traitor in MI5.
Intellectual spy thriller, above the heads of the mass audience but cherished by cultists.

w Arthur Hopcraft, *novel* John Le Carré *d* John Irvin *ph* Tony Pearce-Roberts *m* Geoffrey Burgon

ALEC GUINNESS, Bernard Hepton, Terence Rigby, Michael Aldridge, Ian Richardson, Alexander Knox, George Sewell, Ian Bannen, Michael Jayston, Nigel Stock, Anthony Bate, Hywel Bennett, Siân Phillips

† A sequel, *Smiley's People*, appeared in 1982.

PP: 'Guinness's was an extraordinary performance among a collection of exceptional performances. Guarded, nervous of intimacy, saying little and expressing less, he nevertheless built up with a thousand tiny inflections an indication of the pain of public cuckoldry within him – nearest to the surface in the final, long-deferred meeting with the lady in question, but even then inextricably bound up with the larger weariness of being involved in the affairs of a second-class power which by an accident of history has still to play in the first division of skulduggery.'

Tinniswood, Peter (19 –). British novelist and comedy writer, into TV via radio and *TWTWTW*. At one time in partnership with David Nobbs. Several sitcoms from good to dire, and *Stoker Leishman's Diaries*, *I Didn't Know You Cared* (from his Carter Brandon novels), *The Home Front*, *Tales from a Long Room*, *South of the Border*.   PP

Tiny Revolutions *
GB 1981 110m colour
Granada (Brian Armstrong)

Dramatized account of the arrest, imprisonment and eventual release of Jan Kalina, a Czech professor (of theatre arts) who collected jokes against the regime, published them and put them into a cabaret show at the Tatra Hotel in his home town of Bratislava. At once the most depressing picture of a police state since *1984* and the bravest, or anyway the funniest, demonstration of the individual standing up to it.

w/d Michael Beckham

Freddie Jones, Andrée Melly, Ronald Lacey
                                                                                                          PP

Tiny Tim (1930–) (Herbert David Khoury). Downright weird American falsetto singer who enjoyed some kind of TV fame in the sixties.

Tipton, George Aliceson (1932–). American composer who supplied the themes for *The Courtship of Eddie's Father*, SOAP, *Benson*, *It's a Living*.

'Tis Pity She's a Whore *
GB 1980 120m colour
BBC (Richard Broke)

John Ford's gamey Jacobean tragedy bundled into Victorian dress, presumably to reinforce modish notions about it being rooted in an exaggerated regard for property, while illogically retaining an austerely Jacobean setting. Liberties had also been taken with the text. But a handsome production with an affecting Annabella from Cherie Lunghi and one characterization – Tim Pigott-Smith as the sinister major-domo, Vasques – that did make sense of the Victorianization. As I said at the time: 'With thinning hair, chilly eyes, frock coat and the real manipulation of the household in his hands alone, there was no mistaking him: he would collect his references, change his name and set off for Eaton Square to become Mr Hudson.' Also with Colin Douglas, Kenneth Cranham. Directed by Roland Joffé; photographed by Nat Crosby.   PP

The Titans *
GB 1962 2 × 60m bw
BBC (Therese Denny)

Equally unflattering profiles of the two super-powers, Soviet Russia and the United States, backed up by exceptional film research and caustic commentaries by Malcolm Muggeridge. Who else would have likened starry-eyed Moscow pilgrims like Shaw and Wells to 'vegetarians giving thanks in an abattoir'? PP

T. J. Hooker
US 1982–5 78 × 50m colour
ABC/Columbia/Aaron Spelling

Cases of a detective sergeant and his young associates.
Absolutely routine cop show on the comic-strip level, with tolerability depending on the amount of action packed into each segment. The pilot was shown as *The Protectors* (qv).
William Shatner, Adrian Zmed, Heather Locklear
'A load of clichés, full of stale Spelling–Goldberg trademarks.' – *TV Guide*

To All My Friends on Shore
US 1971 74m colour TVM
Bill Cosby

A black businessman discovers his young son has a fatal illness.
One wonders how dying has suddenly acquired such an appeal. This one is such a star weepie that it's hard to be sympathetic.
w Allan Sloane *d* Gilbert Cates
Bill Cosby, Gloria Foster, Dennis Hines

To Build a Fire *
GB 1970 60m colour
BBC (David Cobham)

Literally chilling little film from a Jack London story, about a Gold Rush prospector in the Klondyke whose survival depends on his lighting a fire. He does, but it goes out . . .
Ian Hogg in the part. PP

† Thirteen years later the film inspired the Canadian series *Tales of the Klondyke*, for which David Cobham acted as consultant and a director.

To Catch a King
US 1984 96m colour TVM
HBO/Gaylord (Robert E. Fuisz)

In 1940 Lisbon, an American café owner defeats a plan to kidnap the Duke and Duchess of Windsor.
Wooden exploitation movie with many similarities to *Casablanca*.

w Roger O. Hirson, *novel* by Harry Patterson *d* Clive Donner *ph* Denis Lewiston *m* Nick Bicat
Robert Wagner, Teri Garr, Horst Janson; John Standing and Barbara Parkins (as the Windsors)
'The idea's great; the execution is numbing.' – *Daily Variety*

To Find My Son
US 1979 96m colour TVM
CBS/Columbia/Green–Epstein (Harry Thomason)

A young man struggles to adopt a small boy. Drawn-out drama with an apparently aberrant hero.
w Sandor Stern *d* Delbert Mann *ph* Gerald Perry Finnermann *m* Ralph Grierson
Richard Thomas, Justin Dana, Molly Cheek, Julie Cobb, Allyn Ann McLerie, Steve Kanaly

To Kill a Cop *
GB title: *Streets of Fear*
US 1978 2 × 96m colour TVM
Columbia/David Gerber

A black terrorist begins a wave of cop killings. Above average crime melodrama.
w Ernest Tidyman, *novel* Robert Daley *d* Gary Nelson
Joe Don Baker, Lou Gossett, Patrick O'Neal, Desi Arnaz Jnr, Christine Belford, Scott Brady, Eddie Egan, Alan Fudge, Eartha Kitt

To Race the Wind
US 1980 96m colour TVM
CBS/Viacom/Walter Grauman (William Kayden)

A blind young man enters university and finds a girl friend.
However authentic, these events are insufficiently dramatic to fill two television hours.
w Carmen Culver, *autobiography* of Harold Krents *d* Walter Grauman *ph* Vincent A. Martinelli *m* John Rubinstein
Steve Guttenberg, Barbara Barrie, Randy Quaid, Mark L. Taylor, Lisa Eilbacher
'I really do believe this movie accomplishes something . . . there's a special spirit in it.' – Harold Krents

To Rome With Love
US 1969–70 48 × 25m colour
CBS/Universal/Don Fedderson (Edmund Hartmann)

A widowed college professor takes his family to live in Rome.

Rather uneasy attempt at a realistic sitcom shot on location.

John Forsythe, Kay Medford (first season), Walter Brennan (second season), Peggy Mondo, Vito Scotti

To See How Far It is
GB 1968 3 × 75m colour (VTR)
BBC *Theatre 625* (Michael Bakewell)

Trilogy by Alan Plater contrasting the attitudes to life of a timorous loner (Norman Rodway) and an extrovert glad-boy (Nigel Davenport) thrown together on an ocean cruise. At the end I wrote: 'In retrospect it was more satisfying than it had been at the time, which is certainly better than the other way round. Nigel Davenport, all teeth and moustache and relentless charm, must be commended for a definitive portrait.' Directed by Roderick Graham, Gilchrist Calder, Naomi Capon.

† The trilogy was rerun in 1970 in the *Play for Today* outlet.   PP

To Serve Them All My Days *
GB 1980 13 × 50m colour
BBC (Ken Riddington)

The life and career of a schoolmaster. Absorbing dramatization for all those who loved *Goodbye Mr Chips*.

w Andrew Davies, *novel* R. F. Delderfield d Ronald Wilson m Kenyon Emrys-Roberts
John Duttine, Frank Middlemass, Alan MacNaughtan

To Tell the Truth (US 1956–66). Half-hour quiz show for CBS, in which contestants had to guess which of three people best fitted MC Bud Collyer's description.

To the Ends of the Earth *
GB 1983 96m colour
Armand Hammer (Kenneth Locker)

An account of the three-year trek, including the north pole, of the Trans-Globe Expedition led by Sir Ranulph Fiennes. A documentary as good as the restrictions of the journey would allow.

w,d WILLIAM KRONICK ph MIKE HOOVER
narrator Richard Burton

To the Lighthouse *
GB 1983 120m
BBC/Colin Gregg Films (Alan Shallcross)

Virginia Woolf's autobiographical novel lovingly and languidly filmed, with Rosemary Harris as the serene centre of the holiday household, Michael Gough its irascible but warm-hearted head, and World War I grimly intervening towards the end.

w Hugh Stoddart d Colin Gregg
Rosemary Harris, Michael Gough, Suzanne Bertish, Pippa Guard, Lynsey Baxter, Kenneth Branagh, T. P. McKenna   PP

To the Manor Born * (GB 1979–81). Vehicle for Penelope Keith following her acclaim in *The Good Life* which quickly demonstrated a life of its own. The imperious Miss Keith was now a widowed lady of the manor who had to sell up and move to a dower house nearby, Peter Bowles the *nouveau riche* who occupied her old home. Created by Peter Spence; produced by Gareth Gwenlan; for BBC.   PP

LH: 'Although I always found Miss Keith eminently resistible, the series probably deserves its star for Peter Bowles, also for zooming to the top of the ratings and staying there.'

Tobias, George (1901–80). American character actor. TV series: *Hudson's Bay*, *Adventures in Paradise*, *Bewitched*.

Today. NBC's easy-going morning news and chat show, which airs each weekday between 7 a.m. and 9 a.m.

Today's F.B.I.
US 1981 96m colour TVM
ABC/Columbia/David Gerber (Fred Caruso)

The owner of a Boston shipping company is threatened by union mobsters.
Comic-strip bang-bang adventure pointing up the infallibility of Uncle Sam's men. The resulting series ran, or limped along, to 13 × 50m episodes.

cr Jerry Ludwig d Virgil Vogel
Mike Connors, Joseph Cali, Tony Lo Bianco, Carol Potter, Paul Sorvino

Todd, Bob (1922–). Beaming, balding, gurgling British comic actor who was a popular stooge to Benny Hill and others but failed in his own series *In For A Penny*.

Tolstoy, Count Leo (1828–1910). The classic author who peculiarly belongs to the screen age, the circumstances of his death in a lonely Russian railway station having been recorded on one of the earliest bits of *vérité* film ever shot. It turns up regularly in historical compilations and may have inspired J. B. Priestley's TV play *Now Let Him Go*. More orthodoxly, *War and Peace* and *Anna Karenina* have been expensive BBC serials,

but probably the finest single piece of transference to the screen is Russian TV's *A Prisoner in the Caucasus* shown by the BBC. Tolstoy has been twice assessed on television by Malcolm Muggeridge, in *Riches to Rags* (BBC 1972) and *The Third Testament* (CBC, 1974).   PP

The Tom and Jerry Show
US 1975 17 × 22m colour
Hanna–Barbera

Debased version of the classic cartoon characters: poor drawing, no violence, bad jokes. The original cartoons, thankfully, remain in circulation.

Tom, Dick and Mary (US 1964). Shortlived half-hour comedy which ran as part of *90 Bristol Court*. Don Galloway and Joyce Bulifant were a young couple who eked out their finances by boarding the husband's best friend (Steve Franken).

The Tom Ewell Show *
US 1960 26 × 25m bw
CBS/Four Star/Ewell/Carroll/Martin

Misadventures of a real estate agent whose home has 'wall-to-wall women'.
Friendly, competent and amusing domestic sitcom.

TOM EWELL, Marilyn Erskine, MABEL ALBERTSON

Tom Sawyer
US 1975 74m colour TVM

Adventures of a trouble-prone small boy in a town on the banks of the Mississippi.
A plain, even homely, version of the famous tale by Mark Twain.

w Jean Holloway *d* James Neilson

Buddy Ebsen, Jane Wyatt, Vic Morrow, John McGiver, Josh Albee, Jeff Tyler

Toma *
GB title: *Man of Many Faces*
US 1972 74m colour TVM
ABC/Universal (Earl A. Glick, Trevor Wallace)

Adventures of an undercover cop with a penchant for disguise.
Effective police melodrama with plenty of action sequences.

w Edward Hume, Gerald di Pego *d* Richard T. Heffron

Tony Musante, Susan Strasberg, Simon Oakland, Nick Colasanto, Abe Vigoda, Dave Toma

† There followed a series of 24 × 50m episodes (producers: Roy Huggins, Jo Swerling, Stephen J. Cannell), after which the star resigned and the project was redesigned as *Baretta*.

Tombstone Territory *
US 1957–9 91 × 25m bw
ABC/Ziv

A sheriff and an editor combine to tame 'the town too tough to die'.
Absolutely standard western, quite pleasantly made.

Pat Conway, Richard Eastham

Tomlin, Lily (1939–). American character comedienne who became known in *Laugh-In*; in 1972 won an Emmy for her own comedy special.

Tomorrow's World *. A 25-minute BBC studio series which every season from 1957 presented instances of advanced scientific gadgets which would eventually aid the public. For more than 20 years Raymond Baxter was the linkman.

Tongues of Fire (GB 1985; 6 × 60m). Contemporary poets (Seamus Heaney, Peter Levi, Czeslaw Milosz, Craig Raine, D. M. Thomas, Derek Walcott) reading their choice of poems before a captive audience. Presented by Karen Armstrong, produced by Bruce Pulling for Griffin Productions/C4.

The Tongues of Men *
GB 1977 120m colour
BBC

Impressive speculation by the formidable George Steiner as to why human speech had fragmented into so many thousands of different tongues, and assessment of the prospect of a universal language evolving – or rather the threat of same, for the likeliest candidate he saw emerging was the flat, lifeless American–English of international jargon: the 'Great Bulldozer', he called it. PP

Tonight. This title has been used for many magazine programmes, notably the BBC's light-hearted early evening one of the fifties, with Cliff Michelmore, and its more sober late evening version of the seventies. In America since 1954 it has heralded a late-night chat show, first with Steve Allen, then with Jack Paar, and from 1961 with Johnny Carson.
PP: 'The BBC's early-evening version (1957–65) produced by Donald Baverstock and Alasdair Milne, introduced an entirely new, breezy approach to topical affairs, and also set

on their way such reporters as Alan Whicker, Derek Hart and Fyfe Robertson, such film-makers as Jack Gold and Michael Tuchner. In 1982 the programme's beginning was marked by a 25th anniversary special produced by Tom Savage, when I wrote: "I once called *Tonight* the BBC's Geisha, meaning that its function was to welcome the homecoming worker and to soothe him with gossip, jokes, tid-bits of interest so that he would remain contentedly watching the same channel the rest of the evening. I no longer think this image very apt, especially after learning from *The Shogun Inheritance* that the Geisha's sexual favours can on occasion be purchased. I am sure this was not true of the *Tonight* team. But it is interesting that Cliff wound up this memoir with a nice phrase about the programme's eight-year 'conversation' with its audience. It did have that, it did." '

Tony Bennett at the Talk of the Town
GB 1972 13 × 30m colour (VTR)

Thames lured him over for a series with guest stars and occasional bits of British scenery, with a view to exporting it back to America. At the time I wrote: 'The last of the gang that sang its way out of the ghettos, an old-fashioned he-man for whom hitting the right note is as throwing a punch or driving a ball or treating a lady friend to a little male chauvinism: something to be done squarely and truly and apparently without effort.'   PP

The Tony Randall Show
US 1976–7 44 × 25m colour
ABC/Mary Tyler Moore

The professional and home life of a widowed judge.
Nothing new, and the star seemed a little uneasy in this extreme contrast from his Felix in *The Odd Couple*.

cr Tom Patchett, Jay Tarses
Tony Randall, Allyn McLerie

Too Far to Go *
US 1979 96m colour TVM
CBS/Sea Cliff (Robert Geller)

Scenes from the dissolution of a 20-year marriage.
Unusual, slim but effective adult concept based on 17 stories by John Updike.

w William Hanley *d* Fielder Cook *ph* Walter Lassally *m* Elizabeth Swados
Michael Moriarty, Blythe Danner

Too Late to Talk to Billy * (GB 1982; 85m). Kenneth Branagh, later to be a much-hailed Royal Shakespeare actor,

played the name part in this first instalment of Graham Reid's trilogy of plays about growing up in embattled Northern Ireland, much praised for their fidelity. Also with James Ellis (as Billy's father), Brid Brennan and (in the final piece) Gwen Taylor. The two following plays were: *A Matter of Choice for Billy*, 1983, and *A Coming to Terms for Billy*, 1984. Directed by Paul Seed, produced by Chris Parr, for BBC Northern Ireland. PP

Too Long a Sacrifice * (GB 1984; 120m).
Deceptively tranquil Northern Ireland documentary in which ordinary citizens, both Nationalist and Loyalist, murmur liberal – even acceptant – sentiments about finding peace. Film-maker Michael Grigsby achieved it by returning to the same corner of County Derry over a two-year period. At the time it seemed a hopeful as well as a beautiful film; two years on, it begins to lose both qualities. For Central.   PP

Too Long a Winter **
GB 1973 52m colour
YTV (Barry Cockcroft)

Famous documentary directed by Barry Cockcroft about life in upland Yorkshire: a spinster farming 80 bleak acres single-handed, Hannah Hauxwell, became an overnight folk heroine. My 1973 review: 'The glimpses of this extraordinary ordinary life, all alone in a farmhouse without electricity or water, were tantalizingly brief – but it was truly beautifully filmed by the good old Yorkshire cameraman Mostafa Hammuri and a perfect example of a regional company striking gold in its own back-yard.'   PP

Too Many Thieves
US 1966 95m colour TVM
Filmways/Mayo (Richard Alan Simmons)

A New York attorney helps ransom a priceless Middle Eastern treasure stolen from its shrine.
Would-be-funny rigmarole that outstays its welcome, adapted from episodes of a TV series *The Trials of O'Brien*.

w George Bellak *d* Abner Biberman
Peter Falk, Britt Ekland, Elaine Stritch, David Carradine, Nehemiah Persoff, Joanna Barnes, Pierre Olaf, George Coulouris, Ludwig Donath

Took, Barry (1928–). Endearing British humorist, originally a stand-up comic and radio writer. For TV wrote *The Army Game*, *Bootsie and Snudge* and *Marty* with Marty Feldman; *Horne a Plenty* for Kenneth Horne, adapted Beachcomber and other Fleet Street humorists, was briefly head of light entertainment at LWT. Now best known as presenter of *Points of View*.   PP

Toomey, Regis (1902–). Familiar Irish–American character actor, in Hollywood from the early thirties. TV series: *Hey Mulligan*, *Richard Diamond*, *Shannon*, *Dante*, *Burke's Law*.

Top Cat *
GB title: *Boss Cat*
US 1961–2 30 × 25m colour
ABC/Hanna–Barbera

Life among the alley cats of New York City. An amusing take-off of Sergeant Bilko, with draughtsmanship from the company's better days.

Top Cs and Tiaras (GB 1983; 60m). Non-stop songfest of numbers drawn from operetta and musical theatre, with opera star Julia Migenes-Johnson leading the company. One of Channel 4's first popular successes, spawning *Top Cs and Tiaras II* later the same year and a series in 1984. PP

'To find the ultimate thrill you must take the ultimate risk!'
The Top of the Hill
US 1980 2 × 96m colour
Operation Prime Time/Paramount/
 Fellows–Keegan (John Cutts)

Deserted by his wife, an adventurous executive finds new life at a ski lodge.
Soap opera study of an unlikeable hero, competently presented and instantly forgettable.

w Eric Bercovici, *story* Irwin Shaw *d* Walter Grauman *ph* Andrew Laszlo *m* George Duning
Wayne Rogers, Elke Sommer, Adrienne Barbeau, Sonny Bono, Peter Brown, J. D. Cannon, Paula Prentiss, Mel Ferrer, Gary Lockwood, Macdonald Carey

'Close to substantial if not commanding.' – *Daily Variety*

Top of the Pops (GB since 1963). BBC weekly pop charts review, for many years an institution, these days just another outlet for pop videos. Most typical presenter: Jimmy Savile. 1000th edition, May 1983. PP

Top of the World (GB 1982). Intercontinental quiz show clearly modelled on *Mastermind* but with contestants in London, Sydney and Miami linked by satellite and a final section in each round in which they competed against each other; special delay circuits had to be incorporated so that all three would hear the question and be able to signal a reply simultaneously. Despite this elaborate technology and the ultimate prize of a vintage

Rolls-Royce the contest failed to command the esteem accorded to *Mastermind* and never returned. Eamonn Andrews put the questions. Devised and produced by Malcolm Morris; for Thames. PP

Top Secret
US 1978 96m colour TVM
NBC/Sheldon Leonard/Jemmin

An art dealer is really a superspy doing work the CIA won't touch.
Dreary, witless spy capers against exotic backgrounds.
w David Levinson *d* Paul Leaf *ph* Gabor Pogany *m* Ted Macero, Stu Gardner
Bill Cosby, Tracy Reed, Sheldon Leonard, Gloria Foster

† In GB the title was used for *I've Got a Secret* in 1983.

Top Town. Quaint BBC tournament, held annually in the late fifties, between municipal teams of amateur entertainers. My verdict at the time: 'Lots of spurious "production", lots of scurrying around to music, all the emphasis on effect and hardly any on performance.' PP

Topper *
US 1953–4 78 × 25m bw
CBS/Bernard L. Schubert

A respectable banker has ghostly friends.
Reasonably fair copy of the movies: it seemed the height of sophistication when it came out.
Leo G. Carroll, Robert Sterling, Anne Jeffreys, Lee Patrick, Thurston Hall, Kathleen Freeman

Topper
US 1979 96m colour TVM
CBS/Kate Jackson, Andrew Stevens

A staid, henpecked lawyer is harassed by two jovial ghosts.
No real match for the old movies, this bid for a second series simply lacked the necessary style.
w George Kirgo, Maryanne Kasica, Michael Scheff *d* Charles Dubin
Kate Jackson, Andrew Stevens, Jack Warden, Rue McClanahan

Torn Between Two Lovers
US 1979 96m colour TVM
CBS/Alan Landsburg (Tom Kuhn)

A happily married woman falls in love with a suave architect.
Superior sudser depending entirely on the acting; the story would fit on the back of a postage stamp.

w Doris Silverton *d* Delbert Mann *ph* Ron Lautore *m* Ian Fraser

Lee Remick, George Peppard, Joseph Bologna, Murphy Cross

'Ripped from the pages of a 1939 *Redbook* or *Cosmopolitan*.' – *Daily Variety*

Tors, Ivan (1916–). Hungarian–American independent producer whose series have usually involved animals or scientific gadgetry: *The Man and the Challenge*, *Sea Hunt*, *Ripcord*, *Flipper*, *Daktari*, *Primus*, etc.

Totter, Audrey (1918–). Sharp-edged American leading lady of the forties. Later in TV series: *Cimarron City*, *Our Man Higgins*. TV movies: *The Outsider*, *UMC*, *The Nativity*.

A Touch of Grace (US 1973). Half-hour situation comedy for ABC, with Shirley Booth and J. Pat O'Malley as an old couple falling in love. Based on the British (Thames) series *For the Love of Ada*.

A Touch of Scandal *
US 1984 96m colour TVM
CBS/Columbia/Doris Keating

An LA lady counsellor making a bid for the attorney generalship becomes involved in an old scandal.
Watchable suspenser with various unsavoury characters including a stalking killer.

w Richard A. Guttman *d* Ivan Nagy *ph* Fred Koenekamp *m* Sylvester Levey

Angie Dickinson, Tom Skerritt, Jason Miller, Don Murray, Robert Loggia, Stephen Shellen, Lois Foraker, Marta Kober

'No one's going to switch this one off.' – *Daily Variety*

A Touch of the Jumbos ** (GB 1970). American super-tycoon invites his restive European executives aboard a chartered Boeing 747 for a jaunt to Chicago, holding court in the upstairs bar and periodically keeping an eye on the main cabin via closed-circuit TV. The only memorable contribution to an LWT anthology series dreamed up by Wilfred Greatorex to the title of *Big Brother*, and a strikingly original play in its own right by Peter Draper. My 1970 review: 'There's a bravura performance by David Bauer as Rook and a beautifully calculated one by Robert Hardy as his eventual opponent. The dialogue is tough and bouncy and epigrammatic. It's no masterpiece, but masterpieces have always been thin on the ground, and short of a masterpiece I'd soon as have a play like this

as any: imaginative, articulate, cleanly constructed and unafraid to have ideas above its station.'   PP

The Toughest Man in the World
US 1984 96m colour TVM
CBS/Guber–Peters (John Cutts)

A tough guy takes over a youth centre abandoned by a heartless school system.
Empty comedy-drama designed purely as a vehicle for a star who can't act and isn't required to do so.

w James Sangster, Richard A. Guttman *d* Dick Lowry *m* Bill Goldstein

Mr T, Dennis Dugan, John P. Navin Jnr, Lynne Moody, Peggy Pope

Toughlove
US 1985 96m colour TVM
ABC/Charles Fries (Ervin Zavada)

An organization helps parents whose children have teenage drug problems.
Well acted but very predictable propaganda.

w Karen Hall *d* Glenn Jordan *ph* Gayne Rescher *m* Paul Chihara

Lee Remick, Bruce Dern, Jason Patric, Eric Schiff

'Often compelling drama.' – *Daily Variety*

Tourist
US 1980 96m colour TVM
Operation Prime Time/TCF/Castle Combe (David Lawrence)

Adventures of American tourists in Europe.
A failed hope for a series à la *Love Boat*: writing, acting and direction are alike rudimentary.

w Norman Hudis *d* Jeremy Summers *ph* Norman Langley *m* Jack Smalley

Lee Meriwether, Bradford Dillman, Lois Nettleton, Adrienne Barbeau, David Groh, John Ireland, Marisa Berenson

Towards 2000
GB 1964–5 35 × 25m bw
Rediffusion (Guthrie Moir)

Guthrie Moir jumped the gun by some 25 years when he keyed this ambitious adult-education series to the coming second millennium. It was in fact a history of four centuries of technological innovation and how same had influenced ordinary life. But there was some looking ahead to future possibilities, and with its direct exposition by unstuffy academics such as Steven Watson and John Hales, plus a back-up of prescribed reading, viewers' seminars and an optional correspondence course, it anticipated many of the features of the Open University.   PP

'A story of overpowering emotions; a production of overwhelming proportions!'

A Town Like Alice **
Australia 1981 4 × 75m colour

Women are taken prisoner by the Japanese shortly before the fall of Singapore, and a love story blossoms to be fulfilled years later in Alice Springs.
Sufficiently intelligent and supple version of a key novel of World War II.

w Rosemary Anne Sisson and Tom Hegarty, *novel* Nevil Shute d David Stevens

Helen Morse, Bryan Brown, Gordon Jackson, Dorothy Alison, Yuki Shimoda

Townley, Toke (1912–84). British general-purpose actor, often seen as rustics, especially in *Emmerdale Farm*.

T. R. Sloane
aka: *The Man Called Sloane*
US 1981 96m colour TVM
NBC/Quinn Martin (Cliff Gould)

America's answer to James Bond is the number one agent for UNIT, a counter-espionage team reporting directly to the President.
There you have it, or nearly; in fact the expected hit series ran to only 22 episodes.

cr Philip Saltzman

Robert Logan, Ji Tu Cumbuka, Clive Revill, Maggie Cooper, Ann Turkel, Peter Nyberg

Trackdown
US 1957–8 71 × 25m bw
CBS/Four Star

Adventures of an 1870s Texas Ranger.
Adequate action western.

Robert Culp

Trackdown: Finding the Goodbar Killer
US 1983 96m colour TVM
CBS/Columbia/Sonny Grosso, Larry Jacobson

New York police solve the case of the murdered schoolteacher whose story was told in the film *Looking for Mr Goodbar*.
Long-drawn-out case history, with too much spare footage allotted to the problems of the leading cop.

w Albert Ruben d Bill Persky ph Fred Murphy m Stephen Lawrence

George Segal, Shelley Hack, Alan North, Shannon Presby, Tracy Pollan

The Trackers
US 1971 73m colour TVM
Aaron Spelling

A posse depends on a black man to find a murderer.
Unremarkable western.

w Gerald Gaiser d Earl Bellamy

Sammy Davis Jnr, Ernest Borgnine, Julie Adams, Jim Davis, Connie Kreski, Arthur Hunnicutt

Traitor *
GB 1971 75m colour

Dennis Potter's play not about Philby but the kind of person who might have behaved as Philby did. Not wholly convincing, nevertheless a play thick with ideas and images (astonishingly, Potter's 17th), with John le Mesurier side-stepping carefully from his haunted comedy performances to this haunted–serious one and, by being such a familiar of the screen, giving the whole thing a curious and rather valuable quality of being about someone whose picture really was on the front pages a while ago. Directed by Alan Bridges; produced by Graeme McDonald; for BBC (*Play for Today*).   PP

Transplant
US 1980 96m colour TVM
CBS/Time–Life/Douglas Benton

At 35, a forceful executive needs a heart transplant.
Urgent but undramatic case history involving more operational detail than most viewers will be able to stomach. There seems no reason at all to present this in extended fictional form.

w John Gay, *book* Philip Dossick d William A. Graham ph Jordan Cronenweth m Fred Karlin

Kevin Dobson, Melinda Dillon, Granville Van Dusen, Ronny Cox, Bibi Besch

'Wheels spin, blood flows through plastic tubing, the heart itself is exposed to the camera.' – *Daily Variety*

'The intentions are noble, the result unsatisfying.' – *TV Guide*

Trapped **
GB theatrical title: *Doberman Patrol*
US 1973 74m colour TVM
Universal (Richard Irving, Gary L. Messenger)

Department store doors close on a man who has been mugged, and he finds himself at the mercy of vicious guard dogs.
Rather silly but suspenseful melodrama.

w/d Frank de Felitta

James Brolin, Susan Clark, Earl Holliman

Trapped beneath the Sea
US 1974 100m colour TVM
ABC Circle

Four men are running out of oxygen at the bottom of the sea in a mini-sub.

Predictable, well-managed suspenser.

w Stanford Whitmore d William Graham

Lee J. Cobb, Martin Balsam, Joshua Bryant, Paul Michael Glaser

Trauma Center
US 1983 96m colour TVM
ABC/TCF/Glen E. Larson (William F. Phillips)

Cases of a mobile ambulance unit and emergency surgical services attached to a large city hospital.

A show so noisy it's a wonder the patients can hear the doctors' advice: the medics are always yelling at each other. Not a winner at all; the one-hour series lasted 13 episodes.

w Glen Larson, Jerry McNeely d Thomas Carter

James Naughton, Dorian Harewood, Wendie Malick, Bill Randolph, Eileen Heckart, Lou Ferrigno, Arlen Dean Snyder, Jack Bannon

'As for quality, the turkey raffle says it all.' – *Daily Variety*

Travanti, Daniel J. (1940–). American leading actor now familiar as the kingpin of *Hill Street Blues* (Emmy 1982). Also: *A Case of Libel*, *Adam*, *Murrow*.

Travellers in Time (GB 1984; 6 × 30m).
Early exploration and travel films, e.g. the Americans Osa and Martin Johnson on *Flying Safari* through Africa in 1934. Presented by Duncan Carse, produced by Richard Robinson, for BBC.

Travellers' Tales. BBC programme of the late fifties, edited by Brian Branston, which was unique in relying on contributed material, much of it from amateurs – sometimes Branston even loaned out cameras and provided film stock. But if the traveller failed to bring back footage up to professional standards, no show. When BBC2 arrived it was superseded by *The World About Us*.   PP

Travelling Man * (GB 1984–5; 13 × 52m; VTR). Busted police detective wanders the canals of Middle England in a narrow boat in search both of missing drop-out son and of the villain who framed him. Two semi-series cleared up both quests and brought in some sharp incidental adventures among Britain's semi-secret, drug-ridden travelling community. With Leigh Lawson; written by Roger Marshall, produced by Brian Armstrong, for Granada.   PP

The Travels of Jamie McPheeters *
US 1963 26 × 50m bw
ABC/MGM

A young boy's experiences on an 1840s wagon train.

Carefully mounted re-creation of frontier days; emphasis on character rather than action prevented popularity.

From the novel by Robert Lewis Taylor

Kurt Russell, Dan O'Herlihy, Charles Bronson

Travis Logan DA
US 1970 100m colour TVM
Quinn Martin

A DA upsets a murderer's careful plans.

Adequate courtroom job.

d Paul Wendkos

Vic Morrow, Hal Holbrook, Brenda Vaccaro, George Grizzard

Travis McGee
US 1983 96m colour TVM
ABC/Warner/Hajeno (George Eckstein)

An ex-private eye lives on a Florida houseboat; he goes to help a friend and falls for the friend's sister.

Dreamy pilot which aims to be long on atmosphere and short on action, which was disappointing to those expecting mystery and suspense. The anticipated series did not materialize.

w Sterling Silliphant, *novel The Empty Copper Sea* by John D. MacDonald d Andrew V. McLaglen ph Jack Whitman Jnr m Jerrold Immel

Sam Elliott, Gene Evans, Katharine Ross, Richard Farnsworth, Barry Corbin, Geoffrey Lewis, Amy Madigan, Vera Miles, Marshall Teague

'Travis misses the boat.' – *Daily Variety*

Travolta, John (1955–). American leading man who before *Saturday Night Fever* played in several series including *Welcome Back Kotter*, and one TV movie, *The Boy in the Plastic Bubble*.

Treasure Hunt **
Original title: *Chasse au trésor*
GB since 1982 52 × 60m
C4/Chatsworth Televison (Peter Holmans, Malcolm Heyworth)

TREASURE HUNT. One of television's most spectacular game formats came from France and was avidly grabbed by Channel Four. Kenneth Kendall prompts the guests in the studio on the working out of clues which send Anneka Rice off by helicopter in search of hidden treasure. Spectacular aerial views were naturally a feature.

Engagingly elaborate game show in which the contestants at base radio-control a helicopter-borne 'skyrunner' along a trail of clues leading to a modest reward. Adapted from a French (Télé-Union Paris) model, it maintains one of C4's highest ratings and has made a star of the callipygous Anneka Rice, who does the running. With Kenneth Kendall in charge at base plus (latterly) Wincey Willis as adjudicator.   PP

LH: 'Apart from the charms of Miss Rice, the show should gladden the hearts of tourist boards around the country.'

A Tree Grows in Brooklyn
US 1974 74m colour TVM
TCF

A thoughtful young girl grows up in the New York slums at the turn of the century, and watches her ne'er-do-well Irish father die of drink.

Unaffecting remake of the famous film, all too brightly coloured.

w Blanche Hanalis, *novel* Betty Smith *d* Joseph Hardy

Cliff Robertson, Diane Baker, Nancy Malone, James Olson, Pamela Ferdin, Michael-James Wixted

Trethowan, Sir Ian (1922–). British journalist and administrator, director-general of the BBC 1977–82. Originally a political columnist in Fleet Street, into television by way of ITN. BBC *Panorama* and *Gallery*. Managing director, BBC Television, 1975–7, when he acquired his reputation as a steady but cautious leader – 'the first of the small spenders', I wrote in 1976.   PP

Autobiography *Split Screen*, 1984

Trevor, William (1928–). British-domiciled Irish novelist and playwright with a particular understanding of women and old people. *The Old Boys*, from his novel of the same name dramatized by Clive Exton, broke the ice. Since then, a steady stream of plays of his own: *The Baby Sitter* (1965), *The Mark Two Wife* (1969), *The General's Day* (with Alastair Sim, 1972), *Elizabeth Alone* (trilogy, 1981), *Autumn Sunshine* and *Ballroom of Romance* (1982), *Mrs Silly, One of Ourselves* and *The Blue Dress* (1983), *Broken Homes* (1985).

Trevor was subject of a *South Bank Show* study 1983 and of a *Bookmark* interview, by Ian Hamilton, 1986.   PP

The Trial of Chaplain Jensen *
US 1975 74m colour TVM
ABC/TCF (Ron Preissman for Paul Monash)

A naval chaplain is courtmartialled for adultery.
True-life courtroom drama, discreetly scripted.
w Loring Mandel, *book* Andrew Jensen *d* Robert Day
James Franciscus, Joanna Miles, Charles Durning, Lynda Day George

The Trial of Dr Fancy
GB 1964 50m bw (VTR)
ABC (Sydney Newman)

Clive Exton's black comedy actually made in 1962 but not transmitted (for *Armchair Theatre*) until the nation's morale was considered strong enough (or its morals lax enough), when it proved to be a mild lampoon on the law, medicine and human gullibility in which the only questionable taste lay in having a character with a dreadful stammer. But the impediment of two ABC scripts on grounds of taste (the other, *The Big Eat*, was sold to the BBC instead) had the effect of driving Exton away from television for some years, he has said.
d Ted Kotcheff
Nigel Stock, Ronald Hines, Dandy Nichols, Peter Sallis   PP

The Trial of Lee Harvey Oswald *
US 1978 2 × 96m colour TVM
Charles Fries (Richard Freed)

The film supposes that Oswald was never shot by Ruby and that his trial proceeded.
Rather flashy and dramatically suspect fantasy which plays about with facts and despite excellent cameos doesn't really succeed as entertainment.

w Robert E. Thompson, *play* Amram Ducovny, Leon Friedman *d* David Greene *ph* Villis Lopenieks *m* Fred Karlin
Ben Gazzara, Lorne Greene, Frances Lee McCain, Lawrence Pressman, John Pleshette, Marisa Pavan, Mo Malone

The Trial of Richard III ***
GB 1984 225m
LWT (Richard Drewett)

Did he or did he not murder the little Princes in the Tower? The dock was empty, but otherwise the evidence for and against Richard's guilt was put and tested with the full rigour of a high-court trial, a former Lord Chancellor presiding and eminent, if unnamed, QCs engaged. 'A tale from the Madame Tussaud's department of history,' I wrote, 'grippingly re-examined.'
d Graham C. Williams
† Richard was acquitted   PP

Trial Run
US 1969 98m colour TVM
Universal (Jack Laird)

An ambitious lawyer overreaches himself.
Overlong courtroom drama.
w Chester Krumholz *d* William Graham
James Franciscus, Leslie Nielsen, Janice Rule, Diane Baker

The Trials of O'Brien *
US 1965 20 × 50m colour
CBS/Filmways (Richard Alan Simmons)

A flamboyant defence lawyer seems always to get into trouble.
Amusing light mystery series.
Peter Falk, Elaine Stritch, David Burns, Joanna Barnes, Ilka Chase

Triangle. Septet of plays from Granada (1964), each of which was made up of three segments furnished by three different writers. Philip Mackie masterminded. Also the title for a BBC soap opera (1981–4), set aboard usually empty North Sea ferry plying triangular schedule; the first fiction series to put lightweight portable video gear to use, but alas not to any rewarding effect. Luyansha Greer created the format.   PP

The Triangle Factory Fire Scandal *
US 1979 96m colour TVM
NBC/Alan Landsburg/Don Kirshner

In 1911 dozens of people perish in a sweatshop because of poor precautions.
Detailed account of a real incident, worked out like *The Bridge of San Luis Rey*. Compelling period reconstruction.

w Mel and Ethel Brez *d* Mel Stuart *ph* Matthew F. Leonetti *m* Walter Scharf

David Dukes, Tovah Feldshuh, Lauren Frost, Janet Margolin, Tom Bosley, Stephanie Zimbalist, Larry Gelman, Stacey Nelkin

The Tribe
US 1974 74m colour TVM
Universal (George Eckstein)

Problems of cro-magnon man.
Some Universal executive must have had a brainstorm: the result isn't highbrow, it's paralysingly boring.

w Lane Slate *d* Richard A. Colla

Victor French, Warren Vanders, Henry Wilcoxon, Adriana Shaw

Tribes *
GB theatrical title: *The Soldier Who Declared Peace*
US 1970 74m colour TVM
TCF/Marvin Schwarz

A hippie is called up and has a varying relationship with his drill sergeant.
Mildly amusing contemporary comedy.

w Tracy Keenan Wynn, Marvin Schwarz *d* Joseph Sargent *ph* Russell Metty

Darren McGavin, Jan-Michael Vincent, Earl Holliman

Trikonis, Gus (19 –). American director. *The Darker Side of Terror*, *The Last Convertible*, *She's Dressed to Kill*, *Flamingo Road*, *Elvis and the Beauty Queen*, *Twirl*, *Dempsey*, *First Affair*, *Malice in Winderland*.

Trilogy of Terror
US 1975 74m colour TVM
ABC Circle/Dan Curtis

Women have the problems in three strange stories.
Grab-bag of hauntings and neuroses; not exactly compulsive.

w William Nolan, Richard Matheson *d* Dan Curtis

Karen Black (in four roles), Robert Burton, John Karlin, George Gaynes

Trinder, Tommy (1909–). Cheerful British cockney comedian whose prime TV work was as the first host of *Sunday Night at the London Palladium*. In 1981 told his story in *The Old Boy Network*.

Trinity Tales *
GB 1975 6 × 50m colour (VTR)
BBC (David Rose)

Six supporters on their way to a cup final tell tall stories.
A cheeky updating of Chaucer with moments of charm but an overall inability to keep up the pace. Half the length would have been twice as good.

w Alan Plater *d* Tristan de Vere Cole

Bill Maynard, Francis Matthews, Colin Farrell, Susan Littler, Paul Copley

The Tripods *
GB/Australia/US 1984–5 26 × 25m
BBC (Richard Bates)/Channel 7/Talbot

Towering metal creatures rule a future Europe which has reverted to 18th-century rusticity, the people made docile subjects by thought-control implants under the scalp. A few rebels who have escaped the 'capping' ritual strive to overthrow the Tripods.
Effective science fiction serial, especially for the bright-child audience, owing much to solid visual effects.

w Alick Rowe (1984), Christopher Penfold (1985), *novels* John Christopher *d* Graham Theakston, Christopher Barry, Bob Blagden *visual effects* Robin Lobb, Steven Drewett

PP

Tripper's Day (GB 1984; 6 × 25m). Leonard Rossiter's last sitcom (and last appearance of any kind), as an embattled supermarket manager. Written by Brian Cooke, produced by Anthony Parker, for Thames. In the US the idea became *Check It Out*, with Don Adams. PP

The Triumph of the West *
GB 1985 13 × 50m
BBC (Christopher Martin)

How a comparatively small corner of the northern hemisphere impressed its ideas, cults and sciences over the whole world, and continues to do so. A fresh and wider-eyed look at the European ascendancy Lord Clark took for granted in *Civilization*, delivered by Dr John Roberts, historian and university administrator. PP

Trodd, Kenith (19 –). Outstanding British producer, campaigner for filmed drama rather than electronic, and critic of all institutions. A founder member of the independent production unit Kestrel in 1968 and again of PFH Productions in 1978. Responsible for almost all Dennis Potter's plays from *Moonlight on the Highway* onwards, also Jim Allen's *United Kingdom*, *Shadows On Our Skin*, *Caught on a Train*, *The Aerodrome*, etc, etc. PP

trompe l'oeil. Literally, 'deceives the eye'. In television any programme, but usually a play, which appears to be one thing and sooner or later reveals it's something else altogether. *Long Past Glory* (1963), *Heydays Hotel* (1976), *Psy Warriors* (1981).   PP

Tropic
GB 1979 6 × 50m colour
ATV (Greg Smith)
Best-selling novelist Leslie Thomas's novel of exurbanite goings-on, *The Tropic of Ruislip*, was the basis of a serial which so famously bombed in the ratings that programme controllers still blench to remember it. In fact it merely failed to survive being interrupted by the fatuous ITV strike of 1979 and restarted many months later.
d Matthew Robinson
Ronald Pickup, Ronald Lacey, Hilary Tindall, Hilary Pritchard   PP

Tropical Moon Over Dorking. See Home Video

Trouble Comes to Town
US 1972 73m colour TVM
ABC Circle (Everett Chambers)
Racial problems erupt in a small southern town.
Obvious social melodrama.
w David Westheimer *d* Daniel Petrie
Lloyd Bridges, Pat Hingle, Hari Rhodes, Janet McLachlan, Sheree North

Trouble for Two (GB 1958; 4 × 30m). Bizarre sitcom teaming comic reporter Jacqueline Mackenzie and Australian entertainer Lorrae Desmond (decades later to be lynch-pin of the antipodean soap *A Country Practice*) as bachelor girls sharing a flat. Donald Churchill bravely intruded as a male char. Partly written – or re-written – by la Mackenzie and full of unscheduled overtones, it ran to only four of the six episodes originally planned, probably to the relief of the producer Ronnie Marsh; for BBC.   PP

Trouble in High Timber Country
US 1980 96m colour TVM
ABC/Warner/Witt–Thomas (Robert A. Papazian)
The widowed head of a foresting and mining family in the northwest has three sons and a daughter, not to mention numerous grandchildren.
All would have been ready to make storylines if a series had resulted, which it

didn't: the level of writing and characterization was far too low.
w Jeb Rosebrook *d* Vincent Sherman
ph Edward R. Plante *m* George Aliceson Tipton
Eddie Albert, James Sloyan, Belinda Montgomery, Kevin Brophy, Martin Kove, Joan Goodfellow, Robin Dearden, James Sikking, Bettye Ackerman
† The intended series was to be called *The Yeagers*, and there had also been a one-hour pilot starring Andy Griffith

Trouble Shooters
US 1959 26 × 25m bw
NBC/Meridian
Adventures of construction gangs on difficult jobs.
Poor action series: scope too limited.
Keenan Wynn, Bob Mathias

The Trouble With Father
aka: *The Stu Erwin Show*
US 1953–5 126 × 25m bw
Hal Roach Jnr/Roland Reed
The family life of a high school principal.
Predictable star sitcom.
Stuart Erwin, June Collyer

The Troubles
GB 1981 4 × 50m colour/bw
Thames (Richard Broad, Ian Stuttard)
The alternative to Robert Kee's longer and more personal Irish history which went out concurrently on BBC TV. This one, directed by Richard Broad, was terse and cold in tone, if the more powerful of the two. My reaction at the time: 'A professional actress, Rosalie Crutchley, delivers the commentary in a severe, chiding voice, as if the whole sorry chronicle was to have been expected from *men*, and if only women had been in charge it would never have happened. The text, credited to Taylor Downing but drawing on the work of a team of researchers, sometimes skids towards Marxist jargon – "History is called upon to justify", for instance, used twice in one episode. In the same episode there was a real mischievous, misleading usage, that of the contemporary term "security forces" for the British army sent to put down the United Irish rising of 1798. That was done with extreme harshness: the temptation concealed in the words is to think of the British army in Northern Ireland today as equally repressive.'
† The title had previously (1963) been used by Granada for a one-off action-stills history of Ireland 1916–23, produced by Jeremy Isaacs.
                                              PP

The Troubleshooters: see Mogul

Troughton, Patrick (1920–   ). Stocky, tight-lipped British character actor who once played *Dr Who*.

True *
originally known as: *General Electric True*
US 1962 33 × 25m bw
CBS/Jack Webb
Stories from the files of *True Magazine*.
Adequate anthology: the stories, one suspected, were not *quite* true.
host Jack Webb

True Grit: A Further Adventure
US 1978 96m colour TVM
ABC/Paramount (Sandor Stern)
Rooster Cogburn and Mattie Ross continue on their way to Monterey.
Uninspired sequel to a western which was overpraised to begin with. Understandably, no series resulted.
w Sandor Stern *d* Richard Heffron *ph* Steve Larner *m* Earle Hagen
Ben Johnson, Lisa Pelikan, Lee Meriwether, James Stephens
'Charitably, a mistake . . . a ponderous tale, it's told ploddingly.' – *Daily Variety*

Truman at Potsdam: see Meeting at Potsdam

The Truth Game (GB 1983; 52m). The perfectly respectable, if answerable, case against nuclear arms – and their justification to free peoples – ruined by John Pilger's usual accusatory style and self-cancelling arguments. Produced by Alan Lowery, for Central.
† It was answered, effectively, by Max Hastings in the companion-work *The War about Peace*. PP

The Tube (GB since 1982). Raucous but up-to-the-minute rock magazine which goes out live on Channel 4 early Friday evening (the old 'weekend starts here' spot established in the sixties by *Ready Steady Go!*), with occasional specials such as a five-hour *Midsummer Night's Tube*, 1983. Presented by Jools Holland, Paula Yates, Muriel Gray, Gary James. Produced by Tyne-Tees (Malcolm Gerrie and Paul Corley) from Newcastle. PP

Tuchner, Michael (1934–). British director, former film editor, first directing fun items for the early evening *Tonight*, later

documentaries with Whicker, Muggeridge and others. Crossed to drama in 1969 with *Sling Your Hook*. Since then many credits on both sides of the Atlantic, including *Easy Go* (1974), *Barmitzvah Boy* (1976), *The One and Only Phyllis Dixey* (1978), *Summer of My German Soldier* (US 1978), *Parole* (US, 1981). Returned to Whickerwork to shoot the doomed *Fast Boat to China* (1984). PP

Tucker, Colin (1941–). British freelance drama producer, formerly story editor. Several 4 × 25 mini-mini-serials under umbrella title of *Love Story* from late seventies; *Jury* and *The Gathering Seed*, 1983; *Drummonds*, 1985. PP

Tucker, Forrest (1919–). Burly American character actor, ex-vaudevillian. TV series: *Crunch and Des*, *F Troop*, *Dusty's Trail*, *Ghost Busters*.

Tucker's Witch
US 1982 13 × 50m colour
CBS/TCF/Hill–Mandelker (William Bast, Steve Kline, John Thomas Lenox)
A husband is confused when his wife uses her powers of witchcraft to solve murders.
Muddled combination of *Bewitched* and *The Thin Man*; not as good as either.
cr William Bast, Paul Huson
Tim Matheson, Cathryn Hicks, Barbara Barrie
† The original pilot had different actors and was called *The Good Witch of Laurel Canyon*

Tugboat Annie: see The Adventures of Tugboat Annie

Tully
GB 1974 78m colour (16mm) TVM
Thames/Euston Films (James Gatward)
A high-powered insurance investigator chases a gang leader across the world.
Routine pilot for a series which didn't happen.
w Ian Stuart Black *d* James Gatward
Anthony Valentine, Barbara Neilsen, Kevin Miles

Turn of Fate *
US 1957 38 × 25m bw
ABC/Four Star (Robert Fellows)
An anthology series of suspense melodramas which now seem distinguished because of their casts, the original four stars of the production company having amply fulfilled their promise to contribute.
The episodes were as follows:

The Danger by Night (*w* Frederic Brady; *d* Peter Godfrey; with David Niven)

The Tinhorn (*w* Frederic Brady, Floyd Beaver; *d* Lewis Allen; with David Niven, Michael Pate)

On Edge (*w* Frederic Brady, Pat Frank; *d* Tom Gries; with Robert Ryan, Edward Binns)

Circumstantial (*w* Leonard Freeman, Alex Coppel; *d* Andrew McCullough; with David Niven, Angie Dickinson)

Voices in the Fog (*w* Robert Bloomfield; *d* Tay Garnett; with Jack Lemmon)

Silhouette of a Killer (*w* Palmer Thompson, T. E. Brooks; *d* Alvin Ganzer; with Robert Ryan, Beverly Garland)

The Face of Truth (*w* John Q. Copeland; *d* Alvin Ganzer; with Robert Ryan, Catherine McLeod)

Encounter on a Second Class Coach (*w* Robert G. Dennis; *d* Tay Garnett; with Jane Powell, Steve Geray, Stuart Whitman)

Hurricane (*w* Harold Swanton; *d* Tay Garnett; with Jane Powell, Douglas Dick, Virginia Gregg)

Crowd Pleaser (*w* Frederic Brady, William R. Cox; *d* Louis King; with Robert Ryan, Stuart Whitman)

Guests for Dinner (*w* Alec Copple; *d* Robert Sinclair; with Charles Boyer)

Music in the Night (*w* Frederic Brady, Peggy and Lou Shaw; *d* Tay Garnett; with Jane Powell, Peter Hanson)

Days of November (*w* Frederic Brady, Mark Rogers; *d* Alvin Ganzer; with Jack Lemmon, Richard Jaeckel)

In the Dark (*w* Bob Barbash; *d* Robert Florey; with David Niven, Barbara Lawrence)

Night Caller (*w* Philip Saltzman; *d* Robert Florey; with David Niven, Henry Daniell)

Cupid Wore a Badge (*w* Leon Ware; *d* Byron Haskin; with Jane Powell, David Janssen)

The White Flag (*w* Frederic Brady; *d* Robert Florey; with Robert Ryan, Whit Bissell)

Hidden Witness (*w* Bob Barbash; *d* Robert Florey; with Robert Ryan, Michael Pate)

The Victim (*w* Marc Brandel; *d* Robert Florey; with Jack Lemmon, Doe Avedon)

The Lady Takes a Stand (*w* Irving Elman, Philip Salzman; *d* Robert Florey; with Jane Powell, Keith Andes)

The Fatal Charm (*w* George Slavin, Paul Franklin; *d* Thomas Carr; with David Niven, Nita Talbot)

The Loudmouth (*w* Christopher Knopf; *d* Donald McDougall; with Jack Lemmon, Harold J. Stone)

Even a Thief Can Dream (*w* Laszlo Gorog; *d* Robert Florey; with Charles Boyer)

The Seventh Letter (*w* Charles B. Smith; *d* Robert Florey; with Robert Ryan, Virginia Gregg)

A Frame for Mourning (*w* T. E. Brooks; *d* Thomas Carr; with Jane Powell, John Baragrey)

The Clock Struck Twelve (*w* Leonard Freeman, Fred Freiburger; *d* Robert Florey; with Charles Boyer, Nestor Paiva)

My Wife's Next Husband (*w* George F. Slavin; *d* Robert Florey; with David Niven, Jane Daly)

The Giant Step (*w* Leonard Freeman, Floyd Beaver; *d* Robert Florey; with Robert Ryan, Michael Landon)

Most Likely to Succeed (*w* Bob Barbash; *d* Robert Florey; with Jack Lemmon, King Donovan)

The Perfectionist (*w* George F. Slavin; *d* Robert Florey; with Robert Ryan, Frances Rafferty)

Decision by Terror (*w* George F. Slavin; *d* Robert Florey; with David Niven, John McIntire)

Disappearance (*w* Christopher Knopf; *d* Robert Florey; with Jack Lemmon, William Talman)

Johnny Risk (*w* Fred Freiberger; *d* Donald McDougall; with Michael Landon, Alan Hale Jnr, Lew Ayres)

Decoy Duck (*w* John Robinson, Frederic Brady; *d* Robert Florey; with Jane Powell, David Janssen)

Three Years Dark (*w* Fred Freiberger; *d* Robert Florey; with Barbara Stanwyck, Gerald Mohr)

Turnabout (US 1979). Very shortlived attempt to make a 25-minute comedy series out of Thorne Smith's novel about a man and wife who swap bodies. The one joke got it through a feature film, but wasn't enough for a series, especially not with John Schuck and Sharon Gless. Written by Steven Bochco; produced by Sam Denoff; for Universal/NBC. 'A series that might have given our minds a spin settles for easy laughs.' – *TV Guide*

The Turning Point of Jim Malloy **
aka: *Gibbsville*
US 1975 74m colour TVM
NBC/Columbia/David Gerber (Peter Katz)

A troublesome youth settles down as reporter on his hometown paper, in 1940s Pennsylvania.

Thoroughly competent blend of *Peyton Place* and *King's Row*, with fast pace, excellent acting, and most of the old Hollywood skills in evidence. A series resulted in 1976, but disappointed. See *Gibbsville*.

w/d FRANK D. GILROY, *novel* John O'Hara

JOHN SAVAGE, GIG YOUNG, Biff McGuire, Kathleen Quinlan, Janis Paige

Turnover Smith
US 1983 74m colour TVM
ABC/Wellington/William Conrad (Everett Chambers)

A specialist in criminal law seeks a chess-playing killer.

Misfired pilot about a legal Nero Wolfe. Contrived but amiable.

w Richard Jessup d Bernard L. Kowalski ph Matthew F. Leonetti m Bernardo Segall
William Conrad, Belinda J. Montgomery, Hilly Hicks, James Darren, Michael Parks, Cameron Mitchell, Tracy Reed, Nehemiah Persoff, Nita Talbot

Turns (GB 1982; 6 × 40m). Music hall greats of the thirties and forties recalled by an enthusiast, comedy writer Jimmy Perry. Produced by Donald Sayer, for BBC.

Turtle's Progress (GB 1979). ATV series about comic crooks who nick a hoard of safe-deposit boxes from a bank. Opening up one in each episode they sought to profit (by blackmail or otherwise) from the contents, thus setting up a fresh little story. With John Landry, Michael Attwell. Written by Edmund Ward.   PP

Tusa, John (1936–). Czech-born British reporter-presenter, into TV via radio's *The World Tonight*. *Newsweek* and *Newsnight*, 1978–86, *Timewatch*, 1982–4. Now heads BBC's External (radio) services.   PP

Tutin, Dorothy (1930–). 'Elfin British actress who grew positively voluptuous in the service of the classics,' I said after her Goneril in the Olivier/Granada *Lear*. Other credits over the years range from *Antigone* and *Colombe* in the fifties through *South Riding* and *Sister Dora* to *Ghosts*, *The Father* and *A Kind of Alaska* in the eighties.   PP

TV Eye (GB 1978–86). Pointless change of title for the respected *This Week* after 22 years. My opinion at the time: '*TV Eye* sounds like a fashionable ophthalmic affliction or the chat column in back copies of the *TV Times*. The first bumper number devoted to the extra-uterine conception baby Louise Taylor was nicely done but mainly a triumph for whoever signed the cheque that gave Thames the rights.'   PP

† In 1986 the wheel swung full circle and it was replaced by a new version of *This Week*.

TV Hour of Stars: see The Twentieth Century-Fox Hour

Twelve O'Clock High *
US 1964–5 78 × 50m bw (last 17 in colour)
ABC/Quinn Martin/TCF

Pressure problems for officers commanding USAF squadrons in Britain during World War II.

A fair copy of the movie, but the long run brought many irrelevant episodes.

Robert Lansing (first 31 films), Paul Burke (after that)

Twentieth Century (US 1957–70). Long-running current affairs series for CBS, hosted by Walter Cronkite.

The Twentieth Century Remembered (GB 1985). Memoirs by various elders, usually over 2 × 35m, e.g. Dora Russell (Bertrand's surviving wife), coaxed by Sally Hardcastle, Barbara Cartland talking to Donald McCormick. Produced by John Walker.

The Twentieth Century-Fox Hour
aka: *TV Hour of Stars*
US 1955 49 × 50m bw
CBS/TCF

Allegedly an anthology of mini-features, this in fact contained many thirties second features chopped down to length. New productions largely consisted of hasty retreads of successful Fox movies such as *Portrait for Murder* (*Laura*), *City in Flames* (*In Old Chicago*), *The Hefferan Family* (*Chicken Every Sunday*), *Lynch Mob* (*The Ox Bow Incident*), *Meet Mr Kringle* (*Miracle on 34th Street*), *Death Paints a Legacy* (*Christopher Bean*), *Operation Cicero* (*Five Fingers*). The stock footage was more entertaining than the new shooting.

28 Up ** (GB 1984; 1 × 28, 2 × 75m). A re-run of Derek Granger's 1964 *Seven Up* in which 14 assorted seven-year-olds lisped their innocent expectations, followed by two progress reports drawing on interim up-dates

(*Seven Plus Seven* in 1971, *Twenty One* in 1978) and new footage as the subjects were entering their 28th year. All but two co-operated; many had fulfilled their predictions for themselves with uncanny precision, but for half the sample life had taken unexpected turns, if none quite so dramatic as those that had elevated the humble researcher on the original programme and director of all the follow-ups, Michael Apted, to eminence as a Hollywood moviemaker. He still came back to make this one. BAFTA Robert Flaherty Award.   PP

The 25th Man/Ms.
US 1981 74m colour TVM
ABC/Universal/Jack Webb (William Stark)
A trainee policewoman is stalked by a Peeping Tom killer.
Not a pretty sight; a woefully inept pilot with an impossible title.
w Sean Baine d Daniel Haller
Ellen Regan, Pepe Serna, Robert Lee Jarvis, Ed Winter

24-Hour Call (GB 1963). Stage Three in ATV's tradition of medical fiction which endured from *Emergency – Ward 10* in 1957 to *General Hospital* in 1979. Here, the family doctors of *Call Oxbridge 2000* were shoved into group practice – shiny new surgery, two-way car radio, much diagnostic bickering, same old plots.   PP

24 Hours. BBC nightly current affairs show from 1965 until it was replaced by *Midweek*, going out Tuesday, Wednesday and Thursday only. The usual mix of film stories, interviews, discussion and 'down the line' links to provincial and foreign centres was held together by a succession of anchormen, of whom Cliff Michelmore, Kenneth Allsop and Ludovic Kennedy were the most resilient. The final change of designation was to *Tonight*. PP

Twenty-One. A quiz show popular in America and Britain in the fifties, vaguely based on blackjack and involving rival contestants in sealed booths. A major scandal was unleashed when it was revealed that in order to maintain suspense some contestants had been told the answers beforehand. On NBC; the British version ran on Granada.

21 Beacon Street
US 1959 34 × 25m bw
NBC/Filmways
A private eye has two young assistants.
Absolutely routine detection hokum.
Dennis Morgan, Brian Kelly, Jim Mahoney

21 Hours at Munich
US 1976 96m colour TVM
ABC/Filmways/Moonlight (Edward S. Feldman)
A reconstruction of the attack on Israeli athletes at the 1972 Olympic games.
Rather less thrilling, and much less thought-provoking, than the real thing.
w Edward Hume, Howard Fast d William A. Graham
William Holden, Franco Nero, Richard Basehart, Shirley Knight, Anthony Quayle, Noel Willman

26 Men
US 1957–8 78 × 25m bw
Russell Hayden/NBC
True stories of the Arizona Rangers around 1900.
Adequate western adventures.
Tris Coffin, Kelo Henderson

Twenty-Twenty Vision (GB 1982–3). Channel 4's weekly 'flagship current affairs programme' came at first from an all-women outfit, okay on timeless topics but not hard-nosed enough about being newsy. Its place was taken by *Diverse Reports*. Produced by Lyn Gamble and Claudia Milne.   PP

Twice a Fortnight
GB 1967 approx. 12 × 30m bw
BBC (Tony Palmer)
Wild and woolly comedy series con-temporaneous with *At Last the 1948 Show* and from the same radio roots. But its leading clowns, Bill Oddie, Graeme Garden and Tim Brooke-Taylor, developed rather differently, becoming The Goodies.   PP

Twice in a Lifetime
US 1974 74m colour TVM
Martin Rackin
A retired navy cook in San Pedro operates his own salvage tugboat.
Easy-going family comedy–drama.
w Martin Rackin d Herschel Daugherty
Ernest Borgnine, Della Reese, Arte Johnson, Slim Pickens, Herb Jeffries, Vito Scotti

twice-done TV plays. Of the thousands of good, bad and indifferent British television scripts over the years only a handful of single plays and serials have been produced at different times with different directors and different casts.
They include:

28 UP. Three wives/mothers see themselves at 14 . . . and also, in the programme, at seven, for Granada's cameras have been following them every seven years since then.

Iain McCormick: *The Liberators* (1954/64); Nigel Kneale: *1984* (1954/64); Kenneth Hyde: *The Last Reunion* (1955/65); Arthur Hailey: *Flight into Danger* (1956/62) and *Time Lock* (1958/72); Alun Owen: *No Tram to Lime Street* (1959/65 plus musical version 1970), *The Rose Affair* (1961/65) and *Park People* (1967/78 *); Clive Exton: *Where I Live* (1960/65) and *Hold My Hand Soldier* (1960/65); Harold Pinter: *Night School* (1960/78 *), *The Collection* (1961/76) and *The Lover* (1963/78); Peter Nichols: *Ben Spray* (1961/72); David Mercer: *For Tea on Sunday* (1963/78); Ray Jenkins: *The Bonus* (1968/78 *); Antony Skene: *The File on Harry Jordan* (1967/78 *); Paul Jones: *The English Climate* (1967/78 *); John Mortimer: *A Voyage Round My Father* (1969/82); Ronald Eyre/Nikolai Leskov: *A Crack in the Ice* (1964/85).

Those marked * were produced the second time by Peter Willes, retiring YTV head of drama, as a deliberate series of revivals. Among serials were Giles Cooper's version of *Madame Bovary* (1964/75), and Donald Wilson's *The Six Proud Walkers* (1954/62).

PP

Twilight Zone **
US 1959–63 134 × 25m, 17 × 50m bw
CBS/Cayuga
Stories of space, time and the imagination. Despite a good deal of repetition, this was a series with real mood, skill and intelligence, the kind of pacy imaginative entertainment which TV has since forgotten how to do. The series borrowed fearlessly from such writers as H. G. Wells and John Collier, and was probably most at home in dealing with time warps. Two typical, and excellent, episodes are *Where Is Everybody*, in which an astronaut

imagines he is the only person on earth (he is spending a week in a space test capsule) and *A Hundred Yards Over the Rim*, in which Cliff Robertson, as a covered wagonner stranded in the desert, comes across a modern roadside café and takes back some aspirin to cure his daughter's fever. The one-hour episodes didn't work, whereas *The Outer Limits*, a series similar in intent, was more at home with the extra length.

cr/host ROD SERLING

The half-hour episodes, in sequence, were as follows:

Where Is Everybody? (*w* Rod Serling; *d* Robert Stevens; with Earl Holliman)

One for the Angels (*w* Rod Serling; *d* Robert Parish; with Ed Wynn)

Mr Denton on Doomsday (*w* Rod Serling; *d* Allen Reisner; with Dan Duryea)

The Sixteen Millimeter Shrine (*w* Rod Serling; *d* Mitchell Leisen; with Ida Lupino)

Walking Distance (*w* Rod Serling; *d* Robert Stevens; with Gig Young)

Escape Clause (*w* Rod Serling; *d* Mitchell Leisen; with David Wayne)

The Lonely (*w* Rod Serling; *d* Jack Smight; with Jack Warden)

Time Enough At Last (*w* Lynn Venable; *d* John Brahm; with Burgess Meredith)

Perchance to Dream (*w* Charles Beaumont; *d* Robert Florey; with Richard Conte)

Judgment Night (*w* Rod Serling; *d* John Brahm; with Nehemiah Persoff)

And When the Sky Was Opened (*w* Richard Matheson; *d* Douglas Heyes; with Rod Taylor)

What You Need (*w* Lewis Padgett; *d* Alvin Ganzer; with Steve Cochran)

The Four of Us Are Dying (*w* George Johnson; *d* John Brahm; with Harry Townes)

Third from the Sun (*w* Richard Matheson; *d* Richard Bare; with Fritz Weaver)

I Shot an Arrow in the Air (*w* Madeleine Champion; *d* Stuart Rosenburg; with Edward Binns)

The Hitchhiker (*w* Lucille Fletcher; *d* Alvin Ganzer; with Inger Stevens)

The Fever (*w* Rod Serling; *d* Alvin Ganzer; with Everett Sloane)

The Last Flight (*w* Richard Matheson; *d* William Claxton; with Kenneth Haigh)

The Purple Testament (*w* Rod Serling; *d* Richard Bare; with William Reynolds)

Elegy (*w* Charles Beaumont; *d* Douglas Heyes; with Cecil Kellaway)

Mirror Image (*w* Rod Serling; *d* John Brahm; with Vera Miles)

The Monsters Are Due on Maple Street (*w* Rod Serling; *d* Ron Winston; with Claude Akins, Jack Weston)

A World of Difference (*w* Richard Matheson; *d* Ted Post; with Howard Duff)

Long Live Walter Jameson (*w* Charles Beaumont; *d* Tony Leader; with Kevin McCarthy, Estelle Winwood)

People Are Alike All Over (*w* Paul Fairman; *d* Mitchell Leisen; with Roddy McDowall)

Execution (*w* Rod Serling; *d* David Orrick; with Albert Salmi)

The Big Tall Wish (*w* Rod Serling; *d* Ron Winston; with Steven Perry)

A Nice Place to Visit (*w* Charles Beaumont; *d* John Brahm; with Sebastian Cabot)

Nightmare as a Child (*w* Rod Serling; *d* Alvin Ganzer; with Janice Rule)

A Stop at Willoughby (*w* Rod Serling; *d* Robert Parrish; with James Daly)

The Chaser (*w* Robert Presnell Jnr; *d* Douglas Heyes; with John McIntire)

A Passage for Trumpet (*w* Rod Serling; *d* Don Medford; with Jack Klugman)

Mr Bevis (*w* Rod Serling; *d* Robert Parrish; with Orson Bean)

The After Hours (*w* Rod Serling; *d* Douglas Heyes; with Anne Francis)

The Mighty Casey (*w* Rod Serling; *d* Alvin Ganzer; with Jack Warden)

A World of His Own (*w* Richard Matheson; *d* Ralph Nelson; with Keenan Wynn)

King Nine Will Not Return (*w* Rod Serling; *d* Buzz Kulik; with Bob Cummings)

The Man in the Bottle (*w* Rod Serling; *d* Don Medford; with Luther Adler)

Nervous Man in a Four Dollar Room (*w* Rod Serling; *d* Douglas Heyes; with Joe Mantell)

A Thing About Machines (*w* Rod Serling; *d* Douglas Heyes; with Richard Haydn)

The Howling Man (*w* Rod Serling; *d* Douglas Heyes; with John Carradine)

The Eye of the Beholder (*w* Rod Serling; *d* Douglas Heyes; with Joanna Hayes)

Nick of Time (*w* Richard Matheson; *d* Richard Bare; with William Shatner)

The Lateness of the Hour (*w* Rod Serling; *d* Jack Smight; with Inger Stevens)

The Trouble with Templeton (*w* E. Jack Neuman; *d* Buzz Kulik; with Brian Aherne)

A Most Unusual Camera (*w* Rod Serling; *d* John Rich; with Jean Carson, Fred Clark)

Night of the Meek (*w* Rod Serling; *d* Jack Smight; with Art Carney)

Dust (*w* Rod Serling; *d* Douglas Heyes; with Thomas Gomez)

Back There (w Rod Serling; d David Orrick McDearmon; with Russell Johnson)

The Whole Truth (w Rod Serling; d James Sheldon; with Jack Carson)

The Invaders (w Richard Matheson; d Douglas Heyes; with Agnes Moorehead)

A Penny for Your Thoughts (w George Clayton Johnson; d James Sheldon; with Dick York)

Twenty Two (w Rod Serling; d Jack Smight; with Barbara Nichols)

The Odyssey of Flight 33 (w Rod Serling; d Justus Addiss; with John Anderson)

Mr Dingle, the Strong (w Rod Serling; d John Brahm; with Burgess Meredith)

Static (w Charles Beaumont; d Buzz Kulik; with Dean Jagger)

The Prime Mover (w Charles Beaumont; d Richard Bare; with Dane Clark, Buddy Ebsen)

Long Distance Call (w Charles Beaumont, William Idelson; d James Sheldon; with Philip Abbott)

A Hundred Yards Over the Rim (w Rod Serling; d Buzz Kulik; with Cliff Robertson)

The Rip Van Winkle Caper (w Rod Serling; d Justus Addiss; with Simon Oakland)

The Silence (w Rod Serling; d Boris Sagal; with Franchot Tone)

Shadow Play (w Charles Beaumont; d John Brahm; with Dennis Weaver)

The Mind and the Matter (w Rod Serling; d Buzz Kulik; with Shelley Berman)

Will the Real Martian Please Stand Up? (w Rod Serling; d Montgomery Pittman; with John Archer)

The Obsolete Man (w Rod Serling; d Elliot Silverstein; with Burgess Meredith)

Two (w/d Montgomery Pittman; with Elizabeth Montgomery, Charles Bronson)

The Arrival (w Rod Serling; d Boris Sagal; with Harold J. Stone)

The Shelter (w Rod Serling; d Lamont Johnson; with Larry Gates)

The Passers-By (w Rod Serling; d Elliot Silverstein; with James Gregory)

A Game of Pool (w George Clayton Johnson; d A. E. Houghton; with Jack Klugman)

The Mirror (w Rod Serling; d Don Medford; with Peter Falk)

The Grave (w/d Montgomery Pittman; with Lee Marvin, Strother Martin, Lee Van Cleef)

It's a Good Life (w Rod Serling; d James Sheldon; with Cloris Leachman)

Deathshead Revisited (w Rod Serling; d Don Medford; with Joseph Schildkraut)

The Midnight Sun (w Rod Serling; d Tony Leader; with Lois Nettleton)

Still Valley (w Rod Serling; d James Sheldon; with Gary Merrill)

The Jungle (w Charles Beaumont; d William Claxton; with John Dehner)

Once Upon a Time (w Richard Matheson; d Norman Z. McLeod; with Buster Keaton)

Five Characters in Search of an Exit (w Rod Serling; d Lamont Johnson; with William Windom)

A Quality of Mercy (w Rod Serling; d Buzz Kulik; with Dean Stockwell)

Nothing in the Dark (w George Clayton Johnson; d Lamont Johnson; with Gladys Cooper, Robert Redford)

One More Pallbearer (w Rod Serling; d Lamont Johnson; with Joseph Wiseman)

Dead Man's Shoes (w Charles Beaumont; d Montgomery Pittman; with Warren Stevens)

The Hunt (w Earl Hamner; d Harold Schuster; with Arthur Hunnicutt)

Showdown with Rance McGrew (w Rod Serling; d Christian Nyby; with Larry Blyden)

Kick the Can (w George Clayton Johnson; d Lamont Johnson; with Ernest Truex)

A Piano in the House (w Earl Hamner; d David Greene; with Barry Morse, Joan Hackett)

To Serve Man (w Rod Serling; d Richard Bare; with Richard Kiel, Hardie Albright)

The Last Rites of Jeff Myrtlebank (w Montgomery Pittman; d Lamont Johnson; with James Best)

The Fugitive (w Charles Beaumont; d Richard Bare; with J. Pat O'Malley)

Little Girl Lost (w Richard Matheson; d Paul Stewart; with Sarah Marshall, Robert Sampson)

Person or Persons Unknown (w Charles Beaumont; d John Brahm; with Richard Long)

The Gift (w Rod Serling; d Allan Parker; with Geoffrey Horne)

The Little People (w Rod Serling; d William Claxton; with Claude Akins)

Four O'Clock (w Rod Serling; d Lamont Johnson; with Theodore Bikel)

The Trade-Ins (w Rod Serling; d John Brahm; with Joseph Schildkraut)

Hocus Pocus and Frisby (w Rod Serling; d Lamont Johnson; with Andy Devine)

The Dummy (w Rod Serling; d Abner Biberman; with Cliff Robertson)

The Changing of the Guard (*w* Rod Serling; *d* Robert Ellis; with Donald Pleasence)

Young Man's Fancy (*w* Richard Matheson; *d* John Brahm; with Phyllis Thaxter, Alex Nicol)

I Sing the Body Electric (*w* Ray Bradbury; *d* James Sheldon; with Josephine Hutchinson)

Cavender Is Coming (*w* Rod Serling; *d* Robert Ellis; with Jesse White, Carol Burnett)

In Praise of Pip (*w* Rod Serling; *d* Joseph M. Newman; with Jack Klugman)

Steel (*w* Richard Matheson; *d* Don Weis; with Lee Marvin)

Nightmare at 20,000 Feet (*w* Richard Matheson; *d* Richard Donner; with William Shatner)

A Kind of Stop Watch (*w* Rod Serling; *d* John Rich; with Richard Erdman)

The Last Night of a Jockey (*w* Rod Serling; *d* Joseph M. Newman; with Mickey Rooney)

Living Doll (*w* Charles Beaumont; *d* Richard Sarafian; with Telly Savalas)

The Old Man in the Cave (*w* Rod Serling; *d* Alan Crosland; with James Coburn)

Uncle Simon (*w* Rod Serling; *d* Don Siegel; with Cedric Hardwicke)

Night Call (*w* Richard Matheson; *d* Jacques Tourneur; with Gladys Cooper)

Probe 7 – Over and Out (*w* Rod Serling; *d* Ted Post; with Richard Basehart)

The 7th Is Made Up of Phantoms (*w* Rod Serling; *d* Alan Crosland Jnr; with Warren Oates)

Ninety Years without Slumbering (*w* George C. Johnson; *d* Roger Kay; with Ed Wynn)

Ring-a-Ding Girl (*w* Earl Hamner Jnr; *d* Alan Crosland Jnr; with Maggie McNamara)

You Drive (*w* Earl Hamner Jnr; *d* John Brahm; with Edward Andrews)

Number Twelve Looks Just Like You (*w* Charles Beaumont; *d* Abner Biberman; with Suzy Parker, Richard Long)

The Long Morrow (*w* Rod Serling; *d* Robert Florey; with Robert Lansing, George Macready)

The Self-Improvement of Salvatore Ross (*w* Henry Slesar and Jerry McNeeley; *d* Don Siegel; with Don Gordon)

Black Leather Jackets (*w* Earl Hamner Jnr; *d* Joseph M. Newman; with Lee Kinsolving, Shelley Fabares)

From Agnes with Love (*w* Barney Scofield; *d* Richard Donner; with Wally Cox)

Spur of the Moment (*w* Richard Matheson; *d* Elliot Silverstein; with Diana Hyland, Marsha Hunt)

Stopover in a Quiet Town (*w* Earl Hamner Jnr; *d* Ron Winston; with Barry Nelson, Nancy Malone)

Queen of the Nile (*w* Charles Beaumont; *d* John Brahm; with Ann Blyth)

What's in the Box (*w* Martin Goldsmith; *d* Dick Baer; with Joan Blondell, William Demarest)

The Masks (*w* Rod Serling; *d* Abner Biberman; with Robert Keith)

I Am the Night, Colour Me Black (*w* Rod Serling; *d* Abner Biberman; with Michael Constantine)

Caesar and Me (*w* A. T. Strassfield; *d* Robert Butler; with Jackie Cooper)

The Jeopardy Room (*w* Rod Serling; *d* Richard Donner; with Martin Landau)

Mr Garrity and the Graves (*w* Rod Serling; *d* Ted Post; with John Dehner)

The Brain Center at Whipple's (*w* Rod Serling; *d* Richard Donner; with Richard Deacon)

Come Wander with Me (*w* Tony Wilson; *d* Richard Donner; with Gary Crosby)

The Fear (*w* Rod Serling; *d* Ted Post; with Mark Richman, Hazel Court)

The Bewitchin' Pool (*w* Earl Hamner Jnr; *d* Joseph M. Newman; with Mary Badham)

† Serling's opening spiel was as follows: 'There is a fifth dimension beyond that which is known to men. It is a dimension as vast as space and as timeless as infinity. It is the middle ground between light and shadow, between science and superstition, and it lies between the pit of man's fears and the summit of his knowledge. This is the dimension of imagination. It is an area we call the twilight zone.'

PP (1983): 'For all its esteem, its cult following, its immensely valuable role in opening up popular American TV fiction to the imagination, it belongs forever to the era of the small screen, the 30-minute format, the anecdotal plot with a quick, flip ending.' But at the time it more than earned its four stars. Channel 4 re-ran early episodes in their original playing order in 1983–4 and further ones in 1986.

The Twilight Zone
US 1985   × 50m colour
CBS (Philip de Guere)

An anthology of supernatural stories with twists in the tail.
The Rod Serling series of the fifties was not all good; this rejuvenated attempt has even more of the curate's egg about it because it aims too obviously for a higher intellectual

plane which it often fails to attain. But some of the pieces (usually three to an hour) have a distinct quality.

'If you enjoy letting your imagination run loose every so often, you'll find this an intriguing change from standard weekly series.' – Don Merrill, *TV Guide*

Twin Detectives

US 1976 74m colour TVM
ABC/Charles Fries (Everett Chambers)

An unusual pair of private eyes expose a psychic con group and solve a murder.
A rather shoddy production doesn't help a pilot for a series which didn't happen featuring two leads who may be twins but not actors.

w Robert Specht *d* Robert Day *ph* Earl Rath *m* Tom Scott

Jim and Jon Hager, Lillian Gish, Patrick O'Neal, Michael Constantine, Otis Young, Barbara Rhoades

Twist in the Tale: see Tales of the Unexpected (US)

Two by Forsyth

Eire 1984 50m colour
Tara/Mobil (Morgan O'Sullivan)

A portmanteau of stories by Frederick Forsyth, quite carefully done. A series was projected.

w Michael Feeney Callan *d* Michael O'Herlihy

Dan O'Herlihy, Shirley Ann Field, Cyril Cusack, Milo O'Shea, Gayle Hunnicutt

Two Faces West

US 1960 39 × 25m bw
Columbia

A doctor and an irresponsible cowboy are twin brothers.
Acceptable western series which didn't really know what to do with its gimmick.

Charles Bateman

Two Fathers' Justice

US 1985 96m colour TVM
NBC/A. Shane (Robert Long)

Newlyweds are murdered by gunmen, and the two fathers, from different classes and hating each other, go after vengeance.
A strained situation develops into a rousing melodrama, but the two halves of the plot don't really connect.

w David J. Kinghorn *d* Rod Holcomb *ph* George Kohut *m* Jan Hammer

Robert Conrad, George Hamilton, Brooke Bundy, Catherine Corkill

The Two-Five

US 1978 74m colour TVM
Universal (R. A. Cinader)

Two New York cops are accident-prone.
Failed attempt at a softened *Freebie and the Bean.*

w R. A. Cinader, Joseph Polizzi *d* Bruce Kessler *ph* Frank B. Beascoechea *m* Peter Matz

Don Johnson, Joe Bennett, George Murdock, John Crawford

Two for the Money *

US 1971 73m colour TVM
Aaron Spelling

Two policemen become private detectives and hunt down a mass murderer.
Adequate failed pilot.

w Howard Rodman *d* Bernard L. Kowalski

Robert Hooks, Stephen Brooks, Walter Brennan, Neville Brand, Catherine Burns, Mercedes McCambridge

Two Kinds of Love

US 1983 96m colour TVM
CBS (Peter Nelson, Arnold Orgolini)

A young boy is disturbed when his mother dies of cancer.
We have been here before, many times; for those who can stand it, it is decently done.

w Peter Nelson, *novel* by Peggy Mann *d* Jack Bender *ph* James A. Crabe *m* Mark Snow

Lindsay Wagner, Ricky Schroder, Peter Weller, Evan Richards, Allyn Ann McLerie

'A moving, intimate telefilm that shows the faces of hurt.' – *Daily Variety*

The Two Lives of Carol Letner

US 1981 96m colour TVM
CBS/Penthouse One (Robert A. Papazian)

An ex-callgirl is recruited by the police to comfort a nervous squealer.
Unsavoury melodrama with very little to commend it.

w Annie Scott *d* Philip Leacock *ph* Dennis Dalzell *m* Roger Kellaway

Meredith Baxter Birney, Don Johnson, Dolph Sweet, Salome Jens, Robert Webber

Two Marriages

US 1983 74m colour TVM
CBS/Lorimar (Carroll Newman)

A blue-collar worker and a chief of surgery are neighbours.
Pilot for a soap opera which faltered after a few episodes.

cr Carol Sobieski

Karen Carlson, Tom Mason, Michael Murphy, Janet Eilber, John McLiam

Two of a Kind
US 1981 96m colour TVM
CBS/Lorimar (Stanley Kallis)

A senile old man in a nursing home is brought back to caring by his grandson, who has his own problems.

The switch happens too quickly, and what starts as serious drama erupts into farce; but it all holds the attention, more or less.

w James Sadwith   *d* Roger Young
ph Edward R. Brown   *m* James Di Pasquale
George Burns, Robby Benson, Barbara Barrie, Cliff Robertson, Frances Lee McCain

The Two of Us (US 1981). 25-minute comedy series based rather insecurely on LWT's *Two's Company* and given a New York setting. It provided enough easy laughs to please the American public. With Peter Cook, Mimi Kennedy. Written by Charlie Hauck and Arthur Julian; produced by Charlie Hauck; for ITC.

Two on a Bench
US 1971 73m colour TVM
Universal/Link–Levinson

One of two eccentrics is known to be a spy, so the CIA brings them together and watches. Muddled comedy.

w Richard Levinson, William Link   *d* Jerry Paris

Patty Duke, Ted Bessell, Andrew Duggan, John Astin, Alice Ghostley

Two People (GB 1979). Earnest serial of teenage love set in the social stratum of coach lamps by the front door and bronze pictures in the lounge. Written by Alick Rowe and Julian Bond, it just about took its place in an honourable tradition of painstaking middle-class realism plodded previously by London Weekend with *Helen* and *Intimate Strangers*.   PP

The Two Ronnies. Little RONNIE CORBETT and big RONNIE BARKER took this title for a series of BBC comedy variety shows in the seventies, after being teamed in various shows by David Frost. Their trick was to endear themselves to the respectable middle-class and then get away with an immense amount of smut; but they are highly accomplished, professional and intelligent performers and several of their sketches are classics, while their fake news

items, borrowed from Frost and contributed by many hands, have so far filled three paperback books. The format continues unchanged into the eighties, and the Ronnies have occasionally attempted silent film comedies running forty minutes or so, under such titles as *Futtock's End*, *The Picnic* and *By The Sea*. These have generally disappointed.

Two Stars for Comfort (GB 1977). Kenneth More cosily cast as the amiable, amorous proprietor of a riverside hotel who has his annual fling at regatta-tide, when the wife is always away and the pretty girls compete to be Regatta Queen. Set in Coronation Year, John Mortimer's play rather dimly provided ATV with their Jubilee drama. Judy Parfitt and newcomer Sheridan Fitzgerald played wife and girl. Produced by David Reid.   PP

The Two Worlds of Jenny Logan
US 1979 96m colour TVM
CBS/Charles Fries/Joe Wizan

A married woman finds that an antique gown transports her 80 years back in time to the arms of a 19th-century lover.

Amusing romantic kitsch borrowed from *Berkeley Square* and its contemporary imitation *Somewhere in Time*. Really not bad.

w/d Frank de Felitta, *novel Second Sight* by David Williams   *ph* Al Francis   *m* Glenn Paxton

Lindsay Wagner, Alan Feinstein, Marc Singer, Linda Gray, Henry Wilcoxon, Joan Darling

'Romanticists will turn starry-eyed; others will simply wonder why the central character doesn't practice more restraint.' – *Daily Variety*

Two's Company **
GB 1976–8   × 25m colour (VTR)
London Weekend

An American authoress in London takes on a very British butler.

Patchily written but generally delightful comedy vehicle for two splendid personalities who, when the author lets them, splendidly convey an acerbic love–hate relationship.

cr/w Bill McIlwraith
ELAINE STRITCH, DONALD SINDEN

† An American version turned up in 1981 as *The Two of Us*.

TV Guide said of it: 'The mark of an insecure comedy is that it will sacrifice a character for a joke.'

The Tycoon
US 1964 32 × 25m colour
ABC/Danny Thomas (Charles Isaacs)

An old corporation chairman can dominate his business but not his family.
Competent but forgettable star comedy vehicle.

Walter Brennan, Jerome Cowan, Van Williams, Janet Lake

Tycoon (GB 1978). BBC super-soaper set up (by John Sichel) to rival ATV's *The Foundation*, with Diane Cilento as the newly widowed Diana Clark, doing her glossy best to protect her industrialist husband's reputation . . . the plummy cast included Jean Kent, Christopher Gable and Norman Rodway.   PP

Tynan, Kenneth (1927–80). British critic whose place in the history of television seems doomed to be a footnote recalling that he was the first man to pronounce the word 'fuck' on the air. In fact his contribution was far from negligible: appeared in two editions of *Round the World with Orson Welles* (1955); competed

in *The 64,000 Question* (1956), answering questions on jazz; produced two ATV blockbusters on The Method (in acting) (1958), and Dissent in America (1960); originated and edited the arts programme *Tempo* (1961–2). *One Pair of Eyes* (1968). PP

Subject of a *Reputations*, 1981.

Tyrer, Alan (19 –). Veteran British film editor whose career included responsibility for all the *Monitor* arts films on which many young directors cut their teeth.

Tyson, Cicely (1933–). Distinguished black American actress. TV movies: *Marriage Year One*, THE AUTOBIOGRAPHY OF MISS JANE PITTMAN (Emmy 1974), *Just an Old Sweet Song*, *Roots*, *Wilma*, *King*, *A Woman Called Moses*. Series: *East Side West Side*.

Tyzack, Margaret (1933–). British character actress. TV work includes *The First Churchills*, *The Forsyte Saga* (BAFTA best actress 1969), *I, Claudius*.

UFO *
GB 1970 26 × 50m colour
ATV/Gerry Anderson

In the 1980s, SHADO is a defence organization against alien invaders.

Lively, well produced, rather humourless science fiction adventures, too early to catch the public fancy.

Ed Bishop, George Sewell

'*The Ugliest Girl in Town* actually began at 3 o'clock one morning when one of Hollywood's most talented and original writers was lying awake thinking, "What if Twiggy is really a boy?" '

The Ugliest Girl in Town
US 1968 20 × 25m colour
ABC/Columbia/Harry Ackerman

For rather complex reasons (none of which hold water), a Hollywood talent agent must pose as a female model in order to join his fiancée in London.

A bottom-of-the-barrel fiasco.

cr Robert Kaufman

Peter Kastner, Patricia Brake, Gary Marshal, Jenny Till

Ullman, Tracy (19 –). British comedienne and actress who seems destined for great things. Series: *Three's Company* (1980–1), *Kick Up The Eighties* (1981–2), *The Young Visiters* (1984).

Ulster. The troubles in Northern Ireland have been assiduously covered by television, if never analytically (i.e. accusingly) enough to please those for whom the divide between Protestant and Catholic is attributable only to capitalism or colonialism. The apter questions to ask of the coverage are whether it has been sufficiently free or, conversely, sufficiently responsible; whether it has poked back far enough in history; whether it has been as imaginative as it could have been in conveying the nature of things in Ulster to the rest of the British Isles.

Censorship and cries of 'Censorship' have certainly arisen. Under successive UK governments, interviews with terrorists or scenes of paramilitary forces drilling have been restricted or, in the case of a 1971 *World in Action*, actually banned by the IBA. In 1972 Home Secretary Reginald Maudling sought to persuade the BBC not to transmit a blockbuster debate, *The Question of Ulster*, though this was partly due to a semantic blunder: a draft outline had unwisely referred to the format of the programme as a tribunal, implying it would sit in judgement. In 1985 another Tory Home Secretary, Leon Brittan, did succeed in influencing the BBC governors to ban a *Real Lives* film, which see. The programme went out three months later.

Charges that the presence of news cameras actively encourages demonstrations of violence were heard increasingly in the seventies, with accusations that foreign film crews in particular were bribing children to throw stones at British troops. More seriously, it was undeniable – and undenied – that television's appetite for action rather than negotiation was exploited by extremists on both sides. But a common Leftist complaint that the historical roots of the impasse were never examined was answered by two detailed series, Robert Kee's *Ireland: a Television History* (BBC/RTE) and Thames's *The Troubles*, both 1981.

In 1980 the academic critic Richard Hoggart asked why there had not been more TV plays about Northern Ireland, on the premise that fiction was often a more subtle as well as a more popular means of engaging an audience only too liable to switch off at the mere mention of Belfast or Derry. He rather overlooked the contribution of non-political or indirect features which also helped; but in the next five years the numbers of both sorts would increase dramatically. At the time of the *Real Lives* hoo-hah in 1985 I noted that its producer, Paul Hamann, had made no less than eight films about different aspects of life in the embattled province and been associated with two more.

Notable examples of fiction from all sources include: *Your Man from the Six Counties*; *I'm a Dreamer, Montreal*; *Shadows on Our Skin*; episodes from *Spearhead*; *Harry's Game*; *Chance of a Lifetime*; *The Fire at Magilligan*; *Contact*; *We'll Support You Evermore*; *Ties of Blood*.

Non-fiction: *Children in Crossfire* and up-date 10 years later, *A Bright Brand New Day*; *Creggan*; *Christians at War*; *The Bomb Disposal Men*; *Too Long a Sacrifice*; *The Surgery of Violence* and follow-ups; 'The Soldiers' for *This Week* (1972), 'A Company' and 'On the Edge of the Union' for *Real Lives* (1984–5). PP

'He loves, he fights, he lives like no other man alive!'
The Ultimate Imposter
US 1979 96m colour TVM
CBS/Universal (Lionel E. Siegel)

A man with no memory can be computerized by the CIA to become an expert on anything . . . but he forgets his knowledge in 72 hours. Strained attempt to create yet another superhero. This time the audience forgot.

w Lionel E. Siegel, *novel The Capricorn Man* by William Zacha Snr d Paul Stanley ph Vincent Martinelli m Dana Kaproff

Joseph Hacker, Keith Andes, Macon McColman, Erin Gray, Tracy Brooks Swope, John Van Dreelen

Ultra Quiz (GB 1984). Bloodless English version of the Japanese game show of roughly the same title in which competitors are eliminated ruthlessly, and with frequent humiliations, as the action moves halfway across the world. David Frost and Willie Rushton, both lacking the hangman's touch, were in charge. Produced by Tony McLaren, for TVS. PP

umbrella title. One billed to hold together otherwise disparate units; e.g. *Million Dollar Movie*, *The Big Event*, *World Première*.

UMC: see Operation Heartbeat

An Uncommon Love
US 1983 96m colour TVM
CBS/Lorimar (Seth Freeman)

A divorced teacher of marine biology falls for one of his students who works part time in a massage parlour.
And lives to regret it. Those who care for this kind of story will care for this movie.

w Seth Freeman d Steven Stern ph Isidore Mankofsky m Miles Goodman

Barry Bostwick, Kathryn Harrold, Connie Needham, Holly Hunter, Kenneth Gilman

Uncommon Valor
US 1983 96m colour TVM
CBS/Brademan–Self/Sunn Classic (Mark Rodgers)

An arsonist fires a hospital.
Pilot for a series about firefighters. Luckily it didn't catch on.

w Mark Rodgers d Rod Amateau ph Stephen W. Gray m Bob Summers

Mitchell Ryan, Ben Murphy, Rick Lohman, Barbara Parkins, Norman Fell, Gregory Sierra, Salome Jens

Under Fire (GB 1956–9; 83 × 15m). Typically Granadan exercise whereby two figures representing authority in a London studio were challenged by an audience in Manchester. The latter could see the former on a projection screen, in the opposite direction there was only a sound link. It worked quite well, if over-restricted to MPs as the most available victims. Stephen McAdden, a Tory, was a regular participant. Among those making occasional appearances were Enoch Powell, Tony Benn, Keith Joseph, George Brown and Geoffrey Rippon. PP

Under the Same Sky (Europe 1984; 13 × 30m). Children's version of the idealistic Largest Theatre in the World. Thirteen European countries each contributed one film, always named after its young hero or heroine. Participating networks could use as many or as few as they liked. ITV took nine, including *Danny* from Australia, which for this series was tacked on to Europe. Executive producer for the EBU, Joy Whitby. Further season of 11 films, 1986. PP

Underground
GB 1958 52m bw (live show)
ABC (Sydney Newman)

Nuclear cautionary tale in the *Armchair Theatre* slot which earns a macabre place in the annals as the live production during which one of the actors suffered a heart attack and died. Luckily, he had already played his big scene.

w James Forsyth, *story* Harold Rein d Ted Kotcheff

Donald Houston, Patricia Jessel, Andrew Cruikshank, Gareth Jones PP

The Underground Man
aka: *Archer*
US 1974 100m colour TVM
Paramount (Philip L. Parslow)

A private eye seeks a missing husband and father-in-law.
Dull adaptation of a John Ross Macdonald novel. A series, *Archer*, ensued but was quickly scuttled.

w Douglas Heyes *d* Paul Wendkos
Peter Graves, Celeste Holm, Sharon Farrell, Jim Hutton, Jack Klugman, Kay Lenz, Vera Miles, Judith Anderson

Understanding Opera (GB 1982; 4 × 60m). Bright but uncondescending guide to enjoying the spectacle of grown men and women singing secrets to each other; written and presented by Stephen Oliver. Produced by Rod Allen, for LWT.   PP

Underwater Car: see Manhunt

Unfair Exchanges (GB 1985; 75m). Weird and whizzing thriller in which the telephone system finally turns into a malignant force, leading Julie Walters into increasingly dreadful events. Also with David Rappaport, Malcolm Terris, Robert Kingswell. Written by Ken Campbell, directed by Gavin Millar, produced by Kenith Trodd, for BBC.

Union Pacific *
US 1958 39 × 25m bw
NBC
Adventures of a railway construction boss in the 1880s.
Good action series.
Jeff Morrow

Union World (GB since 1982). Worthy undertaking to give trade union affairs a regular weekly programme, introduced by Gus Macdonald, with reports by Anne Lester and Julie Hall (originally Bob Greaves). Until 1985 it was the only national series to come from Liverpool; it was then transferred to Manchester. Produced by David Kemp, for Granada/C4.   PP

United Kingdom (GB 1981; 90m; colour). Misbegotten epic by Jim Allen about a North-East council which rebels against government spending cuts and suffers first a ministry overlord then a police intervention masterminded by Colin Welland as a heavy-handed Chief Constable. Seemed to have been cobbled together from several sources, including earlier and, sadly, unproduced Allen works. Directed by Roland Joffé; produced by Kenith Trodd; for BBC. With Ricky Tomlinson, Peter Kerrigan, Val McLane, Bill Patterson, Rosemary Martin.
                                                              PP

'It does for marriage what *M*A*S*H* did for war!'
United States **
US 1980 13 × 25m colour
NBC/Viacom/OTP
A realistic look at a contemporary marriage. Much heralded and well intentioned comedy drama series which was simply above the heads of the public. So was the punning title.
cr Larry Gelbart
Helen Shaver

Unity *
GB 1981 105m colour
BBC (Louis Marks)
The story of the Mitford sister who went to Germany in 1934 and fell in love with Adolf Hitler.
The trouble with this kind of subject is that no one can ever be sure what went on in the people's minds; but the script makes intelligent guesses and the production is handsome.
w John Mortimer, *book Unity Mitford: A Quest* by David Pryce-Jones *d* James Cellan Jones
Lesley-Anne Down, Nigel Havers, Jeremy Kemp, Ernst Jacobi (as Hitler), James Villiers
PP: 'After the cosy fictionalized account of the Mitford family in *Love in a Cold Climate*, John Mortimer's biopic had a welcome astringency. Anne Down was beautiful, wilful, spoiled. She gave Unity a very credible upper-class impermeability. It's not her fault that Unity's whole involvement with the Nazis was banal beyond belief, and that as a person she was no more interesting than the rest of her over-publicized family, from whose carryings-on we might now be given some relief.'

University Challenge. British general knowledge quiz, produced by Granada since 1962, with Bamber Gascoigne as sole question master presiding over university teams. Based on the American *College Bowl*, with an extremely high level of erudition required.
PP (in early days): 'The questions range enterprisingly over the field of useless information (surveying, cybernetics, publishing jargon and the Beatles were among topics last time). Bamber Gascoigne presides with the buoyant high spirits of someone who still can't believe he's getting paid for doing what he enjoys.'
† An early member of a Cambridge team was Clive James, later to be critic and performer.

The Unknown War
US 1978 20 × 50m colour
Syndicated/Air Time International/Fred
 Weiner (Isaac Kleinermann)

Extraordinarily long documentary series recapitulating the war on the Russo-German front in World War II. Burt Lancaster is on the spot to deliver the narration, but it's a long haul despite the fascinating chunks of Russian archive material. Written by Roman Karmen, John Lord; directed by Roman Karmen.

The Untouchables ***
US 1959–62 117 × 50m bw
ABC/Desilu/QUINN MARTIN

An élite squad of the Chicago police tracks down the criminals of the prohibition era. Much criticized for its violence, this well-made series now seems rather tame. Its music, its commentary and its star all helped to keep the world tuned in for four seasons, and of all TV series it has had the best re-run life.

commentary WALTER WINCHELL

ROBERT STACK, NEVILLE BRAND (as Al Capone), BRUCE GORDON (as Frank Nitti); Jerry Paris, Abel Fernandez, Steve London, Nick Georgiade, Anthony George, Paul Picerni (the Untouchables)

The Scarface Mob was shown theatrically in most countries. Here are the other episodes, with guest star(s):

The Empty Chair (with Bruce Gordon as Frank Nitti, Nehemiah Persoff as Jake Guzik)

The George 'Bugs' Moran Story (with Lloyd Nolan as Moran, Jack Warden as Halloran)

Noise of Death (with J. Carrol Naish as Joe Bucco)

Ma Barker and Her Boys (with Claire Trevor)

You Can't Pick a Number (with Darryl Hickman)

The Jake Lingle Story (with Jack Lord as Bill Hagen)

Ain't We Got Fun (with Cameron Mitchell as Johnny Pacheck)

The Vincent 'Mad Dog' Coll Story (with Clu Gulager as Coll)

Mexican Stakeout (with Vince Edwards as Nick Delgado)

The Artichoke King (with Jack Weston as Terranova)

The Tri-State Gang (with William Bendix as Leganza)

The Dutch Schultz Story (with Lawrence Dobkin)

Underground Railway (with Cliff Robertson)

Syndicate Sanctuary (with Anthony Caruso, Jack Elam)

Star Witness (with Jim Backus, Marc Lawrence)

One Armed Bandit (with Harry Guardino)

The St Louis Story (with David Brian)

The Big Squeeze (with Dan O'Herlihy)

Little Egypt (with Fred Clark, John Marley)

Unhired Assassin (two-parter) (with Robert Middleton, Joe Mantell – distributed theatrically as The Gun of Zangara)

The White Slavers (with Betty Field)

Three Thousand Suspects (with Peter Leeds)

The Doreen Maney Story (with Anne Francis)

Portrait of a Thief (with Edward Andrews)

The Underworld Bank (with Thomas Mitchell, Peter Falk)

Head of Fire, Feet of Clay (with Jack Warden, Madlyn Rhue, Patsy Kelly, Nehemiah Persoff)

The Frank Nitti Story (with Bruce Gordon, Myron McCormick)

A Seat on the Fence (with John McIntire)

The Jack 'Legs' Diamond Story (with Steven Hill)

The Rusty Heller Story (with Elizabeth Montgomery)

The Waxey Gordon Story (with Sam Gilman)

The Mark of Cain (with Eduardo Ciannelli, Henry Silva)

The Otto Frick Story (with Jack Warden, Francis Lederer)

Nicky (with Luther Adler, Michael Ansara)

The Big Train (two-parter) (with Neville Brand, Bruce Gordon – distributed theatrically as Alcatraz Express)

The Purple Gang (with Steve Geray, Steve Cochran, Werner Klemperer)

The Kiss of Death Girl (with Jan Sterling, Robert H. Harris)

The Larry Fay Story (with June Havoc, Sam Levene)

The Tommy Karpeles Story (with Harold J. Stone, Madlyn Rhue, Joseph Wiseman)

The Masterpiece (with Rip Torn, Robert Middleton, George Voskovec)

Augie 'The Banker' Ciamino (with Keenan Wynn, Sam Jaffe)

The Organization (with Richard Conte, Susan Oliver)

Jamaica Ginger (with Michael Ansara, Brian Keith, James Coburn)

The Underground Court (with Joan Blondell)

The Nick Moses Story (with Harry Guardino)

The Antidote (with Joseph Wiseman, Telly Savalas)

The Lily Dallas Story (with Norma Crane, Larry Parks)

Murder Under Glass (with Luther Adler)

Testimony of Evil (with David Brian)

Ring of Terror (with Harold J. Stone, Viveca Lindfors)

Mr Moon (with Victor Buono)

Death for Sale (with James MacArthur)

Stranglehold (with Ricardo Montalban)

The Seventh Vote (with Nehemiah Persoff, Bruce Gordon)

The Nero Rankin Story (with Will Kuluva, John Dehner)

The King of Champagne (with Robert Middleton, Barry Morse, Michael Constantine

The Nick Acropolis Story (with Lee Marvin)

90 Proof Dame (with Steve Cochran, Steve Geray)

Tunnel of Horrors (with Martin Balsam)

Power Play (with Wendell Corey, Albert Salmi, Carroll O'Connor)

The Matt Bass Scheme (with Telly Savalas)

Loophole (with Jack Klugman)

The Troubleshooters (with Peter Falk, Murray Hamilton)

The Genna Brothers (with Marc Lawrence, Frank Puglia)

Hammerlock (with Harold J. Stone)

Jigsaw (with James Gregory, Bruce Gordon)

Mankiller (with Ruth Roman)

City without a Name (with Bruce Gordon, Paul Richards)

Canada Run (with Arthur Hill)

Fall Guy (with Herschel Bernardi)

The Silent Partner (with Charles McGraw, Allyn Joslyn)

The Gang War (with Bruce Gordon, Victor Buono)

The Whitey Steele Story (with Henry Silva, Eduardo Ciannelli)

Takeover (Luther Adler, Robert Loggia)

The Death Tree (with Charles Bronson, Barbara Luna)

The Stryker Brothers (with Nehemiah Persoff)

Element of Danger (with Lee Marvin, Victor Jory)

The Maggie Storm Story (with Patricia Neal)

Man in the Middle (with Martin Balsam, Tom Drake, Cloris Leachman)

Downfall (with Steven Hill, Simon Oakland)

The Case Against Eliot Ness (with Pat Hingle)

The Ginnie Littlesmith Story (with Phyllis Love)

The Contract (with Harry Guardino)

Pressure (with Harold J. Stone, Darryl Hickman)

The Monkey Wrench (with Dolores Dorn, Claude Akins)

Arsenal (with Bruce Gordon, George Matthews)

The Chess Game (with Richard Conte)

The Night They Shot Santa Claus (with Ruth White, Nita Talbot)

The Pea (with Frank Gorshin)

Cooker in the Sky (with Milton Seltzer, J. D. Cannon, Anne Jackson)

The Economist (with Joseph Sirola)

A Taste of Pineapple (with Jeremy Slate)

The Snowball (with Bruce Gordon, Robert Redford)

Elegy (with Barbara Stanwyck, Peggy Ann Garner)

Bird in the Hand (with Dane Clark)

Come and Kill Me (with Dan Dailey)

The Eddie O'Hara Story (with Michael Connors)

An Eye for an Eye (with Jack Klugman)

Search for a Dead Man (with Barbara Stanwyck, Ed Asner)

A Fist of Five (with Lee Marvin)

The Floyd Gibbons Story (with Scott Brady, Dorothy Malone, Stuart Erwin)

Doublecross (with Nehemiah Persoff, Harry Morgan)

The Speculator (with Telly Savalas)

Jake Dance (with Dane Clark)

Blues for a Gone Goose (with Kathy Nolan, Robert Duvall)

Globe of Death (with Bruce Gordon)

Junk Man (with Pat Hingle)

Man in the Cooler (with J. D. Cannon)

The Butcher's Boy (with Frank Sutton, John Larkin)

The Spoiler (with Rip Torn, Claude Akins)

One Last Killing (with Don Gordon, Harold J. Stone)

The Giant Killer (with Paul Richards, Peggy Ann Garner)

The Charlie Argos Story (with Patricia Owens, Robert Vaughn)

The Jazz Man (with Simon Oakland, Robert Emhardt)

The Torpedo (with Charles McGraw)

Line of Fire (with Ed Nelson)

Unwed Father

US 1974 74m colour TVM
David Wolper (Lawrence Turman, Stan Margulies)

A teenager wants custody of his illegitimate child.

What will they think of next? Something more entertaining, one hopes.

w W. Hermanos, Carol McKeand *d* Jeremy Kagan

Joe Bottoms, Kay Lenz, Joseph Campanella, Beverly Garland, Kim Hunter

Up Pompeii *. A BBC comedy series of the early seventies, plainly borrowed from *A Funny Thing Happened on the Way to the Forum*. Frankie Howerd, the host, was a Roman slave who masterminded his owner's household and commented intermittently on the farcical action. It was vulgar but funny; the film versions which followed, including *Up the Front* and *Up the Chastity Belt*, were merely crass.

Up the Junction

GB 1965 70m bw
BBC (James MacTaggart)

Nell Dunn's *Wednesday Play* from her own sketches of life lived to the full in Battersea created a stir at the time, especially an abortion undergone by one of the girls. But in retrospect its real importance was that for the first time the BBC's advance guard of young directors managed to shoot virtually the entire story on film, thus setting a precedent which would lead to about 50 per cent of single plays being filmed by the mid-seventies.

d Kenneth Loach

Carol White, Geraldine Sherman, Vickery Turner   PP

The Upchat Line (GB 1976). My reaction at the time: 'Sitcom from the Hope Springs Eternal department of Thames Television with John Alderton as hard-pressed writer freeloading his way round London from the permanent address of a baggage locker in Marylebone station . . . pleasantly unraucous and quite funny: the problem is going to be to stretch out the basic joke of Alderton having to extricate himself from self-made gaffes.' Scripts by Keith Waterhouse did well enough to sustain two seasons followed by a sequel *The Upchat Connection* with Robin Nedwell.
                                                                            PP

Upstairs, Downstairs ****

GB 1970–5 75 × 50m colour (VTR)
London Weekend (JOHN HAWKESWORTH)

In a London house between 1900 and 1930, the lives of masters and servants intermingle.

A simple but very clever concept which was aided by astute casting and a highly professional sheen in all departments, this highly agreeable series was a national institution in Britain and a surprising success (via PBS) in America.

cr Jean Marsh, Eileen Atkins

GORDON JACKSON (Hudson), ANGELA BADDELEY (Mrs Bridges), JEAN MARSH (Rose), DAVID LANGTON (Mr Bellamy), SIMON WILLIAMS (James Bellamy); and intermittently NICOLA PAGETT, John Alderton, Pauline Collins, Raymond Huntley, Christopher Beeny, Lesley-Anne Down

Urge to Kill

US 1984 96m colour TVM
CBS/Metromedia/Jerry London (Lee Rafner)
aka: *With Intent To Kill*

After serving a sentence for the murder of his girlfriend while of unsound mind, a young man returns to his home town and begins to wonder whether he really did it.

An adequate suspense melodrama, rather confusingly told to begin with, but gripping when it gets into its stride.

w,d Mike Robe

Karl Malden, William Devane, Shirley Knight, Paul Sorvino

Urich, Robert (1948–). American leading man who became popular in the seventies. *Bob and Carol and Ted and Alice*, *SWAT*, *Killdozer*, *The Specialists*, VEGAS, *Leave Yesterday Behind*, *Fighting Back*, *The Killing at Hell's Gate*, *Take Your Best Shot*, *Gavilan*, *Princess Daisy*, *Invitation to Hell*, *Mistral's Daughter*, *His Mistress*, *Scandal Sheet*, *Spenser for Hire*.

Urquhart, Robert (1922–). Scottish general purpose actor whose gentle manner has been underused except in a brief series, *The Awful Mr Goodall*. Series: *Pathfinders*; recent credits: *Bookie*.

Us Against the World

US 1975 96m colour TVM
CBS/Columbia (Chris Morgan)

Problems in the lives of female interns at a large city hospital.

Nothing to be said about this that hasn't been said before.

w Rita Lakin *d* Paul Wendkos

Christine Belford, Meredith Baxter Birney, Donna Mills, Theodore Bikel, Sam Groom, Linda Purl

UPSTAIRS, DOWNSTAIRS.   The Bellamys and their faithful domestics pose for a happy family group.

The Users
US 1978 122m colour TVM
ABC/Aaron Spelling, Douglas S. Cramer
(Dominick Dunne)

A call girl marries a has-been film actor and
takes him back to the top.

Emasculated from the original, but still a
pretty lively peek at the new Hollywood, or at
least the one the gossip columnists see.

w Robert J. Shaw, *novel* Joyce Haber d
Joseph Hardy *ph* Richard L. Rawlings *m*
Maurice Jarre

Jaclyn Smith, Tony Curtis, Red Buttons, Alan
Feinstein, Joan Fontaine, John Forsythe,
George Hamilton, Darren McGavin, Carrie
Nye, Michelle Phillips

✳ **Ustinov, Peter** (1921–). British actor,
director, raconteur, playwright. Emmys 1957
for playing Samuel Johnson in *Omnibus*; 1966
for playing in *Barefoot in Athens*; 1969 for
playing in *A Storm in Summer*. In Britain,
most of his TV appearances have been as
narrator or in talk shows.

PP: 'His participation in more ambitious
undertakings has usually been unfortunate,
from a live BBC production of *Peer Gynt* in
1955 which flummoxed the then single-
channel audience to a dotty attempt to explain
the Theory of Relativity, with Ustinov as a
space traveller, in 1980. In *Ustinov in Orbit*
(ATV, 1967 – no connection with the
foregoing) he compared the British theatre
with its opposite numbers in Germany,
Holland and Switzerland. Joint narrator of
The Mighty Continent (1975), and of an
ill-timed tour of *The Hermitage* (Leningrad)
as Russian troops were invading Afghanistan
in 1980.'

The U-2 Affair
US 1960 50m bw
NBC White Paper (Irving Gitlin)

Graphic history of Captain Francis Gary
Powers's disastrously unfinished flight across
Russia in a spy plane, though a little suspect in
its mixture of actuality and reconstructed
scenes. Shown by the BBC in 1961.   PP

'V' **
US 1983–4 5 × 96m colour
NBC/Warner/Blatt–Singer (Kenneth Johnson, Dean O'Brien)

Aliens invade Los Angeles, allegedly on a peace mission but actually in search of human food. When their true nature is known and they have occupied California, an underground is set up.

And it turns into Nazis versus the Maquis, with flying saucers and some horrifying make-up thrown in. Special effects variable, acting elementary, but a fair amount of action makes suspense inevitable.

w Kenneth Johnson, Brian Taggert, Lillian Weaver, Faustus Buck, Diane Frolov, Peggy Goldman, others *d* Richard Heffron *ph* Stevan Larner *m* Barry de Vorzon, Joseph Conlan *pd* Mort Rabinowitz

Jane Badler, Michael Durrell, Robert Englund, Faye Grant, Richard Herd, Thomas Hill

'Thrilling, thought-provoking, and paced like a motor race.' – *Washington Post*
'The rise of the Nazis done as a cautionary science-fiction fable.' – *New York Times*
'An imaginative first-class thriller of substance and social significance.' – Judith Crist

† In the 1984–5 season a one-hour series followed, to far less interest. Marc Singer was added to the remaining cast, Paul Monash wrote the opener and Paul Krasny directed. 22 episodes were made.

A Vacation in Hell
US 1980 96m colour TVM
ABC/David Greene/Finnegan Associates

Four men and a woman on a tropical holiday get stranded in a rain forest.
Repetitive adventure thriller with lots of danger but not much suspense.

w Shelley Katz, D. B. Ledrov *d* David Greene *ph* Harry May *m* Gil Melle

Michael Brandon, Priscilla Barnes, Barbara Feldon, Andrea Marcovici, Maureen McCormick

'Concept for a taut, spellbinding horror yarn is jettisoned when the folk in the script begin to talk.' – *Daily Variety*

Vaccaro, Brenda (1939–). Spunky American actress who pursued a good career in all media. TV series: *Sara*. Emmy 1973 for *The Shape of Things* (special). TV movies: *Travis Logan DA*, *What's a Nice Girl Like You*, *Honor Thy Father*, *Sunshine*, *Dear Detective*, *The Pride of Jesse Hallam*, *The Star Maker*, *A Long Way from Home*, *Paper Dolls*, *Deceptions*.

Valentine
US 1979 96m colour TVM
ABC/Malloy–Phillips/Edward S. Feldman

Two residents at an old people's home fall in love.
Thin, protracted whimsy with little relation to life and little that's interesting for its stars to do.

w Merrit Malloy, Lee Phillips *d* Lee Phillips *ph* Charles F. Wheeler *m* Lee Holdridge

Jack Albertson, Mary Martin, Loretta Swit, Danny de Vito, Lloyd Nolan

'Pedestrian writing, adolescent concepts and *outré* characters.' – *Daily Variety*

Valentine, Anthony (1939–). British leading actor with a rather sinister smile. Series include *Justice*, *Raffles*, *Colditz*; and he played the Ivor Novello role in *The Dancing Years*.

Valentine, Karen (1947–). American leading lady, a pert Debbie Reynolds type who hasn't quite hit the ultimate heights. Series: *Room 222*, *Karen*. TV movies: *Gidget Grows Up*, *The Daughters of Joshua Cabe*, *Coffee Tea or Me*, *The Girl Who Came Gift-Wrapped*, *Having Babies*, *Murder at the World Series*, *Go West Young Girl*, *Eischied* (pilot).

Valentine Magic on Love Island
US 1980 96m colour TVM
NBC/Dick Clark/Osmond TV

Four pairs of people sort themselves out on a Hawaiian holiday island.
Very thin pilot with attractive backgrounds. Even *Love Boat* and *Fantasy Island* did better.

w Madeline B. David, Robert Hilliard, John Kurland *d* Earl Bellamy *ph* Ken Lamkin *m* Peter Matz

Adrienne Barbeau, Bill Daily, Howard Duff, Dody Goodman, Lisa Hartman, Rick Hurst, Christopher Knight, Janis Paige

'Backgrounds look fine, but it's what's up front that counts, and this one doesn't make it.' – *Daily Variety*

Valentine's Day
US 1964 34 × 25m bw
ABC/TCF/Savannah–Yorktan

The love life of a bachelor editor.

Very moderate, rather tiresome New York comedy.

cr Hal Kanter

Tony Franciosa, Jack Soo, Janet Waldo, Patsy Kelly

Valerie
US 1985 13 × 25m colour
NBC/Lorimar (Ronny Hallin)

Domestic trials of a career woman.

Archetypal sitcom, quite well done but instantly forgettable.

Valerie Harper, Jason Bateman, Josh Taylor, Jeremy Licht, Danny Ponce

The Valiant Man (GB 1965; 300m; bw). The title adopted in subsequent commemorative literature for ITV's coverage of Sir Winston Churchill's funeral, generally accepted as a masterly outside broadcast. Commentary by Brian Connell with other narration by Sir Laurence Olivier, Paul Scofield and Joseph C. Harsch. Produced by Peter Morley for the ITV network using the resources of nine companies. PP

The Valiant Years ***
GB/US 1960 26 × 25m bw
Columbia/JACK LE VIEN

Documentary series recalling World War II through newsreel footage and Churchill's own words (from his memoirs).

An excellent job of work and a valuable demonstration of how history can be popularized through TV.

narrator Richard Burton

Valley of Mystery
US 1967 90m colour TVM
Universal

Survivors of a plane crash fight for survival in a South American jungle.

Or, *Five Came Back* and back and back and back. . . This version isn't even entertaining.

w Dick Nelson, Lowell Barrington *d* Josef Leytes

Richard Egan, Peter Graves, Joby Baker, Lois Nettleton, Harry Guardino, Julie Adams, Fernando Lamas

Valley of the Dinosaurs *
US 1974 16 × 22m colour
Hanna–Barbera (Iwao Takomoto)

Boating on the Colorado river, a family is swept away into a lost prehistoric valley.

Nicely styled cartoon series with good sense of pre-history.

Valley of the Dolls
US 1981 2 × 96m, 1 × 50m colour
CBS/TCF/Irving Mansfield (Renee Valente)

Four women seeking Hollywood fame meet success and tragedy.

Would-be daring mini-series, marginally more entertaining than the dreary film version.

w Leslie Stevens, Laurence Heath, *novel* Jacqueline Susann *d* Walter Grauman

Catherine Hicks, Lisa Hartman, Veronica Hamel, Jean Simmons, James Coburn, Gary Collins, Bert Convy, Britt Ekland, Steve Inwood, Camilla Sparv

Vampire
US 1980 96m colour TVM
ABC/MTM (Steven Bochco)

A vampire causes trouble in San Francisco.

Stylish but slow-moving horror chiller which spurns logic and moves in a curiously stilted way.

w Steven Bochco, Michael Kozoll *d* E. W. Swackhamer *ph* Dennis Dalzell *m* Fred Karlin

Richard Lynch, Jason Miller, Kathryn Harrold, E. G. Marshall, Jessica Walter, Barrie Youngfellow

'Two things are missing: a good scare, and please pass the garlic.' – *Daily Variety*

Van der Valk *
GB 1972 13 × 50m colour (VTR)
Thames

Cases of a Dutch police inspector.

Likeable cops and robbers with a 'different' background, from the character created by Nicholas Freeling. The filmed series of 13, which followed in 1977, was a disappointment, the stories seeming very thin.

Barry Foster

PP: 'There was also a filmed series made in West Germany using Freeling's published plots, with Frank Finlay as Van der Valk.'

VALLEY OF THE DOLLS. Gary Collins and Veronica Hamel in the miniseries version of the successful film, a millgirl's dream of Hollywood romance.

Van Dyke, Dick (1925–). American comic actor who had an enormous personal success in THE DICK VAN DYKE SHOW during the years when he played opposite Mary Tyler Moore, but failed to make the same grade a few years later in *The New Dick Van Dyke Show.* Meanwhile he had temporarily established for himself a niche as film actor and star of specials, but his appeal in these fields also waned. TV movies: *The Morning After, Drop Out Father, Found Money, The Wrong Way Kid, Breakfast with Les and Bess.*

Van Dyke, Jerry (1931–). American comic actor, brother of Dick; never in the same class, he did star in two series, *My Mother the Car* and *Accidental Family.*

Van Gyseghem, Joanna (19 –). British actress whose upper-crust good looks and brittle voice have enriched several sitcoms and were crucial to the fluttering romantic pretensions of Linda in DUTY FREE. Previously *Pig in the Middle,* 1983.   PP

Van Patten, Dick (1928–). Plump American TV actor, a household word for his long-running role in *Eight Is Enough.* Also: *I Remember Mama, The Dick Van Dyke Show, Arnie, When things Were Rotten.*

Van Patten, Joyce (1934–). American comedy actress. *The Bravos, The Martian Chronicles, Eleanor First Lady of the World, The Demon Murder Case, In Defense of Kids, Malice in Wonderland.*

Vance, Vivian (1907–79). American comedy actress whose greatest hour came when she played the wise-cracking neighbour in *I Love Lucy.* TV movies: *Getting Away from It All, The Great Houdinis.*

Vanished **
US 1970 2 × 98m colour TVM
Universal

The President's top adviser goes missing and is revealed as a homosexual.
Reasonably absorbing, well acted and sharply written political melodrama on the lines of *Seven Days in May.*

w Dean Riesner, *novel* Fletcher Knebel *d* Buzz Kulik

Richard Widmark, Robert Young, James Farentino, Skye Aubrey, Tom Bosley, Stephen McNally, Sheree North, Larry Hagman, Murray Hamilton, Arthur Hill, Robert Hooks, E. G. Marshall, Eleanor Parker, William Shatner

† Important as the forerunner of the 'Best Sellers' mini-series fashion, generally thought to have begun with *Rich Man, Poor Man*.

Vanishing Army * (GB 1978; 78m; colour). Plaintive BBC *Play for Today* by Robert Holles about an old sweat sergeant-major (Bill Paterson) trying to come to terms with civilian life after tours in Northern Ireland. Really a lament for lost virtues and growing up and growing old. PP

Vanoff, Nick (1929–   ). American producer of musical specials who won an Emmy for *The Julie Andrews Hour*.

Varney, Reg (1922–   ). British cockney comedian who was popular on TV in THE RAG TRADE and ON THE BUSES, but fared less well when he left both in the hope of being a star of films and specials.

Vas, Robert (1931–78). Hungarian documentary director, formerly a critic, who came to Britain after the 1956 rising. Of many films he made the best remembered will be his treatments of two World War II tragedies: one about the Katyn massacre, and *Orders from Above* (1975), dealing with the forced repatriation of Russian prisoners of war, slave workers and other strays. BBC tribute, *Robert Vas, Film-Maker* (1978). PP

Vaughan, Frankie (1928–   ) (Frank Abelsohn). British popular singer ('give me the moonlight, give me the girl') who remains a staple of TV variety shows but never really made it in any other form.

Vaughan, Norman (*c* 1928–   ). British stand-up comic with a nervous manner; popular from 1962 when he took over as compere of *Sunday Night at the London Palladium*, but his career subsequently faltered.

Vaughan, Peter (1924–   ). Heavily built British character actor; TV series include *The Gold Robbers*, *Porridge*, *Fox*.

Vaughn, Robert (1932–   ). Serious-faced American actor who despite his dramatic ambitions is best known as star of *The Lieutenant*, *The Man from UNCLE* and *The Protectors*. Also played the Haldeman figure in *Washington Behind Closed Doors*. TV movies: *The Woman Hunter*, *Kiss Me Kill Me*, *Captains and the Kings*, *The Islander*, *Centennial*, *Backstairs at the White House*, *The Rebels*, *Dr Franken*, *The Gossip Columnist*, *City in Fear*, *Mirror Mirror*, *The Day The Bubble Burst*, *A Question of Honor*, *Inside the Third Reich*, *The Blue and the Gray*, *Intimate Agony*, *Silent Reach*, *The Return of the Man from UNCLE*, *The Last Bastion*, *Evergreen*, *Private Sessions*, *International Airport*.

Vegas *
US 1978 74m colour TVM
ABC/Aaron Spelling (E. Duke Vincent)

A private eye in Las Vegas solves a murder case.

Brisk, bright, old-fashioned mystery à la Chandler, with good local colour.

w Michael Mann *d* Richard Lang *ph* Arch Dalzell *m* Dominic Frontiere

Robert Urich, Tony Curtis, June Allyson, Edd Byrnes, Red Buttons, Jack Kelly, Will Sampson, Greg Morris

'After three days in Las Vegas I would kill to get out, so I am not surprised at the violence in this series – some of the characters have been there for *weeks*.' – Robert MacKenzie, *TV Guide*

† A successful series of 50m episodes resulted and ran three seasons.

Velvet
US 1984 96m colour TVM
ABC/Warner/Aaron Spelling (Richard Lang)

International aerobics studios serve as a front for a government intelligence agency.

Not only 20 years behind the girls from UNCLE, but even missing the bus on aerobics, this tired spoof didn't have a hope of becoming a series.

w Ned Wynn *d* Richard Lang

Leah Ayres, Shari Belafonte-Harper, Mary Margaret Humes, Sheree J. Wilson, Polly Bergen, Andrea Marcovicci, Michael Ensign

The Velvet Glove
GB 1977 6 × 75m colour (VTR)
BBC (Anne Head)

Biodramas of celebrated Victorian and Edwardian women: Edith Cavell, Marie Stopes, Annie Besant, etc. But only three of the writers were women, and not a single director. My reaction to one episode: 'Beryl Bainbridge, pithy novelist, made rather an unpithy job of Annie Besant. A few bursts of shorthand narrative only emphasized the lengthiness of the passages in which the characters helpfully explained their beliefs to each other.'   PP

Vendetta (GB 1966). Dopey BBC attempt, created by Brian Degas and Tudor Gates, to crash the international market with a co-production series propelling a lone Italian hero (Stelio Candelli) against the Mafia, whose power, as I said at the time, was nothing to that of the Trashia, that vast international conspiracy to flood the television networks of the world with filmed thuggery.   PP

The Verdict Is Yours **
GB 1958–9 70 × 30m bw (VTR)
Granada (Denis Forman)
Adaptation of an ingenious American format in which real-life attorneys pleaded unscripted cases before a real judge and jury; only the defendant and witnesses were played by actors. Under British legal protocol all roles had to be entrusted to actors, including a few with legal experience such as the former police prosecutor David Ensor who presided as 'Mr Justice Ensor'. Each case was prepared by professional writers in the form of a scenario of events, together with dossiers on all leading participants, but the outcome was genuinely left to a jury recruited from Granada viewers. Actors taking part, whether as counsel or laymen, sometimes became so deeply involved that unpremeditated breakdowns and weepings occurred, and on one occasion a fist-fight, fortunately off the set. Directed by Herbert Wise. The function of the lay jury was revived in the later but conventionally scripted *Crown Court*.   PP

Verdugo, Elena (1926–). American character actress. TV series: *Meet Millie*, *The New Phil Silvers Show*, *Marcus Welby MD*.

Vereen, Ben (1946–). Energetic black American dancer and actor. TV movies: *Louis Armstrong Chicago Style*, ROOTS. Series: TENSPEED AND BROWN SHOE.

Verité **
GB 1973 50m colour (VTR and film)
Hilarious first play by Howard Schuman – first to get on the air anyway – about a progressive American film-maker in London, complete with final glimpse of his absurd handiwork. My 1973 review: 'Tim Rice was hideously accurate as the film-maker, a phoney homing unerringly on to fellow-phoneys, latching on to any fad, untroubled by self-doubts, yo-yoing between extravagant elation and extravagant despair. He picked up at one stage a delicious fellow-American (Beth Porter) given to tap-dancing and the expression of approval *brillante* – the transatlantic idiom was very crisp throughout.' Also with Christopher Morant, Anabel Leventon. Directed by Piers Haggard; produced by Joan Kemp-Welch; for Thames (*Armchair Theatre*).   PP

Vernon, Richard (1924–). Dignified British actor of the old school, most at home in plays by Lonsdale or Maugham. His many TV series include *The Men in Room 17*, *The Liars*, *The Duchess of Duke Street*, *Something in Disguise*.

Vernon, Tom (19 –). British traveller of generous build who made his name cycling round the world for a radio series *Fat Man on a Bicycle*. For television, conducted an agreeable cooking-cum-travel series *Fat Man in the Kitchen*, 1985. *Spirit of Whitby*, 1986.   PP

Vertue, Beryl (19 –). British entre-preneur, formerly agent, who specializes in exporting British formats to America: Alf Garnett became Archie Bunker; Steptoe and Son, Sanford and Son. *Upstairs Downstairs* was – unsuccessfully – transformed into *Beacon Hill*, *It's a Knockout* into *Almost Anything Goes*.   PP

Very Like a Whale (GB 1980). Nine-year-old John Osborne screenplay finally taken off the shelf to yield a TV film, and a pretty boring one, about the last hours of a tycoon for whom wealth, success and prestige have turned to wormwood. With Alan Bates, Gemma Jones, Leslie Sands. Directed by Alan Bridges; for ATV.   PP

A Very Missing Person
aka: *Hildegarde Withers*
US 1972 73m colour TVM
Universal (Edward J. Montagne)
A lady sleuth and her policeman friend follow the disappearance of a young woman.
A bad stab at recasting the old Hildegarde Withers films.
w Philip Reisman d Russell Mayberry
Eve Arden, James Gregory, Julie Newmar, Skye Aubrey

The Victim **
aka: *The Storm*
US 1972 73m colour TVM
Universal (William Frye)

A girl visits her sister during a storm, and finds a dead body and a lurking killer.
A very adequate *Psycho*-ish chiller using all the old tricks.

w Merwin Gerard *d* Herschel Daugherty

Elizabeth Montgomery, George Maharis, Sue Ann Langdon, Eileen Heckart

'More terrifying than rape . . . the threat that it could happen again!'

Victims

US 1982 96m colour TVM
ABC/Warner/Hajeno (Douglas Benton)

Rape victims plot their own revenge.
Arrant melodrama which fails to make any point and is more unpleasant than exciting.

w William Wood, Conrad Bromberg *d* Jerrold Freedman *ph* Robert Steadman *m* Lalo Schifrin

Ken Howard, Kate Nelligan, Madge Sinclair, Jonelle Allen, Howard Hesseman, Amy Madigan

'Subject is too important to be handled in such a clumsy, contrived manner.' – *Daily Variety*

Victims for Victims *

US 1984 96m colour TVM
NBC/Orion/Daniel L. Paulson/Loehr Spivey (Harry R. Sherman)

Theresa Saldana is half-murdered by a deranged assassin and forms an association to help victims of violent crime.
Re-enactment of a genuine case, with the victim playing herself. Gripping and fairly moving.

w Arthur Heinemann *d* Karen Arthur *ph* Jan Kiesser *m* Paul Chihara

Theresa Saldana, Adrian Zmed, Leila Goldoni, Lawrence Pressman, Linda Carlson

Victor, David (*c* 1920–). American producer of such series as *Dr Kildare*, *Marcus Welby*, *Lucas Tanner*.

Victor, James (1939–). Dominican general-purpose actor in American films and television. *Viva Valdez*, *Condo*, *Robert Kennedy and His Times*.

10
Episodes:
Design for War
The Pacific Boils Over
Sealing the Breach (Atlantic anti-submarine warfare)
Midway is East
Mediterranean Mosaic
Guadalcanal

Rings around Rabaul
Mare Nostrum
Sea and Sand (North Africa)
Beneath the Southern Cross (the battle of the Graf Spee)
Magnetic North (German bases in Norway)
The Conquest of Micronesia
Melanesian Nightmare
Roman Renaissance
D Day
The Killers and the Killed (U-boats)
The Turkey Shoot (the Marianas)
Two if by Sea (Pacific islands)
The Battle for Leyte Gulf
Return of the Allies (Luzon)
Full Fathom Five (Japanese ships sunk)
The Fate of Europe
Target Suribachi
The Road to Mandalay
Suicide for Glory (Okinawa)
Design for Peace (the atom bomb)

The Victorian Chaise-Longue *

GB 1962 40m bw
BBC Studio Four (Roger Smith)

Effective if rather abrupt adaptation by James MacTaggart, who also directed, of Marghanita Laski's story of a young woman haunted by a previous occupant of the day-bed on which she is convalescing, and typical of the Studio Four style. Two production touches which impressed me were the use of ceilings (still quite rare in television sets) and the persistent tick of the clock, both used to emphasize the enclosed stuffiness of the Victorian room. With Frances White. PP

Victorian Scandals

GB 1976 7 × 50m colour (VTR)
Granada (Michael Cox)

Seven plays about headline-making incidents of the Victorian era.
Oblique narrative prevented these dramatizations of fact from being compelling drama.

The Victorians *

GB 1963 8 × 50m bw
Granada (Philip Mackie)

Anthology of 19th-century well-made plays by Tom Taylor, Pinero, etc, cut down but otherwise played straight, as the Victorians themselves might have seen them had television been invented then. PP

Victory at Entebbe

US 1976 150m colour (VTR) TVM
David Wolper (Robert Guenette)

How the Israelis rescued a planeful of hostages held by terrorists at Entebbe.

Instant all-star re-creation of a famous event. At best competent, at worst fatuous.

w Ernest Kinoy *d* Marvin J. Chomsky *ph* James Kilgore *m* Charles Fox

Helmut Berger, Theodore Bikel, Linda Blair, Kirk Douglas, Richard Dreyfuss, Julius Harris, Helen Hayes, Anthony Hopkins, Burt Lancaster, Christian Marquand, Elizabeth Taylor, Jessica Walter, Harris Yulin

'It succeeds only in diminishing what it sets out to glorify.' – *Monthly Film Bulletin*

Victory at Sea ***
US 1952 26 × 25m bw
NBC (Project 20)

The battle for sea power during World War II. Absorbing documentary series put together from newsreel footage. A major achievement of its time.

Vidal, Gore (1926–). American author, a member of the Kennedy circle and a contributor to the 'Golden Age' of American TV drama in the fifties. His plays included *Visit to a Small Planet* and *Please Murder Me*, which was done in Britain by *Armchair Theatre* in 1958. Also edited collection of Golden Age scripts, *Best Television Plays*, Ballantine Books 1956.

In the seventies and eighties became a fairly frequent visitor on chat shows and arts programmes, airing a silky wit. *Vidal in Venice* (GB 1984) was a two-part series produced by Peter Montagnon for Antelope Films/C4, in which Vidal explored the city from which his family had originally come, and towards which he seemed increasingly proprietorial. 'What was that absurd name of his,' I wondered, 'but an anagram of RIVAL DOGE?'   PP

Videostars (GB 1983). A cable channel opens itself up to all comers, allowing secret, outrageous and impossible entertainers to flourish. Disappointing video play about video from Howard Schuman, possibly because what should have been an up-to-the-minute media fable had been kept waiting too long, shuttled from BBC to ITV and back before finally being aired. In the meantime the concept of an 'access' channel – much mooted before Cable got going – had been overtaken by commercial realities. Directed by Colin Bucksey, produced by Kenith Trodd.   PP

Vietnam. The first major war to be fought with full television coverage and, according to prevailing American opinion, to be lost because of television coverage. It is argued that nightly displays of increasingly vain warfare in the news shows finally destroyed any appetite for victory on the part of the American public. In his history of American television, *Tube of Plenty*, Erik Barnouw dates the process from as early as 1965, when viewers were shocked by a report from the CBS correspondent Morley Safer in which GIs casually set fire to a Vietnamese village accused of having aided the Vietcong. Two years later a special by the same reporter called *Morley Safer's Vietnam* provided further food for thought. Also in 1967 CBS commissioned a documentary on 'the other side' from the British traveller Felix Greene which, though they declined to screen it themselves, was seen on the national educational network under the title *Inside North Vietnam*.

British television produced several important reports on the war from the very early *The Quiet War* of 1963 to the terminal despatches of the BBC's Brian Barron, plus his special, *The Day the War Ended*, ten years later. Pierre Schoendorffer's *The Anderson Platoon* (France) brilliantly brought home the flavour of the campaign. *America on Trial* was a 1968 two-hour inquiry into the legality of the Americans' conduct of the war, produced by the BBC in conjunction with West Germany and, characteristically, the Americans themselves. Since the end of the war in 1975 there have been two plays about the last days, *The Last Day* and *Saigon – Year of the Cat*. Central co-produced the 12-part history *Vietnam* for C4. C4 also ran the Canadian series *Vietnam: the 10,000 Day War*.   PP

Vietnam *
US/GB/France 1983 12 × 50m
WGBH Boston/Central/Antenne 2 (Richard Ellison)

Encyclopedic history of the 30-year war in Indo-China, but going back even farther in search of its roots, to the French colonial heyday and World War II. Which made the abrupt cut-off as the Americans quit Saigon all the less satisfactory. A 13th episode might have brought in the Boat People as a reminder that not all was sweetness and light as the Vietnamese settled down to rule themselves at last.

Until then, only praise. The roll call of star witnesses ranged from ex-President Ford and Henry Kissinger to General Vo Nguyen Giap. British producer Martin Smith, who had worked on *The World at War*, demonstrated the same ability to survey great events from a proper distance while also catching the feel of what it was like to be there in the thick of it.

p and *d* Martin Smith   PP

Vietnam: the Ten Thousand Day War
Canada 1984 26 × 25m
Cineworld (Ian McLeod)

An alternative and almost as well-documented history. In Britain, both were shown by Channel 4.

w Peter Arnett *narrator* Richard Basehart

Vigoda, Abe (*c* 1919–). Gaunt American character actor who after small film roles (e.g. *The Godfather*) became well known in the TV series *Barney Miller* and starred in *Fish*. TV movies include: *The Devil's Daughter*, *Toma*, *The Story of Pretty Boy Floyd*, *How to Pick Up Girls*.

Vikings!
GB 1979 10 × 30m colour
BBC (David Collison)

Magnus Magnusson chronicling the rowdy history of the Norsemen who raided large areas of Europe and the Middle East and left a permanent mark on many of them. Mainly of interest to other Vikings.   PP

The Villa Maroc ** (GB 1972). Mordant Willis Hall comedy about a family holiday in Tangier. My view at the time: 'Funny, scathing about the English abroad, ultimately bitter and in odd way rather more salutary than any of the weightier examples of tribal self-criticism to be found on the air just now.' With George A. Cooper, Thora Hird, Anne Beach. Directed by Herbert Wise; produced by Irene Shubik; for BBC (*Play for Today*).
PP

Village Hall *
GB 1975 14 × 50m colour (VTR)
Granada (Michael Dunlop)

An anthology of plays all set in the same village hall, which is put to various uses.
A bright idea produced generally bright comedy–dramas, including contributions by Jack Rosenthal, Willis Hall and Kenneth Cope.

Villechaize, Herve (1943–). French–American dwarf actor, a fixture of FANTASY ISLAND.

Vincent, Jan-Michael (1944–). American leading man. TV movies: *Tribes*, *The Catcher*, *Sandcastles*, *Deliver Us from Evil*, *The Winds of War*, *Airwolf*.

Vinton, Bobby (1935–). American pop rock singer who has had several minor series of his own.

The Violation of Sarah McDavid
US 1981 96m colour TVM
CBS Entertainment (Nancy Malone)

A dedicated teacher is attacked and assaulted in her classroom.
Another rape story: not badly made, but does anybody need it?

w Joan Marks, Lois and Arnold Peyser *d* John Llewellyn Moxey *ph* Robert L. Morrison *m* Robert Prince

Patty Duke Astin, Ned Beatty, James Sloyan, Vernee Watson, Fran Bennett, Richard Venture

Virginia Fly is Drowning * (GB 1982; 60m; colour). Middle-aged virgin blurts out the truth about herself in a trendy TV programme, with predictable but touching consequences. Anna Massey gave another consummate performance in this dramatization by Angela Huth of her own novel. Directed by Mark Cullingham; produced by Anne Head; for BBC *Playhouse*.
PP

The Virginia Hill Story *
US 1974 74m colour TVM
RSO (Aaron Rosenberg)

After the 1947 killing of gangster Bugsy Siegel, his girl friend testifies before the Kefauver Commission.
Well-written crime exposé with good performances.

w Joel Schumacher, Juleen Compton *d* Joel Schumacher

Dyan Cannon, Harvey Keitel, Allen Garfield, Robby Benson

The Virginian *. This series of 74-minute TV westerns ran seven seasons, from 1962 to 1969, and though mostly boring it did recruit a large number of interesting guest stars who held the attention, despite leisurely production and strong family ambience. It had little to do with the original story: the Virginian (James Drury) was a slightly mysterious but impeccably natured ranch foreman, Trampas (Doug McClure) was an impulsive pal rather than a villain, and most of the stories centred on the judge, played first by Charles Bickford, then by Lee J. Cobb. Executive producer: Norman MacDonnell; producers: Howard Christie, Paul Freeman, Jim McAdams. Here is a selection of the more interesting episodes and guest stars:

The Brazen Bell: George C. Scott

Impasse: Eddie Albert

The Dream of Stavros Karas: Michael Constantine

Roar from the Mountain: Jack Klugman
The Executioners: Hugh O'Brian
The Small Parade: David Wayne
The Accomplice: Bette Davis
It Takes a Big Man: Ryan O'Neal
The Evil That Men Do: Robert Redford
The Big Deal: Ricardo Montalban
The Nobility of Kings: Charles Bronson
Men with Guns: Telly Savalas
Old Cowboy: Franchot Tone
The Invaders: Ed Begley
A Time Remembered: Yvonne de Carlo
Strangers at Sundown: Harry Morgan
Duel at Shiloh: Brian Keith
It Tolls for Thee: Lee Marvin
The Fortunes of J. J. Jones: Pat O'Brien
† The series ran on NBC throughout and led to a sequel series with a different cast and title: *The Men from Shiloh*.

Visions *
aka: *Visions of Death*
US 1972 73m colour TVM
CBS/Leonard Freeman
A clairvoyant professor has a vision of a building being dynamited, and though the police scoff he is suspected when it comes true. Adequate, predictable TV suspenser.
w Paul Playdon *d* Lee Katzin
Monte Markham, Barbara Anderson, Telly Savalas, Tim O'Connor

The Visit *
GB 1983–5 12 × 50m
BBC Scotland (Desmond Wilcox)
Originally four separate documentaries, with Des dogging people caught up in the process of making an important visit, e.g. a family to their mentally-handicapped daughter. One of the episodes featured the efforts of a Scottish surgeon to restore the face of a little Peruvian boy, eaten away by disease. A further programme followed the surgeon's wife to South America to try to arrange their adoption of the boy. In 1985 these two films were re-run, plus a third cliffhanger episode in which the adoption was sanctioned in the nick of time before new legislation would have blocked it.
A parallel strand of programmes followed the struggles of an injured London policeman to recover the use of his legs with the aid of new treatment and new technology in America. Finally some new stories were added, including a supposedly comic account

of an Irish gambler trying his game at the poker championships in Las Vegas.
No one would deny the bravery, kindness and determination Wilcox captured in the Boy David trilogy. 'The most moving TV I've seen in years,' said the Glasgow *Sunday Post*. Equally, there's no gainsaying the crassness with which he intruded on the P.C. Olds sequence or dressed up the silly poker stunt. Like his wife Esther Rantzen, he seems immune to self-criticism.
d Alex McCall   PP

Viva Valdez
US 1976   × 25m colour
ABC/Columbia/Rothman–Wohl/Stan Jacobson
Mishaps of a Chicano family in Los Angeles. Forgettable ethnic comedy.
cr Jacobson, Rothman, Wohl *d* Alan Rafkin
Carmen Zapata, Rodolfo Hoyos, James Victor

Vive Judson McKay: see Don't Call Me Charlie

Vogel, Virgil (19 –). American director who filmed a lot of episodes of *Wagon Train*, *Bonanza* and *The Big Valley*. TV movies, all pilots, include *The Return of Joe Forrester*, *Law of the Land*.

A Voice in the Darkness – Christabel Bielenburg (GB 1985). She was an English debutante who married a young German and spent the whole of World War II in Germany. Her reminiscences to Peter Williams for a local TVS programme, later expanded for C4, made one of the best accounts of ordinary life in Hitler's Germany. 'It was the oddness and unexpectedness of some of her stories,' I noted, 'which gave them such a strong smell of the way things happen.'   PP

Voices * (GB since 1982). Uncompromisingly egghead discussions of political and cultural trends by speakers drawn from academic life and the higher reaches of the novel, though Martin Amis has figured. Others include Umberto Eco, Kurt Vonnegut, Saul Bellow, Günter Grass. One season, two will take part at a time; another, the number will rise to three or four. By 1986 there had been four batches of six or seven, usually an hour long. Produced by Udi Eichler, for Brook Productions/C4.
                                                        PP

Von Zell, Harry (1906–81). Rotund American announcer and comic dupe on *The Burns and Allen Show*.

Vote, Vote, Vote for Nigel Barton (GB 1975). Dennis Potter's second Nigel Barton play, with his hero now standing for Parliament and cordially detesting it. Directed by Gareth Davies; produced by James MacTaggart; for BBC (*Wednesday Play*).   PP

vox pop. TV slang for random opinions gathered in the street by news or documentary film crews, from the Latin *vox populi*, voice of the people. Hence *Vox Pop*, a rather silly 1983 series built on the edited remarks of the population of Darwen, Lancs. Produced by Paul Watson, for BBC.
PP

The Voyage of Charles Darwin ***
GB 1978 6 × 50m colour
BBC (Christopher Ralling)
Splendid historical reconstruction obtained by sailing a near replica of HMS *Beagle*, with the actors aboard, over much of the same route Darwin took on the scientific voyage that was to lead him to the Theory of Evolution. As I wrote at the time, 'The *Beagle* is small, crowded, buffeted by the waves. The uniforms look lived-in, worn, and tarnished by time and tide rather than by a quick burst from the aerosol sea-spray spray.'
w Robert Reid *d* Martyn Friend *m* Wilfred Josephs
Malcolm Stoddard, Andrew Burt, Robert Stephens, Joseph Blatchley   PP
LH: 'First-class visualization of a dusty chapter of history.'

Voyage of the Heroes (GB 1985; 4 × 40m). Explorer Tim Severin and crew retrace the journey of Jason and Argonauts from classical mythology, rowing all the way. Written and narrated by Libby Purves; produced by John Miller, for BBC Manchester.

The Voyage of the Yes *
US 1972 73m colour TVM
Fenady–Crosby
Teenagers embark on a dangerous sea journey.
Mildly pleasing adventure with racial overtones.
w William Stratton *d* Lee H. Katzin
Desi Arnaz Jnr, Mike Evans, Beverly Garland, Skip Homeier, Della Reese

A Voyage Round My Father *
GB 1969 120m colour
BBC
John Mortimer's affectionate autobiographical play about his father Clifford Mortimer who despite losing his sight continued to plead in court as a successful divorce counsel; with Mark Dignam and Ian Richardson. Directed by Claude Whatham. The play later became a stage success and in 1981 was filmed by Thames Television with Laurence Olivier ageing marvellously as the father, Elizabeth Sellars as his wife and Alan Bates miscast as the young John Mortimer. Apart from one flicker of life in a courtroom vignette, I found he looked bored and blank for the rest of proceedings, beneath a thatch of hair that, for the forties scenes, anyway, was quite wrong. Since they used John Mortimer's own house and went back to his old school for this otherwise luminous production you'd have thought they would also have cast around for a reasonably convincing lookalike for the source of it all. Directed this time by Alvin Rakoff.   PP

Voyage to the Bottom of the Sea **
US 1964–7 110 × 50m colour
ABC/TCF/Irwin Allen
An atomic submarine scours the ocean bed for villains and monsters.
Among the best-produced juvenile series of its kind, this very watchable slice of hokum also benefited from agreeably zany script ideas and kept its tongue firmly in its cheek.
cr IRWIN ALLEN *m/d* Lionel Newman
Richard Basehart, David Hedison, Robert Dowdell, Terry Becker

Episodes:
First season:
Eleven Days to Zero
The City beneath the Sea
The Fear Makers
The Mist of Silence
The Price of Doom
The Sky Is Falling
Turn Back the Clock
The Village of Guilt
Hot Line
Submarine Sank Here
The Magnus Beam
No Way Out
The Blizzard Makers
The Ghost of Moby Dick
Long Live the King
Hail to the Chief
The Last Battle
Mutiny
Doomsday

The Invaders
The Indestructible Man
The Buccaneer
The Human Computer
The Saboteur
Cradle of the Deep
The Amphibians
The Exile
The Creature
The Enemies
Secret of the Loch
The Condemned
The Traitor

Second season (note the increasing suggestion of horror):
Jonah and the Whale
Time Bomb
And Five of Us Are Left
The Cyborg
Escape from Venice
The Left Handed Man
The Deadliest Game
Leviathan
The Peacemaker
The Silent Saboteurs
The X Factor
The Machines Strike Back
The Monster from Outer Space
Terror on Dinosaur Island
Killers of the Deep
The Deadly Creatures Below
The Phantom
The Sky's on Fire
Graveyard of Fear
Dead Men's Doubloons
The Death Ship
The Monster's Web
The Menfish
The Shape of Doom
The Mechanical Man
The Return of the Phantom

Third season (note the increasing proliferation of weird monsters):
The Monster from the Inferno
The Werewolf
The Day the World Ended
Night of Terror
The Terrible Toys
Day of Evil
Deadly Waters
The Thing from Outer Space
The Death Watch
The Deadly Invasion
The Haunted Submarine
The Plant Man

The Lost Bomb
The Brand of the Beast
The Creature
Death from the Past
The Heat Monster
The Fossil Men
The Mermaid
The Mummy
The Shadow Man
No Escape from Death
Doomsday Island
The Wax Men
Deadly Cloud
Destroy Seaview!

Fourth season (note the running out of ideas):
Fires of Death
The Deadly Dolls
Cave of the Dead
Journey with Fear
Sealed Orders
Man with Many Faces
Fatal Cargo
Time Lock
Rescue
Terror
A Time to Die
Blow Up
The Deadly Amphibians
The Return of Blackbeard
The Terrible Leprechaun
The Lobster Man
Nightmare
The Abominable Snowman
Secret of the Deep
Man Beast
Savage Jungle
Flaming Ice
Attack
Edge of Doom
The Death Clock
No Way Back

Voyagers!
US 1982 22 × 50m colour
NBC/Universal/Scholastic/James D.
   Parriott (Robert Bennett Steinhauer)
A young orphan has adventures with a time traveller.
Feeble fantasy series on the comic-strip level, with pretensions to be educational.
cr James D. Parriott
Jon-Erik Hexum, Meeno Pelluce

VTR. Video Tape Recording.

The Wackiest Ship in the Army
US 1965 29 × 50m colour
NBC/Columbia/Harry Ackerman (Herbert Hirschman)

During World War II in the Pacific an officer finds himself in charge of the only ship ever commissioned by the army.
Rather tired version of a rather tired film. It would have been funnier at half an hour.

cr Danny Arnold

Jack Warden, Gary Collins, Mike Kellin

† One episode title demands to be quoted: 'I'm Dreaming of a Wide Isthmus'.

Wacky Races
US 1968–9 52 × 25m colour
Hanna–Barbera

Stories of a cross-country car race, with villain Dick Dastardly trying to outdo all the other contestants.
Moderately pleasing cartoon series obviously inspired by *The Great Race*.

Waggoner, Lyle (1937–). American model and announcer (for Carol Burnett) who became a reasonably successful actor in *The New Adventures of Wonder Woman*.

Wagner *
West Germany/Hungary/GB 1983 10 × 50m or 1 × 300m
Richard Wagner Film GmbH/Hungaro Film and MTV Budapest for London Trust Productions (Derek Brierley)

The life and loves and battles of the composer, from heady revolutionary days in 1848 to the building of Bayreuth, the triumph of *The Ring* and his death in 1883.
Tony Palmer's sprawling epic which in popular myth went over budget, over the top and on for ever, though only some European audiences had the opportunity to judge for themselves from the full serial version. In Britain the single five-hour lump was chosen, a test of stamina at the best of times, never mind the belated midwinter scheduling C4 finally awarded it. With colds and 'flu about and metabolism running low, I hazarded, it probably took a couple of days off thousands of innocent lives.

There was some perverse casting – Vanessa Redgrave uninteresting as Cosima, the over-icing of the cake in enlisting Olivier, Richardson and Gielgud to play King Ludwig's three ministers. Richard Burton was himself too close to death to give Wagner the driving force of his middle years. 'But when you were caught up,' I wrote, 'as at the horrific first night of *Tannhäuser* – well, that was being put under some considerable spell, and spells aren't to be sniffed at.'

w Charles Wood   *ph* Vittorio Storaro
d Tony Palmer

RICHARD BURTON, VANESSA REDGRAVE, GEMMA CRAVEN, LASZLO GALFFI, EKKEHARD SCHALL, JOHN GIELGUD, Ralph Richardson, Laurence Olivier, Ronald Pickup, Richard Pasco, Marthe Keller, Franco Nero, Bill Fraser, Arthur Lowe, Prunella Scales, Corin Redgrave, Barbara Leigh-Hunt, Christopher Gable, Andrew Cruikshank, Stephen Oliver, Niall Toibin, Gabriel Byrne, John Shrapnel and Cyril Cusack   PP

Wagner, Lindsay (1949–). American leading lady, star of BIONIC WOMAN, which won her an Emmy in 1976. TV movies: *The Incredible Journey of Dr Meg Laurel*, *The Two Worlds of Jenny Logan*, *Callie and Son*, *Memories Never Die*, *I Want to Live*, *Passions*, *Princess Daisy*, *Two Kinds of Love*.

Wagner, Robert (1930–). Durable American leading man of many films. TV series: *It Takes a Thief*, *Colditz*, *Switch*, *Hart to Hart*. TV movies: *How I Spent My Summer Vacation*, *City Beneath the Sea*, *Cross Current*, *Killer By Night*, *Madame Sin*, *The Streets of San Francisco*, *The Affair*, *The Abduction of St Anne*, *Death at Love House*, *Cat on a Hot Tin Roof*, *The Critical List*, *Pearl*, *To Catch a King*, *Lime Street*.

Wagner's Ring (GB/West Germany 1982; 865m). The complete cycle recorded in Bayreuth, conducted by Pierre Boulez, directed by Brian Large. BBC2 and most other networks screened it over 10 weeks, with the whole of the opening *Rheingold* as the longest helping (145m) and Act One of *Valkyrie* and Act Two of *Götterdämmerung* the shortest, at 65m each.   PP

Wagon Train **
aka: *Major Adams, Trailmaster*
US 1957–61 approx. 120 × 50m bw
US 1963 32 × 74m colour
NBC (later ABC)/Revue

Stories of the people on an 1840s wagon train heading west.

A highly popular family series which showed that the western can be bent to any purpose: its scripts included rewrites of *Pride and Prejudice* and *Great Expectations*. It tended to be studio-bound, and one tired of the same shot of four wagons rounding a bend; the interest was in character, and luckily a stranger turned up every week, played by a famous star. The colour longforms didn't work at all: they looked too realistic for the material.

ROBERT HORTON (later Robert Fuller), WARD BOND (who died and was replaced by John McIntire)

The one-hour episodes were as follows:

The Jean Lebec Story (*w* Dwight Newton; *d* Sidney Lanfield; with Ricardo Montalban)

The Willy Moran Story (*w* William Fay, William R. Cox; *d* Herschel Daugherty; with Ernest Borgnine)

The Nelson Stack Story (*w* John Dunkel; *d* Don Weis; with Mark Stevens, Joanne Dru)

The Clara Beauchamp Story (no details to hand)

The Mary Halstead Story (*w* Robert E. Thompson, Leo Lieberman; *d* Justin Addis; with Agnes Moorehead)

The Les Rand Story (*w* Robert Florey; with Sterling Hayden)

The Emily Rossiter Story (*w* Richard Collins; *d* Sidney Lanfield; with Mercedes McCambridge, Susan Oliver)

The Charles Avery Story (*w* Aaron Spelling; *d* Bernard Girard; with Farley Granger, Chuck Connors)

The Zeke Thomas Story (*w* Halsted Welles; *d* John Brahm; with Gary Merrill, Janice Rule, K. T. Stevens)

The John Cameron Story (*w* E. Jack Neuman; *d* George Waggner; with Michael Rennie, Carolyn Jones, Claude Akins)

The Charles Maury Story (*w* Robert Yale Libott; *d* Allen Miner; with Charles Drake, Wanda Hendrix)

The Ruth Owens Story (*w* Robert E. Thompson; *d* Robert Florey; with Shelley Winters, Kent Smith)

The John Darro Story (*w* Adrian Spies; *d* Mark Stevens; with Eddie Albert, Margo, Sidney Blackmer)

The Riley Gratton Story (*w* William Fay; *d* John Brahm; with Guy Madison, Karen Steele, Jean Carson)

The Julie Gage Story (*w* Aaron Spelling; *d* Sidney Lanfield; with Anne Jeffreys, Robert Sterling)

The Luke O'Malley Story (*w* William Fay; *d* Mark Stevens; with Keenan Wynn, Carlos Romero)

The Cliff Grundy Story (*w* Aaron Spelling; *d* George Waggner; with Dan Duryea, Russell Johnson)

The Jesse Cowan Story (*w* Dwight Newton; *d* Sidney Lanfield; with George Montgomery, Lee Van Cleef)

The Annie MacGregor Story (*w* Frank W. Marshall; *d* Mark Stevens; with Jeannie Carson)

The Mark Hanford Story (*w* Turnley Walker; *d* Jerry Hopper; with Tom Tryon, Kathleen Crowley)

The Gabe Carswell Story (*w* John Dunkel; *d* Earl Bellamy; with James Witmore, Scott Marlowe)

The Bill Tawnee Story (*w* Rik Vollaerts, Dwight Newton; *d* David Butler; with Macdonald Carey, Joy Page)

The Marie Dupree Story (no details to hand)

The Conchita Vasquez Story (*w* Harry Von Zell; *d* Aaron Spelling; with Anna Maria Alberghetti)

The Bije Wilcox Story (*w* Milton Krims; *d* Abner Biberman; with Chill Wills, Onslow Stevens)

A Man Called Horse (*w* Leo Townsend; *d* Sidney Lanfield; with Ralph Meeker, Michael Pate)

The Dora Gray Story (*w* E. Jack Neuman; *d* Arnold Laven; with Linda Darnell, John Carradine, Michael Connors, Dan Blocker)

The Tobias Jones Story (*w* Harry Von Zell; *d* Herschel Daugherty; with Lou Costello, Beverly Washburn)

The Liam Fitzmorgan Story (*w* Robert E. Thompson; *d* Herschel Daugherty; with Cliff Robertson, Audrey Dalton)

The Sally Potter Story (*w* David Butler; with Vanessa Brown. Martin Milner, Lyle Bettger)

The Jeb Drummond Story (w Rudy Makoul, Lester Burke; d Richard Bartlett; with Gene Evans, June Lockhart, William Talman)

The Bernal Sierra Story (w Richard Maibaum; d David Butler; with Gilbert Roland)

The Major Adams Story (w Frank W. Marshall; d Mark Stevens; with Virginia Grey, Douglas Kennedy)

The Ralph Barrister Story (w Norman Jolley; d Richard Bartlett, with Charles Bickford, Roger Smith)

The Dan Hogan Story (w William Fay; d Richard Bartlett; with Jock Mahoney, Judith Ames)

The Cassie Tanner Story (w Paul Savage; d Mark Stevens; with Marjorie Main, George Chandler)

The Juan Ortega Story (w/d David Swift; with Dean Stockwell, Robert Simon)

The Rex Montana Story (w Warren Wilson; d Jesse Hibbs; with James Dunn, Joe Vitale)

The Ruttledge Munroe Story (w Norman Jolley; d Richard Bartlett; with John Drew Barrymore, Mala Powers)

The John Wilbot Story (w Richard Maibaum; d Mark Stevens; with Dane Clark, Audrey Dalton)

The Last Man (w Larry Marcus; d James Neilson; with Dan Duryea, Judi Meredith)

The Monty Britton Story (w Thomas Thompson; d Mark Stevens; with Ray Danton, Mona Freeman)

The Flint McCullough Story (w Harry Von Zell; d Allen Miner; with Everett Sloane)

Around the Horn (w Ted Sherdeman; d Herschel Daugherty; with William Bendix, Osa Massen)

The Sacramento Story (w Thomas Thompson; d Richard Bartlett; with Marjorie Main, Linda Darnell, Dan Duryea, Margaret O'Brien)

The Millie Davis Story (w Leo Townsend; d Jerry Hopper; with Evelyn Rudie, Nancy Gates, James Coburn)

The Dick Richardson Story (w Martin Berkeley, Clark E. Reynolds, Gene L. Coon; d David Butler; with John Ericson, Lyle Talbot)

The Doctor Willoughby Story (w Harry Von Zell; d Allen Miner; with Jane Wyman, Alan Marshal)

The Beauty Jamison Story (w Frank L. Moss; d Richard Bartlett; with Virginia Mayo, Russell Johnson)

The Jennifer Churchill Story (w Robert Yale Libott; d Jerry Hopper; with Rhonda Fleming)

The Steve Campden Story (w Robert Yale Libott; d Christian Nyby; with Torin Thatcher)

The Clara Duncan Story (w Richard Collins, Warren Wilson; d Jerry Hopper; with Angie Dickinson, Eduardo Ciannelli)

The Jasper Cato Story (w Robert Yale Libott; d Arthur Hiller; with Brian Donlevy, Allen Case)

The Sakai Ito Story (w Gene L. Coon; d Herschel Daugherty; with Sessue Hayakawa)

The Annie Griffith Story (w Kathleen Hite; d Jerry Hopper; with Jan Sterling)

The Matthew Lowry Story (w Paul David; d Jack Arnold; with Richard Anderson, Cathleen Nesbitt, Dorothy Provine)

The Ben Courtney Story (w Gene L. Coon, Rik Vollaerts; d Abner Biberman; with Stephen McNally, Kay Stewart)

The Tent City Story (w Norman Jolley; d Richard Bartlett; with Wayne Morris, Audrey Totter)

The Hunter Malloy Story (no details to hand)

The Mary Ellen Thomas Story (w Gene L. Coon, Harry Junkin; d Virgil Vogel; with Patty McCormack)

The Litty Angel Story (w Leonard Praskins; d James Neilson; with Anne Baxter, Henry Hull)

The Vincent Eaglewood Story (w David Swift; d Jerry Hopper; with Wally Cox, James Bell)

The Vivian Carter Story (w Peggy and Lou Shaw; d Joseph Pevney; with Phyllis Thaxter, Lorne Greene, Patric Knowles, Jane Darwell)

The Ella Lindstrom Story (w/d Allen H. Miner; with Bette Davis)

The Old Man Charvanaugh Story (w Arthur Browne Jnr; d Virgil Vogel; with J. Carrol Naish)

The Swift Cloud Story (w Donald S. Sanford; d Virgil Vogel; with Rafael Campos, Johnny Washbrook)

The Kate Parker Story (w Leonard Praskins; d Tay Garnett; with Virginia Grey, Warren Stevens)

The Jenny Tannen Story (w Kathleen Hite; d Christian Nyby, with Ann Blyth)

Chuck Wooster, Wagonmaster (w Nat Tanachuck, Arthur Browne Jnr; d Virgil Vogel; with Douglas Kennedy, Harry Carey Jnr)

The Sister Rita Story (*w* Gerry Day; *d* Joseph Pevney; with Vera Miles)

The Duke Le May Story (*w* Robert Fresco; *d* Virgil Vogel; with Cameron Mitchell, Edward Platt)

The Jose Maria Morgan Story (*w* Joe Stone, Paul King; *d* Tay Garnett; with Robert Loggia, Audrey Dalton)

The Honourable Don Carlos (*w* Oscar Millard; *d* David Butler; with Cesar Romero)

The Steele Family Story (*w* Jean Holloway; *d* Christian Nyby; with Lee Pàtrick, Lori Nelson, Dan Tobin) NB. This was the episode that borrowed the plot and characters of Jane Austen's *Pride and Prejudice*.

The Rodney Lawrence Story (*w* Gerry Day; *d* Virgil Vogel; with Dean Stockwell)

The Andrew Hale Story (*w* Jean Holloway; *d* Virgil Vogel; with John McIntire, Louise Fletcher, James Best)

The Vittorio Antonelli Story (*w* Jean Holloway; *d* Jerry Hopper; with Gustavo Rojo, Elizabeth Montgomery)

The Danny Benedict Story (no details to hand)

The Felizia Kingdom Story (*w* Leonard Praskins, Sloan Nibley; *d* Joseph Pevney; with Judith Anderson)

The Countess Olga Baranof Story (no details to hand)

The Estaban Zamora Story (*w* Halsey Melone; *d* Bretaigne Windust; with Ernest Borgnine)

The Lita Foladaire Story (*w* Jean Holloway; *d* Jerry Hopper; with Diane Brewster, Kent Smith)

The Cappy Darin Story (no details to hand)

The Elizabeth McQueeny Story (*w/d* Allen H. Miner; with Bette Davis)

The St Nicholas Story (*w* Jean Holloway; *d* Bretaigne Windust; with Robert Emhardt)

The Ruth Marshall Story (*w* Jean Holloway; *d* Richard Bartlett; with Luana Patten)

Trial for Murder, parts one and two (no details to hand)

The Ricky and Laurie Bell Story (*w/d* Allen H. Miner; with James Gregory, June Lockhart)

The Amos Gibbon Story (no details to hand)

The Joshua Gilliam Story (no details to hand)

The Jonas Murdock Story (no details to hand)

The Leslie Ivers Story (no details to hand)

The Dick Jarvis Story (no details to hand)

The Robert Farnsworth Story (no details to hand)

The Colter Craven Story (*d* John Ford; with Carlton Young, Anna Lee, John Carradine, John Wayne as General Sherman)

The Weight of Command (*w* Harold Swanton; *d* Herschel Daugherty; with Dan Riss, Jeanne Bates)

The Renie Webster Story (no details to hand)

The Sam Elder Story (no details to hand)

The Barnaby West Story (no details to hand)

About 20 other episodes of which details cannot currently be obtained from the distributors were completed before Ward Bond died on location. Robert Horton had opted out almost a season previously. John McIntire took over as wagonmaster; Terry Wilson and Frank McGrath remained. It was with this cast, plus Robert Fuller as scout, that a 74-minute version was launched in 1963, and the series was seen for the first time in colour. Somehow its appeal had faded despite the refurbishing. The 74-minute episodes were:

The Molly Kincaid Story (*w* Gene L. Coon; *d* Virgil Vogel; with Barbara Stanwyck, Ray Danton)

The Robert Harrison Clarke Story (*w* Gene L. Coon; *d* William Witney; with Michael Rennie, Henry Silva)

The Gus Morgan Story (*w* Norman Jolley; *d* Virgil Vogel; with Peter Falk, Tommy Sands)

The Fort Pierce Story (*w* John McGreevey; *d* William Witney; with Ronald Reagan, Ann Blyth)

The Andrew Elliott Story (*w* John Kneubuhl; *d* Herschel Daugherty; with Scott Miller, Everett Sloane)

The Sam Spicer Story (*w* Norman Jolley; *d* R. G. Springsteen; with Clu Gulager, Ed Begley)

The Sandra Cummings Story (*w* Norman Jolley; *d* Virgil Vogel; with Rhonda Fleming)

The Kate Crawley Story (*w* Norman Jolley; *d* Virgil Vogel; with Barbara Stanwyck, Michael Burns)

The Zebedee Titus Story (*w* Norman Jolley; *d* Virgil Vogel; with Neville Brand)

The Pearlie Garnet Story (*w* Leonard Praskins; *d* Herschel Daugherty; with Marilyn Maxwell)

The Kitty Pryor Story (*w/d* Allen H. Miner; with Diana Hyland, Bradford Dillman)

The Michael Malone Story (*w* Gerry Day; *d* Virgil Vogel; with Michael Parks, Joyce Bulifant)

The Cassie Vance Story (*w* Betty Andrews; *d* Joseph Pevney; with Laraine Day, Richard Carlson)

The Fenton Canaby Story (*w* Thomas Thompson; *d* Joseph Pevney; with Jack Kelly, Barbara Bain)

The Myra Marshall Story (*w* Peter B. Germano; *d* Joseph Pevney; with Suzanne Pleshette)

The Whipping (*w* Leonard Praskins; *d* Virgil Vogel; with Martin Balsam)

The Widow O'Rourke Story (*w* Leonard Praskins, Sloan Nibley; *d* Joseph Pevney; with Carol Lawrence)

The Geneva Balfour Story (*w* Ken Trevey; *d* Sutton Roley; with Sherry Jackson, Robert Lansing)

The Sam Pulaski Story (*w*/*d* Allen H. Miner; with Ross Martin, Annette Funicello)

The Ma Bleecker Story (*w* Ted Sherdeman; *d* William Witney; with Joan Blondell, Ed Nelson)

The Eli Bancroft Story (*w* Steve Ritch; *d* R. G. Springsteen; with Leif Erickson)

The Story of Cain (*w*/*d* Allen H. Miner; with Roy Hayes)

The Jed Whitmore Story (with Neville Brand)

The Grover Allen Story (*w* Jack Curtis; *d* Joseph Pevney; with Burgess Meredith, Nancy Gates)

The Melanie Craig Story (*w* John McGreevey; *d* Joseph Pevney; with Myrna Fahey, Jim Davis)

The Trace McCloud Story (*w* John McGreevey; *d* Virgil Vogel; with Larry Pennell, Audrey Dalton)

The Ben Engel Story (*w* Betty Andrews; *d* Joseph Pevney; with Clu Gulager, John Doucette)

The Santiago Quesada Story (*w* Gerry Day; *d* Virgil Vogel; with Joseph Wiseman)

The Duncan McIvor Story (*w* Norman Jolley; *d* Herschel Daugherty; with Ron Hayes, John Larkin)

The Link Cheney Story (with Charles Drake)

The Stark Bluff Story (*w*/*d* Allen H. Miner; with Ray Danton)

The Last Circle Up (*w*/*d* Allen H. Miner; with Arthur Space, Joe de Santis)

Wainwright, James (1938–). Tough-looking American general purpose actor. Series: *Jigsaw*, *Beyond Westworld*. TV movies: *Once Upon a Dead Man*, *The President's Plane Is Missing*, *Killdozer*, *Bridger*, *A Woman Called Moses*.

Wait 'Til Your Father Gets Home **
US 1972–3 48 × 22m colour
Hanna–Barbera

Domestic problems of a suburbanite.
This cartoon half-hour, drawn with UPA-like economy, is also an agreeable satirical comedy with more than a passing reference to *All in the Family*. Thoroughly amusing, and not for kids.

Wait till Your Mother Gets Home
US 1983 96m colour TVM
NBC/Blue–Greene (Albert Salzer)

A football coach bets his wife he can mind the kids and the house for two months while she takes on a summer job.
Elementary role-reversal comedy-drama, reasonably well mounted but running out of steam early on.

w D. Eyre, Bill Persky *d* Bill Persky
ph Frank Stanley *m* Ken Harison

Paul Michael Glaser, Dee Wallace, Peggy McKay, David Doyle, Lynne Moody, James Gregory

Waite, Ralph (*c* 1937–). American general purpose actor, hardly known until he became a national figure as Dad in *The Waltons*. TV movies: *The Borgia Stick*, *The Secret Life of John Chapman*, *Red Alert*, *Roots*, *Angel City*, *Gentleman Bandit*, *A Good Sport*. 1983: starred in a series, *The Mississippi*, which was less than a resounding success.

Wake Me When the War Is Over
US 1969 74m colour TVM
Spelling–Thomas

In the closing days of World War II an American is captured by a German baroness, who keeps him in luxury long after the war. Smoking room story, a little funnier than *Situation Hopeless But Not Serious*; though not much.

w Frank Peppiatt, John Aylesworth *d* Gene Nelson

Ken Berry, Eva Gabor, Werner Klemperer, Jim Backus, Hans Conried

Wakelam, Stephen (19 –). British writer who came to notice with *Brother to the Ox* (1982). Also *Gaskin* (1983), *Punters* (1984), etc.

Walden, Brian (1932–). Presenter of LWT's *Weekend World* current affairs show 1977–86; until then, a Labour MP for 13 years. As an interviewer displayed a rare gift to lead politicians through sometimes uncomfortable scenarios of things to come.
PP

Walden, Robert (1943–) (R. Wolkowitz). American general-purpose actor. *Shirts/ Skins*, *The Great Ice Ripoff*, *Larry*, *The Marcus-Nelson Murders*, LOU GRANT (as the chief reporter), *Enola Gay*, *Brothers*.

A Walk in the Desert * (GB 1960). Injured, sorry-for-self provincial (Kenneth Haigh) takes it out on girl who calls mistakenly at his house (Tracey Lloyd). Why? At the time, I thought: 'She was a natural enemy, optimistic, someone on the march. He was none of those things, an aimless wanderer in the desert. They clashed, recognized each other, parted, that was all. But it had been some sort of encounter, a landmark in the desert, something to remember. . .' John Whiting's eloquent needling match inaugurated a season of 20 new works put on by the BBC in somewhat belated recognition of the need to have purpose-written plays on TV. Other contributors included Alun Owen (*The Ruffians*), Elaine Morgan, John Osborne (*A Subject of Scandal and Concern*), Leo Lehman, Jack Pulman, John Hopkins, John Elliot and Donald Wilson. PP

A Walk in the Forest *
GB 1980 90m colour
BBC

Play by Jeremy Paul based on his own involvement, as a member of the British Writers' Guild, with a dissident Russian, enabling him to chart with honesty the quickenings, fadings, shifts and affectations of a do-gooder doing good.

d Jack Gold *ph* John McGlashan *m* Carl Davis

John Alderton, Lynn Farleigh, John Bird, Jeremy Kemp PP

Walk Up and Die: see Banyon

Walk With Destiny
US title: *The Gathering Storm*
GB 1974 75m colour (VTR)
BBC/Jack Le Vien (Andrew Osborn)

The life of Winston Churchill in the years preceding his appointment as prime minister. Interesting but much decried drama documentary with impersonations of historic figures too much the centre of attention.

w Colin Morris *d* Herbert Wise

Richard Burton, Virginia McKenna, Angharad Rees (Sarah), Clive Francis (Randolph), Robert Beatty (Beaverbrook), Robin Bailey (Chamberlain), Thorley Walters (Baldwin), Ian Bannen (Hitler), Ian Ogilvy (Edward VIII)

Walker, Clint (1927–). Massive American leading man who came to fame via TV in the series *Cheyenne*; later in *Kodiak*. TV movies: *Yuma, Hardcase, The Bounty Man, Scream of the Wolf, Killdozer, Snowbeast, Centennial.*

Walker, Nancy (1921–) (Ann Swoyer). Pint-sized American comedienne who appeared in a handful of seventies series. *McMillan and Wife, Rhoda, The Nancy Walker Show, Mrs Blansky's Beauties.* TV movies: *Every Man Needs One, Thursday's Game, Death Scream, Human Feelings.*

Walking Tall (US 1981). Originally promoted as *Part Two Walking Tall*, this rather unhappy one-hour series was produced by David Gerber for Columbia. It told the supposedly true story of vigilante sheriff Buford Pusser, who had already featured in 3 feature films, and tried unsuccessfully to sanitize the violence by treating him as some kind of national hero. Bo Swenson starred; only 7 episodes were made.

Walking Through the Fire
US 1979 96m colour TVM
CBS/Time–Life (Stan Hough)

When a woman finds she is suffering from cancer, her husband is not the support she might hope.
Case history with vague but depressing details; a film which seems to have absolutely no purpose.

w Sue Crafton, *book* Laurel Lee *d* Robert Day *ph* Richard C. Glouner *m* Fred Karlin

Bess Armstrong, Tom Mason, Richard Masur, Swoosie Kurtz, June Lockhart, Bonnie Bedelia, J. D. Cannon

The Wall
US 1982 142m colour TVM
CBS/Time–Life/David Susskind (Harry R. Sherman)

Jews die in the 1943 Warsaw Ghetto uprising. One would like to applaud this mini-*Holocaust*, but the treatment is doleful and protracted and the plot seldom rises above Hollywood cliché.

w Millard Lampell, *book* John Hersey *d* Robert Markowitz *ph* Brian Tufano *m* Leonard Rosenman *ad* Jerzy Maslowsky

Tom Conti, Lisa Eichhorn, Eli Wallach, Gerald Hiken, Rachel Roberts, Philip Sterling

Wallace, Mike (1918–). American newscaster and host who became known in the fifties for his abrasive interviews.

Wallach, Eli (1915–). Sharp-eyed American stage actor who has not despised other media. TV movies: *A Cold Night's Death, Indict and Convict, Seventh Avenue, The Pirate, The Pride of Jesse Hallam, The Poppy Is Also a Flower, Skokie, The Wall, The Executioner's Song, Anatomy of an Illness, Christopher Columbus, Our Family Honor.*

'He sacrificed everything in the name of love!'
Wallenberg: a Hero's Story
US 1985 2 × 96m colour miniseries
NBC/Paramount/Dick Berg/Stonehenge (Richard Irving)

During World War II a Swedish diplomat saves hundreds of Hungarian Jews from extinction by the Nazis, but is himself eventually imprisoned by the Russians and never seen again.

An appalling true story which was more gripping on the printed page than in pictures, where it comes out as just another war suspense thriller.

w Gerald Green *d* Lamont Johnson *ph* Charles Correll *m* Ernest Gold

Richard Chamberlain, Bibi Andersson, Melanie Mayron, Alice Krige, Kenneth Colley, Stuart Wilson

Walston, Ray (1917–). American comedy character actor, star of TV series *My Favorite Martian*. TV movie: *Institute for Revenge.*

Walter **
GB 1982 75m
Central/Randel Evans Productions (Nigel Evans) for C4

A mentally-retarded young man who has been lovingly brought up by his mother is flung into the harsh world of institutional care when she dies. Nigel Evans's deliberate shocker, shirking neither the realities of morning body-washing nor homosexual assault, gave Channel 4's viewers an opening-night promise – or threat – of what to expect. Some of them may not have realized, either, that it depicted conditions back in the fifties. But it marked the summation of a long struggle by Nigel Evans, as an independent producer, to bring home the needless indignities accompanying physical and mental handicap, and with Ian McKellen's extraordinary performance – contorting his head in an effort to comprehend what was required of him – it could only be a good deed.

w David Cook *d* Stephen Frears *ph* Chris Menges *m* George Fenton

Ian McKellen, Barbara Jefford, Tony Melody, Arthur Whybrow

Walter and June followed six months later, bringing in Sarah Miles as a sweet simple girl who gives Walter great joy and great sorrow. *Loving Walter*, also 1983 (*p* Richard Creasey), was a 120m amalgamation of the two films. PP

† In Central's own area the original transmission of *Walter* was preceded by a film about its making, *A Perfectly Ordinary Person . . .*, *d* and *p* Patricia Ingram.

Walter, Harriet (19 –). Intelligent British actress who came to notice in the otherwise misconceived *The Imitation Game*; since then, *The Cherry Orchard*, as Amy Johnson in *Amy* and a powerful performance in THE PRICE, 1985. PP

Walter, Jessica (1944–). Stylish American leading lady, busy in films and TV. Series: *Amy Prentiss, Wheels*. TV movies: *The Immortal, Three's a Crowd, They Call It Murder, Women in Chains, Home for the Holidays, Hurricane, Having Babies, Victory at Entebbe, Black Market Baby, Wild and Woolly, Dr Strange, Secrets of Three Hungry Wives, Vampire, She's Dressed to Kill, Miracle on Ice, Scruples, Thursday's Child, Bare Essence, The Return of Marcus Welby, The Execution.*

Walters, Barbara (19 –). American interviewer and newscaster who made headlines in 1977 when she left NBC's *Today* for a million-a-year contract with ABC.

Walters, Julie (1950–). British comedienne, the thinner, darker, straighter one of Wood and Walters; also famed for *Educating Rita* on stage, screen and TV excerpts; other credits include *Happy since I Met You, Intensive Care, The Boys from the Blackstuff, Unfair Exchanges* and *The Secret Diary of Adrian Mole* (as his mum). PP

Walton, Kent (1925–). Canadian sports commentator in Britain, the voice of wrestling for many a year.

The Waltons ***
US 1972–81 approx. 220 × 50m colour
CBS/Lorimar

Problems of a family in the Appalachian mountains during the Depression years.
The original novel by Earl Hanmer Jnr also formed the basis of a film, *Spencer's*

WALLENBERG: A HERO'S STORY. They changed the title several times, but this downbeat story could never be a top grosser. Richard Chamberlain's fans, however, enabled it to achieve decent ratings.

Mountain, and a TV movie, *The Homecoming*. The series rapidly became the seventies equivalent of the Hardy family movies, and one could not fault the writing or production.

RALPH WAITE, MICHAEL LEARNED, WILL GEER, ELLEN CORBY, RICHARD THOMAS

† The series included a number of episodes combined to make longforms under such titles as *The Waltons' Crisis*.

PP: '*The Waltons' Crisis* was in fact an example of the series at its worst, the grave disability which struck the materfamilias being sunnily overcome with no real hardship. But maverick screenwriters would often field heart-felt individual episodes, e.g. one by "Colly Cibber" (a pseudonym) about a gnarled old author who had talked his books away in bar-rooms rather than putting them down – many a screenwriter's own story.'

Wambaugh, Joseph (1937–). American novelist, an ex-cop who writes exclusively about what he knows. *The New Centurions*

formed the basis for *Police Story*, which spun off into *Police Woman*; meanwhile he had got a long TV movie and a series out of *The Blue Knight*.

Wanamaker, Sam (1919–). American actor domiciled in Britain since the Parnell Johnson witchhunt in the US in the late 1940s. Has appeared on TV, if sparingly, since *The Power and the Glory*, 1958. Also directed one or two plays for A-R.   PP

Wanted Dead or Alive *
US 1958–60 98 × 25m bw
CBS/Four Star/Malcolm

Adventures of a western bounty hunter. Competent series which helped to create one of the sixties' biggest stars.

Steve McQueen

Wanted, the Sundance Woman *
US 1976 75m colour TVM
ABC/TCF (Ron Preissman)

The wife of the Sundance Kid tries to find another identity in the old west.
Pretty good action pilot, certainly better than the previous attempt at this subject, *Mrs Sundance*.

w Richard Fielder *d* Lee Philips *m* Fred Karlin

Katharine Ross, Steve Forrest, Stella Stevens, Michael Constantine, Hector Elizondo

The War about Peace (GB 1983; 52m). The argument for keeping the nuclear deterrent as the most effective safeguard not only against another world war but against any kind of nuclear war, too. Ably presented by Max Hastings, with contributions from George Bush, Michael Heseltine, Vladimir Bukovsky, Eugene Rostow, et al. Directed and produced by David Gerard, for Central.

War and Peace ***
GB 1963 150m approx. bw (VTR)
Granada

Tolstoy's novel compressed and adapted for the studio, with a master of ceremonies. Trail-blazing, Emmy-winning compendium of television techniques.

w R. D. MacDonald *d* Silvio Narizzano

John Franklyn Robbins, Kenneth Griffith (as Napoleon), Daniel Massey, Clifford Evans, Valerie Sarruf

War and Peace *
GB 1972 20 × 45m colour (VTR)
BBC

Solemn, expensive, beautiful, reverent adaptation. Unfortunately it was too slow, too complex and too long.

w Jack Pulman *d* John Howard Davies

Rupert Davies, Anthony Hopkins, Faith Brook, Morag Hood

† BBC2 has also shown the full 4 × 2 hr version of Sergei Bondarchuk's epic Russian version, much cut on its cinema release.

The War between the Tates *
US 1977 75m colour TVM
NBC/Talent Associates (Frederick Brogger)

A study of a marriage on the point of breaking up.
Good solid matrimonial drama with satisfactory performances.

w Barbara Turner, *novel* Alison Lurie *d* Lee Phillips *m* John Barry

Richard Crenna, Elizabeth Ashley, Granville Van Dusen

The War Game ** (GB 1965 – not transmitted). Peter Watkins's alarming, indeed misanthropic vision of Britain under nuclear attack, made for, but not transmitted by, the BBC. The official view put forward by the then director-general, Sir Hugh Greene, was that it might seriously harm the old, the simple or the out of touch who lit upon it without prior warning; instead the BBC made it available to the British Film Institute for theatrical release: an elegant but not really satisfactory solution. Even if it meant a late late late showing hedged with provisos, it should have gone out on the medium for which it was intended.   PP
† It did finally in 1985.

A War of Children *
US 1973 73m colour TVM
Tomorrow (Roger Gimbel)

Problems of an Irish family in the present troubles.
Well-made but astonishingly anti-British lowlife drama.

w James Costigan *d* George Schaefer

Vivien Merchant, Jenny Agutter, John Ronane, Anthony Andrews

The War of the Springing Tiger (GB 1984; 50m). Indians who in World War II were tempted to join or support the Indian National Army, fighting on the Axis side. An extremely well-researched documentary (Candida Tunbridge) which Granada made and scheduled just ahead of *The Jewel in the Crown* in the hope of instructing the audience in advance about this little-known – but vital to the *Jewel's* narrative – bit of history. Produced by David Boulton.   PP

War School
GB 1980 4 × 50m colour
BBC

Serial report by Michael Cockerell on the British army's staff college at Camberley, overshadowed by the fame (or notoriety) of its commandant at the time, Major-General Sir Frank Kitson, whose text-book on peace-keeping operations had been attacked by the Left. My initial impression: 'He seemed to be an unsentimental person with an unexpected quick-change aptitude, rolling up to the College in jumper and slacks and a moment later addressing the students in full service dress. Or was this just another accident of the restlessness with which this opening instalment, at all events, had been put together?
'Never quite certain whether to dwell on the bogeyman or the sample of young officers the series will follow through their course, it came to grips with neither.'

† A previous one-off documentary on the staff college was Westward's *This Is My Contract* (1971). PP

Ward, Bill (19 –). Pioneer British producer and executive from the seat-of-the-pants days in television, director of programmes at ATV until his retirement in the mid-seventies. The telerecording of his production of the Moscow state circus (1959) is preserved in the archives as a classic live television relay. PP

Ward, Burt (1945–) (Herbert Jervis). American juvenile actor who became famous as Robin in *Batman*.

Ward, Jay (19–). American animator and producer, creator of *Bullwinkle* and *Fractured Flickers*.

Warden, Jack (1920–). American character actor. TV series: *The Asphalt Jungle*, *The Wackiest Ship in the Army*, *NYPD*, *The Bad News Bears*. TV movies: *The Face of Fear*, *Brian's Song*, *What's a Nice Girl Like You*, *Man on a String*, *Lt Schuster's Wife*, *Remember When*, *The Godchild*, *Journey from Darkness*, *They Only Come Out at Night*, *Raid on Entebbe*, *A Private Battle*, *Hobson's Choice*, *Helen Keller: The Miracle Continues*, *Robert Kennedy and His Times*, *A.D.* New series 1985: CRAZY LIKE A FOX.

Warhol
GB 1973 50m colour
ATV
Supposedly scandalous documentary by the photographer David Bailey about the *avante-garde* painter and film-maker Andy Warhol, delayed first by a busybodies' lawsuit, then by corporate doubts. When finally shown it proved to be unexceptional save for Joe d'Allessandro shaving in the bath – could he possibly steer his way through the acne unscathed? The whole thing was distinctly seedy: there is nothing like ill-shot Eastmancolor to bring up rashes, pimples, warts and all. PP

Waring, Eddie (1909–). British north country rugby league commentator who in later years was also familiar on *It's a Knockout*.

Waring, Richard (*c* 1930–). British comedy writer whose series include *The Marriage Lines*, *Not in Front of the Children*, *Bachelor Father*, *Miss Jones and Son*.

Warner Brothers Presents: see Casablanca, King's Row, Cheyenne

Warner, David (1941–). Tall, bony British character actor, in all media. TV movies: *Holocaust*, *SOS Titanic*, *Masada*, *Marco Polo*, *A Christmas Carol*, *Hitler's SS*. British series: *Charlie*, *Hold the Back Page*.

Warner, Jack (1895–1981) (Jack Waters). British character actor, the beloved DIXON OF DOCK GREEN. He also made light entertainment appearances as a comedian and singer.

Warner, Lavinia (–). Resourceful British story editor and producer who originated *Tenko* for the BBC, produced *G.I. Brides* and *Jailed by the British* as an independent, and steered Maria Aitken first into her chat show *Private Lives*, then up the Amazon in *Lizzie* (1986).

Warren, Lesley Ann (1948–). American leading lady. TV movies: *Seven in Darkness*, *Love Hate Love*, *Assignment Munich*, *The Daughters of Joshua Cabe*, *The Letters*, *The Legend of Valentino*, *Betrayal*, *79 PARK AVENUE*, *Pearl*, *Beulah Land*, *Portrait of a Showgirl*, *Evergreen*.

The Wars of the Roses (GB 1964; 11 × 60m; bw). Shakespeare's *Henry VI* and *Richard III* in the RSC's Stratford serialization by John Barton and Peter Hall. For TV the directors were Michael Hayes and Robin Midgley. The casting retained celebrated performances by David Warner, Peggy Ashcroft, Donald Sinden and Ian Holm. Produced by Michael Barry; for BBC. PP

Warship *
GB 1973–8 approx. 39 × 50m colour
BBC (Anthony Coburn)
Life aboard a Royal Navy frigate in the seventies, involved in the Cold War, Cod Wars, NATO exercises, foreign troubles of all sorts, very good on the curious pressures on the servicemen in times of frozen war but tending to dwell on internal bickerings so obsessively that in the end the entire ship's complement was on the edge of a nervous breakdown. A succession of actors commanded HMS *Hero*: Donald Burton, Bryan Marshall, Derek Godfrey. Created by Ian Mackintosh; written by Ian Mackintosh, Allan Prior, others. PP

Washington: Behind Closed Doors **
US 1977 6 × 96m colour
Paramount (Norman Powell)

A fictionalization of the Nixon regime. Parts of this extension of John Erlichman's book *The Company* are as gripping and well produced as anything made for TV, and the acting is of a high standard, but in the end one wonders whether the mixing of fact and fiction can in any way be justified, especially as the plot does not vary sufficiently from the known facts to be worth considering on its own account.

w DAVID W. RINTELS with ERIC BERCOVICI *d* Gary Nelson

JASON ROBARDS JNR, Cliff Robertson, Stefanie Powers, Robert Vaughn, Barry Nelson, Andy Griffith, Lois Nettleton, Harold Gould, Tony Bill, John Houseman

PP: 'On the contrary I thought the original Erlichman plot about the CIA chief the least interesting element. The expanded material with Robards as a Nixonish president and Robert Vaughn as his hatchet man was fascinating.'

Washington Mistress
US 1981 96m colour TVM
CBS/Lorimar (Karen Mack)

A senator's aide bears a child for an ambitious Washington lawyer who can't get a divorce.
Corny melodrama with a political background.

w Audrey Davis Levin *d* Peter Levin *ph* Robert Caramico *m* Billy Goldenberg

Lucie Arnaz, Richard Jordan, Tony Bill, Pat Hingle, Dorothy Fielding, Peter Hobbs

'Old-fashioned woman's-picture nonsense.' – Hollywood *Reporter*

Watch Mr Wizard (US 1951–4). Half-hour children's instructional series in which Don Herbert conducted simple scientific experiments.

Watch the Woman (GB 1985; 6 × 45m). Shrill women's magazine of the air, predictably (on Channel 4) obsessed with women's rights and scoring off men. 'The sort of thing they say on this programme is that on this programme Lesbianism will never be a term of abuse, which is like Israel affirming that it doesn't go in much for anti-semitism.' Presented by Jenny Lecoat, Lucy Mathen and Bert McIver (token male), with Tina Baker as reporter. Produced by Carol Sarler for Carol Sarler Productions/C4.   PP

The Water Margin (Japan 1978). Medieval epic serial of oriental chivalry which became a cult favourite in Britain when anglicized by David Weir and Michael Bakewell in 7 × 45m episodes. Originally directed by Nobuo Nakagawa for NTV Tokyo.   PP

Water World
US 1973–4 52 × 25m colour
Syndicast

Film snippets of water sports, linked by Lloyd Bridges (first 26) and James Franciscus (second 26). The hosts occasionally participate.

Waterfront
US 1954–5 78 × 25m bw
Roland Reed

Adventures of a tugboat captain in San Pedro harbour.
Adequate low-key melodrama with a family background.

Preston Foster

Waterfront (Australia 1985; 6 × 50m). Jack Thompson as a happy-go-lucky Melbourne docker is nudged by circumstances into leading his union against grasping shipowners and luckless immigrant scabs during the bad times of 1928, plus Warren Mitchell as a run-down Pommie music-hall comedian striking gold by inventing the political satire which counterpoints the action. All a bit black-and-white but, as I said, this is a country still stumbling on its own history as raw material, and getting it down while it's still raw. With Greta Scacchi, Ray Barrett, John Karlsen. Written by Mac Gudgeon, directed by Chris Thomson, produced by Bob Weis, for Waterfront Pty. Shown in Britain by C4 in 3 × 100m helpings.   PP

Waterhouse, Keith (1929–   ). British writer and journalist whose work for television, apart from a dramatization of his novel of childhood, *There is a Happy Land*, used to be mostly in comedies often with Willis Hall: *Inside George Webley* (1968), *Queenie's Castle* (1970), *Budgie* (1971–2), WORZEL GUMMIDGE (1978–81), *The Upchat Line* (solo) (1977–8). Lately into screenplays: *This Office Life*, 1984; *Slip-Up*, 1986. Subject of a *South Bank Show* assessment, 1983.

Waterloo Sunset (GB 1978). Mistakenly lauded tract by Barrie Keeffe in which an old lady played by Queenie Watts, former music hall and pub entertainer, fled the old people's home whither her bourgeois son had condemned her and found happiness with a

West Indian family – a praiseworthy sentiment on Keeffe's part made impossible to accept by his vitriolic picture of all whites. and particularly the police. A BBC *Play for Today*.   PP

Waterman, Dennis (1948–). Amiable British actor and true product of the television age, in *Member of the Wedding* (1959) and *All Summer Long* (1960) as a juvenile, as well as William in the original TV version of *Just William*; these days best known for *The Sweeney* and *Minder*. Also writes and sings, and in 1982 part-financed as well as starred in the TVM *World Cup: a Captain's Tale*.   PP

Waters, Joe (1926–). Veteran British fiction producer, on BBC staff until 1984, freelance since. Credits go back to *Dixon of Dock Green* and all the way forward, via DON'T FORGET TO WRITE and *Squadron* (1982), to *My Brother Jonathan* (1985) and *Strike It Rich* (1986). To come: Gerald Durrell's *My Family and Other Animals* and Frances Brett Young's *Portrait of Clare*.

Waterston, Sam (1940–). American actor, in all media. *Friendly Fire, Oppenheimer, QED, Games Mother Never Taught You, In Defense of Kids, Dempsey, Finegan Begin Again, Love Lives On*.

Watford, Gwen (c 1929–). British leading actress, in the sixties one of the most popular on TV, in many single plays including *The Greeting, A Provincial Lady, Aren't We All*.

Watkins, Peter (1936–). Gifted British film-maker who came to fame with *Culloden* (1964); on its strength given free hand to make *The War Game* the following year, only to have this alarming vision of a nuclear attack on Britain denied transmission by the BBC. It was released instead to a limited cinema audience. Watkins made a couple of features, worked in Scandinavia and has since had only one TV film shown in Britain: *Edvard Munch* (1976), made for Norwegian Radio and SRT, Sweden.   PP

Watson, Paul (1942–). British documentary producer, famous or infamous for *The Family* in 1974. Recent credits include fairly dotty *Vox Pop* series (1983), a remarkable *Real Lives* (1985) of a space shuttle mission and an even more remarkable *Forty Minutes* (1986) chronicling a 'Fishing Party' enjoyed by a quartet of rich slobs.   PP

Watts, Queenie (1920–80). British East End pub owner, former singer, whose appearances in *Stars and Garters* led to her turning character actress in plays such as *Waterloo Sunset* and series such as *Yus My Dear*.

Waverly's Wonders (US 1968). Half-hour comedy series from Lorimar for NBC, about a school basketball team; with Joe Namath. It was cancelled after three weeks.

Wayne, David (1914–) (Wayne McKeekan). American character actor with many film credits. TV series: *Norby, The Good Life* (US), *Ellery Queen, Dallas, House Calls*. TV movies: *The Catcher, The FBI vs Alvin Karpis, Ellery Queen, Once an Eagle, In the Glitter Palace, Black Beauty, Murder at the Mardi Gras, Loose Change, The Gift of Love, The Girls in the Office*.

We Bring You Live Pictures (GB 1982; 4 × 30m). The great and gorblimey days of the live outside broadcast recalled by Peter Dimmock, Berkeley Smith, S. J. de Lotbinière, T. H. Bridgewater and other exponents, and illustrated with telerecorded examples. These ranged from notable genuines – Coronations, Cup Finals, the Oxford boat sinking into the Thames – to such potty contrived occasions as a train crash on a length of army railway. 'After 25 years you still held your breath as the unmanned train approached its doom, whereupon there was a teeny bang, the engine steered itself and its coaches off the rails and came to an unhurried stop alongside them. "What a grand old lady," said commentator Bob Danvers-Walker resourcefully, "still on her wheels."' Presented by Martin Bell, for BBC.   PP

We Dissent
GB 1960 90m bw (VTR)

Comprehensive array of dissident Americans assembled by Kenneth Tynan to voice their disapproval of materialism, John Foster Dulles's foreign policy and the Bomb. But why only Americans? Shouldn't candour like charity have begun at home? For ATV.   PP

We Got It Made
US 1983 22 × 25m colour
NBC/MGM/InterMedia/Farr/Fred Silverman

A blonde live-in maid gets a job with a pair of Manhattan bachelors.
One-set farce with a stupid premise; acting and situations to match.

cr Gordon Farr, Lynn Farr Brao

Teri Copley, Tom Villard, Matt McCoy, Stepfanie Kramer, Bonnie Urseth

'Looks iffy.' – *Variety*

'This bit of fluff has been panned from coast to coast, but that's not the only reason I decided to like it. It features the cutest blonde in television, and who needs a better reason than that?' – Robert MacKenzie, *TV Guide*

We Love TV (GB since 1984). Viewers versus celebs in a panel show about popular television, presided over by Gloria Hunniford. Produced by Brian Wesley, for LWT.

We, the Accused *
GB 1980 4 × 75m colour
BBC (Jonathan Powell)

Meek schoolmaster murders oppressive wife and absconds with fellow teacher; a powerful serialization by Julia Jones of an Ernest Raymond novel set between the wars. My review at the time: 'It turns into an on-the-run story with the lovers trying desperately to keep one step ahead of police and public though they know it can't be for ever, which has been good for pathos from Tess and Angel's brief idyll in Hardy to Arthur and Eileen's in *Pennies from Heaven*. What gives this one extra potency is the extraordinary intensity of the performances of Ian Holm and Angela Down: he, grey and bristly and curiously (but honestly) unrepentant; she, working out what she must do from her newly awakened instincts. It's buttoned down, thought-out, essential television acting.' PP

We Think the World of You: see Secret Orchards

We Want an Answer (GB 1956–9). Schoolchildren, or occasionally university students, quizzed celebrities and mandarins, usually one at a time, sometimes in pairs. They included: Dr Hewlett Johnson, Randolph Churchill, Len Hutton, Harold Wilson, Humphrey Lyttelton, A. P. Herbert, Lord Beveridge, Antonia Fraser, Billy Butlin, John Braine, Edith Sitwell, Nancy Spain, Godfrey Winn, David Low and Moira Shearer. Produced by Barrie Heads; for Granada. PP

Wearing, Michael (19 –). British drama producer who came to the fore with *Bird of Prey* and stayed there with *Edge of Darkness*.

The Weather in the Streets
GB 1984 125m TVM
BBC (Alan Shalcross)

Unexciting adaptation from Rosamund Lehman's 1936 novel and bits of a previous one, possibly prompted by early glimmerings of now-fashionable feminism in the text. 'The usual little steam train did its stuff, shining and spotless period motor-cars drove warily along the street as if to proclaim their hire cost . . .'

w Julian Mitchell *d* GAVIN MILLAR *ph* John Hooper *m* Carl Davis

Michael York, Lisa Eichhorn, Joanna Lumley, Rosalind Ayres, Faith Brook, Isabel Dean PP

❋ **Weaver, Dennis** (1924–). American character star, one of TV's busiest actors and almost exclusive to the medium. Series: *Gunsmoke, Gentle Ben, Kentucky Jones, McCloud, Stone*. TV movies: *The Forgotten Man, Duel, Rolling Man, Female Artillery, The Great Man's Whiskers, Terror on the Beach, Intimate Strangers, The Islander, Centennial, Pearl, Ishi: the Last of his Tribe, The Ordeal of Patty Hearst, The Ordeal of Dr Mudd, A Cry for Justice, Amber Waves, The Day the Loving Stopped, Don't Go To Sleep, Cocaine, Emerald Point, Going for the Gold*.

Weavers Green
GB 1966 50 × 25m bw (VTR)
Anglia

Twice-weekly soaper of rural life created by Peter Lambda, centred on veterinary partnership, pub, village shop, etc. Anglia broke new ground by recording it on mobile VTR equipment but failed to get adequate placings for it on the ITV network, they said, and wound the experiment up after six months. PP

The Web
US 1956 13 × 25m bw
CBS/Columbia/Goodson–Todman

Stories of people trapped by circumstantial evidence.

Unremarkable suspense series.

W.E.B. (US 1979). Much-heralded one-hour series which, following the success of *Network*, was to expose the corruption in the upper echelons of television. Executives steeled themselves against its revelations quite unnecessarily, as the public weren't interested and it was cancelled after two episodes. Regulars were to have been Pamela Bellwood, Alex Cord, Richard Basehart, John Colicos, Andrew Prine and Zalman King; producer, Lin Bolen; chief writer, David Karp; for TCF/NBC.

✳ **Webb, Jack** (1920–82). Busy American character actor who turned producer. Internationally known as the flat-talking Joe Friday ('All we want is the facts, ma'am') in *Dragnet*, he seldom acted thereafter but turned out via his Mark VII Productions such series as *True*, *Pete Kelly's Blues*, *Adam 12*, *Emergency*, *O'Hara US Treasury* and *Hec Ramsey*.

Webster
US 1983–   × 25m colour
ABC/Paramount
A Chicago sports commentator with a new wife finds he has a black godson on his hands.
Uneasy rip-off of *Diff'rent Strokes*: a smile, a message, and perhaps a tear. Yucky.
cr Stu Silver
Alex Karras, Susan Clark, Emmanuel Lewis

The Wedding **
GB 1984 120m TVM
Tyne-Tees (Keith Richardson)
As one daughter marries, Farmer Tom Bell browbeats the remaining one to stay at home, keep him company and help on the farm, rather than go off to university; but a pleasing alternative solution emerges during the course of the wedding-day revels.
'Cheerful, funny, boorish, believable and welcomely masculinist,' I thought at the time.
w Thomas Ellice, *story* V. S. Pritchett *d* Gordon Flemyng *ph* Dave Dixon
Tom Bell, Meg Wynn Owen   PP

A Wedding on Saturday ***
GB 1964 60m bw (VTR)
Granada (Norman Swallow)
The first use of mobile VTR facilities for a documentary essay, going on the air just a week after the first successful application of this technique to drama, a BBC production of *Murder in the Cathedral* recorded in Canterbury Cathedral. Though hardly encouraging spontaneity (it required parking space for massive vans, and an hour's warm-up for the equipment), mobile VTR proved its capacity to achieve beautiful pictures from ordinary lighting. The wedding in *A Wedding* was of a Yorkshire miner, filled out by Norman Swallow in partnership with Denis Mitchell. Italia Prize, 1965. My reaction at the time: 'With its brimming pints and pithead showers and Bingo and plump bride and Sean Connery-esque groom it must have been the most robust, least condescending bit of sociology ever shown.'   PP

The Wednesday Play. The BBC's prime outlet for newly written TV drama after 1964, changed to *Play for Today* when the transmission day was altered. My 1969 assessment (in *Radio Times*): 'No play series was more innocuously named than the *Wednesday Play*. None established its fame – or infamy – more quickly. The *Wednesday Play* became synonymous with all that was exciting or alarming or revolutionary in television. In fact this reputation stemmed from a comparatively small number of productions by the team of Tony Garnett, Kenneth Loach & Co whose free-wheeling social commentaries like *Up the Junction* or *Cathy Come Home* gained tremendously in impact from being almost wholly filmed, an expensive facility then not generally available. The truth is that most of the *Wednesday Play*'s solid achievement was built up by individual writers (e.g. David Mercer, Peter Nichols, Michael Frayn, James Hanley, Jim Allen) and individual directors (Alan Bridges, Charles Jarrott, Waris Hussein, Gil Calder) whose only common factors were adventurousness and professionalism.'   PP

A Week in Politics (GB since 1982). Admirable end-of-the-week summing up of Parliament and politicking on C4, presented latterly by Peter Jay and produced by Ann Lapping for Brook Productions.   PP

A Week with Svetlana (GB 1982; 60m; colour). Stalin's daughter Svetlana Alliluyeva, resident in the US since the sixties, converses with Malcolm Muggeridge and his wife at their home in Sussex. The talk naturally comes round to Papa quite often. Produced by Jonathan Stedall, for BBC.   PP

The Weekend Nun
US 1972 74m colour TVM
Paramount
A young nun is a parole officer during the week.
Beyond comment: some people will like it.
w Ken Trevey *d* Jeannot Szwarc
Joanna Pettet, Vic Morrow, Beverly Garland, Ann Sothern, James Gregory, Barbara Werle, Kay Lenz

Weekend of Terror *
US 1970 74m colour TVM
Paramount
Two young killers accidentally kill a hostage and search for a lookalike to replace her. Fast-moving suspenser.
w Lionel E. Siegel *d* Jud Taylor
Robert Conrad, Lois Nettleton, Lee Majors, Carol Lynley, Jane Wyatt

Weekend World (GB 1972–). London Weekend's regular current affairs show, commanding much respect despite its noonday transmission. Presented until 1977 by Peter Jay, from 1977 to 1986 by Brian Walden, since then by Matthew Parris. Those most influential behind the scenes have included John Birt, Barry Cox.   PP

The Weekly's War (Australia 1984; 2 × 80m). World War II as seen by staff and correspondents of Australia's only national magazine at the time, *The Australian Women's Weekly*. A nice idea given rather soap-operatic treatment by writers Stephen Ramsey and John Edwards, with Noni Hazlehurst, Jane Harders, Jacqueline Kott and Pat Thompson playing the leading parts. Directed by Stephen Ramsey, produced by Suzanne Baker, for Film Australia and the Nine Television Network. C4 showed it in GB in 1985 as a single 160m blockbuster. PP

Weeks, Alan (1923–). British sports commentator, who rose by way of 'fringe' sports – ice hockey, snooker, etc. Since then all major events, including Olympics, soccer World Cup, etc.

Weir, David (–   ). British writer chiefly associated with *The Onedin Line*, though had also done many *Troubleshooters*. Responsible for BBC version of *The Water Margin*.

Weis, Don (1922–). American director who filmed many episodes of *Perry Mason*, *Burke's Law*, *It Takes a Thief* and *Ironside*. TV movies: *The Longest Hundred Miles*, *Now You See It Now You Don't*, *The Millionaire*.

Welcome Back Kotter
US 1975–79 approx. 80 × 25m colour (VTR)
ABC/David Wolper (James Komack)
A Jewish primary school teacher has trouble with tough kids.
Formalized 'realistic' comedy with a marked resemblance to *Please Sir*. The studio audience makes it seem funnier than it is: the characters are really a bunch of morons.
cr Gabriel Kaplan, Alan Sacks, Peter Myerson *m* John B. Sebastian
Gabriel Kaplan, John Travolta, Marcia Strassman, John Sylvester White

Welcome Home Johnny Bristol *
US 1971 100m colour TVM
Cinema Center 100 (Arthur Joel Katz)

A wounded Vietnam veteran seeks the hometown he dreamed of, but finds only mystery.
A gripping puzzler with a disappointing explanation.
w Stanley R. Greenberg *d* George McCowan *ph* Robert L. Morrison *m* Lalo Schifrin
Martin Landau, Jane Alexander, Brock Peters, Forrest Tucker, Martin Sheen, Pat O'Brien, Mona Freeman

Welcome to Our Night
retitled after network: *Final Jeopardy*
US 1985 96m colour TVM
NBC/Telepictures/Shooting Star/Frank Von Zerneck
A well-heeled young couple find themselves on the run from street gangs in a no-go area of downtown Detroit.
Grotesquely funny in the unreeling, this surely has to be an exaggeration.
w Shirl Hendryx *d* Michael Pressman
Richard Thomas, Mary Crosby, Jeff Corey

Weld, Tuesday (1943–). American leading actress. TV movies: *Reflections of Murder*, *F. Scott Fitzgerald in Hollywood*, *A Question of Guilt*, *Madame X*, *The Winter of Our Discontent*, *Scorned and Swindled*.

Weldon, Fay (1932–). British playwright and novelist, formerly advertising wizard, making her initial impact with plaintive comedies of life and love and weight-watching in London NW. Later became more overtly feminist in tone. A side claim to fame is that she wrote the very first episode of *Upstairs, Downstairs*. *The Fat Woman's Tale* and *A Catching Complaint* (1966); *Poor Cherry* (1967), contribution to *Happy Ending* (1969); *Splinter of Ice* (1972), *Life for Christine* and serialization of *Pride and Prejudice* (1980); subject of a *South Bank Show* study the same year. Contributed to *Out of the Undertow* (1984).

Welk, Lawrence (1902–). American bandleader whose old-fashioned but enjoyable show was popular on ABC from 1955 until 1970.

Well Being (GB since 1984). Periodic health and safe-living series, produced for C4 by Holmes Associates.

We'll Get By
US 1974 5 × 25m colour (VTR)
CBS

Problems of a New Jersey lawyer and his family.
Modestly pleasing upper-crust comedy.
cr Alan Alda
Paul Sorvino, Mitzi Hoag

We'll Meet Again
GB 1982 13 × 50m colour
LWT (Tony Wharmby)
Wasted opportunity to construct a saga of the US airmen in World War II who, as the show's tactless posters put it, dropped their bombs on Germany and their pants in England. The stereotyped characters included Susannah York as a Mrs Miniverish figure with a glum husband (Ronald Hines) doomed to paraplegia and cuckoldry, in that order; the Ivy League American major who loved her; and an absurd caricature of a wartime spiv. One B-17 Flying Fortress, painted the wrong colours, represented the might of air power, along with model shots and footage from William Wyler's authentic combat documentary *The Memphis Belle*.
cr David Butler *w* David Butler, David Crane, John Gorrie *d* Tony Wharmby, Christopher Hodson, Peter Cregeen, John Reardon
Susannah York, Ronald Hines, Michael J. Shannon, Lise-Ann McLaughlin, Ray Smith, Christopher Malcolm, Joris Stuyck   PP
'Leaden plot and incredible dialogue.' – Sean Day-Lewis, *Daily Telegraph*
† *Return of the Enemy*, same year, 30m, chronicled the flight of the same B–17 to a West German air show – the first time one has been seen in Germany since World War II. *w* and *d* Ian Masters, *p* Michael Hill, for BBC East.

We'll Support You Evermore **
GB 1985 75m
BBC (Brenda Reid)
The father of a young officer murdered by the IRA travels to Belfast to try to find out how and why it happened. Seen almost wholly through the visitor's eyes, Douglas Livingstone's film left the audience to decide for itself whether the boy had been about to desert, on an undercover mission, or torn between both. 'What really mattered in the end,' I wrote, 'were an uncomplicated man's grief and puzzlement, both conveyed so subtly by the formidable John Thaw . . . Livingstone's film joins the half-dozen television fictions now which seem to have captured the Northern Ireland impasse better than any of the documentaries.'
w and *d* Douglas Livingstone.
John Thaw, Anthony Milner, Sheila Ruskin, Colette O'Neil, Nicholas Le Prevost   PP

Welland, Colin (1934–). Good British actor and better writer, formerly an art teacher (hence his play *Roll on Four O'Clock*). Became a familiar of the screen in *Z Cars* and later *Cowboys*. Notable appearances in *Jack Point*, *Blue Remembered Hills*. His TV plays include *Bangelstein's Boys* (1969), *Roll on Four O'Clock* and *Say Goodnight to Your Grandma* (1970), *Kisses at Fifty* (1973), *Jack Point* and *Leeds United* (1974), *The Wild West Show* (series, 1975), *Your Man from the Six Counties* (1976). Into the cinema with *Yanks*.   PP

Welles, Orson (1915–85). Rotund American director and actor whose television credits include *King Lear* for CBS (1953), *The Orson Welles Sketchbook* for the BBC (six chats to camera, 1956), *Round the World with Orson Welles* for Rediffusion (1955), Ben Hecht and Charles MacArthur's play *Twentieth Century* for CBS (1956), *The Method* for ATV (1958), *Orson Welles Great Mysteries* for Anglia (1973), and of course those sherry commercials for Domecq.   PP
† *The Orson Welles Story*, a 1984 two-part BBC Arena special by Alan Yentob and Leslie Megahey was built round an extended interview with Welles by Megahey. Repeated on his 70th birthday and again on his death. 'The greatest performance Welles has ever given, whatever the size of the screen.' – *The Times*

Wells Fargo: see Tales of Wells Fargo

Welsh, John (1914–). Irish-born actor familiar in august roles: *The Forsyte Saga*, *Oh Brother!*, *Duchess of Duke Street*, etc.

Wendkos, Paul (1922–). American director, one of the most accomplished TV practitioners. Series episodes include *The Untouchables*, *Naked City*, *The Invaders*. TV movies: *Fear No Evil*, *The Brotherhood of the Bell*, *Travis Logan DA*, *A Tattered Web*, *A Little Game*, *A Death of Innocence*, *The Delphi Bureau*, *The Family Rico*, HAUNTS OF THE VERY RICH, *Footsteps*, *The Strangers in 7A*, *Honor Thy Father*, *Terror on the Beach*, *The Legend of Lizzie Borden*, *Death Among Friends*, *The Death of Richie*, *Secrets*, *Good*

Against Evil, 79 Park Avenue, Betrayal, A Woman Called Moses, The Ordeal of Patty Hearst, A Cry for Love, The Five of Me, Golden Gate, Farrell for the People, Cocaine, Intimate Agony, Celebrity, Scorned and Swindled, The Bad Seed, The Execution.

Wendy and Me *
US 1964 34 × 25m bw
Warner/Natwill (George Burns)

An apartment house owner has one particularly dizzy lodger.
The star takes kind of a back seat to a substitute Gracie. The result is mildly appealing and quite stylish.
George Burns, Connie Stevens, Ron Harper

Wenham, Brian (1937–). British executive, by turns an ATV researcher, ITN producer and *Panorama* editor before heading BBC current affairs. Since 1978 Controller of BBC2, 1978–82. Director of Programmes 1983–6. Now heads BBC radio.
PP

We're Fighting Back
US 1981 96m colour TVM
CBS/Warner/Highgate (Linda Gottlieb)

Four young New Yorkers form a guard unit to catch the hoodlums who terrorize people in subways.
A milder form of *Death Wish*, not terribly interesting apart from its locations.
w T. S. Cook d Lou Antonio ph Richard Brooks m Fred Karlin
Kevin Mahon, Paul McCrane, Elgin Jones, Ellen Barkin

Wesker, Arnold (1932–). British dramatist who has twice favoured television with an original script, neither time to set the nation buzzing. *Menace*, 1967, was an abstract piece about life under the imminent prospect of a nuclear attack; *Love Letters on Blue Paper* ten years later was a lachrymose play about a retired trade union leader.
PP

Wessex Tales
GB 1973 6 × 75m colour
BBC (Irene Shubik)

Elegant dramatizations of Thomas Hardy's short stories by various writers including David Mercer, Dennis Potter. Directors included David Jones, Michael Tuchner.
PP

West, Adam (1929–) (William Anderson). American light leading man who scored an unexpected success as *Batman*. Also appeared in *The Detectives*.

West Country Tales (GB 1983; 7 × 30m). A successor to *Sea Tales* from the same BBC West source. Various authors; produced and directed by John King.

❊ **West, Timothy** (1934–). Hardworking and distinguished British character actor, the Charles Laughton of his day. *Hard Times, Edward the Seventh* (title role), *Churchill and the Generals* (as Churchill), *An Evening with Thomas Beecham, Oliver Twist* (as Bumble), *Masada, Brass, Florence Nightingale.*

The Western
US 1983 13 × 25m colour

A compilation series effectively put together by Adlon/New York Times, with Bob Thomas as narrator/reporter.
Episodes:
In the Beginning
The Sound of Silents
Talkies: Emergence of an Art
King of the Bs
The Western Woman
John Ford: Master of the Western
The Comedy Western
John Wayne: the Ultimate Cowboy
The Vanishing American
The Western Reborn
Stuntmen, Sidekicks and Heavies
The Western on Television
Westerns: a Musical Roundup

The Westerner *
US 1960 13 × 25m bw
NBC/Four Star/Winchester (Sam Peckinpah)

Experiences of a wandering ranch-hand in the 1870s.
Intelligent low-key western which didn't take.
Brian Keith
'An unusually good show.' – Don Miller

Westheimer, Dr Ruth (1929–) (Karola Ruth Siegel). Diminutive German-American sex counsellor whose programme *Good Sex with Dr Ruth* was in 1985 a nationwide American hit.

Weston, Jack (1926–). Roly-poly American character comedian. Series: *Rod Brown of the Rocket Rangers, The Hathaways.* TV movies: *Fame Is the Name of the Game, Now You See It Now You Don't, I Love a Mystery, Deliver Us from Evil, 79 Park Avenue.*

Westside Medical (US 1977). Shortlived one-hour drama series about three dedicated young doctors, created by Barry Oringer for ABC; with James Sloyan, Linda Carlson, Ernest Thompson.

Westward. British ITV company serving the South-West of England from 1958 until 1981. Most of the time under the idiosyncratic chairmanship of Peter Cadbury. Replaced on 1 January 1982 by TSW.   PP

Wet Gold
US 1984 96m colour TVM
ABC/Telepictures (Bill Coker)
Four unrelated characters seek gold in the Bahamas.
Scrappy, undeveloped outdoor melodrama which fails to justify its initial air of mystery.
w David Sherin, Otis Jones d Dick Lowry
ph Jorden Klein m John Scott
Brooke Shields, Burgess Meredith, Tom Byrd, Brian Kerwin, William Bronder, Dave Cass
'The glossy finish isn't enough to disguise lackluster acting in roles of little or no interest.' – *Daily Variety*

We've Got Each Other
US 1977 22 × 25m colour
CBS/Viacom
Misadventures of two married misfits.
Less endearing than was intended.
Oliver Clark, Beverly Archer

A Whale for the Killing
US 1980 140m colour TVM
ABC/Playboy/Beowulf (Robert
  Lovenheim)
A whale strands itself in the lagoon of a remote Canadian fishing village, and a holidaymaker defends it against would-be slaughterers.
Heavy-going moral tale, recounted at unnecessary length but of a high standard in all departments.
w Lionel Chetwynd, *book* Farley Mowat d Richard T. Heffron ph Edmund Koons m Basil Poledouris
Peter Strauss, Dee Wallace, Richard Widmark, Kathryn Walker, Ken James, Bruce McGill, David Ferry, Bill Calvert

Whalley, Joanne (19   –   ). Young British actress who came to everyone's notice as the daughter in *Edge of Darkness*, 1985, but she had previously been the female lead in *A Kind of Loving* (1982). Latest role: in Dennis Potter's *The Singing Detective*, 1986.
                                                     PP

What Are Best Friends For?
US 1973 74m colour TVM
ABC Circle
A man thrown out by his wife moves in with his best friends.
Underwritten treatment of a pleasant idea.
w Rubin Carson, J. A. Vapors d Jay Sandrich
Ted Bessell, Lee Grant, Larry Hagman, Barbara Feldon, Nita Talbot

What Really Happened to the Class of '65?
(US 1977). Shortlived one-hour series from Universal for NBC; an anthology of stories about the careers of young graduates; with Tony Bill as one of them, a teacher.

What the Papers Say ***. A 15-minute British programme in which since 1956, by courtesy of Granada TV, a leading journalist each week has wittily reviewed the performance of his colleagues, these days on C4.
PP: 'Has easily the longest unbroken run of any current affairs show anywhere in the world, reaching its silver jubilee (and 1,242nd edition) on 5 November 1981. Peter Mullings had directed 542 of them.'

What the Public Wants (GB 1962). Historically, the first satire show to get on television, but overshadowed and out-dared by *TWTWTW* when that muscled in only a week or two later. With the ITA and the Rediffusion management scrutinizing every line, the tilts were either at generalized types or individuals safely beyond the pale, e.g. convicted spies. With Clemence Bettany, Jean Hart, Aubrey Woods.   PP

Whatever Happened to the Likely Lads? British comedy series which won BAFTA's 1973 award for producer James Gilbert. See *The Likely Lads.*

What's a Nice Girl Like You. . . ? *
US 1971 73m colour TVM
Universal (Norman Lloyd)
A working girl impersonates a socialite and is drawn into an elaborate plot.
Sharply written and acted gangster comedy.
w HOWARD FAST, *novel* E. V. Cunningham d Jerry Paris
BRENDA VACCARO, Vincent Price, Jack Warden, Roddy McDowall, Edmond O'Brien, Jo Ann Worley

What's Happening? (US 1976–7). Half-hour comedy series for ABC, about three black urban kids perpetually in scrapes.

What's My Line? **. A Goodson–Todman game show, immensely popular in the fifties, in which the panel had to guess the occupation of the contestant by asking roundabout questions. The American host was John Daly, with Dorothy Kilgallen, Arlene Francis and Bennett Cerf as panellists. In Britain (where the show was briefly revived in the seventies) Eamonn Andrews was in the chair, and residents included Isobel Barnett, David Nixon, Gilbert Harding and Barbara Kelly.
† It was revived again in 1984, but by Thames instead of the BBC. Only Eamonn Andrews (in the chair) and Barbara Kelly survived from the original team. George Gale took over the grouchy Gilbert Harding role and Eric Morecambe the amiable egghead contribution of David Nixon. Jilly Cooper was rather miscast as the Lady of the Shires (previously Isobel Barnett) and for some reason a fifth member was added to the panel: Patrick Mower. Producer: Malcolm Morris.
For a further run in 1986, Ernie Wise took Eric Morecambe's seat and motorcyclist Barry Sheene replaced Patrick Mower.   PP

Wheelbase. Successful BBC2 motoring magazine from the mid-sixties, replaced by *Top Gear* when the subject was transferred to Birmingham.   PP

Wheeler and Murdoch *
US 1970 70m colour TVM
Paramount
Seattle private eyes take on an assignment to guard money that proves to belong to the Syndicate.
Routine cops and robbers with an agreeably fresh and rainy location and a whiff in the script of *The Maltese Falcon*. It didn't make a series for all that.
w Jerry Ludwig, Eric Bercovici *d* Joseph Sargent
Jack Warden, Christopher Stone, Van Johnson, Charles Cioffi, Jane Powell, Diane Baker

Wheeler, Charles (1923–). Authoritative British journalist, former Washington correspondent, who has presented *Panorama* and other BBC current affairs programmes. A brilliant special in 1985, *The Battle for Berlin*.   PP

Wheeler, Sir Mortimer (1890–1976). British archaeologist and TV personality of the fifties, especially on the panel game *Animal, Vegetable and Mineral*.

Wheelie and the Chopper Bunch (US 1974). 13 × 22-minute cartoons detailing the unexciting adventures of talking Volkswagens and motor cycles. Not for the discriminating. From Hanna–Barbera; for NBC.

Wheels *
US 1978 6 × 96m colour
Universal/Roy Huggins
Lots of problems crop up for Adam Trenton, senior executive in a Detroit car factory.
Busy, competent but somehow not very interesting novelization. Good production, boring characters and situations, good performances.
w Millard Lampell, Hank Searls, *novel* Arthur Hailey *d* Jerry London
Rock Hudson, Lee Remick, Blair Brown, Ralph Bellamy, Tim O'Connor, Gerald S. O'Loughlin, Tony Franciosa, John Beck, James Carroll Jordan

The Wheeltappers' and Shunters' Social Club
GB 1974–6 39 × 50m colour
Attempt to do for club acts what *Stars and Garters* had done for pub entertainers, i.e. present them in a fictitious and larger-than-life club setting. Thanks to a droll running performance by Colin Crompton as the entertainments committee chairman and insults from ex-*Comedians* comic Bernard Manning it became popular viewing. There were also one or two special (e.g. New Year) editions and a seaside outing. Directed by Dave Warwick; produced by John Hamp; for Granada.   PP

✻ **Wheldon, Sir Huw** (1916–86). Welsh producer, performer and inspirer, into TV via publicity and press and children's programmes. Edited and presented *Monitor* 1957–64, commissioning their first film work from Ken Russell, John Schlesinger and Humphrey Burton. Became controller of programmes and then Director of Television in the BBC's last great expansionist era. On retirement, back to programmes with *Royal Heritage* (co-writer and presenter) and *Destination D-Day*.   PP

When Day Is Done
GB 1974 78m colour (16mm) TVM
Thames/Euston Films (Reg Collin)
A disillusioned musician finds that life holds too many problems, and his wife tries to bring him back to optimism.
Rather muddled character drama with good acting.

w John Kershaw *d* Reg Collin

Edward Woodward, Rosemary Leach, Patricia Maynard, Jeremy Hawk, Julia Goodman

When Dreams Come True
US 1985 96m colour TVM
ABC/Telepictures/I & C (Hans Proppe)

An art museum tour guide finds the menaces of her nightmares appearing in real life. Intriguing mystery which leaves far too many details unexplained.

w William Bleich *d* John Llewellyn Moxey *ph* Jack Richards *m* Gil Melle

Cindy Williams, David Morse, Lee Horsley, Jessica Harper, Stan Shaw

When Every Day Was the Fourth of July *
US 1978 96m colour TVM
Dan Curtis

A small town is rocked by a brutal murder. Interesting reconstruction of a real murder case.

Dean Jones, Louise Sorel

When Havoc Struck: see Havoc

When Hell Was in Session *
US 1979 96m colour TVM
NBC/James T. Aubrey, Robert Hamner (R. J. Louis)

An American naval commander suffers horrific treatment as a Vietnam prisoner-of-war.
Agonized semi-documentary of man's inhumanity to man; generally well done.

w Jake Justiz, *book* Rear Admiral Jeremiah A. Denton Jnr *d* Paul Krasny *ph* Robert Hauser *m* Jimmie Haskell

Hal Holbrook, Eva Marie Saint, Mako, Ronne Cox, Renne Jarrett, Richard Evans

When Michael Calls **
US 1971 74m colour TVM
TCF (Gil Shiva)

A woman is terrorized by phone calls which appear to come from a dead child.
Chilling suspenser which plays pretty fair and moves smartly along.

w James Bridges *d* Philip Leacock

Michael Douglas, Ben Gazzara, Elizabeth Ashley, Karen Pearson

When She Says No
US 1983 96m colour TVM
ABC/Metromedia (Gerald I. Isenberg)

A university professor claims she was gang-raped by three colleagues; they say she submitted willingly.
Who cares, but the movie paints an odd picture of customs and practices at American universities.

Kathleen Quinlan, Rip Torn, Jane Alexander, Kenneth McMillan, David Huffman

When She Was Bad
US 1979 96m colour TVM
ABC/Henry Jaffe (Michael Jaffe, David Ladd)

A well-to-do wife unaccountably gets depressions in which she ill-treats her children. A welter of the new psychology, all very predictable in its development and, if anything, too slickly written and photographed.

w Carmen Culver *d* Peter Hunt

Cheryl Ladd, Robert Urich, Eileen Brennan, Dabney Coleman

When the Actors Come (GB 1978). Play written and directed by Don Taylor for BBC. It was set, as I said in my review at the time, 'in that post-revolutionary Hungary of the 1850s which on the critic's map is warningly marked as a location where people stun each other with speeches for two hours before implementing the revenge, or whatever it is, on their minds. Taylor, it must also be said, doesn't believe in surprises. His troupe of revolutionaries-turned-actors declared their intentions early on, to murder the patrician who had engaged them, together with his family, at the conclusion of the performance. But thanks to some gripping scenes only distantly borrowed from *Hamlet*, and some great performances, the play held you. Alec McCowen had a beard, Patrick Stewart had hair! – as, respectively, the Count and the leader of the troupe.' PP

When the Boat Comes In *
GB 1975–7 26 × 50m colour (VTR)
BBC (Leonard Lewis/Andrew Osborn)

Life for the Seaton family in the north-east during the Depression.
Love on the Dole in another setting: impressive serial drama for those who care to remember.

w James Mitchell (with episodes from Sid Chaplin, Tom Hathaway, Alex Glasgow)

James Bolam, Susan Jameson, John Nightingale, James Garbutt, Jean Heywood

'A thrill of pleasure is consistently renewed at the sheer consistency of the performances.' – *The Times*

When the Kissing Had to Stop *
GB 1962 2 × 78m bw
Rediffusion (Peter Willes)

Better-than-the-book dramatization (by Giles Cooper) of Constantine FitzGibbon's cautionary shocker about a Russian takeover of Britain. From my 1962 review: 'First-rate apocalyptic thriller . . . the shot of civilian-clothed Soviet "inspectors" marching in step across the lonely Essex airfield to close the first half of the production and open the second remains one of the most pregnant television scenes I can remember . . .'

d Bill Hitchcock

Denholm Elliott, Peter Vaughan, Douglas Wilmer   PP

When Things Were Rotten
US 1974 13 × 25m colour
ABC/Paramount/Mel Brooks

Robin Hood has more than his share of trouble with the idiocies of his merry men as well as with King John.
Campy spoof which is neither campy, spoofy nor funny enough; usually just embarrassing.

cr Mel Brooks

Dick Gautier, Misty Rowe, Bernie Kopell, Dick Van Patten, Richard Dimitri

'She's looking for a few good men – and finding lots of eager recruits!'
When Your Lover Leaves
US 1983 96m colour TVM
NBC/Henry Winkler, Ron Howard

A recently divorced woman is rejected by her married boyfriend and plans life on her own.
Well-dressed soap opera of no consequence. The title is pure come-on.

w Michael Lesson d Jeff Bleckner

Valerie Perrine, David Ackroyd, Betty Thomas, Dwight Schultz, Merritt Buttrick

'Eccentricity is a comic staple; lunacy is amusing only in minute doses.' – Daily Variety

Where Adam Stood **
GB 1976 76m colour
BBC (Kenith Trodd)

Dennis Potter play taken from incidents in Edmund Gosse's Father and Son about a stern Victorian papa agonizing over Darwin's Theory of Relativity. As a leading natural scientist of the day he recognizes its force, as a fundamentalist Christian he is committed to the literal truth of the Bible; his motherless son unwittingly sharpens the dilemma. On any estimation one of the half-dozen best things Potter has done – intellectually faultless, warm, tender and sly.

d Brian Gibson

Alan Badel, Ronald Hines, Max Harris   PP

Where Angels Fear to Tread (GB 1966). E. M. Forster's other novel was produced as a BBC Play of the Month by Cedric Messina, with Alec McCowen, Anna Massey, Wendy Hiller, Norah Swinburne; directed by Naomi Capon.

Where Are They Now? A favourite and sometimes valuable television exercise is to chase up the personage of some previous film or programme and see what has befallen them, e.g. the follow-ups to Granada's Seven Up, revisiting the seven-year-olds at 14, 21 and 28, the same company's Timothy's Second Diary, Michael Croucher's updating of Citizen '63 for the BBC, Robert Reid's The Broken Bridge and the two progress reports on two British soldiers first encountered in a Belfast casualty hospital with appalling injuries. An extension of the idea is to pick some more arbitrary group for similar research. Don Haworth tracked down the faces in a group photograph picked at random from a grammar school prefects' room, the playwright Hugh Whitemore his classmates (including Susannah York) at drama school for Twenty Years On (1979).
† Inevitably a series called Where Are They Now? was hatched (by the BBC) in 1979 with David Jacobs wanly digging up half a dozen names from the recent past each week and choosing two for interview.   PP

Where Do We Go From Here? (US 1978). Shirley Maclaine special whose big joke was the Ballet Trockadero, the louche misspelling of the name being a perfect indicator of the funny but rather endearing and wholly American style of this drag ballet troupe.
The rest of the entertainment, as its title implied, was vaguely about the future. It might have been written by James Burke, but was in fact the work of Digby Wolfe, an English comedian long lost to America.   PP

Where Harry Stood *
GB 1974 50m colour
ATV (Anthony Thomas)

Life and times of a Scottish steelworker, using only one or two brief film clips, plus some longer passages of recorded sound, otherwise relying entirely on the recollections of its 70-year-old subject. Directed by Anthony Thomas; photographed by Stan Evill.   PP

Where Have All the People Gone? **
US 1974 74m colour TVM
ABC/Metromedia/Jozak/Alpine (Gerald I.
Isenberg)

Coming down from a mountain holiday, a
family discovers that almost everybody has
been killed by a lethal virus set off by
radiation.

Sharply made and quite inventive
contemporary thriller.

w Lewis John Carlino, Sandor Stern d John
Llewellyn Moxey ph Michael Marguilies m
Robert Prince

Peter Graves, Verna Bloom, George
O'Hanlon Jnr, Kathleen Quinlan, Michael-
James Wixted

Where I Live
GB 1960 50m bw
ABC (Sydney Newman)

Who's to look after old Dad? Daughter Jess
and her easy-going husband or ambitious son
George and his dreadful wife? The five people
concerned shout themselves into an answer
which can only mean despair all round. One of
the first essays (for Armchair Theatre) in what
was to become a well-worn theme (the
American Tad Mosel's Other People's Houses
was done by ATV only a few days later). Clive
Exton's forceful play was re-produced by the
BBC in 1965.

d Ted Kotcheff

Ruth Dunning, Madge Ryan, Robert Brown,
Lloyd Lamble, Paul Curran   PP

Where in the World.
British travel quiz of
the early seventies (BBC) which was revived
by HTV in 1984 for transmission on Channel
4, with the same captains, John Carter and
John Julius Norwich, leading teams of
celebs. Michael Parkinson was the original
chairman, later Ray Alan, who also joined
the revival. Produced (BBC) by Cecil Korer,
(HTV) by Derek Clark.   PP

Where the Difference Begins
GB 1961 90m bw
BBC (Don Taylor)

David Mercer's first play: gnarled old railway
worker's Socialist ideals are put to the test
when his successful grown-up sons come home
to be with their dying mother.

d Don Taylor

Leslie Sands, Nigel Stock, Barry Foster,
Hylda Baker   PP

Where There's Life
(GB since 1981). Pop
medical matters series presented by Drs Rob
Buckman and Miriam Stoppard. Though
often valuable, the chat show atmosphere
and applauding studio audience – even when
the subject is terminal illness or euthanasia –
is hard to take. Produced (1985) by Liz
Brice, Irene Garrow, David Poyser, for
YTV.   PP

Where's Raymond?:
see The Ray Bolger
Show

※ Whicker, Alan (c 1923–). British
commentator with a distinctive voice and
chatty manner. First popular in the fifties on
BBC's Tonight, he went over to Yorkshire
TV and has produced many series of
Whicker's World and is fast running out of
places to visit. Back to the BBC for Living
with Uncle Sam, 1985.

PP (1966): 'Whicker is the Plain Man's Guide
to anything. Whether it's Paris or Paraguay, a
millionaire's castle or an Indian's wigwam, he
marches in with the solid, unshatterable
insularity of the Englishman abroad.
Anything that looks odder or costs more than
it does in Shepherd's Bush astonishes him for
a moment, then is superseded by a fresh
distraction. Home again, he tries to re-create
the moment by means of a script laced with
extravagant slogans and puns.'

† His productivity is prodigious: in his first
ten years with YTV he made no fewer than 83
documentaries. In 1982 25 years of Whickeric
were celebrated with retrospective
compilations by both YTV and the BBC.
Autobiography, Within Whicker's World,
same year.

Whiplash
GB 1960 34 × 25m bw
ATV

In the 1840s, an American forms Australia's
first stagecoach line.

Quite well made, rather unjustly derided
down-under western.

Peter Graves

The Whip Hand *
(GB 1975). Excellent
improvised drama-doc by Leslie Blair about
an apprentice jockey and stable-lad (Sean
Flanagan). Prettily photographed by Phil
Meheux; produced by Kenith Trodd; for
BBC.   PP

Whirlybirds
US 1954–8 111 × 25m bw
Desilu/CBS (N. Gayle Gitterman)

Two young pilots own and operate a charter
service.

Adequate juvenile action series.

Kenneth Tobey, Craig Hill

Whispering Smith
US 1958 25 × 25m bw
Whispering Smith Company
Cases of the old west's first private detective.
A promising but rather disappointing series.
Audie Murphy, Guy Mitchell

The Whistler *
US 1954 39 × 25m bw
Columbia
Anthology of suspense stories with twist endings.
Not a bad collection on a purely hokum level. The title merely referred to a theme tune which was whistled briefly at the beginning of each story.

White, Betty (1924–). American character comedienne who has been around as long as TV and had her own show as recently as 1977. TV movies: *Vanished, With This Ring, The Best Place to Be.* In 1985 came back to the fore as one of the stars of *Golden Girls.*

The White Bird Passes * (GB 1980). Dramatization of Jessie Kesson's memoir of her childhood in the North-East of Scotland, brought up by a fondly remembered mother who happened to be a prostitute. Rather a soulful production with lots of dragging woodwind music and carefully composed pictures, but an impressive return to the screen by Isobel Black, pretty young star of the sixties. Written and directed by Mike Radford; for BBC Scotland.   PP

The White Guard. Mikhail Bulgakov's drama set during the civil war that followed the Russian Revolution, and said to be Stalin's favourite play, has had two powerful productions on BBC TV: by Rudolph Cartier in the fifties, and by Louis Marks (*d* Don Taylor) in 1982.   PP

White Hunter
GB 1958 39 × 25m bw
Bernard L. Schubert
Hero vs villain in the African bush.
Abysmally made and acted hokum adventures.
Rhodes Reason

White Mama *
US 1979 96m colour TVM
CBS/Tomorrow (Jean Moore Edwards)
A young black car thief befriends his ageing, impoverished court-assigned guardian.
Only the acting is of any interest in this sentimental character study.

d Jackie Cooper
Bette Davis, Ernest Harden Jnr, Eileen Heckart

The White Rabbit (GB 1967). BBC serial from Bruce Marshall's biography of the wartime SOE hero Wing Commander Yeo-Thomas, with Kenneth More in the part. My 1967 review: 'Too many bad, stiff-upper-lip war films have made war subjects suspect and Kenneth More has acted in too many of them. But underneath the actor's heroic Jolyon Mask the real knobbly human face is still available . . . this is his best and most affecting performance for some time.'   PP

The White Shadow
US 1978 61 × 50m colour
CBS/MTM (Mark Tinker)
A former pro-basketball player is injured and turns coach for a ghetto high school basketball team.
Yawnworthy sporting variation on *The Blackboard Jungle* and *Welcome Back Kotter.*
w Mike Post, Pete Carpenter
Ken Howard, Jason Bernard, Joan Pringle

White Water Rebels
US 1984 96m colour TVM
CBS (Doris M. Keating)
A rugged canoeist helps a photojournalist who has uncovered local corruption.
Routine adventure melodrama with well-photographed sporting sequences.
w Jim Kouf *d* Reza Badiyi *ph* William F. Geraghty *m* Ken Thorne
Catherine Bach, James Brolin, Pepe Serno, Richard Lynch, Lai Wulff

Whitehall Wonders (GB 1949). Distant early forerunner of *Yes Minister* – an original comedy for TV by J. B. Priestley set in the conference room of one of the new post-war ministries. With Edward Chapman, Michael Gough, William Mervyn, Eleanor Summerfield, Patrick Troughton. Produced by Ian Atkins, for BBC – there was no other network then.   PP

Whitehouse, Mary (1910–). British moral reformer who became well known in the sixties and seventies for her attacks on the corrupting influence of TV. Her influence has been generally beneficial.
PP: 'I couldn't disagree more. Though the lady's courage is formidable and she is always pleasant to meet face to face, her campaign   against   television   and

television people, especially in the early days, was ignorant, bigoted and vindictive. She attacked the truly beautiful *Country Matters* anthology, for instance, because of a brief nude bathing scene which was absolutely vital to one story, H. E. Bates's *Breeze Anstey*, and in any case involved two women without a man in sight. She sniped endlessly at Sir Hugh Greene, the best Director-General the BBC has ever had. Yet she was silent about the mindless violence of imported series or the celebration of greed in give-away shows. Needless to say she was made a CBE in 1980 while a critic such as Peter Black, who had done more than anyone to goad TV to higher standards, went unrewarded.'

Whitelaw, Billie (1932–). Spunky British character actress in radio drama as a child, into TV via the pioneering *Pattern of Marriage* and the Colin Morris drama-doc *Without Love* (about prostitution), then the throbbing social realism of *No Tram to Lime Street* and *Lena, O My Lena*. Many and varied performances since (BAFTA award for *Sextet*, 1972) and has become particularly associated with the plays of Samuel Beckett. What did she do to deserve that?   PP

Whitemore, Hugh (1936–). British playwright, trained as an actor, at one time so prolific – both as an originator and an adapter – that he was dubbed 'Hugh Writemore'. But a highly sensitive craftsman once past some early stridencies: *Dan Dan the Charity Man* (1966), *Party Games* (1968), *Killing Time* (1970), *Act of Betrayal* (1971), *Dummy* (1977), *I Remember Nelson* (1982) plus such classic dramatizations as *Country Matters* (two episodes) and the 1979 BBC2 version of *Rebecca. The Boy in the Bush*, 1984.   PP

The Whiteoaks of Jalna
Canada 1972 13 × 50m colour (16mm)
CBC
Four generations of the Whiteoaks family. The popular stories by Mazo de la Roche are made unnecessarily complicated by intercutting present and past, and despite the general high quality there is some decidedly bad acting. On the whole the series lacked the Ancient Mariner touch.

Paul Harding, Kate Reid

Whitfield, June (1927–). British comedy actress, a stalwart of radio's *Take it from Here* and a highly professional worker with all the major comedians. Got her own series in the seventies: *Happy Ever After*.

Whiting, John (1917–63). British dramatist whose brief and stormy career might have gained from dwelling sooner on TV. In fact he only wrote twice for television: the 30-minute *Eye Witness* and the more substantial *A Walk in the Desert* (1960), both for the BBC. Also eloquently took part in a *Monitor* devoted to his stage play (and later, movie) *The Devils*.
                                                                         PP

Whitman, Stuart (1936–). American leading man. Series: *Cimarron Strip*. TV movies: *The Man Who Wanted to Live Forever, City Beneath the Sea, Revenge, The Woman Hunter, The Man Who Died Twice, The Cat Creature, Go West Young Girl, The Pirate, Women in White, The Last Convertible, The Seekers*.

Whitmore, James (1921–). Leading American character actor with long film career and penchant for one-man shows in which he impersonates famous figures (Harry Truman, Will Rogers). TV series: *The Law and Mr Jones, My Friend Tony, Temperatures Rising*. TV movies: *The Challenge, If Tomorrow Comes, I Will Fight No More Forever, The Word, Mark I Love You, Rage*.

Whitmore, Richard (1933–). British newsreader, for BBC.

Whitney, John (1930–). British entrepreneur, producer and executive, formerly TV writer with Geoffrey Bellman (*The Verdict is Yours, Surrender Value*); after a founding role in commercial radio, Director-General of the IBA since November 1982.   PP

Whiz Kids
US 1983   × 50m colour
CBS/Universal (Philip DeGuere)
Bright teenagers fighting evil are immeasurably helped by their computer. Flashy adventures for juveniles, not far removed from *The Hardy Boys* but with equipment fashionable in the wake of *War Games*.

ph Philip DeGuere, Bob Shayne

Matthew Laborteaux, Todd Porter, Jeffrey Jacquet, Andrea Elson, Melanie Gaffin

Who Are the Vandals?
GB 1967 bw
BBC (Jill Craigie)
Swingeing and (as things turned out) prescient attack by director Mrs Michael Foot on public building policies, with special reference to

tower blocks, though its vigorous demolition work wasn't matched by constructive ideas of the same weight. Written by John Chisholm.

PP

Who Dares Wins *
GB 1984 9 × 50m
Who Dares Wins Ltd (Denise
O'Donoghue, Andy Hamilton)

Overall the wittiest and most genial of the 'alternative' comedy shows. 'Something really funny and intrepid and out on a limb,' I said of the original (1983) live one-off called *Who Dares Wins a Week in Benidorm*. The series followed, and another in 1985. Between them came *The Unrepeatable Who Dares Wins* edited down to 7 × 30m from the first batch.

w legion

Julia Hills, Rory McGrath, Jimmy Mulville, Phil Pope, Tony Robinson   PP
† 'Who Dares Wins' is the motto of the crack army outfit, the SAS.

Who Do You Do? A variety format devised by Jon Scoffield for London Weekend in the seventies: impressionists' acts are intercut so that joke follows joke with great rapidity and freshness; trains of thought and running gags can also be arranged. The contributors included Freddie Starr, Paul Melba, Little and Large, Peter Goodwright.

Who Fought Alone * (GB 1959). Why should a child of the Glasgow slums, in and out of prison, victim of the Slump, fight a lone action in World War II as if he had the most precious heritage in the world at stake? Moultrie Kelsall's epitaph on a Scottish soldier, originally a radio play, failed to produce the whole answer, but undeniably this was a moving television document charting 25 years of bitter social history with just the right kind of understatement. With Frank Wylie. Directed and produced by James Crampsey; for BBC Scotland.   PP

Who Is the Black Dahlia? *
US 1975 96m colour TVM
Douglas S. Cramer

The unsolved 1947 murder case of a 22-year-old girl found dead on waste ground.
Interesting and well made, but like all unsolved cases a bit of a let-down.

w Robert W. Lenski   *d* Joseph Pevney

Lucie Arnaz, Efrem Zimbalist Jnr, Ronny Cox, Macdonald Carey, Linden Chiles, Mercedes McCambridge, Tom Bosley, Gloria de Haven, John Fiedler, Rick Jason, Henry Jones, June Lockhart, Donna Mills

Who Killed Miss USA? *
aka: *McCloud: Who Killed Miss USA?*
GB title: *Who Killed Merri-Ann?*
US 1971 98m colour TVM
Universal (Leslie Stevens)

A New Mexican marshal loses a murder suspect in New York, but recovers him and stays for further training in metropolitan methods.
Based on the cinema film *Coogan's Bluff*, this is the pilot for one of *Mystery Movie*'s more popular segments; the plot makes no great sense, but technically it is well put together.

w Stanford Whitmore, Richard Levinson, William Link   *d* Richard A. Colla

Dennis Weaver, Craig Stevens, Mark Richman, Diana Muldaur, Julie Newmar

Who Killed the Lindbergh Baby? (GB 1982; 50m). Ludovic Kennedy re-opens the case of Bruno Hauptmann, electrocuted in 1932 for the kidnap and murder of Charles Lindbergh's baby son, and finds some very flimsy evidence to support that stroke of justice. From his own book *The Airman and the Carpenter*, for BBC.   PP

Who Killed the Mysterious Mr Foster?
aka: *Sam Hill: Who Killed the Mysterious Mr Foster?*
US 1973 98m colour TVM
Universal (Jo Swerling Jnr)

A western sheriff finds the body of the town's new minister.
Failed comedy western pilot which never really gets going.

w Richard Levinson, William Link   *d* Fielder Cook

Ernest Borgnine, Judy Geeson, Will Geer, J. D. Cannon, Bruce Dern, Sam Jaffe, John McGiver, Slim Pickens, Jay C. Flippen

Who, Me? **
GB 1959 55m bw (VTR)
BBC

Three men are interviewed by police after a robbery.
Trim little dramatic set piece, one of the pilots which led to the long-running *Z Cars*.

w Colin Morris   *d* Gilchrist Calder

Brewster Mason, Lee Montague, Maxwell Shaw, Neil McCarthy

Who Raised His Voice Against It?
GB/West Germany 1968 bw
BBC/BR (Lawrence Gordon Clark)

German resistance to the Nazi regime: a documentary perhaps over-emphasizing the churches' part and curiously (considering it was a Bavarian co-production) omitting any reference to the Munich 'White Rose' movement; otherwise a cool, annotated, unsensational approach to the subject. Written by Lawrence Gordon Clark, Bridget Winter.   PP

Who Were the British? * (GB 1966). Six half-hours of archaeology from Anglia TV; an excellent piece of popular research.

'Life is running out for Lucile Fray. She had enough love to bear ten children. Now she needs enough love to give them all away.'
Who Will Love My Children? *
US 1983 96m colour TVM
ABC (Paula Levenbach, Wendy Riche)
Learning that she has cancer, an invalid's wife sets about getting her children adopted. Real-life tearjerker, not badly done for those who can stand this kind of thing.

w Michael Bortman   d John Erman   ph Thomas Del Ruth   m Laurence Rosenthal

Ann-Margret, Frederic Forrest, Cathryn Damon, Donald Moffat, Lonny Chapman

Who'll Save Our Children?
US 1980 96m colour TVM
CBS/Time–Life (George Schaefer)
Adopted children are claimed when teenagers by their natural parents.
Emotional drama which will satisfy its intended audience.

w William Hanley, book Rachel Maddux d George Schaefer ph Don Wilder

Shirley Jones, Len Cariou, Cassie Yates, David Hayward, Conchata Ferrell

Whoops Apocalypse! (GB 1982; 6 × 28m). Knockabout political satire in which ex-actor US President, oft-cloned Soviet leader and supermanic British prime minister bring the world to the brink of disaster. A cult for some, baffling to others. Directed by John Reardon; produced by Humphrey Barclay, for LWT.

Who's the Boss? (US 1985–). Half-hour comedy series about a widowed ex-baseball player who with his nine-year-old daughter becomes live-in housekeeper to a scatty lady executive. Light, amusing stuff dependent on personalities. Tony Danza, Katherine Helmond. Created by Martin Cohan and Blake Hunter. Produced by Embassy for ABC.

Who's Watching the Kids? (US 1978). Unsuccessful half-hour comedy series for NBC, originally transmitted as *Legs*, and a development of *Blansky's Beauties*. It concerned Las Vegas showgirls attempting to look after their young brothers and sisters.

Who's Who? One-hour peak-time magazine show tried out unsuccessfully by CBS in the 1976 season. It usually consisted of three rather slackly handled interviews with people of passing interest.

Whose Life Is It Anyway? *
GB 1972 50m colour
Granada (Peter Eckersley)
Brian Clark's début, directed by Richard Everitt; later a successful stage play and movie. My 1972 review: 'Scratchy young sculptor languishes in hospital after a road smash, paralysed from the neck down and virtually certain to remain so. He decides rationally, calmly that he would rather not remain alive under such circumstances and agitates to be discharged – which would mean death within six days. Thanks to a very good line in bitter humour by playwright Brian Clark, a matching performance by Ian McShane and a plot that doesn't shirk lots of brisk development, it's not nearly as morbid as it sounds and makes a much better discussion about euthanasia than most discussions.'   PP

Why Me?
US 1984 96m colour TVM
ABC/Lorimar (Bob Papazian)
A happy, pregnant wife has a car accident in which her face is badly injured.
Surgical soap opera in which the lady falls for her doctor. Not a pretty sight.

w Dalene Young, novel by Leola May Harmon d Fielder Cook

Glynnis O'Connor, Armand Assante, Craig Wasson

Wiard, William (19 –). American director. *Ski Lift to Death, The Girl the Gold Watch and Everything, Fantasies, Help Wanted Male, Deadly Lessons, Kicks.*

Wichita Town
US 1959 39 × 25m bw
NBC
Marshal Mike Dunbar keeps law and order.
Adequate potted western of its time.
Joel McCrea, Jody McCrea

Wickes, David (1940–). British director specializing in action. Shot some of the best *Sweeney* episodes plus the feature film of the same title; also *Target*, *The Professionals*, etc. Produced *Marlow – Private Eye* as an independent. PP

The Wide Country
US 1962 28 × 50m bw
NBC/Revue/Gemini

A rodeo rider tries to prevent his young brother, who travels with him, from following in his footsteps.
Boring modern western.
Earl Holliman, Andrew Prine

Widmark, Richard (1914–). Cold-eyed American leading man and character actor with extensive film career. TV series: *Madigan*. TV movies: *Vanished*, *Brock's Last Case*, *The Last Day*, *Mr Horn*, *All God's Children*, *A Whale for the Killing*.

Widow *
US 1975 96m colour TVM
NBC/Lorimar (John Furia Jnr)

The first year of widowhood for an attractive woman with a family.
Glossy but moving domestic drama.
w Barbara Turner, *book* Lynn Caine *d* J. Lee-Thompson
Michael Learned, Bradford Dillman, Robert Lansing, Louise Sorel, Farley Granger, Carol Rossen

Widows **
GB 1983 7 × 52m
Euston Films (Linda Agran) for Thames

Three London gangsters die when a hold-up plan is spectacularly wrecked by mischance. Their wives decide to carry out their next job according to notes left behind by the gang's mastermind, recruiting a fourth girl along the way.
A clever feminization of the classical heist thriller with a sombre twist to the ending and the implausibilities smoothed over by an outstanding piece of characterization from Ann Mitchell as the ringleader.
A second series of 6 × 52m (1985) picks up the women in Rio as life in the sun starts to go wrong and one of the late husbands turns out to be not so dead after all.
w Lynda La Plante *d* Ian Toynton
Ann Mitchell, Maureen O'Farrell, Fiona Hendley, Eva Mottley (replaced in sequel by Debby Bishop). Maurice O'Connell, David Calder, Paul Jesson, Stanley Meadows PP

Wilcox, Desmond (1931–). British anchorman, long on *Nationwide* and *Man Alive*; his own series include *Americans*, *The Golden Vision* (American jewry) and *The Visit*. BAFTA awards 1967 and 1971.

Wilcox, Larry (1947–). American leading man, co-star of CHIPS. TV movies: *Mr and Mrs Bo Jo Jones*, *The Great American Beauty Contest*, *The Girl Most Likely To*, *Death Stalk*, *Sky Heist*, *Relentless*, *The Last Ride of the Dalton Gang*.

Wilcox, Paula (*c* 1950–). Saucer-eyed British leading actress, a comedy specialist. Series: *The Lovers*, *A Man About the House*, *Miss Jones and Son*.

Wild and Woolly
US 1978 96m colour TVM
Aaron Spelling/Douglas Cramer (Earl W. Wallace)

Three female convicts escape from Yuma in 1903 and expose a plot to kill the President.
An alleged adventure comedy with precious little of either commodity; very unprofessionally thrown together in the apparent hope of creating 'Charlie's Angels Out West'.
w Earl W. Wallace *d* Philip Leacock
Elyssa Davalos, Susan Bigelow, Christine de Lisle, Vic Morrow, Doug McClure, David Doyle, Paul Burke, Charles Siebert, Jessica Walter

The Wild and the Free
US 1980 96m colour TVM
CBS/Marble Arch (Paul Radin)

A scientist raises chimpanzees to the level of human behaviour.
Unconvincing but undeniably cute telefilm in which the animals steal the show.
w Michael Berk, Douglas Schwartz *d* James Hill *ph* Neil Roach *m* Gerald Fried
Granville van Dusen, Linda Gray, Frank Logan, Sharon Anderson

Wild Bill Hickok
US 1951–4 113 × 35m bw (39 colour)
Columbia

Sheriff Hickok fights for law and order.
Cheerful, competent juvenile western.
Guy Madison, Andy Devine

'Today there's a place where a man can be free . . . and he'd risk everything for the life he loves!'
Wild Horses
US 1985 96m colour TVM
CBS/Telepictures/Wild Horses (Hunt Lowry)

WIDOWS. In the old days of Hollywood you could never have a villain for a hero, much less a villainess for a heroine. In this popular Thames series of the eighties, however, the burglarous ladies have survived one series and are now setting off on another caper. Ann Mitchell, Maureen O'Farrell, Fiona Hendley, Debby Bishop.

A retired rodeo rider takes part in a wild horse round-up in Wyoming and foils a deal to send the animals to a meat packer.

Pleasant open-air melodrama with echoes of *The Misfits*.

w Rod Taylor, Daniel Vining   *d* Dick Lowry   *ph* Keith Wagstaff   *m* Kenny Rogers

Kenny Rogers, Pam Dawber, Ben Johnson, Richard Masur, Richard Farnsworth

'As fresh as the Wyoming air where it was filmed.' – *Daily Variety*

Wild Times

US 1980 2 × 96m colour TVM
Golden Circle/Metromedia/Rattlesnake (Douglas Netter)

A western gunman has various adventures and becomes the star of a wild west show.

Peripatetic action yarn clearly based on Bill Cody; good to look at, but its narrative grip is insecure.

w Don Balluck, *novel* Brian Garfield *d* Richard Compton *ph* John C. Flinn *m* Jerry Immel

Sam Elliott, Ben Johnson, Pat Hingle, Dennis Hopper, Leif Erickson, Trish Stewart, Cameron Mitchell, Bruce Boxleitner, Harry Carey Jnr

'A dime novel stretched over four hours.' – *Daily Variety*

The Wild Wild West *

US 1965–8 104 × 50m colour (26 bw)
CBS/Fred Freiburger, John Mantley (Bruce Lansbury)

Special government agents in the old west have their own specially equipped train.

A James Bond spoof which outlasted its welcome and had some terribly dud episodes; but people kept watching in the hope of a stunt or a laugh.

Robert Conrad, Ross Martin

The Wild Wild West Revisited
US 1979 96m colour TVM
CBS Entertainment (Jay Bernstein)

Daring agents track down a villain who has substituted clones for the crowned heads of Europe.

Amiable reprise of the series.

w William Bowers d Burt Kennedy ph Robert Hauser m Jeff Alexander

Robert Conrad, Ross Martin, Paul Williams, Henry Morgan, René Auberjonois, Trisha Noble, Shields and Yarnell

'A frolicsome, good-humoured piece of tongue-in-cheekery.' – Daily Variety

Wild Women
US 1970 74m colour TVM
Aaron Spelling

Army engineers on a secret mission disguise themselves as a wagon train and use women borrowed from the local jail.

Oddball comedy western, not really very good.

w Vincent Fotre d Don Taylor

Hugh O'Brian, Anne Francis, Marilyn Maxwell, Marie Windsor

'Their men left them without guns . . . but what ammunition!'

The Wild Women of Chastity Gulch
US 1982 96m colour TVM
ABC/Warner/Aaron Spelling (Shelley Hull)

A young lady doctor during the Civil War finds that she is to inherit a fortune from her small-town aunt . . . who is also the local brothelkeeper.

Wacky comedy–drama which aims to fire on all cylinders but soon chokes on its own exhaust.

w Earl W. Wallace d Philip Leacock ph Richard L. Rawlings m Frank de Vol, Tom Worrall

Priscilla Barnes, Joan Collins, Lee Horsley, Howard Duff, Pamela Bellwood, Phyllis Davis, Jeanette Nolan, Morgan Brittany, Donny Osmond

The Wilde Alliance (GB 1978; 13 × 50m).
Not-very-successful attempt by YTV to marry the talents of the stars of separate previous series: Julia Foster of Good Girl, John Stride of The Main Chance. They played a sporty husband and wife who solved a few mysteries.
PP

Wilder, John (1936–) (Keith Magaurn).
American producer in Hollywood: STREETS OF SAN FRANCISCO, Most Wanted, CENTENNIAL, The Devlin Connection, Spenser for Hire, etc.

Wildlife on One. Periodic seasons of BBC
programmes, self-explanatory in scope, presented by David Attenborough since 1979. Produced by Peter Bale.
PP

Wilfred and Eileen (GB 1981; 4 × 30m;
colour). A Love Story mini-serial by Robin Chapman from a true story by Jonathan Smith concerning a badly wounded World War I officer hauled back to sentient life by his determined fiancée. With Judi Bowker, Christopher Guard. Directed by David Green; produced by Colin Shindler; for BBC.
PP

Will – C. Gordon Liddy
US 1982 96m colour TVM
NBC/A. Shane/Joan Conrad (John Ashley)

How the Watergate burglar came to grow up with criminal tendencies.

Tedious and unconvincing psychological mumbo-jumbo applied to a man who simply did it for the dough.

w Frank Abatermarco d Robert Leiberman

Robert Conrad, Kathy Cannon, Gary Bayer, Peter Ratray

Will Shakespeare
GB 1978 6 × 50m colour (VTR)
ATV (Lorna Mason, Peter Roder, Cecil Clarke)

Shakespeare's adventures in and around the Globe Theatre.

An extremely ill-advised concept which, with all its undisciplined noise and bustle, and lack of sympathy for its leading character, must have set back the Shakespeare cause quite a bit.

w John Mortimer d Peter Wood

Tim Curry, Ian MacShane, André Morell, Nicholas Gray, Patience Collier

PP: 'Oh what a busy, bustling Elizabethan London! From holding playgoers' nags at the opening of the first episode, young Will was into the players company by the first break and lying in his bed inditing Henry VI, Part One, in Part Two. They were performing Part Two in Part Three, and Will was named the next great poet and play-maker by the dying Marlowe. But it steadied later.'

Will the Real Mr Sellers . . . (GB 1969).
Ingeniously put together (by Tony Palmer) but objectionable profile of Peter Sellers which turned out to be promoting his movie The Magic Christian. My review at the time: 'What an anti-climax! Our old friend the Free

Plug Circuit in full operation, if on a rather higher-minded, indeed at times quite stratospheric level. This was more than television's habitual adoration of the entertainer. It was the attempted Christification of Peter Sellers. He was to be regarded not as a gifted comedian and mimic with a compulsion to work too hard and without sufficient discrimination, but as some archetypal Victim of the Age doomed – like the Wandering Jew or the Flying Dutchman – to roam the world in search of the undiscoverable.' Produced by Denis O'Dell; for BBC/Grand Films.   PP

Will There Really Be a Morning?
US 1983 143m colour TVM
CBS/Prion (Everett Chambers)

The tragic life of Frances Farmer, the midwestern girl who became a thirties film star and couldn't take it.
Irritatingly overwrought and slow-paced real-life tragedy, unnecessary because an inevitably more polished movie version was in theatres at the same time.

w Dalene Young, from Frances Farmer's *autobiography* d Fielder Cook *ph* Michael Hugo

Susan Blakely, Lee Grant, Royal Dano, Joe Lambie, John Heard, Melanie Mayron

Willa
US 1979 96m colour TVM
CBS/Dove Inc/Gerry Leider (Michael Viner)

A deserted, pregnant wife learns to be a truckdriver.
Slight but lively character study with nice location work.

w Carmen Culver d Joan Darling, Claudio Guzman *ph* Matthew F. Leonetti *m* John Barry

Deborah Raffin, Clu Gulager, Cloris Leachman, Nancy Marchand, Mary Wickes, Bob Seagren

'It affords several performers fine opportunities, but eventually just spins its wheels.' – *Daily Variety*

Willes, Peter (1913–). British producer and executive, formerly Hollywood feature player (*The Dawn Patrol, Idiot's Delight*). Successively head of children's programmes, light entertainment and drama at Rediffusion; head of drama at YTV until 1978. Devised anthology series *The Seven Deadly Sins, Seven Deadly Virtues, Ten Commandments*; mounted first TV plays by Pinter, Joe Orton, Christopher Fry and his driver Charley Humphreys.   PP

William Tell: see The Adventures of William Tell

Williams, Andy (1930–). American ballad singer who through the sixties and seventies had several musical series to himself.

Williams, Bill (19 –). American leading man. Series include *A Date with the Angels, Kit Carson, Assignment Underwater*.

Williams, Cindy (1948–). American comedienne best known as co-star of *Laverne and Shirley*.

Williams, Dorian (1914–84). British equestrian commentator, recently retired.

Williams, Emlyn (1905–). Eminent Welsh actor and playwright who wrote occasionally for TV in the early days and forgettably on one or two later occasions, e.g *The Power of Dawn* for YTV, 1976. Popped up as an actor in *Rumpole of the Bailey* as late as 1983.

Williams, Kenneth (1926–). Frail, flaring-nostrilled British comic actor (all the *Carry On* films, etc) and professional chat-show guest with a line in perpetual outrage.   PP

Williams, Michael (1935–). Amiable British actor best known for *A Fine Romance* in which he partnered his wife Judi Dench.   PP

Williams, Nigel (19 –). Documentary writer and director of cultural programmes, e.g. the five-part *Arena* series on George Orwell, 1984.

Williams, Paul (1940–). Diminutive American songwriter and performer. TV movies: *Flight to Holocaust, The Wild Wild West Revisited, The Fall Guy*.

Williams, Robin (1955–). American entertainer. His material being on the zany side, he was a cinch to play the confused alien in MORK AND MINDY.

Williams, Simon (1946–). British leading man who was a hit in *Upstairs Downstairs* and again in *Agony*.

Williams, Treat (19 –). American leading actor. *Dempsey, A Streetcar Named Desire*.

ROBIN WILLIAMS. An instant hit as the comic alien in *Mork and Mindy*, he found more normal parts hard to find, and between unsuccessful movies returned to the night-club circuit.

Williams, Van (19 –). American leading man who didn't get far in films but on TV played *The Green Hornet*. TV movies: *The Runaways, Night Rider*.

Williamson, Nicol (1938–). Dour Scottish actor impressive in *Horror of Darkness*, 1965, but a woebegone Macbeth in the BBC Shakespeare and a suburban Lord Louis in *Mountbatten – the Last Viceroy*, 1986.   PP

Willie's Last Stand (GB 1982; 55m; colour). Gentle comedy by Jim Allen about a self-employed builder's itch in middle life to have a last little masculine adventure, foiled by a bad conscience and too nice a wife. With Paul Freeman, Colette O'Neill, Diana Davies. Directed by Brian Parker; for BBC *Play for Today*. PP

Willis, John (1945–). British writer, director and producer, son of Ted, best known for *Johnny Go Home* (1975) and other YTV social documentaries. *Rampton, The Secret Hospital*; *Alice – a Fight for Life* (asbestosis); *From the Cradle to the Grave* (series): *Churchill's Few, Return to Nagasaki*. PP

Willis, Ted (*c* 1918–) (Lord Willis). British 'working-class' TV playwright notable for *Woman in a Dressing Gown* and *Dixon of Dock Green*.

PP: 'A conscious pioneer of the school of social realism who sent to America for Paddy Chayevsky's book of TV scripts and sat down to do the same for Britain. His own collection, *Woman in a Dressing Gown*, was published in 1959. Soon drifted away to write terrible make-believe series like *Mrs Thursday* but also the respectable *Hunters Walk* and some good thrillers. Did much to advance the cause of TV writers.'

Willy (US 1954). Shortlived half-hour comedy series for CBS, with June Havoc as a lawyer settling in her home town in New Hampshire.

Wilma
US 1977 96m colour TVM
NBC/Cappy (Bud Greenspan)
A physically handicapped girl becomes an Olympic track sprinter.
A well-intentioned if overlong piece of 'faction', but some of the black accents are impenetrable.
w/d Bud Greenspan *ph* Arthur Ornitz *m* Irwin Bazelon
Shirley Jo Finney, Cicely Tyson, Jason Bernard, Joe Seneca

Wilsher, J. C. (John Wilsher) (1947–). British writer, formerly academic historian and sociologist, with a gift for the imaginative dramatization of computer technology and other horrors of the imminent future. *The Quiz Kid*, 1979; *Sin with Our Permission*, 1981; *Athens Without the Slaves*, unproduced. PP

Wilson, Sir Angus (1913–). British novelist and academic who wrote directly for television in the early days of ABC's Armchair Theatre (*After the Show*, 1959; *The Stranger*, 1960; *The Invasion*, 1962), but thereafter was represented by serializations of his novels: *Late Call*, 1975; *The Old Men at the Zoo*, 1982. Also wrote television criticism and a rather respectful book *Tempo: the Impact of Television Arts* (Studio Vista 1984) geared to ABC's *Tempo* series.

Wilson, Dennis Main (19 –). Veteran British producer of comedy shows from *The Goon Show* through to *Till Death Us Do Part*. BAFTA award 1969.

Wilson, Donald (1910–). British writer, script editor and producer, especially of BBC drama serials. BAFTA award 1967 for *The Forsyte Saga*. Also: *The Six Proud Walkers* (1954/62); *The Royalty* (1957); *No Wreath for the General* (1960); *The First Churchills* (1969); *Anna Karenina* (1977).

Wilson, Flip (1933–) (Clerow Wilson). Black cabaret comedian who was a number one TV attraction in a one-hour musical series in the early seventies, after which his appeal faded somewhat. Reappeared 1985 as *Charlie in Charge*.

Wilson, Sir Harold (1916–). During his premiership nursed strange animosity against the BBC, culminating in his imposition of Lord Hill as chairman, while at the same time displaying undignified eagerness to appear on ITV, including cross-talk acts with Ena Sharples and Morecambe and Wise. On retirement from active politics presented *A Prime Minister on Prime Ministers* (1977), and notoriously hosted two editions of the chat show *Friday Night . . . Saturday Morning*. Actually he wasn't bad. PP

Wilson, Richard (1936–). Scottish actor-director lately seen in *Strangers, Poppyland, The Last Place on Earth*. Directed *Under the Hammer*, 1984. PP

Wimbledon. In 1967 Wimbledon tennis furnished the first colour broadcast in Britain. By 1980 my verdict was: 'The annual tennis tournament is also an annual orgy of coverage on BBC TV, despite the fact that this event has long declined into a benefit for visiting players, ranging from the actively unpleasant to the merely Australian, with the natives restricted to the roles of worried hosts and squealing spectators.' PP

Winch, Arden (19 –). Reliable British TV playwright and novelist with flair for crime and action subjects, best realized in hugely compelling 1981 serial *Blood Money*. Earlier titles include *Tarnish on a Golden Boy* (1964), *The Bad One*, and contributions to many series. Provided the ideas for *Skorpion* and *Cold Warrior*.

Winchell, Paul (1924–). American ventriloquist popular in the fifties with his dummy Jerry Mahoney.

Winchell, Walter (1897–1972). American columnist of the fast-talking, hard-hitting school, a national institution through the thirties and forties. He made several less successful forays into TV, and will be best remembered in this medium as commentator for *The Untouchables*.

Winchester 73
US 1967 96m colour TVM
NBC/Universal (Richard E. Lyons)
Brother opposes brother for possession of a repeating rifle.
Flat rehash of a famous big-screen movie.
w Stephen Kandel, Richard L. Adams *d* Herschel Daugherty *ph* Bud Thackery *m* Sol Kaplan
Tom Tryon, John Saxon, Dan Duryea, John Drew Barrymore, Joan Blondell, John Dehner, Barbara Luna, Paul Fix

The Wind in the Willows (US 1984; 96m; colour; TVM). Japanese animated version of a story too familiar and too English. Not a success. Produced by Rankin–Bass for Telepictures. 'Yet another case where the original soars above its flatterer . . . if the sad lip-synchs and plastic individuals aren't enough to stiffen anyone's spine, the tunes should do the trick.' – *Daily Variety*

Windmill (GB 1985; 13 × 60m). Misspent dips into the BBC's hoard of video and celluloid programmes going back 50 years. Fidgety, uninformed presentation by the normally admirable Chris Serle robbed the compilations of both historical and intrinsic interest. Produced by Nigel Hannel, for BBC.
† The title came from the address of the BBC film and video archive in Windmill Road, Brentford.   PP
LH: 'I'd rather have an uninformed presentation of choice titbits from the past than none at all.'

Windom, William (1923–). American character actor who must have played in more TV guest spots than anyone. Series include *The Farmer's Daughter*, *My World and Welcome to It*. TV movies: *Prescription Murder*, *UMC*, *The House on Greenapple Road*, *Assault on the Wayne*, *Escape*, *A Taste of Evil*, *Marriage Year One*, *The Homecoming*, *Second Chance*, *A Great American Tragedy*, *Pursuit*, *The Girls of Huntington House*, *The Day the Earth Moved*, *The Abduction of St Anne*, *Journey from Darkness*, *Guilty or Innocent*, *Bridger*, *The Missing 24 Hours*, *Once an Eagle*, *Seventh Avenue*, *Hunters of the Deep*, *Blind Ambition*, *Leave 'Em Laughing*, *Side Show*, *The Rules of Marriage*, *Why Me?*

Window on Main Street
US 1961 36 × 25m bw
CBS/FKB (Robert Young)
A novelist returns to write about his home town.
Modest, agreeable drama.
Robert Young, Constance Moore

The Winds of Kitty Hawk *
US 1979 96m colour TVM
NBC/Lawrence Schiller/Charles Fries
An account of the Wright Brothers' first motorized flight, to mark the 75th anniversary.
A quality production which suffers from a flat script and flatter acting.
w Jeb Rosebrook, William Kelly *d* E. W. Swackhamer *ph* Dennis Dalzell *m* Charles Bernstein
Michael Moriarty, Tom Bower, David Huffman, Robin Gammell, Scott Hylands, John Hamilton, Eugene Roche
'There are times when the telefilm gets too heavy for air.' – *Daily Variety*
PP: 'An evidently much more successful version of the same exploit was *Orville and Wilbur* (1972), written by Arthur Barron, with the brothers Stacy and James Keach in the parts and superb flying sequences by Jack Lambie. Produced by NET, America, in association with a local North Carolina station and the BBC.'

The Winds of War ***
US 1983 8 × 96m colour
ABC/Paramount/Dan Curtis
An American naval officer is involved at top level in international events leading up to World War II.
Almost unbeatably impressive as a piece of American television, this generally absorbing

story, filmed all over the world, lets itself down only in the sub-plot dealing with the plight of a rather irritating American Jewess in Europe.

w HERMAN WOUK, from his novel d DAN CURTIS ph Charles Correll m Bob Cobert pd JACKSON DE GOVIA

ROBERT MITCHUM, POLLY BERGEN, JOHN HOUSEMAN, Ali MacGraw, Jan-Michael Vincent, Lisa Eilbacher, David Dukes, Topol, Ben Murphy, Peter Graves, Jeremy Kemp, RALPH BELLAMY (as Roosevelt), VICTORIA TENNANT, Elizabeth Hoffman, Anton Diffring, Ferdy Mayne, Edmund Purdom, Gunter Meisner (as Hitler), Rene Kolldehoff (as Goering), Howard Lang (as Churchill).

PP: 'The wind of war the hero chiefly suffered was brought on by his quasi-diplomatic duties, eating and drinking his way round the chancelleries of Europe.'

Windsor, Frank (1926–). Forthright north country British actor who rose to fame as Inspector Watt in *Z Cars.*

Wine of India * (GB 1970). It's AD 2050 and life has been totally tamed by science. Birth, death, health, happiness and all creature comforts are effortlessly programmed. Until a skeleton turns up, almost literally, at the feast. Nigel Kneale's vision of the future has enlightened humanity subscribing to a life-contract of 75 years; the old crone who long ago opted out of the scheme is sent along by the authorities to reassure those about to take their leave that they are doing the right thing. With Brian Blessed, Annette Crosbie, Catherine Lacey. Directed by Gilchrist Calder; produced by Graeme McDonald; for BBC (*Wednesday Play*).   PP

The Wine Programme * (GB since 1983). Admirable unstuffy guide to wine-bibbing, written and presented by Jancis Robinson; we have quite forgotten she mistakenly did a coffee commercial after the first series. Script consultant Tim Aspinall, directed and produced by Paul Fisher, for Telekation/Goldcrest/C4.   PP

Wine, Women and War: see The Six Million Dollar Man

Wings
GB 1976–7 26 × 50m colour (VTR)
BBC (Peter Cregreen)
Stories of the Royal Flying Corps in World War I.
Rather dull series with good flying sequences.

cr Barry Thomas m Alexander Faris
Tim Woodward, John Hallam, Nicholas Jones, Michael Cochrane

Wings of Fire
US 1967 99m colour TVM
Universal (David Lowell Rich)
The daughter of an air freight service owner enters an air race.
Moderate old-fashioned romantic drama with aerial trimmings; rather a bore.
w Sterling Silliphant d David Lowell Rich
Suzanne Pleshette, James Farentino, Lloyd Nolan, Juliet Mills, Jeremy Slate, Ralph Bellamy

❋ **Winkler, Henry** (1946–). American character actor who unexpectedly became a national celebrity as the bumptious but likeable Fonzie in *Happy Days*; otherwise rather difficult to cast. TV movies: *Katherine, An American Christmas Carol.*

A Winner Never Quits: the Pete Gray Story
US 1985 96m colour TVM
NBC/Columbia/Blatt–Singer (James Keach, Lynn Raynor)
The career of a one-armed baseball player. Yes, really. And of great interest to others similarly handicapped.
w Burt Prelutsky d Mel Damski ph Joe Biroc m Dana Kaproff
Keith Carradine, Mare Winningham, Dennis Weaver, Huckleberry Fox, Jack Kehoe, Fionnula Flanagan

Winner Take All
US 1975 100m colour TVM
NBC/Jozak (Nancy Malone)
A housewife becomes addicted to gambling. Domestic drama moving in well-defined grooves.
w Caryl Ledner d Paul Bogart
Shirley Jones, Laurence Luckinbill, Sam Groom, Joan Blondell, Joyce Van Patten, Sylvia Sidney

Winner Take All
US 1977 50m colour
CBS/Quinn Martin (John Wilder)
A police lieutenant is helped by an insurance investigator.
So-so crime pilot which didn't go.
w Cliff Gould d Robert Day m John Elizalde
Michael Murphy, Joanna Pettet, Clive Revill, Mark Gordon, David Huddleston, Signe Hasso

THE WINE PROGRAMME. Jancis Robinson on Channel Four eyes the red lifeblood as the wine waiter does his stuff.

The Winning Streak
GB 1985 6 × 52m
YTV (Michael Russell)

Two brothers jostle for leadership of the family garage business, one a ruthless commercial go-getter, the other a ruthless rally driver. 'It is difficult,' I noted, 'to imagine a fiction series compounded so unerringly from everything that is mercenary, phony, noisy and smelly about life today.'

w Michael J. Bird d Frank Smith, Richard Holthouse   PP

Winston Churchill – the Wilderness Years **
GB 1981 8 × 50m colour
Southern/Mark Shivas, Richard Broke

How Churchill bided his time in the thirties, when his advice went unheeded.
Ambitious and moderately satisfactory reconstruction which proved caviare to the general.

devisors Martin Gilbert, Richard Broke d Ferdinand Fairfax m Carl Davis
ROBERT HARDY (Churchill), Siân Phillips (Clementine), Peter Barkworth (Baldwin), Eric Porter (Chamberlain), Edward Woodward (Hoare), Sam Wanamaker (Baruch)

A Winter Harvest
GB 1984 3 × 50m
BBC Bristol (Colin Goodman)

Novice farmer's wife is plunged into the deep end when her husband has to go into hospital. Cheryl Campbell stayed crisp and fresh whatever the task, but the relationships between husband and wife, wife and hired hand, hired hand and nature, were nicely understated.

w Jane Beeson d Colin Goodman
Cheryl Campbell, Mark Wing-Davey, Mark Elliott, Sheila Ruskin   PP

Winter Kill **
US 1974 100m colour TVM
ABC/MGM (Burt Nodella)

Inexplicable but connected murders strike a mountain resort community.
This fairly gripping, nicely photographed and vividly narrated murder mystery was intended as a pilot for a series which never happened, Adams of Eagle Lake. It was inspired by the movie They Always Kill their Masters but took its plot without permission from an old Sherlock Holmes movie The Scarlet Claw.

w John Michael Hayes d Jud Taylor
Andy Griffith, Sheree North, John Larch, John Calvin, Tim O'Connor, Louise Latham, Joyce Van Patten

The Winter of Our Discontent
US 1983 96m colour TVM
CBS/Lorimar (R. W. Goodwin)

A New England clerk determines to regain control of his father's store.
Unsuccessful piece of cultural uplift for a network which really needed it.

w Michael de Guzman, story by John Steinbeck d Waris Hussein ph Robbie Greenberg m Mark Snow
Donald Sutherland, Teri Garr, Tuesday Weld, Michael Gazzo, Richard Masur, E. G. Marshall
'A wrenching yarn of a man entrapped in his own hypocrisy.' – Daily Variety

Winter Sunlight
GB 1984 4 × 60m
Limehouse Productions (Susi Hush)/C4

In late life a woman leaves her husband to seek happiness, but it isn't easy to cut all ties . . . Superior soap, superiorly done.

w Alma Cullen d Julian Amyes
Elizabeth Sellars, Derek Francis, Patrick Hayes, Betty Marsden, Derek Farr, Polly Adams, Michael Byrne   PP

Winters, Mike (1930–) and **Bernie** (1932–). British music hall crosstalk act patterned after Abbott and Costello (and Martin and Lewis). TV appearances sporadic. The act split up in 1978. Bernie subsequently had his own shows and was a first-rate Bud Flanagan in Bud 'n' Ches.

Winters, Shelley (1922–) (Shirley Schrift). Cheerful, often heavyweight American character actress who likes to keep working. Emmy 1963 for Two Is the Number (Chrysler Theatre). TV movies: Revenge, A Death of Innocence, The Adventures of Nick Carter, The Devil's Daughter, Big Rose, The Sex Symbol, The Initiation of Sarah, Elvis.

Wire Service
aka: Deadline Action
US 1956 39 × 50m bw
ABC/Sharpe–Lewis

Adventures of international reporters.
The stars alternated, but the stories were the same old hokum.

George Brent, Mercedes McCambridge, Dane Clark

'Not very far removed from the Grade B movie melodramas of the 1930s.' – Don Miller, 1957

Wisdom, Norman (1920–   ). British singing comic, a would-be Chaplinesque droll who in the fifties was big at the movie box office but anathema to the intellectuals. On TV he starred in several variety-oriented comedy series and eventually went straight in *Going Gently*.

✳ **Wise, Ernie** (*c* 1925–). British comedian, the less zany half of Morecambe and Wise and the one with the short fat hairy legs.

Wise, Herbert (1924–   ) (H. Weisz). British director of long standing. Recent credits: *Walk with Destiny*, *I, Claudius*, *The Norman Conquests*, *Rumpole of the Bailey*, *Skokie*, *Pope John Paul II*, *Reunion at Fairborough*.

Wiseman, Frederick (19   –   ). American documentarist who specializes in *cinéma vérité* looks at life's less attractive side, and especially at American institutions such as schools, hospitals and law. His films were all commissioned by public television. *Titicut Follies* 1967. *High School* 1968. *Law and Order* 1969. *Hospital* 1970. *Basic Training* 1971. *Juvenile Court* 1973. *Welfare* 1975; etc.

Wish You Were Here. ITV's long-running seasonal travel programme, from Thames, with Judith Chalmers, Chris Kelly.

Wishman (US 1983; 50m). Risible pilot ripped off from *E.T.*, about a weird but amiable biological specimen on the run from his creators. Poor special effects killed it almost stone dead, and the script did the rest. Created by Bob Christiansen and Rick Rosenberg for Viacom. With Joseph Bottoms, Linda Hamilton, James Keach.

With This Ring *
US 1978 96m colour TVM
ABC/Paramount/Jozak (Bruce J. Sallan)

Three couples about to get married have second thoughts.

Intercut comedies apparently inspired by *Plaza Suite*. Quite witty on occasion.

w Terence Mulcahy *d* James Sheldon *ph* Roland S. Smith *m* George Aliceson Tipton

Joyce de Witt, Scott Hylands, Tony Bill, Betty White, John Forsythe, Tom Bosley, Deborah White

Withers, Googie (1917–   ) (Georgette Withers). Stately British character actress with a long early career as movie heroine. Her most notable TV appearance was as the prison governor in *Within These Walls*.

Within These Walls * (GB 1974–7). British one-hour drama series (from LWT) about life in a prison for women. In general, responsible stuff, but pretty heavy going as entertainment. The governors were played successively by Googie Withers, Katharine Blake and Sarah Lawson.

Witness for the Prosecution
GB/US 1982 96m colour TVM
CBS/MGM/Norman Rosemont

An ailing barrister takes on a murder defence, but despite success is himself tricked.

Tepid rehash of the famous courtroom thriller; clearly it could never be as good as the Billy Wilder film of 1957.

w John Gay, *play* by Agatha Christie *d* Alan Gibson *ph* Arthur Ibbetson *m* John Cameron

Ralph Richardson, Deborah Kerr, Diana Rigg, Beau Bridges, Donald Pleasence, Richard Vernon, Wendy Hiller, David Langton, Peter Sallis, Michael Gough

Wizards and Warriors
US 1982 4 × 50m colour
ABC/Warner/Don Reo (S. Bryan Hickox)

Prince Erik and his loyal vassal oppose the evil wiles of Prince Dirk.

Short-lived, cheaply made offshoot of the fashion for Sword and Sorcery. For grown-up children.

cr Don Reo

Jeff Conaway, Clive Revill, Water Olkewicz, Duncan Regehr, Julia Duffy

WKRP in Cincinnati (US 1978–81). Half-hour comedy for CBS, from MTM. Life in a radio station which is slightly out of touch; with Gary Sandy, Gordon Jump, Loni Anderson.

✳ **Wogan, Terry** (1938–   ). Cheerful Irish man-about-British-television, credited with making *Dallas* a hit by constantly knocking it on his radio show. Television shows as presenter include *Blankety Blank* and *You Must Be Joking*, but one senses that his best is yet to come.

PP: 'After two seasons of his thrice-weekly chat show *Wogan* (BBC) we're still waiting.'

Wolff, Heinz (1928–). British (Austrian-born) demon professor and director of the Institute for Bioengineering at Brunel University who conducts *Ze Great Ek Race* (see *The Great Egg Race*) for BBC. 'With trousers high off his shoes, his bow-tie, his accent, his unquenchable glee, Wolff is wonderful. One of the teams, he ruled last week, would score less more marks than the others.' PP

Wolper, David (1928–). American documentarist who turned executive and formed the Wolper Organization to make non-fiction programmes, a few movies and eventually half-hour comedies (*Welcome Back Kotter, Chico and the Man*), TV movies and the smash success *Roots*. Merged with Warner in 1976.

The Woman at No. 10 (GB 1983; 52m). Courteous call on Mrs Thatcher by writer and traveller Sir Laurens Van der Post, leading to a tour of the premises and polite conversation. 'A cordial occasion contrived for Mrs Thatcher with an elder of her liking,' I said, but went on to point out that such programmes (others have included Jackie Kennedy showing off the White House, President Pompidou playing billiards in the Elysée Palace) can tell you more about someone's style of power than all the tough interview sessions put together. Directed by Michael Gill, produced by Peter Bevan, for Central. PP

A Woman Called Golda
Emmy 1982: best limited series

A Woman Called Moses
US 1977 2 × 96m colour TVM
NBC/IKE/Henry Jaffe (Ike Jones, Michael Jaffe)
The story of black slave Harriet Ross Tubman, who escapes north with a price on her head and returns to lead her people to the same freedom.
Grimmish picture of ante-bellum life in the south, made hard to follow by unfamiliar accents. Slow to start but generally well acted.
w Lonne Elder III, *book* Marcy Heidish *d* Paul Wendkos *ph* Robert Hauser *m* Coleridge-Taylor Parkinson
Cecily Tyson, Mae Mercer, Jane Wainwright, Will Geer, Judyann Elder, Dick Anthony Williams, Robert Hooks, Orson Welles (narrator)

The Woman Hunter
US 1972 74m colour TVM
Jerome L. Epstein
An international jewel thief and murderer seems to be on the trail of a wealthy woman. Crime in the luxury classes, suffering from obscure narration.
w Brian Clemens *d* Bernard L. Kowalski
Barbara Eden, Robert Vaughn, Stuart Whitman, Sydney Chaplin, Larry Storch

Woman in a Dressing Gown
GB 1956 50m bw (live show)
Associated-Rediffusion (Peter Cotes)
Slovenly wife nearly, but not quite, loses husband to younger woman. Ted Willis's first essay in absolutely everyday drama, inspired by reading a book of Paddy Chayevsky TV plays, plus essays by the same writer, which Willis had had sent from America; and in its way a little landmark in British television. Made into a movie the following year.
d Peter Cotes
Joan Miller   PP

A Woman of Substance *
GB 1983 3 × 96m colour
Operation Prime Time/Artemis Portman (Diane Baker)
A Yorkshire servant girl is driven by ambition and becomes the owner of a chain of American department stores.
Reasonably attractive adaptation of a gutsy novel, hampered only by the need to have the central role played by two actresses to cover the age span.
w Lee Langley, *novel* by Barbara Taylor Bradford *d* Don Sharp *ph* Ernest Vincze *m* Nigel Hess *pd* Roy Stannard
Deborah Kerr, Jenny Seagrove, Barry Bostwick, Diane Baker, George Baker, Peter Chelson, John Duttine, Peter Egan, Christopher Gable, Gayle Hunnicutt, Megs Jenkins, Barry Morse, John Mills

Woman of the Year
US 1975 100m colour TVM
CBS/MGM (Hugh Benson)
A sports writer tames and marries a politically conscious lady.
Disappointing TV remake of the cinema film . . . as what remake wouldn't be?
w Joseph Bologna, Renee Taylor, Bernie Kahn *d* Gene Kelly
Renee Taylor, Joe Bologna, Dick O'Neill, Anthony Holland

Woman to Woman (GB since 1985). 'Occasional' conversations with female high achievers by the high-achieving Dr Miriam Stoppard, launched with a cosy 40 minutes *chez* Mrs Thatcher, who revealed that her political appetite began round the old cracker-barrel in the family grocery store. PP

Women at West Point
US 1979 96m colour TVM
NBC/Columbia

A raw recruit learns how to be tough at America's military academy for women.
Tolerable if melodramatic army drama with familiar plot progression.

w Ann and Leslie Marcus *d* Vincent Sherman

Linda Purl, Andrew Stevens, Jameson Parker, Leslie Ackerman

Women in Chains
US 1971 74m colour TVM
Bernard Kowalski (Edward J. Mikis)

A probation officer has herself imprisoned to help research, but her only confidant dies . . .
Not exactly a new plot, but the old melodramatics suffice.

w Rita Lakin *d* Bernard Kowalski

Ida Lupino, Lois Nettleton, Jessica Walter, Belinda Montgomery, John Larch, Penny Fuller

Women in White
US 1978 2 × 96m colour
NBC/Universal/Groverton (David Victor)

Problems of doctors and nurses at a Miami general hospital.
Old-hat intercutting of medico melodramas, which haven't changed much since the days of *Dr Kildare*.

w Robert Malcolm Young, Irving Pearkberg, *novel* Frank G. Slaughter *d* Jerry London *ph* Michael Marguilies *m* Morton Stevens

Susan Flannery, Kathryn Harrold, Howard McGilling, Sheree North, Patty Duke Astin, Robert Culp, Aldo Ray, Stuart Whitman, Maggie Cooper

'There aren't enough new ailments or cures to make the house calls worth while . . . it wouldn't hurt to drain the blood and start over.' – *Daily Variety*

Women of Courage *
GB 1980 4 × 50m colour
YTV (Peter Morley, Kevin Sim)

Four follow-ups to the same producers' *Kitty*, each profiling a heroine of World War II.

Hiltgunt Zassenhaus (German humanitarian), Maria Ratkiewicz (Poland), Sigrid Lund (Norway), Mary Lindell (British agent).   PP

Women of San Quentin
US 1983 96m colour TVM
NBC/MGM/David Gerber (R. W. Goodwin, Stephen Cragg)

Women guards are recruited for a top American male gaol.
It apparently happened, however daft it sounds, but it doesn't make for riveting drama.

w Mark Rodgers *d* William A. Graham *ph* Robert Steadman *m* John Cacavas

Stella Stevens, Debbie Allen, Hector Elizondo, Amy Steel, Rosana DeSota, Gregg Henry, Yaphet Kotto

'It drags from cliché to cliché with little vigour.' – *Daily Variety*

The Women of Willmar: see A Matter of Sex

The Women's Room
US 1980 140m colour TVM
ABC/Warner/Philip Mandelker (Glenn Jordan)

An apparently happy and well-heeled housewife explains why a woman's lot is not a happy one.
Curious, soapish, feminist tract which at this length can't survive even with good production and acting.

w Carol Sobieski, *novel* Marilyn French *d* Glenn Jordan *ph* Terry K. Meade *m* Billy Goldenberg

Lee Remick, Colleen Dewhurst, Patty Duke Astin, Jenny O'Hara, Tovah Feldshuh, Kathryn Harrold, Tyne Daly, Lisa Pellikan, Marc Willingham, Gregory Harrison

'Emotional binges add up to detergent opry stuff loaded with ersatz suds.' – *Daily Variety*

Wonder, Stevie (1950–) (Steveland Morris). Blind American songwriter and performer.

Wonder Woman
US 1974 75m colour TVM
ABC/Warner

Wonder Woman leaves Paradise Island to undertake a special mission for the CIA.
Abysmal comic strip adventures lacking in logic or even action.

w John D. F. Black *d* Vincent McEveety

Cathy Lee Crosby, Ricardo Montalban, Andrew Prine, Kaz Garas

† The subsequent one-hour series started very hesitantly, changed both its format and its network after one season, and was much derided, but struggled on for several seasons with Lynda Carter and Lyle Waggoner in the leads.

Woobinda, Animal Doctor: see Animal Doctor

Wood and Walters ** (GB 1981–2). Television's first teaming of Victoria Wood and Julie Walters in a comedy series; produced by Brian Armstrong for Granada.

Wood, Charles (1932–). British stage- and screenwriter, formerly a regular cavalry soldier (hence *Prisoner and Escort*, 1962, *Drill Pig*, 1963, and the trilogy *Death or Glory Boy*, 1974). Went through experimental phase e.g. *Drums Along the Avon* (1967), before settling down to work a rich vein of comedy usually set in or around the writer's trade: contributions to *The Root of all Evil* (1969) and *The Ten Commandments* (1971); *Love-Lies-Bleeding* (1977), and of course *Don't Forget to Write* (series, 1977–9). *Red Monarch*, 1983; *Wagner* (epic) 1983; *Puccini*, 1984.

Wood, John (1932–). Versatile British actor who was particularly important to television in the early sixties: *The Victorians* (series), *The Hooded Terror*, *The Three Sisters*, *Maupassant*, *The Duel*, all within one year (1963). Since then, more occasional appearances. PP

Wood, Michael (1948–). British writer–presenter of popular archaeology programmes, e.g. *In Search of King Arthur* (and Boadicea, Robin Hood, etc), 1982; *In Search of the Trojan War*, 1985. Also brought his boyish good looks to episodes of *Great Little Railway Journeys* and *Great River Journeys*, all for BBC. PP

Wood, Natalie (1938–81) (Natasha Gurdin). American star actress, occasionally appeared on the small screen. TV movies: *Cat on a Hot Tin Roof*, *The Affair*, *From Here to Eternity*, THE CRACKER FACTORY, *The Memory of Eva Ryker*.

Wood, Peggy (1892–1978). American character actress whose TV pinnacle was as *Mama* in the early fifties.

Wood, Peter (1928–). British theatre director under contract to ATV-Tennents in the fifties and early sixties: *All Summer Long*, *The Pets*, *The Enormous Shadow*, *Children Playing*, etc. Since then, occasional but regular TV productions, including serial *Will Shakespeare* (1978). PP

Wood, Victoria (1954–). Plump, chirpy British playwright and lyricist who likes to seed little songs through her plays, which are funny, sad, funny again and full of marvellous lines. *Talent* (1979), *Happy Since I Met You* (1981). Also in entertainment with Julie Walters, *Wood and Walters* (1980–2), *Victoria Wood as seen on Television* (1985). BAFTA awards for star and show, 1986.
PP

Woodentop (GB 1983; 52m). First day on duty at a London police station for a young probationary copper, played by Mark Wingett. The title came from the derisive nickname for a uniformed constable used by the plain-clothes CID men. A try-out in Thames's *Storyboard* season neat enough to lead to series in 1984–5 under the title *The Bill* (cockney slang for the police in general). Written by Geoff McQueen, directed by Peter Cregeen, produced by Michael Chapman. PP

Woodhouse, Barbara (1910–). Bossy British dog trainer who became an eccentric heroine of the public on the strength of *Training Dogs the Woodhouse Way* (1980), followed by *Barbara's World of Horses and Ponies* and many chat-show appearances. PP

Woods, Peter (1930–). Pouch-eyed British newsreader, former foreign correspondent.

Woodward, Edward (1930–). British general purpose actor who scored a major hit as *Callan* and found later roles few and far between because he was so identified with the character. 1978: *1990*, *The Bass Player and the Blonde*. 1981: *Wet Job* (Callan), *Winston Churchill: The Wilderness Years* (as Sir Samuel Hoare). 1985: *The Equalizer*.

Woodward, Joanne (1930–). Leading American actress, wife of Paul Newman. TV movies: *Sybil* (Emmy 1976), *See How She Runs*, *A Christmas to Remember*, *The Shadow Box*, *Crisis at Central High*.

Woody Woodpecker. The cartoon bird with the maniacal laugh, created for the cinema by Walter Lantz, turned up on TV in half-hours which were collections of the old cartoons with new bridges.

JOANNE WOODWARD. One of the distinguished actresses whose television appearances were always an occasion. Here in *Do You Remember Love* she plays a victim of Alzheimer's Disease.

Wooldridge, Ian (1932–). British sports reporter and television writer–narrator associated with disreputable Michael Begg specials: *The Great Fishing Race, The Golden Maggot, The Birdman of Jacksonville*; also straight sporting specials on American soccer, Superbowl football, US Masters golf tournament, etc; and service documentary series *Behind the Lines*, 1985. BBC interview series *Ian Wooldridge Interviews* (p Malcolm Adams) 1982–3. Clients included Joan Collins, Jeffrey Archer and Laurie McMenemy.   PP

Wooldridge, Susan (19 –). British actress daughter of Margaretta Scott, who deservedly zoomed to fame in THE JEWEL IN THE CROWN; thereafter in *Frankenstein* and as Scott's liberated wife in *The Last Place on Earth*.   PP

Wooller, Mike (1927–). Capable British director, producer and executive, ex-Granada and now working with them again. In between came *All in a Day* for the BBC, editorship of *Omnibus*, overlording documentaries at Thames (*Palestine*, *Creggan*, *The One and Only Phyllis Dixey*, *Hollywood*, *The Troubles*) and setting up the major independent Goldcrest Television (managing director 1981–5).   PP

The Word
US 1978 4 × 96m colour TVM
CBS/Stonehenge/Charles Fries

A publisher travels the world trying to prove the authenticity of a so-called fifth gospel.
A complex, meandering story spread over four nights is too much for this unusual mini-series despite its star cast and intriguing basis.

w Dick Berg, Robert L. Joseph, S. S. Schweitzer, Richard Felder, *novel* Irving Wallace *d* Richard Lang *ph* Michel Hugo *m* Alex North

David Janssen, James Whitmore, Florinda Bolkan, Eddie Albert, Geraldine Chaplin, Hurd Hatfield, Ron Moody, John Huston, John McEnery, Diana Muldaur, Kate Mulgrew, Janice Rule, Martha Scott, Nicol Williamson

'Starts out as a grabber, loses momentum, and settles for dramatic as well as narrative indecision.' – *Daily Variety*

Word of Honour
US 1981 96m colour TVM
TCF/Georgian Bay (John C. Dutton)

A journalist gets into trouble for refusing to reveal his sources in what turns out to be a murder case.
Well-acted though quite predictable melodrama which stands or falls by the performance of its star.

w David Accles, Howard Krantz, I. C. Rapoport *d* Mel Damski *ph* Jules Brenner *m* Bruce Langhorne

Karl Malden, Rue McClanahan, Ron Silver, Largo Woodruff, Jaqueline Brooks, Henderson Forsythe, John Marley

'Fine detailing gives it life.' – *Daily Variety*
† This was the pilot for a series about a small-town reporter and his family, but it didn't go.

Working Stiffs (US 1979). Feeble comedy series with Michael Keaton and Jim Belushi as bumbling janitors. Seven episodes only; for Paramount.

working title. One which is used during production but is likely to be changed.

The World – a Television History (GB 1983–5; 26 × 28m). Ambitious but rather arid television version of the *Times Atlas of World History*, using a lot of graphics. Produced by Nicholas Barton for Goldcrest/C4.

The World About Us. Long-standing umbrella title for BBC2's Sunday evening one-hour documentary about animals or exploration.

The World at War ***
GB 1975 26 × 50m bw
Thames (Jeremy Isaacs)

A history of World War II.
Major in undertaking and achievement, this great enterprise was impeccably executed. If it had a fault it was that it somehow missed the elation which was felt by the winning side even in the midst of the horror.

w various *d* various, but Peter Batty made five episodes, David Elstein three, Phillip Whitehead and Michael Darlow two apiece *assoc p* Jerry Kuehl

PP: 'A magnificent undertaking which consistently took a fitting attitude to the violent events of nearly 30 years before, relying on the personal recollections of survivors of all ranks even when their testimony disagreed with official document-based history.'

The World Cup: a Captain's Tale *
GB 1982 90m TVM
Tyne-Tees (Laurie Greenwood)

True story of how an obscure amateur team from the Durham coalfields carried off the very first World Cup for soccer, offered in 1910 by Sir Thomas Lipton.
A funny, robust version with all the old workingmen-abroad jokes newly dusted off, from encounters with the bidet to the brothel to the spaghetti.

w Neville Smith *d* Tom Clegg

Denis Waterman, Andrew Keir, Richard Griffiths, Derek Francis   PP

World in Action ***. A title devised in 1963 by Granada for its Monday night half-hours of investigative journalism in a punchy, hard-hitting style comparable with that of the popular press (but rather better informed). The series has run for the best part of each year since.

† In 1985 *W. in A.* celebrated 21 years with a special compilation. Among nearly 90 producers in that time were Tim Hewat (who started it), Granada's managing director David Plowright, *Brideshead* director Charles Sturridge, film-makers Michael Apted, John Goldschmidt and Denis Mitchell; Mike Wooller, John Birt and Ray Fitzwalter. PP

The World of Beachcomber (GB 1972). Evangelical attempt by Barry Took and John Junkin to transfer the much-loved humour of J. B. Morton to the screen, introduced by Spike Milligan. Funny, faithful and nostalgic. PP

The World of Darkness
US 1977 50m colour
CBS/Warner/David Susskind

A sportswriter becomes involved in solving supernatural problems.
Occult series never go, but producers keep trying.
w Art Wallace *d* Jerry London *m* Fred Karlin
Granville Van Dusen, Beatrice Straight, Gary Merrill

The World of Hugh Hefner
GB 1974 52m colour
YTV (Tony Palmer)

Profile of the *Playboy* millionaire. My review at the time: 'An act of worship rather than information, but a little leaked out, mostly between the lines . . . We learned that young ladies in Hefnerland may take their clothes off in front of a camera but wear bikinis in the bath, and that Hefner goes to imperious lengths to save time which he then expends on backgammon or table-top soccer. We did not learn how an apparently intelligent man can bear to surround himself with dumb broads. To tell the truth, we didn't much care.' PP

The World of Mr Sweeney. A quarter-hour series starring Charles Ruggles as the kindly proprietor of a small-town store. After exposure on the NBC network in 1954, it totalled 345 episodes in daytime.

World of Sport. British independent television's main weekend sports broadcast, the opposition to BBC's *Grandstand*. Originally hosted by Eamonn Andrews, since 1968 by Dickie Davies. PP

World of Television (GB 1981). Whizzing survey of the incongruities of TV round the world conducted by Denis Norden rather as an extension of his LWT *It'll Be Alright on the Night* compilations. In Australia soap opera had discovered sex with the dogged thoroughness of a lepidopterist ticking off variations. In India a solemn pronouncement sanctioned the use of the studio harmonium again after 40 years. New Zealand had a truly funny commercial, weather forecasts were funny everywhere. A macabre American game show rubbed its hands over the visible dissolution of a marriage. Korea had *Upstairs*, *Downstairs* in Korean.

Drawn from the bread and butter television of the various countries rather than their festival treats, the programme had some instructional value, but the ravaging of 500 hours of television to yield this one hour couldn't help smelling of *bonne boucherie*. PP

The World of Wooster (GB 1965–8). The first of a BBC sequence of comedy series from the stories by P. G. Wodehouse. This was probably the best, with Ian Carmichael as the bone-headed Bertie Wooster and Dennis Price the resourceful manservant Jeeves; produced by Michael Mills. In 1967 the title was varied to *The World of Wodehouse* to take in further Wodehouse characters, notably Lord Emsworth as played by Ralph Richardson. Later still: *Wodehouse Playhouse*. PP

World Première. An umbrella title given by NBC to its 96m TV movies which filled two-hour slots in the late sixties. *Movie of the Week* covered the 90m slots.

The World That Summer *
Original title: *Die Welt in Jenem Sommer*
West Germany 1980 90m bw
WDR (P. Canaris)

Half-Jewish boy growing up in Hitler's Germany, torn between fear and admiration of the regime; the British writer Robert Muller's semi-autobiographical story stunningly re-created in the authentic velvety monochrome of the period; directed by Ilse Hofman. My 1980 review: 'The film's great novelty, and what makes it so valuable, is its picture of ordinary life under the Nazis; no pogroms, no set-piece confrontations as in the opening episode of *Holocaust*, scarcely a jackboot in view. Life is well ordered and, for the majority, enjoyable. It is only gradually and between the lines, in little details of behaviour inextricably mixed up with the

SUSAN WOOLDRIDGE, one of the new generation of actresses for the eighties, made her mark in *The Jewel in the Crown* but was less memorable in subsequent roles such as that of Kathleen Scott in *The Last Place on Earth*.

ordinary shifts and treacheries of boyhood, that the unresisting acceptance of a hideous creed becomes evident.'   PP

World Theatre (GB 1958). BBC season of 14 heavyweight stage plays which finally threw up an undisputed masterpiece of TV production: John Jacobs's 2 × 90-minute version of O'Neill's *Strange Interlude*, with Diane Cilento, David Knight, Noel Willman and William Sylvester.   PP

The World Walk * (GB 1984; 45m). Alec McCowen as the 'reformed' Nazi minister Albert Speer who whiled away his prison term in Spandau by trudging round the exercise yard and counting every kilometre to work out where he would have reached on an imaginary walk around the Earth. Interesting little drama by Jonathan Smith, directed by Sarah Hellings, produced by Brenda Reid, for BBC.   PP

World War II. Except for the infant French TV service transmitted from the Eiffel Tower which the Nazis restored for a while to amuse their occupation troops (it was duly monitored by British intelligence via an outsize aerial on Beachy Head), the last major conflict to be waged innocently of television. In retrospect it has, not unexpectedly, inspired a vast amount of fact and fiction. NBC's *Victory at Sea* (1952) was the first great documentary hit anywhere in the world. In Soviet Russia *The Great Patriotic War* was required viewing, in every sense. In Britain it was, curiously, not until nearly 30 years after the end of hostilities that Thames TV mounted *The World at War*.   PP
LH: 'Aspects of it were explored dramatically in such series as *Manhunt*, *A Family at War*, *Ike*, *We'll Meet Again*, *Dad's Army*, *Secret Army*, *A Man Called Intrepid*, *Court Martial*, *Private Schulz* and *Kessler*.'

World War III
US 1982 2 × 96m colour
NBC/Finnegan Associates/David Greene
(Bruce Lansbury)

Russians send an invasion force into Alaska, and the Americans fight back while attempting not to start a war.
Tedious horror story for our time: the action scenes look like offcuts from *Ice Station Zebra* and the romantic scenes are tediously irrelevant.

w Robert L. Joseph   d David Greene
ph Stevan Larner   m Gil Melle

Rock Hudson (as the President), David Soul, Brian Keith, Cathy Lee Crosby, Robert Prosky, Katherine Helmond

World's End (GB 1981; 12 × 30m; colour). Rather odd little serial written by the esteemed playwright Ted Whitehead, put out at a late hour on BBC2 but quite openly observing all the conventions of popular soap opera, including the choice of the local pub to act as a focus for the goings-on of assorted transients in the bed-sitter corner of Chelsea known as the World's End. With Neville Smith, Primi Townsend, etc. Directed by Pedr James; produced by Colin Tucker.   PP

The Worlds of Mr Wells
GB 1966 55m bw
Granada (Patricia Lagone)
Centenary (of his birth) documentary about H. G. Wells, using his own words over 'action-stills' pictures. Directed by Michael Beckham.
† The BBC's equivalent programme was *Whoosh!*   PP

Worldvision. Distribution company formed after the demise in 1971 of ABC Films, the networks having been forced to divest themselves of subsidiaries.

Worldwide. Useful BBC series of the seventies presenting reports on, and samples from, television services around the world. Produced by Maryse Addison.   PP

Worth, Harry (1920–). British variety and sketch comedian who in the sixties perfected his character of an amiable bumbler who confused not only himself but everyone with whom he came in contact. More recent series: *How's Your Father*, *O Lucky Band!*

Worsnip, Glyn (1938–). Quizzical British reporter, with *That's Life* and *Nationwide*.

Worzel Gummidge
GB 1978–81 approx. 52 × 30m colour
Southern (James Hill)
Pleasing family series based on the children's stories about a characterful scarecrow and his friends.
w Keith Waterhouse and Willis Hall   d James Hill
Jon Pertwee, Una Stubbs, Geoffrey Bayldon and Norman Bird as regulars, plus guest stars   PP

Wrather, Jack (1918–84). American independent producer particularly associated with *Lassie* and *The Lone Ranger*.

Write Away (GB 1980). Useful adult educational series for sub-literates, brightly and sympathetically presented by Barry Took, with back-up tutoring available in many areas. Produced by Caroline Pick; for BBC. PP

The Writing on the Wall *
GB 1985 7 × 60m
Brook Productions (Phillip Whitehead) for C4

Excellent, imaginative study of politics – in the widest sense – in Britain during the seventies, with changing attitudes to law and order, the family, employment and welfare bulking as large as changes in government. 'A masterly exercise,' I said, 'in creative hindsight.'

w and narrator Robert Kee p Cate Haste, Ben Shephard

WTVA. British group of television professionals and enthusiasts drawn together to gain 'Wider TV Access' – meaning to the backlog of classic TV series held in archives and company vaults. They have engineered screenings and publish a quarterly periodical *Primetime* devoted to scholarly articles and check-lists on *The Prisoner*, Hancock, *Out of the Unknown*, even *The Professionals*. Through a production company called Illuminations also responsible for occasional TV programmes on television, e.g. *The Prisoner File* and *Cat among the Lions*, both shown on C4. PP

Wuthering Heights. Emily Brontë's oft-dramatized romance has cropped up on BBC Television alone half-a-dozen times since the service resumed in 1946. Rudolph Cartier did it twice to a single play adaptation by Nigel Kneale, the second time with Keith Michell as Heathcliffe and Claire Bloom as Cathy. The most recent is a five-part serial of 1978 directed by Peter Hammond, with Ken Hutchison (later to star in the tough thriller *Hideaway*) and Kay Adshead. The most often remembered production, unhappily for Eng.-Lit., is Monty Python's hilarious semaphore version, c 1972. PP

The Wuzzles (US 1985; 13 × 22m). Stories of a land where all the animals are combinations: a bumbelion, an eleroo, a cowcat and a frogdog. Better in concept than actuality, but new Disney cartooning is always better than anyone else's. For CBS.

WWN. It stood for Wales, West & North, the little company awarded commercial television's least viable franchise. It lasted only eight months in 1961–2; Sian Hinds, star of *Babytime*, a series set up to follow a child's progress from ante-natal days to its first birthday, was made redundant at the age of seven weeks. The area was divided between TWW and Granada, and Wales did not have a wholly Welsh service again until S4C was set up 20 years later. PP

Wyatt Earp: see The Life and Legend of Wyatt Earp

Wyatt, Jane (1912–). American leading lady who after a rather desultory movie career became famous in the long-running *Father Knows Best*. TV movies: *See How They Run*, *Weekend of Terror*, *You'll Never See Me Again*, *Tom Sawyer*, *Katherine*, *Amelia Earhart*, *Superdome*, *A Love Affair*, *The Nativity*, *The Millionaire*.

Wyatt, Will (1942–). British producer and executive, rising via book programmes and the 1978 literary investigation, *B. Traven: a Mystery Solved*, to succeed Desmond Wilcox as head of the BBC's documentary features department in 1980. PP

Wyatt, Woodrow (1918–). British politician, journalist and newspaper publisher who had brief but effective spell as a *Panorama* reporter in the late fifties. He conducted a famous exposé of ballot-rigging in the Electrical Trades Union and pioneered the forthright personal summing-up of an issue. PP

Wyman, Jane (1914–) (Sarah Jane Faulks). American star actress with a long and satisfying Hollywood career. Series: *The Jane Wyman Show*, *Falcon Crest*. TV movies: *The Failing of Raymond*, *The Incredible Journey of Dr Meg Laurel*.

Wymark, Patrick (1926–70) (A. K. A. Cheeseman). Powerful British actor who became famous as the domineering Wilder of *The Plane Makers* and then *The Power Game* during the sixties. Also: *They Hanged My Saintly Billy* (in which he played Palmer the poisoner, 1960), *Malatesta* (1964). PP

Wynette, Tammy (1942–) (Virginia Wynette Pugh). American popular singer.

Wynn, Ed (1886–1966) (Isaiah Edwin Leopold). American vaudeville comedian known as 'the perfect fool'. His many appearances in TV's early years included a domestic comedy series *The Ed Wynn Show*.

Wynn, Keenan (1916–). American character actor, son of Ed Wynn. Series: *Trouble Shooters*, *The Westerners*. TV movies include *The Young Lawyers*, *Assault on the Wayne*, *Cannon*, *Terror in the Sky*, *Hijack*, *Hit Lady*, *Target Risks*, *The Quest*, *The Bastard*, *The Billion Dollar Threat*.

Wynn, Tracy Keenan (19 –). American writer, son of Keenan Wynn. His best-known TV scripts include *Tribes*, *The Autobiography of Miss Jane Pittman*, *The Glass House*, *The Quest*.

Wynne and Penkovsky
GB/US 1984 3 × 55m
BBC (Innes Lloyd)/Arts Network
True story of the British spy Greville Wynne who worked behind the Iron Curtain under cover of his own (genuine) export business.

Penkovsky was the Russian informant he was to bring to the West on what turned out to be his last mission.
An uncomfortable, unheroic version, with David Calder as a close lookalike Wynne.

w Andrew Carr, from Wynne's *books*
d Paul Seed
David Calder, Christopher Rozycki (as Penkovsky), Fiona Walker, Frederick Treves   PP

Wynter, Dana (1930–) (Dagmar Wynter). British leading lady in Hollywood. TV movies: *Companions in Nightmare*, *Any Second Now*, *Owen Marshall*, *The Connection*, *The Questor Tapes*, *The Lives of Jenny Dolan*, *Backstairs at the White House*, *M Station Hawaii*.

Wyver, John (1955–). British critic and commentator influential in the academic and institutional perusal of TV. Formerly TV editor of *Time Out*. Founder member of WTVA (which see) and producer of archive specials on *The Prisoner* and MTM for Channel 4.   PP

The XYY Man (GB 1977). Granada thriller series featuring an ex-villain (Stephen Yardley) trying to go straight but plagued by the extra chromosome in his make-up which gave the show its title. It also continued the rise and rise of George Bulman, later to have his own series.   PP

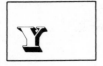

Yancey Derringer
US 1958 34 × 25m bw
CBS/Sharpe—Lewis

Experiences of an adventurer in post-Civil-War New Orleans.

Competent and quite forgettable.

Jock Mahoney, X Brands, Julie Adams

Yanks Go Home
GB 1976 13 × 25m colour (VTR)
Granada (Eric Prytherch)

Stories of a USAAF base in Lancashire during World War II.

A good idea which somehow didn't take: the interplay was all too forced and strident to be funny.

w various *d* Eric Prytherch

Lionel Murton, Stuart Damon, Richard Oldfield, Alan MacNaughton, Bruce Boa, Meg Johnson

Yarwood, Mike (1941–). Favourite British impressionist of the seventies and eighties.

Yeah! Yeah! Yeah!
aka: *The Beatles in New York*
GB 1964 35m bw
Granada (Derek Granger, Peter Eckersley, Dick Fontaine)

Lively account of the Beatles' conquest of New York with pioneer *cinéma vérité* footage by the American cameramen Albert and David Maysles, often quoted in subsequent programmes.   PP

A Year at the Top (US 1977). Briefly seen Norman Lear half-hour comedy for CBS, about two rock musicians who are offered success – at a price – by an agent who is really the devil. With Greg Evigan, Paul Shaffer, Gabriel Dell.

A Year in the Life of . . .
GB 1969 12 × 50m colour
BBC (Paul Watson)

A dozen subjects monitored by camera over the same twelve months between July 1968 and July 1969 – new MP, newly married couple expecting their first baby, hopeful pop group. Only eight years after the pioneering *vérité* efforts of Drew and Leacock the surprises already seemed lacking. As I wrote at the time: 'Nowadays we're too knowing (as subjects). We've been half expecting the cameras for some time. It's long past our turn. We compose the performance we've been rehearsing subconsciously for years.'

† The title was revived in 1981 for one or two isolated programmes, including *A Year in the Life of* Viscount Weymouth, tedious peer. PP

Year of the French (GB 1982). Twelve portraits of representative citizens (peasant farmer, scholarly train guard, wildlife warden, etc) arranged to follow the cycle of the seasons. Shot by various directors, produced by Edward Mirzoeff, for BBC. PP

The Year of the French
Ireland/France 1982 6 × 60m
RTE/FR3 (Niall McCarthy)

Elegiac costume serial from Thomas Flanagan's novel of the 1798 Irish uprising encouraged by – as things turned out – some rather evanescent French revolutionary help.

w Eugene McCabe, *novel* Thomas Flanagan *d* Michael Garvey *m* The Chieftains

Robert Stephens, Jean Claude Drouot, Niall O'Brien, Oliver Cotton, Anne Louise Lambert, Keith Buckley, T. P. McKenna, François Perrot, Jeremy Clyde.   PP

Year Zero (GB 1979). John Pilger report from wartorn Cambodia which prompted huge donations to the British relief fund but raised many misgivings about his methods and the selectivity of his attack – hence my 1979 review: 'As a revelation and an exclamation of dismay, *Year Zero* was salutary. May it have prompted a million contributions to the Cambodia Fund . . . Those children's faces will not be easily forgotten. I just wish that Pilger's relentless accusatory tone, frequent repetitions and gross partiality hadn't left me with the ignoble suspicion that their plight had been made use of.' Directed by David Munro; for ATV.   PP

Years Ahead (GB since 1982). Magazine show for the elderly presented by retired newsreader Robert Dougall. A welcome innovation by Channel 4, produced for them by Skyline (Steve Chambers).   PP

The Yellow Rose
US 1983 17 × 50m colour
NBC/Warner/Nightwatch/American Flyer
(John Wilder, Michael Zinberg)
Family intrigues after the style of *Dallas* on a modern Texas ranch.
A well-done soap opera which rather surprisingly didn't take, despite its cast of well-known faces.
cr John Wilder
Sam Elliott, David Soul, Susan Anspach, Cybill Shepherd, Edward Albert, Noah Beery Jnr, Ken Curtis, Will Sampson

Yes, Honestly: see No, Honestly

Yes Minister *** (GB 1980–5). BBC comedy series rooted so accurately in the Whitehall manoeuvrings of government and Civil Service that Cabinet Ministers rate it their favourite programme. It's also quite funny. With Nigel Hawthorne, Paul Eddington. Written by Antony Jay and Jonathan Lynn; produced by Peter Whitmore.   PP
LH: 'I'd give it four stars at least.'
† After five seasons a special at Christmas 1985 had Jim Hacker (Eddington) unexpectedly facing the possibility of becoming Prime Minister, which led to the entry below.
†† Only previous attempt at Civil Service sitcom was *If It Moves, File It* (1970), written by Troy Kennedy Martin; with John Bird, Dudley Foster.

Yes Prime Minister ***
GB 1986 8 × 25m
BBC (Sydney Lotterby)
In a logical development of *Yes Minister* Jim Hacker becomes Prime Minister and has to cope with Whitehall manoeuvrings even funnier, more intricate and more accurate than before – by a fluke of scheduling he tangled with his Defence Secretary the very day Michael Heseltine resigned from that post in real life.
w Antony Jay, Jonathan Lynn   PP
Sample Sir Humphreyisms:
'The purpose of our defence policy is to make the British people believe Britain is defended. Not the Russians. The Russians *know* it's not.'

'It's safer to be heartless than mindless. The history of the world is the history of the triumph of the heartless over the mindless.'
'Things are only disastrous if people find out.'

Yes, Yes, Nanette
aka: *The Nanette Fabray Show*
US 1961 26 × 25m bw
NBC/BJ
Stories of a Hollywood writer and his ex-actress wife.
Mild comedy series supposedly inspired by the star's own life with husband Ranald McDougall, and written by him.
Nanette Fabray, Wendell Corey, Doris Kemper

Yesterday's Child
US 1977 74m colour TVM
NBC/Paramount/William Kayden
A woman returns to claim her inheritance and finds her life in danger.
A hoary plot dusts off quite entertainingly.
w Michael Gleason, *novel Night of Clear Choice* by Doris Miles Disney *d* Corey Allen
Shirley Jones, Geraldine Fitzgerald, Claude Akins, Ross Martin, Stephanie Zimbalist

Yesterday's Men (GB 1971; 50m). Sardonic documentary on Labour cabinet ministers who had lost office in the 1970 election, and how they were faring. The style, the mocking music by the pop group The Scaffold and a question put to Harold Wilson about his earnings from his instant memoirs of Downing Street 1964–70 (though not included in the final programme) led to the threat of lawsuits, an outsize political row and the setting up of the Broadcasting Complaints Commission. Written and presented by David Dimbleby, produced by Angela Pope.   PP

Yesterday's Witness. Generic title of an occasional series of documentaries produced by Stephen Peet for BBC2. The general aim was to put on record the recollections of days gone by from elderly people who led interesting lives.

Yogi Bear *
US 1958–62 123 × 25m colour
Hanna–Barbera
Cartoon series featuring a friendly bear in Jellystone National Park; also *Snagglepuss* and *Yakky Doodle Duck*.
† Yogi became the most popular Hanna–Barbera character of all.

Yogi's Gang
US 1973 19 × 22m colour
Hanna–Barbera

Yogi and his friends set out on a crusade to protect the environment.
Inferior workmanship marks this sequel.

York, Susannah (1941–). Tomboyish British actress discovered by ABC Armchair Theatre in 1959. After a movie career back into TV with the series *Prince Regent, Second Chance, We'll Meet Again*. Latest credit, alas, *Macho*, 1986.

Yorkin, Bud (1926–) (Alan Yorkin). American producer–director who after years in light entertainment teamed with Norman Lear in Tandem Productions to make the smash hits *All in the Family*, *Maude* and *Sanford and Son*.

You Are There **
US 1954–6 65 × 25m bw
CBS

Re-enactments of historical incidents in terms of modern reporting: the trial of Joan of Arc, the death of John Dillinger, etc.
Carefully researched information series in a format which was certainly an influential TV first. It was briefly revived in the early seventies, but by then the freshness had worn off.
host Walter Cronkite
† The BBC borrowed the format and title in the late fifties, to no great effect.

You Bet Your Life. A so-called quiz show which, cheaply made, was really an excuse for Groucho Marx to interview and mildly insult a variety of contestants. The ·impromptu humour was a little strained at times, but the show became a national institution. (A British version, *Groucho*, failed miserably.) The show ran from 1956 to 1961, was produced by John Guedel and hosted by George Fenneman; for NBC.

You Can't Go Home Again
US 1979 96m colour TVM
CBS Entertainment (Bob Markell)

Fragments from the short and unhappy life of Thomas Wolfe.
Unexpectedly literate, if slightly falsified, televersion of an autobiographical novel by one of America's oddest literary figures, a writer of the thirties who died at 38 of tuberculosis of the brain.
w Ian McLellan Hunter *d* Ralph Nelson *ph* Jack Priestley *m* Charles Gross

Lee Grant, Chris Sarandon, Hurd Hatfield, Tammy Grimes, Christopher Murney, Roland Winters, Paul Sparer
'CBS has at least had the courage to take a stab at something from literature, instead of working over yet another disease-racked victim or another detective yarn.' – *Daily Variety*

You Lie So Deep My Love
US 1975 74m colour TVM
Universal (David Lowell Rich)

Murder results when a girl is convinced that her husband is a crook and philanderer.
Muddled and slow-starting suspenser.
w William K. Stuart, Robert Hammer, John Neufeld *d* David Lowell Rich
Barbara Anderson, Don Galloway, Walter Pidgeon, Angel Tompkins

You Must Be Joking (GB 1981). Estimable BBC panel show in which teams from male and female wings of fire service, army, etc, compete to decide whether proffered jokes, hoaxes and bizarre tales did in fact happen. Presided over with great good humour by Terry Wogan; produced by Marcus Plantin.
PP

You Take Over (GB 1958). Airport controller, Fleet Street news editor, race team manager cope with routine crises, each situation seen through his eyes only. Geoffrey Bellman's and John Whitney's experimental drama-doc series marked television's only sustained flirtation with the subjective camera. Because the TV cameras of the day could not imitate the quick shifts of focus of the human eye, it worked convincingly only when the viewpoint was the sedentary one of a tetchy police court magistrate. This led to a successful spin-off series the following year, *The Case Before You*.
PP

Youens, Bernard (1914–). Heavyweight British character actor forever identified with the idle, beer-swilling Stan Ogden in *Coronation Street*.

You'll Never Get Rich ****
aka: *The Phil Silvers Show; Bilko*
US 1955–8 138 × 25m bw
CBS

At a remote army post, the fast-talking motor pool sergeant is full of clever schemes.
Smartly written and performed vehicle for a star who as Ernie Bilko created an unforgettable comic character and became a national institution.

cr NAT HIKEN *m* John Strauss

PHIL SILVERS, PAUL FORD (Colonel Hall), MAURICE GOSFIELD (Doberman), Elizabeth Fraser (Sgt Hogan), Joe E. Ross (Ritzik), Harvey Lembeck (Barbella), Allan Melvin (Henshaw), Billy Sands (Paparelli), Hope Sansberry (Mrs Hall)

You'll Never See Me Again
US 1973 74m colour TVM
Universal (Harve Bennett)
A wife disappears after a quarrel and may have been murdered.
Standard suspenser.
w William Wood, Gerald di Pego *d* Jeannot Szwarc

David Hartman, Joseph Campanella, Jane Wyatt, Ralph Meeker, Jess Walton, Bo Swenson

Young, Alan (1919–) (Angus Young). British character comedian in America: after some success as nervous type in films he became a variety star on TV and especially scored in the series MISTER ED.

Young and Gay: see The Girls

The Young and the Restless. CBS daily soap opera which premièred in 1973 and puts its main focus on teenage problems.

Young at Heart
GB 1980 13 × 25m colour
Sir John Mills as a humble pottery worker facing retirement after 50 years of toil, and sounding rather like Mr Harold Macmillan when he used to insert a playful 'ain't' into his speech. Sentimental sitcom by Vince Powell, with Megs Jenkins as the missus. Directed and produced by Stuart Allen; for ATV.   PP
LH: 'Watchable, but not exactly a sparkler.'

Young, Sir Brian (1922–). British executive, director-general 1970–82 of the Independent Broadcasting Authority.

Young, Collier (1908–80). American writer–producer who created *The Rogues*, *One Step Beyond* and *Ironside*.

The Young Country *
US 1970 74m colour TVM
Universal (Roy Huggins)
A young gambler gets worried when he finds a fortune in a saddlebag and no one will acknowledge ownership.
Pleasant light western.

w/d Roy Huggins
Roger Davis, Walter Brennan, Joan Hackett, Wally Cox, Pete Duel

Young Dan'l Boone
US 1977 8 × 50m colour
CBS/TCF
An attempt to refurbish an old warhorse with youth appeal, this location adventure series failed rather miserably.
Rick Moses, John Joseph Thomas, Devon Ericson

Young Dr Kildare
US 1972 24 × 25m colour (VTR)
MGM
A cheap taped retread of a famous series.
Gary Merrill, Mark Jenkins

Young, Gig (1913–78) (Byron Barr). Debonair American leading man of the fifties, latterly character actor, especially associated with tipsy roles. TV series: *The Rogues*, *Gibbsville*. TV movies: *Companions in Nightmare*, *The Neon Ceiling*, *The Great Ice Rip-off*, *The Turning Point of Jim Malloy*, *Sherlock Holmes in New York*, *Spectre*.

Young, Jimmy (19 –). British pop musician turned disc jockey who introduced political interviews into his cosy Radio 2 show, whereupon politicians started to court him and he became a serious personality. Hence *The Jimmy Young Television Programme*, periodic chat and audience join-in show (YTV) related to a topic of the day.   PP

'Torn between his family, who demanded greatness, and a woman who wanted only his love, he risked it all in one defiant moment of glory.'
Young Joe, the Forgotten Kennedy
US 1977 96m colour TVM
ABC Circle (William McCutchen)
The eldest son of Joseph Kennedy, killed in World War II, is presented as an ambitious and romantic young man.
So-what biopic leaves us not much the wiser and very thinly entertained.
w M. Charles Cohen, *biography The Lost Prince* by Hank Searls *d* Richard T. Heffron
ph Stevan Larner *m* John Barry
Peter Strauss, Barbara Parkins, Stephen Elliott, Darleen Carr, Simon Oakland, Asher Brauner, Gloria Strook

The Young Lawyers
US 1969 74m colour TVM
ABC/Paramount

A Boston corporation lawyer takes over a legal aid office run by students.
A very predictable pilot.

w/d Harvey Hart

Jason Evers, Louise Latham, Keenan Wynn, Michael Parks, Anjanette Comer

† The ensuing series lasted 24 × 50m films and starred Lee J. Cobb with Judy Pace and Zalman King.

❋ **Young, Loretta** (1913–) (Gretchen Young). American leading lady of the thirties and forties who later became famous on television for wearing a different gorgeous dress each week on *The Loretta Young Show* (Emmy for best series actress 1954, 1956, 1958).

Young, Muriel (*c* 1928–). British presenter, especially associated with children's programmes. In the seventies she became head of children's programmes for Granada TV.

The Young Ones (GB 1982–4). Pioneering 'alternative' comedy show supposedly featuring a spectacularly unsavoury household of eternal students and drop-outs. 'What they are inviting you to laugh at or be shocked by,' I wrote, 'is a lurch through life without any saving graces or niceties. Watching them is like watching the monkeys at the zoo: there is just the chance they might do something really original involving a passing archdeacon, but mostly it's the usual little habits from which you avert the children's gaze.' Never mind, it had its moments and all the Young Ones went to other things: Rik Mayall, Adrian Edmondson, Nigel Planer and the worrying normal Christopher Ryan. Written by Ben Elton, Rik Mayall and Lise Mayer, Alexei Sayle (who also dropped in); directed by Geoff Posner, produced by Paul Jackson, for BBC. PP

Young Pioneers *
US 1975 100m colour TVM
ABC Circle

In 1873, newlywed teenagers travel west.
Standard pioneering saga, well enough made.

novels Rose Wilder Lane *d* Michael O'Herlihy

Roger Kern, Linda Purl

† A second 96m episode, *The Young Pioneers' Christmas*, was aired in 1977, and in 1978 two one-hour films were made but no series resulted.

'Together they operate as a kind of "colonial" Mod Squad, working to create their own kind of world.'

The Young Rebels
US 1970 15 × 50m colour
ABC/Columbia/Aaron Spelling (Jon Epstein)

During the War of Independence, a young guerrilla band fights the British.
Unappetizing historical adventure.

cr Harve Bennett

Rick Ely, Lou Gossett, Philippe Forquet, Alex Henterloff, Will Geer

Young, Robert (1907–). American movie star of the thirties and forties who also had great TV success with *Father Knows Best*, *Window on Main Street* and *Marcus Welby*. TV movies: *Vanished*, *All My Darling Daughters*, *My Darling Daughters' Anniversary*, *Little Women*.

Young Shoulders (GB 1984; 75m). First television play (in fact a film) in the fullness of his years by John Wain, seminal novelist of the fifties and lately Professor of Poetry at Oxford. It turned out to be a sensitive but rather dreary study of growing up and coming to terms with parents, bereavement, being abroad. With David Horovitch, Jennifer Piercey and Andrew Groves as the boy undergoing it all. Directed by Silvio Narizzano, produced by Bernard Krichefski, for BBC Pebble Mill. PP

Young, Stephen (*c* 1931–) (Stephen Levy). Canadian leading man, occasionally in Hollywood. Series: *Seaway*, *Judd for the Defence*. TV movies: *The Mask of Sheba*, *Death Squad*.

The Young Visiters ** (GB 1984). Very good shot at capturing the blissful innocence of Daisy Ashford's child's-eye view of posh goings-on at the turn of the century, as set down in the story she wrote at the age of nine. Of Tracey Ullman as the heroine Ethel I wrote, 'No one can register such fine variations of aspiration, anticipation or quiet satisfaction at the way things are turning out.' Also with Kenny Ireland (Mr Salteena), John Harding (Bernard), Carina Radford (Daisy). Written, directed, produced by James Hill, for C4. PP

The Younger Generation
GB 1961 11 × 60m bw (VTR)
Granada (Peter Wildeblood)

Plays by young writers performed by mostly young actors, who incidentally constituted TV's first stock company, each appearing in several of the episodes. Among those that went on to make names for themselves were authors Robert Holles, Tim Aspinall, Patrick Garland, Adrian Mitchell and Maureen Duffy; from the actors, Judy Cornwell, Ronald Lacey, Mary Miller and John Thaw.

PP

Your Life in Their Hands.

Surgical case-histories in a BBC format of the fifties successfully revived, with little change, in the 1980s. My review of the later series: 'Essentially, it is a reassurance show. You meet the patient, suffering from some unpleasant complaint. You meet the surgeon, who proposes what he proposes. You see the operation and invariably, as far as I remember – I may be wrong – you see or hear of the happy outcome; six months later, patient leading new life.' Producer (1980-1): Fiona Holmes; series editor: David Paterson.

PP

Your Man from the Six Counties

GB 1976 94m colour
BBC *Play for Today* (Kenith Trodd)

12-year-old Belfast boy who has never known anything but bombs and hatred is sent to stay with an aunt and uncle in the Republic. Until the same producer's *Shadows on Our Skin* four years later, perhaps the most sensitive play about the Northern Ireland impasse. Written by Colin Welland; directed by Barry Davis.

PP

Your Money or Your Wife

US 1972 74m colour TVM
Bentwood

A scriptwriter's plot turns into an almost perfect crime.

Rather talkative comedy suspenser.

w J. P. Miller, *novel If You Want to See Your Wife Again . . .* by John Gay *d* Allen Reisner

Ted Bessell, Elizabeth Ashley, Jack Cassidy, Betsy Von Furstenberg

Your Place or Mine

US 1983 96m colour TVM
CBS/Lorimar/Finnegan Associates

A lady psychiatrist is devastated when her lover leaves her.

Modern comedy of the tables turned; not bad but very elongated.

w Terry Louise Fisher, Steve Brown *d* Robert Day

Bonnie Franklin, Robert Klein, Tyne Daly, Peter Bonerz

Your Show of Shows.

American variety show which ran on NBC on Saturday nights from 1949 to 1954 and made stars of Sid Caesar and Imogene Coca. Among the writers were Neil Simon, Mel Brooks and Woody Allen; producer–director was Max Leibmann. Some grainy kinescopes were edited into a 1976 movie release, *Ten from Your Show of Shows.*

Your Witness

GB 1967 4 × 75m bw

BBC attempt to conduct a television debate on such subjects as euthanasia within the formal rules of a tribunal, each side fielding evidence and calling witnesses but no head-on confrontations. For once there was no manic cutting-off of arguments in mid-flow.

PP

You're Not Watching Me, Mummy *

GB 1980 50m colour
YTV

John Osborne's uncharitable backstage comedy. Funny, mean and parochial in about equal proportions but always a delight to the ear or, rather, the stuff between the ears.

Anna Massey, Peter Sallis

PP

You're Only Young Twice

GB 1977-8 14 × 26m colour

Peggy Mount and Pat Coombs in a YTV sitcom set among the elderly, one of several so disposed about this time. Written by Pam Valentine and Michael Ashton.

PP

Yuma *

US 1970 70m colour TVM
ABC/Aaron Spelling

A tough lawman tackles the wildest town in the old west.

Conventional, enjoyable western.

w Charles Wallace *d* Ted Post *m* George Duning

Clint Walker, Barry Sullivan, Edgar Buchanan, Kathryn Hays

Z Cars ***. A BBC series which emerged from Elwyn Jones's drama documentary department and ran from 1960 until 1978, covering 667 one-hour episodes. When it began, with a simple play called *Jacks and Knaves*, based on the experiences of Liverpool detective Jack Prendergast (the series format based on the crime cars was by Troy Kennedy Martin) it seemed to have all the hallmarks of the new realism, showing crime and low-life from the police point of view in two kinds of Liverpool suburb. The leading policemen, played by Stratford Johns, Frank Windsor, Joseph Brady, Jeremy Kemp, James Ellis, Terence Edmond, and later Brian Blessed and Colin Welland, soon became familiar faces. Leading writers over the years were John Hopkins, Robert Barr, Alan Plater, Allan Prior. Spin-offs included *Softly Softly* and *Barlow*; the influence on other crime series was immense.

Z Channel. One on which, for a fee, the American viewer can see up-to-date uncut movies without commercials.

Z for Zachariah (GB 1984; 120m). After the nuclear unthinkable has happened . . . into the remote Welsh valley inhabited solely (it seems) by a young girl strays Anthony Andrews as a survivor from other parts, trailing his private anti-contamination gear behind him. A protracted, presumably symbolic yawnie which made the predicament of the two characters oddly unreal and even oddlier unimportant. Also with Pippa Hinchley. Written and directed by Anthony Garner, for BBC.   PP

Zane Grey Theatre *
US 1956–60 156 × 25m bw
Four Star

Western anthology, hosted by Dick Powell. A competent production with excellent guest stars, providing the kind of middlebrow entertainment hard to find in the eighties.

The Zany Adventures of Robin Hood
US 1983 96m colour TVM
CBS/Charles Fries/Bobka (Andrew Donally)

In King Richard's absence at the Crusades, Robin Hood holds the throne for him.
The kind of awful spoof which makes talent look like no talent. A positive pain to sit through.
w Robert Kaufman *d* Ray Austin *ph* Jack Hildyard *m* Stanley Myers
George Segal, Morgan Fairchild, Janet Suzman, Roddy McDowall, Kenneth Griffith, Michael Hordern, Melvyn Hayes, Tom Baker, Robert Hardy, Roy Kinnear, Robin Nedwell, Fenella Fielding
'Lamentable attempt at getting laughs out of the legend ends up looking like something washed up on *Gilligan's Island*.' – *Daily Variety*

Zavaroni, Lena (1963–). Scottish child entertainer, a hit at the age of ten on *Opportunity Knocks*; later in her own specials.

Zero One *
GB 1962 39 × 25m bw
MGM/BBC
Cases of an airline detective.
Polished crime entertainment.
Nigel Patrick, Katya Douglas

Zetterling, Mai (1925–). Swedish actress many years resident in Britain. In several productions of Ibsen, etc, also a witless sitcom, *My Wife and I* (A–R, 1958), adapted from an American radio series. *One Pair of Eyes* (1969). As a director made a gloomy documentary about her native land for the BBC, *The Prosperity Race* (1962).   PP

Ziegfeld: The Man and His Women
US 1978 150m colour TVM
NBC/Columbia/Mike Frankovich (Buzz Kulik)

The women in the life of the great showman give their assessment of him.
Despite a large budget by TV standards, this hefty biopic looks like a dry run, notably lacking in slickness and professionalism. Its facts appear to be accurate, but its presentation of them seems shifty, and the performances leave much to be desired. Only the musical numbers raise a mild flicker of interest.

LENA ZAVARONI, a child star who made it to adult popularity, though not without a few problems on the way. Here she revels in her appearance in a 1984 charity gala.

w Joanna Lee *adviser* Patricia Ziegfeld *d* Buzz Kulik *ph* Gerald Perry Finnermann *a/d* John de Cuir *m/d* Dick de Benedictis *choreo* Miriam Nelson

Paul Shenar, Samantha Eggar (Billie Burke), Barbara Parkins (Anna Held), Pamela Peadon (Marilyn Miller), Valerie Perrine (Lillian Lorraine), David Opatoshu, Nehemiah Persoff, Richard B. Shull, Inga Swenson (Nora Bayes), David Downing (Bert Williams), Richard Shea (Eddie Cantor), Dan Tullis Jnr (singer of 'Old Man River'), Catherine Jacoby (Fanny Brice)

Zimbalist, Efrem Jnr (1918–). American star actor of comfortable presence. Series: *77 Sunset Strip*, *The FBI*. TV movies: *Who Is the Black Dahlia?*, *A Family Upside Down*, *Terror out of the Sky*, *The Best Place to Be*.

Zone of Occupation
GB 1982 5 × 60m colour/bw
BBC (Patricia Meehan)

Guiltier-than-thou history of the British occupation of Germany after World War II, unrecognizable to anyone who had served in that country and making some questionable use of archive footage, e.g. an old German pushing his belongings on a handcart through an early-days ruined street scene with the implication that he had been dispossessed to make room for a British service family – something which did not start to happen until later in the Occupation. But Reginald Steed defended the series in *Encounter* Magazine, April 1982.

w Patrick O'Donovan   PP

Zoo Gang *
GB 1973 6 × 50m colour
ATV (Herbert Hirschman)

Members of a wartime resistance group meet again 30 years later to use their special skills in combating modern crime.

Curiously abortive star-studded series which had good things but failed to catch the imagination.

cr Paul Gallico, from his novel *m* Paul and Linda McCartney

Lilli Palmer, John Mills, Brian Keith, Barry Morse

Zoo Time (GB 1958–65). Prolonged Granada series (331 programmes) of animal films, some known under different titles such as *A to Zoo* and *Breakthrough*, obtained under controlled conditions by a Granada unit at the London Zoo. By some imaginative casting the producer for much of the time was the theatre critic Milton Shulman, with Derek Twist. PP

Zorro (US 1957–8). Half-hour black-and-white series by Walt Disney for ABC, based on the several films about the masked avenger of Old California. With Guy Williams, Gene Sheldon.

Zuma Beach
US 1979 96m colour TVM
NBC/Warner/Edgar G. Scherick

A singer–songwriter tries to get fresh inspiration by returning to the beach where she grew up.

Blah comedy–drama for the youth audience, wherever it is.

w William Schwartz *d* Lee H. Katzin *ph* Hector Figueroa *m* Dick Halligan

Suzanne Somers, Mark Wheeler, Michael Biehn, P. J. Soles, Steven Keats, Kimberly Beck

Alternative Titles for TV Movies
(not including pilots for subsequent series – these are cross-referenced in the text)

The Adventures of Freddie *see* The Magnificent Magical Magnet of Santa Mesa
Alias Sherlock Holmes *see* The Return of the World's Greatest Detective
Anna, Anna *see* The Seven Deadly Sins
Ants! *see* It Happened at Lake Wood Manor
Archie Bunker's Place *see* All In the Family
As I Rode Down from Laredo *see* The Return of the Gunfighter

Behind the Badge *see* A Killing Affair
The Big Dragnet *see* Dragnet
The Big Train *see* Alcatraz Express
Brahmin *see* The Invasion of Johnson County

The Cable Car Murders *see* Crosscurrent
The Caper *see* The Heist
Cat and Mouse *see* Mousey
Chasse au Trésor *see* Treasure Hunt
Christmas Miracle in Caulfield USA *see* The Christmas Coal Mine Miracle
Circumstantial Evidence *see* Mallory
City of Fear *see* Panic on Page One
The Comeback *see* Love Is Forever
The Companion *see* The Betrayal
Culpepper *see* The Asphalt Cowboy

The DA: Conspiracy to Kill *see* Conspiracy to Kill
Danger Grows Wild *see* The Poppy Is Also a Flower
The Dark Side of Innocence *see* The Hancocks
Deadly Roulette *see* How I Spent My Summer Vacation
Death Dive *see* Fer de Lance
Doberman Patrol *see* Trapped
Don't Steal My Baby *see* Black Market Baby

The Egghead on Hill 656 *see* The Reluctant Heroes
End of the Line *see* A Cry for Help
Enter Horowitz *see* Conspiracy of Terror
Escape of the Birdmen *see* The Birdmen

The Faceless Man *see* The Counterfeit Killer
Fathers by Sons *see* Mothers by Daughters
The FBI versus the Ku Klux Klan *see* Attack on Terror

The Fifth Victim *see* Jane Doe
Fifty Fifty *see* Partners in Crime
Fitzgerald and Pride *see* Heat of Anger
Flying into the Wind *see* Birth of a Nation
Four Days in Dallas *see* Ruby and Oswald
Further Adventures of Lucky Jim *see* New Adventures of Lucky Jim

The Gathering Storm *see* Walk with Destiny
The Girl in the Park *see* Father Brown, Detective
The Gravy Train *see* The Dion Brothers
The Guardians *see* Incident on a Dark Street

Happiness Is a Warm Clue *see* Charlie Chan: Happiness Is a Warm Clue
Hildegarde Withers *see* A Very Missing Person
The Hunter *see* Scream of the Wolf

Incident in a Dark Alley *see* Incident on a Dark Street
Inside Job *see* The Alpha Caper
Intensive Care *see* Objects of Affection
Intimate Strangers *see* Battered (1977)
Island of Sister Theresa *see* The Mysterious Island of Beautiful Women

James Michener's Dynasty *see* Dynasty
Joshua Tree *see* The Courage and the Passion

Kenny Rogers as the Gambler *see* The Gambler
Kisses on the Bottom *see* I Can't See My Little Willie

Lady in Danger *see* The Last Song
The Last Key *see* Crime Club (1975)
L.A.T.E.R. *see* The Life and Times of Eddie Roberts
Law of the Land *see* The Deputies
The Legend of Machine Gun Kelly *see* Melvin Purvis G-Man
Life of the Party: the Story of Beatrice *see* Beatrice
The Lost Honor of Kathryn Beck *see* Act of Passion
Love Trap *see* Curse of the Black Widow

Made in Britain *see* Birth of a Nation
Making a Living *see* It's a Living
Man at the Crossroads *see* A Great American Tragedy
The Man Called Sloane *see* T. R. Sloane
The Man Who Wanted to Live Forever *see* The Only Way Out Is Dead
Marshal of Sladetown *see* The Rousters
A Masterpiece of Murder *see* A Nice Pleasant Deadly Weekend
Midnight Oil *see* Now You See It, Now You Don't
Million Dollar Face *see* Kiss of Gold
Mrs Columbo *see* Kate Loves a Mystery
Mrs R *see* Death Among Friends
Murder Me, Murder You *see* Mike Hammer

The Murder of Sherlock Holmes *see* Murder She Wrote
My Darling Daughters' Anniversary *see* All My Darling Daughters' Anniversary
My Undercover Years with the KKK *see* Freedom Riders

New Orleans Force *see* Dead Man on the Run
Nice Night for a Hanging *see* Charlie Cobb: Nice Night for a Hanging
Nick Carter *see* The Adventures of Nick Carter
Nobody's Perfect *see* Hart in San Francisco

Off Sides *see* The Pigs vs the Freaks
Once They Marched Through a Thousand Towns *see* Skokie
Once Upon a Murder *see* Chiefs
One Hour to Doomsday *see* City Beneath the Sea
Only One Day Left Before Tomorrow *see* How to Steal an Airplane
Our Winnie *see* Objects of Affection

Panic at Lake Wood Manor *see* It Happened at Lake Wood Manor
The Paramedics *see* The New Healers
The Power and the Passion *see* The Courage and the Passion
A Private Investigation *see* Missing Pieces

Raising Daisy Rothschild *see* The Last Giraffe
The Raving Beauties *see* In the Pink
Rehearsal for Armageddon *see* Ring of Passion
The Rivermen *see* The Runaway Barge

Sam Hill: Who Killed the Mysterious Mr Foster? *see* Who Killed the Mysterious
  Mr Foster?
Sarge: The Badge or the Cross *see* The Badge or the Cross
Search (1972) *see* Probe
Set This Town on Fire *see* The Profane Comedy
Sewers of Gold *see* Dirty Money
Shamus *see* A Matter of Wife and Death
Sierra *see* The Rangers
The Silent Lovers *see* Moviola
The Sixth Column *see* The Love War
The Soldier Who Declared Peace *see* Tribes
A Special Kind of Love *see* Special Olympics
SST: Death Flight *see* SST: Disaster in the Sky
The Storm *see* The New Healers
The Storm (1972) *see* The Victim
The Story of Pretty Boy Floyd *see* Pretty Boy Floyd
Streets of Fear *see* To Kill a Cop
The Strong Man *see* The 500 Pound Jerk
Suspected Person *see* The Heist

They've Kidnapped Anne Benedict *see* The Abduction of St Anne
This Man Stands Alone *see* Lawman without a Gun
Three Faces of Love *see* Rex Harrison Presents Three Stories of Love
Today is Forever *see* Griffin and Phoenix: A Love Story
Tropical Moon Over Dorking *see* Home Video

The UFO Incident *see* The Interrupted Journey

Visions of Death *see* Visions

Westward the Wagon *see* Hitched
With Intent to Kill *see* Urge to Kill
The Woman Who Cried Murder *see* Death Scream
The Women of Willmar *see* A Matter of Sex

Postscript (1986)

by Philip Purser

An unedifying episode between January 1985 and March 1986 neatly packages nearly all that's worrying about British television these days. While the BBC was still playing footsy over the price to be paid for the next series of *Dallas*, Thames Television's managing director Brian Cowgill nipped in and bagged the insane super-soap for ITV. This little coup blew back in Cowgill's face in grisly fashion. Reviled by his opponents, assailed by his fellow programme controllers, disowned even by his own board, he was driven from his job and today sitteth on the right hand of Robert Maxwell as head of that publishing tycoon's cable and video interests.

His offence in the eyes of the other commercial companies is not to be gainsaid. He had cut across a well-established collective buying operation efficiently administered, as all readers of this book must know, by Leslie Halliwell. To introduce impulse purchases and risk having ITV company bid against ITV company would inevitably drive up prices and reduce the range of products affordable.

He had also breached a gentlemen's agreement between ITV and BBC not to try and poach each other's regular bought-in series. This is perhaps a dodgier arrangement, a gentlemen's agreement being polite English for what Americans prefer to call a cartel. But however legitimate or otherwise their grievance, nothing excuses the fury which the BBC vented at the time – as if Mrs Thatcher had just learned her Trident missiles had been sold to France instead – nor the absurd welcome they lavished on *Dallas* when they finally got it back. Joy shall be in heaven over one Ewing which was lost and has returned to the fold, more than ninety and nine Carringtons which never strayed.

Terry Wogan was appointed to usher the initial feature-length dollop on to the air, turning his regular chat show over to long-distance interviews with its stars and ending with a trick he'd played once before, which was to bring up the *Dallas* titles on a monitor screen by his side. Whereupon everyone's screens changed to fresh – or rather, stale – variations on the same old jockeyings of JR and Sue-Ellen and Cliff and Donna.

The BBC moguls (Bill Cotton, managing director; Michael Grade, controller of BBC1) were proclaiming that the purchase and promotion of *Dallas* and its terrible twin *Dynasty* are now of more moment than the production of the BBC's own programmes. Worse still, they weren't even pretending that there was any worth in the goods they were shipping in. Wogan had long been famous for mocking *Dallas*, in particular, while professing to be fascinated by it. He made his name teasing it every day on his radio show. By having him preside over the great return Grade and Cotton were also saying that it didn't matter if people thought the show junk; as long as they watched it, that was enough.

The use of Wogan's show to perform such a function is, incidentally, another admission of something which it might be wiser not to admit. That chat shows have long depended on the free plugs they can offer celebrities with a new book or record or film to advertise is a smelly fact of life, but it is depressing to see it publicly endorsed by the BBC whenever it wants to promote something itself.

One reassuring sign emerges from the incident, if Brian Cowgill will forgive its mention. The cable and satellite industry which he joined has not yet taken over the world. The old-fashioned universal dispensation of broadcast television is still what most people watch most of the time. The shared experience of everyone seeing the same thing at the same time and talking about it next day is still a potent force.

As I write, the live broadcast of the British Academy Awards has just come up fourth in the ratings, and even the fairly dotty relay of the Giotto spacecraft's encounter with Halley's Comet – late at night and reducing to still pictures of what looked like a sliced Scotch Egg – made 84th place with a UK audience of 5.75 million. Nor does the programme have to be a live programme. The occasion of its transmission can be an event if enough people are watching it at the same time, wondering about it, talking it over with everyone else the next day. You need think only of the night *The Day After* went out in America, or the final episode of *Edge of Darkness* in Britain, the resolution of Ken and Deirdre's marital crisis in *Coronation Street*, the transmission of *Holocaust* in Germany.

Take with a pinch of salt those forever mourning a lost 'Golden Age'. There was a Golden Age – indeed there were many Golden Ages in the fifties and the sixties and the seventies, all full of marvellous things. What the mourners forget, for the very good reason that it was eminently forgettable, is the great mass of nothing very much swilling along with the goodies. In the eighties there are still plenty of candidates for four stars in this *Companion* – from me *Rumpole of the Bailey*, *The Boat* and *Duty Free*.

What has been lost, maybe, is the adventurousness of the pioneers, the bravado with which Ed Murrow, long before satellites existed, would have statesmen in three continents discussing world affairs over a radio link while separate film crews filmed them, or Rudolph Cartier staged the destruction of half London in Studio D at Lime Grove. As the resources have become greater and greater, so the use of them has become safer and safer. To reverse a much misquoted dictum by the late Sir Huw Wheldon, the aim is no longer to court triumph, it is to avoid failure.

Not that failure is avoided, of course. But the more expensive shows, anyway, are now so wrapped up in co-production deals and pre-production sales that the book-keeping counts for more than the audience's appreciation. *Time After Time*, a routine Irish country-house comedy which went out on BBC2 early in 1986, might just have made sense as a studio production – the action was pretty well confined to the house. Under the barmy economics of the day it was filmed, with an all-star cast, to a budget that would have paid for three or four good little dramas.

Though Leslie and I don't altogether see eye to eye on this, the shift to making bad little movies instead of intelligent television plays seems to me to be one of the disasters of the decade. Apart from the economic consideration it hands over to the director what was a writer's medium; the visual image is suddenly all that matters. At worst, the camera creeps interminably through acres of empty landscape, or alternatively bucks from shot to shot like a startled horse. Scripts reduce to a few cryptic exchanges, plots simply don't make sense.

Is this really what the public wants? I doubt it, and support comes, symmetrically, from the terrible twins with which we began. *Dallas* and *Dynasty* are both filmed, but never in any self-consciously filmic way. Excursions beyond a few familiar settings are few; and seldom well done. For what it's worth the drama comes from the exchange of 'lines of naïve bitchery', as Leslie terms them in his Introduction. In other words, *Dallas* and *Dynasty* are driven along by the things that have always driven drama along – dialogue, predicament, characterization, and to be fair some good strong acting from one or two of the players involved. These qualities, plus imagination and humour and fellow-feeling, are precisely what once made the TV play a phenomenon of popular culture. They could do so again.

LH: 'But, Philip, we *do* see eye to eye about preferring intelligent television plays to bad little movies. What I bemoan is the lack of television plays which speak with wit, clarity and discretion to the large audience instead of restricting themselves to a minority of would-be highbrows. As for the "gentleman's agreement", life would be impossibly and needlessly complicated if every series had to be auctioned whenever a few new episodes were ordered. We simply insist that the original buyer gets first chance.'